THE OXFORD COMPANION TO

Women's Writing

IN THE UNITED STATES

THE OXFORD COMPANION TO
Women's Writing
IN THE UNITED STATES

Editors in Chief

Cathy N. Davidson   Linda Wagner-Martin

Editors

Elizabeth Ammons   Trudier Harris
Ann Kibbey
Amy Ling   Janice Radway

New York   Oxford
OXFORD UNIVERSITY PRESS
1995

OXFORD UNIVERSITY PRESS

Oxford   New York
Athens   Auckland   Bangkok   Bombay
Calcutta   Cape Town   Dar es Salaam   Delhi
Florence   Hong Kong   Istanbul   Karachi
Kuala Lumpur   Madras   Madrid   Melbourne
Mexico City   Nairobi   Paris   Singapore
Taipei   Tokyo   Toronto

and associated companies in
Berlin   Ibadan

Library of Congress Cataloging-in-Publication Data
The Oxford companion to women's writing in the United States / editors
in chief, Cathy N. Davidson, Linda Wagner-Martin ; editors,
Elizabeth Ammons . . . [et al.].
p. cm.
Includes bibliographical references and index.
ISBN 0-19-506608-1
1. American literature—Women authors—Dictionaries.   2. American
literature—Women authors—Bio-bibliography.   3. Women and
literature—United States—Dictionaries.   4. Women authors,
American—Biography—Dictionaries.   I. Davidson, Cathy N.
II. Wagner-Martin, Linda.   III. Ammons, Elizabeth.
PS147.094   1995
810.9'9287'03—dc20
[B]   94-26359

ISBN 0-19-506608-1

85410

1 3 5 7 9 8 6 4 2

Printed in the United States of America
on acid-free paper

CONTENTS

INTRODUCTION

The Oxford Companion to Women's Writing in the United States is, by design, a volume for both general readers and specialized academic critics. It is addressed to anyone who has ever been intrigued by the enormous range and vitality of writing produced by American women. Whether penning diaries, advice books, epic poems, or scientific treatises, women have contributed abundantly to the intellectual output of the nation. And, as every publisher has known since at least the late eighteenth century, women comprise the greater portion of the American reading public. At its most basic level, the *Oxford Companion* is a tribute to the literate convictions (as writers and readers) that fuel American women's lives.

Despite a long tradition of women's reading and writing, only in the last two decades has women's writing entered the American academy as a subject for classroom teaching and as a topic for extensive scholarly attention. Since then, an entire generation of students has taken courses on "Women and Literature" and its many subfields, including "American Women Writers." Students today study a rich and exciting body of work, from the poems of Anne Bradsteet in the seventeenth century to the fiction of Toni Morrison, who was awarded the Nobel Prize for Literature in 1993. Women writers have worked in a remarkable variety of forms, breaking down traditional boundaries between literary genres, testing the relationship between popular and elite forms of writing, and exploring new topics and areas that previously had not been considered "legitimate" topics for literature.

Precisely because of the boundary-breaking nature of women's writing, *The Oxford Companion to Women's Writing in the United States* is a different kind of reference book. It does not duplicate the efforts of the many excellent resources currently available, but, rather, seeks to build upon their strengths in the process of charting new directions. The original letter sent to prospective contributors to the *Oxford Companion* proposed that essays should "redefine U.S. literary history from a diversity of female and feminist perspectives by questioning traditional literary historiography: categories, genres, theories, periods, and canons." Reading the assembled volume five years later, the editors realize how very much we asked of the five hundred scholars who participated in this project. Those critics discovered whole new genres of writing and did original research never published before in any source. With gratitude and even awe, we thank them for contributing all that—and much more.

The field of women's literary criticism and scholarship is now old enough to have its own body of knowledge, references, networks, key sources, canonical (and noncanonical) texts, and even its own generation gaps and concomitant theoretical disagreements. The burgeoning of the study of women's literature that began at the end of the 1960s and early in the 1970s continues with the participation of a new generation of scholars who went through an educational system marked by women's studies programs, a new canon of writing that included works by women of all races, and, significantly, the presence of women as university teachers and scholars. The very things for which the first generation of women's literary scholars fought are what the current generation of women scholars can often take for granted in their own education.

Yet scholars who have come of age in the late 1980s or 1990s have had other problems to grapple with, including the vastness and richness of the field and the philosophical disagreements inevitable in a vital, changing, and significant discipline. These younger scholars have had to theorize a "feminism" that could encompass, for example, both anti-pornography activists and the exuberant sexualities of *On Our Backs*, a magazine celebrating the varieties of female desire. They have had to contend with seeming contradictions, such as feminists who are pro-choice as well as self-identified feminists who oppose abortion but demand full female participation in the legal process. They have dealt with issues central to the lives of white middle-class women as well as issues brought to the fore by women of color or by lesbians (of any race) who sometimes felt excluded from the women's movement of the 1970s. They have had to analyze theoretical issues as disparate as feminist psychoanalytic criticism and the "woman spirit" (female spirituality) movement, or feminist film theory and women's social history.

Even in purely literary terms there are complexities because, as the canon of women's writing has changed, so have definitions. Does a term such as "women's literature" really encompass writing that uses traditional (or even conservative) literary forms and themes as well as radically avant garde or experimentalist writing? In our own era, for example, how does one talk about both Alice Walker and Kathy Acker as late-twentieth-century "women writers"? Are terms such as "women's studies" expansive enough to account for all the forms of women's written expression that this particular women's movement has encouraged?

We think so. And we think it is a tribute to the pioneering women scholars of the late 1960s and early 1970s that there is so much to talk about (and to argue about) at this point in American literary history. It requires a volume as thick as the present one to begin to map out the contours of U.S. women's literary culture as a field. Indeed, the editors of this book are convinced that the differences of perspective that mark women's literary scholarship in 1994 are precisely what have allowed us to go back to the beginnings of U.S. history to rethink and rediscover women's writing in its many forms and contradictions. We would not need this thick volume if U.S. women's writing could be described (and discounted) with an aphorism. If there is a single point we hope to make with *The Oxford Companion to Women's Writing in the United States*, it is that there is no one "woman's" point of view. As this volume proves—

abundantly and even joyously—there never has been such a single view, and there most assuredly never will be.

Readers outside the academy, specialists in women's studies (in all its disciplinary scope), feminist theorists, and women's rights activists will all find much of interest within this volume. We also hope that this volume might help to explain the different forms that women's writing has taken historically and is taking now. In practical terms, the theoretical, ideological, and generational differences among scholars of women's literature have yielded a plethora of approaches, theories, and political stances that the editors of this volume embrace. Rather than a "generation gap," we see a generational flourishing as the mothers of this wave of feminism watch their daughters address issues such as "performativity" and "queer theory," concepts that were not invented yet when many of the contributors to this book began graduate school (but which are included as entry terms in the present volume). Essays on "deconstruction and feminism" or "object-relations theory" explain in clear and readable terms new critical approaches that many, both inside and outside of the academy, have found difficult and sometimes even incomprehensible. We realize that some people feel lost in the thicket of proliferating feminisms; it is another goal of the *Oxford Companion* to make some sense of the present state of women's literary scholarship by including terminologies and topics representative of the various generations and sub-generations of the past quarter century. For some readers, this book may serve as a road map—or survival guide—to many of the current forms of feminist criticism.

SCOPE OF THE PROJECT

As a collective, the editors and advisers on this project found ourselves thinking seriously and deeply about the scope of the project, which meant weighing carefully the words we chose for our title. We decided to use the word "women's" (as opposed to "woman's") because it suggests the variety of writing produced by persons who happen to be biologically female. We chose "writing" rather than "literature" to acknowledge that women write in the genres that have been esteemed and canonized in our present day educational system (poetry, fiction, drama, essays), but also in a range of genres that are still not recognized as *belles lettres*—from advice books to recipes to newspaper columns to film scripts. And "United States" is a term we chose in contrast to "America" because it is no longer clear to us what the term "America" includes and excludes. Canada? The Caribbean? Latin America? Given the plethora of superb women writers who live in the United States but were born elsewhere (everyone from Susanna Rowson who wrote *Charlotte Temple*, "America's" first bestseller in 1791, to Trinh T. Minh-Ha who creates films and feminist theory in 1994), we also questioned the word "American" (implying citizenship if not a more deeply inculcated—and suspect—notion of what it means to be native-born). Thus, in choosing the term "United States" we have consciously limited ourselves to the geographical United States and, in colonial times, those areas that would be incorporated into the United States.

What should be clear by now is that by focusing on writing, not just literature, *The Oxford Companion to Women's Writing in the United States* is comprehensive in new ways:

- It provides full chronological coverage, with articles on specific periods in literary history (colonial era writing, contemporary poetry) as well as on authors and topics covering four centuries of literary history.
- It provides comprehensive geographical surveys, including essays on regionalism and on writing in the South, the West, New England, and New York.
- It approaches themes and topics from a truly multicultural perspective, providing quantities of new information, whether the subject be grandmothers in literature, women's newspapers, or beauty and fashion. It also provides separate essays on a wide array of ethnic literatures (Filipino-American, Irish-American, South Asian-American, Caribbean-American, and many others), as well as those traditions that are the mainstays of multiculturalism—African-American, Asian-American, Chicana, Latina, Native American, and Jewish-American writing.
- It presents significant new studies in genres such as domestic fiction, ghost stories, travel writing, war novels, humor, folklore, recipe books, biography, spiritual narratives, reportage, and other (sometimes disregarded) kinds of women's writing.
- It includes essays on women writers in such diverse fields as anthropology, leisure studies, linguistics, art history, theater criticism, journalism, sociology, and speech communication.
- It offers discussion of more than a hundred theoretical and philosophical concepts and issues, including separatism, essentialism, black feminism, feminist film theory, ecofeminism, deconstruction, theories of gender, poststructuralism, gynocriticism, and psychoanalysis and women.
- It provides a means for the reader to explore the interplay between women's writing and a wide array of cultural and historical issues: marriage laws, the civil rights movement, exoticization, immigration, class, disabled women's writing, religion, sexual harassment, abolition, women's movements, the Federal Writers Project, the Chicago Renaissance, and countless others.
- It insists that personal issues are worthy of serious scholarly attention, both as important themes in women's writing, and as issues affecting the lives of women and the literary productivity of women writers. Included are essays on eating disorders, body and health, adolescence, family, aging, hysteria, menopause, romantic love, birth control, kinship, gossip, and many other topics.
- It focuses on the process of writing: writing spaces, authorship, naming,

collaboration, storytelling, gender and writing, politics and writing, canon formation, and others.

- It explores the reading/publishing "circuit," with essays on women's bookstores, readership, women's clubs, women's presses, publishing outlets, lesbian publishing, readers' circles, and others.
- And, besides the hundreds of women mentioned in various essays (and included in the work's index), it provides separate biographies of more than four hundred women, from Abigail Adams and Maya Angelou to Hisaye Yamamoto, Anzia Yezierska, and Zitkala-Ša.

Finally, early in the project, we made an editorial decision to allow contributors to the volume to choose the voice in which they wished to write. While most entries are in the familiar encyclopedic voice of the reference volume, others are written in a distinctly autobiographical mode. "The personal is the political," says one feminist maxim, and we decided not to censor those authors who felt they could write more persuasively in their own voice.

HOW TO USE THIS BOOK

Because *The Oxford Companion to Women's Writing in the United States* approximates, in its range and its scope, the complexity of American women's writing, you might want to begin by perusing the index to discover the wide variety of people and ideas contained therein. If you are interested in a specific author, you can turn to the alphabetically arranged entry on her work. From there, you might go to a substantive genre essay (is she a poet? a short story writer? a novelist?) or perhaps to an essay that deals with similar subject matter (let's say, motherhood or anti-war movements). The substantive entry on that topic provides asterisks (*) before any word denoting the title of another entry to be found elsewhere in the book. At the end of the entry, you will find further cross references to related entries, and those new entries take you to still others.

Like a mobius strip that loops back upon itself, each entry leads to another entry, which leads to another, which might well lead back to the original essay. Every entry is a beginning as well as an ending because that, we believe, is how writing works. From "Abolition" to "Women's Studies Programs," various non-literary entries were conceptualized in a way that would be most helpful to readers of women's writing. How to be profitably multidisciplinary became a conceptual problem as we asked ourselves, "What do readers wonder about as they are reading books by women?" or "What do people want to know about as they are preparing to teach women's literature or women's studies courses?" Read Toni Morrison's *Beloved*, and of course you want to know about slavery, the Middle Passage, abolition, the Underground Railroad, slave narratives, folklore, and the various histories and traditions of African-American women's writing. You might also think about childbirth, friendship, spirituals, race, racism, and maybe even "whiteness" and what it means (a category brought to our attention by Morrison's own collected essays, *Playing in the Dark: Whiteness in the American Literary Imagination*). All of these topics have entries in this book. Each leads to still other topics. An individual woman's writing is presented within a varying network of concerns and relationships—ranging over personal, theoretical, historical, and aesthetic issues. Additionally, the timelines in the back of this volume allow you to locate any specific writer (Louisa May Alcott or Joyce Carol Oates) within a constellation of social, historical, cultural, political, medical, and artistic events.

ACKNOWLEDGMENTS

The bibliography at the end of this volume provides a list of the many excellent sources available to readers interested in women's literature, and acknowledges the remarkable efforts of generations of scholars, without whom this book could not exist.

Too many individuals to be named here have contributed to the making of this volume in various ways but the editors would especially like to thank the members of the Editorial Board, the Advisory Board, and the following scholars for their advice and consent: Jeanne Holland, Susan Koppelman, Robert A. Martin, Carla Mulford, and Dana D. Nelson. Dianne Chambers, Cynthia Davis, Catherine Taylor, and Kathryn West served as invaluable research assistants, with Cynthia and Kathryn also conceptualizing and compiling the timelines and Dianne providing the bibliography. The members of the Trade Reference Division of Oxford University Press—especially Linda Halvorson Morse, Marion Osmun, Ann Toback, and Margaret A. Hogan—have been unfailingly supportive of this project. More generally, we thank all of the contributors to this book, particularly for their enthusiasm and their knowledge.

At the end of the process of assembling this reference work, even more than at its expectant beginnings, we are aware that this collective effort has resulted in a volume that celebrates the excitement, diversity, complexity, and excellence of writing by U.S. women authors. It is a thick volume that pays homage to what has been omitted from many standard literary histories, the specific contributions of women writers. Like U.S women's writing in general, *The Oxford Companion to Women's Writing in the United States* refuses to walk meekly beside (or five paces behind) standard histories. Rather, it navigates its own course—and invites the reader to come along for an interesting, and sometimes unexpected, ride.

Cathy N. Davidson
Linda Wagner-Martin
Editors in Chief

DIRECTORY OF CONTRIBUTORS

Sandra Adell, *Professor of English, University of Wisconsin at Madison*
African-American Writing: Fiction

Marjorie Agosin, *Associate Professor, Department of Spanish, Wellesley College, Massachusetts*
Latina Writing: Poetry

Susan Albertine, *Assistant Professor of English, Susquehanna University, Selingsgrove, Pennsylvania*
Industrialization

June M. Aldridge, *Professor of English, Emerita, Spelman College, Atlanta, Georgia*
Margaret Danner

Elizabeth Ammons, *Professor of English and American Literature, Tufts University, Medford, Massachusetts*
Progressive Era Writing

Adelaide P. Amore, *Professor of American Literature and Women's Studies, Southern Connecticut State University, New Haven*
Captivity Narratives; Midwifery; Religion: To 1700; Mary Rowlandson; Silence Dogood; Mercy Otis Warren

Chris Andre, *Department of English, Duke University, Durham, North Carolina*
Expatriate Writers

Joyce Antler, *Associate Professor, Department of American Studies, Brandeis University, Waltham, Massachusetts*
Jewish-American Writing: Overview

Frances R. Aparicio, *Associate Professor of Spanish and Latino Studies, University of Michigan, Ann Arbor*
Latina Publishing Outlets

Nancy Armstrong, *Nancy Duke Lewis Professor of Comparative Literature, English, Modern Culture, and Media, Brown University, Providence, Rhode Island*
Daughters

Amittai F. Aviram, *Associate Professor of English and Comparative Literature, University of South Carolina, Columbia*
Gender Theory

Marilou Awiakta, *Memphis, Tennessee*
Grandmothers

Rebecca Ann Bach, *Lecturer, University of Pennsylvania, Philadelphia*
Subaltern

Eleanor J. Bader, *Director, Student Services, Eugene Lang College, New School for Social Research, New York City*
Women's Newspapers

Brooke DuPuy Baker, *Department of Speech Communication, University of North Carolina at Chapel Hill*
Speech Communication Professionals

Helen M. Bannan, *Associate Professor of History; Director, Women's Studies Center, Florida Atlantic University, Boca Raton*
Helen Hunt Jackson

Marleen S. Barr, *Associate Professor of English, Virginia Polytechnic Institute and State University, Blacksburg*
Feminist Fabulation

Milly S. Barranger, *Professor of Dramatic Art, University of North Carolina at Chapel Hill*
Theater Critics

Regina Barreca, *Associate Professor of English, University of Connecticut, Storrs*
Social Comedy

Dale M. Bauer, *Professor of English, University of Wisconsin at Madison*
Beauty; Hysteria; Politics and Writing

Peter G. Beidler, *Lucy G. Moses Professor of English, Lehigh University, Bethlehem, Pennsylvania*
Native American Writing: Fiction

Eileen T. Bender, *Professor of English, Indiana University at South Bend*
Joyce Carol Oates

Bernard Benstock, *Professor of English, University of Miami, Coral Gables*
Little Magazines

Betty Ann Bergland, *Assistant Professor of History, University of Wisconsin at River Falls*
Racism

Jacqueline Berke, *Professor of English, Drew University, Madison, New Jersey*
Violet Weingarten

Dorothy Berkson, *Professor of English, Lewis and Clark College, Portland, Oregon*
Adolescence; Catharine Beecher; Alice James

Amanda Berry, *Department of English, Duke University, Durham, North Carolina*
AIDS; Lois Gould; Jill Johnston

Ellen E. Berry, *Associate Professor of English; Director, Women's Studies Program, Bowling Green State University, Ohio*
Gender and Writing

Deborah Bice, *Willoughby, Ohio*
Fannie Hurst

Nguyen Ngoc Bich, *Formerly Lecturer of Vietnamese Literature, Culture, and Civilization, George Mason University, Fairfax, Virginia*
Southeast Asian-American Writing

Karen J. Blair, *Professor of History, Central Washington University, Ellensburg*
Club Movement

Mutlu Konuk Blasing, *Professor of English, Brown University, Providence, Rhode Island*
Poetry: 1850 to 1976

Rachel Blau DuPlessis, *Professor, Department of English; Women's Studies Affiliated Faculty, Temple University, Philadelphia, Pennsylvania*
Poetry: Contemporary Women's Poetry

Sophia B. Blaydes, *Professor of English, West Virginia University, Morganstown*
Amy Lowell

Margaret Bockting, *Professor of English, North Carolina Central University, Durham*
Djuna Barnes

Tony Bolden, *Harvey, Louisiana*
Maya Angelou

Thomas Bonner, *Professor of English, Xavier University of Louisiana, New Orleans*
Creole and Acadian Writing

Linda J. Borish, *Assistant Professor of History, Western Michigan University, Kalamazoo*
Suffrage Movement

Hamida Bosmajian, *Professor of English, Seattle University, Washington*
Laura Ingalls Wilder

Candice Lewis Bredbenner, *Assistant Professor of History, Arizona State University West, Phoenix*
Citizenship; Political Organizations: 1900 to 1960

Virginia Brereton, *Professor, The Divinity School, Harvard University, Cambridge, Massachusetts*
Spiritual Narratives

Carol Brightman, *Professor of English, University of Maine at Augusta*
Mary McCarthy

Kate Bristol, *Professor of English, University of California at Santa Cruz*
Architects

Virginia Broaddus, *Morgantown, Virginia*
Geneva Stratton-Porter

Linda Brodkey, *Associate Professor of Literature, University of California at San Diego*
Storytelling

Jacqueline Vaught Brogan, *Professor of English, University of Notre Dame, Indiana*
June Jordan

Mary Hughes Brookhart, *Associate Professor of English, North Carolina Central University, Durham*
Ellease Southerland

Marty Brooks, *Department of English, Duke University, Durham, North Carolina*
Mary Boykin Chesnut

Alanna Kathleen Brown, *Associate Professor of English, Montana State University, Bozeman*
Mourning Dove

Barnsley Brown, *Department of English, University of North Carolina at Chapel Hill*
Race; Racial Identity

Susan Brown, *Assistant Professor of English, University of Guelph, Ontario, Canada*
Alta; Jane Rule; Sappho

Tracy E. Brown, *Department of English, Princeton University, New Jersey*
Gothic Fiction

Elizabeth Brown-Guillory, *Associate Professor of English, University of Houston, Texas*
Louise Meriwether; Arthenia J. Bates Millican; Carlene Hatcher Polite

Dickson D. Bruce, Jr., *Professor of History, University of California at Irvine*
Antilynching Campaign; Angelina Weld Grimké

Maria Bruno, *Associate Professor of American Thought and Language, Michigan State University, East Lansing*
Italian-American Writing

Dana Brunvand Williams, *Professor of English, University of Utah, Salt Lake City*
Frontier Writing

Harriette C. Buchanan, *Associate Professor of Interdisciplinary Studies, Appalachian State University, Boone, North Carolina*
Lee Smith

C. Beth Burch, *Assistant Professor of English Education, University of Alabama, Tuscaloosa*
Jewish-American Writing: Fiction

Judith Burdan, *Professor of English, James Madison University, Harrisonburg, Virginia*
Frances Hodgson Burnett

Kathleen Burrage, *English Instructor, Washington State University at Vancouver*
Prison Writing

Keith E. Byerman, *Professor of English, Indiana State University, Terre Haute*
Toni Cade Bambara; Gayl Jones

Laura Byra, *Department of English, Duke University, Durham, North Carolina*
Step-parents and Stepchildren

Eileen Cahill, *Instructor of English, Marlborough School, Los Angeles, California*
Kinship

Laura M. Calkins, *Professor of History, Oglethorpe University, Atlanta, Georgia*
Antiwar Movements

Ardis Cameron, *Associate Professor, American and New England Studies, University of Southern Maine, Portland*
Ecofeminism; Immigration

Jane Campbell, *Associate Professor of English, Purdue University, West Lafayette, Indiana*
Sarah Moore Grimké and Angelina Grimké Weld; Frances Ellen Watkins Harper; Historical Fiction; Pauline Elizabeth Hopkins; Margaret Walker

Nancy D. Campbell, *Dakar, Senegal*
Visual Art and Writing

Oscar V. Campomanes, *Assistant Professor of English and American Literature, University of California at Berkeley*
Filipino-American Writing; Jessica Tarahata Hagedorn; Ninotchka Rosca; Linda Ty-Casper

Cordelia Candelaria, *Professor of English, Stanford University, California*
Chicana Writing: Poetry; La Llorona; La Malinche; Latina Writing: Overview

Kelly Cannon, *Adjunct Professor of English, North Carolina Central University, Durham*
Sara Teasdale

Jane Caputi, *Associate Professor of American Studies, University of New Mexico, Albuquerque*
Ranting

Anne Marie Carey, *Senior Teaching Assistant, Brown University, Providence, Rhode Island*
Erotica

Lynette Carpenter, *Assistant Professor of English, Ohio Wesleyan University, Delaware*
Ghost Stories

Mary Wilson Carpenter, *Associate Professor of English, Queen's University, Kingston, Ontario, Canada*
Masquerade

Glynis Carr, *Assistant Professor of English, Bucknell University, Lewisburg, Pennsylvania*
Friendship

Jean Ferguson Carr, *Assistant Professor of English, University of Pittsburgh, Pennsylvania*
Collaboration

Steven R. Carter, *Professor of English, Salem State College, Massachusetts*
Adrienne Kennedy

JoAnn E. Castagna, *Assistant to the Dean, College of Liberal Arts, University of Iowa, Iowa City*
Mary Daly

Dianne Chambers, *Assistant Professor of English, Elmhurst College, Illinois*
Dorothy Parker; Constance Rourke

Deborah G. Chay, *Assistant Professor of English, Dartmouth College, Hanover, New Hampshire*
Essentialism; The Other

Dianne Chisholm, *Assistant Professor of English, University of Alberta, Edmonton, Canada*
French Feminism

Linda K. Christian-Smith, *Associate Professor of Curriculum and Instruction, University of Wisconsin at Oshkosh*
Romance Novels

Keith Clark, *Assistant Professor of English, George Mason University, Fairfax, Virginia*
Lorraine Hansberry; Anne Spencer

Jan Cohn, *Professor of English and American Studies, Trinity College, Hartford, Connecticut*
Mary Roberts Rinehart

Constance Coiner, *Assistant Professor of English, State University of New York at Binghamton*
Class

Eugenia W. Collier, *Professor, Department of Language and Literature, Coppin State College, Baltimore, Maryland*
Kristin Hunter; Georgia Douglas Johnson

Kay K. Cook, *Department of English, University of Colorado at Boulder*
Beth Henley; Marsha Norman; Megan Terry

Martha E. Cook, *Professor of English, Longwood College, Farmville, Virginia*
Harper Lee

Allene Cooper, *Professor of English, Arizona State University, Tempe*
Maria Susanna Cummins; Anne Home Livingston; Sarah Wentworth Morton

Angelo Costanzo, *Professor of English, Shippensburg University of Pennsylvania*
African-American Writing: Literary Criticism

Nancy F. Cott, *Stanley Woodward Professor of History and American Studies, Yale University, New Haven, Connecticut*
Mary R. Beard

Susan M. Coultrap-McQuin, *Professor of Women's Studies and Humanities, University of Minnesota, Duluth*
Pseudonyms; Publishing Business

Pattie Cowell, *Professor and Chair, Department of English, Colorado State University, Fort Collins*
Ann Eliza Bleecker

Marilyn B. Craig, *Assistant Professor of English, Southern University, Baton Rouge, Louisiana*
Pinkie Gordon Lane

Julie Crawford, *Philadelphia, Pennsylvania*
Andrea Dworkin

Margaret Cruikshank, *Professor, English Studies Department and Gay Studies Department, City College, San Francisco, California*
Lesbian Writing: Nonfiction; Lesbian Writing: Overview

Paul Crumbley, *Assistant Professor of English, Niagara University, New York*
Emily Dickinson

Laurie Crumpacker, *Professor of History; Director, Master of Arts Program in Liberal Studies, Simmons College, Boston, Massachusetts*
Elizabeth Cady Stanton

Kate Cummings, *Associate Professor of English, University of Washington, Seattle*
Bisexuality; Heterosexuality; Lesbianism; Sexualities

Kirk Curnutt, *Assistant Professor of American Literature, Troy State University, Montgomery, Alabama*
Short-Story Cycles

Karen A. Dandurand, *Associate Professor of English, Pennsylvania State University at Indiana*
Susan Hale; Separate Spheres

Arnold E. Davidson, *Research Professor of Canadian Studies, Duke University, Durham, North Carolina*
Woman Chief

Cathy N. Davidson, *Professor of English, Duke University, Durham, North Carolina*
Jane Addams; Amazon; Androgyny; Bookstores; Canon Formation; Betty Friedan; Goddess; Hermaphrodite; Immigrant Writing; Letters; Marriage Laws; Menopause; Menstruation; Kate Millett; Novel, Beginnings of the; Romantic Love; Sentimental Novel; Sexual Harassment; Silences; Jane Smiley; Spirituality; Wendy Wasserstein; Whiteness

Cynthia J. Davis, *Department of English, University of South Carolina, Columbia*
Laurie Anderson; Gloria Anzaldúa; Birth Control; Carrie Catt; Civil War; Conservatism; Identity Politics; Cherríe Moraga; Pornography; Psychoanalysis and Women: Early Dissent; Psychoanalysis and Women: Object Relations Theory; Woman-Identified Woman

James Davis-Rosenthal, *Curriculum Specialist and Lecturer, University of Colorado, Boulder*
Rita Mae Brown; Angela Davis

Deborah De Rosa, *Department of English, University of North Carolina at Chapel Hill*
Womanism

Alice A. Deck, *Associate Professor of English and Afro-American Studies, University of Illinois, Urbana*
Pan-Africanism

Celeste Fraser Delgado, *Assistant Professor of English, Pennsylvania State University, University Park*
Family; Housekeeping; Reproduction

Kathryn Zabelle Derounian-Stodola, *Professor of English, University of Arkansas at Little Rock*
Jarena Lee; Sally Wister

Elin Diamond, *Professor of English, Rutgers University, New Brunswick, New Jersey*
Drama

Margaret Dickie, *Helen S. Lanier Distinguished Professor of English, University of Georgia, Athens*
Poetry: Long Poem

Robert DiGiulio, *Assistant Professor of Education, Johnson State College, Vermont*
Widowhood

Jill Dolan, *Chair, Department of Theatre and Drama, University of Wisconsin at Madison*
Lesbian Writing: Drama

Jane Donawerth, *Associate Professor of English; Affiliate Faculty of Women's Studies, University of Maryland, College Park*
Science Fiction

Reade W. Dornan, *Professor of English, University of Michigan at Flint*
Playwrights: 1975 to Present

Cathy Downs, *Department of English, University of North Carolina at Chapel Hill*
Laura Z. Hobson

Jennifer B. Doyle, *Department of Literature, Duke University, Durham, North Carolina*
Queer Theory

Mylène Dressler, *Vaughan Graduate Fellow, Rice University, Houston, Texas*
Harriet Monroe; Lucretia Mott

Julia Dryer, *Professor of English, University of Toronto, Ontario, Canada*
Rosellen Brown

Wendy M. DuBow, *Chapel Hill, North Carolina*
Anaïs Nin; Tess Slesinger

Ann duCille, *Chair, Center for Afro-American Studies, Wesleyan University, Middletown, Connecticut*
African-American Writing: Overview

Carolyn M. Dunn, *Lecturer, Native American Studies, Humboldt State University, Arcata, California*
Native American Writing: Song and Poetry

Connie Eble, *Professor of English, University of North Carolina at Chapel Hill*
Louise Pound

Belinda Edmondson, *Assistant Professor, Rutgers University, Newark, New Jersey*
Caribbean-American Writing

Leigh H. Edwards, *Department of English, University of Pennsylvania, Philadelphia*
Olga Broumas; Aurora Levine Morales; Milcha Sanchez-Scott; May Swenson

Marilyn Elkins, *Assistant Professor of English, California State University, Los Angeles*
Kay Boyle; Fashion; Elizabeth Spencer

Marcus Embry, *Department of Literature, Duke University, Durham, North Carolina*
Josefina Niggli

Sabine Engel, *Department of English, Duke University, Durham, North Carolina*
Violence

John Ernest, *Assistant Professor of English, University of New Hampshire, Durham*
Underground Railroad

Mark W. Estrin, *Professor of English, Rhode Island College, Providence*
Lillian Hellman; Musicals

John Evelev, *Department of English, Duke University, Durham, North Carolina*
Rachel Crothers

Elisa Linda Facio, *Assistant Professor of Sociology and Chicana Feminist Studies, University of Colorado at Boulder*
Chicana Rights Movements

Julia S. Falk, *Professor of Linguistics, Michigan State University, East Lansing*
Linguists

Susan Faludi, *Los Angeles, California*
Backlash

Cecilia Konchar Farr, *Assistant Professor of English, Brigham Young University, Provo, Utah*
E. M. Broner

Elizabeth Faue, *Associate Professor of Urban, Labor, and Metropolitan Affairs, Wayne State University, Detroit, Michigan*
Marxist-Feminism

Kathy A. Fedorko, *Professor of English, Middlesex County College, Edison, New Jersey*
Janet Flanner

SallyAnn H. Ferguson, *Associate Professor of English, University of North Carolina at Greensboro*
Dorothy West; Sarah Elizabeth Wright

Thomas J. Ferraro, *Assistant Professor of English, Duke University, Durham, North Carolina*
Catholic Writers

Judith Fetterley, *Professor of English and Women's Studies, State University of New York at Albany*
Alice Cary

Anne Marsh Fields, *Reference Librarian, Columbus State Community College, Ohio*
Nicholasa Mohr

Lisa M. Fine, *Associate Professor of History, Michigan State University, East Lansing*
Women's Movement

Shelley Fisher Fishkin, *Professor of American Studies, University of Texas, Austin*
Reportage

Jane Flax, *Professor of Political Science, Howard University, Washington, D.C.*
Subjectivity

Blythe Forcey, *Lecturer, American Literature, North Carolina State University, Raleigh*
Domestic Fiction; Domestic Ideology; Epistolary Novel; Motherhood; E.D.E.N. Southworth

Rhonda Denise Frederick, *Department of English, University of Pennsylvania, Philadelphia*
Ethnic Consciousness Movement

Nancy Fredricks, *Assistant Professor of Humanities, University of Colorado at Boulder*
Etiquette Books and Columns

Jan Freeman, *Taos, New Mexico*
Jane Bowles; Muriel Rukeyser; Ruth Stone

Traci Freeman, *Department of English, University of Pennsylvania, Philadelphia*
Carolyn Forche; Gloria Steinem

Donnalee Frega, *Assistant Professor of English, University of North Carolina at Wilmington*
Eating Disorders

Ellen G. Friedman, *Professor of English; Director, Women's Studies, Trenton State College, New Jersey*
War Novel

Marilyn Frye, *Professor of Philosophy, Michigan State University, East Lansing*
Separatism

Sarah B. Fryer, *Director, Student Affairs and Advising, College of Arts and Letters, Michigan State University, East Lansing*
Zelda Fitzgerald

Judith E. Funston, *Associate Professor of American Literature, State University of New York College at Potsdam*
Travel Writing

Lilian R. Furst, *Marcel Bataillon Professor of Comparative Literature, University of North Carolina at Chapel Hill*
Realism

Joanne V. Gabbin, *Professor of English, James Madison University, Harrisonburg, Virginia*
Nikki Giovanni; Sonia Sanchez

Joan Gabriele, *Department of English, University of Colorado at Boulder*
June Arnold; Beth Brant

Jane Gallop, *Distinguished Professor of English and Comparative Literature, University of Wisconsin at Madison*
Psychoanalysis and Women: Jacques Lacan

Patricia M. Gantt, *Fairview, North Carolina*
Federal Writers Project; Margaret Mitchell

Judith Kegan Gardiner, *Professor of English and Women's Studies, University of Illinois at Chicago*
Gynocriticism

Mary A. Gardner, *Professor Emerita of Journalism, Michigan State University, East Lansing*
Journalists

Joanna B. Gillespie, *Adjunct Associate Professor, Bangor Theological Seminary, Hanover, New Hampshire*
Judith Sargent Murray; Martha Laurens Ramsay

Sander L. Gilman, *Goldwin Smith Professor of Human Studies, Cornell University, Ithaca, New York*
Stereotypes

Thomas Gladsky, *Professor of American Literature, Central Missouri State University, Warrensburg*
Polish-American Writing

Mimi Gladstein, *Professor of English and American Literature, University of Texas at El Paso*
Ayn Rand

David Golumbia, *Department of English Language and Literature, University of Pennsylvania, Philadelphia*
Philosophers

Charlotte Goodman, *Professor of English, Skidmore College, Saratoga Springs, New York*
Edith Summers Kelley; Jean Stafford

Suzanne Gossett, *Professor of English, Loyola University, Chicago, Illinois*
Sarah Josepha Hale

Amy Gottfried, *Department of American Literature, Tufts University, Medford, Massachusetts*
Rituals and Ceremonies

Sandra Y. Govan, *Professor of English, University of North Carolina at Charlotte*
Gwendolyn B. Bennett; Octavia Butler

Janet Gray, *Lecturer in Literature, Rutgers University, New Brunswick, New Jersey*
Grace Greenwood

Sally Greene, *Adjunct Professor of Legal Writing, Van Hecke-Wettach School of Law; Instructor of English, University of North Carolina at Chapel Hill*
Susan Sontag

Barbara Grier, *Tallahassee, Florida*
Lesbian Publishing Outlets

Beverly Guy-Sheftall, *Anna Julia Cooper Professor of Women's Studies; Director, Women's Research and Resource Center, Spelman College, Atlanta, Georgia*
African-American Publishing Outlets; African-American Reading Network

Kathy D. Hadley, *Adjunct Visiting Assistant Professor of English, Albion College, Michigan*
Betty MacDonald

K. Graehme Hall, *Dayton, Ohio*
Confessional Nonfiction

Thelma Hall, *Professor of English, Chair, Division of Humanities, Shorter College, Rome, Georgia*
Elizabeth Hardwick

Christine Hanks, *Professor of English, Columbia College, South Carolina*
Katherine Anne Porter

Barbara Harlow, *Associate Professor of Humanities, University of Texas at Austin*
Gayatri Spivak

Donna Akiba Sullivan Harper, *Assistant Professor of English, Spelman College, Atlanta, Georgia*
Black English

Mary Turner Harper, *Associate Professor Emerita of Literature, University of North Carolina at Charlotte*
Mildred Delois Taylor; Joyce Carol Thomas

Sharon M. Harris, *Associate Professor; Graduate Chair of English, University of Nebraska at Lincoln*
Elizabeth Hanson

Susan K. Harris, *Professor of English, Pennsylvania State University, University Park*
Augusta Jane Evans

Trudier Harris, *Augustus Baldwin Longstreet Professor of American Literature, Emory University, Atlanta, Georgia*
Ba-ad Woman; Conjure Woman; Toni Morrison; Passing; Sharecropping; Taboos, Literary; Alice Walker; Ida B. Wells-Barnett

Beth J. Harrison, *Instructor of English, College of Charleston, South Carolina*
Marriage

Heather A. Hathaway, *Assistant Professor of English and American Studies, Trinity College, Hartford, Connecticut*
Caroline W. H. Dall

Mary Hawkesworth, *Professor of Political Science, University of Louisville, Kentucky*
Liberal Feminism

Terri S. Hayes, *Department of English, University of North Carolina at Chapel Hill*
Zitkala-Ša (Gertrude Simmons Bonnin)

Elaine Hedges, *Professor of English; Director, Women's Studies, Towson State University, Baltimore, Maryland*
Rebecca Harding Davis; Charlotte Perkins Gilman

Kathryn Hellerstein, *Lecturer in Yiddish Literature and Language, Department of Germanic Languages, University of Pennsylvania, Philadelphia*
Jewish-American Writing: Poetry

Karla A. Henderson, *Professor of Leisure Studies and Recreation Administration, University of North Carolina at Chapel Hill*
Leisure Studies

Louise Levitas Henriksen, *Department of English, Wesleyan University, Middletown, Connecticut*
Anzia Yezierska

Diane Price Herndl, *Assistant Professor of English, New Mexico State University, Las Cruces*
Invalidism

Anne Herrmann, *Associate Professor of English and Women's Studies, University of Michigan, Ann Arbor*
Cross-Dressing; Transsexuality

Kristin Herzog, *Durham, North Carolina*
Native American Oral Traditions

Marina Heung, *Assistant Professor of English, Baruch College, City University of New York*
Amy Tan

Marianne Hirsch, *Professor, Department of French and Comparative Literature, Dartmouth College, Hanover, New Hampshire*
Mothers and Daughters

Sylvia D. Hoffert, *Associate Professor of History, Southwest Missouri State University, Springfield*
Mothers Manuals

Hilary Holladay, *Assistant Professor of American Literature, University of Massachusetts at Lowell*
Rita Dove; Ann Petry

Jeanne Holland, *Assistant Professor of English, University of Wyoming, Laramie*
Jenny Fenno; Susannah Willard Johnson

Donna Hollenberg, *Assistant Professor of English, University of Connecticut, Storrs*
Edna St. Vincent Millay

Karla F. C. Holloway, *Professor of English, Duke University, Durham, North Carolina*
Zora Neale Hurston

Martha Stoddard Holmes, *Department of English, University of Colorado, Boulder*
Ann Beattie; Carolyn Heilbrun

Sally C. Hoople, *Associate Professor of Humanities and Communications, Maine Maritime Academy, Castine*
Tabitha Tenney; S.S.B.K. Wood

Helen R. Houston, *Professor of English, Tennessee State University, Nashville*
Lucille Clifton; Marita Golden

Ted Hovet, Jr., *Department of English, Duke University, Durham, North Carolina*
Zoë Akins; Suffragist Plays

Ruth Yu Hsiao, *Lecturer in American and Asian-American Literature, Tufts University, Medford, Massachusetts*
Mary Antin; Awiakta

Dolan Hubbard, *Assistant Professor of English, University of Tennessee, Knoxville*
Charlotte Forten Grimké; Gloria Naylor

Angela E. Hubler, *Assistant Professor of English and Women's Studies, Kansas State University, Manhattan*
Sexism

Joonok Huh, *Associate Professor of English and Women's Studies, University of Northern Colorado, Greeley*
Asian-American Writing: Nonfiction

Patricia Hunt, *Affiliated Scholar, Beatrice M. Bain Research Group, University of California at Berkeley*
Bilingualism

Claudia Ingram, *Lecturer, Writing Program, University of California at Los Angeles*
Mixed Ancestry, Writers of

Caren Irr, *Assistant Professor of English, Pennsylvania State University, University Park*
Edith Abbott

Lorna Irvine, *Professor of English, George Mason University, Fairfax, Virginia*
Colonialism

Nancy Isenberg, *Professor of History, University of Northern Iowa, Cedar Falls*
Political Organizations: Nineteenth-century Organizations

Daniel Itzkovitz, *Department of Literature, Duke University, Durham, North Carolina*
Jewish-American Writing: Nonfiction

Annette Jaimes, *Instructor/Lecturer, American Indian Studies at The Center for Studies of Ethnicity and Race in America, University of Colorado at Boulder*
American Indian Rights Movement

Kelly Jarrett, *Department of Religion, Duke University, Durham, North Carolina*
Incest

La Vinia DeLois Jennings, *Assistant Professor of American Literature, University of Tennessee at Knoxville*
Alice Childress

Alisa Johnson, *African and Afro-American Studies Program, University of North Carolina at Chapel Hill*
Marita Bonner Occomy

Ronna C. Johnson, *Director, Women's Studies; Lecturer in English, Tufts University, Medford, Massachusetts*
Cynthia Ozick

Diane Brown Jones, *Lecturer, Department of English, North Carolina State University at Raleigh*
Elizabeth Blackwell

Jill C. Jones, *Professor of English, Tufts University, Medford, Massachusetts*
Harriet Spofford

Robin Jones, *Department of Multi-Cultural Literature, University of Colorado at Boulder*
Sandra Cisneros; Elaine Goodale Eastman; E. Pauline Johnson

Suzanne W. Jones, *Associate Professor of English; Coordinator of Women's Studies, University of Richmond, Virginia*
Alice Adams

Nancy Carol Joyner, *Professor of English, Western Carolina University, Cullowhee, North Carolina*
Olive Tilford (Fielding Burke) Dargan

Jane Kamensky, *Assistant Professor of American History, Brandeis University, Waltham, Massachusetts*
Colonial Court Papers

Leela Kapai, *Associate Professor of English Studies, University of the District of Columbia*
Henrietta Cordelia Ray

Eleanor Kaufman, *Department of Literature, Duke University, Durham, North Carolina*
Tama Janowitz

Gloria Kaufman, *Professor Emerita of English, Indiana University, South Bend*
Womb Envy

Samira Kawash, *Assistant Professor of English, Rutgers University, New Brunswick, New Jersey*
Pat Califia; Ethnicity and Writing; European Immigrant Writing; Lesbian Pulp Fiction

David Kellogg, *Senior Fellow, Department of English, University of North Carolina at Chapel Hill*
Babette Deutsch

Colleen Kennedy, *Assistant Professor of English, College of William and Mary, Williamsburg, Virginia*
Politics and Writing

Deborah Kent, *Chicago, Illinois*
Disabled Women's Writing

Katie Kent, *Department of English, Duke University, Durham, North Carolina*
Ann Bannon; Coming Out; Girl Scouts; Heterosexism; Homophobia; Lesbian Writing: Fiction; Male-Identified Woman

Carol Farley Kessler, *Professor of English, American Studies Department, Women's Studies Department, Pennsylvania State University, Delaware County, Media*
Matriarchy; Elizabeth Stuart Phelps; Elizabeth Stuart (Ward) Phelps

Cheryl L. Keyes, *Professor of Ethnomusicology and Systematic Musicology, University of California at Los Angeles*
Rap

Lee Cullen Khanna, *Professor of English, Montclair State College, New Jersey*
Utopias

Ann Kibbey, *Professor of English, University of Colorado at Boulder*
Anne Hutchinson; Identity; Prejudice; Witchcraft

Elaine H. Kim, *Professor of Asian-American Studies, University of California at Berkeley*
Theresa Hak Kyung Cha; Ronyoung Kim; Korean-American Writing

Michael S. Kimmel, *Associate Professor of Sociology, State University of New York at Stony Brook*
Men and Feminism

Mary Klages, *Assistant Professor of English, University of Colorado at Boulder*
Censorship

Abby Wettan Kleinbaum, *Professor, Department of Social Sciences, Manhattan Community College, New York*
Woman Warrior

Katherine Kleitz, *Stow, Massachusetts*
Susan B. Anthony

Wendy K. Kolmar, *Department of Women's Studies, Drew University, Madison, New Jersey*
Ghost Stories

Susan Koppelman, *St. Louis, Missouri*
Anthologies; Fannie Hurst; Short Story; Alix Kates Shulman; Martha Wolfenstein

Virginia M. Kouidis, *Associate Professor of English, Auburn University, Alabama*
Patriarchy

Harriet Davis Kram, *Professor of History, Queens College, Flushing, New York*
Political Organizations: 1960 to the Present

Cheris Kramarae, *Professor of Speech Communication, Sociology, and Women's Studies, University of Illinois at Urbana-Champaign*
Language, Women's: Women's Language

S. Lillian Kremer, *Assistant Professor of English, Kansas State University, Manhattan*
Holocaust Writing

Randi Gray Kristensen, *Department of English, University of Louisiana, Baton Rouge*
African-American Writing: Nonfiction

Arnold Krupat, *Professor of Literature, Sarah Lawrence College, Bronxville, New York*
Orality

Jane Kuenz, *Department of English, Duke University, Durham, North Carolina*
Imagist Movement

Peter Kurth, *New York, New York*
Dorothy Thompson

Amy Schrager Lang, *Associate Professor of American Studies, Emory University, Atlanta, Georgia*
Alice Morse Earle

Esther F. Lanigan, *Associate Professor of English, College of William and Mary, Williamsburg, Virginia*
Mary Austin

Phil Lapsansky, *Research Librarian, The Library Company of Philadelphia, Pennsylvania*
Leonora Sansay

Joan Larkin, *Shelburne Falls, Massachusetts*
Lesbian Writing: Poetry

Denise M. Larrabee, *Reference Librarian, The Library Company of Philadelphia, Pennsylvania*
Anne Hampton Brewster

Charles R. Larson, *Professor of Literature, American University, Washington, D.C.*
Nella Larsen

Kelli A. Larson, *Assistant Professor of English, University of St. Thomas, St. Paul, Minnesota*
Sylvia Beach

Estella Lauter, *Frankenthal Professor of Humanities, Department of Humanistic Studies, University of Wisconsin at Green Bay*
Diane Wakoski

Mary Lawlor, *Assistant Professor of English, Muhlenberg College, Allentown, Pennsylvania*
Exoticization

Valerie Lee, *Associate Professor of English and Women's Studies, Ohio State University, Columbus*
Folklore

George S. Lensing, *Professor of English, University of North Carolina at Chapel Hill*
Elizabeth Bishop

Russell C. Leong, *Editor, Amerasia Journal, Asian-American Studies Center, University of California at Los Angeles*
Janice Mirikitani

Neal A. Lester, *Assistant Professor of English, University of Alabama, Tuscaloosa*
Ntozake Shange

Shirley A. R. Lewis, *Department of English, Spelman College, Atlanta, Georgia*
Black English

Diane Lichtenstein, *Associate Professor of English, Beloit College, Wisconsin*
Antisemitism

Shirley Geok-lin Lim, *Professor of English and Women's Studies, University of California at Santa Barbara*
Asian-American Writing: Poetry

Amy Ling, *Associate Professor of English; Director, Asian-American Studies Program, University of Wisconsin at Madison*
Eileen Chang; Chinese-American Writing; Sook Nyul Choi; Maxine Hong Kingston; Wendy Law-Yone; Hazel Ai Chun Lin; Tai-Yi Lin; Han Suyin; Onoto (Winnifred Eaton) Watanna; Jade Snow Wong

Tess Lloyd, *Department of English, University of North Carolina at Chapel Hill*
Alice Brown

Beverly Whitaker Long, *Department of Speech Communication, University of North Carolina at Chapel Hill*
Speech Communication Professionals

Tricia Lootens, *Assistant Professor of English, University of Georgia, Athens*
Shirley Jackson

Tiffany Ana López, *Department of English and Women's Studies, University of California at Santa Barbara*
Latina Writing: Drama

Carol Schaechterle Loranger, *Assistant Professor of English, Wright State University, Dayton, Ohio*
Annie Dillard; Ursula Le Guin

Lisa Lowe, *Associate Professor of Comparative Literature, University of California at San Diego*
Asian-American Writing: Overview; Multiculturalism; Orientalism

Margaret A. Lukens, *Assistant Professor of American Literature, University of Maine at Orono*
Paula Gunn Allen; Ethnopoetics; Diane Glancy; Estela Portillo-Trambley; Vickie L. Sears; Leslie Marmon Silko; Anna Lee Walters; Sarah Winnemucca

Juanita Luna Lawhn, *Professor of English, San Antonio College, Texas*
Judith Ortiz Cofer

Jean Marie Lutes, *Department of English, University of Wisconsin, Madison*
Beauty

Juliet Flower MacCannell, *Professor; Director, Comparative Literature, University of California at Irvine*
Psychoanalysis and Women: Sigmund Freud

Ruth K. MacDonald, *Professor of English; Associate Dean of Academic Affairs, Bay Path College, Longmeadow, Massachusetts*
Louisa May Alcott

Lisa Watt MacFarlane, *Associate Professor of English, University of New Hampshire, Durham*
Harriet Beecher Stowe

Billie Maciunas, *Department of Portuguese and Romance Languages, University of North Carolina at Chapel Hill*
Meridel Le Sueur

Laurie F. Maffly-Kipp, *Assistant Professor of Religious Studies, University of North Carolina at Chapel Hill*
Religion: 1700 to the Present

Carol Maier, *Professor of Spanish, Department of Modern and Classical Language Studies, Kent State University, Ohio*
Translators

Michael Maiwald, *Department of English, Duke University, Durham, North Carolina*
Laura Jean Libbey

Lois A. Marchino, *Associate Professor of English, University of Texas at El Paso*
Western Women's Writing

Reginald Martin, *Professor of English and Special Assistant to the President, Memphis State University, Tennessee*
Black Aesthetic; Black Arts Movement

Robert A. Martin, *Professor of American Literature, Michigan State University, East Lansing*
Martha Gellhorn

Julian Mason, *Professor of English, Emeritus, University of North Carolina at Charlotte*
Phillis Wheatley

Judith Mayne, *Professor of French and Women's Studies, Ohio State University, Columbus*
Feminist Film Theory

Charlotte S. McClure, *Associate Professor of English, Emerita, Georgia State University, Atlanta*
Gertrude Atherton

Patrice McDermott, *Assistant Professor of American Studies, University of Maryland, Baltimore County, Catonsville*
Journals, Academic

Sheila Smith McKoy, *Assistant Professor of English, Vanderbilt University, Nashville, Tennessee*
Civil Rights Movement; Alice Ruth Moore Dunbar-Nelson

Jacquelyn Y. McLendon, *Associate Professor of English, College of William and Mary, Williamsburg, Virginia*
Protest Writing

Sheryl L. Meyering, *Associate Professor of English, Southern Illinois University, Edwardsville*
Caroline Chesebrough; Louise Glück; Aimee Semple McPherson

Helena Michie, *Professor of English, Rice University, Houston, Texas*
Body and Health

Bruce Mills, *Assistant Professor of American Literature, Kalamazoo College, Michigan*
Lydia Maria Child

Elizabeth McGeachy Mills, *Professor of English, Davidson College, North Carolina*
Taylor Caldwell

Toril Moi, *Professor of Literature and Romance Studies, Duke University, Durham, North Carolina*
Simone de Beauvoir

E. Jennifer Monaghan, *Professor, Department of Educational Services, Brooklyn College, City University of New York*
Textbooks by and for Women

Patricia L. Morse, *Professor, Department of American Thought and Language, Michigan State University, East Lansing*
Marilyn French; Marietta Holley; Minimalism

Gail L. Mortimer, *Professor of English, University of Texas at El Paso*
Eudora Welty

Rosalind Urbach Moss, *Twentieth-century Historian and Curator of Photographs, The Valentine Museum, Richmond, Virginia*
Spinsterhood

Carla J. Mulford, *Professor of English, Pennsylvania State University, University Park*
Early National Writing; Annis Boudinot Stockton

Molly H. Mullin, *Visiting Assistant Professor of Cultural Anthropology, Duke University, Durham, North Carolina*
Irish-American Writing; Native American Writing: Overview

José Esteban Muñoz, *Assistant Professor of Performance Studies, New York University*
Chicana Writing: Fiction

Joseph Murphy, *Department of English, New York University*
Protestantism

Lisa Myers, *Lecturer, Department of English, University of Pennsylvania, Philadelphia*
Poetry: Love Poetry

Gwen L. Nagel, *Athens, Georgia*
Annie Fields; Zona Gale

William R. Nash, *Department of English, University of North Carolina at Chapel Hill*
Andrea Lee

Charlotte Nekola, *Assistant Professor of English, William Paterson College, Tenafly, New Jersey*
Activism

Dana D. Nelson, *Associate Professor of English, Louisiana State University, Baton Rouge*
Diaries and Journals; Frances Anne Kemble; Sarah Kemble Knight; Rebecca Rush

Adele S. Newson, *Associate Professor of English, University of Miami, Florida*
Abolition; African-American Oral Tradition

Greta Ai-Yu Niu, *Department of English, Duke University, Durham, North Carolina*
Self-Help Books

Perry Nodelman, *Professor of English, University of Winnipeg, Manitoba, Canada*
Children's Literature: 1900 to the Present

Jeanne R. Nostrandt, *Professor of English, James Madison University, Harrisonburg, Virginia*
Hortense Calisher

Lisa Maria Burgess Noudehou, *Department of English, University of Pennsylvania, Philadelphia*
Latina Writing: Fiction and Nonfiction

Karen Oakes, *The University of Hull, United Kingdom*
Rose Terry Cooke

Jean F. O'Barr, *Director, Women's Studies, Duke University, Durham, North Carolina*
Women's Studies Programs

Sharon O'Brien, *Professor of English, Dickinson College, Carlisle, Pennsylvania*
Willa Cather

Margaret Anne O'Connor, *Associate Professor of English and American Studies, University of North Carolina at Chapel Hill*
Flannery O'Connor

Priscilla D. Older, *Social Sciences Librarian and Head of Public Services, Mansfield University Library, Pennsylvania*
Libraries

Margarite Fernandez Olmos, *Professor of Spanish, Brooklyn College, City University of New York*
Puerto Rican Writing, U.S.

Taimi Olsen, *Department of English, University of North Carolina at Chapel Hill*
Pearl Buck

Gregory Orfalea, *Editor, Resolution Trust Corporation, Washington, D.C.*
Arab-American Writing

Kossia Orloff, *Chapel Hill, North Carolina*
New York Writers; Performance Art

Elaine Orr, *Department of English, North Carolina State University, Raleigh*
Motherhood

Nell Irvin Painter, *Edwards Professor of American History, Princeton University, New Jersey*
Sojourner Truth

Phyllis Palmer, *Associate Professor of American Studies and Women's Studies, George Washington University, Washington, D.C.*
Black Feminism

Jennifer Parchesky, *Department of English, Duke University, Durham, North Carolina*
Marjorie Kinnan Rawlings

James W. Parins, *Professor of English, University of Arkansas at Little Rock*
Jane Johnson Schoolcraft

Patricia Parker, *Professor of English, Salem State College, Massachusetts*
Susanna Rowson

Raymond R. Patterson, *Professor of English, Emeritus, City College of New York*
Helene Johnson

Linda Peckham, *Berkeley, California*
Trinh T. Minh-ha

Scott Peeples, *Department of English, Louisiana State University, Baton Rouge*
Women's Clubs

Jane C. Penner, *Department of English, University of Pennsylvania, Philadelphia*
Proletarian Writing

Kathy A. Perkins, *Professor of Theatre, University of Illinois, Urbana*
Shirley Graham (Du Bois)

Linda M. Perkins, *Associate Professor of Educational Foundations, Hunter College, City University of New York*
Anna Julia Cooper; Fanny Marion Jackson Coppin

Priscilla A. Perkins, *Department of English, Rutgers University, New Brunswick, New Jersey*
Experimental Writing

Alice Hall Petry, *Professor and Head, Department of English, Rhode Island School of Design, Providence*
Dorothy Day

Joyce Pettis, *Associate Professor of English, North Carolina State University, Raleigh*
Paule Marshall

William M. Phillips, *Department of English, University of North Carolina at Chapel Hill*
Caroline Gordon

Lynn Pifer, *Assistant Professor of English, Mansfield University, Pennsylvania*
Middle Passage

Diana Pingatore, *Associate Professor of English, Lake Superior State University, Sault Ste. Marie, Michigan*
Diane DiPrima; Edna Ferber

Della Pollock, *Professor, Department of Speech Communication, University of North Carolina at Chapel Hill*
Performativity

Mary Poovey, *Professor of English, The Johns Hopkins University, Baltimore, Maryland*
Poststructuralism

Deborah Pope, *Associate Professor of English, Duke University, Durham, North Carolina*
Adrienne Rich

Constance J. Post, *Associate Professor of English, Iowa State University, Ames*
Catherine Drinker Bowen; Hannah Mather Crocker

Sheila Post-Lauria, *Assistant Professor of American Literature, University of Massachusetts, Boston*
Women's Magazines

Michelle Powe, *San Antonio, Texas*
Spiritualism

Annis Pratt, *Birmingham, Michigan*
Bildungsroman and Küntslerroman; Myths: Overview

Peggy Whitman Prenshaw, *Fred C. Frey Professor of English, Louisiana State University, Baton Rouge*
Fathers

Alan Price, *Associate Professor of English, Pennsylvania State University, Hazleton*
Dorothy Canfield Fisher

Marjorie Pryse, *Professor of Women's Studies, State University of New York College at Plattsburgh*
Mary Wilkins Freeman; Mary Murfree

Bernetta Quinn, O.S.F., *Rochester, Minnesota*
Poetry: Religious Poetry

Paula Rabinowitz, *Associate Professor of English and American Studies, University of Minnesota, Minneapolis*
Anarchism; Communism

Lisa Radinovsky, *Jacob K. Javitz Fellow, Department of English, Duke University, Durham, North Carolina*
Lorna Dee Cervantes

Brian Abel Ragen, *Associate Professor of English, Southern Illinois University at Edwardsville*
Mary Gordon

Brian Railsback, *Assistant Professor of American Literature; Director, Professional Writing, Western Carolina University, Cullowhee, North Carolina*
Native American Publishing Outlets

Diana C. Reep, *Professor of English, University of Akron, Ohio*
Margaret Deland

Jeanne Campbell Reesman, *Associate Professor of English, University of Texas at San Antonio*
Spiritualism

Ann Reuman, *Professor of English, Tufts University, Medford, Massachusetts*
Cross-Racial Relations

Carol Reuss, *Professor of Journalism and Mass Communication, University of North Carolina at Chapel Hill*
Dorothy Dix

Kathryn L. Rios, *Assistant Professor of English, University of Colorado, Boulder*
Chicana Writing: Overview

Evelyn M. Rivera, *Professor of Zoology, Michigan State University, East Lansing*
Science Writing

Eliana Rivero, *Professor of Spanish-American Literature, University of Arizona, Tucson*
Cuban-American Writing

Susan L. Roberson, *Instructor of English, Auburn University, Alabama*
Marriage Manuals

Nancy L. Roberts, *Associate Professor of Journalism and Mass Communication, University of Minnesota, Twin Cities, Minneapolis*
Newspaper Columns

Lawrence R. Rodgers, *Assistant Professor of English, Kansas State University, Manhattan*
Migration

Valerie Rohy, *Department of American Literature, Tufts University, Medford, Massachusetts*
Louise Bogan

Judith Roof, *Associate Professor of English, University of Delaware, Newark*
Lesbian Literary Theory

Rosamond Rosenmeier, *Watertown, Massachusetts*
Anne Bradstreet; Colonial Era Writing

Laura H. Roskos, *Modern Studies Program, University of Wisconsin at Milwaukee*
Vocational Advice Literature

Cheri Louise Ross, *Assistant Professor of English, Pennsylvania State University, Mont Alto*
True Woman; The Woman Question

Lois Rudnick, *Professor of English; Director, American Studies Program, University of Massachusetts, Boston*
Crystal Eastman; Mable Dodge Luhan; New Woman

Kathy Rudy, *Research Fellow, Center for the Study of American Religion, Princeton University, New Jersey*
Abortion

A. LaVonne Brown Ruoff, *Professor of English, University of Illinois at Chicago*
Sophia Alice Callahan; Myths: Native American Mythological Figures

Leila J. Rupp, *Professor of History, Ohio State University, Columbus*
Lesbian Feminism

John Rury, *Associate Professor, School for New Learning, DePaul University, Chicago, Illinois*
Education

Ona Russell, *Department of English, University of California at San Diego*
Consciousness-Raising

Roshni Rustomji-Kerns, *Professor of India Studies, Emeritus, Hutchins School of Liberal Studies, Sonoma State University, Rohnert Park, California*
Meena Alexander; Bharati Mukherjee; Tahira Naqvi; Santha Rama Rau; Usha Saksena-Nilsson; Bapsi Sidhwa; South Asian-American Women Writing; Sara Suleri

Barbara T. Ryan, *Post-Doctoral Fellow, Department of English, University of Michigan, Ann Arbor*
Elizabeth Oakes Smith

Linda Ann Saladin, *Associate Professor of English; Director, Certificate Program in Critical Theory, Florida State University, Tallahassee*
Medical Practice and Women

Dorothy C. Salem, *Professor of History, Cuyahoga Community College, Cleveland, Ohio; Adjunct Faculty, Cleveland State University*
Temperance Movement

Rosaura Sanchez, *Associate Professor of Latin American and Chicano Literature, University of California at San Diego*
Chicana Writing: Nonfiction

Leslie Catherine Sanders, *Associate Professor of Humanities and English, Atkinson College, York University, Toronto, Ontario, Canada*
African-American Writing: Drama

Chéla Sandoval, *Assistant Professor of Chicano Studies and English, University of California at Santa Barbara*
Third World Feminism, U.S.

Gayle K. Fujita Sato, *Associate Professor of English, Deio University, Yokohama, Japan*
Japanese-American Writing; Clara Mitsuko Jelsma; Yoko Kawashima Watkins; Hisaye Yamamoto

Timothy H. Scherman, *Assistant Professor of English, Northeastern Illinois University, Chicago*
Authorship; Lydia Huntley Sigourney

Ellen Schiff, *Professor of French and Comparative Literature, Emerita, Massachusetts State College, North Adams*
Jewish-American Writing: Drama

Pamela Schirmeister, *Assistant Professor of English, New York University*
Assimilation

Mary Lea Schneider, *President; Professor of Religious Studies, Cardinal Stritch College, Milwaukee, Wisconsin*
Theologians

Paul Ryan Schneider, *Department of English, Duke University, Durham, North Carolina*
Catharine Sedgwick; Slave Narratives

Meg Schoerke, *Assistant Professor of English, San Francisco State University, California*
Maxine Kumin; Other Woman, The

Elizabeth Schultz, *Professor of English, University of Kansas, Lawrence*
Ann Allen Shockley; Sherley Anne Williams

Bonnie Kime Scott, *Professor of English, University of Delaware, Newark*
H. D.

Joyce Hope Scott, *Associate Professor of English, Massachusetts Maritime College, Buzzards Bay*
Slavery

Dorothy M. Scura, *Professor of American Literature, University of Tennessee, Knoxville*
Doris Betts; Southern Women's Writing

Robert P. Sedlack, *Professor of English, DePauw University, Greencastle, Indiana*
Naomi Long Madgett

Margot Sempreora, *Somerville, Massachusetts*
Maria Amparo Ruiz de Borton

Judith L. Sensibar, *Department of English, Arizona State University, Tempe*
Women Writing on Men

Adrienne Lanier Seward, *Professor of English, Colorado College, Colorado Springs*
Testifying

Sarah Way Sherman, *Professor of English, University of New Hampshire, Durham*
Sarah Orne Jewett; Myths: Greek and Roman Mythological Figures

David S. Shields, *Professor of English, The Citadel, Charleston, South Carolina*
Elizabeth Graeme Fergusson; Janet Schaw; Anna Young Smith; Lucy Terry

Kayann Short, *Department of English, University of Colorado, Boulder*
Louise Erdrich; Linda Hogan; Postmodern Writing; Presses, Women's; Helena Maria Viramontes

Carol Siegel, *Assistant Professor of English, Washington State University, Pullman*
Homosocial Relationships

Carol J. Singley, *Assistant Professor of English, Rutgers University, New Brunswick, New Jersey*
Sisterhood

Linda Ching Sledge, *Assistant Professor of English, Westchester Community College, Valhalla, New York*
Asian-American Writing: Fiction

Lorna J. Smedman, *Adjunct Lecturer of English, Hunter College, City College of New York*
Susan Howe

Bonnie G. Smith, *Professor of History, Rutgers University, New Brunswick, New Jersey*
Historians

Carolyn H. Smith, *Associate in English; Director, Freshman and Sophomore Writing, University of Florida, Gainesville*
Composition

Erin A. Smith, *Program in Literature, Duke University, Durham, North Carolina*
Pioneer Women

Rebecca Smith, *Associate Professor of English, Barton College, Wilson, North Carolina*
Ellen Gilchrist

Sidonie Smith, *Professor of English, Comparative Literature, and Women's Studies, State University of New York at Binghamton*
Autobiography

Susan Belasco Smith, *Associate Professor of English, California State University, Los Angeles*
Margaret Taylor Goss Burroughs

Geneva Smitherman, *University Distinguished Professor of English; Director, African-American Language and Literacy Program, Michigan State University, East Lansing*
Nonstandard English; Signifying

Mary Ellen Solt, *Professor, Department of Comparative Literature, Indiana University, Bloomington*
Poetry: Concrete Poems

Daphne Spain, *Associate Professor of Urban and Environmental Planning; Associate Dean, School of Architecture, University of Virginia, Charlottesville*
Gendered Spaces

Bes Stark Spangler, *Professor of English and American Literature, Peace College, Raleigh, North Carolina*
Clare Boothe Luce

Rajini Srikanth, *Lecturer of English, Tufts University, Medford, Massachusetts*
Margaret Mead

Jamie Stanesa, *Assistant Professor of English, Iowa State University, Ames*
Julia Ward Howe

Ann Folwell Stanford, *Assistant Professor, School for New Learning, DePaul University, Chicago, Illinois*
Gwendolyn Brooks; Barbara Chase-Riboud

Linda O. Stanford, *Professor of History of Art, Michigan State University, East Lansing*
Art Historians

Helen Winter Stauffer, *Martin Chair Professor of Literature, Emerita, University of Nebraska at Kearney*
Mari Sandoz

Elizabeth Steele, *Toledo, Ohio*
Rachel Carson

Karen F. Stein, *Professor of English and Women's Studies, University of Rhode Island, Kingston*
Names and Naming

Louise L. Stevenson, *Associate Professor of History and American Studies, Franklin and Marshall College, Lancaster, Pennsylvania*
Reading Circles

Katherine Stubbs, *Department of English, Duke University, Durham, North Carolina*
Martha Wadsworth Brewster; Gossip

Deborah Tannen, *University Professor, Department of Linguistics, Georgetown University, Washington, D.C.*
Language, Women's: Communication between the Sexes

Laura E. Tanner, *Assistant Professor of English, Boston College, Chestnut Hill, Massachusetts*
Rape

Michele Lise Tarter, *Department of English, University of Colorado at Boulder*
Prophesyings

Catherine Taylor, *Department of English, Duke University, Durham, North Carolina*
Exploration Narratives; Native American Writing: Drama; Native American Writing: Nonfiction; Helena Wells

David Teal, *Professor of English, North Carolina State University, Raleigh*
Margaret Craven

Mary Thom, *Brooklyn, New York*
Ms. Magazine

Amy M. Thomas, *Assistant Professor of English, Montana State University, Bozeman*
Abigail Adams; Literacy; Readership

Ardel Thomas, *Department of English, University of Colorado, Boulder*
Cheryl Clarke; Pat Parker

Nicole Tonkovich, *Assistant Professor of Literature, University of California at San Diego*
Advice Books; Elizabeth Ellet

Marianna Torgovnick, *Professor of English, Duke University, Durham, North Carolina*
Anthropologists

Cheryl B. Torsney, *Associate Professor of English, West Virginia University, Morgantown*
Constance Fenimore Woolson

Emily Toth, *Professor of English, Louisiana State University, Baton Rouge*
Kate Chopin

Ann Trapasso, *Department of English, University of North Carolina at Chapel Hill*
Audre Lorde

Marlene Tromp, *Professor of English, University of Florida, Gainesville*
Anna Cora Mowatt

Roberta Uno, *Pelham, Massachusetts*
Asian-American Writing: Drama; Velina Hasu Houston; Momoko Iko; Wakako Yamauchi

Susan Updike, *Department of English, University of North Carolina at Chapel Hill*
Emma Goldman

Marie Mitchell Olesen Urbanski, *Professor of American Literature, University of Maine, Orono*
Margaret Fuller

Kathy Scales Vandell, *Visiting Assistant Professor of American Studies, University of Maryland, Baltimore County, Catonsville*
Literary Criticism

David Kirk Vaughan, *Associate Professor of English, Air Force Institute of Technology, Dayton, Ohio*
Anne Morrow Lindbergh

Michael W. Vella, *Associate Professor of English, Indiana University of Pennsylvania*
Hannah Adams

Deborah Viles, *Lecturer, University Writing Program, University of Colorado, Boulder*
Judy Grahn; Susan Griffin; Bobbie Ann Mason; Marge Piercy; May Sarton; Anne Sexton; Anne Tyler

Jill Wacker, *Department of English, University of Pennsylvania, Philadelphia*
Children's Literature: 1650 to 1900; Girlhood; Health Books, Pamphlets, and Reference Guides

Andrea Wagner, *School of the Arts, New York University*
Tina Howe

Wendy Wagner, *Adjunct Instructor, Department of English, Pace University, New York*
Jessie Redmon Fauset; Reconstruction

Linda Wagner-Martin, *Hanes Professor of English and Comparative Literature, University of North Carolina at Chapel Hill*
Biography; Ana Castillo; Michele Cliff; Mari Evans; Flapper; Gibson Girl; Ellen Glasgow; Susan Glaspell; Poetry: To 1850; Local Color Fiction; Modernism; Sylvia Plath; Recipe Books; Regionalism; Gertrude Stein; Suicide; Virginia Woolf

Candace Waid, *Professor of English, Yale University, New Haven, Connecticut*
Edith Wharton

Gayle Wald, *Department of English, Princeton University, New Jersey*
Julia Fields

Ann Walker, *Assistant Professor of English, Rockford College, Illinois*
Carolyn Kizer; Mona Van Duyn; Elinor Wylie

Lisa Walker, *Department of English, Louisiana State University, Baton Rouge*
Deconstruction and Feminism

Nancy Walker, *Professor of English; Director, Women's Studies Program, Vanderbilt University, Nashville, Tennessee*
Humor

Jo-Ann Wallace, *Associate Professor of English, University of Alberta, Edmonton, Canada*
Laura Riding

M. O. Wallace, *Department of English, Duke University, Durham, North Carolina*
Spirituals

Kathryn Ward, *Associate Professor of Sociology, Southern Illinois University at Carbondale*
Sociologists

Susan Ward, *Professor of English, St. Lawrence University, Canton, New York*
Naturalism

Michele S. Ware, *Assistant Professor of English, Wake Forest University, North Carolina*
Josephine Herbst

Robyn R. Warhol, *Professor of English, University of Vermont, Burlington*
Feminism

Joyce W. Warren, *Associate Professor of English; Director, Women's Studies, Queens College, City University of New York*
Fanny (Sara P. W. Parton) Fern

Kazuko Watanabe, *Kyoto Sangyo University, Japan*
Eliza Lucas Pinckney

Delese Wear, *Professor, College of Medicine, Northeast Ohio University, Rootstown*
Birth

Kitty Wei-hsiung Wu, *Associate Professor of English and American Literature, Bowie State University, Maryland*
Diana Chang; Bette Bao Lord

Jane Weiss, *Adjunct Lecturer of English, Hunter College, City University of New York*
Susan Warner

Abby H. P. Werlock, *Associate Professor of English, St. Olaf College, Northfield, Minnesota*
Carson McCullers; Tillie Olsen

Craig Hansen Werner, *Professor of Afro-American Studies, University of Wisconsin at Madison*
Chicago Renaissance; Harlem Renaissance

Kathryn West, *Assistant Professor of English, Bellarmine College, Louisville, Kentucky*
Hannah Webster Foster; Mystery and Detective Fiction; Frances Newman

Barbara A. White, *Professor of Women's Studies, University of New Hampshire, Durham*
New England Women's Writing

Mary Wheeling White, *Assistant Professor of English, Longwood College, Farmville, Virginia*
Harriette Arnow; Evelyn Scott

Annette White-Parks, *Assistant Professor of English, University of Wisconsin at La Crosse*
Sui Sin Far (Edith Eaton)

Nancy Whittington, *Chapel Hill, North Carolina*
Needlework

Margaret B. Wilkerson, *Professor and Chair, African-American Studies Department, University of California at Berkeley*
Alexis Deveaux

Patricia C. Willis, *Elizabeth Wakeman Dwight Curator of American Literature, Beinecke Rare Book and Manuscript Library, Yale University, New Haven, Connecticut*
Marianne Moore

Doni M. Wilson, *Instructor, Department of English, University of North Carolina at Chapel Hill*
Crone; Hag

Judith Bryant Wittenberg, *Professor of English, Simmons College, Boston, Massachusetts*
Anita Loos; Women Writing on Men

Helena Woodard, *Professor of English, University of Texas at Austin*
Mary McLeod Bethune; Harriet (Linda Brent) Jacobs; Terry McMillan; Harriet E. Wilson

Ann M. Woodlief, *Associate Professor of English, Virginia Commonwealth University, Richmond*
Elizabeth Madox Roberts

Jon Woodson, *Associate Professor of English, Howard University, Washington, D.C.*
Johari Amini-Hudson; Jayne Cortez; Carolyn M. Rodgers

Kathleen Woodward, *Director, Center for Twentieth Century Studies; Professor of English, University of Wisconsin at Milwaukee*
Ageism

Anne M. Wyatt-Brown, *Assistant Professor of Linguistics, University of Florida, Gainesville*
Aging

Mary Wyer, *Hillsborough, North Carolina*
Mentors; Scribbling Women

Marilyn Yalom, *Senior Scholar, Institute for Research on Women and Gender, Stanford University, California*
Madness

Yvonne Yarbro-Bejarano, *Associate Professor of Spanish, Stanford University, California*
Chicana Writing: Drama

Kristine A. Yohe, *Department of English, University of North Carolina at Chapel Hill*
J. California Cooper; Jamaica Kincaid

Reggie Young, *Assistant Professor of African-American Literature and Creative Writing, Louisiana State University, Baton Rouge*
African-American Writing: Poetry

Ming-Bao Yue, *Professor, Department of East Asian Languages and Literature, University of Hawaii at Manoa*
Marginality; Post-Colonialism

Elizabeth Yukins, *Department of English, University of Pennsylvania, Philadelphia*
Lesbian Herstory Archives; Joan Nestle

Sandra A. Zagarell, *Professor of English, Oberlin College, Ohio*
Community; Caroline Kirkland; Elizabeth Drew Barstow Stoddard

Janet Zandy, *Assistant Professor of Language and Literature, Rochester Institute of Technology, New York*
Agnes Smedley

Mary B. Zeigler, *Associate Professor of English, Georgia State University, Atlanta*
Nanina Alba

Susan J. Zevenbergen, *Fort Collins, Colorado*
Kathy Acker; Joan Didion; Marilyn Hacker; Erica Jong; Denise Levertov; Grace Paley; Marilynne Robinson; Joanna Russ

Suzanne M. Zweizig, *Department of English, University of North Carolina at Chapel Hill*
Elizabeth Ashbridge; Maria Weston Chapman

THE OXFORD COMPANION TO

Women's Writing

IN THE UNITED STATES

A

ABBOTT, Edith (1876–1957), American feminist, economist, and educator, grew up in Grand Island, Nebraska. Her college-educated mother, Elizabeth Griffin, was a school principal before marrying Othman Abbott, a lawyer and first lieutenant governor of Nebraska. Both parents advocated feminism and the abolition of slavery. After alternating between attending and teaching school, Abbott graduated from the University of Nebraska in 1901. In 1905, she received her Ph.D. in economics from the University of Chicago; her thesis explored unskilled labor in the United States.

While researching labor conditions at the Women's Trade Union League in Boston and at the London School of Economics, Abbott committed herself to serving the poor. In 1908, she and her sister, Grace Abbott, moved into Jane Addams's Hull House in Chicago where they lived for ten years, actively campaigning for the rights of the working class, immigrants, and women. Between 1921 and 1934, when Grace headed the federal Children's Bureau, they struggled to restrict child labor and implement efficient, humane relief programs.

From 1908 to 1942, Abbott and her close friend and frequent coauthor, Sophonisba Breckinridge, ran the Chicago School of Civics and Philanthropy, a training school for social workers that merged with the University of Chicago in 1920. During her tenure as professor of social economy and later as dean, Abbott insisted social workers investigate the legal, medical, industrial, and psychological factors influencing poverty. Abbott's program encouraged the use of scientific methods and statistics; she also advocated public services over voluntary agencies.

Together, Abbott and Breckinridge founded an influential professional journal, the *Social Service Review*, in 1927. Abbott wrote over seventy-eight articles, fifteen books, and innumerable government bulletins, editorials, reviews, and political pamphlets. Her most significant works include *Immigration* (1924); *Report on Crime and the Foreign Born* (1931); *Social Welfare and Professional Education* (1931); *The Tenements of Chicago, 1908–1935* (1936); and *Some American Pioneers in Social Welfare* (1937). Her first book, *Women in Industry* (1910), was reprinted through the 1970s.

As an economist and educator, Abbott shaped both her profession and public policy. She worked so persistently to unite scholarship and social advocacy that the year after her death Elizabeth Wisner, one of her former students, wrote: "I do not recall that she ever talked about methods of social action, but one felt involved in the causes in which she was engaged and ready to do battle by her side."

• Helen Wright, "Three against Time: Edith and Grace Abbott and Sophonisba P. Breckinridge," *Social Service Review* (March 1954): 141–153. Elizabeth Wisner, "Edith Abbott's Contributions to Social Work Education," *Social Service Review* (March 1958): 1–10. Stephen J. Diner, "Scholarship in the Quest for Social Welfare: A Fifty-Year History of the *Social Service Review*," *Social Service Review* (March 1977): 1–66. Lela B. Costin, *Two Sisters for Social Justice: A Biography of Grace and Edith Abbott* (1983).

Caren Irr

ABOLITION, the crusade for the emancipation of slaves, was a process begun with the sentiments contained in the Bill of Rights and African-Americans' contribution to the Revolutionary War. Though individuals and the clergy (especially Quakers) had long maintained that *slavery was a hateful institution contrary to the laws of nature, it was not until the Revolutionary War, with its eloquent doctrines on the rights of man, that the antislavery movement began in earnest. The movement was slowed, both in the North and South, by the conservatism that followed the Revolution.

During the early decades of the nineteenth century, there appeared a visible increase in antislavery sentiment in the North. Antislavery papers, pamphlets, poetry, and resistance narratives multiplied and increasingly called for direct action. Considered the most radical of early written protests penned by an African-American, David Walker's *Appeal* attacks both white racism and African-American acquiescence. Nat Turner led slaves in the Southampton rebellion, which resulted in the killing of over 55 whites in a period of less than 48 hours. William Lloyd Garrison assumed a strident but nonviolent posture against slavery in his editorials in the *Liberator*. Together, the 1829 publication of Walker's *Appeal*, Turner's 1830 revolt, and Garrison's publication constituted the catalysts that would forever catapult the antislavery debate into the public eye.

From the very beginning of the crusade, polarity was inherent among members of antislavery societies. In 1831, the New England Anti-Slavery Society was formed, led by Garrison. In 1833, the American Anti-Slavery Society was organized; it too was largely controlled by Garrison. The goal of both societies was immediate and uncompensated abolition. Other, less progressive, members believed that a gradual end to slavery via political means was the best route, while colonization would solve "the Negro problem." By 1840, the American and Foreign Anti-Slavery Society was founded to provide a forum for the less-than-progressive abolitionists.

Garrison and his progressive group objected to slavery on the grounds that it was contrary to both Christian teachings and to the principles that formed the foundation of democracy. They also believed that dominion over another human debased the nature of the owner. Further, they considered slavery an economically unsound institution and a threat to the peace and security of the country. In 1833, Lucretia Coffin * Mott, a Philadelphia Quaker, helped to found the Philadelphia Female Anti-Slavery Society. After the formation of this parallel group, Garrison began to admit women into his society, while many conservative groups continued to spurn women.

Surprisingly, in a nineteenth-century setting in which relatively few people read, and in which the cult of * true womanhood restricted the activities of the females who were literate, the voices of women rang in support of abolition. They were not without their models, however. In a famous letter to her husband, Abigail * Adams wrote of the irony of a people who would fight for the inalienable rights of man, while themselves sanctioning slavery. In 1782, Belinda (an African slave in her late seventies) petitioned the Massachusetts State Legislature for reparations. An as-told-to account, "Petition of an African Slave, to the Legislature of Massachusetts" (dictated in 1787), narrates the story of a young girl who was abducted from her home in present-day Senegal while in prayer and enslaved for some seventy years.

Nineteenth-century women abolitionists, inspirited by reform movements concerning temperance, women's rights, and labor, wrote letters, journals, speeches, poetry, and prose. In 1848, Elizabeth Cady * Stanton organized the first women's rights convention at Seneca Falls, New York, in response to the exclusion of women delegates at the World Anti-Slavery Convention in London. Always a staunch abolitionist, she was also instrumental in separating issues of slavery and other reforms from women's rights issues.

Perhaps the best-known of the abolitionist women writers was Harriet Beecher * Stowe. Her famous antislavery work, *Uncle Tom's Cabin, or Life Among the Lowly*, was published as a novel in 1852. First published in serial form in the antislavery journal *National Era* in 1851 and 1852, the book became the most sensational best-seller of its time. The literary conventions of the Victorian era made it necessary for Euro-American women writers to encase their antislavery messages in polite prose. Yet Stowe's depiction of the hateful slave system generated adverse response from Southern leaders who questioned the veracity of the abject cruelty of the controlling class and the suffering of the slave class depicted in Stowe's work. Her response to her critics culminated in *A Key to Uncle Tom's Cabin* (1853), a work that was longer than the novel itself and less popular, and through which Stowe sought to document the claims made in her novel about the system. Moreover, by 1840, fugitive slaves moved to the forefront of the antislavery crusade. The African-American's interest in emancipation had been long-standing and varied. But according to Lerone Bennett, Jr., in his work *Before the Mayflower* (1968), white abolitionists conceived of the African-American as a talking exhibit, used in testifying to the cruelty of slavery and the individual's misuse by Southern slaveholders. Olaudah Equiano and Frederick Douglass eventually grew out of such use and emerged as their own articulate heroes, providing an enduring prototype in African-American literature.

The resistance narrative (a fused form of the Western * autobiography and the African storytelling tradition) had become a very popular genre by 1840. It offered a chronological account of an enslaved person's attempts to escape from slavery and recounted the perils and disasters associated with the flight to freedom. Such stories were solicited, collected, and published by antislavery societies, the members of which were often extremely pious and at times victims of cultural arrogance. Because the authors were made to depict themselves in stereotypical roles (pious, God-fearing, victimized, asexual, childlike) that were acceptable to their European and Euro-American readers, the conventions governing the resistance narrative made it necessary for authors to embed their stronger messages indirectly within the text.

As a general rule, women writers were subject to inventing strategies for encoding the truth of their experiences and inviting interpretation beyond the surface message. This is particularly true of reports of the rampant sexual abuse suffered by African-American women at the hands of their owners. Perhaps the best-known account of such abuse is contained in Harriet * Jacobs's *Incidents in the Life of a Slave Girl* (1861). Jacobs's narrative is an adventure in encoded messages. A consideration of what she reveals and what she omits proves as much a challenge as the text itself.

[*See also* Middle Passage; Slavery; Underground Railroad; Antilynching Campaign; Liberal Feminism.]

• Belinda, "Petition of an African Slave, to the Legislature of Massachusetts," in *American Museum, or Repository of Ancient and Modern Fugitive Pieces, Prose and Poetical* 1 (June 1787): 538–540. Lerone Bennett, Jr., *Before the Mayflower: A History of the Negro in America: 1619–1964*, revised ed. (1986). John Hope Franklin, *From Slavery to Freedom: A History of Negro Americans*, 4th ed. (1974). Bert James Loewenberg and Ruth Bogin, eds., *Black Women in Nineteenth-Century American Life: Their Words, Their Thoughts, Their Feelings* (1976). Carol Ruth Berkin and Mary Beth Norton, *Women of America: A History* (1979). Bell Hooks, *Aint I a Woman? Black Women and Feminism* (1981). Mary Frances Berry and John Blassingame, *Long Memory: The Black Experience in America* (1982). Paula Giddings, *When and Where I Enter: The Impact of Black Women on Race and Sex in America* (1984). Joanne M. Braxton, *Black Women Writing Autobiography* (1989).

Adele S. Newson

ABORTION. In 1962, Shery Finkbine, a middle-class mother of four, became pregnant while using the tranquilizer thalidomide, a drug that had been found to produce severe birth defects in the fetus. Although in her home state of Arizona abortion was permitted only to save the life of the mother, Finkbine's physician nonetheless recommended the procedure. Finkbine's case gained quick publicity and her unusual pregnancy brought the issue of abortion to the forefront of American politics. Although she was forced to leave the country to obtain her abortion, Finkbine's story, and subsequent others similar to it, lent significant attention and credibility to the growing abortion rights movement. In the struggle for rights and equality, legalized abortion has become one of the most significant issues affecting women's independence.

On 22 January 1973, the Supreme Court of the United States, deciding the case of *Roe v. Wade*, legalized elective abortion in the first trimester, while applying restrictions to protect maternal health in the second, and the potentially viable life of the fetus in the third. Justice Harry Blackmun, writing in support of the Court's decision, claimed that a woman's right to terminate her pregnancy was protected by the fundamental right to privacy. Justice Potter Stewart, also concurring with the decision of the majority, cited as precedent the Fourteenth Amendment's due process clause, which guarantees every individual a general right to freedom. Although the decision has been accepted by the majority of Americans, many subsequent court cases have attempted to erode a woman's right to abort. The most significant challenges have come from *Webster v. Reproductive Health Services* (1989), a decision that allows states to restrict abortions if fetal viability can be established, and *Hodgson v. Minnesota* and *Ohio v. Akron Center for Reproductive Health* (both 1990), decisions that restrict minors' rights to obtain abortions.

Since the beginning of the abortion rights movement in the early 1960s, a significant number of historians have examined the status of abortion in American history. Such works as James Mohr's *Abortion in America* (1978), Linda Gordon's *Woman's Body, Woman's Right* (1974), and Carl Degler's *At Odds* (1980), have demonstrated that the American criminalization of abortion in the late nineteenth century was produced by concrete political struggles between factions contending for the control of medical discourse, not hazardous health conditions, as they claimed. These historical works help us understand that abortion was an acceptable part of everyday life in the first two centuries of the nation, and has been practiced by women throughout all eras.

Feminists from a variety of other disciplines have contributed major scholarly works to the abortion discussion. In *Abortion and the Politics of Motherhood* (1984), sociologist Kristin Luker shows how the issue of abortion shifted from a "medical problem" (that is, one that could only be evaluated by a licensed physician) to a moral and public one. Luker suggests that in the 1960s, shifts in attitudes regarding human rights enabled some women to organize around the issue of abortion. Women's involvement in the movement, Luker argues, was conditioned by their "world view," life circumstances, and perceived career options. With her ethnographic work, Luker discovers that those who place a higher value on careers for women are often pro-choice in their political convictions. Conversely, women whose futures mainly entail motherhood locate themselves within the pro-life movement. Luker persuasively concludes that the current abortion debate can also be understood as a representation of the conflict regarding women's role in society.

Also published in 1984, Rosalind Petchesky's *Abortion and Women's Choice* offers one of the most influential and analytical works on the subject. Petchesky argues that efforts to control abortion are implemented not only to control fertility, but also to control the organization and collective power of women. More importantly, Petchesky persuasively denaturalizes all aspects of the fertility process, detailing the social conditions for many aspects of women's concrete abortion decisions. Writing from a Marxist-feminist perspective, she argues that no reproductive experience is unmediated by social circumstances. In this analysis, variations in rates and availability of abortion always occur inside complicated social and economic systems. Through sociological analysis, Petchesky elucidates how shifts in economic conditions as well as in social attitudes help dictate to what degree, and under what conditions, abortion is acceptable. Petchesky's inquiry also investigates how well various concrete social and economic systems are able to absorb unwanted and unintended pregnancies, and then tracks abortion against that level of tolerance. In her work, the meaning of the abortion is dependent on the particular community in which it occurs.

Faye Ginsburg's *Contested Lives: The Abortion Debate in an American Community* (1989) details the events surrounding the full-scale controversy that arose around the 1981 opening of the first abortion clinic in Fargo, North Dakota. Her ethnographic research displays the concrete contextual nature of the political involvement of people on both sides of the debate. Although both the pro-life and pro-choice movements were organized originally to overturn or support specific Supreme Court decisions regarding abortion, Ginsburg suggests that the activities of both of these groups have been focused largely on the delivery of abortion services. Involvement in the abortion debate, as she chronicles, entails donating endless amounts of time and resources to the protection or elimination of a specific clinic. Furthermore, although the pro-life and pro-choice movements see each other as ideological enemies, Ginsburg's work demonstrates that participants from opposing sides of the debate often work together to help a pregnant woman find the care and support she desires.

Judith Wilt's *Abortion, Choice and Contemporary Fiction* (1990) offers a psychoanalytic analysis of abortion, suggesting that the Lacanian transformation from the imaginary to the symbolic paradigmatically occurs as women, choosing abortion, experience fragmentation and incompleteness. Abortion, then, becomes a representation of consciousness, signified against the wholeness represented in prelinguistic and prepregnant stages. Wilt provocatively suggests that this twentieth-century narrative of development is presaged by nineteenth-century stories of infanticide. *Abortion, Choice and Contemporary Fiction* is the

only monograph dealing exclusively with readings of fictional representations of abortion. Also published in 1990, Marlene Gerber Fried's collected volume, *From Abortion to Reproductive Freedom: Transforming a Movement*, attempts to unify the diverse voices active in the current reproductive rights movement. The volume consequently cuts across class and racial barriers and presents feminism's activity in the movement as a multicultural montage. Contributors include Angela Davis, Ellen Willis, and Alice Walker, as well as anonymous contributions from such sources as the Chicago-based illegal abortion provider "Jane." This book bridges the gap between academic and cultural activist factions of feminism.

Serious convictions on both sides of the issue regarding the value and quality of life have created oppositions that seem to preclude compromise. Additionally, participants in the controversy conduct their political activities with unparalleled passion. In a politically inactive era, the fact that the activity surrounding the abortion debate regularly makes the headlines testifies to the intensity with which this issue strikes at our hearts. These fierce disagreements are produced by deep commitments to beliefs about gender, reproduction, life, and death.

[*See also* Birth Control; Reproduction.]

• Beverly Harrison, *Our Right to Choose: Toward a New Ethic of Abortion* (1983). Louise Kapp Howe, *Moments on Maple Avenue: The Reality of Abortion* (1984). Mary Ann Glendon, *Abortion and Divorce in Western Law* (1987). Catherine MacKinnon, "Privacy v. Equality: Beyond *Row v. Wade*," in *Feminism Unmodified: Discourses on Life and Law*, ed. Catherine MacKinnon, (1987), pp. 93–102. Marian Faux, *Roe v. Wade* (1988). Celeste Michelle Condit, *Decoding Abortion Rhetoric: Communicating Social Change* (1990). Laurence Tribe, *Abortion: The Clash of Absolutes* (1990). Angela Bonavoglia, *The Choices We Made: Twenty-Five Women and Men Speak Out about Abortion* (1991). Peter Wenz, *Abortion Rights as Religious Freedom* (1992).

Kathy Rudy

ACADIAN WRITING. See Creole and Acadian Writing.

ACKER, Kathy (b. 1948), novelist, grew up in Manhattan and attended college mainly at Brandeis and the University of California, San Diego. She lived a "split life" as a poetry hippie and a sex-show worker on New York City's Forty-second Street. Although she studied the Black Mountain poets, the main influences in her development as a novelist were William Burroughs and Jack Kerouac. Her early novel, *The Childlike Life of the Black Tarantula by the Black Tarantula* (1975), made use of autobiographical material to explore the notion of identity. Many of her later novels, particularly

Great Expectations (1983) and *Don Quixote* (1986), use appropriated male texts in the search for a female voice. Acker's other works include *The Adult Life of Toulouse Lautrec by Henri Toulouse Lautrec* (1975), *Hello, I'm Erica Jong* (1982), *Blood and Guts in High School* (1984), and *Empire of the Senseless* (1988). Acker lived in London as an American expatriate from 1984 to 1990 and now resides in San Francisco.

Kathy Acker considers herself a feminist as well as a *postmodernist writer. Like other postmodern work, Acker's novels subvert the assumptions of fiction: narrative line, so-called originality, authorial distance, and so on. By deliberately "plagiarizing" everything from Freud to the venerable texts of literary history, Acker hopes to provoke the reader into a revolutionary consciousness that cannot cease to question the status quo. Acker also considers herself a political writer, one for whom it is necessary to "present the human heart naked so that our world, for a second, explodes into flames" ("A Few Notes on Two of My Books," the *Review of Contemporary Fiction*, Fall 1989). The language necessary to be truly political is that of the body, which, according to Acker, can tell no lies. While feminists have been especially troubled by what some consider "pornography" in Acker's work, Ellen Friedman claims that, for Acker, "sadistic men victimizing slavish, masochistic women represents conventional sexual transactions in society, the underlying paradigm for normal relationships in patriarchal culture" (" 'Now Eat Your Mind,' " the *Review of Contemporary Fiction*, Fall 1989). Only through making her readers uncomfortable by glorifying the taboo, does Acker see any possibility of creating a "new myth" through which women can become empowered.

• Leslie Dick, "Feminism, Writing, Postmodernism," in *From My Guy to Sci-Fi: Genre and Women's Writing in the Postmodern World*, ed. Helen Carr (1989), pp. 204–214. Kathleen Hulley, "Transgressing Genre: Kathy Acker's Intertext," in *Intertextuality and Contemporary American Fiction*, eds. Patrick O'Donnell and Robert Con Davis (1989), pp. 171–190. Larry McCaffery, "The Artists of Hell: Kathy Acker and 'Punk' Aesthetics," in *Breaking the Sequence: Women's Experimental Fiction*, ed. Ellen G. Friedman (1989), pp. 215–230. Richard Walsh, "The Quest for Love and the Writing of Female Desire in Kathy Acker's *Don Quixote*," *Critique* 32, no. 3 (Spring 1991): 149–168. Carol Siegel, "Postmodern Women Novelists Review Victorian Male Masochism," *Genders* 11 (Fall 1991): 1–16.

Susan J. Zevenbergen

ACTIVISM in the literature of American women writers can be discussed on many levels. A literary text can accomplish the work of raising political consciousness and inspiring political action, thereby having an "activist"

effect on its audience. In this sense, any literature that serves to enrich the political consciousness of the reader, with regard to issues of gender, class, race, ethnicity, international politics, or other issues, can be said to be activist literature. Literary works may also portray or address specific political movements and issues. Categories of literary works by American women that define, expand, and provoke political thinking include *captivity narratives; *slave narratives; temperance novels; the literature of *abolition and suffrage; *working-class literature; early and contemporary feminist literature; literature of socialist, *utopian, and leftist radical movements; literature of the *Harlem Renaissance and the civil rights movement; literature of self-determination (African-American, Chicano, Native-American, and so on); antiwar protest literature; literature of the labor movement; literature of feminism and lesbianism; *ethnic and immigrant literature; and literature concerning women's involvement in international politics.

The activist effect of a particular author's work can change over time, as different historical audiences examine a particular work. Kate *Chopin's *The Awakening*, for example, was dismissed by many at its publication in 1899 as a scandalous account of a woman's sexual awakening; it later became a key text for investigating the entire premise of white middle-class womanhood when it was eagerly reread in the 1970s and later. Some audiences read Zora Neale *Hurston's *Their Eyes Were Watching God* in 1937 as an example of narrative in the black story-telling tradition; it was later recognized in the 1970s as an important inquiry into race and gender issues as well. Activist authors of the radical left in the 1930s who wrote novels depicting women's participation in domestic strikes and international revolutions found a like-minded audience of 1930s leftists, and in the 1980s they also gained a new audience of feminists who recognized a radical extension of their own developing politics.

The term *activist* may apply to an author's work in many contexts. Some authors have taken on social issues, as did Harriet Beecher *Stowe in her depiction of slavery in *Uncle Tom's Cabin*, Charlotte Perkins *Gilman in her exploration of gender issues in *Herland*, or Carolyn See in her portrayal of nuclear warfare in *The Golden Years*. Some women writers' works revealed the economics of working-class life, such as Rebecca Harding *Davis's *Life in the Iron Mills*, Anzia *Yezierska's *Breadgivers*, or Tillie *Olsen's *Yonnondio*, or portrayed class conflict, as in Elizabeth Stuart *Phelps's *The Silent Partner*, or Josephine *Herbst's *Rope of Gold*. Other authors served an activist purpose in another literary capacity, as did Jessie *Fauset by editing *Crisis*, the literary and political journal of the Harlem Renaissance, or Lola Ridge, by combining community activism with writing poetry on international concerns in the 1910s and 1920s. In the 1930s, it was the express purpose of revolutionary literature to incite political action, as seen in the poetry of Genevieve Taggard or Josephine Johnson, or the songs of Aunt Molly Jackson, which encouraged protests and urged workers to unite. A text could also depict a character's involvement in international political issues, as in Barbara Kingsolver's *Animal Dreams* or Valerie Miner's *Blood Sisters*.

Works that bring previously invisible groups into full relief through characterization also serve an activist purpose, as does Elmaz Abinader's depiction of Arab-American women in *Children of the Roojme*, Christina Garcia's portrayal of Cuban-American women in *Dreaming in Cuban*, or Maxine Hong *Kingston's treatment of Asian-American women in *Woman Warrior*. Authors become activists by deepening their audience's understanding of an already-discussed social issue, as with Toni *Morrison's reexamination of the mental, emotional, physical, and historical cost of slavery in *Beloved*.

Another category of political activism in literary works can be found in texts that portray and explore the political involvements of female characters. Toni Cade *Bambara's heroine in *The Salt Eaters*, for example, works for the civil rights movement, and the speakers in Denise *Levertov's poetry contemplate their role in Vietnam War protests.

Recurring issues often surface throughout texts that examine the strategies and consequences of political activism. Within a story or poem, political activism may become the outspoken expression of an otherwise silent speaker. A conflict between political work, personal relationships, and domestic labor often emerges—a concern that may distinguish women's literature of activism from its male counterpart, since women explore the conflict between, for example, caring for children and attending political meetings. The difference between the "body" work (food, children, sex) and the "mind" work (strategy, theory, organizing) necessary for political action, and how these roles are assigned on the basis of gender, is often discussed. Works may also debate the position of women who belong to the same political organizations but may be divided from each other on the basis of class, race, ethnicity, or sexual orientation. The link between an author's actual political activity in her daily life, and how her political commitment works into the literature she produces, is also a source of discussion. Often valued throughout these works is the comradery and complexity of friendship between women. Forging relationships between self, the local community, and the global community continues to challenge activist women authors and readers alike.

[*See also* Political Organizations; Women's Movement; Protest Writing; Civil Rights Movement; Antiwar Movements; American Indian Rights Movement; Antilynching Campaign.]

• Tillie Olsen, *Silences* (1983). Charlotte Nekola and Paula Rabinowitz, eds., *Writing Red: An Anthology of American Women Writers, 1930–1940* (1987). Hazel Carby, *Reconstructing Womanhood: The Emergence of the Afro-American Woman Novelist* (1989). bell hooks, *Yearning: Race, Gender, and Cultural Politics* (1990). Michelle Wallace, *Invisibility Blues: From Pop to Theory* (1990). Paula Rabinowitz, *Labor and Desire: Women's Revolutionary Fiction in Depression America* (1991).

Charlotte Nekola

ADAMS, Abigail (1744–1818), letter writer and advocate for women's rights, was born in Weymouth, Massachusetts, to William Smith, a Congregationalist minister, and Elizabeth Quincy. Abigail Smith never attended school, and instead was educated by her grandmother and through her own reading in the family library. In October 1764, when she was 20, Smith married John Adams, a lawyer who was to become the second president of the United States. During the first ten years of their marriage, the Adamses had five children. As John Adams's involvement in politics deepened, Abigail Adams became increasingly responsible for managing their home. In 1774, John Adams became a delegate to the first Continental Congress, beginning what was to be a ten-year separation for the married couple. Abigail Adams became solely responsible for managing the family farm and financial matters, in addition to raising and educating her children.

Though self-conscious about her unrefined handwriting and poor spelling (the result of her lack of formal schooling), Abigail Adams nevertheless frequently chose to write to her husband, relatives, and friends. From an early age, she viewed letter writing as a means of education. She often wrote about her own lack of education and protested the condition of women's education. Perhaps her most famous letter was written on March 31, 1776, to her husband, when he was a delegate at the Continental Congress; she admonished him to "Remember the Ladies" by improving married women's legal rights.

The earliest editions of Adams's letters were heavily edited by her grandson, Charles Francis Adams. In *Letters of Mrs. Adams* (1840) and *Fa-*

miliar *Letters of John Adams and His Wife, during the Revolution* (1876), Charles Adams corrected his grandmother's spelling and deleted content that he perceived as unseemly for the wife of a president, such as her descriptions of her pregnancies and child rearing, and her accounts of household management and business concerns. *The Book of Abigail and John* (1975), edited by L. H. Butterfield, et al., restores these deletions, thereby providing an accurate record of Abigail Adams's writing style and the spectrum of her concerns as a woman living in the late eighteenth and early nineteenth centuries. *New Letters of Abigail Adams* (Stewart Mitchell, ed., 1947; reprint, 1973) reprints Adams's letters to her sister, Mary Cranch, and provides another view of Adams as a writer: she sent her sister first-draft letters, rather than the edited and corrected final versions of letters she sent to friends.

• *The Adams Family Correspondence*, ed. L. H. Butterfield (1964–1973). Edith B. Gelles, *Portia: The World of Abigail Adams* (1992).

Amy M. Thomas

ADAMS, Alice (b. 1926), novelist and short story writer. The author of eight novels, four collections of stories, and one travel book about Mexico, Alice Adams has often mined her life for fictional material. Born in Fredericksburg, Virginia, she was the daughter of a frustrated writer, Agatha Boyd Adams, and a Spanish professor, Nicholson Adams. She grew up in a farmhouse near Chapel Hill, North Carolina, which has provided the setting for some of her most moving stories: "Verlie I Say Unto You," "Home Is Where," and "Roses, Rhododendron" in *Beautiful Girl* (1979); "Truth or Consequences" in *To See You Again* (1982); "New Best Friends" in *Return Trips* (1985); and "Child's Play" in *After You've Gone* (1989). A memoir, "My First and Only House" (in *Return Trips*) which describes the permanent "imprinting" of that farmhouse on her life, testifies to Adams's visceral response to her environment, a sense she deftly conveys to readers no matter what her setting is.

After graduating from Radcliffe College in 1946, Adams worked in publishing in New York City, as does a character in *Superior Women* (1984). In 1947, Adams married Mark Linenthal, Jr., and accompanied him to Paris for his graduate work at the Sorbonne. They moved to California, where their only child, Peter Adams Linenthal, was born in 1951. While Mark Linenthal taught English at San Francisco State University, Alice Adams wrote stories. Her first published story, "Winter Rain," appeared in *Charm* in 1959, the year after her divorce. Adams's first three novels, *Careless Love*

(1966), *Families and Survivors* (1974), and *Listening to Billie* (1978), are about traditional, upper-middle-class white women struggling to be emotionally and financially independent from men. Her protagonists are frequently artistic women whose search for self-realization often means giving up what Adams has termed "the kind of addictive love affair that is so all-consuming that it makes sex an excuse for delaying the things that matter, like getting down to work" (*Publisher's Weekly*, January 16, 1978). In *Rich Rewards* (1980), *Superior Women* (1984), and *Caroline's Daughters* (1991), Adams rewards her female protagonists who find themselves through fulfilling work with meaningful lives and loves. In *Almost Perfect* (1993), she explores the effect a woman's professional success can have on her lover's relationship to her. *Second Chances* (1988), which several reviewers have deemed her strongest work, focuses on the friendships of men and women in their sixties and seventies.

The reviews of Adams's fiction have been mixed, and literary critics have virtually ignored her work. While reviewers have praised Adams's fluid writing style, her frank depictions of female sexuality, and her adroit social observations, they have faulted her plots for their unbelievable coincidences and events borrowed from soap operas, and complained that her tone should be more clearly ironic. Although reviewers complain that Adams's works document how people act rather than how they feel, they readily grant that Adams's novels make for a good read.

• Cara Chell, "Succeeding in Their Times: Alice Adams on Women and Work," *Soundings: An Interdisciplinary Journal* 68, no. 1 (Spring 1985): 62–71. Larry T. Blades, "Order and Chaos in Alice Adams' *Rich Rewards*," *Critique: Studies in Modern Fiction* 27, no. 4 (Summer 1986): 187–195. Lee Upton, "Changing the Past: Alice Adams' Revisionary Nostalgia," *Studies in Short Fiction* 26, no. 1 (Winter 1989): 33–41.

Suzanne W. Jones

ADAMS, Hannah (1755–1832), researcher, historian, and writer. Hannah Adams was born in Medfield, Massachusetts, on 2 October 1755, the third of five children of Elizabeth Clark and Thomas Adams, Jr., a distant cousin of President John Adams. Personal and material loss punctuated Adams's childhood: At ten her mother died, as did later her closest, eldest sister Elizabeth. Unable to keep his family from penury, Adams's father unprofitably ran the family farm, and unsuccessfully operated an English goods and book shop. Hungry for knowledge, Hannah read his library and inventory, and learned Greek and Latin from boarders he lodged to relieve debts.

That Adams supported herself during the Revolution by weaving bobbin lace is less important than her continued research in religious history and theology, despite many obstacles during this time in her life. She often had to conduct research in bookshops whose texts she could not afford to buy. When her father left the family house and property to his son, John Wickliffe Adams, whose own family dislodged Hannah, she was forced to support herself, and she at one point became a schoolmistress who resided with the families of her students. Her research yielded *An Alphabetical Compendium of the Various Sects . . .* (1784). The *Compendium* sold out its four hundred subscriptions, yet Adams and her father had contracted for royalties on only fifty copies, a scant profit for her labors. Having secured copyright for the *Compendium* under the new Massachusetts law in 1783, however, she increased her income from better-contracted later editions. The *Alphabetical Compendium* appeared in expanded second and third editions as *View of Religions* (1790, 1801), and in a substantially expanded fourth edition as *A Dictionary of All Religions and Religious Denominations, Jewish, Heathen, Mahometan and Christian, Ancient and Modern* (1817).

Adams then began her *Summary History of New England* (1799). Financial losses through the late 1790s, however, forced her to print it privately and to abridge it as a textbook for New England schools. When Adams learned through Salem's Cushing and Appleton's Bookstore that Cushing was printing a competing text written by Jedidiah Morse and Elijah Parish, a conflict was begun whose intensity only increased when Adams's *Abridgement of the History of New England* appeared (1805). Allegations fraught with ideological, theological, and gender implications passed between Adams and Morse, resulting in litigation beginning in 1804 and lasting nearly a decade. In response to the conflict, Adams wrote *A Narrative of the Controversy Between the Rev. Jedidiah Morse, D.D., and the Author* (1814). Adams completed *History of the Jews* in 1812. Her *Letters on the Gospels* (1824) aimed at the spiritual edification of young female readers; she wrote her last work, *Memoir* (1832), for the financial support of her infirm and aging younger sister. *Memoir* testifies to the difficulty of female authorship in this period of American literary history.

Adams died at the age of seventy-six in Brookline, Massachusetts. She is buried in Mount Auburn Cemetary, Cambridge, Massachusetts.

• Jedidiah Morse, *Appeal to the Public* (1814) contains many of the documents of the Adams-Morse litigation, including Adams's correspondence. Major holders of Hannah Adams's manuscripts and papers include the Boston Public Library; the New England Historic and Geneaological Society; the Massachusetts Historical Society; Yale University; the New York Public Library; the Schelsinger Library; and the Boston Atheneum.

Michael W. Vella

ADDAMS, Jane (1860–1935), social worker, peace advocate. One of the most important social reformers of the late nineteenth and early twentieth centuries, Jane Addams eloquently wrote about and fought for the working poor, particularly in Chicago. She founded Hull House in 1889 when she and her classmate from Rockford Female Seminary, Ellen Gates Starr, moved into decaying Hull mansion, located in the infamous Nineteenth Ward of Chicago, one of the city's worst ghettos. Hull House became a meeting place for dozens of political and civic groups, attracting some two thousand weekly visitors. Here Addams lectured on her own theories of social reform through settlement. "Settlement" meant that educated social workers literally settled into poor areas, living in communal dormitorylike houses in order to be in the midst of the community they served. Settlement workers preached health care and hygiene to the poor but, equally important, publicized the plight of the poor to the nation's elite.

Addams used the printed word to spread her message nationally. *Democracy and Social Ethics* (1902) analyzes American industrialization and its effects on immigrants and the urban poor. *Newer Ideals of Peace* (1907), *The Spirit of Youth and the City Streets* (1909), and *A New Conscience and an Ancient Evil* (1912) explore social ethics, urban sociology, and the cycle of poverty and prostitution among poor urban women. Her autobiography, *Twenty Years at Hull-House* (1910), was a best-seller and is now a classic of reform literature. It details the cultural, political, and educational activities at Hull House.

A pacifist during World War I, an internationalist in the 1920s, and a civil libertarian, Addams was increasingly considered a radical by many Americans. Her *Peace and Bread in Time of War* (1922) was reviled by critics for its "extremist" views. However, in 1931 she was named corecipient of the Nobel Peace Prize.

• Peggy Stinson, "Jane Addams," in *American Women Writers*, ed. Lina Mainiero, vol. 1 (1979), pp. 20–23. Ursula Lehmkuhl, "The Historical Value and Historiographic Significance of Jane Addams' Autobiographies 'Twenty Years at Hull-House' and 'Second Twenty Years at Hull-House,' " in *Reconstructing American Literary and Historical Studies*, ed. Gunter H. Lenz, Hartmut Keil, and Sabine Brock-Sallah (1990), pp. 285–297. Rebecca L. Sherrick, "Addams, Jane," in *Handbook of American Women's History*, ed. Angela Howard

Zophy (1990), p. 8. Lois Rudnick, "A Feminist American Success Myth: Jane Addams's *Twenty Years at Hull-House*," in *Tradition and the Talents of Women*, ed. Florence Howe (1991), pp. 145–167. Judith Ann Trolander, "Settlement House Movement," in *Women's Studies Encyclopedia*, ed. Helen Tierney, vol. 3 (1991), pp. 405–407.

Cathy N. Davidson

ADOLESCENCE. Fictions and autobiographies of adolescence comprise one of the largest and most diverse categories of American literature. As Patricia Meyer Spacks has observed in *The Adolescent Idea* (1981), the "idea of adolescence" has a particularly strong hold on the Western imagination, embodying as it does the values of "exploration, becoming, growth, [and] pain." There are distinctly different patterns for the female * bildungsroman in the nineteenth and twentieth centuries, as there are for the fictions and autobiographies of adolescence written by women of different classes, races, and sexual orientations. In *Woman's Fiction: A Guide to Novels by and about Women in America, 1820–1870* (1978), Nina Baym notes that early fiction by women such as Catharine * Sedgwick, E.D.E.N. * Southworth, Susan * Warner, Maria * Cummins, and Mary Jane Holmes tells "a single tale" of a young woman "faced with the necessity of winning her own way in the world," whose story "exemplifies the difficult but successful negotiation of the undifferentiated child through the trials of adolescence into the individuation of sound adulthood," and finally to the "formation and assertion of a feminine ego." Although adolescence in these fictions inevitably ends in marriage, Baym argues this heroine is not passive; rather, facing the inevitable failure of patriarchal authority figures to protect her, the female adolescent is forced to become "a self-made woman."

Like the literature of these mid-nineteenth-century women writers, the stories of adolescence told by middle-class white women writers of the last half of the nineteenth and the first half of the twentieth century reveal the degree to which the psychological pressures of female adolescence are the products of patriarchal culture. In the past several decades, feminist scholarship, often anticipating or relying on the insights of psychologists like Nancy Chodorow in *The Reproduction of Mothering* (1978) and Carol Gilligan in *In a Different Voice* (1982), revealed the rich diversity of the female bildungsroman. For the heroines of Elizabeth * Stoddard's *The Morgesons* (1862), Louisa May * Alcott's *Little Women* (1868), Carson * McCuller's *The Heart is a Lonely Hunter* (1940), and Harper * Lee's *To Kill a Mockingbird* (1960), these fictions of middle-class adolescence reveal a common theme of the loss of childhood freedom and the closing in of the repressive sexual and social mores of "the feminine mystique" as these protagonists realize that, unlike their brothers or male peers, their experience of life will shrink rather than grow as they pass into adulthood and face the inevitable expectation that they marry and become mothers. Many of these fictions, like Sylvia * Plath's *The Bell Jar* (1963), reveal the extreme psychological consequences of the pressures and contradictions of female adolescence, which sometimes result in a descent into madness.

Many of the nineteenth-century fictions of middle-class adolescence also reveal the richness of women's culture and female bonding. From the deep friendships between adolescent friends in *The Pearl of Orr's Island* (1869) to the ambivalent but deep bond of the March sisters in *Little Women*, writers like * Stowe and * Alcott celebrate the "female world of love and ritual" that Carroll Smith-Rosenberg describes as a central aspect of female adolescence in the middle-class culture of the mid- to late nineteenth century. For some nineteenth-century writers, the onset of adolescence seemed so dangerous because it signified the dreaded advent of sexuality, which clashed with the middle-class Victorian values of female purity, and they killed off their heroines to preserve that purity, as do Stowe in *Uncle Tom's Cabin* (1852) and Mary Wilkins * Freeman in "Old Woman Magoun" (1902). Other writers, like Willa * Cather in *O Pioneers!* (1913) and *The Song of the Lark* (1915), provide glimpses of female adolescents who were able to transcend the restrictions of women's culture to achieve individuation and success in traditionally male modes.

From the mid-nineteenth century on, African-American women writers explored the complexities and trials of growing up female in a patriarchal, racist, slave-owning culture. Although few African-American women had the luxury of experiencing adolescence as a period relatively free of responsibility, Harriet E. * Wilson's *Our Nig* (1859) and Harriet * Jacobs's *Incidents in the Life of a Slave Girl* (published under the name Linda Brent in 1861) reveal that the worst dangers for young African-American women, whether free or slave, were distinctly gender-bound, since they became sexual prey for powerful white men and servants to be exploited by white women. * Zitkala-Ša, in her autobiographical *American Indian Stories* (1921), provides insight into the complexities of entering adolescence on a reservation and then being sent away to school and thrust into the dominant culture, deprived of family support and cultural rituals. In both her autobiographical essay, "Leaves from the Mental Portfolio of an Eurasian" (1909), and some of her fiction, collected in *Mrs. Spring Fragrance* (1912), * Sui Sin Far reveals the way Chinese-American women were caught between two cultural stereotypes of women as they negotiated the difficult task of forming an identity in the crucial adolescent years.

One would expect that images of adolescence in post-1960s women's fiction would show dramatically different patterns in the wake of the second wave of feminism. If anything, the patterns become even more various as the fictions and autobiographies of adolescence acknowledge and even celebrate the way cultural and sexual diversity shape a girl's voyage to womanhood. In "Exiting from Patriarchy: The Lesbian Novel of Development" in *The Voyage In* (1983), Bonnie Zimmerman argues that "the paradigmatic lesbian novel of development, in many ways, is closer to the classic *Bildungsroman* than is the heterosexual feminist novel of awakening," because the mythic journey of the "young [wo]man from the provinces" is translated into the journey out of patriarchy into "the new world of lesbianism." Working-class writers like Marge * Piercy, deeply influenced by an earlier generation of writers such as Tillie * Olsen, have explored the interlinking of classism and sexism for working-class female adolescents. Asian-American writers like Maxine Hong * Kingston in *The Woman Warrior* (1975) and Amy * Tan in *The Joy Luck Club* (1989) have written powerful works about the complexities of adolescents caught between two cultures. Perhaps the greatest outpouring of contemporary fiction on female adolescence has come from African-American women writers such as Paule * Marshall, Maya * Angelou, Toni * Morrison, and Alice * Walker. In their autobiographies and novels (*Brown Girl, Brownstones*, 1959; *I Know Why the Caged Bird Sings*, 1969; *The Bluest Eye*, 1970, and *Sula*, 1973; and *The Color Purple*, 1982), these African-American women are writing with explosive power about the devastating impact of the dominant culture's racism and sexism on young black women trying to negotiate the identity crises of adolescence. They also have taken on the difficult and painful issue of sexism within African-American culture itself. The list of contemporary fictions of adolescence, and the rich variety of settings, themes, and social environments they reveal, from two young adolescents in the Pacific Northwest trying to understand their mother's suicide and their aunt's rootlessness in Marilynne * Robinson's *Housekeeping* (1980), to a protagonist's trying to grasp the significance of the "American Dream" in a barrio in Sandra * Cisneros's *The House on Mango Street* (1985), to a southern adolescent trying to deal with the loss of her father in the Vietnam War in Bobbie Ann * Mason's *In Country* (1989), increasingly reveal the greater variety of women's lives in the wake of the second wave of feminism.

[*See also* Girlhood; Children's Literature.]

• Barbara Welter, "Coming of Age in America: The American Girl in the 19th Century" (1969), reprinted in *Dimity Convictions* (1976). Barbara T. Christian, *Black Women Novelists: The Development of a Tradition* (1980). Elizabeth Abel, Marianne Hirsch, Elizabeth Langland, eds., *The Voyage In: Fictions of Female Development* (1983). Beverly R. Voloshin, "The Limits of Domesticity: The Female *Bildungsroman* in America, 1820–1870," in *Women's Studies: An Interdisciplinary Journal* 10, no. 3 (1984): 283–302. Carroll Smith-Rosenberg, "Puberty to Menopause: The Cycle of Femininity in Nineteenth-Century America," in *Disorderly Conduct: Visions of Gender in Victorian America* (1985). Katherine Dalsimer, *Female Adolescence: Psychoanalytic Reflections on Works of Literature* (1986). Geta Leseur, "One Mother, Two Daughters: The Afro-American and the Afro-Caribbean Female *Bildungsroman*," in *Black Scholar* 17, no. 2 (March–April 1986): 26–33. Elizabeth Ammons, *Conflicting Stories: American Women Writers at the Turn into the Twentieth-Century* (1991).

Dorothy Berkson

ADULTERY. *See* Marriage Laws.

ADVICE BOOKS are texts concerned with prescribing proper behavior for their readers. The locus of this concern may be any combination of outward actions and inner moral or psychological states. Subgenres of advice books include almanacs, books of * etiquette, domestic economies (* cookbooks, * marriage and child-rearing advice), guides to citizenship and republican behavior, funeral and mourning literature, urban guidebooks, books of self-instruction, * vocational advisors, medical manuals (physiologies and books of sexual advice), and psychological handbooks. Advice books offer education, articulate (and conserve) social ritual, encourage self-regulation, and prescribe the characterological traits of the desirable individual. Although their readers vary according to historical period and by subgenre, they are generally young, white, middle-class, largely urban, English-speaking, and literate.

The earliest American advice books were reprints or adaptations of British conduct books, which, in their turn, derived from Continental courtesy books. In the eighteenth century, two models prevailed: those that emphasized manners, read mainly by southern planters who wished to model their lives after British country gentry; and those that stressed moral probity, favored by northern colonists. Most of these earliest manuals assumed that mannerly behavior derived from moral character, and that character was inseparable from the privileges of social status predicated by blood line. The notable exception to this pattern was Lord Chesterfield's *Letters to His Son* (1774), a book that advocated adapting one's behavior to elicit the social responses most favorable to one's own advancement. Although many Americans, including Abigail *Adams, condemned Chesterfield's apparent unconcern for authenticity of character, his work (often expurgated of its advice on seduction) went through dozens of American printings.

In the 1820s, the number of American advice books burgeoned, the result of technological innovations in printing and transportation; the increasing availability of a variety of manufactured goods (and thus a need for guides to their purchase, use, and social significance); and, in the North, the concentration in cities of a diverse and mobile population with widely varying standards of behavior. American advice books written before the Civil War maintained a paradoxical outlook on this fluid social situation: Their function is clearly monitorial, prescribing a code of behaviors designed to contain social mobility; yet they imply that in a democracy people can, by following the books' advice, raise their social standing. The blatant exception to this situation is advice written by and for southern slave owners (see James O. Breeden's collection of *Advice Among Masters: The Ideal in Slave Management in the Old South*, 1980). Early nineteenth-century advice books present morally grounded codes of behavior characterized as natural "law," and promise that adherence to these "laws" will smooth social interaction. The advent of mandatory common schooling, whose required subjects included deportment, effected the dispersion of conduct-book values. More women than men wrote advice texts during this period, and they included novelist Catharine *Sedgwick (*Morals of Manners; or, Hints for Our Young People*, 1846); editor Sarah Josepha *Hale (an almanac, *Manners; or, Happy Homes and Good Society All the Year Round*, 1868); educator Catharine *Beecher (*A Treatise on Domestic Economy*, 1841, and *Letters to Persons Who Are Engaged in Domestic Service*, 1842); physician Elizabeth Blackwell (*The Laws of Life with Special Reference to the Physical Education of Girls*, 1852); and Irish-Spanish actress Lola Montez (*The Arts of Beauty*, 1858). Not coincidentally, most of these women were highly educated, white, New England writers and/or professionals.

After the Civil War, as social classes became more sharply differentiated, and as an expansion of scientific knowledge produced professionals who felt entitled to prescribe the proper management of home, mind, and body, the rhetoric of American conduct books changed significantly. Twice as many advice books were published during this period, peaking in 1900–1910 at seven books per year. Magazines and newspapers began to include advice features, among the first of which was Dorothy *Dix's (pseudonym of Elizabeth M. Gilmer) column in the New Orleans *Daily Picayune* (1895). This increase signaled a greater concern for social monitoring, as immigrants and newly rich families sought social respectability by consulting etiquette books for directions on how to consume and display the panoply of consumer goods their wealth made available to them. The tone of this advice, unlike that written earlier in the century, was less egalitarian, stressing manners over moral probity and equating proper behaviors with an ineffable quality called "taste." Unlike the earlier books, which assumed smooth social intercourse to be the result of monitoring one's relation to others, books of this period prescribe how one might manufacture a self that would be intelligible to others who already understood the codes of proper conduct. Advice books written by women during this period signaled a new concern with physical and mental culture: see, for example, Genevieve Stebbins's *Society Gymnastics and Voice-Culture Adapted from the Delsarte System* (1888); Julia Thomas's and Annie Thomas's *Psycho-Physical Culture* (1892); and Martha L. Pratt's *The New Calisthenics: A Manual of Health and Beauty* (1889). Most widely read was Marion Harland (pseudonym of Mary Virginia [Hawes] Terhune), who wrote twenty-five such books, including *Eve's Daughters; or, Common Sense for Maid, Wife, and Mother* (1882).

After 1865, for the first time, advice was addressed to readers of nondominant social classes and races with the purpose of assimilating their behaviors to dominant values and social usages. The Woman's Foreign Missionary Society published the *Heathen Woman's Friend;* the Women's National Indian Association published the *Indian's Friend*. Several books were written for newly emancipated African-Americans, among them Clinton B. Fisk's *Plain Counsel for the Freedmen* (1866) and Elias M. Woods's *The Negro in Etiquette: A Novelty* (1899). Mary Frances Armstrong's *On Habits and Manners* (1888) was first written for and distributed to students of Hampton Institute (a school established in 1868 for the education of freed slaves; now Hampton University), and later sold publicly. The Japanese Association of America (founded in 1908) published a *Guide for Newly Coming Women*, an etiquette book distributed to immigrants during their passage.

Immigrants were addressed, as well, through penny press newspapers, illustrated Sunday supplements, and illustrated magazines. For example, Abraham Cahan's *Jewish Daily Forward* included an advice column written in conversational Yiddish.

World War I slowed the publication of advice books; but by the 1920s, the rate of publication had again increased. At this time, the advice book genre began to blur the distinctions between areas conventionally understood as "private" (the home, domestic, and personal/psychological behaviors) and "public" arenas, such as business and international relations. Domesticity became increasingly aligned with consumer culture. In *Selling Mrs. Consumer* (1929), Christine Frederick, a pioneer of the scientific homemaking movement, turned her attention to marketing consumer goods to the newly professionalized homemaker. Etiquette books, like Emily Post's *Etiquette, the Blue Book of Social Usage* (1922), endorsed a new democratic attitude and simplicity of manners. As the United States engaged in colonial expansion, "American" social usages were grafted onto colonized territories under United States domination (see, for example, the series of *Civico-Educational Lectures* published by the Philippine Bureau of Education, 1917). After World War II, this attitude modified, as witnessed by a series of "pocket guides" for military personnel (and their adaptation in diplomatic and business handbooks and tourist literature), instructing readers in the fine points of social relativism and prescribing that international travelers assume an attitude of tolerance and respect for differing social usages.

Probably the largest change in advice books had its roots in the 1890s' preoccupation with the mind's workings. New Thought, a nondenominational religious movement, and the "mind cure," which sought to remedy psychogenic illnesses by correcting "erroneous thinking," were supplemented in the new century by the science-based discourse of psychology, whose insights informed almost all subsequent books of advice. Businessmen in the Great Depression read Napoleon Hill's *Think and Grow Rich* (1937), and in the fifties consulted Norman Vincent Peale's *The Power of Positive Thinking* (1952). Dale Carnegie's *How to Win Friends and Influence People* (1937), the first paperback best-seller, inaugurated a flood of inexpensive and mass-marketed advice.

Psychology entered the domestic realm with Marie Stopes's *Married Love: A New Contribution to the Solution of Sex Difficulties* (1918), a British book that circulated widely despite attempts at censorship. The post–World War II baby boom created a new market for child-rearing advice, whose tenor modified from a disciplinary stance based in behaviorism to a new "permissiveness" promoted by Yale's Gesell Institute studies in the 1940s and Dr. Benjamin Spock's *The Pocket Book of Baby and Child Care* (1946).

The 1960s marked yet another change in the rhetoric of advice literature, with the advent of the Human Potential Movement of Abraham Maslow, Gordon Allport, and Carl Rogers. This movement, which establishes the self as the locus of values, was foundational to sixties attitudes of self-actualization. From this point, self-help books addressed to those who could not afford professional treatment proliferated, focusing on both private and professional relationships. Books authorizing women as eroticized heterosexual partners (Mirabel Morgan's *The Total Woman*, 1975; and "J's" *The Sensuous Woman*, 1969) shared shelf space with Margaret Fenn's *Making It in Management: A Behavioral Approach for Women Executives* (1978), a guide to manufacturing the self as a consumer product essential to wage labor. The nascent feminist movement produced many self-help books designed to give women alternatives to "expert" advice that positioned them as mindless consumers (for example, the Boston Women's Health Collective's *Our Bodies, Ourselves*, 1976). Current trends in self-help books address readers wounded by nonfunctional family systems (Melody Beattie, *Codependent No More*, 1989) and seek to redress a purported failure in the educational system by outlining programs of "cultural literacy." To focus only on books, however, overlooks a variety of other advice genres: in daily newspaper columns, groups and seminars, on radio, television, audio cassette, and videotape, advisors address topics ranging from business success to thin thighs.

Since a major function of advice books has been to invent, prescribe, and normalize gendered behaviors, their study is an important part of women's literary history. Women have been associated with advice literature in the United States from the beginning. In an era in which their participation in public discourse was proscribed, they found the often-pseudonymous or -anonymous genre inviting; when they wrote under their own names, they often did so with more authority because of cultural ideologies that assigned women monitoring functions associated with "taste," manners, and interpersonal relations. Nancy Armstrong's *Desire and Domestic Fiction: A Political History of the Novel* (1987) posits that eighteenth-century British conduct books redefined the ideal woman, replacing nobility and entitlement as desirable qualities with the ideals of private domesticity. This reinscription preceded and occasioned the emergence of the British middle class. Gender-based analyses suggest that as women writers entered this discourse of advice giving, traditionally associated with politics and statecraft, they participated in an important political process of class management by defining middle-class values. Those women writers inscribed and disseminated the codes of class and social power for themselves and others; their readers were, in turn, made responsible for their own self-fashioning and self-regulation.

Tracing the production of manners and character in American advice books suggests that the democratic impulse conventionally ascribed to the "American" character has dimensions of both social mobility and repression. In the nineteenth century, advice books fueled class mobility, providing patterns whereby upwardly mobile citizens might invent their character; at the same time, however, they functioned as effective monitors of eccentric behavior, as grammars by which counterfeit or unentitled social climbers might be identified. These books commonly linked "correct" manners with a uniquely "American" character and, by extension, deviant behaviors with foreignness. Thus they contributed significantly to the creation of a political national identity. In the current period, by contrast, they deflect attention from social or political circumstances, centering their attention on the personal deficiencies of the reader and placing responsibility for their remedy solely with that reader (subject, of course, to the expert's advice). In all periods they have simultaneously produced and questioned the idea of character. By assuming that it exists, and by articulating its attributes, they construct character; by codifying its components, they ensure its reproducibility and at the same time attest to its artifice.

[See also Etiquette Books and Columns; Health Books, Pamphlets, and Reference Guides; Housekeeping Books; Marriage Manuals; Mothers' Manuals; Self-help Books; Vocational Advice Literature.]

• Arthur M. Schlesinger, *Learning How to Behave: A Historical Study of American Etiquette Books* (1946). Donald Meyer, *The Positive Thinkers* (1965). Barbara Ehrenreich and Deirdre English, *For Her Own Good: 150 Years of the Experts' Advice to Women* (1978). Anita Clair Fellman and Michael Fellman, *Making Sense of Self: Medical Advice Literature in Late Nineteenth-Century America* (1981). Karen Halttunen, *Confidence Men and Painted Women: A Study of Middle-class Culture in America, 1830–1870* (1982). George L. Dillon, *Rhetoric as Social Imagination* (1986). Nancy Armstrong and Leonard Tennenhouse, eds., *The Ideology of Conduct* (1987). Karen Lystra, *Searching the Heart: Women, Men, and Romantic Love in Nineteenth-Century America* (1989). Steven Starker, *Oracle at the Supermar-*

ket: The American Preoccupation With Self-Help Books (1989). John F. Kasson, *Rudeness and Civility: Manners in Nineteenth-Century Urban America* (1990).

Nicole Tonkovich

ADVOCACY WRITING. *See* Protest Writing.

AFFIRMATIVE ACTION. *See* Liberal Feminism; Women's Movement.

AFRICA. *See* Pan-Africanism.

AFRICAN-AMERICAN ORAL TRADITION.

"I thought about the tales I had heard as a child. How even The Bible *was made over to suit our vivid imagination"* —Zora Neale Hurston

The African-American oral tradition is, in part, a product of the tradition of * story telling inherited from a West African tribal group or groups. It is also, in part, a product of the African-American's limited access to literacy in North America. In her article "Arts of the Contact Zone" (*Profession*, 1981), Mary Louise Pratt offers the term "transculturation" to explain the process by which members of a subordinated culture select and invent from materials of a dominant culture. The African-American oral tradition might then be viewed as the process by which African-Americans revise and create materials from Euro-American culture while using the African constructs of story telling. The constructs posit the dynamics of the story and the dynamics of the storyteller as central to the act of revision and creation.

Tribal West Africa featured many oral forms, including the choreo-performance, the chant, the trickster tale, and the proverb. What individuals knew, they related orally—including knowledge of religion, heritage, traditions—via the story. In *African Folktales: Selected and Retold* (1983), Roger D. Abrahams has suggested that the vitality of story telling is a function of two characteristic elements: first, the seizure of the role of narrator and the maintaining of it; second, the constant audience commentary and periodic introduction of call-and-response. The African oral tradition regards the narrator as one who performs and creates simultaneously and holds the story as a dynamic, variable, and participatory phenomenon.

Captured Africans were, through a series of black codes, systematically disenfranchised and segregated as labor pools. The African tradition of story telling prevailed because of such dictates. The result, as Richard Dorson explained in his *American Negro Folktales* (1967), is an oral subculture with a story-telling tradition, including its own unwritten history and literature. The early products of the African-

American oral tradition included various manifestations of story telling: the proverb; mother wit; the folktale; the animal tale; the trickster tale (featuring John and Ol Massa); and various musical forms—the *spiritual, the blues, and jazz. The hybrid of the story and the song, the folk sermon, also thrived in this subculture. Later, as a protective measure and, in part, because language is not static, the oral tradition spawned such forms as the blues, the urban blues, the dozens, and rap.

These are distinctive cultural products of the African-American folk experience. Yet it would be a mistake to imagine the oral tradition as solely a function of opposition to specifically Western oppression, or of opposition to Western cultural hegemony. More likely, it is a function of opposition to oppression in its various forms. One of the oldest tales found in Africa is that of "The Talking Skull." In the account, collected by anthropologist Leo Froebenius in *African Genesis* (1983), a hunter goes into the bush and finds a talking skull that admits: "Talking brought me here." The hunter reports his discovery to his king, who orders his guards to accompany the hunter to the site of the skull and to kill the hunter if he has lied. The skull refuses to speak; the hunter is killed according to the king's command, and only after the hunter is decapitated does the skull ask, "What brought you here?" The dead hunter's head replies, "Talking brought me here!"

In the account contained in Gerald W. Haslam's work *Afro-American Oral Literature* (1975), the setting is the antebellum South, and John replaces the hunter, while Ol Massa replaces the king. In this account, the bleaching skeleton tells John that "Tongue brought me here." John returns to the plantation and convinces the Ol Massa to accompany him back to the woods to hear the skull talk. The skull says nothing. The results parallel those in the strictly African tale. The tale evolves to caution New World Africans against offering too much information to whites.

Zora Neale *Hurston provides a literary adaptation of the familiar lesson in her anthropological work *Mules and Men* (1935) to gain both authority (seizing and maintaining control as narrator) and credibility (as storyteller). In her introduction to the book, Hurston explains why white ethnographers met with little success in collecting southern African-American *folklore: Essentially, the experience garnered from the oral tradition and life informed the would-be subject's evasiveness. No one was willing to risk becoming a talking skull.

Alice *Walker set out to study Hurston for information related to folklore and found Hurs-

ton's works and life to be a model of the possibilities and pitfalls of the African-American woman writer. A staunch believer in the richness of the African-American folk tradition and a transformer of the constructs of that tradition, Hurston is one of the first writers to convert the African-American oral tradition into a literary tradition with distinguishing features. The literary applications of the oral tradition manifest themselves in a number of ways, including a revision of a story presumably familiar to the audience; a participatory narrator who is moved to maintain an intimate connection with the story, thereby lending the story a sense of immediacy; and the use of multiple narrators in a kind of mock call-and-response performance.

Zora Neale Hurston's *Mules and Men* and her novel *Their Eyes Were Watching God* feature all of these revisionary applications. Jane Phillip's *Mojo Hand* (1966) uses the blues tradition to render her story about the overthrow of patriarchal constructs. Toni Cade *Bambara's *The Salt Eaters* (1970) features the nonlinear, circular story to suggest a multiplicity of ways for African-Americans to be in the world. Gloria *Naylor's *Mama Day* (1989) offers multiple narrative voices and African cosmology to address the endurance of love. More recently, Toni *Morrison's *Jazz* (1992) features a participating narrator and multiple narrators to tell the story of a woman who seizes her husband from the clutches of despair, and Alice Walker's *Possessing the Secret of Joy* (1992) features the notion of story telling as a transformer of reality.

[See also Orality; Native American Oral Tradition; Folklore.]

• Richard Dorson, *American Negro Folktales* (1967). Gerald Haslam, *Afro-American Oral Literature* (1975). Zora Neale Hurston, *Mules and Men* (1935; reprint, 1978). Mary Louise Pratt, "Arts of the Contact Zone," in *Profession* (1981). Roger D. Abrahams, *African Folktales: Selected and Retold by Roger D. Abrahams* (1983). Leo Frobenius and Douglas C. Fox, *African Genesis* (1983).

Adele S. Newson

AFRICAN-AMERICAN PUBLISHING OUTLETS. When Samuel Cornish and John B. Russwurm founded the first black newspaper in 1827, a new phase in the struggle for African-American liberation began. The opening editorial of *Freedom's Journal* underscored the significance of the establishment of the independent black press in the United States, a major goal of which was the *abolition of slavery: "We wish to plead our own cause. Too long have others spoken for us. Too long has the public been deceived by misrepresentation in things which concern us dearly." Similarly, Frederick

Douglass's weekly newspaper, the *North Star*, founded twenty years later, loudly advocated racial solidarity and the eradication of oppression and discrimination based on skin color. These publishing outlets, mainly newspapers, provided black women with an important forum for the expression of antiracist and antisexist sentiments, as well as a platform for focusing on their particular plight of the triple burden of *race, *class, and *gender. By 1900, with the establishment of fifty newspapers and forty periodicals published by blacks, women were playing a significant role in the black publishing world.

However, the extraordinary saga of black women publishing is less well known and scantily documented in African-American and women's history, although I. Garland Penn, the first historian of the black press, paid tribute to "Our Women in Journalism" in his *The Afro-American Press and Its Editors* (1891). Mary Shadd Cary's pioneering publishing efforts in the 1850s marks the beginning of black women's leadership roles in journalism; she was the first black woman newspaper editor in North America. Similarly, Charlotta Bass is considered the first black woman to own and publish a newspaper in the United States; after beginning a writing career with the *California Eagle* in 1910, she purchased the paper two years later and remained its editor for forty years. Publications of the black church, such as *Repository of Religion and Literature and of Science and the Arts*, an African Methodist Episcopal Church journal founded in 1858, provided black women with their earliest publishing opportunities as well. Mary Cook, whose pen name was Grace Ermine, wrote for the *American Baptist* in her role as secretary of the Baptist Woman's Educational Convention. The black women's *club movement in the late nineteenth century also provided a major publishing outlet for black women; it attracted large numbers of writers whose major theme was racial uplift, self-help, and the empowerment of black women. *Woman's Era* (1894), the official organ of the National Federation of Afro-American Women, and the *National Association Notes*, founded in Tuskegee, Alabama (1897), and edited by Margaret Murray Washington until 1922, was the official organ of the National Association of Colored Women (NACW). They were the two periodicals most receptive to black women's opinions.

Church papers and women's publications were not the only publishing outlets for black women, however. They were also regular contributors, as essayists, reviewers, poets, and writers of fiction, to the independent black press, including such prominent newspapers as

the *New York Age*, the *New York Globe*, the *Boston Advocate*, the *Pittsburgh Courier*, and the *Chicago Daily News*. Equally important were the independent projects black women undertook in the form of pamphlets or broadsides, which they self-published and distributed. Phillis *Wheatley has the distinction of being the first black person to publish a book in this country (*Poems on Various Subjects, Religious and Moral*, 1773). The first *slave narrative published by a black woman was *The History of Mary Prince, a West Indian Slave* (1831). In 1849, Mary Shadd (Cary) published the pamphlet *Hints to the Colored People of the North*, which urged black independence and self-respect. Ida *Wells-Barnett published a number of political treatises, including twenty thousand copies of *The Reason Why the Colored American Is Not in the Columbian Exposition* (1893), and many *antilynching pamphlets, including *On Lynching: Southern Horrors* (1892) and *A Red Record* (1895). Numerous black women also published and distributed their own *autobiographies or *biographies, including Jarena *Lee's *Journal* (1849); Sojourner *Truth's *Narrative* (1850); and Anna Julia *Cooper's *Personal Recollections of the Grimké Family and the Life and Writings of Charlotte Forten Grimké* (1951).

Black magazine or periodical publishing began with Thomas Hamilton, Sr.'s, *Anglo-African Magazine*, published from 1858–1865, in New York City. The *A.M.E. Church Review* (1887) was the prestigious journal of the African Methodist Episcopal Church. The earliest effort on the part of black women was the founding in 1887 of a monthly literary journal, the *Joy*, by A. E. Johnson, a Baltimore poet; it published for three years. In 1891, Lucy Parsons, the first black woman to play an important role in radical Left struggles, published and edited *Freedom: A Revolutionary Anarchist-Communist Monthly*, a short-lived newspaper that focused on women's issues such as divorce, *rape, and the oppression of women under capitalism. In the same year, pioneering journalist Julia Ringwood Coston published and edited *Ringwood's Afro-American Journal of Fashion*, which had the distinction of being the only illustrated journal for black women in the world; from 1893–1895, she published a second journal, *Ringwood's Home Magazine*. The former included departments such as "Plain Talk to Our Girls," which were edited by competent black women journalists.

In 1900 in Boston, the Colored Cooperative Publishing Company was founded, which was responsible for publishing *Colored American Magazine* (1900–1909), a monthly literary periodical that covered a range of topics of interest to the black community. Pauline *Hopkins was hired to edit its women's section, and three years later became its literary editor, during which time she published four of her novels in serial form in the magazine. Four years later, another prominent monthly magazine was founded: the *Voice of the Negro*, edited by J. Max Barber, which included numerous contributions by black women. During this period three additional periodicals were founded by black women: *Women's World* in Fort Worth, Texas; *Colored Women's Magazine*, a monthly family magazine, in Topeka, Kansas, in 1907; and the *Helper* (1900–1907), which focused on child care, *religion, and temperance. In 1940, Sue Bailey Thurman became founding editor of *Aframerican Women's Journal*, the official publication of the National Council of Negro Women (NCNW). In 1942, one of the most successful publishing ventures within the African-American community began with the establishment of the Negro Digest Publishing Company, founded in Chicago in 1942 by John H. Johnson. It published *Negro Digest* and eventually *Ebony* magazine, both of which provided publishing outlets for black women.

A pivotal moment in black women's publishing history occurred with the founding of *Woman's Era*, a major vehicle for the articulation of women's political aspirations at the turn of the century. It was also a critical publishing outlet for black club women. In 1893, Josephine St. Pierre Ruffin, club woman, abolitionist, and *women's rights crusader, founded the New Era Club in Boston, and initiated a monthly publication, *Woman's Era*. In 1895, the first national convention of black women, later named the National Association of Colored Women (NACW), was called in Boston by Ruffin. The national association was brought about by the consolidation of the Women's League of Washington, D.C., and the Woman's Era Club of Boston, which Ruffin had also founded. *Woman's Era* was eventually designated the official organ of the NACW. The first issue came out March 24, 1894, and twenty-four issues were published through January 1897. Each issue included from sixteen to twenty-four pages, and the subscription price was one dollar per year. Since *Woman's Era* was founded, edited, and published by Ruffin, who was active in the Massachusetts woman suffrage movement, it is not surprising to find a strong advocacy of woman suffrage, especially for black women, in the publication.

The front page of the first issue carried a portrait and feature article on the woman's rights leader Lucy Stone, which set the tone for the publication. The first issue also contained an article on the closing meetings of the New England Woman Suffrage Association, of which Ruffin was a member. There was also strong advocacy for black women entering the public arena in order to solve their unique problems. An awareness of the dilemma that black women faced as a result of the "double jeopardy" of race and sex is apparent throughout *Woman's Era*, a major publishing outlet for the political views and aspirations of black women during the *"Progressive" era.

There were six African-American women born in the nineteenth century whose professional careers were substantially, though not exclusively, devoted to publishing, and who were pioneering journalists: Mary Ann Shadd Cary (1823–1893); Josephine St. Pierre Ruffin (1842–1924); Pauline Elizabeth *Hopkins (1856–1930); Victoria Earle Matthews (1861–1907); Ida *Wells Barnett (1862–1931); and Jessie Redmon *Fauset (1885–1961). There were also numerous other less well known southern black women journalists (because of the proliferation of southern black newspapers): Rosa Bowers, Mary E. Britton, Mary Virginia Cook, A. E. Johnson, Josephine Turpin Washington, to name a few.

Shadd, known primarily for her editorship in Ontario, Canada, of the *Provincial Freeman*, heralded as the best of the fugitive slave newspapers, was a writer, teacher, editor, lawyer, abolitionist, and suffragist. She also has the distinction of being the first black woman newspaper editor in North America. Born in Wilmington, Delaware, to free parents, she migrated to Canada with her brother after the passage of the Fugitive Slave Act in 1850, and published *A Plea for Emigration, or Notes on Canada West, in its Moral, Social and Political Aspect* (1852), a guide for fugitive slaves in the United States concerning what to expect in Canada. A year later, she embarked upon a journalism career and solicited the help of Samuel Ringgold Ward, abolitionist and fugitive slave, in the founding of the *Provincial Freeman*, whose motto was "Self Reliance Is the True Road to Independence." Its main audience was the fugitive slave community in Canada. Shadd was the editor and publisher of this excellent weekly, Canada's first antislavery organ. In 1856, along with H. Ford Douglass and her brother Isaac Shadd, she assumed the responsibility of coeditor until the paper ceased publication two years later. After moving back to the United States in 1855, she became principal of a school, wrote for Frederick Douglass's the *New National Era* and John W. Cromwell's the *Advocate*, and became an outspoken abolitionist on the lecture circuit.

In 1893, Ruffin began her career as an editor with the *Boston Courant*, a black weekly; during this time she also became a member of the New

England Women's Press Association. In 1894, along with her daughter, Florida Ridley, and Maria Baldwin, a principal in the Boston city schools, she founded the Women's Era Club, which was affiliated with the Massachusetts State Federation of Women's Clubs. Her role in the publication of *Woman's Era* led to membership in the Women's Press Club of Boston, of which she was the only black member.

Pauline Hopkins, writer, editor, and playwright, became editor in 1900 of the *Colored American*, a monthly magazine published by the Colored Cooperative Company. She was a passionate advocate of the need for blacks to write their own histories, and wrote a series of biographical sketches of blacks for the *Journal of Negro History*, founded by Carter G. Woodson in 1916. She was inspired by the noted historian William Wells Brown to pursue a writing career after winning a prize in high school for her essay on "The Evils of Intemperance and Their Remedies." In 1900, her first novel, *Contending Forces, A Romance Illustrative of Negro Life North and South*, was published by the Colored Cooperative Publishing Company of Boston; she promoted book sales by reading excerpts to women's clubs throughout the country. The publication of her first novel led to her position as editor of *Colored American Magazine;* the first issue included her short story, "The Mystery Within Us." Subsequent issues also included two of her serialized novels, *Winona: A Tale of Negro Life in the South and Southwest* (1902), and *Of One Blood; or, the Hidden Self* (1902–1903); several short stories, most of which focused on interracial relationships; twenty-one sketches on "Famous Men of the Negro Race" and "Famous Women of the Negro Race," including Frederick Douglass, Harriet Tubman, Sojourner *Truth, and Booker T. Washington; and biographical profiles of prominent white men. A novella, "Topsy Templeton," was published in *New Era Magazine* in 1916. In 1904, she was forced to retire as editor when the magazine was purchased by a Booker T. Washington supporter with whom she did not get along. Her career as a journalist continued when she became a contributor to *Voice of the Negro*, a major outlet for the writings of black women. Her illustrated article on the New York subway appeared in the December 1904 issue, and during 1905 she wrote four articles on "The Dark Races of the Twentieth Century." In 1905, she founded her own publishing firm, P. E. Hopkins and Company, and published in the same year a thirty-page booklet, *A Primer of Facts Pertaining to the Early Greatness of the African Race and the Possibility of Restoration by Its Descendants, with Epilogue*. Some years later she became editor of *New Era*, a monthly magazine published by the New Era Publishing Company in Boston, similar in format to *Colored American Magazine*. Because of competition with William E. B. Du Bois's the *Crisis*, it was unsuccessful. A letter to the *Boston Guardian* in 1906 revealed her awareness of the *sexism that would prohibit her from achieving the recognition she deserved among her contemporaries as a fine journalist.

Victoria Earle Matthews, a self-taught writer and club woman, began her career as a substitute for reporters employed by the large New York daily newspapers—the *New York Times*, *The Herald Mail and Express*, the *Sunday Mercury*, the *Earth*, and the *Photographic World*. She was the New York correspondent for the *Detroit Plaindealer*, the *Southern Christian Recorder*, and the *National Leader*, and wrote for the following black newspapers: the *Washington Bee*, the *Richmond Planet*, the *New York Globe*, the *New York Age* (a leading newspaper founded by Timothy Thomas Fortune), the *New York Enterprise*, the *Boston Advocate*, the *Catholic Tribune*, and the *Cleveland Gazette*. Her fiction appeared in the *Family Story Paper*, the *Waverly Magazine*, and the *New York Weekly*. She coedited briefly with Fortune his paper, the *Atlanta Southern Age*, and during an 1895 tour of the South, she also edited for Fortune a collection of Booker T. Washington's speeches, *Black-Belt Diamonds* (1898); Fortune was Washington's ghostwriter. In 1893, she also published a novella, *Aunt Lindy*.

Perhaps the best-known and most influential of these journalists is Ida *Wells-Barnett, whose international antilynching crusade made her legendary among black political activists. Her career as a journalist began in Memphis, Tennessee, when she assumed the editorship of a black weekly newspaper, the *Evening Star*. Shortly thereafter, she began to write a weekly column under the pen name "Iola" for another weekly, *Living Way*. It was in 1889, when she became co-owner (and later editor) of the *Memphis Free Speech and Highlight* in order to broadcast the plight of black schoolchildren in the public schools, that her career reached a new plateau. After writing a controversial editorial in *Free Speech* about southern white women's sexual interest in black men, she was forced to leave town when the offices of the paper were destroyed. She joined the editorial staff of the *New York Age* and continued her investigative reporting of lynching.

Jessie *Fauset, a *Harlem Renaissance novelist, is also important because of her role as literary editor of the *Crisis*, the official organ of the National Association for the Advancement of Colored People (NAACP), which began publication in 1919 and lasted until 1926. She attracted the attention of its editor, William E. B. Du Bois, because of her earlier literary contributions to the magazine. In her role as literary editor, she became a mentor for large numbers of creative writers, and in 1920 she was made literary editor of the *Brownies' Book*, the NAACP's monthly magazine for young people; she regularly contributed poems, short stories, and plays, as well as children's literature, to this publication. Fauset also solicited and published the works of such prominent writers as Nella * Larsen.

Black book publishing began in 1817 with the establishment of the A.M.E. Book Concern, a project of the African Methodist Episcopal Church. The second-oldest black book publisher was also a project of a religious denomination—the A.M.E. Zion Publishing House, founded in 1841 by the A.M.E. Zion Episcopal Church in New York City. During the contemporary period, six book-publishing projects are significant. The first is Broadside Press, founded by Dudley Randall in 1960 in order to publish black poetry, including volumes of poetry of a number of black women, such as Nikki * Giovanni, Gwendolyn * Brooks and Margaret * Walker. In 1967, Third World Press was launched on the South Side of Chicago by Haki Madhubuti and several friends, and published a number of black women, including Margaret Walker, Gwendolyn Brooks, and Sonia * Sanchez; it is now the official publisher of the works of Gwendolyn Brooks. In 1972, Naomi Madgett * Long founded Lotus Press in Detroit, which provided another outlet for black women poets. Wild Trees Press, a publishing firm founded by writer Alice * Walker and Robert Allen in 1984, also provided, during its short life, an outlet for such new and largely unknown women writers as J. California * Cooper, whose short story collection, *Piece of Mine* (1984), launched her literary career. Kitchen Table: Women of Color Press was founded for the purpose of publishing mainly feminist women of color. Howard University Press, which published its first title in 1896, is the only press of a historically black college/university, and has been a publishing outlet for black women, especially in the 1970s and 1980s.

The first scholarly journal devoted exclusively to the experiences of women of African descent in the United States and throughout the world was founded in Atlanta, Georgia, in 1984, by Patricia Bell-Scott and Beverly Guy-Sheftall. Sage Women's Educational Press, Inc., has as its primary project the publication of *SAGE: A Scholarly Journal on Black Women*. To date, SAGE, housed at Spelman College's Women's Research and Resource Center, has published fourteen, mostly thematic, issues. This biannual, black feminist publication is now a major publishing outlet for black women scholars. Its mission is to provide an interdisciplinary forum for critical discussion of issues relating to black women; to promote feminist scholarship about black women; and to disseminate new scholarship about black women to a broad audience.

Within the popular media, *Essence* magazine, founded in 1970, is the most successful magazine ever published for black women, with a circulation of a nearly a million. It was founded by a group of black men with an initial operating budget of $1.5 million, and supported in its infancy by the white publishing establishment. Its earliest editors were Ruth Ross, Ida Lewis, and Marcia Gillespie, with Susan Taylor assuming the position of editor in 1981. A publishing outlet for prominent black women writers, it also provided opportunities for new writers to express their opinions on a broad range of issues of particular concern to contemporary black females.

• Frederick Detweiler, *The Negro Press in the U.S.* (1922). Ishbel Ross, *Ladies of the Press* (1936). Martin Dann, ed., *The Black Press, 1827–1890* (1971). Penelope Bullock, *The Negro Periodical Press in the United States, 1838–1901* (1981). Gloria Wade-Gayles, "Black Women Journalists in the South, 1880–1905," *Callaloo* 9 (February/October 1981): 138–52. Stella Dong, "Kitchen Table Press: Publishing for Third World Women," *Small Press* (January/February 1983): 17–20. Paula Giddings, *When and Where I Enter: The Impact of Black Women on Race and Sex in America* (1984). Barbara Belford, *Brilliant Bylines: A Biographical Anthology of Notable Newspaperwomen in America* (1986). Donald Joyce, "We Wish to Plead Our Own Cause": Black-Owned Book Publishing in the United States, 1817–1897 (1988). Darlene Clark Hine, ed., *Black Women in America: An Historical Encyclopedia*, 2 vols., 1993.

Beverly Guy-Sheftall

AFRICAN-AMERICAN READING NETWORK. Projects designed to make visible the writings of African-Americans date back to 1827 with the founding of the first black periodical, *Freedom's Journal*, and Carter G. Woodson's *Journal of Negro History* (1916) and *Negro History Bulletin* (1937). These publishing outlets, an obvious manifestation of the self-help movement, emerged in part because blacks were denied access to mainstream publications. Blacks also formed organizations to document, promote, and preserve their cultural heritage; one such organization was the Philadelphia Library of Colored Persons (1833), which housed books and sponsored lectures, debates, and concerts. Another, nearly a century later, was Woodson's Association for the Study of Negro Life and History (1915). The church was also one of the major vehicles for fostering group cohesiveness and promoting self-help and self-improvement among African-Americans shut out of mainstream activities and organizations. It promoted education, social welfare, cultural and spiritual uplift, and the formation of literary societies.

In the antebellum years, free women of color established their own literary, benevolent, and antislavery societies. Concerned about their cultural, moral, and intellectual development, and the absence of educational and artistic outlets, they organized the African Female Benevolent Society of Newport, Rhode Island (1809); the Minerva Literary Association of Philadelphia (1814); the Colored Female Religious and Moral Society of Salem, Massachusetts (1818); the Female Literary Association of Philadelphia and the Afric-American Female Intelligence Society in Boston (both 1831); and the Ladies Literary Society and the Female Literary Society of New York (1834 and 1836). The emergence of black periodicals in the early 1900s—the *Atlanta Independent*, the *Voice of the Negro*, the *Colored American Magazine*, and the *Crisis*—contributed significantly to the development of the black intelligentsia. An important aspect of these nineteenth-century periodicals is their documentation of a black female literary tradition, since much of their creative literature was written by women.

In the 1960s and 1970s, with the emergence of black studies, the academic arm of the black liberation struggle, a movement began to resurrect and reprint lost, ignored, or marginalized writing by African-Americans in order to reconstruct and reclaim their rich intellectual tradition in the Americas. The Black Periodical Literature Project, which identifies creative literature in periodicals during the period 1827–1940, was conceived in 1980 at Yale University by professors John Blassingame, Charles T. Davis, and Henry Louis Gates, Jr. When Gates moved to Cornell University in 1985 he took the project with him, and it is now housed at Harvard University where Gates teaches. The project has recorded 12,544 pieces of fiction, 28,740 poems, and 45,000 book reviews and literary notices published by black writers; the project will be published on microfiche. A subsequent project, *The Schomburg Library of Nineteenth-Century Black Women Writers* (30 volumes), published by Oxford University Press in 1991, was sparked by what Gates uncovered with respect to the lost work of black women writers during the periodicals project. Gates's forward to this extraordinary collection of the published writings of African-American women during the nineteenth century credits Phillis *Wheatley with having "launched two traditions at once—the Black American literary tra-

dition *and* the Black woman's literary tradition." It also calls attention to the facts that Ann Plato was the first black to publish a book of essays (*Essays*, 1841) and that Harriet E. *Wilson was the first black to publish a novel in the United States (*Our Nig*, 1859). The collection also includes Anna Julia *Cooper's *A Voice from the South* (1892), the first black feminist text, and Frances E. W. *Harper's *Iola Leroy* (1892), the second novel to be published by a black woman. This collection is a collaborative project between Oxford University Press and The Schomburg Center for Research in Black Culture, the research unit of The New York Public Library, and the repository of one of the world's largest collections on people of African descent. The Schomburg Center has a long history of collecting, documenting, and preserving the history and cultural heritage of peoples of African descent throughout the world. The oldest book in its collection is an Ethiopian Coptic Tunic, which dates from the eighth or ninth century.

A similar project, whose mission is the reprinting of forgotten literary gems of African-Americans, was initiated by Richard Yarborough, associate professor of English and chair of the B.A./M.A. degree programs in Afro-American studies at UCLA. It reprints genre fiction by African-American writers for the Northeastern Library of Black Literature, an imprint of Northeastern University Press. To date, eleven books have been reprinted, including George Samuel Schuyler's *Black Empire* (1938), a science fiction novel written under the pseudonym Samuel I. Brooks. Two science fiction novellas by Schuyler were identified and edited by Robert Hill and R. Kent Rasmussen, editor and coeditor, respectively, of the Marcus Garvey Papers. The novellas ("Black Internationale" and "Black Empire") were serialized in the *Pittsburgh Courier* between 1936 and 1938. This effort signals a growing trend in reprint projects that draw from fictional work previously published in black newspapers and periodicals. Also included in the series are Schuyler's *Black No More* (1931); Gayl *Jones's *White Rat* (1977); and William E. B. Du Bois's *The Quest of the Golden Fleece* (1911).

In 1989, the Project on the History of Black Writing (HBW), previously the Afro-American Novel Project (1983), moved to Northeastern University in Boston from its original home at the University of Mississippi (Oxford). The founding director of the Project, Maryemma Graham, had as her original goal to identify all published novels written by African-Americans. Its first study guide, *The Afro-American Novel: A Guide for Teachers and Students*, was published in 1986. Supported by the National Endowment of the Humanities (NEH), a major component of the project is the "Checklist of the African American Novel, 1853–1990," which was published by Greenwood Press in Westport, Connecticut, in 1993; the project also publishes *HBW News*, a quarterly newsletter. There are also satellite projects in three states: in Texas, research on writer Clarissa M. Thompson Allen and other Texas writers is being coordinated by Shirley Moore (Texas Southern University); in Kentucky, David Deskins is completing a biography on "recovered" poet Effie Waller Smith; in South Carolina, a group of scholars is working on lost texts by Carolina black women writers. As of 1991–1992, the database holdings of the Afro-American Novel Project are complete for the novel from 1853–1990. Activities of the expanded project include gathering information related to the African-American novel, its criticism, and history of production; developing anthologies, bibliographies, and reference books; preparing book manuscripts for publication; conducting research and writing biographies; and working with specific projects such as the Richard Wright Circle, founded in 1990 by Jerry Ward (Tougaloo College).

Like the Schomburg Library reprints, there have been several projects in recent years designed to celebrate the historical and literary contributions of African-American women and promote the development of black women's studies. Beacon Press of Boston, Massachusetts, initiated the Black Women Writers Series, with Deborah McDowell as the series editor. Its goal was to reprint previously published but out-of-print fiction; to date, reprints include Marita *Bonner's *Frye Street and Environs: The Collected Works of Marita Bonner Occomy* (1987); Octavia E. *Butler's *Kindred* (1979); Alice *Childress's *Like One of the Family* (1953); Frances E. W. Harper's *Iola Leroy* (1892); Gayl Jones's *Corregidora* (1975) and *Eva's Man* (1976); Ann *Petry's *The Narrows* (1953) and *The Street* (1946); and Charlene Hatcher *Polite's *The Flagellants* (1967).

Carlson Publishing Series initiated the project *Black Women in United States History: From Colonial Times to the Present* (16 volumes), with Darlene Clark Hine as editor. The project, based in Brooklyn, New York, reprinted pioneering scholarly essays intended to make a significant contribution to analyses of the intersection of race, class, and gender in American history. The series also includes five dissertations and the conference proceedings from the historic gathering in Atlanta in October 1988 on "Women in the Civil Rights Movement: Trailblazers and Torchbearers, 1941–1965." Similarly, Carlson Publishing, with Hine as editor, released the comprehensive *Black Women in America: An*

Historical Encyclopedia (2 volumes; 1993), which includes over 800 entries and over 450 photographs. The entries range from biographical essays on individual women (prominent and obscure) to broad thematic essays on such subjects as slavery, education, and abolition. It has been heralded as the standard reference work on black women from the time of slavery to the post–civil rights era.

The massive, comprehensive *Notable Black American Women* (1992), edited by Jessie Carney Smith of Fisk University, contains 500 biographical essays and is a major contribution to the reconstruction of black women's history. A condensed paperback version, released a year later and also edited by Smith, was entitled *Epic Lives: One Hundred Black Women Who Made a Difference.*. This biographical dictionary is reminiscent of earlier efforts to document the lives of black women, most notably in Hallie Quinn Brown's *Homespun Heroines and Other Women of Distinction* (1926); M. A. Majors's *Noted Negro Women: Their Triumphs and Activities* (1893); Gertrude Mossell's *The Work of the Afro-American Woman* (1894); Sadie Iola Daniell's *Women Builders* (1970); and Sylvia Dannett's *Profiles of Negro Womanhood* (1964).

Other activities, most notably the Organization of Black American Culture Writer's Workshop, the Melvin Butler and Phillis Wheatley poetry festivals, and the periodic Black Women Writers Conferences held at Jackson State University, have helped to institutionalize efforts to document the creative and intellectual tradition of African-Americans, particularly black women.

[*See also* African-American Publishing Outlets.]

• Penelope Bullock, *The Afro-American Periodical Press, 1838–1909* (1981). Donald Franklin Joyce, *Gatekeepers of Black Culture: Black-owned Publishing in the United States, 1817–1981* (1983). Stella Dong, "Kitchen Table Press: Publishing for Third World Women," *Small Press* (January/February 1983): 17–20. Darlene Clark Hine, ed., *Black Women in America: An Historical Encyclopedia*, vol. 1 (1993).

Beverly Guy-Sheftall

AFRICAN-AMERICAN WRITING. *This entry consists of six essays that survey the generic and historical range of African-American writing. The entry begins with a personal overview of African-American women's writing that assesses both the impact and meaning of this literature for women of color. This article is followed by more-detailed discussions of the literature arranged by genre:*

Overview
Drama
Fiction
Nonfiction

Poetry
Literary Criticism

For further information, please refer to African-American Publishing Outlets; African-American Reading Network; Caribbean-American Writing; Chicago Renaissance; Ethnicity and Writing; Harlem Renaissance.

Overview

A Great Day. At almost precisely the same moment in the fall of 1993, poet Rita *Dove was officially installed as Poet Laureate of the United States and novelist Toni *Morrison was announced as the winner of the Nobel Prize in Literature. Both writers had previously won Pulitzer Prizes: Rita Dove in 1987 for *Thomas and Beulah* (1986), a collection of interrelated poems that artfully chronicles the lives and loves of a black man and woman, and Toni Morrison in 1988 for *Beloved* (1987), a deeply and painfully historical novel of slavery and salvation, murder and memory, and murder of memory—perhaps literature's most haunting narrative of the loves, losses, and legacies of the "Sixty Million and more" claimed by the slave trade and the "peculiar institution."

The awarding of these prestigious prizes and posts were momentous events in American letters to be sure, but few who track such things failed to note their significance for African-American literary history. And few (if any) of the myriad media reports of these events failed to note that the recipients of literature's highest honors were not only black but women. Even as the *New York Times* quoted the Swedish Academy's description of Toni Morrison's work as a kind of lustrous poetry that seeks "to liberate language from the fetters of race," its cover story went on to point out that Morrison was the first black woman to receive the Nobel Prize. Rita Dove, journalists and scholars alike reminded us repeatedly, was not only the youngest writer to be named the nation's Poet Laureate but the first African American—male or female—to be chosen for the position.

Addressing the communal significance of Morrison's award, Henry Louis Gates, Jr., noted literary scholar, observed, "This is a great day for African-Americans and for Americans in general." Toni Morrison seemed to agree that the award and the glory thereof were not hers alone. Eloquent, elegiac, and ecumenical even in the throes of this greatest of all literary accolades, Morrison spoke the afternoon of the announcement not of her own personal accomplishment but of public, national, and racial honor—of the many communities of which she as an African-American woman is a part and with which she shares the prize. "I am of course profoundly honored," she said. "But what is most wonderful for me, personally, is to know that the prize at last has been awarded to an African-American. Winning as an American is very special—but winning as a black American is a knockout."

A knockout. A great day. On that great day as Americans celebrated for and with both Toni Morrison and Rita Dove—as we danced in the streets of Lorain, Ohio; Princeton, New Jersey; Charlottesville, Virginia; and even Middletown, Connecticut—some of "us" whirled and twirled and stamped and hollered all the harder because we knew that, for African Americans, this great day had come after a long and difficult night.

The Long Night. Perhaps nowhere have the trials and triumphs, joys and sorrows, hurts, haunts, and hardships of the long night of blacks in these United States been more vividly recorded than in the literature of African Americans—women no less so than men. From the plaintive cries, songs, testimonies, and tales of anonymous, illiterate slaves, to the carefully crafted prose and poetry of a developing black intelligentsia, the earliest texts of African American women are framed by the historical circumstances of slavery and its aftermath, miscegenation, migration, and the northern urban experience. Indeed, from Lucy Terry's 1746 eyewitness account of what historians have called an "Indian raid" in Deerfield, Massachusetts; to the classical verse of Phillis *Wheatley (ca. 1743–1784) and Charlotte Forten *Grimké (1837–1914); to the rich public orations of Maria Stewart (1803–1879) and Sojourner *Truth (1797–1883), the political poetry and prose of Frances Ellen Watkins *Harper (1825–1911), and the autobiographical fiction of Harriet *Wilson (ca. 1807–1870); as well as in the personal narratives and "secret histories" of Jarena *Lee (1783–?), Nancy Gardener Prince (1799–?), Harriet *Jacobs (1813–1897), and Elizabeth Hobbs Keckley (ca. 1824–1907), we hear echoed in the voices of the few the cries of the multitude who lived their lives under the lash.

But more than just a record of adversity, the poetry and prose that are the founding, enabling texts of African-American letters are an aesthetic chronicle of a long night's journey into day. They are an artful affirmation of the courage, faith, wisdom, will, and "word work" that have carried a people from illiteracy to belles lettres, from auction block to the academy, and from Lorain, Ohio, to Stockholm, Sweden.

With the exception of slave or freedom narratives, which began to appear in the 1730s, the earliest written expressions of African-American women were in the form of poetry and political prose: the formal verse of Phillis Wheatley in the eighteenth century, for example, and the religious and often decidedly proto-feminist essays and speeches of Maria Stewart and Frances Harper in the nineteenth. And while historians have generally characterized slave narratives as a primarily male form of expression, few would disagree that in poetry the voices of black women were first, if not always as foremost or as critically celebrated as those of black male poets such as Paul Laurence Dunbar, James Weldon Johnson, and later Langston Hughes.

Often criticized for its alleged mimicking of classical European forms, the inaugural poetry of the African-American literary tradition employed the master's tongue in a campaign for literacy and liberty that some contemporary scholars have begun to define as subversive—in the same camp with what black feminist critic Harryette Mullen calls the resistant orality of the slave narrative. For eighteenth and nineteenth-century black Americans, mastery of the King's English, as it were, was a political tool, which, while it might not entirely dismantle the big house, might at least help unlock the back door. As most slave narratives and other early writings make clear, the desire for literacy was both part and parcel of the demand for freedom and a sign of entitlement to that liberty and citizenship—to what Frederick Douglass called "manhood rights" but what Sojourner Truth, in "Ain't I a Woman" (1851) and elsewhere, argued were the rights of black women as well as black men.

Just as early black women poets drew on the verse forms of the white European and Anglo-American traditions, so too did early writers of autobiographical prose and so-called sentimental fiction. But they also appropriated and put to creative use the uniquely American form of the slave narrative. Combining elements of both the black slave narrative and the white sentimental novel, nineteenth-century writers such as Harriet Wilson (*Our Nig; or Sketches from the Life of a Free Black, in a Two-Story House, North, Showing That Slavery's Shadows Fall Even There*, 1859), Harriet Jacobs (*Incidents in the Life of a Slave Girl, Written by Herself*, 1861) and Frances Harper (*Iola Leroy; or Shadows Uplifted*, 1892) merged the properties of an oral tradition rooted in resistance with those of a literary tradition grounded, at least in part, in the piety, purity, submissiveness, and domesticity of what historian Barbara Welter has called the Cult of True Womanhood. It is important to note, however, that while many African-American women writing in the nineteenth century claimed for black women the virtue and even the domesticity of their white counterparts,

few, if any, embraced the principle of submission to men in marriage or to male authority in general that was perhaps the most prescriptive facet of true womanhood ideology.

Perhaps no early written text bears out this resistance more dramatically than Frances Harper's short story "The Two Offers" (1859), believed to be the first published short story by an African American. In this brief tale, the multi-talented Harper juxtaposes the life of Janette Alston, a politically active career woman, against that of her cousin Laura Lagrange, who suffers through an unfortunate union to a worthless man for whom marriage was nothing more than "the title deed that gave him possession of the woman he thought he loved." Laura dies alone, calling in vain for the husband who fails her in death as he did in life. Her cousin Janette, on the other hand, unencumbered by the bonds of either matrimony or motherhood, lives an active and productive life as a writer and abolitionist—a life that brings her the love and respect of the many men, women, and children whose lives she alters with her political activism and her literary offerings.

"The Two Offers" is a kind of parable whose title may refer both to the two marriage proposals Laura Lagrange is considering at the start of the tale and to the cousins' ultimately quite different offerings to society. Stepping from narration into exposition (as fiction writers of her time often did), Harper argues quite pointedly for the education and higher training of women that would allow them to make of themselves something more than mere friends, companions, and servants of man. "The true aim of female education," she maintained, "should be, not a development of one or two, but all the faculties of the human soul, because no perfect womanhood is developed by imperfect culture" ("The Two Offers," 1859).

While sentimental fiction was certainly one of the major vehicles that helped to carry into the public consciousness the ideology of domesticity, it was also, as Harper's story demonstrates, one of the principal sites of contestation of that ideology for both white and black women writers. In fact, the challenges to patriarchal authority written between the lines of white women's fiction such as Catharine * Sedgwick's novels *Hope Leslie* (1827) and *The Linwoods* (1835) were part of what made the sentimental form attractive to early black writers. Beginning with William Wells Brown's *Clotel; or, The President's Daughter* in 1853 and continuing in such turn-of-the-century novels as Harper's *Iola Leroy* (1892) and Pauline * Hopkins's *Contending Forces* (1900), black writers, men as well as women, appropriated the formula of the marriage plot (what I have called elsewhere "the coupling convention")—the staple of sentimental fiction—and used it to explore and expose the limitations and the racial particularity of such would-be American notions as female deference, genteel femininity, and marital protection.

In *Contending Forces*, for example, as in so many African-American novels of the period, black womanhood—even in the "whiteface" of the ubiquitous light-skinned mulatta heroine—receives none of the deference, protection, and respect from white patriarchy that the system accorded white women. Instead, a fourteen-year-old girl's black blood makes her the easy target of incestuous rape, impregnation, and concubinage at the whim of her white uncle, a would-be southern gentleman and state senator. Moreover, the black family has little or no recourse against such assaults on its daughters or, as the novel also demonstrates, against the lynching of black men. Like other African-American women writers and activists of her era such as Ida B. *Wells-Barnett (*Southern Horrors: Lynch Law in All Its Phases*, 1892) and Anna Julia *Cooper (*A Voice from the South*, 1892), Hopkins links capitalism, sexism, and racism as the motivating factors behind the rape of black (rather than white) women, the destruction of black businesses, and the lynching of black men.

But while severely and profoundly critical of the white patriarchal social order, novels like *Contending Forces* ultimately offered a hopeful and instructive message to the black readers who were their intended audience. For with the support of an understanding black family (often a metaphor for the wider black community) and the love of a good black man, Hopkins's heroine Sappho Clark gains entitlement to the respectability and bourgeois marriage that her sexual history, under the Victorian tenets of the day, would otherwise deny her. Despite the psychic and physical violence she endures and the "illegitimate" child she bears as a consequence, Sappho Clark, in keeping with the romantic form Hopkins has appropriated and revised, eventually marries Mr. Right (or, in this case Dr. Smith) and presumably lives happily ever after with a true partner, devoted like her to uplifting the black race.

Such romantic fictions and even such happy endings were part and product of the same political activism that black feminist cultural critic Hazel Carby calls a shared discourse among African-American clubwomen, intellectuals, and artists at the turn of the century. It is no accident that some of the era's leading public figures—those who fought longest and loudest for the equal rights of women and for the civil rights of all African Americans—are also the best-known and most prolific women writers of the age: Harper, Hopkins, Cooper, Wells-Barnett, and Victoria Earle Matthews. But in addition to the poetry, fiction, essays, and anti-lynching manifestoes of these activists, turn-of-the-century black women fought gender and racial oppression through the establishment of female training schools, black suffrage societies and temperance unions, and an extensive network of women's clubs that ultimately resulted in the formation of the National Association of Colored Women (NACW) in 1896. *Woman's Era* (later *National Notes*), the official publication of the club movement, regularly printed essays and articles by Mary Church Terrell, first president of the NACW; Victoria Earle Matthews, a cofounder of the Association; and Fannie Barrier Williams, Josephine St. Pierre Ruffin, and Josephine Bruce, all active clubwomen; as well as Cooper, Wells-Barnett, and many others. Like other black feminist writing of the time, these articles took up such topics as the status and potential of African-American women, the black family, and both race and gender relations.

Whatever the topic, the overriding concern of black clubwomen, in and out of print, was defending both the name and the bodies of African-American women against verbal and physical assaults. Mrs. N. F. Mossell (Gertrude E. H. Bustill, 1855–1948) took up this task in her collection of poems and essays *The Work of the Afro-American Woman* (1894), which paid tribute to black women's accomplishments in literature, education, journalism, business, music, etc. Decidedly feminist in its politics, *The Work* represents an early effort on the part of an African-American woman to acknowledge and to celebrate the contributions of her black sisters engaged in uplifting the race or, as the clubwomen themselves put it, "lifting as we climb."

Even the far from overtly political fiction of black female evangelical writers like Emma Dunham Kelley (*Megda*, 1891, and *Four Girls at Cottage City*, 1898) and Amelia Johnson (*Clarence and Corinne; or God's Way*, 1890, and *The Hazeley Family*, 1894), some critics contend, contributed to the cause of racial uplift by calling both white and black Americans to the saving, elevating grace of Christianity. But while writers and activists like Harper and Hopkins (and Jacobs and Truth before them) sought to revise—to "blacken," as it were—impossible standards of white womanhood and femininity, writers like Kelley and Johnson used "whiteness" as a signifier of the transcendent grace and purity open to all good Christians. In this regard, they were less a part of the black feminist project of their contemporaries and predecessors than of the literary evangelism practiced by such white women writers as Harriet Beecher *Stowe and Elizabeth Stuart *Phelps.

The Harlem "Error." It is important to note that many of the texts mentioned in the preceding section have become readily available only recently, through reprint editions known collectively as the *Schomburg Library of Nineteenth-Century Black Women Writers*. Under the general editorship of Henry Louis Gates, Jr., this Oxford University Press series, published in conjunction with the Schomburg Library, has made available since 1988 dozens of previously lost or long out of print nineteenth-century texts by African-American women. In his foreword to the Schomburg collection, Gates notes that between 1890 and 1910, black women published more works of fiction than black men had published in the previous half century. Yet, as Gates also notes, nineteenth-century literary studies, until very recently, has focused the lion's share of its attention not on the prodigious literary production of black women but on the work of black men.

Much the same can be said of the second great flowering of African-American letters: the 1920s, the era known as the Harlem Renaissance, which has been characterized as the age of exceptional black men and bodacious blues women. Black women writers such as Jessie *Fauset (1882–1961) and Nella *Larsen (1891–1964), whose fiction is often said to focus too narrowly on the middle class, have frequently been overlooked entirely or pushed to the margins of the literary movement, to what white literary critic Robert Bone calls the "rear guard" of the Renaissance era. This posterior positioning is meant to suggest that these writers lagged behind such authentically black male artists as Langston Hughes, Countee Cullen, and Claude McKay and such sexually uninhibited blues singers as Bessie Smith and Ma Rainey.

Far from merely "bringing up the rear" in the literary movement of the 1920s, however, writers like Fauset and Larsen actually helped shape the cultural climate of the period. Both as literary editor of the NAACP's influential journal *Crisis* from 1919 to 1926 and as the author of four novels in fewer than ten years, Jessie Fauset was a particularly formidable force among the Harlem literati. In fact, the publication of her first novel *There Is Confusion* in 1924 became a kind of media event—a gathering of more than a hundred writers, critics, editors, and publishers—that historian David Levering Lewis has called the dress rehearsal for the Harlem Renaissance. Black intellectuals such as Charles Johnson at *Opportunity* and George Schuyler at the *Messenger* immediately recognized the potential market value of Fauset's book. Jean Toomer's *Cane*, published the year before *There Is Confusion*, had been a critical success but a commercial disappointment. Johnson, Schuyler, and other members of the black intelligentsia understood that it was profit, not mere praise, that would keep white publishers interested in the work of black writers; accordingly, they encouraged black readers to help make Fauset's book a bestseller. The publication of *There Is Confusion*, a new novel by a "New Negro," may have been a small step for one black woman, but if the book sold well it would be a giant leap for a new generation of young black writers struggling to find their way into the mainstream literary marketplace.

In her role as literary editor of the *Crisis*, Fauset guided the careers of a number of these young black writers, including Langston Hughes (who credited her, Alain Locke, and Charles Johnson at *Opportunity* with having midwifed the renaissance into being), Jean Toomer, Georgia Douglas *Johnson, and Nella Larsen. Though not so prolific as Fauset, Larsen, too, left her imprint on the era. Her two novels—*Quicksand* (1928) and *Passing* (1929)—though well received in their own time, languished in relative obscurity until they were rediscovered in the 1970s and reclaimed as feminist texts. Indeed, Larsen's innovative explorations into the female psychosexual self link her work both thematically and stylistically to that of contemporary black feminist writers, even as her rendering of the crisis and conflicts of her day places her squarely within the renaissance era.

While many of their black male contemporaries looked to an imaginary African and a romanticized rural South for subject matter, Fauset and Larsen focused their attention on the here and now of the burgeoning and burdened black communities around them and on many of the issues most pertinent to modern African-American women: gender, race, and social relations; men, marriage, and motherhood; sexuality; labor, love, and leisure. Like their nineteenth-century predecessors, they were concerned with defending the name of black women, but they also attempted to assert and insert into the public consciousness a new sense of a vital, passionate (rather than passionless) black womanhood. Much of the writing of African-American women of the period is rooted in the paradox of these competing impulses: the need to paint the portrait of a black lady on the one hand and the desire to knock her off her pedestal on the other.

Fauset and Larsen were hardly alone in trying to work through on paper these complex and contradictory imperatives, but the essential conflicts of the era are perhaps best played out in the six novels these two women published between 1924 and 1933: Fauset's *There Is Confusion* (1924), *Plum Bun* (1929), *The Chinaberry Tree* (1931), and *Comedy: American Style* (1933), and Larsen's *Quicksand* (1928) and *Passing* (1929). Both individually and jointly, these novels and other texts of the period such as the poetry, plays, essays, and short fiction of Alice *Dunbar-Nelson (1875–1935), Angelina Weld *Grimké (1880–1956), Georgia Douglas Johnson (1880?–1966), and Marita Bonner (1899–1971), offer an at times scathing critique of the very conservatism and bourgeois materialism so often attributed to their authors.

Though by no means as sexually explicit, raunchy, and risque as the lyrics of their blues-singing sisters, the poetry and prose of the would-be rear guard writers made their own tentative forays into the forbidden realm of black female desire. This is particularly true of *Plum Bun*, where Fauset blends brilliantly nursery rhyme and sexual innuendo, and of *Passing*, where—according to black feminist critic Deborah McDowell—Larsen introduces the possibility of a lesbian attraction between her two heroines Clare Kendry and Irene Redfield. Sex and sexuality are recurrent, perhaps even unrelenting themes in the diary and personal letters of Alice Dunbar-Nelson, but once again the issue of sexuality—heterosexuality, bi-sexuality, and lesbian desire—receives a far more oblique treatment in her published work, as in the poetry, drama, and fiction of her contemporary Angelina Weld Grimké.

The poetic and prosaic accomplishments of a variety of black women who wrote during the 1920s, 1930s, and 1940s—including poets Gwendolyn Bennett, Helene Johnson, Margaret Danner, and Margaret Walker—have long been overshadowed not only by the achievements of black men but also by the luminary presence of novelist and folklorist Zora Neale *Hurston. Like Jessie Fauset, Hurston published four novels in a relatively short span of time: *Jonah's Gourd Vine* (1934), *Their Eyes Were Watching God* (1937), *Moses, Man of the Mountain* (1939), and *Seraph on the Suwanee* (1948). But the rediscovery of *Their Eyes* in the 1970s and its reclamation as a black feminist text have brought Hurston and her work a degree of attention that neither Fauset nor Larsen nor any black women writer except Toni Morrison and Alice *Walker has received.

A kaleidoscope of complex and often contradictory impulses and imperatives—the bourgeois and the bohemian, the reserved and the risque, the sensible and the sensual—the Harlem Renaissance and its cultural production defy easy assessment or summary. I hope it will suffice to say that the renaissance era in particular and literary studies in general take on a different character entirely when African-American women are positioned not as spectators in a male-driven anomalous moment but as active participants in a cultural coup that began in the nineteenth century and is still going on.

Contemporary Black Feminist Texts. The 1940s and 1950s have received far less attention as periods or as defining moments in African-American literary history than the decades that surround them. Yet these years, too, produced a wealth of important work in poetry, drama, autobiographical narratives, and especially fiction. From the Pulitzer Prize-winning poetry of Illinois's longtime poet laureate Gwendolyn *Brooks (for *Annie Allen* in 1950) to the Obie Award-winning drama of Alice *Childress (for *Trouble in Mind* in 1956) and Lorraine *Hansberry's *A Raisin in the Sun* (which won the New York Drama Critics Circle Award in 1958), African-American women carried on in the 1940s and 1950s the furious literary activity that had been the hallmark of preceding decades. Time and space allow for little more than a list, but among the many names and texts of note are Margaret Walker, perhaps best known for her stirring extended poem *For My People* (1942) and her monumental historical novel of slavery and reconstruction *Jubilee* (1966); and the less well-known Marian Minus (1913–1973) and Marita Bonner (1899–1971), whose short stories, essays, and reviews appeared frequently in *Crisis* and *Opportunity*. (Through the scholarly and editorial efforts of Joyce Flynn and Joyce Occomy Stricklin, Bonner's works were published by Beacon Press as *Frye Street and Environs: The Collected Works of Marita Bonner* in 1987, part of the Black Women Writers series, edited by Deborah E. McDowell.)

Among the many novels to come out of the 1940s and 50s are Ann *Petry's *The Street* (1946), *Country Place* (1947), and *The Narrows* (1953); Dorothy *West's *The Living Is Easy* (1948); Hurston's *Seraph on the Suwanee;* Gwendolyn Brooks's *Maud Martha* (1953); and Paule *Marshall's *Brown Girl, Brownstones* (1959). Though vastly different works, most of these women's novels of the 1940s and 1950s are united by their explicit concerns with gender relations and sex roles and in their figuring and refiguring of woman as wife, as object of desire, attempting to assert both her own sexuality and her own individuality. Glory Roane in *Country Place;* Cleo Judson in *The Living Is Easy;* Arvay Henson in *Seraph on the Suwanee;* Lutie Johnson in *The Street;* Silla Boyce in *Brown Girl, Brownstones;* Maud Martha in Brooks's novel of the same name; and, from the preceding decade, Janie Crawford in *Their Eyes Were Watch-*

ing God are all willful wives who in quite different ways rebel against the "proper," particular roles society has determined for them.

In the turbulent, tumultuous, tongue-loosening 1960s, these heroines were joined in their rebellion and resistance—in their willfulness and inexplicable wanting—by such memorable women characters as Kristin *Hunter's Rosalie Fleming in *God Bless the Child* (1964) and Margaret *Walker's Vyry Brown in *Jubilee* (1966). But they are tied as well to the new breed of heroine who emerged in bold face on the pages of black feminist fiction beginning in 1970 with the publication of such pivotal texts as Alice Walker's *The Third Life of Grange Copeland*, Toni Morrison's *The Bluest Eye*, and Louise *Meriweather's *Daddy Was a Number Runner*, followed by Rosa Guy's *The Friends* and Morrison's *Sula*—both published in 1973—Ann Allen *Shockley's *Loving Her* (1974) and Gayl *Jones's *Corregidora* (1975) and *Eva's Man* (1976). These texts ushered in a wave of black feminist fiction concerned with sexism, sexual politics, and the historical effects of racism and patriarchal gender ideals on the lives of black women and children.

It would be a mistake for me not to note, however, that these "womanist" (to use Alice Walker's term) texts of the 1970s and 1980s were enabled at least in part by the civil rights movement and feminist activism of the 1960s. Like their nineteenth-century predecessors, black women artists, activists, and intellectuals of the 1960s discovered, in the midst of the civil rights and women's liberation movements, that the causes they supported frequently silenced or erased them. While women in general were often assigned a marginal status within the male-dominated civil rights movement, black women experienced a particular kind of ostracism, rooted, some of them complained bitterly, in the sexism of their black "brothers." As historian Jacqueline Jones has argued, "too often male Black Power advocates—from activists to scholars—wanted their female kin to get out of the white man's kitchen and *back* into their own" (*Labor of Love, Labor of Sorrow*, 311–312 [my emphasis]). Jones's observation speaks to another problematic aspect of the much misunderstood historical particularity of black women's position in relation to both racial and gender politics. However black men may have perceived the role of "their female kin," and however much white feminists may have been represented reductively as simply wanting out of the kitchen, for black women liberation was neither a matter of getting *out of* or *back to* the kitchen: for while they had historically been forced to work outside their homes, they had never left their own kitchens.

Moreover, it often was (and is) the labor of black and other women of color domestic workers that made it possible for white women to work outside the home. This double-edged labor issue is only one of the many sociohistorical particulars that separated black feminists from white in the 1960s. Dominated by white women on the one hand and by black men on the other, neither the feminist movement nor Black Power activism afforded African-American women much of a sense of presentness, place, or voice.

Black women refused to lie "prone and silent," however, as Stokely Carmichael reportedly suggested. Their voices were raised in some of the most fiery writing of the era. From the often fervently political poetry of Nikki *Giovanni, Sonia *Sanchez, Jane *Cortez, Audre *Lorde, June *Jordan, and Sherley Anne *Williams; to the fiery speeches, essays, and activism of Angela *Davis and Michele Wallace and the autobiographical testimonies of Ann Moody and Maya *Angelou; to the compelling fiction and drama of Toni Cade *Bambara and Ntozake *Shange, as well as Walker, Jones, Morrison, Marshall, and later Gloria *Naylor, black women helped write the text of changing times and helped transform the character of the country.

If the decade of the 1970s represents yet another renaissance in black women's writing, that resurrection continues in the work of contemporary African-American women—too numerous to name—writing within and across a variety of genres. I would be remiss, however, if I failed to note that in addition to the fiction, poetry, drama, and essays that came out of the 1970s, the decade gave rise as well to a new discipline: black feminist criticism. Initially devoted to reclaiming lost texts and to defining a tradition of black women's writing, black feminist criticism has helped transform the contours of the historically white and/or predominantly male Anglo- and Afro-American literary traditions.

While the seeds surely had been germinating since the 1890s, the publication of Toni Cade Bambara's anthology *The Black Woman* in 1970 marks the formal beginning of what has become known as black feminist criticism. *The Black Woman*, which showcased the prose and poetry of writers such as Giovanni, Lorde, Marshall, Walker, and Williams, stands with essays by Mary Helen Washington, Barbara Christian, and Barbara Smith as foundational black feminist texts. Decades have not dulled the sharpness of Washington's critiques, which began appearing in *Black World* in 1972, or of Barbara Smith's pivotal essays "Toward a Black Feminist Criticism (1977)—a black lesbian feminist critical manifesto that named and defined politically the perspective from which Bambara and Washington had been writing. Barbara Christian's first book, *Black Women Novelists: The Development of a Tradition, 1892–1976* (1980), which brilliantly analyzed the work of black women writers from Frances Harper to Marshall, Morrison, and Walker, also remains a foundational text. Alice Walker, too, has played a pivotal role in the development of black feminist studies, through her fiction, her essays—especially "In Search of Our Mothers' Gardens"—and her efforts to recover the once lost texts of Zora Neale Hurston.

Limited space does not allow for a full appraisal or summary of the field of black feminist literary criticism, but among the many names that must appear on even a partial list of pioneering black feminist scholars are those of Hazel Carby, Thadious Davis, Frances Smith Foster, Trudier Harris, Mae Henderson, Gloria Hull, Joyce Joyce, Deborah McDowell, Nellie McKay, Patricia Bell Scott, Valerie Smith, Hortense Spillers, Claudia Tate, Gloria Wade-Gayles, and Cheryl Wall, as well as Christian, Washington, Smith, and many many others. As an inspiration to aspiring young black women writers, as an editor at Random House in the 1970s, and as critic, Toni Morrison, too, has played a particularly dramatic role in opening up spaces for and directing critical attention toward African-American women.

So in a sense, I end where I began: not only with Toni Morrison's and Rita Dove's awards (and, I should add, Maya Angelou's poem read at the 1993 presidential inauguration) but with a "great day" or, rather, a series of them—with a wealth of black women who have written and are writing so much more than I could begin to address in this introduction. To all of those unnamed here, I offer both apologies and gratitude for generations of word work. Henry Louis Gates has speculated that the flowering of black women's writing in the 1890s may have been precipitated by an 1886 essay which said that the great American novel would be written by an African-American woman (Foreword to the Schomburg series, xii–xiii). And perhaps it has been.

Ann duCille

Drama

Nineteenth-century American theatre confined African-American characters to minstrelsy, vaudeville and the musical, demeaning forms utterly uncongenial to women. The more remarkable, then, is the pioneering theatrical career of writer, lecturer and editor Pauline *Hopkins (1859–1930). Her musical drama *Slaves* *Escape; or The Underground Railroad*, was performed in Boston in 1880 by Hopkins's Colored Troubadours, a company which included several members of her family. and which starred the author. More typical of early African-American women writers is Katherine Davis Chapman Tillman (1870–193?) whose several plays, published but probably unproduced, convey the impact of slavery and its aftermath on African Americans. Denied access to the professional theatre by virtue of both race and gender, African-American dramatists wrote for church, school and community productions, or for a reading audience.

Early twentieth century activity responded to several influences: one was the call by W. E. B. Du Bois for a little theatre movement and for "race" plays; that is, plays directed at racial uplift and social change. To this end, the Drama Committee of the NAACP was established in 1915, and two African-American magazines, *Crisis* and *Opportunity*, sponsored literary contests in 1925, 1926 and 1927. As well, in 1926 Du Bois organized the Krigwa Players, a short-lived but influential group that formed units in several cities. Another, equally important, was the activities of the Howard Players at Howard University in Washington, D.C., whose founders, Alain Locke and Montgomery Gregory, promoted folk drama, plays depicting African-American life on its own terms. Finally, Carter G. Woodson, founder of the Association for the Study of Negro Life and History, called specifically for plays depicting African-American history. Many of the plays so inspired came from the pens of women, particularly from a talented network of women in Washington, D.C., all in some way connected to Washington's Dunbar High School or influenced by the program at Howard University.

Angelina Weld *Grimké's full-length play *Rachel*, first performed in Washington in 1916 by the NAACP Drama Committee, was a powerful, if melodramatic, rendering of the effect of lynching on an African-American family, particularly on a daughter's decision to reject a suitor and not to have children. Its concentration on the impact of racism on women and children presaged a central issue for subsequent plays by women. Encouraged by literary contests and by the beginnings of organized community and collegiate drama, writers such as Georgia Douglas *Johnson, Mary P. Burrill, May Miller, Eulalie Spence, Zora Neale *Hurston, Ruth Gaines-Shelton, Myrtle Smith Livingston, Eloise Bibb Thompson, Shirley *Graham, and Marita Bonner wrote plays on a variety of social issues, including lynching, blacks and the military, miscegenation, birth control, poverty and education. An element in all their work is the creation of credible and dignified portraits of African-American women, correcting and refuting prevalent stereotypes of black women as mammies, maids and whores, stereotypes in which the black woman either is sexualized or neutered, largely depending on age and position. Symptomatic of this effort are the ways in which miscegenation figures in several of the plays. For example, in Johnson's *Blue-Eyed Black Boy*, a lynching is averted by state troops because the intended victim is the governor's son; the mother is not diminished by the secret she has kept for 21 years, but rather thanks God for her reform and redemption. Somewhat humorously, in Johnson's *Blue Blood*, true love triumphs and class pretension is undermined when, just before the wedding, it emerges that the groom's haughty mother and the charming and unpretentious mother of the bride were raped by the same white man. The face-saving resolution is the bride's elopement with a faithful suitor.

Not all plays focused on oppression, social issues and the need for change. Spence, for example, preferred to provide dramatic entertainment: *Undertow*, about a love triangle and *Her*, about a haunting. Other plays depicted historical figures of African descent; for example, Harriet Tubman and Sojourner * Truth, Frederick Douglass and William and Ellen Craft, the Haitian rulers Christophe and Dessalines. Most plays employed realism as medium; a notable exception in this period is the expressionist work of Marita Bonner's *The Purple Flower* and *Exit: An Illusion*. None of their work was professionally produced.

As dramatist in this period, the most accomplished was Shirley * Graham, not surprising because she alone of the writers pursued a career in the theatre, as composer, designer and director, as well as playwright. Her opera *Tom-Tom* was the first all-black opera to be professionally produced (in Cleveland in 1931); her brilliant work as head of the Negro Unit of the Chicago Federal Theatre (1936–1938) led to a Rosenwald Fellowship to Yale University where she wrote several plays, all of which explored class, racial, or social issues. Graham's theatrical work ended with her marriage, in 1951, to W. E. B. Du Bois, whose political persecution then consumed her energies.

The 1950s marked a breakthrough for African-American women dramatists. In 1955, Alice * Childress's *Trouble in Mind* won an Obie; in 1959, Lorraine * Hansberry's *Raisin in the Sun* opened on Broadway to much acclaim. The play won the New York Drama Critics Circle Award, making its author both the first African American and the youngest person so honored; the play and its author are now per-manently inscribed in American theatrical history. Alice Childress's contributions, as performer and playwright, began in the 1940s and span the next forty years. Hopkins aside, she is the first African-American woman to have a play professionally produced; her twelve plays and television scripts have attracted international audiences. Speaking to white audiences as well as to black, Childress's plays depict African-American women in a variety of circumstances, their vulnerability and strength, despair and resilience. Nor does she shy away from the controversial; in *Wedding Band*, she portrays an interracial love affair; in *Wine in the Wilderness*, an artist who romanticizes an ideal black woman, but is contemptuous of the real woman who serves as his model.

Following on the achievements of these writers, and on the more general flowering of African-American theatre in the 1960s in New York and in African-American communities throughout the country, as well as on the revitalization of American regional theatre, a generation of African-American women saw drama as a genuine avenue of expression for their many talents. Best known from the 1960s and early 1970s are Adrienne * Kennedy and Ntozake * Shange, the first for such dense and disturbing expressionist theatre pieces as *Funnyhouse of a Negro*, *The Owl Answers*, and *A Rat's Mass*, which explore anguished attempts to construct a gendered sense of self from a biracial historical and cultural heritage. Shange is best known for her much celebrated and highly controversial *for colored girls who have considered suicide/when the rainbow is enuf*, a remarkable performance piece for seven women, whose various monologues move from laughter to frustration, pain, rage, and anguish, yet culminate in hope and a renewed sense of self.

This generation works in a multiplicity of dramatic styles, seeking structural principles in music, particularly jazz and gospel, ritual, and various symbolically patterned expressionistic forms, as well as in conventionally structured realistic drama. Moreover, developing from the 1960s poetic experimentation with the linguistic richness particularly of African-American urban speech, younger writers delineate their characters with language far more variegated than the dialect and standard English distinctions of their predecessors. J. E. Franklin's *Black Girl*, Elaine Jackson's *Toe Jam*, and Martie Charles's *Black Cycle*, while formally relatively conventional, eloquently explore the difficulty of being mother and daughter within a variety of family and social arrangements. Sonia * Sanchez's *Sister Son/ji*, a dramatic monologue, recalls a woman's life; her *Uh, Huh;*

But How Do It Feed Us? challenges the Black Power movement's cult of masculinity. Also important is work in musical theatre; particularly Vinnette Carroll's *Don't Bother Me I Can't Cope,* and *Your Arms Too Short to Box with God.*

Striking in contemporary work is the freedom with which writers render and explore African-American women's sexuality and desire, this freedom a mark of the space women artists have declared for themselves, in defiance of the sexist and racist gaze. At times the tone is satirical and celebratory, for example, in Elaine Jackson's *Paper Dolls;* at others, agonized, for example, P. J. Gibson's *Brown Silk and Magenta Sunsets* and *Long Time Since Yesterday;* or conflicted, Alexis DeVeaux, *The Tapestry.* In *The Brothers,* Kathleen Collins views the hopelessness of African-American men through the eyes of wives, sisters and mothers who care for them, and whose own desires are muted and denied. Although varied in class focus, most plays assume a generic urban setting. Distinctive, then, are the many plays of Sybil Kein's which depict Louisiana Creole language and culture. Most remarkable for elegance and originality of structure and language is the work of Aishah Rahman; her *Unfinished Women Cry in No Man's Land While a Bird Dies in a Gilded Cage* is widely regarded as an underground classic. Various and exciting, African-American women's drama commands critical attention.

• Jeanne-Marie A. Miller, "Black Women Playwrights from Grimké to Shange: Selected Synopses of Their Works," in *All the Women Are White, All the Blacks Are Men, But Some of Us Are Brave,* eds. Gloria T. Hull, Patricia Bell Scott, and Barbara Smith (1982). Margaret Wilkerson, ed., *Nine Plays by Black Women* (1986). Nellie McKay, " 'What Were They Saying?': Black Women Playwrights of the Harlem Renaissance," in *The Harlem Renaissance Re-examined,* ed. Victor A. Kramer (1987). Elizabeth Brown-Guillory, *Their Place on the Stage: Black Women Playwrights in America* (1988). Helene Keyssar, "Rites and Responsibilities: The Drama of Black American Women," in *Feminine Focus: The New Women Playwrights,* ed. Enoch Brater (1989). Kathy A. Perkins, ed., *Black Female Playwrights: An Anthology of Plays before 1950* (1989). Elizabeth Brown-Guillory, ed., *Wines in the Wilderness: Plays by African American Women from the Harlem Renaissance to the Present* (1990). Leo Hamalian and James V. Hatch, eds., *The Roots of African American Drama: An Anthology of Early Plays, 1858–1938* (1991). Eileen Joyce Ostrow, ed. *Centre Stage: An Anthology of Twenty-one Contemporary Black-American Plays* (1991). Margaret B. Wilkerson, "Music as Metaphor: New Plays of Black Women," in *Making a Spectacle: Feminist Essays on Contemporary Women's Theatre,* ed. Lynda Hart (1991).

Leslie Catherine Sanders

Fiction

In March 1975, * *Ms Magazine* published Alice * Walker's "In Search of Zora Neale * Hurston" and inaugurated a new era in African-American literary studies—the era of black women novelists. To be sure, prior to this date there had been other published essays by African-American women which spotlighted the achievements of black women writers of fiction, but none of them had as strong an impact on the literary mainstream as Walker's essay.

Two years after the publication of the article, Walker again carved out an opening in the literary mainstream by offering a course on black women writers at Wellesley College. By 1980, a number of colleges and universities across the country had also begun, albeit reluctantly, to offer courses on black women writers. And at the top of their reading lists was Zora Neale Hurston's *Their Eyes Were Watching God* (1937). Indeed, for many undergraduate and graduate students alike, Hurston symbolizes the Great Foremother of African-American women novelists. But with the publication in 1988 of the *Schomburg Library of Nineteenth-Century Black Women Writers,* a much longer tradition of black women writers of fiction, beginning with Harriet * Wilson's *Our Nig; or, Sketches from the Life of a Free Black* (1859), has begun to take shape.

Like much of the fiction written by African-Americans during the mid-nineteenth century, Wilson's *Our Nig* must be measured in terms of the historical context in which it was produced. Thematically, the novel transgresses the code of silence on antebellum Northern racial prejudice by presenting a domestic scene in which Frado, a young "mulatta" servant, must struggle against the tyranny of her powerful white mistress, Mrs. Bellmont. As Hazel Carby remarks in *Reconstructing Womanhood* (1987), this "domestic realm," in which Mrs. Bellmont is represented as the "ultimate power," was the "terrain of struggle" in which other members of the Bellmont family fought and lost the battle over how Frado, and by extension all black people, should be treated. Drawing on the conventions of the slave narrative and the sentimental novel, *Our Nig* is as much an indictment of the hypocrisy of Northern abolitionism as it is a quasi-autobiographical account of Harriet Wilson's life. Claudia Tate argues in *Changing Our Own Words* (1989) that these popular antebellum narrative strategies allow Wilson to write critically about the abuse of black women by white women without offending the Northern abolitionists who were undoubtedly her intended audience, despite her solicitation in her preface for the support of her "colored brethren."

Wilson obviously received little support from either group, for as Tate points out, the novel fell into obscurity almost immediately after its publication. One can only speculate, as Tate does, that *Our Nig*, and the works of Frances *Harper (*Iola Leroy; or, Shadows Uplifted*, 1892) and Pauline *Hopkins (*Contending Forces*, 1899), to name two other nineteenth-century black women novelists, failed to attract the kind of attention given to fiction written by black men because they emphasize the domestic sphere as the locus of social protest. One must also take into consideration the fact that these novels are not without their literary shortcomings. They were written by black women for mainly extra-literary purposes. For example, in the preface to *Our Nig*, Wilson explains that she wrote the novel in hopes that it would provide extra income for herself and her ailing child. Frances Harper, who by 1892 had already established herself as a widely published poet and lecturer, wrote *Iola Leroy* with the intention of inspiring black youth "to rise in the scale of character and condition." And Pauline Hopkins describes her novel as an attempt to "raise the stigma of degradation from my race." Social conditions in the nineteenth century made it difficult, if not impossible, for black women writers to give careful attention to the literariness of their work and to engage in the act of writing as a form of self-expression. It would take several decades after the publication of *Our Nig* for black women writers to begin to acquire for themselves the social and psychological space that literature—indeed, that all artistic creativity—demands.

The period in African-American literary history popularly known as the Harlem Renaissance ushered in a new generation of black women writers, among whom Nella *Larson and Jessie *Fauset figure most prominently. This era provided black women writers with the space they needed in order to explore, in their fiction, such *intraracial* concerns as discrimination based on caste and color, the prevalence of "passing" (for white) as a form of resistance to racial oppression, and the impact of the great Negro migration on an emergent urban black bourgeoisie. In fact, Fauset, who from 1919 to 1926 was the literary editor of *Crisis* magazine, almost singlehandedly ensured that the group of young African-American writers and intellectuals known as the "New Negroes" received the critical attention she felt they deserved. Ironically, Fauset often did not receive the recognition she deserved for her efforts or for her own prodigious literary output. Her first novel, *There Is Confusion* (1924), went practi-

cally unnoticed. Fauset remained undaunted, however. Although she did not receive the kinds of accolades that were bestowed upon her male contemporaries, Fauset never lost her passion for literature. She resigned her position with *Crisis* magazine in 1926, but continued to write, and by 1933 had produced three more novels: *Plum Bun* (1929), *The Chinaberry Tree* (1931), and *Comedy: American Style* (1933).

Thematically, Fauset's novels have much in common with those of her female predecessors, particularly with regard to her representations of African-American women. To cite just one example, in *There Is Confusion* her female characters all strive, in various ways, to be virtuous and morally upright. They also consider marriage an important, if not a "fixed," purpose of their lives. What distinguishes Fauset's work from those of the earlier black women novelists is her treatment of those themes. *There Is Confusion* is a carefully crafted novel. Although it has its share of social protest, that aspect of the work does not interfere with the overall structure of the novel as it does in Harper's *Iola Leroy*, for example. But neither does the novel offer a cogent analysis of the snobbish fictional universe of the pre-World War I African-American middle-class society it depicts. It simply asserts that universe as a model to be emulated in the interest of uplifting the race.

Nella Larsen also focuses almost exclusively on the black middle class. But her novels, *Quicksand* (1928) and *Passing* (1929), introduce a new theme in African-American women's fiction: the theme of feminine sexuality and desire. Larsen's female characters struggle, but in vain, with their sexual desire and against the moral and ethical imperatives that demand that their desire be repressed. In *Quicksand*, Larsen's Helga Crane, who Hazel Carby in *Reconstructing Womanhood* correctly identifies as "the first truly sexual black female protagonist in Afro-American fiction," tries in several ways to assert herself as an independent and sexual being, only to end up as defeated by her own sexuality.

In *Passing*, Larsen develops a complex relationship between two women that subtly suggests lesbianism, a theme that would be explored more fully in the fiction of Alice Walker (*The Color Purple*, 1982), Gloria *Naylor (*The Women of Brewster Place*, 1982), Audre *Lorde (*Zami*, 1982), and Ntozake *Shange (*Sassafrass, Cypress and Indigo*, 1982). Irene Redfield is irresistibly attracted to Clare Kendry, despite the threat she believes her beautiful friend poses to her marriage. Clare, who has spent many years passing as a white woman married to a successful white businessman, Mr. Bellew, convinces Irene to help her get reacquainted with Harlem's "Negro Society." Irene reluctantly agrees, and the result is deadly. Irene becomes obsessed with Clare's beauty and with the idea that her friend is having an affair with her husband, Brian. She also fears Clare's independence and her willingness to risk everything, including her marriage to Mr. Bellew, for the pleasure of doing what she pleases whenever she pleases. Irene, like most of the female characters in novels written by black women prior to Hurston's *Their Eyes Were Watching God*, needs to feel secure. She needs to be sure that Brian will remain by her side. And it is for the sake of her marriage, her children—her security—that Irene represses her own sexual desire and precipitates Clare's tragic end. Nella Larsen's message, in *Passing* and *Quicksand*, seems to be that in the 1920s, the independent and desiring black middle-class woman is indeed a tragic (mulatta) figure, a woman who, for the sake of conformity, is not allowed to thrive.

Hurston's *Their Eyes Were Watching God* marks a radical shift in black women's fiction in a number of ways. The most significant is Hurston's rendering of Janie as a member of a poor and rural community who goes against convention and succeeds in determining for herself the conditions of her existence. For instance, Janie rejects her privileged community status as Mayor Jody Stark's widow and marries Tea Cake, a man thirteen years younger than she who can only offer her the precariousness of life on the muck. After she kills Tea Cake in self-defense and is exonerated, Janie returns to her town unperturbed by the ugly utterances and insinuations of the local "porch" people. She is, for some critics, the prototype for such female characters as Alice Walker's Shug *(The Color Purple)*, Toni *Morrison's Sula (Sula, 1973)*, and the disturbing figure of Eva Canada in Gayl *Jones's Eva's Man* (1976). What each of these characters shares with Hurston's Janie is a certain antipathy towards the traditional role of women as lovers, wives, and mothers. Although some of them fail, these and many of the other modern(ist) female figures who inhabit the fictional worlds of black women writers seek new ways of defining themselves as women. As Ann *Petry shows in her powerful novel *The Street* (1946), those who fail do so because the racism and sexism with which they must contend prohibit any possibility for such self-realization. In *The Street*, Petry's Lutie Johnson and her young son both fall victim to the scheming people around her until finally, after having killed a hustler named Boots Smith for trying to prostitute her to the local white con man, Lutie is forced to leave Harlem. In so doing, Lutie breaks an unwritten code of

(African-American) maternal conduct: she sacrifices her son, by abandoning him in a Harlem reform school, in order to save herself. Petry wrote two other novels, *Country Place* (1947), and *The Narrows* (1953), a tale of interracial love which is as violent and pessimistic as *The Street*.

According to Gloria Wade-Gayles (*No Crystal Stair*, 1984), between 1946, when Ann Petry published *The Street*, and 1976, when Gayl Jones's *Eva's Man* and Alice Walker's *Meridian* appeared, black women produced twenty-six major novels. Of these, Wade-Gayles selects twelve that she feels cut "most brilliantly through layers of institutionalized racism and sexism and take us to the core of black women's humanity." Her list includes Petry's *The Street*, Dorothy West's *The Living Is Easy* (1948), Gwendolyn Brooks's *Maud Martha* (1953), and the early novels of Paule *Marshall (*Brown Girl, Brownstones*, 1959), Toni Morrison (*The Bluest Eye*, 1970), and Alice Walker (*The Third Life of Grange Copeland*, 1970).

Much of what is presently being hailed as a new era in African-American fiction can be attributed to the prodigiousness of these latter three novelists. Marshall, who in 1992 became a recipient of the prestigious MacArthur Foundation Award, has, since the publication of her first novel, written four more: *Soul Clap Hands and Sing* (1961); *The Chosen Place, The Timeless People* (1969), *Praisesong for the Widow* (1983), and *Daughters* (1991). Morrison gained national attention when her third novel, *Song of Solomon* (1977) was named a Book-of-the-Month Club selection. According to Nellie McKay, who edited the first volume of critical essays on Morrison, *Song of Solomon* was "the first [novel] by a black writer to receive such attention since Richard Wright's *Native Son* in 1940" (*Critical Essays on Toni Morrison*, 1988). Morrison's more recent novels—*Tar Baby* (1981), the 1988 Pulitzer Prize winning *Beloved* (1987), and *Jazz* (1992)—have firmly established her as a major American writer.

McKay remarks in her introduction to *Critical Essays* that Morrison shares a "special link" with Jessie Fauset in the "chain" of black women's literary tradition in that, as a senior editor at Random House, Morrison "discovered" and brought onto the publisher's list several black writers, including Gayl Jones, whose first novel, *Corregidora*, was published in 1975, and Toni Cade *Bambara (*The Salt Eaters*, 1980). As McKay remarks, "[Morrison's] interest in promoting black writers, as was Fauset's, was her desire to participate in the development of a canon in black literature in which writers 'can get down to the craft of writing . . . [as] black people talking to black people.' " As the 1993 recipient of the Nobel Prize for Literature, Morrison represents the avant-garde of Black American writers who are presently making their mark on the international literary scene.

Another "special link" in the "chain" of black women's literary tradition was forged by Mary Helen Washington when, in 1975, she edited *Black Eyed Susans*, an anthology of short fiction. She published a second anthology, *Midnight Birds*, in 1979. These anthologies, which have recently been reissued as a single volume, remain the definitive anthologies of black women's short fiction. They include excerpts from novels by Morrison, and short stories by Alice Walker, Toni Cade Bambara, and a number of equally talented, but less well known, black women writers who have chosen the short story as their preferred genre.

Black women writers have been trying, with varying degrees of success, to "get down to the craft of writing" fiction and more specifically, the novel, for over a century, despite the exigencies of their race and gender. The result at the end of the twentieth century is that the works of Morrison, Alice Walker (*The Temple of My Familiar*, 1989; *Possessing the Secret of Joy*, 1992), Gloria *Naylor (*Linden Hills*, 1985; *Mama Day*, 1988; *Bailey's Cafe*, 1992), Terry *McMillan (*Mama*, 1987; *Disappearing Acts*, 1989; *Waiting to Exhale*, 1992), Marita *Golden (*A Woman's Place*, 1986; *Long Distance Life*, 1989; *And Do Remember Me*, 1992), Thulani Davis (*1959: A Novel*, 1992), J. California *Cooper (*Family*, 1991) Rita *Dove (*Through the Ivory Gate*, 1992), Xam Cartier (*Muse-Echo Blues*, 1991) and other black women writers too numerous to mention here across the variables of caste and class and present a myriad of African-American women's fictional experiences richer than anything their foremothers could ever possibly have imagined or written. These writers' appeal to a broad and heterogeneous audience is proof positive that a new era in African-American women's fiction, indeed, in African-American literature itself, is well under way.

• Roseann Bell, et al. *Sturdy Black Bridges: Visions of Black Women in Literature* (1979). Claudia Tate. *Black Women Writers at Work* (1983). Mari Evans. *Black Women Writers (1950–1980): A Critical Evaluation* (1984). Hazel Carby. *Reconstructing Womanhood* (1987). Nellie McKay, ed., *Critical Essays on Toni Morrison* (1988). Craig Werner. *Black American Women Novelists* (1989). Mary Helen Washington, ed., *Black-Eyed Susans/Midnight Birds*. (1990).

Sandra Adell

Nonfiction

The appearance of autobiographies like Jill Nelson's *My Experience as an Authentic Negro* (1993) serve as a reminder that not only have black women had to struggle to express themselves in print, but they have often had to control the production of that print in order to find expression. The nonfiction writings of black women—journalism, autobiography, and transcribed oratory—reflect a dynamic of persistent exclusion from, and insistent participation in, the cultural and political life of the United States. Often, this required the establishment of independent institutions that produced publications that reached audiences of all races. Hence, black women's writing, organizing, and struggle for civil rights have been inextricably connected. The first example of this connection, "Belinda, or the Cruelty of Men Whose Faces Were Like the Moon," was published in 1787, after being presented to the Massachusetts Legislature in 1782 as an autobiographical appeal for freedom in old age.

In the first half of the nineteenth century, black women who did write claimed their authority from spiritual or virtuous sources. Maria Stewart, the first American-born woman to speak publicly, felt authorized by her Christian faith to uphold the morality of the Victorian ethic of true womanhood. Simultaneously, she challenged its racist and classist assumptions by ascribing morality and virtue to external dynamics, not internal or inherent qualities (*Productions of Mrs. Maria W. Stewart*, 1835). Jarena *Lee, in *The Life and Religious Experience of Jarena Lee, A Coloured Lady* (1836), documents her extensive travels and speechmaking. Lee is the first of the spiritual autobiographers, among them Rebecca Jackson and Amanda Smith, whose religious faith provided justification and protection for their literacy and written expression. Along with the writers of the slave narratives, such as Harriet *Jacobs (1861), Elizabeth Keckley (1868), and Sojourner *Truth (1878), they solidified the connection between writing and social responsibility that continues to characterize black women's writing.

The first black woman to publish a newspaper was Mary Ann Shadd Cary, whose abolitionist *The Provincial Freeman* appeared in Canada (1850–1860). She was also the first to establish the link between black women writers and independent organizations. After her return to the United States, she founded the Colored Women's Progressive Association (1880), which was also to publish a newspaper.

Ida B. *Wells-Barnett, columnist and co-owner of the newspaper *Free Speech*, Memphis, Tennessee, more than ably followed in Cary's impressive footsteps. By the 1880s, her columns were serialized in the Detroit *Plaindealer*, the New York *Age*, and the *Indianapolis Freeman*, among the best of the nearly 200 black newspapers then being published. She undertook a campaign to document the lynch-murders of black people in the South and was forced, amid the arson of her newspaper and death threats, into exile in the North in 1892. She moved to New York and purchased a one-fourth share of *New York Age* in exchange for the *Free Speech* subscription list, and continued to publish her findings. A group of prominent black women raised the funds for the publication of her research in a booklet (1892). Many of these women went on to participate in the founding of black women's clubs and national organizations that in turn generated newspapers in which black women writers documented their lives and advocated the improvement of conditions for black women and men.

The most prominent publications included *Women's Era* (1894), edited by Josephine St. Pierre Ruffin, the official paper of the National Federation of Afro-American Women (1895), and *National Notes* (1897), the publication of the National Association of Colored Women and successor to *Women's Era*. In their pages, women such as Mary Church Terrell, Margaret Murray Washington, Fannie Barrier Williams, and many others advocated a philosophy of social uplift characterized by the motto "Lifting As We Climb." Recognizing the role of women in acculturation, black women club leaders urged the black woman to provide a stable home and moral structures for her family in order to raise black people from a position of degradation and vulnerability to white prejudice. At the same time, club leaders recognized the tremendous economic and physical strains black women in general labored under, and organized to provide kindergartens and nutritional and hygienic education for their less-privileged sisters. In general, their preoccupations reflected those of Anna Julia *Cooper, whose *Voice of the South by a Black Woman from the South* (1892) was the first black feminist analysis of the condition of blacks and women in the United States.

Despite the proliferation of publication opportunities, the first black woman to make a living from journalism was Alice *Dunbar-Nelson (1875–1935). Significantly, she published in both black and white newspapers, signalling the shift in black women's energies that took place after the turn of the century. Black women had been able to sustain the tension of advocating for both the cult of true womanhood and suffrage; the struggle for suffrage had made clear the intransigence of race as social boundary. As a result, black women refocused their energies on antilynching laws, through the male-led National Association for the Advancement of Colored People (NAACP), and renewed efforts at inter-racial cooperation. By 1922, *National Notes* was no longer, and the cult of true womanhood and other Victoriana was eclipsed by the glamourization of femininity in the age of the flapper.

A single outstanding exception in this period was Amy Jacques Garvey, editor of the Women's Page in the United Negro Improvement Association (UNIA) newspaper, *Negro World*. Her writings reflected attitudes shared with turn of the century clubwomen, although they appealed to a working-class, mass-movement oriented audience. Another UNIA supporter, Charlotte Bass, owned and published the *California Eagle* (1912) in Los Angeles for nearly forty years.

Despite Bass's newspaper, black women's nonfiction appears to have entered an eclipse from the onset of the Depression until the beginning of the Civil Rights movement. The demise of black women's organizations and official publications and the creation of a class of educated black readers allowed black women writers to turn to other forms, particularly the novel, during the intervening years. Many of these novels, however, continue to join social responsibility with the written word in their depiction of black women's lives. One of the few non-fictionalized autobiographies to appear during this time was Zora Neale *Hurston's *Dust Tracks on the Road* (1942), commissioned by her publisher, and restrained by its commitment to a factual account of her life.

The emerging Civil Rights movement once again lent motivation to black women to document their lives, comparable to the abolitionist and religious motivations that had inspired an earlier generation. Women who had achieved success on either a national or community level began to write of their lives to provide examinations of their culture, explanations of their choices and, most importantly, examples to a coming generation. Marian Anderson's *My Lord, What a Morning* (1956), Billie Holiday's *Lady Sings the Blues* (1956), Ethel Waters's *His Eye Is on the Sparrow* (1951), Eartha Kitt's *Tuesday's Child* (1956), and Althea Gibson's *I Always Wanted to Be Somebody* (1958) appeared alongside Effie Kay Adams's *Experience of a Fulbright Teacher* (1956), Ella Earls Cotton's *A Spark for My People: A Sociological Autobiography of a Negro Teacher* (1954), and Reba Lee's (pseud.) *I Passed for White* (1955).

The growth of the Civil Rights and Black Power movements prompted a wave of testimonies from activists, among them Septima Clark's *Echo in my Soul* (1962), Daisy Bates's *The Long Shadow of Little Rock* (1970), and Angela *Davis's *An Autobiography* (1974). Maya

*Angelou's *I Know Why the Caged Bird Sings* (1970) began a testimony to a contemporary life that has continued through four volumes. In addition, creative writers like Gwendolyn Brooks, Nikki *Giovanni, Lorraine *Hansberry, and Audre *Lorde have written autobiographies that explore the role of creativity in black women's lives.

Many of these same writers are also essayists of note, and increasing numbers of collections have been appearing since the early 1980s, such as June *Jordan's *Civil Wars* (1981) and *On Call* (1985), Audre Lorde's *Sister Outsider* (1984), Alice *Walker's *In Search of Our Mother's Gardens* (1983); and the many works of bell hooks.

An emerging form is the collective autobiography, generally organized around a particular aspect of identity or experience, featuring nonfictional prose selections from a number of authors. Two of the most popular and influential works in this form are *This Bridge Called My Back: Writings by Radical Women of Color* (1981) and *Home Girls: A Black Feminist Anthology* (1983). Both volumes also represent a return to self-publication for black women, although the form's proliferation has attracted the interest of white publishers.

Nonetheless, nonfiction writing by black women continues to unite the written word with political and spiritual purpose. *Essence,* the black women's magazine, fulfills a more varied function than *National Notes,* but remains substantially dedicated to advising the black woman on how best to insist on her participation in a culture that still strives to exclude her by providing resource lists and acting as a clearinghouse for organizations and services geared to black women. Black women remain woefully underrepresented in white media, and those who can be found there are apparently waiting to get out, like Jill Nelson, before telling their stories.

• Mary Burgher, "Images of Self and Race in the Autobiographies of Black Women" in *Sturdy Black Bridges: Visions of Black Women in Literature,* ed. Roseann P. Bell, Bettye J. Parker, and Beverly Guy-Sheftall, (1979), pp. 107–122. Jean Fagan Yellin, "Afro-American Women, 1800–1910: Excerpts from a Working Bibliography" in *All the Women Are White, All the Blacks Are Men, But Some of Us Are Brave: Black Women's Studies,* eds. Gloria T. Hull, Patricia Bell Scott, and Barbara Smith, (1982), pp. 221–244. Paula Giddings, *When and Where I Enter: The Impact of Black Women on Race and Sex in America* (1984). Sandi Russell, *Render Me My Song: African-American Women Writers From Slavery to the Present* (1990). Beverly Guy-Sheftall, *Black Women in United States History* (1990). Darlene Clark Hine, ed., *Black Women in America: An Historical Encyclopedia,* 2 vols. (1993).

Randi Gray Kristensen

Poetry

The tradition of African-American women as poets dates back to the mid-eighteenth century when Lucy *Terry (1730–1821) composed the first known poem written by an African in America. Although biographical information on Terry is limited, it is known that she was taken from Africa as a child and sold in America as a slave. Her "Bars Fight" records a skirmish in 1746 between settlers in her village of Deerfield, Massachusetts, and Native Americans. The poem was handed down orally for more than a century, surviving in the oral tradition because of its significance to New England colonial history. "Bars Fight" is of historic value today only because it is credited as the first poem by an African American and not due to its literary value.

The works of Phillis *Wheatley (ca. 1753–1784), whose career as a writer peaked a few decades after Terry composed her historic poem, marks the beginning of both the African-American formal literary tradition and the African-American women's literary tradition. Wheatley, the most popular African-American poet of the eighteenth century and the most successful until Paul Laurence Dunbar emerged in the late nineteenth century, was the first African-American poet of real literary significance, and the first to publish a book of verse. Like Terry, Wheatley was also a native of Africa who was kidnapped from her family and homeland at the age of five or six and sold into North American slavery. In 1761, she was purchased by the family headed by Susanna and John Wheatley, a Boston merchant. Aided by informal tutoring sessions conducted by members of the Wheatley family, she learned to speak and read English at an accelerated pace. By the time she was ten she could translate Ovid's tales from Latin and by her early teens she wrote poetry in fluent English. She published her first poem at the age of seventeen, and issued her *Poems on Various Subjects, Religious and Moral* in 1773, although racial attitudes in this country forced her to go to England to find a publisher. Several African-American critics in years past have complained of Wheatley's failure to speak out loudly against the practice of slavery in her poetry, but more recent studies have found her to be one of the first African Americans to express formally her love for freedom for all people and to protest to high-ranking authorities concerning the plight of slaves.

After Wheatley's premature death in her early thirties, few of the African-American women poets who followed in the eighteenth and nineteenth centuries are well known today—with the possible exception of Frances Ellen Watkins *Harper (1825–1911), who is also remembered for many of her other achievements—although a number did express themselves in verse. Through much of the century a large amount of the imaginative work by African-American writers that successfully found its way into print attempted to further the abolitionist cause. As a result, those who wrote slave narratives, speeches, and essays of moral appeal were better able to place their works, while those who wrote poetry, especially women who wrote about more personal concerns, were generally neglected by publishers. Harper was the most important African-American woman writer of the nineteenth century and the most popular African-American poet from Wheatley to Dunbar. In a career that spanned the critical period in American history from abolition to women's suffrage, her popularity as a poet was largely a result of her performances of her work in front of large audiences who were moved by her combination of oratorical skill and political message. She reportedly sold more than fifty thousand copies of her various volumes and numerous broadsides and tracts, with most sold at the various meetings and rallies where she spoke during her tours to support causes such as the abolition movement, temperance, women's suffrage, literacy during Reconstruction, and the anti-lynching issue.

Throughout the eighteenth century, African-American women found it nearly impossible to find presses willing to publish their collections of poems; in fact, before 1890 there were virtually no book-length collections of poems by African-American women published in this country other than Harper's. Most of the women who did publish during this time, up until the mid-twentieth century, did so in local magazines, newspapers, club gazettes, and in church bulletins. Several important research projects in recent years have discovered the identities of women poets who were not previously known and have made their works available to modern scholars and students for the first time. Several of the poets who did receive notice during the nineteenth century other than Harper were: Ann Plato (1820–?), who as a teenage girl published a collection of moral essays, biographical sketches, and poems entitled *Essays: Including Biographies and Miscellaneous Pieces, in Prose and Poetry* (1841); Charlotte Forten *Grimké (1837–1914), one of the few African-American women to have a book-length diary published and whose poems appeared in the leading African-American journals during the latter half of the century; Henrietta Cordelia *Ray (1850/1852?–1916), a prolific and well-known poet who published 146 poems in her collections

Sonnets (1893) and *Poems* (1919); Mary Weston Fordham (1862–?), whose volume of verse, *Magnolia Leaves* (1897), was introduced by Booker T. Washington; and Priscilla Jane Thompson (1871–1942), who published seven volumes of poems with her sister and brother between 1899 and 1926 on topics such as Christian faith and morality, love, and racial pride.

At the beginning of the twentieth century, Harlem, New York, developed as the center of African-American artistic and cultural expression, and writers from around the country flocked to New York where the best publishing opportunities existed. During this period, however, only a few women writers were promoted, and the best known, such as Nella *Larsen (1891–1964), Zora Neale *Hurston (1891–1960), and Jessie *Fauset (1888–1961), were recognized for their fiction, drama, and work in other areas. (Fauset also wrote poetry but is best known for her novels and her work as literary editor of the NAACP's *Crisis* magazine.) Some of the best-known women poets of this period are Angelina Weld *Grimké (1880–1958; Charlotte Forten Grimké's niece by marriage), Alice *Dunbar-Nelson (1875–1935), Ann Spencer (1882–1975), Georgia Douglas *Johnson (1886–1966), Effie Lee Newsome (1885–1979), Gwendolyn *Bennett (1902–1981), and Helene Johnson (b. 1906). However, despite the significant developments in African-American literature from Dunbar through the Harlem Renaissance period, especially in poetry, not one woman emerged as a major African-American poet, although several are of great interest. Georgia Johnson, for example, produced three books of verse during this period, making her the most important African-American woman poet after Harper; Spencer was considered to be one of the Renaissance's most innovative and highly imaginative poets; Bennett was an artist and poet, and her artistic influence showed in some of the detailed scenes she wrote into her poems; Angelina Weld Grimké, who was also a dramatist and short fiction writer, was from a family with an important literary heritage. Due to several factors, including chauvinism among the male writers and others of literary influence during the Renaissance, few of the women poets were able to situate themselves among the literary elite during an era when poetry was the most popular form of African American creative expression. Of the women poets of the Renaissance, few were a part of the movement's mainstream. Georgia Johnson, despite her published volumes, received little of the promotion the published male writers received; and like many of the other women, she did not live in New York. Her residing instead in the Washington, D.C., area limited her interactions with the editors of the popular journals that published and promoted Renaissance writers. Not living in New York also limited her interactions with the leading male poets. In fact, for the women poets who comprised the core of the lower echelon of Renaissance writers, the nation's capital was a more significant setting since the majority of them lived in close proximity to Washington and Douglas Johnson's parlor, where she held regular literary gatherings involving the writers who lived in that area and others who traveled through it.

From the beginning of the contemporary period to the present, African-American women poets have ranked among the major poets of the literature. In fact, their ranks have increased to a number equal to, if not exceeding, that of the major African-American male poets. Margaret * Walker Alexander's (b. 1915) collection, For My People (1942), is possibly the most important single book of verse published by an African-American woman until that time. As a graduate student in the School of Letters of the University of Iowa, Walker wrote the poems that appeared in the volume as her master's thesis. It was later published in the Yale Series of Younger Poets, one of the most prestigious nonracial honors given to an African-American poet at the start of a career. Three years later, Gwendolyn * Brooks (b. 1917) published her first collection, A Street in Bronzeville (1945). Her second collection, Annie Allen (1949), won the 1950 Pulitzer Prize, making her the first African American to receive that honor. Near the close of the century, Brooks is arguably the most important poet in the African-American and African-American women's literary traditions. Predicted by her mother to become the lady Paul Laurence Dunbar at the age of seven, she has been one of the nation's most prolific poets, and she is the most highly recognized African-American poet of her time. She has received two Guggenheim fellowships, was the first African-American woman elected to membership in the National Institute of Arts and Letters, was the first selected as Consultant in Poetry to the Library of Congress, was awarded the Frost Medal from the Poetry Society of America, has served as Poet Laureate of Illinois since 1968, and has been awarded more than seventy honorary degrees. Like many of the African-American writers of the time, her early works were written in the academic language of the literary mainstream, although the poems were about the lives of African-Americans confined to living in kitchenette apartments in northern urban communities such as the area of Chicago she characterizes as "Bronzeville." However, in these early collections she explores intimate aspects of the lives of African-Ameri-

can women which had seldom been discussed in literature before, especially in verse. In her third collection, The Bean Eaters (1960), some critics in the literary mainstream, black and white, accused her of forsaking lyricism for polemics, and sharply criticized the work's social content. By the mid-1960s, Brooks had metamorphosed herself from what she describes as a "Negro poet" to a "new Black" poet. Although she continued to write (and still does) some of the most carefully crafted poems of any of her contemporaries, after attending a black poetry conference in 1967, she experienced what she describes as a racial "awakening," and after remaking herself as a "black poet," her involvement lent credibility to the * Black Arts Movement of the 1960s and Black Aesthetic thought.

Along with the women poets of the Renaissance period, Walker and Brooks, Margaret * Danner (b. 1915), Margaret Gross * Burroughs (b. 1917), Naomi Long * Madgett (b. 1923), and others who wrote in what is generally considered the lull in African-American literary production in the years following the * Harlem Renaissance, are the foremothers to the African-American women's poetry who made contributions to the literature during the Black Arts Movement despite facing the same literary chauvinism that confronted the women poets of the Renaissance. Among the poets who joined with the still active Walker and Brooks and emerged as some of the leading poets of the period were Maya * Angelou (b. 1928), Audre * Lorde (1934–1992), Sonia * Sanchez (b. 1934), June * Jordan (b. 1936), Jayne * Cortez (b. 1936), Lucille * Clifton (b. 1936), Pinkie Gordon * Lane (b. 1939), Toi Derricotte (b. 1941) Carolyn * Rodgers (b. 1942), Nikki * Giovanni (b. 1943), and Alice * Walker (b. 1944). Most of these poets are still active today. They have been joined by younger poets such as Rita * Dove (b. 1952), 1987 Pulitzer Prize recipient for her collection Thomas and Beulah and current Poet Laureate of the United States, * Ai (b. 1947), Ntozake * Shange (b. 1948), Angela Jackson (b. 1951), Nzadi Keita (b. 1956), Kimmika L. H. Williams (b. 1959), Patricia Smith (b. 1955), Jean Towns (b. 1959), and others who are still contributing to a flourishing and vibrant literary tradition.

• Dudley Randall, ed., The Black Poets (1971). Roseann P. Bell et. al., eds. Sturdy Black Bridges: Visions of Black Women in Literature (1979). Erlene Stetson, ed., Black Sister: Poetry by Black American Women, 1746–1980 (1981). Amiri Baraka (LeRoi Jones) and Amina Baraka, eds., Confirmation: An Anthology of African American Women (1983). Mari Evans, ed., Black Women Writers (1950–1980) (1983). Gloria T. Hull, Color, Sex, and Poetry: Three Women Writers of the Harlem Renaissance (1987). Joanne M. Braxton and Andree Nicola McLaughlin, eds., Wild Women in the Whirlwind: Afro-American Culture and the Contemporary Lit-

erary Renaissance (1990). Joan R. Sherman, ed., *African American Poetry of the Nineteenth Century* (1992). Frank N. Magill, ed., *Masterpieces of African-American Literature* (1992).

Reggie Young

Literary Criticism

The feminist movement in the United States has gained ascendancy and has created branch organizations that are proceeding forcefully with their own agendas. Since the early 1970s, feminist literary critics have been devising new standards for use in fairly evaluating works by contemporary women writers and their foremothers, most of whom have been ignored because of gender bias and narrow criteria usually applied by the dominant school of literary theory.

Thus, the activity in feminist criticism involves a strong concern for issues of race, gender, and class. One of the benefits of this interest in American diversity and equality has been the continuing reclamation of minority literatures. The impetus for this activity began in the 1960s, when the *civil rights movement sparked a revolution in black arts that led to the rediscovery and subsequent publication of many forgotten African-American texts.

However, the reprintings of minority novels, poems, and essays have given rise to a series of difficult questions and possible explanations by scholars examining the previous rejection of these works by the literary establishment. Many theoretical studies and polemical pieces have appeared that center on the political, racial, and sexist reasons for the lack of serious critical review of women's writing in the past. Developing from the recent scholarship have been attempts by critics to set new standards for measuring the previously neglected literature in a more effective and equitable manner.

At the beginning of the feminist movement, many African-American women tried to conduct their struggles within the general framework of the women's organizational aims. However, by the mid-1970s, many young women of color who had entered the nation's graduate schools during the years of civil rights had begun their professional careers and were considering more specific feminist goals.

It soon became apparent to many scholars dealing with the literature of women of color that there was a need for a separate area of study because of the twofold nature of the battle that involves gender and race. Critics such as Barbara Smith (whose 1977 essay, "Toward a Black Feminist Criticism," made a strong impact) and Barbara Christian called for an independent concentration of critical thought on black women's works. This focus would consider that most of society's literary dictates reflect the bias of its patriarchal composition, and also that black women's artistic efforts, along with those of black men, suffer from the racial views expressed by predominantly white schools of criticism.

A strong motive that forced women of color to strike out on their own is the fact that white feminists have not always supported black women's special concerns. In the nineteenth century, many white women in the suffrage groups did not welcome, and sometimes even expressed hostility toward, their black sisters. Hazel Carby in *Reconstructing Womanhood* (1987) documents the difficulties encountered by black women activist speakers and writers, such as Frances *Harper, Pauline *Hopkins, Anna Julia *Cooper, and Ida *Wells. However, the twentieth century's feminist movement has been characterized more by a lack of understanding and scant interest in black issues than by much racial antagonism.

Black feminist criticism became a highly qualified and important field of study in the 1980s, and continued to gain momentum in the 1990s. Critical assessments of the works by women of color have become important academic endeavors for many of the nation's well-known and highly respected literary scholars. The information from numerous books and journal articles (on such themes as lesbianism, male-centered views in literature, and the question of what constitutes *black feminist writing) flows into the widening pool of knowledge that helps readers to understand and appreciate the recent literary achievements of African-American women. In addition, many critics have turned their attention to the long-neglected works written by women of color from the eighteenth and nineteenth centuries. Many of those texts became accessible in 1988 upon publication of *The Schomburg Library of Nineteenth-Century Black Women Writers*.

Black feminist critics have been examining these reclaimed works to reveal the key characteristics of the existing tradition of writing by women of color. The literary foremothers are strongly admired today for their struggles to be heard, and they are credited with founding the themes and devising the forms later used by well-known contemporary black women authors. The newly recognized literary patterns and devices are enabling scholars to construct an aesthetic set of criteria for judging the literature by women of color.

Much of this work has been accomplished by well-respected black feminist critics. In addition to Christian and Smith, writers whose studies have been influential include Alice *Walker, Deborah McDowell, Claudia Tate,

Valerie Smith, Jean Fagan Yellin, Nellie McKay, Hazel Carby, Mary Helen Washington, Barbara Johnson, and Mae Henderson. Many little-known and unappreciated black women authors have been brought to the attention of the literary world through the persistent efforts of these scholars.

Two notable examples are the studies done by Yellin and Walker. Yellin's effort in calling attention to the authenticity and merit of Harriet * Jacobs's 1861 veiled autobiography, *Incidents in the Life of a Slave Girl*, has contributed to the understanding of how a woman's description of the slave experience differed in emphasis and expression from a male's account of bondage. What is revealed in Jacobs's work is a life story involving sexual integrity, familial attachments, and a sense of community—themes found in many of the later texts of women of color. In Walker's case, she successfully resurrected the literary achievement of Zora Neale * Hurston and pointed out the independent figure of the woman protagonist in Hurston's *Their Eyes Were Watching God* (1937).

Certainly, what has given a strong impetus to the black women critics today is the number and quality of novels, poems, plays, and essays published by African-American women. Much of the feminist criticism has centered on the powerfully effective works of Alice Walker, Toni * Morrison, Gloria * Naylor, Paule * Marshall, Maya * Angelou, Toni Cade * Bambara, Gayl * Jones, Ntozake * Shange, Audre * Lorde, Nikki * Giovanni, and Gwendolyn * Brooks. Many of these accomplished writers have themselves contributed to the pronouncements, critical debates, and aesthetic findings of the literary productions by women of color.

[*See also* African-American Oral Tradition; African-American Publishing Outlets; African-American Reading Network.]

• Gloria T. Hull, Patricia Bell Scott, and Barbara Smith, eds., *All the Women Are White, All the Blacks Are Men, But Some of Us Are Brave* (1982). Alice Walker, *In Search of Our Mothers' Gardens* (1983). Mari Evans, ed., *Black Women Writers* (1984). Barbara Christian, *Black Feminist Criticism* (1985). Josephine Donovan, ed., *Feminist Literary Criticism*, 2d ed, (1989). Henry Louis Gates, Jr., ed., *Reading Black, Reading Feminist* (1990).

Angelo Costanzo

AFROCENTRISM. *See* Pan-Africanism.

AGEISM. The term ageism was coined in analogy with racism and sexism by psychiatrist and leading gerontologist Robert N. Butler in 1968 to name the widespread discrimination against the elderly in the United States, which, Butler explained, is rooted in part in people's personal fears of their own aging and death ("Age-ism:

Another Form of Bigotry," *Gerontologist* 9 [1969]). Although ageism theoretically can refer to any systematic prejudicial behavior toward or favored treatment of people based on chronological age (adolescents, for example), it has come to be associated in the United States with old age, which is linked culturally with disease, dependency, decay, and death.

Although she does not use the term *ageism*, pioneering French feminist Simone de * Beauvoir, in her important but largely ignored book *The Coming of Age* (1972), offers a trenchant indictment of Western culture for its shameful, indeed "criminal," treatment of the elderly; Beauvoir locates the sources of this behavior in both the economic system of capitalism, which values only certain kinds of labor as productive, and in existential concerns.

In the United States, aging is a women's issue. Statistically, women live, on the average, seven years longer than men, and older women constitute the fastest-growing poverty group. Of the 8.8 million elderly in the United States who live alone, 81 percent are women, most of whom live in poverty (American Association of Retired People, 1988). Since the primary caretakers of old men are women, the effects of ageism on men are to a certain extent neutralized by women.

To make matters worse, the intersection of ageism and sexism results for women in what Susan * Sontag has called the double standard of aging (*Saturday Review*, 23 September 1972). Older women, more vulnerable than older men to the stigma attached to age, suffer more from negative cultural stereotypes (the spinster/old maid, the little old lady, the wicked witch). Female attractiveness has long been associated with youth, for example, and the older woman is thought of negatively as "postmenopausal," that is, as no longer able to bear children and thus fulfill biologically the role of * motherhood (cross-cultural studies, on the other hand, suggest that the status of women rises after menopause in some non-Western cultures). The ageism experienced by women, in other words, is embedded in sexism, which is the very foundation of patriarchy. Barbara Macdonald, in *Look Me in the Eye: Old Women, Aging and Ageism* (1983), astutely observes that "youth is bonded with patriarchy in the enslavement of the older woman. There would, in fact, be no youth culture without the powerless older woman."

Insidiously, ageism is a form of prejudice that many if not most women have internalized and directed against themselves and other women. Ageism infects women when, as Maggie Kuhn of the Gray Panthers puts it, "we despise our powerlessness, wrinkled skin and physical limitations" (*New Life for the Elderly*, 1974). The entrenched ageism within feminism itself has gone virtually unacknowledged and unanalyzed. An exception is Baba Copper's incisive analysis in *Over the Hill: Ageism Between Women* (1988). She argues that ageism between women derives substantially from the traditional model of the mother-daughter relationship, in which the mother (always the older woman) is expected to devote all of her attention and energy to those younger than herself.

In recognizing ageism and in repudiating our culture's negative, trivializing stereotypes of women who are old, we must take equal care, however, not to produce a similarly limiting repertoire of "positive" stereotypes that ignore the realities of the vicissitudes of old age. Just as importantly, we need to devote more attention to analyzing the roots of ageism (social, psychological, cultural, economic) and to tracing the history of ageism in the United States.

• Robert N. Butler, "Psychiatry and the Elderly: An Overview," *The American Journal of Psychiatry* 132 (September 1975): 893–900. Kathleen Woodward, "Simone de Beauvoir: Aging and Its Discontents," in *The Private Self: Theory and Practice of Women's Autobiographical Writings*, ed. Shari Benstock (1988), pp. 90–113. Evelyn R. Rosenthal, ed., *Women, Aging and Ageism* (1990). Lois W. Banner, *In Full Flower: Aging Women, Power, and Sexuality* (1992). Thomas R. Cole, *The Journey of Life: A Cultural History of Aging in America* (1992). Germaine Greer, *The Change: Women, Aging, and the Menopause* (1992). Betty Friedan, *The Fountain of Age* (1993). Anne M. Wyatt-Brown and Janice Rossen, eds., *Aging and Gender in Literature: Studies in Creativity* (1993).

Kathleen Woodward

AGING. The subject of aging has often been a central feature of women's literature since the late nineteenth century. The theme can best be understood if divided into two categories: stories of the aging other—parents, grandparents, and elders in the community—and those of the aging self—the heroine, narrator, or writer as subject. In the first group, the speaker or narrator is young or middle-aged, but has some compelling reason for observing elders or listening to their stories. In the second, aging is something that is happening to the writer, heroine, or narrator herself.

In portraying the aging other, writers have demonstrated how by custom and convention the aged are often deprived of power and placed at the margin of society. The southern writer Eudora *Welty exemplifies this point in "Old Mr. Marblehall" (1941), a story of an aging bigamist, as well as in "A Worn Path," a tale concerning Phoenix, a heroic black grandmother (1941). Although both characters go almost unnoticed in their communities, Welty presents them as worthy of our attention.

Writers have also treated aging characters as points of significant reference to their young protagonists. The young are often forced to overcome parental barriers of reticence and shame to discover exactly who their elders were and therefore who they are themselves. For example, at an early age, Margaret Gower in Gail Godwin's *Father Melancholy's Daughter* (1991) becomes an amateur detective of the past. Such a search for personal identity, by reaching into the past of elders, has special meaning for African-American, Asian-American, and Latina writers like Toni *Morrison, Alice *Walker, Maxine Hong *Kingston, Amy *Tan, Lorna Dee *Cervantes, and Sandra *Cisneros, whose cultural traditions differ from the mainstream. The strategy helps the figures to negotiate the treacherous currents of a pluralistic society. For Native American writers—such as Paula Gunn *Allen or Wendy *Rose—the figure of the *grandmother draws on strong cultural traditions of respect and reverence for elders; the clash between Indian and white attitudes toward old age is often a subject in Native American writing.

The aged often play inspirational or redemptive roles by rescuing young protagonists from indecision or desperation. For instance, Mrs. Todd in Sarah Orne *Jewett's *The Country of the Pointed Firs* (1896) is an oracle and healer, a source of solace and wisdom for the middle-aged narrator, as is the title character of Gloria *Naylor's *Mama Day* (1988) for her young relative, Cocoa.

Death of the old is sometimes treated as a public rather than a personal loss. For example, colonial poets Anne *Bradstreet and slave-born Phillis *Wheatley celebrate the accomplishments of the great men they eulogize rather than dwell on grief over their deaths. Nonetheless, in Bradstreet's elegy for her three-year-old granddaughter and namesake, feelings of loss outweigh the consolations of religious faith.

In considering the aging self, that is, whenever the main character or the author is the person aging, the definition of growing old changes radically. Most American women dread the loss of youth. Such middle-aged writers as Kate *Chopin in *The Awakening* (1899) and Edith *Wharton in *The House of Mirth* (1905) write movingly of women in their late twenties who, finding little possibility for emotional survival, commit suicide. This variety of alienation persists in contemporary society, but writers can treat it comically, as does Anne *Tyler in *Breathing Lessons* (1988). Maggie, the forty-eight-year-old heroine suffering from an unrecognized malaise just before her daughter departs for college, acts with eccentric poignancy.

Midlife can provide a turning point toward celibacy or a new fulfillment. Ellen Douglas in *A Lifetime Burning* (1982) describes the painful disintegration of a contemporary marriage. Willa *Cather in *The Professor's House* (1925) and Pearl *Buck in *Pavilion of Women* (1946) depict marriages in which one person emotionally deserts the other for psychological reasons that bewilder them all. The protagonists of all three authors reconstruct their lives without sexual companionship.

In other works, characters are offered a second chance, one that compensates for youthful agonies. Such midlife progress novels include Zora Neale *Hurston's *Their Eyes Were Watching God* (1937); Louise Field Cooper's *Summer Stranger* (1947); Alison Lurie's *Foreign Affairs* (1984); Anne Tyler's *Saint Maybe* (1991); and Toni Morrison's *Beloved* (1987) and *Jazz* (1992). Most of the characters, however, first undergo a journey of remembrance, a life review. Moreover, surviving the transition necessitates accepting the natural rhythms of life and cultivating a saving sense of humor, qualities exemplified by Mona *Van Duyn in *Near Changes* (1990).

Fear of dependency terrifies the elderly and their families. Ellen Douglas's *Apostles of Light* (1973) and May *Sarton's *As We Are Now* (1973) are cautionary tales about the possible horrors in nursing homes when those in authority disrespect their charges. Even under better circumstances, institutionalization can be irksome. Joyce Horner's *That Time of Year: A Chronicle of Life in a Nursing Home* (1982) describes the purgatorial aspects of being mentally capable but physically infirm. In contrast, the detective story writer Jane Langton's *Good and Dead* (1986) reveals that demented patients may find pleasures that elude distressed relatives. Life is no easier, however, when elders are cared for at home. Madeleine L'Engle's *The Summer of the Great-Grandmother* (1974) and Tina *Howe's *Painting Churches* (1982) portray the trials and bravery of both parties, caretakers and dying relatives alike.

For the aging observer, witnessing death becomes experiential. Emily *Dickinson challenges the conventional wisdom that religion comforts the bereaved. "I heard a Fly buzz—when I died" (c. 1862) describes the final stages of dying, while in "The last Night that She lived" (c. 1866) the subject's death shatters the speaker's equipoise. In contrast, Willa Cather's *Death Comes for the Archbishop* (1927) recounts the archbishop's peaceful end; he dies sustained by reveries of early days. The distress of bereavement permeates May Sarton's eulogy to her friend Judy (*Letters from Maine: New Poems*, 1984), Maxine *Kumin's poems about Anne

*Sexton (*Nurture*, 1989, and *Looking for Luck*, 1992), and A. G. Mojtabai's novel *Autumn* (1982).

Despite the trials of life, writers attest to the saving grace of creativity. In "A Village Singer" (1891) and "A Poetess" (1891), Mary Wilkins *Freeman suggests that artists require an appreciative audience. Willa Cather's *The Song of the Lark* (1915) and Madeleine L'Engle's *A Severed Wasp* (1982) stress that creativity can compensate for much pain. The poems of Adrienne *Rich in *Time's Power* (1989) and Lola Haskins in *Forty-four Ambitions for the Piano* (1990), as well as May Sarton's recent journals, *Endgame: A Journal of the Seventy-ninth Year* (1992) and *Encore: A Journal of the Eightieth Year* (1993), reveal the gratification of prolonging creativity into later life.

• Margaret Morganroth Gullette, *Safe at Last in the Middle Years: The Invention of the Midlife Progress Novel* (1988). Dorothy Sennett, ed., *Full Measure: Modern Short Stories on Aging* (1988). Dorothy Sennett, with Anne Czarniecki, *Vital Signs: International Stories on Aging* (1991). Sandra Martz, ed., *When I Am an Old Woman I Shall Wear Purple*, 2d ed. (1991). Lois W. Banner, *In Full Flower: Aging Women, Power and Sexuality* (1992). Thomas R. Cole, David D. Van Tassel, and Robert Kastenbaum, eds., *Handbook of the Humanities and Aging* (1992). Diane Hume George, " 'Keeping Our Working Distance': Maxine Kumin's Poetry of Loss and Survival," in *Aging and Gender in Literature: Studies in Creativity*, eds. Anne M. Wyatt-Brown and Janice Rossen (1993), pp. 314–338. Margaret Morganroth Gullette, "Creativity, Aging, Gender: A Case Study of Their Intersections, 1910–1935," in *Aging and Gender in Literature*, pp. 19–48.

Anne M. Wyatt-Brown

AIDS (Acquired Immune Deficiency Syndrome) is a breakdown of the immune system that is thought to be caused by the Human Immune Deficiency Virus (HIV). According to the Center for Disease Control (CDC), as of March 1992, 22,607 cases of AIDS in adult and adolescent women had been reported in the United States. Of all American women with AIDS, 53% are black, 26% are white, and 21% are hispanic. Asians, Pacific Islanders, and Native Americans make up less than 1% of reported cases in women. Also according to these figures, women make up 10% of all reported AIDS cases. The CDC groups People with AIDS (PWAs) into categories according to the ways in which those people have contracted the disease. For women, these categories include intravenous drug use (11,350); heterosexual contact (7,781); blood transfusion (1,752); undetermined transmission (1,682); and hemophilia (42). Any person of any gender, race, class, or sexual identity can contract AIDS by sharing needles or practicing unsafe sex, that is, sex in which bodily fluids are exchanged.

There are two extremely informative, broad-ranging, and inclusive anthologies on women and AIDS: *AIDS: The Women* (1988) and *Women, AIDS, and Activism* (1990). Both collections treat AIDS from a variety of perspectives relevant to the relationship of women to AIDS. These perspectives include those of women with AIDS and HIV; friends, lovers, and relations of PWAs or HIV-infected people; caregivers; AIDS activists; and AIDS educators. The latter of the two anthologies, which was written by the Women and AIDS Book Group of the AIDS Coalition to Unleash Power (ACT UP) in New York, does a thorough job of providing information about HIV testing, AIDS in relation to issues of race and class, and lesbians and AIDS. Unlike the former collection, which emphasizes experiential narratives, *Women, AIDS, and Activism* provides explicit information about HIV transmission, treatment, and preventative practices. It also ends on a decidedly active note, advocating "translating issues into action."

The literature of women and AIDS, like all AIDS literature, varies in approach and form. This literature is not written exclusively by PWAs, although there have been several first-person accounts written by women living with AIDS. These narratives vary widely in attitude and style, from Iris de la Cruz's "Sex, Drugs, Rock-n-Roll, and AIDS" (excerpted in *Women, AIDS, and Activism*) to some of the essays in Cookie Mueller's *Walking through Clear Water in a Pool Painted Black* (1990) to Tema Luft's short essay on being diagnosed with ARC (AIDS-related Complex) symptoms, "Going Public" (in *AIDS: The Women*).

Other contributions to AIDS literature by women writers include Barbara Peabody's *The Screaming Room: A Mother's Journal of her Son's Struggle with AIDS* (1987), Carol Pearson's *Good-bye, I Love You* (1986), in which a wife describes her husband's struggle with AIDS, and "Life and Death with Joan," in which Jennifer Brown discusses her lesbian lover's death by suicide after her AIDS diagnosis (included in *AIDS: The Women*).

AIDS activist and educator Cindy Patton has written several books that treat the topic of women and AIDS: *Sex and Germs: The Politics of AIDS* (1985), *Making It: A Woman's Guide to Sex in the Age of AIDS* (with Janis Kelly, 1987), and *Inventing AIDS* (1990). She has also published numerous articles on the subject. Journalist, novelist, and AIDS activist Sarah Schulman has also written several articles that consider women and AIDS, among them "AIDS and Homelessness: Thousands May Die In the Streets" (*Nation*, 10 April 1989) and "Lesbians Respond to AIDS Hysteria" (*New York Native*, 2 December 1988). Her most recent novel, *People in Trouble* (1990), also portrays PWAs and AIDS activism.

Amanda Berry

AKINS, Zoë (1886–1958), poet, novelist, dramatist, and screenwriter. Zoë Akins had a successful literary career on both coasts, achieving fame and respect as a playwright on Broadway and as a screenwriter in Hollywood. Akins was born and raised in Missouri, and gained an affection for the stage while living in St. Louis during her adolescence. Her breakthrough came in 1919 with the New York production of her play *Déclassée*, starring Ethel Barrymore. During the 1920s, she had nearly a dozen original plays and adaptations produced in New York, making her one of the leading figures in the dramatic world. Her highest official honor came in 1935, when she won the Pulitzer Prize for her stage adaptation of Edith *Wharton's novella *The Old Maid*.

In 1930, she relocated to California from New York to write screenplays for Paramount and later MGM. Akins's penchant for creating dazzling upper-class settings and intense personal conflicts was attractive to Hollywood, which had already brought some of her plays to the screen in the 1920s. During the 1930s, Akins wrote or cowrote thirteen screenplays, including the famous Greta Garbo vehicle *Camille* in 1936, and four adaptations for Dorothy Arzner, the leading female director of the time: *Sarah and Son* (1930), *Anybody's Woman* (1930), *Working Girls* (1931), and *Christopher Strong* (1933). In the 1940s, she returned to writing plays and also one novel, *Forever Young* (1941), which she described as a welcome "release" from the world of cinema.

Akins, who was proud of her reputation for creating strong roles for actresses, wrote plots that frequently focused on great emotional and social stresses faced by a central female character. Her original work and adaptations explored marital infidelities and betrayals (*Daddy's Gone A-Hunting*, 1921; *Déclasée; Christopher Strong*), the "fallen" woman (*The Varying Shore*, 1921), illegitimate children (*Sarah and Son, The Old Maid*), and even comedic treatments of so-called gold-digging (*The Greeks Had a Word for It*, 1930). As Jennifer Bradley argues in "Zoë Akins and the Age of Excess" (*Modern American Drama: The Female Canon*, ed. June Schlueter, 1990), Akins's plots may be seen as potentially exceeding the conventions in which they are steeped. Though the popularity of her output reflects in part the interest that male-dominated cultural industries had in exploiting stories of "female problems," her works often use the many trials of her female characters to expose pressures and double-standards imposed on women by conventional morality. Her success also helped to further open doors for other women writers in both Broadway and Hollywood.

• Zoë Akins's papers are held in the Huntington Library in San Marino, California. A collection of her manuscripts exists in the Department of Special Collections, University Research Library, University of California at Los Angeles. See also Melissa Sue Kort, "'Shadows of the Substance': Women Screenwriters in the 1930s," in *Women and Film*, ed. Janet Todd (1988), pp. 169–185. Felicia Hardison Londré, "Zoë Akins," in *Notable Women in the American Theater*, eds. Alice M. Robinson, Vera Mowry Roberts, and Milly S. Barranger (1989), pp. 11–13.

Ted Hovet, Jr.

ALBA, Nanina (1915–1968), poet, short story writer, and professor. Alba was born in Montgomery, Alabama, to the Reverend and Mrs. I. C. Champey. By blending the first and last syllables of her given name, Nannie Williemenia, Alba renamed herself Nanina.

Nanina Alba attended Haines Institute in Augusta, Georgia, and then Knoxville College, from which she received an A.B. in 1935. On 27 November 1937, she married Reuben Andres Alba; they had two daughters, Panchita and Andrea, the elder of whom, as Pan Adams, illustrated Alba's poetry collection *Parchments II* (1967). In 1955, Alba received an M.A. in education from Alabama State College. Between 1935 and 1968, Alba taught music, French, and English in the public schools of Alabama, and was a professor of English at Tuskegee Institute (now University) in Alabama. Alba pursued graduate studies at Indiana University during the summers of the late 1950s, and began to write poetry seriously.

Her first published works appeared in the early 1960s in the journals *Crisis, Phylon*, and *Negro Digest*. Alba is noteworthy as a poet of the 1960s because her work solidly presents the best characteristics of the highly acclaimed black writers working inside the Euro-American tradition, and reflects the innovative aesthetics of the new *black arts movement of the 1960s.

In technique, Alba utilized the jazz rhythms and motifs of the black arts movement, inspired by Langston Hughes's 1950s bebop rhythms (as in "Holy Blues," 1963). Her methods employed *Black English vernacular to give voice and introspective cultural commentary to the personae of her poems and the narrator of her Miss Lucy stories. Alba manipulated classical Western figures and *myths in allusions to Daedelus, Antigone, and Medusa, and incorporated Afri-

can-American figures in allusions to literary mentors like James Baldwin (as in "For Malcolm X," 1965).

Alba's themes reflect black literary tradition and innovation in their universal appeal and in their specific reference to an African-American context. Turning to her experiences as an African-American, Alba, the daughter of a Presbyterian minister, uses her religious and deeply spiritual background in the subjects of her poems ("Prayer," 1967, "The Holy Blues") and in the titles of her poetry collections, *Parchments* (1963) and *Parchments II*. She commented on the events that affected the family to whom she was devoted by lamenting the conditions of greed, poverty, and loneliness ("Tria Juncta," "Psychosis," 1967) and by protesting the Vietnam War ("Shades of the Ardennes, Et Al. (For Private Milton Olive, III, et al.," 1966). Having avidly supported and participated in the civil rights movement in Montgomery, Alba urged blacks toward ingenuity and the surmounting of adversity ("Be Daedulus," 1967), and she celebrated their stoic, indomitable leadership and accomplishment ("For Malcolm X").

Most of Alba's works were published between 1963 and 1967. In 1968, Nanina Alba died of cancer, her writing career having just begun to accelerate.

• James A. Emanuel and Theodore L. Gross, eds., *Dark Symphony: Negro Literature in America* (1968), p. 373. Dudley Randall and Margaret G. Burroughs, *For Malcolm: Poems on the Life and Death of Malcolm X* (1969), p. 95. Eugene B. Redmond, *Drumvoices: The Mission of Afro-American Poetry, A Critical History* (1976), pp. 319, 332, 333. Arthur P. Davis, J. Saunders Redding, and Joyce Ann Joyce, eds., *The New Calvalcade: African American Writing from 1760 to the Present*, vol. 2 (1992), pp. 4–9.

Mary B. Zeigler

ALCOTT, Louisa May (1832–1888), fiction writer for children and adults. Born in Germantown, Pennsylvania, she and her family moved to Boston and then Concord, Massachusetts, in her early years, where their neighbors were the Hawthornes, the Emersons, and Henry David Thoreau. The second of four daughters of the famous transcendental philosopher and utopianist Amos Bronson Alcott and his wife Abba May Alcott, Louisa was forced to take on the burden of supporting her family early in life, most frequently through writing.

In her teens, Alcott began writing short stories, some for children, while others were potboilers or gothic thrillers published under a pseudonym. Her authorial break came with *Hospital Sketches* (1863), a collection of letters to her family while she was a nurse during the

Civil War in Washington, D.C. Her first and personal favorite novel, *Moods* (1864, rev. 1881), brought some attention but little money.

Her landmark novel, *Little Women* (1868), based loosely on her own family's life, is domestic fiction for teenaged girls. That the book now seems so conventional is a credit to its originality at the time. The girls in the book, especially the autobiographical Jo, stand as models for the heroines that were to follow in girls' fiction— flawed, imperfect, lively young women, yet not object lessons in depravity. Their home life is warm, but not uniformly harmonious. They aspire to be more than wives and mothers; the novel encourages readers and characters to pursue greatness and public service.

Alcott's novels remain popular because they deal with continuing perplexities in women's lives: how to have successful careers and happy home lives; how to balance housewifery and professional obligations; how to be supportive wives, mothers, and daughters without being subordinate. Although Alcott's other books for children are derivative and less successful, they are still satisfying domestic fiction, perhaps too sentimental and sweet for contemporary tastes.

Her adult fiction is less noteworthy and successful. Trading on sensational topics such as drug abuse and forged identities, and set in exotic places, the potboilers give an expanded sense of Alcott's potential as a writer. Her novels, especially *Moods*, dwell on transcendentalist notions of spousal appropriateness. While interesting experiments, the adult works pale in literary worth, longevity, and commercial success beside the fiction for children.

• Martha Saxton, *Louisa May: A Modern Biography of Louisa May Alcott* (1977). Nina Auerbach, *Communities of Women* (1978). Madelon Bedell, *The Alcotts: Biography of a Family* (1980). Ruth K. MacDonald, *Louisa May Alcott* (1983). Sarah Elbert, *A Hunger for Home: Louisa May Alcott and Little Women* (1984).

Ruth K. MacDonald

ALEXANDER, Meena (b. 1951), poet, novelist, essayist, social activist, educator. Born in Allahabad, India, Meena Alexander moved to Khartoum with her parents when she was four. She frequently visited her ancestral home in Kerala, South India, until she returned to live in India at the age of twenty-two. She studied at the University of Khartoum and received her Ph.D. from Nottingham University. She is associate professor of English and creative writing at Hunter College and at the Graduate Center of the City University of New York. She also teaches in the writing program at Columbia University.

Alexander develops the images, writing techniques, and sociopolitical concerns displayed in one of her earliest works, a book of poetry entitled *The Bird's Bright Wing* (1976), with great skill and immense sensitivity in nearly all of her later works. For example, *The Bird's Bright Wing* concludes with the image of a wounded mouth; just as her first novel, *Nampally Road*, published nearly fifteen years later in 1991, ends with an image of the wounded mouth of an abused woman slowly healing.

Another recurring image in Alexander's works is that of her grandmothers. She introduces her autobiographical work, *The Storm* (1989), thus: "The stiff palmyra fans grandmother had hung to the wall." The memories of her grandmothers, one of them gradually going blind, the other eternally kneeling on thresholds, appear, disappear, and reappear like dream images in the poems and prose pieces of *House of a Thousand Doors* (1988).

In *Nampally Road* (1991), the protagonist, Mira Kannadical, returns to Hyderabad, India, after four years of graduate study in England. She finds herself personally enmeshed in the social and political betrayal of contemporary, independent India. The central episode of the novel focuses on the involvement of Mira with Rameeza, a woman gang-raped by a group of policemen and then imprisoned by her rapists. The plot is based on a real incident that happened in Hyderabad in 1979. Again, Alexander repeats and reworks the story of Rameeza from her earlier work *House of a Thousand Doors*, where it appears as a short poetic narrative, "Mosquitoes in the Main Room."

Alexander's *Fault Lines: A Memoir* (1993) is a lyrical work in which she portrays what it means to be born in a female body in a world that is continually changing and constantly enacting dramas of abuse and injustice.

Meena Alexander's uncompromisingly honest perception of herself and her world, and her involvement with the world of poetry and politics, are presented through exquisite imagery and language. She transcends rigidly drawn boundaries of cultural, political, or literary concerns, and can be ranked among the best writers in English today.

Roshni Rustomji-Kerns

ALLEN, Paula Gunn (b. 1939), poet, critic, educator, and novelist. Born in Albuquerque, New Mexico, Paula Gunn Allen is of Laguna Pueblo, Sioux, and Lebanese descent. She grew up in Cubero, New Mexico, a member of both the Laguna and Acoma Pueblo Indian communities.

Allen has a doctorate in American studies from the University of New Mexico. She has taught at San Francisco State University, the University of New Mexico, Fort Lewis College in Durango, Colorado, the University of California at Berkeley, and is currently a professor of English at the University of California, Los Angeles. Her work has brought her much recognition, including a National Endowment for the Arts Fellowship for Writing in 1978, the Susan Koppelman Award from the Popular and American Culture Associations in 1990, and the Native American Prize for Literature in 1990.

Allen includes among the influences on her writing, besides her * Roman Catholic and * Native American backgrounds, such writers as Gertrude * Stein, the English Romantic poets, the Beats, and her contemporaries, Adrienne * Rich, Audre * Lorde, Denise * Levertov, and Judy * Grahn. Allen began writing poetry in the 1960s with the instruction of Robert Creeley, and to date has published seven volumes of poetry, including *Shadow Country* (1982), *WYRDS* (1987), and *Skins and Bones* (1988). In her novel *The Woman Who Owned the Shadows* (1983), Allen creates a racially-mixed heroine, Ephanie, who validates her own lesbianism through a spiritual and emotional quest; Ephanie empowers herself by forging a connection between events of her personal past and mythic aspects of her tribal heritage.

Allen is also well known for her scholarship in Native American studies: *The Sacred Hoop* (1986) seeks to recuperate the feminine aspects of tribal cultures erased by Anglo-European representations of Indians and applies her gynecentric tribal perspective to contemporary Native American literature; *Grandmothers of the Light* (1991) brings together a collection of myths and stories "central to a woman's spiritual tradition." She has edited two anthologies, *Studies in American Indian Literature: Critical Essays and Course Designs* (1983), and *Spider Woman's Granddaughters* (1989), a collection of short fiction by Native American women, which received the American Book Award in 1990. A third anthology, the two-volume *Voice of the Turtle: A Century of American Indian Fiction* is forthcoming. Her poetry, fiction, and criticism are widely anthologized.

Allen is a longtime activist in the antiwar, antinuclear, and American feminist movements; she has also spoken and written on the role of gays and lesbians in contemporary society and world history. Her ongoing interest centers around the feminine ritual traditions of Native America.

• Joseph Bruchac, *Survival This Way: Interviews with American Indian Poets* (1987). Brian Swann and Arnold Krupat, eds., *I Tell You Now: Autobiographical Essays by Native American Writers* (1987). A. LaVonne Brown Ruoff, *American Indian Literatures* (1990).

Margaret A. Lukens

ALTA (b. 1942), poet, publisher, fiction writer, essayist, and editor. Alta, who discarded her surname, Gerrey, was born and raised in Reno, Nevada. She began her disobedient writing career at the age of four by creating a newspaper that detailed what the grown-ups were saying about each other. Alta studied literature at the University of California, Berkeley, and, in addition to writing, has worked various tedious jobs, taught creative writing, and worked in video, film, and television. Central to the West Coast women's poetry renaissance of the seventies, Alta initiated the first women-only poetry readings in the San Francisco Bay area. Alta has published more than a dozen works in numerous genres, and contends that she is best-known as a poet simply because it was easiest to be published in alternative poetry magazines of the late sixties. Her second husband, editor John Oliver Simon, published her first volume of poetry, *Freedom's in Sight*, in 1969. Interest in her second volume, the often-erotic *Letters to Women* (1970), was withdrawn when publishers learned of its subject. When she left Simon, Alta took with her the printing press on which *Freedom's in Sight* had been printed and founded Shameless Hussy Press, one of the longest-running feminist presses in the United States, where she published work by Susan * Griffin, Pat * Parker, Ntozake * Shange, and herself, at prices women could easily afford.

Alta began writing from a desire to represent her own experience: working-class, white, female, bisexual, and that of a sometime suburban housewife, tranquilizer addict, mental hospital survivor. Her poetry includes ironic aphorisms, trenchant political analysis, and free-flowing eroticism, always starting from personal positions, voices, or narratives. Her language and rhythm are unapologetically colloquial American, her poetic form as resistant to convention and category as her spelling and her attitudes; she is bitter, funny, and irreverant. Her sparse, expressive prose narratives, such as *True Story* (1973), confirms the self-avowed influence of Ernest Hemingway, Dorothy * Parker, and Gertrude * Stein. *Momma: A Start on All the Untold Stories* (1974)—she has two daughters—chronicles obstacles to combining writing with motherhood. *The Shameless Hussy: Selected Stories, Essays and Poetry* (1980) collects much now-scarce early material with newer work; in her introduction to the book, Judy * Grahn calls Alta's "the finest poetic reporting of modern times." Recent works include *Deluged with Dudes* (1989).

Alta considers writing against * sexism, * racism, * ageism, * homophobia, war, and other cruelty historically specific and necessary, arguing, "WE MUST WORK TOWARDS OUR OWN OBSOLESCENCE" ("Tell It Like It Is," *Small Press Review*, 1971).

• Suzanne Juhasz, "The Feminist Poet: Alta and Adrienne Rich," in *Naked and Fiery Forms: Modern American Poetry by Women* (1976), pp. 177–204.

Susan Brown

AMAZON. Once a derogatory term, *Amazon* has been resuscitated by some feminists as a general term for the original, powerful, pre-patriarchal female. Lineages for the Amazon have been variously attributed to a matriarchal Indo-European clan and to the nation of female warriors of Scythia (near the Black Sea). Comparisons have also been made to the African Amazons of Dahomey or to American Indian tribes, in which some women took on traditionally male roles as fierce warriors and hunters. In all feminist * myths, the Amazon is a strong, inspirational force capable of defending herself and other women against the violence of patriarchy.

[*See also* Woman Chief; Woman Warriors.]

Cathy N. Davidson

AMERICAN INDIAN RIGHTS MOVEMENT. Women have formed the very core of indigenous resistance to Euroamerican domination since the first moment of conflict between Indians and European invaders. A traditional Cheyenne saying claims that "A people is not defeated until the hearts of its women are on the ground." Today, the tradition is continuing with the reemergence of native women leadership, as council chair*women* of their respective tribes, among them Twila Martin Kekahbah, Turtle Mountain Chippewa, and Wilma Mankiller, leader of the Cherokee Nation. In addition, American Indian women in the U.S. throughout the twentieth century have been in other not-so-visible leadership positions as well, in Indian education and community development, land and resource resistance struggles. Traditionally then, female leadership is not a new phenomenon since native women have always held important and influential positions in their communal societies; among them the Creek and Cherokee Nations and the Haudenosaunee's Iroquois Confederacy in New York State. The latter formed the "Longhouse" type of government with "clan mothers" who selected male council leaders. Others included the Narraganset of Rhode Island and the Delawares, among the Algonquin peoples along the Atlantic coast, the latter generically referring to themselves as "women," which was meant to be supremely complimentary. This same govern-

mental tradition, albeit in varied forms, can also be found among the Southwest tribes, such as the Navajos (Dine) and Pueblos, and in the Northwest as well as other regional groups.

Native women's leadership is contrary to those images of meekness, docility and subordination to males that have been typically portrayed by the dominant culture's books and movies, in early descriptions by anthropologists and other racistly based and sexist-oriented scientists, and among political ideologues of both rightist and leftist persuasions. It was customary for American colonists to portray Indian women, for example, as "beasts of burden" among the "nomadic" Plains peoples, and therefore treated not much better than dogs. There are numerous other racist/sexist * stereotypes, from the derogatory "squaw" to the equally denigrating "Cherokee princess." It has been well-documented that the reduction of the status held by women within indigenous nations was a first priority for European colonizers eager to weaken and destabilize target societies. Despite their post-contact disempowerment by European chauvinism, North American indigenous women have continued to resist their negation, if not oblivion, in Euroamerican history. Actually, these traditional societies were either matrilineal or patrilineal regarding descendancy in varied *kinship systems. They included matrifocal and patrifocal spheres of influence and persuasion, as power-bases, in what was likely the closest state of egalitarianism in human society. Hence, such sociocultural communal structures were designed to balance out any internal conflicts among the membership.

These native women were typically accorded a greater social value in indigenous tradition, primarily because of their biological ability to bear children with traditional procreation rights, and therefore tended to be noncombatant to a much greater degree than men. Yet, there was the other side of this scenario. As a case-in-point, Lakota women traditionally maintained at least four warrior societies of their own. Among the Cherokees and the Piegans, there was also a women's military society and leadership. This, then, serves to debunk the grossly misleading and derisive male/female, war-like/peaceful dichotomies deployed by others.

This leadership for traditional rights is practiced today by American Indian women in the forefront of "grassroots" movements, in land, resources, and rights struggles throughout the U.S. Marie Lego, an elder, provided crucial leadership in the Pit River Indian land claims "settlement" dispute in northern California in the 1970s. In Washington State, women such as

Janet McCloud (Tulalip) and Ramona Bennett (Puyallup) had leading roles in the "fish-in" rights struggles of the 1960s. In South Dakota during the early 1970s, elder Oglala Lakota women such as Ellen Moves Camp and Gladys Bissonette assumed the leadership in establishing what was called the Oglala Sioux Civil Rights Organization (OSCRO) on the Pine Ridge Reservation. This was the result of the Wounded Knee seige in 1973, when federal authorities came in with machine guns, and Bissonette became a primary negotiator for what was called the Independent Oglala Nation. At Big Mountain, in the former "Navajo-Hopi Joint Use Area" in Arizona, where the federal government is even now attempting to relocate forcibly more than 10,000 Dine (Navajos) in order to open the way for corporate exploitation of the rich coal reserves underlying their land, it is again usually elder women who have stood at the forefront of resistance, refusing to leave their homes and lands. Among them is Pauline Whitesinger, who was the first to resist relocation, followed by elder leadership, among them Roberta Blackgoat and Katherine Smith who met the federal authorities with armed resistance. Such women have constituted a literal physical barrier blocking consummation of the government's relocation/mining effort for more than a decade. Younger activist Indian women, Lorelei Means and Madonna Thunderhawk in South Dakota have organized for self-determination in Indian health and water rights, including the coordination of international forums to support indigenous rights in North America. These same women are founders of Women of All Red Nations (WARN), a national organization that calls for the "decolonization" of Indian peoples. A young Winona LaDuke (Anishinabe) has been in the forefront of the White Earth Land struggle to restore her peoples' tribal landbase, due to the federally imposed allotment program. She is now living in Canada and is still very much an activist in the environmental movement, specifically focused on James Bay and "the Water Plot," between Canadian and U.S. government authorities. She is also a key organizer in the Indigenous Women's Network, an international organization that is Canadian based.

The costs of such uncompromising, and uncompromised, * activism have often been high, for both the living and the dead. Both native men and women, as American Indian Movement (AIM) members, have paid dearly with their own lives. One among them was Anna Mae Aquash (Canadian Micmac), who was found murdered execution-style in South Dakota in the aftermath of Wounded Knee in 1973, and with suspicion of FBI complicity in her death.

She was also a mother who left behind two little children when she became an involuntary martyr for the movement. Many similar stories, all of them accruing from the past quarter century, could be told in order to demonstrate the extent to which Indian women have galvanized in the center of contemporary native resistance.

As individual women and also as mothers, grandmothers, and sisters, North American Indian women have always been in the forefront of their people's land and life struggles for their children's, family's, and tribal community's rights more so than for their own individual rights. This collective orientation is one reason why there are not more Native American women involved in the mainstream women's movement and feminism in general. Many native women are too busy working and surviving in their own * communities to afford to engage in dialogue with the U.S. women's movement. Yet, as writers, poets, artists, teachers, scholars, and political leaders, Indian women have found many ways to assert their traditional rights and preserve indigenous traditions.

• Johanna Brand, *The Life and Death of Anna Mae Aquash* (1978). Rayna Green, ed., *Native American Women: A Contextual Bibliography* (1983). G. M. Bataille and K. M. Sands, *American Indian Women: Telling Their Lives* (1984). M. A. Jaimes with Theresa Halsey, "American Indian Women: At the Center of Indigenous Resistance in Contemporary North America," in *The State of Native America*, ed. M. A. Jaimes (1992).

Annette Jaimes

AMINI-HUDSON, Johari (b. 1935), poet. Born in Philadelphia, Johari Amini-Hudson (Jewel Lattimore) was an extremely gifted child who sped through her early education and married young. She pursued her literary career as a member of the Chicago's group of black cultural nationalist writers. Coming under the tutelage of Haki Madhubuti during her first term at the University of Chicago, Amini-Hudson was one of the founding members of the Third World Press. One of the press's first releases was Amini-Hudson's first book of poems, *Images in Black* (1967). Amini was also a key figure in the founding of another important literary organization, the Organization of Black American Culture (OBAC), which sponsored writers' workshops and published the influential literary magazine *Nommo* beginning in 1967. Amini-Hudson wrote and read in the style created by OBAC, which stressed black colloquial language, dynamic delivery, typographical experimentation, the rejection of universalism and art for art's sake in favor of protest, and the expression of African values. In 1968, she published new poems, *Black Essence*, and made two contacts that were to greatly influence her development as a poet: She began an association with the Kuumba Performing Arts Company of Chicago, and, along with the members of OBAC, she began to attend the Gwendolyn *Brooks Writer's Workshop. The association with Brooks was close and influential, leading Brooks to write some appreciative introductory notes to Amini-Hudson's third book of poems, *Let's Go Somewhere* (1970). Like the work of the other OBAC poets, Amini-Hudson's work was divided between personal expressions and a more didactic strain that focused on black cultural nationalism. The didactic side of Amini-Hudson's work first emerged in 1969, when she published in pamphlet form and publicly performed *A Folk Fabel* [sic] *(for My People)*. An essay that had been published in *Black World* magazine was reprinted as a pamphlet by the Institute of Positive Education in 1972. "An African Frame of Reference" sets forth Amini-Hudson's views about the operation of the dialectic of thought that distinguishes European from African thought and culture. She develops a scheme for the "re-definition" of concepts and values that will result in different patterns of behavior. In this vein, Amini-Hudson also published essays in *Black World* and in *Black Books Bulletin*, which she helped to found in 1973 and edit. In the 1970s, Amini-Hudson continued her education but was not as active in literary circles as she had been, publishing only a broadside, *A Hip Tale in the Death Style* (1970), and new poems in periodicals. Poems by Amini-Hudson appear in eighteen anthologies of African-American literature.

• Stephen Henderson, ed., *Understanding the New Black Poetry* (1973). Eugene B. Redmond, *Drumvoices: The Mission of Afro-American Poetry—A Critical History* (1976). Maria K. Mootry, "The OBAC Tradition: Don L. Lee, Carolyn Rodgers and the Early Years," in *Nommo: A Literary Legacy of Black Chicago, 1967–1987: Anthology of OBAC—Writers Workshop*, ed. Carole A. Parks (1987), pp. 2–10.

Jon Woodson

ANARCHISM. No state, no property, no authority, absolute freedom. Simply put, this is the philosophy of anarchism, which flourished in the United States between 1870 and 1920. Arguably the most thoroughly American of political theories and yet its most subversive, anarchism has a European pedigree. First articulated in the 1840s by French printer Pierre-Joseph Proudhon, anarchism proclaimed the freedom of the individual from the restrictions of an increasingly bureaucratic state. In the United States, this radical individualism resonated with transcendentalism to become the foundation of Benjamin Tucker's journal *Lib-*

erty: Not the Daughter but the Mother of Order (1881–1908), which appealed to a mostly middle-class, native-born population. In 1871, the uprising of Parisian workers that led to the Paris Commune sparked the dreams of revolutionaries worldwide, giving birth to communist-anarchism, which attracted the impoverished eastern and southern European immigrants crowding America's cities. Its most adept theorists, the Russians Mikhail Bakunin and Peter Kropotkin, reiterated Proudhon's declaration that "property is theft."

Although small in numbers, the anarchists' militance insured their infamy in the American cultural imagination. Stock images of black-bearded foreigners toting sticks of dynamite were sinister emblems of rapid urbanization, industrialization, and immigration during this volatile era. But it was the image of the anarchist woman that threatened the very fiber of Victorian America. *Red Ruin; or the Romance of Anarchy*, an 1888 dime novel about the Chicago Haymarket "riot," in which police were killed when a bomb exploded during a worker's demonstration, portrayed Lucy Parsons as a "shrieker and a termagent," carrying her "anarchist sucklings" as she marched through the city streets denouncing the rich and advancing free love.

Ex-slave, worker, organizer, and writer, Parsons—denounced as the "dynamite-eating wife" of Albert Parsons, one of the four Haymarket martrys—detailed in "To Tramps" (1884), an essay in the socialist periodical the *Alarm*, communist-anarchist Johann Most's theories of direct action to inspire workers to overthrow the capitalist state. Parson's and Most's calls for "propaganda of the deed" were mostly rhetorical, but some individual anarchists did resort to bombings and assassinations. In 1892, a young Russian-Jewish immigrant, Alexander Berkman, with the aid of "Red Emma" *Goldman (both then followers of Most), attempted an *Attentat*, a political assassination, on Henry Clay Frick to avenge the company-ordered shootings of striking steel mill workers.

The anarchist ideals of individual freedom spoke to middle-class as well as working-class women confined by sexual and economic dependence on men. In essays and novels, Voltairine de Cleyre ("The Gates of Freedom," 1891), Lois Waisbrooker (*Nothing Like It*, 1879), Florence Finch Kelly (*Frances: A Story for Men and Women*, 1889), and Goldman ("The Traffic in Women," 1911) insisted that marriage restrained a woman's body in much the same ways that the state restricted personal freedom. They connected the corrosive effects of private property to the stifling of human sexuality, demanding safe, effective birth control. Goldman, for instance, influenced by literary modernism, rejected woman's suffrage, arguing in her journal *Mother Earth* that women's freedom was tied to economic and sexual autonomy, not to the vote.

As cultural radicals, anarchists called for revolution in all phases of life. After World War I, the government increased its repression of "terrorists," jailing, deporting, and executing activists, and anarchism's influence waned. Its legacy continued, however, among Greenwich Village bohemians and Industrial Workers of the World syndicalists, to be resurrected in the movements of the 1960s.

• Voltairine de Cleyre, *Selected Works* (1914). Emma Goldman, *Anarchism and other Essays* (1917; reprint, 1969). Emma Goldman, *Living My Life*, 2 vols. (1931; reprint, 1970). Carolyn Ashbaugh, *Lucy Parsons* (1976). George Woodcock, ed., *The Anarchist Reader* (1977). Paul Avrich, *An American Anarchist: A Life of Voltairine de Cleyre* (1978). David De Leon, *The American As Anarchist* (1978). Margaret S. Marsh, *Anarchist Women, 1870–1920* (1981).

Paula Rabinowitz

ANDERSON, Laurie (b. 1947), performance artist, composer, sculptor, violinist, poet, photographer, comedienne, singer. Of all the descriptions for what it is Laurie Anderson does, Anderson herself prefers narrator or *storyteller. Born in Wayne, Illinois, the second child in a family of eight storytellers, Anderson was encouraged at an early age to develop her artistic abilities. She began playing the violin at age five, eventually performing with the Chicago Youth Symphony, but quit at age sixteen to "learn other things."

Anderson chose New York City as the place to do this learning: she received a B.A. in art history from Barnard College (1969) and an M.F.A. in sculpture from Columbia University (1972). Anderson supplemented her income from sculpting by working as a free-lance art critic and interviewer for journals such as *Art Forum* and *Art News*, and, briefly, as an instructor at the City College of New York in art history and Egyptian architecture. Eventually, a series of grants enabled Anderson to devote herself more fully to her craft.

Anderson soon grew fascinated with the possibilities of multimedia performance art. In one of her earliest street performances, "Duets on Ice" (1974–1975), she played a duet with herself (via a prerecorded tape built into her violin) while her skated feet were frozen in blocks of ice. When the ice melted, the show was over.

International attention did not come to Anderson until she recorded "O Superman" (1981), which included a series of doom-filled telephone answering machine messages. The single, which Anderson made for $400, eventually grossed over one million dollars and reached number two on England's charts.

Anderson's subsequent decision to sign five records with Warner Brothers was seen by many in the art world as a sellout. Anderson contends that commercial venues enable her to produce works that are accessible to more than just the very rich. Anderson's first album with Warner Brothers, *Big Science* (1981), includes "O Superman" and other excerpts from Anderson's epic *United States Part I–IV*. In this six-hour-long performance, Anderson explores the four themes of transportation, politics, money, and love, through stories, songs, music, and over 1,200 photos, cartoons, and films. Inspired by Anderson's attempts to explain her country to foreign audiences, *United States Part I–IV* premiered in 1983 at the Brooklyn Academy of Music to over 85,000 fans. The performance was ultimately recorded on a five-record set entitled *United States Live*.

Anderson is a prolific artist with numerous performances, sculptures, and recordings to her credit. American characters and themes dominate her works, which also reflect her preoccupation with words, autobiography, and technology. Anderson tours her performances—the most recent of which is *Empty Places* (1989)—around the world, often for six months a year. Famous for her cropped, spiked, "vaselined" hair and petite figure, Anderson is one of the few performance artists who is known and liked outside avant-garde art circles.

In recent years, Anderson presented a Grammy Award to Cyndi Lauper; collaborated with rocker Peter Gabriel, guitarist Andrew Belew, and Beat writer William S. Burroughs on the album *Mister Heartbreak*; produced several works with the Trisha Browne Dance Company; served with Harry Belafonte on the board of Performing Artists for Nuclear Disarmament; appeared on the Johnny Carson show; and made a commercial for Reebok.

• Mel Gordon, "Laurie Anderson: Performance Artist," *The Drama Review* 34 (June 1980): 51–55. Adam Block, "Laurie Anderson: In Her Own Voice," *Mother Jones* 10 (August–September 1985): 42–45. Jamie Diamond, "Bio: Laurie Anderson," *People Weekly* 33, no. 18 (7 May 1990): 137–142.

Cynthia J. Davis

ANDROGYNY. The term derives from the Greek *andros* (male) and *gyne* (female), and it is precisely the placement of the female after or subordinate to the male that makes the term problematic. In classic psychology, such as that of Carl Jung, emphasis typically falls on ways to humanize men; the female androgyne is mostly an afterthought. Furthermore, although androgyny hopes, ideally, to erase gender barriers, the androgyne is based on a combination of the most conventional or traditional identities of "male" (aggression, strength, rationality) and "female" (compassion, nurturing, intuition). Many feminists would rather discard these stereotypes altogether.

• Carolyn G. Heilbrun, *Toward a Recognition of Androgyny* (1973). June Singer, *Androgyny: Toward a New Theory of Sexuality* (1976).

Cathy N. Davidson

ANGELOU, Maya (b. 1928), autobiographer, poet, educator, actress, dancer. Responding to her granddaughter Maya Angelou's decision to stop talking after being raped by her mother's boyfriend when she was seven and a half, Annie Henderson told Angelou that she did not care one bit about what neighbors were saying about her—that she was either crazy or a moron or an idiot. Speaking in the repetitive cadences of the old black oral tradition, she repeated that she did not care. She *knew*—she was absolutely certain—that Angelou would eventually belong to that most articulate group of human beings: she would be a preacher. And Annie Henderson was right. While Angelou did not become a preacher in the traditional sense of the term, she did become a messenger of truth. And her sermons, in lieu of the preacher's chants and cries, have come to us in the form of poems and narratives that speak with the emotional power of the preacher.

Angelou was born Margurite Johnson on 4 April 1928, in St. Louis, Missouri. Her mother, Vivian (Baxter) Johnson and her father, Bailey, divorced shortly afterwards. Consequently, the three-year-old Angelou and her four-year-old brother, Bailey, were sent to Stamps, Arkansas, to live with "Momma" Henderson.

After her graduation from the eighth grade, Angelou and her brother went to live with her mother in San Francisco. Once, while visiting her father, she fought with his girlfriend, and ran away. She lived in a junkyard with other homeless children for a month. When she later returned to San Francisco, she became the city's first black streetcar conductor, and at age sixteen gave birth to her son, Guy, shortly after graduating from high school.

Before gaining notoriety as a writer, Angelou worked as a creole cook, a madam, a prostitute, a dancer, an actress, a singer, a songwriter, and a social activist. At the request of Martin Luther King, Jr., she served as northern coordinator for the Southern Christian Leadership Council in 1960 and 1961, thus establishing her commitment to the struggle for black freedom.

Meanwhile, she was launching her career as a writer. She joined the Harlem Writers Guild, which included such writers as James Baldwin and Paule Marshall, and learned the importance of discipline and technique. After her return from Ghana in 1966, Angelou joined James Baldwin for an evening with Jules and Judy Feiffer. Relaxed by the atmosphere created by casual drinking and talking, Angelou felt comfortable enough to tell her life story. Judy Feiffer was so intrigued that she contacted a friend who worked at Random House. He, in turn, contacted Angelou and encouraged her to write her autobiography. Initially, Angelou refused. But after her future editor noted the difficulty of the autobiographical form, Angelou responded to the challenge and consented.

Her first volume of autobiography, *I Know Why the Caged Bird Sings* (1970), was an instant success. It became a best-seller and was nominated for the National Book Award. Since then, she has published five more volumes of autobiography, including *Gather Together in My Name* (1974), *Singin' and Swingin' and Gettin' Merry Like Christmas* (1976), *The Heart of a Woman* (1981) and *All God's Children Need Traveling Shoes* (1986). In addition, she has published five collections of poetry: *Just Give Me A Cool Drink of Water 'fore I Diiie* (1971), *Oh Pray My Wings Are Gonna Fit Me Well* (1975), *And Still I Rise* (1978), *Shaker, Why Don't You Sing?* (1983), and *I Shall Not Be Moved* (1990). In 1993, her memoir *Wouldn't Take Nothing for My Journey Now* was a Book-of-the-Month Club featured selection.

In a crowning achievement, Angelou was selected to read the inaugural poem on President Bill Clinton's Inauguration Day. The poem, "On the Pulse of the Morning," is both a celebration of life and an appeal to listeners and readers to help America live up to its promise of genuine democracy.

And so it was that on 20 January 1993 Maya Angelou fullfilled her grandmother's prophecy. Standing before the entire country, she paid homage to the word and spoke the truth. Granted, Maya Angelou has had a multifaceted career. In 1954 and 1955, she toured Europe and Africa as a cast member in a production of *Porgy and Bess*. She was nominated for an Emmy in 1977 for her role in the television production of Alex Haley's *Roots*. And in 1981, she received a lifetime appointment as Reynolds Professor of American Studies at Wake Forest University. But despite her many achievements in other artistic and intellectual spheres, she will always be best remembered as a writer.

• Maya Angelou's papers are located in the Z. Smith Reynolds Library at Wake Forest University. "Prominent Southern-born Author Talks about the South, Southerners, and the Long Road Home," *Ebony* (February 1982): 130–134. Lynn Z. Bloom, "Maya Angelou." in *Afro-American Writers after 1955: Dramatists and Prose Writers*, eds. Thadious Davis and Trudier Harris (1985), pp. 3–12. Maya Angelou, *Conversations with Maya Angelou*, ed. Jeffrey M. Elliott (1989). Dolly A. McPherson, *Order Out of Chaos: The Autobiographical Works of Maya Angelou* (1990). Nancy Caldwell Sorel, "Maya Angelou and Billie Holiday," *Atlantic Monthly* (September 1990): 61. Grace E. Collins, "Maya Angelou," in *Notable Black American Women*, ed. Jessie Carney Smith (1992), pp. 23–27. Kathleen Thompson, "Maya Angelou," in *Black Women in America* (1993), pp. 36–38.

                                        Tony Bolden

ANGER. *See* Ranting.

ANOREXIA. *See* Body and Health; Eating Disorders.

ANTHOLOGIES are compilations of the personal visions and individual styles of writers, and can and should be judged as unified works. The "parts" of the anthology—including the stories and whatever additional material is included, such as a preface, introduction, and headnotes—function both separately and together. The anthology is a genre in which the synergistic interaction of the parts is the controlling characteristic. It is the expression of an anthologist's coherent and intentionally expressed vision.

Behind each anthology is a controlling "I," called an editor, an anthologist, or a compiler. The editorial "I" has ideas about what gives a work of literature value, what constitutes a genre, and how short works of literature can interact with other short works of literature— poems, essays, letters, stories—so that each piece is enhanced by the others. In all cases, anthologists' choices of writings grow out of their personal and professional history and identity, and their individual temperaments, biases, preferences, reading experiences, and hidden agendas.

The individuality of the choosing anthologist has often been disguised by a title that makes claims to some sort of universality or inevitability for the collection. The titles of short story collections seldom if ever make clear that the collection is the product of a deliberate, conscious, and discriminating agency.

Short story collections are put together by people who have to make two kinds of decisions: (1) They must choose what sources they will investigate and what sources they will ignore to find stories to choose among for inclusion in their collection; (2) and they must decide which stories from their chosen sources they will include and which they will exclude.

The criteria on which they base these two sets of choices, taken together, are "the editorial rationale." Anthologists are literary critics creating theory-about-literature in the form of an object, that is, an anthology.

There are many kinds of short story anthologies. Historically, anthologies tend to develop from the general to the increasingly specialized, from the multigeneric to the generically specialized, from the historically inclusive to the contemporary, from the thematically nondiscriminatory to the thematically particularized.

Carol Farley Kessler's collection, *Daring to Dream: Utopian Stories by United States Women, 1836–1919* (1984), is a thematic anthology with specific gender, geographical, and historical boundaries. Other kinds of thematic anthologies are based on relationships, such as *Between Mothers and Daughters: Stories across a Generation* (1985) and *Women's Friendships: A Collection of Stories* (1991), both edited by Susan Koppelman; or on shared experiences, such as the short story collection *The Other Woman: Stories of Two Women and a Man*, edited by Susan Koppelman (1984), and the multigeneric collection *Wall Tappings: An Anthology of Writings by Women Prisoners*, edited by Judith A. Scheffler (1986); or on shared circumstances, such as *Old Maids: Short Stories by Nineteenth Century U.S. Women Writers* (1984), edited by Susan Koppelman.

The multiplication of specifying considerations of anthologies has two implications: the first is that the general body of literature from which the collected materials have been drawn is rich, varied, and abundant; the other is that the audience for such tightly circumscribed material is large enough to justify publication.

In other thematic collections, the stories are all contemporary (with each other) with no apparent attempt to illustrate historical development; rather, the focus is on breadth of current literary interpretation of a particular topic. Among such anthologies are Lonnie Barbach's *Pleasures: Women Write Erotica* (1984) and *The Things That Divide Us: Stories by Women*, edited by Faith Conlon, Rachel da Silva, and Barbara Wilson (1985), which includes writing by contemporary women of a variety of races, United States regions, sexualities, religions, and ages, and concentrates on the role of diversity in women's personal lives.

Some anthologies represent the breadth of experience and variety of sensibilities of the members of a group identified by a feature that has had historical saliency, usually as the excuse for oppression. For instance, Mary Helen Washington attends to race in her two collections of black women's writings, *Black-Eyed Susans: Classic Stories by and about Black Women* (1975) and *Midnight Birds: Stories by Contemporary Black Women Writers* (1980). Other anthologies, such as Elly Bulkin's *Lesbian Fiction* (1981), address sexual identity, while Judy *Grahn's two-volume *True to Life Adventure Stories* (1978; reprint, 1981) focuses on class issues and experiences. Anthologies that examine ethnicity include *The Woman Who Lost Her Names: Selected Writings of American Jewish Women,* edited by Julia Wolf Mazow (1980) and *Cuentos: Stories by Latinas,* edited by Alma Gomes, Cherrie Moraga, and Mariana Romo-Carmona (1983). Nationality provides the frame for *Reclaiming Medusa: Stories by Contemporary Puerto Rican Women,* edited and translated by Diana *Velez (1988), as well as for the multigeneric *Dream Book: An Anthology of Writings by Italian American Women,* edited by Helen Barolini (1985). Attention to disabilities draws together the works anthologized in *With the Power of Each Breath,* edited by Susan Browne, et al. (1985) and *With Wings: An Anthology of Literature by and about Women with Disabilities,* edited by Marsha Saxton and Florence Howe (1987). *New Stories by Southern Women,* edited by Mary Ellis Gibson (1989), is one example of an anthology organized according to geographic region.

Some collections focus on the ways in which women writers' imaginations have used a particular subgenre, such as Pamela Sargent's *Women Of Wonder: Science Fiction Stories by Women about Women* (1974; reprint, 1975) and Vonda N. McIntyre and Susan Janice Anderson's *Aurora: Beyond Equality* (1976). Other anthologies that are organized around particular subgenres include *Womansleuth Anthology: Contemporary Mystery Stories by Women,* edited by Irene Zahava (1988; 1989; 1990), the *Sisters in Crime* series, edited by Marilyn Wallace (1989; 1990; 1990), *"May Your Days Be Merry and Bright" and Other Christmas Stories by Women,* edited by Susan Koppelman (1988; reprint, 1989), and *Companions of Our Youth: Stories by Women for Young People's Magazines, 1865–1900,* edited by Jane Benardete and Phyllis Moe (1980).

Some anthologies of women's writings are based on propinquity or provenance, such as *It's a Woman's World: A Collection of Stories from Harper's Bazaar,* edited by Mary Louise Aswell (1944). Contemporary anthologies based on propinquity are *The Lesbians' Home Journal* (1976), a collection of stories that all originally appeared in the *Ladder,* and *Fine Lines: The Best of Ms. Fiction,* edited by Ruth Sullivan (1981). Collections such as Susan Cahill's two-

volume *Women and Fiction* (1975; 1978) refer to undefined standards of literary greatness, advertising themselves as bringing readers "more of the finest short stories by women writers from around the world." The collection of eighteen stories by women and twelve by men edited by Barbara Solomon, *The Experience of the American Woman* (1978), promises readers "a century of great fiction about the place and the role of women in America."

Rediscovery: 300 Years Of Stories by and about Women (1981) promises readers "experiences all women share—from the beginnings to the ends of their lifetimes." This collection, edited by Betzy Dinesen, is international in scope and does indeed include stories from three centuries. The rationale behind the temporal and geographical dimensions of the collection is that their breadth serves to undergird the claim to the "female" universality of the subject—women's life cycle. Another life-cycle, international, multiracial, multiethnic, and multigeneric collection is *I'm On My Way Running: Women Speak on Coming of Age,* edited by Lyn Reese, Jean Wilkinson, and Phyllis Sheon Koppelman (1983).

A group that has previously had minimal representation in general anthologies begins to demonstrate its literary presence with multigeneric anthologies of the voices of its members, such as *I Am the Fire of Time: The Voices of Native American Women,* edited by Jane B. Katz (1977), *That's What She Said: Contemporary Poetry and Fiction by Native American Women,* edited by Rayna Green (1984), and *Spider Woman's Granddaughters: Traditional Tales and Contemporary Writing by Native American Women,* edited by Paula Gunn *Allen (1989). Each of these collections is increasingly more specific generically and chronologically, as if, as time passes, the members of the group, whatever the group is, grow more insistent upon the importance of their individualities, specificities, and diversities, and celebrate those identifiers. *Making Waves: An Anthology of Writings by and about Asian-American Women,* edited by Asian Women United of California (1989), will no doubt be followed by collections of writing within a single genre by women from specific Asian nationalities.

The women's liberation movement has stimulated the rediscovery and interest in many women's voices. Much of the personal and political work of the women's liberation movement has taken place in the context of consciousness-raising groups whose work could not have been accomplished without many voices speaking and being heard. Because of the multivocal nature of the women's liberation movement, the anthology seems to be its paradigmatic literary manifestation.

Susan Koppelman

ANTHONY, Susan Brownell (1820–1906), pioneer woman's rights leader. Born in Adams, Massachusetts, to Daniel Anthony, a mill owner, and Lucy Read, Susan Anthony grew up in an atmosphere filled with Quaker ideas of human equality and service. The Anthonys and their eight children moved to Battenville, New York, in 1826, and it was there that Susan attended a school that her father ran in his home for the benefit of his own children and those of his mill workers. From 1839 to 1849, after financial reverses forced her father to close his mill, Anthony taught school, notably at Canajoharie Academy in New York State. She then returned home, ostensibly to manage the new family farm in Rochester. With the support of her family, she devoted the rest of her life to reform work.

Anthony worked first for the cause of temperance, until, as a woman, she was denied permission to speak at a temperance convention. Beginning in 1852, she campaigned for the abolition of slavery; after the Emancipation Proclamation of 1863, she concentrated on woman's rights. Criticized for her racism, in the 1860s and 1870s Anthony refused to support black male suffrage (guaranteed by the Fifteenth Amendment in 1870) before woman suffrage (guaranteed by the Nineteenth Amendment in 1920). She fought sexism and pursued women's issues, such as the right to vote, better working conditions, and equitable marriage laws, but many felt that she did not take black women's issues seriously.

An immensely charismatic and persuasive speaker, Anthony traveled around the United States for over fifty years lecturing on woman's rights. Her erect figure, clothed in black and wrapped in a red shawl, became well known as a symbol of the independent woman, and she gathered about her many admiring disciples. She decided at an early age never to marry and was therefore free of the family restraints that hampered many colleagues. Her lifelong devotion to the reformer Elizabeth Cady * Stanton (1815–1902), who was married and the mother of seven children, also provided Anthony with an immensely effective political partnership. Together, they founded the National (American) Woman Suffrage Association and joined Matilda Gage (1826–1898) in writing the initial four volumes of the *History of Woman Suffrage* (1881–1882).

By the end of the nineteenth century, Susan B. Anthony held a position of international fame and respect. Although she died with her goal of woman suffrage unfulfilled, she deserves much of the credit for the final passage of the Nineteenth Amendment.

• Anthony's personal papers are located in a variety of places, including the Library of Congress, the Schlesinger Library of Radcliffe College, and the Susan B. Anthony Memorial in Rochester, New York. See also Ida H. Harper, *The Life and Work of Susan B. Anthony*, 3 vols., 1898–1908. Alma Lutz, *Susan B. Anthony* (1959). Ellen Carol Dubois, ed., *Elizabeth Cady Stanton, Susan B. Anthony: Correspondance, Writings, Speeches* (1981). Kathleen Barry, *Susan B. Anthony* (1988).

Katherine Kleitz

ANTHROPOLOGISTS. Women were present in the discipline of anthropology practically from its beginnings. Matilda Coxe Stevenson and Alice Cunningham Fletcher are early examples of women anthropologists; they wrote about the Zuni and Omaha Indians, respectively. In 1903, forty-nine women were founding members of the American Anthropological Association, among them Elsie Clews Parson, who would teach Ruth Benedict and send her to Columbia, where she would in turn teach Margaret * Mead. These two women, Benedict and Mead, remain the most famous American women anthropologists, and are among the truly important women writers in the United States.

Benedict and Mead reached huge reading publics. Benedict's *Patterns of Culture* (1934) was influential in founding the culture and personality school in anthropology, which believes in the interplay of social and personal history— a view often shared by women writers in anthropology. A twenty-five-cent paperback in 1946, this study of Zuni culture as "Apollonian" and Kwakiutl culture as "Dionysian" was a best-seller whose ideas were assimilated by the general public; it remains a standard text in college courses and a classic statement of cultural relativism, the belief that cultural norms vary and that the anthropologist, "insofar as he [Benedict's pronoun] is an anthropologist . . . is bound to avoid any weighting of one in favor of the other."

Benedict's 1946 study of Japan, *The Chrysanthemum and the Sword: Patterns of Japanese Culture*, was similarly widely read by a public curious about the United States' recent opponent, though its thesis of "national character" was respected less by the profession. Her 1940 book, *Race: Science and Politics*, and the numerous pamphlets derived from it, circulated in public schools for more than a decade, promoting the idea that race is a constructed and often meaningless concept, and that biological differences imply neither superiority nor inferiority.

Similarly, Mead's *Coming of Age in Samoa*

(1928) and later works became best-sellers and touchstones in discussions of adolescence, male-female relations, and similar themes in American life. Over the decades, Mead became a popular columnist, talk show guest, and cultural guru on matters ranging from race relations to the sexual revolution. Her portly frame and grandmotherly, bespectacled face became familiar cultural symbols for more than a generation.

They were powerful creatures, these mothers of anthropology—powerful creatures, but also victims in a profession that defined itself as the study of Man, and where the anthropologist (as in the brief quotation from Benedict, above) is generically a "he." Benedict began to teach at Columbia University in 1921, but she did not hold a full-time assistant professorship until 1931, and only then by the efforts of her mentor, the powerful Franz Boas. She was already well known by the time she wrote *Patterns of Culture*, but she remained an assistant professor for years. Benedict experienced humiliating defeat when Boas retired, and she, as a woman, was overlooked as possible chair of her department for Robert Linton, whose name survives only in this context.

Mead, like Benedict, was also undervalued by the academic establishment. Although she was and remains the most famous American anthropologist, Mead's work was never widely respected in the profession, and she too had trouble obtaining full-time work in universities. She supported herself for most of her life working part-time for both Columbia University and the American Museum of Natural History. Her popularity was turned against her by the academic establishment, which saw her work as "unscientific" at a time when anthropology was debating its role as a social science and increasingly choosing to de-emphasize subjectivity and accessible style in favor of "hard" data.

Both Mead and Benedict were bisexual and brought to their work a veiled desire to remove homosexuality from the category of abnormal behavior; to this end, they collaborated with rebel psychoanalysts like Karen Horney. Benedict wanted to integrate and defend the full range of her sexuality in her work, though coming out as a lesbian (Mead and others warned) would jeopardize her position at Columbia. Under the pseudonym Anne Singleton, Benedict wrote and published poetry with the Lyricist group associated with Lousie * Bogan and Edna St. Vincent * Millay, poetry that made her sexuality and feelings clear. But as an anthropologist, she had to work through indirection, as in the following passage from the first page of *Patterns of Culture:* "The distinguishing mark of anthropology among the social sciences is that

it includes for serious study other societies than our own. For its purposes any regulation of mating and reproduction is as significant as our own." Like Mead, Benedict wanted to show how "the individual was the creature of culture and so was in no way responsible for the discomfort of his position if he was accidentally bred to deviance." Yet in this passage from *Patterns of Culture*, she still speaks in terms of "deviance." The trap resembles that which ensnares her when all anthropologists are subsumed under the masculine pronoun.

These two famous women anthropologists set a pattern for the concerns and styles of many women writers in anthropology, whether lesbian or heterosexual. The writing of the best women anthropologists is often guided by the following imperatives: chose the unusual topic; espouse the underdog's agenda; write your work in clear and lucid prose accessible to generalists; protect cultural relativism and freedom of choice; write about culture with a woman's eye and a woman's heart; court the public; and also, sadly, expect to be overlooked or denigrated by many men who dominate the profession.

Benedict and Mead's intellectual legacy influenced the literary style and personal voice cultivated by Barbara Myerhoff in *Number Our Days* (1979), a beautifully written account of a community of aged Jews in California, struggling to maintain *Yiddishkeit* (Eastern European Jewish culture) in the modern United States. It also appears, in different ways, in female anthropologists like Michelle * Rosaldo, Barbara Tedlock, Ruth Behar, and Virginia Dominguez, some of whom write traditional ethnographies, but with a choice of subject, style, or perspective that places them in the tradition of women writers in anthropology.

Women are a full part of anthropological writing today; feminist anthropologists form almost one-twelfth of American Anthropological Association membership. Still, two important recent essays by female anthropologists show that men's concerns and views still dominate the profession. In a recent *Signs* article, Frances E. Mascia-Lees, Patricia Sharpe, and Colleen Ballerino-Cohen show how postmodern anthropology remains blind to women's issues and deftly excludes feminism from the category of "theory" ("The Post-Modern Turn in Anthropology: Cautions from a Feminist Perspective," Autumn 1989). Anthropologist Catherine Lutz's important essay, "The Erasure of Women's Writing in Sociocultural Anthropology" (*American Ethnologist* 17, 1990), shows how women anthropologists, though representing a large percentage in the field of anthropology and publishing as much as their male colleagues, are underrepresented in networks of citation that confer prestige. From the beginning, women anthropologists have been strong and brave, articulating the cutting-edge perceptions in their field. From the beginning, they have been swamped by the generic "he" and struggled to be heard in "his" discipline.

• Margaret Mead, *Blackberry Winter: My Earlier Years* (1972; reprint, 1975). Michelle Rosaldo and Louise Lamphere, eds., *Woman, Culture, and Society* (1974). Nannerl Keohane, Michelle Rosaldo, and Barbara Gelpi, eds., *Feminist Theory: A Critique of Ideology* (1982). Judith Schacter Modell, *Ruth Benedict: Patterns of a Life* (1983). Mary Catherine Bateson, *With a Daughter's Eye: A Memoir of Margaret Mead and Gregory Bateson* (1984). Jane Howard, *Margaret Mead: A Life* (1984). Henrietta Moore, *Feminism and Anthropology* (1988). Margaret M. Caffrey, *Ruth Benedict: Stranger in this Land* (1989).

Marianna Torgovnick

ANTI-ABORTION. *See* Abortion.

ANTIESSENTIALISM. *See* Essentialism.

ANTILYNCHING CAMPAIGN, a movement to end mob violence against African-Americans—particularly the summary execution of individuals accused of crime (often the rape of white women)—in the southern United States during the period from the 1880s to the 1940s. The antilynching campaign, led by such organizations as the National Association of Colored Women (NACW), the National Association for the Advancement of Colored People (NAACP), the Council for Interracial Cooperation (CIC), and the Association of Southern Women for the Prevention of Lynching (ASWPL), sought to fight lynching through education or legal action, or by securing federal legislation against it.

Women played a major role in the campaign. The most effective leader in its early development was Ida B. *Wells-Barnett. An African-American teacher and journalist, Wells-Barnett was moved initially by the 1892 Memphis lynching of three black businessmen whose success had outraged their white competitors. Responding with a series of newspaper columns, later expanded into the widely circulated pamphlet *Southern Horrors: Lynch Law in All Its Phases* (1892), Wells-Barnett documented the innocence of many victims of lynching, especially those charged with rape, while denouncing the failure of leading white southerners to act forcefully against the evil. In 1895, she published a larger investigative work, *A Red Record*, which served as a major resource for the campaign itself. Wells-Barnett led legal efforts to prevent lynchings and worked through both the NACW and the NAACP (an organization that she helped found) to secure antilynching legislation. It was through these organizations that other black women, including the writers Angelina Weld *Grimké and Georgia Douglas *Johnson, also became active in the effort.

Beginning in the 1920s and 1930s, an increasing number of white women, especially in the South, joined the antilynching movement. Revolted by the brutality of lynching, and resenting the white southern defense of lynching based on the "protection" of white womanhood, women such as Jessie Daniel Ames and others worked through the CIC and, after 1930, the ASWPL to try to bring the practice to an end. Focusing on education and the courts—and ambivalent about federal legislation—they worked to create a climate of opinion among white southerners that would lead to lynching's demise.

Although both the CIC and the ASWPL chiefly involved women activists rather than writers, those organizations provided a background for the work of one of the most eloquent white literary opponents of lynching, and of racial injustice in general, the Georgia writer Lillian Smith. In such major works as her 1944 novel *Strange Fruit* and her 1949 collection of essays *Killers of the Dream*, Smith elaborated on arguments developed by ASWPL activists that linked lynching to a larger system of racial and sexual pathology and exploitation in the South.

With a decline in lynching in the 1940s, most of those involved in the campaign began to focus on other issues. Nevertheless, the campaign itself provided an important background to the larger battle against racism and segregation that ultimately took shape in the southern United States.

[*See also* Abolition; Activism; Reconstruction; Wells-Barnett, Ida B.]

• Morton Sosna, *In Search of the Silent South: Southern Liberals and the Race Issue* (1977). Jacquelyn Dowd Hall, *Revolt Against Chivalry: Jessie Daniel Ames and the Women's Campaign Against Lynching* (1979). Robert L. Zangrando, *The NAACP Crusade Against Lynching, 1909–1950* (1980). Paula Giddings, *When and Where I Enter: The Impact of Black Women on Race and Sex in America* (1984). Trudier Harris, comp., *Selected Works of Ida B. Wells-Barnett* (1991).

Dickson D. Bruce, Jr.

ANTIN, Mary (1881–1949), writer. Mary Antin was born Maryashe Antin in Polotzk, Russia, and renamed Mary soon after her family's immigration to Boston in 1892, during the mass migration of eastern European Jews in the late nineteenth century. A gifted and precocious child, she attended public school and collected prizes in writing. She prepared for college at the Boston Girls Latin School, but did not go on to college. Instead, she married William Grabau in 1901 and moved to New York City, where her husband taught science at Columbia University.

Antin's published works include *From Plotzk to Boston* (1899), originally a letter to her uncle about the family's exodus from Europe; *They Who Knock at Our Gates* (1914), a defense of immigration at a time when anti-immigration sentiment was gathering force; and "House of the One Father" (1941), her last published essay, which reveals an abiding solidarity between her and the people of Polotzk. But her career as a writer depended chiefly on her autobiography *The Promised Land* (1901). It enjoyed sensational success, with eighty-five thousand copies sold in thirty-four printings. This success was due partly to Antin's uplifting and reassuring tone, which served as an antidote to the fears and social unrest following the Spanish American War. More important, Antin's first-person, insider's story established a warm relationship between the despised and misunderstood immigrant and her reader, whom she addresses as "my American friend."

The uplifting tone of *The Promised Land* stems in part from its reassurance that the American Dream is realizable. Even though Antin's father suffers many financial setbacks, Mary fulfills his dream of giving his children an education. As the family fortune spirals downward, Mary's academic and social performance takes off on an upward course. She crosses boundaries undreamed of in the old world, exclaiming: "The world as I knew it was not large enough to contain all that I saw and felt." As she sees it, the slum her family lives in cannot imprison her; America is her fairy godmother, and it will lead her out of poverty.

In New York, Antin also was determined to transcend the confines of the immigrant world, and she took her cue from her friends the Lazarus sisters. Josephine Lazarus, who carried on her sister Emma's work in fusing Judaism with secular philosophies, became Antin's mentor and encouraged her to write her autobiography for self-exploration and self-realization. Antin's patriotic effusions may grate on late-twentieth-century sensibilities, but this Jewish-American book's adulation of America and the new Self created by it capture a significant moment in immigrant experience.

• Evelyn Avery, "Oh My 'Mishpochal': Some Jewish Women Writers from Antin to Kaplan View the Family," *Studies in American Jewish Literature* 5 (1986): 44–53. Steven Rubin, "Style and Meaning in Mary Antin's *The Promised Land:* A Reevaluation," *Studies in American Jewish Literature* 5 (1986): 35–43. William Proe-friedt, "The Education of Mary Antin," the *Journal of Ethnic Studies* 17, no. 4 (1990): 81–100.

                                                    Ruth Yu Hsiao

ANTINOMIANISM. *See* Colonial Era Writing; Hutchinson, Anne; Prophesying; Religion, *article on* Religion to 1700.

ANTI-SEMITISM. Anti-Semitism in the United States has been characterized not so much by the violence of Russian pogroms or a Holocaust as by an ambivalent attitude toward Jews. This attitude, which stems in part from America's ideals of tolerance and religious freedom, has been evident since the first Jews arrived in New Amsterdam in 1654. The ambivalence has revealed itself in stereotyping as well as in exclusionary practices, such as the scheduling of school exams on Jewish holy days. Since the middle of the nineteenth century, overt anti-Semitism has increased, fueled in part by the rise in the number of Jews in America (200–300 in 1700; 1,600–2,500 in 1800; 938,000–1,058,000 in 1900; 5,800,000 in 1992), and by the popularity of nativism and Know-Nothingism in the nineteenth century, and of the Ku Klux Klan and neo-Nazis in the twentieth.

Christian American women writers have reflected and contributed to the ambivalent attitude toward Jews. In the nineteenth century, Harriet Beecher *Stowe, for example, praised the productive, self-sufficient Katy Scudder in *The Minister's Wooing* (1859) by calling her a "Mother in Israel," but then had Eva Van Arsdel in *My Wife and I: or, Harry Henderson's History* (1871) learn that Jews are "good" not through direct contact, but through the mediation of a Quaker. Other writers, including C. A. Ogden and Harriette N. W. Baker, wrote novels that only thinly veiled their mission to convert Jews to Christianity. Early in the twentieth century, Edith *Wharton portrayed a Jew, Simon Rosedale in the *House of Mirth* (1905), as stereotypically obsessed with money, but also as sympathetic in his relationship with Lily Bart. More blatant in her xenophobic and anti-Semitic stance was Charlotte Perkins *Gilman, who declared in her 1935 autobiography, *The Living of Charlotte Perkins Gilman*, that New York is an "unnatural city" because the native-born American is an exile, and one-third of the inhabitants are Jews.

Jewish American women writers have been highly conscious of their special, yet vulnerable, position as Jews in America. Believing in the opportunities for free expression that America offered, nineteenth-century women such as Nina Morais Cohen, Alice Hyneman Rhine, Emma Lazarus, and Emma Wolf wrote (in essays, poetry, and fiction) about the anti-Semitism they observed around them. For example, in 1887, Rhine told non-Jewish readers of the *Forum* that "Christian dislike" of Jews stemmed from "the obstinacy with which Jews deny the Messiahship of Jesus," and that Christian infants imbibed hatred and contempt for the Jew with their mothers' milk (*Forum* 3). Five years later, Wolf reminded readers of her 1892 novel, *Other Things Being Equal*, that Christians never let Jews forget that they are different (and, by implication, inferior). In the twentieth century, Jewish women have fought against not only the ambivalence of non-Jews, but of Jews as well. Edna * Ferber and Anzia * Yezierska, among others, have confronted the self-hatred of assimilated Jews who see their Jewish identities as a liability. Most recently, Letty Cottin Pogrebin, Irena Klepfisz, and Grace * Paley have begun to examine the anti-Semitism within the women's movement.

[*See also* Holocaust Writing; Jewish-American Writing.]

• Louis Harap, *The Image of the Jew in American Literature* (1974). Charlotte Baum, Paula Hyman, and Sonya Michel, *The Jewish Woman in America* (1975). Nathan Belth, *A Promise to Keep: A Narrative of the American Encounter with Anti-Semitism* (1979). Susanna Heschel, ed., *On Being a Jewish Feminist* (1983). Jonathan Sarna, ed., *The American Jewish Experience* (1986).

Diane Lichtenstein

ANTIWAR MOVEMENTS. Women activists, including writers and speakers whose ideas have been made available to a larger public through published tracts and pamphlets, have acted as both consciences and catalysts for movements opposing the variety of conflicts that have marked American history. As often as not, these individuals have acted without external support or formal affiliations or positions, and their works have served to expand and elucidate popular definitions of war, violence, and their victims.

Throughout the colonial and Revolutionary period and into the era of the War of 1812, the complex relationship between revolutionists and loyalists in America was further complicated by the activities of a third, albeit smaller, grouping, the religious pacifists. Individual women pacifists, like Sarah Hodkins, published letters and editorials during this period that decried the practical effects of men's enlistment in the armed forces upon the family and its finances, but there was also a broader, more idealistically based movement defined by its attempt to selectively apply the Christian gospel to matters of state and policy. Centered first in the New England Quaker communities and later spreading to the cities of that region, the pacifist movement gained momentum through its rejection of the more aggressive elements of Calvinist teaching. The rapidly proliferating "peace societies" in the 1820s and 1830s criticized the "evils of warfare," especially offensive war, and advocated peaceful, and even self-sacrificial resolutions of all conflicts.

Many abolitionist activists, like Elizabeth Buffum Chace, had their intellectual roots in this pacifist movement, but a minority began to question its reliance upon the notion that government policies reflected God's will. Sarah and Angelina * Grimké, speaking and writing in the 1830s and 1840s, pointed to the inconsistency between the Creator's perfect state and contemporary United States government policy, especially in domestic affairs, where they condemned as a "violation of human rights" the "violent seizure and confiscation" of women's rights to autonomy and democratic participation. The Grimkés were among the first to identify as a "war" political and social inequality within the country itself, and to oppose the violence that might be directed or tolerated by the state against its own members.

This broadened definition of conflict played an important role in the rise of the abolition movement in the 1840s. The persistent threat of open civil conflict over the terms of admission to the Union for new territories, the potential for another war with Britain over boundaries in the Pacific Northwest, and the war with Mexico prompted the formation of new peace advocacy groups in which women played crucial roles. Lydia Maria * Child had sacrificed her career as a novelist in 1833 by publishing a tract critiquing slavery and racism, and throughout the succeeding antebellum years she wrote for a variety of abolitionist newspapers, advocating nonparticipation in "corrupt" civil institutions that permitted slavery and racial inequality to persist.

By the late 1850s and early 1860s, the intensity of feeling over the slavery issue overwhelmed the pacifist and resistant strains within the abolition movement; realizing that full disengagement from social institutions was for the most part neither productive nor possible, abolitionists began to shift their focus toward support for a "righteous" war to end slavery. Harriet Beecher * Stowe's fiction and Julia Ward * Howe's lyrics for the "Battle Hymn of the Republic," drawn from the Book of Revelation, contributed to the development of this phenomenon. Like other women writers who were quite young during the Civil War, including such southerners as Rebecca Latimer Felton of Georgia, Howe later became a leader in the peace advocacy and women's suffrage movements of the late nineteenth century. Meanwhile, it became clear that the closing of the Civil War in 1865 was in fact a prelude to the expansion of military conflict against Native Americans in the western territories, an extended war criticized by women writers like Belva Bennett Lockwood. Likewise, the end of the century was marked by a resurgent violent racism, including not only discrimination against, but also lynchings of African-Americans, especially in the South. African-American women speakers and writers such as Ida B. *Wells-Barnett and Mary Church Terrell brought attention to these injustices, the latter as part of her leadership of a growing international peace advocacy movement. At the same time, in the Far West, Chinese laborers and their families encountered discriminatory laws and mob violence fueled by economic hardship and Sinophobic racism. *Sui Sin Fan (Edith Eaton) authored short stories describing these conflicts and defending the Chinese immigrants. Although not as popular as it had been during the antebellum period, absolute pacifism also gained new adherents in the late 1800s, in part because of the writings of Quaker polemicists like Antoinette Doolittle.

The emergence of global war during World War I was accompanied by international movements advocating civil disobedience, socialist pacifism, and disarmament. Women writers and activists were in the forefront of these movements in the United States: the poet Angela Morgan, education advocate May Wright Sewall, socialist speaker Kate O'Hare Cunningham, and political advocates Jane Addams and Carrie Chapman *Catt all wrote and spoke against the war and its effects, the latter in fact organizing the Women's Peace Party in 1915. Others, such as Laura Puffer Morgan and Dorothy Detzer, advocated new forms of international organizations, including world government, to prevent future global conflict. After the war, many of the same women were active in the women's suffrage and prohibition movements.

During World War II, pacifist advocacy was less prevalent than during the Great War, in part because improved communications technologies made knowledge of and propaganda about the nature of the enemy easier to transmit. In fact, in the work of poet Muriel *Rukeyser, criticism of the new war-related technologies themselves became one of the most effective points of antiwar protest. The early postwar period was marked by the emergence of the cold war, and women writers were among the foremost critics of the strident anticommunism and antipacifism that characterized national political life: writers Alice Hamil-

ton, Lillian *Hellman, and Pearl S. *Buck each contributed to the discourses of tolerance and peaceful coexistence that developed during the late 1940s and 1950s. Others, including authors Helen Keller and Helen Clarkson, criticised the use of atomic weapons against Japan and the continued testing of such weapons and their radioactive fallout.

While the civil rights and students' movements grew during the late 1950s, so did the United States' military deployments in support of the South Vietnamese government in Saigon. By 1965, main force military units had been committed to the conflict against the Vietnamese Communists, and a new antiwar movement emerged, drawing its strength from the civil rights, students', and later, women's rights movements. Women writers whose initial politicization had been within these other movements, including Barbara Deming and Emma Gelders Sterne, soon joined with those whose writings had as their primary political focus criticism of United States involvement in the Vietnam conflict. This latter group included essayist Mary *McCarthy, poet Denise *Levertov, and author Frances FitzGerald, whose nonfiction work, *Fire in the Lake*, underscored the fragility and corruption of the South Vietnamese regime being supported by the United States, and influenced moderate public opinion in favor of antiwar sentiment.

As United States force deployments to Vietnam declined in the early 1970s and were terminated in 1973, the focus of antiwar activism moved again toward a critical examination of both the continuing cold war, now increasingly defined by nuclear weapons and the strategy of "mutually assured destruction," and domestic social and political inequities that prevented women from influencing United States policies on peace and war. Physician Helen Caldicott and poet Sharon Olds contributed to the revitalization of the anti–cold war movement in the United States by discussing and describing the effects of nuclear conflict, while Pam McAllister explored the relationship between new conceptions of feminism, pacifism, and nonviolent political action. Distinctions between men's and women's roles in war became more blurred in the 1991 Gulf War, in which both men and women were deployed as part of the all-volunteer United States military and saw action in both combat and combat-support capacities. Although the brief conflict had substantial public approval, women writers, including contributors to such journals as *off our backs*, the *Nation*, and *Ms.*, directly opposed or questioned the motives and the utility of American participation in the war.

The study of the complexities of women's

connections with antiwar movements has been greatly assisted by the growth of women's studies as an accepted academic discipline in the United States. Scholars from a wide range of disciplines have focused on women's political activism, and a group of specialists emerged in the late 1980s and early 1990s to produce a new body of scholarly literature on women and war. Jean Bethke Elshtain, Harriet Hyman Alonso, Valerie Ziegler, and Sybil Oldfield have all taken leading roles in the scholarly reexamination of the questions of war and peace in America and in recovering the histories, ideas, and writings of the women who have explored those questions for themselves and for others.

[*See also* Protest Writing.]

• Angela Morgan, *The Hour Has Struck: A War Poem, and Other Poems, by Angela Morgan* (1914). May Eliza Wright Sewall, *Women, World War and Permanent Peace* (1915). Carrie Chapman Catt, *Why Wars Must Cease* (1935). Emma Gelders Sterne, with Mario Ginsberg and Essy Kay Rasmussen, *Blueprints for the World of Tomorrow: A Summary of Peace Plans Prepared for the International Federation of Business and Professional Women* (1943). Barbara Deming, *Two Essays: On Anger, New Men, New Women: Some Thoughts on Nonviolence* (1982). Milton Meltzer and Patricia G. Holland, eds., *The Collected Correspondence of Lydia Maria Child, 1817–1880* (1982). Helen Broinowski Caldicott, *Missile Envy: The Arms Race and Nuclear War* (1984; rev. ed., 1986). Harriet Hyman Alonso, *The Women's Peace Union and the Outlawry of War, 1921–1942* (1989). Sybil Oldfield, *Women Against the Iron Fist: Alternatives to Militarism 1900–1989* (1989). Valerie H. Ziegler, *The Advocates of Peace in Antebellum America* (1992).

Laura M. Calkins

ANZALDÚA, Gloria. Poet, essayist, editor, and feminist Chicana lesbian. Gloria Anzaldúa has emerged as one of the most influential spokespersons against oppression and for coalition of contemporary times. Anzaldúa is the author of numerous poems and polemical essays, anthologized, among other places, in the collection she coedited with Cherríe Moraga, *This Bridge Called My Back* (1981), in her solely authored *Borderlands/La Frontera: The New Mestiza* (1987), and in *Making Face, Making Soul—Haciendo Caras* (1990), an anthology for which she acted as both editor and contributor.

A self-identified "border woman," Anzaldúa sets out to raise consciousness by calling attention to the exhilarating but often precarious (and even life-threatening) balancing act required of those living on the geographical, cultural, and subjective borders/margins of white elite (hetero)sexist society.

Pride in her rich cultural heritage and hope for an even richer future permeate all aspects of Anzaldúa's work. Her lush poetic images help to graphically depict her own personal struggles, hardships, and joys, as well as those of other women/Chicanas. Many of her poems and essays weave the daily and often isolated or trivialized activities and experiences of those living at the margins into an intricate web of commonality, of tentative community.

Often, if not always, in her poetry and prose, Anzaldúa will intertwine both Spanish and English words and phrases, allowing fellow Chicanas easier access to the written word. This strategy also simultaneously forces anglos to experience the alienation of reading in a foreign tongue and of not always being the implied audience. More to the point (as she outlines in *Borderlands* and in such important essays as *Making Face, Making Soul's* "La Conciencia de la mestiza: Towards a New Consciousness"), these linguistic shifts highlight the perpetual and inevitable clash of voices, the constant cultural collision, the essential multiplicity evidenced by a multicultural society and embodied in "la mestiza."

A mestiza herself, Anzaldúa draws on her own experiences as a straddler of cultures—a straddling at once oppressive and potentially liberatory—to promote both activism and alliances between diverse peoples brought together by their commitment to change, to healing the splits that divide us, and to creating new worlds in which diversity is not merely acknowledged, but celebrated.

Cynthia J. Davis

ARAB-AMERICAN WRITING. Although by 1970, women from the Arab world had been in the United States for a century, it was not until the early part of the decade that two pathbreaking poets, Etel Adnan and D. H. Melhem, and one fiction writer, Consuelo Saah Baehr, began to publish in English. Adnan, an immigrant from Lebanon, had published earlier material written in French. Melhem, the New York–born daughter of Greco- and Syro-Lebanese immigrants, published *Notes on 94th Street* in 1972, the first poetry collection in English by an Arab-American woman. Baehr's first book, *Report from the Heart* (1976), is a novelistic account of twenty-four hours in the life of one family—hers.

It should be mentioned, however, that one early woman immigrant to the United States, Afifa Karam (1883–1924), did write and publish novels in Arabic. Karam's first novel, *Badiyah and Fuad* (1906), was a romance that was still popular with teenagers years later in Lebanon, the country from which she had immigrated. Her last work was the autobiographical *The Girl from Amshit* (1913). Though a resident of Louisiana, Karam's Arabic publisher was the al-Hoda press in New York City, which published some of the early writings of the Pen League of Ten (all male) authors gathered by renowned poet and parable writer Kahlil Gibran in New York in the 1920s. Karam also served as editor of the *New World, A Ladies' Monthly Magazine*, published by al-Hoda from 1910 through 1913.

Born in Beirut in 1925, Etel Adnan explains, "Looking west at the sunsets it was natural that I would have a life of explorations, journeys, and exiles" (*Grape Leaves*, 1988). But she sees a symmetry between her two worlds: "Americans are a nomadic people." Among her works in English is the intriguing book of poetic contemplations, *Journey to Mt. Tamalpais* (1986), where her love of color prompts her to further Descartes, "I exist because I see colors," and to skewer television as "white, pale as God," the very opposite of the mountain. The San Francisco Beat movement of the 1950s and 1960s influenced Adnan's most renowned work, "The Beirut-Hell Express" (self-translated from *L'express Beyrouth-Enfer*, 1973), a long poem that foreshadowed the sixteen-year Lebanese civil war. Adnan's work is filled with a sweeping sense of cataclysm, of history and time. She has lived and taught in San Francisco for several decades.

D. H. (Diana Helen) Melhem, who was born in Brooklyn in 1926, presents a tamer, more spatially centered, but no less socially conscious work than Adnan's. Two collections of her poetry deal with her "longtime Muse, the multiethnic West Side" (*Grape Leaves*, 1988) of New York City, *Notes on 94th Street* (1972) and *Children of the House Afire* (1976). The latter was turned into a musical drama in 1991. Her work is marked by compassion, whether for those starving in Ethiopia or for those who will lose homes to construction of gentrified, expensive high-rise apartments. Most accomplished is a book-length poem about her immigrant mother, *Rest in Love* (1975), which ends with an actual poem of her mother's, written on arrival at Ellis Island in 1922. A critic of American black poetry, Melhem turned a Ph.D. dissertation into *Gwendolyn Brooks: Poetry and the Heroic Voice* (1987), and won the American Book Award for her *Heroism and the New Black Poetry: Introductions and Interviews* (1990).

Born in El Salvador in 1934, the romantic novelist Consuelo Saah Baehr is a descendant of the Saahs, a distinguished Palestinian Christian family that immigrated to Washington, D.C., in the 1930s. A resident of Long Island, Baehr has published three novels, the latest and most ambitious of which is *Daughters* (1988). It has been translated into ten languages. Throughout the work, three generations of Palestinian women move in uneasy passage between Jerusalem/Nazareth and Washington, D.C.

In the 1980s, the work of two younger poet-essayists, Naomi Shihab Nye and Elmaz Abinader, and two younger novelists, Mona Simpson and Diana Abu-Jaber, began to be published. Nye, whose grandmother still lives on the West Bank, is the daughter of a Palestinian Muslim immigrant journalist from Jerusalem. She is one of the most distinctive poetic voices of her generation. Born in St. Louis in 1952, Nye published three books of poetry full of life, liberty, and the pursuit of responsibility: *Different Ways to Pray* (1980), *Hugging the Jukebox* (1982), and *Yellow Glove* (1986). A graceful solidity permeates her writing, a search for spiritual groundwater that gazes with sunlight in the darkest of niches. Nye has a magical command of the language, a suppleness that is the sign of a natural writer. In the oft-anthologized poem, "My Father and the Fig Tree" (1980), Nye catches her father picking a fig in Dallas, fixing the scene beautifully as a cipher of a lost world.

Although only fourteen or fifteen poems in Nye's published volumes have a recognizable Arab or Palestinian content—many more deal with the Hispanic Southwest, where she lives—Nye has written some pieces on the agonizing Palestinian/Israeli conflict, and on the courageous stoicism and sense of continuity of the Palestinians.

Born in 1954 to Lebanese immigrant parents in the coal-mining town of Carmichaels, Pennsylvania, and currently a professor of English at Mills College in Oakland, California, Elmaz Abinader is more avowedly feminist than Nye. Her poem "Women of Power Who Write Poetry" won the Academy of American Poets First Prize in 1984. But Abinader, like all Arab-American writers, is obsessed with family and parentage, and her obsession took penetrating form in her family memoir, *Children of the Roojme* (1991). The *roojme* is a stone terrace situated at the conjunction of the homes of the Abinader clan in the Lebanese mountain village of Abdelli, overlooking the Mediterranean. Abinader's tale of deprivation, betrayal, and longing is a classic, and part of a fine tradition of Arab-American immigrant memoirs, though Abinader uses time shifts and other fictional techniques to tell her family's story. In 1991, *Publisher's Weekly* said the work made "one family's saga emblematic of a nation torn apart." The most heartrending passages in *Roojme* do not concern the recent Lebanese civil war, however, but rather the ravages of World War I, when Lebanon lost one-quarter of its population to starvation.

Modesty; a fear of *ayb* (shame) at speaking too boldly, cast into most children of Arab parents; and a historic willingness to disappear as a "benevolent stranger" into the American hinterland (see Gregory Orfalea's *Before the Flames, A Quest for the History of Arab Americans,* 1988) staved off most Arab-American writers—men or women—from asserting a point of view until recently. It's no surprise, then, that Abinader's mother insisted that her real name not be used in the *Roojme* memoir.

Fathers, even in absence, loom large for these women writers; this is especially true of Mona Simpson. Born in the United States in 1957 to Syrian immigrants from Homs, Simpson began writing as a poet. Her novels are filled with Americana, powered by the identity search omnipresent in American fiction. In her first novel, *Anywhere But Here* (1986), about an American divorcée who carts her daughter around the country in search of stardom, the Egyptian father Hisham remarries, changes his name to John, and soon disappears. He is briefly shown as a rather hapless vacuum cleaner salesman and hotel waiter in the zany, poignant chapter "Las Vegas, Disneyland, Egypt." The last the daughter sees of him is at Disneyland. The father figure remains fantastical, though more a central concern from afar, in *The Lost Father* (1991), in which the narrator admits, "I'd always been suspicious of ethnics. Especially those who, like me, didn't look it . . . I liked to topple people's pride." *The Lost Father* has been read with great interest by the intelligentsia of the Arab world, and has achieved critical acclaim in America as well.

Diana Abu-Jaber, born in Syracuse, New York, in 1959, has also written a coming-of-age first novel, titled *Arabian Jazz* (1993). Neither Abu-Jaber nor her heroine Jem Ramoud are Saudi Arabian, but rather Arab, from Jordan. Abu-Jaber's fictional family is more fixed than Simpson's—in upstate New York, to be exact. They are shopkeepers among self-described (by a neighbor) "white trash." Hers is a book of hilarity and warmth, utilizing a double heritage to good effect, as when Jem's sister remarks in Arabic straight to the face of the first man to French-kiss Jem, "Well, he looks like the biggest horse's ass I've ever seen." Abu-Jaber is the niece of the foreign minister of Jordan, Kamel Abu-Jaber, who played a seminal role in the peace talks with Israel begun in Madrid in 1991. A scholar of third world literature who has published critical essays on writers such as Louise Erdrich and Jamaica Kincaid, Abu-Jaber has written and spoken sensitively about her own ethnic community.

In the 1990s, anthologies of Arab-American women's writing, as well as new scholarly attention by critics such as Evelyn Shakir and Mary Zoghby, will introduce the work of other writers such as Doris Safie, Adele NeJame, Kathryn Abdul-Baki, Lisa Suhair Majaj, and Therese Saliba. This literature of Arab-American women is new, exciting, compassionate, and as colorful as the crossroad of civilization from which it descends.

• Evelyn Shakir, "Starting Anew: Arab American Poetry," *Ethnic Forum* (1983): 9–13. Gregory Orfalea and Sharif Elmusa, eds., *Grape Leaves: A Century of Arab American Poetry* (1988). Bryce Milligan, "Writing to Save Our Lives: An Interview with Naomi Shihab Nye," *Paintbrush* (Spring 1991): 31–49. Mary Zoghby, "Memory, Image and Identity in Arab American Poetry," *Paintbrush* (Spring 1991): 21–30. Joanna Kadi, ed., *Food for Our Grandmothers: Writings by Arab-American and Arab-Canadian Feminists* (1994).

Gregory Orfalea

ARCHITECTS. Women have had tremendous difficulty gaining acceptance in the male-dominated realm of the American architecture profession. Though women in architecture have made tremendous strides in the past twenty years, their level of influence and numbers within the profession remain very small. Therefore, it should not be surprising that the number of women architects who have written about their profession is even smaller still. The major writing contributions by women in architecture have come not from the center of professional debates, but rather from two subfields considered by the mainstream to be of only peripheral importance: domestic architecture and architectural criticism.

Women's segregation into the "female" area of domestic architecture began in the Victorian era as the logical outgrowth of the rigid separation of home and work spheres and the ideology of female supremacy in the home, which characterized the period. The foremother of women's writing on the architecture of the home was Catherine *Beecher, who with her sister Harriet Beecher *Stowe published *The American Women's Home* in 1898. This seminal text argued that the home should be designed according to a model of domestic efficiency that placed the kitchen and other mechanical services in the center of the plan—an idea that would prove to have a tremendous impact on suburban house design in the twentieth century. During the first decades of the twentieth century, the domestic science movement gained momentum as a number of women writers began to apply Frederick Taylor's ideas about scientific management to the home. Women recognized that Taylor's methods for rationalizing factory floor plans and standardizing workers' paths of movement were directly applicable to the designs of kitchens. Christine Frederick, Helen Lukes Grant, and Una Nixson Hopkins were among those who contributed important articles in this period to the *Ladies' Home Journal*, the definitive publication on the subject.

In the 1930s and 1940s, as Franklin Roosevelt's New Deal brought the federal government into the business of constructing public housing, women architects and planners were able to expand their influence into the realm of housing policy. One of the most highly respected experts on low-income housing was the planner Catherine Bauer. Based on research she conducted in Europe, in 1934 Bauer published *Modern Housing*, an analysis of the socialized housing experiments of England and Germany and a recommendation that the United States work towards similar ends. Another major figure in this period was the architect Elizabeth Coit, who in the 1940s and 1950s carried out housing studies for the American Institute of Architects and federal housing agencies concentrating on the quality of housing design from the perspective of the tenant. Today, this tradition is carried on by designers like Clare Cooper Marcus, whose 1986 study, *Housing As If People Mattered*, is widely considered one of the most important recent texts on housing design.

The second major area in which women architects have been able to find a voice is architectural history and criticism. When Louise Tuthill published her *History of Architecture*, the first history of American architecture ever written, in 1848, it marked the beginning of a fifty-year period in which women critics aided the relatively new profession of architecture by writing popular articles that helped translate the architects' views to a lay audience. One of the most prolific of these critics was Mariana Van Rensselaer, whose 1888 book *Henry Hobson Richardson and His Works* was the first architectural monograph written in the United States; she also wrote extensively on architectural issues in the *Century* in the 1880s.

The twentieth century has also seen its share of great female critics. When the *New York Times* hired Ada Louise Huxtable in 1963, she became the first architecture critic appointed by a major American newspaper. Throughout her career Huxtable wielded tremendous influence, since her opinion pieces affected decisions in areas ranging from zoning ordinances to historic preservation. Similarly, Jane Jacobs's classic 1962 critique of modern architecture and planning, *The Death and Life of Great American Cities*, has had a tremendous impact on the theory and practice of urban design. In the 1970s and 1980s, women began making faster progress toward gaining acceptance within the profession, yet there still remain few publications by prominent contemporary practitioners. One notable exception is Denise Scott Brown, who with her husband Robert Venturi coauthored the seminal postmodern architectural treatise *Learning from Las Vegas* in 1976. In addition, there are a number of notable female architectural professionals who have written on the problems of women in architecture, four of whom are listed in the following bibliography.

• Susana Torre, ed., *Women in American Architecture: A Historic and Contemporary Perspective* (1977). Gwendolyn Wright, "On the Fringe of the Profession: Women in American Architecture," in *The Architect: Chapters in the History of the Profession*, ed. Spiro Kostof (1977), pp. 280–308. Dolores Hayden, *Redesigning the American Dream* (1984). Ellen Perry Berkeley, ed., *Architecture: A Place for Women* (1989).

Kate Bristol

ARCHIVES. *See* Libraries.

ARNOLD, June (1926–1982), novelist and publisher. Born June Davis in South Carolina, June Arnold is known as a southern regional writer, as well as a writer of feminist—and specifically lesbian—fiction. Arnold attended Vassar and Rice colleges, later establishing herself as one of the first experimental feminist writers of the second wave of the feminist movement to manipulate gender and language in her work. Her novels include *Applesauce* (1966; reprint, 1977); *The Cook and the Carpenter* (1973); *Sister Gin* (1975; reprint, 1989); and *Baby Houston* (1987), which was published posthumously. Currently, both *Applesauce* and *The Cook and the Carpenter* are out of print. While *Applesauce* provides its feminist critique thematically by focusing on androgyny, *The Cook and the Carpenter* deconstructs gendered language in its use of the neutral pronoun "na" as a substitute for he and she. The blurring of gender is further reinforced by Arnold's frequent use of androgynous names in her work. Arnold develops her critique of sexual politics further in her later novel, *Sister Gin*, which takes on racism and white lesbian privilege. The book is perhaps best known for its bold portrait of an aging woman going through menopause, a portrait considered by some critics to be unsurpassed. Mother-daughter relationships are the central theme of Arnold's last book, *Baby Houston*, which draws heavily on her own life and times growing up in Houston, Texas.

Arnold's literary contributions are not limited to her feminist writing. Together with her partner, Parke Bowman, she founded Daughters, Inc., one of the earliest and most successful feminist presses; its most famous publication was Rita Mae *Brown's *Rubyfruit Jungle*. Now defunct, Daughters was committed to "discovering and working with new women writers

to develop . . . 'the radical feminist novel'"
(Lois Gould, "Creating a Women's World," *New
York Times Magazine,* 2 January 1977). In the
words of June Arnold in the same article, such
a commitment was necessary to "maintain control over our future . . . [to] spend the energy of
our imaginations and criticisms building feminist institutions that women will gain from,
both in money and skills." Working out of Vermont and later New York City, Arnold and
Bowman were important figures in the early
days of the feminist press.

June Arnold's literary career was tragically
cut short in 1982 when she died from cancer in
Houston. Besides Bowman, she also left four
children from an early marriage.

• June Arnold, "Feminist Presses and Feminist Politics," *Quest: a feminist quarterly* 3, no. 1 (Summer
1976): 18–26. June Arnold, "Lesbians and Literature
[MLA Panel]," *Sinister Wisdom* 1, no. 2 (Fall 1976): 28–
30. June Arnold and Bertha Harris, "Lesbian Fiction:
A Dialogue," *Sinister Wisdom* 1, no. 2 (Fall 1976): 42–
51. Ellen Morgan, "The Feminist Novel of Androgynous Fantasy," *Frontiers* 2, no. 3 (Fall 1977): 40–49.
Bonnie Zimmerman, "Exiting from Patriarchy," in
The Voyage In: Fictions of Female Development (1983),
pp. 244–257. Jan Hokenson, "The Pronouns of Gomor-
rha: A Lesbian Prose Tradition," *Frontiers* 10, no. 1
(1988): 62–69. Jane Marcus, Afterword, "Under Review: How to Read a Hot Flash," in *Sister Gin* by June
Arnold (1989), pp. 217–236. Bonnie Zimmerman, *The
Safe Sea of Women: Contemporary Lesbian Feminist
Fiction* (1989).

Joan Gabriele

ARNOW, Harriette Simpson (1908–1986), novelist and social historian. Arnow is chiefly
known for her novels portraying the poor
whites of Appalachia and is considered a writer
of the Southern Renaissance. Born Harriette
Louisa Simpson in Wayne County, Kentucky,
Arnow found in this region of her youth the
subject matter for much of her literary work.
Groomed by her parents to be an educator, Arnow nevertheless felt a calling to write. Upon
completing two years' instruction at Berea College, she began teaching in an impoverished
area near her childhood home, a locale she
would later re-create in her first novel, *Mountain Path* (1936). After two years of teaching,
Arnow decided to finish her bachelor's degree
at the University of Louisville. She taught again
after graduation in 1930, but soon moved to
the Midwest to pursue her dream of writing. In
Cincinnati, she finished *Mountain Path* and met
Harold Arnow, a journalist, whom she married
in 1939 in Kentucky. The Arnows lived there
briefly but soon moved to Michigan, settling
first in Detroit and then in Ann Arbor, where
Arnow wrote *Hunter's Horn* (1949), also set in

Kentucky. Her next and most successful novel
was *The Dollmaker* (1954), the story of a Kentucky wife transplanted with her family to Detroit, where her husband is employed. A best-
seller, *The Dollmaker* was beaten out for the
1955 National Book Award by William Faulkner's *A Fable.* Arnow's social histories, *Seedtime
on the Cumberland* (1962) and *Flowering of the
Cumberland* (1963), describe the beginnings of
the Appalachian region of her youth through its
pioneer days. Her next novel, *The Weedkiller's
Daughter* (1970), is again set in Detroit, but this
time centers around a city girl. Arnow completed one more novel, *The Kentucky Trace*
(1974), and another Kentucky history, *Old
Burnside* (1977), before her death in 1986. Arnow's ability to tell a fine story is enough to
make her works highly readable. More significant, though, is her fiction's ability to present
the truth about a region and its people. From
her first novel on, her literary goal is not the
romantic sentimentalism of the regionalists
and local colorists, but the realistic depiction of
human beings as individuals, rather than stereotypes. Her work in no way takes part in the
"hillbilly" characterization of the people of her
homeland; what Arnow's work accomplishes is
the honest portrayal of a people in the midst of
debilitating socioeconomic circumstances.

• William Eckley, *Harriette Arnow* (1974).

Mary Wheeling White

ART. *See* Visual Art and Writing.

ART HISTORIANS. The contributions of
American women art historians to modern culture are related to the maturation of art history
as an academic discipline and to changing professional and institutional practices.

The role of women in art history was affected dramatically by an intellectual crisis in
the late 1960s that transformed the discipline.
Artists, art or architectural historians, and critics challenged the decades-old modernist conception of art history as the study of style in the
context of the linear development of European
and American avant-gardism. They also lamented the cultural and political exclusivity of
art exhibitions that focused solely on modernist
art. Many women art or architectural historians and critics viewed this decline in the hegemony of * modernism as an opportunity to recognize the breadth of accomplishment of many
women and minorities who were previously un-
acclaimed. Specifically, they began recovering
a forgotten heritage of women in the visual arts.

While the first publications by women art
historians appeared in Europe after 1820, the

earliest work by American women appeared in mid-century. Elizabeth *Ellet published *Women Artists in All Ages and Countries* in 1859 as a continuation of her interest in the contribution of women to history. In 1886, Clara Erskine Clement Waters enlivened the nineteenth-century fascination for iconography with her *Handbook of Christian Symbols and Stories of the Saints as Illustrated in Art.* Two years later, the prolific Mariana Griswold Van Rensselaer, known as the first American woman art critic, completed *Henry Hobson Richardson and His Works.* This pioneering monograph still enhances our understanding of a well-known architect. As upper-class women, Ellet, Waters, and Van Rensselaer all worked alone and achieved success by assuming the roles of educators and preservers of cultural tradition. Each left the issue of the position of women in that tradition essentially unchallenged.

From 1890 to 1940, art history matured as a discipline. Women emerged who were university educated, and, later, employed in women's colleges or art museums. Georgiana Goddard King founded the art history department at Bryn Mawr College in 1913. In *The Way of Saint James* (1917), she interwove literary sources with her historical tracing of medieval pilgrimage routes leading to Santiago de Compostela. Helen Gardner taught art history at the Art Institute of Chicago and, in 1926, wrote *Art Through the Ages* for her classes. This unpretentious historical survey of primarily Western art is still assigned, in subsequent editions, to thousands of undergraduates. Beginning in the mid-1930s, Dorothy C. Miller served as a curator at the newly established Museum of Modern Art in New York City and authored many exhibition catalogs, including *Fourteen Americans* (1946). In this time period, King and Gardner wrote respectively on topics of specialty and general interest while Miller documented the achievements of living avant-garde artists, including a few women.

After 1945, the literature reveals the significant contribution of women scholars who emigrated from Europe. One was Rachel Bernstein Wischnitzer, who in 1948 published *The Messianic Theme in the Paintings of the Dura Synagogue* as a study of the ideological foundation for synagogue decoration. In 1957, Elizabeth Gilmore Holt became known for the second edition of *A Documentary History of Art*, which contains indispensable documents previously unavailable in English. During the next decade, Barbara Novak offered a fresh perspective on the interrelationship of art and literature in *American Painting of the Nineteenth Century* (1969). In 1967, Barbara Rose wrote *American*

Art since 1900, a lucid exploration of the lineage of modernism. By the mid-1970s, the number of publications by women art or architectural historians and critics had increased considerably. In their monumental 1976 catalog and exhibition, *Women Artists: 1550–1950*, Ann Sutherland Harris and Linda Nochlin offered an important foundation for the rediscovery of European and American women artists. Susana Torre helped discover women architects when, in 1977, she edited *Women in American Architecture: A Historic and Contemporary Perspective.* C. Kurt Dewhurst, Betty MacDowell, and Marsha MacDowell presented American folk artists in *Artists in Aprons* (1979). These pioneering works were complemented by new feminist art criticism, such as Lucy Lippard's collection of essays *From the Center* (1976).

In the 1980s, research by independent or institutionally affiliated scholars flourished. Charlotte Streifer Rubinstein offered a multicultural survey, *American Women Artists*, in 1982. Gwendolyn Wright expanded readers' grasp of architecture in relation to the social role of women in *Moralism and the Model Home* (1980). In 1985, Shifra Goldman and Tom Ybarra-Frausto presented a comprehensive analysis of a particular ethnic group in *Arte Chicano.* This was also the decade for art historians to reassess the women's art movement and the beginnings of feminist art criticism. Thalia Gouma-Peterson and Patricia Mathews completed "The Feminist Critique of Art History" for the September 1987 issue of the *Art Bulletin.*

Today, contemporary women art or architectural historians and critics continue to grapple with the historiographical approaches and theories that inform the study of art from any time period or culture. Over twenty years ago, in *Art and Sexual Politics*, a 1971 book edited by Thomas Hess and Elizabeth Baker, Linda Nochlin asked, "Why Have There Been No Great Women Artists?" Since that time, writers such as Whitney Chadwick in *Women, Art, and Society* (1990) have explored the interplay between *feminism as a political ideology that addresses relations to power and art history as a discipline that produces knowledge. Here are the essential questions: What is the paradigm that shapes art history? And, what is the role of ideological, social, and economic power in relation to visual representation? Griselda Pollock, a British art historian, asked these questions in her book, *Vision and Difference* (1988). The response of Americans to these issues is most apparent in books such as *Impressionism: A Feminist Reading* (1991), an art-historical *gender study by Norma Broude, and in anthologies that feature diverse perspectives on multicultural women artists, such as *Yesterday and Tomorrow: California Women Artists* (1989), edited by Sylvia Moore.

• Gwendolyn Wright, "On the Fringe of the Profession: Women in American Architecture," in *The Architect*, ed. Spiro Kostof (1977), pp. 280–308. Claire Richter Sherman, *Women as Interpreters of the Visual Arts, 1820–1979* (1981). Eleanor Tufts, *American Women Artists, Past and Present*, vol. 1 (1984), vol. 2 (1989). Arlene Raven, *Crossing over: Feminism and Art of Social Concern* (1988). Arlene Raven, Cassandra L. Langer, and Joanna Frueh, eds., *Feminist Art Criticism* (1988). Ellen Perry Berkeley, ed., *Architecture: A Place for Women* (1989). Mara R. Witzling, ed., *Voicing Our Vision: Writings by Women Artists* (1991). Judy Seigel, ed., *Mutiny and the Mainstream: Talk That Changed Art, 1975–1990* (1992).

Linda O. Stanford

ASHBRIDGE, Elizabeth (1713–1755), Quaker preacher. Born in England and raised in the Anglican church, Elizabeth Ashbridge used to wish as a young child that she was a boy so that she could become a minister. Although barred from the ministry by most denominations, Ashbridge's ambitions were eventually fulfilled in her adulthood when she converted to Quakerism, in which women were granted the authority to preach. Her *spiritual autobiography, *Some Account of the Fore Part of the Life of Elizabeth Ashbridge*, published posthumously in 1774, documents Ashbridge's spiritual journey toward Quakerism and her struggle to claim her religious authority in a society where cultural prejudices against women and Quakers were strong.

Ashbridge's personal narrative, the primary source for biographical information, is lively and picaresque, and in it she paints herself as an independent and adventurous young woman. Born Elizabeth Sampson, she eloped at age fourteen. Widowed shortly thereafter, she traveled to America by herself in 1732 and worked as an indentured servant for three years. She then entered into what she called another "cruel servitude"—marriage to a man she names only as Sullivan. Ashbridge's conversion to Quakerism several years after her marriage greatly displeased her violent and abusive husband, who tried to prevent her from attending Quaker meetings and, most importantly, from preaching, as Ashbridge was increasingly wont to do. Ashbridge persisted, however, formally entering the ministry in 1738. Two years later, Sullivan deserted her to join the military; however, he writes her from his deathbed that he has finally accepted Quakerism. Here Ashbridge concludes her autobiography, vindicating her wifely disobedience with her husband's conversion. Ashbridge continued preaching, however, rising to some prominence as a speaker. In 1746 she married Aaron Ashbridge, and in 1753 she embarked on a preaching tour of Great Britain, where she died in 1755.

Influential and widely read among Quakers in colonial America, Ashbridge's narrative remains an important example of Quaker spiritual autobiography, and also of women's autobiography. Among the earliest of American women's autobiographies, it reveals how Ashbridge's Quakerism enabled her to construct a public self and assert an autobiographical voice, despite cultural oppositions to women's speech and public identity. Moreover, in describing the harshness of her indenture, the prejudice she endures for her Quakerism, and her poverty, Ashbridge's autobiography offers a perspective of colonial life seldom seen in the literature of early America.

• Daniel Shea, *Spiritual Autobiography in Early America* (1968). Howard H. Brinton, *Quaker Journals* (1972). Daniel Shea, "Elizabeth Ashbridge and the Voice Within," in *Journeys in New Worlds: Early American Women's Narratives*, ed. William L. Andrews et al. (1990), pp. 119–146.

Suzanne M. Zweizig

ASIAN-AMERICAN WRITING. *This entry consists of five essays. The first provides an overview of the history of Asian-American writing and the others discuss Asian-American writing by genre.*

Overview
Drama
Fiction
Nonfiction
Poetry

For further information, please refer to Chinese-American Writing; Citizenship; Ethnicity and Writing; Filipino-American Writing; Immigrant Writing; Japanese-American Writing; Korean-American Writing; Polynesian-American Writing; South Asian-American Writing; Southeast Asian-American Writing.

Overview

Asian-American writing by women may not be best generalized through the criteria of traditional literary study. That is, due to the heterogeneity and diversity of work comprised by the category "Asian-American women's writing," to describe it exclusively by means of period, style, or genre may be less effective than to give attention to the social classifications of generation, class, region, religion, sexuality, ethnicity, or national origin. Since the majority of the first generation of Asian women who immigrated to the United States in the late nineteenth century had difficult lives of labor that prevented them from writing their life narratives—like Lalu Nathoy (1865–1933), whose life is narrated in the fictionalized reconstruction by Ruthann Lum McCunn, *Thousand Pieces of Gold* (1981)—what is recognized as Asian-American women's writing begins with turn-of-the-century work by Eurasian immigrants such as *Sui Sin Far and Onoto *Watanna (Edith and Winnifred *Eaton), includes early twentieth-century narratives by Etsu Sugimoto or Jade Snow *Wong, but is largely comprised of writing by contemporary women, some of whom are first-generation immigrants like Indian-American fiction writer Meena *Alexander, Philippine exile novelist Ninotchka *Rosca, or Vietnamese-American short fiction writer Monique Thuy-Dung Truong. Other contemporary Asian-American writers are several generations removed from their original Asian cultures, such as *sansei* (third-generation Japanese-American) poet Janice *Mirikitani, second-generation Chinese-American novelist Maxine Hong *Kingston, or second-generation Korean-American writer *Kim Ronyoung. Another equally important area of Asian-American writing by women is constituted by the critical writing of contemporary scholars: King-kok Cheung, Elaine Kim, Shirley Geok-lin Lim, Amy Ling, Trinh T. *Minh-ha, Sau-ling C. Wong, Shelly S. Wong, and others. Asian-American women writers are descendant from cultures as diverse as Chinese, Japanese, Korean, Philippine, Indian, Pakistani, Lao, and Vietnamese; some came to the United States as refugees or exiles, some immigrated to join already settled family, a number came for education or employment, others fled colonialism or neocolonial persecutions. In the case of Hawaiians and Pacific Islanders, these writers may not be immigrants at all, but colonized and deracinated people in their own homelands. Asian-American women are of exclusively Asian parents and of mixed race; hail from different class backgrounds; are Christian, Buddhist, Hindu, and Muslim; are married, widowed, unmarried, heterosexual, and lesbian. In other words, while there are strong reasons to discuss Asian-American women's writing as a distinct body of work—for these women share a common history of discrimination against Asians as a minority group, as well as a common relationship to United States policies of immigration, labor laws, and institutional policies regarding women of Asian descent—any generalizations about the group must also stress the very specific social differences among Asian-origin women. The range and spectrum of contemporary Asian-American women's writing is illustrated in four recent literary anthologies: *The Forbidden Stitch: An Asian American Women's Anthology*, edited by Shirley

Geok-lin Lim, Mayumi Tsutakawa, Margarita Donnelly (1989); *Making Waves: An Anthology of Writings by and about Asian American Women*, edited by the Asian Women United of California (1989); *Home to Stay: Asian American Women's Fiction*, edited by Sylvia Watanabe and Carol Bruchac (1990); and *Sister Stew: Fiction and Poetry by Women*, edited by Juliet Kono and Cathy Song (1991). Sucheng Chan's *Asian Americans: An Interpretive History* (1991) and Sucheta Mazumdar's introduction to *Making Waves* are two approaches to the comparative history of Asian women in the United States.

The remainder of this entry will first consider the question of the relationship of Asian-American women's writing to the canon of American literature, and then, in turn, will discuss Asian-American women's writing in relation to the emergent canon of Asian-American literature. Rather than seeking to be a comprehensive survey of all writing by Asian-American women, this discussion will make some observations about important critical dimensions of the writing, suggesting the diversity of the writing by briefly focusing on a few examples that illustrate critical issues.

The formalization of the classification "Asian American" was a product of the 1970s and the social movements that sought to extend the rights of Asian-Americans and other people of color. These movements necessarily challenged the concept of an American society comprised solely of peoples of Anglo-European descent, not only by revealing the history of exclusions and discriminations against populations of color, but also by securing spaces for the study of Asian-American, Afro-American, Native-American, and Chicano/Latino cultures. From the perspectives of these social movements, the study of Asian-American literature within the university, along with the development of interdisciplinary programs of ethnic studies, was one part of a project of institutional transformation. For this reason, the establishment of Asian-American literature historically has had a critical relationship to the traditionally exclusive canon of American literature; institutionally, its marginal location, or "minor" status, has paradoxically provided a space from which to critically reevaluate the "major" tradition. This critical institutional location has an analogous expression in the formal aspects of the literature: Asian-American texts exemplify a different relation to traditional notions of aesthetic unity and autonomy, and therefore may be said to function differently in the production of culture. If the function of canonization with respect to American literature is to represent a formally autonomous and aesthetically unified tradition through the selection of genres and authors whose works elicit the identification of the reading subject with that unified tradition, we can observe that Asian-American literature has never expressed this traditional canonical imperative. On the one hand, the inclusion and exclusion of works has not functioned primarily to unify Asian-American culture through defining a uniform narrative of the Asian-American subject's development. On the other hand, most scholars have not conceptualized Asian-American literature as a supplement or contribution to the majority canon as a representation of "American culture": works have not been selected in order to establish Asian-American approximations of major canonical genres, such as the tragedy, the lyric poem, or the * bildungsroman. Furthermore, Asian-American literature has not been conceived as an aesthetic domain that reconciles the contradictions of Asian-American experiences through eliciting the identification of the reading subject; Asian-American writing does not offer the possibility of separating culture from the material relations of its production.

Rather than either resolving texts into a unified definition of ethnic minority culture or assimilating Asian-American writing into the majority culture, the study of Asian-American literature historically has been an endeavor committed to a consideration of the work in terms of its material contexts of production and reception. In this regard, Elaine Kim's immeasurably important first critical study, *Asian American Literature: An Introduction to the Writings and Their Social Context* (1982), emphasizes "how the literature elucidates the social history of Asians in the United States," rather than choosing an exclusive focus on "the formal literary merit" of those works. Kim makes clear that her decision to interrogate Asian-American literature as an expression of social context is not due to the literature's lack of stylistic or rhetorical complexity, but is owing rather to the way in which the literature itself captures a "movement between social history and literature." Monica Sone's *Nisei Daughter* (1953), for example, portrays the treatment, during World War II, of the Japanese Americans who were named Japanese enemies by the government if they did not assimilate to American culture and repudiate any Japanese cultural affiliation. Featuring a narrator who concludes that "the Japanese and American parts of me were now blended into one," yet juxtaposing this wishful conclusion with depictions of anti-Japanese racism, employment segregations, immigration restrictions, and ultimately internment, the novel's literary resolution mirrors the social demand for individual resolution, but in doing so sets that demand against the material contradictions that make such individual resolution and integration into American society impossible. To the degree that the narrative captures the complex, unsynthetic constitution of the Asian-American female subject exposed to contradictory pressures and demands, the novel itself betrays the premature resolution in the final declaration of "blending," and formally defies the closure and reconciliation demanded by the bildungsroman form. Sone's novel, one example of Asian-American women's fiction, demonstrates Kim's "movement between" the literary demand and historical contradiction, a dialectical movement that resists the formal abstraction of aestheticization and canonization. If we evaluate Asian-American literary expression in canonical terms, it reveals itself as an aesthetic product that cannot repress the material inequalities of its conditions of production; its aesthetic is not defined by sublimation, but rather by contradiction, whereby discontent, nonequivalence, and irresolution call into question the project of abstracting the aesthetic as a separate domain of unification and reconciliation. It is a literature which, if subjected to a canonical function, dialectically returns a critique of that function. Thus, the study of Asian-American literature institutionally occupies an oppositional site in relation to the tradition of American literature, while its texts formally exemplify critically different relationships to notions of genre, aesthetics, and canon upheld by that tradition.

In light of the history of Asian-American literature as an oppositional "canon" in relation to American literature, Asian-American women's writing has also historically served a critical function within the emergent field of Asian-American literature. In the context of the need to establish a concerted critical Asian-American voice, early definitions of the literature tended to stress less the heterogeneity of Asian-American experience and to be more concerned with establishing the singular character of Asian-American literary expression. Among its projects was the replacement of fraudulent, racist, emasculating stereotypes of Asians with more realistic, self-determined, empowered representations. To this end, early definitions of Asian-American literature emphasized male-authored texts, and favored realist or naturalist notions of representation and privileged narratives of development. One of the first volumes of Asian-American literature, *AIIIEEEEE!: An Anthology of Asian-American Writers*, edited by Frank Chin, Jeffrey Paul Chan, Lawson Fusao Inada, and Shawn Wong (1974), precisely formalized these emphases. Since this groundbreaking volume brought together a collection of writings of which many had been previously unavailable or unheralded, it virtually constituted the "canon." The work of Carlos Bulosan, Frank Chin, Louis Chu, John Okada, Toshio Mori, Shawn Wong, and woman writer Hisaye *Yamamoto, along with others collected in *AII-IEEEEE!*, formed the basis of an oppositional Asian-American literature that effectively challenged the exclusivity and dominance of the American canon.

During the 1980s, the predominantly male profile of this early construction of Asian-American writing was challenged, particularly by women writers and critics, who made arguments for diversifying definitions and broadening access to publication in order to account for the heterogeneity of Asian Americans. This challenge did not exclusively voice the argument that many women authors had been overlooked and women's experiences excluded; rather, the critique also stressed the need to appreciate the heterogeneous composition of Asian Americans in terms of national origin, class, and sexuality, as well as gender. In this sense, the social context that gave rise in the 1980s to the critique of the male-dominated early definitions of Asian-American literature, and to the more vigorous attention given to Asian-American women's writing, was produced by the convergence of a variety of determinants: not only did the United States women's movement and the feminist theories of white women, women of color, and Third World women influence this project in very important ways, but the post-1975 immigration from South and Southeast Asia that greatly shifted and diversified the class composition and national origin of the Asian-American constituency informed the critique as well.

Asian-American women's writing has also displaced some of the formal conventions privileged by the earlier definition of Asian-American literature. While some Asian-American women's writing makes use of realist or naturalist representation, linear or developmental narrative, a male protagonist, and single point of view, it is frequently the case that the writings by women revise or depart from these conventions. Nonlinear narrative, multiple perspective, antimimetic representation, and uneasily classified genres characterize many of the writings. These formally heterogeneous women's writings have radically altered the definitions of the Asian-American field; they give rise to different questions about the relationships between gender and genre, language and subjectivity, and personal and popular memory. For example, Joy Kogawa's *Obasan* (1982) situates its narrator in 1972, three decades after the internment and relocation of the Japanese Canadians, but the text weaves back and forth between different time periods, making use of private memory, dreams, diaries, letters, and documented histories in order to dramatize the *nisei* narrator's project of reconstructing the events that led to the loss of her mother, father, and grandparents, and the dispersal of other family and community during the relocation and internment years. Rather than a unitary, linear development, *Obasan* narrates the life of the female subject through a modernist recomposition of fragments, shifting from first-person to third-person narration, from personal flashback to official documents. Theresa Hak Kyung *Cha's *Dictée* (1982) is a Korean-American woman's text that even more radically challenges Asian-American conventions of representation, genre, style, and development; *Dictée* provides neither a linear narrative of development, nor an ethical resolution at the text's conclusion. In combining autobiographical and biographical fragments, photographs, historical narrative, calligraphy, and lyric and prose poems in a complex, multilingual piece, Cha's *Dictée* blurs genre and narrative authority, troubling the formal categories upon which canonization depends. Furthermore, *Dictée* challenges the notion of a discrete typology of "Asian-American experience," for it evokes a Korean-American subject who is not only the product of multiple determinations—gender, language, religion—but she bears the traces of differentiated layers of Japanese colonial and American imperial dominations as well. Jessica *Hagedorn's *Dogeaters* (1990) exemplifies a further multiplication and diversification of perspectives and styles. *Dogeaters* is a multiperspectival novel that juxtaposes a kaleidoscopic collection of extremely different voices. The testimonies of a schoolgirl, a mixed-race hustler, and the President's wife are interrupted by excerpts from daytime television melodramas, historical accounts, and newspaper articles; military generals, movie stars, wealthy Philippine society wives, and revolutionaries are the central characters of interspersed third-person narratives. *Dogeaters* does not resolve or reconcile these heterogeneous textures of Philippine society, but out of their numerous contradictions builds both rapidly and jaggedly to a climax.

In summary, both the institutionally and formally critical positions of Asian-American women's writings have been of crucial importance to the diversified construction of Asian-American identity, both on the level of the individual subject and in terms of group formation. While the emergence of Asian-American literature in the 1970s served as a critical revision of the American literary canon, Asian-American women's writings have more recently shifted the institutional, political, and literary definitions of that Asian-American field.

Lisa Lowe

Drama

As the youngest genre of Asian-American literature, Asian-American drama, particularly by women writers, has become visible only in the last two decades. This is not to imply that it is a literature without a historic tradition. To the contrary, through production and publication, a theater has become visible that is a natural extension and formalization in American terms of theatrical traditions that have crossed the Pacific engraved in the cultures of Asian immigrants. However, the use of Western forms of theater by Asian Americans to reflect their experience in the United States has been slowed by the lack of access those writers have had to the means of production. While negative and stereotypical images of Asians have abounded on the American stage and in its media, the opportunity for Asian-American writers to have their work produced did not viably exist until the post–civil rights era founding of ethnically specific theaters such as the East West Players of Los Angeles, Pan Asian Repertory Theater in New York City, the Asian American Theater Company in San Francisco, and the Northwest Asian American Theater Company in Seattle. These largely actor-driven theaters, which sought to provide alternatives to artistically unchallenging and humanly demeaning roles, have been joined in the last decade by regional and commercial theaters seeking to be inclusive of multiculturalism. The result is the present American theater environment—one that provides the possibility that the Asian-American woman dramatist will flourish.

The list of contemporary Asian-American women playwrights is headed by pioneering writers Momoko * Iko and Wakako * Yamauchi, followed by a second generation of playwrights including Velina Hasu * Houston, Genny Lim, and Jessica * Hagedorn. Other writers who have amplified the body of theatrical literature by Asian-American women include Rosanna Yamagiwa Alfaro, Jeannie Barroga, Bernadette Cha, Kitty Chen, Maria Feleo Gonzales, Linda Faigao Hall, Lionelle Hamanaka, Karen Huie, Akemi Kikumura, Cherylene Lee, Nikki Nojima Louis, Elizabeth Wong, Karen Yamashita, and Gerri Igarashi Yoshida. Also significant are works by actresses turned writers/performance artists, such as Brenda Wong Aoki, Amy Hill, Jude Narita, Marilyn Tokuda, and Patty Toy. The aforementioned playwrights are of Chinese,

Japanese, Filipino, and Korean heritage, with a greater representation of Japanese- and Chinese-American writers. As in the larger literature by Asian-Americans, this representation corresponds with the length of time each group has been in the United States, Chinese and Japanese having the longest histories in this country. Dramatic writing by Korean, Filipino, South Asian, and Southeast Asian-Americans is in a nascent stage and newer theaters, such as the Filipino American Teatro Ng Tanan (Theater for the People) in San Francisco and the Korean American Silk Road Playhouse in New York City, are giving birth to a new generation of playwrights.

Significant works by Asian-American women playwrights include Momoko Iko's *Gold Watch* (1970), which was the first play by an Asian-American woman to be given a professional production in the United States. Produced by the Inner City Cultural Center in Los Angeles in 1972, the play dramatizes the plight of a Japanese-American family and community in turmoil before their internment during World War II. Wakako Yamauchi's *And the Soul Shall Dance* (1974) is another early work of importance. This drama poetically examines the lives of Japanese living in pre–World War II rural California, and focuses on the inability of a Japanese woman to adjust to an arranged marriage. Genny Lim's *Paper Angels* (1978) departs from traditional naturalism, utilizing impressionistic techniques to tell the story of Chinese immigrants on Angel Island who are awaiting admittance to the United States. Jessica Hagedorn's *Mango Tango* (1978) fuses music, poetry, movement, and theater in an autobiographical epic. *Mango Tango* and Wakako Yamauchi's *The Music Lesson* (1980), a drama about a widowed Japanese woman running a farm during the Great Depression, were the first plays by Asian-American women to be produced by the New York Public Theater's Shakespeare Festival. Velina Hasu Houston's *Tea*, a drama surrounding a suicide in a community of Japanese war brides, has had numerous productions, effectively breaking the barriers to productions of Asian-American women's work by white regional and commercial theaters. Among the many theaters that have produced *Tea* are the Manhattan Theater Club, the Old Globe Theater in San Diego, and New Jersey's Whole Theater. Full-length plays by Asian-American women that have been published include *Bitter Cane* and *Paper Angels* by Genny Lim; *And the Soul Shall Dance, The Music Lesson, The Chairman's Wife,* and *12-1-A* by Wakako Yamauchi; *Gold Watch* by Momoko Iko; *Tea* and *Asa Ga Kimashita* by Velina Hasu

Houston; *Walls* by Jeannie Barroga; *Tenement Lover: No Palm Trees/In New York City* and *Teenytown* by Jessica Hagedorn (with Laurie Carlos and Robbie McCauley); and *Letters to a Student Revolutionary* by Elizabeth Wong.

It is important to mention that the contemporary body of literature by Asian-American women is predated by earlier developments. In 1903, *A Japanese Nightingale*, a novel by Chinese-American author Winnifred * Eaton, was adapted for a Broadway production and competed with David Belasco's "Madame Butterfly," which ran for five years. In the mid-1910s, Eaton collaborated with French dramatist Claude Anthelme on the play *L'honneur Japonnais*, which was performed at the Odean Theater in Paris. From 1924 to 1936, Eaton wrote scripts for Hollywood films. Another early example of an Asian-American woman's writing for the stage is Gladys Li's *The Submission of Rose Moy* (1928), which dramatizes a Chinese-American girl's rejection of an arranged marriage. During this same time, a pioneering group of Asian-American playwrights was encouraged by the University of Hawaii's Department of English to focus on the Asian experience in Hawaii , and to express that experience in uniquely Asian-American dialogue. Among the Asian-American women playwrights who wrote during these early decades, finding publication in *College Plays*, the *Hawaii Quill Magazine*, and *Theater Group Plays*, are Gladys Li (*The Law of Wu Wei*, 1929; *The Submission of Rosie Moy*, 1928; *The White Serpent*, 1932); Wai Chee Chun (*For You a Lei*, 1937; *Marginal Woman*, 1937); and Bessie Toishigawa (*Nisei* and *Return of Sam Patch*, 1966–1967 and *Second Choice*, 1959). Primarily one-act plays, most of these works were never produced, or if given productions, were limited to amateur performance on the college stage. It is only from the 1970s on that a sustained body of literature by Asian-American women dramatists has emerged, one that has been supported by production and publication.

• G. M. Lee, "One in Sisterhood: Asian Women," *Asian Women's Journal* (1971): 119–121. Jessica Hagedorn, "Chiquita Banana," in *Third World Women* (1972). Lori Higa, *Calamity Jane Meets Suchi Mama and the B.V.D. Kid: or, . . . Lady Murasaki Rides the Wild, Wild West* (1976). Santha Rama Rau, *A Passage to India* (1961; reprint, 1976). Meena Alexander, *In the Middle Earth* (1977), pp. 125–126. Clara Kubojiri, "Country Pie," in *Talk Story: Big Island Anthology*, Stephen H. Sumida and Martha Webb, eds. (1979). Elaine Becker, "The Best of Both Worlds (act one only)," in *Hanai: An Anthology of Asian American Writing* (1980). Merle Woo, "Balancing (act one only)," in *Hanai: An Anthology of Asian American Writing* (1980). Diana W. Chow, *An Asian Man of a Different Color* (1981), pp. 39–50. Ly-

nette Amano, "Ashes," in *Kumu Kahua Plays*, Dennis Carroll, ed. (1983), pp. 3–46. Besse Toishigawa Inouye, "Reunion," in *Kumu Kahua Plays*, Dennis Carroll, ed. (1983), pp. 47–62. Alba Cota, "A Better Way," in *Toronto South Asian Review* 3, no. 1 (1984): 29. Uma Parameswaran, "Rootless but Green are the Boulevard Trees," in *Toronto South Asian Review* 4, no. 1 (1985): 62–103. Joanne Y. Yamada, excerpts from "Shizue's World," *Bamboo Ridge* 25 (1985): 38–63. Marina Feleo Gonzalez, *A Song for Manong* (1988). Misha Berson, *Between Worlds: Contemporary Asian American Plays* (1990). Laurie Carlos, Jessica Hagedorn, Robbie McCauley, "Teenytown," in *Out From Under: Texts by Women Performance Artists*, Lenora Champagne, ed. (1990), pp. 89–118. Velina Hasu Houston, ed., *The Politics of Life: Four Plays by Asian American Women* (1992). Roberta Uno, *Unbroken Thread: An Anthology of Plays by Asian American Women* (1993).

Roberta Uno

Fiction

Fiction by Asian-American women enjoys a rich century-long tradition that has culminated in an abundant crop of gifted contemporary writers, among them award-winning Maxine Hong * Kingston and Bharati * Mukherjee, and the publishing phenomenon Amy * Tan. The persistence of such a tradition is particularly admirable, given the relative scarcity of Asian women in the United States until the 1943 repeal of the Exclusion Acts (enacted against Chinese in 1882 and expanded to all "aliens" in 1924) and the double bind of gender and race that these writers have perennially endured.

Pioneers. The first Asian-Americans to publish fiction in English were the * Eaton sisters, Edith and Winnifred. Born to a Chinese mother and an American father in the late nineteenth century, an era of anti-Chinese agitation and pro-Japanese zeal, the sisters assumed conflicting Asian identities as a means of endorsing the ethnic motives of their writing. Taking the Chinese pen name * Sui Sin Far ("Narcissus") in the short story collection *Mrs. Spring Fragrance* (1912), Edith wed humor and irony to the extravagant style of her day to affirm the humanity of immigrants from Canton at a time when common wisdom regarded them as "subhuman pets incapable of morality." In contrast, the more prolific and commercially successful Winnifred assumed the pseudo-Japanese identity of Onoto * Watanna to capitalize on the public's fascination with Japan. Most of her fifteen enormously successful romance novels, among them *A Japanese Nightingale* (1901), *The Wooing of Wisteria* (1902), and *Sunny-San* (1922), typically brought together Japanese heroines and their caucasian lovers in a stylized setting more generically "oriental" than authentically Japanese. Although it is tempting to praise the steely

Edith's pioneering fiction and discount the shrewd Winnifred's literary exotica, both women were seminal figures in the history of Asian-American fiction. Many salient issues in Asian-American women's literature—the complexities of interracial romance, the intergenerational tensions in immigrant families, the emotional rootlessness of the Eurasian, the hazards of assimilation, the self-doubt caused by conflicting notions of beauty—were first articulated by Sui Sin Far and Onoto Watanna.

World War II. After the outbreak of World War II, America's long-standing antipathy towards China and sympathy towards Japan underwent a sea change. Political realignment inevitably marked the fortunes of writers of Chinese and Japanese ancestry, as well as the nature of their fiction. So numerous were the pro-West war accounts by expatriate Chinese women that these works constituted a subgenre interpreting China to Americans. The World War II novels of China-born Lin Tai-Yi (*War Tide*, 1943), Han * Suyin (*Destination Chungking*, 1942), Helena Kuo (*Westward to Chungking*, 1944), and Mai-mai Sze (*Silent Children*, 1948), China citizens with residencies of varying duration in the United States, found an audience sympathetic to a people under siege. An offshoot of this same vein of political fiction are the more recent expatriate novels of Eileen * Chang (*Rice Sprout Song*, 1955; *The Naked Earth*, 1956; *The Rouge of the North*, 1967) and Yuan Tsen Chen (*The Dragon's Village*, 1980), which depict ordinary Chinese citizens forced by Communist officialdom to question their ideals.

Pro-China sentiment during the war years kindled an accompanying curiosity about Chinese immigrant family life, as the huge success of Jade Snow * Wong's seminal autobiography, *Fifth Chinese Daughter* (1945), demonstrated. Oddly enough, no significant work emerged in the postwar years to offer in fiction the same trenchant analysis of immigrant family life from a woman's perspective as Jade Snow Wong's true-to-life account. Works of a minor order occasionally surfaced in print, such as Virginia Lee's nostalgic Chinatown novel, *The House that Tai Ming Built* (1963); however, it would take an upheaval in gender roles and in ethnic politics before the definitive Chinese immigrant novel would be written.

Whereas China apologists in the 1940s and 1950s enjoyed a wide national audience, anti-Japanese paranoia stifled the nascent literary tradition of *issei*, Japan-born women writing poems and stories for Japanese-language publications. Paradoxically, *nisei*, or American-born Japanese, found inspiration in the very act of injustice that muted their *issei* mothers: Executive Order 9066, which consigned over one hundred thousand Japanese Americans to internment camps as potential collaborators of enemy Japan. The early stories of Hisaye * Yamamoto, set in the detention center at Poston, Arizona, showed how internment tore asunder the already precarious lives of immigrant wives and American daughters. In the haunting story "The Legend of Miss Sasagawara" (1950), the inspired eccentricities of the camp madwoman confounded her more conventional neighbors in Block 33. Yamamoto's contemporary, Wakako * Yamauchi, offered a similarly rare portrait of immigrant life in the *nihonmachi*, the isolated towns poised on the bleak rural landscape of prewar Japanese America. Yamauchi's searing "And the Soul Shall Dance" (1974), a short story transformed into an award-winning drama in 1977, depicted the doomed Mrs. Oki dancing in lonely abandon in defiance of her loveless marriage and isolation from other *issei*.

Postwar Hiatus. While redressing the imbalance of the sexes, the repeal of the anti-Asian Exclusion Acts in 1943 did little to augment the Asian population in the 1950s and 1960s, composed largely of descendants of Chinese and Japanese who had immigrated before the turn of the century. Little wonder that in the absence of compelling new voices and because of the conservativism of third- and fourth-generation Asians more intent on assimilation than self-examination, no marked advancement in indigenous fiction by Asian-American women occurred. Instead, there were occasional expatriate memoirs and scattered translations from Chinese, vestiges of the now-attenuated war novel genre. Except for Chang Hua's *Crossings* (1968), a richly allusive yet overlooked gem of a novel examining the interior life of a peripatetic Chinese woman, only the protean voice of Eurasian writer Diana * Chang filled the relative void of these decades. Chang is an important transitional figure whose fiction links the China novels of the war years to the feminist works of the 1970s. Ethnicity inspires yet does not define Chang. Continually inventing herself anew in fiction, she has moved from the semiautobiographical *Frontiers of Love* (1958), a novel depicting disenchanted Chinese and Eurasian youth in postwar Shanghai, to the wry and sophisticated urban love stories of more recent date, none of which has embraced ethnic characters or situations (*A Woman of Thirty*, 1959; *A Passion for Life*, 1961; *Eye to Eye*, 1974).

The Impact of Feminism. Fiction by Asian-American women sprang to vigorous, new life in the 1970s with the burgeoning ethnic self-consciousness of Asian Americans coming of age in the era of civil rights and antiwar unrest. A key event making possible the current efflorescence of female writing was the landmark anthology *AIIIEEEEE! An Anthology of Asian American Writers* (1974), which introduced Sui Sin Far and Hisaye Yamamoto to young Asian Americans seeking to redeem the forgotten sources of their history. Yet the single galvanizing influence on Asian-American fiction was the women's movement, which provided the rationale, the audience, and a writer with the gifts to turn unfocused generational angst into compelling literature. With the publication of Maxine Hong *Kingston's paired memoirs, *Woman Warrior* (1976) and *China Men* (1980), Asian-American writing moved to the forefront of national letters. In these works, Kingston mixed history, myth, personal narrative, and the immigrant oral lore called "talk-story," thus infusing the memoir form with the allusiveness of fiction. Because Kingston's works have been in part an exposure of the misogyny in Chinese families, she was denounced by the male editors of *AIIIEEEEE!*, chiefly by the playwright Frank Chin, who, in the revised edition of the anthology, *The Big AIIIEEEEE! An Anthology of Chinese and Japanese American Literature* (1989), disparaged Kingston's "authenticity." The long-standing feud between Kingston and Chin has divided Asian-American scholars and led both Kingston and Chin to a writerly revenge: turning the other into fiction. Chin has parodied *Woman Warrior* and *China Men* in the afterword of his collection of stories, *The Chinaman Pacific and Frisco R.R. Co.* (1989). Similarly, Kingston has endowed her protagonist Wittman Ah Sing with Chin's bombastic machismo in the exuberant, satirical *Tripmaster Monkey* (1989).

Despite its heat, the gender war surrounding Kingston has strengthened her role as touchstone for a generation of Asian-American women who model her mythmaking and feminist concerns. Her voice has echoed with particular force in the pages of short story anthologies, where many emerging writers are first seeing print. Foremost in the tribe of Kingston's emulators mining the field of talk-story has been the novelist Amy Tan, whose *The Joy Luck Club* (1989) and *The Kitchen God's Wife* (1991) reclaim the old-world secrets of her mother's generation for self-doubting American-born daughters. Yet unlike the mythopoeic and fragmentary structures of Kingston's works, Tan's plots are straightforward, her characters anchored in reality, and her individual chapters taut enough to stand alone as separate short stories. This latter quality reflects the unique system of refinement inherent in the writers' group process from which *The Joy Luck Club* springs.

More recent novels depicting immigrant life have veered from feminist themes to focus instead on families traumatized by assimilation as "bachelor" and clan societies give way to Western-style nuclear families. Gish Jen's mismatched lovers in *Typical American* (1991); Kim *Ronyoung's rancorous tribe of Korean-Americans in *Clay Walls* (1986); Cynthia Kadohata's rootless clan of indigent *nisei* and *sansei* laborers in *The Floating World* (1989); and Fae Mienne Ng's trio of sibylline sisters in the spare, sophisticated suicide narrative *Bone* (1993) are proof of the unpredictable, often disastrous falling away of old-country values.

The New Immigrants. Besides feminism, the other significant factor contributing to the post-1970s resurgence of fiction by Asian-American women was the influx of new voices from across Asia in the aftermath of the Vietnam War. Whereas American daughters like Kingston and Tan might yearn for spiritual connection with the motherland and feel keenly the limitations of an America they know too well, the immigrant novelist might lament the corruption of the old country while affirming the openness of the new. The young protagonist of Burmese novelist Wendy *Law-Yone's *The Coffin Tree* (1983) suffers incalculable misfortunes as a result of America's random cruelty, yet is profoundly moved by the primal image of America as frontier. In *Dogeaters* (1990), Philippine-born Jessica *Hagedorn turns a penetrating eye at the country of her birth and offers a raunchy, explosive dissection of wayward youth under Marcos.

No American writer has depicted the developing global consciousness of America in the 1980s with the keenness of "semi-assimilated Indian" Bharati Mukherjee. Her gallery of ethnic misfits, drawn with Dickensian sharpness, exposes the volatile clash of disparate elements in the multicultural stew (*Darkness*, 1985; *The Middleman and Other Stories*, 1988; *Jasmine*, 1989). Ethnicity for Mukherjee has been less a fact of birth than a metaphor for wrenching social change. Hers is a quintessential Third World perspective, lacking in mainstream envy and claiming kinship with every disenchanted newcomer languishing in the margins of American society.

Contemporary Asian-American women writers of fiction continue to work in a multiplicity of subgenres and display an extraordinary stylistic range, from the tightly drawn psychological riddles of Canadian-Japanese Joy Kogawa (*Obasan*, 1980); the prose-poems of Theresa Hak Kyung *Cha (*Dictee*, 1982); the ample canvases of historical novelists Bette Bao *Lord (*Spring Moon*, 1981), Ruthann Lum McCunn (*A Thousand Pieces of Gold*, 1981), Linda Ching Sledge (*Empire of Heaven*, 1990) and Leslie Li (*Bitter-

sweet, 1992); to Cynthia Kadohata's futuristic parable (*In the Heart of the Valley of Love*, 1992). Their prolixity belies the continued cost of their art, for Asian women writers have always been, by necessity, iconoclasts who in order to delineate the life of their community must defy a central cultural tenet—the still-potent notion of feminine decorum. This singular perspective has permitted them to hear with surprising clarity what Mukherjee in *Darkness* describes as the voice of the American outsider "singing even in the seams of the dominant culture."

• Elaine H. Kim, *Asian American Literature: An Introduction to the Writings and their Social Context* (1982). Hisaye Yamamoto, *Seventeen Syllables and Other Stories* (1988). Amy Ling, *Between Worlds: Women Writers of Chinese Ancestry* (1990). Sylvia Watanabe and Carol Bruchac, eds., *Home to Stay: Asian American Women's Fiction* (1990).

Linda Ching Sledge

Nonfiction

The scope of Asian-American nonfiction is wide: from the writings of highly educated women to illiterate immigrant women; from first-generation Asian women to the American-born, American-educated "American daughters"; from wealthy, high-status women to poor factory and farm workers. Often in the form of autobiography, Asian-American women's nonfiction tells the history of their survival in America and the process of their maturity in a collective sense. For Asian Americans and for women, it is only natural to ask "Who am I? Where is my place?" In the United States, they started out as demure, courteous "Oriental girls" but were then assimilated as successful American daughters. Finally, they have become women on their own terms, transcending labels. Their doubly marginalized status—of gender and race—has forced them to move beyond socially defined boundaries and thus enabled them to create the space in which both their new and old worlds, their past and present, can exist together without conflict.

Asian-American women's writings began to appear in the mid-nineteenth century. Until the mid-twentieth century, these early writings were very limited in number: they consisted of a few autobiographies of educated Asian or Asian-American women and scattered autobiographical pieces produced by those who struggled with survival in the United States. Most early immigrant women were not educated and received no encouragement to write. In addition, their hard lives—as wives of patriarchal husbands, as mothers of several children, or as laborers—did not offer them the luxury of writing. In many cases, the fragmented information

about their discontent, discomfort, and disappointment in the new country was transmitted orally to their daughters and not compiled until very recently.

The writings of a few elite women protective of their home countries in Asia and at the same time courteous toward their new place tells a different story. It is rare to find any bitterness in their accounts. *A Daughter of the Samurai* (1925), written by Etsu Inagaki Sugimoto, is a good example. Sugimoto was a Japanese language and history teacher at Columbia University. It is clear that she chose to present both her Asian world, Japan, and her new American world in the best possible light. While praising Sugimoto's "ceremonial" writing about both Japan and America, Christopher Morley, in his introduction to the book, suggests that Sugimoto was "even a little too generous toward the America she adopted."

The America of the two Eaton sisters was somewhat different from that of Sugimoto. Born of a Chinese mother and an American father who was disowned by his wealthy parents because of his marriage, Edith and Winnifred * Eaton describe their lives as Eurasians in the early twentieth century. Edith, the second of fourteen children, briefly recounts her life in "Leaves from the Mental Portfolio of an Eurasian" (1909), a short protest piece against class and gender biases in the United States. On the other hand, Winnifred describes her first year away from home in her lengthy autobiography, *Me, a Book of Remembrance* (1915). As Amy Ling points out in her *Between Worlds: Women Writers of Chinese Ancestry* (1990), Winnifred focuses on gender issues rather than race; indeed, she was very obscure about racial issues, which may explain why she was more popular among readers than her rather critical sister.

As the number of Asian immigrants increased, so did hostility and prejudice against Asians and Asian Americans, whom many viewed as "the yellow peril." World War II certainly contributed to the negative image of Asians in the United States, especially that of the Japanese. American-born Asian daughters had to struggle with a negative, stereotyped image. Unlike their Asian-born parents, they were better educated, they spoke English, and they ate American food. It was their wish to make their way in U.S. society and they felt that their success would be gauged by how much they became part of America.

A second-generation Chinese American, Jade Snow * Wong, and a second-generation Japanese American, Monica Sone, recorded their experiences as young women who became successful American daughters. *Fifth Chinese Daughter*

(1945) starts with Wong's Chinese elementary school and ends with her successful American education at Mills College. This is truly a story of the American Dream. Wong expresses no bitterness, no serious questions about her Asian-American identity. Sone's *Nisei Daughter* (1953) presents a more skeptical picture of being Japanese American. The autobiographical Kazuko's experience in a relocation camp during World War II especially illustrates Sone's obsession with the question, "What is my place in the world?" Nevertheless, the conclusion of the book is rather compromising in its doubts about the principle of assimilation. At the end, Kazuko returns to "Wendell College with confidence and hope." She writes, "I had discovered a deeper, stronger pulse in the American scene. I was going back into its mainstream, still with my Oriental eyes, but with an entirely different outlook, for now I felt more like a whole person instead of a sadly split personality. The Japanese and the American parts of me were now blended into one."

Farewell to Manzanar (1973), which appeared twenty years after *Nisei Daughter*, shows a similar effort to assimilate into the American dominant culture on the part of the Japanese-American writer Jeanne Houston. It is the story of her father, who represents her Japanese past, and her own life in the American present. Although the father's daughter's lives intersect in the book, they are not part of each other's life; in fact, the daughter's life starts as the father's life ends. The father remains Japanese while the daughter accepts an American identity. As Elaine Kim says, the book was written for an American audience.

Since the 1970s, young Asian-American women writers try to find, in Julia Kristeva's term, "a signifying space," in which everyone, regardless of gender, race, class, or any difference, can exist without confronting a ranking hierarchy. In this space, socially defined boundaries cease to exist; the writers feel comfortable to bring their past and present together, their old and new worlds. By piecing together the lost past and the fragmented present and by connecting the two worlds over the Pacific Ocean, the writers are able to understand who they are without having to choose one identity over the other.

Maxine Hong *Kingston's *Woman Warrior: Memoirs of a Girlhood among Ghosts* (1975) is truly a book of reconciliation of differences— in this case between a Chinese mother and a Chinese-American daughter, between the Chinese identity and the American one, between widely differing cultures. Only gender remains outside Kingston's reconciling picture. (In an interview with Bill Moyers in 1991, Kingston remarked that if she were to rewrite the book, she would include gender in her reconciling effort.) By the end of *The Woman Warrior*, Kingston not only understands who she is but sends a message of transcendence.

Since the past is crucial in understanding their identity, more and more young Asian-American women writers go back to their "mothers' gardens" to rewrite their American lives. Daughters speak up for the lost and buried old-world lives of their mothers and grandmothers in collections such as *Making Waves: An Anthology of Writings by and about Asian American Women* (1989) and *The Forbidden Stitch: An Asian American Women's Anthology* (1989). Li Ling Ai's *Life Is for a Long Time* (1979) explores the chronicle of a Chinese immigrant family in Hawaii. In *Through Harsh Winters: The Life of a Japanese Immigrant Woman* (1981), Akemi Kikumura writes of her mother's life after immigrating to the United States. While Kingston interwove her own story with her mother's, Kikumura's purpose is to present her mother's life in both Japan and the United States. The preface makes her intentions clear: "In an attempt to capture [her] spirit and to learn more about my own cultural heritage, I had decided to write a life history of my mother, using her own words (as I translated them) to tell a story about an Issei woman's experience in America."

It is significant that newly rising Asian-American women are also writing novels based on their own, their parents', or historical characters' life stories: Kim Ronyoung's *Clay Walls* (1987), Amy Tan's *Kitchen God's Wife* (1991), and Ruthanne Lum McCunn's *Thousand Pieces of Gold: A Biographical Novel* (1981) are some examples. The fact that they write autobiographical novels, or fictionalized biographies, indicates that they no longer have to cry out loudly in a straight autobiographical form; instead, they enjoy creating stories out of their once-painful experiences.

Like their counterparts a century earlier, Asian-American women writers are still struggling with the dominant question, "Who am I?" Although they may remain on the margins of American society, their own view of their identity, place, past, and future does not seem grim. They have found their identity in the space they created. Their writings prove their struggle, strength, and achievements.

• Elaine H. Kim, *Asian American Literature: An Introduction to the Writings and Their Social Context* (1982). Julia Kristeva, "Women's Time," in *The Kristeva Reader*, ed. Toril Moi (1986), pp. 187–213. Shirley Geok-lin Lim, "Twelve Asian American Writers: In

Search of Self-Definition," *MELUS: Society for the Study of the Multi-Ethnic Literature of the United States* 13, nos. 1 and 2 (Spring/Summer 1986): 57–77. Asian Women United of California, ed., *Making Waves: An Anthology by and about Asian American Women* (1989). Shirley Geok-lin Lim, Mayumi Tsutakawa, and Margarita Donnelly, eds., *The Forbidden Stitch: An Asian American Women's Anthology* (1989). Amy Ling, *Between Worlds: Women Writers of Chinese Ancestry* (1990).

Joonok Huh

Poetry

Although individual poets have attracted some attention, little has been written about Asian-American women's poetry as a category. The reason for this disciplinary neglect is partly that Asian-American women poets seem to constitute a bewilderingly heterogeneous group, representing not only the usual differences between women but also a vast diversity of national origins, cultural sites, multilingual influences, regional contexts, immigration histories, sexual orientations, and generational positions, so that a study of this category frustrates any attempt to see it as a congruent whole. Also, until the 1970s, Asian-American women did not publish much poetry; the lack of a readily identifiable body of work together with the diversity of voices made it easy to assume that the field was both submerged and fragmentary.

In the 1990s, however, Asian-American women's poetry emerged strongly both in number of publications and in the shape of recurrent themes and stylistic "schools" that these publications together suggest and construct. The "sudden" visibility of this work is related to the success of the civil rights movements of the fifties and sixties that sought to integrate diverse cultures into the mainly white, English-speaking U.S. culture. Ethnic texts began to appear in mainstream publishing, and Asian Americans gained greater access to higher education and arts endeavors. The growing body of Asian-American work is perhaps strongly related to changes in U.S. immigration laws in 1965. Race quotas were replaced with a policy of equitable representation based on national origins, an amendment that has resulted in a dramatic increase in the presence of Asian Americans in the United States, from about .7 percent of the U.S. population in 1970 to almost 3 percent of the population in 1990.

Until the 1970s, Asian Americans were chiefly of Chinese, Japanese, and Filipino descent. Recently, immigration from Korea, Vietnam, and South and Southeast Asia, has resulted in an expansion of ethnic variations in the U.S. Asian-American population, a subtlety often lost in the federal government's treatment of *Asian* as a distinct homogeneous ethnicity. This diversity has been accompanied by a growing internal recognition of the necessity for intraethnic coalition for political representation and empowerment. All of these sociohistorical forces are evident in Asian-American women's poetry, as political themes and as the materiality that explains the forms and language zones exhibited in the poems.

Japanese-American Women Poets. Among the first poems published in the United States by a Japanese-American are those by Toyo Suyemoto who, influenced by the strict forms of Japanese-language poetry as a young woman, began writing while interned by U.S. authorities during World War II (1941–44). After the war, Suyemoto worked as a librarian in Ohio and continued to write brief, lyrical poems that combined Western and Asian conventions in their use of sensuous observations of nature fused with a moral sensibility. Her lyrics, so out of step with Modernist *vers libre*, take their stanzaic formality from the Romantic tradition and from the elegant economy of the haiku, hokku, and tanka, the common Japanese poetic forms. Suyemoto's poems, however, are not an elegiac deadend; rather, in their insistence on formal continuity, they participate in the memory and translation projects that more contemporary Asian-American women poets are undertaking. As she writes, even as the poet demands answers from Asian ancestral sources, she recognizes that she "must go on ... inventing translations."

The drive to rescue cultural materials from memory, to invent a reusable past that is different from Anglo-American history, is closely related to the themes of identity conflicts. Sometimes, these themes result in poems of simple celebration of ethnic identity, associated with rituals, families, and kinship bonds. Asian-American women poets of all national origins share in this theme: Filipinas such as Myra Pena-Reyes (*The River Singing Stone*, 1984), Chinese Americans such as Amy Ling (*Chin-America Reflections*, 1984), Japanese Americans such as Patricia Ikeda (*House of Wood, House of Salt*, 1978) write praise poems to their family members, marking the loyalty, love, and stability of the family unit as a cultural value. Yet these praise poems can be highly ironic, for they also suggest or openly criticize a hostile countersociety that makes the family a necessary sanctuary against its depredations.

Many women poets who began publishing in the 1970s deployed the politically oppositional positions of the civil rights activists. Because of their experiences of U.S.-sanctioned racism during the Japanese-American internment, which was created by President Roosevelt's Executive Order 9066 of 1941, Japanese-American women poets tend to be among the most radical, refusing to separate the political from the literary. Japanese-born Mitsuye Yamada and American-born Janice *Mirikitani reimagine the Japanese-American internment experience as a means to record their community's history and as part of the struggle against racism and violence in their nation. Yamada's *Camp Notes* (1976) contain poems written during her involuntary stay at Camp Minidoka. Later poems in her second collection, *Desert Run* (1988), elaborate on her political education in American racism and her struggles to understand her Japanese cultural identity when it is interrogated by both American and Japanese prejudice. Mirikitani's poems in *Awake in the River* (1978) and *Shedding Silence* (1987) are rawer, invoking a rage against many social evils including racism, U.S. militarism in Vietnam, and patriarchal abuse of women. Her poems are performed as much as written, and their open topographical arrangements, repetitions, and "moveable" feet testify to their oral quality. Kimiko Hahn's *Air Pocket* (1989) enlarges the field of her protest poetry to include U.S. militarism in Nicaragua; like the two older poets, she also speaks from the position of woman to indict, for example, patriarchy in its global manifestâtions in "Resistance: A Poem on Ikat Cloth."

Japanese-American women poets have also been willing to explore other facets of experience and to approach poetic language less as an instrument of protest than for its own sake. Kyoko Mori, a Japanese-born poet based in the Midwest, shows an imagistic power in poems that sharply imagine an individual's interior emotions; while family and Japanese cultural motifs are also important components, her work is less politicized and more allusively implicated in the language of poetic presence.

Chinese-American Women Poets. Similar differences—between, on the one hand, overtly politically conscious poetry that appeals to nostalgia for an ethnic community's past and proclaims indignation at shared histories of oppression, and on the other, Modernist and Postmodernist concerns with language as elliptical signification that encompasses self-consciousness, irony, playfulness, allusiveness, obscurity, opaqueness, a distrust of transparency and authority (including the authority of the past and of community)—exist among Chinese-American women's poetry. This is not to say that the first kind of poetry lacked those language attributes or that the second was empty of sociopolitical content.

The women's poems that form part of the anthology, *American Born and Foreign* (1979), demonstrate the dynamic between sociopoliti-

cal urgencies and language play that exceeds if not obscures the political dimension. The anthology is organized thematically ("Working Mothers and Fathers," "Rituals," "Chinatown," "Alienation," etc.), suggesting the overt message-driven context for the poetic discourse. Within these not-so-subtle ideological constraints, individual Asian-American women's poems strike a range of notes that encapsulate their divergent styles in their later collections.

Nellie Wong's poems, for example, insist on a plainness of language, even in metaphorical usage, that emphasizes sociopolitical issues over linguistic matters. In the same way, her language in later collections, such as *The Death of a Long Stem Lady* (1986) and *Dreams in Harrison Railroad Park* (1977), possesses a referential dimension that assumes a transparent relation between words and their significance as political statement. Lacking the self-consciousness and irony of word play, Wong's language operates as sentimental, unproblematically oppositional, and self-righteous discourse, acknowledged as "this language, this tiresome but necessary chant" ("Under Our Own Wings"). At their best, the poems offer a caustic commentary from the point of view of the marginalized, particularly on themes of class and race divisions.

In contrast, the vivid diction and elaborate details in Mei-mei Berssenbrugge's poems (*Summits Move with the Tide*, 1974; *Random Possessions*, 1979) are woven with deliberate syntactical flexibility so as to reconstruct ancestral and community memory and to present interior states as ironical, unstable, fragmented, and intense in their partiality. Diana *Chang's poems (*The Horizon Is Definitely Speaking*, 1982; *What Matisse Is After*, 1984; *Earth Water Light*, 1991) are perhaps even more self-conscious in their economical and intense treatment of the fragile boundary between subject (consciousness) and the language (words) through which the subject constitutes itself.

Younger Chinese-American poets such as Marilyn Chin (*Dwarf Bamboo*, 1987) and Carolyn Lau (*Wode Shuofa*, 1988) enlarge this poetics of identity to include the indeterminacies that result from the intersections of national histories, cultures, and languages. In "Art Wong Is Alive and Ill and Struggling in Oakland California," Chin imagines the incongruency between classical Chinese literature as portrayed by Ezra Pound's idealization of Chinese civilization and the contemporary American art scene; she asks for a "marriage between / ... the diaspora and the yearning sea." Shirley Geok-lin Lim addresses similar postcolonial fractures between a Malaysian-Chinese history and an uneasy Asian-American present in *Mod-*

ern Secrets (1989) and in her earlier collections, *Crossing the Peninsula* (1980) and *No Man's Grove* (1985). Hilary Tham, another Malaysian-born Chinese-American poet, also explores the particularities of this ethnic community. She mines rich intraethnic content in poems that speak about her conversion to Judaism in *Bad Names for Women* (1989). Lau, Lim, and Tham are also among the most openly feminist in their sympathies, Lau through enigmatic narrative lines, Lim through explorations of experiences that are gendered as female (sexuality, loss, motherhood), and Tham through the fiction of women characters whose voices tell loudly of oppression.

The jazzy rhythms and urban images of Fay Chiang's *In the City of Contradictions* (1979) and Genny Lim's *Winter Place* (1989) have a good deal more in common with the Filipina-American writer, Jessica *Hagedorn (see her *Dangerous Music*, 1975; *Petfood and Tropical Apparitions*, 1981). All three poets are concerned with the ethnic negotiation of metropolitan culture. Either didactically or stylistically, through reliance on city images, themes, and dialects, all of their poems celebrate an ethnic urban culture composed of people of color, working-class citizens, and the marginalized individual—all persons who have become dehumanized in their identification with America's inner cities. So Genny Lim, echoing Walt Whitman, writes, "I heard the breath of Harlem / her fingers reached for a needle of sky," and Hagedorn defiantly imagines the woman riding in underground trains with "rats / strung out on methadone."

Filipina-American Poets. Hagedorn is the most experimental voice among the growing number of Filipina-Americans who are appearing in print. A noted novelist, her early volumes of poetry already show the influence of American Beat poetry (her mentor was Kenneth Rexroth). In *Dangerous Music*, her dark humor and deliberate constructions of a Brechtian metropolitan persona are witty and often touching. Virginia Cerenio's *Trespassing Innocence* (1989) is a collection in the tradition of social realism and shares its attributes of sentimentality and moralizing and its virtues of community portrayals and political persuasion based on a cataloging of details and close social observations.

Korean-American Women Poets. Korean-American women poets, while having appeared more recently, have made a tremendous contribution in challenging conventions of genre, form, and stylistics. Theresa Hak Kyung *Cha's *Dictee* (1982), a richly Postmodernist text that has been read as a novel and as poetry, treats the intersecting positions of the Korean-American woman artist, whose circumstances are situated in the political division of North and South Korea, the relations of Korea and the United States, and the divide between the Korean language and the English language. Through her use of a highly allusive vocabulary that condenses French, Korean, and English associations, that repeats and circles around motifs and images, that disrupts and interrupts itself, Hak Kyung Cha in *Dictee* has created a work whose power as text is inseparable from its power as language; the signifier and the signified are inextricably saturated with each other's presence. It is the only Asian-American poetic work to have an entire study devoted to it (see Norma Alarcon and Elaine H. Kim, eds., *Writing Self, Writing Nation*, forthcoming). Myung Mi Kim's *Under Flag* (1991) shares Hak Kyung Cha's penchant for the powerfully indeterminate image, her concern with the condition of the "interlingual" or "between languages" diasporic writer, and her exploration of Korean national history and fractured postcolonial identity. Kim's yoking of vivid concrete images with teasing abstractions both addresses and constitutes the metastylistics of a "slurred and taken over / Diaspora."

Hawaiian Women Poets. Cathy Song, whose first book, *Picture Bride* (1983), received the Yale Younger Poets Award, is a very different kind of Asian-American writer. Of Korean and Chinese descent, born in Hawaii, her poetry shows the influence of the island landscapes and culture. Her work is grounded in sensuous observations of nature and the serious moral feeling that encompasses the tensions of the individual woman in relation to valued family and community ties. Her second collection, *Frameless Windows, Squares of Light* (1988), expands on these pastoral and familial themes with a quiet meditative rhetoric that persuades through an appeal to contemplative conviction.

Song's success in mainstream American poetry publishing has encouraged other women poets in Hawaii to strike their particular regional notes. Juliet S. Kono's *Hilo Rains* (1988) shifts the attention from Oahu, site of Song's island pieces, to her native island of Hawaii, and draws from a more rural, working-class body of experiences than the more cosmopolitan Song, as in her poem, "Rice Bag Sheets and Pillow Cases." Examples of Hawaiian (a term here that includes women of Asian descent and those of indigenous ancestry) women's poetry are found in collections such as *Malama* (1985), numerous collections of the periodical *Bamboo Ridge*, and the recent *Sister Stew* (1991). A major stylistic innovation is the move to exploit the musicality, color, and immediacy of pidgin, the dialect of English spoken on the islands, as seen in Lois-Ann Yamanaka's poem, "Sista: Boss of the Food" (*Bamboo Ridge* no. 47, Summer 1990). Many native Hawaiian women write in their native language, often using a convention of Hawaiian literature known as the *mele*.

Asian-American Lesbian Poets. Welcomed by the second wave of feminism in the United States in the 1970s, these poets have published poems that boldly celebrate their sexuality, criticize homophobia in their communities, and construct a solidarity or sisterhood based on working-class and feminist life rather than on race sympathies. Merle Woo (*Yellow Woman Speaks*, n.d.), Barbara Noda (*Strawberries*, 1978), Michiyo Fukaya (*Lesbian Lyrics*, 1981), Willyce Kim (*Eating Artichokes*, 1972; *Under the Rolling Sky*, 1976), and Kitty Tsui (*The Words of a Woman Who Breathes Fire*, 1983) are the best known of these poets.

Stylistic and Thematic Connections. Some Hawaiian women poets are weaving native Hawaiian words and phrases into English-language poems in efforts that parallel the incorporation of Asian language phrases in the work of many Asian-American women. This linguistic intertextuality vivifies the ethnic poets' position, and identifies their location within two simultaneous but different cultural worlds, the Asian culture often being untranslatable into an American vocabulary. Thus, many Asian-American women poets show a keen awareness of the struggle with languages, with the reconstitution of ethnic identity through forcing English to express a different-language culture. They explore the resources of a second language/mother tongue, of pidgin and dialect, and of syntactical play and grammatical fractures to achieve either indeterminacy and a nonstandard English or a linguistic ethnic consciousness.

This stylistic inventiveness is also related thematically to the writers' content and images. Living in the United States, American-born and first-generation immigrants, their poems are sometimes located as "from Asia" (Mori, Chin, Lim, Tham, Hagedorn, Cerenio, Cha, and Kim, e.g., are all first-generation American). But "Asia" in the poems has already been mediated through the agency of the English language and American literary culture. Their poems are therefore at least a doubled form; the presence of Asia is evoked even as it is American circumstance that shapes their writing, and in many cases this duality forms the locus of their social struggles. Two anthologies, *The Forbidden Stitch* (1989) and *Making Waves* (1989), provide useful sociological, historical, literary, and bibliographical materials to understand Asian-American women's positions and works. *Without Ceremony*, a special issue of the journal *Ikon* (no. 9, 1988), offers a more New York–based collection. The poems of South Asian Meena *Alexander and Chitra Divakaruni's *Black Candle: Poems about Women from India, Pakistan, and Bangladesh* (1991), like many of the works discussed so far, also illustrate the difficulty in assigning simple identity categories to works of the imagination that, the more powerful and successful they are, elude the nets of race and nation. Do these first-generation Asian-American women's revivification of Asia within a feminist ideology and free-verse practice mark their work as an American cultural product? Or do they point forward to the induction of a global women's literature on which common feminist ideological lines and a "universal" female sensibility can be traced? Like every fresh body of literature, Asian-American women's poetry will lead to crucial questions and controversies.

• Dexter Fisher, *The Third Woman: Minority Women Writers of the United States* (1980); Shirley Geok-lin Lim, Review-essay, "Cathy Song's Picture Bride," *MELUS* 10, no. 3 (1983): 95–99; Shirley Geok-lin Lim, "Reconstructing Asian-American Poetry: A Case for Ethnopoetics," *MELUS* 14, no. 2 (Summer 1987): 51–63; Stephen Sumida, "Sense of Place, History, and the Concept of the 'Local' in Hawaii's Asian/Pacific Literatures," in *Reading the Literatures of Asian America*, ed. Shirley Geok-lin Lim and Amy Ling (1992), 215–37.

Shirley Geok-lin Lim

ASSIMILATION. Both the historical process of assimilation and the literature that represents and enacts this process turn on a curious paradox. Assimilation is not only central to any definition of American cultural experience but also a fragmentary dynamic that resists coherent, historical definition. In the simplest sense, assimilation designates a relation between marginal groups or cultures and the central or dominant culture within which they function; it is a dialectic between inside and outside. To be outside, however, is to be inside, for as works like *Walden* and *The Great Gatsby* remind us, dominant and canonical American culture is and has always been a culture of the outsider. We began as a nation of immigrants and created a culture inscribed from the start with otherness and marginality. The centrality of the marginal has put the female ethnic American writer in a unique position. As Carolyn *Heilbrun remarks, the ethnic American woman is an outsider twice over. And, if her very marginality marks her as most centrally American, her literature thus describes not just female or ethnic experience in America, but, potentially, American cultural experience itself.

But the relation between margin and center itself has a history, and the theorizing of assimilation thus has focused on whether a marginal culture can have a literature of its own, or whether it must always respond to the conventions of the dominant. This question has often been approached through an examination of certain themes such as generational conflict, *marriage and miscegenation, all of which recur across various ethnic boundaries, perhaps because they provide apt and general tropes for the relation between margin and center, both in terms of *ethnicity and *gender.

More recently, *language itself has become the crucial issue in the study of female ethnic American writing, for the appropriation of language at the most literal level defines the relation of the individual to his or her culture. Mary *Antin, for example, writes in They Who Knock at Heaven's Gate (1914), "the ghost of the Mayflower pilots every immigrant ship and Ellis Island is another name for Plymouth Rock." The Puritan errand into the wilderness thus becomes the prototype for the immigrant struggle in the urban jungle, and implicitly, the immigrant becomes yet another child of the Founding Fathers. Antin's project is one of mediation and it occurs at a thematic and, more importantly, a rhetorical level. Her story thematizes the desire to become part of the American family, but it also unquestioningly appropriates the familial dimension of American political rhetoric. To learn American rhetoric is to earn American *identity.

Antin's text is uncritical and straightforward in its attempt to naturalize itself in an American language, but the appropriation of language tends to generate a complexity of responses and results. Cogewea (1927), by *Mourning Dove, is no less accepting of a dominant rhetoric than Antin, but here, the mixture of discourses and ideologies results in a kind of linguistic and cultural schizophrenia. Mourning Dove's work, in its confusion of the ends and purposes of particular rhetorics, anticipates the double consciousness that will inform later ethnic writing, particularly that of *the Harlem Renaissance. This work exhibits far more ambivalence towards the values of assimilation but its language remains caught between two cultures, genders, and ideologies.

Perhaps the crucial lesson that emerged from the Harlem Renaissance was that militant rejection or acceptance of dominant cultural rhetoric and ideology was neither effective nor desirable. The most instructive figure here is perhaps Zora Neale *Hurston whose work continues to influence contemporary black literature and which participates in the many complications that surround female ethnic authorship. Provided for by white patrons, enmeshed in the debate between aesthetics and politics and working within a welter of discourses, Hurston was in her own time criticized by both blacks and whites, women and men, seemingly representative of both and neither. But Their Eyes Were Watching God (1937) is indisputably an American literary classic, not least of all because it accepts its own double consciousness and forcefully interrogates the relation between cultures and discourses without attempting to appropriate, mediate or denounce. What emerges is a work that transcends the conflicts it embodies and that creates a language and world of its own. In this respect, Hurston's work looks forward to contemporary novelists such as Alice *Walker and Toni *Morrison whose writings clearly resist the pull of assimilation but which nonetheless have become a dominant presence within the canonical tradition. No longer attempting to learn a language that precedes them or to become part of a family that would exclude them, these writers are giving birth to a new language spoken by and within a new American *community. Both female and ethnic, their work redefines our conception of both.

Contemporary female ethnic writing, especially in its diversity, has in some sense been responsible for the recent and massive upheaval in our current views and theorizing of assimilation. There is an increasingly persistent sense among writers and literary historians that no coherent female ethnic literary tradition exists, and this, at least partially, because no single process of assimilation exists. In keeping with its etymological meaning, "to liken to," assimilation supposes separate and often oppositional identities made similar. Such a notion, however, assumes that identities, be they national or gender specific, marginal or dominant, could be isolated and defined, and it is an idea that has come under increasing scrutiny. The phrase "ethnic American women's writing" may illustrate the problem.

The word "American" reminds us that one aspect of assimilation entails confrontation with a national identity, whether this identity is accepted, mediated or rejected. The last decade, however, has seen a movement in American Studies from consensus to dissent. What was once a shared belief in a unified national identity, and in the unique national literature that both participates in and helps to define that identity, has been disputed on both ideological and intellectual grounds. It is no longer assumed that American culture or literature can or should be defined by its unique nature, and consequently, it becomes difficult to speak of a dialectic between marginal and dominant. This difficulty is augmented by the fact that at the so-called margins, different cultural identities themselves resist unification under any single rubric; ethnicity itself is a shifting concept. And, even if ethnic identities could be defined in relation to some dominant culture, we would do better to speak of ethnic identities and literatures rather than attempt to collapse their variety into a single tradition.

If national cultural identities have been called into question at both the nominal center and at the margins, so, too, feminist literary theory has begun to interrogate its own forms of *essentialism. The writer of feminist literary history, like the historian of national literature, faces a complex task. She must be wary of any single paradigm of women's history, culture, or consciousness and articulate the interplay of *gender, *race, and *class. In attempting to examine the forces of assimilation in female ethnic American literature, feminist scholars have paid increasing attention to the particular relation between gender and ethnicity, which, while structurally similar, remain wholly distinct concepts. And, even if each of these concepts could be isolated as conditions to be assimilated or marginalized, more recent feminist theory questions the very structure of gender opposition, in which case the whole notion of "women's" writing needs to be rethought.

Lastly, the phrase "ethnic American women's writing" presupposes that we know what writing is. But both earlier and contemporary examples of ethnic American women's texts tend to destabilize the concepts of genre and authorship so favored by literary historians. As Mary Dearborn has pointed out, our earliest and most canonical story of assimilation, that of Pocahontas, was first written by John Smith, but this does not necessarily disqualify it as an ethnic American woman's story. Similarly, many Afro-American texts of the late nineteenth century were "mid-wived" into the world with the help of white patrons so that the question of authorship becomes problematic. The definition of genre poses similar problems. Leslie *Silko's Ceremony (1977), for example, incorporates legend and poetry and implicitly defends oral story-telling in such a way that generic boundaries and definable authorship collapse. The questions posed by such a work are twofold: are the women who transmit these stories authors or transcribers, and to what generic group do their writings belong?

As national, ethnic and gender identities fragment, and as concepts of authorship and genre come to be rethought, it has grown increasingly difficult to speak of a coherent history of ethnic American women's writing, and, consequently, to trace a definable process of assimilation. The Afro-American of the 1870s, the Native American of the 1920s, and the Chinese American of the 1970s may all experience and represent the dialectic of assimilation in their works, but these experiences may bear little relation to each other, or to the experiences of writers from the same ethnic background but from different historical periods. The possibilities and limitations of this fragmentation have increasingly come to dominate both ethnic American women's writing and the work of its critics and theorists.

[See also Ethnicity and Writing.]

• John Higham, Strangers in the Land: Patterns of American Nativism 1860–1925 (1963). Milton Gordon, Assimilation in American Life: The Role of Race, Religion and National Origins (1964). Nathan Glazer and Daniel P. Moynihan, eds., Ethnicity: Theory and Experience (1975). Edith Blicksilver, The Ethnic American Woman (1978). Carolyn Heilbrun, Reinventing Womanhood (1979). Stephen Thernstrom, ed., The Harvard Encyclopaedia of American Ethnic Groups (1980). Kristen Herzog, Women, Ethnics, and Exotics: Images of Power in Mid-Nineteenth Century Fiction (1983). Mary V. Dearborn, Pocahontas's Daughters: Gender and Ethnicity in American Culture (1986). Louise Kaplan, Female Perversions (1991).

Pamela Schirmeister

ATHERTON, Gertrude (1857–1948), novelist and short fiction writer. Born in California, Gertrude Atherton was informally educated but well-read. She was unhappily married for eleven years, and after the death of her husband left provincial (to her) California to begin her writing career in New York, London, and other cities in Europe and America. When her first novels featuring unconventional heroines were scorned by American reviewers, she sought and attained serious attention in London, where she began her fictional chronicle of California with The Doomswoman (1892). Depicting California hacienda and city life that Bret Harte, Mark Twain, and Ambrose Bierce ignored, Atherton, between 1895 and 1907, portrayed a new self-conflicted woman, endowed with Californian vitality and ambition. She also wrote a biographical novel about Alexander Hamilton (The Conqueror, 1902), which was praised for its original form. With Black Oxen (1923), she achieved her goal of writing a best-seller; in The Immortal Marriage (1927), she recreated classical figures such as Aspasia and Pericles. Returning to California in 1932 as a permanent resident and with a primary reputation as a California author, Atherton at 75 wrote a candid memoir, Adventures of a Novelist, and climaxed her career with two novels depicting the fortunes of her aspiring new woman in postwar San Francisco (The House of Lee, 1940; The Horn of Life, 1942) and with two reminiscing biographies of her birth city's environs and personalities. She died in 1948.

Out of the contradictions of her personality and her ambition to be an authentic historian of her times, Atherton produced thirty-four novels, seven short fiction and short-story collections, six history-based books and essays, and many newspaper and magazine articles on feminism, politics, war, and other popular issues. Her California novels such as *The Californians* (1898), *Ancestors* (1907), and *Perch of the Devil* (1914) offer credible analysis of the problems of love and marital relationships and the fear of and restrictions on the full development of women and men because of traditional social roles. With a style both romantic and realistic, Atherton illuminated tensions for women in an expanding society. Scorning William Dean Howells's thin realism and formulaic writing, she was influenced by her contemporaries, Mary Wilkins * Freeman, Edith * Wharton, Ellen * Glasgow, and Willa * Cather as well as by Twain, Bierce, and Harte. Recent critical attention acknowledges her fictional analysis of psychosocial factors in the lives of women and men in an urban civilization.

- Kevin Starr, "Gertrude Atherton: Daughter of the Elite," in *Americans and the California Dream, 1850–1915* (1973), pp. 345–364. Charlotte S. McClure, "Gertrude Atherton (1857–1948): A Checklist of the Writings of and about Gertrude Atherton," *American Literary Realism* 9 (1976): 95–162. Charlotte S. McClure, *Gertrude Atherton*, Western Writers Series (1976). Charlotte S. McClure, *Gertrude Atherton* (1979). Emily Leider, *California's Daughter: Gertrude Atherton and Her Times* (1991).

Charlotte S. McClure

AUSTIN, Mary Hunter (1868–1934), nature writer, poet, novelist, short-story writer, dramatist, and journalist. She published more than thirty books and hundreds of articles and stories centering on her interests in nature, the environment, and the American West and its inhabitants, principally the Indians of the West and the Southwest. The daughter of George Hunter, an English immigrant to Illinois, and Susanna Savilla Graham Hunter, whose ancestors had been among the earliest settlers of Carlinville, Illinois, where Mary was born, she grew up in a household diminished by the untimely deaths of her father and sister in 1878. Her mother's early support of Frances Willard and the Women's Christian Temperance Union (WCTU) exposed her to * feminism at an early age. She graduated from Blackburn College in 1888, setting out later in the year to homestead with her family in the southern Joaquin Valley of California. On the journey from Los Angeles to the homestead, she wrote *One Hundred Miles on Horseback* (1889; 1963). The *Overland Monthly* published her first short story, "The Mother of Felipe," in 1892.

Initially working as a teacher, Mary Hunter began writing before her marriage in 1891 to Stafford Wallace Austin, a failed viticulturist, mining engineer, and school superintendent. Together they moved to the Owens Valley, northwest of Bakersfield, where their retarded daughter, Ruth, was born. The Mojave Desert inspired her to write *The Land of Little Rain* (1903; 1987), a collection of nature essays that was serialized in the *Atlantic Monthly* and that launched her literary career. Ruth died, institutionalized, in 1918; the Austins divorced in 1914.

In the 1900s and 1910s Austin enjoyed a modicum of literary success. Living in the Carmel community and traveling abroad, she wrote realistic short stories about the desert, which are collected in *The Basket Woman* (1904) and *Lost Borders* (1909). Fascinated by the habits of those whose lives were regulated by the rhythms of the land, her prose assumed an oracular, distanced voice in her stories and in nature works such as *The Flock* (1909; 1973), a sustained reflection on sheep and shepherds. In 1910 her play, "The Arrow-Maker," about a female shaman, was produced in New York, while her novel, *A Woman of Genius*, about the life of a Mary Austin alter ego, appeared in 1912 (reprint, 1977). She divided her time between New York City and California until the early 1920s, when she decided to settle in Santa Fe, New Mexico, where she was deeply involved with the rights of American Indians and the preservation of the Hispanic arts. Although she yearned for the reputation of a recognized novelist, writing *Isidro* (1905), *Santa Lucia* (1908), *The Ford* (1917), and her New York feminist novel, *No. 26 Jayne Street* (1920), her reputation resides in her nature works, including *Land of Journey's Ending* (1923; 1983); her final novel, set in New Mexico, *Starry Adventure* (1931), may be her most important fiction, although it is little known. She completed her * autobiography, *Earth Horizon* (1932; 1991), shortly before her death.

- Papers (letters, manuscripts, and photographs) reside in the Mary Austin Collection, Huntington Library, San Marino, California. See also T. M. Pearce, *Mary Austin* (1965). Augusta Fink, *I—Mary: A Biography of Mary Austin* (1983). David Wyatt, "Mary Austin:Nature and Nurturance" in *The Fall into Eden* (1986). Lois Rudnick, "Re-Naming the Land: Anglo Expatriate Women in the Southwest," in *The Desert Is No Lady,* eds. Vera Norwood and Janice Monk (1987). Esther Lanigan Stineman, *Mary Austin: Song of a Maverick* (1989).

Esther F. Lanigan

AUTHORSHIP. For more than two centuries "authorship" has been conceived by American readers in Romantic terms—that is, as the creation, by a stable and individual consciousness, of an original idea or literary work. Over the last three decades, however, developments in both literary theory and the historical study of literature and culture have exposed the limits of this conception. These developments are of special concern to scholars interested in women writers and women's writing in the United States, for, to challenge the Romantic conception of authorship is also to challenge the gender assumptions built historically into the Romantic ethos itself, in which the elements of authorship—creation, stability, and individuality—were seen as specifically male qualities defined in contradistinction to corresponding female qualities of reception or procreation, emotion, and self-effacement. Although challenges to this conception have not produced a new dominant paradigm of authorship, they have brought forth new debates that have helped scholars redefine the status of American women writers and their writing in earlier periods—especially the nineteenth century. What follows is a description of two general positions in the most contested and vexing of these debates—that between feminist scholars and poststructuralist literary theorists over the material status of the author—and an outline of new directions in the study of women's writing currently preparing the practical grounds from which a post-Romantic conception of authorship might emerge.

Death and Resurrection. Over the past three decades, post-structuralists have attacked the stability and individuality of the Romantic author, arguing that the origin of literary texts—and even what we call consciousness—is ultimately never discoverable, but rather only traceable in a constantly shifting field of language. The most well-known of these attacks was made in 1967 by Roland Barthes in an essay pronouncing the "death of the author," and the precession of the infinite possibility of "writing," defined as "that oblique space . . . where all identity is lost, starting with the identity of the body writing." In this view, what speaks to us in a literary work is not the voice of a unique and creative consciousness, but the cumulative effect of a multitude of past voices, which present readers, in a cocreative capacity, continually recombine in an infinite variety of harmonic and dissonant chords.

Still, not all post-structuralists shared Barthes's conception. In 1969, cultural anthropologist Michel Foucault delivered a response to Barthes's essay in an address whose title—"What Is an Author?"—implied the author's resurrection. Accepting Barthes's claim for the

death of the Romantic author, Foucault insisted on the practical and theoretical necessity of continuing the study of the authorship on broader historical grounds. The "author" had lived, and would continue to live, he argued, as a construction or "function" of written texts indicating an unlocatable origin outside texts; however, while earlier studies of authorship had identified this origin with a unique and creative consciousness, studies which recognized the "death of the author" would focus on the historical conditions and modes of discourse that have enabled or disabled this very process of identification.

Feminist Critique. If some feminists were tempted to welcome Barthes's radical critique, which in its wholesale leveling of all subjectivities seemed to place the male-identified Romantic concept of authorship in serious question, many others argued that Barthes had gone too far. Foreclosing discussion of all writing "identities" during a period in which a reinvigorated feminism and new women's studies programs were beginning to bring the identities of women writers eclipsed by a male canon back into view, Barthes seemed to have only displaced the Romantic principle of male transcendental creativity with an equally oppressive, if neutral, transcendental anonymity of text. Indeed, for many of these scholars, Foucault's ostensible differences with Barthes made no difference. If one of the chief goals of feminist literary and historical scholarship was to recover the thoughts, desires, and experiences of women through evidence of their writings, for them Foucault's poststructuralist premise—that no one "originating" consciousness could be located beyond any text—seemed just as hostile to the feminist project as ever; worse still, the flippant concluding remark of his address, "What matter who's speaking?" seemed to imply that finally the material differences between male and female experiences of writing did not matter anyway.

But even as some feminists were resisting post-structuralist attempts to undermine the position of the Romantic author before female figures had the opportunity to occupy it, others saw the dangers of arguing for a position that had emerged within and in terms of a patriarchal tradition. If such an authorial position claimed for women the same voice as men, did it not also deny myriad historical differences in men's and women's relation to institutions which had given women's voices a character distinct from men's? Would a female conception of authorship differ from a male conception only in the sex of the author, claiming, along with the creative faculty of the Romantic author, the uniqueness that might underpin her claim to individuality but simultaneously deny her any relation to a community of writers and readers? Not all feminists wished to borrow the pretense of the self-centered Romantic author's "independence": if no one need be spoken to, and no one need listen, indeed, "what matter who's speaking?"

Unfazed by postmodern parlance, those feminists who had long studied literature in historical contexts saw that Foucault had only made theoretical virtue of practical necessity: all he had declared impossible was the pure transcendence of voice that would make anything like literary-historical recovery unnecessary. In fact, once the stable self-presence of Romantic authorship was revealed as an illusion, the only author remaining viable in Foucault's conception was a decentered and unstable figure that depended for its existence on a variety of historical forces—social, legal, economic, cultural—ultimately beyond the writer's control. It is in this sense that Nancy K. Miller has suggested that claims for the "death of the author" did not apply to the study of women writers, for Foucault's author, in old Romantic terms, was already "female."

Authorship and Recognition. Since the 1970s, scholars of women's writing in the United States have begun to demonstrate what Foucault and others only theorized by building new historical frameworks in which "authorship" is seen as the result not only of a writer's original creation, but of the cultural recognition of that creation in her own time and in ours. In effect, by broadening the focus of author-study to include the conditions enabling or disabling the conversion of certain women writers into "authors," these scholars are not only describing but participating in a process of recognition that means not "death" but rebirth for women writers whose status has fallen outside the bounds defined by the male or "independent" creative Romantic mold.

One of the major goals of this new approach has been to reconstruct the material and ideological conditions informing women's reading and writing during the nineteenth century, when the rise of the publishing industry elevated writing from avocation to profession. As Nina Baym, Mary Kelley, and Susan Coultrap-McQuin have shown, during this period authorship offered many women not only a gainful income, but also an opportunity to move from the bounds of a socially and legally prescribed private or domestic sphere onto the public stage of print. Recovering the assumptions of reading communities to which the most successful women writers spoke, these critics have reestablished terms for the recognition of female voices the Romantic literary ethos once dismissed as merely "popular."

Other critics such as Cheryl Walker, Sandra Gilbert, and Susan Gubar have focused more closely on the costs of such recognition by a patriarchal literary tradition. Reminding us that the predominantly male publishers of nineteenth-century literature produced work reflecting women's experiences as authorized by patriarchy rather than women's experiences "as such," these critics have set out to recover ironic modes common to women's writing in the nineteenth century in which the authorized voice of selfless acceptance gives way to subtexts registering authentic, if not authorial, anxiety, desire, and frustration.

Since the early 1980s, the fastest-growing area in studies of women's authorship has been autobiography, in which scholars have set out to question the critical assumptions that have made autobiography an almost exclusively male genre. Expanding the archive of women's autobiographical writing to include letters, diaries, scrapbooks, and other unpublished or "private" documents, this scholarship has discovered not a female equivalent of the traditionally centered, exemplary male autobiographical subject, but a subject whose sense of individuality is fundamentally communal.

The woman author was never dead, but she is only now being recognized as a key to the reconception of authorship. Far from simply reclaiming a Romantic conception of authorship or exchanging women's authorial position for an equally oppressive "abstract indeterminacy," studies in the wake of this reconception now offer scholars of women's writing a critical site where the results of research in the history of the book and of the publishing industry in the United States, gender politics, and new theories of the self and subjectivity may be effectively combined.

• Roland Barthes, "The Death of the Author," in *Image—Music—Text*, ed. and trans. Stephen Heath (1977) pp. 142–148. Michel Foucault, "What Is an Author?" in *Textual Strategies: Perspectives in Post-Structuralist Criticism*, ed. Josue V. Harari (1979), pp. 139–148. Sandra M. Gilbert and Susan Gubar, *The Madwoman in the Attic: The Woman Writer and the Nineteenth-Century Literary Imagination* (1979). Estelle C. Jelinek, ed., *Women's Autobiography: Essays in Criticism* (1980). Mary Kelley, *Private Woman, Public Stage: Literary Domesticity in Nineteenth-Century America* (1984). Nancy K. Miller, "Changing the Subject: Authorship, Writing and the Reader," in *Feminist Studies/Critical Studies*, ed. Teresa de Lauretis (1986), pp. 102–120. Bella Brodzki and Celeste Schenk, eds., *Life/Lines: Theorizing Women's Autobiography* (1988). Cheryl Walker, "Feminist Literary Criticism and the Author," *Critical Inquiry* 16 (Spring 1990): 551–571. Susan Coultrap-

McQuin, *Doing Literary Business: American Women Writers in the Nineteenth Century* (1990). Nina Baym, *Women's Fiction: A Guide to Novels by and about Women in America, 1820–1870*, 2d ed. (1993).

Timothy H. Scherman

AUTOBIOGRAPHY. Assuming her experiential history as referential base and point of departure, an autobiographer represents her life story in order to share it with others. Her "experience" and the "memory" through which it is routed are already interpreted phenomena and thus at least once removed from any pure facticity. After all, autobiographers sometimes take liberty with that most elementary fact, the date of birth, choosing for themselves a more propitious moment or purposefully confusing the date. And memory is selective and untrustworthy. What truth we come to know in reading autobiography derives not from the *facts* of a life truly remembered, though they may be of interest if we can find them, but from the *meanings* the autobiographer assigns to and extracts from the representation of her life. She is reading meaningful reality into her life and we are reading her reading. Because of the interpretive nature of any autobiographical act, then, the distinction between autobiographical narrative and fiction remains elusive. Autobiography is always an intricate web of historical facts and fiction.

The meanings the autobiographer reads into her life are historically and culturally contingent. Telling her story, she negotiates, sometimes with little, sometimes with discerning self-consciousness, the subjectivity culturally provided to her, the discourses of *identity circulating around her, and the narrative frames commonly used to tell stories. The identities and frames provided by the dominant culture establish what goes into the text, as part of an intelligible and official story, and what remains outside, as unintelligible and unofficial excess—a kind of noise troubling conventional meanings. In effect, then, she is reading her life through her readings of other life stories.

But discourses within the dominant culture are multiple, their calls to normative subjectivity often contradictory, their effects on a specific autobiographical subject unpredictable. And each specific autobiographical subject speaks not from a single location within the community but simultaneously, from multiple locations determined by *gender, *race, *class, *nationality, *ethnicity, *religion, and *sexuality among other markers of identity. Moreover nondominant communities conserve their own alternative discourses of identity and modes of *storytelling. They too circulate heterogeneous calls to subjectivity. Given this multiplicity of the "real," the autobiographical subject does not necessarily imitate prevailing cultural scripts in passive conformity. (And in fact, an imitation by a marginalized subject creates its own kind of noise in the system.) From her specific location within a complex experiential history she may quietly contest, critically adjust, or actively resist normative autobiographical meanings. The impact of her autobiographical mediation depends on the narrative adjustments she makes as she pursues her narrative act, her audience, the models available to her, her social context and historical circumstances. These theoretical remarks, then, preface the history of women's participation in autobiographical acts in America.

The history of "America" and the history of autobiographical practices are intimately connected. Autobiographical writing emerges as a compelling cultural activity in the West at approximately the same historical moment that European colonists and enslaved Africans began settling into the space described as "the New World." This New World, laid out in all its abundance before the colonists, invited ever-new opportunities for recreating self and community. America called for autobiographical subjects. Of course, the earliest first-person narratives were accounts of travel and travail through which male Europeans mapped their encounters with and projections of new geographies, new peoples, new experiences, and new identities. Adventure narratives thus became one potent medium through which the "feminized" land and peoples were domesticated, through which colonization could be turned into the founding *myth of America.

In the Puritan colonies, self-scrutiny saturated the environment as what Daniel B. Shea calls the "ur-narrative of God's saving activity in time," a salvation history at once personal and communal, justified and sustained the beleaguered community ("The Prehistory of American Autobiography," in John Paul Eakin, *American Autobiography*, 1991). In these close communities, soul searching and community building coincided. Individual lives affirmed and secured communal norms; those norms organized the spiritual lives of individuals, including the lives of women, for whom *marriage was an economic necessity and public anonymity the mark of God-given *femininity.

Despite the feminine subjectivity assigned to them in this old world of gender relations, women left accounts of their lives. Autobiographical forms—the poetry of Anne *Bradstreet, the *captivity narrative of Mary *Rowlandson (1682), the *diaries of Sarah Kemble

*Knight (1704–1705) and Elizabeth House Trist (1783–1784), the journal of Esther Edwards Burr (1754–1757), the spiritual testimonies of Quakers Jane Hoskens (1771) and Elizabeth *Ashbridge (1774)—provided ready and intimate vehicles through which colonial women simultaneously heeded the cultural call to feminine subjectivity and negotiated their personal and often eccentric response to unsettling experiences. These are the autobiographical inscriptions of women undomesticated, if only temporarily, by captivity, by travel, or by ministry. Traversing new, often hostile, assuredly fluid environments, these undomesticated I's end up disputing communal constructions of femininity. Disputatious subjects, they adventure through a frontier of their own, reinventing femininity.

By the late eighteenth century, heterogeneous autobiographical forms circulated through the vast space of what was becoming a new republic. These included *conversion narratives, spiritual journals, adventure narratives, travel diaries, captivity narratives, sea adventures, gallows narratives (or criminal confessions), and *slave narratives—all of which contributed powerful cultural myths and communal models of identity to a colony becoming a nation with its own incipient identity. The most influential of these personal narratives was The Autobiography of Benjamin Franklin begun in the 1770s, but not published as a complete work until 1868. Through his adroit manipulation of the rhetoric of self-fashioning, Franklin creates an exemplary type of American subject: the self-made man, bourgeois, optimistic, flagrantly individualistic, and decidedly masculine. The legacy of his model American continued throughout the nineteenth century. But another autobiographical mode emerged, influenced by Romanticism and Transcendentalism that celebrates an intensified, sometimes secularized, antinomianism in which the autobiographical I as creator of the world defies all provided frames and selves. In either mode, the autobiographical subject assumes its participation in the making of an American history.

Not everyone in the nineteenth century, however, had equal access to the official status of the new republican subject or assumed equal access to the making of autobiography and, with autobiography, the making of history. The republican subject remained normatively white, male, and bourgeois even in its rebellions. Its exclusions were manifold and manifest: bourgeois white women, Native Americans, slaves, ex-slaves, Mexican Americans, recent immigrants, and members of the working class. When such marginalized subjects turned to autobiographical writing, then, they brought to the official stories unofficial and eccentric histories.

The *cult of true womanhood emerged as the prevailing ideology affecting white bourgeois women during the nineteenth century. Properly feminine forms of autobiographical writing were assigned to the true woman: *letters, *diaries, *journals. These sheltered scribblings were intimate, personal, and colloquial. They focused on the quotidian and were circulated within a private circuit of exchange rather than the marketplace. Certain bourgeois women, however, publicized their "lives": Lydia *Sigourney in Letters of Life (1866), Elizabeth Cady *Stanton in Eighty Years and More: Reminiscences, 1815–1897 (1898), Lucy Larcom in A New England Girlhood: Outlined from Memory (1889), Julia Ward *Howe in Reminiscences 1819–1899 (1899), and Jane Addams in Twenty Years at Hull House (1910). Not entirely domesticated, these women were publicly active and vocal. But their narratives testify to the cultural pressures of official bourgeois femininity. In each narrative, the autobiographical subject has to constitute femininity as well as republican subjectivity and to construct it in such a fashion as to legitimize the claim to narrative authority.

Nineteenth-century narratives of *African-American, *Native American, and Mexican-American women raise other complex issues. While the majority of slave narratives were written by men, several important narratives by women have survived, including Harriet *Jacobs's Incidents in the Life of a Slave Girl (1863). Jacobs addresses her narrative to Northern women, those "true women" to whom she appeals for support as a "sister" in bondage and for social action. But her revelation of the unspeakable history of her *body introduces a narrative threatening to true womanhood. In telling her story, Jacobs challenges the ideological grounds of multiple narrative frames, from the sentimental novel to *domestic fiction, that create the true woman as the free, white, bourgeois woman. Instead, she insinuates an alternative notion of the true woman, one informed by the material history of *slavery. The postbellum narratives of Elizabeth Keckley, Behind the Scenes; or, Thirty Years a Slave, and Four Years in the White House (1868), and Anna Julia *Cooper, A Voice from the South (1892), shift the emphasis away from the horrors of slavery and the moral dilemma of the black woman's sexual concubinage, to the representation of the black woman as an independent self-supporting member of an emerging black bourgeoisie desirous of participating in the Franklinian myth. Autobiographical narrative becomes a means to affirm the subject's identification with the mainstream values of American life.

Although there were indigenous forms of *oral and pictographic personal narratives in Native American cultures (Hertha Wong, *Sending My Heart Back across the Years*, 1992), only after contact with white Americans did written autobiography by Native American women emerge. Thus whether written solely by a literate Native American or through *collaboration with a white amanuensis/editor, the autobiographical act is bicultural. The narrator constitutes herself as an autobiographical subject not as an autonomous individual but through what Arnold Krupat calls a synecdochic sense of self "where narration of personal history is more nearly marked by the individual's sense of himself in relation to collective social units or groupings" ("Native American Autobiography and the Synecdochic Self," in John Paul Eakin, *American Autobiography*, 1991). This communal identification is signaled in the titles of such narratives as Catherine Brown's *Memoirs of Catherine Brown, a Christian Indian of the Cherokee Nation* (1824) and Sarah *Winnemucca Hopkins's *Life among the Paiutes: Their Wrongs and Claims* (1883). Yet the narrator weaves this alternative notion of subjectivity through narrative patterns influenced by those culturally current in the dominant culture. Brown is influenced by Christian conversion narratives; Winnemucca may be influenced as much by protest narratives as by traditional coup tales that establish communal stature (David Brumble, *American Indian Autobiography*, 1988). In both cultural contexts they engage ideologies of gender that differentiate the narrative spheres of men and women.

The personal testimonies of nineteenth-century Mexican-American women are only now being recovered from various archives, the primary one being the archive of Hubert H. Bancroft, a historian who collected over one hundred personal narratives (most in oral history form) of native Californios in the 1870s. Forty of these histories are women's personal narratives, which, according to Genaro M. Padilla, reveal common preoccupations: the affirmation of a distinct cultural heritage and a way of life forever changed by the anglicization of California; the recording of the personal experiences of cultural disruption; the braiding of domestic and social histories. But Padilla also notes that these women variously reflect upon and critique the gender arrangements deployed in the community and affirm their ability to find forms of empowerment within the constraints of a patriarchal society ("The Recovery of Chicano Nineteenth-Century Autobiography," *American Quarterly* 40, 1988).

Many autobiographical narratives of culturally eccentric subjects emerged through collaborative ventures. Often the narratives had to be authenticated by white patrons/editors who testified to their veracity and thereby legitimated the "life." In other cases, the autobiographical occasion became entirely collaborative. White editors, whether amateur political activists or (later) professional anthropologists, collected the narrative, framed it, organized it, and in the process conformed both narrative mode and autobiographical subject to their ideological agenda. Nonetheless, autobiographical acts, even if collaborative, also became a medium of cultural critique and resistance. Women like Harriet Jacobs implicitly challenged the exclusionary bases upon which cultural notions of white feminine identity rest, bases implicating racial, ethnic, and class identifications. In the process these subjects reproduced different forms of femininity. They thereby undermined the naturalness of sexual and racial differences. And they simultaneously affirmed and troubled the meaning of American lives, turning their own specific lens upon the process of forced Americanization.

By the early decades of the twentieth century great masses swelled the populations of urban centers, including large numbers of immigrants who established ethnic communities in America's cities. Like African Americans, Native Americans, and Mexican Americans, these immigrants and their children struggled with hyphenated identities and the different histories determinative of those identities. Thus each group of immigrants and each generation of ethnic Americans confronted the dynamic tension between assimilation to a normative American identity that degraded cultural differences and the immigrant's allegiance to the culture of origin with its indigenous traditions. Autobiographies of immigrant and ethnic women reveal how these tensions are exacerbated by multiple gender histories. Gender arrangements line up differently in different cultural contexts, their effects on women influenced by generational position, class status, ethnic group, and racial identification. Autobiographers negotiate competing histories of normative femininity and, in those negotiations, make gender adjustments. The destabilizing possibilities of adjustments to and in a new land, to and in a multicultural identity, are evident in the succession of names Mary *Antin adopts in her autobiography, *The Promised Land* (1915), as well as in the undoing and reinvention of identity in Lillian Wald's *The House on Henry Street* (1915), Anzia *Yezierska's *Children of Loneliness* (1923), Jade Snow *Wong's *Fifth Chinese Daughter* (1945), and Monica Sone's *Nisei Daughter* (1953).

The first half of the twentieth century brought radical changes in American life: the macrocosmic and microcosmic revolutions in physics and psychology, exposure to impersonal warfare, transformative technologies, women's suffrage, immigration and migration, the Depression, unionization, the emergence of the United States as a world power, the beginning of modern consumer culture. Increasing numbers of women assumed public roles—as artists, intellectuals, teachers, revolutionaries, social activists—and many wrote autobiographies. The 1930s and early 1940s alone produced a heterogeneous array of autobiographical works: Emma *Goldman's *Living My Life* (1931), Frank Linderman's collaborative life history of Pretty Shield, *Red Mother* (1931), Ida B. *Wells's *Crusade for Justice: The Autobiography of Ida B. Wells* ([1928–34] 1970); Gertrude *Stein's *The Autobiography of Alice B. Toklas* (1933), Charlotte Perkins *Gilman's *The Living of Charlotte Perkins Gilman* (1935), Ruth Underhill's *Autobiography of a Papago Woman* (1936), Zora Neale *Hurston's *Dust Tracks on a Road* (1942). Radically different as are the personal histories and the narrative strategies, each of these texts challenges the mainstream ideology of bourgeois femininity.

Modernist writers such as Stein looked critically at autobiography both as an old father's tale that inscribed patriarchal relationships and as an elastic medium through which to resist that master narrative of identity. In *The Autobiography* she both camouflages and reveals a culturally transgressive lesbian coupling that splits the autobiographical subject in "two" rather than situating it in the singular *I*. Zora Neale Hurston turns the laborious task of writing autobiography for an interested white audience into a disappearing act. Refusing to be fixed in specific identity content, such as "Negro" or "woman," or in the chronological time of history, she becomes so elusive that she almost disappears altogether from the text, except as the voice of ethnographer, artist, and cultural necromancer, playfully and yet seriously specifying.

Political activists such as Goldman, Gilman, and Wells understood that a phantom shadowed their autobiographical act, the public construction of "Red Emma" and "Charlotte Perkins Gilman" and "Ida B. Wells." Goldman and Gilman were notorious because they flagrantly violated bourgeois norms of feminine behavior and criticized that founding institution of bourgeois society, the bourgeois *family. Wells was notorious for her aggressive crusade against lynching. The autobiographical act as they conduct it becomes a means to reaffirm the legitimacy of their public *activism and to ameliorate the negative characterizations of the public persona. Significantly, all three affirm the inextricable link between subjectivity and history, between personal identity and social, intellectual, political, and economic events. The reconstruction of the autobiographical subject becomes a reconstruction of women's history as undomesticated history.

The narratives of Pretty Shield and Maria Chona belong to the continuing tradition of collaborative narratives through which the lives of Native American women "go public." As Hertha Wong points out, collaboration is not a one-way act of appropriation but rather an act of transculturation in which influence moves in two directions, creating a frontier of narrative *(Sending My Heart)*. Pretty Shield and Maria Chona narrate stories that take women as central actors within their community and that rewrite communal history through a woman's perspective. They push back against the constraints imposed by the editor's questions and expectations. In this way, both the white editor and Native American subject make narrative adjustments.

In the last half of the twentieth century, the *civil rights and feminist movements have influenced contemporary autobiographical practices. Ever malleable and adjustable, autobiography has continued to provide a vehicle through which women may chart the relationship between consciousness, history, identity, and the body. The strands of contemporary autobiographical practice are multiple. There are, of course, vast numbers of popular narratives in which women who have achieved public recognition tell their stories. These are model "lives" that sustain the liberal dream of America. Then there are those autobiographical works that chart the emergence of various kinds of feminist consciousness. In a culture that represses female sexuality, devalues the contributions of women, and contains women and their sexuality through the discourses of bourgeois femininity, autobiographical acts become occasions for self-recovery of the body, for the body, and by the body. In such works, the autobiographer attempts to uncover, recover, and discover what she calls her "true" self, a self overwritten by a false consciousness imposed by patriarchal institutions. In the process she emphasizes the representative nature of her personal confession, affirming her identification with all women as women.

If works in the 1970s, such as Kate *Millett's *Sita* (1977), followed the dictum that the personal is political and celebrated the expression of intimate details of female desire, works of the 1980s and 1990s use autobiographical occasions to critique any essentialist notion of woman, to historicize the cultural construction of the body and desire, to theorize the dynamics of the social construction of gender, race, and class, and to personalize the political. Thus the number of autobiographical works by women from indigenously colonized groups has proliferated. Through autobiographical acts, women become not merely subject to the dominant history of America, but history-making subjects who rewrite their relationship to the history of this country, including its history of multiple oppressions. Through various textual strategies Maxine Hong * Kingston (*The Woman Warrior*, 1977), Leslie Marmon * Silko (*Storyteller*, 1981), Cherríe * Moraga (*Loving in the War Years*, 1983), Audre * Lorde (*Zami*, 1983), Adrienne * Rich (in such works as *Of Woman Born*, 1976, and *On Lies, Secrets, and Silence*, 1979), Minnie Bruce Pratt (in her essay in *Yours in Struggle: Three Feminist Perspectives on Anti-Semitism and Racism*, 1984), and Gloria * Anzaldúa (*Borderlands/La Frontera*, 1987) map the cultural terrain of multicultural subjects through an exploration of multiple discourses of identity.

Contemporary autobiographical writers challenge the hegemony of any stable notion of an autobiographical subject, that master narrative of the white, male, Western subject secured by stable gender, race, and class identifications, and explore instead the ways in which the autobiographical subject is multiply situated; as such this subject negotiates heterogeneous discourses of identity, sometimes congruent, contradictory, and confused. This postmodern autobiographical subject undermines the very ideology and discourse of traditional autobiography as a master narrative of American identity and as a form that conforms white women and people of color to oppressive individualistic norms of identity and to a compulsory heterosexuality. Contemporary autobiographers also explore multicultural histories that generate alternative notions of subjectivity to normative individualism, such as "the new mestiza" of Anzaldúa's *Borderlands/La Frontera*. In fact, in the 1990s the borderland becomes a new metaphor for multicultural subjects situated at the intersections of multiple identities, an intersection where balancing takes priority over crossing from one side to the other.

Contemporary autobiographical practices generate hybrid forms for hybrid subjects. Autobiographical texts combine many and diverse forms: poetry, essay, photograph, dream, or vision. Fragmented, these multiforms crack the notion of a coherent, unified autobiographical subject, the meaning of whose "life" can be contained in progressive chronology. Body, imagination, intellectual analysis, memory, cultural discourses including media and * myth—all

provide different ways of knowing, interpreting, shaping a "life." Then there are a significant number of women who turn out multiple-volume autobiographies, among them Anaïs * Nin, Lillian * Hellman, Maya * Angelou, and Nancy Mairs. In these successive forays into self-fashioning, the autobiographical subject resists any final fixing in a stable history and a stable identity. Other autobiographical acts emphasize the communal construction of identity as autobiography metamorphoses sometimes subtly, sometimes dramatically, into biography, family chronicle, autoethnography, or alternative mythology. Finally, artists explore issues of subjectivity, identity, and the social construction of gender, race, class, ethnicity, and sexuality through various media. The postmodern manifestos Barbara Kruger plasters on billboards, the story quilts of Faith Ringgold, the photographs of Cindy Sherman, the performances of Laurie * Anderson, the comics of Lynda Barry can all be read as autobiographical acts.

Heading into the twenty-first century, America is in turmoil and transition. It is an increasingly multicultural country in a contentiously global environment. The institutions that hold it together seem fragile and inadequate to the task. Its people struggle with the tensions between individual freedoms and communal responsibilities. Its generations stretch further and their relationships fray. * Racism, * homophobia, * sexism, and religious intolerance permeate everyday life. But America has always been a country in the making. And its history is written every time someone tells the story of his or her life. In this fractious, mobile, multicultural environment, autobiographical * storytelling becomes one means of simultaneously communicating differences and affirming the need for community. It also becomes one means of ensuring that all people, including all women, participate in the interpretation of their own and their country's history and thus in the making of its future.

[*See also* Diaries and Journals; Biography; Confessional Nonfiction.]

• William L. Andrews, *To Tell a Free Story: The First Century of Afro-American Autobiography, 1760–1865* (1986). Bella Brodzki and Celeste Schenck, *Life/Lines: Theorizing Women's Autobiography* (1988). David Brumble, *American Indian Autobiography* (1988). Genaro M. Padilla, "The Recovery of Chicano Nineteenth-Century Autobiography," *American Quarterly* 40 (September 1988): 286–306. Joanne M. Braxton, *Black Women Writing Autobiography: A Tradition within a Tradition* (1989). Rita Felski, *Beyond Feminist Aesthetics: Feminist Literature and Social Change* (1989). Françoise Lionnet, *Autobiographical Voices: Race, Gender, Self-Portraiture* (1989). Felicity A. Nussbaum, *The Autobiographical Subject: Gender and Ideology in*

Eighteenth-Century England (1989). Timothy Dow Adams, *Telling Lies in Modern American Autobiography* (1990). William L. Andrews, ed., *Journeys in New Worlds: Early American Women's Narratives* (1990). Paul John Eakin, *American Autobiography: Retrospect and Prospect* (1991). Margo Culley, *Fea[s]ts of Memory: The Autobiographical Writings of American Women* (1992). Sidonie Smith and Julia Watson, *De/Colonizing the Subject: The Politics of Gender in Women's Autobiography* (1992).

Sidonie Smith

AWIAKTA, also Marilou Awiakta (b. 1936), a Cherokee-Appalachian poet. Awiakta was born in Knoxville, Tennessee, of Scotch-Irish and Native American heritage and grew up nearby in Oak Ridge, the city built as the headquarters of the Manhattan Project. This pattern of intertwined influences in her childhood followed her to college at the University of Tennessee, marriage with Paul Thompson, and work as an interpreter for the U.S. Air Force in France. She is a writer for whom the mystery of nuclear fission in the hallowed home of her Cherokee and Scotch-Irish forebears has become an emblem. In her art Awiakta emphasizes her connection to her Cherokee muse of Little Deer, a spirit of reverence, and Selu, Grandmother Corn—the First Woman in the traditional genesis story. She explains that from them she receives the wisdom of seeing with the inner eye, of balancing male and female strengths, and of understanding the unity of all life. Her name *Awiakta*—"the eye of the deer" in Cherokee—acknowledges this source of wisdom.

Awiakta's writing touches on important concerns of modern society: the environment, *gender relations, *abortion, preservation of native cultures, and nuclear energy. Her first work is the collection of poetry, *Abiding Appalachia: Where Mountain and Atom Meet* (1978), which begins with her quest for roots and takes us to her growing awareness of the healing that comes from tapping both the Cherokee-Appalachian heritage and the Western scientific tradition. The poems in *Abiding Appalachia* chronicle the history of her people—the removal of the Cherokee, the coming of the Scotch Irish—as well as trace her personal journey to attain a holistic vision of the disparate worlds that make up her life. The two journeys, communal and personal, follow a spiraling path that leads to healing and reunification in the end. This collection was followed by a second book in 1983, *Rising Fawn and the Fire Mystery: A Story of Heritage, Family, and Courage, 1833*. Her third book, *Selu: Seeking the Corn-Mother's Wisdom*, a collection of "seed-thoughts for the twenty-first century," was published in 1993.

Ruth Yu Hsiao

B

BA-AD WOMAN. This is a two-word phrase in which pronunciation obviously conveys attitude. "Ba-ad woman" is used to denote black women who do not conform to the mores of their communities and can be either positive or negative depending on context. Literary treatment may romanticize the type, as in Gwendolyn *Brooks's "A Song in the Front Yard" (1945): the speaker wants to destroy what the ba-ad woman represents, as the community wants done to the poem's Sula.

In literature, such women appear in Dorothy *West's *The Living Is Easy* (1948), in which Cleo Judson schemes and plots against her husband and uses whatever means necessary to assist her freeloading sisters. Ann *Petry's *The Narrows* (1953) features Mamie Powther, whose blatant *sexuality is just too much for the staid, churchgoing Abbie Crunch. The three whores in Toni *Morrison's *The Bluest Eye* (1970) are other manifestations of the type; they may nurture Pecola, but the churchwomen would never approve of them. A ba-ad woman will sleep with and discard her neighbors' husbands or put her grandmother in an old folks' home, as the title character does in Morrison's *Sula* (1974). She may also plot against her neighbors, as Ruby does in Gloria *Naylor's *Mama Day* (1988) with her plan to kill Cocoa, or she may literally bring about death, as Eva does in Gayl *Jones's *Eva's Man* (1976).

On the healthier, more positive side, such women may be perceived as evil by adults, but may in fact serve a positive role in the lives of children. An example is Suggie Skeete in Paule *Marshall's *Brown Girl, Brownstones* (1959). And such women may simply bask in the *beauty and health of being black; a striking example is Nikki *Giovanni's "Ego-Tripping" (1973), where, after a litany of proud assertions, the speaker ends by claiming that she can fly "like a bird in the sky."

Trudier Harris

BACKLASH. The word *backlash* has a double meaning, depending whether you read it forward or backward. In the context of women's rights, one's reading depends in good measure on *gender. Women tend to read *backlash* forward, men backward. Women experience a backlash against their efforts to achieve equality as if, literally, their backs are being lashed, as a slave feels the whip. For women, the backlash feels like an unfair, unwarranted sneak attack, in which more powerful male figures creep up from behind to administer blows. Because the attack comes from the back, because they are unprepared, unsure of their assailants and overcome by their own perception of defenselessness, many women will react to the backlash by covering their heads and cowering, by appeasing the attacker, by denying their affiliation with the cause of *women's rights, by saying and doing anything, in short, to stop the pain.

Men, on the other hand, especially men who participate directly in working against women's independence, perceive the backlash simply as an effort to defend themselves from forceful female invaders. In the male version of backlash, they were out in the fields minding their own business when women came out with whips. It is the men who have been accosted and, out of self-defense, are lashing back. Men see themselves as the original victims in this drama. (Hence, the sarcastic labeling of *women's studies as "victim studies" by male scholars hostile to the incursion of women on campus. To these men, women's studies is actually triumphal studies, and the defused male *canon is the female scholars' conquest.) As the victorious women run roughshod, the wounded male struggles to his feet, swinging a feeble blow to save his own hide. Or, as more than one man has put it when talk of backlash arises within earshot: "Backlash? What backlash? The only backlash I see is the backlash against *men.*"

Of course, reading the meaning of the backlash against women's rights in either direction is skewed—although authentic enough to the players in either camp. Women see themselves as weaker and less threatening than they really are; men see women as stronger and more encroaching than they are. These clashing perceptions generate the basic paradox that drives backlash. The men who are the most aggressive agents of backlash believe they have the least agency; in fact, it is their loss of standing and authority, their bitter sense of disenfranchisement, that has made them so resentful and avenging. "The politics of despair in America has typically been the politics of backlash," political scientists Seymour Martin Lipset and Earl Raab observe in *The Politics of Unreason: Right-Wing Extremism in America, 1790–1970* (1970). At the same time, women see how little progress they had made before men tried to stifle them—and, as a consequence, they despair and are overwhelmed by a sense of powerlessness. The backlash, in short, serves to transfer men's emotional despair to women. Men who feel vanquished manage to square their shoulders and stand tall by causing women's shoulders to sag with defeat. Men's expression of anger, backed by the threat of * violence, can cause women to swallow their own political anger and convert it to internal and isolating depression.

Understanding this his-and-hers experience is essential to understanding the seemingly mysterious "overreaction" of men in a backlash climate. It explains why men repeatedly and, it would seem, almost ludicrously, complain that "women are taking over" when women barely have their feet in the door. Contemporary male students protest that the curriculum is crammed with "politically correct" feminist studies courses and female professors—at universities that offer only a few women's studies classes and employ so few women that they can be counted on one hand. Male employees complain bitterly of a "feminized" workforce when women's proportions in the office are still absurdly tiny. In the early 1990s, company after company, university after university, had discontinued affirmative action efforts to hire women when women's representation in the higher ranks hit a lowly 20 or 30 percent—or, at one university, less than 10 percent. The last round of American backlash against female independence followed the meager gains of working women during World War II, when the postwar media made much of, in the words of *Look* magazine, "female dominance" in the corporate world. Women are grabbing "authority-wielding executive jobs," this male-edited magazine insisted in 1949, from the depths of the "feminine mystique" era. Or, even more ridiculous in retrospect, Cato declared in 195 B.C., after a few Roman women sought to gain the right to ride in chariots, "Women have become so powerful that our independence has been lost in our own homes and is now being trampled and stamped underfoot in public."

These allegations are not ridiculous to the men who express them; they feel real. To a woman, a woman in a chariot is just a woman in a chariot—and a reminder of how few women own chariots, much less hold the reins. But through the lenses of male glasses, one woman in a chariot becomes an Amazonian army. "Men view even small losses of deference, advantages, or opportunities as large threats," sociologist William Goode wrote in his essay "Why Men Resist" (*Rethinking the Family*, eds. Barrie Thorne with Marilyn Yalom, 1982).

This gender difference in perceiving the backlash grew out of another gender gap—that of changing and challenging assigned sex roles. In the last twenty-five years in particular (and, more subtly, since the 1840s) women have vastly transformed their own vision of their role in society. Modern women's perception of themselves as public actors, individuals deserving of equal opportunity, freedom, and authority in the public sphere, represents a dramatic departure from their designated role as private helpmeets and hearth angels. Women have barreled out of the literal and psychological domestic circle while—and here's the rub—men have stood still. The research available on male attitudes (woefully little, to date) indicates that in the same period in which women were shedding their sex roles like old skins and moving on, men were clutching theirs ever closer. Even as the cloak of socially constructed masculinity has become increasingly outmoded and threadbare—few men in the service-dominated economy can fulfill the "manly" expectation to play the role of sole provider, physical prowess has little application to modern occupations, and the warrior designation has only frightening and lethal implications in today's world—men have been loathe to set it aside, much less press on to find another, better-fitting garment. The perceptual difference between women and men, then, is essentially a problem of motion. Men see the women's movement as moving too fast, while women see the movement's progress as too slow. This is because men are standing still as the movement passes while women are running alongside the parade—maybe not quite as fast as the most radical feminist marchers but waving their flags and cheering nonetheless.

If the struggle for women's rights is ever to transcend repeated bouts of backlash, it must first find a way to bring men along. The opposition to the feminist revolution will continue so long as men refuse to challenge the confinement of their own socially ordained roles. Only when men are unstuck, moving forward, will they begin to view the movement of women as something other than a mob trampling their own stationary status. Only when men and women are marching together—suffrage-style, shoulder to shoulder—will the guarding of fixed "male" territory seem an unnecessary, even unhealthy, holding action—a stalling tactic that serves to block the progress of men's, as well as women's, liberty.

[*See also* Conservatism; Liberal Feminism; Radical Feminism.]

Susan Faludi

BAMBARA, Toni Cade (b. 1939), African-American novelist, short-story writer, essayist. Born to Helen Cade in New York City, Bambara attended various public schools in New York and New Jersey. She received a bachelor's degree from Queens College in 1959, studied in Florence and Paris, and then returned to New York, where she received a master's degree from City College (CCNY) in 1964.

Bambara has been a community activist and an educator as well as a writer, teaching English and Afro-American Studies at CCNY, Livingstone College, and Spelman College. More recently, she has written screenplays and worked in community-centered cultural organizations.

She established her reputation as a short-story writer with *Gorilla, My Love* (1972), which focused primarily on the experiences of black women told in the voices of first-person narrators of various ages, from either the inner city or the rural South. The stories are generally inspirational in that they encourage caring and responsibility within the black * community.

The stories in *The Sea Birds Are Still Alive* (1977) are more diverse and also more ambivalent than those in the first book. The title story, for example, is set in Southeast Asia. Here, the author demonstrates that within the black community there is much more and deeper conflict both over political issues and between men and women than exists in the larger society. The heroic figures in this collection are community activists and women who try to care for the alienated and often violent men in their lives. But these stories lack the confidence that caring and community values make a difference.

The Salt Eaters (1981), her American Book Award–winning first novel, extends this theme. Velma Henry, an activist frustrated over the divisiveness within the black community, has attempted * suicide. With her is Minnie Ransom, a traditional healer who believes that the way to health is through identification with * folk values. The novel's ultimate message is that life is change, that there is no secure, fixed place. Community and self must be constantly recreated.

In addition to these works, Bambara edited *The Black Woman* (1970), a collection of essays and poems concerning the "double jeopardy" of being black and female, and *Tales and Stories for Black Folk* (1971), a collection of both traditional black folklore and revisions of European materials. Toni Cade Bambara has attempted in both her writing and her community activities to create a positive sense of black community without simplifying or ignoring its real problems.

• Mari Evans, ed., *Black Women Writers (1950–1980): A Critical Evaluation* (1984), pp. 41–71. Alice Deck, "Toni Cade Bambara," in *Dictionary of Literary Biography*, vol. 38, eds. Trudier Harris and Thadious Davis (1985), pp. 12–22. Keith Byerman, *Fingering the Jagged Grain: Tradition and Form in Recent Black Fiction* (1986), pp. 105–128.

Keith E. Byerman

BANNON, Ann, is the pseudonym of a lesbian writer now living on the West Coast, where she is an associate dean of a university. She grew up in the Midwest and married immediately after college. At the time she wrote the Beebo Brinker series, she was a housewife and mother.

Bannon's books were originally published in the late 1950s and early 1960s by Gold Medal Books, a division of Fawcett Publishing. As reports attest, the series played an essential part in establishing a sense of lesbian community and identity in America. *Odd Girl Out* (1957) begins the series and details the development of a relationship between two of the main characters, Beth Cullison, an outgoing, vivacious college senior, and Laura Landon, a shy freshman. The novel portrays women who are struggling against the restrictions placed on white middle-class girls of the 1950s as they have illicit lesbian affairs and heterosexual sex without birth control, and try desperately to combat the pressure to fulfill traditional gender roles. *I Am a Woman* (1959) follows Laura to New York where she is introduced to Jack, a gay man; he facilitates her entry into the life of Greenwich Village. Eventually Laura meets Beebo Brinker, a young "butch," and they set up house together. In *Women in the Shadows* (1959) Beebo and Laura's relationship is falling apart. Beebo is brutally assaulted and raped, a scene that, like many others in the series, vividly portrays the abuse suffered by lesbians during this time. Eventually, Laura marries Jack and has a baby by artificial insemination.

Beebo Brinker (1962) tells Beebo's story as she leaves her small, isolated hometown for New York and comes out as a butch lesbian. *Journey to a Woman* (1960) focuses on Beth, who is trapped in an unhappy marriage. In describing how she leaves her husband and children, the book dramatizes the difficult choices lesbians face while at the same time asserting the legitimacy of Beth's decision to leave her family. Beth seeks out Laura and, in the end, gets together with Beebo.

After being reissued once in the 1970s by

Arno/New York Times Press, Bannon's novels were reprinted by the Naiad Press, a lesbian publishing company, in the early 1980s. While some have faulted the series for what they feel are negative images of lesbians, recent critiques of Bannon's writing have demonstrated the ways in which her novels challenge normative sexual and *gender identities and present visions of "queer" families, butch/femme sensibility, and *sexuality, and have praised them for their honest portrayals of lesbian life as it was before the Stonewall incident precipitated the "coming out" revolution of the late twentieth century.

• Roberta Yusba, "Odd Girls and Strange Sisters: Lesbian Pulp Novels of the '50s," *Out/Look* 12 (Spring 1991): 34–37.

Katie Kent

BARD, Anne Elizabeth Campbell. *See* MacDonald, Betty.

BARNES, Djuna (occasional pseudonym Lydia Steptoe; 1892–1982), novelist, poet, playwright, journalist, satirist, artist, and author of short stories. Born in Cornwall-on-Hudson, New York, to Wald and Elizabeth Chappell Barnes, she spent most of her childhood on a Long Island farm, where she grew up in a polygamous household. She received almost no formal schooling. Educated at home by her father and his mother, Zadel Gustafson, Barnes learned to play musical instruments and was exposed to a range of literary styles and to her grandmother's *feminism and mysticism. After escaping an arranged marriage (1909), she moved to New York City (1912) and began a career in journalism and creative writing. In 1915, fellow Greenwich Village resident Guido Bruno published a chapbook of her poems, *The Book of Repulsive Women* (reprinted 1989). The Provincetown Players performed three of her plays in the 1919–1920 season. With the publication of *A Book* (1923), the first broad collection of her poems, stories, plays, and drawings, she became a well-known and respected writer.

Barnes spent the 1920s among expatriates in Europe. She bought an apartment in Paris that she shared for several years with her lover, the American artist Thelma Wood, on whom she modeled the character Robin Vote in her best-known novel, *Nightwood* (1936). While in Europe, she wrote *Ryder* (1928) and *Ladies Almanack* (1928). The latter, a comic satire and celebration of Natalie *Barney's lesbian circle, was privately published and distributed. *Ryder* appeared in expurgated form with a foreword in which Barnes attacked censorship for its mutilation of art. Like the work of her friend James Joyce, her books offended conventional middle-class audiences by their explicit, often bawdy,

treatment of sexual desire and their graphic description of bodily functions.

After returning to New York, she wrote for *Theatre Guild Magazine* from 1929 to 1931. She spent the 1930s in England, North Africa, and France. By the 1940s she resided at Patchin Place, Greenwich Village, which remained her home until her death in 1982. In her later years, Barnes was a recluse; she suffered from asthma and chronic pain and wrote poetry, very little of which has been published. Her last major publication, the verse play *The Antiphon* (1958), examines the theme of *family and the genre of tragedy. This play displaces significant struggle from its conventional sites in contests between men, or between men and women, to focus on the clash between a *mother's and daughter's conflicting claims to knowledge, worth, and creative power.

• The Barnes papers reside at the University of Maryland. See also Douglas Messerli, *Djuna Barnes: A Bibliography* (1975). Louis F. Kannenstine, *The Art of Djuna Barnes* (1977). Andrew Field, *Djuna: The Life and Times of Djuna Barnes* (1983). Mary Lynn Broe, ed., *Silence and Power: A Reevaluation of Djuna Barnes* (1991).

Margaret Bockting

BARNETT, Ida B. Wells. *See* Wells-Barnett, Ida B.

BEACH, Sylvia (1887–1962), publisher, translator, and bookshop owner. Beach was born in a parsonage in Baltimore, Maryland, the daughter and granddaughter of Presbyterian ministers. Though chronic health problems as a child prevented Beach from being formally educated, she devoured a range of authors in private reading and study. Beach's early eclectic taste in literature may account in part for her later openness to such experimental writers as James Joyce and T. S. Eliot. According to most sources, the Beaches were close, but their family intimacy was sometimes oppressive, and Sylvia moved to Paris in her late twenties partly to escape it. With her early devotion to books serving as a kind of literary apprenticeship, she established Shakespeare and Company in 1919, the first American lending library and bookshop in Paris. For over two decades, Beach's shop, servicing mainly the expatriate literary community, filled the gap for those seeking English-language texts ranging from *Beowulf* to the avant-garde.

During the decade before Beach's arrival on the literary scene, Paris had become the center of the international artistic *community. Soon her bookshop would become the visible center within that center, frequented by both the famous and soon-to-be-famous, including Ernest Hemingway, Gertrude *Stein, F. Scott Fitzgerald, T. S. Eliot, Ezra Pound, and others. She influenced their reading, provided them with the newest in *experimental literature, and brought them and their works to the attention of one another and the French public. Perhaps of equal importance to her intellectual nurturing, however, was her commitment to meet as best she could their practical needs. To this end, she arranged low-cost accommodations, secured financial backing, and loaned money. She found printers and translators for her writers, circulated their manuscripts to publishers and editors, and even received their mail.

Though some might doubt that she earned a place in literary history through her unfailing support of all those who crossed her threshold, few would deny that her publication of Joyce's originally suppressed *Ulysses* constituted a contribution to modern literature of the first magnitude. Most of her own literary efforts consist of translations of such authors as Eliot, Whitman, and Michaux. Her memoirs, fittingly entitled *Shakespeare and Company* (1959), provide a comprehensive view of those who frequented her shop, some of this century's greatest writers. Long after the expatriate community had returned home, Sylvia Beach died alone in her apartment on the Left Bank at the age of seventy-five.

• The Princeton University Library houses the Sylvia Beach Papers. See also Noel Riley Fitch, *Sylvia Beach and the Lost Generation* (1983). Shari Benstock, *Women of the Left Bank* (1986).

Kelli A. Larson

BEARD, Mary Ritter (1876–1958), suffragist, independent scholar, and historian. Born and reared in comfort in Indianapolis, Indiana, Beard was one of six children of Narcissa Lockwood and Eli Foster Ritter. Her high school's valedictorian, she went on to De Pauw University, where she obtained the Ph.B. (1897) and met Charles Austin Beard, whom she married in 1900. The couple's first two years together were spent in Oxford and Manchester, England, where Mary Beard saw *working-class poverty and formed commitments to cooperative socialism, workers' *education, and the improvement of wage-earning women's lives through the ballot—this last determination influenced by close association with Emmeline Pankhurst.

Returning to New York City in 1901, Mary Beard combined care of her young family (a daughter born in 1901 and a son in 1907) with organizational work for socialism, wage-earning women's unionism, and *woman suffrage. In 1913 Alice Paul and Lucy Burns sought her out for the inner circle of the Congressional Union, a militant *suffrage group that became the National Woman's Party. While an active

suffragist, Beard also completed her first book, a detailed overview of the accomplishments of contemporary women's voluntary associations, called *Women's Work in Municipalities* (1915). She wrote a second book, *A Short History of the American Labor Movement* (1920), for the Workers' Education Bureau that she and her husband helped found.

When Charles Beard resigned his professorship at Columbia University in 1917, the family moved to New Milford, Connecticut. Mary Beard henceforth saw herself as a writer. She became known first through the U.S. history books that she wrote with her husband—especially the much-acclaimed two-volume *Rise of American Civilization* (1927)—and then through her own groundbreaking works. She collaborated with Charles Beard on the sequential historical works, *America in Midpassage* (1937) and *The American Spirit* (1942), as well as on three textbooks—and on all of these he received the lion's share of the credit. At the same time, she also pressed insistently for the recovery of women's past. In rapid succession she brought out *On Understanding Women* (1931), a history of women's participation in constructing Western civilization, and two anthologies of women's documents, *America through Women's Eyes* (1933) and *Laughing Their Way: Women's Humor in America* (1934). Between 1935 and 1940 she headed an ultimately unsuccessful effort to found the World Center for Women's Archives, for the collection and preservation of women's documents; she composed, for the American Association of University Women, a syllabus entitled "A Changing Political Economy as It Affects Women" that was a *women's studies course before its time; and she attempted to revise the *Encyclopedia Britannica* to include women's roles more adequately. Her most ambitious and best-known work, *Woman as Force in History* (1946), like her earlier ones, was laced with acid criticism of male historians' oversights and motivated by her belief in women's creative historical accomplishments. Although she produced two more books, *The Force of Women in Japanese History* (1953) and *The Making of Charles A. Beard* (1955), it was *Woman as Force* that outlived her and inspired a later generation.

• Berenice A. Carroll, "Mary Beard's *Woman as Force in History*: A Critique," *Massachusetts Review* (1972). Ann J. Lane, *Mary Ritter Beard: A Sourcebook* (1977). Barbara K. Turoff, *Mary Beard as Force in History* (1979). Bonnie Smith, "Seeing Mary Beard," *Feminist Studies* 10 (1984). Nancy F. Cott, *A Woman Making History: Mary Ritter Beard through Her Letters* (1991).

Nancy F. Cott

BEATTIE, Ann (b. 1947), short-story writer and novelist. Born in Washington, D.C., Beattie received her B.A. from American University (1969) and her M.A. from the University of Connecticut (1970). Her stories have appeared in *The New Yorker* and other prominent magazines since 1973. In addition to story collections and novels, Beattie has written a critical study of painter Alex Katz (*Alex Katz*, 1987). She has taught at Harvard and the University of Virginia. Beattie is married to painter Lincoln Perry (m. 1988).

From the concurrent publication in 1976 of her first novel (*Chilly Scenes of Winter*) and first story collection (*Distortions*), Beattie's fiction has received reductive appraisals. Critics who hailed her as chief chronicler of the Woodstock generation's anomie a decade later often failed to look past this label to the actual variety of Beattie's characters or the aesthetic, rather than sociological, texture of her work. Others attacked Beattie's fiction for its lack of obvious moral center and its characters' passivity, often mischaracterizing philosophical differences as artistic flaws.

A similar combination of acclaim and controversy met Beattie's novels *Falling in Place* (1980) and *Love Always* (1985), and her story collections *Secrets and Surprises* (1978) and *The Burning House* (1982). Even detractors, however, acknowledged Beattie's increasing skill. She has been consistently championed by chronicler of privileged malaise John Updike, with whom she shares a (chiefly male) literary genealogy from Hemingway and Fitzgerald through Cheever and Salinger. Beattie's fictional mode is also close to those of postmodernist Donald Barthelme and "minimalist" Raymond Carver, making her style difficult to categorize.

Beattie is famous for evoking situations of missed emotional connection with economical but telling particulars; she has an artist's eye for visual detail and a remarkable ear for dialogue. While her flat diction and emotional detachment have been criticized, many readers find Beattie's style all the more emotionally charged for its restraint.

Beattie's most recent publications are *Picturing Will* (1990), arguably her best and most intricately crafted novel to date, and two collections of stories, *Where You'll Find Me and Other Stories* (1986) and *What Was Mine* (1991). Critical notice for these works has been quieter because less politically charged; Beattie has thwarted attempts to reduce her to the voice of her generation. While the later work offers no more major truths nor moral certainties than its predecessors, the surfaces Beattie evokes have grown increasingly resonant, full of emotionally luminous objects like the vase in her story "Janus."

• Pico Iyer, "The World According to Beattie," *Partisan Review* 50, no. 4 (1983): 548–553. Larry McCaffery and Sinda Gregory, "A Conversation with Ann Beattie," *Literary Review* 27 (Winter 1984): 165–177. Carolyn Porter, "Ann Beattie: The Art of the Missing," in *Contemporary American Women Writers: Narrative Strategies*, eds. Catherine Rainwater and William J. Scheick (1985), pp. 9–28. Daniel G. Marowski, ed., *Contemporary Literary Criticism*, vol. 40 (1986). Christina Murphy, *Ann Beattie* (1986).

Martha Stoddard Holmes

BEAUTY. The concept of beauty in American literature has been a vexed one. Beauty has been distrusted because it ostensibly seduces believers away from spiritual matters, as it did for the Puritans, or because beauty represents a patriarchal ploy to keep women focused on individual rather than collective change, or because dominant white standards have been used to judge racial and ethnic others as inferior. Juliet Flower MacCannell and Dean MacCannell identify the feminine beauty system as the institutionalization of the process by which women appear to be committed to making themselves beautiful for men (see "The Beauty System" in *The Ideology of Conduct*, ed. N. Armstrong and L. Tennenhouse, 1987). Recent feminist critics argue that beauty standards are the discipline through which women are kept in check through observation and moral-sexual control, internalizing their subordinate position (see Sandra Bartky, *Femininity and Domination*, 1990; Wendy Chapkis, *Beauty Secrets: Women and the Politics of Appearance*, 1986). American women writers have constructed, enforced, challenged, and revised beauty standards, grappling with problems that range from being prohibited from attraction to natural beauty to being proscribed as the created or "made-up" sex, whose beauty is artificial. Many American women writers have rejected the assumption that it is women's desire to be beautiful by patriarchal standards, choosing to redefine the concept of beauty altogether and refusing the equation whereby traditional beauty equals economic security with men.

Physical beauty was a temptation, not an attainment, to the Puritan church members who established the Massachusetts Bay Colony in the 1630s. The human *body and its corrupt desires were to be denied, not dressed up to please others. Showing interest in personal beautification was akin to publicly confessing one's earthly vanity and possibly relinquishing one's claim to salvation. The Puritans' continuing struggle to wean their affections from this world required them to pursue spiritual—not physical—grace; however, attraction to beauty proved difficult to eradicate, as Anne Bradstreet showed in her "rapt" attention to the beauty of the world in "Contemplations" (1678).

The work of America's first published poet, Bradstreet, often addresses the conflicts between her attachment to worldly things and her desire to renounce them. Bradstreet's dialogue poem, "The Flesh and the Spirit," reveals her own distrust—and her fascination—with physical beauty. Flesh challenges her sister, Spirit, asking, "What liv'st thou on / Nothing but Meditation?" Spirit refuses to argue with her earthbound sister, asserting loftily that she sees rewards that are beyond Flesh's "dull Capacity." Spirit may be alluding to a divinely inspired standard of beauty, but she does not distinguish it clearly from the temporal beauty that Flesh represents. Although Spirit wins the argument, by the end of the poem she has failed to provide an alternative to earthly beauty standards. The good sister imagines her eternal life only as an extension of her temporal life. When she tells Flesh that in heaven no "withering age shall e're come there, / But beauty shall be bright and clear," she unwittingly implies that the difference between salvation and damnation lies not in how beauty is judged, but rather in how long it will last.

Standards of beauty were more often used to make secular decisions, and they became a way to marginalize Native American, African-American, and all other women. When early English settler Mary *Rowlandson wrote the story of her abduction by Narraganset Indians in 1676, she insulted one of her female captors by calling attention to her enemy's beauty regimen: "A severe and proud Dame she was: bestowing every day in dressing herself near as much time as any of the Gentry of the land; powdering her hair and painting her face, going with her Necklaces, with Jewels in her ears, and bracelets upon her hands." By comparing her captor to English gentry, Rowlandson implies not only that the Narraganset woman is vain, but also that her actions are absurd because a woman of color could never attain the ideal of white beauty upheld by the English upper class. The "other" women's artificial beauty is taken as a sign of their barbarism.

The early republic held to the Enlightenment version of the beautiful and the sublime. Boston businesswoman Sarah Kemble *Knight takes a more worldly approach to her natural surroundings in the *diary of her round-trip from Boston to New Haven in 1704. When Knight becomes frightened as she follows her guide through a dark forest, she suddenly reflects that she has neglected her call, or spiritual vocation. However, as soon as she makes it to the top of the hill where the moonlight allows her to see more clearly, she is inspired to "very divirting tho'ts" by the moon's beauty. The late-eighteenth-century author Hannah Webster *Foster presents an argument for beauty and pleasure in The Coquette (1797). If the culture advocated passive virtue as the ultimate beatific state for women, Foster's heroine Eliza *Wharton adopted an active pursuit of her own desires. Also in this vein, Margaret *Fuller addresses female beauty in Woman in the Nineteenth Century, her 1845 treatise advocating equal rights for women. Fuller argues that a woman may "express publicly the fulness of thought and creation, without losing any of the peculiar beauty of her sex." Beauty, for Fuller, need not be gender specific since everyone has both masculine and feminine traits and there are "men of far more beauty than power." She entreats American women to clear their souls "from the taint of vanity" and to focus on developing their minds instead of developing their appearances.

Arguably the most damaging theory of beauty came from Edgar Allan Poe in Poe's notion in "The Philosophy of Composition" (1846). His statement that "the death of a beautiful woman is, unquestionably, the most poetical topic in the world" seems confirmed in many nineteenth-century fictions by women. Nineteenth-century sentimental novelists, as Jane Tompkins and others argue, redefined the coordinates of beauty. Focusing on the internal beauty of influence and matriarchal interests, Harriet Beecher *Stowe—like other writers—inverted the long-established hierarchy of physical and spiritual beauty in her portrayals of Rachel Halliday and Marie St. Clare. Rachel Halliday epitomizes Stowe's ideal of maternal influence, a power that belonged to women who established their influence through the home and family. In Uncle Tom's Cabin, Stowe poses a rhetorical question that a generation of nineteenth-century *domestic novelists answered: "So much has been said and sung of beautiful young girls, why don't somebody wake up to the beauty of old women?" Although beautiful by conventional standards, Marie St. Clare is plagued by overreliance on fashion and on antimatriarchal ideals, as well as by illness. Clarina Howard Nichols, an early women's rights activist, argued in "The Responsibilities of Women" (1851) that she "could not believe that God had created so many homely women, and suffered all to lose their beauty in the very maturity of their powers, and yet made it our duty to spend our best efforts in trying to look pretty." Her rhetoric echoes Stowe's insistence that women be taken off the pedestal and enfranchised to fulfill their duties. The same revision of values is articulated in the fiction of Elizabeth Stuart *Phelps's The Story of Avis,

Louisa May *Alcott's "Behind a Mask" and *Work* (see especially chapter 20, "At Forty"), and Fanny *Fern's *Ruth Hall*. Ruth's mother-in-law laments the passing of her " 'woman's seven beauties' including the 'dimple in the chin.' " The dilemmas for nineteenth-century culture were fashion and its effects on republican, virtuous women and the ethic of sincerity to which "republican motherhood" gave rise.

As American society made the transition into modern industrial work, the cult of domesticity gave women a special responsibility to counteract the hypocrisy of the working women outside the home. As Karen Halttunen suggests, sincerity became so highly valued in the 1830s and 1840s that any appearance of artificiality was shunned. Standards of beauty were adapted to the female role as a perfectly sincere homemaker. *Advice writers disparaged women who painted their faces or succumbed to the extravagant whims of fashion (see Karen Halttunen's *Confidence Men and Painted Women*, 1982, 33–60). "The Fatal Cosmetic," a short story by Caroline Lee *Hentz published in *Godey's Lady's Book* (1839), suggests that beauty aids disguise—and further pollute—the corrupt interior of misguided young women. The heroine, honest Margaret Howard, is so sincere that she informs a social gathering that the young woman who just played the piano has no musical talent. The villain, Mary Ellis, who flatters even bad pianists, is a consummate hypocrite. Mary carelessly misplaces a poisonous cosmetic she bought to treat a facial blemish, and the potion ends up in a medicine chest. The next day, the cosmetic is accidentally administered to a beautiful visitor who has fainted. The woman dies. In conclusion, Hentz implores her readers to "reflect on the consequences of Mary Ellis's moral delinquency and tremble at the view." The rising middle-class women who read such stories and bought conduct manuals needed a way to define themselves as part of the emerging bourgeoisie of the 1800s; meeting prescribed beauty standards helped to consolidate their newly acquired status. The restrictive code of absolute sincerity could not last, however, and as Halttunen notes, social relations among the middle class became more theatrical in the latter half of the century. As the idea of cultivated—even manufactured—beauty became more accepted, advice writers spent less time detailing the dangers of insecurity and more time prescribing potentially poisonous potions, like arsenic for beautifully pale skin.

Dominant standards of beauty were often even more dangerous for oppressed women. In chapter 3 of *Uncle Tom's Cabin*, Stowe refers to the trials of beauty in terms of Susan's trying to disguise her daughter Emmeline's beauty before they went to the auction block. As early as 1861, Harriet *Jacobs, in *Incidents in the Life of a Slave Girl*, suggested how beauty made life difficult for black women slaves. Jacobs's narrator, Linda, states that "if God has bestowed beauty upon [the black woman slave], it will prove her greatest curse." In *Of One Blood, or the Hidden Self*, Pauline *Hopkins details the plight of the tragic mulatta whose beauty is at the heart of her ambivalence and complicated, tragic life. Novels such as Nella *Larsen's 1929 *Passing*, in which light-skinned women of color are accepted as members of the larger society, treat the heroine's confusion of choice between white standards and Afrocentric ones as a forced cultural determination.

In the late nineteenth century, standards of beauty reflected the general shift from a Protestant desire for salvation through self-denial to what Jackson Lears calls a "therapeutic ethos" that focuses on self-realization in this world. In order to accept remediation and develop their beauty, women first had to admit that they needed help. Beauty guides such as Susan D. Power's *The Ugly-Girl Papers* (1874) prescribed "cures" for their presumably ugly readers, and associated lack of beauty with physical and mental illness. The therapeutic ethos, with its reassuring evocation of medical authority and convenient usefulness for selling products, lent authority to conduct manual writers. In an increasingly secular society, the ritualistic nature of the beauty regimen replaced the ritualistic nature of religious worship: just as seventeenth-century church members had to reiterate constantly their own sinfulness to attain salvation, the late-nineteenth-century woman had to reiterate constantly her own ugliness to attain beauty. The woman who is not obsessed with her looks will never be beautiful, thus spending too much time worrying about her appearance; the woman who is obsessed with her looks is already spending too much time worrying about her appearance, so that she is not, as the author of *The Ugly-Girl Papers* puts it, "at liberty to devote herself successfully to others."

By the end of the century and along with the rise of industrial capitalism, beauty itself had become commodified, a packaging that continues into the late twentieth century. Like Henry James's *Portrait of a Lady*, John Singer Sargent, among others, made a fortune on the consumer desire for realistic, not romanticized, pictures of well-to-do women such as Isabella Stewart Gardner and the Boit daughters. James's *Daisy Miller* set the standard for realist arguments about the construction of standards of beauty and conduct. Constance Fenimore *Woolson, Kate *Chopin, and Charlotte Perkins *Gilman challenged the more conventional paradigms of female beauty. In Edith *Wharton's *The House of Mirth* (1905), Lily Bart—who has been taught to view her good looks as "the raw material of conquest"—manipulates her appearance in order to manipulate men. For Wharton's heroine, beauty is not a passive attribute, but rather a cleverly packaged asset necessary for survival on the marriage market. Lily's "raw" physical beauty is on bold display when she participates in a *tableau vivant* at a society party, scorning elaborate costumes and "trusting to her unassisted beauty." Gertrude *Stein's "Melanctha" in *Three Lives* (1909) redefined the standards of beauty—and subjectivity—through her experiments in form and aesthetics. Gilman offers an alternative vision in *Herland* (1915), in which she describes a feminist *utopia where all women possess beauty and power, as well as absolute freedom from patriarchal oppression, since physical beauty does not mean economic security.

Other contemporary works address the monolithic standard of beauty proffered by consumer culture. Like Emily *Dickinson before her, poets such as Adrienne *Rich redefine the concept of beauty away from its heterosexual norms. While Emily Dickinson contested dominant ideologies of fashion in her unorthodox vision of beauty ("A face devoid of love or grace" and "I died for beauty, but was scarce"), Sylvia *Plath's poems "The Ravaged Face" and "The Face Lift" (1961) explore the ugliness of the body considered grotesque by the culture and a popular surgical means for restoring youthful female beauty. These poems attack a culture obsessed with women's bodies and confront the vulnerability women feel about self-exposure, especially in the face of male *violence and threats of assault. "The Face Lift" details the self-obliteration involved in beautification and a cultural violence internalized and directed against the self—a self denied the chance to "age gracefully" and compelled to submit to the requirement of youth. The novelist, poet, and short-story writer Joyce Carol *Oates criticizes modern standards of beauty in a variety of ways as she writes about troubled female characters who find themselves unable to fulfill—or maintain—the role of the beautiful woman. The transience and packaging of beauty is the subject of a 1978 poem entitled "Former Beauty Queen, Dying of Cancer, Watches an Old Movie of Hers at a Film Festival in San Francisco." In Oates's 1990 novel, *Because It Is Bitter, and Because It Is My Heart*, one of the main characters watches her mother, a strikingly beautiful woman, cling desperately to the remnants of seedy glamour and ultimately drink herself into a fatal illness.

Toni *Morrison's 1970 novel *The Bluest Eye* directly confronts white standards of beauty. All around the little girl who desires blue eyes is popular culture, which proclaims that blond hair and blue eyes—as represented by Shirley Temple—are the ideal traits to which all must aspire. The little girl's mother, Pauline Breedlove, inherits her dream from the movies, where she learns about romantic love and the touchstone of physical beauty—the latter of which Morrison declares to be "probably the most destructive idea in the history of human thought." Pauline's failure to become the image of her desire leads her to displace that anger on her family, which also fails to live up to the ideal of the American nuclear family. Morrison challenges the *race and *class bias inherent in the dominant beauty system of American culture. Similarly, Alice *Walker's *The Color Purple* (1982) also explores Celie's rejection of the patriarchal definition of beauty and its judgment against her leveled by Mr.: Celie's "pore, black, and a woman." In discovering her *sexuality and compatibility, Celie also learns to value her talents beyond patriarchal evaluation.

The first chapter of Maxine Hong *Kingston's 1975 *The Woman Warrior* tells of the "no name woman"—the narrator's aunt—who paid too much attention to her looks and rejected a "commonplace loveliness." Her search for individual beauty, the narrator's mother suggests, caused her expulsion from the community. The narrator internalizes the lesson of this family story and tries to become "American-feminine," a mode that seems far less vexed with contradictions than her aunt's rejection of "Chinese-feminine." Contemporary novelist Amy *Tan dramatizes the damaging effects of rigid beauty standards in *The Joy Luck Club*, her 1989 novel about Chinese immigrant mothers and their Chinese-American daughters. Suyuan Woo insists that her nine-year-old daughter, Jing-Mei, can become a prodigy and live out the mythic American dream. Hoping to make Jing-Mei into a "Chinese Shirley Temple," Suyuan takes her to a beauty training school, where disaster ensues. The hoped-for transformation never comes, of course, and Jing-Mei becomes increasingly alienated from her mother and from the society whose beauty standards deny her own heritage.

Susan Faludi's *Backlash* (1991) is a work on contemporary culture that confronts the effects of the American beauty industry on women. Fearing that beauty has become medicalized, the author challenges the idea of beauty as an abstract ideal and suggests that beauty has become politicized, a construction that benefits the male medical establishment and the cosmetic industry especially. For example, Gertrude *Atherton's 1923 bestseller *Black Oxen* details an older woman's transformation "via the Steinach treatment," which included x-ray stimulation to the reproductive organs to reinvigorate the patient. Faludi argues that the late Victorian ideal of beauty as the enervated invalid is not so far from the ideal today. Naomi Wolf also demythologizes the cult of beauty in America, pointing to its roots in women's political "sedation" (*The Beauty Myth*, 1991). The main feminist critique of the beauty system is against the contradictions that it forces women to inherit and the belief that women are essentially ugly and must be "made" beautiful. Writers have used the paradoxical notion of "natural beauty"—the doctrine that requires women to work at being beautiful and, at the same time, to hide all evidence of such work—to draw class distinctions as well. In contemporary culture, female celebrities can be ridiculed or categorized as "tacky" if their appearance is too artificial; women such as Cher and Dolly Parton have committed themselves to the "masquerade" of femininity, making their attempts at beautification visible and sometimes parodic. Exposing the work of beauty can be an effective strategy for disempowering the worker herself.

[*See also* Fashion; Body and Health.]

• Caroline Lee Hentz, "The Fatal Cosmetic," *Godey's Lady's Book* 18 (June 1839): 265–273. Karen Halttunen, *Confidence Men and Painted Women* (1982). T. J. Jackson Lears, "From Salvation to Self-Realization" in *The Culture of Consumption*, ed. Richard Wightman Fox and T. J. Jackson Lears (1983). Jane Tompkins, *Sensational Designs* (1985).

Dale M. Bauer and
Jean Marie Lutes

BEAUVOIR, Simone de (1908–1986), French intellectual, author of *The Second Sex* (1949). In 1929 Beauvoir became the ninth woman in France to pass the prestigious *agrégation* exam in philosophy, coming second only to Jean-Paul Sartre (who, incidentally, had failed the same exam the year before). Beauvoir belonged to the first generation of European women to receive a formal university *education on a par with men. Self-taught or educated at home, women intellectuals before her, such as Madame de Staël, George Sand, George Eliot, or Virginia *Woolf, never found themselves competing with men in the educational sphere. Given their pioneering status, Beauvoir and her contemporaries came to experience with emblematic force many of the conflicts and contradictions that still leave their mark on the lives of intellectual women in ostensibly egalitarian institutions.

With the existentialist notion of freedom as their point of departure, Beauvoir's writings focus on the question of how to reconcile a woman's desire for social and economic independence with her fundamental need for love and sexual fulfillment. In their exploration of these themes, novels such as *She Came to Stay* (1943) and *The Mandarins* (1954; winner of the Prix Goncourt) are as significant as the more theoretical discussions of the same issues in Beauvoir's pathbreaking essay on women's oppression, *The Second Sex*. In her own autobiographical works (*Memoirs of a Dutiful Daughter*, 1958; *The Prime of Life*, 1960; *Force of Circumstance*, 1963; *All Said and Done*, 1972), she paints a fascinating—albeit not always utterly truthful—picture of her own Catholic childhood in Paris, her struggle to free herself from her parents, her more or less successful attempts to pioneer new sexual and emotional arrangements in her own life, her political development, and her determination to become a published writer.

On its publication in France in 1949, *The Second Sex* was greeted with outrage: "What a festival of obscenity!" Beauvoir commented in *Force of Circumstance*. "Unsatisfied, cold, priapic, nymphomaniac, lesbian, a hundred times aborted, I was everything, even an unmarried mother. People offered to cure me of my frigidity or to satisfy my ghoulish appetites." The Vatican quickly placed *The Second Sex* on its Index, a list of books unsuitable for Catholics, and Albert Camus accused Beauvoir of having committed the crime of making the French male look ridiculous. But women flocked to buy it: the first volume sold twenty thousand copies in two weeks.

In *The Second Sex* Beauvoir shows that, under patriarchy, women are cast as the *other in relation to men. Instead of accepting women as free, acting subjects in their own right, our civilization imposes upon them an alienated, objectified image of themselves. Rooted in the earliest childhood experiences of the little girl, the process of alienation often succeeds in making the woman internalize and identify with the patriarchal image imposed upon her. In the context of this analysis, Beauvoir goes on to discuss history, psychoanalysis, and biology, before launching into detailed analyses of topics such as childhood, *heterosexuality, *lesbianism, *marriage, childbirth, *menopause, housework, *abortion, contraception, women's work outside the home, women's creativity, and women's efforts to combine independence with authentic sexual freedom. It is remarkable to consider that, although there was no women's movement in France in 1949, *The Second Sex* nevertheless succeeded in raising all the issues that were to become central to feminists from the late 1960s onward.

This is not to say that Beauvoir's arguments have met with no opposition. Feminists committed to various theories of women's fundamental difference from men, for instance, have denounced their precursor for hating the female * body, glorifying maleness, and for lacking any sympathy or understanding for traditional female pursuits, including marriage and motherhood. Implacably opposed to any form of * identity politics, Beauvoir's brand of feminism remains controversial in the 1990s. The strongest legacy of *The Second Sex* is the fact that all its analyses are placed within a powerful narrative of liberation. By taking as her point of departure a story of historical and social transformation—or, in other words, by giving feminism an end, by imagining a society in which there would no longer be any need to *be* a feminist—Beauvoir provided women around world with a vision of change. This is what gives her essay such power and such a capacity to inspire its readers to action, and it is also the reason why *The Second Sex* remains the founding text of materialist feminism in the twentieth century.

In her later career, Beauvoir published two popular texts of fiction (*Les Belles Images,* 1966; *The Woman Destroyed,* 1968) and a pioneering exploration of aging (*Old Age,* 1970), as well as the moving account of her mother's death (*A Very Easy Death,* 1964) and the spare, understated text of mourning for her life-long companion, entitled *Adieux: A Farewell to Sartre* (1981).

[*See also* French Feminism.]

• Elaine Marks, ed., *Critical Essays on Simone de Beauvoir* (1987). Deirdre Bair, *Simone de Beauvoir: A Biography* (1990). Michèle Le Doeuff, *Hipparchia's Choice: An Essay Concerning Women, Philosophy, etc.* (1991). Simone de Beauvoir, *Letters to Sartre* (1992). Toril Moi, *Simone de Beauvoir: The Making of an Intellectual Woman* (1993).

Toril Moi

BEECHER, Catharine (1800–1878), educator. Born at East Hampton, Long Island, into the noted Beecher family, she was the daughter of Roxana Foote (1775–1816) and the noted Calvinist minister Lyman Beecher (1775–1863), and the sister of the novelist Harriet Beecher * Stowe (1811–1896), the suffragist Isabella Beecher Hooker (1822–1907), and the minister Henry Ward Beecher (1813–1887). She radically changed the direction of * education for women in her work and her writings about the education of women. She began a school for girls in 1823 that eventually became the Hartford Female Seminary. When the Beecher family moved to Cincinnati, she and her sister Harriet began the Western Female Institute in 1832. She was the author of dozens of articles and books about female education that radically challenged patriarchal values. Jeanne

Boydston, Mary Kelley, and Anne Margolis argue in *The Limits of Sisterhood: The Beecher Sisters on Women's Rights and Women's Sphere* (1988) that Beecher, in *Suggestions Respecting Improvements in Education* (1829), "recast both the teacher and the mother as female counterparts of the minister, charged, not only with education of the mind, but with the perfection of the soul." Her *Treatise on Domestic Economy for the Use of Young Ladies at Home and at School* (1843) espoused her views on a curriculum for women and the centrality of domesticity in the moral and political life of the nation. Many of her educational reforms were quite radical for her day. She advocated calisthenics and physical education for women, and she believed that women should be provided with the same classical education as men. She also believed that women should be trained in domestic economy and should learn rational skills for running a home. Along with Harriet, she believed that the family and the home were the moral center of society and that the private sphere and women's culture provided a moral antidote to the corruptions of the public sphere. Unlike her sister Isabella, she did not believe in female suffrage, for she feared the corrupting influence of the public sphere on women and * domesticity. The eldest and favorite child of her famous father, she broke with his evangelical Calvinism after the death in 1822 of her fiancé, Alexander Metcalf Fisher, who had not experienced a conversion and thus, according to Lyman Beecher, could not be counted among the elect, or saved. Like her sister Harriet, Catharine found Calvinism authoritarian, patriarchal, and opposed to the maternal philosophy of women's values that she saw as an alternative moral foundation of the culture.

• Lyman Beecher Stowe, *Saints, Sinners and Beechers* (1934). Kathryn Kish Sklar, *Catharine Beecher: A Study in Domesticity* (1973). Milton Rugoff, *The Beechers: An American Family in the Nineteenth Century* (1981).

Dorothy Berkson

BENNETT, Gwendolyn B. (1902–1981), poet, short-story writer, columnist, journalist, illustrator, graphic artist, arts educator, teacher and administrator on the New York City Works Progress Administration Federal Arts Project (1935–1941). Gwendolyn Bennett was one of the most versatile figures to participate actively in both the 1920s Black American arts movement, which was designated the *Harlem Renaissance, and in the 1930s arts alliance formed among African-American graphic artists that was called the Harlem Artists Guild.

Although born in Giddings, Texas, much of Bennett's childhood was unsettled as her family continually moved, eventually settling in

Brooklyn, New York. Artistic and multi-talented as a child, Bennett continually felt the pull of two career goals—to be a writer and to become an artist. Her literary skills and artistic aptitude were first recognized at Brooklyn's Girls' High (1918–1921). The first Negro to join the literary society, she participated in the drama society, and won first place in an art contest with a poster design. Upon graduation, Bennett attended first Columbia University (1921) and then Pratt Institute (1922–1924), preparing to teaching art at either the secondary or college level; her initial teaching position was at Howard University (1924).

The first journals to accept her work were the NAACP's *The Crisis* and the National Urban League's *Opportunity*. In December 1923, while she was still a student, *Opportunity* accepted her poem "Heritage" and *The Crisis* carried a cover illustration. From 1923–1931, twenty-two Bennett poems appeared in journals of the period: *Crisis, Opportunity, Palms,* and *Gypsy.* Additionally, other poems were collected in William Stanley Braithwaite's *Anthology of Magazine Verse for 1927 and Yearbook of American Poetry* (1927), Countee Cullen's *Caroling Dusk* (1927), and James Weldon Johnson's *The Book of American Negro Poetry* (1931). During the twenties Bennett's poetry reflected either the shared themes and motifs of the Harlem Renaissance—celebrating racial pride, rediscovery of Africa, recognition of Black music and dance—or, she penned romantic lyrics, the poetry of personal statement. In 1926, the short-lived *Fire!!,* which Bennett served as an editor, carried "Wedding Day," her first published short story; "Tokens," her second story, appeared in Charles S. Johnson's *Ebony and Topaz: A Collectanea* (1927).

The twenties were fruitful for Bennett; she spent a year studying art in Paris (1925) and in 1927, along with Aaron Douglass, she received a scholarship to study art at the Barnes Foundation. Additionally, she wrote book reviews for several New York newspapers and *Opportunity* carried her "Ebony Flute" arts news column, 1926–28. Yet despite a facility for both poetry and prose, Bennett never devoted her full attention to writing. She married Alfred Jackson in 1928; he died in 1936. Subsequently, she focused less on her own creative work, writing or painting, and instead concentrated on facilitating the artistic development of others. She joined the Harlem Artists Guild; from 1938 to 1941 she directed the Harlem Community Art Center (largest of the Federal Art Projects); she served on the Board of the Negro Playwright's Guild; and she directed the development of the George Washington Carver Community School. In all these capacities Bennett nurtured and fostered the talents of countless young African-American artists.

• Arna Bontemps, ed., *The Harlem Renaissance Remembered* (1972). Ronald Primeau, "Frank Horne and the Second Echelon Poets of the Harlem Renaissance" in *The Harlem Renaissance Remembered,* ed. Arna Bontemps (1972), pp. 247–267. Walter C. Daniel and Sandra Y. Govan, "Gwendolyn Bennett," in *The Dictionary of Literary Biography, Afro-American Writers from the Harlem Renaissance to 1940,* Vol. 51, ed. Trudier Harris (1987), pp. 3–7. Sandra Y. Govan, "After the Renaissance: Gwendolyn Bennett and the WPA Years," in *The Middle Atlantic Writers Association Review* 3, no. 2 (December 1988): 227–231.

Sandra Y. Govan

BETHUNE, Mary Jane McLeod (1875–1955), educator and college administrator, a founder of Bethune-Cookman College, organizer of the National Council of Negro Women, director of the Division of Negro Affairs for the Franklin D. Roosevelt administration, and lobbyist for civil and women's rights for African-Americans.

Bethune was born July 10, 1875, near Mayesville, South Carolina, the fifteenth of seventeen children born to Patsy McIntosh McLeod and Samuel McLeod. Her parents and many of her siblings had been slaves at the time of the *Civil War.

In 1885, Bethune attended a school for blacks, opened by the Board of Missions for Freedmen, a Trinity Presbyterian organization. In June 1894 she entered Scotia Seminary (now Barber-Scotia College), a school for black women at Concord, North Carolina. After graduation (5 July 1894) Bethune enrolled in missionary training school at the Moody Bible Institute in Chicago; she was the only black student at that time. But her hopes of becoming a missionary in Africa were dashed when the Mission Board of the Presbyterian church determined that no openings existed for black missionaries in Africa.

Following this disappointment, Bethune returned to the South and taught at the Haines Institute in Augusta, Georgia. She later taught at the Kendall Institute in Sumter, South Carolina, where she met her future husband, Abertus Bethune, whom she married in May 1898. Their only child, Albert McLeod Bethune, was born 3 February 1899. But the couple separated after eight years of marriage, though they remained legally married until Abertus's death in 1918.

In 1900, Bethune founded a Presbyterian school in Palatka, Florida. Four years later she established the Daytona Educational and Industrial Institute, modeling it after Scotia Seminary. Students worked on local farms to help raise revenue for the school's operations. In addition, Bethune received financial support from

Daytona's black leadership and from white philanthropists, including James M. Gamble of the Proctor and Gamble Manufacturing Company. In 1923, Bethune merged the Daytona Normal and Industrial Institute with the Cookman Institute in Jacksonville to create the Bethune-Cookman College. Meanwhile, Bethune assumed the presidency of the National Association of Colored Women (NACW) in 1924. As a result of her work in education and on behalf of women's rights, Bethune was awarded the Spingarn Medal by the National Association for the Advancement of Colored People (NAACP) in 1935.

Bethune favored a strong, centralized organization particularly for women, that addressed social, economic, and political concerns of blacks in both the United States and in international politics. To achieve these and other goals, Bethune organized the National Council of Negro Women (NCNW) on 5 December 1935. She was NCNW president for fourteen years (1935–1949). Bethune's accomplishments include convincing the Women's Army Auxiliary Corps (WAAC) to include African-Americans in their ranks. In addition, she sought ten percent black representation in WAAC's officer training school.

Bethune was appointed special assistant to Roosevelt's secretary of war in order to select prospective female officers. Her affiliation with the National Youth Administration, established in 1935, provided a wedge in President Franklin D. Roosevelt's "New Deal" administration. The Civil Service Commission officially recognized Bethune's directorship of the Division of Negro Affairs for the Roosevelt administration in January 1939. Frequently in partnership with Eleanor Roosevelt, Bethune contributed substantially to the banning of discrimination in government and industry employment and in the creation of the Fair Employment Practices Commission.

Bethune died of heart failure 18 May 1955.

• Owen Peare, *Mary McLeod Bethune* (1951). Rackham Holt, *Mary McLeod Bethune: A Biography* (1964). B. Joyce Ross, "Mary McLeod Bethune and the National Youth Administration: A Case Study of Power Relationships in the Black Cabinet of Franklin D. Roosevelt," *Journal of Negro History* 60 (January 1975): 1–28. Elaine M. Smith, "Mary McLeod Bethune," in *Notable Black American Women*, ed. Jessie Carney Smith (1992), pp. 86–92.

Helena Woodard

BETTS, Doris (b. 1932), novelist, short-story writer, and educator. Born in Statesville, North Carolina, the only child of Mary Ellen Freeze and William Elmore Waugh, a cotton mill worker, Betts grew up surrounded by an ex-tended family, attending the Associate Reformed Presbyterian Church, and reading widely. She found her vocation early, as a young girl, composing poetry and fiction. She attended Woman's College of the University of North Carolina at Greensboro for two years and the University of North Carolina for a year, although she never completed a degree. In 1952 she married Lowry Betts, a lawyer, who is now a District Court Judge in Chatham and Orange Counties. The Bettses have three grown children and live on their farm, Araby, in Pittsboro, where they raise Arabian horses. Doris Betts is an elder in the Presbyterian Church, a Democrat, and active in community affairs.

Betts began teaching creative writing part time at the University of North Carolina at Chapel Hill in 1966; and has moved up the academic ladder, holding several administrative positions. A prize-winning teacher, Betts is now Alumni Distinguished Professor of English and has served two terms as Chairman of the Faculty, the first woman to enjoy that distinction.

She is the author of three books of short fiction and four novels. Her first book is *The Gentle Insurrection* (1954), a collection of twelve short stories that was published when she was twenty-two. It won the Putnam Prize and received fine reviews. A second volume of short fiction, *The Astronomer and Other Stories* (1966), includes seven short stories and a novella, the title story, considered by a number of critics to be Betts's masterpiece. Among the nine stories in *Beasts of the Southern Wild* (1973) is the frequently anthologized "The Ugliest Pilgrim." "Violet," an American Film Institute short film of this story, won an Academy Award in 1982.

Betts is a natural short-story writer whose work is uniformly excellent; she is frequently compared to Katherine Anne *Porter and Flannery *O'Connor. Her style is rich, allusive, metaphorical, and economical, and her ear for spoken language is true. Most of her characters are lower and middle *class, and place—North Carolina—is always significant in her work. Her themes have remained consistent as she has written about children and old people, about women's lives, about love and death, and about the relationship of diverse races. She writes frequently about isolated people, about the submerged life of characters, and about the difficulties of communication; Betts has said that her main themes are "time and mortality."

Her five novels echo these themes. *Tall Houses in Winter* (1957) is an apprentice work about a middle-aged, cancer-stricken English professor who comes home to North Carolina to come to terms with his family and his past. With more characters and a wider scope, *The Scarlet Thread* (1964) is an historical novel, set at the turn of the century, which tells the story of the Allen Family and of their small North Carolina village as it is affected by a new cotton mill. *The River to Pickle Beach* (1972), set in 1968, features a happily married couple and focuses on the problem of violence as the assassinations of Martin Luther King, Jr., and Bobby Kennedy echo in the background. A woman is the protagonist for the first time in Betts's fourth novel, *Heading West* (1981). Complex and richly layered, this novel tells of Nancy Finch's kidnapping and subsequent journey across the country; it is also a profound account of the protagonist's inner life. Betts' 1994 novel, *Souls Raised from the Dead*, like her other recent works, focuses on the presence of evil in life, a topic that interests Betts more and more.

• Doris Betts's papers are at Boston University. See also George Wolfe, "The Unique Voice: Doris Betts," in *Kite-Flying and Other Irrational Acts*, ed. John Carr (1972), pp. 149–173. Elizabeth Evans, "Negro Characters in the Fiction of Doris Betts," *Critique: Studies in Modern Fiction* 17 (1975): 59–76. Dorothy M. Scura, "Doris Betts at Mid-Career: Her Voice and Her Art," in *Southern Women Writers*, ed. Tonette Bond Inge (1990), pp. 161–179. Sue Laslie Kimball and Lynn Veach Sadler, eds., *The Home Truths of Doris Betts* (1992; includes complete bibliography and a full list of Betts's writings).

Dorothy M. Scura

BILDUNGSROMAN AND KÜNSTLERROMAN. These literary terms define novels of development *(Bildung)* in which the hero ventures forth to develop herself fully and to win adult membership in her * community. The künstlerroman (*Künstler* is German for artist) narrates the development of an artist's vocation. In the American woman's bildungsroman there is a rich and varied tradition for depicting heroes of many backgrounds trying to develop talents and capacities according to values women hold especially dear: the love of nature, exuberant creativity, joyous * sexuality, and the desire for significant work within one's community. Although novels of male development perceive these values as good when men pursue them, women authors show female heroes punished for trying to achieve the same goals. Whereas a white male hero's sexuality is taken as evidence of his maturing, for example, "giving in" to her natural sensuality often lands woman heroes from the same ethnic group in serious social trouble. And although the bildungsroman values a young man's development of significant vocational choices, women heroes of the genre encounter disapproval when they display a wide range of talents and capacities.

Early novels in which heroes' rebellions lead to the atrophy of their development, insanity, and even death include Susanna * Rowson's *Charlotte Temple, A Tale of Truth* (1790) and Hannah * Foster's *The Coquette* (1797). Later bildungsromans also depicted heroes punished for having even the appearance of a sex life (Kate * Chopin's *The Awakening* in 1899; Edith * Wharton's *The House of Mirth* in 1905). Even twentieth-century heroes continue to grow down rather than up, as in Mary * McCarthy's *The Group* (1954) and Sylvia * Plath's künstlerroman of a young writer, *The Bell Jar* (1963). These bildungsromans do not uphold victimization as their norm; instead, the authors express rebellion by satirizing how patriarchal society dwarfs their heroes' full human development.

Many works in the bildungsroman tradition describe young female heroes who refuse to renounce their love of nature or to repress their talents. Short-story writers such as Alice * Brown in *Meadow-Grass, Tales of New England Life* (1895), Sarah Orne * Jewett in *Deephaven* (1877) and "A White Heron" (1896), and Mary Wilkins * Freeman in "A New England Nun" (1891) describe young women whose love of nature and distaste for subordinating themselves to men led them to choose a single life over marriage. They inspired twentieth-century characters like Willa * Cather's Alexandra in *O Pioneers!* (1913) and Ellen * Glasgow's Dorinda in *Barren Ground* (1925).

The lesbian bildungsroman, pioneered by Gertrude * Stein's *Things as They Are (Q.E.D.)* in 1904, also ranges from punitive plots, which satirize patriarchal bigotry against women loving women (Naomi Royde-Smith's *The Island* in 1930, and Shiela Donisthrope's 1931 *Loveliest of Friends*), to novels in which young lesbians struggle more successfully (Isabel Miller's *Patience and Sarah* and Rita Mae * Brown's *Rubyfruit Jungle* in 1973; and Sharon Isabel's *Yesterday's Lessons* and Elana Nachman's *Riverfinger Woman* in 1974). Two lesbian künstlerromans exemplify the novel whose hero wants to become an artist in a society that is uncomfortable with talented, creative women: Gale Wilhelm's *We too Are Drifting* (1935), about a sculptor, and May * Sarton's *Mrs. Stevens Hears the Mermaids Singing* (1965), about a poet.

Punishments influence the artistic development of heroes in such heterosexual künstlerromans as Elizabeth Stuart * Phelps's *The Story of Avis* (1877), in which Avis's marriage atrophies both her creativity and her health, and Charlotte Perkins * Gilman's "The Yellow Wallpaper" (1892), in which the narrator is driven mad by the tension between her creativity and the demands of motherhood and marriage. Women artists as different as the singer Thea Kronberg in Willa Cather's *The Song of the Lark* (1915), Harriet * Arnow's Kentucky woodcarver Gertie in *The Dollmaker* (1954), and Erica * Jong's Isabella Wing in *Fear of Flying* (1973) are similarly constrained. Gail *Godwin's *Violet Clay* (1978), in contrast, depicts an artist's achieving her goals, but only after struggling to survive marriage and divorce.

Growing up female in America is different in the *African-American community in ways that reflect the oppression of *racism but which also demonstrate distinct strengths of African-American cultural history. Ntozake *Shange describes the development of three sister creators in her triple künstlerroman *Sassafras, Cypress and Indigo* (1982): although all three must first overcome significant white patriarchal obstacles, they are richly empowered by their mother's artistry and that of women mentors to become a dancer, an artist-weaver, and a musician-healer.

African-American women heroes accept their bodies, including their sexuality, as attributes of strength: in her important historical bildungsroman *Jubilee!* (1966) Margaret *Walker uses her family's oral narratives of their nineteenth-century experiences to show an African-American hero surviving *slavery, the *Civil War, and Reconstruction on the strength of self-pride instilled by the African-American women who reared her. Some young African-American heroes, like Angela in Jessie Redmon *Fauset's *Plum Bun* (1929), set out to pass into the white world, only to become disgusted with its values and return to their community. Other novelists, such as Ann *Petry in *The Street* (1946) and Toni *Morrison in *The Bluest Eye* (1970), develop tragic narratives that deplore what happens when their heroes try to survive as young black females in America.

Authors of the African-American women's bildungsroman neither idealize the African-American community nor wholly reject African-American men: Alice *Walker's Celie must survive abuse from her stepfather in *The Color Purple* (1982), for example, but when she discovers the empowering community of African-American women, she is able to transcend patriarchal constraints and to welcome African-American men, including her stepfather, into a new collective.

Although expectations for female development vary from tribe to tribe, most *Native American bildungsromans celebrate feminine sexuality and generativity as *gender powers important to a young woman's quest for identity. Gender difference is marked not to oppress women but to achieve a gender complementarity important to theologies that emphasize harmony and balance. In the Native American bildungsroman young women learn to pay attention to the traditions preserved for them by their elders, and they seek identity in these stories, poetry, drawings, music, and *ritual activities. Okanogan writer *Mourning Dove's *Cogewea, the Half Blood* (1927), for example, interweaves white western-style adventure stories with Okanogan legends and history; Leslie Marmon *Silko narrates *Storyteller* (1981) using family photographs along with stories and legends from her Sioux and Laguna Pueblo heritage; Mohawk writer Beth *Brant uses a cycle of interrelated poems and stories in *Mohawk Trail* (1985), and Louise *Erdrich builds her trilogy—*Love Medicine* (1984), *The Beet Queen* (1986), and *Tracks* (1988)—out of a variety of narrative voices based on her white ancestors as well as her Ojibway forebears. Ephanie, in Laguna Pueblo/Sioux/Lebanese writer Paula Gunn *Allen's *The Woman Who Owned the Shadows* (1983), achieves her identity through the medium of the Yellow Women cycle of stories she received from her Keres forebears, but this occurs only after she recovers from illness and insanity brought on by conforming to white norms for women.

Heroes of the *Chicana bildungsroman come up against male domination and violence inherited from the colonial history of Spanish patriarchy, a history founded on *rape and perpetuated in permission for male violence. Chicana bildungsromans share Native Americans' joyous celebration of feminine sexuality, closeness to nature, and empowerment through community identity. They rely on similarly strong *oral traditions and are often structured on cycles of stories, ballads, and family memories, which are powerful helpers in heroes' quests: Helena María *Viramontes' *The Moths and Other Stories* (1985), Ana *Castillo's *The Mixquiahuala Letters* (1986) and Denise *Chavez's *The Last of the Menu Girls* (1986) are similarly structured. The importance of identifying with the female community is illustrated in Sandra *Cisneros's künstlerroman *The House on Mango Street* (1985): here, Esperanza is inspired by the poet Minerva, who writes in spite of suffering beatings from her husband. Esperanza grounds her hope in a specific house within the Chicana community. An example of the Chicana lesbian bildungsroman is Cherríe *Moraga's *Giving up the Ghost* (1986).

*Asian-American bildungsromans are also marked by tension between traditions of male domination and young women's desires for development. Early examples of the genre are Chinese-American Jade Snow *Wong's *Fifth Chinese Daughter* (1945) and Diana *Chang's *Frontiers of Love* (1956) and Japanese-American Monica Sone's *Nisei Daughter* (1953). Maxine Hong *Kingston structures *The Woman Warrior* (1975), which she subtitles *Memoirs of a Girlhood among Ghosts*, so that she circles back to embrace ancestral myths and adventures that empower her present-day identity. Amy *Tan's *The Joy Luck Club* (1989) is built on traditional narratives and the adventures of four immigrant mothers, which four Chinese-American daughters use to construct blended Chinese-American identities.

[*See also* Novel, Beginnings of the; Short Story]

• Grace Stewart, *A New Mythos: The Novel of the Artist as Heroine, 1877–1977* (1979). Elaine H. Kim, *Asian American Literature: An Introduction to the Writings and Their Social Context* (1982). Elizabeth Abel, Marianne Hirsch, and Elizabeth Langland, eds., *The Voyage In: Fictions of Female Development* (1983). Linda Huf, *A Portrait of the Artist as a Young Woman: The Writer as Heroine in American Literature* (1983). Barbara Christian, *Black Feminist Criticism: Perspectives on Black Women Writers* (1985). Barbara Anne White, *Growing Up Female: Adolescent Girlhood in American Fiction* (1985). Paula Gunn Allen, *The Sacred Hoop: Recovering the Feminine in American Indian Traditions* (1986). Maria Hererra-Sobek and Helena María Viramontes, eds, *Chicana Creativity and Criticism: Charting New Frontiers in American Literature* (1988). Patricia Hill Collins, *Black Feminist Thought: Knowledge, Consciousness, and the Politics of Empowerment* (1990). Laura Sue Fuderer, *The Female Bildungsroman in English: An Annotated Bibliography of Criticism* (1990).

Annis Pratt

BILINGUALISM. The use of two languages among women writers and critics in the United States occurs in tandem with biculturalism. Some bilingual-bicultural writers are children of immigrants whose primary language was not English (Maxine Hong *Kingston and Monica Sone), while others are themselves immigrants (Anzia *Yezierska, Bharati *Mukherjee, Kim Chi-won, Jessica *Hagedorn). Bilingualism also figures in the writings of women whose experience is not that of the immigrant, but of the colonized within this country, such as Native Americans (Louise *Erdrich, Leslie Marmon *Silko) and Latinas, including Chicanas (Sandra *Cisneros, Mary Helen Ponce) and Puertorriqueñas (Luz María Umpierre-Herrera). Bilingualism entails not only the writer's or critic's knowledge of the mother tongue; comprehension of cultural history, for example, Native American *mythology, informs much of the work of these writers and enables the bicultural literary critic to illuminate their subtexts. In addition to nonstandard vocabulary, most bilingual-bicultural women writers interweave the rhythms, melodies, and syntax of other languages with those of English. The retention of bilingual-bicultural customs is usually dependent on geographical regrouping within the United States, as in the Chinatowns of San Francisco and New York or the Spanish-speaking *barrios* throughout the Southwest. Bicultural-bilingual literature encodes cultural confrontation and the history of the confrontations between native and immigrant cultures and the dominant culture of white America. Many bilingual women writers directly address the economic and social conditions of this dominance; others also write about patriarchal dominance within their own communities. Louise Erdrich's novels (such as *Love Medicine*, 1984) examine the economic oppression and political contradictions inherent in Chippewa reservation life. Knowledge of Native American mythologies, religions, and tribal governing structures enables Native American critic Paula Gunn *Allen to comprehend Erdrich's debt to the traditional Anishinabeg (Chippewa) story, "Oshkikwe's Baby," in her story "American Horse" (1983). Erdrich's use of the myth in Albertine American Horse's story emphasizes how U.S. government policies have precipitated the invasion and fragmentation of Chippewa familial and cultural structure.

Sandra *Cisneros also writes about the alienating effects of Anglo-American culture; in "Never Marry a Mexican," the narrator recounts her mother's warning "not to marry a Mexican" or any Hispanic man. By the story's end we know that the narrator is a Chicana artist exploited in a love affair with an older Anglo male artist and that she feels emotionally and culturally abandoned by her now-dead Mexican-American mother who did not speak Spanish. Male dominance, however, is a destructive aspect of both cultures. Cisneros's "Woman Hollering Creek" (1991) depicts a young Mexican woman's battering at the hands of her Mexican-American spouse, and her escape with the help of two *comadres*. Cisneros peppers her work with Spanish words and phrases, as well as cultural references such as the Virgin of Guadelupe and the *telenovela Tú o Nadie*.

Bilingualism encodes the experience of living in two worlds, often manifested as a sense of not feeling at home in either culture. The immigrant characters of early twentieth-century Jewish writer Anzia Yezierska speak an English that replicates the cadence and syntax of Yiddish. In Yezierska's "The Fat of the Land" (1919), Hannah Breineh embodies the Old World's encounter with the materialism of the United States, at one point lamenting that her language separates her from her Americanized children. *Dogeaters* (1990), a novel by the Filipino-American writer Jessica Hagedorn, portrays the complexity of being an immigrant from a culture that is already multilingual.

While not denying the significance of the quotidian racial prejudice experienced by bilingual people, nor the enormity of the genocidal policies that the U.S. government directed against indigenous North Americans, bilingual women writers illuminate the incalculable impact of their cultures on American identity. In *The Sacred Hoop* (1986), Allen writes about the influence of Native American tribal systems on democracy and the ways in which "white feminism" is rooted in matrilineal native cultures. The cadence and idioms of Yiddish permeate Eastern urban speech particularly, and the forms and vocabulary of African-American dialects, rooted in West African languages, must be considered constitutive of American English as a whole. Moreover, numerous works by African-American women writers invite the bilingual-bicultural paradigm for African-American versus standard American language and culture. Geographical features (mesa, canyon) and place names of the Southwest are heavily Spanish, and geographical names across the country transliterate the words of native languages. While works of bilingual-bicultural women constantly address change in and preservation of non-Anglo language and culture, they also demonstrate that the United States has incorporated far more non-Anglo traditions than the hegemony admits to. The attention to bilingual-bicultural women writers comes with the understanding of the debt the *norteamericano/a* owes to this multicultural heritage.

[*See also* Language, Women's; Black English; Nonstandard English; Latina Writing; Translators.]

• Geneva Smitherman, *Talkin and Testifyin: The Language of Black America* (1977). Leslie Marmon Silko, "Language and Literature from a Pueblo Indian Perspective," in *English Literature: Opening the Canon*, eds. Leslie A. Fiedler and Houston A. Baker, Jr. (1981), pp. 54–72. Elaine Kim, *Asian American Literature: An Introduction to the Writings and Their Social Context* (1982). Cherríe Moraga and Gloria Anzaldúa, eds., *This Bridge Called My Back: Writings by Radical Women of Color*, 2d ed. (1983). Cynthia Ozick, *Art and Ardor* (1983). Paula Gunn Allen, *Spider Woman's Granddaughters: Traditional Tales and Contemporary Writing by Native American Women* (1989). Asunción Horno-Delgado, Eliana Ortega, Nina M. Scott, and Nancy Saporta Sternbach, eds., *Breaking Boundaries: Latina Writing and Critical Readings* (1989). Amy Ling, *Between Worlds: Women Writers of Chinese Ancestry* (1990).

Patricia Hunt

BIOGRAPHY. Through literate history, people have written, or told, biographies. The lives of real people have always been more interesting than stories about fictional characters; we can temporarily believe in the exploits of imaginary human beings, but biography wears better. From the time of the 1579 translations of Plutarch's *Parallel Lives*, through Izaak Walton's *Life of John Donne* (1640) and, in this country, Cotton Mather's *Magnalia Christi Americana*, his 1702 biographies of New England worthies, readers have found biography a means to both moral instruction and entertainment.

Modern biography in the English speaking world began with James Boswell's *The Life of Samuel Johnson* in 1791. Diligent as he was about copying down Dr. Johnson's witty conversation, Boswell himself became a metaphor for the dedicated biographer—one who lives to make another's life an art object. But while Boswell was creating Dr. Johnson, in 1771 in America, Benjamin Franklin began creating himself: *The Autobiography of Benjamin Franklin*, unfinished at the time of his death, was published in 1868. Throughout American literary history, *autobiography has been a more appealing form than biography—and innumerable narratives of conversion, *slavery, travel, captivity, and other exploits were written and published. Some of these were written by women; more often, the writer was a man. While published writing was more often male-authored, women writers spent their time writing *diaries, journals, and *letters.

While Americans wrote autobiography, biography in the States grew slowly, and continued to mimic the form of the genre popular in England: lives of prominent male subjects, written with an emphasis on the external, historical events of their lives, praising the subject rather than questioning events or character. Biographers were often men, and their subjects were nearly always male. When American women did write biography, as Lydia M. *Child did during the 1830s, it was sometimes denigrated as being unprofessional. When Ednah D. Cheney published *Louisa May *Alcott, Her Life, Letters and Journals* (1889); Annie *Fields, *Life and Letters of Harriet Beecher *Stowe* (1897); and Alice *Brown, *Mercy *Warren* (1896), the works were often called panegyrics. Women writing about women were suspect.

Women's interest in their subject's motivation and inner life rather than in simple history made them move toward the kind of biography that was to revolutionize the genre during the early twentieth century. British biographer Lytton Strachey is credited with modernizing biography with his *Eminent Victorians* (1918) and *Queen Victoria* (1921), but in the States Gamaliel Bradford's attempts to build what he called a "psychograph" of the subject from his prodigious research paralleled Strachey's method. Among Bradford's many works were such collections of women's biography as *Portraits of Women, Portraits of American Women*, and *Daughters of Eve* (books published 1916 through 1930); and *Jenny Lind* (1931), a biography by his pupil, Edward C. Wagenknecht, which showed the method in a longer format.

This change to a more psychoanalytic biography attracted women writers, as well as women readers, and by the second decade of the twentieth century, women were writing biographies of women with élan and success. In 1920 Katharine Anthony published *Margaret *Fuller: A Psychological Biography*, using psychology to show motivation that would otherwise be lost. Her *Catherine the Great* (1925), *Queen Elizabeth* (1929), and *Marie Antoinette* (1932) continued to emphasize the inner lives—and often the sexual behaviors—of her subjects; unfortunately, these were lives that might have benefited from being treated with more attention to external event. Her turn away from lives of American women also suggested that she agreed with readers' interest in subjects who had led more historically interesting lives. The kind of biography that validated and valued women's inner lives—domestic and private—did not yet exist, for all the popularity of biography during the 1920s.

Constance *Rourke tried to shape biography so that she could write about inner characterization. In 1927, her *Trumpets of Jubilee* combined portraits of nineteenth century figures—including Harriet Beecher *Stowe—to suggest interrelationships among intellectual and family life. In 1928 her biography of the gold rush actress *(Troupers of the Gold Coast; or, the Rise of Lotta Crabtree)* continued her success in grounding psychological understanding of a subject in wide cultural history. (Rourke's later biographies were of Davy Crockett, Audubon, and the artist Charles Sheeler; she also wrote important cultural studies of humor and of the American character.) Mrs. Dorothie Bobbé's short biographies, *Abigail *Adams, the Second First Lady* (1929) and *Mr. and Mrs. John Quincy Adams; an Adventure in Patriotism* (1930), were good meldings of external and internal event, and her method worked even better in *Fanny Kemble* (1931), a reasonably complex drawing of the actress. Bobbé worked from Kemble's memoirs and other personal papers, bringing a method formerly used to write biography of men to women's narrative.

Freed from the necessity that the subject of biography be an important historical or public figure, many women turned to writing biography—and they sometimes wrote biographies of women subjects. During the 1920s and early 1930s, American biography—including a substantial representation of women's lives—came into its own. Rheta L. Dorr's *Susan *Anthony, the Woman Who Changed the Mind of a Nation* (1928); Alice S. Blackwell's *Lucy Stone* (1930); Ruth Finley's *Lady of Godey's: Sarah Josepha*

Hale (1931); and Fleta C. Springer's *According to the Flesh; A Biography of Mary Baker Eddy* (1930) dealt sensibly with women subjects. Some very capable women biographers dealt again with the life stories of women writers—Genevieve Taggard and Josephine Pollitt wrote new biographies of Emily *Dickinson (both 1930); Marie H. Howe and Elizabeth W. Schermerhorn presented George Sand from new perspectives (both 1927); and Caroline Ticknor wrote *Louisa May Alcott; a Memoir* in 1928. Martha Dickinson Bianchi had published *The Life and Letters of Emily Dickinson* in 1924; Vivian Burnette wrote *Romantick Lady (Frances Hodgson Burnett)* in 1927. In 1930 when Margaret Bell tried the technique of having Margaret Fuller "speak" her writings in a novelistic Fuller biography, critics decided they preferred biography straight. Agnes Repplier, Emanie L. Sachs, Edith Curtis, Helen Augur, and Winifred K. Rugg also wrote biographies about women subjects.

One of the best biographies of this period was Susan *Glaspell's book about her husband, *Road to the Temple: The Life of George Cram Cook*, 1927. The modernist poet Amy *Lowell (with her two-volume biography of John Keats), investigative reporter Ida M. Tarbell, and historical novelist Honore W. Morrow also joined the group of women biographers who chose to write about male subjects: Agnes R. Burr, Mary Agnes Best, Elizabeth Cutting, Temple Bodley, Catherine D. Mackenzie, Clara Barrus, Lucy Cable Bikle, Dorothy Dudley, Margaret Goldsmith, Julia E. Harris, Elsie Gluck, Mary E. Phillips, Katherine M. Roof, Anna B. Dodd, Emily Easton, Clara G. Stillman, Helen H. Grant, and others.

Interest in women's lives burgeoned so that a number of collections of shorter biographies of women subjects—written by men—were also published during the 1920s (among them, *Forgotten Ladies, Gallant Ladies*, and *Uncommon Americans*). Besides the expected Presidents' wives, subjects here included Mary Baker Eddy, Susan B. Anthony, Emily Dickinson and Anne *Bradstreet. In 1929 F. O. Matthiessen's *Sarah Orne *Jewett* revived interest in her and her fiction.

During the 1930s and the 1940s, the depressed economy and World War II put an end to experimental publishing, and the niche that women biographers had found in the expanding marketplace disappeared. Catherine Drinker *Bowen, Margaret L. Coit, and a few other women biographers continued to publish (Mary Gray Peck's *Carrie Chapman Catt*, 1944, was a bright spot in the period), but activity diminished to such an extent that Carolyn *Heilbrun may be right when she claims that contemporary women's biography as today's readers know it began with Nancy Milford's *Zelda* in 1970. In her sympathetic portrayal of F. Scott Fitzgerald's problematic wife, Milford told the couple's story from the woman's perspective and thereby led several generations of readers to re-assess the better known male writer's history. In Milford's book, Zelda was not just one of a pair; she was a sentient and talented woman in her own right.

This use of what poet Adrienne * Rich called "re-visioning," bringing different perspectives to the historical events as they had already been defined and recognized, has come to characterize the rich period of the writing of biographies of women, the last twenty-five years. Many of the more important life stories published during the 1970s and 1980s were re-tellings of biographies already known, but presented differently because of the author's insightful understanding of family structure, gender roles, medical history, and cultural circumstances. Through the Louisa May Alcott readers, as they came to be known—the biographies of Martha Saxton (*Louisa May: A Modern Biography*, 1978), Madelon Bedell (*The Alcotts: Biography of a Family*, 1980), Sarah Elbert (*A Hunger for Home: Louisa May Alcott and Little Woman*, 1984), and the work of such other women scholars as Judith Fetterley and Ann Douglas—a life profile emerged that privileged Alcott's *Work* and her dissenting fictional voice over her more predictable, money-making books for adolescents. Similarly, to the staid expatriate Mrs. * Wharton, whose long novels had all but disappeared from the * canon of American texts, R. W. B. Lewis's prize-winning *Edith Wharton, A Biography* in 1975 brought both new attention and new understanding. Followed two years later by a more intensely psychological reading, Cynthia Griffin Wolff's *A Feast of Words, The Triumph of Edith Wharton*, these good biographies in tandem reversed the downward spiral of Wharton's reputation, and she became the most often taught, and most often read, of the early modernists. Shari Benstock's new biography of Wharton, fifteen years after this dual re-visioning, draws on an even greater quantity of unpublished materials, and makes use of the contemporary reader's ability to understand Wharton's conflicts—social, sexual, and economic. Judith Thurman's *Isak Dinesen: The Life of a Storyteller* (1982) had the same kind of revitalizing effect on Dinesen's reputation.

Emily Toth's *Kate * Chopin* (1990) also re-writes earlier existing biographies of the Southern woman, with new attention to her social and sexual life after she was widowed. In each case of the literary biography providing new kinds of personal information, the biographers'

attention to the subject's work is also enriched appreciably by the changing biographical emphasis. Successive enriching has been the result of the various biographies of American novelist and short story writer Jean * Stafford, whose most recent biographer, Ann Hurlburt, has written a superlative biography in *The Interior Castle, The Art and Life of Jean * Stafford* (1992).

Gioia Diliberto's 1992 *Hadley*, the Hadley Richardson story, re-tells the narrative of Alice Sokoloff's *Hadley: The First Mrs. Hemingway* (1973). The difference, in the twenty year interval, was Diliberto's access to much new correspondence, readers' readiness to appreciate Hadley's being willing to live alone, and some reliance on an intermediate telling, Bernice Kert's *The Hemingway Women* (1983).

Sharon O'Brien's first volume of *Willa * Cather* does more than tell a new version of the woman writer's story; it illustrates a woman biographer using the genre in order to educate her readers. Because much of O'Brien's understanding of Cather depends on her relationship within her family, and her self-imaging of a life role, which includes what O'Brien calls * "lesbianism," the biography provides readers with recent sociological, sexual, and feminist information necessary to understand the biographer's approach. While such inclusion is somewhat digressive, O'Brien handles her tactic capably, and subsequent women's biographies have benefited from the information the Cather book helped to circulate—as have two 1990 important biographies of Cather: Hermione Lee's *Willa Cather: Double Lives* and Merrill Maguire's *After the World Broke in Two: The Later Novels of Willa Cather*, which is an intellectual biography.

Women biographers are also telling new stories. Noel Riley Fitch's seminal *Sylvia * Beach and the Lost Generation* (1983)—to be followed soon by her biography of the difficult to categorize, and to appreciate, Anaïs * Nin—provided a quantity of information about * Beach and other women in the Paris expatriate world. In the case of Gertrude * Stein, whose life had been told by several male biographers as well as Elizabeth Sprigge and Janet Hobhouse, her story is now being contextualized in the framework of her family's story by Linda Wagner-Martin. In 1977 Linda Simon told a good share of Stein's story in *The Biography of Alice B. Toklas*, and the current narrative of expatriate women's lives is also composed of valuable insights from Meryle Secrest's *Between Me and Life: A Biography of Romaine Brooks* (1974), Anne Chisholm's *Nancy Cunard* (1981), Karla Jay's *The Amazon and the Page* (1988), and Thadious Davis's *Nella Larsen* (1994).

Women who write women's biographies are

now less concerned about their identity as women, and about their subject's identity as a woman. All the censure, all the prevarication, all the taboo topics have gone by the board (although the recent controversy over Louise DeSalvo's focus on Virginia *Woolf's sexual abuse by her half-brothers in her 1988 *Virginia Woolf* suggests that practical reception is not quite so ideal as theorists would have readers believe). Women biographers can therefore be more honest, more explicit, and more genuine in emphasizing what they believe readers should find central to interpretation. (Brenda Maddox's 1988 *Nora* includes a number of letters that, even ten years ago, might not have seen print because of their being in questionable taste—regardless of the fact that James Joyce wrote them.)

For all the self-congratulation about how far women's biography has come, and how wide a readership is following it and its progress, the critic or the writer of biography must ask, how much has changed since biography was defined as the adulatory recounting of external events in the life of a male subject. That narrative began with his birth and ancestry, followed the events of his public life, and ended with his death. Even though women's lives often break out of these conventional patterns and time frames, and speak for their own emphases—their own "event"—are the biographers of women really free to use structures that are different from traditional paradigms? Will the reading public honor the biographer's mandate to tell the story entire, without omitting or shading parts of the truth—even if the story is unpleasant or in poor taste?

Carolyn Heilbrun has noted that "the woman who writes herself a life beyond convention, or the woman whose biographer perceives her as living beyond conventional expectations, has usually early recognized in herself a special gift without name or definition." Whether living beyond or outside marriage or other approved women's options—or writing about women living controversial roles—the woman writer must expect criticism. Guardians of the literary establishment will chastise her because she seems *not* to know the rules, and neither fiction nor biography is now an appropriate place to write a prolegomenon about the writer's intention. On one hand, the very reason a woman becomes an interesting subject to treat in biography—her life's difference from the expectations of her culture—may make a standard linear narrative of external events unsuitable. On the other, too experimental a structure, or too little emphasis on those external events that may be less significant than the subject's internal life, leaves the biography as a book open to criticism. What should be most compelling about the woman as subject, to return to Heilbrun's comment, is her possession of "a special gift without name or definition."

One wishes it were possible to be more explicit about what constitutes greatness, or even specialness, in either a woman or a biography. Undoubtedly, Heilbrun's vagueness is meant to suggest that some mystery be allowed the achieving woman, and that her story be told in whatever mode seems appropriate to her own sensibility. Luckily, recent biography of women has given us wonderful and varied examples of how narratives of women's lives might be told: Jean Chalon, *Portrait of a Seductress: The World of Natalie Barney* (1979), Mary A. Hill, *Charlotte Perkins *Gilman: The Making of a Radical Feminist, 1860–1896* (1980), Susan Stanford Friedman, *Psyche Reborn: The Emergence of *H.D.* (1981), Joan Givner, *Brave Voyage: The Life of Katherine Anne *Porter* (1981), Elizabeth Young-Bruehl, *Hannah Arendt* (1982), Alice Wexler, *Emma *Goldman: An Intimate Life* (1984), Sharon O'Brien, *Willa Cather* (1987), Linda Wagner-Martin's and Anne Stevenson's biographies of Sylvia *Plath (1987 and 1989), Esther Lanigan Stineman, *Mary *Austin: Song of a Maverick* (1989), Roxana Robinson, *Georgia O'Keeffe, A Life* (1989), Phyllis Rose, *Woman of Letters: A Life of Virginia Woolf* (1978) and *Josephine Baker* (1990), Diane Wood Middlebrook, *Anne *Sexton, A Biography* (1991), and Blanch Weisen Cook, *Eleanor Roosevelt*, volume one (1992).

Unlike American women's autobiography, however, women's biography has just begun to be recognized as a genre in itself. Current research concentrates on mapping the territory; important theoretical work about the practice of writing women's biography remains to be done.

• Edward H. O'Neill, *A History of American Biography, 1800–1935* (1968). Mary Hiatt, *The Way Women Write* (1977). Anthony M. Friedson, ed. *New Directions in Biography* (1981). Dennis W. Petrie, *Ultimately Fiction, Design in Modern American Literary Biography* (1981). Leonore Hoffman and Margo Culley, ed. *Women's Personal Narratives; Essays in Criticism and Pedagogy* (1985). William Zinsser, ed. *Extraordinary Lives, The Art and Craft of American Biography* (1986). Carolyn G. Heilbrun, *Writing a Woman's Life* (1988). Eric Homberger and John Charmley, eds. *The Troubled Face of Biography* (1988). Rita Felski, *Beyond Feminist Aesthetics: Feminist Literature and Social Change* (1989). Gail Porter Mandell, *Life Into Art, Conversations with Seven Contemporary Biographers* (1991). Ann Fehn, Ingeborg Hoesterey, and Maria Tatar, eds. *Neverending Stories, Toward a Critical Narratology* (1992).

Linda Wagner-Martin

BIRTH. Childbirth, as a subject of women's writing across genres in the United States, has taken many forms, from silences or oblique references to the subject, to jubilant defiance of its medicalization. The following three categories provide a frame for tracing the ways birth has been portrayed historically by women both in fact and in attitude: I. Conceived in Sin (colonial period), II. Don't You Worry Your Pretty Little Head (post-colonial through the twentieth century), and III. What Do Women Want? (contemporary).

Conceived in Sin. Oversight of *pregnancy and birth in the colonies followed patterns established by male-dominated European societies, professions, and social constructs. Until the development of the forceps (early 1600s) and new market possibilities for opportunistic physicians, events associated with female reproduction were of little interest to male practitioners. Women, especially midwives, counselled pregnant women, prepared them for birth with personal stories and anecdotes, and attended deliveries. The patriarchal society, church, and government, which had assigned strict domestic roles to women, regarded pregnancy as a private female matter.

Although women writers, in general, are barely present in the early literary history of this nation, writing about a topic as "private" as birth would have violated prevailing standards of propriety. Not surprisingly, very little written discourse by women about pregnancy and birth has been discovered. Sociologists conclude that a rich oral literature must have sustained women during these times, but find only oblique, socially correct references in writing.

Diaries, Journals, and Letters. Prior to the nineteenth century few women wrote for publication. They wrote privately, in forms that were inclusive, fragmentary, and interrupted, an embodiment of the uncertainties and responsibilities of daily life. The entries, however, in these private *diaries, journals, and *letters are themselves circumspect: they reveal only veiled accounts of pregnancy and birth with little suggestion of physical changes during the nine months and not many descriptions of labor and delivery.

Religious settlers brought with them stern biblical injunctions about Eve's ignominy in the Garden; the presence of pain during labor represented to men and women alike an infliction by God for women's assumed perdition and moral frailty. As Cotton Mather's solemn and frightening words to expectant mothers suggest, childbirth was a serious travail with high infant mortality rates: mothers might "need no other linnen . . . but a *Winding Sheet*, and have no other chamber but a *grave*, no neighbors but *worms*." Private writings show an acceptance of pain as punishment and the fear and terror it inspired; they also show that in private and profound loneliness women adhered obediently to conventional impositions. Few wrote about their fears of death. We assume that women talked out these fears rather than writing: "nine months of gestation," says historian Judith Walzer Leavitt, "was always a possible death sentence." Sylvia D. Hoffert's careful study of attitudes about birth during this period reviews personal comments in private writings: Sally Hughes wrote that she was in a state of "constant depression"; Millicent Hunt was "depressed in spirit"; and Elizabeth Parker said of her pregnant friend, she "looks so weak and miserable, I dread to see the end thereof."

Public Writings. Domestic poems written by Anne *Bradstreet (1612–1672) illustrate rare confidence and brave struggle between the poet's feelings and religious sanctions. The poems articulate her desires and passions within a context of rigid censorship and admonition. The mother of eight children, Bradstreet understood the conditions of pregnancy and childbirth. She acknowledges, for example, in "The Four Ages of Man" that she was "conceiv'd in sin," a "mean beginning, blushing cann't reveale." Her mother's "breeding sickness" was marked by suffering, but the pain of that birth, she advises, "cann't be told by tongue." For centuries, even women writers like Anne Bradstreet accepted the supposed sinfulness of sex, and the guilt imposed on them by unrelenting patriarchs.

Don't You Worry Your Pretty Little Head. When transfer of control shifted from midwife to physician, women remained understandably silent. For example, the shift from "meddlesome midwives" to professional males reduced reliance on personal narratives by women, introduced unfamiliar and intimidating medical jargon, and—by virtue of male intrusion into an intensely private, previously female situation—promoted modesty, delicacy, and the bothersome corollary, submission. The medical profession looked with self-serving disdain on the model of care and comfort provided by midwives; physician control weakened connections among women and increased dependency on male providers. Traditionally, pregnancy and birth had brought women in different socioeconomic classes together because all women, regardless of social *class, relied on the practical knowledge and skills of experienced midwives. Physicians struggled persistently, even to costuming themselves as women, for acceptance and eventual dominance, using newly formed professional organizations to challenge and subordinate *midwifery. Gradually but decisively, pregnancy and birth were refigured from being considered a natural part of the life process to being a medical event, a pathology in need of both physician supervision and management.

Considering women's continuing subjugation during these decades of struggle for medical dominance and control, the prudish taboos about feminine matters, and the imposed disorientations accompanying the introduction of physician-managed pregnancy and birth, any inclination for honest reflection and literary expression about birth was suppressed.

The entire process from admission, to medication, to delivery-positioning, accentuates and accommodates the attending physician who oversees with paternalistic efficiency the "machinery" of childbirth (analgesics, enema, shaving, episiotomy, stirrups, anaesthesia, etc.). In *The Woman in the Body* Emily Martin reviews medicine's obsession with the uterus as machine, physician as efficient foreman, and the resulting depersonalized language and imagery for describing birth. "Medical imagery," says Martin, "juxtaposes two consistent pictures: the uterus as a machine that produces the baby and the woman as the laborer who produces the baby." In an extreme but common occurrence, the abuses associated with cesarean sections represent the most vivid example of medically constructed births.

Women's dissatisfaction with the medical model is expressed often. In *No Longer Patient*, Susan Sherwin outlines from a feminist perspective concerns about technological intervention in reproduction (technophilia) that disregard women's autonomy, informed consent, and decision-making functions. As Regina Morantz-Sanchez points out *(Science and Sympathy)*, women in the twentieth century were freed by the "industrial order into more sophisticated forms of degradation."

In all cases and by whatever delivery approach, any subject dealing with matters below the waist has remained for too many centuries unsuitable for written commentary by ladies. Reformists, on the other hand, protested vigorously so that their concerns and bold positions about improving women's conditions created rebellious sparks that eventually would ignite.

What Do Women Want? During the twentieth century a number of circumstances shifted to allow new opportunities for women. The ability to control reproduction represented new freedoms, and sometimes, burdens. Due to public health measures, improved sanitation, and water safety, family size diminished, maternal deaths declined, and newborns thrived. When insured women became pregnant, it became routine for physicians to confirm the expectation and prescribe a schedule of visits and examinations. Except for the poor and the otherwise marginalized, American women embraced the medical model and the rationale for more technologies. Women were able to manage families and careers; pregnancies were no longer capricious events; parents could be assured of fetal wellness and sex; deliveries could be scheduled according to preferred physician hours; and fertility subspecialties proliferated.

As women reflected on their situations and began to use their voices to reframe personal experiences, questions arose about their loss of power and identity in matters dealing with themselves and their bodies. Recent writings about pregnancy and birth tend to abandon paternal parameters, choosing instead to validate and authenticate the women's long subverted inner feelings and emotions. In literature, thoughts wander along uncharted paths loosely, playfully, expansively. Today, little is taboo.

No Longer Silent. While many women contentedly adhere to the inherited model of physician control, others are searching for something beyond patriarchal patterns. Modern writings, therefore, are revolutionary: women no longer hesitate to tell the story of birth and pregnancy through their own eyes. Anne *Sexton, Joyce Carol *Oates, Sharon Olds, Jane *Smiley, Linda Pastan, Ellen *Gilchrist, Ellen Bryant Voigt, and others push old restraints aside to describe subjectively the concerns, joys, and difficulties that accompany each birth. From them readers gain an enhanced understanding of what childbirth entails, and means, in different but similar circumstances.

Freedom to express honestly is epitomized in "She Understands Me" by Lucille *Clifton. The poem is refreshingly vivid and real: "it is all blood and breaking," she announces, an infant dropping "out of its box." She speaks of "wetness," "emptying," and "squalling" without regard for medicine's aseptic whiteness and sterility or longstanding commitments to privacy and delicacy.

Ellen Gilchrist, in *The Annunciation*, questions the New Testament's story of Mary's passive role in the immaculate conception. In Gilchrist's story , the protagonist, Amanda, experiences childbirth as it has always been. Instead of angels there are street-savvy nuns to guide her through the real-life circumstances of labor and delivery: "gauze pads," "blood," "hemostats," "slipperyness," "mucus," and "sinewy cords." Women writers have discovered disparate tones for telling the truth about shared experiences. Linda Pastan's poem "Notes from the Delivery Room" focuses on birth directly but with unexpected imagery: the speaker, who is in labor—"strapped down" and "crowning"—is released by her imagination. She transforms herself to become a magician pulling "a rabbit from [her] swollen hat." While many women may be disturbed by medicine's continuing use of straps and stirrups, the speaker soars freely and creatively. About sex, Sharon Olds is similarly direct. In the audaciously titled "A Woman in Heat Wiping Herself," she speaks of "the hole," "gold grease," "follicles," "solemn spillage," and "glittering threads," boldly ignoring former language constraints.

The Doctor Is Enamel. In "Unknown Girl in the Maternity Ward," an important and painfully provocative poem by Anne Sexton, the speaker lingers over her "illegal" child, a "small knuckle" lying on the bed. The mother has carried the child, "my sin," to term in defiance of conventions about unmarried women's pregnancies. In spite of the hospital's cold and disapproving atmosphere, the beautiful, loving words whispered by the mother to the child reveal powerful ambivalence about her choice. She wonders what her baby sees, calls her "funny face," but the nagging background remains: "You trouble my silence." Still, it is not just the baby's presence that is troubling; her caregivers are critical of her situation. Wanting only facts, doctors become "enamel" and staff "scold" her. All the while she is struggling alone with her ultimate decision to send her baby off, this baby who is her "sin and nothing more." Sexton is charting new ground by giving readers an honest portrayal of complexities that can accompany pregnancies and births.

"The Pleasure of Her Company" by Jane Smiley contains two women's discussion about the loss of a baby. While they talk in the kitchen about Frannie's dead baby, readers learn that the mother's undetected illness resulted in a tragic labor and, probably preventable, outcome. Frannie's evaluation of her physician's incompetence suggests a new irreverence for paternalistic figures: "The doctor was an ass."

Somewhere in Alabama. For minority women, silence remained profound. Not only were they mute, they were invisible. Deprived of social, political, and economic existence, these women had to face hopelessness, abuse, and despair. Their particular trials and celebrations have been given voice by Toni * Morrison, Alice * Walker, Nikki * Giovanni, Sandra * Cisneros, Judith Ortiz * Cofer, and Louise * Erdrich. From them we know the terms of survival, the cultural fictions that define and liberate.

"Eyes" by Lucille * Clifton is not about the physicality of birth, but about inequities and deprivation. Here she speaks of a black girl giving birth "somewhere in Alabama" in a "tarpaper room." Nowhere in medical texts is there reference to such a birthing room; Clifton's lines force disturbing confrontations with the circumstances of birth for disadvantaged populations. The deprived, shivering girl sings with pathos a song of guarded hope. Clifton lays out for the reader fragments of a story of an uncomfortable reality. If white women have been managed and controlled, black women have been ignored.

Now women of all colors are speaking for themselves with compelling intensity. The portrayal of a black woman in labor in Toni Morrison's *The Bluest Eye* is not easily forgotten. The physician rounding with his residents dismisses her as one of "these here women you don't have any trouble with." She is teaching material, a faceless body for learning about medicine. Her voice describes the shameful treatment. The "old one was learning the young ones about babies." Without looking her in the eye or addressing her as a vulnerable human being dependent on the medical establishment, the physician demonstrates the calumnies of professional abuse: he jellies his glove and rams his hand between her legs. Morrison gives the indigent patient words for describing how she is treated and how she feels. As readers, we are stunned and outraged by the professional arrogance. More important, however, we are grateful for the empowering, descriptive voice that once suffered in silence.

Regardless of race, women are writing increasingly about difficult issues such as miscarriage and * abortion; other related topics including birth defects and technology interventions are reflected in "Birth" by Constance Urdang, "Damage" by Ellen Bryant Voigt, and "Written on Learning of Arrhythmia in the Unborn Child" by Judith Skillman. In "The Abortion," a short story by Alice Walker, and "The Wide and Varied World" by Ellen Bryant Voigt, women writers deal with personal and emotional subtleties beyond controversial headlines and court actions.

By asking essential questions and considering real and imaginary responses, literature contributes to vision, freedom, and understanding for all human beings. Writings by women enable us to think anew, to explore other possibilities.

[*See* Body and Health.]

• Barbara Katz Rothman, *In Labor: Women and Power in the Birthplace* (1982). Mary Field Belenky et al., eds., *Women's Ways of Knowing: The Development of Self, Voice, and Mind* (1986). Emily Martin, *The Woman in the Body: A Cultural Analysis of Reproduction* (1987). Marta Weigle, *Creation and Procreation: Feminist Reflections on Mythologies of Cosmogony and Parturition* (1989). Anne Sexton, "Unknown Girl in the Maternity Ward," *The Naked Astronaut.* Susan Sherwin, *No Longer Patient: Feminist Ethics and Health Care* (1992).

Delese Wear

BIRTH CONTROL. The term *birth control* was coined by feminist Margaret Sanger during her early-twentieth-century crusade to legalize contraception and allow for "planned parenthood." But while the term itself emerged only in 1914, the methods—some more reliable than others—have been in existence for centuries.

For as long as women have sought to control their lives, their bodies, and their choices, they have sought to control their reproductive cycles. Popular preventative methods have included abstinence, withdrawal, potions, douches, pills, prophylactics, and pessaries (a nineteenth-century term for diaphragm-like devices).

Once pregnant, many women have sought out abortive methods ranging from surgical procedures to homemade remedies, some of which bordered on the hazardous or even fatal, such as ingesting poisons, throwing themselves from heights, or undergoing invasive procedures by unskilled practitioners.

Although the Supreme Court's 1973 *Roe v. Wade* decision legalizing abortion should have made such drastic measures obsolete, the fact that there are still deaths from self-induced abortions (not to mention medically sanctioned ones) reveals that birth control has been and remains a life-and-death matter for women.

As John D'Emilio and Estelle B. Freedman document in *Intimate Matters: A History of Sexuality in America* (1988), in the 1800s the medical profession began to intervene in contraceptive matters, once considered the concerns solely of organized religion and/or midwifery. By mid-century, it was fairly common for pamphlets, guides, advertisements, and lecturers to circulate, dispensing advice as to the "best" prophylactic methods. For the most part, however, women seeking answers turned to perhaps the most reliable source: other women. Just as their mothers did and their daughters and granddaughters continue to do, many nineteenth-century women confided in other women when it came to learning the hows and how-not-tos of birth control.

The relative freedom with which such information was exchanged was soon countermanded with the passage of the so-called Comstock Law in 1873, which prohibited the circulation of contraceptive devices or information through the mail (a law that was not fully overturned until the Supreme Court's 1965 *Griswold v. Connecticut* decision). It took the efforts of early twentieth-century crusaders like Sanger (who was herself arrested for violating the Comstock Law) to bring the topic of contraception back out into the open and onto the public agenda.

Sanger should be given ample credit for her pioneering work in birth control, work that is continued today by the organization she founded, the Birth Control Federation of America, eventually renamed Planned Parenthood. However, her project was not without its limitations—in part due to both her own and many of her followers' belief that birth control was not only an individual issue of choice, but also a means of population control. For instance, Sanger's efforts were targeted primarily at the working class, and while truly sympathetic and committed to their needs for contraception, her desire to reduce lower-class births was at times tainted with a middle-class abhorrence of what many saw as ever-increasing broods of impoverished urchins. Additionally, some of the later national efforts of her Birth Control Federation were explicitly racist, including its 1939 Negro Project, intended to halt the "careless" and "disastrous" breeding it believed many blacks engaged in.

Just as birth control's history is not without controversy, so too is its use for most women. For instance, following the invention of the birth control pill in the early 1960s, a veritable sexual revolution was declared. But because the "free love" that was the buzzword of that period often translated into sex on demand, many women who lived through those times have questioned whether that love came as freely to the women involved as to the men. Even now, for many heterosexual women, the realization that both men and women are involved in making babies but that women alone are frequently handed sole responsibility for preventing conception or birth provides glaring evidence that the double standard is still alive. Additionally, as many users of oral contraceptives or surgically implanted devices—especially the early high-estrogen pill and the intra-uterine device known as the Dalkon Shield—will attest, where research into birth control is concerned, women often function as experimental guinea pigs.

New and safer contraceptive methods are clearly mandatory, and despite conservative political and religious attempts to ban or impede birth control research, the 1990s have seen the invention of the female condom and federal approval of both Norplant implants and of research on the controversial "abortion pill," R.U. 486. As more and more women continue to demand more and better means of birth control, birth control itself is being redefined by women to mean not just reproductive choice, but reproductive choices.

Despite this country's renowned Puritan modesty, birth control has been featured in a surprising number of American novels, especially contemporary ones such as Sylvia Plath's *The Bell Jar* (1963), Philip Roth's *Goodbye, Columbus* (1959), Lisa Alther's *Kinflicks* (1976), Erica *Jong's *Fear of Flying* (1973), Gloria *Naylor's *The Women of Brewster Place* (1982), Alice *Walker's *The Color Purple* (1982), and Jane * Smiley's *A Thousand Acres* (1992). Marge *Piercy's *Woman on the Edge of Time* (1976) provides perhaps the most utopian literary take on birth control; although Piercy's late-nineteenth-century hispanic protagonist is forced to undergo a hysterectomy, her visits to the year 2137 hold out the promise that a time will come when the genetic and cultural ties that bind women and reproduction are broken, leaving men and women equally free and willing to "mother." The question remains: how do we get there from here?

[See also Abortion; Birth; Reproduction.]

• Margaret Sanger, *My Fight for Birth Control* (1931). Linda Gordon, *Woman's Body, Woman's Right: A Social History of Birth Control in America* (1976). James Reed, *From Private Vice to Public Virtue: The Birth Control Movement and American Society since 1830* (1978). The Boston Women's Health Book Collective, *The New Our Bodies, Ourselves: Updated and Expanded for the '90s* (1992).

Cynthia J. Davis

BISEXUALITY. Women have been attracted to members of both sexes throughout American history. Although the majority of them do not appear to have enacted "bisexuality" in their choice of sexual partners, a few assuredly did. Indirect historical evidence of female "bibehavior" is provided by a 1655 New Haven sodomy statute criminalizing "unnatural acts" between women whose marital status might reasonably be inferred from the colonists' God-given mandate to reproduce. Direct evidence of cross-sexual behavior can be found in private memoirs of women who represent themselves as having had sex with women and men.

I have placed these inscriptions of bisexuality within quotes so as to mark their anachronistic use. The fact is, the category of sexuality we now take for granted did not come into being as a separate domain, with distinct properties and rules particular to it, until the mid-nineteenth century, when new medical technologies made it possible to systematize bodily processes and behaviors in heretofore unheard of ways. Another fifty years passed before this relatively diffuse sexual field was subdivided into the antithetical sexual territories of homosex and heterosex. For a number of decades thereafter, bisexual behavior was defined extrinsically as a deviation from one or the other norm.

Women who enacted bisexuality under the rule of two sexual types differed widely. Numbers must have internalized these typologies, if only because there were socially compelling reasons to do so. Think, for instance, of the women who acted in isolation without bibehavioral role models or bisexual community support; for these women the pressure to understand oneself as others did must have been intense. Consider also the operation of "heterosexual privilege," which surely induced some women who were having sex with women to prove they were real(ly) heterosexuals participating in a "fling." Despite these definitional and societal constraints, many women did participate in bisexual behaviors without apology. Among them are Almeda Sperry, a social activist, sex-worker, and passionate friend of Emma *Goldman; Ma Rainey and Bessie Smith, who represented bisexuality, lesbianism, and male homosexuality through the medium of the blues, while enacting bisexuality in their choice of sexual partners; an array of Greenwhich Village artists, including the poet Edna St. Vincent *Millay, who slept with women and men; and a number of American expatriates, one of whom, *H.D., brought the experience of bisexuality to her therapeutic sessions with Sigmund Freud. These women were subsequently cross-identified as lesbian (circa the 1970s) and bisexual (circa 1992) by populist historiographers representing either of the two sexual communities. However, with the sole exception of H.D., there is no evidence that any of these women ever identified as being any sexuality whatsoever. It behooves the sexual ethnographer to take these women on their own terms, since to do otherwise is to confound the very meaning of sexual identity, which, while incorporating erotic choices, feelings, and practices, remains irreducible to any or all of the above enactments. For unlike sexual enactments, which exist in and of themselves, sexual identity requires an inaugural act of self-recognition/self-naming, whose grammatical expression is "I am," as opposed to "I do" or "I have." Under this definition, H.D. is a bisexual woman who understood her sexuality as psycho-sexual androgyny, which was also the core of her identity as an artist.

Historically speaking, H.D. belongs to an exceptional group of women who publicly represented themselves as bisexual prior to the 1970s, when the second wave of feminism provided a women's community and androgynous ideology that made it possible for many more women to come out. For a time it seemed as though bisexuality was here to stay. However, for a variety of reasons, the most important being the lack of incentive to build a bi-community or movement, the phenomenon was short-lived. Many of the women who saw themselves as bisexual went on to identify as lesbians or returned to identifying as heterosexuals, while those who continued to think of themselves as "bi" found little support in either sexual community. Without it they were all but silenced—until 1990–1991, when unprecedented numbers of women and men went on record as being bisexual and a multicultural bicommunity was formed. This formation was due in part to the proliferation of bisexual coming-out narratives, a collection of which appeared in 1991 under the title *Bi Any Other Name: Bisexual People Speak Out.*

A number of conditions enabled the emergence of a collective bi identity, the first and most important of which was the established existence of a gay-lesbian community. Many "new" bisexual women had previously identified as lesbians, and those who had been political activists brought their skills to bear in organizing bisexuals. When erotic experiences with, or in some cases, fantasies about the opposite sex prompted these women to redefine their sexuality, they did so on their own terms, as bi-identified subjects whose sexuality was inalienably queer. Thus, against extrinsic definitions of female bisexual behavior as discrete manifestations of lesbian-sex and heterosex, bi women claimed to enact "queer sex" in their relations with women and men. By insisting on their queer identity, biwomen sought to avoid accusations of heterosexual privilege and to win a place in the gay-lesbian community. By the end of 1992, they had met with limited success. Generally speaking, bi support is highest among younger (or new) lesbians and gays, who also tend to identify as queer, and lower among older members of the community. The *AIDS crisis has also played a formative role in the new bi movement. In the first place, AIDS united lesbians and gay men despite the divisions of the 1970s and early 1980s. Though gender differences remained a source of tension, political bonds, friendships, and love relationships were forged as individuals from the two groups worked, mourned, and celebrated together. In the second place, throughout the eighties, bisexuals were repeatedly blamed for "spreading AIDS" to "innocent populations." Without question, most of the scapegoating came from heterosexuals who charged the presence of HIV/AIDS in "the heterosexual community" to bisexual men, but some of it also came from lesbians who attributed AIDS in "the lesbian community" to women who used intravenous drugs and/or slept with (gay) men. These bi attacks inspired bi defenses, which in turn prompted bi solidarity. The third condition enabling the recent emergence of bisexuality is strictly related to the sharp increase in bisexual subjects quite apart from any political movement they might organize. The general name for this condition is postmodernity. Two features of postmodernity are of particular relevance: one is represented by the proliferation and commodification of styles, sexual styles being a case in point; the other by a breakdown in the "old categories," and thus the erosion of sexual identity itself. This is not to say that sexual identity has disappeared under postmodernism, at least not for most. However, it is to say that identities of all sorts have generally fallen under suspicion. In this situation it is possible, perhaps chic, to hold on to sexual identity as a necessary sociopolitical fiction, while recognizing—if only in principle—the fluidity and/or uncategorizability of sexuality itself.

[*See also* Heterosexuality; Lesbianism; Sexualities; Transsexuality.]

                                        Kate Cummings

BISHOP, Elizabeth (1911–1979), poet, was born on 8 February 1911 in Worcester, Massachusetts. Her father died before her first birthday, and her mother suffered a series of nervous collapses and was committed to a mental hospital when Bishop was five, thus being permanently removed from the life of her only child. From ages three to six, Bishop lived in Great Village, Nova Scotia, with her mother's parents, and was then taken in by her father's family in Worcester and Boston. She attended Walnut Hill School near Boston during her high-school years, followed by four years at Vassar. By way of the Vassar librarian, in New York Bishop met the poet Marianne *Moore, twenty-four years her senior, and their friendship quickly flourished. Her earliest work, which was influenced by George Herbert, Gerard Manley Hopkins, and Moore, appeared in the Vassar undergraduate magazine she had helped to found. Having briefly considered a career in medicine, she turned to poetry with the encouragement of Moore, who published a handful of her poems in an anthology called *Trial Balances* in 1935. In residence in New York for a year, she wrote her first mature poems, including "The Map" and "The Man-Moth." She then lived intermittently in Europe for three years before purchasing a house in Key West, Florida, in 1938. After being rejected by several New

York publishers, the first of her four volumes of poetry, *North and South*, was finally published in 1946. The next year she was introduced by Randall Jarrell to Robert Lowell, who became a lifelong friend.

In 1951, the geographical displacement in her life continued when she took ill on a trip to South America; left behind by a freighter in Brazil, she made that country her home for the next eighteen years. Her lesbian relationship with Lota de Macedo Soares gave her life stability and love, and she established residences in Rio de Janeiro, nearby Petrópolis, and, later, Ouro Prêto. *A Cold Spring*, her second volume of poetry, appeared in 1955. Brazil became the setting for many of the poems that were collected a decade later in *Questions of Travel* (1965).

After the suicide of Lota de Macedo Soares, Bishop increasingly began to live in the United States, and became poet-in-residence at Harvard University in 1969. A close friendship with Alice Methfessel began in 1971 and continued until the time of Bishop's death in 1979. Her final poetry volume, *Geography III*, was published in 1976.

Bishop often spent many years writing a single poem, working toward an effect of offhandedness and spontaneity. Committed to a "passion for accuracy," she re-created her worlds of Canada, America, Europe, and Brazil. Shunning self-pity, the poems thinly conceal her estrangements as a woman, a lesbian, an orphan, a geographically rootless traveler, a frequently hospitalized asthmatic, and a sufferer of depression and alcoholism. "I'm not interested in big-scale work as such," she once told Lowell. "Something needn't be large to be good."

• Manuscript holdings are at the Houghton Library, Harvard University; the Rosenbach Museum and Library, Philadelphia, Pennsylvania; the Vassar College Library; and the Washington University Libraries. See also Elizabeth Bishop, *The Complete Poems, 1927–1979* (1983). Elizabeth Bishop, *The Collected Prose*, ed. Robert Giroux (1984). Thomas Travisano, *Elizabeth Bishop: Her Artistic Development* (1988). David Kalstone, *Becoming a Poet: Elizabeth Bishop with Marianne Moore and Robert Lowell*, ed. Robert Hemenway (1989). Bonnie Costello, *Elizabeth Bishop: Questions of Mastery* (1991). Laurie Goldensohn, *Elizabeth Bishop: The Biography of a Poetry* (1992). Brett C. Miller, *Elizabeth Bishop: Life and the Memory of It* (1993).

George S. Lensing

BLACK AESTHETIC. The most fervent years of the black aesthetic may be measured along a political time line, beginning roughly with the 1964 Civil Rights Act and the publication in that same year of Martin Luther King, Jr.'s, "Letter from Birmingham Jail," and ending with the wholesale flight of American forces and their sympathizers from Vietnam in the fall of 1975. By that time, the best works by the leading aestheticians had been published. Other than Carolyn Gerald, no black female critics were among the group who were later to be called the new black aesthetic critics.

It is especially between 1967 (when "A Black Criteria" was published by Clarence Major) and 1971 that the new black aesthetic is refined into several different and singular visions by its adherents. In addition to his detailed definition of the black aesthetic already published in 1967, Major had written the introduction to *The New Black Poetry* in 1969, asserting that writing by blacks was the only humanistic writing of the period; all other writing had become mere artifice because of its disdain for human uplift.

Addison Gayle's best-known works, *The Black Aesthetic* (1971) and *The Way of the New World: The Black Novel in America* (1976), were also seminal. In *The Black Aesthetic*, Gayle laid the foundation of any set of principles that attempts to label itself as a black aesthetic: "A critical methodology has no relevance to the black community unless it aids men in becoming better than they are."

In the past, the term *universal* had always been used as a way of disavowing the literary validity of works by black authors. It was said that black authors worked with too much of an introverted ethnic flourish to appeal to non-black or non-American audiences, and this objection was offered as the excuse for not publishing black authors and as a reason for the lack of sales of books already in print. Major negates this idea by asserting that the term "universal" was too much of a "European cultural judgment" to be fairly applied to texts by black artists. This is another basic tenet of the new black aesthetic: to have black writers judged by unique indexes created from their own experiences and by the new black aestheticians themselves.

Key to Gayle's thinking in *The Way of the New World* is the idea that literature by blacks must always do something to better the collective good if it is to be considered valid writing. This component would later be a major point of disagreement between the New Black Aesthetic Critics and such black female writers as Alice *Walker and Gayl *Jones. Most of the women writers who were to become prominent in the mid- to late-1970s, such as Walker and Toni *Morrison, ignored the movement known as the black aesthetic, labeling it as both too restrictive and too male-specific to use as a critical grid for their works. It is during the late 1970s that black feminist criticism begins to surface, such as Mary Helen Washington's introduction to *Black Eyed Susans* (1975) and

Mari *Evans's *Black Women's Writings* (1981), which argued for more specialized grids for properly judging black women's writings. Those grids would include the concepts of an aesthetic of grace purportedly not to be found in the writing of black men and a textual reliance on the previous writings of black female authors.

But Gayle, Houston Baker, Gerald, Clarence Major, and Amiri Baraka saw their ideas as above and better than both the women writers' criticism and the mainstream critics' silence about their ideas. Their emphasis on social responsibility put the black aesthetic squarely in opposition to most, if not all, current trends in literary criticism. Innate in the new black aestheticians' stance on the social responsibility of art was their belief that mainstream criticism had always tried to dehumanize art so that it could not be used as human expression to better the social lot of both the artist and the receiver of the art. And thus, the new black aesthetic critics continue to propose their critical ideas as valid and workable long after their most thoughtful works had gone out of print.

And how did the black women writers of the time fare under the new black aesthetic rubric? Gerald seems to have been the only principal female critic in the black aesthetic movement, and her writings, while not so well known as those of Baraka, Baker, or Gayle, contributed to having the school's tenets examined by scholars and noticed by creative writers. But what of female creative writers and their association with black aesthetic principles?

In 1970 the first novels of both Alice Walker and Toni Morrison were published. Walker's *The Third Life of Grange Copeland* would seem to maintain most of the ostensible requirements of the black aesthetic; that is, that the work be socially uplifting in some way and that the book enumerate the horrors of being black and American. There was little critical fuss about this book from the new black aesthetic critics. Walker had had poetry published by a major publishing house before (*Once*, 1968), and perhaps the critics expected to see only another volume of poetry.

The Bluest Eye (1971) by Morrison seemed to catch the new black aesthetic critics off-guard also. Some have proposed that this was because the new black aesthetic elite were not accepting of black female writers who performed at a high level, by their own rules, and who, moreover, included unflattering portraits of black men in their novels (see an example of this by-now-classic exchange in the June *Jordan/Houston Baker/Henry Louis Gates, Jr. disagreement in *New Literary History*, 1987).

But Morrison's second novel, *Sula* (1973), did not escape notice. Gayle blasted the book at the Second Annual National Conference of Afro-American Writers held at Howard University in Washington, D.C., in 1976. Also during 1976, Gayle criticized Gayl Jones's *Eva's Man* as anti-black male and "bizarrely sadistic" *(Books)*. Thus, it would appear that there were certain aspects of these novels—the treatment of black men, the negative images conveyed of blacks in general—that could not fit comfortably under Gayle's black aesthetic.

Of other male and female writers who appeared later in the 1970s, the black aesthetic critics find none they can wholeheartedly embrace, returning again and again to Richard Wright as the exemplar of what a black writer should be and do. Besides the excellence of his texts, Wright is a favorite of the new black aestheticians for unspoken reasons. Certainly, he became the black literary voice of his time, with the publication in 1940 of his most famous book, *Native Son*. But he was also almost the only black voice to receive major promotion and acceptance during that period. The same degree of attention was not given to Margaret *Walker Alexander's *For My People* (1942) or Gwendolyn *Brooks's *A Street in Bronzeville* (1945). In his article "Afro-American Literature and Class Struggle," Amiri Baraka would say of Ntozake *Shange's work that it was "confused," and that Michelle Wallace's work was "not advanced" (*Black American Literature Forum* 12, 1982). Baraka insists that only writers who get to the crux of the problem, that is, monolithic, monopoly capitalism, are truly doing justice to black people and to a black aesthetic.

But the artists themselves seem to pay little attention by this time to the outlines of what the critical elite say is good and what is a sell-out. Baraka asserts that the black authors in the public eye in the 1980s are "Hollywood"; that is, commercial for the sake of being commercial, and that they, thus, are ferrying true black issues down the river of betrayal. Shange wrote that she seldom, if ever, read critics (*Geography* 6, 1983), and David Bradley, author of the prize-winning *The Chaneysville Incident* (1981), wrote that he worked from a base that he called "achromism," which operated under the critical assumption that no matter the merit of a text he wrote, his blackness would always outweigh his work when critical judgments were rendered, and that the negative effects his color would bring outweighed any critical opinion. By 1973, Major, in *Interviews with Black Writers*, had crystallized his ideas about the things black writers should do. Major writes that he is "against any artistic limiting by critics," and that the new black aesthetic did, unfortunately, serve in a limiting way.

The authors who were ignoring, or simply not reading, the requirements of the new black aesthetic critics—or reading any criticism for that matter—were proving Major's earlier premise correct. Something had crystallized by the middle to late 1970s, but it had solidified in the psyches of the creative artists who had drawn up standards of their own. The black aesthetic period showed that, despite what others may have assumed, black writers and critics had proven themselves to be as diverse—and as talented—in artistic thought and production as any other group on the contemporary scene.

[See also African-American Writing.]

• Clarence Major, "A Black Criteria," *Journal of Black Poetry* (Spring 1967): 23–25. Amiri Baraka, *Raise, Race, Rays, Rage: Essays since 1965* (1971). Addison Gayle, *The Black Aesthetic* (1971). Walter Shepperd, "An Interview with Clarence Major and Victor Hernandez Cruz," *New Black Voices*, ed. Abraham Chapman (1972), p. 545. Addison Gayle, *The Way of the New World: The Black Novel in America* (1976). Houston Baker, Jr., *The Journey Back* (1980). Amiri Baraka, "Afro-American Literature and Class Struggle," *Black American Literature Forum* 14, no. 1 (Fall 1980): 12. David Bradley, "Black and American in 1982," *Esquire* (May 1982): 60. Amiri Baraka, *The Autobiography* (1984). June Jordan, Houston Baker, and Henry Louis Gates, Jr., "Patriarchy and Rereading the Canon," *New Literary History* (Winter 1987): 17–23.

Reginald Martin

THE BLACK ARTS MOVEMENT

Background. A central problem in the paradigmatic development of art and literary "history" has always been whose ideas of art and literature will be empowered and, thus, whose ideas will be used to judge what is "good" or "bad" art. The question of who empowers and validates certain literary critical trends is beyond the scope of my inquiry here. But such battles are historically frequent in the sometimes purposely stagnated progression of art "theory." The problems that the progenitors of the Black Arts Movement faced were merely synecdochal of the many traditional and frequent battles in art and literary history fought to decide whose ideas will be censored and whose ideas will be validated and propagated. In other words, stipulative skirmishes have always been fought within the larger battleground of general censorship to decide whose ideas will be codified as a part of the taught *canon of art history and criticism. The trials of museum director Dennis Barrie in Cincinnati in the Mapplethorpe controversy and the rap group 2 Live Crew (Luther Campbell, Mark Ross, Christo-

pher Wongwon) in Florida are other similar and related skirmishes. Those whose art triumphs over others' art know that the spoils of that war are certificates of deposit and cold hard cash, not whether one songwriter's love-making lyrics are more acceptable than another's, nor whether nude heterosexual images should preclude nude homosexual images.

History and Development. The precursors to what is now called the Black Arts Movement (ca. 1962–1971) are many and interwoven. One could reasonably argue that there had been a call for a separate black letters in the American literary mainstream since Frederick Douglass's "What the Negro Wants" (1868). But the literary events that took place in the 1960s, influenced by social events from the 1950s and 1960s, overshadowed all work in black letters that had gone on before.

During this volatile period, LeRoi Jones (later Amiri Baraka) wrote in his essay "The Myth of a 'Negro Literature'" (1962) that "a Negro literature, to be a legitimate product of the Negro experience in America, must get at that experience in exactly the terms America has proposed for it in its most ruthless identity," and that the Negro, as an element of American culture, was "completely misunderstood by Americans." In discussing why, in his opinion, there was so little black literature of merit, Jones wrote,

… in most cases the Negroes who found themselves in a position to pursue some art, especially the art of literature, have been members of the Negro middle class, a group that has always gone out of its way to cultivate any mediocrity, as long as that mediocrity was guaranteed to prove to America, and recently to the world at large, that they were not really who they were, i.e., Negroes.

Further, Jones wrote that as long as the Negro writer was obsessed with being accepted, middle class, he would never be able to "tell it like it is," and, thus, would always be a failure, because America made room only for white obfuscators, not black ones. It was from such thoughts by Jones and the thoughts of many like-minded theoreticians such as Hoyt Fuller, that the Black Arts Movement (BAM) took its origins.

In 1969, during his black nationalist period, Baraka laid concrete boundaries for a "nationalistic art." Baraka wrote in "nationalism vs. Pimpart":

The Art is the National Spirit. That manifestation of it. Black Art must be the Nationalist's vision given more form and feeling, as a razor to cut away what is not central to National Liberation. To show that which is. As a humanistic expression it is itself raised. And these are the poles, out of which we create, to raise, or as raised.

In this difficult passage, Baraka was proposing (in typical 1960s rhetoric) specific and limited boundaries for acceptable art. Though a writer on all aspects of the BAM, Baraka's areas of greatest interest were the related arts of literatures and literary criticism, and it was, indeed, the debate on the content of black letters that would fuel the heat of the BAM from 1969 to its last official flickerings in 1974, when Baraka wrote his amazing essay "Why I Changed My Ideology." After Baraka formally announced that he was a socialist, no longer a black nationalist, his guidelines for "valid" black writing changed, but his new requirements, with slightly different emphases (liberation of all classes, races, genders) and a slightly different First Cause (Monopoly Capitalism), were as rigid as his prior requirements. And at this time, Baraka was powerful enough to influence others to codify his vision of acceptable art.

Baraka saw certain black writers as disrupting the essential and beautiful Black Arts Movement of the 1960s and early 1970s. Baraka called these writers "capitulationists," and says their movement was simultaneous with and counter to the Black Arts Movement. Baraka felt that the simultaneity was no accident. In his long essay "Afro-American Literature and the Class Struggle" in *Black American Literature Forum* (Summer 1980), Baraka, for the first time, made several strong, personal attacks on Ishmael Reed, the fiction writer and poet, and also attacked several black female writers whom he felt fit into the capitulationist mold. And, again, Baraka reiterated that he believes that the groundbreakers in the Black Arts Movement (among them, the new black aesthetic literary wing, including Addison Gayle, Houston Baker, and Clarence Major) were doing something that was new, needed, useful, and black, and those who did not want to see such a flourishing of black expression were "appointed" to the scene to damage the movement.

Naming Reed and Calvin Hernton as "conservatives," Baraka wrote:

Yes, the tide was so strong that even some of the "conservatives" wrote work that took the people's side. (The metaphysical slide [sic] of the BAM [Black Arts Movement] even allowed Reed to adopt a rebellious tone with his "Black power poem" and "sermonette" in *catechism of d neo-american hoodoo church*, 1970, in which he saw the struggle of Blacks against national oppression as a struggle between two churches: e.g., "may the best church win. shake hands now and come/out-

conjuring." But even during the heat and heart of the BAM, Reed would call that very upsurge and the BAM "a goon squad aesthetic" and say that the revolutionary writers were "fascists" or that the taking up of African culture by Black artists indicated such artists were "tribalists."

Much of the labeling of Reed as a conservative and a "house nigger" began with the publication of *The Last Days of Louisiana Red*, in which a group of characters Reed labeled as "moochers" loiter around Ed Yellings, a small black business owner who is making active efforts to earn a living and who, through practicing voodoo, finds a cure for cancer. Critics interpreted "the moochers" as being stipulative of some of the BAM group. Supposedly, *The Last Days of Louisiana Red* contains autocratic figures who do little more than emphasize Reed's definition of moochers, and who continually reenact negative, black stereotypes. Ed Yellings, the industrious black, is killed by black moocher conspirators. Does this mean blacks will turn against what Reed believes to be the good in their own communities? Ed Yellings is a business and property owner. Baraka wrote,

Ishmael Reed and Stanley Crouch both make the same kind of rah-rah speeches for the Black middle class. Reed, in fact, says that those of us who uphold Black working people are backwards . . . Focus on the middle class, the property owners and music teachers, not the black masses (Ralph) Ellison tells us. This is the *Roots* crowd giving us a history of the BLM [Black Liberation Movement] as a rags-to-riches, Horatio Alger tale in brownface, going off into the sunset and straight for Carter's cabinet or the National Book Award. . . .

Baraka also set up a dichotomy for a "white arts movement" and a "black arts movement," but while defining the two—one would assume toward the end of endorsing one or the other—Baraka shows only the failings of each and discusses his points of divergence from the "Black Aesthetic Crowd."

In Baraka's dichotomy, the "white aesthetic is bourgeois art—like the 'national interests' of the U.S. at this late date when the U.S. is an imperialistic superpower." Immediately following this passage, Baraka seemed to defend the black aesthetic group over Ellison's negative criticism of them. Baraka wrote that Ellison said of the black aesthetic crowd that they "buy the idea of total cultural separation between blacks and whites, suggesting that we've been left out of the mainstream. But when we examine American music and literature in terms of its themes, symbolism, rhythms, tonalities, idioms, and images it is obvious that those rejected 'Negroes' have been a vital part of the mainstream and were from the beginning." Baraka responded, "We know we have been exploited, Mr. Ralph, sir; what we's arguing about is that we's been exploited! To use us is the term of stay in this joint. . . ." Baraka's point is that it makes no difference if the corrupt personage is black; the issue is still corruption, and it is a double insult to the oppressed when that corrupt person turns out to be black. But it is at that point that Baraka separated himself from others in the new black aesthetic movement:

Where I differ with the bourgeois nationalists who are identified with the "Black Aesthetic" is illuminated by a statement of Addison Gayle's: "An aesthetic based upon economic and class determinism is one which has minimal value for Black people. For Black writers and critics the starting point must be the proposition that the history of Black people in America is the history of the struggle against racism" ("Blueprint for Black Criticism," *First World*, Jan.–Feb. 1977, p. 43). But what is the basis for racism; i.e., exploitation because of one's physical characteristics? Does it drop out of the sky? . . . Black people suffer from national oppression: We are an oppressed nation, a nation oppressed by U.S. imperialism. Racism is an even more demonic aspect of this national oppression, since the oppressed nationality is identifiable anywhere as that regardless of class.

Baraka reminded the reader that his disagreement with the new black aesthetic elite was not to say that there was no such thing as a black aesthetic, but that his conception of a black aesthetic manifested itself in his definition of it differently than it did for others. For him it was "a nation within a nation" that was brought about by the "big bourgeoisie on Wall Street, who after the Civil War completely dominated U.S. politics and economics, controlled the explanters, and turned them into their compradors." Further, black aesthetic ideas had to be subsumed under the larger category of the Black Arts Movement so that its ideas would be in concert with those black ideas from drama, dance, and graphic arts.

Baraka claimed that several women writers, among them Michelle Wallace and Ntozake Shange, like Reed, had their own "Hollywood" aesthetic, one of "capitulation" and "garbage." Toward the end of his article, Baraka said that the "main line" of his argument had been that "class struggle is as much a part of the arts as it is any place else." His pleas and support were reserved for those artists who were "struggle oriented," those who were trying to "get even

clearer on the meaning of class stand, attitude, audience, and study, and their relationship to our work."

And, thus, Baraka's argument is epanaleptic, as it turns back for support upon the same core of arguments of the other black aestheticians with whom he has said he is in disagreement; those arguments form a complete circle with Baraka's stated premise that black literature, black art must do something materially positive to help black people. Art must be socially functional.

The heat and heart really left the BAM after Baraka changed from black nationalist to Leninist/Socialist (1974) and after the death of Hoyt Fuller (1971). Baraka was by far the strongest voice in the movement, and when he changed his ideas and said that before he had been absolutely wrong about his views on black art and that now his Leninist/Marxist vision was absolutely correct, many of his adherents lost faith. The basic tenets of the movement included the ideas that art by black Americans could never be accepted by white Americans, and separate criteria needed to be developed by black artists to appraise properly the talent of black artists. Also, all art should be toward a political/humanistic end that would elevate all people—but especially black people—to a higher consciousness and a better life. In a retrospective on this artist/censor exchange, W. Lawrence Hogue wrote in "Literary Production: A Silence in Afro-American Critical Practice" from his book *Discourse and the Other: The Production of the Afro-American Literary Text* (1986) that the writers of the BAM:

in using literature to further their political ends . . . understand the political function of literature. Their strategy is to promote those Afro-American texts that present an aesthetic theory of literature. But that strategy is silent completely on how established literary institutions and apparatuses, throughout American literary history, have affected the production of Afro-American literature. . . . Of course, such a discussion would cause these black aestheticians to confront openly the ideological nature and function, and therefore the constraints and exclusions, of their own cultural nationalist critical practices.

Thus, at least in theoretical discussion, an expansive, stylistically, thematically, and racially absorptive and syncretic "aesthetic" would put itself arguably above what Hogue calls the "nationalistic criteria" of the BAM regimen. In theory, a racially syncretic aesthetic would even absorb any facets of the BAM platform it could find useful, transform them, and produce new "discursive formations" (Foucault) that helped to explain itself or explain any kind of art text it chose. It is partly the syncretic idea that the proponents of the BAM fought against. For them, the only way to artistic purity was through separation from the mainstream.

Most recently, Baraka has reassessed Leninist/Marxist theory as an applicable filter for African-American literature. He now finds that, while perhaps a Leninist/Marxist grid is not the best way to assess and form the black arts, he still feels that at the root of any authentic black art endeavor must be the love of black people and the love of self-affirmation.

[See also Black Aesthetic.]

• Leroi Jones, "The Myth of a 'Negro Literature,' " in Black Expression: Essays by and about Black Americans in the Creative Arts, edited by Addison Gayle (1969), pp. 187–210. Ishmael Reed, Yellow Back Radio-Broke Down (1969). Amiri Baraka, Raise, Race, Rays, Essays since 1965 (1971). Addison Gayle, The Black Aesthetic (1971). Ishmael Reed, The Last Days of Louisiana Red (1974). Michel Foucault, Language, Counter-Memory, Practice, edited with an introduction by Donald F. Bouchard (1977). Henry Louis Gates, Jr., "The History and Theory of Afro-American Literary Criticism, 1773–1831: The Arts, Aesthetic Theory, and the Nature of the African," Ph.D. diss., University of Cambridge (1978). Ntozake Shange, Nappy Edges (1979). Michelle Wallace, Black Macho and the Myth of the Superwoman (1979). Amiri Baraka, The Autobiography (1984). Lawrence Hogue, "Literary Production: A Silence in Afro-American Critical Practice," in Discourse and the Other: The Production of the Afro-American Text (1986), pp. 1–22.

Reginald Martin

BLACK ENGLISH. Black English is primarily an oral form, but some features of it can be captured in writing. It is identifiable by particular syntactical ("sure you're right" for "you are surely right"), phonological ("ho' de do' " for "hold the door"), lexical ("smooth" for "well done"), or grammatical ("I ain't gonna tell you nothin' ") usage. An examination of Black English usage reveals not a monolithic linguistic pattern, but at least three varieties of usage: Vernacular Black English or VBE (typified by the examples of "Black English" listed above), Standard Black English or SBE (identifiably "Black" by intonation and inflection, but essentially "correct" and "standard" in grammar and syntax), and Network English or NE (not identifiably "Black," but spoken by Blacks). Shirley A. R. Lewis and Mary R. Hoover discuss these types in some detail in their research memoranda Teacher Training Workshops on Black English and Language Arts Teaching (1979).

Normative descriptions such as "standard

English" and "nonstandard English" draw condemnation from linguistic analysts who connect such terminology with political domination. Indeed, many expressions in spoken English stray from conventional grammar but have become commonly accepted and therefore "standard." Such hypocrisy in terminology weakens the value of labels.

Educational debate weighs the benefits and disadvantages of responding to Vernacular Black English in the classroom. Children who participated fully in the VBE language and culture in the 1960s grew alienated from the school system. This trend led to Herbert L. Foster's two editions of Ribbin', Jivin', and Playin' the Dozens, subtitled The Unrecognized Dilemma of Inner City Schools (1974) and The Persistent Dilemma in Our Schools (1986). Typically, African-Americans and educators of every background agree that in school children should learn the patterns of English that represent "correct" grammar in standardized tests. However, modern trends urge teachers to appreciate the structure and nuances of Black English dialects, so that they can view VBE speakers as culturally enriched rather than culturally deprived.

Whereas teachers and researchers in the 1960s sometimes interpreted Vernacular Black English as evidence of inferiority, since the 1970s linguists have agreed that VBE is a structural dialect, not a conglomeration of errors. Furthermore, recent examinations of the varieties of Black English and of the numbers of persons using such dialects suggest that bidialectalism is a desirable goal for Black English speakers because those speakers must be able to communicate in the speech variety that is most appropriate and effective for a given audience and situation.

This same philosophy applies to literature. Since many speakers vary their use of Black English, writers who mirror a healthy reality would present in their dialogues one or more varieties of Black English. A single character might use VBE at a sports event and use SBE or NE when greeting a multiracial public on the job. Such a shift would not take the individual out of character, but would instead represent the flexible dialectic skill of that individual.

Belletristic writings by post-Emancipation African-American authors employ a range of dialects. For example, Paul Laurence Dunbar, Charles Chesnutt, Zora Neale *Hurston, Langston Hughes, Sterling Brown, and June *Jordan all gained recognition for their use of Black dialect. All of these authors also published works that employed no discernible Black English, and, conversely, works that revealed a spectrum of dialects. Such a range of dialects faithfully represents the spoken language of African-Americans.

A writer who habitually avoids any signs of dialect in a work that claims to capture the African-American experience reveals some negative associations and even shame regarding these distinctively African-American patterns of expression. In her novel *Linden Hills* (1985), Gloria * Naylor broaches the negative repercussions of bleaching Black nuance from language and culture. Rather than bleaching Black nuance, authors tend to include discernible features of the spoken dialect in dialogue between African-American characters. Furthermore, even "standard" English can be rendered "Black" by intonation and body language. Thus, some elements of Standard Black English may be difficult to capture in written dialogue alone. However, a concerned writer could add descriptions of sound and delivery to indicate that Standard Black English is being spoken. For example, Paule * Marshall effectively employs both dialogue and description in *Brown Girl, Brownstone* (1959) to capture Barbadian accents.

Any writer alleging to portray the African-American experience would need to present realistic members of this community, including those who speak mainly Vernacular Black English, those who are bidialectic, those who speak Standard Black English, and those who speak mostly Network English. Such broad presentations in literature can assist educators in reaching students previously alienated from the school system.

[See also Nonstandard English; Language, Women's.]

• J. L. Dillard, *Black English: Its History and Usage in the United States* (1972). William Labov, *Language in the Inner City: Studies in the Black English Vernacular* (1972). Jim Haskins and Hugh F. Butts, *The Psychology of Black Language* (1973). M. E. R. Hoover, *Appropriate Use of Black English by Black Children as Rated by Parents* (1975). William Labov, "The Logic of Nonstandard English," in *Black American English: Its Background and Its Usage in the Schools and in Literature*, ed. Paul Stoller (1975), pp. 89–131. Geneva Smitherman, *Talkin' and Testifyin': The Language of Black America* (1977).

Donna Akiba Sullivan Harper
and Shirley A. R. Lewis

BLACK FEMINISM. African-American women have always asserted their own worth as women and allied with black men to defend their group against the dominant society's demeaning racial oppression. After their forced settlement in America, black people suffered enslavement in a world where white people created elaborate cultural and legal systems to justify denying black people humanity. In the twentieth century, deprivation of full standing as citizens and as people sparked black protests. Black feminists supported these struggles and also focused attention on black women's unique experiences, combating a singular black male vision when necessary.

Most black women in antebellum America lived under legalized terror and coercion in slavery; twentieth-century scholars have named slave women's resistance as feminist. In a system where an owner could meet an enslaved woman's refusal to work or her complaints about enforced sex with beatings and decisions to sell her children, black women denied compliance with a worldview that asserted their bestiality as workers, as mothers, and as women. Jacqueline Jones's *Labor of Love, Labor of Sorrow* (1985) recounts how women demanded reduced fieldwork for real or feigned menstruation and pregnancy; cared for children even though those children might be stolen from them by the slavers; and often defended themselves from sexual connections with dominant whites, a story told in Harriet * Jacobs's *Incidents in the Life of a Slave Girl* (1860), pseudonymously authored by former slave Linda Brent. Women's care for children kept them from seizing opportunities for physical flight, but did not humble them.

Most free black women in the North and South suffered lack of education and low incomes because dominant whites stigmatized all black people as kin of slaves and excluded women and men from good employment. Cultural degradation assaulted even those rare women from households with money and education. Black women took up abolition as their first cause in the years before the Civil War. But always, alongside this great political fight, they formed societies and clubs in autodidactic efforts to compensate for their educational deprivation. From Maria Stewart's 1832 Boston speeches to the Afric-American Female Intelligence Society and beyond, black feminists spurred their sisters to speak, think, and act like women worthy of the respect denied them by white enslavement and racial opprobrium.

For a brief time in mid-century, women such as the escaped slave Sojourner * Truth offered a bridge between the liberation movements of African-Americans and of white women. Her classic "Ain't I a Woman?" speech at the 1851 Akron Women's Rights Convention claimed respect for women who physically labored and saw their children sold, and not just for protected "angels in the house." Women's rights alliances to end all forms of oppression shattered in Civil War and Reconstruction politics, when former allies divided over supporting or opposing the Fifteenth Amendment, which would guarantee suffrage only to former slave men.

During the harsh Reconstruction years and their culmination in the segregationist, Jim Crow America of the first two decades of the twentieth century, black women volunteered to educate freed slaves; sought and achieved professional training for themselves; organized civic services for growing communities of urban refugees from rural peonage; and allied with white women in temperance and women's suffrage groups, despite the dominant group's reluctance to challenge segregation and to see political violence like lynching as a woman's cause.

In novels such as Frances Ellen Watkins *Harper's *Iola Leroy* (1892) and in books of essays such as Anna Julia *Cooper's *Voice from the South* (1892), black women asserted their goals of universal justice, which required "racial uplift" in partnership with black men, and uniquely for women, of defense against attacks on their morality, a legacy of many women's sexual vulnerability under slavery. These interests fused in 1892 when journalist Ida B. *Wells-Barnett published documented reports that whites used lynching to intimidate blacks; she further speculated, to the fury of white feminists, that assaults on black sexual morality disguised white women's interest in black men. Prominent black women defended the journalist and formed an array of clubs, which united in 1896 as the National Association of Colored Women (NACW), under the presidency of Oberlin graduate Mary Church Terrell. In the NACW and its later manifestation, the National Council of Negro Women, founded by educator Mary McLeod *Bethune in 1935, black women fought first for the vote and then for public authorities to allow them to exercise it. Black women helped found early civil rights groups such as the National Association for the Advancement of Colored People (1910), and became local leaders in the great post–World War II struggles to overturn the nation's history of racial oppression and segregation. The 1960s second wave of feminism, emerging from the civil rights crusade, inspired black women to protest common demands that they be acquiescent helpmeets to black men leaders. In Toni Cade *Bambara's anthology *The Black Woman* (1970), women asserted their worth independent of family roles and proclaimed women's liberation as essential to human justice. After this first statement, black feminist thought unfolded into a rich diversity characteristic of new opportunities: Marxian, anti-racist, lesbian, Third World, and experiential/phenomenological.

Angela Y. *Davis, 1960s heroine of Black Power militancy, penned a Marxist-socialist analysis, *Women, Race & Class* (1981), which indicted capitalism and the exploitation of labor in domestic and factory work. bell hooks's *Ain't I A Woman* (1981), the first of a prolific oeuvre, charged that white women's racism and black men's dominance negated black women's feminism, as seen in polls where black women regularly showed greater support for "women's" issues than did white women. Writer/organizer Barbara Smith issued *Home Girls: A Black Feminist Anthology* (1983) to counter the *homophobia that equated black lesbianism with rejection of the black community.

Black feminism in the 1980s and early 1990s replicated the world tension between global allegiances and particularistic loyalties. An upsurge of organization and writing among other racial minority women, and the stimulus of the United Nations' Decade for Women (1975–1985), led black feminists to identify shared interests as women of color; *This Bridge Called My Back: Writings by Radical Women of Color* (1981), edited by Cherríe Moraga and Gloria *Anzaldúa, became an instant classic. Patricia Hill Collins studied everyday actions and writings of American women of African descent to infer a coherent and distinctive *Black Feminist Thought* (1990).

Black law professor Anita Hill's charge of *sexual harassment against black Supreme Court nominee Clarence Thomas during his 1991 Senate confirmation hearings revealed the persistent difficulties black women face. Allied with white feminists on the harassment issue, black women found themselves charged with sexual irregularity and racial disloyalty. Black feminists refused allegiance to either group. Once again, black women claimed that when American democracy could respect a woman of color, then all women and all men of color would find security as well.

[*See also* Feminism; Womanism; Women's Movement.]

• Barbara Smith, Gloria T. Hull, and Patricia Bell Scott, *All the Women Are White, All the Blacks Are Men, but Some of Us Are Brave: Black Women's Studies* (1982). Alice Walker, *In Search of Our Mothers' Gardens: Womanist Prose* (1983). *Sage: A Scholarly Journal on Black Women* (1983–). Paula Giddings, *When and Where I Enter: The Impact of Black Women on Race and Sex in America* (1984). Dorothy Sterling, ed., *We Are Your Sisters: Black Women in the Nineteenth Century.* (1984).

Phyllis Palmer

BLACKWELL, Elizabeth (1821–1910), first woman to receive a medical degree in the United States, physician, educator, essayist, lecturer. Blackwell was born in Bristol, England, and at age eleven emigrated to the United States with her family. Experiences as a teacher in Ohio, Kentucky, North Carolina, and South Carolina proved unsatisfactory for Blackwell, and the idea of a medical career slowly took shape. Blackwell's autobiography, *Pioneer Work in Opening the Medical Profession to Women* (1895; reprint, 1977), conveys the determination of a woman willing to challenge gender bias in the medical profession. After numerous rejections from other medical schools, Blackwell was admitted to the Geneva Medical School in New York, where she matriculated from November 1847 through January 1849. Her recollections from this period reveal her sense of herself as setting a course for others to follow. While training at Blockley Almshouse in Philadelphia, she arranged her work table so that curious female patients might see her at her studies. Believing that her reform goals would demand lecturing, she practiced public speaking before imaginary audiences. After graduation, Blackwell pursued further study in Paris and London. While studying obstetrics and gynecology at *La Maternité* in Paris, she contracted ophthalmia and permanently lost sight in her left eye. Consequently, her subsequent studies no longer included training to become a surgeon.

Blackwell's professional achievements in the United States from 1851 through 1869 included opening her own medical practice (1851); the New York Dispensary for Poor Women and Children (1854); the New York Infirmary for Women and Children, with her sister, Dr. Emily Blackwell, and Dr. Maria Zakrzewska (1857); and the Woman's Medical College of the New York Infirmary for Women and Children, with Emily Blackwell (1868), where Elizabeth Blackwell briefly held the Chair of Hygiene. Her European travels during this period facilitated her becoming, in 1859, the first woman listed in the Medical Register of the United Kingdom. In 1869, Blackwell made a permanent move to England and opened a medical practice in London. In 1874, she aided in opening the London School of Medicine for Women, the first medical school for women in the United Kingdom.

Blackwell's essays and lectures, most of which are available in *The Laws of Life* (1852; reprint, 1986) and *Essays in Medical Sociology* (1902; reprint, 1972), reflect her alignment of medical practice with moral and social reform. She consistently iterated a program of preventive medicine and hygiene; advocated reduced use of surgery; spoke out against experimentation on animals, bacteriology, and vaccination; and encouraged opening additional professions to women. With her sister, Blackwell coauthored *Medicine as a Profession for Women* (1860).

• Blackwell family papers are in the Library of Congress and the Schlesinger Library, Radcliff College. Additional Elizabeth Blackwell documents are held in the Columbia University Library; the Fawcett Society Library, London; the Sophia Smith Research Room, Smith College; the Library of Hobart and William Smith Colleges, Geneva, New York; the Boston Public Library; the New York Infirmary; the Medical Library at St. Bartholomew's Hospital, London; and the Royal Free Medical School Library, London. See also Dorothy Clark Wilson, *Lone Woman: The Story of Elizabeth Blackwell, the First Woman Doctor* (1970). Nancy Ann Sahli, "Elizabeth Blackwell, M.D. (1821–1910): A Biography" (Ph.D. diss., University of Pennsylvania, 1974). Mary Roth Walsh, M.D., Introduction to *Pioneer Work in Opening the Medical Profession to Women*, by Elizabeth Blackwell (1977). Regina Markell Morantz, "Feminism, Professionalism, and Germs: A Study of the Thought of Mary Putnam Jacobi and Elizabeth Blackwell," in *Women and the Structure of Society: Selected Research from the Fifth Berkshire Conference on the History of Women*, eds. Barbara J. Harris and Jo Ann K. McNamara (1984), pp. 170–185.

Diane Brown Jones

BLACK WRITING. *See* African-American Writing.

BLEECKER, Ann Eliza (1752–1783), poet, fiction writer, and correspondent. Most of what is known of Bleecker's life and works derives from a memoir written by her daughter, Margaretta V. Faugeres, and from Bleecker's letters to family and friends. Both memoir and letters, along with the extant portions of her verse and fiction, are collected in *The Posthumous Works of Ann Eliza Bleecker* (1793; reprint, 1970). Written without thought to publication, those portions of Bleecker's work to reach print in the *New-York Magazine* (1790–1791) and in the aforementioned collection were all published posthumously. Born in New York City to Margareta Van Wyck and Brandt Schuyler, even as a child Bleecker was an avid reader and writer of verse. Although she shared her early work with family and friends, it was only after her marriage to John J. Bleecker in 1769 that she began to collect her writing. Eventually settling in Tomhanick, New York, eighteen miles north of Albany, Bleecker wrote many of her poems and letters with the purpose of describing a rural environment to friends and family unfamiliar with country living. These early works reveal both her attraction to the pastoral qualities of her adult home and her ambivalence about being so far removed from the urban activities of her youth.

Bleecker's later work focuses on her struggle to continue writing: "Amidst domestic cares to rhyme/I find no pleasure, and I find no time" ("To Miss M. V. W.," 1780). Many of her difficulties resulted from the isolation and vulnerability that were the products of the Revolutionary War as it swept upstate New York. In 1777, General John Burgoyne's invasion forced Bleecker to flee her home on foot with her two small daughters. She was soon reunited with her husband, who had been in Albany during the attack, but the strain of the flight contributed to the youngest daughter's death from dysentery during their further retreat. Bleecker's mother and sister also died soon after.

The lighthearted, even teasing, qualities that mark Bleecker's early verse—invitations to friends, condescending portraits of less-educated neighbors, pastoral descriptions of home and gardens—disappear from her writing during the Revolutionary War, and are replaced by a melancholy that forms an almost constant backdrop for her later work. After Burgoyne's defeat, Bleecker returned to her home, but she was forced to leave again in 1779. In 1781, John Bleecker was captured by the Tories; his relatively quick rescue did not prevent Ann Bleecker from approaching nervous collapse: the fetus she was carrying at the time was stillborn. These experiences frame *The History of Maria Kittle* (1779), a fictionalized and sentimental captivity narrative set during the French and Indian War. In 1783, shortly after the Treaty of Paris officially ended the American Revolution, thirty-one-year-old Ann Eliza Bleecker died. Throughout her struggles, Bleecker's writing continued to give voice to her experience, shaping one woman's Revolutionary War for later readers.

• Lewis Leary, "Ann Eliza Bleecker," in *Notable American Women*, vol. 1 (1971), pp. 177–178. L. W. Koengeter, "Ann Eliza Schuyler Bleecker," in *American Women Writers from Colonial Times to the Present*, ed. Lina Mainiero, vol. 1 (1979), pp. 176–178. Pattie Cowell, ed., *Women Poets in Pre-Revolutionary America, 1650–1775: An Anthology* (1981). Lucy M. Freibert and Barbara A. White, eds., *Hidden Hands: An Anthology of American Women Writers, 1790–1870* (1985), pp. 103–115.

Pattie Cowell

BODY AND HEALTH. Feminists have long seen the female body as a contested site of institutional and personal power, and much nineteenth- and twentieth-century feminism has focused on the necessity for women to control access to and deployment of their bodies. While such an emphasis is usually associated with individualist feminism or with what legal scholars have called "rights" discourse, control of how bodies get to be defined, used, and represented is a pervasive issue for most feminists.

An account of the relation between women and the body must begin with the fact that, as Genevieve Lloyd has pointed out, in Western culture women have traditionally been defined *as* body. Each term—"women" and "body"—gets contaminated by cultural uneasiness with the other. While liberal feminists have been consistently suspicious of the woman/body equation, others, including matriarchal feminists, have found empowerment in the association of women with the corporeal. Many contemporary feminists, from Hélène Cixous to Mary *Daly, have chosen to support the idiom of the body and what they see as an especially close and productive—if culturally denigrated—relation between women and the body.

In a specifically American context, the female body has, as Annette Kolodny delineates in *The Lay of the Land* (1975), a special place in the American cultural imagination, which has figured the American wilderness as a female body and the conquest and civilizing of that wilderness—the foundational gestures of American identity—as a conquest or a rape of that body. If this is the case, and the "civilizing" of America is inscribed in a tradition of sexual conquest, it is imperative to outline the place of women writers in that civilization.

Much of the literature produced by women in the United States in the eighteenth and nineteenth centuries has labored under the critical category of the *"sentimental." Itself a word inflected by the discourse of the body and feeling, *sentimental* has, until recently, been used as a term of denigration. Robyn Warhol has shown that some of the cultural anxiety about sentimentality has focused on its presumed ability to produce changes (usually figured as tears) in the body of the (usually figured as female) reader. Nina Baym, in *Novels, Readers, and Reviewers* (1984), exposed the link between antisentimental discourse and a fear of contagion from "feverish" or "poisonous" texts to their readers. Thus, through the trope of the sentimental, the reader's body becomes a crucial locus of critical discourse. Warhol has also noted that the body of the female writer occupies an anxious place in the critical discourse surrounding women's literature; the position of the woman writer was often conflated with the spectacularly public position of the female lecturer, whose body, according to this discourse, was voluptuously open to the public gaze. Mary

Kelley, in *Private Woman, Public Stage* (1984), explores the issue of publicity, in all its senses, for women constructing careers as writers.

The role of the female body in the nineteenth-century American women's novel is, of course, a complex one. While American fiction does not seem as populated as the Victorian novel with sickly heroines, feminine illness does figure textually in many works of the period. The famous death scenes of girl heroines such as Little Eva in Harriet Beecher * Stowe's *Uncle Tom's Cabin* (1850) and Beth March in Louisa May * Alcott's *Little Women* (1869) are embedded in a tradition that also produced books for women and children like the evangelical *Elsie Dinsmore* (1868) by Martha Finley, in which the titular heroine, presumed dead on account of the cruelty of her father, comes miraculously to life to convert him and to spawn a series of great-grandchildren and numerous sequels. The broader cultural fascination with and feminization of death and its surrounding rituals, outlined in Ann Douglas's landmark *The Feminization of American Culture* (1977), also serves as a background for these repeated scenes of dying. The nonsectarian "cemetery movement," which affirmed the importance of the body after death, produced a series of "consolation texts," such as Elizabeth Stuart * Phelps's *The Gates Ajar* (1868), which stressed the material and corporeal continuity between life in heaven and life on earth.

Embodiment then, becomes a provisional form of power in much writing by women; ironically, of course, that embodiment is usually made possible by death or ill health, which allow for the textual and cultural representation of the otherwise—to use D. A. Miller's term—"unnarratable" female body.

More unnarratable than even the white female body is the body of the female slave, a body even more subject to * rape and to violence. Sander Gilman (1988) has shown how representations of the black female body called upon a lexicon of the public and the grotesque.

The literary female body—ill, enslaved, or dying—is of course only one of many cultural representations of the relation between women and health. The nineteenth century constituted a crisis in the understanding of illness and health. It was during the middle of that century that women's health first began to be seen as the province of doctors; previously, what came to be thought of as "women's diseases" (the management of pregnancy, labor, and birthing), were largely in the hands of nurses and midwives. The development of medicine as a profession, culminating in the institutionalization of the American Medical Association, sepa-

rated pregnant and birthing women from a traditional network of midwives and placed them in the control of doctors—often, at least in the early years of this tradition, with terrible results for the well-being of individual women.

If illness and death are the primary loci of nineteenth-century women's literature's depiction of the female body, twentieth-century women's literature multiplies those loci to include contestations of female bodily autonomy, from madness to suicide to rape. *The Yellow Wallpaper* (1892) by Charlotte Perkins * Gilman, the poetry and fiction of Sylvia * Plath, and the poems of Anne * Sexton suggest connections between madness, suicide, and female sexuality. All can be read as critiques of the institutional discourses of medicine, which conflate illness, madness, and the feminine and overdetermine female ill health. More contemporary literature about rape and incest, from Toni * Morrison's *The Bluest Eye* (1970) to Alice * Walker's *The Color Purple* (1982), vividly represent the connections between power, violence, race, and sexuality as they are inscribed upon the female body. Texts about eating and anorexia, like Margaret Atwood's *Lady Oracle*, represent yet another contested bodily site, another bodily location of the cultural construction of femininity.

There is by now a rich primary literature on female sexuality, from the liberationist novels and poems of the early sixties and seventies, like those by Marge * Piercy, to the lesbian-feminist texts of Adrienne * Rich, Audre * Lorde, and more recently, Lisa Alther. Lesbian and gay theory has also made a series of paradigm-shifting interventions in ongoing feminist debates about sexuality. Debates about lesbian sadomasochism, butch-femme role-playing, safe sex, and sexual styles have helped to define emergent fields of sexuality studies and to challenge the heterosexual norms that have traditionally governed discourses of sex and sexuality.

The most recent studies of all aspects of the representation of the female body, especially in terms of sexuality, have been deeply influenced by the work of French philosopher Michel Foucault, and by the emergence of the interdiscipline known as cultural studies. Foucault's displacement of the locus of power from the state apparatus to more diffuse and local cultural sites, including the family and the individual subject, have been useful in re-articulating feminist links between the personal and the political, as well as between the individual body and the culture that shapes and is in turn shaped by it. While even Foucauldian feminists disagree about Foucault's usefulness in enabling political change, most find compelling his descriptions of the internalization and incorporation of power as well as, for example, his observation, in *The History of Sexuality*, that the body is a primary site of cultural "policing."

Cultural studies as a discipline has also been helpful in producing analyses of the role of the female body; because of its emphasis on links between "high" and "low" culture, cultural studies has enabled the juxtaposition of, for example, high canonical literary texts with representations of women in the media, in sex education classes, in prenatal clinics. Recently, a great deal of criticism on reproduction, and in particular on reproductive technology, has benefited from a Foucauldian and cultural studies perspective. Jana Siwicki's *Disciplining Foucault* (1992) provides an accessible introduction to such perspectives on the reproductive body.

Late-twentieth-century representations of female health cannot be understood without an account of the struggles of the women's movement, specifically of the women's health movement. From the germinal formation of The Boston Women's Health Collective, which came together to produce the self-help manual *Our Bodies, Ourselves* (1971), to women's health groups currently intervening in the theory and practice of nutrition, pregnancy, childbirth, and other aspects of women's care, the feminist movement has produced a series of local challenges to the disciplining of the female body.

[*See also* Eating Disorders; Health Books, Pamphlets, and Reference Guides; Hysteria; Leisure Studies; Madness.]

• John S. Haller and Robin M. Haller, *The Physician and Sexuality in Victorian America* (1974). Barbara Ehrenreich and Dierdre English, *For Her Own Good: 150 Years of the Experts' Advice to Women* (1978). Genevieve Lloyd, *The Man of Reason: "Male" and "Female" in Western Philosophy* (1984). Robyn Warhol, *Gendered Interventions: Narrative Discourse in the Victorian Novel* (1990). Lynn R. Higgins and Brenda R. Silver, eds., *Rape and Representation* (1991). Emily Martin, *The Woman in the Body* (1991).

Helena Michie

BOGAN, Louise (1879–1970), poet, reviewer, and short fiction writer. Born in Livermore Falls, Maine, to middle-class Irish Catholic parents, Bogan attended the Girls' Latin School in Boston, where she began writing poetry at the age of fourteen. She studied at Boston University for one year, then turned down a Radcliffe scholarship to marry Curt Alexander in 1916. At the start of World War I, Alexander was sent to Panama, and Bogan joined him there. Her daughter was born in Panama in 1917, and marital difficulties followed; shortly after their return to the United States in 1918, the couple separated. When Alexander died of pneumonia in 1920, Bogan settled in New York City and entered literary circles. Her first book of poems, *Body of This Death*, was published in 1923, followed, in 1929, by *Dark Summer*.

In 1931, Bogan became poetry critic for the *New Yorker* magazine, a position she held for thirty-eight years. She published two more volumes of poetry, *The Sleeping Fury* (1937) and *Poems and New Poems* (1941), in addition to several collections of critical essays, including *Achievement in American Poetry, 1900–1950* (1951) and *Selected Criticism: Poetry and Prose* (1955). Bogan underwent periods of psychiatric treatment and recovery throughout her life, and in her later years produced new poems infrequently; her collection *The Blue Estuaries: Poems 1923–1968*, published two years before her death in 1970, contained just over one hundred poems.

Formally rigorous, compact, and controlled, Bogan's poetry tends to be epigrammatic rather than descriptive; her poems often inhabit stark, dreamlike landscapes, and, reflecting her interest in psychology, attempt to explore the workings of the unconscious. With regard to poetic form, Bogan occupies an ambiguous position: she situates herself between the female lyric tradition and male modernism, rejecting the sentimentalism of the former, but finding grounds for difference from the latter. Although she resisted definition as a woman poet—and, indeed, her work was praised by Theodore Roethke, among others, for its lack of "feminine" qualities—Louise Bogan's poetry frequently addresses cultural constructions of gender. In poems such as "A Tale" (1921), "Medusa" (1922), "The Sleeping Fury" (1937), and the ambivalent "Women" (1923), Bogan revises masculine mythology, anatomizes heterosexual love, and explores the relation of femininity to speech and silence, masks and masquerade, in ways that would powerfully influence later poets, including May Sarton and Sylvia *Plath.

• Jacqueline Ridgeway, *Louise Bogan* (1984). Martha Collins, ed., *Critical Essays on Louise Bogan* (1984). Elizabeth Frank, *Louise Bogan: A Portrait* (1985). Gloria Bowles, *Louise Bogan's Aesthetic of Limitation* (1987).

Valerie Rohy

BONNER, Marita. *See* Occomy, Marita Bonner.

BONNIN, Gertrude. *See* Zitkala-Sa.

BOOK CLUBS. *See* Women's Clubs.

BOOKSTORES. In cities and university towns, especially where there is an active women's community, one can usually find women's bookstores. Owned and operated by women, these businesses feature books written by women, often covering a wide spectrum of interests, including liberal or radical feminist pamphlets, magazines, and newspapers; works on *spirituality or New Age topics such as healing or *witchcraft; *erotica; the full range of books by women of color; poetry, fiction, and nonfiction by lesbian writers; and, in some stores, such mainstream genres as *romances or *detective novels. According to Carol Seajay, there are now over one hundred women's bookstores across the United States and Canada, with some of the stores carrying up to eighteen thousand titles.

While women have run bookstores for a long time (one thinks of Sylvia *Beach's famous Shakespeare and Company in Paris), the 1960s and 1970s saw an explosion in bookstores owned by women and featuring women's books, just as those same decades saw the burgeoning of women's presses such as the Feminist Press, Kitchen Table Press, and Naiad Press as well as series of women's books from both university and commercial presses. One part of the women's movement focused on books—writing them, reprinting them, and, most important, making them available to the widest possible women's readership. Women's bookstores are thus part of the whole process of *canon formation that has changed our conception of what is women's literature or, even more basically, what is literature.

Without the specialized attention and energy supplied by the owners of women's bookstores, it is possible that many independent feminist periodicals and publishing companies would fail. The bookstores do not just sell books; they promote them, typically in an environment that is welcoming to women readers. Women's bookstores are community gathering places. Most host readings by women authors, and virtually all include bulletin boards where women can exchange information about upcoming events, political as well as literary. Some offer a children's corner where kids can browse through nonsexist juvenile books. Often women's bookstores are owned and run collectively, sometimes as cooperatives. The lesbian community has been especially energetic in supporting women's specialized literary enterprises.

As Seajay notes, despite the ninety percent failure rate of most small businesses, feminist bookstores have done surprisingly well: more than half of the seventy-three feminist bookstores listed in the September 1983 issue of *Ms. magazine are still viable in 1993, and new bookstores open all the time. While indi-

vidual stores may not be making millions for their owners, women's bookstores are now a multimillion-dollar industry. The National Women-in-Print Conference and the International Feminist Bookfair have become important gathering places for store owners and women publishers while Feminist Bookstore News (edited and published by Seajay) and Feminist Bookstores Network facilitate communication and promote public sponsorship of women's bookstores.

Antigone Books (Tucson, Arizona), Giovanni's Room (Philadelphia), Judith's Room (New York), Old Wives' Tales (San Francisco), New Words Bookstore (Cambridge, Massachusetts), Women and Children First (Chicago), A Room of One's Own (Madison, Wisconsin), and Southern Sisters (Durham, North Carolina) are just a few of the women's bookstores working to transform the literary landscape.

[See also Literacy; Publishing Business; Reading Circles.]

• Carol Seajay, "Twenty Years of Feminist Bookstores," Ms. (July–August 1992): 60–63.

Cathy N. Davidson

BOWEN, Catherine Drinker (1897–1973), biographer. The author of more than a dozen books, Bowen was born in Haverford, Pennsylvania. She started out by writing fiction, but then shifted to biography, which remained the focus of a career spanning almost five decades. Married twice and the mother of two children, Bowen was also a skilled violinist who wrote about chamber music in Friends and Fiddlers (1935), and unsurprisingly chose musicians as the subjects of her earliest biographies, Beloved Friend: The Story of Tchaikowsky, with B. von Meck (1937), and Free Artist: The Story of Anton and Nicholas Rubinstein (1939).

In the 1940s, however, her interest turned to law, a field she admitted was far removed from her training, although both her father, Henry Sturgis Drinker, and a brother, Harry, were lawyers. (They and other members of her family are carefully delineated in her 1970 book, Family Portrait.) She began writing about the subject with Yankee from Olympus: Justice Holmes and His Family (1944), and followed it with John Adams and the American Revolution (1950), but Bowen capped these studies with The Lion and the Throne: The Life and Times of Sir Edward Coke, 1552–1634 (1957).

By Bowen's own admission, the Coke biography was a watershed. No longer would she write fictionalized biography, a device she said she would be less prone to condemn so severely had she not relied on it so extensively in her earlier work. In her work Biography: The Craft and the Calling (1969), Bowen says, "I turned once and for all to writing biography that contained no fictional devices and documented every quotation." Subsequent biographies support her claim; these include *Francis Bacon: The Temper of a Man* (1963), a study of Coke's greatest rival; *Miracle at Philadelphia: The Story of the Constitutional Convention, May to September 1787* (1966), a group portrait of its fifty-five participants; and *The Most Dangerous Man in America: Scenes from the Life of Benjamin Franklin* (1974).

Bowen also wrote two books on the art of biography, *Adventures of a Biographer* (1959) and *Biography*, as well as many essays. Above all, Bowen believed the business of a biographer is to excite the reader, which she was widely praised for doing by her grasp of historical detail, her ability to render the subject in dramatic terms, and her skill in evoking the spirit of the age. Her dedicated work earned her the National Book Award in 1957 for *The Lion and the Throne*, membership in the American Philosophical Society, and the frequent choice of her biographies as Book-of-the-Month Club selections.

• Bowen's papers are at the Library of Congress. William Zinsser, ed., *Extraordinary Lives: The Art and Craft of American Biography* (1986).

Constance J. Post

BOWLES, Jane (1917–1973), short story writer, novelist, and dramatist. Bowles was born in New York City to middle-class Jewish parents. With Elsie Dinsmore as her childhood hero, Bowles grew up in New York City and Woodmere, Long Island. After the sudden death of her father in 1930, Bowles and her mother, Claire Sager Auer, moved from Long Island to an apartment in Manhattan. Bowles briefly attended the Stoneleigh School in Greenfield, Massachusetts, but left the institution after breaking her leg in a horseback-riding accident. At the age of fifteen, she contracted tuberculosis in the knee, and spent the next two years in a sanatorium in Leysin, Switzerland. On Bowles's transatlantic journey back to the United States, she met Louis-Ferdinand Celine, whose book, *Voyage au Bout de la Nuit*, she was reading; following their encounter, Bowles decided that she, too, would become a writer.

Once back in New York City, Bowles underwent ankylotic surgery on her leg, and then, with characteristic determination, embarked on a life of avid socializing. During this period, she frequented the Greenwich Village bars and the Askew Salon, where she was introduced to many composers, artists, writers, and theater celebrities of the 1930s. In 1938, on the day before her twenty-first birthday, she married the composer and writer Paul Bowles. During their honeymoon, the Bowleses visited Paris and Central and South America, and it was in Mexico that Jane Bowles began *Two Serious Ladies* (1943), a novel that mixes fantasy with autobiographical material from her honeymoon and her experience of living on Staten Island, New York.

Although she remained married to Paul Bowles until her death, Jane Bowles's romantic involvements were primarily lesbian. As reflected in *Two Serious Ladies* and the long short story, "Camp Cataract," Bowles's fiction reveals her interest in the female psyche and the relationships between women. Her associative writing style intersperses shifting segments of time and place with the lives of quirky female characters who struggle, as Bowles did, with issues of intimacy and independence. Although she produced a relatively small body of work, the humor, surprise, and precision of her fiction created a cultlike following during her lifetime, and included writers such as Tennessee Williams, John Ashbery, and Truman Capote.

During the 1940s, Bowles's most productive period, she wrote and published several short stories, the puppet play "A Quarreling Pair," "Camp Cataract," and the first act of the play *In the Summer House*. In 1948, she left the Vermont farmhouse that she shared with the writer Helvetia Perkins and traveled to Morocco, where Paul Bowles had settled the year before. Once in Morocco, she befriended a young Arab woman, Cherifa, and the two established a complex relationship of romance, companionship, and servitude that lasted until Jane Bowles's departure from Morocco in 1969. In 1957, at the age of forty, she suffered the first of several strokes, which left her temporarily partially paralyzed and blind. For the next sixteen years, she moved in and out of hospitals in England, the United States, and Spain, where she was treated for neurological and psychiatric conditions. During this time, Bowles suffered from extended periods of writer's block, and though she wrote and rewrote fragments of stories, she completed few. In 1966, after editorial assistance from Paul Bowles, *Plain Pleasures*, a collection of Jane Bowles's short stories, was published by an English press. That same year, *The Collected Works of Jane Bowles* was published in the United States. The final five years of Bowles's life were spent almost entirely in the Clinica de Los Angeles in Málaga, Spain. She died in 1973 and was buried beneath an unmarked grave in the San Miguel Cemetary in Málaga. In 1978, *My Sister's Hand in Mine*, a new and enlarged edition of Bowles's *Collected Works*, was published.

• Millicent Dillon, *A Little Original Sin: The Life and Work of Jane Bowles* (1981).

Jan Freeman

BOYLE, Kay (1902–1992), novelist, short story writer, poet, essayist, and memoirist. Born in Saint Paul, Minnesota, and reared in Cincinnati, Ohio, Boyle studied briefly at the Cincinnati Conservatory, the Ohio Mechanics Institute, and Parson's School of Design in New York City. In 1922, she married Richard Brault, a French engineer, and worked with the Australian poet Lola Ridge at *Broom*, an avant-garde magazine.

Boyle and Brault moved to France in 1923. Mistakenly diagnosed as suffering from tuberculosis, in 1926 Boyle went to Grasse, France, at the invitation of Ernest Walsh, editor of *This Quarter*, with whom she lived. When Walsh died within the year, Boyle was pregnant with his child. She lived briefly in Paris in Raymond Duncan's artists' colony; signed the "Revolution of the Word" issue of *transition*, which declared "The plain reader be damned" (1929); and published *Short Stories* (1929), *Wedding Day and Other Stories* (1930), and the novel *Plagued by the Nightingale* (1931).

After divorcing Brault, Boyle married Laurence Vail in 1932, and together they had three children. They spent the 1930s in France, England, and Austria, with Boyle writing prolifically. Her works from this time, *Year before Last* (1932) and *My Next Bride* (1934), are experimental, lyrical novels; they inscribe a woman's right to inhabit and combine the worlds of expatriatism, artistic endeavor, sexual discovery, and heterosexual love. Three other novels vary in subject; *Gentlemen, I Address You Privately* (1933; rev. ed., 1991) treats homosexuality uncritically; *Death of a Man* (1936) indicts Nazism; and *Monday Night* (1938) chronicles the failed aspirations of a hack writer. Two novellas, *Bridegroom's Body* (1938) and *Crazy Hunter* (1940), critique marriage, while the novel *1939* (1948) questions nationalism.

In 1941, Boyle returned to the United States. She divorced Vail in 1943, and married Baron Joseph von Franckenstein, with whom she had two children. She completed the novel *Primer for Combat* (1942), set in Nazi-occupied France, and also finished two novels about the French Resistance, *Avalanche* (1944) and *A Frenchman Must Die* (1946). In 1947, Boyle joined her husband, then a United States Foreign Service Officer, in Germany; there she worked as a correspondent for the *New Yorker* and wrote the novel *His Human Majesty* (1949) and stories about occupied Germany, *The Smoking Mountain* (1951). Because of McCarthyite loyalty charges, Franckenstein was dismissed from the

Foreign Service, and the couple moved to Connecticut. They taught school while fighting his dismissal. Boyle continued to produce novels; *Seagull on the Steps* was published in 1955, and *Generation without Farewell* in 1960.

Reinstated to his position in 1962, Franckenstein died a year later. Boyle moved to San Francisco, and until her retirement, taught at San Francisco State University. Boyle's writing continued, most significantly with *Being Geniuses Together* (1966), which alternated her 1920s memoirs with Robert McAlmon's, and *The Underground Woman* (1975), which fictionalized her involvement in student protests. In 1978, she was elected to the Henry James Chair of the American Academy of Arts and Letters, and in 1980, she was awarded a National Endowment of the Arts Senior Fellowship. *Fifty Stories* (1980); *Words That Must Somehow Be Said: The Selected Essays of Kay Boyle, 1927–1984* (1985); and *Collected Poems* (1991) contain her best work in these genres.

• Sandra Spanier, *Kay Boyle: Artist and Activist* (1986). Hugh Ford, *Four Lives in Paris* (1987). Suzanne Clark, *Sentimental Modernism: Women Writers and the Revolution of the Word* (1991). Elizabeth Bell, *Kay Boyle: A Study of the Short Fiction* (1992). Marilyn Elkins, *Metamorphosizing the Novel: Kay Boyle's Narrative Innovations* (1993).

Marilyn Elkins

BRADSTREET, Anne (c. 1612–1672) was the first published poet in America. Born Anne Dudley in Northampton, England, in 1612 or 1613, she was the second oldest in a family of five children. She began her education early, being taught, no doubt, by her mother, Dorothy Yorke Dudley. By age six or seven, Anne was reading Scripture. For her education in Latin, poetry, religion, and natural science, she was especially indebted to her father, Thomas Dudley. During Anne's preteen years, she had use of the castle library at Sempringham, Lincolnshire, where Thomas was steward to the earl of Lincoln. Because girls did not attend school, Bradstreet probably was tutored by the tutors to the earl's children. In her work, she pays allegiance to Sir Philip Sidney, Edmund Spenser, Sir Walter Raleigh, and the anatomist, Helkiah Crooke. Sidney's sister, the countess of Pembroke, and his eldest daughter, Lady Mary Wroth, both poets, may have served as role models. Bradstreet's poetic discipleship of the French Protestant poet Du Bartas may be attributed to medical practitioner and erstwhile poet and playwright Thomas Lodge, who tutored at Sempringham and translated a commentary on Du Bartas's *Semaines* in 1620. Two of the Dudleys' four daughters, Anne and Mercy, were poets, and one, Sarah, was a preacher in England. Clearly, the Puritan Dudleys believed in educating daughters. In 1630, two years after Bradstreet's marriage to her childhood friend, Simon Bradstreet, the couple and the Dudley family emigrated to New England to help found the Massachusetts Bay colony. After a year in Charlestown, Massachusetts, the Bradstreets and Dudleys moved to Cambridge, and from there, in 1635 or 1636, to distant Ipswich. Ipswich was settled by John Winthrop, Jr., the physician son of the famous governor—a very different man from his father. An adept at hermetic lore, practiced, of course, for Christian purposes, the younger Winthrop had the largest alchemical library in colonial New England.

Some scholars emphasize that outlying Ipswich was limiting in its isolation; it was also the location of Bradstreet's primary interpretive community and an environment protected by its isolation. Ipswich was home to an unusually learned group of Puritans, including Nathaniel Ward, John Norton, and Nathaniel and John Rogers, all of whom had high praise for Bradstreet's poetry. This group, including Simon Bradstreet, would soon be at odds politically with powerful Boston over various issues, such as allowing non–church members the vote. In addition, their interests in applied science, alchemy, medicine, and the arts set them apart. Anne Bradstreet shared these interests. Natural science was one of her chief poetic and prose subjects, and from alchemy she borrowed key metaphors for growth processes of all kinds. Just as alchemists believed "affliction," or the grinding of the soul, precedes its transformation, so too, in Bradstreet's finest poem, "Contemplations," is Christ the Philosopher's Stone with which God grinds the creation to perfect it. The poet's task in "Contemplations" is to bear witness to and assist in this process—both in the microcosm of the individual and family life and in the macrocosm of universal nature and history.

This ambitious view of the poet's role seems to have been shaped in Anne's childhood by John Dod, the minister who converted her father, married her parents, and perhaps baptized Anne. Although Dod remained in England, his work and his later tolerationism were demonstrable influences on Bradstreet. Her Lincolnshire education in science, colored, no doubt, by the ideas of the Czech John Amos Comenius, whose radical pedagogy favored the education of girls, and by Dod's interpretations of the feminine presence in biblical wisdom, supported a belief in women's powers of mind and expression.

A supportive audience for poetry was but one factor contributing over the next three decades of her life, beginning with the elegy to Sir Philip Sidney dated 1638. Separation from parents may have been another. Soon after Anne *Hutchinson's trials for heresy in 1637–1638, Dorothy and Thomas Dudley left Ipswich for Roxbury, near Boston, so that Thomas could take a more active role in government. At about this time, Bradstreet must have begun work on the major poems of The Tenth Muse, including the so-called quaternions—descriptions of human and natural history and physiology, presented to her father in 1642.

Additionally, during these years Bradstreet bore eight children—the first, Samuel, was born in Cambridge in 1633, and the last, John, was born in Andover in 1652. For Bradstreet, these procreative years were a time of remarkable poetic energy. In "The Author to her Book" and "In Reference to her Children," childbearing is associated with poetry. As the mother had given birth, so the poet expected her words to engender rebirth. In "A Dialogue between Old England and New," dated 1642, Bradstreet portrayed Old England's suffering during its civil war as a mother-daughter dialogue. Sarah Dudley, then in England preaching, was apparently caught up in the country's religious enthusiasm. Against this background of physical separation, theological difference, and even dissension among the Dudley family members, Bradstreet's poems stand as reenactments of the parental legacy, forging connections between science and Puritan piety, between Old England and New, parents and daughters, past and future. Internal struggle is evident. In "Of the vanity of all worldly creatures," the poet's aspirations to religious devotion are confronted by her uncompromising intellect. Bradstreet was frank about her religious doubts. Her autobiographical letter to her children, "To my dear children," the chief source of information about Bradstreet's life, and an example of "mother's legacy," describes her religious rebelliousness in adolescence and her "blocks" to belief in her mature years. Dorothy Dudley's death in 1643 would provide yet another reason for Bradstreet to address themes of continuity in the midst of change.

By 1647, the Bradstreets had moved to the yet more distant town of Andover, Massachusetts, where their minister was John Woodbridge, Mercy Dudley's husband. The Woodbridges took a sheaf of Bradstreet's poems with them to England, and, with Nathaniel Ward's help, arranged for publication of The Tenth Muse. John Woodbridge's dedication suggests that all this activity took place without Bradstreet's knowledge. Whether or not this is actually so, it is known that Bradstreet did not guide either of her volumes through to publication. She died in Andover in 1672. Six years later, her *Several Poems*, which republished the *Tenth Muse* poetry as well as presenting eighteen new poems, was compiled, probably by John Rogers. In 1867, a complete works, *The Works of Anne Bradstreet in Prose and Verse*, edited by John Harvard Ellis, contained, for the first time, Bradstreet's and her son Simon's manuscript writings, among these her prose, "Meditations divine and moral," her poem, "Contemplations," and her letter, "To my dear children."

Bradstreet's contemporaries valued *The Tenth Muse* poems, but her nineteenth- and twentieth-century critics preferred the later and more generally accessible work: the personal, rather than the formal elegies, and the poems to and about family members, particularly the five devoted to her relationship with her husband. "Contemplations," probably written in the mid-1660s, return in a much-transformed way to the subjects of history and nature with which her career began.

Bradstreet's poetic universe is filled with female presence (Elements; Humours; Old and New England; Flesh and Spirit; Queen Elizabeth; and the daughter, wife, and mother personae of the later poetry), and this universe is marred by dissension, disappointment, and loss. Yet Bradstreet's feminism is directly related to her expectation of a worldwide transformation, a "Day" when, as she tells us in her elegy to Queen Elizabeth (1643), women will be restored to equal power. In the marriage poems, her identity as wife coexists in a complex amalgam with her identity as her husband's equal. This strategy has led critics, depending on their views of Bradstreet, to ascribe ambivalence, duplicity, or an intended doubleness to her self-portrayals.

Bradstreet's talent has been perceived as held in check by her Puritan piety and/or familial obligations. Poststructuralist feminists problematize Bradstreet's situation, as woman and as artist, in terms of a conflict with Puritan patriarchy. Others have seen in her work an intentional artist, effectively deploying such resources as her time and place provided.

• Jeannine Hensley, *The Works of Anne Bradstreet* (1967). Elizabeth Wade White, *Anne Bradstreet: "The Tenth Muse"* (1971). Ann Stanford, *Anne Bradstreet: The Worldly Puritan* (1974). Joseph R. McElrath and Allan P. Robb, eds., *The Complete Works of Anne Bradstreet* (1981). Pattie Cowell and Ann Stanford, eds., *Critical Essays on Anne Bradstreet* (1983). Wendy Martin, *An American Triptych: Anne Bradstreet, Emily Dickinson and Adrienne Rich* (1984). Raymond F. Dolle, *Anne Bradstreet: A Reference Guide* (1991). Rosamond Rosenmeier, *Anne Bradstreet Revisited* (1991).

Rosamond Rosenmeier

BRANT, Beth (b. 1941), also known as Degonwadonti, short fiction writer, poet, essayist, editor, and activist. Brant, a Bay of Quinte Mohawk from Theyindenaga Mohawk Territory in Ontario, Canada, was born in 1941 in Detroit, Michigan. She was married at seventeen and then became mother of three daughters. As she explains in an interview in *Visibilities*, Brant began writing at age forty after an encounter with a bald eagle in Mohawk Valley, New York, left her feeling that "there was something [she] was supposed to do." Brant has been published in numerous Native American and feminist journals in both the United States and Canada, and has works in various anthologies, including Gloria *Anzaldúa's anthology of writings by women of color, *Making Face, Making Soul: Haciendo Caras*. Brant has edited *A Gathering of Spirit: A Collection by North American Indian Women* (1988), and written two other books, *Mohawk Trail* (1985), a selection of prose and poetry, and *Food and Spirits* (1991), a book of short stories. Brant may be best known for *A Gathering of Spirit*, which was originally printed as a special double edition of the feminist journal *Sinister Wisdom*, and later made into a book by Sinister Wisdom Press and titled *A Gathering of Spirit: A Collection of Writing and Art by Native American Indian Women* (1984). This collection brought together for the first time the writing and art of a wide variety of Native American women from North America and Alaska. The work was reprinted by Firebrand Books in 1988 with its present title. *A Gathering of Spirit* has also recently been published in Canada by The Women's Press. Brant's other two books comprise her own writing, which tells stories from a wide range of Native American experience, including her own as a North American Indian lesbian.

In addition to her writing, Brant has been an activist and advocate for Native American communities in a variety of ways. She is cofounder with Denise Dorsz of Turtle Grandmother, an archive and library of information on Native American women and a clearinghouse for unpublished and published manuscripts by Indian women. She is also involved in *AIDS activism and has worked with AIDS survivors in the Native American community. A mother and grandmother, Brant resides in Detroit, where she lives and writes with her life partner, Denise Dorsz.

• Maureen Brady, "Turtle Grandmother Books [An interview with Beth Brant and Denise Dorsz]," *off our backs* 12 (December 1982): 18+. Beth Brant, "Grandmothers of a New World," *Woman of Power* 16 (Spring 1990): 40–47. Christian McEwen, "Beth Brant: Native American Writer," *Visibilities* 5, no. 3 (May/June 1991): 4–7.

Joan Gabriele

BRENT, Linda. *See* Jacobs, Harriet.

BREWSTER, Anne Hampton (1818–1892), fiction writer and foreign correspondent. Born in Philadelphia, Brewster was the second child of Maria Hampton and Francis Enoch Brewster. She was an Anglo-American Protestant of the middle class, and primarily educated by her mother, who taught Brewster that she could derive happiness and financial security through intellectual pursuits. Brewster never married, choosing to live alone and support herself by writing. She began by composing poetry in 1837, but officially launched her prolific writing career in 1845 by publishing short fiction in Philadelphia periodicals under the pseudonym Enna Duval. By 1849, Brewster had published at least twenty-two short stories and the novel *Spirit Sculpture* (1849), and she had also converted to Catholicism, an empowering act that emotionally distanced Brewster from her family. She was an editor at *Graham's American Monthly Magazine* from March 1850 until May 1851, publishing many of her own poems, short stories, and reviews. Brewster also assumed the domestic responsibilities in the house she shared with her older, unmarried brother, Benjamin Harris Brewster, from 1853 until 1856, when she challenged the validity of their father's will in a lawsuit against him, hoping to gain authority over her portion of the family estate, but having to reluctantly settle for control only over her inherited property. She remained estranged from him the rest of her life. In 1857, Brewster traveled to Switzerland and Italy, returning to the United States in 1858 to settle in Bridgeton, New Jersey, where she would supplement her income from teaching by publishing fiction under her true name. Brewster kept journals for most of her life and drew heavily from those she wrote in during her European trip when she was composing her later novels, *Compensation, or, Always a Future* (1860) and *Saint Martin's Summer* (1866). Like most of Brewster's short fiction, these novels feature heroines who must choose between marriage and celibacy, as well as provide commentary on history, music, literature, and art, which critics generally praised; *Compensation* warranted a second edition in 1870. Brewster moved to Rome in 1868, becoming one of the earliest female foreign newspaper correspondents from the United States. With income from her inheritance being at best unreliable, she needed a more profitable vocation than fiction writing, and in 1869 accepted her first newspaper engagement—writing weekly "letters" for the *Philadelphia Evening Bulletin*. A unique combination of gentility, self-revelation, and scholarship endeared Brewster to her audience, making her one of the most popular foreign correspondents of the time. She would write for at least twelve newspapers in the United States in her nineteen years in journalism, during which she reported on political, religious, and archaeological events in Rome, and the artistic, literary, and musical accomplishments of her friends and acquaintances, including other Anglo-American women in Italy. Brewster was a member of Arcadia, the poetical academy in Rome, and hosted a highly celebrated weekly salon, in which she entertained sculptors, painters, musicians, and writers, including Sarah Lippincott, Louise Chandler Moulton, and Julia Ward *Howe. Financial problems arose in the 1880s; income from her inheritance dropped considerably and her journalism career suffered because of changes in journalistic writing styles. In 1889, Brewster moved to Siena, Italy, where she could meet her expenses without additional income from her writing. She died there in 1892.

• The Anne Hampton Brewster Manuscript Collection, Library Company of Philadelphia, contains personal incoming correspondence, journals, commonplace books, copybooks, and miscellaneous article drafts, as well as clippings of Brewster's newspaper correspondence, reviews of her novels, and obituaries of friends and family. The Lloyd P. Smith Papers, Library Company of Philadelphia, contains outgoing correspondence. See also Estelle Fisher, *A Gentle Journalist Abroad: The Papers of Anne Hampton Brewster in The Library Company of Philadelphia* (1947). Nathalia Wright, *American Novelists in Italy. The Discoverers: Allston to James* (1965). Denise M. Larrabee, *Anne Hampton Brewster: Nineteenth-Century Author and "Social Outlaw"* (1992).

Denise M. Larrabee

BREWSTER, Martha Wadsworth (dates unknown), colonial poet. Little is known about the life of Martha Wadsworth Brewster, who was one of only four colonial women to publish a volume of poetry before the American Revolution. Brewster lived in Lebanon, Connecticut, and, according to town records, she purchased and sold land in her own name and with her husband Oliver Brewster, whom she is thought to have married in 1732. Apart from town records, Brewster's poetry is the only source of information about her life, and much of this information concerns not Brewster herself, but her immediate family.

Brewster's only volume of verse, *Poems on Divers Subjects*, was first published in 1757 in New London, Connecticut, and then republished a year later in Boston. The volume, containing seventeen poems and four acrostics, displays Brewster's facility with a wide range of poetic forms, as well as letters and a prose passage describing a dream in which Brewster meets her dead father. While conventional religious and familial themes recur throughout Brewster's work, critics have noted Brewster's occasional departure from traditional subject matter. In "To the Memory of That Worthy Man Lieut. Nathaneal Burt of Springfield" and "Braddock's Defeat, July 9, 1755," Brewster displays a willingness to address issues of military conflict and violence, themes rarely discussed in literature by women at that time. In "To the Subjects of the Special Grace of God and Its Oppressors Compos'd August 1741," Brewster explores the changes heralded by New England's Great Awakening.

Brewster's poetry is often compared to that of Anne *Bradstreet, in part for stylistic reasons—both poets wrote in heroic couplets and both used a broad variety of poetic materials—but also because there are so few colonial female poets with whom to compare Brewster's work. It is not known whether Brewster ever read Bradstreet's work, and recent critics have argued that far from being imitative, Brewster at times exhibits an independent and experimental poetic style. Evidence of this experimentation is provided in the opening line of Brewster's elegy for Nathaneal Burt, which reads, "Oh!—he—is—gone."

Martha Brewster shared with Anne Bradstreet an early American environment intensely hostile to the efforts of female poets. In the introduction to *Poems on Divers Subjects*, Brewster acknowledges that "rare it is to see a Female Bard." One of the most striking passages of the volume relates an incident in which Brewster was accused of plagiarism and to prove her innocence was made to publicly and extemporaneously translate a scriptural passage into verse. Aware of the many barriers restricting colonial women's consumption and production of poetry, Martha Brewster urged her daughter to "increase in Learning" and "delight in Reading," and in her own poetic endeavors set an example for succeeding generations of female poets.

• Emily Stipes Watts, *The Poetry of American Women from 1632 to 1945* (1977). Pattie Cowell, "Martha Wadsworth Brewster," in *American Women Writers*, ed. Lina Mainiero (1979), pp. 231–232. Pattie Cowell, *Women Poets in Pre-Revolutionary America, 1650–1775* (1981). Mindy Janak and Maurice Duke, "Martha Wadsworth Brewster," in *American Writers before 1800*, eds. James A. Levernier and Douglas R. Wilme (1983), pp. 206–208.

Katherine Stubbs

BRONER, E. M. (b. 1930), author of essays, fiction, and drama. A native of Detroit, Michigan,

Esther Masserman Broner was born to Paul Masserman, a journalist and Jewish historian, and Beatrice Weckstein Masserman, a onetime actress in Yiddish theater in Poland. Married to artist Robert Broner and the mother of four children, Broner often writes in the autobiographical mode about her Jewish heritage and about mothering and personal relationships. Broner was also educated in Detroit, at Wayne State University, where she received her B.A. and M.A., and also where she has been a professor and writer-in-residence. She is a literary scholar as well, having received her Ph.D. from Union Graduate School in 1978.

Broner is a significant figure in contemporary American feminist fiction and in Jewish literature. Her early works, including *Summer Is a Foreign Land* (1966) and *Journal/Nocturnal and Seven Stories* (1968), depict assertive female characters making decisions about their lives in clearly defined contexts of ethnic, historical, and social influences. Her later works continue in that vein, with strong Jewish-feminist heroines in *A Weave of Women* (1978) and *Her Mothers* (1975). Her most recent book, *The Telling* (1993), relates the story of four Jewish women who meet annually for a Passover seder. Her writing is experimental and innovative, with underpinnings in traditional myth and tragedy.

Broner's two most-recognized novels, the utopian *A Weave of Women* and the bildungsroman *Her Mothers*, rewrite the mother-daughter relationship and renegotiate women's place in patriarchal religious and social structures. Both works value the rituals of women's lives, their births and initiations, myths and visions. Both are also significant in their use of what has been called "female language," the non-linear, rhythmic prose found in some of the most influential contemporary women's writings.

Broner has written numerous critical essays for such publications as the *New York Times Book Review* and *Commentary*. She also edited, along with Cathy N. Davidson, *The Lost Tradition: Mothers and Daughters in Literature* (1980), an important feminist critical text. Indeed, as a frequent lecturer at women's studies conferences and as a contributor to *Ms.*, Broner's influence on contemporary feminist studies is notable.

Broner now lives in New York City, where she continues to publish fiction and essays and to teach creative writing.

• Ruthann Robson, "A Conversation with E. M. Broner," *Kalliope* 7, nos. 1–2 (1985): 51–57. "Interview with E. M. Broner," *Dispatch* 7, no. 1 (Fall 1988): 23–26. E. M. Broner, "My Mother's Madness," *Ms.* 2 (July/August 1991): 49–54. Cecilia Konchar Farr, "Her

Mother's Language," in *Narrating Mothers*, eds. Maureen Reddy and Brenda Daly (1991), pp. 94–108.

Cecilia Konchar Farr

BROOKS, Gwendolyn (b. 1917), poet, novelist, and autobiographer. The first African-American to win a Pulitzer Prize (1950), Brooks's career has been characterized by a commitment to and celebration of the black community—its ordinary lives, and the realities of oppression. Her early writing, while appealing to a mostly white audience trained in the tenets of modernism and New Criticism, contains a carefully crafted but powerfully resistant voice that scrutinizes and challenges existing racial and sexual oppression. The work written in the 1960s and beyond is more directly political, and the veiled critique that was embedded in the early work becomes more blatant, and is combined with an intensified focus on black solidarity and freedom.

Gwendolyn Brooks was born in Topeka, Kansas, but has lived virtually all of her life in the south side of Chicago. The daughter of David Brooks and Keziah Corine Wims, as a young girl Brooks began writing and reading poetry widely. Her mother told her she would become the "*lady* Paul Laurence Dunbar," and encouraged her literary pursuits, taking Gwendolyn to poetry readings to meet writers such as James Weldon Johnson and Langston Hughes. Brooks began publishing poetry as a teenager in the *Hyde Parker* and *American Childhood*, and became a regular contributor to the *Chicago Defender*'s column, "Lights and Shadows," publishing some seventy-five poems there.

Brooks graduated from Wilson Junior College in 1937, and became involved in the NAACP Youth Council, an involvement that led to an invitation to join a poetry workshop for blacks conducted by wealthy socialite Inez Cunningham Stark (later Boulton) at Chicago's South Side Community Center. Stark, who had been a reader for *Poetry* magazine, emphasized the techniques of the modernist poets, sharing back issues of *Poetry* magazine and volumes of recently published poetry with the class, thereby adding to the already impressive range of poets Brooks had read. Brooks has been married to Henry Lowington Blakely, Sr., since 1939; they have two children.

In 1943, Brooks began to achieve national recognition, winning the Midwestern Writers' Conference Poetry Award in Chicago, as well as awards at that same conference in 1944 and 1945. She was selected as one of *Mademoiselle* magazine's "ten Young Women of the Year" in 1945, the same year Harper & Row published her first volume, *A Street in Bronzeville*. Best known for their sensitive portraits of urban blacks and their lives, the poems of *Bronzeville* frequently contain a resistant voice, one that is embedded in a fine modernist technique. Her sonnet sequence, "Gay Chaps at the Bar," written in the voices of World War II soldiers, links the dynamics of war with the rampant racism in the United States. "The Sundays of Satin Legs Smith," ostensibly portraying a day in the life of an urban zoot-suiter, includes an apostrophized reader/critic whom the narrator chastises throughout the poem for his or her blindness and inability to understand the realities of Satin Legs's (and other American blacks') urban experiences. Brooks's concern for women's lives is evident in *Bronzeville* in poems like "the mother," which unapologetically examines the complexities of the speaker's choice to abort her children, and "the ballad of chocolate Mabbie," in which the focus is provided by a young woman's experience of intraracial discrimination, among many others.

The focus on women in Brooks's poetry intensifies with the appearance of *Annie Allen* in 1949, the volume for which Brooks won the Pulitzer prize in 1950. In many of these poems, war signifies the struggle of a people confined by racism, as well as the struggle between men and women who are confined to a romanticized, oppressive, and unworkable notion of love. Feminized by its title and content, *Annie Allen* (which includes the mock epic "The Anniad") carries forward from *Bronzeville* the resistance to male co-optation, to female passivity, and to the sexual politics that frequently characterize relations between the sexes.

In 1953, Brooks's novel, *Maud Martha*, was published. Under two-hundred pages long and written in short chapters, it represents something of a departure from the conventional novel, and was enthusiastically reviewed. In this lyrical, partly autobiographical story of a dark-skinned black woman's marriage and motherhood, Brooks addresses gender and racial identity.

The increasing social tumult of the 1950s influenced many of the poems in Brooks's next major volume of poetry, *The Bean Eaters* (1960), which addresses racial injustice and the violence of white prejudice more directly than her earlier volumes. The poems of *The Bean Eaters* are less autobiographical, but contain the same technical adroitness of *Bronzeville* and *Annie Allen*.

Nineteen sixty-three marked the publication of *Selected Poems*, which included poems from *Bronzeville*, *Annie Allen*, and *The Bean Eaters*, as well as several new poems. Five years later, *In the Mecca* (1968) was published. The long title poem recounts the protagonist's, Mrs. Sallie's, frantic search for her lost child, Pepita, through the decaying halls of the once-beautiful Mecca Building in Chicago (in which Brooks herself had once worked), mapping the contours of urban poverty through the quiet heroism of Mrs. Sallie.

While Brooks's primary publisher was Harper & Row, she had been publishing small volumes with the black-owned and -controlled Broadside Press in Detroit since 1966. In 1971, Harper published its last Brooks volume, *The World of Gwendolyn Brooks*, a collection that included *Bronzeville, Annie Allen, Maud Martha,* and *In the Mecca*. Although Brooks's relationship with Harper & Row had remained cordial, Brooks's increasing commitment to the black arts movement, and her desire for more control over publication kept her from renewing her contract with Harper after 1971.

In 1967, Brooks attended the momentous Second Fisk University Writers Conference in Nashville, where she encountered the *black arts movement face-to-face, meeting many of its most influential spokespersons, including John Killens, Hoyt Fuller, Ron Milner, and Amiri Baraka. Although her early poems articulate a powerful resistance to oppression, Brooks's poetic vision had not undergone what she calls in her autobiography, *Report from Part One* (1972), a "surprised queenhood in the new black sun," which an awakened black consciousness provided her. She stated that her new goal was "to write poems that will somehow successfully 'call' all black people: black people in taverns, black people in alleys, black people in gutters, schools, offices, factories, prison, the consulate."

Brooks began to publish her own work in 1980, first establishing the Brooks Press and then the David Company of Chicago, which has published *The Near Johannesburg Boy and Other Poems* (1986), *Gottschalk and the Grande Tarantelle* (1988), and *Winnie* (1988), a long poem celebrating the life of Winnie Mandela. Once rights reverted to her from Harper & Row, Brooks produced the omnibus collection of her work, *Blacks*, in 1987. Her most recent book, *Children Coming Home*, was published by the David Company in 1992.

In honor of Brooks's seventieth birthday, Haki Madhubuti edited *Say That the River Turns: The Impact of Gwendolyn Brooks* (1987). The book is a warm tribute from over seventy writers—many of whom have been Brooks's students—that attests to the powerful artistic and social impact Brooks has had on the black community and beyond. The recipient of more than fifty honorary degrees, Brooks has published over twenty-five books of poetry and fiction. She has won numerous prizes and honors, among them two Guggenheim Fellowships, an

American Academy of Arts and Letters Grant in Literature, the Shelley Memorial Award, the Frost Medal, the first Kuumba Award, and a Senior Fellowship in Literature from the National Endowment for the Arts. In 1988, Brooks was elected an honorary fellow of the Modern Language Association. She was the first black woman to be elected to the National Institute of Arts and Letters, as well as the first black woman to be appointed consultant in poetry to the Library of Congress. After Carl Sandburg's death, Brooks was appointed poet laureate of Illinois (1968). In 1993, the Gwendolyn Brooks Center for Black Literature and Creative Writing was established at Chicago State University, where Brooks is Distinguished Professor of English, continuing her many outreach and awards programs throughout the United States.

• R. Baxter Miller, *Langston Hughes and Gwendolyn Brooks: A Reference Guide* (1978). Harry B. Shaw, *Gwendolyn Brooks* (1980). D. H. Melhem, *Gwendolyn Brooks: Poetry and the Heroic Voice* (1987). Maria K. Mootry and Gary Smith, eds., *A Life Distilled: Gwendolyn Brooks, Her Poetry and Fiction* (1987). George E. Kent, *A Life of Gwendolyn Brooks* (1990). D. H. Melhem, "Gwendolyn Brooks" in *Heroism in the New Black Poetry* (1990) pp. 11–38.

Ann Folwell Stanford

BROUMAS, Olga (b. 1949), poet, translator. Broumas's powerful and lucid poetry displays stunning language, unforced rhythms, and an unflinching eroticism. Writing with straightforward lyricism about female sexuality, Broumas uses a poetry rooted in the senses to explore lesbian feminist themes. Her goal is often to find new language with which to convey formerly inexpressible and invalidated experience.

Born in Greece, Broumas moved to the United States at eighteen to become a student, and published her first book of verse, *Restlessnesses* (1967), which was written in Greek. She earned her B.A. in architecture from the University of Pennsylvania in 1970, and her M.F.A. from the University of Oregon in 1973. Broumas has held teaching positions at various academic institutions, including Boston University, Brandeis University, and Freehand, a learning community of women artists that she helped to found in 1982 in Provincetown, Massachusetts. Broumas has also published translations of two books by the Greek writer Odysseas Elytis. Recognitions of her work include a National Endowment for the Arts grant, a Guggenheim Fellowship, and the Yale Series of Younger Poets Award.

Caritas (1976), a chapbook of five love poems, was Broumas's first volume to appear in English. *Beginning with O* (1977), her best-known volume and the text that won the

Younger Poets Award, establishes her voice and themes more fully. The work opens with a series of poems written in 1975 for a two-media piece with painter Sandra McKee. The poems envision Greek goddess myths in a contemporary context, showing their continuity with modern times. Notably, in "Demeter," Broumas charts her modern literary heritage through Anne * Sexton, Sylvia * Plath, Virginia * Woolf, and Adrienne * Rich. The volume's final section features feminist reworkings of Hans Christian Andersen's fairy tales, in the vein of Sexton's *Transformations* (1971).

The poems in *Soie Sauvage* (1979) focus on the human body and interior and exterior landscapes, often employing interior monologue and pared-down syntax. *Pastoral Jazz* (1983) turns on language full of fluid, musical progressions. *Black Holes, Black Stockings* (1985), a series of prose poems written in collaboration with Jane Miller, chronicles dreamlike journeys through Mediterranean countries. *Perpetua* (1989), her most recent work, continues Broumas's sensual lyricism and foregrounds her interrogation of language as a political tool. As elsewhere, this poetry is animated by Broumas's intelligence, her attention to language, and the visceral authority of the body.

• Karla Hammond, "An Interview with Olga Broumas," *Northwest Review* 18, no. 3 (1980): 33–44. Ellen Cronan Rose, "Through the Looking Glass: When Women Tell Fairy Tales," in *The Voyage in: Fictions of Female Development*, eds. Elizabeth Abel, Marianne Hirsch, and Elizabeth Langland (1983), pp. 209–227. Mary J. Carruthers, "The Re-Vision of the Muse: Adrienne Rich, Audre Lorde, Judy Grahn, Olga Broumas," *Hudson Review* 36, no. 2 (Summer 1983): 293–322.

Leigh H. Edwards

BROWN, Alice (1857–1948), short story writer, novelist, dramatist, poet, and essayist. Born in Hampton Falls, New Hampshire ("Tiverton" in the regionalist short fiction for which she is best known), Alice Brown was highly active in New England literary life throughout her long, prolific, and varied career. Educated at Robinson Academy in Exeter, New Hampshire, Brown taught in a country school before moving to Boston in 1880 to work on various magazine staffs. In Boston, she joined the literary network that included Sarah Orne * Jewett, Annie * Fields, and William Dean Howells.

Brown's "Boston marriage" with Louise Imogen Guiney was long lasting, although reconstructing the friendship and its possible sexual dimensions is difficult since Brown, reticent about making her private life public, burned all of Guiney's letters to her after Guiney's death in 1920. Brown and Guiney collaborated on *Three Heroines of New England Romance* (with Harriet Prescott * Spofford; 1894) and *Robert Louis Stevenson: A Study* (1896). They also founded the Women's Rest Tour Association (1891) and the magazine *Pilgrim Scrip* (1892) to promote women's travel abroad.

In her regionalist short fiction, especially *Meadow-Grass: Tales of New England Life* (1895) and *Tiverton Tales* (1899), Brown sensitively and affectionately portrayed rural, independent women. Typically middle-aged or elderly, Brown's heroines retain their independence by rejecting suitors or importunate family members, but without sacrificing their vital connection to the community. Often, these women demonstrate a sustaining mystical response to nature.

Eventually, Brown rejected the New England tale, perceived as a feminine (thus, secondary) genre, for the masculinist discourse of the realist novel. In her novels, she tended to draw women characters conventionally, reserving the privileged role of artist for male characters. Brown also wrote dramas (*Children of the Earth: A Play of New England*, 1914, won the $10,000 Winthrop Ames Prize), poetry, and biographical studies of Mercy * Warren (1896) and Guiney (1921).

Brown's regionalist fiction was enthusiastically received; Howells compared her favorably with Jewett and Mary Wilkins * Freeman. Later, Robert Frost and Thornton Wilder acknowledged having read Brown's stories with interest. But Brown lived to see her reputation dwindle with the rise of modernism, even though she continued to publish until four years before her death in 1948 in Boston. In her relationships, her literary career, and her ambivalent responses to women's issues, Brown is representative of the changing attitudes toward and opportunities for women on the cusp of the twentieth century.

• Susan Toth, "More than Local-color: A Reappraisal of Rose Terry Cooke, Mary Wilkins Freeman and Alice Brown" (Ph.D. diss., University of Minnesota, 1969). Susan Toth, "Alice Brown (1857–1948)," *American Literary Realism, 1870–1920* 5, no. 2 (Spring 1972): 134–143. Dorothea Walker, *Alice Brown* (1974). Margaret Ann Baker, "Alice Brown: A Bibliography of Books and Uncollected Prose," *American Literary Realism, 1870–1920* 17, no. 1 (Spring 1984): 99–115. Beth Wynne Fisken, "Alice Brown (1857–1948)," *Legacy: A Journal of Nineteenth-Century Women Writers* 6, no. 2 (Fall 1989): 51–57.

Tess Lloyd

BROWN, Rita Mae (b. 1944), novelist, poet, screenwriter, and humorist. Born in Pennsylvania, and then adopted, Brown was raised in a poor family in York, Pennsylvania, and was encouraged to write at a young age by her family's friends and teachers. As a girl, she was a frequent reader at the town library. In 1955 her family moved to Fort Lauderdale, Florida, where she attended public schools, and in 1962 she attended the University of Florida at Gainesville. She enrolled in New York University in 1964 and became very absorbed in the theater. By age twenty-two Brown had published two books of poetry and many political articles. In the late sixties and early seventies, she was involved in civil rights activism, lesbian and gay liberation, and the early feminist movement.

Brown's first published book of poetry was *The Hand That Cradles the Rock* (1971). Her first novel was the semiautobiographical *Rubyfruit Jungle* (1973), a tremendously popular book that was republished in 1977 and translated into many languages. *Rubyfruit Jungle* is one of the first American novels to portray a lesbian character in a liberated way and has been a standard in lesbian literature and in women's studies courses for many years. Though often thought of as lesbian, Rita Mae Brown is bisexual. In 1974, she published her second novel, *In Her Day*, and in 1977, with the help of a fiction grant from the National Endowment for the Arts, she published *Six of One*. Brown is also a screen and television writer, and includes such scripts to her credit as *Sweet Surrender*, and a spoof on horror films called *Sleepless Nights*, which was produced by Roger Corman as *Slumber Party Massacre*. Her other books include the novels *Southern Discomfort* (1982), *High Hearts* (1986), and *Bingo* (1988), and a 1987 collection of poetry.

A voracious reader and a tremendously popular and prolific writer, Brown has quirky and unusual perspectives on writers and writing, which she discusses in her 1988 autobiographical book, *Starting from Scratch: A Different Kind of Writers' Manual*. It contains advice about how a writer should live to be successful and healthy, and also outlines her philosophy about the use of the English language, the development of plot, character, and dialogue, and advice about how to survive financially as a writer. *A Plain Brown Rapper* (1976) is a collection of her early essays.

• Lois Marchino, "Rita Mae Brown," in *American Women Writers: A Critical Reference Guide from Colonial Times to the Present*, ed. Lina Mainiero (1979), pp. 257–259. Carol Marie Ward, *Rita Mae Brown* (1993).

James Davis-Rosenthal

BROWN, Rosellen (b. 1939), poet, novelist, short fiction writer, and educator. The youngest of three children, Brown was born in Philadelphia to Jewish parents. The family moved around considerably during her childhood, the pursuit of economic security and advancement taking them to various locations in the Northeast, and, for a brief period, as far as Los Angeles. Not surprisingly, as she says in "What I Do When I Write," Brown sees "perpetual rootlessness" as a recurring theme in her writings. Her adult years have been characterized by a similar mobility. After earning a B.A. at Barnard College (1960), and an M.A. in literature at Brandeis (1962), Brown married Marvin Hoffman, a psychologist. They have since lived in California, Massachusetts, Mississippi, New York, New Hampshire, and Texas, where Brown, since 1982, has taught in the University of Houston's Creative Writing Program.

During the latter part of the civil rights movement (1965–1967), Brown and her husband lived in Tougalou, Mississippi, where they taught at a black college. It was here that Brown had her first child, Adina (1967), and wrote most of her first book, *Some Deaths in the Delta* (1970). Set in both the South of the civil rights movement and in Brooklyn, New York, this collection of poems situates sharply etched personal portraits and individual voices against a highly charged political backdrop. Brown achieved a similar balance in *Street Games* (1974), a collection of short stories set on the Brooklyn block where she and her family lived in the late sixties, and where her daughter Elana was born (1970).

Brown's first novel, *The Autobiography of My Mother* (1976), explores the painful and often paradoxical relationship between an estranged mother and daughter. The novel continues to interest feminist scholars, with recent articles ranging from a psychoanalytic reading of mother-daughter relations to a treatment of the protagonist's struggle with the patriarchal legacy of her Jewish background.

As she says in a 1986 *Contemporary Literature* interview, Brown brings to her works a strong sense of what she calls the "conflict between ideology in a pure form and the messy details of everyday life." This tension is played out most compellingly in her novel *Civil Wars* (1984), which depicts the daily existence and family life of a white couple who met and married while active in the civil rights movement. The narrative's central point of view—that of the female protagonist—reflects Brown's wish "to present a woman's insight" into traditionally male-centered discourses.

In her most recent novel, *Before and After* (1992), Brown manipulates the conventions of the murder mystery to uncover the darkness that belies the seemingly charmed existence of an upper-middle-class American family.

• Melissa Walker, "An Interview with Rosellen Brown," *Contemporary Literature* 27, no. 2 (1986): 152. Rosellen Brown, "What I Do When I Write," *Women's*

Review of Books 6, nos. 10–11 (July 1989): 24–25. Dee Seligman, "Jewish Mothers' Stories: Rosellen Brown's *The Autobiography of My Mother*," in *Mother Puzzles: Daughters and Mothers in Contemporary American Literature*, ed. Mickey Pearlman (1989), pp. 115–122.

Julia Dryer

BUCK, Pearl Sydenstricker (1892–1973), Nobel Prize winner in literature, novelist, biographer, short fiction writer, essayist, and humanitarian. Born in Hillsboro, West Virginia, to Presbyterian missionaries Absalom and Caroline Stulting Sydenstricker, Pearl, at three months old, moved with her family to Chen-Chiang, China, and did not return to the United States until 1910. Learning Chinese before English (she always said that she thought in Chinese), Pearl absorbed Chinese folk tales from her "amah" (nurse) and wrote articles with her mother's encouragement. In 1914, she graduated from Randolph-Macon Woman's College in Lynchburg, Virginia, and then returned to her family in China. After her 1917 marriage to agricultural specialist John Lossing Buck, Pearl put aside her writing to care for her daughter Carol, who was mentally disabled, her adopted daughter Janice, and her aging parents.

Hoping to solve pressing financial problems, Pearl Buck published her first novel, *East Wind: West Wind* in 1930. *The Good Earth* (1931), a novel about the rise of peasant Wang Lung, was an immediate best-seller and Pulitzer Prize winner. *The Mother* (1934) portrays a Chinese peasant woman as a universal mother. *Sons* (1932) and *A House Divided* (1935) completed the Wang Lung trilogy. In 1936, Pearl published *The Exile* and *Fighting Angel*, biographies of her mother and father, respectively.

In 1938, Pearl Buck received the Nobel Prize for literature—the first woman to do so—"for rich and genuine epic description of Chinese peasant life and for biographical masterpieces" (*American Winners of the Nobel Literary Prize*, 1968). In her Nobel lecture "The Chinese Novel," she explained the influence of eastern literary standards on her writing, such as the novel's basis in popular oral traditions and the importance of story line. Popularity indicated to Buck that she was communicating to ordinary readers; the literary establishment, however, criticized the award's being given to a popular writer, as well as to a recently expatriate American. Other critics, such as Malcolm Cowley, defended *The Good Earth* in particular on the basis of its universal appeal.

By 1935, Pearl was settled in America, having divorced Buck and married her publisher, Richard Walsh. In 1949, she founded Welcome House, an adoption agency for Asian-American children, and in 1964, the Pearl S. Buck Foundation, to aid Asian-American children and their mothers overseas. Buck played a central role in changing social attitudes about and legal barriers to adoptions that created multiracial families. She continued to write novels, stories, essays, and plays (her least-successful genre). Pearl S. Buck died of lung cancer on 6 March 1973, in Danby, Vermont, having published over one hundred works and received over three hundred humanitarian awards.

• Paul A. Doyle, *Pearl S. Buck* (1965). Nora Stirling, *Pearl Buck: A Woman in Conflict* (1983). Dody Weston Thompson, "Pearl Buck," in *American Winners of the Nobel Literary Prize* (1968), pp. 85–110. Lucille S. Zinn, "The Works of Pearl S. Buck: A Bibliography," *Bulletin of Bibliography* 36 (1979): 194–208.

Taimi Olsen

BULIMIA. *See* Body and Health; Eating Disorders.

BURKE, Fielding. *See* Dargan, Olive Tilford.

BURNETT, Frances Hodgson (1849–1924), author of over fifty stories and novels for adults and children, of which five were best-sellers and thirteen were adapted for the stage. The daughter of a lamp manufacturer, the young Frances Hodgson lived in Manchester, England, until 1865, when her widowed mother moved the impoverished family to Tennessee. In 1874, Frances married Dr. Swan Burnett, with whom she had two sons. She divorced Burnett in 1898; from 1900 to 1902 she was married to Stephen Townesend. From 1887 to 1924 she maintained residences both in England and America. She died at her Plandome, Long Island, home in 1924.

Burnett's writing is marked by the conflicting desires to write both social criticism and romance. Her early realistic novels, *That Lass o' Lowrie's* (1877), *Haworth's* (1879), and *Through One Administration* (1883), in which she treats class and gender issues, were favorably compared to the works of George Eliot, Elizabeth Gaskell, William Dean Howells, Henry Adams, and Henry James. Through diverse female characters, Burnett explores the roles of women as socialites, workers, wives, and mothers, and illustrates the ways in which women are empowered or rendered powerless by those roles. In *Through One Administration*, for example, Bertha Amory is torn between exercising her feminine social power as a political lobbyist and her equally strong desire to remain at home and be the perfect mother. Proud, hard-bitten Joan Lowrie in *That Lass o' Lowrie's* must relinquish her working-class independence and transform herself through feminine and domestic education in order to become worthy of Fergus Derrick.

In most of her novels, however, Burnett depends upon popular romance formulas and fairy-tale plots, in which all conflicts are benignly resolved. *Little Lord Fauntleroy* (1886), *A Fair Barbarian* (1881), and *The Shuttle* (1907) each retells the Cinderella story of an American protagonist who is transplanted into British society and there proves his or her superior worth. In *The Making of a Marchioness* (1901), Emily Fox-Seton, an incongruous heroine of large heart and large feet, unconsciously wins the affections of a British nobleman by allowing herself to be exploited by everyone around her.

Burnett is perhaps best known, however, for her children's stories. In 1886, she published the best-selling *Little Lord Fauntleroy*, whose hero was based on her younger son, Vivian. The success of this book and two other novels for children—*A Little Princess* (1902) and *The Secret Garden* (1911)—earned Burnett her continuing reputation as a writer for children. In these works, and in *The One I Knew Best of All* (1893), the autobiography of her childhood, Burnett creates an idealized version of a childhood inhabited by nearly perfect children, whose goodness and good nature has transformative power.

• Vivian Burnett, *The Romantick Lady* (1927). Ann Thwaite, *Waiting for the Party* (1974). Francis J. Molson, "Frances Hodgson Burnett (1848–1924)," *American Literary Realism* 8 (Winter 1975): 35–41. Phyllis B. Koppes, "Tradition and the Individual Talent of Frances Hodgson Burnett: A Generic Analysis of *Little Lord Fauntleroy*, *A Little Princess*, and *The Secret Garden*," *Children's Literature* 7 (1978): 191–207. Phyllis Bixler, *Frances Hodgson Burnett* (1984).

Judith Burdan

BURROUGHS, Margaret Taylor Goss (b. 1917), poet, educator, artist, editor, and museum director. The title of one of Margaret Taylor Goss Burroughs's earliest books, *What Shall I Tell My Children Who Are Black?* (1968), poses a question about the significance of her African-American heritage that Burroughs has been answering in a variety of ways throughout her career. Born in rural Louisiana on 1 November 1917, Burroughs was the child of parents who migrated to Chicago after World War I to find better economic opportunities. Deciding to become a teacher, she graduated from Chicago Normal College with an elementary school certification, and later earned an advanced degree in art education from the Art Institute of Chicago. Actively engaged as a teacher at the Dusable High School, Burroughs was also a working writer and artist. Her first book, *Jasper, The Drummin' Boy* (1947), an illustrated book for children, was published in the same year that she won her first prize for one of her paintings.

In the 1950s and 1960s, Burroughs began writing and collecting poems (including prose poems) as a way of finding new expression for the political activism in which she participated in Chicago. She edited *Did You Feed My Cow? Rhymes and Games from City Streets and Country Lanes* in 1955, and, with Dudley Randall, edited *For Malcolm: Poems on the Life and Death of Malcolm X* (1967), an anthology that included some of her own works as well as the works of important black poets such as Gwendolyn *Brooks, Amiri Baraka, and Margaret *Walker. Her first collection of poems, *What Shall I Tell My Children Who Are Black?*, reflects Burroughs's ongoing concern with the oppression of her people. Generally regarded as her finest poetry (and written after her first travels to Africa and Europe), the eighteen poems of *Africa, My Africa* (1970) form the narrative of an African-American who visits Africa in search of an identity.

Throughout her career as a teacher, artist, and writer, Burroughs's abiding concern has been to preserve her African-American heritage. With her second husband, Charles Gordon Burroughs, she established in 1961 a small museum in their Chicago home, the Dusable Museum of African American History. Under Burroughs's direction, the collection has grown to include over ten thousand books, papers, and manuscripts on African-American history and culture. As its emeritus director, Burroughs continues to create art, preserve history, and foster the talents of other African-Americans.

• Elaine Stetson, ed., *Black Sister: Poetry by Black American Woman, 1946–1980* (1981), pp. 118–122, 301. Harry A. Ploski and James Williams, eds., *The Negro Almanac: A Reference Work on the African American* (1989), p. 1047.

Susan Belasco Smith

BUTLER, Octavia (b. 1947), African-American novelist and short story author specializing in science fiction. In 1984, she won science fiction's Hugo Award for her 1983 story "Speech Sounds," and received both a Hugo and a Nebula Award for her story "Bloodchild" in 1985. Butler has become one of the most respected and admired writers of the genre, and that Butler is a black woman successfully negotiating a literary terrain long dominated by white men, a territory where few other black writers have ventured, further highlights her accomplishments.

Born in Pasadena, California, the only child of Laurice Butler and Octavia M. (Guy) Butler, the young Octavia led a rather insulated life. Her father died when she was an infant; she was raised by her mother and grandmother in a racially integrated and culturally diverse community in Pasadena, whose inhabitants were African-American, Asian-American, Hispanic, and white. She did not experience strict racial segregation, either in school or within her neighborhood, nor racial discrimination, except on those occasions when she accompanied her mother to her job as a maid. Tall for her age, quiet, and isolated in a largely adult world, Butler did not mix well with other children. Yet because her mother frequently took in older people as boarders to supplement the family income, a certain social and cultural diversity was also present in her home. This socially constructed, extended family gave the young Butler access to various adult role models.

Octavia Butler's career as a writer began in her childhood. She had been a shy and solitary child who read avidly from the juvenile selection in her local library's children's reading room. As a preteen, she was drawn to stories of wild horses, fairy tales, and romance fiction; her earliest attempts at fiction imitated the conventions of those forms. By age twelve, she discovered science fiction. She found that she enjoyed it; it offered more freedom than other genres, and she believed that she could write stories at least as well as those she saw televised. Thus, in junior high school, with the aid of a supportive science teacher, Butler began crafting her own stories and submitting them to pulp magazines, in her bid to become a published writer.

Despite the rejection of her initial tales, Butler persevered. Through high school, she continued to read widely in science fiction. On her early reading list was Robert Heinlein's science fiction for young readers; Butler subsequently found the fiction of Zenna Henderson, Theodore Sturgeon, John Brunner, and Marion Zimmer *Bradley. Some of science fiction's best authors—Arthur C. Clark, Isaac Asimov, Ursula K. *Le Guin, A. E. Van Vogt, Harlan Ellison, and Frank Herbert, among others—were writers whose works she devoured. Apart from the novels and story collections in libraries, Butler discovered the science fiction pulp magazines that were still flourishing in the late 1950s and early 1960s: *Amazing; Fantastic; Fantasy and Science Fiction; Galaxy.* An eclectic reader, her tastes in this period also included the irreverently satirical *Mad* magazine, as well as comic books— DC's *Superman,* and the various superheroes of Marvel comics.

Following her 1965 high school graduation, Butler enrolled at Pasadena City College, graduating in 1968. She then briefly attended California State University at Los Angeles, but withdrew because the program lacked sufficient creative writing offerings. As a consequence, in 1969 and 1970, she also took some writing courses at UCLA and at the Writers' Guild of America West. At the Writers' Guild classes, Butler met Harlan Ellison, already an established writer and editor; he became her teacher and a mentor. Butler deemed Ellison her first honest critic, not a teacher merely offering encouragement to the novice, but a professional writer giving blunt constructive criticism. In the summer of 1970, Ellison also encouraged Butler to attend the Clarion Science Fiction Writers' Workshop, held in Clarion, Pennsylvania. The workshop was an intensive six-week program that featured established science fiction writers and editors who taught and talked about the particular requirements of the genre. Extremely valuable to her because of the practical advice she garnered there, Butler regarded Clarion as one of the best writer workshop experiences of her life.

Butler's only stand-alone novel, *Kindred* (1979), is a text she views more as a grim historical fantasy rather than as science fiction because "it has no science in it." The story involves Edana Franklin, called Dana, an African-American woman from twentieth-century Los Angeles, whose life becomes linked to that of a white child who is mysteriously able to call her to his side, across both time and distance (specifically, to nineteenth-century antebellum Maryland), when he needs her assistance. Five novels, *Wild Seed* (1980), *Mind of my Mind* (1977), *Patternmaster* (1976), *Clay's Ark* (1984), and *Survivor* (1978), comprise Butler's extended Patternist saga. This series was well received by science fiction fans, black and feminist readers, and scholars of the genre because of its complexities, interweaving as it does dystopian visions of the future with questions of race; culture; political, ethical, and social issues; and feminist concerns. Butler's second series is the Xenogenesis trilogy, beginning with *Dawn* (1987) and followed by *Adulthood Rites* (1988) and *Imago* (1989). In this series, readers are able to explore with Butler an imaginative scenario for survival after the nuclear holocaust, a recurrent science fiction theme. Additionally, the trilogy marks what is possibly literature's most traumatic meeting of humans and an alien species, in this case, the Oankali, rescuers determined to preserve humanity's remnants, but at a price—the mixing of genes to create a new species. Here, in addition to continuing an emphasis on a restructured political, social, and anthropological matrix, Butler further develops an interest in biology and genetic engineering, thus adding more "hard science" to her fiction. The trilogy was critically acclaimed by Butler's already established audience, science fiction fans, black readers, and feminist scholars alike.

Although her short stories appear infrequently, they are highly regarded for their power and intensity. "Speech Sounds" recounts a world where anarchy reigns and where almost everyone is afflicted by a communications deficit. "Bloodchild," depending on the reader's perspective, is either a story of human enslavement by aliens or a "pregnant man" story. "The Morning and the Evening and the Night" explores the nightmarish horrors of a bizarre genetic disease. Introducing the story in *The Year's Best Science Fiction* (1988), Gardner Dozois called it a "chilling tale of despair, resignation, and most painfully, hope."

Butler's appeal as one of the most esteemed science fiction writers of her generation lies not only in her altered or alien landscapes, but in character delineation and the interplay of her motifs as well. From the Patternist saga through the Xenogenesis trilogy, she confronts issues of gender, power, isolation, alienation, slavery, survival, control, change, compromise, adaptation, and difference. Butler also uses such social sciences as anthropology, political science, and sociobiology. She borrows from the physical sciences as well, emphasizing biology and genetic engineering, symbiosis, and human mutation. She also manipulates the pseudosciences—parapsychology, psionic ability, telepathy, and telekinesis. Yet throughout her differing, largely dystopian, futures, several characteristics remain virtual constants—strong women of African-American or racially mixed heritage are protagonists or heroines; a family unit, either extended, altered, or reconfigured, remains; nothing is absolute; change is necessary, and balance, essential.

• Veronica Mixon, "Futurist Woman: Octavia Butler," *Essence* 9 (April 1979): 12–15. Frances Smith-Foster, "Octavia Butler's Black Female Future Fiction," *Extrapolation: A Journal of Science Fiction and Fantasy* 23, no. 1 (Spring 1982): 37–49. Sandra Y. Govan, "Connections, Links, and Extended Networks: Patterns in Octavia Butler's Science Fiction," *Black American Literature Forum* 18 (1984): 82–87. Ruth Salvaggio, "Octavia Butler and the Black Science-Fiction Heroine," *Black American Literature Forum* 18 (1984): 78–81. Thelma J. Shinn, "The Wise Women: Black Women Mentors in the Fiction of Octavia Butler," in *Conjuring: Black Women, Fiction, and Literary tradition*, eds. Marjorie Pryse and Hortense Spillers (1985), pp. 203–215. Frances M. Beal, "Black Women and the Science Fiction Genre: Interview with Octavia Butler," *Black Scholar* 17, no. 2 (March–April 1986): 14–18. Interview with Butler in *Across the Wounded Galaxies: Interviews with Contemporary Science Fiction Writers*, ed. Larry McCaffery (1990), pp. 54–70. Hoda M. Zaki, "Utopia, Dystopia, and Ideology in the Science Fiction of Octavia Butler," *Science Fiction Studies* 17, no. 2 (July 1990): 239–251. Frances Bonner, "Difference and Desire, Slavery and Seduction: Octavia Butler's Xenogenesis," *Foundation: The Review of Science Fiction* (Spring 1990): 48, 50–62. Sandra Govan, "Octavia Butler" in *Notable Black American Women* (1991), pp. 144–147.

Sandra Y. Govan

C

CADE, Toni. *See* Bambara, Toni Cade.

CAJUN WRITING. *See* Acadian and Creole Writing.

CALDWELL, Taylor (1900–1985), novelist. The author of thirty-eight internationally best-selling novels, Caldwell also used the pseudonyms Max Reiner and Marcus Holland.

Born in Prestwich, Manchester, England, Caldwell described her austere upbringing in her collection of autobiographical essays, *On Growing Up Tough* (1971). Caldwell's family was dominated by a mother who "believed in rearing girls exactly as boys were reared, and no nonsense about the weaker sex and the softer yearnings in a girl's heart." Although her family was financially secure after their immigration to Buffalo, New York, in 1906, Caldwell's mother urged her to withdraw from school at fifteen and to begin working in a factory, where Caldwell claimed she displayed "too much independence of manner, too much self-assurance, too much of an appearance of confidence" to attract the protective husband she desired. Women in Caldwell's fiction reflect her view of "the sole and natural business of women: To be good wives and prudent mothers, soothers of the masculine brow, good cooks, pleasant companions, and truly feminine."

Married in 1919 to William Fairfax Combs, whom she divorced in 1931, Caldwell had one daughter, Mary Margaret; her marriage to Marcus Redback in 1931 produced a second daughter, Judith Ann. Caldwell's other marriages were to William E. Stancell in 1972 and to William Robert Prestie in 1978.

Before publishing her first novel in 1938, Caldwell worked as a court reporter for the New York State Department of Labor (1923–1924) and served as secretary of the Board of Special Inquiry of the U.S. Immigration and Naturalization Service, U.S. Department of Justice (1924–1931). She earned her A.B. in 1931 after attending night school at the University of Buffalo. A Roman Catholic and a Republican, Caldwell received several awards for her writing, including a Gold Medal from the National League of American Penwomen (1948), the Grand Prix Chatrain, Paris (1956), and the Daughters of the American Revolution National Award (1956).

The subjects of Caldwell's novels fall into three main categories. The first group depicts tough and often ruthless men. *Dynasty of Death* (1938) begins a trilogy dealing with magnates from the munitions and steel industries. *The Eagles Gather* (1940) and *The Final Hour* (1944) complete the saga of powerful American industrialists and their dependent families. *The Strong City* (1942), *This Side of Innocence* (1946), *Never Victorious, Never Defeated* (1954), and *Bright Flows the River* (1978) also concern bold men working out their complicated destinies. The second subject Caldwell develops involves a historical figure enmeshed in an invented world. Genghis Khan in *The Earth Is the Lord's* (1940), Richelieu and Louis XIII in *The Arm and the Darkness* (1943), Cicero in *A Pillar of Iron* (1965), and Aspasia and Pericles in *Glory and the Lightning* (1974) exemplify her blend of historical fact with pure fiction. Caldwell's third subject is the hidden life of biblical characters, such as the disciple Luke in *Dear and Glorious Physician* (1959), Paul in *Great Lion of God* (1970), and Judas in *I, Judas* (1978). Her novels *Testimony of Two Men* (1968) and *Captains and the Kings* (1972) were serialized for television.

The *New York Times*, the *Saturday Review of Literature, Books and Bookmen*, as well as other publications, consistently reviewed Caldwell's novels, but no scholarly study of her work has been written. Reviewers criticized Caldwell's full-throttle style, citing its blaring verbs surrounded by glaring adjectives and adverbs. They remarked on her lack of subtle characterization, and after the publication of her autobiographical essays, Caldwell's use of fictional characters as mouthpieces for her political views became undeniable. In her world, simple and predictable dichotomies revealed what she claimed as "natural" divisions: male/female, rich/poor, conservatives/liberals, west/east, heroes/villains, God/Satan. Although specialists found inaccuracies in Caldwell's historical and biblical novels, and other reviewers criticized her plots as simplistic and formulaic, Caldwell's works entertained general readers; before her death from lung cancer on 30 August 1985, she had sold over thirty million volumes.

Elizabeth McGeachy Mills

CALIFIA, Pat (b. 1954), writer, poet, columnist, sex educator, and activist. Califia was one of the founding members of Samois, a group of sadomasochist (S/M) lesbians who joined together in San Francisco in the late 1970s in an effort to increase the visibility and acceptability of the lesbian S/M community. Califia defines S/M as "a sexual experience in which the participants have agreed to act out a fantasy in which one of them controls the sex and the other is sexually submissive" (*Gay Community News*, 15 August 1981). Between 1978 and 1982, some of the most virulent debates in American feminism centered on women's sexuality and pornography. Some groups within the feminist community, most notably the organization Women against Violence in Pornography and the Media (later Women against Pornography), sought to determine and enforce boundaries around properly "feminist" sexuality and sexual consciousness. Samois's members believed feminism need not exclude a variety of sexual preferences and practices, and they organized to counter prejudices that viewed S/M sexuality as a sickness, and equated lesbian S/M with battery, rape, mutilation, or the pornography industry. Califia's first book, *Sapphistry: The Book of Lesbian Sexuality* (1980), an informative, frank, affirming account of the diversity of desires and practices that make up lesbian sexuality, was written partly as a response to the negative attitudes of some feminists towards sexuality.

Califia has devoted much of her creative energy to educating and informing different communities about lesbian S/M. Numerous articles and interviews on lesbian sexuality and S/M have appeared in the gay press in the 1980s and 1990s. *The Lesbian S/M Safety Manual* (1988), which Califia edited, is a responsible how-to book that is still the only source of reliable, comprehensive information on this subject. In addition, Califia has contributed a column to the gay magazine the *Advocate* for several years. In it, she dispenses advice to gay men on a virtually unimaginable range of sexual questions. Those columns have been collected in *The Advocate Adviser* (1991).

Califia is perhaps best known for her erotic fiction, especially the short story collection *Macho Sluts* (1988) and the novel *Doc and Fluff* (1990). Her short fiction has also appeared in many magazines. Califia's pornography breaks down boundaries of gay and straight, acceptable and deviant, to bring to light the fear, excitement, pleasure, and danger of outlawed desires. In her introduction to *Macho Sluts*, Califia states that she aims to entertain and to arouse, but also to create "a vision of the woman of the future, including her ideas about what 'sexy' means and looks like, and what 'pleasure' is, and what it's worth."

• Laura Lederer, ed., *Take Back the Night: Women on Pornography* (1980). Nancy Wechsler, "Gayle Rubin and Pat Califia Talk about Sadomasochism," *Gay Community News* (15 August 1981): 6. Samois, ed., *Coming to Power: Writings and Graphics on Lesbian S/M* (1981). Thomas Weinberg and G. W. Levi Kamel, eds., *S and M: Studies in Sadomasochism* (1981). Feminist Anti-Censorship Task Force, *Caught Looking: Feminism, Pornography, and Censorship* (1986). Amy Scholder and Ira Silverberg, eds., *High Risk: An Anthology of Forbidden Writings* (1991).

Samira Kawash

CALISHER, Hortense (b. 1911), novelist, short story writer, autobiographer. Born in New York City on 20 December 1911, Calisher graduated from Hunter College High School and received an A.B. in philosophy from Barnard College in 1932. Her first marriage, to H. B. Heffelfinger in 1935, produced a daughter and a son. Her second marriage in 1959 was to Curtis Harnack, who became director of Yaddo in Saratoga Springs, New York, in 1971; they lived in a converted art studio on the grounds until 1986. Her work as an investigator with the New York Department of Public Welfare (1933–1934) yielded material for her later fiction, and her home at that time (East Twenty-third Street in Manhattan) appears in her story "The Woman Who Was Everybody" (1951).

Though she has held many temporary teaching positions, Calisher is not associated with any one educational institution; her most recent appointment was as a professor at Brown University (1986). She was president of the American branch of PEN (1986) and of the American Academy of the Institute of Arts and Letters (1987–1990). Her many honors include Guggenheim Fellowships (1952, 1955); grants from the Department of State Specialists (1958), the American Academy of Arts and Letters (1967), and the National Endowment for the Arts (1967); an honorary doctorate from Skidmore College (1980); and the Lifetime Achievement Award from the National Endowment for the Arts (1989).

In the Absence of Angels (1951) was Calisher's first book; it contains semiautobiographical stories, as well as others, reflecting her interest in the human psyche, which is also characteristic of her later writing. Her images and characters are often of New York, but her work defies regional labels. She examines the human experience in all its complexity, especially those episodes in which a character's survival depends on both an understanding of self and relationships with others. Her fictional landscape is interior; it journeys into the thoughts and feelings of her characters. Critics find her short fiction more successful than her novels because it has more plot focus. In addition to her first book, her short fiction collections include *Tale for the Mirror* (1962), *Extreme Magic* (1964), *The Railway Police and the Last Trolley Ride* (1966), *The Collected Stories* (1975), and *Saratoga, Hot* (1985). The range of her characters extends from children to the aged; the tone of her stories is often sad, melancholy or nostalgic. Scenes extend from urban everyday places (*The New Yorkers*, 1969) to outer space (*Journal from Ellipsia*, 1965, and *Mysteries of Motion*, 1983).

Through her subtle but definite verbal humor, Calisher examines the human condition with exactness and depth. If the rhetoric sometimes slows action, the prose is so finely woven that readers forgive the pace. Her other novels are *False Entry* (1961), *Textures of Life* (1963), *Queenie* (1971), *Standard Dreaming* (1972), *Eagle Eye* (1973), *On Keeping Women* (1977), *The Bobby-Soxer* (1986), and *Age* (1987). Her autobiographical works are *Herself* (1972) and *Kissing Cousins* (1988). She published a lecture, *What Novels Are* (1969), and, with Shannon Ravenel, edited *The Best American Short Stories, 1981*. Calisher lives in New York City.

• Emily Hahn, "Calisher, Hortense," in *Contemporary Novelists*, ed. James Vinson, 2d ed. (1976), pp. 232–235. Eugene Ehrlich and Gorton Carruth, "Middle Atlantic States," in *The Oxford Illustrated Literary Guide to the United States* (1982), p. 135. Bruce Kellner, "Calisher, Hortense," in *Reference Guide to American Literature*, ed. D. L. Kirkpatrick, 2d ed. (1987), pp. 129–130. "Calisher, Hortense," in *The Writers Directory, 1992–94*, 10th ed. (1991), p. 149. Kathleen Snodgrass, *The Fiction of Hortense Calisher* (1993).

Jeanne R. Nostrandt

CALLAHAN, Sophia Alice (1868–1894), author of *Wynema, A Child of the Forest* (1891), one of the earliest novels by a Native American woman. Born near Sulphur Springs, Texas, Alice was the daughter of Samuel Benton Callahan and Sara Elizabeth Thornberg Callahan. One-eighth Creek, Samuel was the captain of a company of the First Creek Regiment of the Confederate Army, and was elected in 1862 and 1864 to represent the Creeks and Seminoles at the Confederate Congress at Richmond, Virginia. During his absence, marauders raided the prosperous trading post and ranch he had established in the Creek Nation in Indian Terri-

tory, located in present-day southeastern Oklahoma. Sara fled with her children to friends in Sulphur Springs. After the Civil War, Samuel held many important positions within the tribe, often serving as a delegate to Washington. He also edited the *Indian Journal* and was superintendent of the Wealaka Boarding School for Creek children near Tulsa, Oklahoma. Samuel made and lost several fortunes as a merchant, rancher, and farmer.

Little is known about Alice's life. She spent her early years in Sulphur Springs. Although her father returned to the Creek Nation in approximately 1865 to start a ranch near Okmulgee, Indian Territory, his family remained in Sulphur Springs. In 1885, they joined him in Okmulgee, capital of the Creek Nation. By 1887, the family had relocated to Muskogee, Indian Territory, south of Tulsa. For ten months, Alice attended the Wesleyan Female Institute in Staunton, Virginia, from which she returned in June 1888. When *Wynema*, her only book, was published in 1891, she was teaching at Muskogee's Harrell International Institute, a Methodist high school. In 1892–1893 she taught at the Wealaka School. In late 1893 she moved back to Harrell. Callahan planned to return to the Female Institute in 1894 to complete her studies so that she could open her own school. However, before she could fulfill her plans, she died of pleuresy on 7 January 1894 at age twenty-six.

Callahan's *Wynema* focuses on the acculturation of a genteel southern woman, Genevieve Weir, to life as a teacher in the Creek Nation, and the gradual evolution of her favorite pupil, Wynema, into a sophisticated young lady equally at home among her people or in white society. The first two parts of the romance describe Creek culture and contemporary politics. The second part also argues strongly for women's rights, which reflects Callahan's ardent support of the 1890s movement to gain equality for women. Part three, undoubtedly inspired by contemporary news reports, focuses on the events in the Sioux Nation in what is now South Dakota that led up to Sioux unrest, the murder of Sitting Bull, and the massacre at Wounded Knee in late 1890. In this section, Callahan staunchly defends the Sioux and excoriates whites for their treatment of the Sioux and of Indians in general.

• Carolyn Thomas Foreman, "S. Alice Callahan," *Chronicles of Oklahoma* 33 (1955): 306–315, 549. "Samuel Benton Callahan," Appendix, *Chronicles of Oklahoma* 33 (1955): 314–315. A. LaVonne Brown Ruoff, "Justice for Indians and Women: The Protest Fiction of Alice Callahan and Pauline Johnson," *World Literature Today*, Contemporary American Indian Literature Issue, 66, no. 1 (1992): 249–255.

A. LaVonne Brown Ruoff

CANON FORMATION. According to the *New American Heritage Dictionary*, the canon is composed of "the books of the Bible officially recognized by the Church." In the late sixties and early seventies, literary critics began to apply this ecclesiastical term to literature as a way of describing the process by which certain works come to be taught in universities and, to a lesser extent, secondary schools. Analogous to the biblical canon, the literary canon includes books officially recognized by the academy.

Ask any literary scholar over the age of, say, forty or forty-five and she will tell you that such famous women writers as Willa *Cather, Kate *Chopin, Zora Neale *Hurston, Flannery *O'Connor, Gertrude *Stein, or Edith *Wharton were not part of the canon when she was an undergraduate; often such authors were omitted even from specialized graduate reading lists in American literature. Once the syllabus of great books was termed canonical, everything started to change, for the very terminology questioned the authority by which certain books were included and others excluded. Groundbreaking studies such as Jane Tompkins's *Sensational Designs: The Cultural Work of American Fiction, 1790–1860* (1985) charted the process of canon formation, examining the ways in which authors' reputations are made and how they are sustained by the literary academy. Cathy N. Davidson's *Revolution and the Word: The Rise of the Novel in America* (1986) showed that the American novel, although typically taught as a masculine genre, actually began as a women's form, while Linda Wagner-Martin's *The Modern American Novel, 1914–1945: A Critical History* (1990) showed how even that most "masculine" cultural phenomenon—Modernism—was influenced profoundly by both white women and women of color.

Presses such as The Feminist Press were established with the explicit intention of bringing back into print great works of literature by "lost" women writers while Indiana University Press, University of North Carolina Press, Rutgers University Press, and other mainstream academic outlets inaugurated important series specializing both in reprinting the work of women writers and in publishing scholarly monographs about women and gender. Additionally, Beacon Press, Kitchen Table Press, Aunt Lute Press, Crossing Press, and Naiad Press all brought back into print books by women of color, including a number of lesbian writers who had been all but forgotten. A book cannot be canonized unless it is available, and the new process of canonization could not have occurred without this industrious publishing activity.

It must be emphasized that the process of canon formation is never fixed—and never has been. Long before feminists and multicultural critics began asking about the writers who had been excluded from the canon, white male critics were in the business of finding and "resurrecting" lost writers. The most famous case is Herman Melville, who was all but lost to literary history until he was rediscovered in the late 1920s by modernist critics and writers. Edgar Allan Poe has been lost and found several times. Other writers go in and out of favor; for example, William Dean Howells and Frank Norris are suddenly receiving attention again after a decade of inattention, partly because of the recent critical interest in *realism and "the body." The same complicated and sometimes fortuitous processes that favor the introduction of texts by women and minority authors are constantly at work for white male writers too.

Not coincidentally, the "reconstructed" canon has gained currency in universities just as there are more and more women professors in university literature departments. Also, the U.S. college population is now almost sixty percent female, and the general literate book-buying readership is also largely female. There is now an active and interested body of readers for rediscovered classics such as Harriet *Wilson's *Our Nig* (1859), one of the first novels published by a black woman, or Harriet A. *Jacob's *Incidents in the Life of a Slave Girl* (1861), which has yielded sales of over seventy-five thousand dollars for Harvard University Press. The Schomburg Library of Nineteenth-Century Black Women Writers and the Early American Women Writers series (both published by Oxford University Press) have made texts available to libraries worldwide as well as to classroom teachers, with individual texts such as Susanna *Rowson's *Charlotte Temple* (1791) selling some fifty thousand copies. The monumental two-volume Heath *Anthology of American Literature* (1990) is perhaps the single most important text for transforming the canon at American colleges and universities.

Together, these and other texts help to present the full and complex story of American literary history—not just a white, male, New England literary history. The new canon allows us to read again the books that women have written and made popular through the centuries.

Similar processes of canon formation have occurred in all disciplines—history, sociology, even science—that have also reexamined their own historiography for gender or racial biases and omissions. The expanded canon corrects previous aesthetic misconceptions (such as the idea that there were no black women writers before the 1970s) or ideological ones (for example, that *feminism is merely a late-twentieth-century fad, a notion belied by the work of earlier writers such as Judith Sargent *Murray, Margaret *Fuller, Marietta *Holley, or Ida B. *Wells).

The process of canon formation has always been evolutionary and will continue to be. Reference works such as the *Oxford Companion to Women's Writing in the United States* consolidate the canon at a specific historical moment by documenting the history of women's writing and, ideally, inspiring new scholars and critics to make their own canonical additions (and deletions).

[*See also* Education; Women's Studies Programs.]

• Dale Spender, ed., *Men's Studies Modified: The Impact of Feminism on the Academic Disciplines* (1981). Nina Baym, "Melodramas of Beset Manhood: How Theories of American Fiction Exclude Women Authors," in *The New Feminist Criticism: Essays on Women, Literature and Theory,* ed. Elaine Showalter (1985). Hazel Carby, *Reconstructing Womanhood* (1987). Patricia Hill Collins and Margaret L. Andersen, *An Inclusive Curriculum: Race, Class, and Gender in Sociological Instruction* (1987). Susan Hardy Aiken et al., *Changing Our Minds: Feminist Transformations of Knowledge* (1988). Elizabeth Minnich, Jean O'Barr, and Rachel Rosenfield, eds., *Reconstructing the Academy* (1988). Paul Lauter, *Canons and Contexts* (1991). Henry Louis Gates, Jr., *Loose Canons* (1992).

Cathy N. Davidson

CAPTIVITY NARRATIVES. Historically, men have written of their heroic battles, struggles, and trailblazing adventures. For women, the struggle was more often with private doubts, prayer, and resolution. New forms of these external and internal adventures occurred when colonial women, taken captive by North American Indians, had their own tales of terror, torture, subservience, and ridicule to tell. Early captivity narratives emphasized God's role in spiritual conversion and deliverance; later ones focused more on woman captives' attempts to cope or to flee through their own wits. Women such as Mary *Rowlandson and Susannah *Johnson wrote their own narratives; others, such as Hannah Duston, Elizabeth *Hanson, and Jane A. Wilson, had their narratives recorded or reported by ministers or military officers as part of religious or historical records.

Mary Rowlandson's narrative, *The Sovereignty and Goodness of God, Together with the Faithfulness of His Promises Displayed; Being a Narrative of the Captivity and Restoration of Mrs. Mary Rowlandson* (1682), focuses on her experiences as a deeply religious Protestant who saw herself as part of the New Israel's Elect. Thus, when she and her three children were captured in 1675 in Lancaster, Massachusetts, she turned to God and the Scriptures for mercy and deliverance. She records events in the same way biblical scholars did, and presents the wilderness as hell and the Indians as kin to Satan. Removed from her "civilized" world, she learns more about her own animal nature; her concerns for food dominate her as she sees herself cherish a moldy piece of cake for which she bartered. She suffers the death of a young daughter and dreads the fate of her other two children, John and Mary. But her religious sense dominates all she experiences. Throughout her trial, Rowlandson prays for deliverance, and when it is granted through ransom, she sees her freedom as an act of God.

Hannah Duston's captivity, as recounted in her "Narrative of a Notable Deliverance from Captivity," first published in Cotton Mather's appendix to *Humiliations Followed with Deliverances* (1697), bears similarities to Rowlandson's. Taken in an attack at Haverhill, Massachusetts, five days after childbirth, she marched one hundred miles into the wilderness with her friend, Mary, and a young boy, Samuel Lennardson. Allegedly, she prayed for mercy and deliverance, but taking matters into her own hands, she reportedly killed her captors and brought home ten scalps, for which she received a bounty of twenty-five pounds. Cotton Mather saw her spiritual and physical efforts as a biblical reenactment of Jael upon Sisteria (Judges 4), and he reported this in sermons and in his classic *Magnalia Christi Americana* (1702). Duston became an instant heroine who was compared to Jael. Just as her biblical sister had become God's instrument and saved Israel, so had Duston saved the New Israel.

Susannah Johnson's August 1754 first-person narrative, *A Narrative of the Captivity of Mrs. Johnson* (1796), deals with her seizure by Indians in what is now Charlestown, New Hampshire. Her narrative details the capture of her family (including her husband, three children, and sister) and their subsequent march north to Lake Champlain. Susannah's experiences bring her to realizations about the Indian world. She reports that she gave birth to her daughter Captive "in the open wilderness rendered cold by a rainy day," upon which followed the nine day's march to Lake Champlain and the Indian camps nearby. Although Susannah had the initial security of her family to support her, she learned that the Indians planned to sell them as slaves as soon as they reached Montreal, where they were sold into slavery.

Her family's capture altered Susannah's life forever. It appears her husband had inadvertently broken parole because he was captured;

thus, when he was released by the Indians, he was sent to prison in Montreal and Quebec. The governor of Quebec eventually responded to petitions for Susannah's release. He permitted her and two of her daughters to sail to England in an exchange of prisoners there. Finally, she returned to New York in 1757 to reunite with her husband, but he was killed shortly thereafter at the Battle of Ticonderoga. Although a Christian, her work has a decidedly different tone than Mary Rowlandson's. Johnson reports in an openly realistic manner and without religious reference, that "on viewing myself, I found that I too was naked," like the Indians.

Elizabeth Hanson's captivity narrative, *God's Mercy Surmounting Man's Cruelty* (1728), displays her Quaker humanist virtues of patience and long-suffering kindness. Captured in Dover, New Hampshire, in August 1724, she also struggled with hunger and cold on her twenty-six day journey to Canada, but she consciously made the effort to befriend Indian women who helped her save her baby by showing her a recipe for pap made from cornmeal and walnut kernels. Like other captives, Hanson was beaten by her Indian master, who eventually sold her to the French. She told her story to a preacher visiting New Hampshire, who recorded it. In his version, during her captivity she consistently held the view that "God will avenge the weak and powerless." After six months in captivity, her prayers were answered when her husband John found and rescued her.

Women's captivity narratives changed with the eighteenth-century movement west. The narratives shift to a more biographical format, which also emphasizes the pioneer spirit. The unattributed introduction to *The Thrilling Narrative of the Sufferings of Mrs. Jane Adeline Wilson during Her Captivity Among the Comanche Indians* (1853) calls it "unquestionably one of the rarest items of Western history." Recorded by Major Carleton and a newspaper correspondent, L. Smith, the narrative presents Wilson almost as a sentimental heroine of a series of tragic adventures. Wilson's early tragic experiences include the death of her parents, the parceling out of herself and her siblings to neighbors, and her early arranged marriage to a man she did not love.

On her journey west with a wagon train, Indians murder Wilson's husband during an attack. After a short grieving period, she sets out again, only to be captured. This time, they cut her hair and used it for decorative purposes. Wilson reports: "I was mortified to see [my hair] decorating the heads of the heartless savages." During her captivity, she learned to ride bareback, chase animals through the briars,

carry wood, and catch her own mule. Beaten regularly when she could not work quickly enough, she also complains of starvation and thirst.

Eventually, with a trading party's assistance, Wilson escapes. Her tale of struggle does not present her as calling upon God. Her closing statement appears to support the male ideal of a factual report; it reads, "I have related nothing but facts."

History fails to provide a clear record of Indian women who were killed, held captive, or suffered at the hands of white men.

[*See also* Autobiography; Religion, *article on* Religion to 1700.]

• Kathryn Zabelle Derounian and David L. Greene, "The Publication, Promotion and Distribution of Mary Rowlandson's Indian Captivity Narrative in the Seventeenth Century," *Early American Literature* 23, no. 3 (Fall 1988): 239–261. Frances Roe Kestler, comp., *Indian Captivity Narratives* (1990). Tara Fitzpatrick, "The Figure of Captivity: The Cultural Work of the Puritan Captivity Narrative," *American Literary History* 3, no. 1 (Spring 1991): 1–26.

Adelaide P. Amore

CARIBBEAN-AMERICAN WRITING. The immigration of Caribbeans into the United States is not a late-twentieth-century phenomenon, as recent discussion might suggest. As early as the turn of the twentieth century, the first wave of Caribbean immigrants—or West Indians, as they were then, and are still called—poured into the United States, mostly through New York. Many settled in Harlem, and in so doing reshaped the character of the black community in the city. The West Indian influence is to be found in the literature of the *Harlem Renaissance (1919–1929), in the writings of such Caribbean-American authors as Jamaican-born Claude McKay (1889–1948), who situated themselves as subjects of both black America and the Caribbean. In that the vast majority of Caribbean immigrants were black, they became aligned with African-American culture for both socioeconomic reasons—all black people in the United States were immediately put at the bottom of social and economic ladders—as well as for political ones. Yet they also struggled to retain their cultural heritage, something that was considered incompatible with "Americanness." This frisson between race and culture, Americanness and West Indianness, is at the heart of writings by the first generation of West Indian–American writers.

It is important to understand the legacy of this generation when considering the literature of the second generation of Caribbean-American authors, who may concern themselves with similar themes and yet define them differently. The historical era in part explains the differences; equally important is the gender difference between the two generations. While the first generation of Caribbean-American writers was male, the second generation is almost entirely female. These writers are usually anthologized as African American, and their oeuvres are considered in light of the themes of African-American feminist literature. Criticism of the works tends to focus heavily on race, then on class and gender, usually as those issues are understood and defined within the American context. Yet, while it is important to situate these writers as part of American society, the totality of their ideas on these critical variables is missed without situating them within the canon of Caribbean narrative. These women writers are poised, in varying degrees, between two cultures, and of necessity must draw from both in their assessments of society. Furthermore, while Caribbean-American literature by women is an integral part of the body of African-American female-authored literature that exploded onto the literary scene in the 1970s, 1980s, and 1990s, it is important to make the critical distinction that this is also the work of immigrants whose perceptions of race and society are often shaped by another culture. Because Caribbean perceptions of race, class, and gender diverge so widely from the American, one must consider the writers' point of origin when interpreting the narratives.

The most prominent Caribbean-American female authors are Audre * Lorde, Jamaica Kincaid, Paule * Marshall, and Michelle * Cliff. These authors all have their roots in the English-speaking Caribbean and were either born in or first immigrated to New York City. Consequently, their narratives bear witness to similar experiences of growing up West Indian in urban America. Yet there are important differences as well.

Of these, Audre Lorde is the only author not primarily a novelist, having written only *Zami: A New Spelling of My Name* (1982), which she labelled not fiction but rather a "biomythography," conflating as it does her own history, her literary depiction of her own history, and myth. Born in Manhattan in 1934 of Grenadian parents, she was a poet, a professor at Hunter College, an essayist, and an activist for black, lesbian, and women's causes until 1993, when she died of the cancer she had fought so valiantly for years, a struggle she chronicles in one of her best-known works, *The Cancer Journals* (1980).

In *Zami*, the young Lorde, growing up in New York City, struggles to articulate her newly conscious lesbian identity within her traditional Caribbean household. She attempts to meld her intrinsically incompatible lesbian and Caribbean identities by re-envisioning the Carriacou homeland (a small island off the coast of Grenada) of her mother, whose approval she ardently desires, as a place where the kinship of the women who work together is a distinctively Caribbean, nonsexual form of lesbianism. Zami, the Carriacou word for women who work together as friends and lovers, embodies this fusion for her, and she takes it as her own name, thus recreating and sustaining both her Caribbean and American heritage.

Lorde's technique of redefining the social and historical parameters of Caribbean society in order to "rebirth" herself as a Caribbean-American lesbian, as it were, can be seen working to similar effect in the literature of Michelle Cliff, particularly in her first heavily autobiographical novel, *Abeng* (1984). Michelle Cliff, born in 1946 in Kingston, Jamaica, grew up in both Jamaica and the United States. That a significant portion of her formative years were spent on the island influences both the vision and setting of her novels, which take place mostly in Jamaica.

Like Lorde, Cliff is also lesbian, and uses literature to effect a reconciliation between her Caribbean, American, and lesbian identities using a conflation of history and myth. In *Abeng*, the character of Mma Alli is an obvious appropriation of the historical Maroon leader Nanny, the first and only female Jamaican national hero. (The Maroons are descended from the groups of slaves who escaped the plantations and fled to the mountains, where they formed communities, fought the British, and won.) The historical Nanny led the Maroons in their fight against the British in the Maroon wars of the eighteenth century and was reputed to use obeah, one of the African-derived religious practices of the island (pejoratively known in the United States as "voodoo"). In the novel Mma Alli is a nineteenth-century lesbian obeah woman who counsels women and leads the slaves on the plantation of Judge Savage into rebellion. By recreating the historical figure of Nanny into a woman warrior and healer, Cliff is inserting a wedge into the masculinist vision of Jamaican history that will allow women, lesbian and otherwise, to see themselves as a natural part of the historical landscape. This is particularly important for Caribbean-born lesbians in that homosexuality is still seen by Caribbean societies as alien, a reviled import from the United States and Europe.

Perhaps more importantly, however, *Abeng* and its sequel, *No Telephone to Heaven* (1987), are concerned with issues of race and how racial categories as symbols of class and caste shift parameters depending on political and cultural affiliations. The protagonist of both novels, Clare Savage, a member of the privileged "brown" class in the Caribbean who is able to pass for white in the United States and Europe, attempts to retrieve her Afro-Caribbean cultural identity from the invisibility to which her father, Boy Savage, a descendant of a white slave owner, has consigned it. That Boy has trouble "passing" in the States makes it all the more important for him to emphasize European origins in Clare, who as the lighter of his two daughters is designated his heir, while her darker-skinned sister is the favorite of Clare's mother, who is a more obviously black woman. Whiteness in these narratives is associated with Clare's patrilineal, "masculine" heritage: European colonization of the island and the suppression of the cultural and historical legacy of the black and indigenous Caribbean populations. Blackness, on the other hand, is associated with her mother's African-descended heritage and values. In this manner the racial signifiers confer both gender and political positions. Thus Clare herself embodies the essential contradictions inherent in Caribbean society.

Like Cliff, Jamaica Kincaid also spent a significant portion of her formative years in the Caribbean, on the island of Antigua, where she was born in the capital, St. John's, in 1949 as Elaine Potter Richardson. She migrated to the United States in 1965, shortly after her sixteenth birthday, to work as an au pair girl for an American family, and later moved to New York where she studied photography and worked as a journalist at *Seventeen* and later at the *New Yorker*, which published many of her first short stories. Kincaid's novels also have an autobiographical component, from her first—and perhaps most famous—novel, *Annie John* (1985), which chronicles a young Antiguan girl's passage to adulthood and separation from her beloved yet hated mother, to *Lucy* (1990), the story of a West Indian au pair who works for an American family. *Lucy* appears in many ways to be a sequel to *Annie John* in the continuation and elaboration of the mother-daughter conflict.

Perhaps the most purely lyrical of Caribbean-American writers, Kincaid writes novels that are deceptively simple stories of young women's personal sojourns into maturity. They do not appear to investigate overtly political themes or to carry a feminist worldview. Indeed, Kincaid herself has said that while "I think I owe a lot of my success . . . to this idea of feminism," she still does not "really want to be placed in that category" (*Caribbean Women Writers*, 1990).

To conclude that this is in fact the case, however, is to misinterpret Kincaid's work. Issues of power and dominance are worked out in intensely personal exchanges between mother and daughter, white female employer and black female employee in both *Annie John* and *Lucy*. The relationships between women (male characters generally have little emotional impact in Kincaid's novels) often function as metaphors for the historical legacy of colonialism within the culture of women. The conflictual relationship between mother and daughter functions as a symbolic commentary on the dislocation between the daughter/island from the mother/country, both in terms of the female Caribbean immigrant in the United States and the colonial Annie John, whose connection to her African and Native Carib ancestry is refracted through the distorting prism of a colonial ethos that seeks both to tame and to negate her.

In Kincaid's first book of nonfiction, *A Small Place* (1988), she effects a more deliberately political critique of colonialism and its aftereffects in her observations on her return to Antigua. If we consider this critique in the light of her more obliquely critical novels, it becomes clear that Jamaica Kincaid defines politics differently, as she herself has explained: "When I write I don't have any politics. I am political in the sense that I exist" (*Out of the Kumbla*, 1990).

Paule Marshall is the most prolific of the four novelists and the earliest, in that her works have spanned three decades, beginning with her first novel, *Brown Girl, Brownstones*, first published in 1959. Like the protagonist of *Brown Girl*, Marshall was born in New York City in 1929 of Barbadian parents, and one senses an autobiographical element in the conflict Marshall's female protagonists face in trying to achieve success in their new country while reconnecting themselves to the old.

Marshall's second novel, *The Chosen Place, The Timeless People* (1969), follows the life of Merle Kimbona, a young woman from Bourne Island (which bears a striking resemblance to Barbados) who has returned to her homeland from London to teach the children their real history, and not the history of imperial European victories thrust upon them by the colonial education system. The motif of the returning islander is a constant in Marshall's fiction; it also appears in her fourth novel, *Daughters* (1991), which investigates the meaning of Caribbeanness and Americanness through mother/daughter relationships.

A similar weaving of Caribbean and United States locales is employed in Marshall's most-analyzed and third novel, *Praisesong for the Widow* (1983). The protagonist, Avey Johnson, is a middle-aged African-American widow from New York City who grew up on the South Carolina islands. Her husband literally worked himself to death striving to achieve the American dream, and indeed Avey is financially comfortable enough to take a cruise to the Caribbean. In the Caribbean Avey rediscovers, through the African-based cultural rituals there, her links to her rural, African-derived heritage, a memory she had repressed as she became a respectable middle-class black woman. She returns to the mainland spiritually whole, determined to preserve and nurture these links to her homeland.

The American dream in these fictions is associated with a masculine quest for money and power at the expense of inner life, while black culture and spirituality is passed down through the maternal characters. Thus the United States and the Caribbean take on gendered characteristics in this symbolic representation. This characterization of America lends itself to a reading of the text as an allegory of the author's anxieties about her relationship to the United States as a second-generation Caribbean, immigrant, where the pursuit of Americanness in the form of American economic wealth means the loss of Caribbeanness. It also means that on subsequent journeys to the Caribbean the Caribbean emigrant will inevitably suffer a "sea change," such that she can never travel back across the sea as the same person she was at the beginning of the immigrant journey because she now carries the baggage of First World economic and social status.

Although Lorde, Cliff, Kincaid, and Marshall are strikingly different in both ideological and structural terms, their novels carry critical thematic similarities in the way they negotiate gender and race, culture and citizenship. In this way they can be said to have forged a new cultural identity and literary canon that belongs to both the United States and the Caribbean.

[See also African-American Writing; Assimilation; Citizenship; Ethnicity and Writing; Immigrant Writing.]

• Giovanni Covi, "Jamaica Kincaid and the Resistance to Canons," in Out of the Kumbla: Caribbean Women and Literature, eds. Carole Boyce Davies and Elaine Savory Fido (1990), pp. 345–354. Selwyn R. Cudjoe, "Jamaica Kincaid and the Modernist Project: An Interview," in Caribbean Women Writers: Essays from the First International Conference, ed. Selwyn R. Cudjoe (1990), pp. 215–232.

Belinda Edmondson

CARSON, Rachel (1907–1964), nonfiction writer, conservationist. Rachel Carson grew up on a farm near Springdale, Pennsylvania. An early, fervent concern for nature conservation was reinforced by her mother, Maria (McLean) Carson, who, as Carol Gartner documents, had the same concern and was a strong believer in "mother-daughter bonds." Rachel also imagined becoming a professional author, and wrote several pieces for the children's journal St. Nicholas.

Misfortune struck with the deaths of Carson's father, Robert W. Carson, in 1935, and her sister, Marian, in 1936. Maria Carson convinced Rachel to help her raise Marian's two young girls, and so, armed with an M.A. from Johns Hopkins University, Rachel moved to Silver Spring, Maryland, with her widowed mother and the children. In order to support this brood, Rachel began a fourteen-year stint as a writer of pamphlets and radio scripts for the U.S. Fish and Wildlife Service, eventually becoming editor in chief of the service's publication program.

Meanwhile, Carson composed two books: Under the Sea-Wind (1941), a vivid account of lives in the sea, and the dramatic The Sea Around Us (1951), which details the ocean's formation, creatures, and all-important contribution to the planet. The latter's success—it won the National Book Award, spent eighty-six weeks on the best-seller list, and was translated into over thirty languages—allowed Carson to resign her job and become a full-time writer. Less picturesque but still much-admired, The Edge of the Sea, a metaphorical move inland, followed in 1955.

No sooner had Carson risen to prominence than her adopted niece Marjorie died in 1957, leaving a son to raise, a duty Carson assumed, although her own mother was dying. Marked by constant mental exertion, the next five years tested Carson's endurance.

Olga Huckins, a writer for the Boston Post, asked Carson to help combat damage to birds caused by Massachusetts's widespread aerial pesticide spraying to extinguish mosquitoes. The plea inspired Carson, in January 1958, to begin her renowned work Silent Spring (1961). This dynamic denunciation of chemical pesticides marked the summit of Carson's career as a national benefactor. Despite criticism by pesticide advocates, including Secretary of Agriculture Orville Freeman, President John Kennedy appointed a committee to investigate the matter, and the first antipesticide bills were introduced.

While writing Silent Spring, Carson met and corresponded with other authors, illustrators, and reformers. Most germane was her rapport with Dorothy Freeman, near whose cottage Carson lived during summers in Maine, and to whom Carson "gave herself completely," as Paul Brooks notes.

The creed of mercy permeates Silent Spring, showing how persistence, tact, and good will may counter malicious attitudes toward nature.

This motif reappears in *The Sense of Wonder* (1965), inspired by actual outdoors adventures with Carson's young great-nephew Roger.

Though weakened by an operation in 1960, Carson continued writing. Her television speech on "CBS Reports" defending *Silent Spring* against attacks from the chemical industry, and her preface to *Animal Machines* by Ruth Harrison, describing the cruelties of intensive livestock raising—both in 1963—rallied supporters of these causes to battle. To the very end, Rachel Carson's brief life was creative.

[*See also* Ecofeminism.]

• Yale University Library is the repository of the Rachel Carson Papers. Frank Graham, Jr., *Since Silent Spring* (1970). Paul Brooks, *The House of Life: Rachel Carson at Work* (1972). Carol B. Gartner, *Rachel Carson* (1983). L[ewis] J. A[mster], "Carson, Rachel Louise," in *American Reformers*, ed. Alden Whitman (1985), pp. 149–151. H. Patricia Hynes, *The Recurring Silent Spring* (1989).

Elizabeth Steele

CARY, Alice (1820–1871), writer of regionalist sketches, poet. Born on a farm eight miles north of Cincinnati, Ohio, Alice Cary chose the nearby crossroads village of Mt. Healthy as the site and scene for her most significant fiction—*Clovernook; or, Recollections of Our Neighborhood in the West* (1852); *Clovernook, Second Series* (1853); and *Pictures of Country Life* (1859). Her sketches, dedicated to gaining recognition for what she called the farming class, share with her female contemporaries, such as Caroline *Kirkland, a commitment to realism, and with her male contemporaries, such as Nathaniel Hawthorne, an understanding of fiction as psychic exploration and dream work. Her fiction distinguishes itself from the work of contemporaries, both female and male, however, by her willingness not only to advocate for a class misrepresented by the prejudices of uninformed writers, but also by her willingness to use her art to privilege a female consciousness, located in the narrative "I" of the sketches.

Death and deprivation marked Cary's childhood. A beloved older sister, from whom she learned the art of story telling, died in 1833, and her mother died two years later. Cary had only the rudiments of formal schooling, and few resources outside of school. Yet she evidently began writing poetry at an early age, publishing her first poem in 1838, and achieving national recognition by 1849 with her inclusion in Rufus Griswold's *The Female Poets of America*. With the publication in 1850 of *Poems of Alice and Phoebe Cary*, Cary had a sufficient sense of her own economic and personal possibilities to leave her father's house in Ohio and move to New York City, where she established, with her younger sister Phoebe, a household of her own, later famous for the Sunday evening receptions the sisters hosted there. Cary spent the rest of her life in New York, publishing several volumes of poetry and occupying, for many years, the poet's corner in the *New York Ledger*. She died at home on 12 February 1871 and was buried two days later in Greenwood Cemetery in Brooklyn, New York.

Though Alice Cary's reputation during her lifetime derived from her poetry, her regional fiction provides the source of contemporary interest in her work, both for its own literary merits and as part of a larger tradition. Her sketches offered a model to subsequent regionalist writers interested in focusing on character rather than plot, in foregrounding the fragment rather than the "complete" story, and in writing of rural communities from a sympathetic and participatory stance rather than from that of a superior urban observer.

• Mary Clemmer Ames, *A Memorial of Alice and Phoebe Cary, with Some of Their Later Poems* (1873). W. H. Venable, *Beginnings of Literary Culture in the Ohio Valley* (1891). Janice Pulsifer, "Alice and Phoebe Cary, Whittier's Sweet Singers of the West," *Essex Institute Historical Collections* 109 (January 1973). Annette Kolodny, *The Land before Her* (1984). Judith Fetterley, Introduction to *Clovernook Sketches and Other Stories*, by Alice Cary (1987).

Judith Fetterley

CASTILLO, Ana (b. 1953), poet, novelist, and teacher. Chicago-born Ana Hernandez Del Castillo graduated from Northeastern Illinois University in 1975, the same year that she published her first book of poems, *Zero Makes Me Hungry*. In the next few years, she published three more collections, *I Close My Eyes (to See)* (1976); *Otro canto* (1977); and *The Invitation* (1979). In her use of mixed Spanish and English, she forces recognition of the power of bilingualism, and its validity as literary expression.

With her 1981 collection, *Keats, Poe, and the Shaping of Cortazar's Mythopoesis*, she took on critics who claimed Spanish was not a "literary" language. Her membership in ethnic groups—the Chicago-based Association of the Latino Brotherhood of Artists, Movimiento Artístico Chicano, La Junta de Sociólogos, and others—also showed her conviction to identifying as an important Chicana writer. With the 1984 publication of *Women Are Not Roses*, she moved into a more strident voicing of Chicana women's experience, but she muted that voice in her best-known work, *The Mixquiahuala Letters*, published in 1986 by Bilingual Press.

Letters has been viewed as both an epistolary novel and a series of prose poems. It poses as letters written by Teresa, a California Chicana poet, to her white friend Alicia, a New York artist, during the ten years following their graduation from college. Relentlessly fragmentary (only one side of the correspondence appears, and gaps in narrative are prevalent), Castillo's text suggests the women's changing attitudes toward themselves and each other, toward work and sexuality. Experience is the narrative, but Castillo prevents oversimplification by providing alternative arrangements of the forty letters: the several tables of contents, titled "Conformist," "Cynic," and "Quixotic," lead to different plot resolutions.

In her 1990 *Sapogonia*, Castillo continues her use of fragmented and sometimes surreal episode, moving more clearly toward magical realism. Both this novel and *Letters* are utopian/dystopian fictions, with place-names referring to imaginary locations where people of mixed racial backgrounds have value and power, as with Sapogonia, described by Castillo in the novel as "a distinct place in the Americas where all mestizos reside, regardless of nationality, individual racial composition, or legal residential status." Each work challenges conventional genre distinctions and form, as in the case of *Sapogonia*, which is subtitled *An Anti-Romance in 3/8 Metre*. With the fantasized (or real) murder of Pastora, whose story is being told, on page two, Castillo announces the chimera her fiction is, a Barthian fun house filled with erotica, outrage, and realistic pain.

In 1988, Castillo published *My Father Was a Toltec: Poems* and saw the publication of a new edition of the influential anthology *This Bridge Called My Back: Writings by Radical Women of Color*, which she had coedited with Cherríe Moraga and Gloria Anzaldúa in 1981.

Linda Wagner-Martin

CATHER, Willa (1873–1947), novelist, essayist, and writer of short fiction. Although Cather is associated with the midwestern landscape that she celebrated in novels such as *My Ántonia* (1918), she was born in a small farming community in Virginia's Shenandoah Valley, the eldest child of Charles and Virginia Cather. She found her first introduction to narrative in the *storytelling of women who came to the Cather's farmhouse, Willow Shade, to help out with canning, preserving, and quilting, and later paid tribute to this first exposure to women's creativity in her last novel, *Sapphira and the Slave Girl* (1940), her only book set in the Virginia of her childhood.

In 1883, when Willa was ten years old, Charles and Virginia Cather decided to join Charles's brother and parents, who were farming on the Nebraska Divide. Cather at first found the transition from Virginia's sheltered landscape to the raw openness of the Nebraska prairies a painful one, and she later said she did not know how she survived. But this transition from the relatively homegenous culture of the Shenandoah Valley to the rich ethnic mix Cather found on the Divide—where Scandinavians, French, Russians, Bohemians, and Germans farmed alongside native-born Americans—was ultimately a gift to Cather's creativity. In many of her novels and short stories she recorded the lives of Nebraska's immigrant settlers, who had introduced her to cultures and histories that first directed her gaze from America to Europe.

Charles Cather did not take to farming, and in 1884 the family moved into the small prairie town of Red Cloud, where he found work in real estate. Willa Cather's awakening imagination found many resources in the town—she attended school, acted in amateur theatricals, attended plays at the opera house, studied Greek and Latin with a town storekeeper, and found neighbors who introduced her to European literature. In 1888, she rejected the constraints of Victorian *femininity by adopting a male persona: she wore male dress, cropped her hair, and proclaimed herself "William Cather, Jr." or "William Cather, M.D." (she then wanted to be a surgeon). She maintained this appearance for four years.

In September 1890 she moved to Lincoln and enrolled as a second-year student in the Latin School, the two-year preparatory school of the University of Nebraska, eventually graduating from the university in 1896. Among her friends and fellow students were Dorothy Canfield (later Dorothy Canfield *Fisher), who eventually became a novelist and the only woman judge for the Book-of-the-Month Club, and Louise *Pound, who later became a well-known folklorist and linguist and first woman president of the Modern Language Association.

In college, Cather became more interested in literature, and she began writing book and drama reviews for local newspapers; she also published her first short story, "Peter," in a Boston magazine. She also wrote several stories that appeared in the university literary magazine, although her criticism showed contempt for women writers and preference for the "manly" ideology of *masculinity popular at the time.

Ironically enough, Cather's first job was editing a woman's magazine, the Pittsburgh-based *Home Monthly*, which she took over in the summer of 1896. During her ten years in Pittsburgh, she worked as editor, newspaper-woman, and high school teacher of English and

Latin. These were productive years, professionally and personally. Cather wrote book and drama reviews for both the Lincoln and Pittsburgh papers, placed several short stories in national publications, among them *Scribner's*, *McClure's*, and *Cosmopolitan*, and published a collection of poems, *April Twilights*, in 1903. Her fiction caught the attention of the powerful S. S. McClure, who published her short story collection *The Troll Garden* in 1905.

Cather's maturing craft and steady productivity were owing in part to the happy domestic life she found in Pittsburgh. In 1899, she met Isabelle McClung, daughter of a wealthy and prominent Pittsburgh judge. Drawn together by their shared interests in literature, arts, and the theater, they began a lifelong intimacy; Isabelle would be the romantic love of Cather's life. In 1901, Cather began living with Isabelle and her family, and the McClung home became a nurturing space where she could combine intimacy and creativity.

In 1906, Cather accepted a job offer from S. S. McClure and moved to New York City to begin work at *McClure's* as a staff writer; in 1908, she became managing editor. She began sharing an apartment with Edith Lewis in the same year, although she also made frequent trips to Pittsburgh to see Isabelle. These were years of heady accomplishment in which Cather succeeded in the male world of publishing and journalism, but they were also years of exhaustion and, eventually, depression when she feared her literary powers, drained by the work of editing, were not maturing.

In order to find a quiet and supportive environment for her writing, Cather took a leave of absence from the magazine in 1911, and spent three months in Cherry Valley, New York, with Isabelle McClung. There she revised the manuscript of what was to be her first novel, *Alexander's Bridge* (1912), and wrote "The Bohemian Girl" and the short story "Alexandra," which would be the seed for *O Pioneers!*. Encouraged by this resurgence of her creativity, Cather decided not to return to the magazine. She stayed in Pittsburgh with Isabelle during the fall of 1912 and found that *O Pioneers!* (1913)—the novel in which she took the "road home" to her Nebraska past—seemed to write itself.

After this turning point, Cather found literary and economic success as a novelist, never returning to journalism. In the next three decades she published *The Song of the Lark* (1915), *My Ántonia* (1918), *Youth and the Bright Medusa* (1920), *One of Ours* (1922), *A Lost Lady* (1923), *The Professor's House* (1925), *My Mortal Enemy* (1926), *Death Comes for the Archbishop* (1927), *Shadows on the Rock* (1931), *Obscure Destinies* (1932), *Lucy Gayheart* (1935), *Not Under Forty* (1936), *Sapphira and the Slave Girl* (1940), and the posthumously published *The Old Beauty and Others* (1948).

Cather's first novels were hailed as bringing a fresh voice to American fiction by such prominent critics as H. L. Mencken and Edmund Wilson. Her literary reputation continued to rise throughout the 1920s; she won the Pulitzer Prize for *One of Ours*, received honorary degrees from major universities, and was elected to the National Institute of Arts and Letters. In the 1930s, when left-wing critics like Granville Hicks were praising socially conscious fiction that addressed contemporary issues, Cather found herself attacked for "escapism" and "romanticism," and her reputation slipped. But she never lost her wide readership, and all her books have continued to stay in print.

By the 1990s, Cather was reinstated, along with Edith *Wharton, as a major twentieth-century novelist. Once viewed simply as a celebrator of the American past, she is now considered a writer who employs a complex and shaded emotional palette and whose work explores the darker tones of American life—incompleteness, change, loss. But Cather's fiction, even when sombre, is not pessimistic. Against the forces of pettiness, materialism, and mortality, she places the human desire to make meaning through work, family, religion, art, domestic crafts, and—perhaps most important to Willa Cather—through story telling.

Sharon O'Brien

CATHOLIC WRITERS. The established litany of twentieth-century Catholic women writers, limited to the exploration of theological issues and the institutional Catholic church on the one hand and to English-department constructions of belles lettres and its modernist refinements on the other, is very short: Flannery *O'Connor, Mary *Gordon, and less well known writers Maureen Howard and Elizabeth Cullinan. All of Irish extraction, they are also all postwar writers of fiction with classical leanings, and their profound strengths are their roots in philosophical and moral discourse, the nineteenth-century novel of manners, and the Anglo-American essay. The reconstruction of modern American Catholic literary history must begin by expanding consideration to the ethnic diversity of "Roman" Catholicism and by opening up the literary pool to religious tracts and scholarship; to the occasional writing of nonprofessionals, including poetry, letters, and journals; to inspirational and young people's literature; to treatises in the social sciences and the social work professions; and, above all, to sociologically oriented fiction and autobiography.

The genre of religious writing in the United States has a recognized Catholic dimension because of the achievements in the twentieth century of convert Dorothy *Day (whom James T. Fisher places at the center of "the Catholic counterculture in America") and of radical feminist theologian Mary *Daly. But church-sponsored work by nuns and active laity is virtually unknown. For instance, the monograph series of the United States Catholic Historical Society features a half-dozen books by women on church history, with subjects ranging from St. Patrick's Cathedral to immigrant colonization to missionary work in Cuba. Collections of inspirational verse, authored overwhelmingly by women, include *Our Lady's Choir* (1931; all by nuns), *Drink from the Rock* (1944), and *Arrows of Gold* (1941), an anthology of black Catholic voices. Elizabeth Laura Adams, an African-American whose mother was a Paris-trained artist from Madagascar, published a conversion narrative, *Dark Symphony*, in 1942.

During the interwar heyday of doctrinal fiction, Lucille Papin Borden, Kathleen Thompson Norris, and Ethel Cook Eliot were prominent. Borden's *The Candlestick Makers* (1923) and Norris's *Margaret Yorke* (1930), both typical of their many novels, treated the new-womanhood issues of divorce, birth control, and sexual freedom catechistically—in stark contrast to Kate *Chopin's feminist breakthrough novel of adultery in Catholic New Orleans, *The Awakening* (1899). Eliot's *Her Soul to Keep* (1935) examined the spiritual emptiness of an agnostic university professor facing his wife's death. After World War II, Sister Mariella Gable, literary critic at the College of St. Benedict in St. Joseph, Minnesota, helped lead a drive to improve the quality of American Catholic fiction. Mary *McCarthy's semiscandalous *Memories of a Catholic Girlhood* appeared in 1957, and was, with telling irony, more warmly received by the clergy than by the laity.

Flannery O'Connor's *Wise Blood* (1952) dramatized redemption among the seemingly unredeemable of the poor white South and was the harbinger of a corpus of her texts (a second novella, short story collections, a miscellany) at once doctrinally sophisticated, satirically macabre, and radically humane. Since 1960, Maureen Howard has published one or two novels a decade, between which she produced her most acclaimed work, the exorcistic autobiography *Facts of Life* (1978), detailing her Bridgeport, Connecticut, childhood, her schooling there at the Academy of Our Lady of Mercy, and her initiation as an assistant professor's wife into the academy and publishing. Mary Gordon's first three novels—*Final Payments* (1978), *The Company of Women* (1980), and *Men and Angels*

(1985)—explore tangles of faith, ethics, and art in the wake of both Vatican II and second-wave feminism. In *Good Boys and Dead Girls* (1991), an essay collection, Gordon analyzes American Catholic literary history as reflecting the double linguistic colonization (by English and by church Latin) of the Irish.

The most undervalued subgenre of American Catholic literature is the representation, in whatever mode, of *immigration, cultural persistence/mobility, and ethnic interaction. How have Catholics fared, as Catholics, in America? Immigrant women and their descendants have responded, not always in dissent, to the long-standing charge of sociologists that the Catholic poor are poor *because* they are Catholic, that is, because they are fatalistic, obsessively familial, deaf to the virtues of the Protestant work ethic, anti-intellectual by nature, and, above all, because they are female dominated or mother centered. To read Hasia Diner's social history *Erin's Daughters in America* (1983); Mary Doyle Curran's memoir *The Parish and the Hill* (1948); or the novels of Mary Anne Sadlier (a famine-era U.S. series); Elizabeth Cullinan (*House of Gold*, 1969); and Gordon (especially her 1989 family saga, *The Other Side*) in tandem with Virginia Yans-McLaughlin's social history *Family and Community* (1977); the oral history *Rosa* (1970), transcribed by Marie Hall Ets; or Helen Barolini's multigenerational epic *Umbertina* (1976) is to be struck by certain convergences in immigrant Catholic women's conditions and immigrant Catholic women's compensatory strategies.

But to read Catholic women's literature across ethnic lines is also to be confronted, full force, with reproduction in the New World of the Old World's inexorable division between the semi-Protestantism of the North (where Christ is Vindicator-King, In the Beginning was the Word, and sexuality takes to the underground) and the semi-Paganism of the South (where Mary is the Virgin Intercessor, image and icon supersede language, and the body is vessel to the spirit). The fact that the Irish won control of the American Catholic Church in the nineteenth century (along with Germans and, later, Poles in the Midwest), reversing European hierarchy, is significant. Partaking of a less-sanctioned American Catholic sensibility have been not only the Italians but the East-Coast Portuguese, the Californian Spanish, the Cajuns and Creoles of Louisiana, as well as the Afro- and Indo-Hispanics of the Caribbean Rim. For Catholics with a Mediterranean bent, facing Irish-American hegemony has meant either renewing the anti-institutionalism characteristic of peasant Catholicism outside of Northern Europe (by means, paradoxically, of national-origin parishes) or else assimilating to mainstream American Catholicism—itself on the way, after Vatican II especially, to increasingly Protestant form. Acts of anti-institutional populism have been both strenuously imaginative and forcefully feminizing: the dedication of cults to Mary (most extravagantly, Mexico's Virgin of Guadalupe, but also East Harlem's Madonna of 115th Street); the increasing conversion, especially by women of color, to evangelical Protestantism; and the renewal of fading folk elements (be they from pre-Christian Europe, Indo-America, or Africa), many of them gynomythic—as illustrated, most notoriously, by the pop icon whose own mother named her Madonna. The strategy of the upwardly mobile has been to work within mainstream American Catholicism in the name of Catholicism's universalist vision: a reconfiguration that has characteristically conceded much of women's remarkable consecration in Marian culture, but with it, less regrettably, the concomitant burdens of the Old World.

American Catholic women writers have not only investigated but also enacted forms both of resistant preservation and conciliatory change. In Mari Tomasi's *Like Lesser Gods* (1949), for example, Piedmontese immigrants in Vermont are seen to achieve blue-collar security and incorporation into the Yankee community of Granitetown, but only at the cost of Marianist bloodletting: Maria of the Pietà is transformed into a celibate male nursemaid who fancies himself a guardian angel, Christ of the Bleeding Heart turns into a cold, colorless, Passion-denying tombstone of granite. This Catholic self-transformation is performed (at least in part) by Tomasi herself, without the compensatory development of modern feminist consciousness, but with an insistence on preserving the dignity of labor, on allaying ethnic tensions, and on instituting companionate child-centered marriage. In *The Dream Book* (1985, ed. Helen Barolini), Tomasi is anthologized along with fifty-five other Italian-American women writers—many of whom (the poets particularly) struggle for or against woman's place in Marianist culture.

On those occasions when it has treated Catholicism, mainly Marie-Clair Blais's *Une saison dans la vie d'Emmanuel* (1966) and Anne Hébert's *Les enfants du sabbat* (1975), French-Canadian women's literature has focused on clergy, convents, and the socialization of the young with a dark humor reminiscent of O'Connor, J. F. Powers, and the Irish/Anglican Church debunkers before them.

The story of Catholicism on this continent predates, of course, the arrival of the European working classes, but it is a story we are only just beginning to recover. The role of Catholicism in colonization is open for examination in the literature of the missions. Occasionally, it has been scripted by European women, such as Sister Blandina Segale in *At the End of the Sante Fe Trail* (serial, 1870–1880; book, 1932); and it was also made the vehicle of anti-Puritan romance in works such as Willa *Cather's three late novels (especially her elegy to a desert Catholic aesthetic, *Death Comes for the Archbishop*, 1927). More recently, the issue of a specifically Catholic colonial legacy has begun to surface in the "American" literatures of the Caribbean Rim, the Mexican borderlands, and of pre-Columbians, including Judith Ortiz *Cofer's *Silent Dancing* (1990), Sandra *Cisneros's stories, Gloria *Anzaldúa's *Borderlands/La Frontera* (1987), as well as Louise *Erdrich's important *Tracks* (1988). In various ways, these texts address fundamental postcolonial problematics, from third-world Catholicism's longstanding preservation of non-European forms of spirituality to the latest developments in liberation theology.

[*See also* European Immigrant Writing; Immigrant Writing; Religion; Theologians.]

• Sister Mary Anthony Scally, *Negro Catholic Writers, 1900–1943: A Bio-Bibliography* (1945). Paul R. Messbarger, *Fiction with a Parochial Purpose: Social Uses of American Catholic Literature, 1884–1900* (1971). Rose Basile Green, *The Italian-American Novel: A Document of the Interaction of Two Cultures* (1974). Robert Anthony Orsi, *The Madonna of 115th Street: Faith and Community in Italian Harlem, 1880–1950* (1985). James Terence Fisher, *The Catholic Counterculture in America, 1933–1962* (1989). Donna R. Gabaccia, *Immigrant Women in the United States: A Selectively Annotated Multidisciplinary Bibliography* (1989). Charles Fanning, *The Irish Voice in America: Irish-American Fiction from the 1760s to the 1980s* (1990). Arnold Sparr, *To Promote, Defend, and Redeem: The Catholic Literary Revival and the Cultural Transformation of American Catholicism, 1920–1960* (1990). Anthony Julian Tamburri et al., eds., *From the Margins: Writings in Italian Americana* (1991).

Thomas J. Ferraro

CATT, Carrie Chapman (1859–1947), suffragist and peace advocate. Susan B. *Anthony and Elizabeth Cady *Stanton may be the two names most commonly associated with woman suffrage, but Carrie Chapman Catt should spring just as readily to mind. A recurring favorite on turn-of-the-century media lists of "the ten most famous American women," Catt deserves to be remembered today for her dedication to women's rights, woman suffrage, and world peace.

Catt was born in Wisconsin, but grew up, attended college, and taught school in Iowa. She began her public career as a suffragist in

1885 by speaking and writing on woman suffrage, and by attending local suffrage conventions. Her two devoted husbands—newspaper editor Leo Chapman, who died from typhoid fever during the first year of their marriage, and engineer George Catt, who died in 1905—shared Catt's commitment to suffrage. After George's death, Mary Garrett Hay, a sister suffragist, became Catt's live-in companion.

Catt's brilliant oratory skills and her personable ways soon brought her to the attention of Susan B. Anthony, who picked Catt as her successor as president of the National American Woman Suffrage Association (NAWSA) in 1900. In 1902, while still president of NAWSA, Catt formed the International Woman Suffrage Alliance (IWSA), providing a forum for women around the world to exchange strategies on attaining the vote. In 1904, Catt resigned as NAWSA president (only to be elected vice-president) and began to tour the globe as an advocate for universal suffrage.

Catt is the author of numerous articles, pamphlets, forewords, introductions, and books, most of which address three cherished subjects: her struggle for women's suffrage in the United States (especially in New York, where she presided over several hard-fought campaigns); her duties as president of the IWSA; and her increasing involvement in the peace movement. From her first book, *The Ballot and the Bullet* (1897), through her articles in *Harper's Magazine*, the *New York Times Magazine*, *Ladies Home Journal*, and other journals, to her last book, *Woman Suffrage and Politics: The Inner Story of the Suffrage Movement* (with Nettie Rogers Shuler; 1923), Catt illustrated her ongoing dedication to women's rights.

In 1915, Catt was asked to put the international suffrage and peace movements on the back burner for a while in order to resume the presidency of NAWSA. It was widely felt that suffrage in this country could only be achieved under Catt's able leadership. This feeling proved correct, and when the Nineteenth Amendment guaranteeing women's suffrage was finally ratified in 1920, Catt was feted in a victory parade through the streets of New York. On the eve of ratification, Catt proposed the formation of the still-influential League of Women Voters, designed to insure that women would cast educated and informed ballots.

With the battle for suffrage finally won, Catt devoted most of her energies to attaining global peace. She helped found the Woman's Peace Party (1915), organized the Committee on the Cause and Cure of War (1925), and formed the Protest Committee of Non-Jewish Women Against the Persecution of Jews in Germany (1933). On 9 March 1947 the eighty-eight-year-old Catt died quietly in her sleep, hoping that the outcome of the battles she had seen and participated in throughout her long life would be lasting peace between and for women and men worldwide.

• Mary Gray Peck, *Carrie Chapman Catt: A Biography* (1944). Library of Congress, Manuscript Division, *The Blackwell Family, Carrie Chapman Catt, and the National American Woman Suffrage Association* (1975). Robert Booth Fowler, *Carrie Catt: Feminist Politician* (1986). Jacqueline Van Voris, *Carrie Chapman Catt: A Life* (1987).

Cynthia J. Davis

CENSORSHIP. Most studies define censorship as the formal legal mechanisms for prohibiting performances or the production and distribution of printed materials, and most exclude any mention of women writers as subjects of censorship, with the implication that women writers' works only rarely reach the point where the criminal justice system imposes sanctions against them. Rather, women writers have historically been affected by more informal mechanisms of censorship, including self-imposed silences, familial pressures, and economic and political coercion. For women writers, the term censorship must encompass any means by which women writers have been pressured or restrained in what or how they write.

Traditional discussions define three categories of censorship, which become prevalent in three distinct eras of United States history: religious censorship, which dominated the United States during the Puritan era, when blasphemy and sacrilege were civil crimes; political censorship, which arose during the Revolutionary era, when sedition and treason against the established government became prosecutable; and moral or cultural censorship—the question of what is immoral, obscene, or pornographic—which has preoccupied American culture from the early decades of the nineteenth century to the present day. Most accounts of censorship locate women writers largely in this third category, but usually as censors, not as the censored. Such groups as the Society for the Suppression of Vice, the Watch and Ward Society, the Clean Books League, and other groups established as guardians of purity in literature in the nineteenth and early-twentieth centuries were backed by numerous women, both individually, and in groups like the Women's Christian Temperance Union, the Daughters of the American Revolution, and many other women's clubs.

The role of women as censors of literature stems from the nineteenth-century Cult of *True Womanhood, which defined white middle-class women as inherently innocent and pure, and thus elevated them to the status of guardians of public and private morality while removing them from participation in the sordid activities of the public sphere. When some of these white middle-class women became published "authoresses" in the mid-nineteenth century, this ideology of innate moral purity served as a mechanism for self-censorship. Concerned that writing anything for public consumption (especially fiction, which was still considered vaguely immoral) would mark them as "unwomanly," most women authors were doubly careful to present only moral tales and ideas that supported the Victorian values of piety, chastity, submission, and obedience for women. Male family members were often ready to censor these women writers when they suspected that the self-censorship inherent in the ideology of True Womanhood was insufficient; for example, Samuel Gridley Howe forbade his wife, Julia Ward *Howe, to publish her poetry because he would not permit his wife to become a public figure. If all else failed, male editors and publishers could intervene before a book was published to prevent any supposed immorality from appearing under a woman author's name (or pseudonym). Novelist E.D.E.N. *Southworth broke with her publisher over this issue, because he insisted that she not mention any vices or villainies at all, lest weak-minded readers (defined as women, children, working-class people, Negroes, Indians, and immigrants) imitate the wicked behavior.

Many women writers had to tolerate varieties of censorship for economic survival, because writing was one of the few careers open to respectable women until well into the twentieth century; so, they had to write what publishers would print, and what would sell. The women factory workers at the Lowell mills censored their own writings for publication in the *Lowell Offering,* knowing that criticisms of factory life or calls for strikes in that newspaper could cost them their jobs. Similar economic pressure forced Helen Keller to cease her political writing and speaking on behalf of socialism as a condition for being hired as a paid spokesperson and fund-raiser for the American Foundation for the Blind in 1924. Political censorship has also been an issue for many women writers of color, including Harriet *Jacobs, whose *Incidents in the Life of a Slave Girl* (1861) was published because it fulfilled abolitionist needs and met dominant-cultural sentimental conventions about womanhood and Christianity; her contemporary Harriet *Wilson's *Our Nig* (1859), which overturned these conventions, was not found acceptable by white publishers and reviewers, and was effectively erased from literary history. Native-American writer

*Zitkala-Sa experienced similar pressure to shape her writings to the dominant-cultural audience in the early twentieth century, and toned down her autobiographical essays to make them less critical of American Indian policies.

The forms of censorship imposed by True Womanhood and by economic and political pressures have, in the nineteenth and twentieth centuries, largely prevented women writers from publishing works that might be liable to prosecution for obscenity. Exceptions include Victoria Woodhull and Tennessee Claflin, who were tried for obscenity in 1873 for publicizing the adultery scandal of a prominent minister; Margaret Sanger, whose writings about birth control were banned in the early twentieth century under the Comstock Laws, which prohibited sending "obscene" materials through the United States mail; Margaret Anderson and Jane Heap, whose *Little Review* was banned as obscene when they published excerpts from James Joyce's *Ulysses* in 1920; and Radclyffe Hall, whose *Well of Loneliness* became a test case for obscenity laws when it was published in the United States in 1929. Obscenity charges against women novelists, as this last example suggests, usually were employed to censor depictions of "deviant" sexuality, especially lesbianism, which were seen as threats to the family and to the state. Many lesbian writers censored themselves by expatriation, publishing their works in France rather than risking obscenity trials in the United States.

Most twentieth-century debates about censorship focus on the morality or obscenity of pornography, the key issue for a culture that depends on textual representations and discursive constructs for its conceptions of sexuality. Certain feminist schools of thought define pornography as violence against women, and thus deny that women could be willing producers or consumers of sexually explicit texts. This perspective favors the legal censorship of pornography as a means of protecting women from patriarchal violence. Feminist groups that oppose such censorship argue that the issue at stake is freedom of choice, and the right to decide for oneself what one will or will not read or write.

A final important aspect of contemporary censorship is the power wielded by groups that decide who gets funding for art projects. The National Endowment for the Arts, for example, a government-sponsored agency supported in part by tax dollars, has been increasingly unwilling to provide funds for projects that seem to contradict conservative views of proper sexual, familial, and national attitudes. In the face of the withdrawal of funds, many writers and artists who do not fit the conservative ideal are forced to censor themselves, to disregard their sexually or politically explicit pieces when applying for funding. Thus, for the woman writer today, as for her sisters in the nineteenth century, the main issue in censorship lies not in the legal procedures or definitions of what is obscene, but rather in economics: Can she say what she wants to say, what she needs to say, and still survive?

[*See also* Erotica; Pornography.]

• Robert W. Haney, *Comstockery in America: Patterns of Censorship and Control* (1960). John McCormick and Mairi MacInnes, eds., *Versions of Censorship* (1962). Paul S. Boyer, *Purity in Print: The Vice Society Movement and Book Censorship in America* (1968). Evelyn Geller, *Forbidden Books in American Public Libraries, 1876–1939: A Study in Cultural Change* (1984). Varda Burstyn, ed., *Women against Censorship* (1985). Robert Emmet Long, ed., *Censorship* (1990). Jewelle Gomez, "The Economics of Censorship," *Ms.* 2, no. 6 (May/June 1992): 74–76.

Mary Klages

CEREMONIES. *See* Rituals and Ceremonies.

CERVANTES, Lorna Dee (b. 1954), poet, editor, teacher. A feminist of Native American and Mexican ancestry, Cervantes was active in the Chicano movement of the 1970s. In the middle of the decade she founded a small press, Mango Publications, to publish the work of Chicano writers. At that time, she edited and published the literary magazine *Mango*, worked on her own writing, and published her poems in a number of literary magazines. Cervantes received grants from the National Endowment for the Arts, which helped her to complete two collections of her poetry in 1981 and 1991. Receiving her B.A. from California State University at San Jose in 1984, Cervantes was a graduate student in the History of Consciousness program at the University of California at Santa Cruz through 1988. She is now the editor of *Red Dirt*, a magazine of multicultural literature, and a creative-writing teacher at the University of Colorado at Boulder.

The title of Cervantes's first book of poetry, *Emplumada* (1981), winner of the 1982 American Book Award, combines the Spanish words for "feathered" and "pen flourish" to link her frequent use of bird metaphors to her concern with language. The first section of her book focuses on women's relationships with each other and on violence against working-class Chicana and Native American women. Section two considers language as both problem and solution and meditates on conflicts over Chicana identity. The last section, with its birds and love poems, hints that the struggle with silence and lack of understanding may be resolved by writing (tellingly, Spanish words are translated in a glossary). *Emplumada* is a collection of free verse in simple diction that creates intense images and moods.

Like Cervantes's first book, her second frequently combines the concrete and the abstract, the personal and the general. In *From the Cables of Genocide: Poems on Love and Hunger* (1991), Cervantes's style is denser and more complex, featuring surrealist and stream-of-conscious passages. The occasional Spanish words are no longer translated. The "cables" in the title may be interpreted as ropes, clotheslines, messages, and telegram conductors that bind and liberate, connect and divide lands and people, pointing to the themes of the book: love and death, hunger, injustice, communication, genocide, and Native American history and culture. Section III differs from the rest of the collection in containing less obscure, formally tighter, and yet lyrical love poems that deal with colonization and power struggles; in them dreams and love are linked to hate and death as well as to life and joy.

• Bernadette Monda, "Interview with Lorna Dee Cervantes," in *Third Woman* 2, no. 1 (1984): 103–107. Marta Ester Sánchez, "The Chicana as Scribe: Harmonizing Gender and Culture in Lorna Dee Cervantes' "Beneath the Shadow of the Freeway," in *Contemporary Chicana Poetry: A Critical Approach to an Emerging Literature* (1985), pp. 85–138. John F. Crawford, "Notes toward a New Multicultural Criticism: Three Works by Women of Color," in *A Gift of Tongues: Critical Challenges in Contemporary American Poetry*, eds. Marie Harris and Kathleen Aguero (1987), pp. 155–195. Roberta Fernández, "Lorna Dee Cervantes," in *Dictionary of Literary Biography*, vol. 82, eds. Francisco A. Lomelí and Carl R. Shirley (1989), pp. 74–78. Agueda Pizarro Rayo, "From the Cables of Genocide: Poems on Love and Hunger," *Latin American Literature and Arts* 45 (July–December 1991): 103–105.

Lisa Radinovsky

CHANG, Diana (b. ca. 1934), author and poet. Born in New York City to a Chinese architect and his Eurasian wife, Diana Chang grew up in China, where she and her family lived until the end of World War II. She then returned to New York to attend high school and college. Her literary talent first won recognition when she was an English major at Barnard College; her early poems were published in such literary jounals as *Poetry* and *Voices* when she was still in college. After graduating from Barnard and receiving a John Hay Whitney Foundation Fellowship, she completed her first novel, *The Frontiers of Love* (1956), which garnered impressive critical accolades and established her reputation as a fiction writer. Since then she has published five more novels—*A Woman of Thirty* (1959), *A Passion for Life* (1961), *The Only*

Game in Town (1963), *Eye to Eye* (1974), and *A Perfect Love* (1978)—as well as three books of poetry, *The Horizon Is Definitely Speaking* (1982), *What Matisse Is After* (1984), and *Earth Water Light* (1991). More recently, her radio play "Falling Free," adapted from her short story of the same title, has been broadcast over National Public Radio in more than thirty-five cities across the United States. A professor of creative writing at Barnard College until 1989, Chang has also been active as an editor and painter, whose works of acrylics, pastels, and watercolors have been exhibited at various galleries in New York.

Although Chang has a remarkable understanding of the Chinese way of life, neither her fiction nor her poetry conveys a Chinese sensibility. Though the protagonists of her first novel are Eurasians, the rest of her novels are peopled with Caucasian characters. The bulk of her fiction—from *The Frontiers of Love* to "Falling Free"—bears the imprint of existentialism, which not only forges her angle of vision but also informs the themes of her work. Preoccupied with the question of being and becoming, Chang has given voice to an existential view of the human condition through her fictional characters' quest for identity, love, self-knowledge, and meaning in their lives. By exploring their consciousnesses and by presenting their existential encounters in open-ended narrative structures, Chang succeeds in dramatizing a contemporary angst and in demonstrating that life is a constant improvisation. This modern sensibility not only informs her fiction—it pervades her poetry as well. Rich in startling imagery, concise in language, and often cryptic in meaning, her poems issue invitations to perceive freshly and to rediscover reality through feeling and form. Chang's imagination is, in her own words, "closer to lilacs blooming in doorways than to moon gates and lotus pods" ("A Hyphenated Condition," *Asian Journal*, Spring 1982).

• Dexter Fisher, ed., *The Third Woman: Minority Women Writers of the United States* (1980). Amy Ling, "Writer in the Hyphenated Condition: Diana Chang," *MELUS* 7, no. 4 (1980): 69–83. Shirley Geok-Lin Lim, "Twelve Asian American Writers: In Search of Self Definition," *MELUS* 13, nos. 1–2 (1986): 57–77. Wei-hsiung Kitty Wu, "Cultural Ideology and Aesthetic Choices: A Study of Three Works by Chinese American Women—Diana Chang, Bette Bao Lord, and Maxine Hong Kingston" (Ph.D. diss., University of Maryland at College Park, 1989). Amy Ling, *Between Worlds: Women Writers of Chinese Ancestry* (1990).

Wei-hsiung (Kitty) Wu

CHANG, Eileen (b. 1921), novelist, short story writer, dramatist. Already an acclaimed author in China whom critics believed to be the most gifted writer of her generation, Eileen Chang immigrated to the United States in 1955, translated into impeccable English her brilliant novel *The Rice Sprout Song* (1955), and had it published by Scribners to glowing reviews. Chang has written two other novels in English, *The Naked Earth* (1956), and *The Rouge of the North* (1967), an elaboration of her much-praised novella, *The Golden Cangue* (1943).

Eileen Chang grew up in Tienjing and Shanghai in a well-to-do but disrupted and decadent family. Chang's mother left behind her two small children (Eileen and a younger brother) when she went to France to study, returning only years later to divorce her husband. Her father was a domestic tyrant and an opium addict, and her stepmother was no better. Chang had a difficult time escaping from this oppressive household, a struggle she later retold in "The Golden Cangue." In 1939, she enrolled in Hong Kong University, where she studied English until the Japanese invasion in 1942, whereupon she returned to Shanghai. The years that followed (1943–1947) were productive; she wrote a series of essays, a collection of short stories, and several plays, all of which were well received.

Since moving to the United States, she has led a reclusive life, refusing interviews and not answering correspondence. She married Ferd Rehyer, and for a while worked at the Center for Chinese Studies at the University of California, Berkeley. Now widowed, she has retired to Southern California.

As a skilled writer in both Chinese and English who lived through the Chinese revolution, Chang was in the unique position of being able to re-create these experiences for the West. She captured the oppressive atmosphere of a decadent, feudal family in pre-Communist China in *Rouge of the North*, and, in her other two novels, the terror and tragedy experienced by ordinary peasants and cadres under a Communist regime gone awry. Eschewing crude propaganda, Chang's masterpiece, *The Rice Sprout Song*, simply and effectively evokes the tragedy of human suffering through selected details and resonant images. The novel was inspired by a newspaper article Chang read in which a Communist cadre, finding himself shooting at peasants assaulting a granary during a famine, questions his orders; these were the very people whose labor had filled the government granary and for whom, as a soldier of the Communist revolution, he had fought.

• Ching I Shueh, *Chang Ai-ling de Shao Shuo Yi Shu* (The Art of Eileen Chang's Stories) (1973). C. T. Hsia, *History of Modern Chinese Fiction* (1979) Joseph Lau et al., eds., *Modern Chinese Stories and Novellas, 1919–*

1949 (1981). Amy Ling, *Between Worlds: Women Writers of Chinese Ancestry* (1990).

Amy Ling

CHAPMAN, Maria Weston (1806–1885), abolitionist writer and editor. Born in Weymouth, Massachusetts, to Warren and Anne Weston, both descendants of old Massachusetts families, Maria Weston Chapman spent part of her childhood in England, where she was educated in a genteel fashion. Returning to Boston in 1828, Chapman taught school until 1830, when she married Henry Chapman, whose family was very wealthy and extremely dedicated to the abolitionist cause. Chapman also committed herself wholeheartedly to abolitionism through her work as a writer, editor, organizer, and fund-raiser. Firm in her convictions and a formidable opponent to those who disagreed with her, Chapman's leadership and influence in the American abolitionist movement were profound.

Chapman aligned herself firmly with William Lloyd Garrison in the antislavery debates; she advocated immediate emancipation and favored moral reform over political action. Named to the executive board of the American Anti-Slavery Society in 1840, Chapman occasionally helped to edit its newspaper, the *Liberator*, and in 1844 she helped found and coedit the *Anti-Slavery Standard*. Despite the controversy surrounding women's presence in the abolitionist movement, Chapman firmly defended her work. Her pamphlet *Right and Wrong in Massachusetts* (1839) condemns clergy for disapproving of women's participation in the abolitionist movement.

Chapman also helped found and lead the Boston Female Anti-Slavery Society in 1832. There she wrote and edited the group's annual reports, *Right and Wrong in Boston*, from 1836 to 1838. Beginning in 1834, she also conceived and organized the yearly Boston antislavery fairs to raise money for the abolitionist cause. At the 1839 fair, Chapman debuted *The Liberty Bell*, an annual gift book that she edited and sold at the fairs.

In many ways, *The Liberty Bell* was similar to other contemporary gift books; bound handsomely and printed on good paper, it contained stories, poetry, and essays by various contributors. However, it differed significantly from these other volumes in its polemical nature and in its open criticism of the United States. It featured the work of many leading abolitionist writers, and Chapman herself usually contributed an essay or a poem for the volume. Although *The Liberty Bell* and the fair were successful money-makers, Chapman discontinued both in 1858 to pursue even more profitable fund-raising activities.

As the antislavery movement became more politically oriented, Chapman and Garrison agreed to disband the American Anti-Slavery Society in 1860. In 1870, she published her friend Harriet Martineau's two-volume autobiography, to which she herself added another volume of reminiscences about Martineau. She died in Weymouth in 1885.

• Ralph Thompson, *"The Liberty Bell* and Other Anti-Slavery Gift Books," the *New England Quarterly* 7 (March 1934): 154–168. Jane H. Pease and William H. Pease, *Bound with Them in Chains: A Biographical History of the Anti-Slavery Movement* (1972).

Suzanne M. Zweizig

CHASE-RIBOUD, Barbara (b. 1936), poet, novelist, and sculptor. The author of three novels, two books of poetry, and several essays, Barbara Chase-Riboud has lived in Paris since 1961. Her sculpture and writing have won her worldwide acclaim. Born in Philadelphia, Pennsylvania, Chase-Riboud received a B.F.A. from Temple University in 1957 and an M.F.A. from Yale University in 1960, and studied in Rome on a John Hay Whitney Foundation Fellowship (1957–1958).

After gaining significant recognition as an artist, Chase-Riboud turned to poetry and fiction. In 1974, she published a volume of poems, *From Memphis and Peking* (1974). Travel, as well as spiritual and psychic journey, figures as a central motif in this work, and indeed, the poet's own travels to Egypt and China provided much of the inspiration for the book. While the Memphis of the book is placed in Egypt, Africa and black America are joined in the poem "Memphis," with its blues refrain, "I'm going to Memphis, I won't be back this way." Another book of poems, *Portrait of a Nude Woman as Cleopatra* (1988), which Chase-Riboud describes in the book's preface as a "verse novel about Cleopatra," consists of fifty-seven sonnets rendered in the voices of both Cleopatra and Antony. Quotations from Plutarch's historical account of the famous love affair are woven together with Chase-Riboud's look at grand passion and sexual politics.

In 1979, Chase-Riboud's *Sally Hemings*, a novel that links slavery and the oppression of women in America, was published. Drawing on the work of historian Fawn Brodie, Chase-Riboud constructed a story around the rumored and highly plausible twenty-eight-year relationship between Thomas Jefferson and the beautiful slave woman Sally Hemings. The novel met with mixed reviews, but has been translated into eight languages and won the Janet Heidinger Kafka Prize for Excellence in Fiction by American Women in 1980.

Chase-Riboud's other two novels also tie history to contemporary concerns. *Valide: A Novel of the Harem* (1986) focuses on women in the eighteenth- and nineteenth-century Ottoman Empire, and *Echo of Lions* (1989) looks at the successful slave rebellion on board the Spanish ship *Amistad* in the early nineteenth century. For *Echo of Lions*, Chase-Riboud was cited by the Connecticut State Legislature and governor for excellence and achievement in literature.

Chase-Riboud and her husband live in Paris and Rome. Influenced by her travel and such experiences as her participation in a 1969 Pan-African festival in Nigeria, Chase-Riboud's writing consistently draws on history and dramatizes themes that examine power dynamics and constructions of race, class, and gender.

• Theresa A. Leininger, "Barbara Chase-Riboud," in *Notable Black American Women*, ed. Jessie Carney Smith (1992), pp. 177–181.

Ann Folwell Stanford

CHA, Theresa Hak Kyung (1951–1982), producer; director; performer; creator of video and film productions, installations, performances, and published texts. Cha was born in Pusan, Korea, on 4 March 1951. She was third of five children of Cha Hyung Sang and Huo Hyung Soon, both of whom had been raised in Manchuria and educated as teachers before returning to Korea during World War II. In 1962, the Cha family moved to the United States. After several years in Hawaii, they settled in San Francisco, where Theresa attended Catholic schools, studying the French language as well as Greek and Latin classical literature. After attending the University of San Francisco, she transferred to the University of California at Berkeley, where she earned a B.A. in comparative literature in 1973, a B.A. in art in 1975, and an M.F.A. in art in 1977. She also attended the Centre d'Etudes Americaine du Cinema in Paris in 1976.

Cha's performance art pieces include *Barren Cave Mute* (1974), *A Secret Spill* (1974), *A Blé Wall* (1975), *Aveugle Voix* (1975), *Life Mixing* (1975), *Vampyr* (1976), and *Reveille Dans La Brume* (1977). Cha used slides and video in her performances, which were often lit by candles. Her mother frequently stitched the fabrics for the sets. Cha's black-and-white videos include *Mouth to Mouth* (1975), *Passages Paysages* (1978), *Re Dis Appearing* (1980), and *Exilee* (1980). The videos focus on the splice, in order to expose the apparently seamless quality of film and video. By revealing the process of film, Cha hoped to point out the interdependent relationships between the film, the filmmaker, and the viewer of the film. In Cha's films and videos, French, Korean, and English often overlap, with words sometimes spoken in two languages simultaneously to express layered identities. Memory is invoked with images of empty rooms and the sound of rain.

Cha's published work includes a mail art piece, *Audience Distant Relatives* (1978), a series of six folded sheets of paper with short texts; *Apparatus/Cinematographic Apparatus: Selected Writings* (1980), a collection of essays Cha edited that includes works by Vertov, Baudry, Huillet, Kuntzel, Augst, Metz, and others, as well as a piece by Cha herself ("Commentaire"); "Pravda/Istina" (1982); and *DICTEE* (1982). Cha received a number of grants, fellowships, and awards, including the Eisner Prize for Video and Film at UC Berkeley (1975), the Stuart McKenna Nelson Memorial Award for the Photographic Medium (1977), a prize in the University of Nevada Film/Video Competition (1977), and a National Endowment for the Arts Fellowship (1981). Cha used the NEA Fellowship, together with a University of California Chancellor's Post-Doctoral Fellowship, to go to Korea to begin shooting a film about buried memories. She tentatively titled the film *White Dust from Mongolia*.

During the last year of her life, Cha, then living in New York, was beginning to gain wider recognition for her work: she received a Beard's Fund Award and was selected to be artist in residence at the Nova Scotia College of Art and Design in Halifax. Her video *Passages Paysages* was exhibited in New York City and at the Hague. But tragically, on 5 November 1982, Cha was murdered by a stranger in New York. At the time of her death, Cha had been working on the film about memory, a book, a critique of advertising, and a piece on the representation of hands in Western painting for a four-person exhibition scheduled to open the following month at Artists Space in New York. Cha's work, particularly *DICTEE*, has attracted and influenced the work of Korean and other Asian-American women writers, including Myung Mi Kim and Trinh T. *Minh-ha, and visual artists such as Jin S. Lee and Jinme Yoon.

• *In Honor of Theresa Hak Kyung Cha* [a collection of poetry, personal statements, and images of and by Cha put together by relatives and friends] (1983). Michael Stephens, "Korea: Theresa Hak Kyung Cha," in *The Dramaturgy of Style: Voice in Short Fiction* (1986), pp. 184–210. Susan Wolf, "Theresa Cha: Recalling Telling Re Telling," *Afterimage* 14 (Summer 1986): 10–13. Also in *Fire Over Water*, ed. Reese Williams (1986), pp. 101–111. Stephen-Paul Martin, "Theresa Cha: Creating a Feminine Voice," in *Open Form and the Feminine Imagination: The Politics of Reading in Twentieth-*

Century Innovative Writing (1988), pp. 187–205. Rob Wilson, "Falling into the Korean Uncanny: On Reading Theresa Hak Kyung Cha's *DICTEE*," *Korean Culture* 12 (Summer 1991): 33–37. Norma Alarcon and Elaine H. Kim, eds., *Writing Self, Writing Nation: Essays on Theresa Hak Kyung Cha's DICTEE by Hyun Yi Kang, Elaine H. Kim, Lisa Lowe, Yong Soon Min, and Shelley Sunn Wong* (1993).

Elaine H. Kim

CHESEBROUGH, Caroline (1825–1873), novelist and short story writer. Born in Canandaigua, New York, Chesebrough was educated at Canandaigua Seminary. At age twenty-three, using the name Caroline Chesebro', she began to write articles and short fiction for magazines such as *Harper's*, *Putnam's*, *Knickerbocker*, and the *Atlantic Monthly*. Her first published volume was a collection of short tales called *Dream-Land by Daylight* (1852), and over the next twenty years she remained a prolific and successful writer, publishing novels and collections of stories at an astounding rate: *Isa, a Pilgrimage* (1852), *The Children of Light* (1853), *The Little Cross-Bearers* (1854), *Susan, the Fisherman's Daughter* (1855), *The Beautiful Gate, and Other Stories* (1855), *Victoria* (1856), *Philly and Kit* (1856), *The Sparrow's Fall* (1863), *Peter Carradine* (1863), *Amy Carr* (1864), *The Glen Cabin* (ca. 1865), and *The Foe in the Household* (1871).

Throughout her career, Chesebrough generally maintained the formula observed by several other nineteenth-century American women writers, constructing primarily domestic and sentimental plots that end with an obvious moral. Further, in nearly every work, Chesebrough presents her women characters as something akin to angels, who through their righteousness, long-suffering, and compassion redeem other characters and remedy whatever dreadful situation has been created in the plot, usually by rigid, merciless men. Typically, these women are finally rewarded for their uncomplaining self-sacrifice and simple goodness. Chesebrough's children's stories are examples of another nineteenth-century convention—the inclusion of an orphaned, destitute, abused or otherwise-suffering young person as the central character.

Religion also plays a dominant role throughout Chesebrough's fiction. In many ways, however, she is out of step with the dogmatic, doctrinal Protestantism of her time. Instead, she demonstrates her belief that God has purposely chosen women to be his emissaries on earth, and that he speaks to women through their dreams. Possessed solely by women, this spiritual knowledge is to be used to modify those religions that emphasize justice over mercy and rigid doctrine over compassion. This powerful spiritual inner life of women was one of Chesebrough's primary interests, and she ignored almost completely the social and political upheavals that occurred during her lifetime. She spent her last years, from the mid-1860s until her death in 1873, teaching rhetoric and composition at Packer Collegiate Institute in Brooklyn, New York.

• Nina Baym, *Woman's Fiction* (1978). Juliann E. Fleenor, "Caroline Chesebrough," in *American Women Writers*, vol. 1, ed. Lina Mainiero (1979), pp. 346–348. "Caroline Chesebro'," in *Hidden Hands*, eds. Lucy M. Freibert and Barbara A. White (1988), pp. 322–323.

Sheryl L. Meyering

CHESNUT, Mary Boykin (1823–1886), memoirist and diarist. In mid-February 1861, when Mary Chesnut wrote her first journal entries, she was thirty-seven years old and the wife of James Chesnut, a South Carolina senator who had recently resigned his office to align himself with the Confederacy. Over the next four years, she would follow her husband from Montgomery, Alabama, where she observed bickering over the Confederate constitution; to Charleston, South Carolina, where she watched the siege of Fort Sumtner; to Richmond, Virginia, where she entertained General Davis and other Confederate officers; and eventually back to South Carolina, where she would flee Sherman's troops before returning to her husband's devastated family plantation. How diligently she maintained her journals during these years, it is difficult to say; seven volumes (covering approximately seventeen months) are extant, and critic C. Vann Woodward speculates that five more once existed. These journals, her wartime remembrances, were the basis of her "revised" diary, which, when published posthumously, established her literary reputation.

She would begin this "revision" sixteen years after the Civil War. During the interim years, despite a heart condition and her role as mistress of her husband's Camden, South Carolina, estate, she wrote steadily. She composed unsuccessful drafts of three novels and began numerous projects, including her husband's memoirs. By the time she rewrote her war diaries in 1881–1884, Chesnut was a practiced writer who used her skills to rearrange incidents and add new material, expanding her journals. She also edited for the sake of the public, deleting scathing critiques, references to her father-in-law's slave children, and boastful passages. Maintaining a diary format, she creates a story in which daily social exchanges are foregrounded and the war becomes a backdrop that progressively intrudes upon and shapes society life. Chesnut also creates a complex self-portrait: she is at once a voracious reader who refuses to accept that George Eliot is a "fallen woman"; a self-proclaimed "abolitionist" who is repulsed by "dirty" negroes; and a denouncer of patriarcial power who espouses southern chivalry.

After her death in 1886, her "revised" diary (comprised of 460 copybooks) was left in the care of Isabella Martin, a respected friend. In 1905 and 1949, two extensively edited and condensed versions of this work were published under the title *A Diary from Dixie*. Deceived by this appended title and the book's format, historians and literary critics regarded and praised Chesnut as a diarist until the 1981 publication of *Mary Chesnut's Civil War*. In the introduction to this complete edition of her 1880s work, the editor, Woodward, notes Chesnut's extensive rewriting. Her wartime journals were later published as *The Private Mary Chesnut* (1984).

• Elisabeth Muhlenfeld, *Mary Boykin Chesnut: A Biography* (1981). C. Vann Woodward, "Mary Chesnut in Search of Her Genre," the *Yale Review* 73, no. 2 (Winter 1984): 199–209.

Marty Brooks

CHICAGO RENAISSANCE. An important step toward adequate recognition of black women writers, the Chicago Renaissance has attained increasing acceptance as a center of African-American culture between the end of the * Harlem Renaissance (c. 1935) and the civil rights movement of the early 1950s. Described by Robert Bone (*Callaloo*, Summer 1986) and George Kent (*A Life of Gwendolyn Brooks*, 1990), the idea of a black Chicago Renaissance has gradually supplanted definitions emphasizing proletarian writing, protest literature, the movement toward universalism, or, most problematically, the school of Richard Wright. Although the sociological vocabulary emanating from the University of Chicago contributed to the contemporary attacks on and historical suppression of Zora Neale * Hurston (1891–1960) and Ann * Petry (b. 1908)—neither of whom had strong Chicago connections—recognition of the movement establishes the importance of black women such as Marita * Bonner Occomy (1898–1971), Dorothy * West (b. 1907), Katharine Dunham (b. 1910), Shirley * Graham (1896–1977), Margaret * Walker (b. 1915), Lorraine * Hansberry (1930–1965), and Gwendolyn * Brooks (b. 1917) in African-American literary history.

Like the Harlem Renaissance, the Chicago Renaissance originated in the Great Migration of blacks from the rural South to the urban North, a movement championed by Robert Abbots's newspaper *Chicago Defender*. Carried to the South by railroad employees, the *Defender* contrasted the brutalities of lynching and sharecropping with the economic opportunity of Chicago's factories and stockyards. However, as Richard Wright's introduction to Horace Cayton and St. Clair Drake's sociological classic *Black Metropolis* (1945) makes clear, for most black migrants the harsh realities of Chicago's South Side "Black Belt" belied Abbott's utopian images. Representing a major current of Renaissance thought, Cayton and Drake belonged to a group of black intellectuals who had received graduate training at the University of Chicago, where they were influenced by the ideas of sociologist Robert Park. Focusing on conditions in American cities, Chicago sociologists traced a race relations cycle moving from contact and conflict to accommodation and eventual assimilation into a raceless American melting pot. Even before the Great Migration, however, Chicago-based social activists, black (Ida * Wells-Barnett) and white (Jane * Addams), recognized that the intensity of conflict dominated the experience of both black and European immigrant workers.

Despite these very real problems, Chicago provided a rich cultural setting for African-American writers. Although both were associated with the Harlem Renaissance, Nella * Larsen (1891–1964) and Marita Bonner anticipated the concerns of Wright's Chicago classic *Native Son* (1940). In *Quicksand* (1928), Chicago-born Larsen focused her portrait of bleak urban conditions on her native city. Written both before and after she moved to Chicago in 1930, Bonner's "Frye Street" stories, which were not published in book form until 1987, deserve recognition as the first major work of the Renaissance. Although Bonner and Larsen had little direct contact with the younger generation, Harlem Renaissance writers such as James Weldon Johnson and Langston Hughes frequently visited Chicago during the 1930s. Hughes was particularly supportive of young writers, encouraging Brooks and introducing Walker to Wright. In addition, many younger writers interacted with white Chicago Renaissance novelists (Theodore Dreiser, James Farrell) and poets (Edgar Lee Masters, Carl Sandburg). The single most important American poetry magazine, the Chicago-based *Poetry*, edited by Harriet * Monroe, advanced the careers of both Hughes and Brooks. Equally important for young black writers was the Chicago musical scene, in which southern black music was being transformed into the most influential forms of twentieth-century vernacular music: gospel and the urban blues. Generally absent from the male-dominated interracial Chicago jazz scene of the 1920s, black women—Mahalia Jackson, Roberta Martin, Big Mama Thornton, and KoKo Taylor—were central figures in the predominantly black churches and bars that established the aesthetic base for popular musical forms, including soul and rock.

The reorientation from Harlem to Chicago was expressed by Dorothy West, who edited the transitional periodical *Challenge* (1934–1937) and coedited *New Challenge* (1937) with Richard Wright and Marian Minus. Acknowledging that *Challenge* had "come in for considerable dispraise" as a result of its focus on Harlem Renaissance writers, West announced in 1937 that she had "become greatly interested in a young Chicago group," which would receive "a special section in a forthcoming issue" (*Propaganda and Aesthetics*, 1979). The result was *New Challenge*, which published four poems by Margaret Walker alongside Wright's influential "Blueprint for Negro Writing," the primary aesthetic statement of the era. Subsequently, Chicago-based publications assumed a central position in black culture. Known primarily for Abbott's political activism, the *Defender* published the classic "Jesse B. Simple" stories in Langston Hughes's regular column. In addition to her essay in the 1950 issue of *Phylon* on "The Negro in Literature," *Defender* staff writer Era Bell Thompson (1906–1986) published an autobiography, *American Daughter* (1946). Gentle and humorous, Thompson's book is a necessary complement to the bleak portrait of black Chicago in Wright's *American Hunger* (written 1944, published 1987). The most widely circulated black magazine of the period, *Negro Digest* (first series, 1942–1951), published excerpts from many prominent black novels. Perhaps the most significant Chicago magazine, however, was *Negro Story* (1944–1946), published out of the South Side home of Alice Browning, a central figure in African-American literary history who has received very little recognition. In contrast to the proletarian aesthetics of the Communist-affiliated magazines *Left Front* and *Negro Quarterly*, *Negro Story* encouraged experimental writing on racial themes, publishing Walker and Brooks alongside Ralph Ellison and Chester Himes.

For most black women writers, the Renaissance was centered in specifically black cultural institutions. The South Side Writers' Group, organized by Wright, brought together early Renaissance writers, including Walker, Fern Gayden, Dorothy Sutton, Frank Marshall Davis, and Theodore Ward. Later, Inez Cunningham Stark, a white patron of *Poetry*, conducted poetry workshops at the South Side Community Center, which were attended by Brooks, Margaret Danner (b. 1915), and Margaret Taylor Burroughs (b. 1917), all of whom helped pass the Renaissance legacy to younger Chicagoans. Brooks's work with Chicago gangs and Burroughs's work with the DuSable Museum nurtured writers, artists, and musicians, including poets Carolyn *Rodgers (b. 1945), Angela Jackson (b. 1951), Johari *Amini (Jewel Latimore; b. 1935), Sharon Scott (b. 1951), and singer-composer Amina Claudine Myers (b. 1943). Lorraine Hansberry, a central figure in post-Renaissance African-American drama, graduated from the same high school as Brooks.

Black women occupied somewhat less prominent positions in the interracial organizations of the period. The Communist-supported John Reed Clubs, which played a major role in advancing Wright's career, provided no support for black women writers. In contrast, both the *Works Progress Administration Writers' Project and the Chicago branch of the Federal Theater Project brought together white Chicagoans (Nelson Algren, Saul Bellow), black male writers (Wright, Willard Motley, Frank Yerby) and black women writers (Walker, Katherine Dunham). Although playwright Shirley Graham (better known as an activist who later married W. E. B. Du Bois) dismissed Chicago as a city lacking cultural life, she directed the Negro unit of the Federal Theater Project from 1936 to 1938, and was instrumental in productions of Ward's *Big White Fog*, and Charlotte Chorpenning's *Little Black Sambo* and *The Swing Mikado*. The most influential interracial contacts of the Renaissance, however, focused on the University of Chicago, where the Department of Sociology, supported by black alumni such as Charles S. Johnson and E. Franklin Frazier, encouraged the academic study of racial tensions. Of equal importance to the Renaissance, the Chicago University–based Julius Rosenwald Fund was the major source of patronage for black intellectuals of the 1930s and 1940s. Under the direction of Edwin Embree, the Fund's fellowship program supported Marian Anderson and Hurston, as well as the Chicago-based Dunham and Walker.

Despite the very real contributions of the Chicago sociologists to the support of black intellectuals, and of their progressive policy agenda that culminated in the 1954 *Brown v. Board of Education* Supreme Court decision mandating desegregation of public schools, those sociologists' impact on African-American women's culture must be viewed with ambivalence. Reinforced by the unprecedented public response to *Native Son*—which was understood almost entirely by white contemporaries to be a "protest" novel presenting black Chicago as a "problem" to be solved—the application of sociological methods to cultural criticism allowed white readers and critics to underestimate both the individuality and the complexity of black women's expression. To a disturbing extent, the sociological premises established during the Renaissance continue to dominate discussions of African-American culture, reducing complex attempts to negotiate situations that are both personal and communal to "representative" expressions of social unrest. As June *Jordan observes in "Notes toward a Black Balancing of Love and Hatred" (in *Civil Wars*, 1987), the emphasis on Wright—and on the subsequent "rebellions" of literary sons Ralph Ellison and James Baldwin—resulted in the loss of Zora Neale Hurston's specifically black, woman-centered, and celebratory vision, a vision extended by Walker's *For My People* (1942), Brooks's *A Street in Bronzeville* (1945), and Hansberry's autobiographical *To Be Young, Gifted and Black* (1969). Focusing on the Chicago Renaissance as a central movement in African-American literary history resists the inordinate emphasis on Wright and helps establish Brooks, Bonner, Hansberry, and Walker as major figures. Unless the sociological premises of the movement receive adequate attention, however, their further reformulation risks contributing to the continuing repression of significant aspects of the black women's tradition.

[*See also* African-American Writing; Harlem Renaissance.]

• Gwendolyn Brooks, *Report from Part One* (1972). Michel Fabre, *The Unfinished Quest of Richard Wright* (1973). Abby Arthur Johnson and Ronald Maberry Johnson, *Propaganda and Aesthetics: The Literary Politics of Afro-American Magazines in the Twentieth Century* (1979). Trudier Harris, ed., *Afro-American Writers, 1940–1955* (1988). Margaret Walker, *Richard Wright: Daemonic Genius* (1988). Lorraine Elena Roses and Ruth Elizabeth Randolph, *Harlem Renaissance and beyond* (1990).

Craig Hansen Werner

CHICANA WRITING. *This entry consists of four essays that discuss Chicana writing by genre.*

Drama
Fiction
Nonfiction
Poetry

For further information, please refer to Assimilation; Chicana Rights Movement; Citizenship; Cuban-American Writing; Ethnicity and Writing; Immigrant Writing; Latina Writing; Puerto Rican Writing.

Drama

In 1965, El Teatro Campesino (The Farmworkers' Theater) emerged amid the grape strike of the United Farmworkers' Union at Delano, California. The theater movement that developed under the influence of this company was oppositional, an arm of the Chicano movement to resist the cultural and economic domination that have marked the experience of people of Mexican ancestry in the United States since 1848. The initial goals of the Chicano theater movement were those of the cultural project of the movement as a whole: to create an alternative to the dominant mode of production of mainstream theater, to make theater accessible to a working-class Chicano audience, to validate popular cultural forms, and to represent Chicanos' historical and social experiences. At its peak in the mid-seventies, the Chicano theater movement was a vigorous, grass-roots, amateur theater movement of national, even international, proportions.

The *teatros*, or theater groups, were microcosms of the conflicts and contradictions of the larger movement. The cultural nationalism that predominated in the movement defined Chicano identity in terms of an oppositional relationship between Chicanos and the dominant society, leading to a static view of culture, reinforcing male dominance, and effectively excluding gay and lesbian as well as Chicana feminist subjectivities. While many *teatros* succeeded in replacing the privileged male protagonist of mainstream theater with a working-class male subject of color, they continued to represent woman as object and to perpetuate stereotyped roles for female actors.

The work of El Teatro de la Esperanza (Theater of Hope) in Santa Barbara, California, informed by a materialist rather than a cultural nationalist analysis, attempted to decenter the male subject of representation through the use of collective protagonists (*Guadalupe*, 1974) and by placing a weak, contradictory male character in dialectical relation to active female characters who possessed a clearer vision of the economic and social forces composing the dramatic conflict (*La victima [The Victim]*, 1976; *Hijos [Children], Once a Family*, 1979; *El pulpo [The Octopus]*, 1980).

Chicanas working within the theater movement attempted to counter male domination in their representations as well as in the material conditions of theater production. Yolanda Broyles-González has studied the imaginative strategies of the female members of El Teatro Campesino in circumventing subordinate roles and casting by "type," including the development of ungendered roles such as *La Muerte* (Death). In 1978, Chicanas established a women's caucus called W.I.T. (Women in Teatro) within TENAZ, the theater movement's national organization, in response to the widespread perception that TENAZ was not addressing itself effectively to the specific needs of female theater workers. W.I.T. provided a much-needed communication network and support base, organized workshops during TENAZ seminars and festivals, and helped women just beginning to work in *teatros* to deal with their specific problems.

Another response to male domination was the formation of all-women *teatros*. These groups tended to favor the narrative representation of America's history through *teatropoesia*, a collage of poetry, prose, music, dance, and pantomime. In 1974, Dorinda Moreno, with *Las Cucarachas*, performed a *teatropoesia* piece called *Chicana* (San Francisco, Mexico City); in 1981, Valentina Productions presented *Voz de la mujer* (Woman's Voice) in San Francisco. Both texts place the contemporary Chicana last in a line of female figures from Mexican history, including the pre-Columbian Native-Indian woman; the remarkable intellectual/nun from colonial times, Sor Juana Inés de la Cruz; and the *Adelita*, or woman soldier of the revolution.

At Mills College in Oakland, California, in 1981, Barbara Brinson-Pineda, together with Antonio Curiel, scripted the *teatropesia* piece *Tongues of Fire*, which focused Chicana subjectivity in relationship to sexuality, "race," class, and writing. Binson-Pineda used Gloria * Anzaldúa's "Speaking in Tongues: A Letter to Third World Women Writers" to foreground the importance of Chicana writers' "tongues of fire" in remembering their history, denouncing social injustice, confronting restrictive gender roles within their culture, and expressing their dreams and visions. By placing the individual Chicana subjectivity of the various pieces in a dialectic with collective identity, *Tongues of Fire* avoided the romanticization of "a" Chicana identity. The accumulative effect of the text was the impression of many different voices engaged in a dialogue about what it means to be Chicana.

More recently, Josefina López's *Real Women Have Curves* refracts concerns of class and immigration, treated in such movement plays as El Teatro de la Esperanza's *La victima*, through a feminist lens, incorporating issues of female corporality. The play's large-figured women, who labor in a sweatshop in Los Angeles to produce expensive, petite-sized party dresses, live in the shadow of *la migra* (the INS), and share their various struggles—the search for a voice as a writer, domestic violence, and the self-negating internalization of the "feminine ideal." *Real Women* formed part The Group Theater's regular season in Seattle (March 1992), and the KPBS production of López's *Simply Maria, or, the American Dream* won a Gold Award from the Corporation for Public Broadcasting (1990). Denise Chávez, in collaboration with four other Chicanas, drew on New Mexican cultural traditions of storytellers and *ofrendas* (collages of religious and personal objects constructed for All Souls Day) to produce the nine monologues of *Novena Narrativas y Ofrendas Nuevomexicanas*. Under the beneficent auspices of a clay Madonna, the characters, ranging in age from seven to seventy-eight, give voice to their unique experiences, hopes, and devotions. The play toured the Southwest after its first performance in Taos, New Mexico, in 1986.

Cherríe * Moraga's first play, *Giving up the Ghost* (1986), broke a twenty-five-year silence in the Chicano theater movement by placing Chicana lesbian desire center stage. *Ghost*, a two-act verse play, juxtaposes the monologues of three characters (Marisa, a Chicana lesbian; Corky, Marisa's younger self; and Amalia, a heterosexual Chicana) to explore the ways Chicanas' sexuality and subjectivity have been affected, for better or for worse, by their culture and class. By the end of the play, they are still struggling with their private ghosts, although Marisa dreams of a community based on the loyalty of women to women, of "making familia from scratch." Moraga's second play, *Shadow of a Man*, was performed in 1990 at San Francisco's Eureka Theatre (and co-produced by Brava! for Women in the Arts). Besides examining Chicanas' negotiations of their culture's privileging of males, *Shadow* also explores the harmful impact of machismo on Chicano men. Set in the late 1960s in Los Angeles, the play tells the story of the Rodriguez family, which is torn apart by the dark "secret" of the father Manuel's obsession with his *compadre* Conrado, who represents the masculine ideal Manuel both desires and fails to embody. At issue is not whether Manuel is gay; instead, the audience is invited to consider sexuality along a continuum, to explore the intersections and contradictions of homosociality and homosexuality. Moraga's new play, *Heroes and Saints*, was presented by Brava in April 1992. In its engagement of pesticide poisoning of farmworkers, sexuality, and female subjectivity, Moraga continues the project of creating a "healing" theater that offers the possibility of transformation by addressing Chicano reality in all its complexity.

• Jorge Huerta, *Chicano Theatre: Themes and Forms* (1982). Yolanda Broyles-González, "Women in El Teatro Campesino: 'Apoco Estaba Molacha La Virgen de Guadalupe?' " in *Chicana Voices: Intersections of Class, Race, and Gender*, eds. Teresa Córdova et al. (1986). Yvonne Yarbro-Bejarano, "Cherríe Moraga's *Giving up the Ghost*: The Representation of Female Desire," *Third Woman* 3 (1986): 113–20. Yvonne Yarbro-Bejarano, "The Female Subject in Chicano Theatre: Sexuality, 'Race,' and Class," *Theatre Journal* 38 (December 1986): 389–407. Denise Chávez, "Novena Narrativas y Ofrendas Nuevomexicanas," in *Chicana Creativity and Criticism*, eds. Maria Herrera-Sobek and Helena María

Viramontes (1987). Yolanda Broyles-González, "Toward a Re-Vision of Chicano Theatre History: The Women of El Teatro Campesino," in *Making a Spectacle: Feminist Essays on Contemporary Women's Theatre*, ed. Lynda Hart (1989). Jorge Huerta, ed., *Necessary Theater* (1989).

Yvonne Yarbro-Bejarano

Fiction

Terri de la Peña's 1992 novel *Margins* opens with a scene of Chicana pedagogy. The novel's protagonist, Veronica Meléndez, meets with her Chicana studies professor, who has assigned the young Chicana writer a text featuring "a pre-Columbian motif on the book's black and gold cover." This cover is familiar to readers and writers of Chicana fiction as the groundbreaking collection *Cuentos: Stories by Latinas*. The 1983 volume, over a decade after its publication, is considered one of the best collections of Latina fiction. Editors Alma Gómez, Cherríe *Moraga, and Mariana Romo-Carmona describe the power of Latina fiction as "writings which put the concerns and struggles of the Latin woman first." Fueled by powerful political forces such as the Chicano and women's movements, Chicana writers have put the Chicana and her experience first, forging over the last three decades an important emergent American literature.

While Chicana feminist poets have produced highly regarded books of poetry, the Chicana novel has not garnered the same kind of critical attention. Active Chicana poets outnumber Chicana fiction writers, and there have always been greater opportunities for the publication of poems in various *Raza* and Latina/o journals and newspapers. Still, these fictional works represent a variety of styles and narrative strategies that form a collective body worthy of further critical attention.

Some critics have credited *We Fed Them Cactus* (1953) by the New Mexican writer Fabiola Cabeza de Baca as the first Chicana novel. Cabeza de Baca led a long and productive life as a writer, folklorist, and educator and worked with UNESCO and the Peace Corps. *We Fed Them Cactus* mixed fiction, personal narrative, historical chronicle, and folklore to tell the story of Latino life on the plains of the Southwest. The book received positive attention in newspaper reviews and was later rediscovered by Chicano literary historians. Although condemned by some critics as not being politically progressive, Chicana feminists have celebrated Cabeza de Baca's display of concern for the effects of North American cultural influence on her beloved region.

More widely regarded as the first Chicana novels, Berta Ornelas's *Come Down from the Mound* (1975) and Isabella Ríos's *Victuum* (published in 1976 and copyrighted in 1974) were written at the historical convergence of the women's and the Chicano movements, allowing a sharp focus on specifically feminist Chicana concerns. Appearing at a juncture in the Chicano literary renaissance when an interest in experimental writing began to reshape the themes of social realism and the quest for identity that had dominated earlier texts, both Ornelas and Ríos turned away from more traditional narrative forms. *Come Down From the Mound* narrates a heterosexual romance complicated by politics. Aurora, a student-teacher with a radical background who has decided to work within the system, falls in love with Chuy, am unscrupulous city commissioner. As the novel's agent of social change, the female protagonist eventually wins the battle of the sexes by having her lover renounce his crooked political career. Ríos's novel *Victuum*, the earliest Chicana bildungsroman, tackles metaphysical concerns through science fiction, tracing the trajectory of the protagonist's psyche through encounters with psychic phenomena. Both texts de-emphasize plot and focus instead on the political and psychic dimensions of Chicanas's lives.

Chicana novels flourished in the 1980s and 1990s. Gina Valdés's novelette *María Portillo*, in her collection *There Are No Madmen Here* (1981), reveals her concerns with social issues in Latina communities: bilingualism, multiculturalism, class injustice, consumerism, and the plight of the undocumented worker. Named after the narrative's garment worker protagonist, the novel documents María Portillo's dissatisfaction with her low status and her transition to tequila smuggler. The novel scrutinizes the traditional Latino family and concludes that many of its support systems are false ones. In 1982, Sheila Ortiz Taylor published the first Chicana lesbian novel, *Faultline*. Often blinded by homophobia, certain critics have faulted Ortiz Taylor not focusing on "real" Chicanos, neglecting the explicit and implicit connections between the protagonist's struggles as a Latina lesbian and those of all Latinas. *Faultline* posits a reconstructed and extended family unit based on lesbian love. The utopian impulse of *Faultline* reappears in Ortiz Taylor's second novel *Spring Forward/Fall Back* (1985).

Award-winning dramatist Estela Portillo *Trambley's first novel, *Trini*, narrates the life of an undocumented Tarahumara Indian woman, who succeeds within the Anglo-American patriarchal culture while retaining some of her traditional spirituality after crossing the border to give birth to her child in the United States. These themes of the conflict between

U.S. cultural imperialism and traditional cultural understanding also animate Trambley's early collection of stories *Rain of the Scorpions and Other Writings* (1975). In the collection's title story, "Rain of the Scorpions," a gang of Chicano boys set out on a quest to discover Azaltán, the Chicano mythical garden of paradise and homeland. The story ends with a collective epiphany in which the boys discover that Azaltán has always been within them.

Another highly regarded Chicana dramatist from New Mexico became a novelist in 1986. Denise Chávez published *The Last of the Menu Girls*, a novel composed of seven interrelated stories. Chávez's text was concerned with giving voice to different disenfranchised social players such as nurse's aids, gardeners, and janitors. In telling the story of her protagonist Rocio Esquibel, Chávez employed multiple narrators and experimented with dialects and accents, an experimentation with linguistic codes prevalent in Chicana fiction. *Puppet* (1985), a novel by Margarita Cota-Cárdenas is perhaps the best example of code-switching, a narrative technique employed by many U.S. Latina and Latino authors. *Puppet*'s narrative structure forsakes traditional linear development and instead employs a system of symbolic and linguistic juxtapositions as an organizational rubric through the device of Spanish/English code switching in the various interior monologues and dialogues that loosely structure the text. The highly autobiographical novel tells the story of Petra Leyva, a Chicana professor of Spanish who responds to the death of a young Chicano boy nicknamed Puppet by writing a novel. The coming into social consciousness of the Chicana woman is an important theme in much Chicana literature.

Many Chicana fiction writers, like their male counterparts, have focused on the experience of young people growing up in *el barrio*. Some of the stories in Helena María *Viramontes's *The Moths and Other Stories* (1985) are considered to be among the most powerful fictional testaments to what it means to grow up female, poor, and Chicana. The title story, "Moths," recounts a young girl's mourning for her *abuela* (grandmother) and the strength that this gives her to defy patriarchal institutions such as the church as well as her overly strict father. "Growing" is another of the collection's rite-of-passage stories in which the protagonist, Naomi, is forbidden to play baseball by her strict Mexican-born parents. Detailing the ways Naomi challenges her father's patriarchal belief system, the story links the young girl's situation to that of larger patriarchal oppressive structures. Viramontes is equally gifted at narrating

the lives of older Chicanas, as in her story "Neighbors," which conveys an older woman's loss of control over her body due to the aging process. The story annexes the seventy-three-year-old woman's narrative to a larger political survey of the death of her barrio due to the "progress" of urban renewal.

Like Viramontes, Beverly Silva is also adept at portraying Chicanas and Chicanos across the age spectrum. Silva's collection *The Cat and Other Stories* (1986) represents aspects of Chicana lives, including small-town life, student protests, childhood, graduate-student life, and romantic relationships through an intensely personal voice often infused with touching nostalgia. This looking back also infuses one of the best-known collections of Chicana short fiction, Sandra *Cisneros's *The House on Mango Street* (1985). Broken up into forty-four brief, compressed narratives, the award-winning volume meditates upon the time and space of childhood through the narrator Esperanza's return to her childhood experience in a Chicago barrio. This intensely feminist space reflects both the gender inequality of patriarchy and the empowerment supplied by relationships between women. Cisneros's most recent collection of stories, *Woman Hollering Creek* (1991), explores a similar emotional terrain through a wider range of narrative techniques and voices.

One of the most prolific and distinguished Chicana writers in the 1980s and early 1990s, Ana *Castillo has published various poetry collections and three important novels. Castillo dedicates her first novel *The Mixquiahula Letters* (1986) to Latin American "Boom" writer Julio Cortázar. Like Cortázar's masterpiece *Hopscotch*, this epistolary novel is not meant to be read in a prescriptive linear fashion, but according to three different reading sequences: one for the Conformist, one for the Cynic, and one for the Quixotic. The letters written by Teresa to her friend Alicia meditate on the women's travels on both sides of the Mexican/U.S. border and muse upon issues of love, courtship, and sexual difference. The epistolary structure functions as a narrative device that shuttles the narrative and the reader back and forth from one country to another and from one topic to another. Castillo's second novel, *Sapogonia (An Anti-Romance in 3/8 Meter)* (1990), narrated from the perspective of a would-be modern conquistador who agonizes over his inability to seduce the female protest singer Pastora Aké, focuses on the familiar themes of sexual miscommunication, difference, and indifference. Her third novel, *So Far from God* (1993), is clearly influenced by the Latin American literary style known as *lo real marvilloso* or magic realism, pioneered by writers such as Cortázar, José María Arguedas, María Luisa Bombal, Alejo Carpentier, Clarice Lispector, and Gabriel García Márquez. The influence of this literary style is equally detectable in the work of other Chicana writers such as Portillo Trambley and Viramontes. *So Far from God* is the story of Sofía and her four martyred daughters who are subjected to the societal threats that prey on Chicana women in the United States such as rape, lethal working conditions, and the devastating AIDS epidemic. Although some of her children return as ghostly visitors, Sofía is essentially the sole survivor in this narrative's matriarchy. While her daughters and their deaths represent the dangers of being Chicana and female in a racist and sexist culture, Sofía and her perserverance stand for the Chicana's amazing strength and survival skills. While readers have commented on a submerged lesbian dynamic between the protagonists in *The Mixquiahula Letters*, there is nothing submerged about the lesbian characters that populate *So Far from God*. With this latest novel, Castillo incorporates lesbianism not as a spectacle or an issue, but as an everyday reality of Chicana life.

Another novel that insists on representing the Chicana lesbian as part of everyday Latina life, De la Peña's *Margins* portrays the Chicana lesbian as daughter, sister, aunt, student, writer, friend, and lover. *Margins* is dedicated to Anzaldúa, Cisneros, Moraga, and Viramontes, four Chicana writers who de la Peña credits with making her artistic production possible. De la Peña and the coming generations of Chicana novelists will retrieve a particular ethos from the Chicana literature that paved the way for them, which critic Yvonne Yabaro-Bejarano has described as "the courageous move to place Chicana subjectivity in the center of literary representation." Indeed, if there is one unifying factor in Chicana fiction beyond the writers' identity, it is clearly the move to bring Chicana subjectivities from the margins of other discourses to their very own discursive, emotional, and ideological center.

• Francisco A. Lomelí, "Chicana Novelists in the Process of Creating Fictive Voices," in *Beyond Stereotypes: The Critical Analysis of Chicana Literature*, edited by María Herrera-Sobek (1985), pp. 26–46. Tey Diana Rebolledo, "Tradition and Mythology: Signatures and Landscapes in Chicana Literature," in *The Desert Is No Lady*, edited by Vera Norwood and Janice Monk (1987), pp. 96–256. Sonia Saldívar-Hull, "Feminism on the Border: From Gender Politics to Geopolitics," in *Criticism in the Boderlands: Studies in Chicano Literature, Culture, and Ideology*, edited by Hector Calderón and José David Saldívar (1991), pp. 221–237. Yvonne Yabaro-Bejarano, "Chicana Literature from a Chicana Feminist Perspective," in *Chicana Creativity and Criticism: Charting New Frontiers in American Literature* (1988), pp. 139–147.

José Esteban Muñoz

Nonfiction

Issues of ethnicity and class have been central to both the fiction and nonfiction production of Chicanas since 1848, when residents of the Mexican territory invaded and conquered by the United States, became citizens and, thereafter, part of a subordinated and increasingly marginalized national minority. Yet gender discourses have always underpinned the social, economic, and political concerns of these writers, for it has always been as minority *women* of Mexican origin that have addressed their collective oppression in Chicanas discourses that fall within three historical periods.

Discourses of Structural Displacement (1848–1910). The nineteenth century was a period of social, political, and economic transformation in the Southwest, which for the conquered population meant dispossession, structural displacement, and oppression. With the shattering of that population's political and economic structure, new constructs of ethnicity and race were generated. María Amparo Ruiz de Burton, for example, in a letter today housed in the Huntington (California) Library, refers to the importance of loyalty to the Latin race crushed by the Anglo invaders. Resentment against the United States government, which had reneged on promises of full citizenship rights, is a key issue in the earliest historical narratives by women, but equally prominent are romantic discourses both of nostalgia for a pastoral past and in defense of the colonial missions and missionaries. Within these texts are interspersed a number of personal reminiscences in which these women revealed their subordinate roles in patriarchal families, and also disclosed their exploitive roles in relation to the Indian labor force, whether as housekeepers of missionaries or as wives of landowners and merchants. However, nineteenth-century women of Mexican origin do not question the patriarchal system in their writings. On the contrary, women like Angustias Guerra de Ord, in her testimonial, are eager to show that no decision was taken without consulting husbands, fathers, brothers, or missionaries.

The earliest nonfiction works by Chicanas are testimonials, letters, diaries, memoirs, and newspaper articles. Most of the testimonials, although not in print, are accessible to researchers at various libraries and archives, including the Bancroft, Huntington, San Diego Historical Society, and University of New Mexico (Albuquerque) libraries, and the Benson Collection at the University of Texas, Austin. The majority of texts are available only in Spanish, although the Bancroft Library published part of Eulalia Pérez's "An Old Woman and Her Recollections" in *Three Memoires of Mexican California* (1988), and the Academy of American Franciscan History published a translated edition of Angustias Guerra de Ord's *Occurrences in Hispanic California* (1956).

Discourses of Marginalization (1910–1960). The end of the nineteenth century signaled increased immigration of Mexicans to the United States for work in mining, ranching, railroad, and farming. The Mexican Revolution of 1910 also served to push out of Mexico both those fleeing from the Díaz regime and those escaping from revolutionary armies. Among the former were a number of revolutionaries, like the Flores Magón brothers, whose cause attracted a number of Chicana/Mexicana women. Especially in border towns, women like the newspaper writers Sara Estela Ramírez in Laredo, Texas, Isidra T. de Cárdenas in El Paso, Texas, Andrea Villarreal in San Antonio, Texas, and Jovita Idar in Laredo, urged women to participate in revolutionary struggle. In her autobiography, *La Rebelde*, Leonor Villegas de Magnón details her life story and the participation of other women in the Mexican Revolution. Most of these women were first-generation Chicanas, concerned as much with revolutionary causes in Mexico and the discrimination of the Mexican-origin population in the United States as with gender issues. Ramírez, for example, exhorts women to reject romantic constructs of femininity and become active participants in revolutionary struggle.

Following the Mexican Revolution, concrete social issues within the United States became dominant themes in Chicana writings. In the period after 1930, the war effort, the growth of agribusiness, and increased industrialization of the Southwest accelerated immigration from Mexico (both documented and undocumented), urbanization, and a migration of Chicanos to California, as well as a gradual shift from agricultural to service and blue-collar employment. Urbanization and concentration of Chicanos in large segregated barrios increased marginalization and interethnic conflicts, like that of the Los Angeles Zoot Suit Riots of 1943. The diversity within the Chicano communities of today, in terms of origin, generation, residence, occupation, and language choice were mapped during this second period, and that diversity significantly affected subsequent generations of Chicana women and, in particular, Chicana writers.

Ethnic discrimination in the areas of law, labor, and education were crucial issues addressed by Chicanas like Emma Tenayuca, Luisa Moreno, and Josefina Fierro de Bright in the 1930s and 1940s. Their writings in newspapers and journals advocated the organization not only of women workers, but of all Latino workers, many of whom had been excluded from racist unions. By the 1950s, many Chicanos involved in labor organizing would face harassment and deportations, among them Luisa Moreno.

Discourses of ethnicity, class, and gender (1960–present). The period from 1960 to the present has witnessed the highest degree of production by Chicanas in the fields of sociology, history, political science, health, law, linguistics, education, and literature, with the formation of small but outspoken groups of academics who have undertaken an active campaign of research into numerous issues affecting women. Since the 1960s and the Chicano movement, Chicanas have organized not only as members of an oppressed minority, but as women. The creation of Chicana organizations has given rise to a number of publications in which writers grapple with concrete problems of health, sterilization, abortion, wife abuse, rape, drug addiction, employment, and education (especially bilingual education), as well as with theoretical issues of gender identity in relation to class and ethnicity, and the differences that separate Chicanas from mainstream feminists. More recently, works such as Gloria *Anzaldúa's *Borderlands/La Frontera* (1987) have begun to deal as well with issues of sexuality and alternative life-styles.

From 1970 to 1990, a concerted effort to record the experiences of older Chicanas and to reconstruct the history of women of Mexican origin in the Southwest has led to projects that have generated case study and oral history research and publications, such as Vicki Ruíz's *Cannery Women, Cannery Lives* (1987), and the publication of numerous anthologies and special journal issues with critical essays by Chicanas on a variety of women's concerns. Despite the publication of many anthologies of Chicana poetry and fiction, single works about Chicana writers, like Marta Sánchez's *Contemporary Chicana Poetry* (1985), are rare. There is no denying that the corpus of Chicana nonfiction publications is small, but it is greater today than it has ever been. With this growth has come a concomitant diversification of Chicana positions on basic issues of class, ethnicity, gender, and sexuality, ideological differences that are shared by the larger heterogeneous Chicano communities.

• Rosaura Sánchez and Rosa Martínez Cruz, eds., *Essays on La Mujer* (1977). Magdalena Mora and Adelaida del Castillo, eds., *Mexican Women in the United States* (1980). Emilio Zamora, "Sara Estela Ramírez: Una rosa roja en el movimiento," in *Mexican Women in the United States*, eds. Magdalena Mora and Adelaida R. Del Castillo (1980), pp. 163–169. María Herrera-Sobek, ed., *Beyond Stereotypes: A Critical Analysis of Chicana Literature* (1985). Luis Leal, *Aztlán y Mexico* (1985). Teresa Córdova et al., eds., *Chicana Voices: Intersections of Class, Race, and Gender* (1986). María Herrera-Sobek and Helena María Viramontes, eds., *Chicana Creativity and Criticism: Creating New Frontiers in American Literature* (1988). Mario Garcia, *Mexican Americans. Leadership, Ideology, and Identity, 1930–1960* (1989). Clara Lomas, "Mexican Precursors of Chicana Feminist Writing," in *Multiethnic Literature of the United States: Critical Introductions and Classroom Resources*, ed. Cordelia Chávez Candelaria (1989), pp. 17–27. Gloria Anzaldúa, *Making Face, Making Soul/Haciendo Caras* (1990). Adelaida Del Castillo, ed., *Between Borders: Essays on Mexicana/Chicana History* (1990).

Rosaura Sánchez

Poetry

Mexican-American women have played a vital part in configuring the feminisms of the Americas and the ideology of Chicana/Chicano consciousness known as *chicanismo*. Chicana activists have helped forefront the distinctive experience of women vanquishing multiple societal inequities, including the challenge of women's in-group subordination by machismo and its persistent traditions. This requires what scholar Rosaura Sánchez calls considering the "multiple subjectivities" of gendered identity, ethno-racial experience, and material class situation in any "subject-identified" analysis. Defining themselves from within Chicana experience, not solely in relation to the dominating political and societal hegemonies, whether of the empowered dominant group or their subordinated in-group, Chicana writers and artists offer such subject-identified perspectives in their creative work. They reinvent Chicana identity by re/visioning Chicana/o topics and themes such as Aztlán (originally the legendary northern homeland of Mesoamerican Indians, which was heralded in the 1960s as a Chicano political space and *mestizaje* (the Spanish/Indian racial and cultural syncretism basic to Mexican-American consciousness), as well as by creating Chicana-defined views of gender and feminism. Their work usually does not privilege gender over race or ethnicity, but comprehends sex/gender/race/ethnicity as intertwined constructions of socioeconomic class and material history. However, a significant part of Chicana creative expression does emphasize gender and sexuality in recognition that in patriarchy fundamental issues of identity and power unavoidably derive from, and reside in, primary notions of femaleness, maleness, and their effects.

Chicana poets in particular have added to the literature of the Americas, at least since the Chicano Renaissance of the 1960s and 1970s, a library of writings nuanced by these concerns. Recent scholarship reveals, however, that the sources of Chicana poetry trace back to the sixteenth- and seventeenth-century European exploration and colonization in the western hemisphere, particularly in Mexico. Among the best-known of these sources are the historical woman *La Malinche and the folkloric character *La Llorona. Considered together, these two figures comprise meanings of woman, sexuality, power, and culture that have affected the cultural identity of all Mexicanas/Chicanas. As cultural icon, La Malinche is crucial to comprehending the hemisphere's ingrained systems of gendered hierarchy and misogyny. More formally, Mexican-American women's literary heritage (currently being recovered) dates back to the preeminent colonial poet, Sor Juana, arguably the Americas' first published feminist, and continues to the present. Due to space limits, Chicana antecedents are discussed here only if directly relevant to the highlighted writers (Ana *Castillo, Lorna Dee *Cervantes, Sandra *Cisneros, Lucha Corpi, Cherríe *Moraga, Carmen Táfolla, and Bernice Zámora) or to the themes and techniques characterizing the poetry in general.

Ana Castillo (b. 1953) has contributed a unique signature to Chicana/o literature since the early 1970s, for she was one of the first poets to express publicly a genuinely woman-identified alternative to the machismo of the early Chicano Movement's cultural nationalism. Her work in the last decade has evolved to question the applicability of liberal bourgeois feminism to Chicanas and other women of color. From her chapbooks of poetry (*Zero Makes Me Hungry* [1975] and *I Close My Eyes (To See)* [1976] to *My Father Was a Toltec* [1988]) to her recent novels (the award-winning *The Mixquiahuala Letters* [1986] and *Sapogonia* [1990]), Castillo's writings disclose the imagination, language, and style of an artist intent on an uncensored chronicling of her universe(s) and the process of that effort.

Emerging from her apprenticeship in the early chapbooks, Castillo's vision and writerly skills are clearly evident in *My Father Was a Toltec*. The volume's closing poem, "In My Country," declares a utopian vision that exposes the ironic truth about the sexism of her country. Castillo employs irony to expose facile idealizations, regardless of ideology. In "Someone Told Me," her homage to Chile's revolutionary singer Violeta Parra, she captures both the singer's feminism and the tragedy of her suicide. This grappling with the complexity of romantic love, its sexual expression, and its relation to the prevailing ideologies of power energizes Castillo's vision. Her achievement in writing "Chicana" in its multiple re/presentations looks ahead to its expanded explorations in her fiction.

Also working the demanding genre of poetry with acclaimed skill is Lorna Dee Cervantes (b. 1954), who in 1983 was described by the distinguished poet Alurista as "probably the best Chicana poet active today" (Chicano Poetry). Her vigorous record in alternative publishing (such as the Flor y Canto anthologies, Mango, Quarry West, and Red Dirt) has further established her central place in Chicana/o literature. Her first published volume, Emplumada (1981), is one of the most highly regarded post–Chicano Renaissance titles, and it has been widely reprinted. The title image of Emplumada recognizes the fragility of lived experience by marrying life's fleeting temporal aspect (the bird plumage [plumado] that molts with the passing of seasons) with the prospect of the conquest of time by the pen (pluma) and its permanent inscriptions.

With striking new configurations, Bird Ave. extends the bird motif introduced in Emplumada. Inspired by a San Jose street sign, the book's title reveals the poet's fresh creativity as she teases the allusion to the Latin ave (hail), which calls up sacred hosannas to the Virgin Mary, out of the more mundane than profane abbreviation for avenue. She fills the title poem with tropes that play off one another to texture an image, to contest an idea, and to syncopate rhythm, language, and line—complex techniques distinguishing the volume. The poem's muscular technique and dense figuration evoke a world of bittersweet vitality, street violence, and the paradoxes of urban life. Also re/presenting chicanismo with her dramatic voice(s) of complex Chicana sensibility, the poems in From the Cables of Genocide: Poems on Love and Hunger extend Cervantes's range as a poet and thinker. Here she explores the mother-daughter bond, treating both the mother loss and mother found themes through interconnected poems.

Best-known for her novella of vignettes The House on Mango Street (1985), Sandra Cisneros (b. 1953) has also written an evocative volume of poems, My Wicked Wicked Ways (1987). Like the references to physical space as a mirror of personal identity, which characterize her prose fiction, Wicked Ways contains location metaphors. Two of the volume's four sections bear place-name titles, and two sections open with epigraphs alluding explicitly to place, a concern with Aztlán that threads throughout Chicana/o literature.

Another writer who has imaged Aztlán as both material place and symbolic space, is Lucha Corpi (b. 1945). Her "Veracruz" and "San Luis Potosí" (1980) exemplify her use of place and cultural context to "establish the metaphors for the conflicting pressures between sexuality and prohibition [facing women]," as scholar Marta Sánchez notes. A published poet since the mid-1970s, Corpi began publishing fiction in the 1980s, yet her narrative bent was apparent in her verse, especially in her four-poem Marina cycle, where story and characterization are plotted with the same care given to poetic elements. A recuperation of the Mexicana/Chicana icon, La Malinche, the Marina poems examine the history and legend of Cortes's guide/interpreter/mistress Doña Marina to reveal her germinal effect on the hemisphere's gendering of culture. Originally written in Spanish, the poems reinterpret the history of the Conquest through the "autobiography" of Doña Marina, the woman Octavio Paz described as "la chingada [whore] de Mexico," but who some Chicana feminists have recovered as a key foremother of "herstory." This recovery goes well beyond her individual victimization as a woman, both by the conquering Spaniards and later by Mexican politicians seeking an indigenous scapegoat for the Conquest, to address the pervasive sexism at the root of the culture, politics, and history of the Americas. Another important participant in contemporary Chicana feminist discourse is writer Cherríe Moraga, who first gained a national audience for her anthology This Bridge Called My Back: Writings by Radical Women of Color (coedited with Gloria Anzaldúa; 1981) and for her well-received autobiographical prose poem Loving in the War Years: Lo que nunca paso por sus labios (What Was Never Spoken [through her lips]; 1983). Among the factors explaining the success of Loving are the recognition Moraga received for This Bridge, as well as for her explicit foregrounding of gender, race, and economic class as inseparable markers of identity. In the section of Loving headed "We Fight Back with Our Families," she writes:

> The strategy for the elimination of racism and sexism cannot occur through the exclusion of one problem or the other. . . . I remain amazed at how often so-called 'Tercer mundistas [third world women]' in the U.S. work to annihilate the concept and existence of white supremacy, but turn their faces away from male supremacy. Perhaps this is because when you start to talk about sexism, the world becomes increasingly complex. The power no longer breaks down into neat little hierarchical categories.

A major part of the work's power in "talking about sexism" is Moraga's depiction of her own lesbian identity in a heterosexist world—the agony, the confusion, the wonder, and the joy. Also accounting for the book's success is her experimentation with form in its quilting together of techniques and genres (essay, poetry, personal narrative, and vignettes of experience) as if to celebrate *mestizaje* through bold disregard of literary conventions.

Also exploiting the multiplicity of *mestizaje* as a literary element, Carmen Táfolla (b. 1951) has expanded Chicana/o creativity with what scholar Yolanda Broyles Gonzales describes in the *Dictionary of Literary Biography* as Táfolla's "most characteristic and powerful" technique, the voicing of "barrio personalities to life" through her "rare sensitivity" to the many "registers of barrio speech." Like Lucha Corpi, she wrote one of her apprenticeship works on La Malinche (*Encuentro Artistico Femenil*, 1978), although her best-known volume may be *Get Your Tortillas Together* (1978), a collection of poetry she edited that includes the work of two Chicano poets. Her most recent book, *Sonnets to Human Beings* (edited by literary scholar and publisher, Ernesto Padilla, 1992) continues her chronicling of Mexican America with a collection of some previously published titles of poetry and prose, the appearance of new work, and the inclusion of a dozen critical essays about her work.

Another writer considered among the most able Chicana poets, is Bernice Zámora (b. 1938), who, despite a modest publishing record, has been an active presence in Chicano/a letters for over three decades. Zámora's reputation rests primarily on the strength of *Restless Serpents* (1976), a collection marked by "occasional brilliance" and a "multiplicity of subjects and themes that range from Aztlán motifs to frequent allusions to art, religion, and politics" (*Chicano Poetry, A Critical Introduction*). The intertextual framework of the book, which was revised and expanded in 1992, structures a great many of her images, techniques, and themes.

Many other Chicana writers have contributed their voices to the poetry of Aztlán. Among them are Gloria Anzaldúa, whose *Borderlands/ La Frontera: The New Mestiza* (1987) asserts that Chicana identity cannot be separated from landbase and place, and Angela De Hoyos, whose *Chicano Poems for the Barrio* (1975) examines the oppression of *raza* in urban barrios by showing how the land "belongs" to no one, even though it must be respected as if it "belong[s] to all." Poets who have published extensively in Spanish include Miriam Bornstein, Margarita Cota Cardenas, Yolanda Luera, and Gina Valdez. Gaining critical notice in the 1980s are Cordelia Candelaria, Alicia Gaspar de

Alba, Demetria Martinez, Alma Villanueva, and Helena Maria *Viramontes, writers who have also been recognized for their work in other genres. Along with Sylvia Gonzales, Inez Hernandez, Pat Mora, Dorinda Moreno, Marina Rivera, Evangelina Vigil, and Xelina, these and the seven poets highlighted in this entry prove what critics as diverse as Norma Alarcon, Juan Bruce-Novoa, Maria Herrera-Sobek, Ramon Saldivar, and Charles Tatum have all observed: that one of the most vital and prolific areas of Chicana/o literary expression is that written by Chicana feminists.

Cordelia Candelaria

CHICANA RIGHTS MOVEMENT. Chicana/o history of resistance and self-determination centers on struggles over land and national boundaries. Ancestors of today's Chicanas/os were members of the many different Indian nations who inhabited the lands now known as Mexico and the American Southwest. During the sixteenth century, Spanish invaders conquered these indigenous peoples. Sexual relations, many of them forced, between Spanish men and indigenous women produced a mestiza/o population. Through colonization and settlement, the Spanish extended their territories north. The vast country of Mexico was formed after independence from Spain in 1821, stretching from what is known today as Guatemala up through Texas, California, Arizona, Colorado, New Mexico, Nevada, and even into parts of Oregon, Utah, and Idaho. In the early nineteenth century, Anglo settlers from the deep South migrated to Texas, sowing the seeds for a war between Mexico and the United States that eventually led to the annexation of almost half of Mexico's territories in 1848.

Confronting colonization, exploitation, and repression characterizes Chicana/o struggles in the Americas. One of the most-noted eras of contemporary struggle was the 1960s *Movimiento*. During the sixties, American society witnessed the birth of a Chicano rights movement, a social movement characterized by a politics of protest.

Chicanas participated actively in struggles ranging from social justice, equality, and educational reforms to political and economic self-determination for Chicano communities in the United States. The Chicana/o movement was an important source of Chicana *feminism. Chicanas found opportunities for activism and leadership in the movement, but also encountered sexist behavior and assumptions. Chicana feminists were accused of splitting the movement and repudiating *la raza*. Chicanos argued that it was inappropriate and dangerous for Chicanas to utilize concepts like women's liberation, *sexism, and male chauvinism, because these terms had originated in the Anglo women's movement, were imbued with Anglo individualism, and were antithetical to Chicana/o culture and traditions.

During this period, Chicana feminist consciousness emerged from a struggle for equality with Chicanos and from a reassessment of the role of the family as a means of resistance to oppressive societal conditions. In feminist organizing and writing, Chicanas have had the difficult task of both supporting the Chicana/o family as vital to Chicana/o culture, *community, and economic survival, and criticizing it when it was oppressive to women.

At the same time as Chicanas were active in the student movement, electoral parties, and the Chicana feminist movement, organizing continued among poor Chicanas. Chicanas participated actively in the National Welfare Rights Movement of the late 1960s, which demanded higher benefits and an end to humiliating and restrictive requirements for women on welfare. In 1967, Alicia Escalante founded the East Los Angeles Welfare Rights Organization, as well as the Chicano National Welfare Rights Organization, to represent the interests of Chicana welfare receipients.

Chicana/o political activity during the 1960s and 1970s also drew attention to the plight of migrant farm workers. Jessie Lopez De La Cruz, a farm worker active in union organizing, together with Dolores Huerta and César Chavez, organized Mexican farm workers throughout the Southwest into the United Farm Workers (UFW). The UFW achieved contract gains in pay and benefits during this time. In addition, the UFW was instrumental in passing laws that had an enormous impact on working conditions for California farm workers, including regulations governing occupational safety and pesticide use. The UFW employed many innovative techniques, such as hunger strikes and a national consumer grape boycott, to challenge successfully the firmly entrenched power of California's growers.

During the 1970s and 1980s, Chicana labor force participation rates continued to grow. In 1985, over half of American Chicanas were in the labor force. Relative to Anglo women and men, however, Chicanas still remained concentrated in low-paying seasonal jobs. In spite of many obstacles, Chicanas, as well as other racial/ethnic groups, have militantly struggled for their right to unionize.

In 1991, Chicanas once again found themselves struggling against big business. Over six hundred former garment workers of a closed Levi Strauss & Company plant in San Antonio, Texas, organized a boycott of all Levi products. The plant's move to Costa Rica resulted in the loss of 1,150 jobs, of which 90 percent belonged to Chicanas/Mexicanas. Levi's runaway plants have caused the loss of about seven thousand jobs since 1985. Responding to the crisis, Chicana/Mexicana sisters banned together to form *Fuerza Unida.*

With respect to health care, the National Latina Health Organization, founded in March 1986, was formed to raise Latinas' consciousnesses about their health and health problems, in an effort to begin to take control of their health and lives. Chicana activists point to the many cases where Chicanas' rights have been abused by doctors and hospital administrators. In one instance, Los Angeles County Hospital performed numerous sterilizations in the early 1970s without appropriate consent, often on women with poor English-language skills who were not advised of the risks or the irreversibility of the operation. The NLHO is actively involved in reproductive issues, advocating the expansion of *abortion rights to include all reproductive issues such as family planning, prenatal care, education on *sexuality, *birth control, sterilization abuses, and above all, access to all health services. In early 1990, NLHO created a project entitled "Latinas for Reproductive Choice." The project was launched in San Francisco on October 3, the anniversary date of the death of Rosie Jimenez, the first women to die as a result of an illegal abortion after the cutoff of Medicaid funds for legal abortions.

Chicanas face great challenges in the years ahead. The English-only movement threatens the future of bilingual education, and Chicanas must work even harder to maintain their rich cultural heritage. Poverty is growing among Chicanas. Declines in manufacturing jobs and an employer offensive against unions have worsened the bargaining power of Chicana/o workers. In assessing the achievements and limits of Chicana/o participation in the Movimiento, noted writer and veteran Chicana activist Elizabeth Martinez (1992) notes that despite "promising organizational concepts, such as an alternative electoral party (La Raza Unida) [and] transnational working class unity (CASA/Centro de Accion Social Autonomo)," such problems as *homophobia, sexism, and sectarianism threaten women's efficacy.

• Maria L. Apodaca, "The Chicana Woman: An Historical Materialist Perspective," *Latin American Perspective* 12–13 (Winter/Spring 1977). Marta Cotera, *Diosa y Hembra: History and Heritage of Chicanas in the U.S.* (1977). Ellen Cantarow, Susan Gushee O'Malley, and Sharon Hatman Strom, *Moving the Mountain: Women*

Working for Social Change (1980). Rosalinda M. Gonzalez, "Chicanas and Mexican Immigrant Families 1920–1940: Women's Subordination and Family Exploitation," in *Decade of Discontent: The Women's Movement 1920–1940,* eds. Lois Scharf and Joan M. Jensen (1982). Maxine Baca Zinn, "Familialism Among Chicanos: A Theoretical Review," *Humboldt Journal of Social Relations* 10 (Fall/Winter 1982/1983). Laurie Coyle, Gail Hershatter, and Emily Honig, "Women at Farah: An Unfinished Story," in *A Needle, a Bobbin, a Strike: Women Needleworkers in America,* eds. Joan M. Jensen and Sue Davidson (1984). James Cockcroft, *Outlaws in the Promised Land: Mexican Immigrant Workers and America's Future* (1986). Gloria Anzaldúa, *Borderlands/La Frontera: The New Mestiza* (1987). James Cockcroft, and Frank Bardacke, "Watsonville: A Mexican Community on Strike," in *Reshaping the U.S. Left: Popular Struggles in the 1980s,* eds. Mike Davis and Michael Sprinker (1988). Vicki L. Ruiz, " 'And Miles to Go . . .': Mexican Women and Work, 1930–1985," in *Western Women: Their Land, Their Lives,* eds. Lillian Schilissel, Vicki L. Ruiz, and Janice Monk (1988). Alma Garcia, "The Development of Chicana Feminist Discourse, 1970–1980," *Gender and Society* 3 (June 1989). Arnoldo Garcia, "Revelations of a Movement," *Crossroads* (February 1992): 16–19.

Elisa Linda Facio

CHILDBIRTH. *See* Birth.

CHILDHOOD. *See* Girlhood.

CHILD, Lydia Maria (1802–1880), novelist, short fiction writer, editor, abolitionist. Child was the youngest of seven children born to Susannah Rand and Convers Francis, a prosperous baker and strict Calvinist. When her mother died in 1814, Lydia moved from her home in Medford, Massachusetts, to Norridgewock, Maine, to live with her sister, Mary Preston. In 1824, two years after returning to the Boston area to live with her brother, Convers, she utilized the American social and geographical landscape in writing *Hobomok* (1824). This historical novel established her literary reputation, even though it offended readers by portraying the miscegenation of a Puritan woman and a Native American. By the time of her marriage in 1828 to lawyer and abolitionist David Lee Child, she had written another novel (*The Rebels,* 1825) and founded and edited the nation's first children's magazine (*Juvenile Miscellany,* 1826). In the next decade, she published *The Frugal Housewife* (1829), a domestic manual that went through thirty-three American editions, and the *Ladies' Family Library,* a collection of five books that included historical accounts of such figures as Madame de Staël and Lady Russell as well as, in the last two volumes, *The History of the Condition of Women, in Various Ages and Nations* (1835)—an account that would become a source for early feminists such as Sarah *Grimké. Celebrated by the *North American Review* (July 1833) as the nation's foremost woman writer, Child was the second woman to be granted access to the Boston Athenaeum.

In 1833, Child dramatically entered the abolitionist ranks by writing one of the first book-length calls for immediate emancipation, *An Appeal in Favor of That Class of Americans Called Africans.* Because of her views, she was denied use of the Athenaeum and was forced to give up editorship of *Juvenile Miscellany.* Moving to New York in 1841, she continued to promote the abolitionist cause as editor of the *National Anti-Slavery Standard.* Under her two-year tenure, the newspaper expanded readership and thus broadened sympathy for antislavery principles. While not entirely at ease with transcendental views, Child echoed many of them in one of her most popular works, *Letters from New York* (1843), a collection of journalistic essays first published in the *Standard,* on topics ranging from women's rights to prison reform to mesmerism. Estranged from her husband during the 1840s, she remained in New York, writing short fiction for the *Columbian* and *Union* literary magazines.

After reuniting with her husband in 1850, she moved back to the Boston area and soon returned to the forefront of the antislavery movement. In 1856, Horace Greeley's *New York Tribune* interrupted the serialization of Dickens's *Little Dorrit* to run instead Child's "The Kansas Emigrants," a story depicting the conflict between pro- and antislavery forces in Kansas and Missouri. After giving up her attempt to join the imprisoned John Brown and serve as his nurse, Child was forced to defend her actions and the abolitionist cause in *Correspondence between Lydia Maria Child and Gov. Wise and Mrs. Mason, of Virginia* (1860). In 1860, she also edited Harriet *Jacobs's *Incidents in the Life of a Slave Girl* (1861). After the Civil War, Child continued to write and edit numerous books, including *The Freedmen's Book* (1865), *A Romance of the Republic* (1867), and *An Appeal for the Indians* (1868).

• Milton Meltzer and Patricia G. Holland, eds., *Lydia Maria Child: Selected Letters, 1817–1880* (1982). Carolyn L. Karcher, ed., Hobomok *and Other Writings on Indians* (1986). Jean Fagan Yellin, *Women and Sisters: The Antislavery Feminists in American Literature* (1989). Deborah Pickman Clifford, *Crusader for Freedom: A Life of Lydia Maria Child* (1992).

Bruce Mills

CHILDREN. *See* Family; Mothers and Daughters.

CHILDREN'S LITERATURE. *This entry is divided into two parts, the first surveying the history of U.S. children's literature from its beginnings to 1900, and the second assessing twentieth-century children's literature:*

1650 to 1900
1900 to the Present

For further information, please refer to Adolescence; Girlhood.

1650 to 1900

It is almost impossible to trace women's involvement in writing and publishing for children before the end of the eighteenth century in America. In the seventeenth and eighteenth centuries, children's reading was for the most part limited to religious and educational tracts. What number of primers and prayer books may have been written or edited by women remains unknown. The American women writers who began to address young people in the eighteenth century devoted their energies to the most popular of American genres at that time, tales of seduction and treatises on education. Both genres often dealt with the depravity of European modes of conduct and the threat such conduct posed to young people in America, and both genres would hardly be considered children's literature by the standards of the twentieth century. Susanna * Rowson, author of the seduction novel *Charlotte Temple* (1794), argued that her novel was written for moral edification, as did Hannah Webster * Foster, whose epistolary *The Coquette; or, The History of Eliza Wharton* (1797) details the tragic seduction of a young woman uneducated in proper conduct. Hannah * Webster also wrote more directly about the importance of educating girls, describing an eighteenth-century school for girls and encouraging reading in the anecdotal survival manual *The Boarding School; or, Lessons of a Preceptress to Her Pupils* (1798). Other similar tracts include *Mrs. Chapone's Letters on the improvement of the mind, addressed to a young lady* (1786) and Mrs. Pilkington's *Mirror for the female sex* (1799). Another popular female author of this period whose work was aimed at young people was Mrs. Pinchard, whose *The Blind Child* (1793) told the story of an unfortunate but pious child and was followed by *The Two Cousins* (1796), *Dramatic Dialogue for the Use of Young Persons* (1798), and *The Little Trifler* (1798).

The market for conduct manuals for girls grew with the dawn of the nineteenth century, and a slew of * advice books formed the bulk of what women writers published on the subject of girlhood. Eliza W. Farrar's *The Young Lady's Friend* (1836) and Lydia H. * Sigourney's *Letters to Young Ladies* (1837) are typical of this genre, and include essays on dress, reading, education, health, cooking, and housekeeping. Lydia Maria * Child, a novelist and abolitionist, edited *The Juvenile Miscellany* and was the author of *The Girl's Own Book* (1853), a compendium of articles on conversation, manners, and amusements. Perhaps because it was not deemed appropriate for women to address men in print, many women authors limited their explicit aims to the improvement of women and children.

Church-sponsored publishing consortiums such as the American Tract Society and the American Sunday School Union produced numerous female-authored sentimentally pious pamphlets and books early in the nineteenth century. These religious publishing organizations represented many denominations and attempted to provide all children with suitably educational reading material both at school and at home. The Union published hundreds of volumes as well as thousands of tracts, magazines, and journals, which generally were cheerful in tone and provided instruction about religious matters, the importance of charity to the poor (increasingly important in nineteenth-century America's overflowing cities), kindness to animals, the dangers of idleness, and the virtues of work.

Sentimental fiction went hand in hand with practical advice in this period. Susan * Warner's *The Wide, Wide World* (1850) deals with the education of Ellen Montgomery, a girl who must learn to endure what she cannot change. In 1852, abolitionist Harriet Beecher * Stowe's *Uncle Tom's Cabin*, not written for children but later adopted by them, appeared. Stowe's book tells the story of Tom, a slave who saves the life of Eva St. Clair, a tiny girl who then convinces her wealthy father to buy him. Little Eva dies, Tom is sold to the cruel Simon Legree, blamed for the escape of two other slaves, and flogged to death. The book ends with the voice of George Shelby, who has learned of Tom's end and is now a confirmed abolitionist, giving his slaves their freedom. Retellings of this timely tale written for children soon began to appear, and in abridged form the book quickly became a children's classic. *The Lamplighter* (1857), by Maria * Cummins, tells the story of a girl who faces life's hardships "with the simplicity of a child, but a woman's firmness; with the stature of a child, but a woman's capacity; the earnestness of a child, but a woman's perseverance." These books centered around the growth of girls into women and encouraged girl readers toward self-dependence, but were popular with a much larger audience composed primarily of adult women. Martha Finley wrote about 100 children's books during the nineteenth century, among them those of the *Elsie Dinsmore* series. Elsie, whose mother is dead and whose father is absent in Europe, is being brought up by relatives who show her a limited affection similar to that experienced by Ellen Montgomery of Susan Warner's *Wide, Wide World*. Waiflike, meek Elsie eventually wins the affection of her returned father and marries a man of her father's age.

A woman—popular novelist Ann St. Stephens—wrote the first of the American dime novels often popular among children, the sensational *Malaeska; the Indian Wife of the White Hunter*, published by Irwin Beadle and Co. in 1860. Stephens's story was atypical of the dime novel as it would later develop, for it was a story of *Native American life. But it was full of action, sold 300,000 copies, and was translated into five languages within five years.

The late nineteenth century saw a steady growth in the number of children's magazines in the United States, and many women writers were frequent contributors. *The Riverside Magazine for Young People* (1867), *Harper's Young People* (1879), and *St. Nicholas* (1873) encouraged both the growth of child readership and female authorship. Mary Elizabeth Mapes Dodge began to write children's stories to support her two sons, and had many contributions accepted by magazines before she completed her best-known book, *Hans Brinker* (1865). In 1870 she became children's editor of a magazine called *Hearth and Home*, and three years later was appointed editor of *St. Nicholas*, the leading high-end children's periodical of its day. Louisa May *Alcott was soon contributing serials like *Eight Cousins* and *Jack and Jill* to *St. Nicholas*; in 1886 Frances Hodgson *Burnett's tale of American animosity for the British class system, *Little Lord Fauntleroy*, made its first appearance in the magazine. Other children's magazines that featured the work of women writers were *Our Young Folks* (published out of Boston between 1865 and 1873 and edited by Lucy Larcom and Mary Abigail Dodge) and *Wide Awake* (published from 1875 until 1893 by Lothrop and containing contributions from such writers of girls' stories as Elizabeth Stuart *Phelps, author of *Gypsy Brenton*, and Mrs. A. D. T. Whitney, author of the very popular *Faith Gartney's Girlhood* [1862]). A magazine called *Youth's Companion* counted Annie Johnston as a contributor at the beginning of her literary career; she later made her name as an author of children's books through a series begun with *The Little Colonel* (1895).

Louisa May Alcott's *Little Women* (1868) is perhaps the most enduring work of juvenile fiction of the nineteenth century. It offered, like most popular fiction for girls, a story line that revolved around homes, family, and personal relationships. In the character of Jo March, however, Alcott created a rough, tomboyish, ambitious girl uncommon in other fiction of the day. The book describes several months in the lives of the March sisters, in a Massachusetts home run by the girls' mother, Marmee, while their father is away serving as an army chaplin during the Civil War. Fifteen-year-old Jo's singularity is offset by her sisters' stock attributes: sixteen-year-old Meg is pretty; thirteen-year-old Beth is "good" and destined for martyrdom; twelve-year-old Amy is vain and slightly selfish. Departing from the cues of fiction by and for women of the day, Alcott refused to marry appealing, energetic Jo March to the neighborhood suitor, Laurie, who would have in any other novel been her match. When readers wrote to ask who the girls would marry, Alcott refused to endorse marriage as the only idea of female success, replying, "I won't marry Jo to Laurie to please any one." Jo rejects Laurie's proposal and marries the older and foreign teacher, Dr. Bhaer. Alcott's writing for children did not end with *Little Women*. Her next novel, *An Old-Fashioned Girl* (1870), was the story of a girl struggling to support herself in Boston as had Alcott herself; *Little Men* (1871) is set at the Plumfield School, run by Jo March and her husband; *Jo's Boys* (1886) finds Jo the wife of a college president.

Little Women encouraged many American writers to try their hand at family stories; one of the first and best results was *What Katy Did* (1872) by Susan Coolidge (Sarah Woolsey). *Five Little Peppers and How They Grew* (1881), by Harriet Lothrop, was another popular example. Coolidge later returned to the exploits of the Carr family in *What Katy Did Next* (1886), which describes a tour of Europe, *Clover* (1888), and *In the High Valley* (1890). Lucretia Hale published a series of comic stories in *St. Nicholas* about a fictional family named Peterkin. *The Peterkin Papers* was published as a book in 1880. The stories, told in deadpan fashion, recorded the stupidities of Mrs. Peterkin and her children, and the help they almost always enlist from "the lady from Philadelphia," who invariably rescues them with common sense. The stories are partly a satire on Boston society and its desire for self-improvement. Many of the women writers of the nineteenth century who were involved in social reform wrote children's fiction as well as material for adult consumption. Helen Hunt *Jackson wrote *Nelly's Silver Mine* (1878), the story of a sister and brother whose family moves to Colorado mining country. Sarah Orne *Jewett is famous for her strong, independent New England women, and wrote about girls with the same qualities in *The Country Doctor* (1884).

[*See also* Adolescence; Girlhood.]

• Joseph F. Kett, *Rites of Passage: Adolescence in America, 1790 to the Present* (1977). Mary Kelley, ed., *Woman's Being, Woman's Place: Female Identity and Vocation in American History* (1979). Patricia Meyer Spacks, *The Adolescent Idea: Myths of Youth and the Adult Imagination* (1981). Humphrey Carter and Mari Pritchard, eds., *The Oxford Companion to Children's Literature* (1984). Barbara A. White, *Growing Up Female: Adolescent Girlhood in American Fiction* (1985). Cathy Davidson, *Revolution and the Word: The Rise of the Novel in America* (1986).

Jill Wacker

1900 to the Present

Written, marketed, and most often purchased by people well past childhood, children's books represent adult fantasies about being young more than they reflect the experiences of children. Nevertheless, children often accept what their teachers and parents want them to believe: that they are or ought to be like the imaginary children in the books they read.

Furthermore, because of traditional assumptions about women's primary responsibility for children, most of the American adults who have been attracted to the business of writing, editing, selling, reviewing, and buying children's books throughout this century have been women. Consequently, the powerful images of childhood in children's books have most often been products of women's imaginations, and represent women's desire.

The fantasy children of American children's books come in three main types. The first is blissfully innocent, the second, dangerously ignorant. The third is an attempt to balance the other two. Not surprisingly, most representatives of the first type are male children, imagined by male authors. Understood as faith in one's power to be and to do whatever one likes, innocence is hard to distinguish from the American ideal of manhood. But the American ideal of womanhood has traditionally tempered that democratic ideal with a more gender-specific need for responsibility to others; and most of the books of the second type, from Sunday school parables of earlier decades to contemporary fables encouraging nonsexism and ecological correctness, have been produced by women.

These didactic books, by far the largest proportion of the literature produced for children in this century, always preach some version of the same message: the necessary limits of desire, the extent to which the delights of innocence might also be the dangers of ignorance. While the implied audience for that idea is usually children in general, the message resonates most profoundly in terms of our expectations for girls. But that doesn't mean there have been no utopian visions of innocent desire triumphant for girls.

At the beginning of the century, alongside popular adventure series about all-conquering males like the Outdoor Chums, the Khaki Boys, the Auto Boys, and the Hardy Boys were others about all-conquering females like the Girl Aviators, the Adventure Girls, the Khaki Girls, and the Motor Girls. While the authors' names on these books' covers were female, the texts of these volumes were often turned out by anonymous writers working from plot outlines. We can't know if they actually represent female desire. Nevertheless, Harriet Adams, daughter of the mass-market entrepreneur Edward Stratemeyer, claimed late in life to have been the Carolyn Keene credited with Stratemeyer's Nancy Drew series; and as the continuing popularity of Nancy Drew, who first appeared in 1930, reveals, these books do represent one version of desirable femininity.

Clever and attractive, Nancy solves crimes without mussing her stylish outfits or evoking anything but unqualified adoration from everyone she meets. The evildoers, meanwhile, tend to be disturbingly hairy males who speak in foreign and lower-class accents—nightmarish figures girls might desire and ought to fear.

The many books for girls about boys also offer both fulfillment of readers' utopian desires for self-indulgent triumph—in this case, romantic triumph—and messages about the dangers of desire. Maureen Daley's *Seventeenth Summer* (1942) celebrates almost the same version of male-besotted female adolescence that informs the widely read "teen romances" produced decades later, in the 1980s, in series like Sweet Valley High (created by Francine Pascal). In both cases, love, here defined as the wish to submit passively to the implacable male desire one has aroused, becomes acceptable only when its object is a safely "nice" boy, instead of a disturbingly exciting one from a different class or culture.

If romance fiction represents the accommodation of desire to social pragmatism, the novels produced for older children from the 1960s through the 1980s and identified as representing a "new realism" perform the opposite trick: they represent the accommodation of reality to the utopian desires of innocence. Each of the protagonists of these books faces just one real psychological or social problem: the onset of menstruation (Judy Blume's *Are You There, God? It's Me, Margaret*, 1970; obesity (E. M. Kerr's *Dinky Hocker Shoots Smack*, 1972); a growing awareness of one's homosexuality (Nancy Garden's *Annie on My Mind*, 1982). But while the novels offer practical advice, they are also classic wish-fulfillment stories: underdog children triumph over uncomprehending or repressive parents. Furthermore, they all offer the same solution to their various problems—a theoretically educational message that confirms a desire-requiting self-indulgence: to grow is to accept yourself as you already are.

Anne M. Martin's *Babysitter's Club* series, the best-selling children's books of the 1990s, if not of the century, also confirms self-acceptance as the correct response to just about any problem imaginable, from romance to cancer. But in these cynical times, psychological growth pales in comparison to what *really* matters: getting ahead in business. In their blissfully unfailing financial acumen, the Babysitters not only satisfy an intensely contemporary form of desire, they also represent role models for young entrepreneurs-in-the-making.

This combination of wish-fulfillment and business advice is merely the latest version of the most enduring characteristic of American women's writing for children. Boys in children's books by men often have adventures without learning anything but the rightness of their self-confidence; but in Nancy Drew and the Babysitters, in even the most utopian visions of female desire fulfilled, there is almost always a message. And more often than not, the message qualifies the desirability of desire fulfilled: even the cash-crazy Babysitters pay lip service to the idea that money can't buy happiness. As a result, the fantasy children in children's books by women almost all represent the third type outlined earlier: attempts to balance desire and didacticism.

The most characteristic stance of books written across the decades and for children of all ages is a nostalgia for that which the author nevertheless finds lacking—a celebration of the joys of childhood qualified by an insistence on the limitations of childlike perception. Thus, children's poets like Eve Merriam, Kaye Starbird, Myra Cohn Livingston, and Karla Kuskin often ask readers both to enjoy and see beyond the limitations of the childlike voices they evoke. The texts of picture books intended for the youngest audiences—from classics like Wanda Gag's *Millions of Cats* (1928), Margery Flack's *Story about Ping* (1933), Virginia Lee Burton's *Little House* (1942), and Margaret Wise Brown's *Runaway Bunny* (1942), through more contemporary tales like Judith Viorst's *Alexander and the Terrible, Horrible, No Good, Very Bad Day* (1972) and Ann Jonas's *The Quilt* (1984)—describe comfortingly cozy worlds in pleasurable rhythms; but they all imply or assert the danger of the childlike desires of innocent people, animals, or objects.

So do many novels. In the early years of the twentieth century, the qualified nostalgia emanated from books about deliciously ingenuous heroines: Kate Douglas Wiggin's *Rebecca of Sunnybrook Farm* (1904), Gene Stratton Porter's *Girl of the Limberlost* (1909), Eleanor Porter's *Pollyanna* (1913). While the innocent optimism of these girls delights everyone they meet, they must also learn the limitations of imaginative freedom: it can transform the world, but only when what they want to transform it into is a conservative idyll of domestic bliss.

A focus on the limitations of innocence continues in the most characteristic form of American women's writing for children through the decades—the nostalgic family story. Eleanor Estes's *The Moffats* (1941), Elizabeth Enright's *The Saturdays* (1941), Beverly Cleary's *Henry Huggins* (1950) and *Ramona and Her Father* (1979), E. L. Konigsburg's *From the Mixed-Up Files of Mrs. Basil E. Frankweiler* (1967), Ilse-Margaret Vogel's *My Twin Sister Erica* (1976) and *My Summer Brother* (1981)—all focus on young children making foolishly ignorant but endearingly innocent mistakes. While the children claim to learn from their errors, they usually manage to be innocent again in the next episode.

The conflict between pleasure in childhood innocence and the didactic urge to end it is characteristic of American women's writing for children because it is characteristic of American mothering. As *advice manuals have insisted throughout the century, mothers must both love children as they are and work constantly to change them into something better. Novels by women that focus on male children are particularly intense expressions of maternalism. They often work to undermine conventional images of machismo by celebrating boys who are less the dangerous males women supposedly find sexually attractive than the docile ones they would actually like to mother.

Novels as different as Paula Fox's nostalgic *One-Eyed Cat* (1984), Katherine Paterson's realistic *Come Sing, Jimmy Jo* (1985), and Madeleine L'Engle's science fictonal *Time Trilogy* (1979) describe boys considered effeminate or ineffectual by other youngsters, whose apparent weakness turns out to be a strength. Many other novels celebrate the taming of more traditionally masculine boys. In Virginia Hamilton's remarkable *M. C. Higgins, the Great* (1974), for instance, a backwoods boy turns from sitting in splendidly masculine antisocial isolation on top of the phallic pole erected by his father to the more communal (and traditionally female) task of holding his family together. Surprisingly often, the taming requires physical mutilation: in Marguerite d'Angeli's *The Door in the Wall* (1949), a crippling disease turns a medieval squire from macho knighthood to gentle musicianship, and in both Esther Forbes's tale of the American Revolution, *Johnny Tremain* (1943), and Ursula * Le Guin's fantasy, *Wizard of Earthsea* (1968), a cocky youngster undergoes accidental self-maiming as the first step in learning service to others.

The taming of male children takes an ugly turn in books by mainstream women that deal with foreign or minority children. In Elizabeth Foreman Lewis's *Young Fu of the Upper Yangtze* (1932), an American woman missionary persuades a Chinese boy that his traditional culture is repressively superstitious. Middle-class women perform the same culture-effacing miracle for African-American and Hispanic boys in works written by white women through the decades; in these colonizing books, as in Nancy Drew, being foreign is just a particularly unfortunate form of machismo.

If the taming of male children represents a maternal wish-fulfilment, the taming of female ones is less a matter of fantasy than a social imperative, and a battalion of tomboys learn to temper their independence with concern for others. The surprising thing about books as diverse as Laura Ingalls Wilder's nostalgic Little House series (1932–1943), Eleanor Cameron's fantasy, *Court of the Stone Children* (1973), and Cynthia Voigt's contemporary reworking of the Odyssey in terms of a young female Odysseus, *The Homecoming* (1981), is not that they sensibly balance freedom with responsibility; it's that they always start with independent girls instead of repressed ones, and therefore move to their happy endings by qualifying independence, rather than vice-versa. Surely most real children move in the opposite direction.

But not all tomboys get tamed. In her outrageous masterpiece *Harriet the Spy* (1964), Louise Fitzhugh craftily pushes her notebook-keeping protagonist toward what seems like the usual compromise between self-fulfilment and the needs of others—and then offers no compromise. The would-be writer Harriet keeps on writing, and learns no more than the subversive and useful skill of being just hypocritical enough to continue her work of expressing herself in safety.

Meanwhile, the African-American heroine of the white Fitzhugh's *Nobody's Family Is Going to Change* (1974) is one of the few black female protagonists of children's fiction who ends a story of defiance of adult values still defiant. When black girls in novels by African-Americans, such as Virginia Hamilton's *Arilla Sun Down* (1976) and *A White Romance* (1987), Rosa Guy's *Ruby* (1976) and *Edith Jackson* (1978), and Mildred Taylor's *Roll of Thunder, Hear My Cry* (1976), find their need for freedom hedged

by their perception of limits, it means something different, more pragmatically necessary, and more painful than when white characters are urged to make the same move. These books imply a revealing correspondence between the attitudes demanded by life in an intolerant society and conventional American ideals of femininity.

It is not surprising that the children's books American women have written in this century mirror the conflicts women have faced, both in their own self-definition as nurturers and in their definitions of the children they nurture. What is surprising is the range of uniquely pleasurable reading material they have produced while doing so: the utopian delights of Porter's *Girl of the Limberlost;* the technicolor exuberance of Forbes's *Johnny Tremain;* the delicious irony of Fitzhugh's *Harriet the Spy;* the simple but deeply resonant prose of Margaret Wise Brown's picture book texts; of Wilder's *Little House* series; of novel after astonishing novel by Virginia Hamilton. This brief roll call of excellence merely suggests the depth and range of a significant literary enterprise—surely one of the major triumphs of American women's writing.

• John Cech, ed., *American Writers for Children, 1900–1960* (1983). Alethea Helbig and Agnes Regan Perkins, eds., *Dictionary of American Children's Fiction, 1859–1959* (1985), *1960–1984* (1986). Donnarae MacCann and Gloria Woodard, eds., *The Black American in Books for Children,* 2d ed. (1985). Glen Estes, ed., *American Writers for Children since 1960: Fiction* (1986). Linnea Hendrickson, *Children's Literature: A Guide to the Criticism* (1986). Elizabeth Segel, " 'As the Twig Is Bent . . .': Gender and Childhood Reading," in *Gender and Reading: Readers, Texts and Contexts,* eds. Elizabeth A. Flynn and Patricinio P. Schweikart (1986). Perry Nodelman, "Children's Literature as Women's Writing," *Children's Literature Association Quarterly* 13 (Spring 1988): 31–34. Lissa Paul, "Enigma Variations: What Feminist Theory Knows about Children's Literature," in *Children's Literature: The Development of Criticism,* ed. Peter Hunt (1990). Peter Hunt, *Criticism, Theory and Children's Literature* (1991). Perry Nodelman, *The Pleasures of Children's Literature* (1992).

Perry Nodelman

CHILDRESS, Alice (b. 1920), playwright and author. The great-granddaughter of a slave, Alice Childress was born 12 October 1920 in Charleston, South Carolina. At the age of five her parents separated, and she was sent to live in Harlem with her maternal grandmother, Eliza White. Childress attended Public School 81, the Julia Ward Howe Junior High School, and Wadleigh High School, but she did not complete her secondary education. Both her mother and grandmother died, and she had to go to work to support herself. Largely self-educated, Childress attributes her success as a literary artist to female empowering: her grandmother Eliza urged her to write.

In 1941, Childress joined the American Negro Theatre in Harlem. By the decade's end she had written *Florence*, a one-act play that launched her writing career and led to her more than eighteen published and unpublished plays and five novels for adults and adolescents. She holds the distinction of being the only African-American woman whose plays have been written and professionally produced over four decades. One of her early plays, *Gold through the Trees* (1952), which deals with Africans who ultimately become slaves, was the first play by a black woman to be professionally produced on the American stage. Childress is also the first female playwright to win the Obie Award for the best original Off Broadway play (*Trouble in Mind*, 1955).

Childress primarily portrays the truthful experiences of the African-American female, void of stereotypes. Only two of her main works, *A Hero Ain't Nothin' But a Sandwich* (1973) and *Those Other People* (1989), feature male protagonists. Attacking the dramatic arts' neglect of the black female's story, Childress wrote in a 1966 essay, "A Woman Playwright Speaks Her Mind," that "the Negro woman has almost been omitted as important subject matter in the general popular American drama, television, motion pictures and radio." When depicted she is either "the constant but empty and decharacterized faithful servant" or the strong matriarchal figure, the black wife or mother who dominates and emasculates her husband and son. In Childress's plays, however, black women are strong and feminine.

Childress's work falls into three distinct phases. From 1949 until the mid-1960s, interracial conflicts inform *Florence* (1949), *Trouble in Mind* (1955), *Like One of the Family . . . Conversations from a Domestic's Life* (1956), and *Wedding Band* (1966).

In 1969–1970, Childress turned briefly to the exploration of intraracial conflicts in *Wine in the Wilderness* (1969), *String* (1969), and *Mojo: A Black Love Story* (1970). Probing the racial self, Childress indicts classism and white acculturation as artificial and destructive social appropriations that undermine collective acceptance and understanding among black people.

More at home with intraracial themes, Childress devoted the third phase—the decade of the 1970s and early 1980s—to plots involving and directed toward black children and adolescents: *The African Garden* (1971), *A Hero Ain't Nothin' But a Sandwich* (1973), *When the Rattlesnake Sounds* (1975), *Let's Hear It for the Queen* (1976), and *Rainbow Jordan* (1981). Their message, however, transcends racial boundaries. *A*

Hero Ain't Nothin' But a Sandwich and *Rainbow Jordan*, adolescent novels, examine the dangerous lures and pitfalls of inner-city life for young black teenagers.

A Short Walk (1979), although published two years before *Rainbow Jordan*, serves as a culmination of all three phases. *Those Other People* (1989) extends the exploration of racism and sexism to the sphere of young adults.

Being African-American, female, and a literary forerunner in examining and exposing the inequities of race, class, and gender at a time when integrationist fiction was in vogue did not enhance Childress's chances of receiving critical acclaim. Moreover, her unwillingness to compromise her art for commercial purposes or to make it more palatable to white audiences further hindered her rise to Broadway. Though Alice Childress has contributed much to American literature and theater, her name is seldom recognized by members of either fields. Even she refers to herself as "one of the best known of unknown persons."

• Alice Childress, "The Negro Woman in American Literature," *Freedomways* 6 (Winter 1966): 14–19; reprinted as "A Woman Playwright Speaks Her Mind," in *Anthology of the American Negro in the Theatre: A Critical Approach*, ed. Lindsay Patterson (1968), pp. 75–79. Gayle Austin, "Alice Childress: Black Woman Playwright as Feminist Critic," *Southern Quarterly* 25 (Spring 1987): 53–62. Alice Childress with Elizabeth Brown-Guillory, "Alice Childress: A Pioneering Spirit," *Sage* 4 (Spring 1987): 66–68. Elizabeth Brown-Guillory, *Their Place on the Stage: Black Playwrights in America* (1988).

La Vinia Delois Jennings

CHINESE AMERICAN WRITING. A literature defined by the ethnicity of its authors leads to complications as various as human vagaries. Intermarriage, for example, results in hybrids who are of two ethnicities. Which one should be considered the identifying ethnicity? Is this a matter to be left to individual choice? What if mixed-blood siblings make different choices? What if a person chooses a third ethnicity or nationality into which she has not been born or chooses the ethnicity that is only one-quarter her heritage and which does not show on her face? What about travel and changing residencies and naturalized citizenships? Should a particular text be classified as Chinese American by the "authenticity" of its "sensibility," by its language, by its the setting, by its theme, by the ethnicity of its characters? All these are questions with which the scholar of Chinese American literature must wrestle and which have been answered in various ways.

Though the terms *Chinese American* and *literature* have been multiply and controversially interpreted, Chinese American literature, simply and most inclusively defined, encompasses biography, autobiography, short stories, novels, poetry, and plays written by Americans of Chinese ancestry, as well as by Chinese residing in the United States. The texts may be written in Chinese or English. Although scholars such as Marlon Hom and Sau-ling Wong have worked on Chinese language texts, most of the texts themselves, as well as their scholarly and critical interpretations, have been written in English. The author may be an immigrant Chinese writing of experiences in China, such as Nien Cheng in *Life and Death in Shanghai* (1986), or an American-born Chinese American writing of experiences in the United States, such as Maxine Hong *Kingston in *The Woman Warrior* (1976). As with British and American literature, a specific text in itself, particularly an older one, may be of greater historic than aesthetic value, but its inclusion in the history and tradition of Chinese American literature provides a base by which to measure the growth and development of the field.

Although Chinese American literature has a hundred-year history dating almost as far back as Chinese people have been living in the United States, interest in this literature may be traced to the political and social events and movements of the 1960s and 1970s. This period saw a dramatic and widespread change of consciousness. The war in Vietnam was the third war in three decades that the United States fought in Asia, both with and against Asians. The daily sight of Asians on television as victims of gunfire and Asian homelands as sites of napalm bombings created complex, ambiguous reactions in many Asian Americans. Furthermore, the civil rights and women's liberation movements set the example for community coalition and self-definition. Such self-assertion ran directly counter to the Taoist philosophy of Lao Tze, of camouflage and "lying low," that had seen many Chinese in America through periods of extreme sinophobia. In this changed and charged atmosphere, Asian American students at San Francisco State University joined the Third World Coalition Student Strike in 1969, demanding courses relevant to their own history and culture. The strike lasted five months, and though hundreds were jailed, courses in Asian American studies resulted at San Francisco State University and on the Berkeley and Los Angeles campuses of the University of California. Publications began to appear tracing Asian American history, and in the early 1970s, three anthologies of Asian American literature marked the birth of a new field of research and production.

The first of these, *Asian American Authors* (1972), compiled by Kai-yu Hsu and Helen Pa-

lubinskas, included stories and poems by Chinese Americans, Japanese Americans, and Filipino Americans. In 1974, two additional anthologies appeared: *Aiiieeeee! An Anthology of Asian-American Writers*, edited by Frank Chin et al., and *Asian American Heritage: An Anthology of Prose and Poetry*, edited by David Hsin-fu Wand. Each editor differed in his definition of Asian American literature. Hsu and Palubinskas gave priority to an authors' citizenship and length of residence in the United States; Chin and his group required an "authentic Asian American sensibility," unadulterated by "racist" assimilationism. Wand's definition was the broadest, extending the boundary of Asian America to include the South Pacific. In the two decades since then, Asian American literature in all its branches has grown in both directions; the literature of the past is being continually uncovered, and new writers, encouraged by the critical and popular acclaim given such authors as Maxine Hong Kingston and Amy *Tan, are rapidly emerging.

As far as research has uncovered to date, Chinese American fiction began with the work of two Eurasian sisters, Edith Maud *Eaton (1865–1914), who published her stories under the pseudonym *Sui Sin Far, and her sister, Winnifred *Eaton (1875–1954), author of seventeen novels and hundreds of short stories under the pseudonym Onoto *Watanna. Daughters of an impoverished English landscape painter and his Chinese wife, both sisters were typists and journalists before they turned to writing fiction. Sui Sin Far's stories were the first by a person of Chinese ancestry to show the Chinese residents of North America in a sympathetic light, a stance that ran counter to the blatant sinophobia of the period. Her focus on Chinese immigrant women and children and on Eurasians introduced new subjects to American readers. In spite of the Chinese Exclusion Act of 1882, repeatedly renewed until its repeal in 1943, her stories were published in major national periodicals and collected in one volume, *Mrs. Spring Fragrance*, in 1912. Her correspondence indicates the existence of a novel in manuscript, which disappeared after her death.

Since Edith Eaton was already writing about the Chinese, and since the Japanese were much more highly regarded at the turn of the century, Winnifred Eaton chose to write stories with Japanese settings and Japanese characters and gave herself a Japanese persona to authenticate her work. Her first novel, *Miss Nume of Japan* (1899), was followed by sixteen others, most of which were best-sellers. *A Japanese Nightingale* (1901) went through three editions; sold two hundred thousand copies; was translated into Hungarian, Swedish, and German;

and was adapted for a Broadway production in 1903. Between 1924 and 1932, Winnifred Eaton wrote scripts for Hollywood film studios before retiring to Calgary, Alberta. Although her plots tended to be formulaic, her lively Japanese and Japanese Eurasian heroines, her exotic settings, her skillful portrayal of burgeoning love, and the twists and turns of her plots accounted for her striking successes. Her career and the camouflaging of her ethnicity provide an interesting barometer of the social climate and the popular taste of her day.

A group of pioneering Chinese American women students were encouraged in the 1920s and 1930s by the Department of English at the University of Hawaii to write about the Asian experience in Hawaii. The works of Gladys Li (pen name of Li Ling-Ai), "The Submission of Rosie Moy" (1928), "The Law of Wu Wei" (1929), and "The White Serpent" (1932), and Wai Chee Chun's "For You a Lei" (1937) and "Marginal Woman" (1937) are notable among these writers and plays.

In the period surrounding World War II, Americans needed to distinguish foes from allies, and this need may well account for the large number of books published by Chinese Americans and immigrants from China. The writer who dominated the scene throughout this period was Dr. Lin Yutang, who published nearly two dozen books, including novels, collections of essays, and translations. Although he lived for many decades in the United States and received his higher education there, Lin Yutang considered himself a spokesperson for China. Encouraged as children to write, his daughters, while still in their teens, collaborated on two books: *Our Family* (1939) and *Dawn over Chungking* (1941). Adet Lin, the eldest, went on to write a novel, a love story set in war-torn China, *Flame from the Rock* (1943). The second daughter, Anor, using the pen name her father gave her, *Lin Tai-yi, became a successful writer, publishing five novels. Her first, *War Tide* (1943), a brilliant piece of work, written when she was only seventeen, depicts the strength of the teenage daughter of a Chinese family in a China torn loose by war. Of her successive novels, only *The Eavesdropper* (1958) is partially set in the United States. It is the story of a Chinese in conflict as he moves back and forth between China and the United States. Her other novels, though all published in the United States, have only Chinese characters and Chinese settings: *The Golden Coin* (1946), *The Lilacs Overgrow* (1960), and *Kampoon Street* (1964).

Other immigrants from China published autobiographies and novels during this period. Journalist Helena Ching Ch'iu Kuo wrote *Peach Path* (1940), a collection of essays with a feminist slant; *I've Come a Long Way* (1942), tracing her life journey from a childhood in Macao to her arrival in the United States at the invitation of Eleanor Roosevelt; and *Westward to Chungking* (1944), a novel about the effects of war on a family in China. Mai-mai Sze, daughter of Ambassador Alfred Sze, published a poignant, existential autobiography, *Echo of a Cry* (1945), and a surrealistic novel, *Silent Children* (1948), about a band of homeless children surviving by wit and cunning in an imaginary country.

In contrast to books focused on war-torn China written by Chinese in America, American-born Chinese American Jade Snow *Wong's *Fifth Chinese Daughter* (1945) stands apart during this period as the unique story of a girl growing up in San Francisco's Chinatown in a family dominated by an extremely traditional Chinese father. Wong apologizes for her boldness in writing an autobiography at the age of twenty-four, and refers to herself in the third person in order to give honor to her father and to demonstrate that she has no ego as long as he is alive. Only after his death can she refer to herself by the first-person pronoun. The surface tone is polite and restrained; however, Wong's selection of details and anecdotes makes clear her awareness of sexism and racism, though she does not use these terms. Although much less outspoken and explicit in her expression of these conflicts than would be the writers of the 1970s and 1980s, and criticized by some in this later generation for the mildness of her tone, Wong's *Fifth Chinese Daughter* is certainly part of a major theme in Chinese American literature. The theme of identity and cultural conflict, introduced a generation earlier in the work of the Eaton sisters, became in Wong's book a model for the work of later authors like Maxine Hong Kingston and Amy Tan.

The 1950s and 1960s saw a continued predominance of work by Chinese in America rather than American-born Chinese Americans. Han *Suyin's *A Many-Splendored Thing* (1952), an extremely popular novel set in Hong Kong and depicting a Eurasian doctor and an English journalist, was purchased by Hollywood and, as a popular film starring William Holden and Jennifer Jones, gained an international audience. Although born in the United States, Diana *Chang spent her formative years in China, and her first novel, *Frontiers of Love* (1956), reflects this experience in its exploration of Eurasian identity in Shanghai during the Japanese Occupation. With one exception, Chang's later novels, all set in the United States, are not concerned with Chinese or Chinese American characters: the protagonists are all WASPs. By contrast, Hazel *Lin, who practices medicine in Jersey City, New Jersey, has set all four of her novels in China, from her first, *The Physicians* (1951), to her last, *Rachel Weeping for Her Children Uncomforted* (1976). Despite its Beijing setting, cross-cultural conflicts are in evidence in *The Physicians*, in that the heroine studies Western medicine against the wishes of her grandfather, a practitioner of Chinese medicine. At the novel's end, the two are reconciled when each learns that the medicine practiced by the other has knowledge complementary to his/her own.

Virginia Lee is notable as one of the first United States–born Chinese American women novelists, and her novel, *The House That Tai Ming Built* (1963), set in San Francisco in the early 1940s, continues the theme of interracial marriage introduced by Sui Sin Far (Edith Eaton) several decades earlier. In the period between Sui Sin Far's stories, set in the 1890s, and Virginia Lee's, set in the 1940s, nearly half the states in the nation had passed anti-miscegenation laws. California was one of these. Thus the interracial (Chinese/Caucasian) relationship in Lee's novel could only come to a tragic end. Although this novel, like Wong's *Fifth Chinese Daughter*, predated the era of outspoken protest, it makes a quiet statement about the indignity and injustice of anti-miscegnation laws.

Although there are still books by immigrants about life in China, most notably Eileen *Chang's novels, in the past three decades, literature focused on life in the United States and on the struggle to achieve a bicultural identity has experienced a virtual explosion in comparison to what came before. All genres seem to be flowering, and many texts have garnered prestigious national awards. Towering above all others, however, is the work of Maxine Hong Kingston, whose first book, *The Woman Warrior: Memoirs of a Girlhood among Ghosts*, won the National Book Critics Circle Award for Best Nonfiction of 1976. Four years later, Kingston's second book, *China Men*, won the American Book Award, and her latest, a novel, *Tripmaster Monkey* (1990), won the Pen West Award. In *The Woman Warrior*, Kingston explores the struggles of a young Chinese American woman to achieve a sense of self and coherence when caught between American traditions of independence and individualism and Chinese traditions of dependence and community responsibility. Building on the audience prepared by Kingston's work and by the feminist movement, Amy Tan's novels, *The Joy Luck Club* (1989) and *The Kitchen God's Wife* (1991), continue to explore the theme of generational struggle, as Chinese mothers and American daughters strive to understand each other. Gish

Jen's *Typical American* (1991) presents the comic side of a Chinese American family's efforts to attain the American Dream, while Fae Myenne Nq's beautifully pared-down novel *Bone* (1993) depicts a family's tragic struggles to come to terms with the suicide of one of its daughters.

Among poets, May Wong has three books: *A Bad Girl's Book of Animals* (1969), *Reports* (1972), and *Superstitions* (1978), although her work does not deal directly with Chinese American themes. Poets whose work does explicitly concern itself with these themes are Mei-mei Berssenbrugge, Fay Chiang, Marilyn Chin, Amy Ling, Kitty Tsui, and Nellie Wong.

In drama, Mei-mei Berssenbrugge has a one-act play about mother/daughter relationships entitled *One, Two Cups* (1974). Genny Lim has written several plays, one of which, *Paper Angels* (1991), about internees on Angel Island in San Francisco harbor, was produced on PBS television in 1985. And finally, Elizabeth Wong is a promising playwright whose *Letters to a Student Revolutionary* premiered in New York in 1991 and went on an international tour the following year. Her second play, *Kimchee and Chitterlings* (1993), treats a timely subject, the black boycott of Korean stores in New York. Both Lim and Wong are included in *Unbroken Thread: An Anthology of Plays by Asian American Women* (1993).

In addition to the exploration of a bicultural identity, another major theme in Chinese American literature is the retrieval and revisioning of Chinese American history. Kingston's *China Men*, for example, inverts the disparaging Chinese coolie image by describing as heroic labors the building of the Hawaiian sugar plantations and the construction of the transcontinental railroad. On the basis of this history, she counters the notion of Chinese as sojourners and aliens by emphasizing their claims as "founding fathers" of America. Ruthann Lum McCunn, in a fictionalized biography, *Thousand Pieces of Gold* (1981), demonstrates the heroism of a pioneering nineteenth-century Chinese woman homesteader, who had been abducted as a child, shipped across the Pacific, and sold as a slave on the auction block in the Far West. In *Sole Survivor* (1985), McCunn recreates the 133-day ordeal of the Chinese American sailor who holds the Guiness world record for survival at sea. In these revisions of history and stereotypes, Chinese Americans are finding their own voices, retrieving their past, and expressing the variety and complexities of their bicultural identities.

[*See also* Asian-American Writing; Assimilation; Citizenship; Ethnicity and Writing; Immigrant Writing.]

• David Hsin-fu Wand, *Asian-American Heritage: An Anthology of Prose and Poetry* (1974). Amy Ling, "A Perspective on Chinamerican Literature," *MELUS* 8, no. 2 (1981): 76–81. King-kok Cheung and Stan Yogi, *Asian American Literature: An Annotated Bibliography* (1988). Amy Ling, *Between Worlds: Women Writers of Chinese Ancestry* (1990). Frank Chin et al., eds., *The Big Aiiieeeee!* (1991). Shirley Lim and Amy Ling, eds., *Reading the Literatures of Asian America* (1992). King-kok Cheung, *Articulate Silences: Hisaye Yamamoto, Maxine Hong Kingston, Joy Kogawa* (1993). Roberta Uno, ed., *Unbroken Thread: An Anthology of Plays by Asian American Women* (1993). Sau-ling Cynthia Wong, *Reading Asian American Literature: From Necessity to Extravagance* (1993).

Amy Ling

CHINESE EXCLUSION ACT. *See* Citizenship; Immigrant Writing; Racism.

CHOI, Sook Nyul (b. 1937), novelist, memoirist, children's author. Born in Pyongyang, North Korea, Sook Nyul Choi immigrated to the United States in 1958 to further her education. After graduating from Manhattanville College, having studied European history, French, and art, she taught for nearly twenty years in New York City schools and reared two daughters. She now lives in Cambridge, Massachusetts, where she spends most of her time writing.

The harrowing experiences of her early childhood in Korea, first under Japanese colonial rule and then Russian domination, are recorded in her first book, *Year of Impossible Goodbyes* (1991). Both her grandfather and father were scholars and teachers of Korean history and Chinese and Korean literature; such teaching and scholarship, considered acts of sedition by the Japanese, brought them years of imprisonment and torture. Her three older brothers spent years in hard labor in Japanese camps. Her mother supervised a small factory on the family's property, manufacturing socks for the Japanese army. The young female workers from this factory were forcibly removed to serve as "comfort women" for the Japanese soldiers at the front. At age ten, Choi and her younger brother escaped from Russian-dominated North Korea, digging under the barbed wire of the 38th Parallel to the south. These events form the subject of *Year of Impossible Goodbyes*, fictionalized only in that names were changed and the brutality of the actual events was considerably softened. Written in a style both simple and eloquent, and relating a part of history unknown to most Americans, the book has attracted great attention from both young and adult readers, and has garnered positive reviews in major publications, national speaking engagements for the author, and numerous awards. The book has been translated into Korean and French.

A sequel, *Echoes of the White Giraffe* (1993), continues the story of Sookan, recounting her life in Seoul until the point of her departure for the United States. The author is at work on a third book, which will focus on Sookan's life in the United States. A forthcoming children's picture book, *Halmoni and the Picnic*, is Choi's response to the 1992 Los Angeles riots, her contribution to building bridges between races.

[*See also* Watkins, Yoko Kawashima.]

Amy Ling

CHOPIN, Kate (1850–1904), novelist and short fiction writer. Kate O'Flaherty, born 8 February 1850 into a bourgeois family in St. Louis, Missouri, had many of the prerequisites for literary achievement. She grew up in a community of women who stressed learning, curiosity, and financial independence; she shared girlhood reading and writing with a lively and intelligent best friend, Kitty Garesché; she received a rigorous education at the St. Louis Academy of the Sacred Heart, where literature and science were emphasized; and she was nurtured by a gifted high school teacher who recognized her writing talent.

Kate's parents, Eliza Faris and Thomas O'Flaherty, had married when Eliza was sixteen and Thomas thirty-nine, and after Thomas's death in a railroad accident when Kate was five, Eliza became a wealthy widow who never remarried. (In her 1894 work "The Story of an Hour," Chopin describes the sadness and exhilaration of a woman who hears that her husband has died in a railroad crash: she will miss him, but loves her freedom more.)

Young Kate's household was run by vigorous widows: her mother, grandmother, and great-grandmother, Victoire Charleville, who schooled Kate to love music, French, and gossip. There were also four slaves, and when the Civil War broke out at the time of Kate's First Communion (May 1861), the O'Flaherty household supported the Confederacy. During the war years, Kate was almost arrested for tearing down a Yankee flag on the porch; her great-grandmother and her half-brother, a Rebel soldier, both died; and her friend Kitty's family was banished for their Confederate sympathies. After the war, Madam Mary O'Meara, of the Sacred Heart nuns, assigned Kate to keep a commonplace book, in which the thoughtful adolescent recorded themes that appear in her later fiction, among them women's roles (homemakers vs. "blue stockings") and the conflict between desire (her "dear reading and writing") and duty (the "general spreeing" expected of a belle). Kate O'Flaherty graduated from the Sacred Heart Academy in 1868, and on 9 June 1870 married Oscar Chopin, the son of a Louisiana planter. Her diary of their three-month European honeymoon records her detailed, clever observations of women, houses, and food, as well as her own delight in walking, cigarette smoking, and solitude.

Kate Chopin had the gift, the discipline, and the early encouragement to be a writer, but marriage and motherhood filled her twenties and thirties. During the New Orleans years (1870–1879), she gave birth to five sons. Although she kept diaries and wrote long, entertaining letters, none of them survives. When Oscar's business failed, the Chopins moved to Cloutierville ("Cloochyville"), a tiny French village in Natchitoches ("Nak-i-tush") Parish in north Louisiana; there, Kate Chopin found the literary material she needed. She gave birth to her last child and only daughter, Lélia, in 1879 in Cloutierville, where she also amazed villagers with her flamboyant clothes and citified ways. Oscar owned a general store, and Kate listened avidly to their customers' dramatic stories. (The Chopins' Cloutierville house is now the Kate Chopin Home/Bayou Folk Museum.)

When Oscar died of malaria on 10 December 1882, he left Kate $12,000 in debt; but she came from a family of resourceful women. She sold some properties, successfully ran Oscar's remaining plantations, and had a scandalous romance with a married local planter, the charming but brutal Albert Sampite ("Sam-pi-tay"): he became the model for the character Alcée in several of her stories. Chopin left him and Cloutierville in 1884 to return to her mother's home in St. Louis; after Eliza O'Flaherty died a year later, Kate bought a new home, left the Catholic church, and began writing about Louisiana people, especially women in unhappy marriages.

Starting late—her first story, "A Point at Issue!," was published when she was thirty-nine—Kate Chopin was an instant success. Her first novel, At Fault (1890), about a Louisiana widow who loves a man married to another woman, drew national attention; her first short story collection, Bayou Folk (1894), was praised everywhere for its charm, local color, and deft characterization. Although her second collection, A Night in Acadie (1897), puzzled some readers with its decadent atmosphere and inconclusive stories, it was lauded by the critics Chopin admired most. Her prose style was always lucid and unadorned; her stories were ironic, lush, and sensual in a manner more French than American.

Meanwhile, she had become the center of St. Louis's literary colony, and each Thursday she held a salon at her home, where artists, editors, and literati would visit. Her friends included avant-garde, European-oriented women of the day, among them the journalist Florence Hayward, the translator Thekla Bernays, and the editor Rosa Sonneschein, founder of the American Jewess, to the first issue of which Chopin was the only gentile contributor.

When she published her second novel, The Awakening (1899), in which a Louisiana wife and mother has two lovers, Chopin was unprepared for its nationwide condemnation by male critics who found it "unwholesome." Although women, recognizing Chopin's celebration of women's individuality, wrote letters of praise and invited her to give readings, the men who controlled publishing made it clear that Kate Chopin should not publish what she knew of life and love and sinful desire.

Chopin never attempted to publish her most graphic short story, "The Storm" (eventually published in 1969); her publisher cancelled her last short story collection, A Vocation and a Voice (eventually published in 1991). In just thirteen years, Chopin had written nearly a hundred small pieces (short stories, essays, translations, poems, one play, and one polka), but after The Awakening's hostile reception, she wrote only eleven more stories before her death on 22 August 1904, of a cerebral hemorrhage. She was buried in St. Louis's Calvary Cemetery and mostly forgotten—until the 1960s, when a Norwegian scholar, Per Seyersted, rediscovered her.

Besides The Awakening, Chopin is now best known for stories about women who learn startling secrets about themselves and their men, especially "The Story of an Hour," "Désirée's Baby," and "At the 'Cadian Ball," and "The Storm." Some of her best stories are about women's friendships, among them "Odalie Misses Mass" (about a very old black woman and an adolescent white girl); "Lilacs" (depicting a Sacred Heart nun and a Parisian actress); and "Fedora" (a sly exploration of homophobia). She wrote gently and subtly about many social problems, including venereal disease ("Mrs. Mobry's Reason"); prostitution ("Dr. Chevalier's Lie"); and wife beating ("In Sabine"). Chopin is one of the few white writers of her day to write sympathetically about the anguish of black single mothers ("La Belle Zoraïde") as well as white ones ("Miss McEnders"). In many ways a writer ahead of her times, Kate Chopin is now a woman for all seasons.

• Chopin's personal papers are housed at the Missouri Historical Society, St. Louis; a few are also in the Cammie G. Henry Research Center, Eugene Watson Memorial Library, Northwestern State University, Natchitoches, Louisiana. Daniel S. Rankin, *Kate*

Chopin (1932). Per Seyersted, *Kate Chopin* (1969). Barbara Ewell, *Kate Chopin* (1986). Bernard J. Koloski, *Approaches to Teaching Kate Chopin's "The Awakening"* (1988). Emily Toth, *Kate Chopin* (1990). Lynda S. Boren and Sara deSaussure Davis, eds., *Kate Chopin Reconsidered: Beyond the Bayou* (1992).

Emily Toth

CIRCULATING LIBRARIES. *See* Libraries.

CISNEROS, Sandra (b. 1954), Chicana activist, poet, fiction writer. Cisneros was born in Chicago and grew up in Humboldt Park, Illinois, the only girl in a family of six boys. Her mother is Mexican-American and her father is from Mexico. She completed her undergraduate work at Loyola University and is a graduate of the writing program at the University of Iowa. She has been writer in residence at the University of Michigan in Ann Arbor, the University of California at Irvine, and the University of New Mexico in Albuquerque. Cisneros is the author of two collections of poems, *Bad Boys* (1980) and *My Wicked Wicked Ways* (1987). Her book *The House on Mango Street* (1984) won the Before Columbus American Book Award and was reissued by Vintage Contemporaries. *Woman Hollering Creek* (1991) is a collection of stories which, like *Mango Street*, concentrates on the Chicana experience in the United States.

In her writing, Cisneros explores and transcends borders of location, ethnicity, gender, and language. Location or "place" is a key element for understanding meaning, or ways of knowing, particularly for women. In *The House on Mango Street*, the narrator Esperanza Cordero is influenced just as much by an environment filled with poverty and racism (a Chicago barrio), as by the humor and warmth of her Chicana/o culture and neighboring community. To Cisneros, community is a bridge to selfhood. She relies on the Chicana experience of growing up with other women to dismantle the power sexism, racism, and classism have on influencing identity. To quote Gloria Anzaldúa, Cisneros "makes the invisible, visible" by centering the lives of Chicanas, their relationships with their families, their religion, their art, and their politics. The characters and situations she creates are complex and diverse, and reflect the multiplicity and not the stereotypes of the United States.

Cisneros writes in lyrical yet deceptively simple language. Her bilingualism enriches her stories and poems, exemplifying the varied experiences of women of Mexico and the United States. Disliking traditional forms of short stories, Cisneros's writing combines the sound of poetic language with oral story telling, creating her own innovative style with song, poetry, and prose.

Cisneros writes as a Chicana feminist, criticizing the academic or mainstream feminism for its racism: "A vagina is not enough to make someone my sister. A woman earns the right to be called my sister by learning my culture as well as I've learned hers" (*Elle*, August 1991). She concentrates not only on her writing, but also on the politics of publishing. Being published by a mainstream press is not a personal success as much as an opening for other Chicana(o) writers: "Any success by one of us is a collective success." To Cisneros, "our familia is our culture."

• Alvina Eugenia Quintana, "Chicana Discourse: Negations and Meditations," Ph.D. diss. (1990). Pilar E. Rodriguez Aranda, "On the Solitary of Being Mexican, Female, Wicked and Thirty-Three: An Interview with Writer Sandra Cisneros," *Americas Review* 18, no. 1 (Spring 1990): 64–80.

Robin Jones

CITIZENSHIP. In the post–World War II era, citizenship has assumed a narrower range of popular meaning in the United States. But as movements for civil rights and debates over immigration policy attest, citizenship has not lost its political relevance.

Judith Shklar writes: "There is no notion more central in politics than citizenship, and none more variable in history, or contested in theory" (*American Citizenship*, 1991). The meaning of citizenship that has achieved the greatest currency, but not the greatest significance, is associated with badges of political and economic power, specifically rights of voting and earning. This definition and Shklar's other three representations of citizenship ("citizenship as nationality, as active participation or 'good' citizenship, and . . . ideal republican citizenship") form the basic structure of this entry. Given American women's long struggle for equal political and civil rights, gender is a compulsory category of analysis for critiquing these notions of citizenship.

Despite its democratic tradition, the United States' bestowal of the rights and privileges of citizenship on women and minorities has often been illiberal. Throughout the pre-enfranchisement period, dissenting women challenged their gender's second-class citizenship, charging that it was a consequence of an oppressive patriarchy. Yet, the written record left by many of these protestors reveals that they still believed the functions of women's citizenship were complementary to rather than identical to that of men. In speaking of "woman's citizenship," they exalted difference while promoting equality.

This particular attribute of women's writings on citizenship, most pronounced before

1920, can be interpreted as an effort by disenfranchised women to claim public power and recognition as citizens despite their lack of conventional political influence. What emerges from this literature is an idealized image of the female citizen that capitalizes on woman's presumed superior moral authority as well as her biological and social maternal functions. In the early national period this popular model emerges as the "republican mother," the country's primary inculcator of moral values in America's youth. As Linda Kerber notes, "[m]otherhood was discussed almost as if it were a fourth branch of government" (*Women of the Republic*, 1980). Throughout the nineteenth and well into the twentieth century, republican motherhood reappeared in various contexts to serve popular appeals to female civic virtue and patriotism.

Circumscribed in their ability to vote, to serve in the military, or to hold public office, women aspiring to "good" citizenship were judged foremost by their personal rather than public affiliations. Citizen mothers were to train their male children to assume a public station with no female counterpart. From the Revolutionary to Second World War, patriotic rhetoric bade American women at home to sacrifice and labor for soldier sons and husbands. Suffragists defended their cause by arguing that they required the ballot to effectively fulfill their cardinal duty as women to protect domestic institutions. Other female reformers who overleaped the mythic boundary between the public and private spheres justified their activism with similar appeals to women's moral mission to preserve the home. Devotion, sacrifice, and virtue were chief attributes of the "good" citizen, but the institutions and services through which those characteristics were illumined depended on the sex of the actor.

The belief that a woman's public loyalties were extensions of private ties of affection or obedience contributed to the domestication of female citizenship and inhibited women's function as citizens. Thus, generations of woman suffragists had to combat the argument that giving women the vote would prompt a dramatic rise in the divorce rate, or that married women would not vote independently of their husbands. Champions of the Equal Rights Amendment proposed in 1923 were declared enemies of the family. That charge has never lost popular appeal. Perhaps the most overt legislative proclamation of woman's status as dependent citizen arrived in 1907, when the federal government ordered the expatriation of any American woman who married an alien. Lawmakers assumed that a woman could not

(and preferred not) to maintain her allegiance to the United States if she wed a foreign man.

The treatment of women of color under nationality law further compromised women's status as citizens. In the 1857 *Dred Scott v. Sanford* decision, the United States Supreme Court declared that African-Americans were not national citizens. The Fourteenth Amendment (1868) subsequently acknowledged native-born blacks' citizenship, but basic constitutional protections continued to be denied to racial minority groups. For Native Americans, who view themselves as sovereign peoples forced to function as wards of a foreign government, the meaning and implications of assuming United States citizenship have been very problematic. It should be noted, nevertheless, that the federal government did not recognize all Native Americans as United States citizens until 1924.

Nationality laws in effect from 1790 to 1952 maintained racial standards for naturalization, leaving many foreign-born women of color ineligible for American citizenship. Naturalization policy from 1907 to 1931 added to this burden of discrimination; with the exception of African-Americans, citizen women of color faced permanent forfeiture of their United States citizenship if they married alien men. They lost their status as Americans by marrying noncitizens and were thus rendered aliens racially ineligible for naturalization.

Much contemporary writing on women and citizenship serves as feminist critique of Western political theory or assessments of women's status based on the distribution of social and economic resources. Feminists such as Jean Elshtain have ventured to renew and defend the linkages between maternalism, virtue, and citizenship. Other commentators evoke liberal ideals to argue for a rights-based, nongendered theory of citizenship (which the proposed Equal Rights Amendment asserted). However, feminists such as Mary Dietz and Kathleen B. Jones have explored the limitations of liberalism's individualist definition of citizenship; and, for Marxist feminists, liberalism's conception of citizenship is too enmeshed in capitalism's patriarchal ideology to be valuable.

Women's writings on the meaning of citizenship are richly diverse and often polemical, expressive of the patriotism, pride, prejudice, disillusionment, anger, and vision women have experienced as American citizens. Their words remind us that citizenship, in theory and practice, has never truly been a gender-neutral concept.

[*See also* Assimilation; Immigrant Writing.]

• Catheryn Seckler-Hudson, *Statelessness: With Specific Reference to the United States: A Study in Nationality and Conflict of Laws* (1934). Carole Pateman, *The Disorder of Women: Democracy, Feminism and Political Theory* (1980). Jean Bethke Elshtain, *Public Man, Private Woman: Women in Social and Political Thought* (1981). Virginia Sapiro, "Women, Citizenship, and Nationality: Immigration and Naturalization Policies in the United States," *Politics and Society* (1984): 1–26. Mary G. Dietz, "Context Is All: Feminism and Theories of Citizenship," *Daedalus* 116 (Fall 1987): 1–24. Kathleen B. Jones, "Citizenship in a Woman-friendly Polity," *Signs* 15 (Summer 1990): 781–812.

Candice Lewis Bredbenner

CIVIL RIGHTS MOVEMENT, THE. The movement spans two decades of African-American history beginning in the mid-1950s, with the Montgomery Bus Boycott as one of its christening moments. Despite the fact that historians have generally focused on the role of male civil rights leaders, women, as writers and activists, shaped the boycott, as well as the civil rights movement as a whole. From the time of the civil rights movement's birth through the black power movement of the mid-1960s, African American women writers explored experiences of struggle in a literary movement that was matched only by the political gains of the era.

The period abuts the protest period, known for its naturalistic formations. Many of the themes of naturalism prevail in the civil rights texts. These writers considered the dynamics of *race, *ethnicity, environment, migration, sexuality, and *gender within the framework of the social changes of the period, whose dates are usually set between 1954 and 1955. However, since such historicism does not account for literary movement, which is more fluid than legalized notions of time, it is useful to consider those writers who published on the fringes of the period.

Many of the writers of this period, having published during the protest period of the 1940s, explored similar problems in the era of social change. Ann *Petry, author of *The Street* (1946), *Country Place* (1947), and numerous short stories and articles, examined the problems of interracial life in a white world in *The Narrows* (1953). Playwright Alice *Childress also spanned these moments in her work. Five years after she wrote *Florence* (1950), Childress's *Trouble in Mind* was the winner of the 1955–1956 Obie Award for the best original off-Broadway play. She addressed the same issues in *Like One of the Family: Conversations from a Domestic's Life* (1956). Zora Neale *Hurston was the last of the writers connected to the earlier period. Near the end of her career she published *Mule Bone* (1964), a drama coauthored by Langston Hughes. Due to copyright disagreements between Hurston and Hughes, this play was not produced during the period.

There were a number of African-American women writers who published for the first time in this era. Significantly, many continued to publish during the black power movement and beyond. Gwendolyn *Brooks, a novelist and playwright, drew from her own experiences to write *Maud Martha* (1953). The novel turns on the conflict of being an artist in a society that defines black womanhood in terms of domesticity. She also uses episodes of violence, marches, and martyrdom within the movement in a poetry collection, *Selected Poems* (1964). Paule *Marshall, drawing upon her experiences as a West Indian transplant in New York, produced more than any other woman writer of the period in both the novel and the short story form, including "The Valley Between" (1954), *Brown Girl, Brownstones* (1959), *Soul Clap Hands and Sing* (1961), "Reena" (1962), and "Gone Get Wasted" (1964). Of her publications, *Brown Girl, Brownstones* best encapsulates the experience of being doubly marginalized, as an immigrant and as a black woman.

Lorraine *Hansberry explodes in her portrayal of the Younger family in *A Raisin in the Sun* (1959). Winner of the New York Drama Critics Circle Award for the best play of the 1958–1959 theater season, *Raisin* was the first play written by an African American and only the fifth play written by a woman to be mounted on Broadway. Hansberry, whose father filed and won a suit against racially restrictive housing convenants in Illinois that was heard in the U.S. Supreme Court, tapped into the physical and mental aspects of such struggles in her portrayal of the Younger family's attempts to move beyond the confines of the ghetto. Hansberry continued to develop these themes in *The Movement: Documentary of a Struggle for Equality* (1964) and *The Sign in Sidney Brustein's Window* (1965). Her work beyond this period included the posthumously published *To Be Young, Gifted and Black* (1969), which drew on the energy and thematic concerns of the early 1960s.

Jane J. Phillips's *Mojo Hand* (1960) is one of the first texts to be included in the black literature offerings of the 1960s. This, Phillips's only published effort, was written while the author was in jail in North Carolina at the height of the civil rights demonstrations. Drawing on both the blues and the "orphic tale," as the novel's subtitle indicates, Phillips used poetic language to construct a novel about the need for African-American women to define the self in the midst of social upheaval. Playwright Adrienne *Kennedy also posed questions about the black self in *Funnyhouse of a Negro* (1962) and *A Rat's Mass* (1965).

African-American women writing during the civil rights movement considered how questions of identity evolve in an era of social disruption. As such, their writings reflected the concerns of African-American women of that historical moment. Through their writings, they drew attention to the limitless possibilities of African-American female subjectivity in their texts and provided a context from which the writings of the late 1960s could grow.

Sheila Smith McKoy

CIVIL WAR. Mention the Civil War to most Americans, and they will envision men in blue or shades of gray, marching, fighting, dying. Mention Civil War fiction and no doubt it will also be mostly men who come to mind, writers such as Stephen Crane, Ambrose Bierce, perhaps William Faulkner, or even Charles Chesnutt. Historically, women and war, and by extension, women and war fiction, have been seen as fundamentally opposing terms: woman's place, both in fact and in fiction, was (and often still is) perceived to be not the front but the homefront.

And yet, of course, there were numerous women who witnessed, participated in, survived, and wrote about the war between the North and the South. Margaret * Mitchell's *Gone with the Wind* (1936) is not the only proof that this is so. Although Mitchell's riveting story—especially after its dramatization on the big screen—represents for many citizens the quintessential Civil War novel, it is but one story, and Mitchell but one of many women storytellers.

Most of the women who wrote made explicit the profound connections between the two fronts—home and war—proving the war to be truly a domestic conflict. Many women writers took up their pens as weapons on behalf of their side's cause. For example, Harriet Beecher * Stowe's *Uncle Tom's Cabin* (1852) evangelized against southern slavery and was praised by President Lincoln, only half jokingly, as the book that "made this great war."

Other writers documented the war's effect on those left at home; Louisa May * Alcott's *Little Women* (1868; 1869), for instance, traces the March girls' struggles to endure a variety of hardships while their father is off preaching at the front. Although Mr. March eventually survives and returns to his "little women," in Alcott's *Work, A Story of Experience* (1873) the protagonist's boss dies in combat, leaving the heroine to take charge of business at home.

Works such as Alcott's are representative in suggesting that wartime victories, struggles, and casualties were not limited to the battlefield.

Writing from and for the South, Mary * Chesnut explored her innermost thoughts and the intimate details of Confederate life in her often-excerpted diaries. Southern novelists such as Augusta Evans, Mary Virginia Terhune, and Caroline Gilman frequently used fiction to educate Northerners about the South, vilify Northern customs, and defend, even glorify, the peculiar institutions and charms of the Southern way of life.

For writers such as Harriet * Jacobs and Frances * Harper, what was peculiar was that anyone could find charms in a system that objectified and oppressed other human beings because of the color of their skin. Writing before emancipation, Jacobs bore witness to the horrors of slavery in *Incidents in the Life of a Slave Girl* (1861).

Although Harper's *Iola Leroy* (1892) is set in part during wartime, as Elizabeth Young has argued, the novel actually contains no battle scenes. Rather, the war serves as the context through which Harper underscores the heroism of the black men who fought for freedom, and places black women—as mothers, nurses, and the glue that holds families together—at the center of both the conflict and its resolution.

Fiction about the Civil War continues to be generated even after many of those who actually lived through it have died. Recently, in *Beloved* (1987), Toni * Morrison chose the years surrounding the Civil War as the setting for her exploration of the extremes of maternal love. Sharing with Harper a belief in the powerful bonds between mother and child, Morrison gives a compelling account of how an institution like slavery can so pervert such bonds that the ultimate act of mother love becomes the murder of one's own children.

With so many rich narratives about the Civil War by women authors, why have they been virtually ignored in classrooms, in studies such as Edmund Wilson's *Patriotic Gore: Studies in the Literature of the Civil War* (1962), and in anthologies, including *Classics of Civil War Fiction* (1991)? Broadly speaking, it may very well be that the historical gendering of war is so excessively masculine that "feminine" narratives, perspectives, and experiences not only are, but must be, excluded. According to this logic, not only is war to peace what man is to woman, but war is to man as peace is to woman. Judging by these culturally produced syllogisms, women who fight in, fight for, and/or write about war are, quite simply and wrongly, acting like men.

And yet, "acting like men" is not uncommon

during war time: think of the Rosie the Riveters who so skillfully handled "men's jobs" during World War II. Such role reversals are not uncommon themes in women's Civil War fiction. As Margaret Higonnet suggests, with men away, the women (real and fictional) left behind were forced to become heads of households, "masters" of plantations, and both emotional and material providers. In many women's Civil War novels, the women who take on such roles succeed admirably, even though not a few simultaneously insist that they are eager to rescind them when their men come marching home.

The question of what kind of homes the men would return to is central to many of these fictional works. As Kathleen Diffley contends, the Civil War itself may have been less about a "house divided" than a "house invaded," in that the North's victory was in large part due to the control and plundering of Southern homes. *Gone with the Wind* stands as testament to such an invasion and its consequences, as do the later novels of Ellen Glasgow, which explore the spiritual and literal destitution of the once proud Dixieland.

All told, most of these women's novels expand the definition of war to include the home front. As such, their stories put dual emphasis on both "civil" and "war" and suggest that, ultimately, it is this awkward coupling of civility and bloodshed, more than the pairing of women and war, that proves the real contradiction in terms.

[*See also* Abolition; Slavery; Southern Women's Writing; Underground Railroad.]

• Margaret R. Higonnet, "Civil Wars and Sexual Territories," in *Arms and the Woman: War, Gender, and Literary Representation*, eds. Helen M. Cooper, Adrienne Auslander Munich, and Susan Merrill Squier (1989), pp. 80–95. Kathleen Diffley, "Where My Heart Is Turning Ever: Civil War Stories and National Stability from Fort Sumter to the Centennial," *American Literary History* 2, no. 4 (Winter 1990): 627–658. Elizabeth Young, "Warring Fictions: *Iola Leroy* and the Color of Gender," *American Literature* 64, no. 2 (June 1992): 273–297.

Cynthia J. Davis

CIXOUS, Hélène. *See* French Feminism.

CLARKE, Cheryl (b. 1947), essayist, critic, short fiction writer, editor, and poet. Born in Washington, D.C., Cheryl Clarke has become one of the most influential African-American lesbian activists and authors of the present day. Her books of poetry include *Narratives: Poems in the Tradition of Black Women* (1982), *Living As a Lesbian* (1986), and her most recent volume, *Humid Pitch: Narrative Poetry* (1989).

These books, along with her two essays, "Lesbianism: An Act of Resistance" in *This Bridge Called My Back* (1982) and "The Failure to Transform: Homophobia in the Black Community" in *Home Girls* (1983), confront and examine both homophobia in the African-American community and racism in the too often predominantly white gay and lesbian community. Clarke writes with anger and irony about being caught on the cultural borders because she is both African-American and lesbian. At the same time, her works envision an African-American gay and lesbian movement.

Cheryl Clarke is one of the most widely anthologized African-American lesbian authors. Her short story "Women of Summer" in *Home Girls* juxtaposes the harsh realities of growing up African-American and lesbian in the inner city with the different realities of being African-American and lesbian in a small town in the South. In this story she explores different levels of racism encountered throughout the United States, and presents a final vision of empowerment for the African-American lesbian.

In addition to her essays, poetry, and short fiction, Clarke also served on the editorial collective for the journal *Conditions* from 1981 through its final issue. She has also written reviews for *Conditions* and *Sinister Wisdom*.

Clarke's latest book of poetry, *Humid Pitch*, focuses particularly on the subject of the Diaspora and all of its metaphoric implications for both the author and other African-American gays and lesbians. Through such writing, which becomes political activism, Clarke continually attacks both racism and homophobia in the United States' societal structure.

The writings of Cheryl Clarke have greatly expanded and influenced the scope of lesbian writing, which historically has been primarily Anglo-centered. Clarke's poetry and essays are an important part of forming what will become a broad base of African-American lesbian theory, for not only are her works creative, but they carry with them theoretical and political messages about how we must all work together to shape a diverse, multicultural future if we are not only to survive, but to flourish.

Ardel Thomas

CLASS.
1930s * Proletarian Writing. During the Depression, working-class writing was identified as "proletarian." During this period of heightened class consciousness in the U.S., many Leftists envisioned art's immediate task as helping to build an American working-class movement. To put matters simply, Left literary debates during the 1930s were shaped out of two distinct

sets of assumptions about the possibility of "proletarian art." Although there were many differences about the particulars of their views of art, one group of writers, many of them associated with *New Masses*, the American Communist Party's literary journal, assumed that proletarian art was not only possible, but imminently realizable. Some, but by no means all, *New Masses* contributors argued that would-be proletarian writers must reject modern bourgeois experiments with form and develop new, unborrowed forms for proletarian literature. Such a belief led them to propose techniques that would clearly distinguish proletarian art from bourgeois art. Another group of writers, many of whom clustered around *The Partisan Review*, considered it necessary to explore those techniques of bourgeois literature that could most productively be borrowed and adapted to the purposes of a working-class literature. Despite these fundamental tensions, from roughly 1928 to 1935 the American Communist Party (CP) promoted what it referred to as "proletarian culture."

As part of its focus on working-class writing, the CP also promoted *reportage, a generic sibling of proletarian realism. A form of journalism, reportage attempted to detail Depression conditions from the perspective of those most acutely suffering them—the hungry, unemployed, and homeless. *Reportage, which was published by *The Nation* and *New Republic* in the early 1930s, was a mainstay in *The Working Woman*, a CP publication, although *The Working Woman* (1929–1935), along with its successor, *Woman Today* (1936–1937), have been nearly obliterated from America's cultural memory.

During this period, however, the literary world, even on the Left, was chiefly a male preserve. Men generally staffed editorial boards of Leftist journals of literature and criticism, although a few women writers, like Meridel *Le Sueur, Josephine *Herbst, and Grace Lumpkin, contributed regularly. While Daniel Aaron, James Burkhart Gilbert, and Richard Pells have contributed valuably to the history of literary radicalism, they focused on "the head boys," to borrow Herbst's term (*Proletarian Writers of the Thirties*, edited by David Madden, 1968), and on the period's most prominent Left publications, such as the *Daily Worker, New Masses,* and *Partisan Review*. For the writings of women and people of color, we must also examine more obscure Left journals from the period; in *Labor and Desire* (1991; pages 186–187), Paula Rabinowitz provides a useful list of now-eclipsed Left journals from the period.

Michael Gold, probably America's best-known Communist writer and critic during the early 1930s, challenged proletarian writers (in "Notes of the Month," *New Masses*, September 1930) to "write with the courage of [their] own experience." Addressing himself to machinists, sailors, farmers, weavers, tanners, ditch-diggers, and hobos, Gold thought he was speaking broadly, inclusively. Ironically, it is as if women writers such as Tillie *Olsen, Le Sueur, and Herbst took Gold at his word and wrote "with the courage of [their] own experience." It is as if they knew that the man on an East Side soap-box whose revolutionary oratory awakened the boy at the end of Gold's autobiographical novel *Jews Without Money* (1930) was, in Gold's actual experience, a woman (Elizabeth Gurley Flynn, then a Wobbly orator). Many 1930s working-class women writers subverted the party's productivism and *sexism, legitimating the point of *re*-production. These women writers implicitly questioned the Marxist theory of the primacy of production, which defines production as *the* distinctively human activity and encodes activities carried out in the home, to which women have historically been disproportionately consigned, as less valuable than men's outside it. Yet writers such as Olsen and Le Sueur acknowledge a tremendous debt to the party for fostering their writing; indeed, Le Sueur credits it for her very survival as a writer. Moreover, the party's John Reed Clubs, in existence from 1932–1934, warmly encouraged working-class writers, including women writers such as Le Sueur and Olsen.

Neither those affiliated with the Party nor those on the anti-Stalinist Left had been prepared for the complexity of history's unfolding events. The Moscow Trials (1936–1938) and the Nazi-Soviet Non-Aggression Pact (1939) brought on a debilitating disillusionment. By the end of the decade, proletarian literature became the subject of a number of obituaries, and proletarian literature was, in effect, blacklisted for decades.

Recent Attention to Working-Class Women's Writing. We now have in print a discrete body of work that can be identified as writing by or about U.S. working-class women. However, I must preface my discussion of some of the working-class writing now available to us by suggesting that working-class writing has, potentially, far broader categorical parameters than many people recognize—and far broader parameters than, in the interest of economy, I can employ in this entry. Working-class writing often coincides with other literary categories; frequently, writings by Euro-American women, people of color, and ethnic minorities also qualify as "working-class," even though readers and critics usually identify the texts only in terms of *gender, *race, or *ethnicity. For example, anthologies such as *This Bridge Called My Back: Writings by Radical Women of Color* (1983), edited by Cherríe Moraga and Gloria Anzaldúa, and *Making Face, Making Soul/Haciendo Caras* (1990), edited by Anzaldúa, illuminate ways in which race, ethnicity, and sexual orientation intersect with class to produce distinctive narratives of working-class women's lives. And writing by immigrants such as the Jewish writer Anzia *Yezierska is often "working-class" as well as "ethnic" or *"immigrant" writing. Conversely, *Calling Home: Working-Class Women's Writing* (1990), edited by Janet Zandy, features many women of color as well as white working-class women, lesbians as well as heterosexuals, and could be as accurately termed a "multicultural" anthology as a "working-class" anthology. In *Sex, Class, and Culture* (1978; 1986), Lillian Robinson rightly argues that working-class women's writing "gives form to the experiences of the *majority* of women" (emphasis added).

The Feminist Press, founded in 1970 by Florence Howe and Paul Lauter, has a distinguished history of publishing and reprinting working-class women's writing, including, among numerous other titles, Rebecca Harding *Davis's *Life in the Iron Mills*, the first significant portrait in U.S. literature of industrial workers' lives (1861; 1972; a 1985 edition contains additional stories by Harding Davis); Agnes *Smedley's *Daughter of Earth* (1929; 1973; 1987); *Women Working: An Anthology of Stories and Poems* (1979), edited by Nancy Hoffman and Florence Howe; Paule *Marshall's *Brown Girl, Brownstones* (1959; 1981) and *Reena and Other Stories* (1984); Meridel Le Sueur's *Ripening: Selected Work, 1927–1980*, edited by Elaine Hedges (1982; 1990); Josephine Herbst's *Rope of Gold* (1939; 1984); and *Writing Red: An Anthology of American Women Writers, 1930–1940* (1987), edited by Charlotte Nekola and Paula Rabinowitz.

West End Press, largely through the efforts of John Crawford, has since 1976 published and reprinted working-class women's writing, including Le Sueur's; and Arno Press has reprinted, among other working-class women's writing, two of Herbst's novels, *Money for Love* (1929; 1977) and *Nothing Is Sacred* (1928; 1977). The ILR Press (the press of the School of Industrial and Labor Relations at Cornell University) has begun a Literature of American Labor Series that includes Theresa Serber Malkiel's *The Diary of a Shirtwaist Striker* (1910; 1990). A note in texts published in the ILR series explains its purpose: to "bring back into print some of the best literature that has emerged from the labor movement" in the U.S. and Canada. "We are defining literature broadly," the note continues,

to include "novels, biographies, autobiographies, and journalism."

Tillie Olsen's *Tell Me a Riddle* (1961) and *Yonnondio: From the Thirties* (1974) are prominent among working-class texts. Moreover, Olsen has tirelessly encouraged and promoted working-class women writers—with poet Linda McCarriston (*Eva-Mary*, 1991) and fiction-writer Fae Myenne Ng (*Bone*, 1993) providing only two recent examples. Other noteworthy texts by working-class women writers include Harriette *Arnow's *The Dollmaker* (1954; 1972); Meredith Tax's *Rivington Street* (1982); Bobbie Ann *Mason's fiction, including *Shiloh and Other Stories* (1982) and *In Country* (1985); Carolyn Chute's *The Beans of Egypt, Maine* (1985) and *Letourneau's Used Auto Parts* (1989); Denise Giardina's *Storming Heaven* (1987) and its sequel, *The Unquiet Earth* (1992); and Dorothy Allison's *Trash* (1988) and *Bastard Out of Carolina* (1992).

The Politics of Literature: Dissenting Essays on the Teaching of English (1973), edited by Louis Kampf and Lauter, raised issues still relevant for readers and critics of working-class writing, who are "up against the great tradition," to borrow the title of one of the collection's essays. And since its inception in 1975, the journal *Radical Teacher* has consistently supported working-class studies, as has the Modern Language Association's Radical Caucus. Since 1968 the Caucus has organized convention sessions addressing working-class concerns, including working-class women's writing.

The pioneering work of the Feminist Press, *Radical Teacher*, and the Radical Caucus has been furthered by collections such as *Working Classics: Poems of Industrial Life*, edited by Peter Oresick and Nicholas Coles (1990), and essays such as Coles's "Democratizing Literature: Issues in Teaching Working-Class Literature" (*College English*, November 1986) and Pam Annas's "Pass the Cake: The Politics of Gender, Class, and Text in the Academic Workplace" (*Working-Class Women in the Academy: Laborers in the Knowledge Factory*, edited by Michelle Tokarczyk and Elizabeth A. Fay [1993]). Moreover, biographies of Herbst (by Elinor Langer, 1984), Agnes Smedley (by Janice R. and Stephen R. MacKinnon, 1988), and Mary Heaton Vorse (by Dee Garrison, 1989) have appeared. Both *Radical Teacher* and *Women's Studies Quarterly* are currently preparing special issues devoted to working-class studies.

Such publications signal that working-class writing may be emerging as a visible, if not yet "legitimate," category of literary studies. Promoting working-class writing is linked to and extends the efforts of those expanding the literary *canon and examining the aesthetic and political bases on which it is constructed; it is also linked to the published or current work of scholars re-visioning the 1930s, including James Bloom, Barbara Foley, Laura Hapke, James Miller, Cary Nelson, David Peck, Rabinowitz, Deborah Rosenfelt, Jon Christian Suggs, Harvey Teres, and Alan Wald. Among other pertinent works, the following may be cited: *Revisioning Thirties' Culture*, edited by Sherry Lee Linkon and Bill V. Mullen, forthcoming from the University of Illinois Press; a series of reprints, also forthcoming from Illinois, titled "The Radical Novel in the U.S. Reconsidered" (Alan Wald, series editor); and Constance Coiner's *Better Red* (Oxford University Press, 1995).

In "Working-Class Women's Literature—An Introduction to Study," a pioneering essay first appearing in *Radical Teacher* (1979) and later reprinted in *Women in Print I* (1982), Paul Lauter deliberately employs "relatively loose definitions" and "broad categories" for working-class literature. He discusses texts "by *and* about the working class," written and oral forms, "high," "popular," and "mass" culture. He designates as members of the working class "those who sell their labor for wages; who create in that labor and have taken from them 'surplus value,' to use Marx's phrase; who have relatively little control over the nature or products of their work; and who are not 'professionals' or 'managers.'" Lauter refers "to people who, to improve their lot, must either move in *solidarity* with their class or leave it (for example, to become managers)," and he includes not only factory workers but also slaves, farm laborers, and those who work in the home. Zandy draws on Lauter's definition in her introduction to *Calling Home*, but since the anthology's publication Zandy has said she limits her attention largely to writings that evince a working-class *consciousness*.

To legitimate working-class literature, we need a broader definition of "literature." As Martha Vicinus has observed in her study of British working-class writing, *The Industrial Muse* (1974), "what we call literature, and what we teach, is what the middle class—and not the working class—produced. Our definitions of literature and our canons of taste are class bound; we currently exclude street literature, songs, hymns, dialect and *oral story telling, but they were the most popular forms used by the working class." Lillian Robinson also unmasks the class-bound nature of what universities consider "literature" and calls for "a radical redefinition" of the term. She offers an alternative standard for literature, shocking for its simplicity and its revolutionary implications: It "should help us learn about the way things are,

in as much depth and fullness as possible and by any means necessary."

While there are differences among the few scholars attempting to theorize working-class writing, they generally share the recognition that canonical views of the nature and status of "literature" have seriously impeded attempts to understand and value working-class discourse. These scholars have variously argued that we must look through something other than aesthetic lenses when evaluating working-class writing. I suggest that all these scholars are looking through various pragmatic lenses: that is, not unlike their 1930s predecessors, they are looking at connections between discourse and society, asking, among other questions, how society shapes discourse and how discourse shapes society. To avoid the trap of trying to evaluate writings by the very standards those writings challenge, we should examine those works and ways of reading them, not from an aesthetic perspective, but from a pragmatic one.

Long-standing principles of aesthetic reading practices aim to assure that individual readers become passive receivers and appreciators of canonical discourses and the cultural values they embody, and of "aesthetic" devices peculiar to an "elevated" literary realm. Pragmatic reading strategies, on the other hand, require close scrutiny of language structures such as figuration—but structures viewed not as *aesthetic* components but as tools with which writers and readers make texts do various sorts of social or cultural work. Denoted by "cultural work" is the work any text does, implicitly or explicitly, to support or subvert the dominant culture. (Both supporting and subverting elements are often present in any text, even one clearly intent on subversion.) The working-class discourse with which some of us are concerned disrupts passivity by demanding that readers become active interrogators of texts and cultural values, at times questioners and critics of meanings, at times participants in constructing meaning. Most scholars theorizing working-class writing are concerned with formal experiments as they attempt to subvert traditional notions of bourgeois individualism and promote collective social change.

Because theorizing working-class women's writing at points coincides with the materialist-feminist approach to culture outlined in Judith Newton and Deborah Rosenfelt's introduction to *Feminist Criticism and Social Change* (1985), it is a good starting point for approaching working-class women's writing. Working-class studies, committed as much to historic and economic concerns as to *gender relations, often lies within the province of materialist-feminism, opposing the flight from history evident in much literary theory. Scholars approaching working-class writing have often done so dialectically, embracing contradictions and locating "in the same situation," as Newton and Rosenfelt have put it, both "the forces of oppression and the seeds of resistance."

The Obfuscation of Class as a Category of Literary Analysis. Whereas many 1930s intellectuals mistakenly subordinated all social issues to those of class, at this historical juncture class is not a fashionable category of analysis among literary critics. Despite its place in the now-familiar list—race, gender, class, ethnicity, and sexual orientation—class is often the least addressed of these issues.

While some teachers and students rightly exert pressure on literature departments to consider gender, race, and sexual orientation as interpretive categories and to include texts by women, people of color, and gays and lesbians in college courses, few protest exclusions based on class. Indeed, few students seem even to *see* class markers, typically identifying Rita Mae *Brown's *Rubyfruit Jungle* (1973), for example, as a "lesbian," but not also as a "working-class" novel; Sandra *Cisneros's *Woman Hollering Creek* (1991) as both "Latina" and "women's" short stories but not additionally as "working-class" texts; Ann *Petry's *The Street* (1946) or Alice *Walker's "Everyday Use" (1973) as both "African-American" and "women's" writing but not as "working-class" fiction as well. Even so, reading and analyzing multicultural working-class writing encourages alliances across identities of race, ethnicity, gender, and sexuality and fosters a political consciousness capable of decoding the middle-class myth and building coalitions to give ordinary people better life chances.

[*See also* Proletarian Writing.]

• Walter Rideout, *The Radical Novel in the United States 1900–1954* (1956; reprint 1992). Jayne Loader, "Women in the Left, 1906–1941: A Bibliography of Primary Sources," *University of Michigan Papers in Women's Studies* 2 (1975): 9–82 (catalogued in libraries under the series title). Paul Lauter, "Working-Class Women's Literature—An Introduction to Study," *Women in Print I,* eds. Joan E. Hartman and Ellen Messer-Davidow (1982). Cherríe Moraga and Gloria Anzaldúa, eds., *This Bridge Called My Back: Writings by Radical Women of Color,* 2nd ed. (1983). Mari Jo Buhle, *Women and the American Left: A Guide to Sources* (1983). Janet Zandy, ed., *Calling Home: Working-Class Women's Writing* (1990). Paula Rabinowitz, *Labor and Desire: Women's Revolutionary Fiction in Depression America* (1991). Laura Hapke, *Tales of a Working Girl: Wage-Earning Women in American Literature, 1890–1925* (1992). Jon Christian Suggs, *American Proletarian Culture: The Twenties and Thirties,* vol. 11 of the Documentary Series of the *Dictionary of Literary Biography* (1993).

Constance Coiner

CLASSICAL MYTHS. *See* Myths.

CLIFF, Michelle (b. 1946), poet and prose writer. An American citizen who was born in Kingston, Jamaica, Cliff was educated at Wagner College (A.B., 1969) and the Warburg Institute in London (M. Phil., 1974). The international flavor of her work stems from her identification as a light-skinned Jamaican woman, a product of the pressures of both British colonialism and American racism. In her writing, Cliff questions the roles of both the privileged and the victimized within the anglocentric patriarchy.

In 1969 Cliff worked as a researcher and journalist in New York City; in 1970 she became production supervisor of the Norton Library Series, and by 1979 was a manuscript and production editor of the series, specializing in history, politics, and women's studies. In 1980 Cliff published her first collection of poems, *Claiming an Identity They Taught Me to Despise.* From 1981 through 1983, she was copublisher and editor of *Sinister Wisdom,* a lesbian feminist journal. With fellowships from the MacDowell Colony and the National Endowment for the Arts in 1982, and the Massachusetts Artists Foundation and the Yaddo Writers Colony in 1984, she wrote both poetry and fiction. *Abend: A Novel* appeared in 1984, followed three years later by its sequel, *No Telephone to Heaven.* This project, a kind of emotional autobiography, traces the life of Clare Savage and her darker-skinned friend Zoe as they come to maturity in Jamaica. In the second book, Clare, now in her thirties, rejects the privileged colonialist role and experiments with choices to find the sense of wholeness missing from her life. In 1985, Cliff's *The Land of Look Behind: Prose and Poetry* explored many of these questions about place, class, language, and sexuality in prose poems that marked her as an important postmodernist. Poems from this work, such as "Passing," "Obsolete Geography," "Love in the Third World," and "If I Could Write This in Fire, I Would Write This in Fire" are evocative prolegomena for the questing woman in today's world. In 1993, her novel *Free Enterprise* was published; a fictionalized biography of an abolitionist who spirited escaping slaves along the Underground Railroad through use of her family's hotels, the book forces readers to question generic borders.

Cliff has interwoven teaching experience throughout her professional life, giving courses at the New School for Social Research, Hampshire College, the University of Massachusetts at Amherst, Vista College, Norwich University, the Martin Luther King, Jr., Public Library in Oakland, California, the University of California at Santa Cruz, and Trinity College in Hartford, Connecticut. She has combined a politically active life with high achievement in her own writing, and continues to voice her awareness of the similarities among women's roles in West African, Jamaican, and United States cultures.

Linda Wagner-Martin

CLIFTON, Lucille (b. 1936), educator, poet-author, poet laureate of Maryland. Born in Depew, New York, she attended Fredonia State College and Howard University. She began writing early; she was first published in 1969, when she was the mother of six children under the age of ten. Mari Evans notes that Clifton's writing reflects her childhood in a strong, loving family and the early lesson "that being very poor . . . had nothing to do with lovingness or familyness or character" (*Black Women Writers [1950–1980]*, 1984). This lesson, combined with her optimism, disregard for the mediocre and pleasing the crowd, and respect for the past permeate both Clifton's poetry and her books for young people.

Clifton has been likened to Gwendolyn * Brooks, Walt Whitman, and Emily * Dickinson in her style. Her poems are spare in form, deceptively simple in language, complex in ideas, and reflective of the commonplace, the everyday. As Evans remarks, her poetry reflects optimism, an emphasis on "the qualities which have allowed us to survive," and the belief that we have the ability to make things better. It is peopled with strong characters and historical and biblical figures. Her female characters represent known and unknown heroes who have taken responsibility and stands, and reflect the strength of the Dahomey woman who was the founder of Clifton's family in America. Her black males are strong, healthy, and treated with love and respect; this results from her positive male relationships and models, beginning with her father. Her collections of poetry include *Good Woman: Poems and a Memoir 1969–1980* (1987), *Next: New Poems* (1987), and *Quilting: Poems 1987–1990* (1991). Mari Evans observes that "the 'place' of her poetry and prose is essentially urban landscapes that are examples of most Black communities in this country." Her poetry "is often a conscious, quiet introduction to the real world of Black sensitivities."

Clifton's books for young people reflect the same themes, views, and landscapes as her poetry. Clifton addresses the fears, joys, and pain of children, reassures them, teaches them self-reliance, self-acceptance, and the assumption of responsibility for their actions. Her writing for

children is honest and lacks condescension. Sharon Malinowski has written that these works "are designed to help them understand their world" and "facilitate an understanding of Black heritage specifically, which in turn fosters an important link with the past generally" (*Black Writers*, 1989). Her most sustained character is Everett Anderson, who always uses his entire name, is six or seven years old, and lives with his mother in an apartment in the city. These books include *Some of the Days of Everett Anderson* (1970), a book of nine poems; *All Us Come Cross the Water* (1973), which links Everett Anderson with his past; *Everett Anderson's Year* (1974), which celebrates one year in verse; *Three Wishes* (1976, 1992); *Everett Anderson's 1-2-3* (1977), which details his mother's remarriage; *The Lucky Stone* (1979), stories; *My Friend Jacob* (1980), which describes a friendship with a retarded neighbor; *Everett Anderson's Goodbye* (1983), which details stages of grief after his father's death; *Everett Anderson's Christmas Coming* (1991), which are poems describing the five days before Christmas. Clifton celebrates life, emphasizes home, and remains positive.

• Wallace R. Peppers, "Lucille Clifton," in *Dictionary of Literary Biography: Afro-American Poets since 1955*, vol. 41, eds. Thadious M. Davis and Trudier Harris (1985), 55–60. Sharon Malinowski, "Clifton, (Thelma) Lucille," in *Black Writers: A Selection of Sketches from Contemporary Authors*, eds. Linda Metzger et al. (1989), 111–115.

Helen R. Houston

CLUB MOVEMENT refers to the phenomenon of American women's literary and civic reform clubs whose heyday spanned from the * Civil War to World War II. Middle-class women throughout the nation formed voluntary associations devoted largely to self-improvement and to municipal reform of their communities. While many of these organizations still exist, they enjoyed their greatest influence in the early twentieth century.

Although the roots of this popular women's activity lie in such antebellum endeavors as Margaret * Fuller's Boston Conversations of the 1830s, two post–Civil War clubs are generally credited with launching the women's literary club movement. In 1868, Jane Cunningham Croly, a New York City journalist, founded Sorosis, and Julia Ward * Howe, a Boston reformer, founded the New England Woman's Club. Both invited forward-thinking women to join, collecting those bold enough to defy the popular dictum that "woman's place is in the home." Antagonizing those who objected to a public voice for women, members prepared papers on subjects of literary and historical interest and on current events. They also launched reform projects to benefit women, children, and the general community.

The idea of the women's club spread quickly throughout the nation, and by 1912 women in large cities and small towns across America had formed thousands of clubs, totalling one million members. State and local federations and a national alliance, the General Federation of Women's Clubs, linked clubs to share resources and to call for social change, providing women with an effective collective public voice long before they were awarded the vote. Membership in clubs peaked in the mid-1920s.

Most clubs selected a theme each year, such as American poetry, English women novelists, or French playwrights. Every member would take her turn providing a program for one of the ten to forty meetings each year by delivering a twenty-minute speech on her topic. For many women this was their first experience at public speaking, and the quality of the presentations varied widely. Listeners were generally supportive rather than critical and expected that practice would strengthen women's researching, writing, and rhetorical skills. The knowledge and talents women built in the club setting caused the organizations to be nicknamed "universities for middle-aged women."

In time, a number of clubs, especially those that grew in size to several hundred or even several thousand members, expanded their literary offerings and invited writers, critics, and professors to deliver speeches. William Butler Yeats, Upton Sinclair, and Charlotte Perkins *Gilman were among those who appeared on the club circuit. Some women's societies also instituted weekly book review discussions for members particularly fond of reading. In the 1920s, clubs often sponsored play- or poetry-writing workshops for members, often hiring an instructor to lead the sessions and offering competitions with cash prizes for the winners.

While some groups remained content to offer a literary curriculum for members' enjoyment and edification, most became involved in projects to bring literature to wider audiences. Many clubs established the first public libraries in their towns, as Helen Santmyer's novel, *And the Ladies of the Club*, records. The success of these enterprises often triggered local support for more ambitious government funding for regular library staff or book purchases or even eligibility for one of Andrew Carnegie's library buildings. Other clubs sent reading materials to rural schools, prisons, lumber camps, and other facilities remote from books. In Evanston, Illinois, the Reading Circle invited similar groups to assemble in Chicago in 1910 to create the Drama League of America, which became a vast network of amateur community theater groups.

Several clubs donated money to build the cottages at the MacDowell Colony in Peterborough, New Hampshire, so professional writers and composers could hide away to create in peace. Others offered theater and puppetry workshops for school children. In Providence, New York, and Boston, clubwomen pressured major private universities to open Pembroke, Barnard, and Radcliffe Colleges for women.

Professional women in the arts also founded clubs, for the purpose of networking. Women's Press Clubs in many cities enabled journalists to share career advice with their peers. Local branches of the National League of American Penwomen provided acquaintanceship among composers, writers, and painters.

The social conscience of the early-twentieth-century middle-class inspired many women's club members to spend more and more energy on municipal improvements, such as pasteurized milk, free health clinics, kindergartens, streetlights, playgrounds, and parks. The clubs in the National Association of Colored Women's Clubs agitated against racism. But few associations of women abandoned literary interests altogether. The National American Woman Suffrage Association and National Woman's Party, both devoted to securing the vote for women, used pageants and plays to raise money and publicize their cause. Local branches of the American Association of University Women (formerly the Association of Collegiate Alumnae) engaged in book discussions even while they lobbied for better salaries for teachers and better educational facilities for women students. The literary component has been critical to the members of the women's club movement throughout its long history.

• Jane Cunningham Croly, *The History of the Woman's Club Movement in America* (1898). Mary I. Wood, *The History of the General Federation of Women's Clubs* (1912). Elizabeth Lindsay Davis, *Lifting as They Climb: The History of the National Association of Colored Women* (1933). Mildred White Wells, *Unity in Diversity: The History of the General Federation of Women's Clubs* (1953; Diamond Jubilee Edition, 1965, vol. 2, 1975). Karen J. Blair, *The Clubwoman as Feminist: True Womanhood Redefined, 1868–1914* (1980). Paula Baker, "The Domestication of Politics: Women and American Political Society, 1780–1920," *American Historical Review* 89 (June 1984): 620–647. Karen J. Blair, *The History of American Women's Voluntary Organizations, 1810–1960: A Guide to Sources* (1989).

Karen J. Blair

COLLABORATION The issue of collaborative writing calls into question many traditional notions about authorship, texts, and textual production, notions that have been instrumental in evaluating women's writing in the United States. Multiple authorship challenges the trope of the patriarchal author, of the genius who singly produces a creation that is owned and that can be traced to others in lines of influence or resistance. It re-situates acts of writing in social contexts, raising questions about originality and authorial control. Because of the critical pressure to determine who wrote what, prefaces and commentaries about coauthored texts usually foreground issues of the processes of writing and of power and hierarchy more submerged in the idealized narratives of singular creative genius. It is often claimed, for example, that one of the authors was primary, and the other a helper or editor. Coauthored texts make more visible the necessary negotiations between authors and those involved in textual production, dissemination, and reception. The changing critical approaches necessary to account for such a social model of literary culture may well make the position of women writers more visible as well.

The preface to a reissue of the 1869 *American Woman's Home* (ed. Joseph Van Why, 1987) illustrates the difficulties of accounting for collaborative texts, for it shows how such texts provoke awareness of the social conditions of authorship. The modern editor describes the book as reflecting the moral philosophy of Catharine *Beecher, explaining that it is "in large measure an expansion" of her earlier *Treatise on Domestic Economy*. Yet the editor must then explain why she is listed as coauthor with her sister, Harriet Beecher *Stowe:

> It is probable that Mrs. Stowe's fame as author of *Uncle Tom's Cabin* and many other books and her practical experience as a mother of seven children led Catharine to conclude that having her sister as co-author would enhance the reputation and sale of the book. Despite her knowledge and previous works on domestic economy and child care, Catharine was shrewdly aware that the public might question a spinster woman in her late sixties writing authoritatively on such subjects.

The editor identifies authorship by discerning whose ideas are primary, whose are "suggestive" or "contributory." Yet there are other complications of establishing "authority": matters of gender, age, experience, reputation, and social position also shape the authoring of a text, making one name more valuable in selling a book than another. The double authorship of *American Woman's Home* suggests the problems of being perceived by the reading public, by critics and publishers, by literary historians, as "writing authoritatively."

Collaboration sometimes describes a joint project of work undertaken by coequals, both of whom receive credit for their work. The nineteenth-century poets Alice and Phoebe *Cary, for example, published their separate poems in coauthored volumes, thus enhancing the visibility of each. Margaret *Fuller and Ralph Waldo Emerson collaborated on editing the influential periodical the *Dial* (1840–1844). But, as Jack Stillinger has detailed, co-authors have come in many forms, some less equal or visible than others: "a friend, a spouse, a ghost, an agent, an editor, a translator, a publisher, a censor, a transcriber, a printer." Women collaborators often suffer practical or political complications from such shared or mutual work. Women coauthors are less likely to be recognized as "the author," and are more frequently a silent partner. Exceptions occur usually when the woman is clearly the more established author of the couple, as was the case of Elizabeth Stuart *Phelps, who cowrote two novels with her relatively unknown husband in the 1870s (Phelps's name appears first on the title pages and, perhaps more telling, hers is the only name listed on the covers and spines). Few women writers succeed both on their own and in collaboration, as did Mary *Beard, who wrote histories on women's issues, including *Woman: Co-Maker of History* (1940), and whose "co-operative efforts" with her husband Charles produced the four-volume *Rise of American Civilization* (1927–1942). Literary daughters, like Ellen Emerson or Susan Fenimore Cooper, have usually been approved of by literary historians for their dutiful support. Wives, like Mark Twain's "civilizing" wife, Livy, or Herman Melville's wife, Elizabeth, are more commonly castigated for curtailing literary genius or for producing egregious textual errors as they copy or proofread manuscripts.

Women's collaboration has often been instigated by unequal access to publication or critical circuits. Some form of collaboration was often a precondition for women to offer a manuscript to the public. Not all were as adamant as Harriet Beecher Stowe, who credited God with writing her novel *Uncle Tom's Cabin*. But women routinely wrote prefaces insisting their venture into the literary marketplace was urged or helped by "friends," and was not an act of self-assertion. Early women writers often emerged as anonymous—as exemplary of their class or experience, disguised or protected by *pseudonyms. They often had to share their title page or prefatory pages with editors, translators, or eminent introducers. Indeed, their names are often secondary, so that the texts come to "belong" to those who can negotiate the dominant culture's terms and practices. Even when a book like *The History of Mary *Prince* (1831) is "related by Herself," it may have a "Supplement" by the editor or an editorial glossary, as does Mary *Antin's novel *The Promised

Land (1912). As in the cases of *Scenes in the Life of Harriet Tubman* (1869) and *The Narrative of Sojourner Truth* (1850), books are transcribed from oral to written form or even ghostwritten by more established authors.

As Mary Dearborn has written, the practice of "midwifing" texts "by such devices [as] prefaces, appendices, explanations and authentications" was especially prevalent for ethnic writers for whom "the tradition of . . . authorship is a tradition of mediation." The nature and extent of such "midwifing" varies considerably. Women often needed insistent readers to authorize, inspire, or encourage them, as was the case with Maimie Pinzer, whose autobiographical "papers" describing her life as a prostitute in turn-of-the-century Philadelphia were written as *letters to a wealthy patron and only recently published in book form (*The Maimie Papers*, ed. Ruth Rosen and Sue Davidson, 1977). The writings of *African-American, *immigrant, *working-class, and *Native American women were often made available to the reading public by intermediaries: abolitionists who certified the "truth" or "accuracy" of an escaped slave's narrative, sociologists or reformers who interviewed and validated the experiences of tenement dwellers or factory workers, and anthropologists who collected and arranged the ceremonial songs of Native American *ritual. Women trying to break into print often worked with editors or established men of letters who could "translate" them into the proper form for public approval. As Gretchen Bataille and Kathleen Sands have discussed (*American Indian Women: Telling Their Lives*, 1984), editors and anthropologists were involved in the collecting, recording, and publishing of the life stories of Native Americans. Even a modern novel by a Native American woman (*Co-ge-we-a* by Humishuma or *Mourning Dove, 1927) is produced through the mediation of a promoter, annotator, and editor. Harriet *Jacobs's *Incidents in the Life of a Slave Girl* (1861) is "written by herself," but the title page names only the book's "editor," Lydia Maria *Child, the white abolitionist who helped negotiate Jacobs's book contract and reassure readers of the narrative's authenticity. Harriet *Wilson's novel *Our Nig* was published in 1859 with authenticating letters and reissued in 1983 with an authenticating introduction. The eighteenth-century poet Anne *Bradstreet's first book was accepted when her brother-in-law, without consulting her, took her poems to a London publisher. Emily *Dickinson's first book (*Poems*, 1890) was published with the editorial oversight of Mabel Loomis Todd and Thomas W. Higginson, the eminent editor and essayist with whom Dickinson had corresponded about her work. Powerful

editors like Frank Leslie, James T. Fields, and William Dean Howells encouraged women to write—suggesting the kinds of tales desirable, commenting on manuscripts, offering topics and outlines for characters, and requesting changes in names or settings. Even in the twentieth century, women writers, especially of "popular" texts, received elaborate editorial "assistance." As Stillinger reports, Jaqueline Susann's 1966 best-seller *Valley of the Dolls* was substantially "reconstructed" by an editor given "carte blanche" to "cut, compress, and edit (interlinear as well as surgical)."

Collaboration can also take more public and more extended forms, as in the case of the experimental novels written by groups of six or even twenty authors: for example, *Six of One by Half a Dozen of the Other* (1872, by Harriet Beecher Stowe, among others), *The Sturdy Oak* (1917, by fourteen authors), and *The Bobbed Hair* (1925, by twenty authors, including Dorothy *Parker). Such projects can reveal cultural and political tensions about collaboration more often endured in private. *The Whole Family*, a novel written by twelve authors and serialized in *Harper's Bazaar* (1907–1908; reprint, edited by Alfred Bendixen, 1986), foregrounds the complicated *gender politics of working in tandem, as writers jostled for position within the fictional and literary "family."

Since the nineteenth century, women scholars have used collaborative or collective writing in seeking collegial support and in trying to diminish the effects of differences in class, race, or academic status. Anne Ruggles Gere has shown the importance of *writing groups both inside and outside of academia, and Theodora Penny Martin has written about nineteenth century study clubs in which women gathered to read, discuss, present papers, and write essays. Susan B. *Anthony collaborated with other women to produce a *History of Women's Suffrage* (1881–1887). Fellow suffragist Elizabeth Cady *Stanton organized a committee of thirty women who "took sweet counsel together" to produce *The Woman's Bible* (1895–1898), a contentious project critiquing and revising those biblical passages "directly referring to women, and those also in which women are made prominent by exclusion." More recently, women have coauthored pieces for such feminist journals as *Signs* and *Sojourner;* they also have collaborated on projects of curricular reform (see the course syllabi reprinted in *Feminist Studies* in the 1970s, or the ground-breaking collection of materials on "Black Women's Studies" in *But Some of Us Are Brave*, edited by Gloria T. Hull, Patricia Bell Scott, and Barbara Smith, 1982). Such cooperative acts have, appropriately, produced studies about women's literacy and collaborative writing, as, for example, the group-authored volume investigating *Women's Ways of Knowing* (1986) and the coauthored book investigating collaborative writing as a mode of writing and learning, *Single Texts/Plural Authors* (1990). Sandra Gilbert and Susan Gubar articulated the value of egalitarian collaboration in their preface to *The Madwoman in the Attic* (1979): "We feel our book represents not just a dialogue but a consensus. . . . [T]he process of collaboration has given us the essential support we needed to complete such an ambitious project." Collaboration thus serves, for many women writers, as a literary and political gesture, an experiment that challenges what Gilbert and Gubar call "metaphors of literary paternity" and that proposes the virtues of "sweet counsel," of collectivity, of shared custody.

[*See also* Authorship.]

• Mary F. Belenky, Blythe M. Clinchy, Nancy R. Goldberger, and Jill M. Tarule, *Women's Ways of Knowing* (1986). Mary V. Dearborn, *Pochahontas's Daughters: Gender and Ethnicity in American Culture* (1986). Anne Ruggles Gere, *Writing Groups* (1987). Theodora Penny Martin, *The Sound of Our Own Voices: Women's Study Clubs, 1860–1910*. Shirley Marchlonis, ed., *Patrons and Protégées: Gender, Friendship, and Writing in Nineteenth-Century America* (1988). Wayne Koestenbaum, *Double Talk: The Erotics of Male Literary Collaboration* (1989). Lisa Ede and Andrea Lunsford, *Single Texts/Plural Authors: Perspectives on Collaborative Writing* (1990). Jack Stillinger, *Multiple Authorship and the Myth of Solitary Genius* (1991).

Jean Ferguson Carr

COLONIAL COURT PAPERS are not, strictly speaking, women's writings. These documents—a wide array of materials filed in connection with civil and criminal actions heard by magistrates in British North America circa 1607–1776—were generally written by men and used by exclusively male judges and juries in a legal system that prohibited most women from owning property or suing on their own behalf. Yet these texts are among the most important sources for understanding the lives of early American women. For if colonial court papers are not truly women's *writings*, they offer unusually direct access to women's *voices*.

The typical white woman in British North America did not write. Though women shared in Anglo-American print culture, broadly defined (they regularly heard the Bible read aloud, for example), their literacy rates lagged far behind those of men until after the American Revolution. Even in text-centered, introspective Puritan New England, few Euro-American women left written records of their lives. Anne Bradstreet, a self-styled poet in seventeenth-century Boston, commented in verse on the uniqueness of public writing for even a high-status Englishwoman. Women's private writings, such as diaries and letters, are also rare before the mid-eighteenth century. Relying on women's writings to uncover female lives in early America thus makes the majority of white women's voices faint, and the voices of black and Native American women virtually inaudible.

If few women actually wrote about their lives in early America, a surprising number of ordinary female voices became part of written history through the colonial legal system. Since we in the late twentieth century are likely to consider going to court a costly, contentious, and preferably unusual experience, it is difficult for us to understand the prominent role courts played in the daily lives of men and women in seventeenth- and eighteenth-century America. Far from the formal judicial establishment we experience, colonial courts were local institutions concerned with the social and moral governance of all aspects of community life. Particularly in New England, where Puritan authorities considered watching over and reporting on one's neighbors to be a duty to God and society, an exceptional variety of the business of daily living came before the courts. The sluggish work habits or foul language of a neighbor, the depredations of runaway livestock, the sullenness of a servant, and the date of conception of a bastard child all fell within the purview of local court magistrates.

Thus, though colonial American women rarely wrote descriptions of their own lives, court papers afford a glimpse of them literally caught in the act of living and making sense of their worlds. Although their voices are filtered through a male screen—the court clerks who recorded their words, the magistrates who interrogated them—ordinary women of varying social classes, ethnicities, and races literally speak through these records.

Often women's voices emerge in the act of witnessing, pleading, or occasionally, suing. Serving as witnesses in civil and criminal actions ranging from debt to murder, female deponents describe in amazing detail the fabric of their daily lives: what tasks they were performing at home or in the field when they overheard a dispute between neighbors; with whom they were talking when they noticed the constable's drunkenness. In addition to this level of immediacy, women's court testimony gives us evidence of their systems of values, their ways of ordering their experiences. As midwives called to testify in cases of suspected illegitimacy or infanticide, they describe the social nexus of childbirth for the community of women. As victims of slander, they enforce the parameters of acceptable discourse in their society. As accused slanderers, they raise their voices, using speech to claim moral authority. Petitioning for divorce, they define their expectations of marriage and family.

In addition to female testimony, colonial court papers encompass other kinds of documents that fill in this picture of ordinary women's lives. Indenture contracts specifying the reciprocal duties of masters and servants offer clues about social expectations for women's work and about the relationship between race, gender, and servitude. Women's wills (unusual because few early American women owned property outright) reveal women ordering their affairs, making their wishes known by passing on property and life lessons to their survivors. Inventories of the property and belongings of deceased women show how women arranged the physical space they lived in, preparing their larders for the winter, their finished goods for market, their kitchens for the noonday meal.

Taken together, these varied kinds of records afford rare glimpses of the self-consciousness of ordinary women in an era when female opinions were seldom sought and even more rarely preserved for posterity. Though colonial court papers cannot typically be called examples of women's writing, they are evidence of a kind of authorship: women's efforts to inscribe their own sense of order on the narrative of their lives.

• William Jeffrey, Jr., *Early New England Court Records: A Bibliography of Published Materials* (1954). Kenneth A. Lockridge, *Literacy in Colonial New England* (1974). Hendrik Hartog, "The Public Law of a County Court: Judicial Government in Eighteenth-Century Massachusetts," *American Journal of Legal History* 20, no. 4 (October 1976): 282–329. William Jeffrey, Jr., "Early American Court Records—A Bibliography of Printed Materials: The Middle Colonies," *University of Cincinnati Law Review*, vol. 39 (1976): 685–710. Laurel Thatcher Ulrich, *Good Wives: Image and Reality in the Lives of Women in Northern New England, 1650–1750* (1980). Rhys Isaac, *The Transformation of Virginia, 1740–1790* (1982), chaps. 5 and 6. Mary Beth Norton, "Gender and Defamation in Seventeenth-Century Maryland," *William and Mary Quarterly* 3d ser., 44, no. 1 (January 1987): 3–39. Helena M. Wall, *Fierce Communion: Family and Community in Early America* (1990). Mary Beth Norton, "Gender, Crime, and Community in Seventeenth-Century Maryland," in *The Transformation of Early American History*, James A. Henretta et al., eds. (1991).

Jane Kamensky

COLONIAL ERA WRITING. In the period extending from the 1630s, when Anne *Bradstreet wrote her first poems, to 1779, when Judith Sargent *Murray argued for legal, economic, and educational rights for women, we find a multiplicity of genres and purposes for writing. Even though most extant writing by women in the colonial period in America comes from New England, it is nevertheless difficult to define a single tradition in women's writing prior to the nineteenth century. It is tempting to try to simplify the multiplicity by selecting out works according to genre—creating a list that might include, for example, Mary *Rowlandson's captivity narrative, some of Bradstreet's and Phillis *Wheatley's elegies, Mercy Otis *Warren's poetry, satires, and plays. But that sorting would leave out an immense and significant noncanonical plethora of other writing—*diaries, letters, journals, almanac interleavings, hymns, memorials, *travel accounts, *spiritual narratives, legacies, and more. Some of these kinds of writing were eventually published, but most were apparently not intended for publication. Some is just now coming to light.

The absence of a women's literary tradition in the colonial period is no doubt related to the absence of a female audience for literature, such as would exist in the nineteenth century. By the end of the eighteenth century most men in New England were literate. Women's literacy lagged significantly behind men's despite the argument made in the early republic that duties of citizenship required that women read, and despite a similar Puritan argument that literacy was a necessary means to knowing Christ. (Puritan women were encouraged to study scripture and to keep a journal of God's workings in their lives.) Some journal-keepers (Esther Edwards Burr, for example) developed an audience of intimates for their writing, but not until a small group of well-educated, self-conscious writers began to see literature as an enhancement to the culture of the new republic did women begin to exchange work and become an audience for each other's efforts. Even so, the intended audience for these republican women's published work was predominantly male.

Except for such rare cases as the poets Anne Bradstreet and Jane Colman Turrel, who were encouraged to literary accomplishment by family members, the sanction for most women's writing came from the immediate circumstances of their lives. The letters of Abigail *Adams came about because of frequent separations from her husband, John. Journals were essential to many kinds of work. Women used pocket almanacs to record household and bodily cycles; the need to record carefully was a practical and a spiritual necessity since daily life was infused with evidence of the Holy Spirit. Thus, almanac entries were sometimes interleaved with a biblical verse, a thanksgiving, or a providential interpretation. Spiritual narratives, in which the writer sought to find God's hand in events, required accuracy and specificity of detail.

For colonial women needlework and writing seem to have been alternative forms of symbolic expression. In the Middle Atlantic states, where a tradition of women's preaching existed among the German settlers, women turned to handwork more often than to writing, except for Moravian women, who were celebrated hymnodists. Among the English there, many of the same kinds of writing existed as in New England, but Quaker women, who also preached, were encouraged to write and publish their spiritual autobiographies as tools for evangelism. Elizabeth *Ashbridge's *Account* of her life narrates the development of her faith as a legacy to those within and without her community.

Similarly, Puritan fathers and mothers left legacies to their children. The so-called mother's legacy, books of advice to children who might be left motherless, were generally written in anticipation of both a child's birth and the mother's death. The fact that at childbirth the mother's life was at risk endowed that moment with great significance. Colonial women had large families, and they were expected to assist in each other's deliveries (traditionally, men were excluded from the birth chamber). Women also prepared the dead for burial. Thus, both as bearers of children and as attendants at death and birth, women mediated between life and death. As Bradstreet's poem "Before the Birth of one of her Children" suggests, childbirth opened a glimpse both into and from the hereafter. It offered the mother and writer a special perspective on mortal life.

In the mother's legacy, female creative and procreative powers are associated. At the Second Coming of Christ, and at their own deaths, women expected to emerge as equal members of Christ's kingdom. Thus, in the birth/death process both mother and child are born into new life. And so too will the writer's words be perfected when these are read and brought to life by future generations. The mother's legacy embodies a transformative moment. The mother gives the gift of her words and of her special point of view, spoken on the verge of birth/death.

This complex stance toward the world and the world to come manifested itself in various ways. To those such as Anne *Hutchinson, who argued that the millennium was at hand, full equality and liberation could seem almost within reach. Women's two-way involvement in this world and the next can account, too, for the ambiguity, tension, and convoluted style said to characterize women's writing under patriarchy. For example, Mary Rowlandson's narrative of her captivity among the Narragansetts, as Amy Lang points out, begins with a kind of death: "a violent end to the daily rounds of the Puritan wife and mother." Spoken from a place literally and figuratively beyond the pale, the narrative weaves realistic ethnography and Puritan dogma into a journey toward the rebirth of self. In Rowland's "wilderness" the mother's two-way (and at times contradictory) perspective is fully evidenced.

A century later, Phillis Wheatley, the African who as a child was taken into slavery and sold to a prosperous Boston family, would find sanction for writing poetry both in the approbation of eighteenth-century Boston and in the conviction that she too spoke from the other side of "redemption." She navigated the boundary between this world (which she calls Africa) and the next (America). Having survived her rebirth ordeal, she lived to correct those who "view our sable race with scornful eye": ultimately blacks, like women, would be equal members of the Resurrection. Wheatley's dense neoclassical imitativeness, like the Puritan's dense referencing of biblical and doctrinal authority, may be attributable, in part, to the ambiguity of roles she adopted; sold into oppression as a slave, she is redeemed and transformed into an accomplished poet who feels herself joined to the company of angels. Wheatley suggests that writing itself provided a means of reconciling both realms and both identities.

America as the land of the already reborn was a motif common to men and women writers of Wheatley's time who used the amused distance of the eighteenth-century narrator to instruct more often than to console. *Humor emerged as a means of persuasion, for example, in the political satires of Mercy Otis Warren. Humor colors the special perspective adopted in Sarah Kemble *Knight's description of her 1704 trip from Boston to New Haven. Knight's journey is not a Christian pilgrimage, and yet it has the anecdotal particularity of much Puritan writing. An ironic, sometimes sardonic observer who is both inside and outside the scene, she records the facts but does not find in them the hand of an inscrutable Providence. Knight's New England is no neoclassical Eden or "favoured land." For Knight, not only has the millennium not arrived, it appears to be irrelevant. Knight implies that the important challenges that meet modern women on the road of life are how to find a good meal and a clean bed—challenges of this world, not of the next.

It is tempting to place Knight's journal suggestively between a Puritan seventeenth and a republican eighteenth century. But a work such as Martha Ballard's eighteenth-century diary serves as a caveat. Laura Ulrich points out that although midwife Ballard records the events of the Revolution, her life was far more affected by having to cross the river eight times to deliver Tabitha Sewall: "Her life had been altered by the Revolution, but her identity was unrelated to the ritual of republicanism." Well into the eighteenth century, then, colonial women's writing continued to mean multiplicity. If there are features in common, they may have to do with similarities in how these women's lives were lived and their assigned roles defined. There are features to the literature (its formulaic quality, for example) that we have yet to interpret. As Cheryl Walker reminds us, there may well be "secrets" hidden in these texts, and codes that we have not yet learned how to crack.

[See also Antinomianism; Early National Writing; Spiritual Narratives.]

• Lyle Koehler, A Search for Power: The "Weaker Sex" in Seventeenth Century New England (1980). Laurel Thatcher Ulrich, Good Wives: Image and Reality in the Lives of Women in Northern New England, 1650–1750 (1980). Pattie Cowell, Women Poets in Pre-Revolutionary America, 1650–1775, An Anthology (1981). Cheryl Walker, The Nightingale's Burden: Women Poets and American Culture before 1900 (1982). William L. Andrews, ed., Journeys in New Worlds: Early American Women's Narratives (1990). Katherine M. Rogers, ed., The Meridian Anthology of Early American Women Writers from Anne Bradstreet to Louisa May Alcott, 1650–1865 (1991). Laurel Thatcher Ulrich, The Life of Martha Ballard, Based on Her Diary, 1785–1812 (1991).

Rosamond Rosenmeier

COLONIALISM. During the last two decades of the twentieth century, many literary scholars in the United States have turned their attention to the ways in which inequitable distributions of power affect literary production and reception. Renewed interest in colonization, imperialist expansion, and neo-colonization have resulted also in attention to the appropriations, parodies, and subversions of postcolonialism, with its perplexed connections to nationalism, multiculturalism, and globalism. Making use of feminist, deconstructive, psychoanalytic, and Marxist theory, students of colonialism and postcolonialism investigate the postmodern collapse of traditionally dominant Western narratives, questioning their political, economic, and cultural hegemony, and examining marginalized perspectives affected by gender, race, class, and ethnicity. This decolonized approach to literary studies unsettles established canons by broadening literary genres, filling in and emphasizing gaps in representation, and focusing

on formerly ignored writings both in the United States and in third- and second-world countries where writers look at power differently and are intimately involved in developing national identities. Some critics view the development of the literature of the United States as paradigmatic of colonial/postcolonial positioning.

Because they are focused on rethinking the meaning of subjectivity and representation, feminist literary theorists and critics are particularly interested in studying colonialist and postcolonialist discourse. Some investigate indigenous literatures, teasing out the resistances, subversions, and interventions of native writings, exposing the problematic tensions between Western, metropolitan theorists, and the native writers they sometimes subsume. Some examine the rhetorical strategies apparent in literary constructions of the "other," a concept that reveals colonizers' attitudes to the colonized. In general, whether chronologically or structurally aligned, studies of colonialism and postcolonialism emphasize rhetorical strategies such as irony and parody, and structural and contextual literary characteristics such as hybridization, discontinuity, and dislocation. They also document the often subtle complicities between colonizer and colonized.

Literary representations of women (whether in fiction, poetry, or drama) sometimes metaphorically connect or contrast female bodies with landscapes, reproduction with labor, and women's private, local lives with more public, politicized existence. For example, the oppression of female bodies, critics argue, reverberates in the rape of the land so that many studies concentrate on the politics of exploration, mapping, and tourism. Other feminist approaches also critique the neocolonizing tendencies of first-world feminists toward the work of marginal peoples. Many critics argue that both traditional and nontraditional women's writing operates in a postcolonial mode, for example connecting orality and literacy, appropriating the language and forms of various oppressors, and employing tactical strategies designed to subvert colonizing gestures and genres.

Certain theoretical studies have been particularly influential. In Resistance Literature (1987), Barbara Harlow demonstrates that language choice (English, for example) constitutes part of a writer's political statement, that different genres use specific methods of resistance—poetry often attacks through stripped and sparse language, while narrative, with its historical perspective, creates controversial endings—and that marginalized forms such as prison memoirs and women's autobiographies can effect political change. Other feminist theorists concentrate on imperialist narratives, investigating their colonizing strategies. Gayatri * Spivak, in *In Other Worlds* (1987) and in a collection of interviews, strategies, and dialogues, *The Post-Colonial Critic* (1990), seeks out the colonized object in several canonized texts. She also reads and annotates writing by third-world women, emphasizing various levels of discourse. Spivak's attention to the subaltern has encouraged critics to pay renewed attention to the heterogeneity of women's writing in the United States, and to the problems that arise when women with some power speak for those with none. She argues against monolithic approaches to the third world and the treacherous benevolence of some imperialist approaches to marginalized literatures.

Trinh * Minh-ha, in *Woman, Native, Other* (1989) and *When the Moon Waxes Red* (1991), describes hegemonies—of states over one another, of men over women, of the first world over the third—that operate often through consensual arrangements. She emphasizes the overlapping of old forms with new as fictions struggle to replace each other. Stories, she insists, are never passive reflectors of reality, but active mediations. Like Spivak, Minh-ha castigates the colonizer's pretense of seeing into the minds of the colonized, and tries to demolish divisions between insider and outsider. Borders and margins are, she insists, always indeterminate.

Focused more on the constructed subjects and objects of specific discourses, Donna Haraway, in her collection of essays, *Simians, Cyborgs and Women* (1991), and Mary Louise Pratt in *Imperial Eyes* (1992) demonstrate how to question such fundamental concepts as "nature." Attempting to break open dualisms, Haraway presents the cyborg as an ironic image of the inappropriate/d other (a term used by Minh-ha), while Pratt investigates travel writing as it creates the world from the perspective of imperialist powers. Both Haraway and Pratt argue that nineteenth-century natural histories tried to assert authority over the whole planet. Women's writing, they suggest, often resistant to imperial takeovers, commonly displays strategies that can be called postcolonial.

In the United States, female theorists of colonialist and postcolonialist discourse use North American women writers in exemplary ways. Frequently referenced is the work of Leslie Marmon * Silko, the Canadian Margaret Atwood, Paule * Marshall, Toni * Morrison, and Alice * Walker, writers who are conscious of the doubly colonized position of women of color, native women, ethnic minorities and, particularly in Atwood's case, of national marginalization. These writers, as Linda Hutcheon suggests about others in "Circling the Downspout of Em-

pire" (1990), constructively seek social change, responding, through the subject positioning of powerful female characters, to imperialist and colonialist histories.

[*See also* Post-colonialism.]

• Chandra Talpade Mohanty, "Under Western Eyes: Feminist Scholarship and Colonial Discourses," *Boundary 2* 12/13, no. 3/4 (Spring/Fall 1984): 333–358. Biddy Martin and Chandra Talpade Mohanty, " Feminist Politics: What's Home Got to Do with It?" in *Feminist Studies/Critical Studies*, ed. Teresa de Lauretis (1986). *Inscriptions*, "Feminism and the Critique of Colonial Discourse," no. 3/4 (1988) and "Travelling Theories, Travelling Theorists," no. 5 (1989). Published by the Group for the Critical Study of Colonial Discourse and the Center for Cultural Studies. Bill Ashcroft, Gareth Griffiths, and Helen Tiffin, eds., *The Empire Writes Back: Theory and Practice in Post-Colonial Literatures* (1989). *Modern Fiction Studies*, "Special Issue: Narratives of Colonial Resistance," 35, no. 1 (Spring 1989). Ian Adam and Helen Tiffin, eds., *Past the Last Post: Theorizing Post-Colonialism and Post-Modernism* (1990). Teresa De Lauretis, "Eccentric Subjects: Feminist Theory and Historical Consciousness," *Feminist Studies* 16, no. 1 (Spring 1990): 115–150. Laura Ann Stoler, " 'In Cold Blood': Hierarchies of Credibility and the Politics of Colonial Narratives," *Representations*, "Imperial Fantasies and Postcolonial Histories," no. 37 (Winter 1992): 151–89.

Lorna Irvine

COMBAHEE RIVER COLLECTIVE. *See* Black Feminism; Lesbian Feminism.

COMING OUT. Traditionally, to "come out" meant to make one's debut socially. The term conjured up images of white, upper-middle-class and upper-class young women, clad in rustling, full-length gowns, descending the wide sweeping staircases of southern mansions or high-priced local hotels. While this kind of coming out continues, albeit a little abashedly, around the United States, in the last twenty-five years the queer definition of coming out has become part of the vocabulary of the culture at large. Coming out, in the gay and lesbian context, is shorthand for "coming out of the closet," and involves acknowledging one's sexual preference to one's self, one's family, one's employers, and the world at large. As Eve Kosofsky Sedgwick has noted, gays and lesbians (as well as many others outside the definitional safety net of reproductive heterosexuality) are constantly reenacting the moment of coming out of the closet as they meet new people and make decisions about how much of themselves to reveal. In addition, Sedgwick explains that while declaring one's sexuality may propel one from a private realm into a public one, there may be very different consequences and effects of privately acknowledging one's sexuality and publicly doing so. Since the Stonewall rebellion, both private and public acts of coming out have taken on the status of a political imperative within the modern gay and lesbian civil rights movement.

In *Epistemology of the Closet* (1990), perhaps the most extensive and complex discussion of the philosophical and political effects of coming out, Sedgwick traces the history of this term. Following the French philosopher Michel Foucault, she argues that at the turn of the century there was a shift in the discourses that described and regulated sexuality. Instead of focusing on acts, descriptions of sexuality began to focus on identities. Out of this shift developed the previously unimaginable identities "homosexual" and "heterosexual." Along with these identities came descriptions of being "in the closet" or "out," acknowledging one's sexuality, or keeping it a secret.

Since the late 1960s, a genre of oral and written autobiographical narratives that chart various coming outs has developed. Many of these narratives concentrate almost completely on the steps that lead up to the moment of sexual self-recognition. Often they involve a rewriting of one's personal history, an interpretation of major life events in light of one's sexual preference. Other narratives detail a specific coming out moment, for example, to parents or to one's children. Encoded in many of these accounts is the assumption that in discovering one's homosexuality, one has uncovered or fully realized the truth of one's self.

The first volumes written entirely by women that attempt to document a variety of coming out experiences are *The Lesbian Path: Thirty-seven Lesbian Writers Share Their Personal Experiences, Viewpoints, Traumas and Joys*, edited by Margaret Cruikshank, and *The Coming Out Stories*, edited by Susan J. Wolfe and Julia Penelope Stanley, both of which appeared in 1980. These books contain a wide sampling of coming out narratives and serve both as documents of lesbian social history and as handbooks for women questioning their sexuality.

While these volumes may have inaugurated the genre, since then numerous other works that contain the same kinds of narratives, including a book devoted specifically to nuns who realized they were lesbians (*Lesbian Nuns: Breaking Silence*, 1985), as well as collections by lesbians whose identities are also impacted by race, ethnicity, disability, religion, or class, have been published. For example, *Chicana Lesbians: The Girls Our Mothers Warned Us About* (1991) includes prose as well as poetry from a number of differing perspectives. Both of these anthologies also illustrate another kind of coming out encoded in the books themselves: in the former, the outing of the profession of nun, and

in the latter, the outing of an ethnic group. Furthermore, for lesbians of color there is a sense that making coming out as a lesbian the central event in one's identity may not be enough. Many lesbians of color refuse to put primary emphasis on sexual self-recognition, and instead elucidate how racial and ethnic self-recognition is crucial to and inseparable from sexuality. In so doing, they widen the parameters of coming out to include coming out as a racial or ethnic person.

Most of these accounts are autobiographical and fall into the realm of nonfiction. Both in poetry and in prose, however, there are many notable examples of coming out experiences. Adrienne *Rich's poetry (*The Dream of a Common Language: Poems 1974–1977*, 1978) and Alice *Walker's story of a young African-American woman's discovery of her self through her sexual and emotional relationship with another woman, *The Color Purple* (1982), are two important works that represent a woman's experiences coming out.

In the late eighties and early nineties, women within the lesbian community have begun to challenge what they feel are the restricted narrative, political, and sexual conventions of the coming out genre. For example, Jan Brown, in her essay "Sex, Lies, and Penetration: A Butch Finally 'Fesses Up," (*The Persistent Desire: A Femme-Butch Reader*, 1992), uses the idea that the coming out genre reveals the truth of one's sexuality and one's essential being to push at the limits of what are considered acceptable lesbian sexual desires and behaviors. She purports to tell the truth about butch desires, to argue that, in fact, some butches do want to be men, and do desire women in ways that have often been labeled "masculine" or "violent" by the lesbian community.

Jan Clausen, in "My Interesting Condition," "fesses up" to another supposed transgression (*Out/Look: National Lesbian and Gay Quarterly*, 1990). She uses the conventions of the coming out narrative against itself to describe her realization of her desire for a man, and the ways in which this both threatened her status as "lesbian" and brought on a wave of anger from the lesbian community of which she felt herself a part. Both of these examples challenge the narrative conventions that grounded the coming out genre and, in particular, the idea that the genre reinforced the political imperative that (usually, a certain sanctioned version of) lesbian sexuality was *the truth* of an individual's life.

[*See also* Lesbianism; Lesbian Writing.]

• Michel Foucault, *The History of Sexuality: Volume 1: An Introduction* (1978). Cherríe Moraga and Gloria Anzaldúa, *This Bridge Called My Back: Writings by Rad-

ical Women of Color (1981). Audre Lorde, *Zami: A New Spelling of My Name* (1982). Barbara Smith, *Home Girls: A Black Feminist Anthology* (1983). Adrienne Rich, *The Fact of a Doorframe: Poems Selected and New, 1950–1984* (1984). Minnie Bruce Pratt, *We Say We Love Each Other* (1985). Mab Segrest, *My Mama's Dead Squirrel: Lesbian Essays on Southern Culture* (1985).

Katie Kent

COMMUNICATIONS BETWEEN THE SEXES. *See* Language, Women's, article on Communications Between the Sexes.

COMMUNISM. "A specter is haunting Europe," Karl Marx and Friedrich Engels announced in the *Communist Manifesto* (1848). That specter, communism, viewed history as the unceasing struggle between classes—slave and slave owner, serf and master, worker and capitalist—until the rising revolutionary movements of the proletariat could overthrow capitalism. However, class struggle means more than workers rebelling against exploitative working conditions: revolution changes all aspects of life. For instance, under capitalism, the bourgeoisie determines the economy; more importantly, because the "ideas of the ruling class are in every epoch the ruling ideas" (*The German Ideology*, 1846), bourgeois ideology controls the family, the state, and culture as well. Through ideology "men become conscious of this conflict and fight it out" ("Preface to *A Contribution to the Critique of Political Economy*," 1859).

Marxism is little understood in America, and the recent demise of communism in the USSR and Eastern Europe only seems to confirm its irrelevance to American culture. Yet, for a time, communism emerged as a powerful force in American political and cultural life. Its very vitality produced, in part, its vilification during the cold war. The hysteria of 1950s anticommunism led to blacklists and purges in unions, universities, Hollywood, and the government as the House Un-American Activities Committee, the FBI, and local "red squads" harrassed, jailed, deported, and executed known or suspected communists. Opportunistic politicians such as Joseph McCarthy and Richard Nixon carved out careers by orchestrating smear campaigns against opponents, instilling a mass fear of the "communist menace." Perhaps the most egregious travesty of this *Scoundrel Time* (1976), as Lillian *Hellman called it, was the execution of Ethel and Julius Rosenberg as spies.

Communism as an idea is ultimately inseparable from its institutions. In 1919, a few leftwing socialists formed a small American Communist Party (CPUSA). After the shock waves of the 1929 stock market crash rippled into the Great Depression, however, communism emerged briefly as a force in America; Marxism seemed to account for the plight of workers and farmers. While the Party maintained its extreme leftism during the early years of the depression, its militant organizing on behalf of the unemployed, industrial workers, sharecroppers, farmers, and African Americans inspired an entire generation. By the end of the 1930s, the CPUSA grew from a small movement of several thousand members into a mass organization attracting millions of "fellow travelers."

As artists and intellectuals confronted the horrors of the depression and the dust bowl, communism profoundly influenced culture. Literary radicals invented a new form of narrative—reportage—combining personal testimony and social critique; it influenced the fiction, drama, and poetry of the decade and provided women writers with a genre that could wed domestic fiction to political commentary and historical analysis. Josephine *Herbst's *Rope of Gold* (1939), Mary Heaton Vorse's *Strike!* (1930), and Myra Page's *Moscow Yankee* (1935), among others, weave reports from Cuban soviets, the Gastonia strike, and Russian factories into novels about intimate relations between radical couples. Black and white working-class women's life stories were published in *Working Woman, Woman Today*, and the women's pages of the *Daily Worker*. Because literary radicalism explored working-class experience, women novelists such as Agnes *Smedley (*Daughter of Earth*, 1929), Fielding *Burke (*Call Home the Heart*, 1932), and Meridel *Le Sueur (*Salute to Spring*, 1940) could detail the pain of growing up poor *and* female in America. Their feminized proletarian fiction described the powerful solidarity women felt when they joined the communist movement.

But communism's glory days were shortlived. From its inception, American communism has been riven by contradictions as it tried to impose European theories of class onto America's racially and ethnically divided cultures. Despite Communist Party leader Earl Browder's 1936 presidential campaign declaration that "Communism was twentieth-century Americanism," the Party never really achieved an American face, because it adhered to Stalin's brutal program of collectivization, gulags, and pronatalism to create "socialism in one state." Many supporters deserted after the Hitler-Stalin pact was signed in 1939. What was left of the Party all but disappeared after Stalin's horrors were publicly denounced in Krushchev's 1956 address to the Twentieth Party Congress. The confluence of Party members' disaffection with and government repression of communism during the 1950s helps explain the historical amnesia obscuring communism's place in America.

Feminism has also forgotten the importance of the CPUSA to women during the lean years between its first and second waves. Women's relationship to communism has always been ambiguous. As a theory analyzing the degradation of personal life under capitalism and a practice struggling to end the subjugation of oppressed people, communism appeals to radical women. Yet as a revolutionary theory that argues for the primacy of class analysis, communism maintains gender and ethnicity as secondary to its social critique. Therefore, women and national minorities remain peripheral to its organization. For instance, when Mary Inman (*In Women's Defense*, 1940) cogently criticized sexism within the Party, she was purged from the CPUSA for her outspokenness. Still, as early as the *Manifesto*, communism helped to raise "the woman question."

Engels had found the *Origins of the Family, Private Property and the State* (1884) in the sexual division of labor resulting from women's childbearing and foresaw women's inevitable freedom with capitalism's overthrow. The first few years after the 1917 Bolshevik revolution seemed to confirm this for many American observers. Writers such as Ella Winter (*Red Virtue*, 1933) and Ruth Gruber (*I Went to the Soviet Arctic*, 1939) reported on women's tremendous gains in the new Russia—equal pay and educational opportunities, full employment, free birth control and abortion, easy access to divorce. As American feminism waned following suffrage, communism kept alive the discussion of sex and gender inequalities by providing a new model of women's roles.

The possibilities of answering the "woman question" by actually entering the historical process like their Soviet sisters attracted both working- and middle-class women to the CPUSA. While only one woman, Elizabeth Gurley Flynn, sat on the Central Committee, women made up 40 percent of Party membership by World War II. Some African-American women, such as Claudia Jones in the 1930s and Angela *Davis in the 1960s, emerged as national leaders, but despite organizing efforts in Alabama and Harlem during the depression, the Party never achieved wide influence in the black community. Still, women were instrumental in organizing Unemployed Councils, working against racism, and challenging "male supremacy" in the movement. For many women the connection to a world-historical movement—one willing to fight against fas-cism's first battle in Spain and stand up for the poor and oppressed at home—meant that for a time they could transcend gender restrictions by associating with working-class struggle.

As a source of theories about the operations of capitalism and ideology, Marxism remains a powerful explanatory tool influencing today's feminist, anti-imperialist, antiracist, gay liberation, and ecology movements even as they resist and reshape Marxism. As the largest radical organization in twentieth-century America the CPUSA's legacy, even to women, is substantial.

[*See also* Marxist Feminism; Socialist Feminism.]

• Theodore Draper, *The Roots of American Communism* (1957). Peggy Dennis, *The Autobiography of An American Communist* (1977). Jessica Mitford, *A Fine Old Conflict* (1977). Robert Shaffer, "Women and the Communist Party, U.S.A., 1930–1940," *Socialist Review* 45 (May–June 1979): 73–118. Angela Davis, *Women, Race, and Class* (1981). Mark Naison, *Communists in Harlem during the Depression* (1983). Harvey Klehr, *The Heyday of American Communism* (1984). Ellen Schrecker, *No Ivory Tower: McCarthyism and the Universities* (1986). Charlotte Nekola and Paula Rabinowitz, eds., *Writing Red: An Anthology of American Women Writers, 1930–1940* (1987). Robin D. G. Kelley, *Hammer and Hoe: Alabama Communists during the Great Depression* (1990). Dorothy Healey and Maurice Isserman, *Dorothy Healey Remembers: A Life in the American Communist Party* (1990). Paula Rabinowitz, *Labor and Desire: Women's Revolutionary Fiction in Depression America* (1991).

Paula Rabinowitz

COMMUNITY. In attesting to the significance, and often the vitality, of community life, American women writers have long asserted their own enduring commitment to influencing both the nation's image of itself and the forms its inhabitants' lives take. Before the *Civil War, women's fictional representations of American communities mainly conformed to the formulas of the popular village sketch. Like similar work by male writers, sketches by Harriet Beecher *Stowe, Sarah *Hale, Fanny Forrester, and others affirmed the American community as fixed, stable, and homogeneous (and usually located in New England) just when the nation was expanding geographically and becoming more ethnically diverse. A few women explicitly liberalized this image—Eliza Lee by portraying differences among women in *Sketches of a New England Village* (1838), Lydia *Sigourney by emphasizing racial and religious differences in *Sketch of Connecticut* (1824), Caroline *Kirkland by showing the formation of cross-class communities in the West in *A New Home* (1839). Even in modes that did not depict community, writers often actively elicited readers' sense of community with each other. The literature linked with antebellum (white) women's culture—*domestic fiction and sentimental poetry—united women readers in a translocal, gender-based community that valorized their particular values and experiences. At mid-century, as *class tensions intensified and civil war loomed, some women drew on women's culture's ethos to fuse readers into politically engaged communities: Rebecca Harding *(Davis) by soliciting middle-class readers on behalf of industrial workers in *Life in the Iron Mills* (1861), Stowe by activating white women (and men) against *slavery in *Uncle Tom's Cabin* (1852), Harriet *Jacobs by appealing to white women's *sisterhood with enslaved black women in *Incidents in the Life of a Slave Girl* (1861).

Following the Civil War and into the twentieth century, as urbanization, class stratification, and the diversification of the nation's population intensified, women's representations of community tended to be more self-consciously reflective of their class, race, and, often, region. The New England narratives of Stowe, Alice *Brown, *Jewett and others built on the village sketch tradition, exhibited great artistry in portraying everyday community life and representing it as woman-centered, and also displayed a nativist bias in their emphasis on the Americanness of pre-industrial Protestant New England communities. Some, such as Rose Terry *Cooke and Mary E. Wilkins *Freeman, adapted the tradition to stress a New England provincialism in which local communities stifled individualism, particularly among women. As women from nondominant groups entered print in greater numbers, they often wrote about and for their own communities, situating them within *racism and oppression while asserting their unique histories, cultures, and traditions. The writing of Frances *Harper, Pauline *Hopkins, Mrs. N. F. Mossell and other African Americans detailed the ravages of white supremacy but stressed African-American resilience, including women's achievements, and encouraged readers' pride in and commitment to African-American community. Native American women sought to enlist white support for their communities (such as Sarah *Hopkins's *Life Among the Prairies*, 1883), and to preserve Native American culture (such as *Zitkala-Sa's *Old Indian Legends*, 1901). Asian-American fiction writer *Sui Sin Far reflected Chinese Americans' negotiations between traditional life and assimilationist pressures in the pieces collected in *Mrs. Spring Fragrance* (1912), drawing a composite, albeit implicit, portrait of the new community emerging from these negotiations. African American Alice *Dunbar-Nelson took a multicultural stance, juxtaposing vignettes of members of several racial and ethnic groups in urban New Orleans in *The Goodness of St. Rocque* (1899) to indicate that community must comprise the unique circumstances of a diversifying America.

Until recently, community was a vexed subject in much literature by twentieth-century women, many of whom concentrated on women's attainment of selfhood. In narratives recounting women's efforts at self-realization by such middle-class white writers as Kate *Chopin, Willa *Cather, Edith *Wharton, Carson *McCullers and Shirley *Jackson, community was often associated with stifling obligations and roles. For many others for whom the question of individualism was inflected by a commitment to and association with racial, ethnic, and/or working class communities—including Anzia *Yezierska, Nella *Larsen, Agnes *Smedley, Edith Summers *Kelley—the tensions between protagonists' communities of origin or societal ascription and their desires for individualized selfhood were often unresolvable. Some writers did remain more immersed in community. Among these, some sought to preserve *folk culture or indigenous life—Zora Neale *Hurston by rendering black vernacular southern communities, Che-Na-Wah Weitch-Ah-Wah by recording the history and lifeways of California's Klamath River Indians, for example. In *Bronzeville* (1945), poet Gwendolyn *Brooks cultivated black cultural resistance and pride, celebrating the versatility and vitality of blacks' adaptation to urban ghetto life, while the activist Meridel *Le Sueur illuminated the oppressive circumstances of urban white *working-class women, hoping to forge readers into communities dedicated to structural change.

When community began reemerging as a more widely honored concept in the 1960s and 1970s, women's portrayals of community life reflected a deepening complexity and variety. Helen Hooven Santmyer draws conservatively on the village sketch tradition to depict an American community whose stability inheres in traditional family structure and group homogeneity. Others, while commemorating the culture and history of a specific group, equate community with diversity. Frequently weaving stories and sketches into extended narratives, and frequently portraying the community as a reconfigured family, they foreground community members' disparate ways of negotiating between ethnic or racial traditions and the dominant culture and society. This approach is prominent among Native Americans such as Leslie Marmon *Silko and Louise *Erdrich; African Americans such as Alice *Walker, Gloria *Naylor, and Toni *Morrison; Asian Americans, including Maxine Hong *Kingston and Amy *Tan; Latina writers going back to Josephina *Niggli's *Mexican Village* (1945); such Jewish-American writers as Tillie *Olsen. Several regional writers—Joan Chase, Barbara Kingsolver—also fashion community narratives around multiple voices and reconstructed families, indicating that community must be grounded in difference.

Still other contemporary works, such as the story collections of Grace *Paley, suggest that community must be forged among different ethnic, racial, and political groups, to each of which Paley's collections give voice. Such sophisticated versions of community take on extra political urgency for writers such as Audre *Lorde and Cherríe *Moraga, who push their racial/ethnic communities to come to terms with unsettling differences in expressing both their claims to community membership and the multiplicity of members' identities, including their *lesbianism. In collections such as *This Bridge Called My Back* (1981), Lorde, Moraga, and others also continue the mid-nineteenth-century tradition of urging all readers into communities committed to a more egalitarian nation. In short, whether emphasizing the virtues of community or disputing them, American women writers have long drawn attention to connections between the composition and conduct of community and the character and quality of life in the nation.

[*See also* Gendered Spaces.]

• Ida Honaker Herron, *The Small Town in American Literature* (1939). Nancy Cott, *The Bonds of Womanhood: Women's "Sphere" in New England, 1780–1835* (1977). Nina Auerbach, *Communities of Women: An Idea in Fiction* (1978). Thomas Bender, *Community and Social Change in America* (1978). Dexter Fisher, ed., *The Third Woman: Minority Writers of the United States* (1980). Judith Fetterley, ed., *Provisions: A Reader from Nineteenth-Century Women* (1985). Carroll Smith-Rosenberg, *Disorderly Conduct: Visions of Gender in Victorian America* (1985). Mary V. Dearborn, *Pocahontas's Daughters: Gender and Ethnicity in American Culture* (1986). Joseph Allen Boone, *Tradition Counter Tradition: Love and the Form of Fiction* (1987). Sandra A. Zagarell, "Narrative of Community: The Identification of a Genre," *Signs: Journal of Women in Culture and Society* 13, no. 3 (1988): 498–527. Elizabeth Ammons, *Conflicting Stories: American Women Writers at the Turn into the Twentieth Century* (1991).

Sandra A. Zagarell

COMPOSITION. Olive Songhurst, a Quaker from Philadelphia, was the first woman in the republic permitted to teach rhetoric and composition, in 1702, followed by Mary McAllester, head of a boarding school for girls in Philadelphia in 1767. From 1792 to 1833 at her Litchfield Female Academy in Connecticut, Sarah

Pierce (1767–1852) taught composition in light of Hugh Blair's *Lectures on Rhetoric* (1783), and she defended her curriculum for women in her commencement addresses. While teaching in Middlebury, Vermont, Emma Hart Willard (1787–1870) proposed in *Plan for the Improvement of Female Education* (1819) the first school where women could take courses such as rhetoric on levels close to those of men's college courses.

Willard opened her school in Troy, New York, in 1821. Three other women soon had similar schools: a former Pierce student, Catharine *Beecher (1800–1878), founder of the Hartford Female Seminary in 1823; Zilpah Grant Banister (1794–1874), head, Adams Female Academy, Londonderry, New Hampshire, from 1824 to 1827, and Ipswich Female Seminary, Massachusetts, from 1828 to 1839; and Mary Lyon (1797–1849), co-head with Grant at Ipswich and founder of Mount Holyoke in 1837. Like Willard, they trained other women to assign and comment on weekly compositions following principles of argument and audience appeal in college-level rhetorics, specifically Samuel Newman's *Practical System of Rhetoric* (1827), for first- and second-year students, and Richard Whately's *Elements of Rhetoric* (1828), for advanced students. Like Willard in her essays, Beecher in such writings as *An Essay on the Education of Female Teachers* (1835) and Lyon in *Principles and Design of the Mount Holyoke Female Seminary* (1837) persuasively defended their plans by adapting rhetorical patterns and tropes advocated by the rhetoricians they taught.

The students obviously felt empowered by their rhetorical training. Many became highly praised teachers, heads, and school founders, as did students trained in rhetoric, composition, and other subjects at the Institute for Colored Youth in Philadelphia under Fanny Jackson *Coppin (1837–1913). Coppin began teaching there after receiving her A.B. at Oberlin in 1865, in the men's rhetorically focused classical course; from 1869 to 1901, she was the head principal at the institute, the first African American with such a position. She used her rhetorical training in class teaching, reports on her innovative programs, and speeches urging support for education for African Americans.

In the post–Civil War era, beliefs in industrial efficiency and scientific objectivity led to the view that rhetoric is not persuasion but an objective presentation of information in clear and grammatically correct sentences organized by modes. In writing classes, topics were narrowed to historical backgrounds and explications of literary works. Among the few to break from this narrowing was Clara Frances Stevens

(1855–1934), head of rhetoric at Mount Holyoke from 1881 to 1921. She instituted the first undergraduate major in rhetoric, with electives involving persuasive writing and debates on contemporary issues, and she designed the first college journalism course, as noted by John Wozniak (*English Composition in Eastern Colleges, 1850–1940*, 1978). In *The Ethics of English Work* (1903), she argues that composition topics should engage both writer and audience.

Another reformer was Gertrude Buck (1871–1922), the first woman in the United States to receive a doctorate in rhetoric and to publish rhetorics, all reformist: two on argumentation (1899, 1906), one defining exposition as a fusion of description and interpretation (1899), and one extending the rhetorical narrative mode to include creative writing (1906). She published essays as well as books while head of the rhetoric program at Vassar from 1899 to 1922. She wrote collaboratively, twice with Elisabeth Woodbridge Morris (1870–1964), a Vassar colleague with a doctorate from Yale. They viewed composing as interaction between writer and reader on shared concerns.

This view was also held by the National Council of Teachers of English (NCTE), founded in 1911, of which Stevens and Buck were among the earliest woman members. Emma J. Breck of Oakland High School, California, was elected at the founding meeting as first vice president. Essie Chamberlain (1875?–1948) of Oak Park High School, Illinois, was the first woman to serve as acting president and to give the presidential address (1924); Rewey Belle Inglis (1885–1967) of University High School, Minneapolis, became the first woman president in 1929. All were classroom teachers who also published essays in the *English Journal* on teaching writing from kindergarten through twelfth grade. The University of Minnesota's Dora Valentine Smith (1893–1985), NCTE president in 1936, has been considered the primary leader in English education because of extensive publications, training courses and workshops for K–12 teachers, and work on key NCTE committees. Although NCTE membership was open, hotel segregation policies kept most minority teachers from attending conferences. Not until 1977 was the first African-American president elected, Charlotte K. Brooks (b. 1918), advocate of African-American literature and author of *They Can Learn English* (1973).

A number of women pioneered reforms in modern college composition teaching: Mina Shaughnessy (1925?–1978), whose work in the 1960s with basic writers at New York University led to her *Errors and Expectations: A Guide for the Teacher of Basic Writing* (1977), the first book to analyze causes of basic writing problems; Josephine Miles (1911–1985), who in the 1960s helped plan and write about the Bay Area Writing Project, the first forum for interchange of ideas between kindergarten through high school composition teachers; and Janet Emig (b. 1928), whose publications in the 1970s were the first to give case studies and language development research supporting the view that composition instructors should not assign rhetorical modes but let students discover their own in the process of writing.

• Emily Noyes Vanderpoel, comp., *Chronicles of a Pioneer School from 1792 to 1833, Being the History of Miss Sarah Pierce and Her Litchfield School*, ed. Elizabeth C. Barney Buel (1903). Willystine Goodsell, ed., *Pioneers of Women's Education in the United States: Emma Willard, Catherine* [sic] *Beecher, Mary Lyon* (1931). Thomas Woody, *A History of Women's Education in the United States*, 2 vols. (1966). J. N. Hook, *A Long Way Together: A Personal View of the NCTE's First Sixty-Seven Years* (1979). James Berlin, *Rhetoric and Reality: Writing Instruction in American Colleges, 1900–1985* (1987). Albert R. Kitzhaber, *Rhetoric in American Colleges, 1850–1900* (1990). Jeanne Marcum Gerlach and Virginia R. Monseau, *Missing Chapters: Ten Pioneering Women in NCTE and English Education* (1991).

Carolyn H. Smith

CONCRETE POEMS. See Poetry, article on Concrete Poems.

CONFESSIONAL NONFICTION. From a tradition of * spiritual autobiography rooted in the religious act of confession, confessional writing by women has continued to evolve in the nineteenth and twentieth centuries as self-conscious narratives of personal development. Twentieth-century writers of confessional nonfiction often explore and restructure the chaos of the past or the present as it lives within them, transforming their struggles through language into a unified structure that may, in the end, serve as part of their mythology of self. * H.D.'s struggle within herself regarding her relationships with Ezra Pound and Frances Gregg is recorded in *HERmione* (completed 1927, published 1981); Kate * Millett's *Flying* (1974) is another example of a personal and self-aware journey. The act of writing may serve as confession or as a narrative of one's internal struggle with inner or outer oppressive forces, and may function as part of the author's process of healing or survival. As Pam Brown writes in the anthology *The Stories We Hold: Tales of Women's Spiritual Development* (1986), "I am writing to save my life."

Jarena * Lee believed that her own record of the experience of God's work in and through her, *The Life and Religious Experiences of Jarena Lee, a Coloured Lady*, would convert others to Christianity and thus save them (1836). *Amanda Smith's Own Story* by Amanda Smith (1893) and *Dark Symphony* by Elizabeth Laura Adams (1942) also reflect personal and spiritual quests. Dorothy * Day writes in her introduction to *The Long Loneliness* (1952), titled "Confession," "I can write only of myself, what I know of myself, and I pray with St. Augustine, 'Lord, that I may know myself, in order to know Thee.' " A more recent spiritual autobiography is Annie * Dillard's *Pilgrim at Tinker Creek* (1974).

Confessional writing has been particularly important for women as a means of exposing the problems and narrow strictures of their lives. Ann Eliza Young shocked the nation in 1875 with the publication of her book *Wife No. 19, or The Story of A Life in Bondage*. As the nineteenth wife of the Mormon prophet Brigham Young, she sought a divorce in 1873. Young dedicated her book to the Mormon wives of Utah, saying she "was driven . . . by sheer desperation" to tell their tale. A more recent exposé is Wanwadee Larsen's *Confessions of a Mail Order Bride: American Life through Thai Eyes* (1989), which drew attention to a practice many Americans thought discontinued.

In popular culture the role of confessional nonfiction has been important both in magazines (i.e., *True Story, True Confessions, Modern Romances*) and books. In recent years there has been a trend toward publishing stories by women who have endured painful experiences common to women, providing important resources for others in similar circumstances. Examples include Jennifer Barr's *Within a Dark Wood: The Personal Story of a Rape Victim* (1979), Sylvia Fraser's *My Father's House: A Memoir of Incest and Healing* (1987), and Betty Rollin's *First, You Cry* (1976). Works such as *Lesbian Nuns: Breaking Silence* (1985), edited by Rosemary Curb and Nancy Manahan, confront the societal mythology—and misinformation— about who women really are.

The confessional nature of a work is often only one of its strains, as most confessional writing can be classed into several literary categories. Confessional nonfiction does, however, defy pretense. The author must make sense of the experience, first to herself and then to her readers, illuminating both the writer's and the reader's understanding of female experience.

[*See also* Autobiography; Prison Writing.]

• Alma Gómez et al., eds., *Cuentos: Stories by Latinas* (1983). Margaret Cruikshank, ed., *New Lesbian Writing* (1984). Carol Bruchac et al., eds., *The Stories We Hold Secret: Tales of Women's Spiritual Development* (1986). Sue E. Houchins, ed., *Spiritual Narratives* (1988).

K. Graehme Hall

CONFESSIONAL POETRY. *See* Poetry.

CONJURE WOMAN. A term used to refer to a woman in African-American communities believed to have extranatural powers. She can use these powers for good or for evil, as long as the supplicant is willing to pay the price that she requests. Usually separated geographically from the communities in which they wield their powers, these women have precedents in African healers and the tradition of Vodun that was transmitted from Dahomey by way of Haiti. It entered the United States by way of New Orleans, where Vodun's fame grew with its greatest practitioner, Marie Laveau.

In African-American literature, conjure women range from Charles W. Chesnutt's *The Conjure Woman* (1900) into contemporary poetry and fiction. Margaret * Walker's "Molly Means" (1942) has the power to make her love rival howl like a dog; Toni * Morrison's M'Dear (*The Bluest Eye*, 1970) can simply look at the stool of an ill person and name the cause of their sickness; Alice * Walker's Tante Rosie in "The Revenge of Hannah Kemhuff" (1973) brings modern methods of discovery and a conspicuous knowledge of human psychology to her conjuring powers; Minnie Ransom in Toni Cade * Bambara's *The Salt Eaters* (1980) can converse with the dead; and Gloria * Naylor's *Mama Day* (1988) can raise a lightning storm to strike down the house of her grandniece's enemy. Numerous in the works of contemporary black women writers, conjure women seem to be as respected in their fictional representations as they were and are in African-American history.

Trudier Harris

CONSCIOUSNESS-RAISING, or CR as it came to be known, was a group practice by which predominately white, middle-class women during the late 1960s and 1970s became aware of their common oppression. Through a collective sharing of individual experiences, such women soon discovered the similarity of their lives and began to see how that similarity was connected to their gender, to the condition of being female in a male-dominated society. Indeed, it was in the consciousness-raising groups of this period that women began to understand the broader dimension of their "personal" problems, learning to see many of those problems as the effects of an inequitable patriarchal system.

Although frequently identified with the early contemporary feminist movement, the concept behind consciousness-raising originated in the *civil rights movement of the 1960s, during which people were encouraged to "tell it like it is." It was believed that talking about one's personal experience could have a radicalizing effect because it could lead to the kind of self-awareness necessary for change. For the African American, this meant discovering "the black within the negro," an identity that had been stripped away by years of white oppression. For women, it meant realizing, for example, that the long-standing taboo against female self-assertion, rather than being a natural law, was really a convenient way to keep women "in their place." In both cases, it was believed that the possession of such knowledge would promote reform; the implied assumption was that individual experiences could have public consequences, that the personal could, in fact, be political.

Many of the central architects of the early contemporary feminist movement and CR were indeed prompted to take political action because of personal experience. Most of them had been involved in the civil rights movement, the New Left, or such liberal student political organizations as the Student Nonviolent Coordinating Committee (SNCC) and the Students for a Democratic Society (SDS), and it was their experiences of gender discrimination there that led to the development of their own political agenda. Indeed, what these women came to realize was that these groups, despite their egalitarian ideals, often lacked a critical consciousness of gender relations. They were, for instance, dominated by men, while women members were often delegated conventionally female work. They also continued to adhere to a sexual double standard in spite of their official call for "free love." Moreover, the concerns that women expressed over such inequities were often dismissed as trivial, and it was this dismissal, perhaps more than anything else, that prompted women to form a coalition that would specifically address their needs.

Consciousness-raising groups brought more women into this coalition by helping them to recognize the deleterious effects of unequal distribution of power. In small, active discussion groups women gathered to talk about a range of problems from competitiveness with other women to unequal pay at work, seeing—often for the first time—the diverse and insidious manifestations of patriarchy. They often read and discussed novels that mirrored some of these problems as well, novels such as Erica *Jong's Fear of Flying, which portrayed a woman's struggle to achieve an identity outside

proscribed patriarchal codes. It was hoped that by gaining an awareness of the interrelationship of these problems and the underlying system that contributed to their formation, women would take an active stance and would begin dismantling the system by challenging it at its most local level.

Despite the fact that they indeed inspired many women to resist the limitations imposed upon them, consciousness-raising groups were short-lived. There were both external and internal reasons for this. To begin with, the concept was contested by an entire segment of the feminist movement that had strong ties with the New Left and believed that these groups were apolitical and essentialistic—apolitical because they focused on the personal; essentialistic because in emphasizing the personal they reinforced the notion that feelings are exclusively a woman's domain. The groups were also hindered by racial, class, and heterosexual biases, and were criticized particularly by women of color and lesbians for failing to take into consideration the full range of female experience.

Most significant among the problems that led to the groups' dissolution was weak organization. In trying not to replicate a hierarchical power structure, groups often refused to assign leaders; leaders emerged anyway, but through the assertion of will instead of democratic process. Egos clashed and group members found themselves engaged in the very kind of power struggles to which they were ideologically opposed. This situation led to fragmentation and prevented the groups from continuing to serve as effective vehicles for change.

[See also Women's Movement.]

• Kathie Sarachild, "A Program for Feminist Consciousness Raising" in Notes from the Second Year: Women's Liberation; Major Writings of the Radical Feminists (1968; reprinted in Women Together, ed. Judith Papachristou, 1976). Pam Allen, "Free Space" in Notes from the Third Year (1970; reprinted in Radical Feminism, eds. Anne Koedt, Ellen Levine, and Anita Rapone, 1973). Sookie Stambler, ed., Women's Liberation: Blueprint for the Future (1970). Kathie Sarachild, Feminist Revolution: Redstockings of the Women's Liberation Movement (1978). National Organization for Women, NOW Guidelines for Feminist Consciousness Raising (1982). Anita Shreve, Women Together, Women Alone (1989). Alice Echols, Daring to Be Bad: Radical Feminism in America (1989).

Ona Russell

CONSERVATISM. In The Handmaid's Tale (1985), Margaret Atwood depicts a dystopian world in which conservatism is the prevailing dogma. In Atwood's vision of tomorrow, the conservative ideological belief in preserving established traditions is made manifest through control of the female *body. Women are allotted roles based on their reproductive/domestic functions: A woman's place, by official mandate, is in the home, or else.

Although set in the future, Atwood's fictional world is nonetheless anchored in contemporary North American culture. In her futuristic city of Gilead, Atwood represents as nightmare what could be considered the dreams and long-term aspirations of such conservative icons as Moral Majority's Jerry Falwell, former president Ronald Reagan, talk-show host Rush Limbaugh, media pundit Pat Buchanan, and founder of Operation Rescue Randall Terry.

Perhaps more ominously (or, depending on your point of view, promisingly), the conservative movement in the United States includes a number of prominent and powerful women, including one-time antigay spokesperson Anita Bryant, author Marabel Morgan, columnist Midge Decter, conservative pundits Phyllis Schlafly and Connie Marshner, and Concerned Women for America's founder, Beverly LaHaye. While countless explanations ranging from consciousness-raising to man-hating have been offered to explain why and how women become feminists, the reasons women adopt conservative positions are less frequently discussed. Are right-wing women born or made?

In *Right-Wing Women* (1983), Andrea *Dworkin argues that they are made, or rather, that these women are forced to take up conservative positions because they are the only safe ones in a society intrinsically hostile to women. Girls, Dworkin argues, are taught by their mothers to conform to patriarchal, conventional norms and mandates in exchange for protection from endemic male *violence. What's more, Dworkin asserts, a woman who evidences this self-destructive faith in a system out to demean her comes to be seen and, in the only way allowed to her, valued by men as the(ir) ideal woman.

Dworkin suggests that the political-ideological-religious Right offers these conforming women several key benefits: black-and-white order in the midst of chaos, shelter in the form of a home defined as her "place," safety from her rightful fears of violence, inexorable rules by which to conform, and the promise of love—God/Man's—in exchange for her unswerving obedience. In a male-dominated, woman-hating world, the right-wing woman's position is, Dworkin concludes, eminently logical.

A more nuanced theory is worked out by Deirdre English in her article, "The Fear that Feminism Will Free Men First." As does Dworkin, English considers antifeminism to be a means of survival in an ever-hostile environment. While feminists go on the offensive vis-à-vis this hostility in hopes of a better future, right-wing women, English suggests, adopt a more defensive strategy in hopes of returning to a romanticized past. Examining anti-abortion, antifeminist women in particular, English argues that these women believe freedom of choice will obviate a man's moral responsibility when it comes to sex, freeing him from his responsibility to marry the woman/women he impregnates. According to English, sexually conservative women believe that the "sexual revolution" has forced many women to abdicate their "power" to withhold sex in exchange for *marriage—an exchange which, historically, has for many women been an economic and political necessity. English concludes that the coincidental rise of *feminism and divorce rates, not to mention the increasing feminization of poverty, only stoke the antifeminist woman's fears that feminism really does free men first.

In her recent book *Backlash: The Undeclared War against American Women* (1991), Susan Faludi devotes a chapter to the strategies, motivations, and motivators of the conservative "New Right." While Faludi does not exclusively focus on women, she shares Dworkin's and English's belief that the Right never misses a chance to attack feminism by holding it responsible for the modern woman's alleged unhappiness.

In contrast to Dworkin, Faludi does not see the Right as merely extending its entrenched dominance over women but as struggling to keep what little influence and power is still allotted to it. As such, the backlash against feminism, Faludi contends, is less a power-play by the already powerful than it is the last gasp of an endangered species. While the greater percentage of this species, according to Faludi, is male, not female, she does contend that the New Right shrewdly employs right-wing women to launch its most direct attacks against feminism. It is Faludi's argument that, as these women deliver public speeches and earn respect for their words and actions, they often unintentionally express and enjoy many of the feminist positions and accomplishments they set out to oppose.

As Faludi suggests, right-wing women are more than capable of speaking for themselves and hence rightfully deserve to be heard here. As Marabel Morgan and her "Total Woman," Phyllis Schlafly and her "Positive Woman" and even Midge Decter and her fabulous "Liberated Women" all attest, conservative women share a common belief that a woman's proper sphere of influence is in the traditional home as a committed wife and mother. The woman who puts her family first is not a disempowered victim of false consciousness nor a traitor to her sex. Instead, according to these conservative authors, she is a powerful shaper of our country's moral future through her daily interactions with her children and the support she gives her spouse. She, unlike the at times misguided, macho, or even man-hating feminists whose model she should and does reject, is doing the right thing, not only for her self and family but for the nation.

The importance attached to traditional marital and familial relationships is reflected in Midge Decter's critique of the sexual revolution—as not allowing women the freedom *not* to have sex—as well as in her doubts as to why a woman would choose to work on assembly lines or other jobs filled with "routine drudgery" when she could be doing the far more essential work of tending to her family. It is perhaps nowhere more evident than in Morgan's *The Total Woman* (1973), where the author vows that the route to true marital bliss and family accord is for the wife to accept, support, surrender to, and even worship her husband.

Even when the *family is not the direct topic of conversation, conservative women continue to stress the importance of maintaining traditionally defined *gender roles. For instance, Phyllis Schlafly grounds her opposition to women in military combat on the idea that men are born to fight, women to nurture. Hence, any divergence from these roles should be viewed as cause for grave concern and protest. Schlafly argues that the idea of women/mothers fighting in enemy combat is a barbaric, disrespectful, and unnatural practice that degrades both women and men as well as the nation. She concludes her lecture by arguing that no man can be respected if he allows a woman to "do his fighting for him." Many liberals, of course, might counter that Schlafly herself could qualify as one such woman fighter, and there can be no doubt that conservative women such as Schlafly are more than capable of combat.

Combat, in fact, is a favorite metaphor of one of the more vocal conservative women of the 1990s. Although Camille Paglia self-identifies as a feminist, the fact that this media cause célèbre is the darling of conservatives signals that her allegiances may actually lie on the other side of the fence. Paglia, who believes in the "truth in sexual *stereotypes," in many ways embraces the conservative ideology outlined by Dworkin—with a twist. While she sees *patriarchy as the protective, civilizing force that operates to shelter women from male violence and bodily harm, Paglia assigns women's purported base sexual nature the blame for that harm. In Paglia's world-view it seems, women are sexual creatures who are "asking for it," and who should just accept this fact of nature.

Further, Paglia rails against feminism for misleading women about the true cause of their oppression and for pretending that women can ever be agents of social change, can ever be the skilled, organized aggressors that men essentially are.

In making her claims—in her books, articles, reviews, on talk shows, and in interviews—Paglia has demonstrated that she is an aggressive exception to her own rule, only further proving the point that conservative women, despite their disclaimers, are not only extremely competent on the battlefield, but fighting to win. Even with the end of the Reagan-Bush era in 1992, the odds are that these skirmishes between liberals and conservatives will, like old soldiers, never die; but nor is it likely that they will just fade away.

[*See also* Liberal Feminism; Radical Feminism; Backlash.]

• Midge Decter, *The Liberated Woman and Other Americans* (1971). Marabel Morgan, *The Total Woman* (1973). Phyllis Schlafley, *The Power of the Positive Woman* (1977). Deirdre English, "The Fear that Feminism Will Free Men First," in *Powers of Desire: The Politics of Sexuality*, ed. Ann Snitow, Christine Stansell, and Sharon Thompson (1983), pp. 477–483. Camille Paglia, *Sexual Personae: Art and Decadence from Nefertiti to Emily Dickinson* (1990).

Cynthia J. Davis

CONSTRUCTIVISM. *See* Essentialism.

CONTRACEPTION. *See* Abortion; Birth; Birth Control; Reproduction.

CONVERSION NARRATIVES. *See* Spiritual Narratives.

COOKBOOKS. *See* Recipe Books.

COOKE, Rose Terry (1827–1892), short fiction writer. The psychic terrain of Rose Terry Cooke's stories is often as rugged as the hills of Wethersfield, Connecticut, where she was born. Cooke's privileged upbringing concluded with the reversal of her family's fortunes in her mid-teens. After teaching and serving as a governess, Cooke returned home (now Hartford) to begin a successful writing career.

Although she published poetry, a play, children's stories, and novels, Cooke's short fiction, collected in *Somebody's Neighbors* (1881), *Root-Bound and Other Sketches* (1885), *The Sphinx's Children and Other Stories* (1886), and *Huckleberries Gathered from New England Hills* (1891), speaks most powerfully to contemporary readers. Her versatile voice, enhanced by pungent New England dialect, combines granitic realism ("Too Late"), delicate romanticism ("Dely's

Cow"), and subversive sentimentalism ("Clary's Trial"); grinding tragedy ("Mrs. Flint's Married Experience") and athletic comedy ("Cal Culver and the Devil"). Her characters mirror their time and place, from men departing to the Civil War ("My Thanksgiving") and West to find fortune ("A Black Silk"), to the more fully portrayed women who remain behind, in Cooke's ambiguous concept, "at home."

Widely admired by influential contemporaries such as William Dean Howells, Harriet *Spofford, Harriet Beecher *Stowe, John Greenleaf Whittier, and Annie *Fields, Cooke has often been reductively assigned to a "*local color" tradition, although her range exceeds geographical boundaries. Among her important contributions to American literature are subversive old women heroines like Aunt Huldah in "Freedom Wheeler's Controversy With Providence" and Celia in "How Celia Changed Her Mind." The hidden heroes of human existence, such characters form the connective tissue of the social body, perform ordinary tasks in remarkable and unremarkable ways, and affirm the enduring value of human relationships.

Although Cooke explores issues of social class ("Doom and Dan"), sexuality ("My Visitation"), and race ("Too Late"), she illuminates most brightly the dark corners of women's experiences. She parallels many perceptions of her contemporary, Emily *Dickinson, whom she did not know. For example, her metaphor of "stillness" encodes the traditional repressions of her own observant Calvinism, of which she offered piercing critiques ("Some Account of Thomas Tucker"). One of Cooke's most potent messages for women, rendered poignant by her financially ruinous marriage at forty-six to a man sixteen years younger, was the power of women's speech and the danger of their silence. Cooke's voice echoes forward into the twentieth century, from the work of Edith *Wharton (*Ethan Frome*, 1911; *Summer*, 1917) to that of working-class Maine writer Carolyn Chute (*The Beans of Egypt, Maine*, 1985).

• Jean Downey, "A Biographical and Critical Study of Rose Terry Cooke," Ph.D. diss., University of Ottawa (1956). Evelyn Newlyn, "Rose Terry Cooke and the Children of the Sphinx," *Regionalism and the Female Imagination* 4 (Winter 1979): 49–57. Katherine Kleitz, "Essence of New England: The Portraits of Rose Terry Cooke," *American Transcendental Quarterly* 47–48 (Summer–Fall 1980): 127–139. Josephine Donovan, *New England Local Color Literature: A Women's Tradition* (1983). Elizabeth Ammons, Introduction, *"How Celia Changed Her Mind" and Selected Stories* (1986). Cheryl Walker, "Rose Terry Cooke, 1827–1892," *Legacy: A Journal of American Women Writers* (Fall 1992): 143–150.

Karen Oakes

COOPER, Anna Julia Haywood (ca. 1858–1964), educator, feminist, writer, pan-Africanist. Born in Raleigh, North Carolina, of a slave mother and slave-owner father, Anna Haywood Cooper was in one of the first classes of students admitted to the newly established Episcopal St. Augustine Normal School and Collegiate Institute (which opened in Raleigh for African-American students in 1868). After she completed her studies at the institution in 1877, Cooper remained as a tutor. That same year, Anna married George A. C. Cooper, a professor and theology student at St. Augustine. During their marriage, George Cooper was ordained as an Episcopal Priest, but died shortly thereafter in September of 1879.

After spending nearly fourteen years at St. Augustine, Anna Cooper entered Oberlin College in Ohio in 1881 and received a bachelor's degree in 1884. After graduating from Oberlin, Cooper taught for one year at Wilberforce University, a black college in Ohio, and returned the following year to Raleigh to teach mathematics, Latin, and German at St. Augustine. By the fall of 1887, Cooper had earned a master's degree from Oberlin in mathematics and moved to Washington, D.C., to become a teacher at the only black public high school in the city, the Preparatory High School for Colored Youth (later M Street and Dunbar high schools).

In 1892, Cooper published *A Voice from the South: By a Black Woman from the South*, a collection of essays and speeches primarily concerning women's rights and the conditions of black women. Cooper served as principal of M Street High School from 1902 to 1906. Under Cooper's principalship, M Street students received scholarships to prestigious Ivy League and New England colleges. The D.C. Board of Education sought to reduce the classical offerings of the high school and Cooper refused. She was replaced as principal.

From 1906 to 1910 Cooper served as chair of the Department of Languages at Lincoln University in Missouri. She returned to the M Street school in 1910 as a teacher of Latin, a post she would hold until 1930. Cooper studied at the Guilde Internationale in Paris during the summers of 1911 through 1913 and at Columbia University during the summers of 1914 through 1917. At the age of sixty-six she earned a doctorate at the Sorbonne in France. From 1930 to 1940, Cooper was president of Frelinghuysen University in Washington, D.C. Frelinghuysen was an adult-education college for employed African Americans. The school offered collegiate, law, and religion courses and maintained an all-volunteer faculty.

Cooper took part in activities involving the

"uplift" of her race. In 1900 she attended the first Pan-African Conference in London, where she presented a paper, "The Negro Problem in America." Cooper died at the age of 105 in Washington, D.C.

• The Anna J. Cooper Papers are housed at the Moorland-Spingarn Research Center at Howard University, Washington, D.C. See also Louise Daniel Hutchinson, *Anna J. Cooper: A Voice from the South* (1981). David W. H. Pallow, "Anna Julia Cooper," in *Notable Black American Women* (1992).

Linda M. Perkins

COOPER, J. California, playwright, short fiction writer, novelist. Born in Berkeley, California, Joan California Cooper now lives in rural Texas. She has one daughter, Paris A. Williams, to whom, among others, all of her fiction is dedicated.

The author of seventeen plays, Cooper has had her work performed on public television and radio, as well as before live audiences. Her dramatic work is anthologized in Eileen J. Ostrow's *Center Stage* (1981). Cooper's play *Strangers* earned her the title Black Playwright of the Year in 1978.

A Piece of Mine, Cooper's first book of fiction, was published in 1984 with a foreword by Alice *Walker. A collection of twelve stories, *A Piece of Mine* indicates through its folksy diction, reminiscent of oral story telling, the path that Cooper's fiction would continue to follow. Cooper next published *Homemade Love* (1986), a grouping of thirteen tales that received the American Book Award in 1989. Through first-person narration and colloquial language, this work demonstrates Cooper's gift for imbuing the written word with dynamics of the spoken. *Homemade Love* typifies Cooper's writings by focusing on African-American women and their relationships.

A year after *Homemade Love*, Cooper produced *Some Soul to Keep* (1987). A collection of five long stories, *Some Soul to Keep* received mostly favorable reviews. While pointing out weaknesses such as the overuse of punctuation and occasional preachiness, critics still praised *Some Soul to Keep* and identified it as genuine— a response engendered by all of Cooper's writing.

Perhaps the most enthusiastic praise has come with *Family* (1991), Cooper's first novel. Set amid the atrocities of slavery, *Family* is told by the slave Clora—after she has killed herself. Like her mother before her, Clora decides to escape slavery through suicide, and, in a move reminiscent of Toni *Morrison's *Beloved* (1987), she tries also to kill her children. While this work succeeds as a novel, it retains much of the flavor of Cooper's earlier collections of short fiction because it consists of the related stories of Clora's children as narrated in Clora's own voice.

Losing no time after *Family* was published in January 1991, Cooper produced *The Matter Is Life* the following summer. In this work, a collection of eight tales, Cooper returns to the form with which she seems most comfortable. Like her preceding books, *The Matter Is Life* depicts modern-day fables of mostly rural black women.

Although perhaps not yet in the literary mainstream, Cooper's work has been honored repeatedly. In 1988, she was recognized as a Literary Lion by the American Library Association. And that same year, she also received the James Baldwin Writing Award.

• "J. California Cooper," in *Contemporary Literary Criticism*, vol. 56, ed. Roger Matuz (1989), pp. 69–72.

Kristine A. Yohe

COPPIN, Fanny Marion Jackson (1837–1913), educator, lecturer, and civic, religious, and feminist leader. Born a slave in Washington, D.C., Fanny Marion Jackson was twelve when her freedom was purchased by an aunt. She was raised by various family members and grew up in New Bedford, Massachusetts, and Newport, Rhode Island. Jackson attended the Rhode Island State Normal School in the late 1850s and later enrolled in Oberlin College in Ohio in 1860. She earned a baccalaureate degree at Oberlin in 1865, becoming the second African-American woman to achieve such a distinction.

After her graduation, she was appointed principal of the Female Department of the Institute for Colored Youth (ICY) in Philadelphia. ICY was a prestigious Quaker-founded private preparatory high school for African Americans, with a classical curriculum. Jackson's reputation as an outstanding teacher and administrator resulted in her being appointed principal of the entire school in 1869—a rare accomplishment for a woman of her era. Jackson spent her entire career as principal of ICY until her retirement in 1902. The institution grew during her administration, attracting a national and international student body. Deeply concerned with making quality education available to African Americans of all classes, Jackson successfully campaigned to have tuition abolished at the Institute in 1877. She was also instrumental in establishing an Industrial Department at the institution in 1889; its aim was to prepare African Americans for the growing number of industrial occupations emerging in the north. ICY was located in the heart of Philadelphia's African-American community, near the Mother Bethel African Methodist Episcopal (AME) Church.

Jackson frequently wrote children's stories for the *Christian Recorder*, the newspaper of the AME Church. In 1878, she also began writing a regular column in the paper, entitled the "Women's Department." In this column, Jackson reported on the activities and achievements of women in education and employment. She also reported on cases of employment discrimination against African-American women.

In 1881, Fanny Jackson married Levi Jenkins Coppin, an AME minister. After her marriage to Coppin, she joined the AME Church. Subsequently, she was elected president of the local Women's MITE Missionary Society and later became national president of the Women's Home and Foreign Missionary Society of the AME Church. In 1888, she represented the organization at the Centenary of Missions Conference in London. Very active in women's issues, Coppin was elected one of the first vice presidents of the newly organized National Association of Colored Women in 1897. She also served on the Board of Managers of the Home for Aged and Infirmed Colored People in Philadelphia for over thirty years (1881–1913). Coppin died at her home in Philadelphia on 21 January 1913. Coppin State College in Baltimore, Maryland, is named in her honor.

• Fanny Jackson Coppin, *Reminiscences of School Life, and Hints on Teaching* (1913). Levi Jenkins Coppin, *Unwritten History* (reprinted 1968). Linda M. Perkins, *Fanny Jackson Coppin and the Institute for Colored Youth, 1865–1902* (1987).

Linda M. Perkins

CORTEZ, Jayne (b. 1937), poet and performer. Born in Arizona, Cortez grew up in the Watts section of Los Angeles, California, after her family moved there in 1944. Her family loved books, and from an early age Cortez read the Bible and children's books. Later she explored her family's reference books, dictionaries, medical books, and encyclopedias for new words, which she kept in notebooks. She also wrote down the stories that she heard told by the members of her extended family. Cortez was an avid reader of African-American poetry and newspapers. Her family owned a large record collection of jazz and blues, and her mother sang to her. She took piano lessons as a child, played the bass and cello, and also studied harmony and theory. Cortez regularly attended local jam sessions and wrote and drew as she listened to the music. At a session in 1951 she met the avant-garde saxophonist Ornette Coleman, with whom she had a seven-year marriage.

In 1962 the examples of the charismatic leaders of the civil rights movement, Malcolm X and Martin Luther King, Jr., inspired Cortez to begin performing seriously. She joined an acting workshop, where she was exposed to the poetry of Langston Hughes and Federico García Lorca. In 1967 Cortez and her son Denardo moved to New York, where she became active as a politically engaged poet in an emerging scene that included Amiri Baraka, whom Cortez considers to be an accomplished reader and a major influence on political poetry. She published her first book of poems *Pissstained Stairs and the Monkey Man's Wares* in 1969. Cortez publishes her own works, which allows her both control and access to an audience, since recognized presses have shown little interest in her work. Her books include *Festivals and Funerals* (1971), *Scarifications* (1973), *Mouth On Paper* (1977), *Firespitter* (1982), *Coagulations: New and Selected Poems* (1985), and *Poet Magnetic* (1991). She has also released five recordings and a videotape on which she reads her poetry with her jazz group, the Firespitters. Her poetry has become increasing political since *Scarifications*, with her style being characterized by surprising associations; shocking, exotic, and unfamiliar words; and original insights. Cortez's mastery of the jazz poetry pioneered by Langston Hughes, Ted Joans, and Amiri Baraka, her use of the politically engaged surrealism of García Lorca, Amiri Baraka, and the Negritude poets, and her willingness to use music and multimedia have effectively expanded the range of possibilities open to contemporary poetry.

• Eugene B. Redmond, *Drumvoices: The Mission of Afro-American Poetry—A Critical History* (1976). Quincy Troupe, Clyde Taylor, Stanley Crouch, Charles Davis, and Eugene Redmond, "The Poetry of Jayne Cortez," *Yardbird Reader* 5 (1976): 91–117. Barbara T. Christian, "There It Is: The Poetry of Jayne Cortez," *Callaloo* 9, no. 1 (1986): 235–238.

Jon Woodson

COUVADE. *See* Womb Envy.

CRAVEN, Margaret (1901–1980), novelist, short fiction writer, journalist. Born in Montana and raised in the Puget Sound area of Washington, Margaret Craven wrote stories that demonstrate traditional twentieth-century American themes: her protagonists struggle against their social roles or personal fears or both, searching for identity and stability in a rapidly changing, increasingly impersonal modern world. Although her stories usually mourn conservative values, Craven compassionately examines complex gender, class, and racial conflicts.

Except for *I Heard the Owl Call My Name*, a highly praised novel that was made into a television movie in 1973, Craven's work has been largely ignored by critics. Most reviewers accuse her of simply reinforcing traditional values because her narrative and thematic structures (especially in her short fiction) are sometimes formulaic. These reviewers often overlook the variety and complexity of the stories' settings, as well as their thematic depth. Many of Craven's stories privilege romantic love, compassion, loyalty, and stoic endurance and self-discipline in the face of sometimes unpleasant duties, but usually not at the expense of her characters' self-knowledge.

A representative sampling of Craven's short stories is collected in *The Home Front* (1981). Published originally in popular magazines such as *Ladies' Home Journal, Collier's,* and the *Saturday Evening Post,* these stories reflect the years of national social turmoil between 1941 and 1962 as their characters discover, usually through some initiation experience, enduring humanist qualities—hard work, self-reliance, personal courage, and independence, as well as the sustaining values of self-sacrifice, heritage, and community. In several stories her women characters face troubling conflicts as they move, in large numbers, into the workplace during and after World War II, but Craven avoids sentimentality and reinforces her themes about identity by having her "long-suffering" women find the men of their dreams after the women have already established their own inner sense of worth separate from that man.

Her first published novel, *I Heard the Owl Call My Name* (1973), traces a British Columbian Indian tribe's gradual acceptance of a conscientious young Anglican vicar, Mark Brian, who ministers to the tribe's remote village. As modern decadence (marked by oily motorboats and alcohol abuse) overtakes the traditional Native American culture, Brian is led to an understanding of human values that endure, regardless of the culture from which they arise, so that he can eventually face his own mortality with dignity and grace. As lyrical as a Native American chant, it is a sparse, modernist lament for lost values.

Similar themes but less delicate handling mark Craven's second novel, *Walk Gently This Good Earth* (1977). In *Again Calls the Owl* (1980), a memoir of imagistic fragments, Craven recalls defining moments of her life: her father's death; her years at Stanford; loss of much of her eyesight in an automobile accident; lifelong friendships with injured war veterans whose stoic and humorous endurance she much admired; and a career as a journalist and fiction writer. Nearly half of the book recounts her four months among the Kwakiutl people, many de-

tails of which appear only thinly disguised in *I Heard the Owl Call My Name.*

• Timothy Foote, "A Swimmer's Tale," *Time* (28 January 1974): 73. Jennifer Farley Smith, "Fiction: 'I Heard the Owl Call My Name,' " *The Christian Science Monitor* (30 January 1974): F5. Elizabeth Schmidt, "Family Saga Concentrates on Strengths," *Christian Science Monitor* (28 December 1977). Joyce Flint, "Margaret Craven," in *American Women Writers,* vol. 1, ed. Lina Mainiero (1979). Andrea Lee Shuey, "Fiction: 'The Home Front,' " *Library Journal* 106 (1981): 812.

David A. Teal

CREOLE AND ACADIAN WRITING. From the eighteenth century through the present, Acadian women and Creole women, mostly in New Orleans and southern Louisiana, have explored their cultures in imaginative and nonimaginative literature. Despite the ease with which many people substitute the terms Creole and Acadian ('Cajun) for each other, important distinctions remain, especially in Louisiana. Creole refers to native-born descendants of French and Spanish colonists, some of whom may also have African, American Indian, Anglo-American, or additional European ancestry. Local debate on the term Creole, its definition, and application often evokes heated emotions.

While the Creoles frequently trace their origins to the arrival of the French explorers in the late-seventeenth century, the Acadians were relative latecomers, arriving from Nova Scotia in 1763 after their expulsion by the British. These people had a less-aristocratic background than the Creoles, for they farmed, fished, and trapped along the coastal bayous of Louisiana, south and southwest of New Orleans. Over the years since their arrival, the Acadians have intermingled with other ethnic groups in the region, including the Creoles. Roman *Catholicism has exerted a strong influence on both cultures in the observed pieties, icons, and customs.

When France ceded Louisiana to Spain in 1762, the French population successfully resisted the imposition of Spanish culture. Few Spaniards colonized, and as result, the cultural impact was minimal, with the exception of the architecture of New Orleans's French Quarter, rebuilt because of fire under Spanish rule. By 1802, Spain had ceded Louisiana back to France, and by 1803, France had sold it to the United States.

During these years of significant political change, women wrote very little. The earliest writing appears in the 1727 letters of Madeline Hachard to her father in France. An Ursuline nun involved in teaching the young and caring for the ill, she describes the life and times of the earliest years of the colony in New Orleans. As with Hachard's letters, writing in Louisiana was largely in French until the Civil War in 1861, when English began to dominate. The difficult subtropical climate, yellow fever epidemics, and the traditional responsibilities of childbearing and housekeeping limited women's literary contributions through the mid-nineteenth century.

In 1850, Emilie Lejeune, a Creole, published in New Orleans retold stories, songs, and folklore, including those by people of African descent. *Les Cenelles* (1845), a collection of poems dedicated to the women of Louisiana by Creole men of color, is the first collection of poems by African-Americans on this continent, but no comparable volume by Creole women of color exists. Many Creole women, however, wrote memoirs, some of which were published after their deaths. Celine Frémaux Garcia, who was born in Donaldsonville, Louisiana, wrote an account of her life in the years 1850–1871; it was published as *Celine: Remembering Louisiana, 1850–1871* in 1987. Julia LeGrand kept a Civil War journal. A Creole of Jewish ancestry, Adah Isaacs Menken (née Théodore), born in Milneburg (near New Orleans), wrote poems (the collection *Infelicia* appeared in 1868) and essays in New York and Cincinnati newspapers.

The aftermath of the Civil War brought on a renaissance of writing by Creole women, especially in poetry and fiction. The subject of Acadian and Creole life also came into fashion at publishing houses, especially those in the Northeast. As a consequence, some writers who were neither Acadian nor Creole became so identified because of their subjects; an example is Grace Elizabeth King, whose *Balcony Stories* (1892) provides one of the best views of postbellum Creole life "as told" by ladies conversing on a balcony overlooking the ebb and flow of street life. Similarly, Ruth McEnery Stuart represents this period in her short fiction and sketches in dialect, published in periodicals. Kate *Chopin, who can lay marginal claim to being Creole on her mother's side and by marriage, wrote two novels, *At Fault* (1890) and *The Awakening* (1899), as well as over fifty stories exploring both Creole and Acadian life, which she collected in *Bayou Folk* (1894) and *A Night in Acadie* (1897). Due to her nearly unique position in Creole society because of her mixed Irish and Creole heritage, she drew clear and sharp distinctions between Creoles and Acadians, particularly regarding social status.

French continued to be a literary language after the Civil War. Sidonie de la Houssaye (1820–1894), its foremost practitioner, was influenced by Zola, Lamartine, and Dumas. Her most widely known novel, *Pouponne et Balthazar* (1888), a romance set in the Acadian country, delineates that region's marital customs. A Creole from Franklin, Louisiana, she is but one of many Creoles who found the Acadians charming and interesting as literary and artistic subjects. Besides writing fiction, she made translations and contributed to the newspaper *L'Abeille*. Furthermore, she corresponded with George Washington Cable on literary matters.

Most Creole women writing in English took advantage of the popular interest in the region. Marie Marguerite Bonnet, born in New Orleans, wrote the local color novel *Clotilde* (1903); Margaret Janvier penned the romance *Clover Beach* (1880). Creoles of color also wrote actively. Alice Dunbar *Nelson, the wife of the poet Paul Lawrence Dunbar, wrote *The Goodness of St. Rocque* (1899), stories of life in New Orleans. Louise R. Lamotte, born in New Orleans and educated in France, spent nearly forty years there before returning to her place of birth. Like the Creole of color Victor Sejour, she earned her reputation as an expatriate in Abbeville, France, where she edited *Revue*, a literary magazine.

The twentieth century brought a decline in women writers identified as Creole and a dramatic increase in Acadian women writers, notably after 1945. Some interest in Creoles and Acadians as subjects of literature continued by authors beyond these groups, including Ada Jack Carver and Frances Parkinson Keyes.

Leona Queyrouse Barel, who had published poems in French in the New Orleans newspapers *L'Abeille* and *Compte-rendus*, wrote *The Idyll, My Personal Remembrance of Lafcadio Hearn* (1933). An example of the Creole writer in transition, she worked in French and English while pursuing subjects both personal and regional. Nathalie Bouligny Smyth also wrote lyric poems, most of which were published posthumously in 1923. And Carmalite Janvier captured the images of the city in the fictionally framed *Whimsical Madam New Orleans* (1928). Elma Godchaux of Napoleonville, Louisiana, dominated Creole fiction prior to 1941 with short stories in *Harpers* and the *Atlantic*. Her novel *Stubborn Roots* (1936), with its Becky Sharp–like heroine, explores the sugar cane country below New Orleans. Simone Delery's and Gladys Renshaw's *France d'Amerique* (1932) reflects continuing interest by Creoles in their heritage. Creoles of color have had the most recent impact in this area: Sybil Kein's *Gombo People: Poesie Creole de la Nouvelle Orleans* (1981) and Fatima Shaik's collection of novellas, *The Mayor of New Orleans: Talking Jazz* (1987).

Acadians developed an oral culture over the years. Songwriters like Cleoma Falcon and Shirley Bergeron were active during the 1920s and 1930s with works aimed at social gatherings. Increased access by the rural citizens of Acadiana to towns and cities after 1945 enabled more women to write. Writing books for young readers proved popular; Mary Alice Fontenot of Eunice, Louisiana, created Clovis Crawfish in 1962 as the hero for a series of books whose purpose was reviving Acadian culture. Muriel Fontenot Blackwell explores life on an Acadian farm in *The Secret Dream* (1981) and the threats to it by World War II and oil companies in *The Dream Lives On* (1984). Acadian women, like Beryl Sauce Styles, also wrote columns on local culture for newspapers; her writings are collected in *A Cajun's Persuasions* (1977). Other notable women writers include Julie Hebert, author of the plays *Purgatory* (1983) and *Almost Asleep* (1985), and Elizabeth Nell Dubus, who wrote the novels *Cajun* (1983) and *Acadian* (1984). With the establishment of writing programs at universities in the region, there promises to be a wider range of Acadian women's writing.

Acadian and Creole writing has roots in the colonial impulse to document experience, in the realist tendency to explore it, and in the local practice of popularizing it. Even writers on the margins of these heritages, like Berthe Amoss, Shirley Ann Grau, and Brenda Osbey, continue to be drawn to these exotic subjects.

• Lizzie Carter McVoy and Ruth Bates Campbell, *A Bibliography of Fiction by Louisianaians and on Louisiana Subjects* (1935), is out of print, but is partially superseded by Brown and Ewell. Harry Hanson, *Louisiana: A Guide to the State* (1971). Rodolphe Lucien Desdunes, *Our People and Our History*, translated by Sr. Dorothea Olga McCants (1973). Dorothy Brown and Barbara Ewell, *Louisiana Women Writers* (1992).

Thomas Bonner, Jr.

CRIME FICTION. *See* Mystery and Detective Fiction.

CRITICISM. *See* Literary Criticism; Theatre Critics.

CROCKER, Hannah Mather (1752–1829), essayist and early champion of women's rights. Crocker's *Observations on the Real Rights of Women, with Their Appropriate Duties, Agreeable to Scripture, Reason and Common Sense* (1818) is one of the first books on women's rights written by an American to be published in America. Dedicated to the British writer Hannah More, Crocker's book demonstrates an impressive familiarity with a wide range of authors in its survey of the history of women. Her desire for inclusiveness somewhat abates in later chapters as she considers her own views in the light of Scripture, reason, and common sense. Anticipating criticism of her treatise on women, Crocker provides an appendix that lists the contributions of men.

A book of multiple arguments of which few are adequately sustained, *Observations* is nevertheless a revealing document about a white, middle-class woman's attitudes in early nineteenth-century America. One of many surprises is Crocker's defense of Mary Wollstonecraft as "a woman of great energy and a very independent mind" at a time when Wollstonecraftism in America was synonymous with licentiousness. Crocker parts company with her on the matter of "the total independence of the female sex" but does so out of the conviction that women's rights are inextricably linked to mutuality, whether between spouses, neighbors, or citizens. Crocker argues, moreover, that the American Revolution has made the United States more congenial to women's rights and insists that American genius is already evident among its women.

Also evident in *Observations* is the willingness of its author both to challenge and confirm the beliefs of the New England family from which she sprang and to which she refers as "the four-fold line of Mathers." The same holds true of her earlier works. In *A Series of Letters on Free Masonry* (1815) written by "A Lady of Boston," Crocker defends the Society of Free Masons against a charge in 1810 of carousing in Boston lodges, although she recognizes "that it will be thought by many, a bold attempt for a female to even dare enter on the subject at all." In contrast, *The School of Reform, or Seaman's Safe Pilot to the Cape of Good Hope* (1816) cautions men against the excesses of drinking and places that concern within the larger framework of the public good, a practice for which there was ample precedent in the writings of her family.

The daughter of Samuel and Hannah Hutchinson Mather, Hannah married Joseph Crocker, a graduate of Harvard and a captain in the revolutionary army, in 1779. The mother of ten, she did not pursue her writing until her children were grown; she had, as she put it, reached an age at which "the well informed mind, if still in full vigour, is now fully ripe for composing." Crocker insisted that women like herself "must have a right to unbend their minds in well digested thoughts for the improvement of the rising generation," a concern that aligns her with the Matherian strain in New England even though she often departed from her forebears about what those improvements should include. Among her papers are several sermons; a play, "The Midnight Beau"; reminiscences about Boston and its traditions; and some poetry.

• The papers of Hannah Mather Crocker are at the American Antiquarian Society in Worcester, Massachusetts, and the New England Historic Genealogical Society in Boston. Hannah Mather Crocker, *Observations on the Real Rights of Women, with Their Appropriate Duties, Agreeable to Scripture, Reason and Common Sense* (1818). Microform ed., *History of Women*, 1975 (Reel 114, No. 747). Robert Riegel, *American Feminists* (1963). Eleanor Flexner, *Century of Struggle: The Women's Rights Movement in the United States* (rev. ed., 1975). Sara M. Evans, *Born for Liberty: A History of Women in America* (1989).

Constance J. Post

CRONE. The crone traditionally appears as the female version of the old man. Associated with courage, power, strength, and wisdom, crones serve as a symbolic reference to aging, death, and other forms of decline that precede regeneration. Creativity, destruction, cyclic existence, and various modes of appearances characterize some of the crone's aspects. Examples include Kali the Destroyer, Hecate, Persephone, Minerva, Athena, and Medusa. Barbara Walker (*The Crone: Woman of Age, Wisdom and Power*, 1985) identifies the crone as a representation of a female worldview, an archetypal challenge to patriarchal authority. Mary *Daly suggests (*Gyn/Ecology*, 1979; *Pure Lust*, 1984) that crones are long surviving hags, and that "croneographers" are those who oppose sexist language. Crones provide a female alternative from traditional and patriarchal models.

Doni M. Wilson

CROSS, Amanda. *See* Heilbrun, Carolyn.

CROSS-DRESSING means dressing in the clothes of the opposite sex for the purposes of "passing" as a man, signaling a (homo)sexual identity, engaging in stage impersonation, or experimenting with poetic personae.

Women have "passed" as men primarily to escape poverty or an abusive marital situation, and in order to appropriate male gender roles, such as soldier or lover. The first American woman known to have disguised herself was Deborah Sampson (1760–1827), who enlisted as Robert Shurtleff in the Continental army during the Revolutionary War. Lucy Brewer (1793–?) was the first woman to write about her experiences in a disguise autobiography, a genre ranging in length from eight to forty-eight pages that describes the successful deception for a curious audience. In *The Female Marine* (1815), Brewer describes how an unwanted pregnancy forced her into prostitution until she

donned the uniform of a seaman in the War of 1812. Lucy Ann Lobdell (1829–?), in the *Narrative of Lucy Ann Lobdell, the Female Hunter of Delaware and Sullivan Counties, N.Y.* (1855), suggests that women wear pants in order to receive equal wages. She eventually entered an insane asylum; in 1883 her case became one of earliest reports of female "sexual perversion" (lesbianism) in the United States. Disguise autobiographies proliferated during the Civil War, including William Craft's *Running a Thousand Miles for Freedom; or, the Escape of William and Ellen Craft from Slavery* (1860) which describes how the light-skinned slave Ellen Craft masqueraded as the white southern master of her dark-skinned husband William on their flight north, and *The Woman in Battle: A Narrative of the Exploits, Adventures, and Travels of Madame Loretta Janeta Velazquez, Otherwise Known as Lieutenant Harry T. Buford, Confederate States Army* (1876) by a Cuban-born patriot of the Southern cause who worked as a spy. Rita Mae *Brown recaptures this epoch in *High Hearts* (1986), the story of a woman who enlists in the Confederate army to be with her newly married husband.

Mary Walker (1832–1919), after serving as a Confederate surgeon (for which she adopted the same uniform as her fellow officers), published her views on dress and other social reforms for women in an autobiography entitled *Hit* (1871). In 1902 Walker was considered "the most distinguished sexual invert in the United States," although it remains unclear whether her regular appearance in masculine evening dress was a sign of her sexual proclivities. The romantic attachments of Willa *Cather (1876–1947), who in her youth cut her hair short, donned a Civil War cap, and called herself "Willie," remain equally ambiguous. Her writing, nevertheless, manifests cross-gendered personae in the male narrators of such novels as *My Ántonia* (1918).

For the American expatriates in Paris in the 1920s, cross-dressing clearly functioned as a sign of (homo)sexual identity, captured in the studio portraits of Romaine Brooks, who portrayed the women of Natalie Barney's circle in aristocratic clothing—tuxedos, top hats, and monocles—at a time when female-to-male cross-dressing was illegal. Radclyffe Hall's heroine in *The Well of Loneliness* (1928), Stephen Gordon—modeled on Brooks—serves as the prototypical "mannish lesbian," a congenital invert marked by character traits of the opposite sex. In Djuna *Barnes's *Nightwood* (1936) the cross-dresser represents not just an inversion but another example of artifice, joining the freak, the dandy, the clown, as part of the Parisian underworld in the male transvestite Dr. O'Connor and Robin Vote, who habitually dresses as a boy for the role of female Don Juan. Gertrude *Stein (1847–1946) figures prominently because of her cropped hair and idiosyncratic dress—Greek sandals, large overcoats, brocade vests—as well as her masculine identification as artist when she invokes her role as Defoe at the end of *The Autobiography of Alice B. Toklas* (1933). In 1920s and 1930s Harlem, Gladys Bentley (1907–1960), a nightclub entertainer and recording artist, performed to acclaim in a tuxedo, although she later renounced her identity as "bulldagger" in her autobiographical sketch, "I Am a Woman Again" (*Ebony*, August 1952).

In the 1940s and 1950s, butch/femme roles dominated the lesbian bar scene frequented by working-class women, where cross-dressing was equated not with class privilege but with an erotic partnership based on female sexual autonomy. Joan Nestle (b. 1940) defends this scene in *A Restricted Country* (1987) by arguing that it promoted cultural visibility for lesbians, while the participation of African American women is recorded in Audre *Lorde's "mythobiography" *Zami* (1982) and in a historical novel by Cherry Muhanji entitled *Her* (1990). By the 1970s lesbian-feminists rejected such role playing in favor of the figure of the androgyne. Several popular novels written by and for lesbians nevertheless incorporate cross-dressing plots, of which the best known is Isabel Miller's *Patience and Sarah* (1968). There, even as masculine clothing eroticizes the relationship between two women, it finally is discarded because of the gendered hierarchies it reintroduces into an egalitarian same-sex relationship. Butch-femme roles have recently reemerged on stage, particularly in the plays by Holly Hughes for the theater troupe Split Britches. In *Dress Suits for Hire* (1989) the influence of gay male camp emphasizes the parodic imitation of gender roles primarily through the role of the femme, revitalized by the postfeminist figure of the "lipstick lesbian."

Women poets have experimented with cross-gender identities, as in Adrienne *Rich's "Diving into the Wreck" (1973), where the roles of both "mermaid" and "merman" serve to uncover a masculine culture the speaker knows only through its oppressive myths. In "Exchanging Hats" (1956), Elizabeth *Bishop plays with gender identity in terms of clothes by appropriating "the headgear of the other sex" to recover the thoughts underneath the mismatched hat.

Cross-dressing has also played an important role in feminist literary criticism, beginning with Sandra Gilbert and Susan Gubar's reading of it as a metaphor for literary modernism. Elaine Showalter coined the term "critical cross-dressing" to refer to men who appropriate feminist scholarship, while Sue-Ellen Case theorizes lesbian subjectivity in terms of a "butch-femme aesthetic." Most recently Marjorie Garber has reexamined the transvestite as a figure of crisis that confounds categories of culture besides those of male and female.

[*See also* Performativity.]

• Jonathan Katz, "Passing Women 1782–1920," in *Gay American History* (1976), pp. 209–279. Elaine Showalter, "Critical Cross-Dressing" in *Men in Feminism*, ed. Alice Jardine and Paul Smith (1983; reprint, 1987), pp. 116–132. Shari Benstock, *Women of the Left Bank: Paris, 1900–1940* (1986). Estelle Jelinek, "Disguise Autobiographies: Women Masquerading as Men," *Women's Studies International Forum* 10, no. 1 (1987): 53–62. Sandra Gilbert and Susan Gubar, *No Man's Land: The Place of the Woman Writer in the Twentieth Century; Vol. 2: Sex Changes* (1989). Sue-Ellen Case, "Toward a Butch-Femme Aesthetic" in *Making a Spectacle: Feminist Essays on Contemporary Theatre*, ed. Lynda Hart (1989), pp. 282–299. Lillian Faderman, *Odd Girls and Twilight Lovers: A History of Lesbian Life in Twentieth-Century America* (1991). Marjorie Garber, *Vested Interests: Cross-Dressing and Cultural Anxiety* (1992).

Anne Herrmann

CROSS-RACIAL RELATIONS. Historically, cross-racial relations among women in the United States have often been marked by exclusion, exploitation, and appropriation. In the fight for women's equality, many white women refused to form meaningful alliances with women of color and poor women in order to achieve social change for all women. Suffragists such as Elizabeth Cady *Stanton and Susan B. *Anthony claimed that female enfranchisement and the race question were separate issues, while during the same period Sojourner *Truth protested discrimination against women of color and Fannie Barrier Williams charged that black women's mothers could not protect them and white women would not. White *women's clubs early in the twentieth century opposed admission of women of color, leading to two separate club movements, one black and one white; the Women's Christian Temperance Union denied admittance of black women to its southern branches; and the Young Women's Christian Association refused to include women of color on its board.

Racial relations among women today, during the third wave of the women's movement, are no less complicated, as contemporary women writers indicate. Beth *Brant, editor of *A Gathering of Spirit* (1984), criticizes the feminist movement that has seemed to forget that Native American women exist except in romantic fantasies of earth mother and of women-as-victims; and Audre *Lorde in *Sister Outsider*

(1984) asks the radical feminist Mary *Daly why non-European women are mentioned in her 1978 *Gyn/Ecology* only as victims and not as women of power. bell *hooks, Cherríe *Moraga, Carol Lee Sanchez, Barbara Smith, Mitsuye *Yamada, and Merle Woo have protested the burden placed on women of color to teach white women about *racism, and they have urged white feminists to question the format and focus of conferences which no women of color attend. In "The Incompatible *Ménage à Trois:* Marxism, Feminism, and Racism" (1981), Gloria Joseph criticizes the necessity of white "endorsement" to validate voices of women of color. Maxine Baca Zinn, Lynn Weber Cannon, Elizabeth Higginbotham, and Bonnie Thornton Dill, coauthors of "The Costs of Exclusionary Practices in *Women's Studies" (1986), note the failure of feminist journals, universities, and professional associations to include significant representation of women of color in positions of power.

As these examples suggest, and as most appearances of interracial relations in literature by women attest, the women in the United States have not had a history of female alliance across color lines. Harriet *Wilson spoke out against the racism of Northern white women through her detailed descriptions of Mrs. Bellmont's brutal treatment of Frado in *Our Nig* (1859). Harriet *Jacobs in *Incidents in the Life of a Slave Girl* (1861) noted the cruelty and betrayal of black women by several white women. Frances Ellen Watkins *Harper similarly indicted white women's complicitous and overt racism in *Iola Leroy*, citing instances of white mistresses having black women whipped, white working girls protesting the employment of a peer because she was black, and white Christian women refusing to receive black girls into their boarding houses and asylums established to aid young women. Anna Julia *Cooper's *A Voice From the South* (1892) faulted Susan B. Anthony for the refusal of women's culture clubs, of which she was a part, to admit women of color; she criticized the polarization of women and the negative depiction of Indians and African Americans in Anna B. Shaw's "Woman Versus the Indian"; and she questioned middle-class white girls writing of the safety and comfort of American rail travel without considering the differences *race made for women traveling alone. Kate *Chopin's *The Awakening* (1899), often considered by white feminists to be a groundbreaking piece on women's liberation, entirely disregarded the oppression of black and Mexican women by the privileged, white female protagonist. Charlotte Perkins *Gilman, acclaimed for her progressive exploration of alternative social organizations

to free women from domestic subservience, ignored the implications of her ideas for women of color. Similarly, her 1915 *Herland* proposed a "perfect" world which included no women of color. *Sui Sin Far's 1912 *Mrs. Spring Fragrance* subtly criticized the ethnocentricity, arrogance, and classism of white women who failed to see cultural differences. *Zitkala-Ša in her 1921 *American Indian Stories* spoke out against the white women who mistreated her: the rude stares of white women on trains; the paleface woman at the Bureau of Indian Affairs school who tossed her into the air like a puppet, and the white woman who cut her hair, never considering the cultural significance of her action. And in "A Warrior's Daughter," a 1902 story included in this collection, she challenged white notions of ideal womanhood by offering the character of a clever and courageous Indian girl who saves a Sioux warrior from death by rescuing him from an enemy camp. More recently, Audre *Lorde noted the unabashed racism of white Sisters of Charity at a young women's Catholic school, of white forewomen in companies that hired and kept women of color only for health-hazardous jobs, of white waitresses who refused to serve ice cream to black girls, and of white lesbians who refused to acknowledge the racist discrimination accorded their peers (*Zami*, 1982). Louise *Erdrich in "American Horse" (1983) indicted a white woman social worker who stole an Indian woman's child in order to "salvage" him; and Vickie Sears in "Grace" (1989) wrote about a Native American girl briefly cared for by an elderly white woman after a childhood of sexual abuse by a white orphanage lady.

White writers who have attempted to include "other" women more often than not have betrayed their own racism. Harriet Beecher *Stowe's 1852 abolitionist novel *Uncle Tom's Cabin* depicted most black characters in racist terms, awarding the most positive traits to the lightest skinned African-American protagonists. When Harriet Jacobs asked Stowe to endorse *Incidents*, the leading white abolitionist wrote that if Jacobs's story were true, she would use it herself in her *Key to Uncle Tom's Cabin*; and in an article written for the 1863 *Atlantic Monthly*, she undermined her praise of Sojourner Truth by including overtly racist descriptions of the "Libyan Sibyl" and her grandson. Gertrude *Stein in her 1909 *Three Lives* portrayed black women as shiftless, promiscuous, and childish and used the black female character Melanctha to talk guardedly about her own *sexuality. Ellen *Glasgow condemned racism yet perpetuated it in *Barren Ground* (1925) by drawing a romantic picture of a black and white woman working side by side on a farm and neglecting to see the power imbalance in the relationship; just as in real life, as the poet Adrienne *Rich has pointed out, Glasgow consigned to illiteracy Lizzie Jones, the black woman who raised her and nurtured her writing. Willa *Cather's *The Song of the Lark* (1915), *My Ántonia* (1918), *The Professor's House* (1925), and *Death Comes for the Archbishop* (1927) submerged the stories of black, Mexican, and Indian women to tell the stories of white women artists (whose comfort and art were made possible by laboring women of color). Further, in her final novel, *Sapphira and the Slave Girl* (1940), a novel supposedly written to celebrate the shared struggle of black and white women, Cather not only used vague, racist *stereotypes to depict the black characters in the book and showed a white mistress plotting the *rape of a black servant girl but also appropriated the heroism of the black woman to give it to a white woman and her daughter, and, indeed, to herself.

Inseparable from such recurrent instances of ethnocentrism, exclusion, and brutal racism are images of women in literature who have crossed racial barriers to form meaningful alliances and relationships. Catharine Maria *Sedgwick in her 1827 novel *Hope Leslie* portrays heroic Native American women and offers a feminist gesture of solidarity in the two scenes in which a white female protagonist helps two Indian women. Harriette *Arnow's *The Dollmaker* (1954) shows how hatred of people from different races, ethnicities and geographic locations erodes the sense of *community among women; and she includes in her novel several instances of individual women overcoming individual differences to help other women. June *Arnold acknowledges in *Sister Gin* (1975) her complicity in colonizing others and ends the novel by trying to set a black woman's voice free. Paula Gunn *Allen's 1983 novel, *The Woman Who Owned the Shadows*, offers glimpses of meaningful connections between a Chicana and *Native American girl, and between a young Native American woman and her white lesbian partner, even as she shows the "benign" racism of "liberal" white feminists and divisions among women of color.

Women's cross-racial relations in the U.S. also have had significant bearing on the very possibility of writing. Some white women, for example, have used their positions of power to help women of color voice their own stories. Susanna Wheatley encouraged Phillis *Wheatley to revise her manscripts and arranged to have them published with the help of the Countess of Huntingdon in 1773. Olive Gilbert transcribed and edited the *Narrative of Sojourner Truth* (1850), sales of which helped support Truth as she toured the states delivering speeches; and, although she did so for her own ends, Stanton encouraged Truth after the *Civil War to speak for female enfranchisement and recorded her public addresses in *The History of Woman Suffrage* (1881–1886). Cornelia Grinnell Willis, whose husband had employed Harriet Jacobs to care for their baby, later bought Jacobs in order to set her free; and antislavery feminist Amy Post, who became a friend of Jacobs, urged her to write *Incidents* and agreed to endorse Jacobs's story so that it could be published. Charlotte Mason, though heavily compromised in her patronage of African-American arts by the racist expectations and prohibitions she set for her protégées, nevertheless financed Zora Neale *Hurston's travel to the South to collect material which established her as a folklorist and led to her 1937 publication of *Their Eyes Were Watching God*. More recently, Adrienne *Rich rejected the National Book Award in 1974 as an individual, accepting it instead, in a statement written with Alice *Walker and Audre Lorde, in the name of all women; Rich also as editor along with Michelle *Cliff of Sinister Wisdom supplied Beth Brant with the postage, printing, and photocopying needed to make possible *A Gathering of Spirit: A Collection by North American Indian Women*.

Statements by women also testify to connections between individual writers across racial lines. Jessie Redmon *Fauset in 1923 said that young African Americans should read "the great writers and stylists" like Edith *Wharton. Contesting the 1936 sermon of Reverend Francis Grimké who condemned Charlotte Perkins *Gilman for ending her life and failing to bear her afflictions with Christian patience, Anna Cooper felt that Gilman's life was full of interest and inspiration. Mirtha Quintanales, in a 1980 letter to Barbara Smith, thanked her for sharing literature of the black lesbian/feminist experience, and particularly noted how Lorraine Bethel's "What Chou Mean *We* White Girl?" gave form and meaning to the experiences of many Latina women she met with during a visit to San Francisco. Gloria *Anzaldúa in "Speaking In Tongues: A Letter to 3rd World Women Writers" (1980), said that it was women like Genny Lim and Luisah Teish who empowered others and dispelled the loneliness of writing. Jill Lewis, in a preface to *Common Differences* (1981), gave special thanks to Toni Cade *Bambara and Barbara Smith for helping her to dislocate "the static areas" of her white feminism. Cherríe Moraga acknowledged in a letter to Barbara Smith the powerful effect of Ntozake *Shange's public reading and its influence on her own writing, and in "La Guera" (1981) noted her pleasure in seeing Maxine Hong * Kingston's description of fear and alienation as "white ghosts" rather than as a "dark" unknown. In her 1983 *In Search of Our Mothers' Gardens*, Alice Walker claimed that it was Muriel * Rukeyser who helped Walker find the courage to become a writer and commented that Tillie * Olsen, in her generosity and honesty, literally saved lives. Cathy Song named several of her poems in *Picture Bride* (1983) after Georgia O'Keeffe's floral paintings and dedicated "From the White Place" to the modern American artist. Paula Gunn Allen in her acknowledgments to *The Woman Who Owned the Shadows* thanked Gloria Anzaldúa and Judith McDaniel for their helpful responses and commitment to her 1983 novel; noted the influence of Gertrude Stein and Mary Daly on her work; and expressed particular indebtedness to Judy Grahn for her time, support, and love. In turn, * Grahn gave special acknowledgment to Allen whose ideas, library resources, and critical eye gave Grahn "a place to stand" in the tribal traditions of America in her writing of *Another Mother Tongue: Gay Words, Gay Worlds* (1984); and she thanked Ann Allen Shockley and Pat * Parker for their work. Joan * Nestle specially notes the support of Jewelle Gomez and Cheryl Clarke in making the completion of *A Restricted Country* (1987) possible. As such inscriptions make clear, much of women's writing has not occurred in isolation.

In the last few years several presses and books also attest to cross-racial * collaboration among women. Publishing companies such as Kitchen Table: Women of Color Press, Spinsters/Aunt Lute, Firebrand Books, and Third Woman Press have developed out of interests in women's works across racial lines. Many women have also edited volumes that represent writings by women of different races and ethnicities. Janice * Mirikitani edited *Third World Women* (1973) and *Time to Greez! Incantations from the Third World* (1975). Gloria I. Joseph and Jill Lewis coedited *Common Differences: Conflicts in Black & White Feminist Perspectives* (1981). Moraga and Anzaldúa coedited *This Bridge Called My Back: Writings by Radical Women of Color* (1981). Mitsuye Yamada, founder of Multi-Cultural Women Writers of Orange County, edited with Sarie Sachie Hylkema *Sowing Ti Leaves: Writings by Multicultural Women* (1990). In addition to such anthologies, individual articles, such as Virginia R. Harris's and Trinity A. Ordoña's "Developing Unity Among Women of Color: Crossing the Barriers of Internalized Racism and Cross-Racial Hostility" coauthored for Anzaldúa's 1990 *Making Face, Making Soul: Haciendo Caras: Creative and Critical Perspectives by Feminists of Color*, also show increasing collaboration across racial lines.

As the history of interracial relations among women in the U.S. suggests, there has been no easy * sisterhood; yet many women writers have crossed racial barriers to create meaningful dialogue based on difference and a shared commitment to work for equal rights for all. In the process, these women have shown ways in which race relations have affected their work in significant ways; they have reconceptualized American notions such as "self-reliance," * "true womanhood," * "feminism," and "the * woman's movement" to include more multicultural perspectives; and they have challenged traditional literary genres and * myths of authorship.

[*See also* Assimilation; Ethnicity and Writing; Mixed Ancestry, Writers of; Passing; Race.]

• bell hooks, *Ain't I A Woman: Black Women and Feminism* (1981). Cherríe Moraga and Gloria Anzaldúa, eds, *This Bridge Called My Back: Writings by Radical Women of Color*, 2d ed. (1983). Paula Giddings, *When and Where I Enter: The Impact of Black Women on Race and Sex in America* (1984). Hazel V. Carby, *Reconstructing Womanhood* (1987). Gloria Anzaldúa, *Making Face, Making Soul: Haciendo Caras: Creative and Critical Perspectives by Feminists of Color* (1990). Elizabeth Ammons, *Conflicting Stories: American Women Writers at the Turn into the Twentieth Century* (1991).

Ann E. Reuman

CROTHERS, Rachel (1878–1958), Broadway playwright, producer, director, actress. Crothers was born the youngest child of two doctors in Bloomington, Illinois. Her mother's difficulties in becoming and practicing as a doctor in a small midwestern town had a great impact on Crothers's writing. Many of her plays would reexamine Dr. Marie Crothers's decisions regarding a woman's choices between career and family.

Writing and performing from an early age, Crothers pursued a theatrical career against her parents' wishes. In 1897, after studying acting in Boston and returning to teach speech and drama in Bloomington for a number of years, Crothers moved to New York, teaching acting and performing professionally. First producing and writing one-act plays for her acting students, she went on to success for over thirty years on the New York stage, primarily as a playwright, but also as a producer, director, and actress.

In the years before World War I, Crothers wrote a number of plays, all classifiable as social problem plays, which dealt with the double standard in society against women and the limited options available to them. In plays like her first professionally produced *The Three of Us* (1906), *A Man's World* (1909), and *He and She*

(1911), Crothers depicted intelligent and capable women, often artists, and examined the difficulties of balancing independence with the demands of the roles of wife and mother.

After the war, Crothers enjoyed greater success writing social comedies, still concentrating on women's problems but resolving them happily. Many of her plays of the twenties, such as *Nice People* (1921) and *Mary the Third* (1923), attacked women's economic dependence and defended (with reservations) the flapper's flouting of traditional values.

In the thirties, Crothers continued to write comedies of manners. In plays like *As Husbands Go* (1931) and *When Ladies Meet* (1932) and her last professionally produced *Susan and God* (1937), Crothers examined sexual mores and codes of behavior among high-society women in a light and crowd-pleasing manner.

From her own day up to contemporary times, Crothers's ambivalence toward the freedom of the New Woman versus women's traditional roles has led to critical debates as to whether she should be categorized as a feminist writer or not. In any case, Crothers's focus on women's perspectives and concerns remained constant throughout her lengthy career and her work remains an important signpost for American attitudes toward women's issues through the early decades of the twentieth century.

• Lois Gottlieb, *Rachel Crothers* (1979). Sharon Friedman, "Feminism as Theme in Twentieth-Century American Women's Drama," *American Studies* 25, no. 1 (Spring 1984): 69–89. Doris Abramson, "Rachel Crothers: Broadway Feminist," in *Modern American Drama: The Women's Canon*, ed. June Schlueter (1989), pp. 55–65.

John Evelev

CUBAN-AMERICAN WRITING. The history and trajectory of Cuban American writing in the United States—and that certainly includes women—is fraught with chronological and cultural ambiguities. The main wave of immigration from Cuba to the continental United States occurred from 1959 through the early 1960s, but a second generation of writers also left the island country in the early 1980s during the so-called Mariel exodus (named after the Cuban sea port from which refugees set sail on small boats for Key West or Miami). The first group included women authors that had already started writing careers in Havana, and who identified themselves as part of the growing number of exiled writers that Latin America sent to American shores during the political and social upheavals of the sixties and the seventies; the novelist and short fiction writer Hilda Perera (b. 1926) and the poet Pura del Prado (b. 1926) are two examples. These women

had begun publishing in Havana, and have continued to produce novels, short stories, and books of poetry, written in Spanish and published in Spain and Miami. That first immigration wave also spawned a new batch of writers who learned their literary skills while growing up in an immigrant community, and these children of exile were indeed more bilingual and bicultural than their parents. The second wave brought several writers and artists to America, not many of whom were women. The best known among them is Belkis Cuza Malé (b. 1944), who now codirects Linden Lane Magazine and Linden Lane Press in Princeton, New Jersey, publishing works by Cuban and Cuban American authors.

Many observers and critics have dubbed as Cuban American writers those who really consider themselves "Cubans in exile," and a controversy of sorts has arisen about the identity of the "real" Cuban Americans as a group. Are they those Cubans who have lived the experience of hybridity intrinsic to young first-generation immigrants, and whose processes of maturation and acquisition of linguistic skills have approximated those of other ethnic minority writers in the American tradition? Or are they simply those Cuban exiles who write and continue to publish in the United States, in their native language or in English translation? Some literary historians gather all groups under the title "Cuban American" (Silvia Burunat and Ofelia García, *Veinte años de literatura cubanoamericana* [Twenty years of Cuban American literature], 1988), whereas others argue that "Cuban Americanness" is an identity marker whose main features are constituted not only by a deep self-awareness of "otherness" but also by bilingualism beyond functionality— and mainly by a profound sense of cultural hybridity: these features are only exhibited by the "children of exile." This is maintained by Carolina Hospital in "Los hijos del exilio cubano y su literatura" (The children of Cuban exile and their literature, *Explicación de Textos Literarios* 15, no. 22, 1986–1987), and by Eliana Rivero ("(Re)Writing Sugarcane Memories: Cuban Americans and Literature," *Paradise Lost or Gained? The Literature of Hispanic Exile*, 1990, 164–182). But even those who tend to describe Cuban Americans as the most homogeneous Hispanic group, and perhaps the one that most suggests assimilation with nonethnic American society, concede that Cubans in the United States appear to be divided between those possessing traditional Cuban culture and mores and who still think about an eventual return to the island, and those who, while maintaining some linguistic and cultural autonomy, consider themselves "new Americans" (David Foster, ed., *Sourcebook of Hispanic Culture in the U.S.*, 1982).

All the women writers in these groups, whatever their cultural affiliation, are immigrants: they were born in Cuba as early as 1926 and as late as 1960. However, many critics now seem to agree that the works published by the oldest, written in Spanish and steeped in what has been called the Cuban nostalgia discourse, do not belong in a discussion of Cuban *American* writing. Nevertheless, many of the younger women authors also write in Spanish, and some in a bilingual mode or in English since the mid-1970s: Lourdes Casal (1938–1981), Uva Clavijo (b. 1944), Magali Alabau (b. 1945), Maya Islas (b. 1947), Alina Galliano (b. 1950), Carlota Caulfield (b. 1953), Iraida Iturralde (b. 1954), Lourdes Gil (b. 1955), Mercedes Limón (b. 1957), Mercedes Cortázar (b. 1960). These writers are mostly poets, with the exception of Mireya Robles (b. 1934), who in addition to being a poet of lyric introspection and gifted insights (*Tiempo artesano/Time the Artisan*, 1975) has published short stories and an acclaimed novel, *Hagiografía de Narcisa la Bella* (Hagiography of Narcisa the beautiful, 1985). Casal, who publicly supported the Cuban Revolution after many years in New York, distinguished herself as the moving force behind return visits to Cuba of those children of exile who wanted to recover their historical and cultural roots. Before she died, after a long illness during a return trip to Cuba, she distinguished herself by her essays and short stories (*Los fundadores: Alfonso y otros cuentos* [The founders: Alphonse and other stories], 1973), and her book of poems *Palabras juntan revolución* (Words gather revolution, 1981) won posthumously the prestigious Casa de las Américas prize in Havana. Clavijo, better known as a poet and short fiction writer (*Versos del exilio* [Verses in exile], 1974; *Ni verdad ni mentira y otros cuentos* [Neither truth nor lie and other stories], 1977; *No puedo más y otros cuentos* [I can't take it any longer and other stories], 1989), has now made her English debut as a playwright: *With All and for the Good of All* (1990), a title highly suggestive of a well-known speech by the revered Cuban patriot, José Martí. Along with Casal, but on the opposite end of the political spectrum, Clavijo illustrates in her works the cultural plight and emotional uprootedness of the Cuban exile in Miami. These two women writers are good examples of a discourse that has since the mid-1970s begun to assimilate American cultural icons and English phraseology; their texts manifest the process of transition—from immigrants to ethnic minority writers—in which their authors are engaged.

Some of the women who began publishing in the mid- to late-1970s also manifested a growing feminist consciousness in their writing. The playwright, actress, director, journalist, and poet Dolores *Prida (b. 1943) is one such example, also typifying the best of Cuban American women authors coming into their own as full-fledged members of the community of Latina writers in the United States. Her better-known plays are either bilingual or entirely in English (*Beautiful Señoritas*, 1977; *Coser y cantar* [singing and sewing]: *A One-Act Bilingual Fantasy for Two Women*, 1981; *Savings* [*A Musical Fable*], 1985). Most recently, *Pantallas* (Screens, 1986) and *Botánica* (Botanical store, 1990), addressed to Spanish audiences both in the United States and Latin America, poke gentle fun at generational cultural gaps and the mass-media addiction of Latina women: soap operas.

The thematic richness evidenced in the works by Cuban American women authors is nevertheless permeated by a uniting thread: their experience of an "ex-centric" life. That is, their existence as Latina women is functional within the American system but not at the center, which makes for the representational paradoxes of their biculturalism and bilingualism—most characters in their fiction and stage works are trapped in a dual world of hybrid identity, in the dilemma of being/nonbeing: Cuban and yet American. The nostalgia discourse of earlier generations of writers has been replaced by the subtle malaise of marginality awareness; many of the works reflect a sense of how, in their view, the majority of Anglo women cannot possibly understand their condition.

And yet, thematic similarities with not only other Latina writers but also with feminist and lesbian writers from the "mainstream" are also appearing. In the works of Achy Obejas (b. 1956), a poet, short fiction writer, and playwright, a profound sense of community with her adopted Chicago and its Latino population has been present since her texts began to appear in the 1970s. Obejas illustrates the transformation of a young writer who begins thematically oriented toward immigrant motifs such as flight from the mother country and life in the ethnic ghettos (see her short stories "The Escape" and "The Living," and her bilingual poem "Sugarcane") and evolves to a consideration of women's lives in all their complexities ("Polaroids"). Nevertheless, Obejas continues to focus her attention on Latino life in the United States, and more recently on her short fiction on lesbian themes ("Acts of Charity"). She has also coauthored and produced two plays in Spanish: *Carnicería Rodríguez* (Rodríguez meatmarket) and *Las Brisas de Marianao* (The breezes of Marianao). Both play heavily on

Cuban traditions and the lore of public establishments.

Perhaps the most Cuban American of all these women authors are those who not only write in English, but have incorporated into their literary worldview a more American "meltingpot" culture. In recent years, the name of Carolina Hospital (b. 1957) has appeared on pages that depict in poetry and nonfiction prose the rites of passage that a Cuban-born, Havana/San Juan, Puerto Rico–raised, Miami-residing Cuban woman traverses as a human being trying to root herself in her own cultural history: her poems attest to that (*Los Atrevidos*, 165–169). But she is also an anthologist, compiler, and critic; her work as an essayist and historian of the Cuban American "condition" can be said to have blazed the trail, in the mid- and late-1980s, for those others who continue to observe the literary phenomenon of most children of Cuban exiles.

And last but not least, there is the fully assimilated immigrant—born in Havana on the fourth of July, 1958, and having left Cuba at the age of two—who is touted by reviewers and critics as "the most American of Cuban authors": Cristina Garcia. Her novel *Dreaming in Cuban* (1992) bespeaks her New York upbringing, but only in her skillful knowledge of American ethnic realities (raised in Brooklyn Heights, she lives in Los Angeles with her half-Japanese, half-Jewish journalist husband). Still, Garcia goes along with the popularization of nostalgia for the fifties that won a Pulitzer Prize for her (less Cuban) male counterpart, Oscar Hijuelos (*The Mambo Kings and Their Songs of Love*, 1989). Her excellent prose work, however, focuses more directly on the daily lives of a single, divided family of Cubans, also described by American reviewers as "the Waltons of Santa María del Mar" (a suburban beach east of Havana).

The nostalgia ever-present in the young Cuban American's parents' generation has given way to a split, hybrid cultural consciousness in the daughters of exile, although their works still exhibit subtle remnants of the past. These women are eloquently writing themselves into the present panorama of U.S. Latino/Hispanic literature.

[*See also* Immigrant Writing; Latina Writing.]

• Naomi Lindstrom, "Cuban American and Continental Puerto Rican Literature," in *Sourcebook of Hispanic Culture in the United States*, ed. David Foster (1982), pp. 221–245. Eliana Rivero, "Hispanic Literature in the United States: Self-Image and Conflict," in *International Studies in Honor of Tomás Rivera*, ed. Julián Olivares (1985), pp. 173–192. María del Carmen Boza, Beverly Silva, and Carmen Valle, eds., *Nosotras:* *Latina Literature Today* (1986). Carolina Hospital, ed., *Los Atrevidos: Cuban American Writers* (1988). Eliana Rivero, "From Immigrants to Ethnics: Cuban Women Writers in the U.S.," in *Breaking Boundaries: Latina Writings and Critical Readings* (1989), pp. 189–200. Rodolfo Cortina, ed., *Cuban American Theater* (1990). Marc Zimmerman, "U.S. Latino Literature: History and Development," in *U.S. Latino Literature: The Creative Expression of A People*, ed. M. Zimmerman (1990). Judith Weiss, ed., *Dolores Prida: Beautiful Señoritas and Other Plays* (1991).

Eliana Rivero

CULT OF TRUE WOMANHOOD. *See* True Woman.

CUMMINS, Maria Susanna (1827–1866), novelist, author of *The Lamplighter*. Cummins was born in Salem, Massachusetts, to David Cummins and Maria Franklin Kittredge. Her father, a judge of the court of common pleas, directed her early studies and encouraged her literary pursuits. Later, Cummins attended the fashionable Young Ladies School of Mrs. Charles Sedgwick in Lenox, Massachusetts, where she had frequent opportunities to meet Mrs. Sedgwick's sister-in-law, novelist Catherine Sedgwick, as well as other literary personalities. After her schooling, Cummins spent her life at the family residence in Dorchester, Massachusetts. She remained single.

In her early twenties, Cummins published her first works, short stories that appeared in the *Atlantic*. In 1854, she wrote *The Lamplighter*. Forty thousand copies sold within the first two months and 100,000 in the first decade, making the novel second in popularity only to *Uncle Tom's Cabin*. The novel's success prompted Nathaniel Hawthorne to write his now-famous complaint concerning the "d——d mob of scribbling women" to his publisher William Ticknor in 1855. *The Lamplighter* was also published in England and translated into French, German, Danish, and Italian.

The Lamplighter tells the story of a passionate-tempered orphan girl, Gerty, who is mistreated by a cruel caretaker and subsequently adopted by a kindly old lamplighter, Trueman Flint. Through his love and the religious teachings and loving example of a well-to-do blind woman, Gerty learns to control her emotions and grows to virtuous womanhood. In the end, after silently suffering many afflictions, she is rewarded by being married to her childhood friend and confidante and by being reunited with her father, long thought dead.

Although *The Lamplighter* was frequently translated and published as a children's book and is still studied as such, its moralistic lessons for women on the power of love and the in the genre of sentimental domestic fiction. In addition, Cummins's rich depictions of minor characters, city and suburban life, and Boston's poor and middle classes foreshadow the emerging realism that came to dominate this country's fiction.

Cummins wrote three more novels before her death at age thirty-nine in 1866. Their lessons range from the irrevocability of moral corruption in the wealthy class in *Mabel Vaughan* (1857) to the praiseworthiness of the heroine's exotic bravery and sensuousness in *El Fureidis* (1860) to the unhappy consequences of thoughtlessness in *Haunted Hearts* (1864). The variations on women's themes in Cummins's works remind twentieth-century readers that, as Nina Baym has noted in the Introduction to her edition of *The Lamplighter* (1988), "the vision of women and their potential" could differ even in the works of a single nineteenth-century author.

• Allen Johnson and Dumas Malone, eds., *Dictionary of American Biography* (1934). Frank Luther Mott, *Golden Multitudes: The Story of Best Sellers in the United States* (1947). Edward T. James, ed., *Notable American Women: 1607–1950*. (1971). Nina Baym, *Woman's Fiction* (1978). Mary Kelley, *Private Women, Public Stage* (1984).

Allene Cooper

D

DALL, Caroline W. H. (1822–1912), writer, lecturer, historian, and reformer. Dall was an influential nineteenth-century feminist and prolific writer who advanced women's rights. Born in Boston, she received a superior education from private tutors and at Joseph Hale Abbot's school for young women in her hometown. Dall's literary career began at age thirteen with the publication of her essays on moral and religious issues in newspapers and periodicals; some of these are included in *Essays and Sketches* (1849), a collection of her early work. During her adolescence, Dall was primarily committed to reform, and served as a Sunday school teacher, relief worker, and director of a nursery school for children of working women. In 1841, she attended Margaret *Fuller's weekly "Conversations," where she met important transcendentalists, including Ralph Waldo Emerson, Theodore Parker, and Elizabeth Peabody. She later published a record of these meetings titled *Margaret and Her Friends* (1895), as well as a lecture on *Transcendentalism in New England* (1897), which includes a discussion of Fuller's significance to the movement. In 1842, financial difficulties stemming from the Panic of 1837 forced Dall to help support her family, and until 1844 she acted as vice principal of a girls' school in the Georgetown section of Washington D.C. In 1844, Dall married Reverend Charles Henry Appleton Dall, and until 1854, she shared his ministerial duties in Baltimore; Boston; Portsmouth, New Hampshire; and Toronto, Canada. During this decade, Dall became increasingly involved with antislavery activities, including writing for the *Liberty Bell*, a gift book promoting abolition. In 1854, Dall returned to Boston, where she coedited with Paulina Wright Davis the *Una*, an important forum of feminist thought. In 1855, she helped to coordinate and lectured at the women's rights convention in Boston; in 1859, she organized the New England Woman's Rights Convention and was one of its principle speakers. In 1865, Dall cofounded the American Social Science Association, in which she remained an important figure until 1905, serving as librarian, director, and vice president. In 1879, Dall moved to Washington, D.C., the home of her son, where she continued to write and teach until her death in 1912.

Dall's writings include historical essays, children's stories, biblical studies, biographies, and political tracts. In addition to those mentioned above, her most significant works include *Historical Pictures Retouched* (1860), revisionist interpretations of famous women in history, and *The College, the Market, and the Court; or, Woman's Relation to Education, Labor, and Law* (1867), her most important feminist tract, which argues that women have a right to equal opportunity in all areas, and particularly in education, employment, and law.

• Dall's personal papers are located at the Schlesinger Library, Radcliffe College, and at the Massachusetts Historical Society in Boston. See also Barbara Welter, "The Merchant's Daughter: A Tale from Life," *New England Quarterly* 42, no. 1 (March 1969): 3–22. Stephen Nissenbaum, "Caroline Wells Healey Dall," in *Notable American Women, 1607–1950*, vol. 1, ed. Edward T. James (1971), pp. 428–429. Susan Phinney Conrad, *Perish the Thought: Intellectual Women in Romantic America, 1830–1860* (1976). Susan Sutton Smith, "Caroline Wells Healey Dall," in *American Women Writers*, vol. 1, ed. Lina Mainiero (1979), pp. 448–450. William Leach, *True Love and Perfect Union: The Feminist Reform of Sex and Society* (1980).

Heather A. Hathaway

DALY, Mary (b. 1928), theologian and philosopher. Mary Daly received her B.A. from the College of St. Rose (1950), an M.A. from Catholic University of America (1952), and a Ph.D. from St. Mary's College, Notre Dame (1954). After teaching for five years at Cardinal Cushing College in Massachusetts, she went to the University of Fribourg, Switzerland, where she earned doctorates in theology (1963) and philosophy (1965). She began teaching at Boston College in 1966. Her first book, on Jacques Maritain (1966), was followed almost immediately by *The Church and the Second Sex* (1968; rev. ed., 1985). As the title suggests, the text responds to the work of Simone *de Beauvoir and is deeply critical of the Catholic Church's attitudes and practices toward women. In *Beyond God the Father* (1973; 2d rev. ed., 1985) Daly characterized Christian soteriology as "necrophilic" and rejected all attempts to reconcile Christianity with feminism. But she did not abandon theological questing, and in *Gyn/Ecology: The Metaethics of Radical Feminism* (1978) and *Pure Lust: Elemental Feminist Philosophy* (1984) she attempts to define an essentially female religious understanding. Central to her undertaking is a reexamination of language: as she says in *Gyn/Ecology*, "Gynocentric writing means risking. Since the language and style of patriarchal writing simply cannot contain or carry the energy of women's exorcism and ecstasy . . . I invent, dis-cover, re-member." In *Pure Lust*, she posits an understanding of God/dess/es as "Verb," different "Powers and manifestations of Be-ing." *Gyn/Ecology* includes an index to nearly two hundred new words/phrases/meanings. Daly has continued the task of re-creating and reinventing womanspeech in *Websters' First New Intergalactic Wickedary of the English Language* (with Jane Caputi, 1987).

Some critics see in Daly's theology a Gnostic-like dualistic construction identifying the feminine and the masculine as fundamentally opposed. Audre * Lorde ("An Open Letter to Mary Daly," 1979) and others have noted her dependence on Western models and mythologies and scant attention to women's traditions and culture outside of the European tradition. But Daly's writing has been transformative within both academic circles and the wider feminist community. Her books were essential components of the development of feminist theory in the United States and the nurturing of spiritual life in feminist politics. Her uncompromising critique of male-created culture and male-inspired religious imagery has made her later work most welcomed by those interested in Goddess spirituality and those involved in the creation and development of new concepts of lesbian identity.

• Emily Erwin Culpepper, "Philosophia in a Feminist Key: Revolt of the Symbols," Th.D. diss., Harvard University (1983). Amanda Porterfield, "Feminist Theology as a Revitalization Movement," *Sociological Analysis* 48, no. 3 (1987): 234–244. Wanda Warren Berry, "Feminist Theology: The 'Verbing' of Ultimate/Intimate Reality in Mary Daly," *Ultimate Reality and Meaning* 11, no. 3 (September 1988): 217–232.

JoAnn E. Castagna

DANNER, Margaret (1910–1984), poet. Born to Caleb and Naomi Danner in Chicago where she lived most of her life, she was married first to Cordell Strickland, with whom she had a daughter, and later to Otto Cunningham. Danner won her first of several poetry prizes in the eighth grade. She later studied to be a poet by taking courses at Chicago colleges and attending a poetry workshop conducted by Inez Stark Boulton. From 1951 to 1957 Danner worked at *Poetry* magazine where in 1956 she became the first African-American to become assistant editor. Under the influence of Karl Shapiro and Paul Engle she published four

poems in *Poetry* entitled "Far From Africa" during that period. She later recalled her association with *Poetry* as being one of the most rewarding experiences of her life.

The 1960s proved to be the most productive years of Danner's career as a poet. In 1961 she went to Detroit as a poet in residence at Wayne State University and stayed to found Boone House, a community arts center, in 1962. Assisting Danner was poet Dudley Randall, whose Broadside Press published her *Impressions of African Art Forms* (1960) and *Poem Counterpoem* (1966) of which Randall was coauthor. Other poets who assisted her at Boone House included Robert Hayden, to whom she later dedicated her most important collection of poetry, *The Down of a Thistle* (1976). The opportunity to work with other poets in Detroit was for Danner a beautiful and fruitful experience.

Margaret Danner's most distinctive poetry utilized African art forms as a lodestar to focus on the beauty and value of the African transmittals in African-American life. Often anthologized, such poems as "The Small Bells of Benin," "Through the Caribbean Sea," "The Slave and the Iron Lace," "This Is an African Worm," and "Garnishing the Aviary" employ the inherited gifts of Africa, which are often misunderstood or unappreciated by Americans. Critics who extol Danner's poetry note her exotic and exact images, her subtle protest poems, and her pervasive message that African-Americans should preserve, appreciate, and most of all, celebrate their African heritage.

• June M. Aldridge, "Margaret Esse Danner," *Dictionary of Literary Biography: Afro-American Poets since 1955*, eds. Trudier Harris and Thadious Davis (1985), pp. 84–88. Erlene Stetson, "Dialectic Voices in the Poetry of Margaret Esse Danner," in *Black American Poets Between Worlds, 1940–1960*, ed. R. Baxter Miller (1986). June M. Aldridge, "Benin to Beale Street: African Art in the Poetry of Margaret Danner," *College Language Association Journal* 31, no. 2 (December 1987): 201–209.

June M. Aldridge

DARGAN, Olive Tilford (1869–1968), also known as Fielding Burke, novelist, short story writer, poet, dramatist.

Born in Kentucky of abolitionist parents four years after the Civil War, Olive Tilford acquired early an enthusiasm for literature and a sympathy for the politically and economically underprivileged. Educated first at her father's academy in Arkansas and later at Peabody and Radcliffe colleges, she held a variety of teaching and secretarial jobs before her marriage in 1898 to Pegram Dargan. The couple went to New York to pursue writing careers, but in 1906 they moved to Almond, North Carolina, because of

Pegram's health. She lived in London from 1911 to 1914, publishing three books there. After Pegram drowned in 1915 she returned to the Appalachians and lived in Almond or Asheville until her death in 1968.

Dargan's literary career is remarkable in its length and diversity. In 1904 she published *Semiramis*, the first of four collections of closet dramas. *Path Flower* (1914) was her first volume of poetry; her last one, *The Spotted Hawk* (1958), won three poetry awards. Her fiction, which includes two collections of short stories and three novels, is her most enduring claim to literary recognition.

Highland Annals (1924), later reprinted with photographs as *From My Highest Hill* (1941), is a series of sketches that appear to be autobiographical, all presenting the peccadilloes of mountain people from the perspective of the newcomer/landowner. They are basically local color stories, generally sympathetic to the Almond residents but viewing them as a breed apart.

The proletarian novels for which she is best known were published under the pseudonym Fielding Burke. Both *Call Home the Heart* (1932) and *A Stone Came Rolling* (1935) feature Ishma Waycaster, a strong woman who comes down from the hills to work in a cotton mill. After observing the exploitation of workers, she helps to organize a union and is accused of being a communist. Based on the violent mill strikes of 1929 in Gastonia and Marion, North Carolina, the novels are noted for their socialist sympathies. Nevertheless, the portrayal of Ishma as a complex individual with complicated relationships makes the books more than political vehicles. A third novel, *Sons of the Stranger* (1947), features a male labor organizer for mine workers in a fictional western state.

While Dargan was never a member of the Communist Party, she considered herself a Marxist and a feminist. In 1907, she wrote Alice Stone Blackwell, "I find I have been a socialist for some time" and she allowed Party members to hold meetings in her home in Asheville. Her entry in the 1914 *Women's Who's Who* includes the statement, "strongly favors woman suffrage." Evident throughout her works is her unfaltering championship of liberal causes.

• Carol Bird, "Write for the Future: An Interview with Fielding Burke," *Writers' Markets and Methods* (February 1950): 6–7. Virginia Terrell Lathrop, "Olive Tilford Dargan," *North Carolina Libraries* 18 (Spring 1960): 68–76. Sylvia J. Cook and Anna W. Shannon, Afterwords in *Call Home the Heart: A Novel of the Thirties* by Fielding Burke (1983 ed.), pp. 433–462.

Nancy Carol Joyner

DAUGHTERS. In a creole culture, where marriage outside a group invariably threatens that group's ties to the country of origin, daughters are especially problematic. To maintain an English identity in North America, it was necessary for English settlers to develop new rules for exchanging women. Insofar as bloodlines provided an imaginary link with people back in England, however, new ways of constituting a household necessarily called the English identity of the group into question. This conflict at the very heart of the concept of Anglo-America accounts for the peculiar treatment daughters often receive in colonial accounts of Indian captivity. But the attempt to figure out our national identity in terms of daughters does not end there. Indeed, one can read a number of important literary texts as attempts to deal with this conflict.

In one of the earliest examples of a specifically colonial genre, Mary *Rowlandson describes the trials she endured as a captive. Embodied in this solitary woman, colonial culture itself seemed to be under assault. When English culture was cast in this feminine position, however, it acquired a form of legitimation peculiarly suited for a colonial situation. English men had to conquer Native American men for the sake of English women and children; colonialism was both a paternal and a patriotic obligation. The demands of this ideology should have been satisfied once Rowlandson tells us she is safely enfolded in her husband's embrace and they have bought back both her son and her sister's son from the Indians. Indeed, as far as Cotton Mather was concerned, the *captivity narrative was over. His *Magnalia Christi Americana* (1702) tells Rowlandson's story from her husband's point of view. Her captivity tested Reverend Rowlandson, and her return proves his faith stronger than the evil of her heathen captors.

In telling her own story, however, Rowlandson emphasizes her daughter's return. Her separation from and reunion with her child mark the beginning and end of her trials in the wilderness, and her family is not a family until her daughter is restored to them under notably miraculous circumstances: "Thus she traveled three days together, not knowing whither she was going, having nothing to eat or drink but water and green hirtleberries. At last they came into Providence where she was kindly entertained by several of that town. The Indians often said that I should never have her under twenty pounds. But now the Lord hath brought her in upon free cost and given her to me the second time." The miraculous return of Rowlandson's daughter ensures that she remains her father's daughter. Only he can give her away. His Englishness descends to her and through her into the family of other Englishmen, thereby ensuring the Englishness of the community in the New World. Under these circumstances, the daughter functions as what anthropologist Annette Weiner has called an "inalienable possession." Such an object is so vital to the identity of the group that it can neither be taken nor traded away without threatening that group's very identity. To protect against this threat, groups can decide to endow this kind of object with a metaphysical identity. Daughters who are so invested with the power of culture-bearers tend to die whenever they leave the family. Thus we may find them returned through death to their father's home, as in Samuel Richardson's *Clarissa* (1747–1748), the British prototype for American sentimental fiction, or reborn through the daughter's daughter, as in Susanna * Rowson's *Charlotte Temple*, *Clarissa*'s American counterpart (1791). In these cases, the dead daughter proves to be the true one because she cannot survive outside the family.

What happens to a colonial culture when the daughter goes native and survives? Mary Jemison's account of her life among the Senecas was transcribed from her oral testimony in 1823. In this testimony, she speaks as the daughter who never returned, because she was miraculously singled out for survival among the Indians. Her mother left her with these parting words: "Alas, my dear! my heart bleeds at the thoughts of what awaits you; but, if you leave us, remember my child your own name, and the name of your mother and father. Be careful and not forget your English tongue. If you shall have an opportunity to get away from the Indians, don't try to escape; for if you do they will find and destroy you." Heeding this practical advice, Jemison allows herself to be adopted into an Indian family, marries, produces a number of children, all the while helping others like herself to survive among the Senecas. She takes considerable pride in the household she created under these adverse circumstances: "I live in my own house, and on my own land, with my youngest daughter Polly, who is married to George Chongo, and has three children."

This statement reveals the consequences of going native in two different ways. Jemison's reward is one that eighteenth-century English culture might well have considered more appropriate for men than for women. She became head of household at the expense of her femininity, and her daughter married outside the English community, which sets the entire Jemison family forever apart from the "rich and respectable people, principally from New-England," who eventually inhabited "the whole country around her." Her ability to reproduce

an English household without an English husband distinguishes members of the Jemison household from creole families who relied on intermarriage to preserve an English identity. The daughter's capacity to reproduce herself in others is no doubt why fiction and cinema— from Natty Bumppo, Huck Finn, and Ishmael to Jack Kerouac in *On the Road* (1957) and Ethan Edwards (John Wayne) in John Ford's film *The Searchers* (1956)—generally cast men in the role of the educated person who has gone so far native that he cannot be reintegrated in domestic life. The hybrid male is not allowed to reproduce.

Concealed within the commonplace assumption that men want their daughters pure are certain questions that need to be addressed: Of what do we want to keep our daughters pure? How does the nation's identity hinge on their being so? And how can any kind of national purity exist in a colonial setting where its ability to reproduce itself outside of England is necessary to the survival of English culture? To answer these questions, we have to think of the two different options for the daughter in colonial captivity narratives as two different models of social reproduction. According to the Rowlandson model, transmission of English culture takes place through the family. Indeed, the English family is virtually the same as culture itself and will be perpetuated so long as its descendents intermarry with their kind. Such a culture abhors a mixture. It prefers a dead daughter to an ethnically impure one. According to the Jemison model, however, English culture is reproduced within the household, and there is nothing pure about it. That is precisely its virtue. No matter who makes up this household or where they came from, it can incorporate, imitate, reenact, parody, or otherwise reproduce whatever appears to be most English about the English family. Such a household creates a family peculiar to settler colonies.

Harriet Beecher * Stowe's *Uncle Tom's Cabin* (1851–1852) demonstrates how profoundly the conflict between these two bases for national identity has shaped our literature. Stowe asks us to think of the two daughters Eva and Topsy "as representatives of the two extremes of society." Next she asks us to translate their social positions directly into race: "There stood the representatives of their races. The Saxon, born of ages of cultivation, command, education, physical and moral eminence; the African, born of ages of oppression, submission, ignorance, toil, and vice." However, as Hortense Spillers was the first to note, Stowe challenges this absolute difference between white and black daughters whenever she reveals the playfully sensual character of Eva's affection for Tom. Stowe does something perhaps still more curious with Topsy. In a scene that anticipates the spectacle of Eva's deathbed in all respects, Eva engages Topsy in an exchange that empties the black girl of her animating spirit and replaces her illegible—presumably African—elements with English sentimentality. "Yes, in that moment," declares the narrator, "a ray of real belief, a ray of heavenly love, had penetrated the darkness of her heathen soul!" This exchange of interiorities inaugurates Eva's rapid decline, which detaches all African sensuality from the white daughter's body and uses it as a metaphor for her religious ecstasy.

Topsy, in contrast, lives out the logic of cultural assimilation: "the child rapidly grew in grace and in favor with the family and neighborhood. At the age of womanhood, she was, by her own request, baptized, and became a member of the Christian church in the place; and showed so much intelligence, activity, and zeal, and desire to do good in the world, that she was at last recommended, and approved, as a missionary to one of the stations in Africa." This peculiar way of blanching Topsy appears to accomplish much the same thing that the miraculous return of Mary Rowlandson's daughter did. It removes her from the exchange of women. In contrast with the daughters of colonial captivity narratives, however, Topsy has virtually no cultural identity to preserve— no mother, no father, no known relatives at all. Her blood has been mixed with that of her captors, and her culture deliberately reduced to an uncanny force that spasmodically animates her little body. Her options as a daughter therefore differ significantly from those of her Anglo-American prototypes. The novel offers Topsy a way out of the slavery system through cultural assimilation, only to remove her to Africa so that she can reproduce the culture of her captors there.

By way of contrast, Stowe deals with the white daughter in much the same way a feudal aristocracy dealt with their hereditary holdings whenever they deeded them over to the Church. To remove certain objects from the vicissitudes of economic history was to freeze their symbolic identities; those objects became what Weiner describes as inalienable possessions, objects capable of preserving the identity of the group even after the death of its members. If her enormous popularity with readers is any indication, then Eva's symbolic identity was similarly fixed by her extravagantly sentimental death. Refusing to let her grow up as a refined and debilitated Southern beauty, Stowe turned her heroine into a purely literary type, an imported ideal of womanhood that presided

over a culture that was by then not only creolized but also hybrid.

In what may be read as an aggressive rewriting of Stowe's comparison of Eva and Topsy, Harriet * Jacobs recalls, "I once saw two beautiful children playing together. One was a fair white child; the other was her slave, and also her sister. When I saw them embracing each other, and heard their joyous laughter, I turned sadly away from the sight. I foresaw the inevitable blight that would soon fall on the little slave's heart." In writing the autobiographical *Incidents in the Life of a Slave Girl* (1861; reprint 1987), Jacobs draws on the sentimental tradition in order to put the slave girl in much the same relation to Anglo-American culture as the English was to Native Americans. She puts herself in the white captive's position in order to demonstrate that white narrative alternatives are not available to slaves. There is no father to whom she can return, since her father *is* her captor. Nor does the narrative allow her to avoid the negative consequences of the seduction narrative by way of an exalted death. Yet she has all the capacity for virtue and affection that were necessary to guide and protect an English girl. Indeed, the language in which she tells her story could easily be confused with that of Mary Rowlandson: "For years, my master had done his utmost to pollute my mind with foul images, and to destroy the pure principles inculcated by my grandmother, and the good mistress of my childhood." Jacobs even tries to remove herself from the system of sexual exchange by giving herself to another white man in order to avoid sex with her master.

By making this, the only move open to her save suicide, she not only loses her place as the heroine of a sentimental captivity narrative but also fails to reap the rewards allowed to a practical heroine like Mary Jemison. "Reader," she tells us, "my story ends with freedom; not in the usual way, with marriage." Upon her release from captivity, the heroine's options fall significantly short of those enjoyed by both Rowlandson and Jemison: "I and my children are now free! We are as free from the power of slaveholders as are the white people of the north; and though that, according to my ideas, is not saying a great deal, it is a vast improvement on my condition. The dream of my life is not yet realized. I do not sit with my children in a home of my own." Jacobs uses the narrative paradigm of Anglo-American literature to represent her own experience as a slave girl, only to demonstrate that its options do not obtain for her. The means of social reproduction are systematically withheld. In place of a family, hybrid or pure, Jacobs' version of the captivity narrative produces a social unit that has been ruptured, polluted, and dismembered so systematically that rupture, pollution, and dismemberment have become its identifying traits.

Although modern industrialized cultures tend to displace daughters by sons and to subsume them in mothers, daughters are nevertheless crucial to group identity (whether of nation, race, ethnicity, or class), to the social reproduction of that identity, and hence to the position of the group in an increasingly multiethnic and transnational conceptual map of the world's population. Daughters are most likely to reveal discriminations, subordinations, eradications. This cultural logic generates the desperately irrational narrative of Willa * Cather's *Sapphira and the Slave Girl* (1940), a novel that—as Toni * Morrison explains in *Playing in the Dark* (1992)—"has been virtually jettisoned from the body of American literature by critical consensus." The reason is pretty clear. Sapphira is a genteel invalid patiently attended by the devoted female slave Till. The consequences of the fact that the two actually constitute only one woman—Anglo-American whims and commands, African-American body and labor—becomes unmistakably clear when Sapphira gets it into her head that her husband yearns for her slave's pubescent daughter. Operating on the assumption that to own the mother's labor is to own the daughter's sexuality, Sapphira arranges for her nephew to rape the girl in a scheme that plays out the distinctively American logic of racism. Having delegated her labor to an enslaved population, the white woman has handed over her sexuality as well. Why should a nephew not take the place of the father in a family where a servant's daughter might very well have taken the place of his wife? This second substitution simply completes the narrative logic of Stowe—a doubling process that symbolically drains black bodies of their own desires and disembodies white women in order to keep them pure.

It was at an enormous cost, then, that the family was made to bear the burden of cultural transmission. We have considered two captivity narratives that define this burden as one borne by women, implying that Englishness itself was in danger whenever they were exposed to alien ways and other men. For the household to have the character of a world complete unto itself—a world, what is more, with a woman displaying English refinement at its center—required the labor of others. Thus the paradox that organizes *Sapphira and the Slave Girl:* The preservation of the English family in America required the very thing that most threatened its claims to autonomy. Other people were brought into the household not only to perform the most basic forms of labor but also to serve as the objects of lust. African-American bodies were both prosthetic devices for Sapphira's body and all the body she had. Her very existence was threatened, not by her husband's attraction to the daughter of a slave, but by the alliance between Till and her daughter that Cather hints at but never allows to intervene in the narrative. The novel has Sapphira's sister, a white women, remove the slave's daughter from the system of exchange that defines her as the object of white desires. The * slave narrative differs structurally from other captivity narratives, then, because it records how African Americans were systematically cut off from the means of social reproduction available to other groups within American culture. If they could never be their fathers' daughters, as Mary Rowlandson and her daughter were, then neither did they have the means to create their own version of the Anglo-American household, as Mary Jemison did. This is perhaps the one conviction that Stowe, Jacobs, and Cather share.

A more sustained examination of the daughter in American culture would reveal how the sentimental conventions of the family actually divided a national population into racial, ethnic, and regional groups that existed in a peripheral relationship to an elite core whose values are both universalized and critiqued in canonical literature. A focus on the figure of the daughter in American literature necessarily raises questions about group identity and how such identities are forged in diaspora. It seems unlikely, however, that we would now be willing to consider the daughter capable of providing the key to such an extensive conceptual map of our culture without the work of contemporary women writers. Indeed, since the 1980s we have witnessed a veritable explosion of fiction by women from racial, ethnic, or regional groups. With significant regularity these women write as daughters confronting something like the dilemma that once confronted Englishwomen captured by Native Americans: whether to remain their father's daughters or to mix with another culture and reproduce their mothers' households according to new rules.

As if to confirm the fictionality of the English core of American culture, Jane * Smiley's *A Thousand Acres* (1991) has the all-American girl retell the story of *King Lear* from the perspective of one of the bad daughters. Ginny Cook grows up in Zebulon County, Iowa. She describes her life in perfectly transparent, dialect-free English, making sure that all ethnographic information divulged locates her at the heart of a patriarchal family in the heart of the midwestern United States. The story takes up her life when her father decides to deed the farm over to his daughters so that they can toil and raise their own families on land that they own. But what begins as a tale that seems, by virtue of its commitment to the work ethic and traditional family values, hardly worth the telling, soon enough reveals uncanny traces of the slave's narrative. How can this be? Is Smiley drawing on a totally inappropriate narrative tradition in describing how Ginny [Goneril] and Rose [Regan] Cook grew up within a typical American family in a country that seems to be made entirely of such families? Not at all. The narrator realizes, in the telling of her story, that she is an incest victim who has remained within her father's house in order that her younger sister Caroline [Cordelia] can survive and go away to school. Ginny also reveals that the very land on which she labored to perpetuate the illusion of the American family has poisoned her. Having rendered the all-American girl biologically incapable of having children, the chemically saturated soil of the heartland allows sister Rose to have two daughters before killing her off with breast cancer. The sexually amputated bodies of the sisters come together to form a patchwork maternal body, as Ginny leaves Zebulon county to raise her sister's children elsewhere. By redefining the story of the father's daughter as something more like a slave's narrative, Smiley redefines our national story as one of pollution and hybridization under conditions of captivity.

If these contemporary versions of the captivity narrative prompt us to rethink the American literary tradition all the way back to Rowlandson and Jemison from the perspective of an ethnically mixed and therefore dangerous periphery, then Toni Morrison's *Beloved* (1988) is a large part of the reason why. Morrison's novel is surely the most self-conscious literary examination of the daughter's centrality in American culture that we have. It displays elements of the kind of magical realism we generally associate with Latin American novels in which colonial European culture has trouble mixing with residual indigenous cultures. As the name attached to a daughter murdered lest she fall into enemy hands, *Beloved* is about this suppressed history and its apotheosis in contemporary literature. The daughter's murder simply literalizes her social death. Her sinister reappearance as a grown woman, complete with the scar recording the moment long ago when her mother slit her throat, transforms what was social non-being into a positive cultural category, the more potent for its having a purely fabulous basis independent of our scientific and legal definitions of the body. Produced by the uncanny traces of a body cancelled out, this position is perhaps what currently lends the

African-American woman writer a privileged vantage point from which to explain American culture to itself.

By resurrecting the story of the daughter who returned miraculously undefiled ("She was my best thing," says Sethe, a former slave, about her daughter), Morrison brings the slave narrative home to roost. She uses it to break open a profound cultural contradiction between family and household that American fiction tends either to resolve or else to suppress. The only pure daughter would have had to be a dead one for most American readers, few of whom stayed either European or Anglo-American for very long. This fact of belonging to a colonial culture is at least part of the explanation for such works as Edgar Allan Poe's "Fall of the House of Usher" (1839–1840), Nathaniel Hawthorne's "Rappaccini's Daughter" and "The Birthmark" (both 1846), and Herman Melville's *Pierre* (1852). It was in this ultimately negative way that she represented their relationship to some original family. According to the tradition of the slave narrative, however, a pure daughter could not even be a dead one. If she were not her father's daughter, then the very idea of cultural purity in the English sense was nothing but a fiction from the very beginning. Certain fictions, however, acquired a life of their own, and the fiction that only pure forms of cultural identity are transmitted through the patriarchal family was certainly one of them.

As the pure daughter—dressed, significantly, in white—Beloved is not simply one more fiction but a gloriously violent disembodiment of the ruling idea that cultural identity depends on remaining true to one's origins. The novel rejects this basis for identity, insisting at the beginning and end of Sethe's narrative that "It was not a story to pass on." Why remember a family that never did exist, if that memory exists at the expense of one's actual household? When Morrison brought the pure daughter back to life and killed her off a second time, the residual tradition of the daughter's narrative gained ascendancy not only over the narrative of the slave girl but over the twofold fantasy of household autonomy and cultural purity as well. Morrison brought back the pure daughter, paradoxically, in order to locate value in the real one: "She's still with me, my Denver," says Sethe, finally acknowledging this other daughter as the true one.

[*See also* Mothers and Daughters.]

• James E. Seaver, *A Narrative of the Life of Mrs. Mary Jemison* (1824; reprint, 1992). Leslie Fiedler, *Love and Death in the American Novel* (1966). Ann Douglas, *The Feminization of American Culture* (1977). Mary Rowlandson, "The Sovereignty and Goodness of God," in *Puritans among the Indians: Accounts of Captivity and*

Redemption, 1676–1724, eds. Alden T. Vaughan and Edward W. Clark (1981), pp. 29–76. Benedict Anderson, *Imagined Communities: Reflections on the Origin and Spread of Nationalism* (1983). Jane Tompkins, *Sensational Designs: The Cultural Work of American Fiction, 1790–1860* (1985). Hazel Carby, *Reconstructing Womanhood: The Emergence of the Afro-American Woman Novelist* (1987). Patricia Nelson Limerick, *The Legacy of Conquest: The Unbroken Past of the American West* (1987). Hortense J. Spillers, "Changing the Letter: The Yokes, the Jokes of Discourse, or, Mrs. Stowe, Mr. Reed," in *Slavery and the Literary Imagination*, eds. Deborah E. McDowell and Arnold Rampersad (1989), pp. 25–61. Annette Weiner, *Inalienable Possessions: The Paradox of Keeping-While-Giving* (1992). Ann duCille, *The Coupling Convention: Tradition and the Black Female Talent* (1993).

Nancy Armstrong

DAVIS, Angela (b. 1944), activist, educator, philosopher, critic. Born in Birmingham, Alabama, Davis is a committed activist and philosopher, dedicated to the liberation of oppressed peoples. Her 1974 *Angela Davis, An Autobiography* focused particularly on the political significance of her first twenty-six years and on the development of her revolutionary consciousness. Her experience of racism and white supremacy in Birmingham and New York and an acute awareness of class, color, and sex discrimination were a part of her early consciousness. Well educated, she attended Elisabeth Irwin High School in New York and Brandeis University, where she first began to study philosophy with Herbert Marcuse. She spent her junior year in France and after graduating with honors from Brandeis, she went to Frankfurt to study philosophy with Theodor Adorno and other philosophers at the Institut für Sozialforschung.

Upon returning to the United States in 1967, Davis worked on her doctoral degree at the University of California, San Diego, with Marcuse and was hired in 1969 by the University of California, Los Angeles, to teach philosophy. In San Diego and Los Angeles, she became a grassroots organizer for Black Liberation, for prisoner's rights, and against the Vietnam War. She joined the Communist Party in 1968; after traveling to Cuba in the summer of 1969, Governor Ronald Reagan and the U.C. Regents tried to fire her from her UCLA teaching job for being a Communist. While fighting for her job, she was accused of conspiring in a courtroom uprising because of her activism for prisoner's rights in the Soledad Brothers Defense Committee. In 1972, she was acquitted on three death penalty charges of murder, kidnapping, and conspiracy. She helped to compile and edit an anthology about prisoner's rights and political prisoners called *If They Come in the Morning* (1971).

Always conscious of the intersections of oppressions, Davis's *Women, Race, and Class* (1981) is an important historical study which critiques the feminist movement for race and class biases. In 1980 and 1984 she ran on the Communist Party ticket as a vice-presidential candidate. A respected lecturer, she has taught at Berkeley and at the History of Consciousness program at Cal-Santa Cruz. Though sometimes criticized for her educational privilege, she has been a consistent grassroots activist, serving on the National Committee of the Communist Party, the National Alliance Against Racist and Political Repression, and the National Black Women's Health Project. A very accessible writer, she is also the author of *Women, Culture and Politics* (1989) and numerous articles.

• Michele Wallace, *Black Macho and the Myth of the Superwoman*, 2d ed. (1978; reprint, 1990), pp. 160–167.

James Davis-Rosenthal

DAVIS, Rebecca Harding (1831–1910), novelist, short fiction writer, journalist. Raised in the industrial town of Wheeling in what is now West Virginia, Rebecca Harding was the oldest of the five children of Richard W. and Rebecca Leet Harding. Until she was thirty she led the conventional life of a well-to-do middle-class white unmarried woman of her time. Taught at home by tutors and her mother, she also attended Washington Female Seminary in Pennsylvania, graduating in 1848 at the age of seventeen. For the next fourteen years she lived at home, helping with housework and the education of her younger siblings. With the publication of "Life in the Iron Mills" in the *Atlantic Monthly* (1861) she dramatically emerged as an important new literary voice. The novella was the first extended depiction of the desperate and deprived lives, the "soul starvation," of workers in the nation's new mills and factories, based on what Harding had seen in Wheeling's mills and iron foundries. The story introduced new elements of realism and naturalism into American fiction, and it brought Harding fame and the attention of the New England literary establishment. In the novel *Margaret Howth* (1862) she further explored the crippling material, emotional, and spiritual effects of industrial capitalism, and announced her antiromantic credo, "to dig into this commonplace, this vulgar American life, and see what is in it."

In 1863, Harding married L. Clarke Davis, a Philadelphia journalist. In the four decades that followed, while managing a home and raising three children, she continued to publish steadily, although never again equalling the achievement of "Iron Mills." Her prolific output—ten novels, over 100 short stories, essays, journalism, and children's literature—included both serious fiction and melodramatic and sentimental potboilers written to help support her family. Although economic and esthetic compromises marred much of her work, she continued to explore new and often controversial subject matter, addressing important issues of race, class, and gender in American society. *Waiting for the Verdict* (1868) dealt with injustice against blacks in the aftermath of emancipation; *Earthen Pitchers* (1873–1874) described women beginning to earn their own living professionally; *John Andross* (1874) was one of the first novels to treat corruption in government. Meanwhile many of her stories, such as "The Wife's Story" (1864), treated the anguish of women caught between the demands of family and creative work, a conflict she never resolved. Her last critical success was a group of realistic short stories, *Silhouettes of American Life* (1892).

By 1904, when she published the autobiographical *Bits of Gossip*, Harding Davis had been largely forgotten. At her death in 1910 she was remembered more as the mother of the famous journalist Richard Harding Davis than as the author whose work, in the words of the writer Tillie * Olsen, who first returned Harding Davis's work to contemporary attention, had "extended the realm of [American] fiction" in important ways.

• The Rebecca Harding Davis Papers are in the Clifton Waller Barrett Collection at the University of Virginia Library in Charlottesville. Other material on Davis is in the James T. Fields Papers, Huntington Library, San Marino, California. See also Gerald Langford, *The Richard Harding Davis Years: A Biography of Mother and Son* (1961). Tillie Olsen, "A Biographical Interpretation," Afterword to *Life in the Iron Mills*, by Rebecca Harding Davis (1972). Jean Fagan Yellin, Afterword, in *Margaret Howth. A Story of Today* (1990). Jean Pfaelzer, "Rebecca Harding Davis, 1831–1910," *Legacy* 7, no. 2 (Fall 1990): 39–45.

Elaine Hedges

DAY, Dorothy (1897–1980), liberal Catholic activist and journalist. Though born in Bath Beach, New York, to an Episcopal family, Day from an early age felt an attraction to Catholicism, which took the form of activism on behalf of the poor and homeless. At sixteen, she entered the University of Illinois, where she engaged in political activism and wrote for the *Daily Illini*. In New York in 1916, she wrote for a socialist newspaper, the *New York Call*, and in the following year she participated in the rally in support of the Russian Revolution at Madison Square Garden; marched against President Wilson's institution of the military draft; and was arrested for supporting a group of militant suffragists.

At this juncture, Day had not yet committed herself to Catholicism, and her political activ-

ism coexisted with an unorthodox lifestyle. Indeed, Day first came to national attention in 1924 with the publication of her sizzling semi-autobiographical novel, *The Eleventh Virgin*. In March 1927, Day gave birth to a daughter, Tamar Teresa, by her atheistic common-law husband, biologist Forster Batterham. When Day finally made her commitment to Catholicism by insisting on baptism for her child and herself, the relationship with Batterham ended. After a brief 1929 stint as a Hollywood screenwriter, Day and her daughter moved to Mexico. In the summer of 1930, they returned to the United States, where they apparently were supported by Day's father.

In late 1932, Day went to Washington, D.C., to write about the "hunger march"; while there, on 8 December 1932, she prayed at the National Shrine of the Immaculate Conception for God's guidance in directing her energies toward helping the poor. The following day she met French activist Peter Maurin (1877–1949); thereafter they worked closely together and shared a life of voluntary poverty. Maurin urged Day to create a newspaper committed to social Christian values that would serve as an alternative to the Marxist *Daily Worker*. The first issue of Day's the *Catholic Worker*, a four-page penny tabloid, was sold on 1 May 1933; as of 1993, the *Catholic Worker* was still being published. Maurin also worked with Day to establish self-sustaining farm communes, plus "hospitality houses" offering food and shelter to the homeless. Day recorded their activities in *House of Hospitality* (1939).

Through the pages of the *Catholic Worker*, Day spoke against the military-industrial complex and opposed both World War II and Vietnam. Her books include *On Pilgrimage: The Sixties* (1972); *Loaves and Fishes* (1963), her account of the Catholic worker movement; and *Therese* (1960), a life of St. Therese of Lisieux. Day's personal writings include *From Union Square to Rome* (1938), an account of her conversion; and *The Long Loneliness* (1952), her autobiography. She died in New York on 29 November 1980.

• Robert Coles, *A Spectacle unto the World* (1973). William D. Miller, *A Harsh and Dreadful Love* (1973). William D. Miller, *Dorothy Day: A Biography* (1982). Robert Ellsberg, ed., *By Little and by Little: The Selected Writings of Dorothy Day* (1983). Nancy L. Roberts, *Dorothy Day and "The Catholic Worker"* (1984). Anne and Alice Klejment, *Dorothy Day and "The Catholic Worker": A Bibliography and Index* (1986). Robert Coles, *Dorothy Day* (1987).

Alice Hall Petry

DECONSTRUCTION AND FEMINISM are two late-twentieth-century movements connected by their shared interest in critiquing established Western philosophical and political traditions. The relationship between feminism and deconstruction is complicated because each movement calls the strategies of the other into question. While some feminist writers reject deconstructive criticism, primarily on the basis of its antihumanist premises, others argue that examining the distances between feminism and deconstruction can be productive to the development of feminist politics. In the United States in particular, such disparities within the feminist movement can be attributed to very different interpretations of both feminism and deconstruction.

There are as many "deconstructions" and "feminisms" as there are critics who write about them. But for the purpose of describing the relationship between the two movements, the concepts of deconstruction can be outlined as follows: In American literature departments, the term "deconstruction" is often used loosely to refer to a critical practice of reading for points of contradiction within a text in order to subvert the text's implicit claims to a unified meaning. Challenging the concept of writing as a mimetic representation of the world or of the author's experience, deconstruction locates texts within systems of linguistic constructs and analyzes the processes by which they produce the illusion of truth or realism.

There term deconstruction has it origins in French philosopher Jacques Derrida's (b. 1930) critique of Western metaphysics, from which the understanding of deconstruction as a critical practice is adapted (some would argue reductively). Derrida's work is based on his rereadings of German philosophers (primarily Nietzsche and Heidegger), Swiss linguist Ferdinand de Saussure, and Sigmund Freud, among other intellectuals. Some of the key concepts of Derridean deconstruction for feminism are the notions of *binary opposition* and *différance*.

The notion of binary opposition comes from structuralism, which argues that Western thought is structured by oppositions such as nature/culture, identity/difference, and man/woman, in which the meaning of each term rests on its opposition to the other. Derrida complicates structuralism's linguistic analysis by exposing the hierarchical relationship between the two terms in which the first is given priority while the second is represented as negative or derivative. In general, these binaries favor self-identity, unity, and presence over difference, multiplicity, and absence. Derrida's critique of Western thought hinges on a two-part method of deconstructing binary oppositions: reversal and displacement. Reversal gives priority to the second term over the first

in order to overturn the hierarchy of the dominant discourse. The aim of deconstruction, however, is not to establish a new hierarchy but to displace the system of oppositions by demonstrating that difference always exists within the supposedly unitary categories of binary thinking.

The paradigm of binary oppositions is useful to feminism because it denaturalizes identity by exposing its structural aspects. Feminists have used deconstructive strategies to challenge traditional definitions of gender and to analyze the opposition male/female as a cultural construct that gives precedence to the masculine and marginalizes the feminine. This construct not only defines human subjects as "male" and "female," but also extends to other kinds of representations that do not initially appear to be tied to gender. For example, the binaries culture/nature, intellectual/emotional, and political/personal can all be read as gender-coded pairs in which the second terms are associated with the feminine. This kind of analysis enables feminists to identify the mechanisms of oppression in ideologies that are not obviously about sex and gender but which are produced within a patriarchal value system.

While deconstruction's critique of the essentialist underpinnings of identity is useful to feminism, deconstruction does not necessarily share feminism's concerns. Derridean deconstruction identifies "woman" as a privileged object of analysis, but it is not interested so much in the specificity of women's oppression as it is in how the category "woman," defined by lack and negation, consolidates the "phallocentric" (male-engendered) nature of Western discourse, and how, as a figure of indeterminacy, the metaphor of woman is useful in deconstructing that discourse. While such an analysis does offer a critique of phallocentrism, it also appropriates the feminine to define its own theory and ignores women's historical experience of social relations. In fact, the logic of deconstruction avoids the social criticism based on women's experience in which feminism is grounded because that criticism re-establishes the category of identity. Deconstruction's antihumanist undermining of identity clashes with women's claim to identity through the women's movement, raising the question of who the subject of feminism will be if identity is deconstructed. Some feminists see deconstruction as a threat because it severs the notion of "woman" from women as a social category made up of historically "real" subjects and so disempowers them as agents of social change.

Feminist critics have attempted to negotiate the tensions between the philosophical movement of deconstruction and the social movement of feminism by adapting the Derridean concept of *différance* to theorize the disruption of binary oppositions in a way that might enable political change. The term plays on the two meanings of the French verb *differer*: to differ and to defer. It approaches the logic of the binary by accounting for the inscription of difference within identity (marked by the dependency of the dominant term on the subordinate one for definition) and the resulting deferral of self-presence or determinate meaning.

The adaptation of *différance* to negotiate the link between deconstruction's philosophical critique (of the dominant ideology's definition of difference in terms of opposition and hierarchy) and feminism's social critique (of the effects of that ideology on women) takes different forms within feminist theory. One of the most influential theories, both on the continent and in the United States, is what has come to be referred to as "French feminism," which is concerned with the acquisition of gendered subjectivity through language. Some key figures of French feminism are Hélenè Cixous, Luce Irigaray, and Julia Kristeva, whose projects are founded on rereadings of Derrida and of French psychoanalyst Jacques Lacan. In their work, female sexuality is the figure for *différance* that disrupts phallocentric discourse by celebrating multiplicity and diffusion. Although the French feminists have been accused of essentialism because their theory appears to be based on a return to biology, their criticism continues to inform new deconstructive feminisms.

Lesbian feminism (now referred to along with gay criticism under the rubric "queer theory") often reads the French feminists as part of an effort to push the deconstruction of gender/sexuality beyond the biological by suggesting that the anatomical categories "male" and "female" on which gender identities are based are themselves as culturally constructed as gender. Judith Butler (*Gender Trouble*, 1990), for example, argues that bodies are sexed not in nature but in discourse, and suggests that categories of sex and gender might be multiplied beyond the duality of the anatomical. *Queer theory also considers the binary opposition between heterosexuality and homosexuality, and the construct "bisexual," which is often positioned as a third term but which can be read as a recontainment of the binary masculine/feminine within a single term (Eve Sedgwick, *The Epistemology of the Closet*, 1990).

Feminisms that rely less heavily on psychoanalysis than do French feminism and lesbian feminism tend to move from the philosophical concept of *différance* to a more politically grounded understanding of difference. Materialist feminism, for example, makes a point of balancing the analysis of gender as a discursive construct with an analysis of gender as a historically changing set of social relations. It is also interested in oppressions based on differences of race and class. Materialist feminism frequently draws on Michel Foucault's (*The History of Sexuality*, 1976) deconstruction of power relations because it combines discourse theory with historical analyses of the way power is deployed through institutions that structure social relations (e.g., medicine, psychiatry, the penal system). Rather than conceiving of patriarchy as a monolithic entity (a tactic that only offers a partial analysis of oppression and so only suggests partial points of resistance), a feminism based on Foucauldian deconstruction looks at the multiplicity of power relations in which women are oppressed.

Feminist women of color have also complicated the notion of *différance* by suggesting that the category "woman," as it is traditionally employed in both Derridean and white feminist deconstructions, reductively considers gender over other social determinants. While white Western deconstructions analyze different figures within the category woman (e.g., Madonna/whore), the analysis is often interested in these figures as metaphors that replicate binary thinking about gender through which masculinist discourse defines itself. Deconstructions that incorporate the point of view of women of color, on the other hand, are interested in disrupting the falsely unified category of woman. They argue that different women occupy that category differently and that power relations among women themselves must be put under scrutiny. Gayatri *Spivak, who established herself as a deconstructive critic translating Derrida and later developed feminist readings of his work, addresses this issue in "French Feminism in an International Frame" (*Yale French Studies* 62 (1981): 154–184), where she argues that First World feminists must stop theorizing for women of color and learn from them instead.

The relationship between feminism and deconstruction remains uneasy but can no longer be described as distant, primarily because feminism's somewhat wary interest in the efficacy of deconstructive strategies as a means of social change has brought the two projects in contact. At worst, the two movements threaten each other's premises. At best, their contact enables feminism to challenge its essentialist underpinnings and deconstruction to specify its political goals.

[*See also* Post-structuralism.]

• Frances Bartowski, "Feminism and Deconstruction: A Union Forever Deferred," *Enclitic* 4 (Fall 1980): 70–77. Gayatri Spivak, "Displacement and the Discourse of Woman," in *Displacement: Derrida and After*, ed. Mark Krupnick (1983), pp. 169–195. Alice Jardine, *Gynesis: Configurations of Woman and Modernity* (1985). Toril Moi, *Sexual/Textual Politics* (1985). Elizabeth Meese, *Crossing the Double-Cross* (1986). Barbara Johnson, *A World of Difference* (1987). *Feminist Studies*, special issue on deconstruction, 14, no. 1 (Spring 1988). Diana Fuss, *Essentially Speaking* (1989). Norma Alarcón, "The Theoretical Subject(s) of This Bridge Called My Back and Anglo-American Feminism," in *Making Face, Making Soul: Haciendo Caras*, ed. Gloria Anzaldúa (1990), pp. 356–369.

Lisa Walker

DELAND, Margaret (1857–1945), novelist, short story writer, and poet. Born in Allegheny, Pennsylvania, Deland was orphaned as an infant and raised by relatives. Determined to earn her own living, she studied drawing and then taught art at The Girls' Normal School in New York (later Hunter College). In 1880, she married Lorin Deland of Boston and became active in social work, taking dozens of unwed mothers and their babies into her home until the women could be placed in jobs. Deland's activities convinced her that women needed sex education and birth control, and her fiction often dealt with the problems of unwed mothers.

After publishing *The Old Garden and Other Verses* (1886), a highly successful poetry collection, she turned to serious fiction. Her first novel (*John Ward, Preacher*, 1888) rejected religious orthodoxy and stressed the dangers of fanaticism. That book and her next novels (*Sydney*, 1890; *Philip and His Wife*, 1894) embroiled Deland in controversy; she was accused of attacking Christian values and advocating free love. However, Deland charmed readers with her stories and novels set in Old Chester, a rural Pennsylvania village she created and filled with appealing characters. Deland's use of social detail and finely drawn characters won her short story collections (*Old Chester Tales*, 1898; *Dr. Lavendar's People*, 1903; *Around Old Chester*, 1915; *New Friends in Old Chester*, 1924) comparisons to the works of Jane Austen. Many stories and her mid-career novels (*The Awakening of Helena Richie*, 1906; *The Iron Woman*, 1911; *The Rising Tide*, 1916) dealt with women facing financial or moral crisis and suggested a new feminine ideal—a woman with intellect, strength, and independent moral judgment.

After Deland's husband died in 1917, she visited France and wrote essays supporting the Allies and war relief efforts. Her last novels (*The Vehement Flame*, 1922; *The Kays*, 1926; *Captain Archer's Daughter*, 1932) dealt with failed marriages. Two autobiographies (*If This Be I, As I Suppose It Be*, 1935; *Golden Yesterdays*, 1941) followed. In 1926, Deland was elected to the National Institute of Arts and Letters, along with Edith Wharton and Mary Wilkins *Freeman. Deland's writings are valuable for the ways in which they reflect changes in women's issues and societal moral dilemmas from the nineteenth century to the twentieth century. Her major themes—fanaticism, women's independence, and individual responsibility—remain current.

• Barbara Welter, *Dimity Convictions: The American Woman in the Nineteenth Century* (1976). Herbert F. Smith, *The Popular American Novel, 1865–1920* (1980). Diana C. Reep, *The Rescue and Romance: Popular Novels before World War I* (1982). Diana C. Reep, *Margaret Deland* (1985). Susan Albertine, "Breaking the Silent Partnership: Businesswomen in Popular Fiction," *American Literature* 62, no. 2 (June 1990): 238–261.

Diana C. Reep

DETECTIVE FICTION. *See* Mystery and Detective Fiction.

DEUTSCH, Babette (1895–1982), poet, translator, critic, and novelist. Babette Deutsch was in many ways a representatively modernist poet. Like many of her generation, she wrote free as well as formal verse; worked in longer, mixed forms (*Epistle to Prometheus*, 1931); and supplemented what she perceived as her primary career in poetry with work as a teacher, editor, translator, critic, and novelist.

Born in New York City, Deutsch remained a New Yorker until her death, receiving her education there and teaching at Columbia University for more than twenty-five years. Perhaps the cosmopolitan atmosphere of the city as she experienced it, as well as her own German-Jewish ethnic heritage, contributed to her eclectic and wide-ranging tastes, her iconoclastic political progressivism, and her sympathy with children, the elderly, and other marginalized members of society.

Deutsch began her professional career as a poet while a student at Barnard College (B.A., 1913), and published *Banners* in 1919. The title poem of this book directly celebrates the Russian Revolution, though Deutsch's political views would make few other appearances in her poems. More characteristic was the imagistic style of *Banners* and her next two books, a style which might seem opposed to the often philosophic or historical content of the poems. *Epistle to Prometheus*, which Deutsch later disowned, was an explicitly philosophical book-length poem; again here, the surface similarity to other modernist long-poem projects (such as Pound's *The Cantos* or Eliot's *The Waste Land*) is belied by the accessibility and humane progressivism of the work. Most of her later books of poetry concentrated on short poems in both free and formal verse. In all she would maintain a cool and restrained voice, not without emotion but capable of admitting abstract reflection into an imagistic setting.

As a translator, Deutsch sometimes collaborated with her husband, Avrahm Yarmolinsky. She also translated from Rilke (*Poems from "The Book of Hours,"* 1941), Pushkin (*Eugene Onegin*, 1943), and Pasternak (*Selected Writings*, 1949), among others. She was an astute critic; *Poetry in Our Time* (1952, revised 1963), though it gave little space to women poets and bore a typically New Critical distrust of political poetry, was nonetheless a monumental survey of modern verse. And her *Poetry Handbook: A Dictionary of Terms* (1957, 4th edition, 1974) is still in print as a standard reference.

Deutsch's work as a poet, though highly regarded by her peers, has largely been ignored in recent histories of the modernist verse revolution. Yet this representative modernist both exemplifies the possibilities of that revolution and refuses its excesses, its pretensions, and its inflated claims.

• Deutsch's manuscript papers are in the New York Public Library. Babette Deutsch, *The Collected Poems of Babette Deutsch* (1969). Jean Gould, *American Women Poets: Pioneers of Modern Poetry* (1980), pp. 293–301. William Drake, *The First Wave: Women Poets in America, 1915–1945* (1987).

David Kellogg

DEVEAUX, Alexis (b. 1948), poet, playwright, novelist, essayist, and performance artist. An activist-artist in the tradition of Lorraine *Hansberry, Alexis Deveaux has successfully produced in many genres. As Editor-at-Large of *Essence* magazine (1978–1990), she wrote numerous feature articles on the psychological, social, and economic contradictions faced by African Americans and third world peoples. Despite her strong, progressive political views, her fictional works avoid didacticism, instead creating compassionate treatments of black women whose relationships are a microcosm of complex national and international relations.

Deveaux became involved in community service early on in her native New York City. Before earning her bachelor's degree (1976) from Empire State College, State University of New York, she worked in numerous community projects, including the Frederick Douglass's Creative Arts Center (New York), where she taught English and creative writing. She also cofounded the Coeur de l'Unicorne Gallery, which exhibited her paintings.

Her major accomplishments as a playwright include "Tapestry" and "Circles," produced for KCET-TV's *Visions* (1976); "A Season to Unravel," produced by the Negro Ensemble Company in New York City (1979); "No," produced

by the New Federal Theatre in New York City (1981); and "Elbow Rooms," written for and produced at Wabash College (a men's college) in Crawfordsville, Indiana (1987). In these works, black women are presented in relation to their sexuality and seek to comprehend their political and social selves. Poetic dialogue and nonlinear narrative enhance the effect of these works.

Her fictional biography of singer Billie Holiday, *Don't Explain: A Song of Billie Holiday* (1980), was praised as a graceful manipulation of biographical and sociohistorical materials that led to new narrative modes and won honorable mention for the Coretta Scott King Award presented by the American Library Association (1981). Several of her short stories have been anthologized ("Adventures of the Dread Sisters," in *Memory of Kin, Stories about Family by Black Writers* [1991], and "The Riddles of Egypt Brownstone" and "Remember Him A Outlaw" in *Midnight Birds: Stories by Contemporary Black Women* [1990], both edited by Mary Helen Washington). Her poems have appeared in nationally known journals and anthologies; "Everyone Is Nicaragua" was included in *The Black Scholar* (vol. 19, nos. 4 and 5, 1988), and "The Sisters," in *Love Poems by Women: An Anthology*, edited by Wendy Mulford (1990). Deveaux's books for children, among them *Na-Ni* (1973), won her the Brooklyn Museum's Art Books for Children Award in 1974 and 1975.

Currently, Deveaux is a Visiting Assistant Professor in the American Studies Department at the State University of New York at Buffalo, where she earned her Ph.D. in American Studies in 1992.

• Thadious M. Davis and Trudier Harris, eds., *Afro-American Writers after 1955: Dramatists and Prose Writers (Dictionary of Literary Biography)*, vol. 38 (1985), pp. 92–97. Margaret B. Wilkerson, ed., *Nine Plays by Black Women* (1985), pp. 135–137.

Margaret B. Wilkerson

DIARIES AND JOURNALS. Feminism has produced an extraordinary interest in women's pasts and issues concerning the interface of women's private lives and public concerns. Scholars from various disciplines have become interested in and energized by exploring women's diary and journal literature. Many of these materials have been reprinted, and often excerpted in collections (see below). While many initially assumed that this material would be scanty, scholars have discovered a wealth of these writings in archives and private collections across the nation.

The United States has had a rich legacy of diary-keeping, from the conversion and spiritual diaries of Puritan culture to wartime journals of the Revolution, the Civil War and the two world wars; from the family and social chronicles of frontier diaries to highly self-conscious psychologizing journals; from romance and courtship diaries to work journals of professional women of all kinds. Readers have long enjoyed the works of such prominent women diarists and journalists as Sarah Kemble * Knight, Abigail * Adams, Fanny * Kemble, Mary Boykin * Chesnut, Alice * James, Helen Keller, and Sylvia * Plath, but only recently have we gained access to works by women like Elizabeth * Ashbridge, Charlotte Forten, and Alice * Dunbar-Nelson, and begun to appreciate the writings and lives of hundreds of other women who did not previously achieve public notice. To date, writings by Anglo-American women have been most fully explored, and the majority of academic collections, commentary, and bibliography concerns those materials.

For students of literature, the act of considering diaries and journals as literature has mandated canon expansion. Elizabeth Meese argues that this body of writing "present[s] a standard by giving us an idea of a whole culture—history, socialization, texture, preoccupations—from which a literature emerges and within which the literary canon should be established" ("The Whole Truth," in *Teaching Women's Literature from a Regional Perspective*, 1982). In a larger sense, the increasingly sophisticated use of these materials has served to broaden our notions of what counts as a literary text. While many have discredited diaries as literature, Robert Fothergill argues that the idea of keeping a diary in itself is "produced out of a respect for the diary as a literary form" (*Private Chronicles*, 1974); Margot Culley agrees that "calling this form of autobiographical writing 'literature' identifies the many examples of fine writing contained in diaries and journals and also acknowledges that this periodic life-writing springs from the same sources as the art created for a public audience: the urge to give shape and meaning to life with words, and to endow this meaning-making with a permanance [sic] that transcends time" (*A Day at a Time*, 1985).

Exploring American women's journals and diaries has provided a powerful corrective for our knowledge of women's history; as Elizabeth Hampsten has observed, our understanding of women's experiences has been obscured by the exclusion of women's private writings from scholarly consideration. Mary Jane Moffat notes in her introduction to *Revelations* (1975) that diaries and journals have often been a woman's only outlet for honest expression in societies that have devalued women's experiences. Harriet Blodgett agrees: "The diary, by its nature as a genre of personal record, by the opportunity it offers the diarist to record what is important to her, and by the daily time that it claims for itself, counters the patriarichal attack on female identity and self-worth" (*Centuries of Female Days*, 1988).

Diaries have provided women not only a way to claim a space of their own, but also imaginative and actual links to other women. Scholars like Susan Armitage have noted the frequency with which women actually kept diaries as records to send to female friends and relatives (" 'Aunt Amelia's Diary,' " in *Teaching Women's Literature from a Regional Perspective*, 1982), or personified the diary itself as a female friend, like Helen Ward Brandreth (1862–1905), who named her diary after the famous writer Fannie * Fern (pen name of Sara Payson Willis). In her study of nineteenth-century American women's diaries and letters, Carroll Smith-Rosenberg traces female rituals and emotional links that excluded men entirely, and were therefore hidden from traditional male-centered histories. As Smith-Rosenberg observes, such documents offer a "unique opportunity to hear women's words directly, not filtered through a male record" (*Disorderly Conduct*, 1985).

Researchers such as Lillian Schlissel have cautioned that we must not read the diary as a transparent document, for "diaries also conceal information" ("Diaries of Frontier Women," in *Woman's Being, Woman's Place*, 1979). Careful scholars must learn to read such material with sensitivity to silences and gaps, working to discern patterns in omissions, not only about expected materials, like the omission of discussions of sexuality and records of pregnancies in nineteenth-century Anglo-American middle-class writings, but silences as well about women's actual achievements. Schlissel herself studies the curious fact that frontier diarists "permitted themselves to record moments of weakness, moments of despair, but not moments of strength and independence."

Resisting reading, to use Judith Fetterley's well-known phrase, may be especially important for assessing the diaries and journals of women of color, as Genaro Padilla has urged in his work on Chicana autobiography. "What happens," Padilla queries, "when the autobiographic impulse finds its self-constitutive means undermined by the very discursive practices that make autobiographic textualization possible?" ("Imprisoned Narrative?" in *Criticism in the Borderland*, 1991). These issues might be highly salient to the examination of journals and diaries of boarding-school–educated Native American girls, for example.

Raised in cultures that emphasized *orality rather than *literacy, and community and kinship over individuality, young Native American women were thrust into an environment that demanded they adopt values that were "foreign, if not also repugnant," as Brian Swann and Arnold Krupat put it in their introduction to *I Tell You Now* (1987). Obviously such "private" writings demand readings that are sensitive to issues of cultural imperialism as well as cultural exchange.

Although there has been much study of the autobiographical writings of Native, Asian, and African-American women and Chicanas, very little work has been done specifically on the journals and diaries of women of color. Along with generic differences between autobiographic and diary literature—in terms of intent, chronology, and authorial positioning in relation to the material—autobiographies written by racial and ethnic minorities have traditionally aimed their stories at the dominant Anglo culture. Diary literature clearly has a different positioning, and its serious pursuit could offer important correctives to women's history and literature with the same vitality that the study of Anglo-authored diaries originally provoked. Such work must continue at the level of the archive, since most minority groups in America have not had the same easy access to English written literacy, the same kinds of material circumstances of wealth and residential stability that would enable them to preserve private writings within families, or the same cultural status that would lead libraries to seek such materials. Further, as Gloria Hull (editor of Alice Dunbar-Nelson's diary, *Give Us Each Day*, 1984; see also her essay on same in *But Some of Us Are Brave*) and Carmen del Rio observe, minority groups often choose not to make family writings public for reasons of cultural resistance, privacy, and even self-preservation. These issues, as well as cultural preferences for different autobiographical expression (such as oral legend), make this area of study problematic in a way that only a few scholars have begun to probe.

Sources. Far and away the most important collection is Margo Culley's *A Day at a Time: The Diary Literature of American Women from 1764 to the Present* (1985). Culley's introduction to the subject matter is the best general discussion available. The volume includes several selections by African-American women and one by a Native American. Her bibliography is essential for anyone interested in American women's journals and diaries. Other important collections include: Lillian Schlissel's *Women's Diaries of the Westward Journey* (1982), which excerpts from four diaries in an appendix, ana-

lyzes numerous others, and provides a helpful bibliography; Dorothy Sterling's *We Are Your Sisters: Black Women in the Nineteenth-Century* (1984), which surveys and excerpts from a variety of documents, including journals and diaries, and provides lengthier sections of four African-American women's diaries in an epilogue, two from authors born in slavery, two born free; William Andrews et al., eds., *Journeys in New Worlds: Early American Women's Narratives* (1990), a collection of four narratives, including the travel diaries of Sarah Kemble Knight and Elizabeth Ashbridge, with helpful critical material by the editors; Lyn Lifshin, *Ariadne's Thread: A Collection of Contemporary Women's Journals* (1982), which includes journal excerpts by a number of American women from various professional fields, and provides a helpful critical introduction; Mary Jane Moffat and Charlotte Painter's *Revelations* (1975), a survey of women's diaries that includes many selections by well-known American women as well as a limited bibliography; Laurel Holliday's *Heart Songs* (1978), a collection which excerpts from "intimate" diaries of young girls, including one American, "Kathie Gray" (pseudonym); and Steven Kagle's three-volume series, *American Diary Literature* (1979), *Early Nineteenth-Century American Diary Literature* (1986), and *Late Nineteenth-Century Diary Literature* (1988), all of which contain excerpts by women and useful selected bibliographies.

Perhaps the most important bibliographical source is Andrea Hinding et al., comps., *Women's History Sources: A Guide to Archive and Manuscript Collections in the U.S.* (2 vols., 1979), which has located "hundreds of collections" containing diaries and journals by American women from all periods and all regions of the U.S., including holdings on minority women. Other useful bibliographical sources include: "Additional References and Resources" in Gloria T. Hull et al., eds., *But Some of Us Are Brave* (1982); Patricia K. Addis, comp., *Through a Woman's I: An Annotated Bibliography of American Women's Autobiographical Writings, 1946–1976* (1983); Laura Arksey et al., comps., *American Diaries: An Annotated Bibliography of Published American Diaries and Journals* (2 vols., 1983); Jane Dupree Begos, comp., *Annotated Bibliography of Published Women's Diaries* (1977, Supplement I, 1984), ed., *Women's Diaries: A Quarterly Newsletter*; "Bibliography" in Adelaida Del Castillo, ed., *Between Borders* (1990); A. LaVonne Brown, *American Indian Literatures* (1990); King-Kok Cheung and Stan Yogi, *Asian American Literature* (1988); Cheryl Cline, ed., *Women's Diaries, Journals and Letters: An Annotated Bibliography* (1989); Jill Conway, *The Female Experience in Eighteenth-*

and *Nineteenth-Century America* (1982); Rayna Green, comp., *Native American Women: A Contextual Bibliography* (1983); Eugenie Andruss Leonard et al., eds., *The American Woman in Colonial and Revolutionary Times, 1565–1800* (1962); Gerda Lerner, bibliographical essay in *Black Women in White America* (1972); William Matthews, *American Diaries: An Annotated Bibliography of American Diaries Written prior to the Year 1861* (1945) and *American Diaries in Manuscript, 1580–1954* (1974); Barbara J. Robinson and J. Cordell Robinson, comps., *The Mexican American* (1980); Virginia Terris, ed., *Woman in America: A Guide to Information Sources* (1980); Elizabeth Tingley and Donald Tingley, eds., *Women and Feminism in American History: A Guide to Information Sources* (1981); Jean Fagan Yellin's "Afro-American Women 1800–1910: A Selected Bibliography" in *But Some of Us Are Brave* (1982), reprinted in *Black Women in United States History*, vol. 2 (1990).

Important critical treatments of journals and diaries include: Virginia Walcott Beauchamp, ed., *A Private War* (1987); John Mack Faragher, *Women and Men on the Overland Trail* (1979); Elizabeth Fox-Genovese, *Within the Plantation Household* (1988); Elizabeth Hampsten, *Read This Only to Yourself* (1982); Leonore Hoffman and Margo Culley, eds., *Women's Personal Narratives* (1985); Leonore Hoffman and Deborah Rosenfelt, eds., *Teaching Women's Literature from a Regional Perspective* (1982); Julie Roy Jeffrey, *Frontier Women* (1979); Annette Kolodny, *The Land Before Her* (1984); Thomas Mallon, *A Book of One's Own* (1984); Sandra Myres, *Westering Women* (1982); and Carroll Smith-Rosenberg, *Disorderly Conduct* (1985).

Women's diaries and journals have proven useful in classrooms as documents and as models for composition, the latter of which can, as John Schilb notes in his article "The Usefulness of Women's Nontraditional Literature" (in *Women's Personal Narratives*, 1985) make both writing and history more accessible for students. For other useful guides to studying and teaching women's diary literature, see: essays on using personal narrative in the classroom by Gillikin, Stitzel, Waugh, Kissel, Ward, and Bell in *Women's Personal Narratives: Essays in Criticism and Pedagogy* (Hoffman and Culley, eds., 1985); Ruth Saxton's "Letters and Diaries: Demystifying Archival Research for Undergraduates," as well as the helpful appendixes on curriculum materials in *Teaching Women's Literature from a Regional Perspective* (Hoffman and Rosenfelt, eds., 1982); and John Faragher's "Notes on Method" in *Women and Men on the Overland Trail* (1979).

[*See also* Autobiography; Biography; Confessional Nonfiction; Frontier Writing; Letters; Narratives; Pioneer Women.]

Dana D. Nelson

DICKINSON, Emily (1830–1886), poet. Emily Dickinson's poetic accomplishment was recognized from the moment her first volume appeared in 1890, but never has she enjoyed more acclaim than she does today. Once Thomas H. Johnson made her complete body of 1,775 poems available in his 1955 variorum edition, *The Poems of Emily Dickinson*, interest from all quarters soared. Readers immediately discovered a poet of immense depth and stylistic complexity whose work eludes categorization. For example, though she frequently employs the common ballad meter associated with hymnody, her poetry is in no way constrained by that form; rather she performs like a jazz artist who uses rhythm and meter to revolutionize readers' perceptions of those structures. Her fierce defiance of literary and social authority has long appealed to feminist critics, who consistently place Dickinson in the company of such major writers as Anne *Bradstreet, Elizabeth Barrett Browning, Sylvia *Plath, and Adriënne *Rich.

Dickinson was born 10 December 1830, in Amherst, Massachusetts, where she lived until her death from Bright's disease on 15 May 1886. There she spent most of her life in the family home that was built in 1813 by her grandfather, Samuel Fowler Dickinson. His role in founding the Amherst Academy in 1814 and Amherst College in 1821 began a tradition of public service continued by her father, Edward, and her brother, Austin. All the Dickinson men were attorneys with political ambitions; the Dickinson home was a center of Amherst society and the site of annual Amherst College commencement receptions. The effect of growing up in a household of politically active, dominant males can be heard in Dickinson's 1852 letter to her close friend and future sister-in-law Susan Gilbert during a Whig convention in Baltimore: "Why can't *I* be a Delegate to the great Whig Convention?—dont I know all about Daniel Webster, and the Tariff and the Law?" As the confidence and frustration of this letter attests, the Dickinson family tradition had prepared the poet for a life of political activity and public service, only to deny her that life because of her sex.

By the time she wrote this letter, Dickinson had graduated from Amherst Academy and completed a year of study at Mount Holyoke. Though she was referred to by her close friend Samuel Bowles as "the Queen Recluse" in an 1863 note to Austin, her life was not nearly so sheltered as these terms imply; the "Queen" portion of Bowles's appellation should perhaps receive the greater emphasis. Accounts of her earliest years with Austin and her younger sister Lavinia depict a healthy, happy girl whose precocious intelligence did not prevent her from enjoying a normal childhood. From the time she started school, Dickinson distinguished herself as an original thinker who, in her brother's words, dazzled her teachers: "Her compositions were unlike anything ever heard—and always produced a sensation—both with the scholars and Teachers—her imagination sparkled—and she gave it free rein."

During the 1847–1848 year she spent studying under Mary Lyons at Mount Holyoke Female Seminary, Dickinson acquired limited notoriety as the one student unwilling to publicly confess faith in Christ. Designated a person with "no hope" of salvation, she keenly felt her isolation, writing her friend Abiah Root in 1848, "I am not happy, and I regret that last term, when that golden opportunity was mine, that I did not give up and become a Christian." In 1850, she would share similar sentiments with her friend Jane Humphrey: "Christ is calling everyone here, all my companions have answered, even my darling Vinnie believes she loves, and trusts him, and I am standing alone in rebellion."

Such resistance to conversion at a time when friends and family were making public confessions reflects a lifelong willingness to oppose popular sentiment. The experience at Mount Holyoke may well have brought to the surface an independence that fueled Dickinson's writing and led her to cease attending church by the time she was thirty. Following her return to Amherst in 1848 and after the religious awakening that peaked there around 1850, she began to write seriously. The magnitude of her output was not clear until after her death, when her sister Lavinia discovered a cherry-wood cabinet containing some 1,147 poems in fair copy. In the meantime, Dickinson increasingly withdrew from public view, participating in commencement receptions but little else after the early sixties. Despite her withdrawal, however, she maintained correspondence with a wide community of friends and associates, including such well-known literary figures as Helen Hunt *Jackson. The 1,150 letters in *The Letters of Emily Dickinson*, edited by Thomas H. Johnson and Theodora Ward in 1958, represent a fraction of what she actually wrote.

Much critical attention has been devoted to the years of Dickinson's greatest poetic production, when her output is estimated to have accelerated from 52 poems in 1858 to 366 poems in 1862, and then declined to 53 poems in 1864.

What provoked such a sudden and rich abundance of creativity? And why did Dickinson take the time to carefully gather fair copies of 1,147 poems and bind 833 of them in the individual packets known as the fascicles? Early scholarship sought evidence of a failed love interest in the late fifties to account for this sudden burst of energy. Speculation about her possible lovers has at one time or another touched on almost every person for whom she felt deeply, from her brother, her sister-in-law Susan Gilbert, and her friend Kate Scott Anthon, to Charles Wadsworth, Thomas Wentworth Higginson, Samuel Bowles, and Judge Otis Lord. These various studies reveal that Dickinson felt great passion for her family and friends and that at times her feelings were distinctly sexual. There is no solid evidence linking her romantically to anyone.

Most recent scholarship has abandoned the search for Dickinson's romantic inspiration. Finding in the poetry the reflection of a complex, multifaceted mind, critics have hesitated to simplify her achievement by inscribing it within a single master narrative. Though the suddenness and the intensity of Dickinson's most productive years still excites scholarly interest, the focus has shifted from questions related to motive and origin to those concerned with style and practice. The fascicles, especially, together with Dickinson's refusal to publish when she had ample opportunity in later life, have provoked close examinations of both her manuscripts and her communication with other literary figures.

The likelihood that updated variorum and readers' editions of the poems will shortly appear has intensified debate over the way Dickinson's writing should appear in print. As scholars explore methods for translating her chirography onto the printed page, more is learned about the range of possible readings suggested by her fair copies. Respecting Dickinson's punctuation, use of variants, and lineation will have a major influence on the way her poems are read and understood. Feminist scholarship has convincingly demonstrated her resistance to patriarchal authority and stimulated interest in the revolutionary nature of the self presented in her work. With the advent of the *Emily Dickinson Journal* (1992), students of her poetry gained an invaluable tool for monitoring these and other issues that characterize a rapidly expanding field of research.

• Major collections of Dickinson manuscripts are located at the Houghton Library of Harvard University and the Jones Library at Amherst. See also Richard B. Sewall, *The Life of Emily Dickinson* (1974). R. W. Franklin, ed., *The Manuscript Books of Emily Dickinson*, 2 vols. (1981). Suzanne Juhasz, ed., *Feminist Crit-*

ics *Read Emily Dickinson* (1983). Barton Levi St. Armand, *Emily Dickinson and Her Culture: The Soul's Society* (1984). Cynthia Griffin Wolff, *Emily Dickinson* (1986). Cristanne Miller, *Emily Dickinson: A Poet's Grammar* (1987). Judy Jo Small, *Positive as Sound: Emily Dickinson's Rhyme* (1990). Mary Loeffelholz, *Dickinson and the Boundaries of Feminist Thought* (1991). Martha Nell Smith, *Rowing in Eden: Rereading Emily Dickinson* (1992). Sharon Cameron, *Choosing Not Choosing* (1992).

Paul Crumbley

DIDION, Joan (b. 1934), novelist, journalist, and screenwriter. Joan Didion was born in Sacramento, California, and is nostalgic for her pre–World War II agrarian life. Didion received her B.A. from the University of California at Berkeley, then moved to New York City after winning the Vogue Prix de Paris writing competition. While in New York, Didion worked at *Vogue* and wrote her first novel, *Run River* (1963), married John Gregory Dunne and then moved back to California. Dunne and Didion have one daughter, and they have collaborated for many years on columns and screenplays. Didion's other novels are *Play It as It Lays* (1970), *A Book of Common Prayer* (1977), and *Democracy* (1984). Her journalistic works are *Slouching Towards Bethlehem* (1968), *The White Album* (1979), *Salvador* (1982), *Miami* (1987), and *After Henry* (1992).

Didion has said, "I write entirely to find out what I'm thinking" (*The Writer on Her Work*, 1980). Clearly her journalistic works, the first two compiled from columns she wrote for *Esquire*, *New West*, and other publications, embody this thinking process. She is best known for her essay on the hippie culture in *Slouching Towards Bethlehem*, but her critical eye has covered a myriad of subjects with brutal honesty. Because of her tendency to reveal personal information, one critic considers Didion almost "the journalistic equivalent of a confessional poet" (Mark Royden Winchell, *Joan Didion*, 1991).

While she herself has criticized postmodernism as solipsistic, Didion's novels have tended in later years towards the same self-referentialism that those writers practice. *Democracy*, particularly, circles around "Joan Didion" the author as she tries to collate and focus her memories into a narrative structure. But narcissism is little evident in this process; instead one feels the same impulse that informs Didion's essays, that of the self-deprecatory author who calls herself "neurotically inarticulate" in person.

Didion was influenced by Conrad, James, and especially Hemingway, whose stamp can be seen in her spare, terse style. Her characters are, as is Didion herself, nostalgic for a childhood when the myths of America—upward mobility, scientific progress—still held. Her work explores the tension between the chaotic universe and naïve optimism. Didion has been contemptuous of feminism, seeing it as victimizing women by emphasizing their mistreatment at the hands of men (*The White Album*). But by blurring the lines between journalism and fiction—and daring to take on any subject, political or personal—Didion has opened up new possibilities for writers of both sexes.

• Katherine Usher Henderson, *Joan Didion* (1981). Ellen G. Friedman, ed., *Joan Didion: Essays and Conversations* (1984). Katherine Usher Henderson, "Joan Didion: The Bond between Narrator and Heroine in Democracy" and "A Bibliography of Writings about Joan Didion," in *American Women Writing Fiction*, ed. Mickey Pearlman (1989), pp. 69–93.

Susan J. Zevenbergen

DILLARD, Annie (b. 1945) essayist, novelist, poet, naturalist, and mystic. In *An American Childhood* (1987), Annie Dillard describes her extraordinarily ordinary childhood in the homogenous middle-class urban America of the 1950s. Social issues of the decade—racial tension, enforced conformity, and ambivalence toward corporate life—are masked behind tales of learning how to tell a joke or conducting smelly experiments with a chemistry set. The tensions between affluence and fear, and individualism and conformity that informed the period's social criticism (in such works as *Man in the Gray Flannel Suit*, *The Feminine Mystique*, and *One-Dimensional Man*), appear in Dillard's child's-eye retrospective as part of the remarkable warp and woof of life. This emphasis on pluralistic ways of knowing and a balance of tensions dominates Dillard's work.

Pilgrim at Tinker Creek (1974) established Dillard as a major American naturalist. Published when Dillard was twenty-nine, *Pilgrim* received the Pulitzer Prize and earned Dillard a contributing editorship at *Harper's*, which she continues to hold. Unlike the roughly contemporary *Silent Spring*, *Pilgrim* is largely unconcerned with eco-disaster but is instead a work of mystical naturalism, allusive and imagistic, exploring the tension between nature's fertility and violence, between inclusiveness and isolation. As Lynn Ross-Bryant remarks ("The Silence of Nature," in *Religion and Literature*, vol. 22, Spring 1990), Dillard's pluralism includes discontinuity, deriving spiritual weight from that tension. *Pilgrim*'s structural similarities to Thoreau's *Walden* invite comparison between the two works. Both combine careful observation of natural phenomena with a cyclic narrative structure—the turn of the year, progression of the seasons and days—investing observation with the mythic import of eternal return. But where *Walden* is essentially a work of social philosophy addressing communal relations through a series of metaphoric encounters, *Pilgrim* is, in Dillard's words, "really a book of theology," focusing on the relation of the self to the spirit (later, in *Holy the Firm* [1977], she explores self and creator). Pond and creek make abstract speculation concrete, but Thoreau's pond is emblematic of the self in ecological relation to society while Dillard's creek is a locus for communication with the web of life. Though essentially utopian, Dillard's theology is not free of horror. *Pilgrim*'s opening essay describing a water bug sucking a frog dry emphasizes the essential ambiguity of the spiritual, and the precarious balance struck between body and soul, culture and nature, humans and gods.

Teaching a Stone to Talk (1982), *Living by Fiction* (1982), and *Writing Life* (1989) continue the theme, though without the careful structure of *Pilgrim*, as if to suggest that even emblematic structuring of experience hampers pluralistic knowledge. With *The Living* (1992), Dillard has established herself as a labor novelist in the regionalist, Stegnerian mode, but, characteristically, she adapts the genre to her major philosophical themes. Few extensive bibliographic or critical studies of Dillard's work exist, partly because the work defies categories, but also, perhaps, because Dillard's philosophy demonstrates the inadequacy of categorization.

[*See also* Ecofeminism.]

• Joseph Keller, "The Function of Paradox in Mystical Discourse," *Studia Mystica* 6, no. 3 (Fall 1983): 3–19. William S. Scheick, "Annie Dillard: Narrative Fringe," in *Contemporary American Women Writers: Narrative Strategies*, ed. Catherine Rainwater and William S. Scheick (1985), pp. 51–67. Susan M. Felch, "Annie Dillard: Modern Physics in a Contemporary Mystic," *Mosaic* 22, no. 2 (Spring 1989), pp. 1–14. Suzanne Clark, "Annie Dillard: The Woman in Nature and the Subject of Nonfiction," in *Literary Nonfiction: Theory, Criticism, Pedagogy*, ed. Chris Anderson (1989), pp. 107–124.

Carol Schaechterle Loranger

DIPRIMA, Diane (b. 1934), poet, playwright, publisher, and translator. Born in Brooklyn, New York, to Italian-American parents, DiPrima attended Swarthmore College from 1951 to 1953, when she withdrew to begin her odyssey as poet and seer of the counterculture. Her *Memoirs of a Beatnik* (1969) presents an ironic retrospective look—in graphic language—at her early rebellions and her associations with such representatives of the Beat Generation as Jack Kerouac and Alan Ginsberg. Her first collection of poems, *This Kind of Bird Flies Backwards* (1959), announces her lifelong preference for the unconventional and the nonconformist. In

poetry as in politics, she is, like her grandfather, an anarchist. For DiPrima, the power of poetry lies in its magical transformational, not its rational, properties. This attraction to the mystical explains her later explorations of Eastern religions.

Her 25-odd volumes of poetry attest to her search for enlightenment along many paths, from the mystic to the revolutionary. Important works from the 1960s are *The New Handbook of Heaven* (1963), *Poems for Freddie* (1966), *Earthsong: Poems 1957–59* (1968), and *Revolutionary Letters* (1969), the latter written after her move to California, where she raised her five children. DiPrima's publishing ventures also express her disaffiliation from the mainstream. With LeRoi Jones, she edited the *Floating Bear* newsletter from 1961 to 1970, promoting the work of such contemporaries as William Burroughs and Gary Snyder. She founded Poets Press (1964–1969), which issued several volumes of her poems, as well as her translations of Jean Genet and love poems from Middle Latin; her publishing activity resumed in 1974 when she established Eidolon Editions. While associated with the New York Poets Theatre, she wrote and produced six of her eight plays.

In the 1970s, after a divorce from Alan Marlowe, DiPrima began to study Zen and teach poetry workshops in such nontraditional settings as reform schools, prisons, and Zen centers. When a three-year marriage to Grant Fisher ended in 1975, DiPrima extended her interest in the magical and healing arts through formal study and began working as a psychic healer.

The publication of *Selected Poems: 1956–57*, the first major collection of DiPrima's works in 1975 (reissued in 1977), brought only tentative recognition of the quality of her work. Although many readers still denigrate her nonintellectualism, later readers noted the blend of the mythic and the personal in her poetry. With the appearance of *Loba, Parts I–VII*, DiPrima won recognition as a woman writer tracing her work to prehistorical traditions. *Loba* examines the complexity of female experience through this mythical she-wolf, who represents all womanhood from Lilith to Hindu goddesses. In this broader context, DiPrima's guerilla tactics acquire a significance beyond that of youthful rebellion. Ignored by the literary establishment that embraced the works of her male contemporaries in the fifties and sixties, DiPrima's mystical vision now has resonance with those readers seeking alternatives to rational, mainstream behaviors.

• DiPrima's manuscripts are housed in the Manuscript Collection at Southern Illinois University, Carbondale. David Meltzer, "Diane di Prima," in *Contemporary Po-*

ets, ed. James Vinson (1980), pp. 380–383. "Diane Diprima," in *Dictionary of Literary Biography: American Poets since World War II,* vol. 5, ed. Donald J. Greiner (1980), pp. 202–205. Anne Waldman, "Interview with Diane DiPrima," *Rocky Ledge* 7 (February–March 1981): 35–49. "Diane DiPrima," in *Dictionary of Literary Biography: The Beats: Literary Bohemians in Postwar America,* vol. 16, ed. Ann Charters (1983), pp. 149–160. "Diane DiPrima," in *The Feminist Companion to Literature in English,* eds. Virginia Blaine, Isobel Grundy, and Patricia Clements (1990), pp. 296–297.

Diana R. Pingatore

DISABLED WOMEN'S WRITING. In 1853, a woman who signed herself only as "Emma" wrote a series of letters to the *Una,* a small suffragist magazine. Emma described herself as "a cripple." In the earliest letters (as cited in *A Voice of Their Own: The Woman Suffrage Press, 1840–1910,* edited by Martha M. Solomon, 1991), Emma expresses a deep sense of worthlessness. Yet over the ensuing months, her writings undergo a change. She recognizes that her life has intrinsic value, value that has been denied by society. Gradually she comes to feel herself a part of the struggle of all women against oppression. Emma's metamorphosis mirrors the evolution of disabled women's writing over the past century, from self-negation to a search for autonomy and self-respect.

Women with disabilities have been doubly devalued, both for being female and for having bodies that differ from the desired norm. Like her nondisabled counterparts, the woman with a disability is expected to be passive, dependent, and frail. But in addition, she is perceived as unattractive to men and incapable of caring for children—unable to fulfill a woman's traditional roles. Thus she is regarded as a burden to others, and of little use to herself.

Depictions of women with disabilities by most nondisabled writers reflect these negative attitudes. In *Ethan Frome* (1911), Edith *Wharton depicts Mattie Silver, a whining, demanding invalid who saps the strength of her caretakers. Laura Wingfield, the crippled young woman in Tennessee Williams's *The Glass Menagerie* (1944) is emotionally isolated and locked in a fragile world of fantasy. The reverse side of the passive, helpless image appears in *The Street* (1946), by African-American novelist Ann *Petry: Mrs. Hedges, a woman covered with disfiguring scars, is a tough survivor of the urban ghetto. Her distorted body symbolizes her sinister, twisted soul.

Generations of women with disabilities felt powerless to change these stereotypes. Some wrote about a wide variety of topics but avoided direct autobiography. Yet, obliquely, their writing reveals their personal experiences. Ellen *Glasgow, who became deaf during adolescence, writes feelingly of nondisabled women who cope with crushing loss and disillusionment. In her best-known work, *Barren Ground* (1925), a young woman's life is damaged when her lover abandons her. Flannery *O'Connor, who developed lupus as a young woman, rarely wrote from the viewpoint of a woman with a chronic illness, but when women with disabilities appear in her fiction, they are generally outcasts, living on the fringes of society. Huldah in "Good Country People" is lonely and embittered after the loss of a leg; her only encounter with a would-be lover ends in pain and humiliation.

On the other hand, a number of women with disabilities wrote autobiographies. Generally these works are inspirational in nature, celebrating the author's triumph over adversity. Undoubtedly the most famous is Helen Keller's *The Story of My Life* (1904). Keller's writings on social and political issues are nearly forgotten today, as is *Midstream* (1931), a later memoir. The public revered her as the miracle child, but had trouble accepting her as a mature woman.

One autobiography that reaches beyond the inspirational is Katherine Butler Hathaway's *The Little Locksmith* (1943). This richly textured work resounds with the full range of human emotion, from warmth and merriment to the depths of loneliness.

Women with disabilities have found it especially hard to express "negative" emotions when writing about their lives. Too often the world interprets their hurt and sadness as self-pity, and their anger as unbecoming bitterness. In the 1980s and 1990s, women with disabilities created safe places for the expression of their most intimate feelings. They shared their lives with one another in periodicals such as *Womyn's Braille Press Newsletter* and *Hikane: The Capable Womon.* These publications made little attempt to reach nondisabled women or men; almost exclusively, their readers and contributors were women with disabilities.

The 1980s also saw the publication of two major collections of disabled women's writing. *With the Power of Each Breath: A Disabled Women's Anthology,* edited by Susan E. Browne, Deborah Connors, and Nanci Stern (1985), features poetry and personal essays by women previously unknown outside the disabled community. *With Wings: An Anthology of Literature by and about Women with Disabilities,* edited by Marsha Saxton and Florence Howe (1987), draws upon the work of widely recognized writers as well as those with few prior publications. *With Wings* includes previously published pieces by several writers who are not generally regarded as having disabilities: Adrienne *Rich, Vassar Miller, Muriel *Rukeyser, and

Alice *Walker. In "Beauty: When the Dancer Is the Self," Walker resolves her feelings about being blind in one eye. In "Transit," Rich describes an encounter between herself, "the cripple," and the vigorous, active woman she might have been if she had never had polio. The works in these anthologies reflect frustration, disappointment, and anger. But, as in the case of Alice Walker, there is also growth and self-acceptance.

Adrienne Rich, Alice Walker, and other "mainstream" writers addressed disability long after they earned their reputation in other spheres. Yet at last they incorporated their disabilities into their public personas. Disability does not define them or their work. It is one more human experience to be explored, as valid as any other.

These periodicals and anthologies opened the way for other literary efforts by women with disabilities. Disability is a key theme in the work of several poets. *Herb Woman* by zana (1983) and *Past, Present, and Future Passions* by Barbara Ruth (1987) explore the impact of a newly acquired disability. Nanci Stern's *Visions Incognito* (1978), Mary McGinnis's *Private Stories on Demand* (1988), and Sue Tullos's *A Pink Disregard for Decorum* (1988) examine how disability affects relationships and self-perceptions.

Nancy Mairs's collection of personal essays, *Plaintext* (1986), ranges over a wide array of topics, including the realities of life with multiple sclerosis and clinical depression. In 1989, Jean Stewart published her first novel, *The Body's Memory*, shaping compelling fiction from the pain and eventual empowerment of an orthopedically disabled woman. Women with disabilities appear frequently as forceful characters in Anne Finger's 1988 short story collection, *Basic Skills*. In all of these works, women with disabilities write for a broad audience, seeking connection with all women.

The old image of the disabled woman did not die out entirely, but even a few nondisabled writers began to search beyond stereotypes. In her *In This Sign* (1973), Joanne Greenberg creates a memorable couple, both deaf. Many of Toni *Morrison's novels also offer strong, positive portrayals of women with disabilities. In Morrison's work, damage to the physical body often symbolizes the spiritual damage resulting from racism. In *Sula* (1973), Eva Peace amputates her own leg to collect insurance money with which to buy food for her children. She is a figure of creation, rebuilding the world for her descendants. In *Tar Baby* (1981) the wet-nurse, Therese Foucault, is a nurturing figure with mystical powers. Her blindness is only one aspect of her self. Sethe in *Beloved* (1987) bears the scars of a brutal beating, a testament to the hardships she has survived and finally cast behind her.

Considering that some twenty million American women are disabled, the literature of disability is appallingly scant. Yet as increasing numbers of women with disabilities venture to write honestly about their lives, disabled women can begin to tap their own strength. Like Emma, they are learning to value themselves, and fearlessly sharing their truest thoughts with the rest of the world. With a deepening understanding born of openness, disabled and nondisabled women can discover their commonalities, and work to dispel the fears and misconceptions that have too long kept them apart.

[*See also* Invalidism.]

• Jacob Twersky, *Blindness in Literature* (1955). Adrienne Asch and Lawrence H. Sacks, "Lives Without, Lives Within: Autobiographies by Blind Women and Men," in *Journal of Visual Impairment and Blindness* 77, no. 6 (June 1983). Alan Gartner and Tom Joe, *Images of the Disabled, Disabling Images* (1987). Deborah Kent, "In Search of a Heroine: Women with Disabilities in Fiction and Drama" in *Women with Disabilities: Essays in Psychology, Culture, and Politics* (1988).

Deborah Kent

DIVORCE. *See* Marriage Laws.

DIX, Dorothy, pen name of Elizabeth Meriwether Gilmer (1861–1951), columnist, reporter, author. She was born in Montgomery County, Tennessee, the daughter of William D. and Maria Winston Meriwether. Educated at home and at the Female Academy in Clarksville, Tennessee, she completed one term at the Hollins Institute in Virginia.

Elizabeth married George O. Gilmer in 1882, but two years later he had a breakdown, from which he never recovered fully, so Elizabeth supported him the rest of his life. The reality of the situation affected her health and several months after George's first hospitalization she went to Mississippi to recuperate. There she wrote short stories to distract her from her problems and by chance met Eliza Holbrook Nicholson, poet and owner-publisher of the New Orleans *Daily Picayune*, who encouraged Elizabeth to continue writing and helped her get a job at the *Picayune* in 1894.

Elizabeth took newspaper work seriously and studied reporting and writing on the job and in her free time. In 1895 she began a weekly column under the pen name Dorothy Dix. Within months it was "Dorothy Dix Talks" and in time, the world's longest-running column, read by millions of men and women who sought Dorothy Dix's practical advice about life and love. In 1901 she went to the New York *Journal*, where she continued her column three times a week and became a masterful reporter of human tribulations and a fixture at murder trials that involved women. She returned to New Orleans in 1917 and for more than 30 years, except for time to cover the Hall-Mills murder in 1926, she wrote six columns a week. Her columns were direct, full of common sense, and often based on readers' letters, which she burned regularly to protect their identities. The columns overflowed to two popular books, *Every-day Help for Every-day People* (1926) and *How to Win and Hold a Husband* (1939). A disciplined writer, Elizabeth kept a three-month supply of columns, regularly updated, in a safety-deposit box so she could work and travel without fear of missing deadlines. When she became ill in 1949, associates continued the column but, as stipulated in her will, it ended when she died in 1951.

Elizabeth also wrote fiction (*Mirandy*, 1914; *Mirandy Exhorts*, 1922) travel (*My Trip around the World*, 1924), and autobiography (*Dorothy Dix, Her Book*, 1926).

Carol Reuss

DODGE, Mabel. *See* Luhan, Mabel Dodge.

DOMESTIC FICTION, didactic and exemplary fiction centered in the "woman's sphere" and focusing on the concerns of women's lives, was the best-selling literary genre of nineteenth-century America. Hawthorne's notorious "scribbling women" created and perpetuated a literary form that dominated from roughly the 1830s through the 1870s, the period in which domestic ideology provided a persuasive vision of domestic power and influence for the women of the rising urban/suburban middle class.

Like the ideology that it both perpetuated and was the product of, domestic fiction aims to convert and reform its readers with an address to their hearts. Assuming that women are designated by God to foster and preserve morality, love, virtue, and happiness in America, domestic writings illustrate how women might accomplish their moral mission in a world bent on foiling their attempts. Though its plots, settings, and characters vary greatly, domestic fiction tends to be idealistic and sentimental in its intended effects while it remains quite realistic and pragmatic in its conflicts, characters, and scenes. In fact, as one of the most potent tools of conversion and reform was believed to be weeping, domestic authors would often structure their plots around a series of poignant, heart-wrenching episodes designed to enlist readers' sympathies and thereby effect their reform.

Though the roots of domestic fiction are planted firmly in the emergence of republican motherhood in late-eighteenth–century America, the full articulation of the form appears to have paralleled the growth of the burgeoning market for women's magazines in the 1830s and 1840s. *Godey's Lady's Book*, edited by Sarah Josepha *Hale, was the most notable of these periodicals; in its pages many earlier works of domestic fiction were first published in serial form. Whether short story or novel, most domestic fiction appeared first in a periodical and was republished later if demand seemed assured. As the market for domestic fiction expanded, so did the number and type of periodicals in which it appeared. Both *Harper's Monthly* (first published in 1850) and *The Atlantic Monthly* (first published in 1857), for example, rose to quick prominence largely from their support of this genre.

From the periodical evidence, it appears that in its heyday the market for domestic fiction crossed gender and class boundaries and managed for some years to sustain a remarkably varied and loyal audience. The decline of the form seems to have begun during the Civil War, even though domestic fiction continued to be published with great frequency until nearly the end of the nineteenth century. As realism, naturalism, and the bleaker view that they reflected and promoted began to become the more dominant worldview, domestic fiction and its vision of human perfectibility and women's divine agency began to seem naïve, lachrymose, archaic, saccharine, simplistic, and over-sentimental. While the genre has never died out, it became an object of near-constant disdain in the first half of the twentieth century as it was made the icon of everything that modern literature strove *not* to be.

While such early works as Susanna *Rowson's *Charlotte Temple* (1794), *The Coquette* (1797) by Hannah *Foster, and even Anne *Bradstreet's poetry (1650–1678) can be seen to contain elements of the genre, the novel that best marks the first full articulation of the form was *A New England Tale* (1822) by Catharine *Sedgwick; she was also later to write *Redwood* (1824), *Clarence* (1830), and *Home* (1837). Sedgwick was joined by Sarah Josepha Hale with *Northwood: A Tale of New England* (1827); Hale also would continue to write novels even as she began to edit *Godey's*, contributing *The Lectress: or, Woman's Sphere* (1839), *Keeping House and Housekeeping: A Story of Domestic Life* (1845), and *Boarding Out* (1846). The success of these novels encouraged others to join this first group of domestic authors. Most notably, Caroline Gilman contributed *Recollections of a Housekeeper* (1834), *Recollections of a Southern Matron*

(1838), and *Love's Progress* (1840); Mary Jane McIntosh, *Woman an Enigma* (1843); Mrs. A. J. Graves, *Girlhood and Womanhood* (1844); Susan Fenimore Cooper, *Elinor Wyllys* (1846); Caroline Lee Hentz, *Linda . . . : A Tale of Southern Life* (1850), *Rena* (1851), and *The Planter's Northern Bride* (1853); and Elizabeth Stuart *Phelps, *The Sunny Side* (1851).

Mid-century, the three most successful and renowned authors of domestic fiction emerged nearly simultaneously. Susan *Warner wrote *The Wide, Wide World* in 1850; this novel was to remain one of the best-loved and most widely read novels in America for some years, and it still provides an excellent model of domestic fiction in its purest form. Early in the following year, Harriet Beecher *Stowe wrote *Uncle Tom's Cabin* (1851) in the domestic form and it became the most sensational best-seller America had yet known. Later that same year, E.D.E.N. *Southworth contributed *The Mother-in-Law* (1851). Though Southworth's fame did not match Stowe's or Warner's at first, she soon rose to equal prominence as readers responded with enthusiasm to her sensational Gothic interpretation of the domestic form. While her output was prolific, *The Hidden Hand* (1859) became her most widely known work.

Shortly after this critical era, the genre reached the apex of its popularity. While most of the above-mentioned authors continued to lead the field, several others worthy of note emerged. Maria Susanna Cummins contributed *The Lamplighter* (1854); Mary Virginia Terhune, *Richmond* (1854) and *The Hidden Path* (1855); Sara *Parton [Fanny Fern], *Ruth Hall* (1855); and Augusta Wilson, *Inez* (1855) and, particularly, *St. Elmo* (1867). Just as its beginning could be marked by Sedgwick's *New England Tale*, the end of the genre's dominance might well be marked by Louisa May *Alcott's *Little Women* (1869). While this novel still celebrates women's domestic role and promotes a sentimental and idealistic vision of the world, its heroine Jo March carried with her the nascent image of the "new woman" to whom the genre would no longer appeal. When Charity Royalle, the heroine of Edith *Wharton's anti-romance, *Summer* (1917), can only use a moldering copy of *The Lamplighter* to wind her poorly executed crocheted lace, it seems a clear statement that the classic domestic novels did not serve the needs of the new women of the new century.

[*See also* Novel, Beginnings of the; Sentimental Novel.]

• Nina Baym, *Women's Fiction: A Guide to Novels by and about Women in America, 1820–1870* (1978). Sandra M. Gilbert and Susan Gubar, *The Madwoman in the Attic: The Woman Writer and the Nineteenth-Century Literary Imagination* (1979). Mary P. Ryan, *The Empire*

of the Mother: American Writing about Domesticity, 1830–1860 (1982). Nina Baym, *Novels, Readers, and Reviewers: Responses to Fiction in Antebellum America* (1984). Mary Kelley, *Private Woman, Public Stage: Literary Domesticity in Nineteenth-Century America* (1984). Jane Tompkins, *Sensational Designs: The Cultural Work of American Fiction, 1790–1860* (1985). Cathy N. Davidson, *Revolution and the Word: The Rise of the Novel in America* (1986). Susan Coultrap-McQuin, *Doing Literary Business: American Women Writers in the Nineteenth Century* (1990). Gillian Brown, *Domestic Individualism: Imagining Self in Nineteenth-Century America* (1990).

Blythe Forcey

DOMESTIC IDEOLOGY. Linked to the decline of agrarianism and the rise of the urban-suburban middle-class during the early nineteenth century, domestic ideology exalted the position of the Victorian mother and homemaker. As "angels in the home," middle-class women could combine their faith in God with their "natural purity and goodness" to create a potent redeeming and reforming environment within the "woman's sphere." Domestic ideology could become quite radical in its implications, as some believed it could lead to a millennial "Age of Women" in which the force of feminine love and virtue could unite to eradicate all male vice and aggression.

[*See also* Domestic Fiction; Motherhood; Reproduction; Sentimental Novel.]

Blythe Forcey

DOMESTIC VIOLENCE. *See* Violence.

DOOLITTLE, Hilda. *See* H.D.

DOUBLE CONSCIOUSNESS. *See* Assimilation.

DOVE, Rita (b. 1952), poet and fiction writer. Named Poet Laureate in 1993, Rita Dove is the first African-American to hold the prestigious position at the Library of Congress. She is the author of four books of poetry, a novel, and a collection of short fiction. Her third volume of verse, the narrative sequence *Thomas and Beulah* (1986), received the 1987 Pulitzer Prize for Poetry.

Dove was born on 28 August 1952 to Ray and Elvira Dove of Akron, Ohio. The second of four children, she grew up in a middle-class home and attended the city's public schools. Both her father and paternal grandfather worked for Akron's Goodyear Tire and Rubber Company. Her father started out as an elevator operator, but, after earning a master's degree, eventually became Goodyear's first black chemist.

After graduating summa cum laude in 1973

from Miami University in Ohio, Rita Dove traveled to Germany on a Fulbright Scholarship. She attended the University of Tübingen and then returned to the United States to earn an M.F.A. in creative writing from the University of Iowa in 1977.

Her European travels invigorated her poems and expanded her worldview. Although *Thomas and Beulah* (based on the lives of her grandparents) chronicles the courtship and marriage of a black working-class couple in Ohio, her poetic subject matter goes far beyond her own heritage and personal experience. In *The Yellow House on the Corner* (1980), *Museum* (1983), and *Grace Notes* (1989), as well as in *Thomas and Beulah*, her often impressionistic poems juxtapose the personal with the political, the aesthetic with the historical. Many poems also reflect her fascination with what she calls "the ways in which language can change your perceptions."

Her forays into short fiction—*Fifth Sunday* (1985) and the novel *Through the Ivory Gate* (1992)—illustrate her interest in narrative and her continuing devotion to seeing the world from as many angles as possible. She has also published a play, *The Siberian Village*, in the spring 1991 issue of *Callaloo*.

Dove has taught at several universities, most recently the University of Virginia, where she holds a professorship in creative writing. She is married to Fred Viebahn, a writer from Germany, and they have a daughter, Aviva.

A popular speaker on the poetry-reading circuit, she is beginning to receive critical attention as well as admiring reviews for her emerging body of verse. Her post as Poet Laureate will no doubt inspire more analysis of her work, while securing her position as a poet known outside and inside the academy.

• The following all appear in *Callaloo* 14, no. 2 (1991): Mohamed B. Taleb-Khyar, "An Interview with Maryse Condé and Rita Dove," pp. 347–366. Bonnie Costello, "Scars and Wings: Rita Dove's *Grace Notes*," pp. 434–438. Ekaterini Georgoudaki, "Rita Dove: Crossing Boundaries," pp. 419–433.

Hilary Holladay

DRAMA. The contribution of drama to the making of a national literature in the United States is both fundamental and elusive. We know that drama helped define nationalist aspirations in the Revolutionary War period, yet scores, possibly hundreds, of plays printed for circulation have been lost. The work of women dramatists is even more elusive. As eighteenth-century Europe prepared the ideological ground for the bourgeois revolutions of the nineteenth century, it reaffirmed the gender divide through de facto and de jure enforcement of * "separate spheres" for women and men. Women received minimal education, and if they lacked a father or husband, they had no legal status. Such a restriction did not, of course, keep women from writing. But since the advent of print, women writers, especially those who chose to circulate their work, were regarded as morally tainted.

The woman dramatist was especially culpable. Unlike the novelist, who could choose a pseudonymous identity, the woman playwright would eventually be forced into public view—at which point her gender became the preeminent issue. Aphra Behn (1640–1689), England's first successful woman dramatist, inspired attacks like this one: "For punk [whore] and poetess agree so pat, You cannot be this and not be that." Not surprisingly, the first colonial woman playwright, Mercy Otis *Warren (1728–1814), apologized for going "so much out of the road of female attention." But worse attacks on women dramatists were those based on the "scientific" belief, touted since Aristotle, that women were congenitally inferior to men. As recently as the 1930s, the influential U.S. drama critic George Jean Nathan insisted that women were "generically" incapable of writing "tough" (read "great") plays.

Before turning to Mercy Warren and her "inky-fingered sisterhood," a word about the focus of this article. When, in 1692, the Puritan patriarch Cotton Mather noted the bicentennial of Columbus's transatlantic passage of 1492, he reaffirmed the spiritual promise of America as "a new heavens, a new earth." Such language fortuitously obscured the secular, imperialistic foundations of the United States. In mapping the early drama of the United States, we must stress at the outset how much of this continent's indigenous drama remains obscure. Writing has existed for the last six or seven thousand years, but *oral traditions and the *ritual enactments accompanying them are far older. "Drama," from its Greek root, *dran*, "to do," implies more than fictions in dialogue; it suggests cultural acts or *performances, some suppressed by European imperialism—Native American tribal rituals, for example—and some ironically created by that imperialism, as in the community-binding rites of enslaved Africans. Although these topics are beyond the purview of this article, they suggest at the very least that "drama" should extend beyond the play-text to theatrical activity in the culture at large.

Historically, American culture has had contradictory reactions to theatrical display. Of all the literary forms, drama is closest to the *body, and the body with its irrational desires is precisely what Puritans feared most. Thus, while the libraries of wealthy colonists (including those of Increase and Cotton Mather) contained the classics of Western drama, the ban on theater in Puritan New England, in New Netherlands, and in Quaker Pennsylvania was unabated from the 1620s to the mid-eighteenth century. In the South, less burdened by theocratic rule, the climate for theater was better; indeed, there is evidence of a play being performed there in 1703. As the colonial population burgeoned (over two million by 1776), and as printing presses became available (by 1763 each colony had one), the appetite for drama grew. English actor-managers Lewis Hallam and David Douglass toured plays in Virginia, Maryland, New York, and occasionally New England after 1750, and yet a Boston performance of Thomas Otway's *The Orphan* in 1750 brought such loud protests from the local clergy that the General Court of Massachusetts passed an Act to Prevent Stage-Plays, and other Theatrical Entertainments. In 1774, the First Continental Congress in Philadelphia resolved against "every species of extravagance ... horse-racing and all kinds of gaming, cockfighting, exhibition of shews, plays. ..." This was followed in 1778 by a warning that "any person holding an office under the United States would be dismissed if he "shall act, promote, encourage or attend [stage-]plays." Nevertheless, such prominent patriots as Benjamin Franklin and George Washington enjoyed the theater, and in 1778, Washington had Addison's *Cato* performed for his officers at Valley Forge.

As the nationalist cause intensified, sermon writing, the dominant literary form between 1639 and 1729, gave way to polemical tracts and dialogues that argued the merits of revolution. Playwriting, especially the dramatic satire, was considered to be an effective form of persuasion and propaganda: between 1770 and 1776, the Whigs alone published five dialogues and six political satires.

It was, she claimed, her pious devotion to liberty that drew Plymouth-born Mercy Otis Warren into public notice, first with poetry, then political satire in the popular press. Named "the Pen woman of the American Revolution," Warren was educated along with her brother, and had read Milton, Shakespeare, and Moliere. Clearly, she viewed the events of her time as riveting theater, for she titled her first play *The Adulateur; a Tragedy; As It Is Now Acted in Upper Servia.* A ponderous blank verse tragedy à clef about the Boston Massacre, it was printed in two installments in the Massachusetts *Spy* in 1772. In *The Group* (1775), printed on the day before the battle of Lexington, Warren castigates the sixteen Tories ("the venal herd") who, in accepting appointments on the Massachusetts Council, preempted the rights of the colonial electorate. Although she claimed to worry about violating the honor of the women's sphere, Warren actively sought approval for her efforts from her circle of male friends, John Adams, Alexander Hamilton, and later Thomas Jefferson, and even asked Adams, two years before her death, to validate her authorship of *The Group* at Boston's Atheneum library when it was misattributed to a male author. Other works of the Revolutionary years include *The Motley Assembly* (1779) and possibly *The Blockheads* (1776), a farce whose scatological language has made attribution controversial. In 1790, Warren published *Poems, Dramatic and Miscellaneous*, which included two tedious tragedies, *The Ladies of Castile* and *The Sack of Rome.*

Unlike her friend Abigail *Adams, Mercy Otis Warren was no feminist; she opposed many of the views of Mary Wollstonecraft's *A Vindication of the Rights of Women* (1792). Not so the Bostonian Judith Sargent *Murray (1751–1820), who made Wollstonecraft's ideas the inspiration for the anonymously published *The Gleaner* (1792), a collection of fictional letters, short stories, and essays. Her two plays *The Medium; or Happy Tea Party* (1795) and *The Traveller Returned* (1796) are less well known than her "Panegyric on the Drama," in which she imagines a theater from which "Young persons ... will learn to think, speak, and act with propriety."

Different from both Warren and Murray, Susanna Haswell *Rowson (1762–1824), was a self-made professional writer, famous on both sides of the Atlantic for *Charlotte: A Tale of Truth* (1791). English-born, Rowson worked as an actress, singer, and dancer in America to support her profligate husband. She wrote five original dramas, though only *Slaves of Algiers; or a Struggle for Freedom* (1794), a comedy in which she acted, was published. Loosely based on the public anger over capture of American ships by Algerian pirates and the enslavement of American sailors, the play features a Jewish-Algerian heroine who draws together the themes of slavery, women's rights, and republican ideals.

By the 1790s, the remaining bans on building theaters were lifted; joining the Park Theater in New York and the Chestnut in Philadelphia were Boston's Haymarket and Federal Street Theatres; by the turn of the century, Gloucester, Newport, Providence, Hartford, and Portland each had a theater. Equally vital to the spread of drama were the intrepid itinerant troupes who followed the pioneers westward, playing on makeshift stages in the flourishing waterfront towns of Pittsburgh, Cincinnati, and St. Louis.

By the 1820s, the hegemony of the big city theater managers was being challenged by free-market capitalism, which inspired star performers like Edwin Forrest and Charlotte Cushman to become self-representing entrepreneurs and demand top salaries. In this period of increased competition and democratization of the marketplace, the public demanded new kinds of entertainment. On a summer's night in the 1820s, New Yorkers could watch a melodrama, an equestrian drama, circuses, fireworks, balloon ascents, Shakespeare, and any number of concerts. Nostalgic and conservative "fairy tale" melodramas (Payne's *Therese*, 1822, and *Clari; or, the Maid of Milan* 1823) became popular. These focused on saintly daughters, symbols of the *cult of true womanhood, whose loyalty to paternalistic hierarchies of family, village, and country was rewarded in tableaux at the final curtain.

Powerful women in the antebellum professional theater became exceptions to the true womanly role. In the 1820s and 1830s, Louisa Medina (d. 1938) transformed romantic novels into millenarian melodramas for the working-class audiences of Thomas Hamblin's Bowery Theatre. The actress Charlotte Cushman (1816–1876), who was equally respected in classical male or "breeches" parts (Hamlet, Romeo) as in melodramatic roles (Meg Margulies), outdrew all her contemporaries with the exception of Edwin Forrest. Julia Ward *Howe (1819–1910), author of "The Battle Hymn of the Republic," wrote a typical tearjerker in *Leonora; or the World's Own* (1857), in which an innocent orphan is befriended, seduced, and then abandoned by an evil nobleman. Despite its foreign setting, this plot anticipates Mrs. Henry Wood's best-selling *East Lynne* (1861, adapted for the American stage in 1863). Laura Keene (1819?–1873), besides being a celebrated touring star, was the first woman in the United States to manage a theater. Her Laura Keene's Theater, known for its sumptuous interiors and for lavish efforts at authenticity, relied on the star system, but Keene also initiated the policy of the long run, and became the first manager to offer awards for the best play written by an American. Anna Cora *Mowatt (1819–1870), who cultivated her true-womanly affect when she did theatrical readings to support her ailing husband, wrote one of the most celebrated antebellum plays: *Fashion* (1845), a comedy of manners satirizing a nouveau riche family, the Tiffanys, who flaunt their ignorance as well as their wealth.

From the 1850s to the 1870s, an increasing appreciation of decorum and manners led to the construction of smaller, elegant, more comfortable theaters, built to accommodate bourgeois "business-class" audiences and their families. The bourgeois classes who laughed knowingly at Mowatt's Tiffanys began celebrating their own sense of theatrical self-invention in amateur theatricals, which swept middle-class parlors in the 1850s and 1860s.

But other theatricals were also taking place, not to consolidate patriarchal bourgeois hegemony, but to change it forever. As the abolitionist campaigns (the American Anti-Slavery Society in 1833, the Female Anti-Slavery Society in 1837), the Women's Rights and Suffrage campaigns in Seneca Falls (1848) and later the Woman's (Temperance) Crusade (1873–1874) were launched, demonstrations, town meetings, and yearly conventions became social dramas that American women staged with ever-increasing effectiveness. Sojourner *Truth's famous "Ain't I a Woman?" intervention at the 1851 women's rights convention in Akron, Ohio, emphatically politicized the cadenced oratory spoken from mid-century pulpits and theaters.

The temperance campaigns, or "women's whiskey wars," brought theatrical melodrama to the small-town streets of Ohio and Missouri. Standing in for the innocent heroine were bonneted middle-class women who entered saloons, knelt, prayed, sang, and lifted rapturous faces to hardened drinkers to rescue them from sin. If the temperance campaign died quickly, suffrage agitation continued until the ratification of the Nineteenth Amendment in 1920. In 1923, the radical Women's Party proposed the first Equal Rights Amendment to the Constitution and in the same year, at Seneca Falls, mounted a pageant to commemorate the seventy-fifth anniversary of the first women's rights convention, complete with processionals to the lake, banner carriers arriving on barges, and, at nightfall, women representing Lucretia Mott and Elizabeth Cady *Stanton reading the "Declaration of Sentiments" to trumpet fanfares and fireworks.

In the late nineteenth century, the drama written for legitimate theaters tried with limited success to keep pace with these increasingly complex social currents. Women playwrights and second-generation suffragists coming of age in the nineties were part of the migration of young people from small towns to urban centers. In the 1890s, feminist actresses in London, especially the American Elizabeth Robins, embraced Ibsenite social realism, and in the United States, Minnie Maddern Fiske (1865–1932), an actress who adopted and promoted the new realist style, acted in *Hedda Gabler* at her Manhattan Theater on 5 October 1903. The event has been called the beginning of twentieth-century theater in the United States.

Fiske's acting innovations prepared audiences for Rachel *Crothers's (1878–1958) feminist social dramas, the best of which were written and performed between 1908 and 1914: *Myself Bettina* (1908); *A Man's World* (1914); *Young Wisdom* (1914), and *He and She* (1911), plays that featured strong, opinionated women (clearly older than the nineteenth-century ingenue) who both confront their status as women and cultivate associations with other women. Through such relationships Crothers broached hot feminist issues like the double standard, the "new woman," free love, trial marriage, and woman's evolution.

While Crothers, who often directed her own plays, worked the commercial venues, Susan *Glaspell (1882–1948), born and trained as a reporter in Davenport, Iowa, devoted herself to modernist experimentation through the Provincetown Players. The Players not only gave Eugene O'Neill his start, but about a third of their plays were by women, including Djuna *Barnes, Edna *Ferber, Louise Bryant, Edna St. Vincent *Millay (especially *Aria da Capo*, 1919), and of course, Glaspell herself, whose *Trifles* (1916) has become a feminist classic.

Zona *Gale's *Miss Lulu Bett* (1920), a darkly comic play about small-town repression, set, amusingly, in "the middle class," was the first play by a woman to win a Pulitzer Prize—although Gale romanticized the open-ended conclusion in the original to make the play more satisfying for audiences. Sophie Treadwell's *Machinal* (1928), like Glaspell's *The Verge* (1921), embraced modernist experimentation over conventional realism. Influenced by Elmer Rice's expressionist techniques in *The Adding Machine* (1921), *Machinal* is a feminist parable depicting in nonrealistic scenes the demise of the Young Woman. Alice Gerstenberg's *Overtones* (1916), in which the unconscious aggression of two women is embodied by two separate performers, is a crude but earnest attempt to theatricalize women's psyches.

If white women found few theatrical outlets for the complexity of their experience, African-American women had even fewer, for they had to contend with vicious stereotyping—the "wench" role—in white-produced minstrel shows (1820s to early 1900s) and with the image of the shiftless illiterate or beloved "mammy" servant of hundreds of stage families since the early nineteenth century. (Anna Cora *Mowatt's *Fashion* makes satirical hay off the bumbling black servant Zeke, whom the pretentious Tiffanys clothe in full livery; Mowatt's racism was, of course, socially acceptable and theatrically conventional.)

If pre- and early twentieth-century plays by women are difficult to locate, the texts of black women, usually denied production as well as publication, are nearly impossible to find. Pauline Elizabeth *Hopkins's musical play *Slaves' Escape: or the Underground Railroad* (Boston, 1800) was perhaps the first work by an African-American woman to be produced in this country. Angelina Weld *Grimké's *Rachel*, billed as "a race play in three acts," is given honors as the first full-length drama written by a black woman. Having opened on 3 March 1916 in Washington, D.C., under the auspices of the NAACP Drama Committee, the play centers on idealistic Rachel Loving, who, reacting to the depth of white racism—the lynching of her father and stepbrother in the South, the harassment of black children in the North—renounces her dream of marriage and motherhood.

The Little Negro Theatre Movement in Harlem in the early 1920s was promoted by NAACP founder W. E. B. Du Bois, whose *Crisis* magazine, along with the Charles S. Johnson's Urban League *Opportunity* magazine, sponsored playwrighting contests for the best one-acters in 1925, 1926, and 1927. Female entrants to these contests outnumbered male, and among the winners were Zora Neale *Hurston for *Colorstruck* and *Spears* (1925); Marita *Bonner for the vibrantly anarchic *The Purple Flower* (1926), which pits "Us's" against the "Sundry White Devils" in a blend of folk mysticism and surrealist imagery; and the poet Georgia Douglas *Johnson, whose *Plumes* (1927), about a mother choosing between a suspect operation for her dying daughter or plumes for a fancy funeral, resembles Glaspell's *Trifles* in its careful observation of women's culture.

There has been a tendency to divide, perhaps too neatly, "race plays," written in response to Du Bois's urging that black writers smash stereotypes and write plays "About us ... By us ... For us ... Near us," from "folk plays," depictions of rural black life that were designed to delight and educate rather than politicize audiences. Promoted by Howard University professors Montgomery T. Gregory and Alain Locke, whose teachings were so influential to *Harlem Renaissance artists, folk plays (according to Gregory) provided "a wonderful opportunity ... to win a better standing in the community." But distinctions blur in Hurston's *Color Struck* and in Johnson's *Plumes*, in *A Sunday Morning in the South* (1925) (about the horror of lynching), and in *Blue Blood* (1926). For the "folk" characters in these plays, *racism constantly threatens and destroys. In the 1930s, while the Federal Theatre Project's Negro Unit briefly hired Zora Neale Hurston as a drama coach, the FTP produced neither Hurston nor Johnson, though the latter submitted some of her best work.

Like Laura Keefe and Susan Glaspell, but ultimately with more power, Hallie Flanagan (1889–1969) changed the shape of American theater in the 1930s. As a director at Vassar, she was the first to use the Constructivist techniques she witnessed firsthand in Russia. But she is best known for heading the Federal Theater Project and for nurturing the Living Newspaper, a documentary revue combining pantomime, skits, song, and simulated radio broadcasts, always from the worker's perspective: *Triple-A Plowed under* (1936), a Living Newspaper on American agriculture, *Power* (1937), on power company profiteering, and *One-Third of a Nation* (1937), inspired by a line from Roosevelt's second inaugural speech ("one-third of a nation ill-housed, ill-clad, and ill-nourished"). Critically acclaimed as those productions were (FTP produced the American premiere of *Murder in the Cathedral*, for example), Flanagan, in control of the money, drew heat both from the socialist Left and from the red-baiting Right, the latter charging that the government was funding communist propaganda. Flanagan faced hostile questioning at HUAC hearings in September 1938, and in 1939, funding for the Federal Theatre Project was officially terminated.

From 1930 to 1960 feminist gains in the public sphere were being reversed by a growing tide of political and cultural conservatism coupled by reductive applications of Freudian theories of female sexuality (such as anatomy is destiny). Some women playwrights from this period worked to turn well-made realism to women's issues. Claire Boothe *Luce's *The Women* (1935) is a witty, sour satire on society women's dependency on men. In Lillian *Hellman's (1905–1984) *The Children's Hour* (1936), two young schoolteachers base their career ambitions on their friendship, which collapses when they are rumored to be lesbians and are forced to close their school. Supposedly an exposé of civic hypocrisy and witch-hunting, Hellman has the "real" lesbian commit suicide at the end, thus assigning her the obligatory death of "fallen women" since the early nineteenth century. Hellman's *The Little Foxes* (1939) and *Another Part of the Forest* (1946) are southern gothic portraits of inbred familial sadism; in *Watch on the Rhine* (1946), set in 1940, Hellman attacks fascism by having fascism attack the American family, although in this archly up-to-date political play, gender conventions hardly budge.

Anatomizing the African-American family in a racist society, Lorraine *Hansberry's (1931–1965) *Raisin in the Sun* (1959) reaffirms the durability of the family drama even as it explodes the racist stereotypes that so disgusted her in the mainstream theater of the 1940s and 1950s: ". . . [the] whole body of material about Negroes. Cardboard characters. Cute dialect bits. Or hip-swinging musicals from exotic sources" (quoted in Kathy A. Perkins, ed., *Black Female Playwrights*, 1989). As the United States moved into the 1960s, Hansberry used the Younger family's travails to explore identity, racism, abortion, and gender relations in the black family. She made theater history as the youngest American and the first black playwright to win the New York Critics' Best Play Award for *Raisin in the Sun*. While realism remains the effective chosen medium of such fine playwrights as Alice *Childress, others were committed to destroying realism's grip on the theater.

Political upheavals from the mid-1950s to the mid-1970s—the civil rights, Black Power, second-wave feminism, anti–Vietnam war, free speech, and student movements—provided the turbulent contexts for counterculture revolutions in music, the visual arts, and theater. Distrust of authority, including the authority of the text, shifted focus from the theatrical product sold for consumption (Brecht's hated "culinary" theater) to the performance process in which personal exploration of psyche and body became the motive and content of art making. Judith Malina and Julian Beck's Living Theater (1951) was a visionary, noncommercial alternative to the aesthetic dominance of realism. While Gertrude *Stein's collaborations with Virgil Thompson—*Four Saints and Three Acts* (1934) and *The Mother of Us All* (1946)—had been produced, Beck and Malina were among the first to attempt her earlier wholly antireferential landscape plays. Later, influenced by Antonin Artaud, the Living Theater strove for "cruel" spectacle, staging their *Paradise Now* (1968) not only to engage, but to provoke audiences. An appropriate mantra for the turbulence of 1968, the last part of *Paradise Now*, called "The Permanent Revolution," had the company lead spectators into the street, chanting: "The theater is in the street. The street belongs to the people. Free the theater. Free the street. Begin."

The Open Theater (1963), directed by Joseph Chaikin, developed what were to become celebrated techniques of collective creation for many alternative groups: improvisation, psycho-physical exercises, and transformation (actors becoming, instantaneously and fluidly, any object, any fiction). Structuring material from company improvisations, founding member Megan *Terry wrote the antiwar *Viet Rock: A Folk War Movie* (1966), the Open Theater's first success. In New York, Ellen Stewart's Cafe LaMama dedicated itself to producing new playwrights (*Viet Rock* opened there), and is still hanging on, as are many of the most innovative groups from the 1960s and 1970s: The San Francisco Mime Troupe, The Wooster Group (previously The Performance Group), The Ridiculous Theatre Company, The Women's Project (American Place Theater), El Teatro Campesino, Theater Rhinoceros, the Ontological-Hysteric Theater, At the Foot of the Mountain, Spiderwoman Theater, El Teatro de la Esperanza—all producing some of this country's best alternative theater work.

Women playwrights since the 1960s, whether or not they call themselves feminists, have benefited from the social-consciousness raising of women's advocacy groups in every aspect of American political and cultural life. Beth * Henley's *Crimes of the Heart* (1979), Wendy * Wasserstein's *Uncommon Women and Others* (1978) and the Pulitzer prize-winning *The Heidi Chronicles* (1989), and Marsha * Norman's finely crafted *'Night Mother* (1982) have been Broadway successes offering mainstream audiences formally conventional, palatable images of women learning to speak and think as autonomous beings. Most feminist playwrights, however, worked experimentally in noncommercial venues, seeking to challenge the barrier between art and life. "The personal is political" was the rallying cry of sixties and seventies feminism; for women playwrights, "the personal" was an aesthetic mandate to explore women's multilayered identities, histories, rage, and vision, as well as the culture's sexism, racism, and (more recently) homophobia without concern for realism's normalizing logic. The first wave of still-productive feminist playwrights, including Megan * Terry (in *Calm Down, Mother*, 1964, and *Approaching Simone*, 1969), Adrienne * Kennedy (in *Funnyhouse of a Negro*, 1964, and *The Owl Answers*, 1965), Maria Irene Fornes (in *Fefu and Her Friends*, 1977), and Ntozake * Shange (in *for colored girls who have considered suicide when the rainbow is enuf*, 1976), along with Myrna Lamb, Rochelle Owens, Rosalyn Drexler, and Wendy Kesselman used surreal and often grotesque imagery, explosive language, and bodily transformations to shock, move, and even politicize their audiences. Shange's *Spell #7* (1979) recuperates minstrelsy (with Mr. Interlocutor) and the trickster/mask of folk tradition to structure a dynamic monologue-cum-ensemble.

Recuperation in the sense of "return to health" has been the spirit behind recent black feminist theater work. In *Re/Membering Aunt Jemima: A Menstrual Show* (1991), Glenda Dickerson, with Breena Clarke, has sought to de-iconize and empower Aunt Jemima, she "whose jolly accommodating laugh hides her fat hand as she sprinkles poison in the stew." In *The Death of the Last Black Man in the Whole Entire World* (1991), Suzan-Lori Parks places characters called "Black Man with Watermelon," "Black Woman with Fried Drumstick," "And Bigger and Bigger and Bigger," and "Old Man River Jordan" in rhythmic designs that juxtapose history and iconography, chorus and solo, using language reminiscent of Shange, Kennedy, and Gertrude Stein.

Like Rochelle Owens's sodomy-celebrating *Futz* (1965) and Myrna Lamb's satirical soap opera *The Mod Donna* (1970), Joan Schenkar's *Signs of Life* (1979) has become a landmark of feminist alternative theater. One of the first playwrights to explore * hysteria, Schenkar interweaves scenes of Alice * James and a sadistic late-Victorian doctor with P. T. Barnum's freak show, whose main attraction is Jane Merritt, an Elephant Woman. *Cabin Fever* (1983), *The Last of Hitler* (1985), and *Fulfilling Koch's Postulate* (1986) probe the American psyche for other dark, dirty secrets.

Lesbian drama has ranged from the well-made realism of Jane Chambers's celebrated *Last Summer at Blue-Fish Cove* (1980), to Cherríe * Moraga's poetic investigations of the evolution of Chicana lesbian consciousness in *Giving Up the Ghost* (1986), to the improvisation-based, cabaret styles of the WOW Cafe in New York City (founded 1982), the site of the first performances of Holly Hughes's *The Well of Horniness* (1983) and *Lady Dick* (1985). Performers in Hughes's *Dress Suits to Hire* (1987), WOW founding members Lois Weaver and Peggy Shaw plus Deb Margolin became the theater company Split Britches, naming it for their first text, a witty folk-play with songs, *Split Britches* (1981). Along with other WOW performers, Split Britches worked through the 1980s to cauterize old gender stereotypes, to tangle politics with irony and sensuous stage images. *Beauty and the Beast* (1982) and *Upwardly Mobile Home* (1984) are witty, lesbian feminist cabarets peopled by pop cultural icons and zanies—Weaver's Tammy Whynot, Shaw's lipsynched Perry Como, Margolin's peripatetic rabbi. Following *Little Women* (1987), in 1992 Margolin wrote *Lesbians Who Kill* for Weaver and Shaw, and the latter performed with the gay male troupe Bloo Lips in an Obie award–winning satire on Williams's *Streetcar*, *Belle Reprieve* (1991).

Mixing art and activism for over three decades, the San Francisco Mime Troupe's commedia-styled, comic-strip-inspired scripts, often authored by Joan Holden, have been seen in parks, schools, auditoriums, and arts festivals throughout the United States and Europe. Starting in 1970, the Mime Troupe has built each play around a political issue: in 1970, the issue was feminism, for which Holden wrote (and later revised) a melodramatic farce, *The Independent Female, or A Man Has His Pride!*, which is sometimes performed by other groups. El Teatro de la Esperanza (founded 1971) developed a docudrama style in such works as *La victima* (The victim, 1976) and *El Pulpo* (The octopus, 1980) to anatomize the oppression of Chicanos, while the musical revue *La muerte viene cantando* (Death comes singing, 1984) made gender and sexual power relations the centerpiece. Spiderwoman Theater (founded 1976), with a core group of three Cuna-Rappahannock Native-American women, creates pieces drawing on Native-American oral traditions and feminist consciousness. *Women in Violence* (1976) combined anger and slapstick to expose street violence and domestic battering, while the recent *Winnetou's Snake Oil Show from Wigwam City* (1988) mocks New Age shamanism as the latest example of expropriation of Native-American culture.

Through the 1980s into the 1990s, three feminist performers have honed innovative performance styles based on an activist commitment to fighting the ubiquitous racism and sexism in contemporary American culture. Anna Deveare Smith began *On the Road: A Search for American Character* in 1985 as a form of performance research; she would interview people, shape solo theater pieces from tape-recorded interviews, and invite the interviewees to see themselves performed. In her award-winning *Fires in the Mirror* (1991), based on interviews with African Americans and Lubovitcher Jews after the Crown Heights, New York, riots in 1990, Smith's multivocal solo performance became a cathartic means of bringing together groups generally too angry, fearful, and culturally myopic to listen to one another. In the recent *Twilight: Los Angeles, 1992* (1993), Smith again gathers materials from famous and unknown witnesses or participants in the Los Angeles riots that were sparked by the acquittal of policemen involved in the March 1991 beating of Rodney King. Robbie McCauley confronts racism through family history in pieces combining story telling, enactment, and music and visual effects. *My Father and the Wars* (1985) and *Indian Blood* (1988) look at American history through her grandfather's military career, and her Obie award–winning *Sally's Rape* (1990), with Jeannie Hutchins, explores the rape of McCauley's enslaved great-great grandmother Sally in the context of relations between black and white women today. Karen Finley's explosive pieces bypass enactment; she makes her body the object of patriarchal violation by smearing it (in recent pieces) with foodstuffs to simulate sperm and excrement. (When in 1990, Finley, Hughes, and two gay performers had their NEA funding withdrawn by the U.S. Congress for alleged obscenity, Finley's sense of victimization was confirmed.) In performance, Robbie McCauley's voice is measured, loud, angry, clear. In *A Constant State of Desire* (1988) and *We Keep Our Victims Ready* (1990), Finley shouts, turning monologues into incantations whose violent images protest the continual violation of the culturally marginalized—gays, lesbians, people of color, people with AIDS, and, at the most fundamental level, women.

To end on this note of outrage is to recall the timorous self-presentation of Mercy Warren, and to realize that notwithstanding feminine modesty about taking up the pen, Warren's prorepublican polemic contained a good deal of the shout. Indeed, a shout can be heard throughout U.S. women's drama, sometimes in the self-satisfied mainstream, but most often at its experimental edges, summoning an imagined community, a cult of new womanhood: embodied, spectacular, ever-transforming.

[*See also* Social Comedy; Suffragist Plays; Theatre Critics; Performance Art; Playwrights; *also article on Drama in the following composite entries:* African-American Writing; Asian-American Writing; Chicana Writing; Jewish-American Writing; Latina Writing; Lesbian Writing; Native American Writing.]

• Arthur Hobson Quinn, ed., *Representative American Plays* (1917). Eleanor Flexner, *Century of Struggle: The Woman's Rights Movement in the United States* (1970). Victoria Sullivan and James Hatch, eds., *Plays by and about Women* (1973). Walter J. Meserve, *An Emerging Entertainment: The Drama of the American People to 1828* (1977). Carol Hymowitz and Michaele Weissman, *A History of Women in America* (1978). Judith Barlow, ed., *Plays by American Women, 1900–1930* (1981). Helen Krich Chinoy and Linda Walsh Jenkins, *Women in American Theatre* (1981). Theodore Shank, *Alternative American Theatre* (1982). Karen Halttunen, *Confidence Men and Painted Women: A Study of Middle-class Culture in America, 1830–1970* (1982). Helene Keyssar, *Feminist Theatre* (1985). Sue-Ellen Case, *Feminism and Theatre* (1988). N. Scott Momaday, "The Native Voice"; Wayne Franklin, "The Literature of Discovery and Exploration"; Barbara Kiefer Lewalski, "English Literature at the American Moment"; Sacvan Bercovitch, "The Puritan Vision of the New World"; Sargent Bush, Jr., "Sermons and Theological Writings"; Thomas Philbrick, "The American Revolution as a Literary Event"; and Ruby Cohn, "Twentieth-Century Drama," in Emory Elliott, gen. ed., *Columbia Literary History of the United States* (1988). Kathy A. Perkins, ed., *Black Female Playwrights: An Anthology of Plays before 1950* (1989). Bruce A. McConachie, *Melodramatic Formations* (1992).

— Elin Diamond

DUNBAR-NELSON, Alice Ruth Moore (1875–1935), poet, short story writer, journalist, essayist, educator, and suffragist. Born in New Orleans, Louisiana, on 19 July 1875, Alice Ruth Moore was the daughter of Patricia Wright, a seamstress, and Joseph Moore, a merchant marine, and, due to her middle-class social status and racially mixed appearance, she enjoyed the diverse culture of the city. She graduated Straight University (now Dillard University) in 1892 and began her career as a teacher in the public school system of New Orleans. In 1895, Dunbar-Nelson published her first collection of short stories and poems, *Violets and Other Tales.* Although many of the pieces were obviously marked by her inexperience, "Titee," "A Carnival Jangle," and "Little Miss Sophie" reveal her gift for capturing the language, setting, and pathos peculiar to New Orleans life at the turn of the century. She married Paul Laurence Dunbar after a courtship of letters that began when Dunbar saw her picture accompanying one of her poems published in the *Monthly Review* in 1897. They married in 1898 in a secret ceremony in New York, where she was teaching at the White Rose Mission (later, the White Rose Home for Girls in Harlem), which she helped to found. After her marriage, Dunbar-Nelson moved to Washington, D.C., with her husband.

Dunbar-Nelson continued to write and, in 1899, published *The Goodness of St. Rocque and Other Stories*, which included a revision of "Titee" (one with a happier ending), "Little Miss Sophie," and "A Carnival Jangle." Aside from the ending of "Titee," the revisions of these stories heralded the problems that she faced with later manuscripts. Publishers, eager for dialect stories such as those that made Paul Laurence Dunbar famous, opted for versions of these stories in which the characters spoke with pronounced creole dialects. Dunbar-Nelson's published fiction dealt exclusively with creole and anglicized characters; difference was characterized not in terms of race, but ethnicity. Many of her manuscripts and typescripts, both short stories and dramas, were rejected when Dunbar-Nelson explored the themes of racism, the color line, and oppression. This, coupled with the fact that *Violets* and *St. Rocque*, published so early in her career, were, until recently, the only published collections of her work, have made it difficult for both readers and critics to access Dunbar-Nelson's work.

When Dunbar-Nelson's marriage ended in 1902, she moved to Wilmington, Delaware, where she taught at Howard High School, and, during summer sessions, at the State College for Colored Students (Deleware State College) and at Howard University. Although she never saw Dunbar again after their volatile separation, Dunbar-Nelson continued to publish under the name of Alice Dunbar even after Dunbar died in 1906. During the years that she taught high school in Wilmington, Dunbar-Nelson chiefly published poetry, essays, and newspaper articles. In 1909, *Modern Language Notes* carried "Wordsworth's Use of Milton's Description of Pandemonium." Dunbar-Nelson entered into her second marriage, with Arthur Callis, in 1910; the couple was subsequently divorced. She acted as coeditor and writer for the *A.M.E. Review*, one of the most influential church publications of the era, from 1913 to 1914. Dunbar-Nelson published *Masterpieces of Negro Eloquence* (1914).

Dunbar-Nelson addressed the issues that confronted African-Americans and women of her time. In 1915, she served as field organizer for the woman's suffrage movement for the Middle Atlantic states; she was later field representative for the Woman's Committee of the Council of Defense in 1918 and, in 1924, campaigned for the passage of the Dyer Anti-Lynching Bill. Following her third and final marriage to Robert J. Nelson in 1916, Dunbar-Nelson published chiefly in the periodical press. "People of Color in Louisiana" *(Journal of Negro History)* in 1917 was followed by her poetry, which was published in the NAACP's *Crisis, Ebony and Topaz*, and the Urban League's *Opportunity.* Countee Cullen also included three of her most popular poems, "I Sit and I Sew," "Snow in October," and "Sonnet," in his collection of African-American poets, *Caroling Dusk* (1927). In 1920, Dunbar-Nelson edited and published *The Dunbar Speaker and Entertainer*, a literary and news magazine directed toward a black audience, and, with Nelson, coedited the Wilmington *Advocate.* Her press publications included "The Colored United States" *(Messenger*, 1924), "From a Woman's Point of View" (later, "Une Femme Dit," column for the Pittsburgh *Courier*, 1926), "As in a Looking Glass" (column for the Washington *Eagle*, 1926–1930), and "So It Seems to Alice Dunbar-Nelson" (column for the Pittsburgh *Courier*, 1930). Economic conditions precluded Dunbar-Nelson from concentrating solely on her writings; however, her corpus stands as a major achievement. She died on 18 September 1935 in Philadelphia.

• Erlene Stetson, ed., *Black Sister* (1981). Gloria T. Hull, *Color, Sex, and Poetry: Three Women Writers of the Harlem Renaissance* (1987). Ann Allen Shockley, *Afro-American Women Writers, 1746–1933* (1988; reprint, 1989). Gloria T. Hull, ed., *The Works of Alice Dunbar-Nelson*, 3 vols. (1988).

Sheila Smith McKoy

DWORKIN, Andrea (b. 1946), lesbian-feminist activist, essayist, novelist, short story writer.

Born in Camden, New Jersey, to Jewish parents, Dworkin earned her B.A. from Bennington College in 1968, and after a short marriage to a batterer, moved to New York, where she has spent most of her life. One of the most outspoken Radical Feminists, a group that includes Kate *Millett and Robin Morgan, Dworkin's political roots lie in the *civil rights and antiwar movements of the 1960s.

Dworkin's writing focuses on systemic sexual *violence against women. Best known for her antipornography *activism, radicalism, and epigrammatic writing ("Romance . . . is rape embellished with meaningful looks"), Dworkin feels "censored out of the Amerikan press" because of her politics. Her style is often one of outrage, at both the sexually violent *patriarchy and collaborating liberals.

Her first book, *Woman Hating* (1974), connects fairy tales, *pornography, and literature with the *sexism of cultural practices, such as Chinese foot binding. In *Pornography: Men Possessing Women* (1981), Dworkin analyzes pornography's role in the sexual abuse and oppression of women, and in *Right-wing Women: The Politics of Domesticated Families* (1983), she discusses how the fear of male violence compels women to seek safety in the status quo. *Letters from a War Zone: Writings, 1976–1987* (1988) includes her important 1986 testimony before the United States Attorney General's Commission on Pornography.

In *Pornography and Civil Rights* (1988), coauthored with law professor Catharine MacKinnon, pornography is defined as the sexually explicit subordination of women through pictures and words. The two women initiated legislation in 1983–1984 to make pornography legally actionable as sex discrimination. Although eventually vetoed as a violation of the First Amendment, this bill opened a nationwide debate on pornography.

Dworkin's fiction is semiautobiographical, sexually graphic, and stylistically innovative. Her first novel, *Ice and Fire* (1988), portrays a young woman who endures sexual violence, eventually finding freedom as a feminist writer. *Mercy* (1991), chronicling a nine-year-old victim of sexual violence who grows up to be mankiller, is designed both to shock and to move to action.

Like Millett's *Sexual Politics* (1970), Dworkin's most controversial book, *Intercourse* (1987), is both literary and cultural analysis. Focusing on the act of heterosexual intercourse as the basis of women's oppression ("Coitus is punishment"), *Intercourse* was criticized for conflating the metaphorical and literal, and sexual acts with social organizations. Yet Dworkin does not apologize for her polemic; her politics, like her writing, are not there to entertain. She says: "I am a feminist, not the fun kind."

• Mary Kay Blakely, "Is One Woman's Sexuality Another Woman's Pornography?," *Ms.* 13 (April 1985): 37–38. Louise Armstrong, "Dissident for the Duration" (Interview), the *Women's Review of Books* 3, no. 8 (May 1986). Alison Assiter, *Pornography, Feminism and the Individual* (1989). Virginia Blain, Patricia Clements, and Isobel Grundy, eds., *The Feminist Companion to Literature in English: Women Writers from the Middle Ages to the Present* (1990). Andrea Dworkin, Letter to the *New York Times Book Review* 97 (3 May 1992): 15–16.

Julie Crawford

DYSTOPIAS. *See* Utopias.

E

EARLE, Alice Morse (1851–1911), social historian. Christened Mary Alice, Alice Morse Earle was born in Worcester, Massachusetts, to Edwin Morse, a prominent businessman, and Abby Mason Clary of Waterville, Maine. Earle was educated at Worcester High School and at Dr. Gannett's boarding school in Boston. In 1874, she married Henry Earle, a New York stockbroker, and moved to Brooklyn Heights, where her four children were born and where she lived until her death.

Growing up in a household of collectors, Earle shared an avid interest in colonial antiques with her half-brother and sister. On the death of her husband, Earle launched her writing career with an account of her forebear's church in Chester, Vermont. Her extremely popular first book, *The Sabbath in Puritan New England* (1891), disregards the political focus of professional history of the time. Concentrating instead on the material conditions of Puritan worship, from the size and shape of the meetinghouse to the design of its pews, it sets the pattern for her later work. Over the next twenty years, Earle produced sixteen volumes of colonial history and at least thirty signed articles.

Writing in the period of the Colonial Revival in architecture and the rise of the Arts and Crafts movement, Earle produced work that shares with these movements a belief in "the true dignity which comes from simplicity in living" *(Margaret Winthrop)*. As a historian, however, Earle rejected the utopian strain in these movements, insisting instead on a clear-eyed appraisal of concrete colonial practices and an attention to "real things." Earle's acknowledgement of disparities arising from gender and social status (though not from race) reflects her interest in women's rights. A member of the Daughters of the American Revolution and kindred groups, Earle supported temperance and immigrant exclusion.

Some of Earle's work focuses on specific artifacts of early New England (such as *Two Centuries of Costume in America, 1620–1820*, 2 vol., 1903). Of greater interest are the detailed and heavily illustrated accounts of everyday life in the colonies based on court records, diaries, correspondence, and other primary sources: *Colonial Dames and Good Wives* (1895), *Margaret Winthrop* (1895), *Colonial Days in Old New York* (1896), *Curious Punishments of Bygone Days* (1896), *Home Life in Colonial Days* (1898), *Child Life in Colonial Days* (1899), and *Stage-Coach and Tavern Days* (1900). Unusual for their attention to domestic life, Earle's lively accounts are among the first social histories of the American colonies.

• Earle's papers are in the Sophia Smith Collection at Smith College and the American Antiquarian Society in Worcester, Massachusetts. Esther C. Averill, "Alice Morse Earle," *Old-Time New England* 37 (January, 1947): 73–78. Edward T. James, ed., *Notable American Women, 1607–1950*, vol. 1 (1971), pp. 541–542.

Amy Schrager Lang

EARLY NATIONAL WRITING. Shortly after the Constitution reached its ratification vote, George Washington wrote on 31 August 1788 to Annis Boudinot * Stockton, a well-known New Jersey poet and longtime supporter, "The felicitations you offer on the present prospect of our public affairs are highly acceptable to me. . . . I think you Ladies are in the number of the best Patriots America can boast. And now that I am speaking of your Sex, I will ask whether they are not capable of doing something towards introducing foederal fashions and national manners? A good general government, without good morals and good habits, will not make us a happy People; and we shall deceive ourselves if we think it will." Washington was speaking according to the general attitudes of the day—attitudes promulgated especially in circles of elite and middle-class white Euro-Americans—which said that while men were searching for the best mode of federal government, women were to do their parts in governing the domestic realm, because good "citizens" of the household, the argument went, would become good citizens of the state.

It is easy to understand why Washington might have worried about domestic governance and focused upon the importance of women in educating a dutiful citizenry. Revolutionary women had experienced life-wrenching circumstances that called upon them to take on duties ranging from farming to accounting, smithing to printing, while their husbands, sons, or other male heads-of-households were fighting in the colonial militia (as Whigs or Patriots or, from the British perspective, Rebels), in British regiments (as Tories or Regulars), or in border skirmishes (where relations among Native Americans, Euro-American whites, and African Americans were less driven by the international concerns of the Revolutionary War than by the more local concerns of land rights and sustenance). The Revolutionary War experiences significantly altered men's and women's formerly rather low expectations about women's abilities to manage by themselves. That "middling" and elite women were able to take on greater household and business burdens during the war while sustaining their own activities brought about, for them, a paradoxical situation when the war was over. It was a situation not unlike that faced by United States women after World War II: in war time, women had proven their abilities to do more than men had formerly expected of them; after war time, the question became, what would happen to these capable and confident women.

Some women writers questioned the submerged ("femme covert") status of women foisted upon them when they married. They insisted that, as the war years had proven, women were equal partners in *marriage. Like the *Matrimonial Republican* of 1790, they argued that "marriage ought never to be considered as a contract between a superior and an inferior, but a reciprocal union of interest. . . . The obedience between man and wife is, or ought to be mutual." Despite their arguments, however, women did not receive the same legal status as men after the Revolutionary War. Abigail *Adams's famous plea in a letter to her husband, John—that the men of Congress "Remember the Ladies" while settling the laws for the new nation—went largely unheard by the group of men (who have been called the "Founding Fathers" of the United States) she sought to convince. As Washington's letter to Stockton and as the terms "Ladies" and "Founding Fathers" seem to suggest, an ideology of domestic relations, relations both familial and political, dominated literary transactions. That is, whether one reads William Hill Brown's *The Power of Sympathy*, Charles Brockden Brown's *Wieland*, *Edgar Huntly*, or *Jane Talbot*, or whether one reads Hannah Webster *Foster's *The Coquette*, Susanna *Rowson's *Charlotte Temple*, Judith Sargent *Murray's *The Story of Margaretta*, Tabitha *Tenney's *Female Quixotism*, or Rebecca *Rush's *Kelroy*, the key issues most frequently treated in the literary medium most accessible to the readership—novels—are familial relations (especially those between parents and children), marital situations, and moral or ethical choices that will affect personal freedom, government, and/or social status in the world-at-large.

Both the international and domestic political situation of the new government was precarious. In the absence of already codified laws, elite white men and women seem to have sought protective standards that would enable them to retain their status even while "instructing" the broader—and growing—populace about good federal and good domestic government. Whether they were writing fictional *captivity narratives or domestic fictions, women writers of the middling and elite group faced a difficult situation: in order to get published, they would have to reflect the traditional social mores that would keep potential subversion (both of government and family) in check, yet some seem to have found ways to question precisely those traditional mores that would keep women subjugated. This twofold effort—an effort that would seem to contain and edify, even as it called into question social roles and attitudes—was first noted in Cathy N. Davidson's ground-breaking study, *Revolution and the Word: The Rise of the Novel in America* (1986). Because novels were considered potentially suspect (as vehicles of entertainment rather than edification), writer after writer insisted in her opening lines that the narration to follow would be a "Tale of Truth," or a tale "founded in fact," the insistence upon truth telling at once serving to justify the fiction and enhance the seeming potentialities of edification. On one level, most of the novels by women ended either in the witnessing of "happy" marital relations (with good prospect for children, if not with children born within the fictional line) or in the total demise, in unhappy death or dementia, of women whose behaviors (usually in evading "good" parental advice and/or taking up with seductive partners whom they did not marry) were considered socially questionable and abhorrent. It would seem that, in the larger fictional story line, the women's "good" behaviors (obeying good parents and marrying appropriate partners) were rewarded and women's "bad" behaviors punished. Yet even within these fictive worlds, elements of subversion—or at least elements that called into question the traditional roles for women—revealed the uneasy tension that women of the middling and elite group might have experienced in their own lives. To take one example, in the fictive world she inhabits, Eliza Wharton, the central character in Foster's *The Coquette*, dies a miserable death, a seeming "just punishment" for her transgressions, which included avoiding marriage to her boring suitor and entering clandestine relations with another man. On the other hand, that Wharton dies such a fictionalized death effectively calls into question the constrained roles and expectations foisted upon middling white women by a patriarchal and authoritarian social and governmental system.

Women novelists were perhaps the most exploratory of the writers in this era, but this is not to suggest that novels were the only genre of writings in which women found voice. Many middling and elite women continued to write drama and poetry, the privileged genres for much of the eighteenth century, during this era of political and social change. In New England, Mercy Otis *Warren and Sarah Wentworth *Morton were perhaps the most celebrated poets. Yet Annis Boudinot Stockton and Elizabeth Graeme *Fergusson were perhaps the best known of a rather large group of published women poets of this era. Stockton and Fergusson knew the elite men who were key politicians of their era; they each hosted literary salons, sometimes of women alone but often with men and women, in the Middle Atlantic area (Princeton and Philadelphia), at a time when key political questions—such as the location of the nation's capital and the development of a national mint—were being addressed. Their verse, like that of Anna Young *Smith and Isabella Oliver Sharp, a rural Cumberland County (Pennsylvania) poet, addressed issues from family relations to governmental transactions, marital restrictions to Fourth of July celebrations. Unlike their novelist counterparts, these women tended toward the clear implementation of the status quo in both familial and governmental questions. Yet that they wrote poetry at all is a sign of their growing sense of importance to United States society and their strong sense of ability in the face of those who might chastise them for their poetic attempts.

It has sometimes been suggested that women were reticent to publish their writings because of the potential disregard, registered in men's (and sometimes women's) criticisms of their "vanity" or their "presumption" in publishing. To some extent, this supposed reticence seems available in the poems themselves, as this preface to Martha Wadsworth *Brewster's *Poems on Divers Subjects* (1757) would seem to indicate: "Pardon her bold Attempt who has reveal'd/Her thoughts to View, more fit to be Conceal'd/Since thus to do was urged Vehemently,/yet most no doubt will call it Vanity." The reticence, however, is merely a seeming reticence, an acknowledgement that women were not expected to speak rather than an acknowledgement that they had nothing to say. Annis Stockton's poem "To the Visitant [a pseudonymous journalist], from a Circle of Ladies" (first published in 1768; reprinted, 1788) clearly indicated the source of women's seeming reticence. The poem questions "How many [women] would surmount stern custom's laws,/ And

prove the want of *genius* not the cause [of their not writing];/ But that the odium of a *bookish fair,*/ Or *female pedant*, or *"they quit their sphere,"*/ Damps all their views, and they must drag the chain,/ And sigh for sweet instruction's page in vain." Although they were writing in the privileged medium of their day and thus reinforcing traditional values, these poets were nonetheless—in the very act of writing and/or in the public display of a questioning of these values—interrogating the social norms that kept women subjugated and uneducated.

More than any other group of women poets, the *African-American poets Lucy *Terry (or Luce Bijah, as she was called) and Phillis *Wheatley most clearly confronted the sexist and racist standards of the era. Both poets were brought to North America as young slave children, and both became free as they reached maturity. Terry's "Bars Fight" existed in the oral tradition for nearly 100 years before it was first published in 1855. Wheatley's *Poems on Various Subjects, Religious and Moral* (1773) received public attention; the volume likewise was ridiculed by men from the dominant white establishment like Thomas Jefferson, whose *Notes on the State of Virginia* (1787) belittled Wheatley's tremendous accomplishment. One wonders if it was that Jefferson feared most what Wheatley marked as "liberty" in "America," a poem not published in her lifetime: "Thy power, O Liberty, makes strong the weak,/And (wondrous instinct) Ethiopians speak/Sometimes by simile." White women might have had to learn to speak in indirection; African-American women seem to have recognized from the start that a seeming indirection was both ennobling and liberating.

Many women poets of the early national era chose to remain unpublished in their lifetimes. Yet some poets, such as Mercy Otis Warren and Judith Sargent Murray, wrote and published their poems while writing for the theater as well. Theirs was an especially bold insertion of women's abilities in the public domain, for dramatic activity had been proscribed by the Continental Congress during the Revolutionary War, and the residual distrust of the theater in New England (where these women lived) must have indicated to them that drama writing, like novel writing, was suspect and potentially profligate. In an era when print culture was on the rise, it is not surprising that theatrical representation—even representation of the patriotic political and domestic status quo—held less public attention than novels, poems, and essays.

Perhaps more than the other genres, the genre of the nonfiction essay became the preeminent means by which middling and elite white women explicitly voiced their social and political concerns. The issues they elected to address—marital strife, wedded bliss, home cures, infant and children's concerns, and women's *education (from literacy to the study of history and the fine arts, as well as accounting)—suggest the level of personal investment on the part of these women to better their own social circumstances even as incomes, like literacy and the infant survival rate, began to rise during the first part of the nineteenth century. Most white women essayists could hardly be called self-centered, however. Some of the first essays on prohibition, the poor and children's relief, *abolitionism, and the necessity for multiracial and multiethnic equality came from women's pens during this era. Some writers, such as Sarah Pogson Smith, Isabella Marshall Graham, and Hannah Mather *Crocker argued in behalf of many of these issues according to traditional religious and social attitudes. Others, like Judith Sargent Murray (on occasion), Mercy Otis Warren, Helena *Wells, the *Grimké sisters, and Lydia *Sigourney challenged received notions and directly called into question the reigning attitudes of men in influential social stations. Theirs was a complex task: because they were writing essays, no masking of intention could occur in fictional or poetic devices; and their ability "logically" to "reason" (an ability more frequently attributed by men to themselves, while women were credited with "sensibility") challenged men's views of themselves and their public and patriarchal roles.

In the face of patriarchal governmental and religious institutions, it is not surprising that many women preferred the privacy of *diary writing, frequently in a variety of genres. The private writings by many women of the era were religious in orientation. Some women's private or family writings were published posthumously. Posthumously published writings—like those by Bridget Richardson Fletcher, Ann Eliza *Bleecker, Sarah Prince Gill, and Sarah Ewing Hall—could procure for the writer some little contemporaneous reputation while retaining power over public censure, because few people would care to challenge a writer who was already deceased. In the absence of known private writings in this era by African-American and *Native American women (there are no known public writings by Native American women from this time), twentieth-century readers must learn about these groups' cultural attitudes from the points of view of white aristocrats—specifically, from the diaries of Janet *Schaw, who wrote her travels to Antigua, St. Kitts, North Carolina, and Portugal; and Eliza Lucas Pinckney, whose private papers detail her management of plantations, and cultivation of indigo in South Carolina.

Between the years 1776 and 1820, the social formation within what came to be called the United States of America transformed dramatically from primarily regionally oriented, separate nation-states to a much larger and amorphous national body. Although many of the writings by women of the era seem concerned with personal religious and/or regional issues, many more of these writings evince women's recurrent concerns, across *class and racial lines, with finding voice in a world dominated politically and domestically by men who seemed to have less concern than did women about the welfare of women, children, the poor, and the generally underrepresented. It seems that women were indeed trying to "introduce foederal fashions and national manners, . . . good morals and good habits," as Washington had suggested they should. The problem seems in part to have been that the men weren't listening: What might have been a glorious revolution became a *Civil War, mid-century.

[*See also* Colonial Era Writing; The Novel, Beginnings of.]

• Elizabeth Ellet, *Women of the American Revolution*, 3 vols. (1848–1850). Nancy F. Cott and Elizabeth H. Pleck, eds., *A Heritage of Her Own: Toward a New Social History of American Women* (1979). Linda K. Kerber, *Women of the Republic: Intellect and Ideology in Revolutionary America* (1980; reprint, 1986). Mary Beth Norton, *Liberty's Daughters: The Revolutionary Experience of American Women, 1750–1800* (1980). Lee Virginia Chambers-Schiller, *Liberty, A Better Husband: Single Women in America, the Generations of 1780–1840* (1984). Carla Mulford, *"Only for the Eye of a Friend": The Poetry of Annis Boudinot Stockton* (1994).

Carla J. Mulford

EASTMAN, Crystal (1881–1928), journalist, lawyer, and social investigator. Born in upstate New York, of parents who were both ministers and suffragists, educated at Vassar, Columbia, and New York University Law School, Eastman spent her life, according to Wiesen Cook, "in the vanguard of every major movement for social change": industrial democracy, women's rights, civil rights, and world peace.

Eastman drafted New York's first worker's compensation law, which was used as a model by other states (see her book *Work Accidents and the Law*, 1910). She was founder and chair of the Woman's Peace Party of New York (1914), and a cofounder of the National Women's Peace Party (1915), which became the Women's International League for Peace and Freedom (1922). She was executive secretary of the American Union Against Militarism (1916), and cofounder of the Civil Liberties Bureau (1917), out of which the American Civil Liberties Union developed. An active member of the National Women's Party (1916), which introduced the Equal Rights Amendment into Congress (1923), Eastman opposed protective legislation for working women on the basis that it was grounded in arguments for women's biological inferiority and "natural dependence" on men. From 1918 to 1922, she coedited the *Liberator,* the successor to the radical journal the *Masses,* which had been suppressed by government proscriptions on freedom of the press during World War I. Under her leadership, the magazine took a stronger stand on black civil rights than its predecessor, publishing African-American poetry as well as articles on the international socialist movement.

Eastman was a militant socialist feminist, with a strongly articulated vision of the equal necessity for social and sexual revolution. As a child, she insisted on the equal division of household labor, a principle she elaborated on later when she called for mothers to bring up "feminist sons." She also argued for state-funded "motherhood endowments" for women, in recognition of the importance of child rearing to society at large. Although she became an ardent proponent of communism after the Bolshevik Revolution, she recognized that socialism did not guarantee women's equality, which would have to continue to be fought for on its own grounds.

Eastman brought to her antimilitarist work a similar independence of thought. The cogency of her analysis of the U.S. government's imperialism and self-interest in regard to military preparedness and entrance into the war place her with the leading antiwar journalists of her era (John Reed, Randolph Bourne). Her willingness to break ranks with her more moderate pacifist colleagues (Jane *Addams, Lillian Wald) over public advocacy for conscientious objectors and war resisters was a mark of her commitment to civil liberties, perhaps her most enduring legacy.

• Eastman's papers from the World War I era are in the Swarthmore College Peace Collection. See also Max Eastman, *Enjoyment of Living* (1948). June Sochen, *The New Woman: Feminism in Greenwich Village, 1910–1920* (1972). Blanche Wiesen Cook, ed., *Crystal Eastman on Women and Revolution* (1978). Elaine Showalter, ed., *These Modern Women: Autobiographical Essays from the Twenties* (1978). Nancy Cott, *The Grounding of Modern Feminism* (1987).

Lois Rudnick

EASTMAN, Elaine Goodale (1863–1953), novelist, poet, editor, educator, and activist for Native American causes. Eastman is remembered as her husband's wife more than anything else. She was married to Santee Sioux Dr. Charles A.

Eastman (Ohiyesa) and collaborated on works with him and edited his manuscripts. But her own life and works deserve a revisionary examination. Her biography and writing can be seen as historical accounts of Anglo involvement with Native Americans. Further, she is the epitome of the influence of domesticity and gendered idealism in the struggle and formation of a woman's identity.

Her youth resembled that of Louisa May *Alcott, in that she was raised amid literature and freethinking parents on "Sky Farm," a vaguely transcendental homesite in Massachusetts. She and her sister published a collection of poems in 1879 when she was 15, *Apple Blossoms: Verses of Two Children.* At age 20, Eastman began to teach Sioux Indians at the Hampton Institute in Virginia, beginning her lifelong involvement with Native Americans and education. She was a strong supporter of missionary work and boarding schools among the Native American tribes. The detrimental results of such white interests and establishments are documented by such contemporary Native American writers as Linda *Hogan and Louise *Erdrich. Eastman did attempt a more active engagement with tribes. She spoke Dakota, dressed and lived similarly to her companions while in their company, and attempted to record the lifestyle of the Native American.

She was present at the 1890 Wounded Knee Massacre and nursed the wounded. Her article on the Ghost Dance and Massacre can be found in *Nebraska History* (1945). Eastman had concentrated her energy on writing and teaching on reservations and advocating for government intervention and protection for Native Americans. While thus occupied she met and soon married Charles Eastman, a Sioux educated at Dartmouth and Boston University. After marriage, her commitment was divided between these interests and her growing family. She still wrote, but was now more motivated by a need for financial success, completing three "potboilers" for a popular readership. Upon separating from her husband in 1921, Eastman continued to write, producing a last and more rounded final novel, *One Hundred Maples,* in 1935, which deals with marriage and responsibility to family.

Eastman's work is frequently overlooked, even more so because it is usually out of print. A closer examination, however, would reveal the complex social structures that motivated her reform and education work, her awareness of literary genres, and her conflict with identity, in an era when women lived more for others than for self.

• Elaine Goodale Eastman, *Sister to the Sioux: The Memoirs of Elaine Goodale Eastman, 1885–1891,* ed. K.

Graber (1978). Ruth Ann Alexander, "Elaine Goodale Eastman and the Failure of the Feminist Protestant Work Ethic," *Great Plains Quarterly* 8, no. 2 (Spring 1988): 89–101.

Robin Jones

EATING DISORDERS. Women's eating habits have long been recognized as a form of discourse, a complex metaphoric language of victimization, physicality, eroticism, and empowerment. In the Middle Ages, an age of hunger, gluttony was both a social and moral transgression; thus the medieval woman's ability to distribute food entitled her to the status of patriarch and her fasting was a sacrifice of social and religious significance. Caroline Walker Bynum points out (in *Holy Feast and Holy Fast: The Religious Significance of Food to Medieval Women*, 1987) that in refusing food, the saintly woman simultaneously fed others and nourished herself spiritually.

In *Never Satisfied: A Cultural History of Diets, Fantasies and Fat* (1986), Hillel Schwartz argues that throughout American history, dieting has similarly symbolized charity yet has contradicted the American belief in rightful surplus. *Anorexia epitomizes this contradiction, allowing women self-proprietorship and self-expression through renunciation. Susie Orbach (*Fat is a Feminist Issue*, 1978; *Hunger Strike*, 1986), Kim Chernin (*The Hungry Self: Women, Eating, and Identity*, 1985; *The Obsession: Reflections of the Tyranny of Slenderness*, 1981), and Sandra Gilbert and Susan Gubar (*The Madwoman in the Attic*, 1979) write that female eating disorders constitute women's response to a misogynistic society that values the thin, subordinate female body both for aesthetic reasons and as an exemplification of the logic of patriarchal capitalism. Anorexia thus can represent a loathing of society transferred to one's flesh and to one's self-enclosed art. Writers such as Mary *Gordon (*Final Payments*, 1978) and Anne *Tyler (*Dinner at the Homesick Restaurant*, 1982) thematize women's struggles to accommodate unrealistic social expectations through starving or overeating. Immigrant writers such as Anzia *Yezierska (*Hungry Hearts*, 1920) have particularly relied on hunger and orality to express discontent with the role of women in American capitalist society.

In adolescent literature, anorexic protagonists often feel unloved, fear sexual maturity, and have a distorted image of their bodies and unrealistic expectations of themselves. These issues are explored by fiction writers Deborah Aydt (*Katie*, 1980), Karen Dean (*Maggie Adams, Dancer*, 1980), Deborah Hautzig (*Second Star to the Right*, 1981), Emily Hudlow (*Alabaster Chambers*, 1979), Rebecca Josephs (*Early Disor-

ders*, 1980), Ivy Ruckman (*The Hunger Scream*, 1983), and Anne Snyder (*Goodbye Paper Doll*, 1980). Autobiographical treatments of anorexia include Aimee Liu's *Solitaire* (1979), Sheila MacLeod's *The Art of Starvation: A Story of Anorexia and Survival* (1982), and Cherry O'Neill's *Starving for Attention* (1982). Judy Blume's *Blubber* (1974) thematizes children's cruelty to an obese classmate.

Feminist critics have drawn on the work of eating specialist Hilde Bruch (*Eating Disorders: Obesity, Anorexia Nervosa, and the Person Within*, 1973; *The Golden Cage*, 1978) to argue that food negation may suggest not rejection but plenitude, an articulation of female creativity. Writers such as Emily *Dickinson may thus have translated literal starvation into spiritual and creative intensity. Southern writers in particular have thematized the ritual nature of meals in a postagrarian society. The novels of Jill McCorkle (*The Cheerleader*, 1984; *Crash Diet*, 1992), Kaye Gibbons (*A Virtuous Woman*, 1989), and Fannie Flagg (*Fried Green Tomatoes at the Whistle Stop Cafe*, 1987), and the drama of Marsha *Norman (*Getting Out*, 1977; *'Night, Mother*, 1983) rely particularly on metaphors of consumption and the ability to serve or reject food as an indication of social status in modern American society.

[See also Body and Health.]

• Heather Kirk Thomas, "Emily Dickinson's 'Renunciation' and Anorexia Nervosa," *American Literature* 60, no. 2 (May 1988): 205–225. Gillian Brown, "Anorexia, Humanism, and Feminism," *Yale Journal of Criticism* 5, no. 1 (Fall 1991): 189–215. Evelyn J. Hinz, ed., *Diet and Discourse: Eating, Drinking and Literature*, special edition of *Mosaic*, vol. 24, nos. 3–4 (Summer/Fall 1991). Lilian Furst and Peter Graham, *Disorderly Eaters: Texts in Self Empowerment* (1992). Peggy Whitman Prenshaw, ed., *The Texts of Southern Food*, special edition of *Southern Quarterly* (Winter–Spring, 1992).

Donnalee Frega

EATON, Edith. *See* Sui Sin Far.

EATON, Winnifred. *See* Watanna, Onoto.

ECOFEMINISM. Writing in the first issue of *Audubon Magazine* in 1887, New England writer and poet Celia Thaxter railed against the Victorian penchant for stuffing the bodies of birds and wearing their feathers in fashionable hats. Entitled "Woman's Heartlessness," the article called attention to the "indifference and hardness" among educated and enlightened women who, argued Thaxter, erroneously believed that birds, like mosquitoes, were too abundant to ever be missed. Writing almost a century before the term *ecofeminism* was coined by the French writer Francoise d'Eaubonne in 1974, Thaxter nevertheless captured two of the central tensions inherent in the modern ecofeminist movement: the relationship between women and nature and the role of ecology in feminist philosophy and politics.

In contrast to Thaxter's concern over "woman's heartlessness," contemporary ecofeminism celebrates women's special relationship with nature, arguing that both tradition and biology have situated women in a position to bring about an ecological revolution to ensure the future of the planet. While some ecofeminists refuse the dualities of Western culture (whereby the "female is to male as nature is to culture"), others embrace women's closeness to nature and see it, not as degrading or limiting to women, but as a source of spiritual empowerment and political activism.

Because both women and nature stand at the center of ecofeminist analysis, it can rightly claim a variegated and diverse heritage. Celia Thaxter might balk at the centrality of essentialist thinking, but she would have recognized the political imperatives so central to contemporary ecofeminism. Unlike many so-called nature writers, authors as diverse as Thaxter, Josephine Johnson, Rachel *Carson, Alice *Walker, and Starhawk nourished ecofeminism through their insistence on the interconnectedness of all "things"—of humans and plants, of science and everyday life, of trees and the air we breathe. For these writers, nature was never simply a mysterious source of wonder, but rather a material reality—a thing that was simultaneously natural and made up.

Fashion, in other words, could alter nature. And birds, like mosquitoes, would be painfully missed, for to kill the latter would, as Rachel Carson stunningly argued, condemn us all to a *Silent Spring* (1961). Like her previous works, *The Sea Around Us* (1951) and *The Edge of the Sea* (1955), *Silent Spring* demonstrated Carson's deep commitment to both the interconnectedness of living things and the necessity for political action. As she told her biographer Paul Brooks, "There would be no peace for me if I kept silent." The need to speak out provoked as well the lyrical and moving works of Josephine Johnson. Both *Now in November* (1934) and *The Inland Island* (1969) inveigh against a warring world of senseless destruction and exploitation and, like ecofeminism, seek to awaken and mobilize an insurgent spirit.

If the works of Thaxter, Johnson, and especially Carson (who is generally credited with initiating the modern environmentalist movement) politicized nature by calling attention to the consequences of careless human intervention, writers like Annie *Dillard, Starhawk, and Lynn Andrews spiritualized nature—seeking within it new ways to live in an increasingly "unnatural" world. For Dillard, in particular, nature is more a vehicle for spiritual insight than for ecological revolution and it is as a sojourner in search of revelation that she confronts the natural world at Tinker Creek. In *A Pilgrim at Tinker Creek* (1974), as well as in *Holy the Firm* (1977) and *Teaching a Stone to Talk* (1982), Dillard accentuates the mystical and life-affirming power of nature, whose beauty and horror is viewed as both ordinary and divine. Like the Romantic seekers William Wordsworth, Henry David Thoreau, and John Muir, Dillard writes of a God that is to be sought, even stalked, so that nature becomes less an arena of social struggle than a place of moral and metaphysical conflict. Identifiably Judeo-Christian, Dillard's spirituality remains too closely attached to the androcentric biases of Western culture to appeal to ecofeminists who are committed to rethinking and transforming the relation of humanity and divinity to nature. Emphasizing the intrinsic value of all living things, writers like Starhawk and Lynn Andrews alternatively attempt to replace the Western duality of man/nature with a nature-based religion, usually (and to the criticism of indigenous peoples) by appropriating the symbols and practices of Native-American cultures, or by celebrating a pre-Christian goddess.

Far from a monologue, ecofeminism is perhaps best understood as a babel whose intellectual roots are grounded in the centrality of nature and the insurgent spirit. Arguing against the mutual denigration of both women and nature in traditional Western thought and culture, activists put ecology at the center of feminist politics, simultaneously reclaiming and redefining "nature" writing.

[*See also* Feminism.]

• Carolyn Merchant, *The Death of Nature: Women, Ecology, and the Scientific Revolution* (1980). Ann Bookman and Sandra Morgan, *Women and the Politics of Empowerment* (1988). Irene Diamond, *Reweaving the World: The Emergence of Ecofeminism* (1990). Elizabeth Jane Harrison, *Female Pastoral: Women Writers Re-visioning the American South* (1991). Anne Primavesa, *From Apocalypse to Genesis: Ecology, Feminism, and Christianity* (1991). Robert Sessions, "Deep Ecology versus Ecofeminism: Healthy Differences or Incompatible Philosophies?," *Hypatia* 6, no. 1, (Spring 1991). Anne E. Simon, "Ecofeminism: Information and Activism," *Women's Rights Law Reporter* 13, no. 1 (Spring 1991). Scott Slovic, *Seeking Awareness in American Nature Writing: Henry Thoreau, Annie Dillard, Edward Abbey, Wendell Berry, Barry Lopez* (1992).

Ardis Cameron

ECRITURE FEMININE. *See* French Feminism.

EDUCATION. Few aspects of American institutional life have changed as dramatically in the past three hundred years as women's education. While women today enjoy access to a wide range of educational opportunities, this was not always true. By and large, changes in women's education have mirrored basic shifts in women's status and the changing definitions of female roles in American culture. But education itself has contributed to changes in the lives of American women, and has affected different groups of women in different ways. Education has enhanced the status and power of some women, while others have struggled to succeed without it.

Colonial Beginnings. Women were largely excluded from formal education in the seventeenth and eighteenth centuries, a fact that was linked to their being restricted from positions of power and authority in public life. The early common schools of New England, which taught children primarily to read the Bible and participate in the political and cultural life of the community, generally served a male clientele. The same pattern held true for other regions, where formal systems of schooling were even less developed. There is evidence that some schools educated girls and young women, particularly schools in urban areas, but historians agree that men generally received a good deal more schooling than women throughout this period. Women were barred from the colonial colleges, and hence from any real prospect of participation in the social or political leadership of the colonies. The effect of this policy has become clear: historians have calculated that illiteracy was twice as high among women in colonial New England than it was among men, a direct consequence of differences in education.

Because women did not go to school does not mean, of course, that they were uneducated. There is evidence of a widespread system of training in household tasks and other domestic duties for young women at this time, amounting to a form of female apprenticeship. Young women were sent to other households under agreements to exchange work for such training. Again, this system seems to have been especially well developed in New England, but may have existed in certain other parts of the colonies as well. These arrangements often were formalized by contracts, with clearly stipulated expectations for the transmission of certain skills. Historians have estimated that a third of all households in seventeenth-century New England contained young women performing domestic duties, many of them as servants but others as household apprentices.

For most women in colonial America, then, education was rather informal. Many undoubtedly learned from their mothers, sisters, and neighbors, acquiring the complex skills they would need to maintain a household in a preindustrial era. Informal education certainly characterized the lives of black women, most of whom were slaves, and white female indentured servants, sizable and growing segments of the population in southern colonies. For these women, and indeed most others, the prospect of a literate life was quite remote.

The Era of Republican Motherhood. Women's education changed dramatically in the years following the Revolutionary War, reflecting new views of women's roles and status in the emerging republican political and social order. Because elected governments called for an informed populace, particularly among male voters, national leaders came to place great importance on popular education in the years following the revolution. Many observed that women had a critical role to play in fostering democratic values and respect for learning in succeeding generations if the American experiment in republican government was to succeed. And to do this, they reasoned, women themselves needed education. As mothers, then, American women would become responsible for the upbringing and education of the nation's future leaders. Historians have labeled this general conception of women's role as "republican motherhood," and it sparked a veritable revolution in female education. In the century to follow, women's schooling, taken as a whole, would develop significantly.

Things did not change overnight. The period immediately following the revolution was a time of experimentation, with a number of new schools for women being founded in different parts of the country by pioneering reformers. Most of these schools were organized as academies, and served a rather affluent—and therefore limited—clientele. More fundamental change occurred with the gradual development of local and state systems of common schooling, which extended into the opening decades of the nineteenth century. As David Tyack and Elisabeth Hansot have noted (*Learning Together*, 1991), most of these schools appear to have been coeducational from early on, reflecting Yankee preferences for simplicity and economy in the development of local institutions. Tyack and Hansot suggest that coeducation seemed a natural extension of relations between children in the family and the church, the two other popular institutions most Americans were familiar with at this time. And the prospect of constructing parallel school systems for boys and girls in a country with a widely dispersed population was too costly. Thus, the growing acknowledgment that women ought to be educated resulted in a widespread development of coeducational schooling in the United States.

The impact of these developments, though gradual, was manifold. Perhaps the most important result of these changes was the growth of women's literacy. In every region except the South, female literacy rates had reached parity with or surpassed male rates by 1850. This development was clearly linked to the appearance of a large female reading public in the nineteenth century, and to the development of the nation's first identifiable generation of popular women writers. At the same time, the growth of widespread common schooling for women spurred the development of secondary and collegiate education for women as well. The first half of the nineteenth century was characterized by yet more experimentation in education for teenage girls and young women. Such leading women educators as Emma Willard, Mary Lyon, and Catharine *Beecher (and a number of others) established schools and wrote influential books about women's education. Women were also admitted to a limited number of colleges at this time. Beginning with Oberlin in 1837, and extending to Antioch, the University of Michigan, and others in the 1850s, a number of institutions experimented with coeducation.

The women who benefited from these developments, however, were white, of middle-class status, and largely from the North. In the South, school systems were poorly developed and illiteracy among women remained relatively high. While wealthy white women were often tutored privately, most women in the South received little education. Even in the North, women from poor families generally did not attend school beyond the primary level, if at all. Black women were largely excluded from formal education, particularly in the South, where the vast majority of blacks were slaves in this period. There were notable efforts to extend formal education to blacks in the North (Prudence Crandall's ill-fated school for black women in Connecticut was a highly publicized example), but outside of such major urban centers as New York, Philadelphia, and Boston, these ventures were limited in duration and impact. For women from these groups, education continued to be informal and largely conducted in domestic settings, and so, these women were generally excluded from the growing literary culture of American women.

Controversy and Expanding Opportunities. In the closing decades of the nineteenth century, the development of women's education became a point of national controversy, as primary education expanded to the South and West and even larger numbers of women enrolled in high schools and colleges. In 1872,

Boston physician Edward Clarke wrote a widely circulated book arguing that advanced education was dangerous to the health of American women, and by implication, threatened future generations. Similar arguments would be made in the years that followed, particularly as nativist concerns about declining birthrates among educated, middle-class whites mounted. Even so, female enrollment at all levels of schooling continued to grow. By the 1890s women outnumbered men by nearly two to one in public high schools, and were attending college in ever larger numbers.

Despite the efforts of Clarke and other critics of women's education, opportunities for women in higher education expanded enormously in the years following the Civil War. Most educators endorsed women's education because it was a great source of enrollments essential to the growth of school systems across the country. New colleges and universities were established in all regions of the country, most of which admitted women (although most scholarships and other forms of student support went to men). Other institutions, particularly those in the midwestern and western states, opened their doors to women as well. All-women colleges were established to provide opportunities when established institutions proved unwilling to change their policies. The best-known of these were the famous "seven sisters" women's colleges in the Northeast, which were established in the decades between 1870 and 1900 to provide opportunities to young women aspiring to attend elite eastern universities (particularly Ivy League schools) that refused to admit female students.

The years following the Civil War were also marked by significantly expanded educational opportunities for black women, particularly in the South. In the immediate aftermath of the war, schools were established for ex-slaves, men and women, by missionaries from the North, and public school policies were changed to provide schooling for blacks. Literacy rates for blacks, including black women, improved dramatically as a result. Although few blacks could attend existing colleges, a number of important colleges and universities were established for blacks in the late nineteenth century, most of which were coeducational. A number of colleges for black women were established in southern states at this time as well (Spelman Seminary was the best known).

The closing decades of the nineteenth century were a time of massive immigration to the United States, a process linked to rapid industrialization and urban growth. For thousands of immigrant women living in industrial cities, education beyond the primary level was not a viable option. Most of these women entered the labor force in their teens, taking jobs in shops, factories, or as domestics to help support their struggling families. Women from some immigrant groups demonstrated a higher propensity to attend school than others (this was true, for example, of Jewish women). But for the families of most working-class immigrant women in these settings, extended education was simply beyond their means.

Growth and Differentiation. The opening decades of the twentieth century were a time of continued growth in American education, and a period of reform. Influenced by the ideas of John Dewey and other proponents of Progressive Education, high schools and colleges became more concerned with vocational education. The numbers of women enrolled in secondary schools, colleges, and universities continued to grow, and women began attending graduate and professional schools in modest but significant numbers. Consequently, the first generation of female professionals (scholars, lawyers, medical doctors, social workers, and others) began to affect their fields. These years, however, were marked by the development of clear curricular differences in the education of men and women, and growing distinctions between the schooling available to women from different social and economic backgrounds.

As high schools began to develop curricula to prepare adolescents for the world of work, new courses began to distinguish male and female education. While growing numbers of boys enrolled in industrial education, girls were encouraged to take home economics, sewing, and cooking classes. Developed because of the concern that young women were losing touch with domestic skills, by the second decade of the twentieth century these courses had been established in high schools across the country. Large numbers of women also enrolled in typing, stenography, and bookkeeping classes in these years, in direct response to opportunities in the growing field of clerical employment. Before long, large numbers of young men and women were studying different curricula in the nation's high schools.

As in earlier years, large numbers of working-class immigrant and black women were excluded from secondary and higher education in the early decades of the twentieth century. This meant that women in these groups generally were unable to participate in such new fields of female employment as clerical work, teaching, and the professions of social work and nursing. Indeed, immigrant and black women became even more overrepresented in manual labor after 1900 than they had been before. Throughout most of the South (and isolated instances elsewhere), segregated schools existed for blacks, often with curricula for women focused largely on home economics or related subjects. In the plains and western states, Native-American children attended federal boarding schools and mission schools, most of which featured home economics or domestic crafts curricula for women. Black, Native-American, and immigrant women often faced discrimination in higher education, even from institutions outside the South. There were few avenues to fields of white-collar employment for these women.

For middle-class, white women born in the United States, however, these were years of continued expansion of educational opportunities, although important obstacles still remained. By 1920, women constituted nearly half of all college students in the country, a mark they would not reach again until the late 1970s. Women filled about 80 percent of the nation's teaching positions at that time, and dominated a number of other professions. But they remained critically underrepresented in the most prestigious professional groups (such as medicine and law). Even on college campuses, nearly 60 percent of all women faculty members at coeducational institutions held appointments in home economics. Even with large numbers of women in college, important distinctions between men's and women's education persisted.

A Continuing Search for Equity. In the decades following 1920, the number of women enrolled in colleges and universities continued to grow, albeit at a slower rate than male enrollments until the 1960s and 1970s. High school enrollment became nearly universal after 1950, but important differences in completion rates distinguished women in various social and economic groupings. By and large, women from high-status groups continued to enjoy greater access to education than others. But these differences appear to have narrowed in the years after 1960, at the same time that women began to make inroads into areas of professional and technical education once dominated by men.

It was in the decades after 1920 that curricular differences in the education of men and women began to exert a toll. In high schools and colleges, women were more likely to enroll in literature and languages, as well as home economics, while men dominated mathematics, the sciences, and political studies. Large numbers of women went through college with few aspirations beyond marriage or perhaps teaching. One such graduate, Betty *Friedan, discovered in the 1950s that many other women shared her dissatisfaction with these roles. Recognition of this dissatisfaction was an important catalyst to the women's movement of the sixties and seventies.

Important changes have started to occur in women's education in the years since 1960. Inspired by the civil rights and women's movements, and spurred by federal civil rights legislation, educators have created new opportunities for women in high schools, colleges, and universities. With increased scholarships and other forms of support, the number of women enrolled in colleges had surpassed the number of men by 1980. While women continued to be underrepresented in math and science, they began to appear in larger numbers in law and medical schools. New fields of scholarship and teaching were created under the rubric of women's studies, and the number of women enrolled in graduate school increased dramatically. Important differences in the education of men and women, it appears, are finally beginning to disappear.

Perhaps the biggest problems in women's education today revolve around the issue of equity in access for different groups of women. Women from middle- or high-income backgrounds continue to enjoy greater access to higher education than others. While important gains have been made in the education of black women, attainment levels still lag behind those of whites, particularly with regard to graduate and professional training. Women from other groups, especially the new immigrant groups of the past several decades, are poorly represented at all levels of achievement (although Asian-American women are an important exception to this pattern). While college-educated women have made inroads in a wide variety of fields once monopolized by men, and have succeeded in establishing new female career patterns, large numbers of women who have not benefited from higher education remain mired in poverty and dependency.

There can be little doubt that women's education has advanced enormously since colonial times, when women were generally excluded from extended formal education. And as women's education has developed, women have come to play a wider range of roles in society at large. Important differences between men's and women's education, however, continue to reflect inequities in gender roles, regardless of rapid advances in recent years. And the vast differences that still mark the educational—and working career—opportunities of women from varied social and economic backgrounds poses a difficult challenge for the future.

[See also Literacy; Historians; Women's Studies Programs.]

• Margaret Szasz, American Indian Education: The Road to Self Determination, 1928–1973 (1974). Linda Kerber, Women of the Republic: Intellect and Ideology in Revolutionary America (1980). Barbara Miller Solomon, In the Company of Educated Women: A History of Women and Higher Education in America (1985). John L. Rury, Education and Women's Work: Female Schooling and the Division of Labor in Urban America, 1870–1930 (1991).

John Rury

EIGHTEENTH-CENTURY WRITING. See Early National Writing.

ELLET, Elizabeth (ca. 1812–1877), early historian of U.S. women, poet, and translator of European historical and literary texts, was born in Sodus Point, New York, and was educated at the Aurora (New York) Female Seminary, under the direction of Susanna Marriott, an English Quaker. Elizabeth Lummis married William Henry Ellet in about 1835.

While still in her teens, Lummis began publishing poetry in the American Ladies' Magazine. Her early literary reputation was established with her verse translations from Italian, a literary/historical appreciation of Schiller, and a collection of German legends (Evenings at Woodlawn, 1849). Like the work of other women translators, such as Margaret *Fuller and Mary Booth, Ellet's books fueled the New England Romantic interest in Continental texts; their work also broadened the reading of literate women untrained in foreign languages.

Between 1848 and 1850, Ellet completed what is considered her major work, a three-volume history of the American Revolution. Rather than focus on traditional political history, these volumes establish the domestic context for that event, taking as their focus the involvement of women in the conflict. Ellet particularly chronicles women of the middle states and the South, areas neglected in more traditional studies. Significantly, she relied on documents, letters and interviews, making hers the first study to be based wholly on authenticated primary sources. Reprinted several times during her lifetime and at least three times during the twentieth century, The Women of the American Revolution (1848–1850) is still respected by historians as a landmark document in social history, although its conservatism has disturbed some feminist scholars. Ellet followed this trilogy with a volume of narrative history drawn from the same sources, Domestic History of the American Revolution (1850).

Ellet wrote several more histories of women, including Pioneer Women of the West (1852), also based on authenticated primary sources. The Queens of American Society (1867), a subscription book, is an encyclopedia of the socially prominent women of the Northeast; The

Court Circles of the Republic (1869) presents biographical accounts of the female relatives of eighteen U.S. presidents. Ellet's interest in women's history and Continental art coincided in her encyclopedic *Women Artists in All Ages and Countries* (1859).

A prolific writer, Ellet also published hundreds of essays and poems in the literary quarterlies of her day, several volumes of poetry, a book of domestic economy, a volume of historical fiction, and a travel book.

• Sidney P. Moss, *Poe's Literary Battles* (1963). Susan Phinney Conrad, *Perish the Thought* (1976). Jill K. Conway, *The Female Experience in Eighteenth- and Nineteenth-Century America* (1982).

Nicole Tonkovich

ENVIRONMENTALISM. *See* Ecofeminism.

EPISTOLARITY. *See* Letters.

EPISTOLARY NOVEL. Although American women have produced few epistolary novels, the literary significance of those that exist is much greater than simple numbers would suggest. Since an epistolary novel is composed of an exchange of *letters, a correspondence among its characters, it does not contain the explicit guiding, framing, and potentially dominating presence of a narrative persona. The epistolary novel offers readers direct and potentially equal access to the voices of its characters. For this reason, the epistolary novel has served as a vehicle for authors who wish to present voices marginal to the dominant cultural experience—voices traditionally muted or submerged. From Hannah Webster *Foster's *The Coquette* (1797), to Alice *Walker's *The Color Purple* (1982), Ana *Castillo's *The Mixquiahuala Letters* (1986), and Lee *Smith's *Fair and Tender Ladies* (1988), the epistolary novel has offered women writers a way to privilege voices that might not otherwise be heard.

The epistolary novel emerged in eighteenth-century Europe from the tradition of genteel exchanges of private letters. Significantly, the earliest epistolary novels, modeled on Samuel Richardson's classic epistolary tomes, *Pamela* (1740) and *Clarissa* (1747–1748), told and retold stories of young, powerless women beset, seduced, and often abandoned. Thus, as these novels traced the abuse and eventual effacement of young women, they also provided potentially voiceless women with a voice, and ensured that their stories would be heard. Since the American republic emerged in the heyday of epistolarity, it is not surprising that the first American novels followed the Richardsonian model and adopted the epistolary form. Foster's *The Coquette*, a classic epistolary tale of seduc-

tion and betrayal, was the first widely read American novel.

In the less orderly world of early republican America, however, the epistolary novel could not be depended on to provide the powerless with voice. As cultural conventions blurred, multiple readings became possible, and the greatest strength of the epistolary novel, its ability to project the unmediated voice of the powerless, became its greatest weakness. The interaction of the reader with the text became a disempowering liability as readers not well schooled in the traditional cultural codes could as easily misread the novel as read it according to the author's design. Susanna *Rowson appears to have realized this because, while penning *Charlotte Temple* (1794), America's first genuine best-seller, she chose to enter the text of the novel and use her narrative voice to protect and amplify the voice of the weak and abused heroine. While the novel contains and reproduces many of Charlotte Temple's letters, few reach their intended recipients. The narrator preserves the letters and weaves a narrative that compensates for their misdirection as she restores and protects the voice that they contain. Thus, from its roots in epistolarity, the American women's novel quickly veered in a direction that would better protect and amplify the voices of powerless women and result in the dominance of the strongly narrated domestic novels of the nineteenth century.

Nevertheless, while the main current of literary history moved in other directions, a thin stream of epistolarity remained, and in this stream women continued to voice less often heard concerns. In early epistolary novels by Susanna Rowson, Ann Eliza *Bleeker, Eliza Vicery, Mrs. Hassall, and a "Lady of Philadelphia," the voices of widows, young girls, and chambermaids are recorded unmediated. As the nineteenth century progressed, Catharine Maria *Sedgwick, Mrs. A. M. Diaz, Anne Stephens, Kate Douglas Wiggin, Amelie L'Oiseau, and Myrtle Reed wrote epistolary novels of note. These novels remain significant for the chronicle they provide of the lives and crises of ordinary women of this time. Letters allow readers to construct their own narrative framework as they experience the voice of the characters in more intimate proximity and share more of the "trivial" daily occurrences of characters' lives.

In the early twentieth century, the stream of epistolary novels widened somewhat as writers sought new forms in an era of literary experimentation. Some of the epistolary authors of the period were Mrs. Wilson, Lady Helen Pole, Laura Livingston, Mrs. Poultney Bigelow, Aurelia I. Sidner, Sarah Biddle, Bettina Baroness Van Hutten, Hildegarde Hawthorne, M. J. Lanen and Cally Ryaland, Zora Putnam Wilkins, Jean Chamblin, Adelaide L. Rouse, Irene Osgood, Frances Little, Mary Ridpath Mann, Elizabeth Cooper, Ruth McEnery Stuart, Florence Elizabeth Summers, Grace Zaring Stone, and Kay Cleaver Stone. Many of the epistolary novels penned in this period chronicle the freedom and mobility of the "New Women" of the era, documenting exchanges between women traveling to far corners of the world and engaged in exciting new careers. However, even as epistolarity offered a forum for women forging frontiers, it continued to be a forum for the abandoned sweetheart or the disaffected widow, thereby providing voice for the less often heard voices on both ends of the newly expanded continuum of women's experience.

As the twentieth century progressed and telecommunications developed apace, the epistolary novel fell into a state of some decline, paralleling that of the private letter. Nevertheless, while few epistolary novels were published in the second half of the century, several of note emerged. In 1978, Elizabeth Forsythe Haily published *A Woman of Independent Means*, a chronicle of the life of an admirable woman who insisted on controlling her own destiny. Alice Walker's *The Color Purple* appeared in 1982 and was acclaimed for revealing the heart of the experience of African-American women. Ana Castillo, in her extraordinary and experimental *The Mixquiahuala Letters*, explores the relationship between two Chicanas. Castillo adds a new element to the epistolary form by numbering the letters and then, in three tables of contents, suggesting different orders of approach for "the conformist," "the cynic," and "the quixotic," thereby heightening the interactive mutability of the form and the role of the reader of an epistolary novel as de facto narrator of the text. Most recently, Lee Smith has added *Fair and Tender Ladies* to the epistolary oeuvre. Through the correspondence of Ivy Rowe, the matriarch of an Appalachian family, Smith records and preserves several generations of the voice of the Virginia hills.

These three recent examples exhibit the continuance of the most important use of the epistolary form, and the reason why the fundamental elements of the genre are not likely to die. From the earliest American novels, the epistolary form has served admirably as a vehicle for the clear transmission of voices submerged by the dominant culture. Further, without the guiding and directing voice of the active narrator, the epistolary novel offers the reader the powerful if disquieting role of narrator of the text. It is from the epistolary novel, through such explicitly hybrid forms as Castillo's *The Mixquiahuala Letters*, that the narrative role of the reader is expanding further in such fascinating new genres as interactive fiction, which appears to be the literary offspring of electronic mail, much as the epistolary novel was the literary offspring of the traditional letter.

[*See also* Letters; Novel, Beginning of the.]

• Ian Watt, *The Rise of the Novel* (1957). Godfrey Frank Singer, *The Epistolary Novel: Its Origin, Development, Decline, and Residuary Influence* (1963). Ruth Perry, *Women, Letters, and the Novel* (1980). Janet Gurkin Altman, *Epistolarity: Approaches to a Form* (1982). Alistair Fowler, *Kinds of Literature: An Introduction to the Theory of Genres and Modes* (1982). Cathy N. Davidson, *Revolution and the Word: The Rise of the Novel in America* (1986). Elizabeth Goldsmith, ed., *Writing the Female Voice: Essays on Epistolary Literature* (1988). Linda S. Kauffman, *Special Delivery: Epistolary Modes in Modern Fiction* (1992).

Blythe Forcey

ERDRICH, Louise (b. 1954), Chippewa/German-American fiction writer and poet. Although first published as a poet, Louise Erdrich considers herself a storyteller: "I began to tell stories in the poems and then realized that there was not enough room . . . But I think in the book you try to make the language do some of the same things, metaphysically and sensuously, physically, that poetry can do" (*Winged Words*, 1990). Erdrich's fiction has been critically acclaimed for its lyrical prose and humor, beginning with *Love Medicine* (1984), which won the National Book Critics Circle Award. Chickasaw writer Linda *Hogan credits Erdrich with pointing *Native-American writing in a new direction by "telling the plain stories of people and their lives without pity, judgment, opinion or romanticization" (*This Is About Vision*, ed. William Balassi, et al., 1990).

Erdrich was raised in North Dakota, where her parents worked for the Wahpeton Indian School. Her mother encouraged her to enter the first coeducational class at Dartmouth College in 1972 through the Native American Studies program, where she met her future husband and collaborator, Michael Dorris, the program's director. After graduation, she returned to North Dakota and held a variety of jobs, including Poet in the Schools. In 1979, she earned a master's degree in creative writing from Johns Hopkins University, and became a writer in residence at Dartmouth, marrying Dorris in 1981.

In 1982, Erdrich won the Nelson Algren fiction competition with the story "The World's Greatest Fisherman," which became the first chapter of *Love Medicine*, the first novel in a tetralogy that includes *The Beet Queen* (1986), *Tracks* (1988), and *Bingo Palace* (1994). Each of the novels interweaves self-contained short stories told by different narrators and chronicles three generations of Native-American and European-immigrant families in a fictionalized region of North Dakota from 1912 to the present. Cyclical in structure, the novels move toward resolution through discovery of individual identity in relation to "people in a small community who have to get along with each other over time and who know all of each other's stories" ("An Interview with Louise Erdrich and Michael Dorris," *Missouri Review* 11, 1988).

Erdrich's first book of poetry, *Jacklight*, was published in 1984, and was followed by a second collection, *Baptism of Fire*, in 1989. Although Erdrich and Dorris always write collaboratively, *The Crown of Columbus* (1991) was the first work to be published under both their names. Erdich's work has appeared in such periodicals as *Ms.*, the *New Yorker*, and *Harper's*, among others, as well as in numerous anthologies, including *That's What She Said* (1984) and *Spider Woman's Granddaughters* (1989). She and Dorris live in New Hampshire with their five children.

• Jan George, "Interview with Louise Erdrich," *North Dakota Quarterly* 53 (1985): 240–246. Hertha D. Wong, "An Interview with Louise Erdrich and Michael Dorris," *North Dakota Quarterly* (1987): 196–218. Kay Bonetti, "An Interview with Louise Erdrich and Michael Dorris," *Missouri Review* 11 (1988): 79–99. Louise Erdrich, "Conversions," in *Day In, Day Out: Women's Lives in North Dakota*, ed. Elizabeth Hampsten (1989), pp. 23–27. Laura Coltelli, ed., *Winged Words: American Indian Writers Speak* (1990).

Kayann Short

EROTICA. Erotica and *pornography are controversial terms that are often used interchangeably, and little consensus has been reached over their use. While a common practice has been to define one or both terms as simply that which is intended to arouse, historically much literature in these categories has been intensely degrading to women. Thus, the debate has important implications, for just as the power to control underlies the definitions, so the power to control the terms has definite social and political consequences.

Etymologically, erotica derives from Eros, the Greek god of passionate love. Pornography combines the Greek words "graphos," meaning writing about or description of, and "porno," meaning prostitution. It follows that value distinctions have conventionally been made among pornographic/erotic texts, where those considered to portray socially acceptable sexual practices are termed erotica, and those judged obscene or deviant, pornography (or exotica). In a parallel distinction, erotica has generally been used to denote texts considered to have literary merit, as opposed to pornography.

Such distinctions are problematic because they include the fundamental dispute of what makes a text literary. Similarly, dividing erotica from pornography/exotica into "normal" and "deviant" patterns of sexuality begs the question of what exactly is normal or deviant. A more useful distinction, according to Gloria *Steinem, foregrounds the importance of sexual politics in the terms: erotica is about sexuality, whereas pornography is about power, with social issues of domination and control at its base. Historically, this domination has been almost exclusively that of men over women.

One of the aims of women's erotica, therefore, has been to reclaim the female body and female pleasure from subjection to a male viewpoint. Male erotica and/or pornography generally centers on the actions, sometimes abusive, performed on a passive, silent female body. Women's erotica does not simply reverse this formula, but attempts to rewrite it entirely in order to erase the imbalance of power, or, more radically, to redefine power in a nonbinary fashion. Textual as well as sexual politics become issues: How does one write about the female body without merely echoing masculine texts? Do we need a new, female language free from the binary oppositions of phallocentric discourse? Whatever the answer, we may conclude that women's erotica is by nature transgressive, because it violates not only previous sexual, but textual standards as well.

Until the twentieth century, only a small amount of American erotica existed, although European erotica was available even in the colonial period. Benjamin Franklin, for one, maintained a collection, as did Thomas Jefferson. Despite cultural proscriptions, erotica became a flourishing minor industry, and by the time of the Civil War, public outcry and government response against growing amounts of this material resulted in the Comstock Act and other actions aimed at suppressing the growing popularity and publication of "obscene" books.

This is not to say that mainstream American literature was devoid of erotic content, however. Examples as early as the didactic bestsellers *Charlotte Temple* (1794) by Susanna *Rowson and *The Coquette* (1797) by Hannah Webster *Foster were attractive at least in part for portraying the violations of young women—both of their virginity and, more subtly, women's violation of social standards—even though punishment for female sexual dalliance in the novels was inevitable and heavy.

The radical questioning of textual methods and theories that began in the early twentieth century with modernism provided room for newer, more open exploration of eroticism in literature. Gertrude *Stein's prose and poetic works are deeply concerned with expressing the female body through language, particularly in lesbian relations. In *experimental texts such as "Lifting Belly" and *Tender Buttons* (1914), Stein produces a female erotics that does not depend on masculine sexual and textual standards. The poetry of *H. D. (Hilda Doolittle) also transforms the erotic by breaking down traditional cultural assumptions about female sexuality. According to critic Eileen Gregory, the poetry of *Hymen* (1921), for instance, posits a multiple female sensuality that exists apart from male control.

The culture and politics of the modern era also provided an atmosphere open enough for the first large-scale attempts to publish erotic literature. The Obelisk (later Olympia) Press in Paris, as well as the Grove Press and Essex House in America, published erotica and pornography almost exclusively by and for men, although some women, such as Deneen Peckinpah and Mary Sativa, wrote for the houses. When the Supreme Court loosened censorship in the late 1960s, publication of erotica began to increase significantly.

At the same time that publishers in the United States were producing erotica and pornography for a male audience, romantic and erotic novels written almost exclusively by and for women were becoming a major component of the publishing industry, reaching their height in the 1970s and 1980s. Whereas the conventional view of the modern formula *romance is that it reinforces traditional conservative values, newer scholarship, notably by Carol Thurston, suggests that more recent examples of these texts, particularly the overtly erotic bodice rippers, more often challenge than uphold conservatism, presenting heroines whose autonomy and power, sexual and otherwise, are well established before the romantic liaison takes place.

Aside from the somewhat older genre of the romance novel, development of women's erotica in America has mainly occurred within the historical and cultural context of the American women's movement of the 1970s and 1980s. Erica *Jong's *Fear of Flying* (1973) is often seen as a milestone in the female erotic novel. Its bawdy, earthy language and the protagonist's fantasy of guiltless, anonymous, and polygamous sex shocked many reviewers and readers. A partially autobiographical *bildungsroman, *Fear of Flying* portrays heroine Isadora Wing's exploration of female sexuality and Jewishness, inverting and complicating themes of guilt, love, and freedom in male-female relationships. To a certain degree, the novel evolves from the pornographic tradition of Henry Miller; Jong's appropriation of the male language of obscenity is, however, both ironic and aware.

A germinal work in the lesbian erotic novel also appeared in 1973: The energetic, exuberant, and sometimes humorous heroine Molly Bolt in Rita Mae *Brown's *Rubyfruit Jungle* broke through many destructive stereotypes about lesbianism. Quite different from the specular scenes of lesbianism in texts by men, Brown's depiction of lesbianism does not depend on male viewing, but instead relies on a woman's genuine desire for other women based on erotic attraction.

Two collections of women's sexual fantasies, short stories, and other various pieces appeared in 1984: Lonnie Barbach's *Pleasures: Women Write Erotica* and the Kensington Ladies' Erotica Society's *Ladies Home* (later *Own*) *Erotica.* Working within the context of revisionist research on women's sexuality by Shere Hite and others, both attempt to redefine what women find to be erotic, although many readers and critics find *Pleasures* to rely more on the traditional model of male sexual control, which defines male pornography.

The most recent important development in women's erotica is the emphasis on the interrelation of class, race, and ethnicity with sexual and textual issues. The poems in Cherríe *Moraga's *Loving in the War Years: Lo que nunca pasó por sus labios* (1983) express the difficulties of constructing a lesbian Chicana identity within a web of racial, cultural, and class oppressions. Ana *Castillo also explores these issues in her collection of erotic poems *The Invitation* (1979) and epistolary narrative *The Mixquiahuala Letters* (1986). The growing body of erotica by women of color emphatically demonstrates that erotica concerns the social, cultural, and political power to define oneself.

[*See also* Censorship; Pornography.]

• Michael Perkins, *The Secret Record: Modern Erotic Literature* (1976). Gloria Steinem, "Erotica and Pornography: A Clear and Present Difference," in *Take Back the Night: Women on Pornography*, ed. Laura Lederer (1980), pp. 35–39. Catharine R. Stimpson and Ethel Spector Person, eds., *Women: Sex and Sexuality* (1980). Maurice Charney, *Sexual Fiction* (1981). Susan Rubin Suleiman, "(Re)writing the Body: The Politics and Poetics of Female Eroticism," *Poetics Today* 6, nos. 1–2 (1985): 43–65. Peter Michelson, "Women and Pornorotica," *Another Chicago Magazine* 16 (1986): 131–176. Carol Thurston, *The Romance Revolution: Erotic Novels for Women and the Quest for a New Sexual Identity* (1987). Lucienne Frappier-Mazur, "Marginal Canons: Rewriting the Erotic," *Yale French Studies* 75 (1988): 112–128. Peter Wagner, *Eros Revived: Erotica of the Enlightenment in England and America* (1988). Patricia Yaeger, *Honey-Mad Women: Emancipatory Strategies in Women's Writing* (1988).

Anne Marie Carey

ESSENTIALISM. Beginning with Aristotle's challenge to the Platonic doctrine of the immutability of forms, the history of Western philosophy has developed through the successive critique and establishment of different foundational systems, each of which derived its authority from that which it claimed to be essential. Essentialism occupies a central place in feminist discourse because feminism itself is crucially bound up in this conceptual history, even though the object of feminist critique is often the Western philosophical tradition itself. While essentialism is often cited as if it were a unitary doctrine, it actually accounts for at least three major philosophical tendencies: Platonic, Aristotelian, and Cartesian-type essentialisms. According to Plato, essences, or forms, are the universal truths our sensory perceptions can only approximate. All aesthetic and moral judgment consists in estimating the accuracy of the physical world's imitation of "true existence" or "reality"—that is, of imperceptible and eternal essences. Aristotelian essentialism also posits a mimetic relation between appearances and forms, but locates "real essence" in the process by which the physical is manifested or generated by the ideational. Whereas Platonic essentialism is based on the doctrine of the immutability of forms, Aristotelian essentialism takes change to be the fundamental condition of essence, which resides in the principle of internal generation and causality. Our modern understanding of essentialism as a question about the nature of the individual subject emerged with Descartes, and has been elaborated in the philosophical writings of Locke, Kant, Husserl, and Sartre.

Women's relationship to essentialist doctrine of all kinds has always been deeply ambivalent and it is this same deeply ambivalent relation that drives feminist intellectual and political production. Women have had to contend with essentialist philosophy's accounts of women's nature, which, in assigning women such qualities as irrationality, disloyalty, and cunning, pronounce them unfit to enjoy civil and political rights granted on condition of the capacity for responsible citizenship. The strategies women have used to gain political and social power within such prejudicial conditions have followed two primary logics. One has been to challenge the prevailing wisdom by arguing that, indeed, women do possess reason, loyalty, and all other male-identified characteristics, and therefore deserve equal treatment under the law and in society. Another strategy has been to accept but to revalue the features attributed to women: emotionalism, closeness to nature, and so on. These two types of arguments are both central to the history of feminist thought, and have coexisted (sometimes compatibly, sometimes contentiously) at least since

Christine de Pizan launched the *querelle des femmes* at the end of the fourteenth century.

The feminist debate over essentialism today reflects these long-standing political and philosophical concerns, often quite self-consciously. During the 1980s, for example, American feminists, such as philosopher Elizabeth V. Spelman (*Inessential Woman*, 1988) and literary theorist Diana Fuss (*Essentially Speaking*, 1989), have sought to elaborate the philosophical context and credentials of the feminist discourse on essentialism by reference to essentialist thinkers such as Plato, Aristotle, Kant, and Locke. As their contemporary writings make clear, the political stakes of feminist debate on essentialism are not simply reducible to the status of women in male-dominated society, but include such issues as the different status of black and white women and men within a racist economy of gender, and the different status of lesbians, gays, and straights within a heterosexist gender economy. Can lesbians be women? Can straights? If they can, is it because, despite, or regardless of their sexuality? Are some women more women than others? Such questions, which go to the heart of any feminist politics, have been met with a variety of responses, many (though not all) of which rely in some way on an idealist or metaphysical account of identity. While some of these accounts are biological and some are cultural/historical, they share the belief that there is a reality prior to and beyond social identity, a Woman behind every woman. It is this faith that links the feminist projects of Mary *Daly and Elaine Showalter, Barbara Christian and Luce Irigaray, each of whom has at various times been called an essentialist.

In the United States, where the rhetoric of the melting pot and universal rights has always complemented social policies of slavery and segregation, exclusion and extermination, feminist advocacy and opposition to essentialism carry a distinctive historical burden. In a society where ideologies of white womanhood have left black women without a claim to any gender privilege—entitled neither to the power accorded white men nor to the protection afforded white women—it is little wonder that the protestations of black feminist critic Barbara Christian against the deconstruction of identity have been echoed by so many others for whom identity—racial, sexual, or otherwise—has never been a sanctuary anyway. In her essay "The Race for Theory," Christian argues that "the new literary-critical theory of relativity is so prominent" precisely because the writings of black women, for example, have become a more powerful and popular force in literature and culture. In Christian's view, the very concept of identity is under attack by anti-essentialists and other kinds of literary-critical relativists for the very reason that those who had historically been the most injured by its terms are finally gaining access to some of its advantages.

Christian's argument demonstrates the political urgency of philosophical questions of essentialism, and constitutes a uniquely potent defense against antiessentialism. Claiming that one's position is essentialist is something like claiming that one's position is ideological: essentialism is almost by definition the other feminist's error. This is not to suggest that feminists habitually defend themselves against charges of essentialism by denying they are essentialists; more often they do as Barbara Christian did in "The Race for Theory" essay, and redefine their own positions outside and against the entire critical discourse of essentialism and antiessentialism. Many American feminists have identified this discourse with French feminism, which they consider "theoretical"—uniformly and probably deliberately obscurantist and elitist. French feminists and their adherents, it is argued, betray women by privileging "male" philosophy and science over "women's ways of knowing." In the United States, this charge of elitism bears the magnified burden of the history of nonwhite women's exclusion not only from male preserves of power such as philosophy and government, but from the white women's movement and feminist theory as well.

Many of the feminist positions that are considered essentialist are based on appeals to the "authority of experience." Some essentialist feminists understand experience primarily as a cultural or historical category, while others use the term to organize biological or physiological phenomena. But since biology has a history and history contains biological assumptions, the two orientations tend to coalesce. It is their common history that Barbara Smith urges black women writers to recognize and reflect as their unique "experience" in her well-known essay, "Toward a Black Feminist Criticism." Yet the criteria by which readers are to recognize themselves as included or excluded in Smith's account of black women's common history are clearly biological. Similarly, the biological orientation of French philosopher Luce Irigaray's feminism is thoroughly and often explicitly grounded in a history of philosophical writing that employs the gendered body as a metaphor for power and consciousness. The authority of experience is a concept that unites the essentialist projects of theoretical feminists such as Irigaray with the essentialist projects of

antitheoretical feminists such as Smith and Christian.

Feminist antiessentialists believe that identity is not a stable phenomenon, but a historically variable social formation. One of the effects of the identity formation may be precisely that it appears natural or universal; this, antiessentialists argue, is one of the principal contributing factors in the construction and persistence of racism, sexism, and other forms of domination. Women have always been subordinate to men; white people have always governed nonwhite people. Such contingent observations can be and are easily misconstrued as aspects of some natural order; according to antiessentialists, such an interpretation is both misguided and dangerous, regardless of whether the reader supports the status quo or objects to it.

For many feminists, antiessentialism is mainly a matter of favoring social explanations over natural ones. In her account of feminist standpoint epistemologies, for example, Sandra Harding argues that their "social experience" provides women with the necessary "oppositional consciousness" to confront the essentialist beliefs that support their political subordination (*The Science Question in Feminism*, 1986). Harding is an antiessentialist, but like many essentialist feminists, she privileges the category of experience. But where essentialist feminists look to experience for information about and evidence of essential qualities of woman-ness, Harding sees experience as a basis for challenging prevailing (naturalizing) definitions of woman.

Many feminists who object to the idealist philosophy of essentialism are nonetheless reluctant to declare themselves conclusively antiessentialist for fear of the possible political ramifications of such a position. How, they ask, can one make a case for special legal provisions for women (such as protections against domestic violence and affirmative action policies) if one agrees with Lacan that "There is no such thing as Woman"? Some of these feminists have adopted what they consider a compromise position by advocating a "strategic" form of essentialism. Originally proposed by feminist theorist Gayatri Chakravorty *Spivak as a way of relating to the universalizing tendencies of one's own feminist practice, strategic essentialism has become popularized as, in Spivak's words, an "alibi to essentialism"—a pragmatic way to simultaneously occupy both the theoretical and political positions that, although not incommensurable, continue to constitute a central problem for feminist thought on essentialism: how to construct a practical vision of social change for women out of the political and ideological circumstances at hand.

[*See also* Lesbianism.]

• Jonathan Culler, "Reading as a Woman," in *On Deconstruction* (1982), pp. 43–64. Luce Irigaray, *This Sex Which Is Not One*, trans. Catherine Porter with Carolyn Burke (1985). Elaine Showalter, ed., *The New Feminist Criticism: Essays on Women, Literature, and Theory* (1985). Julia Kristeva, "Women's Time," in *The Kristeva Reader*, ed. Toril Moi (1986), pp. 187–213. Barbara Christian, "The Race for Theory," *Cultural Critique* 6 (Spring 1987): 51–63. Michèle Le Doeuff, "Women and Philosophy," in *French Feminist Thought*, ed. Toril Moi (1987), pp. 181–209. Denise Riley, *"Am I That Name?": Feminism and the Category of "Women" in History* (1988). *The Essential Difference: Another Look at Essentialism*, issue title of *Differences* 1, no. 2 (Summer 1989). Gayatri Chakravorty Spivak, *The Post-Colonial Critic: Interviews, Strategies, Dialogues*, ed. Sarah Harasym (1990). Donna J. Haraway, *Simians, Cyborgs, and Women: The Reinvention of Nature* (1991).

Deborah G. Chay

ETHNIC CONSCIOUSNESS MOVEMENT.
* Stereotypes of people of color in the United States that grew out of Euro-American * racism toward and oppression of * African Americans, * Asian Americans, * Chicano/as, * Latino/as, and * Native Americans were naturalized in the discourse surrounding these groups, leading many ethnic and racial minorities to accept social and cultural positions subordinate to those of the dominant culture. The * civil rights movement of the 1960s marked a shift in the extent to which these ethnic minorities accepted Euro-American-defined images and offered a counterdiscourse that moved the idea of ethnic identification from stigma to a basis for group pride and unity. Through ethnic consciousness movements, ethnic minorities sought to unify their members around group-specific sociocultural attributes and, through this unity, attain self-respect both within the group and from those in the dominant population. Through this group solidarity, ethnic and racial groups would challenge past Euro-American economic and political exploitation and other group concerns.

Each ethnic movement used culturally specific ideologies that addressed their experiences as an oppressed group, as well as incorporated successful strategies from the civil rights movement. Consider, for example, Asian-American use of the yellow-and-black-striped bee as a symbol of group pride and alliance with the African-American community, as well as the Chicano/a organization *La Raza*, established in response to the

success of organizations like the Student Nonviolent Coordinating Committee, which promoted group advancement through collective action.

Although the goals of the different ethnic consciousness movements varied according to the needs of each specific group, African-, Asian-, and Native American, Chicano/a and Latino/a movements shared similar goals. Once membership was defined, each movement set out to confront issues salient to the group. Ethnic and racial stereotypes held by the dominant culture were replaced by group-defined, self-affirming and empowering images. Each movement addressed historical conceptualizations of their members' roles in American history and culture, defying the silence surrounding ethnic participation in all aspects of American life and subverting the notion that ethnic and racial minorities served roles subordinate to those of Euro-Americans.

These revisions of ethnic stereotypes and American history fueled the movements, enabling them to address economic, political, and cultural oppression experienced by their members. As collective bodies, these ethnicities addressed local and national concerns regarding inequality, political disenfranchisement, and economic isolation to enact social change.

In every respect, the face of America changed dramatically as a result of each ethnic movement, pointing to the significant influence racial and ethnic minorities had on this country. Yet their struggle was by no means easy. In the early stages of the movements, increased ethnic identification made adherents more visible; they were, therefore, easy targets for those daunted by the growing economic and political strength of these ethnic groups as well as for ethnics who chose * assimilation as a means of acceptance in the dominant culture. Those who perceived a threat to their livelihood, social status, or political position quickly reverted to racial/ethnic stereotyping, isolation, and sometimes violence. Fortunately, overcoming these short-term difficulties usually led to further achievements.

The system of higher * education in the United States was profoundly influenced by the addition of ethnic studies. Departments of African- and Asian-American, Latino/a and Chicano/a literature and studies, not to mention programs of study in Native American literature and culture, continue to strengthen the mosaic that is American culture. Literatures by and about these ethnic groups greatly enhanced the artistic exploration of an American consciousness, questioning Euro-American, male-authored classics on their representations of a homogeneous and monolithic American identity and their depictions of all ethnic groups. The increased participation of ethnic and racial minorities in local, state, and federal governments permanently influenced the ways in which this country conducted its business. Additionally, ethnic agitation in labor movements improved the physical and economic lives of all workers.

Yet in the attempt to forge group solidarity around ethnicity and/or cultural nationalism, adherents ignored or effaced the oppressive features of this ideology. As E. Frances White notes in her article "Africa on My Mind" (1990), to combat racism, leaders of ethnic consciousness movements achieved consensus around an idealized and often homogeneous model of ethnic life. It is in this way that definitions of ethnicity and the subsequent goals of the movements served to collapse intra-ethnic difference.

White further notes that although they were radical in relation to the Euro-American power structure, traditional movements were often conservative with regard to the internal organization of their communities. These movements failed to address issues of *gender and *sexuality, and instead favored issues of racism, for racism was considered the greatest threat to the group. Alma Garcia, in her article "The Development of Chicana Feminist Discourse, 1970–1980" (1989), has shown that the response to issues of gender and sexuality within the movements and as part of their national agendas was threefold: If sexism and heterosexism existed within the movement, they were the result of the dominant and oppressive system; gender and sexuality issues were white people's problems that could potentially undermine the movement's main goal; and women's roles within ethnic movements were within the family, as nurturing wives and mothers, and any other role was inauthentic.

These dynamics, in addition to the increased gender consciousness inspired by the civil rights movement, stimulated ethnic women's *feminism. Women played vital parts in civil rights and ethnic movements, either within or outside of established gender roles, but their experiences as women of color in America were not fully addressed.

Ethnic women were effected by race, gender, sexuality, and *class, each working separately and together to delimit women's full participation in many facets of American life. Traditional ethnic movements failed to recognize these layers and their impact on women and the group as a whole, thereby blocking a potential avenue toward the successful attainment of the movement's goals. However, the layered experiences of American women of color demonstrated that one-dimensional approaches to redress racial and ethnic inequality and define ethnic identity would be ineffective. Women's activism forced members of ethnic groups and the larger society to recognize that binaries that set whites and people of color, or ethnic women and "inauthentic" ethnic women as their endpoints could no longer hold. Relationships between people and the natures of experiences were more complex than binaries allowed. Any approach that attempted to define identity, counter intra- and inter-ethnic perceptions, or combat racism and oppression had to deal with these concerns simultaneously. For example, ethnic women could not claim to be ethnic first and women second; their experiences in this country impacted upon them as women *and* as members of their ethnic/racial groups.

Faced with resistance from members of their ethnic group and struggling against oppression from the dominant group, women of color questioned their former roles within the larger movement and inserted agendas specific to their needs. As E. Frances White notes, they revised former ways of thinking to counter racism and avoid sexist pitfalls. Not only interested in changing women's experiences of oppression, they questioned gender-specific roles and their effects on the group as a whole; when Chicanas' roles were defined as the Virgin Mary and Chicanos' as macho, significant numbers of people who did not fit these roles were excluded, their voices silent. Culture-specific gender roles further circumscribed ethnic women; Alma Garcia has shown that in the beginning of African- and Asian-American women's activism, women rarely organized separately from men. Addressing this subordination was a goal of ethnic women's feminism.

Ethnic women who challenged the ways their cultural movements operated were frequently baited. They were accused of allying themselves with the white power structure/feminists and, therefore, against their ethnic groups. Issues that specifically addressed their concerns were viewed as divisive and a threat to the larger movement; the mere act of voicing their concerns and rejecting traditional women's roles was enough to circumscribe their behavior. Garcia suggests that traditional Chicano cultural nationalists constructed an image of the family as the center of their movement; women who rejected gender-specific roles rejected the family, and, as a result, were false ethnics. Lesbian women of color, their life-styles and politics, were labeled abnormal. The binaries that the mere existence of women of color challenged were reified in the attacks on feminist and lesbian agitation; ethnic women were either with the larger movement or against it, promale or antimale, prowhite or pro-ethnic. Women were further circumscribed by being defined as lesbian—*lesbian* and *feminist* were used interchangeably.

Coming out of larger civil rights movements, cultural nationalism and women of color's feminism sought to counter discourses that physically and mentally delimited the lives and livelihood of group members. Women of color confronted additional problems due to the impact of sexism and heterosexism both within their ethnic movements and in the larger society. However, their fight highlighted the complexity of American relationships and forced people to recognize that difference takes on many forms and requires a multifaceted means of redress.

[*See also* Consciousness-Raising.]

• Elizabeth J. Ordonez, "Narrative Texts by Ethnic Women: Rereading the Past, Reshaping the Future," *Journal of the Society for the Study of the Multi-Ethnic Literature of the United States (MELUS)* 9, no. 3 (1982): 19–28. Miriam J. Wells, "Power Brokers and Ethnicity: The Rise of a Chicano Movement," *Aztlan* 17, no. 1 (1986): 47–77. Richard J. Jensen and Cara J. Abeyta, "The Minority in the Middle: Asian American Dissent in the 1960s and 1970s," *Western Journal of Speech Communication* 51, no. 4 (1987): 402–416. John Gledhill, "Agrarian Social Movements and Forms of Consciousness," *Bulletin of Latin American Research* [Great Britain] 7, no. 2 (1988): 257–276. Alma Garcia, "The Development of Chicana Feminist Discourse, 1970–1980," *Gender and Society* 3, no. 2 (1989): 217–238. E. Frances White, "Africa on My Mind: Gender, Counter Discourse and African-American Nationalism," *Journal of Women's History* 50, no. 2 (1990): 73–97.

Rhonda Denise Frederick

ETHNICITY AND WRITING. While the Greek word *ethnos* originally meant nation or people, its usage in the New Testament and later came to refer to gentile Christians, and subsequently to heathens, people neither Christian nor Jewish. Etymologically, then, ethnicity might be considered as both something that everyone has by virtue of belonging to a specific people or nation, and as a quality particular to some groups that are different from "nonethnic" peo-

ple. Hence, the difficulty of determining the applicability and limitations of the term *ethnic* or *ethnicity* derives from the paradox at the core of the term, by which it is both universal, applicable to everyone, and minoritizing, specifying some as different from others.

Ethnicity has had different meanings and implications in American culture in the twentieth century. In common usage in the 1950s and early 1960s, ethnicity was used as a minoritizing term that referred to the cultural differences of relatively recent European immigrants, as compared to "mainstream" American culture. Ethnically distinct groups were expected to slowly assimilate into the melting pot of American culture. At the same time, American social scientists substituted the term *ethnicity*, in its universal sense, for *race* as a category for investigating and explaining cultural difference. The scientific racisms of the eighteenth and nineteenth centuries (which claimed to prove racial superiority or inferiority as a function of biology), and the genocidal eugenics of the German Nazi regime in the 1930s and 1940s, had amply demonstrated the dangers of equating cultural differences with genetic differences.

The emergence of the "new ethnicity" in the 1960s began not with European immigrants or their descendants, but with African Americans. The revaluation of cultural difference, which accompanied the social reform movements of the civil rights era, directly challenged the ideology of assimilation. Mexican Americans, Asian Americans, and Native Americans quickly followed the lead of African Americans in asserting pride in their different cultural heritages. White ethnic groups—Jews, Italians, Irish, and others of European descent—also joined in the general resurgence of the assertion and positive valuation of cultural difference. The image of America as a cultural melting pot, in which newcomers would slowly assimilate to the dominant culture, gave way to an image of America as a land of cultural pluralism, in which ethnic differences are powerful and enduring.

Ethnic literature is frequently defined as literature written by and about the experiences of an ethnic group in America, written by a member of that ethnic group. This conventional definition presupposes the existence of an essentially unique ethnic experience or perspective, and the unique ability of an "insider" to express or represent that experience. Hence, critical valuation of ethnic literature has been based on its perceived authenticity. The personal consciousness and lived experience of the author authorize a literary representation as "true to life."

This traditional approach assumes that

there is an ethnic essence that can be represented in, and thus garnered from, literary and cultural artifacts. Thus, one might argue that Greek-American ethnicity is characterized by certain beliefs, values, and practices which are specific to that ethnic group and which provide the group with coherence and meaning. One might turn to Mary Vardoulakis's *Gold in the Streets* (1945) or Roxanne Cotsakis's *The Wing and the Thorn* (1952) to appreciate the unique experiences of Greek immigrants and their second- and third-generation descendants.

An ethnic approach to literary studies has been aligned with larger issues surrounding the social and cultural representation of non-Anglo portions of the population. Understanding and tolerance will increase, this position reasons, if members of society learn to value and appreciate difference. Thus, the inclusion of ethnic literature as the representation of cultural difference is intended to increase multicultural awareness. At the same time, however, the focus on identity and authenticity tends to reproduce structures of difference that devalue ethnic literature in relation to American literature, as well as reinforce a tendency to stereotype an ethnic group in terms of some singular ethnic identity.

In response to the critical and political shortcomings of an approach to ethnic literature predicated on a stable or essential ethnic identity, recent critics have suggested that the idea of ethnicity, as well as the constitution of particular ethnic groups, are social constructions determined by specific historical conditions. Language plays a primary role in this construction, and therefore literary texts are a crucial site for discovering the ways in which ethnicity is constructed and how it functions socially.

Some theorists of American ethnicity, especially those who advocate a constructivist approach, increasingly argue that *race ought to be considered as one especially salient component of the larger and fully encompassing category of ethnicity. Ethnicity in this sense thus includes both white ethnicities (Irish-American, French-American) and racially oppressed groups (African-American, Mexican-American).

Opposing the subsumption of race under the category ethnicity are those who argue that although European ethnic groups have suffered at different times and in different ways from prejudice and discrimination, African, Asian, Native, and Mexican Americans have suffered from an oppression different not merely in degree, but in kind. While the discursive structures underlying white ethnicity and third world ethnicity may be the same, the difference in political implications for these two frameworks suggests that it may be too soon to collapse the latter into the former.

Rather than a group-by-group approach, which is concerned with authentic experience and cultural heritage, a discursive or constructivist approach examines changing historical conditions and dynamic interactions. This approach is thus not limited to authors sharing particular identities, or texts bearing particular topical markers. Rather, this approach is attentive to textual constructions of Americanness and otherness: family, community, history, ancestry, inheritance, tradition, culture; in short, this approach presumes that ethnicity is itself a cultural artifact, and that the attribution and maintenance of ethnic difference relies first on the possibility of ethnicity as an abstract idea.

At its most useful, ethnicity, when applied to literary texts or writers, is not a reductive category, but a partial, historically specific characterization that can be both recognized and critically complicated. Transforming the domain of American literature in the academy and in popular culture may require the use of ethnicity as a category for recovering texts and restoring them to their place in American literary history; however, these texts need not be considered therefore as simply or only ethnic. In addition to expanding the boundaries for cultural and literary inquiry, attention to the discursive production of ethnicity or race in a wide range of texts, especially those that have not traditionally been considered ethnic, promises to increase our understanding of the production and circulation of prejudice, racism, and discrimination—issues whose importance extends far beyond the walls of the classroom.

[*See also* Assimilation; European Immigrant Writing; Immigrant Writing; Mixed Ancestry, Writers of; Whiteness.]

• Steven Steinberg, *The Ethnic Myth: Race, Ethnicity, and Class in America* (1981). Mary V. Dearborn, *Pocahontas's Daughters: Gender and Ethnicity in American Culture* (1986). Henry Louis Gates, Jr., ed., *"Race," Writing, and Difference* (1986). Werner Sollors, *Beyond Ethnicity: Consent and Descent in American Culture* (1986). Ronald Takaki, ed., *From Different Shores: Perspectives on Race and Ethnicity in America* (1987). Alan Wald, "Theorizing Cultural Difference: A Critique of the 'Ethnicity School,'" *MELUS* 14, no. 2 (1987): 21–33. Werner Sollors, ed., *The Invention of Ethnicity* (1989). Lawrence J. Oliver, "Deconstruction or Affirmative Action: The Literary-Political Debate over the 'Ethnic Question,'" *American Literary History* 3, no. 4 (1991): 792–808. Thomas J. Ferraro, *Ethnic Passages: Literary Immigrants in Twentieth-Century America* (1993).

Samira Kawash

ETHNOGRAPHERS. *See* Anthropologists.

ETHNOPOETICS. The term *ethnopoetics*, first coined by Jerome Rothenberg in the late 1960s, asks for a definition of the "other" by the "other." Ethnopoetic criticism locates authority for interpretation within the culture that produced the text, rather than in the politically empowered perspective of traditional Anglo-European literary criticism. An alternative to the traditional critical approach is necessary because adherence to certain standards of taste, judgment, and genre have frequently influenced readers to assume superiority vis-à-vis works of ethnic literature, regarding the texts as inferior, quaint, and decidedly outside the Great Books tradition. Ethnopoetics regards the text as culturally centered, thus requiring the application of the methods of both literary criticism and cultural studies; it also permits consideration of a more widely defined group of texts, some of which are oral rather than written, performative rather than static.

Margaret A. Lukens

ETIQUETTE BOOKS AND COLUMNS. Writers of etiquette books in America have had to mediate between an American ideology of democratic egalitarianism and a European tradition rooted in an aristocratic social order. During the colonial period in America, most etiquette books were imported from Europe and stressed knowing one's place in a rank-based order. In the wake of the American Revolution, the call went out for a new American etiquette. Etiquette writers rejected former references to "inferiors" and "superiors" and the idea that the lower classes owe an attitude of deference to their "betters." Use of the word *servant* was avoided and replaced with *help*. American etiquette was redefined as an expression of regard for one's fellow human being. During this time of rapid social change, the production of etiquette books soared, and many American women writers entered the market.

The most popular etiquette books by women in the antebellum period were *Letters to Young Ladies* (1833) by Lydia * Sigourney, *The Young Lady's Friend* (1837) by Eliza Farrar, *Morals of Manners; or, Hints for Our Young People* (1846) by Catherine * Sedgwick, and *Miss Leslie's Behavior Book* (1853) by Eliza Leslie. Sarah J. * Hale reached a large audience as editor of *Godey's Lady's Book*, and eventually distilled her etiquette advice in the book *Manners; or Happy Homes and Good Society All the Year Round* (1867). Catherine * Beecher included discussions of etiquette in her books on domestic economy. These early writers of etiquette books generally upheld the ideal of republican virtue. Eliza Farrar claimed to recognize no distinctions but those founded on character and morals. Catherine Sedgwick urged her readers to forget European nonsense about traditional birthright and the use of silver and pewter spoons according to rank. In America, she asserted, we can all use silver spoons if we wish. While professing the virtues of democracy, these writers were also concerned that many Americans, in their democratic zeal, were mistaking republicanism for rudeness. Early etiquette books were not only concerned with the proper techniques for making introductions, writing letters, conversing, dining, visiting, and shopping; they treated the whole personality and stressed the development of character.

With the increasing prosperity of the middle class after the Civil War, a more complex structure of etiquette emerged, which derived its form from the model provided by the European aristocracy. The two most popular books of the time, *Sensible Etiquette of the Best Society* (1878) by Clara Sophia Jessup Moore (writing under the pseudonym Mrs. H. O. Ward) and *Manners and Social Usage* (1884) by Mary Elizabeth Wilson Sherwood, were addressed primarily to the upwardly mobile middle classes who were either aspiring to become or suddenly found themselves wealthy. This was a time of increased formalism, in which etiquette was viewed as a system of laws that one had to obey in order to be granted entry into the company of the elite. While these authors were caught up in the dazzle of the Gilded Age, there were still a few who continued the republican tradition. One such writer was Florence Marion Howe Hall, a suffragist and daughter of Julia Ward * Howe, who wrote *Social Customs* (1881) and *The Correct Thing in Good Society* (1888). Even more of an egalitarian was Agnes H. Morton, who professed little interest in "society," and wrote her *Etiquette* (1892) for the average person, believing that the teacher, the stenographer, and the bookkeeper belonged in society as much as the banker's daughter. She was one of the first etiquette writers to sanction invitations by telephone (in a 1911 edition of her book).

Mary Frances Armstrong wrote *On Habits and Manners* (1888), a book of etiquette originally written for the students of Hampton Institute and later adapted for a general black readership. While emphasizing good character as the true mark of a lady or a gentleman, Armstrong provides her readers with the information they need to move comfortably into middle America. In addition to advice on such topics as table manners, grooming, underwear, and behavior while traveling, she includes information on buying property, running a farm, and cooking, all aimed towards the cultivation of self-pride and self-sufficiency. Two magazines for black women, *Ringwood's Afro-American Journal of Fashion* and *Ringwood's Home Magazine*, edited by Julia Ringwood in the late 1890s, included etiquette advice for young girls and mothers.

In the early part of the twentieth century, a reaction against what many saw as the wasteful and decadent extravagances of the Gilded Age can be seen in Marion Harland's *Everday Etiquette* (1905). Then, the early 1920s witnessed a revolution in the world of etiquette books. With Prohibition and the advent of the automobile, many were lamenting the decline of manners in the Jazz Age. Sensing a need, publisher Nelson Doubleday hired a young copywriter, Lillian Eichler, to develop an aggressive ad campaign to sell some old copies of Emily Holt's *Encyclopedia of Etiquette* (1901). The campaign was a great success, but people complained that the book was outdated. Eichler decided to write her own updated *Book of Etiquette* (1921), which actually had little new to say. Eichler's success indicated a vacuum in the market, however, which was soon filled by the woman whose name has come to personify etiquette, Emily Post.

At first reluctant to write a book of etiquette (she had considered Mary Sherwood a traitor to her class), Emily Post eventually came to rule a vast etiquette empire. She ran a syndicated column, broadcast a weekly radio program, established the Emily Post Institute, and wrote one of the most comprehensive and authoritative books on etiquette ever published, *Etiquette in Society, in Business, in Politics, and at Home* (1922). Born into wealth and position, Post began her career by defending the old order. She soon adapted to the market, however, and acknowledged the right of every generation to interpret social law for themselves. She had a flair for the dramatic (she was also a novelist) and filled her book with amusing fables built around an extensive cast of characters with names like Mrs. Craven Praise, Mrs. Clinker, the Bobo Gildings, and the Smarthingtons.

The assault on the old order continued with Alice Leone Moats's loosening of the rules on smoking, kissing, slang, and informal parties in *No Nice Girl Swears* (1933). A genre of business etiquette books emerged and taught the new female work force proper behavior for the office and retail shop. The authority of Emily Post remained unchallenged until Amy Vanderbilt's extensive *Etiquette* (1952). Eleanor Roosevelt wrote an etiquette book, *Common Sense Etiquette* (1962), in which she rejected excessive formalism and returned to the moral and democratic tone of early nineteenth-century etiquette books. The idea that proper etiquette could help ease racial tensions is given humorous treatment in *How to Get Along with Black People: A Handbook for White Folks and Some Black Folks Too* by Sheila Rush and Chris Clark (1971). The current reigning authority on etiquette is "Miss Manners," the self-effacing persona of Judith Martin, a popular syndicated columnist and author of *Miss Manners' Guide to Excruciatingly Correct Behavior* (1979) and *Miss Manners' Guide for the Turn-of-the-Millennium* (1982).

[*See also* Advice Books.]

• Dixon Wecter, *The Saga of American Society* (1937). Russell Lynes, *The Domesticated Americans* (1963). Arthur M. Schlesinger, *Learning How to Behave: A Historical Study of American Etiquette Books* (1946; reprint, 1968). Esther B. Aresty, *The Best Behavior* (1970). John F. Kasson, *Rudeness and Civility* (1990).

Nancy Fredricks

EUROPEAN IMMIGRANT WRITING. It is only in the last decade that critics have begun to focus their attention on writing by European immigrants, and European ethnics in general, as literary and cultural texts, rather than as sociological or historical data. Nevertheless, interest in immigrant women's writing has generally been subordinated to interest in writing about immigrant women. The most comprehensive and extensive study to date, Maxine Seller's *Immigrant Women* (1981), collects both first- and third-person accounts of various aspects of immigrant women's lives, including European as well as Asian- and Latin-American women. Similarly, Donna Gabaccia's extensive annotated bibliography, *Immigrant Women in the United States* (1989), includes immigrant women's autobiographical writings, and writings that include images of immigrant women in fiction, but makes no effort to catalogue immigrant women writers in general. Although this work attempts to restore immigrant women to their proper place as important participants in the history of the United States, it effectively replicates the sexist bias of traditional historiography by presenting immigrant women as only the passive objects of representation, rather than as creative producers of and participants in their own cultural world.

In the period that is commonly known as the "great wave of migration," from about 1860 to 1924, the ratio of foreign-born to native-born residents in the United States remained a relatively stable one in seven. While immigrants were coming from Asia, Canada, and Latin America, by far the largest numbers were coming from Europe. The traditional approach to European immigrant history is that the "old migration," before around 1880, was primarily Protestant northwestern Europeans, easily assimilable into American cultural and economic life, while the "new migration" was increasingly Jewish or Catholic, from eastern or southern Europe. While this division corresponds with the data, it neglects other shifts in immigration patterns that may be especially relevant in considering women immigrants' lives, and the possibilities for the emergence of immigrant women's writing. Of special interest is the gender composition of different immigrant groups, and the way it changed over time. For example, although males emigrating from Ireland before 1880 outnumbered females, after 1880 the ratio shifted to a slight female preponderance. On the other hand, male immigrants from southern and eastern Europe outnumbered female immigrants by five to one in the early twentieth century. Settlement patterns also shifted in the late nineteenth century, becoming increasingly urban. For women as well as men, access to educational opportunities, the possibilities for participation in a literary culture, and a concentrated community that could support publication would be much more available in an urban setting than in rural or frontier areas. The socioeconomic status of immigrant groups was also an extremely important determinant for the development of a literary culture. Greek and Portuguese immigrants, arriving in the 1890s and 1900s, were mainly from rural backgrounds and were not likely to be literate. At the other extreme, political refugees from Germany or Russia were often well-educated urban intellectuals eager to produce and participate in literary and cultural life.

Writing by immigrant women has fallen through the cracks between critical histories of American women's writing, which focuses on native-born American women, and immigrant writing, which focuses on writing by men. The experiences and opportunities available to European immigrant women were often different from those of their male counterparts. Fewer jobs were available or open to women, and typically, women's wages were lower. Many women were wives and mothers, adding housework and child care to their responsibilities. If women had access to any educational opportunities at all, they were usually inferior to those available to men. While Americanization programs for men offered training in English literacy and industrial trades, similar programs for women were limited to domestic skills and only as much English as was deemed necessary to run a household.

Recovering writing by first- and second-generation immigrant women is difficult. There has been no consideration of the private writings of these women; *journals, *diaries, and *letters, which are perhaps buried in archives and attics around the country and which may give insight into the literary and creative imagination of immigrant women. Even writing that has been published may be lost to the current generation: immigrant women may have written under Americanized names, or written material that does not seem "ethnic," and therefore have escaped critical attention. Immigrant women also may have contributed poetry, essays, and articles to the ephemeral publications of the popular immigrant and ethnic presses that thrived from 1880 to 1940.

More than three hundred French-language newspapers have been published in the United States since the American Revolution. A systematic survey of the poetry, fiction, and essays that have appeared would undoubtedly uncover contributions by women. The many poems, essays, and works of fiction published in Greek magazines and newspapers, or published privately or by the Greek press, has not been studied systematically. The Polish press of the late nineteenth and early twentieth centuries did not support Polish-American writers, preferring to publish well-known Polish writers. Thus, most first-generation immigrant Polish-American poetry and fiction appeared in ephemeral newspapers and periodicals. The great bulk of Portuguese immigrant writing appeared in Portuguese immigrant newspapers. Although the numbers of immigrants from the Scandinavian countries of Norway, Denmark, and Sweden was small compared to other immigrant groups, Scandinavian immigrants to the United States published a large amount of native-language material in many forms. Because the Scandinavians were a highly literate group, they were well-equipped to contribute to the rapid development of their own immigrant literature. Native-language periodical, book, and newspaper publishing flourished from the 1880s to World War I, when antiforeign hysteria curtailed Scandinavian-language publications.

Many immigrant women published works of poetry, fiction, and autobiography. Some combined community and political activism with their creative efforts. Poet and novelist Mathilde Anneke was an advocate for equal legal rights for women in Germany and in America, and inspired many with her political and creative energies. Klara Hollos and Agota Illés contributed short stories to the Hungarian-language socialist press in the 1930s, focusing on the struggles of working immigrant women. Polish-born Maria Kuncewiczowa (b. 1897) resided in the United States after World War II, and was the founder of the International P.E.N. Club Centre for Writers in Exile in England. Several of her novels have appeared in English translation, as has *The Olive Grove* (1963), written originally in English. Romanian writer Eglantina Daschievici (b. 1903) came to the United States as an exile from the communist regime in 1956. Her nationalist poems and songs, mostly written in Romanian, reflect her political commitments. Rose Pesotta (b. 1896), a Russian Jew who emigrated in 1913, used her eight-year experience as a labor organizer as the basis for her autobiographical *Bread Upon the Waters* (1944). Theresa Serber Malkiel (b. 1874), also a Russian Jew, was active in socialist and labor politics at the turn of the century. Her *Diary of a Shirtwaist Striker* (1910) provides a fictionalized account of the New York shirtwaist-makers' strike.

Anzia *Yezierska is perhaps the best-known immigrant woman writer. A Russian Jewish immigrant, she published two collections of short stories, four novels, and an autobiography. *Bread Givers* (1925) is especially well known. Hungarian Teréz Stibran came to the United States as a young girl to work in a Cleveland factory; her novel *The Streets Are Not Paved with Gold* (1961) traces the struggle of immigrants and their children arriving in America at the turn of the century. Greek-American novelist Roxanne Cotsakis's sole work, *The Wing and the Thorn* (1952), details Greek customs extensively. Nina Fedrova, born in Russia in 1895, moved into China in 1919 and finally to the United States in 1938. *The Children* (1942) continues the story, begun in her first novel, *The Family* (1940), of a White Russian family trying to survive in China during the Japanese invasion of 1937. Both books were translated into Russian. Russian-born Irena Kirk was another postrevolution self-exile. She has received numerous awards for her fiction; *Born with the Dead* (1963) is a novel about the tragedy of self-exile. Edita Morris and Flora Sandström were Swedish-born novelists who published work in English in the 1930s and 1940s. Martha Ostenso was born in Norway and came to the United States at the age of two. Her first novel, *Wild Geese* (1925), is her best known. She published sixteen novels, some of which may have been ghostwritten by her Anglo-Canadian husband. Hungarian-born Kate Seredy (1896–1975) was both an illustrator and a writer. She emigrated alone to the United States in 1922, where she wrote several novels, set in both Hungary and the United States, including *The Good Master* (1935) and *The Singing Tree* (1939).

Several Scandinavian immigrants specialized in short stories. Swedish-born Anna Olsson (1866–1946) came to the United States with her family at the age of three. She wrote humorous short stories in Swedish-American dialect, as well as stories for children that were published in Swedish-language periodicals. Dorthea Dahl,

born in Norway, also came to the United States as a baby. Equally competent in both languages, her first collection of short stories was in Norwegian, and her second in English. She also wrote a novel in Norwegian.

Immigrant women have also written literature for children. Born in Poland in 1927, Maia Wojciechowska is an award-winning writer of children's books in English. Claire Bishop emigrated from France in the 1930s. She opened the first children's library in France, and in the United States was both a story teller and writer of children's books in English. Several Scandinavian-born women published children's books in the 1940s and 1950s: Helen Foster Anderson, Clara Ingram Judson, Erna Oleson Xan, Nina Morgan, and Ellen Turngren.

Many immigrant women writers have been recognized as distinguished poets, both in English and in their native languages. Irish immigrant Mary Blake (1840–1907) was a popular poet in Boston's Irish-Catholic community in the 1880s. She also published accounts of her travels and political pamphlets. Russian-born Marya Zaturenska (b. 1903) fled czarist Russia with her family when she was a child. Her second book of poetry, *Cold Morning Sky*, won the Pulitzer Prize in 1938. Lola Ridge (1873–1941) was born in Ireland, grew up in Australia and New Zealand, and emigrated to the United States in 1907. Her first book of poems, *The Ghetto* (1918), was very well received. Subsequent poetry collections include *Firehead* (1929), considered her masterpiece, and *Dance of Fire* (1935). The first Norwegian woman to earn a doctoral degree, Agnes Mathilde Wergeland emigrated to the United States in 1890 when she could find no employment as an academic in Norway. In addition to her scholarly work, she wrote two volumes of poetry in Norwegian. Also writing in her native language, contemporary poet Anna Frajlich-Zazac is known for the work she has published in Polish-language periodicals in New York and London. Olga *Broumas (b. 1949) immigrated from Greece to continue her university education. Her poems, collected in *Caritas* (1976) and the award-winning *Beginning with O* (1977), fuse lesbian eroticism and a sense of connection with Greek tradition.

Gabaccia provides a comprehensive annotated bibliography of immigrant women's autobiography, the most common form of writing by immigrant women. One Portuguese woman writer of note is Laurinda C. Andrade. Her autobiography, *The Open Door* (1968), recounts her experience of emigrating to America alone in 1917. Mary *Antin, a Russian Jewish immigrant, recounts in *The Promised Land* (1912) the story of her own assimilation. *The Italics Are

Mine, Nina Berberova's 1969 autobiography, recalls life in the Russian intellectual émigré colony in Paris in the 1920s; she emigrated to America after World War II. Autobiographies by other Russian aristocrats who fled the revolution include Princess Catharine Radziwill's *It Really Happened* (1932) and Kyra Govitzina's *Service Entrance: Memoirs of a Park Avenue Cook* (1939). Martha Heywood (1812–1873) immigrated to the United States from Ireland in 1834. Her recently published diary, *Not by Bread Alone: The Journal of Martha Spence Heywood* (1978), recounts her life in a Mormon settlement in Utah territory in the years 1850–1856. Writers such as Swedish-born novelist Thyra Ferré Bjorn and Norwegian Kathryn Forbes used their life experiences to write semiautobiographical fiction. Forbes's *Mama's Bank Account* (1943) won success on stage and screen as *I Remember Mama*.

[*See also* Assimilation; Catholic Writing; Citizenship; Ethnicity and Writing; Immigrant Writing; Irish-American Writing; Italian-American Writing; Jewish-American Writing; Polish-American Writing.]

• Dorothy Skardal, "The Scandinavian Immigrant Writer in America," *Norwegian American Studies* 21 (1962): 14–63. Helen M. Bannan, "Warrior Women: Immigrant Mothers in the Works of Their Daughters," *Women's Studies* 6, no. 2 (1979): 165–177. Lina Mainiero, ed., *American Women Writers*, 4 vols. (1981). Robert J. DiPietro and Edward Ifkovic, eds., *Ethnic Perspectives in American Literature: Selected Essays on the European Contribution* (1983). Werner Sollors, "Immigrants and Other Americans," in *Columbia Literary History of the United States* (1985), pp. 568–588. Thomas J. Ferraro, "Ethnicity and the Marketplace," in *Columbia History of the American Novel* (1991), pp. 380–406.

Samira Kawash

EVANS, Augusta Jane (1835–1909), novelist and journalist. Biographical research on Evans has not been updated since William Perry Fidler's 1951 biography. In it, he says Evans was born in Columbus, Georgia, on 8 May 1835 to Sarah Howard and Matt Evans. The Evanses' fluctuating fortunes took them and their eight children to San Antonio, Texas (1845–1849), and to Mobile, Alabama (1849–1855). A loyal southerner, during the Civil War Evans was active as a nurse, a journalist, and a political influence on the Confederate government. She married Colonel Lorenzo Madison Wilson on 2 December 1868, and moved into his imposing home, Ashland, near Mobile, Alabama, where she lived until his death in 1891.

In all, Evans published an undetermined amount of journalism and nine novels: *Inez: A Tale of the Alamo* (1855); *Beulah* (1859); *Macaria* (1863); *St. Elmo* (1866); *Vashti; or, Until Death Us Do Part* (1869), *Infelice* (1875); *At the Mercy of Tiberius* (1887); *A Speckled Bird* (1902); *Devota* (1907). Immensely popular, most remained in print into the 1950s; *St. Elmo* was also adapted into a moderately successful play (1909) and movie (1914). With the exception of *St. Elmo*, which was reissued in 1992, all her works are currently out of print.

Evans's novels are marked by Byronic love plots, lavishly overdetermined language, and apparent antifeminism. A self-consciously Southern Lady, she created heroines whose innate class and competence, and acquired erudition, win them a public recognition that their ideology of feminine reticence rejects. Interestingly, the contradiction between Evans's heroines' deeds and their words is precisely the arena that has sparked the interest of recent feminist critics, who have retrieved her, noting her plots' appeal for contemporary women. Among these critics, one has suggested that in *Macaria*, a Civil War novel, the Confederacy becomes a metaphor for women's rebellion against restricting social roles. Another has argued that for women readers, the power accrued by the heroine of *St. Elmo* provides an effective counterplot to the novel's antifeminist denouement. Evans's papers are listed variously as at the University of Alabama, the University of Virginia, and the University of California at Los Angeles.

• William Perry Fidler, *Augusta Evans Wilson, 1835–1909: A Biography* (1951). Helen Waite Papashvily, *All the Happy Endings: A Study of the Domestic Novel in America, the Women Who Wrote It, the Women Who Read It, in the Nineteenth Century* (1956). Nina Baym, *Woman's Fiction: A Guide to Novels by and about Women in America, 1820–1870* (1978). Anne Goodwyn Jones, *Tomorrow Is Another Day: The Woman Writer in the South* (1981). Mary Kelley, *Private Woman, Public Stage: Literary Domesticity in Nineteenth-Century America* (1984). Jan Bakker, "Overlooked Progenitors: Independent Women and Southern Renaissance in Augusta Jane Evans Wilson's *Macaria; or Alters of Sacrifice*," *Southern Quarterly* 25, no. 2 (Winter 1987): 131–142. Susan K. Harris, *Nineteenth-Century American Women's Novels: Interpretive Strategies* (1990). Diane Roberts, Introduction to *St. Elmo*, by Augusta Jane Evans (1992).

Susan K. Harris

EVANS, Mari (b. 1923), poet and dramatist. Born in Toledo, Ohio, where she attended the University of Toledo, Evans did technical editing, which she combined with homemaking and the rearing of her two sons, until 1969, when she began teaching creative writing and African-American literature at Purdue University at Indianapolis. Her poem collections, *Where Is All the Music?* and *I Am a Black Woman*, appeared in 1968 and 1970, and as one of the earliest black women writers in the new Renaissance, Evans was a compelling, influential poet. Between 1970 and 1978, she taught at Indiana University, Bloomington, and also wrote, produced, and hosted the weekly television program "The Black Experience," which aired for five years. Evans later taught at Cornell University, Washington University in St. Louis, and the State University of New York, Albany.

Committed to participation in her community, Evans served in a number of capacities in Indianapolis. She was active in YMCA work, a member of the Indiana Corrections Code Commission, chair of the Statewide Committee for Penal Reform, and an adviser in ethnic and minority publishing projects. During the 1970s, she wrote books for children (*J.D.*, 1973; *I Look at Me*, 1974; *Rap Stories*, 1974; *Singing Black*, 1976; and *Jim Flying High*, 1979); during the late 1970s, she wrote the plays *Portrait of a Man* (1979), *The Way They Made Beriani*, the one-woman show *Boochie* (1979), and the choreopoem *River of My Song* (1977). She also wrote musicals—*Glide and Sons* and *Eyes* (1979)—the latter adapted from Zora Neale *Hurston's novel *Their Eyes Were Watching God* (1937)—as well as a children's musical *We're Going to Make a New World*.

In 1981, Evans published *Nightstar*, a collection of new poems; in 1984, she edited and contributed materials to *Black Women Writers, 1950–1980: A Critical Evaluation* (1984). Her most recent book of poems is *A Dark and Splendid Mass* (1991). Throughout her work, she combines an idiomatic language with an organic form that is sometimes playful and even humorous. On the other hand, Evans has long been a critic of modern, patriarchal, Anglo life and power.

Among her awards are grants from the Woodrow Wilson Foundation, the John Hay Whitney Association, the MacDowell Colony, and the Yaddo Writers Colony. She has received the Black Arts Celebration Poetry Award, an NEA fellowship, the Black Liberation Award from Kuumba Theatre Workshop in Chicago, and a prize from the Black Academy of Arts and Letters. She has also been a Copeland Fellow at Amherst College. Her poems have appeared in nearly three hundred textbooks and anthologies, many of them translated into foreign languages.

• Mari Evans, ed., *Black Women Writers, 1950–1980: A Critical Evaluation* (1984), pp. 165–202. Trudier Harris and Thadious Davis, eds., *Dictionary of Literary Biography: Afro-American Poets since 1955* (1985), pp. 117–123.

Linda Wagner-Martin

EXOTICIZATION. In literary terms, exoticization is a process by which a human figure is cast as foreign, not in the concrete sense of belonging to a foreign country or ethnic group, but in the phenomenological and ethical sense of being "other." The other is considered an object of interest and contemplation for the viewing subject, who presumably represents a cultural norm. The hallmark of exoticization in European and American literature is the construction of the other as strange and mysterious—often in some desirable or attractive but nevertheless distanced way—as if she did not exist within a plausible cultural or psychological context.

Probably the earliest and most well known instance of this mode in European-American writing is the representation of the Algonquian woman, Pocahontas, by John Smith in *A True Relation of . . . Virginia* (1608) and *Generall Historie of Virginia, New England and the Summer Isles* (1624). Smith introduces Pocahontas as a "nonpareil," the beautiful and spirited daughter of the emperor Powhatan. Eventually baptized a Christian and married to an Englishman, she travels to England, where for all of the obvious influences of European ideas on her person, her significance is as an emblem of heathen Virginia, whose exotic beauty and fertility are associated with her own. The strangeness that really constitutes Pocahontas's character for Smith always remains in view, and the function of her mystery is to elicit English desire for a wilderness, where some form of self-regeneration—monetary, social, or otherwise—is possible.

Pocahontas's role in Smith's histories is similar to those played by Native women in many narratives of European colonial expansion in what became the United States. Like Pocahontas, the Shoshoni woman Sacagawea becomes an emblem of the wilderness for the Lewis and Clark expedition of 1804–1806. As guide and translator, however, Sacagawea acts and speaks in Lewis's and Clark's journals only for the expedition; her status as its representative is palpable because of the strangeness that her figure bears whenever the explorers refer to her. Sacagawea's liminal quality, as well as her silence, work like Pocahontas's wild beauty to signal mystery and seduce the reader's imagination to believe that the world she stands for is unknown, unspoken for, and thus rich with possibilities for European profit.

Through the nineteenth century, images of exotic women of other cultures appear in Euro-American fiction with various rhetorical functions, although they often carry the symbolic burden of ideas by which narrators and Euro-

American characters are driven (see Leslie Fiedler, *Love and Death in the American Novel*, 1966, and Annette Kolodny, *The Lay of the Land*, 1975). This mechanism of exoticization is not restricted in the history of American literature to white male writings about women of other cultures, although such representations are probably models for literary exoticization practiced by men and women of all ethnic backgrounds in the United States up to the present.

In the middle of the nineteenth century, the often mutually supportive rhetorics of abolitionism, feminism, and sentimentalism resulted in many narratives that illustrated the tragic denials resulting from slavery and the actual exoticization of women, as, for instance, Harriet * Jacob's history of her life in *Incidents in the Life of a Slave Girl* (1861), introduced by the abolitionist and novelist Lydia Marie * Child; Mary Prince's *The History of Mary Prince: A West Indian Slave* (1831); and Harriet Beecher * Stowe's *Uncle Tom's Cabin* (1852), just to list a few. While demonstrating the psychological and cultural contexts of figures susceptible to erotic exploitation and exoticization, these texts nevertheless depend upon the "otherness" of the experiences of slavery, madness, and homelessness for a middle-class reader to achieve a palpable, moving narrative and provoke political action against slavery.

For later Native American women, the history of exoticization has often been a stimulus for revisionary representation. In Maria Chona's autobiography, *Papago Woman* (1936), and in *Mountain Wolf Woman . . . The Autobiography of a Winnebago Indian* (1961), the speakers narrate their lives in terms of their own cultures' images, values, and social codes. Both of these texts, like many other late nineteenth- and early twentieth-century Native American autobiographies, were produced through the transcribing and editing work of European-American anthropologists, in these cases, Nancy Lurie and Ruth Underhill. The contextualizing of Chona's and Mountain Wolf Woman's lives makes them seem understandable and in some ways even analogous to Euro-American lives. But Underhill's and Lurie's disciplinary interests in documenting the beliefs and practices of people understood as different from and unknown by white academic audiences require that they keep the fact of their subjects' cultural distance in view.

In recent American fiction, many efforts have been made to de-exoticize images of women whose cultural sources are not entirely European. Even in their revisionary effects, however, these retorts often reproduce exoticization rather than eliminate it. It can be ar-gued, for instance, that Maxine Hong * Kingston's *The Woman Warrior* (1976) poses substitute figures, like the powerful Ts'ai Yen and Fa Mu Lan, as alternatives to more conventional Chinese female images, which emphasize otherness in shyness and superstition. Toni * Morrison's *Sula* (1974) and *Beloved* (1987) take the production of black female images out of the hands of men and turn them over to women characters who, in order to revise and break those images and to thus take possession of themselves, often produce highly idiosyncratic self-designs whose peculiarities virtually re-exoticize the images. In Louise * Erdrich's *Tracks* (1988) and *Love Medicine* (1984), Fleur Pillager, Marie Lazarre, and other Chippewa women are constructed so that their shamanistic knowledge and mixed cultural identities are made plausible for a general readership; but the maintenance of tradition and its otherness to Euro-American culture is both the works' major narrative problem and a source of allure that establishes the characters' distinctions.

These comments are not to condemn the procedures of Kingston, Morrison, and Erdrich, but to suggest that what they participate in is a contest of exoticizations, rather than a defusing of this complicated mode. To represent someone in or because of cultural and ethnic difference and the interesting stories these conditions create is to almost automatically call up the process and action of exoticization. These writers go a long way to revise the processes of exoticization, so that the figures they represent do have both a cultural and psychological integrity. Their fictions are valuable commentaries on portraits of exoticization, such as those found in the examples of Sacagawea and Pocahontas.

• Bernard DeVoto, ed., *The Journals of Lewis and Clark* (1953). Edward Said, *Orientalism* (1978). Elaine H. Kim, *Asian American Literature: An Introduction to the Writings and Their Social Context* (1982). Kristin Herzog, *Women, Ethnics and Exotics: Images of Power in Mid-Nineteenth-Century American Fiction* (1983). Gretchen Bataille and Kathleen Sands, *American Indian Women: Telling Their Lives* (1984). Peter Hulme, *Colonial Encounters* (1986). Arnold Krupat, *The Voice in the Margin: Native American Literature and the Canon* (1989).

Mary Lawlor

EXPATRIATE WRITERS. Expatriation by women from the United States has largely been a twentieth-century phenomenon, in which a spatial shift often produced a complicated matrix of related social detachments. In choosing geographical and national dislocation, expatriate women from the United States challenged forms of privilege, whether cultural, economic, educational, political, or sexual. The cultural estrangement of a foreign setting, coupled in many cases with an acute sense of linguistic difference, served as the foundation for frequent attempts by women to create lives unrelated to those that had previously dictated their actions. "The dilemma that they had once been children," to paraphrase Descartes, became a primary concern for these expatriated women, for patriarchal structures seemed to resurface at every level of their lives; expatriated women often unwittingly reproduced, in their writing and their lives, the dominant social structures of the United States. Shari Benstock has argued that the experience of women in the United States under the patriarchy of the nineteenth and early twentieth centuries was essentially one of internal expatriation, an interior awareness of difference and separateness (*Women of the Left Bank*, 1986); expatriation from the United States served as both a literalization of this difference, and a project of redefinition and internal integration.

Expatriated women were able to find, in the writing process and the public sphere of publishing, a space in which to articulate the debilitating nature of patriarchy and to examine various alternate modes of self-representation and of life. A number of women were both expatriates and writers, especially during the period between World War I and the Great Depression; the most visible and influential of these were Gertrude * Stein, Edith * Wharton, * H. D. (Hilda Doolittle), Djuna * Barnes, and Kay * Boyle. Beyond being American women writing abroad, this group had little in common; attempts to define an "essential" expatriate women's experience have often relied on highly schematic, singular notions that included only those writers in specific lesbian or modernist communities.

Like many of the expatriate women of this period, Gertrude Stein (1874–1946) combined iconoclasm and conservatism in a highly individual synthesis. While living with her brother Leo in Paris, she published her first major literary work, *Three Lives* (1909), and also produced *The Making of Americans* (written in 1906–1911; published in 1925). In this monumental work, she articulated her desire to overthrow not the concept of America, for she felt herself to be very much an American, but rather the patriarchal order that dominated social life in America. Her expatriation was social rather than political, a response to the puritanical character of American culture. As she later said, "It was not what France gave you but what it did not take away from you that was important." In *Tender Buttons* (1914), Stein con-

structed a form of prose poetry that decentered the syntax associated with patriarchal society (in the "Objects" and "Food" sections), and then obliquely explained this new syntax as a critical, antipatriarchal practice (in "Rooms").

Stein's understanding of rooms as extensions of patriarchy that enclose women within "a climate, a single climate" is quite similar to that expressed by Edith Wharton (1862–1937). Wharton moved to Paris after her divorce in 1912, seeking a cultural setting different from New York's, where she found herself "too intelligent to be fashionable." Wharton's Paris salon, located on the edge of the aristocratic Faubourg St. Germain, was to become a haven for refugees, in a temporal sense, from the nineteenth century in much the same way that Stein's salon was resolutely committed to the zeitgeist of the twentieth century; *The Age of Innocence* (1920) displays Wharton's cultural nostalgia, in both its realism and its apparent idealization of the period of Wharton's childhood.

Expatriates born late in the nineteenth or early in the twentieth century tended to have a different relationship to movements and salons than did the older figures of Stein and Wharton. H. D. joined Ezra Pound in London in 1911 as part of the new * Imagist movement, and maintained relations with it until its disintegration in 1917. Her investment in the movement was primarily personal rather than artistic, and after 1917 she remained aloof from artistic communities. Writing from London, Vienna, Paris, and New York, Kay Boyle (1902–1992) consistently privileged political and international concerns above matters of what might be considered purely individual interest. Her strongest writing, such as "Effigy of War" (1940) and "Winter Night" (1946), emerges from the intersection of international politics and daily life. Boyle's internationalism put her at theoretical odds with expatriate writers who, with Stein, considered themselves primarily "Americans," while at the same time making Boyle a respected figure in the international modernist community.

Djuna Barnes (1892–1982) maintained a steady relationship with Natalie Barney's salon throughout her stay in Paris (1919–1941), but she seems to have remained consistently detached from the world of the salon, both in terms of her life and especially her writing. *Nightwood* (1936), the most famous of Barnes's works, diagrams various modes of internalized difference, figures of social control and domination etched into the lives of those marginalized by patriarchal culture. When her character Dr. O'Connor tells of his experience in a cellar during wartime, of the time when he put his hand on a cow and it seemed to be running on the inside, he articulates the alienation that society can produce in those considered "different": "There are directions and speeds that no one has calculated" inside people as well as cows. Barnes's characters are the complicated result of these internal trajectories. Like these characters, the expatriate experience was often one of "running on the inside," of settling in a foreign environment while still being moved to internal flight by residual experiences and structures of United States culture. The writing of expatriate women often reflected this conflict while attempting to produce a new level of experience that would transcend and eliminate the need for flight.

• Andrew Field, *The Life and Times of Djuna Barnes* (1983). Sandra M. Gilbert and Susan Gubar, *No Man's Land* (1988). Amy Kaplan, *The Social Construction of American Realism* (1988). Mary-Lynn Broe and Angela Ingram, eds., *Women's Writing in Exile* (1989). Mary-Lynn Broe, ed., *Silence and Power* (1991). Suzanne Clark, *Sentimental Modernism* (1991).

Chris Andre

EXPERIMENTAL WRITING. Since the mid-nineteenth century, some women writers in the United States have developed and employed experimental literary techniques, in part as a response to the political, social, and artistic marginalization women often experience. Experimental strategies can be subtle or radical, and they can focus on form, subject matter, or both. Depending on the writer's purposes, experimental techniques may serve to encode and turn a writer's private, often sexual, experiences into socially acceptable literary expression; other experimentalists maximize the political effectiveness of their texts by combining "high" and popular literary forms in ways that appeal to traditionally neglected audiences.

Most women experimentalists share a desire to reshape structures of consciousness by interfering with the way their readers encounter literary language. Recent critical interest in experimental writing has coincided with the introduction of Americans to controversial French theories of "feminine writing." The theories of Hélène Cixous and Julia Kristeva, themselves written in an experimental prose style, have encouraged some critics to view nonlinear or otherwise nontraditional writing as evidence of a desire to "write the body" of woman, to escape phallocentric structures in favor of an essentially "womanly" aesthetic. In their original form, these theories focused on the achievements of such male modernist writers as James Joyce and Jean Genet; their applicability to the historically wider range of experimental writing by women remains questionable.

Emily *Dickinson's massive and consistently innovative body of poetry, which dates to the early 1850s but which began to appear publicly only in the years after her death in 1886, continues to challenge readers. Her first audiences were startled by Dickinson's eccentric punctuation and capitalization, as well as by her unusual prosody, an amalgamation of Protestant hymnbook measures and her own complicated, conceptually demanding rhyming practices. Contemporary readers must confront what critic Alicia Ostriker calls (in *Stealing the Language*, 1986) the subversive "duplicity" of Dickinson's vision: in poems about religion, love, and literary authority, Dickinson creates tension between contradictorily submissive and defiant responses to patriarchal structures.

Pauline *Hopkins, whose novels were published serially in the *Colored American Magazine* between 1901 and 1903, manipulated the often problematic conventions of formula fiction in order to make plain the racist ideologies of the dominant white culture. As Hazel Carby shows in her introduction to the recently collected *Magazine Novels of Pauline Hopkins* (1988), Hopkins uses the technique of direct authorial address in ways that disrupt narrative expectations, and which challenge her readers, in turn, to question the political assumptions behind such conventional narrative resolutions.

For decades, the innovations of expatriate modernists like Gertrude *Stein, *H.D., and Djuna *Barnes were ignored or denigrated by critics and literary historians. Between 1905 and 1912, Stein produced some of the most radically experimental writing in the English language; in *Three Lives* (1909), *The Making of Americans* (written in 1906–1908, published in 1925), and *Tender Buttons* (1914), Stein uses repetition, ruptured grammar, and antirealist notions of characterization to create new literary methods for representing consciousness. Her influence on such male modernists as Ernest Hemingway and F. Scott Fitzgerald is well documented; her importance to modern composers (like John Cage), dramatists, and postmodern poets is less well known. Some theorists of the postmodern argue that Stein's experiments anticipate the deconstructive practices of Jacques Derrida and other poststructuralists.

Djuna Barnes's highly stylized novels *Ryder* (1928) and *Nightwood* (1937) included frank treatments of lesbian life at a time when most discussions of female sexuality were still taboo. H.D.'s poetic experiments with palimpsest, a revisionary layering of mythological and scriptural representations of women, are as significant as her early association with the Imagist movement. H.D.'s narratives, including *Bid Me to Live* (written in 1939, published in 1960) and *HERmione* (published in 1981), are genre-crossing productions that combine elements of fiction, autobiography, and intensely sensual language.

Critic Shari Benstock claims that "for women, the definition of patriarchy already assumes the reality of expatriate *in patria*" ("Expatriate Modernism," in Broe and Ingram, eds., *Women's Writing in Exile*, 1989). Distance from their homeland may have given Stein, Barnes, and H.D.—lesbian or bisexual women in a rigidly heterosexist culture—the social freedom and emotional space they needed in order to carry out their experimental projects. At the same time, their expatriation highlights the feelings of alienation from culture and language that lead women writers in many situations to forge new literary forms.

In recent years, experimentalists have altered traditional genres to accommodate explorations of racial, cultural, and sexual identity. Both African-American dramatist Adrienne * Kennedy and Asian-American fictionist Maxine Hong * Kingston present themselves as radically historicized women who are constructed, in part, by internalized ideologies of racial or cultural inferiority. The protagonist of Kennedy's surreal, sometimes violent *Funnyhouse of a Negro* (1960) calls the idea of unified selfhood a "lie": Kennedy's characters repeat each other's speeches with only minimal changes, a tactic that reinforces the nonmimetic quality of her dramaturgy. Kingston's *The Woman Warrior: Memoirs of a Girlhood among Ghosts* (1976) mixes autobiography with Chinese mythology to produce a two-edged examination of both the misogyny of her traditional culture and the anti-Asian prejudice of her family's adopted home.

Like Adrienne Kennedy, novelist Kathy * Acker rejects the sense-making potential of traditional realism. Acker manipulates concepts of identity and authorship—an early novel, *The Childlike Life of the Black Tarantula* (1973), has "The Black Tarantula" listed as its author—and experiments with plagiarism, sometimes incorporating long passages from Freud or Dickens into her texts. Influenced by writers like William S. Burroughs and Charles Bukowski, Acker has been a literary exponent of the cynical, sometimes pornographic, technologically oriented punk aesthetic that also produced some of the most interesting music of the 1970s and 1980s.

Ntozake * Shange, whose best-known work is a choreopoem called *for colored girls who have considered suicide/when the rainbow is enuf* (1976), employs poetry, drama, music, dance, and narrative; Shange frequently performs in productions of her works. A recent performance piece, *The Love Space Requires* (1991), addresses elements of urban African-American culture in both English and Spanish. Shange asks her audiences to consider the ways that poverty, AIDS, and drug abuse distort the erotic and affectionate ties that lead people to seek and preserve community.

[*See also* Postmodern Writing.]

• Thomas H. Johnson, ed., *The Complete Poems of Emily Dickinson*, 3 vols. (1955). Marianne DeKoven, *A Different Language* (1983). Hélène Cixous and Catherine Clément, *The Newly-born Woman*, trans. Betsy Wing (1986). Rachel Blau DuPlessis, *Writing Beyond the Ending: Narrative Strategies of Twentieth-Century Women Writers* (1985) and *H.D.: The Career of That Struggle* (1986). Shari Benstock, *Women of the Left Bank: Paris, 1900–1940* (1986). Ellen G. Friedman and Miriam Fuchs, eds., *Breaking the Sequence: Women's Experimental Fiction* (1989).

Priscilla A. Perkins

EXPLORATION NARRATIVES. In the history of American literary criticism, exploration narratives traditionally referred to writings by men of European descent who explored the New World frontier from its earliest existence in the woods of New England to its later incarnation in the Far West. These narratives often referred to the land of the New World as both "maternal" and "virgin" territory, invoking a metaphorically feminized landscape. From the first reports sent to Sir Walter Raleigh in 1584, in which the land was described as "a country that hath yet her maidenhead" ("Discovery of Guiana," 1595), to John Smith's 1616 praise of New England as a place whose "treasures have-(ing) yet never been opened, nor her originals wasted, consumed, nor abused" ("A Description of New England") to Thomas Morton's 1632 verse depicting the land as "like a faire virgin, longing to be sped, / and meete her lover in a Nuptial bed" ("New English Canaan . . .), early English male settlers promoted a vision of the land as feminine and pure, which influenced the subsequent history of the emergent United States. In these narratives, the land is subjugated and civilized merely by calling it female.

The conception and construction of America as "virgin land," which, like many other European acts, clearly worked to erase the native inhabitants of the country, was (and is) a powerful mythology inextricably linked with the notion of America as paradise, through which its explorers partake in what R. W. B. Lewis called "the noble but illusory myth of the American as Adam." But this was paradise with a twist; in the narratives, "Eve" rarely figured, and paradise could always be found again. Even as the land became despoiled through civilization and, in the nineteenth century, industrialization, there remained the promise of a new frontier further west, at least for a while.

The figure of a New-World Adam found an early and enduring personification in the exploration tales of Daniel Boone. Boone was first introduced as a literary character in John Filson's 1784 work *The Discovery, Settlement, and Present State of Kentucke*, to which was added *The Adventures of Col. Daniel Boon, One of the First Settlers*. Boone's legendary love of the wilderness and his insistence on facing the dangers of the woods alone became a common theme, recurring most significantly in the work of James Fenimore Cooper. Cooper's backwoodsman, Natty Bumppo, is in many ways the epitome of American literary wilderness explorers, and Cooper's description of the American land both conforms to and continues earlier projections of nature as feminine and virginal. For example, in *The Prairie* (1827) he compares the loss of nature to the construction of the town of Templeton with "some sad spoiler of a virgin's fame."

Inevitably, the metaphorics of a feminized land conditioned the ways in which individuals acted within the physical and figural landscape. The paradoxical image of the land as both mother and maiden made "her" available for metaphorical and actual adoration, incest, conquest, and, of course, rape. Annette Kolodny, in her impressive and ground-breaking works, *The Lay of the Land; Metaphor as Experience and History in American Life and Letters* (1975) and *The Land before Her: Fantasy and Experience of the American Frontiers, 1630–1860* (1984), analyzes the correlations between the ways Americans described and acted toward their new land. Kolodny explores feminizing metaphors as "both personalized and transpersonalized (or culturally shared) expressions of filial homage and erotic desire" (*The Lay of the Land*, 1975) viewing "the landscape [as] the most immediate medium through which we attempt to convert culturally shared dreams into palpable realities" (*The Land before Her*, 1984).

In *The Land before Her*, Kolodny broadens the exploration narrative rubric to include women's writings, in particular white women's promotional writings, domestic fiction of the western frontier, and captivity narratives. Interestingly, these women writers typically use different metaphorics than their male contemporaries. Pioneer women of the eighteenth and nineteenth centuries, writing to encourage their middle-class peers to join their migration westward, often see the land as an actual or potentially cultivated garden, around which a community could live and grow. *Captivity narratives, accounts by white women captured by Native Americans and later released or rescued, offered still different visions of the land. Traveling with their captors, these women were often the first white settlers to see the land through which they journeyed, and their narratives often detail the geographic locations they saw. Their descriptions vary widely, depending on when they were written. The earliest (seventeenth- and early eighteenth-century) captivity narratives often give fearful descriptions of an unrelentingly harsh wilderness. No kind mothers, no fair maidens. Later (late eighteenth- and nineteenth-century) writers are more likely to dispassionately catalogue the various parts of the country that might prove profitable to settle. As Richard Slotkin has convincingly argued in his book *Regeneration through Violence: The Mythology of the American Frontier, 1600–1860* (1973), the earlier Puritan captivity narratives, among other religious and social functions, worked to justify genocidal wars against the Indians under the guise of protecting Puritan communities, especially their women, from marauding savages. The captivity narratives of the later western frontier still implicitly advocate the destruction of the native peoples, but now only for the purpose of acquiring the potentially valuable land surveyed by the captives.

The history of the genre of "exploration narratives" presents several problems. First, analyses either of a largely male tradition, and even those that address female accounts, are still limited to narratives written by those in a position to be published, namely white men and women of the wealthier and educated classes. People of color and all those without the ability to write are categorically excluded. Second, and more fundamental, is the failure to question one of the central premises of the exploration narrative genre itself: that all of these writers were the first to see these allegedly "new" lands. What of the narratives of the peoples who were on the continent long before English was spoken here? Early written Spanish accounts, such as Alvar Núñez Cabeza de Vaca's 1542 *Relacion*, telling of his journey through Florida and the American Southwest, are just now entering the academic canon; Native-American and other silenced narratives, however, have yet to be accounted for by this "literary" classification. Beyond its existence as an artifact of literary history, perhaps the value of the exploration narrative genre lies as much in its ability to self-destruct once we ask "Who is exploring?" and "What does it mean to explore?" For

F

FABULATION, FEMINIST. Even though women enjoy an influential position within the *science fiction (SF) community, it may be suggested that most of them are not writing SF. "Feminist SF" has become a term inadequate and distorting. It is time to redefine feminist SF, to ensure that this literature's subversive potential is not nullified (and shunned by most Anglo-American feminist theorists) because of a generic classification connoting literary inferiority.

This insistence upon a new term for feminist SF writers' work stems from realizing that SF is not feminist; SF is divided into separate women's and men's worlds. Most male SF writers imagine men controlling a universe once dominated by nature; most female SF writers imagine women controlling a world once dominated by men. SF writers of both genders who present new feminist worlds move beyond merely creating woman-oriented versions of a genre that appeals to men, not women.

Women tend not to like male SF writers such as Robert Heinlein and Isaac Asimov—and women fail to associate SF with feminist visions. Coining the correct descriptive term for feminist SF writers' work, then, is pedagogically as well as theoretically compelling. William Sims Bainbridge signals that establishing this new definition is also a pressing civic responsibility:

> Examination of the new activism of women in science fiction will allow us to see how this field of popular fiction may shape and reflect changing conceptions of the roles available to women in the real world. . . . Women authors have made science fiction a medium for analysis of current sex roles and for advocacy of change. . . . Women authors' science fiction has become an important medium for public discussion of the disadvantages of contemporary sex roles and consideration of options for the future. ("Women in Science Fiction," *Sex Roles* 8, 1982)

Since "women authors' science fiction" is a catalyst for social change, feminist literary scholars should surely strive to affect society by introducing these imaginative texts to colleagues, to students, and to the general public.

To coin and define a new, more appropriate term to replace feminist SF, one can look to Robert Scholes, who, twenty years ago, spoke about the lack of terminology to describe a new literary mode. Scholes explains that "much of the trouble comes from inadequate understanding of this new literary mode I have called fabulation. The trouble is aggravated by the absence of terminology in which to discuss it" (*The Fabulators*, 1967). Now that *fabulation* is a recognized term, I call upon it to quell trouble caused by present-day inadequate understanding of a new feminist literary mode. Further, I ask the critical community to accept feminist fabulation as an important contribution to the postmodern literary canon.

What is the appropriate name for feminist SF, for literature's new women's worlds? *Science*, in the sense of technology, should be replaced by a term that has social connotations and focuses upon new sex roles, not new hardware. One such term, Thomas Kuhn's *paradigm shift*, is applicable to women's social roles and to fiction written by feminist SF authors. Feminist SF writers encourage readers to contemplate a paradigm shift regarding human relations. Virginia Allen and Terry Paul, through a discussion of Betty *Friedan, link feminist SF to Kuhn's notion of paradigms. Allen and Paul explain that when

> Betty Friedan defined "the problem that has no name" as sexism, she generated a scientific revolution in Kuhn's terms. The problem had been around long before she named it, and many sensitive and observant feminists had grappled with it. But Friedan did for sexual politics what Galileo had done for cosmology: She brought forward so much anomalous data that they could no longer be ignored. ("Science and Fiction: Ways of Theorizing about Women," in *Erotic Universe: Sexuality and Fantastic Literature*, ed. Donald Palumbo, 1986)

Feminist SF writers approach the fantastic to generate names for "the problem that has no name." They bring forth a great deal of anomalous data about women that can no longer be ignored.

For example, in Ursula *Le Guin's "Daddy's Big Girl" (*Omni*, 9 January 1987), Jewel Ann is a character who becomes anomalous data. Jewel Ann (like the ponderous protagonist of "Jack and the Bean Stalk") is a giant; she cannot fit within patriarchal social space; she cannot enact feminine gender roles, which require women to be small and unobtrusive. She can destroy a particular repressive domestic system, the house that imprisons her and her mother: "If she had stretched and pushed and wanted to, she could have pushed out the back wall of that house, pushed it down like the side of a paper box." Jewel Ann, though, does not want to demolish the house. Instead, she continues to grow in another reality beyond the inhibiting boundaries of patriarchal space and stories. Her situation suggests that reality should be changed to accommodate "giant," expansive women. In the manner of Le Guin, feminist SF writers produce metaparadigmatic literature as they venture outside women's reality and imagine a social revolution directed toward changing patriarchy.

Sheila Finch follows the example set by Le Guin. Her *Infinity's Web* (1985), which moves beyond existing sexist paradigms to envision new horizons for women, is a feminist metaparadigmatic novel. Ann, Finch's protagonist, encounters different versions of herself who inhabit alternative realities. Opportunities to confront these differing identity possibilities enrich Ann's daily life. Finch's novel, which explores women's inner space (instead of the male-controlled domain of outer space) is not science fiction. Rather than emphasizing technology, this novel presents a new feminist behavioral paradigm: women who celebrate their own potential instead of applauding men who send phallic machines into the sky.

Infinity's Web points out that sexist societies are artificial environments constructed by patriarchal language, which defines sexist as normal. The contrived nature of patriarchal reality, the fiction about women's inferiority and necessarily subordinate status, is best confronted by metafiction, which, according to Patricia Waugh, explores "the possible fictionality of the world outside the literary fictional text" (*Metafiction: The Theory and Practice of Self-Conscious Fiction*, 1984). Waugh explains that "literary fiction (worlds constructed entirely of language) becomes a useful model for learning about the construction of 'reality' itself." Feminist SF writers create metafiction, fiction about patriarchal fiction, to unmask the fictionality of patriarchy. When these authors use language to construct nonsexist fictional worlds, they develop useful models for learning about how patriarchy is constructed. Feminist SF metafictionally facilitates an understanding of sexism as a story authored by men's power to make women the protagonists of patriarchal fictions. Feminist metafiction is a relevant artistic form for contemporary feminists who are beginning

to gain awareness of precisely how patriarchal values are constructed and legitimized.

SF writers who create feminist metafiction magnify institutionalized—and therefore difficult to view—examples of sexism. These writers seem to peer into metaphorical microscopes while playing at being scientists—artful practitioners of soft sciences who expand women's psyche and unearth an archaeology of new feminist knowledge. They refresh embattled feminists by using language artistically to create power fantasies and to play (sometimes vengefully) with patriarchy.

Feminist metaparadigmatic fiction and feminist metafiction (terms to replace describing power fantasies written for feminists as feminist SF) are components of a wider literary area: feminist fabulation, an umbrella term for describing overlapping genres. Feminist fabulation includes feminist speculative fiction and feminist mainstream works (which may or may not routinely be categorized as postmodern literature) authored by both women and men.

Here Scholes's "fabulation" is claimed for feminist theory and feminist fiction. Scholes defines fabulation as "fiction that offers us a world clearly and radically discontinuous from the one we know, yet returns to confront that known world in some cognitive way" ("The Roots of Science Fiction," in *Science Fiction: A Collection of Critical Essays*, ed. Mark Rose, 1976). Feminist fabulation is feminist fiction that offers us a world clearly and radically discontinuous from the patriarchal one we know, yet returns to confront that known patriarchal world in some feminist cognitive way. It provides "cognitive estrangement" (Darko Suvin's term) from the patriarchal world by depicting feminist visions that confront the patriarchal world. Feminist fabulation is a specifically feminist corollary to Scholes's definition of structural fabulation. Scholes states that

> in works of structural fabulation the tradition of speculative fiction is modified by an awareness of the nature of the universe as a system of systems, a structure of structures, and the insights of the past century of science are accepted as fictional points of departure. . . . It is a fictional exploration of human situations made perceptible by the implications of recent science. ("The Roots of Science Fiction")

He continues: "Man must learn to live within laws that have given him his being but offer him no purpose and promise him no triumph as a species. Man must make his own values, fitting his hopes and fears to a universe which has allowed him a place in its systematic working, but which cares only for the system itself and not for him. Man must create his future himself." Structural fabulation addresses man's place within the system of the universe; feminist fabulation addresses woman's place within the system of patriarchy.

Or, in terms of Scholes's language, feminist fabulation modifies the tradition of speculative fiction with an awareness that patriarchy is an arbitrary system that constructs fictions of female inferiority as integral aspects of human culture, and the insights of this century's waves of feminism are accepted as fictional points of departure. Feminist fabulation is a fictional exploration of woman's inferior status made perceptible by the implications of recent feminist theory. Woman has been forced to live within patriarchal laws that define her as subhuman, offer her no purpose beyond serving men, and promise her no triumph as a human. Woman must make her own new values, fitting her new objectives to a patriarchal system that gives her a secondary place in its systematic working—and that certainly does not care for her. Woman must create her future herself.

Female feminist fabulators, located outside a literary status system that functions by passing recognition from one male generation to the next, do not shine as brightly as the male structural fabulators Scholes discusses. Many feminist writers (especially feminists who create the literature Doris Lessing calls "space fiction") are shut out of the postmodern literary system's space. It is desired here to reclaim postmodern canonical space for feminists by broadening the definition of postmodern fiction to include the subject matter and structures characterizing contemporary feminist writing.

Feminist fabulation retells and rewrites patriarchal stories, points toward incalculable feminist futures, and thinks the as yet unviable thought of effectively transforming patriarchal society. Reality is made of words; women must nurture their own definitions. Only then will feminist fabulation become empowered reality and patriarchal stories fade as things of the past.

A new openness toward feminist fabulation is probably best exemplified by Doris Lessing. She is not afraid to break through the barrier separating the mainstream from the fantastic, to let go of man's world. Near the conclusion of her *Memoirs of A Survivor* (1975), walls dissolve and possibilities expand:

We were in that place which might present us with anything . . . walls broken, falling, growing again. . . . Beside Emily was Hugo, and lingering after them Gerald. Emily, yes, but quite beyond herself, transmuted, and in another key, and the yellow beast Hugo fitted her new self: a splendid animal, handsome, all kindly dignity and command. . . . Both walked quickly behind that One who went ahead showing them the way out of this collapsed little world into another order of world altogether. . . . They all followed quickly on after the others as the last walls dissolved.

Anglo-American feminist theory might fruitfully shift some emphasis from the age of established patriarchal realism to the place of fabulative feminist potential, a place that might present us with anything. We can allow feminist fabulators to guide us into a completely other order of world. Feminist theorists and feminist fabulators can, together, let go of current reality and penetrate barriers that inhibit creating new reality. As inhabiters of this alternative reality, like Emily's transmuted self, women can move beyond their present selves and become splendid, dignified selves. Feminists can theorize about dissolving walls that imprison women within a sexist reality they—with few exceptions—have not made. Readers, fiction writers, and theorists can begin to construct new feminist paradigms, viable feminist futures. Reinventing the canon coincides with reinventing womanhood. We can claim that feminist fabulative works are important examples of postmodern fiction. The force is with us.

[*See also* Postmodern Writing; Science Fiction.]

• Marleen Barr, *Future Females: A Critical Anthology* (1981). Natalie M. Rosinsky, *Feminist Futures: Contemporary Women's Speculative Fiction* (1984). Thelma J. Shinn, *Worlds Within Women: Myth and Mythmaking in Fantastic Literature by Women* (1986). Marleen Barr, *Alien to Femininity: Speculative Fiction and Feminist Theory* (1987). Marleen Barr and Patrick D. Murphy, eds., "Feminism Faces the Fantastic," *Women's Studies*, Special Issue, 14 (1987). Anne Cranny-Francis, *Feminist Fiction: Feminist Uses of Generic Fiction* (1990). Marleen Barr, *Feminist Fabulation: Space/Postmodern Fiction* (1992). Marleen Barr, *Lost In Space: Feminism/Speculative Fiction/Postmodernism* (1992).

Marleen S. Barr

FAMILY. "I had eight birds hatcht in one nest," begins Anne *Bradstreet—the first British colonist in North America to publish a book of poetry—in her poem "In Reference to Her Children, 23 June 1659." Bradstreet's poems and meditations describe the concerns of the wife and mother of a large colonial family in an early Puritan settlement. If there is a traditional American family, we might find it here, husband-children-wife in one nest, perched on the foundations of the nation and the national literature. However, Bradstreet's extended metaphor of the family in flight resonates with a rich variety of traditions, literatures, and family structures in the United States. The travels of Raven, a trickster figure in the oral tales of many Native American tribes, reveals the broad sense of community included in indigenous conceptions of the family. The passing on of the African-American myth of the Flying Africans at Ibo Landing speaks to another sense of family, in which survival under the violent conditions of slavery depended upon non-kin affiliations.

No one structure has ever uniformly or consistently characterized the organization of family life in the United States, making a sustained and vehement campaign necessary to maintain the fictions of domestic bliss proclaimed by the cult of domesticity in the nineteenth century, and the ideology of the "traditional family" in the twentieth. This campaign solicited the participation of women as readers and writers in ways that other political campaigns did not. These fictions domesticated hostile class, gender, and race relations and naturalized them as the ways of blood kin. Women writing the "traditional family" in the United States have alternately subverted, supported, and put to strategic use received notions of the domestic scene.

If the family, at the beginnings of poetry in the British colonies, had a husband as its head, the first big-selling novels in the newly formed nation, also written by women, figured a more attenuated family that began outside of matrimony and ended at the early grave of mother and child. The seduction plot in Susanna * Rowson's *Charlotte Temple* (1794) and Hannah * Webster's *The Coquette* (1797) showed up the failure of a husband-headed household to guarantee the rights not written for women in the Constitution. The seduction of Rowson's and Webster's heroines forced them into independent (outcast) status without providing them independent means of support. The heroines' deaths soon after childbirth—a fate not demographically uncommon in the early period of the Republic—is not merely mimesis, but an indication of the failure of the nation to incorporate the rights or needs of women as citizens.

The ideal of the family in ascendence in the 1830s and 1840s promised middle-class white women access to more power in the home, a separate sphere of consumption under the newly industrialized economy. No longer an amorphous band of kin and other cohabitants, the family came to mean an isolated unit presided over economically by a father employed outside the home, and spiritually by a mother who took her family's gratification as her only recompense. Ironically, the development of the cult of domesticity paid women writers well,

because they alternatively structured and subverted what would become, with time and much insistence, the "Traditional Family." A burgeoning literature developed to naturalize this ideal. Women's magazines, made widely available by new print and distribution technologies, outlined a role for their readers/consumers as the spiritualizing force of capitalism in poems, stories, essays, and how-to's, such as "Woman as She Should Be" (*Ladies' Wreath*, 1847), "Home and Women" (*The Ladies' Keepsake*, 1851), and "Make Home Beautiful" (*The Ladies' Home*, 1866). "Woman as She Should Be" is the queen of the home, for "there she reigns—mother, daughter, wife, / Strews with fresh flowers the narrow paths of life." Catherine * Beecher, in her *Treatise on Domestic Economy* (1841), extended the housekeeper's reign out into the world, declaring a well-kept house the condition for a well-kept nation.

By the 1860s, the cult of domesticity had settled into common sense and the education of children. Plotting the progress from rambunctious girlhood to * True Womanhood, the domestication of Louisa May * Alcott's energetic heroine at once sanctions and reveals the cost of this transformation for *Little Women* (1868), as Jo learns from her mother Marmee to control her anger, and from her artistic sister Amy to transfer her desire to write to the care of her family. Emily * Dickinson suggests the ambiguous nature of this bargain in her poems beginning "She rose to his requirements / Drop't the playthings of her life" (1863) and "Title Divine—is mine! / The Wife without the Sign" (1862), suggesting that many have assumed the physical confinement of marriage metaphorically in order to create poems rather than children, and avoid the wife's progress, which Dickinson recasts as "Born—Bridalled—Shrouded." The association of the bride with the bridle finds further expression in Elizabeth * Stoddard's work. *The Morgesons* (1862) anticipates *Little Women* in portraying the domestication of Cassandra, a child "possessed" by mischief at the opening of the novel. Stoddard's gothic style makes Cassandra's transformation less sanguine by depicting Cassandra's mother's suffering as neurosis, not patience, and her sister's artistic sacrifice as producing not only children, but a listless, incommunicative state. Shifting focus from housekeeper to domestic, Harriet * Wilson's early novel *Our Nig, or, Sketches from the Life of a Free Black* (1859) exposes the ideology of domesticity as a means for white women to obtain power over black domestic workers. Feigned frailty serves "Nig's" white female employer as an alibi for overworking and severely beating Frado, while other members of the household justify their lackluster intervention on Frado's behalf as a bow to the queen of the home.

Despite limitations, the ideology of domesticity provided a means by which to enter political debates otherwise closed to women. Lydia Maria * Child's novel *Hobomok* (1824) opposed the national policy of removal and extermination of Native Americans with a romance of assimilation in which her Puritan heroine "civilizes" a noble savage through marriage. The condemnation of slavery in Frances E. W. * Harper's poem "The Slave Mother" (1857) rests upon sympathy for the disruption of the domestic ideal with the separation of mother from child. Harriet Beecher * Stowe's wildly popular appeal for abolition in *Uncle Tom's Cabin* (1852) transported this same sentiment from enslaved mother and child to white Little Eva, the epitome of the domestic ideal of woman—not just childlike, but a child; not just sick with sympathy, but dead. In the slave narrative *Incidents in the Life of a Slave Girl* (1861), Harriet * Jacobs adapts the domestic script to justify her escape, with the famous closing line: "Reader, my story ends not in the usual way, in marriage, but in freedom." Freedom in conjunction with marriage sets the scene for the postbellum novel *Iola Leroy, or, Shadows Uplifted* (1892), as Frances Harper here integrates African-Americans into a reconstructed ideal of domesticity in which women as wives and mothers fulfill the triple duty of uplift of family, race, and nation.

By the turn of the century, the politics of the feminist movement licensed a sharper critique of the idealized family. Writers like Charlotte Perkins * Gilman, Kate * Chopin, and Nella * Larsen concluded their heroines' progress through the domestic plot in madness or death. Gilman's autobiographical and allegorical story "The Yellow Wallpaper" (1896) exposes the ideal of wife as invalid as leading to madness attributable to domestic confinement, where the nursery becomes the setting for horror. Kate Chopin's "The Story of an Hour" (1894) also dramatizes confinement as a woman falsely informed of her husband's death drops dead herself when the revelation of his narrow escape cuts short her dreams of a widow's freedom. Gilman's 1915 *Herland* enlarges rather than escapes the domestic sphere in rendering the ideology of motherhood into a kind of sexless socialism in a feminist utopia populated by women who reproduce through parthenogenesis. The adventures of the hapless fin-de-siècle explorers expose sex as a masculine malaise. The "civilization" of the narrator through chaste heterosexual union with a Herland wife demonstrates Gilman's alternative vision. By contrast, Chopin's novel *The Awakening* (1899) uses the device of realism to portray the constraint on sexuality within the ideology of motherhood as suffocating. The sensual Edna Pontellier defies pressures that would make her a "motherwoman," but ultimately neither she nor Chopin can successfully integrate nonprocreative sexuality and creativity into the plot of her life as the novel engulfs Edna and scandal engulfs Chopin's career.

In *Quicksand* (1928), Nella Larsen embeds the dynamics of domestic constraint within those of race as the spirited Helga Crane first rejects teaching and marriage premised on racial uplift through assimilation to the white family ideal in favor of the glamorous life of the Harlem Renaissance. Unable to live with either the assimilated moral traditions of the South or the new, masculine-defined morality of Harlem, Helga hopes for spiritual sanctuary through marriage to a revivalist minister who ultimately smothers her spirit by confining her body to the bearing and care of five children. In Larsen's *Passing* (1929), the figure of Clare Kendry shows up the dependence of women upon their husband's status through her marriage to a white man. Clare moves clandestinely through Harlem circles, dancing on the edge of racial and domestic propriety, until she is pushed out of the plot through a Harlem window.

After World War II, the ideology of domesticity returned as the "Traditional Family," to which women were encouraged to "return" after participating in the paid labor force during the war. Nevertheless, the number of married women working outside the home increased throughout this period and has continued to increase to the present day. As documented in Betty * Friedan's landmark critique *The Feminine Mystique* (1963), the revival of the ideology of domesticity affected mostly educated women of privilege: "Women who had once wanted careers were now making a career out of having babies." One such educated woman and poet, Adrienne * Rich, departs from her personal anguish as a young mother in the 1950s and 1960s who had experienced rage and depression in her separate sphere for an investigation of motherhood "in feminist terms" in her prose study *Of Woman Born: Motherhood as Experience and Institution* (1976). A second feminist movement had intervened in the years between Rich's diary entries detailing her frustration with child rearing and her published meditation on what mothering could become, as advances in contraceptive technology in the 1960s, the legalization of abortion in 1973, and the beginning of the gay rights movement promised greater control of reproduction and suggested new paradigms for sexuality.

Public policy and the discourse of sociology ran counter to the demographic development of U.S. families, inventing a second, supposedly traditional family structure in the United States. The "Black Matriarchy" served as a foil to the standard of white "Traditional Family"—a foil described as "dysfunctional" or "pathological." Where the cult of domesticity proclaimed the purity of women, the myth of the "Black Matriarchy" portrayed women as promiscuous and unfit mothers. Much of the literature of black women writers in the late twentieth century has had to negotiate between this racist pathologizing of the woman-headed household and a reactionary idealization of the black family headed by men. The controversy surrounding such writers as Ntozake * Shange, Toni * Morrison, Alice * Walker, and Gloria * Naylor has centered on an alleged betrayal of black men that ultimately seeks to contain black women's writings within the parameters of an assimilated ideology of the traditional white heterosexual family. In a novel written in 1946, Ann * Petry enacts the breakdown of the domestic script in the tale of the attempted seduction of an abandoned wife and mother. Racism and economic desperation force Lutie Johnson out of the "confinement" of the home into *The Street*, where she loses her nine-year-old son to the machinations of a lustful landlord and an insensitive city government. Significantly, this critique of the domestic ideal does not end in the heroine's death or madness, but in her murder of the pimp who would seduce and trap her into a life of prostitution with white men. Gloria Naylor's *The Women of Brewster Place* (1982) and Toni Morrison's *Sula* (1973) and *Song of Solomon* (1977) all protray strong households headed by multiple women in which the generations of care black women take for each other cannot be characterized as mere deviations from a white norm.

The Canadian author Margaret Atwood has most chillingly plotted out the implications of the ascendance of the "Traditional Family" in the near future of the United States in her feminist dystopia *The Handmaid's Tale* (1985). Force makes the "Traditional Family" fact, not only ideology, with the exploitation of domestic workers exposed by Harriet Wilson and the separation of mother from child in Harper's "The Slave Mother" here figured into a political structure dependent upon rigid social roles and forced reproductive labor. Marilynne * Robinson's anticult of domesticity, *Housekeeping* (1981), portrays nostalgia for the "Traditional Family" as a yearning that cannot be satisfied, and the attempt to impose that nostalgia as norm the catalyst in a continuous process of loss, which narrator Ruth and her Aunt Sylvie can only escape by burning down their house.

Just as no family structure can actually claim to be traditionally American, the family unit, father-mother-children, can also be the site of the articulation of difference from U.S. cultural norms. Maxine Hong * Kingston's fictionalized autobiographies *The Woman Warrior* (1975) and *Chinamen* (1977) recount the conjunction and conflict of Chinese traditions with U.S. customs as the mixed strength and torment bequeathed her by her mother and her father. Katherine Dunn's *Geek Love* (1983) forges the family as difference, as a family of circus freaks valorizes divergence from the norm until the bid for power of would-be patriarch and cult leader Arturo threatens to cut future deviations into the debilitating pattern of his own limbless norm. Cherríe * Moraga's *Loving in the War Years: Lo Que Nunca Pasó por Sus Labios* (1983) intimately explores the imbrication of sexuality and identity within the home, as she assesses the place of the home provided her by her Chicana mother and Anglo father in her adult life as a gay woman of color. The vignettes in Sandra * Cisneros's *The House on Mango Street* (1984) comprise a loving chronicle of narrator Esperanza's girlhood neighborhood. Inspired by her father's tears, mother's songs, and her neighbor's struggles and triumphs, this chronicle places the family as unit of parents and children (house) within the context of the community (street). The "Traditional Family" can speak many traditions.

[*See also* Fathers; Grandmothers; Kinship; Marriage; Mothers and Daughters; Spinsterhood; Widowhood.].

• Leslie A. Fiedler, *Love and Death in the American Novel*, rev. ed. (1966). Cathy N. Davidson, *Revolution and the Word: The Rise of the Novel in America* (1986). Deborah E. MacDowell, "Reading Family Matters," and Claudia Tate, "Allegories of Black Female Desire; or, Rereading Nineteenth-Century Sentimental Narratives of Black Female Authority," in *Changing Our Own Words: Essays on Criticism, Theory, and Writing by Black Women*, ed. Cheryl A. Wall (1989), pp. 75–127. Ramón Saldívar, *Chicano Narrative: The Dialectics of Difference* (1990).

Celeste Fraser Delgado

FASHION. If a woman's clothing and use of cosmetics reflect the ideals of mainstream culture, her appearance affords her an easier entry into marriage and/or the male-dominated workplace. She may don society's costume as necessary camouflage. Consequently, a woman's regard for accoutrements rarely constitutes a litmus test for character, and women writers usually avoid an either/or attitude toward fashion, acknowledging its double-edged effect on women's lives.

Reflecting the values of their Puritan society, early writers characterize the wearer of finery—as is clear in Mary *Rowlandson's *The Narrative of the Captivity and Restoration of Mrs. Mary White Rowlandson* (1682) and in Sarah Kemble *Knight's journal (1825)—as barbarian or frivolous. Yet early authors also acknowledge their ambivalence toward dress: in *Desultory Thoughts upon the Utility of Encouraging a Degree of Self-complacency, Especially in FEMALE BOSOMS* (1784), Judith Sargent *Murray instructs her daughter to "adorn" her mind rather than her body in order to engender "worthy respect," but she adds, "it behooves us to render ourselves as pleasing as possible" through awareness of fashion.

Certainly, Ellen Montgomery of Susan *Warner's *The Wide, Wide World* (1851) learns that a dowdy bonnet can inspire contempt. While Louisa May *Alcott in *Little Women* (1868) provides Jo with a special "scribbling suit," effectively liberating her from "female" roles, she also depicts Meg's thwarted attempts at fashion sympathetically. In her short story "A Pair of Silk Stockings" (1896), Kate *Chopin treats Mrs. Summers's shopping spree empathetically, illuminating her "sense of belonging to the well-dressed multitude." In "The Gala Dress" (1891), Mary E. Wilkins *Freeman illustrates the inevitable connection between economics, class, jealousy, and fashion within women's friendships. The Babcock sisters share one black silk dress, on which they alternate removable, signature trims to prevent its recognition and the public confirmation of their suspected poverty. Charlotte Perkins *Gilman's utopian *Herland* (1915) emphasizes that love of finery is learned behavior. The women of Herland wear cropped hair and sexless costumes, but the male interlopers choose "highly decorated" clothing for their own attire.

Mirroring the real world, writers have situated characters in fashion-related jobs ranging from the factory to the design studio. Rebecca Harding *Davis's *Margaret Howth* (1862) and Elizabeth Stuart *Phelps's *The Silent Partner* (1871) detail the unhealthy, pinched lives of women textile workers. Alcott's novel *Work* (1873) depicts the tedium of life as a seamstress: Christie resolves not to sew "till every thing else failed." Willa *Cather, however, created characters whose fashion skills provide rewarding lives. Lena Lingard, the most ragged of the immigrant Black Hawk "hired girls" in Cather's *My Ántonia* (1918), parlays her sewing skills into a successful San Francisco career as dress designer. Having sewn for the St. Peter family for many years, Augusta of Cather's *The Professor's House* (1925) shares the professor's office as her sewing room—symbolically connecting her sewing and his writing as creative acts. Significantly, it is Augusta's practicality that helps Professor St. Peter survive his self-doubt.

Being fashionable motivates many of Edith *Wharton's heroines; her narratives critique the speciousness of society, but suggest that women who ignore fashion are either naive or foolish. Having grown up in a fashionable milieu and having written about interior design (*The Decoration of Houses*, 1897), Wharton knew the vagaries of style. She contrasts the cultivated with the popular to define class and character. Her narrator's tone suggests that Lily Bart's understated taste (*The House of Mirth*, 1905)—that of the "perfect lady," to use Elaine Showalter's term—is superior to Undine Spragg's voracious appetite for show (*The Custom of the Country*, 1913). Yet Lily's taste does not insure her success at millinery; her suicide is a wry comment on the future of understated elegance. The acquisitive, ostentatious Undine survives. In *The Age of Innocence* (1920), Madame Olenska's style—a self-proclaimed "fashion of one's own," lived with elegant simplicity in an "unfashionable quarter"—defies Old New York's standards and leads to her banishment.

As their literature suggests, immigrant women see fashion as both salvation and bane. In *The Promised Land* (1912), Mary *Antin says an immigrant must wear "real American machine-made garments" or be taunted. In her fictionalized autobiography *Red Ribbon on a White Horse* (1950), Anzia *Yezierska works in a sweatshop, sewing buttons on clothes that she cannot afford. She marks her eventual ability to dress "like the American-born" as a turning point; it frees her to develop a literary voice.

For immigrants and first-generation women of color, depicting the relationship between a woman's self-esteem and fashion is decidedly more complicated. The heroines of Maxine Hong *Kingston's (*Woman Warrior*, 1976), Amy *Tan's (*The Joy Luck Club*, 1988), and Gish Jen's (*Typical American*, 1991) all detail the necessity of adopting American fashion. There can, however, be compensations: Jen's character Theresa has less difficulty finding attire for her 5'7" frame and proportionately-sized feet than she did in China. In Helena *Viramontes's short story "Miss Clairol" (1991), Arlene's daughter Champ clips photographs of honey-haired Miss Breck models, while Arlene applies hair dye, eyeliner, "Ripe Plum nail enamel," and "chalky beige lipstick" so she can spin "herself into Miss Clairol, only stopping when it is time to return to the sewing factory." The narrator of Pat Mora's poem "Sonrisas" (1986) contrasts a room of "beige" business women with a room of "señoras in faded dresses" to illustrate the dilemma of the woman who inhabits the cultural "doorway" between.

The culture-bound aspects of fashion are no less disconcerting for American Indians. Gertrude Bonnin (* Zitkala-Sa) finds the dress code of the white boarding school she attends confusing. In her culture, "short hair was worn by mourners, and shingled hair by cowards"; she feels immodest in tight-fitting clothing, but without it she must miss social gatherings among the Americanized teenagers of her tribe (*The School Days of an Indian Girl*, 1900). Louise * Erdrich's *Love Medicine* (1984) echoes this incident in its portrayal of Marie's childhood.

Perhaps fashion gets its most complex treatment by African-American women; they certainly capture its simultaneous tyranny and beauty. As M. Teresa Tavormina points out, making fashion is part of an African tradition in which "arts of needle, thread, loom, and cloth are more than mere crafts . . . as the makers of medieval tapestries knew." African-American literature often features female fashion artists. Jessie * Fauset's *The Chinaberry Tree* (1931) and *Comedy: American Style* (1933) contain positive female characters who become successful fashion designers; in *Comedy*, Fauset juxtaposes Teresa's need for high fashion and a rich husband (and her subsequent "fall") with Phebe's rise as fashion designer. Alice * Walker's Celie in *The Color Purple* (1982) gains economic and artistic freedom through her business, "Folkspants Unlimited," creating clothing which, as Mary Jane Lupton stresses, can be worn by either sex. In her play *for colored girls who have considered suicide/when the rainbow is enuf* (1975), Ntozake * Shange celebrates the variety of black women's clothing and hair design, as does Terry * McMillan in *Waiting to Exhale* (1992).

Following the 1960s black-is-beautiful movement, fashion was often seen as political. Alice * Childress's play "Wine in the Wilderness" (1969) argues against such easy distinctions: "If my hair is straight, or if it's natural, or if I wear a wig, or take it off, . . . that's all right; because wigs, shoes, hats, bags are just . . . accessories." In her story "Everyday Use" (1971), Walker satirizes Dee's (Wangeroo's) attempt to secure family heirlooms for their fashion value and her ready adoption of Muslim styles solely because they are fashionable; and Toni Cade * Bambara's story "My Man Bovanne" (1972) ridicules the younger generations' overemphasis on fashion as political statement.

The African-American writer also presents fashion as detrimental to self-esteem—especially when it rests upon white standards. It can induce the shame expressed by Helga Crane in Nella * Larsen's *Quicksand* (1929) that "evidently there were parts of her she couldn't be proud of," or it can leave one yearning, as the heroine of Andrea * Lee's *Sarah Phillips* (1984) does, to fit in with the "gold-bangled popular girls, shimmering in their Fair Isle sweaters."

Toni * Morrison's novels explore these effects with great sensitivity. Pauline Breedlove's marriage begins to flounder after she undertakes her "white" fashion quest to gain other women's admiration (*The Bluest Eye*, 1970); when Sula returns to her hometown dressed "as close to a movie star as anyone would ever see," she alienates the community (*Sula*, 1974); Hagar's shopping binge for cosmetics and clothing, which her mother financed by selling her diamond, leads to death rather than the anticipated "beauty that would dazzle" Milkman (*Song of Soloman*, 1977); Jadine, a "high yallow" model whose clothing and makeup emphasize her whiteness, feels "lonely and inauthentic" compared to the African woman in African dress with "too much hip, too much bust" (*Tar Baby*, 1981); Sethe scavages to create her wedding dress, concocting it from pillowcases, a dresser scarf, an old sash, and mosquito netting (*Beloved*, 1988); Dorcas "knows that a badly dressed body is nobody at all" (*Jazz*, 1992). As Morrison particularizes African-American women's need for visible symbols of acceptance and empowerment, she condemns society's reification of the fashionable as "white" through its magazines and movies.

Because fashion magazines provide a major outlet for publishing women's writing, that market has undoubtedly influenced what authors can safely incorporate into their texts. While popular novelists such as Judith Krantz and Danielle Steel subvert regalia from its initial use by Puritan writers, it continues to be used negatively, as it is in Lorine Niedecker's poetry and fiction, prompting Reginald Abbott to argue that she attacks fashionable women merely to demonstrate her own moral superiority. Feminist scholars such as Naomi Wolf and Susan Faludi argue, however, that fashion constitutes a key ingredient in male domination and is antithetical to feminism, and Sandra Lee Bartky calls for "a revolutionary aesthetic" that would ridicule and eliminate the "fashion-beauty complex." But the writers of women's literature rarely vilify or glorify their characters for attention to dress. Instead, they strive to capture women's conflicted relationships with fashion.

[*See also* Beauty.]

• Quentin Bell, *On Human Finery* (1976). Anne Hollander, *Seeing Through Clothes* (1978). Allison Lurie, *The Language of Clothes* (1981). Roland Barthes, the *Fashion System* (1983). M. Teresa Tavormina, "Dressing the Spirit: Clothworking and Language in *The Color Purple*," *Journal of Narrative Technique* 16, no. 3 (Fall 1986): 220–230. Mary Jane Lupton, "Clothes and Closure in Three Novels by Black Women," *Black American Literature Forum* 20 (Winter 1986): 409–421. Reginald Abbot, "All Fashions Feud," *Sagetrieb* 8 (Spring–Fall 1989): 149–174. Sandra Lee Bartky, *Femininity and Domination* (1990). Susan Faludi, *Backlash* (1991). Elaine Showalter, *Sister's Choice* (1991). Naomi Wolf, *The Beauty Myth* (1991).

Marilyn Elkins

FASHION MAGAZINES. *See* Beauty; Fashion; Magazines, Women's.

FATHERS. When Europeans emigrated to the North American continent, they brought with them an image of a Judeo-Christian God who was creator and lawgiver—above all, masculine authority, the Father. For women writers in the United States, especially those of European ancestry, the figure of the father has been deeply problematical. Manifest as God, the Father provides the underpinning of a belief system that subjugates women to men and socializes women to silence their tongues and abjure their pens. As Sandra Gilbert and Susan Gubar have observed, in a culture that predicates * authorship upon male sexuality and power, the female writer finds herself in a weakened, if not impossible, state. In order to write, she must oppose or somehow circumvent the Father (often a literal as well as metaphysical one); in the face of his absence, she may inscribe her voice through exercise of will and imagination.

Anne * Bradstreet illustrates the constraining presence of the father in Puritan society in poetry expressing humility before God the Father, indebtedness for her literary gifts to her biological father ("To Her Father with Some Verses"), and wry disclaimers ("The Author to Her Book") in which she images the poet as a mother of "feeble brain" and the book of poems as fatherless.

By contrast with the Judeo-Christian tradition, many Native-American explanations of creation posit an Earth Mother and Sun Father who jointly and reciprocally created the inhabitants of earth. These origin myths do not include accounts comparable to "original sin" or "Eve's betrayal," and one does not find in the writings of Native Americans such equivocal portraits of fathers and daughters as one finds in the European tradition.

Despite the dominance of the image of the patriarch in the Euro-American colonies, and its continuing prevalence later, many cultural conditions in the growing and changing United States worked to modify assumptions about the superiority of the father (man) and the inferiority of the mother (woman). For example, the value placed in individualism and democratic institutions mitigated the aggrandizement of human fathers' prerogatives. Trust in the "inner light" for religious instruction had, since Anne * Hutchinson's time, moderated the influence of Protestant male preachers, especially in the Northeast. And slave-owning fathers in the South, who professed belief in Christian family values, were portrayed as hypocrites by writers like Harriet * Jacobs, who had been a slave herself, or Harriet Beecher * Stowe in *Uncle Tom's Cabin* (1852). In these books, powerful fathers are absent, ineffectual, aloof, or abusive, and benevolent fathers, such as Augustine St. Clare in *Uncle Tom's Cabin*, are converted to goodness by angelic daughters like Eva.

Nineteenth-century novelists Caroline Lee Hentz, Susan * Warner, E.D.E.N. * Southworth, Augusta Evans Wilson, and Louisa May * Alcott similarly created stories in which heroines typically have little for which to thank fathers. Their struggles, albeit arduous and painful, are accomplished largely because they do not have fathers—or husbands—to rely on, having been left by men who die or go to war, the legislature, or "out West." Irreligious fathers saved by Christian daughters continue as an occasional motif: Martha Finley's protagonist in *Elsie Dinsmore* (1867) faints at the piano rather than obey her father's command to play on a Sunday. Among supportive fathers, some notable ones are surrogates, such as Stowe's Uncle Tom, and Sarah Orne * Jewett's Dr. Leslie of *A Country Doctor* (1884).

The most compelling nineteenth-century interrogation of the father figure is Emily * Dickinson's, in poems in which she images God as a human father who is not only powerful, but cruel: "Burglar! Banker—Father!" in "I never lost as much but twice," and in " 'Heavenly Father'—take to thee," a creator of "supreme inequity" must answer to "Duplicity." Among twentieth-century poets, one finds comparable intensity in Sylvia * Plath's "Daddy" and in Adrienne * Rich's poetry, with their portraits of oppressive human fathers.

In fiction of the twentieth century, one continues to find a line of weak, failed, or absent fathers. Since most women writers have observed fathers chiefly in the context of the family—women's sphere—it is not surprising to find they portray fathers in secondary roles. For example, in novels of the rural South, Ellen * Glasgow (*Barren Ground*, 1925), Elizabeth Maddox * Roberts (*The Time of Man*, 1926), and Harriette * Arnow (*The Dollmaker*, 1954) show fathers who are outmatched by nature's forces and the willfulness of strong wives. In *O Pioneers!* (1913) and *My Ántonia* (1918), Willa *Cather portrays struggling immigrants whose daughters are more competent and hopeful than their fathers. Ellen Glasgow (*The Sheltered Life*, 1932) and Katherine Anne *Porter in the Miranda stories depict fathers and grandfathers who are evasive, absent, or both, and Edith *Wharton's Newland Archer in *The Age of Innocence* (1920) seems less a responsible father than a victim of genteel respectability. Tillie *Olsen's Jim Holbrook of *Yonnondio: From the Thirties* (1974) is harsh, even brutal, toward his family, but in this account of a destitute family of the Great Depression, the blame falls upon a merciless economic machinery. Social forces that similarly pervert contemporary lives and blight fathers' relations with children are widely depicted by Joyce Carol *Oates.

The African-American fathers of Zora Neale *Hurston (*Dust Tracks on a Road*, 1942) and Paule *Marshall (*Brown Girl, Brownstones*, 1959) bequeath their daughters their adventurousness, but it is mothers and grandmothers who are their mentors. The abusiveness of fathers and stepfathers described by Maya *Angelou, Toni *Morrison, Ntozake *Shange, and Alice *Walker show that the father's presence may be dangerously, even murderously threatening, although this figure of the African-American father is significantly ameliorated in Morrison's *Beloved* (1987). The Asian fathers explored by Maxine Hong *Kingston in *China Men* (1980) emerge as fierce mysteries, oppressive in their silence, rage, and unarticulated power.

Of course, portrayals of nurturing, significant fathers do exist. Harper *Lee's Atticus Finch (*To Kill a Mockingbird*, 1961) and Marjorie K. *Rawlings's Penny Baxter (*The Yearling*, 1938) are widely known, especially by young people. There are also compelling, largely sympathetic portrayals of complex relationships between adult daughters and aging fathers in such works as Caroline *Gordon's *Aleck Maury, Sportsman* (1934), Eudora *Welty's *The Optimist's Daughter* (1972), Grace *Paley's "A Conversation with My Father" (1974), and Beverly Lowry's *Daddy's Girl* (1981). But to regard the whole spectrum of fathers in works by American women writers, one must conclude that many writers created the psychological space to compose lives in books by withholding textual space from fathers.

[*See also* Motherhood; Mothers and Daughters.]

• Harriet A. Jacobs, *Incidents in the Life of a Slave Girl* (1861; reprint, 1987). Louisa May Alcott, *Little Women* (1869). Joyce Carol Oates, *Marriages and Infidelities* (1972). Sandra M. Gilbert and Susan Gubar, *The Mad-woman in the Attic* (1979). Ursula Owen, ed., *Fathers: Reflections by Daughters* (1983). Mary Kelley, *Private Woman, Public Stage* (1984). Wendy Martin, *American Triptych: Anne Bradstreet, Emily Dickinson, Adrienne Rich* (1984). Adrienne Rich, *The Fact of a Doorframe; Poems Selected and New, 1950–84* (1984). John Demos, *Past, Present, and Personal: The Family and the Life Course in American History* (1986). Jane Miller, ed., *Women Writing about Men* (1986).

Peggy Whitman Prenshaw

FAUSET, Jessie Redmon (1882–1961), author, critic, editor, and teacher, is considered one of three major figures who "midwifed" the Harlem Renaissance into being. Aside from writing four novels and several poems, short stories, and essays, Fauset was an editor for the *Crisis* during the peak of the Renaissance.

Fauset was born near Philadelphia, the daughter of an African Methodist Episcopal minister. After graduating with honors from the Philadelphia High School for Girls in 1900, she applied to Bryn Mawr College, but her application was denied; however, arrangements were made for her to receive a scholarship to Cornell University. In 1905, she became the first black woman to graduate from Cornell. She also received an M.A. from the University of Pennsylvania, and studied at the Sorbonne.

After teaching high school French for many years, Fauset became the literary editor of the *Crisis*, the journal of the National Association for the Advancement of Colored People. At *Crisis* from 1919 to 1927, Fauset discovered and encouraged several young African-American authors. In 1920 and 1921, she edited and contributed to the *Brownie's Book*, a children's magazine. She also published several poems, short stories, and essays, including two articles on her experiences at the Second Pan-African Congress in 1921.

Fauset is best known for her four novels: *There Is Confusion* (1924); *Plum Bun* (1929); *The Chinaberry Tree: A Novel of American Life* (1931); and *Comedy, American Style* (1933). These novels, conventional in form and style, treat with subtlety and complexity the problems of black middle-class women.

There Is Confusion examines the lives of two characters, Joanna Marshall and Peter Bye, and their struggles to overcome racial discrimination in their quest for respectability and success. By exploring the tangled genealogies and internal prejudices of the black middle class, Fauset exposes the ways race is socially constructed, not biologically determined.

Plum Bun centers on the life of a young, middle-class black woman and her pursuit of the American dream. Inspired by the fairy tales told by her mother, Angela Murray decides to cut herself off from her family and "pass" as a white woman in order to achieve her dreams. After a disastrous relationship with a wealthy white man, Angela decides to accept her identity as a black woman.

The Chinaberry Tree depicts the prejudices of a small black community, which ostracizes a woman, Aunt Sal, and her daughter Laurentine because of Laurentine's illegitimate origins. However, the chinaberry tree, which grows in Sal's yard, represents the power of natural forces, of life and love, to transcend the social fictions of race and class.

Comedy American Style focuses on a light-skinned black woman, Olivia Cary, who is obsessed with being white. Olivia's obsession has disastrous effects on her family: she manipulates her daughter into an unhappy marriage and drives her youngest son to suicide when he realizes the extent of his mother's hatred of his dark skin.

As the Renaissance waned, so did interest in novels by African-Americans, and Fauset returned to teaching. She died having never published another novel.

Wendy Wagner

FEDERAL WRITERS' PROJECT. In 1935 the United States Congress authorized the formation of its most ambitious piece of New Deal legislation, the Works Progress Administration (WPA; later known as the Works Projects Administration). Its four arts components—the Federal Art Project, the Federal Music Project, the Federal Theatre Project, and the Federal Writers' Project—comprise significant milestones in the growing prominence of American women in the arts. The WPA was pragmatic evidence of Franklin D. Roosevelt's democratic ideal, aimed simultaneously at providing jobs for artists already on relief and at assuring federal subsidy for the arts, the first such funding this country had known. Harry L. Hopkins, director of the WPA from 1935 to 1939, agreed with Roosevelt that these programs could not only assist the economy, but give the average American greater access to the arts. Projects were set up by geographic regions, with plans to reach small towns having limited cultural opportunities as well as metropolitan centers. During the nine years the WPA existed, it employed thousands of writers, some of whom were later to achieve international acclaim. Zora Neale * Hurston was active as a dramatic coach in the Theatre Project in New York and as an editor in the Florida Writers' Project; Eudora * Welty photographed rural Mississippi while a WPA publicity agent. Many WPA writers, such as folklorist Bernice Kelly Harris, collected oral histories from a wide variety of Americans—midwives, ex-slaves, elevator operators, and textile workers, in addition to judges or similar socially prominent individuals. Other writers, like Richard Wright, were funded to pursue creative projects of their own.

One of the chief contributors to women's recognition in the arts was Hallie Flanagan, national director of the Federal Theatre Project (1935–1939). Flanagan, long active in little theater, was working as head of Vassar's Experimental Theater when Hopkins selected her to run the FTP. As the Library of Congress Catalog to the FTP Archives notes, Hopkins challenged Flanagan to produce "free, adult, uncensored theatre," and supported her in doing so. Flanagan was an innovator who gave women and minorities the opportunity to have their works produced and their voices heard—at least on the public stage. The list of plays Flanagan mounted ranges from classic theatrical productions centering on female characters (such as *Medea*) or featuring all-black casts (such as *MacBeth*) to dramatizations of more modern works by women (such as Harriet Beecher * Stowe's *Uncle Tom's Cabin*) or FTP dramas focusing on modern women's concerns (such as *A New Deal for Mary*). A number of women wrote original plays for the Project as well. Prominent among these was Betty * Smith, whose novels, including *A Tree Grows in Brooklyn* (1943), would bring her fame. When Congress withdrew funding from the FTP after four very active years, Flanagan had staged more than 8,000 productions in sites as varied as Manchester, New Hampshire; San Francisco, California; and Waterloo, Iowa.

• The Federal Writers' Project Collection is in the National Archives, Washington, D.C. See also Jane Dehart Mathews, *The Federal Theatre, 1935–1939* (1967). Jerre Mangione, *The Dream and the Deal: The Federal Writers' Project 1935–1943* (1972). Richard D. McKinzie, *The New Deal for Artists* (1973). Monty Noam Penkower, *The Federal Writers' Project: A Study in Government Patronage of the Arts* (1977). Archie Hobson, ed., *Remembering America* (1985). Federal Theatre Project Collection, George Mason University (On loan from the Library of Congress, which has a published catalog, 1987).

Patricia M. Gantt

FEMININITY. *See* Gender; Psychoanalysis and Women, article on Sigmund Freud.

FEMINISM. In the 1990s, feminism does not exist as a singular entity. There are only feminisms, as the titles of more than one recent book on the subject suggest. Even the attempt to define feminism poses problems, because contemporary feminist theory calls into question the possibility of fixing stable, objective meanings. As a feminist scholar, I am explicitly aware that I speak from a particular institutional and experiential position (that of a female, middle-class, white, heterosexual, late twentieth-century American academic, to mention only the categories of sex, class, race, sexual preference, era, nationality, and profession, all of which have—among others—become categories within feminist analysis), and that my understanding of the phrase "as a feminist scholar" will carry the marks of my position, with all its social and cultural privileges and disadvantages. I am also aware that it is unusual to write in the first person in encyclopedic entries, but I do so as a specifically "feminist" gesture, to emphasize that I speak as one voice participating in an ongoing dialogue about feminism, rather than explaining it definitively. I am aware, too, that I have not used any form of the word *feminism* in this paragraph in a sense that all persons calling themselves feminists would endorse.

Historically speaking, feminism has been associated in the United States with the struggle for women's political enfranchisement. The women's suffrage movement of the nineteenth and early twentieth centuries—building on the philosophical foundations established by the British social theorist and novelist Mary Wollstonecraft, author of *A Vindication of the Rights of Woman* (1792)—is known as the first wave of feminism in America. The efforts of American women to garner the right to vote were intimately interconnected in the nineteenth century with abolition, temperance, and social reform movements, and are chronicled in the three-volume *History of Woman Suffrage*, edited in 1881 by Elizabeth Cady * Stanton, Susan B. * Anthony, and Matilda Joslyn Gage.

Since the time that women received the vote (through the passage of the Nineteenth Amendment to the Constitution in 1920), feminism has persisted in attempting to achieve equal rights for women. Feminist positions within American politics occupy a broad range of stances, from liberal feminists (sometimes called mainstream feminists) who advocate "working within the system" to achieve equality; to Marxist feminists, who espouse a fundamentally socialist view of the interworkings of gender and class; to Black, Latina, Native-American, Asian-American, and other "minority" feminists, who speak from a position outside the mainstream to emphasize the relations between ethnicity, race, and gender; to radical feminists, known in some connections as separatists, who eschew cooperation with the patriarchy (or the system granting political power to men) altogether (see Alice Echols, *Daring to Be Bad: Radical Feminism in America, 1967–1975*, 1989). The second wave of feminism has been operating on the American political scene since the women's movement (also called women's liberation) began in the late 1960s, raising the issues of equity in the workplace, reproductive rights, and female representation in government. A related concept is what Alice * Walker (*In Search of Our Mothers' Gardens*, 1984) has called womanism, a "pro-human" position " 'committed to the survival of entire people,' female *and* male, as well as to a valorization of women's works in all their varieties and multitudes" (Sherley Anne * Williams, "Some Implications of Womanist Theory," in *Reading Black, Reading Feminist*, ed. Henry Louis Gates, Jr., 1990).

Generally speaking, feminism is a political, social, and cultural stance that is prowoman. That does not necessarily mean, as many who participate in the * backlash against feminism (see Susan Faludi's 1991 book on the subject) suggest, that a feminist is antiman. Most feminists espouse a politics of coalition that brings people together in a collective resistance of gender-based oppression, and most feminists agree that it is important to celebrate women and their works. What keeps feminism in a constant state of dialogue, however, is the fact that feminists do not necessarily agree about the definition of terms as basic as *woman*, let alone what it would mean, precisely, to be prowoman. While critics outside the movement may see such ongoing debate as the sign of a systemic problem within feminism, many feminists appreciate bell hooks's suggestion that we think of it not as *the* feminist movement, but rather as feminist movement, a process that "keeps the thing going while things are stirring," to borrow a phrase from nineteenth-century black feminist Sojourner * Truth.

One prominent theme in contemporary feminism is the idea that "the personal is the political," or that politics must be understood as a realm much broader than the merely electoral or governmental, and must include every action bearing upon power relations. Feminism thus draws heavily on experience as well as theory, because many persons come to feminism through their own experience of gender oppression, or in response to other women's testimonies of experience. Much feminist energy is directed toward ameliorating the material realities of gender-based oppression, in terms of economics (where women consistently earn and own less than men, as a group), social and familial arrangements (where domestic violence and rape victimize more women than men), and mass culture (where pornography and high fashion perpetuate the notion that women's bodies, more than men's, are sexual objects). The movement known as *ecofeminism draws parallels between the exploitation of women and abuse of the planetary environment. Feminism provides both a ground for framing and critiquing such realities, and for proposing and celebrating alternatives.

Feminism can be thought of as an ideology (that is, an intellectual system for explaining why things are the way they are) that has operated in political and social theory, epistemology, psychology and psychoanalysis, spiritual and religious studies, linguistics, cultural studies, literary theory and criticism, and daily experience for at least as long as the United States of America has existed. The modern British novelist Rebecca West both highlighted and sidestepped the problem of defining it when she said, "I myself have never been able to find out precisely what feminism is: I only know that other people call me a feminist whenever I express sentiments that differentiate me from a doormat or a prostitute" (*The Young Rebecca*, ed. Jane Marcus, 1982). West raises the question of whether one can identify oneself as a feminist or whether it is a label that will be affixed by others; she nevertheless clearly communicates that for her, a feminist position asserts a woman's right to resist being used as a tool or an object by others.

To joke, as West does, or to take a playful stance in the face of the institutional necessity of self-definition has been a common feminist strategy, from the often hilarious ironies of Virginia *Wolf's extended essay on women writers, *A Room of One's Own* (1929), to Hélène Cixous's virtuoso experiments with *écriture féminine* (a style of writing designed to be distinct from traditional, logical rhetorical norms, and purported to be specific to woman) in *The Laugh of the Medusa* (first published in English in 1975), to the wryly funny anti-institutional gestures in the essays of the African-American feminist who signs herself bell hooks, to the airily autobiographical resistance to theoretical academic discourse in Jane Tompkins's essay about her personal relation with feminism and literary theory, "Me and My Shadow" (*Gender and Theory*, ed. Linda Kauffman, 1989). Each of these feminist theorists, like countless others, "dances through the minefield" (to use Annette Kolodny's famous phrase) of opposition to feminism and opponents within feminism by writing in a feminist style that announces itself as different from academic models for writing.

Difference between, Difference within. In its American origins, feminism insisted that women and men were fundamentally different from each other, thus participating in the dominant ideology of gender prevalent in the nineteenth century. Men and women were supposed to occupy *"separate spheres," with men assigned to the world of commerce and politics, and women assigned to the home. Whereas men would be necessarily tainted by the competitive, self-promoting practices of capitalism, women's "frailer bodies" and "finer moral natures" were supposed to be protected and preserved within the domestic sphere. Of course, this ideology excludes from the category of woman all those women who did factory work, domestic work, or other forms of labor for pay; all those who were literally enslaved; and those few middle-class and upper-class women who ventured outside the home to pursue professions. In this view, women's power was to be exerted by personal influence over husbands and children. A similar ideology can be found among conservative American women today who espouse the discourse of "family values," but this position is no longer associated with feminism. The suffrage movement and the modern period brought an androgynist ideal to feminism, arguing that women and men are more alike than different, and that social insistence on gender differentiation is both arbitrary and damaging to both sexes. This position, too, continues to have proponents, most of whom would today call themselves feminists. But not every feminist holds androgyny as an ideal. Many feminists today emphasize the differences between men's and women's bodies and men's and women's experiences, with the goal of valorizing the female and feminine elements that had previously disqualified women from full participation in culture and society.

Difference has become an important term for contemporary feminist discourse in two senses that Barbara Johnson (writing from the traditions of psychoanalysis and deconstruction in *A World of Difference*, 1987) has identified: the difference between and the difference within. If American feminism began, as Nancy Cott argues, in a nineteenth-century debate over women's "sameness as" and "difference from" men and the ramifications of that sameness and difference for women's political status (*What Is Feminism?*, eds. Juliet Mitchell and Ann Oakley, 1986), it has come more recently to recognize that generalizing about women erases diversity among them. Whereas the differences between women and men are still an area of inquiry, the differences within woman are now in the foreground. Such locations of difference as sexual preference, ethnicity, class identification, nationality, and age have come to signify "otherness" among women, and the psychoanalytic theory of split subjectivity suggests that difference exists not only within the group of women but also within each individual woman herself. Some feminists refer to the negotiation of such differences in feminism as identity politics.

While the denotation of woman remains debatable within feminist theory, feminism seems generally to have settled on usages for the key terms *sex* and *gender*, and their corresponding terms, *female/male* and *feminine/masculine*. Contemporary feminist discourse uses *sex* to refer to the biological categories of male and female, which—in most people's cases—can be applied unambiguously on the basis of physical features: a female human has a vagina and uterus, a male has a penis; a female menstruates, a male does not. (Of course, there are anatomical and hormonal exceptions that make even this seemingly obvious binary opposition questionable.) *Gender*, by contrast, does not refer to biological attributes, but to culturally constructed notions of what is appropriate to persons of either sex. Gender, unlike sex, varies from one context to another. To borrow a helpful illustration from Susan Brownmiller (*Femininity*, 1984), modern American culture attributes a gendered difference to body hair. Whereas both male and female human bodies grow hair in the armpit, the dominant culture in America (reflected, for instance, in images in the mass media) holds that it is masculine to leave it there and feminine to shave it off. Similarly, American culture assigns masculine gender to such traits as intelligence, ambition, and aggressiveness, feminine gender to intuition, self-effacement, and nurturing. The gender identification of individual persons exists within a spectrum, or on a sliding scale, so that masculine and feminine do not, in analysis, necessarily serve as discrete and opposing poles.

Some feminisms argue that differences between men and women are based in anatomy (a position known as biologism); others take a social constructionist stance, holding that gender, not sex, should be the primary category of analysis. Depending on the disciplinary approach, gender arrangements can be attributed to ego development within a psychoanalytic frame (as in the work of psychologists Nancy Chodorow and Carol Gilligan, or those critics of literature and of film who have adapted the theories of Sigmund Freud and Jacques Lacan, such as Jane Gallop, Laura Mulvey, and Kaja Silverman), to social experience within historical contexts (as in studies conducted by such historians as Nancy Cott, Gerda Lerner, Carroll Smith-Rosenberg, Joan Wallach Scott, and Barbara Ehrenreich), to linguistic patterns (as studied by Barrie Thorne and Nancy Henley, Robin Lakoff, and Deborah Tannen), to parenting practices (for example, Dorothy Dinnerstein's *The Mermaid and the Minotaur*, 1976), to the perpetuation of literary conventions (as in images of woman criticism), or to any number of other causes.

In most feminisms' vocabularies, sex is not to be confused with sexuality and sexual preference, which refer to an individual's pattern of erotic attraction. Nor does gender correspond in any obvious way to sexuality: a person of the female sex who is erotically attracted primarily to persons of her own sex (who may or may not refer to herself as lesbian, another term whose definition is under debate within feminism) might be either strongly feminine or strongly masculine in her gendered self-presentation, or—most likely—her gender identity would, like most heterosexual persons, be made up of a complicated combination of gendered "differences within."

Just as some definitions of woman take differences into account, so do many current definitions of feminism. Teresa de Lauretis identifies points of difference that had become central to debates over feminism by the mid-1980s: "The debate on culturalism vs. biologism in the social sciences. . . ; the issue of 'identity politics' with the attendant problems of racism and anti-Semitism in the representation and definition of feminism; the difficult relation of feminist scholarship to the practice-oriented component of the women's movement, a relation often summed up (falsely, in my opinion) as an opposition of theory to practice" (*Feminist Studies/Critical Studies*, 1986). De Lauretis warns against thinking of feminism as a "coherent ideology, a set of dogmas and rules of conduct." She argues that the "image . . . of a homogeneous, monolithic Feminism—whether white or black or Third World, whether mainstream or separatist, academic or activist—is something that must be resisted." Her point hinges on the arguments of American-based theorists whose life experiences and theoretical stance bring a third world perspective to their work, as well as theorists who speak from within Asian-American, black, Native-American, Latina, or other American ethnicities or lesbian experience, all of whom protest against feminism's having been, until recently, predominantly a white, middle-class, heterosexist politics of exclusion. As Trinh T. *Minh-ha puts it, "There cannot be any grand totalizing integration without massive suppression, which is a way of recirculating the effects of domination" (*When the Moon Waxes Red*, 1991).

From Margin to Center. Feminist scholarship in America had its beginnings in the late 1960s and early 1970s in what it conceived as the study of women per se, taking female experience out of the margins of historical, social, and literary analysis, where they had been placed by patriarchal scholarly tradition, and putting women and their works in the center of the academic field of vision. More recently, feminist academic writing has felt the impact of such theorists as Trinh T. Minh-ha, Gayatri *Spivak, Chandra Mohanty, bell hooks, Gloria *Anzaldúa, Audre *Lorde, Barbara Smith, Paula Gunn *Allen, Judith Butler, Biddy Martin, and many others who bring forward the concerns of "other" women, those who have been relegated to the margins of modern feminist discourse by its emphasis on the experience of white, middle-class, American heterosexuals. These theorists may embrace the margin as a new center, a new focal point (as in hooks's *Feminist Theory: From Margin to Center*, 1984), but in doing so they point to "the irreducibility of the margin in all explanations," to use Spivak's phrase. Even when it is adopted to draw attention to the margin, the language of margin and center can operate to perpetuate oppressive structures, according to some feminist points of view.

The effect of bringing feminism to bear on academic inquiry has been to alter the paradigms that structure scholarly research. Broadening the data base available as evidence for philosophical, social, or literary generalization can change the shape of the generalizations themselves. Taking women's experiences, women's texts, women's subjectivity, and women's priorities into account alters the set of questions raised within scholarly fields.

The study of women's writing in America is a notable example. In evaluative forms of literary criticism, feminism has raised such questions as "Why are so few female-authored texts featured in the 'canon' of 'great American books'? Who established the standards by which 'great books' are judged, and whose interests do those standards serve? How has the gender of individual authors, and individual readers, colored the reception of texts?" Descriptive forms of criticism ask, "In what ways, if any, are women's texts different from men's? Do women write with 'a different voice,' and, if they do, what does that voice sound like, what does it say?" And interpretive criticism asks, "What does 'gender' signify in literary texts written by women or by men? How does a contextual understanding of women's historical experience affect our understanding of texts written in different periods? What bearing does the author's, reader's, or character's gender have on our interpretations of what a text means?" Paradigms shift again when the critic brings into focus questions of class (as in Marxist feminism); race and ethnicity (as in Paula Gunn *Al-

len's *The Sacred Hoop: Recovering the Feminine in American Indian Traditions*, 1986; Cherríe *Moraga and Gloria Anzaldúa's *This Bridge Called My Back: Writings by Radical Women of Color*, 1983; Asunción Horno-Delgado et al.'s collection *Breaking Boundaries: Latina Writing and Critical Readings*, 1989; Barbara Christian's *Black Feminist Criticism*, 1985; and Barbara Smith's *All the Women are White, All the Blacks Are Men, But Some of Us Are Brave: Black Women's Studies*, 1982); sexual identity (as in Bonnie Zimmerman's *The Safe Sea of Women: Lesbian Fiction, 1969–1989*, 1990; and Lillian Faderman's *Odd Girls and Twilight Lovers: A History of Lesbian Life in Twentieth-Century America*, 1991); or the legacy of colonialism (as in Gayatri Spivak's *The Post-Colonial Critic*, 1990, *Selected Subaltern Studies*, 1988, and *In Other Worlds: Essays in Cultural Politics*, 1987).

As a subject of academic study, feminism has been approached in at least three ways: it can be presented synchronically, as a fixed paradigm operating across historical periods; diachronically, as a movement that has evolved through time; or oppositionally, as a set of issues under debate at any given moment in history. As applied to women's writing in the United States through literary theory and criticism, feminism continues to be approached in each of these three ways. Because I resist assigning a definitive meaning to feminism, I propose instead to outline here some of the ways the term has been defined in synchronic, diachronic, and conflictual feminist theories of writing that have originated or been studied in the United States in the past three decades. I will also point out aspects of each approach that are controversial within the broader realm of feminism, or that have been criticized from within the rubric of feminist theory.

Synchronic Definitions. Some theorists propose synchronic definitions of feminism that are presented as being universally applicable. A useful example is Catharine Stimpson's list of four basic principles of feminist criticism. For Stimpson, a critic who is a feminist must (1) agree that "we cannot understand history, politics, and culture until we recognize how influential the structures of gender and sexual difference have been"; (2) believe that "men, as men, have controlled history, politics, culture," and, in so doing, have "relegated women, as women, to the margins of culture, if not to silence and invisibility"; (3) insist that "we must also act, politically and culturally, in order to change history"; and (4) assert "the need to seek out and then to codify texts women have produced" (*Feminist Issues in Literary Scholarship*, ed. Shari Benstock, 1987). A year earlier, Maggie Humm proposed three basic assumptions for "all critics writing what they call 'feminist criticism' ": (1) the belief that literature and criticism are "ideological since writing manipulates gender for symbolic purposes"; (2) the assumption that "there are sex-related writing strategies"; and (3) the conviction that "the continuing tradition of literary culture, like the economic and social traditions of which it is a part, uses male norms to exclude or undervalue female writing and scholarship" (*Feminist Criticism*, 1986). What these two synchronic descriptions of feminism in literary criticism have in common are the beliefs that gender is significant for the production, interpretation, and evaluation of writing; that women, per se, have been and still are oppressed; and that writing by women deserves more attention than it has traditionally received in the academy.

Writing in the introduction to *Feminisms: An Anthology of Literary Theory and Criticism* in 1991, Diane Price Herndl and I proposed a synchronic characterization of the assumptions behind the fifty-eight essays of feminist theory and criticism collected in that anthology:

Feminist critics generally agree that the oppression of women is a fact of life, that gender leaves its traces in literary texts and on literary history, and that feminist literary criticism plays a worthwhile part in the struggle to end oppression in the world outside of texts. When they turn their attention to social history, most feminists agree that oppression of ethnic and racial minorities, gay men and lesbians, and working class people is closely tied to the oppression of women. Of course, not all feminist critics ground their work in material history. But even when they focus on such comparatively abstract matters as discourse, aesthetics, or the constitution of subjectivity, feminists are always engaged in an explicitly political enterprise, always working to change existing power structures both inside and outside academia. Its overtly political nature is perhaps the single most distinguishing feature of feminist scholarly work.

To say that feminists "always" do anything is to propose an essence of feminism, a highly debatable concept.

Synchronic definitions of feminism, while they gesture toward consensus and seek to lend manageability to an enormous body of textual material, come under interrogation for their tendency toward essentialism, or the assumption that certain aspects of gender arrangements, whether biologically or culturally determined, are permanent and unchanging. This assumption is couched in a concept of patriarchy as a universal (Western) system by which cultures and societies operate to oppress women and privilege men. As Judith Butler explains, "The political assumption that there must be a universal basis for feminism, one which must be found in an identity assumed to exist cross-culturally, often accompanies the notion that the oppression of women has some singular form discernible in the universal or hegemonic structure of patriarchy or masculine domination." However, Butler critiques the notion of a "universal patriarchy" for its

failure to account for the workings of gender oppression in the concrete cultural contexts in which it exists. Where those various contexts have been consulted within such theories, it has been to find "examples" or "illustrations" of a universal principle that is assumed from the start. That form of feminist theorizing has come under criticism for its efforts to colonize and appropriate non-Western cultures to support highly Western notions of oppression, but because they tend as well to construct a "Third World" or even an "Orient" in which gender oppression is subtly explained as symptomatic of an essential, non-Western barbarism. The urgency of feminism to establish a universal status for patriarchy in order to strengthen the appearance of feminism's own claims to be representative has occasionally motivated the shortcut to a categorial or fictive universality of the structure of domination, held to produce women's common subjugated experience. (*Gender Trouble*, 1990)

The more inclusive a synchronic definition of feminism attempts to be, the more questionable will be its applicability to "other" women.

Diana Fuss has recently suggested seeing essentialism as "neither good nor bad, progressive nor reactionary, beneficial nor dangerous" in itself. She elaborates: "The question we should be asking is not 'is this text essentialist (and therefore "bad")?' but rather 'if this text is essentialist, *what motivates its deployment?*' How does the sign 'essence' circulate in various contemporary critical debates? Where, how, and why is it invoked? What are its political and textual effects?" Fuss's book *Essentially Speaking: Feminism, Nature, and Difference* (1989) investigates the purposes and functions essentialism plays within various discourses, without assuming that essentialism is, by definition, oppressive. However, her approach, like Butler's, insists upon attention to context, and in that respect moves away from the synchronic approach.

Diachronic Definitions. Feminist scholarship has produced many diachronic accounts of the development of feminist criticism in America. Such histories of feminist criticism propose an evolutionary model of feminism, showing how each successive movement within feminist literary theory grows out of (and implicitly improves upon) its predecessors. These chronological accounts offer alternative means of defining feminism, conceiving it as a process, rather than a static entity.

Most diachronic accounts of feminism in literary studies cite two texts as early inspirations: Virginia Woolf's *A Room of One's Own* (1929)—an extended essay on the history of British women writers, the social position of modern middle-class women, and the androgynous possibilities for the future of women's writing—and Simone * de Beauvoir's *The Second Sex* (1949)—a social and philosophical analysis of how women came to be defined as "other" from men, who are held to be the norm. Neither Woolf nor de Beauvoir declares herself to be practicing feminist criticism, but both take broad questions of women and literature into account in their analyses. Two other, more recent texts that are almost invariably cited as among the first works of feminist criticism are Mary Ellman's *Thinking about Women* (1968) and Kate * Millet's *Sexual Politics* (1969). Both books expose negative stereotypes of women in male-authored literature; Ellman's book also explores alternative portrayals of women in female-written texts.

A highly influential diachronic account of feminism in literary criticism is the one sketched out by Elaine Showalter in a series of essays about feminist critical methodology. Before the women's movement took hold in the 1960s, Showalter states, literary criticism of women's writing "took the form of an androgynist poetics, denying the uniqueness of a female literary consciousness, and advocating a single or universal standard of critical judgment which women writers had to meet" ("A Criticism of Our Own," *The Future of Literary Theory*, ed. Ralph Cohen, 1989). With the women's movement, came two forms of feminist criticism, which she calls the "feminist critique of male culture"—in projects such as Ellman's and Millet's that identify the phallocentric or androcentric biases in mainstream literature and criticism—and the "Female Aesthetic," a celebration of women's "distinct female consciousness" and its effect within women's writing. Invoking Adrienne * Rich as an example, Showalter calls this a "phase of intellectual rebellion, gynocentrism and critical separatism"; she also places the writing of French feminists Julia Kristeva, Hélène Cixous, and Luce Irigaray within this movement, acknowledging that their psychoanalytically inspired theories grew out of "radically different intellectual sources." For Showalter, the "French feminist project of 'writing the body' is a particularly strong and revolutionary effort to provide women's writing with an authority

based in women's genital and libidinal difference from men." After the "Female Aesthetic" comes the 1970s movement Showalter herself named gynocriticism, the study of the history of women's writing, focusing on "the multiple signifying systems of female literary traditions and intertextualities." Her *A Literature of Their Own* (1977) and Sandra Gilbert and Susan Gubar's *The Madwoman in the Attic* (1979) have become landmarks of gynocriticism, tracing nineteenth-century middle-class white women authors' revisions of and responses to one another's work, as well as their relation to the parallel masculine literary tradition. Showalter identifies gynesic criticism (after Alice Jardine's 1985 book *Gynesis*) as the next phase, drawing upon the poststructuralist theories of Jacques Derrida, Jacques Lacan, and the French feminists, and focusing upon "the feminine" in history and discourse. Such studies turn away from biographical considerations to concentrate on text, dismantling traditional binary oppositions associated with gender arrangements, and calling into question the concept of the unified subject (the "self") on which so much previous feminist work had been built. Showalter sees the late 1980s as moving into gender theory, an approach insisting "that all writing, not just writing by women, is gendered." This approach opens up masculinity as well as femininity for feminist analysis, and serves as "a constant reminder of the other categories of difference that structure our lives and texts."

Showalter's is only one of many narratives of the history of feminist criticism. Some competing diachronic accounts of feminism can be found in Carol T. Neely, "Feminist Criticism in Motion" (*For Alma Mater*, eds. Paula Treichler et al., 1985); Carolyn Allen, "Feminist Criticism and Postmodernism" (*Tracing Literary Theory*, ed. Joseph Natoli, 1987); Ellen Messer-Davidow, "The Philosophical Bases of Feminist Literary Criticism" (*New Literary History* 19, 1987); Teresa de Lauretis, "Eccentric Subjects: Feminist Theory and Historical Consciousness," (*Feminist Studies* 16, 1990); and in the introductions to such anthologies of feminist criticism as Catherine Belsey's and Jane Moore's *The Feminist Reader* (1989) and Mary Eagleton's *Feminist Literary Criticism* (1991). Each account places different stress on the various practices of feminist criticism, and each implies that feminism progresses through time as it becomes more inclusive and more theoretically sophisticated.

Oppositional Definitions. Some theorists conceive of feminism not as a developing, unified entity, but rather as a field of conflict in which diverse points of view struggle for institutional priority. These theorists set up oppositions within contemporary feminist theories of literature, often arguing for the superiority of one view. One such opposition sets poststructuralist theories against the kind of critical pluralism advocated by such American critics as Annette Kolodny and Nina Baym; another places theoretically-oriented criticism in opposition to politically-engaged activism. Critics writing from the "margins" of feminism sometimes oppose their commitment to studying race, class, and sexual preference with the practices of feminists in the "mainstream."

A conflict that structured much debate within literary feminism in the past decade is the opposition between Anglo-American and French feminist approaches, as set out in Toril Moi's influential book *Sexual/Textual Politics: Feminist Literary Theory* (1985). Moi severely criticizes "images of woman criticism" and gynocritics as they had been practiced in America for participating in traditional liberal humanism (which she characterizes as a patriarchal system that seeks to universalize human experience) and for treating the relations between texts and lived experience in an overly literal, naive way. She places such American critics as Showalter, Gilbert and Gubar, and Kolodny in opposition to the French feminists Kristeva, Cixous, and Irigaray, whose psychoanalytically inspired treatments of woman and the feminine take into account the poststructuralist problematics of language, text, and the self. Moi privileges the French feminists for what she sees as their superior resistance to "phallogocentrism," the patriarchal location of power in "the phallus" and "the law of the father" (as theorized by Lacan). Janet Todd answers Moi's arguments in *Feminist Literary History* (1988), reproducing the opposition between French feminist and Anglo-American feminist criticism, but celebrating the latter for its refusal to separate feminist literary criticism from the feminism operating in the world outside of texts.

Feminism in literary studies has placed itself in alliance with and opposition to other, broader critical movements, including Marxism (see Nancy Fraser's *Unruly Practices*, 1989, and the books of Michele Barrett, including *Women's Oppression Today*, 1980, *The Politics of Diversity*, 1986, and *Destabilizing Theory*, 1992), the theories of Michel Foucault about the deployment of social power and the history of sexuality (see *Feminism and Foucault*, eds. Irene Diamond and Lee Quinby, 1988), and the theories of Freud and Lacan about the role gender plays in ego formation and the effects it has on writing (see Madelon Sprengnether, *The Spectral Mother: Freud, Feminism, and Psychoanalysis*, 1990; Richard Feldstein and Judith Roof,

eds., *Feminism and Psychoanalysis*, 1989; and Marleen Barr and Richard Feldstein, eds., *Discontented Discourses: Feminism/ Textual Intervention/ Psychoanalysis*, 1989). Last—and perhaps not least—feminism looks at the role of *Men in Feminism* (as Alice Jardine and Paul Smith named a 1987 collection on the subject), as allies within the movement and as opponents to female colleagues.

[*See also* Black Feminism; Conservatism; Deconstruction and Feminism; Ecofeminism; French Feminism; Gender Theory; Gynocriticism; Lesbian Feminism; Liberal Feminism; Marxist Feminism; Men and Feminism; Radical Feminism; Socialist Feminism; Third World Feminism.]

• Joanna Russ, *How to Suppress Women's Writing* (1983). Janice A. Radway, *Reading the Romance: Women, Patriarchy, and Popular Literature* (1984; reprint 1991). Susan Rubin Suleiman, ed., *The Female Body in Western Culture: Contemporary Perspectives* (1986). Evelyn Fox Keller, *Reflections on Gender and Science* (1985). Elizabeth Flynn and Patrocinio Schweickart, eds., *Gender and Reading* (1986). Christie Farnham, ed., *The Impact of Feminist Research in the Academy* (1987). Elizabeth Spelman, *Inessential Woman: Problems of Exclusion in Feminist Thought* (1988). Dale Spender, *The Writing or the Sex? or, Why You Don't Have to Read Women's Writing to Know It's No Good* (1989). Cheryl Wall, ed., *Changing Our Own Words: Essays on Criticism, Theory and Writing by Black Women* (1989). Deborah Rhode, ed., *Theoretical Perspectives on Sexual Difference* (1990). Karla Jay and Joanna Glasgow, eds., *Lesbian Texts and Contexts: Radical Revisions* (1990). Elizabeth Fox Genovese, *Feminism without Illusions: A Critique of Individualism* (1991). Jane Gallop, *Around 1981: Academic Feminist Literary Theory* (1992). Helena Michie, *Sororophobia: Differences among Women in Literature and Culture* (1992).

Robyn R. Warhol

FEMINIST FILM THEORY. *See* Film Theory, Feminist.

FEMINIST PRESS. *See* Presses, Women's.

FEMINIST THEORY. *See* Feminism; Women's Movement.

FENNO, Jenny (ca. 1765–?), author of *Original Compositions in Prose and Verse on Subjects Moral and Religious* (1791; repub. 1803). Little biographical information is known about Jenny Fenno. She may have been the "Jennet Fenno" born in Boston in 1765; evidence within her book indicates that she was a member of Boston's Second Baptist Church. *Original Compositions* is mostly sixty-nine heroic couplet poems, including several elegies, and fifteen short didactic essays. Fenno's writing reveals the influences of early romanticism, especially graveyard poetry. Traditional piety and joyful assurance in her salvation dominate her themes, which range from religious to pastoral and neoclassical. Her repeated encomia to Elizabeth Singer Rowe suggest that she views Rowe as an enabling poetic model.

Published in the wake of the Revolution, Shay's Rebellion, and the Boston fire of 1787 (the latter of which she writes about), the volume implicitly promotes harmony and the reestablishment of order. In "Filial Love and Obedience," Fenno exhorts deference from children and servants, kindness from parents and masters. She reinforces the pervasive cultural maternalization of patriarchal authority: "If God does hear young ravens when they cry, / His children's wants he surely will supply." In a prose dialogue between a minister and a shepherd, the minister laments, "O how can I bear the thought, that one of [my flock] should be lost eternally?" Interested in shaping a prudent citizenry, Fenno praises Reason (as did Mercy Otis Warren in 1790) as the crucial attribute of humanity and a necessary check on sensuality.

Fenno shrewdly negotiates late eighteenth-century proscriptions that forbid a woman's publishing. In the preface, her humility *topos* displays proper feminine submissiveness and self-deprecation. Because she is single, "Miss J. Fenno" cannot fulfill the ideologically sanctioned roles of republican wife and mother. To justify her unseemly intrusion into the public sphere, Fenno explains that providential intervention impelled her work: "I expected ere now to have launched out into the shoreless ocean; but just as I was expecting to change worlds, the scene was changed, and I was sent back by unerring wisdom to finish this work I had begun to do." She associates herself with biblical poet and underdog David, stating, "I doubt not that this book may appear in the eyes of the learned world, like an insignificant pebble. But happy shall I be, if it may be so slung as to smite one philistine." This quietly rebellious strain is amplified in "David's Victory Over Goliath [sic]," the book's longest poem and centerpiece where Fenno details an account of the shepherd's courageous triumph over the brute.

Jeanne Holland

FERBER, Edna (1885–1968), novelist, playwright, short story writer. The publication of her first short story, "The Homely Heroine," in 1911 signaled the beginning of a long, prolific career for Ferber as one of America's most popular writers early in the twentieth century. The appearance of her first novel, *Dawn O'Hara: The Girl Who Laughed*, also in 1911, launched the fifty-year career during which Ferber published 12 collections of short stories, 12 novels, two autobiographies, and in collaboration, 9 plays. Twenty of her novels, short stories and plays were adapted to film, some several times.

Despite her tremendous commercial and literary success (she received the Pulitzer Prize for the novel *So Big* in 1925), her writings always reflected her inauspicious beginnings. She retells the same story again and again: that of her own realization of the American Dream. Born in Kalamazoo, Michigan, to Jewish parents, Ferber acutely felt the stings of anti-Semitism in the family's frequent moves around the Midwest; later she attributed her insights into the American success story, and especially into the plight of American women, to her Jewish experience. Although only *Fanny Herself* (1917) and *A Peculiar Treasure* (1939) address that heritage directly, anti-Semitism remains a subtext of almost all of her writings; adversity makes her heroes, but more often heroines, strong.

Her early work as a journalist, as the first woman reporter for the *Appleton Daily Crescent* and later for the *Milwaukee Journal* and *Chicago Tribune*, trained her eye for detail that she later used effectively in her fiction. Her typical approach to such popular successes as *Cimarron* (1929), *Giant* (1952), *Come and Get It* (1935), *Great Son* (1945), and *Ice Palace* (1958) was to conduct historical research on site, either in Texas, Oklahoma, the Midwest, the Northwest, or Alaska, respectively, and then write her traditional story (the American success story or some version of it).

Her place in American letters is somewhat uncertain. While she is generally dismissed by critics who insist on innovative style or technique, others value her ability to chronicle accurately American life early in this century. Perhaps her lack of education beyond high school accounts in part for her failure to change stylistically. Yet she knew all the famous writers of her time, and belonged to the Algonquin Round Table circle.

It is her role as social critic that causes most consternation; just as her heroines are reformers of one sort or another, so Ferber herself found the world of fiction a proper place to advocate for the values she thought crucial. Didacticism often intrudes in her fictional world. In this respect, and in her ongoing concern for the working class, her work resembles that of her nineteenth-century predecessors in the novel, especially the female ones.

• Ferber's papers are housed at the Wisconsin State Historical Society. William White, "A Friend's Story of Edna Ferber," *English Journal* 19, no. 2 (February 1930): 101–106. Louis Bromfield, "Edna Ferber," *Saturday Review of Literature* 12 (13 June 1935): 10–13.

Mary Rose Shaughnessy, *Women and Success in American Society in the Works of Edna Ferber* (1977). Julie Goldsmith Gilbert, *Ferber* (1978).

Diana R. Pingatore

FERGUSSON, Elizabeth Graeme (1737–1801), poet who presided over the most distinguished intellectual salon in British America. Born in Philadelphia to Anne Diggs and Dr. Thomas Graeme, Elizabeth Graeme was trained at home by her father, an adherent to the doctrines of the Scottish enlightenment. By age fifteen, she could write passable Latin, converse in French and German, argue theology and philosophy, and extemporize English couplets. In 1757, she accepted a proposal of marriage from William Franklin, the son of Benjamin Franklin. Her courtship was captured in a verse exchange with Franklin. In 1759, the romance unraveled when young Franklin's affections wandered during a trip to England. She responsed by immersing herself in society and organizing her literary acquaintances into a salon, based on the French model that met weekly. Its membership included Jacob Duché, Hannah Griffitts, Nathaniel Evans, Annis * Stockton, Thomas Coombe, William and Mary Smith, her sister Anna Stedman, her niece Anna Young Smith, Benjamin Rush, and Francis Hopkinson—the most talented aggregation of writers to form in colonial America.

Elizabeth Graeme excelled at composing vers de société and * letters. From 1752 onward, she circulated manuscript writings designed to elicit social pleasure—songs, travel accounts, occasional pieces, and impromptus—under the cognomen "Laura." Among the wittiest was "Lines Written in Smith's Theory of Morals," twitting provost William Smith's incapacity to see how desire directed Louis XIV's policies. In 1764, poor health prompted her to visit England. The journal of her visit, now lost, was by all accounts a masterful portrait of metropolitan manners. She achieved some celebrity in England, delighting the novelist Laurence Sterne with her wit, securing an introduction to George III, and winning the friendship of Dr. John Fothergill. Her ode "To Doctor F———l," displayed a striking talent for physicotheological speculation.

Her convalescence was curtailed in 1765 by the deaths of her mother and sister, and to alleviate depression, she undertook several ambitious literary projects—a translation of Fenelon's *Telemaque* (1765–1768), a series of biblical paraphrases (1767), and "The Dream of the Philosophical Farmer" (1768), a political vision justifying an American embargo on British commerce. In 1772, Elizabeth secretly married

Henry Hugh Fergusson, an educated but propertyless Scot whose ardent Tory politics were at odds with her and her dying father's Whiggery. In 1777, Henry convinced Elizabeth to convey to George Washington a treasonous letter from loyalist Jacob Duché. Henry Fergusson decamped, abandoning Elizabeth. She retained his name, but published poems advertising her patriotic feelings. For the remainder of her life, Elizabeth Graeme Fergusson divided her energies between public verse and manuscript communications with a network of women in the Delaware valley. Serving as both example and instructor, she encouraged the literary abilities of Anna Young Smith, Hannah Griffitts, Annis Stockton, the Willing sisters, and Susanna Wright. No other author did as much to encourage womens' writing in eighteenth-century America.

David S. Shields

FERN, Fanny (1811–1872), pseudonym of Sara Payson Willis Parton, novelist and journalist, first American woman newspaper columnist, and originator of the saying, "The way to a man's heart is through his stomach." Born in Portland, Maine, on 9 July 1811, Fern grew up in Boston. She graduated from Catharine * Beecher's Hartford Female Seminary in 1831, and in 1837, she married Charles Eldredge, a cashier at the Merchants' Bank in Boston. Her first child, Mary, was born in 1838, and died in 1845. She had two other children, Grace (b. 1841) and Ellen (b. 1844). In 1846, Eldredge died insolvent, and in 1849, under pressure from her family, Fern entered into a marriage of convenience with Samuel Farrington, a widower with two children. The marriage was, as her daughter Ellen later said, "a terrible mistake," and in 1851, Fern left Farrington and attempted to earn her own living, first by sewing and then by writing.

Fern began writing for the Boston *Olive Branch* and *True Flag* in 1851. Sometimes tender, but more often sharply satirical, Fern's articles were immensely popular. In 1852, she became a regular columnist for the *New York Musical World and Times*, and the following year published a collection of her essays, *Fern Leaves from Fanny's Portfolio*, an immediate best-seller. In 1853, Farrington obtained a divorce on the grounds of desertion, and Fern moved to New York, becoming a regular columnist for the Philadelphia *Saturday Evening Post*. In 1854, she published *Ruth Hall*, an autobiographical novel. The novel was very successful, but Fern was criticized for her "unfeminine" satirical portrayal of her relatives, who had refused to help her when she was left in poverty after her husband's death.

Robert Bonner, the enterprising editor of the *New York Ledger*, offered Fern twenty-five dollars a column to write a serialized story. When Fern refused, Bonner raised his offer until Fern accepted the then-unprecedented fee of one hundred dollars a column, which made her the most highly paid newspaper writer of the time. Fern's story, "Fanny Ford," began appearing in June 1855, and Fern then signed a contract to write an exclusive column for the *Ledger*. Her first column appeared on 5 January 1856, the date on which she married James Parton, the biographer. Fern continued to write a weekly column for the *Ledger* for the rest of her life. Her last column appeared on 12 October 1872, two days after her death. Her oeuvre includes a second novel, *Rose Clark* (1856), six collections of essays, and three books for children.

A pioneer in the use of the vernacular and understatement, Fern was acclaimed by *Harper's* in 1854 as the welcome harbinger of a new writing style, which, the editors hoped, marked the end of the "stilted rhetoric" and "parade and pomp" of literature. Thematically, Fern was a pioneer noted for her courageous and independent stance. She was the first woman to praise Whitman's *Leaves of Grass* in print; she wrote fearlessly on such taboo subjects as venereal disease, prostitution, and divorce; she questioned male authority and conventional marriage patterns; and she advocated economic independence for women, a revolutionary concept at the time.

• Fern's private papers are in the Sophia Smith Collection, Smith College. The only full-length biography of Fern is by Joyce W. Warren, *Fanny Fern: An Independent Woman* (1992).

Joyce W. Warren

FICTION. See Novel, Beginnings of the; Short Story.

FIELDS, Annie (1834–1915), biographer and diarist, literary hostess, wife of publisher James T. Fields, companion to Sarah Orne *Jewett. Annie Adams Fields, the wife of James T. Fields, one of the founders of the Boston publishing firm of Ticknor and Fields and editor of the *Atlantic Monthly*, was the foremost literary hostess during the last half of the nineteenth century. She was educated at the George B. Emerson School for Young Ladies in Boston, where she was encouraged to cultivate her intellect, devote herself to charitable work, and keep diaries. Annie married Fields in 1854, and their house on fashionable Beacon Hill in Boston became a cultural center. Annie also became inti-

mately involved with James's editing duties, giving critical advice on manuscripts and encouraging many aspiring women writers.

Annie fulfilled some of her own literary ambitions as well. Her only novel, *Asphodel*, anonymously published in 1866, was followed by several volumes of poems, including *The Children of Lebanon* (1872) and *The Return of Persephone* (1877). Her other collections of verse reveal her continuing interest in both transcendental and classical themes: *Under the Olive* (1881), *The Singing Shepherd* (1895), and *Orpheus* (1900).

Her *diaries and literary memoirs, however, represent her most lasting contribution to American literature. Both James and Annie drew from the diaries she kept during the 1860s and 1870s, James for his lectures and literary reminiscences. After Fields's death in 1881, Annie published a memoir of her husband (1881). Her *Shelf of Old Books* (1894) was followed by *Authors and Friends* (1896), a very popular collection of essays about literary friends. She published biographies of Whittier (1893), Harriet Beecher *Stowe (1897), Hawthorne (1899), and Charles Dudley Warner (1904), and in 1895, she edited the letters of the poet Celia Thaxter. Mark A. DeWolfe Howe published a selection of Annie's diaries in *Memories of a Hostess* (1922).

Annie also devoted herself to social service. One of the founders of Associated Charities of Boston (1879), Annie buttressed her administrative work with *How to Help the Poor* (1883), a best-selling guide to centralizing charitable work.

After James died, Sarah Orne Jewett became Annie's companion. Their "Boston marriage" lasted until Jewett's death in 1909. Annie's last book was a heavily edited volume of the letters of Sarah Orne Jewett (1911). Annie, who died in 1915, was at the center of the literary world of Boston in the last half of the nineteenth century and greatly affected the course of American publication. Her diaries and memoirs are a continuing source of interest to researchers in American literature.

• Important collections of Fields's papers are at the Huntington Library in San Marino, California; the Houghton Library at Harvard University, Cambridge, Massachusetts; the New York Public Library; the Boston Public Library; and the Massachusetts Historical Society, Boston. See also Josephine Donovan, "Annie Adams Fields and Her Network of Influence," in *New England Local Color Literature: A Women's Tradition* (1983), pp. 38–49. Rita K. Gollin, "Annie Adams Fields, 1834–1915," *Legacy* 4, no. 1 (Spring 1987): 27–33. Rita K. Gollin, "Subordinated Power: Mrs. and Mr. James T. Fields," in *Patrons and Protegees*, ed. Shirley Marchalonis (1988), pp. 141–160. Sarah Way Sherman, *Sarah Orne Jewett: An American Persephone*

(1989). Judith A. Roman, *Annie Adams Fields: The Spirit of Charles Street* (1990).

Gwen L. Nagel

FIELDS, Julia (b. 1938) is an African-American poet, fiction writer, and dramatist who emerged in the early 1960s with the *black arts movement. Born in Bessemer, Alabama, Fields grew up cutting cotton, attending church on Wednesdays and Sundays, and working as a shepherdess, a waitress, a vegetable peddler, and a telephone operator. By her own account, Fields, one of eight children of farming parents, "spent her childhood in streams and wild flowers," whose beauty inspired her to take up painting and writing. While an English major at Knoxville College in Tennessee, Fields met Rosey Pool, who later selected two of Fields's poems, "I Heard a Young Man Saying" and "Madness One Monday Evening," to appear in the 1962 collection *Beyond the Blues: New Poems by American Negroes.* Fields subsequently attracted the attention of Langston Hughes, who, along with African-American poet Georgia Douglas *Johnson, served as an important artistic mentor. She also drew inspiration from the black freedom fighters of the '60s, including Medgar Evars, Martin Luther King, Jr., and Malcolm X, whom she eulogized in "Poem," a work of 1968. The same year, Fields published a short story, "Not Your Singing, Dancing Spade," in LeRoi Jones's and Larry Neal's influential *Black Fire* anthology, and produced her own first book of poetry, *Poems.* While issues of black cultural, social, and political identity are central to her poetry, Fields has never been primarily associated with the black arts movement or its themes of cultural nationalism and black separatism. In poems such as the well-known "High on the Hog," first published in *Negro Digest* in 1969, she even derided the movement's romanticization of suffering. Fields's work is noted for both its representation of black politics and its commitment to incorporating elements of southern black folk culture. Although Fields has at different times lived and worked in New York City, at the University of Edinburgh in Scotland, and at the Bread Loaf School in Vermont (where she received an M.A. in 1972), she has lived most of her life in the South, teaching high school in Birmingham, Alabama, and teaching and writing poetry at Hampton Institute, East Carolina University, Howard University, and North Carolina State University. She has also written a full-length play, *All Day Tomorrow,* which was performed at Knoxville College in 1966. Fields's two most recent works are *Slow Coins* (1981), a book of poems, and *The Green Lion of Zion Street* (1988), a children's book in verse.

• Don L. Lee (Haki Madhubuti), *Dynamite Voices: Black Poets of the 1960s* (1971). Clarence Major, *The Dark and Feeling: Black American Writers and Their Work* (1974). Mary Williams Burger, "Julia Fields," in *Afro-American Poets since 1955,* ed. Trudier Harris and Thadious M. Davis (1985), pp. 123–130. "Julia Fields," in *Black Writers: A Selection of Sketches from Contemporary Authors,* ed. Linda Metzger (1989), p. 197.

Gayle Wald

FILIPINO-AMERICAN WRITING. Much of notable Filipino-American literary production in recent years must be credited to women writers. Ninotchka *Rosca, Jessica *Hagedorn, and Linda *Ty-Casper have been the most active artists, and together account for the bulk of the new writings. Emerging talents such as Cecilia Manguerra Brainard (*Woman with Horns and Other Stories,* 1988) and Michelle Cruz Skinner (*Balikbayan,* 1988) already exhibit similar productive energies, their first efforts winning awards and acclaim. This plenitude of women's writing is observable for other emergent postcolonial and American literatures, including Asian-American literature, which counts Filipino-American writing among its tributaries.

These new utterances take their varied accents from American women's, ethnic, and social movements in the 1960s, and post–World War II national liberation struggles. Hence, their categorizations as Asian-American, ethnic, postcolonial, or women's literatures remain contested, even as they find the space for amplitude and legitimation under such rubrics. Among the new canons, Asian-American literature has yet to be conceptualized adequately to match the spread of its territorial claims. At least seven subcultural traditions are supposedly covered by the category, but Chinese- and Japanese-American writings still provide its theoretical nuclei. This is partly due to the uneven development of both Asian-American studies and the historical and cultural geography of various Asian immigrant communities. Epifanio San Juan, Jr., ("The Filipino Writer in the U.S.A.," *Journal of Ethnic Studies* 19, no. 1, 1991) and Lisa Lowe ("Marking Asian American Differences," *Diaspora* 1, no. 1, 1991) call for revising the current wisdom, given the heterogeneous and specific texts, traditions, cultural groups, and histories. Otherwise, Asian-American literature as a category would abet Western ideologies, which reduce Asian and Asian-descended cultures into a homogenized otherness (see Edward Said, *Orientalism,* 1978).

Filipino-American writing is assumed to be more a preconstituted plank of the larger literature than examined for its descriptive reach by American critics and scholars. As presently conceived, it encompasses the works of such first-generation male writers as Carlos Bulosan (1911–1956), José García Villa (b. 1906), Bienvenido Santos (b. 1911), and NVM Gonzalez (b. 1915), with those of women writers as recent additions. The tentative efforts of some second-generation Filipino Americans, mostly poets who trace their emergence to the 1960s yellow power movement, constitute the slim middle between these major cohorts. Debates over key questions have yet to thrive. How have these writers identified themselves? To what specific historical and cultural measures is their creative work cut? What distinguishes their stances and writings from those of other ethnotyped legacies in the United States?

The available writings, by both men and women, tend to take the Philippines and Philippine history as the origin or terminus of their aesthetic references. Spanish and subsequent United States colonization of the Philippines renders Filipino life in the United States irreducible to the telos of citizenship and the logics of the immigrant epic. Although Filipino migration followed Chinese immigration (1850s–present) and Japanese immigration (1880s–1930s), the American colonial period in the Philippines (1899–1941) and American neocolonialism decisively contour Filipino-American texts, identities, and experiences. Except for Bulosan's pieces on the Filipino migrant workers, Santos's or Gonzalez's short fiction on middle-class cultural expatriates, Villa's universalist poetry, which shirked ethnic affinity altogether, or Jeff Tagami's eulogies to the working-class descendants who inspired him and the second-generation poets, most other texts—particularly by the women writers—turn to Philippine themes, landscapes, personas/characters, literary conventions, and sociocultural details.

Such writings and their historical inflections synchronize with changes in the composition of the migrant Filipino population in the United States, and can be distinguished in their exilic stances by generation and gender. The first major wave of migrants (1903–1930s) was heavily male. It consisted of Filipino peasants (Pinoys) recruited for agricultural and cannery work in Hawaii and the Pacific Coast states, and upper-class Filipinos sponsored coterminously by the American colonial government as political and cultural apprentices (pensionados). The canonized male writers may be identified with either stream, and their writings from the 1940s onward adverted to such historical sources for narrative viewpoints and aesthetic motifs. As American colonial policy foresaw, class divides among Filipinos were reinforced when the pensionados dominated the professions, business, and government upon their return to the Philippines. The emergence of Filipino English writers (conventionally dated from 1925) paralleled this development in the literary sphere and eclipsed the vernacular writings. American colonialism, after succeeding in its war against Filipino resistance (1899–1903), dissipated the national unity achieved in the 1896–1898 Filipino revolution against Spain in these ways.

A consequence of the American imposition of English as the lingua franca in the colony, English proficiency became both the symbol and the mode of social or historical alienation among Filipinos. Indeed, male writers commonly lamented or admitted their linguistic expatriation from countercolonial Philippine history, vernacular cultures, and even readers after this period. Yet, a common nativist thread weaves through their texts, irrespective of their creative creeds and in spite of their indebtedness to Western canonical literatures. Extended residence in the United States usually gave precision to their sense of exile and longing for a precolonial past. One can divine a similar pattern in the work of indigenous writers who sojourned in the United States after World War II in the manner of the early pensionados. Such ambivalent subject-positions are characteristic of how these writers outlined the problem of identity as a search for "essence," or the authentic.

The second major migratory wave came after the 1965 liberalization of American immigration laws, which emphasized family reunification and skilled workers and professionals. Recent research reveals a mostly female profile (60 percent) that also recasts the current Filipino-American population as 70 percent foreign-born, with projections that Filipino-Americans would treble their 1980 census numbers to 2.1 million by the year 2000. This demographic imbalance by gender and origin stems from the preferential immigration policies shaped historically by race and nativist movements in the United States, and explains the smallness of the Filipino-American second generation. Yet it also coextends with the emergence of women's and second-generation writing by the 1970s, even as it elaborates the exilic bent of the earlier migrants and writers with the ancestral romanticism characteristic of first/second generations. But whereas the older and male writers explored social history or nativism for identification and material (typical of incipient nationalist styles, according to Terry Eagleton et al. in *Nationalism, Colonialism, and Literature*, 1990), the women writers, especially in their historical fiction, rewrite Philippine colonial history and engage its manifold mediations.

The second-generation writers tend to mime

the older writers in turning to nativism, perhaps because of their liminality in the overdetermined contexts of American life. They often oscillate between Filipino and Filipino American as terms of identity politics. They prefer the ethnic modifier Pilipino on the thesis that the *f*-sound does not occur in the indigenous alphabets and is a linguistic transfer from the Spanish and American colonial eras. Frank Denton and Victoria Villena-Denton argue that, in consequence, Filipinos in the United States remain politically indeterminate, regarding Filipino American as an uneasy pair of names for themselves, or claiming Filipino and American binationality as an alternative (*Filipino Views of America*, 1986). *Filipino* is thus a term that simulates the flux of Philippine nationalism and community formation in the United States, which is sure to continue multiplying the purviews of Filipino-American identities and literary efforts.

[*See also* Asian-American Writing; Assimilation; Citizenship; Ethnicity and Writing.]

• Antonio Manuud, ed., *Brown Heritage: Essays on Philippine Cultural Tradition and Literature* (1967). Lucila Hosillos, *Philippine-American Literary Relations, 1898–1941* (1969). Sam Solberg, "Introduction to Filipino American Literature," in *Aiiieeeee! An Anthology of Asian American Writers*, eds. Frank Chin et al. (1974; reprint, 1983), pp. 49–64. Edilberto Alegre and Doreen Fernandez, eds., *Writers and Their Milieu* (1987). Epifanio San Juan, Jr., "Pacifying the Boondocks," in *Ruptures, Schisms, Interventions* (1988), pp. 21–37. Delia Aguilar, *The Feminist Challenge* (1988). Dolores Stephens Feria, "Filipino Writers in Exile," in *Red Pencil, Blue Pencil: Essays and Encounters* (1991), pp. 179–189. Oscar Campomanes, "Filipinos in the United States and Their Literature of Exile," in *Reading the Literatures of Asian America*, eds. Shirley Geok-lin Lim and Amy Ling (1992), pp. 49–78.

Oscar V. Campomanes

FILM THEORY, Feminist. Most feminist film theorists and critics use the language of "before" and "after" to characterize the evolution of the field. Before, there were "images of women," and after, there was "feminist film theory." The befores usually include groundbreaking studies in the early 1970s, especially Molly Haskell's *From Reverence to Rape* (1972) and Marjorie Rosen's *Popcorn Venus* (1973), as well as feminist demands from the same time period for more and better female role models on film and television screens. But the very notion of feminist film theory is predicated on the assumption that it is not enough to bring a feminist perspective to the study of cinema; rather, the very foundations of cinema as an art form and as an institution require thorough analysis and critique.

Feminist film theory emerged in the mid-1970s as a critical examination of woman as image. It is insufficient, feminist film theorists argued, to insist on "better" images if one has not examined the complex and often invisible ways in which such images are produced and consumed. Some feminists praised Katharine Hepburn or Mae West as offering powerful alternatives within Hollywood; others heralded the new feminist documentaries, like *Growing Up Female* (Julia Reichert and James Klein, 1969) and *Janie's Janie* (Geri Ashur, 1971), as offering images of women created by and for women. Feminist film theorists, however, brought skepticism to such claims by insisting that all images are ideological, thus challenging the very idea of a positive image.

Psychoanalysis was a crucial dimension of this challenge of feminist film theory to any notion of positive feminist images. Following the examples set by theorists in France and Great Britain in particular, for whom psychoanalysis offered a means of understanding not only individual psyches but textual and cultural obsessions, feminist film theorists insisted that the language of the cinema needed to be approached as Freud approached the dreams and speech of his patients—symptomatically. And the language of psychoanalysis was, for emerging feminist film theory, a crucial—and controversial—means of analyzing how images function.

Here another before and after enters into play. It is common to describe two different kinds of feminism—the images of women approach and feminist film theory—as the two stages of feminist film studies. Less commonly noted is that feminist film theory was shaped by the new film theory of the 1970s as much as it was by feminism. For the study of cinema was influenced by the advent of new theories of representation—a combination of semiotics and psychoanalysis, exemplified in the changing interests of French theorists Christian Metz and Raymond Bellour, both of whom began as "pure" semioticians of the cinema and then eventually became committed to the analysis of the cinema in semiotic and psychoanalytic terms. Kaja Silverman traces the shift from semiotics to psychoanalysis as a history of the subject in film theory (*The Subject of Semiotics*, 1983), and she regards this shift as the foundation for feminist film theory.

The influence of French psychoanalyst Jacques Lacan is often cited in this context, particularly given the striking parallels between the regressive pleasures of the cinema and the Lacanian imaginary (what Metz would call the "imaginary signifier"), or the dynamics of the gaze, central both to Lacan's writings and to the cinema. In more general terms, the historical parallels between the cinema and psychoanalysis have been described as "no coincidence"; both are late nineteenth-century "inventions" that functioned, in however different ways, to articulate the fantasies of white, middle-class culture.

Two concepts emerged as particularly crucial to 1970s film theory, both on its own terms and as it was later challenged by feminist film theorists: the cinematic apparatus and the gaze. If cinema worked as a powerful ideological medium, it was due in large part, film theorists argued, to its status as an apparatus, that is, as a machine capable of positioning its viewers in precise ways, of articulating desire and resolution, of reinforcing patterns of order and coherence. An understanding of the cinema as apparatus led to emphasis on how the cinema worked as a textual system capable of producing strong effects of identification and investment vis-à-vis the spectator. Hence the importance of the gaze. If cinema is primarily a visual medium, then the gaze is what draws the spectator into the dramas of seeing and being seen, and what creates the fundamental narrative and visual components of the cinema, from point-of-view shots to rules of continuity.

Another important feature of 1970s film theory was the distinction between dominant and alternative cinemas. Analyses of the apparatus and the gaze took classical Hollywood cinema as the point of departure. The term *classical Hollywood cinema* refers most specifically to Hollywood films from the late 1920s (with the advent of sound film) to the 1950s (with the demise of the studio system), but more generally and commonly to cinema that draws the spectator into a seamless, fictional world of narrative crisis and resolution. Theorists like Metz and Bellour were concerned almost exclusively with the classical cinema, but for others, the point of analyzing the classical cinema was to better understand the features necessary for a truly alternative cinema. Jean-Luc Godard's films were important examples, for they offered demonstrations of many of the points made by film theorists. Godard's work took up many of the issues at stake in film theory—the nature of the cinematic apparatus, the pleasures and discomforts of looking and being looked at, the relationship between seamless and fractured narratives. Godard's films highlighted the stark opposition between dominant and alternative film that was assumed in much film theory, and offered the possibility of a theoretically sophisticated alternative cinema.

It does not require too much imagination to see, in the preoccupations of 1970s film theory, issues that would be central to feminist inquiry in general. Indeed, virtually independently of 1970s film theory, feminists had called for alternatives to dominant cinema, even if the alternatives offered by feminist documentaries were quite different from the alternatives offered in Godard's cinema. And if the apparatus and the gaze suggested the institutional quality of the cinema, it follows that the institution in question can be seen as a profoundly patriarchal one. What was not entirely clear to many feminists was the necessity of the psychoanalytic dimension.

In 1975, Laura Mulvey published an essay that both summarized existing theories of the cinema and moved them into new territory, and the case Mulvey makes for psychoanalysis as a "political tool" has remained influential to this day. In "Visual Pleasure and Narrative Cinema" (*Screen* 15, no. 3), Mulvey argued that the unique pleasures of the cinema come from its combination of fetishism (fragmentation and display of the body, especially the female, maternal body) and scopophilia (pleasure in looking, especially male pleasure in looking at women), both of which reactivate early traumas of loss. Most important, Mulvey queried and foregrounded what had been assumed but rarely problematized by most theorists of the gaze: that the spectator theorized by 1970s film theory is a male spectator, and that the classical cinema is therefore an apparatus made to the measure of male desire and male crises of identification.

Mulvey is a filmmaker as well as a theorist, and her essay was also a manifesto for an avant-garde cinema that would reject the trappings of classical cinema. Indeed, if the classical cinema is fully informed by and dependent upon the objectification of woman, as Mulvey argued, then the only possibility for feminist cinematic alternatives was the creation of a radically new film aesthetic. In Mulvey's own 1975 film *Riddles of the Sphinx* (made with Peter Wollen), for instance, 360-degree pans destabilized the relationship between viewer and screen by refusing both the objectification of the female body and the familiarity of point-of-view shots.

Mulvey's essay focused theoretical attention on male spectatorship and feminist alternative film, setting the terms of the discussion for the next decade and a half. Two book-length introductions to feminist film theory, Annette Kuhn's *Women's Pictures* (1982) and E. Ann Kaplan's *Women and Film: Both Sides of the Camera* (1983), are concerned centrally with the gaze (a chapter in Kaplan's book is entitled "Is the Gaze Male?"), and the opposition between dominant and alternative film structures both books. Increasingly, however, Mulvey's analyses of spectatorship became more foregrounded than her discussions of feminist avant-garde cinema.

Indeed, if there is a single preoccupation that has characterized feminist film theory from Mulvey's ground-breaking 1975 essay to the present, it is female spectatorship, whether defined as a contradiction in terms or as a necessary revision of the implications of psychoanalytic film theory. Attention to female spectatorship has involved an accompanying move away from large generalizations about the male gaze and classical cinema toward more specific examples. In feminist work, this attention has emerged from the desire to understand the institutions of cinema less as generalized monoliths and more as particular sets of forces shaped by a variety of cultural and ideological factors. For instance, Mary Ann Doane, in *The Desire to Desire* (1987), demonstrates a dominant film practice that effectively denies the possibility of female cinematic pleasure in any but patriarchal terms, and in that sense she follows Mulvey's account. But she does so by examining a very particular genre (the "woman's film") at a particular juncture of American history (the 1940s).

Other critics have examined periods of film history that have been underrepresented in feminist work, precisely because they lie outside of the realm of the dominant cinema, as it is generally understood. Patrice Petro's study of Weimar cinema, *Joyless Streets* (1989), is a historical investigation of female spectatorship that examines the relations between film and other forms of mass culture. At the same time, many feminist film theorists have sought to problematize the absolute division between dominant and alternative film. Lucy Fischer's study of dominant cinema and works by women filmmakers, *Shot/Countershot: Film Tradition and Women's Cinema* (1989), may seem from its title to perpetuate the opposition, but this is far from the case; Fischer is concerned, rather, with rethinking the relationship between women filmmakers and the institutions of cinema as an "intertextual dialogue."

Since feminist film theory has responded to film theory as much or more than to other developments in feminist theory and criticism, historically it has not been particularly influential vis-à-vis other fields. In the last several years, however, this has begun to change, and feminist film theory has become more visible within feminist literary criticism in particular. Nancy K. Miller's *Subject to Change* (1988) includes a chapter entitled "Performances of the Gaze," an analysis of the female gaze in Madame de Staël's *Corinne, or Italy* (1807); the influence of feminist film theory is clearly in evidence. At a plenary session of the 1989 National Women's Studies Association convention, Catherine Stimpson spoke about the development of feminist literary criticism and theory, and acknowledged the importance of the work of feminist film criticism and theory in warning against the dangers of the seductive powers of realism and the image.

Such references suggest that the cinematic questions addressed by feminist film theorists have a much wider frame of reference than was previously the case. The works of two feminist film theorists, Teresa De Lauretis and Trinh T. *Minh-ha, are particularly representative of current directions in the field. If feminist film theorists in the 1970s criticized film theory's marginalization of sexual difference, De Lauretis, in *Alice Doesn't: Feminism, Semiotics, Cinema* (1984) and *Technologies of Gender* (1987), has extended the critique further to explore issues of race and sexuality outside the heterosexual paradigm. Similarly, De Lauretis's work suggests that feminist alternative cinema raises questions for theory that have been insufficiently addressed. Trinh T. Minh-ha is a filmmaker as well as a theorist; her writings, from *Woman, Native, Other* (1989) to *When the Moon Waxes Red* (1991), like her films (*Reassemblage*, 1982; *Naked Spaces-Living Is Round*, 1985; *Surname Viet Given Name Nam*, 1989; and *Shoot for the Contents*, 1991) do not fall into any easily identifiable categories, and in that sense represent a new kind of challenge to feminist film theory. De Lauretis and Trinh examine critically the theoretical foundations of feminist film theory, including psychoanalysis. In so doing, they investigate areas that previously were marginalized in feminist film theory, and difference in their work is understood as an entity as complex and contradictory as the cinema itself.

• Karyn Kay and Gerald Peary, eds., *Women and the Cinema: A Critical Anthology* (1977). Mary Ann Doane, Patricia Mellencamp, and Linda Williams, eds., *Re-vision: Essays in Feminist Film Criticism* (1984). Philip Rosen, ed., *Narrative, Apparatus, Ideology: A Film Theory Reader* (1986). Constance Penley, ed., *Feminism and Film Theory* (1988). Laura Mulvey, *Visual and Other Pleasures* (1989). Janet Bergstrom and Mary Ann Doane, eds., special issue on The Spectatrix, *Camera Obscura*, nos. 20–21 (1990). Patricia Erens, ed., *Issues in Feminist Film Criticism* (1990). Annette Kuhn with Susannah Radstone, eds., *Women in Film: An International Guide* (1990). Judith Mayne, *The Woman at the Keyhole: Feminism and Women's Cinema* (1990).

Judith Mayne

FIRST AMENDMENT. *See* Censorship.

FISHER, Dorothy Canfield (1879–1958), novelist, short story writer, essayist, educational leader. Born in Lawrence, Kansas, Dorothea Frances Canfield was educated in public schools in Kansas and Nebraska, where her father held teaching and administrative positions at state universities. While attending high school in Lincoln, Nebraska, she began a lifelong friendship with Willa *Cather. Dorothy Canfield completed her undergraduate education at Ohio State University and her doctorate in French at Columbia University, where her dissertation focused on translations of Corneille and Racine. Declining a university teaching post, she cared for her aging parents in New York City and began publishing stories and poems in magazines and newspapers. In 1907, she married John Fisher, and the couple moved to her family home in North Arlington, Vermont.

Following a visit to Maria Montessori's Casa dei Bambini in Rome in 1911, Fisher introduced the Montessori method through two books and a series of articles on child rearing. Her popular children's book *Understood Betsy* (1916) celebrates the values of independence and Montessori self-discovery when Betsy learns that not only can she take care of herself, but she is also capable of taking care of others.

During the First World War, Fisher participated in civilian relief activities in France. *Home Fires in France* (1918), dedicated to her old geometry teacher General John Pershing, is a collection of propagandistic sketches describing life in wartime France. Later, she used her experiences in the novel *The Deepening Stream* (1930).

Fisher's novels and stories are frequently set in a small Vermont village. They are rich studies of character set against contemporary social concerns, such as racial *prejudice, anti-Semitism, the role of women, the rise of fascism, and experimental theories of *marriage and child rearing. Her major novels include *The Bent Twig* (1915), *The Brimming Cup* (1921), *Her Son's Wife* (1926), *The Home-Maker* (1924), *Bonfire* (1933), and *Seasoned Timber* (1939).

She published twenty-two works of fiction under the name Dorothy Canfield, and eighteen books or collections of nonfiction under Dorothy Canfield Fisher. Fluent since childhood in French and Spanish, she also translated two Italian books. Despite her productivity and contemporary reputation, her work has been the subject of only two recent scholarly articles. As an original member of the Book-of-the-Month Club's selection committee, Fisher shaped the reading of the country's most popular book club. She discovered and recommended Pearl *Buck's *The Good Earth* (1931) and Isak Dinesen's stories, and contributed a preface to Richard Wright's *Native Son* (1940).

• Canfield's personal papers and manuscripts are in the Bailey-Howe Library, University of Vermont, and the Paul Reynolds Collection, Columbia University. See also Ida H. Washington, *Dorothy Canfield Fisher: A Biography* (1982). Mark J. Madigan, *Keeping Fires Night and Day: Selected Letters of Dorothy Canfield Fisher* (1993). Mark J. Madigan, "Profile: Dorothy Canfield Fisher," in *Legacy: A Journal of American Women Writers* vol. 9, no. 1 (1992): 49–58. Alan Price, "Writing Home from the Front: Edith Wharton and Dorothy Canfield Fisher Present Wartime France to the United States: 1917–1919," in the *Edith Wharton Newsletter* vol. 5 (Fall 1988): 1–8.

Alan Price

FITZGERALD, Zelda (1900–1948), perhaps best known as F. Scott Fitzgerald's zany Jazz Age wife, had brief but noteworthy successes of her own as a writer, artist, and dancer. Her public antics with Scott in the early days of their marriage contributed to their reputation for unconventional behavior, extravagance, and intoxication. Zelda was a source of tremendous inspiration for Scott throughout his career, but she was frustrated in her efforts to develop her own talents fully; she spent much of her adult life under psychiatric care in various mental institutions.

Zelda Sayre was born in Montgomery, Alabama. Her father was a judge, and she led a privileged life. She met Fitzgerald at a Montgomery country club dance in 1918, while he was a lieutenant in an army unit stationed nearby. They were married in New York in 1920, just after *This Side of Paradise*, his first novel, appeared. Their only child, a daughter named Frances Scott Fitzgerald, but whom they called Scottie, was born a year later.

The spectacular success of Scott's first novel, which exposed the rapidly changing morals of the early twentieth century, thrust the young couple into the limelight. Both Scott and Zelda were soon seen as spokespersons for the youth of postwar America; during the early 1920s, magazines eagerly interviewed both Fitzgeralds, and they coauthored several magazine articles and short stories. Zelda also wrote some of her own, although several of these were published under Scott's name, apparently to command greater pay.

Zelda's lasting influence on American literature was first apparent in Scott's stories and novels. She was the model for many of the women in his fiction, including Gloria in *The Beautiful and Damned* (1922), Daisy in *The Great Gatsby* (1925), and Nicole in *Tender Is the Night* (1934). Zelda once candidly told an interviewer that she recognized portions of her diary in *The Beautiful and Damned,* and Scott readily acknowledged his reliance on her experience and perceptions.

When Zelda expressed interest in launching an independent career as a writer, Scott vehemently opposed the idea. He claimed that he had exclusive rights to the literary expression of their shared experiences, because he was the "professional" writer. As Scott's career flourished, the marriage deteriorated. While they were living in Europe after the publication of *The Great Gatsby* (1925), Zelda began professional ballet training. She had been a gifted dancer in her teens, and ballet later figured prominently in her only published novel, *Save Me the Waltz* (1932).

From the late 1920s until her death in 1948, Zelda struggled relentlessly with mental illness. She was hospitalized repeatedly for long periods, both in Europe and in the United States. Her illness and her interaction with her psychiatrists contributed greatly to Scott's depiction of psychotherapy in *Tender Is the Night* (1934).

As a psychiatric patient, Zelda resumed writing. She wrote *Save Me the Waltz* (1932) in six weeks while she was hospitalized, dedicating it to one of her doctors, Mildred Squires. Scott was outraged when Scribners accepted the autobiographical novel, and insisted on editing it.

Save Me the Waltz was neither a critical nor a financial success. As an artistic achievement, it is uneven, but it is important in its portrayal of a young woman's determination to develop her own career and a meaningful life for herself apart from her husband. Alabama Beggs Knight, the protagonist, responds to her husband's womanizing by throwing herself into belated training to become a ballerina. Her excessive zeal ultimately leads to an incapacitating foot infection, which prevents her from reaching her goal, much as Zelda's mental illness crippled her. Frustrated and despondent, Alabama reluctantly resigns herself to her familiar, empty life with her pompous husband and young daughter. *Save Me the Waltz* was Zelda Fitzgerald's greatest personal literary achievement, but her influence on Scott Fitzgerald's *Tender Is the Night* was also substantial.

After Scott's death in 1940, Zelda continued to require psychiatric care. She wrote a second novel, *Caesar's Things*, in the 1940s, but it was never published. In addition to her writing and dancing, Zelda cultivated a lifelong interest in art. An exhibit of her paintings and drawings attracted little attention in the early 1930s, but samples of her works are sometimes displayed in books and discussions about her life with Scott. In 1948, she died with several other patients in a fire that engulfed the North Carolina nursing home where she lived.

• Nancy Milford, *Zelda: A Biography* (1970). Sara Mayfield, *Exiles from Paradise: Zelda and Scott Fitzgerald* (1971). Matthew J. Bruccoli and Margaret M. Duggan, eds., *The Correspondence of F. Scott Fitzgerald* (1980). James R. Mellow, *Invented Lives: F. Scott and Zelda Fitzgerald* (1984). Sarah Beebe Fryer, *Fitzgerald's New Women: Harbingers of Change* (1988).

Sarah B. Fryer

FLANNER, Janet (1892–1978), journalist and essayist. Flanner is best known for her twice-monthly column, "Letter from Paris," which appeared in the *New Yorker* from October 1925 to September 1975, and which she wrote under the pseudonym "Genêt," a name given her by the magazine's founder, Harold Ross. The letters were later collected in *Paris Journal: 1944–65* (ed. William Shawn, 1965), *Paris Journal: 1965–71* (ed. William Shawn, 1971), and *Paris Was Yesterday, 1925–1939* (ed. Irving Drutman, 1972).

Witty, vividly detailed observations of life in France, the letters deal with topics as varied as Sylvia *Beach's publication of James Joyce's *Ulysses*, the January white sales, the presidency of Charles de Gaulle, a Brigitte Bardot television show, and a Pablo Picasso retrospective. Crime, theater, politics, art, photography, literature, film—all are discussed with the eye of a social historian and journalist in an epigrammatic yet personable style. Clearly evident in the letters are Flanner's delight with language and life, her keen moral sense, and her unstinting craftsmanship.

Darlinghissima: Letters To a Friend (1985), a collection of letters written to her literary agent and lover, Natalia Danesi Murray, comments more bluntly on many of the same topics published in the *New Yorker* and reveals more of Flanner's passion, humor, and vulnerability.

Flanner was born in Indianapolis, Indiana, to Quaker parents, Francis and Mary Ellen Hockett Flanner. She attended the University of Chicago from 1912–1914, and three years later, in 1917, became art critic for the *Indianapolis Star*, fulfilling her childhood ambition of being a professional writer. The next year, 1918, she began publishing a movie column for the *Star*, now thought to be the first film criticism ever written.

Though Flanner published a novel, *The Cubical City*, in 1926, she quickly realized that her strengths were in the kind of essay reporting she would do as a foreign correspondent in Paris for the *New Yorker*. When Paris was occupied by the Germans in 1940, Flanner lived in New York City, where she prepared *An American in Paris: Profile of an Interlude between Two Wars* (1940), an anthology of her *New Yorker* profiles, including a riveting one on Adolf Hitler, and crime pieces written for other magazines.

Flanner received the French Legion of Honor in 1947 for her "Letter from Paris" column, an honorary Litt. D. from Smith College in 1958, and the National Book Award in 1966 for *Paris Journal: 1944–1965*.

• Brenda Wineapple, *Genêt: A Biography of Janet Flanner* (1989).

Kathy A. Fedorko

FLAPPER. Dating from the 1920s, the term *flapper* named the attractive, giddy, and slightly unconventional adolescent American women who epitomized the new freedoms of the Jazz Age. They were characterized by cartoonist John Held as wearing galoshes worn with the buckles unfastened so as to create the greatest possible "flap." Drawing attention to themselves was one of their primary motivations. Criticized by H. L. Mencken, as well as by preachers and parents throughout the country, the flapper was thought to be "a somewhat foolish girl, full of wild surmises and inclined to revolt against the precepts and admonition of her elders" (William and Mary Morris, *Dictionary of Word and Phrase Origins*, 1962). F. Scott Fitzgerald memorialized them as flat-chested lovelies in rolled-down hose, living it up at house parties and in the backseats of roadsters. They disappeared at the end of the 1920s—in the economic debacle of the Wall Street crash—as quickly as they had arrived.

• George E. Mowry, ed., *The Twenties, Fords, Flappers and Fanatics* (1963).

Linda Wagner-Martin

FOLKLORE. Although most literatures show evidence of folk elements, the writings from communities of color are especially strong in interweaving folk and written traditions. Because folklore can foster ethnic pride, clarify cultural values, and maintain cultural unity, African-American, Asian-American, Latina, and Native-American writers often use it to inform, center, or frame their narratives. Women from these groups celebrate the literary possibilities of folklore, incorporating in their narratives and poems a full range of folk genres.

Because these are cultures with hyphenated existences, their literatures use folklore to explore their ethnic heritage and its American permutations, constructing a self from the intersection of two sources. Although the specific origins of much of the lore are debatable, what is clear is that these are traditions that have a long history of preserving wisdom and cultural identity through story telling as a communal act. The writers use grandmothers, shamans, *curanderas* (women healers), and female tricksters to show the polarity between their culture's values and mainstream American values. Folklore becomes an appropriate vehicle to enhance a literature that deals with place, displacement, and cultural memory. Dismissing boundaries and artificial distinctions between high art and folk art, the women writers use lore to energize a wide range of writings, from folk poems to postmodern narratives.

Having survived the *Middle Passage, the *oral tradition permeates African-American literature. Its first major literary use by a woman is Zora Neale *Hurston's *Their Eyes Were Watching God* (1937), a novel full of folk wisdom, mother wit, animal tales, folk beliefs, and folk language. In the novel's turning point, the protagonist, Janie, gains a voice by playing the dozens, a game of ritualized insult, against her husband. Also included in this pivotal work are folk proverbs, arguments, and signifying, which Hurston's *Mules and Men* (1935) explains as "de inside meanin' of words." After all of Janie's ordeals, she ends up telling her story to her best friend, Phoebe. It is a story strong enough to make Phoebe feel taller. Janie's story uses folklore as text and context.

Following most directly in Hurston's steps is Alice *Walker. In one of Walker's stories, "The Revenge of Hannah Kemhuff" (1973), the root worker consults her bible, *Mules and Men*, and uses the rhetorical power of hoodoo to avenge the slights suffered by her black client at the hands of a white woman. The ultimate power of hoodoo is in its threat of power; the news of root working kills the offender. This story, as with so many of Walker's stories, is a retelling of her mother's stories. Walker's *The Color Purple* (1982) uses black vernacular speech, and *The Temple of My Familiar* (1989) is a story about stories told over the course of five hundred thousand years, experienced through the many different forms of Miss Lissie, a goddess in whom healing, memory, and story telling converge.

Another African-American writer whose narratives significantly use the oral tradition is Toni *Morrison. *Song of Solomon* (1977) collapses Greek myths, Western fairy tales, biblical stories, and African and African-American myths to form a work that is both folk/oral and postmodern. Children's rhymes and songs become folk communal aids in the process of self-discovery. *Tar Baby* (1981) uses folk myths, legends, and dreams to discuss Afro-Caribbean women's relationships to "ancient properties," as does Paule *Marshall's *Praisesong for the Widow* (1983). *Beloved* (1987) embraces African concepts of the living dead. The syncopation and improvisations of *Jazz* (1992) build upon the early attempts of Xam Wilson Cartier's *Be-Bop, Re-Bop* (1987) and some of Ann *Petry's short fiction to capture folk musical forms in narratives.

Other examples from African-American women's literature abound: Ntozake *Shange's *sassafrass, cypress & indigo* (1982), a narrative about femaleness, art, sexuality, and heritage, interweaves recipes, spirituals, menstruation rites, dance, and music to create new narrative possibilities; Gloria *Naylor's *Mama Day* (1988) pits folk healing, beliefs, and southern magic against science, logic, and urban experience. *Mama Day's* Sapphira Wade is a conjure woman who passes her folk gifts to Miranda Day, who, like Tina McElroy Ansa's Lena in *Baby of the Family* (1989), Toni Cade *Bambara's Maggie ("Maggie of the Green Bottles," 1967), and Bambara's Minnie Ransom (*The Salt Eaters*, 1980), has special powers; Sherley Anne *Williams's *Dessa Rose* (1986) turns a rebellious, pregnant slave woman awaiting her hanging into the ultimate trickster figure.

Characteristically oral, African-American poetry, too, uses folklore. Known as much for her ballads as for her sonnets, Gwendolyn *Brooks blends ancient forms with contemporary politics. Her Emmett Till ballads question historical portraits of villains and damsels in distress. In "how i got ovah" (1976) Carolyn *Rodgers makes use of spirituals; both Audre *Lorde and Lucille *Clifton write about black female goddesses; and many of the poets record oral histories of their families: Marilyn Waniek's *The Homeplace* (1989); Rita *Dove's *Thomas and Beulah* (1986), and several of Clifton's collections.

*Spirituals, blues songs, jazz rhythms, conjuring tales, hoodoo workers, animal tales, etiological tales, dozens rituals, and the call and response antiphonal structure of black folk sermons are all folk elements that African-American women writers transform to energize their writings. With such a large number consciously using the lore and using it extensively, the writers talk to each other through a type of intertextual folk talk, or as Henry Louis Gates, Jr., points out, they "signify" upon each other (*The Signifying Monkey*, 1988).

Asian-American women writers, too, have at their disposal a strong oral tradition that bridges two worlds, creating an American revision of their native lore. In *The Woman Warrior: Memoirs of a Girlhood among Ghosts* (1976), Maxine Hong *Kingston rewrites the traditional Chinese tale of the woman warrior, Fa Mu Lan, merging it with events from her own life. Kingston weaves together a new tale that bridges the ocean between China and America, empowering her both as a Chinese American and as a woman. The book follows this rhythm throughout, creating a tension between the overly romanticized power of Chinese lore and the comparatively dull reality of America. Folk proverbs such as "girls are maggots in the rice" and "it is more profitable to raise geese than daughters" war against the image of Fa Mu Lan, the legendary warrior. Kingston explores both faces of the lore—the empowering and the debilitating. Her last chapter revises the traditional tale of Ts'ai Yen, the woman poet abducted by barbarian warriors. The narrator tells us that the beginning of this story is her mother's, but the ending is hers. Through her revision of this traditional tale, Kingston finds a way to understand and retell her mothers' language and stories.

Amy *Tan's 1989 novel, *The Joy Luck Club*, is a collection of sixteen separate but related tales told between four pairs of mothers and daughters. As in Kingston's work, the stories are told and retold to bridge the distances between mother and daughter, as well as between China and America. Tan's work, too, seems to demystify and de-exoticize Chinese culture and lore. Each section begins with an epigrammatic tale that merges Chinese lore with American reality. In one, a mother warns her daughter not to ride her bike around the corner because a book of Chinese folklore, *The Twenty-Six Malignant Gates*, says something bad will happen if she leaves the protection of the house. The daughter protests, denounces the book, rides away on her bike and, in fact, falls off. Other folk elements include folk wisdom, folk jokes, and the myth of the moon goddess, Chang-O. Although Kingston and Tan have received most of the critical attention, several other Asian-American women authors, Diana *Chang, Mitsuye Yamada, Nellie Wong, and Hisaye Yamaoto, are combining maternal "talk-stories," legends, and myths into their writings.

Although the number of Latina writers combining lore and literature is not as large as the number of African-American or Asian-American women doing so, their lore is more focused, centering around *La Llorona, *La Malinche, and *La Virgen de Guadalupe/Tonantzin*. The legendary native woman who commits infanticide, *La Llorona* wanders the streets at night wailing, becoming an important cultural symbol of loss and suffering. One modern revision of this legend is Victoria Moreno's "La Llorona, Crying Lady of the Creekbeds, 483 Years Old, and Aging" (1980). In Morena's poem/legend, the welfare office takes *La Llorona's* children because her style of life does not represent the ideal household and her wailing is hard to hear without the necessary telephone.

Often associated with *La Llorona* is *La Malinche*, violated mother, the Indian woman who translates the Maya and Aztec languages for

Cortés and through their union gives birth to the *mestizo*. Although some of the legends blame *La Malinche* for cooperating with the oppressor and speak of her children as *los hijos de la Chingada* (the children of the Sacred Whore), Chicana writers are reclaiming *La Malinche* as a symbol of female power and cultural nationhood, as evidenced in "Chicana Evolution," a poem by Sylvia Gonzales.

La Virgen de Guadalupe, the bronze spiritual mother associated with Tonantzin, the Aztec goddess of fertility, is a third major folk character. Estela Portillo Trambley's *Trini* (1986) is the story of a Tarahumara Indian woman who illegally leaves Mexico to chase her dreams in the United States. Devoted to the *La Virgen de Guadalupe*, Trini gives birth in a church with the images of the Virgin in sight. The narrative mixes Indian and religious images. Women in the work teach Indian ways, stories, customs, and games; collect herbs with medicinal and spiritual powers; and ritualize the eating of folk foods. This emphasis on folklore and its effect on the community of women can also be seen in the writings of Pat Mora, Cherríe *Moraga, Lorna Dee *Cervantes, De Carmen Tafolla, and Josefina *Niggli. Sandra *Cisneros's *Woman Hollering Creek and Other Stories* (1990) contains legends of "witch women" and other stories of border women. A work that synthesizes the legends, goddesses, *cuentos* (stories), and *corridos* (ballads) together with present realities of living as a border woman is Gloria *Anzaldúa's *Borderlands/La Frontera: The New Mestiza* (1987).

Rich in lore, Native-American literature deals with mythology in a fragile world, where myths and ceremonies are needed for healing and wholeness. The work most prominent for its integration of folk material (Laguna Pueblo) is Leslie *Silko's *Ceremony* (1977), the story of Tayo, a shell-shocked World War II veteran in need of ritual chants, however modified. His is a world where the stories of Corn Woman, Reed Woman, and Spiderwoman/Thought-Woman are all needed. A story about stories and interconnectedness, *Ceremony* has no boundaries or chapters, just transitions, as one story moves into another. As with Silko's story, "Yellow Woman" (1981), time immemorial and time present merge into one fluid reality. Another Silko story, "Storyteller" (1981), examines the relationship of teller to audience, raising questions about the nature and function of telling stories, the importance of telling one's own story. It is a story of a woman who uses stories to free herself. Silko's latest work, *The Almanac of the Dead* (1992), continues her interest in keeping alive ancient wisdom.

Additionally, Paula Gunn *Allen's (Laguna Pueblo/Sioux) canon merges literature and lore; Louise *Erdrich recaptures the oral nature of Chippewa narratives in *Tracks* (1988) and the role of shamans in *Love Medicine* (1984). Other writers who adapt chants, coyote tales, Grandmother Spider stories, traditional prayers, and a wide range of other folk materials include Judith Ivaloo Volborth (Apache/Comanche), Joy *Harjo (Creek), Anita Endrezze-Danielson (Yaqui), Anna Lee Walters (Pawnee/Otoe), Nia Francisco (Navajo), Mary TallMountain (Koyukan), Beth *Brant (Mohawk), and Janet Campbell Hale (Coeur d'Alene). Wendy *Rose's (Hopi) "For the White Poets Who Would Be Indian" (1980) and Elizabeth Cook-Lynn's (Crow-Creek Sioux) "The Power of Horses" (1986) deal with the appropriation and theft of the lore and culture.

Comparative analyses of the writings from all these traditions reveal several similarities: an emphasis on circular or cyclical movement, rather than sequential or linear; the centrality of the transmission of tales between mother and daughter; fluid versus dichotomous realities; and a worldview framed by gender and ethnicity. The writers keep the oral traditions healthy by their historical reconstructions, constantly recontextualizing and revising the lore for both personal and political use.

[*See also* Orality.]

• Dexter Fisher, ed., *The Third Woman* (1980). Paula Gunn Allen, *Studies in American Indian Literature* (1983). Marjorie Pryse and Hortense J. Spillers, *Conjuring: Black Women, Fiction, and Literary Tradition* (1985). Paula Gunn Allen, ed., *Spider Woman's Granddaughters* (1989). Amy Ling, *Between Worlds* (1990). Gloria Anzaldúa, ed., *Making Face, Making Soul/Haciendo Caras* (1990). Gayl Jones, *Liberating Voices: Oral Tradition in African American Literature* (1991).

Valerie Lee

FORCHÉ, Carolyn (b. 1950), poet, journalist, and translator. Born to middle-class parents in Detroit, Michigan, and the oldest of seven children, Carolyn Forché entered the Justin Morrill College at Michigan State University on a scholarship in 1968. There, she majored in creative writing, minored in English literature and French, and studied international relations and several foreign languages, including Russian, Spanish, Serbo-Croatian, and Tewa (Pueblo Indian). She received her masters of fine arts at Bowling Green State University in 1975.

Forché's first book of poetry, *Gathering the Tribes* (1976), received the Yale Series of Younger Poets Award. In this selection of short narrative poems, she explores the nature of *kinship through her Slavic ancestors, her childhood friends, and her spiritual family, the Pueblo Indians; she reflects on her own development in relation to these influences.

In 1977, with a fellowship from the National Endowment of the Arts, Forché traveled to Spain, where she translated the work of exiled Latin American poet Claribel Alegria, published in Alegria's *Flowers from the Volcano* (1982). In Spain, Forché developed an interest in the politics of Latin America, an interest that found expression in the United States through her involvement in Amnesty International and other human rights organizations. When she received a Guggenheim Fellowship in 1978, she was urged by Alegria's nephew to spend time writing in El Salvador.

Forché's experience in El Salvador led to her second book of poems, *The Country between Us* (1981). Honored as the Lamont Selection of the Academy of Poets (1981) and nominated for the *Los Angeles Times* Book Award (1982), *The Country between Us* further explores Forché's personal growth, focusing particularly on the development of her social conscience. Its publication earned her both critical recognition and the problematic label of "political poet."

In addition to her own books of poetry and translations, Forché, working with William Kulik, has translated *The Selected Poems of Robert Desnos* (1991), and has written the texts for a series entitled *El Salvador: The Work of Thirty Photographers* (1983), and for *Shooting Back: Photography by and about the Homeless* (1991). She has recently edited an anthology of twentieth-century political poetry called *Against Forgetting: Twentieth Century Poetry of Witness* (1993). Forché currently teaches English and creative writing at George Mason University. She remains active in human rights causes, travels, and gives frequent poetry readings. Her third volume of poetry is forthcoming.

• "Carolyn Forché," in *Contemporary Literary Criticism* vol. 25, ed. Jean C. Stine (1983), pp. 168–172. David Montenegro, "Carolyn Forché: An Interview by David Montenegro," *American Poetry Review* (November/December 1988): 35–40. "Carolyn Forché," in *Critical Survey of Poetry* ed. Frank N. Magill (1992), pp. 1153–1160.

Traci Freeman

FOSTER, Hannah Webster (1758–1840), alias "A Lady of Massachusetts," novelist. Little is known of her childhood, although it is generally believed she was well educated for her time and gender. In 1785, she married John Foster, minister of First Church in Brighton, Massachusetts, and a leader in social and literary activities. They had six children.

Foster is known for authoring (anonymously, until 1866) one of the first and most popular novels in early America, *The Coquette; or, The History of Eliza Wharton* (1797). Foster based the novel on the story of Elizabeth Whitman, who, like the fictional heroine, died in a tavern in Danvers, Massachusetts, after giving birth to a stillborn child. Both Eliza Wharton and Elizabeth Whitman were the daughters of respected ministers and were known among their friends for their wit, intelligence, and charm. While there is no consensus as to how closely Foster adhered to the Whitman case, contemporary and later readers have read *The Coquette* as a true story, drawing on its subtitle, *Founded on Fact*, and on the knowledge that Foster might have had access to unpublished information, since Whitman was a cousin of Foster's husband.

The Coquette is an epistolary sentimental novel in the Richardsonian tradition and is widely considered to be a skillfully executed example of the genre. The heroine, like Clarissa, is more of a rebel and more learned than most sentimental heroines. Foster complicates the typical choices of the sentimental plot and adds sympathy to Eliza's situation by providing two possible suitors. Major Sanford, who succeeds in seducing Eliza, is an arrogant, unprincipled rake. Yet Reverend Boyer, although respectable, would be no more suitable due to his condescension, pedantry, and hints of unrestrained temper.

One of two best-sellers in the United States prior to 1800, *The Coquette* eventually appeared in at least thirteen editions. It was reprinted eight times between 1824 and 1828. In 1802, it was dramatized as *The New England Coquette* by Horatius Nichols.

Only one edition of *The Boarding School; or, Lessons of a Preceptress to Her Pupils* (1798) was published. It combines moral reflections with letters. Considered overly didactic, it shows the preceptress educating young women to fulfill their expected roles through a curriculum of needlework, reading, composition, dance, and "sentimental song." The work is notable for its attack on the double standards regarding sexuality, as the preceptress argues for greater punishment for seducers and more tolerance for their victims. Foster's only other published works consisted of short newspaper articles.

• Jane E. Locke, Preface to *The Coquette* by Hannah Webster Foster (reprint, 1855). Caroline H. Dall, *The Romance of the Association; Or, One Last Glimpse of Charlotte Temple and Eliza Wharton* (1875). Herbert Ross Brown, Introduction to *The Coquette* (Facsimile Edition, 1939). Herbert Ross Brown, *The Sentimental Novel in America, 1789–1860* (1940). Cathy N. Davidson, *Revolution and the Word: The Rise of the Novel in America* (1986). Cathy N. Davidson, Introduction to *The Coquette* (reprint, 1987).

Kathryn West

FREEDOM LIBRARIES. *See* Libraries.

FREEMAN, Mary Wilkins (1852–1930), New England regionalist, short story writer, and novelist. Born in Randolph, Massachusetts, Freeman moved at the age of fifteen to Brattleboro, Vermont, where her family declined economically, and her sister, mother, and father all died by the time she was thirty-one. In 1884, she returned to Randolph to live for almost twenty years with childhood friend Mary Wales. During this period, with the support of editor Mary Louise Booth of *Harper's Bazaar*, she wrote the regionalist short stories that established her reputation. Later collected in *A Humble Romance* (1887) and *A New England Nun* (1891), Freeman's stories from this decade often focus on the lives of aging, unmarried, and homeless *New England village women who struggle for social and economic self-determination. Unlike the writers of *local color who were her contemporaries—Bret Harte, Hamlin Garland, and Mark Twain—Freeman wrote not in order to entertain an urban Eastern audience, but to give regional characters voice and to portray the dignity of their lives. Following Booth's death in 1889, Freeman turned away from the subject matter of her early short fiction, taking as the plot of her most successful novel, *Pembroke* (1894), an old family story about a broken engagement.

On New Year's Day, 1902, after a decade of acquaintance and a series of her own broken, then renewed, engagements, forty-nine-year-old Mary E. Wilkins married Charles Manning Freeman, a New Jersey physician who never practiced medicine, and moved to Metuchen, New Jersey. By all critical evaluations, the quality of her writing diminished after this move, and in her novel *By the Light of the Soul* (1906), which contains autobiographical elements, she appears to reconsider the wisdom of marriage; indeed, by 1909, Charles had begun to enter sanitariums for alcoholism, and, after institutionalizing her husband in 1919, Freeman would eventually secure a formal separation.

Freeman wrote prolifically throughout her career, publishing fourteen collections of stories, including *ghost stories and experimental fiction, thirteen novels, children's books, a play, and poems for children and adults. Her circle of friends and acquaintances included Hamlin Garland, William Dean Howells, Rudyard Kipling, Julia Ward *Howe, Sarah Orne *Jewett, and Mark Twain. In April 1926, she received the Howells Medal for Fiction from the American Academy of Arts and Letters; later that year, she and Edith *Wharton were among the first women to be elected to membership in the National Institute of Arts and Letters in New York. She died of a heart attack in Metuchen.

• Edward Foster, *Mary E. Wilkins Freeman* (1956). Abigail Ann Hamblen, *The New England Art of Mary Wilkins Freeman* (1966). Perry D. Westbrook, *Mary Wilkins Freeman* (1967). Josephine Donovan, *New England Local Color Literature: A Women's Tradition* (1983). Brent L. Kendrick, *The Infant Sphinx: The Collected Letters of Mary E. Wilkins Freeman* (1985). Marjorie Pryse, "Mary E. Wilkins Freeman," in *Modern American Women Writers*, ed. Elaine Showalter (1990), pp. 41–53.

Marjorie Pryse

FRENCH CREOLE WRITING. *See* Acadian and Creole Writing.

FRENCH FEMINISM is a style of feminist practice having roots in French antihumanist philosophy and marking a departure from feminist thought based in Marxism and existentialism. Closely associated with the *Mouvement de Libération des Femmes (MLF)*, the name the French press invented to identify radical groups of women who took part in the student uprisings of May 1968, the new feminism generated a heterogeneous front against patriarchal ideology, which persisted in even the most revolutionary activity. One founding group, *Psychanalyse et politique*, outlined a dialectical application of psychoanalysis and historical materialism to women's struggle, and became the *MLF*'s cultural and intellectual center after setting up its publishing house, *éditions des femmes*. Other groups emerged: the lesbian separatist *Feministes révolutionnaires* in 1970 and the militant *Ligue du droit des femmes* (led by Simone de *Beauvoir) in 1974. Mobilizing consciousness through intellectual terrorism, the new feminism circulated powerful manifestos in feminist journals such as *Le Torchon Brule* (in the early 1970s), *Nouvelles féministes* (the *Ligue*'s newspaper, 1974–1977), *Le Quotidien des femmes* (*Psyche et po*'s newspaper, started in 1975), *Questions féministes* (started under Beauvoir's editorship in 1977), and special issues of *Partisans* (July–October 1970), *Les temps modernes* (April–May 1974), and *L'Arc* (no. 61, 1975).

Elaine Marks and Isabelle de Courtivron's anthology *New French Feminisms* (1980) introduced English speakers to writers and activists, their different political affiliations in the *MLF*, and the general history and context of feminism in France. Selective translation and selective critical commentary (notably Toril Moi's 1985 *Sexual/Textual Politics*, one of the first studies to read French and American feminisms in their very different intellectual contexts), familiarized English-speaking feminists most particularly with the writings of Hélène Cixous, Luce Irigaray, Julia Kristeva, and Monique Wittig. While each has her own distinct writing practice, English interpreters read them together, perceiving them to share such text-based projects as the radical critique of phallogocentrism and the promotion of *ecriture feminine* (feminine writing/writing the feminine). They do share an education in Hegel, Marx, and Freud; in structuralist linguistics, anthropology, and psychoanalysis (Ferdinand de Saussure, Claude Levi-Strauss, Jacques Lacan); in avant-garde poetics (Stéphane Mallarmé, Surrealism); in narrative theory and dialogism (Mikhail Bakhtin); in deconstructive philosophy (Jacques Derrida); in textual semiotics (Roland Barthes); in discourse formation (Michel Foucault); and in the phenomenological, ideological, and linguistic subject (Martin Heidegger, Louis Althusser, Emile Benveniste). From these contexts they derive related analyses of master discourses, or mainstream philosophy, whose binary logic and figurative language is said to form the structural and generative framework of Western thought. They draw most heavily on Lacan's phallocentric description of symbolic organization and on Derrida's critique of Lacan, questioning Lacan's assumption that the phallus or masculine signifier is the structural center or monosexual standard of subjectivity and exchange in the symbolic universe. Their deconstruction of psychoanalytic, philosophical, and anthropological language exposes a systemic ideological privileging of the masculine in the very genealogy and structure of discourse, in its grammar (the hierarchy of gender opposition); its figures (masculine figures always being positive, feminine, negative); its narrative plots (Oedipal, paternal, patriarchal); its subject of enunciation (the universal masculine singular); and even its syntax, the copula being analogous to phallomorphology (that is, as a rule, the subject is predicated to indicate identity, unity, autonomy, solidity, and order erected against "feminine" heterogeneity and fluidity). Their purpose is to "unwrite" this discursive privileging of masculinity, which inevitably, in patriarchal society, translates into institutional power for men as the predestined bearers of the phallus. They deploy a variety of textual strategies, collectively known as *écriture feminine* or "writing the body," to destabilize, decenter, and dis*organize* the phallocratic order.

For all four feminists, the feminine refers to a repressed semiotic potential that has been exiled to the cultural margins since the Greeks. Cixous, Irigaray, and Kristeva attempt to recover the feminine from the residues and reserves of Western discourse in a subversive application of psychoanalysis's reading for the "other" in the gaps and slips of speech. Conversely, from outside the psychoanalytic circle Wittig maintains that the feminine cannot be recuperated, that it can only signify the repressed, the enslaved, the inferior, and is wholly useless for feminist practice. The psychoanalytic feminists proceed with a radical "archeology": Cixous and Kristeva re*orient* the discourse of woman toward Eastern (Egyptian, Chinese), primitive (prehistoric), or poetic (pre-Oedipal, transhistoric) writing, while Irigaray systematically recovers figures of feminine spatiality, fluidity, and heterogeneity from the (back)ground of philosophical textuality, against which masculine figures are erected in positive relief. They reinscribe Freud's/Lacan's Oedipal narrative, shifting the focus from castration (as the privileged imaginary site of [masculine] subjectivity, where maternal attachments are severed in exchange for symbolic autonomy and sexual identity) to sites of pre-Oedipal resistance. The eruption of pre-Oedipal expressivity into discourse signifies the uncanny and/or hysterical return of repressed incestuous phantasies, including the most primitive, most disruptive, and most repressed mother-daughter phantasies comprising the unconscious "feminine" (p)reserve of signifying power. But while Cixous and Irigaray "write the feminine" as a countercultural strategy to displace and overthrow male-centered or hom(m)osexual discourse in its various (political, economic, legal) manifestations, Kristeva traces the most successful "feminine writing" in men's avant-garde poetry and in the writing of pregnant women who, hypothetically, heretically desire the Law (castration, the incest taboo) to demarcate and symbolize the maternal subject. Kristeva confines revolutionary feminism to the signifying process of poetic practice, whereby masculine discursivity is disrupted and transformed but never displaced by "maternal" semiotic impulses. She rejects collective feminism as an alternative theology deriving from regressive homosexual phantasies of the "phallic mother," and hence, is counterrevolutionary.

Consistent with their antihumanism, all French feminists espouse antifeminism, agreeing that *woman* cannot be defined, that *she* does not exist either as pure essence or pure difference. Cixous denounces the movement for political identity and equality as phallofeminism, calling instead for women to write themselves into history by figuring their sex, their joy, their love in excessive violation of patriarchal taboos. Irigaray appeals to women to assemble amongst themselves to learn to speak (as) woman in gestural and syn*tactical* turns of phrase, which mime women's morphological and cultural differences and forge the foundations for a woman's society. Having been exiled by patriarchy to a state of social and symbolic dereliction, women, she argues, must create a sacred (but not sacrificial) knowledge of woman's divinity. Wittig questions the use of the word *feminist* for a militant practice that aims at the total destruction of the sex/gender system, including such politically disabling categories as feminine and woman. As a "materialist lesbian," Wittig perceives the primary material cause of women's oppression to be the linguistic regime of (hetero)sexual opposition, hegemony, and forced coupling. To subvert this regime, she writes fictions that figure only lesbian embraces and exchanges, attacking patriarchal propriety, like Georges Bataille, with avant-garde pornography. Adapting motifs from classical literature to foreground their perversity, she radically reinterprets the primitive and sacred texts of "the straight mind." Rather than promote minority (homosexual) literature, she deploys lesbian writing as a "war machine" to explode the mainstream canon.

Though not aligned with Wittig's lesbian feminism, Kristeva, Cixous, and Irigaray could also be called "materialist" feminists. Kristeva's revolutionary semiotics locates the source and power of its transformative action in the generative interstices of bodily drives and textual layers. Cixous inscribes her metaphorical figure of a "feminine libidinal economy" against the capitalist notion of accumulation and debt. Drawing on Marcel Mauss's and Bataille's concept of "the gift," she calls for a women's practice of "giving the mother to the other woman" to counteract the masculine economy that has robbed women of a mother's unconditional love, while blinding both sexes to the (m)other in men. Irigaray appropriates Marx's economics to demonstrate how women function as commodities in patriarchal capitalism. With Levi-Strauss's structural account of exogamy, she demonstrates how women might subvert the market structure: the exchange of women, like the exchange of signs, occurs between men, unless women, as potential signmakers, begin to signify (for) themselves. She promotes a *parler entre femme*, a speaking between women, ex-centric to patriarchal exchange.

While thus feminizing "the libidinal economy," French feminism also reinscribes the conventional discourse of love. In Lacan's caricature of woman's orgasm or *jouissance* as "the other face of God," they trace a strategic as well as an ecstatic "negative capability," which, while sublimely exceeding the bounds of representability, marks the limits of masculine desire. Cixous reads in particular for the "other bisexuality" (the engaging *jouissance* of woman's repressed masculinity and man's repressed femininity) in Shakespeare, Kleist, and others. Wittig explores "total" *jouissance* through an imaginary lesbianism, whose violent, visceral couplings dissolve the individual in the corporeal, in boundless consummation and regeneration of love's body. Irigaray presents such amorous figures as the "fecundity of the caress," the "mucosity" and intimacy of woman's lips ever "touching" at the "threshold" of sexual and oral intercourse, to subvert and displace the figure of the erect, untouched, and transcendent subject of patriarchal lover's discourse. She critiques Hegel's discourse on sexual ethics, according to which it is woman's civic duty to subject herself to man's desire while denying the cultivation and expression of her own. She forsees a society in which men and women cultivate their desires independently, so that a true heterosexuality can find expression in love.

American interest in French feminism over two decades reflects a departure from textual criticism toward ethics and politics. Following enthusiastic reception by psychoanalytic and literary audiences, Kristeva has met with severe criticism by sociological feminists, while Cixous and Irigaray enjoy renewed affirmation from legal, philosophical, and postcolonial feminists. Wittig attracts primarily lesbian audiences: her first wave of transatlantic reception in the seventies, when political lesbianism was at its height, has been succeeded by a second with the recent arrival of Queer Theory. She continues to serve on the editorial board of the American journal *Feminist Issues*.

[*See also* Simone de Beauvoir; Feminism; Gynocriticism.]

• Gayatri Chakravorty Spivak, "French Feminism in an International Frame," *Yale French Studies* 62 (1981): 154–184. Jane Gallop, *Feminism and Psychoanalysis* (1982). Claire Duchen, *Feminism in France* (1986). Toril Moi, ed., *French Feminist Thought* (1987). Elizabeth Gross, *Sexual Subversions* (1989). Judith Butler, *Gender Trouble* (1990). John Fletcher and Andrew Benjamin, eds., *Abjection, Melancholia and Love: The Work of Julia Kristeva* (1990). Morag Shiach, *Hélène Cixous: A Politics of Writing* (1991). Margaret Whitford, *Luce Irigaray: Philosophy in the Feminine* (1991). Drucilla Cornell, *Beyond Accommodation* (1991). Gayatri Chakravorty Spivak, "French Feminism Revisited: Ethics and Politics," in Judith Butler and Joan W. Scott, eds., *Feminists Theorize the Political* (1992), pp. 54–85. Nancy Fraser and Sandra Lee Bartky, eds., *Revaluing French Feminism* (1992). Kelly Oliver, *Ethics, Politics and Difference in Julia Kristeva's Writings* (1992). Carolyn Burke, Naomi Schor, and Margaret Whitford, eds., *Engaging with Irigaray: Feminist Philosophy and Modern European Thought* (1994).

Dianne Chisolm

FRENCH, Marilyn (b. 1929), novelist and social critic. Born Marilyn Edwards in New York City and educated at Hofstra University (B.A., 1961) and Harvard University (M.A., 1964, and Ph.D., 1972), French is best known for *The Women's Room* (1977), a novel that captured its cultural moment and became a controversial best-seller. Based on French's own movement from the life of a white, suburban wife and mother in the 1950s to that of a graduate student at Harvard in the 1960s, it traces the growth of Mira toward independence. Around this story, French accumulates case history after case history of middle-class women betrayed by men and society, culminating in the figure of Val, who seems to have reached a comfortable independence within patriarchal society until her liberated daughter is raped by a black man and then betrayed by the justice system. Val rejects masculine society and is gunned down as she attempts to free a black woman, who had resisted rape, from prison. The relentless outrage and long, consciousness-raising conversations drew some complaints from reviewers, but the book's raw emotion and form is its strength.

None of French's other works have had the same cultural impact, although they pursue two of the same issues: how to heal the wounds caused by patriarchy, and how mothers can protect their daughters from those wounds. *The Bleeding Heart* (1980) investigates the failed love affair between Dolores, a divorced feminist mourning her daughter's suicide, and Victor, a married executive with traditional values. *Her Mother's Daughter* (1987) explores four generations of mothers and daughters, from the silence of the Polish immigrant grandmother, through the mother who repeats that silence and the emotional abuse it perpetuates, to the daughter, Anastasia, who tries to break the silence with her own daughter, Franny.

In *Beyond Power: On Women, Men, and Morals* (1985), French attempted to rethink civilization by tracing the defeat of prehistoric, mother-centered society, based on the pursuit of pleasure, by historic, masculine society, based on the pursuit of power. She concluded this sweeping and speculative world history of human suffering and environmental degradation with the hope that this history could be redeemed through a feminist revolution of values, resulting once more in human equality and harmony with nature. French has also written conventional literary criticism—*The Book as World: James Joyce's* Ulysses (1976) and *Shakespeare's Division of Experience* (1981).

• Linda W. Wagner, "The French Definition," *Arizona Quarterly* 38, no. 4 (Winter 1982): 293–302. Janet Todd, ed., *Women Writers Talking* (1983). Mary Rose Sullivan, "Breaking the Silence: Marilyn French's *Her Mother's Daughter*," in *Mother Puzzles: Daughters and Mothers in Contemporary American Literature*, ed. Mickey Pearlman (1989).

Patricia L. Morse

FREUD, Sigmund. *See* Psychoanalysis and Women, article on Sigmund Freud.

FRIEDAN, Betty (b. 1921), feminist nonfiction writer, journalist, activist, social psychologist. Born in Peoria, Illinois, Friedan attended Smith College, where she studied psychology. After a year of graduate work at Berkeley, she dropped out to become a reporter in New York and to marry Carl Friedan. When she was fired from her newspaper position after requesting a second maternity leave, she began free-lancing for women's magazines, but became disillusioned when she noticed that her articles were repeatedly edited to exclude any reference to women's careers. These personal experiences, along with material gleaned from interviews with housewives, mostly Smith graduates, became the core of her classic *The Feminine Mystique* (1963). *The Feminine Mystique* argued that middle-class American white women had been duped (by education, advertising, the media, sociology, and psychology) into accepting the notion that marriage and motherhood were the sole means of happiness for women. Friedan pinpointed "the problem that has no name," the angst suffered by women who, supposedly, have everything—home, husband, children— but who feel dissatisfied with their lives. The book has been credited with marking the beginning of the most recent wave of U.S. feminism.

In 1966, Friedan cofounded the National Organization for Women (NOW) and became its first president. NOW was founded on the ideal that women should be able to enjoy full political, economic, and sexual equality with men. However, under Friedan's leadership, NOW also strove to represent itself as an organization for white, middle-class heterosexual women, and thus came under attack for being conservative as well as hierarchical. Under fire, Friedan retired as president of NOW in 1970 and went on to organize the Women's Political Caucus, the National Association to Repeal Abortion Laws, and the First Women's Bank.

In 1976, Friedan published *It Changed My Life: Writings on the Women's Movement*, and, in 1981, *The Second Stage*, a book that reiterated what Friedan has called her "middle American pragmatism." Her approach has won both admirers and detractors. Friedan continues to lecture widely and remains active in a variety of women's business and professional associations.

• Billie J. Wahlstrom, "Betty Friedan," in *American*

Women Writers, ed. Lina Mainiero, vol. 2 (1980), pp. 90–92. Susan Salter, "Friedan, Betty," in Contemporary Authors New Revision Series, eds. Linda Metzger and Deborah A. Straub, vol. 18 (1986), pp. 154–156. Barbara McGowan, "Friedan, Betty," in Handbook of American Women's History, ed. Angela Howard Zophy (1990), pp. 221–222. "Betty Friedan," in Contemporary Literary Criticism, ed. Thomas Votteler, vol. 74 (1993), pp. 89–113.

Cathy N. Davidson

FRIENDSHIP. When the witty and sharp-eyed narrator of Virginia * Woolf's A Room of One's Own (1929) turned from the fiction of the past to consider books written by women in this century, she was shocked and astounded to discover that "Chloe liked Olivia." Woolf's fundamental literary historical insight was that women had been represented almost exclusively in their relationships to men, and as a consequence, both literary tradition and readers' imaginations were sorely impoverished. In her hunger to peer into the "serpentine caves" of unrepresented women's experience, that "vast chamber where nobody has yet been," Woolf's narrator anticipated a later generation of women readers. Influenced by the women's liberation movements, these women would clamor for books written beyond the ending of nineteenth-century romance, for writers to reinvent the stories that shape our lives. Consequently, since the 1970s, women's friendship has been the centrally focused subject of more novels and short stories than can be counted, as well as popular films and even television series, from "Cagney and Lacey" to Thelma and Louise. Woolf's Room also set the agenda for U.S. feminist scholarship of the 1970s. Quickly constructing friendship as a paradigm of ideal relations among women, scholars began to investigate it, only to find that Woolf had been wrong.

When feminist readers shifted their focus of vision to allow the "background" (women's relationships with each other) to displace the conventional "foreground" (women's relationships with men), virtually every tradition of fiction, drama, and poetry suddenly teemed with images of women's friendship. Similarly, the lives of women writers themselves assumed fascinating new dimensions in the work of revisionist biographers. In an essay that exemplifies the dramatic revision of perspective that occured during the 1970s, Annis Pratt and Andrea Loewenstein named friendship as one of the Archetypal Patterns in Women's Fiction (1981). Several other studies of friendship in literature, while not exclusively treating U.S. or women writers, supply provocative insights on the subject (Nina Auerbach's Communities of Women,

1978; Janet Todd's Women's Friendship in Literature, 1980; Pauline Nestor's Female Friendships and Communities, 1985; and Tess Cosslett's Woman to Woman, 1988). To cite only two biographical studies, Ellen Moers's Literary Women (1977) was a ground-breaking exploration of the international network linking women writers to each other as collegial friends, and Josephine Donovan documented the productive friendships of publisher Annie * Fields's circle, which included such notable U.S. writers as * Stowe, * Jewett, * Cooke, * Alcott, * Phelps, * Freeman, * Wharton, and * Cather (New England Local Color Literature, 1983).

Such work revealed the truth that "women have always cherished friendships with women, and women writers have always told stories in which women's friendships are central realities." With these words, Susan Koppelman introduces her anthology of short stories by multiethnic U.S. women writers, Women's Friendships (1991), a work of "literary archeology" that establishes friendship as an important theme throughout two centuries of literary history. In an afterword, Koppelman provocatively explores the complexity of female friendship and its significance for women at various stages of life and under various conditions of oppression. She finds in women's literature a definition of female friendship, valid across cultures, founded on an ethics of equality, reciprocity, and mutual support. However brief or long-lived, "intrinsic to all friendships is mutual reflection for the friends of images of themselves they cherish, visions of their best selves." Women's friendships are thus crucial to women's psychological and emotional growth—and because friends exchange material resources, they are often necessary merely to survive. Significantly, Koppelman also explores "the things that divide us"—"ideas about propriety and status" and the social inequalities created by racism and class oppression—finding that "there must be a balance of power or privilege between or among the participants in the relationship. That is, the friends must be equally in and subject to each other's power." Friendships that cross the politically and emotionally charged lines of racial or class difference can be radically oppositional and transformative, but they are also the most fragile of female friendships. Friendships end when there is nonreciprocity and unequal status. Studies of interracial friendship by Schultz and Porter elaborate this point.

The trope of friendship is formally as well as thematically significant. Women writers, for example, often cast a female friend as the heroine's foil, a strategy of characterization that emphasizes differences among women and, sometimes, the underside of friendship, which includes competition, manipulation, and jealousy. A powerful literary convention is to use the trope of friendship to explore women's choices: two friends are poised at a moment of decision and choose differently; their subsequent fates allow readers to explore the limits, possibilities, and consequences of choice.

Friendship between women is also productively understood in the larger context of the history of sexuality. Because friendship is often defined within and against notions of family, historical changes in sex-role divisions of labor, sexual practices, and family configuration exert a significant impact on women's friendships. Not surprisingly, the social history of Anglo-American women is better documented than that of other groups. Carroll Smith-Rosenberg's essay, "The Female World of Love and Ritual" (1975), inaugurated a line of inquiry that would alter forever our understanding of relations between women in the highly sex-segregated society of the nineteenth century, "a world in which men made but a shadowy appearance" to women. The friendships Smith-Rosenberg describes were supportive, intensely emotional, and deviant by today's sexual standards. The significance of these passionate "romantic friendships" has been hotly debated, especially the questions of whether or not they should be described as lesbian and whether they complemented or antagonized the institution of marriage. Lillian Faderman has made the fullest application of this material to literary studies. Her *Surpassing the Love of Men* (1981) discusses romantic friendship in literature from the Renaissance to the present.

A number of historians describe the radical revision of the gender system at the turn of the twentieth century, which culminated in the sexual revolution of the 1920s and drastically altered certain practices of female friendship. Christina Simmons's essay, "Companionate Marriage and the Lesbian Threat" (1979) and Sheila Jeffreys's "Women's Friendships and Lesbianism" (1985) are good entries into this material. As the ideology of *separate spheres disintegrated and women made progress in education and the professions, a new sexual ideology emerged, which achieved cultural hegemony by the 1930s. The new ideology had two keys: 1) an imperative that marriage be companionate, that is, that one's spouse rather than another woman be one's best friend, and 2) a powerful taboo against the older practices of romantic friendship, now relabeled lesbian and deviant. Not until the 1930s, then, did U.S. women's friendships assume their contemporary shape.

The intertwined history of sexuality and women's friendship challenges the notion that contemporary sexual categories and practices are "natural" rather than socially constructed, which has been both productive and problematic for lesbian studies of friendship. Many feminist theorists blur distinctions between friendship and lesbianism, a strategy that has the advantages of normalizing the term *lesbian* and demonstrating the presence of lesbianism throughout history. Adrienne *Rich, for example, advances the notion of a "lesbian continuum" to understand the historical continuity of women's relationships in the context of "Compulsory Heterosexuality" (1980). The most important study of friendship in this tradition is Janice G. Raymond's *A Passion for Friends* (1986). But Rich's paradigm has been sharply criticized on the basis that it aggrandizes the category of lesbian to virtual meaninglessness, ironically rendering invisible the very women Rich would have us reperceive, women for whom lesbianism is a sexual matter rather than a more diffuse inclination toward other women and homosociality. Bonnie Zimmerman's overview of lesbian feminist literary criticism, "What Has Never Been" (1981), effectively summarizes the lesbian debates concerning friendship, and argues, against Rich, that definitions of lesbianism ought not be conflated with female friendship generally, but should instead be historically specific and discriminating.

The history of friendship among women of color is even more problematic. Although friendship is a crucial theme in the literature of women of color, when one attempts to synthesize the scattered impressions of one's reading and compare it to the historical record, what one faces is not so much controversy as an enormous blank in existing scholarship. Angela *Davis was among the first scholars to question the absence of black women as subjects in history. Her article, "Reflections on the Black Woman's Role in the Community of Slaves" (1971), broke ground for historians such as Deborah White, whose work on African-American women during slavery includes a fascinating chapter on friendship (1985). A volume of *Conditions* (5: 1982) is much concerned with African-American women's friendship, but the histories of friendship for Hispanic, Native-American, and Asian-American women remain unwritten. Research in these sorely neglected areas is required.

Psychoanalytic studies of friendship in women's literature are rare. Elizabeth Able's "(E)Merging Identities" (1981) is an important work, not only for Able's insights into the psychological processes at work between friends—processes by which women's identities tend to merge with those of their friends—but also because she discovers new psychoanalytic concepts in women's literature rather than merely applying established concepts to it.

[*See also* Cross-racial Friendship.]

• Christina Simmons, "Companionate Marriage and the Lesbian Threat," *Frontiers* 4, no. 3 (1979): 54–59. Elizabeth Abel, "(E)Merging Identities: The Dynamics of Female Friendship in Contemporary Fiction by Women," *Signs* 6, no. 3 (1981): 413–435. Annis Pratt, with Andrea Loewenstein, "Love and Friendship between Women," in *Archetypal Patterns in Women's Fiction* (1981), pp. 95–112. Bonnie Zimmerman, "What Has Never Been: An Overview of Lesbian Feminist Criticism," in *The New Feminist Criticism: Essays on Women, Literature, and Theory,* ed. Elaine Showalter (1985), pp. 200–224. Sheila Jeffreys, "Women's Friendships and Lesbianism," in *The Spinster and Her Enemies: Feminism and Sexuality 1880–1930* (1985), pp. 102–127. Elizabeth Schultz, "Out of the Woods and into the World: A Study of Interracial Friendships between Women in American Novels," in *Conjuring: Black Women, Fiction, and Literary Tradition,* eds. Marjorie Pryse and Hortense J. Spillers (1985), pp. 67–85. Deborah Gray White, "The Female Slave Network," in *Ar'n't I A Woman? Female Slaves in the Plantation South* (1985), pp. 119–141. Nancy Porter, "Women's Interracial Friendships and Visions of Community in *Meridian, The Salt Eaters, Civil Wars,* and *Dessa Rose,*" in *Tradition and the Talents of Women,* ed. Florence Howe (1991), pp. 251–267.

Glynis Carr

FRONTIER WRITING. Because frontier literature begins with the first encounters by Europeans with the New World and continues well beyond the official closing of the frontier in 1890, and because every part of America has been the frontier at some point in history, it is difficult to make meaningful generalizations about frontier women. Their roles were as diverse as the land itself.

Among the earliest of women's frontier writing is New England Puritan Mary *Rowlandson's 1682 account of her captivity by Native Americans, *The Narrative of the Captivity and Restoration of Mrs. Mary White Rowlandson.* Hers is the first book-length example of the *captivity narrative, a unique American genre that remained popular both in factual and fictional forms until the early twentieth century. Rowlandson describes her ordeal as a religious test of faith. Later narratives, many by or about women, emphasize the cruelty of the captors, and were used to justify aggression toward Native peoples, or focused on the self-reliance of the victims. Some captives chose to remain with their captors, and their stories, by contrast, present a sympathetic and informative view of Native-American life.

Writings by Native-American women of the frontier are scarce, but some exist. Sarah *Winnemucca Hopkins's autobiography and tribal history, *Life among the Piutes: Their Wrongs and Claims* (1883), was part of the author's ongoing effort to gain increased rights for her people. Other notable works include autobiographical collaborations between Native-American women and white interviewers/interpreters, such as Frank B. Linderman's interviews with a Crow woman, *Pretty-Shield: Medicine Woman of the Crows* (1932), and *Autobiography of a Papago Woman* (1936), written by Ruth Underhill from interviews with Maria Chona. Both women were in their seventies when interviewed, so their autobiographies include their perceptions of the frontier era.

Many pioneer women came west reluctantly, as the wives or daughters of homesteaders, miners, or soldiers. Often their diaries and letters reveal lives of loneliness, homesickness, and hard work, though some express appreciation for the beauty of the land or for the opportunities available to women on the frontier. For example, in *Letters of a Woman Homesteader* (1914), Elinore Pruitt Stewart describes her homesteading experience in Wyoming. She worked hard and suffered setbacks, but saw homesteading as a means to economic independence; she wrote in part to encourage other women to follow her example. Journals and letters by Mormon pioneer women, collected by modern-day Mormon historians, are unique because of the writers' religious motivation for moving west, and because of early Mormonism's acceptance of polygamy.

Women's accounts of military life, such as Martha Summerhayes's *Vanished Arizona: Recollections of the Army Life of a New England Woman* (1908) and Frances M. A. Roe's *Army Letters of an Officer's Wife* (1909), show the realities of daily existence in the frontier army. After General Custer was defeated at Little Big Horn, his wife Elizabeth Custer glorified his memory in three widely-read books published in 1885, 1890, and 1893. Her writing also gives a clear picture of her responsibilities and privileges as the wife of a senior officer, and of her perceptions of frontier life.

Some women came west not to stay, but as travelers. Susan Magoffin's *Down the Santa Fe Trail and into Mexico* (1926) recounts her 1846–1847 journey and provides one of the most detailed early descriptions of the Santa Fe trail. Englishwoman Isabella Bird describes her 1873 hiking trip to Colorado with precise, vivid images in *A Lady's Life in the Rocky Mountains* (1888).

Helen Hunt *Jackson, who traveled extensively in Colorado and the Southwest, used her observations for the purpose of social reform. A strong advocate of Native-American rights, she wrote *A Century of Dishonor* (1881) as a chronicle of the mistreatment of Native people by the U.S. government and an attempt to influence Congress to make amends. With her novel *Ramona* (1884), she hoped to convey the message to a wider audience.

As Sherilyn Cox Bennion writes in *Equal to the Occasion: Women Editors of the Nineteenth-Century West* (1990), from the 1850s onward, opportunities arose for women as contributors to or editors of newspapers and periodicals. Although most publications were conventional small-town weekly newspapers, others were directed toward a female audience, or specialized in topics such as religion or temperance, and some published fiction. The number of serials published in the West grew steadily throughout the nineteenth century, improving the publishing and professional prospects for women writers.

Western women also published works of natural history. As Marcia Meyers Bonta explains in *Women in the Field: America's Pioneering Women Naturalists* (1991), women made valuable contributions to such fields as ornithology and botany. Mary *Austin took a literary approach to nature. In *The Land of Little Rain* (1903), *Lost Borders* (1909), and *The Land of Journey's Ending* (1924), she explores the desert lands of California and the Southwest in knowledgeable, artistic essays, also interpreting human interaction with nature through the lore of ranchers, sheepherders, and Native Americans.

The frontier also inspired postfrontier writers. Willa *Cather draws on the settlement history of Nebraska in her novels *O Pioneers!* (1913) and *My Ántonia* (1918), and the history of the Southwest in *The Professor's House* (1925) and *Death Comes for the Archbishop* (1927). Mari *Sandoz wrote *Old Jules* (1935), a biography of her father, a Swiss immigrant who homesteaded in Nebraska in the 1880s. This portrait of a poor, isolated family dominated by a tyrannical father provides a contrast to the popular image of the tight-knit pioneer household. Sandoz also looks realistically at conflicts between white settlers and Native Americans, and at the history of white settlement of the frontier in the five books of her Great Plains series (1942–1958). Notable in children's literature is Laura Ingalls *Wilder, who shaped her memories of homesteading into the popular *Little House on the Prairie* series (1932–1943).

Since the 1970s, growing interest in women's frontier history has led to an increase in reprints of frontier literature, publication of women's personal writing, and works reexamining women's roles. Contemporary writers continue to revise the myths of the frontier through scholarship and fiction.

[*See also* Diaries and Journals; Exploration Narratives; Pioneer Women; Western Women's Writing.]

• Patricia Y. Stallard, *Glittering Misery: Dependents of the Indian Fighting Army* (1978). Claudia Bushman, ed., *Mormon Sisters: Women in Early Utah* (1980). Helen Winter Stauffer and Susan J. Rosowski, eds., *Women and Western American Literature* (1982). Kenneth L. Holmes, ed. and comp., *Covered Wagon Women: Diaries and Letters from the Western Trails, 1840–1890*, vols. 1–8 (1983–1988). J. Golden Taylor et al., eds., *A Literary History of the American West* (1987). Frances Roe Kestler, comp., *The Indian Captivity Narrative: A Woman's View* (1990). Ruth B. Moynihan, Susan Armitage, and Christine Fischer Dichamp, eds., *So Much to Be Done: Women Settlers on the Mining and Ranching Frontier* (1990). James C. Work, ed., *Prose and Poetry of the American West* (1990).

Dana Brunvand Williams

FULLER, Margaret (1810–1850), writer. Although Margaret Fuller came to rebel against the Boston Brahmin class into which she was born in 1810, the values of her elite heritage gave her the intellectual foundation and self-discipline that later enabled her to question the politics of power.

Tutored by her father, Timothy, a Harvard-educated lawyer who served in the Massachusetts State Legislature and the United States Congress, Fuller, by the age of six, recited her Latin translations to him nights, after he returned home from his office. Her mother bore eight more children, but found time to support her precocious daughter's aspirations, including her earliest literary efforts, the letters she composed as a child. When her intellectual precocity became too marked even for Cambridge, her parents sent her to a girls' school in Groton, to be socialized into the proper conduct for a "young lady." Her father's death in 1835 was a major life crisis, forcing her to confront women's financial powerlessness and to struggle with an unsympathetic uncle for control of her father's limited estate.

Fuller taught school, but found it more satisfying and more lucrative to conduct seminar-style "Conversations" for establishment-class women. Many of the aspirations and dissatisfactions expressed by Boston's "non-traditional students" were later developed by her in her writing.

Throughout her life, Margaret Fuller had a furious hunger for ideas and answers. She taught herself German in order to read Goethe, and then translated German poetry and prose. She first sought Ralph Waldo Emerson as her mentor, but as their relationship progressed, it developed into one of mutuality. She was chosen by members of the Transcendental Club to edit their journal, the *Dial*. Her *Summer on the*

Lakes, published in 1844, attracted the attention of Horace Greeley, who offered her a position as literary critic and feature writer on the New York *Tribune*. Her work for the paper was so successful that when she left for Europe, she was able to continue serving as the *Tribune*'s foreign correspondent. After traveling in England and France, Fuller settled in Italy, where she became involved in the Italian revolutionary cause and took as her lover an Italian nobleman, Marchese Giovanni Angelo Ossoli. After their baby was born, Ossoli joined Mazzini's forces, who fought to free Rome from the secular power of the papal state. When the short-lived Roman Republic was defeated, the couple fled to Florence with their son. Soon, they embarked for the United States. During a storm, the family was lost at sea.

After Fuller's untimely death in 1850, so much emphasis was given to her dramatic life as a revolutionary radical that her literary genius was often overlooked and even denigrated. Her writing about highly controversial subjects so threatened traditionalists that, instead of dealing directly with her ideas, patriarchal apologists discredited them by disparaging Fuller's ability as a writer, additionally attacking her personality, her sexuality, and her physical appearance.

Extraordinarily imaginative and versatile, Margaret Fuller wrote critical essays about social problems and the promise of American democracy, in addition to her letters, poetry, experimental fiction, and German translations. She covered the cultural scene of a parochial United States with articles on art and music, but her literary criticism is the most significant. Her travel narrative, *Summer on the Lakes*, raised disturbing questions about exploitation of Native Americans, the uses of the environment, and the treatment of pioneer women. She continued her acute assessment of social turmoil and of the politics of power in the dispatches she sent to the New York *Tribune* from Europe. However, *Woman in the Nineteenth Century* (1845) is her literary masterpiece. She suggests the androgynous nature of sexuality and demands that all barriers to women be removed, that vocations traditionally male, such as sea captain, be opened to them. Her treatise adheres to the chief tenets of transcendentalist philosophy, which acknowledged the power of intuition as a guide and the godlike ability of the human spirit to transform the self. In 1883, Julia Ward *Howe stated that nothing subsequently written had made Fuller's teaching superfluous.

Woman in the Nineteenth Century served as the feminist manifesto that gave courage to those writing the "Declaration of Sentiments" at Seneca Falls in 1848. In *History of Woman Suffrage*, edited by Elizabeth Cady *Stanton and others, it is said that Fuller had "vindicated a woman's right to think." Others inspired by Fuller, such as Thomas Wentworth Higginson, Mary A. Livermore, Ednah Dow Cheney, and Caroline Healey *Dall, continued to carry forward Fuller's message throughout the nineteenth century, as did new generations in the twentieth.

• Fuller's manuscripts are housed at the Houghton Library, Harvard University, and the Boston Public Library. See also Joseph Jay Deiss, *The Roman Years of Margaret Fuller* (1969). Bell Gale Chevigny, *The Woman and the Myth: Margaret Fuller's Life and Writing* (1976). Marie Mitchell Olesen Urbanski, *Margaret Fuller's Woman in the Nineteenth Century: A Literary Study of Form and Content, of Sources and Influence* (1980). Joel Myerson, ed., *Critical Essays on Margaret Fuller* (1980). Marie Mitchell Olesen Urbanski, "Margaret Fuller: Feminist Writer and Revolutionary," in *Feminist Theorists: Three Centuries of Key Women Thinkers*, ed. Dale Spender (1983), pp. 75–89. Robert N. Hudspeth, ed., *The Letters of Margaret Fuller*, 5 vols. (1983–1988). Margaret Fuller, *Summer on the Lakes, in 1843*, ed. Susan Belasco Smith (1991).

Marie Mitchell Olesen Urbanski

G

GALE, Zona (1874–1938), novelist, short fiction writer, and Pulitzer prize–winning playwright for *Miss Lulu Bett*. Zona Gale was a midwestern writer whose portraits of small-town life ranged from sentimental to starkly realistic. Born in Portage, Wisconsin, in 1874, Gale attended the University of Wisconsin, where she earned two degrees. She worked as a reporter for the New York *Evening World* before moving back to Portage, where she lived until her death. Her first novel, *Romance Island* (1906), and *The Loves of Pelleas and Etarre* (1907), a short story cycle, are sentimental and romantic. In *Friendship Village* (1908), Gale found her literary vocation as chronicler of midwestern village life. The main character, Calliope Marsh, is a wise, old storyteller whose humor and good sense permeate the book. Gale published four more volumes of stories, two novels, and a play about Friendship Village.

Gale supported a variety of liberal causes, including women's suffrage, social welfare, and education reform. *Heart's Kindred* (1915) is a propagandistic novel supporting pacifism; *A Daughter of the Morning* (1917) concerns labor conditions for women. Gale was also an outspoken champion of Senator Robert La Follette, a Progressive Republican.

With the publication of *Birth* (1918) and *Miss Lulu Bett* (1920), Gale shifted from idealization of the village to realism. The latter novel is a terse depiction of the disillusionment and rebellion of its heroine. Gale dramatized *Miss Lulu Bett*, adding a controversial happy ending; the play won the Pulitzer Prize in 1921. *Faint Perfume* (1923), another realistic portrait of village life, was a best-seller. Later works, such as *Preface to a Life* (1926), *Borgia* (1929), and *Papa La Fleur* (1933), reveal Gale's interest in mysticism and the occult. Two collections of stories, *Yellow Gentians and Blue* (1927) and *Bridal Pond* (1930), include some of her strongest realistic tales.

In the last decade of her life, she published *Portage, Wisconsin, and Other Essays* (1928) and a biography, *Frank Miller of Mission Inn* (1938). In 1928, she married William Breese, a Portage businessman, and adopted a child. She continued to publish short fiction and dramatized several of her Friendship Village stories for radio. *Light Woman* (1937) is set, uncharacteristically,

in upstate New York. Her novel *Magna* (1939) appeared posthumously.

Zona Gale first won success as a nostalgic apologist for village life; toward the end of her career her work is infused with mysticism. Her literary reputation, however, rests most solidly on the regional realism of her middle years.

• Important collections of Gale's papers are at the State Historical Society of Wisconsin, Madison, and the Ridgely Torrence Collection in the Princeton University Library. See also Ima Honaker Herron, *The Small Town in American Literature* (1939). August Derleth, *Still Small Voice: A Biography of Zona Gale* (1940). Harold P. Simonson, *Zona Gale* (1962). Katherine A. White, "*Miss Lulu Bett* Revisited," *Turn of the Century Women* 1 (Winter 1984): 38–40. William Maxwell, "Zona Gale," *Yale Review* 76 (March 1987): 221–225.

Gwen L. Nagel

GELLHORN, Martha (b. 1908), novelist, short story writer, journalist, and foreign correspondent. Born into a socially prominent family in St. Louis, Martha Gellhorn attended the John Burroughs School (1923–1926) and Bryn Mawr College (1926–1929), which she left before finishing her degree to pursue a career as a journalist. After brief employment at the *Times Union* in Albany, New York, in 1930 Gellhorn left for Paris, where she worked at a variety of writing assignments, among them a position on the Paris staff of *Vogue*. As a freelance reporter, she traveled widely in Europe. From 1933 to 1935 she was married to French journalist Bertrand de Jouvenel. Returning to the United States, Gellhorn became a field investigator for the Federal Emergency Relief Administration, headed by Harry L. Hopkins. Outraged by conditions she saw in the South and in New England, Gellhorn considered resigning but was advised by Hopkins to give her eyewitness account directly to Eleanor Roosevelt and President Roosevelt. This meeting proved to be important for Gellhorn, who was thereafter a welcome guest at the White House. Her field reports formed the basis for a collection of her short stories, *The Trouble I've Seen* (1936).

In 1936, a chance meeting with novelist Ernest Hemingway led to her reportage during the Spanish Civil War as a correspondent for *Collier's* magazine and her eventual marriage to Hemingway (1940–1945). An avid supporter of the Loyalist cause, Gellhorn gave numerous talks in the United States to help raise money for supplies. After a brief residence with Hemingway in Havana, Cuba, Gellhorn accepted an assignment from *Collier's* to travel to Finland and report on a probable Russian invasion. Following a trip to China with Hemingway in 1942, Gellhorn's journalistic urge to see for herself led to a *Collier's* assignment to cover the European front from 1943 to 1945. Following her divorce from Hemingway, Gellhorn moved permanently to London, England. Since that time she has reported on wars in Java, Vietnam, the Middle East, and Central America. From 1954 to 1963 she was married to Tom S. Matthews, a retired *Time* editor, and she has one adopted son. She has published over 150 articles and short stories; her journalism has been collected in *The Face of War* (1988) and *The View from the Ground* (1988). A volume of nonfiction, *Travels with Myself and Another*, was published in 1983.

Her fiction is distinguished by its acute and penetrating style and powers of observation. Her novels include *What Mad Pursuit* (1934), *A Stricken Field* (1940; reissued 1986), *Liana* (1944; reissued 1987), *The Wine of Astonishment* (1948; reissued 1989), *His Own Man* (1961), and *The Lowest Trees Have Tops* (1967). In addition, she has published six collections of short stories. One of Gellhorn's lifelong passions is her conviction that all wars are futile; another is her intellectual contempt for those she calls "apocryphiers," that is, "liars who make up apocryphal stories." Gellhorn currently resides in London and Wales. She continues to travel and write with remarkable enthusiasm and cogency of world issues, as always from a personal perspective.

• Jacqueline Orsagh, "A Critical Biography of Martha Gellhorn," Ph.D. Diss., Michigan State University (1978). Bernice Kert, *The Hemingway Women* (1983). Carl Rollyson, *Nothing Ever Happens to the Brave: The Story of Martha Gellhorn* (1990).

Robert A. Martin

GENDER AND WRITING. The influence of sexual difference upon writing, of gender upon genre, has been vigorously debated by feminist literary critics throughout the past two decades. The variety and complexity of these debates might be suggested by situating them in relation to the concept of difference itself, as it has been constituted and deployed within them. Each specific use of the term implies a distinct notion of the nature of women's relation to language and to larger discursive structures and of the project of feminist literary criticism itself.

Among Anglo-American critics in particular,

difference typically refers to gender (and power) asymmetry between men and women—themselves conceived as relatively unproblematic categories. The feminist critic—figured as an archivist or a revisionary reader—aims to locate instances of this gender asymmetry (most often images of gender stereotypes in male-authored texts); to trace its consequences (including the identification of male bias in assigning literary value and the resultant devaluation of women's writing); and to theorize the specificity of women's writing as the female-authored text dynamically interacts with dominant literary traditions. In these ways psychosexual and political differences are translated into a variety of literary differences of genre, structure, voice, and style. The influence of other variables such as race or class positioning may be included within efforts to trace the evolution of a female literary tradition and to construct a poetics of women's writing, but the emphasis usually falls on the continuities and interrelations that connect women to each other over time and geographical distance. This has led to the charge that the approach encourages an ahistorical universalizing on the basis of women's experience and a general return to those humanist categories and values that feminist criticism should disrupt. On the other hand, the archival approach has effectively challenged the pretense of neutrality of the literary canon, rescued a great number of lost works from obscurity, and allowed critics to emphasize women's agency in the construction of culture.

In a second meaning, one most often associated with the poststructuralist theories of Jacques Lacan and Jacques Derrida, difference is a condition of identity itself, figured as divided, contradicted, unstable, dispersed, and constructed through and by the workings of language. Within a patriarchal symbolic order, "feminine" difference functions not as an essence but as an otherness within identity and language, existing outside of current systems of representation but evident in the gaps, silences, and paradoxes of discourse. A feminist practice in this context is not constructive but deconstructive, aiming to disclose the function and expose the traces of the (textually) feminine inscribed within the meaning-production processes of culture. Because women always speak an alien tongue in which they cannot represent themselves as women, the argument goes, the search also becomes one for a new feminine language and textual practice—produced on an analogy with a feminine unconscious and libidinal economy—with which women may write themselves into history. As Hélène Cixous puts it in "The Laugh of the Medusa" (1976), "If woman has always functioned [as an otherness] within the discourse of man ... it is time for her to dislocate this within, to explode it, to invent for herself a language to get inside of." Within Cixous's psycholiterary experiment, women's writing (a woman writing) is itself disruptive, troubling the smooth functioning of official discourse, and, according to her, capable of becoming the springboard for actual sociocultural and political change. This last claim and Cixous's tendency to essentialize the female have proved problematic for many critics as has her tendency to locate women's writing as a future possibility, thereby ignoring the radical signifying practices that women have already produced. Cixous's texts and those of other French feminists such as Luce Irigaray and Catherine Clement are in fact excellent examples of these dazzling new reading and writing strategies.

Difference conceived as gender asymmetry or as a radical instability within identity may, in the end, limit feminist analyses of writing by women by confining it within the parameters of a universal male/female opposition. Such an emphasis minimizes differences among women based on experiential diversity as well as on diverse relations to power and privilege; it obscures the heterogeneity of women as a class whose members are multiply constructed and divided through their different experiences of race, sexual preference, age, nation, and so on. This relatively recent emphasis on relational differences among women emerged from a critique—largely by U.S. Third World feminists—of the hegemony of white academic feminism. In taking white middle-class heterosexual experience as the norm, hegemonic feminism has, at the very least, distorted understandings of the variety and complexity of those cultural productions that emerge from "a lived experience of difference from white feminism" in Chela Sandoval's words ("Oppositional Consciousness," *Genders* 10). The critical writings of U.S. Third World feminists have encouraged analyses of exclusionary practices among hegemonic feminists, leading to a new self-consciousness about one's critical location. They have promoted the construction of new interpretive strategies capable of disclosing relations among inscriptions of race, class, ideology, and gender determinants within literary texts. Thus, they have transformed understandings of the nature and development of female literary traditions (and not *a* female literary tradition). These efforts to incorporate differences among women in culture, language, race, and ideology have transformed existing feminist knowledge. They may also suggest the need for a radical paradigm shift within hegemonic feminism, one

"capable of rescuing its theoretical and practical expressions from their exclusionary and racist forms" (Sandoval), and aligning these revised practices with different spheres of theoretical and practical activities for the transformation of culture.

[*See also* Authorship; Collaboration; Silences.]

• Sandra Gilbert and Susan Gubar, *The Madwoman in the Attic* (1979). Elaine Marks and Isabelle de Courtivron, eds., *New French Feminisms* (1981). Cherríe Moraga and Gloria Anzaldúa, eds., *This Bridge Called My Back* (1981). Elizabeth Abel, ed., *Writing and Sexual Difference* (1982). Rachael Blau DuPlessis, *Writing Beyond the Ending, Narrative Strategies of Twentieth-Century Women Writers* (1985). Judith Newton and Deborah Rosenfelt, eds., *Feminist Criticism and Social Change: Sex, Class and Race in Literature and Culture.* Margaret Homans, *Bearing the Word: Language and Female Experience in Nineteenth-Century Women's Writing* (1986). Elizabeth A. Meese, *Crossing the Double-Cross: The Practice of Feminist Criticism* (1986). Nancy K. Miller, ed., *The Poetics of Gender* (1986). Shari Benstock, ed., *Feminist Issues in Literary Scholarship* (1987). Patricia Yaeger, *Honey-Mad Women: Emancipatory Strategies in Women's Writing* (1988). Cheryl Wall, ed., *Changing Our Own Words: Essays in Criticism, Theory, and Writing by Black Women* (1989). Marianne Hirsch and Evelyn Fox-Keller, eds., *Conflicts in Feminism* (1990). Gloria Anzaldúa, ed., *Making Face, Making Soul/Haciendo Caras: Creative and Critical Perspectives by Women of Color* (1990).

Ellen E. Berry

GENDERED SPACES. Virginia *Woolf may have needed a room of her own in which to write, but for many other women the greatest productivity results from the opportunity to exchange ideas with other women. Places in which women deliberately gather to pursue common interests, separate from men, can provide the setting for many literary accomplishments. The key to the positive effect of separation, however, is choice. Gender segregation may be negatively associated with women's status when it is legally or culturally imposed.

When women and men are spatially separated from one another in schools and workplaces by custom or legal decree, one of the consequences may be lower status for women. Enforced gender segregation does more than create physical distance between men and women; it also affects the distribution of knowledge that women could use to change their position in society. The greater women's access to socially valued resources (such as formal education and prestigious occupations), the greater their potential for equality with men.

American history holds several examples of the relationship between gendered spaces and women's status. Seventeenth-century dame schools and eighteenth-century masters' schools were largely closed to girls; if they attended, it was at different times of the day or year from boys, or in separate rooms. Seminaries and academies of the nineteenth century perpetuated this gender segregation, as did the first women's colleges. The common thread among all these institutions was that different curricula were associated with different places: boys learned Latin, Greek, and mathematics in preparation for a public life, while girls learned reading, writing, and domestic skills in preparation for a private life.

It was not until the Morrill Act of 1862 legislated coeducation in land grant colleges that middle-class women had the opportunity to share the same space—and the same curriculum—with college men. Over half of all colleges were coeducational by 1910. Although many schools wavered in their commitment to coeducation (such as the University of Chicago in its 1902 attempt to create a separate junior college for women, with separate courses, laboratories, and chapel, after many years of full coeducation), the stage had been set for gender integration in college classrooms and curricula. The educational access accorded women was soon followed by a major improvement in women's status: the right to vote granted by the Nineteenth Amendment in 1920.

Comparable conditions existed in the workplace. In the nineteenth century, when few free women worked outside the home and few occupational choices existed, there were basically two types of jobs open to women: those that kept them in a homelike environment and brought them into contact only with other women and children (teaching and domestic service) and those that took them out of the home and into contact with men (factory and clerical work). Factory and clerical jobs paid better than teaching or domestic service and also exposed women to the technologies of the industrial era in gender-integrated places. Concomitantly, legislation such as New York's Married Women's Property Acts of 1848 and 1860 were granting women the right to their own property and wages.

Such examples demonstrate one possible outcome of institutional gendered spaces. Another possibility, connected more closely with women's writing, is that optional gendered spaces may create nurturing environments within which women's talents blossom. That has certainly been the argument in favor of women's colleges for over a century. Self-selected separation from men, according to this perspective, has positive effects for women because they are removed from sexual and intellectual competition with men. At the same time, relative isolation from men encourages

solidarity among women, which is conducive to creativity. Two historical examples illustrate this point: *reading circles of the nineteenth century and *consciousness-raising groups of the middle twentieth century.

Reading circles originated hand in hand with industrialization. The Merrimack Manufacturing Company of Lowell, Massachusetts, began recruiting rural middle-class women to its factories in the early 1820s. By 1845, the city had grown to thirty thousand people (from its original two hundred), and the image of the "Lowell girls" epitomized the textile industry. In an attempt to avoid the British mill village system in which entire families worked for the company, Francis Cabot Lowell built strictly supervised boarding houses to attract a rotating group of young women. Matrons insured that the girls observed curfews, attended church, and abstained from alcohol and sex.

Women were attracted to Lowell by its high wages and also by its opportunities for informal education. In 1843, there were at least five "Improvement Circles" in Lowell in which women talked about current events and shared their original essays and poetry. The outgrowth of one of these reading circles was the *Lowell Offering*, the first literary magazine entirely written and edited by women. The *Offering* painted a generally rosy picture of factory life and thus was endorsed by management as a recruitment tool. It was a novelty that attracted attention from such literary personalities as Charles Dickens, Harriet Martineau, and George Sand. Contributors to the *Lowell Offering* parlayed their talents into public achievements later in life. Among its "graduates" were teachers, missionaries, a sculptor, an acting U.S. treasurer, and newspaper and magazine editors and writers.

Although management may have approved of the *Offering*, its contributors were quite radical for their era. Harriet Robinson, former "Lowell girl" and author of *Loom and Spindle; or, Life among the Early Mill Girls* (1898), chronicled women's status and the changes wrought by the factory system: "For the first time in this country woman's labor had a money value. She had become not only an earner and producer, but also a spender of money, a recognized factor in the political economy of her time." The all-female boarding houses in which meetings of the *Lowell Offering* staff occurred became places that encouraged progressive thought and action among independent women.

More than a century later, such reading circles would be considered quaint. Yet their legacy persisted and was reincarnated in the form of consciousness-raising groups in the 1960s and 1970s.

Consciousness-raising groups were part of the women's liberation movement that emerged in the 1960s, which grew partially out of women's dissatisfaction with their roles in the civil rights movement, just as the suffragist movement had been spawned by Elizabeth Cady *Stanton and Lucretia *Mott's exclusion from the 1840 World's Anti-Slavery Convention. Drawing on their ties to the radical Left, this new wave of feminists emphasized grass-roots organization to heighten women's political awareness of their secondary status. Consciousness-raising groups provided women everywhere with a sympathetic circle in which to redefine the roles of women. By 1970, hundreds of consciousness-raising groups existed in major cities and college towns. They encompassed white women and women of color, straight and lesbian, old and young; adopted striking names (such as WITCH, or Women's International Terrorist Conspiracy from Hell); and published newsletters such as *off our backs*.

If the *Lowell Offering* was the bible of textile mill women, Robin Morgan's *Sisterhood is Powerful* (1970) was its equivalent for late twentieth-century feminists. Subtitled *An Anthology of Writings from the Women's Liberation Movement*, it was a six-hundred-page collection that contained pieces that have become classics: an excerpt from Kate *Millet's doctoral dissertation, *Sexual Politics*, and Pat Mainardi's "The Politics of Housework." This volume was required reading in consciousness-raising groups across the country; its cover helped popularize the clenched fist in the womb as the symbol of the women's movement. While Betty *Friedan's *The Feminine Mystique* (1963) can be credited with igniting the women's movement, *Sisterhood Is Powerful* fed the flames with stories from the trenches.

Like reading circles, consciousness-raising groups fostered the careers of various women of achievement. Eleanor Holmes Norton and Florynce Kennedy were two African-American contributors to *Sisterhood Is Powerful* who became nationally recognized advocates for children's rights and reproductive control, respectively. Authors Rita Mae *Brown and Gloria *Steinem were also veterans of the consciousness-raising era. More important, perhaps, than famous women were the thousands who were encouraged to succeed by the support they received in these groups.

Both nineteenth-century reading circles and twentieth-century consciousness-raising groups are examples of social places in which women chose to gather to exchange information and from which women writers drew inspiration. Both types of groups emerged spontaneously from shared experiences in women's lives, and created environments (outside the institutions of school or workplace) in which women expressed progressive ideas. Members were independent women for whom the group provided an outlet for action in a world otherwise dominated by men. Although participants were largely white and middle-class, they were pioneers whose accomplishments set the stage for future women's rights. In sum, the presence of such self-selected gendered spaces as reading circles and consciousness-raising groups has contributed to a women's community supportive of literary creativity and political action.

[See also Community; Education; Sisterhood.]

• Harriet Jane Hanson Robinson, *Loom and Spindle; or, Life among the Early Mill Girls* (1898; reprint, 1976). John Phillips Coolidge, *Mill and Mansion: A Study of Architecture and Society in Lowell, Massachusetts, 1820–1865* (1942). Miriam Schneir, ed., *Feminism: The Essential Historical Writings* (1972). Daphne Spain, *Gendered Spaces* (1992).

Daphne Spain

GENDER THEORY. Since the 1970s, feminists have often distinguished between sex and gender. *Sex* refers to one of the (usually) two categories of the biologically observable human body, female and male; *gender*, to the categories of social expectations, roles, behaviors, and values into which each such body is placed. While sex is a mere physical matter, gender is the social area in which men and women are differently—and unequally—raised, treated, and valued. Gender is thought of as something that society *constructs* on top of the biological facts. This *constructionism* implies that "masculine" and "feminine" traits are not expressions of any natural, universal, eternal *essence* of men and women, but rather conventionally accepted fictions, such as Santa Claus. The opposing view, that gender and sex are connected and natural, is *essentialism*. From a constructionist view, precisely because gender is socially constructed, we can imagine altering the gender system in some way in order to make the genders more equal and to liberate women (and perhaps men) from a sexist system.

The word *sex*, from Latin, has through the ages been connected with the categorization as male and female, especially in breeding farm animals. *Gender* came into feminist discourse, apparently, from the social sciences in the mid-sixties. Historically, *gender* has meant the grammatical category of nouns and their modifiers in languages such as Latin and French. So whereas *sex* has always been associated with biology and reproduction, *gender* has been associated more with words—symbols, signs, and social meanings.

This opposition between sex and gender is put in conveniently simple terms—something like nature vs. culture. The real issues are more complicated. The "construction" of gender implies more than a culture's teachings: gender is an aspect of the general construction of the subject, and implies a theory wherein individual speaking, thinking, acting, and perceiving subjects are not born as such, but are formed with culturally-specific traits in an unconscious developmental process.

If gender is constructed, is sex really natural? What is *nature*? How do we know what to call "female" and "male," if not by means of already socially constructed categories of perception? If all societies construct gender, then can we get rid of it, or can we only change it? Can we even change it by conscious action—since we are all already part of the gender system, grew up within it, and have our thoughts influenced by it? If we can consciously change it, how? What changes would ensure greater equality, freedom, and justice?

Recent writings by American women show a spectrum of approaches to these issues. The word *gender* has become popular; the past decade has given us countless publications and talks with *gender* in the title. This article can only point out a few current trends, key terms, and concepts. Judith Butler, for instance, argues not only that gender is inauthentic and factitious, but that even what we call *sex*—the physical attributes of female and male bodies—is the product of our interpretive perceptions of otherwise multiple, varied phenomena. Gender is thus an element of our epistemology. But we cannot perceive the world at all without some epistemology, whether conscious or unconscious, and gender is a part of how we perceive. Since we cannot just get rid of gender, freedom, for Butler, can be found in a strategy of continual ironic and subversive play against gender norms and perceptions. At an opposite extreme, the reactionary Camille Paglia reasserts the validity of gender stereotypes as social expressions of essential, biological truths, such as the aggressiveness of the male sex and the passivity (or even masochism) of the female sex.

Many writers, such as Gayle Rubin, view sex differences as real but small compared with the differences within each sex and the similarities among all humans as compared with other animals. There are sex-specific attributes for each sex on the average, but there is a large area of overlap in each category—some women are taller, stronger, or hairier than some men, etc. Gender exaggerates and stereotypes these differences between the average traits of the two sexes, focuses on particular attributes while ignoring others, and interprets these differences in ways that are specific to each culture but which, for the most part, oppress women across cultures and history. In addition, according to such writers as Butler, Rubin, and Adrienne *Rich, the reduction of human difference to two internally homogenous genders may be connected to a system of compulsory heterosexuality, in which sexuality is regulated in order to structure society and to reproduce that structure without regard to real differences in desire and activity.

Given this view, we can find at least two distinct but complementary goals for the critique of gender in relation to sex. One is to challenge the hierarchical placement of feminine gender attributes (passivity, cooperativeness, an orientation toward relationships, etc.) as inferior to masculine attributes (aggressivity, competitiveness, an orientation toward public rules and laws, etc.). Much of the oppression of women is not just in coercing them to live the stereotype of femininity but in devaluing that very stereotype, even if it has some potentially positive contributions to make to society. The other goal is to reduce or remove the coercion, so that women and men can freely be as "masculine" or "feminine" as they wish to be individually, and so that the plurality, multiplicity, and complexity of real people can be recognized and valued, rather than the narrowness of the binary masculine/feminine opposition. (Rubin, Butler, and Donna Haraway share this goal.) Since much of society's induction of the individual into this gender binarism is unconscious, simply talking and writing about it may help us to be somewhat free of it, as suggested by Catharine MacKinnon in her discussion of consciousness-raising. Toward this second goal, there are at least two different approaches. One is to have men and women become more like each other, so that gender difference can be effaced or abolished, as proposed by Dorothy Dinnerstein. Another is to ironize gender stereotypes through cultural practices such as styles of dress, behavior, and a self-conscious self-dramatization of gender on the model of comic theater—an aspect of what Butler calls gender as "performance." All of these latter methods of irony work to deprive gender binarism of its credibility (Butler).

The critique of gender today should be seen against the background of the history of modern American feminism. In the late nineteenth and early twentieth centuries, two different approaches could be discerned in the women's movement, especially toward the chief goal of the day, women's right to vote. Some feminists saw their suffrage in the context of a larger pursuit of equality with men, finding voices in, for example, the English writer Mary Wollstonecraft and the American Charlotte Perkins *Gilman. Other supporters of women's suffrage argued, by contrast, that men and women really were different, and that women should be given the vote because they could help to improve America with the contribution of feminine values such as peace and charity. This second group is now largely credited with the eventual success of the movement in persuading men to give up their monopoly at the ballot box. This group would today be considered essentialist; the first group anticipated modern constructionists.

Some writings from 1960s feminism onward register the universality of women's oppression (Adrienne Rich, Mary *Daly). Some also draw on a sense of physical and experiential commonality among all women for strength in fighting social oppression (Rich, Audre *Lorde). But partly under the influence of French existentialist Simone *de Beauvoir's observation that "one is not born, but made, a woman," other American feminists have pursued a strategy that challenges any essentializing or naturalizing definition of *woman*. One constructionist critique of essentialist feminism as a whole is that it may ignore or marginalize important and numerous cultural differences among women: Which definition of *woman* is the "universal" one? Who is the "real" woman? (Rich and Lorde, however, both stress the importance of diversity and difference. However, the charge of universalism can be leveled against constructionists too.) Constructionists also view essentialism as a trap, leading one to repeat the obfuscatory maneuvers of oppressive patriarchy by making social habits appear natural and thus unchangeable.

Because constructionist theory has sought to analyze and criticize the unconscious reproduction of the social institution of unequal gender within each individual as an apparently inherent aspect of the subject, it has tended to bring together, in various combinations, psychoanalysis, structuralist anthropology, the Marxist critique of "nature" as ideology, and Marxist analyses of oppression. Catharine MacKinnon draws on a feminist analysis of women's oppression and on the feminist practice of consciousness-raising to correct the inadequacies of Marxist concepts of labor and revolution. In later writers, the psychoanalytic component has ranged in specific approach from object-relations theory (Rubin, Chodorow) to Lacan's poststructuralist rereading of Freud (Butler and many others). The latter particularly emphasizes the social fiction involved in the construction of the gendered subject, which is integrated into a "phallic economy" of social values

just as a word or sentence forms part of a language.

More recently, Butler has used the pragmatic model of language to analyze gender, wherein speaking something makes it so. "I thank you" is such a performative utterance. So too would then be "I am a woman," or the suburbanite father's charge to his little-leaguer son to "be a man." This latter case supports Butler's punning shift from *performative* to *performance* as the model of gender—it is all an act. And hence, once we become conscious of our pre-scripted parts, although we are not free to quit the stage (drop out of society altogether), we can subvert the force of those parts through pastiche, an ironic parody.

The very opposition between constructionism and essentialism that gives rise to the pair gender/sex raises many philosophical problems. Although constructionists often argue as if essentialism were automatically reactionary, naive, and sexist, both essentialist and constructionist positions offer their own respective political advantages, as suggested by Diana Fuss and Steven Epstein. Essentialism affords a sense of group identity grounded in an appeal to lived, physical experience, whereas constructionism's emphasis on multiplicity and contingency may seem to undermine group solidarity in political practice. But constructionism also undermines the power of gender stereotypes. The construction/essence opposition itself is somewhat fictitious—somewhat *constructed*. Constructionism always depends on some essentializing concepts, including its concept of "essentialism" as a single, eternal error; while any particular essentialism is itself constructed, a little differently for each moment and each context (Fuss). Accordingly, gender constructionism may artificially isolate one attribute (gender) while not considering its interaction with other, equally constructed categories, such as race and class.

Furthermore, neither essentialism nor constructionism *necessarily* offers more or less freedom. While sex as an essence may seem like a biological determinant, one could imagine many ways of dealing with biological givens. Conversely, the construction of gender may imply such thorough social determination of the subject that one must wonder what bits of a somebody are left to pursue any freedom—for even one's picture of freedom would always be already determined by the same culture that constructed gender to begin with. Thus some constructionisms can begin to appear a bit reactionary. Finally, both essentialism and constructionism, when taken to an extreme, may come full circle to where gender and sex are, after all, the same thing. If sex as essence is real, then gender cannot but reflect it; if gender is entirely an arbitrary fiction, then so must sex be—indeed, it is what gender is called by the naive.

Some writers do address some of these problems, at least in part. Rubin effectively avoids the whole problem by referring to the "sex/gender system" within a moderately constructionist analysis that assumes some real, if undefined, physical difference between men and women. Haraway addresses the problem of political solidarity in constructionism by advocating "affinity" as opposed to "identity" politics. Several constructionists explore race and class and their interactions with gender in the social construction of subjectivity and difference (e.g., Carby, Fuss). Finally, Butler begins to address the problem of just who can be free if everything is already constructed, by suggesting an element of our beings that is not quite the same as the socially active subject. This would be the agency that makes pastiche possible. Perhaps it is necessary that we leave this agency relatively unanalyzed—for as soon as we begin to describe it, we are starting to construct a subject, with its attendant baggage.

But there remain other potential problems with the postmodern focus on the construction of gender as a liberatory strategy. Many women, despite their wish to have equal pay and equal access to social and political power, seem rather attached to some elements of gender, including a complex of feelings and experiences associated with motherhood and the female body. The insistence that these traits are mere social fictions may itself seem alienating and even oppressive. Furthermore, American culture today cannot be said to suffer from an overabundance of authenticity. Both women and men struggle to find some connection with their bodies and with the physical, natural world; constructionist theory poses the danger of allowing people to feel even more disembodied, lost in language and fictional images. A need for some sense of authentic connection with a physical reality beyond the images and words that so often deceive may help to explain the popularity of essentialists such as Paglia. In another development, American feminists have recently shown interest in the writings of the French psychoanalytic feminist Luce Irigaray, whose essentialist writings are somewhat mythic and have immediate political implications—in other words, her essentialism is consciously constructed (Fuss). Irigaray emphasizes an inclusive logic, which may include both essence and construct, both gender and sex. Perhaps the task that lies ahead for American

feminist theory will be to develop such inclusive modes of discourse, which would help empower women (and men) to acknowledge and enjoy the benefits of some sort of sex/gender while at the same time they affirm their diversity, individuality, and freedom to struggle for change.

[*See also* Feminism.]

• Simone de Beauvoir, *The Second Sex*, trans. H. M. Parshley (1953; reprint, 1974). Gayle Rubin, "The Traffic in Women: Notes on the 'Political Economy' of Sex," in *Toward an Anthropology of Women*, ed. Rayna R. Reiter (1975), pp. 157–210. Dorothy Dinnerstein, *The Mermaid and the Minotaur: Sexual Arrangements and the Human Malaise* (1976). Nancy Chodorow, *The Reproduction of Mothering: Psychoanalysis and the Sociology of Gender* (1978). Mary Daly, *Gyn/Ecology: The Metaethics of Radical Feminism* (1978). Carol Gilligan, *In a Different Voice: Psychological Theory and Women's Development* (1982). Catharine A. MacKinnon, "Feminism, Marxism, Method, and the State: An Agenda for Theory," *Signs* 7 (1982): 515–544. Adrienne Rich, "Compulsory Heterosexuality and Lesbian Existence," in *Powers of Desire*, eds. Ann Snitow, Christine Stansell, and Sharon Thompson (1983), pp. 177–205. Audre Lorde, *Sister Outsider: Essays and Speeches by Audre Lorde* (1984). Donna Haraway, "A Manifesto for Cyborgs: Science, Technology, and Socialist Feminism in the 1980s," *Socialist Review* 15 (1985): 65–107. Hazel Carby, *Reconstructing Womanhood* (1987). Steven Epstein, "Gay Politics, Ethnic Identity: The Limits of Social Constructionism," *Socialist Review* 17 (1987): 9–54. Diana Fuss, *Essentially Speaking: Feminism, Nature & Difference* (1989). Rosemarie Tong, *Feminist Thought: A Comprehensive Introduction* (1989). Camille A. Paglia, *Sexual Personae* (1990). Judith Butler, *Gender Trouble: Feminism and the Subversion of Identity* (1990).

Amittai F. Aviram

GHOST STORIES. American women writers produced ghost stories throughout the nineteenth and twentieth centuries. Practitioners of the genre include such well-known writers as Edith * Wharton, Ellen * Glaskow, Sarah Orne * Jewett, Mary Wilkins * Freeman, Zora Neale * Hurston, Shirley * Jackson, Cynthia * Ozick, and many popular or less well-known writers, among them E.D.E.N * Southworth, Gertrude * Atherton, Elizabeth Stuart * Phelps, Mary * Austin, Mary Elizabeth Counselman, Annie Trumbull Slosson, and Josephine Daskam Bacon. In recent decades the tradition has been broadened and enriched with the incorporation of supernatural elements from African, Native American, and Asian cultures in contemporary fiction by such American women of color as Toni * Morrison, Paule * Marshall, Maxine Hong * Kingston, Louise * Erdrich, and Toni Cade * Bambara.

Most historians of the ghost story genre in

the United States trace its roots to the eighteenth-century English Gothic novel, a genre in which women writers were prominent if not dominant. English Gothic novels were widely available in the United States from the late eighteenth century on, often in Minerva Press reprints. Ann Radcliffe, the most popular of Gothic writers, was only one of many Englishwomen whose work was reprinted in the United States. In the latter half of the nineteenth century, such American magazines as the *Eclectic* also made available works of supernatural and sensation fiction by such Englishwomen as Mary Braddon and Charlotte Riddell. Central to much English female Gothic and supernatural fiction was a concern with the dangers for women of life in the patriarchal home. Charles Brockden Brown's *Wieland* (1798), which translated this familiar Gothic plot of domestic terror into an American setting and gave it a female narrator, probably also contributed to the American women's tradition. American women writers would have been conscious, too, of the supernatural tales written by their major male contemporaries and predecessors, particularly Washington Irving, Nathaniel Hawthorne, and Edgar Allan Poe. However, the work of these male writers, usually credited with the development of the American supernatural tale, seems to have been less important as an influence on American women's ghost stories than the work of their British sisters.

In the United States as in England, the popularity and the availability of ghost stories in the 1850s and 1860s were enhanced by the proliferation of new periodicals, both middle-class monthlies and cheaper weeklies. From the high-toned *Atlantic Monthly* and *Harper's New Monthly Magazine* to the more sensational *Frank Leslie's Illustrated Weekly* and *The Flag of Our Union*, periodicals nourished native contributions to the genre. The Christmas numbers of many magazines, as well as publishers' Christmas annuals and gift books, provided particularly popular outlets for ghost stories. Many of these periodicals also catered to the rapidly growing audience of female readers.

Victorian culture's sentimental fascination with death undoubtedly also contributed to the popularity of supernatural literature. This fascination was expressed in many ways: through elaborate domestic mourning rituals, regular outings to the cemetery, a fashion for mourning pictures and brooches, and quantities of sentimental poetry about dead children. In the latter decades of the century, interest in *spiritualism and parapsychology also fed the popular enthusiasm for ghost stories. In each case, women played a critical role: they were largely responsible for the domestic aspects of mourning; they also made up the majority of the enthusiasts for seances and spiritualism.

The ghost story was one of several nineteenth-century popular genres that spoke particularly to a female readership and that drew key concerns from women's culture. Often women's stories mix the supernatural with elements of these other genres. *Local color writing frequently incorporated supernatural elements, perhaps in part because of the prominence of ghosts in much regional *folklore. More importantly, however, local color realism was dominated by women writers, and its themes were strongly woman-centered as a consequence. Local color writers Alice *Cary, Harriet Beecher *Stowe, Rose Terry *Cooke, Mary Wilkins Freeman, Annie Trumbull Slosson, Charles Craddock (Mary Ann *Murfree), Marietta *Holley, Jeanne de Lavigne, and Mildred Haun all wrote ghost stories. Consolation literature, which articulated the Victorian fascination with death and claimed a considerable female readership by the mid-nineteenth century, also demonstrates clear affinities with the ghost story; many of the stories of Annie Trumbull Slosson are excellent examples of the genre.

In the twentieth century, with the decline of the classic ghost story as a mainstream form, women writers continued to produce supernatural literature. Some incorporated supernatural elements into the realist novel and short story. Others wrote ghost stories for newer, more specialized outlets, such as the periodicals *Weird Tales* and *Amazing Stories* and publishers such as Arkham House and Strange.

Ghost stories by women writers have often been measured against critical definitions and standards based on classic men's stories and have been found anomalous. Yet the women's tradition has emerged as distinct, often in conscious counterpoint to the masculine tradition. In women's stories, for example, while the supernatural event may occasion surprise, even horror or terror, such responses are rarely central to the story's meaning, because these stories present a worldview that is not sharply dichotomized into natural and supernatural. Many characters in women's stories continue personal relationships across the "boundary" between life and death as in Edith Wharton's "The Lady's Maid's Bell" (1904) or Toni Morrison's *Beloved* (1987).

Reason and rationality, those faculties valorized by the classic ghost story, only prevent the characters in many women's stories from perceiving the continuum of life and death, natural and supernatural. Women's stories often target those professional men who incarnate reason, exposing the limits of their imagination. The alienist Dr. Stanchon of Josephine Daskam Bacon's *The Strange Cases of Dr. Stanchon* (1913) and the doctors of Ellen Glasgow's stories collected in *The Shadowy Third and Other Stories* (1923) typify the breed.

Stories by American women often suggest that sympathy, rather than terror or horror, is the most useful response to a supernatural visitation, and the property superior to reason in enabling perception of the supernatural. Sympathy often permits a woman character to see ghosts invisible to others, as in stories by Glasgow and Counselman. Some ghosts return in need of affection or guidance; others return because they have messages or missions for the living. In a few cases, ghosts return to claim justice or revenge, or to continue a romance or romantic rivalry. But by far the dominant motifs in women's stories is of women who contact each other across the boundary that divides the living from the dead to share a common experience or to join in resisting patriarchal oppression and domestic violence from lovers who seduce and abandon, and from cruel fathers and husbands who abuse, imprison, and even murder the women and children in their households. Harriet Prescott * Spofford's *Sir Rohan's Ghost* (1860), with its multiple ghostly women victims, dramatizes the likelihood that women living in the same house will inherit a legacy of domestic tragedy. Ghost stories provided many women writers with an outlet for some of their most scathing attacks on * domestic ideology. One need only remember that Charlotte Perkins * Gilman's feminist classic *The Yellow Wallpaper* (1892) was first anthologized in collections of supernatural stories to appreciate the possibilities of the ghost story genre for women writers.

[*See also* Gothic Fiction; Magazines, Women's; Short Stories.]

• Edith Birkhead, *The Tale of Terror: A Study of the Gothic Romance* (1921; reprint, 1963). Donald Ringe, *American Gothic: Imagination and Reason in Nineteenth Century Fiction* (1982). Everett F. Bleiler, *The Guide to Supernatural Fiction* (1983). Howard Kerr, John W. Crowley, and Charles L. Crow, eds., *The Haunted Dusk: American Supernatural Fiction, 1820–1920* (1983). Alfred Bendixen, ed., *Haunted Women: The Best Supernatural Tales by American Women Writers* (1985). Jessica Amanda Salmonson, ed., *What Did Miss Darrington See?: An Anthology of Feminist Supernatural Fiction* (1989). Lynette Carpenter and Wendy K. Kolmar, eds., *Haunting the House of Fiction: Feminist Perspectives on Ghost Stories by American Women Writers* (1991).

Lynette Carpenter and Wendy K. Kolmar

GIBSON GIRL. Created by *Life* illustrator Charles Dana Gibson in 1896, the Gibson Girl was a dignified beauty, impeccably dressed in a sailor middy, neat hose, and a skirt that came to the knee. Modern and smart, this idealized young woman could move freely and, therefore, could be athletic. She neither drank nor smoked, was delicate as well as strong, and helped to create a whole new standard of romance. Modeled on Gibson's sister Josephine and his wife, the former Irene Langhorne, the Gibson Girl imaged the fresh, appealing American woman so different from her European counterpart, who was much more sexual. Unfortunately, the code of Gibson Girl dress and behavior tended to infantalize the American woman, who could not stay innocent forever.

• Jessie Edith Gibson, *On Being a Girl* (1927). Charles Dana Gibson, *The Gibson Girl and Her America: The Best Drawings* (1969).

Linda Wagner-Martin

GILCHRIST, Ellen (b. 1935), novelist, short fiction writer, poet, scriptwriter. Born in Vicksburg, Mississippi, Gilchrist grew up at Hopedale Plantation in Grace, Mississippi. At nineteen, she ran away to be married and had three sons by this first of four husbands, all of whom she divorced. After earning her B.A. in philosophy at Millsaps College in 1967, Gilchrist began her professional career at the age of forty, when she began work for *Vieux Carre Courier*, a New Orleans newspaper. She simultaneously sent poems to poet and novelist Jim Whitehead, who invited her to join his writing class at the University of Arkansas in Fayetteville. Tired of upper-class snobbery, Gilchrist flourished in this unpretentious environment and in 1979 published a collection of poetry, *The Land Surveyor's Daughter*. Subsequent fictional works chronicle the decline of southern aristocracy through tragicomic narratives describing women who escape the restrictions of their upper-class lives with sometimes destructive behavior.

Gilchrist won popular and critical acclaim with her first collection of short stories, *In the Land of Dreamy Dreams* (1981). In these New Orleans stories, as well as in the novel *The Annunciation* (1983), Gilchrist's realistic style captures a social milieu of class consciousness, racism, and confining gender roles. These and later works focus on the psyche of women who love, lust, manipulate, and dream while they seek self-realization and wholeness, a goal they sometimes achieve through their own creativity.

Gilchrist won the American Book Award for Fiction for *Victory Over Japan* (1984), a gathering of interrelated stories about spirited female protagonists, some of whom appear elsewhere in her oeuvre. Subsequent works include *Drunk with Love*, collected stories (1986); *Falling*

Through Space, The Author's Journals (1987); *The Anna Papers*, a novel (1988); *Light Can Be Both Wave and Particle*, collected stories (1989); *The Blue-Eyed Buddhist*, collected stories (1990); *I Cannot Get You Close Enough*, three novellas (1990); and *Net of Jewels*, a novel (1992). Gilchrist won a national scriptwriting award for her play *A Season of Dreams*, based on the short stories of Eudora Welty.

Compared with Carson *McCullers and Flannery *O'Connor for her creation of idiosyncratic, pitiable characters, Gilchrist nonetheless avoids the moral fervor of southern gothic. Her work resembles that of such other contemporary southern women writers as Lee *Smith, Lee Zacharias, and Bobbie Ann *Mason, but she creates her own voice through an energetic yet low-key style. Her bold characterizations of feisty, untrammeled adolescent and adult women living rather traditional southern women's lives are memorable.

• Jeanie Thompson and Anita Miller Garner, "The Miracle of Realism: The Bid for Self-knowedge in the Fiction of Ellen Gilchrist," *Southern Quarterly: A Journal of Arts in the South* 22, no. 1 (Fall 1983): 101–114. George Garrett, "The Year in Fiction," in *Dictionary of Literary Biography Yearbook*, ed. Jean W. Ross (1984), pp. 144–159. "Ellen Gilchrist—*Victory Over Japan:* The American Book Award: Fiction," in *Contemporary Literacy Criticism*, vol. 34, ed. Sharon K. Hall (1985), pp. 164–166. Margaret Jones Bolsterli, "Ellen Gilchrist's Characters and the Southern Woman's Experience: Rhoda Manning's Double Bind and Anna Hand's Creativity," *New Orleans Review* 15 (Spring 1988): 7–9. Virginia Blain, Patricia Clements, and Isabel Grundy, eds., *The Feminist Companion to Literature in English: Women Writers from the Middle Ages to the Present* (1990).

Rebecca Smith

GILMAN, Charlotte Perkins Stetson (1860–1935), feminist, author, and lecturer. Widely known in her own time for her incisive, broadranging analyses of women's role and status in society, Charlotte Perkins Gilman was considered the preeminent intellectual in the woman's movement at the turn of the century. Born in Hartford, Connecticut, to Mary Fitch and Frederic Stowe Perkins (through whom she was related to Harriet Beecher *Stowe), Gilman as a child suffered from her father's abandonment of the family and the need to move, with her mother and older brother, some nineteen times in eighteen years as her mother sought work or the help of relatives. This, and her mother's witholding of physical affection in order to prepare her children for possible future disappointment, may have influenced her decision early in life to be independent and self-supporting. After some formal training at the Rhode Island School of Design, she taught art

and designed greeting cards for a living. In 1884, despite concern over combining marriage and professional work, she married Charles Stetson, a Rhode Island artist. In 1885, the birth of a daughter, Katherine, was followed by depression and emotional collapse, for which she sought treatment from the prominent neurologist, Dr. S. Weir Mitchell. However, Mitchell's regimen—widely applied at the time to middle-class white women thought to be suffering from *"hysteria"—of complete bed rest and no intellectual stimulation, and his advice that she lead a life totally devoted to domesticity, led Charlotte, as she said, to the brink of "utter mental ruin."

After a trial separation from her husband, Gilman moved to California in 1888, and in 1894 she and Stetson were amicably divorced, although she was widely condemned both for the divorce and for giving her daughter to Stetson and his second wife to raise. A second marriage in 1900 to her cousin, George Houghton Gilman, endured happily until his death a year before her own.

In California, at the time a center of progressive social thought, Gilman began to write and lecture on issues related to women, labor, and social reform. She also became interested in the ideas of Edward Bellamy, whose immensely popular *Looking Backward* (1888) described a future world based on socialist and egalitarian principles. In 1890, the poem "Similar Cases," a witty satire on opponents of social change, brought her recognition, as did a volume of verse, *In This Our World* (1893). In 1892, she had published in *New England Magazine* the short story "The Yellow Wall-Paper." Based on her own experience with Dr. Mitchell, it is a harrowing depiction of a woman driven to madness by the well-meant but destructive ministrations of her doctor husband—an indictment of the sexual politics of marriage and medicine in the nineteenth century that is today considered a classic of feminist literature.

In 1898, Gilman published her major work, *Women and Economics*. Drawing on history, sociology, anthropology, and psychology, it used an evolutionary perspective to explore women's subordinate status in society in the past and present, tracing it to their economic dependence within marriage. Women were underdeveloped as social beings, Gilman argued, because their energies were focused on pleasing a husband on whom they relied for economic support. And they were undervalued because the essential work they performed of cooking, cleaning, and child care was unpaid. Her proposed reforms included socializing the work of the home through the establishment of nurseries and kitchens run by trained professionals, thereby releasing women for paid, productive work in the public world, where they would contribute to social progress.

Eventually translated into seven languages, *Women and Economics* brought fame to Gilman, and she continued to lecture widely in the decades that followed, both at home and abroad. In addition, despite recurrent bouts of depression, she published prolifically. In *Concerning Children* (1900), *The Home* (1903), *Human Work* (1904), *Man-Made World* (1911), and *His Religion and Hers* (1923), she explored the androcentric nature of society and its institutions, and continued to argue for the importance of trained, professional care for children as society's most precious resource and for the importance of work to human fulfillment. From 1909 to 1916, Gilman also published a monthly magazine, *The Forerunner*, for which she wrote most of the copy, including editorials, news articles, poems, some two hundred short stories, and three utopian novels—an output that she estimated was the equivalent of twenty-eight books. The *utopia *Herland* (1915) describes an all-female society (with reproduction by parthenogenesis) in which women's qualities of nurturing and caring have created a peaceful, prosperous, rationally ordered and ecologically sound world, focused on the collective raising of children.

Gilman's death in 1935 was self-induced. She took chloroform when the breast cancer from which she had suffered for three years threatened to make her a burden to others. By then, with the decline of the organized woman's movement and the popularity of new ideas, including the belief in women's emancipation and personal fulfillment through sexual liberation, she had outlived her reputation and her books were out of print. Her autobiography, *The Living of Charlotte Perkins Gilman* (1935), appeared posthumously. Since the mid-1960s the importance of her ideas has been newly recognized, and many of her works are back in print.

• The Gilman Papers are housed in the Schlesinger Library, Radcliffe College, Cambridge, Massachusetts. Elaine Hedges, Afterword to *The Yellow Wallpaper*, by Charlotte Perkins Gilman (1973). Mary A. Hill, *Charlotte Perkins Gilman* (1980). Gary Scharnhorst, *Charlotte Perkins Gilman: A Bibliography* (1985). Sheryl L. Meyering, ed., *Charlotte Perkins Gilman: The Woman and Her Work* (1989). Ann J. Lane, *To "Herland" and Beyond: The Life and Work of Charlotte Perkins Gilman* (1990). Carol Farley Kessler, "Charlotte Perkins Gilman, 1860–1935," in *Modern American Women Writers* ed. Elaine Showalter (1991), pp. 155–169. Catherine Golden, ed., *The Captive Imagination: A Casebook on "The Yellow Wallpaper"* (1992). Larry Ceplair, ed., *Charlotte Perkins Gilman: A Nonfiction Reader* (1992).

Elaine Hedges

GIOVANNI, Nikki (b. 1943), poet. The dialectic of change permeates the poetry of Nikki Giovanni and is the soul force at the core of the poet's sensibility. Nikki Giovanni, one of the most noted poets to emerge during the 1960s, was born Yolande Cornelia Giovanni, Jr., in Knoxville, Tennessee. Assertive, outspoken, impatient with ignorance, Giovanni brought to her first books, *Black Feeling, Black Talk* (1967) and *Black Judgement* (1968), a sensibility that had been shaped by nurturing middle-class parents; by Louvenia Terrell Watson, her maternal grandmother who gave her spiritual fiber; and by a radicalized period that demanded activism and a struggle for social justice in American society. These books include poems aimed at jarring the complex double consciousness of blacks and the safe complacency of whites. "The True Import of Present Dialogue, Black vs. Negro" asks the question "Nigger / Can you kill?" They also include poems like "Nikki Rosa," which signal the controlled, piercing, irony-laced voice heard so often in her later poetry, in which the speaker hopes that whites will never write about her "because they never understand Black love is Black wealth and they'll probably talk about my hard childhood and never understand that / all the while I was quite happy."

Her early poetry brought Giovanni critical attention and a following among those in the black liberation movement. Buoyed by her success, she produced works in rapid succession: *Re-Creation* (1970), her third volume of poetry; *Gemini: an Extended Autobiographical Statement on My First Twenty-Five Years of Being a Black Poet* (1971); *Spin a Soft Black Song* (1971), which was dedicated to her two-year-old son Thomas Watson Giovanni; and "Truth Is On Its Way," a best-selling record album on which she reads her poetry accompanied by gospel music sung by the New York Community Choir. Her prose and her poetry shared the characteristics of political savvy, intimacy of speech, and mother wit.

By the time *Re-Creation* was published, critics had already noticed the poet's divergence from the militant, often scatological, language that punctuated some of the earlier poems, and much critical debate focused on what was perceived to be the tempering of her militant voice. In *My House* (1972) Giovanni attempts to put the issue to rest. "I'm into a very personal thing, now, and I have a two-and-a-half-year old son, and I'm more settled." She continues, "only a fool doesn't change." *My House, Ego-Tripping and Other Poems for Young People* (1973), *The Women and the Men* (1975), and *Cotton Candy on a Rainy Day* (1978) evidence an artistic sensibility that has turned to matters of family, celebration of men and women in relationships, the fantasy world of children, and the transitory quality of life and happiness. Giovanni confidently affirms her right as an artist to resist being confined or restricted by ideological precepts or critical blueprints, no matter whose they are. In the preface to *Those Who Ride the Night Winds* (1982) she writes: "Art . . . and by necessity . . . artists are on the cutting edge . . . of change. The very fact . . . that something has been done . . . over and over again . . . is one reason . . . to change. Everything . . . must change."

Evoking the soulful lyrics of Nina Simone's song, "Everything must change," Giovanni embraces change as the rejuvenating force of her work. In "Hands: For Mother's Day," the poet also reveals the essence of her consistent and strong appeal: the moral and spiritual fiber that give her work power.

"My grandmother washed on Mondays . . . every Monday. . . . mostly in the dark . . . frequently in the cold . . . certainly alone . . . you heard on the back porch . . . some plea to higher beings for forgiveness and the power to forgive."

From *Black Feeling/Black Talk* to her most recent collection of prose, *Sacred Cows and Other Edibles* (1988), Giovanni has reveled in the power of language to lift the veil of ignorance, to engage the heart as well as the mind, and to affirm the human spirit. Her work exhibits a dynamism that reflects her insistence upon change and growth as natural consequences of freedom.

Joanne V. Gabbin

GIRLHOOD. The American women writers who began to address the lives of young women and girls in the eighteenth century devoted their energies to the most popular of American genres in that era: tales of seduction and treatises on education. Some women, like Judith Sargent *Murray, wrote straightforward calls for female liberty and improvements in the quality of education offered girls. Many of the other women who wrote about girlhood, however, took for their subject matter the depravity and corruption of European modes of conduct and the threat such conduct posed to young women in America. Susanna *Rowson, author of the seduction novel *Charlotte Temple* (1794), and Hannah Webster *Foster, who wrote the epistolary *The Coquette; or, The History of Eliza Wharton* (1797), detail the tragic seduction of young women uneducated in proper conduct. Hannah Webster Foster also wrote more directly about the importance of

educating girls, describing an eighteenth-century school for girls and encouraging reading in the anecdotal survival manual *The Boarding School; or, Lessons of a Preceptress to Her Pupils* (1798).

*Advice books and conduct manuals formed the bulk of what nineteenth-century women writers published on the subject of girlhood. Eliza W. Farrar's *The Young Lady's Friend* (1836) and Lydia H. *Sigourney's *Letters to Young Ladies* (1837) are typical of this genre, as is Lydia Maria *Child's *The Girl's Own Book* (1853), a compendium of articles on conversation, manners, and amusements. Conduct-of-life tracts aimed at young ladies of quality between 1840 and 1860 contained none of the exhortations that marked comparable tracts intended for young men.

Later in the century, *autobiography and fictionalized autobiography took precedence as effective genres for communicating the perils of girlhood. Harriet *Jacobs's autobiographical *Incidents in the Life of a Slave Girl*, published in 1861, provides a remarkable window on the experiences of an enslaved woman who escapes to freedom in the North. The title of the Jacobs narrative, and its insistence on framing her experiences within a condescending version of American "girlhood" (witness the chapter titled "The Trials of Girlhood"), create a kind of dissonance around the real story: subjected to unrelenting sexual harassment by her master, Jacobs became pregnant by a white neighbor at sixteen in the hope that it might win her freedom. After the Civil War, Frances *Harper re-created in fiction the periods of slavery and Reconstruction she had lived through as a young woman in *Iola Leroy* (1892), the story of a girl separated from a mother sold back into slavery at the death of her planter husband.

Many of the women writers of the nineteenth century who were involved in social reform wrote children's fiction as well as material for adult consumption. The best-selling *Uncle Tom's Cabin* (1852), by Harriet Beecher *Stowe, tells the story of Tom, a slave who saves the life of Eva St. Clair, a girl who convinces her wealthy father to buy him. Retellings for children of this tale were numerous, and in abridged form the book quickly became a children's classic. Helen Hunt *Jackson, another reformer and author of *Ramona*, wrote *Nelly's Silver Mine* (1878), the story of a sister and brother whose family moves to Colorado mining country. Sarah Orne *Jewett wrote about strong, independent New England girls in *The Country Doctor* (1884).

At the same time that journalistic and autobiographical stories of girlhood sought to score moral and political points with adult readers, stories written specifically for girl audiences began to succeed in America with female writers such as Elizabeth Stuart Phelps *Ward, whose tomboyish *Gypsy Breynton* (1866) initiated a series; Martha Finley, whose weepy *Elsie Dinsmore* (1867) reaped twenty five titles; and Rebecca Sophia Clarke, whose "Little Prudy" stories premiered in the 1860s. Louisa May *Alcott's *Little Women* (1868) centered around the lives of four sisters, especially the rebellious, tomboyish Jo March, whom Alcott modeled on her own girlhood self. At the turn of the century, a slew of brighter, more positive girl heroines appeared in books such as Kate Douglass Wiggin's *Rebecca of Sunnybrook Farm* (1903), Jean Webster's *Daddy Long-Legs* (1912), and Eleanor Hodgman Porter's *Pollyanna* (1913). Around this time, new ideas about adolescence filtered into the world of reading and writing about girls in America. Female adolescence began to merit attention in fiction after 1900, as the position of girls in Victorian families began to change and new social and medical discourse offered female adolescence as a period of anticipation, change, and self-reflection. Edith *Wharton's *Summer* (1917) is one of the first novels about adolescent girls to give its main character, Charity Royall, an extensive inner life. Female adolescents predominate in the fiction of Ruth Suckow, whose *The Odyssey of a Nice Girl* (1925) portrays a dreamy teenager coming to grips with growing up. By the 1940s, Carson *McCullers introduced an even younger adolescent heroine in *Member of the Wedding* (1946). At twelve, Frankie Addams confronts "the decision to be a woman at all."

In the early twentieth century, women writers continued to use autobiography and fictionalized autobiography to tell stories about girlhood, often with strong political motives. At the turn of the century, boys' reading about great men and inventors was often matched by books about famous women aimed at girls. Frances Hodgson *Burnett, the popular author of children's literature, published a memoir called *The One I Know Best of All, A Memory of the Mind of a Child* (1893), and Helen Keller's *The Story of My Life* (1903) was enshrined as the premiere account of girlhood triumph over adversity.

The most numerous and powerful girlhood stories to be told in the early twentieth century were those of recent immigrants, ethnic minorities and residents of the Western frontier. In *My Ántonia* (1918), Willa *Cather refigured her own Nebraska childhood with that of the self-sacrificing, fictional Bohemian immigrant girl Ántonia Shimerda. Similar difficulties and awakenings were later echoed in Laura Ingalls

*Wilder's popular series of children's books. From the Wisconsin woods girlhood of *Little House in the Big Woods* (1932), to the young married status of *The First Four Years* (1971), Wilder's accounts of her own daily life grow progressively more sophisticated, anticipating the linguistic progress of a child reader making her or his way through the collection. In *The Bread Givers* (1925), Anzia *Yezierska created the fictional voice of an urban immigrant waif who pulls herself up from poverty through "wit and hard work." Sioux *Zitkala-Sa's *American Indian Legends* (1921) include autobiographical accounts of the author's painful girlhood experiences at a Quaker missionary school in Indiana as well as her difficult return home. The second chapter of Zora Neale *Hurston's *Their Eyes Were Watching God* (1933) details the self-discovery of Janie, a West Florida girl who fails to recognize herself at age six among white playmates in a photograph and exclaims in shocked tones, "Aw, I'm colored!" Girlhood ends at sixteen when her grandmother discovers her kissing a boy at the front gate.

At midcentury, such authors as Sylvia *Plath, Jean *Stafford, Mary *McCarthy, and Anne *Sexton mined girlhood and motherhood for moments of powerful honesty on the subject of female identity. Plath's novel *The Bell Jar* (1963) narrates the crippling effects of intellect and artistic imagination on a young woman of the 1950s, a girl taught by her mother, her schools, and the magazines she reads to accept a domestic and diminished role. McCarthy's *Memories of a Catholic Girlhood* (1957) is only one of her autobiographies, and one in which girlhood is a state of awareness that allows for the narration of adult hypocrisies. Sexton's poetry confronts the struggles and relationships of mothers and daughters powerfully, particularly in "Little Girl, My Stringbean, My Lovely Woman" (1966). Stafford's *The Mountain Lion* (1947) is the tale of a bookish girl in Colorado crushed under the weight of adolescence, a wise child unwilling to cope "with all the tommyrot with which people were constantly trying to ruin her life."

In the same period, American girls read more and more of the Nancy Drew mystery stories, lessons in accommodation first published in the 1920s and couched in the girl detective's brilliant mastery of ballet, nursing, flower-arranging, archaeology, and sleuthing. Contradictory impulses toward adventure and domesticity are at the core of so much of this writing, still the site of a conversation about girls' place that stretches far back into the nineteenth century. Patricia Meyer Spacks has argued, however, in an essay titled "What Have 60 Million Readers Found in Nancy Drew?," that the

Nancy Drew stories "insist that growing up provides no unmanageable difficulties, that adolescence is even for girls a time of freedom and power, not a time of dangerous sexuality, and that young people can play a meaningful part in society."

More recently, many women writers in America have returned to the politics of sex, power, and ethnicity in writing, often autobiographically, about girlhood. Maya * Angelou's autobiographical *I Know Why the Caged Bird Sings* (1969) is filled with bittersweet humor as well as the devastation of child sexual abuse. Autobiography, myth, fantasy, and fiction come together in Maxine Hong * Kingston's *Woman Warrior: Memoir of a Girlhood Among Ghosts* (1976). Through the Chinese legends and family stories that have marked her childhood and the customs insisted on by her mother, and Kingston's own poetically and politically inclined experience of Northern California in the 1960s, *The Woman Warrior* details the complexities and difficulties in Kingston's development as a woman and as a Chinese American. Kingston protests the sexism of traditional Chinese culture, exemplified in such misogynist sayings as "It is better to feed geese than girls" and in such acts as the binding of girls' feet and the selling of girl slaves. Kingston's collage of genres and story of a female, first-generation American upbringing has inspired countless female American authors since it appeared in 1976. One of those authors may be Amy * Tan, whose *Joy Luck Club* (1989) tells the story of Chinese-American women and their families, and the significance of the mother-daughter bond in one young woman's self-creation.

Turning through girlhood in the new South to the politics of national identity, Bobbie Ann * Mason's *In Country* (1985) presents the lives of a group of Vietnam veterans through their encounters with a teenage girl. Mason is an author fascinated with girlhood, and has also published a critical book on her own girlhood reading, a study called *The Girl Sleuth: A Feminist Guide to the Bobbsey Twins, Nancy Drew, and Their Sisters* (1975). Paule * Marshall's first major work, *Brown Girl, Brownstones* (1959), considers the coming of age of a young West Indian girl in New York and simultaneously explores the black immigrant experience in America. Toni * Morrison's *Sula* (1973) deals with the lives of two girls growing up together in Ohio. One, Nel Wright, chooses to marry and raise a family in their hometown. The other, Sula Peace, escapes to college and city, only to return and reinvolve herself in the life of her childhood friend. Born in Antigua, Jamaica * Kincaid now lives in the United States, and has written a novel about the process of growing up in the West Indies, *Annie John* (1985); stories like "Girl" from *At the Bottom of the River* (1984), in which a young girl hears the voice of a long tradition of advice from elders; as well as stories about the experiences of young, female West Indian immigrants in the United States. Louise * Erdrich's *The Beet Queen* (1986) follows the intrigues of Native and European Americans in the upper Midwest, culminating in the end of the main character's girlhood and her crowning in the local sugar beet festival. The work of Latina writer Sandra * Cisneros is filled with young girls coming of age, often straddling Mexican and American geography and culture, as in *The House on Mango Street* (1989). More recently, Lorene Carey's autobiographical *Black Ice* (1991) tells the story of the author's experiences as a lone African-American student at an elite New England prep school.

[*See also* Adolescence; Children's Literature.]

• Joseph F. Kett, *Rites of Passage: Adolescence in America, 1790 to the Present* (1977). Mary Kelley, ed., *Woman's Being, Woman's Place: Female Identity and Vocation in American History* (1979). Patricia Meyer Spacks, *The Adolescent Idea: Myths of Youth and the Adult Imagination* (1981). Humphrey Carter and Mari Pritchard, eds., *The Oxford Companion to Children's Literature* (1984). Barbara A. White, *Growing Up Female: Adolescent Girlhood in American Fiction* (1985). Cathy N. Davidson, *Revolution and the Word: The Rise of the Novel in America* (1986).

Jill Wacker

GIRL SCOUTS. Originally known as the Girl Guides, the Girl Scouts was founded in 1912 by Juliette Gordon Low, a native of Georgia and a close friend of the British founder of the Boy Scouts and his wife, Lord and Lady Baden Powell. Designed as the American equivalent of the British Girl Guides and the female counterpart of the newly formed Boy Scouts, the Girl Scouts at its inception embodied both the conservative and militaristic ideology of turn-of-the-century America and the ideals of the burgeoning feminist movement.

In his book *Bodies and Machines* (1992), Mark Seltzer outlines some of the contemporary events and anxieties that led in part to the founding of the Boy Scouts. Central among these were the closing of the frontier, the subsequent worries about the future of American expansion, and a new philosophy of character that combined the technological with the natural in asserting that boys could be "made into men."

The Girl Scouts took on much of this ideology, with the added problem of adapting these "masculine" Boy Scout ideals to programs for girls without threatening white middle-class standards of femininity. Like the Boy Scouts, the Girl Scouts combined the missionary and imperialist zeal of the middle-class charity movements with a more liberal view toward global understanding and exchange. Thus, in the early years of the movement the Girl Scouts worked to expand their recruitment of girls within the United States and to pass on the ideology of Scouting to girls and women around the world. This expansion was often blatantly classist, racist, and imperialist. However, along with an emphasis on patriotism, duty, religiosity, and purity came the establishment of a social sphere for women in which they could wield power, assume male military titles, aid in national defense, and participate in physical activities formerly denied them.

Today the Girl Scouts is the largest nonpolitical organization for women in the world. Unlike the Camp Fire Girls, which has gone coed, the Girl Scouts remains a single-sex organization. In recent years the Scouts have declared themselves a feminist organization, and at a time when the Boy Scouts are being sued for their heterosexist practices, the Girl Scouts have issued statements claiming that they do not discriminate on the basis of sexual preference.

There is little writing on or analysis of the Girl Scouts except for that published by the Girl Scouts themselves.

• *Scouting for Girls* (1920). Anne Hyde Choate and Helen Ferris, eds., *Juliette Low and the Girl Scouts: The Story of an American Woman, 1860–1927* (1928).

Katie Kent

GLANCY, Diane (b. 1941), poet, fiction writer, playwright, educator. Although her ancestry is only one-eighth Cherokee, Diane Glancy credits her Cherokee grandmother with influencing her to write and feels "even that small part has leavened the whole lump." Glancy's rising sense of herself as "Indian" and as poet, possessed of the "medicine bundle" of language, coincided with the death of her influential grandmother during her own adolescence. Later in life her path brought her to live in Oklahoma, near the site of her great-grandfather's birth.

Glancy is a prolific writer who has won numerous prizes for her poetry, fiction, and plays. In 1982, she received a first-place award from the National Federation of State Poetry Societies; the same year she won first prize in the American Indian Theater Company playwriting contest. In 1984, she received the playwriting prize and became the 1984–86 laureate of the Five Civilized Tribes. The Oklahoma Federation of Writers gave her chapbook of poetry *Brown Wolf Leaves the Res* (1984) its 1985 Pegasus

award, and her next collection of poetry, *One Age in a Dream* (1986), received the Lakes and Prairies Prize. She has published three more books of poetry: *Offering* (1988), *Iron Woman* (1990), for which she received the Capricorn Award, and *Lone Dog's Winter Count* (1991). Her fiction is collected in two recent volumes: *Trigger Dance* (1990), for which she was the recipient of the Nilon Excellence in Minority Fiction Award, and *Claiming Breath* (1992), winner of the University of Nebraska Press Native American Prose Award.

Glancy has a B.A. from the University of Missouri and an M.F.A. from the University of Iowa. She started her own fine arts press, MyrtleWood, in Tulsa, Oklahoma, where she was poet-in-the-schools and writer-in-residence at the Heller Theater. She has also been artist-in-residence for the State Arts Councils of Oklahoma and Arkansas. Glancy received a fellowship from the NEA and the Minnesota State Arts Board in 1990; she currently teaches creative writing and Native American literature at Macalester College in St. Paul, Minnesota.

• Joseph Bruchac, ed., *Songs from This Earth on Turtle's Back* (1983). Brian Swann and Arnold Krupat, eds., *I Tell You Now* (1987). Craig Lesley, ed., *Talking Leaves* (1991).

Margaret A. Lukens

GLASGOW, Ellen (1873–1945), was a novelist, essayist, and short story writer whose work characterized women of the nineteenth and twentieth centuries living in a protective southern culture. Although "Miss Ellen's" fiction was often said to chronicle the South, it was more accurately a depiction of white women of various classes trying to live within that paternalistic society. The acerbity that surfaced in novels that appeared to be traditional mark Glasgow's work as ironic, and often subversive of the values of southern culture.

Glasgow's fiction dominated best-seller lists in America between the turn of the century and the late 1930s. Born to a prominent Richmond, Virginia, family, Ellen Anderson Gholson Glasgow was the seventh of eight children. "Born without a skin," as her family said, the delicate child was educated largely at home. She disliked her Scottish father's staunch Presbyterianism and his dictatorial methods of running his household. When her mother discovered her husband's long-term affair with a woman of color, the breakdown she experienced alienated Ellen still more from her father, and she abandoned all religious practices. After her mother died in 1893, Glasgow suffered depression and hearing loss. She destroyed a novel in progress, though she soon began another, against her family's wishes (women of her class neither went to college nor had professions).

Glasgow learned about modern philosophy—Darwin, Malthus, Spencer, Mill, others—from Walter McCormack, her sister Cary's husband, who committed suicide a few years into the marriage. Cary and Ellen's grief was a bond between them, and they often lived together until Cary's death from breast cancer. Glasgow's reading and her early life experiences fed her tendency to a brooding skepticism evident in her first novel, *The Descendant*, which appeared anonymously in 1897. Critics attributed it to Harold Frederic, author of *The Damnation of Theron Ware*.

When *Phases of an Inferior Planet* (1898) and *The Voice of the People* (1900) were published under her own name to good reviews, her career was made. The young Glasgow was a realist, a writer intent on presenting real characters—unconventional women as well as strong, if poor, men. Glasgow wrote about the South without romanticizing it, an accomplishment during the years when Thomas Nelson Page's work set the pattern for southern fiction.

During the next six years, Glasgow traveled often to Europe and New York, where she became acquainted with Thomas Hardy, Joseph Conrad, Hugh Walpole, Henry James, and others. Because of her hearing loss, she usually traveled with one of her sisters or friends. She made money from her novels, but she was still dependent—as she would always be—on her family. Because she was in love with a married man, her travels allowed her to be with him circumspectly. According to Glasgow's autobiography, *The Woman Within* (1954), rather than his wife's freeing him so that they could marry, Glagow's lover died. *The Battle-Ground* (1902) and *The Deliverance* (1904) are romances, with strong women protagonists overcoming adversity to lead happy lives in marriage. By 1906—the end of Glasgow's romance—the character Laura Wilde, the realistic poet of *The Wheel of Life*, counters her doomed love with reliance on Eastern thought.

Glasgow continued to write and publish: *The Ancient Law* appeared in 1908, *The Romance of a Plain Man* in 1909, and *The Miller of Old Church* in 1911. Following the literary practice that serious fiction was to be about male characters, the two later novels had strong male protagonists, who were rewarded with the love of women above them in class. *The Miller of Old Church*, filled with unconventional southern women characters, emphasizes that *friendship among women is essential. Even though Glasgow was embittered over the deaths of her favorite siblings, Cary and Frank

(a suicide), in 1913 she wrote one of her best novels, *Virginia*, in memory of her sister and mother. Begun as an ironic treatment of the traditional woman who gave up everything for the love of a good man, the novel became a sympathetic account of Virginia Pendleton, married to and finally abandoned by a playwright, despite her dedication to the roles of wife and mother.

When the novel appeared in 1913, Glasgow was living in New York, trying to sever ties with her father. She remained there until 1916, but she wrote best in Virginia and soon returned to Richmond. Her quiet life sometimes disguised her feminism, but in 1916 she published her most feminist novel, *Life and Gabriella*. Subtitled *The Story of a Woman's Courage*, the novel showed Gabriella Carr empowered by her own will and intellect.

Once in Richmond, Glasgow was wooed by a neighboring lawyer and politician, Henry Anderson. Although the two became engaged, after Anderson went with the Red Cross to Europe, Glasgow realized that she could not marry him, probably because of his fascination with younger women. The rupture was painful, however, and she overdosed on sleeping pills upon his return. She survived, and the two remained close throughout their lives. *The Builders* (1919) focused fondly on Anderson, whereas *One Man in His Time* (1922) describes the beautiful, if aging, Corinna Page, who decides she does not want to marry; several of Glasgow's stories echo the theme of women's choosing to remain single. By 1925, when Glasgow published *Barren Ground*, she understood well the relative power of men and women in the love relationship. The betrayed Dorinda Oakley's vengeance leads to her economic and social triumph as a farmer; and though her sense of herself as nonsexual disappoints some readers, Dorinda finds stability through withdrawing from erotic passion.

Glasgow wrote out all aspects of her angst in the three novels that followed, which are usually considered comic. The relentless irony of *The Romantic Comedians* (1926), *They Stooped to Folly* (1929), and *The Sheltered Life* (1932) brought her new critical recognition. *The Romantic Comedians* was a Book-of-the-Month Club selection; *They Stooped to Folly* was a Literary Guild choice; and *The Sheltered Life* was fifth on the best-seller list in 1932. Glasgow's shocking denouement to this Queenborough trilogy—the anguished southern lady killing her betraying husband—was softened in her 1935 *Vein of Iron*, when both male and female protagonists triumphed through moral, upright lives. In 1942 she won the Pulitzer Prize for fiction for *In This Our Life;* in 1966 its short sequel, *Beyond Defeat,* was published posthumously.

Incapacitated with a heart ailment, Glasgow lived until November of 1945. She completed her autobiography, *The Woman Within,* to be published after her death, and was happy with the honors her last decade brought her. She was the sixth woman member of the American Academy of Arts and Letters; she received the Howells Medal for Fiction, a special award from the *Saturday Review of Literature,* and several honorary doctorates. She was the only American writer whose fiction was published in two special matched sets, the 1929–1933 *Old Dominion Edition of the Works of Ellen Glasgow* from Doubleday and *The Virginia Edition of the Works of Ellen Glasgow* in 1938 from Scribner's. For the latter publication, she wrote the prefaces that comprise *A Certain Measure: An Interpretation of Prose Fiction* (1943).

Known by her peers as a southern writer, Glasgow is accessible today as a woman writer who cared about families, *community, and strong individual women and men. The dynamic of her best fiction was its capability to reflect the passion and endurance of all human life. In her writing, she moved beyond whatever geographical constraints her southern subjects might have imposed on her imagination

• Glasgow's papers are in the Alderman Library, University of Virginia. See also Blair Rouse, ed., *Letters of Ellen Glasgow* (1958). Frederick P. W. McDowell, *Ellen Glasgow and the Ironic Art of Fiction* (1963). William W. Kelly, *Ellen Glasgow: A Bibliography* (1964). Julius Rowan Raper, *Without Shelter: The Early Career of Ellen Glasgow* (1971), *From the Sunken Garden, The Fiction of Ellen Glasgow, 1916–1945* (1980), and ed., *Ellen Glasgow's Reasonable Doubts* (1988). E. Stanly Godbold, Jr., *Ellen Glasgow and the Woman Within* (1972). Linda W. Wagner, *Ellen Glasgow: Beyond Convention* (1982). Elizabeth Jane Harrison, *Female Pastoral: Women Writers Re-Visioning the American South* (1991). Lynette Carpenter, *Haunting the House of Fiction: Feminist Perspectives on Ghost Stories by American Women* (1991).

Linda Wagner-Martin

GLASPELL, Susan (c. 1882–1948), playwright, novelist, memoirist. Born in Davenport, Iowa, Glaspell graduated in 1899 from Drake University as an outstanding journalism student. She worked for Des Moines newspapers until she began publishing short stories and her first novels, *The Glory of the Conquered* (1909) and *The Visioning* (1911). In 1913, she married George Cram ("Jig") Cook after his divorce was final. Glaspell and Cook lived first in Chicago, where they saw the work of the Irish Players; they soon followed the migration of other freethink-

ers to Greenwich Village and then to Provincetown, Massachusetts. In 1915, with the help of Hutchins and Neith Boyce Hapgood, Djuna *Barnes, Louise Bryant, Edna St. Vincent *Millay, and others, they founded the Provincetown Players, an experimental theater group that introduced work by serious new playwrights.

Glaspell and Cook wrote *Suppressed Desires,* a satirical one-act that was produced in 1915. Glaspell's first play, written in fewer than ten days, was *Trifles,* a one-act remarkable for its use of silences and offstage protagonists, and its provocative treatment of gender and women's anger. Now a classic of feminist literature, *Trifles* appeared in a short story version as "A Jury of Her Peers." It was followed in 1917 by *The People, Close the Book,* and *The Outside.* In 1918, *Woman's Honor* was produced; in 1919, her first three-act play, *Bernice.* In 1921, Glaspell's *Inheritors* was compared with Ibsen's work, and that same year's *The Verge,* a psychological study of women, was brilliantly experimental.

Glaspell often acted in her own plays, but she saw her primary role, with Cook, as a nurturer for young playwrights. Their most famous discovery was Eugene O'Neill, who learned much about innovative drama from Glaspell's work; the Provincetown Players produced his *Bound East for Cardiff, The Emperor Jones, The Hairy Ape,* and *Desire Under the Elms.* In 1922, Glaspell and Cook moved to Greece. Cook died in 1924 (Glaspell's biography of him, *The Road to the Temple,* appeared in 1926). In 1925, she married Norman Matson, and in 1927, they wrote *The Comic Artist;* their marriage broke up in 1932.

Glaspell's other work includes the plays *Chains of Dew* (1922) and *Alison's House* (1930), a retelling of Emily *Dickinson's story, which won the Pulitzer Prize for drama; the novels *Brook Evans* (1928), *Fugitive's Return* (1929), *Ambrose Holt and Family* (1931), *The Morning Is Near Us* (1939), *Cherished and Shared of Old* (1940), *Norma Ashe* (1942), and *Judd Rankin's Daughter* (1945); and fifty short stories. In the 1930s, she grew depressed and stopped writing for the stage, though between 1936 and 1938 she was head of the Midwest Play Bureau of the Federal Theatre. She then returned to Provincetown, where she died of pneumonia and pleural embolism in 1948.

• Jean Gould, *Modern American Playwrights* (1966). Arthur E. Waterman, *Susan Glaspell* (1966). C. W. E. Bigsby, Introduction to *Plays by Susan Glaspell* (1987), pp. 1–33. Jane Schlueter, ed., *Modern American Drama: The Female Canon* (1990).

Linda Wagner-Martin

GLÜCK, Louise (b. 1943), poet. Born in New York City, Louise Glück was educated at Sarah

Lawrence College and Columbia University. Among the many universities where she has taught are the University of North Carolina at Greensboro; the University of Iowa; the University of California at Berkeley, Davis, and Irvine; and Columbia University. She has been on the faculty of Williams College in Williamstown, Massachusetts, since 1984.

To date, Glück has published seven volumes of poetry. The earliest, *Firstborn* (1968), reveals the influence of Glück's former Columbia professor, Stanley Kunitz, as well as that of Robert Lowell, Sylvia *Plath, and Anne *Sexton. The poems in this volume are somewhat self-conscious and stylized, displaying the poet's concern with craft. With her second volume, *The House on Marshland* (1975), Glück finds and commands her own voice, although vestiges of Plath's and Sexton's influence may still be felt, perhaps because the poems are confessional in tone. The dominant theme of this volume is the pain of lost or damaged relationships, especially with men. In *The Garden* (1976), Glück includes a series of five closely related yet essentially independent poems about fear and loss. Her fourth volume also has a unifying theme, which is implied by its title, *Descending Figure* (1980). The poems depict various forms of descent: drowned children, a child's impression of a dead sister's figure descending, and expressions of mourning for the lost or fallen city of Jerusalem, for example. Glück's knowledge of and reliance on Greek myth is evident in her fifth volume, *The Triumph of Achilles* (1985), as is the voice of a much more mature woman than that heard in the earlier poems. The poems in *Ararat* (1990) concern the child's painful awareness of separation from the parent and the desperate but futile struggle for reunion. Glück's latest book, *The Wild Iris*, was written in a ten-week whirlwind of creative activity in the summer of 1991, and published in 1992.

Glück's awards and prizes include a Rockefeller Fellowship, NEA and Guggenheim Fellowships, Academy of American Poets Prize, American Academy Award, the Sara Teasdale Memorial Prize, and the Pulitzer Prize in poetry, 1992.

• Calvin Bedient, "Four American Poets," *Sewanee Review* 84 (Spring 1976): 351–364. Helen Vendler, "The Poetry of Louise Glück," *New Republic* (17 June 1978): 34–37. Liz Rosenberg, review of *The Triumph of Achilles* in *New York Times Book Review* (22 December 1985): 22–23. Stephen Dobyns, review of *Ararat* in *New York Times Book Review* (2 September 1990): 5. James K. Robinson, "Louise Glück," in *Contemporary Poets*, ed. Tracy Chevalier (1991), pp. 349–350.

Sheryl L. Meyering

GODDESS. As during earlier political movements for women's equality, in the 1970s many women expanded their political convictions to the spiritual realm. A romantic evocation of a matriarchal past, drawing its sustenance from worship of the Goddess, became the basis for a feminist spirituality. Whether or not an actual Great Mother or Goddess existed in some pre-patriarchal past is a matter for speculation. More important is the sense of "empowerment," "connectedness," and "wisdom" (crucial words for the "womanspirit" movement) that some women find in rejecting patriarchal religion with its single male God as the hierarchical model for humanity. Goddess worshipers prefer a nurturant, whole, courageous, collective divinity.

[*See also* Spirituality; Theologians.]

• Merlin Stone, *When God Was A Woman* (1976). Una Stannard, *Mrs. Man* (1977). Susan Griffin, *Woman and Nature: The Roaring Inside Her* (1978). Carol P. Christ and Judith Plaskow, eds., *Womanspirit Rising: A Feminist Reader in Religion* (1979). Rosemary Radford Ruether, *Womanguides: Readings towards a Feminist Theology* (1985).

Cathy N. Davidson

GOLDEN, Marita (b. 1950), journalist, poet, essayist, novelist, educator, founding member of the African American Writers' Guild, creator of the Zora Neale *Hurston/Richard Wright Award. Born in Washington, D.C., and educated at American University and Columbia University, Golden sees herself as one who "cannot be complacent," therefore, one who must work to raise the people's political consciousness, and as one of the generation of blacks having "both black identity and skill from the white world [which she must use for] institution building." These goals resulted from her home life and from her becoming "politically conscious" in the 1960s and centered in America.

This philosophy has informed her writing. Her autobiography, *Migrations of the Heart* (1983), presents her search for self in the tribulations of American life, her marriage to a Nigerian, and her move to Nigeria to live and work. Golden came to realize that the marriage, not the time spent in Africa, was a mistake. The text introduces concerns that have permeated her work: the black working and middle class and the affirming relationships between women, the need for someone to talk to and listen to, the empowerment of women, and women's pain often inflicted by other women.

These issues and many more surface in her first novel, *A Woman's Place* (1986). This is a novel of the friendship begun in college between three black women. Each character represents a vestige of Golden's experience as she confronts a problem of today and makes her own search and meaning. Serena, as the passionate radical, seeks a life of political commitment. Faith marries a Muslim and contends with the pressures of his tradition. Crystal works through an interracial relationship. These women, their families, and their friends take turns telling the story.

Her second novel, *Long Distance Life* (1989), a generational work, is set in a segregated Washington, D.C., in the 1920s. It presents middle-class and upwardly mobile black people and major movements from the 1920s to the 1980s such as Marcus Garvey, the migration north, and the civil rights movement. Depicted are the struggle for justice, race pride, and a self-sufficient intellectual black society. The narrative is told in the third person with musings from Naomi, the matriarch, interspersed.

Golden builds on and goes beyond Alice *Walker, Toni *Morrison, and Paule *Marshall. She remains concerned with black women. She is more concerned with *community building than community defining. In "Word Star" (*Essence*, November 1989), she says her women characters "find themselves negotiating the tension between personae and political choices and are compelled to leave home to further their self-definition." Her reaction to a lack of multifaceted black males in literature and the varied responses to urban America is illustrated in Logan and Nathaniel in *Long Distance Life*. Golden's concerns are finding self, and the responsibility of individuals to self and the community.

• Marita Golden, "Word Star," *Essence* 20 (November 1989): 32. Katherine Boo, "The Golden Standard," *City Paper* (8–14 December 1989): 24–32. "Golden, Marita 1950–," in *Black Writers: A Selection of Sketches from Contemporary Authors*, eds. Linda Metzgar et al. (1989), p. 224. Maria Koklanaris, "Reaching Back to Lend a Hand," *The Washington Post* (5 May 1991).

Helen R. Houston

GOLDMAN, Emma (1869–1940), anarchist, feminist, autobiographer, lecturer, essayist, and editor. Born on 27 June into a Jewish lower-middle-class family in Lithuania, Goldman emigrated to America in 1885 and became Red Emma, labeled by J. Edgar Hoover as "the most dangerous woman in America." First working in a garment factory in Rochester, New York, Goldman closely followed the events of the violent Chicago Haymarket strike and the 1887 execution of the four Haymarket martyrs. This pivotal event moved her to devote her life to *anarchism.

Goldman moved to New York in 1889, where she met anarchist Alexander Berkman and came under the influence of Johann Most, an advocate of violence. Most, recognizing Goldman's talent for public speaking, encouraged

her to become active in the anarchist movement. In 1892, Goldman helped her lover Berkman plan the unsuccessful assassination attempt on Henry Clay Frick in retaliation for his brutal suppression of the Homestead steel mill strike, for which act Berkman received a twenty-two-year prison sentence.

Goldman continued lecturing and was sentenced to one year in prison in 1893 for inciting a riot. During her stay in Blackwell's Island Penitentiary, Goldman became fluent in English and developed an independent political philosophy for social revolution that combined an insistence upon complete individual freedom with her passion for justice, but now renounced violence. Goldman also trained in nursing at Blackwell's and then studied midwifery in Vienna. Observing the suffering women endured from unwanted pregnancies led Goldman to define marriage as an institution of sexual oppression that exploits women through pregnancy, and she began lecturing on birth control.

Goldman began a nationwide lecture tour on free love, atheism, birth control, and free speech in the 1890s, but it was cut short in 1901 when her name was connected with Leon Czolgosz's assassination of President McKinley. Resurfacing in 1906, Goldman founded *Mother Earth* magazine, a forum for radical political, philosophical, and literary essays. Now recognized as a forceful public speaker, she began a second lecture tour in 1910; many of these speeches were collected in *Anarchism and Other Essays* (1911). A self-taught student of art, Goldman recognized the importance of modern European drama and introduced Ibsen, Shaw, and Strindberg to America in *The Social Significance of the Modern Drama* (1914).

A series of jail sentences in 1916 and 1917 for dispensing birth control information and encouraging draft resisters resulted in Goldman's deportation to Russia with Berkman in 1919 as undesirable aliens. At first enthusiastic about the Bolshevik government, she later denounced its abuses and violence, publishing *My Disillusionment in Russia* (1922) and *My Further Disillusionment in Russia* (1924). She left Russia in 1921 to lecture in Europe and England. Goldman published her autobiography, *Living My Life* (1931), before returning to the United States in 1934 for a last lecture tour. While working in England in support of the Spanish Loyalists, she died of a stroke on 14 May 1940, and was buried in Chicago.

Goldman maintained a passionate commitment to the nonviolent attainment of individual human rights and personal freedom, especially women's escape from their sexual bondage to men.

• Richard Drinnon, *Rebel in Paradise: A Biography of Emma Goldman* (1961). Alix Kates Shulman, *To the Barricades: The Anarchist Life of Emma Goldman* (1971). Emma Goldman, *Red Emma Speaks: Selected Writings and Speeches* (1972). John Chalberg, *Emma Goldman: American Individualist* (1991). Martin B. Duberman, *Mother Earth: An Epic Drama of Emma Goldman's Life* (1991).

Susan J. Updike

GORDON, Caroline (1895–1981), novelist, short fiction writer, critic, and teacher. Born in Kentucky, Caroline Gordon was given a thorough education in the classics by her father James Morris Gordon, who conducted a classics school, and she graduated from Bethany College (A.B., 1916). Gordon was involved with the Nashville Agrarians and married the Fugitive poet Allen Tate in 1924, with a daughter, Sally, born in 1925. Gordon converted to Catholicism in 1947. Gordon and Allen Tate divorced in 1959.

Gordon served as Ford Madox Ford's secretary while in New York (1924–1928), and he assisted her with her first novel, *Penhally* (1931). It is a family history involving two sets of brothers—the sons of the family founder and their contemporary descendants—and contains themes that run throughout Gordon's fiction: the conflict between the heroic and the selfish, the agrarian and the mercantile, and the *community and the individual. The novel also illustrates Gordon's emphasis on classical style, dramatic presentation, and unobtrusive narration.

Aleck Maury, Sportsman (1934) details the life of a new southern male, steeped in tradition yet devoted to hunting and fishing, often to the detriment of his family. Her third novel, *None Shall Look Back* (1937), continues her exploration of southern tradition, the *Civil War, and the agrarian movement. *Green Centuries* (1941) deals with a heroic pioneer, Rion Outlaw, who is tragically separated from the larger community. *The Garden of Adonis* (1937) and *The Women on the Porch* (1944) both explore the contemporary South, focusing on agrarian values.

After Gordon's conversion to Catholicism, her novels increasingly emphasize grace and salvation. *Strange Children* (1951) and *The Malefactors* (1957) set the power of Christian redemption against the immorality of the modern world. Gordon spent the last years of her life working on a fictionalized autobiography and family history, and published one more novel, *The Glory of Hera* (1972), a narrative in which Heracles is seen as precursor to Christ.

Gordon also wrote many essays and two books of criticism: the *House of Fiction* (1950), written with Allen Tate, and *How to Read a Novel* (1957). Both books show Gordon's emphasis on craft and style, as well as her knowledge of classical myth. In her later years she taught creative writing at the University of Dallas. Gordon maintained a close relationship with Flannery *O'Connor and has influenced other southern writers, including Walker Percy. Her work has enjoyed a devoted critical following for its highly developed craft and controlled style.

• Caroline Gordon's manuscripts and personal papers are at the Princeton University Library. See also *The Collected Stories of Caroline Gordon* (1981). Rose Ann C. Fraistat, *Caroline Gordon as Novelist and Woman of Letters* (1984). Ann Waldron, *Close Connections: Caroline Gordon and the Southern Renaissance* (1987). Veronica A. Makowsky, *Caroline Gordon: A Biography* (1989).

William M. Phillips

GORDON, Mary (b. 1949), novelist, essayist, and short fiction writer. Born on Long Island, Mary Gordon was the child of devout Catholic parents, her mother an Irish-American, her father a convert from Judaism. She was educated at Barnard College (B.A., 1971) and Syracuse University (M.A., 1973). She has taught at several colleges, including Amherst and Barnard, where she is now professor of English.

Gordon has published four novels as well as a collection of essays, *Good Boys and Dead Girls* (1991), a book of short stories, *Temporary Shelter* (1987), and a set of three novellas, *The Rest of Life* (1993). Her fiction is marked by both a Catholic sensibility and a feminist worldview. *Final Payments* (1978), which was awarded the Kafka Prize, records the development of a young woman entering the world after spending years caring for her reactionary Catholic invalid father. The new sorts of unhappiness she finds in the wider world lead her to return to a life of fruitless self-sacrifice, caring for an unlovable old woman, until she is saved by the intervention of her women friends and an alcoholic priest. *The Company of Women* (1981) describes another young woman entering the world. Felicitas is the daughter of one of the four female disciples of a fiercely conservative priest. Felicitas rejects her mother's circle and, trading one patriarchy for another, devotes herself to a Columbia professor who sums up all that was worst about sixties radicalism. In this novel Gordon begins the experiments in point of view that mark her later work. *Men and Angels* (1985), a less overtly Catholic novel, continues to explore the issues raised in the earlier works: How can the unlovable be loved? Is self-sacrifice always good? The novel is told from the points of view of Anne Foster, an art historian, and Laura Post, a religious fanatic who cares for Anne's child while she pursues her research. Like the painter who is her subject, Anne must balance her love for her child with her devotion to her work. Laura displays an insane self-sacrificing love—finally killing herself—that brings nothing but misery. Gordon's most recent novel, *The Other Side* (1989), is her most complicated treatment of point of view. The narrative moves in and out of the minds of several generations of a family who have adapted to America in widely different ways since coming to New York from Ireland.

• David Lodge, "The Arms of the Church," *Times Literary Supplement* (1 September 1978): 965. Margaret Drabble, "The Limits of Mother Love," *New York Times Book Review* (31 March 1985): 1, 30–31. Carol Iannone, "Fiction: The Secret of Mary Gordon's Success," *Commentary* (June 1985): 62–66. Susan Rubin Suleiman, "On Maternal Splitting: A Propos of Mary Gordon's *Men and Angels*," *Signs* 14 (Autumn 1988): 25–41.

Brian Abel Ragen

GOSSIP. The practice of gossip, historically associated with women and traditionally considered to be a harmful habit, has in recent years been reevaluated by scholars interested in exploring the rich complexity of what appears to be only "idle talk." In her 1985 book *Gossip*, Patricia Meyer Spacks argues that investigating the dynamics of gossip can reveal much about the content and narrative structure of literature and can serve as a model for the relationship between the writer and the reader of a text. Literature, in turn, can illuminate the power and seductiveness of gossip. By using gossip as a model with which to examine literary texts, Spacks is able to stress the link between narrative technique and everyday social discourse. In so doing, she opens the way to a serious consideration of the importance of gossip in the lives of women.

When gossip is represented in literature, it often serves as an instrument of the plot—a way for the writer to introduce or emphasize information to the reader. But much of real gossip's power lies not in the actual information imparted but in the process of exchange—the give-and-take dialogue and emotional connection between the participants. Gossip is an oral form and as such is highly unstable, subject to transmission and transformation beyond any single individual's control. This flexibility means that gossip can be the instrument of radically opposed ends, a duality that Spacks has identified as lying at the heart of the practice. The most widely recognized function of gossip is its regulatory capacity; gossip frequently serves as an articulation of a dominant social group's values, a way of keeping people "in their place." But gossip can potentially become a highly subversive practice.

For women restricted to a subordinate position within society, gossip can serve as a medium for exploring their own victimization—a way of understanding oppression by breaking the silence surrounding it. Gossip thus offers an escape into a realm of relative freedom, an arena in which women can form close emotional associations apart from men, forging an alternative discourse. Such a connection is often a source of intense pleasure, an intimate temporary alliance in which the participants can explore their feelings about a wide range of subjects while ostensibly considering meaningless trivialities. Gossip—a discussion of other people and their lives—becomes a way of imaginatively traversing the distinction between the private sphere and the public realm, a way of relating individual incidents to systemic social realities.

There are countless examples in American literature of the negative side of gossip, its capacity to enforce restrictive societal norms. Sarah Orne *Jewett's "The Foreigner" (1900) takes as one of its subjects the prejudice of a small Maine town against a woman from the West Indies. Gossip is the agent of exclusion and provincial insularity in Jewett's tale, as public opinion condemns the outsider for her behavior at a church social, her Catholicism, and her purported ability to weave spells. In Willa *Cather's *A Lost Lady* (1923), gossip serves to expose and condemn a woman's sexual behavior and social pretensions. When the small town of Sweet Water discovers evidence of Marian Forrester's extramarital affair, the community relishes the signs of her downfall— the illness of her husband is judged to be just retribution for her transgressions. At one point in the story, a group of neighborhood women commandeer Mrs. Forrester's house and openly discuss her failings among themselves, eagerly criticizing her possessions, her housekeeping, her drinking habits, and her mental faculties. In yet another example of gossip's regulatory power, Frances Watkins *Harper's *Iola Leroy* (1892) depicts the way in which a community's gossip serves to enforce notions of racial identity. In Harper's story, it is gossip that creates and polices the distinction between "white" and "black," thus ensuring the subordination of those deemed "black," regardless of the color of their skin.

But literature also contains examples of the other side of gossip, its powerful subversive potential. A salient example of this is Susan *Glaspell's *Trifles* (1916), in which two women investigate a murder simultaneously with an official criminal investigation. In Glaspell's play, the women discover the truth of the situation by relating seemingly meaningless anecdotes about other people and themselves, dwelling on what appear to be trivial domestic details at the scene of the crime, and slowly piecing these together. Tentatively testing each other's reaction to every new discovery, the two women uncover a series of clues indicating the murdered man's mistreatment of his wife. Explicitly identifying with the wife's situation ("I know how things can be—for women," one of the women declares), the protagonists tacitly agree to conceal what they have learned, thereby protecting the farm wife who has strangled her husband. *Trifles* is thus a compelling example of the way in which what appears to be a trivial gossip session can operate as a complex alliance between women, effectively subverting the channels of the official male power structure.

Katherine Stubbs

GOTHIC FICTION. The American female Gothic tradition has created works of darkness and terror that reflect the gendered experience of the female self responding to and often in conflict with the psychological, social, cultural, and physical structures within which she lives. As Michelle A. Masse has emphasized (*Signs*, 1990), conventional accounts of eighteenth- and nineteenth-century Gothic plots are familiar territory. The basic plot, originating with the works of Ann Radcliffe, is a "terror-inflected variant of Richardsonian courtship narrative" in which a young female heroine finds herself entrapped in a menacing space such as a castle or ruins, beset by various horrifying events and scenes. Charles Brockden Brown, one of the first American novelists, wrote the Gothic novel *Wieland* (1798), with its besieged heroine Clara Wieland; his later novel *Edgar Huntly* (1799) relocated the Gothic from the castles and ruins of a European landscape to an American wilderness filled with Indians and dark forests.

Ostensibly the conventional Gothic plot revolves around the solving of a mystery at the core of both the haunted castle and story, but the energy of the plot also circulates around an elaborate marriage tale. The wedding ceremony restores the narrative to the rational from the supernatural that threatened the domestic, and reinscribes the castle as the domain of the pleasures of domesticity. The American female Gothic tradition works within and against the earlier Gothic tradition, which was first developed in England and Europe during the eighteenth and nineteenth centuries by Horace Walpole, M. G. Lewis, C. R. Maturin, Ann Radcliffe, and Mary Shelley. The Radcliffe and Shelley models of Gothic narrative are important to both early and contemporary women writers of Gothics. Judith Fleenor, in the collection she edited, *The Female Gothic* (1983), has defined this genre in terms of texts such as *Udolpho* and *Frankenstein*, claiming that it is formless save as a guest. The spatial symbolism of the enclosed castle or room, as in the red room that Jane Eyre is thrust into in Charlotte Bronte's *Jane Eyre*, symbolizes not simply the heroine but culture as well. Like Ellen Moers before her, Fleenor calls attention to the terror, awe, and often self-loathing that are directed toward the female role, self, and sexuality. Claire Kahane has argued (1985) that the forbidden center of the female Gothic is the "presence of the dead-undead mother," a ghost who signifies "the problematics of femininity which the heroine must confront."

Like their British sisters, nineteenth- and early twentieth-century American women writers often wrote in the Gothic mode. For writers such as Harriet Beecher * Stowe, Mary Wilkins * Freeman, Sarah Orne * Jewett, Louisa May * Alcott, Kate * Chopin, Helen Hull, Georgia Wood Pangbourne, and Edith * Wharton, many of whom have * ghost story collections to their credit, the Gothic genre offered a unique space from which feminist ideas could be forwarded. In embracing this genre's conventions, these authors could write subversively about issues at odds with traditional ideas about domesticity and sentimentality. Nineteenth-century authors such as Stowe, Freeman, and Jewett, who have been critically understood in terms of their commitment to * realism and * regionalism, explored areas such as abolitionism and love between women by writing in terms of the supernatural, not the natural. Later writers, including Pangbourne and Hull, wrote ghost stories that addressed the horrors of enforced heterosexuality and abusive marriages. The Gothic mode allowed women to speak about taboo subjects—to symbolize what should be unspeakable and unknowable to a "true" woman.

Mary Shelley's *Frankenstein* (1818) is an important ur-text for the American female Gothic tradition. Shelley assumed that we would perceive the horror of being trapped within a body that evokes disgust. "God in pity made man beautiful," says the monster, "but my form is a filthy type of yours, more horrid even from the very resemblance." If we accept Sandra Gilbert and Susan Gubar's thesis in *The Madwoman in the Attic* (1979) that the monster is an Eve figure, then the monster's solitary suffering is akin to the female experience written about in the female grotesque novel, an important component of the female Gothic genre. Twentieth-century writers such as Carson * McCullers, Flannery * O'Connor, Shirley * Jackson, and

Katherine Dunn have explored what it means to perceive through the lens of the female grotesque, gazing with horror at the female body, often distorted and denied. Freaks are central to the stories and novels of these writers, symbolizing the uncanny quality of the female body when it is strange and estranged.

Contemporary female Gothics authored by the aforementioned as well as by Toni *Morrison, Leslie Marmon *Silko, Louise *Erdrich and Joyce Carol *Oates are often politicized, redrafting the genre to include female and feminist concerns. Morrison's *Beloved* (1987), for example, places a maternal haunting within an Afro-American context, bringing the history of slavery to the list of concerns of the female Gothic. In the case of Morrison, she works against an American literary tradition dating back to Nathaniel Hawthorne that tends to locate blackness as the source of sin. Louise Erdrich and Leslie Marmon Silko resist the way Native Americans have also been seen as horrifying; unlike the haunted landscapes of Charles Brockden Brown or James Fenimore Cooper, which are haunted because of the presence of Indians, the ghostly landscapes of Silko or Erdrich are haunted because of the absence of Native Americans.

Contemporary American female Gothic narratives also confront the violence and often violent sexuality that have been a part of the literary Gothic and horror tradition as well as of the reality of women's lives. The Gothic genre remains an important means of accounting for the anger that erupts from the violation of the female self by the world. Authors such as Diane Johnson and Joyce Carol Oates deal frankly with the sexuality and violence that were gothicized in earlier American Gothic narratives. The Gothic mode remains as popular as it was in the eighteenth century. Supermarket Gothics, written and read primarily by women, are directly related to the novels of the Brontë sisters. Anne Rice, V. C. Andrews, Mary Higgins Clark, and Jewelle Gómez are among other contemporary women writers who have successfully combined horror and gothicism.

[See also Novel, Beginnings of the; Short Stories.]

• Ellen Moers, *Literary Women* (1977). Sandra M. Gilbert and Susan Gubar, *The Madwoman in the Attic: The Woman Writer and the Nineteenth-Century Literary Imagination* (1979). Judith Fleenor, ed., *The Female Gothic* (1983). Claire Kahane, "The Gothic Mirror in The (M)other Tongue: Essays in Feminist Psychoanalytic Interpretation*, eds. Shirley Nelson Garner, Claire Kahane, and Madelon Sprengnether (1985). Michelle A. Masse, "Gothic Repetition: Husbands, Horrors, and Things That Go Bump in the Night," in *Signs* 15, no. 4 (1990).

Tracy E. Brown

GOULD, Lois, journalist, novelist, essayist, and children's book author, was born in New York City, where she still lives. She received her B.A. from Wellesley College. She has been married twice and has two children.

Her early career included journalism (she reported for the *Long Island Star Journal*), essay writing, and editorial work. She is a former editor and columnist for both *Ladies' Home Journal* and *McCall's*, became a columnist for the *New York Times* in 1977, and founded *Insider's Newsletter*. She has lectured and taught at Wesleyan University, Northwestern University, and New York University. She writes a column entitled "Hers" for the *New York Times* and continues to contribute to several periodicals, including *Ms., Newsday,* and *New York*. She is a board member of the Wesleyan Writers Conference.

Gould has written two nonfiction books about *childbirth and mothering, both under the name Lois Benjamin (*Sensible Childbirth: The Case Against Natural Childbirth*, with Waldo L. Fielding, 1962, and *So You Want to be a Working Mother!*, 1966). Her later works, under the name Lois Gould, are a children's story (*X: A Fabulous Child's Story*, 1978), a collection of essays (*Not Responsible For Personal Articles*, 1978), and seven novels.

Critics describe Gould as a novelist comfortable with the use of symbolism, allegory, and fairy tales. Her children's story is perhaps the best example of her allegorical treatment of *gender issues. But Gould is noted for portraying a range of issues, including but not strictly limited to gender and gender roles. *La Presidenta* (1981), based on the story of the Perons of Argentina, explores the complicated relationship between media representation and political power. In *Subject to Change* (1988), which has been described as distanced and dreamlike, the cast of characters includes a king, a queen, a dwarf, and a sorcerer who live in an imaginary kingdom beset by financial problems.

Perhaps Gould's most successful novel, certainly the novel most relevant to the representation of sex and gender roles in society, is *A Sea-Change* (1976). The novel chronicles the life and changes of the character Jessie Waterman, who moves to an isolated island and undergoes a sex-role transformation. Although some critics fail to recognize what is the explicitly lesbian content of the novel, it has been described by Doris Grumbach as "an entirely meaningful study, in contemporary terms, of being a woman" (*New York Times Book Review*, 19 September 1976).

Gould's other novels are *Such Good Friends* (1970), *Necessary Objects* (1972), *Final Analysis* (1974), and *Medusa's Gift* (1991).

• Doris Grumbach, "Intricate, Important Allegory in the Eye of Lois Gould's Storm," in *Chicago Tribune Book World* (19 September 1976). Linda Mainiero, ed., *American Women Writers: A Critical Reference Guide from Colonial Times to the Present in Four Volumes*, vol. 2 (1985), pp. 163–164. Hal May and James G. Lesniak, eds., *Contemporary Authors: A Bibliographical Guide to Current Writers in Fiction, General Non-Fiction, Poetry, Journalism, Drama, Motion Pictures, Television, and Other Fields*, vol. 27 (1990), pp. 178–179. Barry Unsworth, "The Creature Below," in *New York Times Book Review* (27 October 1991).

Amanda Berry

GRAHAM (Du Bois), Shirley (1896–1977), playwright, composer, activist, biographer, and novelist. Shirley Graham's role as the wife of W. E. B. Du Bois, whom she married in 1951, has overshadowed her significant contributions to the arts and humanities. Shirley Lola Graham was one of few African-American women prior to the 1950s to pursue a career in the professional theater as a playwright and composer. While all of her plays received professional productions, few have been published. During the mid-1940s, Graham embarked on a career as a writer of children's books.

Graham was raised throughout the country in parsonages by her parents, Reverend David and Etta B. Graham. In the early 1920s, Graham studied music at the Sorbonne in Paris, and from 1929 to 1931, she headed the music department at Baltimore's Morgan State College. In 1931, she enrolled at Oberlin College to study music. At Oberlin, she wrote a three-act opera called *Tom-Tom*. The opera, which traces how African music came to America, was produced in 1932 at the Cleveland Stadium in Ohio, the first all-black opera to be produced professionally in America.

After graduating from Oberlin in 1935 with A.B. and M.A. degrees, Graham became head of the Fine Arts Department at Tennessee A. & I. State College in Nashville. In 1936, she was director of the Chicago Negro Unit of the Federal Theatre Project, where she remained until 1938. Due to her success in Chicago, Graham was awarded a Rosenwald Fellowship in creative writing to study at Yale. While at Yale from 1938 to 1940, Graham wrote five plays— *Elijah's Raven, Dust to Earth, I Gotta Home, It's Morning,* and *Track Thirteen*—all of which explore class, social, or racial issues.

After leaving Yale, Graham was appointed to a YWCA-USO camp in Fort Huachuca, Arizona. There her interest in the arts waned and was eclipsed by an interest in civil rights activism that grew out of her experiences on the base, where she observed the blatant discrimination against African-American soldiers. She moved to New York in 1942 to become a field secretary for the National Association for the Advancement of Colored People. Simultaneously, Graham began writing biographies about African-American heroes. From 1944 to 1975, she wrote twelve biographies and one novel. In 1960, she became the founding editor of *Freedomways* magazine. Shirley Graham died in Beijing, China, on 27 March 1977.

• The Shirley Graham Papers are in the W. E. B. Du Bois Manuscript Collection, University of Massachusetts, Amherst. The Washington Conservatory of Music Collection in the Moorland-Spingarn Research Library, Howard University, Washington, D.C., also has material on Graham. See also Kathy A. Perkins, "Shirley Graham," in *Dictionary of Literary Biography: Afro-American Writers, 1940–1955*, vol. 76 (1988), pp. 66–75. Kathy A. Perkins, ed., *Black Female Playwrights: An Anthology of Plays before 1950* (1989). Leo Hamalian and James V. Hatch, eds., *The Roots of African American Drama* (1991).

Kathy A. Perkins

GRAHN, Judy (b. 1940), poet, novelist, feminist theorist. Born in Chicago, Judy Grahn was raised in New Mexico, where she began writing poems at age ten or eleven. In the 1970s, several small presses began publishing her work. Grahn has also acted as publisher for her own and other women's poetry, which would have had no other outlet.

Grahn's experience as a lesbian is central to her work, although she would rather not be labeled a lesbian writer. In fact, she feels she must be taken for granted as a lesbian before people can begin to see beyond the lesbian label.

The Work of a Common Woman, collected and published in 1980, is Grahn's best-known work. The poems have been reprinted more than half a million times in many languages. Their wide appeal is a tribute to Grahn's ability to bridge gaps between women. The *Common Woman* poems, written after Grahn attended a consciousness-raising group, examine social, political, and sexual issues confronting both lesbian and working-class women. The poems are at once powerful social commentary and celebratory of ordinary women.

This focus on ordinary women is what characterizes much of Grahn's creative work. In *The Queen of Wands* (1982) and *The Queen of Swords* (1987), Grahn engages in revisionist mythmaking. The poems in both books re-infuse goddess figures with the power they have lost in traditional history. Though neither Helen of *Wands* nor Ereshkigal of *Swords* is drawn as entirely ideal, both are women for whom power is natural, woven into the fabric of their everyday lives. *Wands* is interesting structurally because it creates a kind of narrative without using a controlling narrative device. The voices of each poem resonate together but never speak directly to one another, allowing a reader to seek connections to her own life. *Swords*, too, is interesting because Grahn frames the poems within a play and because the goddess is a lesbian bar-owner.

Grahn is also a feminist critic and historian. Her nonfiction writing, such as *Another Mother Tongue*, focuses on women's history as well as gay history.

Common to all her work are the many voices and faces women assume. What these voices share is a sense of connectedness—a shared history, a collective memory—and these features are more important than any single characteristic in drawing women together.

• "Judy Grahn," in *Women Writers of the West Coast*, ed. Marilyn Yalom (1983), pp. 93–101.

Deborah Viles

GRANDMOTHERS. Who is the grandmother? What does she signify—to her community and to the writer? Shaped primarily by culture, concepts vary widely. Although there is a common understanding of the grandmother as a source of survival wisdom—spiritual strength, endurance, heritage and continuity—her place in literature, as in life, depends on whose relative she is. Writers with tribal roots give her precedence.

In the work of indigenous women, grandmothers are central and pervasive, and embody a web of relationships that includes mothers of parents, aunts, elders, foremothers, spirit beings, and this center, described by Paula Gunn * Allen in *The Sacred Hoop: Recovering the Feminine in Native American Traditions* (1986): "In the beginning was thought, and her name was Woman. The Mother, the Grandmother . . . to her we owe our lives and from her comes our ability to endure." She thought Mother Earth and all that lives into existence and extended her thought through spirit beings such as White Buffalo Calf Woman and Selu, Grandmother Corn, who taught the people how to maintain the Web of Life in balance and harmony. On the human plane, women continue this role of teaching and healing—in the family, as well as in the public spheres of ceremony, medicine, art, and, in many tribes, government. Wisdom and esteem increase with age and the title "Grandmother" evokes the entire web of relationships.

This tradition of the sacred understanding of womanhood as an expression of spirit informs the writing of indigenous women, who have no need to turn to the complementary grandfather tradition for entitlement. Allen says, "Acknowledging that the violation of the Mothers' and Grandmothers' laws of kinship, respect, balance, and harmony brings about social, planetary, and personal illness, women writers give their energies to healing by restoring the balance within themselves and their communities." In all genres, they weave the grandmothers into their work, both as central figures and as underlying voices. This paradigm holds from * Humishuma, the first Native woman to publish a novel (*Cogewea*, 1927), to contemporary writers such as Allen, Leslie * Silko, Joy Harjo, Rayna Green, Linda * Hogan, Louise * Erdrich, Beth * Brant, and Anna Lee Walters.

The African-American grandmother has been a pivotal figure in black life and literature. Despite slavery, racism, and sexism, she has tenaciously continued her function, role, and importance, which were traditional in West African society (where the grandfather tradition was equally strong). In both family and community, she has revered status as a preserver of her extended family and the race, a communicator of heritage, lore, and wisdom, and a source of spiritual strength. In this context she appears as a central character in numerous novels, autobiographies, short stories, plays, and poems.

Among African-American writers, especially in the twentieth century, it is the women who have consistently brought the grandmother to the fore—writers such as Lorraine * Hansberry, Margaret * Walker, Maya * Angelou, and Toni * Morrison. In her collection of essays *In Search of Our Mothers' Gardens* (1983), Alice * Walker uses the tribal definition of mother/grandmother, which includes aunts, elders, and foremothers, to portray women who are spiritual guides for love and survival, for shaping a just society, and for creating art. They are the "sisters who, in their time, shone like gold," the mothers and grandmothers who have, "more often than not anonymously, handed on the creative spark."

In the South, where Native, African, and Euro-Celtic traditions reinforce one another, the grandmother in the latter culture may be seen as a transitional figure. Having spent two-thirds of her life deferring to the patriarchal system, she emerges, like the Celtic clan mothers of old, to take her central place in family and community. In *Southern Ladies and Gentlemen* (1975), humorist Florence King accurately portrays this grandmother within the "belle" society.

But it is in the mountains of Appalachia, where Celts settled in the 1700s and remained fairly isolated until the 1930s, that her prototype is most clearly defined and the language/cultural link established. In her classic study, *The Spirit of the Mountains* (1905), Emma Bell

Miles describes these older women as the race's roots of survival: "Old prophetesses . . . repositories of tribal lore—tradition and song, medical and religious learning . . . their wisdom commands the respect of all." Family and community confer on them the title "Granny," "Granny Woman," or "Old Aunt" ("old" as in "venerable"). Such heroines are in Wilma Dykeman's *The Tall Woman* (1962), Lee *Smith's *Oral History* (1983), and Denise Giardina's *The Unquiet Earth* (1992).

Elsewhere in American literature, women writers generally have followed the patriarchal norm that defines the grandmother only in biological terms, and relegates her to the personal realm, almost out of sight. Lacking a female tradition that integrates private and public spheres, they have focused primarily on mother/daughter conflicts, especially when the daughter moves into what is culturally the male domain. Nevertheless, when the grandmother does appear, her essence is intact: "These things you taught me—/think seriously/always go ahead / never stop learning/*live*," says the Jewish writer, Irene Reti, in her poem "A Modern Woman" (1989). Madeleine L'Engle, who has European roots, contemplates a similar legacy in *The Summer of the Great-Grandmother* (1974).

Although the grandmother is not prominent in the writing of Asian- and Mexican-American women, three novels reflect a trend toward her emergence, a trend that appears to be national in scope. In Jade Snow Wong's *Fifth Chinese Daughter* (1950), the grandmother appears only long enough to teach her granddaughter a truth about growing plants and people: "The ones who do not try are left behind." In Wendy *Law-Yone's *The Coffin Tree* (1983), the grandmother and aunts have greater roles, but the heroine still turns to father and brother as models in the public sphere. Sandra *Cisneros, in *The House on Mango Street* (1989), speaks through the voice of Esperanza, "my great-grandmother. I would've liked to have known her. She was a wild horse of a woman, so wild she wouldn't marry. Until my great-grandfather put a sack over her head and carried her off . . . She looked out the window her whole life, the way so many women sit their sadness on an elbow." Although Esperanza wars against that fate by living "like a man," in the end it is "the aunts, the three sisters, *las comadres*," who give her the circular vision for her path, a vision rooted in the tradition of strong women.

In literature as in life, the grandmother is ingeniously resilient. If the indigenous definition of her is applied to American women's writing, strands of thought that have seemed related but separate connect in a web: Feminist theology, ecology, archaeology, and anthropology, for example; and searches, for the *goddess, for other female mythology, and for matrilineage—both familial and literary—are all present in these representations. It is evident that, as Native people have long been saying, "The Grandmothers are coming back."

[*See also* Mothers and Daughters.]

• Ignatia Broker, *Night Flying Woman* (1983). Rayna Green, ed., *That's What She Said: Contemporary Poetry and Fiction by Native American Women* (1984). Juanita Lawhn, "Victorian Attitudes Affecting the Mexican Woman Writing in *La Prensa* during the Early 1900s and the Chicana of the 1980s," in *Missions in Conflict: Essays on U.S. Mexican Relations and Chicano Culture*, eds. Renate von Bardeleben, Dietrich Briemeister, and Juan Bruce-Novoa (1986), pp. 67–71. Mildred Hill-Lubin, "The Grandmother in African and African-American Literature: A Survivor of the African Extended Family," in *Ngambika: Studies of Women in African Literature*, eds. Carole Boyce Davies and Anne Adams Graves (1986), pp. 257–270. Sandra Gilbert and Susan Gubar, *No Man's Land* (1988). Paula Gunn Allen, ed., *Spider Woman's Granddaughters: Traditional Tales and Contemporary Writing by Native American Women* (1989). Lesléa Newman, ed., *Bubbe Meisehs by Shayneh Maidelehs: An Anthology of Poetry by Jewish Granddaughters about Our Grandmothers* (1989). Maya Angelou, *I Shall Not Be Moved* (1990).

Marilou Awiakta

GREEK AND ROMAN MYTHOLOGICAL FIGURES. *See* Myths, article on Greek and Roman Mythological Figures.

GREENWOOD, Grace (1823–1904), journalist. Among the first American women travel writers, Greenwood published one of the earliest American children's magazines and was the second woman to report on politics as a Washington correspondent. She was born Sara Jane Clarke, the youngest of Dr. Thaddeus Clarke and Deborah Baker Clarke's eleven children. Through her theologian father she was descended from Sarah and Jonathan Edwards, the Puritan theologian; her mother was of Huguenot descent. A native of Onondaga County, New York, Clarke was educated in Rochester. As a child she wrote lugubrious verse, which she published in local papers under her own name. At nineteen she moved to New Brighton, Pennsylvania, coined her alliterative pen name, and began her career as a journalist, spending most of her time away from home in Philadelphia, Washington, and New England. She served as junior editor of *Godey's Lady's Book* until she was fired for writing antislavery pieces for *National Era*, an abolitionist journal. Her popular letters on assorted high-minded topics as well as parodies of well-known writers (such as *Sigourney, *Child, Melville, Poe), published in periodicals during the 1840s, were collected in *Greenwood Leaves* in 1850. In 1852 she went to Europe and England. An indefatigable traveler, she sent back to American newspapers vivacious descriptions of Dickens, Browning, Vesuvius, the Pope, and sights of interest. These pieces were collected in *Haps and Mishaps of a Tour in Europe* (1854). Upon her return, she and Leander K. Lippincott married and started *Little Pilgrim*, a magazine for children. She became interested in women's issues in the 1850s and lectured on various topics concerning reform. She read and lectured to soldiers in camps and hospitals during the Civil War, earning the praise of President Lincoln, who called her "Grace Greenwood, the Patriot." After the war she moved to Washington and, as correspondent for the *New York Times*, became one of the first women to cover political issues for a general audience. She went West in 1871, lecturing, touring, and writing; *New Life in New Lands* (1873) records her observations of Rocky Mountain life. She traveled in Europe again in the 1870s; in the 1880s she lived in New York and Washington and wrote a newspaper column. During her last years she lived with her only daughter in New Rochelle, New York. *Greenwood Leaves* and *Haps and Mishaps* were her most popular books; others of note are *Stories and Legends of Travel* (1858), *Stories from Famous Ballads* (1860), *Stories and Sights of France and Italy* (1867), and *Victoria Queen of England* (1883).

• John S. Hart, *The Female Prose Writers of America* (1852). Frances E. Willard and Mary A. Livermore, *American Women*, vol. 2 (1897). Ishbel Rosh, *Ladies of the Press: The Story of Women in Journalism by an Insider* (1936). Marion Marzolf, *Up from the Footnote: A History of Women Journalists* (1977). William L. Vance, "The Sidelong Glance: Victorian Americans and Baroque Rome," *New England Quarterly* 58 (December 1985): 522.

Janet Gray

GRIFFIN, Susan (b. 1943), poet, playwright, feminist theorist. A native Californian, Susan Griffin graduated from San Francisco State University in 1965. Her knowledge of scientific theory, feminist theory, and mysticism is evident in her poetry and prose. Griffin has devoted herself to feminism and the changes feminism can effect.

Griffin credits her commitment to feminism and nature to her upbringing and education in California, which she has said were probably less traditional than might have been the case elsewhere and allowed her the freedom to explore feminist theories.

Her poems, most recently collected in *Unremembered Country* (1987), are often called spare and imagistic. They, like all her work, are carefully crafted; Griffin crosses out all the words in a draft except those that really move her, and then starts over. The poems in this volume are often very personal, exploring female spirituality, as well as the terror of living in a nuclear world. While definitely feminist, her poems are not dogmatic.

Fond of the theater, Griffin has also written a drama, *Voices* (1975), which won an Emmy Award that same year. She considers *Voices* an "active poem," in which the characters evolve through their language, developing in terms of how they "feel" their stories.

Perhaps her best-known work is *Woman and Nature: The Roaring Inside Her* (1978). In it she explores male and female language and how each influences one's connection to nature. Griffin has called *Woman and Nature* an extended prose poem, commenting that poetry is the mother of language and thought. In the first half of the book, Griffin focuses on a detached, authoritative, patriarchal voice, which abdicates responsibility by using phrases like "it is said" or "it is decided." Such detachment provides an excuse for a system which exploits both women and nature. When the female voice emerges, it moves from silence toward transformation and power. The striking differences between the voices are that the female voice takes responsibility, using the more personal "she" and "us," and the voices strive to find common ground, instead of dividing through dominance and submission as the patriarchy does.

Griffin insists in much of her work that women *are* nature, but that nature must be defined outside the patriarchal culture. She theorizes that there is a deep fear of women and the earth which is related to a fear of mortality and change. Her writing begins to explain the fear and to provide that new definition.

• "Susan Griffin," in *Women Writers of the West Coast*, ed. Marilyn Yalom (1983).

Deborah Viles

GRIMKÉ, Angelina Weld (1880–1958), African-American poet and writer. Born in Boston, Grimké was the daughter of black leader Archibald Grimké (nephew of the noted abolitionist Grimké sisters) and Sarah Stanley Grimké. She attended integrated schools in Hyde Park, Massachusetts, Carleton Academy in Minnesota, and, finally, the Boston Normal School of Gymnastics, later part of Wellesley College. Graduating in 1902, Grimké began a career as a teacher in the Washington, D.C., schools. She continued to teach until 1926 when, for health reasons, she retired. After her father's death in 1930, Grimké moved to Brooklyn, where she lived for the remainder of her life.

Angelina Grimké began her literary efforts while quite young, her first published poem appearing in Hyde Park's Norfolk County *Gazette* in 1891. Throughout her youth, and at several points thereafter, she considered pursuing a full-time literary career, but was ultimately unable to do so. Nevertheless, even though much of her writing remains unpublished, several of her works brought her wide notice.

Probably best known of these works was a short play entitled *Rachel*, first presented in 1916 and published in book form in 1920. Offering a tragic view of race relations, the play was sponsored by the NAACP for several performances in Washington, New York, and Boston as a response to D. W. Griffith's notoriously racist 1915 film, *The Birth of a Nation*.

But Grimké's most influential work was as a poet. Her earliest poetry fit within the larger framework of late nineteenth-century black verse, conservative in form and sentimental in theme. However, in the early years of the twentieth century, Grimké began to display an interest in experimentation, in both form and content, that looked toward the post–World War I *Harlem Renaissance. Indeed, despite residing in Washington during the 1920s, she has often been identified with that movement, and a few of her poems appeared in such major documents of the renaissance as Alain Locke's *The New Negro* (1925) and Countee Cullen's *Caroling Dusk* (1927).

Grimké was not destined to be a major figure in the Harlem Renaissance, and her writing actually began to taper off during the 1920s. Following her retirement from teaching and, especially, her move to Brooklyn, her literary activity came to a virtual end. But, for her time, Grimké's writing represented an important step in the development of an African-American literary tradition.

• The Angelina Weld Grimké Papers are in the Manuscript Division, Moorland-Spingarn Research Center, Howard University, Washington, D.C. See also Gloria T. Hull, *Color, Sex and Poetry: Three Women Writers of the Harlem Renaissance* (1987).

Dickson D. Bruce, Jr.

GRIMKÉ, Charlotte Forten (1837–1914), abolitionist, school teacher, poet, and diarist. Born into a distinguished African-American family of Philadelphia, Charlotte L. Forten's early life was typical for a daughter of America's nineteenth-century industrial bourgeoisie; it included private tutors, a New England education, and an abiding interest in nature. The daughter of Robert Bridges Forten and Mary Wood Forten, she spent much of her childhood in the elegant Philadelphia home of her crusading grandfather, James Forten, a shipping magnate.

In 1854, her father sent her to Salem, Massachusetts, to continue her formal education. Upon her graduation from Salem Normal School in July 1856, she was appointed as the first African-American teacher in the Epes Grammar School of Salem.

After the outbreak of the Civil War, Forten received permission from the Philadelphia Port Royal Relief Association to teach runaway slaves, classified as "contrabands of war." In October 1862, with a number of other Northern teachers, she sailed to St. Helena Island, South Carolina. Here she made her home for the next two years as the first African-American teacher to participate in educating the exslaves.

Eventually she moved to Washington, D.C., where she met and married Princeton graduate Francis James Grimké. From this union, there was one daughter, Theodora Cornelia, who was born on 1 January 1880 and died six months later. Forten, who became an invalid in 1887, died in Washington.

Forten is important to African-American literary history because of her journal, an illuminating portrait of a young woman determined to prove the intellectual competence of black people. Her five manuscript diaries (covering the years from 1854 to 1864 and from 1885 to 1892) document her commitment to excellence, her dedication to the causes of social justice, her observations on the bravery of black soldiers, her forays into ethnography, and her bouts with illness and depression; they provide us with a rare glimpse by a member of America's black elite into a world where contact with the famous (William Lloyd Garrison, William Wells Brown, Lydia Maria *Child, John Greenleaf Whittier, and Ralph Waldo Emerson were all known to her) was as casual as attending a lecture, and where politics and life were synonymous.

Her journal is comparable in historical importance to *A Diary from Dixie* (1905), kept by Mary Boykin *Chesnut, and provides us with a dignified counterweight to the numerous autobiographies and narratives of former slaves. Through her efforts to find a voice to call her own, Charlotte Forten initiated a tradition of black women's writing in the United States.

• Charlotte L. Forten Grimké's manuscripts are in the Moorland-Spingarn Research Center of Howard University. Anna Julia Cooper, *Personal Recollections of the Grimké Family* (1951). Ester M. Doughty, *Charlotte Forten: Free Black Teacher* (1971). Joanne M. Braxton, "Charlotte Forten Grimké and the Search for a Public Voice," in *The Private Self: Theory and Practice of*

Women's Autobiographical Writings, ed. Shari Benstock (1988), pp. 254–271.

Dolan Hubbard

GRIMKÉ, Sarah Moore, and Angelina Grimké Weld, public lecturers, abolitionist agents, feminist *activists, authors. Daughters of prominent Charleston, South Carolina, slaveholders, Sarah (1792–1873) and Angelina (1805–1879) Grimké renounced their family's values to become fervent abolitionists, touring New England with Theodore Weld's Band of Seventy in the 1830s. Leaders of the female antislavery movement, Sarah and Angelina were the first female abolitionist agents and the first white women to denounce publicly the "peculiar institution" at a time when speaking before "promiscuous audiences" of both sexes was prohibited for women. So exceptional was their courage at breaking that *taboo, and so effective was their oratory, that audiences would walk ten miles to hear them.

Denied formal education, the Grimké sisters did have access to their father's library. Sarah secretly taught herself law; she later addressed her frustration and rage at being prevented from practicing her chosen profession in her manuscript "The Education of Women." Rebelliousness and independence also characterized Angelina, dubbed "Devilina" by her opponents. Her *Appeal to the Christian Women of the South* (1836) enunciated the decidedly unpopular belief that white southern women should publicly commit themselves to eradicating *slavery.

Throughout their lives, the two sisters were condemned for their unconventional, often radical beliefs and actions. The Grimkés were attacked as un-Christian and unwomanly by the Council of Congregationalist Ministers of Massachusetts, and Angelina was chastised in an essay by educator Catharine *Beecher for venturing beyond the domestic domain. In response, Angelina published a pamphlet entitled *Letters to Catharine Beecher in Reply to an Essay on Slavery and Abolitionism Addressed to A. E. Grimké* (1837), in which she equated those forbidden to express themselves with slaves.

Although both sisters were abolitionists and feminists, and both equated slavery with women's oppression, Angelina considered the "woman question" as less pressing than *abolition. Sarah, on the other hand, penned the first *women's rights pamphlet in the United States: *Letters on the Equality of the Sexes and the Condition of Women* (1838). This work influenced such feminists of her day as Lucretia *Mott, Elizabeth Cady *Stanton, and Lucy Stone. Moreover, *Letters* wrestles with comparable worth, women's *spirituality, and marital oppression, prefiguring late twentieth-century *feminism. Throughout Sarah's life, she addressed women's rights in her writing, though her later works were unpublished.

Sarah turned down two proposals of *marriage, in part because of her dissatisfaction with the institution, and when Angelina married Theodore Weld in 1838, Sarah moved in with them. This date marked the sisters' retirement from public life, but not the end of their political commitment. Throughout Sarah's life, she addressed women's rights in her writing, though her later works went unpublished. And when Sarah was seventy-eight and Angelina was sixty-five, they led a suffrage demonstration, marching fifty-eight women through a snowstorm, an act befitting the careers of two sisters who virtually defined women's movement into the public sphere.

• Gerda Lerner, *The Grimké Sisters from South Carolina: Rebels Against Slavery* (1967). Katherine Du Pre Lumpkin, *The Emancipation of Angelina Grimké* (1974). Elizabeth Ann Bartlett, ed., *Sarah Grimké: Letters on the Equality of the Sexes and Other Essays* (1988). Larry Ceplair, ed., *The Public Years of Sarah and Angelina Grimké: Selected Writings, 1835–1839* (1989). Jean Fagan Yellin, *Women and Sisters: The Anti-Slavery Feminists in American Culture* (1989).

Jane Campbell

GYNOCRITICISM. The feminist study of women's writings. The term is sometimes used to mean any literary criticism devoted to works written by women. More often, it designates a body of literary criticism principally produced by academic feminists in the United States between the mid-1970s and the mid-1980s that sought to characterize imaginative writing by women in contrast to canonical literature written by men. Gynocriticism celebrated a distinctive "voice" in women's literature across genres and periods that it explained in terms of women's cultural position as an oppressed group; of women's experiences, especially experiences of male domination and of female bonding; and of psychological traits supposedly typical of women such as empathy and fluid ego boundaries. This approach, sometimes simplistically labeled "American feminist criticism," pioneered feminist literary history and established a *canon of women's literature influential in teaching, publishing, and scholarship. By broadly endorsing women's creativity, gynocriticism overlaps "cultural feminism."

Gynocriticism's most important precursor is Virginia *Woolf's *A Room of One's Own* (1929), which posed influential questions about "women and literature." Following Woolf, American feminists of the late 1960s and thereafter saw imaginative literature as an important force affecting women. While some scholars attacked male writers for stereotyping women, other feminists sought role models and found energizing identifications in female characters drawn by women writers. For example, in 1972 Nancy Burr Evans rejoiced to see her "own experiences mirrored" in fiction by women (in *Images of Women in Fiction*, ed. Susan Koppelman Cornillon). Similarly, Louise Bernikow's *Among Women* (1980) and Rachel Brownstein's *Becoming a Heroine* (1982) emphasized the satisfactions of reading women writers who portrayed female friendships and women's search for identity.

In "Toward a Feminist Poetics" (1979), Elaine Showalter coined the term *gynocritics* for the study of women writers. One exemplar of this tradition was her book, *A Literature of Their Own* (1977), which situated English women novelists in terms of "a common heritage" that concerned itself with the deliberate "articulation of women's experience." In 1976 Ellen Moers's *Literary Women* tracked "the deep creative strategies of the literary mind at work upon the fact of [being] female." Another widely influential text was Sandra Gilbert and Susan Gubar's *The Madwoman in the Attic* (1979), which derived common themes and images in "a distinctively female literary tradition" from cultural strictures on female expression, creativity, and authority. "Toward a Feminist Poetics" further distinguished *feminist critique*, the tough, demystifying practices of women reading sexist men, from *gynocritics*, the study of "*woman as writer* . . . with the history, themes, genres, and structures of literature by women." This distinction apparently pitted critical reading against creative writing, although gynocritics was, like feminist critique, a feminist reading strategy that assumed women would find personal resonance reading texts by women. In a related essay, "Feminist Criticism in the Wilderness" (1981), Showalter stressed "the *difference* of women's writing" from men's, asking, "How can we constitute women as a distinct literary group?," answering that women developed a "double-voiced discourse" from their "muted" position in male-dominant culture. In *The New Feminist Criticism* (1985), she championed gynocritics as offering "the most exciting prospect for a coherent feminist literary theory" independent of male models and congratulated it for the "massive recovery and rereading of literature by women from all nations and historical periods." By 1989 in *Speaking of Gender*, Showalter placed gynocriticism as a past "phase" of feminist criticism that had moved on to a broader concern with gender. However, feminist analysis of women's writings continues to flourish.

Some opponents charged that gynocritical practice was too restrictive because it selected some women writers over others, preferring poets who rejected marriage to sentimentalist encomiasts, for example, or condemning prudish novelists in favor of sexually explicit ones according to prescriptive notions of women's liberation. However, the most common attacks against gynocriticism fault the category of "writing by women" on which it is based. Some people believe this category is meaningless because differences in writing are individual, not sex specific. Pseudonymous authors prove that readers cannot reliably tell authors' sexes, and no experiments find definitive markers of female style. Some scholars argue that gynocriticism falls into the "essentialist" error of assigning definitive characteristics according to authors' biological sex, although gynocritics reply that being a woman is always culturally defined. Others agree that literature is gendered, but not necessarily to match authorial sex. Thus proponents of "*écriture féminine*" claim this practice maintains an antipatriarchal, feminine "subject position" even under male authorship. Another view sees gender implicit in literary genres and audience expectations, not authors, so that, for example, Harlequin romances are "feminine" no matter who writes them.

For many feminists of color, lesbians, and postmodernists, the category "women's writing" too often generalizes from privileged white women to all women and their literature, whereas most feminists now agree that women are not a unified category but are divided by *class, *race, language, sexual practices, and many other factors, and that their writings must be contextualized in historically and culturally specific ways. Some radical feminists fault Showalter's version of gynocriticism from another direction, claiming it is not specific enough to women, especially to women's sexual oppression, but rather applies a paradigm of "dominant" and "muted" powers so that all oppressed groups follow parallel paths of imitation, resistance, and autonomy. In contrast, these theorists point out that each group has its unique history, character, and interests, and any writer or reader is shaped and responsive to multiple, complexly interacting, and possibly contradictory and conflicting forces.

Although some early gynocriticism now seems naive, feminist criticism of writing by women is currently thriving. It does not automatically reject theories by men or idealize writing by women, though it continues to find women's works personally important and politically relevant to female readers. The most fruitful practice in this area uses the hypothetical categories of (some kinds of) writing by (some) women to group texts in order to analyze whether or not, and how, they exhibit a gendered coherence, for example, in studies of the female gothic novel. As feminist scholars range more broadly, they discover women's literary traditions in many times and cultures without insisting that they resemble those nineteenth-century English novels central to early gynocriticism. Some women's traditions, like European Renaissance women's love lyrics, modify dominant male forms. Women's literature from more sex-segregated societies, like Persian manuscripts by and for women, may assume more autonomous shapes, and some contemporary literature, like African-American fiction by women, may set standards for writing by men, rather than the reverse.

[*See also* French Feminism; Feminism.]

• Josephine Donovan, ed., *Feminist Literary Criticism* (1975). Patricia Meyer Spacks, *The Female Imagination* (1975). Elizabeth Abel, ed., *Writing and Sexual Difference* (1982). Sandra M. Gilbert and Susan Gubar, eds, *The Norton Anthology of Literature by Women* (1985). Elaine Showalter, "Toward a Feminist Poetics" and "Feminist Criticism in the Wilderness," in *The New Feminist Criticism*, ed. Elaine Showalter (1985). Toril Moi, *Sexual/Textual Politics* (1985). Judith Kegan Gardiner, *Rhys, Stead, Lessing, and the Politics of Empathy* (1989). Elaine Showalter, *Sister's Choice: Tradition and Change in American Women's Writing* (1991). Jane Gallop, *Around 1981: Academic Feminist Literary Theory* (1992).

Judith Kegan Gardiner

H

HACKER, Marilyn (b. 1942), poet. Marilyn Hacker was born in Bronx, New York, on Thanksgiving Day, 1942. Her first book of poems, *Presentation Piece* (1974), received the National Book Award and was a Lamont Poetry Selection of the Academy of American Poets. Her other volumes include *Separations* (1976), *Taking Notice* (1980), *Assumptions* (1985), *Love, Death and the Changing of the Seasons* (1986), and *Going Back to the River* (1990). Hacker has been awarded many grants, including those from the National Endowment for the Arts and the John Simon Guggenheim Foundation. She lives in Manhattan and Paris and is the editor of the *Kenyon Review*.

Marilyn Hacker has earned renown for a poetic style that weds traditional forms, such as the sonnet and the sestina, with "confessional" content: the graphic imagery of everyday life. "I like the tension in a poem that comes from the diction of ordinary speech playing against a form," she states in an interview in *Frontiers* (Fall 1980). She is admired for sheer technical ability—she breaks the rules only deliberately and for comic effect—and, as "another Jewish lesbian in France," for her divulgence of detailed sexual and political exploits. Her poems, therefore, simultaneously elevate the vernacular and deflate the pomposity of strict rhyme and meter, one moment ecstatic and the next, conspiratorially bawdy, inviting the response of the reader as well as that of the implied recipient of her letter-poems.

As a lesbian poet, Hacker's primary subject is the relationships between women, not only on the personal level but on the sociopolitical as well. "Everything is propaganda," she maintains, adding, "any piece of writing that doesn't suggest or imply change, or criticize, by statement or scrutiny, that which needs changing, is by definition propaganda for the status quo" (*Frontiers*). She includes among her influences Marie Ponsot, Adrienne *Rich and *H.D., though, like many women writers, she discovered these long after an education in the male modernist poets. Among her contemporaries, Hacker feels special affinities with Judy *Grahn and Audre *Lorde.

Marilyn Hacker's innovations as a poet include a "verse novel," *Love, Death and the Changing of the Seasons*, and a sequence of poems that revises the Snow Queen fairy tale, found in *Assumptions*. She can be credited with inspiring younger women poets to experiment with traditional forms, which, she claims, have been used by many women poets throughout literary history, in spite of their absence in the canon.

• "Interview with Marilyn Hacker," *Dispatch* 7, no. 1 (Fall 1988): 16–19.

Susan J. Zevenbergen

HAG. The hag often appears as an ugly, demanding, fat, and magically powerful woman, a symbol of female power. The word *hag* stems from ancient cognates designating wisdom and holiness. A source of reference for female wisdom, the hag is commonly associated with words of power, sacred texts, spiritual authority, witchcraft, deviltry, and matriarchy. In some cultures, hags are represented as death goddesses and moon priestesses. Mary *Daly (*Gyn/Ecology*, 1979) defines hags as counter-identities to patriarchal models of cultural authority. Hags serve as models for harpies, witches, female demons, furies, and evil-looking, old women. Daly celebrates hags in an effort to move society toward female-identified kinds of writing. Daly notes that the word *hag* exposes the sexism and ageism inherent in patriarchal language; moreover, the definitions of *hag* reveal the cultural resistances hags represent.

Doni M. Wilson

HAGEDORN, Jessica Tarahata (b. 1949), novelist, poet, multimedia and performance artist. Jessica Tarahata Hagedorn had been in the United States for only three years (after moving from the Philippines at age thirteen) when her poems caught the attention of Kenneth Rexroth. Rexroth, a San Francisco–based artist, encouraged her to hone her writing and edited the book that first featured her poetry, *Four Young Women* (1973). Forged in the heat of the early 1970s ethnic revival, her early forays into poetry, playwriting, and short fiction employed the psychedelic and rebellious idioms particular to that period. Anthologized in *Mountain*

Moving Day (1973), *Third World Women* (1973), and *Time to Greez!* (1975), she soon produced her first collection of poetry and fiction, *Dangerous Music* (1975).

While in San Francisco, Hagedorn took acting lessons and subsequently developed an interest in the performing arts that was to steer her into multimedia work. Her experience as a lyricist for a band configured her poetry as one of effect and rhythm, proving congenial to her interest in interpretive readings and theater. After Joseph Papp produced her collaboration with Thulani Davis and Ntozake *Shange, *Where the Mississippi Meets the Amazon* (1977), she moved to New York to work as a playwright and musician, involvements that stamped her poetry with distinctively performative strains. Papp produced her first play, *Mango Tango*, in 1978. She then mounted a score of productions in New York, from *Tenement Lover* (1981) to *Holy Food* (theater: 1988; radio: 1989), as well as one in San Francisco, *Teenytown* (1990).

Pet Food and Tropical Apparitions (1981), a novella that incorporates a surreal vignette and seven musical poems, distinguished her as an eclectic and highly experimental artist. It won her the American Book Award for the same year and helped her secure Macdowell Colony Fellowships in 1985 and 1986. Another Macdowell fellowship in 1988 allowed her to complete work on *Dogeaters* (1990).

Pet Food clearly contained the seeds for *Dogeaters;* this accomplished, hilarious, and hyperreal, novella is driven by two memorable cinematic moments. A starlet recounts the sordid sequence of her newest skin flick in which a virtuoso pianist plays "A Moonlight Sonata" while she performs sex with an anteater and five West Indians on top of a grand piano. George Sand, the youthful but hardbitten protagonist-poet, gives form to her morbid desire for patricide and suicide in cross-cut images of Filipino guerillas slaughtering her politically powerful father and her alter ego. Character sketches for the top, middle, and bottom "dogs" that populate Philippine society in *Dogeaters* inhabit this novella's world of maladjusted migrant youths and social deviants. What one critic described as "the cinematext of a Third World scenario that might be the Philippines" in *Dogeaters* is first seen in this ensemble of deftly-spliced "rushes."

The cinematic metaphors are apt since Hagedorn has acknowledged Manuel Puig as an influence and has now moved into video- and filmmaking. Included in sixteen anthologies of women's, ethnic, and third world writing since 1975, Hagedorn made her debut as a screenwriter with *Wasteland* (the title was subsequently changed to *Fresh Kill*), a feature film produced and directed by Shu Lea Chang.

• Robert Rydell, *Visions of Empire* (1984). "Interview with Jessica Hagedorn," *Dispatch* 6, no. 1 (Fall 1987): 14–18. Epifanio San Juan, Jr., "Mapping the Boundaries: The Filipino Writer in the U.S.A.," *Journal of Ethnic Studies* 19, no. 1 (1991): 117–132. Shirley Geoklin Lim et al., eds., *The Forbidden Stitch: An Asian American Women's Anthology* (1989).

Oscar V. Campomanes

HALE, Sarah Josepha (1788–1879), author, biographer, and editor of *Godey's Lady's Book* from 1837–1877. As editor of *Godey's* for forty years, Sarah Hale was the most prominent American woman engaged in literary enterprise in the mid-nineteenth century. Widowed suddenly, with five children to support, she turned to writing (*Northwood*, a novel published in 1827) and assumed editorship of the Boston *Ladies' Magazine*. The goals she established for that journal—that contributions be original and when possible by Americans and by women—she took with her to Philadelphia when she merged her journal with *Godey's* in 1837.

Through her "Editor's Table" Hale articulated personal philosophy, social concerns, and literary criticism. While admonishing women against "blue-stockingism" or usurpation of male authority, over her lifetime she encouraged women's activism. *Northwood*, a description of life in New England including details of customs such as Thanksgiving, weddings, and town governance, reveals that she believed a women's role in the family to be fundamental to the political order of the republic. She was deeply patriotic and led successful campaigns for a Bunker Hill Monument, the purchase of Mount Vernon, and a national Thanksgiving day. She also organized support for the families of seamen, for improved female education, and for greater job opportunities for women.

Debate continues about the nature of Hale's feminism. Some scholars criticize her as a proponent of "women's sphere"; as a believer in women's moral superiority she expected women to provide spiritual leadership for western civilization and for the Christianization of the world. Thus she used her position to advance the careers of women missionaries and teachers. She disliked women public speakers, abolitionists, and women's rights proponents. Yet, she advocated property rights for married women, female doctors, and, in her later life, support for working women.

Her constant literary goal was the promotion of women authors, through publication in *Godey's* and other collections (*The Ladies'*

Wreath, 1837) and even in her great compendium, *Woman's Record; or, Sketches of all Distinguished Women, from the Creation to A.D. 1868*, which appeared in three editions (1853, 1855, 1872). While entries include Eve and Mary, Queen Victoria and Pocohontas, the true focus is stated in the heading of the fourth (the modern) era: "of living female writers." Hale was not a great writer herself: *Northwood* is her best work, much better than stories written to deadlines and as filler for *Godey's*, but she supported and encouraged several generations of authors, especially women but also such men as Poe. She was the first of the great "lady editors."

• Ruth E. Finley, *The Lady of Godey's* (1931). Isabelle Webb Entrikin, *Sarah Josepha Hale and 'Godey's Lady's Book'* (1946). Paul S. Boyer, "Sarah Josepha Buell Hale," in *Notable American Women 1607–1850*, eds. Edward P. James, Janet Wilson James, and Paul S. Boyer, 4 vols. (1971), vol. 2, pp. 110–114. Barbara Ann Bardes and Suzanne Gossett, "Women and Political Power in the Republic: Two Early American Novels," *Legacy* 2 (1985): 13–30. Nina Baym, "Onward Christian Women: Sarah J. Hale's History of the World," *New England Quarterly* 63 (1990): 249–270. Barbara A. Bardes and Suzanne Gossett, "Sarah J. Hale, Selective Promoter of Her Sex," in *A Living of Words: American Women in Print Culture*, ed. Susan Albertine (1995).

Suzanne Gossett

HALE, Susan (1833–1910), writer, editor, painter, lecturer, and reader. The youngest of eight children of writer and translator Sarah P. Everett Hale and editor and publisher Nathan Hale, Susan Hale was born into a family where writing and editing were commonplace activities. At seventeen, Hale was reviewing books for her father's *Boston Daily Advertiser*. Throughout her life she continued writing for newspapers and magazines, primarily nonfiction prose. Although her family retained its place in Boston upper-middle-class society, in the 1840s and 1850s they faced financial difficulties. By the time she was twenty, Hale was contributing to the family's income by running a school for boys with her sister Lucretia P. Hale, and giving private lessons in classics and French to young women; she made her living by teaching for almost twenty years. In the late 1860s, after the family home was broken up following her mother's death, she rented rooms in Boston for her residence and studio. In 1872 she went to France and Germany to study art for a year, on her return painting and giving lessons.

During the last three decades of her life, Hale traveled regularly, sometimes going as companion, guide, and translator. She subsidized trips by writing newspaper travel letters and gathering material for books, supplementing observations with research on history,

archeology, anthropology, and geography. Her most successful book in this genre was *The Story of Mexico* (1889). She wrote books for younger readers such as *A Family Flight through Spain* (1883), and as coauthor with her brother Edward Everett Hale wrote other *Family Flight* volumes. Her publications also include *Self-Instructive Lessons in Painting* (1885) and *Men and Manners of the Eighteenth Century* (1898). Her editorial work included several fundraising newspapers (such as *Baloon-Post*, 1871).

During the 1880s and early 1890s she gained celebrity, and income, giving readings throughout the United States. Her best-known series, "Readings from the Early English Novelists," drew from works by six authors, four of them women. She also created and performed one-woman productions, the most popular being "The Elixir of Youth," and lectured on literary subjects and places she had visited.

A prolific correspondent, Hale excels in the genre of the personal letter. More than 200 published letters (*Letters of Susan Hale*, 1918) and hundreds more in manuscript, spanning almost seventy years, are notable for their distinct voice, vivid descriptions, and humor; many are illustrated with sketches. The protagonist is a sometimes flustered but always essentially competent, energetic, adventurous woman whose self-reliance and love of outdoor activities defies the stereotype of the parlor-bound Victorian lady.

• Letters and Miscellaneous Papers of Susan Hale, 1842–1910, Hale Family Papers, are in the Sophia Smith Collection, Smith College, Northampton, Massachusetts. See also Edward E. Hale, Jr., Introduction to *Letters of Susan Hale*, ed. Caroline P. Atkinson (1918).

Karen A. Dandurand

HANSBERRY, Lorraine (1930–1965), playwright. Regarded by many as the foremother of African-American drama, Lorraine Hansberry shares with novelist Ralph Ellison the distinction of having achieved greatness on the basis of a single work. When *A Raisin in the Sun* opened at the Ethel Barrymore Theatre in New York City on 11 March 1959, Hansberry assured her place in the pantheon of American and African-American dramatists. Her premature death at thirty-four marked the silencing of a compassionate and prescient voice.

Lorraine Vivian Hansberry was the fourth child of Carl Augustus Hansberry, a realtor, U.S. marshal, and civil rights activist, and Nannie Perry, a teacher and ward committeewoman. Lorraine's parents fostered their daughter's artistic development at an early age, entertaining such luminaries as W. E. B. Du

Bois, Duke Ellington, and Paul Robeson. At the University of Wisconsin from 1948 to 1950, Hansberry saw Sean O'Casey's *Juno and the Paycock*, a drama about Irish peasants' dashed hopes and deferred dreams that would spark her creation of the Younger family. Other significant events included working for Paul Robeson's "radical" *Freedom* magazine, where she served as associate editor in 1952. Hansberry's participation in marches and demonstrations also led to another crucial encounter: she met a white New York University graduate, Robert Nemiroff, and they married on 20 June 1953. With Nemiroff's intellectual and emotional support, Hansberry's fertile literary imagination produced the play on which her reputation would rest.

The significance of *A Raisin in the Sun* (1959) in American and African-American literary canons is unquestioned. After a successful trial run in New Haven, Philadelphia, and Chicago, the play opened on the Great White Way with a stellar cast featuring Sidney Poitier, Claudia McNeil, Ruby Dee, Diana Sands, and Glynn Turman. The plight of the Youngers—Mama Lena, her son Walter Lee, Jr., daughter Beneatha, daughter-in-law Ruth (Walter's wife), and grandson Travis—epitomizes the black struggle for equality and dignity. The action centers around the family's inheritance of a $10,000 insurance policy upon the death of Walter Lee, Sr. The characters' reactions to the money reveal their buried hopes. The drama's critical and popular acclaim secured Hansberry the New York Drama Critics Circle Award for Best Play of 1959 (over Eugene O'Neill's *A Touch of the Poet* and Tennessee Williams's *Sweet Bird of Youth*), making her the youngest winner ever, as well as the first black and first woman to receive the honor. Two years later the play was made into a film with the same cast; Nemiroff subsequently produced *Raisin*, a musical version that garnered the Tony Award in 1974; and the Yale Repertory Theatre produced a 25th anniversary version in November 1983.

Hansberry's only other full-length completed play, *The Sign in Sidney Brustein's Window* (1964), is a "drama of ideas" whose characters resemble the white Greenwich Village denizens with whom Hansberry and Nemiroff lived in the fifties and sixties. The play opened on 15 October 1964 at the Longacre Theatre to mixed reviews, and closed on 12 January 1965—the date of Hansberry's death. In 1959 NBC commissioned Hansberry to write a drama commemorating the 100th anniversary of the Civil War, but *The Drinking Gourd*, which the network executives judged "superb," was put "away in a drawer" (*Lorraine Hansberry:*

The Collected Last Plays, 1983), because of its unsentimental treatment of slavery. The never-produced short "fable," *What Use Are Flowers?* (1962; published in 1972), examines the aftermath of nuclear war.

Although the couple divorced secretly in March 1964, Nemiroff continued Hansberry's artistic legacy. He adapted *To Be Young, Gifted and Black*, a work consisting of excerpts from Hansberry's plays, interspersed with published and unpublished materials—letters, journal entries, speeches, and poetry. The play opened on 2 March 1969, at the Cherry Lane Theatre in New York and featured Cicely Tyson. Hansberry's political play *Les Blancs* (1970) was completed by Nemiroff and produced posthumously. Set in "a Mission Compound in Africa," it focuses on Tshembe Matoseh, an African expatriate residing in London with his white wife and son. Tshembe's guilt about deserting his country's struggle is exacerbated when he returns for his father's funeral. After an excruciating inner struggle, Tshembe accepts if not embraces violence to defeat the implacable white colonialists. As was the case with *Brustein*, the play received lukewarm reviews, and closed after forty-seven performances. Hansberry also left an unpublished novel, "All the Dark and Beautiful Warriors."

Lorraine Hansberry's work serves as a beacon for black dramatists, from the black nationalist Amiri Baraka to the black feminist Ntozake * Shange. Epitomizing the inextricable connection between art and life, she led the vanguard of black aestheticians who recognized that all art must serve that entity both absurd and beautiful, the human being. As her life and work so poignantly attest, the conundrum of the human heart provides the impetus for all art.

• C. W. E. Bigsby, *Confrontation and Commitment: A Study of Contemporary American Drama, 1959–1966* (1968). Doris E. Abramson, *Negro Playwrights in the American Theatre, 1925–1959* (1969). *Lorraine Hansberry: The Black Experience in the Creation of Drama*, video (1975). Jean Carey Bond, ed., "Lorraine Hansberry: Art of Thunder, Vision of Light," *Freedomways* 19, special issue devoted to the author (1979). Anne Cheney, *Lorraine Hansberry* (1984). Elizabeth Brown-Guillory, *Their Place on the Stage: Black Women Playwrights in America* (1988). Stephen R. Carter, *Hansberry's Drama: Commitment Amid Complexity* (1991).

                                      Keith Clark

HANSON, Elizabeth Meader (1684–1737), author of a Quaker captivity narrative. On 27 August 1724, a party of French and Indian allies attacked the Hansons' isolated farmhouse at Cocheco in Dover Township, New Hampshire; Hanson's oral narrative, *God's Mercy Sur-*

mounting Man's Cruelty (1728), recounts her five-month captivity with the Indians and a sixth month with the French at Port Royal. On the day of the raid, two of her younger children were killed and scalped; Hanson, four remaining children, and a woman servant were taken captive. In addition to twenty-six days of continuous travel and lack of food that led to her inability to nurse her infant, Hanson also had to face the emotional stress of separation from her two daughters and the female servant.

In a factual manner, Hanson details the hardships of her captivity, which were exacerbated by the fact that she had given birth to her fifth child only two weeks before the raid. Although Hanson, like earlier captives, attributes any acts of assistance and kindness by her captors to God's mercy and recounts the harsh cruelties of one of her "masters," she often acknowledges the kindnesses that were also paid to her by her Indian captors, especially the Indian women who repeatedly demonstrated their concern for her welfare. She also recognizes that the Indians' celebration upon reaching their destination is their own form of giving thanks to God for a safe and prosperous journey. Thus, in spite of the danger and violence with which she was confronted, Hanson maintained her pacifist values throughout her captivity. Hanson's husband was able to ransom her and the three youngest children but died before he could locate their sixteen-year-old daughter, Sarah, who eventually married a captain in the Canadian militia and thus remained in Canada.

Unlike the earlier Puritan tradition of captivity narratives, Hanson's account focuses on her personal experiences rather than presenting herself as a representative of her community. Thus the text offers a more fully developed sense of the individual writer as a woman and the hardships she endured. The overall effect is of a more secular rendering of captivity; it is in this capacity that *God's Mercy* had its greatest influence: it opened the door to the rise of fictional, sentimentalized captivity narratives that became popular later in the century. Modern critics' recognition that *God's Mercy* was altered (and often sentimentalized) by editors of later editions has, to some extent, overshadowed the power of the original text itself.

• Richard VanDerBeets, ed., *Held Captive by Indians: Selected Narratives, 1642–1836* (1973). Alden T. Vaughan and Edward W. Clark, eds. *Puritans among the Indians: Accounts of Captivity and Redemption, 1676–1724* (1981). Laurel Thatcher Ulrich, *Good Wives: Image and Reality in the Lives of Women in Northern New England, 1650–1750* (1982). James A. Levernier and Douglas R. Wilmes, eds., *American Writers before 1800: A Biographical and Critical Dictionary*, vol. 2 (1983).

Sharon M. Harris

HARASSMENT. *See* Sexual Harassment.

HARDWICK, Elizabeth (b. 1916), novelist, short story writer, essayist, teacher, and editor. Born in Lexington, Kentucky, Hardwick attended the University of Kentucky and Columbia University. She has spent most of her life in New York City, where she was a professor at the Columbia School of the Arts and founded *The New York Review of Books*. She was married in 1949 to the poet Robert Lowell (they divorced in 1972); they have one daughter, Harriet.

Hardwick is the author of three collections of essays: *A View of My Own* (1962); *Seduction and Betrayal: Women and Literature* (1974), nominated for the National Book Awards; and *Bartleby in Manhattan and Other Essays* (1983). Her novels are *The Ghostly Lover* (1945); *The Simple Truth* (1955); and *Sleepless Nights* (1979), nominated for the National Book Critics Circle Award. She was editor of *The Best American Short Stories* (1986), and *The Best American Essays* (1986). Other awards include the George Jean Nathan Award for dramatic criticism.

In *Seduction and Betrayal*, Hardwick writes of the artistic and personal struggles, loves, and betrayals of both real and fictional characters, ranging from the Brontë sisters, to Ibsen's Nora and Hedda, to Sylvia * Plath. With impeccable taste and style, she maintains objectivity while enabling her readers to feel sympathy, regret, and respect for the real and fictional lives portrayed. Essays in *Bartleby in Manhattan and Other Essays* take an astonishing variety of subjects, ranging from a Rolling Stones concert, to Billy Graham, to contemporary manners and fiction, to Memphis after the assassination of Martin Luther King, Jr. The style is expressive, intelligent, and lucid.

Hardwick's novel, *A Simple Truth*, offers an ironic analysis of truth in presenting characters who cannot distinguish reality from appearance. About *Sleepless Nights*, Laurie Stone writes in "Hardwick's Way" in the *Village Voice* (7 May 1979) that the novel "is about romance with memory"; the narrator, Elizabeth, "a feminist who is also heterosexual," is revealed by what she remembers from the past.

Summarizing a major concern in Hardwick's works, Joan * Didion writes in "Meditations on a Life" in the *New York Times Book Review* (29 April 1979) that "in certain ways, the mysterious and somnambulistic 'difference' of being a woman has been, over 35 years, Elizabeth Hardwick's great subject, the topic to which she has returned incessantly. . . ." Didion says, "She has chronicled again and again the undertow of family life, the awesome torment of being a daughter ... the ways in which women compensate for their relative physiological inferiority."

Thelma Hall

HARLEM RENAISSANCE. Sometimes labeled the New Negro Movement, the Harlem Renaissance has traditionally been seen as the first successful assertion of a specifically African-American presence in American literature. Although historians have suggested that the renaissance began in 1915 and ran through the middle 1930s, the movement clearly culminated in Harlem during the 1920s. Originating in a complex of forces including the Great Migration of blacks from the rural South to the urban North, the death of Booker T. Washington (1915), and the return of black veterans from World War I, the Harlem Renaissance fell into decline when the Great Depression undercut its economic foundation. Highly aware of their connections with a larger group of women writers who did not move to Harlem, Zora Neale *Hurston (1891–1960), Jessie *Fauset (1882–1961), Nella *Larsen (1893–1963), and Georgia Douglas *Johnson (1886–1966) were among the major contributors to this complex interracial movement. They associated with both black male writers (Langston Hughes, Claude McKay, Wallace Thurman, W. E. B. Du Bois) and Euro-American modernists (Ezra Pound, *H. D., Eugene O'Neill, William Carlos Williams, and Carl Van Vechten, one of the movement's major patrons). Defined by the March 1925 "Harlem number" of *Survey Graphic* (edited by Alain Locke and reprinted in expanded form as *The New Negro*, 1925), the Harlem Renaissance centered on an interrelated set of debates over white patronage; art vs. propaganda; the meaning of Africa for black Americans; and the tension between the "genteel" black middle class and either the "folk" or the "bohemians." Frequently remembered as a golden age of black letters, the Harlem Renaissance has assumed a central role in subsequent discussions of African-American cultural history.

Although women's presence during the renaissance was noted in Nathan Huggins's ground-breaking *The Harlem Renaissance* (1971), early accounts portrayed them primarily as part of the social scene surrounding the more serious literary activity of the predominantly male circles of Locke and Van Vechten. Many highlight the "exotic" sexuality of performers such as Josephine Baker (1906–1975),

Bessie Smith (1894–1937), and Florence Mills (1895–1927), the "colorful" personality of Zora Neale Hurston, and the parties hosted by A'Lelia Walker (1885–1931), daughter of Madame C. J. (Sarah Breedlove) Walker (1867–1919), who amassed a substantial fortune marketing beauty products to black women. Numerous memoirs of the era condemn Hurston's role-playing for white patron Charlotte Osgood Mason and recall Walker's party at which black guests dined on champagne and caviar while aristocratic white guests were seated separately and served chitterlings and bathtub gin.

Most surveys of the renaissance briefly acknowledge black women's work in various cultural forms. Some contributions, notably the diary of Alice *Dunbar-Nelson (1875–1935; diary published 1984), remained unknown to the public during the era. Others, such as the blues performed by Ma Rainey (1886–1939), Bessie Smith, Gladys Bentley (1907–1960), and Ida Cox (1889–1967) were not taken seriously. Many black women, however, worked effectively in established genres. Although the novels of Lillian Wood (*Let My People Go*, 1922), Zara Wright (*Black and White Tangled Threads*, 1920) or Sarah Fleming (*Hope's Highway*, 1917) have attracted few readers, Nella Larsen (*Quicksand*, 1928; *Passing*, 1929), Jessie Fauset (*There Is Confusion*, 1924; *Plum Bun*, 1929) and Hurston (*Jonah's Gourd Vine*, 1934) rank with the era's most substantial novelists. Larsen, Hurston, Gwendolyn *Bennett (1902–1981) and Marita *Bonner (1899–1971), who was later to play a germinal role in the *Chicago Renaissance (1936–1950) all published short fiction. Following Angelina Weld *Grimké (1880–1958), whose *Rachel* (1916) was the first full-length black play produced in the twentieth century, Bonner (*The Purple Flower*, 1928), Georgia Douglas Johnson (*A Sunday Morning in the South*, 1924; *Plumes*, produced by the Harlem Experimental Theater in 1927), Eulalie Spence (1894–1981; *Hot Stuff*, 1927; *Episode*, 1928), May Miller (b. 1899; *Riding the Goat*, 1929), and Mary Burrill (1884–1946; *They That Sit in Darkness*, 1919) all published work during the renaissance. Although few of these plays were produced, several deserve serious attention. Bonner's use of surrealist techniques recalls the experimental work of Eugene O'Neill, and Spence's plays on the domestic tensions generated by Harlem economic conditions compare favorably with those of Willis Richardson, the leading black male playwright of the era.

In part because many editors considered lyric poetry the proper form for women writers, a much larger number of black women published poetry during the 1920s. Some received substantial attention, winning major prizes in the prestigious contests sponsored between 1925 and 1927 by both *Opportunity* and *Crisis*, published by the Urban League and the National Association for the Advancement of Colored People respectively. As literary editor of *Crisis* from 1919–1926, Fauset encouraged many poets, including Angelina Grimké, Alice Dunbar-Nelson, Georgia Johnson, Helene *Johnson (b. 1907), Anne *Spencer (1882–1975), and Gwendolyn Bennett (1902–1981), whose monthly column "The Ebony Flute" appeared in *Opportunity* from 1926–1928. As Gloria Hull (*Color, Sex, and Poetry: Three Women Writers of the Harlem Renaissance*, 1987), Maureen Honey (*Shadowed Dreams: Women's Poetry of the Harlem Renaissance*, 1989), and Tony Martin (*Literary Garveyism: Garvey, Black Arts and the Harlem Renaissance*, 1983) have established, black women of the area did not limit themselves to lyric forms or domestic themes. Honey draws attention to the explicitly lesbian poetry of Mae Cowdery (1909–1953) and Gladys Mae Casely Hayford (1904–1950), who was born in Sierra Leone. Martin emphasizes the broad concerns of the poetry written by sculptor Augusta Savage (1882–1962), and Ethel Trew Dunlap, the most frequently published poet in the Garveyite newspaper *Negro World*.

Throughout the renaissance, black women writers encountered both limited publishing opportunities and a public discourse that usually failed to take the unique qualities of their work into account. To be sure, black women's writing appeared in every substantial African-American periodical and anthology of the era: Locke's *The New Negro*, Cullen's *Caroling Dusk* (1927), Richardson's *Plays and Pageants of Negro Life* (1930), along with the special "Negro" numbers of the University of North Carolina literary journal *Carolina Magazine*, and the single issue literary journals *Fire!* and *Harlem*. Although Fauset with *Crisis*, Hurston and Bennett with *Fire!*, and Dorothy *West (b. 1908), with *Challenge* and *New Challenge* during the 1930s, were active as editors, they worked within the terms established by male contemporaries such as Locke, *Crisis* editor W. E. B. Du Bois, *Opportunity* editor Charles S. Johnson, and James Weldon Johnson, whose *Book of American Negro Poetry* (1922) defined the task of the "new negro" poet as the employment of the folk tradition to break away from the racial stereotypes associated with dialect poetry. This formulation was particularly problematic for black women, who were confronted with a different set of stereotypes than those faced by black men. As many black women critics have observed, stereotypes of the Mammy and the sexually promiscuous Sapphire excluded black

women from "respectability" as defined by the "Cult of *True Womanhood." Reflecting the necessity of resisting these stereotypes, the published work of most black women writers—Hurston is the notable exception—was characterized by relatively conservative prosody and genteel thematic content. As a result, it attracted little interest from the prestigious mainstream publications that introduced the work of young black (male) writers to a white audience interested in experimental modernist themes and techniques. Only a single poem by a black woman—Helene Johnson's "Bottled" *(Vanity Fair)*—was published in a mass market magazine during the decade. Far more important to black women's writing than *Poetry* or *The Atlantic Monthly*, which published work by Hughes, Cullen, and novelist Rudolph Fisher, were the Philadelphia-based *Black Opals* and the Boston-based *Saturday Evening Quill*. Despite their genteel aspirations, these journals provided important alternative outlets for women who viewed their work as part of an ongoing struggle to "uplift the race."

Placing African-American women at the center of literary history suggests that the phrase "Harlem Renaissance of the 1920s" is deceptive both chronologically and geographically. Hull's work on Georgia Johnson, Grimké, and Dunbar-Nelson emphasizes that three of the most important women of the "Harlem Renaissance" were well-established long before 1920. In addition, novelist Pauline *Hopkins (1859–1930), who had played a major role with *Colored American Magazine* during the first decade of the century, anticipated the concerns of *Opportunity* and *Crisis* in *New Era*, which she edited during 1916. Among its regular features was a column titled "Helps for Young Artist" by sculptor Meta Warrick-Fuller (1877–1968), whose papers include a large number of unpublished poems and plays. Again reflecting the limitations of conventional chronology, the major work of many of the younger women associated with the renaissance—Hurston, Marita Bonner, and Dorothy West are the obvious examples—was not published until the late 1930s or 1940s.

Several geographical factors also contributed to de-emphasizing the importance of the Harlem Renaissance to black women. Many critics have noted that the importance of Harlem during the 1920s resulted from its status as gathering place for writers and intellectuals from throughout the hemisphere. Hughes was raised in the midwest; McKay in Jamaica; Wallace Thurman in Utah; James Weldon Johnson in Florida. The women writers, too, came from a variety of geographical backgrounds; Georgia Johnson was raised in Atlanta and educated in Ohio; Fauset was part of Philadelphia's long-established black middle class; Eulalie Spence moved from the West Indies to New York; Anne Spencer was born in Virginia; the Florida-born Hurston was one of many writers who studied for a time at Howard University in Washington, D.C. Of this group, however, only Fauset and Hurston spent much time in Harlem. Reflecting the demands placed on black women as wives and mothers, their limited opportunity for travel or relocation should not be seen, however, as a sign of cultural isolation. Black women in fact created a sequence of alternative local centers for interaction and support. Part of a network with important centers in Boston and Philadelphia, the most important of these was probably Washington, D.C. There, Georgia Johnson's S Street Salon brought together Fauset, Bonner, Dunbar-Nelson, May Miller, Grimké, Hurston; black men including Locke, Du Bois, James Weldon Johnson, Cullen, and Hughes; and prominent white writers Rebecca West, H. G. Wells, Edna St. Vincent *Millay, Vachel Lindsay, and Waldo Frank. Seen from this perspective, African-American women's culture of the era is more accurately characterized as a multigenerational network than as a geographically-centered movement of a "new generation."

Recognizing this decentralized network of black women writers helps clarify their significance both in relationship to the Harlem Renaissance and to African-American women's culture. Building on their unique perspective on the relationship between race, gender, and class oppression, these foremothers resisted the dominant terms of discussion of the Harlem Renaissance and provided a foundation, as Alice *Walker and Toni Cade *Bambara have acknowledged, for the redefinition of African-American cultural traditions by black women writers of the 1970s and 1980s. Women's writing of the 1920s did, of course, share numerous thematic concerns with black male expression. Like Crisis editor W. E. B. Du Bois, Fauset was concerned with the proper relationship between "art" and "propaganda"; Georgia Johnson wrote numerous "protest" or "problem" plays; Gwendolyn Bennett ("Heritage") and Helene Johnson ("Bottled," "Magalu") wrote poems responding directly to the question raised in Cullen's "Heritage": "What is Africa to me?" Almost every writer of the period, male or female, expressed concern over the impact of color prejudice within the African-American community. Finally, most literary figures of the period—Hurston and Hughes were the primary dissenters—viewed cultural activity as a way of raising the black masses out of their misery. Georgia Johnson and Fauset would certainly have endorsed the classic formulation from

Locke's "The New Negro" (1925): "He [sic, i.e., the Negro] now . . . lays aside the status of a beneficiary and ward for that of a collaborator and participant in American civilization. . . . The especially cultural recognition they win should in turn prove the key to that revaluation of the Negro which must precede or accompany any considerable further betterment of race relationships."

Beyond the general agreement, however, black women's expression was consistently informed by an understanding of "triple jeopardy," the multiplicative interaction of race, gender, and class oppression. Although no theoretical essay written by a black woman received serious attention at the time, Marita Bonner's "On Being Young—A Woman—and Colored" (Crisis, 1925) and Elise Johnson McDougald's "The Task of Negro Womanhood" (The New Negro, 1925) emphasize the impact of racial and gender stereotypes on their experience. McDougald emphasizes the diversity of black women's experience and presents a four-level model that resists the standard middle class/masses formulation. Like the numerous black women who devoted their energies to the women's club-based National Association of Colored Women, or to the Universal Negro Improvement Association, in which Amy Jacques Garvey played a major leadership role, McDougald bases her vision on the perception that "even in New York City, Negro women are of a race which is free neither economically, socially nor spiritually." Despite the now-discredited stereotypes of Fauset and others as middle-class women who uncritically perpetuated white values and social structures, black women consistently directed their energies toward what McDougald calls "enterprises of general racial interest."

This understanding was not limited to "political" activities. Both Gwendolyn Bennett and Hurston created a body of commentary that encourages a fundamental redefinition of the African-American cultural tradition in a way that highlights the experience and expression of "excluded" groups, including working women and lesbians. The importance of Hurston's essays on the aesthetics of African-American oral expression must be understood in relation to the widespread association of "Africa" with "primitivism," derived from Euro-American modernist interest in African masks and white stereotypes of jazz as "jungle music." Although the classic expression of Hurston's insights was not published until 1936 ("Characteristics of Negro Expression," "Shouting," and "Spirituals and Neo-Spirituals" in Nancy Cunard's anthology Negro), throughout the Renaissance she asserted the aesthetic importance of African-American oral culture, especially that of the working class. Although Hazel Carby properly cautions against using Hurston's rural focus to evade the economic tensions developing in Harlem and other urban black communities, Carby's brilliant essay "It Jus Be's Dat Way Sometime: The Sexual Politics of Women's Blues" (in *Unequal Sisters*, ed. Carol DuBois and Vicki L. Ruiz, 1990) demonstrates the fundamental importance of oral forms to a full understanding of black women's culture of the 1920s. A nuanced understanding of Hurston, Larsen, and Fauset leads inexorably, and not particularly ironically, to the recognition that any list of Harlem Renaissance masterworks should include Bessie Smith's "Backwater Blues" and "Young Woman's Blues"; Ma Rainey's "Hustlin Blues" and "Prove It On Me Blues," one of many explicit assertions of lesbian identity in the blues of the period; and Ida Cox's "Wild Women Don't Get the Blues" and "One Hour Mama." To draw an arbitrary line separating literature and music—a line that Hurston clearly reveals as meaningless in African-American aesthetics—is to exclude both the most powerful statements on the impact of triple jeopardy on poor black women *and* the most joyous celebrations of black women's strength. The fact that Bessie Smith, Ma Rainey, and countless other singers of both sacred and secular music reached an audience far larger than that of their literary sisters—in the tent shows of Mississippi and Georgia as well as the clubs of Harlem and Washington—simply reenforces the conclusion that, in relation to African-American women, the "Harlem Renaissance" was only the shadow of a more substantial reality.

[*See also* African-American Writing; Chicago Renaissance.]

• Nathan Huggins, ed., *Voices from the Harlem Renaissance* (1976). Amritjit Singh, *The Novels of the Harlem Renaissance* (1976). Abby Arthur Johnson and Ronald Maberry Johnson, *Propaganda and Aesthetics: The Literary Politics of Afro-American Magazines in the Twentieth Century* (1979). David Levering Lewis, *When Harlem Was in Vogue* (1981). Jervis Anderson, *This Was Harlem* (1982). Victor Kramer, ed., *The Harlem Renaissance Re-examined* (1986). Bruce Kellner, ed., *The Harlem Renaissance: A Historical Dictionary for the Era* (1987). Trudier Harris, ed., *Dictionary of Literary Biography: Afro-American Writers from the Harlem Renaissance to 1940* (1987). Cary D. Wintz, *Black Culture and the Harlem Renaissance* (1988). Elizabeth Brown-Guillory, ed., *Wines in the Wilderness: Plays by African-American Women from the Harlem Renaissance to the Present* (1990).

Craig Hansen Werner

HARPER, Frances Ellen Watkins (1825–1911), poet, novelist, orator, essayist. Frances Ellen Watkins was born in Baltimore, Maryland. Her parents were free; she was their only child. When Frances was only three, her mother died, and she moved into her aunt and uncle's home. As a child, Frances learned about and witnessed slavery in Maryland, and she attended a school owned by her uncle, William J. Watkins, a minister and abolitionist. Although economic pressures ended Frances's formal schooling at thirteen, her intelligence and thirst for knowledge resulted in an extraordinarily active career as a writer and lecturer lasting into her seventies.

After a two-year stint as a teacher in Ohio and Pennsylvania, Watkins embarked on her life's work when William Grant Still, the renowned African-American abolitionist, influenced her to join the *Underground Railroad in 1854. Soon after she began traveling for the Maine Antislavery Society, and her oratorical gifts quickly became evident. In 1860, at the age of thirty-five, Frances married Fenton Harper, a widower with three children. Fenton and Frances had one child of their own, Mary, and in 1864, Fenton died, leaving Frances penniless. Thereafter, Harper continued to support herself, and her children, as well, with the grueling career of traveling lecturer.

Often subjected to danger and ridicule for her militant speeches, Harper refused to yield to despair. Throughout her life, she insisted on a bright future for African-Americans and emphasized interracial harmony. After the Civil War, Harper focused her oratorical talents on the subject of equal rights for black men and women, denouncing lynching and supporting educational and economic opportunity. A staunch feminist, she was a key figure in numerous predominantly white organizations, such as the Women's Christian Temperance Union and the American Women's Suffrage Association, despite the racism she faced from white members.

Harper's career as an activist continued until 1901, when failing health and age began to slow her down. She died on 22 February 1911 of heart failure.

A brilliant orator able to speak for two hours without notes, Harper was also a phenomenally prolific and versatile writer, publishing poetry, short stories, sketches, and essays. She published numerous letters on political subjects in such newspapers as the *National Anti-Slavery Standard* and the *Liberator*. Known as the "Bronze Muse," Harper has long been considered the pre-eminent African-American poet of the nineteenth century. Moreover, she was the first popular black protest poet.

Harper's most popular collection, *Poems on Miscellaneous Subjects*, first published in 1854, went through twenty printings during her lifetime. Containing abolitionist poems such as

"The Slave Mother," biblical retellings such as "Ruth and Naomi," feminist pieces such as "Advice to Girls," and temperance poems such as "Drunkard's Child," *Poems on Miscellaneous Subjects* encompasses many of Harper's themes and concerns.

"Bury Me in a Free Land," one of Harper's best-loved poems, was first published in the *Anti-Slavery Bugle* in 1858. Expressing the anguish of slavery, the poem has also been said to reflect the physical and psychological toll of Harper's career.

Harper's story "The Two Offers" appeared in an 1859 issue of *The Anglo-African Magazine*, a publication aimed at black audiences. The first published story by an African-American, "The Two Offers" explores the theme that women may choose other options besides marriage. The two characters, Laura and Janette, embody the traditional and feminist perspectives, respectively, with Janette avoiding the loss and disappointment accompanying a failed marriage. Janette, like Harper, enjoys a career as a writer and activist.

Harper's 1869 work *Moses: A Story of the Nile* is a forty-page blank verse poem that probably equates Abraham Lincoln with Moses. Harper's optimism embodies post–Civil War sentiments that emancipation prefigures a new age for African-Americans. *Sketches of Southern Life* (1872) is a collection of poems, many of which are narrated by Aunt Chloe, a courageous survivor of slavery who insists on learning to read. Speaking dialect, Aunt Chloe represents Harper's belief that black feminism has its roots in folk culture.

Harper's novel *Iola Leroy; or, Shadows Uplifted* (1892), one of the earliest-known novels by an African-American, is a historical romance that begins during the Civil War. Iola, a feminist heroine despite her sentimental treatment as a tragic mulatta, survives a series of catastrophes including enslavement and separation from her family. Freed from slavery, Iola becomes a Civil War nurse and heroically refuses a white doctor's proposal to marry him and pass for white. Subsequently, Iola reunites her family and marries an African-American doctor, dedicating her life to crusading for her race.

Frances Harper's writing, be it fiction, poetry, essays, or oratory, reflects her lifelong commitment to equality between blacks and whites, between women and men. A reliance on oral devices and rhetorical techniques infuses her work. Her emphasis on protest resurfaces in such poets as Sonia * Sanchez, Nikki * Giovanni, and Audre * Lorde. Her use of folk ballads, biblical themes, and lyrics can be seen most obviously in the poetry of Margaret * Walker. Finally, Harper anticipates the feminist themes of Nella * Larsen, Alice * Walker, and Gloria * Naylor. Nearly 150 years after she began her career, Frances Harper's literary reach is irrefutable.

• Frances Harper's papers are housed at the Moorland-Spingarn Research Center of Howard University and at the New York Public Library's Schomberg Center for Research in Black Culture. See also Jane Campbell, *Mythic Black Fiction: The Transformation of History* (1986). Maryemma Graham, "Frances Ellen Watkins Harper," in *DLB: Afro-American Writers Before the Harlem Renaissance*, eds. Trudier Harris and Thadious M. Davis (1986), pp. 164–173. Hazel Carby, *Reconstructing Womanhood: The Emergence of the Afro-American Woman Novelist* (1987). Frances E. W. Harper, *The Complete Poems of Frances E. W. Harper*, ed. Maryemma Graham (1988). Frances E. W. Harper, *A Brighter Coming Day: A Frances E. W. Harper Reader*, ed. Frances Smith Foster (1990). Barbara Christian, *Black Women Novelists: The Development of a Tradition, 1892–1976* (1990). Frances Smith Foster, "Frances E. W. Harper," in *African American Writers*, ed. Valerie Smith (1991), pp. 159–175.

Jane Campbell

H. D. (Hilda Doolittle, 1886–1961), poet, novelist, autobiographer, critic, filmmaker, and hermetist. Having rejected Victorian norms for modern experiments, H. D. repeatedly launched out from instructors found among the early canonized male modernists. She developed new lyric, mythic, and mystical forms in poetry and prose, and an alternative bisexual lifestyle that were little appreciated until the 1980s. Her literary contacts included Ezra Pound, Marianne * Moore, William Carlos Williams, Ford Madox Ford, May Sinclair, Dorothy Richardson, Richard Aldington, Bryher, D. H. Lawrence, T. S. Eliot, Djuna * Barnes, Gertrude * Stein, Amy * Lowell, Norman Douglas, Edith Sitwell, and Elizabeth Bowen. She was the literary editor of the *Egoist* (1916–1917), and admired the work of James Joyce and Virginia * Woolf. Younger poets like Robert Duncan, Allen Ginsberg, May * Sarton, and Denise * Levertov took her as a mentor. H. D.'s literary papers are at Beinecke Library, Yale University.

Autobiographies. H. D. was born into the Moravian community of her artistic, musical mother, Helen (Wolle), in Bethlehem, Pennsylvania, and reared in Upper Darby, a Philadelphia suburb convenient to the University of Pennsylvania. Her astronomer father, Charles, was director of the Flower Observatory there. *The Gift* (written 1941–1944; published 1982) is cast in the inquiring voice of a child, who is cognizant of several generations of her family, and of her own dreams and fantasies. Her grandmother ultimately bestows a sense of her self-enabling heritage or "gift," and its mystical connection to the Moravians. Mystical access to the past through visions and the reading of "signets"—signs or heiroglyphs requiring patient deciphering—is essential to all of H. D.'s autobiographical writing.

H. D.'s autobiographical writings from the middle years of her life are invaluable to the study of the gendered politics of experimental modernism, and the place of the female analysand in psychoanalysis. Ezra Pound entered her life while she was still a schoolgirl in Pennsylvania. In verses written for her, Pound gave her the persona of the "dryad," which persisted among her many self-concepts. They were twice engaged. Barbara Guest has suggested that his tutelage interfered with her studies at Bryn Mawr, which she quit in her second year. She did meet another as yet undeclared poet, Marianne Moore, while there (1904–1906). H. D. joined the same literary circles Pound traveled in when she moved to London in 1911. In a famous incident of 1913, he sent some of her verse to Harriet * Monroe's *Poetry Magazine*, appending the signature "H. D., *Imagiste.*" They served as models of the new poetry he was promoting. *End to Torment: A Memoir of Ezra Pound by H. D.* (written 1958; published 1979) explores this relationship.

With *Bid Me to Live* (written 1933–1950, published 1960), H. D. writes herself out of what Rachel Blau DuPlessis has called "romantic thralldom" with two other literary men. She married the British poet, Richard Aldington, in 1913. Having enlisted in World War I, his fictional counterpart called for her sustaining letters to the front, yet resented her sharing verses with "Rico," the D. H. Lawrence counterpart, and flaunted his infidelities. Lawrence had a charismatic effect upon H. D. during the war years in London, but discouraged her creation of male subjects in her poetry, and objected to her relationship with Cecil Grey, the painter whom she joined in Cornwall. Grey became the father of her only surviving child, Frances Perdita Aldington (born 1919). H. D. had been anguished over the still-birth of a daughter fathered by Aldington in 1915, and the death of her brother Gilbert at the front. *Bid Me to Live* was part of a "madrigal cycle," including also *Paint it To-Day* and *Asphodel* (neither yet fully published). All of these works intertwined the painful demands of war and love relationships, as does the brilliant long poem, *Trilogy* (written 1944–1946), with its images of rebirth taken from classical, Egyptian and Christian sources.

Tribute to Freud (written 1944; published gradually from 1945–1985) offers a third creative re-vision of male-inspired paradigms. H. D. was analyzed by Freud in 1933 and 1934, in an attempt to overcome writer's block. She also underwent analysis with Hans Sachs in the 1930s, with Erich Heydt in the 1950s, and was treated with intervenous shock therapy, following a major breakdown in 1946. Freud encouraged her to write straight history to break out of the personal crisis she experienced during World War I. With *Bid Me to Live* she felt she was escaping also from the influence of psychoanalysis; she did revise Freud's role as analyst to something more like a medium. * Spiritualism became an overriding interest in the 1940s. Communication with the dead and projections from another realm were regular tropes in her writing, including her last writing, *Hermetic Definition*.

Bisexuality. H. D.'s troubled alliance with Pound was mingled with her love of Frances Josepha Gregg, a student at the Pennsylvania Academy of Fine Arts, and the recipient of some of her earliest poems. Gregg and her mother were H. D.'s companions on the 1911 trip to London. Prefiguring other bisexual triangles she would involve herself in, H. D. planned to accompany Gregg on her honeymoon, but was prevented from doing so by Pound. The strains between lesbian and heterosexual attractions, experienced over the Gregg relationship, entered into H. D.'s novel *HERmione* (written 1927, the year before Radclyffe Hall's lesbian novel, *The Well of Loneliness*, was the subject of an obscenity trial; published 1981).

The novelist and editor Bryher (Winnifred Ellerman, an heiress to a shipping fortune), was the most significant companion of her mature life. Their relationship survived until H. D.'s death in 1961, spanning Bryher's two marriages of convenience to Robert McAlmon and Kenneth Macpherson, in circumstances that included significant travel and residences mainly in London and Switzerland. H. D. has credited Bryher with saving her life during the final months of her pregnancy in 1919, when she was struck with influenza. Bryher and H. D. traveled to the Scilly Islands together in June 1919, for a month of idyllic companionship; they went to Greece (sailing by Lesbos) with H. D.'s mother in 1922, and traveled to Egypt the next year. The women made a creative trio with the artist and filmmaker Kenneth Macpherson from 1927 to 1932; Macpherson became H. D.'s lover, and Bryher's husband, and the married couple adopted H. D.'s daughter Perdita. Their collaborations included photomontages, the film journal *Close Up*, to which H. D. supplied poetry and reviews, and *Borderline*, a film in which H. D. starred with Paul Robeson. The project is one indication of H. D.'s literary connections to the Harlem Renaissance, and her attraction to the margins of modernism. Much of H. D.'s poetry published in the 1930s and 1940s appeared in *Life and Letters Today*, edited by Bryher.

H. D. was well informed about contemporary theories of homosexuality, due both to her analysis by Freud, who pronounced her bisexual, and her friendship with sexologist Havelock Ellis, whom she met in 1919. But she was not limited to their views, particularly in *HER*. Her shift in interest to mother-daughter dynamics in *Notes on Thought and Vision* may have been a transference out of Freud's influence. However, Ellis failed to appreciate her revolutionary "bell jar" experiences of pregnancy and the unconscious, recorded in *Notes on Thought and Vision*, and his lack of enthusiasm may have discouraged her publishing it.

Critical Repositioning and Feminist Criticism. For many years H. D. was known chiefly for the stark, chiseled images and experimental rhythms of her earliest work, collected as *Sea Garden* (1916). This fit the imagist program of Ezra Pound. She also had a limited reputation as a classicist and translator of Greek. Feminist critics, led by Susan Stanford Friedman and Rachel Blau DuPlessis, have studied H. D.'s works for feminine, lesbian, and bisexual discourses. Since the early 1980s H. D.'s epic and prose writing have received more attention, and work self-suppressed in her own lifetime has been recovered and studied. H. D.'s frequent recourse to the palimpsest can be seen as an escape from binary and hierarchical thinking associated with patriarchy. The term denotes a parchment that retains partially erased parts of earlier writings, which strain productively with new text. She titled a three-part story sequence *Palimpsest* (written 1923–1924), but the term also applies to her rewritings of her own selfhood in autobiographies, and to her rewritten myths. H. D. can be credited with anticipating the maternal semiotic of Julia Kristeva, and with giving a female voice to classical myths. Sandra Gilbert ("H. D.? Who Was She?," *Contemporary Literature* 24 [1983]: 496–511) suggests that she developed a "woman's mythology" in *Trilogy, Helen in Egypt*, and *Hermetic Definition*. Alicia Ostriker ("Thieves of Language," *Signs* 8, no. 1 [1982]: 68–90) includes H. D. among women poets who construct new myths to include their selves. H. D.'s Greek texts, culminating in *Helen in Egypt*, explore the divinity of the goddess, the sexually ecstatic Eleusinian mysteries, and the female version of patriarchal epics. A criticism from Lawrence S. Rainey ("Canon, Gender and Text," *Representing Modern Texts*, ed. George Bornstein, [1991]) is that in recent years H. D.'s work has been studied for the sake of content

conducive to feminist solidarity, rather than aesthetic value. Yet this criticism neglects feminist critics' remarks on the formal devices of mythic mask, palimpsest, and return of the repressed, characteristic of life-writing cure, that moved H. D. beyond confinement to the divisive gender stereotypes of her day.

• Susan Stanford Friedman, *Psyche Reborn: The Emergence of H. D.* (1981). Barbara Guest, *Herself Defined: The Poet H. D. and Her World* (1984). Rachel Blau DuPlessis, *H. D.: The Career of That Struggle* (1986). *H. D. Newsletter*, ed. Eileen Gregory (1987–). Michael King, ed., *H. D.: Woman and Poet* (1987). Gary Burnett, *H. D. between Image and Epic: The Mysteries of Her Poetics* (1990). Susan Stanford Friedman, *Penelope's Web* (1990). Susan Stanford Friedman and Rachel Blau DuPlessis, eds., *Signets: Reading H. D.* (1990). Dianne Chisholm, *H. D.'s Freudian Poetics: Psychoanalysis in Translation* (1992). Richard Aldington, *Richard Aldington and H. D.*, ed. Caroline Zilboorg (1992).

Bonnie Kime Scott

HEALTH. *See* Body and Health.

HEALTH BOOKS, PAMPHLETS, AND REFERENCE GUIDES. Most of the health books, pamphlets, and reference guides published in America have been written by men. Female authors of such guides often wrote only in response to what they saw as particularly wrong-minded arguments about the health of women and children set forth initially by male "experts." In colonial America, health advice and health care had for the most part been the province of female healers. By the nineteenth century, however, the New England writer Sarah Orne *Jewett produced a nostalgic sketch about Mrs. Goodsoe, an aging healer whose practice had long been overtaken by professionalized medicine and physicians, most of whom were male. In the early part of the nineteenth century, "Ladies' Physiological Societies," in which women learned about female anatomy and health, sprang from the social climate produced by workingmen's parties and early feminist agitation. Fighting against sex and class injustice, early feminists like Fanny Wright brought women's health issues to the forefront in newspapers such as the *Free Enquirer*.

Books written between 1840 and 1900 are largely the work of women whose activity in the health field was combined with involvement in other reform movements, such as temperance, sex education, and dress reform. Catharine Esther *Beecher took as her chief concern the health of women and children, and in *Physiology and Calisthenics* (1856) warned against the era's tendency toward chronic invalidism among middle-class women. *Letters to the Public on Health and Happiness* (1855) was packed with rambling statistics on the poor health of hundreds of women, and included Beecher's own stories of poor health care: she admitted that she had consumed sulphur and iron, submitted to blistering, and subjected herself to animal magnetism and the water cure. *Housekeeper and Healthkeeper* (1873) offered striking evidence for the conviction of many women that their grandmothers enjoyed better health than they did. Mary Grove Nichols was one of several women who lectured to women audiences about medicine and physiology at mid-century. An advocate of hydrotherapy, she wrote *Lectures on Anatomy and Physiology* (1844) and together with her husband published *Nichols' Journal of Health, Water-Cure and Human Progress* in the 1850s. Harriot Hunt, a home-trained Boston practitioner, published the autobiographical *Glances and Glimpses* in 1856. Like Catharine Beecher, Hunt was appalled at the poor care and unnecessary treatments many women received at the hands of male physicians.

Some readers sought spiritual answers for the medical problems that plagued them. Despite the increasingly secular nature of medical care in America, religiomedical activities and publications flourished. Mary Baker Eddy, founder of the Church of Christ, Scientist, published a pamphlet entitled *The Science of Man, By Which the Sick Are Healed* (1870), and the textbook of Christian Science, *Science and Health* (1875). Seventh-Day Adventist Ellen White's first book on health reform was the antimasturbation tract *An Appeal to Mothers: The Great Cause of the Physical, Mental and Moral Ruin of Many of the Children of Our Time* (1864). In 1905, with her church well established, she published her last major work on health, *The Ministry of Healing*.

Much of the medical rhetoric of the nineteenth century that equated women with their reproductive organs was contained in appeals to parents to guard their daughters against the dangers of excessive activity or mental application. Parents who pushed their girls ahead in school only hastened their decline, warned Elizabeth Blackwell (herself one of the first women to attend medical school in the United States) in *The Laws of Life, With Special Reference to the Physical Education of Girls* (1852). She argued that for women, every epoch of development had its appropriate application. In girlhood, priority had to go to bodily growth and the storing up of energy. Failure to follow a course of rest in youth would be punished by a frail maturity. Blackwell also sounded ominous warnings against city life, fashion, and stimulating diet.

E. H. Clarke's *Sex in Education; or, A Fair Chance for the Girls* (1873), the product of a male physician, was a lightning rod for women writing about health in the nineteenth century. Clarke argued against coeducation, illustrating some of the health-bound prejudices concerning female adolescence in nineteenth-century America. Like Blackwell, Clarke insisted that menstruation required that young girls follow a schedule of long periods of rest, so long as to make coeducation impossible. Coeducational colleges, argued Clarke, ran the risk of damaging young women's procreative capabilities. Clarke's treatise against coeducation was met with a slew of written protest from prominent women, including Julia Ward *Howe's Sex and Education: A Reply to Dr. E. H. Clarke's Sex in Education* (1874), Anna C. Brackett's *The Education of American Girls, Considered in a Series of Essays* (1874), and E. B. Duffey's *No Sex in Education; or An Equal Chance for Girls and Boys* (1874). Mary Putnam Jacobi was one of the most brilliant doctors of her day, and her monograph *The Question of Rest for Women During Menstruation* (1877), an answer to Clarke, won the Harvard Boylston Medical Prize. Sarah Stevenson, also writing in response to the climate that produced Dr. Clarke in *The Physiology of Woman, Embracing Girlhood, Maternity and Mature Age* (1881), noted that "the unerring instincts of woman have been an eloquent theme for those who do not know what they are talking about."

The birth-control movement in the United States met with controversy from the start, and early proponents of birth control often couched their activism in the popular rhetoric of eugenics. Books on perfectionism, or race improvement, were some of the most popular early tracts on birth control. Eliza Barton Lyman's *The Coming Woman: or, The Royal Road to Physical Perfection* (1880), Lois Waisbrooker's *From Generation to Regeneration: or, The Plain Guide to Naturalism* (1887), and even Charlotte Perkins *Gilman's Women and Economics* (1898) appealed not to right or morality but to evolutionary theory. Women's confinement to domestic activities, she claimed, had made them more primitive and less developed than men. Ellen Key's 1909 best-seller, *The Century of the Child*, proposed a eugenicist approach to parenting in which women, by dint of the effort of several generations, might produce a superior race. Voluntary motherhood was a more radical idea, similar to free love and espoused by Tennessee Claflin in *The Ethics of Sexual Equality* (1873) and *Virtue, What It Is and What It Isn't; Seduction, What It Is and What It Is Not* (1872) and Alice Stockham, whose *Tokology: A Book for Every Woman* (1883) proposed deliberate sexual coldness as birth control. Many other marriage manuals and sex-education volumes authored by women appeared at the turn of the century, including Mrs. P. B. Saur's *Maternity: A Book for Every Wife and Mother* (1891), Ida Craddock's *Letter to a Prospective Bride* (1897), Alice Stockham's *Karezza: Ethics of Marriage* (1898), Juliet Severance's *Marriage* (1901), Emma Frances Angell Drake's *What a Young Wife Ought to Know* (1901), and Dr. Edith Bell Lowry's *Herself: Talks with Women Concerning Themselves* (1911). Margaret *Sanger, popularly perceived as the mother of birth control in the United States, pushed it in her socialist/feminist journal *The Woman Rebel*, as well as the *Birth Control Review* she sold on the streets of New York in 1915. In *Woman and the New Race* (1920), Sanger blamed motherhood for all of the world's ills, positing birth control and the elimination of the unfit as the only answer.

Germ science and a frustrated female chemist, Ellen Richards, created the new discipline of home economics with her *Euthenics: The Science of Controllable Environment* (1912). Earlier books on the science and medicine of cleanliness included Mrs. H. M. Plunkett's *Women, Plumbers and Doctors, or Household Sanitation* (1897), filled with fears of contagion from the poor, outlined women's responsibilities as sanitation officers in their own homes; and Helen Campbell's *Household Economics* (1907), which described how the old domestic crafts had gradually been taken over by men, leaving only cleaning as women's art. Margaret Reid's *Economics of Household Production* (1934) was a popular later volume in this vein.

In the 1970s, a burgeoning feminist movement produced innumerable advice books and exposés of medical practice in the United States. The most durable of these has been *Our Bodies, Ourselves* (1976), published by a consortium of female health practitioners calling themselves the Boston Women's Health Collective. No health book by women has been so widely read since Mrs. Max West's *Infant Care* ceased to be produced by the Government Printing Office in the late teens. A large-format volume, *Our Bodies, Ourselves* includes first-person accounts of women's passage through various stages of maturation, professional analysis of such case histories, photographs, and illustrations. Social and economic issues that influence women's health are also covered as some of the chapter titles from the original edition indicate: "Our Changing Sense of Self," "Living With Ourselves and Others," "In Amerika They Call Us Dykes," "Rape," "Self Defense," "Venereal Disease," and "Coping, Organizing and Developing Alternatives."

More recently, Jane Brody, a *New York Times* columnist, has written a great deal on health, nutrition, and fitness. Pediatrician Perri Klass, another frequent contributor to the *Times*, also writes on issues of concern to the health of women and children. America's increasing reliance on televised media for the dissemination of information has created the need for a number of telegenic female medical experts who cross over into print media. Psychiatrist Dr. Joyce Brothers was one of the first counselors to become a household name, and Dr. Ruth Westheimer has become familiar in recent years for her candid discussions of sex.

Much attention has also been focused on the health issues surrounding women's appearance. Naomi Wolf's *The Beauty Myth* (1991) deals with topics such as anorexia and bulimia, plastic surgery, and sexual violence against women. Wolf also drew renewed attention to a phenomena first addressed by Betty *Friedan in *The Feminine Mystique* (1963): the power of family and women's magazines to influence women's mental health and self-image. Just as women of the fifties and sixties had learned to bring their babies up "by the book," Wolf argues, women of the eighties and nineties learn to aspire to medically impossible physical forms.

[*See also* Advice Books; Body and Health.]

• Barbara Ehrenreich and Deirdre English, *Complaints and Disorders: The Sexual Politics of Sickness* (1973). Mary S. Hartman and Lois Banner, eds., *Clio's Consciousness Raised: New Perspectives on the History of Women* (1974). Linda Gordon, *Woman's Body, Woman's Right: A Social History of Birth Control in America* (1976). Barbara Ehrenreich and Deirdre English, *For Her Own Good: 150 Years of the Experts' Advice To Women* (1979). Judith Walzer Leavitt, ed., *Women and Health in America* (1984). Carroll Smith-Rosenberg, *Disorderly Conduct: Visions of Gender in Victorian America* (1985).

Jill Wacker

HEILBRUN, Carolyn Gold (b. 1926). Born in East Orange, New Jersey, Carolyn G. Heilbrun graduated Phi Beta Kappa from Wellesley College (1947). Heilbrun earned her M.A. (1951) and Ph.D. (1959) from Columbia University, where she has been a full professor of English since 1972. She and James Heilbrun (m. 1945) have three children.

After two biographical studies (*The Garnett Family*, 1961, and *Christopher Isherwood*, 1970), Heilbrun wrote her best-known critical works, all essays that develop their theses through extensive literary examples. *Toward a Recognition of Androgyny* (1973), which was inspired by Virginia *Woolf's *A Room of One's Own*, problematizes social constructions of *gender and suggests ways of escape. *Reinventing Womanhood* (1979) explores women's difficulty imagining themselves as autonomous beings and suggests women appropriate some models of masculine behavior. *Writing a Woman's Life* (1988) examines the shaping of women's lives in *biography, *autobiography and their own imaginations. Heilbrun's refusal of an impersonal academic style and articulation of her personal relation to her scholarly material make all three books accessible to a variety of readers.

Amanda Cross's detective novels evoke and often satirize literary-academic milieus (particularly English departments) through protagonist Kate Fansler, English professor and sometime sleuth. All ten novels are marked for their multi-layered literariness, from allusive dialogue to plots equally concerned with manuscripts and murder. Cross's attention to the manners of the socially and intellectually privileged works as an affectionate parody of classic detective novels, especially those of Dorothy L. Sayers. Cross's most famous novel is *Death in a Tenured Position* (1981), in which Fansler investigates the apparent murder of Harvard's only tenured woman English professor. The others are *In the Last Analysis* (1964), *The James Joyce Murder* (1967), *Poetic Justice* (1970), *The Theban Mysteries* (1971), *The Question of Max* (1976), *Sweet Death, Kind Death* (1984), *No Word from Winifred* (1986), *A Trap for Fools* (1989) and *The Players Come Again* (1990).

The fact of a *pseudonym whose secrecy has expired invites comparisons between Heilbrun and Cross, who might seem on opposite ends of the continuum from elite to popular culture. In fact, there are significant overlaps. The two writers share a sustained interrogation of gender issues—most significantly, women's lives, *friendships and self-images after the age of fifty—and a concern with the process and genre of biography. Most recently, Heilbrun's *Hamlet's Mother and Other Women* (1990) includes essays on gender and genre in detective fiction, and Cross's *The Players Come Again* is more concerned with feminine authorship and the lives of a group of remarkable women than with detection *per se*.

• Steven R. Carter, "Amanda Cross," in *Ten Women of Mystery*, ed. Earl Bargainnier (1981), pp. 269–296. Diana Cooper-Clark, *Designs of Darkness: Interviews with Detective Novelists* (1983). Laura Marcus, "Coming Out in Print: Women's Autobiographical Writings Revisited," *Prose Studies* 10, no. 1 (May 1987): 102–107. Maureen Reddy, *Sisters in Crime: Feminism and the Crime Novel* (1988). "The Feminist Counter-Tradition in Crime: Cross, Grafton, Paretsky, and Wilson," in *The Cunning Craft: Original Essays on Detective Fiction and Contemporary Literary Theory*, ed. Ronald G. Walker, June M. Frazer, and David R. Anderson (1990), pp. 174–187.

Martha Stoddard Holmes

HELLMAN, Lillian (1905–1984), playwright, screenwriter, memoirist. Despite her claim that she detested the theater, thirty-two of Lillian Hellman's fifty unusually public years in American letters were devoted primarily to dramatic writing. Arguably the most significant American dramatist next to Eugene O'Neill in the first half of the twentieth century, Hellman shifted her writing mode entirely when she was in her mid-sixties, initiating in 1969 a series of memoirs which kept her in the public eye until her death. She appeared to court controversy and, by the final decade of her life, drew such extremes of praise and vituperation that virtually everything printed about her work led to a discussion of Hellman herself.

In addition to eight original plays and four adaptations for Broadway, Hellman wrote seven produced screenplays, directed three Broadway productions of her work, reported for newspapers and magazines on a broad range of issues, edited the letters of Anton Chekhov (*The Selected Letters of Anton Chekhov*, 1955) and the stories of Dashiell Hammett (*The Big Knockover*, 1966), and, in her plays and her memoirs (*An Unfinished Woman*, 1969; *Pentimento*, 1973; *Scoundrel Time*, 1976; *Maybe*, 1980), provided the source material for another five films and an opera. She had already reinvented herself as a writer before she switched to the memoir form, turning from the Ibsenite structure and topicality of her most familiar plays (*The Children's Hour*, 1934; *The Little Foxes*, 1939; *Watch on the Rhine*, 1941; *Another Part of the Forest*, 1946) to Chekhovian character analysis in *The Autumn Garden* (1951) and *Toys in the Attic* (1960) and experimentation with dramatic form in her four stage adaptations (*Montserrat*, 1949; *The Lark*, 1955; the Leonard Bernstein operetta *Candide*, 1956, for which she wrote the libretto; and *My Mother, My Father and Me*, 1963).

The only child of Julia Newhouse and Max Hellman, Hellman lived in New Orleans until age six, when business failure precipitated the family's move to Manhattan. For the next decade Hellman spent half the year in New York, the other in the New Orleans boardinghouse run by two paternal aunts, attending school in both cities. She studied at New York University (1922–1924) and, briefly, Columbia (1926) without completing a degree. A series of early jobs included manuscript reader for publisher Horace Liveright, press agent, play reader, and book reviewer for the *New York Herald-Tribune*. She married press agent Arthur Kober (1925), with whom she traveled to Europe and, in 1930, to Hollywood, where she read scripts for Metro-Goldwyn-Mayer and met novelist Dashiell Hammett (1894–1961). Hammett remained the central figure in her life for what Hellman called "thirty-one on and off years" of a stormy relationship frequently idealized in her writing.

She and Kober divorced in 1932 and she never remarried.

Following the opening of *The Children's Hour* on Broadway, she wrote screenplays for Samuel Goldwyn (including *The Dark Angel*, 1935; *These Three*, 1936—a laundered version of *The Children's Hour*; *Dead End*, 1937; and *The Little Foxes*, 1941). Among many lifelong political acts, she coproduced (with Ernest Hemingway and others) the documentary film *The Spanish Earth* (1937) in support of antifascist Loyalists fighting in the Spanish Civil War. She wrote articles on that war and numerous other topics during her frequent travels. With the exceptions of *Days to Come* (1936), her second play, and *My Mother, My Father and Me* (1963), her last, Hellman's plays enjoyed successful Broadway runs and international productions; most were adapted to the screen. *Watch on the Rhine* and *Toys in the Attic* won the New York Drama Critics' Circle Award as best American play for their respective years.

Blacklisted in Hollywood in 1948 for alleged pro-Communist sympathies, Hellman was subpoenaed to appear before the House Committee on Un-American Activities. In a highly publicized letter to the Committee using a metaphor with which she became permanently identified, she expressed a willingness to speak about herself but refused to answer questions concerning others: "I cannot and will not cut my conscience to fit this year's fashions [of naming names]. ...." She felt compelled to invoke the Fifth Amendment during her testimony (21 May 1952), but her letter was entered into the record. She escaped contempt charges—on a legal "technicality," she later maintained—but suffered serious financial hardship from her continued blacklisting.

Her reputation soared in the 1960s and, particularly, the 1970s, following publication of her memoirs. After a long hiatus, she wrote one final screenplay (*The Chase*, 1966). Admitted into the American Academy of Arts and Letters in 1963, she received numerous honorary degrees, taught at major universities, and won prestigious awards, including the Gold Medal for Drama from the National Institute of Arts and Letters (1964), the National Book Award for *An Unfinished Woman* (1970), and the Edward MacDowell Medal (1976). She played a central role in the formation of the Committee for Public Justice (1970), a group dedicated to the protection of civil liberties against government abuse.

Despite her enormous popular success, Hellman was often misunderstood or patronized as a playwright, even in her theater heyday. The furor surrounding her inclusion of lesbianism as a thematic concern led to the banning of *The Children's Hour* in Boston, Chicago, and London, and obscured the play's primary subject: the incalculably destructive power of gossip. Modeled on her mother's wealthy family, the rapacious Hubbards of *The Little Foxes* and its sequel *Another Part of the Forest* were intended as a composite portrait of the comic and evil elements in greed and cheating but her satiric thrust was mistaken, Hellman said, as "straight stuff." Critics misread her abhorrence of sentimentality (a unique quality in the American theater of her time) as unyielding rigidity; and they frequently condemned her for excessive reliance on conventions of the well-made play, seldom perceiving the original twist she gave those conventions.

Hellman created strong, independent women characters in an era when American drama marginalized women by representing them onstage primarily as dutiful wives and mothers. Her plays are characterized by a Marxist, Depression-influenced treatment of wealth and a conviction that the meek are destined to disinherit the earth, elements intended to goad the audience toward political action. But she possessed scant faith in that audience's capacity for sustained moral commitment. Thus, while prodding it to correct society's ills, Hellman simultaneously indicted her audience for complicity in their perpetuation.

Throughout her playwriting career, critics persisted in calling Hellman a *woman* playwright, an identification she loathed. Characteristically, however, she would later deny that her memoirs certified her as a feminist. *An Unfinished Woman* and *Pentimento* were nevertheless embraced by the women's movement, contributing to Hellman's reemergence as a cultural heroine twenty years after her blacklisting. "I believe in women's liberation," she told an interviewer in 1974, [but] "I think it all comes down to whether or not you can support yourself as well as a man." Properly praised for their narrative virtuosity and compelling sense of drama, the memoirs rekindled the type of adulation she experienced early in her career, but the critical accolades of the seventies, hailing her as accomplished prose stylist and "super-literate Humphrey Bogart," shifted by the decade's end toward a backlash of derision at "the canonization of Saint Lillian."

Scoundrel Time reminded readers of her courageous stand before the House Committee on Un-American Activities but the memoir's allegations against "anti-Communist writers and intellectuals" of the McCarthy period unleashed a barrage of counterclaims accusing Hellman of pro-Stalinist distortion. Her response in *Three* (1979), the collected edition of her memoirs, escalated the level of rancor and led to more damaging attacks in the early eighties, three of which particularly undermined the credibility of Hellman's memoir self-portraits: Her literary rival Mary *McCarthy (whom Hellman sued for libel) called her a liar during a television interview; writer Martha *Gellhorn (a witness to events described by Hellman), while focusing specifically on the Spanish Civil War section of *Unfinished Woman*, alleged that virtually all of Hellman's memoirs were fictions; and Muriel Gardiner, a psychoanalyst who never met Hellman, suggested in her memoirs (*Code Name Mary*, 1983) that Hellman had appropriated *her* life for the story of the woman called "Julia" in *Pentimento*. Hellman died before her libel suit against McCarthy was tried. Publicly, she denied or ignored the other charges made against her.

The fragility of truth, the *unverifiability* of memory, is an issue explicitly pondered in Hellman's memoirs, where she repeatedly struggles to sort out images of the past which have replaced or clouded earlier ones. *Maybe*, her last memoir, is subtitled *A Story*, and may therefore be considered a fiction, not a memoir at all. Yet, it appears to contain Hellman's most candid self-portrait, one in which she movingly confronts the terror of impending death.

She is herself a dramatic construct in a film (*Julia*, 1977, adapted from *Pentimento*) and three plays: William Luce's *Lillian* (1986), based on Hellman's memoirs; Richard Nelson's *Sensibility and Sense* (1989), in which characters loosely based on Hellman and Mary McCarthy confront their feuding relationship; and, notably, Peter Feibleman's *Cakewalk* (1993), a complex portrayal of Feibleman's own intimate relationship with Hellman, adapted from his candid reminiscences (*Lilly*, 1988).

• Hellman's papers are in The Lillian Hellman Collection, Humanities Research Center, University of Texas at Austin. Lillian Hellman, *The Collected Plays* (1972). Manfred Triesch, *The Lillian Hellman Collection at the University of Texas* (1966). Doris V. Falk, *Lillian Hellman* (1978). Katherine Lederer, *Lillian Hellman* (1979). Mark W. Estrin, *Lillian Hellman: Plays, Films, Memoirs—A Reference Guide* (1980). Mary Marguerite Riordan, *Lillian Hellman, A Bibliography: 1926–1978* (1980). Martha Gellhorn, "On Apocryphism," *Paris Review* 79 (Spring 1981): 280–301; reprinted in *Critical Essays* (see below). Bernard F. Dick, *Hellman in Hollywood* (1982). Jackson R. Bryer, ed., *Conversations with Lillian Hellman* (1986). William Wright, *Lillian Hellman: The Image, The Woman* (1986). Carl Rollyson, *Lillian Hellman, Her Legend and Her Legacy* (1988). Mark W. Estrin, ed., *Critical Essays on Lillian Hellman* (1989).

Mark W. Estrin

HENLEY, Beth (b. 1952), playwright. Beth Henley's play *Crimes of the Heart* won the Pulit-

zer Prize for drama in 1981; the award marked the first time the prize has been awarded prior to a play's Broadway opening. Besides *Crimes of the Heart*, Henley's plays include *Am I Blue?* (1972), *The Miss Firecracker Contest* (1979), *The Wake of Jamey Foster* (1983), *The Debutante Ball* (1985), *The Lucky Spot* (1986), and *Abundance* (1989).

Henley attended Southern Methodist University and the University of Illinois and was an actress before becoming a playwright. She had, however, written her first play, *Am I Blue?* as part of a drama class assignment while an undergraduate at Southern Methodist.

Henley explores the broken lives of southern families, especially southern women, who have been left to their own resources and who must collectively gather courage to fight against the culture that entraps them. Her style has been described as "southern Gothic," a regional literary idiom that combines dark humor with the grotesque to achieve an effect of laughter tempered with tragedy. In *Crimes of the Heart*, (her best-known and most widely produced play), for example, the occasion for the reunion of three sisters is the youngest sister's arrest after shooting her abusive husband. The play is set in the kitchen of the house where they were raised by their grandfather; food and drink are central metaphors for the way the sisters either displace their emotional pain or celebrate their unity.

Henley's work is often compared to Marsha *Norman's (Pulitzer winner for '*night Mother* in 1983). Although they are both from the South, Henley explores the unique identity formation of the southern woman, while Norman prefers to deregionalize her settings and characters. Their commonality lies in their domestic settings, their exploration of female relationships, and their dramatic strategy of employing food and eating as a means to understanding the characters.

Henley's dramatic technique has been described (along with Marsha Norman's and Wendy *Wasserstein's) as traditional, a strategy that, according to some critics, affords women playwrights a voice in mainstream theatrical productions. Although Henley works with a traditional three-act structure and realistic staging, many critics contend that regional theater (such as The Actors Theater of Louisville, where both Henley and Norman have been produced) affords women playwrights the opportunity to present female characters that challenge traditional Broadway, male-oriented stereotypes. Of her work, Henley has said, "I like to write characters who do horrible things, but whom you can still like. . . . because of their human needs and struggles" (*Interviews with Contemporary Women Playwrights*, 1984).

• Nancy D. Hargrove, "The Tragicomic Vision of Beth Henley's Drama," *The Southern Quarterly* 22, no. 4 (Summer 1984): 54–70. Karen L. Laughlin, "Criminality, Desire, and Community: A Feminist Approach to Beth Henley's *Crimes of the Heart*," *Women and Performance* 3, no. 1 (1986): 35–51. Billy J. Harbin, "Familial Bonds in the Plays of Beth Henley," *Southern Quarterly* 25, no. 3 (Spring 1987): 81–94. Joanne B. Karpinski, "The Ghosts of Chekhov's *Three Sisters* Haunt Beth Henley's *Crimes of the Heart*," *Modern American Drama: The Female Canon*, ed. June Schlueter (1990), pp. 228–245.

Kay K. Cook

HERBST, Josephine Frey (1892–1969) novelist, journalist, and social historian. She is best known for her novels chronicling the political, economic, and social struggles of America during the 1920s and 1930s. Born and raised in Sioux City, Iowa, Herbst decided early in life to make a living as a writer. After she graduated from the University of California at Berkeley, Herbst moved to New York City in 1919 and pursued a literary career. Like many other American writers, she was drawn to Europe; she settled for a short time in Germany and Italy before traveling to Paris in 1924, where she met her future husband, John Herrmann. There Herbst worked to complete her never-published first novel, "Following the Circle." After her return to America in 1925 with Herrmann, and their marriage in 1926, Herbst published *Nothing is Sacred* (1928), a novel based loosely on her Sioux City background. At a stone farmhouse in Erwinna, Pennsylvania, which she made her permanent home, Herbst completed *Money For Love* (1929), a rather experimental novel in terms of its purposefully lean characterization and stripped-down style. Her growing political awareness developed into activism in the late 1920s and propelled Herbst into journalism. During the 1930s, she reported on the Scottsboro Trial for *New Masses*, wrote of agrarian protests in the Midwest, and reported sympathetically on the revolutionary movement in Cuba following the general strike of 1935. Herbst also traveled as a correspondent to Nazi Germany and to Spain during the Spanish civil war, consolidating her reputation as an anti-Fascist, radical intellectual.

As her biographer Elinor Langer points out, Herbst's reputation today rests upon her depression-era trilogy about the Trexler-Wendel family: *Pity Is Not Enough* (1933), *The Executioner Waits* (1934), and *Rope of Gold* (1939). Herbst's trilogy explores the development of American society from the Civil War to the depression through the story of a single family. Often compared to John Dos Passos' *USA*, the novels are collective and panoramic, and Herbst provides an ironic counterpoint to her family narrative with prose inserts that chronicle actual historical events. Most critics consider these three novels to be a significant contribution to social realism and the radical fiction of the 1930s. After her divorce from John Herrmann in 1940, Herbst wrote two more novels, *Satan's Sargeants* (1941) and *Somewhere The Tempest Fell* (1947), works considered less successful than her 1930s novels. In 1954, Herbst turned to new genres, publishing *New Green World*, a biography of American naturalists John and William Bartram, and a novella, *Hunter of Doves*, now considered to be one of her finest literary efforts. During her later years, Herbst published three short memoirs about her life in the 1920s and 1930s, "The Starched Blue Sky of Spain" and "A Year of Disgrace" (in *Noble Savage*, 1960, 1961), and "Yesterday's Road" (in *New American Review*, 1968). She died in New York City of cancer in 1969.

• Josephine Herbst's personal papers, correspondence, and the manuscripts of some of her novels are in the Collection of American Literature in the Beinecke Rare Book and Manuscript Library of Yale University. See also Elinor Langer, *Josephine Herbst* (1984). Winifred Farrant Bevilacqua, *Josephine Herbst* (1985).

Michele S. Ware

HERMAPHRODITE. Possessing the sex organs and some of the secondary sexual characteristics of both the male and the female, the hermaphrodite is the literal or physical embodiment of androgyny (the psychological blending of both sexes). In different mythological traditions, the hermaphrodite has been celebrated as representing the merging of opposites or despised for its anarchic potentialities. In the modern Western psychoanalytic tradition, the hermaphrodite has been the subject of much clinical investigation and speculation, especially in the work of Carl G. Jung. Recent speculative fiction, most notably Ursula *Le Guin's *Left Hand of Darkness* (1969), has made the figure of the hermaphrodite a starting place for examination of the cultural construction of gender differences.

[*See also* Androgyny; Transsexuality.]

• Marie Delcourt, *Hermaphrodite: Myths and Rites of the Bisexual Figure in Classical Antiquity* (1961). Wendy Doniger O'Flaherty, *Women, Androgynes, and Other Mythical Beasts* (1980).

Cathy N. Davidson

HETEROSEXISM. The term *heterosexism* emerged out of the combined traditions of the feminist and the gay/lesbian liberation movements. Building on the root word *sexism*, it implies the effects of both a system of gender inequality and compulsory heterosexuality, and emphasizes the way these two forms of oppression are often crucially and inextricably linked. Heterosexism can be distinguished from homophobia in that it is not based on individual fears, but on an individual or institutional privileging of heterosexuality over any other sexuality. Heterosexist acts include establishing heterosexuality as the "natural" sexuality and discriminating against homosexuals.

Katie Kent

HETEROSEXUALITY. Heterosexuality is both the least adequately theorized and the most highly visible *sexuality in American literature. When it emerged as a distinct sexual category around 1900, American women had been writing about heterosexual institutions and experiences for approximately 200 years. Twentieth-century women writers extended this tradition—writing, for the most part, with a knowledge of sexual variance and consciousness of sexual categories their predecessors lacked. On the whole, these documents represent the (hetero)sexual understandings, attitudes, and experiences of American women whose material circumstances allowed or encouraged them to write in the first place and whose (seeming) adherence to prevailing ideologies enabled them to be published in the second.

The cultural predisposition to view heterosexuality as though it were the only sexuality (a perduring perspective) or the natural outcome of human sexual development (a modern notion) has inhibited heterosexuals from analyzing heterosex as such. This is not to say there are no theories of heterosexuality in American women: however, it is to say the theories are recent, scarce, and incomplete. For instance, in the 1970s, feminists produced a powerful analysis of institutionalized heterosexuality which not only addressed the social privileges and legal rights accrued by heterosexual women but also the virtual omnipresence of heterosexual images in American culture. The obvious merits of this analysis are its ability to account for the widespread presumption of heterosexuality within the United States and the sociopolitical incentives that lead American women to become heterosexual. Heterosexuality can never be explained solely as the effect of cultural conditioning. Rather, the theorist must always ask how desire comes into play. For heterosexuals, the question of desire has only begun to be raised. It must be accompanied by other questions that attempt to think heterosexuality in relation to *race, *ethnicity, and *class. These relations assume the salience they do because white middle-class women have habitually spoken for and about women whose sexual experiences, norms, and self-understandings they do not necessarily share. Consider the following example from the nineteenth century.

With the exception of the first few agrarian decades, the dominant meaning of (hetero)sexuality during the nineteenth century was informed by the socioeconomic interests and racial ethos of white middle-class women, many of whom were married. These women wrote about a variety of sexual subjects including courtship, married life, *pregnancy, *childbirth, prostitution, and *rape. The (hetero)sexual meanings they brought to these subjects and the standard of sexuality they extended in writing was based upon a *gender system in which the sexual drive and sexual license were coded as male, while maternal instinct and morality (defined by chastity outside of *marriage and, at minimum, the subordination of sexual desire to "higher ends" within marriage) were coded as female. In effect, this gendered construction of sexuality produced the "naturally asexual woman" and her sexed antithesis, the "naturally licentious man." By deploying this antithetical couple, white middle-class women lay claim to a moral superiority that worked to secure their influence at home and abroad. Certainly, their definition did not operate to the advantage of all women; indeed, it operated to the indisputable disadvantage of some. At the very least, the material circumstances of women who were neither white nor middle class and the potentially different sexual experiences to which these circumstances gave rise were rendered invisible as all sexualities were assimilated to the sexuality of the "socially pure woman."

The social reformers' construction of the female prostitute as a "tragic victim" of man's lust is an evident case in point, since it denies the historical existence of women who chose to earn their living as prostitutes. At worst, the social purity definition did violence to women who could not be expected to share the privileges of white middle-class women but were held accountable to the same social norm. This is the existentially impossible position from which Harriet *Jacobs wrote and published *Incidents in the Life of a Slave Girl.* Jacobs' access to an audience (via mass publication), her ability to mobilize it against the slave system, and her claim to womanhood (social purity) depended on her use of the white middle-class trope. And use it she did. For as Hazel Carby and other contemporary critics have shown,

Jacob's strategic deployment of the "pure woman" turned the tables on those who would define her by exposing the particularity of their class and racial ethos, which could not be applied cross-culturally without denying the material conditions in which slave women were compelled to live ("I feel that slave women ought not to be judged by the same standards. . . .") and by claiming the right to define herself ("I knew what I did [in taking a lover] and I did it with deliberate calculation, . . . [since] it seems less degrading to give one self [to one man] than to submit to [a slave master's] compulsion").

Disquieting similarities link the past century to our own. Thus, on a number of occasions and in response to different events, white middle-class women have assumed that the sexuality of female prostitutes was the mirror image of their own. This assumption has motivated several antithetical articulations. One, representing prostitutes as like victims of male lust and/or * pornography, attained some popularity during the 1970s and early 1980s. The other, depicting them as sources of sexual disease, emerged near the turn of the century when the national incidence of syphilis sharply increased and again in the 1980s under the aegis of * AIDS. The first of these constructions most nearly approximates that of the 19th-century social reformers in content and effect. In particular, the metaphoric substitution of "sexual victim" for sex-workers displaces the different self-understandings of prostitutes themselves, who effectively disappear behind the mask of white middle-class women's heterosexuality. The last two constructions are but the flip side of the first. Not only do these images of the prostitute as a "sexual monstrosity" work to establish her difference from the sexually disciplined white middle-class heterosexual, they also function as proofs of her inhumanity: that is, of nonbeing itself.

Why has women's sexuality been stereotyped as white heterosexual? These are complicated questions. However, two partial explanations might be advanced. First, * racism and * classism motivate these constructions on covert and overt levels. Second, the proliferation of sexual understandings, "lifestyles," and experiences in the twentieth century, along with the emergence of sexual identities and the growing visibility of sexual minorities, have produced an understanding of "authentic" female sexuality that judges sexual variation as a threat.

[See also Bisexuality; Lesbianism; Pornography, Prostitution; Sexualities; Transexuality]

Kate Cummings

HISPANIC-AMERICAN WRITING. See Assimilation; Chicana Writing; Citizenship; Cuban-American Writing; Immigrant Writing; Latina Writing; Puerto Rican Writing.

HISTORIANS. Of the thousands of women who have written significant history in the United States, Hannah Adams (1755–1831) of Massachusetts is credited with being the first. Her histories of Christian sects (1784) and of New England (1799) were commercially successful. Taught Latin, Greek, and other languages by a succession of student boarders, Adams, like many other women, had financial motives for writing: "It was poverty . . . that first induced me to become an author." Mercy Otis * Warren (1728–1814), Adams's contemporary and a member of New England's political elite, wrote copious political satire, plays, verse, and tracts during the American Revolution, but her enduring fame came from the spirited defense of republicanism in her three-volume history of the Revolution (1805). Not writing from any institutional base, these authors set some of the themes for the next century of women's historical writing.

To the theme of patriotism subsequent authors added the theme of women themselves and thus produced the kind of heroic narrative that amateur men were also writing. Like may other women historians Elizabeth * Ellet (1812?–1877) wrote in multiple genres, but Women of the American Revolution (1848), Pioneer Women of the West (1852), The Queens of American Society (1867), and many other works of history overshadowed her other writing. Fascinated with the republican tradition, Lydia Maria * Child (1802–1880) wrote The Rebels, or Boston before the Revolution (1825), Memoirs of Madame de Stael and of Madame Roland (1832), Good Wives (1833), and a two-volume History and Condition of Women in Various Nations (1835). Child wrote prodigiously to support her family, and as an active member of social-reform groups, she fostered writing about Native Americans and the slave experience. Pauline Wright was among the first to produce a history of feminism in her History of the National Woman's Rights Movement (1871), a work that was followed by histories of the movement in individual states and by the encyclopedic History of Woman Suffrage (1881).

From the mid-nineteenth century, American men, influenced by the new historical science practiced in German universities, began focusing on political history, organizing professional training in universities, and stressing archival research in their work. But the amateurs continued to push their work in social history. Martha Lamb (1829–1893), editor of the Magazine of *American History*, made sophisticated forays into describing social life, especially in her *History of New York* (1877). Alice Morse *Earle (1851–1911) wrote many histories of colonial America, detailing its household artifacts, child life, customs, and women's and household work, among other topics. Earle is only one of the most accomplished of many similar women social historians writing outside the academy.

Women also played an important role as local and regional historians, collecting artifacts, *diaries, and *letters, organizing local historical societies, taking down oral histories, preserving historic buildings, writing important histories , and editing regional historical journals. Societies such as the Daughters of the American Revolution, Society of Colonial Dames, and United Daughters of the Confederacy, all of them founded late in the nineteenth century, sought to promote one or another version of the American past. In most cases these societies were racist and concerned about preserving white power in the face of increasing immigration and rapid social change. One of the most active of the many local historians, Mildred Rutherford (1851–1928) wrote as teacher and principal of Lucy Cobb Institute many textbooks and most notably *The South in Literature and History* (1907), a work arguing that southern history had been slighted and twisted in most versions of the American past.

Meanwhile, women, too, began receiving graduate training at universities across the country, Kate Ernest Levi being the first woman who earned the doctorate in 1893. Levi took her degree at the University of Wisconsin because midwestern universities were most receptive of women scholars. Between 1893 and the mid-1930s, women earned 16 percent of all Ph.D.s in history, but by the late twenties they were receiving some 22 percent. However, because of discrimination against women in the profession, they held few of the positions in universities, with most opportunity confined to positions in women's colleges. Thus, women with advanced training in history looked for other jobs, notably in high schools, welfare organizations, libraries, and government research. When they did find college jobs, women had very heavy teaching loads, which, along with restrictions on their entering such research facilities as Widener library at Harvard, hampered their writing. In addition, the American Historical Association, which held its first annual meeting in 1884, discriminated against women by including few as speakers or as officers of the association, and by restricting social functions at the annual and other meetings to men only. In response, women historians banded together to form the Lakeville Conference in 1930; in 1936, the group became the Berkshire Conference of Women Historians. After more than a decade lobbying, these women succeeded in getting Nellie Neilson of Mount Holyoke College elected president of the AHA in 1943.

Many women historians in the academy before World War II clustered in traditional fields of expertise such as medieval and English history, but they also worked in Latin American, western American, and modern European history. While most adopted the standards for archival work and political topics, others like Lucy Maynard Salmon (1853–1927), who stressed the seminar method in her teaching at Vassar College, began laying the foundations for a professionalized women's history. Having written a prize-winning study of the appointing power of the U.S. presidency, Salmon next wrote on domestic servants and by the early twentieth century was composing such essays as "On Beds and Bedding," "The Family Cookbook," and "Ode to the Kitchen Sink." Her "History in a Backyard" proposed that historical material could be found outside the archive and even in domestic space, while her two-volume study of the newspaper (1921–1923) compared the much-undervalued newspaper with traditional historical material. Salmon's merger of professional standards with eccentric material was matched in innovation by the historical work of Mary *Beard (1876–1921), who from outside the academy inserted cultural material and information on women into the vast History of American Civilization series (coauthored with her husband Charles). Beard also wrote documentary histories of women that dramatically revised U.S. history, while her *Woman as Force in History* (1946) also challenged the then-current feminist belief that women had made few contributions to history because of past oppression.

These pioneering works were inspirational to the sudden eruption of women's history from the late 1960s on, but the more important motivation for change came from the rebirth of feminism and the *civil rights movement during those years. Many aspects of the amateur tradition remained—for example, the production of historical novels and the work in local history societies—but the percentage of women in the profession began mounting again after reaching a low point in the 1950s and early 1960s, and increasing numbers of women historians turned their attention to women's history. They continued to work in social history, but the attention the academy as a whole now gave to this field validated their efforts. Anne Firor Scott wrote *The Southern Lady*; Gerda Lerner studied white reformers of the antebellum period and relations between black and white women; Natalie Zemon Davis looked at charivaris and rituals of sexual misrule in the early modern period; and Joan Kelly explored the condition of women to ask "Did Women Have a Renaissance?" These women and many others also started women's history courses, circulating mimeographed bibliographies and syllabi across the continent, and in 1973 the Berkshire Conference of Women's Historians held its first conference on women's history, some of whose papers were published in *Clio's Consciousness Raised* (1974, eds. Mary Hartman and Lois Banner). By the 1990s, there were professional journals, thousands of courses, majors and minors, and even endowed chairs in women's history. Still active across the intellectual spectrum of the discipline, women historians served as department chairs and officers of professional associations: as the AHA entered its second century, Natalie Z. Davis was elected the second woman president in 1985, and in 1992, Louise Tilly became the third.

Women's history, however, continued to attract the most interest, and as the genre matured some challenged the focus on social history, including the study of working women, prostitutes, and the needy. *But Some of Us Are Brave* (1982, eds. Gloria Hull, Patricia Bell Scott, and Barbara Smith) contended that both black and women's history neglected African-American women, and subsequently Paula Giddings, Darlene Hines, Nell Painter, and others produced both synthetic works and monographs. At a 1988 conference about graduate education in U.S. women's history, Rosalyn Terborg-Penn, in a speech of a single sentence, maintained: "I have only one thing to say: Race." Claims that issues of sexual orientation were crucial to historical understanding led to such important works as Estelle Freedman and John d'Emilio's *Intimate Matters* (1988) and *Hidden from History* (1990, ed. Martha Vicinus). Finally, Joan Scott, who became the first woman historian on the faculty of the Institute for Advanced Study, challenged the direction taken by women's history in "Gender: A Useful Category of Historical Analysis" (1986), which proposed exploring the production of masculinity and femininity as intertwined concepts. Scott's forceful argument led many women historians to adopt gender as their major theoretical focus, a move that also took them into literary theory much as the work in earlier women's history had spawned connections with anthropology.

In 1991, women received 37.5 percent of the doctorates in history and women of color formed 8.8 percent of those recipients. But these historians had changed the discipline beyond their numbers. They were bringing gender to a range of subfields, for instance, Londa Scheibinger rewriting the history of science, Asuncion Lavrin rewriting Latin American history, or Margaret Strobel rewriting the history of imperialism from a gendered perspective. Besides gender women historians were at the forefront of acquainting historians with postmodernist theory and even in pioneering new subfields, as with Lynn Hunt and the "new cultural history." Women historians were active in international meetings and were especially important in forging international ties among women scholars globally.

[*See also* Art Historians.]

• Kathryn Kish Sklar, "American Female Historians in Context, 1770–1930," *Feminist Studies* 3, nos. 1–2 (1975–1976): 171–184. Bonnie G. Smith, "The Contribution of Women to Modern Historiography in Great Britain, France, and the United States, 1750–1940," the *American Historical Review* 89 (June 1984): 709–732. Nancy F. Cott, *A Woman Making History: Mary Ritter Beard through Her Letters* (1991). Jacqueline Goggin, "Challenging Sexual Discrimination in the Historical Profession: Women Historians and the American Historical Association, 1890–1940," *American Historical Review* 97 (June 1992): 769–802. Judith Zinsser, *A Glass Half Full: The Impact of Feminism on History* (1993).

Bonnie G. Smith

HISTORICAL FICTION. Diversity is the key word to describe historical fiction written by African-American, white middle-class, Native American, Latina, and Asian-American women. Without simplifying the techniques and themes of this rich genre, one might characterize American women's historical fiction as that in which historical events are pivotal, fiction in which the multiple historical roles women have played are revealed. Women's historical fiction has explored women's connection with the public arena as well as their relationships to and reflections on history within private and inner spaces.

As it emerged during the nineteenth century, African-American women's historical fiction struggled to counter negative stereotypes imposed on blacks for generations at the same time as the fiction sought to celebrate women's roles in history. Harriet *Wilson's *Our Nig; or Sketches from the Life of a Free Black* (1859), the first novel by an African-American woman, underscores the courage and integrity of women consigned to indentured servitude. Most early African-American historical fiction, although inspired by narratives such as Harriet *Jacobs's *Incidents in the Life of a Slave Girl* (1861), nevertheless shied away from graphic depictions of slavery. Frances *Harper's *Iola Leroy*, rather than detailing Iola's experiences as a slave, focuses on the heroism Iola exhibited in nursing wounded soldiers during the * Civil War, and her success at reuniting her own family, separated by slavery. Pauline * Hopkins's *Winona: A Tale of Negro Life in the South and Southwest* (1902) is a historical romance involving slave trading, the * Underground Railroad, and John Brown's Free Soilers. Hopkins's *Contending Forces* (1900) explores African-American women's historical contributions after Emancipation, highlighting, for example, the Black Women's * Club Movement, which actively fought against discrimination and lynching. Furthermore, Hopkins suggests the historical impact of less visible women's gatherings such as sewing circles, where political discussions involve such subjects as African-American women's sexual exploitation by white men. Hopkins also explores the inner, psychological impact of slavery and racism.

Early twentieth-century black writers Nella * Larsen, Zora Neale * Hurston, and Ann * Petry did not take history as their primary subject. In the 1960s, however, women's historical fiction reemerged. In 1966, Margaret * Walker published *Jubilee*, illustrating the fortitude and transcendence of Walker's great-grandmother during slavery and its aftermath. Paule * Marshall's *The Chosen Place, the Timeless People* (1969) conveys the oppression of African-Caribbean people yoked by neocolonialism on an imaginary Caribbean island. Alice * Walker's *Meridian* (1976) reenacts the * civil rights era and the psychology and politics of relationships between blacks and whites. Harper's and Hopkins's concern with slavery and its legacies are voiced anew by contemporary writers Sherley Anne * Williams and Toni * Morrison. Williams's *Dessa Rose* (1986) fictionalizes the relationship between a white woman and a pregnant black woman who led an 1829 slave uprising. In Morrison's *Beloved* (1987) the reader shares a mother's haunted life, as she wrestles with her own spiritual and ethical challenges and tries to reconcile with the ghost of the daughter she killed to prevent the child's reenslavement. Morrison's earlier novel *Song of Solomon* (1976) explores the positive aspects of African-American family history, as does Alice Walker's *The Color Purple* (1982), an epistolary novel which retells and revises Walker's grandmother's life. In fact, much of Walker's fictional canon might be considered historical, including *The Third Life of Grange Copeland* (1970) and *Possessing the Secret of Joy* (1992).

Historical fiction by white women has been said to begin with two early nineteenth-century novels. Catherine * Sedgwick's *Hope Leslie* (1827), a historical romance set in seventeenth-century Massachusetts, concerns the lives not only of white immigrants but also of Mohawk peoples, whose customs and lifeways Sedgwick took care to research. Lydia Maria * Child's *Hobomok* (1824) fictionalizes an interracial marriage between a Puritan woman and a Native American man, allowing Child to indict the early settlers' racism and ethnocentrism. At the middle of the nineteenth century, the tradition of fiction looking back at Puritan life was picked up by Harriet Beecher * Stowe in *The Minister's Wooing* (1859), a novel deeply rooted in issues of Puritan theology. Late in the nineteenth and early in the twentieth century, historical fiction by white women enjoyed wide popularity. Edith * Wharton's first novel, *The Valley of Decision* (1902), is a long, ambitious fiction set in Renaissance Italy. A number of Ellen * Glasgow's early novels, which are interesting to compare with Harper's and Hopkins's treatments, set for themselves the project of looking at southern history, in Glasgow's case from a relatively privileged, racially moderate, white feminist point of view.

In the teens and into the 1920s, Willa * Cather consistently turned her attention to the past, imagining the lives on the western United States frontier of white pioneer and eastern European immigrants in books such as *O Pioneers!* (1913) and *My Ántonia* (1918); in 1927 her historical novel *Death Comes for the Archbishop* sympathetically portrays the establishment of European hegemony in the Southwest through imagining the lives of two French priests in what is now New Mexico, and Cather's last novel, *Sapphira and the Slave Girl* (1940) looks back to pre–Civil War Virginia to tell the tale of a ruthless and powerful white woman's failed attempt to victimize a young slave woman through plotting her rape.

Women's historical romances have always been extremely popular, and the contemporary industry of formulaic historical romances for mass female audiences speaks to the continuing popularity of the genre. Nineteenth-century writers such as Lydia Maria Child and Pauline * Hopkins infused this popular romance with serious political and social messages. Twentieth century writers have continued to mine the historical romance for its ability to politicize a wide audience. While Margaret * Mitchell's *Gone with the Wind* (1937) has boasted huge sales and continuous republication, it now stands in juxtaposition to Walker's *Jubilee*, a best-selling realistic novel that recasts Mitchell's glorified South from an African-American perspective. Artistically ambitious and politically challenging explorations of the popular romance also exist in the work of authors such as Joan Chase, who in 1983 published her retrospective about rural white women's experience, *During the Reign of the Queen of Persia*.

Native American literature, by all rights the quintessential American literature, reflects Euro-American oppression by the very invisibility the literature has suffered until recently. Beginning with *Mourning Dove's 1927 novel *Cogewea*, Native American women's fiction communicates suppressed history of non-Western lifeways and values on the North American continent. Ethnologist Ella Cara Deloria's *Waterlily*, a novel written in 1944 but not published until 1988, recreates the lives of the Dakotas, or Sioux, before the white man colonized the western plains. An early Native American novel written from a women's perspective, Deloria's novel was intended for a wide audience and reveals women's challenging roles, especially in relation to family and culture. Leslie Marmon *Silko's *Ceremony* (1977) shows the struggles of a former Japanese prisoner during World War II who returns to his Laguna Pueblo reservation hoping for peace and sanctuary. Silko's protagonist must instead investigate his cultural history in order to find tranquility. Louise *Erdrich's *Love Medicine* (1984), spanning the years between 1934 and 1984, focuses on three Chippewa families and the relationships among them. Its successor, *The Beet Queen* (1986), is more concerned with Euro-American than Native American characters; Erdrich's determination to use historical fiction to retell the past from Indian points of view reemerges in *Tracks* (1988). Continuing this tradition of historical fiction, Linda *Hogan penned *Mean Spirit* in 1990. Hogan's epic, like its precursors, bespeaks the deep connection with nature that infuses her culture, as Hogan portrays Euro-American exploitation of Indians during the Oklahoma oil boom in the 1920s.

As with most writing by women of color, an intertwined artistic and political mission permeates contemporary Chicana and Latina writing. Works such as Gloria *Anzaldúa's *Borderlands/La Frontera* (1987) freely intermingle Spanish and English to infuse fiction with the historical biculturality experienced by Chicanas. Contrastingly sharply with Nicholasa *Mohr's *El Bronx Remembered* (1975), which details the poverty and oppression of Puerto Ricans struggling to realize the American Dream in the barrio during the 1940s, are two works about women whose families have left the homeland primarily for political reasons. Julia Alvarez's novel of interlocking stories, *How the Garcia Girls Lost Their Accents* (1991), captures the experience of newly immigrated Latinas from the Dominican Republic, as Alvarez looks

back to 1956 and the terrors of Trujillo's reign. Cristina Garcia's *Dreaming in Cuban* (1992), moves back and forth between Cuba and Brooklyn, her characters trying to understand the effects of Castro's 1959 revolution.

Historical fiction by Asian-American women writers has burgeoned since the Second World War in particular. History is a major preoccupation in the work of Maxine Hong *Kingston. Her novel *The Woman Warrior* (1976) entwines a young woman's coming-of-age story with wide-ranging historical matter and myth from both the United States and China. *China Men* (1980) chronicles the exploitation of Chinese labor in the material construction of America and particularly the railroads in the nineteenth century; *Tripmaster Monkey* (1989) is set in 1960s America. Historical themes also appear in Hisaye *Yamamoto's *Seventeen Syllables and Other Stories* (1988), a collection of interlocking stories that fictionalize prewar and postwar lives of Japanese Americans, focusing especially on generational conflicts. Amy *Tan's *The Joy Luck Club* (1989) demonstrates a similar preoccupation with generational conflicts, as Tan moves back and forth between pre-1949 China and the contemporary United States.

Focusing on these particular works should suggest that historical fiction is an enormous, complex body of literature. Increasingly, American women from all cultures and ethnicities, many of whom have not been considered here, are writing fiction about their histories. As authors reconsider the ways in which women have participated in history, so will this canon continue to diversify, enriching our understanding of the history we all, to some degree, share.

[*See also* Novel, Beginnings of the.]

Jane Campbell

HOBSON, Laura Z. (1900–1986), novelist, short story writer, and advertising copywriter for Time, Inc. and other firms. Hobson's Russian Jewish parents, Michael Zametkin and Adella Kean Zametkin, were political activists in New York City. Michael Zametkin was the first editor of the *Jewish Daily Forward*, preceding the more famous Abraham Cahan, and Adella Zametkin gave advice to homemakers in Yiddish in her column in *The Day*. As a child, Hobson was embarrassed by her parents' protests against injustice; however, their teaching stayed with her all her life. Her novels forthrightly protest anti-Semitism, the oppression of women, and bigotry against people of color and gays.

Hobson's novels grew out of her life's experiences. *The Trespassers* (1943), her first novel, describes the asylum movement of World War II, in which Americans sponsored families who were fleeing Nazi terrorism; Hobson herself had successfully sponsored a family. Her 1964 *First Papers* fictionalizes her coming of age in the early years of the century: a newly arrived Jewish family and a Gentile family confront the problems of growing up, xenophobia, and religious and cultural differences. Hobson's 1971 *The Tenth Month* describes the subterfuge in which a single, forty-year-old woman must engage in order to have a child—an experience lived by Hobson herself in 1941. *Over and Above* (1979) was not a critical success; however, this novel about intergenerational love and conflict, in which a grandmother, mother, and daughter learn to live with their differences, is a refreshing study of a subject not often covered in depth.

Hobson wrote her most famous novels at the beginning and end of her career. The first, *Gentleman's Agreement* (1947), tells the story of Phil Green, a reporter with a tough assignment: find a new angle for a series of articles on anti-Semitism. Green decides that, although he is a Gentile, he will tell people that he is Jewish. Green experiences bigotry firsthand; as novel and article unfold, the jokes, racist comments, and stereotyping that "nice people" participate in are revealed. *Gentleman's Agreement*, whose title refers to the way neighborhoods kept themselves free of the "wrong sort," was made into a movie that won the New York Film Critics' Award in 1947, and in 1948, received the Academy Award for Best Picture.

Hobson was seventy-five when she wrote *Consenting Adult*, a novel that explores the relations between a married couple, Tessa and Ken Lynn, and their son Jeff, who has just informed them that he is gay. *Consenting Adult* became a made-for-TV movie in 1985 and won the Alliance of Lesbian and Gay Artists' Media Award.

Besides two westerns written with Thayer Hobson under the pen name Peter Field, Laura Hobson wrote short stories, screenplays, and advertising campaigns for Time, Inc., including "The March of Time," "Life Begins . . ." (which inaugurated *Life Magazine* in 1936), and 1957's "Know" campaign. Her other novels include *The Other Father* (1950), *The Celebrity* (1951), and *Untold Millions* (1982). Her children's books are *A Dog of His Own* (1940) and *I'm Going to Have a Baby* (1964). Hobson's two-volume autobiography is called *Laura Z: A Life* (1983–1986).

Cathy Downs

HOGAN, Linda (b. 1947), Chickasaw poet, fiction writer, playwright, and essayist. Using "in-tuitive and common language," Hogan's writing makes us listen to voices too often ignored—women, Native people, the natural world, the earth itself—and explores their interconnection through concrete, multilayered images. Rather than "telling the truth," Hogan's writing "clarifies the world without muddling life with the bias of fact."

Raised in Colorado and southern Oklahoma, Hogan received an M.A. in Creative Writing in 1978. She has taught at Colorado Women's College and the University of Minnesota, and is currently an Associate Professor at the University of Colorado–Boulder. Hogan is the author of several poetry collections: *Calling Myself Home* (1979); *Daughters, I Love You* (1981); *Eclipse* (1984); *Seeing Through the Sun* (1985), which won an American Book Award from the Before Columbus Foundation; *Savings* (1988); and *The Book of Medicines* (1993). Her fiction includes *That Horse* (1985), *Mean Spirit* (1990), and *Solar Storms* (1994). *Red Clay* (1991) reprints *Calling Myself Home* and *That Horse*. She has also written a play, *A Piece of Moon* (1981), which won the Five Civilized Tribes Museum Playwriting Award, as well as two screenplays, *Aunt Moon* (1986) and *Mean Spirit* (1986). She is the recipient of many awards, including a 1986 NEA fiction grant and a 1991–1993 Guggenheim Fellowship. Her writing has appeared in numerous anthologies, including *Spider Woman's Granddaughters* (1989), *That's What She Said* (1984), and *A Gathering of Spirit* (1988), and she is a co-editor of *The Stories We Hold Secret: Tales of Women's Spiritual Development* (1986). Her next novel centers on fishing treaty rights in Wisconsin.

Hogan's hauntingly suspenseful novel, *Mean Spirit*, chronicles the destruction of Native life that followed the 1920s Oklahoma oil boom. Combining fact and fiction, including stories from her own family, Hogan's complex plot exposes the schemes of murder and deception familiar to indigenous people: how the Dawes Allotment Act of 1887 cheated American Indians out of tribal land; how the forced removal of Native children into government schools severed families; and how white men married Indian women to steal their land. With breathtaking poetry and oral storytelling rhythms, Hogan captures the inevitable clash between a Native world that wanted "nothing more than to be left in peace" and a white world that viewed them as "a locked door to the house of progress." Despite its portrayal of relentless violence, the novel captures the incredible will to survive that has sustained Native cultures through centuries of attempted annihilation.

• Brian Swann and Arnold Krupat, eds., *I Tell You Now: Autobiographical Essays by Native American Writ-*

ers (1987). William Balassi et al., eds., *This Is About Vision: Interviews with Southwestern Writers* (1990). Laura Coltelli, *Winged Words: American Indian Writers Speak* (1990). Janet Sternburg, ed., *The Writer on Her Work*, vol. 2 (1991).

Kayann Short

HOLLEY, Marietta (1836–1926), humorist, novelist, and poet. Holley was born near Adams, New York, a small town near Lake Ontario that she made famous as Jonesville, the home of her popular heroine of twenty-one books, Samantha Allen. Holley, the youngest of seven children, had been forced to leave school at fourteen to help on the family farm. With the early death of her father, Holley sought a means of supporting her beloved mother and reclusive sister. After a number of false starts, she found success with one of the first positive female characters in American comic writing, which she may have created in reaction against Frances Whitcher's Widow Bedott. Holley herself was a shy woman, who remained single, did not move far from her home, and turned down many opportunities to become a public speaker.

Holley has been seen as a bridge between dialect, wise fool *humor, *sentimental novels whose pathos appeared in the anecdotes used by her heroine Samantha, and the regionalist writers of the turn of the century. In her own time, Frances Willard, Susan B. *Anthony, and Clara Barton saw her as the voice of *suffrage, *temperance, and justice, and often sent her suggestions for her episodic stories, which reached a wide audience through magazines as well as books. Samantha, always identified as the hard-working wife of Josiah Allen, a hardscrabble farmer, tests everything against her common sense, in particular the farmer himself, who presents the standard prejudices against women, only to be laughed at by his larger, stronger, and more reasonable wife. For example, she explores what literally being on a pedestal would be like for a woman who still has chores to do. The relationship between Josiah and Samantha made Holley's moderate Christian *feminism acceptable to a wide audience. Samantha's other foils are women like Betsey Bobbet, an old maid made foolish precisely because she accepts society's ideas about women and does not cultivate self-reliance, and even public figures such as Ulysses S. Grant, whom Samantha berates at the Centennial for prosecuting Susan B. Anthony. Holley's best works are her earlier ones, including *Josiah Allen's Wife as a P.A. (Public Advisor) and P.I. (Private Investigator): Samantha at the Centennial* (1877), *Sweet Cicely: Josiah Allen as a Politician* (1885), and the very popular *Samantha at Saratoga* or *"Flirtin' with Fashion"* (1887). *Samantha on the Race Problem* (1894) reveals the difficulty the *women's movement had dealing with the question of voting rights for African-Americans.

• Marietta Holley, *Samantha Rastles the Woman Question*, ed. Jane Curry (1983). Kate H. Winter, *Marietta Holley: Life with "Josiah Allen's Wife"* (1984).

Patricia L. Morse

HOLOCAUST WRITING. American writers were long reluctant to address the Holocaust imaginatively. Ambivalence about whether imagination should or could transform the Holocaust into an artistic form was often resolved by silence. However, the Eichmann Trial, the 1967 Arab-Israeli War, and the increasing accessibility of Holocaust scholarship have led to the emergence of a significant American Holocaust canon. Writing by émigré and native-born American women has been important to its creation.

The experiences and perceptions of Jewish women in the Holocaust have often been obscured or absorbed into accounts and interpretations of male experience. Among the recurrent subjects of Holocaust writing by men and women are ghetto and concentration camp conditions, wartime survival strategies, and postwar survivor syndrome. Female Holocaust writing differs from that by males in its inclusion of gender-specific suffering and coping strategies. It demonstrates how women's Holocaust experience was affected by their biological roles as childbearers and their gender socialization as nurturers and homemakers. Women writers portray female prisoners' heightened vulnerability as sexual beings, as menstruating and pregnant women, as victims of sexual assault and sexually determined medical experimentation, and as mothers. This literature echoes survivor testimonies that attribute women's better survival record to their gender socialization fostering nurturing, bonding, and domestic skills as opposed to the education of men, which stresses independence and competition.

Victims' suffering and coping is presented directly in works set in ghettos and concentration camps across Europe or indirectly through memory, nightmare, and imagery in postwar settings. The danger-filled world of the Jewish fugitive is central to Elzbieta Ettinger's *Kindergarten* (1970). The distinctive circumstances of a "half-caste of the first degree," benefitting from one parent's German status and suffering from the other's Jewish status, is explored by Hana Demetz in the autobiographical novel *The House on Prague Street* (1970). Marge *Piercy charts the tribulations of French Jews subject to the restrictive decrees of the collaborating Vichy government, the massive arrests and deportations of native-born and naturalized French Jews, and their militant response in *Gone to Soldiers* (1987). Susan Fromberg Schaeffer (*Anya*, 1974), Ilona Karmel (*An Estate of Memory*, 1969), and Ettinger chronicle the hardships of the Vilna, Krakow, and Warsaw ghettos, respectively—their overcrowding, abysmal housing, starvation rations, lack of sanitation, slave labor policies, early mass killings, and Jewish resistance efforts. Harold and Edith Lieberman set their play *Throne of Straw* (1972) in the Lodz ghetto to examine the moral dilemma of its Jewish leader and the prisoners who struggle to balance obedience to the German overlords with efforts to save a remnant of the Jewish people. Although Irena Klepfisz's play *Bread and Candy: Songs of the Holocaust* (1991) is staged as a Holocaust memorial and focuses on responses of child survivors in their adult years and on children of survivors, their dialogue and songs depict ghetto adversity and the heroic efforts and achievements of the Vilna partisans. Concentration camp persecution and atrocities are extensively delineated in Karmel's Plaszow and Skarzysko, Schaeffer's Kaiserwald, and Piercy's Dora Nordhausen and Auschwitz. Each writer portrays the systematic efforts to dehumanize the victims before their murder.

Survival trauma is a recurrent theme of American Holocaust fiction and drama. In accord with the psychiatric literature identifying paranoia, emotional isolation, and stress-induced illness as symptoms of survivor syndrome, fictional survivor protagonists maintain emotional and intellectual distance from non-survivors and frequently suffer unbidden memories, nightmares, and free association of unrelated postwar images with wartime trauma. Cynthia *Ozick's *Cannibal Galaxy* (1983) and "Rosa" (1983), Schaeffer's *Anya*, and Barbara Lebow's play *Shayna Maidel* (1985) explore the physical and psychological consequences of Holocaust trauma. Guilt for outliving families and friends, failure to pursue prewar ambitions and professions, and sharply circumscribed lives often characterize fictional survivors.

Complementing the focus on survivor syndrome is the attention of writers to survivor mission. This is manifested politically, in Piercy's and Adrienne *Rich's advocacy of Zionism; culturally, through Schaeffer's and Ozick's protagonists (in Anya's fierce attachment to preservation of the Jewish people and in Hester Lilt's preservation of the Judaic literary legacy in *The Cannibal Galaxy*); and religiously, in survivors' efforts to perpetuate and transmit the Judaic liturgical legacy in Ozick's *Trust* (1966) and "Bloodshed."

Direct expressions of post-Holocaust consciousness are embodied in immigrant-survivor protagonists and their children, who probe moral and intellectual dimensions of the Holocaust. How to live with Holocaust knowledge is examined by Irena Klepfisz in her play, by Rebecca Goldstein in "The Legacy of Raizel Kadish: A Story" (1985), and by Gloria Goldreich in *Four Days* (1980). An elegiac mode and prosecutor's judgment converge in Norma Rosen's novel, *Touching Evil* (1969), which chronicles the enduring impact of Holocaust awareness on two generations of sympathetic American Gentile women, one learning of Holocaust atrocities through photojournalism of camp liberations and the other discovering Holocaust history from the televised Eichmann trial.

Debunking the myth of Jews passively acquiescing to Nazism, these writers depict Jewish spiritual and militant resistance. Active resistance is central to Piercy's heavily researched novel and is accorded attention by Karmel, Schaeffer, and Ettinger. Incorporating many of the resistance roles Vera Laska documents in her anthology, *Women in the Resistance and in the Holocaust*, Piercy's Jewish women engage in missions as hazardous as those men perform, including attacks on the Milice and the German army. The concentration camp inmates of Piercy and Karmel are saboteurs, learning from oldtimers how to debilitate war materials they produce, to slack off at production, and to keep each other alive by stealing food and medicine. Piercy's and Ettinger's women, passing as Christians, work for the resistance in France and on the Aryan side in Poland.

The significance of female bonding to survival is a central theme of women's Holocaust testimony and creative writing. This is especially true in the feminist perspective of Piercy, Schaeffer, and Karmel, where cooperation among women engaged in resistance is crucial. Despite every effort to dehumanize them, women behave humanely. They share food; pick each other's lice; sustain each other through long, painful roll calls; nurse each other through illnesses and pregnancies; share memories, recipes, and literature to bolster their humanity; and strive to evade selection for death. Daughters adopting the maternal role toward their own debilitated mothers and women creating surrogate families after they have lost their own loved ones augment the survival chances and dignity of prisoners.

American elegiac poetry, sometimes inspired by victim testimonies, criminal trials, and Holocaust sites and memorials, mourns the victims as it condemns the perpetrators and their active and passive collaborators. In "The Amsterdam Poem," Maxine *Kumin writes of an American from Germantown, Pennsylvania, making a pilgrimage to Anne Frank's hiding place and juxtaposes Anne's nightmare reality with the tourist's Nazi nightmares. Contrasting a contemporary person's efforts to save a drowning bird with wartime disinterest in saving an endangered Jewish populace expresses the poet's moral outrage for the complicity of uninvolved bystanders. Ruth Whitman's "The Testing of Hanna Senesh," Elaine Mott's "On the Wings of the Wind," and Adrienne Rich's "Letters in the Family" memorialize Senesh, a young woman from Palestine who parachuted behind enemy lines, was brutally tortured, and yet, at her execution, urged continued defiance. Marge Piercy's "The Housing Project of Drancy" and "Black Mountain" chart her feelings during research at these sites, her bitter response to French efforts to obscure the truth of Drancy, and her feelings of sorrow for the fallen resistance fighters at Black Mountain. Denise *Levertov's trilogy, "During the Eichmann Trial," presents Eichmann as the technocrat of radical evil. She employs the image of Eichmann in the protective glass booth to warn of the human capacity for violence and insensibility to others' suffering, juxtaposes the oppressor's consumption of a meal and his order to gas thousands, and evokes the brutality of Crystal Night through the imagery of shattering glass. Anne *Sexton's dramatic speaker despairs of the horrors of Nazi violence, offering a litany of curses while death looks on indifferently in "After Auschwitz." Vividly evoking mountains of personal effects stolen from children in "The Concentration Camps" portion of "The Invocation to Kali," May *Sarton indicts us for putting murdered children and God out of mind. An Adrienne Rich persona in "Sources XVI" relates the vulnerability of Israeli Jews and diasporan Jews' anxiety for Israeli security to memories of the Holocaust and identification with Europe's slaughtered Jews.

Writers in each genre move beyond sorrow to articulate theological, ethical, and social concerns wrought by the Holocaust. They implicitly question how, in the heart of civilized Europe, an educated, rational people with traditional and religious upbringings were capable of pursuing unprecedented evil. They explicitly address the moral dilemmas of the oppressed. The authors consider whether survival of the group supersedes responsibility for individual survival, whether it is appropriate to improve one's own chances for survival if that entails exploiting fellow victims, whether collaboration with the enemy is ever justified, whether resistance is acceptable despite the possibility of massive retaliation, and myriad other quandaries arising from efforts to survive in a uni-verse designed to destroy life. These writers warn us against self-deception and remind us that we reveal our own propensity for evil when we fail to respond to others' humanity.

[See also Anti-Semitism; Jewish-American Writing.]

• Edward Alexander, Resonance of Dust: Essays on Holocaust Literature and Jewish Fate (1979). Sidra DeKoven Ezrahi, By Words Alone: The Holocaust in Literature (1980). Dorothy Seidman Bilik, Immigrant Survivors: Post-Holocaust Consciousness in Recent Jewish-American Fiction (1981). Alan L. Berger, Crisis and Covenant: The Holocaust in American Jewish Fiction (1985). Joan Ringelheim, "Women and the Holocaust: A Reconsideration of Research," Signs, 10, no. 4 (1985), pp. 741–761. Marlene E. Heinemann, Gender and Destiny: Women Writers and the Holocaust (1986). Robert Skloot, The Darkness We Carry: The Drama of the Holocaust (1988). S. Lillian Kremer, Witness Through the Imagination: Jewish American Holocaust Literature (1989).

S. Lillian Kremer

HOME. See Domestic Fiction; Family.

HOME ECONOMICS. See Education; Sociologists.

HOMOPHOBIA. According to the authors of "Male Homophobia" (1981), Stephen F. Morin and Ellen M. Garfinkle, the term homophobia originated in 1967 in a book by Wainwright Churchill, Homosexual Behavior among Males. Churchill actually coined the term homoerotophobia, which he used, in the words of Morin and Garfinkle, "to describe the fear of erotic or sexual contact with members of the same sex." In 1978, in "Scratching the Surface: Some Notes on Barriers to Women and Loving," Audre *Lorde began with this fear and expanded the definition to include the "hatred of [homosexual] feelings in others." In the Encyclopedia of Homosexuality (1990), Wayne Dynes elaborated on these definitions by outlining three different kinds of homophobia: institutional homophobia, individual homophobia, and internalized homophobia. Churchill and Lorde's definitions match most closely that of individual homophobia, which Dynes describes as the extremely hostile and physically, verbally, and emotionally violent behavior of individual persons toward gays and lesbians. Institutional homophobia refers to systems that perpetuate and encourage discrimination against gays and lesbians. Internalized homophobia, which Dynes also terms "self-hatred," refers to the negative images and *stereotypes perpetuated by a homophobic culture that a gay man or lesbian internalizes.

Critics of the term homophobia fault it for its emphasis on the individual. As Eve Kosofsky

Sedgwick (*Between Men: English Literature and Male Homosocial Desire*, 1985) has explained, the use of the word *phobia* to describe individual fear of homosexuals and homosexual desires tends to cover up or draw attention away from the more overarching ways in which homophobia is also concerned with keeping a heterosexist power structure in place. Furthermore, she argues that there is always the danger in reducing homophobia to the level of the individual psyche that violence against gays and lesbians can be excused as a form of illness or pathology, and therefore as out of the control of the perpetrator.

Homophobia can be distinguished from *heterosexism in that homophobia is based on fear of homosexual desires and feelings whereas heterosexism is based on the belief that heterosexuality is a superior form of *sexuality. Homophobia can produce heterosexism, but is not necessarily identical to it.

Recent revisions of the term have begun to try to account for the ways in which homophobia functions not only in terms of an irrational fear and/or hatred of one's own homosexual desires and of gays and lesbians, but also as a way of denying the gay man or lesbian access to his/her culture, family, ethnicity, region, religion, and race. In her book *Borderlands/La Frontera* (1987), Gloria *Anzaldúa discloses that one of her students mistakenly defined homophobia as the "fear of going home." Anzaldúa takes up this definition as one that enables her to describe the ways in which homophobia keeps a gay or lesbian person from feeling "at home" in his/her culture, race, ethnicity, family, and region of origin. In creating this definition of homophobia, Anzaldúa allows for the disparate effects of *race, *ethnicity, and culture on gay and lesbian identity.

[*See also* Lesbianism; Prejudice; Racism; Sexism.]

• Stephen F. Morin and Ellen M. Garfinkle, "Male Homophobia," in *GaySpeak: Gay Male and Lesbian Communication*, ed. James W. Chesebro (1981), pp. 117–129. Cherríe Moraga, *Loving in the War Years* (1983). Audre Lorde, "Scratching the Surface: Some Notes on Barriers to Women and Loving," in *Sister/Outsider* (1984), pp. 45–52. Gloria Anzaldúa, *Borderlands/La Frontera* (1987).

Katie Kent

HOMOSEXUALITY. *See* Lesbianism.

HOMOSOCIAL RELATIONSHIPS. While the success of women writers often derives from their sense of belonging to a female community, literature ordinarily privileges heterosexual bonding. Still, women in the United States have consistently written of the value of their homosocial relationships.

The roots of modern feminism go much deeper than the eighteenth- and nineteenth-century separate female spheres described in Carroll Smith-Rosenberg's "The Female World of Love and Ritual" (1975) and Nancy F. Cott's *The Bonds of Womanhood* (1977). Paula Gunn *Allen's translations demonstrate the importance of accounts of women's interdependence to Native American culture. Women's need for an interpretive community who empathize because of their gender is a recurrent theme in American women's literature, dramatized in Susan *Glaspell's play *Trifles* (1916), in Zora Neale *Hurston's novel *Their Eyes Were Watching God* (1937), in Maxine Hong *Kingston's fictionalized "memoir" *The Woman Warrior* (1976), and in Ana *Castillo's epistolary novel *The Mixquiahuala Letters* (1992), among many other texts.

Early novels, like Harriet Beecher *Stowe's *Uncle Tom's Cabin* (1852) and Sarah Orne *Jewett's *The Country of the Pointed Firs* (1896), and stories of race relations like Pauline E. *Hopkins's *Contending Forces* (1900), tend to imply that the affection and respect linking women offer a redemptive power to the culture as a whole. Texts by female expatriates, Gertrude *Stein's "Ada" (1922) and *H. D.'s *Tribute to the Angels* (1945), for example, suggest that the places where women's lives touch are their only true country.

Such contemporary novels as Marge *Piercy's *Small Changes* (1972), June *Arnold's *Sister Gin* (1975), Marilynne *Robinson's *Housekeeping* (1981), and Alice *Walker's *The Color Purple* (1982) trace the growth of women's creative identity out of their bonding with other women. Some of this bonding is explicitly lesbian, but sexuality is rarely treated as more important than the sharing of a woman-centered sensibility.

Women's homosocial relations are most often depicted as the strong core of female experience and gender identity. Yet just as Eve Kosofsky Sedgwick has shown in *Between Men* (1985), homosocial connection need not be direct, and a number of literary texts offer evidence that women's relations may be triangulated like men's, through rivalry over an opposite sex love object. For instance, in Anne *Sexton's "For My Lover, Returning to His Wife" (1969), Gail Godwin's "False Lights" (1976), and Fay Weldon's *The Life and Loves of a She-Devil* (1983), one woman's obsession with another completely eclipses her involvement with the man. Two texts that complexly mediate between conventional glorification of heterosexual connection and American women's culture's traditional self-referentiality are Eudora *Welty's *Delta Wedding* (1945) and Toni *Morrison's *Sula* (1973). Each provides an intricate portrait of women's bonds within a matriarchal society, which are temporarily disturbed and then strengthened by an otherwise scarcely significant marriage.

• Nina Auerbach, *Communities of Women: An Idea in Fiction* (1979). Louise Bernikow, *Among Women* (1980). Lillian Faderman, *Surpassing the Love of Men: Romantic Friendship and Love between Women from the Renaissance to the Present* (1981). Gloria Anzaldúa, "Speaking in Tongues: A Letter to Third World Women Writers," in *This Bridge Called My Back: Writings by Radical Women of Color*, ed. Cherríe Moraga and Gloria Anzaldúa, 2d ed. (1983), pp. 165–174. Jane Tompkins, *Sensational Designs: The Cultural Work of American Fiction 1790–1860* (1985). Trinh T. Minh-ha, *Woman, Native, Other* (1989). Barbara Smith, "Toward A Black Feminist Criticism," in *The New Feminist Criticism*, ed. Elaine Showalter (1985), pp. 168–186.

Carol Siegel

HOPKINS, Pauline (1859–1930), playwright, novelist, short story writer, essayist, and nonfiction writer. The great-grandniece of the poet James Whitfield, Pauline Elizabeth Hopkins was born in Portland, Maine, to William and Sarah Allen Hopkins. During Pauline's childhood the family moved to Boston, where she graduated from Girls High School.

Pauline won her first writing prize at fifteen for an essay submitted to a contest sponsored by William Wells Brown, the escaped slave, abolitionist, and author. At twenty, she completed her first play, *Slaves' Escape: or the *Underground Railroad*. A year later, in 1880, Pauline and her parents played leading roles in *Slaves' Escape* when it was produced in Boston, inaugurating Pauline's twelve-year stage career with the Hopkins's Colored Troubadours and her ensuing fame as "Boston's Favorite Colored Soprano."

During the 1890s, Hopkins left the stage to become a stenographer so that she might support her writing; she worked at the Bureau of Statistics and developed a career as a public lecturer. In 1900, she helped found *The Colored American Magazine*, a pioneering publication designed to showcase the works of African-American writers, musicians, politicians, and educators. Aimed at a predominantly African-American audience, *The Colored American* was intended to enhance pride in African-American heritage, culture, and achievements. Hopkins edited the magazine, promoted it nationwide through Boston's Colored American League, which she founded, and published three novels, seven short stories, and numerous historical, political, and biographical sketches in its pages between 1900 and 1903.

She left *The Colored American* in 1904. Returning to her stenographic work, Hopkins published two more works, "The Dark Races of the Twentieth Century," a sociocultural series (1905) and *Topsy Templeton*, a novella (1916). There may have been later work that was unpublished, but it burned in the 1930 housefire that killed Hopkins.

Despite Hopkins's prolific output and considerable visibility during her lifetime, later scholars discredited her work. Like so many women writers, Hopkins was until recently either derided as a sentimental romancer or ignored. An examination of her writing reveals a talented woman committed to indicting *racism and *sexism, and to heightening awareness of African-Americans' artistic, historical, and social contributions.

Hopkins is best known for her *historical romance *Contending Forces: A Romance Illustrative of Negro Life North and South*, published in 1900 by the Colored Co-Operative Publishing Company. *Contending Forces* encompasses several generations of an African-American family from their enslavement in the Caribbean and the South to their post-*Reconstruction years in Boston. Hopkins's most feminist novel, *Contending Forces* explores the sexual exploitation of women, the role of *mothers as culture bearers, the influence of the black women's *club movement, and the importance of education and employment for women. Sappho, her heroine, enunciates Hopkins's feminist perspective, while Dora, Sappho's foil, fictionalizes the traditional role.

Like most nineteenth-century women's *romances, *Contending Forces* draws on complication and coincidence, heroic and villainous characters, suspense and high drama. But Hopkins marries these devices with American historical realities: *slavery, *lynching, voting disenfranchisement, and racial *stereotypes. This marriage ensures that her stated intent to "raise the stigma of degradation" from her race will reach a wide audience.

Hopkins's other novels, which were serialized in *The Colored American*, employ similar romance techniques. *Hagar's Daughter: A Story of Southern Caste Prejudice* (serialized from 1901 to 1902) impugns *racism through exploring its effects on a wealthy, "white" mother and daughter who discover themselves to be of African origin. *Hagar's Daughter* bitterly castigates racism, revealed often among liberal white Americans. *Winona: A Tale of Negro Life in the South and Southwest* (serialized during 1902), takes place during slavery. The romance is a fast-paced narrative of the tragic mulatta, Winona, dramatizing slave-trading, the *Underground Railroad, and John Brown's Free

Soilers. Judah, a militant African-American, embodies black resistance against injustice and heroism during slavery. *Of One Blood: or the Hidden Self* (serialized from 1902 to 1903) underscores Hopkins's reverence for her African origins. On a trip to Africa, Reuel, the black protagonist, learns of the superiority of African civilization and culture; *Of One Blood* encourages racial pride and announces a Pan-African vision.

Hopkins's short stories re-voice these themes and motifs. She celebrates blacks' intelligence and ethics, as in "As the Lord Lives, He Is One of Our Mother's Children" and "A Test of Manhood." In "George Washington, A Christmas Story," she celebrates the courage of the young African-American who prevents his gang from committing a burglary.

Complementing her novels and tales, Hopkins's sketches highlight the intelligence, ethics, and contributions of African-Americans. Biographical pieces on Harriet Tubman, Sojourner *Truth, and Frederick Douglass and essays on female African-American literary figures, singers, and professionals comprised much of *The Colored American Magazine.*

Although Hopkins's neglect and consequent invisibility prior to the late 1980s make it difficult to assess her influence, her historical, feminist, and Pan-African concerns prefigure such writers as Jessie *Fauset, Zora Neale *Hurston, Alice *Walker, and Toni *Morrison.

• Hopkins's papers are in Fisk University Library, Nashville, Tennessee. See also Ann Allen Shockley, "Pauline Elizabeth Hopkins: A Biographical Excursion into Obscurity," *Phylon* 33 (1972): 22–26. Dorothy B. Porter, "Hopkins, Pauline Elizabeth," in *Dictionary of American Negro Biography,* eds. Rayford W. Logan and Michael R. Winston (1982), pp. 325–326. Claudia Tate, "Pauline Hopkins: Our Literary Foremother," in *Conjuring: Black Women, Fiction, and Literary Tradition,* eds. Marjorie Pryse and Hortense J. Spillers (1985). Jane Campbell, *Mythic Black Fiction: The Transformation of History* (1986). Jane Campbell, "Pauline Elizabeth Hopkins," in *Dictionary of Literary Biography, Volume 50: Afro-American Writers before the Harlem Renaissance* (1986), pp. 182–189. Hazel V. Carby, *Reconstructing Womanhood: The Emergence of the Afro-American Woman Novelist* (1987).

Jane Campbell

HOPKINS, Sarah Winnemucca. *See* Winnemucca, Sarah.

HORNEY, Karen. *See* Psychoanalysis and Women.

HOUSEKEEPING BOOKS. Around 1830, the Industrial Revolution gave rise to one of the most intimate genres of communication between women in U.S. literature: the housekeep-

ing book. Until that time, books by male authors, such as *Family Receipts, or Practical Guide for the Husbandman and Housewife* (1831) by H. L. Barnum, had engaged both sexes in a tutorial on "rural and domestic economy." The separation of paid production in factories and unpaid labor in the home created new professional questions about an old occupation—the care of house and home. Most often framed as the personal narrative of one woman addressed to other women in the second person, housekeeping books pass on everyday strategies needed by isolated homemakers to survive within the confines of a strict heterosexual and patriarchal script. Lydia Maria *Child established the twin concerns of the genre in the opening line of *The American Frugal Housewife* (1829): "The true economy of housekeeping is simply the art of gathering up all the fragments, so that nothing be lost. I mean fragments of *time* as well as *material.*" Women's desire to save "time" and what would become more narrowly "money"—in a society that demands more work of women for less money than it awards men—remains the constant theme of housekeeping books to the present day.

Child's imperative style provides a philosophy for housework that becomes aphorism in the *Recollections of a Housekeeper* by Mrs. Clarissa Packard [Caroline Howard Gilman] in 1834, written with "windows clear as a good conscience." Unlike Child, who wrote for "those not afraid of economy," Packard speaks for the privileged classes in demanding of legislators a "total system" for preparing good domestic workers for her readers' employ. The tension between the need to "keep" even the most humble house and regarding a certain kind of housekeeping as a sign of cultural superiority divides the genre within itself. Catherine *Beecher's *Treatise on Domestic Economy for the Use of Young Ladies at Home and at School* (1841), the enormously popular forerunner of the "home economics movement," outlines what would become the ideal for middle-class white women at least until the end of the nineteenth century: "qualitative" mothering and "professional" housekeeping. The "peculiar responsibilities of American women" encompass both a nationalist and imperialist mission as well as *Stowe's practical guidelines for keeping house, revealing the pressure on the genre to rescue the image of women working in the home without pay from depreciation in the newly consolidated cash economy. Many subsequent housekeeping books would echo Stowe's evangelical tone, making the mission of housekeeping dependent upon the assumption of other unenlightened and unclean classes, races, or nationalities in need of instruction.

Upper-class African-American women such as Anna Julia *Cooper in *A Voice from the South* (1892; reprint, 1969) took up this mission during *Reconstruction, presenting homemaking as a means of "racial uplift" in reaction against the forced domestic labor under *slavery.

While housekeepers struggling for middle-class "respectability" turned to L. H. Wright's *Six Hundred Dollars a Year, A wife's effort at low living under high prices* (1867; reprint, 1970) and Catherine Owen's [Helen Alice Matthews Nitsch] *Ten Dollars Enough; Keeping House on ten dollars a week; how it has been done; how it may be done again* (1886), word-of-mouth probably provided much of the training for women domestic workers, who earned on average fifty cents a week in 1850 and one to two dollars a week in 1895. Waves of immigration and Emancipation contributed to a pool of principally non-native and African-American domestic workers in the second half of the nineteenth century and of women of color in the twentieth. The housekeeping books of these women primarily take the form of first-person testimonials to the conditions of work projected or collected by college-educated researchers, from the 1901 *Toilers of the Home: The Record of a College Women's Experience as a Domestic Servant* written by Vassar graduate Lillian Pettengill, who took on domestic service due to a combination of economic need and intellectual curiousity, to Susan Tucker's 1988 collection of personal narratives of black domestic workers and their white employers in the South, *Telling Memories among Southern Women*.

On 16 April 1917, President Woodrow Wilson proclaimed: "Every housewife who practices strict economy puts herself in the ranks of those who serve the nation." To show housewives how to serve, Thetta Quay Franks wrote *Household Organization for War Service: America Expects Every Woman to Do Her Duty* (1917) during World War I and Janet Camp Troxell wrote *The Home Front: Five Hundred Ways to Save Time, Labor, and Money* (1941) during World War II. By this time housekeeping, like warfare, had been made "scientific." The 1893 World's Fair in Chicago included the Rumford Kitchen Exhibit, showing a "working man's home" managed on $500 a year according to precise principles of "domestic science." The exhibit and the American Home Economics Association, both presided over by Ellen H. Richards, set the stage for the academic institutionalization of "home economics," licensing a proliferation of technical manuals and textbooks written by women through the next several decades who frequently included their professional affiliation on the title page under their names.

Periodicals such as *Good Housekeeping* (1885–present) have provided professional advice for a practical audience while books such as *The House that Runs Itself* (1929) by Beulah Schenk and Gladys Denny Shultz recognize the distinction between theoretical "home economics" and practical "homemaking"—"it became not so important to wash the dishes the scientific way, as to see that they got washed at all." This disjuncture gave rise to a humorous variation on the genre as in Peg Bracken's popular *I Hate to Housekeep Book* (1977) and Jean Littlejohn Aarberg's *Don't Phone Mother* (1945), which recommends for dirty dishes: "Stack 'em, sisters, stack 'em." Anxiety about the breakdown of the housekeeper's mission in contemporary times prompted such works as *The Joy of Housekeeping* (1975) by Ella May Miller, urging women to "accept your role" because "You no longer are a self-pleaser. You now are a Jesus-pleaser." Meanwhile, Jean Pay Laury's *The Creative Woman's Getting It All Together Handbook* (1977) provides hints for women assumed to work in and outside of the home. Whatever the ideological frame, for nearly two centuries housekeeping books have recognized the unremunerated work of women in their own homes while providing hints for performing that work within the time and economic constraints imposed by women's variable status.

[*See also* Advice Books.]

• Lucy Maynard Salmon, *Domestic Service* (1901). Kathryn Kish Sklar, Introduction to *Treatise on Domestic Economy* (1977).

Celeste Fraser Delgado

HOUSTON, Velina Hasu (b. 1957), playwright. Born in Tokyo, Japan, Houston emigrated at the age of two with her Japanese mother and American G.I. father. The Houston family settled in Ft. Riley, Kansas, one of several bases where the U.S. Army segregated nearly 100,000 "war brides"—Japanese, French, German, Italian, English, and later Korean and Thai women—married to active duty American servicemen between 1946 and 1960. An exploration of the tensions produced by the coming together of her native Japanese mother and African-American/Blackfoot Indian father inspired her first professionally produced plays, a trilogy comprised of *Asa Ga Kimashita* (Morning Has Broken, 1980), *American Dreams* (1983), and *Tea* (1983). *Asa Ga Kimashita*, written while she completed an M.F.A. in playwrighting at University of California at Los Angeles, describes her Japanese mother's decision to marry an African-American/Native American G.I. and leave her ancestral home. *American Dreams* finds the young couple confronted by hostility and intolerance after meeting their African-

American relatives stateside. *Tea* concludes the trilogy, reaching beyond immediate *autobiography to encompass a *community of Japanese women who came to the United States as international brides.

One of the most widely produced Asian-American playwrights, Houston has shifted her work from autobiography to plays that address a wide range of issues. The common thread in all her writing, however, is an ongoing exploration of the politics of culture, *race, and *gender, particularly as they affect interracial relations in America. Of particular interest is what she terms "the Afro-Asian diaspora," broadening the discussion of race in America beyond the black/white confrontation. Her plays examine a set of social dynamics, cultural nuances, and racial problems that reflect aspects of America's troubled plurality. Other works that have been produced are *Amerasian Girls* (1983), *Thirst* (1981), and *Necessities* (1990). Works that have received staged readings include *The Legend of Bobbi Chicago* (1985), *Christmas Cake* (1991), *Kapioplani's Faith* (1991), *My Life, A Loaded Gun* (1988), and *Albatross* (1985). Her play *Tea* was adapted for television by PBS/KPBS in 1991; it is anthologized in *Unbroken Thread: An Anthology of Plays by Asian American Women* (1992). Houston edited *The Politics of Life: 4 Plays by Asian American Women* (1992). Her work has been produced by such American ethnic theaters as the East West Players, Los Angeles; Kumu Kahua, Honolulu; and the Negro Ensemble Company, New York City; as well as by regional and commercial theaters, most notably the Manhattan Theater Club; the Whole Theater, New Jersey; and the Old Globe Theater, San Diego.

Roberta Uno

HOWE, Julia Ward (1819–1910), poet, essayist, social reformer, and author of "The Battle Hymn of the Republic." Born in New York City to Julia Cutler and Samuel Ward, Julia Ward lived a quiet life in Manhattan and in the family's second home in Newport, Rhode Island. Educated largely at home in a close family, Ward read voraciously, studying languages, history, geometry, and European literature. Rarely domestic enough to suit her family, she felt constrained by her father's strict control over her education and envied her brothers' freedom. Her adolescent literary aspirations were fostered only by her brother Sam.

Soon after her introduction to Manhattan society, Julia Ward met Samuel Gridley "Chev" Howe, a social reformer best known for his work with the handicapped and blind at the Perkins Institute. They married in 1843 after a stormy courtship, largely due to Julia's independent spirit. Throughout their marriage, Chev Howe resented his wife's literary aspirations, refused to allow her to manage her own finances, and criticized her management of the household and their six children. Nevertheless, Julia Howe, desperate to establish a reputation of her own, continued visiting her literary acquaintances and writing poetry, publishing *Passion Flowers* anonymously in 1853, followed by a second book of verses, *Words for the Home* (1857), a play, *The World's Own* (1857), and a diary of her travels to Cuba (1859).

Not originally an abolitionist, Howe was converted by the mid-1850s. On the suggestion of a friend, in 1861 she composed lyrics for a stirring camp tune, "John Brown's body lies a-mouldering in the grave." Howe reportedly awoke from a deep sleep to write "The Battle Hymn of the Republic" in its entirety on a scrap of paper. The poem, published in 1862 in the *Atlantic Monthly*, secured her national fame and reputation.

Howe's public life flourished during and after the war, much to her husband's dismay and embarrassment. She published articles, poems, a travel narrative, and a play, delivered sermons and lectures, and became a leading advocate of suffrage, women's ministry, and world peace. Consistently treating marriage as a means for women to broaden their horizons, she generally advocated the ideology of *separate spheres, especially glorifying motherhood.

After Samuel Howe's death in 1876, Julia Howe enjoyed even greater success as a writer and social reformer in her own right. She was a founding member of the American Women Suffrage Association and the New England Woman's Club, and presided over the South Boston Woman's Club and over the Association for the Advancement of Women for nineteen years. Her career culminated in a triumphant lecture tour on the west coast in 1888 and in the publication of her *Reminiscences, 1819–1899* (1899). She died quietly at her home near Newport in October 1919.

• Julia Ward Howe, *Reminiscences, 1819–1899* (1899). Deborah Pickman Clifford, *Mine Eyes Have Seen the Glory: A Biography of Julia Ward Howe* (1978). Mary H. Grant, "Domestic Experience and Feminist Theory: The Case of Julia Ward Howe," in *Woman's Being, Woman's Place: Female Identity and Vocation in American History*, ed. Mary Kelley (1979), pp. 220–232.

Jamie Stanesa

HOWE, Susan (b. 1937), poet and literary scholar. Susan Howe is an iconoclastic American poet-scholar in the tradition of *H. D., Charles Olson, and Robert Duncan. Howe knows intimately the literary and historical narratives she assiduously deconstructs and re-arranges on the page in order to sound out what has been systematically excluded or ignored. The rich historical information she mines provides the occasion to which she brings her own concerns with the lyrical potential and etymology of individual words, and a political commitment to question the dynamics of domination. What ties together these micro- and macro-concerns is a disjunctive poetic style that resists the domination of grammatical logic and reaches toward a distinctive, magical lyricism.

Howe's poetry acknowledges debts to her intellectual and artistic upbringing. She was born in Boston, daughter of an Irish actress and writer, and a Harvard law professor. *The Europe of Trusts: Selected Poems* (1990) brings together three poem sequences that are concerned with European philosophical, historical, and literary roots, most importantly her own Irish heritage. *Singularities* (1990) includes three more recent texts that reflect Howe's preoccupation with early American history, a preoccupation shared with her father.

Howe graduated from the Boston Museum School of Fine Arts in 1961. By 1974, when she published the first of a dozen books of poetry, writing had eclipsed her work in the visual arts, but this earlier training is apparent in her sensitivity to the arrangement of words and space on the page. Increasingly, she has played with breaking the linear expectations we usually bring to reading.

Howe was first recognized and published by other poets who were interested in linguistic experimentation and poststructuralist literary theory. Her work appeared in many small press magazines, including *L-A-N-G-U-A-G-E*. However, her work has reached a wider audience, especially since the enthusiastic reception of her critical study, *My Emily Dickinson* (1985). Howe's rigorous investigation of Dickinson's intertextual reading/writing strategies, and her own experimental prose style have made this an influential model for literary and feminist scholars and critics. Although she is wary of aligning herself with any particular feminist "camp," her critical readings of women writers such as * Dickinson and Mary * Rowlandson, and her attention to * gender in her use of language, history, or literary texts have made solid contributions to feminist knowledge.

Mother of two children, Howe has lived in Guilford, Connecticut, with her second husband, the sculptor David von Schlegell. She is a professor of English at SUNY Buffalo.

• Marjorie Perloff, "Collision or Collusion with History: The Lyric of Susan Howe," *Contemporary Literature* 30 (Winter 1989): 518–533. Edward Foster, "An Interview with Susan Howe," *Talisman: A Journal of Contemporary Poetry and Poetics* 4, special issue on Susan Howe (Spring 1990): 14–38.

Lorna J. Smedman

HOWE, Tina (b. 1937), playwright. The daughter of Quincy Howe, historian and radio and television journalist, and Mary Post Howe, a painter, Tina Howe was born in New York and attended private schools there until her father joined the faculty at the University of Illinois, Urbana. There Howe wrote plays for secondary school productions and studied piano seriously. She then attended Bucknell University for two years and transferred to Sarah Lawrence College to graduate in 1959. At Sarah Lawrence her first one-act play, *Closing Time*, was produced, and in 1960, while studying at the Sorbonne, she wrote her first full-length play.

Returning to the United States in 1961, Howe received a degree in education from Teachers College, Columbia University, and married Norman Levy, a novelist and historian. The couple resided in Illinois, where Howe did further graduate work at the University of Chicago and was an editor for a publishing company. She then taught secondary school English in Maine and Monona Grove, Wisconsin, from 1965 to 1967. In the latter school system, Howe was made head of the drama department and was allowed to produce her own plays. She wrote five one-acts, and claims that the experience of producing those plays formed her craft. A playwright who emphasizes the absurd and the improbable, and draws heavily on the work of Beckett and Ionesco, Howe textualizes her plots with visual metaphor.

After the production of her first professional one-act plays, *The Nest* (1969) and *Birth and After Birth* (1974), Howe explored women's participation in the arts in *Museum* (1976–1977). She continued to focus on women artists and nontraditional settings in her 1979 play *The Art of Dining. Painting Churches*, for which Howe received a *Village Voice* (Obie) Award in 1983, was also awarded the Outer Circle Critics Award and the Rosamond Gilder Award in 1984, was televised on the PBS "American Playhouse" series in 1985, and in 1993, was filmed with Lauren Bacall and Gregory Peck in leading roles. *Painting Churches*, with its female protagonist and an emphasis on working as a part of one's intimate life, was a precursor of her 1986–1987 *Coastal Disturbances* and the recent *Approaching Zanzibar*. Adjunct Professor of Dramatic Writing at the Tisch School of the Arts at New York University since 1983, Howe has also taught at UCLA and Johns Hopkins University. In 1984 she was an NEA fellow; in 1988 she was awarded an honorary degree from Bowdoin

College; and in 1990 she received a Guggenheim fellowship.

• Janet Brown, *Feminist Drama, Definition and Critical Analysis* (1979). Alice M. Robinson, Vera M. Roberts, and Milly S. Barranger, eds., *Notable Women in the American Theater* (1989). Jane Schlueter, ed., *Modern American Drama: The Female Canon* (1990).

Andrea Wagner

HUMISHUMA. *See* Mourning Dove.

HUMOR. Women's literary humor in the United States can be traced to Anne *Bradstreet's witty challenge to those "carping tongues" who preferred a needle to a pen in the hands of seventeenth-century women. For three hundred years, a tradition of American women's humor as a direct response to women's cultural subordination has flourished, although until very recently that tradition was obscured by suppositions about women's passivity and sentimentality that are at odds with the creation of humor. Thus, while the classic (male) tradition of American humor originated in the broad political satires of the colonial period, was transformed by frontier experience into the hyperbole and bluster of the tall tale, and became in the twentieth century urbane and often absurd in the hands of writers such as S. J. Perelman and Woody Allen, women's humorous expression has typically measured the distance between public and private, power and powerlessness, the hearty laugh and the subversive giggle.

Although feminists have been accused of lacking a sense of humor, women writers have used humor as one instrument in the fight for equality since the early days of the republic. During the Revolutionary era, both Mercy Otis *Warren and Judith Sargent *Murray used satire to show the relationship between national independence and full citizenship for members of both sexes. At the end of Warren's patriotic play *The Group*, a female patriot speaks of women's desire for equality with men; and Murray, in essays, comedies, and fiction, turned her considerable wit on male assumptions about women's mental and physical fitness for participation in the political process. The weapon of wit did not help secure women's right to vote for another 150 years, but women continued to use humor to protest inequality; rather than creating absurdity, female humorists have tended to point out existing conditions.

In the early nineteenth century, America's women humorists attempted to counter the popularity of the sentimental novel and what they felt to be its pernicious effects on women's behavior and goals. The usual method of these humorists, which was to create satiric portraits of passive, love-starved women imitating the behavior of foolish fictional heroines, led to the misperception that female humorists targeted women, whereas their actual target was an increasingly genteel culture that encouraged women to be dependent and weak. Tabitha *Tenney's 1801 novel *Female Quixotism* is the earliest of these satires, starting a trend in women's humor that reached its apotheosis in the "clinging vine" figure of Betsey Bobbet in Marietta *Holley's 1872 *My Opinions and Betsey Bobbet's*. Humor that mocked women's acceptance of limiting stereotypes continued into the twentieth century, flourishing especially in the post–World War II domestic humor of such writers as Jean Kerr and Shirley *Jackson.

In the 1830s and 1840s, as the experience of the frontier began to engage the attention of America's male humorous writers, women focused on the sewing circles and quilting bees that reflected the *"separate spheres" ideology. The targets of the satire of Frances Whitcher, whose work appeared in *Neal's Saturday Gazette* and *Godey's Lady's Book* in the 1840s, were the gossiping, social-climbing women whose economic dependence on men is revealed in their competition for husbands. A different version of the trials of domestic life is presented in Caroline *Kirkland's *A New Home—Who'll Follow?* (1839). Set in frontier Michigan rather than in the more settled New York state of Whitcher's sketches, *A New Home* approaches slapstick comedy in Kirkland's depiction of homemaking without most of the amenities of civilized life. Like Tenney and Whitcher, Kirkland makes fun of the overly sentimental woman, whose lack of practicality and common sense are thrown into particularly high relief by the frontier setting.

The critique of women's place in American culture that remains an implication or a subtext in the work of these early humorists became explicit in the work of Marietta Holley, beginning in the 1870s. From this point until 1920, when women won the right to vote, the subject of women's rights was a significant strand in women's humor. Samantha Allen Holley's central character in more than twenty books, speaks in the sort of folksy dialect that characterized much nineteenth-century humor, but she has a sophisticated understanding of issues that still concern feminists—women's participation in the political process and in organized religion, nonsexist childrearing, and the trivialization of housework. By the time Holley published her last "Samantha" book in 1914, America's taste in humor had changed from regional dialect humor to the more urbane wit that would, beginning in 1925, be celebrated and promoted by *The New Yorker* magazine. Prosuffrage humorists such as Alice Duer Miller wrote polished parodies of antisuffrage arguments, and cartoonists such as Lou Rogers provided visual depictions of the hollowness of such arguments.

Even when America's female humorists were not addressing women's place in society and advocating, directly or indirectly, greater freedom and participation, their work reflected their perception that women's lives were centered in the domestic and the relational realms. As early as the 1850s, Fanny Fern (Sara Willis * Parton) wrote her irreverent "Fern Leaves," newspaper columns admonishing women to choose husbands who were generous and not given to drink, and by the turn of the twentieth century Josephine Dodge Daskam addressed the "New Woman" in *Fables for the Fair: Cautionary Tales for Damsels Not Yet in Distress,* advising her that most men were not ready to accept her intellectual achievements and ambitions. Edna St. Vincent * Millay, using the * pseudonym Nancy Boyd in her *Distressing Dialogues* (1924), delivered a similar message, and Florence Guy Seabury warned in *The Delicatessen Husband* that most men preferred home-cooked meals to women with brilliant careers. What has been termed "the war between the sexes" in American humor of the early decades of the twentieth century—featuring E. B. White and James Thurber—was engaged from both sides.

Two best-selling humorous works in the first half of the twentieth century contributed memorable characters to American humor and also presented variations of the concept of domesticity. Anita * Loos's 1925 *Gentlemen Prefer Blondes* has as its narrator and protagonist Lorelei Lee, a "kept" woman who presents an ill-educated exterior but who is a shrewd businesswoman, knowing her worth and insisting on appropriate compensation for her companionship. Twenty years later, Betty * MacDonald (Anne Elizabeth Campbell Bard) published *The Egg and I,* which humorously explodes several myths. One of these is that happiness for a woman consists of supporting her husband in his career; when the narrator's husband decides to raise chickens in a remote area of the Northwest, she finds the isolation daunting and the few neighbors—including the irrepressible Ma Kettle—less than compatible.

The fact that American women's humor often carries a serious message is exemplified in the work of the best-known female humorist of the twentieth century: Dorothy * Parker. In light verse, sketches, and short stories written primarily in the 1920s and 1930s, Parker deplored the faithlessness of men and the dependence of women on their favor. The female

speakers in Parker's work wait beside silent telephones and dance with men they do not like, who step on their toes; her wit lays bare the pain of loneliness. Parker was one of the few women associated with the Algonquin Round Table—a group of writers, critics, and journalists that met frequently at New York's Algonquin Hotel. She was known for her acerbic wit, both in person and in the pages of *Vanity Fair, The New Yorker,* and *Esquire.* Although Parker's writing career ended long before her death in 1967, the witty, pointed laments of her sad ladies continue to be widely anthologized.

Not all of America's female humorists of the early decades of this century participated in the "war between the sexes," however. One of the most popular humorous writers early in the twentieth century was Carolyn Wells, whose work constitutes one of the few forays women writers have made until quite recently into nonsense and absurdity. Wells's light verse abounds in puns and other wordplay that recall Lewis Carroll and Edward Lear, and she delighted in writing parodies of well-known works of literature. Much of Wells's work is topical, addressing popular authors, women's fashions, and other aspects of popular culture. Also widely read in the early decades of the century were the humorous stories of Anne Warner French and Mary Roberts * Rinehart, whose central characters represent quite divergent views of woman's role in American culture. Although both characters are unmarried, French's Susan Clegg reflects nineteenth-century ideals of "true womanhood," while Rinehart's Letitia ("Tish") Carberry more nearly resembles the "New Woman." Susan Clegg lives with and cares for her invalid father; the humor in the stories consists in the daily back-fence gossip between the talkative Susan and her taciturn next-door neighbor. Tish Carberry, in contrast, like her creator, who was a correspondent for the *Saturday Evening Post,* experiences a series of madcap adventures with her friends Lizzie and Aggie.

By the middle of the twentieth century, women humorists had left behind both absurdity and amusing adventures and turned again to depictions of domestic settings. The post–World War II years that saw the growth of the suburbs and the "baby boom" also produced a number of writers that Betty * Friedan, in her 1963 book *The Feminine Mystique,* termed the "housewife humorists." Friedan felt that these writers, by finding humor in everyday domestic situations, encouraged women readers to laugh away their dissatisfactions and thereby assisted in the trivialization of their lives. What Friedan failed to see was that the humor embodied a subversive protest against the numbing routines of suburban life—just as Frances Whitcher's gossiping women criticized the conforming pressures of genteel society.

In such works as Shirley Jackson's *Life Among the Savages* (1953) and *Raising Demons* (1957) and Jean Kerr's *Please Don't Eat the Daisies* (1957) and *The Snake Has All the Lines* (1960), the sewing circles and household drudgery of nineteenth-century women's humor were replaced by PTA meetings and suburban isolation. The concept of separate spheres was revived and reinforced by husbands who commuted to jobs while their wives remained in suburbia to deal with appliance repairmen, *Girl Scout cookie sales, and children's illnesses. The increase in the number and circulation of women's magazines during this period provided publishing opportunities for a number of humorists. Phyllis McGinley began her career by contributing light verse to *The New Yorker*, but by the 1950s her work appeared with more frequency in such magazines as *Good Housekeeping* and *Mademoiselle*. Although McGinley ostensibly celebrated woman's traditional role as homemaker, her poetry, like the work of Jackson and Kerr, revealed the tedium and isolation of suburban life. More overt and more amusing was the work of Peg Bracken, whose *The I Hate to Cook Book* (1960) and *I Hate to Do Housework Book* (1962) encapsulated women's frustrations with enforced domesticity on the eve of the 1960s women's movement.

The postwar period also brought greater racial and ethnic diversity to American women's humor. For the African-American Alice *Childress, the term "domestic" meant not life in the suburbs, but work as a servant in the homes of white people. Childress' 1956 book *Like One of the Family . . . Conversations from a Domestic's Life* uses the conversational method of Anne Warner French's "Susan Clegg" stories, but Childress's narrator tells her friend of the various ways in which she teaches her employers about the hypocrisy of the whites' claim that black domestic servants are "just like one of the family." In the decades that followed, writers such as Judith Viorst and Nora Ephron created humorous writing in which their Jewish heritage played a significant part in the humor.

The political confrontations of the 1960s and 1970s were mirrored in a more confrontational humor by women. Like their predecessors in the pre-suffrage years, women largely abandoned the subversive voice of domestic humor and turned to satire. Erma Bombeck, who began writing her newspaper column, "At Wit's End," in the early 1960s, is a transitional figure in this transformation. Although the speaker in her humor is clearly a homemaker, Bombeck does not depend on her reader to figure out that it is the culture and not the individual woman who is to blame for her dissatisfaction with her role, but instead employs hyperbole and direct statement to challenge the disparity between the reality of women's lives and the myths promoted by popular culture. The title of one of the sketches in her first collection of columns, *At Wit's End* (1965), signals her method: "What's a Nice Girl Like Me Doing in a Dump Like This?" The dilemma of Bombeck's persona is the same as that of the 1950s woman—intelligent and well-educated, but apparently destined to pack lunch boxes; the speaker, however, has declared open warfare on her circumstances. The language of even her early sketches anticipates the rebelliousness of Roseanne Barr's comedy routines of the 1980s and 1990s; in "What's a Nice Girl . . ." she says to one of her children, "So you swallowed the plastic dinosaur out of the cereal box. What do you want me to do, call a vet?"

While feminist ideas and claims had been present in much of women's humor since the mid-nineteenth century—often subversively, but sometimes, as in the work of Marietta Holley and Alice Duer Miller, overtly—the humor of the 1970s and 1980s was more openly political and more apt to deal with subject matter thought to be inappropriate for "ladies" to address. Gloria *Steinem's frequently reprinted essay "If Men Could Menstruate" embodies both tendencies. Steinem's essay addresses directly the issue of male power, suggesting that aspects of human biology associated with subordinate groups are regarded as secret and "dirty," whereas if they were associated with those in power they would receive public support and celebration. Regarded primarily as a political activist, Steinem, the founding editor of *Ms. magazine, wrote television comedy in the 1960s and is an admirer of Dorothy Parker—for her day, an equally irreverent woman.

As the women's movement increasingly recognized the differences among groups of women as well as their common need for equality, the voices in women's humor became more diverse. African-American writers such as Nikki *Giovanni and Ntosake *Shange used humor to address the double bind of racism and sexism, and to undermine clichés about and stereotypes of black women. Gail Sausser, in *Lesbian Etiquette*, similarly used humor to counteract stereotypes and misperceptions of lesbian women. And at a time when detractors commonly accused feminists of lacking a sense of humor, a number of women writers wrote humorously about the women's movement itself.

Judith Viorst, whose light verse chronicles the dilemmas and crises of a woman coming to maturity in the 1950s and then encountering the political turbulence of the 1960s, admits in one poem being torn between the movement's promise of independence and the security of a more traditional lifestyle. Nora Ephron, whose witty essays appeared in such magazines as *Esquire* and *New York*, explored the effect on women's lives of American popular culture. Her essays in *Crazy Salad: Some Things About Women* (1975) confront the paradoxes of the early years of the women's movement, when such things as make-up and the Pillsbury Bake-Off were considered by some to be antithetical to feminist orthodoxy.

Not all women's humorous writing of the past few decades has been politically motivated, although the settings and concerns of women's humor have become increasingly less domestic and more "public." Both Fran Lebowitz and Veronica Geng, for example, write about the particular absurdities of contemporary urban life—specifically, life in New York. Cyra McFadden's *The Serial* is a parody of a soap opera about the residents of Marin County, California. Increasingly, too, women writers are aware that they work in a long tradition of humor that provides a reliable index of women's concerns and perspectives.

• Lois Rather, "Were Women Funny? Some 19th-Century Humorists," in *American Book Collector* 21, no. 5 (1971), pp. 5–10. Emily Toth, "Female Wits," in *Massachusetts Review* 22, no. 4 (Winter 1981), pp. 783–793. Alfred Habegger, *Gender, Fantasy, and Realism in American Literature* (1982). Emily Toth, "A Laughter of Their Own: Women's Humor in the United States," in *Critical Essays on American Humor*, ed. William Bedford Clark and W. Craig Turner (1984), pp. 199–215. Nancy A. Walker, *A Very Serious Thing: Women's Humor and American Culture* (1988). Nancy A. Walker and Zita Dresner, eds., *Redressing the Balance: American Women's Literary Humor from the Colonies to the 1980s* (1988). Regina Barreca, ed., *Last Laughs: Perspectives on Women and Comedy* (1988). June Sochen, ed., *Women's Comic Vision(s)* (1991). Nancy A. Walker, " 'I cant write a book': Women's Humor and the American Realistic Tradition," in *American Literary Realism* 23, no. 3 (Spring 1991), pp. 52–67.

Nancy Walker

HUNTER, Kristin (b. 1931), novelist and short story writer. Born in Philadelphia, Kristin Hunter was reared in Camden and Magnolia, New Jersey, the only child of a middle-class African-American family. Lonely and imaginative, she turned readily to reading and then to writing; during her teen years she wrote a youth column in the *Pittsburgh Courier*. At twenty she earned her B.S. in education from the University of Pennsylvania, after which she became in turn a teacher, an advertising copywriter, an information officer, and a free-lance writer. In 1955 she won the Fund for the Republic Television Documentary for her script *A Minority of One*, which was aired nationwide on the *Lamp under My Feet* series.

She moved into an apartment in Philadelphia's inner city, a block from South Street, a main artery in black Philadelphia. This street appears in nearly all her works and is, as she says, almost a character. In 1964, Hunter published her first novel, *God Bless the Child*, which concerns a young black woman's near-fanatic determination to overcome the incubus of poverty through material success, sacrificing her health and her closest relationships. Two years later, she published *The Landlord*, a novel about a young white man who buys a tenement building and tries to impose his values upon his tenants but instead learns from them and attains maturity. Republic Pictures made it into a successful film, *The Landlord*.

Hunter now turned to writing children's books: Her prize-winning *The Soul Brothers and Sister Lou* (1968) was based upon a group of youngsters who sang beneath her window. Others are *Boss Cat* (1971), *The Pool Table War* (1972), and *Uncle Dan and the Raccoon* (1972).

By then a lecturer teaching African-American literature and creative writing at the University of Pennsylvania, in 1973 Hunter published *Guests in the Promised Land*, a story collection for which she was a National Book Award finalist. In 1975, *The Survivors*, a novel about a friendship between a homeless boy and an aging seamstress, appeared. In 1978, *The Lakestown Rebellion* recounted how a small black town successfully resisted a powerful corporation's attempts to build a highway that would have destroyed the town. Both books are reminiscent of the trickster tradition in African-American culture, in which a physically powerless character outwits a larger and more powerful one. Hunter's latest book is *Lou in the Limelight* (1981).

A skilled storyteller, Kristin Hunter has looked mainly to African-American experience and traditions for her material. She has portrayed the inner city honestly, but with warmth and humor. She shows the ravages of poverty, oppression, and *racism, but she also shows how people can survive, and even triumph, in the contemporary world.

• Tracy Chevalier, ed., *Twentieth Century Children's Writers*, 3d ed. (1989). Linda Metzger et al., eds., *Black Writers* (1989). Anne Commire, ed., *Something about the Author, Autobiography Series*, vol. 10 (1990). Virginia Blain, et al., eds., *The Feminist Companion to*

Literature in English (1990). *The Writers Directory* (1990).

Eugenia W. Collier

HURST, Fannie (1885–1968), novelist, short story writer, and social activist. She represented with empathy and accuracy the tragedies and triumphs between lovers, *mothers and daughters, and working woman in the sex, entertainment, domestic, department store, and fashion industries. Hurst is best remembered for her gripping storytelling and the twenty-nine films made from her fiction, notably: three versions of *Back Street*, two of *Imitation of Life*, and two of *Humoresque*. Born on her grandparent's Hamilton, Ohio, farm, to Rose Kopel and Samuel Hurst, of German-Jewish ancestry, Fannie and her mother rejoined her father in St. Louis, Missouri, where she graduated from Central High School and Washington University (1909) and preferred history and the classics (she was especially taken with Chaucer, Dickens, Masters, Hardy, and Mrs. Oliphant). As an undergraduate, she was active on social and administrative levels and eventually divided her estate between Washington and Brandeis Universities. She married pianist Jacques S. Danielson in 1915, kept their union secret until 1920, and remained devoted to him until his death in 1954. Hurst was awarded, along with T. S. Eliot, an honorary degree from Washington University, was a member of Heterodoxy, and was close friends with Eleanor Roosevelt, Zona *Gale, and Zora Neale *Hurston.

Yet her legacy remains her extensive canon, for between "The Joy of Living" in 1909 and her final published novel *Fool, Be Still* in 1964, she produced a sensitive *autobiography, *Anatomy of Me: A Wonderer in Search of Herself* (1958), thirty novels, her favorite being *Lummox* (1923), and three hundred short stories. Ten were listed in *Best American Short Stories* and five were reprinted; "Humoresque" was included in an O. Henry Prize Award Collection, and twenty-four appeared in anthologies after original publication. Moreover, she frankly addressed wife abuse, *sexual harassment, age discrimination, sex education, the plight of indigent women and children, intergenerational and imigration *assimilation, *birth control, *civil rights and labor issues, and public health horrors, always believing that once a writer discovered a person's "reality," it must be respected, valued, then shared accordingly. Before her death in 1968, Fannie Hurst—author, Renaissance scholar, saloniere, and activist—captivated millions with realistic tales in classic symmetry and with perfect portraiture that will forever recall the struggles for survival, the wistful memories of hopeful times, and the exalted expectations within the framework of interpersonal relationships. Indeed, she was ahead of her time—so much so that she is most relevant in ours.

• Hurst's primary manuscript and correspondence collection are at the Harry Ransom Humanities Research Center, University of Texas at Austin. Significant collections are also at Brandeis and Washington Universities. See also Cynthia Brandimarte, *Fannie Hurst and Her Fiction: Prescriptions for America's Working Women* (1980). Susan Koppelman, ed., *Fannie Hurst— The Woman, The Writer: A Collection of Essays* (1994). *A Fannie Hurst Anthology: Stories Selected and Introduced by Susan Koppelman* (1994).

Deborah Bice and Susan Koppelman

HURSTON, Zora Neale (1891–1960), novelist, short story writer, playwright, and folklorist. When, in the 1980s, scholars discovered that Zora Neale Hurston's claim that she had been born in the early 1900s was off by about ten years, the carefully manipulated tapestry of her life, recorded in her 1942 autobiography, *Dust Tracks on the Road*, became somewhat more knotted than she would have liked. One way of understanding the life and works of this enigmatic American author is to acknowledge her need to maintain such careful and deliberately orchestrated perceptions of both her public and private lives, so that the boundaries between truth and fiction, in both these domains, was often obscured.

When she matriculated at Barnard College, she was not, as she claimed, a young, impressionable coed, but was instead a mature young woman in her late twenties who had learned to manipulate details (like her age) to gain her an immediate objective and a very particular image. Neither was she a youngster when she won her first literary award for the story "Spunk," and used the occasion to move from Washington, D.C., to Harlem in New York City. The year was 1925, a time when Harlem was just beginning to gather together the energies and creative talents of artists of the *Harlem Renaissance.

Hurston was born into the African-American town of Eatonville, Florida, in 1891. Her mother's advice to her children was to "Jump at de sun—and you might at least catch holt to de moon." Hurston's life was a constant battle to achieve beyond the prescribed, to do more (or differently) than what was expected, and to reach insistently for dreams. However scattered the records of her often stunning successes, she cannot be faulted for her persistent and admirable efforts.

Lucy Hurston died when her daughter was eleven. This event, especially her mother's death-bed instructions—"Don't let them be coverin' up de lookin glass"—was a scene later recalled both in Hurston's autobiography and her first novel, *Jonah's Gourd Vine* (1934). What she recalled from this troubled and tragic event, especially the elements of black folk beliefs that surround her memories, was to emerge as the cultural focus that consistently identifies the values and beliefs expressed in her literature and her life.

Hurston's unwavering belief in the beauty of African-American culture was the driving and abiding force in both her literature and in her career. She was, perhaps, America's first "race-woman"—dedicated to living and celebrating the expressive aesthetic culture of African Americans. The writing of her novels, short stories, and drama had the same objective as her efforts to preserve African-American spirituals and the artistry of diaspora cultures of the United States and the Caribbean. Both efforts were to help the world appreciate what it meant to be "gorgeously Negro."

Hurston's decision to mask her age indicates her desire to exercise some control over her public image and there is certainly plenty of evidence that she was able to create and maintain an exciting and dramatic presence in the literary world of the 1920s and 1930s. Her short stint as a secretary and companion to novelist Fannie *Hurst included an episode in which she dressed as an "African princess" to gain entrée to a segregated hotel tearoom. Her appearance at Harlem literary events was often characterized as dramatic and theatrical—her dress, manner, and speech on these occasions made her the center of attention—especially as she had the tendency to announce herself as "Zora, Queen of the Niggerati."

The flamboyance of her early years in Harlem and the riveting episodes of her folklore gathering trips to the American South, Haiti, and the Caribbean contrast sharply with the poverty and obscurity of her later years. In 1960 she died in a welfare home in St. Lucie County, Florida. Few there knew she had initiated herself as a voodoo priestess in Louisiana, told tall tales and held "lying sessions" with the workers in turpentine camps and jook joints, exchanged recipes with root doctors and conjurers across the South, and shared some of these trips in her Chevrolet coupe with Langston Hughes.

Her *folklore was published in a collection she titled *Mules and Men* (1935). Charlotte Mason, her literary patron; the impressive and already well-known Renaissance literary artists Alain Locke and Langston Hughes; and her Columbia University professor, anthropologist Franz Boas—all were members of her conversational and advising circle during the period when she collected data for that book.

The sociopolitical and literary travelogue of her Caribbean adventures is recorded in *Tell My Horse—Voodoo Gods, an Inquiry* (1938). Although it begins with a historical-political survey of Jamaica and Haiti, like *Mules and Men* it eventually centers on the practices of vodun. As a celebrant of her culture, she insisted that her discoveries would not languish in print. To assure this would not be the fate of her research, Hurston directed and produced splendidly elaborate productions of *spirituals, folksongs, and storytelling on the stages of the Harold Golden Theatre in New York City and in auditoriums of historically black colleges across the American South. Even her short story anthologies broke the mold for that traditional form as they inserted the author's presence and voice into both the stories and their telling.

Over 100 manuscripts—plays, short stories, essays, articles, interviews, and reviews—are among Hurston's published and unpublished papers. Her published fiction includes the novels *Jonah's Gourd Vine* (1934), *Moses, Man of the Mountain* (1939), and *Seraph on the Suwanee* (1948). Today, we know of these works largely because of the popularity and acclaim that have come to her 1937 novel, *Their Eyes Were Watching God*.

The controversial reception given to this novel (Alain Locke's and Richard Wright's reviews expressed regret over its folkloric elements) has some relationship to the chaos that generated the story. The novel's love story had a real-life parallel—not in circumstance, but certainly in emotional intensity. Hurston said that she "tried to embalm all the tenderness of my passion" into this story, which recalled her own private relationship with a West Indian college student who was much younger than she. In the novel, Janie Killicks battles sexism and the boundaries of race and class in two unsuccessful marriages before she falls in love with TeaCake Woods, a man seventeen years her junior. The natural world, always an important "character" in Hurston's fiction, contributes to the chaos of love and life that the novel expressively represents. The fury of a hurricane forces the novel's final tragic moment, and the intense passion of the lovers' relationship shifts to the storm's unpredictable rage.

At the conclusion of *Their Eyes Were Watching God*, the character Janie withdraws to an upper room of her home in central Florida to reflect on and remember the confusion of events within her life. The closing scene of Janie's story foreshadows Hurston's own final years.

Although her controversial political views and ever-present financial crises haunted her during these final years, what was most damaging was her forced alienation from the African-American community. A false morals charge made against her in 1948 was trumpeted throughout the black press. Hurston was abandoned by the community that had nurtured her artistic and cultural spirits. She felt she could never recover from the vehemence and persistence of the headline accusations and the public shattering of her carefully constructed image.

Twelve years following her own reclusive return to Florida, where she worked as a librarian and a maid, Zora Neale Hurston suffered a stroke and died in a welfare home. Her burial was a pauper's event, the grave itself unadorned until Alice *Walker reclaimed Hurston's place in African-American literary history. Walker made a pilgrimage to Hurston's gravesite and erected a marker. Its epitaph?

Zora Neale Hurston
"A Genius of the South"
Novelist, Folklorist, Anthropologist

It is with this inscription, which spans the public and the private Hurston, that we remember her artistry and celebrate the force, grace, and skill of her presence in twentieth-century letters.

• Alice Walker, "In Search of Zora Neale Hurston," Ms. (March 1975): 74–79, 84–89. Robert E. Hemenway, Zora Neale Hurston: A Literary Biography (1977). Alice Walker, ed., I Love Myself When I Am Laughing: A Zora Neale Hurston Reader (1977). Cheryl A. Wall, "Zora Neale Hurston: Changing Her Own Words," in American Novelists Revisted: Essays in Feminist Criticism, ed. Fritz Fleischmann (1982), pp. 370–393. Karla F. C. Holloway, The Character of the Word: The Texts of Zora Neale Hurston (1987). Michael Awkward, New Essays on Their Eyes Were Watching God (1990).

Karla F. C. Holloway

HUSBANDS. See Marriage; Fathers.

HUTCHINSON, Anne (1591–1643), religious leader. Anne Hutchinson was the best-known Puritan woman in colonial Massachusetts. Tried for heresy and banished from church and state in 1637–1638, she was the pivotal figure in the colony's first major political and religious crisis, which came to be known as the *antinomian controversy. The wife of a prominent and wealthy Boston merchant and the mother of sixteen children, Hutchinson was a noted midwife and informal spiritual leader—in short, a person of considerable stature in the colony.

She aroused the suspicion of John Winthrop and other political and clerical leaders when she began holding "prophesyings" to discuss the sermons of her minister, John Cotton. Through these informal meetings of lay members of the church, Hutchinson became the head of a religious faction that believed in direct revelations from God or, in their own terms, "assurance of grace." From the clergy's perspective, this belief circumvented ministerial authority over church members. In the state's view, it was a threat to the religious underpinnings of their legislative authority.

Hutchinson and her numerous followers were denounced as antinomian, meaning one who believes that grace has placed them above (and therefore against) the law. Although Hutchinson and others denied that the individual's assurance of grace was an antinomian belief, the accusations against them stuck. The opposing faction, led by Governor John Winthrop and Deputy Governor Thomas Dudley (Anne *Bradstreet's father), succeeded in bringing Hutchinson to trial and banished her for heresy in 1637. Her minister turned against her, as did a large portion of her congregation, the First Church of Boston, which held its own trial the following spring and excommunicated her. After the public slander and banishment of Hutchinson, no other woman ever achieved such authority in the colony.

Hutchinson was named an antinomian by those who opposed her, but they could have more fairly applied this term to themselves. Throughout the trials and the subsequent narratives by her enemies, Hutchinson was vilified as a monstrous threat to public order, the epitome of evil female sexuality unwilling to submit to male authority. A threat to both church and state, she was condemned by Winthrop as "the breeder and nourisher of all these distempers." The language of Hutchinson's enemies linked female sexuality and antinomianism so strongly that Hutchinson's theological beliefs seemed almost irrelevant in the outcome of the trials. The record of the one-sided court trial conveys a sense of public mockery intended to humiliate and punish a powerful woman who challenged the leadership of Puritan men. Later trials of women involved charges of *witchcraft rather than heresy, a cultural shift presaged by the rhetoric of Hutchinson's opponents. By casting female sexuality as itself antinomian, the Puritan men of the antinomian controversy created a systematic prejudice against women in general as evil threats to the social order. Hutchinson's history provided Nathaniel Hawthorne with the inspiration for the character of Hester Prynne in his novel The Scarlet Letter.

[See also Prejudice; Witchcraft.]

• Emery Battis, Saints and Sectaries (1962). David D. Hall, ed., The Antinomian Controversy (1968). Ann Kibbey, The Interpretation of Material Shapes in Puritanism (1986). Amy Schrager Lang, Prophetic Woman (1987).

Ann Kibbey

HYSTERIA is a special pathology attributed to women, whose reproductive system ostensibly causes mental disorders ranging from seizures to schizophrenia. Victorian medical and scientific communities linked women's sexual organs—their "wandering wombs"—to a propensity for insanity. This assumed debility was variously represented in narratives by and about women, most notably in male medical texts that portended dire consequences if women were allowed access to education and in texts by women who wrote of the effects of a stifling patriarchal system. Hysteric narratives are marked by disjunction, heightened anxiety, and inconclusive endings. Pain characterizes hysteric stories, though the symptoms are often vague. Early cases and narratives of hysteria are connected to such diverse "causes" as feminism and melancholia.

The most influential diagnosis of hysteria was offered by Sigmund Freud and Josef Breuer's *Studies on Hysteria* (1893, *Standard Edition* II), which suggests that the hysteric's story is filled with gaps, imperfections, inadequate expressions, feeble motives, and deficiencies. These narrative fissures suggest that a trauma, left unnarrated or lodged in the unconscious, is the origin of the hysteric's condition. As Freud and Breuer claim, the hysteric is plagued by reminiscences. Although the symptoms occur without reference to a source or trauma, these symptoms appear in symbolic configurations. The hysteric's story, then, shifts between narrative and symbol, often without an expressed connection between the two except for subjective association—a disruption of an inadequate patriarchal language that cannot account for women's experience. To analyze the hysteric's narrative, one must unravel the actual figures of speech used from the more subtle narrative codes to locate the original trauma. The hysteric's body becomes the site of the symptoms (and their symbols) and it is here that the traumatic cause and its symptoms are confused. Freud's seduction theory of hysteria—prompted by Dora's case—has led to new feminist work on reinterpreting these narratives.

The "metaphor of illness" for women in stifling patriarchal culture is central to the analysis of women's narratives and experience of hysteria. Is hysteria a choice or rebellion against an oppressive system? or a psychic disorder that symbolizes women's oppression? an ambivalence about gender and class socialization, or an expression of repressed sexuality? This ambiguity is key to the narrative code of hysteria itself: the narrative is disjointed and noncontinuous with the often unidentified trauma. The trauma is just as often related to the cure: Silas Weir Mitchell's "rest cure" for "disordered"

women included enforced bedrest, isolation, and feeding to infantilize the patient and confine her to a "domesticity" that also enforced silence. Middle-class women (in contrast to working-class women, who suffered from overwork, malnutrition, and unassisted childrearing) were most often patients since their inactivity and passivity subjected them to the contradictions of sex roles. As Carol Smith-Rosenberg has pointed out, "hysteric behavior and stereotypic femininity" are often parallel.

Hysteria has been associated with the witchcraft trials in 1692 and has been used to explain the preponderance of women accusing others and themselves of being witches. Early "hysteric" narratives can be found in Cotton Mather's description of witchcraft in *Magnalia Christi Americana* (1702). Many of the witchcraft narratives—like Mather's description of Martha Carrier's offenses against the community—reveal conflicting Puritan sex roles for women; their testimonies suggest how these conflicts submerged Puritan women into a vortex. Puritan psychology portrayed women as the weaker vessel, more susceptible to emotionality and to the madness of sin, as well as more likely to be scapegoats for communal ills.

In the nineteenth century, "hysteric" narratives could be found in many domestic or sentimental fictions representing women's illness (see Fanny *Fern's depiction of the asylum in *Ruth Hall*), as well as in such representative texts as Harriet Beecher *Stowe's portrait of Marie St. Clare and Little Eva in *Uncle Tom's Cabin* (1852), Charlotte Perkins *Gilman's "Yellow Wallpaper" (1892), and Alice *James's *Diary* (1892). Stowe demonstrates how the social system of slavery compels women to react according to bio-political resistance—a resistance embodied in women's physical responses to their imposed cultural identity. Gilman's story connects the medical treatment to the distress manifested in hysterical behavior and narrative. Limited by her choices, Gilman's narrator "chooses" madness over the cure—the passivity forced upon her by her doctor-husband and the medical-legal establishment. The medicalization of women's bodies, or, in other words, the pathologizing of female complaints (like the medicalization of good and bad mothering in the early eugenics movements), led women to search for "scientific" or literal cures for these symptoms rather than the moral, spiritual, or social crises of the culture. Victorians believed that nervous disorders arose from "structural lesions in the brain cortex," as Ellen Bassuk has noted. Alice James's "hysteria" emerges from her drama to enable her to assert a self apart from her brothers' identification and manipulative interpretation of her subjectivity (as it is

I

IDENTITY. Modern U.S. culture idealizes the freedom we associate with individuality, the freedom to have and express one's identity in a personal, individual sense. This basic social idea originated in the cultural upheavals of early modern Europe. In the seventeenth century, the philosophical idea of "identity" (absolute or essential sameness, oneness) merged with the more practical notion of "personal" (what is private or one's own) in the * spiritual autobiographies that developed as a distinctive genre in this period. The idea of personal identity as private property asserted the continuity of individual identity in the midst of massive social change—civil war, immigration to the new world, religious dissent, and radical changes in economic, political, and social structure. Personal continuity was expressed through the linear narrative of an individual life, usually a spiritual narrative of survival through devastating experiences in which one's personal identity was endangered, if not lost altogether.

The first women's writing in the U.S. participated in this cultural development. Women who might otherwise have remained anonymous to history emerge in narratives of personal crisis, like Mary * Rowlandson's narrative of her capture by Indians, a tale of her survival as a Christian persecuted by heathens (*Narrative of the Captivity and Restoration of Mrs. Mary Rowlandson,* 1682). Her struggle to remain herself in the midst of an alien culture was the struggle to maintain her personal identity. According to her account, the threat she faced was not only the physical threat to her life, but also the cultural threat to her identity. Numerous testimonies of Quaker women recount similar struggles to remain themselves in the face of persecution by a hostile society, and often as isolated individuals in the absence of friends, husbands, or children. Although these early * autobiographies cast personal identity in primarily religious terms, as a spiritual crisis, they are the prototype for later autobiographies such as * slave narratives and immigration narratives. Basic to the genre is the tension between the individual and society.

For feminist writers, the genre is especially sensitive to the experience of women who see their identity ignored or distorted by social * stereotypes about women. Implicit in the genre is the notion of identity as private property: the struggle for identity is the struggle to acquire property, often by those who have been dispossessed by emigration, by * slavery, or by laws (implied or actual) against women's holding property.

The autobiography of personal identity is a story of contradictions. It is the narration of the individual's lifelong resistance to social pressures, the struggle to remain oneself. It is also the story of the personal choice to reject oppressive conventions and forge a new social identity suitable to the individual. What is essential and what is changeable in oneself? The concept of personal identity, with all its attendant contradictions, underlies current debates about * essentialism, * identity politics, and the significance of * ethnicity and * race for the individual.

Ann Kibbey

IDENTITY POLITICS. As its name would suggest, "identity politics" emerged as the strategy of groups advocating that politics be grounded in personal identity. Christened in the late 1970s, the idea has become the rallying cry for many whose "identities" have been suppressed within dominant social structures: notably, women, people of color, lesbians/gays, religious minorities, the underprivileged, and, of course, those who define their identities through a combination of one or more of these categories. The movement refuses universalized understandings of "humanity" and argues instead for an attention to, even a celebration of, differences.

According to the logic of identity politics, "difference" is and can be an effective basis for the critical practices necessary to change the very systems that try to mask, deny, or denigrate any identity that is not bourgeois, white, heterosexual and/or male. (It is important to note here, however, that groups like the neo-Nazis also employ a form of identity politics in their pride in the Aryan race and their sense of themselves as an oppressed minority.)

While in a broad sense the roots of a politics of identity are ancient (think of the Jews, the early Christians, and numerous other ethnic or religious groups that have organized around their ostracization), "identity politics" as an identifiable term emerged only within the last thirty years or so. It particularly emerged in feminism, where, to put it simply, woman is the "identity," feminism the "politics." That is, feminist positions, tactics, and goals are typically derived from critical attention to women, their experiences, oppression, and strengths.

Within feminism itself, the origin of "identity politics" is often traced to "A Black Feminist Statement" by the *Combahee River Collective, first issued in 1977 and published in Cherríe *Moraga and Gloria *Anzaldúa's *This Bridge Called My Back: Writings By Radical Women of Color* (1981; 1983). The statement's authors, a coalition of black lesbian feminists, explicitly call for a radical politics stemming from a focus on a specific identity and its oppression—here, from analyzing, discussing, and revaluing the experience of being both black and lesbian. Many of the other contributors to *This Bridge* also proclaim the importance of identity as the source of resistance to the homogenizing and marginalizing gestures that mark their daily lives.

As the Combahee River Collective notes, the feminist motto that "the personal is political" provides one springboard for their own politics of identity. The Collective, in fact, was one of the first voices to provide a critique of such a motto as being too quick to equate "the personal" with white women's experiences alone. Early feminist "*consciousness-raising" sessions were important in providing a space where women's concerns and issues, often dismissed as trivial or isolated, could be voiced, legitimized, and brought together into the makings of a political movement that would, among other things, put the lie to such dismissals. But as even the organizers of these sessions now would acknowledge, there was a tendency to define the "woman" whose experience was being tapped as homogeneous, a definition that failed to recognize the differences between women (differences that identity politics specifically address and rally around).

Perhaps because the concept of identity politics is recognized to be such an empowering one, there is no shortage of warnings as to its dangers. One of the most cogent is Biddy Martin's and Chandra Talpade Mohanty's "Feminist Politics: What's Home Got to Do with It?" (in *Feminist Studies/Critical Studies*, ed. Teresa de Lauretis, 1986). Drawing on Minnie Bruce *Pratt's "Identity: Skin Blood Heart" in *Yours in Struggles: Three Feminist Perspectives on Anti-Semitism and Racism* (1984), Martin and Mohanty challenge the comforting and comfortable notion of not only feminism but all "identities" as "homes"—as safe, romanticized havens

to which one can always return. Pratt, they argue, is exemplary in that she constantly situates and resituates herself and her positions in the social realm. This historicizing process, as Martin and Mohanty argue, also enables Pratt as a white woman to get beyond the "white guilt" that prevents so many white theorists from working with and educating themselves about other races with differently situated identities.

Another important article that grapples with both the significance and problems of identity politics within feminism is Linda Alcoff's "Cultural Feminism Versus Poststructuralism: The Identity Crisis in Feminist Theory" (*Signs: Journal of Women in Culture and Society* 13, no. 3, 1988). After detailing what Alcoff sees as cultural feminism's tendency to define "woman" in the singular and poststructuralism's tendency to refuse any and all definitions, Alcoff promotes a strategy not unlike the one Martin and Mohanty identify in Pratt's work. Alcoff calls for "positionality" based on a historical understanding of identity, one that would frame "identity" as a process, not an essence. Positionality allows for an identity politics that is constantly questioning what identity (gender, race, class, sexual preference, etc.) means at any given moment in any given context.

One of the most powerful critiques of "the personal" as it plays out within feminist "politics" is bell hooks's "feminist politicization: a comment" in her *Talking Back: thinking feminist, thinking black* (1989). Rather than, as was intended, connecting the personal with the political so as to shatter the former's status as private and hence outside of politics, the slogan "the personal is political," hooks maintains, has often led to an exclusive, even narcissistic dwelling on the personal at the expense of politics. Hooks insists that beginning with the personal is a crucial first step in educating individuals for critical consciousness and resistance, especially for those subordinate(d) groups that have as yet had little opportunity to voice their own individual or collective identities. And yet, hooks also insists that the next step must be a politicization that results in a sense of coalition, of working together across differences to insure that the personal is never again depoliticized. "Rapping" about one's unique oppression is not, she maintains, at all the same thing as working collectively to end oppression.

To take one final example from the many persuasive critical analyses available, Diana Fuss's "Lesbian and Gay Theory: The Question of Identity Politics," in her *Essentially Speaking: Feminism, Nature and Difference* (1989), challenges the stability and coherence of not only "identity" but "politics." Beginning with an examination of the struggle over whether gays and lesbians are "born or made," Fuss maintains that arguments for identity politics often lack an understanding of the complicated processes whereby identity is formed: of psychic and social processes that construct fundamentally unstable identities. Fuss also argues that those who try to avoid essentialism by staking their identity claims in "the political" versus "the personal" tend to confer upon political identities the stability they recognize as lacking in personal ones. She concludes that slogans like "the personal is political" risk transforming everything into politics and hence depoliticizes and dehistoricizes politics.

Celebrations of and challenges to identity politics are not solely contained within academic, theoretical treatises. For instance, many works of "women's fiction" grapple with the issues of self, voice, and resistance that are essential to any politics of identity. Works such as Marilyn *French's *The Women's Room* (1977) served for many as powerful consciousness-raising tools despite their relatively uncomplicated notion of woman- and sisterhood and of "women's experience." Novels including Maxine Hong *Kingston's *The Woman Warrior* (1976), Gloria *Naylor's *The Women of Brewster Place* (1982), Louise *Erdrich's *The Beet Queen* (1986), and Sarah Schulman's *After Delores* (1988) are each more careful to "situate" the specific identities and experiences they explore. They illustrate the extent to which all identities are fictional, if still necessary fictions. Furthermore, such works call into question not only the concept of a "woman's" identity or experience but also the notion of a "woman's fiction."

As this entry might suggest, there seem to be more critiques of identity politics than there are calls for them. If so, the question arises as to why such a politics should appear so threatening when it is by no means dominant. As hooks rightly suggests, we need to acknowledge, before we engage in automatic critique or dismissal, that "identity" and "identity politics" might mean different things for "different" people: clearly, it can be used by specific groups as a powerfully strategic tool by which to gain both voice and visibility. More to the point, we need to ask why this rush to deny the importance of identity as ground for a politics of resistance emerged almost simultaneously with the increasing presence of people of color and gays—and, indeed, of multiculturalism and difference as vital issues—on the national stage. By asking such questions, we can situate not just our own identity, our own politics, but our own stances toward identity politics—all necessary steps if the personal is to be truly political and the political to be truly transformative.

Cynthia J. Davis

IKO, Momoko (b. 1940), playwright. Momoko Iko was born in Wapato, Washington. Following the outbreak of World War II, Iko, at the age of two, was interned at Hart Mountain, Wyoming, in one of ten internment camps administered by the Department of Justice. A five-year-old child at the time of her release, Iko relocated with her family to Chicago. Her mother did piecework sewing and her father did factory work; despite economic hardship, the Iko apartment became a gathering place for displaced Japanese Americans seeking to resettle following the war. Of this period Iko states, "As I was growing up, our house was like a center for young Nisei. . . . There were always people coming in and out . . . I know a lot of my stories come out of that period." Despite the fact that Iko was a young child during her internment, the camp experience surfaces as a major thematic motif in her work, directly in *Gold Watch* (1970) and indirectly in such interesting works as *Flowers and Household Gods* (1975), *Boutique Living and Disposable Icons* (1987–1988), *Second City Flat* (1976–1977), *When We Were Young* (1973), and *Old Man* (1972).

Iko began writing fiction at Northern Illinois University and later as she completed her degree in English at the University of Illinois. Though originally intending to be a novelist, Iko became intrigued by the dramatic form after attending a performance of Lorraine *Hansberry's *A Raisin in the Sun*. Her first play, *Gold Watch* (1970), was begun after she read an announcement that the newly formed East West Players in Los Angeles were sponsoring a national playwrighting contest for Asian-American writers. Adapted from a portion of an unpublished novel, *Gold Watch* takes place during the tumultuous days preceding internment. After winning the East West Players contest, it was produced in 1972 at the Inner City Cultural Center in Los Angeles, and has received numerous subsequent productions, including a 1975 adaptation for television by PBS. *Gold Watch* is anthologized in *Unbroken Thread: An Anthology of Plays by Asian American Women* (1992). In addition to the aforementioned plays, she is the author of *Hollywood Mirrors* (1978). Her works have been primarily produced by ethnic American theaters, most notably the Pan Asian Repertory, New York City; the Asian American Theater Company, San Francisco; the North West Asian Theater Company, Seattle; the East West Players, Los

Angeles; and the Inner City Cultural Center, Los Angeles.

Roberta Uno

IMAGINARY, The. *See* Psychoanalysis and Women, article on Jacques Lacan.

IMAGIST MOVEMENT. A movement in American poetry prominent from about 1912 to 1917 that was dedicated to rejuvenating poetic language and form through the objective presentation of visual images. Ezra Pound first used the term *Imagiste* to refer to one of his own poems in a letter to Harriet Monroe, the editor of the newly formed *Poetry*. Several months later, he sent Monroe poems by *H. D. (Hilda Doolittle), to which he had attached the name "H. D., Imagiste." His intent was to launch Doolittle's public career and a new movement, and he did just that: the following March (1913), Monroe published Imagist manifestos by Pound and F. S. Flint; *Des Imagistes: An Anthology* appeared in 1914; it was promptly followed, minus Pound and the French spelling, by three years of *Some Imagist Poets* (1915, 1916, 1917), edited and introduced by Amy *Lowell. After 1917, Lowell decided that the anthologies' goal of introducing new poets to a wider American audience had been accomplished. In this she was right: While the first edition of Louis Untermeyer's important *Modern American Poetry* (1919) included poems by only Pound, Lowell, and H. D., the 1925 third revised edition was expanded to include, besides those three, William Carlos Williams, John Gould Fletcher, T. S. Eliot, and Marianne *Moore, thus reflecting Untermeyer's somewhat begrudging acknowledgement that Imagism was a significant force in American poetry.

Imagism's significance lies in the clean break it announced with past poetic forms and the base it provided for the development of the major tenets of modern poetry. Reacting to what was left of the Fireside poets—Bryant, Lowell, Whittier, and the other household names who dominated nineteenth-century American poetry—and their turn-of-the-century imitators and to the excesses of a poetry seen to have degenerated into a sentimental and vague conventionality, the Imagists drew on T. E. Hulme's theories of metaphor in outlining their own formal requirements for a new American poetry characterized by "hard light, clear edges." They favored precision in word choice to produce concentrated effect, organic rhythms drawn from the subject of the poem and loyal to the musical phrase rather than the metrical foot, complete freedom in choosing a subject matter, and an absolute refusal to make abstract or generalized statements about that subject. In place of such "messages," the Imagists substituted the concise presentation of a concrete image.

In the best Imagist poems, these principles produced a structure undergirded by an implied metaphor, by the juxtaposition, unremarked, of dissimilar objects. Pound's "In a Station of the Metro" and especially H. D.'s paradigmatic "Oread" use this analogical structure as the means by which form itself becomes a source of the poems' discoveries. By forcing readers to define the logic of their own connections, both poems become not the static pictures suggested by the movement's name, but dynamic processes in which meaning is recreated in the reader in the act of reading. For example, the repeated substitution and reversal of pines for waves in "Oread" does not produce a single image at all but the "complex" of effects alluded to in Pound's famous definition: an image is "an intellectual and emotional complex in an instant of time."

A critical look at how Imagism has been historicized within Modernism is crucial to gauging the contributions of its primary female participants, Lowell and H. D., both of whose careers were touched and in some ways marred by Pound's influence. Pound's defection from Imagism to Vorticism after the publication of *Des Imagistes* has been a major point around which Modernism's would-be periodizers continually circulate. While claiming his shift reflected his commitment to the poem as an active process rather than a static picture, Pound's departure seems also intimately connected to the fact that Imagism was taking shape in the United States without his help under the leadership of Amy Lowell. After leaving Pound's company in London in 1913 and taking most of his Imagist followers with her, Lowell was quickly recognized in this country as the spokesperson for Imagism as well one of its leading poets. With Pound's earlier *Poetry* essays, Lowell's "Prefaces" constitute the most explicit and systematic attempts to define Imagism and its intentions for American poetry. Furthermore, whatever success Imagism enjoyed in this country was accomplished largely through her efforts and skill as an editor, fundraiser, and spokesperson.

Amy Lowell's work, however, has been collapsed by literary history under Pound's denigrating title "Amygism," a term of abuse signifying the writing of those for whom, Pound thought, the original principles of Imagism served merely as an invitation to description. Consistent with his tendency to gender feminine whatever he was in the process of walking away from, Pound's label implies Lowell's feminized corruption of his original intentions for Imagism. With its focus on her name, however, Pound's designation also suggests his pique at being replaced as the movement's acknowledged leader.

More importantly, Pound's devaluing of Imagism as a promising literary movement stalled by Lowell's incompetence as a poet has resulted indirectly in superficial readings of H. D.'s work and the underestimation of her contribution to the development of modern American poetry and Modernism itself. Critical discussions of H. D. often stop with the early Imagist poems and fail, even then, to account for their significance in the articulation of Imagist principles. H. D. is presented as the ideal Imagist poet who, unlike her important male contemporaries, never outgrew the movement. Not only does this evaluation inaccurately reflect H. D.'s later work, which both overlaps with and departs from the major texts of High Modernism, but it also misidentifies the importance of her early poetry, which can be read not just as an expression of Imagist principles, but as the model that enabled their articulation. Indeed, Cyrena Pondrom has recently argued (Friedman and Duplessis, 1990) that it was the specific example of H. D.'s poetry that moved Pound from his early attempts in 1912 to define Imagist principles to their full elaboration in his later essays on Vorticism. If such was the case, then H. D. could be said to have originated in practice what Pound advanced in theory.

• Amy Lowell, *Tendencies in Modern American Poetry* (1917). H. D., *Collected Poems* (1925). Stanley Coffman, *Imagism: A Chapter for the History of Modern Poetry* (1951). Ezra Pound, *Selected Prose, 1909–1965* (1975). Janice S. Robinson, *H. D.: The Life and Work of an American Poet* (1982). Richard Benvenuto, *Amy Lowell* (1985). William Drake, *The First Wave: Women Poets in America, 1915–1945* (1987). Susan Stanford Friedman and Rachel Blau Duplessis, eds., *Signets: Reading H. D.* (1990).

Jane Kuenz

IMMIGRANT WRITING. With the exception of the diverse indigenous peoples who have inhabited this land for eons, people living in the United States are all immigrants or descendants of immigrants who came, or were forcibly brought, from somewhere else. While many women have written as "immigrants" defined by a specific ethnic identity, the term is confusing and inexact because it has been applied differently and even pejoratively in various historical eras. English writers, for example, have rarely been called "immigrants." The term needs to be used circumspectly, with an awareness that who is or is not an "immigrant" often changes with a group's increasing assimilation to dominant cultural norms.

[*See also* African-American Writing; Arab-American Writing; Asian-American Writing; Assimilation; Caribbean-American Writing; Catholic Writing; Chicana Writing; Chinese-American Writing; Citizenship; Cuban-American Writing; Ethnicity and Writing; European Immigrant Writing; Filipino-American Writing; Immigration; Irish-American Writing; Italian-American Writing; Japanese-American Writing; Jewish-American Writing; Korean-American Writing; Latina Writing; Polish-American Writing; Polynesian Writing; South Asian-American Writing; Southeast Asian-American Writing.]

Cathy N. Davidson

IMMIGRATION. Between 1820 and 1980 more than forty-six million people entered the United States, the vast majority as immigrants from Europe, Latin America, Asia, and the Caribbean. In the decades before 1920, men accounted, on average, for roughly three out of every five of these newcomers although sex ratios for specific immigrant groups varied widely. Women made up only a small proportion of immigrants in Asian and some eastern European groups while females consistently outnumbered males among the Irish and, after 1920, among West Indians, Bohemians, and Jews. Since World War II the majority of all immigrants have been women.

Until recently, immigrants in general, and immigrant women in particular, were simultaneously viewed as problems and as objects of reform. Portrayed as both passive victims "uprooted" by processes beyond their control and as backward-looking traditionalists resistant to American progress, the foreign-born wife and mother emerged in the first decades of the twentieth century as a figure of pity and danger, a well-meaning but ignorant woman, the "ox without horns." Both the civil rights movement and the women's movement challenged such popular images and by placing women at the center of analysis, a new generation of scholars, many of them descendants of immigrants, called attention to the resourcefulness of women coping with discrimination, poverty, racism, and "culture shock" as well as with ethnic and class prejudice. Reconsidered in the 1970s and 1980s as subjects rather than as objects, immigrant women took on new importance as active participants in the struggle to survive and give meaning to "ethnic" communities they experienced as both empowered and burdened by Old World traditions and values.

For women who left homes to come to America, stories were thus less about making things up than about working things out. What did it mean to be a wife, mother, or daughter in a new world where individual self-realization and -definition collided with Old World traditions of female responsibility and family loyalty? How did one reconcile older patterns of marital relationships with newer codes of sexual behavior and expectations of intimacy? To what extent were the struggles and sacrifices of immigrant mothers a source of empowerment or oppression for their daughters? Whatever the form—*autobiography, fiction, poetry, memoirs, *diaries, life stories, speeches, or family tales—*storytelling helped Old World mothers and New World daughters to make sense of their world and of their place in it. Far from idle fictions, their stories were acts of comprehension. As Isak Dinesen once commented, "I could bear almost anything if I could make it into a story."

Yet immigrant women mobilized their stories not only to understand the world, but to change it. For writers as diverse as Anzia *Yezierska, Mari Tomasi, Maxine Hong *Kingston, Kim Chernin, Rose Winslow, Lucy Robins Lang, Emma *Goldman, and Amy Jacques Garvey, the immigrant saga was as much a story about *possessing* a new world as it was about being uprooted and displaced from an old one. As Maxine Hong Kingston makes clear in *The Woman Warrior: Memoirs of a Girlhood Among Ghosts* (1979), it was both as women and as warriors that immigrant mothers, wives, and daughters confronted the constraints and possibilities of a new world. Against a backdrop of poverty, discrimination, and the ambiguities of America's many promises, immigrant women imagined themselves remade in an America still in the making. Writing in 1922, Anzia Yezierska described her popular stories of Jewish immigrant life on New York's Lower East Side as her contribution to making an America that was not yet finished, and in works like Rose Schneiderman's *All For One*, Emma Goldman's *Living My Life*, Lucy Robins Langs's *Tomorrow is Beautiful*, and especially Yezierska's *Bread Givers*, rebellious women bitterly questioned the limited paths available to them not only in the old but in the new world as well. "We foreigners are the orphans," wrote Yezierska in the midst of the depression, "the stepchildren of America. The old world is dead behind us, and the new world—about which we dreamed . . . is not yet born."

Disrupting popular images of immigrant women as passive victims of landlords, bosses, and social reformers, the stories of immigrant women suggest the degree to which neighborhood life and ethnic communities sustained female collaboration and activism. In the life stories of Jessie Lopez de la Cruz, daughter of Mexican immigrants; Irish-born Mary Harris, "Mother Jones"; Polish-born Rose Winslow; or Puerto Rican immigrant and rent striker Innocencia Flores, immigrant women move in a latticework of relationships where close living arrangements facilitated exchange and the sharing of goods, services, and mutual concerns. Central in the writing of well-known immigrant activists, female patterns of exchange and traditions of reciprocity are the sustaining web through which immigrant women and their children confront American society. In her autobiographical novel *Brown Girl, Brownstones*, Paule *Marshall describes the West Indian community that emerged after World War II in New York City as a tapestry of female neighbors and kin whose lives became the warp around which childhood unfolded. Encouraging mutual support, female efforts in immigrant neighborhoods also enhanced women's concepts of material rights and sustained efforts to negotiate and agitate for economic justice. In her diary of the Harlem rent strike of 1964, Flores records the role that neighborhood women played in arranging meetings, guarding fellow strikers' apartments, and sharing childcare. Like the women continually moving in and out of each other's kitchens in the novels of Yezierska, Harlem women stick their heads in and out of windows to and from meetings, work, and picketing. Such exchanges frequently led to the development of formal political organizations such as the Polish Women's Alliance, which began in the home of immigrant activist Stefania Chmielinska.

Antonia Pola's novel *Who Can Buy The Stars?* (1957) suggests as well the extent to which rituals, such as a child's christening, blurred the lines between kin and neighbor and helped to overcome Old World hostilities. Surprised at the easy mixing of once-fierce enemies from northern and southern Italy, Pola's central character, mother Sasso, explains, "When you are far away from your own country, everybody who comes from there . . . becomes as dear as a close relative." Yet novels like Marshall's, as well as the autobiographies of rebellious women such as Rose Cohn's *Out of the Shadows*, Rose Pesotta's *Bread Upon the Waters*, or Yezierska's *Red Ribbon on a White Horse*, are also poignant testimonials to the constraints of community pressure on women who rejected traditional female responsibilities. Nor was the immigrant community always capable of socializing such customary female responsibilities as childcare in order to give women chances to go to school, earn a wage, or socialize with friends. Unable to pay for childcare and with no other options than to stay at home, one Chinese mother asked in *Longtime Californ'* (1972), "When will it ever be my turn?"

If storytelling, what Maxine Hong Kingston describes in her family as "talkstory," has been central to female strategies of survival, the stories that women tell are themselves varied and complex. Just as women experienced immigration in different ways, their stories speak to the particularity of the immigrant experience as race, class, and ethnicity both shaped and were shaped by immigration. Irish, Italian, Hispanic, West Indian, Polish, Syrian, Jewish, and Anglo women brought with them different cultural understandings of what it meant to be a woman as well as contrasting histories of female participation in the family, the community, and the workplace. Economically assertive and accustomed to late, even reluctant marriage, such Irish immigrants as Louise Imogene Guiney, Katherine O'Keefe, Mary Blake, and Elenor Cecilia Donnelly were well situated to participate in the emerging fields of journalism and popular literature that opened in the late nineteenth century. Riding the crest of Irish nationalism and infused with the sentimental power of Victorian womanhood, works by Rosa Mulholland, Mary Anne Sadlier, and Lelia Hardin Bugg received popular acclaim and brought to the surface of national discourse the hidden world of immigrant shoe workers, factory girls, and domestic servants.

Culturally different, women also entered the United States in uneven patterns, providing dramatically altered landscapes upon arrival. In *Rosa: The Life of An Italian Immigrant* (1970), the unlettered Rosa Cassettari reminds her biographer of how different her life would have been had she not found the services provided by the Chicago Commons, a settlement house in the early twentieth century. Here she learned English, met friends, and found work, all of which gave her confidence to go back to Italy and confront the gentry who had made her life there miserable. So, too, in *Like Lesser Gods* (1949), Mari Tomasi uses the stories of her childhood to imagine a better world for her immigrant parents had they come to America after the quarries had shut or been made safe. Confined by sickness as a child, Tomasi became the bearer of the family story as her immigrant parents told of tales of better times and of an America racked by granite dust, poverty, too many children, illness, fear, and crushed dreams.

Like many daughters of immigrants, Tomasi finds the stories of her ancestors both empowering and burdensome. On the one hand they provide the basis with which to forge a viable adulthood independent of family and freed from the restraints that weighed down her mother. Yet by turning her family stories into fiction, by becoming an American, the immigrant daughter separated herself from her parents' culture: "I had gone too far away from life," lamented Yezierska, "and I did not know how to get back." Like Yezierska, Kingston, and Chernin, Tomasi found in the immigrant story a way to express the self. In this sense, the act of writing was for immigrant women and their daughters simultaneously an act of creation and destruction—a rupture with a culture that subsumes female individuality in the web of patriarchal family life.

Yet such stories are also about forging new meanings of ethnicity and new possibilities for an ethnic and multicultural America. Stories of immigrants are stories of struggle but also of transformation and recreation. Commenting on the story of her immigrant mother's struggle in America, Chernin writes in her autobiography, *In My Mother's House: A Daughter's Story* (1984), "It is a tale of transformation and development—the female reversal of that patriarchal story in which the power of the family's founder is lost and dissipated as the inheriting generations decline and fall to ruin. A story of power." Here the writings of immigrant women offer subversive alternatives to male perspectives in which the boy or man rejects home and family and seeks autonomy by either "making it" in the dominant culture or by participating in a world that is ultimately self-destructive, as in the case of Chicano and Puerto Rican immigrant literature. As Michael Fischer puts it, Bernice Zamora calls forth women's lifegiving traditions in her poetry collection, *Restless Serpents* (1976), as a healing potential to the male barrios depicted by Chicano writers. Like the "bread givers" described by Yezierska, Zamora's lifegiving rituals challenge paradigms that pit assimilation against "ethnicity" and insist on destroying the past in order to build a new identity. Not unlike *Paper Fish* (1980) by Tina De Rosa and *A Cup of the Sun* (1961) by Octavia Waldo, contemporary Chicana women insist that a sense of belonging involves a dialogue with the family and its past rather than a rejection of it. In this sense, as Fischer argues, immigrant stories become the recreation of ethnicity as each generation reinvents and reinterprets its "ethnic" self.

Yet the voices of immigrant mothers and daughters also remind us that women do not invent themselves. The struggle for self-fulfillment frequently meant a life bitterly remembered for its loneliness and guilt. Carmolina's rhetorical question in *Paper Fish*—"They won't ever let us go, will they?"—spoke for many women of the constraints that could never fully be authored out of immigrant lives.

[*See also* Ethnicity and Writing.]

• Victor G. deBarry Nee and Brett de Bary Nee, *Longtime Californ': A Documentary Study of an American Chinatown* (1972). Alice Kessler Harris, Introduction to *Bread Givers*, by Anzia Yezierska (1975). Maxine Schwartz Seller, ed., *Immigrant Women* (1981). Hasia R. Diner, *Erin's Daughters in America: Irish Immigrant Women in the Nineteenth Century* (1983). Helen Barolini, ed., *The Dream Book: An Anthology of Writings by Italian-American Women* (1985). Mary V. Dearborn, *Pocahontas's Daughters: Gender and Ethnicity in American Culture* (1986). Michael Fischer, "Ethnicity and the Post-Modern Arts of Memory," in *Writing Culture: The Poetics and Politics of Ethnography*, eds. James Clifford and George Marcus (1986), pp. 194–233. Mary Jo Bona, "Claiming a Tradition: Italian-American Women Writers," Ph.D. diss., University of Wisconsin, Madison (1989). Virginia Yans-McLaughlin, ed., *Immigration Reconsidered: History, Sociology, and Politics* (1990). *Criticism in the Borderlands: Studies in Chicano Literature, Culture, and Ideology* (1991). Irene I. Blea, *La Chicana and the Intersection of Race, Class, and Gender* (1992).

Ardis Cameron

IMPERIALISM. *See* Colonialism.

INCEST. Finding "incest" in women's writings depends upon the definition with which one begins. Since the late 1970s, feminists have been actively contesting and expanding definitions of incest and the meanings of incest have shifted dramatically in recent years. These shifts in meaning are both problematic and promising for explorations of the relationships between women's writing and incest.

Incest has traditionally been narrowly defined as sexual intercourse between persons too closely related to marry. While this legal interpretation has dominated, many disciplines, including medicine, religion, criminal justice, psychoanalysis, and child protective services, to name only a few, have played a part in constructing the content and meanings of incest. Incest has been categorized in these disciplines under topics such as pedophilia, paraphilia, sexual perversions, sex crimes, and child molesting.

Since the late 1970s the definition of incest has expanded to include both a wider range of relationships (such as stepparents and siblings, unrelated adults living in the home, adult caretakers, etc.) and sexual behaviors and practices not restricted to intercourse (such as exposure and voyeurism, fondling, masturbation, or oral sex). Incest has been increasingly subsumed within the broader categories of sexual abuse or child sexual abuse. Because concepts and categories such as sexual violence, sexual assault, and sexual abuse only began to appear in the mid-1970s, prior to that time the term incest itself was unlikely to turn up much in card catalogs, book indexes, or bibliographies.

These new, broader definitions of incest place power relations and violations of trust at the center of analysis. They also recognize the effects of child sexual abuse (for example, a history of eating or panic disorders, chronic depression, substance abuse, or sexual dysfunction) as indicators of its likely occurrence. This use of effects of abuse as diagnostic criteria is in part a response to the ways in which denial and repression function for survivors, who often report having no conscious memory of their abuse for years. It is also based on a belief that one of the ways in which the existence and prevalence of child sexual abuse has been minimized and denied is through misdiagnosis—treating symptoms rather than identifying and addressing their causes.

In addition to reading between the lines of the disciplines and discourses that construct child sexual abuse, finding incest may also depend on how the content of a text is interpreted. For example, incest or sexual abuse may be explicitly named or clearly recognizable in such texts as Maya *Angelou's *I Know Why the Caged Bird Sings* (1980), Carolyn Chute's *The Beans of Egypt, Maine* (1985), or the poetry of Anne *Sexton. Or we may find incest explicitly in historical documents and texts such as *Religion and Domestic Violence in Early New England: The Memoirs of Abigail Abbot Bailey* (1815). But, if we discover the diary of a woman who reports having run away from home at a very young age and becoming a prostitute, or who describes a history of suicidal thoughts and attempts, who is agoraphobic, or who struggles throughout her life with depression and alcoholism, and so on, have we found incest in a woman's writing? Often the absence of incest in women's writing is as significant as its presence.

The development of feminist antirape and battered women's movements in the 1970s created institutional spaces (such as hotlines, rape crisis centers, and shelters) and developed analytic tools and practices with which to break the silence about sexual and family violence. Participants in these movements simultaneously redefined these forms of violence from the perspectives of victims and survivors while working for institutional and legislative changes that reflected and responded to their needs. Advocates for sexually abused children have followed the pattern of the antirape and battered women's movements, creating alternative definitions and institutions while also working for changes within "legitimate" institutions. There are now, for example, underground networks for abused children and mothers as well as specialized teams within police departments or mental health clinics, each of which attempts to protect sexually abused children in different ways. Representative examples of some of the first writings that contributed to this redefinition of incest are first-person accounts and anthologies (such as Katherine Brady's *Father's Days* and Louise Armstrong's *Kiss Daddy Goodnight*, both published in 1979) and historical accounts that placed incest within the broader context of child sexual abuse (such as Florence Rush's *The Best Kept Secret*, 1980).

Work within social service and advocacy settings is playing a significant role in producing a new body of knowledge about the sexual abuse of children. The publication of self-help books, sexual abuse prevention guides for parents and teachers, bibliographies, research findings, and professional guidelines mushroomed during the 1980s. There has been an increasing stream of newsletters, journal articles, and books, as well as videos, workshops, and conferences on the issue. In addition to these sources, information and writing about incest is likely to turn up in case notes and records from hospitals, mental health clinics, or child protective agencies; police statements; legal records and transcripts; board meeting minutes or volunteer training manuals from rape crisis centers; school curricula (from primary through college/professional schools); or grant proposals.

However, feminist historical and theoretical work based upon the newer definitions of incest and this emerging knowledge being generated is only beginning. The feminist research and theorizing on incest within the academy has tended to be within "applied" disciplines such as psychology, social work, medicine, or law. Thus far there has been relatively little overlap between work outside the academy or within its applied disciplines and contemporary academic feminist theory. Some examples of the forms and directions such work might take are Judith Butler's exploration of the role of the incest taboo in the construction and enforcement of heterosexuality in *Gender Trouble* (1990) and Linda Gordon's work on family violence and child abuse, *Heroes of Their Own Lives* (1988). As things stand now, much of the information and theory on incest that exists is not feminist, much of the feminist work is fairly recent, and the practical, political, and theoretical implications of feminist work on incest and recovery are only beginning to be explored and articulated.

[*See also* Rape.]

• Judith Lewis Herman, *Father-Daughter Incest* (1981). Suzanne Sgroi, *Handbook of Clinical Intervention in Child Sexual Abuse* (1982). Lenore E. Auerbach Walker, ed., *Handbook on Sexual Abuse of Children* (1988). Ellen Bass and Laura Davis, *The Courage to Heal* (1988). Judith Lewis Herman, *Trauma and Recovery* (1992).

Kelly Jarrett

INDIAN RIGHTS MOVEMENT. *See* American Indian Rights Movement.

INDUSTRIALIZATION, with its complex of change that extended gradually throughout social and economic life in the nineteenth century, produced diverse effects on women's writing. For all women of the working class, as for women in slavery, industrialization changed the conditions of labor and domestic life, but factors of class, caste, race, and gender ensured that writing as personal expression or as enterprise was reserved largely for privileged persons. Female laborers had limited access to print culture; the writing they produced remains relatively inaccessible. The voices of the first women to work in the early factories of New England can, however, be heard in archival letters, diaries, and ephemera, and in publications of workers and of labor organizations. According to documents gathered by Mary Blewett (*We Will Rise in Our Might: Workingwomen's Voices from Nineteenth-Century New England*, 1991), female shoemakers, for example, began to organize for higher wages as early as the 1830s; such publications as the *Awl*, newspaper of the Lynn (Mass.) Society of Journeymen Cordwainers, ran a series of letters on the rights and moral position of female shoebinders in 1844–1845. *The Factory Girls* (Philip S. Foner, ed.; 1977), collects letters, reportage, commentary, and poetry by and about workers both militant and genteel, originally published in local newspapers and union journals. The *Lowell Offering* (1840–1845), the most acclaimed of magazines for female "operatives," was written and edited by laborers who had caste advantage and largely genteel values as descendants of the Puritans and daughters of the New England farming class.

The *Offering* was a grassroots publication, purchased in 1842 by two women with mill experience, editors Harriet Farley and Harriot F. Curtis, and drawing its contributors from the mills themselves. Questions remain as to its degree of editorial independence from the mill owners, who gave the magazine various forms of support. In fiction, editorials, letters, articles, and poetry, the *Offering* taught readers to abide their labor through Christian morality, self-discipline, and intellectual self-improvement, and it defended mill workers against charges of immorality. Among the most successful and widely published of its contributors was Lucy

Larcom, whose *A New England Girlhood, Outlined from Memory* (1889) describes Larcom's childhood home in a Lowell boardinghouse and her years of labor in the mills. Her blank-verse novel, *An Idyl of Work* (1875), fondly recalls the early days of Lowell and the character and experience of the mill girls. Contributor Harriet Hanson Robinson, who worked in the mills from age ten until marriage at twenty-three, published *Loom and Spindle; or, Life among the Early Mill Girls* (1898), a nostalgic account of an Edenic Lowell. Eliza Jane Cate published, among other works, *Lights and Shadows of Factory Life in New England, by a Factory Girl* (1843), a novel, typical of others of the period, about a factory worker who devotes herself to helping her needy family and to improving her mind.

Among contemporary critics of the *Offering* was a contributor, Sarah G. Bagley, who founded the Lowell Female Labor Reform Association, published two radical *Factory Tracts* (1845) allegedly rejected by the *Offering*, and wrote in support of the Ten Hour Movement for the activist *Voice of Industry* (published by the New England Workingmen's Association, 1845–1848). The Lowell experiment inspired a number of works of fiction, including Ariel Ivers Cummings's *The Factory Girl; or, Gardez la Coeur* (1847), the anonymous *Anna Archdale; or, The Lowell Factory Girl* (c. 1850), and Sarah Maria Fry's *The Factory Girl; or, "Trust in God"* (c. 1850).

For women of the middle class and above who did not labor in factories or produce "outwork" at home, industrialization meant structural changes in domestic economy and family life. It also meant wider access to print culture in general and a new array of subject matter. Among notable works by middle-class Anglo-American women are the many publications of Catharine *Beecher, whose domestic ideology took shape in reaction to the altered status of women as production moved from home to factory. A visit to Lowell led Beecher to conclude that working women should leave the factories and find teaching positions in the West, in keeping with her larger plan for the redemption and moral progress of the nation, as outlined in *The Evils Suffered by American Women and American Children: The Causes and the Remedy* (1846). Beecher's work on domestic economy draws its emphasis on scientific management and efficiency directly from industrialism; likewise her insistence on the complementary social duties of the housekeeper, as seen in works such as *Principles of Domestic Science as Applied to the Duties and Pleasures of Home* (1870).

Beecher's grandniece Charlotte Perkins *Gilman radically reconsidered many of Beecher's themes in *Women and Economics* (1898), a celebrated polemic on sex relations within the new industrial order, in which Gilman calls for domestic labor to become professionalized and removed from the home. Gilman's friend Helen Stuart Campbell wrote popular home economics textbooks (including *The Easiest Way in Housekeeping and Cooking* [1881]) designed to address the needs of the working poor. In the 1880s Campbell produced investigative journalism, a treatise on the slums entitled *The Problem of the Poor* (1882), and work on the careers of working women, a topic of much women's journalism, including that of Gilman for the Providence, Rhode Island, *People*, beginning in 1887. At mid-century the materialism of the age and the gulf between rich and poor became a theme of Lydia Maria *Child, in journalism collected in *Letters from New York* (first series 1843; second series 1845); Susan B. *Anthony's *The Revolution* (1868–1872) addressed the cause of the woman laborer; and Ida Tarbell's influential career as a muckraker began in 1902, with the first installment in *McClure's* of the series that became *The History of the Standard Oil Company* (1904). An early study of women and industrialism appears in *The College, the Market, and the Court; or, Woman's Relation to Education, Labor, and Law* (1867), a series of lectures by Caroline Wells Healey *Dall. Dall considers women's entrance into nontraditional fields across the social classes, arguing that the inequity between men's and women's earnings is based on long-standing false valuations of women's capacity as human being and laborer. An important later assessment of women's labor is Helen L. Sumner's Congressional *Report on Condition of Woman and Child Wage-Earners in the United States: History of Women in Industry in the United States* (1910). The literature of the settlement house movement also emphasizes the effects of industrial capitalism; among notable works is Jane *Addams's *Democracy and Social Ethics* (1902) and *Twenty Years at Hull House* (1910).

In imaginative writing, industrialism provided both theme and impetus for the work of middle-class women. As the rhetoric of industrial capitalism emerged, changes in the language of women's writings may be widely noted, as in the commercial and mechanical metaphors of Emily *Dickinson's poetry. The *local color fiction of Harriet Beecher *Stowe, Sarah Orne *Jewett, Mary E. Wilkins *Freeman, and others is shaped by desire for a pre-industrial past, as in Stowe's *Oldtown Folks* (1869), and by a need for the revitalizing effects of nature and community outside the urban industrial centers, as in Jewett's *The Country of the Pointed Firs* (1896), in which the decline of the rural New England economy is likewise a theme. The popularity and widespread production of economic fiction—fiction directly addressing the consequences of industrial capitalism—from the *Civil War period through the turn of the century may be suggested by the following representative titles. Best known among early works of fiction to expose the hard reality of the factories is Rebecca Harding *Davis's naturalistic "Life in the Iron Mills" (1861), a novella about a working man who hungers for artistic expression. Davis's *Margret Howth* (1862), the story of a female bookkeeper in a textile mill, contains realistic depictions of factory and slum life; *John Andross* (1874) attacks the evils of stock speculation and the whiskey ring. Elizabeth Stuart *Phelps (the daughter) wrote "The Twelfth of January" (1868), a story about the death by fire of 112 mill women, and *The Silent Partner* (1871), a realistic critique of industrial capitalism and working conditions for women, in which the daughter of a mill owner finds her vocation not in marriage but in a life devoted to social welfare. Amanda M. Douglas's *Hope Mills* (1880) tells the story of a New England mill town wrecked by speculation. Helen Stuart Campbell's *Mrs. Herndon's Income* (1886) describes the impossibility of life on an income of a dollar a day. Ellen Warner Kirk's *Queen Money* (1888) and *A Daughter of Eve* (1889) are didactic novels on the corrupting influence of money and middle-class ambitions. Gertrude Potter Daniels's *The Warners* (1901) is a melodrama about unfair competition and sweated labor. Mary E. Wilkins Freeman's *The Portion of Labor* (1901) concerns the life of a female worker who falls in love with the mill owner. Margaret *Deland's "The House of Rimmon" (in *The Wisdom of Fools*, 1897; reprinted 1969), tells the story of a widow appalled by the exploitation of workers in her brother's factory. Deland's *The Iron Woman* (1911) examines the conflict between the private and public lives of a female industrialist.

[*See also* Class; Proletarian Writing.]

• Walter Fuller Taylor, *The Economic Novel in America* (1942; reprint, 1969). Kathryn Kish Sklar, *Catharine Beecher: A Study in American Domesticity* (1973). Benita Eisler, ed., *The Lowell Offering: Writings by New England Mill Women (1840–1845)* (1977). Mary A. Hill, *Charlotte Perkins Gilman: The Making of a Radical Feminist, 1860–1896* (1980). Thomas Dublin, ed., *Farm to Factory: Women's Letters, 1830–1860* (1981). Alice Kessler-Harris, *Out to Work: A History of Wage-Earning Women in the United States* (1982). Judith Fetterley, ed., *Provisions: A Reader from 19th-Century American Women* (1985). Tillie Olsen, "A Biographical Interpretation," in Rebecca Harding Davis, *Life in the Iron Mills, and Other Stories*, ed. Tillie Olsen (1861; reprint, 1985). Carroll Smith-Rosenberg, *Disorderly Conduct: Visions of Gender in Victorian America* (1985). Ann Schofield, ed., *Sealskin and Shoddy: Working Women in American Labor Press Fiction, 1870–1920* (1988). Teresa L. Amott and Julie A. Matthaei, *Race, Gender, and Work: A Multicultural Economic History of Women in the United States* (1991).

Susan Albertine

INTEGRATION. *See* Civil Rights Movement; Racism.

INVALIDISM. During the nineteenth century, the term *invalid* referred not only to someone who was bedridden (as it does today), but also to someone who was merely weak or predisposed to illness. Despite the fact that most women were healthy, nineteenth-century medical theories classified all women as predisposed to illness, that is, as invalids; this representation of female illness pervades women's fiction in the nineteenth century. Modern critics have read this fictional invalidism in three ways: first, as the result of women's cultural conditioning, patriarchal oppression, and the masculine power to define and control women's bodies (Gilbert and Gubar, Smith-Rosenberg); second, as a *resistance* to such conditioning (Smith-Rosenberg, Showalter); and third, as a kind of power in itself (Tompkins). Of course, these three views are not mutually exclusive. More recently, illness has been read as a specifically political issue of cultural privilege and power in which illness functions alternately to render women powerful and powerless (Price Herndl).

While mid-nineteenth-century male writers often idealize sickliness as beautiful (Edgar Allan Poe claimed that "the death of a beautiful woman . . . is . . . the most poetical topic in the world" in his 1846 "The Philosophy of Composition"), female writers more often use sickness as a plot device to illustrate a point. Illness and the way a character responds to it frequently serve to reveal that character's true innocence and goodness (as it does for Charlotte Temple in Susanna *Rowson's 1794 novel of that name and for Eva St. Clare in Harriet Beecher *Stowe's *Uncle Tom's Cabin* [1852]), but it sometimes works to expose a character's shallowness, vindictiveness, or selfishness (as it does with Eva's mother, Marie St. Clare, in *Uncle Tom's Cabin*). While such representations do sometimes participate in the aestheticizing of illness that led Abba Goold Woolson (in *Woman in American Society*) to describe invalidism as a "pursuit" in 1873, these representations more often serve to raise the question of women's power and powerlessness in American culture; for some nineteenth-century women, illness marked the only means to power. As Jane Tompkins argues in *Sensational Designs* (1985), women used scenes of religious conversions and transcendence at deathbeds to achieve a kind of power for their heroines to redeem their readers and to change the world for the better.

By the late nineteenth century, the faith in "sentimental power" had waned and illness became a metaphor for the cultural dis-ease that many women felt. Perhaps the most famous "invalid" in nineteenth-century women's fiction is the nameless narrator of Charlotte Perkins * Gilman's "The Yellow Wallpaper" (1891), who goes mad when she is confined in the attic bedroom of a hereditary estate by her physician-husband. Suffering from a "nervous ailment," the narrator is denied access to pen and paper and begins to focus obsessively on a wallpaper that seems to represent bars. In "The Yellow Wallpaper," invalidism is represented as both a result of and a protest against such patriarchal restrictions and domination.

In the twentieth century, illness does not disappear from women's texts—as a glance at Sylvia * Plath's *The Bell Jar* (1963 and 1967) or Tillie * Olsen's "Tell Me a Riddle" (1961) and *Yonnondio: From the Thirties* (1974) shows—but it does assume a clearer political stance (society makes women ill) and the ill woman is rarely an actual "invalid."

[*See also* Disabled Women's Writing.]

• Sandra Gilbert and Susan Gubar, *The Madwoman in the Attic: The Woman Writer and the Nineteenth-Century Literary Imagination* (1979). Elaine Showalter, *The Female Malady: Women, Madness, and English Culture, 1830–1980* (1985). Carroll Smith-Rosenberg, *Disorderly Conduct: Visions of Gender in Victorian America* (1985). Jane Tompkins, *Sensational Designs: The Cultural Work of American Fiction* (1985). Diane Price Herndl, *Invalid Women: Figuring Feminine Illness in American Fiction and Culture, 1840–1940* (1993).

                                        Diane Price Herndl

IRIGARAY, Luce. *See* French Feminism.

IRISH-AMERICAN WRITING. In a 1987 short story entitled "Eileen," Mary * Gordon writes of a bond between two young Irish women in New York. One of the women, Nora, achieves economic stability as a clerical worker by virtue of strong literacy skills and a willingness and ability to conform. The other woman, Eileen, struggles unsuccessfully to make a new life for herself and her younger brother. When her brother is killed on the job, Eileen returns to Ireland.

Although in the nineteenth and early twentieth century returning to Ireland was rarely a realistic option for Irish women in America, Gordon's story captures many other aspects of the experiences of women who immigrated during this period. Conformity, Gordon suggests, was often a possibility: although many Anglo-Americans considered the Irish both racially and culturally inferior, the Irish were not so dissimilar in physical appearance. At least physically, they could "fit in." They also had centuries of British colonization behind them as cultural preparation for life in a former British colony.

After Ireland's Great Famine of the late 1840s, millions of Irish immigrated to the United States. Among immigrants from other countries, men outnumbered women, and the women who did immigrate tended to do so in families. Among the postfamine Irish, however, more women immigrated than men, and many of these women were young and single. Escaping the desperation of rural Ireland, where there were almost no opportunities for women to work or marry, they settled in urban areas of the United States, where they often found work as domestic servants or factory workers. Irish women also moved quickly into the professions of nursing and teaching.

One of the first successful Irish-American novelists, Mary Anne Sadlier, initiated a theme common throughout the history of Irish-American writing: economic success is often accompanied by great emotional and spiritual loss. Sadlier, writing largely for other immigrants, was particularly concerned that Irish * Catholics would abandon Catholicism in their drive to succeed among Protestants. One of her most popular novels, *The Blakes and the Flanagans* (1855), contrasted two families, one remaining dedicated to Catholicism, the other sacrificing faith for upward mobility.

Although journalism was a male-dominated field, turn-of-the-century newspapers, which often published serialized fiction, provided opportunities for many Irish-American women to publish their writing. Katherine Conway began her career as a journalist, and eventually published two novels about Irish-American middle-class life, *The Way of the World* (1900) and the partly autobiographical *Lalor's Maples* (1901). Newspapers and other periodicals also provided publishing opportunities for Kate McPhelim Cleary, whose poetry and short stories appeared in *McClure's* and *Harper's*. Cleary's stories are unusual in Irish-American writing in that many are set in rural Nebraska farming country rather than urban neighborhoods.

Two of the twentieth century's most acclaimed Irish-American women writers paid little direct attention to their Irishness. Best known for novels such as *The Company She Keeps* (1942) and *The Group* (1963), about young women in New York of the 1930s, Mary * McCarthy wrote of her alienation from both Catholicism and Irishness in her autobiographical *Memories of a Catholic Girlhood* (1957). Flannery * O'Connor's fiction dealt primarily with religious matters in the American South, considering not just her fellow Catholics, but also southern fundamentalist Christians in such fiction as *Wise Blood* (1952) and *A Good Man Is Hard to Find* (1955).

Many other Irish-American women writers have foregrounded their ethnicity, often focusing less on Catholicism than other aspects of Irish-American identity. Playwright, journalist, and novelist Betty * Smith wrote of Irish Brooklyn tenement houses and of ambitions channeled into "melting pot" education in her autobiographical novel *A Tree Grows in Brooklyn* (1943). Mary Deasy's *The Hour of Spring* (1948) traced three generations of Irish Americans, from 1870 to 1928, in the Midwest. Mary Doyle Curran, who also wrote poetry, examined Irish immigrants in a New England mill town struggling to make their way from the poverty of the "shanty" to the pretensions of the "lace-curtain," in a well-received novel, *The Parish and the Hill* (1948). These writers offer no solutions as easy as those of their predecessor Mary Anne Sadlier, and they also point to psychic losses that offset economic gain: generations are alienated from one another, neighborhoods are fragmented, friendships lost.

In recent decades, Irish-American women have written critically of the dynamics of Irish Catholic families, contrasting the garrulous * story telling, so often associated with Irish people, with a remarkable ability to evade painful truths. Fictional studies of Irish-American * mothers, daughters, and substance abuse include Diana O'Hehir's *I Wish This War Were Over* (1984) and Susanna Moore's *My Old Sweetheart* (1982). Elizabeth Cullinan, whose novels include *House of Gold* (1970), has examined intergenerational conflicts among urban, lower-middle-class Irish Americans and relationships between Irish-American women and Irish men. Both Mary Gordon and Maureen Howard have written memorable portraits of Irish-American women in novels such as Gordon's *The Company of Women* (1981) and Howard's *Grace Abounding* (1982). Important insights into Irish-American identity can be found in Howard's memoir of life among the Irish of Bridgeport, Connecticut, *Facts of Life* (1978), and Gordon's book of essays, *Good Boys and Dead Girls* (1991).

Ellen Currie's novel, *Available Light* (1986), shares the black * humor found in much Irish-American writing, but indicates important changes in Irish-American writing and experience. Currie writes of a cacophonous, fragmented society of urban consumers, a world in which an agoraphobic mother from Belfast

sequesters herself in a house in Queens, while her daughters work in the fashion industry, and live in Westchester and Manhattan, nourishing destructive obsessions.

Although the election of John F. Kennedy to the presidency in 1960 signaled the admittance of Irish Americans to the "mainstream," Irish-American writing continues to explore the particularities of Irish-American experience. The mid-1980s saw a new wave of Irish immigration, predominantly illegal. Future Irish-American writing can be expected to explore the experience of these new immigrants and their vision of what it is to be Irish-American.

[*See also* European Immigrant Writing; Immigrant Writing; Ethnicity and Writing; Citizenship; Assimilation.]

• Daniel Casey and Robert Rhodes, eds., *Irish-American Fiction* (1979) and *Modern Irish-American Fiction* (1989). Marjorie R. Fallows, *Irish Americans: Identity and Assimilation* (1979). Hasia R. Diner, *Erin's Daughters in America: Irish Immigrant Women in the Nineteenth Century* (1983). Charles Fanning, *The Exiles of Erin* (1987) and *The Irish Voice in America* (1990).

Molly H. Mullin

ITALIAN-AMERICAN WRITING. Helen Barolini writes in *The Dream Book: An Anthology of Writings by Italian American Women* (1985) that Italian-American women have a commonality of experience: "They are women who, with rare exceptions, had never before been authorized to be authors (of themselves, of the word)—not by their external world, nor again by their internal one." Restricted by their traditional roles of wives and mothers, and lacking a literary tradition, they were forced into silence in their male-dominated world, where, Barolini suggests, "their ancillary role was rigidly, immutably restricted to home and family." In *Silences* (1978), Tillie * Olsen catalogs many of the overwhelming life circumstances that too often interfere with a writer's "sustained creation." She lists—among others—poverty, illiteracy, the inhibiting standard literary * canon, the cultural denigration of women, and the demands of motherhood. In America, as in Italy, the traditional * family and its survival was the Italian woman's primary concern. Idealized to an almost Madonna-like status symbolizing nurturance and self-sacrifice, she was expected never to utilize her full potential or challenge male authority, which, for the purposes of this essay, includes androcentric art and literature. Coupled with the cultural imperative of *omerta*, or silence, and inhibited by her status as immigrant in a racist America, she was left with a particular legacy that impeded sustained creation.

In addition, just by virtue of her * gender,

she has received a lifetime of cultural and educational messages that label her experiences marginal, unheroic, and "outside" of what is considered real human experience. Coupled with her socialization, which expects her to embrace and protect family, she is caught between her silencing and the urgencies of her spirit, her mind, her self. Moreover, the lack of a literary tradition presents a serious problem for Italian-American women writers. If all writers need to value and speak the truth of their own experience, how can Italian-American women writers value their own selves and embrace what Joanna *Russ calls in *How to Suppress Women's Writing* (1983) "the unlabeled, disallowed, disavowed, not even consciously perceived experience which cannot be spoken about because it has no embodiment in existing art"? An Italian woman, in particular, risks family condemnation and exclusion if she betrays that family's stories and secrets. To violate the cultural imperative of *omerta* is to risk everything. To place self above family is a sin.

Yet many Italian-American women have sought to gain voice and break these culturally imposed silences. Risking male and familial condemnation, many have freed themselves from damaging societal restrictions and messages that denigrate their experiences as women. Mary *Daly writes in *Gyn/Ecology* (1978), "Gynocentric writing is risk taking," and for the Italian-American woman writer, this means risking not only male antagonism, but familial antagonism as well as she struggles against the effects of her socialization.

Barolini compares Italian-American women writers to black women writers. The similarities rest in "the patient strength, tolerance, earthy attitudes, and concern with the life force." She argues that "both Black and Italian American women writers write from passion and emotional commitment, not stylistic chic. Both are reaching for life and positive affirmations. A quest for self-actualization is what characterizes the personages of Italian American writing." Nina Baym writes in "Melodramas of Beset Manhood: How Theories of American Fiction Exclude Women Authors" (1985) that the woman writer "has entered literary history as the enemy." An Italian-American woman writer has to struggle to re-create herself, to gain voice in a culture where silence can be demanded by the wave of her *grandmother's hand.

This is perhaps one reason we have so few extant *letters, *diaries, and journals from Italian-American women writers, as compared to other women in diverse socioeconomic, racial, and ethnic groups. Whereas the commercially popular Italian-American male writers have carved out a niche in action-packed Mafia novels, which play into the prevailing negative *stereotypes of Italian-American culture, the women writers have a series of recurring themes, which include family, *immigration, generational conflict, relationships, religion, *ethnocentrism, and *racism. Noncanonical names such as Sister Blandina Seǵale, Frances Winwar, Grazia Deledda, Sibilla Aleramo, Renata Brunorini, Mari Tomasi, Dorothy Bryant, Diana Cavallo, Barbara Grizzuti Harrison, Anna Quindlen, Diane *di Prima—to name just a few—are all but lost to even current feminist critical studies.

The new generation of Italian-American women writers can become voices no longer hindered by the cultural and familial dictates of *omerta*; they can break *silences and fight the complications of bicultural patriarchal definitions. In order to define themselves as writers, they must struggle to analyze, redefine, and rename the terms of their socialization.

[*See also* European Immigrant Writing; Immigrant Writing; Citizenship; Ethnicity and Writing; Assimilation.]

• Olga Peragallo, *Italian American Authors and Their Contribution to American Literature* (1949). Rose Basile Green, *The Italian American Novel* (1974). Carolyn Balducci, *A Self-Made Woman* (1975). Francesco Cordasco, ed., *Italian Americans: A Guide to Information Sources*, Ethnic Studies Information Guide series, vol. 2 (1978). Raffaele Cocchi, "In Search of Italian-American Poetry in the U.S.A.," *In Their Own Words* 2, no. 1 (Winter 1984): 52 Ferdinando Alfonsi, *Italo-American Poets: A Bilingual Anthology* (1985). Ferdinando Alfonsi, *Dictionary of Italian-American Poets* (1989).

Maria Bruno

J

JACKSON, Helen Hunt (1830–1885), novelist, essayist, and poet, best remembered for works on Native Americans. Born a professor's daughter in Amherst, Massachusetts, and educated in boarding schools, Jackson began writing poetry in the 1860s, after the deaths, at different times, of her husband and children. Her early verses won high praise from Boston's literary establishment. After her remarriage to a Colorado businessman in 1875, Jackson broadened her repertoire of poetry and travelogues to include short stories, novels, and children's books, which she published under various pseudonyms.

In 1879, Jackson attended a lecture in Boston by Ponca leader Standing Bear, protesting the removal of his peaceful tribe from their homeland, and she became an impassioned convert to the Indian policy reform cause. Jackson immediately began the intensive research that led to *A Century of Dishonor* (1881), a fiery indictment of repeated governmental abuses of Native Americans. The book was the first of Jackson's works to bear her name, indicating a new sense of herself as a person with a public voice and identity.

Jackson's continued commitment to Indian affairs transformed an assignment for a travel article on California missions into inspiration for her major work. She secured appointment as a government agent to investigate possibilities for providing land to Mission Indians threatened with homelessness by increasing development. Jackson reworked her investigative material into a novel, *Ramona* (1884), which she hoped would match Harriet Beecher *Stowe's Uncle Tom's Cabin* in arousing public sympathy for a wronged minority.

While the novel was very popular and has been reprinted frequently, *Ramona* was not as effective a propaganda piece as Jackson had hoped. Its sentimentality dampened outrage with tears, and the Indian and Hispanic cultures of California are rather ambiguously and patronizingly presented. Jackson did succeed in drawing the attention of several national organizations involved in Indian affairs to California, resulting in 1891 in legislation to help the few surviving Mission Indians.

Jackson died of stomach cancer less than a year after *Ramona*'s publication, certain that her Indian books constituted her major legacy. While her direct impact on government policy was limited, the rhetorical power of *A Century of Dishonor* and the simultaneously romantic appeal and realistic intent of *Ramona* continue to challenge persistent stereotypical images of Indians as savages. In literary terms, Jackson is also important as a popular writer whose works show the transition from romantic idealism to realism in American literature.

• Major collections of Jackson's papers are at the Huntington Library in San Marino, California, and the Charles Leaming Tutt Library, Colorado College, Colorado Springs, Colorado. See also Thomas Wentworth Higginson, *Contemporaries* (1899). Ruth Odell, *Helen Hunt Jackson (H. H.)* (1939). John R. Byers, Jr., and Elizabeth S. Byers, "Helen Hunt Jackson (1830–1885): A Critical Bibliography of Secondary Comment," *American Literary Realism* 6 (Summer 1973): 197–241. Rosemary Whitaker, *Helen Hunt Jackson* (1987). Valerie Sherer Mathes, *Helen Hunt Jackson and Her Indian Reform Legacy* (1990).

Helen M. Bannan

JACKSON, Laura Riding. *See* Riding, Laura.

JACKSON, Shirley (1919–1965), short story writer and novelist. Although Shirley Jackson's short stories, especially "The Lottery" (1949), are read as American classics, Jackson's critical status suggests the generic limits of fame. Despite growing feminist interest, most literary criticism still relegates both Jackson's humorous writing and her ambitious novels to the unconsidered realms of popular literature.

Jackson's wry *domestic narratives, which appeared in magazines and short story collections, and her books *Life among the Savages* (1953) and *Raising Demons* (1957), seemed to spring directly from her life as the wife of critic Stanley Edgar Hyman and the mother of three children. Her chilling and sometimes scathingly funny evocations of social and supernatural evil did not. Yet the popular paradox of Jackson's life and work was only an apparent one: in Jackson's terms, the comic and the demonic were inseparable.

Jackson's novels satirize her culture even as they attempt to tap its terrors, particularly for women. The supernatural thus joins forces with the respectable cruelties of bigotry and scapegoating or the corruptions and vulnerabilities of *class privilege. *Madness emerges not only from within, but from the sexual, familial, and institutional threats and seductions through which women and children in particular must mediate their unstable senses of identity.

Dangerous relationships between communal values and feminine identities most often stand at her novels' centers. Thus child murder, scapegoating, and *suicide seem less to violate than enact the aggressive respectability of Pepper Street, the upwardly mobile California neighborhood of *The Road through the Wall* (1948). The gifted, emotionally disturbed protagonist of *Hangsaman* (1951) must battle her family's influence, her silenced *rape memories, her traumatic relationships at college, and possibly her own inner demons to achieve a tenuous hold on maturity. Her successor, in *The Bird's Nest* (1954), begins by disintegrating: she moves through and just beyond multiple personality disorder. In the cruelly comic *Sundial* (1958), Aunt Fanny's apocalyptic visions catalyze a manor house's transformation into a survivalist stronghold. Hill House, in *The Haunting of Hill House* (1959), is no ruined *gothic mansion, but a relentlessly ordered home whose "haunting" claims its victim by arousing, mocking, and fatally manipulating her most intimate familial dreams. Finally, personal and social madness meet in *We Have Always Lived in the Castle* (1962), where sisters who have been ostracized as survivors of domestic mass murder ultimately end up as modern *witches; they are counterparts to the subjects of Jackson's politically suggestive nonfiction children's book, *The Witchcraft of Salem Village* (1956).

"Come Along with Me," Jackson's unfinished final novel, appears in a 1968 collection by that name. Other stories, and lectures, are collected in *The Lottery, or, The Adventures of James Harris* (1949) and *The Magic of Shirley Jackson* (1966).

• Lenemaja Friedman, *Shirley Jackson* (1975). Lynette Carpenter, "Domestic Comedy, Black Comedy, and Real Life: Shirley Jackson, A Woman Writer," in *Faith of a (Woman) Writer*, eds. Alice Kessler-Harris and William McBrien (1988). Judy Oppenheimer, *Private Demons: The Life of Shirley Jackson* (1988).

Tricia Lootens

JACOBS, Harriet Ann (c. 1813–1897), author of *Incidents in the Life of a Slave Girl, Written by Herself* (1861), a *slave narrative, one of the first by an African-American woman and former slave published in the United States.

Jacobs was born in Edenton, North Carolina, to Delilah and Daniel Jacobs. After her mother's death in 1819, Jacobs was enslaved by Margaret Horniblow, who taught her to read and sew. After Horniblow's death in 1825, Ja-

cobs was enslaved to Horniblow's three-year-old niece, Mary Matilda Norcom, the daughter of Dr. James Norcom. Jacobs's father, Daniel, died in 1826.

Dr. Norcom repeatedly tried to force young Harriet into concubinage with him. To thwart Norcom's attempts, she began a consensual sexual relationship with Samuel Tredwell Sawyer, a white attorney. She bore him a son, Joseph, in 1829, and a daughter, Louisa Matilda, in 1833. Before Joseph's birth, Jacobs moved into her maternal grandmother's home to escape abuse by Norcom's wife, who knew of her husband's *sexual harassment of Jacobs. Angered, Norcom sent Jacobs to his son's neighboring plantation, where she encountered brutal working conditions. When Jacobs discovered Norcom's plans to sell her children, she escaped.

Aided by family and friends, mostly slaves, Jacobs escaped, at first hiding in a snake-infested swamp. Molly Horniblow, Jacobs's grandmother, whose freedom had been purchased by Hannah Pritchard in 1828, then hid Jacobs in a tiny crawl space in her attic for nearly seven years. In 1835, Sawyer purchased Jacobs's children, along with her brother, John, but did not free them. Aided by abolitionists, Jacobs escaped to the North in 1842, and arranged to have her children sent there. When Dr. Norcom died in Edenton in 1850 (the year the *Fugitive Slave Law passed), his daughter, Mary Matilda Norcom, continued efforts to recapture Jacobs. In 1852, abolitionist Cornelia Grinnell Willis arranged Jacobs's emancipation. Jacobs was grateful but embittered by the legalized monetary exchange for her person.

At the suggestion of feminist abolitionist Amy Post, she began writing *Incidents* in 1853. Jacobs rejected Harriet Beecher *Stowe's offer to integrate *Incidents* as fiction into *Uncle Tom's Cabin* (1851). Lydia Maria *Child edited Jacobs's narrative, making minor grammatical alterations, and a Boston printer published it on 12 April 1861. Jacobs used the pseudonym Linda Brent to protect her identity because, as a single mother, she was considered an impure woman who wrote on the taboo subject of the sexual exploitation of slave women.

In the narrative, Jacobs appeals to readers to view female virtue and purity differently for slave women, in light of their inability to exercise control over their own bodies. *Incidents* contains some traits associated with the *sentimental novel, as popularized by nineteenth-century American women writers. As a former slave woman's *autobiography, *Incidents* particularly exposes black slave women's oppression by white slaveholders, while simultaneously stressing the extended family and familial bonding among slaves. In addition, it addresses authorial autonomy, language and literacy, cultural survival forms, and other slave narrative motifs.

Jacobs aided in the *Civil War relief effort, and twice visited Edenton, North Carolina, before her death on 7 March 1897.

• William L. Andrews, *To Tell a Free Story: The First Century of Afro-American Autobiography, 1760–1865* (1988).

Helena Woodard

JAMES, Alice (1848–1892), diarist and letter writer. Born into the noted James family, she was the fifth child and only daughter of Mary Robertson Walsh and Henry James, Sr., and the sister of novelist Henry James, Jr., and psychologist/philosopher William James. Her childhood was spent in Newport, Rhode Island, and Cambridge, Massachusetts, and traveling in Europe. In spite of her acknowledged brilliance and her political radicalism (she was an avid feminist, Irish nationalist, and advocate of the poor) her position in the family seems to have been shaped largely by her gender. Her brother Henry once remarked that "in our family group girls seem scarcely to have had a chance." Her correspondence with William, six years her senior, reveals a teasing, eroticized relationship, as William variously constructs Alice as a Victorian "angel in the house," a sweetheart, and his baby sister, while Alice, taking her tone from him, changes voices in response to his attitude. From the age of nineteen until the end of her life, Alice James suffered extended bouts of *hysteria, and tragically, as Ruth B. Yeazell argues in *The Death and Letters of Alice James* (1981), illness and dying became "Alice James's chief vocation." In 1873, Alice met another single woman, Katherine Loring, with whom she developed an intense *friendship, often referred to as a "Boston marriage," which lasted until her death. It provided her with the emotional stability and affection she had yearned for all of her life.

Alice James's primary literary testament is *The Diary of Alice James*, which she began in 1889 and continued during the last three years of her life. Vivid and dramatic, it reveals her political radicalism, and draws a complex psychological portrait of a woman who relished the absurdities of life, faced her own pain with immense courage, and yet welcomed the diagnosis of breast cancer that assured her of the death she had wished for since "that hideous summer of '78, when I went down to the deep sea, its dark waters closed over me and I knew neither hope nor peace … now it's only the shriveling of an empty pea pod that has to be completed." She died peacefully in Bourne-mouth, England, attended to by Katharine Loring and by her brother Henry.

• F. O. Matthiessen, *The James Family* (1947). Jean Strouse, *Alice James: A Biography* (1980). R. W. B. Lewis, *The Jameses: A Family Narrative* (1991).

Dorothy Berkson

JANOWITZ, Tama (b. 1957), novelist, short story writer, and journalist. Best known for her novel *American Dad* (1981) and for her collection of short stories *Slaves of New York* (1986), Janowitz maps out territory that is the intersection between the mundane and the offbeat.

Born in San Francisco, Janowitz received her B.A. from Barnard College in 1977, and did graduate work at Hollins College and at Yale. In addition to her writing, she has worked as an assistant art director and as a model with Vidal Sassoon. She has received many fiction prizes and fellowships and has contributed short stories and articles to such magazines as *Interview*, *Rolling Stone*, *Mademoiselle*, *Harper's*, and the *New Yorker*.

American Dad is the coming-of-age story of Earl Przepasniak, a boy smothered by his parents' permissive eccentricities and disturbed by their divorce. Like Janowitz's own parents, Earl's mother is a poet and his father a psychiatrist. After his mother's untimely and accidental death at the hands of his father, Earl escapes to Europe, where he attempts to pursue women and properly bohemian satisfactions.

Slaves of New York is a loosely woven series of episodes chronicling the doings of a drab set of downtown Manhattan artsy characters. One of the recurrent protagonists is Eleanor, a twenty-eight-year-old jewelry maker who feels enslaved to her boyfriend Stash because she lives in his apartment and is constantly afraid of losing her relationship and her home. Eleanor's predicament is typical of Janowitz's women characters: they are both financially relegated to and psychologically trapped in dissatisfying heterosexual relationships. They retain deadpan yet quirky outlooks on life and occasionally muster sufficient energy and nerve to momentarily disturb their fine-tuned veneers of sophisticated monotony.

A Cannibal in Manhattan (1987) is the fictional diary of Mgungu, an aging cannibal from the South Pacific island of New Burnt Norton. Replete with grass skirt, several wives, and a bone through his nose, Mgungu speaks colloquial English and takes up with Maria Fishburn, an American heiress and Peace Corps volunteer.

Janowitz's nearly exclusive topic is the unstructured ramblings of lethargic East Coast intellectuals and artists. In this regard, the form of her writing almost perfectly mirrors the content. Her work is an assemblage of thrown-to-gether yet oddly similar tidbits of a certain strain of American metropolitan life.

Eleanor Kaufman

JAPANESE-AMERICAN WRITING. Japan's emigration policies and U.S. immigration laws targeted at Asians have shaped the contours of the Japanese-American population. Legal immigrants first arrived in Hawaii in 1868, when Japan's Meiji government ended two hundred years of seclusion. Immigration peaked in the early 1900s, then was slowed by the 1907 Gentlemen's Agreement, and essentially was terminated by the U.S. Immigration Act of 1924, not to resume until 1965. As a result of the 1924 cutoff, there developed three distinctive groups—*issei*, or the immigrant generation; *nisei*, their American-born offspring; and *sansei*, children of the *nisei*—which dominate, respectively, three broad phases of economic, political, and cultural history: (1) settlement and adjustment, from 1868 through the 1930s; (2) World War II and its aftermath, comprehending anti-Japanese hostilities prior to Pearl Harbor, their culmination in concentration camps, and structural assimilation into mainstream society during the 1950s and 1960s; and (3) the development of Japanese-American political consciousness and cultural identity, beginning in the 1970s and continuing to the present.

An extensive but relatively uncharted body of *issei* writing in Japanese exists, much of it housed in Japan's libraries. In English, the *issei* voice is accessible primarily through several excellent oral histories, among them anthropologist Akemi Kikumura's biography of her mother, *Through Harsh Winters* (1981); Eileen Sarasohn Sunada's collection of thirty-two interviews representing communities from southern California to Seattle, *The Issei, Portrait of a Pioneer* (1983); and the thousand-page translation of journalist Kazuo Ito's *Issei: A History of Japanese Immigrants in North America* (1973), focused on the Pacific Northwest. These oral histories constitute a seedbed of themes and tropes cultivated by *nisei* and *sansei* writers, especially the collective figure of *issei* pioneers and their daunting stamina, perseverance in the face of hardship, and devotion to family and education.

Etsu Sugimoto's autobiography *A Daughter of the Samurai* (1925; reprint, 1982), a rare example of an *issei* work in English, has been viewed as an apology for American imperialism and cultural hegemony. Owing to Sugimoto's hailing from Japan's social elite as well as her affluent life in Cincinnati, which enabled her to employ black servants, she remained ignorant of the socioeconomic hardships of most Japanese immigrants who went west as farmers or laborers. However, *Samurai* is one of the earliest prose narratives in English to mediate critically between Japanese and American cultural practices and ideas, making the text highly relevant to the bulk of *nisei* and *sansei* writing that shows an abiding concern with intertwined themes of family, filiality, and cultural affiliations. As a narrative of conflict and consensus between Japanese/*issei* and American/*nisei*, *Samurai* initiates a literary project in which almost all subsequent writers have been engaged.

Narratives of wartime incarceration and its aftermath abound. The internment is at once blatantly simple to view as an infringement of civil rights applied to a racially selected population, yet infinitely nuanced in individual experiences. Several key investigations of this period are written by women: Michi Weglyn's *Years of Infamy: The Untold Story of America's Concentration Camps* (1976), a meticulously researched account of the racist motivations behind internment; Masayo Duus's *Tokyo Rose; Orphan of the Pacific* (1979), chronicling *nisei* Iva Toguri d' Aquino's struggle to regain American citizenship and residency after being questionably convicted of broadcasting anti-U.S. propaganda during the war; and *nisei* journalist Muriel Kitagawa's *This Is My Own: Letters to Wes and Other Writings on Japanese Canadians, 1941–1948* (1985), containing material that Canadian *nisei* Joy Kogawa drew upon when writing her award-winning novel *Obasan* (1981), an indispensable touchstone for critical assessment of American writers' political, psychological, and symbolic constructions of "Japanese" ethnicity.

Works from the *nisei* period exhibit a split between those that do and those that do not define Japanese ethnicity as problematic relative to a white social norm. In the latter group, two lesser-known but significant texts are painter Mine Okubo's *Citizen 13660* (1946; reprint, 1983), a wryly illustrated diary of life behind barbed wire, and Shelley Ota's *Upon Their Shoulders* (1951), which Stephen Sumida in *And the View from the Shore: Literary Traditions of Hawai'i* (1991) identifies as the earliest known novel in English based on Japanese-American immigration. Among the most esteemed and widely read *nisei* writers are Hisaye *Yamamoto and Wakako *Yamauchi, whose stories and plays frequently depict the prewar ethnic communities of their childhood and young adulthood. Particularly in light of their steady achievement during the 1930s, when established role models were absent, and during the postwar years, when the community instructed itself to forget the past and concentrate on socioeconomic upward mobility, Yamauchi and Yamamoto were immediately reclaimed as major figures during the early days of Asian-American canon formation in the 1970s.

Equally famous but considered problematic are two autobiographies, Monica Sone's *Nisei Daughter* (1953; reprint, 1982) and Jeanne Wakatsuki Houston's *Farewell to Manzanar* (1973), which have been marginalized from the canon for their assimilationist stance toward white mainstream culture. As with Sugimoto's autobiography, it is important to remember that these works appeared before "Asian American" became a widespread, politicized, affirmative terminology, as spearheaded by the publication of the anthology *Aiiieeeee!* (eds. Frank Chin et al., 1974). Sone and Houston's self-esteem as daughters is clearly audible, however, despite their being told through a racialist discourse that "Japanese" and "American" are in opposition.

Sansei writers came to the fore in 1970–1990. Whereas * autobiography and oral history dominate in the *issei* period, and short fiction and autobiography in the *nisei* period, a blossoming of poetry and drama, together with continued development of prose genres, characterizes the *sansei* group. Literature from the 1970s responded forcefully to major events then reshaping American society and self-reflection—the Vietnam War, * civil rights activism, the development of ethnic and women's studies. Individual volumes of poetry appeared, such as Patricia Ikeda's *House of Wood, House of Salt* (1978) and Geraldine Kudaka's *Numerous Avalanches at the Point of Intersection* (1978), but dozens of fine stories, poems, and excerpts from plays are contained in the anthologies, newspapers, and magazines characterizing literary output during the early Asian-American movement. Janice * Mirikitani's work as poet and editor (*Time to Greez!: Incantations from the Third World*, 1975) is representative of this period's ethnic politicization, revolutionary fervor, and interdisciplinary and international perspectives in art and history. The transition from the eighties to the nineties was marked by a second burst of talent and productivity in all fields of Asian-American art. Among the compelling new Japanese-American voices are playwright Velina Hasu * Houston (*Tea*, 1987) and novelists Cynthia Kadohata (*The Floating World*, 1989), Holly Uyemoto (*Rebel without a Clue*, 1989), and Karen Tei Yamashita (*Through the Arc of the Rain Forest*, 1990). Their multicultural settings and characters, and indirectly expressed or apparent lack of Japanese signifiers, emphasize a long-standing need for theoretical articulations of "Japanese" ethnicity, as Henry Louis Gates in *Figures in Black*

(1987) and others are providing for black identity in African-American literary criticism. The *sansei* period also nurtured *nisei* writers. Clara * Jelsma (*Teapot Tales*, 1981) and Jessica Saiki (*Once, a Lotus Garden*, 1987) render the details of daily life in Japanese communities of specific times and locations. A decade after *Camp Notes* (1976) appeared, Mitsuye Yamada produced *Desert Run: Poems and Stories* (1988), a meatier, wider-ranging volume testifying to her involvement in global, women's, and political issues in the intervening years. The work of all three writers is representative of ongoing efforts to recover the *issei* experience.

The literature from Sugimoto to the present reveals at least two salient themes. One is a definition of *home*, through actual and symbolic mothering, as an ethnically identifiable site of moral values and social behaviors. The valuation of home is so enduring as to encompass even the most uncompromising critiques or deviant arrangements of family life, as in Yamamoto's story of a woman's artistic suffocation in "Seventeen Syllables" (1949) and Kadohata's portrayal of the nuclear family as a "floating world" in her 1989 work by that name. Comparisons with male writers' representations of family life as the site of ethnic subjectivity, equally extensive and vital to a fuller comprehension of women's perspectives on the subject, reveal a complex intertextuality. The dysfunctional mother in John Okada's *No-No Boy* (1957; reprint, 1981) is both critically and compassionately rewritten through the absent-yet-nurturing mother/s in *Obasan*, while Toshio Mori's indulgent narrators in *Yokohama, California* (1949; reprint, 1985) embody a practice of parenting and a theory of social relationships that anticipate feminist analyses of care taking, such as Nancy Chodorow's *The Reproduction of Mothering* (1978) and Carol Gilligan's *In a Different Voice* (1982).

A second pervasive theme is the relationship between American identity and Japanese history and culture, articulated through binary terminology that reveals changing attitudes. Before World War II, various expressions signifying American of Japanese ancestry were generally deployed without imparting a sense of psychic rending. During and after internment, this terminology itself became the focus of confusion and a compulsion to choose sides at the cost of racial and ethnic self-devaluation. The Asian-American movement's call for an integrated, historically determined definition of selfhood to replace the "dual identity" concept of separate and unequally valorized "American" and "Asian" elements often resulted in rejection of any Japanese art, history, language, social practice, mythology, and ideology that was not visibly manifested in everyday life. A fuzzy but widely held distinction existed between (authentic) Japanese-American culture practiced "here at home" and (irrelevant) Japanese culture and history located "over there." However, ambivalence toward the "old country" has given way to freer exploration and expression of Japanese material, such as Kadohata's construction of a "floating world," which evokes yet diverges from Sugimoto's deployment of "samurai." Especially with the aid of recent anthropological studies, *Japanese American* is being theoretically reformulated in terms of nonhierarchical difference, and as a practice of reciprocity between spheres of experience that are structurally and psychically distinct, yet intersecting.

[*See also* Asian-American Writing; Assimilation; Citizenship; Ethnicity and Writing; Immigrant Writing.]

• Takeo Doi, *The Anatomy of Dependence*, trans. John Bester, rev. ed. (1981). Patsy Sumie Saiki, *Japanese Women in Hawaii: The First One Hundred Years* (1985). Sylvia Yanagisako, *Transforming the Past: Tradition and Kinship among Japanese Americans* (1985). Evelyn Nakano Glenn, *Issei, Nisei, War Bride: Three Generations of Japanese American Women in Domestic Service* (1988). Yuji Ichioka, *The Issei: The World of the First Generation Japanese Immigrants, 1885–1924* (1988). Trinh Minh-ha, *Woman, Native, Other: Writing Postcoloniality and Feminism* (1989). Dorinne Kondo, *Crafting Selves: Gender, Power, and Discourses of Identity in a Japanese Workplace* (1990). Mei T. Nakano, *Japanese American Women: Three Generations 1890–1990* (1990). Stephen Fugita and David J. O'Brien, *Japanese American Ethnicity: The Persistence of Community* (1991). Valerie Matsumoto, "Desperately Seeking 'Deirdre': Gender Roles, Multicultural Relations, and Nisei Women Writers of the 1930s," *Frontiers* 12, no. 1 (1991): 19–32.

Gayle K. Fujita Sato

JELSMA, Clara Mitsuko (b. 1931), fiction writer, essayist, educator. Jelsma grew up in the rural farming town of Glenwood, Hawaii, the eighth of nine children born to Umetaro and Iku (Hayashi) Kubojiri, who emigrated from Japan in 1904 and 1920, respectively. She graduated from the University of Hawaii in 1953, earning tuition and board as a maid and waitress. In 1956, she received a master's degree in elementary education from Colorado State Teacher's College and married classmate Dallas Jelsma. Eight years later, having settled in Hawaii, Jelsma exchanged teaching for full-time child rearing, returning to the classroom only when her third child completed high school.

Jelsma's earliest publications are "The Pond" (1953), which appeared in the *Literary Magazine* for University of Hawaii students, and

"Waikiki Wall Slide" (1954), in *Paradise of the Pacific* (forerunner of *Honolulu Magazine*). *Nisei: In Hawaii and the Pacific* took her third story, "The Little Sansei" (1954), and printed two more stories and seven articles on Japanese-American lifestyles in Hawaii and the mainland before ceasing publication in 1956, at which time Jelsma's own literary activity subsided. When it resumed twenty-five years later, Hawaii's writing climate had changed dramatically through the growth of "local literature," a regional manifestation of the Asian-American and ethnic studies movements focused on distinguishing between "native" and "tourist" perspectives.

Teapot Tales and Other Stories (1981) and *Mauna Loa Rains* (1991) are based on the Kubojiri family's life as homesteaders and truck farmers. While similar in content and stylistic approach to fictionalized life histories of Asian-American pioneers, such as Ruthanne Lum McCunn's *Thousand Pieces of Gold* (1981) and Yoshiko Uchida's *Picture Bride* (1987), Jelsma's works reflect Hawaii's specific geography, immigrant history, and ethnic diversity. Like many local writers, Jelsma makes flexible use of pidgin English, the dialect developed as a lingua franca by sugar plantation laborers from various countries. Her comic representation of conflict between Portuguese and Japanese culture in "Country Pie" brings to mind *A Small Obligation and Other Stories of Hilo* (1982) by Susan Nunes, who also draws on family history in writing about Hawaii's multiethnic communities. "Yasuko Rebels," originally published in *Nisei* (1954), evokes Hisaye * Yamamoto's "Seventeen Syllables" (1949) in its depiction of a naive but plucky *nisei* (first-generation American) country girl's first suitor. A combined focus on daily life, forthright representation of racial tensions, and comic point of view (visible especially in the articles submitted to *Nisei* magazine) suggest certain undeveloped affinities with Yamamoto that make Jelsma's quarter-century of dormancy as a writer regrettable.

• Dennis M. Ogawa, *Kodomo no tame ni, For the Sake of the Children: The Japanese American Experience in Hawaii* (1978). Katharine Newman, "Hawaiian-American Literature Today: The Cultivation of Mangoes," *MELUS* 6, no. 2 (Summer 1979): 46–77. Eric Chock and Darrell H. Y. Lum, eds., *The Best of Bamboo Ridge: The Hawaii Writers' Quarterly* (1986). Gayle K. Fujita Sato, "The Island Influence on Chinese American Writers: Wing Tek Lum, Darrell H. Y. Lum, and Eric Chock," *Amerasia* 16, no. 2 (1990): 17–33. Stephen H. Sumida, *And the View from the Shore: Literary Traditions of Hawai'i* (1991).

Gayle K. Fujita Sato

JEWETT, Sarah Orne (1849–1909), novelist. Theodora Sarah Orne Jewett was born on 3

September 1849, in South Berwick, Maine, where she died sixty years later in her family's large Georgian house, as she had wished. Although she had traveled widely and known many of the best writers of her time, it was to this place—the Maine coast, with its small villages, dilapidated harbors, and scattered islands—that she had dedicated her art.

The Jewetts were a privileged family linked to the past. Sarah's grandfather had been a sea captain, merchant, and shipowner. Her father, Theodore Herman Jewett, was a country doctor; her mother, Caroline Frances Perry Jewett, was herself the daughter of a physician. Family income was secure, but there was pride in work and social service. The second of three daughters, Sarah was educated at Miss Raynes School and then Berwick Academy, from which she graduated in 1865. Like many Victorian women, she did not attend college, but her reading was wide and eclectic. She learned from Wordsworth, Tennyson, and Theocritus. Her mother and grandmother introduced her to Austen, Oliphant, and Eliot, while her father, she remembered, showed her how to delight in and depend on books.

Jewett's ties to her mother, sisters, and female friends were strong and lasting, yet she was also drawn to the professional world of her father, whose profession she at one point considered following. Placed at the intersection of several cultures—female and male, rural and urban, past and present, preindustrial folk and professional elite—she once wrote, "there is a noble saying of Plato that the best thing that can be done for the people of a state is to make them acquainted with one another." It was this work of cultural interpretation, ultimately cultural healing, which Sarah Jewett undertook.

She sold her first story when she was eighteen, to the weekly periodical *The Flag of Our Union*. Recognized by the influential editor William Dean Howells, her work began appearing in the prestigious *Atlantic Monthly* in 1869. In 1873, the *Atlantic* published "The Shore House," the first of the linked sketches later collected in *Deephaven* (1877), which describes the *friendship and explorations of two young women summering on the Maine coast. Jewett's emerging reputation soon brought her into Boston literary society, where she found a mentor in one of its leaders, Annie Adams *Fields. After the deaths of Theodore Jewett in 1878 and James T. Fields in 1881, the friendship between the two women deepened. As revealed in their letters, the relationship was neither exclusive nor self-conscious, but loving and open, and accepted by a pre-Freudian society accustomed to *separate spheres and same-sex attachments. It remained central to both their lives.

During these years, Jewett confirmed her commitment to writing. Her struggle against traditional expectations shapes *A Country Doctor* (1884), a novel whose heroine, Nan Prince, rejects a young lawyer and conventional marriage for medical school. In "A White Heron," Sylvy, only nine years old, is tempted but finally refuses to betray the life of a beautiful, rare heron for money and appreciation from a handsome young ornithologist.

The publication of *A White Heron and Other Stories* (1886) marked Jewett's literary maturity, which saw her attention to regional speech, folkways, and character bring her to the forefront of local colorists. Her precise observation, delicate style, and sly humor won her the admiration and friendship of fellow realists such as Henry James. Her circle included an impressive number of women artists and writers, among them, Sarah Wyman Whitman, Celia Thaxter, Alice *Brown, and Louise Imogen Guiney. Jewett typically spent part of each year with Annie Fields in Boston or at Manchester-by-the-Sea, Massachusetts. They traveled together to England, France, and Greece. When in South Berwick, Jewett lived with her sister, Mary, and cared for her mother, who died in 1891.

The Country of the Pointed Firs, the work that secured Jewett's reputation, appeared in 1896. Like *Deephaven*, the book contains linked sketches with a shared fictional setting: Dunnet Landing, a fishing village on the Maine coast. The unnamed narrator takes a room for the summer with a widowed herb-gatherer and healer, Almira Todd. Retelling the stories she has heard and describing the quiet *rituals of family and friendship, the narrator leads readers to an appreciation of what they might have dismissed as provincial, old-fashioned, poor, or feminine. As in much of Jewett's fiction, the conflicts here are subtle—problems of social negotiation, usually resolved through emotional connection—and the narratives often circle around a suggested center instead of marching toward an explicit climax. This technique, grounded in oral and women's traditions, anticipates literary *modernism and gives the apparently simple scenes of *Pointed Firs* a mythopoeic power. Through classical allusion, poetic suggestion, and narrative silence, Jewett calls her readers' imaginations and emotional memories into play. Participants in the story-telling process, they enter the community her art both celebrates and creates.

In 1901, Sarah Orne Jewett received the Litt.D. degree from Bowdoin—the first woman so honored by the college. In 1902, a carriage accident injured her spine and cut short her career. She died in 1909, following a cerebral hemorrhage. Among the many writers who benefited from her influence and advice were Kate *Chopin, Mary Wilkins *Freeman, and Willa *Cather, who dedicated *O Pioneers!* to her in 1913. In Jewett's "beautiful and delicate work," Cather wrote, "there is the perfection that endures."

• The Houghton Library at Harvard University has the largest collection of Jewett's letters and manuscripts. See also Annie Fields, ed., *Letters of Sarah Orne Jewett* (1911). F. O. Matthiessen, *Sarah Orne Jewett* (1929). Willa Cather, "Miss Jewett" and "148 Charles Street," in *Not under Forty* (1953). Richard Cary, ed., *Appreciation of Sarah Orne Jewett* (1973). Josephine Donovan, *Sarah Orne Jewett* (1980). Gwen L. Nagel, ed., *Critical Essays on Sarah Orne Jewett* (1984). Louis A. Renza, *"A White Heron" and the Question of Minor Literature* (1984). *Colby Library Quarterly Special Issue on Jewett,* vol. 22 (March 1986). Sarah Way Sherman, *Sarah Orne Jewett: An American Persephone* (1989). Marilyn Sanders Mobley, *Folk Roots and Mythic Wings in Sarah Orne Jewett and Toni Morrison: The Cultural Function of Narrative* (1991).

Sarah Way Sherman

JEWISH-AMERICAN WRITING. *This entry consists of five essays. The first provides an overview of the history of Jewish-American Writing and the others discuss Jewish-American writing by genre:*

Overview
Drama
Fiction
Nonfiction
Poetry

For further information, please refer to European Immigrant Writing; Antisemitism; Holocaust Writing; Immigrant Writing; Ethnicity and Writing; Citizenship; Assimilation.

Overview

From the nineteenth century to the present, Jewish-American women's voices have been represented in diverse literary genres, including hymns and poetry; short stories, novels, and plays; essays; journalism; theological treatises; history and autobiography. Writing about subjects sacred and secular, about being Jewish, American and female and the conflicts between these identities, they have created a unique literary tradition, distinct from, although related to, the writings of Jewish men and other ethnic women.

Among the first published Jewish women writers were Penina Moise, Rebekah Gumpert Hyneman, Marion Hartog, Celia Moss, Octavia Harby Moses, Rose Emma Salaman, Martha Allen, and Adah Isaac Mencken. Finding an outlet for their work in the Jewish press established

by newly emigrated Central European Jews or in nonsectarian journals, these women wrote of Jewish and often religious themes; at the same time their work not only expressed their loyalty to American values but also celebrated Jewish womanhood.

The most significant nineteenth century Jewish women author was Emma Larazus (1849–1878). Of elite German-Sephardic background, Lazarus was encouraged by her father and a number of celebrated British and American Romantic writers, especially Ralph Waldo Emerson, who became her mentor. Though she enjoyed considerable success, most of her early poems were sentimental and derivative; not until her thirties, after she had translated the work of several medieval Jewish poets, did she regularly incorporate Jewish themes and write in an authentic poetic voice. Her emergence as a Jewish-identified writer coincided with the catastrophic upheavals of eastern European Jewry; transformed by her visits to refugees at Wards' Island in New York, she addressed the "Jewish problem" in over 20 essays in Jewish and general circulation magazines, urging American Jews to aid new immigrants. In "The New Colossus" and other poems, she expressed a woman-centered sensibility that blended the concerns of womanhood with those of her national and ethnic identities.

Emma's older sister, Josephine, published essays on Louisa May *Alcott, Margaret *Fuller, Madame Dreyfus, and her sister, Emma. Her most important work was *The Spirit of Judaism* (1895), which examined Judaism's relationship to Christianity and probed the notion of a universal religion. Josephine Lazarus's primary literary importance, however, was in her mentoring of younger Jewish women: through her influence, Mary *Antin and Jessie Sampter (discussed below) turned to literary careers.

The massive influx of Eastern European immigrants to the United States in the late nineteenth and early twentieth century sparked the development of new forms of Jewish women's writing. Like Mary Antin, whose work, *The Promised Land* (1912), became a classic tale of the immigrant's bittersweet encounter with America, an unusual number of immigrant Jewish women wrote personal chronicles of their struggles for survival in the New World. Rose Cohen's *Out of the Shadow* (1918); Marie Ganz's *Rebels Into Anarchy—And Out Again* (1920); Elizabeth Hasanovitz's *One of Them* (1918), and in later years, Gussie Kimball's *Gitele* (1960), Lucy Robins Lang's *Tomorrow is Beautiful* (1948), Rose Pesotta's *Bread Upon the Waters* (1944) and *Days of Our Lives* (1958), Rose Schneiderman's *All For One* (1967), and Goldie

Stone's *My Caravan of Years: An Autobiography* (1945), are among the many works which record such experiences. These women's accounts of their grueling, yet ultimately successful, encounters with America were usually their sole published works: the publication of so many *autobiographies of often uneducated, *working-class, or politically radical Jewish women suggests that their stories of cultural conflict, and eventual triumph, appealed to many Americans.

Of the women to develop prominent literary careers based on their accounts of immigrant life, Mary Antin, Anzia *Yezierska, and Elizabeth Stern are the most important. Antin's *Promised Land* was an immediate best-seller, catapulting her to fame and establishing her as the creator of one of the first great works of American Jewish literature. By the time of Antin's death in 1949, the book had gone through 34 editions, becoming one of the most popular immigrant autobiographies of all time. Other than her memoir, *From Polotzk to Boston*, published in 1899 when Antin was 18, and *They Knock At the Gates: A Complete Gospel of Immigration*, published in 1914, a plea for continuing unrestricted immigrant admission, Antin published little other work.

For Anzia Yezierska, the struggle to become an American, to realize her potential as a writer and defy the age-old destiny of Jewish women, became the central theme of her fiction and autobiography. Yezierska's short story collection, *Hungry Hearts* (1920), her novel, *Bread Givers* (1925), and several other works of fiction established her as one of the nation's preeminent chroniclers of immigrant life. When Samuel Goldwyn purchased the film rights to *Hungry Hearts* and brought its author to Hollywood, she became known as the "Cinderella of the Sweatshops." But Yezierska left the film capital disillusioned, rejecting the compromises forced on her scripts. By the mid-1930s, with the public tired of immigrant stories, the sales of her fiction diminished. Living apart from the ghetto community that had nurtured her, Yezierska produced little new work other than her fictional autobiography, *Red Ribbon on A White Horse* (1950) and some short stories written in her 80s.

Elizabeth G. Stern, who also wrote under the pseudonym Leah Morton, is the author of 13 books, including *My Mother and I* (1917), and *I Am a Woman—and a Jew* (1926), both of which combine autobiographical material with fictional episodes to tell the story of an East European Jewish immigrant, daughter of a rabbi, who becomes a professional writer estranged from her family. Stern's own background is murky: Ellen Umansky, who edited *I Am a Woman—And a Jew*, believes Stern may have been Christian by birth but adopted by a Jewish family; she spent her last years as a Quaker.

Although they did not consider writing as their primary career, such immigrant Jewish activists as Emma *Goldman and Rose Pastor Stokes produced an impressive body of literature, including criticism, journalism, fiction, autobiography, and drama. A firm believer in the connection between art and politics, Goldman wrote essays on a wide range of topics, including women's rights, modern art, drama and literature. In addition to her autobiographical works, *Living My Life* and *My Disillusionment in Russia*, which told the story of her Russian childhood, her settlement and revolutionary struggles in America, and her unhappy exile, her writings include *Anarchism and Other Essays* and *The Social Significance of the Modern Drama*, and the many contributions she wrote for *Mother Earth*, which she served as editor and publisher. Rose Pastor Stokes, a leading Socialist and Communist agitator, was a columnist for the *Jewish Daily News (Yiddishe Tageglatt)* before her marriage to millionaire James Phelps Graham Stokes. During her political career, she regularly published poems, articles, and reviews in such diverse periodicals as the *Independent, Everybody's, Arena, Century*. With Helen Frank, Stokes translated Morris Rosenfeld's *Songs of Labor and Other poems* from the Yiddish; she also wrote plays on labor and feminist themes, including *The Woman Who Wouldn't*. Her unfinished autobiography, *I Belong to the Working Class*, was published after her death.

In addition to these authors writing in English, several Eastern European immigrants published work in Yiddish, especially poetry. Anna Rapport's political poems appeared in the Yiddish press in the 1890s and early 1900s; a decade later, the radical Yiddish press regularly published the more modernist and experimental work of Fradl Shtok, Anna Margolin, and Celia Dropkin. Along with these prewar poets, the work of Kadya Molodowsky and Malka Heifetz Tussman, who enjoyed more longlasting poetic careers, expressed a developing female Jewish sensibility influenced by both Yiddish and American moderns.

The mass migration of East European Jewry to the U.S. became a literary stimulus for middle-class, second- or third-generation Jewish-American women of German, Sephardic or Central European backgrounds. Seeking to relieve the plight of immigrants, they organized the National Council of Jewish Women, federations of temple sisterhoods and settlement houses, becoming deeply involved in scientific philanthropy, education, and politics. Hannah Greenbaum Solomon, Rebekah Kohut, Maud Nathan, Lillian Wald, Julia Richman, Alice Menken and Celia Rosofsky are among the many Jewish women who published autobiographies or other nonfiction accounts of their experiences working for political and social reform in the * Progressive Era.

As much as they were motivated by the problems of immigration, many of these women also drew inspiration from the women's rights activities of their American-born sisters. In *The American Jewess*, an English-language journal which she founded and edited in the years 1895–1899, Rosa Sonneschein challenged Jewish women to follow the lead of American feminists, who had created a vigorous presence for themselves in public life. Providing a forum for an incipient American Jewish women's movement, she published material of general interest, yet most of the magazine's coverage concerned Jewish life and Zionism; Sonneschein was one of the first Americans to champion publicly a Palestinian homeland.

After the demise of her magazine, the cause was championed most forcefully by Henrietta Szold, primary founder of Hadassah. A commanding intellectual as well as political leader, Szold's literary career took several forms. At age 19 she began writing a weekly column for the *Jewish Messenger* under the pen name, "Sulamith." Later, in her position as Executive Secretary of the Jewish Publication Society of America, Szold brought scores of classic Jewish works to the public, editing (and improving) many works by distinguished male scholars as well as volumes of the *American Jewish Yearbook*. Her work on behalf of Hadassah and the Palestine Executive led her to produce essays, lectures, and articles about Zionism. The writings of Szold's good friend, Jessie Sampter, a New York Jew of German extraction, also helped educate American Jews about Zionism. Under Hadassah's auspices, Sampter penned the popular *Guide to Zionism*, revised and reprinted several times. After 1919, when she became one of the first Americans to reside permanently in Palestine, Sampter wrote articles and poetry about the country for Jewish and secular magazines. Sampter's poems reveal a powerful women's spirituality; they are published in *Brand Plucked From the Fire* (1937).

By the early decades of the twentieth century, a new generation of American-born Jewish women writers began producing popular fiction. Among the most successful were Edna * Ferber and Fannie * Hurst, second- and third-generation midwestern German Americans. Ferber, who won the Pulitzer Prize in 1914 for her novel, *So Big*, was the author of a dozen other novels, included the ever-popular *Show Boat* (1926), and many plays and short stories. Hurst wrote 17 novels, including the best sellers *Back Street* (1931) and *Imitation of Life* (1933), and hundreds of short stories, many of which were made into films; she was one of the highest paid American writers of mid-century. Though neither Ferber nor Hurst experienced the anxieties of immigration and acculturation at first hand, several of their works explored Jewish or immigrant identity; the influence of ethnicity is apparent as well in Ferber's frequent exploration of Americanness and Fannie Hurst's portraits of working women. Another influential writer of German-Jewish descent, Gertrude * Stein, did not identify as a Jew. However, *The Making of Americans* (1911), Stein's great American novel, is a generational saga of an immigrant family. The meaning of America, her femaleness and otherness are continuing concerns in Stein's modernist writings.

Many Jewish women writers who came of age during the thirties were attracted to radical political and literary movements; several explored themes of Jewish identity and anti-Semitism as well. Tess * Slesinger, college-educated daughter of immigrants, wrote for the *New York Evening Post* and the *Menorah Journal*, whose left-leaning Jewish writers she satirized in her novel, *The Unpossessed* (1934). Jo Sinclair (the pen name of Ruth Seid), another second-generation immigrant daughter, also wrote for general circulation and Jewish magazines and newspapers; her novel, *Wasteland* (1946), which won the prestigious Harper Prize, portrays a second-generation Jew struggling to come to terms with his ghetto heritage; the novel includes a sympathetic portrait of the protagonist's lesbian sister, who must confront her own sexual nonconformity. Issues of Jewish identity and discrimination surface in Laura Z. * Hobson's classic novel about anti-Semitism, *Gentleman's Agreement* (1947) and in several short stories and novels by Hortense * Calisher, a college-educated daughter of German Jews. Hobson was the author of nine other novels and shorter fiction and essays. Sinclair wrote *The Changelings* (1956), which brings together the concerns of race, gender and ethnicity, with a teenage Jewish girl as protagonist, and *Anna Teller* (1960), the saga of a Hungarian Jewish family in Europe and the United States told through the story of its matriarch; Calisher wrote 11 novels, including the 1969 *The New Yorker*, which deals with themes of Jewishness, class, sexuality and gender, and several novellas; she is best known for the craft of her short stories, of which she has produced several volumes.

In addition to these novelists, poets such as Muriel * Rukeyser and Marie Syrkin began to publish in the 1930s; Syrkin, a leading Labor Zionist, also wrote essays on Jewish topics for dozens of magazines; she was most prominently associated with *Jewish Currents*. Other leading intellectuals of this period were Trude Weiss-Rosmarin, founder and, for more than 50 years, editor, of the *Jewish Spectator*, and political philosopher Hannah Arendt, the distinguished refugee scholar.

The short stories of two major Jewish women writers, Tillie * Olsen and Grace * Paley, began to appear in the 1950s. Daughters of Russian immigrants who had been active in Socialist politics, both women write deeply personal accounts of the lives of ordinary (and predominantly Jewish) women; their fiction is marked by a vigorous social and political consciousness which connects their protagonists' experience to the often gendered dilemmas of contemporary life. Tillie Olsen's "Tell Me A Riddle" won the O. Henry Award when it was published in 1956; her collection, with the same title, appeared in 1961, followed by *Yonnondio: From the Thirties* (1974), the first chapter of which had been published in 1934 by the *Partisan Review*. Olsen's major nonfiction work is *Silences* (1978), an exploration of the circumstances which influenced women's literary productivity. Grace Paley's first collection of short stories, *The Little Disturbances of Man*, appeared in 1959; Paley has published many other stories, collected in two other volumes, *Enormous Changes at the Last Minute* (1974), and *Later the Same Day* (1985), and much poetry.

Like Paley, Cynthia * Ozick is the Bronx-born daughter of Russian immigrants. As opposed to earlier Jewish women writers concerned with such topics as assimilation and social class conflict, Ozick has been most interested in Judaism as a religious heritage. She is the author of several novels—*Trust*, (1966); *The Cannibal Galaxy* (1983), *The Messiah of Stockholm* (1987); three collections of short fiction— *The Pagan Rabbi and Other Stories* (1971), *Bloodshed and Three Novellas* (1976), and *Levitation, Five Fictions* (1982), and many critical essays, collected in *Art & Ardor* (1983) and *Metaphor and Memory* (1989).

In her stories "The Shawl" (1981) and "Rosa," Ozick has written a searing account of the Holocaust as a physical and emotional reality which lives on in the memories of survivors. Among other women novelists who have focused on the effect of the * Holocaust on women's lives are Ilona Karmel, author of the 1969 novel *An Estate of Memory*, which dramatizes the daily lives of Jewish women in a concentration camp; Susan Fromberg Schaeffer, creator of the epic *Anya* (1974), which recounts the story of a privileged Jewish-Polish girl taken to the camps, her struggle for survival and immigration to America; and Marge * Piercy's *Gone to Soliders* (1987), the story of a group of Americans and Europeans on the home front, at war, and in concentration camps during World War II. In a recent book of essays, *Accidents of Influence: Writing As A Woman and A Jew In America* (1992), novelist Norma Rosen explores her reconnection to Jewish identity that began with her novel, *Touching Evil* (1969), about the effect of the Eichmann trial on two American women. Women's writing on the Holocaust includes many survivor narratives, among them, Gerda Weissman Klein's *All But My Life* (1957), Lore Segal's *Other People's Houses* (1964), Nechama Tec's *Dry Tears: The Story of A Lost Childhood* (1982), and Judith Magyar Isaacson's *Seed of Sarah: Memoirs of a Survivor* (1990), and historical analyses: most important are Lucy S. Dawidowicz's *The War Against the Jews, 1933–1945* (1975) and *The Holocaust and Historians* (1981).

In recent years, encouraged by the contemporary feminist movement, Jewish women have rewritten and revisioned narratives of Jewish women's lives in many genres. Charlotte Baum, Paula Hyman and Sonya Michel's *The Jewish Woman in America* (1975) inaugurated a constantly expanding revision of Jewish women's history. In such works as Meredith Tax's *Rivington Street* (1982) and *Union Square* (1985), Tema Nason's *Ethel: A Fictional Autobiography* (1990), and Norma Rosen's *John and Anzia: An American Romance* (1989) fiction has been used to reimagine historical events and persons. Blu Greenberg's *On Women and Judaism: A View from Tradition* (1981), Susannah Heschel's *On Being a Jewish Feminist: A Reader* (1983), Judith Plaskow's *Standing Again at Sinai: Judaism from a Feminist Perspective* (1990), and Ellen Umansky and Diane Ashton's *Four Centuries of Jewish Spirituality* (1992) reconsider Jewish theology from a women's perspective. Letty Cottin Pogrebin's *Deborah, Golda and Me* (1991) is both a spiritual and secular autobiographical meditation on the author's Jewish identity; other personal memoirs of Jewish experience are Kim Chernin's *In My Mother's House* (1983), Vivian Gornick's *Fierce Attachments* (1987), Faye Moskowitz' *A Leak in the Heart* (1985) and *And the Bridge Is Love* (1991), and Eva Hoffman's *Lost in Translation: Life in A New Language* (1989).

Fiction, playwriting, and poetry by Jewish women authors have been equally prodigious. Among contemporary writers who have written evocatively on Jewish themes, including Israel, family heritage, * assimilation, spiritual growth, women's autonomy, and lesbian Jewish identity, or Jewish characters are novelists Johanna Kaplan (*O My America!*, 1980); Lynne Sharon Schwartz (*Leaving Brooklyn*, 1989) Rebecca Goldstein (*The Mind-Body Problem*, 1983; *The Dark Sister;* 1991); Anne Roiphe (*Loving Kindness*, 1987; *The Pursuit of Happiness*, 1992); Daphne Merkin (*Deep Enchantment*, 1986); and Nessa Rapoport (*Preparing for Sabbath*, 1981); poets Adrienne *Rich, Irena Klepfisz and Marge Piercy, playwrights Wendy *Wasserstein, Myrna Lamb, and Elizabeth Swados. *Lilith*, the Jewish women's magazine which started in 1976, edited by Susan Weidman Schneider, and *Bridges*, a Jewish feminist magazine inaugurated in 1990, attest to the continuing vigor of the Jewish women's movement and Jewish women's writing today.

Joyce Antler

Drama

The first major American Jewish author to deal in depth with a Jewish subject in theatrical terms was Emma Lazarus. *The Dance to Death* (1882) is based on the fourteenth-century massacre of the Jews of Nordhausen, who were accused of poisoning wells to spread the plague. It would be difficult to invent a more appropriate vanguard work or a more representative pioneer. Lazarus ushers in a century of American-born Jewish dramatists whose work is distinguished by a wide range of interest in their Jewish heritage, often including an appreciation of their forebears' journey past the statue whose pedestal bears Lazarus's noble verse. In her poetry, too, Lazarus was a pacesetter. The women who follow her are also frequently versatile, for in addition to achieving success as dramatists, many are either accomplished in more than one literary genre, or talented as actors or directors.

It is convenient to survey the work of a century of Jewish-American women's drama by examining briefly the major subjects that have inspired plays. Here too, *The Dance to Death* serves as a precursor, even though it is only recently that anti-Semitism has become a common subject in American Jewish women's play writing. A notable exception is Rose Franken's *Outrageous Fortune* (1943), which takes on both bigotry and homosexuality. In the last two decades, the American psyche has absorbed the Holocaust sufficiently for it to exercise its imperative on the creative imagination, stimulating a number of plays by women.

Because Emily Mann allows the subject of her one-person play to tell her own story, she entitles it *Annulla: An Autobiography* (1986). In the version originally premiered in 1977, Mann's play was called *Annulla Allen: Autobiog-*

raphy of a Survivor, a title that suggests Mann's awareness of herself as one who, by sheer accident of time and place, was spared the experiences Allen recounted to her. That historical consciousness is explicit in Leeny Sack's *The Survivor and the Translator* (1980), a work the playwright brilliantly performs herself. Sack's subtitle is eloquent: *A Solo Theatre Work about Not Having Experienced the Holocaust, by a Daughter of Concentration Camp Survivors.* Leah K. Friedman, too, looks for her own roots in *Before She Is Even Born* (1982), a fugue-like play involving three generations of Jewish women.

Sounds and images of the Holocaust permeate Susan Yankowitz's *Terminal* and *Slaughterhouse Play* (both 1971). In *White Ashes* (1990), Barbara Blatner interweaves the experience of the Holocaust and sexual abuse, making them metaphors for each other. Susan Nanus tells the chilling, true story of Jack Eisner in *The Survivor* (1980). The heroic life of a young Hungarian resistance fighter who was caught and executed has been reconstructed from her diaries and poems by Lori Wilner and David Schechter in *Hannah Senesh* (1985), a work Wilner often performs. Barbara Lebow's *A Shayna Maidel* (1988) portrays the postwar reunion of two sisters in New York, where one of them grew up in safety (and ignorance), while the second lived through the horrors of the Holocaust.

However vast the differences between the sisters in Lebow's play, they are united in their mixed feelings for their difficult father. Family relationships have traditionally been a major concern of Jewish playwrights. Fannie *Hurst treats the topic in *Humoresque* (1923), in which a mother's hopes that her son's violin virtuosity will reverse the fortunes of a struggling Lower East Side family are doomed by his insistence on serving his country. Hurst's *It Is to Laugh* (1927) depicts changes in the fortunes of the upwardly mobile Goldfish family. Florence Kiper Frank's *Faith of Their Fathers* (1925) is a tongue-in-cheek portrayal of the extent to which first-generation American Jews might go to find an identity with which they feel comfortable, with outrageous results for their second-generation children. Edna *Ferber collaborated with George S. Kaufman to adapt *Minick* (1924) from a Ferber short story about a feisty old man who upsets his children's lives when he comes to stay with them.

The endlessly resourceful Jewish mother dominates any number of these domestic dramas. Only on rare occasion is she impotent against overwhelming odds. For example, in Sam and Bella Spewack's *Spring Song* (1934), a hardworking widow's earnest intentions are defeated by the Depression-induced desperation that leads her daughter astray. More typical is Rebecca Greenberg, who proves the equality of lawlessness and lawfulness, swaying a jury hearing wrongful charges of murder against her son in Elizabeth Miele's *Did I Say No?* (1931). Or Becky Felderman, who steers her four children and their mates around daunting personal and professional obstacles in Sylvia Regan's *Morning Star* (1940). The quintessence of the powerhouse Jewish mother was Molly Goldberg, the creation of Gertrude Berg, who herself had played Molly on "The Goldbergs," a phenomenally popular radio show for almost twenty years before she brought her to the stage in *Me and Molly* (1948). Even Lillian *Hellman was drawn to dramatize the Jewish family. Hellman's materfamilias is a compulsive shopper, insensitive to the increasingly desperate needs of her husband and son. Hellman's *My Mother, My Father and Me* (1963), based on a novel by Burt Blechman, was her least successful play.

Recent playwrights have been busily inverting stereotypes, and the formulaic Jewish mother is one of their most popular targets. In *The Contest* (1975), Shirley Lauro dramatizes the plight of a woman who, undone by feelings of worthlessness exacerbated by widowhood, becomes a compulsive competitor. Corinne Jacker, in *Later* (1979), portrays a widow and her two daughters trying to honor the memory of their recently deceased husband and father, as they struggle to break free of his enduring control over their lives. In what may be the most radical depiction of a Jewish mother to date, in *Brink of Devotion* (1985) Sybil Rosen tells the story of a forty-year-old unmarried entomologist, pregnant by artificial insemination, who acts in loco parentis to a runaway couple.

Jewish women dramatists' interest in family dynamics has frequently drawn them to sensitive theatrical portrayals of young Jewish women. In 1925, the year she became the first Jewish belletrist to win the Pulitzer Prize (for the novel *So Big*), Edna Ferber wrote *The Eldest: A Drama of American Life*. The subtitle is important in this melodrama, whose eponym, taking the place of her invalid mother, sacrifices herself to her family, and her love to her much younger, and therefore privileged sister. Esther Pollack's intrepid heroine in *Lily* (1935) does not let imminent childbirth deter her from leading a sit-in of indigents demanding more support from a Home Relief Bureau office. Rose Franken captured two feminine concerns just coming into prominence in the 40s. In her 1943 *Doctors Disagree*, she depicts a woman criticized by other women for having a career, and disdained by her professional colleagues for being a woman. In *Soldier's Wife* (1945), Franken dramatizes the ambivalence of a wife whose suc-cessful writing career, established while her husband was away at war, threatens their marriage when he returns.

A number of plays recall the experience of growing up Jewish, as seen through the eyes of a young girl: Susan Merson's *Reflections of a China Doll* (1977), and Leah K. Friedman's *The Rachel Plays* (1985) and *Club Soda* (1991) are examples. The influential relationship between grandmothers and granddaughters is explored by Wendy Kesselman in *I Love You, I Love You Not* (1986), and by Susan Sandler in *Crossing Delancey* (1984).

Wendy Wasserstein's *Uncommon Women and Others* (1977) examines the lives of five competent women encouraged to pioneer in unchartered endeavors, who are not altogether prepared to challenge more conventional expectations. In *Isn't It Romantic* (1983), Wasserstein continues the exploration of the challenges faced by her generation of well-educated women, who seek to define themselves and set their goals without jettisoning values they had grown up with.

Numerous playwrights have used the stage for social and political commentary on a gamut of issues. Karen Malpede plumbs history for matters of contemporary relevance. *Rebeccah* (1976) depicts a woman who loses one child in a pogrom, another in the Triangle Shirtwaist Factory fire, then, as a bag lady, founds a shantytown for the homeless. Malpede describes her theme as "the birth of the feminine consciousness." Suzanne Grossman's *Number Our Days* (1982) brings to the theater the rich and sobering experiences anthropologist Barbara Meyerhoff recorded in her work with the elderly population of Venice, California. The punning title of Emily Mann's docudrama, *Execution of Justice* (1984), refers to events surrounding the trial of Dan White for the assassination of Harvey Milk and George Moscone in the fevered climate of San Francisco of the late 1970s. In *Acts of Faith* (1986), Marilyn Felt probes the relationship that develops between an American woman and the Shiite Arab who guards her during a hijacking. The interaction of an Israeli woman lawyer and her difficult Palestinian client is given depth by being interwoven with the struggle of Sarah and Hagar in Merle Feld's *Across the Jordan* (1991).

Jewish women have also demonstrated enormous accomplishments in musical theater. Myrna Lamb's opera, *Apple Pie* (1975), concerns an escapee from Nazi Germany who finds the demands she subsequently makes of the American dream difficult to satisfy. Susan Yankowitz adapted George Eliot's *Daniel Deronda* for the libretto of the opera of that name, whose score was composed by Moshe Cotel. Doubtless, the most prolific creator of musical theater based on Jewish subjects is the multiply talented Elizabeth Swados, whose work includes *The Hagaddah: A Passover Cantata* (1980); *Esther: A Vaudeville Megillah* (1987), *Jerusalem* (based on the poetry of Yehuda Amichai and the Book of Jeremiah, 1988); and *Jonah* (1990).

There is a growing number of women performance artists who write their own material. To the work of Susan Merson and Lori Wilner should be added Rachel Rosenthal's *My Brazil* (1979), which articulates the confusions of the artist's adolescence in South America, to which she and her parents fled from Europe in 1941. In *The Father* (1985), Beatrice Roth pays heartbreakingly poetic homage to the life and death of her parent. Naomi Newman, one of the principals of San Francisco's A Traveling Jewish Theatre, enacts three ages of woman in her *Snake Talk: Urgent Messages from the Mother* (1989).

While the heyday of Yiddish theater in America is over, its influence survives in several forms. Ironically, though women were prominent during the golden era as actresses or star managers, but not as dramatists, it is as writers and composers that they are helping to keep the tradition alive. For instance, three women collaborated with Isaac Bashevis Singer, arguably the last great Yiddish author, to adapt his tales to the English-language stage: Eve Friedman, in *Yentl* (1977); Leah Napolin, in *Teibele and Her Demon* (1978); and Sarah Blacher Cohen in *Shlemiel the First* (1984). Nahma Sandrow, working with Raphael Crystal and Richard Engquist, scored a phenomenal success with *Kuni-leml* (1984), an updating of an 1880 farce by Avrom Goldfadn, the father of the Yiddish theater.

Miriam Hoffman and Rena Berkowicz Borow wrote the libretto, and Rosalie Gerut, the music for *Songs of Paradise* (1989), based on the biblical poetry of Itsik Manger. Originally played entirely in Yiddish, *Songs* so appealed to Joseph Papp that (some English having been added) he brought it to the Public Theatre in New York, where it was a great hit as the première of the Joseph Papp Yiddish Theatre. Such achievements as these, along with the contemporaneous work of other vibrant, young theatrical talents, signal the renewal of a musical Yiddish-American theater.

The work of numerous other important Jewish women dramatists, such as Gertrude Stein, Rosalyn Drexler, and Roberta Sklare, is not mentioned here solely because their themes and subjects are not specifically Jewish. Collectively, American Jewish women have made an enormous contribution to all aspects of the increasingly sophisticated American stage. Their work reflects both the full participation of Jews in American life and the increased opportunities and revised attitudes hard won by the women's movement.

• *The Drama Review*, Jewish Theatre Issue (September 1980). Helen Krich Chinoy and Linda Walsh Jenkins, eds., *Women in American Theatre* (1981; rev. ed., 1987). Bonnie Lyons, "Lillian Hellman: The First Jewish Nun on Prytania Street," in *From Hester Street to Hollywood*, ed. Sarah Blacher Cohen (1983), pp. 106–22. Kathleen Betsko and Rachel Koenig, *Interviews with Contemporary Women Playwrights* (1987). Louis Harap, *Dramatic Encounters* (1987). Ellen Schiff, "The Greening of American-Jewish Drama," in *Handbook of American-Jewish Literature*, ed. Lewis Fried (1988), pp. 91–122. Alice M. Robinson, Vera Mowry Roberts, and Milly S. Barranger, eds., *Notable Women in the American Theatre: A Biographical Dictionary* (1989). Lenora Champagne, ed., *Out from under: Texts by Women Performance Artists* (1990).

Ellen Schiff

Fiction

"I was born, I have lived, and I have been made over," begins Mary *Antin's paean to America, *The Promised Land*, published in 1912. In that autobiography, the immigrant Antin, having come to America only a few years before, speaks directly to her sense of being reborn as an American, of emerging from (as she perceived) the darkness of Jewish orthodoxy in Russia into the enlightened atmosphere of America, *di goldene medine*, the golden, promised land. In many ways, Antin's perception of her experience is emblematic of the social transformation that, repeated thousands of times, made possible the Jewish woman writer in America. For it was primarily in America that Jewish women first found themselves socially able to write, and it was largely in the late nineteenth and the twentieth centuries that Jewish women entered the previously male territory of arts and letters, as June Sochen has written in "Identities within Identities" (*Studies in American Jewish Literature*, 1983).

Antin was one of the two million Jews who crowded into the United States from 1880 to 1924. These were primarily eastern European Jews, who, fleeing pogroms and political and economic discrimination throughout Russia and Austria-Hungary, came to this country searching for religious, economic, and personal opportunity. Jews had, however, been in America for a long time. A small group of Sephardic (Spanish) Jews had come as settlers in the mid-seventeenth century. Although the Sephardi were very successful financially and socially, their numbers were never large, and it was not until a large number of German Jews came to America in the first half of the nineteenth century that Jews became a cultural force to be reckoned with. The German Jews, frequently of the middle and upper classes, were typically enlightened and familiar with the concepts of equality, democracy, and modern political thought.

In the late nineteenth century, many social and political forces converged to create an atmosphere in which Jewish women—from established Sephardic families, from German families, and from eastern European families—wanted to, and could, write. This was the era of the Chautauqua, the settlement house, the women's suffrage movement, and the politicization of women via many kinds of social endeavors. Increasingly, American women were being formally educated, and Jewish women, coming from a culture that highly values the word and the book, were no exception. In 1885, Annie Nathan Meyer enrolled in Columbia College's substitute college program for women. According to Dora Askowith's biography of Meyer in *Three Outstanding Women* (1941), all the time she was going to school she continued to play a nightly game of whist with her father, because she didn't want him to discover her educational pursuits; he believed that educated women intimidated prospective husbands. Yet his studious (and eventually married) daughter, one of the founders of Barnard College, was an avid lecturer and writer, who contributed articles and short stories to many periodicals. Meanwhile, the work of other Jewish women was being published. Rebekah G. Hyneman's short story, "The Lost Diamond," printed in the *Occident*, in 1862, characterized the Jewish woman as central to the welfare and survival of the Jewish people. Emma Wolf's short stories and novels, such as *Heirs of Yesterday* (1900), portrayed Jewish life in California; her work is dominated by the theme of assimilation. In this era (around 1866), the poet Emma Lazarus wrote the famous poem that appears on the Statue of Liberty; her sister Josephine published literary criticism and reviews.

It was, however, the *American Jewess* magazine that drew the work of many of these early writers together. Published first in Chicago, then in New York from 1895 to 1899 by Rosa Sonneschein, the *American Jewess* was partly a vehicle for her fiction, but it also published Kate *Chopin, Rebekah Kohut, Emma Wolf, and Annie Nathan Meyer).

By the early decades of the twentieth century, some Jewish-American women were in print, but an explosion of Jewish women's writing was still to come. Mary Antin's *The Promised Land* appeared in 1912; her short stories and impassioned articles about immigration also appeared in the *Atlantic*, *Century*, and other magazines. Anzia *Yezierska's stories and nov-

els were so popular that Yezierska was invited to Hollywood to try screenwriting. Published during the same years as Yezierska's stories, the immensely popular Emma McChesney stories (1912–1915) by Edna *Ferber typified the experience of many working-class women, whom Ferber glorified as the heart of the country. Fannie *Hurst's novels about heroines who tried to break free of gender stereotypes even as they enacted the American dream (*Stardust*, 1921; *Imitation of Life*, 1933) were widely read. And during the Great Depression, Tess *Slesinger's short stories and novels, such as *The Unpossessed* (1934), explored Jewish life from the perspective of upper-middle-class privilege.

Since 1950, writing by American Jewish women has explored the familiar theme of self-definition against the refrains of the American ideal, the family, personal sexuality, and Jewishness itself, all typically focused through a feminist lens. Drawing on the theme of America as utopia, Johanna Kaplan's *Oh, My America!* (1980) explores the impact of the American ideal upon Merry Slavin, a second-generation American. The ideal of the modern Jewish family is explored in the work of Tillie *Olsen ("Tell Me A Riddle," 1961), whose grandmotherly protagonist is bitter about the loss of herself in the creation and maintaining of her family; of Susan Fromberg Schaeffer (*Falling*, 1973; *Love*, 1980; *The Madness of a Seduced Woman*, 1983), whose mother characters are always peculiarly flawed through cruelty toward their offspring; of Grace *Paley (*The Little Disturbances of Man*, 1959; *Enormous Changes at the Last Minute*, 1974); of Allegra Goodman (*Total Immersion*, 1989), whose Markowitz family is simultaneously traditional and zanily unconventional and contemporary; and of Rebecca Goldstein (*The Dark Sister*, 1991), whose families are sources of *tzuris* and strength, as are all families, Jewish and otherwise.

The theme of *sexuality persists in writing by Jewish women, originating with Emma *Goldman's listing of her lovers and her passion for them in her slightly fictive autobiography, *Living My Life* (1931). Jewish women are unashamed of and believe themselves entitled to sexual pleasure by virtue of Jewish law; perhaps influenced by the notion of freedom in other aspects of American life, Jewish-American women have freely and frequently written about sexuality, which has subsequently become a significant mode for self-definition. In the work of Alix Kates *Shulman (*Memoirs of an Ex-Prom Queen*, 1969), sex designates the significance of events. Erica *Jong's poetry and highly confessional novels, such as *Fear of Flying* (1973), focus upon minutely detailed sexual encounters, by and through which the protagonist knows not only herself, but others. Sexuality and the implications of sexual choices are also predictably prominent themes in the work of Jewish lesbian writers. Evelyn Torton Beck's anthology *Nice Jewish Girls* (1982) includes notable work by Andrea *Dworkin, Adrienne *Rich, and Irena Klepfisz. The problems that lesbian writers address are multilayered; they struggle for acceptance in their families, the Jewish community, and the society at large.

Contemporary Jewish women writers have also been concerned, and even obsessed, with Jewishness itself—not only with the focal events of Jewish history that have occurred within our century—the *Holocaust and the establishment of the state of Israel—but also with the more diffuse issues of Jewish self-definition, tradition, and culture. Laura Z. *Hobson's *Gentleman's Agreement* (1947) condemns the insidiousness of anti-Semitism, and her *Over and above* (1979) questions her Jewishness. E. M. *Broner's work examines Jewishness from an acutely sensitive feminist perspective; *A Weave of Women* (1978), set in Israel, explores the lives and roles of communal Jewish women in a patriarchal environment. Broner's other works reflect a strong Jewish sensibility; among them is the story "The Woman Who Lived for Ten" (1968), about a woman who takes on vicariously the suffering of a Holocaust survivor. Norma Rosen's *Touching Evil* (1969) examines the evil of the Holocaust via the Eichmann trial. Tova Reich's novels and short stories, such as "Solidarity" (1984), reveal the humanness, the idiosyncrasies of the orthodox Jewish community. Faye Moskowitz's autobiographical sketches, collected in *A Leak in the Heart* (1985), contextualize her experience within the Jewish-American community, and illustrate, among other themes, the importance of the idea of Israel in contemporary American Jewish life. In Francine Prose's work (*Hungry Hearts*, 1983; *"Women and Children First" and Other Stories*, 1988), characters alienated from their Jewishness are forced into confrontations with elements of that Jewishness, and as a result, often acknowledge and return to their heritage. Perhaps the female writer whose Jewishness has been not only most problematic, but most evocative, is Cynthia *Ozick. In almost everything Ozick has written, the questions of her Jewishness, first, and her femaleness, second, are central. She is ever aware of being a Jew and a woman in an American culture that has given impetus to the successful self-realization of both Jew and woman, but which in thought and deed still marginalizes both as manifestations of the Other.

• Charlotte Baum, Paula Hyman, and Sonya Michel, *The Jewish Woman in America* (1975). Elizabeth Koltun, ed., *The Jewish Woman: New Perspectives* (1976). Sydelle Kramer and Jenny Masur, *Jewish Grandmothers* (1976). Dorothy Seidman Bilik, *Immigrant-Survivors: Post-Holocaust Consciousness in Recent Jewish American Literature* (1981). Aviva Cantor, *A Bibliography on the Jewish Woman, 1900–1980* (1981). Blu Greenberg, *On Women and Judaism: A View From Tradition* (1982). Sam B. Girgus, *The New Covenant: Jewish Writers and the American Idea* (1984). Susan Weidman Schneider, *Jewish and Female: Choices and Changes in Our Lives Today* (1984). Rachel DuPlessis Blau, *Writing beyond the Ending: Narrative Strategies of Twentieth-Century Women Writers* (1985). Sydney Stahl Weinberg, *The World of Our Mothers: The Lives of Jewish Immigrant Women* (1988). Neil M. Cowan and Ruth Schwartz Cowan, *Our Parents' Lives: The Americanization of Eastern European Jews* (1989). Judith Plaskow, *Standing Again at Sinai: Judaism from a Feminist Perspective* (1990).

C. Beth Burch

Nonfiction

In her memoirs, *Red Ribbon on a White Horse* (1950), Anzia *Yezierska, the chronicler of immigrant Jews on New York's Lower East Side, writes that after attaining fame and wealth and moving from the ghetto, her writing skills dried up. Paralyzed by the guilt and loss of leaving her people behind, and the pervading emptiness of the success she had desperately sought, Yezierska claims to have "lost her soul."

Yezierska describes a theme commonly found in many twentieth-century Jewish-American women writers. In the old country, one's role as both a woman and a Jew was rigidly enforced, but while assimilation and success were possibilities for Jewish-American women, Yezierska suggests that these can occur only at the expense of losing one's community and history.

Yezierska arrived in America as part of the great wave of immigration that brought over two million Jews to America between 1880 and 1914. Most of these immigrants were from shtetls, or Eastern European Jewish villages, where they had lived traditional Jewish lives until anti-Semitic pogroms forced them from their homes. Before this great immigration there were approximately 250,000 Jews in America. Most were of German descent, as well as prosperous and well educated and from a far different background than the new arrivals. Many had abandoned their orthodox religious traditions and embraced Reform Judaism, finding a relatively comfortable place in secular American society.

As nineteenth-century letters and diaries show, Jewish women were already struggling with the conflicting impulses they felt as Jews in a non-Jewish nation. For instance, the letters of the wealthy Philadelphian Rebecca Gratz, the founder, in 1819, of the first American society for Jewish women, show her to be intensely concerned with issues of Jewish identity and women's community. However, they also tell the story of her love for a gentile man. Feeling she had to choose between love and her Jewish identity, Gratz chose to give up her lover rather than marry outside the faith.

Other nineteenth-century Jewish women dedicated themselves to fighting American * slavery and the oppression of women. While the Reform movement released assimilated Jewish women from many of the traditional expectations and constraints of orthodoxy, they were now expected to embody the nineteenth-century American ideals of the cult of * true womanhood. This role entailed not only performing the duties of marriage and household management, but also becoming the source of goodness, virtue, and delicate sensibility. Feminist and abolitionist Ernestine Rose rebelled against this image, and her brilliantly scathing political speeches made her famous across America. Rose was not a practicing Jew, but, calling herself a "child of Israel," her speeches reveal that she used her experience as both a Jew and a woman to identify with others who were oppressed.

As women's status in society shifted in the twentieth century, many Jewish women felt that mainstream America presented an opportunity to break free of stifling traditions. In her immensely popular * autobiography, *The Promised Land* (1912), Russian immigrant Mary * Antin contrasts the possibilities of freedom in modern America with the "medievalism" of both Russia and Judaism. For Antin, American assimilation is rooted in individualism, and means unsentimentally leaving archaic religions and communities behind. Journalist Elizabeth Stern, who published *I Am a Woman— and a Jew* (1926) under the * pseudonym Leah Morton, also tells of rejecting Jewish orthodoxy and traditional feminine roles in favor of assimilation. Her narrative is complicated, however, when she encounters anti-Semitism, and when she feels the powerful yearning to be back within the stable structures of her former life.

Jewish women have always been at the forefront of feminist and other political movements of the twentieth century. Emma * Goldman and Rose Schneiderman were among the many Jewish women who were leading labor organizers and suffragists in the early part of the century. In her autobiography *All for One* (1967), Schneiderman discusses how her early immigrant experiences with poverty, sexism, and anti-Semitism led her to dedicate her life to helping working women. *Living My Life* (1931), the autobiography of the controversial political theorist Goldman, reveals a similar process. Like Antin,

Goldman had a passionate belief in the freedom of the individual, but she believed that American capitalism hindered this freedom.

The revival of the feminist movement in the 1960s and 1970s derives at least in part from the significant theoretical contributions of Jewish women. Betty * Friedan's ground-breaking *The Feminine Mystique* (1963) examines the societal pressures that led promising young women away from college educations and careers, and toward identities as wives and mothers. Like many other political Jewish women, Friedan attributed her awareness of oppression, in part, to her Jewish identity. Other foundational feminist works by Jewish women include Shulamith Firestone's *The Dialectics of Sex* (1970) and Andrea * Dworkin's *Pornography* (1979).

Because Judaism has traditionally silenced women, many women have felt the need to abandon their Jewish identities in order to find a voice. More recent works by Jewish feminists have tried to reconcile a feminist and Jewish identity by articulating Jewish women's traditions and critiquing existing structures. Blu Greenberg's *On Women and Judaism* (1981), Judith Plaskow's *Standing Again at Sinai* (1990), and Letty Cottin Pogrebin's *Deborah, Golda and Me* (1991) all rethink feminism in relation to Jewish identity, ideology, and religious practice. Many essays in anthologies such as *Nice Jewish Girls* (1982) and *The Tribe of Dina* (1989) find striking parallels between the closeting of sexual orientation and the closeting of Jewishness in assimilated America. Finally, historians such as Paula Hyman, Charlotte Baum, and Sonya Michel in *The Jewish Woman in America* (1976) and E. M. * Broner in *The Telling* (1993) have begun to reinsert Jewish women into the telling of Jewish history, and to explore and reinvent the powerful role women play in Jewish ritual and tradition.

• David Philipson, ed., *The Letters of Rebecca Gratz* (1929). Edgar E. MacDonald, ed., *The Education of the Heart: The Correspondence of Rachel Mordecai Lazarus and Maria Edgeworth* (1977). Hanna Arendt, *The Jew as Pariah* (1978). Jacob Marcus, ed., *The American Jewish Woman: A Documentary History* (1981). Jacob Marcus, *The American Jewish Woman, 1654–1980* (1981). Susannah Heschel, ed., *On Being a Jewish Feminist: A Reader* (1983). Christie Balka and Andy Rose, eds., *Twice Blessed: On Being Lesbian or Gay and Jewish* (1989). Judith Baskin, ed., *Jewish Women in Historical Perspective* (1991). Ellen M. Umansky and Dianne Ashton, eds., *Four Centuries of Jewish Women's Spirituality: A Sourcebook* (1992).

Daniel Itzkovitz

Poetry

Before the beginning of the massive immigration of eastern European Jews (1881–1924), relatively little poetry by Jewish women was published in the United States. Although Jews had lived in America since the colonial days, by 1880 they comprised only one-half of one percent of the general population. The first Jews in America were Sephardic (of Spanish or Portuguese origin); those who arrived in the mid-nineteenth century were Ashkenazic and came from Germany, Austro-Hungary, and central Europe. The idea of women writing and publishing poems, although uncommon, was not completely alien to European Jewish culture, for some devotional verse composed by women in Yiddish had appeared since the sixteenth century among the popular Yiddish prayers read as part of daily religious ritual by women who adhered to traditional Judaism in central and eastern Europe. However, the Jewish women who first published poetry in America in the mid-nineteenth century cannot be regarded as direct descendants of that tradition, for as Reform Jews, which many of them were, they were products of the Jewish Enlightenment, and, as middle-class Americans writing in English, they produced poetry that interwove mainstream gentile culture with Jewish values.

This cultural interweaving establishes a model for Jewish-American poetry against which we can contrast the writers who came later. Diane Lichtenstein's *Writing Their Nations: The Tradition of Nineteenth-Century American Jewish Women Writers* (1992) and Ellen Umansky and Dianne Ashton's *Four Centuries of Jewish Women's Spirituality: A Sourcebook* (1992) discuss a number of early writers. For example, Rebekah Gumpert Hyneman of Philadelphia published *The Leper and Other Poems* (1853), which includes "Female Scriptural Characters," a series of poems praising or personifying the matriarchs and other biblical women as examples of nineteenth century American ideals of femininity, patriotism, and faith. Octavia Harby Moses of South Carolina, whose father was a founder of the first Reform congregation in America, wrote poems between 1836 and 1891, which were published posthumously as *A Mother's Verses* (1915). These poems reflect, on the one hand, the daily life of a mother in a large family, and, on the other hand, a woman's staunch Confederate loyalty during the Civil War, tempered by Jewish values, such as *tsedakah* (charity) and maternal nurturing.

Another southern Jewish woman, Penina Moise, composed the first Jewish hymnal in America, *Hymns Written for the Use of Hebrew Congregations* (1856), published by the Reform Congregation Beth Elohim in Charleston, South Carolina. Adah Isaacs Menken, an actress on the American stage notorious for her revealing costumes and her multiple marriages, published both sentimental pious verse in the Reform journal *Israelite*, and, in her volume *Infelicia* (1868), flamboyant, Whitmanesque poems that speak in the voices of such biblical women as Judith. This period culminates in Emma *Lazarus. A descendant of two of the oldest Portuguese and German-Jewish families, Lazarus was regarded as the most distinguished Jewish writer in America by her contemporaries, and is best known today for her 1883 sonnet "The New Colossus," inscribed on the pedestal of the Statue of Liberty in 1903. Influenced profoundly by the American Romantics, especially Ralph Waldo Emerson, who befriended her after her first book appeared in 1866, Lazarus published primarily in secular rather than Jewish magazines. While her 1867 poem "In the Jewish Synagogue at Newport" echoes Henry Wadsworth Longfellow's famous poem "The Jewish Cemetery at Newport" in its regretful contemplation of a Jewish ruin, Lazarus finds in the obsolete synagogue a living force. Her verse drama, *The Dance to Death* (1882), depicts the 1349 slaughter of the Jews in Nordhausen, Germany.

Lazarus's literary elevation deflected the ambivalence felt and expressed in fiction and political writing, and, to a lesser degree, poetry, by her American-Jewish contemporaries in the 1880s and 1890s, as hundreds of thousands of Russian and Polish Jews, escaping anti-Semitism, violence, and poverty, arrived in the United States. These "huddled masses" of eastern Europe, perceived by the middle-class Americanized Sephardic and German Jewish women who volunteered to help educate and socialize them as ignorant and uncultured, were indeed poor, and struggled to make a living as peddlers on the street or as workers in the sweatshops. Yet through the force of the Yiddish culture they brought from Europe, the writers among them dramatically changed the character of Jewish-American poetry, eventually developing a rich, varied, and quintessentially Jewish-American poetry. Initially, Yiddish poetry, a medium for the nascent Jewish labor movement, was influenced as much by European Romanticism as by socialist ideology. While both the Labor Poets and the neotraditionalists wrote poems to serve the collective concerns of the Jewish people, two short-lived modernist movements in the 1910s and 1920s, *Di yunge* (The Young Ones) and *Di inzikhistn* (The Introspectivists), introduced new notions of individualism, aestheticism, symbolism, and expressionism into American Yiddish poetry. However, the destruction of European Jewry during the Second World War interrupted and bankrupted this movement, and many Yiddish poets writing in America since 1939 revived the spokesperson stance.

The earliest Yiddish women poets in America wrote unreflectingly within the didactic conventions of the political poetry of the day. Anna Rapport, a pioneer of Yiddish poetry in America, worked in a sweatshop and published poems in the popular Yiddish press that protested the exploitation of Jewish immigrant workers, particularly women.

Women poets born in the 1880s and 1890s, who came to America and began to publish poems in the socialist, anarchist, and modernist press before 1914, tell a different story. Influenced by and influencing Yiddish modernism, well-read in and translating European and American poetry, and experimenting with forms, Fradl Shtok, Anna Margolin, and Celia Dropkin are all outstanding poets. Shtok wrote lyrics considered shocking for their sensual imagery and their innuendo of the violent reversal of power between the sexes. Anna Margolin's single book, *Lider* (Poems, 1929), contains exquisite, complex lyric poems that defuse the personal voice with dramatic personae and a "hard" poetics. Celia Dropkin experimented with free verse and established an explicit eroticism in her book *In Heysn Vint* (In the Hot Wind, 1935), which undermines truisms about women, poetry, and sex. Other contemporaries include Rochelle Weprinsky, Malka Lee, Berta Kling, and the younger, American-born Hasye Cooperman.

Esther Shumiatcher, Sara Barkan, and Shifre Weiss published in the communist press and wrote poems that conformed to the puritanical correctness of working-class literature, although, as Norma Fain Pratt points out, they protested the oppression of women more vociferously than other radicals did.

In contrast to most of these Yiddish poets, many of whom published only one volume of poems early in life, Kadya Molodowsky in New York and Malka Heifetz Tussman in California had fully developed poetic careers. Molodowsky, who arrived in New York in 1935, had published several books of poems in Poland, and went on to publish three more books of poems, as well as collections of short stories, essays, a novel, and plays in America. Molodowsky's European poems touch on themes of women's lives in cultural flux and poverty, while her American poems turn to themes of exile and Jewish nationalism. She treats these public topics with a distinctly private poetic voice. Tussman, although born in the Ukraine and a contemporary of Molodowsky, is in her way a pure product of America. Having come to Chicago from the Ukraine in 1912, she eschewed the New York Yiddish community and spent her long writing life in the Midwest and California. While her early poems appeared in the New York modernist journals in the 1910s and 1920s, Tussman did not publish a book of poems until 1949, when she was fifty-six years old. Her sixth book of poems appeared in 1977, and she left a seventh volume unpublished at her death. A maverick lyric poet, Tussman's early works show the influence of writers as diverse as Whitman, the great Indian poet Rabindranath Tagore, and Yeats. In her middle poems, a distinctive personal voice evolves. Her poems of the 1970s and 1980s explore the inner life in a compressed, musical, and almost telegraphic style.

These Yiddish poets can be characterized as Jewish-American poets for a number of reasons. In many of their poems, the poets take issue with the tenets of Jewish life and subvert its defining texts—Scripture, commentary, and prayer. The forms and subjects of other poems contend with the immigrant's interweaving of cultures and languages in the new home of America. And in America, their very language changed its character. The Jewish vernacular Yiddish, constructed from the building blocks of traditional belief, custom, practice, and culture, had to be opened to include the new world of secular knowledge: Anna Margolin's poem, "I Was Once a Boy," spoken in the personae of Greeks and Romans, imports latinate diction in order to distance the Yiddish poem from the cultural assumptions of its own medium. Although the Yiddish poets wrote and published in America, their work has remained essentially invisible to American-born Jewish poets. Only in recent years have their poems begun to be translated and studied.

Extrapolating from Gerald Stern's essay "Poetry" (*Jewish-American History and Culture: An Encyclopedia*, 1992), one concludes that the Jewish women, as well as men, writing American poetry during the twentieth century are the heirs of both Emma Lazarus and Gertrude *Stein—the conventional, bourgeois, and the modernist, radical, experimental. They are also (for the most part, unwitting) descendants of the Yiddish poets—their writing from political conviction, their secular devotions, their assertion and redefinition of the female poetic self all have roots in the earlier tradition. The hundreds of Jewish-American poets of this century can be divided into three roughly defined tendencies by which their poetry takes on both a Jewish and an American character. The broadest and least significant group for this discussion (although it includes many fine poets) consists of those whose poems reflect the poet's Jewishness through occasional, often autobiographical references or images. Examples include Grace *Paley, Maxine *Kumin, Linda Pastan, and Denise *Levertov. The second group is defined by the poet's more sustained examination of her Jewish identity, which she uses as a springboard for political statement and historical reflection on nation, gender, and class. Examples include Marie Syrkin and Adrienne *Rich. The third group encompasses poets who at some point in their work grapple directly with Jewish texts (Hebrew, Yiddish, or Ladino)—Scripture, commentary, prayer, folksong, philosophy, poetry—in order to rework, subvert, and redefine Jewish religion, spirituality, and culture in the American language. In this sense, these poets resemble the nineteenth-century hymnist Penina Moise. Among these writers are Eleanor Wilner, in the exquisite, philosophical poetry of *Shekhinah* (1984) and *Sarah's Choice* (1989); Muriel *Rukeyser, in *Collected Poems of Muriel Rukeyser* (1978); Pamela White Hadas, in her monologues *In Light of Genesis* (1980); Alicia *Ostriker, in *Green Age* (1989); as well as Rachel Blau-Duplessis, Marcia Falk, Ruth Whitman, Chana Bloch, and Marge *Piercy. Irena *Klepfisz, in *A Few Words in the Mother Tongue* (1990), writing as a feminist, interlineates her English and Yiddish poems in a bilingual form that, like recent Latina/o poetry, reshapes American language to accommodate Jewish experience. Other poets, such as Kathryn Hellerstein, are engaged in similar projects. The final category contains American poets living and writing in Israel, but publishing in America, examples of whom include Shirley Kaufman, Ruth Finer Mintz, and Linda Zisquit. Significantly, in recent years, a number of these poets have translated Yiddish or Hebrew poetry by women into English. Such acts of translation renew the cycle of tradition.

• Morris U. Schappes, *Emma Lazarus: Selections from Her Poetry and Prose* (1967). Jerome Rothenberg, ed., *The Big Jewish Book* (1978). Howard Schwartz and Anthony Rudolf, eds., *Voices within the Ark: The Modern Jewish Poets* (1980). Norma Fain Pratt, "Culture and Radical Politics: Yiddish Women Writers in America, 1890–1940," in *Decades of Discontent: The Women's Movement, 1920–1940*, eds. Lois Scharf and Joan M. Jensen (1983), pp. 131–152. Benjamin and Barbara Harshav, eds., *American Yiddish Poetry: A Bilingual Anthology* (1986). Irving Howe, Ruth R. Wisse, and Khone Shmeruk, eds., *Penguin Book of Modern Yiddish Verse* (1987). Marcia Cohn Spiegel and Deborah Lipton Kremsdorf, eds., *Women Speak to God: The Prayers and Poems of Jewish Women* (1987). Kathryn Hellerstein, "A Question of Tradition: Women Poets in Yiddish," in *Handbook of American-Jewish Literature*, edited by Lewis Fried (1988), pp. 195–237. Melanie Kaye/Kantrowitz and Irena Klepfisz, eds., *The Tribe of Dina: A Jewish Women's Anthology* (1989). Elaine Marcus Starkman and Leah Schweitzer, eds., *Without a Single Answer: Poems on Contemporary Israel* (1990). Kathryn Hellerstein, "Canon and Gender: Women Poets in Two Modern Yiddish Anthologies," *Shofar* 9, no. 4 (Summer 1991): 9–23. Ellen M. Umansky and Dianne Ashton, eds., *Four Centuries of Jewish Women's Spirituality* (1992).

Kathryn Hellerstein

JIM CROW. *See* Reconstruction.

JOHNSON, E. Pauline (1861–1913), also known as Tekahionwake, Canadian Mohawk (Iroquois) performer and writer of short fiction, essays, and poetry. E. Pauline Johnson was the daughter of George Henry Johnson, a Canadian Native American activist, and the English-born Emily Susanna Howells, cousin of American writer William Dean Howells. She was raised in the Six Nations Reserve at Grand River, near what is now Brantford, Ontario. Educated with a classical literary background by her mother, she learned much of her Mohawk history from her paternal grandfather Smoke Johnson. Both cultures influenced her own writing. Around 1890, Johnson began publishing poems and performing in Toronto literary events. Billed as the "Mohawk Princess," she toured Canada, the United States, and England as Canada's poet laureate. Some of her earlier work appeared in the *Mother's Magazine*, published in Elgin, Illinois, with a circulation of over 600,000, and *Boys' World*. The White Wampum, a collection of poetry and short stories, was published in 1895, with a second collection of poetry, *Canadian Born*, following in 1903. Johnson retired from touring in 1908 and dedicated herself to writing. She died of cancer in 1913.

Johnson exemplifies the problematics of ethnic and gender identity. She was of mixed-blood heritage, from a well-to-do family, with close ties to both white and Mohawk culture. She was also aware of the expectations of the literary audience for women writers concerning *domestic values. With such romanticized stories of life in the wilderness as *The White Wampum* and *Flint and Feather* (1912), Johnson captured the interest and imagination of the popular market. These titles suggest the picturesque setting that attracted an audience, yet Johnson managed to treat Native American issues. She concentrated on the consequences of the white world upon Native Americans, particularly for women involved in heterosexual, multicultural relationships, as seen in the story "A Red Girl's Reasoning."

Johnson's works countered literary and cultural *stereotypes of Native Americans as savage. Instead, her characters are constantly reacting to and challenged by moral dilemmas and spiritual needs, and her stories invoke the importance of *family and home as based in

Indian life as sources of faith, inner growth, and community. Yet with such an agenda, Johnson continued to perpetuate the Victorian domestic ideal for women with her morally virtuous, always beautiful, mixed-blood "Indian maidens." Still, Johnson goes beyond ideals of mother and wife with such stories as "As It Was in the Beginning," in which she examines racist and sexist imperatives of Christian morals and values, and in her depiction of her own politically active *grandmother, in the biographical sketch "My Mother," contained in her semi-autobiographical work *The Moccasin Maker* (1913).

• Mill Library, McMaster University, in Hamilton, Ontario, contains the E. Pauline Johnson Papers. Betty Keller, *Pauline: A Biography of Pauline Johnson* (1981). Carole Gerson, "Some Notes concerning Pauline Johnson," *Canadian Notes and Queries* 34 (Autumn 1985): 16–19. A. LaVonne Brown Ruoff, *American Indian Literatures* (1990). George W. Lyon, "Pauline Johnson: A Reconsideration," *Studies in Canadian Literature* 15, no. 2 (1990):136–159.

Robin Jones

JOHNSON, Georgia Douglas (1877–1966), African-American poet and playwright. A native of Atlanta, Georgia, Camp attended Atlanta University Normal School, Oberlin Conservatory, and Cleveland College of Music. In 1903, she married Henry Lincoln Johnson. In 1910, the Johnsons moved to Washington, D.C., where their home became a mecca in which artists, politicians, and intellectuals frequently gathered.

Her interest in composing music now moved to writing lyrical poetry. In 1918, she published *The Heart of a Woman*, poems exploring themes especially meaningful to women. With this volume, Johnson became the first widely recognized African-American woman poet since Frances E. W. *Harper. *The Heart of a Woman* is about love, longing, disillusionment, and loneliness. The poems reflect frustration with the strictures of women's prescribed roles. In 1922, she published a second volume, *Bronze*, which concerned racial themes.

Henry Lincoln Johnson died in 1925, leaving his widow with two teenage sons. Georgia Douglas Johnson began a lifelong economic struggle, which robbed her of time and leisure. Nevertheless, she continued to write and to sponsor her Saturday night gatherings. By now she was writing plays as well as poems. In 1925, she completed a protest play, *Sunday Morning in the South*. In 1926, her play *Blue Blood* won honorable mention in the *Opportunity* play competition; the following year, her one-act folk play *Plumes* won first prize. She regarded drama as a way to teach; her works included the historical plays *Frederick Douglass* and *William and Ellen Craft*. She wrote twenty-eight plays, but most are lost.

In 1928, she published a volume of poems, *An Autumn Love Cycle*, which returned to her earlier explorations of feminine themes. This volume is considered her best because of its mature treatment of the theme of *romantic love and because of its skillful use of form. Her much-anthologized "I Want to Die While You Love Me" is in this volume.

Johnson continued to write, but publication became increasingly difficult. In 1962, she published *Share My World*, poems containing the wisdom culled from a lifetime of experience. She remained active into her eighties, until she died suddenly of a stroke in 1966. Because her papers were not saved, much of her work was lost.

Georgia Douglas Johnson's poems are skillfully crafted lyrics cast in traditional forms. They are, for the most part, gentle and delicate, using soft consonants and long, low vowels. Their realm is emotion, often sadness and disappointment, but sometimes fulfillment, strength, and spiritual triumph. Yet Johnson herself was never otherworldly. She remained in the forefront of political and social events of her time. Her plays were moving portrayals of the tragic impact of *racism upon African Americans. Frequent themes in both her poetry and drama are the alienation and dilemmas of the person of mixed blood and the goal of integration into the American mainstream.

• Cedric Dover, "The Importance of Georgia Douglas Johnson," *Crisis* 59 (December 1952). Erlene Stetson, "Rediscovering the Harlem Renaissance: Georgia Douglas Johnson, the 'New Negro Poet,'" *Obsidian* 5 (Spring/Summer 1979). Gloria T. Hull, *Color, Sex, and Poetry* (1987). Ann Allen Shockley, *Afro-American Women Writers* (1988).

Eugenia W. Collier

JOHNSON, Helene (b. 1907), poet, attended Boston public schools and, briefly, Boston University. In 1926, with her cousin Dorothy *West, Johnson arrived in New York at the height of the *Harlem Renaissance to launch a literary career. Through its annual contests and award ceremonies, and the efforts of its editor, Charles S. Johnson, *Opportunity*, the journal of the National Urban League, introduced eighteen-year-old Helene to the leading figures of the Harlem Renaissance, and, between 1925 and 1927, published the poems that made her reputation. Wallace Thurman printed Johnson's "A Southern Road" in the magazine *Fire!!* (1926) and cast Johnson and West as Hazel Jamison and Doris Westmore in his satirical Harlem Renaissance novel *Infants of the Spring* (1932). In Boston, William Stanley Braithwaite reprinted "Fulfillment" and "The Road" in his annual *Anthology of Magazine Verse* (1926), finding, in Johnson's "The Road," "the lyrical sincerity and insight of her generation." Reprinting "Fulfillment" in the *Carolina Magazine* (1927), Charles S. Johnson declared that "Helene Johnson has a lyric penetration which belies her years, and a rich and impetuous power." Countee Cullen praised her "more colloquial verse," reprinting eight poems in *Caroling Dusk* (1927), including "Bottled," first published in *Vanity Fair* (1927) with the help of Carl Van Vechten, whom Johnson had met at one of Zora Neale *Hurston's parties. Work at the Fellowship of Reconciliation, an international organization for world peace, in Manhattan was followed by employment with Gwendolyn *Bennett at *Consumer Reports* in Mount Vernon, New York. In 1928, "A Missionary Brings a Young Native to America" appeared in *Harlem*, another magazine venture of Wallace Thurman. In 1929, the year of the stock market crash, Johnson traveled to Detroit and Chicago with a production of Thurman's play, *Harlem*. In 1931, James Weldon Johnson's *The Book of American Negro Poetry* reprinted five of Johnson's poems; he placed her among the younger poets whose race-conscious poems merited praise. Between 1928 and 1934, she published a dozen poems, few of which achieve the level of her earlier work. In 1934, she married William Hubbell; following the birth of a daughter, she stopped writing poetry and did not resume until the mid-1960s.

• Langston Hughes and Arna Bontemps, eds., *The Poetry of the Negro* (1970). T. J. Bryan, "The Published Poems of Helene Johnson," *Langston Hughes Review* 5, no. 2 (Fall 1978): 11–21. Lorraine Elena Rose and Ruth Elizabeth Randolph, *Harlem Renaissance and Beyond* (1990).

Raymond R. Patterson

JOHNSON, Susannah Willard (1729–1810), *captivity narrative author. Johnson's *A Narrative of the Captivity of Mrs. Johnson* (1796) went through ten editions in the fifty years following its initial publication. A poignant tale of hardship and perseverance, the narrative depicts the Johnson family's kidnapping by Abenakis Indians and their more than three years' captivity among the French and Indians. Abducted from her home in Charlestown, New Hampshire, on 30 August 1754, Johnson delivered a daughter (whom she later named Captive) on the second day of captivity. After being held in Canada and transported by boat to England for a prisoner exchange, Johnson returned to America on 10 December 1757.

Johnson trenchantly comments on her cap-

tors' "civilizations." Adopted by the Indians, she spends two-and-a-half relatively pleasant months with them. Relating many proofs of the Abenakis' humanity, Johnson demands, "Can it be said of civilized conquerors, that they, in the main, are willing to share with their prisoners, the last ration of food, when famine stares them in the face? Do they ever adopt an enemy, and salute him by the tender name of brother?" By contrast, Johnson reviles the French bureaucracy that incarcerates her, her husband, and infant in a lice-infested open-air jail for six months. There she and her husband contract smallpox. Transferred to a civil jail and better conditions, in 1756 Johnson bears a stillborn son.

The narrative's pervasive theme is the scattering redefinition and difficult reorganization of Johnson's family. The family is divided among French captors; Johnson doesn't see her oldest son or daughter for four years. Later she is forced to leave behind her husband as she sails abroad. Although they are joyfully reunited, he is killed in battle shortly thereafter (Johnson remarried in 1761). When her son Sylvanus is ransomed, Johnson observed that he had "learnt too many of [the Indians] habits; to civilize him, and learn his native language was a severe task." Her daughter Susanna tearfully returns after leaving the gentle Jaisson sisters, her Montreal captors: "To give her the accomplishments of a polite education had been their principal care, she had contracted an ardent love for them, which never will be obliterated." Coincidentally, in 1759, Johnson meets and tenderly ministers to Sabatis, her Indian "brother," himself captured by the English. The family's reconstitution and Johnson's justifiable pride as survivor and great-grandmother close her narrative: "My aged mother says to me, arise daughter and go to thy daughter, for your daughter's daughter has got a daughter; a command which few mothers can make and be obeyed."

• Mary M. Billings French, *A New England Pioneer* (1926). Frances Roe Kestler, comp., *The Indian Captivity Narrative: A Woman's View* (1990). Kathryn Zabelle Derounian-Stodola and James Arthur Levernier, *The Indian Captivity Narrative, 1550–1990* (1993).

Jeanne Holland

JOHNSTON, Jill (b. 1929), also known as F. J. Crowe, journalist and author, was born in London, England. She has been married and divorced and has two children. Johnston is openly lesbian and has written and spoken about her sexual identity on several occasions. She began a prepared public speech in New York in 1971 with these words: "All women are lesbians except those who don't know it."

Johnston began writing a *Village Voice* column entitled "Dance Journal" in 1959. She has published selections from this column (*Marmalade Me*, 1971); several other nonfiction books that are at least partly autobiographical, among them *Lesbian Nation: The Feminist Solution* (1973) and *Gullibles Travels* (1974); and a two-volume *autobiography entitled *Autobiography in Search of a Father, Volume One: Motherbound* (1983) and *Volume Two: Paper Daughter* (1985). She continues to contribute to the *Village Voice, Art News, Art in America,* and other journals and newspapers.

Johnston's column in the *Village Voice* gained acclaim for its originality and the degree to which it portrayed her personal experiences and attitudes towards a variety of subjects, including, but increasingly not limited to, dance and the performing arts. The *Village Voice* eventually added a column entitled "Dance" when dance criticism disappeared almost entirely from Johnston's own column. In 1970, art critic John Perreault wrote: "If anyone in the future wants to find out about the sixties, he will have to read Jill's column." In the 1960s and 1970s, she associated with many contemporary artists and critics—Yvonne Rainier, Gregory Battcock, Andy Warhol, and Les Levine among them. She was known as an artist in her own right and gained notoriety and praise for both her writing and her public behavior. There is an entire issue of *Culture Hero: A Fanzine of Stars of the Super World,* published in the late 1960s, devoted to Johnston.

Although very little has been written in response to the themes of Johnston's writing—critics consistently emphasize her appearance and her behavior—some writers have compared her style to that of Gertrude *Stein because it is sparse, repetitive, and rhythmic. She is usually described as eclectic and unusual, and is credited for introducing *Wow* as a term of aesthetic approval to the vocabulary of art critics.

• Rosalind Constable, "Johnston Preserved," *New York* 1, no. 21 (24 May 1971): 60–62. Julia Penelope and Susan J. Wolfe, "Consciousness as Style; Style as Aesthetic," in *Language, Gender, and Society,* eds. Barrie Thorne, Cheris Kramarae, and Nancy Henley (1983), pp. 125–139.

Amanda Berry

JONES, Gayl (b. 1949), African-American novelist, poet, and critic. Although she was born in segregated Lexington, Kentucky, Jones benefited from living in a black community in which the oral tradition was very much alive: *story telling was part of her family heritage. Her grandmother wrote plays for the church, and her mother composed stories for the children. Both black speech and strong narratives are markers of Jones's own work. She began writing fiction as a child, although she received little encouragement in school. Nonetheless, she persevered and received several prizes for poetry while an English major at Connecticut College. She then did graduate work in creative writing at Brown University under William Meredith and Michael Harper. Her first novel, *Corregidora* (1975), was published while she was still a graduate student. She taught creative writing and African-American literature at the University of Michigan until 1983, and has lived and continued to write in France and the United States since then.

Her novels and short stories focus on violent sexual, physical, and psychological experiences of black women, and her characters are often at the very edge of sanity. Jones's originality is in giving these women their own voices. *Corregidora* tells of Ursa Corregidora, a blues singer whose abuse from her husband replicates the experiences of her foremothers under slavery. *Eva's Man* (1976) is narrated by Eva Canada, who is confined to an institution for the criminally insane for having poisoned and then bitten off the penis of her abusive lover. The characters in the stories in *White Rat* (1977) speak of their racial and sexual realities in voices that are both obsessive in their concerns and ordinary in their idiom. Jones's later narratives—*Song for Anninho* (1981), *The Hermit-Woman* (1983), and *Xarque and Other Poems* (1985)—are poems that tell stories of slavery and black resistance and community in the New World, primarily Brazil. Her work of criticism, *Liberating Voices: Oral Tradition in African American Literature* (1991), explores folk traditions in the works of major writers of poetry and fiction. Jones's achievement as a literary artist is in her ability to tell stories of violence and madness in the voices of the victims without sacrificing their credibility or humanity.

• Trudier Harris, "A Spiritual Journey: Gayl Jones's *Song for Anninho,*" *Callaloo* 5 (1982): 105–111. Jerry W. Ward, "Escape from Trublem: The Fiction of Gayl Jones," *Callaloo* 5 (1982): 95–104. Claudia C. Tate, "Gayl Jones," in *Black Women Writers at Work* (1983), pp. 89–99. Keith E. Byerman, "Beyond Realism: The Fictions of Gayl Jones and Toni Morrison," in *Fingering the Jagged Grain: Tradition and Form in Recent Black Fiction* (1986), pp. 171–184.

Keith E. Byerman

JONG, Erica (b. 1942), novelist, poet, essayist. Erica Jong grew up in a Jewish family in Manhattan, earned her B.A. from Barnard College, and later received a number of fellowships while pursuing her M.A. in eighteenth-century literature at Columbia University. She divides her time between New York and Connecticut, where she lives with Jonathan Fast and their daughter. She has been married twice and lived for several years in Europe with her second husband. Jong is the author of six volumes of poetry, including *Fruits and Vegetables* (1971); *Ordinary Miracles* (1983); and *Becoming Light: Poems New and Selected* (1991). She is better known, however, for her novels, particularly *Fear of Flying* (1973); *How to Save Your Own Life* (1977); *Fanny, Being the True History of Fanny Hackabout Jones* (1980); and her latest, *Any Woman's Blues* (1990).

Erica Jong's first novel, *Fear of Flying*, began her reputation as a woman writer willing to explore female *sexuality unashamedly and with much *humor, thus claiming the territory that male novelists insisted on as theirs. Jong's female heroes therefore experience the adventures usually reserved for men; they are neither trapped nor fruitlessly rebelling against social constrictions. Instead, they allow themselves to seek a selfhood, notably through artistic expression, which allows them to transcend convention. Jong's third novel, *Fanny, Being the True History of Fanny Hackabout Jones*, transposes this "modern" heroine into the eighteenth-century tradition of picaresque novels by imitating the most famous of those, *Tom Jones* and *Fanny*. Jong does not claim to have all the solutions for women, however: "I do not write about superwomen who have transcended all conflict; I write about women who are torn, as most of us are torn, between the past and the future, between our mothers' frustration and the extravagant hopes we have for our daughters" (*The Writer on Her Work*, 1980).

This same desire to negotiate new territory for women informs Jong's poems, which, beneath their exuberance and humor, give serious consideration to the problems of women in our culture. As Alicia Ostriker points out in her discussion of Jong's poem "Aging," "Humor can effectively spotlight problems which are naggingly real if trivial; the comic-autobiographical mode has become a major option in women's writing" (*Stealing the Language*, 1986). Jong's work is indeed most compelling when she uses a "comic-autobiographical" voice, a voice that sardonically observes the "man's world" still prevalent around us.

• Leland E. Warren, "The True History of the Adventures of Fanny Hackabout-Jones," *Eighteenth Century Life* 6, no. 1 (October 1980): 106–109. Mary Anne Ferguson, "The Female Novel of Development and the Myth of Psyche," *Denver Quarterly* 17, no. 4 (Winter 1983): 58–74. Robert J. Butler, "The Woman Writer as American Picaro: Open Journeying in Erica Jong's *Fear of Flying*," *Centennial Review* 31, no. 3 (Summer 1987): 308–329. James Mandrell, "Questions of Genre and Gender: Contemporary American Versions of the Feminine Picaresque," *Novel* 20, no. 2 (Winter 1987): 149–170.

Susan J. Zevenbergen

JORDAN, June (b. 1936), poet, playwright, novelist, essayist, professor, and political activist. From her novel *His Own Where* (1971), through *Things I Do in the Dark: Selected Poetry* (1977) and *Civil Wars* (essays, 1981), to her recent *Naming Our Destiny* (poetry, 1989) and *Technical Difficulties* (essays, 1992), Jordan's writings are marked by an increasing inclusiveness (from a focus on blacks in America to other countries, other ethnic groups, and women everywhere) and a faith in the power of language to create a redemptive world. This idealism is tempered by an intensity that borders on militant ferocity. As she notes in "White English/Black English" (1972), "as a poet and writer, I deeply love and I deeply hate words"—the love stemming from human communication, the hate from the conscription that language means to those not in control of the "majority" or dominating sentence.

Jordan's work is also marked by a certain consistency. As she notes in "Poem: From an Uprooted Condition," "sometimes the poem tends to repeat itself," a remark that could apply to her entire corpus. Thus, we find recurring themes of love and desire (see *Passion: New Poems, 1977–1980*, 1980), of family, social injustice, suffering, and joy. In fact, her attention to the suffering of blacks, and later to that of other ethnic groups and women, often results in a scream (both in tone and language), while her attention to the possibility of creative redemption modulates toward a visionary faith (see "Thinking about My Poetry," 1977)—hence the strength of the concluding line of "War and Memory": "And I / invent the mother of the courage I require not to quit." In this sense, Jordan's vision strikes a middle ground between those of Toni Morrison and Alice Walker, other black writers who have much in common with Jordan.

The idea of invention, now feministly conceived, may be traced to Jordan's childhood attraction to the biblical passage "In the beginning was the Word." This thesis of John continually fuels her inherent optimism (an optimism all the more courageous given the facts of life she so scrupulously notes). Born in Harlem, raised in the Bedford-Stuyvesant area of Brooklyn, educated in largely white public and private schools, Jordan has proven to be one of the strongest female voices of the last two decades, and has received numerous awards, including a Rockefeller Grant in creative writing, the Prix de Rome in environmental design, a Creative Artists in Public Service grant in creating writing, and an NEA Fellowship. Other important works, in addition to those mentioned above, include *Who Look at Me* (1969); *Some Changes* (1971); *New Days: Poems of Exile and Return* (1974); *New Life: New Room* (1975); and *Living Room* (1985).

• Peter Erickson, "June Jordan," in *Dictionary of Literary Biography*, vol. 38, eds. Thadious M. Davis and Trudier Harris (1985), pp. 146–162. Peter Erickson, "The Love Poetry of June Jordan," *Callaloo* 9 (Winter 1986): 221–234. Joy Harjo, "An Interview with June Jordan," *High Plains Literary Review* 3, no. 2 (1988): 60–76. Richard Abowitz, "Revolution by Search Committee," *The New Criterion* 7, no. 8 (1989): 30–35. Carla Freccero, "June Jordan," in *African American Writers*, ed. Valerie Smith (1991), pp. 245–261.

Jacqueline Vaught Brogan

JOURNALISTS. The history of women journalists in the United States began when the first colonial printing press was installed at Harvard University in 1638 by Mistress Glover, whose husband, the Reverend Jose Glover, had died aboard ship en route to the New World. Historians estimate that at least fourteen women printers were working during colonial times, in addition to providing the meals, candles, soap, clothing, and other essentials for their families.

The intelligent and outspoken women who ran colonial newspapers generally inherited them from their husbands, learning their trade at home. They often faced problems of controlling their businesses because of laws and attitudes of the times. Although Elizabeth Timothy (c.1700–1757) of Charleston was the first woman publisher, it was Mary Katherine Goddard (1738–1816), the daughter of printer Sara Updike Goddard, who printed the first copy of the Declaration of Independence with all the signers' names. An expert in setting type, she subsequently ran newspapers for her brother in Providence, Philadelphia, and Baltimore.

Anne Newport Royall (1769–1854) was probably the first woman to start a newspaper of her own *(Paul Pry* and *The Huntress)*, and Sarah Margaret *Fuller (1810–1850), who edited the *Dial* for Ralph Waldo Emerson, became a member of Boston's Transcendentals and wrote about women's rights. At the *New York Tribune*, Fuller's interviews of women prisoners at Sing Sing and in city hospitals brought her fame. Transferred to Europe as the first woman foreign correspondent, Fuller married an Italian and became embroiled in the Italian Revolution. As they were returning to the States, their ship went down in a storm off Fire Island and they were lost. Cornelia M. Walter (1813–1898) edited the *Boston Transcript* for five years, supporting Frederick Douglass in his arguments for black freedom. Jane Grey Swisshelm (1815–1884), an abolitionist, feminist, and supporter of temperance, edited numerous papers, including the *St. Cloud* (Minn.) *Visiter*. After she tangled with local politicians, vigilantes wrecked the *Visiter;* she responded by starting another newspaper.

After the Civil War, Elizabeth Cady *Stanton (1815–1902) became publisher and Susan B. *Anthony (1820–1906), coeditor of the *Revolution*. They supported equal rights for women and condemned the Fifteenth Amendment because women were not included. Lucy Stone, who was also an abolitionist, felt that the suffrage campaigns for black men and for women should be separated, and so she started the *Woman's Journal*, a moderate newspaper. It lasted until 1914, expressing the views of middle-class professional and club women, while the *Revolution* lasted only two and a half years.

From 1837–1877, Sarah Josepha Buell *Hale (1788–1879) edited *Godey's Lady's Book*, the first important women's magazine, which set the standard for the period in literature, morals, and deportment. With the push west, women continued to use their writing skills to run newspapers. Eliza Jane Poitevent Holbrook Nicholson (1849–1896), who used the pseudonym Pearl Rivers, became owner of the *New Orleans Daily Picayune* upon the death of her first husband. She was an innovator who hired Dorothy *Dix (Elizabeth M. Gilmer) to give advice to the lovelorn, started a sports column, a medical column, and a humor column, and published the writings of such authors as Mark Twain, Emile Zola, and H. G. Wells. Ellen Browning Scripps helped her brothers on newspapers in Ohio and Michigan, wrote a column, and ran their feature syndicate. Piney W. Forsythe took over her father's paper, the *Liberty* (Miss.) *Advocate*, in 1868, and ran it with the help of her two sisters, who were printers.

By 1889, women journalists had become sufficiently prominent that the *Journalist*, a New York City professional publication, devoted its entire issue to fifty women journalists throughout the nation, including ten blacks. Ida Minerva Tarbell (1857–1944) and Ida B. *Wells-Barnett (1862–1931) epitomized the period. Tarbell, renowned as a muckraker, brought the Rockefeller oil trust down with her series of articles in *McClure's*. A college graduate, Tarbell had attended the Sorbonne and had written ten books on Napoleon and Lincoln. Wells-Barnett (Iola), on the other hand, was the daughter of slaves, lost her parents in the yellow fever epidemic of 1878, and held the family together by teaching school. She invested in *Free Speech*, a Memphis newspaper, became one of the owners of the *New York Age*, and later moved to Chicago, where she continued her ongoing fight against lynching. She risked her life covering the Cairo, Ill., riot in 1909, and the one in East St. Louis in 1918. She helped organize the NAACP in 1909, marched in suffrage parades, and served as a probation officer for the Chicago Municipal Court.

Meanwhile, blacks such as Mrs. N. F. Mossell worked for *New York Freeman* and the *Philadelphia Times*; Mrs. W. E. Mathews (Victoria Earle) acted as a sub reporter for many great dailies, including the *New York Times*; Lillian Alberta Lewis (Bert Islew) wrote for the *Boston Herald* and the *Boston Advocate*; and Mary E. Britton (MEB) contributed to the *Lexington* (Ky.) *Herald*, among other papers.

This was also the period of stunt reporters and sob sisters. Among the best was Elizabeth Cochrane Seaman (Nellie Bly, 1865–1922), who wrote about the conditions in New York City's Blackwell's Island (a mental hospital), sweatshops, and jails, disguising herself as one of the victims. She is probably best known, however, as the traveler who went around the world in fewer than eighty days. Winifred Black Bonfils (1863–1936) was bylined as Annie Laurie for Hearst's *San Francisco Examiner;* she investigated a southern cotton mill, a local cannery, and a brothel, but is best remembered as a sob sister for her coverage of the Thaw trial.

In the 1930s and 1940s, women began, slowly, to move into positions of greater responsibility. Dorothy *Thompson (1893–1961) became the first woman to head a major foreign news bureau (Berlin); Rheta Childe Dorr (1866–1948) covered the Russian revolution; Anne "Q" Hare McCormick (1880–1954) served as the *New York Times'* roving foreign correspondent, won the first Pulitzer Prize awarded a woman, and later became the first woman appointed to the *Times* editorial board; and Agness Underwood became city editor of the *Los Angeles Herald-Express* in 1947. In the meantime, Ishbel Ross of the *Herald Tribune*, Doris Fleeson of the *New York Daily News*, Mary McGrory of the *Washington Star*, Sigrid Schultz of the *Chicago Tribune*, Marguerite Higgins of the *New York Herald Tribune*, and Margaret Bourke-White of *Life* magazine were using their talents as reporters, foreign correspondents, and photographers.

The number of women in the profession continued to grow with each decade, but it was not until the 1940s that the proportion of women journalists increased significantly. Some women who had worked the city beat refused to return to the women's section after WWII.

Those who returned to cover women's news chaffed at being pigeonholed by gender. Dorothy Jurney of the *Miami Herald* began to make notable changes in the way women's news was treated, particularly at the *Detroit Free Press* and the *Philadelphia Inquirer*, where she later worked. On smaller papers, women's section editors, such as Beverly Hall of the *Lansing* (Mich.) *State Journal*, began to address issues that interested women, including equal pay, equal rights, and abortion. The affluence of the 1960s and 1970s, women's postponement of marriage, and the increase of women in the field also permitted them more job mobility. Women began to note that their salaries, assignments, and promotions, were less than men received; the inequities inspired some to complain and others to file suit.

The move started in the East, where women at *Time, Newseek*, NBC, the *Ladies' Home Journal*, and large metropolitan newspapers were among the first to complain. At *Newsweek*, women were researchers rather than editors; at the *New York Times* and the Associated Press, women's salaries, assignments, and promotions were markedly lower than men's. Women employees also lodged complaints against CBS, ABC, the *Washington Post, Detroit News, Cleveland Plain Dealer, San Diego Union, Arizona Republic* and *Phoenix Gazette, Sacramento Union, St. Louis Post Dispatch*, and the *Washington Star*, among others. Many magazines and newspapers settled court cases because inequities were obvious. Probably the most successful case was that of Associated Press, which immediately began to implement changes, while at the *New York Times*, the entrenched chauvinism and bureaucracy made change difficult.

In the meantime, women elsewhere began to make it to the top. Allen H. Neuharth of the Gannett chain, a staunch champion of women journalists, not only recruited and hired women and minorities, he promoted them. By 1988, 39 percent of Gannett's news employees were women—twenty-three were publishers, and eighteen held senior editing positions. At the same time, the National Organization for Women began the fight in the electronic media by challenging the licenses of network-owned and -operated stations. It noted that women were underrepresented, underpaid, and underemployed; neither were women's issues being aired.

Most news directors were white males. Only a few women reported important stories, even fewer reported sports, and both unequal pay and sexual harassment were common. On network news in 1990, women filed 13 percent of the stories, down 1 percent from 1989. In short, the problems were basically the same as those faced by women journalists on magazines and newspapers, where in 1990 women constituted 8.2 percent of publishers and 17.7 percent of directing editors. The larger the circulation, the fewer the women.

[See also Journals, Academic; Magazines, Women's; Little Magazines; Reportage; Newspapers, Women's; Newspaper Columns.]

• Marion K. Sanders, Dorthy Thompson: A Legend in Her Time (1973). Maurine Beasley and Sheila Silver, Women in the Media: A Documentary Source Book (1977). Marion Marzolf, Up from the Footnote: A History of Women Journalists (1977). Judith G. Clabes, ed., New Guardians of the Press: Selected Profiles of America's Women Newpaper Editors (1983). Madelon Golden Schilpp and Sharon M. Murphy, Great Women of the Press (1983). Barbara Belford, Brilliant Bylines: A Biographical Anthology of Notable Newspaperwomen in America (1986). Linda Ellerbee, "And So It Goes": Adventures in Television (1986). Kay Mills, A Place in the News: From the Women's Pages to the Front Page (1988). Marlene Sanders and Marcia Rock, Waiting for Prime Time: The Women of Television News (1988).

Mary A. Gardner

JOURNALS. *See* Autobiography; Biography; Confessional Nonfiction; Diaries and Journals.

JOURNALS, Academic. Feminist academic journals are research publications with stated feminist intentions that are housed, financed, or operated under the acknowledged auspices of accredited universities and/or scholarly presses. The journals use academics as editors and consultants, with organizational structures ranging from consensus to traditional hierarchy. The journals adhere to the conventions and style of academic publishing as defined in professional manuals, and are abstracted, indexed, and microfilmed by major academic reference services. However, the journals are distinguished from traditional publications by their intellectual and political commitment to the study of women.

Many of the scholarly journals in *women's studies were founded during the first half of the 1970s. Invigorated by the political intensity of campus life and the fervor of the contemporary *women's movement, early feminist activists first conceptualized their journals as publications of high academic quality and immediate political relevance. Although the Michigan Papers of the University of Michigan, Ann Arbor, appeared as a monograph series in 1969, *Feminist Studies* (1972) at the University of Maryland and *Women's Studies* (1972) at Queens College, New York, vie for the title of first interdisciplinary feminist academic journal. Dale Spender began *Women's Studies International Quarterly* (1978) in London, and Sherri Clarkson founded the *International Journal of Women's Studies* (1978) for Eden Press in Canada.

The explosion of original and significant research on women, which spanned the academy's disciplinary spectrum, transformed this handful of unsupported feminist activists working in isolation on American campuses into an organized field of specialists with professional associations, conferences, research centers, and scholarly journals. By the mid-seventies, a vast selection of academic journals on women had been established: *Women's Rights Law Reporter* (1971); *Concerns: Newsletter of the Women's Caucus of the Modern Languages* (1971); *Women and Literature* (1972); *Women's Studies Newsletter* (1972); *Women's Studies* (1972); *University of Michigan Papers in Women's Studies* (1974); *Frontiers: A Journal of Women's Studies* (1975); *Signs: A Journal of Women in Culture and Society* (1975); *Sex Roles: A Journal of Research* (1975); and *Psychology of Women Quarterly* (1976).

Early editions of these journals were importantly shaped by the political concerns and literary conventions of the contemporary women's movement. In addition to publishing work that challenged and reconceptualized the study of women in traditional disciplines, early editors, such as Ann Calderwood at *Feminist Studies*, Kathi George at *Frontiers*, and Wendy Martin at *Women's Studies*, regularly included movement-influenced discussions of motherhood, *sexuality, reproductive rights, and *violence against women. A few academic journals experimented with non-academic literary forms, poetry, manifestos, and political essays in order to include the writings and interests of nonacademics. Many journals featured a section devoted to current movement events and concerns. Despite these attempts, rationalist modes and academic styles prevailed, and nonacademic journals such as *Quest: A Feminist Quarterly* (1974); *Sinister Wisdom: A Journal for the Lesbian Imagination in the Arts and Politics* (1976); *Conditions* (1977); *Chrysalis: A Magazine of Women's Culture* (1977); *Trivia: A Journal of Ideas* (1982); and *Lesbian Contradiction: A Journal of Irreverent Feminism* (1983) published most of the work by and for women whose politics, literary conventions, or identities were marginalized in academic publishing.

This genre distinction was exacerbated when the growth of women's studies and the recognition of its scholars drew the field's publications further into the university structure, obligations, and networks, and away from activities in the non-academic feminist movement. As feminist influence spread, traditional academic journals began to feature special issues on women. The success of the *American Journal of Sociology* special issue, "Changing

Women in a Changing Society" (1973), led to the creation of *Signs*, now considered by some to be the most-recognized feminist academic journal in the field. *Signs* was consciously molded in strict compliance with academia's most rigorous standards so that scholarly legitimacy for the study of women could be achieved. In order to establish women's studies as an independent academic field, founding editor Catharine Stimpson rejected the politically specific term "feminist scholarship" and promoted the phrase "the new scholarship on women." Despite the widening split between the domains of the university and the women's movement, *Signs* consistently published some of the most politically challenging scholarship on women ever written, including Adrienne * Rich's "Compulsory Heterosexuality and Lesbian Existence" (1979), Heidi Hartmann's "Capitalism, Patriarchy, and Job Segregation by Sex" (1975), Carroll Smith-Rosenberg's "The Female World of Love and Ritual: Relations among Women in Nineteenth-Century America" (1975), and Maxine Baca Zinn, et al., "The Costs of Exclusionary Practices in Women's Studies" (1985).

Throughout the 1980s, feminist academic journals became more plentiful and specialized. Journals servicing various academic constituencies include *Affilia: Journal of Women and Social Work* (1986); *Berkeley Women's Law Journal* (1986); *Feminist Issues* (1980); *Feminist Review* (1979); *Feminist Teacher* (1984); *Gender and Society* (1987); *Hypatia* (1986); *Journal of Feminist Family Therapy* (1989); *Journal of Women and Aging* (1989); *Journal of Women's History* (1989); *NWSA Journal* (1988); *Tulsa Studies in Women's Literature* (1982); *Women and Criminal Justice* (1989); *Women and Therapy* (1982); and *Women and Politics* (1980). In addition, two quarterly guides, *Feminist Collections: A Quarterly of Women's Studies Resources* (1980) and *Feminist Periodicals: A Current Listing of Contents* (1980), are published by University of Wisconsin Women's Studies Librarian Susan Searing. Of the many journals produced in the 1980s, of particular note is *Sage: A Scholarly Journal on

Black Women* (1984). Under the direction of Patricia Bell-Scott and Beverly Guy-Sheftall, *Sage* publishes interdisciplinary work on issues related to black women, and has featured special issues on "Mothers and Daughters," "Artists and Artisans," "Workers," "The Diaspora," and "Health." Two other recent journals, *differences: A Journal of Feminist Cultural Studies* (1988) and *Genders* (1988), reflect a poststructuralist reframing that centralizes the construction of gendered relations, rather than the experiences of women, in feminist scholarship.

Within the university, feminist academic journals are positioned at the point where private speculation about women becomes authoritative and publicly available information. They negotiate new scholarly critiques, articulate the intellectual structures and consequences of movement practices, and sustain the cultural challenge posed by the study of women in the traditional disciplines. The journals have become a crucial vehicle for the production, legitimation, and dissemination of a usable feminist knowledge upon which students, scholars, policymakers, and practitioners rely.

[*See also* Magazines, Women's; Little Magazines; Reportage; Newspapers, Women's; Newspaper Columns; Journalists.]

• Jean Farrington and Cristine Rom, "Feminist Periodicals," *Serials Review* (October/December 1979): 13–24. Catharine R. Stimpson, "The Making of *Signs*," *Radical Teacher* (1980): 23–25. Eileen Boneparth, "Consciousness Raising through Journal Editing," *Women and Politics* 1 (Summer 1980): 97–99. Dale Spender, "The Gatekeepers: A Feminist Critique of Academic Publishing," in *Doing Feminist Research*, ed. Helen Roberts (1981), pp. 186–202. Lynne Spender, "The Politics of Publishing: Selection and Rejection of Women's Words in Print," *Women's Studies International Forum* 6 (1983): 459–473. Charlotta Hensley, "*Sinister Wisdom* and Other Issues of Lesbian Imagination," *Serials Review* (Fall 1983): 7–20. Joan Ariel, "*Frontiers*: A Journal of Women's Studies," *Serials Review* (Winter 1985): 5–8. Patrice McDermott, *Politics and Scholarship: Feminist Academic Journals and the Production of Knowledge* (1994).

Patrice McDermott

JUNG, Carl. *See* Psychoanalysis and Women.

K

KELLEY, Edith Summers (1884–1956), author of two novels about farm life, *Weeds* (1923) and *The Devil's Hand* (1974). She was born in Ontario, Canada. After graduating from the University of Toronto in 1923, she moved to New York City. From 1906 to 1907, she served as Upton Sinclair's secretary at Helicon Hall, an experimental community for intellectuals that Sinclair had founded in New Jersey. Among the writers who visited the community were Charlotte Perkins *Gilman and Sinclair Lewis. Kelley was engaged to the latter briefly, but married Lewis's friend, the poet-novelist Allan Updegraff.

Following the destruction of Helicon Hall in a fire, Kelley and Updegraff moved to Greenwich Village, where she helped to support her writer-husband by turning out what she called "frothy and inconsequential" stories for pulp magazines and by teaching night school. Soon after the birth of their two children, she and Updegraff separated; subsequently, she became the common-law wife of C. Fred Kelley, a sculptor, with whom she lived for more than fifty years. From 1914 to 1916, the Kelleys grew tobacco in Kentucky, like Edith Summers Kelley's protagonists in *Weeds*; between 1916 and 1920, they operated a boardinghouse in Newton, New Jersey, where their son was born; and then, moving in 1920 to southern California's Imperial Valley, the setting for her novel *The Devil's Hand*, they leased a sixty-acre alfalfa ranch. When that venture also failed, they settled on a chicken farm near San Diego; there, when her three children were in school, Kelley wrote *Weeds*.

A female *bildungsroman, *Weeds* movingly portrays the experience of Judith Pippinger, a poor, uncommonly intelligent and creative Kentucky farm girl who feels trapped by marriage and motherhood. Depressed by the tedious, never-ending household chores that she, a female, is expected to perform, she perceives that men in her society have more autonomy than women do. Judith, an artiste manqué, finds an outlet for her creativity only during those rare moments snatched from tending a crying baby or doing the wash, when she sketches the world around her on bits of wrapping paper, which she stores in a dresser drawer. Dissatisfied with her marriage, she has a brief summer romance with an itinerant preacher, which culminates in a self-induced abortion when she discovers she is pregnant. Kelley delineates the toll that life exacts from Judith, a "poppy among weeds," whose energies ultimately are sapped by poverty, biological imperatives, and the ineluctable demands of family life.

Despite the fact that *Weeds* received favorable reviews after Harcourt Brace published it in 1923, the novel was a financial failure; it would have been forgotten if Matthew Bruccoli had not persuaded Southern Illinois University Press to reissue it in 1972; two years later they published *The Devil's Hand. Weeds* was reissued by The Feminist Press in 1982.

• The Edith Summers Kelley Papers are housed at the Morris Library, Southern Illinois University. Charlotte Goodman, "Portraits of the Artiste Manqué by Three Women Novelists," *Frontiers* 5 (1980): 57–59. Charlotte Goodman, "Widening Perspectives, Narrowing Possibilities: The Trapped Woman in Edith Summers Kelley's *Weeds*," in *Regionalism and the Female Imagination*, ed. Emily Toth (1985), pp. 93–106. Elizabeth Ammons, *Conflicting Stories: American Women Writers at the Turn into the Twentieth Century* (1991).

Charlotte Goodman

KEMBLE, Francis Anne (1809–1893), actress, diarist, and essayist. Born in London, the second of Charles and Marie Therese De Camp Kemble's four children, Fanny followed in the footsteps of her many famous relatives, making her acting debut at age nineteen. In 1832, to raise money for her family's crumbling finances, Kemble, her father, and her "Aunt Dall" (Adelaide De Camp) departed on a two-year acting tour of the United States. During their performances in northern and southeastern cities, Kemble kept a journal of her impressions of America, which she published as *Journal of an American Residence* in 1835. Prominent Philadelphian Pierce (Meese) Butler fell in love with Kemble and followed her from city to city during the highly successful acting tour. Kemble consented to marry Butler in 1834, sending her father back to England without her.

Kemble's temperamental differences from Butler were highlighted during her first visit to his inherited Georgia plantations in 1838–1839.

Horrified by what she encountered, she spent her visit interceding with Butler and his overseer on behalf of the slaves, recording her activities and the slaves' travails in a journal she kept for her close friend, Elizabeth Dwight Sedgwick, sister-in-law of the novelist Catharine Maria *Sedgwick. In particular, Kemble worried about the conditions of the slave women who were regularly forced back into field labor three weeks after childbirth. Because of her activities during this visit, Kemble was forbidden by the Butler family to return to the plantations. Deferring to her husband's fervent opposition, she refused Lydia Maria *Child's invitation to publish the journal for the abolitionist cause in 1842, but she did decide to publish it in 1863, hoping to influence Britain away from supporting the Confederacy during the Civil War.

Kemble divorced Butler in 1848, losing custody of both their daughters to him. Thereafter, she supported herself in Britain and America by performing dramatic readings, and publishing poetry, various journals, and essays on society and traveling.

Known for her candid pronouncements on society and public figures, and for her impatience with the restrictions of Victorian womanhood (she insisted on riding horses in men's clothing, for instance), Kemble was throughout her life the subject of both adoration and approbation. Her journals allow readers a window into her lively and independent mind, as well as insight into nineteenth-century American culture. Her attentiveness to the particular plight of slave women, as well as her own battles against gender conventions, provide a valuable commentary on women's history and resistance.

• Leota S. Driver, *Fanny Kemble* (1933). Margaret Armstrong, *Fanny Kemble: A Passionate Victorian* (1938). John A. Scott, Introduction to *Journal of a Residence on a Georgia Plantation, 1838–1839*, by Frances Anne Kemble (1968). Fanny Kemble Wister, ed., *Fanny, The American Kemble: Her Journals and Unpublished Letters* (1972). John A. Scott, *Fanny Kemble's America* (1973). Eleanor Ransome, ed., *The Terrific Kemble: A Victorian Self-Portrait from the Writings of Fanny Kemble* (1978). J. C. Furnas, *Fanny Kemble* (1982).

Dana D. Nelson

KENNEDY, Adrienne (b. 1931), playwright, mystery novelist, short story and nonfiction writer. Born in Pittsburgh, Kennedy grew up comfortably middle-class in Cleveland. Her parents, Cornell Hawkins, executive secretary of the YMCA, and Etta, a teacher, emphasized education and religion. Cordial childhood experiences in Cleveland's multiethnic community ill-prepared her for the hostility she faced as a black student at Ohio State University, though her persistence earned her a degree in education in 1953. After graduation, she married Joseph Kennedy, returning six months later, pregnant, to her parents' home when the army sent her husband to Korea. Lonely during his absence, she began writing plays. After Joseph's return, she and their son, Joseph, Jr., accompanied him to Columbia University, where he pursued graduate work in social psychology and she studied creative writing from 1954 to 1956.

In 1960, on the ship to Ghana where Joseph was to do research, Kennedy wrote her first published work, "Because of the King of France," a short story accepted by *Black Orpheus*. As noted in her memoirs *People Who Led to My Plays* (1987), though inspired by a cousin who ran away to the Virgin Islands, she had her protagonist flee simultaneously to these islands and to the Palace of Versailles, fusing "the real and the unreal," as she would throughout her plays. Moreover, his behavior was affected by the King of France and Chopin, establishing the use of public figures in private psychodramas as another of her artistic hallmarks.

With Joseph away for his research, Kennedy began writing *Funnyhouse of a Negro*. Traveling to Rome in 1961, she continued this play while awaiting the birth of her son Adam Patrice (named for Patrice Lumumba, the recently assassinated African leader who became a character in *Funnyhouse*). As Kennedy's memoirs observe, upon learning during this time of her parents' separation after thirty years of marriage, she found the gentle Jesus they had affirmed turning into a "cruel" Jesus in her play, suggesting the pain underlying her violent imagery.

In 1962, Kennedy submitted her play for admission to Edward Albee's Circle-in-the-Square play-writing course in New York, and, after reflecting on Albee's chastisement of her fear that it exposed too much about herself, permitted him to stage it. When he coproduced it off-Broadway in 1964, she won an Obie for Distinguished Play.

This and subsequent plays, including *The Owl Answers* (1965), *A Lesson in Dead Language* (1966), *A Rat's Mass* (1966), and *A Movie Star Has to Star in Black and White* (1976), laid bare Kennedy's psyche, but also exposed the inner wounds inflicted by *racism, *sexism, religious stifling of *sexuality, and other oppressions. Through surrealistic, opaque, luminously crafted devices, the plays dealt with her adoration of British culture and fear-ridden anger at its racial crimes, her love for classic American movies and pain at their exclusion of black realities, her admiration for male achievements, especially in writing, and agony over the limitations on women, her tormented consciousness of color and class divisions among blacks, and her need for an identity to unify these disparate, conflicting elements.

Kennedy's recent works, still *experimental, include plots and semitraditional characterization. Her *mystery novel, *Deadly Triplets* (1990), includes two solved puzzles, and *The Alexander Plays* (1992) contain resolved stories. The novel's Suzanne Sand and the plays' Suzanne Alexander represent Kennedy, again mixing the real and the unreal. The plays also contain a husband resembling Joseph, from whom Kennedy was divorced in 1966. The references to Frantz Fanon and his politically charged studies of the psychic wounds of colonialism imply Kennedy's own political dimensions, which long went unnoticed. Writers this distinctive evade imitation but broaden the base for new experiments.

• James A. Page, comp., *Selected Black American Authors: A Illustrated Bio-Bibliography* (1977). Adrienne Kennedy, *In One Act* (1988). Bernard L. Peterson, Jr., *Contemporary Black American Playwrights and Their Plays: A Biographical Directory and Dramatic Index* (1988).

Steven R. Carter

KIM, Ronyoung (1926–1987), artist and writer, published *Clay Walls*, one of the first Korean-American novels, in 1987. Born in Los Angeles on 28 March 1926, the fifth of six children, she grew up in the tiny Korean ethnic community that was the geographical starting point for what has now become Los Angeles Koreatown. She attended Korean language school every afternoon, where she studied Korean language and history. Kim's father, Chong-hak Kim, like the father in *Clay Walls*, was a laborer who died when his daughter was twelve. Her mother, Haeran (Helen) Kim, was in many ways like the mother in *Clay Walls*. Educated and highly spirited, she had come to America as a picture bride, and after the death of her husband, raised her four sons and two daughters by taking in sewing, all the while participating actively in the overseas movement for Korean independence.

Ronyoung Kim, inspired by her mother's intellectual energy and interest in writing, attended Manual Arts High School and Los Angeles City College. While a student, she helped her mother make neckties to sell to local department stores. During World War II, she worked at a Disney Studios assembly plant, and, at nineteen, married Richard Hahn, a Korean-American medical student from Chicago.

By 1956, she had given birth to three daughters and a son. As the wife of the first American thoracic and cardiac surgeon in the United States, Kim experienced a dramatic change in social and economic status, especially when her family integrated an exclusive all-white northern Californian community in 1955. Now a suburban housewife and mother, she pursued her interests in art and literature. She painted, sculpted, studied Chinese calligraphy, and wrote poetry, short stories, and personal narratives.

In 1958, she began a decade of efforts to promote Asian art in San Francisco, helping with the acquisition of the Avery Brundage Collection of the San Francisco Asian Art Museum. When her last child finished high school, she decided to study Asian art, literature, and Chinese language at San Francisco State University, receiving a B.A. in 1975. Shortly thereafter, she was diagnosed with breast cancer. This increased the urgency of her desire to write about her parents and their generation. "A whole generation of Korean immigrants and their American-born children could have lived and died in the United States without anyone knowing they had been here. I could not let that happen," she wrote.

Clay Walls was Kim's book about that generation. Divided into three sections, the novel focuses first on Haesu, the immigrant woman, then on Chun, her husband, and finally on Faye, their daughter. Nominated for a Pulitzer Prize, *Clay Walls* gives readers a particularly vivid sense of the nationalist spirit that made possible the psychic survival of early Korean immigrants in their daily struggle with poverty and racism. The book also illustrates how successfully the immigrants passed on their fierce resistance to cultural extinction to their children, who did not directly experience Japanese colonialism because they were born in America. Kim's plan was to turn her attention next to the daughters and sons of the early Korean immigrants. But on 3 February 1987, shortly after her first book was published, she died. A Korean language translation of *Clay Walls* was published in Seoul in 1989.

Elaine H. Kim

KINCAID, Jamaica (b. 1949), short fiction writer, novelist, essayist. Jamaica Kincaid was born Elaine Potter Richardson in St. John's, Antigua. After leaving home in 1965, she traveled to New York, eventually becoming an au pair, a situation she would render fictionally in *Lucy* (1990). A resident of Bennington, Vermont, Kincaid is married to Allen Shawn, a composer; they have two children.

After studying photography at New York's New School for Social Research and attending

Franconia College in New Hampshire, Kincaid did secretarial work in New York. In 1973, she became a magazine writer for *Ingenue*. It was her friendship in the mid-1970s with George W. S. Trow of the *New Yorker* that eventually led Kincaid to publish in that magazine.

Kincaid's first book, *At the Bottom of the River* (1983), a collection of short stories about growing up in Antigua, earned her the Morton Dauwen Zabel Award. More surreal than her later works, *At the Bottom of the River* exhibits Kincaid's hallmarks: an emphasis on autobiography, a keen sense of place, and a fondness for repetition. Repeated phrases inform the rich style, resulting in sentences of seemingly infinite length.

Published in 1985, Kincaid's first novel, *Annie John*, was chosen as one of the best books of the year by *Library Journal*. The work is divided into eight interrelated chapters, which read like the discrete stories they were when originally printed in the *New Yorker*. A finalist for the Ritz Paris Hemingway Award, *Annie John* recounts Kincaid's painful adolescence, especially focusing on her damaging relationship with her mother.

In 1986, the Whitney Museum of American Art published an oversized limited edition book, *Annie, Gwen, Lilly, Pam and Tulip*, with text written by Kincaid and drawings by artist Eric Fischl. Juxtaposed with colorful illustrations of women, a conversation among the title characters comprises the work. The book was issued in a trade edition in 1989.

During the mid-1980s, Kincaid returned to Antigua after an almost twenty-year absence, an experience resulting in her extended essay, *A Small Place* (1988). The shape of this work departs from Kincaid's earlier writing; *A Small Place* overflows with furious polemical invective, indicting colonialism and its residue.

Her most recent book, *Lucy*, is a return to fiction, but in a more continuous narrative than the earlier works. The anger vented in *A Small Place* remains in the title character, Lucy, whose rage toward her mother threatens her growth. Although set in America, this novel also reflects the focus on place prevalent in Kincaid's earlier writing. *Lucy* exhibits Kincaid's emphasis on names, and particularly poignant is the fact that the protagonist goes unnamed—except for the title page—until the last part of the book. And echoing Kincaid's former middle name, Lucy's last name is Potter.

Because Kincaid's works so far have stressed her own biography, it will be interesting to see if the next novels depict a Caribbean woman married to an American man.

• Selwyn R. Cudjoe, "Jamaica Kincaid and the Modernist Project: An Interview," *Callaloo* 12, no. 2 (Spring 1989):396–411. Donna Perry, "An Interview with Jamaica Kincaid," in *Reading Black, Reading Feminist*, ed. Henry Louis Gates, Jr. (1990), pp. 492–509. Leslie Garis, "Through West Indian Eyes: From an Impoverished Antiguan Childhood to Literary Eminence. Novelist Jamaica Kincaid's Odyssey," *New York Times Magazine*, 7 October 1990: 42.

Kristine A. Yohe

KINGSTON, Maxine Hong (b. 1940), memoirist, novelist. Maxine Ting Ting Hong Kingston was born on 27 October 1940 in Stockton, California, the eldest of six children. Her mother, Ying Lan Chew, who had been a doctor/midwife in China, was a laundress and field hand in the United States. Her father, Tom Hong, was a scholar/teacher in China, and a laundryman and gambling house manager in the United States. Kingston studied English literature, graduated from the University of California, Berkeley, in 1962, earned a secondary teaching credential in 1965, and marched against the Vietnam War. She married classmate Earl Kingston, an actor, in 1962; the couple have one son, Joseph. After seventeen years in Hawaii, the Kingstons returned to the mainland. In the fall of 1991, Kingston's house and almost two hundred pages of manuscript were burned in an Oakland fire. She is now professor of creative writing at the University of California, Berkeley.

After *The Woman Warrior* won the 1976 National Book Critics Circle Award for nonfiction, Kingston garnered numerous additional awards, including the rare title of Living Treasure of Hawaii, bestowed by a Buddhist group in 1980. *China Men* (1980) won the American Book Award for 1981; her novel *Tripmaster Monkey* (1990) received the PEN West Award for fiction. Kingston holds four honorary doctorates. Her first two books have been the most frequently taught texts on college campuses by any living American writer. In 1991, the Modern Language Association published *Approaches to Teaching Maxine Hong Kingston's* The Woman Warrior, placing her in a series that includes such authors as Homer, Shakespeare, Chaucer, Dante, Goethe, Milton, * Cather, * Chopin, and Camus.

On publication, *The Woman Warrior: Memoir of a Girlhood among Ghosts* created a sensation in literary and scholarly circles. Prepared by the * civil rights and the women's liberation movements, readers could appreciate Kingston's voice. Though it spoke of being physically weak because of continued devaluation, both by a patriarchal Chinese culture and by white-dominated society, her voice was strong and angry as it protested * sexism and * racism. *The Woman Warrior* was an experiment in genre, an *autobiography that crossed into fiction without recognizing boundaries. It told seemingly outlandish Chinese stories and superstitions; it also made easy reference to Anglo-American authors and traditions. It mixed American slang and striking poetic metaphor. It was a personal sorting out of the author's particular Chinese-American female identity, as well as the story of every second-generation American. It was a voice that was simultaneously exasperated by and proud of its Chinese-American heritage, the voice of a daughter both angry and loving towards her mother. "I learned to make my mind large, as the universe is large, so that there is room for paradoxes" wrote Kingston, and her text itself is composed of such paradoxes.

Readers' responses to Kingston's work have varied. While some Euro-American reviewers have found her work "exotic" and "Chinese," most readers from China find it very "American." Some Chinese Americans have denounced it as unfaithful to Chinese legends, and *assimilationist in tone, while others rejoice that at last someone speaks for them. This spectrum reveals the difficulties Chinese-American authors face in negotiating others' expectations when so few writers are perceived to be representing so many.

Kingston herself, in *The Woman Warrior*, sought to come to an understanding of her own youth and upbringing, which was beset by conflicting standards of behavior: the self-sacrificial filial obligations demanded of Chinese girls versus the independence and self-fulfillment promised to American children. How was she to fit the Chinese *ghost stories and legends her mother funneled into her imagination to the American world of neon and plastic in which she was growing up? How was she to find her own voice and realize her worth with a mother who claimed to have cut her daughter's frenum, and in a society that devalued daughters? How was she to develop her own *story-telling powers when faced with a mother whose own storytelling powers and domineering spirit were so formidable as to be threatening?

In *China Men*, Kingston presents an alternate version of the founding fathers of America. Not only does she shift the geographical locale from New England to Hawaii and California, but she boldly shifts the ethnicity from Englishmen to China Men. She makes founding fathers of the Chinese men whose backbreaking labor cleared jungles to create sugar plantations and broke through mountains to lay tracks for the transcontinental railroad; who, though scholars, took in laundry to support their families; who, though pacifists, served as soldiers in Vietnam. Again, her text is a collage, mixing *myth and history, fictional elaboration

and biographical fact. Hers are composite, communal stories, as well as stories of her own family. To set the context and provide a contrast for her tales of heroism, she gives a central place in her book to "The Laws," a chronological, factual list of America's legislation that predominantly discriminated against the Chinese.

Kingston's most recent work, *Tripmaster Monkey* (1990), is an ambitious and brilliant novel about a 1960s Berkeley graduate, a loud-mouthed, raging Chinese-American playwright, Wittman Ah Sing. An Asian-American *Ulysses*, the novel is richly textured, interweaving literary allusions from Euro-American traditions with those from the Chinese classic *Journey to the West* or *Monkey*, by Wu Ch'en-en. *Tripmaster Monkey* is a comic/tragic/surrealistic portrait of a complex young spokesman for a developing Asian-American consciousness. Fully aware of racism and its humiliations, Wittman Ah Sing screamingly asserts himself, uninhibitedly expresses his contempt for conventions, seeks validation in personal relationships, and finally expresses himself by directing an extravaganza that incorporates all the people of his acquaintance and all the passion and fury of his person.

• Maxine Hong Kingston, "Cultural Mis-Reading by American Reviewers," in *Asian and Western Writers in Dialogue: New Cultural Identities*, ed. Guy Amirthanayagam (1982). Paul John Eakin, *Fictions in Autobiography: Studies in the Art of Self-Invention* (1985). King-Kok Cheung, "'Don't Tell': Imposed Silences in *The Color Purple* and *The Woman Warrior*," *PMLA* 103, no. 2 (1988): 162–174. Susan Stanford Friedman, "Women's Autobiographical Selves: Theory and Practice," in *The Private Self*, Shari Benstock, ed. (1988). Sau-ling Wong, "Necessity and Extravagance in Maxine Hong Kingston's *The Woman Warrior*: Art and Ethnic Experience," *MELUS* 15, no. 1 (1988): 4–26. Linda Ching Sledge, "Oral Tradition in Kingston's *China Men*," in *Redefining American Literary History*, ed. A. LaVonne Brown (1990). Donald Goellnicht, "Father Land and/or Mother Tongue: The Divided Female Subject in Kogawa's *Obasan* and Hong Kingston's *The Woman Warrior*," in *Redefining Autobiography in Twentieth Century Women's Fiction*, eds. Janice Morgan and Colette Hall (1991). Shirley Lim, ed., *Teaching Approaches to Maxine Hong Kingston's* The Woman Warrior. (1991). Amy Ling, *Between Worlds: Women Writers of Chinese Ancestry* (1990). E. San Juan, "Beyond Identity Politics: The Predicament of the Asian Writer in Late Capitalism," *American Literary History* 3, no. 3 (1991): 542–565.

Amy Ling

KINSHIP. Embracing kin, for a woman writer, springs from a deeper impulse. Her writing seeks to define not only her relation to a biological family, but also her place in a literary genealogy. Alice *Walker's *In Search of Our Mothers' Gardens* (1983) looks backward into the history of African-American women for her own artistic heritage, a matriarchal lineage that might validate and inspire her own writing. Yet Walker knows that the life of a slave could never fill Virginia *Woolf's prescription for a room of one's own and economic self-sufficiency. In her own mother's talent for creating magnificent gardens of flowers, Walker discovers the artistry she has inherited. Sandra Gilbert and Susan Gubar also explore the literary dimension of kinship in *No Man's Land* (1988). In place of "the inexorable lineage of the biological family," they substitute the concept of affiliation for both the paternal and maternal traditions. Akin to adoption in the language of the *family, affiliation would allow the writer the choice of parenthood and would also insure continuity of parenting.

If the idea of kinship is undergoing a critical interrogation on the theoretical level, the same query occurs on the thematic level in women's writing and reflects the challenge the traditional family faces in twentieth-century America. The literature often dramatizes relationships that are more than kin and less than kind. The tension of family life is a frequent theme, and women writers tend to restructure the family to highlight a dominant female, to examine families without men, to test the endurance of families under the stress of *immigration, and to imagine alternative families where kinship does not always provide the foundation.

Kate *Chopin's *The Awakening* (1899) startled critics of its day with its presentation of a young wife and mother who seeks to escape from those familial ties to find her own identity and to try her hand as an artist. This interest in the struggle of a female character toward self-definition despite her family recurs in such works as Willa *Cather's *My Ántonia* (1918); Anzia *Yezierska's *Bread Giver* (1925); Lillian *Hellman's *An Unfinished Woman* (1969); Carson *McCullers's *The Member of the Wedding* (1946); Maya *Angelou's *I Know Why the Caged Bird Sings* (1969); Toni Cade *Bambara's *Gorilla, My Love* (1972); Toni *Morrison's *The Bluest Eye* (1972); and Alice Walker's *The Color Purple* (1983). The difficulties of family life that these books describe are perhaps even more evident in women's writing about immigrant families in the United States.

Literature about immigration expands the common struggle to preserve the integrity of a family to include the particular difficulties of survival in a new world. Maureen Crane Wartski's *A Boat to Nowhere* (1980) focuses on the plight of the Vietnamese boat people through one family's escape to another life. In *Across the Great River* (1989), Irene Beltran Hernandez presents a similar struggle in her account of a family's illegal immigration into the United States from Mexico. The immigrant's ambiguous definition of home has inspired, especially in the second half of the twentieth century, yet another theme in literature related to kinship.

In women's writing about the immigrant family, the focus quickly narrows to the clash between native culture and American ways. This theme finds articulation primarily in multi-generational stories. Jade Snow *Wong's autobiographical *Fifth Chinese Daughter* (1959) describes growing up in San Francisco's Chinatown in the 1930s. Similarly, Maxine Hong *Kingston's *The Woman Warrior* (1975) expresses the second-generation Chinese-American's fractured allegiance to the past of China (through her mother's tales), to the present of San Francisco's Chinatown, to her own future as a writer. *The Joy Luck Club* (1989) by Amy *Tan also presents the stories of four Chinese mothers and their Chinese-American daughters. In *Japanese American Women: Three Generations, 1890–1990* (1989), Mei Nakano traces the history of Japanese women who came to the U.S. as immigrant picture brides, and their granddaughters, who seek to realize the American dream. A similar autobiographical novel by Kim Chernin, *My Mother's House* (1983), follows four generations of women from a Jewish shtetl in Russia to Harvard University. Janet Satterfield presents a related perspective in *A Road Well Traveled: Three Generations of Cuban-American Women* (1991). Louise *Erdrich warns of the threat of cultural erosion in her multigenerational trilogy *Love Medicine* (1984), *The Beet Queen* (1986), and *Tracks* (1988). Her novels present the tale of two Chippewa families who learn the necessity of preserving Native-American values both on their North Dakota reservation and in the outside world. Like Erdrich, most of these women writers emphasize the importance of identifying tracks of their native culture within their American identity.

The interest in women's writing to express a cross-generational perspective often tends to center around the *mother-daughter kinship. As with Kingston's and Tan's works, in which the mother represents the traditional ways and the daughter gets caught between the attraction of the new and respect for the old, these stories frequently pay tribute to a strong maternal figure. Willa Cather's *Sapphira and the Slave Girl* (1940), Jamaica *Kincaid's *Annie John* (1986), Janet Kauffman's *Collaborators* (1987), and Paule *Marshall's *Daughters* (1991) expose the conflict between a powerful mother and a daughter not unlike her. Short stories by

Willa Cather and Katherine Anne * Porter also celebrate an older, strong maternal figure. Amy Tan's *The Kitchen God's Wife* (1991) depicts the life of a Chinese-American matriarch. The vigorous women of Toni Morrison's novels *Song of Solomon* (1978) and *Beloved* (1987) reinvigorate the heart of family life and reenvision the constitution of the family.

While most of the investigation of the theme of kinship is set within portraits of nontraditional families, some women's writing offers an even more radical query of family relations. Joyce Carol * Oates's *Marya: A Life* (1986) exposes an abandoned child raised by a family that does not understand her. In Laura Cunningham's *Sleeping Arrangements: A Memoir* (1987), an eight-year-old girl is raised by two bachelor uncles. A boy, his sister, and her friend compose an extended Chinese family newly residing in America in Gish Jen's *Typical American* (1990). Alice Hoffman's *At Risk* examines a family's struggle when their eleven-year-old child contracts AIDS. In this book, the family becomes the community at large.

As women's writing continues to reflect women's lives, the concept of kinship will expand beyond biological relations to incorporate new families created by gay and lesbian couples, by single parents adopting foreign children, by grandparents raising their children's children, and by children integrated through the marriage of two divorced parents. Perhaps, as Gilbert and Gubar suggest, women are rewriting kinship with affiliation.

[See also Family; Marriage; Spinsterhood; Widowhood; Mothers and Daughters; Grandmothers; Fathers.]

• Nancy Chodorow, "Family Structure and Feminine Personality," in *Woman, Culture, and Society*, eds. Rosaldo and Lamphere (1974). Lillian Rubin, *Worlds of Pain: Life in the Working Class Family* (1977). Carolyn Niethammer, *Daughters of the Earth: The Lives and Legends of American Indian Women* (1977). Sara Ruddick, *Rethinking the Family* (1982). Asian Women United of California, eds., *Making Waves: An Anthology of Writings by and about Asian American Women* (1989). Patricia Bell-Scott, ed., *Double-Stitch: Black Women Write about Mothers and Daughters* (1991). Carole Ione, *Pride of Family: Four Generations of American Women of Color* (1991). Mary Helen Washington, ed., *Memory of Kin: Stories about Family by Black Writers* (1991).

Eileen Cahill

KIRKLAND, Caroline (1801–1865), writer of sketches of frontier life, essayist, editor, educator. Raised in a highly literate family, Kirkland received an education that included Latin, French, and other languages, and that encouraged her abilities of expression and her sense of self-sufficiency. Her marriage to William Kirkland in 1828 inaugurated a loving, mutually respectful partnership. They initially established a girl's school in Utica, New York, moved to Detroit in 1835 to head a girl's seminary, then went, in 1837, to the village of Pinckney, Michigan, which was founded on land William purchased. Finding western life culturally barren, but the process of community formation fascinating, Kirkland regaled eastern friends with satiric letters, which served as the impetus for *A New Home* (1839). Written from a woman's perspective and grounded in domestic life, *A New Home* was the first narrative about the development of a western settlement. It portrays the arduous, frustrating, sometimes comic process by which the truculently individualistic "Wolverine" farmers and more recent newcomers, with allegiances to genteel East Coast culture, slowly and reluctantly accommodate each other as the village becomes a functioning community. Kirkland's pseudonym, Mary Clavers, did not protect her from her western neighbors' ire, and she thenceforth adhered more carefully to prevailing conventions about proper feminine discourse; *Forest Life* (1842) and *Western Clearings* (1845) are more descriptive works, displaying little of the satiric edge of her first book.

In 1843, the Kirklands returned to New York, where Caroline taught school, wrote, and raised their five children. When William's sudden death in 1846 made her the family's sole supporter, she became a literary professional. As editor, briefly, of the *Union Magazine* (later *Sartain's*), she proved an able businesswoman, negotiating successfully in the predominantly male publishing world without compromising her standards of femininity or literariness. The essays and sketches that she continued to write until her death reflect her lively intelligence and interest in cultural life, as well as her liberalism. She wrote on behalf of prison reform and abolition (causes in which she was actively involved), played anthropologist with regard to the customs of Victorian America, and commented astutely about women writers. Her *Life of Washington* (1856), written for children, advocates reciprocity between the genders and advances strong antislavery views. The authoritative, wide-ranging cultural analysis and satire that characterize her best work are unusual for an antebellum woman writer; although her pioneer realism was celebrated by Poe and others, her multivocal essayistic narratives are unique.

• Many of Caroline Kirkland's personal papers are located in the Chicago Historical Society. See also Langley Carlton Keyes, "Caroline Matilda Kirkland: A Pioneer in American Realism," Ph.D. diss., Harvard

University (1935). William S. Osborne, *Caroline M. Kirkland* (1972). Audrey Roberts, "The Letters of Caroline M. Kirkland," Ph.D. diss., University of Wisconsin (1976). Annette Kolodny, *The Land Before Her: Fantasy and Experience of the American Frontiers, 1630–1860* (1984). David Leverentz, *Manhood and the American Renaissance* (1989). Sandra A. Zagarell, Introduction to *A New Home—Who'll Follow?* by Caroline M. Kirkland (1990). Stacy L. Spencer, "Literary Profile: Caroline M. Kirkland," *Legacy* 8, no. 2 (Fall 1991): 133–140.

Sandra A. Zagarell

KIZER, Carolyn (b. 1925), poet, educator, and critic. Carolyn Ashley Kizer grew up in Spokane, Washington, and graduated from Sarah Lawrence College. A fellow of the Chinese government in comparative literature at Columbia University, she lived in Nationalist China from 1945 to 1946. Kizer also did graduate work at the University of Washington (1946–1947), where she later studied poetry with Theodore Roethke (1953–1954). In 1948, she married Charles Bullitt, from whom she was divorced in 1954, and with whom she had three children. In 1959, she founded *Poetry Northwest*, which she edited until 1965. Kizer also worked for the United States Department of State as a specialist in literature in Pakistan (1964–1965); she was the first director of the literature program for the National Endowment for the Arts from 1966 to 1970. In 1975, Kizer married John Marshall Woodbridge.

The Ungrateful Garden (1961), Kizer's first major collection, examines the complexities of existence—specifically, the ways that human beings coexist with the natural world and governmental institutions of their own making. These poems reveal that human relationships and poetry ease the terrors of the unknown and uncontrollable aspects of nature and politics. Kizer's imagery here is unflinching, capturing even the most grotesque moments of life and death.

Knock upon Silence (1965), which reveals Kizer's debt to Eastern verse in its title, taken from the *Wên-Fu* of Lu Chi, contains poems that are more relaxed metrically. The volume includes a section entitled "Chinese Imitations," two long poems, "A Month in Summer" and "Pro Femina," and some translations of the eighth-century Chinese poet Tu Fu. Kizer uses Eastern forms to explore the ways that the persona deals with herself and those she loves and to examine the role of the woman writer in modern culture.

Kizer's restrained tone and voice inform *Midnight Was My Cry: New and Selected Poems* (1971), which focuses more sharply on the social, racial, and political gains and losses of the 1960s. Eastern and classical imagery allows Kizer to approach her subjects with measured control; never sentimental, her diction frames the historical moment completely, yet without judgment.

Mermaids in the Basement: Poems for Women (1984), which contains some new work as well as previously published poems, did not receive much critical attention, but *Yin: New Poems* (1984) won the Pulitzer Prize for poetry in 1985. The title, Chinese for the "feminine principle," is apt for a volume that explores the female psyche. "A Muse," the prose section, examines Kizer's relationship with her mother; "Fanny," written in seven-line stanzas in Roman hexameter, is a first-person, diarylike account that describes Robert Louis Stevenson's last years through the eyes of his wife, who nursed him.

The Nearness of You (1986) includes many poems from previous collections (namely, Kizer's first three volumes, which had been out of print). The third section, "Father," opens with "Thrall" and ends with "Antique Father," both published previously in *Yin;* between the poems Kizer positioned a * letter that she wrote about her father after his death. Like the prose section in *Yin,* "Father" allows the persona to express the complex and often contradictory feelings of a child (and an adult) for her parent. Kizer's later poems, while personal, also encompass the broader themes of balancing and sustaining constructive relationships with self, family, friends, and world. *Carrying Over* (1988) includes some of Kizer's poems inspired by her close observations of other cultures, as well as her translations of Chinese, Urdu, Macedonian, Yiddish, and French-African poetry.

• Karl Malkoff, *Crowell's Handbook of Contemporary American Poetry* (1973). Carolyn Kizer, Introduction to *Carrying Over* (1988).

Ann Walker

KNIGHT, Sarah Kemble (1666–1727), diarist, poet, businesswoman, legal amanuensis. Born in Boston to Elizabeth Trerice Kemble and Thomas Kemble, Knight grew up in a merchant's family. Married in 1688 to Richard Knight, Sarah was apparently managing financial and legal matters well before her husband's death in 1706. In 1704, Knight undertook a journey from Boston to New Haven to attend to the settlement of the estate of Caleb Trowbridge, whose widow was possibly Knight's sister. Her account of that trip, probably written for private circulation among friends, has become famous in early American literature. *The Journal of Madam Knight*, first published by Theodore Dwight, Jr., in 1825, is a vivid, informative, and entertaining account of her trip, remarkable for the glimpse it provides into the life of a strong and independent woman in the colonial period. Already missing several pages when Dwight obtained it, the manuscript was all but destroyed, according to Dwight, when a servant mistakenly used it as scrap paper to light a fire.

The version of the manuscript published by Dwight delivers an adventuresome, literate narrator who humorously records her own fears about the venture. The two hundred miles of the journey were treacherous enough, notes Knight at one point, "to startle a more Masculine courage." The narrative blends a descriptive account of the journey with poems and often-biting social critique. Knight clearly loves the range and play of language, alternating literary allusions and poetry with the colloquialisms and cadences of the different classes and regions of people among whom she traveled, and humorously punning descriptions of those same people.

It is clear from the fragments of information gathered about Knight that she was a distinguished woman in Boston in the early 1700s. Nineteenth-century historian Frances M. Caulkins records that Knight "possessed more than a common portion of energy, talent and education. She wrote poetry and diaries, transacted various kinds of business, speculated in Indian lands, and at different times kept a tavern, managed a shop of merchandise and cultivated a farm" (*History of New London, Connecticut*, 1852). After her husband's death, Knight followed her only daughter, Elizabeth Knight Livingston, to Connecticut. She continued dealing in land and running a store in Norwich. She died at the age of sixty-one and was buried in New London.

• Alan Margolies, "The Editing and Publication of *The Journal of Madam Knight*," *Papers of the Bibliographical Society of America* 58 (1964): 25–32. Malcom Freiberg, Introductory Note to *The Journal of Madam Knight*, by Sarah Kemble Knight (1971). Ann Stanford, "Images of Women in Early American Literature," in *What Manner of Woman*, ed. M. Springer (1977), pp. 185–210. William C. Spengemann, *The Adventurous Muse: The Poetics of American Fiction, 1789–1900* (1977). Robert D. Arner, "Sarah Kemble Knight," in *American Literature before 1800*, eds. James A. Levernier and Douglass R. Wilmes (1983), pp. 857–859. Sargent Bush, Introduction to *The Journal of Madam Knight*, in *Journeys in New Worlds: Early American Women's Narratives*, ed. William Andrews (1990), pp. 69–83.

Dana D. Nelson

KOREAN-AMERICAN WRITING. A general overview of Korean-American women's writings immediately reveals how complex Korean-American history is and how diverse Korean-American experiences are, even though the population remained relatively small and unrecognized until recent decades. Published writings by Korean-American women broadly represent the various generations suggested by Korean-American immigration and settlement history.

The experiences of early, mostly working-class Korean immigrant women in Hawaii and on the mainland are described in accounts of immigrant parents' lives written as nonfiction and fiction by their daughters, as well as in oral histories collected by researchers in recent years.

Margaret K. Pai's *The Dreams of Two Yi-Min* (immigrants) (1989), traces five decades in the history of the author's family in Hawaii. In this first-person narrative, Pai tells the story of her picture-bride mother and her inventor/small-business owner father, who migrated in 1912 and 1905, respectively. The book details the mother's participation in the movement for Korean independence from Japanese colonial rule, the father's attempts to succeed in his own business, first as a furniture maker and later as a manufacturer of bamboo draperies, and the subtly strained relations between them as they struggle to establish their livelihood and raise their children in their adopted land. The parents' tale is told with sympathy and respect, and Pai's depictions of community life are richly detailed. Her own voice is muted and her psychic identity remains mostly in shadow. Although it is presented chronologically, Pai's tale is not a simple developmental narrative celebrating the seamless integration of the immigrant into the fabric of American life: at the end of the book, the parents' beloved homeland, no longer occupied by the Japanese, is divided in half as a cold war battleground, and the father's dream of bequeathing a successful business to his children literally goes up in smoke shortly after his death.

Quiet Odyssey: A Pioneer Korean Woman in America (1990) is an autobiographical account of the life of Mary Paik Lee, who immigrated to America with her family in 1905, when she was five years old. The family's odyssey takes them from Hawaii to California, and then all over California's rugged agricultural and mining country in search of a livelihood during times of relentless poverty and race discrimination. The odyssey is quiet not because Paik Lee is given to excessive restraint, but because the experiences and viewpoints of poverty-stricken Asian immigrants in early twentieth-century America have remained on the periphery of most American people's consciousness. The narrative focuses primarily on Paik Lee's early life, through the 1920s. She gives us a vivid sense of her personality, especially her fierce loyalty to her family, the intense satisfaction she derives from hard work, and her appreciation of the subtlest details of nature's beauty. Militantly antiracist, she seems singularly unmoved by current feminist concerns. *Quiet Odyssey* is a book by a woman, but the writer's mentors and comrades are all men. The people Paik Lee focuses on are her father, her brothers, her husband, and her sons. Her mother is barely mentioned, her sisters are dismissed, and most of the worst racists in the book are white women. Though perhaps regrettable, this is not surprising, given both that Korean identity has been traditionally defined as male-centered, and that racism, rather than sexism, is viewed by many women of color as the fiercer and more dangerous source of material and psychic violence.

In her 1987 novel *Clay Walls*, Ronyoung *Kim presents a daughter's perspectives on her immigrant parents' changing and often conflictual notions about what being Korean in California meant in the decades between the two world wars. Of particular interest to today's readers is the portrayal of the mother's mostly successful efforts to carve out a self-determined identity in America as a woman and as a Korean nationalist. Kim hints that this negotiation is possible because Haesu can take advantage of the interstitial position she occupies as a woman of aristocratic Korean background in what is to her, her husband, and her ethnic community a new land.

The literary legacy of the early Korean-American women is being carried on by Hawaii-born, third-generation Korean-American writer Willyce Kim, who now lives and works in northern California. Her two books of poetry, *Eating Artichokes* (1972) and *Under the Rolling Sky* (1976), explore sources of pain and joy in a lesbian's daily life. Kim has also published two wittily erotic mystery-adventure novels, *Dancer Dawkins and the California Kid* (1985) and *Dead Heat* (1988). The main characters are young lesbians who rescue their friends from danger: in *Dancer Dawkins*, Dancer's lover, Jessica, is held in thrall by a diabolical cult, and in *Dead Heat*, a woman jockey is endangered by gangsters who want to fix the horse race outcomes. In both books, the younger characters are assisted by "Ta Jan the Korean," a middle-aged woman from Hawaii and her dog, Killer Shep, whose humanlike—and feminist—thoughts Kim transmits to the reader. Kim's work refuses closed, unitary identities for Korean-American women. Her character Ta Jan has reinvented and renamed herself: born in Oahu as the descendant of a Korean immigrant worker and a picture bride, she is baptized Penelope Frances Lee, a name she detests because, she says, all her ancient Greek namesake ever did was wait and "weave, weave, weave." At the height of the hippie movement, she heads for San Francisco with a suitcase full of marijuana and names herself Ta Jan. Now she operates an all-night diner called The Golden Goose, where she serves omelets, salads, curries, bagels with lox and cream cheese, and Liliuokalani Coolers, as well as drinks named after Martina Navratilova and desserts named after Gertrude *Stein.

The increasing hybridity and heterogeneity of Korean- and Asian-American identities, especially in Hawaii and among the daughters and granddaughters of pre-1965 immigrants, challenges old categories and notions of who can be called a Korean-American writer. For many, what matters is only the wish to be so called, with *Korean American* being but one of many facets of identity. At the same time, post-1965 migration from Korea has reinforced Korean-American ethnic consciousness and interest in Korean and Korean-American history and legacies, which in turn help shape contemporary Korean-American women's writings.

Some of this work continues to make strong reference to Japanese colonial rule in Korea, which gave rise to modern national identity for the Korean diaspora. Even before 1965, there were several published personal narratives written in English by women born in Korea and resident in the United States, chronicling individual experiences of the Japanese occupation and the 1950–1953 Korean War. Many of these works are unabashedly didactic attempts to increase Westerners' knowledge about and political commitment to Korea, to proselytize and spread Christianity, and to counter communism.

Although Sook Nyul *Choi's *Year of Impossible Goodbyes* (1991), a novel for young adults, is set entirely in Korea, it is addressed to Americans, especially Korean Americans who wish to understand the historical roots of the postwar immigrant generation, about half of whom trace their family origins to northern Korea, and many of whose families were permanently separated by the political partition of Korea in 1948. *Year of Impossible Goodbyes* opens at the northern Korean family home of the narrator, ten-year-old Sookan. The time is spring 1945, near the end of World War II, when the Japanese colonizers were intensifying their exploitation of Korean resources and labor as part of their war effort. The young narrator watches in horror as the Japanese load Korean factory girls into trucks that will carry them to the front, where they will be forced to serve the Japanese soldiers as prostitutes. She experiences the harsh cruelty and racism of Japanese colonial schoolteachers. The male members of her family are in the resistance movement: her father is a guerrilla in Manchuria, and her older brothers are imprisoned in Japanese labor camps. When the war ends with Japanese surrender to the Allied forces, Korea is divided in half by the superpowers, and instead of tasting freedom, Sookhan sees northern Korea overrun with Russian soldiers. The novel ends with the family's dramatic escape to southern Korea, where the migration to America of many already-displaced Koreans begins.

Many of the daughters of these migrants belong to what some Korean Americans call the "1.5 generation," a term coined in the late 1970s and early 1980s to denote those who were born in Korea and speak Korean, but who were educated primarily in the United States. Although some of the work of these writers is informed by the kinds of national consciousness forged under colonial rule and civil war in their parents' and grandparents' generations, a key element for the younger writers is their experience of America, which involves the interplay of racial, ethnic, female, and colonial subjectivities. Important among this generation of Korean-American women writers is the late Theresa Hak Kyung *Cha, whose influential DICTEE (1982) and other written and visual artwork has pushed the boundaries of Korean-American literature by insisting on both heterogeneity and a specifically Korean ethnic identity. Producer, director, performer, creator of video and film productions, installations, performances, and published texts, Cha immigrated to the U.S. with her family when she was eleven years old. While a student of art in the mid-1970s, she studied French film theory and produced a number of performance art pieces, utilizing videos that emphasize the splice to challenge the illusion of seamlessness. She hoped that by revealing the process of making video art she could point out the interdependent relationships between the film, the filmmaker, and the viewer. In her films and videos, French, Korean, and English often overlap, with words sometimes spoken in two languages simultaneously to express her layered and multiple identities, as well as the layers of silence imposed by colonial "dictations."

Attracted by Cha's deployment of concepts such as multiplicity and indeterminacy, some post-structuralist critics have written about DICTEE without considering the importance of her Korean-American identity to the text. DICTEE is a subversive book about a specific set of excluded experiences. Indeed, it undermines popularly accepted notions of genre and of history and questions common assumptions about time, place, origins, and identity. By troubling the notion of progress from fragmentation to wholeness or from immigrant to citizen, Cha challenges the U.S. nationalist narrative. And by bringing Korea and Koreans into view after the damage done by Japanese colonization has been glossed over by history, she creates a space for justice as well as for difference.

Cha's work has attracted and influenced the work of Korean- and other Asian-American women writers like Trinh T. *Minh-ha and Myung Mi Kim, whose book of hauntingly beautiful poems, Under Flag (1991), explores the immigrant's loss of homeland and the Korean American's encounters with racism and experiences with the loss of language. Kim's poetry addresses the impossibility of transfer of meaning when the given content becomes alien and estranged in the act of translation. Kim refuses to give in to the demand that her work reflect something or tell a story that adheres to some chronology or trajectory that can be tracked and named. In her poetry, time is not coherent, but unmoored, disjunctive, and splintered, as are memory and, indeed, life itself, and Korean-American identity is not planted in any one place, but multiple and shifting.

Voices Stirring (1992), a new anthology of Korean-American writing, continues to call into question the meaning of American in the late twentieth century. The slim volume is illustrated by visual artist and cultural critic Yong Soon Min, whose essays, prints, installations, and video artworks are informed by her participation in the minjung (folk or common people's) art movement, the Asian-American movement against racism and injustice, and her interest in the affinities between Koreans/Korean Americans and the third world diasporas. Voices Stirring provides a sampling of poetry and prose by young women writers who explore various facets of Korean-American identity in the 1990s, including Joo-Hyun Kang, Diana Song, Mi Ok Bruining, Lisa Simmons, and Marie G. Lee.

An essayist and writer of fiction for adolescents and young adults, Lee writes about how young Korean Americans struggle to find a place for themselves in a society that is ignorant of their cultural roots. Although each of Lee's works focuses on different kinds of Korean-American experiences, all of them address the ways in which Korean Americans struggle against being trapped in false binaries—between white and nonwhite, between Korea and America, between foreign and native. Her first novel, Finding My Voice (1992), is set in the American Midwest, where Lee herself grew up. The protagonist is Ellen Sung, a Korean-American high school student who learns during the course of the novel how to deal with racism and how to understand from where her parents' views and values come. Lee's new novel, If It Hadn't Been for Yoon Jun (1993), is about a seventh-grader who was adopted as an infant by a white American family and who has been successfully crafting her identity as an all-American teenager, despite the disagreements between her father, who wants her to learn about her Korean roots, and her mother, who prefers that she ignore them. Alice's self-concept and desire for her peers' acceptance are brought into a crisis when a "strange, quiet" Korean immigrant student enrolls at her school.

There are * bildungsromanesque elements in both of Lee's novels, which, like so many works of young adult fiction, seem intent on reassuring members of the older generation that in the end youth will refuse to capitulate to peer pressure and learn to appreciate their elders. But Lee is no simple teller of corny tales for teenaged "squares," as evidenced by her 1991 short essay, "We Koreans Need an Al Sharpton." She writes at a specific moment in history, when young Korean Americans are contesting a paradigm of American identity and race relations that allows for their existence only as statements about African- or European-American experiences. Her current work, a sequel to *Finding My Voice*, follows Ellen Sung to college, where she finds herself torn between her politically involved African-American roommate and her Korean-American boyfriend, whose father's market was destroyed during the 1992 civil disaster in Los Angeles. This very specific Korean-American attempt to create a third space cannot be contained in the promise of happiness formula for young adult fiction any more than Korean-American personal narratives can be interpreted only as developmental.

Korean-American women's writing is diverse and multifaceted. Inspired by their literary foremothers, by each other, and by their awareness of their location in a complex landscape of race, class, and gender issues, Korean-American women are showing increasing interest in inscribing themselves in writing and visual artwork. Given the burst of productivity among them during the past few years, we can expect to hear more and more from them from now on.

[See also Asian-American Writing; Assimilation; Citizenship; Ethnicity and Writing; Immigrant Writing.]

• Cathy Song, "Beginnings (for Bok Pil)," *Hawaii Review* 6 (Spring 1976): 55–65. Elizabeth M. Kim, "Detours down Highway 99," *Quilt* 2 (1981): 103–110. Esther Yoon, "Vanishing Point," *Hawaii Review* 16 (Fall 1984): 61–63. Cathy Song, *Frameless Windows, Squares of Light* (1988). Yong Soon Min, "Whirl War," *New Observations* 62 (November 1988). Myung Mi Kim, "A Rose Of Sharon," *The Forbidden Stitch: An Asian American Women's Anthology*, ed. Shirley Geok-lin Lim and Mayumi Tsutagawa (1989): 20. Alison Kim, "Sewing Woman," *The Forbidden Stitch: An Asian American Women's Anthology*, ed. Shirley Geok-lin Lim and Mayumi Tsutagawa (1989): 203. Anne M: Ok Bruining, "To Omoni, In Korea," in *Making Face, Making Soul*, ed. Gloria Anzaldúa (1990): 153–155. Yong Soon Min, "Territorial Waters: Mapping Asian American Cultural Identity," *New Asia: The Portable Lower East Side* 7, no. 2 (1990). Yong Soon Min, "Comparing the Contemporary Experiences of Asian American, South Korean, and Cuban Artists," *Asian Americans: Comparative and Global Perspectives*, ed. Shirley Hune et al. (1991). Anne Mi Ok Bruining, "Challenging the Lies of International Adoption By White Lesbians & Gays," *Color Life!* (28 June 1992): 22–23.

Elaine H. Kim

KRISTEVA, Julia. *See* French Feminism.

KUMIN, Maxine (b. 1925), poet, fiction writer, essayist, and children's author. Born and raised in Philadelphia, Kumin, the daughter of Jewish parents, attended Catholic schools. She received her B.A. in 1946 and her M.A. in 1948 from Radcliffe College. In June 1946 she married Victor Kumin, an engineering consultant; they have two daughters and a son. In 1957, she studied poetry with John Holmes at the Boston Center for Adult Education. There she met Anne * Sexton, with whom she started a friendship that continued until Sexton's suicide in 1974. Kumin taught English from 1958–1961 and 1965–1968 at Tufts University; from 1961–1963 she was a scholar at the Radcliffe Institute for Independent Study. She has also held appointments as a visiting lecturer and poet in residence at many American colleges and universities. Since 1976, she and her husband have lived on a farm in Warner, New Hampshire, where they breed Arabian and quarter horses.

Kumin's many awards include the Eunice Tietjens Memorial Prize from *Poetry* (1972), the Pulitzer Prize for Poetry (1973) for *Up Country*, an American Academy and Institute of Arts and Letters Award for excellence in literature (1980), an Academy of American Poets fellowship (1986), and six honorary degrees. In 1981–1982, she served as the poetry consultant to the Library of Congress.

Kumin is the author of eleven books of poetry: *Halfway* (1961), *The Privilege* (1965), *The Nightmare Factory* (1970), *Up Country: Poems of New England* (1972), *House, Bridge, Fountain, Gate* (1975), *The Retrieval System* (1978), *Our Ground Time Here Will Be Brief: New and Selected Poems* (1982), *Closing the Ring: Selected Poems* (1984), *The Long Approach* (1985), *Nurture* (1989), and *Looking for Luck* (1992). Her fiction includes a book of short stories, *Why Can't We Live Together Like Civilized Human Beings?* (1982), and four novels, *Through Dooms of Love* (1965), *The Passions of Uxport* (1968), *The Abduction* (1971), and *The Designated Heir*

(1974). *To Make a Prairie: Essays on Poets, Poetry, and Country Living* (1980) consists of interviews with Kumin, her reviews of poetry by her peers, and several essays on her own poetry; *In Deep: Country Essays* (1987) offers seasonal meditations on rural life. She has also published over twenty books for children, four of which she coauthored with Sexton.

Critics have often compared Kumin with Elizabeth *Bishop because of her meticulous observations, and with Robert Frost, for she frequently devotes her attention to the rhythms of life in rural *New England. Likewise, because of her autobiographical bent, she has been grouped with confessional poets such as Sexton and Robert Lowell. But unlike Sexton and Lowell, Kumin eschews high rhetoric and adopts a plain style that is often invigorated by her experiments with formal verse, but sometimes flattens into prosaism in her free verse.

Throughout her career as a poet, Kumin has struck a balance between her sense of life's transience and her fascination with the dense physical presence of the world around her. At its worst, this latter impulse causes her to weigh her poetry down with catalogs of material details and an overabundance of similes; such poems seem to be merely exercises in record keeping. But at its best, her poetry offers details whose blend of quirkiness and exactness beautifully ground her meditations on endurance in the face of loss.

• Jean Gould, "Anne Sexton—Maxine Kumin," in *Modern American Women Poets* (1984), pp. 151–175. Deborah Pope, "A Rescuer by Temperament: The Poetry of Maxine Kumin," in *A Separate Vision: Isolation in Contemporary Women's Poetry* (1984), pp. 54–83.

Meg Schoerke

KÜNSTLERROMAN. *See* Bildungsroman and Künstlerroman; Novel, Beginnings of the.

L

LABOR REFORM. *See* Class; Industrialization; Proletarian writing; Working-class Fiction.

LACAN, Jacques. *See* Psychoanalysis and Women, article on Jacques Lacan.

LA LLORONA, the weeping woman of Mexican legend often viewed as the mythic form of the historical woman *La Malinche. The hundreds of variants of the tale share a kernel plot: as punishment for her offenses a woman is condemned to wander forever (often by rivers) in grief-stricken search for her lost children. Variants concern the nature of her offenses, from adultery, infanticide, child abandonment, homicidal revenge, and excessive pleasure-seeking to combinations of these and other transgressions. Often told as a *bruja* (*witch) or *ghost tale to coerce obedience from children (such as, she will steal them to replace the babies she drowned) and adolescent girls (such as, her suffering will be theirs if they emulate her reputed sexual misconduct), some folklorists trace the story to the 1600s in colonial New Spain. She (and La Malinche) has been interpreted as emblematic of the vanquished condition and reputed fatalism of Mexico and its people. However, some writers (Rosario Castellanos, José Limón, Cordelia Candelaria) have sought to rehabilitate her iconography by emphasizing her attributes as a resisting woman (like Antigone) who wills her own destiny by choosing eternal suffering for herself and merciful death for her children over enslavement by unjust classist, sexist laws and conventions.

Cordelia Candelaria

LA MALINCHE, also Malinalli Tenepal, Malíntzin, and Doña Marina (1502–1527?), guide-translator-mistress of Hernán Cortés during the conquest of Mexico, 1519–1521. Born in Aztec-ruled Coatzacoalcos in central Mexico, she grew up on the Yucatan coast after being given to itinerant traders by her mother. Her native speaker's knowledge of Náhuatl (Aztecan language) and Mayan dialects and her rapid grasp of Spanish made her indispensable to Cortés, the father of two of her sons. Although most of what is known about her comes from Bernal Díaz del Castillo's (1492–1584) famous eye-witness chronicle (*The True History of the Conquest of New Spain*, 1632), his single account forms the basis of countless views of her historical role, including those written by writers such as historians William H. Prescott (1842) and Mariano Somonte (1969), social scientist Adelaida R. del Castillo (1979), and literary scholars Cordelia Candelaria (1980) and Sandra Messinger Cypress (1992). This historiography is central to an understanding of her actual life, debased image, and twentieth-century recuperation by feminists. It explains the evolution of her iconography from victim of both conquerors and caciques (leaders of her indigenous societies); to victor as Doña (lady) Marina, the title conferred by the Spaniards because of her wise and loyal service; to the conqueror's mouthpiece, *La Lengua* (Tongue), and later Malíntzin (-*tzin* denotes honor) revered by the native peoples; to the abhorred symbol of political treason and cultural betrayal identified by Nobel laureate Octavio Paz as *"la chingada* (whore) *de México"* and blamed for the conquest; to a woman of remarkable achievement unfairly scapegoated by sexist history. Because of her sui generis role as Cortés's interpreter, she was perhaps the first post-Columbian American to confront on a public stage such *gender, *race, and *class issues as intercultural identity, bilingualism, and competing loyalties between contrasting cultures. Considered the historical source for the *La Llorona legend, she appears frequently as an archetypal traitor and/or scapegoat in Mexican, Chicana/o, and other literature and art.

Cordelia Candelaria

LA MESTIZA. *See* Third World Feminism, U.S.

LANE, Pinkie Gordon (b. 1923), Southern University professor emerita, and Louisiana poet laureate, her writing career spans over thirty years. In 1961, her first published poem appeared in *Phylon*. Subsequent poems have appeared in many publications—*Callaloo*, the *Southern Review, Obsidian, Ms.*, and the anthology *Double Stitch: Black Women Write about Mothers and Daughters* (1991), among others—

and she has published four volumes of poetry: *Wind Thoughts* (1972); *Mystic Female* (1978), which was nominated for the Pulitzer Prize; *I Never Scream* (1985); and *Girl at the Window* (1991). A naturalist, Lane writes picturesque, lyrical verse chronicling personal experiences.

A native of Philadelphia, Lane attended that city's School for Girls, graduating in 1940, the year her father, William Alexander Gordon, died. Her mother, Inez Addie West Gordon, died in 1945. Lane then left her sewing factory job to enter Spelman College in Atlanta. She earned a bachelor's degree in English and art (1949), and began teaching in the public schools of Georgia and Florida. In 1956, Lane received a Master of Arts degree from Atlanta University, and moved to Baton Rouge, Louisiana, where, in 1967, she became the first black woman to receive the Ph.D. degree from Louisiana State University. She taught at now-defunct Leland College (1956–1959) before joining the faculty at Southern University, the place that nurtured her poetic growth. There she rose to full professor and chairperson of the English department before retiring in 1986.

Since 1974, Lane has served as advisory editor for *Black Scholar* and poetry editor of *Black American Literature Forum*. A vice president of South and West, Inc., from 1979 to 1981, she became editor-in-chief of that organization's literary journal. She has participated in numerous workshops and seminars, and has performed on the lecture/poetry reading circuit throughout the United States, in France, and in Africa.

Among her numerous awards are the National Award/Recognition "The Black Caucus Presents," National Council of Teachers of English (1990); "A Tribute to Black Women Writers," Spelman College (1988); the Delta Pearl Award, Delta Sigma Theta Sorority, Baton Rouge Alumnae Chapter (1991); appointment to the Louisiana poet laureateship (1989); and induction into the Louisiana Black Hall of Fame (1991). She was one of fifty-seven Louisiana women honored in the Women's Pavilion at the New Orleans Expo (1984). Lane holds membership in the Poetry Society of America, the Modern Language Association, the National Council of Teachers of English, the College Language Association, the Delta Sigma Theta Sorority, and the Unitarian Church. Widow of Ulysses Simpson Lane, she has one son, Gordon.

• American Biographical Institute, *Community Leaders and Noteworthy Americans* (1974). Earnest Kay, ed., *International Who's Who in Poetry: 1974–1975*, 4th ed. (1974). Trudier Harris and Thadious Davis, eds. *Dictionary of Literary Biography: Afro-American Poets since 1955*, vol. 41 (1985). Curt Johnson and Frank Nipp, eds., *Who's Who in Writers, Editors, and Poets: United States and Canada, 1989–1990* (1989). Chester Hedgepeth, ed., *Twentieth-Century African-American Writers and Artists* (1991).

Marilyn B. Craig

LANGUAGE, WOMEN'S. *This entry consists of two parts. The first essay addresses several linguistic issues that have been of particular and continuing concern to women. The second focuses on the ways in which the contemporary field of "interactional sociolinguistics" analyzes ways in which men and women are trained to talk (or not to talk) to one another:*

Women's Language
Communications Between the Sexes

For further information, please refer to Linguists; Black English; Nonstandard English.

Women's Language

For many years, women have been talking about the problems they have with the English language and with men's talk. For example, in the nineteenth century, women discussed men's use of the false generics (such as the use of *man* for *humans* and *his* for *her and his*); the frequent labeling (in men's novels, jokes, cartoons, and academic treatises) of women's speech as inferior to men's; the belittling terms of endearment (such as, *honey* and *doll*), the renaming of women when they marry (Mrs. Man), and the exclusive language of church and law (such as *brethren* and *our Father*). These remain problems today.

Through the years, women have experienced major restrictions on where, when, how, and with whom they were allowed to speak. Saying nurturing words (as long as they are not too many words) to family members inside the home is encouraged. Saying critical or political words in settings outside the home is not. Women are seldom hired for jobs that involve expert talk to adult men (including professional jobs in universities, churches, central government, or television announcing). In general, the institutions of the nation encourage women to be appreciative and soft-spoken (or, better yet, silent), and men to be evaluative and assertive. Women who are not cooperative in this respect were labeled "noisy scolds," "monsters," "nonwomen," and "perverts" in the nineteenth century, and "man-hater" and "strident feminists" in the twentieth. Older women, especially, are to be quiet or only to talk about topics that are comfortable to others (such as the past, but not problems of the present).

Women's earlier statements and publications on women's speech have not been retained in malestream publications. Thus, in the late 1960s, women who discussed their own talk, and men's critiques of it, did not have a historical base on which to build their own analyses. Part of the research on women's talk has entailed the rediscovery of earlier work. The historical and contemporary accounts now total thousands.

While many communication scholars use the labels of public/private to describe and evaluate talk, feminist scholars point out that this dichotomy is not a natural division, but a paradigm convenient for exaggerating gender differences in political life. In many ways, men discourage women from talking to large, mixed-sex groups—but then decree the absence of women's talk in public arenas as somehow natural. Further, this public/private hierarchical division ignores talk that cannot be categorized as either. Traditional categories for talk need to be critiqued and new topics and approaches considered. For example, Bea Medicine (in *Women and Language in Transition*, 1987) tells of the role that many American Indian women have played as mediators between their own community and white society. The bilingual skills of many women of color, and their dual roles as cultural guardians and as linguistic innovators, have seldom been respected by men in the respective cultures. Further, traditional scholars have shown little interest in the types and functions of silences within conversations and silences of entire groups of people. Severe penalties for speaking languages from Africa meant that slave narratives were often told or written in secret, or not told or written at all. Even now, black women's stories about their ideas and lives are often excluded, or hushed, in the civil rights or women's movements, as are the voices of Native Americans, Hispanics, Latinas, Chicanas, Asian Americans, and other women of color. Gloria Anzaldúa is one of several editors who has brought together women who give fresh evaluations of speakers and topics, including the problems many women of color experience because of the nation's widespread hostility toward languages and speakers other than standard (that is, middle-class, white male) English.

Talk about Health and Body. The twentieth-century consolidation of medical authority into the male-dominated American Medical Association has meant that most women now have to rely on men for both periodical checkups and emergency health care. This has created problems in the ways women's bodies are discussed (such as pregnancy, childbirth, and menopause being treated as diseases) and in the ways patient-doctor interactions are structured (with physicians controlling the conversation through such strategies as trivialization of troubles, interruptions, topic change, and jokes). In recent years, women have published many critiques of physicians' talk, and many accounts of the ways girls and women are talking about generally taboo topics such as menstruation and menopause, along with accounts of the ways medical authorities, corporations, and advertisers have tried to dictate how our bodies are weighed and described.

Conversing at Home. The talk of white, heterosexual couples is often very problematic for the women of those couples, according to Victoria DeFrancisco's studies (see *Discourse and Society*, October 1991). Women work harder to maintain a conversation than do the men, but are less successful. In interviews, women talk about the patronizing, put-down, and teachy behavior of their husbands. Some recent accounts dealing with miscommunication between heterosexual partners have treated difference as if it were a neutral concept, as if they were two "styles" of talk. These accounts ignore the years of research and observations that point to the hierarchical and power relations involved in the expectations and evaluations of women's and men's talk.

Within families, there are often gender-based divisions in talk, with mothers interacting more frequently with daughters, and fathers with son. In white, middle-class families, fathers are heard to use more direct imperatives, while the mothers are more likely to make requests in more indirect ways. Fathers interrupt their children more than mothers do, and are less likely to use politeness terms such as "thank you." Thus, boys and girls are given early training on how to talk "according to gender."

Stranger Talk. All of women's talk is not in private places; for example, they talk with each other in department stores, grocery stores, and in church foyers. However, women, often required to travel through their communities to get to work and to child care facilities, are made to feel uncomfortable and unsafe on many streets and sidewalks. Girls and women don't often comment on, or threaten, the men on the streets, but they are often commented on and often threatened, especially at night. Not only are there very powerful restrictions on the places in which they are encouraged or allowed to talk, there are also often time-of-day restrictions on their face-to-face talk.

Communication Networks. Telephones were developed primarily for men's business. Women, however, have used them to reduce isolation. Talking on telephones has reduced the need for travel to talk with family and friends, and has also allowed women to talk while doing other activities, such as watching children in the home or cooking (common dual activities for women). The telephone in the home can also be a threat, however. The number of abusive calls made to women has increased in recent decades, adding to the number and type of everyday violations to which women can be subjected.

The thousands of electronic networks and bulletin boards are new communication systems providing some women (mostly those employed in universities or large companies) with new ways of "chatting." In daily increasing numbers, electronic networks are being set up for people in communities to "talk" with each other and with other people throughout the country who have access to these forums. For those who cannot afford to buy the computer equipment for their home, equipment at public sites, such as libraries, provides access. However, since the streets are not safe, especially for old women, and since women are often reluctant users of computers (having been well taught not to take risks with machinery), these networks are likely to continue to be what they are now—communication spaces primarily for men. Already, women on the networks tell about sexual harassment (such as sexist jokes directed at specific women or at women in general) in the "talk." Many women have organized women-only bulletin boards in order to get talk-time for themselves and their ideas and concerns.

School Interaction. Barrie Thorne points out the complexities of talk in the classroom and playground, as girls and boys are together and apart, accepting, rejecting, and contesting gender boundaries and institutionalized heterosexuality. Thorne points out that while adults dichotomize children's actions into work and play, the children's reality is that much of the play has serious meanings. For example, boys, who are the frequent disruptive invaders into girls' talk and other activities, often claim a play frame, but the girls often refuse that definition. Gender hierarchies often determine whose version of reality prevails. Playground and classroom peer teasing may signal affection, solidarity, or courtship, but may also be veiled hostility and aggression. In general, girls and women are infrequently called upon in class, and their comments are less likely to be rewarded. They often experience peer harassment, which works to keep them silent in the classroom. While quiet boys and men are of concern to teachers who want to draw them out, teachers seldom consider the silence of a girl or woman as a teaching problem.

These are all very serious and continuing problems, with enormous implications for the future of all talk and writing.

[*See also* Linguists; Black English; Nonstandard English.]

• Barrie Thorne, Cheris Kramarae, and Nancy Henley, eds., *Language, Gender and Society* (1984). Joyce Penfield, ed., *Women and Language in Transition* (1987). Cheris Kramarae, ed., *Technology and Women's Voices* (1988). Alexandra Todd and Sue Fisher, eds., *Gender and Discourse: The Power of Talk* (1988). Yolanda Moses, *Black Women in Academe: Issues and Strategies* (1989). Gloria Anzaldúa, ed., *Making Face, Making Soul/Haciendo Caras: Creative and Critical Perspectives by Women of Color* (1990). Susan L. Gabriel and Isaiah Smithson, eds., *Gender in the Classroom: Power and Pedagogy* (1990). "Women Speaking from Silence," special issue of *Discourse and Society* 2, no. 4, (October 1991). Barrie Thorne, *Gender Play: Girls and Boys in School* (1992).

Cheris Kramarae

Communication between the Sexes

A major academic tradition that has been brought to bear on the question of gender and language use is interactional sociolinguistics, a methodological approach pioneered by anthropological linguist John Gumperz, and named by him to distinguish it from the more common type of sociolinguistics, which typically examines phonological variation. As the name suggests, work in this tradition is concerned with understanding language as it is used in interaction, taking into account social context. It is Gumperz, along with Frederick Erickson, who developed the methodological framework of tape-recording conversations, identifying segments in which trouble is evident, and then looking for culturally patterned differences in signaling meaning that could account for the trouble. This framework was first applied to gendered patterns in ways of speaking by Maltz and Borker, and also provided the theoretical basis for the work of Gumperz's student Deborah Tannen.

Maltz and Borker did not base their conclusions on original research, but rather reviewed research by *linguists, *anthropologists, *psychologists, and *sociologists, and discerned patterns by which boys' and girls' socialization in their peer groups resulted in systematically different approaches to having and interpreting verbal interactions as adults. In other words, they interpreted earlier findings in Gumperz's framework. Thus, for example, Lynette Hirschman found that women provided more "affirmative" listening responses, and nearly all the instances of "mm hmm" in their study (33 were found in the talk produced by the two women, only 1 in the talk produced by the two men). Maltz and Borker suggest that this occurred because women tend to use these signals to show

"I'm listening," whereas men tend to use them to show "I agree," and that women are listening more often than men are agreeing.

The interactional sociolinguistic framework describes a pattern by which boys and girls tend to play in sex-separate groups, and their manner of play tends to differ. Boys are more likely to play in large groups, where their activities are central, and where much of their verbal behavior is geared to jockeying for status. Girls' friendships, on the other hand, are more likely to center around a best friend; they spend more time indoors, talking, and much of their talk is geared toward managing intimacy: how close each one is to the other. This hypothesis has been misinterpreted to imply that girls are not interested in status and boys are not interested in intimacy. On the contrary, the claim is that the socialization process has taught boys to be aware of relative status because boys in groups have been exposed to repeated attempts by other boys to put them down and push them around. Furthermore, as Tannen points out, agreement about appropriate means for interaction in itself creates intimacy and bonding. Thus, boys frequently report that their close friendships began in opposition and may be characterized by friendly fighting, and picking a fight with another boy can be a means to enter into interaction and eventually friendship. For girls, status is negotiated through intimacy: girls in junior high and high school gain status by their closeness to "popular" girls. In a related phenomenon, whereas girls' and women's discourse is not competitive in the same way that boys' and men's is, nonetheless girls can be shown to negotiate competition while observing norms that require them to be cooperative.

The cross-cultural framework applied to gender and language has also been misinterpreted to imply that misunderstanding is meant to replace dominance as the operative dynamic between males and females. Quite the contrary, work in this tradition claims that gendered patterns of communication contribute to the creation of male dominance. For example, according to Tannen (1990), if women often exert energy in a conversation to show interest in the other speaker, and expect their interlocutor to elicit their opinions in good time, and if boys' socialization has prepared many men to exert effort to hold center stage and deflect others' efforts to take it away, then the result is an imbalance by which men frequently lecture to women, a division of labor that frames the listener as subordinate. Similarly, middle-class Anglo girls' avoidance of open conflict puts women at a disadvantage in interaction with those, including many men, who seek conflict, or at least do not eschew it, as a necessary means of struggling for interactional dominance.

Interruption, a conversational strategy that has been much analyzed and discussed, provides an emblematic example of how the "cultural difference" approach dovetails with research on conversational dominance. A frequently cited claim is that men interrupt women in conversation. In a critical review of the literature, Deborah James and Sandra Clarke show that research has resulted in varying findings. For one thing, studies comparing all-female and all-male groups tend to find that women interrupt each other more than men. However, what have been counted as interruptions are often overlaps intended to create rapport: a kind of talking-along to show interest and agreement rather than to take the floor. Furthermore, Tannen (1990) points out that men often end up interrupting women because:

Men who approach conversation as a contest are likely to expend effort not to support the other's talk but to lead the conversation in another direction, perhaps one in which they can take center stage by telling a story or joke or displaying knowledge. But in doing so, they expect their conversational partners to mount resistance. Women who yield to these efforts do so not because they are weak or insecure or deferential but because they have little experience in deflecting attempts to grab the conversational wheel.

Research in this tradition, then, questions the value judgments associated with ways of speaking that have resulted in devaluation of strategies expected of, and frequently observed among, female speakers. The knowledge that Asian interactional styles also eschew open confrontation, value indirectness, and require frequent listener responses, calls into question the association of these ways of speaking with "insecurity," "lack of confidence," or "powerlessness."

[See also Linguistics; Black English; Nonstandard English.]

• William Labov, Language in the Inner City (1972). Frederick Erickson, and Jeffrey Shultz, The Counselor as Gatekeeper: Social Interaction in Interviews (1982). John J. Gumperz, Discourse Strategies (1982). Penelope Eckert, Jocks and Burnouts (1989). Marjorie Harness Goodwin, He-Said-She-Said: Talk as Social Organization among Black Children (1990). Deborah Tannen, You Just Don't Understand: Women and Men in Conversation (1990). Deborah James and Sandra Clarke, "Women, Men, and Interruptions: A Critical Review," in Gender and Conversational Interaction, ed. Deborah Tannen (1993), pp. 231–280. Deborah Tannen, Gender and Discourse (1994).

Deborah Tannen

LARSEN, Nella (1891–1964), novelist and short story writer. Several of Nella Larsen's literary descendants (Marita * Golden, Maya * Angelou, Alice * Walker) have written glowingly of their discovery of her work. Their admiration is easy to understand. As the major novelist of the * Harlem Renaissance, Larsen published novels (*Quicksand*, 1928; and *Passing*, 1929) concerned with one of the predominant issues of contemporary African-American women's writing: the status of the black woman, often educated, in a male-dominated society. If African-American women writers have written about this topic so successfully in recent times, they are indebted to Nella Larsen—and her somewhat later sister, Zora Neale * Hurston—for defining the territory years earlier.

Larsen's career as a writer has been difficult to assess because of the confusion that has shrouded her life and work. To a certain extent, she hindered her future biographers by embellishing and distorting painful aspects of her life. Until recent years, the dates of her birth and death have been conjectural. She was said to have disappeared after the Harlem Renaissance; it was assumed that she had stopped writing after being accused of plagiarizing her short story "Sanctuary" (1931). Writing in 1980, Mary Ellen Washington referred to her as the "Mystery Woman of the Harlem Renaissance."

Larsen was born in 1891, possibly in New York City, the daughter of Mary Hansen, who was Danish, and an African-American or West Indian father. The name Larsen belonged to her stepfather, whom Mary Hansen married in 1893. Almost nothing is known about the trauma of Nella's childhood—except that when she was still young, she was expunged from the Larsen family because of her color. Census records for the family make no reference to her existence; only one child is identified as part of the family (Nella's half sister, Anna). When Nella died in 1964 and her estate fell to her sister as her only surviving relative, Anna is said to have remarked that she did not even know she had a sister.

In 1912, Nella began attending Lincoln Hospital School of Nursing in New York City, and earned her degree in 1915. She practiced as a nurse from that year until 1921 (including a brief period at Tuskegee Institute). Two years earlier she had married Elmer S. Imes, who had a Ph.D. in physics. Early in the decade of the 1920s, Nella and Elmer (by then settled in Harlem) were part of the city's black elite. Among their friends they counted the W. E. B. Du Boises, Jessie and Arthur Fauset, Walter White, and James Weldon Johnson. From 1921 until 1926, Nella worked as a librarian, mostly at the 135th Street branch of the city library. She also began her writing during these years, though her publications were few and far between.

Nella's initial writing appeared under the name Nella Larsen Imes in the *Brownie's Book*, the imaginative children's magazine that Jessie Fauset edited for the NAACP under W. E. B. Du Bois's guidance. In introductory remarks to both pieces ("Three Scandinavian Games" [June 1920] and "Danish Fun" [July 1920]), Larsen claimed that she had learned the games she wrote about during her childhood in Denmark. Passport records kept by the State Department, however, do not support this assertion.

Much more significant are the two stories that Larsen published in 1926 in *Young's Magazine*: "The Wrong Man" (January) and "Freedom" (April). Both stories were published under the pseudonymous anagram Allen Semi. She may have chosen that name because of the dubious distinction of the magazine itself: at best a purveyor of pulp fiction. Race is of no importance in either of these stories, which border on the maudlin, the sentimental, and rely on O. Henry–type surprise endings for their effect. Under the surface, however, both "The Wrong Man" and "Freedom" relate a simple truism: marriage is at best a precarious institution, especially when spouses have been dishonest with one another about their earlier lives.

By the time *Quicksand* and *Passing* were published, Larsen had stopped working as a librarian and begun writing full time. Her health had declined, possibly because of Elmer's philandering. Still, the Harlem Renaissance was in full swing, and, as her correspondence reveals, Nella regarded herself as playing an important part in it.

Quicksand (1928), which won the Harmon Foundation's Bronze Award for Literature, centers on the life of Helga Crane and her ongoing struggle to find a niche for herself within the black world. Despised because of her dark skin, Helga is shunted away from her family and left to fend for herself. The novel begins in the South, where Helga teaches at an all-black school, but even there she feels out of her element. Moving to Harlem and eventually to Denmark, Helga attempts to discover her identity in those disparate locations. By the end of the story, Helga's life has come full circle: she returns to Harlem and finally to the South, where she becomes the wife of the Rev. Mr. Pleasant Green, and her sole function is bearing his numerous children.

Larsen's masterpiece depicts the psychological breakdown of the "despised mulatto" by delicately probing the then-taboo subjects of illegitimacy, of the cultural half-caste, of race. Helga's problem, to a certain degree, is that she herself cannot determine what she wants out of life. Educated and sophisticated, Helga permits herself to be manipulated by others. Her retreat into passion at the end of the story implies a negation of the earlier values she both admired and embraced.

Passing (1929), by contrast, might be described as the swan song of a whole series of earlier African-American novels dealing with the fate of the tragic mulatto. To her credit, however, Larsen adds to the theme an ironic twist. The story is not so much an account of Clare Kendry's duplicitous life of passing for a white woman—and its fatal consequences—as it is the story of Irene Redfield's jealousy and fear that Clare will take her husband away from her. Once again, Larsen's depiction of character is psychologically complex. Taken together, her two novels comprise the most fully developed black American female characters of any writers until that time.

Nella Larsen was the first African-American woman to be awarded a Guggenheim Fellowship, a grant she held in 1930–1931, while living in Portugal and Spain, where she worked on a novel called *Mirage*. By that time, her marriage was in disarray; she had undergone the charges of plagiarism for "Sanctuary"; and she was soon to experience rejection of her latest work. Though she worked on other novels after her return to the United States and her divorce from Elmer (1933), no other of her works was accepted for publication. By 1941, she had returned to nursing, holding a series of largely supervisory positions in New York City hospitals. Her peers described her as a model worker. During all of the later years of her life, she identified herself as Mrs. Nella L. Imes. She was discovered dead in her apartment in Manhattan on 30 March 1964.

• Mary Ellen Washington, "Nella Larsen: Mystery Woman of the Harlem Renaissance," *Ms.* (December 1980): 44–50. Deborah E. McDowell, Introduction to *Quicksand and Passing*, by Nella Larsen (1986). Charles R. Larson, Introduction to *An Intimation of Things Distant: The Collected Fiction of Nella Larsen* (1992). Charles R. Larson, *Invisible Darkness: Jean Toomer and Nella Larsen (1993)*. Thadious M. Davis, *Nella Larsen, Novelist of the Harlem Renaissance* (1994).

Charles R. Larson

LATIMORE, Jewel. *See* Amini, Johari.

LATINA PUBLISHING OUTLETS. In their introduction to *Breaking Boundaries* (1989), Eliana Ortega and Nancy Saporta Sternbach initiate their analysis of Latina literary discourse in the 1980s with the invisibility metaphor. They clearly argue that the dominant U.S. institutions of literary criticism, including Anglo feminism, have systematically excluded Latinas from the *canon. As Eliana Rivero (1989) has pointed out, anthologies such as Gilbert and Gubar's *Norton Anthology of Literature by Women: The Tradition in English* (1985) and Alicia Suskin Ostriker's *Stealing the Language: The Emergence of Women's Poetry in America* (1986) illustrate how segregationist practices are alive and well in academia, even among women. In this light Ortega and Sternbach's title to their introduction, "At the Threshold of the Unnamed: Latina Literary Discourse in the Eighties," takes on meaning.

In reality, Latinas had been writing well before the eighties. Lack of access to publishing houses, issues of language, and a resistance to validate writings by working-class women of color have been, and still are in many cases, major obstacles to the recognition of a Latina literary canon. The emergence of Latino/a journals, Latina and Latino editors and publishing houses, and feminist small presses dedicated to women of color have created alternative paths for many Latinas to publish.

Many well-known Chicana authors writing today—Sandra *Cisneros, Estela *Portillo-Trambley, Ana *Castillo, Cordelia Candelaria, Lorna Dee *Cervantes—began publishing poems, short stories, and essays during the 1970s in regional journals that emerged during the literary and cultural renaissance of the Chicano movement. *Caracol* in San Antonio, Texas; *De Colores* in Albuquerque, New Mexico; *Tejidos: A Bilingual Journal for the Stimulation of Chicano Creativity and Criticism* from Austin, Texas; *Maize* in San Diego; and *El Grito* and *El Grito del Sol* in California served as a forum for Chicano and Chicana voices. This period, however, was characterized by a strong predominance of male voices, as many critics and Chicanas have already pointed out, and publishing practices were not exempt from the prevalent patriarchal stance among Chicano activists, cultural workers, and writers. For example, Philip D. Ortego's *We Are Chicanos: An Anthology of Mexican American Literature* (1973) includes only nine women out of forty-two authors. *Chicano Voices* (1975), edited by a woman, Carlota Cárdenas de Dwyer, presents only three women out of thirty-seven authors. *From the Barrio: A Chicano Anthology*, edited by Luis Omar Salinas and Lillian Faderman (1973), reprinted Enriqueta Longueaux y Vásquez's essay "The Woman of La Raza," the only contribution by a woman among seventeen selections.

These anthologies incorrectly suggest that

Chicana women were not writing. However, strong evidence of female writing activity appears in small journals such as those mentioned above. Among the few spaces available to Chicana writers were the "special issues" devoted to their works, a format that revealed the secondary, token value ascribed to them by their Chicano peers. Yet these special issues—Quinto Sol's *Mujeres en arte y literatura*, edited by Estela *Portillo-Trambley in 1973; *De Colores*'s 1977 *La Cosecha: Literatura y la mujer chicana*—serve now as invaluable sources for a historical overview of Latina writing in the United States.

Puerto Rican women in New York faced the same situation during the flourishing of the Nuyorican literary movement in the 1970s. Only two or three women poets are included in Miguel Algarín and Miguel Piñero's *Nuyorican Poetry: An Anthology of Words and Feelings*, the representative volume of that movement. *Woman Rise* (1978), edited by Louis Reyes Rivera, seems to be the only anthology dedicated to Puerto Rican women writers during this period. Any general bibliography on U.S. Puerto Rican literature from the seventies and eighties reveals the dearth of women authors among Nuyorican publications. Sandra María Esteves and Nicholasa Mohr are the only female names that have appeared with regularity.

Lourdes Gil, editor of the New Jersey–based Cuban literary quarterly *Lyra* (cofounded in 1987 with Iraida Iturralde), believes that the major obstacle for Cuban and Cuban-American women has been the way men publishers segregate them as "women writers," thus defining them a priori on the basis of their biological sex and not on the value or interest of their writings. In her opinion, some women have been included in anthologies, publications, and literary events merely in order to fill a quota.

Chicana, U.S. Puerto Rican, and Cuban women writers have been actively writing, notwithstanding their early absence in print. Their poems have appeared in chapbooks, and their works have been published by small presses. Bernice Zamora's *Restless Serpents* (1976), Margarita Cota-Cárdenas's *Noche despertando In/ conciencias* (1975), Eliana Rivero's *Cuerpos breves* (1977), and Ana Castillo's *Otro canto* (1977) are but a few examples. Luz María Umpierre's *Una puertorriqueña en Penna*, for instance, was first published in San Juan, Puerto Rico, in 1979, while Iris Zavala's poems appeared in Puerto Rico under the title *Escritura desatada: Poemas 1970–1973*. The works of the Cuban writer Uva Clavijo (*Versos de exilio*, 1974), and *Ni verdad ni mentira y otros cuentos*, 1977) remain virtually invisible to an Anglo reading audience. Cuban and Puerto Rican women writers who write in the United States

and in Spanish—Belkis Cuza Malé, Iris Zavala, Eliana Rivero, Rosario Ferré, Carmen Valle, Giannina Braschi—have to publish either in Spain or in Latin America, thus never really participating as writers of the country in which they live. All of these voices in Spanish will remain unread and on the margins until academia is willing to expand the monolingual base of the U.S. literary canon. In conversations, Lourdes Gil has reaffirmed the double axis of language and gender that has been used to prevent those women writing in Spanish from entering the mainstream.

Thus, the so-called explosion of Latina publications during the 1980s should be understood not as a sudden outburst but as a logical consequence of a collective movement of Latinas writing their selves on the margins of the literary establishment. The 1980s was definitely the decade of Latina writing in the United States. Latina writers have transformed the face of Chicano literature and criticism, not only by their presence and their words but also by bringing to the foreground issues of gender, sexuality, language, race, nationalism, and class that had been previously repressed by their male counterparts.

The emergence of Chicana feminist critics such as Gloria *Anzaldúa, Norma Alarcón, María Herrera Sobek, Angie Chabram, Theresa McKenna, and Sonia Saldívar-Hull, among others, is granting academic value and recognition to the outpouring of poetry, narrative, drama, and essays by Chicana writers Sandra Cisneros, Ana Castillo, Denise Chávez, Lorna Dee Cervantes, Pat Mora, Cherríe Moraga, Angela de Hoyos, Lucha Corpi, Helena María *Viramontes, and Roberta Fernández, thus obliging the U.S. literary establishment to pay attention to this community of women writers. As María Herrera-Sobek has pointed out in her introduction to *Chicana Creativity and Criticism* (1987), the initial success of many of these women authors encouraged Latino publishing houses to take the risk of publishing their later works.

The establishment and consolidation of Latino and Latina publishing houses in the 1980s has helped create the national visibility that some of these authors are now enjoying. The gradual movement from national paradigms to Latino organizations has also been a central development during this decade. Arte Público Press, established by Nicolás Kanellos in 1979 at Indiana University Northwest and relocated to Houston in 1980, where it is now based, was a pioneer in this effort. Perhaps due to its Midwest location, *Revista Chicano-Riqueña*, the journal published by Arte Público and first printed in 1972, may have been the first Latino journal to include more than one national group within its pages. While *Revista Chicano-Riqueña* became *The Americas Review* in the late 1980s in order to represent the larger pan-Latino growth in the United States and to embrace Latin American writers as well, Arte Público Press was extremely busy printing *The House on Mango Street* (1985) by Sandra Cisneros, all of the works of Nicholasa * Mohr, Ana Castillo's *Women are Not Roses* (1984), Evangelina Vigil's *Thirty an' Seen a Lot* (1983), Angela de Hoyos's *Woman, Woman* (1985), and Pat Mora's *Chants* (1984) and *Borders* (1986).

Bilingual Review Press, directed by Gary Keller, and presently housed at Arizona State University, Tempe, is the other major Latino publishing house in the United States. Like Nicolás Kanellos, Gary Keller also directs a journal, *The Bilingual Review*, and has been instrumental in publishing works by Latinas. In the eighties, Bilingual Review Press printed, among others, Estela Portillo's *Trini* (1986), Ana Castillo's *The Mixquiahuala Letters* (1986), Judith Ortiz * Cofer's *Reaching for the Mainland* in *Triple Crown* (1987), and two bilingual volumes of creative writing (*Hispanics in the United States: An Anthology of Creative Literature*, eds. Gary Keller and Francisco Jiménez, vol. 1, 1980; vol. 2, 1982). *Nosotras: Latina Literature Today*, edited by María del Carmen Boza, Beverly Silva, and Carmen Valle (1986), was the third anthology published by Bilingual Review Press. Its value lies in its open submissions format that led to inclusion of lesser-known authors next to already well-known names: Chicanas (Anzaldúa, Mora, Viramontes, Castillo, Villanueva), Puerto Ricans (Ortiz Cofer, Magaly Quiñones, Diana Rivera) and Cubans (Raquel Puig Zaldívar, Eliana Rivero, Achy Obejas, Sonia Rivera Valdés).

A number of major anthologies on Latina writing appeared during the 1980s. Dexter Fisher's multicultural anthology, *The Third Woman: Minority Women Writers of the United States* (1980), anticipated the multicultural efforts prevalent today. Arte Público Press published two editions (1983, 1987) of *Woman of Her Word: Hispanic Women Write*, edited by Evangelina Vigil. This anthology is divided by genre, and like *Nosotras*, it includes Latin American women writers in the United States. Along with creative writing, it presents criticism by Luz María Umpierre, Tey Diana Rebolledo, and Julia Ortiz Griffin, and reproductions of the visual arts, a triple format that will characterize many future editions and anthologies by U.S. Latinas. In 1988, María Herrera Sobek and Helena María Viramontes edited *Chicana Creativity and Criticism: Charting New Frontiers in American Literature*, published by

Arte Público Press and the Mexico/Chicano Program at the University of California, Irvine. This anthology includes proceedings from a second conference on this topic held on 22 April 1987 at the University of California at Irvine. It includes poetry by Lorna Dee Cervantes, Lucha Corpi, Denise Chávez, and Evangelina Vigil; prose by Denise Chávez, Helena María Viramontes, and Roberta Fernández; visual art by Carmen Lomas Garza and Enedina Cásarez Vásquez; and critical essays by Norma Alarcón, Tey Diana Rebolledo, Yvonne Yarbro-Bejarano, Julián Olivares, and María Herrera-Sobek. In 1989, *Breaking Boundaries: Latina Writings and Critical Readings* was published by the University of Massachusetts Press, Amherst, and edited by four women scholars: Asunción Horno-Delgado, Eliana Ortega, Nina M. Scott, and Nancy Saporta-Sternbach. This valuable anthology combines statements by Latina and Latin American women writers in the United States with incisive critical essays on Chicana, Puerto Rican and Cuban-American women authors. The bibliography is one of the most complete reference tools on Latinas, and its introductory essay summarizes some of the most salient issues facing Latina writers today.

This flourishing of publications by and about Latinas would not have been possible without the role of women of color presses: Kitchen Table Press, responsible for *This Bridge Called My Back* (1981) and *Cuentos: Stories by Latinas* (1983); and Aunt Lute Books, whose *Reclaiming Medusa: Short Stories by Contemporary Puerto Rican Women*, edited by Diana Vélez (1989), and Anzaldúa's *Borderlands/La Frontera* and *Making Face, Making Soul* (1991) have been used as major anthologies across the nation.

Latina editors are few in number, yet they have been major protagonists in this context: Xelina of Maize Press, Lorna Dee Cervantes of Mango Publications, and Norma Alarcón, editor of Third Woman Press, have had a major impact in promoting works by Latinas. In a written interview, Alarcón recounts the beginnings of *Third Woman*. She initiated her press on a shoestring budget after having attended a Latina writers and artists caucus at a women's studies conference in Chicago. Feeling isolated in the Midwest, she thought that through a journal Latinas could make themselves visible not just to the world out there, but most important, to each other. Inspired by Rosario Castellanos's statement "We must invent ourselves," in 1980 Alarcón prepared the first issue of *Third Woman* journal, with Sandra Cisneros on its cover. Since then, Third Woman has discontinued the journal but has consistently published important editions, anthologies, and books by Latina writers, activists, and cultural workers. The anthology on *Chicana Lesbians: The Girls Our Mothers Warned Us About*, edited by Carla Trujillo, won the LAMBDA prize for best anthology. Along with *The Sexuality of Latinas* (1990), edited by Norma Alarcón, Ana Castillo, and Cherríe Moraga, and Luz María Umpierre's *The Margarita Poems* (1990), Third Woman Press has been central in making prominent issues such as sexuality and lesbianism among Latinas.

As head of a small enterprise, Norma Alarcón has been able to maintain her role as editor within a collaborative paradigm. She shares decision making, selection, and ideas with the women writers and activists interested in preparing an anthology. Thus, Third Woman has embodied in many ways the issues that have been relevant and important to Latina women both inside and outside academia. Also, it has promoted the works of visual artists and of young poets, costly enterprises that many other presses have rejected because of economic constraints.

The difficulties of managing *Third Woman* should not be underestimated. Funds for printing and distribution, the need for staff, and other material limitations do not allow Third Woman Press, as other small presses, to expand and meet the growing needs of a large writing community. Yet they serve as an important first tier for young Latina writers, many of whom go on to bigger presses with more staff and funding. These benefit in some ways from Third Woman's exposure of writers who subsequently have become famous, as in the case of Sandra Cisneros. Thus, there is a publishing path that, although not exclusive to Latinas, reveals an underlying hierarchy. Small presses such as Third Woman, Maize, and others open the doors for writers to enter into larger, established ethnic publication outlets such as Arte Público Press, Bilingual Review, and into feminist publishers such as Kitchen Table, Aunt Lute, and Seal Press. Afterward, some writers go on to larger, mainstream U.S. outlets: Sandra Cisneros moved to Random House, Judith Ortiz Cofer published *The Line of the Sun* with the University of Georgia Press, and Julia Alvarez published *How the García Girls Lost their Accents* with Algonquin Books.

The mainstreaming of these Latina authors and the recanonization of works such as Gloria Anzaldúa's *Borderlands* under the multicultural agenda may help create more visibility for lesser-known authors. Yet it is essential to recognize the important role of small presses, regional journals, and Latino and Latina editors in allowing previously unknown voices to come to the foreground and in substantially building a corpus of U.S. Latina literature.

• María Herrera-Sobek, *Beyond Stereotypes: The Critical Analysis of Chicana Literature* (1985). Tino Villanueva, ed., *Imagine: International Chicano Poetry Journal* 2, no. 5 (Summer 1985). Juanita Ramos, ed., *Compañeras: Latina Lesbians* (1987). María Herrera-Sobek, Introduction to *Chicana Creativity and Criticism* (1987), pp. 9–39. Silvia Burunat and Ofelia García, eds., *Veinte años de literatura cubanoamericana* (1988). Carolina Hospital, ed., *Cuban-American Writers: Los Atrevidos* (1988). Alicia Gaspar de Alba, María Herrera-Sobek, and Demetria Martínez, *Three Times a Woman* (1989). Eliana Rivero, "From Immigrants to Ethnics: Cuban Women Writers in the United States," in *Breaking Boundaries*, eds. Asunción Horno-Delgado, Eliana Ortega, Nina M. Scott, and Nancy Saporta Sternbach (1989), pp. 189–200.

Frances R. Aparicio

LATINA WRITING. *This entry consists of four articles that place Latina writing in relation to traditional categories of literature. The information provides both historical context and helpful descriptions of the many subgroups of Latina literature.*

> Overview
> Drama
> Fiction and Nonfiction
> Poetry

For further information, please refer to Assimilation; Bilingualism; Chicana Writing; Citizenship; Cuban-American Writing; Ethnicity and Writing; Immigrant Writing; Puerto Rican Writing.

Overview

In the United States, Latina writing embraces the work of Chicanas (Mexican-American women), Puerto Ricans, Cubans, and other South American, Central American, and Hispanic women writers. To denote gender and ethnic inclusiveness for these diverse populations the conflation "Latina/o" is used, usually interchangeably with "Hispanic," a term that is controversial, however, because its European etymon excludes indigenous and mestizo roots. *Mestizaje* refers to the mix of racial and cultural Spanish and American Indian elements, a hybrid that refutes the fallacy of racial purity underlying past Eurocentric colonialism and today's lingering racism. Latina writers and artists emphasize the bilingual, multicultural realities and complex figural possibilities of *mestizaje* throughout their creative production.

The female sources of contemporary Latina writing are usually traced back to Sor Juana Inés de la Cruz (1648–95), child prodigy and canonized poet of colonial New Spain, whose

Athenagoric Letter (1690) and *Response to Sor Filotea* (1691) argue for the rights of women by attacking the hegemonic principle *"mulieres en ecclesia taceant"* (women must be silent in church). Her analysis of the negative effects of barring women from full religious rights and participation in the Church and, especially, the lack of access to formal education, remains valid four centuries after her birth, which partly explains the esteem she receives from both revisionary feminists and orthodox canonists. An equal argument can be made for tracing the genesis of an ars poetica for Latinas, and possibly for all women of the Americas, to an even earlier prefeminist foremother: *La Malinche, the interpreter-guide-mistress of the Spanish conqueror Cortés. She was the first post-Columbian American woman forced to confront such difficult issues as competing ethnic loyalties, the balance between public and private roles, and culture-based gendering—still defining issues for Latinas. Due to her high profile in the conquest (1519–21) she was forced to serve both her European master and the norms of her internalized Nahua (Aztec) and Maya identity by interpreting often contradictory languages and cultures. From the very beginning her pivotal role as interlocutor between the Spanish Christian and the Aztec pantheistic empires, coupled with the required sexual service to Cortés, positioned her in the challenging margins of biculturality—like hyphenated American women of color ever since and, indeed, like all women caught between patriarchal strictures and the desire for self-definition. Moreover, her intellect and imagination were keyed to such crucial literary concerns as audience, re/presentation, semantic nuance, and discursive choices, making her pragmatically, if not theoretically, conscious of the gender, racial, and classist inflections of language that still command writerly interest. With her sui generis historical role, these attributes account for her germinal place in the hemisphere's literary history and Latina discourse.

In addition to Sor Juana and La Malinche, other women writers of the Americas have encountered the link between gender and genre and female experience and cultural expression in anticipation of contemporary writers. Two well-known prefeminist examples are the Cuban Gertrudis Gómez de Avellaneda (1814–73), another prodigy whose collected works comprise over a dozen hefty volumes, and the celebrated Chilean educator and diplomat Gabriela Mistral (1889–1957), who was the first Latin American and the first woman poet to receive the Nobel Prize in literature (1945). Other foremothers include the Argentine Alfonsina Storni (1892–1938), whose *Complete Works* (1961) dis-

close a striking oxymoronic blend of feminist and feminine eroticism; the Chicana Josephina *Niggli (b. 1910), whose *Mexican Village* (1945) and *Step Down Elder Brother* (1947) link economic oppression and loss of landbase to the cultural identity of Mexican Americans; the Puerto Rican Julia de Burgos (1914–53), whose poetry and prose (e.g., *Poems in Twenty Furrows* 1938) employ nature and geography to illuminate human experience; and the feminist Mexican writer Rosario Castellanos (1925–74), whose radical feminism fuels all her ideas in prose fiction, essay, drama, and poetry (see the bilingual anthology, *Meditation on the Threshold*, 1988). Marked by the intelligence and subtle crafting typical of pioneer women writers of earlier generations, these and other Latinas challenged the religious and political hierarchies of their societies by attacking in their writings (and often in other arenas) the daily practice of machismo (male superiority), *hembraíso* (idealized femininity), heterosexism, homophobia, and several other unquestioned conventions.

Contemporary U.S. Latinas continue the challenge to such prevailing monomyths by writing in a variety of ways about three broad themes of *mestizaje:* (a) their roots in a culture whose North American heritage antedates that of later immigrants from England and Europe; (b) their altered citizenship after the 1848 Treaty of Guadalupe Hidalgo ended the U.S.–Mexican War and after the diasporas following the Mexican Revolution of 1910 and post–World War II liberation movements; and (c) the interplay between race, ethnicity, class, and gender in the forging of self-identity and creative discourse. The effects of their compound historical identity find poignant expression in, for example, Chicana poet Lorna Dee *Cervantes's "Barco de refugiados" (Refugee Ship, 1981) where her speaker concludes with a sentiment familiar to many Latinas, "I feel I am a captive / aboard the refugee ship. / The ship that will never dock. / *El barco que nunca atraca*." While resulting in the marginalization associated with a hyphenated "Latin-dash-American" experience, this identity also affirms the rich creativity derived from the quotidian texture of a lived *mestizaje* and its several aesthetic possibilities.

Among Mexican Americans (or Chicanas, a more politicized term), El Paso–born Estela *Portillo-Trambley (b. 1936), recipient of the 1973 Quinto Sol Award, was one of the first contemporary women to gain notice during the 1960s Chicano renaissance. Her fiction and drama integrate feminism and ethnicity with traditional literary and mythological themes (e.g., *Day of the Swallows*, 1971), and, as with many other Latina writers, Portillo-Trambley turns physical setting and geography to thematic purpose (especially to explore Chicana identity) throughout her work (e.g., *Rain of Scorpions and Other Writings*, 1975; *Sor Juana and Other Plays*, 1983; *Trini*, 1986). Other Chicanas whose writing feminized the predominantly male Chicano renaissance up to 1980 include Dorinda Moreno, who published one of the first multiethnic feminist anthologies, *La mujer en pie de lucha* (1973); Angela De Hoyos (*Arise, Chicano, and Other Poems*, 1975); Isabella Ríos (*Victuum*, 1976); and Bernice Zamora (*Restless Serpents*, 1976).

Writing strong treatments of the three themes of *mestizaje* outlined above are Ana *Castillo, Lucha Corpi, and Alma Villanueva, three writers whose steady output of well-received titles dates back to the mid-1970s. Castillo's poetry in *I Close My Eyes to See* (1976) and *Otro Canto* (1977) asserts a bold ethnic feminism that anticipates her later novels, *The Mixquiahuala Letters* (1986) and *Sapogonia* (1990), just as Corpi's poetic portraits of La Malinche in her "Marina Poems" (1976) helped define the next decade's Chicana revisionism of the much maligned, sexist-defined mistress and guide of the conqueror Cortés. Equally concerned with cultural origins, Villanueva, whose *Bloodroot* and the award-winning *Poems* (both 1977) exploit autobiography to express political resistance and personal affirmation, has turned to fiction to pursue her vision (e.g., *The Ultraviolet Sky*, 1988).

Enriching the library of Chicana/o literature in the 1980s and 1990s are poet Lorna Dee Cervantes whose acclaimed *Emplumada* (1981, with its often anthologized "Beneath the Shadow of the Freeway") has been joined by *Bird Ave.* (1989) and *From the Cables of Genocide: Poems of Love and Hunger* (1991) to reaffirm her vision as an artist and her skill as a stylist; and poet and playwright Cherríe *Moraga who gave voice to Third World feminism in *This Bridge Called My Back: Writings by Radical Women of Color* (1981, coedited with *Gloria Anzaldúa) and to Chicana lesbianism in the autobiographical *Loving in the War Years* (1983). However, Sheila Ortiz Taylor's lesbian novel *Faultline* (1982) introduced an out Mexican-American perspective a year earlier, and Gloria Anzaldúa expanded Chicana lesbian consciousness in *Borderlands/La Frontera: The New Mestiza* (1987). Also receiving notice in the past decade are three short-story writers: Chicago native Sandra *Cisneros (*The House on Mango Street*, 1985, and *Woman Hollering Creek and Other Stories*, 1991); East Los Angeles–born Helena María *Viramontes (*The Moths and Other Stories*, 1985); and New Mexican Denise

Chávez (*The Last of the Menu Girls*, 1986). Along with poet Carmen Tafolla, whose published work spans three decades (*Sonnets to Human Beings and Other Selected Works* 1992), these writers characteristically employ literary techniques and themes that disrupt received conventions, especially of linguistic choice and discursive method, and assumptions about culture and ideology.

Puerto Rican women share with Chicanas the bilingual, bicultural centrality of *mestizaje*, conquest, and loss of landbase. But the cultural identities of island-born *puertorriqueñas* also derive from their status as citizens of a U.S. commonwealth and their historical ties to New York City, where their socioeconomic subordination mirrors that of Chicanas and other women of color. Puerto Ricans on the mainland, "Nuyoricans," also experience the paradox of split national identity with its negative and positive dualities, particularly concerning the statehood issue, which has divided the island's inhabitants for decades. Promoting an intense sense of place and identity awareness among writers and artists, Puerto Rico's character is sometimes expressed through the myth of Boricua, the pre-Hispanic, pre-American indigenous name for the island that is often invoked (like the Chicana/o "Aztlán" myth) to idealize a self-determining nativist ideology.

Two Puertorriqueñas who helped open the gate for later women writers are Amelia Agostini de Del Río (1896–1980) and Julia de Burgos (1914–53), both prolific and established writers in canonical Spanish American letters. Agostini de Del Río, also a respected scholar, positioned her literary lens on childhood memories of her hometown, Yáuco, to evoke her native land (*Vignettes of Puerto Rico*, 1965, and *Song to San Juan, Puerto Rico and Other Poems* 1974) through the techniques of *costumbrismo* (regionalism). The celebrated de Burgos produced a considerable literary corpus, six books of poetry and three of prose (e.g., *The Sea and You Poems*, 1954), despite a brief, alcohol-shortened life. De Burgos is greatly admired by her Latina/o peers: writer Nicholasa *Mohr calls her work "matchless." Even de Burgos's earliest writing is acutely modern in its use of physical and political imagery to reveal personal psychology, as in *Poems in Twenty Furrows* (1938).

In the contemporary era Puerto Rican women's literature has been inspired by feminist writers Rosario Ferré (b. 1942) and Nicholasa Mohr (b. 1935). Ferré belongs to that handful of Latin American women writers (e.g., the Mexicans Elena Poniatowska and Rosario Castellanos and the Chileans Gabriela Mistral and Isabel Allende) who enjoy an international readership. Cofounder of the influential journal

Zona de carga y descarga in 1971, Ferré traces the roots of her progressivism to her childhood in an aristocratic political family surrounded by poor, disempowered workers. From her best-known feminist story, "The Youngest Doll" (1976), to her interrogation of femininity in *Pandora's Papers* (1976), to her children's literature, Ferré's body of work offers a critique of unexamined classist and gender beliefs. Nicholasa Mohr, unlike her predecessors, writes in English, "the language that gives life to my work." Focusing on New York's Puerto Rican history and sociology, her fiction juxtaposes island cultural tradition with urban naturalism to disclose the complexity and contradictions of the diaspora experience (*Nilda*, 1974, and *El Bronx Remembered*, 1979).

Also manifesting Borinquen literary creativity are the contributions of poets Sandra Estévez (b. 1948) and Luz María Úmpièrre (b. 1939), both active participants in the post-sixties Puerto Rican artistic and political climate. Estévez's oppositional discourse (e.g., *Tropical Rains: A Bilingual Downpour*, 1984) includes a poetic "conversation" with Julia de Burgos that simultaneously acknowledges her literary foremother's importance as mentor while also interrogating the meaning of the alcoholic poet's early death ("To Julia and Me" in *Spearmint: Drawings and Poems*, 1980). Stylistically different, Úmpièrre insists on bold experimentation in language and form, as in her favorably noticed *A Puertorriqueña in Penn* (1978) and *And Other Misfortunes* (1985). Along with Judith Ortiz Cofer (*Peregrina*, 1986), Ana Lydia Vega (*Pasión de historia*, 1987), Carmen Valle (*Glenn Miller and a Few Lives Later*, 1983), and others who have inscribed the concrete immediacy of Puerto Rican experience, these Latinas memorialize the impact of island and mainland *mestizaje* on the psyche, culture, and literature of the Americas.

Cuban-American women writers and artists also explore the texture of a split island/mainland consciousness, but they must contend as well with the evolving effects of the revolution of 1959, which replaced the colonialist Batista dictatorship with Castro's communism, resulting in the hostile U.S. policy of economic sanction. Although the aftermath of revolution and diaspora problematize Cuban personal identity and literary production in uniquely contemporary ways, their underlying themes surface even in the nineteenth-century writings and unorthodox life of Gertrudis Gómez de Avellaneda (1814–73), the canonized Latina of her century. Her abolitionist novel, *Sab* (1841), was published a decade before the North American *Uncle Tom's Cabin*, and she even threaded the plots of her romantic novels with progressive ideas about civil rights for workers and oppressed women (e.g., *Two Women*, 1842, and *The Flowers' Daughter, or Everyone's Crazy*, 1850). Gómez de Avellaneda's iconoclastic life was as extraordinary for her time as her work and included expatriating to Spain for greater personal freedom and electing to raise her child out of wedlock without shame.

Two twentieth-century Cubanas with similar intensity are Lydia Cabrera (1900–90), folklorist and fiction writer, and Lourdes Casal (1938–81), an essayist and occasional fiction writer. Still recognized for her groundbreaking recuperation of Cuba's African heritage, Cabrera studied and recovered Afro-Cuban folklore throughout her career. She published her research as documentaries (e.g., *El Monte: Notes on the Religion, Magic, Superstitions and Folklore of Cuba's Negroes and Creoles*, 1948) and also reworked it into fictional narratives (e.g., *Negro Stories of Cuba*, 1936). Working a different orbit, Casal, an expatriate to the United States, published journalism, literary criticism, and some fiction and poetry (e.g., *The Founders: Alfonso and Other Stories*, 1973). The striking intertextuality of her fiction recreates Franz Kafka, Eliot, Rostand, and other canonical male writers by placing them alongside familiar icons of popular culture in order to write/right herself "always on the margins between these rocks" of patriarchal power (*Words Gather Revolution*, 1981).

Playwright Dolores Prida and poets Mireya Robles and Nancy Morejón further demonstrate the vigor of Cuban creativity. An émigré to the United States, Prida, an active presence in the New York literary scene, situates her plays and poetry in North America in the English language with code switching to Spanish primarily as a metaphor of resistant ideology. Dramatizing the problematics of gender, she animates her vision of *"la liberación femenina"* with music, comedy, parody, and visual imagery (e.g., *Beautiful Señoritas* and the one-act *Coser y cantar* [To Sew and to Sing], 1981). Also an expatriate to the United States, Mireya Robles, a professor of literature, has published poetry that presents the inner and outer landscapes of her immigrant Cuban consciousness (*Artisan Time*, 1973, and *In This Dawn*, 1976). Her novel, *The Hagiography of Narcisa the Beautiful* (1985), explores the aesthetics of femininity and the ironies of conventional attitudes about women, beauty, and the sacred. Unlike Prida and Robles, Nancy Morejón chose to remain in Cuba to try to realize the revolutionary ideals that redefined her homeland after 1959. Writing in Spanish as a woman-identified poet in a Marxist society, she does not emphasize women's oppression or separateness in her work, preferring instead a poetics of collective engagement in which the sources of socioeconomic suffering are shown to be rooted in the tyrannies of the past and strength lies in the will to break away from them (e.g., "Black Woman" and "April," 1985). Even her love poems are resolutely centered in a communal vision that comprehends the "shining moments" and "stony barriers" between lovers as inextricably bound to their struggles within a colonial heritage of interlocked sexism, racism, and classism (*Silences*, 1962, and *Love, Inscribed City*, 1964). These Cuban women (and such other writers as Hilda Perera, Belkis Cuza Male, Hortensia Ruiz del Viso, and artist Ana Mendieta) articulate a Latina identity and literary aesthetic grounded in the fact of their *mestizaje*, emblem of both a split consciousness as well as of a conscious synthesis of their femaleness and ethnicity.

Most of the Latinas discussed or mentioned in this limited space (limitations that prevent inclusion of many other worthies such as Nicaraguans Claribel Alegría and Giaconda Belli, Chilean María Luisa Bombal, Argentine Clarice Lispector, Chicanas Miriam Bornstein, Yolanda Luera, and Inés [Tovar] Hernández) explicitly forefront the multiplicities of Latina identity within societies that may be culturally and geographically diverse but that share Eurocentric, partriarchal history and values. Their individual mythologies of writing reveal evolving configurations of society, self, and other—the latter two often seen as interchangeable—that attest to an amazing creative achievement reaching back to La Malinche and myriad other premodern precursors. Latina writers of the Americas thus both deepen and expand the international feminist project.

[*See also* Assimilation; Chicana Writing; Citizenship; Cuban-American Writing; Ethnicity and Writing; Immigrant Writing; Puerto Rican Writing.]

Cordelia Candelaria

Drama

Theater has become an important artistic arena for Latinas working through issues of women's identity and cultural development, particularly in regard to their representation of two marginalized groups in American society: women and people of color.

Crucial to the development of a specifically Latina theatrical space is María Irene Fornes, the author of more than two dozen works for the stage. Born in Havana in 1930, she emigrated to New York in 1945. Her first play, *Tango Palace*, was produced in 1963, and shortly thereafter she was directing all her own work. Among her notable plays are *Promenade* (1965), *Fefu and Her Friends* (1977), *The Danube* (1982), *Mud* (1983), and *Sarita* (1984). *Cold Air*, Fornes's translation and adaptation of Virgilio Piñera's *Aire frío*, brought her a Playwrights USA Award. Much of her directorial and written work concerns women characters, such as *Cold Air*, set in prerevolutionary Cuba between 1940 and 1958, which centers on a seamstress who struggles to maintain her family in a whirlwind of emotional and political chaos. *Fefu and Her Friends* features eight women who reunite for a weekend retreat and unveil their hopes, regrets, and yearnings.

In addition to her prominence as a playwright and director, she has also been instrumental in teaching and mentoring a generation of Latina dramatists under her direction as Playwrights Lab Director at INTAR (International Arts Relations, Inc.). These dramatists include Lynne Alvarez, Migdalia Cruz, Lorraine Llamas, Cherríe *Moraga, Dolores *Prida, Milcha Sánchez Scott, Ana María Simo, and Caridad Svich, among others. Other important Latina voices of this generation are Denise Chávez, Estella *Portillo-Trambley, Josefina López, Edit Villarreal, Diana Sáenz, and Laura Esparza. All have contributed to a body of work that deals with culturally specific issues and the empowerment of women. Many recurring central themes include political oppression (Sáenz, Esparza, Sánchez-Scott), the relationships women have to traditional customs so often rooted in *patriarchy (Moraga, Cruz, López, Prida), the proscription of familial and cultural roles that constrict one's sense of self (Fernández, Svich, Simo), and the need to create a woman-centered *spirituality (Villarreal, Chávez).

Moraga's work has been groundbreaking in her exploration of lesbianism, sexuality, and the effect of male presences on women's relationships, as illustrated in the title of her play *Shadow of a Man* (1990). *Giving Up the Ghost* (1986) is one of her most significant works that deals explicitly with sexual abuse. The play has also been critically acclaimed for its portrayal of Latina lesbians. Caridad Svich's *Gleaning/Rebusa* (1992) explores the relationship of two Cuban-American women whose thoughts and superstitions reflect the inheritance of their mother's myths. Milcha Sánchez-Scott's plays have forcefully dealt with feminist issues. Her play *Latina* (1980) was critically acclaimed for its demonstration of differences as well as similarities between women from different parts of Latin America. *The Cuban Swimmer* (1984) deals with a striving woman swimming from Long Beach to Santa Catalina Island, and *Dog Lady* (1984) features a female runner who has been given a potion by a *curandera* that makes her run faster than any other woman in the race. The catch, however, is that she must run on all fours. *Roosters* (1986), which the author describes as "a tearing-away-from-home play," was aired by PBS.

Many Latina dramatists produce work that crosses over into related genres such as poetry, the novel, short story, acting, and criticism. Cuban-born Ana María Simo has crossed over into film with her first short feature *How to Kill Her* (1991), based on her novel-in-progress of the same title. She has also worked collaboratively with the Latina filmmaker Ela Troyano. Her play *Going to New England* (1991) charts the accelerating tensions in a Puerto Rican family due to each individual's history of oppression. The playwright and novelist Denise Chávez has recently edited the first anthology devoted entirely to Latina dramatists, *Shattering the Myth: Plays by Hispanic Women* (1992). Chávez's work has been a significant voice in the Southwest. Her *Novena narrativas y ofrendas nuevomexicanas* (1986) documents the collaboration between five women artists intimately tied to the Southwest who appear one by one with their dreams and devotions to a maternal figurehead. Evelina Fernández's *How Else Am I Supposed to Know I'm Still Alive* (1989) deals with the friendship of two women, one whose child has grown, the other who is thrown into a crisis when she believes she is pregnant in her middle age. Her play won the 1989 Nuevo L.A. Playwriting contest and was adapted into a screenplay and filmed for the American Film Institute and Universal's Hispanic Film Project. Josefina López is one of the youngest and most important voices in this generation of playwrights. She wrote her first play at the age of seventeen. Her work includes *If My Mother Knew, Real Women Have Curves, Food for the Dead*, and *Simply María or the American Dream* (1988), which deals with the myth of the American dream and the development of a Mexican woman in the United States.

Two important figures in the history of Spanish-language theater are Silvia Brito (Thalia Spanish Theatre) and Miriam Colón (Puerto Rican Traveling Theatre). When Brito came to New York City in 1961, Spanish-language theater was virtually nonexistent. She and other Latinas made a commitment to change this by establishing theater companies that would address the needs of Spanish-speaking communities. Like Brito, Colón saw a need to "take theater to hundreds of thousands of people trapped in the ghettos who, due to economic limitations, do not have access to theatre." In 1967, she founded The Puerto Rican Traveling Theatre with the goal of establishing a professional, bilingual theater that would emphasize the contribution that Puerto Rican and other Hispanic writers have made to the canons of dramatic literature while highlighting new plays by Hispanic playwrights living in the United States and making these plays accessible to the widest possible range of people. Other Latina producers, directors, and owners of important bilingual theater companies include Carla Pinza (Workshops for Latino Playwrights), Margarita Galván and Carmen Zapata (Bilingual Foundation for the Arts), Norita González (Mascaritas Puppet Theatre), Socorro Valdez (El Teatro Campesino), and Laura Esparza (Teatro Misión).

Spanish-language theater brings together the various cultural groups in metropolitan areas such as New York and Los Angeles where there are large Spanish-speaking populations. Many Latina dramatists provide translations of hallmark works in Latin American theater (Fornes, Alvarez), as well as write plays to directly promote cultural awareness. Esparza's play *I Dismember the Alamo* (1992) deals with the problem of language and culture for those who survived the history of the Alamo as Mexicans having to fight against their own people. Migdalia Cruz's *Rushing Waters* (1992) is a community-centered project for the Cornerstone Theater Company, whose goal is to work in collaboration with ethnically diverse communities across the United States. The play addresses Pacoima, a predominantly African-American and Latino community in Los Angeles, and its shared history, which includes colonization, drug wars, riots, and issues concerning the emerging multicultural family amid a changing California population. There are forty-six members in the cast; the majority are members of the community. By writing local concerns into the script and casting local actors in the roles, Cornerstone and Cruz work to open people's minds and hearts to plays that have been traditionally closed to them. Involving people of all backgrounds in the creative process works to build a new, inclusive American theater.

Other Latinas using theater to promote social awareness include Los Angeles–based Rose Sánchez and Ofelia Fox, who are Cuban-born and have written extensively for radio, television, and the theater. They combine comedy with serious themes, particularly those that affect women and Latinos. In their plays they bring to the surface homosexuality and *AIDS among Latinos, plus the difficulties encountered by immigrants and their expectations and fears. The filmmaker Lourdes Portillo is an important voice in Latina film and video. She and Susana Muñoz in their documentary *Las madres de la Plaza de Mayo* record the sense of unity mothers of *los desaparecidos* (thirty thousand people lost in a wave of kidnappings, torture, and murder in Argentina) gained among themselves by turning personal tragedy into a powerful political voice when they began marching in front of the presidential palace in the Plaza de Mayo in Buenos Aires, demanding to know what had become of their children. Intercutting the mothers' testimony with statements by government officials and background sections on the military, Muñoz and Portillo trace the development of this movement up to 1984, when the internationally recognized group had grown to more than twenty-five hundred members.

* Performance art plays an important role in Latina drama, for it provides a means by which artists can act out history in an autobiographical format, as exemplified by *L.A. REAL*, a one-woman show that explores the mestizo/Mexican (mixed Indian and Spanish) history of Los Angeles during the period from 1774 to 1900 and how this history is remembered. This history is retold through Rose Portillo, a mestiza who warns, "Don't reinvent me on your salsa bottles, your wine labels, your tract-home logos." Alina Troyano is a Cuban comic voice whose character and stage persona, Carmelita Tropicana, tells the story of her emigration from Cuba to become one of the famous dancing girls of Miami's Club Tropicana, which provides a cheeky look at stereotypes associated with the Latina woman. A number of Latina performance artists employ comedy to discuss important cultural issues, particularly those related to sexuality (Marga Gómez, Monica Palacios). Many performance artists are working to address multicultural issues between Latinas and other women of color, as with the work of Nao Bustamante who has performed in Mexico City, and Guadalupe García whose collaborative piece *La china poblana* addresses the pre-Columbian ties between Mexico and China.

There is an East Coast/West Coast dominance in Latina drama due to the nature of cultural production—theater on the East Coast, television and film on the West—and to the differing regional Latino populations. Chicanos comprise a large population in the West, while the East Coast Latino population includes those from Cuba, Puerto Rico, Chile, Colombia, and other Latin American countries. Most Latinas would like their work to be seen as successful within the greater scope of American drama. However, there is still the problem of getting the mainstream press to include Latina productions under American theater rather than in the often ghettoized space of Spanish theater which assumes that coverage by Spanish-language media is enough—a problem considering that many Latina works are either bilingual or in English.

• Linda Feyder, ed., Selections by Denise Chávez, *Shattering the Myth: Plays by Hispanic Women* (1992). María Irene Fornes, *Fefu and Her Friends* (1992), *Promenade and Other Plays* (1987; second printing, 1992), *María Irene Fornes: Plays* (1986). Dolores Prida, *Beautiful Señoritas & Other Plays* (1991). M. Elizabeth Osborn, ed., *On New Ground* (1987). Cherríe Moraga, *Giving Up the Ghost* (1986; second printing 1991). Asunción Horno-Delgado, et al., *Breaking Boundaries: Latina Writings and Critical Readings* (1989).

Tiffany Ana López

Fiction and Nonfiction

One of the strengths of Latina literature derives from each writer's ability to draw on the many traditions and experiences that come together at the crossroads in which she writes. Latina writers draw on the * oral traditions of song and story. They also draw on the written traditions of Latin American, Caribbean, and U.S. literature. Latina prose is exciting to read, in part, because it refuses to let literature and thought stagnate by refusing to limit itself to one standard language, genre, or tradition.

In the United States, Latinas were not considered a group until the 1960s, when the National Census began using the term "Hispanic" for all Spanish-speaking people living in the United States without consideration for racial or national origins. The 1990 census, for instance, records "persons of Hispanic origin" as composing 9% of the U.S. population, of which 52% are white, 3% black, .75% American Indian, 1.25% Asian, and 43% "other race." Of those identifying themselves as Hispanic, 60% are of Mexican origin, 12% of Puerto Rican origin, 5% of Cuban origin, and 23% of "other Hispanic" origin. Because of their significant presence, these three national groups are usually the focus of study in U.S. Latino literature. Since the 1960s, Latinos have fought as a group for civil rights and for recognition as a force within U.S. culture and politics. This fight and the women's movement led Latinas to form alliances with women of other minority groups. Today Latina literature draws inspiration from the post-sixties coalitions, and challenges the literary as well as the social status quo.

The tensions that translate imaginatively into Latina prose have varied over the years according to political, economic, and social changes. The early chronicles, letters, and literature of Cuba, Puerto Rico, Mexico, and other Latin American colonies were written in Spanish and functioned within the political and economic sphere of Spanish imperialism. In the nineteenth century, as the Americas fought for independence from European colonialism, Cubans such as José Martí wrote for U.S. journals and newspapers on behalf of Cuban nationalism. Similarly, Puerto Rican journalists focused on the strengths of their island and people in an effort to support and justify Puerto Rican nationalism. In fact, Puerto Ricans joined forces with Cubans to form revolutionary parties fighting for independence, Antillean unity, and the abolition of slavery. One such group was the Liga Antillana (1888), a working-class, interracial association of Cuban and Puerto Rican women in New York.

In 1898, the tensions changed when the United States won the Spanish-American War and took over the colonial position in such countries as Puerto Rico and Cuba. Puerto Rican and Cuban writers then began to focus on their Spanish heritage or on their mixed (African, Native American, Chinese, and Creole) heritages as a means of distinguishing themselves from the Yankees. Nonetheless, during the early twentieth century, immigration from these and other countries to the United States increased and so augmented both the cultural and economic ties between the United States and the Caribbean. Puerto Ricans, for instance, were sought as cigar and garment makers and as soldiers in the U.S. military.

By the mid-twentieth century the relationships of Puerto Rico and Cuba with the United States were following different trajectories. The Jones Act of 1917 had given Puerto Ricans U.S. citizenship, benefiting industries from Hawaii to New York in need of labor. The year 1948 marked the end of U.S.–imposed governors. Then in 1952, Puerto Rico became a Free Associated State *(Estado Libre Asociado)*, a status that gave the country autonomy within the bounds of a permanent alliance with the United States. This status left Puerto Rico in a liminal zone allowing for free travel between the island and the mainland and the legal movement of labor and goods but denying Puerto Rico representation in the U.S. government.

Since the 1900s, Puerto Rican writers have been divided between focusing on their Spanish heritage and their *jíbaro* (folk) heritage, between nationalism and statehood, and have been divided geographically as island writers and as what have become known as Nuyorican (which initially meant Puerto Rican New Yorker, then Puerto Rican American) writers. While island writers have been primarily from the upper class, interested in preserving their status by focusing on Spanish traditions and concerned about the preservation of *puertorriqueñidad* (Puerto Ricanness), some, especially the generation of the 1970s, have been interested in social change. Such an islander is Rosario Ferré (b. 1942), a short-story writer, poet,

journalist, editor, and literary critic, whose three books of short stories have focused on social change for women.

Puerto Rican authors began to gain prominence in New York between 1917 and 1945. They were usually workers who became involved in the socialist and the suffrage movements, or writers concerned with the political status of Puerto Rico. Luisa Capetillo (1880–1922), for instance, was a feminist labor activist who wrote for labor publications and on behalf of women's rights. Later, the generation of the 1950s focused their writing on the change from rural to urban life and on the immigrant experience. The Nuyorican writers have generally been the children of these working-class immigrants. Writers of the generation of the 1970s were educated during the 1960s. The Cuban Revolution, the civil rights movement, resistance to the Vietnam War, and the women's movement attuned Nuyorican writers to questions of race and class and to women's issues. Nicholasa *Mohr (b. 1935), for example, is a graphic artist who first started writing what became the novel *Nilda* (1973) because there was nothing written by or about Nuyorican women. She has since become one of the most prolific and respected Latina authors in the United States. Nuyoricans such as Mohr find that they have more in common with black, white, Latina, and immigrant writers in the United States than they do with island writers, who view them as outsiders. Critics and authors have argued about the degree of assimilation to U.S. culture in both island and Nuyorican writings. A number, however, now argue that as in Chicano and African-American literature, it is not a question of a minority culture being replaced by a dominant culture, but rather a question of the give and take between two interrelated cultures.

Cubans have had a somewhat different experience than Puerto Ricans. The Teller Amendment (1898) had secured Cuban independence, but after the Spanish-American War, the United States insisted that Cuba adopt the Platt Amendment (1901), thus assuring the United States ultimate authority in the governing of Cuba. The year 1959 marks the Cuban revolution against dictatorships imposed and supported by the United States. The U.S. refusal to recognize Castro, as well as the dynamics of the cold war, led to a polarization of relations. This polarization resulted in an incredible division between those writers who stayed in Cuba and supported the revolution and those who emigrated to the United States and sought the removal of Castro. Most of these immigrants belonged to the intellectual, economic, and/or social elites, which differentiates them from most Puerto Rican immigrants. Since the 1960s, the majority of Cuban émigrés have been those disillusioned with the Castro government. Thus, most Cuban-American writers have focused on the negatives of the Cuban revolution. Only since 1978 have such writers had the opportunity, which Nuyoricans have always had, of going back to visit their homeland.

Cuban writers in the United States consist primarily of Cubans in exile and Cuban-Americans. The generation of the 1950s, or the first generation, consisted of exiles writing nostalgic or anti-Castro literature in Spanish within the framework of magic realism, *negritud*, and other Latin American and Caribbean trends. This generation includes Lydia Cabrera (1900–91), a folklorist and short-story writer who was one of the first Cuban women whose main interests centered on the African-Cuban experience. These immigrants wrote in Spanish and focused primarily on Cuba.

Some of these writers, in living in the United States, changed their focus to include the immigrant experience. The second generation or the generation of 1966 writes in Spanish or English, code switches (writing in more than one language), uses Cuban-American slang, and writes with a consciousness of Latin American experience but from a U.S. perspective. Raquel Puig Záldivar (Cuba, b. 1950), for instance, in her story "Nothing in Our Hands but Age," focuses on the Cuban revolution's intolerance, yet writes in English with a U.S. university as a setting. Other writers of short stories include Uva Clavijo (b. 19), Lourdes Casal (1938–81), and Mireya Robles (b. 1934). The author and critic Eliana S. *Rivero (Cuba, b. 1940) argues that this generation's main difference from exiled Cuban writers is the writers' awareness of double identity and of their identity as an ethnic minority in the United States ("(Re)Writing Sugarcane Memories," *The Americas Review* 18, 3–4, 1990).

The tensions influencing Latina writers with roots in other Latin American countries have followed similar patterns. Writers from Central America, for instance, often emigrated during periods of civil war (in which the United States participated), and belong to the working class as well as to the middle and upper classes. Claribel Alegría (Nicaragua, b. 1924), for instance, immigrated to the United States in 1943. She has written on behalf of Nicaragua, criticizing the torture and violence of the U.S.–installed regime. Many others emigrated as a result of dictators who rose to power in the 1970s (again with the involvement of the United States), and are primarily middle- or upper-class women. Luisa Valenzuela (Argentina, b. 1938), who emigrated to the United States in 1979, has said that she wrote *Cola de lagartija* (The Lizard's Tail, 1983) in order to understand how military regimes came to dominate Argentina. The Chilean-American author Marjorie Agosín (U.S., b. 1955), on the other hand, has written such books as *Scraps of Life: Chilean Arpilleras: Chilean Women and the Pinochet Dictatorship* (1987) on behalf of women who cannot publicly criticize the government.

Frequent issues raised about Latina fiction and nonfiction include genre, language, and the representation of self and community. Latinas can be said to write fictional novels and short stories, and to write nonfictional autobiographies, *testimonios*, and essays. But to understand Latina prose according to these genres is to misunderstand the ways in which they are creating new prose forms. The issue of genre is often raised by critics questioning the line between autobiography and fiction or between narrative and poetry in Latina prose. Rosario Morales (U.S., b. 1930) and Aurora Levins *Morales (Puerto Rico, b. 1954), for example, created a book of short stories and poems, *Getting Home Alive* (1986). It is a dialogue between mother and daughter that sorts out their relations to family and friends, politics, and ethnicities, and grieves for lost people and places. As a whole, it could be defined as a dual autobiography or as an epistolary novel in which two women communicate through poems and stories. Eliana Ortega of Chile and Nancy Saporta Sternbach argue that this new Latina genre allows the voice to speak at the crossroads of poetry, fiction, the short story, the novel, conversation, and literary discourse (*Breaking Boundaries: Latina Writing and Critical Readings* 1989).

The *testimonio* is another genre that doesn't quite fit canonical U.S. categories. It is a first-person autobiography, yet its focus is usually public and communal, rather than individualistic and private. Latina *testimonios* often deal with issues of inequality and voice. Some of the *testimonios* recorded by the Center for Puerto Rican Studies at Hunter College, New York, for instance, are told by garment workers who struggled for good wages and respect in the workplace. The *testimonio* also appears in the form of novels, such as *Plantando* (1981) by Hilda Perera Soto (Cuba, b. 1926), which criticizes the conditions in which Castro's political prisoners are held.

In the 1970s, Latinas of many national backgrounds began to publish both academic and political essays. These essayists include Edna Acosta-Belén (Puerto Rico), Alma M. Gómez (U.S., b. 1953), Nicholasa *Mohr, Eliana Ortega, Eliana S. Rivero, and Iris M. Zavala (Puerto Rico, b. 1936). Many of these authors also write short stories or novels. Articles and essays written by such women follow in the nineteenth and twentieth century traditions of Latino journalism as well as in the tradition of the U.S. academy. These authors have been crucial to the focusing of attention on Latina literature and to the redefinition of the world of U.S. writing and publishing.

The question of language often focuses on cultural and national identity. Some critics argue that in order to be a U.S. writer, one must write in standard English, while others insist that in order to be a Latina writer one must write in standard Spanish. The majority of critics since the 1980s have argued that Latina use of Spanish and English in all their vernacular forms is actually the most successful way in which to represent characters whose lives are enacted in more than one language. Luz María Úmpièrre's (Puerto Rico, b. 1947) "La veintiuna" is written in a poetic prose that focuses on the sounds of Puerto Rican Spanish that surround the main character. Rosario Morales, on the other hand, writes in English, but uses Puerto Rican Spanish and Yiddish to say what can't be said in English.

In terms of the issue of representation of self and community, critics have focused on how Latinas represent the gender, race, and class of individuals and of the Latino community both in themselves and in contrast to the hegemonic U.S. culture. Since the 1970s, critics and authors have valued realism in prose because of the need to combat the negative stereotypes of Latinos and Latinas found in the dominant U.S. culture. But Latinas have refused to let this effort prevent them from writing creatively and imaginatively or from questioning their own culture's norms. In 1971, for instance, Rima de Vallbona (b. 1931) included a story ("Caña hueca/Hollow Cane") about lesbian lovers in *Polvo del camino*. In *El Bronx Remembered* (1975), Nicholasa Mohr wrote about homosexuality and teenage pregnancy in addition to writing about the struggle of immigrants in New York. This questioning of the norms is also respected by literary critics, since writers such as Ana Lydia Vega (Puerto Rico, b. 1946) have been praised for writings that question the norms that restrict women.

This issue of representation encompasses some of the most prevalent themes found in Latina prose. Characters often go through a process of self-naming, in which they gradually reveal to the reader who they are in relation to their community and to the general U.S. population. Women characters, in particular, become the center for reevaluating the roles of women as daughters, wives, mothers, friends,

workers, activists, and artists, as well as for reevaluating the relations of women to other women and to men. Sometimes authors focus on the spatial boundaries, such as kitchen, church, or street, that restrict characters. At other times they focus on the connections between people and between generations that enable a character's survival in a world of economic hardship, discrimination, and conflicting cultures.

In general, Latina prose represents individuals and their community in terms of the marginality of Latinas in patriarchal and Anglo cultures or in terms of their position at the crossroads of American cultures. Latina writers of fiction and nonfiction, like other Latina writers, face a problem of cultural invisibility within the United States that results in an assumption on the part of the hegemony that theirs is an impoverished culture. The excellence and profusion of Latina prose since 1970 should make clear the richness of cultures at the crossroads. This Latina prose has led U.S. academics to redefine concepts of genre. In addition, Latina prose has been a strong voice in the multicultural movement that has led U.S. academics to reevaluate how canons and cultures are formed.

[*See also* Chicana Writing; Cuban-American Writing; Latina Drama; Latina Poetry; U.S. Puerto Rican Writing.]

• Evangelina Vigil, ed. *The Americas Review*, special edition "Woman of Her Word: Hispanic Women Write," 11 (1983): 3–4. César Andreu Iglesias, ed., Juan Flores, trans., *Memoirs of Bernardo Vega: A contribution to the history of the Puerto Rican community in New York* (1984). *Explicación de textos literarios*, special edition "Literatura hispana de los Estados Unidos," 15, 2 (1986–87). Asela Rodríguez de Laguna, *Images and Identities: The Puerto Rican in Two World Contexts* (1987). *The Oral History Review*, special edition "Oral History & Puerto Rican Women," 16, 2 (Fall 1988). *Association of Departments of English Bulletin*, special edition on Puerto Rican literature, 91 (Winter 1988). Nicolás Kanellos, ed., *Biographical Dictionary of Hispanic Literature in the United States: The Literature of Puerto Ricans, Cuban Americans and Other Hispanic Writers* (1989). *Callaloo*, special edition, 15,4 (Sept. 1992). Ramón Gutiérrez and Genaro Padilla, eds., *Recovering the U.S. Hispanic Literary Heritage* (1993).

Lisa Maria Burgess Noudehou

Poetry

The literary production of U.S. Hispanic writers has been too often marginalized and underestimated by American academics and general readers alike. Latina writers have suffered an even greater marginalization, as they are rarely able to publish their works through mainstream publishing houses. Fortunately, this bleak state of affairs has changed dramatically in the last ten years, and the 1980s can be considered the decade of Latina writing in the United States.

The history of Latina writing in this country has often been linked to a political history of colonization and exploitation by the United States. This historical perception reveals itself in literary works that depict the social and political realities of being a minority in a country that once belonged to one's ancestors. However, most Latino immigrants came to the United States on their own for economic or political reasons. The main exception to this trend is the case of the Mexicans of what was once northern Mexico, who in 1848 suddenly found themselves a minority in a foreign country when the United States annexed what is now most of the Southwest after the so-called Mexican War. Puerto Rican immigrants began to arrive in the 1950s and continue to do so, and Cubans have arrived in various waves of immigration since 1898. Of course, there are Latino immigrants of other nationalities residing in the United States, but their numbers and literary output are smaller.

All Latina poets express in their work the need to recuperate a violated identity and to construct their own poetic discourse. The representation of language is a crucial feature among these Hispanic women poets. Bilingualism is one of their commonly used poetic tools that has been criticized by academics. Yet this is one of the most innovative and powerful characteristics of Latina poetry, which through the use of language expresses a bicultural reality and poetic identity.

Latina poetry characteristically reaffirms a powerful Latino heritage and vindicates Latina women who act as mentors and bearers of this heritage. Other salient characteristics that define Latina women's poetry are their homage to their history and their full awareness of the importance of re-inscribing a new future and space in the United States.

The discourses of Mexican-Americans, Puerto Ricans, and Cubans are varied and complex, yet all the Latina poets whose work began appearing in print in the 1970s share an awareness of their colonial past as well as their common concerns for the present. They seek to establish a unique Latina voice that draws strongly from their oral traditions and to then secure the dissemination of their texts through publication by publishing houses with Latino editors.

Among the most distinguished Chicana, or Mexican-American, writers in the United States are Cherríe *Moraga, Evangelina Vigil, and Sandra *Cisneros. To date, Cisneros has been the only Chicana writer to enter the mainstream of North American literature by publishing with a major house her collection of short stories *The House on Mango Street* (1985), for which she won the American Book Award.

Cherríe Moraga writes of the Chicana consciousness in an alien and hostile culture and dares to speak about the experience of being a Chicana lesbian. Moraga's work, first published in the late seventies, has contributed greatly to the awareness of racist issues involving Latina and Anglo women, putting the entire concept of global sisterhood under scrutiny. Her most important collection, *Loving in the War Years* (1989), brings to light these problems of race.

The work of Evangelina Vigil—especially *The Computer Is Down* (1987)—like that of Cisneros and Moraga, explores the difficulties in asserting a Latina identity in an Anglo world that emphasizes her differentness and her biculturalism. She often speaks of communities in her stories, and portrays her own household and its stability as a haven in a hostile world. In order to regain the self, these poets tend to inscribe into their text an almost mythic memory of their childhood that becomes a terrain full of safety and renewal.

Puerto Rican writers reside for the most part in New York City. The mythification of their island homeland becomes a form of resistance against the turbulent place they occupy in Anglo society. The nostalgia Puerto Ricans feel for their home becomes a constant source of energy and poetic imagination. Sandra María Esteves and Luz María Umpièrre, who write in English, are some of the most distinguished Puerto Rican poets.

Esteves is extremely lyrical, and her poetry is almost a poetic geography of her land, abounding with examples of tropical forests and *yerba buena* as in her collection *Yerba Buena* (1980). The tropical landscape also becomes a space for dissent, and her song and lyrics become a voice for rebellion and resistance not only against An anglo environment but also against patriarchal culture.

Luz María Umpièrre, in her poetic production, speaks with eloquence of the labeling of Latina women who, like most Puerto Ricans in the United States, are forced to do menial jobs. Umpièrre, herself an academic, discusses the difficulty of being a Puerto Rican professor in a hostile environment in her powerful collection *Alicia en el país de las maravillas* (1990).

Although Cuban women poets reside in different parts of the United States, most live in Miami. Their identity is less tied to the United States and more related to Latin America and its political turmoil. It has taken many years for Cuban poets to begin to express their double Cuban–North American identity. Most of the Cubans born around the 1940s began only in the 1970s to gain a new feminist awareness that was strikingly different from their middle-class ideology. Maya Islas's story *Sombras de papel* (1978) and Uva Clacijo's *Versos de exilio* (1981) begin exploring this dual reality of an exile living between two cultures.

Magali Alasale is also a very important Cuban poet living and writing in New York City since the 1960s. Her work, along with that of other Cuban women poets such as Eliase Rivero, represents a total distancing from U.S. cultural imperialism. Alabale demonstrates a strong alliance with the Latin American poetic tradition and explores political conflict through highly metaphysical and symbolic language.

According to Eliana Rivero, it was Lourdes Casal who in 1976 began to create a bridge between her life on two different islands, Cuba and New York. For Casal, Havana is the source of her identity and New York City the source of conflict. Her most important work that reveals this condition is *Palabras juntas* (1981).

Political exile echoes through the voices of the Cubans, many of whom fled Castro's communist Cuba after 1959. These poets-in-exile affirm their identity by drawing upon their rich culture of Spanish and African traditions.

Latina poetry in the United States has evidenced a forceful renaissance. The poets, aware of their female identity, bear witness to the women of their past and at the same time try to reinvent diverse landscapes in order to create freely and be recognized.

• Marta Vidal, *Chicanas Speak Out* (1971). Elizabeth J. Ordóñez, "Chicana Literature and Related Sources: A Selected and Annotated Bibliography," *Bilingual Review/Revista Bilingue* 7 (1980): 143–64. Margarite Fernández-Olmos, "From the Metropolis: Puerto Rican Women Poets and the Immigration Experience," *Third Woman* 1 (1982): 40–51. Luz María Úmpièrre-Herrera, *Nuevas aproximaciones críticas a la literatura puertorriqueña* (1983). Eliana Ortega, "Desde la entraña del monstruo," in *La sartén por el mango*, eds. Patricia Elena González and Eliana Ortega (1984), pp. 163–9. Tey Diana Rebolledo, "Abuelitas, Mythology and Integration in Chicana Literature," *Revista Chicano-Riqueña* 11 (1984): 148–58. María Herrera-Sobek, *Beyond Stereotypes: The Critical Analysis of Chicana Literature* (1985). Marta Esther Sánchez, *Contemporary Chicana Poetry: A Critical Approach to an Emerging Literature* (1985). Asunción Horno-Delgado, *Breaking Boundaries: Latina Writings and Critical Readings* (1989).

Marjorie Agosin

LAW-YONE, Wendy (b. 1947), novelist, short fiction writer, book reviewer. Born in Mandalay, Burma, and reared in Rangoon, Wendy Law-Yone is the second of six children born to an Eurasian mother and a Chinese/Burmese father. Her father, E. M. Law-Yone, was the founder and publisher of the *Nation*, Rangoon's leading English-language daily; in 1960, he won the Asian equivalent of the Pulitzer Prize for journalism.

Law-Yone's childhood was a turbulent time, encompassing Burma's independence from British rule in 1948, a military coup in 1962 ending a parliamentary democracy, and her father's imprisonment without charges or trial from 1963–1968. Attempting to escape from the police state in 1967, she too was arrested and held for two weeks' interrogation before being inexplicably allowed to leave the country. She was the first Burmese citizen to leave in two years, and the only passenger on the departing plane.

In 1968, Law-Yone married an American journalist, lived in Southeast Asia for several years, and reared twins. In 1973, she immigrated to the United States. In 1975, she graduated from Eckert College in St. Petersburg, Florida, and obtained a divorce. She began writing free-lance articles for the *Washington Post* and met her second husband in 1980. In 1983, *The Coffin Tree* was published. In 1987, she won a National Endowment for the Arts fellowship for her second novel, *Irawaddy Tango*. In 1989, she visited rebel camps on the Burmese/Thai border, where large numbers of Burmese students were in hiding from the brutal crackdowns following their abortive uprising against the military government the previous year. Her report appeared in December 1989 issue of the *Atlantic*. She now lives in Washington, D.C., with her husband, lawyer Charles O'Connor, and their two children.

The Coffin Tree is a poetic and haunting novel of the negative consequences attendant upon immigration. Arriving in a foreign country is, Law-Yone writes, akin to stepping forth on the moon. The new immigrant's sense of extreme disorientation, isolation, and alienation from all that was familiar and his/her total immersion in all that is strange can be so unsettling as to create serious psychic disorder. The novel's heroine watches her older brother's gradual disintegration and finally his * suicide before she herself succumbs and requires professional attention. Law-Yone tackles the incongruous and the strange with compassion and sympathy, in powerful language and striking imagery.

Amy Ling

LEE, Andrea (b. 1953), African-American novelist and journalist. Born in Philadelphia to a

Baptist minister and a housewife, Lee completed both her B.A. and M.A. at Harvard. In 1978, she traveled with her husband, Tom Fallows, to the Soviet Union for a year, keeping a *diary that became the basis for *Russian Journal* (1981). After returning to America, Lee worked as a staff writer for the *New Yorker*. She published a novel, *Sarah Phillips*, in 1984, and has subsequently published articles in a number of periodicals, including the *New Yorker*, *House and Garden*, and *TV Guide*.

Russian Journal presents Lee's experiences with a host of young Russians. The compilation of these encounters, with everyone from the student-informant Grigorii to the "hippies" who have adopted a version of 1960s-era American values, makes for entertaining reading. The portraits are vivid but not overdone, and Lee conveys the sense that hers is a realistic view of Soviet society. While dated because of recent political change, *Russian Journal* is nevertheless valuable to anyone wishing to learn more about daily life in Russia.

Sarah Phillips is an interesting, if limited, first novel. Somewhat autobiographical, the novel tells the story of a young black minister's daughter growing up in Philadelphia and eventually attending Harvard. The novel opens in Paris, where Sarah is sharing an apartment with her three French lovers (one frequent, two occasional) and then flashes back to chronicle Sarah's life before her departure for France. Originally published as a series of short stories in the *New Yorker*, the novel is more a loose collection of related vignettes than a coherent, unified text. The influence of such major works as James Baldwin's *Another Country* and *Go Tell It on the Mountain* and Alice *Walker's *Meridian* is evident; Lee has a good command of these works, but she does not substantially revise or improve on them, choosing instead to make her voice conform to their visions.

Since the publication of *Sarah Phillips*, Lee has written magazine articles on various subjects. In both the books and the articles, her prose is consistently clear and slightly sentimental. Lee is a capable and informative writer, and while her works may not have an extensive impact on American literature, *Russian Journal* and *Sarah Phillips* offer readers interesting glimpses of one person's reaction to social and political change in the twentieth century.

• Valerie Smith, "Black Feminist Theory and the Representation of the 'Other,'" in *Changing Our Own Words*, ed. Cheryl A. Wall (1989), pp. 38–57.

William R. Nash

LEE, Harper (b. 1926), novelist. Nelle Harper Lee grew up in the small town of Monroeville,

Alabama, and attended its public schools. Her mother, Frances Finch Lee, was a pianist; her father, Amasa Coleman Lee, practiced law in Monroeville until his death in 1962. Lee has two older sisters, Alice Finch Lee, who practiced law in Monroeville, and Louise Lee Conner. Her older brother, Edwin Coleman Lee, died at age twenty-nine.

Lee attended Huntington College in Montgomery, Alabama, and the University of Alabama; she received her bachelor's degree in 1948. She also had a year at Oxford University and some work toward a law degree. Moving to New York, she worked as a reservations clerk for Eastern Air Lines and British Overseas Airways—and wrote. In 1957, Lee submitted the manuscript of a novel to J. B. Lippincott. Enthusiastic editors found the work too episodic, so she spent roughly two and a half years rewriting. *To Kill a Mockingbird* was published in 1960.

Lee's childhood friend Truman Capote used his memories of her to create his character Idabel Thompkins in *Other Voices, Other Rooms* (1948). He, in turn, clearly influenced her character Dill. While waiting for her novel to appear, Lee traveled to Kansas with Capote to aid in his research for *In Cold Blood*. She told *Newsweek* in 1966, "I'm intrigued with crime, and boy, I wanted to go." Capote acknowledged to George Plimpton in an interview in the *New York Times Book Review* how helpful Lee had been, because of "a warmth that instantly kindles most people, however suspicious or dour." Capote and Lee seem to have sustained a warm relationship well into the 1970s.

Now acknowledged as a classic, *To Kill a Mockingbird* garnered generally positive reviews. Lee's greatest achievement is her depiction of a woman's memories of her childhood. Though careless readers are sometimes confused by the voice of Scout in the novel, William Going notes how we see "through the eyes of a child who now recollects with the wisdom of maturity." As in other enduring works of fiction, her themes of innocence and experience are simple, yet profound. Strong autobiographical elements can be seen in the characters of Scout, her brother Jem, and her father Atticus Finch.

To Kill a Mockingbird was a Literary Guild selection and a Book-of-the-Month-Club alternate. It was awarded the Pulitzer Prize for fiction in 1961 and also received the Brotherhood Award of the National Conference of Christians and Jews. The 1962 film version remains popular. According to *Publisher's Weekly* figures, by 1975, the novel had sold over eleven million copies.

Since the publication of *To Kill a Mocking-*

bird, Harper Lee has lived mostly outside the South. Though she has published no other work of fiction, this novel continues to have a strong impact on successive generations of readers who are motivated by a desire to understand the past of this region or who simply have the good fortune to discover a complex, moving story of the universal process of growing up.

• "Literary Laurels for a Novice," *Life* (26 May 1961). Fred Erisman, "The Romantic Regionalism of Harper Lee," *Alabama Review* 26, no. 2 (1973): 122–136. William T. Going, *Essays on Alabama Literature* (1975). Claudia Johnson, "The Secret Courts of Men's Hearts: Code and Law in Harper Lee's *To Kill a Mockingbird*," *Studies in American Fiction* 19, no. 2 (1991): 129–139.

Martha E. Cook

LEE, Jarena (1783–c. 1849), "the first female preacher of the First African Methodist Episcopal Church," as she described herself. She was born in New Jersey to free blacks who hired her out as a servant when she was seven. In 1804, she became a Christian and joined the Bethel African Methodist Episcopal (A.M.E.) Church in Philadelphia. In 1811, she married Joseph Lee, the minister of a black church in Snow Hill, Pennsylvania, and at about the same time, she felt a vocation to preach. But Richard Allen, the founder of the Bethel Church, initially refused his consent for a woman to preach, citing biblical grounds. Only in 1818, when Lee returned to Philadelphia as a widow and renewed her request, did Allen allow her to hold prayer meetings there and then to become a traveling preacher, though she was never ordained. Her journal describes her boundless energy in holding meetings, revivals, and "Love-feasts," and she cites impressive statistics: in 1835, she traveled 721 miles and gave 692 sermons, and in 1836, she traveled 556 miles and preached 111 sermons. Her prophetic power and charismatic preaching led to countless conversions of men and women, blacks and whites, rich and poor.

Originally published in 1836 with the help of an unknown editor, Lee's twenty-page work was titled *The Life and Religious Experience of Jarena Lee.* It included basic biographical information and accounts of her conversion, marriage, and "call to preach the gospel." This brief first edition reads like a unified spiritual autobiography. In contrast, the second edition, *Religious Experience and Journal of Mrs. Jarena Lee* (1849), was enlarged to almost one hundred pages and seems, after the same first section, like a travelogue in which Lee fills in certain repetitive details: the churches and towns where she preached, the types of congregations, the numbers of converted, the weather, her health, and special providences or miracles. Closer attention to the second edition, however,

shows the importance of this information: Sue E. Houchins, introducing Lee's 1849 work in *Spiritual Narratives* (1988), contends, "the travelbook quality of the autobiography emphasizes the theme of the woman preacher's literal search for a locus from which to speak." In their emphasis on the power of God's "poor female instrument"—as Lee called herself—Lee's texts support her feminist and abolitionist agendas.

• The following three texts reproduce part or all of the first (1836) edition of Lee's work and include an introduction and notes: Bert James Loewenberg and Ruth Bogin, eds., *Black Women in Nineteenth-Century American Life* (1976), pp. 135–141; Mary Grimley Mason and Carol Hurd Green, eds., *Journeys: Autobiographical Writings by Women* (1979), pp. 72–87; William L. Andrews, ed., *Sisters of the Spirit: Three Black Women's Autobiographies of the Nineteenth Century* (1986), pp. 27–48. The following text reproduces a facsimile of the second (1849) edition and also has an introduction and notes: Sue E. Houchins, Introduction to *Religious Experience,* in *Spiritual Narratives* (1988).

Kathryn Zabelle Derounian-Stodola

LE GUIN, Ursula K. (b. 1929), novelist, writer of * science fiction, fantasy, and children's tales, essayist. Daughter of American anthropologist Alfred L. Kroeber and writer Theodora K. Kroeber, Le Guin invests her imaginary civilizations with scrupulous anthropological detail. The mythologies, social customs and taboos, and language of cultural groups on such different worlds as Winter (*The Left Hand of Darkness,* 1969), Earthsea (*A Wizard of Earthsea,* 1968; *The Tombs of Atuan,* 1971; *The Farthest Shore,* 1973; and *Tehanu,* 1990) and post-eco-disaster Oregon (*Always Coming Home,* 1985) are presented as the logical result of social and ecological pressures. Against these backdrops, the individual undertakes a quest for self-knowledge within the context of an interconnected universe. Pondering the question "What does it mean to be human?," Le Guin rejects technological contrivance and speculative scientific theory, drawing instead on humanistic studies such as mythography, archaeology, psychology, and theology, as well as telepathy, mind speech, and precognition to demonstrate that humanness is a groping toward connectedness, toward communication without instrumentalities. The ansible, which links the Hainish novels (*Rocannon's World,* 1966; *Planet of Exile,* 1966; *City of Illusions,* 1967; *The Left Hand of Darkness,* 1976; and *The Word for World Is Forest,* 1976), is not so much an instrument as a concentrating field that permits instantaneous communication across space.

The recurrence of the quest motif in Le Guin's fictions, combined with her vision of history as both cyclical and disjunctive, allows her to explore * myth as a redemptive form of communication relevant to contemporary sociopolitical issues. The dystopian *Orsinian Tales* (1976), *The Lathe of Heaven* (1971), and *The Dispossessed* (1974) broaden the quest motif in order to consider the relation of individual conscience to history. *The Word for World Is Forest* can be read loosely as an allegory of American intervention in Vietnam. Widely regarded as Le Guin's most important novel, *The Left Hand of Darkness* is a heuristic foray into gender politics. In it, Le Guin imagines a world of hermaphrodites who experience gender only temporarily during reproduction. As a result of this nongendered environment, Winter's social systems reflect balance and avoid binary thinking. However, while the absence of gender ensures certain judicial and legal freedoms, the individual is as likely to suffer social restrictions on Winter as in a gendered culture. Only rigorous attention to self-knowledge, personal responsibility, and disinterested love *(agape)* permit freedom and redemption.

A self-described Taoist whose vision of the future is essentially optimistic, Le Guin demonstrates in her essays and fiction that even the most repressive conditions can be restored to wholeness through balance and incorporation of opposites.

• Special Le Guin issue, *Science Fiction Studies* 2 (November 1975). Robert Scholes, "The Good Witch of the West," in *Structural Fabulation: An Essay on Fiction of the Future* (1975). George Edgar Slusser, *The Farthest Shores of Ursula K. Le Guin* (1976). Elizabeth Cummins, *Ursula K. Le Guin: A Primary and Secondary Bibliography* (1983). Charlotte Spivak, *Ursula K. Le Guin* (1984).

Carol Schaechterle Loranger

LEISURE STUDIES is a contemporary area of inquiry although the concept of leisure was addressed originally by early Greek philosophers. Leisure connotes a number of meanings but generally, leisure refers to free time, recreation activity, or meaningful experiences. The latter description, which incorporates elements of time and activity, is most agreed upon in scholarly circles today. The general public, however, often identifies particular activities, such as sports, with leisure. Sports, like cultural arts, outdoor activities, or social interaction, are but one facet of the broader social construct called leisure.

Conducting research on people's leisure has been a visible topic of study since the mid-twentieth century. Until the past ten years, except for a few notable exceptions, women have not been visible as scholars/writers within the field of leisure studies nor has a discussion of women's leisure been evident in either the professional or popular literature of the United States.

The emergence of the contemporary women's movement of the late 1960s did not result in increased visibility for women's leisure until the late 1980s. Leisure generally has not had a prominent value in society. When questions were raised about the role of women in society, leisure often was considered less consequential than other important women's issues related to work and family. Assumptions have been made falsely that women's leisure is family leisure or that the work of a full-time homemaker is total leisure. As women are gaining liberation in many aspects of their lives, they also are gaining a sense of entitlement to leisure. Concomitantly, as women have taken control of their own leisure, leisure has become symbolic of the issues that can be addressed in other aspects of their lives.

The typical descriptions of leisure in North American literature related to free time and activity have emanated from a patriarchal view of leisure as the opposite of work. As leisure has been examined by female researchers within a broader context, especially in trying to understand the women's leisure, the definition of leisure as "experience" has evolved. The notion of experience suggests that leisure has meaning because it is freely chosen and because of the intrinsic value of enjoyment. The British perspective has guided contemporary American literature about leisure studies and particularly, the research conducted about women's leisure. The most recent scholarly study by women about women and leisure is the book by North American authors Henderson, Bialeschki, Freysinger, and Shaw (1989) entitled *A Leisure of One's Own*. The purpose of their book was to present a baseline for what is known about women and leisure and to suggest ways to progress in addressing further questions about the value of leisure for women. This most recent book describes a much different view than Pruette's (1924) book entitled *Women and Leisure: A Study in Social Waste* where Pruette argued that mechanical advances were releasing women from household drudgery while continuing sex discrimination had turned their new free time into useless leisure.

The literature written by women concerning leisure studies has paralleled the roles that women have played in American society. For example, during the progressive era in the United States when issues of economic, political, and social reform were paramount and women were realizing their struggle for the right to vote, much was written about the value of leisure for all individuals including girls and women. Jane Addams was one of the most influential writers, although she focused on recreation and leisure as a means for doing social work (see *The Spirit of Youth and the City Streets,* 1909; *Twenty Years at Hull House,* 1910). The period of time after the "roaring 20s" and into the depression, when women were relegated back to the home, was a period when social control of women's leisure was addressed. Authors who wrote about leisure were largely concerned that girls and women were treated appropriately (see Bowers, *Recreation for Girls and Women,* 1934) within the prescribed social roles. The period of the 1950s and 1960s and even into the 1970s resulted in very little written by women or about women and leisure. The leisure studies literature during this time was informed significantly by other sociological, historical, and psychological writing but women researchers were invisible until the 1980s. Then, women became involved in addressing leisure research and in focusing on women's issues pertaining to leisure studies. This focus on the personal leisure of women seemed also to parallel a concern with the "me generation" and with the "coming of age" of the women's movement.

Writers in leisure studies generally have not been sensitive to issues of multiculturalism. Since the study of leisure for women in general is relatively new, the evolution to acknowledge the real differences that exist among women is just now emerging. Neither has acknowledgement of differences between males and females been evident in the leisure literature. The assumption has been that women's leisure was like men's leisure with little questioning of such assumptions until the past 10 years. Further, few authors of color have been visible in leisure studies. The dearth of concern for multicultural issues and the lack of researchers of color, both male and female, is beginning to change and will be reflected in the leisure literature of the next decade.

A number of themes have emanated about women's leisure in both the professional and the popular literature. The *family has been a common theme addressed when describing women's leisure. The home centeredness of women's lives and the assumptions of leisure as it relates to ways women are responsible for family leisure are frequently described. The oppression of women in leisure as it relates to inequality of free time is also a constant theme. The sense of a lack of entitlement to leisure has been further examined by researchers trying to understand women's leisure. Many of these themes relate to *gender obligations that influence the lives of women in leisure as well as in other aspects of their lifestyles.

Much of the literature to date and the writings about leisure done by women have focused on identifying the problems that exist. Writers and researchers are about to embark on the next step of identifying ways leisure can contribute to social change. Solutions to "leisure lack" and ways to find "a leisure of one's own" will be the focus of emerging professional and popular literature as we move into the twenty-first century.

[*See also* Advice Books; Body and Health.]

• Jane Addams, *The Spirit of Youth and the City Streets* (Champaign, Illinois: The University of Illinois Press, 1909; reprint 1972). Jane Addams, *Twenty Years at Hull House* (New York: Macmillan, 1910). Ethel Bowers, *Recreation for Girls and Women* (New York: A. S. Barnes & Co., 1934). Karla A. Henderson, M. Deborah Bialeschki, Susan M. Shaw, and Valeria J. Freysinger, *A Leisure of One's Own: A Feminist Perspective on Women's Leisure* (State College, Pennsylvania: Venture Publishing, 1989). Lorine Pruette, *Women and Leisure: A Study of Social Waste* (New York: E. P. Dutton, 1994).

Karla A. Henderson

LESBIAN FEMINISM. Lesbian feminism is a variety of feminist belief and practice that emerged in the early 1970s in the context of the women's liberation movement. Lesbian feminist writers assert the connection between an erotic and/or emotional commitment to women and political resistance to patriarchal domination. As Nancy Myron and Charlotte Bunch explain in their introduction to *Lesbianism and Feminism* (1975), one of the early lesbian feminist collections, the "essence of lesbian-feminist politics is that lesbianism is political." How to define *lesbianism* and how to formulate lesbian feminist politics have continued to engage those within the lesbian feminist community.

The earliest—now classic—formulation of lesbian feminism appeared in "The Woman Identified Woman," a 1970 statement of the New York group Radicalesbians (reprinted in *Radical Feminism,* 1973). "A lesbian is the rage of all women condensed to the point of explosion," Radicalesbians asserted. "It is the primacy of women relating to women, of women creating a new consciousness of and with each other, which is at the heart of women's liberation. . . ." Early lesbian feminists saw themselves as the vanguard of the women's movement, as evidenced by the most frequently quoted slogan of lesbian feminism: "Feminism is the theory; lesbianism is the practice," attributed to feminist theorist and activist Ti-Grace Atkinson in Anne Koedt's 1971 piece, "Lesbianism and Feminism" (reprinted in *Radical Feminism*). But Sidney Abbott and Barbara Love (*Sappho Was a Right-On Woman,* 1972) report that what Atkinson actually said was that "Feminism is a theory; but Lesbianism is a practice," presumably making a distinction between rather than conflating the two terms.

In any case, the Koedt version has long served as the quintessential expression of the connection between lesbianism and feminism.

Lesbian feminism grew out of the radical feminist critique of *heterosexuality and the feminist principle that "the personal is political." In addition, the explosive emergence of the gay liberation movement out of the Stonewall riots of 1969, when male and female patrons of a Greenwich Village gay bar fought back against police oppression, shaped the emergent tradition. Women who had a long history of erotic attraction to and relationships with other women, along with previously heterosexual feminists in the radical branch of the women's movement, drew on gay pride, the example of black nationalism, and the hippie counterculture, as well as feminist principles, in formulating the lesbian feminist position.

Hostility from both the liberal and radical branches of the women's movement led lesbian feminists to found their own groups, such as New York Radicalesbians (1970) and the Washington, D.C., Furies (1971). Lesbian feminists throughout the country organized local groups in the 1970s and built or worked in a wide range of institutions—*bookstores, battered women's shelters, rape crisis centers, women's music production companies—associated with what came to be called women's culture. The establishment of such alternative institutions has led critics, most notably historian Alice Echols in *Daring to Be Bad* (1989), to portray lesbian feminism's transformation into "cultural feminism," an essentialist, apolitical, separatist retreat from the original principles of radical feminism.

But in fact, both critics such as Echols and those attacked as cultural feminists continue the lesbian feminist tradition, although they disagree about two central questions: What is the nature of lesbianism and what is the appropriate form of political action?

The association of lesbianism with resistance to patriarchy has led some writers to divorce lesbian identity entirely from sexuality. Early on, Ti-Grace Atkinson asserted:

> There are women in the Movement who engage in sexual relations with other women, but who are married to men; these women are not lesbians in the political sense. . . .
>
> There are other women who have never had sexual relations with other women, but who have made and live a total commitment to this Movement; these women are lesbians in the political sense. ("Lesbianism and Feminism," in *Amazon Expedition*, 1973)

Following in this tradition, Adrienne *Rich's classic article, "Compulsory Heterosexuality and Lesbian Existence," introduced the notion of the "lesbian continuum," which embraces women who resist male control but are not sexual with women (*Signs*, 1980).

Such downplaying of sexuality in defining lesbianism gave rise in the 1980s to a vigorous onslaught by advocates of sexual expressiveness, including champions of butch/fem roles and sadomasochism. "Pro-sex feminists" or "sex radicals" called for a resexualization of lesbianism and criticized the notion of "politically correct" sex. A part of the "sex wars" (which broke out over the appropriate feminist response to pornography), this conflict over the meaning of lesbianism takes place within the lesbian feminist community. Both Pat *Califia, who asserts the feminist character of lesbian sadomasochism because it plays with power in an explicit way, and Joan *Nestle, who defends butch/fem roles as complex erotic and political statements, identify as lesbians and feminists (*Heresies*, 1981).

The second major conflict focuses on the nature of political action and the desirability of separatist political organizing. A strong current within lesbian feminism emphasizes differences between women and men, or female and male values. Egalitarianism, collectivism, an ethic of care, respect for knowledge derived from experience, pacifism, and cooperation constitute female values, in contrast to the male values of hierarchy, oppressive individualism, an ethic of individual rights, abstraction, violence, and competition. Philosopher Mary *Daly, in *Gyn/Ecology: The Metaethics of Radical Feminism* (1978), takes this position boldly. She dismisses men as death-dealing necrophiliacs who drain female energy, both figuratively and literally, in order to stay alive. In a spoof of such arguments, Margot Sims's *On the Necessity of Bestializing the Human Female* (1982) purports to prove that women and men belong to different species.

The conviction that women and men differ in fundamental ways, along with discrimination against lesbians in the larger society and within the early women's movement, led to the formation of separatist groups and the formulation of a separatist ideology. For some lesbian feminists, withdrawing from patriarchal society was the ultimate political act. Marilyn Frye (*The Politics of Reality*, 1983) defines feminist separatism as "separation of various sorts or modes from men and from institutions, relationships, roles and activities which are male-defined, male-dominated and operating for the benefit of males and the maintenance of male privilege—this separation being initiated or maintained, at will, *by women*." In this way, women "are assuming power by controlling access and simultaneously by undertaking definition." In a fictional glorification of separatism, Sally Gearhart portrays communities of women fighting the murderous patriarchy with extraordinary "female" mental and physical powers (*The Wanderground*, 1978; "The Chipko," *Ms.*, September–October 1991).

But separatism is controversial within the lesbian feminist community, both because it is associated with lifestyle taking precedence over politics, and because of the *race and *class bias inherent in the assumption that women want to and can separate from men in this way. In the 1977 "Black Feminist Statement," the *Combahee River Collective voiced the latter objection: "Although we are feminists and lesbians, we feel solidarity with progressive Black men and do not advocate the fractionalization that white women who are separatists demand. Our situation as Black people necessitates that we have solidarity around the fact of race, which white women of course do not need to have with white men. . . ." (*But Some of Us Are Brave*, 1982).

Thus, the lesbian feminist impulse to separate, based on the conviction of female/male difference, ran up against the increasing recognition of differences among women. As black lesbian feminist Audre *Lorde framed the issue in an open letter to Mary Daly, criticizing Daly's Eurocentric vision in *Gyn/Ecology*, "The oppression of women knows no ethnic nor racial boundaries, true, but that does not mean it is identical within those differences" (*Sister Outsider*, 1984). A rich vein of writing by African-American, Asian-American, Latina, Native American, Jewish, and *working-class women—Cherríe *Moraga and Gloria *Anzaldúa's *This Bridge Called My Back: Writings by Radical Women of Color* (1981); Evelyn Torton Beck's *Nice Jewish Girls: A Lesbian Anthology* (1982); Barbara Smith's *Home Girls: A Black Feminist Anthology* (1983); and Carla Trujillo's *Chicana Lesbians: The Girls Our Mothers Warned Us About* (1991)—explores the differences among women who identify as lesbians and as feminists.

As a result, lesbian feminism has increasingly shifted from separatism as an end in itself to limited separatism as a strategy for providing support in the ongoing struggle against women's oppression. Women of color, working-class women, and Jewish women who have charged white, middle-class, Christian, lesbian women with failing to recognize their interest in working politically within their own race, class, and ethnic communities themselves argue for separate space to organize and express solidarity. Separately organized caucuses or groups based on specific identities may work

politically with women of different interests or with men; coalitions across the lines of sexual identity and gender are increasingly common. Lesbian feminists in the 1990s play important roles not only in the women's movement, but also in the gay and lesbian, *AIDS, antiracist, antiapartheid, Latin American solidarity, environmental, antinuclear, peace, animal rights, and union movements.

Lesbian feminism, then, has evolved since the early 1970s, although the core conviction that woman bonding has political consequences for the struggle against male domination remains. The "sex radicals" have resexualized lesbianism, and women of different racial, ethnic, and class backgrounds have pioneered in the deconstruction of the category *lesbian*. Although the term *lesbian feminism* is sometimes used to refer narrowly to those who advocate separatism and downplay the erotic aspect of lesbianism, the tradition, more broadly defined, encompasses a variety of views on the nature of lesbianism and political resistance.

[*See also* Feminism; Queer Theory.]

• Deborah Goleman Wolf, *The Lesbian Community* (1979). Susan Krieger, *The Mirror Dance: Identity in a Women's Community* (1983). Sarah Lucia Hoagland and Julia Penelope, *For Lesbians Only: A Separatist Anthology* (1988). Shane Phelan, *Identity Politics: Lesbian Feminism and the Limits of Community* (1989). Bonnie Zimmerman, *The Safe Sea of Women: Lesbian Fiction, 1969–1989* (1990). Lillian Faderman, *Odd Girls and Twilight Lovers: A History of Lesbian Life in Twentieth-Century America* (1991). Margaret Cruikshank, *The Gay and Lesbian Liberation Movement* (1992). Verta Taylor and Nancy E. Whittier, "Collective Identity in Social Movement Communities: Lesbian Feminist Mobilization," in *Frontiers of Social Movement Theory*, eds. Aldon Morris and Carol Mueller (1992), pp. 104–129. Verta Taylor and Leila J. Rupp, "Women's Culture and Lesbian Feminist Activism: A Reconsideration of Cultural Feminism," *Signs: Journal of Women in Culture and Society* 19, no. 1 (Autumn 1993).

Leila J. Rupp

LESBIAN HERSTORY ARCHIVES. Founded in 1973 by Deborah Edel and Joan *Nestle, the Lesbian Herstory Educational Foundation, as it is officially known, serves as both a repository of lesbian history and a place to preserve lesbian vitality and visibility. Housed at 484 Fourteenth Street in Brooklyn, New York, it is a grass-roots effort that recognizes and memorializes historical changes in lesbian cultures; the archives project also seeks to collect the memoirs, artifacts, letters, tapes, and photos that have told the stories of lesbian life. In contrast to the distortion and erasure of lesbian lives in legal, medical, and religious discourses, the archives were conceived as an effort to reclaim and validate lesbian identity as a vibrant, powerful historical force. The establishment of a specifically lesbian archive holds a political as well as an historical agenda, for it represents not only a radical project to preserve the history of a silenced and persecuted group, but it also challenges social (and often familial) efforts to deny lesbian existence. The archives currently holds the largest collection of lesbian memorabilia in the world, and it continues to collect everything associated with lesbian experience: historical documents, published and unpublished writings, clothing, work-related paraphernalia, news clippings, photographs, and remembrances. The archival space, open to the public and wholly volunteer-run, is meant to serve as a place to browse and to conduct both personal and academic research. Since its inception, the archives has helped bring into existence over five hundred new works of lesbian, feminist, and gay cultural creations, including doctoral dissertations, plays, documentary films, and literary pieces. The archives has also organized a traveling slide show to educate people about the purpose and significance of the communal project, and to encourage women to donate pieces of their own history for preservation. The exhibit offers writings and photos from the archives, and it strives to make clear to women that the archival project was founded as, and continues to pursue, a collective effort to preserve and validate the lives of lesbians of all races, classes, and cultural backgrounds.

• Joan Nestle, "The Will to Remember: The Lesbian Herstory Archives of New York," *Feminist Review* 34 (Spring 1990): 86–94.

Elizabeth Yukins

LESBIANISM. The statement "I am a lesbian" is an act of self-disclosure whose precise meanings, uses, and consequences cannot be determined without prior knowledge of the speaker's psychosexual history and the context, including sociohistorical conditions, in which her utterance is made.

One of the ways in which lesbians currently articulate lesbian identity is framed in the declaration "I fuck women." The verb choice alone links lesbians of the 1990s to lesbian sex-radicals of the late 1970s and 1980s, some of whom would have been identified as lesbian-sadomasochists (as would some lesbians who assert the centrality of sex to their identity today) and all of whom would have foregrounded sexual pleasure, partly as a self-authorizing affirmation of lesbian desire and partly as a counterresponse to the antisex rhetoric of the time. To simplify a complex historical situation, earlier lesbian sex-radicals, who were also feminists, took issue with the desexualized self-

representations of some lesbian cultural feminists and/or the redemptive model of strictly egalitarian lesbian sex they proposed; for by divorcing *sexuality from power, the model operated to exclude butches, femmes, and lesbian sadomasochists from the sexual world of lesbianism. This monolithic definition of lesbian sex prompted numbers of women excluded by it to speak on their own behalf. Among them were Cherríe *Moraga and Amber Hollibaugh in "What Are We Rollin around in Bed with: Sexual Silences in Feminism" and Joan *Nestle in "My Mother Liked to Fuck," from *Powers of Desire* (1983). Speaking from their own locations in *Latina and *working-class communities, these essayists not only expose the foregoing definition of lesbian eroticism as the sexually constraining and white middle-class construction it is, they positively affirm the sociosexual importance of the butch-femme couple to lesbians.

The 1990s lesbian who declares "I fuck women" advances an identity claim that is similar, though far from identical, to that of the 1950s butch. If the two figures are juxtaposed merely as historical models of lesbian sex roles, then, like her exemplary counterpart of the fifties, the conventional neo-butch is a sexual actor whose self-definition asserts "I am the agent of sex." However, unlike the butch whose pleasure resided in pleasing the femme, and decidedly unlike the ideal of the "stone butch" who would not allow being touched, the neo-butch is also something of a femme who, in the butch-fem argot of the fifties, "rolls over" to take her lover's caress and may want her to take the sexual initiative as well. The other salient difference between these two women is that the butch was most often a working-class lesbian whose proscribed role was as much a badge of her sexual identity as it was her *class identity, whereas the neo-butch is more strictly a sexual identity whose claimants are as likely to be middle-class.

In claiming an identity that is emphatically sexual, lesbians of the 1990s are responding to a particular historical situation in which increased "tolerance" for lesbians and gays as a "cultural minority" is coupled with growing hatred and fear of queer sexuality, on the one hand, and denial of lesbian sexuality, on the other. This denial is perhaps most apparent in the flat refusal of the U.S. government to even consider the possibility of HIV transmission among lesbians on the grounds that "lesbians do not have sex" and the widespread resistance of *AIDS Service Organizations in the early 1990s to developing lesbian-specific HIV prevention education, which is at least partly based on the same spurious assumption. In this sociohistorical context, the statement "I fuck women" is as much an HIV transmission alert directed to other lesbians as it is an affirmation of lesbian sexuality directed at nonlesbians who would rather we did not have sex.

The most common articulation of lesbian identity in the 1990s affirms the importance of sexuality in lesbian life while rejecting a definition of lesbianism based solely upon sex. The self-understanding of these lesbians is best represented by the statement: "My primary emotional and sexual commitment is to women." This proposition speaks to the experience of many lesbians for whom the affectional and the sexual are interconnected. It also speaks against the overly inclusive definition of lesbianism implied by Adrienne * Rich under the rubric of a "lesbian continuum" in her 1980 *Signs* essay "Compulsory Heterosexuality and Lesbian Existence." (Rich has since revised much of her earlier thinking and has particularly repudiated the essay's racist assumptions.) In essence, the continuum covers "a range ... of woman-identified experience" throughout human history and across multiple cultures, all of which is supposed to represent a species of lesbianism. In its attempt to unify all women on the basis of our presumptive lesbian likeness, the continuum systematically erased real historical and cultural differences. Not only did it misrepresent African-American women as identifying with women on the basis of gender over and against African-American men, it emptied lesbianism of any meaning whatsoever. In effect, lesbian desire was relegated to the closet; female heterosexual desire was assigned to the realm of the impossible; and all women came to resemble nineteenth-century American "romantic friends."

Carroll Smith-Rosenberg has written extensively about these female couples, as has Lillian Faderman. Employing different approaches, the two document the existence of passionate female attachments throughout the nineteenth century, ranging from intense * friendships between women separated by * marriage (common during the early and mid-century), to long-term female domestic partnerships that emerged with increasing frequency toward the end of the century, as growing numbers of white middle-class women entered the work force. All of these romances were characterized by intense affect and sensuality; some certainly involved sex. Still, it would appear that sex between nineteenth-century women was widely understood in much the same way that female sexuality is represented in the "lesbian continuum"—precisely as an aspect of woman's natural sensuality. Certainly, no romantic friend would have understood a sexual relationship with her female partner as an indication of sexual deviance or lesbian desire, since neither the sexual typologies nor erotic choices and practices they configure were culturally available.

"I am erotically and emotionally committed to women only" represents a significant variation on the second meaning of lesbian, which it repeats in giving equal weight to the sexual and the affectional, and which it revises in replacing "primarily" with "only." It is precisely the iteration "only" that identifies the lesbian separatist. In the 1990s, few lesbians so identify, if only because the sociohistorical conditions out of which lesbian * separatism was born and in which it came of age have changed. On the one hand, early attempts to purge lesbians from the feminist movement (circa 1970) by moderate leaders who saw them as a political liability, coupled with the systematic refusal to consider lesbian concerns as anything other than a "menace" to (heterosexual) sisterhood, sent a clear message that lesbians were not wanted in feminism; on the other hand, lesbian feminists had aspirations of their own, the overarching one being the creation of a "lesbian nation." From these two impulses, lesbian separatism emerged. Its nationalistic excesses and blind spots have all been well rehearsed. Suffice to say, its dream of a "lesbian nation" was impossible from the first, since the charter upon which it was founded said in effect: no woman may pass this border unless she agrees to separate herself emotionally, sexually, and politically from men, the last of which effectively excluded lesbians of color. Outraged by a stipulation that would have them ignore the oppression they shared with men of their race, lesbians of color repudiated lesbian separatism as a racist movement.

The fourth articulation of lesbian identity is a recent cultural phenomenon dating from about 1990. Its newness aligns it with the first articulation, as perhaps does a certain brashness; in most other respects, however, it represents a radical departure from existing lesbian paradigms, including the continuum, a portion of which it repeats. I render this articulation in all of its undecidability: "I sleep with men, but ...." In common practice, of course, women who make this claim end with "I am a lesbian"; however, it is precisely this end point that remains undecidable. What I propose, then, are a set of hypotheticals based on the locations of women identifying as lesbians without specifying what sort of lesbian they intend. Some are married women who claim they have always been sexually attracted to men, but are lesbian no less. I have little to say about this construction of lesbian identity, other than its deployment within the heterosexual institution of marriage is as semantically empty as it is politically naive. A more interesting, and to my mind more plausible, construction of "lesbians who sleep with men" is advanced by women who not only have a history of erotic relations with women, but also maintain psychosocial bonds with other lesbians and political alliances with lesbianism, regardless of their sexual object–choice. When these women say "I am a lesbian," they articulate a psychosocial identity akin to that of the continuum lesbian, for whom emotional commitment to women is paramount. What makes the 1990s lesbian different from her predecessor and excludes her from the continuum itself is her open avowal of opposite-sex desire. What distinguishes her from other sexual identities—heterosexual, bisexual, queer—is finally the lesbian name and the specific communal allegiances thereby implied. Some of the conditions enabling the emergence of "lesbians who sleep with men" can be found under *bisexuality. Two consequences of their emergence are a further splintering of lesbian identity, and, given the foundational definition of lesbianism as same-sex desire, a definitional crisis within lesbianism itself.

[See also Bisexuality; Heterosexuality; Sexualities; Transsexuality; Separatism; Woman-identified Woman; Coming Out; Queer Theory.]

• Karla Jay and Joanne Glasgow, eds., *Lesbian Texts and Contexts: Radical Revisions* (1990). Judith Roof, *A Lure of Knowledge: Lesbian Sexuality and Theory* (1991). Makeda Silvera, ed., *Piece of My Heart: A Lesbian of Colour Anthology* (1991). Joan Nestle, ed., *A Femme-Butch Reader* (1992).

Kate Cummings

LESBIAN LITERARY THEORY. Lesbian literary theories vary widely, depending upon how each theory understands the category *lesbian* and how essentially linked the category is to processes such as reading and writing. Brought continually into question through discussions of major issues such as the definition of lesbian; whether the lesbian is an essential or socially constructed category; how lesbian identifications and identity work; what differences exist among lesbians; and what relations there can be among a lesbian position (however defined), an aesthetic practice, and specific theories of reading and writing, lesbian literary theory is always on the verge of declaring itself impossible, even as it sketches the parameters of what lesbian theories and practices might be.

Lesbian literary theories are premised upon some aspect—position, essence, characteristics, worldview—attributed to a lesbian category treated as an identity or epistemological position. Theories of lesbian reading, writing, literary history, aesthetics, and cultural criticism depend upon the qualities of this lesbian posi-

tion. For this reason, debates in lesbian literary theory tend to take place around the problem of the definition of lesbian, a category that might extend from Adrienne *Rich's "lesbian continuum," representing a range of literal and metaphorical women-identified positions, to Catherine Stimpson's more literal lesbian, who enjoys a carnal relation with other women. Definition is a central issue in lesbian literary theory, both because of the political stake in asserting a definable, identifiable presence, and the emphasis on identity as a primary strategy in lesbian criticism, where identity and definition are linked in processes of reader and writer self-recognition. The problem with definition, however, as both Bonnie Zimmerman (1985) and Jane Gallop (1987) point out, is that it threatens to be either too inclusive or too exclusive. Definition tends to make the lesbian either a completely sexual category dependent upon heterosexual, patriarchal ideologies, or an undifferentiated mass so amorphous as to be useless as an epistemological point. While some definition is desirable for the purposes of founding lesbian literary theories, tracing a tradition of lesbian writing and identifying a lesbian aesthetic, too much definition delimits, becoming itself a disabling point of contest.

The assertion of a distinct lesbian identity often assumes the unproblematic existence of a lesbian reader and/or writer. Lesbian theories of reading and writing depend upon an idea of the lesbian as both outside *patriarchy and more in touch with an inherently female orientation; by virtue of her position and insight, this lesbian problematizes the reading of heterosexual texts and identifies and decodes lesbian texts. The lesbian reader is either alienated from heterosexual texts because of her position within patriarchy or is seduced into identifications antithetical to her position; she must, therefore, become conscious of how alienation or counteridentifications are produced. The lesbian reader is, thus, according to Zimmerman (1985) and Jean Kennard (1986), the conscious reader: she is able to work a double vision and manipulate conflicting identities. The idea of the conscious lesbian reader also underlies theories of lesbian *performativity, where the lesbian's greater consciousness of constructions of gender and sexuality enables her parodic performance of them. This lesbian consciousness is also reflected in Monique Wittig's idea of the lesbian position as that which challenges the heterosexism inherent in language and our conceptions of sex-gender relations.

A lesbian essence also provides the basis for theories of lesbian writing and aesthetics. Premised upon the idea that the lesbian's distinct position in patriarchy and different sexuality produce a markedly different writing, theories of lesbian aesthetics emphasize what are seen as the positive qualities of the interrelation of women: fluidity, mutuality, circularity, multiplicity, generosity. The idea of a lesbian essence that enacts lesbian sexuality produces theories of lesbian writing as an encodement and concepts of the lesbian as intrinsically postmodern. Seeing that the lesbian essence is something that must sometimes be hidden for political reasons, ideas of lesbian encodement assume that lesbian-identified readers will be able to "decode" a lesbian text hidden within a more traditional one. The lesbian text becomes a drag performer known only to those who recognize its costume. Linking the lesbian to contemporary postmodern conditions emphasizes lesbian radicality and ability to enact the fluid multiplicity that challenges modernist logocentrism. From this comes the perception of lesbians as a natural avant-garde, whose very marginality produces a sustained critique of patriarchal oppression while it produces a revolutionary, essentially lesbian writing.

Lesbian literary theories also shift as the result of questioning both the historical constancy of the concept of the lesbian and the assumed homogeneity of the category, whatever its definition. The estimable historical work of Carroll Smith-Rosenberg and Lillian Faderman demonstrates that the practice and perceptions of affectional relations among women and the emergence of the sexualized concept of lesbian itself are linked to social, intellectual, and ideological changes in culture. In so far as the construction of a lesbian history is connected to arguments for a sustained lesbian literary history, tracing the changing perception of women's emotional relations both enables a lesbian tradition by providing a means for identifying and claiming writers as lesbian, and brings such a project into question by showing that modern conceptions of lesbian are relatively contemporary phenomena.

As with any definition, demarcating within one category tends to ignore other differences; understanding the lesbian as a sexual or nonpatriarchal group focuses away from the race, class, age, ethnic differences, and differences in sexual preferences that exist among lesbians, making the lesbian less than a discrete category. Critics such as Barbara Smith and Gloria *Anzaldúa compellingly assert the differing dilemmas of lesbians of color whose positions within culture and community and whose priorities about and understandings of the intersections of sexuality, race, gender, class, and ethnic identity create a critical practice that seeks new ways of understanding and utilizing the visions enabled by a recognition of multiple intersecting positions and qualities. But even as the lesbian category is situated in relation to others, even as it seems sometimes to not exist as a useful point at all, it still embodies a practice of feminist challenge and aesthetics that might extend beyond categories.

[See also Literary Criticism; Queer Theory.]

• Jeannette Foster, Sex Variant Women in Literature (1956; reprint, 1985). Carroll Smith-Rosenberg, "The Female World of Love and Ritual: Relations between Women in Nineteenth-Century America," Signs 1, no. 1 (Autumn 1975): 1–29. Adrienne Rich, "Compulsory Heterosexuality and Lesbian Existence," Signs: Journal of Women and Culture in Society 5 (1980): 631–669. Monique Wittig, "The Straight Mind," Feminist Issues 1, no. 1 (1980): 103–111. Catherine Stimpson, "Zero Degree Deviancy: The Lesbian Novel in English," in Writing and Sexual Difference, ed. Elizabeth Abel (1982), pp. 243–259. Barbara Smith, "Toward a Black Feminist Criticism," in The New Feminist Criticism: Essays on Women, Literature, Theory, ed. Elaine Showalter (1985), pp. 168–185. Bonnie Zimmerman, "What Has Never Been: An Overview of Lesbian Feminist Literary Criticism," in The New Feminist Criticism: Essays on Women, Literature, Theory, ed. Elaine Showalter (1985), pp . 200–224. Jean Kennard, "Ourself behind Ourself: A Theory for Lesbian Readers," in Gender and Reading, eds. Elizabeth Flynn and Patrocinio Schweickart (1986), pp. 63–77. Gloria Anzaldúa, Borderlands: La Frontera: The New Mestiza (1987). Jane Gallop, "The Problem of Definition," Genre 20 (Summer 1987): 111–132. Marilyn Farwell, "Toward a Definition of Lesbian Literary Imagination," Signs: Journal of Women and Culture in Society 14, no. 1 (Autumn 1988): 100–118. Bonnie Zimmerman, The Safe Sea of Women: Lesbian Fiction 1969–1989 (1990). Lillian Faderman, Odd Girls and Twilight Lovers: A History of Lesbian Life in Twentieth-Century America (1991). Judith Roof, A Lure of Knowledge: Lesbian Sexuality and Theory (1991).

Judith Roof

LESBIAN PUBLISHING OUTLETS. Lesbian magazine publishing in the United States began in 1947 with Vice Versa, a short-lived journal written by one woman. In 1956, a major magazine, the Ladder, was produced in San Francisco by the premier lesbian organization The Daughters of Bilitis. The most significant reference point for lesbian life and culture in the fifties and sixties, the Ladder ceased publication in 1972, at almost the same time lesbian book publishing was born as a specific endeavor.

Following the Ladder, from 1972 until the late 1980s, about three hundred lesbian periodicals proliferated, and in many formats—magazines, newspapers, journals, broadsides, and newsletters. In recent years, glossy, slick magazines have emerged, some catering exclusively to lesbian interests, others encompassing lesbian and gay concerns. Deneuve stands out in the former category; the *Advocate* and *Lambda Book Report* are leading publications in the latter.

In the 1990s, magazines and newspapers reflect every facet of lesbian life, and offer unprecedented opportunity for expression to lesbian literary artists across the cultural and political spectrum.

Lesbian book publishing in the United States began in 1972 with the birth of three small companies devoted to literature reflecting the goals of the young, militant lesbian rights movement: Naiad Press, Inc.; Diana Press; and Daughters, Inc. Gay and lesbian rights struggles had always been mirrored in print media, but until 1972, the publications had been in magazine form only, and the change made possible a much wider audience, as well as some semblance of permanence.

In 1974, one book, *Rubyfruit Jungle* by Rita Mae *Brown, was published by Daughters, Inc. This book became a rallying point for lesbians in the entire English-speaking world, and is still widely read today.

Naiad Press, one of the earliest companies, has grown enormously, with 180 books in print, and distribution throughout Europe, Canada, Australia, and New Zealand, as well as Africa and much of the Orient. In its nearly twenty years of life, it has gone from being almost alone in the field to having ten other large lesbian publishing companies with which to work, and twice as many smaller firms, all dealing entirely with women's issues and strongly emphasizing lesbians and their rights.

The themes and subject matter of the earliest work reflected the rigors of the burgeoning civil rights aspects of the movement, with books about lesbians being only one facet of the overall worldwide oppression of women. But in the last dozen years, as the relative position of women in the society at large has improved, the books have begun to reflect some of the general concerns and interests of readers whose lesbian identification is more closely allied to the gay men's rights movement, and also of readers who read for personal identification and affirmation, rather than for political goals.

Accordingly, whole areas of widespread general literary interests are now being accommodated in the publishing of lesbian literature. Genre publishing, including mysteries, *science fiction and fantasy, thrillers and spy novels, romances, serious fiction and an endless array of nonfiction, is commonplace for the many lesbian publishing houses.

In 1985, international attention was focused on the book *Lesbian Nuns: Breaking Silence* (edited by Rosemary Curb and Nancy Manahan), with reviews in newspapers and magazines throughout the world, and foreign-language translations into German, Dutch, Italian, French, and Portuguese, as well as editions in England, Australia, New Zealand, and Ireland. Even the Flemish equivalent of *TV Guide* ran a dozen lengthy excerpts from the book in Flemish. The success of this work attracted a great deal of attention and interest in lesbian publishing in general, and in its publisher, Naiad Press, in particular.

The attention increased the following year, 1986, when the movie *Desert Hearts* was released in the United States (and later in all of Europe and Asia). It was based on the 1983 book *Desert of the Heart* by Jane *Rule, another Naiad author.

The obvious success of such publishing has attracted, in very recent years, the attention of the New York–based mainstream publishing industry, and this interest, though possibly ephemeral, has increased media attention to the phenomena of lesbian and gay publishing, and focused interest in the *civil rights aspects of lesbian works of literature as well.

A surprising and rewarding sidelight of the lesbian and gay publishing explosion is the enormous interest in thrillers and mysteries. The apparently universal language of the mystery, published throughout the world, has been a major force in exposing the concerns for personal freedom in the lesbian movement to the attention of the population in general. In the past seven years, more than fifty such titles have appeared from women's and lesbian publishing houses, and they have been widely accepted and read all over the world, and translated into western European languages and Japanese.

Katherine V. Forrest, the most popular and widely read of all the lesbian novelists, will reach a new plateau in her professional career in the summer of 1994, when noted film director Tim Hunter, together with producer Edward Pressman, begins filming the movie version of her best-selling mystery, *Murder at the Nightwood Bar* (1987), second in the stunning series featuring lesbian detective Kate Delafield of the Los Angeles Police Department.

The single most striking aspect of this flood of lesbian literature into western European languages is the general absence of *censorship and the universal acceptance of the books in society at large.

Considered a growing phenomena, lesbian literature is, in its infancy, a sizable industry in the United States, Canada, England, western Europe, Australia, and New Zealand, as well as just beginning in the Far East. It is clearly just a matter of time before it takes its place throughout the rest of the world.

• Claire Potter, comp. and ed., *The Lesbian Periodicals Index* (1986). Andrea Fleck Clardy, *Words to the Wise: A Writer's Guide to Feminist and Lesbian Periodicals and Publishers* (1986).

Barbara Grier

LESBIAN PULP FICTION. From the mid-1950s to the mid-1960s, a conjunction of social and economic forces produced a wave of widely distributed lesbian pulp novels. Important social factors included a new public awareness of and interest in homosexuality, which was spurred by the Kinsey Reports, as well as the entry of increasing numbers of women into the work force, which created more opportunities to encounter other lesbians and build lesbian communities. The publishing industry was eager to cash in on this new market, and the cheap mass production processes developed for paperback books made pulps widely available. Although many so-called lesbian pulps were written pseudonymously by men and were marketed to men, many others were in fact written by lesbians for lesbians, and represented the first widely available, sexually explicit representations of lesbian desire. The first paperback pulp with significant lesbian content was Tereska Torres's *Women's Barracks* (1950), which was targeted by the 1952 House Subcommittee on Pornographic Affairs. Ann *Bannon is the best known of the lesbian pulp writers (*Odd Girl Out* and *Women in the Shadows*, both 1959; *Beebo Brinker*, 1960). Other writers include Claire Morgan, Ann Aldrich, Kay Addams, Artemis Smith, and Jordan Park.

Explicit sexual content more or less disappeared from lesbian writing in the 1960s and 1970s, as lesbian authors wrote within the terms of *lesbian feminism, emphasizing the emotional aspect of erotic relationships between women, rather than "raw" sexuality and desire. In the 1980s, sex began appearing in mainstream *lesbian fiction; at the same time, a new genre of by-and-for lesbian *pornography emerged. In books, magazines, and increasingly, videos, lesbians as well as sexually adventurous women who do not identify exclusively as lesbians are producing representational and narrative works that have sex as their primary subject and sexual arousal as their primary aim.

The most established and well-known lesbian sex magazine is *On Our Backs*, begun in 1984. The name of this magazine is a play on the feminist newsletter *off our backs*, which served as a forum for many of the debates about sexuality and pornography in the early 1980s. *On Our Backs* features erotic photos and fiction, as well as informative articles, interviews, and reviews, all presented in a slick professional format. Other lesbian erotic magazines have included titles such as *Bad Attitude* and *Black Lace* (especially notable for its emphasis on representing women of color). Several collections of lesbian erotic writing have appeared, such as *Herotica* (ed. Susie Bright, 1988), *Herotica 2* (ed. Susie Bright and Joani Blank, 1992), *The First Stroke* (Cappy Kotz, 1988), *Macho Sluts* (Pat Califia, 1988), and *Bushfire* (ed. Karen Barber, 1991). Lesbian-owned and -operated video production companies are producing explicit amateur and professional pornography, with such titles as *Bathroom Sluts* and *Suburban Dykes*. These productions actively challenge the feminist claim that pornography and sexual representation by definition are oriented toward men and objectify women.

The new pornography is also breaking down the boundaries previously separating lesbian and gay, heterosexual and homosexual. In a recent explosion of small publications circulated through underground networks and alternative commercial enterprises, sexually marginalized voices are articulating oppositional practices, representations, and identifications. Low-profile, often short-lived, amateur magazines, with such titles as *Anything That Moves* and *Frighten the Horses*, stake out the terrain of a "sex radical" consciousness or practice that opposes the social hierarchy of sexual identities and acts (such as hetero is better than homo, monogamy is better than multiple partners, with a partner is better than masturbation, etc.) and that also challenges the stability and consistency of sexual and social identities. For example, *Taste of Latex* promises "an omnisexual magazine—all sexual flavors with no bitter after-taste of apology." *Taste of Latex* constructs its readership in terms of an attitude (sex-positive and adventurous) rather than a particular sexual or social identity. For comparison, *On Our Backs* is marketed to an explicitly lesbian audience, billing itself as "Entertainment for the Adventurous Lesbian."

The increase in sexually explicit material has coincided with the growth of the *AIDS epidemic, making the issue of safer sex central to a consideration of the function and role of this new pornography. Much of the new pornography incorporates safer sex information. For example, descriptions and photographs of oral sex in *On Our Backs* increasingly include a latex barrier, signifying that saliva and vaginal fluid are not being exchanged. Books like *Susie Sexpert's Lesbian Sex World* (Susie Bright, 1990) and *Sapphistry: The Book of Lesbian Sexuality* (Pat Califia, rev. ed. 1988) offer advice and information on sexual matters to women in a context that is both sex-positive and safer-sex-positive.

[*See also* Lesbian Writing, *article on* Lesbian Fiction; Pornography.]

• Laura Lederer, ed., *Take Back the Night: Women on Pornography* (1980). Amber Hollibaugh and Cherríe Moraga, "What We're Rollin Around in Bed with: Sexual Silences in Feminism," in *Powers of Desire: The Politics of Sexuality*, eds. Ann Snitow, Christine Stansell, and Sharon Thompson (1983), pp. 394–405. Alice Echols, "The Taming of the Id: Feminist Sexual Politics, 1968–83," in *Pleasure and Danger: Exploring Female Sexuality*, ed. Carole S. Vance (1984), pp. 50–72. Monica Dorenkamp, "Sisters Are Doin' It (Lesbians Making Lesbian Porn)," *Outweek* (5 September 1990): 40–49. Roberta Yusba, "Odd Girls and Strange Sisters," *Out/Look* 3, no. 3 (Spring 1991): 34–37.

Samira Kawash

LESBIAN SEPARATISM. *See* Separatism.

LESBIAN WRITING. *This entry consists of five essays, an overview followed by essays that analyze four genres of lesbian writing:*

Overview
Drama
Fiction
Nonfiction
Poetry

Overview

Lesbian images begin with *Sappho, but strictly speaking, lesbian writing does not, because the 6th-century-B.C. poet did not write her lyrics; she sang or recited them. Although several of the extant fragments of her work describe passionate love between women, lesbian writing as such could not flourish until the late 1960s and early 1970s, when the second wave of feminism lifted the veil of secrecy and shame from this love. Before then, writers expressed lesbian feelings—Emily *Dickinson, Virginia *Woolf, and Vita Sackville-West, for example, as well as the circle of expatriate lesbians who gathered around Natalie Barney in Paris in the 1920s and encouraged each other's work—but no political movement existed to affirm lesbian experience, to define a liberating alternative to heterosexuality, or to set lesbian love into an historical context. Lesbian feminism, however, provided that context. Without it, lesbian themes might have continued to appear in women's writing, but no body of work delineating a newly understood emotional and sexual identity would exist. Feminism, and especially *lesbian feminism, ended the isolation of lesbians and created a group consciousness that prompted many to take on the identity of "lesbian writer." At the same time, feminism also created an audience for lesbian work. Before lesbian feminism, the best-known popular image came from Radclyffe Hall's novel *The Well of Loneliness* (1928), which usefully announced the existence of lesbians, but depicted them as a congenitally afflicted.

In the past two decades, lesbian writing has undergone a metamorphosis. From its modest beginnings in a subculture that was invisible to those in the dominant culture, it has grown into a complex body of works that influences thousands of readers-heterosexual as well as lesbian. Several stages in this development can be identified. In the beginning, the very notion of open lesbianism was so daring that those who were out of the closet felt an extremely tight solidarity with all other open lesbians. They not only defended their sexual preference; they urged others to adopt it. The tone of much of their writing was upbeat and celebratory. By the end of the 1970s, however, lesbians of color had identified racism and class bias in the lesbian feminist community and thereafter the community no longer seemed monolithic. In the early and mid-1980s, as more work by and about lesbians became available, their diversity was much more accurately represented than ever before, but serious conflicts and controversies arose. By the late 1980s and early 1990s lesbian writing had begun to proliferate. Keeping track of it all, much less generalizing about it, became increasingly difficult, especially as work from other countries reached the U.S. Greater numbers of lesbian writers gained access to mainstream publishers, among them women who had previously been known only in the lesbian subculture.

Early Days. Lesbian writing began as a grass-roots phenomenon through poetry readings and circulation of work on mimeographed sheets, as with Judy *Grahn's poem "Edward the Dyke," for example. By the mid-1970s several lesbian press collectives began publishing newsletters, printed poems, and political essays.

Characteristically, the poetry made political statements and the political essays contained a great deal of personal narrative. Although periodicals such as *So's Your Old Lady* and *Sinister Wisdom*, which were aimed at a national lesbian audience, were not the first lesbian periodicals—*Vice Versa* in Los Angeles in the 1940s and the more widely circulated *Ladder* in the 1950s and 1960s preceded them—they were among the first to bring a radical perspective to the discussion of lesbian feminism. While much of this early work was ephemeral, it contributed greatly to the visibility of lesbianism, and its wide extent is well documented in Clare Potter's *Index to Lesbian Periodicals* (1987).

Contrasting archetypal themes of American literature—the flight from the city to a pastoral countryside and the flight from the narrowness of small towns to cities—appear in early lesbian writing. Cities were praised as places where sexual difference was more likely to be tolerated than in rural America. On the other hand, writers who settled on lesbian land collectives extolled the virtues of country life. Their city sisters were building women's coffeehouses, bookstores, and women's centers, three places where lesbian writing could be found. In addition, much of the early work took the form of coming-out stories, often fictionalized, as in Rita Mae *Brown's immensely popular *Rubyfruit Jungle* (1973), which was a cult classic among lesbians several years before it reached a mainstream publisher. Typically the coming-out stories were full of irony as the writers revealed a gap between heterosexual expectations and the lesbian lives they eventually adopted. Also ironic was the distance between the myth of tortured, twisted creatures some had internalized from popular prejudice and the women they turned out to be. With the exhilarating new freedom from conventional female roles, however, came the sobering realization that lesbians would have to support themselves for the rest of their lives. Nevertheless, lesbianism was portrayed as a grand moral, psychological, sexual and spiritual adventure.

Much of the writing in the 1970s was overtly political because lesbianism was no longer seen as simply a personal preference. Women who chose women as lovers and life companions characterized themselves as resisters of heterosexism and as builders of a separate women's culture. Headnotes of articles read, "feminism is the theory, lesbianism is the practice." In other words, far from being aberrant, lesbianism was portrayed as the logical consequence of feminist ideology. Thus a major theme of the writing was that large numbers of lesbians existed. Another was that the stigma associated with lesbianism reinforced women's subordinate status.

Lesbian writing of the 1970s typically contained a great deal of angry rhetoric about male domination, *patriarchy, and the erasure of lesbians from the historical record. Still, this work was neither dour nor humorless. Much of it was exuberant, high-spirited, witty, and even zany. Sexual pleasure was extolled. Jokes about the "tender buttons" discovered by Gertrude *Stein and Alice B. Toklas indicate that for all of their emphasis on lesbianism as a political statement, the early writers were keenly aware of participating in a *sexual* liberation movement. Many of them regarded butch-femme roles as an imitation of heterosexual life inappropriate for feminists, a position that was challenged throughout the 1980s by writers who identified as either butch or femme.

Articles in *Lavender Culture* (1978), edited by Karla Jay and Allen Young, reveal some of the concerns of early lesbian writing. Fran Koski and Maida Tilchen describe the fun of reading *lesbian pulp fiction of the 1950s; Jane *Rule recalls early influences on her erotic energy. Julia Penelope and Susan Robbins analyze lesbian humor; Karla Jay pays tribute to pioneering lesbian bibliographer Jeannette Foster; Barbara Grier emphasizes the importance of *coming out of the closet; and Felice Newman argues that bars harm the lesbian community. Ginny Vida's anthology *Our Right to Love*, the first collection of lesbian essays published by a mainstream press (Prentice-Hall, 1978), contains articles on monogamy and non-monogamy; workplace issues for lesbians, including lesbian academics; lesbian culture; lesbians and the media; legal issues; sexuality; lesbian mothers; and several autobiographical sketches.

Diversity. Despite the proliferation of lesbian literature in print during the 1970s, oral transmission of stories and poems remained important because the phenomenon of publicly acknowledged and celebrated lesbianism was still so new. Those who had access to print tended to be white and middle-class and thus their writing could be mistaken for representative lesbian work. The viewpoints and personal narratives of working-class lesbians and lesbians of color were obscured until the publication of a special issue of *Conditions* on black women (1979), Audre *Lorde's *Cancer Journals* (1980), and the anthology *This Bridge Called My Back: Writings by Radical Women of Color* (1981), edited by Cherríe *Moraga and Gloria *Anzaldúa. Working-class women were also well represented in *Lesbian Crossroads* (1980), a book of interviews by Ruth Baetz. The 1980 publication of the first two anthologies of lesbians' autobiographical writing, *The Lesbian Path*, edited by Margaret Cruikshank, and *The Coming Out Stories*, edited by Susan J. Wolfe and Julia Penelope, confirmed the existence of a lesbian storytelling tradition that predated the second wave of feminism but was given a special impetus by it.

This Bridge Called My Back was a landmark publication because it dramatically called attention to racism in the lesbian community and also because it introduced talented new writers. For many lesbians of color, race was as central to identity as sexual preference, and such writers often supported alliances with men who were black, Hispanic, Native American, or Asian American. Lesbians of color felt invisible within the lesbian community and demanded more attention to their issues.

Other writers re-examined their roots in the light of their sexual orientation. Some strove to integrate their lesbianism with their religious tradition—anthologies devoted to Jewish lesbians, Catholic lesbians, and lesbian nuns and ex-nuns were published. A new appreciation of the diversity of lesbians was also furthered as physically challenged lesbians and fat lesbians described the oppression they experienced, lesbian mothers wrote about custody battles, and women fired from their jobs for being lesbians told their stories.

Lesbians could not have spoken with so many different voices in the 1980s if they had not founded their own presses. Among the pioneers in the 1970s were Daughters, Persephone Press, Diana, and Naiad, the largest lesbian publisher. They were later joined by Cleis, Seal, Spinsters Ink, and Firebrand Books. An important question inherent in the work published by these presses was posed by Bonnie Zimmerman in an article on lesbians' personal narratives in a special lesbian issue of *Signs* (1985): "Is there somehow a transcendent lesbian identity, or only particularized identities?" Lesbian writing inspired by a huge annual celebration, the Michigan Women's Music Festival, suggests a transcendent identity, but at the same time, much writing of the 1980s attempts to define a complex identity of lesbian *and*, for example, lesbian and Afro-American, lesbian and Jewish, or lesbian and mother.

Conflicts and Debates in the 1980s. Inevitably, conflicts and debates shaped much of the writing in the 1980s. Women who adjured * separatism debated those for whom it remained viable. Separatists argued that lesbian energy ought to be devoted solely to lesbian causes, while others, including some radical lesbians, favored coalition-building, with pro-choice groups, with gay groups, or with peace activists, for example. Some lesbian feminists zealously took up *AIDS work; others felt their actions were misguided. After Pat *Califia and Gale Rubin wrote a book advocating sado-machism, other lesbians responded with *Against Sado-Masochism*. Those radicalized in the 1970s clashed with moderate lesbians who had come out later, when it was safer, and who preferred conciliation and accommodation to confrontation. Even motherhood was controversial: for many lesbians, the choice to bear children was the ultimate rejection of heterosexual norms, while others viewed childrearing as a form of participation in heterosexual culture and an impediment to building a strong lesbian community.

The most vociferous debate, dubbed "the sex wars," involved definitions of feminism and lesbian feminism. In her history of twentieth-century lesbianism, *Odd Girls and Twilight Lovers*, Lillian Faderman describes the two sides of the controversy as, on the one hand, sex radicals, who advocate a totally free view of sex and believe women should be encouraged to fight sexual repression even to the point of creating lesbian pornography or patronizing lesbian strip shows, and, on the other, cultural feminists who believe that pornography, S&M, and public sex are *not* lesbian issues and that some sexually explicit images of lesbians, far from exemplifying freedom, actually demonstrate that the radicals had internalized patriarchal values about sex. Susie Bright championed the former viewpoint, and the magazines *On Our Backs* and *Bad Attitude* urged lesbians to experiment with sex, including butch-femme roles. British writer Gillian Hanscombe argued, however, that marketing lesbian *erotica is not compatible with feminist values because a lesbian may "excuse anything she does by asserting that it has 'liberated' her" (*An Intimate Wilderness: Lesbian Writers on Sexuality*, 1991). Can any behavior or set of attitudes among lesbians be condemned? This question grounds lesbian writers' debates about explicit sexual imagery and sexual practices.

It was obvious by the mid-1980s that sustaining a lesbian community was more difficult than it had appeared in the heady early days of *lesbian feminism, a decade earlier, when the mere sight of large numbers of lesbians gathered at festivals and rallies inspired lesbian writers to imagine major social transformations. Sally Gearhart's fantasy *The Wanderground* (1984) and Joanna *Russ's science fiction novel *The Female Man* (1975) capture this hopeful spirit. A popular button featured the slogan "An Army of Lovers Cannot Fail." Because of internal conflicts in the lesbian community, however, and because of unrelenting *homophobia and heterosexism, writers by the late 1980s were more somber in their assessments of lesbian feminism. A new button read, "An Army of Ex-Lovers Cannot Fail," a wry allusion to impermanent relationships and to a hard-won realism about movement-building. Painful and difficult aspects of lesbians' lives were now more commonly revealed by writers, the experience of being "trashed," for example. Sarah Schulman's novel *After Dolores* described the revenge fantasies of a woman left by her lover. A few lesbians also wrote about abusive relationships.

Despite the debates and disillusionments of the 1980s, and even though lesbians had lost some of their radical fervor, lesbian feminism was stronger than in the previous decade because of the sheer numbers of women who had come out of the closet, because of the resulting growth of the lesbian subculture, and also because the dominant culture began to take note of lesbianism as an alternative life choice. A movie based on Jane * Rule's novel *Desert of the Heart*, for example, was shown in theaters across America. And the revised edition of the canon-reshaping *Heath Anthology of American Literature* contained lesbian work, including the poem "Sisters" by Amy * Lowell.

In the 1980s it became obvious that lesbian writers were not only producing a body of identifiably lesbian work but were also publishing innovative books on various aspects of *women's* experience. Books imbued with lesbian feminist consciousness include Susan Griffin's *Women and Nature* (1979); Sherry Thomas's *We Didn't Have Much but We Sure Had Plenty: Stories of Rural Women* (1981); Sandy Boucher's *Heartwomen: An Urban Feminist's Odyssey Home* (1983), on Midwestern women; and Judith Niemi's anthology of canoeing women, *Rivers Running Free* (1987).

Proliferation. Since the late 1980s, the number of books classifiable as "lesbian writing" has increased so greatly that it is nearly impossible to find them all, a sharp contrast to the 1970s when a few bookshelves could hold everything in the category. The most revered lesbian writers of the 1970s, Judy * Grahn, Adrienne * Rich, and Audre Lorde in the United States, and Jane Rule in Canada, were joined by hundreds of new writers from many different backgrounds. Lesbians whose voices were first heard in *This Bridge Called My Back* published books of their own.

The types of writing also grew more diverse. One of the most popular was the lesbian mystery story, a lighter genre than those favored by lesbian writers of the 1970s but one that occasionally lent itself to political analysis, as for example in the mysteries of Barbara Wilson. Many mysteries published by Naiad Press were translated into European languages. Naiad writer Katherine Forrest published work in several genres, including romance and mystery. Nikki Baker introduced a black lesbian sleuth. A vampire tale by Jewelle Gomez, *The Gilda Stories* (1991), and collections of lesbian short stories edited by Irene Zahava were very popular. Lesbian humor books also proliferated. *The Lesbian Love Advisor* by Celeste West (1989), for example, offered witty and ironic commentaries on sex, courtship, coupling, and breaking up. As more women appeared to value long-term relationships, books on that topic were published, including Susan Johnson's *Staying Power: Long-Term Lesbian Couples* (1990). Some enthusiastically joined the recovery movement; their personal narratives reflected a desire to heal from alcoholism, drug abuse, childhood sexual assault, and the food disorders that frequently resulted from abuse. Separatists decried this emphasis on personal therapy, however, fearing that it tended to de-politicize women. As old lesbians began organizing, their attacks on ageism within mainstream culture and also within the lesbian community created a new political issue. * Spirituality was a focus for some lesbians, either feminist-created rituals, such as goddess worship or witchcraft, or versions of traditional religion. Buddhism attracted many West Coast lesbians.

Several other developments encouraged or reflected the proliferation of lesbian writing. First, the growth of gay bookstores, women's * bookstores, and lesbian presses increased the audience for lesbian writing. Kitchen Table: Women of Color Press, founded by Barbara Smith and others, published lesbian work. Firebrand introduced several new lesbian writers. Seal Press, Cleis, and Spinsters grew. Naiad's sales increased dramatically in the period 1989–1991. Two of the largest gay bookstores, Lambda Rising and A Different Light, launched book reviews.

Secondly, mainstream publishers belatedly discovered lesbian writing (St. Martin's and New American Library preceded others). Before the late 1980s, lesbian writing was almost entirely a subculture activity, unnoticed by outsiders, except for a few books the mainstream media singled out, notably Kate * Millett's autobiographical works *Flying* (1974) and *Sita* (1977) and autobiographies by Jill * Johnston. The publication of lesbian writing by a few mainstream houses opens doors previously closed to writers. Some who were already known to lesbian feminist readers were able to reach a larger audience, including poets Minnie Bruce * Pratt and Chrystos; fiction writers Dorothy Allison, Valerie Miner, and Irena Klepfisz; archivist/historian Joan * Nestle; Eleanor Roosevelt biographer Blanche Cook; and social historian Lillian Faderman. On the other hand, mainstream publishers are unlikely to choose experimental or visionary work having roots in lesbian feminism, such as Elana Nachman's *Riverfinger Woman* (1974; reissued 1992). Novels about lesbians from mainstream publishers tend to portray upper-middle-class women, typically in Eastern boarding schools, perhaps to suggest that lesbianism can be de-stigmatized if presented in an elitist context. Works by lesbians of color—Doris Davenport's poetry, for example, or subtle, complex political novels like Ann McLeod's *Being Someone* (1991)—are unlikely to attract commercial publishers.

Third, lesbians of color continued to publish innovative, challenging work. Plays by Cherríe Moraga were produced in San Francisco. Juanita Ramos edited *Companeros*, an anthology of Latina lesbian writing (1987). Lesbians of color began to be published in mainstream anthologies: Becky Birtha in *Breaking Ice* (1990), an anthology of African-American fiction, and Paula Gunn * Allen and Beth * Brant in *Talking Leaves: Contemporary Native American Short Stories* (1991). Gloria Anzaldúa edited *Making Face, Making Soul: Creative and Critical Perspectives by Women of Color* (1990). In her essay "En Rapport, In Opposition," Anzaldúa suggests that the anger women of color sometimes turn on each other is only a "phase of the internalized colonization process, one that will soon cease to hold sway over our lives."

Fourth, the growth of gay/lesbian professional organizations stimulated new writing by lesbians. The oldest gay/lesbian caucuses, in the American Library Association and the Modern Language Association, were joined by groups for lesbian and gay historians, anthropologists, and educational researchers. Since its founding in 1977, the National Women's Studies Association has provided a major forum for lesbian scholars, writers, and publishers at its annual conventions. Numerous lesbian books originated in meetings and discussions at NWSA.

A fifth trend is that academic women, who have played a major role in creating lesbian literature, may occasionally now do this work without jeopardizing their careers. A few undergraduate and graduate students have been encouraged to pursue research on lesbian issues in fields as diverse as nursing and physical education. Tolerance has not reached all corners of academe—women are still routinely discouraged from writing doctoral dissertations on lesbian topics—but the few pockets of intellectual freedom for lesbians in the 1990s are a marked contrast to the situation in the 1970s and much of the 1980s. This development is likely to encourage sustained research on lesbian literary and historical topics. On the other hand, some of the recent work is written in the current jargon of specialists and thus is accessible only to a small audience. An exception is Michelle Barale's essay interpreting various covers of *The Well of Loneliness* (in *Inside/Out: Lesbian Theories, Gay Theories*, ed. Diana Fuss, 1991). Lesbians who are not academics feel excluded by the difficult language of some of the current critical writing. They do not object to theory *per se* (as Barbara Christian observes of academic women of color in her essay "The Race for Theory" in *Making Face, Making Soul*), but for them, as for Christian and her colleagues, literature "is not an occasion for discourse among critics but necessary nourishment for their people."

Sixth, for the first time, lesbian writing from countries besides Canada, England, and Australia is becoming available in the United States. Fall 1991 publications included *Two Mujeras*, a novel about Jewish lesbians in Mexico City and *Another Love*, a detective story about a lesbian journalist in Hungary during the 1956 revolt. Increasingly, lesbian writing from the U.S. is being translated into other languages as well.

Finally, a significant development in lesbian writing is the appearance of a new generation of young writers. For some of them, feminism is passé; they were socialized into a gay community rather than a women's community, and thus they tend to regard gay male sexuality as a model. Drawn to militant groups such as Queer Nation or ACT UP, they often take a stand against what they perceive as the political correctness of the 1970s and 1980s. Being hip, irreverent, and very explicitly sexual is highly valued. On the other hand, the ranks of lesbian writers under thirty include many impassioned feminists, including critic and bibliographer Linda Garber.

Visibility. Although the creation of a large body of lesbian literature is one of the most significant developments in small press publishing in the past two decades, this work is not much taught in colleges and universities or sold by mainstream bookstores. It is found in the core curricula of some women's studies programs but even women's studies is not completely open to the voices of lesbian writers. Until this situation changes, students interested in social change, gender issues, or sexuality will not know the range and diversity of lesbian writing. Work by scholars such as Martha Vicinus, Paula Bennett, and Lillian Faderman will be assigned in history and literature courses, but neither political commentary blended with personal narrative by writers such as Elly Bulkin, Barbara Smith, and Judy * Grahn nor explicitly lesbian poetry has reached a large student audience. When notable lesbian writers such as Adrienne Rich, Audre Lorde, or May * Sarton are taught in literature courses, their lesbianism is often unacknowledged.

Tension. As lesbian writing slowly gains a degree of acceptance in the dominant culture, tension inevitably arises between those who welcome mainstream success and those who view it as a sign of dilution or of dangerous assimilationist tendencies. Because of the diversity of the lesbian community, some lesbian writers are basically comfortable with the values and norms of mainstream America (except for their sexual difference), while others emphatically reject them. Loyal to the grass-roots origins of lesbian writing, those who have helped to build lesbian archives, staffed a women's bookstore, or worked on a lesbian press collective may have a very different experience of lesbianism from that of a writer first published by a large New York house. In addition, since white lesbian writers will continue to have far more access to print than lesbians of color, the latter will justifiably feel not only that they are excluded from view but that the whole picture of lesbian life is thereby distorted.

AIDS. What impact has the *AIDS epidemic had on lesbian writing? Many lesbians have lost friends, including former husbands, to AIDS, and many others have become caregivers, hospice volunteers, or participants in support networks for the sick. A few lesbians, notably Cindy Patton, have written books about AIDS. Others have commemorated loved ones in poems and reminiscences. Aside from experiencing grief, many lesbians live with anxiety for their gay male friends who have not been diagnosed with HIV or AIDS. The vulnerability of large numbers of gay men has perhaps influenced some lesbian writers to identify more with the gay liberation movement (as opposed to women's liberation) than would have been likely without the epidemic.

Homophobia. Although lesbian writers today find somewhat more receptive audiences for their work than they did twenty years ago, and although homophobia has been identified as a social problem, fear of lesbians still influences the climate in which they work. When Fanny Flagg's novel *Fried Green Tomatoes at the Whistle Stop Cafe* (1987) was made into a movie, for example, the central lesbian relationship was cut out. Many lesbians who work in the publishing industry are closeted. Compared to the 1970s, it is uncommon for a lesbian writer to use a pseudonym, but even today writers must weigh the possible negative consequences of publishing lesbian work—loss of a child custody battle, expulsion from the military, denial of tenure, or lesser problems such as hostility from colleagues.

Conclusion. Lesbian writers had so little credibility in the dominant culture in the 1970s that the first university press to publish a book on lesbians chose one by a heterosexual author, anthropologist Deborah Wolf *(The Lesbian Community)*. One sign of a more open attitude in the 1990s is that Lillian Faderman's *Odd Girls and Twilight Lovers* was widely reviewed in the mainstream media in 1991 and 1992. The publication of hundreds of books and articles by lesbian writers in the intervening years helped create this change.

When D. H. Lawrence ended "The Fox," his novella about an English lesbian couple during World War I, by having a tree fall on one of the women, he mirrored centuries of hatred for lesbians. This storyline could not be challenged effectively until the revival of feminism and the ensuing growth of lesbian feminism gave women a new subject to write about: their lesbianism. Without this subject, many of them could not have taken on the identity of "writer." The stories they told are not about tragic fates and punishments for deviation but rather about self-discovery, re-definition, and freedom. This radical rewriting of the old story of doomed lesbians has been one of the most significant developments in women's writing in this century. But homophobia and heterosexism remain entrenched, and thus lesbian literature will continue to be, to some degree, a literature of rebellion and defiance. No matter how personal the work is, it inevitably comes to life in a political context. The struggle to be whole women and to create a safe place for themselves will continue to preoccupy lesbian writers.

• Jane Rule, *Desert of the Heart* (1965; resissued 1978, 1982). Judy Grahn, ed., *True to Life Adventure Stories* (1978; vol. 2, 1981). Pat Parker, *Movement in Black* (1978; reissued 1990). Adrienne Rich, *On Lies, Secrets, and Silence* (1979). Mary Meigs, *Lily Briscoe: A Self-Portrait* (1981). Audre Lorde, *Zami* (1982). Barbara Macdonald and Cynthia Rich, *Look Me in the Eye* (1984). Elly Bulkin, Barbara Smith, and Minnie Bruce Pratt, *Yours in Struggle: Three Feminist Perspectives on Anti-Semitism and Racism* (1984). *Signs: Journal of Women in Culture and Society*, The Lesbian Issue (1985). Joan Nestle, *A Restricted Country* (1987). Sarah Hoagland and Julia Penelope, eds., *For Lesbians Only: A Separatist Anthology* (1989). Minnie Bruce Pratt, *Crimes Against Nature* (1990). Carla Trujillo, ed., *Chicana Lesbians* (1991). Lillian Faderman, *Odd Girls and Twilight Lovers: A History of Lesbian Life in Twentieth-Century America* (1991).

Margaret Cruikshank

Drama

The feminist and gay and lesbian liberation movements of the late 1960s in the United States provided theater scholars with the impetus to review the history of lesbians in drama. As critical historians reread plays to find evidence of lesbian desire encoded in texts written by mainstream authors, lesbian playwrights began to express their newly claimed identities on U.S. stages for the first time.

The early second wave of U.S. feminism brought with it vexed definitions of lesbian identity. Adrienne *Rich's early article, "Compulsory Heterosexuality and Lesbian Existence" (1980), proposed a continuum of woman-identification that allowed feminist women to claim lesbian identities not necessarily based on sexual activity. From 1980 to the early 1990s, a more fractious lesbian criticism developed multiple, contrary definitions of lesbian identity, some explicitly along the lines of sexuality. These debates of necessity haunt lesbian drama's development.

Many of the earliest lesbian theater collectives produced plays within the feminist movement, which advocated rights for lesbians. Collective lesbian theaters such as the Lavender Cellar Theatre (Minneapolis, 1973), Red Dyke Theatre (Atlanta, 1974), and Medusa's Revenge (New York, 1976), produced plays about "coming out" and other topics, often for community audiences who directly supported the work through funding. The plays produced by these short-lived theaters are no longer extant, evidence of the site-specificity of this political theater work.

Playwrights affiliated with feminist theaters early in the movement also wrote an occasional lesbian play. Martha Boesing, a founder of At the Foot of the Mountain Theatre (Minneapolis), wrote *Love Song for an Amazon* (1976) as a ritual ceremony to celebrate women's friendships. The one-act play, performed by two women, used transformational drama techniques. Each performer played many roles meant to encourage the female-only audience's identification with the multiple, positive aspects of their gender. Although it was not specifically written as a lesbian drama, its criticism describes it as "woman-identified."

Another feminist theater group that produced lesbian drama was the Women's Experimental Theatre (WET) in New York, whose trilogy *The Daughters Cycle* includes *Electra Speaks* (1980). By revising the myth of the House of Atreus to ask, "What happened to the women?," the WET implicitly describes a lesbian possibility as Electra leaves her father's house to commit her life to women. Although the play could be read as a veiled coming-out narrative, Electra's sexual identity is allied with identification with women, and not specifically marked as lesbian.

The first U.S. playwright to enter mainstream theater discourse as a self-identified lesbian was the late Jane Chambers, whose play *A Late Snow* was produced by Playwrights Horizon in New York in 1974. The play details the conflicting relationships between a college professor and her ex-lover, new lover, and potential lover as they inadvertently meet at an isolated cabin. The play marks the sometimes conflicting demands of gay liberation and feminism.

Chambers, who died in 1983, remains the most popular published lesbian playwright. Her play *Last Summer at Bluefish Cove* (1980) enjoyed a long run in an off-off-Broadway New York theater. Chambers's last play, *Quintessential Image* (1983), indicates her move toward a more complicated, layered theater form in its references to the construction of lesbian identity through the conflicting discourses of heterosexuality, the media, and the family.

The first anthology of lesbian plays, *Places, Please!*, was published by a small lesbian press in 1985. Edited by Kate McDermott, the collection includes seven plays by five white, middle-class lesbian playwrights, which keeps it from representing the racial and class diversity of the U.S. lesbian community. Sarah Dreher, one of the volume's more frequently produced playwrights, wrote the award-winning *8x10 Glossy* (1985), and has since published *Lesbian Stages* (1988), a collection of her plays. McDermott's anthology also includes popular lesbian playwright Terry Baum and Carolyn Meyer's revue, *Dos Lesbos*, which was first performed in a lesbian bar in San Francisco.

Lesbian drama has often been generated within lesbian communities. Playwright/performer Holly Hughes began writing at the WOW Cafe, a lesbian performance space in New York's East Village. Hughes's *The Well of Horniness* (1983) is a parodic romp through lesbian subculture that quotes the conventions of radio drama, murder mysteries, soap operas, and melodrama. Hughes's performance piece, *World Without End* (1989), is a one-woman show, which only she has performed; it is not written as a play that any theater company might produce.

The move away from traditional drama into more experimental forms and * performance art also characterizes work by other lesbian playwrights. Paula Vogel, whose play *And Baby Makes Seven* (1989) is an absurdist look at the fashion for lesbian parenting, tends to write in a non-realist style and appeals to a wider theatergoing audience. Joan Schenkar's *Between the Acts* (1989) borrows famous lesbians from history—including Natalie Barney and Renee Vivien—to enact a fantastical morality tale in which Barney's wealthy capitalist father dies seven different ways in the second act. Playwright Schenkar's subjects range from Nazi Germany to Typhoid Mary to theatrical recreations of historical literary figures, in plays whose perspective is more overtly materialist and feminist than lesbian.

Because of the exigencies of play publishing and producing in the U.S., plays about lesbians by lesbians who also affiliate with a racial or ethnic community remain difficult to locate. Chicana critic, theorist, poet, and playwright Cherríe * Moraga's play, *Giving Up the Ghost* (1984), is a fragmented, episodic, poetic script that evokes a split in its main character as she traces her desire through her past relationships in ways that complicate the play's representation of gender and ethnicity. Alexis * DeVeaux's *No* (1990) is a choreopoem that describes the conflicting position of a lesbian active in African-American politics.

The perpetuation and circulation of lesbian drama—especially plays by lesbians of color and working-class lesbians—confronts enormous challenges. Without a significant production, it remains very difficult to publish a play. Even feminist and lesbian presses have not given due attention to the richness and variety of lesbians writing for theater. The economic and cultural limitations on lesbian drama, and its often site-specific location within relatively insular local communities, pose obstacles to its full consideration and continued generation.

• Adrienne Rich, "Compulsory Heterosexuality and Lesbian Identity," in *Signs: Journal of Women in Culture and Society* 5, no. 4 (1980). Dinah Luise Leavitt, *Feminist Theatre Groups* (1980). Elizabeth Natalle, *Feminist Theatre* (1985). Sue-Ellen Case, *Feminism and Theatre* (1988). Jill Dolan, *The Feminist Spectator as Critic* (1988). Jill Dolan, " 'Lesbian' Subjectivity in Realism," in *Performing Feminisms*, ed. Sue-Ellen Case (1990), pp. 40–53. Lynda Hart, "Canonizing Lesbians?" in *Modern American Drama: The Female Canon*, ed. June Schlueter (1990), pp. 275–292. Sue-Ellen Case, "Tracking the Vampire," *differences: A Journal of Feminist Cultural Studies* 3, no. 2 (1991): 1–20.

Jill Dolan

Fiction

Jeannette H. Foster's *Sex Variant Women in Literature*, originally published in 1956, was the first bibliography of lesbian fiction (and poetry) in the United States and the entire world. This groundbreaking work was followed in 1967 by the first edition of *The Lesbian in Literature*, written by Barbara Grier, the founder of Naiad Press, a lesbian publishing company that is responsible for much of what is considered "lesbian fiction" in the United States today. As its introduction notes, this international bibliography, now in its third printing (1981), includes over 3,000 entries.

Bonnie Zimmerman, whose *The Safe Sea of Women: Lesbian Fiction 1969–1989* (1990) is the first book-length critical examination of what she claims is a specific genre, employs several different criteria for establishing whether or not a work of fiction may be included in the category "lesbian fiction." Among them are: the sexual preference of the writer herself, the inclusion of a "central, not marginal, lesbian character," a focus on the sexual and loving relationship between two women, the placing of men on the margins, and a "woman-centered" narrative. Zimmerman also includes experiments in style that attempt to break down what many feminist theorists have described as the "phallologocentric" language of patriarchy and compulsory heterosexuality. Earlier, Catharine Stimpson's pioneering article "Zero Degree Deviancy: The Lesbian Novel in English" (1981) defined a lesbian as "a woman who finds other women erotically attractive and gratifying," while Ann Allen *Shockley's "The Black Lesbian in American Literature: An Overview," (*Home Girls: A Black Feminist Anthology*, 1983), does not offer a specific definition of lesbian fiction but instead theorizes about why black lesbians in fiction have been for the most part conspiciously absent, including homophobia within and outside the black community and racism within the white lesbian community. These few examples illustrate the wide range of issues surrounding even the delimitation of the genre.

At stake is also the historical parameter within which one may confidently discuss "lesbian" as a recognizable identity in the United States. Any attempt to locate a tradition of self-consciously "lesbian" fiction must in some ways conform to the historical boundaries of what we now consider the rise of lesbian identities. In *The History of Sexuality, Volume 1: An Introduction* (1978), Michel Foucault argues that homosexuality as a distinct identity, as opposed to a variety of practices, is a recent invention, a product of the increasing medical analysis of and surveillance of sexuality that occurred at the end of the nineteenth century. Similarly, Lillian Faderman (*Surpassing the Love of Men*, 1981) traces the development of what we now consider a "lesbian" identity in the United States to the turn of the century, and links it to a tendency to categorize as pathological what were formerly considered "romantic friendships" among women.

With these historical boundaries in mind, then, one of the first women in the United States to write self-consciously "lesbian" fiction was Sarah Orne *Jewett, whose short story "Martha's Lady" (*Old Friends and New*, 1890) is widely recognized as a narrative about the love and desire of a young servant girl for her mistress's young niece. Jewett, who lived for most of her adult life in a "Boston Marriage" with the literary figure Annie *Fields, was also a mentor of Willa *Cather, another lesbian whose writing has recently been shown to include lesbian themes.

In 1928 a book was published that had perhaps the greatest influence in the twentieth century on lesbian fiction in the United States and elsewhere, British writer Radclyffe Hall's *The Well of Loneliness*. As Stimpson notes, lesbians writing after this book were faced with the challenge of either replicating the tragic ending of the novel or creating a new ending that could somehow affirm a lesbian identity. At the same time, another one of Hall's circle, a young American named Djuna *Barnes, privately published her satire of the Paris lesbian salons, *Ladies Almanack* (1928). A witty tour of lesbian identity through the ages that parodies all of English literature along the way, Barnes's *Almanack* provides another paradigm—one of humor and sexual pleasure—for lesbian writing. Her more widely known *Nightwood* (1936) is in part the story of the failed relationship between Nora and Robin, two women. Both novels employ what is now considered a *modernist/ *postmodernist style that some critics have argued also represents a kind of lesbian *écriture*, a challenging of stable meaning that in itself is a lesbian act.

Another writer of the twenties who was part of the modernist movement was Nella *Larsen, who in 1929 wrote *Passing*, a novel about two childhood friends who are reacquainted. One is passing for white while the other is a member of the black bourgeoisie. While at the time the book was not recognized as a lesbian novel, the recent writing of Deborah MacDowell establishes *Passing* in the tradition of lesbian fiction in the United States.

In the thirties, Gale Wilhelm published two novels, *We Too Are Drifting* (1935) and *Torchlight to Valhalla* (1938), which dealt explicitly with lesbian themes. The first book details the relationships of Jan Morale, a young artist. The second book relates a young woman's gradual recognition of her love for another woman. This book, unlike Hall's *The Well of Loneliness*, has a happy ending in which the two women are united.

In the fifties, Patricia Highsmith, writing under the pseudonym Clare Morgan, published *The Price of Salt* (1952). Highsmith portrays a woman who has lost custody of her child because of her sexual preference. While the lesbian characters face tragedy and adversity, they, too, are together at the end of the novel. The fifties and early sixties were also the era of *"lesbian pulp fiction" in the United States. While there are debates about whether or not this writing should be included in a list of lesbian high culture, what is certain is that these books had a tremendous effect on the writers who came after them.

Much of the lesbian fiction of the last twenty years has been intimately tied to the feminist movement, not only by its politics but also by its publication, as many of the publishing outlets established by feminists first published lesbian fiction. As Zimmerman explains, perhaps the first lesbian novel of this period was Isabel Miller's *Patience and Sarah* (1969; originally entitled *A Place for Us*), a book that had an enormous impact on the emerging lesbian community. Similarly, *Rubyfruit Jungle* (1973), Rita Mae *Brown's lesbian *bildungsroman, represents one of the first contemporary lesbian coming-of-age narratives. Bertha Harris, the author of *Lover* (1976), as both Stimpson and Zimmerman explain, is one of the only novelists of this period to experiment with style as well as content, a characteristic that connects her to the lesbian modernists of the early twentieth century. While this period is recognized as the time when lesbian fiction in the United States came of age, much of the writing of the seventies and eighties has been faulted for its didacticism and its failure, as in the feminist and lesbian movements themselves, to include a diversity of women and experiences. Fictional writing by women of color, included in such groundbreaking anthologies as *This Bridge Called My Back: Writings by Radical Women of Color* (edited by Gloria *Anzaldúa and Cherríe *Moraga, 1981), *Home Girls: A Black Feminist Anthology* (Smith, 1983), and more recently, collections such as *Making Faces, Making Soul* (Anzaldúa, 1990) and *Chicana Lesbians: The Girls Our Mothers Warned Us About* (Trujillo, 1991), have widened the perspective of the fiction.

Furthermore, with the sex wars and the recent discussion of what constitutes lesbian sexuality and lesbian identity, a new kind of lesbian writing, one that is less tied to a "politically correct" lesbian (and often separatist) agenda, is emerging. In some ways this writing alludes back to the pulps of the fifties in its portrayal of the seamier sides of the lesbian and other subcultures. This new writing also challenges the boundaries of any definition of genre, as it sometimes overlaps with other forms of writing, such as pornography and the detective novel. Sarah Schulman's novels subvert the sometimes overly romantic vision of lesbian love by portraying young dissatisfied lesbian heroines who occasionally sleep with men and occupy communities that include a variety of racial, sexual and ethnic characters. Jane DeLynn's novel *Don Juan in the Village* (1990) tells the story of a lesbian's search for sex (and not necessarily love) through the New York gay scene, as well as a variety of other locations. Like other recent works of lesbian fiction, it was published by a major publishing house, and reflects the breakthrough of lesbian writers into "mainstream" publishing. This move, while hailed by some as a representation of how far lesbian writing has come in its struggle for critical recognition, is seen by others as a symptom of lesbian writers' abandonment of the alternative presses. At the same time, whole volumes devoted to lesbian literary criticism are also appearing. For example, *Lesbian Texts and Contexts: Radical Revisions* (edited by Karla Jay and Joanne Glasgow, 1990) includes critical essays, interviews with and essays by lesbian authors, and revisions of novels (and poetry) that elucidate their lesbian content. Scholars and critics of lesbian writing hail all of these developments as part of an explosion of lesbian culture in America.

• Jeanette H. Foster, *Sex Variant Women in Literature* (1956). Barbara Smith, "Toward a Black Feminist Criticism," *Women's Studies International Quarterly* 2, no. 2 (1979): 183–194. Gloria Anzaldúa and Cherríe Moraga, *This Bridge Called My Back: Writings by Radical Women of Color* (1981). Lillian Faderman, *Surpassing the Love of Men* (1981). Barbara Grier, *The Lesbian in Literature* (1981). Catharine Stimpson, "Zero Degree Deviancy: The Lesbian Novel in English," *Critical Inquiry* 8, no. 2 (1981): 363–379. Ann Allen Shockley, "The Black Lesbian in American Literature: An Overview," in *Home Girls: A Black Feminist Anthology*, ed. Barbara Smith (1983), pp. 83–93. Gloria Anzaldúa, *Making Faces, Making Soul* (1990). Karla Jay and Joanne Glasgow, *Lesbian Texts and Contexts: Radical Revisions* (1990). Bonnie Zimmerman, *The Safe Sea of Women: Lesbian Fiction 1969–1989* (1990). Carla Trujillo, *Chicana Lesbians: The Girls Our Mothers Warned Us About* (1991).

Katie Kent

Nonfiction

Before the feminist revival of the late 1960s, writers who were lesbians had no context for describing their lives positively except for the periodical *The Ladder*. Lesbianism was viewed as sick or sinful. Feminism provided a rationale for discarding these stereotypes and affirming the value of lesbian lives. By the mid-1970s, lesbian feminists had begun to create a distinctly lesbian literature, including political essays, autobiography, and literary criticism.

The first two categories overlap because the politics of lesbian feminism comes directly from personal experience. Similarly, literary criticism by lesbian feminists exhibits a keen awareness of anti-lesbian and misogynist bias and thus is inherently political.

Among the assumptions common to early political writing by lesbians were that lesbianism is not only a personal choice but a political statement challenging male domination; that a separate women's culture is needed to empower lesbians; and that the shared identity of lesbians transcends differences among women who love women. In an article on lesbian feminist theory published in Ginny Vida's 1978 anthology *Our Right to Love*, Charlotte Bunch describes the "ideology of heterosexism" as the myth that all women want to be economically and emotionally connected to men. Much subsequent political writing by lesbian feminists attacks this ideology—for example, both Adrienne *Rich's frequently anthologized important essay "Compulsory Heterosexuality and Lesbian Existence," first published in *Signs* in 1980, and Minnie Bruce Pratt's *Rebellion: Essays 1980–1991* (1991). Another motif in lesbian nonfiction is the depiction of a place, a group, or a set of conditions that would celebrate lesbian life, not simply as an alternative to heterosexuality but as a new way of being. Articles in lesbian periodicals such as *Conditions, Sinister Wisdom*, and *Common Lives, Lesbian Lives* exemplify this pioneering spirit.

An important shift in political writing occurred when African-American, Native American, Hispanic, and Asian-American lesbians protested their invisibility within the ranks of lesbian feminists by emphasizing their differences from white, middle-class lesbians rather than their similarities and by identifying racism in the lesbian community. The groundbreaking anthology edited by Cherríe *Moraga and Gloria *Anzaldúa, *This Bridge Called My Back: Writings by Radical Women of Color* (2d ed. 1983), revealed that for many lesbians of color, ethnic and racial identity was as significant as lesbian identity and called for more awareness of class differences within the lesbian community. Political writing by lesbian feminists who are women of color often appears in sources not specifically focused on lesbianism; for example, Paula Gunn *Allen, Gloria Anzaldúa, and Michelle *Cliff published essays in *Multicultural Literacy*, edited by Rick Simonson and Scott Walker (1988).

Autobiographical writing by lesbians in the 1970s and 1980s typically emphasizes *coming out. Many obstacles to establishing a healthy lesbian identity exist, and thus self-nurture is a major theme. The struggle to become free of internalized homophobia is portrayed as arduous and perhaps life-long. Sexual explicitness characterizes Kate *Millett's *Flying* (1974) and *Sita* (1977), books that describe episodes in her own life. Three of the first full-length autobiographies are *Lilly Briscoe: A Self Portrait* (1981) by Canadian painter Mary Meigs; *Hindsight* (1982), by Charlotte Wolff, a German psychiatrist who lived in England after escaping from Nazi Germany; and *Zami*, (1982), a powerful work by African-American poet Audre *Lorde. In *The Cancer Journals* (1980), Lorde skillfully blends political analysis with personal narrative. At the age of eighty-six, poet Elsa Gidlow completed her autobiography *Elsa, I Come with My Songs* (1986). More recently, Toni McNaron published the memoir *I Dwell in Possibility* (1992).

Much autobiographical material is contained in the writings of Adrienne *Rich and Barbara Deming, two of the best prose stylists among lesbian writers. Many of the interviews by Ruth Baetz in *Lesbian Crossroads* (1988) describe the lives of working-class lesbians and lesbians of color. Experiences of older lesbians are recounted in *Long Time Passing* (1986), edited by Marcy Adelman. Susan Johnson uses autobiographical sketches extensively in her study of lesbians' long-term relationships, *Staying Power* (1990). The same is true of Lillian Faderman's *Odd Girls and Twilight Lovers: A History of Lesbian Life in Twentieth-Century America* (1991). Although lesbian themes are muted in the journals of May *Sarton, these works movingly depict the life of a lesbian who became a celebrated writer.

All of this work has demystified lesbianism and placed it in the broader context of women's emancipation from constricting roles. At the same time, whether radicals or reformers, separatists or non-separatists, lesbian writers have emphasized their differences from other women and their sense of charting new territory. The anthology form has been especially important in making lesbians visible. Notable anthologies from the past decade include *A Gathering of Spirit* (1984), writings of Native American women, edited by Beth *Brant; *Lesbian Nuns: Breaking Silence* (1985), edited by Rosemary Curb and Nancy Manahan; *Hidden from History: Reclaiming the Gay and Lesbian Past* (1989), edited by Martin Duberman, Martha Vicinus, and George Chauncey, Jr.; and *An Intimate Wilderness: Lesbian Writers on Sexuality* (1991), edited by Judith Barrington.

Lesbian feminist literary criticism constitutes a smaller body of work than either political essays or autobiography. Its tasks are to reinterpret the work of well-known literary figures who were lesbians, to recover lost work, and to encourage the creation of a diverse body of lesbian literature. Jane *Rule's groundbreaking study *Lesbian Images* (1975) deals with well-known mainstream writers such as Amy *Lowell and Ivy Compton-Burnett, while a special issue of *Margins* published in the same year focused on women who identified themselves as lesbian feminist writers. Faderman's *Surpassing the Love of Men: Friendship and Love Between Women from the Renaissance to the Present* (1981) is a landmark in lesbian feminist literary criticism and social history. Subsequent work includes Bonnie Zimmerman's survey of lesbian fiction, *A Safe Sea of Women* (1990), and the anthology of critical articles *Lesbian Texts and Contexts*, edited by Karla Jay and Joanne Glasgow (1991). Among the important works that rescue their subjects from heterosexist misinterpretations and omissions are Paula Bennett's critical study *Emily Dickinson: Woman Poet* (1991) and the biographies *Willa Cather: The Emerging Voice* by Sharon

O'Brien (1986) and *Eleanor Roosevelt* (1992) by Blanche Wiesen Cook. The acceptance of such books by mainstream publishers is a sign that lesbian feminist writing is no longer confined to the lesbian subculture, but these books could not have been conceived without the existence of the subculture, and they were preceded by many years of research by scholars unaffiliated with universities and by academics unable to publish on lesbian subjects, both of whom were sometimes denied access to material.

Today much lesbian nonfiction focuses on subjects relevant to all women such as the breast cancer epidemic, mid-life transitions, recovery from childhood sexual abuse, and ageism. Although the work of some young lesbian writers reflects a very strong identification with gay men and a disparaging view of feminism, separatist work remains popular, and women's studies courses continue to introduce students to a wide range of lesbian political writing, autobiography, and literary criticism.

• Julia Penelope and Susan J. Wolfe, eds., *The Coming Out Stories* (1980, reissued 1989). Margaret Cruikshank, ed., *The Lesbian Path* (1980, rev. ed. 1985). Audre Lorde, *Zami* (1982). Cherríe Moraga and Gloria Anzaldúa, eds., *This Bridge Called My Back*, 2d ed. (1983). Joan Nestle, *A Restricted Country* (1987). *Sinister Wisdom* 43/44, 15th Anniversary Retrospective (Summer 1991). Julia Penelope and Sarah Lucia Hoagland, eds., *For Lesbians Only: A Separatist Anthology* (1991). Lillian Faderman, *Odd Girls and Twilight Lovers: A History of Lesbian Life in Twentieth-Century America* (1991).

Margaret Cruikshank

Poetry

No conscious tradition of lesbian poetry existed in America before 1971, the year that the Women's Press Collective in Oakland printed Judy *Grahn's *Edward the Dyke and Other Poems* and Violet Press in New York printed Fran Winant's *Looking at Women*. This is not to say that no lesbian poems were published before the seventies. There were rare examples, like May *Swenson's "To Confirm a Thing" (*A Cage of Spines*, 1958) and Muriel *Rukeyser's "The Transgress" (*The Speed of Darkness*, 1968): ". . . the revelation/thundering on tabu after the broken/imperative . . ." But such poems concealed their lesbian themes, leaving "the Thing" and "the tabu" unnamed. Not until Swenson permitted the inclusion of "To Confirm a Thing" in the 1975 anthology *Amazon Poetry* (a decision she reaffirmed in 1988, publishing two love poems in *Gay and Lesbian Poetry in Our Time*), and Rukeyser agreed to participate in a lesbian reading at the 1978 Modern Language Association convention, could their poems of the fifties and sixties be understood as lesbian.

The Ladder, a lesbian magazine published from 1956 to 1972, printed poems, but none was by an established poet. Judy Grahn, with experience of the military's witch-hunting of lesbians, hid "The Psychoanalysis of Edward the Dyke," written in 1964, in notebooks for seven years. In 1969, when she wanted to write poems that described ordinary women's lives, the only model she found for her passionate portraits was a lyric ("Suzanne") by male songwriter Leonard Cohen. Lillian Faderman's *Odd Girls and Twilight Lovers: A History of Lesbian Life in Twentieth-Century America* (1991) documents the culture's judgment that love between women was degenerate and dangerous; and Jonathan Katz's *Gay American History* (1976) gives an account of the simultaneous vilification of "perverts" and "subversives" during the McCarthy purges in the 1950s. The atmosphere of bigotry such histories illuminate accounts for the long repression of lesbian themes in poetry. The criminalization and stigmatization of lesbian sensuality demanded self-censorship of lesbian poets, and in any case, neither female sensuality nor women's centrality to themselves had yet emerged as themes in women's poetry.

For some, poetic formalism was a strategy for balancing self-censorship and self-revelation. But the view long held by educated readers that poetry was a hermetic language, a code that could be cracked only with difficulty by a few, had begun to change. Work by the poets associated with the Black Mountain school, the San Francisco Renaissance, and the Beat Generation encouraged the use of open forms and revived the popularity of oral poetry in public readings. Some, like Robert Duncan and Allen Ginsberg, wrote openly about homosexuality. At the same time, the work of * confessional poets like Anne * Sexton and Sylvia * Plath opened the door to women's writing about their physical and sexual lives, * motherhood, * menstruation, * abortion, and abuse. And the anti-war and civil rights movements of the sixties contributed a new urgency to poetry. Muriel * Rukeyser wrote passionately of people's daily suffering during her "lifetime/among wars." In "Käthe Kollwitz" (*The Speed of Darkness,* 1968), she articulated the startling idea that the vision central to her poetry was a woman's: "What would happen if one woman told the truth about her life?/ The world would split open."

With the explosion of feminism in the late sixties and early seventies came a rapid proliferation of woman-owned presses, bookstores, magazines, and distribution networks of which many lesbian poets were a part. Among many others, The Women's Press Collective and Shameless Hussy Press in the Bay Area, Daughters, Inc., in Vermont, Diana Press in Baltimore, Motheroot in Pittsburgh, Out & Out Books in Brooklyn, and feminist journals like *Aphra, Amazon Quarterly, Chrysalis, The Second Wave, Sinister Wisdom,* and *Women: A Journal of Liberation* published a new generation of lesbian writers. Poetry readings were numerous and as important as political meetings and actions; possibly for the first time since Sappho, lesbian poets wrote in the context of a responsive community. They strove for clarity and the integrity of the phrasing of spoken language, producing a vital body of work in which women spoke *to* women, of experience whose details could be seen as pertaining directly to their own memories and moral lives. This was poetry not of accommodation to clichés of gender and culture, and not of consolation, but frequently of anger. It gave presence to a new definition of women's lives that connected women to their own history and to one another.

The search for foremothers was ongoing. Lesbian poets looked to * Sappho, Christina Rossetti, * H.D., Amy * Lowell, Gertrude * Stein, Angelina Weld * Grimké, and singers of blues and work songs; made conjectures about Emily * Dickinson's life; mourned the lost history of women-loving women in Asian-American and Native American cultures (as in Paula Gunn * Allen's 1980 poem "Beloved Women"); and debated whether a broad definition of "lesbian" might include poets like Sara * Teasdale, Elinor * Wylie, and Edna St. Vincent * Millay, who wrote poetry focused on women's experience and were sustained by one another's writing. (The obliteration of most of the history of lesbian writing was discussed in Louise Bernikow's introduction to *The World Split Open* in 1974, and in Elly Bulkin's introduction in 1981 to *Lesbian Poetry: An Anthology.*)

Although not every lesbian poem is feminist, the development of lesbian poetry in America cannot be separated from feminism. The second wave of the women's liberation movement was fueled, challenged, and shaped by writers, perhaps most eloquently by lesbian poets. Adrienne * Rich in "Power & Danger: The Work of A Common Woman" (her 1977 introduction to Judy * Grahn's collected poetry) and "Vesuvius at Home: The Power of Emily Dickinson" (1975), Audre * Lorde in "Poems Are Not Luxuries" (1977), and Grahn in *The Highest Apple: Sappho and the Lesbian Poetic Tradition* (1985) have all insisted on the power language has to transform our vision, our selves, and our world.

The lesbian poet, in their definition, is one who understands this power and who seizes language as an instrument of transformation.

The hundreds of books and chap-books published by lesbian poets of the seventies, most with small presses, include Paula Gunn Allen's *Coyote's Daylight Trip*, Ellen Marie Bissert's *the immaculate conception of the blessed virgin dyke*, Karen Brodine's *Illegal Assembly*, Olga *Broumas's *Beginning With O*, Michelle Cliff's *Claiming an Identity They Taught Me To Despise*, Judy Grahn's *The Work of a Common Woman*, Susan Griffin's *Like the Iris of an Eye*, Marilyn Hacker's *Taking Notice*, Irena *Klepfisz's *periods of stress*, Audre *Lorde's *The Black Unicorn*, Eleanor Lerman's *Armed Love*, Honor Moore's *Leaving and Coming Back*, Robin Morgan's *Monster*, Pat Parker's *Movement in Black*, Adrienne *Rich's *The Dream of a Common Language*, Muriel *Rukeyser's *Breaking Open*, Fran Winant's *Dyke Jacket*—an array of extremely diverse voices.

In addition to poetry about erotic experience and the opression shadowing it, lesbian poets wrote unromanticized portraits of other women; a complex range of self-portraits; poems of self-celebration; poems of black, Asian-American, Native American, Jewish, and working-class identity and experience; poems of motherhood, work, myth, *racism, violence, *holocaust, addiction, *incest, *spirituality, the planet, healing, prophecy. Lesbian poetry in the eighties and nineties has continued to explore such themes with increased complexity and sophistication while continuing to suggest that the personal and the political are one. Women's experience, anger, and visions of change continue to be the lifeblood of this body of work.

In the nineties, woman-owned lesbian feminist presses such as Eighth Mountain Press, Firebrand Books, Kitchen Table: Women of Color Press, Seal Press, and Spinsters/Aunt Lute continue to be responsible for the publishing of most of the lesbian poetry, though some comes from university presses and a few commercial publishers. Some poets, such as New York School–influenced Eileen Myles, have moved from more traditional public poetry readings towards theater and performance art. Recent magazines and anthologies have included poetry by lesbians along with that of gay men, in contrast to past separatism.

*Censorship of lesbian and gay materials still exists, overtly and covertly. Under pressure from Senator Jesse Helms, Congress passed an appropriations bill that forbids federal funding of works that may be considered obscene; the National Endowment for the Arts specifically flagged lesbian writers' fellowship applications for scrutiny, including that of Minnie Bruce *Pratt, whose *Crime Against Nature* (1990) is a sequence of poems about losing custody of her sons after *"coming out" as a lesbian.

Acceptance of lesbian poetry, on the other hand, has sometimes meant erasure through a kind of assimilation. A photograph of nude heterosexual lovers adorns the cover of May Swenson's posthumously collected *Love Poems* (1991); jacket copy mentions "human love"; nothing suggests that the poems were inspired by a lifelong passionate relationship with a woman. In an interview with Elly Bulkin in *Conditions: Two* (1977), Adrienne *Rich spoke of the heterosexualizing of *Twenty-One Love Poems* (1976) by those who wished to find her treatment of love "universal"—ignoring what is specifically lesbian in her vision of two "women outside the law."

The dissident voices of lesbian poets have received some acknowledgement from the literary mainstream. Rich and Lorde, for example, were both nominated for National Book Awards for Poetry in 1973, and Rich again in 1992; Olga Broumas's *Beginning With O* was selected for the Yale Younger Poets Series in 1977. Marilyn *Hacker's first book received the National Book Award and was the Lamont Selection of the Academy of American Poets; Minnie Bruce Pratt's *Crime Against Nature* also was a Lamont Selection. National and regional honors for many more of these poets suggest that the test of language has been met and that lesbian poetry is far from peripheral to American writing.

• Elly Bulkin, "A Look at Lesbian Poetry" and "Lesbian Poetry in the Classroom" in *Lesbian Poetry: An Anthology* (1981), ed. Elly Bulkin and Joan Larkin. Canyon, Nancy Hom, Genny Lim, Kitty Tsui, Nellie Wong, and Merle Woo, eds., *Unbound Feet* (1981). Cherríe Moraga and Gloria Anzaldúa, eds., *This Bridge Called My Back: Writings by Radical Women of Color*, 2nd ed. (1983). Juanita Ramos, ed., *Companeras: Latina Lesbians (An Anthology)* (1987). Christian McEwen, ed., *Naming the Waves: Contemporary Lesbian Poetry* (1988). Carl Morse and Joan Larkin, eds., *Gay and Lesbian Poetry in Our Time: An Anthology* (1988). Will Roscoe, coordinator, *Living the Spirit: A Gay American Indian Anthology* (1988). Minnie Bruce Pratt, *Rebellion: Essays 1980–1991* (1991). David Trinidad, *Open House: New Gay and Lesbian Poetry* (1993).

Joan Larkin

LE SUEUR, Meridel (b. 1900), novelist and political writer. Meridel Le Sueur's writing is painful in its truth about the plight of poor women. In stories written in the 1930s, recorded from the voices of women Le Sueur knew, we recognize women's entrapment by a history that has fostered their invisibility. In her political articles, appearing in the *New Masses*, *Daily Worker*, the *American Mercury*, *Partisan Review*, the *Nation*, and other publications, Le Sueur attempted to make the lives of women real to men—especially men who, though sharing her politics, could not countenance as political women's "personal" stories of sexual battery, unwanted pregnancy, and unpaid domestic labor.

The social and economic invisibility of poor and working-class women, as well as Le Sueur's passionate advocacy on their behalf, guaranteed her relative obscurity as a writer even at the height of the populist and workers' movements. Nor was she embraced by the literary establishment represented by *modernism. Le Sueur's novel, *The Girl*, written in 1932, was not published until 1978. Yet, as Linda Wagner-Martin points out in *The Modern American Novel 1914–1945*, "Le Sueur's writing in *The Girl* (1932) accomplished the fusion of form and function so important to the Modernist aesthetic, and in a way that had not before been broached by the male literary establishment. The clipped, often hackneyed language of *The Girl*, in its poignant mimicry of working-class speech, effects the melding of the writer with her down and out characters."

A composite of stories told by women who were living at the Worker's Alliance in St. Paul, *The Girl*, in Wagner-Martin's words, is "nonfiction fiction," an experimental genre that went virtually unnoticed as a literary achievement in Le Sueur's time.

A high school dropout, Le Sueur recognized the despair inherent in the American myth of individual heroism. In her words, " 'The Waste Land' paralyzed me for several years. It paralyzed a great many of us. People became existentialists. I began to talk against Plato when I was 12 years old. If this is what school is, I said, I'm leaving" (Erika Duncan, "Writing and Surviving," 1982). In place of the already stale patriarchal *myth, Le Sueur set a mythos of woman-centered regeneration and communal nurturing. To some modern women readers, this transcendental vision of a mothering community is implausible. Moreover, Le Sueur's sexual politics seem rooted in heterosexual platitudes, especially those concerning motherhood. Nevertheless, as Paula Rabinowitz has shown, Le Sueur is among the first women writers to help forge a female subjectivity by linking women's "personal" desires with historical processes. In addition, although Le Sueur sees the consciousness of the anonymous girl of the novel as forged through the sexual agency of men, she nevertheless recognizes women's bonding with one another as the key to survival in a world of male violence. Le Sueur's *community of women thus foreshadows the separatist politics of 1970s feminists, as well as Adrienne *Rich's lesbian continuum.

Le Sueur's mother, Marian, may have served as model for Le Sueur's activism on behalf of women, for Marian was a speaker for women's right to *birth control at a time when women were imprisoned for using contraceptives. Through her mother and stepfather, Arthur, Meridel as a girl met and absorbed the ideas of such powerful social reformers as Eugene Debs, Emma *Goldman, Mabel Dodge *Luhan, Margaret *Sanger, Theodore Dreiser, Carl Sandburg, and others. Her works were blacklisted throughout the McCarthy purge for their overtly leftist content; Le Sueur was denied work. In the late 1970s, she enjoyed a revival that is ongoing by feminist publishers and researchers, and as of the 1980s, when she herself was in her eighties, Le Sueur was still speaking on behalf of women, and experimenting with writing forms expressive of the Hopi concept of a natural world far more alive than "the American language" can express ("Writing and Surviving," 1982). Her legacy is an oeuvre that ranges from political articles to novels to children's stories, covering "two generations of radical women, those affiliated with the Old Left and those who came of age with the New Left and the most recent women's movement" (Constance Coiner, "Literature of Resistance," 1990).

• Erika Duncan, "Writing and Surviving: A Portrait of Meridel Le Sueur," in *Book Forum: An International Transdisciplinary Quarterly* 6, no. 1 (1982): 25–36. Paula Rabinowitz, "Maternity as History: Gender and the Transformation of Genre in Meridel Le Sueur's *The Girl*," in *Contemporary Literature* 29, no. 4 (Winter 1988): 538–548. Linda Wagner-Martin, *The Modern American Novel 1914–1945* (1990). Constance Coiner, "Literature of Resistance: The Intersection of Feminism and the Communist Left in Meridel Le Sueur and Tillie Olsen," in *Left Politics and the Literary Profession*, ed. Lennard J. Davis and M. Bella Mirabella (1990), pp. 162–185.

Billie Maciunas

LETTERS. Women's letters have provided biographers and historians with a treasure trove of information about how women of the past lived, thought, and felt. In addition, letters are often, in themselves, a form of literature, frequently beautiful, humorous, poignant, or tragic. However, the letter as history and the letter as literature are sometimes at odds with one another. As recent epistolary theorists have emphasized, a letter is its own literary form, with its own time-bound conventions. Thus, to read the letters of another era may provide some historical insights but, unless we have a prior understanding of that historical period, it is also easy to misread them.

In her classic essay, "The Female World of Love and Ritual: Relations Between Women in Nineteenth-Century America," Carroll Smith-Rosenberg quotes from numerous letters by women who express tenderness, physical affection, and love in terms that we would today recognize as "romantic" or "erotic." Reading through the lens of contemporary epistolary styles, one could interpret these as love letters, even passionate and open avowals of lesbian love. However, Smith-Rosenberg cautions that these women were heterosexual, married women who often considered it improper or immodest to divulge one's emotional nature to a man, even a lover or a husband. Thus passion was reserved for correspondence with one's dearest women friends. Critics of Smith-Rosenberg suggest that some of the women who wrote these letters *were* lesbians and that her explanation glosses over that fact. Still, her point is well taken: there are different conventions for expression in different eras and we must be aware of these as we plumb letters for some record of the past.

The letter is a complicated genre in another respect, too. It is one of the few literary forms where the audience is explicitly designated. A *diary is a personal record; a letter is a personal communication. It is addressed to someone with whom the writer has a prior history—or does not. The biographer or social historian who would turn to letters to discover past attitudes must be cautious about the ways in which writing for another person colors the presentation of events, facts, and attitudes. Is the author writing to persuade or present, to convince or cajole? The purpose of a letter is sometimes hard to divine since frequently intention is the one feature of a letter that is never explicitly stated. An announcement of one's engagement, for example, might take quite a different form in a letter to one's best friend and in a letter to one's former lover. And depending upon the circumstances of either the friendship or the break-up, either letter can take on a variety of tones and styles.

As one discovers from reading myriad letters, facts, too, can change depending on who is writing and who is receiving a given letter. Certainly in love letters we see the ways in which "truth" bends according to the situation of the letter writer and the letter receiver. One does not, for example, look for much that is factually accurate in a seduction letter. Natalie Barney could promise eternal love to Liane de Pougy even as she was flirting with other women. Simone de *Beauvoir wrote over and over to Nelson Algren, telling him of her love but saying she had to stay in Paris to tend "dear Sartre." For over a decade, Sartre provided a convenient excuse (if nothing else) for not becoming Mrs. Nelson Algren of Chicago, Illinois.

For all the limitations of letters as historical evidence, biographers and social historians could not write without the corroborating voice of the letter writer. That is, events can be documented, but social history also depends upon the ways in which ordinary (non-famous) individuals responded to and commented on events. Among the many books by historians that make extensive use of women's letters are Lillian Faderman's *Surpassing the Love of Men: Romantic Friendship and Love Between Women from the Renaissance to the Present* (1981), Linda K. Kerber's *Women of the Republic: Intellect and Ideology in Revolutionary America* (1980), Ellen K. Rothman's *Hands and Hearts: A History of Courtship in America* (1987), and Laurel Thatcher Ulrich's *Good Wives: Image and Reality in the Lives of Women in Northern New England, 1650–1750* (1982).

As Susan Koppelman notes in "Letters to Friends," a letter is more intimate and personal than an essay. By comparison to a letter, an essay is like "sex with a sex therapist." It lacks love, passion, little joking asides, and, most important, any real relationship between the participants.

[*See also* Diaries and Journals; Romantic Love.]

• Linda S. Kauffman, *Discourses of Desire: Gender, Genre, and Epistolary Fictions* (1986). Cathy N. Davidson, *The Book of Love: Writers and their Love Letters* (1992). Susan Koppelman, "Letters to Friends," in *The Intimate Critique: Autobiographical Literary Criticism* (1993).

Cathy N. Davidson

LEVERTOV, Denise (b. 1923), poet, poetic theorist, and translator. Born and raised in Ilford, Essex, in England, Denise Levertov had what she calls a "bucolic" childhood. The daughter of a Russian Jewish father and a Welsh mother, Levertov became a nurse during World War II, then married Mitchell Goodman in 1947 and came to the United States in 1948. She divorced in the 1970s and has one son. Levertov became a U.S. citizen in 1955 and considers herself an American poet, a true follower of William Carlos Williams and *H. D. She was also influenced by Charles Olson and Robert Duncan of the Black Mountain school of poetry, though she remains a poet who defies categorization, including that of "feminist poet." She was the poetry editor of the *Nation* and has taught at Tufts and Stanford Universities. Levertov's many volumes of poetry include *Overland to the Islands* (1958), *With Eyes at the Back of Our Heads* (1960), *The Sorrow Dance* (1967), *Relearning the Alphabet* (1970), *The Freeing of the Dust*

(1975), *Life in the Forest* (1978), *Candles in Babylon* (1982), *Breathing the Water* (1987), and *The Door in the Hive* (1989). She has also published two volumes of essays about poetry, *The Poet in the World* (1973) and *Light Up the Cave* (1981), and has translated works by the French poet Jean Joubert.

In spite of the tremendous output and changing subject matter inevitable in a long career, Denise Levertov's newest poems are admired for the same reasons her early poems were. Levertov's poems combine the sacred and the everyday in a seamless whole, written with the cadences of everyday speech and the metaphors of a probing imagination. While Levertov has never called herself a feminist, her work insists on the place of politics in personal life (and in poetry); her volumes during the Vietnam War first opened her work to the ongoing controversy of whether or not politics can make good poems. Her latest concerns include the potential for nuclear devastation and the situation in El Salvador.

Meditative and evocative, Levertov's poetry concerns itself with the search for meaning. She sees the poet's role as a priestly one; the poet is the mediator between ordinary people and the divine mysteries. Her perspective, however, remains a female one, and her work has been a large factor in the acceptance of domestic life as a subject matter for poetry. Levertov celebrates female spirituality and sexuality in poems such as the "Pig Dreams," first published in *Candles in Babylon*, and her questioning of the status quo necessarily includes the place of women in both myth and culture.

• Denise Levertov, *Collected Poems 1960–1974* (1976). Denise Levertov, *Collected Earlier Poems 1940–1960* (1979). Liana Sakelliou-Schultz, *Denise Levertov: An Annotated Primary and Secondary Bibliography* (1988). Harry Marten, *Understanding Denise Levertov* (1988). Linda Wagner-Martin, ed., *Critical Essays on Denise Levertov* (1990).

Susan J. Zevenbergen

LIBBEY, Laura Jean (1862–1925), popular novelist. Despite the fact that Laura Jean Libbey sold between 10 and 15 million books during her lifetime, little biographical information about her is known. A precocious writer, the fourteen-year-old Brooklyn native came to the attention of Richard Bonner, editor of the *New York Ledger*, who published a short piece of hers, and recommended that she return to him at age eighteen with more material. Libbey followed his advice, and in four years, she regularly began to contribute serialized stories to the *Ledger* and other popular magazines. These serialized works were later collected and printed in cheap paperbound editions costing between 15 and 25 cents each. It was through these collected editions that Libbey achieved her fame as one of the most popular and prolific writers of her day.

In novels such as *Leonie Locke: The Romance of a Beautiful New York Working Girl* (1889), *Willful Graynell; or, The Little Beauty of the Passaic Cotton Mills* (1890), and *Little Leafy, the Cloakmaker's Beautiful Daughter: A Romantic Story of a Lovely Working Girl in the City of New York* (1891), a thoroughly middle-class Libbey presented her urban and immigrant readership with different versions of the same basic story, known as the working-girl novel. These novels tell the story of the working girl's ascent to bourgeois respectability, but not before she must triumph over the unwanted sexual intrigues of the genteel villain. The heroine preserves her "virtue" and is rewarded with marriage to a wealthy young man. Often these novels conclude with the revelation that the working girl is herself an heiress, so that her newfound class status becomes a correlative of the "noble" nature that she had demonstrated while still a member of the working class.

After her death, Libbey vanished into literary obscurity, and the only critical attention she received tended to view her fiction as mass-market pulp devoid of any literary value. More recent critics have even asserted that her novels were complicit with the dominant socioeconomic interests of her day because they provided working-class women with fantasies of class mobility that obscured and repressed their actual conditions. While Libbey's novels can be faulted for their lack of "realism," some other recent critics have located in her novels a redefinition of acceptable social activity for young unmarried women that extended to the public workplace, and a utopic protest, however coded, against the working conditions of these newest urban laborers.

• The Bonner Papers in the N.Y. Public Library contain five letters from Libbey, as well as six travel journals that she kept while on a tour of Europe and Egypt. See also Joyce Shaw Peterson, "Working Girls and Millionaires: The Melodramatic Romances of Laura Jean Libbey," *American Studies* 24, no. 1 (Spring 1983): 19–36. Michael Denning, *Mechanic Accents: Dime Novels and Working-Class Culture in America* (1987), pp. 185–200.

Michael Maiwald

LIBERAL FEMINISM originated in eighteenth-century America in the adoption of republican rhetoric and tactics for the cause of women's rights. Early manifestations of liberal feminism include revolutionary pamphlets like the "Sentiments of an American Woman," published in Philadelphia in 1766, which proclaimed that "women were born for liberty" and that they "refused to be enchained by tyrannic government." As early as 1781, young slave women such as Jenny Slew and Elizabeth Freeman successfully sued for their freedom in state court on the grounds that the Massachusetts Bill of Rights applied to them as "persons." Driven by the conviction that all human beings are equal, proponents of women's rights argued that the inalienable rights to life, liberty, and the pursuit of happiness enshrined in the American Declaration of Independence should recognize no distinctions based on sex or color.

The abolitionist movement launched the first public speakers for women's rights in the United States. In 1832, at a time when custom prohibited the participation of women in public debates, the Afric-American Female Intelligence Society in Boston invited abolitionist Maria Stewart to address a mixed audience of men and women in Franklin Hall. A twenty-nine-year-old free black woman, Stewart delivered a lecture that captured many of the principal themes of nineteenth-century liberal feminism. She argued that apparent differences between slaves and free people, and between men and women, are the product of oppressive customs, which are themselves rooted in physical force. Devoid of any moral legitimacy, such life-destroying practices must be abolished. The law affords the means by which to change intolerable traditions. The scope of legal reform must include elimination of all forms of human bondage; formal equality before the law, including rights to vote and hold office, rights to property and to sue in court; elimination of barriers to full participation in all modes of employment; and educational opportunity without regard to race or sex.

These themes formed the core platform of the 1848 Seneca Falls *Declaration of Rights and Sentiments* and of the 1850 *Resolutions of the Women's Rights Convention* in Worcester, Massachusetts. Linking these demands to democratic arguments for justice, progress, individualism, social utility, self-protection, and self-development, noted women's rights advocates such as Lucretia *Mott, Angelina and Sarah *Grimké, Elizabeth Cady *Stanton, Susan B. *Anthony, Lucy Stone, Antoinette (Nette) Brown Blackwell, Sojourner *Truth, Harriet *Tubman, Mary Ann Shadd Cary, and Frances Ellen *Harper continued to press for equality regardless of race or sex through public speeches, essays, court cases, and through the formation of the American Equal Rights Association. The solidarity among abolitionists and women's rights advocates was shattered during debates over the proposed Fifteenth Amendment to the U.S. Constitution, which afforded voting rights to African-American men, but not to women. The consequences of this rift were manifold: racist arguments surfaced and were used strategically by the new National Woman's Suffrage Association under the direction of Stanton and Anthony; to distance themselves from such racist strategies, Lucy Stone, Nette Blackwell, and Julia Ward *Howe founded the American Woman's Suffrage Association; under the leadership of Mary Ann Shadd Cary, African-American women organized the Colored Women's Progressive Association, which adopted women's rights as a central goal. The splintering of the women's rights movement was accompanied by a narrowing of focus: suffrage supplanted the holistic focus on social, economic, and political equality.

In the twentieth century, the second wave of American liberal feminism is frequently traced to the publication of Betty *Friedan's *The Feminist Mystique* (1963). Denouncing an ideal of femininity that denies women's rationality, restricts women to the home, and deprives society of half the world's talent, Friedan launched a movement to eradicate the continuing vestiges of sex discrimination. Forming the National Organization of Women, Friedan devised a multifaceted agenda that included attainment of equal political rights, increasing the representation of women in elective and appointive office, and mobilization of women as a political force to hold politicians accountable for their votes on women's issues. Over the past thirty years, liberal feminists have worked within the system, using techniques including public demonstrations, lobbying, litigation, and civil disobedience to eliminate obstacles to women's equal participation in society and to win substantive improvements in areas such as affirmative action, pay equity, *abortion rights and reproductive freedom, equitable divorce settlements, job segregation by sex, pension equity, *sexual harassment, child care, *pregnancy discrimination, *rape relief, and domestic *violence.

Liberal feminists acknowledge that despite more than 200 years of struggle, they have not yet attained their goal of sexual equality. Radical feminists, Marxist feminists, and socialist feminists have argued that the liberal feminist agenda can never provide meaningful equality to all women: operating within the confines of a capitalist market economy, it fails to redress the economic inequities that constrain the life prospects of working-class women and women of color.

[*See also* Conservatism; Feminism; Radical Feminism; Women's Movement.]

• Elizabeth Cady Stanton, Susan B. Anthony, and Mathilda J. Gage, eds., *The History of Women's Suffrage*

(1881). Bert J. Loewenberg and Ruth Bogin, eds., *Black Women in Nineteenth-Century American Life* (1976). Linda Kerber, *Women of the Republic: Intellect and Ideology in Revolutionary America* (1980). Paula Giddings, *When and Where I Enter: The Impact of Black Women on Race and Sex in America* (1984). Nancy F. Cott, *The Grounding of American Feminism* (1987).

Mary Hawkesworth

LIBRARIES. The history of women's association with libraries in America is linked to the history of their efforts to educate themselves, to improve their own lives and the lives of others, and to be recognized as scholars, teachers, writers, or simply independent readers. In the last decade of the eighteenth and the early nineteenth centuries, starting in the northeastern United States, middle-class women were gradually freed from the necessity of participating in economic production in the household and became aware of new opportunities for intellectual growth, social action and influence, employment, and fulfilling family and social relationships. Girls received more schooling and women's *literacy rate rose. By the 1830s, women were assuming new economic and social roles—as educators, authors, reformers, and industrial laborers—and their roles as wives and mothers took on new meaning.

During this period, the wider circulation of printed materials, including newspapers and magazines, paved the way for the establishment of more libraries and new types of libraries. The rules and codes of behavior governing women's access to these libraries varied: many excluded women entirely, while others provided separate reading rooms or specified separate hours for women and men, and some were exclusively for women. Typically, a woman could not join a library in her own name, but withdrew books as the family member of a male subscriber. In spite of these barriers, more women—like men—became library users.

Educators and other authorities promoted reading as a means of self-improvement and the carefully selected library as a schoolroom of the people. The concept of self-education was hardly new to women, who were given at most a post–grammar school education in an academy or seminary, and had to rely on themselves if they wanted more. Women who could afford books or whose friends or families owned books pursued their studies in personal or household libraries. Most women who wrote of educating themselves in this way expressed satisfaction and pride at what they had been able to accomplish, but the experience could also be frustrating and lead to heightened awareness of male privilege. Sarah *Grimké, who as a young woman studied law in her father's library, was bitterly disappointed to realize that, because of her sex, she could neither continue her studies in college, as her brothers had, nor practice law.

The thousands of girls and young women who left rural homes to work in the boardinghouse mill towns of New England from about 1820 to 1860 went primarily for the chance to earn a living and perhaps save some money for an academy education or for marriage later, but they also found there opportunities for self-improvement and education. Working as long as thirteen hours a day amid noise and dust, the women created a supportive culture (later exploited by mill owners to paint a rosy picture of mill conditions) that valued and encouraged reading, writing, attending lectures, going to school and church, and belonging to voluntary associations. In this culture some workers developed the consciousness and skills that prepared them for labor movement participation. Elfrieda McCauley, in her unpublished dissertation "The New England Mill Girls: Feminine Influence in the Development of Public Libraries in New England, 1820–1860" (1971), found that, excluded from mechanics' and mill libraries, the women drew heavily from the many Sunday school and commercial circulating libraries in the mill towns. According to former mill worker Harriet Robinson (*Loom and Spindle*, 1898), Lowell's famous circulating libraries were responsible for attracting to and keeping in the mills young women from isolated parts of New England who had no such resources at home.

For nineteenth-century readers of fiction, especially novel readers, circulating libraries were a wonderful resource. The low cost of borrowing a book from a circulating library enabled working as well as middle- and upper-class women to take out books. Both women and men read novels and borrowed from circulating libraries, but in the late eighteenth and early nineteenth centuries, many circulating libraries—usually, but not always, attached to bookstores—had the twin advantages of welcoming women and stocking novels. David Kaser (*A Book for a Sixpence: The Circulating Library in America*, 1980) notes that it was not unusual for a circulating library's proprietor to be a woman and for the library to be attached to an establishment patronized primarily by women, such as a fabric or milliner's shop.

Women not only used libraries, they established them as well. In her research on the history of women's voluntary associations, Ann Firor Scott (*Natural Allies: Women's Associations in American History*, 1991) rediscovered the role of women's organizations in the creation of thousands of libraries throughout the nineteenth century, but especially after 1850, when public libraries began to supersede commercial and semipublic types. *Women's organizations established new libraries, supported existing community libraries, and formed lending libraries for the use of their members. Officers of the Female Literary Association of Philadelphia, organized by free black women in 1831, included a Librarian, who looked after the association's books, and an Agent, who subscribed to and cared for its periodicals. Later, black women's clubs established libraries in the segregated South, where library services for blacks were virtually nonexistent. Women donated libraries, too. In her research, McCauley discovered two women mill workers who had served as librarians in mill town libraries and left their life savings for the founding of public libraries.

Women gained access to academic libraries more slowly than to public libraries. Early in the century, pioneer educators Emma Willard and Catharine *Beecher, drawing on their own experiences, pointed out that owners of schools for girls and young women were unable to afford libraries for their pupils because their schools did not attract the endowments and public support that most schools for boys and young men enjoyed. And because only a few thousand women before 1900 were admitted to colleges, few women ever entered a college or university library. Even when there was no overt denial of access, women encountered barriers. Scholar Joyce Antler tells of one turn-of-the-century Radcliffe student who persuaded her grandmother to accompany her on her visits to Harvard's library to work on her senior thesis because it would have been unthinkable for her to enter this male domain unchaperoned.

If the main problem for women library users before 1900 was access, in this century it has been women's invisibility within libraries. All types of libraries and archives have tended to ignore or dismiss women's cultures and history, their written records, and their creative work. The second wave of feminism and the tremendous renewal of interest in women caused this situation to change. Existing collections by and about women were rediscovered and new collections were born. Feminist librarians, calling attention to the problems of terminology, organization, and institutional indifference that prevented patrons from finding out about women, began to produce displays, written guides, and bibliographies for users.

One of the ways that women have coped with their invisibility has been to establish special libraries of materials relating to women, or special collections within libraries. This strategy has resulted in the development of major

institutions and collections as well as smaller, independent organizations. The Arthur and Elizabeth Schlesinger Library on the History of Women in America at Radcliffe College began as two separate special collections—the Woman's Rights Collection, donated in 1943, and consisting primarily of published and unpublished materials on the history of the woman's rights movement; and papers solicited by historian Mary Ritter *Beard in the late 1930s for a World Center for Women's Archives. Aware that source materials on women's history were not being collected by libraries or archives, Beard established the World Center in the late 1930s, but, unable to find funding, had to discontinue her efforts. In 1945 she donated the materials she had collected to Radcliffe. In the 1960s the two collections and others were brought together under one name and one roof.

Smaller, independent, and sometimes temporary libraries and archives have been developed by grassroots movements to serve the needs of particular communities of library users. The Freedom Libraries established in Mississippi in 1964 and 1965 as part of the *civil rights movement not only provided library services to people excluded from other libraries, but made visible through their collections the history and culture of black Americans. The libraries' resources supported children and adults who were writing for the first time about their experiences as black Americans. The *Lesbian Herstory Archives, founded in 1973 in New York City, is one of several independent lesbian archives and libraries in the country. Established to recover, preserve, celebrate, and share the history of lesbian lives and culture, its collections range from the usual to the unusual—from diaries, letters, and papers of individual lesbians to vertical files on every conceivable lesbian subject and lesbian organization; from unpublished stories to pulp paperback novels; from photographs and graphics to T-shirts and bumper stickers. A community project, it is organized as a lesbian collective, run by lesbian volunteers, and open to all lesbians.

[See also Bookstores; Literacy; Education; Reading Circles; Readership; Women's Clubs.]

• Andrea Hinding, ed., Women's History Sources: A Guide to Archives and Manuscript Collections in the United States (1979). Suzanne Hildenbrand, ed., Women's Collections: Libraries, Archives, and Consciousness (1986). Cal Gough and Ellen Greenblatt, eds., Gay and Lesbian Library Service (1990).

Priscilla D. Older

LIN, Hazel Ai Chun (1913–1986), surgeon and novelist. Born in Foochow, Fukien, China, Hazel Lin earned a B.S. degree from Yenjing University in 1932, an M.D. from the Beijing Union

Medical College in 1935, and an M.S. from the University of Michigan in 1938. Thereafter, she lived in Jersey City, New Jersey, with her husband, chemical engineer Dr. Utah Tsao. She served as an endocrinologist and surgeon at Jersey City Medical Center until her death from a stroke.

In addition to having had a full-time medical career, Lin authored four novels and one piece of nonfiction. Her first book, *The Physicians* (1951), is probably the best and was certainly the best received. Shortly after its publication in New York, translations appeared in Zagreb, Yugoslavia; Allahabad, India; and Verviers, Belgium. It is apparently an autobiographical novel about an orphaned Chinese girl, granddaughter of a famous Beijing surgeon, who studies western medicine. Her grandfather, a practitioner of Chinese medicine, at first disapproves and later is convinced that foreign medicine also has its value. Though the book is at times somewhat cloying in tone, its plot is interesting and various and its cross-cultural perspectives are fresh and engaging.

Lin's second novel, *The Moon Vow* (1958), has a sensational subject and a melodramatic style. A woman doctor seeks to help a newly married sixteen-year-old patient who refuses to consummate her marriage. Probing into the young bride's life, the doctor discovers that the girl's teacher, an older woman who has been her surrogate mother, has forced the young woman to vow not to give up her virginity or the teacher would commit suicide. The teacher belongs to a secret lesbian society that is nefarious and cruel.

Lin's third novel, *House of Orchids*, is a sympathetic portrayal of the tragic life of a beautiful, poor young woman. Sold into prostitution by her destitute family, she falls in love with a young student but is forced to marry a wealthy old man. *Rachel Weeping for Her Children Uncomforted* (1976) tells the sad story of a young Chinese medical student who has an affair with a Caucasian surgeon, becomes pregnant, and has an abortion, succeeded by a nervous breakdown. In contrast to these two sensational novels of women's victimization, Dr. Lin's diary of her own emotional and psychological battle with cancer, *Weeping May Tarry, My Long Night With Cancer* (1980), is refreshingly real and moving.

• Amy Ling, *Between Worlds: Women Writers of Chinese Ancestry* (1990).

Amy Ling

LIN, Tai-yi (b. 1926), novelist, editor, translator, and biographer. The second of three daughters, Lin Tai-yi and her sisters were early encouraged to write by their famous author father, Dr. Lin Yutang. Before the age of sixteen, she had published three books that were coauthored with her sisters: *Our Family* (1939), a humorous account of daily life in the Lin family; *Dawn over Chungking* (1941), a report of their visit to China at war; and *Girl Rebel* (1940), their translation of the * diary of a Chinese girl soldier. By seventeen, Lin Tai-yi had launched her own individual literary career with the publication of her first novel. *War Tide* (1943) displayed stylistic finesse and emotional passion remarkable in any writer, but extraordinary in one so young. This book eclipsed her older sister's first novel, *Flame from the Rock*, which appeared the same year. Lin Tai-yi went on to publish four additional novels: *The Golden Coin* (1946), which pits cold rationality against intuition and idealism in war-torn China; *The Eavesdropper* (1958), about a man with loyalties divided between China and the U.S., and between his brother's wife and his own; *The Lilacs Overgrow* (1960), which contrasts the marriages of two sisters; and *Kampoon Street* (1964), recounting the life of an impoverished family in Hong Kong. In 1965, Lin translated and edited *Flowers in the Mirror*, a nineteenth-century Chinese satire, and she has recently completed a biography of her father.

An international figure, Lin Tai-yi has lived in many lands. Born in Beijing, she spent most of her first decade in Shanghai, then came to the U.S. at age ten. She returned to China for a year in 1945, taught Chinese at Yale University in 1945–1946, studied literature at Teacher's College, Columbia University, from 1947–1949, and married R. Ming (Richard) Lai, a translator for the B.B.C., in Paris in 1949. Between 1954 and 1962 she lived in England and Hong Kong, where she was editor-in-chief of *Readers Digest International*. In 1988, she retired to the U.S. She now lives, as though poised for flight, in a high-rise apartment building overlooking National Airport outside Washington, D.C. Her work, with its deep understanding of the human psyche and its rich variety, has not yet received the recognition it so well deserves.

• Elaine H. Kim, *Asian American Literature: An Introduction to the Writings and Their Social Context* (1982). Amy Ling, *Between Worlds: Women Writers of Chinese Ancestry* (1990).

Amy Ling

LINDBERGH, Anne Morrow (b. 1906), essayist, travel writer, poet. Born in Englewood, New Jersey, the second child of Dwight and Elizabeth Cutter Morrow, Anne graduated from Smith College in 1928 and married Charles Lindbergh in 1929. Her first son, Charles, Jr., was kidnapped from the Lindberghs' Hopewell, New Jersey, home in March 1932 at the age of

20 months, and was later found dead. Lindbergh flew as copilot and radio operator with her husband, and her first two works were accounts of her flights: *North to the Orient* (1935) and *Listen! the Wind* (1938). Prior to World War II, Lindbergh also assisted her husband in his noninterventionist activities, producing a brief but controversial philosophical essay, *The Wave of the Future* (1940). After America entered the war, Lindbergh wrote *The Steep Ascent* (1944), a fictional account of a 1937 European flight; at the end of the war she lived in Connecticut and devoted most of her energy to raising her three sons and two daughters. Her most popular and enduring work, *Gift from the Sea*, was published in 1955. A collection of poetry, *The Unicorn and Other Poems*, appeared a year later, and a novel, *Dearly Beloved*, in 1962. Two longer essays were published under the title *Earth Shine* (1969). Published in five volumes from 1972 to 1980, her diaries and letters describe her life up to the end of World War II. She was widowed in 1974.

In addition to the flying adventures she shared with her husband, other important influences in Lindbergh's literary works included the philosophical outlook of her father, Dwight Morrow, and the writings of Rainier Maria Rilke and Antoine de Saint-Exupéry. While Lindbergh has been widely read (especially *Gift from the Sea* and *North to the Orient*), she merits more critical analysis than she has received. She discerned the value of interior as well as exterior observation, of the observation of self as well as the external world. Thus *North to the Orient* becomes a study of visual perception; *Listen! the Wind* and *The Steep Ascent* become cultural comparisons, *The Unicorn* and *Dearly Beloved* examinations of family values, and *Gift from the Sea* a *Walden*-like consideration of the importance of simplifying one's personal values. The five-volume collection of her diaries and letters may well become the most valued of her writings, both for its descriptions of world events and important personalities, and for the insight it provides into her personal growth as a writer.

• Elsie F. Mayer, *My Window on the World: The Works of Anne Morrow Lindbergh* (1988). David Kirk Vaughan, *Anne Morrow Lindbergh* (1988). Trude Wurz, *Anne Morrow Lindbergh: The Literary Reputation: A Primary and an Annotated Secondary Bibliography* (1988). Dorothy Herrmann, *Anne Morrow Lindbergh: A Gift for Life* (1992).

David Kirk Vaughan

LINGUISTS. Linguistics, the scientific study of language, achieved public autonomy as an academic discipline in the United States in 1924 with the formation of the Linguistic Society of America. Four of the most prominent early LSA members were E. Adelaide Hahn (1893–1967), Elsie Clews Parsons (1875–1941), Louise *Pound (1872–1958), and Ola Elizabeth Winslow (1885?–1977).

Like many other LSA members then and now, Winslow was not actually a linguist. Rather, she was a prolific writer on colonial religious history, producing such works as *Meetinghouse Hill, 1630–1783* (1952; reprint, 1972), *Master Roger Williams* (1957; reprint, 1973), and *John Eliot: Apostle to the Indians* (1968). In 1941 she received the Pulitzer Prize in biography for *Jonathan Edwards, 1703–1758* (1940; reprint, 1972).

Louise Pound, a faculty member in English at the University of Nebraska, was well known among the linguists of her time. Her books (*Poetic Origins and the Ballad*, 1921, reprinted in 1962; *American Ballads and Songs*, 1922) reflect an early interest in music, but it was through her studies of contemporary language usage and American English dialects that she achieved national prominence and influence (*Selected Writings of Louise Pound*, 1949). A senior founder (in 1925) and early co-editor of the journal *American Speech*, Pound was twice vice-president of the Modern Language Association of America (in 1916 and 1925), as well as a director of the National Council of Teachers of English (1915–1919) and president of the American Dialect Society (1938–1944). She served as vice-president of the LSA in 1939, and it is possible that her resignation from the organization at the conclusion of 1942, after eighteen years of membership, was prompted by the society's continued pattern of selecting only male presidents.

A lifelong member of the Linguistic Society, Adelaide Hahn (1893–1967) in 1924 was an instructor in classics at Hunter College in New York; by 1936 she was a professor and head of the department, a position she held until her retirement in 1963. She rarely missed a meeting of the society, often presenting a paper, and always commenting on the papers of others. In 1946 she became LSA president, the first woman to hold that position and, until 1963, the only one. Hahn published scholarly works on Latin, Hittite, and Indo-European (*Subjunctive and Optative: Their Origin as Futures*, 1953; *Naming-Constructions in Some Indo-European Languages*, 1969; and, with her friend and mentor Edgar H. Sturtevant, *A Comparative Grammar of the Hittite Language*, vol. 1, revised edition, 1951). A vivid presence, an active member of the profession, and a strong feminist in a field that was largely male-dominated during her lifetime, Adelaide Hahn is one of the most notable women in twentieth-century American linguistics.

A major goal of American linguistics through the late 1950s was the description of native American Indian languages. Elsie Clews Parsons's work, more anthropological and ethnological than linguistic, complemented this interest. Parsons published many books on Indian culture, but perhaps her most remarkable achievement was *American Indian Life* (1922; reprint, 1967). Describing herself as a "Member of the Hopi Tribe" (an honorary title) in the table of contents, she persuaded the most prominent anthropologists, ethnologists, and linguists of her day to contribute accurate but partially fictionalized accounts ("stories" or "tales") from their knowledge, experience, and contacts with different native peoples. Included among these contributors were five men who, two years later, were to call for the establishment of the LSA: Franz Boas, Alfred L. Kroeber, Truman Michelson, Edward Sapir, and John R. Swanton. In the moving preface to her book, Parsons describes "the wife of the Presbyterian Missionary in an Indian town in New Mexico" whose misconceptions and insensitivity about Indians are drawn from her readings of popular fiction; *American Indian Life* is a response "to the over-abundant lore of the white man about the Indian. In this book the white man's traditions about Indians have been disregarded."

Among the linguists who have conducted empirical observations, scientific analyses, and objective descriptions of Native American languages, one highly regarded woman is Mary R. Haas; her study *Tunica* (1941), on a language of the southeastern United States, is a classic in the field. Haas (b. 1910), the second woman president of the LSA (in 1963), also published extensive teaching materials for Thai (such as with Heng R. Subhanka, *Spoken Thai*, 1945), but her scholarly work (see *Language, Culture, and History: Essays*, 1978) has focused on American Indian languages and their history (*The Prehistory of Languages*, 1969).

Similar interests, but from a different perspective, can be seen in the writings of Eunice V. Pike (b. 1913), who has been associated throughout her career with the Summer Institute of Linguistics. Founded in the mid-1930s, this organization operates with a dual program: the linguistic analysis and description of native languages—especially in Mexico and South America—and the translation of the New Testament into those languages. Eunice Pike is well known professionally for numerous descriptive linguistic studies, but her writings also include three accounts of her experiences as "a missionary linguist" living among the Mazatec-speaking people of Mexico (*Not Alone*, 1956; *Words Wanted*, 1958; *An Uttermost Part*, 1971).

Increasing numbers of women entered the field of linguistics during the 1960s, 1970s, and 1980s. With only two women presidents in its first 55 years (Hahn and Haas), the LSA elected four women to the presidency in less than a decade: Ilse Lehiste in 1980, Victoria A. Fromkin in 1985, Barbara Hall Partee in 1986, and Elizabeth Closs Traugott in 1987. Their different interests reflect some of the changes that were taking place in the discipline during this time, with an increasing focus on linguistic theory rather than description. All have published extensively in professional journals and scientific monographs, but each has also authored or coauthored a major textbook introducing readers to important areas of linguistic study.

Ilse Lehiste (b. 1922) is an internationally recognized expert in phonetics (such as *Suprasegmentals*, 1970) and coauthor with Robert J. Jeffers of *Principles and Methods for Historical Linguistics* (1979). Victoria A. Fromkin (b. 1923) also has worked in phonetics, as well as specializing in the psycholinguistic investigation of speech errors (*Speech Errors as Linguistic Evidence*, 1973; *Errors in Linguistic Performance: Slips of the Tongue, Ear, Pen, and Hand*, 1980); with Robert Rodman she coauthored five editions of a widely adopted textbook, *An Introduction to Language* (1st edition, 1974; 5th edition, 1988). Barbara Hall Partee (b. 1940) has focused on mathematics and linguistics (*Fundamentals of Mathematics for Linguistics*, 1978; coauthor with Alice ter Meulen and Robert E. Wall, *Mathematical Methods in Linguistics*, 1990); her best-known book is probably the edited collection in linguistic theory *Montague Grammar* (1976). Prominent in both linguistics and English, Elizabeth Closs Traugott (b. 1939) has written *A History of English Syntax* (1972) and, with Mary Louise Pratt, *Linguistics for Students of Literature* (1980).

By the early 1990s, well over half the degrees awarded in linguistics in the United States each year were earned by women, and women's writings have influenced every aspect of the discipline. But it is the subject of "women and language" that has most attracted public attention: Robin Tolmach Lakoff's personal and political *Language and Woman's Place* (1975), and her recent *Talking Power: The Politics of Language in Our Lives* (1990); Francine Wattman Frank and Paula A. Treichler's scholarly *Language, Gender, and Professional Writing* (1989); Deborah F. Tannen's best-selling *You Just Don't Understand: Women and Men in Conversation* (1990), and her earlier *That's Not What I Meant! How Conversational Style Makes or Breaks Your Relations with Others* (1986).

[See also Black English; Language, Women's; Nonstandard English.]

• George S. Lane, "E. Adelaide Hahn," *Language* 43, no. 4 (1967): 958–964. Ruth M. Brend and Kenneth L. Pike, eds., *The Summer Institute of Linguistics: Its Works and Contributions* (1977). Peter Hare, *A Woman's Quest for Science: Portrait of Anthropologist Elsie Clews Parsons* (1985). Frederick J. Newmeyer, "The Growth of the Field," in *Linguistic Theory in America*, 2d ed. (1986), pp. 44–51. Robert Channon and Linda Shockey, eds., *In Honor of Ilse Lehiste/Ilse Lehiste Pühendusteos* (1987). Larry M. Hyman and Charles N. Li, eds., *Language, Speech and Mind: Studies in Honour of Victoria A. Fromkin* (1988). William Shipley, ed., *In Honor of Mary Haas* (1988). Julie Tetel Andresen, "Louise Pound (1872–1958)," in *Linguistics in America 1769–1924* (1990), pp. 233–235. Frederick J. Newmeyer, "The Structure of the Field and Its Consequences for Women," and Alice Davison, Walter Cichocki, and David Silva, "The Representation of Women in Linguistics 1989," in *The Cornell Lectures: Women in the Linguistics Profession*, eds. Alice Davison and Penelope Eckert (1990), pp. 43–53 and 72–88, respectively. Rosemary L. Zumwalt, *Wealth and Rebellion: Elsie Clews Parsons, Anthropologist and Folklorist* (1992).

Julia S. Falk

LIPPINCOTT, Sara Jane. *See* Greenwood, Grace.

LITERACY. From the 1600s to the 1900s, women experienced considerable gains in literacy, in large part because of increased access to * education. However, all women did not benefit equally from these changes, for a range of social conditions influenced women's ability to acquire literacy—* race, * class, * ethnicity, region, sex roles, and ideology. Despite what at times have been overwhelming barriers, women have been able to gain the literacy skills necessary for becoming writers, often through self-education.

The literacy histories of three women writers from the Colonial period demonstrate the combination of circumstance and will to learn necessary for achieving higher levels of literacy. Anne * Bradstreet, the first woman to publish a volume of poetry in the United States, received her education before she emigrated from England. Her father was a steward to the Earl of Lincoln, a situation that provided her with access to private tutors and the Earl's library. The first African-American woman to publish a collection of poems, Phillis * Wheatley displayed an interest in learning and was tutored by the Massachusetts family who purchased her when she was seven years old. She quickly learned English and Latin. The educational experience of Abigail * Adams shows that the status of women's education had changed little by the end of the Colonial period. Though born into a prominent New England family, she never attended school. Instead, she was taught by her grandmother and educated herself through her own extensive reading in the family library.

Adams frequently wrote about the poor condition of women's education and she lived to see improved opportunities for women's advanced education during the republican period as seminaries and academies were founded to train women for their new role of educating the young citizens of the republic. Caroline * Kirkland, Elizabeth * Stoddard, Emily * Dickinson, and Harriet Beecher * Stowe attended female seminaries. But this higher education was not available for all. Alice * Cary's education consisted of irregular attendance at a district school; she received her advanced training in literature by reading the "poet's corner" in a religious newspaper to which her family subscribed. Lydia Maria * Child's father believed that one year of an academy education was sufficient for his daughter although he sent his son to Harvard. Child furthered her education by reading her brother's textbooks.

While the antebellum period saw access to public education grow as a result of the common school movement, the educational opportunities of African-Americans became increasingly restricted. Free blacks in the North were often prohibited from attending public schools, but members of the African-American community responded by founding private, benevolent, and church schools. Frances E. W. * Harper attended a school for free black children in Baltimore that was run by her aunt and uncle, who adopted her after her parents died. She supplemented her formal schooling with her reading: at age thirteen she began working as a housekeeper for a family who owned a bookstore and used her few spare moments to read. In the South, legal restrictions against slave literacy increased after the Nat Turner Rebellion in 1832. However, as Janet Duitsman Cornelius notes, many slaveowners subordinated state law to Christian tenets and taught their slaves to read the Bible. Harriet * Jacobs, born in Edenton, North Carolina, in 1813, was taught to read and sew by her mistress.

In the late 1800s, women's access to higher education increased dramatically as women's colleges were established and public institutions began to admit women. Women often used higher education intended for traditional roles and occupations for their own ends. Alice * Dunbar-Nelson graduated from Straight College's teacher program, taught, and then used her training to become a writer. * Zitkala-Sa (Gertrude Bonnin) left the Yankton Sioux reservation in South Dakota when she was eight to attend a Quaker missionary school, one of many institutions established in the late 1800s to

"Americanize" Native Americans, and then attended Earlham College. She used her writing skills to improve the conditions of Native American's lives, both through autobiographical essays and fiction and in her work as a political activist for the Society of American Indians and the National Council of American Indians.

Women who immigrated to the United States at the turn of the century encountered many obstacles to achieving literacy in English. Amy Ling notes in *Between Worlds: Women Writers of Chinese Ancestry* (1990) that the majority of Chinese women who immigrated to the United States in the late nineteenth century were working-class people who lacked the education and the time to write literature. Thus, most Chinese-American women writers were born in China to families of upper- or upper-middle-class backgrounds who educated their children in Western languages. However, the class values that encouraged education also discouraged women from writing because it was seen as an act of disrespect. The experience of * Sui Sin Far (Edith Maud Eaton), the first Chinese-American writer, demonstrates the influence of class, education, individual family values, and history on women's acquisition of literacy. Born into an upper-middle-class family that had lost its money, Sui Sin Far was educated by parents who loved the arts and nurtured their children's artistic interests.

* Immigrant women who sought an education when they arrived in the United States found limited opportunities. Maxine Seller notes in *Immigrant Women* (1981) that fewer educational programs existed for women than for men. These programs taught only the English necessary for mastering the domestic skills that comprised the core of the curriculum. Anzia * Yezierska, whose family emigrated from Russian Poland in the 1890s, began her education by paying a janitor's daughter to teach her lessons from her schoolbooks. She attended night classes at a settlement house to learn English while working during the day in sweatshops and laundries. Demonstrating promise as a student, Yezierska won a scholarship from Columbia Teacher's College to study domestic science, a discipline she disdained but chose to pursue because it was her only option for receiving a higher education.

Women's access to public education has continued to improve throughout the twentieth century, but many of the barriers to literacy faced by Colonial women remain today. However, the impact of * feminism and multiculturalism on education and publishing has improved women's opportunities for reading and writing literature that mirrors the complexity of their lives and identities. Alma Gomez,

Cherríe * Moraga, and Marian Romo-Carmona introduce *Cuentos: Stories by Latinas* (1983) by defining themselves as first-generation writers seeking to record the literary tradition their mothers and grandmothers passed onto them: the "cuentos" told by word of mouth are now preserved in writing, in their languages—Spanish and English.

[*See also* Education; Libraries.]

• Carter G. Woodson, *The Education of the Negro Prior to 1861* (1919; reprint, 1968). James D. Anderson, *The Education of Blacks in the South, 1860–1935* (1988). John Mack Faragher and Florence Howe, eds., *Women and Higher Education in American History* (1988). Ann Allen Shockley, *Afro-American Women Writers, 1746–1933* (1988). Janet Duitsman Cornelius, *"When I Can Read My Title Clear": Literacy, Slavery, and Religion in the Antebellum South* (1991). Carl F. Kaestle, et al., *Literacy in the United States* (1991). Judith Fetterley and Marjorie Pryse, eds., *American Women Regionalists 1850–1910* (1992).

Amy M. Thomas

LITERARY CRITICISM by American women, like all American criticism, has its roots in the nineteenth-century tradition of literary journalism. When criticism was professionalized around the turn of the century, it was redefined to exclude the work of literary journalists, and isolated in the mostly male preserve of the academy. As a result, criticism by women was more prominent in the mass periodical press than in academic journals during the first half of the twentieth century. In the postwar period, an influx of women into higher education and the rise of the modern feminist movement has challenged male dominance of academic criticism and established * feminist criticism as an important field of critical discourse.

Book reviews and critical essays were a common feature of the many periodicals that were produced over the course of the nineteenth century. Contributors to these magazines were expected to conform to the ideal of the writer as a leisured gentleman or lady who wrote (more for pleasure than profit or prestige) in addition to other professional or domestic duties. Critics were expected to be broadly educated, to address social as well as literary issues in their reviews, and to speak to a general audience through the periodical press, ranging from the local newspaper to the *North American Review*.

Susan Coultrap-McQuin has pointed out in her study of nineteenth-century women as professional writers (*Doing Literary Business*, 1990) that social conventions defining and governing the work of writing created a space where women could pursue a profession without violating the Victorian * ideal of domesticity and * "true womanhood." Women like Lydia * Child, Elizabeth Peabody, Louisa * Alcott, Mary Abigail Dodge, Helen Hunt *Jackson, and Elizabeth Stuart *Phelps, and many others were regular contributors to magazines and journals, and their contributions included book reviews and criticism. Sarah *Hale wrote reviews for *Godey's Lady's Book*, and used her critical and editorial powers to promote American authors. In *Novels, Readers, and Reviewers* (1984), Nina Baym estimated that as many as one-fifth of antebellum book reviewers were women, pointing in particular to Hale, Caroline *Kirkland, and Ann Stephens.

The most prominent nineteenth-century woman writing criticism was Margaret *Fuller, who worked as editor of the Transcendentalist journal, the *Dial*, and as a contributor to Horace Greeley's *New York Daily Tribune*. In her 1840 "Short Essay on Critics" and other writings, Fuller proposed that American criticism should be "comprehensive," utilizing the viewpoints of both Scottish common sense philosophy and romanticism in a kind of democratic dialogue.

Women continued to contribute criticism to the periodical press after the *Civil War (Helen McMahon, *Criticism of Fiction*, 1952). But the social conventions governing the work of writing and criticism, and those governing women's lives, were changing during this period, and by the turn of the twentieth century the circumstances of women critics had been substantially altered.

As publishing became more commercialized over the course of the nineteenth century, writing came to be viewed less as the hobby of a leisured gentleman or lady, and more as a full-time profession and source of livelihood. At the same time the ideal of the liberal arts college in education was challenged by and began to give way to the German university model that stressed professional preparation in narrowly defined disciplines, exemplified by the founding of The Johns Hopkins University in 1876. Academic critics formed the first literature departments in the 1880s and established their own professional organization (the Modern Language Association) in 1883. As they gradually defined a specialized, professional audience for their work, they created a chasm between academic criticism and literary journalism. Academic literary criticism at the turn of the century focused on philological analysis and literary history.

This specialized, academic world of criticism was less open to women than the old one of literary journalism, but more open than some of the new professions in the social sciences, science, and engineering. The growth of women's colleges after the Civil War, combined with the impact of the suffrage campaign, led to the emergence of the first generation of women academic critics. One of the first of these professional women was Katherine Lee Bates, who entered Wellesley in 1876, the year The Johns Hopkins University was created, and taught there for many years. She produced a number of critical editions of Elizabethan works, and in 1897 published *American Literature*, a chronological survey and literary history wherein she argued that literature is an outgrowth of national character and life. The community of women scholars at Wellesley at that time included another prominent critic, Vida Dutton Scudder, who argued, in works like *Social Ideals in English Letters* (1898) that literature developed the social conscience.

During the period between the two world wars, the gulf between academic criticism and literary journalism widened. In the 1930s and 1940s the philological approach was challenged by critics who promulgated the principles of "New Criticism," which focused on the formal, intrinsic properties of the literary text itself and eschewed all extrinsic criteria for evaluating literature, including authorial biography and social context or impact. When New Criticism became entrenched in textbooks and literature departments in the 1950s, the old tradition of the critic who addresses the connection between social and literary issues was marginalized within the academy, although it persisted among literary journalists.

At the same time, the flow of women into the academic professions slowed in the wake of the Depression and the stagnation of the women's rights movement. Although many of the relatively few women academics in this period followed the precepts of New Criticism, criticism by women tended to be concentrated in areas that stretched the limits of the strictly formalist approach: myth-symbol criticism, *children's literature criticism, and literary journalism.

The most notable case in point is the work of Constance *Rourke. Rourke's analysis of *American Humor* (1931), which became one of the foundational documents of the Myth-Symbol school of criticism in the postwar years, attempted to extract recurrent formulas and *myths about American culture from non-literary sources such as *folk tales and frontier theater. Although the emphasis on enduring myths reflects the New Critical emphasis on formal and enduring structures intrinsic to the text, the use of popular sources to elicit descriptions of American culture as a whole suggests a sociological approach to literature that New Critics had rejected.

The first professional journal of criticism of children's literature, *Horn Book*, was established in 1924, and women dominated the new field. While most agreed with the New Critics that literature was defined by its intrinsic, timeless, formal properties, they also believed that children's literature played a part in socialization, thus linking literature and society. For this reason, they paid more attention to extrinsic evaluative criteria than the New Critical brethren. From the 1930s on, these critics were particularly concerned with evaluating how children's literature promoted democratic values. In a 1942 essay in *Horn Book*, Florence Crannell Means called for children's books that would portray all of America's regional and racial cultures; the year before, in a controversial *Publisher's Weekly* essay, Eva Knox Evans had pleaded with children's authors not to perpetuate stereotyped "Negro dialect" in their books.

Women were also prominent among the critics who dominated literary journalism from the 1930s to the 1970s. Collectively known as the New York Intellectuals, this group of critics never abandoned the tradition of the literary-social critic who writes for a general (educated) audience. These critics believed that literature was a cultural phenomenon necessitating analysis of both text and context, and application of both intrinsic and extrinsic evaluative criteria. Although this insistence on the importance of sociological, psychological, and historical analysis of literature was grounded in Marxism, many of this group reacted strongly against New Left and postmodern literary theory in the 1960s and 1970s. Through the 1940s and 1950s, however, the women critics of this group, including Mary *McCarthy, Elizabeth *Hardwick, Diana Trilling and Susan *Sontag, were far more influential than women critics in academe. Susan Sontag's work, including her influential essays "Against Interpretation" (1966) and "Aesthetics of Silence" (1967), was particularly important in introducing American critics to continental philosophies of literary criticism.

Between the mid-1960s and the 1980s, American academic criticism was inundated by European philosophies that spawned many schools of critical thought (including existentialism, hermeneutics, reader-response criticism, structuralism, and deconstruction). New schools of criticism also arose out of the New Left, the *civil rights and black power movement, and the second wave of *feminism. There was intense debate within and between these various critical schools about the relationship between literature and society, text and context, with deconstructionists assuming the most extreme stance, which attacked the very idea of representationality in literature. All of them challenged some part of the theoretical assumptions undergirding the New Critical approach to literature, and together they eventually overcame its domination of academic criticism. During this same period, women's enrollment in higher education and attainment of professional degrees was increasing, creating a larger pool of women critics in academe. The work of this new generation of women academics was informed by *feminist theory.

The pioneers of feminist literary criticism were Simone *de Beauvoir (*The Second Sex*, 1953) and Betty *Friedan (*The Feminine Mystique*, 1963), who both included criticism of literature or popular culture in their landmark treatises. Beginning in the 1970s, the new generation of academic women produced critiques of the patriarchal assumptions of criticism in works like Kate *Millett's *Sexual Politics* (1970) and Adrienne *Rich's essay "When We Dead Awaken: Writing as Re-Vision" (1971). Feminist critics also sought to recover and re-evaluate lost and non-canonical works by women writers. Important contributions to this project include Patricia M. Spacks, *The Female Imagination* (1975); Ellen Moers, *Literary Women* (1976); Elaine Showalter, *A Literature of Their Own* (1978); and Nina Baym, *Women's Fiction* (1978). Carolyn *Heilbrun's "Feminist Studies: Bringing the Spirit Back to English Studies" (1979) urged male critics to see these new approaches as a source of vitality, rather than a threat. The culmination of these efforts, signaling a degree of acceptance of the reevaluated women writers into the canon, was publication of the 1985 edition of the *Norton Anthology of Literature by Women*, edited by Sandra Gilbert and Susan Gubar.

In the late 1970s feminist critics began to turn from analysis of the patriarchy to theories of gender difference, arguing that women's biological and/or sociohistorical situations had created a distinct women's subculture that created a separate female aesthetic, which in turn required its own critical conventions. Although these theories were influenced by the French psychoanalytic theories of "feminine writing," they drew more directly on Adrienne Rich's *Of Woman Born* (1976) and Nancy Chodorow's *The Reproduction of Mothering* (1978). Both of these works suggested that a female subculture might be rooted in the earliest child-mother interactions. Critical theories of *gender difference were both indebted to and challenged by the emphasis placed on difference by deconstructionist critics, who pointed to male/female identifications as a logocentric polarity that cried out for deconstruction. Barbara Johnson's 1985 essay, "Gender Theory and the Yale School," deconstructed the gendered critical codes of the deconstructionist critics.

Feminist criticism that grew out of gender

difference theory included Elaine Showalter's 1979 essay, "Toward a Feminist Poetics," which called for what she termed "gynocritics," and Annette Kolodny's analysis of the gendered nature of critical strategies in her influential 1980 essay, "A Map for Rereading: Or, Gender and the Interpretation of Literary Texts." Gender difference was also the focus of reader-response critics like Judith Fetterley, whose study of *The Resisting Reader* (1978) suggested that female readers experience literature differently and produce different meanings than men do, and Janice Radway, who examined the way women readers construct meanings out of pulp romance novels in *Reading the Romance* (1984). Taken together, Annette's Kolodny's two studies, *The Lay of the Land* (1976) and *The Land Before Her* (1984), provide an analysis of the gendered responses of men and women writing about the *frontier.

Ironically, although the concept of the female aesthetic and the female subculture owed much to the critics who espoused *Black Aesthetics, white academic women paid little attention to differences among women in the 1970s. African-American and Third World feminists, including Mary Helen Washington, Alice *Walker, Gloria *Anzaldúa and Cherríe *Moraga, had been engaged in the same tasks of recovering lost texts and creating new critical conventions in relative isolation from their white colleagues. From the mid-1980s to the present, feminist critics of all races have increasingly focused on the particularities of difference among women of different nations, races, ethnicities, classes, and sexual orientation.

More and more contemporary critics recognize that both literary and popular texts are sociocultural events, shaped by social conventions and codes, that must be studied in relation to their specific sociohistorical context. Jane Tompkins's study of cultural determinants of the contemporary importance and subsequent canonization of popular nineteenth-century works in *Sensational Designs* (1985) is one example of such approaches. Feminist critics' emphasis on the social and cultural contexts of literature has played a key role in restoring the issue of the relationship between literature and society to the critical agenda.

[*See also* African-American Writing, *article on* Literary Criticism.]

• Elaine Showalter, *The New Feminist Criticism: Essays on Women, Literature, and Theory* (1985). Edward E. Chielens, ed., *American Literary Magazines: The Eighteenth and Nineteenth Centuries* (1986). Maggie Humm, *An Annotated Critical Bibliography of Feminist Criticism* (1987). Vincent Leitch, *American Literary Criticism from the Thirties to the Eighties* (1988). Ellen Cronan Rose, "American Feminist Criticism of Contemporary Women's Fiction," *Signs* (Winter 1993): 346–375.

Kathy Scales Vandell

LITTLE MAGAZINES. For those literary historians who prefer dating the genesis of *Modernism with an *Imagist movement in London, whether with the 1908 School of Images or Ezra Pound's "discovery" of *H. D., *Imagiste*, in 1912, the documentation inevitably leads to the publication of imagist poems in such periodicals as *Poetry, A Magazine of Verse, The Little Review*, and *The New Freewoman/The Egoist*—periodicals edited by women. Yet, despite the important roles played by such editors and associate editors as Harriet *Monroe, Margaret Anderson, Dora Marsden, Harriet Shaw Weaver, Rebecca West, Alice Corbin Henderson, Jane Heap, and Hilda Doolittle on these seminal journals, the history of women editors of modernist magazines is not an auspicious one, generally characterized by their relegation to subsidiary positions in spite of their persistent efforts and significant achievements. To the ambitious, militant, and aggressive Pound, these women were puppets to be manipulated to serve his grand scheme for "making it new," and to be discarded once they had served his purpose. That some of them managed to withstand his exploitation and survive on their own rankled him to such an extent that by the end of the decade he found that all of the strings had been cut; he devoted himself to concentrating exclusively on the careers of several male writers, notably Wyndham Lewis, T. S. Eliot, James Joyce—and later, such lesser lights as Basil Bunting and Ralph Cheever Dunning. His initial scheme was to infiltrate these new journals, and any others to which he could gain access, and in the role of foreign editor, responsible primarily for discovering European talent, to assure himself of a platform for experimental writing. His success on behalf of literary modernism in these first years was extraordinary, but it was bought at a great expense to both his "minions" and himself.

Although *Poetry* and *The Little Review*, both resident in Chicago, were geographically out of immediate reach for Pound, *The Freewoman* was there in London for his daily attention, and he waged a strategic campaign for domination, first succeeding in having the name changed to *The New Freewoman* (subheaded "An Individualist Review") and later to *The Egoist*. Its editor, Dora Marsden, was essentially interested in philosophical and feminist issues, and was more than willing to share the pages of her journal with the "new poetry" (to complement the emphasis on the "new woman"). So when Pound and his cohorts staged their coup d'etat for the second name change, Marsden was quite acquiescent since *The Egoist, An Individualist Review* suited her philosophical bent. Marsden was pliable but maintained her own province, although she was forced out of her position as editor into a lesser capacity. Harriet Weaver assumed the editorship in June 1914, but Pound's positioning of Richard Aldington as assistant editor shifted the base of power to himself. Rebecca West had been assistant editor, and was at first quite receptive to the revolutionary new poetry, but Pound found her too formidable (and too political) and forced her to resign. Yet Pound lost faith in Aldington and had no control over Harriet Weaver, and within six months of his coup was himself disenchanted with *The Egoist*, which flourished quite well without him. When Aldington went off to the war, he was replaced by his wife, Hilda Doolittle, who had no editorial experience and did very little editing.

Harriet Monroe was the most successful survivor of Pound's campaign of aggrandizement. She started *Poetry* before she ever heard of Ezra Pound and continued on after his defection for over two decades, until her death. Although a moving spirit in the early dissemination of Modernism, she shifted to a central position, publishing the poets she liked, modernists and traditionalists, insisting on steering a middle course. Her first assistant editor, Alice Corbin Henderson, remained faithful to Pound and was instructed by him, but ill health separated her from *Poetry*, and her dismay with Vachel Lindsay and Amy * Lowell, plus her championing of Marianne * Moore, put her at odds with Monroe (Eunice Tietjens proved to be a more compatible assistant editor in the 1920s).

By contrast with Monroe's *Poetry*, Margaret Anderson's *Little Review* became a consistent organ for the avant garde, yet Anderson at first was more a maverick than a devotee, beginning with a strong interest in anarchism (after all, *the* anarchist magazine, *Mother Earth*, had been edited from its inception in 1908 by a woman, the extraordinary Emma * Goldman). If Anderson was lacking in intellectual acumen, the same could not be said for Jane Heap, the coeditor who later exerted a powerful influence on the journal and was a confirmed modernist. Yet when *The Little Review* folded in 1929, Heap despaired of its ever having published anything of lasting value in its fifteen years, with the exception of *Ulysses*.

Predictably, several women served as assistant editors to their more prominent husbands, Dorothy Kreymborg on Alfred Kreymborg's *Others*, and Gene Derwood on Oscar Williams's *Rhythmus*. When Eugene Jolas began to put *transition* together, he sought an associate editor and a secretary, the latter position to be taken by Maria Jolas, who also kept the books, edited copy, and translated from several languages, but insisted on maintaining a low profile. On the other hand, when Lola Ridge was hired as American Editor of *Broom*, she assumed that she had a degree of editorial power, but Harold Loeb countermanded her choices and declared himself solely responsible for every item published, forcing Ridge to resign. Marianne Moore fared a great deal better on *The Dial*, essentially taking over when Scofield Thayer suffered a serious mental breakdown, but the editorial policy was already set and in her five years as the editor she did little to change the scope of the journal. A more pathetic case was that of Ethel Moorhead: she had co-edited the first two issues of *This Quarter* with Ernest Walsh, and after his death edited a third, but then had to sell the journal to Edward Titus, so that the word went out that she had no head for business.

Men like Loeb and Thayer exerted their power by controlling the finances (and when their finances dwindled, *Broom* and *The Dial* folded). The successful women editors were primarily those with financial power; Harriet Monroe from the beginning was an astute fundraiser for *Poetry*; Harriet Weaver had a personal fortune to invest in *The Egoist*; and even the money for *transition* derived from Maria Jolas's inheritance. With a personal fortune of her own, Amy Lowell for a while sought a magazine of her own (but Erza Pound's offers—which included *The Egoist*—always had his particular strings attached, and Lowell refused, although she was a generous contributor to Harriet Monroe's *Poetry*).

As extensive as the role of women poets in the Modernist movement has been, those women rarely acted in a concerted effort, either as a coterie of their own (unlike the all-male Fugitives) or in spearheading a facet of Modernism by editing more than a handful of the hundreds of magazines the movement inspired. Disempowered by the lack of capital or financial connections, they worked on their poetry more often than not in isolation, unless attached in their relationships to men poets. The success of Harriet Monroe or Margaret Anderson is all the more impressive when the overwhelming odds and obstacles are considered.

[*See also* Journalists; Journals, Academic; Magazines, Women's; Newspaper Columns; Newspapers, Women's; Reportage.]

• Archival material is in the Beinecke Library at Yale

University, the Harry Ranson Humanities Research Center at the University of Texas, and the Houghton Library at Harvard University. See also Frederick J. Hoffman, Charles Allen, and Carolyn F. Ulrich, *The Little Magazine: A History and a Bibliography* (1947). Shari Benstock and Bernard Benstock, "The Role of Little Magazines in the Emergence of Modernism," *The Library Chronicle of the University of Texas* 20, no. 4 (1991): 69–88.

Bernard Benstock

LIVINGSTON, Anne Home (1763–1841), diarist. Anne (Nancy) Home Shippen was born into an aristocratic family of colonial Philadelphia. Her father, Dr. William Shippen III, was director of the American military hospitals during the Revolution and afterwards became president of the college of Physicians at the University of Pennsylvania. Anne's mother, Alice, came from the prominent Lee family of Virginia.

As the attractive daughter of a distinguished family, Nancy enjoyed the attentions of several suitors. At age eighteen, she fell in love with and agreed to marry Albert Otto, then a French diplomatic secretary, later to become the Compte de Mosloy. Anne's father, however, pressed her to marry a man whose fortune was already one of the greatest in America, Colonel Henry Beekman Livingston of New York.

Livingston took his bride to New York, where he harassed her and virtually held her prisoner, accusing her of improprieties, even after the birth of their daughter, and bringing his own illegitimate children into the house. In 1783, Anne began writing her tragic *journal (Nancy Shippen, Her Journal*, ed. Ethal Armes, 1935), which recounts the painful events of her marriage to Livingston, including a temporary separation from her daughter and her husband's unwillingness to grant her a divorce (in order to marry the widowed Albert Otto) unless she gave up the daughter permanently. Anne abandoned the idea of divorce but took her daughter to live in Philadelphia. Mother and daughter lived together until Anne's death at age seventy-eight. Margaret lived unmarried and died at age eighty-one.

According to Steven E. Kagle, Anne's diary shows exceptional thematic unity because "it was begun in response to the tension of her tragic situation and terminated with her resignation to it" (Emory Elliott, ed. *American Writers of the Early Republic* 1985). In addition, Livingston's writings are useful as a psychological and historical account of a woman taught to value the opinions of father and husband at her own expense, a woman who eventually learned to decide for herself and take responsibility for her own life.

• Livingston's papers are at the Library of Congress.

See also Steven E. Kagle, *American Diary Literature* (1979).

Allene Cooper

LOCAL COLOR FICTION. Used in conjunction with realism, and to create an analogy with American painters of so-called genre scenes, this term described a literature of specific place and character (i.e., Bret Harte's West, Sarah Orne *Jewett's Maine). At its best a way of emphasizing the importance of particular folkways, speech, and traditions, the term later became pejorative. Minor writers, read only when a region was being studied, found themselves denigrated by the "local color" label. Applied unevenly, the term was often used to describe the work of women writers. For example, although many of Ernest Hemingway's stories are set in Michigan, he was never called a local colorist; Kate *Chopin, conversely, was often so described.

Also called "regional realists," such writers depicted local scenes (often for regions other than New England), never to ridicule but to help the reader understand the culture. The point of view of the narrator was often superior to the folk of the culture, however, so that some tone of condescension might occur.

[*See also* New England Women's Writing; Realism; Regionalism; Southern Women's Writing; Western Women's Writing.]

• Judith Fetterley and Marjorie Pryse, eds., *American Women Regionalists, 1850–1910* (1992).

Linda Wagner-Martin

LONG POEM. See Poetry, article on Long Poem.

LOOS, Anita (1893–1981), novelist, playwright, and scenarist. A prolific writer, Loos is best known for her witty minor classic of 1925, *Gentlemen Prefer Blondes*, which was praised by such writers as William Faulkner, James Joyce, and Edith *Wharton, and widely read by an international audience. Admired for its satiric portraiture, *Gentlemen Prefer Blondes* exposes the materialism underlying the seeming innocence of its fair-haired heroine, Lorelei Lee, and the folly of males so captivated by her beauty that they risk respectability, fortunes, and even lives. The novel is a humorous diary of Lorelei's adventures after escaping from Little Rock, where a hapless suitor "became shot." Throughout her travels in the United States and Europe, Lorelei remains faithful to her belief that romance may be fine, "but a diamond bracelet lasts forever." Followed by a sequel, *But Gentlemen Marry Brunettes* (1928), which focuses on the romantic history of Lorelei's wisecracking sidekick Dorothy, *Gentlemen Prefer*

Blondes was made into a play (1926), a musical (1949), and a movie (1953).

Born in Sissons (now Mt. Shasta), California, Anita Loos began work as a stage actress in San Francisco at age five, appearing in the American premiere of *A Doll House* and other productions. By the age of thirteen she was a correspondent for the New York *Morning Telegraph;* at nineteen, she sold her first scenario to D. W. Griffith's Biograph Company. Between 1912 and 1915, Loos did a hundred more scenarios for Griffith. Subsequently, in collaboration with the director John Emerson (whom she married in 1919), Loos wrote screenplays for Douglas Fairbanks and Constance Talmadge, as well as two books, *How to Write Photoplays* (1920) and *Breaking into the Movies* (1921). After an early "retirement" to New York City was ended by the crash of 1929, Loos returned to Hollywood to work for Irving Thalberg at MGM. Among her numerous screenplays were *Red-Headed Woman* (1932), *San Francisco* (1936), *Saratoga* (1937), and *The Women* (1939), notable for its barbed dialogue and all-female cast.

Loos returned to New York in the mid-1940s and continued to write until her death in 1981. Works from the latter part of her career include plays such as *Happy Birthday* (1946), *Gigi* (1951), and *Cheri* (1959); two novels that satirize Hollywood, *A Mouse Is Born* (1951) and *No Mother to Guide Her* (1961); and a memoir, *The Talmadge Girls* (1978). Loos provided anecdotal overviews of her career and friendships in *A Girl Like I* (1966), *Kiss Hollywood Goodbye* (1974), and *Cast of Thousands* (1977).

Judith Bryant Wittenberg

LORD, Bette Bao (b. 1938), novelist and nonfiction writer. Born in Shanghai of Chinese parents, Lord came to the United States at the age of eight. While growing up in Brooklyn, New York, she was daily instructed by her mother to conduct herself as "a little ambassadress" to the U.S. for the millions of Chinese living in her homeland. She could hardly have known then that one day she would return to her birthplace as the wife of the United States ambassador to the People's Republic of China, Winston Lord. She holds a B.A. degree in political science from Tufts University and an M.A. from the Fletcher School of Diplomacy, where she and Winston were classmates.

Her career as a writer began, in her own words, as a "happenstance," her chance meeting with a publisher at a reception. Subsequently, she wrote *Eighth Moon* (1964) about the ordeal and eventual escape of her younger sister Sansan, who, as an infant, was left in the care of relatives for eighteen years when the Baos left China in 1946 for what they thought would be a brief sojourn in the United States. Encouraged by the warm reception accorded her first book, Lord went on to write *Spring Moon: A Novel of China* (1981), which drew inspiration from her first return trip to China in 1973. A best-seller upon publication, touted as a Chinese *Gone With the Wind, Spring Moon* chronicles the lives of Spring Moon Chang and her relatives from 1892 to the early 1970s and poignantly depicts the effects of civil war and social change on the Chinese aristocracy. Unlike *Eighth Moon*, which is essentially a reworking of Sansan's story recorded on tape, *Spring Moon* attests to Lord's conscious attempt to craft a book that is traditional Chinese in its sensibility, orthodox Chinese in its vision, and classical Chinese in its narrative structure. What Lord affirms in this novel—the resilience and endurance of the Chinese—resonates again in her recent book *Legacies: A Chinese Mosaic* (1989). In *Legacies*, she blends her personal reflections on China and its people with wrenching accounts, obtained while living in China from 1985 to 1989, of how some of these people suffered and survived the inhumane treatment inflicted upon them by the repressive Communist Chinese government during the past forty-two years. She has also published a children's book, *The Year of the Boar and Jackie Robinson* (1984), based on her childhood experience. In her role as a self-appointed literary ambassador, Lord seems to have succeeded in her attempts to explain China to the West.

• "Bette Bao Lord," *The Washington Post,* 28 October 1981, sec. B: 13+. Ronald Evans, Review of *Spring Moon* in *Saturday Review* 8, no. 10 (1981): 75–76. Theresa Pease, "A Bridge Between Cultures: Alumna Bette Bao Lord Is on the Best-Seller List with Her First Novel, *Spring Moon,*" *Tufts Criterion* (1981): 9. Kay Miller, "Moderation, accepting limits women into novel set in China," Review of *Spring Moon* in *The Minneapolis Star* (16 November 1981). Wei-hsiung Kitty Wu, "Cultural Ideology and Aesthetic Choices: A Study of Three Works by Chinese Women—Diana Chang, Bette Bao Lord, and Maxine Hong Kingston," Ph.D. Diss., University of Maryland, College Park (1989).

Wei-hsiung (Kitty) Wu

LORDE, Audre (1934–1992), black lesbian feminist poet and essayist. Recognizing that "imposed silence about any area of our lives is a tool for separation and powerlessness" (*The Cancer Journals,* 1980), Audre Lorde claimed and celebrated all of her selves in order that others could come to find their own voices. Her poetry and prose demonstrate that we need not be afraid of difference, that difference can be a creative force for change. At the forefront of black feminist thought, her work has contributed to an analysis of the interlocking nature of all oppression. As activist and poet, she worked to challenge and transform power relations.

The third and youngest daughter of Linda Gertrude Belmar and Frederic Byron Lorde, Audre Geraldine was born tongue-tied and so nearsighted that she was considered legally blind. She grew up in Harlem during the Depression, hearing her mother's stories about the West Indies. She learned to talk while she learned to read, at the age of four. Her mother taught her to write during this time and Audre "did not like the tail of the Y hanging down below the line in Audrey" and so would omit it; she "love[d] the evenness of AUDRELORDE" (Zami, 1982). This early incident reveals the importance of *naming and self-definition to Lorde, themes that she develops in her later writings.

Influenced by her mother's "special and secret relationship with words" (Zami), Audre appreciated poetry and used it to communicate with others. She said: "Words had an energy and power and I came to respect that power early. Pronouns, nouns, and verbs were citizens of different countries, who really got together to make a new world" (Karla M. Hammond, Denver Quarterly, Spring 1981). If asked how she was feeling, Audre would reply by reciting a poem. When the poems could no longer express what she wanted to say, at about age twelve or thirteen, she began to write her own. Her poetry was "very important to [her] in terms of survival, in terms of living" (Hammond, Denver Quarterly). She explained, "I loved poetry, and I loved words. But what was beautiful had to serve the purpose of changing my life, or I would have died. If I cannot air this pain and alter it, I will surely die of it. That's the beginning of social protest" (Claudia Tate, Black Women Writers at Work, 1983). She saw this tradition of confronting pain and learning from it as particularly African and manifest in the best African-American literature.

Educated at Catholic grammar schools, she faced "patronizing" racism at St. Mark's School and "downright hostile" racism at St. Catherine's School (Zami). At Hunter High School she found a "lifeline" in a "sisterhood of rebels" who were also poets. Writing poetry no longer felt like "a secret and rebellious vice" but "an ordinary effort" (Zami). She became literary editor of the school arts magazine and her first love poem was published in Seventeen. During the 1950s she supported herself at a variety of jobs while attending Hunter College part-time. Deciding to become a librarian in order to "gain tools for ordering and analyzing information" (Sister Outsider, 1984), she began

as a library clerk at the New York Public Library Children's Services in March 1955. She earned a B.A. in English and philosophy in 1959 and an M.L.S. from Columbia University in 1961.

Lorde's poetry was published regularly during the 1960s: in Langston Hughes's 1962 New Negro Poets, USA, in several foreign anthologies, and in black literary magazines. During this time she was politically active in the *civil rights, antiwar, and feminist movements. Wanting to have children, she married Edwin Ashley Rollins on 31 March 1962. (The marriage lasted seven years.) Elizabeth was born the following year and Jonathan eighteen months later. By the end of the decade she was able to devote herself full-time to poetry after receiving a 1968 award from the National Endowment for the Arts. The experience as poet-in-residence at Tougaloo College in Mississippi that same year convinced her that teaching was the work she needed to be doing. She discovered that teaching is similar to writing: "Both became ways of exploring what I need for survival" (Tate, Black Women Writers at Work). At Tougaloo she met her companion of many years, Frances Clayton. Lorde taught English, creative writing, and literature at several universities, including John Jay College of Justice, City College of New York, and Hunter College.

Poems from Lorde's first five volumes of poetry, The First Cities (1968), Cables to Rage (1970), From a Land Where Other People Live (1973), New York Headshop and Museum (1974), and Coal (1976), were collected in Chosen Poems—Old and New (1982), along with several new poems. Poems from The Black Unicorn (1978) were not included in this volume because Lorde felt the sequence, which felt like a conversation between herself and an ancestor Audre, could not be broken. Gloria Hull describes her poetry as "basically a traditional kind of modernist free verse—laced with equivocation and . . . allegory." The poems focus on the particular and personal while exploring political implications and making global connections. Lorde's voice calls us to witness violence, comprehend oppression, recognize differences, honor ancestors, celebrate love, nurture children, and visualize possibilities.

When Lorde was diagnosed with breast cancer in September 1978 and had a mastectomy, she explored the meaning of her experiences from the perspective of a black lesbian feminist in The Cancer Journals (1980). Another project, writing a biomythography of her life through 1959, provided Lorde with a "lifeline through the cancer experience" (Tate, Women Writers at Work). Zami: A New Spelling of My Name (1982), the first full-length *autobiography of an established black lesbian, pays tribute to all women, especially her mother, who taught her survival skills. While she considered herself to be a poet, Lorde may be as well known for her prose. Essays and speeches from 1976 to 1984 collected in *Sister Outsider* (1984) are frequently quoted and anthologized. Lorde identifies "Eye to Eye: Black Women, Hatred, and Anger" and "Poetry Is Not a Luxury" as "the two core pieces of [her] prose writing" (*Callaloo*, Winter 1991). In February 1984, she was diagnosed with liver cancer. Journal entries from this time through 1987 make up two-thirds of the essay collection *A Burst of Light* (1988).

In *Our Dead Behind Us* (1986) Lorde shows herself to be "a mature poet in full command of her craft" (Phillips, *Times Literary Supplement*, 15–20 April 1988). An updated edition of *Chosen Poems* entitled *Undersong: Chosen Poems Old and New* (1992) offers some new poems and stylistic revisions of many others. Many would consider Lorde one of the finest contemporary poets, yet her poetry has received mixed reviews. Lorde herself agrees with Gloria Hull's assessment: "Readers who—by whatever means of experience, empathy, imagination, or intelligence—are best able to approximate Lorde's own positionality most appreciate her work." Lorde died on 17 November 1992 in St. Croix, where she had been living with Gloria I. Joseph. She expressed this hope for her last poetry collection, *The Marvelous Arithmetics of Distance, Poems 1987–1992* (1993): "I want this book to be filled with shards of light thrown off from the shifting tensions between the dissimilar, for that is the real stuff of creation and growth."

• Karla M. Hammond, "An Interview with Audre Lorde," *The American Poetry Review* (March/April 1980): 18–21. Karla M. Hammond, "Audre Lorde: Interview," *Denver Quarterly* 16, no. 1 (Spring 1981): 10–27. Claudia Tate, *Black Women Writers at Work* (1983). Mari Evans, ed., *Black Women Writers (1950–1980)* (1984). Irma McClaurin-Allen, "Audre Lorde," in *Dictionary of Literary Biography: Afro American Poets Since 1955*, vol. 41, eds. Trudier Harris and Thadious M. Davis (1985). Mary K. DeShazer, *Inspiring Women: Reimagining the Muse* (1986). Amitai F. Avi-ram, "*Apo Koinou* in Audre Lorde and the Moderns," *Callaloo* 9, no. 1 (Winter 1986): 193–208. Gloria T. Hull, "Living on the Line: Audre Lorde and *Our Dead Behind Us*," in *Changing Our Own Words: Essays on Criticism, Theory, and Writing by Black Women*, ed. Cheryl Wall (1989). Chinosole, "Audre Lorde and Matrilineal Diaspora," in *Wild Women in the Whirlwind: Afra-American Culture and the Contemporary Literary Renaissance* (1990). "Audre Lorde: A Special Section/Poems, Essays, and an Interview [by Rowell]," *Callaloo* 14, no. 1 (Winter 1991): 37–95.

Ann Trapasso

LOVE. *See* Romantic Love.

LOVE LETTERS. *See* Letters; Romantic Love.

LOVE POETRY. *See* Poetry, article on Love Poetry.

LOWELL, Amy Lawrence (1874–1925), poet, critic, and biographer. Genteel and unmarried, Lowell spent her first twenty-eight years as a member of a prominent family and a Boston debutante would—traveling, performing civic duties, and considering marriage prospects. In 1902, however, she found new purpose after seeing Eleonora Duse on stage: she was inspired to write poetry. In 1912, her life changed again. That year she met Ada Dwyer Russell, who lived with Lowell until the poet's death in 1925; she also published *A Dome of Many-Coloured Glass*, poetry that heralded her allegiance to John Keats and a poetic tradition that she would soon abandon; and she saw Harriet *Monroe's Poetry: A Magazine of Verse*. Within a year, Lowell met Ezra Pound and other Imagists in London through Monroe and became the Imagist's popularizer, leading Pound to coin the word "Amy-gism." Returning to London in 1914, Lowell met D. H. Lawrence and Robert Frost, who became her lifelong friends. Lowell's second volume, *Sword Blades and Poppy Seed* (1914), marked her departure from traditional poetry for *vers libre* and *Imagism and its modes of expression. Her subsequent volumes of poetry reveal her importance to the *Imagist movement, her bond with New England, and her continued poetic, polyphonic experimentation: *Men, Women and Ghosts* (1916); *Can Grande's Castle* (1918); *Pictures of the Floating World* (1919); and *What's O'Clock* (1925). Perhaps as important as her poetry, Lowell's translations and essays in *Six French Poets: Studies in Contemporary Literature* (1915) and *Tendencies in Modern American Poetry* (1917) confirmed her position as a critic. By the time of her death at 51 years of age, Lowell had established herself in literary history. For almost a decade before her death, Lowell suffered from ill health, yet she continued her many literary activities, in particular her biography of Keats, which met with mixed reviews when published in 1925. Before she was able to defend it in England, she died of a cerebral hemorrhage. That year, she was awarded the Pulitzer Prize for Poetry posthumously for *What's O'Clock* and her celebrated poem "Patterns." Despite her achievements, her importance to her contemporaries, and her influence upon later poets, Lowell has been in danger of being more remembered for her lifestyle—her family background, her penchant for cigars and cigarillos, her lifelong companion, and her obesity—than for her literary contributions, the lot of many women writers until recent years.

• Lowell's manuscripts are held at the Houghton Library, Harvard University (36 mss.) and the University of Virginia (11 mss.). See also Louis Untermeyer, *Complete Poetical Works of Amy Lowell* (1955). Samuel Foster Damon, *Amy Lowell, A Chronicle, with Extracts from Her Correspondence* (1969). Clemens David Heymann, *American Aristocracy: The Lives and Times of James Russell, Amy, and Robert Lowell* (1980). Richard Benvenuto, *Amy Lowell* (1985).

Sophia B. Blaydes

LUCE, Clare Boothe (1903–1987), playwright, journalist, politician, and diplomat. More than four decades of writing, lecturing, and political involvement earned Clare Boothe (Brokaw) Luce honorary degrees from Fordham, Georgetown, and Temple Universities and the respect of many of her contemporaries. She was criticized by opponents, however, for her conservative views and privileged life. Appraised retrospectively, her historical importance derives not from her particular convictions but from the fact that she acted upon them.

Although she wrote poetry for the school paper while a student at Cassidy Mason's Castle School for Girls, Clare Boothe did not pursue a career in writing until 1929, when she divorced Henry Brokaw and joined the staff of *Vogue* magazine. Moving to *Vanity Fair* in 1930, she discovered her penchant for satire and developed her abiding interest in politics. Before leaving the magazine in 1934 to write plays, she published a collection of her lampoons in *Stuffed Shirts* (1933).

Abide with Me (melodrama, 1935) folded after a brief Broadway run, but her second play, *The Women* (1936), produced soon after she married publisher Henry Luce, was a popular success (filmed in 1939 and in 1956 as *The Opposite Sex*), and was revived on Broadway in 1973. After successful New York runs, *Kiss the Boys Goodbye* (1938) and *Margin for Error* (1939) were filmed in 1941. Luce returned to stage and screen writing in the late forties with the film story, *Come to the Stable* (1949), which was nominated for an Academy Award; *Child of the Morning* (Boston, 1951; Off-Broadway, 1958); and *Slam the Door Softly* (published in *Life* magazine as "A Doll's House," 1970).

Shifting from * drama to * journalism as European conditions worsened in the 1940s, Luce published *Europe in the Spring* (1940), and, as a war correspondent for *Life* magazine, published interviews with the Chiang Kai-sheks and General Douglas MacArthur as well as a feature story on the Flying Tigers (1941–1942).

As a Representative from Connecticut, Luce made another transition in 1943 when she began writing for the platform, both as political speaker and lecturer. Following two terms in Congress, she served as Ambassador to Italy under Eisenhower (1953–1957).

The death of her daughter Ann in 1944 precipitated a religious crisis that resulted in Luce's conversion to Roman Catholicism. She recounted this experience in a series of articles entitled, "The Real Reason," for *McCall's* magazine in 1947; and in 1952, she edited a collection of favorite essays in *Saints for Now* (1952). Her earlier popularity lead to a contract with *McCall's* in 1959 to write the monthly column "Without Portfolio."

Retiring to Hawaii in 1967 after her husband's death, Luce continued to lecture and to write for periodicals. She returned to Washington, D.C., in the 1970s to serve on the President's Foreign Intelligence Advisory Board (1973–1977; 1982–1987) and remained there until her death.

Although her satire of parasitic women in her 1930s plays suggests a betrayal of her sex, Luce promoted the cause of American women by participating actively in events and movements that shaped the twentieth century, leaving, in the process, an indelible mark on history.

• M. Hoehn, ed. *Catholic Authors: Contemporary Biographical Sketches, 1930–1947* (1952). Stephen Shadegg, *Clare Boothe Luce: A Biography* (1970). "Luce, Clare Boothe," in *Contemporary Authors, 45–48* (1974), pp. 338–339. Lucina P. Gabbard, "Clare Boothe Luce," in *American Women Writers: A Critical Reference Guide from Colonial Times to the Present*, ed. Lina Mainiero (1981), pp. 48–49. Wilfrid Sheed, *Clare Boothe Luce* (1982). "Luce, Clare Boothe," in *Biographical Dictionary of the United States Congress, 1774–1984, Bicentennial Edition* (1989). Ralph G. Martin, *Henry and Clare: An Intimate Portrait of the Luces* (1991).

Bes Stark Spangler

LUHAN, Mabel Dodge (1879–1962), writer, arts patron, salon hostess. Among the scores of Anglo writers, artists, and reformers who visited and moved to Santa Fe and Taos, New Mexico, after World War I, Mabel Dodge Luhan took a leading role in generating a body of literature and art that revised traditional Anglo male perceptions of the West. Here, she claimed, was a "new world" whose terrain, climate, and indigenous peoples offered a model of ecological, spiritual, and artistic integration. Her essays, books, and extensive correspondence, and the myriad works of the artists, writers, ethnologists, and reformers who visited her (among them, D. H. Lawrence, Mary * Austin, John Collier, Georgia O'Keeffe, Willa * Cather, Elsie Clews Parsons, Martha Graham, and John Marin) promoted the ideal of a multiethnic democracy that recognized the long-ignored social, economic, and cultural contributions of women, Hispanics, and Indians to American civilization.

When Luhan came to the Southwest, she left

behind her a past cluttered with causes, lovers, and identities tried and discarded. Nothing had been able to assuage the profound spiritual and emotional malaise that she believed her generation had inherited from a disintegrating Victorian culture. Throughout her adult life, Luhan had worked to create a world that would simultaneously establish her identity and serve as a model for the larger European and American communities in which she lived. She moved from one "cosmos"—as she called them—to the next with the expectation that each would provide an answer to her own and her contemporaries' anomie.

Born in Buffalo, New York, the only child of upper-class parents, she escaped first to Florence, where she tried to reestablish the Renaissance in her Villa Curonia (1905–1912); then to New York (1912–1917), where her Greenwich Village salon became one of the spiritual centers for the prewar political and aesthetic avant-garde; and finally to Taos (1918–1962), where she finally found herself "at home" and married her fourth and final husband, Antonio Lujan, a Pueblo Indian.

While Luhan published in leading avant-garde journals before 1918 and was a leading symbol of the "New Woman" during her New York years, she had seen herself primarily as a "muse" and patron to men of genius. She found her own creative voice only after moving to New Mexico, where she wrote her four-volume memoir, *Intimate Memories,* and her edenic pastoral, *Winter in Taos* (1936). In her compelling account of American social and cultural history from the late Victorian through post–World War I eras, she constructed her life as a paradigm for the decline and fall of Anglo-American civilization—and its potential for rebirth in the Southwest. Although Luhan's romantic primitivism raises serious social and ethical questions, her contributions to American art and literature incorporated the traditions, symbols, and forms of non-Anglo ethnic groups in a way that enriched both her region and the nation.

• Luhan's papers are at the Beinecke Library, Yale University. See also Mabel Dodge Luhan, *Intimate Memories,* vol. 1, *Background* (1933); vol. 2, *European Experiences* (1935); vol. 3, *Movers and Shakers* (1936; reprint, 1985); vol. 4, *Edge of Taos Desert* (1937; reprint, 1987). Christopher Lasch, *The New Radicalism in America* (1965). Lois Palken Rudnick, *Mabel Dodge Luhan: New Woman, New Worlds* (1984). Vera Norwood and Jan Monk, eds., *The Desert Is No Lady: Southwestern Landscapes in Women's Writing and Art* (1987). Adele Heller and Lois Palken Rudnick, eds., *1915, The Cultural Moment: The New Politics, the New Woman, the New Psychology, the New Art, and the New Theatre in America* (1991).

Lois Rudnick

LYNCHING. *See* Abolition; Antilynching Campaign; Middle Passage; Reconstruction; Slavery; Underground Railroad.

M

MACDONALD, Betty (1908–1958), author. Betty MacDonald, born Anne Elizabeth Campbell Bard, wrote several humorous autobiographical books and the "Mrs. Piggle-Wiggle" children's series. Born 26 March 1908, in Boulder, Colorado, MacDonald and her family of eight lived in mining towns in Idaho, Montana, and Mexico, following the career of her father, who was a mining engineer. The family settled in Seattle when Betty was nine years old. Her father, Dairsie Bard, died when she was twelve.

In *Anybody Can Do Anything* (1950), MacDonald describes the succession of jobs she held during the Great Depression, and the influence of her ambitious older sister Mary on her family. Although several jobs lasted only a week or two, MacDonald eventually became the first woman labor adjuster in the National Recovery Administration, in 1931, and was in charge of publicity for the National Youth Administration from 1939 to June 1942. According to MacDonald, her writing career began when Mary made an appointment for her with a publisher's representative seeking material about the Northwest. MacDonald hastily composed an outline about her life on a chicken farm, was fired as secretary for a construction office when her boss learned that she had called in sick to finish the outline, and thus began writing full-time. *Anybody Can Do Anything* also describes the other writers in MacDonald's family: her sister Mary Bard, and her mother, Elsie Bard, who wrote a department store's daily radio serial for a year.

MacDonald's first book, *The Egg and I* (1945), a good-humored account of her trials as the wife of a chicken-rancher in a remote mountain area of Washington in the late 1920s, also exposes both the loneliness and the hardship of that life, as well as her increasing estrangement from her first husband, Bob Heskett, whom she later divorced. (In 1927, she had left college to marry Heskett at age eighteen; she separated from him in 1931, returning to her mother's home in Seattle with her two young daughters.) The book, which became a best-seller, inspired the Ma and Pa Kettle films of the 1950s. In *The Plague and I* (1948), MacDonald describes her stay in a tuberculosis sanatorium at age thirty, from September 1938 to June 1939. Separated from her close-knit family

and her daughters Anne and Joan, and forced to stay immobile for several months, MacDonald nevertheless emerged healthy and able to return to work.

In 1942, she married Donald Chauncey MacDonald. In 1955, she published another autobiographical book, *Onions in the Stew*. Her children's books include *Mrs. Piggle-Wiggle* (1947), *Mrs. Piggle-Wiggle's Magic* (1949), *Mrs. Piggle-Wiggle's Farm* (1954), and *Nancy and Plum* (1952). MacDonald died 7 February 1958.

• Anna Rothe, ed., *Current Biography 1946* (1947), pp. 362–363. Stanley J. Kuntz, ed., *Twentieth-Century Authors: A Biographical Dictionary of Modern Literature*, supp. 1 (1955), pp. 611–612. Hal May, ed., *Contemporary Authors*, vol. 121 (1987), p. 278.

Kathy D. Hadley

MADGETT, Naomi Long (b. 1923), teacher, poet, editor, publisher. Born in Virginia and reared in New Jersey and Missouri, Naomi Long Madgett settled permanently in Detroit, where she worked for *The Michigan Chronicle*, an African-American weekly, and the Michigan Bell Telephone Company between 1946 and 1954.

Her career as a teacher began in the Detroit public schools in 1955; she moved to Eastern Michigan University in 1968 and taught there until her retirement in 1984. Assessing her own life, Madgett believes her greatest influence has been as a teacher of creative writing and, especially, of African-American literature.

She also takes deep satisfaction in having helped bring about the better representation enjoyed by black writers in contemporary textbooks and curricula. Her most recent volume of poetry, *Octavia and Other Poems* (1988), examines Madgett's family in a series of poems and photographs and is required reading in the Detroit public schools.

Madgett began writing verse as a child and published her first collection of poems, *Songs to a Phantom Nightingale* (1941), a few days after graduating from high school. Although the poems in this collection derive from the English romantic tradition, a recent volume, *Phantom Nightingale: Juvenilia* (1981), provides a more inclusive picture of vital black life in pre–World War II St. Louis and reveals early talent in her experiments with language and technique.

Between 1956 and 1978 she published four volumes of poetry: *One and the Many* (1956), *Star by Star* (1965), *Pink Ladies in the Afternoon* (1972), and *Exits and Entrances* (1978). While many of the poems in these collections are personal lyrics, others express her response to the *civil rights movement and black nationalism. Acutely sympathetic with the struggle for equality, she rejects the violent excesses of the period, defending distinguished leaders denounced by militants, admiring the beauty of black women and men, and exploring her own roots and heritage.

During this same period, Madgett and her husband took over the fledgling Lotus Press in 1974, turning it into an important publishing house for a generation of black poets. To celebrate the twentieth anniversary of Lotus Press, she edited an anthology entitled *Adam of Ifé* (1992), affirmative poems by black women about black men.

Widely published, anthologized, and honored, Madgett has forged a remarkable career as teacher, poet, editor, and publisher. Her poetry reveals a sensitive black woman whose strong sense of personal identity and black heritage evolved during a period of social and political upheaval.

• Naomi Long Madgett's papers are deposited in the Special Collections Library at Fisk University, Nashville, Tennessee. See also Robert P. Sedlack, "Naomi Long Madgett," in *Dictionary of Literary Biography* (1988), vol. 76, pp. 104–112.

Robert P. Sedlack

MADNESS. *Madness* is an imprecise term for a variety of abnormal mental states. It is the term of choice for women authors who write about their experience of mental breakdown or who illustrate it in fictive characters. Social scientists use it loosely as synonymous with the medical term *psychosis* and the legal term *insanity*.

Psychiatric nomenclature describes two main clusters of psychoses: major mood disorders and schizoid disturbances, both of which are believed to have a biological basis. Sociological, psychological, and literary theorists, on the other hand, tend to focus on culture and society as causal agents. Works by feminist critics such as psychologist Phyllis Chesler's *Women and Madness* (1972) and literary scholars Sandra Gilbert and Susan Gubar's *The Madwoman in the Attic* (1979) argue that patriarchial socialization sows the seeds of madness for women. Chesler takes the position that women are caught in the double bind of incorporating into their self-images the negative "feminine" qualities that men assign them, or, if they reject traditional sex-roles, they are seen as deviants.

Some of the most relevant scholarship has been produced by feminist thinkers investigating the arena of motherhood. The work of poet Adrienne *Rich, sociologist Nancy Chodorow, and literary critic Dorothy Dinnerstein has called attention to the institution of motherhood as a social construct that often undermines both the mother's and the daughter's mental health. Chodorow (*The Reproduction of Mothering*, 1978) maintains that the strong identification between the female child and her same-sex parent makes the development of an autonomous selfhood harder for girls than for boys. Dinnerstein (*The Mermaid and the Minotaur*, 1976) argues that the malaise of both sexes derives primarily from the fact that women remain in charge of infant and child care.

This influential scholarship of the 1970s focused on what psychiatrists call primary prevention—the removal or alteration of conditions inimical to women as a "target population." In the eighties and nineties, numerous articles and books have created feminist modes of therapy appropriate to women's specific biological, existential, and social situation (See, for example, the journal *Women and Therapy*.)

When we examine the writings of women who "know" madness from experience as opposed to those of scholars who "know about" madness, we find a rich literary corpus extending back a hundred years. The best of these works take the form of autobiographical fiction or poetry, with complex symbolic structures and multiple levels of meaning incorporated into the narrative line.

Charlotte Perkins *Gilman's 1890s story *The Yellow Wallpaper* presents madness as a form of postpartum psychosis and flight from patriarchal strictures. Based on her own experience, Gilman—a pioneer feminist writer—evokes the deterioration of a mother confined to a garret room after the birth of her first child. Following the rest cure devised by the famous doctor, S. Weir Mitchell, the mother is allowed no activity, especially no exercise of pen and paper. Her escape into the life perceived beyond the yellow wallpaper—into the figure of a mysterious woman creeping through the house and out into the garden—collapses her sane and insane self into the kind of compelling double image commonly associated with Dostoyevski and Kafka.

What had appeared in 1890 as an isolated case of the madwoman/author/protagonist developed fifty years later into a subgenre of fiction. From Mary Jane Ward's *The Snake Pit* in 1946 to Kate *Millet's *The Loony-Bin Trip* in 1990, women writers who had endured a psychosis have drawn from their personal histories the raw material for works of art. Although the theme of madness had never been absent from Western literature since Aeschylus and Sophocles, that literary tradition was predominantly male-authored and male-centered. Only now is it possible to speak of the topos of madness as having a large number of female archetypes authored by women.

Within this cluster of twentieth-century works on madness, *The Bell Jar* (1963), Sylvia * Plath's first and only novel, has already become a minor classic. Based on Plath's experience of mental breakdown in her junior year of college, *The Bell Jar* is a prefeminist exposé of the adverse effects of sexist culture on American women in the 1950s and, at the same time, a panhuman myth of death and rebirth. Psychopolitical critics have seen Plath's "schizoid" individual as the direct product of twentieth-century civilization, while feminist critics have emphasized the gender-specific strands of Plath's illness, as embodied in the character of Esther Greenwood. Esther's increasing sense of psychic alienation is symbolized by the image of the bell jar—an image of isolation from the rest of the world. Her attempted suicide by an overdose of sleeping pills and her long, difficult road through therapy back to a state of precarious health mirrored the author's own return to normal life. By the time of Plath's death by suicide in 1963 when she was only thirty, she was acquiring a steady reputation as a poet—a reputation further enhanced by the posthumous publication of her autobiographical novel and the collection of poems titled *Ariel*.

I Never Promised You a Rose Garden (1964) offered a more mysterious vision of madness. For three years the teenaged girl who was to become the writer Joanne Greenberg was kept in a mental institution under the care of an empathetic woman doctor (the analyst Frieda Fromm Reichman). Her successful struggle against the torments of schizophrenia was dramatically portrayed in her best-selling novel, and then given even greater publicity as a film.

The early sixties also saw the first book-length collections of Anne * Sexton, who was to become, for an American readership, the madwoman poet par excellence. From 1961, with the publication of *To Bedlam and Part-Way Back*, until 1974 when she committed suicide at the age of forty-five, Sexton's poetry was rooted in her experience as a mental patient. Throughout her adult life, Sexton was subject to bouts of severe depression requiring numerous hospitalizations. Literary critic Diane Middlebrook, whose biography of Anne Sexton became a surprise best-seller in 1991, traces her metamorphosis from "housewife into poet" by focusing on the interconnections between Sexton's family history, chronic mental illness, experiences

in psychotherapy, and her wild determination to be known and remembered for her distinctive confessional poetry.

Sexton, Plath, and Greenberg made of mental illness an acceptable literary theme for women, comparable in popularity to the works of male writers such as Robert Lowell, J. D. Salinger, and Ken Kesey. For better or for worse, numerous women have followed the model of the madwoman as author and/or subject. Marge * Piercy offered in her novel *Woman on the Edge of Time* (1976) a hallucinatory vision of a woman's life both in and out of the asylum, which is simultaneously a feminist critique of society and a highly original utopia. Maxine Hong * Kingston's dazzling autobiography *The Woman Warrior* (1977) is peopled with numerous crazy women coexisting alongside ubiquitous "ghosts" derived from the author's Chinese American culture.

In one of the stories from *The Women of Brewster Place* (1983), Gloria * Naylor draws an unforgettable portrait of a black woman who falls apart after her only child's accidental death, which is linked in her mind to her husband's repeated cruelties. This pathetic young woman is snatched from the edge of permanent insanity by an understanding older woman, who undresses and bathes her like a baby. In this and in many other woman-centered works, a female-female paradigm asserts itself as a symbol of healing.

[See also Body and Health; Hysteria.]

• Jean Strouse, ed., *Women and Analysis* (1974). Jean Baker Miller, *Toward a New Psychology of Women* (1976). Barbara Hill Rigney, *Madness and Sexual Politics in the Feminist Novel* (1978). Shoshana Felman, ed., *Literature and Psychoanalysis* (1982). Dale Peterson, ed., *A Mad People's History of Madness* (1982). Linda Schierse Leonard, *The Wounded Woman* (1983). Natalie Shainess, *Sweet Suffering* (1984). Elaine Showalter, *The Female Malady* (1985). Marilyn Yalom, *Maternity, Mortality, and the Literature of Madness* (1985). Doris Howard, ed., *The Dynamics of Feminist Therapy* (1986).

Marilyn Yalom

MAGAZINES, Women's. By the last decades of the eighteenth century, approximately fifty years after the appearance of the first American magazine, periodical publishers discovered a potential market in female readers. Editors began to consider the needs of "the fair sex" who, they maintained, deserved the "highest attention." Articles increasingly appeared bearing titles such as an "Elegant Description of Domestic Felicity" (*American Moral and Sentimental Magazine*, 1797). The subject of the woman's sphere presented a growing female audience with cultural prescriptions for female behavior: "To be *lovely* you must be content to be *women*;

to be mild, social, and sentimental" (Noah Webster, *American Magazine*, March 1788).

Two magazines from this period actually referred to female readers in their titles. In the first issue of the Boston *Gentlemen and Lady's Town and Country Magazine* (1 June 1784), the editors directly solicited the support of women not only as readers but also, for the first time, as authors.

These new literary contributions described the world of women. Eulogistic poems celebrated female personages. Some stories described, through the Orientalist genre of the Eastern tale, the sexual exploitation of women subjected to forced male lust, while others focused, through the moral tale, upon illicit sexual relations. Some of the essays published in this magazine treated the subject of women's equality, as did the work of Judith Sargent *Murray.

In the last decade of the century, two new magazines catered to women readers. A second *Gentlemen and Ladies Town and Country Magazine* appeared in the Boston area, published this time by Nathaniel Coverly from February 1789 through August 1790. In 1792, the first magazine that aimed exclusively at a female audience started in Philadelphia. Published by W. Gibbons and edited by a "Literary Society," the *Lady's Magazine and Repository of Entertaining Knowledge* was published semiannually.

The nineteenth century, however, became the century of the woman's magazine. Forty-five periodicals for women emerged between 1800 and 1830, while more than sixty-five others appeared in the marketplace during the twenty-year period, 1840–1860. Journals dealt with a range of women's issues including domestic economy, *fashion, labor, *education, literature, society, and women's social and political status.

And the city of Boston was home to one of the most historically famous yet undersubscribed magazines of the day, the *Dial*. The organ for transcendental thought, the magazine was staffed by two women who proved instrumental in maintaining its life through a rough four-year period. For two years Margaret *Fuller, one of the century's most profound feminist intellectuals, edited *The Dial* and served as one of the most prolific contributors to the journal. One of her most popular writings on the "woman's question"—the 1843 "The Great Lawsuit: Man vs. Men. Woman vs. Women"—was first published in these pages. Fuller was assisted by the celebrated "American Renaissance woman," Elizabeth Palmer Peabody (the founder of the first kindergarten in America and sister to Sophia Peabody Hawthorne), who ac-

tually published the magazine during its last two years.

New York housed its share of women's special-interest magazines. Reform periodicals appeared in the city during the 1830s. One of the more notable was the weekly *Female Advocate* (1832–1833). In addition to the temperance issue, the editors focused upon "the elevation of fair sex," including suggestions for helping prostitutes and the impoverished. The most popular of the New York reform journals was the *Advocate of Moral Reform* (1833–1873); it boasted a national circulation of 16,500 in the later 1830s.

One of the most popular publications in the first half of the century was *The Ladies Companion* (1834–1843), also known as *Snowden's*. The magazine employed several women as editors, including Ann Sophia Stephens (1837), Lydia H. *Sigourney (1843), and Emma C. Embury (1843). Another New York publication, the *Union Magazine of Literature and Art* (1847–1848) sought to popularize interest in art. Though not exclusively aimed at women, the popular female editor Caroline *Kirkland and her impressive list of female contributors, among them Lydia Maria *Child, Elizabeth F. *Ellet, Emma C. Embury, Grace *Greenwood [Sarah Jane Lippincott], Catharine *Sedgwick, and Lydia *Sigourney, provided gendered perspectives on a variety of artistic, cultural, political, and literary issues.

But the publishing center for woman's magazines in this period was certainly Philadelphia, a city that produced the widest range and number of magazines for women. Philadelphia-based periodicals included the woman-edited *Intellectual Female, Or Ladies Tea Tray*, a journal started by Mary Clarke Carr; *Miss Leslie's Magazine* (1843–1844), a publication dedicated to "domestic interests"; the *Philadelphia Album and Ladies' Weekly Gazette*, the magazine that started the rage for full-page color fashion plates; and the *Woman's Advocate* (1855–1860), a journal that presented "the wrongs of women."

This last publication is significant in women's magazine history for several reasons. It was the first journal owned by a joint-stock company of women. It was also edited, typeset, and printed by women who received wages equal to males of the same occupations. Unlike other women's magazines of the day, the *Woman's Advocate* focused upon the interests and the needs of *working-class women. The editor, Anne Elizabeth McDowell, proclaimed in an editorial that the magazine directed itself to the "elevation of the female industrial class." While the magazine expressed a reserved criticism of "transcendental sisters" who urge "windy resolutions" because they did not view the situation of women from the perspective of the "blackened hands" of the working class, the *Woman's Advocate* argued relentlessly for a variety of women's issues, especially those related to the working woman: the need for job training and equal pay.

But the most popular Philadelphia woman's magazine was Louis Godey's and Sarah Josepha *Hale's *Godey's Lady's Book*. This magazine was a marriage of Hale's financially destitute but content-rich *Ladies Magazine* and Godey's own *Lady's Book*. Clearly the most widely read and influential of women's magazines at midcentury, *Godey's Lady's Book* provided an environment that catered to a range of women's issues including "female improvement," domestic economy, dress, education, social status, and literature.

Miscellaneous in nature, *Godey's* contained stories, essays, travel accounts, poetry, and reviews by the greatest and most popular female American authors. Catharine Sedgwick, Lydia Sigourney, Anna Sophia Stephens, and Harriet Beecher *Stowe represent some of the most notable female contributors. Together with popular male writers, these women provided readers with the full range of literary topics. A look through the pages of the monthly reveals varied styles and narrative forms. The subject matter of *Godey's* stories included art, sea life, immigrants, family life, and the lives of the social elite. While readers looked to *Godey's* for what Hale called the "moral tale," this genre assumed a variety of forms in the pages of the magazine. This diversity appealed to a growing general readership who seemed to be characterized, in the words of one antebellum critic, by a "lack of patience for investigation, and a longing after variety."

In *Godey's*, the moral tale—written by both men and women—is frequently shaped by the conventions of *domestic fiction and a *sentimental style (described elsewhere by Nina Baym, Mary Kelley, and Susan Harris). Yet the moral tale reaches well beyond the parameters of domestic fiction and sentimentality. Borrowing elements and forms from working-class literature, writers of the moral tale in *Godey's* also employed the form of adventure stories about characters of reputable social standing, and they often describe the sensational adventures of artists, writers, and other professionals. These stories largely focused upon action, mystery, and intrigue in exotic settings, usually European cities, and, like domestic fiction, were written by both male and female writers. Hale remained editor for some forty years, and at the end of her reign she witnessed new magazines for women eclipse her own *Godey's*.

This increasingly lucrative periodical marketplace attracted the majority of "other" American Renaissance writers, and it served as a major outlet for their work. During the 1840s and 1850s, prominent writers such as Caroline *Chesebrough [Maria Jane McIntosh], Fanny Fern [Sara Payson Willis Parton], Fanny Forrester [Emily Chubbuck Judson], Caroline Lee Hentz, Sedgwick, Harriet Beecher Stowe, and E.D.E.N. *Southworth established their careers by contributing to the magazines.

Many of these writers found the periodical marketplace more critically receptive and economically rewarding than the book market. In a period when the income of many popular authors amounted usually to no more than $500 to $1600 yearly, *Godey's Lady's Book*, in its first few years, paid the popular Lydia Sigourney $500 yearly—over two hundred dollars more than the average annual wage for skilled workers—just to add her name to its list of contributors without actually writing anything.

Women founded their own journals: children's miscellanies, and reform, literary, educational, political, religious, and labor magazines. In many magazines, especially toward midcentury, females occupied the posts of main contributors, book reviewers, literary editors, and even editors-in-chief. Some journals were completely published, edited, and typeset by women, such as the *St. Louis Ladies' Magazine* (1871–1892), *Central Magazine* (1872–1875), the *Chicago Magazine of Fashion, Music, and Home Reading* (1870–1876), and the Indianapolis *Ladies' Own Magazine* (1869–1874). And female writers surpassed male contributors in popularity; female audiences became the mainstay of the most successful magazines. *Godey's Lady's Book* had over 30,000 subscribers in 1842, a readership that swelled to 70,000 by 1851 and to 150,000 by 1861.

At midcentury, several magazines dealt specifically with female emancipation. The dress reformer and feminist Amelia Bloomer founded the earliest periodical in this genre, *The Lily*. Lasting from 1849 to 1856, this magazine argued for both the right to vote and the reform of women's clothing styles. The famous crusader Elizabeth Cady *Stanton published some of her early work in its pages. Dr. Lydia Sayers continued the movement begun by Amelia Bloomer by starting the official organ for the National Dress Reform Association, the *Sibyl: A Review of the Tastes, Errors, and Fashions of Society*. Other journals took up the cause of female emancipation: *Woodhull & Clafin's Weekly; Woman's Journal; Woman's Campaign; Ballot*

Box; the Chicago *Sorosis;* the Nebraska *Woman's Tribune,* the *New Northwest,* out of Portland, Oregon; and the Denver *Queen Bee.*

Two of the most well-known women's rights periodicals were strong competitors. Susan B. * Anthony founded the *Revolution,* a weekly journal that lasted from 1868 to 1872. Edited by Laura Curtis Bullard among others, the weekly hosted a group of well-known women writers, namely Stowe, Pauline Wright Davis, the short-story writer Alice * Cary, and her sister, the poet Phoebe Cary. Focusing on women's suffrage, the journal suffered from ideological divisions among the members of the National Woman Suffrage Association in addition to severe financial problems, and the once-feminist weekly, in new hands, ultimately turned to women's domestic "duties." In 1870 Lucy Stone, who supported the proposed Fifteenth Amendment despite its exclusion of women, started the rival—and more conservative—*Woman's Journal.* This magazine attracted an increasingly large readership.

Other women, most notably Lydia Maria * Child, took up the cause of * abolition. Child edited the *National Anti-Slavery Standard,* while Harriet Beecher Stowe serialized in the *National Era* what came to be the century's most popular attack against the institution of * slavery, *Uncle Tom's Cabin.*

Some magazines focused upon the interests of ethnic women. From their first publication 1828, the * African-American periodical press included female writers and gave significant attention to the special needs of African-American women. During the postbellum years magazines designed exclusively for African-American women appeared, largely in regional centers outside of the Eastern pale. In 1888, Louisville housed the first such magazine, *Our Women and Children.* Several well-known leaders and journalists within the African-American community served as editors for the periodical: Mary Virginia Cook, Ida B. * Wells-Barnett, and Iona E. Wood. *Ringwood's Afro-American Journal of Fashion* soon followed in 1891. Edited in Cleveland by Julia Ringwood Coston, this popular periodical contained home, art, and literary departments in addition to a "Mother's Corner." It counted among its editors and contributors Mary Church Terrell, Molly E. Lambert, Sarah Mitchell, and Adina E. White. In the last decade of the century, Josephine St. Pierre Ruffin started the popular *Woman's Era,* a periodical dedicated to reporting the activities of African-American * women's clubs nationally, organizations that, according to Ruffin, systematically worked "for the uplifting of their race." *Woman's Era* debated current issues such as unemployment, the convict lease system,

lynching, temperance, and the establishment of kindergartens. It contained sections on music, drama, public opinion, the home, and presented biographical sketches on notable women. The journal later became the official organ of the National Federation of Afro-American Women as well as the National Association of Colored Women.

While ethnic presses tended to focus upon the interests of more general concerns of the group, some ethnic magazines concerned the particular needs of women. One of the earliest ethnic magazines for women was published for * Native Americans. The *Cherokee Rose Bud* (1848) treated issues related to the interests of Native American female students enrolled at the Rose Bud boarding school, and its pages reveal subtle references to the sorrows of the Cherokee nation over the subordination of their culture to white American values.

During this period a few journals by and about women appeared within the immigrant German and German-Jewish communities. Anne Metz Byland, the first immigrant German female journalist, edited the New York *Fortschritt,* which covered topics ranging from current events to literature. *Die Deborah,* a Cincinnati publication for German-Jewish women, started in 1855 and ran through the century until 1903. A noted Zionist and Jewish feminist, Rosa Sonnenschein, founded the first English language journal for Jewish women. Called *The American Jewess* (1885–1889), this short-lived periodical catered to the political and literary interests of middle- and upper-class Jewish women. One journal started at the beginning of the next century, *Die Hausfrau* (The Housewife, 1904), boasted a circulation of 44,000 by the mid-1970s.

Since * ethnicity and * class were often inextricably linked, some of these magazines catered to the needs of labor. Emma Pack, one of the many women who participated in the agrarian revolts at the end of the century, edited *The Farmer's Wife* and argued for female suffrage. In 1909, Charlotte Perkins * Gilman started *The Forerunner,* a feminist journal that railed against the inequities found in "women's work" and domestic labor. And in 1918, the Danish and Norwegian magazine *Kvinden* (The Woman), published monthly in Chicago, dealt with women's issues from a socialist and labor-oriented point of view. Two other publications edited by women who dedicated themselves to class and ethnic issues appeared during this time. Emma * Goldman started *Mother Earth,* a periodical so politically challenging that it was banned in 1918. That same year, the celebrated Native American writer and activist * Zitkala-Sa (Gertrude Simmons Bonnin) edited the

American Indian Magazine. The organ of the Society of the American Indian, this publication focused upon the collective identity, needs, and goals of Native Americans.

Within the Finnish immigrant population, three long-lived and relatively successful publications aimed at Finnish women emerged during this period. *Toveritar* (The Woman Comrade), published from 1911 to 1926, enjoyed a circulation that peaked at 12,000, while the weekly *Tyoolaaisnainen* (The Working Woman), a short-lived publication for urban and farm women, had a readership of 10,000 to 14,000 during its four-year life span. *Naisten Viiri* (The Women's Banner), a weekly periodical, had a circulation that ranged from 1,566 to 3,200. Despite its smaller readership, it lasted three decades. It was run largely by female editors: Emma Mattila (1930s–1940s); Emma Tuominen (1950s); and Helen Kruth-Leiviskaa (1970s). Considered to be ideologically sympathetic to Communism, this periodical provided articles on labor, domestic issues, health, literature, and women's issues, such as International Women's Day.

Magazines primarily aimed at middle-class women emerged as "home" magazines, and they have dominated the woman's periodical marketplace from the last decade of the nineteenth century throughout the twentieth century. But even within this essentially domestic realm, these journals went beyond their expected boundaries. When the *Woman's Home Companion* (founded 1897) passed into the editorial hands of Gertrude Balltes Lane in 1911, the magazine significantly enriched the concept of a "home" magazine. Viewing the homemaker as "forever seeking new ideas … ever extending" her horizons, Lane moved to intellectualize the domestic sphere by providing women readers with "the most constructive thought on the vital issues of the day" from what she called "a woman's perspective." Throughout her thirty-year editorship, she published the works of popular women authors, including Willa *Cather, Ellen *Glasgow, Zona *Gale, and Dorothy Canfield *Fisher, the labor journalist and pioneer of Montessori education, Mary Heaton *Vorse, Gilman, and chef Fannie Farmer.

A series of upper-middle-class magazines dedicated to women's fashions started in the last part of the nineteenth century have continued to publish through the twentieth century. One of the earliest—and the longest-lived—of the genre is *Harper's Bazar* (now *Harper's Bazaar*). Founded in 1867 by Fletcher Harper of the formidable Harpers Brothers publishing company, and under the editorship of the historian Mary L. Booth, the magazine provided the latest Continental fashions. *Vogue* entered the fashion stage in 1892, supported financially by some of the most aristocratic New York families. As editor some decades later, Edna Woolman Chase pushed the magazine to the top of elite fashion magazines, a position it has enjoyed through most of the century.

Ladies' Home Journal also proved to be a remarkably versatile magazine. Like its competitors, the *Journal* attempted, in the words of the editors Beatrice and Bruce Gould, to expand the domestic woman's "traditional areas of interest." Articles on political, social, educational, and medical issues regularly appeared, in addition to essays that attempted to elevate and to professionalize housework. The magazine campaigned for the protection of animals and openly discouraged women from adopting a Parisian fashion which involved killing maternal birds (and as a result starving their young) in order to obtain plumes. It also hosted a series of articles by public figures such as Jane *Addams regarding the widespread dangers of venereal disease.

The magazine hosted a prestigious group of contributors, including Louisa May *Alcott, Mary Jane Holmes, Edith *Wharton, Mary *Austin, Marion Harland, journalists (and anti-suffragettes) Ida Tarbell and Dorothy *Thompson, Kathleen Norris, Winefred Willis, columnist Mary Roberts *Rinehart, and illustrator Jessie Wilcox Smith. In later decades, the *Journal* was particularly astute in choosing for serialization future best-sellers. By the mid-1950s, it boasted the largest circulation among women's periodicals: more than five million monthly readers. Throughout its history, the magazine has followed the movement of women's lives from within the home to the workplace. Articles, stories, and columns have discussed from a variety of perspectives the dilemmas women face in balancing the different elements of their lives.

Magazines aimed at working-class women, such as those cast in the genres of romance and confession—*True Story, True Romance*, and *True Confessions*—seldom present the realities of working-class life. Rather, many of these periodicals emphasize middle-class values of individualism and success.

Other magazines aimed at lower-middle-class women appeared in the 1930s, often in the newsstands of grocery stores. *Woman's Day* and *Family Circle* were the most popular of these journals, but *Good Housekeeping, Redbook*, and *McCall's* have fought for the limelight. These and other periodicals changed their look as the women's movement encouraged women to alter their views of themselves. By the late 1970s and early 1980s women's magazines attempted to distinguish themselves by catering to a prescribed socio-economic description of "their" women, groups which ranged from suburban "young married homemakers" *(Good Housekeeping)* through women with "their own careers, their own style," *(Mirabella)* and "the woman who wasn't born yesterday" *(Lear)* to "the baby-boomed women, who are seeking a gracious life, balanced between home and business" *(Victoria).* With this move to grace, the genre of the fashion magazine re-fashioned itself into a magazine of "style."

Some magazines have chosen to specialize in political, social, and socio-economic subjects. While these periodicals suffer from limited distribution and remain largely localized, they focus upon cultural issues of national concern. Some of these magazines focus upon the neglected topic of women's health, such as *Herself* and *Monthly Extract*, while others, such as the Chicana *Encuentro Feminil* (Female Encounter), the pan-Latina *Revista Mujeres* (Women's Magazine), the Native American *Namequa Speaks*, organ of the Native American Woman's Action Council, and the feminist underground publication *off our backs*, treat issues related to *ethnicity, poverty, and *education.

The most widely disseminated of these specialized magazines is the feminist journal. A study by *Ms. Magazine* in the mid-1970s found that feminist publications were less hierarchically structured, more reader-centered, and more advertising-conscious than general periodicals. Starting in the 1960s and 1970s with Gloria *Steinem's revolutionary *Ms. Magazine,* the National Organization of Women's monthly, *NOW Acts,* and the regional *No More Fun and Games* (Boston), feminist periodicals have by the 1990s permeated both the general and the academic markets. Magazines of all ideological stances are represented: *Focus: A Journal for Gay Women; Working Woman; Women: A Journal of Liberation* (a Marxist oriented periodical); *Savvy, Amazon Quarterly: A Lesbian Feminist Arts Journal; Lilith: A Quarterly for Jewish Women* (Seattle); and the *women's studies journals *Chrysalis, Feminist Studies, Signs: A Journal of Women in Culture and Society, Sinister Wisdom, Tulsa Studies in Women's Literature,* and *Women Studies Quarterly.* This well-earned position in the periodical marketplace has resulted in the creation of a separate discipline in periodical scholarship for women's magazines which ensures their importance and continued existence.

[See also Journals, Academic; Journalists; Little Magazines; Newspaper Columns; Newspapers, Women's; Reportage.]

• Bertha Monica Stearns, "Early Factory Magazines in New England," *Journal of Economic and Business History* 2, no. 4, (1930): 685–705. Frank Luther Mott, *A History of American Magazines,* 4 vols. (1957). Lyon N. Richardson, *A History of Early American Magazines, 1741–1789* (1966). Penelope L. Bullock, *The Afro-American Periodical Press, 1838–1909* (1981). James E. and Sharon M. Murphy, *Let My People Know: American Indian Journalism, 1828–1978* (1981). Andrea Fleck Clardy, *Words to the Wise: A Writer's Guide to Feminist and Lesbian Periodicals and Publishers* (1986). Dirk Hoerder, *The Immigrant Labor Press in North America, 1840s–1970s: An Annotated Bibliography* (1987). Patricia Smith Butcher, *Education for Equality: Women's Rights Periodicals and Women's Higher Education, 1849–1920* (1989). Nancy K. Humphreys, *American Women's Magazines: An Annotated Historical Guide* (1989). Mary Ellen Zuckerman, *Sources on the History of Women's Magazines, 1792–1960: An Annotated Bibliography* (1989). John Tebbel and Mary Ellan Zuckerman, *The Magazine in America: 1741–1990* (1991).

Sheila Post-Lauria

MALE GAZE. *See* Film Theory, Feminist.

MALE-IDENTIFIED WOMAN. When the term *male-identified woman* was first employed by the feminist movement, it was used both to describe those women whose sense of self was totally circumscribed by "masculine" standards of *beauty, femininity, *sexuality, and power, those who in other words identified *with* men, and those women who identified *as* men. The latter category included those lesbians who dressed "like men" and/or "passed" for men. The former category included both heterosexual and lesbian women. Lesbians whose partners were "masculine" looking and/or acting ("butch") were accused of being male-identified because of their supposed erotic relation to *masculinity and because of their "femme" style, which often replicated "feminine" norms. And just by virtue of her heterosexuality, a straight woman could be labeled male-identified. Often, however, it was not just heterosexuality itself that was considered male-identified, but also the act of vaginal penetration, no matter by whom.

The political implications of this concept were perhaps first fully articulated in 1970, when the Radicalesbians published their manifesto, "The Woman-Identified Woman." As Alice Echols (*Daring To Be Bad: Radical Feminism in America, 1967–1975,* 1989) explains, the declaration coined a new term, *woman-identified woman,* for women who found primary political, emotional, social, or other support but not necessarily sexual sustenance from women. At the same time, by its echoing of *male-identified woman,* the phrase pitted itself against this position as its feminist alternative. The dichotomy established by these terms was very important for feminist *consciousness-raising and organizing, as it provided a way to define and politicize identity.

With the advent of the sex debates, the realignment of the lesbian community with gay men in the face of *AIDS, and the criticism of the feminist movement by women of color, the general acceptance of the label *male-identified* has been challenged. In her essay, "Coalition Politics: Turning the Century," (1981) Bernice Johnson Reagon rejects the restrictions implied by the term *woman-identified* (and by implication, *male-identified*), in part because women of color cannot afford to let go of their political affiliations with men of color. She advocates a kind of "coalition politics" that goes beyond gender separatism and concentrates on building alliances across oppressions. Joan *Nestle (*A Restricted Country*, 1987) describes the violence done to lesbians (and heterosexual women) whose erotic identities were labeled *male-identified*, and many straight feminists are now reclaiming heterosexuality as not necessarily controlled by *patriarchy. With deconstructions of *gender and *sexuality such as Judith Butler's *Gender Trouble* (1990), feminist and *queer theorists challenge the stability of the categories *masculine* and *feminine*, arguing that butch and femme, for example, are not replications of patriarchal *stereotypes but are instead complicated responses and challenges to the sex-gender system. Furthermore, theorists such as Eve Kosofsky Sedgwick have begun an examination of the process of identification itself, one that is based on the premise that the relationship between one's gender, sexual, and other identities and one's identification as "male" or "female" is much more complicated than the terms *woman-identified* and *male-identified* can accommodate.

[*See also* Woman-identified Woman.]

• Bernice Johnson Reagon, "Coalition Politics: Turning the Century," in *Home Girls: A Black Feminist Anthology*, ed. Barbara Smith (1983), pp. 356–368. Adrienne Rich, "Compulsory Heterosexuality and the Lesbian Continuum," in *Blood, Bread and Poetry: Selected Prose 1979–1985* (1986), pp. 23–75. Eve Kosofsky Sedgwick, "Across Gender, Across Sexuality: Willa Cather and Others," in *Displacing Homophobia: Gay Male Perspectives in Literature and Culture*, eds. Ronald R. Butters, John M. Clum, and Michael Moon (1989), pp. 53–72. Radicalesbians, "The Woman-Identified Woman," in *Out of the Closets: Voices of the Gay Liberation*, eds. Karla Jay and Allen Young, 2d ed. (1992), pp. 172–177.

Katie Kent

MAN. *See* Gender and Writing; Gender Theory.

MARGINALITY. Over the past two decades, the term *marginality* has received much critical attention from feminist scholars in various dis-

ciplines. However, according to the *Oxford English Dictionary*, the word *marginality* as such does not exist. The proper noun is *marginalia*, which means "marginal notes." Standard definitions of *marginal* typically explain that it refers to something that pertains to the edge, border, or boundary. A common second meaning defines the term as something that is on the margin or close to the limit, below or beyond which something ceases to be possible or desirable. It is essentially in this latter definition that the term *marginality* has been rendered useful for current feminist criticism.

Like most key notions that invest current feminist terminology with discursive power, the term *marginality* is employed to problematize the gendered politics of cultural representation. But while mainstream feminist scholarship in the United States has seized upon the philosophical potential of the term to reconceptualize the absence of women from canonical forms of representations, other less Anglo-American centered feminist writers have emphasized the term's political impact. In her influential essay "Explanation and Culture: Marginalia" (1979) Gayatri *Spivak maintains that "marginality" denotes an imaginary or arbitrary political space into which socially disenfranchised groups, particularly women and people of color, are placed by the dominant interest holders of a patriarchal society. According to Spivak, marginality does not so much refer to a "natural" state of being as rather to a "reified" state of political consciousness construed by the hegemonic powers of a given society in order to keep antagonistic interest groups in check. She contends that, as much as the notion of marginality carries the potential to deconstruct patriarchal power, it also might reify a "false" political state of consciousness that guarantees women's continued submission to male dominance.

Because the term *marginality* can be used both to question and to ensure women's silence in patriarchal society, much of recent feminist scholarship has been concerned with not only the exclusion but also the persistent *preclusion* of women from active cultural participation. For most feminist conceptual models, the term *marginality* serves as a vital analytical category that crucially highlights women's precarious status in the structure of patriarchal representation. At the same time as the term *marginality* invokes a politics of exclusion, it may also give rise to "feminist tokenism" that allows for a few "exceptional" women to enjoy male privilege only to leave the inherent misogyny, on which patriarchal favoritism operates, fully intact. What seems like a paradox is in fact a logic that underlies the structure of a margin. To draw on Gayatri Spivak again, marginality always already operates in relation to a center which symbolically excludes what is threatening. In accordance with this understanding, the margin is primarily a symptom of the center's ambivalence towards its own political power, and for that very reason, the margin functions within a designated space always already in relation to the center. Against appearances then, the margin never simply represents a border or an edge, just as the center rarely constitutes the actual center of political power. In short, the state of "being marginal" as defined by marginality denotes a state of impossibility, as the *Oxford English Dictionary* appropriately suggests. With regard to the position of *woman* in culture, *marginality* might be the only way to describe her current status, although it should be emphasized that this, by no means, refers to a permanent condition.

• Teresa de Lauretis, *The Technologies of Gender: Essays on Theory, Film, and Fiction* (1987). Sidonie Smith, *A Poetics of Women's Autobiography: Marginality and the Fictions of Self-representation* (1987). Gayatri Chakravorty Spivak, *In Other Worlds: Essays in Cultural Politics* (1987).

Ming-Bao Yue

MARRIAGE has been a prominent topic in writing by women living in the United States. For some women "marriage" becomes the hallmark of a domestic feminism; for others it represents a nightmare of sacrifice and punishment. Throughout U.S. history, women write to celebrate, define, criticize, and revise the institution.

In the seventeenth and eighteenth centuries marriage was often viewed by New England women writers as a spiritual union of two unequal partners. Obedience to one's husband, as in the Bible, was paralleled to obedience to God. Poems by Anne *Bradstreet (1612–1672) are meditations upon family life and loss. "To My Dear and Loving Husband" and "A Letter to Her Husband, Absent Upon Public Employment" (1678) picture marital love as a joyful, even passionate, union. In Mary *Rowlandson's *Narrative* (1682), about her captivity by Indians, the author is removed from her family but seems to focus most on her own welfare and past sins. She pictures her captivity as a spiritual trial; her triumph will be reuniting with her husband and children once her husband is able to "buy" her back from her Indian master. Unlike Rowlandson's narrative, Elizabeth *Ashbridge's autobiography *Some Account of the Fore-Part of the Life of Elizabeth Ashbridge . . . Wrote By Herself* (1774) depicts the author's spiritual journey as a movement away from her husband as she becomes a devout Quaker. Ash-

bridge's allegiance to God outweighs her obedience to her husband; her candid defiance of her husband's will is unusual in literature of this period. Poets Bridget Richardson Fletcher (1726–1770) and Phillis *Wheatley (1753–1784), who came to Boston as a kidnapped African slave, conform to the conventional view of marriage as a bond of obedience. Fletcher's "Hymn LXX The Duty of Man and Wife" (1773) enjoins the husband to "prize" his wife and the wife to "submit" to her spouse, while in Wheatley's "To a Lady on the Death of her Husband" (1773) the narrator consoles a widow with assurances of marital union in "the hills of light."

Mexican and Native American oral tales originating in this period present marriage as part of the fabric of social life. In the Mexican-American tales "The Llorona, Malinche, and Unfaithful Maria" and "The Devil Woman," women become devil figures who take revenge against their lovers; the importance of legitimized marriage is emphasized. Native American trickster tales also reinforce the social customs of proper marriage. The Tlingit tale "Raven and Marriage" and the Tsimshian tale "Raven Makes a Girl Sick Then Cures Her" both concern social hierarchy and the inappropriateness of a poor man marrying a high-caste woman.

Similarly, in literature of the early Republic, women are valued in a marriage match for the status they can bring to their spouse and punished for sexual relations either before or outside of marriage. Authors Susanna *Rowson (1762–1824) and Hannah *Foster (1758–1840) indirectly criticize social conventions that blame and victimize women for adultery. Rowson's best-selling novel *Charlotte Temple* (1794) concerns the seduction and abandonment of a fifteen-year-old girl. The sympathetic narrator instructs the reader to understand and pity the protagonist's mistakes. In Rowson's play of the same year, *Slaves in Algiers, or a Struggle for Freedom*, a stronger feminist invective than her more popular novel, women are portrayed as involuntarily consigned to serve and obey men. Foster's *The Coquette* (1797) is another seduction story, revealed through letters. The protagonist Eliza Wharton is unwilling to submit to a conventional marriage with a dull husband, but her desire for romance and equality is thwarted when she dies, unwed, in childbirth.

In the early nineteenth century, women writers brought the debate over women's status in marriage to the forefront. Transcendentalist Margaret *Fuller and abolitionists Lydia Maria *Child and Sarah *Grimké argue for egalitarian relationships in their essays and fiction. Fuller's *Woman in the Nineteenth Century*

(1845), Grimké's *Letters on the Equality of the Sexes and the Condition of Women* (1838), and Child's *Letters from New York* #50, "Women's Rights" (1843), advocate women being equal partners to their husbands. Grimké blames scripture for society's oppression of women, and Child and Fuller focus on abolishing assigned gender roles. Elizabeth Cady *Stanton (1815–1902), most renowned for her leadership in women's suffrage, also wrote in support of the Married Women's Property Act, and her "Declaration of Sentiments" revises the "Declaration of Independence" to explain the abuses and lack of rights women have suffered as silent spouses.

Women writing in midcentury and after the *Civil War were often categorized as authors of *sentimental fiction, although their stories and novels frequently depicted protagonists resisting conventional marriages. Louisa May *Alcott's *Little Women* (1868–1869) and her autobiographical *Work* (1873) show the importance of female identity and fulfillment previous to and outside of marriage. *Ruth Hall* (1855), by Fanny *Fern, is the story of a widow who, rather than remarry, struggles for financial security on her own. Fern's novel signals the end of the romantic plot that emphasizes sacrifice and self-denial by women for the sake of marriage. Other women authors focused on a new marriage theme for the late nineteenth century: the dilemma between marriage and career. Sarah Orne *Jewett's *A Country Doctor* (1884) and Elizabeth Stuart *Phelps's *Dr. Zay* (1882) both focus on women protagonists who choose to pursue a medical profession instead of marriage.

Black women writers in this era had other concerns. Equality in society at large was more important to achieve than challenging marriage conventions. In Frances *Harper's *Iola Leroy, or Shadows Uplifted* (1892), the author is concerned with the tragic effects of miscegenation and the status of mulattoes. Pauline *Hopkins, who wrote *Contending Forces: A Romance Illustrative of Life North and South* (1899) to "raise the stigma of degradation" from her race, also emphasizes the "tragic mulatto" theme with her complicated plot of the separation, suffering, and reunion of a West Indian family. Hopkins's later serialized novels *Winona* and *Of One Blood* (1902–1903) are plots about interracial marriage and its negative consequences.

Meanwhile, at the turn of the century, white southern women were writing against the plantation romance tradition that elevated white women as the purveyors of culture and purity. Kate *Chopin's *The Awakening* (1899) scandalized the contemporary reading public with its forthright plot of adultery and female sensuality. More significant, it represented a bid for women's freedom outside marriage and motherhood. Ellen *Glasgow began her writing career criticizing the older order in antiromances like *Virginia* (1911). In the North, Charlotte Perkins *Gilman, Edith *Wharton, Mary Wilkins *Freeman, and others amplified the theme of marriage as imprisoning for women. In Gilman's *The Yellow Wallpaper*, the protagonist is driven to madness inside a stifling marriage, and Susan *Glaspell's play *Trifles* (1916) centers around a woman who chooses to kill her husband rather than continue to suffer emotional abuse. Edith Wharton's *House of Mirth* (1905) and *Ethan Frome* (1911) reveal marriage as both an emotional trap and an economic necessity.

*Modernism, the *Harlem Renaissance, and the rise of writing by women immigrants and regionalists reinforced themes of dissatisfaction in marriage as well as introduced new concerns. Nella *Larsen's *Quicksand* (1928) follows the African-American protagonist back to the South, where she marries a preacher and succumbs to a life of drudgery. Zora Neale *Hurston's fiction, as in her stories "Sweat" and "The Gilded Six Bits," often depicts marriage as a battleground for dominance between husband and wife. In *Sui Sin Far's stories about Chinese-American life in San Francisco, the main character, Mrs. Spring Fragrance, is a matchmaker who helps young women defy the strictures of traditional Chinese arranged marriages to choose American or Americanized husbands. Marriage becomes a means of *assimilation into mainstream American culture. *The Autobiography of Alice B. Toklas* (1933) by Gertrude *Stein presents a lesbian relationship as both a mirror of and answer to conventional heterosexual marriage. Harriette *Arnow's *Hunter's Horn* (1949) reveals the trials of marriage and childbirth for poor Appalachian women.

Since World War II, women writing about marriage have increasingly written about its dissolution in divorce or abandonment. Bobbie Ann *Mason's "Shiloh" (1982) concerns a woman growing out of her marriage as her disabled truck-driver husband tries desperately to hang on to it. Lorna Dee *Cervantes's poem "Beneath the Shadow of the Freeway" contains a narrator who relies on herself and other women to do the "man-work" in the household. Other prevalent themes include marriage as friendship, physical and psychological abuse in marriage, and the decision to live outside of marriage. Poems by Adrienne *Rich, Anne *Sexton, and Denise *Levertov offer sharp critiques of contemporary marriage and romance.

Tillie *Olsen's "Tell Me a Riddle" (1961), a story about an older woman dying of cancer and her relationships with her husband and family, shows how grief and the memories of a life shared together can overcome alienation and allow forgiveness in marriage.

Portraits of contented relationships in contemporary women's literature seem rare. Native-American, Asian, Hispanic, and black women writers increasingly write about female communities where men are hardly featured. Joy *Harjo's "The Woman Hanging from the 13th Floor Window" and Paula Gunn *Allen's "Suicid/ing(ed) Indian Women" reveal the despair of women who are isolated or abandoned by lovers and husbands. Louise *Erdrich's character Dot in *The Beet Queen* (1986) grows up under the care of several adults who act as surrogate parents, perhaps a healthier alternative to traditional marriage and family relationships. Alice *Walker's *The Color Purple* (1982) and Amy *Tan's *Joy Luck Club* (1989) also focus on women's kinship and friendship groups to the exclusion of the romance plot. Reflecting the reality of society in the late twentieth-century United States, many women writers picture marriage not as a desired goal, but as a temporary or optional stage of life. As women are no longer censured from divorce or remaining single, women authors are given new choices and circumstances for plots.

[*See also* Family; Kinship; Spinsterhood; Widowhood.]

• Rachel Blau DuPlessis, *Writing Beyond the Ending: Narrative Strategies of Twentieth-Century Women Writers* (1985). Barbara Solomon, ed., *American Wives: Thirty Short Stories by Women* (1986). Jan Cohn, *Romance and the Erotics of Property: Mass Market Fiction for Women* (1988). Carolyn G. Heilbrun, *Writing a Woman's Life* (1988). Sandra M. Gilbert and Susan Gubar, *No Man's Land: The Place of the Woman Writer in the Twentieth Century*, vol. 1, *The War of the Words*, and vol. 2, *Sex Changes* (1988, 1989). Sybille Kamme-Erkel, *Happily Ever After?: Marriage and its Rejection in Afro-American Novels* (1989).

Beth J. Harrison

MARRIAGE LAWS. The legal status of married women has changed dramatically in the course of American history. Until the mid-nineteenth century, a woman was defined as *feme covert*, an Old French term meaning "hidden woman" and connoting that a woman's legal rights were contained within her father's rights or, after marriage, her husband's rights and that she did not need any legal rights of her own. A woman could not vote, serve on juries, or testify in a court of law; she could not sue or be sued in her own name; husband and wife could not testify for or against each other because, by common law, they were the same person after marriage.

In most states, a wife could not own property and any inherited family property typically came under the ownership of her husband. Even her body "belonged" to her husband in the sense that she could not testify against him and thus had little recourse in the case of physical abuse. Women's legal rights rested on an English Common Law idea that a man and woman are one—and the husband was the one. Implicit was the idea that marriage was also permanent. Divorce was difficult to attain in most of the United States in the early years of the Republic. South Carolina did not grant its first legal divorce until 1868.

By 1865, inspired by the nineteenth-century women's movement, twenty-nine states had passed some form of property laws for women (called the Married Woman's Property Acts). With state-by-state variations, these laws allowed married women to retain control of their real property but typically continued to obligate husbands to pay their wives' debts. A wife was given dower rights to one-third of his property after his death and was granted rights to support after a divorce, although custody of the children was not considered a woman's right in the nineteenth century. The most far-reaching law was the 1860 Earnings Act passed in New York which allowed women not only ownership of real property but also control of their earnings. In eight states originally controlled by France or Spain, "community property" laws decreed that each spouse owned half of the family possessions as well as half of any earnings or accrued property.

As Jo Freeman has argued, it was not until 1971 and the agitations and consciousness-raising of another women's movement that, in the case of *Reed v. Reed*, the Supreme Court altered its interpretation of the Fourteenth Amendment in ways that fundamentally changed woman's rights, responsibilities, and obligations inside and outside of marriage. In a number of related cases, the Court ruled that "sex characteristic frequently bears no relation to ability to perform or contribute to society" and thus deemed illegal any state laws based solely on "sex characteristics."

In 1993, most laws based on a discriminatory view of women have been found unconstitutional. However, certain common-law principles remained intact throughout the twentieth century and continue to be upheld in some states today, specifically tort laws, which prevent one spouse from suing another for an injury, and laws decreeing that criminal rape cannot exist within marriage (since, by law, a man is entitled to his wife's "conjugal services").

Marriage laws have also been bound by racial considerations. Under *slavery, there were no legal consequences for women in marriage since no state (except Louisiana, briefly) recognized the validity of slave marriages. Marriage is also, by most current legal definitions, restricted to members of the opposite sex. The lack of marital status for same-sex couples today has left them legally vulnerable, typically barred from their partner's medical and life insurance benefits, deprived of protection in inheritance and tax statutes, or, as happened in some widely publicized cases, denied visitation rights should one partner be hospitalized or institutionalized.

At present, marriage laws are in flux. Gay marriages and palimony cases (where live-in lovers sue for financial compensation after the end of a relationship) both test current laws. Similarly, as Laura Oren notes, the Uniform Premarital Agreement Acts passed by several states in effect end-run marriage laws by permitting partners to negotiate the specific legal terms of their marriage. Additionally, increasing numbers of professional women who have been forced by the courts to pay excessive alimony or settlement awards or who have lost custody of their children are demanding a reassessment of the state of contemporary marriage laws and customs.

• Nancy F. Cott and Elizabeth H. Pleck, *A Heritage of Her Own: Toward a New Social History of American Women* (1979). Carl N. Degler, *At Odds: Women and the Family in America from the Revolution to the Present* (1980). Jo Freeman, "The Legal Revolution," in *Women: A Feminist Perspective*, ed. Jo Freeman (1989), pp. 371–394. Laura Oren, "Marriage," in *Handbook of American Women's History*, ed. Angela Howard Zophy (1990), pp. 353–355. Linda K. Kerber and Jane Sherron De Hart, eds., *Women's America: Refocusing the Past* (1991).

Cathy N. Davidson

MARRIAGE MANUALS. Judging from their rhetoric, it appears that marriage manuals, like other advice manuals written in the United States, respond to a perceived national anxiety or moral crisis, when previous role definitions and self-concepts come into question and call for new codes of behavior. A sense of moral backsliding informs the advice proffered to young couples, particularly young women, in the hope that a reformation of marriage standards will participate in the larger reformation of society. Particularly in the early decades of the nineteenth century, concerns about the identity of the nation, religion, domesticity, and *gender identification intersect with more or less practical advice about building a marriage and maintaining a household. Although some women wrote advice manuals for the young

wife, the majority of authors, especially before the twentieth century, were men, who as ministers or medical doctors made a career of advising others, specifically those of the middle class or those who aspired to it.

While an early marriage manual, *The American Spectator, or Matrimonial Preceptor* (1797), borrowed the language of revolutionary-war egalitarianism to chart a distinctly American domestic life, manuals of the early nineteenth century, informed by an ideology of progress and the new industrialization, splintered conjugal life into *separate spheres, emphasizing woman's inferiority to man. As the husband marched off to work away from home, to do battle with the demons of the commercial world, the wife was ensconced in the home, her sphere, to make it a refuge from the cares of the world. Her task was "to soften, to cheer, and to refresh that mind on which the weightiest cares of a family press" (James Bean, *The Christian Minister's Affectionate Advice to a Married Couple*, 1815). Called upon to build a Christian refuge from the cares of the world, women nonetheless received conflicting messages. Described as the inferior sex, they were enjoined to submit to their husband's rule, both because of his superior intellectual powers and because of the biblical injunction to obedience. At the same time, women were idealized as creatures of sentiment and religion, who by their loving influence would save the nation of men from crass materialism. Idealizing woman's capacity to love, the manuals both rested the hope for a humanized and moral society on her and restricted her life to the private sphere; she was told that "all women have the same [role in life]. . . . It is, to be a wife, a mother, a mistress of a family" (*The Young Lady's Own Book*, 1832) and that as mother, the "first teacher," she formed "the characters of men" (Catherine Marie *Sedgwick, *Means and Ends: or Self-Training*, 1839). Nonetheless, like other types of advice and etiquette manuals, those directed to the young wife emphasize the external female self, her dress, her duty, her smile, her temper; even her submission demonstrates not her true, inner self, which she is advised to conceal, control, and deny.

While marriage manuals of antebellum America stress Christianity and religion as the foundation for a successful marriage, authors increasingly realized the need for some kind of practical, domestic *education for the young housekeeper and thus provide the reader with hints for maintaining a household, educating children, and overseeing servants. Some of the advice is general, admonishing order, regularity, economy, and industry; other advice, like that found in Mrs. *Child's *The American Frugal

Housewife (1833), contains specific housekeeping hints, recipes, remedies, and lessons on hygiene. Early on, writers began to recognize that an education centered on dancing and painting does not prepare a young woman for her calling in life; nor does it, according to Sedgwick, prepare women to contribute to the harmony of the household and the direction of the country.

As the century progressed, the manuals demonstrate some disaffection with the previous generations' approach to marriage and women's roles. Though most writers were not willing to give up the notion of differentiated roles or spheres of influence, they continue to stress practical education while simultaneously softening the legal inequality of women by describing marriage as a union of souls. The author of *Buds for the Bridal Wreath* (1856) describes woman as "the complement of man;— the completion of his humanity" and marriage as "the union of two souls in conjugal love." The strain of her own marriage in the face of her literary success tells in Harriet Beecher * Stowe's 1866 *Little Foxes: or, The Insignificant Little Habits which Mar Domestic Happiness*, where she begins by reiterating the old admonition to silence but later advises a degree of personal integrity: "Do not always shrink and yield; do not conceal and assimilate and endeavour to persuade him and yourself that you are happy . . . respect your own nature, and assert it; woo him, argue with him; use all a woman's weapons." In *The False and True Marriage* (1861), Mrs. H. F. M. Brown more directly criticizes current marriages of convenience by which women gain a livelihood and men men a "cook, washer-woman, housekeeper" and in which "the humanity of the woman is not recognized in law." Her remedy is informed both by legal reform and by a pseudoscientism that describes a universe of male and female atoms, which, like men and women, seek the union of "kindred hearts." Dr. John Cowan, too, attempts a scientific approach to marriage and includes anatomical diagrams of male and female reproductive organs and discussion of sexuality, a topic untouched by previous advisors. But his "Science of a New Life" is informed by the pseudoscience of phrenology as he advises young men on the look-out for a wife to compare phrenological charts in order to assure the "perfect union—a union of resemblance in mind, soul and body" (*The Science of a New Life*, 1874).

The manuals of the twentieth century make broader, and more accurate, use of scientific theory, borrowing from physiology, Darwinism, Freudian psychology, anthropology, and sociology, making of marriage and family life a separate field of study and the subject of textbooks. Yet the manuals also demonstrate a tension between traditional and modern ways of marriage. Mrs. Emma F. Angell Drake, M.D. (*What a Young Wife Ought to Know*, 1901) fuses medical knowledge with the traditional insistence on woman's role as wife and mother as she instructs the reader in matters of health, reproduction, and child care. Alarmed by the increase in divorces and the apparent revolution in morals, Felix Adler (*Marriage and Divorce*, 1905), founder of Ethical Culture and a leading advocate of liberal religion, denounces the modern trends toward "college education of girls" and the "emancipation of woman," while novelist Floyd Dell (*Love in the Machine Age*, 1930) blames the "relics of patriarchal traditions" for the "neurotic maladjustments" of modern life and advocates "a modern and scientific view of behavior" informed by psychology, sociology, and history. Other writers of the twentieth century were concerned with adapting to modern life and argued for broader roles and education for women and entered the new debate about wives working outside the home. In her essay for *The Good Housekeeping Marriage Book* (1939), Eleanor Roosevelt examines several options for the Depression-era wife, noting the difficulties of holding down two jobs— at home and at the office or mill—without prescribing any particular pattern of marriage, only urging "young people to think over what they want out of life very carefully." Similarly, Evelyn Millis Duvall, writing for the Public Affairs Committee (*Building Your Marriage*, 1946), recognizes the alternatives for women and advises a marriage of cooperation and sexual fulfillment, suggesting that marriage requires "skills" and that couples utilize social institutions such as clubs and churches to strengthen their marriage. Although women at midcentury had not achieved full equality with men, advisors were making gestures to suggest that marriage be a mutually loving and cooperative endeavor.

[*See also* Advice Books.]

• *The Female Friend: or the Duties of Christian Virgins* (1809). Lydia Maria Child, *The Mother's Book*, 2d ed. (1831). William A. Alcott, *The Young Wife, or Duties of Woman in the Marriage Relation* (1837). John Morison, *Counsels on Matrimony* (1842). Arthur Freeling, *The Young Bride's Book* (1845). T. S. Arthur, *Advice to Young Ladies on their Duties and Conduct in Life* (1848). Mrs. L. H. Sigourney, *Whisper to a Bride* (1850). V. B. Ames, *Matrimonial Primer* (1905). Marjory Louise Bracher, *Love Is No Luxury: A Guide for Christian Family Living* (1951). Harold T. Christensen, ed., *Handbook of Marriage and The Family* (1964). Michael Gordon, ed., *The American Family in Social-Historical Perspective* (1978).

Susan L. Roberson

MARSHALL, Paule (b. 1929), novelist and short-story writer. In "Zora Neale *Hurston: A Cautionary Tale and A Partisan View," Alice *Walker refers to Paule Marshall as "unequaled in intelligence, vision, [and] craft by anyone of her generation, to put her contributions to our literature modestly," a comment which not only reflects Marshall's standing in the literary community but also acknowledges the distinctive perspective of her corpus. Marshall's vision, that black people of African descent undergo self-redefinition through reclaiming their cultural integrity as a means of neutralizing the psychological trauma of racial oppression, characterizes her first three novels. *Brown Girl, Brownstones* (1959), *The Chosen Place, The Timeless People* (1969), and *Praisesong for the Widow* (1983), in fact, are considered a trilogy by the author because of their expression of her vision. *Daughters* (1991) shares a thematic relationship with the earlier novels; *Reena and Other Stories* (1983) sustains several ideas of the trilogy. *Soul Clap Hands and Sing* (1961), a collection of four novellas in which spiritually moribund men seek revitalization through women, has its own internal unity.

Although characters, setting, and situation advance Marshall's vision, the creation of complex yet human and enduring women and men is her forte. In *Brown Girl*, Silla and Deighton Boyce, as West Indian immigrants with opposing philosophies who are beset by the difficulties of assimilating into a materialist American culture in New York and by marital problems, illustrate Marshall's skill in presenting formidable characters. Merle Kinbona, West Indian protagonist in *The Chosen Place*, embodies the psychological predicaments that multiple heritages and colonialism cause. Avatara Johnson, middle-class widow in *Praisesong*, confronts cultural instability and the consequences of materialism but is redeemed by reaffirming African cultural values in a journey both literal and metaphorical that takes her from suburban New York to the Caribbean island of Carriacou. Marshall's fiction richly evokes the consequences of a history of displacement for black people; its value lies in positing a potential for spiritual healing which looks back to African origins.

Marshall's intimacy with three cultures resulting from her background uniquely shapes her fiction. Her parents immigrated to New York City, where she was born, grew up, and attended Hunter College. Thus she had first-hand knowledge of allegiance to one culture but the necessity of assimilating to another and the alienation that may ensue from both of them. In her essay "From the Poets in the Kitchen" she credits the women domestic workers like her mother, who gathered in their Brooklyn apartment, with teaching her the artistry in normal conversation, providing her "first lessons in the narrative art," and training her ear.

As the author of four substantial novels, two books of short fiction, and several essays, Marshall's place in literary history seems secure. She occupies, however, a unique position in the tradition of black women's letters largely because her discrete vision of cultural continuity and her rendering of complex black characters of African descent fulfills a significant missing bond among black American women's texts.

• Barbara Christian, "Sculpture and Space: The Interdependency of Character and Culture in the Novels of Paule Marshall," in *Black Women Novelists* (1980), pp. 80–136. Alexis De Veaux, "Paule Marshall—In Celebration of Our Triumphs," *Essence* 11 (May 1980): 96, 98, 123–134. "Paule Marshall: Fiction Writer—A Special Section," *Callaloo* 6, no. 2 (Spring–Summer 1983): 21–84. Eugenia Collier, "The Closing of the Circle: Movement from Division to Wholeness in Paule Marshall's Fiction," in *Black Women Writers, 1950–1980*, ed. Mari Evans (1984), pp. 295–315. Joyce Pettis, "Self-Definition and Redefinition in Paule Marshall's *Praisesong for the Widow*," in *Perspectives of Black Popular Culture*, ed. Harry Shaw (1990), pp. 93–100.

Joyce Pettis

MARXIST-FEMINISM. A theoretical and political stance within the contemporary feminist movement that integrates gender analysis in feminist theory with class analysis in the Marxist tradition. Marxist feminism has its origins in a critical engagement with Left ideologies and political parties, but Marxist-feminist theory production has been limited to specific local contexts. While women in national liberation struggles in Latin America, Asia, and Africa joined in political movements that recognized women's double burden and utilized class analysis, the merging of feminist and Marxist theory remained confined primarily to the United States and Europe.

In late eighteenth- and early nineteenth-century Europe, Mary Wollstonecraft and Flora Tristan combined nascent utopian socialism with analyses of women's status in society. These analyses predated the socialist "Woman Question," which originally was examined in such texts as August Bebel's *Woman under Socialism* (1878; reprinted 1883) and Frederick Engels's *The Origin of Family, Private Property, and the State* (1884). Exploration and critique of Engels's arguments linking women's subordination with the family and private property continues to inform much Marxist-feminist thought on the origins of patriarchy, women's subordination in the family, and the sexual division of labor.

By the twentieth century, such socialist

women as Clara Zetkin, Charlotte Perkins *Gilman, and Alexandra Kollontai established themselves as the foremost analysts of the Woman Question. Their writings extended the theoretical understanding of women's subordination as rooted in the family and private property to everyday struggles around work, sexuality, and political liberation. They were joined by a wide range of women activists engaged in similar efforts within anarchism, the trade-union movement, and social reform. As part of social movements based on class, however, they faced major contradictions in Left practice and theory.

After World War I, the revitalized European Left experimented with sexual liberation and feminist cultural and political activity. Soviet constitutions of the 1920s, for example, not only endorsed equal political and economic rights for women but liberalized divorce laws and reproductive rights. By the 1930s, however, conservatism on sexual issues revoked or modified many of these gains; Communist party (KPD) women's activism in Germany on *abortion and family issues was undermined by the increasing violence of Communist-Nazi conflict and the rise of Hitler to power in 1932.

In the United States, the Great Depression brought the revival of leftist organization through community and labor *activism and a corresponding—though smaller—growth in Communist Party (CPUSA) membership. This revival created both cultural and intellectual space for women leftists in journalism, literature, and theory; and while much of this work was concentrated in *reportage, poetry, and fiction, Mary Inman (In Women's Defense), Grace Hutchins (Women Who Work), and others were able to inject a critical evaluation of male dominance within the party and in the broader society. Agnes *Smedley (Daughter of the Earth), Josephine *Herbst (Rope of Gold), Meridel *LeSueur (The Girl), Tillie *Olsen (Yonnondio), and Leane Zugsmith (A Time to Remember) were representative of the broad movement to create a literary culture on the Left, despite the overwhelmingly masculinist tone of much proletarian literature. In Europe, there was a similar interrogation of gender and class: Nina Roll Anker and Gro Holm of Norway, Moa Martinson of Sweden, and Storm Jameson of Great Britain were only a few leftist writers who explored the dual nature of women's economic and political oppression.

The emergence of contemporary Marxist feminism can be traced to several postwar developments. Simone de *Beauvoir's existentialist reading of woman as "Other" in The Second Sex (1946) drew upon Marxism and Freudian theory; its publication and the revitalization of Marxist theory and practice in Europe and the United States had, by the 1960s, laid the groundwork for a feminist critique of Marxism. Further, women writers involved in national liberation struggles contributed to the critique of Western societies as well as Marxist practice through their exploration of the impact of colonialism, racism, and sex oppression.

*Civil rights activism and the New Left in the United States were the context for the incipient women's liberation movement; the socialist analysis of segregation, racial inequality, and *colonialism were applied in understanding women's oppression. Socialist-feminist women's unions formed from such an understanding; but Marxist analysis had an important influence on feminist theory in general. Shulamith Firestone, for example, in The Dialectics of Sex (1971), relied upon the same tropes and models of analysis as Marxism but remained antagonistic to the New Left version of class analysis. In a different vein, Angela Y. *Davis's essays (later published as Women, Race and Class) owed more to the longstanding "woman question" in the Communist party than to the women's movement.

By the 1970s, the question of *patriarchy—and of the relationship among *gender, *class, and *race identities—took on central importance. Dual systems theory, which defined two autonomous but interrelated systems of oppression in capitalism and patriarchy; the sex/gender division of labor; domestic labor; surplus value; and reproduction were major points of contention in theoretical terms. National liberation struggles in Mozambique, Guinea-Bisseau, South Africa, and Nicaragua raised other troubling questions of theory and practice. Foremost was the question of socialist states' ability to incorporate a feminist agenda, given the assertion of class as always, finally, determinant, even if not dominant. Existing socialist states (Soviet Union, China, Cuba) seemed to suggest the difficulty of merging class and gender agendas, even as they underlined the problematic absence of race and nationalism from the agenda of Marxist and feminist movements in Europe and the United States. The politics and theory of gender were expressed in the proliferation of women's writing cross-culturally.

In recent years, socialist- (or Marxist-) feminist discourse has been marginalized to a great extent both on the Left and in the women's movement. Few women writers and critics openly identify with Marxist feminism as a literary and political tradition, although many have benefitted from the incorporation of Marxist concepts into feminist analysis. Still, in the past decade, there has been a remarkable growth of Marxist-feminist literary criticism and theory in Europe and the United States. The central issues are broad-based criticism of the *canon and the project of canon-reclamation; the ideology of women's subordination within the family and society; the conditions of cultural production and the production of knowledge; the origins of subjectivity and its instability. Beyond this, the question of difference—both from men (or masculinity) and from each other (as women of different races, cultures, and classes)—also has informed Marxist-feminist thought as it does other feminisms.

The emergence of a specifically Marxist-feminist literary criticism coincides with, participates in, and helps constitute other approaches to literary criticism and critical theory, particularly in the adoption of deconstruction and the New Historicism within the academy. Opposition to "totalizing" social theory, in this case Marxism, led to the critical evaluation of its understanding of subjectivity and history. Undermining the philosophical foundations of Marxism, however, did not lead to the dismissal of class as a category of analysis, but rather to its interrogation. Further, psychoanalytic theories of Freud and Lacan were grafted on to Marxist analyses, especially through the critical theories of the Frankfurt School; Marxist feminists Juliet Mitchell and Jacqueline Rose have adopted such frameworks in their analyses of women's oppression; Gayatri *Spivak and others have similarly forged materialist analysis and deconstruction in postcolonial studies of the subaltern. Finally, one finds a reengagement with issues of class and material analysis in the critical theory of such writers as Michelle Barrett, Janet Wolff, and Susan Willis.

[See also Communism; Feminism; Socialist Feminism.]

• Annette Kuhn and AnnMarie Wolpe, eds., Feminism and Materialism: Women and Modes of Production (1978). Lillian Robinson, Sex, Class, and Culture (1978). Zillah R. Eisenstein, ed., Capitalist Patriarchy and the Case for Socialist Feminism (1979). Michelle Barrett, Women's Oppression Today: Problems in Marxist Feminist Analysis (1980). Angela Y. Davis, Women, Race, and Class (1981). Lydia Sargent, ed., Women and Revolution: A Discussion of the Unhappy Marriage of Marxism and Feminism (1981). Judith Newton and Deborah Rosenfelt, eds., Feminist Criticism and Social Change: Sex, Class, and Race in Literature and Culture (1985). Seyla Benhabib and Drucilla Cornell, eds., Feminism as Critique: On the Politics of Gender (1987). Barbara Harlow, Resistance Literature (1987). Charlotte Nekola and Paula Rabinowitz, Writing Red: An Anthology of American Women Writers, 1930–1940 (1987). Gayatri Chakravorty Spivak, In Other Worlds: Essays in Cultural Politics (1987). Jean Franco, Plotting Women: Gender and Representation in Mexico (1989). Patricia Hill Collins, Black Feminist Thought: Knowledge, Consciousness, and the Politics of Empowerment (1990).

Karen V. Hansen and Ilene J. Philipson, eds., Women, Class, and the Feminist Imagination (1990). Michele Wallace, Invisibility Blues, From Pop to Theory (1990). Donna J. Haraway, " 'Gender' for a Marxist Dictionary: The Sexual Politics of a Word," in Simians, Cyborgs, and Women: The Reinvention of Nature (1991), pp. 127–148. Paula Rabinowitz, Labor and Desire: Women's Revolutionary Fiction in Depression America (1991). Susan Willis, A Primer for Daily Life (1991).
                                                      Elizabeth Faue

MASCULINITY. See Gender and Writing; Gender Theory.

MASON, Bobbie Ann (b. 1940), short story writer, novelist. Bobbie Ann Mason grew up in rural Kentucky, and though she hasn't lived in the South for many years, that culture still flavors her fiction. She received her Ph.D. in 1972 from the University of Connecticut, where she wrote Nabokov's Garden: A Nature Guide to Ada, which was published in 1974. Since then, she has published two collections of short stories, Shiloh and Other Stories (1982), for which she won the PEN/Hemingway Award and Love Life: Stories (1989), and two novels, In Country (1985) and Spence and Lila (1988).

Mason's most widely anthologized story, "Shiloh," characterizes her style. The story begins with the surface details of the lives of a long-married couple, Norma Jean and Leroy. Their relationship represents a common theme in Mason's work—the tension in the South between a culture locked in the past and, at the same time, rapidly modernizing. In the story Norma Jean tries to keep up with the times, building her muscles, and learning to write compositions. Leroy, disabled in a trucking accident, represents the regressive culture; he watches TV, and dreams of building a log cabin. As in much of Mason's work, emotion isn't the starting place for the story. Instead, Mason focuses on ordinary details, which interpreted together create emotional tension.

Other elements common to Mason's work are her use of popular culture and her exploration of *working-class life. Both In Country and Spence and Lila study how popular music, television shows, and brand-name products influence the everyday lives of the characters. Sam, the main character of In Country, begins to understand her Uncle Emmett and his trauma in Vietnam through listening to Bruce Springsteen's music. She and Emmett are addicted to reruns of "M*A*S*H"; the show is a major source of communication between them. Some critics argue that Mason's use of popular culture is limiting, but its function seems to be to give voice to working-class people who may not otherwise be able to articulate their own emotions or thoughts. It is fitting that *In Country* is now itself a part of popular culture, having been made into a movie.

Mason's work is also often labeled *minimalist because of its narrow themes and focus on literal detail. But a reader who takes the time to integrate and interpret that detail will find a story rich with undercurrents.

• Leslie White, "The Function of Popular Culture in Bobbie Ann Mason's *Shiloh and Other Stories* and *In Country*," *Southern Quarterly* 26, no. 4 (Summer 1988): 69–79. Robert H. Brinkmeyer, Jr., "Never Stop Rocking: Bobbie Ann Mason and Rock-and-Roll," *Mississippi Quarterly* 42, no. 1 (Winter 1988–1989): 5–17. Barbara Henning, "Minimalism and the American Dream: 'Shiloh' by Bobbie Ann Mason, and 'Preservation' by Raymond Carver," *Modern Fiction Studies* 35, no. 4 (Winter 1989): 689–698. Vincent King, "A Conversation with Bobbie Ann Mason," *Four Quarters* 4, no. 1, second series (Spring 1990): 17–22.

Deborah Viles

MASQUERADE. Traditionally associated with women and gay men in Western culture, masquerade figures prominently in twentieth-century feminist, gay, and lesbian theory. Joan Riviere, in "Womanliness as a Masquerade" (1929), posited that *femininity is a "masquerade" or performance of "womanliness." In her analysis of a successful American woman who was beset by anxiety after public speaking and found herself compelled to seek approval from older men by "flirting and coquetting," Riviere postulated that her patient's "mask" of femininity "was an unconscious attempt to ward off the anxiety which would ensue on account of the reprisals she anticipated from the father-figures after her intellectual performance." Hence, womanliness was a "masquerade." "Femininity" did not represent the truth of woman's desire but was a reaction-formation against feared cultural reprisals for behavior or desires categorized as "unfeminine." (Louisa May *Alcott's 1866 sensation story, "Behind a Mask," in which the heroine's apparent docility and "femininity" turn out to be a "mask" to hide her competitiveness and hard-hitting intelligence, may be read as an uncanny anticipation of Riviere's theory.)

Since Riviere's ground-breaking essay, identifying not only femininity but all *gender identity as masquerade has become increasingly important in critical attempts to counter phallocentrism and heterosexism. French psychoanalyst Luce Irigaray advocates the feminist strategy of "mimesis," which transforms masquerade from a defensive to an affirmative position. A woman "must assume the feminine role deliberately," for "to play with mimesis . . . means to resubmit herself . . . to 'ideas,' in particular to ideas about herself, that are elabo-

rated in/by a masculine logic, but so as to make 'visible,' by an effect of playful repetition, what was supposed to remain invisible: the cover-up of a possible operation of the feminine in language" (*This Sex*, 1985).

Mary Ann Doane exploits the notion of masquerade as a position of active agency for the female viewer of Hollywood cinema. Doane suggests that masquerade resists the production of femininity as closeness or self-presence and that the female spectator may "assume the mask in order to see in a different way." Masquerade has the potential "to generate a problematic within which the image is manipulable, producible, and readable by the woman." Mary Russo draws on Mikhail Bakhtin's theory of carnival and the grotesque to speculate about ways in which women can "make spectacles out of themselves," and to what extent such "spectacles" might effect a "redeployment or counterproduction of culture, knowledge, and pleasure." Russo considers instances of both feminist theory and the female *body as carnivalesque and potentially transgressive, focusing particularly on the mother's body and the aging female body.

Lesbian- and gay-studies theorists have critiqued the heterosexism of feminist theories of masquerade and also elaborated gay "drag" and "camp" (parodic imitation of heterosexual gender identity) as antihomophobic and anti-phallocentric strategies. Sue-Ellen Case criticizes the heterosexism and biologism in both Doane's and Russo's accounts, stating that "the subject in heterosexuality cannot become capable of ideological change." She proposes that the butch-femme couple offers the best potential for radical subjectivity, suggesting that they can be read from within Riviere's perspective as the masquerade of penis possession and of femininity, respectively. Leo Bersani, however, disagrees that either butch-femme masquerade or gay male drag effectively subvert *homophobia and heterosexual power hierarchies, suggesting instead that sexual performance (submission to anal penetration) may constitute a radical political subjectivity through its potential for "self-shattering." Carole-Anne Tyler in turn critiques Bersani for the misogyny she perceives in his discussion of gay male transvestism. In addition, she points to the bourgeois and racist implications of masquerade, in which miming the feminine means impersonating a white, middle-class ideal of femininity.

For Judith Butler, the critical question posed by masquerade is whether it covers an originary desire or whether it may be understood as the performative production of a sexual ontology (*Gender Trouble*, 1990). In "Imitation and Gender Insubordination," she proposes that the practice of drag demonstrates that "all gendering is a kind of impersonation and approximation" because "there is no original or primary gender that drag imitates but *gender is a kind of imitation for which there is no original.*" In her analysis of gay male subjectivities, Kaja Silverman develops the notion of "cultural masquerade" or "double mimesis" in which, in contrast with the distance between mask and subjectivity emphasized by Doane's and Riviere's theories, the colonizer's "masquerade" of the colonized implies a desire to *become* the racial or class Other (*Male Subjectivity*, 1992).

[*See also* Crossdressing; Performativity.]

• Louisa May Alcott, "Behind a Mask," in *Behind a Mask: The Unknown Thrillers of Louisa May Alcott*, ed. Madeleine Stern (1975). Joan Riviere, "Womanliness as a Masquerade," *The International Journal of Psycho-Analysis* 10 (1929): 303–313; reprinted in H. Ruitenbeek, ed., *Psychoanalysis and Female Sexuality* (1966), pp. 209–220 and in Victor Burgin, James Donald, and Cora Kaplan, eds., *Formations of Fantasy* (1986), pp. 35–44. Jacques Lacan, "The Meaning of the Phallus," in *Feminine Sexuality*, eds. Juliet Mitchell and Jacqueline Rose (1982), pp. 74–85. Luce Irigaray, *This Sex Which Is Not One*, trans. Catherine Porter (1985). Mary Ann Doane, "Film and the Masquerade: Theorizing the Female Spectator" (1982) and "Masquerade Reconsidered: Further Thoughts on the Female Spectator" (1988–1989) in *Femmes Fatales* (1991), pp. 17–32, 33–43. Mary Russo, "Female Grotesques: Carnival and Theory," in Teresa de Lauretis, ed., *Feminist Studies/Critical Studies* (1986), pp. 213–229. Sue-Ellen Case, "Towards a Butch-Femme Aesthetic," *Discourse* 11.1 (1988–1989, special issue on "Body/Masquerade"): 55–73; reprinted in Sue-Ellen Case, *Making a Spectacle: Feminist Essays on Contemporary Women's Theatre* (1989). Leo Bersani, "Is the Rectum a Grave?" *October* 43 (1987): 197–222. Terry Castle, *The Culture of Travesty: Sexuality and Masquerade in Eighteenth-Century England* (1988). Judith Butler, *Gender Trouble* (1990). Bad Object-Choices, eds., *How Do I Look?* (1991). Carole-Anne Tyler, "Boys Will Be Girls: The Politics of Gay Drag," in *inside/out*, ed. Diana Fuss (1991), pp. 32–70. Judith Butler, "Imitation and Gender Insubordination," in *inside/out*, ed. Diana Fuss (1991), pp. 13–31. Kaja Silverman, *Male Subjectivity at the Margins* (1992). Marjorie Garber, *Vested Interests: Cross-Dressing and Cultural Anxiety* (1992).

Mary Wilson Carpenter

MATRIARCHY. Positive though the word *matriarchy* may seem in asserting female agency, by analogy to *patriarchy* it suggests both historical reality, and sex-specific (so-called natural or universal) essences, such essences having been discredited by cross-cultural evidence. Existing archaeological evidence neither affirms nor denies the prehistoric existence of either matriarchy or patriarchy. A debate proceeds, then, concerning the interpretation of such evidence, in conjunction with cross-cultural studies of mythology and religion. Feminist evolutionists such as Frances Dahlberg (*Woman the Gatherer*, 1981), and Nancy Tanner (*On Becoming Human*, 1981) find prehistoric foraging societies likely to have been gender-egalitarian, not matriarchal. Thus far, neither archaeological, historical, nor contemporary records reveal the existence of matriarchy in the sense that patriarchy exists: women as mothers have not wielded domestic and political power over the lives of children and men, as have men as fathers over children and women.

Matrilocal, matrilineal, and matrifocal societies, however, have existed. *Matrilocality* refers to a "groom" joining a "bride" to live with her kin group or in her native territory, as for example among southwestern Navajo nation or Keres Pueblos. *Matriliny*, a structure that is disappearing, refers to the passage of inheritance through a female line of descent, from mother to daughter, exemplified by the position of Clan Matron among Iroquois Longhouses. The term *matrifocal* (or "gynocentric," as in Adrienne *Rich's Of Woman Born*, 1976), refers to societies in which women have more central roles, approaching those of men. During the mid-twentieth century, African-American women have been scolded, often by white male analysts, for heading "matriarchal" households, more accurately labeled "matrifocal" (Bettina Aptheker, *Women's Legacy*, 1982).

Nonetheless, the debate over the existence of prehistoric and ancient matriarchies continues. Earlier scholars like Johann Jakob Bachofen, author of *Das Mutterrecht* (MotherRight, 1861), carefully qualified their definitions of matriarchy to be closer to current meanings of matrilocality, matriliny, or matrifocality: their gynocentric theories attempted to explain phenomena otherwise inexplicable through current cross-cultural theory (Hildebrandt). The mid-twentieth century reemergence of a *women's movement has revived interest in questions about women's historical legacy.

Scholars of ancient Egypt, Sumer, Assyria, Israel, and the Hellenistic Mediterranean generally seem to agree that between 3100 and 600 B.C.E. more gender-egalitarian societies became patriarchal as women's social status changed in stages from *goddess-priestess to wife-consort while symbolic status lodged in multiple goddesses was subsumed by one male god (Gerda Lerner, *The Creation of Patriarchy*, 1986). Current cross-cultural studies of historic, preindustrial societies by both Eleanor Leacock (*Myths of Male Dominance*, 1981), and Peggy Reeves Sanday (*Female Power and Male Dominance*, 1981) provide evidence for the existence of societies perhaps matrifocal, surely more gender-egalitarian than the United States. Although not matriarchies, more gender-egalitarian prehistoric societies and less universally male-dominant historical societies exist than has previously been understood.

Related to the ideological debate concerning the position of women in prehistoric human life is the debate over the prehistoric worship of goddess(es). On the basis of cumulative unearthing of neolithic artifacts, both figurative and architectural, Marija Gimbutas in *The Civilization of the Goddess: The World of Old Europe* (1991) describes an Old European culture—extending from the Mediterranean to the Baltic, from the Atlantic to the Black Sea and Dnieper River between c. 6500 and 3000 B.C.E.—as matrifocal, matrilineal, and goddess-worshiping, though not matriarchal. The dilemma for interpretation remains, however: artifacts alone do not reveal their meanings to uninitiated scholars; such "signifiers" have no necessary connection to what is signified (Spretnak). Other feminist "thealogians" [*sic*] such as Rosemary Ruether (*New Woman/New Earth*, 1976) and Emily Erwin Culpepper (Atkinson et al.) advocate plural traditions for a more gynocentric future regardless of whether or which pre- or ancient-historic matriarchies or goddesses existed.

Feminist critique of the concept of matriarchy includes multidisciplinary insights. Anthropologist Joan Bamberger asserts that the "myth of matriarchy" is a mis-"Rule of Women" used to denigrate women's capacities and justify male dominance (Rosaldo and Lamphere). In a similar vein, psychoanalysts find matriarchy an androcentric concept, lodged in infant fears or fantasies of an omnipotent mother, or lodged in men's fear that women would use power as have men over women, a mere substitution of one group of oppressors for another. Karen Horney found male "womb envy" projected as "The Dread of Women" (1932; reprinted in *Feminine Psychology*, 1973). In *The Reproduction of Mothering* (1978), Nancy Chodorow notes the separation difficulties of boys from their mothers, causing boys to deny their "female" qualities in order to assert *masculinity—at least in the absence of a mitigating strong father. Male lack of gender self-confidence results in misogynist projections of fear and envy.

Regardless of actual or hypothetical existence, matriarchy posits women's agency and potency, even though conflating projected patriarchal values with women's desires. Feminist writers have found two alternatives for presenting the agency of a goddess-creatrix, a possible facet of matriarchy: they forge new traditions in works whose creative heroines are artists or are participants in utopian societies.

The figure of the artist typically exemplifies human creativity—whether in art or in society. Such creativity questions boundaries, exists in liminal space plumbing the unknown. For author and reader, creative heroines may express desire for larger freedoms and louder voices than experienced as possible. Most importantly the artist demands autonomous self-expression.

The unsubstantiated concept of matriarchy, mirroring patriarchal values, represents terror of or desire for female empowerment; for the future, why not instead imagine women's independent-artistic or communitarian-utopian creative agency?

[*See also* Myths; Patriarch.]

• Michelle Zimbalist Rosaldo and Louise Lamphere, eds., *Woman, Culture, and Society* (1974). Merlin Stone, *When God Was a Woman* (1976). Charlene Spretnak, ed., *The Politics of Women's Spirituality* (1982). Barbara G. Walker, *The Woman's Encyclopedia of Myths and Secrets* (1983). Linda Huf, *A Portrait of the Artist as a Young Woman* (1984). Paula Gunn Allen, *The Sacred Hoop: Recovering the Feminine in American Indian Traditions* (1986). Clarissa W. Atkinson et al., *Shaping New Vision: Gender and Values in American Culture* (1987). Hans-Juergen Hildebrandt, *Johann Jakob Bachofen: The Primary and Secondary Literature* (1988). Frances Bartkowski, *Feminist Utopias* (1989). Judith Plaskow and Carol Christ, *Weaving the Visions: New Patterns in Feminist Spirituality* (1989). Anthropological overviews in *SIGNS* 1, no. 1 (1975); 1, no. 3 (1976); 2, no. 3 (1977); 4, no. 3 (1979), 5, no. 3 (1980); 8, no. 2 (1982); 17, no. 1 (1991).

Carol Farley Kessler

McCARTHY, Mary (1912–1989), memoirist, novelist, critic. The decisive event in Mary Therese McCarthy's young life was the death of her parents in the flu epidemic of 1918. Almost overnight a comfortable childhood in Seattle was transformed by the loneliness and squalor of orphanhood in Minneapolis, where the four McCarthy children were handed over to cruel guardians. The harrowing experience, not without its comic interludes, is chronicled in McCarthy's most enduring book—*Memories of a Catholic Girlhood* (1957). There one finds her central concern with the mutability of human attachments, against which a fierce respect for fact, for truth, affords her compensation.

In the essays collected in *How I Grew* (1987) and *Intellectual Memoirs: New York 1936–1938* (1992), McCarthy continued to confront those facts of life—including the unpleasant patterns in her own behavior—and then set about transcending them with her ample weapons of candor, wit, and optimism. The autobiographical impulse informs McCarthy's nine works of fiction as well, to entertaining effect in *The Company She Keeps* (1942), her first book and the one that established her reputation for sexual explicitness, and less successfully in *Birds of America* (1971), a novel of ideas.

McCarthy's best-selling novel, *The Group* (1963), whose intimate detail about the lives of eight Vassar graduates in the 1930s foreshadows much women's fiction today, was called a "lady-book" by some writers in McCarthy's circle who rebuked her for writing a novel of manners from a woman's point of view.

Criticism engaged McCarthy's real talent for cutting through mystification and sentimentality. As a * drama critic *(Mary McCarthy's Theatre Chronicles, 1936–1962)*, social commentator *(On The Contrary*, 1961), travel/art writer *(Venice Observed*, 1956; *The Stones of Florence*, 1959), literary critic *(The Writing on the Wall*, 1970), and political journalist *(The Seventeenth Degree*, 1974), McCarthy also established herself as a woman of letters of uncommon range.

Uncomfortable with all "isms"—including *feminism, which she once called "bad for women" because it induced the dangerous emotions of "self-pity, covetousness and greed"—McCarthy remains an enigmatic figure. The most influential woman among the so-called New York intellectuals, she was renowned for her cool intelligence; crisp, epigrammatic prose; and wicked tongue (which sometimes caused her trouble, as when Lillian *Hellman sued her for $2.25 million in 1980 for calling her a liar on "The Dick Cavett Show"). McCarthy was also known for her many affairs and four marriages, the second of which was to critic Edmund Wilson. It was a woman's prerogative if not her pleasure, she felt, to take on any man and beat him at his own game, and she rarely shrank from the challenge. Her softer side found expression in friendship, most notably in a long friendship with the political philosopher Hannah Arendt.

• The Mary McCarthy Papers are in the Special Collections, Vassar College Library. See also Elizabeth Hardwick, "Mary McCarthy," in *A View of My Own* (1962). Carol Gelderman, *Mary McCarthy: A Life* (1988). Carol Brightman, *Writing Dangerously: Mary McCarthy and Her World* (1992).

Carol Brightman

McCULLERS, Carson (1917–1967), novelist, playwright, short-fiction writer, poet. Born Lulu Carson Smith in Columbus, Georgia, Carson McCullers grew up in the South. Although she moved to New York City in 1934, then permanently to Nyack, New York, in 1944, all her major fiction is set below the Mason-Dixon line. McCullers declined the inevitable labels—grotesque, freakish, morbid, Gothic—which critics applied to her characters and subject matter. Instead, she argued, she simply portrayed the normal humanity of "lonely hunters" questing after love and a sense of belonging.

The ambivalent nature of love was a personal as well as a writerly concern. McCullers's emotionally complicated relationship with the alcoholic Reeve McCullers lasted through the sixteen years of their marriage, divorce, remarriage, and Reeve's suicide in 1953. Bisexual, McCullers and her husband engaged in love affairs with both women and men, the complexities of which suggest themselves in McCullers's novel *Reflections in a Golden Eye* (1941) and her novella *The Ballad of the Sad Cafe* (1951). McCullers's exploration of androgyny in much of her work is shown in such ambiguously named young girls as Mick in *The Heart is a Lonely Hunter* (1940) and Frankie in *The Member of the Wedding* (1946, 1951).

To some, McCullers seemed an egotist constantly claiming center stage; however, to her friends she was emotionally responsive and brilliant. She was acclaimed early as a wunderkind, both in Columbus and later in New York, where her first novel, published when she was twenty-two, won instant success. Recipient of two Guggenheim fellowships, she was resident artist at numerous writers' conferences, including Breadloaf and Yaddo. Her fiction includes four novels and a novella, two plays, over two dozen nonfiction pieces, one volume of children's verse (*Sweet as a Pickle, Clean as a Pig*, 1964), twenty short stories and a handful of poems, some published posthumously in *The Mortgaged Heart* (1971), edited by her sister Margarita G. Smith. Characterized by a clear, sculpted style, McCullers's novels were often best-sellers. Her versatility is evident in her 1951 television adaptation of "The Sojourner" for *Omnibus* and in her two plays, *The Square Root of Wonderful* (1958) and *The Member of the Wedding* (1951), the latter amassing over 500 Broadway performances and winning the New York Drama Critics' Circle Award.

McCullers's successes were characterized by an impressive determination and tenacity despite debilitating illnesses from adolescence, including crippling strokes, paralysis, and cancer. Finally, in 1967, she suffered a massive brain hemorrhage followed by a coma from which she never revived. When she died on 29 September, McCullers left behind a distinguished body of work both compellingly timeless and disturbingly contemporary. Yet to be fully plumbed, her two least critically acclaimed works, *Square Root* and *Clock Without Hands* (1961), deserve careful reevaluation. Indeed, McCullers's entire canon is currently undergoing reappraisal in light of recent theory, particularly regarding sexuality, mother-daughter relationships, and the effect of illness on the act of writing.

• Virginia Spencer Carr, *The Lonely Hunter: A Biography of Carson McCullers* (1975). Margaret B. McDowell, *Carson McCullers* (1980). Adrian M. Shapiro, Jackson R. Bryer, and Kathleen Field, *Carson McCullers: A Descriptive Listing and Annotated Bibliography of Criticism* (1980). Harold Bloom, ed., *Carson McCullers* (1986).

Abby H. P. Werlock

McMILLAN, Terry L. (b. 1951), novelist, university professor, screenwriter, editor. McMillan was born 18 October 1951, in Port Huron, Michigan, the daughter of Madeline Washington Tillman and Edward Lewis McMillan, a working-class couple. McMillan was thirteen when her parents divorced, and her mother, a domestic and auto-factory worker, raised five children mostly alone. McMillan received a Bachelor of Science degree from the University of California at Berkeley (1979), and a Master of Fine Arts degree from Columbia University in New York City (1979).

Visiting Writer from 1987 to 1988 at the University of Wyoming, Laramie, in 1988, she became Associate Professor in Creative Writing, University of Arizona, Tucson. In addition, she was a literary fellow for the National Endowment for the Arts, 1988.

McMillan published her first short story in 1976 at age twenty-five. She wrote *Mama* while working as a typist, raising a son alone. (Solomon Welch was born in 1984.) Wary of the fate common to first novels, McMillan promoted it herself; she organized tours and wrote letters to colleges and universities. By publication date, *Mama* had sold out its first printing.

McMillan's second book, *Disappearing Acts*, achieved a first printing of 25,000 copies, and has sold over 100,000 copies in paperback. On sabbatical from the University of Arizona (1992), McMillan completed a screenplay for *Disappearing Acts*, optioned by Tri-Star. In the book, Franklin and Zora are star-crossed lovers who tell their stories, alternately, as first-person narrators while they are plagued, peripherally, by life's struggles. In 1990, McMillan edited *Breaking Ice* to showcase a new generation of black writers representing diverse subject matter, perspectives, and values, whose themes do not focus solely or predominantly on race.

In 1992, *Waiting To Exhale* achieved a first printing of 100,000 copies. Pocket Books paid 2.64 million dollars for paperback rights, and Viking established a $700,000 bidding minimum for movie rights. McMillan's narrative of four well-educated and self-supporting black women found eager readers in its move to best-sellerdom. The women's struggles are recognizable and relevant to readers, particularly African-American women. McMillan's literary style is vernacular-based, witty, and conversational. Reviewers laud her honest, poignant, energetic style, though some criticize characters' liberal use of profanity. Charles Johnson notes the "tough love letter" *Waiting to Exhale* sends to black men, and Spike Lee remarks on the book's humor and honesty and on McMillan's literary craftiness.

• "Waiting To Exhale" (book review), *Publishers Weekly* (23 March 1992): 58. Wendy Smith, "Terry McMillan," *Publishers Weekly* (11 May 1992): 50–51. Sybil Steinberg, *"Disappearing Acts"* (book review), *Publishers Weekly* (16 June 1992): 56. Esther B. Fein, "Fiction Verite: Characters Ring True," *New York Times* (1 July 1992): B1, B5.

Helena Woodard

McPHERSON, Aimee Semple (1890–1944), evangelist and religious writer. Born on an Ontario farm, Aimee Elizabeth Kennedy married Robert Semple, a Pentecostal preacher, at seventeen. A year later, Semple died, leaving his wife with an infant daughter. A second marriage, to Harold S. McPherson, ended in divorce, but not before Aimee had had a son. Once single again, McPherson threw all her energy into evangelism and became known as Sister Aimee. In 1918, she settled in California with her mother and children; her revival meetings there were so successful that she was soon able to move her family into a home built for her free of charge by zealous converts. McPherson continued to travel across country, conducting evangelistic campaigns and preaching the four basic tenets she called her Foursquare Gospel: regeneration, divine healing, the Second Coming of Christ, and the baptism of the Holy Ghost. She presented her beliefs and the story of her ministry in her books, *This Is That: Personal Experiences, Sermons and Writings* (1919), *Divine Healing Sermons* (1921), *In Service of the King: The Story of My Life* (1927), *The Holy Spirit* (1931), and *Give Me My Own God* (1936).

By 1923, McPherson had raised enough money to build Angelus Temple, a 5,000-seat permanent evangelistic center in Los Angeles. Despite her success as a preacher, however, McPherson was embroiled in both legal and sexual scandal. On 18 May 1926, in the midst of widespread rumors of an affair between her and Kenneth Ormiston, the radio engineer at the temple, McPherson walked into the ocean for her daily swim and disappeared. The ensuing search for the body produced nothing. Over a month later, McPherson walked up to a small cottage in Mexico just south of the Arizona border, claiming that she had just escaped from kidnappers, who had abducted her while she was swimming and held her for ransom. The story of her actual whereabouts during her disappearance, although never officially proven, was nevertheless confirmed by overwhelming evidence. McPherson had not been abducted at all, but rather had been staying with Ormiston in Carmel. In the absence of legal proof, however, McPherson simply declared herself exonerated and set out on a "vindication tour." When she returned to Los Angeles, she was greeted by throngs of the adoring faithful. McPherson's empire had survived, and she continued to run it until 1944, when she died of a suspicious barbiturate overdose that was ultimately ruled accidental.

• Nancy B. Mavity, *Sister Aimee* (1931). Lately Thomas, *Storming Heaven* (1970). "Aimee Simple McPherson," in *Dictionary of Religious Biography*, ed. Henry Warner Bowden (1977), pp. 278– 279. Daniel M. Epstein, *Sister Aimee: The Life of Aimee Semple McPherson* (1993). McPherson's life was fictionalized in the character of Sharon Falconer in *Elmer Gantry* by Sinclair Lewis (1927).

Sheryl L. Meyering

MEAD, Margaret (1901–1978), anthropologist. Margaret Mead was born in Philadelphia to Edward Sherwood Mead, an economics professor at Wharton, and Emily Fogg Mead, a sociologist. At Barnard College, Mead came under the influence of Franz Boas, often called the father of American anthropology, and his teaching assistant, Ruth Benedict. Mead's doctoral dissertation on cultural stability in Polynesia began her lifelong interest in the peoples of the South Sea Islands. What established Mead firmly as a public figure was her effort to relate the findings from her fieldwork to the lives of people in the United States. She believed unequivocally in the social relevance of anthropology, and influenced theory and practice in almost every major aspect of American society: education, childrearing, sex, marriage, and mental health, to name a few. She worked primarily out of the American Museum of Natural History in New York City, where she served first as assistant curator and then as full curator.

In 1925, Mead made the first of her many field trips to the South Pacific Islands. The book that grew out of her six-month stay on the Samoan island of T'au, *Coming of Age in Samoa* (1928), was a tremendous success. Written in language accessible to the nonspecialist, this work deals with the subject of *adolescence, attempting to determine to what extent the emotional crises and tensions accompanying this developmental stage are biologically determined and to what extent they are the product of cultural variations in childrearing, family structure, and other nonbiological factors. Mead concluded that adolescence was less

stressful for Samoan girls than for American girls because of more relaxed parenting and sexual permissiveness in T'au. Throughout her career, she would emphasize the strong role of culture in shaping human behavior, but she never ignored the parameters set by biological factors.

The recipient of numerous honorary degrees and awards, Mead's output was monumental. Her more than thirty books include *Growing Up in New Guinea* (1930), in which she studies how primitive children think; *Sex and Temperament in Three Primitive Societies* (1935), where she explores the relative effects of biology and culture on so-called gender differences in personality; *And Keep Your Powder Dry* (1942), a study of American character; *Male and Female* (1949), a discussion of marriage, sex, and divorce in contemporary America; and *Anthropologists and What They Do* (1965). She published over a thousand articles and papers, and was audio- and videotaped extensively.

• Mary Catherine Bateson, *With a Daughter's Eye: A Memoir of Margaret Mead and Gregory Bateson* (1984). Jane Howard, *Margaret Mead: A Life* (1984). Lowell D. Holmes, *Quest for the Real Samoa: The Mead/Freeman Controversy and Beyond* (1987).

Rajini Srikanth

MEDICAL PRACTICE AND WOMEN. Though physicians have diagnosed and treated women's diseases for centuries, such treatment has only been considered part of a thorough scientific endeavor for several hundred years. Physicians have traditionally assumed a paternalistic role towards women and in their most extreme behaviors, they have taken on positions of heroic proportion. Women's discourse about their relationships with physicians and experiences of surgery is understandably varied but tends to reflect the shifting attitudes seen throughout Western societies toward the medical community and its practices.

Initially, although women writers were respectful of attending physicians in *diaries and correspondence, and in the characters they created, there are several voices of dissent that question the paternal authority of the physician. In 1811, British writer Fanny Burney, known for such novels as *Evelina* and *Cecilia*, offered a full account of her mastectomy operation. An indictment of the male medical community, this diary entry details her physician's unwillingness to inform Burney preoperatively about the procedure and his total lack of regard for her suffering during a surgery done without anaesthetic. Alice *James shared Burney's low opinion of the medical community. James felt that the physicians consulting in her case virtually ignored her and, in fact, devalued her because of her infirmities. James noted, in her diaries, that her physicians, like most men, assumed that because she was "victim to many pains, that I was, of necessity, an arrested mental development too" (31 May 1891).

In the nineteenth century, physicians viewed their female patients as both mentally and physically frail. After all, even the healthiest women faced *childbirth, not just once, but often numerous times during their lives. Until the twentieth century, the most likely causes of medical complications were infection and loss of blood, both of which often occur after childbirth and miscarriage. These "normal" surgical procedures were a significant threat to a woman's life. Countless novels mirror this real-life danger by fictionalizing the complications of childbirth, and most show the woman as helpless if not victimized by the procedure. Even if the women survived, the process was debilitating and often led to depression and lethargy. Such works as "The Yellow Wallpaper" by Charlotte Perkins *Gilman describe the medical community's rest cure for these women as well as the way the woman may fight back. Rather than submit to *silence and isolation, the protagonist retreats into permanent psychoses, a means of resisting the male medical community at large.

In the twentieth century, women have attempted to regain control over their bodies and have become increasingly vocal in communicating this desire to the medical community. Such a shift in attitude occurs in the surgical setting as well. Not all women silently accept the opinions of the medical community. Surgeons are now treated ambivalently; they may sometimes still be revered but are often required to answer questions. Anne *Sexton, in her poem "In Celebration of My Uterus," challenges a surgeon's decision to perform a hysterectomy as she pays tribute to her uterus and women at large. This paean to a body part epitomizes the spirited, almost defiant attitude of women who wish to restrain the surgical community or at least express their desire to be seen as more than a diseased organ.

Contemporary *feminist theory provides a positive structure for evaluating women's relations with the medical community. It does so by offering a means for studying the complex relationship between *body and *language or discourse as potential empowerment. When entrusting their bodies to a fundamentally masculine-oriented medical community, women now suggest that they have information heretofore ignored by that community—the feminine perspective on the female body. Consultation thus can function reciprocally, as the physician and the patient pool information and share in the medical process.

Though the relationship between women, literature, and surgery is a complex one, women's writing provides ample evidence of an increasing desire for feminine control in an area where the human body and will are at greatest risk.

• Fanny Burney, *The Diary of Fanny Burney* (1956). Alice James, *Diaries of Alice James*, ed. Leon Edel (1964). Charlotte Perkins Gilman, "The Yellow Wallpaper" (1892), in *The Norton Anthology of Literature by Women*, eds. Sandra M. Gilbert and Susan Gubar (1985), pp. 1148–1161. Anne Sexton, "In Celebration of My Uterus" (1969), in *The Norton Anthology of Literature by Women*, eds. Sandra M. Gilbert and Susan Gubar (1985), pp. 1998–1999. Ann Daily, *Women Under the Knife: A History of Surgery* (1991).

Linda Ann Saladin

MEN AND FEMINISM. While the most common responses by men to women's political, social, economic, or literary efforts have been, and remain, indifference, antipathy, subversion, or exclusion, there is also a less well known tradition of men's support, encouragement, and willingness to struggle for women's rights. From the founding of the nation, these "profeminist" men have supported women's entry in the public sphere—from the ballot box to the classroom to the factory floor—as well as women's rights in the private sphere, including her right to divorce, to retain her own name, and to control her own body. Profeminist men have stood publicly for women's equality, and also have attempted to integrate their public and private lives, to remain more personally supportive of the women in their lives.

The Logic of Male Support. Perhaps the first profeminist man in America was Thomas Paine, who reread the Declaration of Independence in August, 1776, one month after ratification, and observed that women were not included under its liberating charter. Women, he wrote, have an "equal right to virtue." As possessors of the same individuality that was to be protected by the new nation, women, Paine believed, must also be included among its fully endowed citizens. Charles Brockden Brown, America's first professional man of letters, wrote a novel, *Alcuin* (1798), in which an older woman explains patiently the case for woman's rights, especially because "[the existing order] renders the female a slave to the man." And John Neal, founding member of the New England Woman Suffrage Association, tried a rhetorical reversal to make the case in his *Rights of Woman* (1843). Imagine the situation were reversed, Neal suggested, and men were excluded from political life. "What a clamor there would be then, about equal rights, about a privileged class, about being taxed without their own consent, about virtual representation and all that!"

In so writing, Paine, Brockden Brown, and Neal articulated the most common philosophical position by which profeminist men grounded their support of women's equality. Throughout the nineteenth century, and up to the present day, men have supported feminism because women were equally individuals, endowed—biologically, by God, or in civil society—with a natural equality that could not be abridged. Gender inequality was therefore a form of "cruel usurpation," as the abolitionist leader William Lloyd Garrison put it. Women's rights, including woman suffrage, were a matter, as Frederick Douglass put it, of "conscience and common sense."

Later in the century, a group of men sought to ground their support of women's equality not in women's innate individual equality, but in their social superiority. Following their activities in reform, and especially in the Temperance movement, profeminist men urged women's emancipation not because they were *as* moral as men, but because women were *more* moral, and in their role as moralizers, women could redeem men from the "muddle we have made of politics," as Frederic C. Howe, warden of Ellis Island, put it. "I want woman suffrage because I believe women will correct many of these law-made wrongs that man has made," argued Howe.

Individualists were unpersuaded by this logic. "It is a plausible and tempting argument to claim suffrage for woman on the ground that she is an angel," wrote Rev. Thomas Wentworth Higginson, one of the century's most visible profeminists, "but I think it will prove wiser, in the end, to claim it for her as being human," not, as some argue, because she is "man's better half" but because she is "his other half."

In the first few decades of this century, many of the bohemian writers and artists gathered in Greenwich Village articulated a third logic for male support of women's rights: feminism would benefit men, demolishing conventional standards of morality and allowing men to fully develop themselves. "Feminism will make it possible for the first time for men to be free," wrote Floyd Dell, in an article, "Feminism for Men," published in *The Masses* in 1914. Max Eastman, *The Masses* editor, added a brief (and possibly apocryphal) vignette that sums up their position. He describes an interview with the new stenographer at the office:

"Are you a feminist?" we asked the stenographer. She said she was.
"What do you mean by Feminism?"
"Being like men ," she answered.
"Now you are joking!"
"No, I'm not. I mean real independence. And emotional independence too—living in relation to the universe rather than in relation to some other person."
"All men are not like that," we said sadly.
"Then they should join the feminist movement!"

Arenas of Male Support. Profeminist men have supported women's struggles for equality in every arena that women have defined as significant, including education, economic rights, political equality, and social and personal freedom.

The founders and early presidents of women's colleges, for example, Matthew Vassar, Rev. L. Clark Seelye, John Raymond, and Henry Noble MacCracken, supported women's rights to education. Henry Fowle Durant, founder of Wellesley, supported the "revolt" that was women's demand for higher education:

We revolt against the slavery in which women are held by the customs of society—the broken health, the aimless lives, the subordinate position, the helpless dependence, the dishonesties and shams of so-called education. The Higher Education of Women is one of the world battle cries for freedom; for rights against might. It is the cry of the oppressed slave. It is the assertion of absolute equality.

Other profeminists support women's right to enter the professions, and also to attend colleges along with men. When several schools, including Columbia, Harvard, and Wesleyan, decided against coeducation—because male alumni were withdrawing financial support, fearful of feminization of the male student body—Columbia philosophy professor John Dewey argued back that "The kind of man that will be kept from the University simply because he will have to associate upon equal terms with his equals is not the kind the University wants or needs."

On the economic front, profeminist men supported women's rights to work (Horace Greeley), to own property (Robert Dale Owen), to join unions (William Sylvis), to enter the professions (Melvil Dewey, Dr. James Longshore), to receive equal wages for equal work, and to be free of harassment on the job. Songwriters Woody Guthrie ("Union Maid"), James Oppenheim ("Bread and Roses"), and Joe Hill ("The Rebel Girl") all saw women as central actors in early labor struggles. The Industrial Workers of the World (IWW) and the Socialist and Communist parties all supported women's economic equality, at least rhetorically, although the Wobblies and Communists believed that equality could only come through economic transformation. After the revolution, one IWW pamphlet predicted "no woman will need to sell herself, either to the general public, or in marriage to a man she cannot love," while Eugene Debs urged his comrades to "lift woman from the mire where our fists have struck her, and set her by our side as our comrade and equal." That, he argued."will be love indeed."

Politically, profeminist men's energies were, like women's, occupied by the struggle for suffrage. At the First Woman's Rights Convention at Seneca Falls in 1848, Frederick Douglass proclaimed his conviction that "all political rights which it is expedient for man to exercise, it is equally so for woman." If ours is truly to be a government by consent of the governed, "there can be no reason in the world for denying to woman the exercise of the elective franchise, or a hand in making and administering the laws of the land." Other supporters of suffrage included W. E. B. Du Bois, Ralph Waldo Emerson, James Mott, Theodore Parker, Wendell Phillips, Parker Pillsbury, and Theodore Tilton. By the turn of the century, men were actively organizing; the Men's League for Woman Suffrage, founded by Dewey, Eastman, Rabbi Stephen Wise, and George Foster Peabody, among others, organized men's contingents to march in suffrage parades, and even arranged for the New York Giants baseball team to donate profits from an exhibition game to the cause.

Socially, men campaigned for birth control, "sex rights," and the right to divorce, as well as supporting women's equality in the context of their own marriages. For example, Henry Brown Blackwell's draft of a marriage contract for his wedding with Lucy Stone (read and approved by her), refused all legal rights of husband over wife, and urged couples to challenge marriage laws. Poems by Walt Whitman ("A Woman Waits for Me") and essays by writers such as Emerson, Hutchins Hapgood, Walter Lippmann, Upton Sinclair, Thorstein Veblen, and Lester Ward all supported women's social rights. When Margaret Sanger fled to England to avoid prosecution, her husband, William, continued to distribute her birth-control pamphlet, *Family Limitation*, and was arrested by Anthony Comstock. At home he was equally supportive. "You go ahead and finish your writing," she quotes him as saying. "I'll cook dinner and wash the dishes." (She did, however, close the curtains over the kitchen windows of their first-floor apartment so that passersby would not see him doing so.)

For their efforts, profeminist men have often been vilified and harassed. The *Syracuse Daily Star* called Douglass an "Aunt Nancy Man," a nineteenth-century version of a Mama's Boy, and a "political hermaphrodite." Men marching in suffrage parades were routinely jeered, heckled, and occasionally assaulted by angry spectators, who questioned the manhood (and heterosexuality) of any man who would consider supporting women. Ben Reitman was tarred and feathered in Utah when caught putting up posters announcing a birth-control lecture by his lover, Emma * Goldman.

Profeminist Men Today. Today's profeminist men are the men in colleges and universities who are supporting * women's studies programs, working with women's groups and developing workshops for men on date and acquaintance * rape; they are the men who are supporting women's claims in the workplace for comparable worth, parental leave, flex time, and freedom from * sexual harassment; who are supporting women political candidates and the Equal Rights Amendment; and supporting women's reproductive freedom, and working to end men's violence against women. They are famous men like actors Alan Alda, Leonard Nimoy, Ed Asner; political men like Representative Don Edwards; jurists like Justice Harry Blackmun; as well as everyday men who are seeking to develop relationships of equality with the women in their lives. Organizationally, the National Organization for Men Against Sexism commits itself to supporting "the continuing struggle of women for full equality" and promotes a vision of men and women working together "as allies to change the injustices that have so often made them see one another as enemies."

As long as there is inequality based on gender, there will be a feminist women's movement to struggle against injustice, and to promote a vision of equality. And as long as there is a women's movement, there will be profeminist men, working in a multitude of ways, to support women's struggle in bringing that vision to life.

[*See also* Feminism; Women Writing about Men.]

• Michael S. Kimmel and Thomas E. Mosmiller, eds., *Against the Tide: Pro-Feminist Men in the United States, 1776–1990: A Documentary History* (1992).

Michael S. Kimmel

MENARCHE. *See* Menstruation.

MENOPAUSE. As noted in *The Curse: A Cultural History of Menstruation* (1976), the word "menopause" did not exist until the last quarter of the nineteenth century. Seventeenth-century English writers described the "climacter," but it was the critical stage in a man's life, not a woman's. The "change of life" for women became a recurrent theme only in medical literature in the twentieth century.

The cessation of menstruation and ovulation, menopause carries an enormous psychological burden in our culture because of its stigmatization as a medical and even pathologic condition (in library cataloging systems, "menopause" is often listed under "women, diseases of"). As Gloria * Steinem notes in *Revolution from Within: A Book of Self-Esteem* (1992), a 150-country study showed that the negative physiological symptoms of menopause increased in societies when aging women went from more to less social power and mobility, but decreased in societies where women become more powerful and independent with age. Steinem quotes medical anthropologist Yewoubdar Beyenne who came to the United States from Ethiopia and was shocked to learn all of the negative attributes (physical and psychological) assigned to menopause. Rather, in her country, menopause was welcomed as the end of menstrual taboos.

Although many psychological effects of menopause may be culturally conditioned, some women have undeniable and unpleasant physiological symptoms, some of which may be alleviated with either holistic or conventional medical treatments. In 1992, the National Institute of Health launched a three-year, $10-million "Postmenopausal Estrogen-Progestin Intervention" study which should finally yield important information about the necessity, benefits, and side effects of hormone-replacement therapy, currently widely used in the United States. Early findings suggest that, in some women, hormone replacements add to, rather than minimize, postmenopausal depression.

The authors of *The Curse* note that in literature menopause traditionally has been associated with lack of self-control, violence, and the end of sexual desire. In Lillian Smith's *Strange Fruit* (1944), Alma, a doting white mother, can control neither herself nor her children during her menopause. In Betty * Smith's *A Tree Grows in Brooklyn* (1943), one character facing menopause laments that she has not had more lovers (implying that menopause will be the end of her love life). And in a range of books by male authors (notably and most virulently in the works of Henry Miller), menopause is seen as the equivalent of sexual death for women. It is only recently that a number of sexy, feisty, older women—of all races and both heterosexual and lesbian—have spoken out (as has Steinem) about the benefits of menopause, including renewed interest in sexuality for some women who are happy to be free of periods and no longer need fear unwanted pregnancy. The French, historically, have thought that women come into their own after midlife. One thinks of writer George Sand taking a young lover at the age of sixty-seven, a robust, jolly painter whom she called the "Mastodon." When her friend, author Gustave Flaubert, chided her for not acting her age, she wrote back haughtily, "And what, you want me to stop loving?"

[See also Aging; Menstruation.]

• Janice Delaney, Mary Jane Lupton, and Emily Toth, *The Curse: A Cultural History of Menstruation* (1976). Ann M. Voda, Myra Dinnerstein, Sheryl R. O'Donnell, eds., *Changing Perspectives on Menopause* (1982). Emily Martin, *The Woman in the Body: A Cultural Analysis of Reproduction* (1987). Rita M. Ransohoff, *Venus After Forty: Sexual Myths, Men's Fantasies, and Truths about Middle-Aged Women* (1987).

Cathy N. Davidson

MENSTRUATION. The biological definition of "menstruation" is simple: it is a periodic, monthly discharge of the uterine lining. In the United States, menstruation typically begins around age 13 (menarche) and ends around age 50 (menopause). Yet menstruation is one of the most culturally fraught of any of the biological processes and, in many cultures, has been used as the justification for discrimination against women. The reasons for this have been detailed in a remarkable study, *The Curse: A Cultural History of Menstruation* (1976), which presents the facts and the * myths (many of them hilarious) about menstruation.

In many cultures, menstruation has inspired awe and fear since it is blood shed without death and partly corresponds to superhuman patterns such as the cycle of the moon and the tides. As an attempt to control a creature so closely wed to the powers of the universe, many societies have surrounded menstrual bleeding with a host of superstitions and * taboos. At various times in the Western past, menstrual blood has been thought to sour wine or milk, make steel dull, kill bees, and drive dogs mad.

In her classic essay "If Men Could Menstruate" (1981), Gloria * Steinem jokes that, were this basic biological fact gendered male instead of female, it would be the subject for boasting, not shame, and men would brag about the quantity and duration of their periods. Sanitary napkins would be federally funded and distributed free, and famous athletes would endorse prestige commercial brands, such as "Joe Na-math Jock Shields—'For Those Light Bachelor Days.'" Similarly, there would be a rationale for male superiority based on periodic bleeding. If men had periods, it would be argued that women cannot excel in fields that require sensitivity to time or spatial relationships (such as mathematics) since they lack the inherent cyclical, biological signals that attune one to such differences. The point of Steinem's satire is that, now, menstruation is seen as "the curse," a traumatic hormonal episode that causes women to be irrational and thus prevents them from ever being President. If men were the ones who had periods, the whole symbol system would be reversed and menstruation seen as the irrefutable, *natural* sign of superiority.

In fact, research begun as early as 1897 suggests that men do have hormonal cycles. A remarkably thorough study of factory workers in 1929, in which men were interviewed four times a day and given regular physical examinations over the course of a year, revealed both daily (circadian) cycles and monthly (four to six week) cycles, altering moods and physical performance. A 1933 study suggested cyclical episodes of epilepsy in men. In 1969, the Omni Railway Company in Japan studied the accident patterns of its male employees and was able to reduce accidents by one third over a two-year period by making the men aware of these cycles.

At least in modern times, menstruation has been a subject that polite girls and women do not talk about. A host of euphemisms have been invented for menstruation ("my aunt is visiting," is one such coded—and ridiculous—phrase). But, increasingly, women writers have paid attention to their bodies. As discussed in *The Curse,* Erica *Jong's *Fear of Flying* (1973) rewrites male quest stories by having Isadora Wing ascend from the underworld just as her period arrives. In the poem, "Inventing My Life" (1983), Jong explicitly compares writing and menstruating, a theme also present in poems by Sylvia *Plath, May *Sarton, and Anne *Sexton. Mary *McCarthy's autobiographical *Memories of a Catholic Girlhood* (1957) details, in comic terms, the secretiveness surrounding menarche. Menstruation is also in books as diverse as Betty Smith's *A Tree Grows in Brooklyn* (1943), Judy Blume's *Are You There God? It's Me, Margaret* (1970), Toni *Morrison's *The Bluest Eye* (1970), Joyce Carol *Oates's *them* (1970), Alix Kates *Shulman's *Memoirs of an Ex-Prom Queen* (1972), and E. M. *Broner's *A Weave of Women* (1978).

[See also Menopause; Reproduction.]

• Janice Delaney, Mary Jane Lupton, and Emily Toth, *The Curse: A Cultural History of Menstruation* (1976). Gloria Steinem, *Outrageous Acts and Everyday Rebellions* (1981). Emily Martin, *The Woman in the Body: A Cultural Analysis of Reproduction* (1987).

Cathy N. Davidson

MENTORS. Education theorists define a mentor as characteristically a half-generation older than his or her protégé, someone who is not precisely a friend, teacher, or parent figure, but a little of each of these. A mentor is someone from whom one learns how to negotiate transitions, personal or professional; but a mentor is also charged with challenging the protégé and, conversely, providing a role model for appropriate behaviors and attitudes.

Despite this seemingly benign definition, there is growing evidence that the concept of mentoring derives from Anglo-American values and aesthetics that are predicated on the exclusion of women. Traditional understandings of mentoring assume that an elder generation of talent and professionalism can and will transmit knowledge to a younger generation through one-on-one relationships. This assumption inadequately describes the working environment of women writers for several reasons: (1) the vast majority of women who write do so outside of the institutions in which formal mentoring might occur; (2) those few writers working within institutions often find that the conventional white male mentors who typically would provide access to the resources for literary production dismiss the significance of many touchstones in women's lives and undervalue their work; and (3) those women writers who achieve powerful positions may not seek to sustain the key commitments of the elder generation, turning instead to the business of creating new traditions and critical frameworks.

Many women writers have sought to create a mentoring process that is nonhierarchical, multifaceted, communal, and conversational. Toni Cade *Bambara, for instance, credits Addison Gayle and Toni *Morrison for encouraging her at crucial points in her career, but she says that the greatest influence on the shape and content of her work has been a *community of writers. Alice *Walker's search for intergenerational relationships led her to Zora Neale *Hurston (a search described at length by Walker in *In Search of Our Mothers' Gardens,* 1983). She maintains that *mothers and *grandmothers have found unannounced ways to encourage their daughters' creativity and self-esteem in a world hostile to women. Amy *Tan says that writer Molly Giles and the writers workshop to which they both belong made possible the writing of *The Joy Luck Club* (1989). Louise *Erdrich has suggested that she created her own mentor in Lamartine, a character in three of her novels (*Love Medicine*, 1986; *The Beet Queen*, 1987; and *Tracks*, 1988) who speaks as Erdrich says she would like to speak but cannot except in fiction.

Unlike the male mentoring model, this approach to nurturing the work of self and others assumes that change is the goal. Because transition is thus a constant state of being, rather than an isolated crisis in an otherwise steady existence, the adequate mentoring of women writers cannot take place as momentary interventions. Helpful and productive mentoring addresses the lack of support that confronts women daily; it breaches the loneliness and anxiety that promote silence; it gives a young writer a welcoming restorative psychological space in which to work; and it generates and sustains self-determination and self-esteem.

• Alice Walker, *In Search of Our Mothers' Gardens* (1983). Ruth Perry and Martine Watson Brownley, *Mothering the Mind* (1984). Claudia Tate, ed., *Black Women Writers at Work* (1985). Berenice Fisher, "Wandering in the Wilderness: The Search for Women Role Models," *Signs: Journal of Women in Culture and Society* 13, no. 2 (Winter 1988): 211–233. Mickey Pearlman and Katherine Usher Henderson, eds., *Inter/View: Talks with America's Writing Women* (1990).

Mary Wyer

MERIWETHER, Louise (b. 1923), African-American essayist, novelist, short story writer, and biographer. Meriwether, whose work has yet to receive serious critical attention, has distinguished herself as the only black woman writer to elucidate the struggles of a black female and her family in Harlem during the Great Depression. Meriwether's only published novel, *Daddy Was a Number Runner* (1970), received high praise from James Baldwin, who admired Meriwether's narrative skill and depth and opined that her novel should be sent to the White House.

Born in Haverstraw, New York, on 8 May 1923 to Julia and Marion Lloyd Jenkins, Meriwether grew up in a constant state of poverty in Harlem with her four siblings. During the depression, her parents depended upon welfare and her father's job as a numbers runner. Her parents struggled to instill in Meriwether hope for a better life, which she achieved by graduating from Central Commercial High School in Manhattan, earning a bachelor's degree in English from New York University, and a master's degree from the University of California at Los Angeles. Her commitment to getting an education and achieving a modicum of independence figured in her two divorces, one from Angelo Meriwether and a second from Earl Howe.

Meriwether's dissatisfaction with the deplorable conditions under which blacks labored compelled her to become an activist. She mounted a successful protest against a planned movie based upon William Styron's novel *The Confessions of Nat Turner*, a book that Meriwether believed distorted the life of an American hero and black abolitionist. By rallying together the NAACP, the Urban League, the Black Panther Party, churches, black student unions, and other groups, Meriwether was able to prevent the movie from being made, in spite of the fact that that Styron had been paid $600,000 for film rights.

The spirit of Meriwether's life is reflected in her essays, short stories, and novel—her writings generally focus on blacks who survive seemingly impossible odds. Her efforts as an organizer during the * civil rights movement informed her writing. The power which allowed her to convince the movie industry that the black community would not sit idly by and witness the defamation of one of its heroes is the same force that dominates *Daddy Was a Number Runner*, a novel she had set aside for nine months to challenge Styron and Twentieth Century Fox.

Daddy Was a Number Runner examines the pain that Francie Coffin battles with as she witnesses her family's deterioration, including watching her father abandon the family for a younger woman and a carefree existence, her brother become a manager of prostitutes, and her mother resort to begging the welfare workers for food. Francie's mental anguish is skillfully drawn as she struggles not to submit to prostitution, domestic work, or breeding to secure welfare.

Concerned with the absence of black heroes in history books, Meriwether has written three biographies: *The Freedom Ship of Robert Smalls* (1971), which treats a former slave who eventually served five consecutive terms in congress; *The Heart Man: Dr. Daniel Hale Williams* (1972), which tells of the life of the first doctor to perform a heart operation successfully and yet be denied an opportunity to practice in Jim Crow hospitals; and *Don't Ride the Bus on Monday: The Rosa Parks Story* (1973), which recounts the story of the woman who ushered in the civil rights movement when she refused to give up her seat to a white man.

Louise Meriwether, a master craftsperson, writes with conviction. Her passion and vivid portrayal of life on the edge has earned for her a notable place among contemporary black women authors.

• Rita B. Dandridge, "From Economic Insecurity to Disintegration: A Study of Character in Louise Meriwether's *Daddy Was a Number Runner*," *Negro American Literature Forum* 9 (Fall 1975): 82–85. Rita B. Dandridge, "Louise Meriwether," in *Afro-American Fiction*

Writers after 1955, Dictionary of Literary Biography, vol. 33, eds. Trudier Harris and Thadious Davis (1984).
                                    Elizabeth Brown-Guillory

MIDDLE PASSAGE. The middle passage was the route across the Atlantic Ocean from the Old World to the New World. Specifically, it referred to the process of transporting African slaves to the Americas. The slave trade and the slaves' torturous journeys through the middle passage lasted from the early sixteenth century to the nineteenth century.

After a grueling march from the interior of Africa to the coast as well as inadequate food and shelter in holding pens, the slaves were often stripped, branded, and crowded onto the ships that would bear them across the ocean. Slaves on board suffered from malnutrition, disease, cramped conditions, and lack of fresh air as slavers frequently packed as many slaves as possible below deck (often in place of sufficient supplies, such as food and water). Mortality rates were high on the middle passage, which could take three months or longer.

The slavers whipped, branded, and tortured both male and female slaves in an attempt to break their spirit and make them more docile, but the female slaves' experience differed from the males' in that women also experienced sexual exploitation. Whereas the crew tried to keep as much distance as possible between themselves and the male slaves by shackling and locking them below deck, they often put the female slaves in the quarterdeck without shackles. This packing method left the women accessible to *rape. Rape gave the slavers a method to show complete domination over the slaves and to impregnate the women, thus producing more slaves. However, they gave no special treatment to pregnant women or nursing mothers. In fact, these women's condition left them more vulnerable to physical and mental torture.

The middle passage now appears in writing by African-American women both literally and metaphorically. Octavia *Butler does not specifically mention the middle passage in her 1979 novel *Kindred*, but, as Robert Crossley notes in his 1988 introduction to this novel, the middle passage serves as a metaphor for the protagonist's time travel from 1976 California to the antebellum South. Dana becomes dizzy and nauseous and sees her surroundings go dark every time she is about to be transported to the antebellum plantation. In Toni *Morrison's *Beloved* (1987), the middle passage appears as part of the slaves' collective memory as Morrison examines the enslaved woman's response to her children. Sethe is told of her mother's rape by white men on the middle passage and of her abandonment of the child born of that rape. The only child she chose to keep was Sethe, who was fathered by a black man. In *The Temple of My Familiar* (1989), a young girl's experience on the middle passage becomes a site of Alice *Walker's theme of struggle against domination. Lissie Lyles, a character who has lived many previous lives, tells the story of her life as a young African girl who was sold into slavery. Despite her captors' attempts to dehumanize Lissie, including shaving her head, stripping her naked, branding, striking, and repeatedly raping her, this young woman maintains her humanity as she values the contact she is able to make with the other slaves on board.

[*See also* Abolition, Slavery, Underground Railroad.]

• bell hooks, *Ain't I a Woman: black women and feminism* (1981), pp. 15–20. Deborah Gray White, *Ar'n't I A Woman? Female Slaves in the Plantation South* (1985), pp. 63–64. Joseph C. Miller, *Way of Death: Merchant Capitalism and Angolan Slave Trade, 1730–1830* (1988).
                                              Lynn Pifer

MIDWIFERY. The practice of midwifery is an ancient feminist tradition reflecting, opined Susan Stone (1737), "a tender regard one woman bears to another and a natural sympathy in those who have gone through the pangs of childbearing; which, doubtless, occasion a compassion for those that labour under these circumstances, which no man can be a judge of." This historical view emphasizes women's experiential learning and sympathetic temperaments as unique assets enabling them to assist at childbirth. Midwives often enjoyed a trusted place in the *community because of their vast knowledge of herbs as well. Historically, midwives acted autonomously and saw themselves as practitioners of an ancient feminist art guided by experience, intuition, and feeling and as dispensers of natural herbal medications.

A breach in their autonomy occurred as early as the sixteenth century with the development of such instruments as forceps that could be used only by male barber-surgeons. With the development of medical education, and accompanying legal regulations, midwives were excluded from what would eventually become the field of obstetrics. With the advent of "science," midwives found themselves increasingly under attack as witches because of their potions, herbs, poultices, and spells. Science, religion, and the law became curiously confused. Anne *Hutchinson, a noted herbalist and popular midwife, was challenged for her Antinomian beliefs. Antinomians were held suspect because they believed that as Christians under God's grace they were not bound by the Church and the secular law, a view considered seditious. Governor John Winthrop of the Massachusetts Bay Colony described Hutchinson as "a woman of ready wit and bold spirit," who brought with her dangerous errors including the conviction that "the person of the Holy Ghost dwells in a justified person." Some Protestant theologians held that individuals could be justified or freed from penalty of sin by God; therefore, they were not bound to traditional moral laws. Religious leaders of that time were intolerant of public expression of these views. Hutchinson believed herself to be a justified person. Testimony corroborated that view. Consequently, she was found guilty of heresy in 1638 and excommunicated. Temporarily exiled at Aquidneck, she suffered a miscarriage that Winthrop labelled a "monstrous birth." Fearful of heretical forces, Winthrop made the easy step of ascribing evil to her midwifery skills and banished her.

In 1648, the Massachusetts Bay Colony tried its first witch, Margaret Jones. A midwife, she was accused of practicing physic (the profession of medicine) and using herbal medicines and confounding physicians. She was found guilty and hanged.

Laurel Thatcher Ulrich (1990) provides a graphic portrait of an eighteenth-century midwife, Martha Ballard, who recorded 814 deliveries in her * diary. She traversed rivers, had her cloak burned, and risked life-threatening dangers to reach the women she attended.

In spite of the fact that midwives continued to be a powerful presence among poor and immigrant women, they were waging a losing battle against doctors who increasingly sought their licensure and regulation. Obstetrics became an important field to which women gradually gained entry in the twentieth century.

The 1980s saw a revival of interest in natural childbirth and home deliveries, and women turned increasingly to midwives rather than to doctors. Today nurse-midwives or certified midwives may practice under the direction of a licensed physician.

For a time the value of midwives was obscured because of their exclusion from scientific developments, but today their ancient traditions, built not only upon knowledge acquired through books, but also upon the empathy women share experientially are valued. Increasingly, midwives are seen as part of obstetrical teams. The transformation of bringing women back to birthing is taking place as midwives, nurse midwives, and female obstetricians grow in number.

[*See also* Birth, Reproduction.]

• Selma R. Williams and Pamela Williams Adelman, *Riding the Nightmare: Women and Witchcraft from the Old World to Colonial Salem* (1978). Laurel Thatcher Ulrich, *Good Wives, Image and Reality in the Lives of Women in Northern New England, 1650–1750* (1983). Raymond DeVries, *Regulating Birth: Midwives, Medicine and the Law* (1985). Laurel Thatcher Ulrich, *A Midwife's Tale: The Life of Martha Ballard, Based on Her Diary, 1785–1812* (1990). Laura-Mae Baldwin, Heidi L. Hutchinson, and Roger A. Rosenblatt, "Professional Relationships between Midwives and Physicians: Collaboration or Conflict?" *American Journal of Public Health* 82, no. 2 (February 1992): 262–263.
                                    Adelaide P. Amore

MIGRATION. If American male writers have long celebrated in literature the freedom to abandon confining spaces for the open road, the sea, the river, and other locations beyond the reach of constricting civilization, women writers have more often chosen or been forced to write from static vantage points, situated inside a domestic space looking out on the rest of the world. When women have looked beyond a stationary setting and written about migration, they have more often concentrated on themes associated with the long tradition of their own domestic genres than with male-authored migration and journey stories. Showing minimal interest in exploring the liberating powers of the journey itself, women when addressing migration have focused upon both the difficulties and the benefits associated with replacing one home with another.

The primary conflict of women's migration literature is born out of differences between the pre- and postmigration settings. Perched between and betwixt two worlds, the migrant is a liminal figure, and literary migration serves as a double-edged sword. The act of migrating, on the one hand may, like the flight north of the fugitive slave, liberate the migrant from oppressive elements of her former home. On the other hand, migration marks a point of critical separation from her family, friends, and geographic identity that she finds difficult, sometimes impossible, to reclaim. Women's migration literature attempts to come to terms with the spatial, communal, and psychological differences between a migrant's former and present circumstances, which are often associated with polarities such as south and north, east and west, rural and urban, frontier and civilization, industrial and agricultural, liberation and enslavement. Despite the fact that writers, particularly when addressing the frontier, may overromanticize the new setting, the change in location can throw the migrant's personal identity into flux. She frequently demonstrates a woeful lack of preparation for her new environment, which may lead her to a sense of geographic alienation. Her success in adapting to her new surroundings can be measured finally by the degree to which she is able to reinvent and reaffirm the usable aspects of her former community and reincorporate them into her postmigration home.

American women have written about numerous distinct migrations. Although there is no one typical migration, the act of leaving one home behind, through force or volition, to make a home in new, often hostile surroundings is a unifying experience that crosses time, *class, *race, and *ethnicity. The largest unforced American migrant stream began to flow westward from the earliest landing in the New World by Europeans and continued until 1890, when the U.S. Bureau of the Census announced that the frontier was officially closed. The ongoing expansion westward of mostly white homesteaders began in New England and slowly moved across the Mississippi valley reaching the Great Plains by the 1840s and moving through to California in the decades following. During this migration, large Native American populations were either systematically killed by American soldiers or forced to migrate to reservations or to much less desirable homelands in the interior. As many as ten million African slaves were also forced to migrate to the New World between 1451 and 1870. More than eight hundred thousand African-American slaves were sold involuntarily and relocated as a part of the Atlantic and Mississippi valley interstate slave trades. Rough estimates suggest that between 1810 and 1850, more than one hundred thousand slaves valued at more than thirty million dollars found freedom through the *Underground Railroad by migrating north. Since 1890, with the notable exception of Japanese-American relocation in internment camps during World War II, migration can be characterized by various groups representing numerous racial and ethnic categories exercising their freedom of mobility and choosing to move from one part of the country to another or from one part of a city to another.

The most notable women's literature to grow out of the westward migration is the small subgenre of domestic fictions called the *domestic novel of western relocation. Especially popular in the decade before the *Civil War, these novels are for the large part glorifications of a West that never existed outside of the literary marketplace. *Live and Let Live; or, Domestic Service Illustrated*, Catharine Maria *Sedgwick's 1837 story of a young married couple migrating from New York "to the land of promise—the indefinite *West*," Emma Southworth's *India, The Pearl of Pearl River* (1853), and Caroline Soule's *The Pet of the Settlement* (1860) all describe appealing western migration fantasies for their eastern readership. The most notable exception to the conventional romanticized version of the West is Caroline *Kirkland's *A New Home—Who'll Follow? Or, Glimpses of Western Life* (1839). Annette Kolodny, whose *The Land Before Her* (1984) is the most complete study of the genre, describes Kirkland's work as the first realistic treatment of *frontier life in American letters. The genre details the way in which the western migration was particularly difficult for women. Kolodny has noted that while a husband often went to work following migration by farming with the same tools using the same methods, his wife, by contrast, found her new world stripped of the "old familiar means and appliances." The genre by no means disappeared following the closing of the West. Maria Susanna *Cummins's *Autobiography and Reminiscences* (1914) and Laura Ingalls *Wilder's best-selling adolescent novel series commencing with *Little House on the Prairie* (1935) point to the continuing popularity of mythologizing the westward migration.

Although attracting less literary than historical interest, the *diaries, journals, *letters, and reminiscences written by frontier women travelling West have also found reading audiences. Molly Dorsey Sanford's 1857–1866 journal (1959), Sarah Royce's *A Frontier Lady* (reprinted 1977), and Susan McGoffin's *Down the Santa Fe Trail* (1926) are among the better-known published works. Despite the presence of black women on all the American frontiers, they are an almost invisible part of the western literary migration experience (and, in fact, this remains a rich vein of material for contemporary *African-American women writers to mine). *Native American women are an even more notable absence. The original inhabitants of every region to which Euro-American homesteaders settled, Native American women typically populate white migrants' literary landscapes as indefinable "others" who need either conquering or civilizing. On rare occasions they serve as guides. Native American traditions, by contrast, portray women in myths as complex and essential parts of domestic life who served with men as cocreators, although the oral nature of Native cultures would discourage a written legacy of their many migrations. *Zitkala-Sä's (Gertrude Simmons Bonnin) autobiographical writings commencing with "Impressions of an Indian Childhood" (1900) make up the earliest Native American migration story to have been written without a mediating ethnographer, translator, or editor. Separated from her mother and her South Dakota reservation when she is taken by Quaker missionaries to an Indian school in Wabash, Indiana, Zitkala-Sä, "trembling with fear and distrust of the palefaces," arrives at the school where she stays for three years. Upon returning to the reservation, she finds that her assimilationist school training has distanced her from her mother's traditional culture so that, like many displaced migrants, she no longer feels truly at home in either world.

No group of American women have been more shaped by migration than African Americans. From the earliest reference to migration by a black woman in Phillis *Wheatley's 1768 poem, "On Being Brought from Africa to America," where she ironically proclaimed, "Twas mercy brought me from my Pagan land / Taught my benighted soul to understand," through the heart and soul of the written black self, the fugitive slave narrative, to the novels and poetry of the twentieth-century Great Migration, black women writers have viewed migration as an opportunity to obtain their physical as well as spiritual freedom. In their writings, migration is often ineradicably tied to protest. In the best-known women's slave narrative, *Incidents in the Life of a Slave Girl* (1861), Harriet *Jacobs's quest for a new home in the North commences only after seven years of virtual entombment as she hides in her grandmother's storeroom waiting for her chance to migrate to freedom. The liberating power of migration finds no stronger expression anywhere in American women's literature than in the obvious contrast between Jacobs's imprisoning "loophole of retreat" and, following her escape and eventual purchase of her freedom, her northern "home found" (the respective titles of chapters 11 and 23).

Despite the fact that the ongoing black migration from the South to northern cities has had more impact on black life than any other post-Emancipation cultural movement, there is surprisingly little black women's literature on the subject. Dorothy *West's satire of Boston's black middle class, *The Living Is Easy* (1948), was the only notable women's novel on the subject prior to the 1980s. In it the spirited South Carolina–born Cleo Jericho migrates to Boston where she meets and marries Bart Judson, the "black banana king." The novel is a significant text of migration for several reasons. While much male migration fiction echoes the conventions of slave narratives in manifesting a desire for freedom through a heroic response to violent white oppression, West refigures this convention entirely, subsuming her protagonist's migration in the oppression of gender rather than race. Her mother sends her daughter North to guard against the inevitable advances of "coachmen and butlers and porters." Nevertheless, the South remains in Cleo's mind a relationally oriented family paradise, a southern pastoral norm against which West balances her satire of the North. The novel recognizes the mixed blessing of migration. Cleo's move North offers her seemingly unlimited potential for improving her economic and social status, but it also distances her from her racial and family birthright, a price in the author's view that is finally too high to pay. The novel ends with Cleo unable to find in high living, a lavish income, and social prestige the same fulfillment provided by her "happy, happy childhood."

In detailing the move of the Younger family from the inner city to the suburbs, Lorraine *Hansberry's 1958 New York Critics Circle Award–winning play *A Raisin in the Sun* signaled a temporary shift of interest in the 1960s toward intra-urban migration and away from the South to North movement. Recent black women writers who have returned to the Great Migration as a rich subject to explore include Marita *Golden, in her 1987 autobiography, *Migrations of the Heart*, and in her novel *Long Distance Life*; Rita *Dove, whose 1986 poetry collection, *Thomas and Beulah*, won the Pulitzer Prize; and Toni *Morrison, in her 1992 novel of postmigration Harlem, *Jazz*.

For Asian Americans, though some have entered the United States through east coast cities, most of the immigration has been a movement from west to east. The wooden barracks of Angel Island Detention Center in San Francisco harbor, now a national park, bears testimony to the frustration and literary skill of multitudes of Chinese would-be immigrants who carved poems into the walls when detained for months, even years, while immigration officials decided their fates. Genny Lim's play "Paper Angels" (1991) dramatizes this little-known chapter of immigration history. Ruthanne Lum McCunn's *Thousand Pieces of Gold* (1981) is a fictionalized biography of a Chinese woman, abducted as a girl in China, sold on the slave block in California, who ends her life as a homesteader on the Salmon River in Idaho. Kim *Ronyoung's novel *Clay Walls* (1987) presents the struggles of an immigrant Korean family in Los Angeles in the 1930s, while Chuang *Hua's *Crossings* (1968) makes explicit, in the multiple Atlantic crossings of its narrator, the psychic dislocation of a Chinese émigré. Wendy *Law-Yone's powerful novel *The Coffin Tree* (1983) brings its protagonists from Myanmar (Burma) to the United States and compares the immigrant experience to the astronauts' stepping onto the moon. Bharati *Mukherjee's short stories and novels, particularly *Wife* and *Jasmine* (1989), focus on the immigrant from India.

More than 110,000 Japanese, two-thirds of them Japanese Americans, were forcefully relocated from the West Coast to inland barbed wire–fenced camps during World War II. The trauma of this violation of civil rights has found literary expression in such works as Karen Kehoe's *City in the Sun* (1946); Jeanne Wakatsuki and James D. Houston's *Farewell to Manzanar* (1973); two collections of poetry by Mitsuye Yamada, *Camp Notes* (1976) and *Desert Run* (1988); the poetry of Janice * Mirikitani; and the masterly poetic novel by Joy Kogawa, *Obasan* (1981).

[*See also* Immigration; Immigrant Writing.]

• L. L. Lee and Merrill Lewis, eds., *Women, Women Writers, and the West* (1979). Alice Poindexter Fisher, " 'Zitkala-Sä': The Evolution of a Writer," *American Indian Quarterly* 5 (1979): 229–238. Sandra L. Myres, *Westering Women and the Frontier Experience, 1800–1915* (1982). James R. Grossman, *Land of Hope: Chicago, Black Southerners and the Great Migration* (1989).

Lawrence R. Rodgers

MILLAY, Edna St. Vincent (1892–1950), American poet, dramatist, and fiction writer. Born in Rockland, Maine, the first child of Henry Tolman and Cora Buzzelle Millay, who divorced in 1900, Millay was raised by her mother, a practical nurse, who encouraged the ambitions of her three daughters. A precocious young girl, called "Vincent" by intimates, Millay published her first poems in her teens and attracted national attention at twenty with the publication of the long poem "Renascence." This accomplishment led to a scholarship to Vassar, a site of avid feminist activity, where she established herself as a dramatist and actress in her own plays.

After graduating in 1917, Millay moved to Greenwich Village, where she became part of the literary and political avant garde, acting with and writing for the Provincetown Players and joining feminists who favored socialism. With her red hair and green eyes, she was striking, magnetic, and passionate, but she resisted marriage and extolled women's sexual and emotional freedom, an attitude expressed in her popular second book, *A Few Figs for Thistles* (1920). She also wrote short stories and satirical sketches for magazines under the pseudonym Nancy Boyd.

Millay wrote prolifically, publishing seventeen books of poems, four plays, an opera libretto, and a translation of Baudelaire's *Flowers of Evil* (1936). She had published enough serious work by 1923 to receive the first Pulitzer Prize in poetry awarded to a woman. Also that year, having returned to the United States after a three-year sojourn in Europe, she married Eugen Jan Boissevain, the widower of the feminist Inez Milholland. In the late twenties, Millay became involved in the crusade to stay the execution of the anarchists Sacco and Vanzetti, about whom she wrote a number of poems (*The Buck*

in the Snow, 1928). She continued to write socially conscious poems in the thirties, and following the outbreak of war, she began writing verse propaganda. The strain of that endeavor may have contributed to the nervous breakdown she suffered in 1944. After her husband's death in 1949, she continued to live alone at "Steepletop," their farm in Austerlitz, New York, until her own death of heart failure in 1950.

Although Millay received awards and honorary degrees in the twenties, thirties, and forties, her reputation was eclipsed after her death by interest in poetic * modernism, which emphasized formal experimentation and innovation. Even former acolytes, such as Anne * Sexton and Sylvia * Plath, repudiated her as old-fashioned. Her work has endured, however, and has been advanced recently by critics interested in the ways traditional poetic forms such as the sonnet, of which she was a leading exponent, may serve the needs of women poets, and in Millay's radical humanism.

• Millay's manuscripts and personal papers are in the Library of Congress, Manuscripts Division, Washington, D.C. Judith Nierman, *Edna St. Vincent Millay: A Reference Guide* (1977). Jane Starbrough, "Edna St. Vincent Millay and the Language of Vulnerability," in *Shakespeare's Sisters: Feminist Essays on Women Poets*, eds. Sandra Gilbert and Susan Gubar (1978). Norman A. Britten, *Edna St. Vincent Millay* (1982). Debra Fried, "Andromeda Unbound: Gender and Genre in Millay's Sonnets," *Twentieth Century Literature* 32, no. 1 (Spring 1986): 1–22.

Donna Hollenberg

MILLETT, Kate (b. 1934), fiction writer, literary critic. After an early career as a sculptor in both Japan and New York, Millett burst on the literary scene in 1970 with the publication of her Columbia University doctoral dissertation, *Sexual Politics*. Selling 80,000 copies within six months, *Sexual Politics* is a densely argued examination of the patriarchal values that inform much canonical literature. British novelist D. H. Lawrence was ridiculed for his sentimental depiction and celebration of virility while the American writer Henry Miller was attacked as a misogynist. Millett argued that these and other male writers portrayed females in degrading terms. It was the first major book of its kind and the first to apply some of the principles of feminist practice to literary criticism.

Flying (1984) is an autobiographical novel about the media circus that Millett endured after the publication of *Sexual Politics*. The book is also an intimate treatment of her own sexuality, specifically her lesbianism, and a sometimes painful examination of the way her sexual preference became a national media obsession. *Sita* (1977) is another confessional work, which documents her three-year affair with a middle-aged mother and college administrator and the collapse of that relationship as Sita turns to various men for love.

Millett's other books include *The Basement: Meditations on Human Sacrifice* (1979), a painful account of the torture and murder of a sixteen-year-old girl by her landlady, her children, and two local boys. Millett became obsessed with Sylvia Likens's story and spent fourteen years finding out all she could about it in order to understand such unaccountable human cruelty. Her 1980 *The Loony-Bin Trip* is an even more excruciating chronicle of Millett's own mental collapse after she stopped taking Lithium for manic-depression. *The Prostitution Papers* (1971) and *Going to Iran* (1982) are both more sociological in nature.

Millett has been a pioneering force in the women's movement and has also been active in the civil rights movement. She now works as an artist and writer, dividing her time between New York and a Christmas tree farm in upstate New York that also serves as a communal retreat for women artists in the summer. Millett insists that the most basic point of her work was to encourage men to look at the inhuman ways in which women have been treated, to say to men, "Look, brother, I'm human."

• "Kate Millett," in *Contemporary Authors*, ed. Frances Carol Locher, vols. 73–76 (1978), pp. 437–438. Frieda L. Werden, "Kate Millett," in *American Women Writers*, ed. Lina Mainiero, vol. 3 (1981), pp. 188–190. Anne Janette Johnson, "Millett, Kate," in *Contemporary Authors New Revision Series*, ed. James G. Lesniak, vol. 32 (1991), pp. 300–301. "Kate Millett," in *Contemporary Literary Criticism*, ed. Roger Matuz, vol. 67 (1992), pp. 232–263.

Cathy N. Davidson

MILLICAN, Arthenia J. Bates (b. 1920), poet, short-story writer, folklorist, essayist, and novelist. Millican has established herself as one of the best short-story writers and novelists of the 1970s. Her collection of short stories, *Seeds Beneath the Snow* (1969, reprinted, 1975) and *The Deity Nodded* (1973) are outstanding examples of regional writing that links the concerns of black southerners to global issues. Her writing captures the spirit of the poor who refuse to despair but who, instead, press for changes in a racist, sexist, and classist society.

Born on 1 June 1920 in Sumter, South Carolina, to Susan Emma David and Calvin Shepard Jackson, Millican grew up in a religious and class-conscious home where she and her siblings were stimulated by their parents, who were both professionals. After completing Lincoln High School and Morris College, both in Sumter, Millican attended Atlanta University where she studied under Langston Hughes, who encouraged her to write about the poor and disenfranchised, people who could teach her about humanity. Divorced from her first husband in 1956, Millican accepted a teaching post at Southern University in Baton Rouge, Louisiana. In 1969, she married Wilbert Millican and began work on a Ph.D. that she earned from Louisiana State University in 1972.

From the late 1950s until 1980 when she retired as professor emeritus from Southern University, Millican devoted her energies to writing poetry and fiction. Her reputation rests primarily upon her collection of short stories *Seeds Beneath the Snow*, twelve vignettes illuminating the will to survive of destitute rural southerners. Often compared to Paul Laurence Dunbar, Charles W. Chesnutt, and Zora Neale *Hurston, Millican has been praised for her deft handling of characters and is considered to be one of the best short-story writers since the 1950s.

One of the stories from *Seeds Beneath the Snow* eventually found its way into Millican's only novel, *The Deity Nodded*. A *bildungsroman, the novel describes the maturation of a poor black southerner, Tisha Dees, who eventually questions her religious faith and accepts Islamic over Christian dogmas. As she moves into adulthood, the heroine learns that the ostracized poor of her community are far more humane than the pretentious middle-class blacks she had been choosing as role models.

Millican's short story "Where You Belong" won the National Endowment for the Arts award in 1976. "Where you Belong," like Millican's previously published fiction, examines closely the hypocrisy of class exclusion.

Millican's short stories about the South add contours to a region seldom filtered through the eyes of a black female academician.

• Virginia Whatley Smith, "Arthenia J. Bates Millican," in *Afro-American Writers after 1955: Dramatists and Prose Writers*, Dictionary of Literary Biography, vol. 38, eds. Thadious Davis and Trudier Harris (1985).

Elizabeth Brown-Guillory

MINIMALISM. Though the term has long been associated with *modernism, minimalism has become the name for a style of fiction that began appearing in the late 1970s. In *modernism the term applies to experiments in a wide variety of arts, summed up in the dictum "less is more." Expression is pared down to its most elemental forms and impersonal tone in search of purity and strength. In light of the later movement, the most relevant modernist is Gertrude *Stein's pupil, Ernest Hemingway, whose experiments in his earliest stories developed into the technique of the later minimalist school. These stories were written, as Hemingway said, by omitting background information about his characters' pasts and motivations in the belief that its absence would be felt. He hoped that the reader would experience the iceberg effect, the sense that the words were just the tip of an iceberg whose bulk was floating beneath the surface of the story. The reader must work to discover the iceberg's scope and significance.

Like Hemingway's Nick Adams, who is the midwestern survivor of a dysfunctional family, the harrowing experiences of World War I, and the hedonism of expatriate life, the characters of much minimalist fiction are midwestern survivors of dysfunctional families, the Vietnam War, and the aftermath of the sexual and personal freedom of the 1960s. However, Hemingway's modernism, which seeks significance, purity, and power, has given way to *postmodernism. The surface of postmodern fiction is composed of the detritus of commercialized American culture. This surface does not always conceal an iceberg of meaning, though readers may search for it. Brand names, popular songs, movies, television, and malls become the vocabulary that defines the limits of characters' ability to think, leading to one of the nicknames for the movement, K-Mart realism. Because of the ephemeral nature of commercial culture, minimalism is tied to the cultural instant that forms its frame of reference.

A narrative is labeled minimalist when it is detached in tone and laconic in expression; has a plot that is mostly middle without definitive beginnings, climaxes, or endings; is written in the present tense without a sense of personal or social history; focuses on the domestic and the ordinary; and accentuates the details of brand names and ordinary conversations until every detail is equally significant or irrelevant.

In this play of surfaces, suspicion of the past as a source of meaning, and erasure of the boundaries between high and popular or commercial culture, mimimalism is part of postmodernism, although it does not have the irony and self-reference of some of the fictions labeled postmodernist. Rather than literally announcing representation as a problem as the metafictions do, minimalism intensifies representation into an unsettling, disorienting experience. Minimalism has also been called hyperrealism or superrealism, thereby associating it with movements in the visual arts. Minimalist fiction strikes many of its commentators as being photographic, a series of snapshots recording every detail of a moment in time and letting the angle of vision form the commentary. In the traditional distinction between telling and showing, minimalism is all showing. Because the reader must decide what significance the surface conceals or reveals, reaction to minimalist fiction tends to be varied: Is the deadpan juxtaposition of irrelevant detail humorous or debilitating? Is the detached, intense scrutiny condescending or sympathetic?

A number of women writers have been attracted to minimalism, using it to reflect on women's lives in the late twentieth century. Although the emphasis on communication and relationships amid the details of domestic life is a traditional subject of women's writing, in minimalist fiction communication rarely occurs, relationships almost always disintegrate, and the bizarre, the sensational, and the violent often enter the surface minutiae of characters' lives. Bobbie Ann *Mason (b. 1940) is one of the best-known writers of minimalist fiction, while reviewers have identified the characteristic minimalism of Ann *Beattie's (b. 1947) fiction as the voice of her generation, which came of age in the 1960s. Mary Robison (b. 1949) takes a somewhat more comic view of her midwestern, upper-middle-class families. Other women writers who use minimalism to explore the difficulty of maintaining relationships in contemporary life are Amy Hempel (b. 1951), Jayne Anne Phillips (b. 1952), Elizabeth Ann Tallent (b. 1954), and Lorrie Moore (b. 1957). Their work has appeared in magazines (particularly the *New Yorker*), short-story collections, and novels. Though minimalism is hard to sustain in longer forms, shorter works are often praised as well crafted.

[*See also* Novel, Beginnings of the; Short Story.]

• Kim Herzinger, "Minimalism as a Postmodernism: Some Introductory Notes," *New Orleans Review* 16, no. 3 (Fall 1989): 73–81. Arthur M. Saltzman, "To See a World in a Grain of Sand: Expanding Literary Minimalism," *Contemporary Literature* 31, no. 4 (Winter 1990): 423–433.

Patricia L. Morse

MIRIKITANI, Janice (b. 1942), poetry and short fiction writer, editor, and educator. Born in Stockton, California, Mirikitani is a third-generation Japanese-American poet and literary editor. Together with her family, she was incarcerated in 1942 in the Rohwer, Arkansas, internment camp with other Japanese Americans during World War II. After the war, Mirikitani and her immediate family were relocated to Chicago and then resettled at her maternal grandparents' farm in Petaluma, California.

The Japanese-American internment experience and her rural family upbringing—primarily by her *grandmother—were themes that she expanded upon in her two books of poetry and prose, *Awake in the River* (1978) and *Shedding*

Silence (1987). Related themes in Mirikitani's work are the incarceration of peoples of color in the Americas, in Asia, and in Africa; the enslavement of women and the poor by culture, economics, and politics; the relationship of military *violence and violence against women; and the multiple generational identities of Japanese and Asian Americans.

Mirikitani represents the post–World War II generation of west coast Asian-American writers who had the opportunity to pursue higher education and who used English almost exclusively in their writing, reading, and speaking. She attended the University of California at Los Angeles and graduated from there cum laude in 1962, obtaining a teaching credential from the University of California, Berkeley. But it was the student strike for Asian-American and Ethnic Studies at San Francisco State College in 1968 that propelled Mirikitani into becoming an editor for Asian-American writers, while she continued her own writing. A member of the San Francisco–based Asian-American Political Alliance, she was involved in Vietnam War protests and in the Black Power and *civil rights movements. In 1969, Mirikitani became the director of programs at Glide Memorial Church in San Francisco, where she continues to oversee a human services and multicultural arts program.

Mirikitani's poetry takes a variety of literary forms: dramatic monologue and dialogue, lyric, satire, and parody, depending on the subject. "Loving from Vietnam to Zimbabwe" treats the Vietnam War and its aftermath; "Where Is Beauty, Imelda?" parodies Imelda Marcos; "Why Is Preparing Fish a Political Act?" traces her grandmother's response to internment during World War II; "Soul Food" reflects on her marriage to the Reverend Cecil Williams, the African-American pastor of San Francisco's Glide Church; "A Lecherous Poem to Toshiro Mifune," is a satire of the Japanese film actor; "Breaking Tradition" questions *mother and daughter *stereotypes; "Shadow in Stone" describes her journey to Hiroshima, and "Breaking Silence" incorporates her mother's testimony before the 1981 Commission on Wartime Relocation and Internment of Japanese Americans.

In 1970, Mirikitani founded the first Asian-American literary journal, *Aion*, with Francis N. Oka. The two issues of *Aion* included many of the political theorists and literary and cultural Asian-American writers of the 1960s and 1970s, including Alex Hing, Lawson Fusao Inada, Frank Chin, Toshio Mori, Pat Sumi, Sam Tagatac, Mitsu Yashima, Serafin Syquia, Al Robles, George Leong, Jim Dong, E. Jundis, and others.

Mirikitani's work as an editor helped to introduce Asian-American writers to a national readership. As a founding member of Third World Communications, a coalition of black, Raza, American Indian, and Native Island writers and artists, Mirikitani helped to publish and coedit a number of major anthologies of the period, including: *Third World Women* (1972) and *Time to Greeze: Incantations from the Third World*. She was editor of *Ayumi: A Japanese-American Anthology* (1980), which is the first bilingual anthology to include work by four generations of Japanese-American artists and writers. In 1990, Mirikitani coedited *Making Waves: An Anthology of Writings by and about Asian-American Women* (1989). Mirikitani continues to write on Third World communities, cultures, and conflicts as transformed through the visions and writings of women.

• Russell Leong, *Why Is Preparing Fish a Political Act: Poetry of Janice Mirikitani*, videotape (1990).

Russell C. Leong

MIRROR-PHASE. See Psychoanalysis and Women.

MITCHELL, Margaret (1900–1949), novelist and journalist. Margaret Munnerlyn Mitchell was born in Atlanta, Georgia, the city that figures prominently in her writing. Her mother, May Belle Stephens Mitchell, was a founder of the Georgia suffrage movement, and her father, Eugene Mitchell, was president of the Atlanta Historical Society. She had one brother. From childhood she was surrounded with stories and books, and read voraciously.

Mitchell also had an early interest in writing, completing two novels while in her teens. After graduation from Atlanta's Washington Seminary in 1918, she enrolled at Smith College. Her mother's death forced Mitchell to leave Smith after her freshman year and assume responsibilities at home. She married Berrien Kinnard Upshaw in 1922, but they divorced two years later, and she married John Marsh in 1925.

In 1923, Mitchell became a reporter for the Atlanta *Journal*, an unusual step for a woman of her time. While successful as a journalist, she continued to write fiction; these books, like her earlier ones, were not published. After three years with the *Journal*, Mitchell resigned and began writing *Gone with the Wind*, a secret, much-revised project. In 1935, she sent the manuscript to Harold S. Latham at Macmillan Publishing Company, where it was quickly accepted.

The fame of Mitchell's romance of the Civil War and Reconstruction South is legendary:

foreign publishers and Hollywood film studios fought over rights to the book while it was still in galleys; it sold over a million copies in the United States alone in the first six months after its 1936 publication. Although *Gone with the Wind* received the 1937 Pulitzer Prize, it was considered more a popular than a literary triumph until recently, when reassessment based on such contexts as southern agrarianism and feminist criticism began. The 1939 film based on Mitchell's novel won an Academy Award and remains prominent among Hollywood successes.

On 11 August 1949, Mitchell was fatally injured while crossing an Atlanta street. Since Mitchell's death, *Gone with the Wind* has become the best-selling novel of all time, its popularity so entrenched that her estate selected an author to write a new novel about Mitchell's most famous character, Scarlett O'Hara. To commemorate the fiftieth anniversary of the book's publication, the United States Postal Service issued a Margaret Mitchell stamp, acknowledging the impact her writing has had on American culture.

• The Margaret Mitchell Collection is in the Manuscripts Department, University of Georgia. Finis Farr, *Margaret Mitchell of Atlanta* (1965). Richard B. Harwell, ed., *Margaret Mitchell's "Gone with the Wind" Letters* (1976). Anne Edwards, *The Road to Tara* (1983). Darden Asbury Pyron, *Southern Daughter* (1991).

Patricia M. Gantt

MIXED ANCESTRY, Writers of. Several contemporary writers challenge neatly drawn, "naturalized" cultural categories by emphasizing their own mixed ancestry and the multiplicity of their identifications. In *Borderlands/La Frontera* (1987), Gloria *Anzaldúa celebrates the consciousness of the *mestiza* (the woman of mixed ethnicity) for its disturbance of restrictive paradigms. The poet Ai refuses to reduce her identifications to a single *ethnicity and thereby calls cultural boundaries into question. Disturbance of boundaries—though by no means only ethnic boundaries—also characterizes Ai's poetic practice and makes of that practice a powerful cultural critique.

Although reviewers occasionally refer to Ai as a black poet, she does not consider herself to be a black writer. As she pointed out in a 1988 interview, her poetry does not deal primarily with black life and experience. While she characterizes herself as "Japanese and black, or black and Japanese," in this interview she also mentioned Irish, Choctaw, and German forebears and a sense of affinity with the Hopi, Navajo, and Pima people of the American Southwest, where she grew up. Though Ai denies none of these as influences, she calls each of

them into question as *the* category that furnishes her a stable and essential identity. If one cannot escape cultural definition, she implies, one can at least use the very multiplicity of one's identifications to destabilize culture's categories of definition.

Ai's poems have the indirect effect of calling cultural definitions of all kinds into question. A dramatic monologuist, she invents voices for those whose entrapment in their cultural definition is most apparent. The speakers of her poems include the obscure and despised who are usually presumed to have no voice at all and those public figures who have become sheer icon, whose cultural meaning subsumes anything they can be imagined saying. In the crucible of her work, their unbearable identities seem always at the point of being shattered and remade, or simply shattered. The poems' speakers by no means transcend cultural definition, but they speak in such a way as to profoundly unsettle the very positions from which they speak.

The poems achieve these effects by a variety of devices. As Bulgarian literary theorist Julia Kristeva argues, ambiguous images—images that obscure or transgress boundaries—tend to disturb the sense of settled identity. The speakers of Ai's poems often describe themselves breaking the body's boundary through *violence, by transgressing laws and *gender roles, or by crossing from the world of the ordinary into surreal, dreamlike experiences. The poems contain horrifying and unsettling images of the bodily remnants and effluvia that disturb because they seem neither human nor inhuman, as well as characters who disturb by their ambiguity, seeming both innocent and evil. The reader is both deeply engaged and deeply unsettled by the poems' speakers; none of the positions constructed by the poems invites comfortable identification. Thus, the poems have the effect of destabilizing the reader's position as well as the positions of their own speakers. By means of these destabilizations, Ai's work performs a radical critique of the identities constructed by contemporary culture.

[See also Assimilation; Cross-racial Relations; Ethnicity and Writing; Passing; Race; Whiteness.]

• Ai, *Cruelty/Killing Floor* (1973, 1979; reprint, 1987). Julia Kristeva, *Powers of Horror*, trans. Leon S. Roudiez (1982). Ai, *Sin* (1986). Ai, *Fate* (1991).

Claudia Ingram

MODERNISM. Some of America's most important writing was published between 1910 and 1945, including much of the best work of Robert Frost, Ernest Hemingway, Willa *Cather, F. Scott Fitzgerald, William Faulkner, *H.D., Gertrude *Stein, Ezra Pound, Jean

Toomer, Amy *Lowell, Sherwood Anderson, Edna St. Vincent *Millay, John Dos Passos, Albert Maltz, Carl Sandburg, T. S. Eliot, Djuna *Barnes, Anzia *Yezierska, Susan *Glaspell, Janet *Flanner, Eugene O'Neill, Thomas Wolfe, Nella *Larsen, Marianne *Moore, William Carlos Williams, Edith *Wharton, Langston Hughes, e. e. cummings, Robinson Jeffers, Sinclair Lewis, Jessie *Fauset, Mary *Antin, Ellen *Glasgow, Wallace Stevens, Zora Neale *Hurston, and many others. Though current critical opinion often denigrates the period for its elitist subjects and stylistic concerns, modernist writing by both women and men was amazingly varied. Just as it drew on French, Russian, British, and other literatures during its inception, so today one or another of its tendencies has shaped contemporary literature throughout the world.

Modernism was an attitude more than a stylistic emphasis or a historical period. In the search for stability, which resulted from the devastation of belief after scientism and was intensified by the cataclysmic First World War, writers privileged dedication to craft combined with philosophic skepticism. The role of literature became less a traditional one of confirming social vision than of questioning it. The shape of literature changed to reflect its purpose: instead of predictable structures and rhymes, modern writing was chaotic, its structure both ironic and whimsical.

In the absence of religious conviction, the artist and writer took on the role of philosophical authority. Early in the century, Ezra Pound, T. S. Eliot, Amy Lowell, and Ford Madox Ford, who were writing hundreds of essays and reviews, created the figure of artist-god, and in their maxims, made literature supreme: "Literature is news that stays news." "The mastery of any art is the work of a lifetime." The high seriousness of this purpose is reflected in the earnest writing of the time. Although there was a great deal of comedy in graphic art, humorous writers—Djuna Barnes, Anita *Loos, Gertrude Stein, Langston Hughes, Mina Loy, Vachel Lindsay, James Thurber, e. e. cummings—were seldom taken seriously. Experiments with tone were less accepted than those with form, where Pound's injunction to "make it new" led to free verse or *vers libre* in poetry, lyricism, impressionism, or stream of consciousness in fiction, and expressionism in drama. Innovative style reflected changes in philosophical and cultural allegiances, to relativism and an ongoing critique of traditional metaphysics.

Modernist literature was not self-conscious about genre divisions. John Dos Passos, H.D., e. e. cummings, Mina Loy, Djuna Barnes, William Carlos Williams, William Faulkner, Jean Toomer, Langston Hughes, Agnes *Smedley, and certainly Hemingway and Stein (Hemingway, who considered himself first a poet, and Stein, who created new forms of all genres) wrote in all forms, regularly borrowing techniques from one mode to use in another. Reacting against formalized "literary" typos, such *experimentalism allowed women and minority writers to create shapes expressive of their themes: Langston Hughes perfected a jazz poem, as well as a voice-based prose for his ironic essays; Mina Loy, Lola Ridge, and Gertrude Stein used a long-line poetry to comment subversively on the literary and social scene (see Stein's "Patriarchal Poetry"), just as Djuna Barnes's mixed form *A Book* and *Ryder* were scathingly ironic; H.D.'s lyric prose—like Jean Toomer's in *Cane* or *Sui Sin Far's in *Mrs. Spring Fragrance*—forced a psychoanalytic awareness upon the reader.

Expatriation became the heart of modernism: either hiding out in Greenwich Village or Provincetown or Harlem, or the actual move to Paris or London or Florence. Through the catalytic salons of Gertrude Stein, Edith Wharton, and Natalie Barney; the influence of Sylvia *Beach's Paris bookshop; and the power of such *little magazines as *Poetry, Crisis, The Double Dealer, Broom, The Dial, Transatlantic review, American Caravan*, and *Opportunity* modernism attempted to break through convention in every direction.

If modernism is defined exclusively by the work of Eliot, Hemingway, Faulkner, and Stein, its great variety is lost. Anzia Yezierska's *Hungry Hearts* showed poignantly the Russian Jewish family in the stony New York streets. F. Scott Fitzgerald's *The Great Gatsby*, Willa Cather's *A Lost Lady*, and Edith Wharton's *The Age of Innocence*, in seeming to mourn the past, expressed a deeply ironic sense of modernity. Jessie Redmon Fauset's *There Is Confusion* and Nella Larsen's *Quicksand* and *Passing* portrayed black women's complex lives, just as Ellen *Glasgow's *The Sheltered Life* and Katherine Anne *Porter's *Flowering Judas* depicted white women.

The dramatic shift in intention between much high modernist writing during the 1920s (although that by immigrant, racial minority, and women writers was often quite different even in this decade) and so-called *proletarian writing of the 1930s depression years confused literary historians. Responding to the human need of deprivation, some writing of the 1930s abandoned the experimentalism of the modern, with its thematic focus on the development of the individual, for readable studies of *community and of the ways characters interacted with and helped others. Many readers preferred the texts of the 1930s because they were much more accessible, finding form in folk song and refrain patterns rather than abstruse symbolism and fragmented text. Edward Dahlberg's *Bottom Dogs* and Michael Gold's *Jews Without Money* explored poverty, especially among immigrant Americans, and pointed toward political radicalism. Fielding *Burke, Grace Lumpkin, and Myra Page wrote about textile workers in Gastonia, North Carolina; Erskine Caldwell, about the misery of southern sharecroppers; and Meridel *LeSueur, about the lives of desperately poor women during the 1930s. Any recounting of important American writers during the depression should include Josephine *Herbst, Josephine Johnson, Mari *Sandoz, Agnes Smedley, James T. Farrell, Muriel *Rukeyser, Kay *Boyle, Jack Conroy, Leane Zugsmith, Ruth McKenney, Martha *Gellhorn, Genevieve Taggard, Clifford Odets, Lillian *Hellman, Tillie Lerner *Olsen, Zora Neale Hurston, Dorothy *West, Harriette *Arnow, Albert Halper, Arna Bontemps, John Howard Lawson, Tess *Slesinger, Ruth Suckow, John Steinbeck, Mary Heaton *Vorse, Ella Winter, Richard Wright, and Ralph Ellison.

Reading the work of these writers with a concern for technique and style would show a number of traits in common with the writing produced during the 1920s. Yet, because of the peculiarities of literary history, most of the writers named above are considered proletarian rather than modernist. They are supposedly more interested in message than in art, and write from a concern with didacticism instead of formalism. The work itself belies this charge and remains as a treasure for readers familiar only with F. Scott Fitzgerald or Willa Cather. The modernist aesthetic was to waken readers to new insights, new understandings: to bring literature back to a central position in life so that reading would be a means of gaining wider understanding. Forcing the reader's attention through coined words, slanted type, or punctuation used as words was one means of eliciting a response, but by the 1930s, the human subject matter of loss and waste was itself sufficient. Typeface would not change the sorrow, nor would fragmented story lines break into the pathos that was inherent. As with all good writers, these American artists of the 1930s used what was before them with skill and seriousness of purpose and created essential literature that is still in the process of being discovered. A lingering modernist irony is that the writing of this decade—much of it accomplished by a lower economic *class, racial minorities, migrants, and women—has been seen as so different from the privileged, and valued, high modernist texts that few people ever bother to read it.

[*See also* Little Magazines; Postmodern Writing.]

• Richard Ellmann and Charles Feidelson, Jr., eds., *The Modern Tradition: Backgrounds of Modern Literature* (1965). Renato Poggioli, *The Theory of the Avant-Garde*, trans. Gerald Fitzgerald (1968). Paul DeMan, *Blindness and Insight: Essays in the Rhetoric of Contemporary Criticism* (1971). Hugh Kenner, *The Pound Era* (1971). Maurice Beebe, "What Modernism Was," *Journal of Modern Literature*, issue "From Modernism to Post-Modernism," 3 (July 1974): 1065–84. Hugh Kenner, *A Homemade World: The American Modernist Writers* (1975). Matei Calinescu, *Faces of Modernity: Avant-Garde, Decadence, Kitsch* (1977). Fredric Jameson, *The Political Unconscious* (1981). Shari Benstock, *Women of the Left Bank, Paris, 1910–1940* (1986). Andrew T. I. Ross, *The Failure of Modernism* (1986). Morton P. Levitt, *Modernist Survivors* (1987). Sandra M. Gilbert and Susan Gubar, *No Man's Land: The Place of the Woman Writer in the Twentieth Century*, I (1988); II (1989). Linda Wagner-Martin, *The Modern American Novel, 1914–1945* (1989). Bonnie Kime Scott, ed., *The Gender of Modernism* (1990). Fredric Jameson, *Postmodernism, or, The Cultural Logic of Late Capitalism* (1990).

Linda Wagner-Martin

MOHR, Nicholasa (b. 1935), novelist, short fiction writer, screenwriter, educator, and graphic artist. The first Puerto Rican–American woman to write in English about the Puerto Rican–American experience, Mohr was born and raised in *El Barrio* of New York City's South Bronx.

Many of her stories are at least semiautobiographical and, although not expressly written for children, many are told from a child's point of view. Such a narrative stance suits her simplicity of style. She has been praised for the complexity of her Puerto Rican–American characters and, especially, for the vitality of her female characters. She also treats her several homosexual characters with particular sympathy. Mohr began her career as a painter, printmaker, and art educator and made the transition to author in her award-winning first novel, *Nilda* (1973), which she also illustrated. Her graffitilike pen-and-ink illustrations for *Nilda* express the alienation and invisibility that Puerto Rican–Americans feel both in the United States, where they are treated more as unwelcome immigrants than as citizens, and in Puerto Rico, where they are derisively called "Nuyoricans" for having sought better lives in the United States. Through this overall theme, Mohr weaves a number of threads: the tensions caused by ethnicity, gender, generation, class, and language; the nostalgic longing for an impossibly edenic past in Puerto Rico; and the remnants of Puerto Rico's colonial past, its patriarchal culture giving way to a matriarchal culture in the United States as traditional masculine and feminine family roles become obscured.

Answering those critics who question why she does not write in Spanish, Mohr cites her own favorite writers—Alice * Walker, Raymond Carver, Tillie * Olsen, Ishmael Reed, and Denise Chávez—whom she sees as representatives of marginalized social groups and classes whose American English both enriches the English language and promotes social equality. She considers many of the Puerto Rican writers who write in Spanish too concerned with their own social status and with Spain, as evidenced by their lavish use of baroque Spanish.

Since *Nilda*, Mohr has written two juvenile novels, *Felita* (1979) and its sequel, *Going Home* (1986); the short-story collections *El Bronx Remembered* (1975), *In Nueva York* (1977), and *Rituals of Survival: A Woman's Portfolio* (1985); *All for the Better* (1993), a juvenile biography of Evelina Antonetty; and various individual short stories. She also has coauthored (with Ray Blanco) a screenplay, "The Artist." Another novel and a juvenile autobiography are in press.

• Edna Acosta-Belén, "Conversations with Nicholasa Mohr," *Revista Chicano-Riqueña* 8 (Spring 1980): 35–41. Nicholasa Mohr, "Puerto Rican Writers in the United States, Puerto Rican Writers in Puerto Rico: A Separation Beyond Language," *Americas Review* 15 (Summer 1987): 87–92. Nicholasa Mohr, "Puerto Ricans in New York: Cultural Evolution and Identity," in *Images and Identities: The Puerto Rican World in Two World Contexts*, ed. Asela Rodríguez de Laguna (1987), pp. 157–160. Sonia Nieto, "Self-Affirmation or Self-Destruction: The Image of Puerto Ricans in Children's Literature Written in English," in *Images and Identities: The Puerto Rican World in Two World Contexts*, ed. Asela Rodríguez de Laguna (1987), pp. 211–226. Edith Blacksilver, "Nicholasa Mohr," in *Biographical Dictionary of Hispanic Literature in the United States; the Literature of Puerto Ricans, Cuban Americans, and Other Hispanic Writers*, ed. Nicolás Kanellos (1989), pp. 199–213.

Anne Marsh Fields

MONOCULTURALISM. *See* Biculturalism; Multiculturalism.

MONROE, Harriet (1860–1936), poet, editor, playwright, critic. As the founder-editor in 1912 of *Poetry: A Magazine of Verse*, Monroe was perhaps the individual most responsible for the concentration of new talent and the infusion of raw energy that would become known as the * Chicago renaissance in American poetry. Born in the city that would remain central throughout her life, Monroe inherited her early love of literature and the arts from her father, a Chicago lawyer. A convent education in the liberal humanistic tradition fueled her early belief in the beauty and progress represented by human

artistic creation, and in 1888 she published her first poem, "With a Copy of Shelley," in *The Century*. In 1892 she mounted a successful campaign to have a poem included in the opening ceremonies of Chicago's Columbian Exposition, composing "The Columbian Ode," for which she received payment and a laurel wreath. Yet Monroe was only too aware of the largely subordinate and unrecognized role poetry and poets played in American life. Supporting herself precariously throughout the next years as a journalist, art critic, and sometime teacher and lecturer, she had privately published in 1891 her first collection, *Valeria and Other Poems*, and in 1903 a volume of plays, *The Passing Show*.

Monroe's conviction that the true "life" of American poetry lay not in the stale imitation of European models nor in the cheap, space-filling verses that rounded out popular magazines led her in the early 1910s to seek backing for a publication that would attempt to build an audience for American poetry as well as provide a forum for new, challenging poetic voices. With the aid of some of Chicago's leading businessmen, and under the eye of a largely dubious press, Monroe founded *Poetry* and almost immediately garnered the support, encouragement, and contributions of many who would remain in the vanguard of the modern movement, including Ezra Pound, Louise * Bogan, Marianne * Moore, Amy * Lowell, and Wallace Stevens. In 1917 Monroe and coeditor Alice Corbin Henderson published their first anthology of new American works, *The New Poetry*, while Monroe continued to produce her own volumes, including *You and I* (1914), *The Difference* (1924), and *Chosen Poems* (1935). Remaining single throughout her life, Monroe in her autobiography *A Poet's Life* (published posthumously in 1938) suggested that the consolations and rewards of her art had more than filled her life with meaning and purpose. She died in Arequipa, Peru, while returning from a writers' conference.

• The Personal Papers of Harriet Monroe are in the Regenstein Library, University of Chicago. See also Daniel J. Cahill, *Harriet Monroe* (1973). Ellen Williams, *Harriet Monroe and the Poetry Renaissance: The First Ten Years of 'Poetry'* (1977). Ann Massa, " 'The Columbian Ode' and Poetry, A Magazine of Verse: Harriet Monroe's Entrepreneurial Triumphs," *Journal of American Studies* 20, no. 1 (April 1986): 51–69.

Mylène Dressler

MOORE, Marianne (1887–1972), poet, critic, and editor. Born in Kirkwood, Missouri, near St. Louis, at the Presbyterian manse of her grandfather, the Reverend John Riddle Warner, Moore never knew her own father and moved with her mother, Mary Warner Moore, and her brother, John Warner Moore, to Carlisle, Pennsylvania, in 1896. She attended the Metzger Institute, a Presbyterian preparatory school for girls where her mother taught English, and graduated from Bryn Mawr College in 1909 with a major in history, politics, and economics. Not permitted to major in English, she elected a course that concentrated on seventeenth-century prose stylists. She published poems and short stories in Bryn Mawr's periodical *Tipyn o'Bob*, serving on the editorial board.

Moore and her mother visited England and France in 1911, and the young writer gathered material for poems from the Glasgow museums, the Ashmolean Museum, the British Museum, Hampton Court, the Louvre, and Victor Hugo's house, paying particular attention to Pre-Raphaelite paintings, collections of armor, and Elizabethan decorative arts. In London she purchased Ezra Pound's *Personae* and *Exultations* from the publisher Elkin Mathews.

Moore had completed a year at the Carlisle Commercial College, having been told to learn secretarial skills if she wanted a career in publishing. After working for a few months for Melvil Dewey, the creator of the library decimal classification system that bears his name, at Lake Placid, New York, Moore took a post teaching business subjects at the United States Indian School in Carlisle from 1911 to 1914. During these years she submitted poems to little magazines; *Poetry* (Chicago) and *The Egoist* (London) published her first professional work in 1915. By the end of that year, her poems had come to the attention of * H. D. (a classmate but slight acquaintance at Bryn Mawr), William Carlos Williams, and Ezra Pound. H. D. and Bryher published Moore's first book, *Poems* (1921), without permission; it was widely if not always favorably reviewed.

Moore's most famous poem, "Poetry," insists that "I, too, dislike it," referring to the sentimental verse that marked poetry before the modernist movement. In her poem, Moore sets forth the subjects she finds suitable for poetry, including human and animal behavior, science and business—anything that can capture the poet's imagination. She borrows a phrase from Yeats's essay on Blake's illustrations to Dante and then rewrites Yeats, calling for poets to become "literalists of the imagination." Her practice of reworking quotations was to mark her subsequent work.

In 1918, Moore and her mother moved to Greenwich Village, across the street from the Hudson Park Branch of the New York Public Library where Moore worked half days. Soon her literary contacts attracted the interest of Scofield Thayer, editor of the prestigious *Dial*.

In quick succession, Moore published there "A Grave," "New York," and "An Octopus"; she won *The Dial* Award for 1924, published her first American book, *Observations*, and became editor of *The Dial* (1925–1929). Work at *The Dial* was eased by a trip to England (1927) and a visit to George Saintsbury, the aged dean of English literary criticism.

After the *Dial* ceased publication in 1929, the Moores moved to Brooklyn, where Marianne lived until her final move back to Manhattan in 1965. She published no poems until 1932, returning then to syllabic meter and rhyme. This decade saw her second group of major long poems: "The Steeple-Jack," "The Jerboa," "The Pangolin," and "The Plumet Basilisk" among them. She chose not to anthropomorphize these exotic animals but to present them as natural wonders, successful in adaptation and self-protection. Later, critics were to interpret her use of animals as her personal "armoring," a protection against revelation of emotions.

T. S. Eliot, in his introduction to Moore's *Selected Poems* (1935), called her work "part of the body of durable poetry written in our time." As editor at Faber and Faber, he published her books for thirty years. Ezra Pound first wrote about Moore in 1918, citing the "logopoeia" (Pound's term for the intelligent and poetic use of words) in her verse. They were lifelong correspondents, their friendship closing only with a memorial service for her that Pound organized in Venice. William Carlos Williams, in his *Autobiography*, called her the "karyatid" who, with long red braids encircling her head, supported the "building" that the modernist poets were trying to fashion. Moore's return tributes occur in her reviews of these poets' books.

Moore lost her mother, her best friend and critic, in 1947. In anticipation of her loneliness, she undertook to translate all of La Fontaine's *Fables*, completing the project after ten years (1954). After nearly two decades of occasional lecturing and considerable reviewing, Moore gathered her prose in *Predilections* (1955) and again, with poems, in *A Marianne Moore Reader* (1961). Her *Collected Poems* (1951) won the Pulitzer Prize, the Bollingen Prize, and the National Book Award.

Following her mother's death, Moore's poetry focused more frequently on accessible subjects. She addressed the Brooklyn Bridge in "Granite and Steel," a well-known ballet artist in "Arthur Mitchell," America's national pastime in "Baseball and Writing," and a race horse in "Tom Fool at Jamaica." Her *Complete Poems* (1967) marked her eightieth birthday. Although Moore remained a poet's poet, her audience grew through publication in the *New Yorker*, photo essays about her in *Life* and *Look*, and the attention of such sports figures as Cassius Clay (Muhammad Ali) and Joe Garagiola. Her trademark tricorn hat and black cape were seen at public events such as the Boston Arts Festival and on the "Tonight Show." In the full-page obituary run by the *New York Times* after her death, it was made clear that her work had achieved major standing and would, as Eliot had said, endure.

• Patricia C. Willis, ed., *The Complete Prose of Marianne Moore* (1986). Taffy Martin, *Marianne Moore: Subversive Modernist* (1986). Grace Schulman, *Marianne Moore: The Poetry of Engagement* (1986). John Slatin, *The Savage's Romance: The Poetry of Marianne Moore* (1986). Margaret Holley, *The Poetry of Marianne Moore: A Study in Voice and Value* (1987). Patricia C. Willis, *Marianne Moore: Vision into Verse* (1987). Celeste Goodridge, *Hints and Disguises: Marianne Moore and Her Contemporaries* (1989). Charles Molesworth, *Marianne Moore: A Literary Life* (1990). Joseph Parisi, ed., *Marianne Moore: The Art of a Modernist* (1990). Patricia C. Willis, ed., *Marianne Moore: Woman and Poet* (1990).

Patricia C. Willis

MORAGA, Cherríe (b. 1952), Chicana lesbian feminist poet, playwright, author, editor, and teacher. For Cherríe Moraga the personal is truly political. Throughout her career she has sought to transform lessons learned from her own life experiences into potential guidelines for other Chicanas, lesbians, and women as well as for anyone struggling to find a voice, battle oppression, and build community.

Moraga's chosen weapon in this struggle has typically been the written word. In 1981, Moraga coedited and contributed to (along with Gloria *Anzaldúa) the award-winning anthology *This Bridge Called My Back: Writings by Radical Women of Color*. Her poems and essays collected in *This Bridge* are consistently attentive to the joys and sorrows of living at the borders of the dominant Anglo middle-class heterosexual culture, of being neither outsider nor insider but both and more. In her poem "For the Color of My Mother" or her essay "La Güera," for instance, she movingly depicts her own cultural and personal struggles as the fair-skinned, educated child of a darker-skinned Chicana mother and an Anglo father and points to the power of speech in the face of both silence and silencing.

More than just writing about such power, Moraga has worked to increase opportunities to attain it. For instance, in 1981, Moraga helped to establish the Kitchen Table: Women of Color Press, founded to insure all women, but specifically those of color, greater access to print and audiences. The year 1983 was productive for Moraga: in addition to publishing her own *Loving in the War Years: Lo que nunca pasó por sus labios* (1983), she coedited with Alma Gó-

mez and Mariana Romo-Carmona *Cuentos: Stories by Latinas*, to which she also contributed two stories. Throughout her poems, stories, and essays, as well as in her several plays, we witness Moraga's continued focus on issues she knows firsthand: the struggles of subordinate(d) groups—Chicanas and/or lesbians in particular—fighting for their right to be seen, heard, and validated.

Wisely, Moraga questions the power of the written word alone to transform the world and worries that many of the people she most wants to reach—especially other Chicana/os—may never get the opportunity to read her own and other critical work. Just as wisely, she acknowledges that writing is an important starting place. As her own career amply demonstrates, after all, there is such a thing as political writing: writing about difference that can make a difference.

Cynthia J. Davis

MORALES, Aurora Levins (b. 1954), short story writer, essayist, poet. Morales joins a growing number of Latina writers attempting to explore and articulate their own subjectivity. Through a mixture of genres and narrative forms, Morales works towards self-definition across sociocultural and linguistic spaces, marking her identity as a Latina at the borderland of different cultures and histories.

Born in Indiera Baja, Puerto Rico, to a Jewish father and a Puerto Rican mother, Morales spent her childhood in Puerto Rico before moving with her family to Chicago at age thirteen, and later settling in San Francisco. She shares a commitment to political *activism with her parents, describing herself as the daughter of communists and activists. Her father, Richard Levins, has been a farmer in Puerto Rico as well as an American academic. Her mother, Rosario Morales, whose parents immigrated from Naranjito, grew up in New York City and is also a writer. As authors, both Morales and her mother share a belief in the importance of writing in promoting social change.

Morales has published her essays and short stories in various journals and magazines, including the *Americas Review*, *Ms., Coming Up*, and *Gay Community News*. She has works in two important anthologies by women of color: *This Bridge Called My Back: Writings by Radical Women of Color* (1981) and *Cuentos: Stories by Latinas* (1983). Morales has also published *Getting Home Alive* (1986), a collaborative text produced with her mother.

In *Getting Home Alive*, Aurora Levins Morales and Rosario Morales employ a mixture of genres, including *poetry, narrative, epistle,

* diary, and * autobiography, in exploring questions of identity. The two women offer the * mother-daughter bond as an important place from which to begin negotiating complex cultural identities. Both call for collective political action by women, and the celebration of diversity as well as the need for solidarity for self-empowerment. Calling themselves "Latinas at the crossroads," both women indicate their cultural pluralism with their language: English, Spanish, and Yiddish. Aurora Levins Morales writes of her childhood, her ancestors, and Puerto Rican history, interweaving memories and sensory images with considerations of her contemporary life. In this text, as in her other writings, Morales draws on the power of testimonial literature in order to celebrate the diversity of her experience and her history as a Latina, and in order to call her readers to social action.

• Rina Benmayor, "*Getting Home Alive:* The Politics of Multiple Identity," the *Americas Review* 17 (Fall-Winter 1989): 107–117. Lourdes Rojas, "Latinas at the Crossroads: An Affirmation of Life in Rosario Morales and Aurora Levins Morales' *Getting Home Alive,*" in *Breaking Boundaries: Latina Writing and Critical Readings,* eds. Asunción Horno-Delgado, Eliana Ortega, Nina M. Scott, and Nancy Saporta Sternbach (1989), pp. 166–177.

Leigh H. Edwards

MORRISON, Toni (b. 1931), novelist, essayist, editor, short fiction writer, lecturer, educator. If the last two decades of the twentieth century could be called the age of African-American women writers, then Toni Morrison can be credited with creating the yardstick by which others are measured. As much a household name in the 1990s as some of her counterparts were in the * Black Arts Movement of the 1960s, Morrison is author, critic, lecturer, teacher, and public servant. Since she made her debut on the literary scene in 1970 with the publication of *The Bluest Eye,* she has been a paragon of success. Her six novels to date make her one of the most prolific of African-American women novelists, and her international reputation makes her one of the best-known of American writers. Critically acclaimed for her deft use of language and her lyrical writing, Morrison has won the National Book Critics' Circle Award and the Pulitzer Prize. In 1993, she was awarded the Nobel Prize in literature.

Now known as Toni Morrison, Chloe Anthony Wofford was born in Lorain, Ohio, on 18 February 1931 to George Wofford, a shipyard welder, and Rahmah Willis Wofford. Both sides of Morrison's family migrated from the South, her father from Georgia and her mother from Alabama. The second of four children, Morrison would recount in interviews how she grew up in a * story-telling environment, which included tales of the supernatural, that would later inform her works. Her appreciation for African-American folk culture, especially music, grew in part from her mother's having sung in a church choir and her grandfather's having supported his family from violin performances. Her parents instilled a sense of self-sufficiency and pride in Morrison, emphasizing that even poverty should not undermine human dignity; they highlighted their claim to a place in American democracy by writing to Franklin D. Roosevelt to complain about the bug-infested meal they had received while on relief.

Morrison entered the first grade as the only child in her class who already knew how to read, a skill that she would cultivate as an adolescent by reading Russian novels, *Madame Bovary,* and works by Jane Austen. She graduated with honors from Lorain High School and entered Howard University, where she changed her name to Toni (people had trouble pronouncing Chloe) and traveled through the South during summers with the Howard University Players. In 1953, she earned a B.A. in English with a minor in classics; in 1955, she earned a master's degree in English from Cornell University with a thesis on suicide in the works of Virginia Woolf and William Faulkner. Morrison has retained close contact with academia throughout her career.

From 1955 to 1957, Morrison taught at Texas Southern University and at Howard University between 1957 and 1964, where Stokeley Carmichael and Houston A. Baker, Jr., were among her students. It was in 1957 that Morrison began to write, after she returned to Howard as an instructor in English; she joined a group of ten black writers in Washington, D.C., that included Claude Brown (author of *Manchild in the Promised Land*). It was also here that she met and married Harold Morrison, a Jamaican architect. The couple had two sons, Harold Ford and Kevin Slade, before they divorced in 1964. Morrison returned briefly to her parents' home in Ohio before getting an editing job with a textbook subsidiary of Random House in Syracuse, New York, the city to which she moved in 1965. She completed *The Bluest Eye* during this period.

By the time *The Bluest Eye* appeared, Morrison had transferred to the Random House offices in New York City where for the next fifteen years, until 1983, she worked as an editor on *The Black Book* (1974, with Middleton Harris), the autobiographies of Muhammad Ali and Angela * Davis, Gayl * Jones's *Corregidora* (1975), and Toni Cade * Bambara's *The Salt Eaters* (1980).

Morrison held a series of academic appointments during this time. From 1969 to 1970, she was an instructor at the State University of New York at Purchase. From 1975 to 1977, she served as Distinguished Visiting Professor at Yale University and as Distinguished Visiting Lecturer at Bard College from 1979 to 1980. Named Albert Schweitzer Professor of the Humanities at the State University of New York at Albany, she left Random House to assume that position in 1984. She would hold it until 1989, when she moved to Princeton University to accept her second endowed professorship, that of Robert F. Goheen Professor of the Council of the Humanities.

Morrison's second novel, *Sula*, was published in December of 1973 (though in the book the date is listed as 1974). It is the story of Nel Wright and Sula Peace, friends in the black community in the town of Medallion, Ohio, as well as the story of the demise of the community in which they live. Introducing a new breed of female characters into African-American literature, *Sula* enjoyed an impressive critical responses. It was an alternate selection by the Book-of-the-Month Club, *Redbook* excerpted portions of it, and it was nominated for the 1975 National Book Award in fiction.

Based on the myth that Africans could fly, Morrison's next novel, *Song of Solomon* (1977), was a best-seller, with a reported 570,000 copies in print in 1979. It won the fiction award of the National Book Critics' Circle in 1978. Morrison also received the American Academy and Institute of Arts and Letters Award, and she was featured in the PBS series "Writers in America." Emphasizing the need to understand and celebrate ancestry and ancestors, the novel is the story of Milkman Dead, who must journey from his plush middle-class existence in Ohio back through his family history in Pennsylvania and Virginia to come to an understanding of how his great-grandfather could fly and to appreciate the true value of his Aunt Pilate, a spiritual guide who has links to forces beyond Milkman's world.

The publication of *Tar Baby* (1981) put Morrison on the cover of *Newsweek* and catapulted her to even more popular and critical acclaim. The novel, on the *New York Times* best-seller list for four months, traces the clash between African-American middle-classness and folk culture, as reflected in Jadine Childs, a light-skinned model raised by "Phil-a-delphia Negroes" and trained in Paris, and Son Green, a ship jumper who violates the peace of the Caribbean island where Jadine has gone for a respite from her Paris adventures. The two become lovers but are destined to part as the worlds of myth, history, and reality collide and make it unclear whether a past or a future is preferable.

In 1983, Morrison wrote a short story, "Recitatif," for Amiri and Amina Baraka's anthology *Confirmation*. Several years later, Morrison wrote her first play, *Dreaming Emmett*, commissioned by the state of New York. It featured the return of Emmett Till, the fourteen-year-old black boy from Chicago killed in Mississippi in 1955 for whistling at a white woman, to confront the persons responsible for his death. The play has not yet been published or re-produced.

Morrison's singular achievement in fiction occurred in 1987, when she published *Beloved*, for which she would win the Pulitzer Prize in 1988. The story of a black woman who killed one of her children (and tries to kill the other three) in order to prevent them from being remanded to slavery after she has run away, the novel is loosely based on Margaret Garner, a black slave woman who executed the same feat in 1851. Sethe, Morrison's character, manages to kill a daughter who is known only as "Beloved"; that child, seeking reunion and/or revenge, returns eighteen years later to claim the space and identity that are rightfully hers. Themes of history, slavery, guilt, the effect of the past upon the present, and the nature of motherhood make the novel an interesting assemblage of provocative issues. In addition to the Pulitzer Prize, Morrison's recognitions include the Chianti Ruffino Antico Fattore International Literary Prize (Italy, 1990), the Modern Language Association of America's Commonwealth Award in Literature (1989), the Melcher Book Award (1988), and the Elmer Holmes Bobst Award for Fiction (1988).

Morrison's creative output continued in 1992 with *Jazz*. Loosely based on a photograph by James Van Der Zee of a young woman dead in a casket, Morrison weaves the tale of a young woman killed by a much older jealous lover whose wife then attempts to mutilate the girl in her casket. From that rather bizarre beginning, the story treks its way through the whys and wherefores, through the pasts of the principal characters, and back to an attempt on the part of the remaining couple to get on with their lives. Intended to incorporate the rhythm of jazz musical structuring as its raison d'être, the novel instead becomes a story about narrators, about how the voice that creates a story can change it at will, with no accountability to anyone but itself.

Simultaneously with the publication of *Jazz*, Morrison published her first collection of essays, *Playing in the Dark: Whiteness and the Literary Imagination*. Based on the William E. Massey, Sr., lectures that Morrison delivered in 1990, the collection expands her earlier essay,

"Unspeakable Things Unspoken: The Afro-American Presence in American Literature," delivered as the Tanner Lecture at the University of Michigan in 1988 and published in the *Michigan Quarterly Review* (1989).

A much-sought-after lecturer and reader, Morrison has used her reputation to benefit various institutions. She serves as cochairperson of the Schomburg Library's Commission for the Preservation of Black Culture and as a board member of the Center for the Study of Southern Culture.

• Bessie W. Jones and Audrey L. Vinson, *The World of Toni Morrison: Explorations in Literary Criticism* (1985). Karla F. C. Holloway and Stephanie A. Demetrakopoulos, *New Dimensions of Spirituality: A Biracial and Bicultural Reading of the Novels of Toni Morrison* (1987). David L. Middleton, *Toni Morrison: An Annotated Bibliography* (1987). Nellie Y. McKay, ed., *Critical Essays on Toni Morrison* (1988). Terry Otten, *The Crime of Innocence in the Fiction of Toni Morrison* (1989). Michael Awkward, *Inspiriting Influences: Tradition, Revision, and Afro-American Women's Novels* (1989). Elliott Butler-Evans, *Race, Gender, and Desire: Narrative Strategies in the Fiction of Toni Cade Bambara, Toni Morrison, and Alice Walker* (1989). Wilfred D. Samuels and Clenora Hudson-Weems, *Toni Morrison* (1990). *Callaloo* 13 (Summer 1990) contains a special section on Morrison. Trudier Harris, *Fiction and Folklore: The Novels of Toni Morrison* (1991). Gayl Jones, *Liberating Voices: Oral Tradition in African American Literature* (1991). Marilyn Sanders Mobley, *Folk Roots and Mythic Wings in Sarah Orne Jewett and Toni Morrison* (1991). Barbara Hill Rigney, *The Voices of Toni Morrison* (1991).

Trudier Harris

MORTON, Sarah Wentworth (1759–1846), poet. Sarah Morton has been called the chief American woman poet between * Bradstreet and * Dickinson. She was born in Boston to James and Sarah (Wentworth) Apthorp, descendants of two wealthy and distinguished New England families. In 1781, she married Harvard graduate and Boston lawyer Perez Morton. Sarah and her husband actively participated in social and political circles and were friends of the families of John Adams and Governor James Bowdoin.

In 1789, Morton began contributing eulogies and pastoral verses to *Massachusetts Magazine*, first under the pen name "Constantia" and later under "Philenia, a Lady of Boston." Her first volume, published in 1790, was *Ouabi, or the Virtues of Nature, An Indian Tale. In Four Cantos*, an idealized narrative of an American "noble savage," neoclassical in its Popean couplets and romantic in its theme. As her verses continued to be published in the *Columbian Centinel*, the *New York Magazine*, the *Tablet*, and the *Port Folio*, Philenia was hailed as the "American

Sappho." In 1797, following a contemporary trend, Philenia wrote an epic tale of the Revolution, *Beacon Hill, a Local Poem, Historic and Descriptive*. It and a companion poem, *The Virtues of Society: A Tale Founded on Fact* (1799), are iambic pentameter celebrations of the heroic behavior of British and American citizens in the American War of Independence. Morton's last published work is the collection of miscellaneous prose and verse pieces, *My Mind and Its Thoughts* (1822).

Her subjects and themes reveal a woman dedicated to family and country. Although the literary quality of Morton's poetry witnesses an unusual education for a woman of her time, she did not hesitate to contest the women's rights espoused by Mary Wollstonecraft. Morton was also a chief spokesperson for the early abolitionist movement, and her "African Chief" was republished in school books, recited by abolitionists, and quoted in John Greenleaf Whittier's "Snow Bound."

• Emily Pendleton and Milton Ellis, *Philenia: The Life and Works of Sarah Wentworth Morton, 1759–1846* (1931). Emily Stipes Watts, *The Poetry of American Women from 1632 to 1945* (1977). Arlen Gilman Runzler Westbrook and Perry D. Westbrook, *The Writing Women of New England, 1630–1900* (1982).

Allene Cooper

MOTHERHOOD. American women writers' representations of motherhood range from rejection and despair to exultation and joy. Dual conceptions of motherhood exist in earliest Western mythology; Gaea, primal mother and Earth goddess, gives birth to Mnemosyne, goddess of intellect and artistic production. In this early incarnation, the two maternal identities coexist harmoniously. Throughout literary history, however, Mnemosyne's intellect has often displaced Gaea's procreative role. Responding to this inheritance in the context of American history, women writers have successively celebrated, rejected, and reevaluated the subject of motherhood. Defined largely by the voice of the white middle class, these responses correspond roughly with three historical periods: colonial to Civil War, Civil War to World War I, and post–World War I. Within each period, the writings of women outside the white middle class often articulate additional perspectives on the mother even as they are influenced by the norms of the dominant culture.

The first writings about mothers in America valorize the role of the colonial mother and reflect the hardships of early American life. The image of the mother is that of survivor and family protector. Mary * Rowlandson, for example, in *A Narrative of the Captivity and Restauration* of *Mrs. Mary Rowlandson* (1682), draws on the Puritan faith and her maternal identity to reunite her family after an Indian raid. Ironically, while she ingeniously employs her cultural framework to empower a maternal voice, she simultaneously denigrates the Native American mother. From the beginning, then, disjunctions appear between various maternal experiences and dominant ideology.

As America emerged as an independent nation, motherhood remained a key identity for leading women writers. Appropriating the rhetoric of democracy, colonial and early republican women generated the image of republican motherhood. In the seventeenth century, Anne * Bradstreet made domestic love and tutelage the foundation for civic virtue. Judith Sargent * Murray's essays of the revolutionary period answered Abigail Adams' question "what about the ladies?" as she linked the maternal role to the democratic ideal. However, while Murray's essays and Bradstreet's poetry defined the cultural ideal, the best-seller of the day, Susanna * Rowson's *Charlotte Temple* (1794) belies its general applicability. This novel of seduction and betrayal demonstrates that for many, motherhood led to impoverishment and * silence. For example, Phillis * Wheatley, writing as a slave, rejected a maternal framework in her poetry and later faced destitution as a free black mother (*Poems*, 1772).

As the literary marketplace expanded during the nineteenth century and women began to write in great numbers, the valorization of motherhood reached its height. Domestic ideology framed the cultural ideal as the celebration of motherhood in women's writing became standard. Harriet Beecher * Stowe applied the rhetoric of maternity to *Uncle Tom's Cabin* (1852) with compelling efficacy. Using her vision of maternal power, Stowe attempted to enlist the Christian mothers of America into battle against slavery. Other white middle-class women of this era (Louisa May * Alcott, Lydia Maria * Child, Maria Susanna * Cummins, Fanny * Fern, Catharine * Sedgwick, E.D.E.N. * Southworth, Susan * Warner, and others) produced similar transcendent visions of Christian maternal power as they insisted that the "Era of the Woman" had arrived.

Simultaneously, black women (often working with abolition-minded domestic novelists) were collaborating to create another genre, the * slave narrative (Lucy Freeman, Harriet * Jacobs, Mary Prince, Sojourner * Truth). While the * domestic novel extolled the mother-child bond, the power of slave narratives was rooted in sexual abuse of the mother and disruption of the mother-child bond. In *Our Nig* (1859), Harriet E. * Wilson shows that nominally free black mothers faced the same abuses and disruptions. In these writings, the mother's plight is thrown into sharp relief against white cultural norms.

As cultural forces shifted at the turn of the century—the * Civil War and * Reconstruction, the rise of industrial capitalism, the * women's movement—so, too, did narrative articulations of the mother. Women realists provided a transitional moment between valorization and rejection. Many of these writers privileged a maternal intelligence in their narratives. Sarah Orne * Jewett, for example, imbues her mother figures with mystical power, though they survive only in isolation from an emerging industrialism (*Country of the Pointed Firs*, 1896; "The White Heron," 1886). Frances E. W. * Harper (*Iola Leroy*, 1892) looked back to Reconstruction, depicting free black mothers and daughters who must deal with miscegenation and separation. Here the hope for reunion with the mother provides the textual frame. Early in the century, * Zitkala-Sa (Gertrude Simmons Bonnin) published autobiographical sketches representing both the Native American mother's central role in storytelling and the systematic erasure of her cultural and linguistic power by Anglo culture. The work of Mary Wilkins * Freeman is particularly transitional as it neither rejects nor romanticizes motherhood but instead suggests an ironic view of maternal power ("The Revolt of Mother" in *A New England Nun and Other Stories*, 1891).

Other women novelists began, sometimes fiercely, to reject the maternal ideal. Influenced by the rise of capitalism as well as by the widely circulating theories of Marx and Freud, writers faced an increasingly fractured social landscape. Replacing domestic ideology, the emerging women's movement extolled female individuality and independence. Increasingly, the romantic ideal of the mother is superseded by images of maternal insanity, impotence, and narcissistic abuse. Charlotte Perkins * Gilman's "The Yellow Wallpaper" (1892) couples motherhood with madness while Kate * Chopin's fictive mother (*The Awakening*, 1899) prefers death to the self-sacrificing rituals of a maternal life. Edith * Wharton seizes upon the mother as the epitome of societal greed and moral decay (*Custom of the Country*, 1913; *The Age of Innocence*, 1920). In *Summer* (1917) and *Twilight Sleep* (1927), Wharton gives frank attention to the issues of * abortion and technologically assisted birth. Willa * Cather (*Sapphira and the Slave Girl*, 1940) exposes the abuses practiced by white mothers against black mothers.

After World War I, differences in * race, * class, and * ethnicity led to increasingly complex and varied conceptions of motherhood, though, as Tillie *Olsen remarks: "least present is work written by mothers themselves" (*Mother to Daughter*, 1984). The *Harlem Renaissance encouraged more culturally valid representations by black women of African-American motherhood and serious questioning of assimilationist tendencies. These authors depict the mother as a potent source of strength and a locus of abuse. Thus, Zora Neale *Hurston introduces the important pattern of *grandmother as surrogate mother and at the same time indicts this figure for her assimilationist posture (*Their Eyes Were Watching God*, 1937). Nella *Larsen's tragic novella *Passing* (1929) exposes the fallacy of the color line as well as the deadly consequences of this national fiction to the "black" mother.

Among immigrant writers, Anzia *Yezierska (*Bread Givers*, 1925) unsparingly details her mother's cultural marginalization. Other working-class women depicted the violence and oppression of their mothers' marriages and the heroines' often futile efforts at escape (Edith Summers *Kelley, *Weeds*, 1923; Agnes *Smedley, *Daughter of Earth*, 1929).

In *My Ántonia* (1918), Willa Cather describes labor and birth with greater freedom and honesty than most previous writers. Tillie Olsen politicized the "natural" processes of birth with depictions of pregnancy, abortion, and labor (Tillie Olsen, *Yonnondio: From the Thirties*, 1974). She and other writers of the thirties identified the masses with the maternal body (Clara Weatherwax, *Marching! Marching!* [1935] and Meridel *Le Sueur, *The Girl* [1978]), rendering a political maternity quite different from that of the so-called republican mother.

Since the 1950s, representations of motherhood have expanded in both number and diversity. Sylvia *Plath (*The Bell Jar*, 1963; *Collected Poems*, 1981) and Anne *Sexton (*The Complete Poems*, 1981) deplored the anachronistic entrapment of the modern mother. In a world flaunting human advance, the mothers of their poetry and fiction are caught in a timeless solitary confinement. Marsha *Norman's *'night Mother* (1983) confirms the mother's inability to heal herself or her suicidal child. Lorraine *Hansberry (*A Raisin in the Sun*, 1959) introduces the troubled relation of impoverished mother and son, similarly confronting the seduction of white society and the loss of black identity. Harriette *Arnow's *The Dollmaker* (1954) brutally illustrates a mother's agony over a child's bodily mutilation.

In feminist theory, Shulamith Firestone (*The Dialectic of Sex*, 1970) offers a materialist analysis of the mother's entrapment, arguing that an exclusive female maternity could never be reconciled with political advance. Other writers complicated her argument with rigorous and interdisciplinary analyses of the mother in culture. Adrienne *Rich (*Of Woman Born*, 1976) presents an extensive review of the social construction of motherhood in patriarchy while Nancy Chodorow (*The Reproduction of Mothering*, 1978) argues that daughters identify themselves in close relation to mothers and develop a psychology of mothering. Audre *Lorde (*Sister Outsider*, 1988) gives voice to lesbian mothers, and Sallie McFague (*Models of God*, 1987) theorizes the maternity of God. Within a philosophical framework, Sara Ruddick delineates the contours of "maternal thinking" (*Maternal Thinking*, 1989). And in a widely influential essay, Alice *Walker traces a literary maternal ancestry (*In Search of Our Mothers' Gardens*, 1983).

Expanding the boundaries of the American literary *canon, minority women revivify the textual mother. Asian-American writers renew the focus on immigrant mothers (Amy *Tan, *The Joy Luck Club*, 1989; Maxine Hong *Kingston, *The Woman Warrior*, 1976), depicting an indigenous maternal culture and its potential loss in contemporary shifts of language, religion, and custom. Among Chicanos, Alma Villanueva desires a return to the maternal womb and yet portrays the working-class circumstances of Chicana mothers. Cherríe *Moraga calls for a revision of *La Malinche, the maiden given to Cortés and maligned as the mother of a bastard race (*Loving in the War Years*, 1983). In *Mother, May I?* (1978), Villaneuva confronts the issue of a mother's abandonment of her child. Native American writer Louise *Erdrich (*Tracks*, 1988) manifests the position of the Native American mother trapped between two world views. Countering this naturalistic portrayal, Paula Gunn *Allen (*The Sacred Hoop*, 1986) reclaims the Native American myth of Spider Woman, counterpart to Mnemosyne, thus contemporizing the link between motherly generation and intellect.

Contemporary writers work to sustain this maternal link while continuing to deal bravely with postmodern contradictions, including the mother's participation in systems of abuse and neglect (Tillie Olsen, *Tell Me a Riddle*, 1961; Sarah Wright, *This Child's Gonna Live*, 1969; Clara Claibourne Park, *The Siege: The First Eight Years of an Autistic Child*, 1972; Eudora *Welty, *The Optimist's Daughter*, 1972; Rita Mae *Brown, *Rubyfruit Jungle*, 1973; Grace *Paley, *The Little Disturbances of Man*, 1973; Marge *Piercy, *Woman on the Edge of Time*, 1976; Anne *Tyler, *Dinner at the Homesick Restaurant*, 1982; Alice Walker, *The Color Purple*, 1982; Sue Miller, *The Good Mother*, 1986; Octavia *Butler, *Dawn*, 1987; Toni *Morrison's *Beloved*, 1987; Gloria *Naylor, *Mama Day*, 1988; Lee *Smith, *Fair and Tender Ladies*, 1988; Fae Myenne Ng, *Bone*, 1993). Often linking motherhood with the process of writing, and dramatizing social change, contemporary women's writing continues to incorporate the text with significant maternal figures. Even as social roles for women have expanded and more women from diverse backgrounds have found their voice and audience, motherhood continues as a chosen subject and central concern.

[*See also* Birth; Grandmothers; Midwifery; Mothers and Daughters; Object-Relations Theory; Psychoanalysis and Women; Reproduction.]

• Nina Baym, *Woman's Fiction: A Guide to Novels by and about Women in America, 1820–1870* (1978). Minrose C. Gwin, *Black and White Women of the Old South: The Peculiar Sisterhood in American Literature* (1985). Cathy N. Davidson, *Revolution and the Word: The Rise of the Novel in America* (1986). Mary Kelley, *Private Woman, Public Stage: Literary Domesticity in Ninteenth-Century America* (1984). Marianne Hirsch, *The Mother/ Daughter Plot* (1987). Nancy M. Theirot, *The Biosocial Construction of Femininity: Mothers and Daughters in Nineteenth-Century America* (1988). Henry Louis Gates, Jr., ed., *Reading Black, Reading Feminist: A Critical Anthology* (1990). Brenda O. Daly and Maureen T. Reddy, *Narrating Mothers: Theorizing Maternal Subjectivities* (1991). Paula Rabinowitz, *Labor and Desire: Women's Revolutionary Fiction in Depression America* (1991). Debra A. Castillo, *Talking Back: Toward a Latin American Feminist Literary Criticism* (1992).

Blythe Forcey and Elaine Orr

MOTHERS AND DAUGHTERS. Many Native American mythologies associate the creation of the world with the power of mothering and the mother-daughter bond. Central to some Southwest tribal theology is the idea of Woman who creates not through her body but through her powers of thought. Northwest Coastal Indians tell their origin story through the figure of Copper Woman: washed up in an uninhabited land, she creates a manikin from her tears of loneliness by whom she conceives a daughter, Mowita, genetrix of all the peoples of the world.

The patriarchal social organization of the colonial period confined women to the domestic sphere. Of the few who wrote, fewer still emphasized mother-daughter relationships. Anne *Bradstreet, the first "American" poet to publish a volume (1650), began writing as a daughter strongly identified with her influential father, thus setting a pattern for many later women writers. Elegizing her mother, she portrayed her as stereotypically pious and obedient. In her later poetry, however, Bradstreet represented herself in domestic and maternal roles, reconnecting what patriarchal culture severs: women's creativity and procreativity.

During the republican period, the model woman was a mother whose traditional domestic and religious responsibilities were augmented by her obligation to instill in children the new ideology of civic virtue even though she herself was denied full citizenship. Thus, Mercy Otis *Warren, poet, playwright, historian of the Revolution and mother of four, urged women to emulate her cultivation of a double life of domesticity and intellect. This accommodation failed, however; in the period's sentimental fiction, mothers trained in female helplessness were depicted as ineffectual moral guides for their enterprising daughters (Hannah Webster *Foster, *The Coquette*, 1797). Phillis *Wheatley was a slave, poet, and mother, but tragically, the poetic record of her maternal voice is lost.

By the early nineteenth century, the notion of *separate spheres, applied primarily to the white middle and upper classes, created close communities of women that encouraged intense mother-daughter identification. Popular writers, such as Lydia Huntley *Sigourney, recognized the resulting strength of maternal influence and made motherhood a central theme.

However, motherhood became an ideology enshrined in a complex set of gender conventions that bequeathed to daughters a mixed heritage of self-denial and economic dependence that crippled their cultural and expressive agency even while it allowed them to claim a moral superiority. White women writers (Catherine *Sedgwick, Harriet Beecher *Stowe, Catharine *Beecher, Margaret *Fuller, and Elizabeth Cady *Stanton) extol the spiritual virtues and sacrifices of their mothers, but identify with their fathers as models of intellectual and professional ambition. Ironically, the era's most enduring mother-daughter novel is Hawthorne's *The Scarlet Letter* (1850)—male-authored and haunted by its cowardly father manqué.

Culturally prescribed *gender conventions shape the lives of women of all classes, races, and ethnic backgrounds. *Slavery as well as the harsh conditions of immigrant life, however, produced familial structures radically different from the Eurocentric nuclear family. Cultural images of the slave mistress (mother), the tragic mulatta (daughter), and the degraded *working-class woman are considered deviations against which white womanhood was defined, preventing others from even counting as women. Thus, female authors of *slave narratives (Harriet *Jacobs, *Incidents in the Life of a Slave Girl*, 1861) reconnected black womanhood to femininity through a specifically female resourcefulness and maternal affection. Jacobs's casting of her heroine as a *mother*—irreducibly female and owning neither herself nor her children—is precisely what provides the strength of her oppositional voice.

In the second half of the century, mothers resisted passing on the dangerous legacy of "true womanhood," but often fail (Louisa May *Alcott, Little Women, 1869; Elizabeth Stuart *Phelps, The Story of Avis, 1879), or they redefine what they can transmit to artist daughters: continuity, wisdom, and woman-identification (Sarah Orne *Jewett, Country of the Pointed Firs, 1896). The spiritual bankruptcy of ideal womanhood and the ultimate contradiction between maternity and creativity emerged at the end of the century in Charlotte Perkins *Gilman's "The Yellow Wallpaper" (1892) and Kate *Chopin's The Awakening (1899).

Not until the 1920s, with the progress of the women's movement (suffrage, greater educational opportunities, wider availability of contraception, significant decreases in maternal and infant mortality) did women writers begin to refigure the female artist in a mother-daughter story. Yet none can overcome what is perceived as a fundamental contradiction between maternity and self-affirmation. Many stories of the twenties and thirties are fantasies of maternal guilt in which mother-daughter bonding is threatened by heterosexual passion and maternal self-involvement (Edith *Wharton, A Mother's Recompense, 1925; Fannie *Hurst, Imitation of Life, 1933). Maternal powerlessness in the face of daughters' difficult acculturation pervades women's immigrant and depression narratives (Anzia *Yezierska, Bread Givers, 1925; Tillie *Olsen, Yonnondio, 1934/1974, "I Stand Here Ironing," 1961; Kim Chernin, In My Mother's House, 1983). In the postwar years, middle-class housewives were described as an insatiable "generation of vipers" overly invested in their daughters (Sylvia *Plath, The Bell Jar, 1963). As the poetry of Sylvia Plath and Anne *Sexton demonstrated, mothers and motherhood remained serious liabilities for the female artist who is hampered both by her mother and her children, though Plath and Sexton also glimpse inspirational dimensions of their procreativity.

"The cathexis between mothers and daughters—essential, distorted, misused—is the great unwritten story," writes Adrienne *Rich in her groundbreaking Of Woman Born: Motherhood as Experience and Institution (1976), locating herself as a daughter, a mother, and a poet, thereby validating the roles of mother and daughter of mothers. In the early 1970s, *feminism preferred the metaphor of *sisterhood and suffered from so-called matrophobia, seeing the mother as a monstrous and inhibiting force (Lisa Alther, Kinflicks, 1975). Rich and others, however, located a new feminist consciousness and sense of female difference in the quality of pre-oedipal mother-daughter connection (E. M. *Broner, A Weave of Women, 1978), a connection endangered by fathers and patriarchy and, still, by maternal creativity, self-expression, and sexuality (Rosellen *Brown, The Autobiography of My Mother, 1976; Mary *Gordon, Men and Angels, 1985; Sue Miller, The Good Mother, 1986; Anne Roiphe, Lovingkindness, 1987).

The 1970s and 1980s experienced an explosion of writing by African-American, Asian-American, Native American, and Hispanic women, all obsessed with mother-daughter plots. From a shared history of triple oppression based on *race and *class as well as gender, daughter-writers attempt to imagine and understand their mothers' lives, drawing mythic portraits of heroic survival fractured by their own fear and anger. Toni *Morrison's Sethe (Beloved, 1987), for example—a slave mother who can protect her daughter only by killing her—insists that hers is "not a story to pass on." Yet texts such as Alice *Walker's "Everyday Use" (1973) and In Search of Our Mothers' Gardens (1983), Morrison's Sula (1973), Maxine Hong *Kingston's The Woman Warrior (1976), Gloria *Naylor's Women of Brewster Place (1982), Jamaica *Kincaid's Annie John (1986), Louise *Erdrich's Tracks (1988), Amy *Tan's The Joy Luck Club (1989) and The Kitchen God's Wife (1991), Paule *Marshall's Daughters (1991), and Cherríe *Moraga's poems and plays draw power from an ambivalent yearning for mother-daughter connection in the face of a desperate need for separation.

But the 1980s and 1990s also produced more local and straightforward descriptions of women's daily lives in which mothers, passionately engaged in mothering, can be writers and feminists who actively intervene in the world on behalf of themselves and their children (Grace *Paley's stories, poems by Alicia Ostriker, Maxine *Kumin, Sharon Olds, Kate Daniels).

[See also Birth; Grandmothers; Midwifery; Motherhood.]

• Nancy Chodorow, The Reproduction of Mothering: Psychoanalysis and the Sociology of Gender (1978). Cathy N. Davidson and E. M. Broner, eds., The Lost Tradition: Mothers and Daughters in Literature (1980). Anne Cameron, Daughters of Copper Woman (1981). Shirley Nelson Garner, Claire Kahane, Madelon Sprengnether, eds., The (M)Other Tongue: Essays in Feminist Psychoanalytic Interpretation (1985). Paula Gunn Allen, The Sacred Hoop: Recovering the Feminine in American Indian Traditions (1986). Alicia Suskin Ostriker, Stealing the Language: The Emergence of Women's Poetry in America (1986). Marianne Hirsch, The Mother/Daughter Plot: Narrative, Psychoanalysis, Feminism (1989). Mickey Pearlman, ed., Mother Puzzles: Daughters and

Mothers in Contemporary American Literature (1989). Brenda O. Daly and Maureen Reddy, eds., *Narrating Mothers: Theorizing Maternal Subjectivities* (1991). Patricia Bell-Scott, Beverly Guy-Sheftall, Jacqueline Jones Royster, Miriam DeCosta-Willis, Lucie Fultz, eds., *Double Stitch: Black Women Write about Mothers and Daughters* (1992).

Marianne Hirsch and
Ivy Schweitzer

MOTHERS MANUALS were first published in the United States in the eighteenth century. Apparently concerned that traditional sources of advice and information were becoming increasingly inaccessible or inadequate, white middle-class male and female manual writers attempted to provide inexperienced and uninformed mothers with health care information and child-rearing advice. The writing of these advice books exposed a social ideology among manual writers that included the ideas that human effort could influence the future, that parenting was a skill that could be learned, that children were valuable, that they could and should be protected, that their personalities were malleable, and that mothers were the ones most responsible for the physical, social, moral, intellectual, and emotional nurture of children. Over the years, the authors of mothers manuals sought to enhance the status of mothers by emphasizing the specialized and scientific nature of the maternal role as well as its social and political importance. At the same time, they were as involved in self-promotion as they were in social engineering.

The emergence and proliferation of mothers manuals were connected to the development of printing technology and the rise of literacy. Also, because of urbanization and the development of a commercial/industrial economy, middle- and upper-class mothers and children increasingly found themselves isolated from public life. Simultaneously, advances in medical knowledge and technology offered the opportunity to limit infant and maternal mortality and to improve the quality of life. The fall in the birth rate among native-born women throughout the nineteenth century meant that these mothers had the opportunity to invest more emotion and time in their children. The result is that ideal standards of child care became more well defined and mothers were encouraged to become more self-conscious about performing their maternal functions.

The most popular of the early manuals was written by a British doctor, William Buchan, whose *Domestic Medicine* and *Advice to Mothers* were primarily concerned with health care. In 1811 an American woman who had borne eight children in sixteen years published *The Mater-*

nal Physician in New York. Her emphasis was on prevention of disease rather than cure. She tempered her reliance on the medical expertise of Buchan and other prominent British physicians with her insistence that a mother's instincts and experience should take precedence in the care of children. She relied on the common sense of her readers, and her approach to child rearing was relatively permissive. Sensitive to the need to produce well-adjusted citizens, she offered advice regarding moral development as well as health care.

Subsequent manuals published in the first half of the nineteenth century were written by educators such as Catharine * Beecher *(Treatise on Domestic Economy)* and popular writers such as Lydia Maria * Child *(The Mother's Book)* and were filled with wide-ranging advice. Lydia * Sigourney's *Letters to Mothers* was atypical in that it focused almost exclusively on moral * education. Books like *Maternity: A Book for Every Wife and Mother*, written by homeopathic physician Prudence Saur, continued to provide mothers with information on anatomy and physiology as well as advice on health care and strategies for successful child rearing.

One of the most widely distributed mothers manuals in the early twentieth century was Mary Mills West's *Infant Care*, first published in 1914 by the Children's Bureau. West was as concerned with buffering women from the demands that their babies placed on them as she was on disseminating practical advice for rearing children. Her pamphlet advised mothers, for example, to establish fairly rigid schedules for feeding their children and to limit the amount of time they spent comforting and playing with them. The 1921 edition of this manual was written in collaboration with Dr. Dorothy Reed Mendenhall. Their advice was reinforced by Dr. Josephine Hemenway Kenyon whose *Healthy Babies Are Happy Babies* was popular from the 1930s through the 1950s. After 1946, Benjamin Spock's *Baby and Child Care* eclipsed manuals written by women.

A survey of this literature reveals significant changes in attitudes over the course of two hundred years toward how mothers should carry out their responsibilities. Manual writers moved from the belief that children are depraved, dangerous, and need to be controlled to the conviction that children are innocent, benign, and should be indulged. Accompanying this change was their recommendation that mothers use the withdrawal of approval and affection rather than physical discipline to socialize their children. In the twentieth century, advances in medicine and psychology led to a tendency on the part of manual writers to view the nursery as a laboratory and the child as a product. At the same time, child care manuals encouraged parents to be as concerned for the happiness of their children as they were for their welfare.

Mothers manuals had both a positive and a negative impact on American women. They were an important source of health care information. By providing mothers with advice concerning the health and nurture of children, these books encouraged women to make choices and thus assert some autonomy within the domestic sphere. At the same time, however, by emphasizing the importance of child rearing to the exclusion of other activities, they discouraged women from seeking expanded roles outside the home. Mothers manuals also had the potential to induce guilt and anxiety in women by establishing standards for measuring maternal competence and by undermining women's confidence in their ability to carry out their domestic responsibilities without the help of experts. Through their admonitions and warnings, manual writers attempted to control the behavior of mothers as well as that of their children. Because they emphasized the role of mothers in preparing children for citizenship, mothers manuals also helped to politicize the maternal role. By the early twentieth century, government agencies on all levels had joined the effort to help women fulfill their maternal duties.

[See also Advice Books.]

• Robert Sunley, "Early Nineteenth-Century American Literature on Child Rearing," in Childhood in Contemporary Cultures, eds. Margaret Mead and Martha Wolfenstein (1955), pp. 150–167. Martha Wolfenstein, "Fun Morality: An Analysis of Recent American Child-training Literature," in Childhood in Contemporary Cultures, eds. Margaret Mead and Martha Wolfenstein (1955), pp. 168–178. Michael Gordon, "Infant Care Revisited," Journal of Marriage and the Family 30 (November 1968): 578–583. Jay E. Mechling, "Advice to Historians on Advice to Mothers," Journal of Social History 9 (Fall 1975): 44–63. Nancy Pottishman Weiss, "Mother, the Invention of Necessity: Dr. Benjamin Spock's Baby and Child Care," American Quarterly 29 (Winter 1977): 519–546. Nancy F. Cott, "Notes Toward an Interpretation of Antebellum Childrearing," Psychohistory Review 6 (Spring 1978): 4–20. William Graebner, "The Unstable World of Benjamin Spock: Social Engineering in a Democratic Culture, 1917–1950," Journal of American History 67 (December 1980): 612–629.

Sylvia D. Hoffert

MOTT, Lucretia (1793–1880), feminist, abolitionist, minister, advocate for peace and social justice. Widely recognized as one of the most powerful individuals behind the major reform movements of the nineteenth century, Mott was born Lucretia Coffin to Nantucket Quaker parents and received her early education in Boston at a private Quaker school. Rising to the position of assistant teacher, she quickly responded to the Society of Friends' ideals of social, religious, and personal tolerance, learning firsthand of the discrimination leveled against women—she was paid less than her less-qualified male counterparts—and of the fundamental atrocities of the American slavery system. In 1811 she married James Mott, a fellow Quaker and reform-minded friend, and for a time confined herself to her duties as wife and as mother to six small children. As the burdens of her family decreased, however, she sought to become involved in the pressing social concerns surrounding her. In 1818, at the age of twenty-eight, Mott became a minister of the Society of Friends, giving the first of what would become nearly countless public addresses on behalf of women's rights, anti-slavery reform, Native American rights, religious freedom, and personal and social tolerance.

As a woman preaching a "practical Christianity" and an unparalleled and universal tolerance for diversity, Mott met with sustained criticism from both within and outside reform circles. Yet her career is most remarkable for the coalitions she was able to forge. In the 1830s, profoundly influenced by abolitionist William Lloyd Garrison's work and by the formation of the American Anti-Slavery Society, Mott established the Philadelphia Female Anti-Slavery Society, and in 1840 she was named a delegate to the World Anti-Slavery Convention in London. Denied a seat at the convention because of her sex, Mott worked energetically to articulate the link between injustices based on race and those based on gender. She acted as a powerful bridge between the feminist and abolitionist movements and influenced an entire generation of reformers, in particular Elizabeth Cady * Stanton, who later worked with Mott to organize the historic 1848 Seneca Falls meeting for women's rights. Although Mott diverged from some feminists over the issue of suffrage—personal, individual reform must take place, she believed, before political reform—she ultimately worked to reconcile various feminist constituencies and continued her speaking campaigns until the end of her life. Her addresses have been collected in the Complete Sermons and Speeches (1980); her personal papers are today housed at the Friends Historical Library, Swarthmore College.

• Anna Davis Hallowell, ed., James and Lucretia Mott, Life and Letters (1884). Lucretia Coffin Mott, Slavery and "The Woman Question," Lucretia Mott's Diary, ed. Frederick B. Tolles (1952). Otelia Cromwell, Lucretia Mott (1958; reprint, 1971). Blanche Glassman Hersh,

The Slavery of Sex: Feminist Abolitionists in America (1978). Margaret Hope Bacon, *Valiant Friend: The Life of Lucretia Mott* (1980).

Mylène Dressler

MOURNING DOVE, also Humishuma (1882?–1936), author of *Cogewea, the Half-Blood* (1927; reprinted 1981), *Coyote Stories* (1933; reprinted 1934 and 1990), and manuscripts posthumously edited into *Mourning Dove, A Salishan Autobiography* (1990), was one of the first to write extensively from a Native American woman's perspective. Her novel, *Cogewea,* explores the difficulty of being a half-blood woman on the Flathead Reservation at the turn of the century. Central themes of the novel include genocide, as the tragic oral tales of Stemteema (the *grandmother) reveal, and the pressure to assimilate, as the choices of the book's three halfbreed sisters impart. One sister marries a white man and lives only minimally in connection with an Indian identity. Another sister chooses the ways of her traditional grandmother and tries to deny the currents of change. The third, Cogewea, wants to live in both worlds but is not comfortable nor fully accepted in either. This dilemma continued to rend Native Americans throughout the twentieth century.

Coyote Stories is a condensed and altered version of Mourning Dove's original manuscript, *Okanogan Sweathouse,* a collection of thirty-seven Salish genesis legends. Mourning Dove recorded these stories because Indian children were being taught to ridicule and reject Indian spiritual teachings. She hoped that a future generation might return to the tales, even if in English translation. Her final manuscripts, published as *A Salishan Autobiography,* are directed toward white audiences, trying to help them to understand what the first reservation years were like for inland Northwest tribes. Through a series of personal recollections and anecdotes, she discusses the difficulties that occurred within a single generation from 1885 to 1900 on the Colville Reservation as people were required to move from a migratory to a stationary culture, from a communal to a cash-nexus culture, from orderly lives to lives that sustained the shock of white settlement and greed exemplified by a mineral rights run and a homesteaders' run.

The critical issues surrounding Mourning Dove's work turn on the problems of *collaboration. *Cogewea* was ultimately coauthored by her mentor and friend, Lucullus V. McWhorter, who inserted long explanatory ethnographic notations into the dialogue as well as diatribes against Christian hypocrisy and government corruption. Dean Guie altered Mourning Dove's

legends to fit the requirements for juvenile literature of the 1930s, and Jay Miller altered Mourning Dove's final manuscripts in voice and organization. Scholars are just beginning to carefully reproduce her original manuscripts, thus more effectively revealing her *storytelling skills and more accurately recording her transcription of the legends as well as the complexity of her commentary on the assimilation period from 1880 to 1934.

• Correspondence and manuscripts are in the Lucullus Virgil McWhorter Collection, Holland Library, Washington State University, Pullman, Washington, and the Erna Gunther Collection, Archives Division, University of Washington, Seattle. See also Mary Dearborn, *Pocahontas's Daughters, Gender and Ethnicity in American Culture* (1986). Alanna Brown, "The Evolution of Mourning Dove's Coyote Stories," *Studies in Native American Literatures* 4, nos. 2 and 3 (Summer/Fall 1992). Alanna Brown, "Looking through the Glass Darkly: The Editorialized Mourning Dove," in *New Voices in Native American Literary Criticism,* ed. Arnold Krupat (1992).

Alanna Kathleen Brown

MOWATT, Anna Cora (1819–1870), actress, dramatist, and novelist. Mowatt made her debut as a thespian at the age of five in a family production. By twenty-one she had composed, directed, and performed in *Gulzara* (1840) for a circle of friends. Only one year later, her private diversions had become her vocation, and "Lily" made her first professional public appearance. Although she ascended the rostrum out of financial necessity, she displayed what many deemed a shocking degree of forwardness. Mowatt was undaunted by rebuffs; her early poetry recitals and private performances led to the publication of two successful plays—*Fashion; or, Life in New York* (1845), an American comedy of manners, and *Armand* (1847)—as well as a brilliant career on the stage in America and abroad. Along with garnering fame, her professional exertions secured her the respect of a public that doubted a woman of genteel birth could be reputably employed. Her memoir, *Autobiography of an Actress* (1853), recounts the remarkable perseverance she demonstrated throughout her professional and personal life.

Mowatt was born in Bordeaux, France, but her family soon returned to its native New York. Supplied with a cosmopolitan education and a healthy dose of American idealism, she resisted the strictures of feminine passivity, the succor of sickbed (despite frequent illnesses), and the criticism of her youthful poetry. Nor did family restrictions prevent her from eloping with James Mowatt at the age of fifteen. After her marriage, she battled tuberculosis, brain fever, and financial ruin. She remained ever watchful of her increasingly invalid husband and supported him and three adopted children by maintaining a rigorous writing and performance schedule. While appearing in different plays nightly and traveling across Europe and the United States, she managed to author several articles, frequently under the pseudonym of Helen Berkley (*The Fortune Hunter*, 1842, and *Evelyn*, 1845), and her * autobiography. After she retired from the stage in 1854, she continued to write, drawing from her experience as an actress (*Mimic Life*, 1856, and *Twin Roses*, 1857) as well as her faith in the American dream and Swedenborgianism (*Fairy Fingers*, 1865, and *The Mute Singer*, 1866). Her ideals were reflected in the lives of fictional women whose professional tenacity, like hers, was matched only by their religious devotion.

Although Mowatt was venerated primarily for her stage appearances in her lifetime, she has attained literary endurance through the modern performance of her most critically acclaimed piece, *Fashion*, and the 1980 reprinting of her autobiography.

• Marius Blesi, *The Life and Letters of Anna Cora Mowatt* (1938). Eric Wollencot Barnes, *The Life and Theatre of Anna Cora Mowatt* (1954; reprinted as *The Lady of Fashion*, 1955). Margaret Opsata, "Genteel Iconoclast," *American History Illustrated* 18 (February 1983): 40–45.

Marlene Tromp

MS. MAGAZINE. *Ms.* Magazine was founded in 1972, at a time when late-twentieth-century feminism was hitting its stride in the United States. Early in 1971, Gloria * Steinem began to gather other activists and writers in New York City to plan a publication that would reflect the vibrancy of the women's movement, thereby filling a void left by the mainstream media.

There was no dearth of feminist publications in existence during this time—in the five years from 1968 to 1973 more than 560 appeared. However, three-quarters of these were newsletters, and none was designed for wide distribution at newsstands. The women's magazines that did have large audiences were not covering those stories that engaged the writers and editors in the loose group that continued to meet through the first half of 1971: the push for power that led to the founding of the National Women's Political Caucus that summer; the campaigns for legal * abortion, child care, equal access to credit, and welfare rights; the struggle to break down gender barriers in employment; issues of sexual preference; the effort to raise children free of sex-role * stereotypes; the quest for respect and equity in the dynamics of male-female relationships.

Creating a magazine the group wanted to read was one thing, but raising money for the venture was a more difficult matter, particularly if it was to remain both woman-owned and -controlled. After months of unsuccessful efforts to raise capital, Steinem received a generous offer from Clay Felker, the editor of *New York Magazine*, who agreed to finance a preview issue of *Ms.* that would go out on newsstands across the country in exchange for the use of a substantial excerpt from the new magazine in the year-end double issue of *New York*. After the *Ms.* preview sold out in less than eight days, Steinem and Patricia Carbine, the editor of *McCall's* who agreed to come to *Ms.* as publisher, were able to trade 25-percent ownership for $1 million from Warner Communications. *Ms.* began as a monthly in July 1972, with a guarantee to advertisers of a circulation of 250,000. By early 1973, that guarantee had reached 325,000, and it rose by increments to 500,000 later in the decade.

Although *Ms.* was ultimately unable to sustain the advertising revenue needed to compete in the commercial arena—in 1990, it stopped taking ads, substantially increased its subscription cost, and began to rely entirely on reader support—the magazine continued to attract and retain a large and loyal, though sometimes critical, audience. Readers responded enthusiastically to the introduction of such writers as Alice * Walker, Erica * Jong, Mary * Gordon, and Judith Thurman, and they looked to *Ms.* for ground-breaking cover stories on such issues as domestic * violence and * sexual harassment. At the same time, readers complained bitterly at any hint that *Ms.* was conforming to commercial demands, such as excessive cigarette or liquor advertisements, too many celebrities as cover subjects, too little visibility for lesbian women or women of color, and columns that flirted with fashion or other traditional editorial topics. Beyond its own audience, *Ms.* paved the way for inclusion of feminist material in more traditional magazines and for new publications that served such previously neglected audiences as women in the workforce or older women.

[*See also* Magazines, Women's.]

• Anne Mather, "A History of Feminist Periodicals," *Journalism History* 1, no. 3 (Autumn 1974): 82–85. Mary Thom, ed., *Letters to Ms.: 1972–1987* (1987). Gloria Steinem, "Sex, Lies and Advertising," *Ms.* (July/August 1990): 18–28.

Mary Thom

MUKHERJEE, Bharati (b. 1940), novelist, short story writer, essayist, educator. Bharati Mukherjee has stated in recent years that she does not wish to be viewed as a hyphenated,

South Asian–American writer, but as an American writer. The insistence on being known as an American, without acknowledging one's Asian heritage, may grate on those who see the term *American* used today as denoting the Euro-American sociopolitically dominant group only. But Mukherjee defines *multiculturalism* from the outside, from the Euro-American point of view, instead of addressing it from the point of view of the person who has become multicultural due to colonialism in one form or another. She does not discuss the inherent power multiculturalism can demonstrate once it refuses to be marginalized.

Although Mukherjee's novels and most of her short stories deal with Americans of South Asian descent, she sees herself in the tradition of Euro-American *immigrant writers rather than Asian-American writers. Mukherjee's ease with discovering her identity as a mainstream American, her skill with the dialogues and incidents familiar to the dominant society, her refusal to be marginalized, and her absolute mastery of English are not surprising when one looks at her biography. She was born in 1940 in an upper-middle-class family in Calcutta, India. Her early education in India was at a convent school run by Irish nuns. She was also educated in England and Switzerland. She came to the U.S. in 1961 to attend the writer's workshop at the University of Iowa, where she received an M.F.A. in creative writing and a Ph.D. in English and comparative literature. She and her husband, the Canadian writer Clark Blaise, lived in Canada from 1966 to 1980, whereupon they migrated to the United States. Mukherjee teaches in the English department at the University of California, Berkeley.

Mukherjee's first novel, *The Tiger's Daughter* (1971), portrays Tara Banerjee Cartwright, a Western-educated, well-to-do Bengali woman, whose constant nervousness regarding her role as the Bengali wife of an American overshadows her well-intentioned efforts to understand her world of diverse cultures.

Mukherjee's second novel, *Wife* (1975), presents Dimple Dasgupta, a woman who goes to New York with her husband, faces intense loneliness in an incomprehensible and violent city, sinks into the world of television, kills her husband as he eats his bowl of cereal, and waits for him to come to life again as characters do on TV.

In *Days and Nights in Calcutta* (1977), Mukherjee describes the difficulties of being a South Asian writer in Canada, and her search for a secure and familiar place. Her brilliantly written, chilling collections of short stories, *Darkness* (1985) and *Middleman and Other Stories* (1988), and her novels *Jasmine* (1989) and *The*

Holder of the World (1993) extend this discussion into the more violent and grotesque, yet very real, aspects of collisions between cultures.

• Roshni Rustomji-Kerns, "Expatriates, Immigrants and Literature: Three South Asian Women Writers," *Massachusetts Review* issue entitled *Desh-Videsh: South Asian Expatriate Writing and Art* 29, no. 4 (Winter 1988–1989): 655–665. Emmanuel S. Nelson, ed., *Writers of the Indian Diaspora* (1992). Emmanuel S. Nelson, ed., *Bharati Mukherjee: Critical Perspectives* (1993). Inderpal Grewal, "Reading and Writing the South Asian Diaspora: Feminism and Nationalism in North America," in *Our Feet Walk the Sky: Women of the South Asian Diaspora*, eds. The Women of South Asian Descent Collective (1993).

Roshni Rustomji-Kerns

MULATTO. Mixed Ancestry, Writers of. *See* Passing.

MULTICULTURALISM. In the United States, as in Britain and Canada, the recent term *multiculturalism* denotes a concept whose meaning is vigorously contested. Its range of meanings, and more particularly, the authoritative locus of the production of such meanings, continues to be as yet unfixed. Ranging from a valorized notion of a more inclusive society comprising many races, ethnicities, and cultures, to a pejorative projection of cultural diversity that threatens the pure exclusivity of Western civilization, to a construction of an already-achieved pluralist society that risks underestimating the continuing exclusions and inequalities of various racial, gendered, and economic groups—multiculturalism is still in the process of being debated, appropriated, and reappropriated.

The term *multiculturalism* first emerged in the 1980s within the context of debates over university curriculum. In response to arguments by such educational theorists as Allan Bloom, E. D. Hirsch, and William Bennett, who advocated a recentralized study of a singular notion of Western civilization, other educators argued that a diversification of the existing curriculum was necessary not only in order to address the multicultural composition of society in the United States, but also to educate U.S. students about the cultures and civilizations that make up the global society of which the U.S. is only one part. As a consequence of this debate, multiculturalism has become the educational policy rubric under which the demands for greater diversification of the university—of curricula, as well as of faculty and student constituencies—are articulated. To this end, many universities have revised their humanities curricula to include greater attention to the various cultures and social groups who have been historically excluded and marginalized by dominant institutions: African Americans, Chicanos, Latinos, Native Americans, Asian Americans, and women. Literary anthologies—such as the *Heath Anthology of American Literature* (1990) and *New Worlds of Literature* (1989)—reflect the attention given to the greater inclusion of works by women and minority groups.

Thus, multiculturalism, on the level of university policy, is a concept that revises the traditional singular notion of "culture" through a consideration of the many cultures that have historically constituted the United States. However, to the extent that the notion of multiculturalism continues to emphasize culture as the significant terrain for diversification, it remains wedded to a culturalist paradigm that tends to separate culture from material relations, a separation not uncharacteristic of the apparently opposing arguments defending a fixed, autonomous notion of Western culture. In some cases, multiculturalism's emphasis on cultural diversity falls short of considering the different material conditions that have disenfranchised and disaffected particular groups. The enslavement of *African Americans, the forced labor of *Chinese Americans, the internment of *Japanese Americans, *anti-Semitism, *immigration and labor laws discriminating against Chicanos and Latinos, or anti-Arab sentiment during the Gulf War—these very different histories produce material diversities that are inexactly and incompletely represented in the concept of cultural diversity. A multicultural curricula may thematize the pressures that materially diverse immigrant, racial, and ethnic populations bring to the educational sphere, but these pressures are registered only partially and inadequately if only curricular changes reflect cultural diversity while the institution itself remains structurally unchanged; for example, while many universities have added texts by non-Western or female authors to western civilization courses, there are fewer black students attending college today than in 1975. Further, to the extent that multiculturalism is expressed through a pluralist logic that projects American society as a terrain to which all cultures have equal access and on which all are equally represented, it analogizes African Americans, Asian Americans, Native Americans and Chicano/Latinos, suppressing the material differences between these groups, and obscuring the gender, regional, national origin, and economic stratifications within the individual groups.

Outside of the university, representations of multiculturalism have a central place in the popular media, visual arts, and political discourse. From celebratory images of a harmonious multicultural cornucopia, to images of decaying cities engulfed and taken over by Asians, Africans, and Latinos, multiculturalism is represented in both *utopian and dystopian terms. Several narratives about multiculturalism may be read in these popular discourses: developmental ones that, on the one hand, suggest immigrants from Africa, Asia, and Latin America "progress" as they assimilate to mainstream American culture, and on the other, stigmatize those groups who do not "melt," who remain politically and economically outside of the "melting pot"; and nondevelopmental ones, which construct U.S. society as an international postmodern terrain on which all cultures meet, juxtaposing apparently random contrasts between the ancient and the new, the "high" arts of European opera and the "low" arts of graffitti or rap, the Latin and the Asian, the developing worlds and the overdeveloped worlds. While the developmental narrative explicitly privileges the dominant mainstream, the pluralism implicit in the latter narrative also effectively continues to centralize dominant culture by promoting a form of tolerance that leaves the status quo unthreatened—the margins are absorbed into the center, the heterogeneous is domesticated into the homogeneous. Multicultural pluralism levels the unevennesses of racial, ethnic, and immigrant cultures, and erases the exclusions and stratifications.

In this sense, it is the specific differences between racial and ethnic minority groups, and the productive conflicts between these groups and the dominant institutions from which they are disenfranchised, that are often omitted from multicultural representations and narratives. Racial and ethnic groups are often denuded of their specificities. Subject to the leveling operations of both postmodern pastiche and pluralism, African, Asian, and Latino cultures become all equally other, all equally different, all whole without contradiction. Thus, radical theories of social transformation argue that the logic of multiculturalism suppresses tension and contradiction, and overemphasizes resolution and integration; more radical challenges urge that greater attention be given to the profound and urgent gaps, the material inequalities and conflicts, among racial, ethnic, and immigrant groups. The radical critique of multiculturalism suggests that in foregrounding contradiction, U.S. society may begin to address the systemic inequalities built into cultural institutions, economies, and geographies, and that through conflict attention is brought to the process through which these inequalities are obscured by pluralist multiculturalism.

In this sense, multiculturalism may be, for the contemporary period in the United States, a central arena for what Antonio Gramsci called "hegemony," the process by which a ruling group gains "consent" to determine the cultural, ideological, and political character of a state. Multiculturalism may be an ambivalent, contested terrain: on the one hand, multiculturalism provides the means to incorporate racial, ethnic, and class minority groups into the state through the promise of equal participation and representation; and on the other, multiculturalism itself serves as an index of the crisis of a racially hierarchized society, providing the opportunities for counterhegemonic groups to organize and contest that hierarchization.

[See also Biculturalism.]

Lisa Lowe

MURFREE, Mary (1850–1922), Tennessee regionalist, short story writer, and novelist. Born in Murfreesboro, Tennessee, a town named for her great-grandfather, Murfree early enjoyed the privileges of wealth. Her father was a successful lawyer and her mother owned plantations in Tennessee and Mississippi, although the family's fortunes declined after the Civil War. Left permanently lame by an illness at the age of four, Murfree attended boarding school in Philadelphia, which ensured her safety during that war. During the summers her family spent at Beersheba Springs in the Cumberland Mountains, Murfree and her older sister Fanny, her closest companion throughout her life, became acquainted with the mountaineers who would inhabit Mary's regionalist fiction. With her father's encouragement, Murfree began to write during the 1870s, and her first significant publication appeared in the *Atlantic Monthly* in 1878, under the *pseudonym Charles Egbert Craddock. Murfree retained her pseudonym and her male identity (signing her letters "M. N. Murfree") until the spring of 1885, a year after publishing *In the Tennessee Mountains*, a collection of her early stories, to wide acclaim. When Murfree revealed her identity to Thomas Bailey Aldrich in the Boston offices of the *Atlantic*, the event created national publicity; journalists reported that everyone had considered her style to be "masculine."

During this same trip to Boston, Murfree met Annie *Fields and Sarah Orne *Jewett, and she and Fanny paid a visit to Celia Thaxter at the Isles of Shoals. Like *Freeman, Jewett, and other regionalist writers, Murfree presents her characters empathically. However, more than her New England counterparts, Murfree writes with awareness of *class differences. Although her outsiders look at and describe mountaineers in genteel and "literary" language, the mountaineers themselves, with a

voice new to American literature in the 1880s, look back at the outsiders and speak in dialect that, though difficult to decipher, is faithful to the phonetic and stylistic features of southern Appalachian English.

In addition to short stories, Murfree wrote several novels about the Tennessee mountaineers, the best of which include *The Prophet of the Great Smoky Mountains* (1885) and *The "Stranger People's" Country* (1891), as well as historical fiction. Her writing contributed substantially to her family's support. Although she continued to publish as late as 1914, her reputation derives from her work of the 1880s, in particular the mountain fiction she had published as Charles Egbert Craddock. In 1922, she received the degree of Doctor of Letters from the University of the South; later that year she died at home in Murfreesboro.

• Edd Winfield Parks, *Charles Egbert Craddock* (1941). Richard Cary, *Mary N. Murfree* (1967). Nathalia Wright, Introduction to *In the Tennessee Mountains*, by Mary Murfree (1970), pp. 5–33.

Marjorie Pryse

MURRAY, Judith Sargent (1751–1820), American proto-journalist. Sargent was born in 1751 to Gloucester, Massachusetts, seafarers, and educated in the classics with her brother Winthrop. Even as a child she wrote poetry. She was married twice, first to John Stevens, who died in 1786, and in 1788, to the Rev. John Murray, a founder of the Universalist denomination. Thirty-eight years old at the time of her second marriage, she gave birth twice, but only one daughter survived. Her husband's theology made him an enemy of Calvinist clerics and small-town Congregationalist orthodoxy, the narrow predestinarianism Judith Sargent Murray called the very "parent of schism." They served a church in Boston and associated with the nation's leaders in Philadelphia and New York. After her husband's 1815 death, she published *The Life of John Murray, Written by Himself with Continuation by Mrs. Judith Sargent Murray* (1816). She lived until 1820 with her daughter Julia, who had married Mississippian Adam Lewis Bingamon when he was a student at Harvard. Thus, an early Massachusetts writer has her grave, and a recently recovered (1986) archive of some two thousand letters, documents, and poems, in Mississippi. The letterbooks had been preserved because of Murray's explicit hope for a larger future readership, according to Sheila L. Skemp, her biographer.

The need to support an ill husband and child launched Murray's regular public appearance in the *Massachusetts Magazine or Monthly Mu-*

seum from 1792 to 1794, in essays that presented a female version of patriot consciousness for the new "United States of Columbia." To raise more money, she then compiled the essays into three volumes titled *The Gleaner* (1798), to which nearly seven hundred of her fellow citizens, about a third of them women, subscribed. She used her culturally authoritative position as minister's wife to promote the exceptionally liberal ideas of "rationality" in a "Commonwealth of Equality," while defending "order and subordination" in society and promoting "the *appropriate* excellence of my sex." Her particular banner was intellectual independence, for single as well as married women: "The plaudit of my own bosom is of countless worth." A third of *The Gleaner* fictionalizes the "new era in female history." Her style displayed a feminine kind of synthesis, gleaning and constructing her stories and didactic arguments with "a hint from one, an idea from another, a sentence from a third." To expand the "quantity, as well as the quality" of women's contribution, she also wrote plays that were produced in Boston, *Virtue Triumphant* (1795) and *The Traveller Returned* (1796).

Unlike other women of her time, Murray openly stated her desire for "just applause" as "an AMERICAN AUTHOR" (her own block letters) in the early nation. She became part of the authorial stream translating Protestant cultural ideals into fictional argument, making her goal entertainment and enlightenment rather than spiritual threat, allegory rather than sermon. Writing under various noms de plume, including Constantia, Mr. Vergilius, Zephaniah Doubtful, and Penelope Airy, she popularized the new constitution, "the flame of Reason," and high standards for female *education. Amid an extensive repertoire of historical and mythological referents, her imagery is sometimes strikingly feminine, such as her apotheosizing a Massachusetts female farmer as "a complete husbandwoman." She made creative use of the rhetorical image "Columbia" (coined by freed African-American poetess Phillis *Wheatley). While contemporary male writers, and the *Columbian Magazine* itself, attempted to establish a distinctively American iconography around Columbia, Murray feminized it. For her, patriotism and the role of "citizenness" originated from and continuously exalted "the Columbian bosom."

• Murray's papers are held at the Mississippi Department of History and Archives, Jackson, Mississippi. See also Vera Bernadette Field, *Constantia* (1931). Madelon Jacoba, *Prose Writings and Dramas of Judith Sargent Murray: Nurturing a New Republic*, Ph.D. diss., Purdue University, 1987. Sheila L. Skemp, "The Judith Sargent Murray Papers," *Journal of Mississippi History* 8, no. 3 (August 1991): 241–250. Nina S. Baym, Introduction to *The Gleaner*, by Judith Sargent Murray (1992), pp. iii–xx.

Joanna B. Gillespie

MUSICALS. Women writers have made a major collective contribution to the development of the American musical despite a body of evidence initially appearing to suggest otherwise. For in several significant respects, women's roles in the confusing collaborative process of American musical theater (and, in its heyday, the Hollywood musical film) *have* indeed been marginalized.

Until recently, for example, virtually all major composers identified with the development of the Broadway musical have been men (Victor Herbert, George M. Cohan, Sigmund Romberg, Jerome Kern, Irving Berlin, George Gershwin, Cole Porter, Vincent Youmans, Richard Rodgers, Harold Arlen, Leonard Bernstein, Frank Loesser, Jule Styne, Stephen Sondheim, et al.). Moreover, the typical musical spectator or listener rarely bothers to disentangle the vital individual functions of those who preside at a musical's conception—the librettist who writes the book, the lyricist who writes the words to the songs, the composer who writes the music. The natural tendency, even when the libretto and lyrics have been written by others, is to attribute a musical play exclusively to the composer (Kern's *Show Boat;* Bernstein's *Candide;* Herbert's *Naughty Marietta*), or to credit a musical film primarily to the director (Vincente Minnelli's *The Band Wagon;* Bob Fosse's *Cabaret*) or, especially, the star (Fred Astaire and Ginger Rogers's *Swing Time;* Judy Garland's *Wizard of Oz;* Barbra Streisand's *Funny Girl*).

Frequently, the same person writes the libretto and the lyrics. Occasionally, as in the notable examples of Cole Porter and Stephen Sondheim, the same artist writes the music *and* the lyrics. In rare but memorable instances in the American musical's development, a composer and a lyricist/librettist have been declared a tacit pair of equals, their names indelibly linked (Rodgers and Hammerstein; Lerner and Loewe), even when legions of their admirers cannot identify which member of the team wrote the words or which one the music. More often, different people compose the music, write the book, and write the lyrics for a single show—and a significant number of those book and lyric writers have been women. Their names, like those of lyricists and librettists who are men, frequently vanish from public consciousness, implicitly subsumed by repeated proprietary references made casually and exclusively to their shows' composers. A musical's book and lyrics may be memorable but it is usually the name of its melodist that lingers on.

Even in its earliest incarnations, American musical theater occasionally displayed the dark, quasi-tragic subjects it would intermittently embrace in its subsequent development, in landmark musicals as diverse as *Show Boat*, *Porgy and Bess, Carousel, Sweeney Todd*, and *Kiss of the Spider Woman*. In that regard, one of the earliest women musical writers, Anne Julia Hatton (1757?–1796?), wrote the libretto and lyrics for *Tammany; or, The Indian Chief* (1794), a melodramatic defense of the Tammany Society and the Antifederalist cause in a production which bordered on tragic opera—a popular American musical form, as Gerald Bordman notes (*American Musical Theatre: A Chronicle*, 1992), through the nineteenth century.

Other women occasionally participated in the early history of the American musical, among them Olive Logan Sykes (1839?–1909), whose play (with music by various composers) *Newport, or The Swimmer, the Singer and the Cypher* (1879) was produced in New York by the powerful playwright-producer-director Augustin Daly (1838–1899). It was not until the early twentieth century, however, that women emerged as prominent writers for the American musical theater.

Anne Caldwell (1867–1936) began her career as a singer and actor but shifted to play and song writing (initially collaborating on the music as well as the lyrics) both by herself and, until his death in 1914, with her husband James O'Dea. Caldwell co-wrote the libretto for one of Victor Herbert's most innovative and successful musicals, *The Lady of the Slipper* (1912), based on the Cinderella story. She wrote or co-wrote the books and/or lyrics for musicals composed by Jean Schwartz (*When Claudia Smiles*, 1914) and Ivan Caryll (*Chin Chin*, 1914; *Jack O'Lantern*, 1917), and, with P. G. Wodehouse, wrote the lyrics for *The Canary* (1918). One of the few women elected to the songwriters' Hall of Fame, Caldwell began an association with Jerome Kern by providing both book and lyrics for *She's a Good Fellow* (1919), a show praised for its witty book and clever score. Subsequent Kern-Caldwell musicals included *The Night Boat* (1920), *Good Morning Dearie* (1921), *Bunch [sic] and Judy* (1922), featuring Fred and Adele Astaire, *Stepping Stones* (1923), for which Caldwell wrote the lyrics and co-wrote the libretto, and *Criss-Cross* (1926), for which (with Otto Harbach) she wrote the book and lyrics. Also in 1926 with Harbach, she provided the lyrics for *Oh, Please!*, composed by Vincent Youmans. Caldwell wrote two screenplays for silent pictures, one of them, *Marry Me* (1925) based on her own play *The Nest Egg* (1910). She wrote the lyrics for *Three Cheers* (1928), a show starring Will Rogers, then moved to Hollywood to write film lyrics and scenarios.

Rida Johnson Young (1869–1926) also began her career as an actor. Highly prolific, Young wrote more than thirty plays and musical librettos, three novels, and the lyrics to some 500 songs. She collaborated on shows featuring the music of the most successful Broadway composers of her day, including Sigmund Romberg, Victor Herbert, and Rudolf Friml. She wrote the book and lyrics for Herbert's *Naughty Marietta*, one of three Young shows appearing on Broadway in 1910. Probably the most famous of her operetta collaborations, *Naughty Marietta* contained such enduring Herbert-Young songs as "Italian Street Song," "Ah! Sweet Mystery of Life," and "I'm Falling in Love with Someone." Young wrote the book for *The Red Petticoat* (1912), usually credited as the first musical-comedy western, which she adapted from her own non-musical play *Next* (1911). The music was by Jerome Kern, the lyrics by Paul West. *Maytime* (1917), one of two shows on which she collaborated with composer Sigmund Romberg, became her greatest success. Her numerous non-musical plays, now generally forgotten, also enjoyed frequent success; she adapted a number of them for the screen in the early 1920s. Young wrote several original screenplays, one of them derived from the title of her song "Mother Machree" for which she wrote the lyrics. She collaborated again with Victor Herbert on *The Dream Girl* (1924). *Naughty Marietta* (1935) and *Maytime* (1937) were eventually filmed by MGM as vehicles for Jeannette MacDonald and Nelson Eddy.

Dorothy Donnelly (1880–1928), an actor for ten years before she began writing musical librettos, played the title role in the first New York production of George Bernard Shaw's *Candida* (1903) and achieved wide popularity as the star of *Madame X* (1910). She worked as co-librettist on several musicals, traveled abroad to entertain troops in World War I, and returned to write the books and lyrics for Sigmund Romberg's *Blossom Time* (1921) and *The Student Prince* (1924), both extraordinary successes. With Romberg, Donnelly wrote two more musicals, *My Maryland* (1927) and *My Princess* (1927). A significant number of Donnelly-Romberg songs endure, including "Drinking Song," "Golden Days," and "Deep in My Heart, Dear" from *Student Prince*, which was filmed twice (1927, 1954).

Playwright Clare Kummer (1873–1958) wrote numerous books and lyrics for Broadway musicals, sometimes collaborating on the music as well, but she was best known for her non-musical plays. More than twenty of her plays were produced during her thirty-year career. With Guy Bolton, she co-wrote the libretto and some of the lyrics for the Jerome Kern musical *Ninety in the Shade* (1915); and with Sigmund Romberg (music) and Clifford Grey (lyrics) she adapted her farce *Good Gracious, Annabelle!* (1916) into a musical, retitled *Annie Dear* (1924). Kummer also wrote screenplays and several other musicals for Broadway, including *The Three Waltzes* (1937), for which she co-wrote the libretto and lyrics, set to Strauss music.

Fred de Gresac (1867?–1943), a playwright and librettist rarely identified as a woman in musical compendiums, collaborated on several Victor Herbert musicals, including *The Enchantress* (1911) and *Sweethearts* (1913), which contained one of Herbert's finest scores and was subsequently filmed by MGM (1939). Also occasionally cited as Mrs. Victor Maurel, wife of the noted French baritone, de Grasac wrote the libretto for Victor Herbert's operetta *Orange Blossoms* (1922).

Elsie Janis (1889–1956), a major vaudeville and silent film star, wrote the lyrics for Jerome Kern's *Miss Information* (1915), in which she starred. Several of her songs were shifted from that show into Kern's more successful musical *Very Good Eddie*, which premiered later the same year. The author of several books, including *The Big Show* (1919), describing her experiences entertaining American overseas forces during World War I, Janis enjoyed an extensive career as performer, screenwriter, and writer of musical revues in New York and London. The author of the screen adaptation of the George and Ira Gershwin musical *Oh, Kay!* (1928), she wrote the lyrics to the song "Love, Your Magic Spell is Everywhere" for the film *The Trespasser* (1929).

Like Janis and other women cited in this essay, librettist Zelda Sears (1873?–1935) was skilled in various aspects of theater. An actor and director, her books for Broadway musicals frequently outshone the music others composed for them, thus accounting for her relatively obscure status in the development of the form. Among the shows she wrote were *Lady Billy* (1920, music by Harold Levey), *The Clinging Vine* (1922, music by Henry Savage), *The Magic Ring* (1923, music by Harold Levey), and *Lollipop* (1924, music by Vincent Youmans).

Like Dorothy Donnelly, Dorothy Fields (1905–1974) matured in a theater family. Lew Fields, her father, was a vaudeville star and producer; her brothers Herbert (with whom she collaborated on numerous projects) and Joseph a librettist and playwright, respectively. From the late twenties to the early seventies, Dorothy Fields wrote or co-wrote some of the wittiest and most sophisticated lyrics and librettos in the history of the American musical. She wrote the lyrics and composer Jimmy McHugh the music for *Blackbirds of 1928*, which featured the pair's first hit, "I Can't Give You Anything But Love." *Blackbirds*, adapted from a revue she and McHugh wrote for Harlem's Cotton Club, was the first in a series of Broadway revues they would write before leaving for Hollywood in the early thirties to write film music. Among other successful songs from early Fields-McHugh shows was "On the Sunny Side of the Street." With McHugh, Fields wrote songs for both musical and non-musical films. In 1935, the pair teamed memorably with composer Jerome Kern to write the lyrics for new ("Lovely to Look At") and revised ("I Won't Dance") Kern songs especially for the screen version of his hit Broadway musical *Roberta* (1935), featuring Fred Astaire and Ginger Rogers. Alone, she wrote the lyrics for Kern's original film score for *Swing Time* (1936), the most dazzling and enduring of all the Astaire-Rogers musicals. Her lyrics and Kern's music for songs including "A Fine Romance," "Never Gonna Dance," "The Way You Look Tonight" and "Pick Yourself Up" represent one of the finest collaborative achievements in American musical film. Fields wrote the lyrics for another, undervalued Kern film score, *Joy of Living* (1938), and numerous screenplays and lyrics for other films of the 1930s and, later, of the early 1950s.

Back on Broadway, with her brother Herbert, Dorothy Fields wrote the librettos for three Cole Porter musicals (*Let's Face It*, 1941; *Something for the Boys*, 1943; and *Mexican Hayride*, 1944) and the librettos for the stage (1946) and screen (1950) versions of Irving Berlin's *Annie Get Your Gun*. Alone, she wrote the lyrics to Arthur Schwartz's scores for *A Tree Grows in Brooklyn* (1951) and *By the Beautiful Sea* (1954), both starring Shirley Booth. With Herbert Fields, she wrote the librettos for *By the Beautiful Sea* and *Up in Central Park* (1945); she also provided the lyrics for the latter musical's Sigmund Romberg score. Her later contributions to major Broadway musicals included the book and lyrics for *Redhead* (1959, music by Albert Hague) and *Sweet Charity* (1965, music by Cy Coleman), both starring Gwen Verdon. Her last show, *Seesaw* (1973, music by Cy Coleman) was produced a year before her death. Dorothy Fields's associations with Kern, McHugh, and Coleman were especially productive ones.

Betty Comden (b. 1915) and her longtime writing partner Adolph Green have written the books and lyrics for some of the most innovative and acclaimed musical plays and films ever produced. In New York, as two-fifths of a group called The Revuers, Comden and Green wrote and performed songs and sketches in a series of cabaret, radio, and theater shows in the early 1940s. When the group disbanded, they wrote the book and lyrics for the Broadway production of *On the Town* (1944, music by Leonard Bernstein), in which they also acted and which, five years later, they adapted for the screen, their roles now played by others. This early period of their partnership significantly influenced their writing. Comden and Green prepared their own material because The Revuers were initially too poor to hire writers. The episodic nature of the sketch form and their ability to integrate it with satiric songs proved particularly adaptable to the more extended requirements of musical comedy, whose heyday at MGM they helped to shape.

Their magical screenplays for *Singin' in the Rain* (1952) and *The Band Wagon* (1954), for example, emerged from sets of songs they were told to incorporate into each film's storyline, not an uncommon process in the making of a movie musical. Other Comden-Green film musicals include *Good News* (1947), *Take Me Out to the Ballgame* (1949), *The Barkleys of Broadway* (1949, the final Astaire-Rogers film pairing), *It's Always Fair Weather* (1955), and *Bells are Ringing* (1960), adapted from their Broadway hit (1956, music by Jule Styne). They also wrote the screenplay for the non-musical film comedy *Auntie Mame* (1958). Comden and Green's other Broadway work includes lyrics for *Wonderful Town* (1953, music by Leonard Bernstein), Mary Martin's *Peter Pan* (1954, music by Jule Styne and Moose Charlap, other lyrics by Carolyn Leigh), and *The Will Rogers Follies* (1991, music by Cy Coleman); the book for Lauren Bacall's star vehicle, *Applause* (1970, music by Charles Strouse); and the book and lyrics for *On the Twentieth Century* (1978, music by Cy Coleman). The pair have frequently performed their own and others' material, notably in their Obie award-winning revue, *A Party with Betty Comden and Adolph Green*.

Among all musical writers, Comden and Green most successfully exploit the self-reflexivity of American musical comedy in their double-edged delineation of the world of show business. As in *Singin' in the Rain*, *The Band Wagon*, and *Applause* (adapted from the non-musical film *All About Eve*), lead characters in musicals frequently tend to be performers in rehearsal for a musical play or film within the play or film, thus providing "natural" contexts for musical performance. Even when (as in *On the Town*) their main characters are not literally performers, Comden and Green's work is infused with the exhilarating appearance of that "Hey kids, let's put on a show" spontaneity so endemic to the spirit of the classic American musical. Note, for example, the madcap element of carnival embedded in the *Singin' in the Rain* and *Band Wagon* dialogue; or the joyous sense of liberation captured in their lyrics to "New York, New York" as the three sailors disembark for shore leave in *On the Town*. Their deep affection for the world of entertainment is balanced by Comden and Green's satiric pleasure in the industry's absurdities. Their musical screenplays abound with pretentious directors, dollar hungry moguls and egomaniacal stars.

Among the many women who have written only briefly for the American musical, or whose careers as song or libretto writers have been less sustained or prominent than those already cited, several names are especially noteworthy. Vaudeville and Broadway star Nora Bayes (1880–1928) composed songs for her own performances in various shows including "Shine on Harvest Moon," which she wrote for the *Follies of 1908*. Composer Kay Swift (b. 1905) contributed songs (usually collaborating with her lyricist husband Paul James) to a variety of Broadway shows, including the score, her best, to *Fine and Dandy* (1930). June Carroll performed and wrote lyrics, music and sketches for various shows, including the *New Faces* revues produced on Broadway between 1934 and 1968. Playwright and humorist Jean Kerr (b. 1923), best known for her non-musical plays, wrote lyrics and sketches for several revues, including *Touch and Go* (1949). With her husband, drama critic Walter Kerr, she wrote the libretto and lyrics for *Goldilocks* (1958, music by Leroy Anderson), which starred Elaine Stritch. Carolyn Leigh (1926–1983) wrote some of the lyrics for the Mary Martin production of *Peter Pan* (1954) and the lyrics to *Wildcat* (1960, music by Cy Coleman), starring Lucille Ball, and *Little Me* (1962, music by Cy Coleman). Mary Rodgers (b. 1931), daughter of composer Richard Rodgers, has written both music and lyrics for Broadway musicals, including the music for *Once upon a Mattress* (1959, lyrics by Marshall Barer) and *The Mad Show* (1966). Gretchen Cryer (b. 1935) has written the books and lyrics for musicals composed by her collaborator Nancy Ford (b. 1935). Their off-Broadway musicals reflected American social and political issues, including the Vietnam War protest (*Now Is the Time for All Good Men*, 1967) and the struggle for women's equality (*I'm Getting My Act Together and Taking It on the Road*, 1978). Their most successful show to date is the rock opera *The Last Sweet Days of Isaac* (1970).

Composer and lyricist Elizabeth Swados (b. 1951) has worked with some of the most innovative theater directors in the world. With

Andrei Serban she conceived a musical adaptation of Euripides' *Medea*, produced at the off-Broadway experimental theater La Mama in the early 1970s. She toured Africa with Peter Brook's International Theater Group as composer and music director. She later composed music for adaptations of *Electra* and *The Trojan Women* which, with *Medea*, were produced at La Mama under the title *Fragments of a Trilogy*. Swados conceived and performed in the revue *Nightclub Cantata* (1977), a collection of literary pieces set to her original music. *Runaways* (1978), for which she wrote the book, music, and lyrics (and which she also choreographed and directed), and *Dispatches* (1979), the rock musical she adapted from Michael Herr's book on the Vietnam War, were among the works she wrote for Joseph Papp's New York Shakespeare Festival. She composed the music for Garry Trudeau's stage adaptation of *Doonesbury* (1983). Among Swados's numerous other compositions is a song cycle based on Sylvia *Plath's poetry.

Brief but memorable forays into musical theater have been made by playwright Lillian *Hellman (1905–1984, libretto for *Candide*, 1956); Bella Spewack (1899–1990, co-librettist for Cole Porter's *Leave it to Me*, 1938, and *Kiss Me Kate*, 1948); Lueen MacGrath (b. 1914), co-librettist for Porter's *Silk Stockings*, 1955); Anita *Loos (1893–1981, co-librettist, *Gentlemen Prefer Blondes*, 1949, adapted from her novel and play of the same name, 1926); Helen Deutsch (b. 1906, libretto for *Carnival*, 1961; numerous musical and non-musical film screenplays, and lyrics for film songs, including the theme from *Lili*, 1952); Isobel Lennart (1915–1971, lyrics for *Funny Girl*, 1964); Carol Bayer Sager (b. 1947, lyrics for *They're Playing Our Song*, 1979, and for numerous film songs); Carole Hall (b. 1936, music and lyrics for *Best Little Whorehouse in Texas*, 1978); Marilyn Bergman (b. 1929, co-lyricist with Alan Bergman for *Ballroom*, 1978, and for numerous film and television scores, including the Oscar-winning songs "The Way We Were" and "Windmills of Your Mind"); and Sybille Pearson (libretto for *Baby*, 1983).

Recent arrivals on the Broadway musical scene include Pulitzer Prize-winning playwright Marsha *Norman (b. 1947, book and lyrics for *The Secret Garden*, 1991, and *The Red Shoes*, 1993); Susan Birkenhead (lyrics for *Jelly's Last Jam*, 1991); Lucy Simon (music for *The Secret Garden*), and Lynn Ahrens (b. 1948, lyrics for *Once on this Island*, 1990, and *My Favorite Year*, 1992).

In addition to Elsie Janis, Dorothy Fields, and Betty Comden, women with impressive writing credits in film musicals include composer Mabel Wayne (1898–1978), who wrote songs for the earliest sound musicals; Sylvia Fine (1913–1991, music and lyrics for stage revues and films, particularly those starring her husband, Danny Kaye, for whom she wrote special song material); Doris Fisher (b. 1915), who composed songs (with lyrics by Allan Roberts) for a variety of musical and non-musical films of the forties, including "Put the Blame on Mame," sung by Rita Hayworth in *Gilda* (1946); and Ann Ronell (b. 1903), who wrote music and lyrics for numerous films in the thirties and forties and, as a music director, became the first woman to conduct music for film soundtracks.

No compendium of important women writers for Broadway and Hollywood musicals is complete without citation of two women who provided source material for the towering achievements of American musical theater before World War II. *Show Boat* (1927) and *Porgy and Bess* (1935) fulfilled the long-held promise for an intrinsically *American* musical of sweep, depth and texture. Oscar Hammerstein II (book and lyrics) and Jerome Kern (music) convinced a hesitant Edna *Ferber (1887–1968) that, despite its unwieldy structural blend of epic and soap opera, its themes of miscegenation and loss, her novel *Show Boat* (1926) would be appropriate for the Broadway musical stage. Dorothy Heyward (1890–1961) and her husband DuBose Heyward dramatized his novel *Porgy* (1925) for production as a serious, non-musical play, produced in New York by the Theatre Guild in the same season that *Show Boat* opened on Broadway. That play—also entitled *Porgy* (1927)—formed the basis of DuBose Heyward's libretto for *Porgy and Bess* (music by George Gershwin, lyrics by DuBose Heyward and Ira Gershwin). Neither Edna Ferber nor Dorothy Heyward played a direct major role in the writing of the seminal musicals which emerged from their work. But neither *Show Boat* nor *Porgy and Bess* could have been produced as musicals without them.

• Arlene Croce, *The Fred Astaire and Ginger Rogers Book* (1972). Stanley Green, *The World of Musical Comedy*, 4th ed. (1980). Clive Hirschhorn, *The Hollywood Musical* (1981). Ethan Mordden, *The Hollywood Musical* (1981). Cecil Smith and Glenn Litton, *Musical Comedy in America*, 2nd ed. (1981). Ethan Mordden, *Broadway Babies: The People Who Made the American Musical* (1983). Otis L. Guernsey, Jr., ed., *Broadway Song and Dance* (1985). Rick Altman, *The American Film Musical* (1987). Gerald Mast, *Can't Help Singin': The American Musical on Stage and Screen* (1987). Stanley Green, *Broadway Musicals: Show by Show*, 3rd ed. (1990). Gerald Bordman, *American Musical Theatre: A Chronicle*, 2nd ed. (1992). Gerald Bordman, *The Oxford Companion to the American Theatre*, 2nd ed. (1992). Philip Furia, *The Poets of Tin Pan Alley* (1992). Jane Feuer, *The*

Hollywood Musical, 2nd ed. (1993). Virginia L. Grattan, *American Women Songwriters* (1993).

Mark W. Estrin

MYSTERY AND DETECTIVE FICTION. Women writers have been a defining force in the mystery genre since its inception. British women writers (led by Agatha Christie and Dorothy Sayers) dominated the first Golden Age of the mystery (1920–1940), which was followed by the heyday of American male authors of hard-boiled fiction (Raymond Chandler, Dashiell Hammett). American women writers produced significant work in the mystery/detective genre before, during, and after these periods, and, more recently, have been the key figures in creating a New Golden Age of mystery fiction, producing best-selling and critically acclaimed examples of mysteries of all types, from the hard-boiled to the cozy, featuring detectives from the amateur to the professional, from a variety of classes, ethnic backgrounds, and geographic regions.

Among the candidates for first mystery/detective novel by an American woman are Mary Andrews Denison's (1826–1911) *The Mad Hunter* (an 1860 dime novel) and Metta Victoria Fuller Victor's (1831–1886) *The Dead Letter: An American Romance* (1866), which was published under the pseudonym Seeley Regester in *Beadle's Monthly;* both appeared almost two dozen years before Conan Doyle's introduction of Sherlock Holmes in 1887. For many years, the honor of author of the first U.S. mystery/detective novel by a woman was given to Anna Katherine Green (1846–1935) for *The Leavenworth Case: A Lawyer's Story* (1878). The first best-selling mystery by an American woman, it made Green an instant success. When published, it was so praised for its mastery of legal points that the Pennsylvania legislature debated its authorship, considering it "manifestly beyond a woman's powers." Green's novel introduced many elements that would come to be conventional in mystery fiction: a rich old man about to sign a new will, a body in the library, a dignified butler, detailed medical evidence, a coroner's inquest with expert witnesses, a group of suspects, and, included in the text, a diagram of the scene of the crime and a facsimile of a handwritten letter. Green, who eventually wrote thirty-eight mysteries, created two prototypical female detectives, Amelia Butterworth, a spinster sleuth (introduced in *The Affair Next Door,* 1897), and Violet Strange, foremother of Nancy Drew and other girl detectives (introduced in *The Golden Slipper and Other Problems for Violet Strange,* 1915).

Other important early authors include Carolyn Wells (1869–1942) and Mary Roberts

Rinehart (1876–1958). Wells began one of the longest-running detective series in *The Clue* (1909), creating Fleming Stone, who was to appear in a record sixty-one cases; she further influenced the development of the genre with *The Technique of the Mystery Story* (1913). Rinehart initiated the "Had-I-But-Known" mystery with *The Circular Staircase* (1908). A combination of mystery and romance, Rinehart's works have roots in Gothic fiction and feature a closed setting, puzzle clues, suggestions of the supernatural, a young female narrator, and, frequently, a sense of humor. Nurse/detective Miss Pinkerton appears in three Rinehart novels. Mignon G. Eberhart (1899–1948) continued Rinehart's tradition of mixing mystery, romance, suspense, and comedy; her first of sixty novels was *The Patient in Room 18* (1929). She created Susan Dare, a mystery writer/detective. The "Had-I-But-Known" tradition has been carried on most notably by Charlotte Armstrong and Phyllis A. Whitney.

Nancy Drew also got her start early in the century. Begun by Edward Stratemeyer, whose daughter Harriet S. Adams took over after his death in 1930, much of the early series was actually written by Mildred Wirt Benson, who made Nancy independent and capable. Later writers who revised the originals and who are still turning out the *Nancy Drew Files* series have made the teenage detective a pretty figure around whom action happens, taking away much of her cleverness and independent spirit.

Helen McCloy (b. 1904) created the first American psychiatrist detective, Dr. Basil Willing, who first appeared in *Dance of Death* (1938). Beginning in 1946, a twist on the idea of the historical mystery came from Lillian de la Torre (pseudonym of Lillian McCue), with her stories of "Dr. Sam: Johnson, detector of crime and chicane," as narrated by Boswell. The prolific Georgiana Ann Randolph Craig (1908–1957) wrote under the pseudonyms Craig Rice, Michael Venning, and Daphne Sanders, and ghostwrote novels for various celebrities, including Gypsy Rose Lee. Craig was the first woman mystery writer to be featured on the cover of *Time.* She delighted in puns and is often praised for her ability to manage humor without lessening suspense.

The forties through the sixties also saw an increase of the use of region in combination with character. The Cape Cod mysteries of Phoebe Atwood Taylor (1909–1976, pseudonym of Alice Tilton), begun in 1934, featured Asey Mayo, a plainspoken but shrewd jack-of-all-trades. As a New England mystery writer, Taylor is the antecedent to contemporary authors Charlotte Macleod and Lucille Kallen. Dorothy B. Hughes set most of her works in the Southwest and Mexico. They include *The Fallen Sparrow* (1942), *The So Blue Marble* (1940), and *Ride the Pink Horse* (1946), a precursor to contemporary mysteries that examine social problems.

Patricia Highsmith (b. 1921), who published the important lesbian novel *The Price of Salt* (1952) as Claire Morgan, began writing suspense mysteries with a strong sense of the macabre in 1950, with *Strangers on a Train*. Dell Shannon (pseudonym of Elizabeth Linnington), who began publishing in the early 1960s, follows the suave LAPD Lieutenant Luis Mendoza in a series of almost forty fast-paced, semi-hardboiled police procedurals. Linnington also published close to forty more novels under her own name and under the pseudonym Lesley Egan.

Several authors from the 1960s and early 1970s laid the groundwork for the contemporary explosion of mystery fiction by women centering on female detectives. Dorothy Uhnak (b. 1933), a policewoman with the NYPD for fourteen years, in 1964 published *Policewoman: A Young Woman's Initiation into the Realities of Justice*. She followed this with *The Bait* in 1968, which introduces Christie Opara, a policewoman who appears in three novels praised for their depiction of police subculture. In *False Witness* (1981), Uhnak created a female narrator who is an assistant district attorney and a feminist. Lillian O'Donnell introduced a policewoman detective, Norah Mulcahaney, in *The Phone Calls* (1972).

Just as important as these policewoman detectives of the 1970s in heralding the New Golden Age of the 1980s has been Amanda Cross's (pseudonym of Carolyn *Heilbrun, b. 1926) Kate Fansler, an academic sleuth who uses critical techniques to solve mysteries. The Kate Fansler novels are written more or less in the traditional style, but emphasize social conditions as much as the mystery. Marcia Muller, who introduced series private detective Sharon McCone in 1977 in *Edwin of the Iron Shoes*, is cited by many as the instrumental figure in creating a woman as a professional detective. In addition, Muller introduced one of the earliest women ethnic detectives, Elena Oliverez, a museum curator, in *The Tree of Death* (1983).

The 1970s also saw the beginning of the collaboration between Mary J. Latis (an economic analyst) and Martha Henissart (a lawyer) as Emma Lathen, creator of the popular John Putnam Thatcher series. Senior vice president at Sloan Guaranty Trust of Wall Street, Thatcher's cases usually have to do with greed in contemporary sophisticated finance. Dryly humorous with carefully fashioned plots, the Lathen novels tend to depict situations with far-reaching social and political implications.

A major emphasis in mysteries of the New Golden Age is on the professional woman detective. If the protagonist is not a professional private investigator, she is almost always a woman who values her work and her identity—examples include several academics, a lawyer, the head of a nonprofit organization, at least two forensic specialists, a couple of bookstore owners, a caterer, a journalist, an art buyer, several policewomen at various ranks, a meter reader for a power company, and a cleaning woman. Mystery fictions of the New Golden Age cover a geographic range from California to Chicago to New York to various small towns, from farms to inner cities to university campuses to the boardrooms of major corporations. The sleuths are lesbian, heterosexual, white, African-American, Chicana, Polish, Italian, Scotch-Irish, Shoshone, Cherokee, Jewish, Jewish Orthodox, wealthy, poor, struggling, and middle-class. These female detectives are characterized by competence, autonomy, compassion, affiliation, intuition, and, frequently, humor. Most of all, they are independent and determined, and, in many cases, concerned about the larger social issues behind the crimes they investigate.

The seriousness with which these characters take their professions and their sense of justice makes a particularly strong statement in that many of these writers are self-consciously using—and, in the process, rewriting—the conventions of the hard-boiled genre of the mystery, where traditionally women have been portrayed as whores, nymphomaniacs, liars, and betrayers. New Golden Age detectives face down questions as to their right to their professions and interests, resist being taken care of unless the relationship is reciprocal, call on other women for various jobs, and have no illusions at the end of each investigation that the world has been made tidy and just. Mystery novels featuring these new professionals often dramatize gender discrimination, the tension between public and private life, the need for historical consciousness, and the inequities inherent in a capitalist system. These works frequently explore the dynamics of same-sex, multigenerational, and platonic opposite-sex friendships.

Many of the most popular of contemporary women mystery writers are creating series detectives; these include Sara Paretsky's V. I. Warshawski; Sue Grafton's Kinsey Millhone; Margaret Maron's Sigrid Harald and Deborah Knott; Patricia Cornwell's Dr. Kay Scarpetta; Marcia Muller's Sharon McCone; Joan Hess's Arly Hanks; Susan Dunlap's Vejay Haskell, Jill Smith, and Kiernan O'Shaughnessy; Julie Smith's Skip Langdon and Rebecca Schwartz;

with dozens more appearing yearly in the late 1980s and early 1990s. While a specific case will reach closure within one novel, over the course of the series we see the detective and her relationships with various people develop and change. Often the protagonist's past is slowly revealed over the course of several novels.

Less commercially popular (and usually published by small presses) but just as significant are a group of novelists led by M. F. Beal, whose *Angel Dance* (1977), featuring a Chicana lesbian detective, is considered the first self-consciously feminist mystery. In this group are Valerie Miner (*Murder in the English Department*, 1982), Sarah Schulman (*Sophie Horowitz Story*, 1984), Sarah Dreher (the Stoner McTavish series, begun 1985), and Barbara Wilson, whose lesbian detective Pam Nilsen first appeared in *Murder in the Collective* (1984).

In a different vein, Martha Grimes and Elizabeth George have both created extremely popular mystery series set in England. Grimes writes of Inspector Richard Jury and Melrose Plant in mysteries that take the names of actual pubs in the United Kingdom for titles. George writes dark suspense mysteries following the professional and personal lives of Inspector Thomas Lynley and his friends.

Among the general acclaim greeting the New Golden Age of the mystery have been questions about its purported feminism. Kathleen Klein (*The Woman Detective*, 1988) argues that the detective novel is an inherently conservative genre featuring an individualistic protagonist dedicated to the restoration of the status quo, and thus is inevitably at odds with feminism. Others, including Maureen Reddy (*Sisters in Crime: Feminism and the Crime Novel*, 1988) and Carolyn Heilbrun, see these fictions as portraying attempts to work for social justice, validating alternate lifestyles, and implicitly and explicitly questioning gender role expectations, thus projecting a feminist aesthetic.

An outgrowth of the recent boom in mystery fiction by women is the founding of the organization Sisters in Crime (SinC), with the goals of furthering the careers of women in the mystery field, correcting imbalances in the treatment of women writers, and addressing the problem of gratuitous violence toward women in crime fictions. Now a worldwide organization consisting of writers, editors, librarians, literary agents, booksellers, and readers (members do not have to be female), Sisters in Crime began in 1986 with a small breakfast, organized by Sara Paretsky at a Bouchercon Conference. As part of an ongoing study, the first steering committee sent a letter to the *New York Times*, pointing out that in 1985, of the 88 mysteries that the *Times* had reviewed, only 14 (16 per-

cent) were written by women. SinC is also cooperating in a study of violence against women in crime fiction at the University of New Hampshire's Family Research Laboratory. To aid women writers in promoting their work, Sisters in Crime offers a booklet, *Shameless Promotion for Brazen Hussies*.

In addition to those known specifically as authors of genre fiction, many well-known American women authors have published mystery fiction, including Louisa May *Alcott, Mary Wilkins *Freeman, Edith *Wharton, Dorothy *Parker, Edna St. Vincent *Millay, Willa *Cather, Fannie *Hurst, and Joyce Carol *Oates.

• Michele B. Slung, ed., *Crime on Her Mind: Fifteen Stories of Female Sleuths from the Victorian Era to the Forties* (1975). Dilys Winn, *Murderess Ink: The Better Half of the Mystery* (1979). Earl F. Bargainnier, ed., *Ten Women of Mystery* (1981). Jane Bakerman, ed., *And Then There Were Nine . . . More Women of Mystery* (1985). Carolyn Heilbrun, "Keynote Address: Gender and Detective Fiction," in *The Sleuth and the Scholar*, ed. Barbara A. Rader and Howard G. Zettler (1988), pp. 1–8. Victoria Nichols and Susan Thompson, *Silk Stalkings: When Women Write of Murder* (1988). Sara Paretsky, ed., *A Woman's Eye* (1991).

Kathryn West

MYTHS. *This entry consists of three articles that provide readers with essential definitional information about mythology and its presence within representative cultures. Its separate essays are:*

Overview
Greek and Roman Mythological Figures
Native American Mythological Figures

Emphasis throughout is on the literary use made of these myths and the resulting mythological figures.

Overview

Myths are stories and symbols that recur over thousands of years in religion, literature, and the other arts. A mythology is an interrelated set of narratives, while a religion is a mythology in which a specific culture believes. Stories about mythic goddesses and legendary women magicians, adventurers, and warriors empower women by suggesting apatriarchal psychological possibilities for women's lives. They evoke women's inner strengths in response to patterns of behavior that are radically different from the gender norms of twentieth-century American patriarchy.

When feminists first studied myths, they condemned them along with religion as weapons for patriarchy to keep women down. Feminist myth scholars and theologians have subsequently discovered that in myths about *goddesses and powerful women, heroes' reverence for women's intelligence, generativity, military prowess, survival skills, and joyous eroticism can be recovered.

Although in Euro-American culture a classical goddess like Venus/Aphrodite carries both a classical and a contemporary signature of patriarchal distaste for women's sexuality, she also retains preclassical traces to which women and men who are not afraid of women respond positively. Aphrodite/Venus evokes delight in feminine intelligence, prowess, self-sufficiency, and sensuality, qualities that were revered in Sumerian Inanna (c. 2500 B.C.E.) and Assyrian Ishtar (c. 1000 B.B.E.), from whence the Greeks constructed her, along with features of the goddesses of Old Europe (6500–3500 B.C.E.), whose culture the Greeks displaced. Although turn-of-the-century mythologists misinterpreted the many goddesses excavated during the period as manifestations of a single "Great Goddess" (mirroring Judaism and Christianity), feminist myth scholars and theologians posit a polytheism based upon gender complementarity as more typical of the religions monotheism sought to replace.

Even within recent European history, Aphrodite's signature varies according to a period's attitude toward women's sexuality: before 1700 in England, for example, women were considered as sensual as men, though with less control; only later, because of men's desire that their genetic progeny inherit their property, was a sexless chastity featured as normal for women (who might otherwise cuckold their husbands' nests). Although twentieth-century American writers first must work through attitudes left over from the Victorian period, Aphrodite and Venus continue to evoke their delight in women who make their own sexual choices. Similarly, throughout nineteenth- and twentieth-century American women's literature, the Diana/Artemis symbol evokes writers' closeness to the natural world, a quality the goddess retains not only from her preclassical and classical signatures, but also from legends about bands of wild women and solitary woman magicians lurking in the woods, popular for hundred of years in Europe.

These myths, which inspire American writers, are structured on a tension between classical mythology and much more feminist elements from earlier cultural signatures. By a quirk of history, in which the invading Normans brought popular Breton minstrels back to England with them in 1066, English literature retained a rich lode of mythology from the Celtic cultures, which the Anglo-Saxons and Normans had previously displaced. Thus, although few traces of Germanic and Norse mythology survived in English literature, Celtic goddesses like Brih, Annwyn, Rhiannon, and Godiva, and heroines like Queen Guinivere and the Celtic priestess Morgan La Fee remained in English literature.

Although the Christian church and the European ruling classes tried to destroy common people's access to myths and legends that celebrated nature; the human body; and the sexual, medical, and military prowess of women, traces of European pagan culture remained in *folklore, literature, and the arts. After hundreds of years of religious repression and suppression of indigenous cultures by imported classicism, many Europeans and Euro-Americans are unaware of their mythological and their religious heritage.

United States government and ecclesiastical policies for eradicating Native American myths and religions are not only more recent (in the living memory of many present-day Native American's parents and grandparents), but much better documented. In her 1986 book *The Sacred Hoop*, Paula Gunn *Allen theorizes that the United States' Indian policy of the last three centuries has a lot to do with Euro-American patriarchy's need to undercut the subversive power of Indian women. In many Native American theological systems, goddesses created the world and have maintained it ever since. There is Thought Woman of the Keres, Tse che nako, who in the beginning of the world "finished everything, thoughts, and the names of all things. She finished also all the languages." Spider Woman, Corn Woman, Earth Woman, Serpent Woman, First Woman, and Coyote Woman are but a few of her tribal names.

Acknowledgement of women's interwoven spiritual and bodily power underlies many Native American tribal religions:

The tribes see women variously, but they do not question the power of femininity. Sometimes they see women as fearful, sometimes peaceful, sometimes omnipotent and omniscient, but they never portray women as mindless, helpless, simple, or oppressed. And while the women in a given tribe, clan, or band may be all these things, the individual woman is provided with a variety of images of women from the interconnected supernatural, natural, and social worlds she lives in. (*The Sacred Hoop*)

Native American women writers create heroes who seek out goddesses and harmony with nature in quests for both American and tribal identities. Keres Yellow Woman works as an empowering myth for Allen's hero Ephanie in *The Woman Who Owned the Shadows* (1983), to give but one example; and many Native American women fiction writers and poets invoke

Spider Woman and other goddesses to aid them in their quests.

Chicana writers weave similarly complex identities out of their mixed Native American and Hispanic history, which they trace back to the conquistador Cortéz's rape of * La Malinche, "the violated mother" Doña Marinia. Sorrowing mothers are important in Chicana mythology: * La Llorona is a legendary Native American woman, forced to forever wander, weeping, because she killed her children after she found out that her husband had been unfaithful to her. Delving further back into their indigenous background, Chicana writers celebrate the Aztec generative goddess Tonatzin, both in her own name and in the name of the Virgin of Guadalupe, with whom the Roman Catholics syncretized her. Chicana writers build upon a dialectical heritage of Hispanic patriarchy and an indigenous mythology that emphasizes the sexual and generative power of women.

Asian-American women also seek empowerment in ancestral legends and goddess myths: in *The Woman Warrior* (1975), Maxine Hong * Kingston contrasts No Name Woman, driven to death by Chinese patriarchal tradition, to Fa Mu Lan, a legendary * woman warrior. Similarly, in *The Joy Luck Club* (1989), Amy * Tan describes immigrant mothers empowering first-generation Chinese-American daughters through a combination of stories about how they survived Chinese and American patriarchy with legends, like Ying-Ying St. Clair's story about the Moon Lady and her husband, the Master Archer of the Sky.

Native American, Chicana, and Asian-American women live in or have access to their traditional communities. Even Native Americans who were torn from their families and taken to distant boarding schools (where they were abused for speaking their tribal languages or practicing their religions) might eventually get back to their reservations. This was not true for African-Americans, who were abducted from their continent, and then deliberately separated from their tribal and language groups to be sold apart from one another. Given America's history of * slavery, the survival of an African-American culture that retains many African traces is especially remarkable.

African-American women's literature shows women empowered not only by one another, but by myths that present women as strong, holy, intelligent, generative, and inventive. Poets like Gwendolyn * Bennett, Lucille * Clifton, and Nikki * Giovani invoke the Egyptian sphinx as an ancestor-goddess; Audre * Lorde seeks * community and self-empowerment by celebrating the gods and goddesses of her Yoruba

heritage in poems like "October" and "The Winds of Orisha" (*Chosen Poems*, 1982), where she derives power from Oya, Yemanja, and Mother Sebouisa and seeks harmony with male divinities like Oshun and Shango. Toni * Morrison in *Beloved* (1987) and Alice * Walker in *The Temple of My Familiar* (1989) develop heroes whose struggles to survive and flourish within white American patriarchy are forwarded by their grounding in African myth and legend.

Native American writers and religious leaders are deeply offended when Euro-Americans borrow their symbols and myths in their writing, or even try to perform their sacred * rituals. These thoughtless acts of literary and religious colonialism spring from a kind of myth starvation brought about by patriarchy's success in repressing memories of pre-Christian European culture, especially European paganism. Native American, Chicana, African-American, and Asian-American mythologies are attractive because, at a deep level of consciousness, they remind us of lost religions friendly to both women and nature buried within us, almost beyond recall. Once we have recovered these deeply buried Euro-American myths we will be in a better position to teach and write about the many ways myths empower women in a variety of literatures created by our multicultural society.

• Jean Markale, *Women of the Celts*, translated by A. Mygind, C. Hauch and P. Henry (1975). Judith Ochshorn, *The Female Experience and the Nature of the Divine* (1981). Paula Gunn Allen, *The Sacred Hoop: Recovering the Feminine in American Indian Traditions* (1986). Judith Gleason, *Oya: In Praise of the Goddess* (1987). Tey Diana Rebolledo, "Tradition and Methodology—Signatures of Landscape in Chicana Literature," in *The Desert Is No Lady: Southwestern Landscapes in Women's Writing and Art*, ed. Vera Norwood and Janice Monk (1987). Maria Hererra-Sobek and Helena Maria Viramontes, eds., *Chicana Creativity and Criticism: Charting New Frontiers in American Literature* (1988). Marija Gimbutas, *The Language of the Goddess* (1989). Shirley Geok-Lin Lim and Mayumi Tsutakawa, eds., *The Forbidden Stitch: An Asian American Women's Anthology* (1989). Gloria Feman Orenstein, *The Reflowering of the Goddess* (1990). Annis Pratt, *Archetypal Empowerment in Poetry: Medusa, Aphrodite, Artemis, Bears* (1993).

Annis Pratt

Greek and Roman Mythological Figures

In the Western tradition, the myths of Greece and Rome have teased and troubled many thinkers. They have remained an important source of expressive symbols centuries after they ceased to be literally believed. The question of what myths mean is impossible to answer here, and very probably there is no one answer. The founder of psychoanalysis, Sigmund Freud, thought myths represented unconscious psychic forces. His student Carl Jung asserted the existence of a collective unconscious in which patterns of archetypal imagery explained the similarity of myths across cultures. Jung's thesis has been influential, but its *essentialism, or denial of historical and cultural differences, has been challenged by social scientists. At a minimum, we might simply say that mythology offers a symbolic language rooted in a people's oldest traditions.

Although myths always present themselves as immutable, in practice they are always open to new interpretations or, once they have lost their authority, to new variations. Because mythic plots and imagery display the same cultural structures that have shaped a writer's own identity, she can use them to express herself within that culture. She can also use them to talk back to it. By subverting or revising a particular myth, she can assert another vision of the way things are or should be. But, clearly, it is safer to subvert a myth that no longer compels belief. In a Jewish or Christian culture, for example, it is one thing to challenge Zeus, father of the Greek gods, and another to challenge Yahweh, God of the Old Testament.

In the Western tradition, at least since the Renaissance and throughout much of the twentieth century, classical literature has been an important part of liberal education. Familiarity with the mythology of Greece and Rome has long been a mark of learning, albeit sometimes an elitist or exclusionary mark. While access to *education has been historically difficult for women because they were barred from colleges and universities until the founding of schools such as Mount Holyoke in 1837, even in the colonial period some women were able to acquire such learning at home. For example, the poems of Anne *Bradstreet (1612–1672), America's first published poet, are studded with references to Greek and Roman deities, as are those of Phillis *Wheatley (c. 1753–1784), an African-American poet who was once a slave, and whose owners provided her with an education that included Latin writers. Writers as diverse as Edith *Wharton (1862–1937), *H. D., (1886–1961), and Toni *Morrison (b. 1931) have found a rich symbolic language in these stories, a code shared between themselves and their readers.

Classical mythology has been especially important for advocates of women's rights. For example, the early-nineteenth-century feminist Margaret *Fuller (1810–1850) argued that the goddesses of Greece and Rome could serve as ideal images for modern women's own lives and aspirations. In an 1869 *Atlantic* article, "The Greek Goddesses," the influential author Thomas Wentworth Higginson, a champion of

women's writing, asserted that the Judeo-Christian tradition deprived women of divine symbols. Acknowledging that Greece and Rome were patriarchal, he nevertheless applauded them for representing female sources of divinity. Some writers went even further. In *Das Mutterrecht* (1861), German historian J. J. Bachofen posited that Homeric Greece supplanted an older, matriarchal culture, whose mother goddesess survived in figures such as Demeter, goddess of the harvest. Although now disputed by anthropologists, the idea that cultures spring from matriarchal roots has intrigued many feminists, including Elizabeth Cady *Stanton (1815–1902). Whether or not such matriarchies ever existed, contemporary theologians such as Rosemary Radford Ruether, Carol Christ, and Judith Plaskow stress the continuing need for female religious symbolism. It is a need that Greek and Roman mythology has often met.

As for the myths themselves, this article, of course, cannot do justice to their enormous variety. However, a close look at a particular example may demonstrate the continuing vitality of the classical tradition. In many ways, the story of Demeter and Persephone fits the model of the quest myth described by contemporary scholars such as Joseph Campbell. These narratives, found in many cultures around the world, describe a hero's separation from family and society, a journey into the unknown, an encounter with various trials, the receipt of a gift or boon, and a return to society bearing new wisdom. Often the hero, like Ulysses, is male. But classical literature also offers strong female heroes such as Antigone, or, as in the example of Demeter and Persephone, a dual protagonist, a mother and daughter.

Persephone is the daughter of Demeter and Zeus, ruler of the gods. (In Roman mythology, which often simply renamed the older Greek deities, Persephone is Proserpina; Demeter, Ceres; Zeus, Jupiter; and Hades, Pluto.) A girl on the verge of adulthood, Persephone strays from her mother to gather flowers. Suddenly, the earth opens and Hades—Zeus's brother, god of the underworld and the dead—appears in his chariot. He seizes Persephone and descends with her to the underworld. During Demeter's grief-stricken search for her lost daughter, the harvests wither and the earth loses its fertility. Finally, the gods appeal to Zeus, high on Mount Olympus, to intercede, and Hades ultimately agrees to restore Persephone to her mother. However, because she has eaten some pomegranate seeds while in the underworld, Persephone must return to Hades for a third of each year.

With the lost daughter safe in her mother's

embrace, spring returns to the earth. But life now assumes a new cyclical quality, for with Persephone's annual departure, autumn will always come again. And the risen Persephone is no longer a maiden. Fully developed, she presides over all three realms: the heavens, the earth, and the underworld. Through Zeus's decree she is awarded Olympian stature. Through the birth of her child she becomes a mother herself, intimately bound to her own mother and the earth's natural cycles. Finally, through her marriage to Hades, Persephone becomes queen of the dead.

Persephone's is a myth of eternal return, a cyclical vegetation myth of death and rebirth. The ancient Athenians made it the core of the Eleusinian mysteries, one of the classical world's most important initiation rituals. Some modern psychologists, like Erich Neumann, interpreted the myth as the developmental tale of a young girl's sexual awakening, with her abduction and brutal rape by Hades a shattering of the peaceful mother-daughter bond. (In *The Return of Persephone*, first published in 1877, poet Annie *Fields gave that plot an unpatriarchal twist by transforming Hades into a sympathetic husband happy to share his wife's love with her mother.) J. J. Bachofen interpreted the story as an artifact of suppressed matriarchal culture, a feminine creation myth surviving in disguised form, while scholars such as Walter Pater, among others, compared its figures to the Roman Catholic Madonna. In the grieving Virgin's shadows they saw outlines of an older goddess weeping, not for a son, but for a daughter. For some feminists and theologians, now as in the nineteenth century, these goddesses embody a deep respect for the earth and its material processes. Their achievement of a love surpassing death promises transcendence gained within and through the cycles of nature, not in opposition to them. In Sarah Orne *Jewett's *Deephaven* (1877), the thoughts of two young women revolve around this story of divine *mother and daughter. "I knew it all by heart once," one says, "and I am always finding a new meaning in it." Many writers have shared her fascination. In such new meanings old myths live.

• Johann Jacob Bachofen, *Myth, Religion, and Mother Right*, translated by Ralph Manheim (1967). Walter Pater, *Greek Studies* (1894). Edith Hamilton, *Mythology* (1942). Joseph Campbell, *The Hero with a Thousand Faces* (1949). Robert Graves, *The Greek Myths*, 2 vols. (1955). Erich Neumann, *The Great Mother: An Analysis of the Archetype*, translated by Ralph Manheim (1955). Burton Feldman and Robert Richardson, *The Rise of Modern Mythology, 1680–1860* (1972). Mircea Eliade, *Myths, Rites, Symbols: A Mircea Eliade Reader*, edited by Wendell C. Beane and William G. Doty, 2 vols. (1975). William Righter, *Myth and Literature* (1975). K. K. Ruthven, *Myth* (1976). Christine Downing, *The Goddess: Mythological Images of the Feminine* (1982). Alan Dundes, ed., *Sacred Narratives: Readings in the Theory of Myths* (1984). Mark P. D. Morford and Robert Jo Lenardon, *Classical Mythology*, 3rd ed. (1985). Rosemary Radford Reuther, *Womanguides: Readings toward a Feminist Theology* (1985). Martin Bernal, *Black Athena: The Afroasiatic Roots of Classical Civilization*, vol. I (1987). Judith Plaskow and Carol P. Christ, eds., *Weaving the Visions: New Patterns in Feminist Spirituality* (1989). Marilyn Sanders Mobley, *Folk Roots and Mythic Wings in Sarah Orne Jewett and Toni Morrison: The Cultural Function of Narrative* (1991).

Sarah Way Sherman

Native American Mythological Figures

Female deities appear in many origin stories. In the Southwest, the Laguna Pueblo creator is Tse che nako, Thought Woman, who has the power to make whatever she thinks, and who, in early versions of the myth, possesses both male and female characteristics. She creates her sisters, Naotsete and Uretsete, to whom she gives the responsibility for forming the earth and preparing it for human habitation. Nearby Acoma has a similar myth. The genetrix of the Hopi pueblos is Huruing Wuhti, Hard Beings Woman. Though she is of the earth, Hard Beings Woman lives in the heavenly world, where she owns the moon and the stars. Associated with shells, coral, and turquoise, she is responsible for the substance of the earth. She creates, rather than gives birth to, Muingwu, god of crops, and Tuwa'boñtumsi, Sand Altar Woman or Childbirth Water Woman, the goddess of human procreation.

Central to Navajo mythology is Asdzáaaą Nádleehé, Changing Woman or Earth Woman, who is the source and sustenance of all of life on earth; she is especially associated with fertility and fecundity. Her adolescence ceremony was the first and most elaborate ever performed. Impregnated by the sun, she bears the hero twins, Monster Slayer and Child-in-the-water, or, in other versions of the myth, the original members of the basic Navajo clans. In some myths, she is identified with Whiteshell Woman and Turquoise Woman.

The Shawnee of the Southeast also believed that a female deity, called "Our Grandmother," created the universe and everything in it. She watched over all the Shawnee, especially the women. In the origin stories of the Iroquois tribes of the Northeast, a woman also figures prominently. Sky Woman, pregnant in some versions, falls or is pushed by her husband through a hole in the sky to the waters below. To prevent her from drowning, a turtle persuades a series of animals to dive down to the bottom of the waters to get a bit of earth to put on his back. Although several die in the attempt, one animal (often the muskrat) succeeds. The bit of earth expands to become an island, which becomes the land on which Sky Woman and her progeny live.

A number of tribes, such as the Penobscot of the Northeast and the Cherokee of the Southeast, have myths that describe how food, such as corn and beans, originated from the body of a woman who had sacrificed herself for her people. In these myths, a mother of supernatural origin or with supernatural power to produce food instructs her family to kill her and drag her body over the fields so that crops can grow from her body.

An example of a female deity who brings ritual to the tribes is the Oglala Sioux myth of Wohpe, Falling Star, who, during the myth age, falls to earth and lives with the South Wind. After the emergence of the Buffalo Nation from their subterranean homes, she is transformed into Ptehincalasan Win, White Buffalo Calf Woman. During the historical past, she brings to the starving humans the calf pipe, to be used to assure peace between the Sioux and their enemies, and the Seven Sacred Rites. She also instructs them on how to find and kill the buffalo.

Although most of protagonists of Native American trickster stories are male, some, notably among the Hopi, are female. The female tricksters possess the cunning, jealousy, curiosity, insatiable appetites, and unfailing ability to get into the same kinds of trouble as their male counterparts.

A tale that focuses on the adventures of two girls (or one) is the Star-Husband myth, which is widespread on the Plains but found as well among some Woodland tribes of the Midwest and Northeast and as far north as the Yukon. In this myth, the two girls (or sometimes one) wish for a star husband or are lured to a sky world. Lonely for their families, they attempt to return to earth by means of a sky rope. In versions in which there is one heroine, the young pregnant woman dies as a result of falling to earth because the rope was too short. Her child is safely born shortly after she lands. Ojibwa versions often include a segment in which the girls (or girl), after they land in a tree, seduce an animal or give in to his sexual demands to obtain his help in getting down.

Other myths in which a woman temporarily leaves the security of the group are the abduction tales of the Southwest. Among the pueblo tribes, Yellow Woman goes off with a handsome stranger. After becoming pregnant or giving birth, she returns home to bear or rear her children. In the myths of such pueblos as Acoma, Laguna, and Zia, Ko'cinako or Yellow Woman bears the hero or war twins after going off with a stranger.

Spider Woman is a secular figure frequently found in Southwestern myths who is indispensable to the survival of gods and humans alike. She weaves her webs to rescue those in trouble, gives food to the hungry, and provides the information necessary to survive or to conquer enemies. Grandmother Spider also appears in Cherokee mythology. In one story, she steals the sun and brings her people fire. She also teaches them the art of pottery. Native American oral literatures are filled with * grandmother figures who nurture children, especially orphans. Often these children become culture heroes.

An interesting example of a series of myths about young Indian women are the Matchikwewis and Oshkikwe stories told among the Court Oreilles and Lac du Flambeau Ojibwa of Wisconsin. The two are the heroines of the Star-Husband myths told by these tribes. In many of the stories, Matchikwewis, the elder, is often compulsive and greedy, whereas Oshkikwe is better-behaved and more obedient. The stories about them focus on appropriate behavior for Ojibwa women.

Some of the female figures in Native American mythology represent misconduct or evil. A figure who represents both proper and improper sexual conduct in Oglala Sioux mythology is Anukite, Double Face. Originally called Ite, Face, she was the most beautiful of all women until she committed adultery and was transformed into Double Face as punishment. She is synonymous with Sinte Sapela Win, Black-Tailed Deer Woman, because she appears to men in visions, and in the real world, as a deer. An example of an evil female figure among the Navajos is Esdzá Shash Nádleehé, Changing Bear Maiden, a fierce power who embodies evil. She is a contrasting figure to Changing Woman. Among the Colville, one of the most feared evil spirits is Owl Woman, who eats children. As scholars increasingly acknowledge and as this brief survey demonstrates, female figures play complex roles in Native American mythology.

• Gladys A. Reichard, *Navaho Religion* (1950; 2d ed., 1963). Hamilton Tyler, *Pueblo Gods and Myths* (1964). Carolyn Neitheimer, *Daughters of the Earth* (1977). Paula Gunn Allen, *The Sacred Hoop* (1986). Marla N. Powers, *Oglala Women* (1986).

A. LaVonne Brown Ruoff

N

NAMES AND NAMING. Women in the totalitarian world of Gilead in Canadian writer Margaret Atwood's *The Handmaid's Tale* (1985) have lost their names and are known by the names of the men they serve. The novel's narrator, Offred (Of Fred), remembers her former "shining name" as a kind of secret talisman that she never reveals to the reader. After another character, Ofglen, commits suicide, her replacement announces matter-of-factly, "I am Ofglen." This casual acknowledgment of the women's lack of individuality, loss of selfhood, and infinite interchangeability is chilling. Because, in every society, a name is the mark of personhood, this loss of women's identity is horrifying.

And yet, although the loss of women's names in Atwood's novel gives us pause, we take it for granted that in America, every day women gladly give up the surnames they are born with to assume their husbands' names, to exchange the selfhood they have known their entire lives for a new one. Women's identities and names have been fragile in the history of the United States. Contracting their first names to initials, exchanging their surnames for their husbands', or writing under pseudonyms, women's real names have disappeared as if written in invisible ink. Perhaps it should not shock us that fictional women also display this fragility of nomenclature. Names are a means of establishing, defining, and communicating identity. In patriarchy, women have often been robbed of their matrilineage, their names, and their power to name. Indeed, according to Anglo-American convention, a marriageable young nineteenth-century woman was supposed to be virtually invisible, a blank page upon which her husband would inscribe a selfhood based on his desires, and sealed with his name.

The narrator of Charlotte Perkins *Gilman's *The Yellow Wallpaper* (1899) exemplifies the erasure of identity under a husband's control. She is never named, suggesting, first, that she could be any woman, and second, that she could be No Woman. Wishing to "protect" her and to cure her postpartum depression, her physician husband isolates her in a country house and administers the rest cure that surely drives her to a deeper degree of madness. By robbing her of the power to name herself, to tell her story, he exacerbates her illness.

Names have a mythic significance, and to be nameless is to have no identity, no selfhood, no power. "No Name Woman," the first chapter of Maxine Hong *Kingston's autobiographical novel *The Woman Warrior* (1975), is the story of an unnamed woman, the narrator's outcast aunt, a *suicide victim who has lost her name because her extramarital pregnancy (possibly a result of *rape) has brought shame to her family. The narrator's mother tells her the story of her aunt as a warning: "Your father does not want to hear her name. She has never been born." In determining to tell the aunt's tale, the narrator undertakes to free the aunt's wandering ghost, to acknowledge the forgotten woman. In so doing, the narrator acquires the power to name, to tell stories, and thus empowers herself in the process.

If naming oneself or another is an act of empowerment, paradoxically, "unnaming" oneself may become a subversive act of empowerment as well. When Emily *Dickinson wrote "I'm Nobody. Who are you? Are you Nobody, too?" (#288), she was playing with conventions of women's names and identity, turning the lack of a name, a fixed identity, into an excess of possibility. Dickinson refused to be a "blank page." She inscribed her poems and her self by deliberately flaunting namelessness, turning her invisibility into a virtue. In Dickinson's wry assessment, to be named, to be a "Somebody," is a "dreary" life of repetition, stasis, stagnation. To be unnamed is to be unfixed, uncommitted, to be in process, to have room for a larger selfhood, "possibility" (#657). Pamela Annas describes stages of unnaming and renaming in contemporary women's poetry. The woman poet may accept a culturally imposed definition of herself or come to reject that definition (to unname herself) and to redefine or rename herself and the world she perceives. In renaming, she seizes control of language. Dickinson proclaimed the possibilities of unnaming; other writers may express a similar position, or choose to rename themselves.

In "When We Dead Awaken" (1971), Adrienne *Rich wrote: "The very act of naming has been till now a male prerogative. . . . We can begin to see and name and therefore to live afresh." Many women writers use the act of naming as an affirmation of power and possibility for their characters. For example, one fifth of French writer Monique Wittig's novel *Les Guerilleres* (1969) consists of women's names centered on the page in block type in bold capitals, as if to affirm the centrality and significance of asserting women's names.

Like the Anglo-American women's tradition, the African-American tradition also realizes the power of names and the horror of namelessness. Deprived of their birth names, slaves on the middle passage were often invisible to white society until named according to owners' whims. The act of naming oneself was an important self-assertion, a milestone of the journey to freedom and selfhood. Toni *Morrison, drawing upon both an African-American and a woman's tradition, is attuned to the mythical significance of names. Her novel *Sula* (1973) uses names both to satirize major works of black American literature and to juxtapose its characters ironically with Greek and Biblical heroes. Nel, for example, is a reduced form of her mother, Helene, and her shortened name suggests a diminution of Helen of Troy. Sula's grandmother, Eva, evokes the biblical first mother. The novel is an exploration of the meaning of identity, and its heroines, Sula and Nel, assert that true intimacy is achieved when one knows another person's name.

As in the case of the former slaves who defined themselves as free people by changing their names, the choice of names carries a poignant political significance for many African-Americans. In more recent times, the choice of an African name for themselves, rather than a slave name, which derived from white masters, bears witness to their doubled history, their African and American lineages. Such name choices may lead to family tensions. Such is the case when Melanie Browne, a young woman in Gloria Naylor's novel *The Women of Brewster Place* (1982), rejects her middle-class background and takes an African name, Kiswana, as an affirmation of pride in her heritage. Her mother is disturbed by the name change, for she is proud of her more recent family heritage, and named her daughter for an African-American ancestor. She exclaims: "I gave you my grandmother's name, a woman who bore nine children and educated them all, who held off six white men with a shotgun when they tried to drag one of her sons to jail." Similarly, in Alice *Walker's short story "Everyday Use" (1967), Dee changes her name to affiliate with her African ancestry, while her mother and her sister Maggie recognize that they are descendants of Africans who came to America and who are also worthy of memorializing.

Ursula *Le Guin's novel *Always Coming Home* (1985) explores the political significance of naming through a narrator who changes her name repeatedly. Her story is a quest for identity, and her name changes indicate stages in the process. She begins life with a name her mother gives her, North Owl, which attests to the value her mother's society places on nature. She then becomes Terter Ayatyu while traveling with her father. These names, which indicate her social status and her family's patronymic, reveal the patriarchal, hierarchical values of her father's clan. But she finds that her father's society denies written language and personhood to women. Naming herself Woman Coming Home, she recognizes her own power and flees from this inimical culture to return to her mother's country. There she renames herself Stone Telling, and becomes a storyteller, teaching others what she has learned.

A significant moment of Suzy McKee Charnas's novel *Motherlines* (1978) concerns the heroine, Alldera, naming her daughter. Names here represent two antithetical cultures—the oppressive, patriarchal society, the Holdfast, and the matriarchal world of the free Riding Women. In between these two groups are the women who were born into slavery in the Holdfast and are now free. Alldera, like the other women of the Holdfast, was named by men. In contrast, the Riding Women are named by their mothers. They weave self-celebratory songs about their names. When the time comes to name her daughter, Alldera is a center of tension. She is unsure of what to do with such unfamiliar power. When she sees her daughter, freshly cleaned and shining, she reflects on her daughter's ruddy complexion and calls her Roan. By naming her daughter (and, especially, by choosing a name that does not sound like any of the traditional Holdfast names) she asserts her own power and begins a new matrilineage.

The act of naming has been, since ancient times, invested with an often-magical power. To name another or oneself is to assert one's own power and to confirm the unique identity of the one who is named. To know another's name is to gain intimacy and a kind of power. Because patriarchy has often controlled the power of naming, a significant motif in women's writing is the loss and attainment of one's own name. One function of the writer is to assert the power of naming in producing stories. Writers tell us who we are, and this is often a matter of naming. Lucille *Clifton acknowledges this in "the making of poems," claiming that her job is to "give true names." Similarly, Sonia * Sanchez, reflecting on the poet Margaret * Walker, writes that when the poet speaks and reads her poems to the audience, "our names become known to us."

• Odette C. Martin, "Sula," First World (Winter 1977): 35–44. Adrienne Rich, "When We Dead Awaken," in On Lies Secrets and Silence (1979), pp. 33–49. Lucille Clifton, Two-headed Woman (1980). Karen F. Stein, " 'I Didn't Even Know His Name': Names and Naming in Toni Morrison's Sula," Names 26, no. 3 (September 1980): 226–229. Pamela Annas, "A Poetry of Survival: Unnaming and Renaming in the Poetry of Audre Lorde, Pat Parker, Sylvia Plath and Adrienne Rich," Colby Library Quarterly 18, no. 1 (March 1982): 9–25. Kimberly W. Benston, "I yam what I am: the topos of un(naming) in Afro-American literature," in Black Literature and Literary Theory, ed. Henry Louis Gates, Jr. (1984), pp. 151–172. Sonia Sanchez, Homegirls and Handgrenades (1984).

Karen F. Stein

NAQVI, Tahira (b. 1945), short story writer, translator, educator. Tahira Naqvi was born in Abadan, Iran, to Pakistani parents, and moved to Pakistan when she was three years old. She earned a B.A. in English literature from Lahore College, Pakistan (1966), an M.A. in psychology from Government College, Lahore, Pakistan (1968), and an M.S. in education from Western Connecticut State University (1983). She has been an adjunct instructor of English at that campus since 1983, as well as an instructor at the Islamic School of the Islamic Society of greater Danbury. Her short stories and her translations from Urdu have been published in a number of journals, magazines, and anthologies.

Naqvi's works deal with the expatriate and the immigrant experiences of Pakistani-Americans. Her short story "Hiatus" (1989) is about the uneasy compromises between a Pakistani-American woman, the land of her birth, and her family. The protagonist, Fatima, and her family argue endlessly about "the plot," the piece of land that Fatima and her husband had bought in Pakistan before they decided to make America their home. Losing sight of one's previous cultural identity is poignantly revealed when Fatima hears her grandmother's recitation of sacred stories, and the blind prophet's face of the Urdu recitation begins to transform itself in her mind into the face from a Hollywood biblical film: "Charlton Heston's Moses . . . fills Fatima's vision . . . her eyes fill with tears."

"Paths Upon Water" (1990) is told from the point of view of an older woman, a Pakistani mother-in-law, who tries to understand and accept the transformation of her Pakistani-American daughter-in-law and her women friends from traditional wives and mothers into women who explore the freedoms of their lives in America.

One of Naqvi's best and funniest stories is "Thank God for the Jews!" (1991). Cooking and food, which appear in nearly all of her stories, become a central theme in this story. A young Pakistani-American woman panics when an orthodox relative announces a surprise visit. The woman has no "halal" (kosher) meat, and she has not yet mastered the art of cooking fish. She calls on an older, more-experienced Pakistani-American woman for help, and is told that there is no problem whatsoever, and that Jewish kosher meat will be fine. With the deftness of a brilliant cook, Naqvi brings before us our confusing world, in which the politics of love and hate, anger and acceptance cross at odd times and in amazing ways.

Tahira Naqvi's short stories are fascinating in the way they portray characters who travel and live between two cultures, sometimes as visitors, sometimes as residents, but who somehow always courageously and with humor accept their status as expatriates or immigrants.

Roshni Rustomji-Kerns

NARRATIVES. See Captivity Narratives; Exploration Narratives; Slave Narratives; Spiritual Narratives.

NATIVE AMERICAN MYTHOLOGICAL FIGURES. See Myths, article on Native American Mythological Figures.

NATIVE AMERICAN ORAL TRADITIONS. Since European culture considered only literate people civilized, it did not enter the popular consciousness of the early American colonists that American Indian oral traditions might be art. Today we know that people like the Incas developed sophisticated civilizations without literacy, and that the Navajo Night Chant deserves as much scholarly attention as The Odyssey or Beowulf. Problems arise, however, when scholars consider Native American traditions in terms of a pan-Indian worldview, not realizing that of the estimated five hundred languages spoken at the time of European contact, some were as different as Chinese and English, and that tribal identities remain highly distinct today. Nevertheless, these traditions show common themes and forms.

Oral art should not be considered a defunct phenomenon. It continues to live both in and out of American Indian reservations. All of the Native American women authors widely known today incorporate oral traditions into their fiction and poetry, making the fusion of Native and Western elements the most outstanding feature of their writing.

Oral literature, literally a contradiction, refers to what is actually performed in oral *story telling, songs, and *rituals, as well as to the written records of this art, in tribal languages or English, including the pictographic records developed by various tribes. The scholarly interpretation of this complex material is still limited because the cultural roots of surviving tribes were ruthlessly cut off for centuries and because for many tribal languages there are no grammars or dictionaries. Further, Native American women have suffered intensely from having to adjust to Western gender roles, because in many tribes women exercised important ritual and political functions. Through the prevailing strength of their traditions, however, some of these women were able to break into print in the late-nineteenth and early-twentieth century.

The tribes use different categories for their genres. Some distinguish between "true," or sacred, stories and those that are fictional and nonsacred. Others distinguish *myths, which deal with a primal world of animal spirits and monsters, and tales or legends, which describe a culture hero or transformer who orders the world and accomplishes its transition from the mythical age to our historical age of human memory. Creation myths either emphasize the emergence of beings from the underworld, the migration of creatures through a series of worlds, or a "fortunate fall" into the present world. The creating force can be a combination of Sky Father and Earth Mother, a single androgynous being, a culture hero who steals fire, or a creatrix, like Changing Woman, Thought Woman, or Spider Woman, who is never a "fertility goddess," but an intelligent deity bringing mountains, animals, humans, and thought systems into being. The transformer is frequently a trickster in the form of a coyote, raven, or hare, merging divine powers with human folly.

There are some traits that narratives of most tribes have in common: the movement is episodic and circular, not linear; the style and setting are terse and compressed; animals, humans, and deities merge; motives and emotions remain unexplained; sexual matters are described graphically, but are set into the framework of human responsibility; creatures are intimately tied to a landscape; humor and irony are pervasive, but often get lost in translation.

The most important aspect of oral literature is its performance character. It is dialogic and communal. Its origins and goals are ritual, whether it has an educational, historical, medical, or entertaining function. The Word is sacred, an energizing power, a vital enactment of the relationship between humans, deities, and all creation. Recording oral literature on paper does not indicate the gestures, rhythms, silences, tone of voice, encouraging responses from the audience, and the presupposed knowledge of stories by all participants. The teller creatively rearranges inherited formulas, revising and interpreting them with sensitivity for the audience's time and place. Recent translations in lines of poetry re-create some of the artistic flavor of the original.

One of the first Native American women writers was Susette La Flesche (Omaha, 1854–1903). Her oratory astounded New England audiences, but very little of her written work has been identified. Her children's story "Nedawi" (1881), reprinted in Bernd Peyer's *The Singing Spirit* (1989), is interwoven with references to Omaha customs and verbal art.

Life histories and oral poetry by Native women are being discussed in separate essays, but of special interest in our context are those American Indian women who first translated and published tales and legends of their tribes. The Sioux writer *Zitkala-Ša [Gertrude Bonnin] (Sioux, 1876–1938) published *Old Indian Legends* as early as 1901 (reprint, 1985), trying to interest white readers in her tribe's oral heritage. Her later volume, *American Indian Stories* (1921; reprint, 1985), includes autobiographical essays and fiction also referring to oral traditions.

Less interested in fictional presentation than in accurate linguistic and ethnological detail, Ella C. Deloria (Teton Sioux, 1889–1971) published *Dakota Texts* in 1932 (reprint, 1978), a collection of trickster, mythological, and historical tales, painstakingly translated with concern for the storyteller's voice.

A year later, *Mourning Dove [Humishuma] (Okanogan, 1888–1936) published *Coyote Stories* (1933; reprint, 1977, 1990; also published as *Tales of the Okanogans*, ed. Donald Hines, 1976). She had earlier published one of the first known novels by a Native American woman, *Cogewea, The Half-Blood* (1927; reprint, 1981). Her white mentor, Lucullus McWhorter, and an illustrator and editor, Heister Dean Guie, collaborated with her, but *Coyote Stories* is mostly the achievement of Mourning Dove, a poorly educated migrant worker.

All of these writers paved the way for the flowering of Native American women's fiction, beginning in the 1970s. Leslie Marmon *Silko, Paula Gunn *Allen, Louise *Erdrich, and many others have used their oral heritage in unique ways in fiction as well as poetry. Allen also created her feminist literary theory on the basis of woman-centered spiritual traditions. Scholars have commented on surprising similarities between oral Native American and postmodern texts, a fact that facilitates their occasional merging in our time. The two often differ, however. Whenever * postmodernity denies the ethical context of narrative, scholars of Native traditions, like many feminist critics, are countering a "value-free" aestheticism.

[*See also* African-American Oral Tradition; Orality.]

• Michael K. Foster, *From the Earth to Beyond the Sky: An Ethnographic Approach to Four Longhouse Iroquois Speech Events* (1974). Karl Kroeber, ed., *Traditional Literatures of the American Indian: Texts and Interpretations* (1981). Brian Swann, ed., *Smoothing the Ground: Essays on Native American Oral Literature* (1983). Dennis Tedlock, *The Spoken Word and the Work of Interpretation* (1983). Gretchen Bataille and Kathleen Mullen Sands, eds., *American Indian Women Telling Their Lives* (1984). Paula Gunn Allen, *The Sacred Hoop: Recovering the Feminine in American Indian Traditions* (1986). Brian Swann and Arnold Krupat, eds., *Recovering the Word: Essays on Native American Literature* (1987). A. LaVonne Brown Ruoff, *American Indian Literatures: An Introduction, Bibliographic Review, and Selected Bibliography* (1990). Paula Gunn Allen, *Grandmothers of the Light: A Medicine Woman's Sourcebook* (1991). Karl Kroeber, *Retelling/Rereading: The Fate of Storytelling in Modern Times* (1992).

Kristin Herzog

NATIVE AMERICAN PUBLISHING OUTLETS. The Native American press has endured nearly 170 years in the United States as the voice for a native population plagued by devastating foreign diseases, inhuman government removal policies, punitive U.S. military operations, and * assimilation programs designed to wipe out entire tribal cultures. Many of its early writers and editors had to adopt a foreign language and learn a foreign medium (from * oral to printed expression), and overcome extraordinary financial and logistical problems. Despite these obstacles, the Native American press has flourished, and, from its beginning in 1826, Native and non-native American women writers and editors have had a significant role in its development.

The press grew slowly and steadily from 1826 to 1969. James P. Danky and Maureen E. Hady list 1,164 publications by and about Native Americans between 1828 and 1982 (*Native American Periodicals and Newspapers, 1828–1982,* 1984). Nearly half of these date to after 1969. Out of the 1,304 editors listed for the entire period, at least 465 are women (forty-two with Native American surnames; many others are probably Native women with adopted European names).

Although the first tribal newspaper to be published was the *Cherokee Phoenix* of New Echota, Georgia, in 1828, Daniel F. Littlefield and James W. Parins argue that the Native American press began with the *Muzzinyegun,* a literary journal established by Henry Rowe Schoolcraft at Sault Ste. Marie, Michigan, in 1826 (*American Indian and Alaska Native Newspapers and Periodicals, 1826–1924,* 1984). Schoolcraft's Ojibwa wife, Jane, and her mother, Susan, and brother, George Johnston, wrote most of the journal's material. Jane wrote poetry, as well as articles on Ojibwa folklore and history. Another early literary production, established in 1848 and lasting nearly a decade, was *Cherokee Rose Bud* (later *A Wreath of Cherokee Rose Buds*), a school newsletter published irregularly by the Cherokee Female Seminary in Tahlequah, Oklahoma. One of its editors was Nancy E. Hicks (Cherokee), and its focus was Cherokee children, school news, temperance, fiction, and poetry. A small percentage of the writing in *Rose Buds* was in Cherokee.

Following the general trend of the Native American press in the nineteenth and early twentieth centuries, Native and nonnative women editors were often associated with government and mission schools (frequently in the shadow of aggressive programs of acculturation). The *Hallequah,* begun in 1879, was a small school monthly founded by Ida Johnson, Lulu Walker, and Arizona Jackson at the Seneca, Shawnee, and Wyandotte Industrial Boarding School at the Quapaw Agency, Indian Territory; they edited works about various tribal groups, religious issues, and temperance. An early outlet for Creek writers was *Our Monthly,* established in 1870 by a Presbyterian missionary, William S. Robertson, and his daughter, Ann, at the Tullahassee Manual Labor School, Tullahassee Mission, Creek Nation. The *Monthly* was open to Creek students, and was supported by the Creek National Council; it was published in Creek and English. Native women contributed regularly to *Our Monthly;* one such contributor was Angel De Cora (Winnebago), who later became an important illustrator and advocate for Native American art in New York. The *Baconian* was a literary journal published from 1898 to 1907 at Bacone Indian University near Muskogee; it came under the editorship of Mamie Johnson and Laura Edwards in 1903.

In 1898, two Cherokee sisters, Myrta Eddleman Sams and Ora V. Eddleman Reed, emerged as important editors in the development of the Native American press. In that year, Myrta and her husband founded the *Twin Territories* at Muskogee, Creek Nation. Ora edited the newspaper by 1900, and later, with Lura A. Rowland, published it. Ora was an experienced newswoman, having been city editor for her father's *Muskogee Evening Times*. For the *Territories*, Ora contributed fiction under the pen name Mignon Schreiber. She also contributed to "Round the Center Fire of the Wigwam," a department that included Native American stories, poems, *folklore, and *children's literature. In 1900, she was the only female member of the Indian Territory Press Association. From 1905 to 1911, she edited the "Indian Department" of *Sturm's Statehood Magazine*.

One of the longest living Native American periodicals founded by women editors was the *Indian's Friend*, which commenced in Philadelphia in 1888 and continued until 1951. It was a publication of the Women's National Indian Association, founded in 1879 by Amelia S. Quinton and Mary L. Bonney; Quinton was the first editor of the *Friend*, and was assisted by Helen R. Foote. Although largely concerned with Native American rights and education, the *Friend* also published poetry, including pieces by prominent Native American poets E. Pauline *Johnson and Alexander Posey.

As the twentieth century progressed, the proliferation of tribal publications afforded several editorial positions for Native American women. Princess Red Wing edited the *Narragansett Dawn* (1935–1936) for the Narragansett Tribe of Indians, Inc., of Oakland, Rhode Island. The first editors of the *Apache Newsletter* (1952–1956) of San Carlos, Arizona, were Juana Todea and Bernice Green (Kiowa-Apache). Native American women comprise almost all of the editors listed by Littlefield for the *Sioux San Sun* (1951–1973), a monthly publication for the patients at Sioux Sanitarium, U.S. Indian Hospital, Rapid City, South Dakota. The *Smoke Signal* (1947–1978) of Sacramento, a publication of the Federated Indians of California, was highly respected due to its editor, Marie Potts (Maidu). At the American Indian Press Association's first annual convention in 1972, the organization's highest award was named in Potts's honor. "One of the founding members of AIPA," James E. and Sharon M. Murphy write in *Let My People Know, American Indian Journalism, 1828–1978* (1981), "she was considered the dean of Indian journalists." Women editors figured in the history of many other Native American tribal periodicals, including the *Cherokee Nation News*, the *Cherokee Times*, *City Smoke Signals* (Sioux), the *Jicarilla Chieftain* (Apache), and *Si Wong Geh* (Seneca).

Since the 1960s, Native American periodicals have increased dramatically. Littlefield notes that the increase in the 1960s was directly related to the availability of Great Society funds. He also observes a general change in the content of these publications, from mission school assimilation periodicals to more politically active ones that reflect the Native American nationalist movement. "From 1921 to 1970 probably no more than 600 titles were established, most in the 1960s," Littlefield writes. "During the period under consideration here [1971–1985], 1,000 or more were begun." More than outlets for writing by Native American women, some publications made women's issues a focus, such as the *Newsletter* of the Lakota Women's Association (South Dakota), the *Newsletter* of Native Women's Program Development, Inc. (Texas), the *Squaw's Message* of the Sisterhood of American Indians (Washington), and the *Indian News* of United Indian Women, Inc. (Oregon). Several recent publications in the Native American press have had women editors or assistants, including *Akwekon* (New York), the *American Indian Culture and Research Journal* (UCLA), *ATLATL Newsletter* (New Mexico), *Bishinik* (Oklahoma), *Cherokee Advocate* (Oklahoma), the *Circle* (Massachusetts; Louise *Erdrich [Chippewa] was editor in 1979), *Indian Family Defense* (New York), *Hopi Tribal News* (Arizona), *Native Peoples Magazine* (Arizona), *Ni-Mah-Mi-Kwa-Zoo-Min* (Chippewa; Minnesota), and *Studies in American Indian Literatures* (Arizona).

Book publishing, now a widespread and extremely important outlet for Native American woman authors, is a recent development. With a hostile mainstream press, Native American women had to overcome many odds to publish a book (as noted by Paula Gunn *Allen [Laguna Pueblo] in the introduction to *Spider Woman's Granddaughters*, 1989). Sarah *Winnemucca Hopkins (Piute) had to contribute to the printing costs of her *Life Among the Piutes: Their Wrongs and Claims* (1883), as did Hum-Ishu-Ma, or *Mourning Dove (Okanogan), for her landmark novel *Cogewea, The Half Blood* (1927). *Tributes to a Vanishing Race* (1916), an early anthology that includes the work of Irene Campbell Beaulieu (Sioux) and To-wam-pah, or Kathleen Woodward (Osage), was privately printed. Josephine Barnaby (Omaha) published her *The Present Condition of My People* through the American Missionary Association (1880). Some did gain access to the mainstream press, like *Zitkala-Ša, or Gertrude Simmons Bonnin (Yankton Sioux), who had articles in *Harper's* and *Atlantic* and publishing experience as editor of the *Indian Magazine;* she found commercial publishers for her works, *Old Indian Legends* (1901) and *American Indian Stories* (1921).

Particularly in the last two decades, Native American women have had increasing access to Native, university, and mainstream presses.

There are at least a dozen small presses owned and operated by Native Americans, such as the Choctaw Heritage Press (Mississippi) and Indian Country Communications (Ojibwa; Wisconsin). Important college presses include the Navajo Community College Press (Arizona; Anna Lee Walters [Pawnee/Otoe], editor), and the university presses of Nebraska, Oklahoma, and Washington. Perhaps the most important development in the distribution of books is the Native American Authors Distribution Project, begun in 1980 and overseen by Joseph Bruchac III (Abenaki) of the Greenfield Review Press, New York. Its spring 1992 book list includes over 250 titles from more than eighty publishers, including works by over seventy Native American women authors and editors.

• Angeline Jacobson, *Contemporary Native American Literature: A Selected and Partially Annotated Bibliography* (1977). Tom Colonnese and Louis Owens, *American Indian Novelists: An Annotated Critical Bibliography* (1985). Gregory W. Frazier, *The American Indian Index* (1985). Andrew Wiget, *Native American Literature* (1985). A. LaVonne Brown Ruoff, *American Indian Literatures: An Introduction, Bibliographic Review, and Selected Bibliography* (1990).

Brian E. Railsback

NATIVE AMERICAN WRITING. *This entry consists of one overview essay that addresses basic, theoretical issues of concern to Native American writing and then four essays that focus on specific genres of Native American writing:*

Overview
Drama
Fiction
Nonfiction
Song and Poetry

For further information, please refer to Native American Publishing Outlets; American Indian Rights Movement.

Overview

Leslie Marmon * Silko writes, in an essay on "Language and Literature from a Pueblo Indian Perspective" (included in *Critical Fictions: The Politics of Imaginative Writing*, 1991), of a story told among the Pueblos about how Thought Woman and her sisters thought of everything in the world, and in doing so, created it. It is through the telling of stories, stories of Thought Woman and countless others, Silko explains, that Laguna Pueblo people construct their identities as Lagunas and bind one another together through time, from generation to generation. Silko also writes of Thought Woman thinking of, naming, and creating the universe in the poem that introduces her novel *Ceremony* (1977). In a volume of short stories, *The Power*

of Horses (1990), Crow Creek Sioux author Elizabeth * Cook-Lynn writes about a grandmother who tells a child about *Mahpiyato*, also a creator who is female. Paula Gunn * Allen, in books of literary criticism such as *The Sacred Hoop* (1986), and Rayna Green, in the introduction to a collection of contemporary Native American poetry and fiction, *That's What She Said* (1984), also write of tribal stories that center around a woman: Thought Woman, * Spider Woman, Grandmother Spider, White Buffalo Calf Woman. . . . Such stories demonstrate that although written literature may be a category that has accompanied colonial conquest, a conquest still very recent by Native American standards, Native women are strangers neither to story telling nor to the power of language.

Silko's essay urges us to reconsider the boundaries between categories such as "language," "literature," and * "story telling." It is not surprising that Native American writing has often encouraged a reexamination of categories and definitions. The very term *Native American* is problematic in that it obscures tremendous differences—differences of language, belief, history—among the hundreds of tribes that it presumes to encompass. Native American, Indian, Native—all these terms have emerged from European colonization. Note that Silko writes of "Language and Literature from a Pueblo Indian Perspective," and does not attempt to describe a generic "Indian" or "Native American" viewpoint.

Because Native American writing has a relatively recent history, many scholars have questioned whether only written texts should be considered literature. Should traditional tribal stories be considered oral literature? If so, what counts as traditional? Silko argues that family stories of relatively recent origin may be as important in Pueblo experiences of language as those of greater antiquity, and that the sort of story telling that goes on while one is, say, lacing a child's shoes is as important as the language spoken within a formal ceremony. Another problem of definition: If stories considered oral literature are told to someone who writes them down, translates, and edits them, what are they then? Who is the author? How much has been changed or lost in the process of translating, editing, and organizing?

Such questions become especially important in considerations of Native American * autobiography. According to H. David Brumble (*American Indian Autobiography*, 1988), approximately six hundred Native American autobiographical texts have been published; 83 percent of these texts were narrated, in most cases to a non-Indian. In the early twentieth century, for example, Maxidiwiac told stories about her life as a Hidatsa farmer to Gilbert Wilson, who published her narratives in a number of different texts, including *Waheenee: An Indian Girl's Story, Told by Herself* (1921). In 1932, Pretty Shield told her life story to author Frank Linderman, resulting in *Pretty Shield, Medicine Woman of the Crows* (1932). Anthropologist Ruth Underhill interviewed Maria Chona about her life story and produced *The Autobiography of a Papago Woman* (1936). In the late 1930s and early 1940s, anthropologist Elizabeth Colson collected the stories eventually published as *Autobiographies of Three Pomo Women* (1974). More recently, Mary Brave Bird (formerly Mary *Crow Dog) has published an autobiographical best-seller, *Lakota Woman* (1990), and its sequel, *Ohitka Woman* (1993), "with" Richard Erdoes. In many narrated autobiographies, much editing, translating, reordering, and even adding has gone on before publication. Readers are often left ignorant of what questions were asked, the historical context in which the story was told, as well as the relationship between the writer and the narrator. According to some scholars, many narrated autobiographies have been so influenced by the writer that they should more properly be considered biographies. Greg Sarris provides a brief, insightful overview of these issues and interesting critiques of recent scholarship in a discussion of *Autobiographies of Three Pomo Women* in his book *Keeping Slug Woman Alive: A Holistic Approach to American Indian Texts* (1993).

In response to concerns about how much may have been changed or lost in narrated autobiographies, some scholars have begun to produce autobiographical narratives with a minimum of editing, publishing the stories in the order in which they are told and in a form designed to reproduce aspects of their oral telling, sometimes accompanying the texts with a more careful explanation of the context of their production and the relationship between narrator and writer. An example is *Shandaa: In My Lifetime* (1981), narrated by an Athabaskan woman, Belle Herbert, and written in Athabaskan and English on facing pages.

Recent discussion of the problems inherent in narrated autobiographies have encouraged readers to question not just how much recorders and editors have interfered with narratives, but also the ways in which an Indian narrator may have tailored a story for a particular sort of audience, usually a non-Indian one. Many Native American women have narrated their autobiographies to recorders who were not only of a different ethnicity, but also of another gender, leaving readers to wonder how those differences may have influenced what was told and how. Of course, any account, oral or written, is but one subjective and partial account, produced in a specific historical context, with choices made about what to include and exclude. Even without the mediation of a recorder and editor, texts authored by Native women have often been produced for non-Indian readers, and it is useful to consider their historical context and the motivations behind them.

Many of the earliest Native American women writers wrote as a way of attempting to counteract negative perceptions of Native people held by non-Indians and to generate support for Indian political struggles. In 1883, for example, when Sarah *Winnemucca published *Life among the Paiutes*, Native American lands were widely considered by Euro-Americans to be a vacant wilderness, and Native people were considered savages—less than, or hardly human. Winnemucca therefore attempted to persuade Euro-American readers that Native people had rights to land and justice. In her book, Winnemucca combines autobiography with tribal history and a history of Paiute and white relations in the mid-nineteenth century. Born in an area now part of Nevada, Winnemucca was a Paiute woman of many talents and much influence: in addition to writing, she acted on stage, worked as a liaison between the army and militant bands of Paiutes and Bannocks, and went on public speaking tours attempting to dispel popular stereotypes of Indians and to educate non-Indians about her people and the injustices of government policies.

The first known novel published by a Native American woman, Sophia Alice *Callahan's *Wynema: A Child of the Forest* (1891), also represented a protest against government policy regarding Native Americans. Callahan, a well-educated Creek of mixed Indian and white ancestry from Oklahoma, focused her outrage particularly on the United States government's massacre of Native Americans at Wounded Knee in 1890. Her novel also includes mention of Native women's struggles for political equality and critical discussions of the allotment policy, whereby the government broke up communally owned tribal lands and allotted plots to individual owners. Callahan's novel, unfortunately, has only recently acquired scholarly attention and currently is not widely available; A. Lavonne Brown Ruoff provides a useful synopsis in her article "Justice for Indians and Women: The Protest Fiction of Alice Callahan and Pauline Johnson" (*World Literature Today*, Spring 1992).

The allotment policy was part of the United States government's plan of coercing Native American assimilation. At the turn of the twentieth century, many policymakers and Christian missionaries believed that the only way Indian people could survive was if they gave up everything that distinguished them from the Euro-American population—including their homelands, languages, religious practices, and styles of dress. In addition to banning Indian ceremonial dancing, the government attempted to coerce assimilation through the allotment of privately owned land and through education, particularly education at off-reservation boarding schools, where children were often forbidden to speak in any language other than English. For Native American women, boarding school education tended to stress domestic skills such as cooking, ironing, and sewing—an education that prepared them for only the most menial sorts of jobs and often served to alienate them from their own communities.

Nevertheless, some Native American women managed to use the literacy they learned in mission and boarding schools as a tool of political empowerment. In the early nineteenth century, many Native women began finding a forum for their writing in newspapers designed for Native readers, such as the *Cherokee Phoenix*, which began publishing in 1828. Many of these early writers, such as Ora Eddeman, a Cherokee woman, who at twenty years of age became editor of *Twin Territories: The Indian Magazine of Oklahoma*, are both indexed and profiled in *A Biobibliography of Native American Writers, 1772–1924*, by Daniel Littlefield and James Parins (1985).

In the 1920s, Gertrude Simmons Bonnin, a Yankton Sioux, attempted to win non-Indian support for Indian people through her writing, reaching a wide audience of non-Indian readers. Bonnin was educated by Quaker missionaries and attended Earlham College and went on to teach at the Carlisle Indian School in Pennsylvania. Under the pen name *Zitkala-Ša, Bonnin wrote short stories, essays, and poetry. Bonnin published autobiographical essays in the *Atlantic Monthly* and published a collection of essays and short stories, *American Indian Stories* (1921), as well as a collection of traditional stories, *Old Indian Legends* (1901). From 1902 to 1919, Bonnin also edited *American Indian Magazine*. Although a passionate crusader for Indian political rights, Bonnin advocated assimilation and supported government efforts to suppress the peyote religion.

During the same period, Christine Quintasket devoted her writing career to dispelling stereotypes common among non-Indians, her particular target being the assumption that Indians were stoic and unfeeling. In 1927, Quintasket, also known as Crystal Galler and Humishuma, published her novel *Cogewea, the Half-Blood: A Depiction of the Great Montana Cattle Range* (1927) under her pen name,

*Mourning Dove. Quintasket, from the Colville Confederated Tribes of eastern Washington State, also published a collection of Salishan tribal tales entitled *Coyote Stories* (1933). Like Sarah Winnemucca and Gertrude Bonnin, Quintasket was active in politics and public speaking; her writing was often done in evenings, after days of migrant labor. Her unfinished autobiography, *Mourning Dove*, has recently been edited and published, with an informative introduction (including much useful information about the editing process), by Jay Miller (1990).

It was also during the 1920s that Ella Deloria, a Sioux, was trained by Franz Boas as an anthropologist and linguist. Deloria's work also attempted to convince Euro-Americans of Native people's humanity. She was particularly concerned that white Americans, including missionaries and educators, were ignorant of the complexity and richness of tribal life and that they assumed that Indians had nothing to lose in the process of coercive assimilation; Euro-American ways, it was thought, could be poured into Indian lives as if into a vacuum. After beginning her college education at Oberlin College, Deloria enrolled at Columbia Teachers College in Manhattan, where Boas, the leading figure in American anthropology at the time, hired her to translate ethnographic texts from Lakota into English. Throughout the 1920s and 1930s, in addition to working as a teacher and health educator, Deloria continued to work with Boas and with anthropologist Ruth Benedict, collecting ethnographic information (including many women's autobiographies), translating numerous Sioux texts, and producing a Sioux grammar and a Sioux-English dictionary. In 1929, Deloria published an article on the Sun Dance in the *Journal of American Folklore*, and several years later published a bilingual collection of Sioux stories, *Dakota Texts* (1932). Many of the stories she gathered have only recently been published in the collection *Deer Women and Elk Men* (1992). Although Deloria was committed to painstaking, relatively technical, detailed, and "objective" ethnographic scholarship and linguistic analysis—work greatly enhanced, no doubt, by her native facility with the language—in 1944, Deloria used some of the material she had gathered in a book written for a more popular audience, *Speaking of Indians*. Her remarkable novel *Waterlily*, written in the early 1940s but only published in 1988, also attempted to make ethnographic detail much more widely accessible. *Waterlily*, a narrative that is constructed from older ethnographic documents, autobiographical interviews, as well as Deloria's own experience, presents a woman's perspective of Sioux life in the nineteenth century. Carrying on the tradition, Ella Deloria's niece, Bea Medicine, is now a well-known anthropologist who also writes poetry.

Partly as a result of the influence of Native American writers and educators such as Gertrude Bonnin and Ella Deloria, in the early 1930s, government policy regarding Native Americans began to move toward supporting tribal self-determination. The non-Indian population also began developing greater appreciation of anything they could consider "Indian" in art and literature. The Indian "New Deal" thus included a shift away from the earlier policies of assimilation, more often tolerating, even encouraging, the expression of tribal identities. Still, many Native Americans battled poverty and prejudice and fought to protect their land and basic political and civil liberties. In 1973, such struggles culminated in the American Indian Movement's sixty-seven-day standoff with government soldiers at Wounded Knee, South Dakota.

Recent writing by Native American women has continued to attempt to educate non-Indians and to combat stereotypes—whether romantic or derogatory. While earlier writers such as Sarah Winnemucca and Christine Quintasket fought to convince non-Indian audiences of Native people's humanity (an aim perhaps best summed up by the title of Ruth Muskrat's 1947 book, *Indians Are People, Too*), contemporary writers often struggle against the common assumption that Native Americans belong in the past rather than in the modern world. Thus many Native American writers attempt to convey the way that Native Americans continue to maintain distinct tribal identities and connections to the past, while moving toward the twenty-first century. Louise *Erdrich, in her short story "The Bingo Van" (included in *Talking Leaves: Contemporary Native American Short Stories*, 1991), provides the example of a young Native American who maintains a distinctly Chippewa identity, even while living surrounded by non-Indians, in a world of consumers always yearning for new possessions. After Erdrich's protagonist wins a van playing bingo, a group of non-Indian youths attempt to forcibly tattoo him with an image of the state of South Dakota; it is not the tatoo that her character objects to, but the square, straight-edged shape of the state—a shape, the narrator explains, that will not do for a Chippewa, who perceives squareness as an unnatural form.

In addition to bridging boundaries between past and present, the traditional and the modern, Native American women have also begun to express a more explicit feminism in their writing and are specifically challenging predominant assumptions about Native women—both past and present. Feminist perspectives can be found, for example, in a number of edited collections: Paula Gunn *Allen's *Spider Woman's Granddaughters: Traditional Tales and Contemporary Writing by Native North American Women* (1989), Beth Brandt's *A Gathering of Spirit* (1988), and Jane Katz's *I Am the Fire of Time: Voices of Native American Women* (1977).

As writers, Native American women continue to represent not just themselves, but also their tribal communities to non-Indian readers. Such aims have encouraged a blurring of conventional boundaries and a mixing of genres of fiction, nonfiction, tribal stories and histories, myths, poetry, and autobiography. Helen Slwooko Carius, in *Sevukakmet: Ways of Life on St. Lawrence River* (1979), juxtaposes a history of the Sevukakmet Eskimo with her own personal history and illustrations. Leslie Marmon Silko's *Storyteller* (1984) presents a discontinuous autobiography constructed of fragments of stories, both old and more recent, personal and tribal, as they might be heard among Lagunas, along with memories, family photographs, and short stories. Many other Native American women work in and between different genres: Salish-Kootenai painter Jaune Quick-to-See-Smith and Santa Clara potter Nora Naranjo-Morse both write poetry; Wendy Rose, Hopi/Miwok, has worked as an anthropologist as well as a poet; Joy Harjo, Creek, is a filmmaker as well as a highly acclaimed poet; Louise Erdrich, Turtle Mountain Chippewa, has published numerous novels as well as short stories and poetry.

Native American women continue to publish in newspapers and periodicals geared to Indian as well as non-Indian audiences; *Akwesasne Notes*, which began in 1969, is one of the best known and widely distributed; *Indigenous Woman*, the official publication of the Indigenous Women's Association, focuses especially on issues pertaining to Native American women. Articles by and about Native American women writers frequently appear in a number of scholarly journals devoted to Native American issues, including *Wicaza sa Review*, edited by Sioux author Elizabeth Cook-Lynn, the *American Indian Culture and Research Journal*, published through the American Indian Studies Center at the University of California at Los Angeles, and *American Indian Quarterly*, produced through the Native American Studies Program at the University of California at Berkeley.

[See also American Indian Rights Movement.]

• Gretchen Bataille and Kathleen Sands, *American Indian Women: Telling Their Lives* (1981). Kenneth Lincoln, *Native American Renaissance* (1983): Robert A. Trennert, "Educating Indian Girls at Nonreservation Boarding Schools, 1878–1920," in *The American Indian: Past and Present*, edited by Roger L. Nichols (1986), pp. 218–231. Brian Swann and Arnold Krupat, eds., *I Tell You Now: Autobiographical Essays by Native American Writers* (1987). A. LaVonne Brown Ruoff, "Three Nineteenth-Century American Indian Autobiographers" and "American Indian Literature," in *Redefining American Literary History*, edited by A. LaVonne Brown Ruoff and Jerry W. Ward, Jr. (1990), pp. 251–269, 327–352. *World Literature Today*, special issue devoted to "From This World: Contemporary American Indian Literature," 66, no. 2 (Spring 1992).

Molly H. Mullin

Drama

As with many categories having to do with literary approaches to indigenous cultural production, "Drama by Native American Women" is a complicated and often inappropriate label. Native scholar Paula Gunn *Allen (Laguna Pueblo and Sioux) is quick to point out the problems of European-American studies of native peoples in her book *The Sacred Hoop: Recovering the Feminine in American Indian Traditions*, where she states, "The study of non-Western literature poses a problem for Western readers who naturally tend to see alien literature in terms that are familiar to them, however irrelevant those terms may be to the literature under consideration." The European term *drama* is a perfect example of this, and yet, without some such formal grouping, much important work by and about Native American women might be either overlooked or silenced.

Drama will be used in this essay to refer to two major bodies of work, which may sometimes have elements in common, but are also quite distinct. The first group is a huge complex of ceremonies and performances, many of which have a sacred nature, and the second will focus on dramatic works written by Native American women that participate in a European theatrical tradition. The limited bibliographic materials presented here are merely one route into a wealth of tribally specific materials in literary, linguistic, historical, and anthropological disciplines, all of which address the notion of "drama" in some way.

In A. LaVonne Brown Ruoff's *American Indian Literatures: An Introduction, Bibliographic Review, and Selected Bibliography*, Ruoff defines ritual drama as "a very sacred form of oral literature that contains both song and narrative and sometimes includes oratory as well." She also points out that "Although *ritual drama* is the current term most commonly used by scholars to denote ceremonial complexes, tribes usually use the terms *chants* or *chantways, ceremonies,* or *rituals.*" While these dramas are frequently analyzed in terms of European-American dramatic conventions such as actors, audience, costumes, narrative, and so forth, they are obviously part of a very different spiritual or sacred tradition, whose purpose is highly culturally specific. Jeffrey Huntsman writes in his article "Native American Theatre," that "the moment of dramatic event is one of extraordinary significance that envelopes everyone concerned, blurring the distinction, so crucial to Euro-American drama, between actor and audience," and insists that in Native American drama "the fundamental embedding of dramatic elements, whatever their particular character, in the metaphysical substratum of the society gives them an immediate power and importance that Western (in the sense of Euro-American) drama cannot command."

Recently, a number of scholars have expanded the horizon of their studies from so-called ritual drama to anything that might be seen as "performative," thus including a range of storytelling practices that might have been seen as more secular than sacred. The term *performative* is also potentially useful in focusing not just on the text produced, but on the context or the entire event, thus allowing aspects such as healing or social regulation to form part of the discussion.

Pauline *Johnson was one of the most prolific nineteenth century Native writers and performers. Born in 1861 on the Six Nations Reserve near Brantford, Ontario, her father was the prominent Mohawk leader George Henry Martin and her mother, Emily Susanna Howells, was a cousin of American magazine editor and writer William Dean Howells. Also known as Tekahionwake, or Double Wampum, Johnson is now known primarily as a poet and writer—the author of a large number of short stories, many of which were published in children's magazines—but she spent much of her life as a stage performer, reciting her works and acting in dramatic skits throughout the United States, Canada, and England. While her work may now seem sentimental and her flamboyant costumes may seem to play to white stereotypes of the "Indian maiden," some of her work, particularly the short story "A Red Girl's Reasoning," is both sophisticated and subtle in its analyses of race and culture. Extremely popular as a stage performer in Canada, she gave 125 performances in the 1893–1894 season alone.

Another popular nineteenth century writer was *Zitkala-Ša, or Gertrude Simmons Bonnin (of Sioux descent). In addition to her widely published fiction, often based on her own experiences of cross-cultural alienation, and her involvement in a wide range of Indian activism (including vigorous support of Native citizenship), Bonnin wrote one piece that falls into the category of drama, an opera entitled *Sun Dance*, written in 1913. Bonnin had a long history as a musician. She was, in fact, a talented violinist. After leaving the Pine Ridge Reservation in South Dakota and the Quaker boarding school in Indiana to which she had been sent, she studied at the Boston Conservatory of Music and in 1900 accompanied the Carlisle Indian Band as violin soloist on a trip to Paris. *Sun Dance* was one of her many efforts to balance the two worlds in which she lived. It was written in collaboration with William P. Hanson and was named American Opera of the Year by the New York Light Opera Guild in 1937.

Of the many contemporary Native playwrights, one of the most prominent is Maria Campbell, a Canadian Métis, author of the autobiographical *Halfbreed*, and, with Linda Griffiths, *The Book of Jessica: A Theatrical Transformation*. Campbell and Griffiths's work tells of their difficult collaboration on the play entitled *Jessica* (included in the book), which they wrote with Paul Thompson of the radical Canadian Theatre Passe Muraille. *Jessica* evolved from improvisations done by white actress Griffiths based on information from Campbell about her life. The surrounding text is a disjointed conversation and often distraught series of communications between the two women, telling of their struggles to understand and respect one another as Native and white and the ways that their relationship foundered on the same racism and history that they were attempting to describe and expose in their play. It is a moving and troubling piece fraught with disturbing emotions and questions at the heart of postcolonial relations between non-Native and Native peoples.

Among the many other contemporary Native Americans involved in theatre have been playwrights Monica Charles (Klallam) who wrote *Yanowis* and *Mowitch* (both 1968); Geraldine Keams (Navajo) who wrote *Na Haaz Zaan* (1972) with Robert Shorty; Lynda Poolaw (Kiowa) who wrote *Skins* (1973); Linda *Hogan (Chickasaw) a poet and fiction writer known for her deft combinations of the political and the spiritual, whose play *A Piece of Noon* won the Five Civilized Tribes Playwriting Award in 1980, and Muriel Miguel (Rappahannock-Cuna) director of the New York City-based Spiderwoman Theatre Workshop. Still, this list mentions but a few of the many Native American women involved in an immense range of theatrical and dramatic productions.

• Rayna Green, *Native American Women: A Contextual Bibliography* (1983). Jeffrey F. Huntsman, "Native American Theatre," in *Ethnic Theatre in the United States*, edited by Maxine Schwartz Seller (1983), pp. 355–385. Andrew Wiget, ed., *Critical Essays on Native American Literature* (1985). Paula Gunn Allen, *The Sacred Hoop; Recovering the Feminine in American Indian Traditions* (1986). Maria Campbell and Linda Griffiths, *The Book of Jessica: A Theatrical Transformation* (1989). Bernd Peyer, ed., *The Singing Spirit: Early Short Stories by North American Indians* (1989). A. LaVonne Brown Ruoff, *American Indian Literatures: An Introduction, Bibliographic Review, and Selected Bibliography* (1990).

Catherine Taylor

Fiction

Native American women's fiction finds its origins in oral narratives now for the most part lost. Though hundreds of languages were spoken in North America before Columbus "discovered" it, none had a written form. Early oral and dramatic narratives concerned the legends, the myths, and the biographies of tribal members, but they never achieved the fixed permanence that we now associate with written fiction.

Wynema, the first novel by a Native American woman, was published in 1891 (to be reprinted with an introduction by A. LaVonne Brown Ruoff) by Creek writer Sophia Alice *Callahan. *Wynema* is about two women who become close friends: a non-Indian Methodist teacher in the Creek nation, and Wynema, her full-blood pupil. Flawed in many ways, this novel nevertheless set the pattern for much of the fiction that was to follow: a part-white author (Callahan was one-sixteenth Indian) writing fiction that is a combination of history, romance, autobiography, anthropology, protest, and artistry. Another early native writer was *Zitkala-Ša. Born in 1876 as Gertrude Simmons (subsequently Gertrude Bonnin), this Sioux writer published several stories in 1901 and 1902 that were collected later, with her other writings, as *American Indian Stories* (1924; reprinted in 1985 with a foreword by Dexter Fisher). These stories were not distinguished fiction, but they introduced a number of the themes that have become common in native fiction: the conflict between native and Christian religion, the plight of a white-educated Indian who attempts to return to a tribal life, and the place of Indian women both in Indian culture and in the colonizing white culture.

Serious discussion of Native American women's fiction usually begins with a discussion of the Colville woman *Mourning Dove, also known as Humishuma and as Christine Quintasket McLeod Galler. Although Mourning Dove wrote and published a number of the tales she collected from her people—some of them appearing as *Coyote Stories* (1933; reprint, 1990), *Tales of the Ocanogans* (1976), and *Mourning Dove's Stories* (1991)—she is best known for *Cogewea, the Half-Blood* (1927; reprint, 1981). Cogewea is courted by two men on a cattle ranch in the Flathead country of the Pacific Northwest. The first is the glittering tenderfoot Easterner Densmore, who only wants Cogewea's money; the second is the "ordinary" but steady and kind half-breed Jim, who loves her for herself. It is almost impossible now to say whether *Cogewea* was improved or worsened by the contribution of Lucullus Virgil McWhorter, the white collaborator who encouraged Mourning Dove to write, and then edited (rewrote?) her work. Although readers find a disturbing mixture of styles in the novel, *Cogewea* developed motifs that were to be the stock-in-trade of later Native women writers of fiction: the exploitation of Indian women by white men, the plight of the half blood, the search for love and happiness, the grandparent who understands and represents the "old ways," the self-serving white government policies toward Indians, and the use of old tribal stories as elements in the new fiction.

A curious footnote in the history of Indian women's fiction is the Sioux writer Ella Cara Deloria, who worked with anthropologists Franz Boas and Ruth Benedict in studying the lifeways of the Sioux people. They encouraged her to write a novel about the life and history of her people. She did so, completing the manuscript of *Waterlily* in 1944, and then shortening and revising it with Benedict's help in 1948. No publisher for the book could be found until 1988, however, primarily because publishers feared, with some justice, that there would be little readership for a fictionalized ethnographic narrative of the birth, life, troubles, and eventual happiness of an imaginary Sioux woman named Waterlily.

If N. Scott Momaday's Pulitzer Prize–winning *House Made of Dawn* made the literary world in 1968 realize that there were modern Indian fiction writers of distinction, then the short stories of Laguna Pueblo writer Leslie Marmon *Silko made that world realize in 1974 that there were also Indian women writers of distinction. A number of fine stories by Silko appeared in *The Man to Send Rain Clouds* (1974, ed. Kenneth Rosen) and have been anthologized several times since, most notably in *Storyteller* (1981). Silko has earned her most enduring place in American literature, however, with her fine novel *Ceremony* (1977). Although the main character, Tayo, is a young man whose involvement in the Pacific theater of World War II nearly destroys him, women play key roles in the action, and Laguna Pueblo critic Paula

Gunn *Allen not only finds a "feminine landscape" in the novel, but also suggests that in his growth to full manhood Tayo must experience an "initiation into womanhood." Key themes in Silko's stories and novel include Indian soldiers returned home from fighting in white men's wars; Indians as victims both of white aggression and of their own people and personality; the need for a return to nature, to the land, and to an Indian sense of community; the acceptance of death as a necessary and important feature of living; the destructiveness of alcohol in Indian life; the role of the supernatural as a natural part of human existence; and the need for adaptation and change in human life and ceremony. Silko's *Almanac of the Dead* (1991) is a long and multicharactered novel of tragedy, addiction, and corruption that seems to pull back from the humor and optimism of her earlier work.

Allen, a Laguna/Sioux writer and scholar, had already made a strong reputation as a poet and critic, but her novel *The Woman Who Owned the Shadows* (1983) confirmed the variety and strength of her writing. Focusing on the life of Ephanie Atencio, the novel takes this mixed-race woman from a severed childhood friendship with Elena, through her observation of the severed love of two nuns, on to severed relationships with a number of men, one of them a relative and one of them a Japanese American. We explore with Ephanie her own troubled psyche, in part through Gestalt therapy, through the death of one of her children, and through an aborted suicide attempt. The stories of the Indian people provide a rich backdrop to this strange and powerful novel, which is variously called "feminist," "lesbian," and "autobiographical." Allen has also edited *Spider Woman's Granddaughters* (1989), an important collection of tales and fiction by Indian women.

No discussion of Native American women's fiction can exclude Ojibwa Indian Louise *Erdrich, whose stunning *Love Medicine* (1984) won the Critics Circle Award. This novel is made up of a series of interconnected short stories, many of which Erdrich had published earlier separately. Taken together, the fourteen chapters span the years 1934 to 1983 and cover the lives of several families trying to cope with life, love, confusion, and death on the twentieth century Chippewa reservation. Published later but set earlier, Erdrich's *Tracks* (1988) deals with some of the same people and families during the years 1912 to 1919. A third novel in the trilogy, *Beet Queen* (1986), takes place in the town of Argus, North Dakota, during the years 1932 to 1972; it has some native characters, but does not focus on them. A projected fourth novel in the series was postponed while Erdrich and her husband, Michael Dorris, also an Indian writer, wrote the sensational *The Crown of Columbus* (1991). In this novel a part-Navajo Dartmouth professor named Vivian Twostar chances upon some documents that lead to a series of adventures in the Caribbean. Without question, however, Erdrich's reputation as a Native American fiction writer rests on the funny, serious, deep, and loving stories in *Tracks* and *Love Medicine*.

Having been shown the way by their predecessors, other Native American writers have recently been publishing fiction. For example, Janet Campbell Hale, of Coeur d'Alene/Kootenai heritage, has written two novels. *Owl's Song* (1974; reprint, 1991) is juvenile fiction about a fourteen-year-old Indian boy whose family fails to help him grow to manhood. *The Jailing of Cecelia Capture* (1985) is about a thirty-year-old Indian woman who wakes up in the drunk tank of a California jail and then begins the painful recollection of the trail, starting many years earlier, that had carried her there. Pawnee/Otoe Indian Anna Lee Walters has published a fine collection of short stories, *The Sun Is Not Merciful* (1985), and a less successful novel, *Ghost Singer* (1988). The novel is about the ghosts of some nineteenth century Navajo Indians who seek revenge against a series of curators of the Smithsonian, where the scalps and other body parts of Indian peoples are stored. Finally, the Chickasaw writer Linda *Hogan, in addition to publishing poetry and short stories in *Red Clay* (1991), has written the compelling novel *Mean Spirit* (1990). Set in Oklahoma around the time when oil was discovered on land owned by Indians, this novel uncovers the corruption of white people, who seem bent on robbing the Indians yet again. Like many of her predecessors, Hogan explores the cultural confusion of Indians, who struggle to find an authentic place for themselves in the twentieth century.

• Charles R. Larson, *American Indian Fiction* (1978). Peter G. Beidler and Marion F. Egge, *The American Indian in Short Fiction: An Annotated Bibliography* (1979). Tom Colonnese and Louis Owens, *American Indian Novelists: An Annotated Critical Bibliography* (1985). Anna Lee Stensland, *Literature by and about the American Indian: An Annotated Bibliography*, 2d ed. (1979). Alan R. Velie, *Four American Indian Literary Masters: N. Scott Momaday, James Welch, Leslie Marmon Silko, Gerald Vizenor* (1982). Kenneth Lincoln, *Native American Renaissance* (1985). Paula Gunn Allen, *The Sacred Hoop: Recovering the Feminine in American Indian Traditions* (1986). Gretchen M. Bataille and Kathleen M. Sands, *American Indian Women: A Guide to Research* (1991). Laura Cotelli, ed., *Native American Literatures* (1989). Elizabeth I. Hanson, *Forever There: Race and Gender in Contemporary Native American Fiction* (1989). A. LaVonne Brown Ruoff, *American Indian Literatures: An Introduction, Bibliographic Review, and Selected Bibliography* (1990).

Peter G. Beidler

Nonfiction

The heading Native American Nonfiction covers an enormous range of works by women writers, including political journalism, cookbooks, legal writings, history, medicine, anthropology, sociology, geology, literary criticism, and autobiography. Not only would any list of such subheadings be inadequate, but the task of naming representative authors in each, immensely difficult. Thousands of Native American women write and publish every year in the United States alone, and, as with most approaches to Native studies, the reader must look beyond certain contemporary political boundaries which, while significant, are not necessarily relevant to this body of work. Witness the tribes of the Six Nations, whose boundaries—like those of many other tribal groups—cross other political borders, in their case those of the United States and Canada. Thus, our scope widens to include the indigenous peoples of Canada, Mexico, Central and South America. The enormity of the category now verges on the unworkable. In fact, even without challenging the overarching ideological constructions of modern nation states we have to ask, as Arlene Hirschfelder, Mary Gloyne Byler, and Michael Dorris do in their *Guide to Research on North American Indians*, "whether there is such a thing as American Indian literature. Since American Indians came from so many distinct tribes and cultures it is perhaps difficult to justify lumping all of their poetry and stories in one group." In other words, tribal differences are often so great as to demand much further cultural specificity in approaching their various writings. And yet, so as not to entirely gloss over the many individuals who have and do contribute to this field, we will mention a few Native American women who have received scholarly attention, especially in Native American and Literary studies. For further research, the bibliography at the end of this article is one place to begin to investigate this large and varied field—or, rather, multiple fields.

In the nineteenth century, a number of Native American women wrote memoirs and autobiographies. One of the earliest such works to be published was *The Memoirs of Catherine Brown, Christian Indian of the Cherokee Nation*. Primarily a paean to the benefits of Christian education and Anglo lifestyles (with a lot of emphasis on cleanliness), Brown's "memoir" was transcribed and, in part, rewritten by Rufus Anderson in 1824. Sarah *Winnemucca Hopkins's account of her tribe, *Life Among the Paiutes*, published in 1883, also speaks from a Christianized and acculturated point of view, while arguing for better treatment of her tribe. Winnemucca's work is written in the first person in a fairly traditional English style and combines history, tribal stories, treaty information, and commentary on relations with Indian agents and the U.S. government. *Life Among the Paiutes* contains a wealth of detail, particularly her account of the tribe's first encounter with whites, which occurred when she was young. Susette La Flesche (known also as Inshata Theumba or Bright Eyes), born on the Omaha reservation in 1854, wrote many articles on Indian rights in the 1880s. She edited the *Weekly Independent*, a Populist newspaper, and became a popular public speaker after accompanying Luther Standing Bear on his 1879 tour to rally opposition to the removal of the Ponca. Angel De Cora was a Winnebago artist and teacher who graduated from the famed Hampton Institute in 1891. Throughout the late nineteenth and early twentieth centuries, she wrote a number of articles on Indian art and at least two autobiographical sketches, frequently publishing under her Winnebago name of Hinookmahiwi-kilinaka, or Woman Coming on the Cloud in Glory. De Cora was also a book illustrator; her work included Francis La Flesche's *The Middle Five* (1900) and Gertrude Bonnin's *American Indian Legends* (1901), a project which began a long friendship with Bonnin.

Gertrude Bonnin (Sioux), also known as * Zitkala-Ša or Red Bird (1876–1938) is primarily known for her fiction, but was also a prolific writer of nonfiction in her role as Indian activist. Born on the Pine Ridge Reservation in South Dakota to a full-blood Sioux mother and a white father, Bonnin was sent at the age of eight to a Quaker boarding school in Indiana. She later returned to the reservation, but found she had become an outsider there. Caught between two worlds, Bonnin poignantly described these wrenching experiences in a number of articles and stories published in the *Atlantic Monthly* and later republished in her 1921 volume, *American Indian Stories*. Her essay "Why I Am a Pagan" is particularly interesting, given the number of Native American women then publishing Christian conversion narratives. Bonnin was elected secretary of the Society of American Indians in 1916; in 1918 and 1919 she edited the SAI's journal, the *American Indian Magazine*, and she later edited the *Indian Newsletter*. Much of her work focused on reforming the U.S. government's treatment of tribes. She was an ardent supporter of the Indian Citizenship Bill, and, at least initially, of John Collier's reforms at the Bureau of Indian Affairs. One of

her major contributions to the field of nonfiction was a work of investigative journalism co-written with Charles H. Fabens and Matthew K. Sniffen: *Oklahoma's Poor Rich Indians: An Orgy of Graft and Exploitation of the Five Civilized Tribes—Legalized Robbery* (1924).

Continuing the tradition of political autobiography are a number of contemporary writers including Maria Campbell (Métis), whose *Halfbreed* (1973) tells of her struggles with poverty, racism, and the Canadian government. A frank and often radical work, *Halfbreed* searches through Campbell's past to try to make sense of her life, to come to terms with the alcoholism, prostitution, and despair in her own life and in the lives of her people. She writes of her great-grandmother, who told her that:

> When the government gives you something, they take all that you have in return—your pride, your dignity, all the things that make you a living soul. When they are sure they have everything they give you a blanket to cover your shame.

Another contemporary author who weaves the personal and the political is Mary Crow Dog, whose 1990 autobiography, *Lakota Woman*, is an angry and moving account of her battles against cultural genocide as a woman on a South Dakota Reservation, her involvement in the American Indian Movement in the 1970s, and her experiences as the wife of spiritual leader Leonard Crow Dog. The different facets of her life are never separated or compartmentalized; for example, her account of the 1973 takeover at Wounded Knee is punctuated by descriptions of her pregnancy and the birth of her son during the siege. Crow Dog's story also deals with the conflicts she faced as a person of mixed race and as a woman trying to balance her need for both traditional tribal roles and nontraditional feminist positions.

Among the many other contemporary Native American writers, some of the most prominent are: Winona LaDuke (Anishnabe), an activist for native peoples rights, who has written political journalism for a number of magazines; Paula Gunn * Allen (Laguna Pueblo/Sioux), who writes both academic and popular works on Native American studies, often on literature and women's issues; Smithsonian anthropologist and teacher Rayna Green (Cherokee), author of an important and extremely useful bibliography for the field entitled *Native American Women;* and well-known poet Elizabeth Cook-Lynn (Crow Creek Sioux), also a major contributor to the realm of non-fiction through her academic writings on Native American Studies and through her role as editor of the important Native American publication *Wicazo-Sa Review*. Cook-Lynn has said, "Writing is an essential act of survival for contemporary American Indians. I'm not interested in some kind of melancholy reminiscence, though sometimes I think that's what people think I'm talking and writing about. I'm interested in the cultural, historical, and political survival of Indian nations, and that's why I write and teach."

• Sarah Winnemucca Hopkins, *Life Among the Paiute: Their Wrongs and Claims* (1883). Daniel Littlefield, Jr., and James W. Parins, *A Bibliography of Native American Writers, 1772–1924*, vols. 1 & 2 (1981). Rayna Green, *Native American Women: A Contextual Bibliography* (1983). Marilyn L. Haas. *Indians of North America: Methods and Sources for Library Research* (1983). Arlene B. Hirschfelder, Mary Gloyne Byler, and Michael A. Dorris, eds., *Guide to Research on Native American Indians* (1983). Gretchen M. Bataille and Kathleen Mullen Sands, *American Indian Women: Telling Their Lives* (1984). Andrew Wiget, ed., *Critical Essays on Native American Literature* (1985). Paula Gunn Allen, *The Sacred Hoop; Recovering the Feminine in American Indian Traditions* (1986). Bernd C. Peyer, ed., *The Singing Spirit: Early Short Stories by North American Indians* (1989). A. LaVonne Brown Ruoff, *American Indian Literatures: An Introduction, Bibliographic Review, and Selected Bibliography* (1990).

Catherine Taylor

Song and Poetry

Native American women have long been writing poetry and prose. In the modern era, E. Pauline *Johnson, the Canadian Mohawk dancer/actress/poet, and *Zitkala-Ša (Gertrude Bonnin), the Yankton Sioux poet/essayist/activist, began publishing in the late 1800s and continued their output well into the 1930s. Many Native American students enrolled in the government's Indian boarding school system were published in early journals such as Carlisle Indian School's *Carlisle Arrow* and *Red Man*. But it was not until the success of N. Scott Momaday's Pulitzer Prize-winning novel *House Made of Dawn* (1969) and Leslie Marmon *Silko's poetry volume *Laguna Woman* (1972) and novel *Ceremony* (1974) that Native American women began publishing to the extent they are today. Poets Paula Gunn *Allen, Louise *Erdrich, Joy *Harjo, Mary TallMountain, Linda *Hogan, Diane *Glancy, Chrystos, Janice Gould, Gail Tremblay, Nila North Sun, Luci Tapahonso, and many others are publishing works that trace back to the vast Native American tribal oral traditions, which are still alive in modern Native America. However, literary critics, with the exception of Paula Gunn Allen, Kenneth Lincoln, and Lavonne Brown Ruoff, have virtually ignored the importance and value of Native American literature.

What is important to note is that American Indian poetry follows its own aesthetic, its own form, its own virtues. American Indian women's poetry and prose is important in understanding the past, not just of Native Americans, but of non-Natives as well. As Allen comments in *The Sacred Hoop* (1986), stories record myths and translate these myths into rituals for everyday life. For example, in Allen's novel *The Woman Who Owned the Shadows* (1983), the stories of the Laguna deity Iyetiku are retold and brought into the modern world through the protagonist Ephanie's consciousness by the omniscient narrator, itself of the spirit world. In order to survive her existence as a mixed blood, Ephanie must rely upon her stories to provide herself with the necessary daily ritual to connect her with her peoples' living traditions, even if she, some 1500 miles away in San Francisco, is removed from the community.

In *The Sacred Hoop*, Allen notes that Indian literature is classified in generic-, culture-, and language-specific terms by most Anglo-American critics. There is a need for the study of American Indian literature without these literary distinctions, which are mainly pertinent to modern Western men's literature. Applying a Western template to literature based firmly in non-Western traditions steals the work's meanings, and recasts and colonizes it. While Western-American literature is entirely secular, modern American Indian literature, particularly that of American Indian women, is firmly based in Native spiritualism.

To the tribal societies and community members, spirits simply exist, and there is no way to articulate the presence of these spirits using scientific reasoning or theory. Not only do these spirits exist, but they are seen as kin—relatives to all. Inanimate objects such as a rock, a tree, or a cloud are all seen as relatives. The chemical or scientific compound of these objects is not important, but the relationship of these objects to the natural living world is. It is difficult, then, for literary critics, especially those of Indian blood, to explore the possibilities of an Indian literary criticism that excludes the presence of these spirits, a presence acknowledged and alive in the work of writers today. While Native myths and legends have been trivialized, seen as pagan or childlike, or as part of the new mysticism currently sweeping the New Age movement, or given one-dimensional characteristics, as in the film and book *Dances with Wolves*, they are as viable and vital to Native people's literary production as their lives. The modern world has been divided between the sacred and the secular, and into this division fall the *myths and legends and *rituals of native peoples all over the world. Native American myths, in the world of Western empiricism and logical positivism, are viewed as false-hoods, trivialities, quaint curiosities. The Western world seeks to destroy its own myths and those of indigenous cultures because the Western tendency to secularize requires the separation of the "ordinary" from the "extraordinary," the sacred from the perception of reality, the intellect from the emotion. Tribal peoples viewing the world from an aesthetically different viewpoint have been unable to see myths and traditions as truth in the scientific world of Western literary criticism.

Oral traditions were (and still very much are) the bread of life to tribal peoples. Stories and songs of Native America serve to tell mythic origins, and through the telling of these mythic origins cultures survive. The Chickasaw writer Linda Hogan has described the presence of such traditions in her work: "As my interest in literature increased, I realized I had also been given a background in oral literature from my father's family. I use this. It has strengthened my imagination. I find that my ideas and even my work arrangement derive from that oral source. It is sometimes as though I hear those voices when I am in the process of writing" (*Winged Words*, 1990). Modern American Indian women poets are translating the songs and story-telling traditions of their tribal cultures into poetry and prose that speaks of survival in the face of genocide, thus manipulating something very ancient, very powerful in those story-telling traditions into something very modern and very powerful: the new Native American literary tradition.

The Laguna Pueblo poet and storyteller Leslie Marmon Silko, author of the poetry volumes *Laguna Woman* and *Storyteller*, as well as the novels *Ceremony* and *Almanac of the Dead*, calls the oral traditions "culture handed down by ear" (*Winged Words*, 1991). Native women poets are writing and therefore recording traditional myths, stories, and songs onto the page for future generations' very survival. If the stories survive, then the culture survives. For example, Paula Gunn Allen's "Whirlwind Man Steals Yellow Woman" from *Spider Woman's Grand-daughters* (1990) records tribal myths and songs and transforms them into contemporary stories as the written word, the written song. Other Native women poets' works, such as Mary Tall-Mountain's "Good Grease," Joy Harjo's "Deer Dancer," and Leslie Silko's "Storytelling" have followed suit. The poets invite the reader in and provide the reader with an immediate sense of intimacy, which comes from knowing oneself and one's culture to the core of being. The poet/storyteller's role is the role of culture bearer, the one who negotiates stories and songs from

the tribal center and forms them, reworks them, into stories of cultural survival.

Native American women poets sing of birth and life and death as a continuous cycle. Female mysticism in Native American cultures honors the place of women in tribal societies; women as life-givers and sustainers are revered for their feminine power. It is within this feminine cyclical system that contemporary Native women are taking songs and myths of the past and turning them into contemporary poems and prose cycles. These poets are reminding women of their mysticism and power. Joy Harjo's poem "Rainy Dawn" (1990) celebrates the birth of her daughter in poetry and song, honoring her daughter and the generations that will follow and the generations that have passed. Harjo becomes cocreator of her child with her ancestors' memory, her ancestors' dreams of the future. She reminds her daughter of the traditions that have been passed on and on, generation by generation, through the oral tradition (Silko's "culture by ear"), and that now are preserved through a written tradition.

In her poem "Ggaal Comes Upriver" (1991), Mary TallMountain uses the *ggaal* (king salmon) as a metaphor for the ongoing survival and continuation of her Koyukon people. The king salmon, like the Koyukon people, has survived the long fight against colonization, and in returning to the traditions and language of her people, TallMountain records, through the written word, centuries-long traditions and metaphors that will serve to tell future generations that a culture has survived. Paula Gunn Allen, in her "Creation Story" from *Shadow Country* (1982), takes the Laguna creation story of the goddess/creatrix Iyetiku and reforms it into her own words. In the Laguna Pueblo tradition, it is held that Iyetiku created the land and the food, giving corn to the people as a sacred gift, and cementing the relationship between the land, the people, and herself. Allen retells this tradition from stories she heard as a child, and as a poet reforms the oral tradition to a written contemporary piece that ensures survival of that tradition.

The Native American literary tradition is not new. It is indeed old and powerful, and speaks to generations to come about something in the past; written and recorded, it will be read by future generations. Native American women are addressing the strength and ties of the oral tradition through the written word. It is those songs and stories, myths and rituals of Native America that are recorded today; the songs and ceremonies and myths and rituals that speak of continuance, survival, of life. They speak of the power to give life and the power to watch a peoples survive through the eyes of their children and grandchildren. To paraphrase a Muskogee Stomp Dance song, "After I die, this dance will continue/say it again/this dance will continue."

Carolyn M. Dunn

NATURALISM. American literary naturalism grew out of philosophic, scientific, and literary developments in Europe in the seventeenth, eighteenth, and nineteenth centuries. Newton, Comte, Darwin, Spencer, and Marx contributed to the development of philosophic determinism and the notion of the human individual as subject to natural laws. In 1880, Émile Zola in *The Experimental Novel* advanced the idea of the novelist as scientist; this idea and his twenty-volume Rougon-Macquart series, in which he traced the influences of heredity in members of a French family, influenced the development of literary naturalism on both sides of the Atlantic.

The American literary naturalists wrote of characters dominated by forces outside their control, and, often, outside their ken. Although they have been excluded from standard discussions of naturalism, women writers utilized these themes throughout the nineteenth and early twentieth centuries. The interplay of heredity and environment provided a starting point for countless thematic variations. Ellen * Glasgow structured two early novels, *The Descendant* (1897) and *Phases of an Inferior Planet* (1898) around the ideas of Darwin and Spencer. Glasgow (*Barren Ground*, 1925), Willa *Cather (*O Pioneers!*, 1913, and *My Ántonia*, 1918), and others dealt with the theme of inherited character as a component of individual fate. Rose Terry *Cooke (*Somebody's Neighbors*, 1881) and Mary Wilkins *Freeman (*A New England Nun and Other Stories*, 1891, and *Pembroke*, 1894) explored the effects of the New England temperament and harsh living conditions on rural women. Writers like *Zitkala-Ša (*Impressions of an Indian Childhood*, 1900) and Nella *Larsen (*Quicksand*, 1928, and *Passing*, 1929) detailed the struggles of nonwhite Americans attempting to live in equanimity within a white-dominated culture. Still others, such as Cather, *Sui Sin Far (*Mrs. Spring Fragrance*, 1912), Mary *Antin (*The Promised Land*, 1912), and Anzia *Yezierska (*Bread Givers*, 1925), traced the difficulties of nineteenth- and early-twentieth-century immigrants' adjustments to their new culture and physical environment. Will versus fate formed another important theme; Kate *Chopin (*The Awakening*, 1899) and Edith *Kelley (*Weeds*, 1923), for example, depicted woman's struggle against her social

and biological destinies. The struggle for economic survival surfaced as a theme in the works of Kelley, Tillie *Olsen (*Yonnondio: From the Thirties*, 1974), Antin, and Yezierska. Social criticism and reform constituted another naturalistic concern; Rebecca Harding *Davis, writing of hopelessness in the lives of factory workers (*Life in the Iron Mills*, 1861), and Edith *Wharton (*The House of Mirth*, 1905, and *The Age of Innocence*, 1920), analyzing the morals of New York society, provide examples. Finally, the literary naturalists did not shrink from the taboo; Chopin and Larsen wrote of woman's sensuality; Kelley, of childbirth and attempted *abortion; Freeman and Cooke, of self-sufficient spinsterhood; and Charlotte Perkins *Gilman (*The Yellow Wallpaper*, 1892), of the danger of *madness if woman was denied a voice in her own destiny.

An objective presentation of fact is one of the most often-noted hallmarks of the naturalistic style, but critics have also cited the impressionistic, the satiric, and even the sensational as variants within it. The years 1890 to 1940 are usually given as the perimeters of the naturalistic movement in America, but writers began experimenting with its styles and themes far earlier, and some contemporary writers continue to do so.

[*See also* Realism.]

• Lars Ahnebrink, *The Beginnings of Naturalism in American Fiction: A Study of the Works of Hamlin Garland, Stephen Crane, and Frank Norris, with Special References to Some European Influences, 1891–1903* (1950). Charles Child Walcutt, *American Literary Naturalism: A Divided Stream* (1956). Donald Pizer, *Realism and Naturalism in Nineteenth Century American Literature,* rev. ed. (1984); and *Twentieth Century American Literary Naturalism: An Interpretation* (1982). June Howard, *Form and History in American Literary Naturalism* (1985). Lee Clark Mitchell, *Determined Fictions: American Literary Naturalism* (1989).

Susan Ward

NATURE. See Ecofeminism.

NAYLOR, Gloria (b. 1950), novelist. Gloria Naylor was born 25 January 1950 in Tunica County, Mississippi. Her parents, Roosevelt Naylor and Alberta McAlpin, migrated to New York when Gloria was a child. In the wake of Martin Luther King, Jr.'s, death, Naylor, the product of a deeply religious home, translated her former religious zeal as a Jehovah's Witness to African-American literature. By the time she made the transition from studying for a nursing degree at Medgar Evers College to earning her B.A. in English from Brooklyn College (1981), Naylor knew that she wanted to celebrate the black female experience in America. She received her M.A. in Afro-American studies from Yale University (1983).

In 1983, Naylor won the American Book Award for *The Women of Brewster Place* (1982), in which she created a ghetto of her own in an urban cul-de-sac. Set in an unnamed Everycity somewhere in urban America, *Brewster Place* chronicles the fates of seven black women of different backgrounds yoked together by confusion and circumstance, yet emotionally vibrant.

In her second novel, *Linden Hills* (1985), Naylor invokes the blues structure of Dante's *Divine Comedy* (hell, suffering, pain) to describe the experience of the black middle class—lost souls trapped in the American Dream. Driven by obsessive materialism, the people in this affluent enclave violate its embittered founder's intent of creating Linden Hills as a Booker T. Washington model of black self-reliance. Having betrayed the values of black integrity, the residents descend into their own inferno. Naylor explores the possibilities of healing a community affected by the interrelationship of color, sex, and class.

With its roots in Shakespeare's *The Tempest*, Naylor's third and most richly textured novel, *Mama Day* (1988), describes the mythical world of Willow Springs, a fertile island off the southeast coast of the United States. Miranda "Mama" Day, the elderly matriarch, sets out to bring about a reconciliation between the dark forces that threaten the body and soul of her recently married great-niece and her mainland husband, as well as between the African past and New World values. A response to the material call of *Linden Hills*, *Mama Day* challenges us to own our own souls and history.

In her 1992 novel *Bailey's Cafe*, Naylor uses the multiple story/multiple narrator format once more, this time juxtaposing male voices and characters with female. The work shows Naylor's wide technical range, all the while creating a world that is emotionally complex and varied. Its immediacy in setting and character is indelible.

As both a storyteller and prose stylist, Naylor echoes Jean Toomer, Zora Neale *Hurston, William Faulkner, Paule *Marshall, and Toni *Morrison. She establishes a firm basis for celebrating the oral expressive forms rooted in the black church and challenges us to plumb these speech acts for what they reveal about the ambiguity and irony of black life. Naylor adds a distinctly feminine voice to this discourse as she works to free the image of black women from the hegemonic shadow of the racial mountain as defined by black men, and presents the female characters in a variety of roles. The unifying thread that ties these four novels together is the community of nurturing women who are heroic, unforgettable, timeless.

• Barbara Christian, "Trajectories of Self-Definition: Placing Contemporary Afro-American Women's Fiction," in *Conjuring: Black Women, Fiction, and Literary Tradition*, eds. Marjorie Pryse and Hortense J. Spillers (1985), pp. 233–248. Gloria Naylor and Toni Morrison, "A Conversation," *Southern Review* 21 (July 1985): 567–593. Gloria Naylor, "Love and Sex in the Afro-American Novel," *Yale Review* 78, no. 1 (Autumn 1988): 19–31. Gloria Naylor, "The Myth of the Matriarch," *Life* 11 (Spring 1988): 65. Larry R. Andrews, "Black Sisterhood in Gloria Naylor's Novels," *CLA Journal* 33, no. 1 (September 1989): 1–25. Barbara Christian, "Gloria Naylor's Geography: Community, Class, and Patriarchy in *The Women of Brewster Place* and *Linden Hills*," in *Reading Black, Reading Feminist*, ed. Henry Louis Gates, Jr. (1990), pp. 348–373. Jill L. Matus, "Dream, Deferral, and Closure in *The Women of Brewster Place*," *Black American Literature Forum* 24, no. 1 (Spring 1990): 49–64. Karla F. C. Holloway, *Moorings and Metaphors: Figures of Culture and Gender in Black Women's Literature* (1992).

Dolan Hubbard

NEEDLEWORK. From colonial times to the present, women have expressed their creativity, personal style, and social concerns through their needlework. Needlework refers to any of the various devices for carrying thread and making stitches, and includes knitting, crochet and lace making, embroidery, beadwork, plain sewing, quilting, and rug hooking. As recorded in *diaries, *letters, and interviews, women do needlework to be creative, to save money, to keep busy, to make gifts, to earn money, to calm nerves, and to help others in need. Most women who do needlework also express a pleasure in working with their hands to make objects of beauty for themselves, their families, and their homes. It is difficult for us in the twentieth century to understand how central needlework was to women of previous centuries. No woman, whatever her age or social class, grew up without knowing how to use a needle. An entire household's linens and clothing were her responsibility, and included the stitching of all bedding, table linens, and clothing, and the knitting of socks, gloves, and hats. Women embellished these articles with embroidery, lace, and patchwork. Fine handiwork became the hallmark of a woman of leisure, as well as the means by which a woman made beautiful, everyday items when times were hard. As quoted in *America's Heritage Quilts* (1991), one pioneer woman wrote, "I made quilts as fast as I could to keep my family warm, and as pretty as I could to keep my heart from breaking."

Designs for needlework came from a variety of sources, including patterns circulated by teachers and periodicals, as well as family traditions. Popular motifs were flowers, pictorial scenes, and geometric patterns.

Native Americans developed needlework traditions, often using materials obtained at trading posts. Some highly prized techniques include bead working, Pueblo embroidery, ribbon appliqué, and Seminole patchwork.

Until the mid-nineteenth century, needlework was one of the few acceptable creative outlets for women. One of the most creative and dramatic forms of needlework is the patchwork quilt. Like jazz, the patchwork quilt is an indigenous American art form that remains vibrant and innovative. It was, and still is, an art form that expresses joy, sorrow, celebration of family events, and political conviction. In the past, images were freely drawn from nature, the home, architecture, and history, as reflected in the names of some of the patterns: Texas Star, Oregon Trail, Double Wedding Ring, Baby's Blocks, and Log Cabin. Quilt making also fulfilled a uniquely social function. While most quilt tops were pieced individually, the stitching together of top, middle, and backing layers was often done by a group of women. By 1800, these quilting bees were quite a social activity, and provided a reason for women of all ages and backgrounds to meet outside the home to discuss personal, social, and political issues. Quiltmaking has been popular with African Americans as well. Slaves brought from Africa their own stitching techniques and design sensibilities. Combined with quilting techniques taught to them by their mistresses, African Americans developed a rich patchwork tradition reflecting their own aesthetics. Stimulated by the women's movement and the craft revival of the 1960s, needlework thrives as an important form of recreation and artistic creation.

Many literary works and scholarly articles have seen potential for rich metaphors in women's needlework. From Edith *Wharton's use of knitting in her suspenseful short story "Roman Fever," to Celie's colorful hand-sewn garments business in Alice *Walker's *The Color Purple,* women authors have illustrated women's industry, creativity, and even patience by providing their female characters with needle and thread. Writers as diverse as Harriet Beecher *Stowe and Gloria *Naylor both use quilting in their writings to symbolize the bringing together of disparate elements, so often celebrated as a specifically feminine task.

Quilting, weaving, and needlework have also figured as metaphors for feminist critics seeking to describe the unique quality of women's writing and experiences. Examples of feminist works that examine weaving and patching as representative of the creative work of women and women writers include Annis Pratt's analysis in *Archetypal Patterns in Women's Fiction* (1981), Elaine Showalter's "Piecing and Writing" in *The Poetics of Gender,* edited by Nancy K. Miller (1986), and Elsa Barkley Brown's 1989 *Signs* article, "African-American Women's Quilting: A Framework for Conceptualizing and Teaching African-American Women's History."

• Judith Reiter Weissman and Wendy Lavitt, *Labors of Love: America's Textiles and Needlework, 1650–1930* (1987). Eli Leon, *Who'd a Thought It: Improvisation in African American Quiltmaking* (1987). Anne L. MacDonald, *The Social History of American Knitting* (1988). Bets Ramsay and Gail Andrews Treschel, *Southern Quilts: A New View* (1991). Barbara Lee Smith, *Celebrating the Stitch* (1991).

Nancy Whittington

NESTLE, Joan (b. 1940), essayist, historian, editor, educator. Born in the borough of the Bronx in New York City, Nestle grew up in a working-class, single-parent family. She graduated from Queens College, City University of New York, in 1963, and received her masters degree from New York University. Self-described as a Jewish femme, Nestle's work centers on lesbian identity, cultural politics, and the preservation of lesbian history. In 1973, Nestle cofounded, with Deborah Edel, the *Lesbian Herstory Archives of New York City, a grass-roots project dedicated to the collection and preservation of lesbian memorabilia, artifacts, and written works.

Nestle cites the repression of the McCarthy period, the strength of the *civil rights movement, and the political writings of Albert Memmi (*The Colonizer and the Colonized,* 1965) as major influences in her activist work. Memmi's essay on the oppression of colonized people and the erasure of their history prompted Nestle to recognize the silence of lesbian history and to organize a communal project to reclaim and validate lesbian lives. Her political interests compel her writings, in which she chronicles the historical experiences of lesbians within both women's communities and American dominant culture. Her work explores the status of lesbians within a patriarchal, heterosexual social system, and, in particular, the meaning and significance of butch-femme lesbian relationships. Her first collection of essays, *A Restricted Country* (1987), chronicles her childhood experiences, the development of her lesbian sexual and political identity, the power of eroticism in her life, and her desire to write a defiant and proud, working-class, femme and feminist history. Nestle is also coeditor, with Naomi Holoch, of *Women on Women: An Anthology of American Lesbian Short Fiction,* vols. 1 and 2 (1991 and 1993). In 1992, Nestle edited *The Persistent Desire: A Femme-*

Butch Reader, which offers a cross-historical, international collection of butch and femme lesbians' memoirs, biographies, and cultural analyses. Nestle is an assistant professor in English at Queens College, where she has taught in the SEEK (Search for Education, Elevation, and Knowledge) Program since 1966.

• Nestle's work, together with the published and unpublished writings of other lesbians, is collected at the Lesbian Herstory Educational Foundation/Lesbian Herstory Archives in Brooklyn, New York. See also Susie Day, "Joan Nestle: 'Taking Pride in Lesbian Herstory,' " *Sojourner* 14, no. 10 (June 1989): 17–19. Holly Metz, "Interview with Joan Nestle," the *American Voice* 20 (Winter 1990): 72–84. Claire Whatling, "Reading Awry: Joan Nestle and the Recontextualization of Heterosexuality," in *Sexual Sameness: Textual Differences in Lesbian and Gay Writing,* edited by Joseph Bristow (1992), pp. 210–226.

Elizabeth Yukins

NEW AGE RELIGION. *See* Spirituality.

NEW ENGLAND WOMEN'S WRITING. New Englanders dominated the first three hundred years of American women's literature. Of the approximately twelve hundred writers in *American Women Writers,* a quarter grew up and/or resided for a long period in Maine, New Hampshire, Vermont, Massachusetts, Connecticut, or Rhode Island. Many have written about New England and exhibited qualities associated with the region's Puritan heritage: a symbolic habit of mind, seeking meaning in nature and ordinary events, and an active conscience—if not religious, at least socially aware and self-probing.

The Puritan settlers' emphasis on education, once it had trickled down to women, enabled them to pioneer in many types of literature. Anne * Bradstreet, mother of eight, published in 1650 the first volume of poetry written in the British colonies. She was followed by such Bostonian poets as Sarah Wentworth * Morton, who wrote under a pseudonym, and Phillis * Wheatley, who published the first book by an African American. In the seventeenth and eighteenth centuries, many women practiced nonfiction genres, such as * letters (Abigail * Adams), autobiographical narratives (Mary * Rowlandson), journals (Sarah Kemble * Knight), and histories (Hannah Adams, Mercy Otis * Warren).

During the Revolution, Warren contributed political plays, and as the Puritan taboo on drama and fiction relaxed, women became instrumental in developing American fiction. Susanna * Rowson might be termed "the mother of the American novel," having experimented widely and preceded Brockden Brown, the so-

called father. Hannah * Foster also contributed to the genre, as did Maine's Sally Wood and New Hampshire's Tabitha * Tenney. By the 1820s, Wood was struggling to exchange exotic settings for those of her native state, and the talented Catharine Maria * Sedgwick was succeeding; her *A New England Tale* (1822) includes authentic Massachusetts settings and local characters such as Native Americans, Shakers, and spinsters like herself.

The realist tradition was not the most popular in the nineteenth century, however. Their Boston setting was incidental to such best-selling novels as Maria * Cummins's *The Lamplighter* (1854) and Louisa May * Alcott's *Little Women* (1867). The famous poets were also "sentimental" in approach: Lydia * Sigourney, the "sweet singer of Hartford"; Sarah Helen Whitman of Rhode Island (Poe's "Helen"); Julia Ward * Howe; Lucy Larcom; Louise Chandler Moulton; and Frances Osgood. Of course, the greatest New England poet, Emily * Dickinson, published only a few poems in her lifetime and was hardly known until the twentieth century. Some very popular writers managed to combine sentimentalism and protest; Maine's Fanny * Fern and Elizabeth Oakes * Smith both began writing about "The Sinless Child" (a Smith poem), and ended up feminist social critics.

There was a vital tradition to draw on. As early as the 1770s, Judith Sargent * Murray had written "On the Equality of the Sexes," and in 1832, Maria Stewart, a black woman, gave feminist speeches in Boston. The Transcendentalist Margaret * Fuller conducted her famous consciousness-raising "conversations" for women and published *Woman in the Nineteenth Century* (1845). Other writers, like Lucretia * Mott, Lydia Maria * Child, and Maria Chapman, were both feminists and abolitionists, and some, like Sarah Bagley and Abby Morton Diaz (who had been at the utopian Brook Farm), wrote on behalf of labor reform. Economic criticism is a strong current in New England women's writing; even the conservative Sarah Josepha Hale and Hannah Flagg Gould attacked their contemporaries' "inordinate thirst for riches" (Hale). New Hampshire's Harriet * Wilson, the first black person to publish a novel in the U.S., also sounded this theme in her indictment of northern racism, *Our Nig* (1859). Wilson was succeeded in African-American fiction by Pauline * Hopkins, a turn-of-the-century Boston novelist who treated the middle class.

A New England writer who combines the predominant strains of the nineteenth century is Harriet Beecher * Stowe (1811–1896). Her *Uncle Tom's Cabin* (1852), often called the greatest of all protest novels, also belongs to the sentimental tradition. Stowe's other work, such as *The Pearl of Orr's Island* (1862) and *Oldtown Folks* (1869), is set in New England, and she was a precursor of the local color school. Stowe influenced Sarah Orne *Jewett, author of *The Country of the Pointed Firs* (1896), who with her partner Annie *Fields formed a network of writers, including Rose Terry *Cooke, Elizabeth Stuart Phelps *Ward, and the poet Celia Thaxter. In many men's accounts, such as that by Hayden Carruth, the local colorists are usually portrayed as "old maids living out their lives in cheerful desperation," mourning the economic decline of New England. From the point of view of Josephine Donovan and other recent critics, they practiced a "woman-identified realism," which celebrated nonmaterialist values and strong, independent women.

Some local colorists, such as Mary Wilkins *Freeman, Annie Trumbull Slosson, and Alice *Brown, wrote well into the twentieth century, and the movement had a continuing impact through its influence on such writers as Willa *Cather and Edith *Wharton, both of whom lived intermittently in New England. But after World War I, following a brief period when Susan *Glaspell and Mary Heaton Vorse worked with the innovative Provincetown Players, the region lost its preeminence in women's literature. The *modernist preoccupation with the broad and cosmopolitan was at odds with the New England focus on small space and data of ordinary life; modernist critic John Crowe Ransom once dismissed the reclusive Emily Dickinson as "a little home-keeping person." Although some New Englanders, like Edna St. Vincent *Millay and Sylvia *Plath, became known as rebels, many were content to be little home-keeping persons. One thinks of the quiet novels of Vermont's Dorothy Canfield *Fisher and Maine's Mary Ellen Chase, or the nature poetry of Abbie Huston Evans, Barbara Howes, and Maxine *Kumin. With the possible exception of Shirley *Jackson's famous short story "The Lottery" (1948) New England women hardly experienced a "revolt from the village" phase.

A negative aspect of smallness is the relative homogeneity of the writers. Although there has always been a vital African-American tradition in the region, carried on in the twentieth century by such novelists as Dorothy *West, who assailed money-getting in *The Living Is Easy* (1948), and Ann *Petry, who writes primarily of small-town Connecticut, New England writing has not been widely multicultural. (There are always exceptions, like the working-class Franco-American Grace Metalious, whose 1956 *Peyton Place*, a novel firmly in the New England

tradition, was sensationalized by the media.) It may be a sign of the future that three contemporary writers, Marge *Piercy, Adrienne *Rich, and May *Sarton, all "woman-identified realists" who have been successful in more than one genre, were born and brought up outside the region. They identify self-consciously as New Englanders, however, and identification with the region may be the strongest commonality of New England women writers. Even the modernist Amy *Lowell wrote a poem ("Lilacs," 1925) about lilac all over New England, which reads "Lilac in me because I am New England."

[*See also* Local Color Fiction; Regionalism.]

• Ima Honaker Herron, *The Small Town in American Literature* (1939). Hayden Carruth, "The New England Tradition," in *Regional Perspectives*, ed. John Gordon Burke (1973), pp. 1–47. Lina Mainiero and Langdon Lynne Faust, eds., *American Women Writers* (1979–1982). Arlen Gilman Runzler Westbrook and Perry D. Westbrook, eds., *The Writing Women of New England, 1630–1900: An Anthology* (1982). Josephine Donovan, *New England Local Color Literature: A Women's Tradition* (1983).

Barbara A. White

NEWMAN, Frances (1883–1928), novelist, short story writer, translator, critic, librarian. Born in Atlanta to a wealthy, socially prominent family, Frances Newman's experience of the repressiveness of the white southern woman's role engendered the themes that would dominate her literary efforts. She deplored her society for extolling intellectual stupidity in women and for raising women to be sexually attractive while denying them the right to acknowledge and express sexuality.

After studying library science and working as a librarian for several years, in 1923 Newman went to Paris, studied literature at the Sorbonne, and began translating materials (from five different languages) that were to appear in *The Short Story's Mutations: From Petronius to Paul Morand* (1924). This study reflects her preference for experimental writing with psychologically oriented plotting. Also in 1924, Newman won an O. Henry Memorial Award for "Rachel and Her Children."

Newman's first published novel, *The Hard-Boiled Virgin* (1926; reprint, 1980), is the semiautobiographical story of the coming of age and struggle for artistic expression of Katharine Faraday. Newman called it an attempt to tell the truth about how women feel. Experimental in form, the novel was banned in Boston for its mention of puberty, menstruation, venereal disease, and birth control. As the novel tells us, women of Katharine Faraday's class were not supposed to know what a virgin was until they had ceased to be one. Caught between the external demands of the southern code for women and the internal pressures of her own passions, Katharine Faraday feels as though she has been "hard-boiled." The sense of frustration and repression experienced by Katharine Faraday is reflected stylistically through complicated sentence structures, numerous conditionals, multiple negatives, and no dialogue. Katharine Faraday is always referred to by her full name, since nothing more intimate is possible for her, either in naming or relationships. The multiple negatives suggest that she has no choices, but is faced only with things that are not choices. The omission of dialogue speaks eloquently in a work that depicts the agony of being silenced and stifled.

In her second novel, *Dead Lovers Are Faithful Lovers* (1928; reprint, 1977), Newman continued her stylistic experiments, exploring the crippling of women who are taught to depend on a relationship with a man for their own sense of identity. The novel juxtaposes two women, a wife bent on holding her husband by means of physical beauty and sexuality, and her husband's mistress, who attracts him with her intelligence.

Newman died of a mysterious eye ailment shortly after the publication of *Dead Lovers Are Faithful Lovers*. Her translation of *Six Moral Tales from Jules Laforgue* (1928) was published posthumously.

• Hansell Baugh, ed., *Frances Newman's Letters*, foreword by James Branch Cabell (1929). Fay Blake, "Frances Newman: Librarian and Novelist," *Journal of Library History* 16 (Spring 1981): 305–313. Anne Goodwyn Jones, *Tomorrow Is Another Day: The Woman Writer in the South, 1859–1936* (1981). Kathryn Lee Seidel, *The Southern Belle in the American Novel* (1985).

Kathryn West

NEWSPAPER COLUMNS. In the fall of 1852, Sarah Payson Willis ("Fanny *Fern," 1811–1872) became the United States' first woman newspaper columnist when she began to write for the New York *Musical World and Times*. Fern went on to write for the *New York Ledger*, whose readers were so eager to see her latest social and political commentary that they mobbed the newspaper's offices at press time, according to Fern's biographer, Joyce W. Warren.

Through the years, many women have followed in Fern's footsteps, despite the historical reluctance of editors to promote women to such positions. In the late nineteenth and early twentieth centuries, when women reporters were largely confined to sob sister positions, editors seemed especially willing to install women as personal advice columnists. Pioneers include Marie Manning ("Beatrix Fairfax," 1873?–

1945), author of a very successful advice-to-the-lovelorn column that was started in 1898 in Hearst's *New York Journal*, and Elizabeth Meriwether Gilmer ("Dorothy *Dix," 1861–1951) of the *New Orleans Picayune* and subsequently the *New York Journal* (where she also worked as a crime reporter until 1917, when she devoted herself exclusively to her column). The advice column remains a viable form today, as evidenced by the phenomenal popularity of columns by twin sisters Ann Landers and Abigail Van Buren ("Dear Abby"). Contemporary subsets of the advice column include the household hints column (such as Heloise Reese's "Hints from Heloise"), the etiquette column (such as "Miss Manners," Judith Martin of the *Washington Post*), and the business advice column (as popularized by the erudite Sylvia Porter).

In the twentieth century, as women were slowly admitted to the ranks of political reporters, they also began to establish outstanding records as political columnists. Their ranks include Dorothy *Thompson (1893–1961), a European correspondent for the *Philadelphia Public Ledger* and the *New York Post* during the 1920s and early 1930s, who after 1940 wrote a widely syndicated column on international affairs noted for its strong emotional language. Other top-ranking women include Anne O'Hare McCormick (1880–1954), the *New York Times'* first foreign affairs columnist; Doris Fleeson (1901–1970), a veteran *New York Daily News* reporter who began a twice-weekly political commentary for United Features Syndicate in 1945; and Mary McGrory (born 1918), one of the *Washington Post's* most widely read columnists.

In a unique class, perhaps, is the syndicated daily "My Day" column started by First Lady Eleanor Roosevelt (1884–1962) in 1936. Read by millions, it covered a range of subjects, from human-interest stories about the First Family, to the place of women in society, to political thought. That the First Lady would launch such a vehicle is testament to the perceived influence of the newspaper column.

Over the years, different perspectives on the social and political events of the day have been offered in columns by a number of women editors of alternative newspapers. Prominent among them is Dorothy Day (1897–1980), who for nearly fifty years in her New York–based *Catholic Worker* provided thoughtful commentary on topics from spirituality and lay Catholic life to the politics of poverty and pacifism. More than a decade after her death, her column is still reprinted in the *Catholic Worker*. Day is part of a long tradition of U.S. advocacy writing by women in alternative newspapers published by various organizations dedicated to achieving goals that range from woman suffrage to abolition and civil rights for minorities, from world peace to gay and lesbian rights. Another notable example is Molly Ivins, long the editor and political writer for the alternative *Texas Observer*, and now a nationally syndicated columnist. Such alternative-press columns, while not as well known as those in large mainstream metropolitan newspapers, have sometimes reached audiences of many thousands.

Many women have found their strongest, most creative voice in writing about the affairs of home and hearth—but from a clearly articulated political and/or social perspective. Contemporary examples include the thoughtful Anna Quindlen (born 1952) of the *New York Times*, as well as the syndicated humorist Erma Bombeck (born 1927). Ellen Goodman (born 1941) covers a wide array of topics in her syndicated column, from politics and the environment to family and domestic issues. These sorts of columns, along with their lesser sister, the gossip column, remain popular. Why? Perhaps in impersonal mass society, the personal column, like the soap opera, fulfills a need for connection. When such a column is pulled for any reason—as, for example, Joyce Maynard's syndicated column was by many newspapers in the 1980s for its increasingly self-indulgent ruminations on her divorce—newspapers hear emphatically from its loyal following of readers.

[*See also* Journalists; Journals, Academic; Little Magazines; Magazines, Women's; Newspapers, Women's; Reportage.]

• Marion Marzolf, *Up from the Footnote: A History of Women Journalists* (1977). Madelon Golden Schilpp and Sharon M. Murphy, *Great Women of the Press* (1983). Nancy L. Roberts, *Dorothy Day and the* Catholic Worker (1984). Barbara Belford, *Brilliant Bylines: A Biographical Anthology of Notable Newspaperwomen in America* (1986). Maurine H. Beasley, *Eleanor Roosevelt and the Media* (1987). Michael Emery and Edwin Emery, *The Press and America: An Interpretive History of the Mass Media*, 7th ed. (1992). Joyce W. Warren, *Fanny Fern: An Independent Woman* (1992). Maria Braden, *She Said* What? *Interviews with Women Newspaper Columnists* (1993).

Nancy L. Roberts

NEWSPAPERS, WOMEN'S. While women's periodicals include opinions ranging from the liberal to the ultraconservative, their history is tied to the history of the American republic. Indeed, history shows that the ebb and flow of political movements dictates the content and number of women's publications. Charles P. Danky's *Women's Periodicals and Newspapers from the Eighteenth Century to 1981* (1982) lists 1500 entries. Some printed only one issue, while others have flourished for more than one hundred years. Some were created by such well-known feminists as Emma *Goldman and Margaret Sanger, and many were published by organizations, including the National Woman Suffrage Association, the League of Women Voters, the National Organization for Women, and the YWCA.

But much is still not known about women's newspapers; since the history of women's periodicals is not housed in any one text, information must be gleaned by combing the library stacks for references. Often, nothing save a publication name is available, with no detail as to focus, political outlook, or intended audience. What follows, then, is an abbreviated overview of women's periodicals that relies heavily on available anecdotes and secondary sources.

During the late eighteenth and early nineteenth centuries, most explicitly female publications concerned themselves with matters of home, family, and spirituality. Discussion of gender relations, while rare, was more likely to be found in such general audience periodicals as the *Genius of Universal Emancipation* or the *Memphis Advocate*.

It was not until *slavery took central stage, and activists opposed to "the peculiar institution" became galvanized, that women's subservience to men became a fit topic for written debate. As a result, explicitly political periodicals written by women for women sought to rally females around the antislavery cause. Many of the writers were Christians, and virtually all were financially independent and able to fund the printing of their ideas themselves. Literary women contributed poetry and pamphlets, and, while careful to avoid linking antislavery politics to radicalism, helped activate large numbers of women who might otherwise not have been reached.

Most powerful and influential were the *Grimké sisters, Angelina and Sarah, who "urged women to participate in the freeing and educating of slaves" (*An Appeal to the Christian Women of the Southern States*, 1836). Their calls, and especially Sarah's *The Province of Women* (1837) and *Letters on the Condition of Women and the Equality of the Sexes* (1837), were widely circulated.

The Grimkés and other antislavery leaders found themselves at the center of a larger debate about women's participation in public life. While some groups tried to sidestep this issue, others, like the U.S. Society of Friends and the U.S. Missionary Friends, used their newsletters to argue for expanding women's influence. Other magazines, such as the *Dial*, put out by a group of New England spiritualists who became Transcendentalists, began publishing in 1840 and stressed the intellectual equality of women and men. When the American Anti-

Slavery Society split in 1840 over "the insane innovation of allowing women to serve as speakers and officers," the still incipient women's movement got an enormous boost. Women's suffrage became a hot topic.

The debate over suffrage was prompted, at least in part, by debates over giving the franchise to black men. A number of periodicals dedicated to arguing the issues and publicizing ideological differences between prosuffrage forces resulted. Susan B. *Anthony and Elizabeth Cady *Stanton of the National Woman Suffrage Association (NWSA) were on one end of the spectrum. They had accepted money from George Francis Train, a rich adventurer who spent most of his time agitating for Irish independence. The *Revolution*, the paper they founded with Train's money as NWSA's organ, began in 1868 under the banner "Men, their rights and nothing more; Women, their rights and nothing less."

Unfortunately, Train was a liability. While he considered himself a staunch feminist, his racism was legion. His statement "Women first and Negro last" branded him an unsavory ally, and Anthony and Stanton found themselves in an untenable position. Within a year, both the *Revolution* and NWSA were on shaky ground. In 1869, Mary Livermore, a NWSA critic, founded the American Woman Suffrage Association (AWSA) to "unite those who cannot use the methods and means which Mrs. Stanton and Susan use." Unlike NWSA, AWSA promoted a single issue, eschewing debate on broader women's rights questions. It's newspaper, the *Woman's Journal*, began publishing in 1870, with Livermore, Lucy Stone, and Julia Ward *Howe as editors. The *Revolution*, meanwhile, folded in 1870 after Train was jailed for giving a pro-Irish independence talk.

While ideological splits fractured suffrage work nationally, state associations worked hard to win the vote locally. Some had their own publications (such as the *Wisconsin Citizen*, published monthly from 1887 to 1919). In addition, The Church of Jesus Christ of Latter Day Saints published the *Women's Exponent* (1872–1914) to push Mormons to support suffrage. Likewise, the Board of Missions of the Methodist Episcopal Church published the *Women's Mission Advocate* (1880–1910), and organizations like the American Association of University Women (AAUW) responded to the growing number of women academics by starting the prosuffrage *Graduate Women* in 1882.

The years following the Civil War gave antislavery activists a chance to regroup. Some joined populist, labor, or socialist organizations. Others got involved in the highly visible and energetic women's rights movement. According to *Women and the American Left* (1983) by Mari Jo Buhle, few left-of-center women's publications appeared between 1871 and 1900, due principally to the limited resources of radical women. The exceptions were *Farmer's Wife* (1891–1894), connected to the National Women's Alliance, Inc., which addressed farm isolation, household drudgery, the women's movement, the People's party, and urged "equal rights to all, special privileges to none." The second, *Woodhull and Claflins Weekly* (1870–1876), editorialized in support of divorce reform, women's rights, free love, spiritualism, and socialism.

A host of nonpolitical publications geared to homemakers and wives also emerged during this period, from *Everyday Housekeeping* (1894–1907) to *Vogue* (1892–present) and *Good Housekeeping* (1885–present). On the other end of the continuum were right-wing publications: *Remonstrance against Woman Suffrage* (1890–1913) in Boston, and the newsletter of the National Association Opposed to Woman Suffrage, *Woman Patriot* (1918–1932), which changed its focus after woman suffrage was won, and opposed women's groups that "organized for class and sex war."

Among the most charged publications of the 1800s were those advocating *temperance. Mary Livermore's claim that woman suffrage could help end moral decay held great sway, and by the mid-1800s temperance groups were springing up and publishing local and national magazines and newspapers. The *Lily* (1849–1856), founded by Amelia Bloomer after the Seneca Falls Convention, was the most famous. Its masthead urged "the emancipation of women from intemperance, injustice, prejudice and bigotry."

The confluence of the temperance and suffrage movements, alongside the generally soaring number of prolabor groups led by immigrants, anarchists, and socialists, led to a turn-of-the-century burgeoning of women's publications. One of the most notable was the *Forerunner* (1909–1916), published and written by Charlotte Perkins *Gilman, which stressed humanism over feminism, and renounced the class-struggle doctrines of Marxism. Also influential was the *Masses* (1911–1917), published by Floyd Dell and Max Eastman. Explicitly feminist, it included the writing of Dorothy *Day, Elizabeth Gurley Flynn, Mabel Dodge *Luhan, and Mary Heaton Vorse, and discussed everything from birth control to social relations.

Emma *Goldman's *Mother Earth* (1906–1917) appealed to anarchists and included essays on birth control and sexual liberation; it was banned from the mails in 1917. *Socialist*

Woman (1907–1913) was the official women's newspaper of the Socialist party. Although it never surpassed three thousand subscribers, it was influential in advancing arguments for women's independence, political rights, temperance, and social purity. Margaret Sanger published six issues of the *Woman Rebel* in 1914. Ostensibly devoted to legalizing birth control, it spoke in favor of free love, labor militancy, and anticlericalism.

But one did not need to be a radical feminist to have access to women's periodicals. The New Woman of the twentieth century might also have read newsletters put out by one of the many chapters of the Federated Clubs of America, the General Federation of Women's Clubs, or the YWCA. Prosuffrage groups also continued producing media, from the sober *Common Cause* (1909–1920) to *Votes, Votes for Women* (1909–1933), which urged suffrage and women's employment, but ignored the controversy over birth control and abortion. Professional women had *Business Women's Magazine* (1914–1915), the *Woman Worker* (published from 1921 to 1956 by the Women's Bureau) and the *Dill Pickle* (1916–1935; for women journalists), while labor unions eager to organize women also got into the publishing act. Among the most prolific was the International Ladies Garment Workers Union, which produced the English-language *Justice* (1919), the Spanish-language *Justicia* (1919), the Italian-, Yiddish-, and English-language *Ladies Garment Worker* (1910–1918). Polish, Finnish, Czechoslovakian, and Jewish women also started magazines, one of which, *Toveritar*, started in 1911 for Finnish-Americans, is still being produced.

Despite this flurry of activity, by the early 1920s many of these publications had folded. Suffrage had been won and the postwar United States had entered a period of severe repression and backlash. Still, several radical newspapers continued. *Working Women* (1928–1935), published by the Communist party, covered the activities of women and blacks in party-sponsored organizations, and was succeeded by *Women Today* (1936–1938), which sought to bring women into emerging antifascist movements.

Despite the fact that the 1920s ushered in a period of relative inactivity (which basically continued until the late 1960s), many women's organizations continued to publish their own newspapers. Thus, groups like the Daughters of the American Revolution, AAUW, Zeta Phi Beta Sorority, National Women's Army Corp., National Association of Colored Women, National Council of Jewish Women, YWCA, and Business and Professional Women kept news of women's struggles and accomplishments alive.

However, one innovative publication, the *Ladder*, deserves special mention because it defied business as usual when it was created in 1956. Published until 1972 by the Daughters of Bilitis, the *Ladder* gave lesbians across the United States a forum. While early editions urged readers to appear traditionally feminine so as not to arouse negative reactions, it was still a daring attempt in the McCarthyite 1950s.

By the late 1960s, second-wave feminism inspired a wide array of new publications. Although many were short-lived, the range was vast, and for the first time, working-class women, women of color, and lesbians wrote explicitly about their lives, condemning the homophobia, racism, and classism that conspired with sexism to silence them. Their work included: *AEGIS: A Magazine on Ending Violence against Women; Africa Women; Akamai Woman* (Hawaii); *Amazon: A Midwest Journal for Women; Broomstick: Options for Women Over Forty; Momma: The Newspaper for Single Mothers; off our backs; On Our Backs; Ms.; Native Sisterhood: Journal of the Organization of Penitentiary Women; New Directions for Women; La Raza Mestiza; Signs;* and *Sojourner*. In addition, thousands of local newsletters, many of them mimeographed by a handful of women, were circulated. Right-wing women also created publications, including *The Phyllis Schlafly Report* (since 1967).

The last two decades have seen a burgeoning of feminist scholarship that attempts to analyze the interplay of race, class, and gender in women's lives. Yet, while today's analysis is somewhat different from those of the past, we know that women have always used the written word to influence one another's thinking.

[*See also* Journalists; Journals, Academic; Little Magazines; Newspaper Columns; Reportage.]

• Alice S. Rossi, ed., *The Feminist Papers: From Adams to de Beauvoir* (1973). Linda Grant dePauw and Conover Hunt, *Remember the Ladies: Women in America, 1750–1815* (1976). Miriam Gurko, *The Ladies of Seneca Falls: The Birth of the Women's Rights Movement* (1976). David Doughan and Denise Sanchez, eds., *Feminist Periodicals, 1855–1984: An Annotated Bibliography of British, Irish, Commonwealth and International Titles* (1987). Sheila Ruth, ed., *Issues in Feminism: An Introduction to Women's Studies*, 2d ed. (1990). Rita J. Simon and Gloria Danziger, *Women's Movements in America: Their Successes, Disappointments and Aspirations* (1991). Vron Ware, *Beyond the Pale: White Women, Racism and History* (1992).

Eleanor J. Bader

NEW WOMAN. The New Woman (1890–1920), as defined by the mainstream media, was a revolutionary social ideal at the turn of the century that defined women as independent, physically adept, and mentally acute, and able to work, study, and socialize on a par with men. The popular image of the New Woman was related to a new consumer and leisure ethic, to health and dress reforms, to rising pressure from woman's suffrage, to gains that women had made in their access to higher education, and to expanding service and public sector occupations. Women writers of the era produced challenging works of fiction and drama about women's lives that explored the new social and psychological possibilities—and their limitations—including the often-inhibiting realities for many women of race and class biases. The literary images of the New Woman encompass women trapped by social conventions, their lives devastated by lack of choice; women who challenge the racial and political orthodoxies of the day; and women who reimagine history and * myth from feminist perspectives.

Lois Rudnick

NEW YORK WRITERS. New York is where it happens. The city is both influent and effluent, at once open-closed, rigid-fluid, urbane-provincial, suffocating-energizing. It is the haven of the émigré, the ghetto of the immigrant; home for the exclusive and the excluded. It houses ethnic neighborhoods and the United Nations. Everything—person, place, event—is instant metaphor for what is right-wrong with it. New Yorkers are edgy and unflappable. They have seen everything; everything is possible.

New Yorkers are always on the move, sometimes laterally within neighborhoods, sometimes vertically into different economic and social territories. The city, in spite of the rigidity of its grid infrastructure, is in constant flux. Hell's Kitchen is gentrified and renamed Clinton. Lincoln Center destroys a long-established community. Upper West Side brownstones get converted into one-room apartments, downgraded to single-room occupancies, upgraded to condos and co-ops. Yesterday's safe block is today's drug-infested alley. Ethnic neighborhoods, which give their inhabitants a sense of place and home within the abrasive city, are pulled out of shape: Chinatown invades Little Italy; Indian restaurants pervade the Ukrainian section; Hasidim and Hispanics fight bloody territorial battles against blacks. The Metropolitan Museum encroaches on Central Park. A defunct department store is converted into the Mid Manhattan Library. Something is always being torn up or put up. There is no center.

To be a woman and live in this structurally most masculist of cities takes bravery, stamina, imagination. The New York woman writer, present or past, native or transplant, learns to use the city to her own advantage to support

herself, her politics, her art. Shirley Hazzard and Ursule Molinaro work at the UN; Toni Cade * Bambara and Hortense * Calisher, for the Welfare Department. Bambara, Audre * Lorde, Grace * Paley, Muriel * Rukeyeser do teaching stints. Veronica Geng is an editor at the *New Yorker;* Toni * Morrison at Random House. Suzanne Zavrian operates a bookstore near Columbia. Ann * Petry writes for *Amsterdam News;* Kate Simon, for the *Nation;* Paule * Marshall for black publications.

New York women use the system to write against the establishment. Letty Cottin Pogrebin and Gloria * Steinem create * *Ms.* magazine; they replace the patriarchal Passover service and text with their own rites and *Hagadah.* Merlin Stone uses the resources of libraries to write revisionist books about the Goddess. Lucy Lippard is the contemporary art world's feminist critic. Social critic Lois Long writes in the *New Yorker* of the male-dominated fashion industry that, more subtly than the "girlie mag," uses and abuses the female body.

Women find tenements and alternate spaces, factory lofts among them, in which to live and work. By accretion, they create communities: Greenwich Village, SoHo, Tribeca. The Lower East Side, once haven of little nations (China, Italy, Middle Europe) becomes the East Village, where Alice Notley runs The Poetry Project, where Susan Sherman lives and publishes *IKON,* an internationalist-feminist poetry journal that sponsors events supporting Nicaraguan women and children. At the west edge of Greenwich Village, an artists' subsidized community, housed in the old telephone building, is the home of Rukeyser, Bonnie Bluh, Erica Duncan, who conducts The Women's Salon from her apartment. On the Upper West Side, Marilyn Hacker edits *Thirteenth Moon;* Zavrian runs her own press, coordinates the annual New York book fair.

The essence of the New York woman writer's art is her experience of the city. Occasionally a woman is perceived as a New York writer because her most famous work is located in New York: Lorraine * Hansberry's *The Sign in Sidney Brustein's Window* (1964), Ann * Petry's for *The Street* (1946). Zora Neale * Hurston, none of whose fiction is of the city, is considered a New York writer because of her relationship with and effect on the * Harlem Renaissance.

Other women who migrate to the city— Irene Fornés (Havana), Geng (Atlanta), Fannie * Hurst (St. Louis), Tama * Janowitz (San Francisco), Jamaica * Kincaid (Antigua), Denise * Levertov (Wales), Kate Simon and Anzia * Yezierska (Poland)—are recognizably New York writers because the city is both the subject and substance of their art. New York writers document the complex and paradoxical life of the city from their perspective as women. Whether Julia Alvarez, Alice *Childress, Simon, Edith *Wharton, or Yezierska, they write of their neighborhoods and the walls that separate neighborhoods, the systems that keep people in their place. Childress, Sybil Claiborne, Fornés, Levertov, Lorde, Gloria *Naylor, Paley, Rukeyser write as fierce feminists; Simon and Yezierska, from their experience as female immigrants; Marshall, Lorde, Naylor, of the black woman in a racist culture. Hurst champions the Lower East Side working-class woman; Wharton addresses her upper-class society's oppression of its women.

Some New York women write of the city with ironic wit. Geng and Fornés, a pioneer in off-Broadway experimental theater, parody the New York pop culture scene. Cynthia *Ozick and Tess *Slesinger write biting portraits of men who dominate the Upper West Side intellectual milieu; Janowitz, of the remnants of Andy Warhol's East Village empire. Wendy *Wasserstein's women, who come of age in the late 1960s, wryly struggle with old values and new feminism.

The *minimalist talk of the Village women in Paley's stories expresses the tenor of their marginal lives. Through Bambara we hear black street dialect and rhythm. Wharton's elegant prose depicts the suffocation of her well-clad women.

In autobiographical poetry, disguised autobiographical fiction and frankly autobiographical essays, many write of themselves as New York women. Calisher's youthful relationship with parents and brother is the source of her early "Hester" stories; Marshall, through Selina in her first novel, depicts her own struggles to find her identity within the black community. Rukeyser's and Lorde's primal poems are of themselves as women, mothers, daughters. Rukeyser writes of her recovery from a stroke. Lorde's response to her cancer is that of a *woman warrior.

For many the dynamics of the neighborhood are the juices that stimulate the move into larger, political territories. Paley celebrates Greenwich Village women who meet in playgrounds, at PTA meetings, in stores, who from their centers as mothers, demonstrate for peace. Levertov, Paley, and Rukeyser are themselves nonviolent activists. Paley is a founder of the Women's Pentagon Action; Rukeyser goes to Spain, South Africa, Korea; Paley and Rukeyser go to jail; all three go to Vietnam. Petry writes of the 1943 Harlem riots. Bambara fights for civil rights, belongs to Sisters in Support of South African Sisterhood. They bear witness in their essays, poetry, fiction.

To look at the New York woman writer is to look through transparencies of often incompatible portraits; to listen to her is to hear choruses not always harmonious. Yet, wherever-whenever she is born, regardless of class, race, or perspective, she speaks of the city so unmistakably that, when we enter her work, we recognize New York.

Kossia Orloff

NIGGLI, Josefina (b. 1910), dramatist, novelist, and educator, is recognized for her realistic portrayals of Mexican village life and people. She was born 13 July 1910 in Monterrey, Nuevo Leon, Mexico, the only child of Frederick Ferdinand, a Texan who managed a cement plant, and Goldie Morgan Niggli, a concert violinist from Virginia. In 1913, she moved with her mother to San Antonio, Texas. She received a B.A. in 1931 from Incarnate World College, and by that time had published articles in *Mexican Life* and *Ladies' Home Journal*. Her father privately printed her poems under the title *Mexican Silhouettes* (1928; revised, 1931). In 1935, she enrolled in the University of North Carolina, where she received an M.A. in 1937. Her plays during this period are all set in Mexico. The folk plays, some of which were published in *One-Act Play Magazine* and collected in *Mexican Folk Plays* (1938), include *Tooth or Shave* (1935), *The Red Velvet Goat* (1936), and *Sunday Costs Five Pesos* (1936). Her historical plays include *Soldadera* (published in Margaret Mayorga's *The Best One-Act Plays of 1937*), *This Is Villa* (published in Mayorga's *The Best One-Act Plays of 1938*), and her M.A. thesis, *Singing Valley* (1936). She received Rockefeller Foundation fellowships in play writing for the years 1935–1936 and 1937–1938, and worked in theater in Mexico. In 1938, she received the Fellowship of the Bureau of New Plays and moved to New York. In 1939, she returned to Chapel Hill, North Carolina, and during the war began teaching English and drama at the University of North Carolina. She published her best-known work, the novel *Mexican Village*, in 1945. Her second novel, *Step Down, Elder Brother* (1947), not as acclaimed as her first, became a Book-of-the-Month-Club selection. *Pointers on Playwriting* (1945) was widely used in schools and revised in 1967. After working in Hollywood in 1948, fellowships allowed Niggli to spend time at the Abbey Theater in Dublin in 1950, and the Old Vic School in Bristol in 1955. In 1956, she was hired to teach English and drama at Western Carolina University, from which she retired in 1975. Recognized for her human and realistic portrayal of women soldiers in *Soldadera*, Niggli is also known for depicting the people and life of Mexico without the typical United States stereotypes and romanticizations, and thus was an early voice in the literary construction of Chicano identity.

• Rodolfo Usigli, Foreword to *Mexican Folk Plays* (1938). Walter Spearman, *The Carolina Playmakers: The First Fifty Years* (1970). Raymond Paredes, "The Evolution of Chicano Literature," *MELUS* 5 (Summer 1978). Julio A. Martinez, *Chicano Scholars and Writers: A Bibliographical Directory* (1979).

Marcus Embry

NIN, Anaïs (1903–1977), novelist, essayist, diarist, feminist guide. Born in Paris to French-Danish singer Rosa Culmell and Cuban pianist-composer Joaquin Nin, Anaïs Nin considered herself an "international" writer. When her parents separated in 1914, Nin came to New York with her mother, helping with boarders and working as a fashion and artist's model until she was twenty-three. In 1926, she moved to France with her new husband, Hugh Guiler, a banker who later became an accomplished lithographer (Ian Hugo).

In France, Nin became personally and artistically involved with many writers, among them Henry Miller, Lawrence Durrell, and Antonin Artaud. Her first publication in 1932 applauds and analyzes D.H. Lawrence's "unprecedented" content and style. In Paris, she cocreated a short-lived printing press (Siana) and a literary magazine (the *Booster*). Her novels *Winter of Artifice* (1939) and *House of Incest* (1936) were both also originally published in France, but the war stifled their dissemination. In 1933, Nin began psychotherapy with Otto Rank, and in 1934, accompanied him to New York, where she herself became a practicing therapist.

After her brief career as therapist, she returned to her preferred vocation, writing, and started another press (Gemor). She concentrated on not only providing printing outlets for new artists, but also on producing beautifully hand-crafted works. The press closed when costs and labor became overwhelming. For the next twenty years, she published novels, short stories, and erotica. Despite the fact that several publishing houses released Nin's work in the 1940s, 1950s, and 1960s, her writing went largely unappreciated outside her artistic circle.

In 1966, Swallow Press and Harcourt and Brace jointly published parts of Nin's private diary. The subject of rumors and conjecture, her diary consisted, in 1966, of over fifteen thousand hand-written pages. Although widely received as frank personal documents, the published volumes were heavily edited. Her seven adult *diaries were published from 1966

through 1977. During these years, Nin began to be considered—and to consider herself—a spokeswoman for newly liberated women emerging from the second wave of feminism. Whether because she was popular or because she believed in remaining traditionally "feminine" and not alienating men, Nin became an increasingly controversial figure as political proponents of the women's movement found her influence, and attention from the media, disturbing. Nonetheless, lecturing and interviewing in America and abroad from 1971 to 1973, Nin was enthusiastically received. As a consequence, several journals emerged, focusing on her and her coterie, including *Under the Sign of Pisces* and *Anaïs Nin: An International Journal*.

• The majority of Nin's papers are housed in the University of California, Los Angeles; Northwestern University; and the University of Southern Illinois, Carbondale. See also Robert Zaller, ed., *A Casebook on Anaïs Nin* (1974). Evelyn J. Hinz, ed., *A Woman Speaks: The Lectures, Seminars, and Interviews of Anaïs Nin* (1975). Rose Marie Cutting, *Anaïs Nin: A Reference Guide* (1978). Nancy Scholar, *Anaïs Nin* (1984).

Wendy M. DuBow

NONFICTION WRITING. *See* Autobiography; Biography; Captivity Narratives; Confessional Nonfiction; Diaries and Journals; Exploration Narratives; Slave Narratives; Spiritual Narratives.

NONSTANDARD ENGLISH. Celie, Alice *Walker's heroine in her Pulitzer Prize–winning work, *The Color Purple* (1982), speaks from the vantage point of her newly constructed self. After being rescued from the physical and verbal brutality and sexual exploitation of her father and husband, as well as from her own psychic bondage of guilt and self-doubt, she emerges whole, empowered, and free at last. Thus, she is not about to surrender to the foolishness of talking in someone else's tongue, in a language that feels "peculiar" to her mind.

When you talk or write in your own language, you are locating yourself in familiar mental surroundings, permitting the creation of a space for voicing your ideas and concerns. You are enabled to produce writing that is real and true to you, and in so doing, you become empowered. Using your own language is an assertion of your right to exist on your own terms. On the one hand, it is a violation of a social convention, a thumbing of one's nose at the bourgeois mandate that all writing must be in the Language of Wider Communication (LWC; in this country, so-called standard English), an implicit rejection of the culture of power and oppression. On the other hand, it is a conscious assertion of the value, power, and functionality of one's own language.

In the 1970s, the Executive Committee of the Conference on College Composition and Communication (CCCC), an organization of some ten thousand college writing teachers, adopted a language policy (and subsequently published a follow-up monograph) advocating "students' right to their own language," that is, use of the linguistic framework in which we individually find our "identity and style." In virtually the same breath, though, *The Students' Right* called for the use of "Edited American English" in writing. Thus arose an inherent contradiction: one's native tongue is good enough for community and home life, but not good enough for writing and the world—unless, of course, one's *muttersprache* is middle-class European-American English.

Beyond the troubling implications of this contradiction concerning spoken communication was the further issue of the written word. Again, Alice Walker put the troubling question into the mouth of Celie. To paraphrase, if only fools would talk in a syntax and semantics peculiar to their minds, wouldn't only fools also write in such a language? The answer, of course, is yes. Writers, like speakers, must situate their discourse within rhetorically familiar patterns, or they will sound foolish. This is no less true for writers from the LWC community as it is for writers from other linguistic communities.

For, as Berger and Luckmann (1966) argue, reality itself is not simply a social construction, but a sociolinguistic construction. We come to know the world and we perceive it through the lens of whatever our particular language happens to be. Further, if a hierarchy is imposed on this linguistic framework, and the "dominant" language in a society is perceived to harbor the power, it is also a consciously empowering act to resist the linguistic patterns of that dominant language and purposefully retain or take on an individual form of communication.

However, the risks attendant to this resistance are many. Among them is the complete rejection of a nondominant writing form by those in the dominant position, or, a questioning of one's learnedness and intelligence. One becomes intimidated by the possibility of these social consequences in the LWC world, and thus one reluctantly does not take any linguistic risks, plays it safe in terms of topics, and produces boring, mechanical pieces of writing, often abstruse, and ultimately meaningless. The essays must have been the kinds of compositions Langston Hughes produced for his college classes before he wrote his "Theme for English B" (in *Montage of a Dream Deferred*, 1951).

Hughes was right when he said, "A page [that] come[s] out of you will be true." Using one's own language is also a way of writing/righting the world; this kind of writing joins one as a comrade in the creation of a new reality and a new social order, while simultaneously rejecting the status quo. The writer who thus challenges the linguistic * canon also helps to pave the way for other marginalized voices speaking in other tongues.

It is balm for the oppressed to witness this act of linguistic defiance. For American Indians, African-, Hispanic-, and Asian-Americans, European-American women, the working class, and others with a different voice, one who writes in her own linguistic discourse provides inspiration to carry one.

[See also Black English; Language, Women's, *article on* Women's Language.]

• Benjamin Whorf, *Language, Thought and Reality,* edited by J. B. Caroll (1956). Joshua Fishman, *Language and Nationalism* (1973). Ayo Bamgbose, ed., *Mother Tongue Education* (1976). Roger Fowler and Gunther Kress, *Language and Control* (1976). Geneva Smitherman, *Talkin and Testifyin* (1977). Thomas Kochman, *Black and White Styles in Conflict* (1981). William Labov, "Objectivity and Commitment in Linguistic Science: The Case of the Black English Trial in Ann Arbor," *Language in Society* 11 (1982): 165–201. John Baugh, *Black Street Speech* (1983). Jerrie Scott, "Mixed Dialects in the Composition Classroom," in *Language Variety in the South: Perspectives in Black and White,* edited by Michael Montgomery (1986). Hanni U. Taylor, *Standard English, Black English, and Bidialectalism* (1989). Miriam Chaplin, "A Closer Look at Black and White Students' Assessment Essays," *Iowa English Bulletin* 38 (1990): 15–27. Keith Gilyard, *Voices of the Self* (1991). Nancy Sommers, "Between the Drafts," *College Composition and Communication* 43, no. 1 (February 1992): 23–31. Geneva Smitherman, " 'The Blacker the Berry, the Sweeter the Juice': African American Student Writers and the National Assessment of Educational Progress, 1969–1989" (1993).

Geneva Smitherman

NORMAN, Marsha (b. 1947), playwright. Best known for her Pulitzer Prize–winning play *'night Mother* (1983), Norman's dramatic works include *Getting Out* (1977), *Third and Oak: The Laundromat* (1978), *Circus Valentine* (1978), *The Holdup* (1980–1983), *Traveler in the Dark* (1984), *The Secret Garden* (book and lyrics, 1991) and *Sarah and Abraham* (1991). Much of Norman's work examines failed family relationships; often she explores the damages and inadequacies of the * mother-daughter relationship.

Before taking up play writing as a career, Norman attended Agnes Scott College and the University of Louisville, and taught emotionally disturbed children. She also worked as a television writer and journalist. Although from the South, Norman has, in personal interviews, eschewed the title of southern woman writer. In fact, 'night Mother contains specific directorial instructions admonishing the affectation of any accent that would place the two characters in a specific region of the United States.

'night Mother, while receiving acclaim for its powerful impact, is also Norman's most controversial work. Jessie's calm and premeditated suicide, in spite of the protests of her mother (the only other character in the play), questions our culture's social and religious views about *suicide, especially when Norman has defended Jessie's actions as "nearly total triumph" (Interviews with Contemporary Women Playwrights, 1987).

Her second-most-popular play, Getting Out, looks not only at the failed mother-daughter relationship, but also at failed institutions. Arlene is "getting out" of jail because she is "completely rehabilitated"; yet for many reasons, it becomes apparent that Arlene has exchanged one prison for another, larger one. Getting Out won the George Oppenheimer Award, and Norman, the Outer Critics' Award for best new playwright.

Three of Norman's plays deviate from a focus on women and identity: Traveler in the Dark portrays the life crisis of a cancer surgeon; The Holdup is a feminist depiction of the frontier myth; and The Secret Garden, a Tony award-winning musical, is an adaptation from the children's book by Frances Hodgson *Burnett.

Norman's plays are the subject of numerous articles in both the scholarly and popular journals. The structure of her drama is most often compared to that of Chekhov and Ibsen; thematically, she is often aligned with Shepard and Beckett. Many scholars explore Norman's and Beth *Henley's (another Pulitzer Prize winner from the South) common domestic motifs and settings—specifically, their characters' fixation on food and the kitchen as the physical and metaphorical setting of those characters' lives.

• Jenny S. Spencer, "Norman's 'night Mother: Psychodrama of Female Identity," Modern Drama 30, no. 3 (September 1987): 364–375. Irmgard H. Wolfe, "Marsha Norman: A Classified Bibliography," Studies in American Drama 3 (1988): 148–175. Leslie Kane, "The Way Out, the Way In: Paths to the Self in the Plays of Marsha Norman," Feminine Focus, ed. Enoch Brater (1989), pp. 255–274. Patricia R. Schroeder, "Locked behind the Proscenium: Feminist Strategies in Getting Out and My Sister in This House," Modern Drama 32, no. 1 (March 1989): 104–114.

Kay K. Cook

NOVEL, Beginnings of the. Women read novels. Women write novels. This was the case in the late eighteenth century when the first American novels were published and this remains the case in the late twentieth century. Perhaps because the novel is such a loose and flexible literary form (defined, simply, as any extended work of fictional prose), women have written every conceivable kind of novel, using various styles and conventions, and have addressed them to a variety of social causes, political issues, personal aspirations, or group identities.

The American novel began in the early national period, the era following the signing of the U.S. Constitution. The two best-selling novels of the time were both written by women, Susanna Haswell *Rowson's Charlotte, A Tale of Truth (1791; later and popularly known as Charlotte Temple) and Hannah Webster *Foster's The Coquette (1797). Both were about women and explicitly addressed to women. Even the novel now regarded as the first American novel, William Hill Brown's The Power of Sympathy (1789), was published anonymously and was long thought to have been written by a woman. More significantly, Brown notes that in his book "the dangerous Consequences of SEDUCTION are exposed, and the Advantages of FEMALE EDUCATION set forth and recommended." In short, Brown's implied reader is a woman reader.

There are reasons for the intimate relationship between the early American novel and women. First, the novel was an accessible form. It did not require advanced learning in the classical tradition as did many forms of eighteenth-century poetry or essay. Because women were barred from higher *education at that time and received a rudimentary primary education that often concentrated on subjects such as sewing or elocution, the novel could be read by middle-class women and even by women from the working classes. In a number of novels, classical allusions are actually defined in the text, again making the books accessible to readers who did not possess sophisticated literacy skills. Second, the establishment of lending *libraries in even the smallest frontier communities made novels available at prices that women could afford. Typically, for a fee of four or six dollars a year, a woman could borrow as many novels as she wished and could also (as frequently happened) share them among her friends. Many eighteenth-century accounts indicate that one woman would often read aloud from a popular novel while other women embroidered or quilted together, another way of minimizing the cost of books and also weaving (literally) the plots of novels into women's everyday lives.

In early America, women had few rights: they could not vote, serve on juries, make wills, or sign contracts. In most states, a woman's property became that of her husband upon marriage (but not vice versa). Ignored by law and politics in the new nation, women found themselves the center of the world represented in novels. The plots of most novels written before 1820 (including many by men) often revolved around everyday life situations of concern to women. In Rowson's *Charlotte Temple*, a teenage girl runs away from her home in England in the company of a dashing young soldier. Abandoned in the new world, she sinks into dreadful poverty, and then dies, bearing her illegitimate daughter among strangers. Rowson does not condemn Charlotte for her promiscuity; rather, she blames a social system that leaves her so innocent, an easy prey to unscrupulous men. The plot is a good deal more complicated in *The Coquette*, since here the main character, Eliza Wharton, is well-educated and, we learn near the end of the book, in her thirties when she "falls." Yet even in this instance, Foster critiques both the character and the society in which she lives. Under particular attack is the double sexual standard by which a woman's sexual transgressions are punishable by abandonment and even death, whereas a man's are often overlooked as trivial offenses.

From the beginning, the novel addressed a variety of social classes. Although the novel is usually defined as a middle-class form, *working-class fiction for and by women has also existed since the very beginning of the nation. Martha Meredith Read, in *Monima, or the Beggar Girl* (1802), extends her analysis of gender dynamics into the lower classes by making Monima a heroine who withstands abuses that middle-class people (both men and women) heap upon her. Sarah Savage's *The Factory Girl* (1814) examines life in early American factories and even shows the heroine organizing the other factory girls into a study group.

Two of the best novels of the early nineteenth century show that women, early on, were not limited to writing *sentimental novels (a term that was originally meant to be pejorative and that continues to have a condescending or even negative connotation). There is nothing sentimental about Tabitha *Tenney's parodic *Female Quixotism* (1801). On the contrary, the novel satirizes Dorcasina Sheldon and women like her who believe in the fantasies they read about in romances. Tenney urges her fellow fiction writers to produce more serious, sensible, and salutary fiction. She also advocates a well-rounded education for women as an antidote to the tendency toward impracticality and daydreaming that insure Dorcasina's downfall. In

her recommendation for better education for women, Tenney joins the ranks of virtually every woman novelist before 1820.

A different critique of the American social system can be found in Rebecca *Rush's *Kelroy* (1812). This book examines the lack of female earning power and the concomitant need for women to rise in the world through calculated marriages. Mrs. Hammond does what needs to be done to get her two daughters married, but in order to accomplish this goal, she must scheme, connive, and disregard all human feeling, including that of her daughters. Yet, Rush suggests, for all her villainy, Mrs. Hammond is doing exactly what an upper-middle-class mother is supposed to do. *Kelroy* is a picture of society life in early America with all of the gilt and varnish stripped away. The portrait is far more sinister than anything Jane Austen ever penned.

The early American novel ranged widely in subject matter, form, and technique, but consistently advocated better education for women as well as a more equitable sexual and social standard. As a genre, it explicitly addressed the needs and desires of the women who had been left out of the new nation's Constitution.

Many of the features that characterized the early American novel continue throughout its history. In particular, the novel makes possible the joint examination of social issues and human psychology, allowing for a more individualized representation of social problems than would, for example, a tract. At the same time, the novel typically presents an array of characters through which the author can represent the effects of social change on a wide variety of individuals. For these reasons, many recent immigrants to the United States (*see* European Immigrant Writing) find the novel to be an excellent form for investigating the impact of culture shock, *assimilation, and resistance. In addition, America has produced rich traditions of *African-American fiction, *Asian-American fiction, *Chicana and Latina fiction, and *Jewish-American fiction.

The novel comes in every form and addresses a variety of issues. From Rowson's *Charlotte Temple* to Kathy *Acker's *Blood and Guts in High School* (1984) to Toni *Morrison's *Beloved* (1987), the novel has proven flexible enough to represent the range of U.S. women's lives and to accommodate the possibilities of the imagination and talents of U.S. women writers.

[*See also* Bildingsroman and Kunstlerroman; Domestic Fiction; Epistolary Novel; Gothic Fiction; Historical Fiction; Minimalist Fiction; Mystery and Detective Fiction; Romance Novel; Science Fiction; Sentimental Novel; War Novel; Working-class Fiction.]

• Lillie Deming Loshe, *The Early American Novel, 1789–1830* (1907). Henri Petter, *The Early American Novel* (1971). Cathy N. Davidson, *Revolution and the Word: The Rise of the Novel in America* (1986).

Cathy N. Davidson

O

OAKES SMITH, Elizabeth (1806–1893), novelist, poet, journalist, lecturer.

A writer from her childhood days in North Yarmouth, Maine, Elizabeth Oakes Smith married (reluctantly) in 1823. When her husband's newspaper published "Mrs. Seba Smith" 's poetry, histories, legends, and biographical sketches (of Madame de Staël and Charlotte Corday), she gained entrance to Portland literary circles, which hosted local writers such as Ann S. Stephens, John Neal, and Nathaniel Parker Willis.

Though her husband gained national recognition for his "Major Jack Downing" letters, the couple's prosperity dwindled due to ill-advised speculation. In 1839, they moved to New York, where the mother of six wrote for some of America's most prominent magazines, including *Godey's Lady's Book*, *Graham's*, and the *Southern Literary Messenger*. The last was where she scored her first great success, "The Sinless Child" (1842), a poem Edgar Allan Poe regarded highly enough to compare to his *Eureka*. With her fame established, she changed her name to Elizabeth Oakes Smith, and her children legally adopted the surname Oaksmith.

Admired by critics Rufus Griswold and Poe, Oakes Smith contributed to and edited gift books while writing novels, prose sketches, essays, poetry, travel narratives, literary and theater criticism, and collections of children's stories. She also published frontier adventure tales in the young dime-novel industry as well as *The Salamander* (1848), a vaguely transcendentalist meditation on purity and pride, and *Bertha and Lily* (1854), a novel on the nature of womanhood. Her reform novel *The Newsboy* (1854) went through twelve editions in its first year.

Oakes Smith's greatest energies centered on women's issues. A recognized leader at Seneca Falls and a succession of women's conventions, Oakes Smith discussed marriage, gender issues, and suffrage in her pamphlet *Woman and Her Needs* (1851). She contributed to the *Una*, an early women's paper, and lectured on women's and labor issues, garnering admirers such as Henry David Thoreau and Bronson Alcott. The latter asked Oakes Smith's advice on Louisa May Alcott's short stories.

Up until the mid-1880s, Oakes Smith lectured on women's rights and on figures ranging from Cleopatra to Margaret * Fuller.

• Mary Alice Wyman, ed., *Selections from the Autobiography of Elizabeth Oakes Prince Smith* (1924; reprint, 1980). Mary Alice Wyman, *Two American Pioneers: Seba Smith and Elizabeth Oakes Smith* (1927).

Barbara T. Ryan

OATES, Joyce Carol (b. 1938), novelist, short story writer, poet, essayist, playwright, educator, publisher.

Working in virtually every literary genre, writing on subjects as varied as feminism, censorship, sexual harassment, and boxing, Oates is a true contemporary American woman of letters. A chaired professor at Princeton University, Oates has readers both within the academy and outside it; her work is accessible to a diverse audience in America and abroad.

Oates grew up in rural Erie County, New York, outside of Buffalo, a region she later transformed into her fictional "Eden County." She graduated from Syracuse University as valedictorian, and earned a master's degree at the University of Wisconsin. After her marriage to Raymond Smith (with whom she directs Ontario Review Press), Oates began a career of university teaching and writing. Her first collection of short fiction, *By the North Gate*, appeared in 1963. She has since published more than seventy-five volumes of fiction, essays, plays, and poems. (Several of her monographs are illustrated with her own line drawings.) Oates's essays appear frequently in the popular press as well as in literary quarterlies.

Working in so many media has made Oates a critical conundrum. Initially, she was dismissed as "popular," or regarded with incredulity because of her productivity. However, by the 1980s, Oates had won considerable critical respect for her uncompromising vision of the human person caught in the violent upheavals of American life. She has received professional honors, including election to the American Academy and Institute of Arts and Letters (1978). Book-length studies and scholarly essays on her work have registered her prominence and influence.

Oates has been viewed primarily as a novelist, with (as of 1992) nineteen novels and novellas published under her own name, and—curiously enough—five others under pseudonyms. One of her novels, *them*, won the National Book Award in 1969; others, including *Because It Is Bitter and Because It Is My Heart* (1990), have been nominated for that award.

Oates has also won distinction in other genres. After many successive years of writing award-winning short stories, the O. Henry Award committee gave Oates a special prize for continuing achievement. Her stories are widely anthologized; two have been made into films. Oates often explores what she calls her "horizontal obsessions" in her short fiction, studies to be further developed in her longer work. Oates's thematic concerns resurface in her poetry and plays, which have been produced off-Broadway and on campuses. She also has published a half-dozen volumes of collected literary and cultural criticism. Her characterization of the recent flood of psychological biographies as "pathography" has been widely quoted. Although some have objected to her fictional portraits of female victims, Oates defines herself as a feminist, offering revisionary readings, and wrestling with the problematic status of the *(Woman) Writer* (essays, 1988).

As Ellen Friedman (*Joyce Carol Oates*, 1980) suggests, Oates believes the artist has a pivotal cultural role. In a May 1973 essay in *Psychology Today*, Oates speaks out against "the myth of the isolated artist," which she believes distorts the relationship of art and world. Unlike the contemporary critic Harold Bloom, Oates does not regard "influence" as an Oedipal demon. Instead, she calls for artists to acknowledge their literary heritage.

In her 1972 collection of short fiction, *Marriages and Infidelities*, Oates dramatizes her own intertextual intentions. She retells a group of classic short stories, including "The Metamorphosis," "The Turn of the Screw," and "The Lady with the Pet Dog," as fables of modern American life, working in an eclectic postmodern spirit.

Although much of her work is hauntingly allusive, it was initially read as a continuation of American realism, as defined by Dreiser and Steinbeck. Her first novel, *With Shuddering Fall* (1964), is set in "Eden County," her own rural birthplace; it is also a contemporary *Paradise Lost*. Like Faulkner, with whom she has been compared (Creighton, 1979), Oates revisits that fictive locale in subsequent fiction. She also sets her characters in motion against other realistic/mythic backdrops: the halls of the academy, the corridors of power, Eastern Europe, even the boxing ring. But her central focus is not on social change or regional myth. Oates is concerned with the self's hallucinatory shadow show, the "phantasmagoria of personality."

As several readers have noted, Oates plays a revisionary game with her own fiction. Repositioning characters, Oates reimagines their struggles for self-realization in pairs and sequences of novels. *them* (1969), a novel of urban violence, is one part of a trilogy about life in twentieth-century America, which includes a surrealistic drama of the migratory underclass, *A Garden of Earthly Delights* (1967), and a wryly satirical existential novel about suburbia, *Expensive People* (1968).

In an important pair of early novels, Oates follows the trajectory of male and female fugitive heroes through the turmoil of the 1960s, with very different results. In *Wonderland* (1971), Oates tracks the hero's flight through a world recognizable as a child's nightmare, peopled by kidnappers, predators, and tricksters. Oates later suggested that *Wonderland* represented a critical transition in her work, and she eventually revised it, replacing a dreamlike final scene with a harsh confrontation between runaway daughter and pursuing father. In *Do with Me What You Will* (1973), Oates shifted the odyssey of selfhood from a patriarchal quest for power and control to a drama of female captivity and resistance.

Oates turns to many sources for what Joanne V. Creighton calls her "middle" novels (1992). These novels are more freely structured and experimental; Oates revisits earlier fiction and develops new imaginative forms. *The Assassins* (1975), a novel of political conspiracy, is subtitled *A Book of Hours*, a secular offertory. *Childwold* (1976), a novel of adolescence, is Oates's rereading of *Lolita*. Both unfold in a succession of interior monologues. *Son of the Morning* (1978) is a singular confession of a Pentecostal fanatic. *Cybele* (1979) evokes the ancient classical myth. *Unholy Loves* (1979) is Oates's first academic novel, a satiric picture of writers in residence. *Angel of Light* (1981), another novel of contemporary political intrigue, is a modern *Oresteia*.

Interestingly, American literature itself provides the allusive framework for Oates's second trilogy: *Bellefleur* (1980), *A Bloodsmoor Romance* (1982), and *Mysteries at Winterthurn* (1984). Extravagantly narrated, these novels reanimate the subversive strategies of nineteenth-century woman writers and offer Oates's own flagrantly feminist reading. *Bloodsmoor*, for example, is Oates's *Little Women*, retold with grotesque comic effect.

Oates's next two novels are even more explicitly feminist. In *Solstice* (1985), the intimate relationship between two women, an artist and a writer in residence, twists and uncoils like Ariadne's thread. *Marya, A Life* (1986) is even more autobiographical. It represents an imaginative bridge between Oates's Eden County fiction and her more recent focus on modern woman's coming of age.

In her later novels, Oates continues to explore many of these characteristic themes—the torturous paths of adolescence (*You Must Remember This*, 1987), the flawed rituals of the academy (*American Appetites*, 1989). She has become more intently focused on feminist concerns. Two novellas tell stories of "outlaw" women (*I Lock My Door upon Myself*, 1990; *The Rise of Life on Earth*, 1991). *Because It Is Bitter and Because It Is My Heart* dramatizes the murderous nature of contemporary sexual and racial relationships.

Because of her extraordinary artistic productivity, Joyce Carol Oates has been resistant to easy critical classification; but there is little doubt that she has become a major contemporary literary figure. Her work offers an important index to the tumultuous, multiform, pluralistic culture of late-twentieth-century America.

• Eileen T. Bender, "Autonomy and Influence: Joyce Carol Oates's *Marriages and Infidelities*," *Soundings* 58 (1975): 390–406. Linda W. Wagner, *Critical Essays on Joyce Carol Oates* (1979). Gary F. Waller, *Dreaming America: Obsession and Transcendence in the Fiction of Joyce Carol Oates* (1979). Joanne V. Creighton, *Joyce Carol Oates* (1979). Ellen Friedman, *Joyce Carol Oates* (1980). Francine Lercangee, *Joyce Carol Oates: An Annotated Bibliography*, Prefaced and annotated by Bruce F. Michelson (1986). Greg Johnson, *Understanding Joyce Carol Oates* (1987). Harold Bloom, ed., *Joyce Carol Oates* (1987). Eileen T. Bender, *Joyce Carol Oates, Artist in Residence* (1987). Elizabeth Lennox Keyser, "*A Bloodsmoor Romance*: Joyce Carol Oates's *Little Women*," *Women's Studies* 14 (1988): 211–223. Anne Hiemstra, "A Bibliography of Writing by Joyce Carol Oates," in *American Women Writing Fiction: Memory, Identity, Family, Space*, ed. Mickey Pearlman (1989), pp. 28–35. Perry Nodelman, "The Sense of Unending: Joyce Carol Oates's *Bellefleur* as an Experiment in Feminine Storytelling," in *Breaking the Sequence: Women's Experimental Fiction*, ed. Ellen Friedman and Miriam Fuchs (1989), pp. 250–264. Joanne V. Creighton, *Joyce Carol Oates: Novels of the Middle Years* (1992).

Eileen T. Bender

OBJECT RELATIONS THEORY. *See* Psychoanalysis and Women, article on Object Relations Theory.

OCCOMY, Marita Bonner (1899–1971), dramatist, short story writer, and essayist. Occomy epitomized the creative furor and passion of her era, the *Harlem Renaissance. Highly creative, her works were published and praised in maga-

zines such as the *Crisis* and *Opportunity: A Journal of Negro Life*. A frequent literary prize-winner in both magazines, Bonner was undoubtedly a compelling model for a readership eager for fresh black voices, and her literary impact has yet to be fully accessed.

Born to Joseph Andrew and Mary Anne Bonner in Boston in 1899, Marita Bonner was also educated in that city. Her literary interest began early, and during high school she was a frequent contributor to the student magazine. In 1918, she entered Radcliffe College, where she was an active member of the student body, and, according to reports, founded the college's chapter of black sorority Delta Sigma Theta. Bonner began teaching high school while in college, and continued to teach after her graduation, holding positions in Bluefield, West Virginia, and Washington, D.C. She met and married William Almy Occomy in Washington in 1930, and moved to Chicago, where she spent the rest of her life rearing three children and eventually resuming her teaching career.

Bonner's literary career began in Washington, D.C. A member of Georgia Douglas *Johnson's S Street Salon, Bonner was exposed to some of the most popular African-American writers of her time. Her early short stories, while noticeably short in length and often simplistic in structure and form, clearly reflect the concerns that would permeate the rest of her writings—the struggle of the individual against restrictive, often insurmountable external forces, primarily class and race, with a particularly cogent focus on the unique challenges faced by black women. These themes remain a constant in Bonner's later, more technically sophisticated writings, many of which are set in Chicago and depict the obstacles often created by the multiethnic and multicultural makeup of the city. Her 1933 two-part story "Tin-Can," which won the literary prize for fiction from *Opportunity*, preempts Richard Wright's *Native Son* in its examination of the effects of poverty-ridden urban life on the development of an individual personality.

But it is her 1928 play, *The Purple Flower*, which best epitomizes Bonner's art. This expressionistic allegory of American race relations, which has lost little of its dramatic impact over time, reveals her sophistication as an artist, and her willingness to experiment with form in order to best address the racial and political challenges of her age.

Unfortunately, in her later years Marita Bonner had less time to devote to her writing, and ceased publishing after 1941. Bonner died in Chicago in 1971 of injuries suffered in a fire. A notebook of unpublished short stories was found after her death, and is currently housed, along with some of her other papers, at Radcliffe College's Schlesinger Library in Cambridge, Massachusetts.

• Doris E. Abramson, *Angelina Weld Grimké, Mary Burrill, Georgia Douglas Johnson, and Marita O. Bonner: An Analysis of Their Plays* (1985). Joyce Flynn, *Marita Bonner Occomy* (1987). Lorraine Roses and Ruth Randolph, *Marita Bonner: In Search of Other Mothers' Gardens* (1987). Lorraine Roses, *Harlem Renaissance and Beyond: Literary Biographies of One Hundred Black Women Writers, 1900–1945* (1990).

Alisa Johnson

O'CONNOR, Flannery (1925–1964), novelist and short fiction writer. O'Connor's career spanned years of great change to the region and the religion that most shaped her perspective on the world. As a Roman Catholic writing in the years immediately preceding the great changes of Vatican II, and as a southerner responding to the social changes of integration and the civil rights movement, O'Connor's work reflects the tensions of the times. In the postwar era, when America was simultaneously defining and extolling the virtues of the nuclear family, O'Connor wrote, instead, of multigenerational households and fragmented families— grandparents rearing a second generation of offspring just as poorly as they had reared the first, widows supporting ungrateful adult children, single fathers neglecting their children, parents completely ignoring children because of their own self-absorption, or couples not wanting children at all. Her work has been labeled black humor, southern Gothic, or southern grotesque in order to describe the humor that emerges from these stories despite the tragedy or pathos of their plots.

For all the attention her work has received, O'Connor wrote comparatively little. Before her death at thirty-nine, she published only two short novels—*Wise Blood* (1952) and *The Violent Bear It Away* (1960)—and one collection of stories, *A Good Man Is Hard to Find and Other Stories* (1955). Her posthumously published work, however, has been of equal, if not greater interest to readers, literary critics, and theologians: a second collection of stories titled *Everything That Rises Must Converge* (1965); an edition of lectures and essays titled *Mystery and Manners* (1969), edited by Sally and Robert Fitzgerald; a selection of letters with biographical headnotes by Sally Fitzgerald called *The Habit of Being* (1979); a collection of O'Connor's reviews for several Catholic journals, compiled by Leo J. Zuber and titled *The Presence of Grace and Other Book Reviews* (1983); and a collection of O'Connor's interviews, *Conversations with Flannery O'Connor* (1987), edited by Rosemary M. Magee.

Born in Savannah, Georgia, on 25 March 1925, Mary Flannery O'Connor was the only child of Edward and Regina Cline O'Connor. When she was thirteen, her father was diagnosed as having lupus erythematosus, and in the three years before his death the family moved inland, eventually to Milledgeville, Georgia, to be near the Cline relatives. O'Connor received a degree in sociology from Georgia State College for Women (now Georgia College) in Milledgeville in 1945. In both high school and college, O'Connor drew cartoons for student newspapers and honed the tools she used for her satiric writing; like the political cartoonist, she learned to rely on exaggeration and humor to make a point. Her undergraduate efforts at fiction won her a fellowship to the University of Iowa, where she earned an M.F.A. in creative writing in 1947. In 1948 another prize brought her to Saratoga Springs, New York, where she worked to expand the stories of her thesis into her first novel. Her brief stay at Yaddo put her in the company of many well-established writers, including poet and convert to Roman Catholicism Robert Lowell.

As her letters make clear, O'Connor's response to her early success was to move to the Northeast to be near the publishing world and the group of Roman Catholic writers and intellectuals that had so enthusiastically accepted her. She spent several months in New York City, and then moved to Connecticut to live with her new friends Sally and Robert Fitzgerald and their large family. Her close friendship with the Fitzgeralds is an important part of O'Connor's current literary reputation, since both parents have edited volumes of her works, and several of the children were instrumental in producing *Wise Blood*, director John Huston's 1979 classic film adaptation of her novel.

Returning to Milledgeville for Christmas in 1950, O'Connor suffered her first attack of lupus, the same disease that had killed her father a decade earlier. The cortisone used in her treatment eventually led to her spending her final years on crutches. The severity of the first attack and impossibility of predicting future ones prevented O'Connor from returning to her life in Connecticut. Though she made occasional trips outside Georgia to give lectures and receive honorary degrees—at her family's insistence, she even flew to Europe to seek a cure at Lourdes—she remained on the farm, Andalusia, in her mother's care until her death on 3 August 1964.

O'Connor's two novels both deal with characters who have been told they are destined to become evangelical Christian preachers. Much as Jonah tried to escape the prophetic role of God's messenger and was swallowed by a great fish while trying to flee, World War II veteran Hazel Motes of *Wise Blood* and twelve-year-old Francis Marion Tarwater of *The Violent Bear It Away* run from their fates. Founding the godless Church Without Christ cannot protect Hazel from his grandfather's prophesy, however. He dies a penitent; having blinded himself, he fills his shoes with stones and wraps barbed wire around his chest to expiate his guilt. Francis Marion is the age of Huck Finn and Holden Caulfield, and like them, he wants to break from the mold an older generation is forcing upon him. Francis Marion fares no better than Hazel in his attempt to escape his destiny. His great-uncle Mason Tarwater, the fundamentalist fanatic who reared him, charges the boy to bury and to baptize; responding to an inner voice, the boy tries to avoid performing these rites, but fails. His journey of initiation leads him to commit murder and to be raped. Again, the despairing fugitive cannot escape the call, but this time the novel's final image suggests he not only survives, but goes on to bring the violent message his experience has taught him to the city he sees ahead of him.

The stories in O'Connor's two collections were included with several other pieces in *The Collected Stories of Flannery O'Connor* (1971), an edition that remains the standard text for her short works. The rural Georgia setting O'Connor knew best predominates, but Atlanta and New York also appear. In many other ways, the stories reflect O'Connor's particular vantage point on the world. Many stories present the situation of O'Connor and her mother, widows living alone on farms, often with adult children in their care. Important stories such as "The Life You Save May Be Your Own," "Good Country People," "Greenleaf," "The Enduring Chill," "Everything That Rises Must Converge," and "The Comforts of Home" all begin with this situation. Often the adult child is, like O'Connor, forced to return from the city due to illness and to leave behind an exciting life of the mind discovered there, one that is missing from the solitary existence of rural life. Joy/Hulga in "Good Country People," for instance, takes out her bitterness at the loss of her leg on her indomitably cheerful mother. Ridiculing all her mother represents, the young nihilist is left, quite literally, without a leg to stand on at the end of the story. O'Connor is a part of the fallen world of pain and suffering she so often appears to mock in her stories.

Flannery O'Connor felt herself to be outside the mainstream of postwar American culture. A Roman Catholic in the Protestant Bible Belt, she felt an affinity toward her fundamentalist neighbors because she shared with them a set of priorities that made gaining salvation the focus of their lives. The handicapped, the elderly, the very young, the widowed, and the orphaned are all at the center of her fictions, but none receives the polite sympathy from the stories' narrators that modern readers have come to expect. Perhaps this sharp-edged vision explains why O'Connor attracts the critical attention of more scholars each year than any other twentieth-century American woman writer.

• Miles Orvell, *Invisible Parade* (1972; reprinted as *Flannery O'Connor: An Intrduction*, 1991). Robert E. Golden and Mary C. Sullivan, *Flannery O'Connor and Caroline Gordon: A Reference Guide* (1977). Melvin J. Friedman and Beverly Lyon Clark, eds., *Critical Essays on Flannery O'Connor* (1985). Arthur Kinney, *Flannery O'Connor's Library: Resources of Being* (1985). Louise Westling, *Sacred Groves and Ravaged Gardens* (1985). Jill P. Baumgaertner, *Flannery O'Connor: A Proper Scaring*, Foreword by Frederick Buechner (1988). Suzanne Morrow Paulson, *Flannery O'Connor: A Study of the Short Fiction* (1988). Robert H. Brinkmeyer, Jr., *The Art and Vision of Flannery O'Connor* (1989). Stephen G. Driggers et al., *The Manuscripts of Flannery O'Connor at Georgia College* (1989). Richard Giannone, *Flannery O'Connor and the Mystery of Love* (1989).

Margaret Anne O'Connor

OLD AGE AND AGING. *See* Aging.

OLSEN, Tillie (b. 1913), novelist, short fiction writer, nonfiction writer, poet. Tillie Lerner was born in 1913 in Wahoo, Nebraska, to Russian Jewish immigrant parents, and was educated through the eleventh grade at Omaha Central High School. Her socialist upbringing, concern for the poor, and love of language became hallmarks of her small but distinguished body of work. Olsen's fiction affirms the humanity of underprivileged individuals who frequently fail to realize their potential because of subsistence-level drudgery, children, and minimal amounts of time and space. She focuses particularly on working-class women and their often heroic ability to endure.

After leaving school, Olsen, a member of the Young Communist League and the Communist party, was twice briefly jailed for participating in strikes, including the famous Bloody Thursday maritime strike in San Francisco, where she had moved in 1933. Olsen married Jack Olsen, a warehouseman and printer, in 1943, and is the mother of four daughters; she still lives in San Francisco, the setting of much of her fiction.

Her work falls roughly into three periods: the activist political publications of the 1930s; the polished, highly praised short fiction of the 1950s and 1960s; and the feminist-humanist nonfiction writing, teaching and public speaking from the 1970s to the present. In the 1930s,

Olsen published several polemical essays, including "The Strike," "Thousand Dollar Vagrant," and "Literary Life in California" (1934); she also wrote two poems, "There Is a Reason" and "I Want You Women Up North to Know" (1934), a powerful evocation of poverty-stricken Mexican women. Her unfinished novel *Yonnondio: From the Thirties*, begun in 1932, remained unpublished until 1974.

In the 1950s and 1960s, Olsen entered the greatest period of her fiction writing. After enrolling in a creative writing course at Stanford University, she published "I Stand Here Ironing" (1956) to critical acclaim, quickly following it with "Hey Sailor, What Ship?" (1957), "O Yes," and the enormously successful "Tell Me a Riddle" (1961). All four stories, written in Olsen's densely rich, imagistic, innovative style, and republished as *Tell Me A Riddle* (1962), delineate the difficulties of poverty, illness, loneliness, bigotry, and exclusion, and center on the relationships of mothers and daughters, ultimately celebrating their accomplishments.

Since 1970, aided by time at such retreats as the MacDowell Writers Colony, Olsen has published the first of a two-part story, "Requa I" (1970); the rediscovered fragment of her Great Depression novel, *Yonnondio* (1974); and the now-classic *Silences* (1978), her explanation of the relatively small number of women writers and suggestions for correcting the imbalance. *Silences* also reprints Olsen's afterword to the 1972 republication of Rebecca Harding Davis's *Life in the Iron Mills*, and Olsen's 1972 essay "Women Who Are Writers in Our Century: One out of Twelve." In the eighties, she edited two collections: *Mother to Daughter, Daughter to Mother* (1984), which includes "Dream Vision," the briefly eloquent tribute to her mother; and *Mothers and Daughters: That Special Quality* (1987).

Perhaps even more significant than her writing in these last two decades is Olsen's personally powerful impact on current views of women writers and women's studies: a recipient of prestigious fellowships and grants, Olsen has held numerous visiting professorships at universities both in the United States and abroad, and continues to be in great demand as a reader and speaker who possesses a gift for galvanizing her audiences. Although she correctly perceives herself as a humanist, encouraging more diversity in curricula and more attention to the voices of "silenced" people, her influence on women has been truly profound.

• Miriam Elaine Neil Orr, *Tillie Olsen and a Feminist Spiritual Vision* (1987). Mickey Pearlman and Abby H. P. Werlock, *Tillie Olsen* (1991). Joanne Frye, *Tillie Olsen* (1994).

Abby H. P. Werlock

ORALITY. *Primary orality*, a condition in which information is communicated and preserved without any reliance upon writing, is known partly from ethnographic description, but mostly from logical operations in which we deduce what orality must have been like from what we know of its paired term, *literacy*.

Oral cultures tend to merge the knower and the known, interpretation of data with the data itself. Because oral communication requires the copresence of both speaker and audience, the oral is always oral-aural, mouth to ear, and thus integrative (it connects) rather than dispersive. Privileging the subjective mutual experience of speech events in time, orality makes understanding a function of situations and occasions: comprehension is never only a matter of words, but of abundant nonverbal context. Orality shows an almost total commitment to narrativization, for, as Walter Ong states in "Writing Is a Technology That Restructures Thought" (1986), "Categories are unstable mnemonically. Stories you can remember." Ong further explains that the narratives circulated in oral cultures "use the past to explain the present, dropping from memory what does not serve this purpose"; hence, orality's present is, as Jack Goody terms it, "homeostatic" with the past.

Current interest in orality arises from our present condition of a "transition" to—again in Ong's term—a "secondary orality," a shift away from print media as central to cultural maintenance. In this transitional moment, academic literary theory has explored the relation and meaning of *voice* and *text* from an essentially logical-philosophical perspective, one which has unfortunately tended to ignore the empirical data increasingly provided of late by researchers in anthropology, linguistics, psychology, and sociology, and the establishment of a number of interdisciplines variously called sociolinguistics, the ethnography of speaking, and *ethnopoetics. There has also been a (somewhat) popular, as well as academic interest in a variety of oral history projects, concerned with recording the life stories of illiterate or marginally literate people, whose illiteracy (or preference for oral expression) seems a function of their racial, class, or gendered subject-positions. Some have called selected examples of this expression *orature*, a positive term invented to undo the paradoxical or oxymoronic implications of *oral literature*.

In its relation to literacy, orality has been the subordinate term. Literacy is modern, advanced, and superior; orality is ancient, retrograde, and inferior. Partly this perception derives from our common experience of learning to speak before we learn to write. Freud's evolutionary narrative of an infantile orality developing by stages to a mature genitality also remains a factor. This means, too, that literacy and textuality are "male," while orality and speech are "female," although, so far as the characterization of American writers is concerned, biological gender does not determine the tendency to write orally. Thus, Whitman, who "sings" to "celebrate" himself, insisting upon presence, immediacy, and "I"-to-"you" dramatic communication, is an oralist, while *Dickinson, with her absent audience, indirection and abstraction, eye rhymes and puns, is a textualist.

Recent attempts to broaden the traditional canon of American literature to include the work of Native Americans, African Americans, ethnic Americans, and women generally have also focused attention on orality. There exists already a considerable body of critical work demonstrating the persistence of oral traditions in the writing of contemporary Native American and African-American writers, while attention to Asian-American writers has highlighted the importance of "talking story" in their written literature. Interestingly, there is a preponderance of women writers among these latter three groups. Similarly, publication and study of women's *diaries, *letters, and journals have touched on the writers' commitment to such traditionally oral values as immediacy, personal experience, and interpersonal relations.

[See also African-American Oral Tradition; Folklore; Native American Oral Tradition.]

• Ruth Finnegan, *Oral Poetry* (1977). Sylvia Scribner and Michael Cole, *The Psychology of Literacy* (1981). Walter Ong, S. J., *Orality and Literacy* (1982). John M. Foley, *Oral Tradition in Literature* (1986). Eric Havelock, *The Muse Learns to Write: Reflections on Orality and Literacy from Antiquity to the Present* (1986). Walter Ong, S. J., "Writing Is a Technology That Restructures Thought," in *The Written Word: Literacy in Transition*, ed. Gerd Bauman (1986), pp. 23–50. Jack Goody, *The Interface between the Written and the Oral* (1987).

Arnold Krupat

ORIENTALISM includes the scholarly, literary, and discursive practices by which Western cultures define their coherence and centrality by opposing themselves to the representations of exotic otherness in the Orient and the oriental. The tradition of orientalism has been well documented and analyzed in Edward Said's *Orientalism* (1979). In Anglo-European and American discourses, orientalism constitutes one means by which Western nations exercise colonial and neocolonial domination over territories and peoples constituted as oriental. Orientalist *topoi* include the representation of

Western culture as morally purer and aesthetically superior to the imperfect oriental culture. At times this opposition takes the form of a narrative of development, in which an unenlightened East is caught in a primordial past imagined as anterior to Western civilization; Arabs or Asians are represented as superstitious and backward, in need of Western rationalism, religion, and philosophy. At other times, the justification of colonial rule is reproduced in the representation of Western nations as the modernizing protector and educator of commercially and technologically unsophisticated oriental colonies; this relationship is naturalized in the trope that figures the empire as father and the oriental object as its child.

The orientalist tradition also often genders the relationship between Occident and Orient, casting the relationship within the romantic narrative that figures the Western subject as masculine and eroticizes the Orient as a feminine object. Orientalist literature is replete with images of the oriental woman as immoral seductress, beguiling traitor, or exotic odalisque, courtesan, or dancer. Alternately passive, enchanting, and threatening, these *stereotypes serve to construct, and to subordinate, a figure at once racially and sexually other to coherent, univocal Western masculinity. Within the history of American society, factors that form the context for such stereotypes include shifts in *class, *gender, and racial definitions, due to changes in *immigration, rapid *industrialization or deindustrialization, or war; these shifts give rise to national anxieties about defining the boundaries of the nation, anxieties symptomatized by stereotypes, such as the oriental woman, which fix and exclude elements projected as threatening to the social order. In this regard, American popular culture and literature has produced the characters of the childlike enchantress Suzie Wong, the endangering Dragon Lady, and the childlike Lotus Blossom.

Recent Asian-American literature has, in turn, refunctioned orientalism against itself, satirizing the stereotype of the passive oriental woman by thematizing its paradoxical construction. David Henry Hwang's *M.Butterfly* (1988), for example, inverts the relationship of the Western desiring male subject and the feminine oriental site and object of desire in a drama that reveals the oriental opera singer to be a transvestite. In Jessica *Hagedorn's *Dogeaters* (1990), the Philippine beauty queen Daisy Avila pronounces a feminist critique of beauty pageants and ultimately takes up a crucial role in the armed struggle against a corrupt dictatorship. In both instances, the figures of the oriental woman are refunctioned in ways that appropriate the stereotype in order to rewrite it as a site of powerful agency in the critique of orientalism.

Lisa Lowe

ORTIZ COFER, Judith (b. 1952), one of many Hispanic women whose work is altering the *canon of American literature by integrating the Puerto Rican American perspective. Cofer was born in Hormigueros, Puerto Rico, and presently lives in Athens, Georgia. Her books include *Silent Dancing* (1990), *The Line of the Sun* (1989), *Terms of Survival* (1988), *Reaching for the Mainland* (1987), *Peregrina* (1986), and earlier poetry chapbooks.

In 1974, Ortiz Cofer received a B.A. in English from Augusta College. With an M.A. in English from Florida Atlantic University, she was an English Speaking Union of America Fellow at Oxford University, England, Summer Graduate School in 1977.

Her work has been anthologized in *The Heath Anthology of American Literature, The Anthology of American Verse and Yearbook of American Poetry, Best American Essays*, and others. She has received fellowships from the National Endowment for the Arts, the Witter Bynner Foundation for Poetry, the Florida and Georgia Councils for the Arts, and the Bread Loaf Writers' Conference. She has taught at Broward College, the University of Miami, Macon College, the University of Georgia, and other colleges. Currently, she is Visiting Professor of English and creative writing at the University of Georgia, Athens.

Ortiz Cofer's work combines fiction with nonfiction to tell her story as a writer and as a Hispanic woman in the United States. Her writing, while not strictly autobiographical, uses much autobiographical data to create a strong sense of an identity influenced by the need to return to the island for a time. Once there, however, she always comes back to the United States. Consequently, the setting of her narratives continually switches from Puerto Rico to Paterson, New Jersey, her barrio *community in the United States.

Like many contemporary writers, Ortiz Cofer focuses her creative ability on creating vibrant images of her mother and grandmothers. As she creates these images, she perfects her own art. In the preface to *Silent Dancing*, Cofer states:

> Much of my writing begins as a meditation on past events. But memory for me is the 'jumping off' point; I am not, in my poetry and my fiction writing, a slave to memory. I like to believe that the poem or story contains the 'truth' of art rather than the factual, historical truth that the journal-

ist, sociologist, scientist—most of the rest of the world—must adhere to. Art gives me that freedom.

• Juan Bruce-Novoa, "Judith Ortiz Cofer's Rituals of Movement," *The Americas Review* 19, nos. 3–4, (Winter, 1991): 88–99. Juan Bruce-Novoa, "Ritual in Judith Ortiz Cofer's *The Line of the Sun*, *Confluencia* 8, no. 1, (Fall, 1992): 61–69.

Juanita Luna Lawhn

OTHER, The. Questions regarding the status of "the Other" are central to American literary and social thought. The nation's very foundations were laid through processes of exclusion that entailed the political differentiation and subjugation of "others": colonies from home countries, indigenous peoples from settlers, slaves from masters. Writers as diverse as Harriet *Jacobs, Mary *Antin, Margaret *Fuller, and Anna Julia *Cooper recognized that white male power was maintained through the creation and control of groups of Others, variously defined as blacks, immigrants, women, and so on. Yet it was not until the 1960s that what might be termed the "politics of the Other" emerged as a significant conceptual framework for describing sexual power relations in the United States. During this period, feminist critics increasingly began to depict the social and political condition of American women in terms derived from French existentialist philosophy and psychoanalysis. A whole generation of American women writers and political thinkers (sometimes known collectively as the second wave) was especially influenced by the definition of the Other proposed by French feminist philosopher Simone *de Beauvoir in *The Second Sex* (1949). Betty *Friedan and Kate *Millett, for instance, whose very different books *The Feminine Mystique* (1963) and *Sexual Politics* (1969) were landmarks in the development of the American women's liberation movement in the 1960s and 1970s, both drew on de Beauvoir's account of woman as the not-human Other to man's human Self, object to his subject, nature to his culture. For de Beauvoir, the sexual status quo was crucially maintained through the discourse of femininity, which identified characteristics such as coquetry, docility, and mothering as not only natural, but constitutive of women as a gender. Constrained by this ideological system from engaging in projects in the outside world (for existentialists, a condition for humanity), women's frustrated desires were manifest as house-pride, vanity, and inappropriate ambitions on behalf of their children. According to de Beauvoir and a generation of sympathetic feminist readers, the liberation of women depends on the achievement of economic independence: only then will women be free to pose and engage in their own projects, instead of existing to fulfill the projects of men.

During the 1970s and 1980s, this statement of the way political subordination was effected in the name of the Other was criticized by feminists who argued two main points: 1) that men did not make women Other by denying them opportunities to engage in significant activities, but by denying the significance of activities in which women in fact engaged; and 2) that the repertoire of social practices considered oppressive was culturally specific and failed to account for the ways in which African-American women, Chicanas, and lesbians, for example, were constituted as Other.

The first challenge was associated with the emergence of a still-powerful tendency within American feminism, one that philosopher Iris Marion Young, among others, has described as "gynocentrism." Theologian Mary *Daly (Gyn/Ecology: The Metaethics of Radical Feminism, 1978) and psychoanalyst Nancy Chodorow (The Reproduction of Mothering, 1978) are two examples of feminists who are concerned with revaluing and affirming what they see as women's real differences from men: If women are stereotyped as unreasonable, for instance, a gynocentric response might be to celebrate the quality of unreason rather than to seek a way to provide women with the tools to acquire reason (or to challenge the attribution). In this case, the traditional definition of woman-as-Other is challenged at the level of value rather than social practice: for gynocentric feminists, the problem is the social overvaluation of activities typically associated with men (such as wage earning and war making), rather than the social restrictions that confine women to such activities as homemaking and mothering.

The other major challenge to de Beauvoir's strategy for redressing the condition of woman-as-Other was issued by black feminists, who charged that in characterizing women's Otherness in terms of traditional notions of femininity, mainstream American feminism ignored and denied the particular historical experience of African-American women. The idea that women were physically weak and morally virtuous, for example, was never used to justify the confinement of black women to the home; by contrast, an ideology of physical and sexual prowess was developed to better control and exploit black women as a source of productive and reproductive labor. Black women's early and powerful criticisms have been a major contributing factor in making historical specificity and respect for differences among women the key issues for American feminism today.

Other groups of American women have joined black feminists in registering the particular ways in which they have been identified as Other. Some of their arguments have underscored and expanded on the connections between accounts that treat sexual inequality in terms of the category of the Other, and theories of racial domination and colonialism that depict nonwhite peoples as the Other of the agents of white power. This trend has contributed to the expansion of the Other into a concept that is now often expressed through the popular terminology of "the margins." Like the Other, the margin suggests a position outside the centers of identity and power. Some critics prefer a model of margin and center (in economic terms, core and periphery) to the traditional model of Other and Same on the grounds that the spatial metaphor facilitates thinking about a more heterogeneous array of social practices of discrimination than is generally indicated by the concept of the Other, and that it thus permits more creative consideration of the possibilities of resistance. Through the languages of margins and center, "difference," "alterity," and "the subaltern" (to name a few), the Other persists as a central organizing metaphor for women's experience in the United States.

• Jean Paul Sartre, Being and Nothingness (1943). Frantz Fanon, Black Skin, White Masks (1967). bell hooks, Ain't I a Woman: Black Women and Feminism (1981). Juliet Mitchell and Jacqueline Rose, eds., Feminine Sexuality: Jacques Lacan and the école freudienne (1983). Fredric Jameson, "Periodizing the 60s," in The 60s without Apology, eds. Sohnya Sayres, Anders Stephanson, Stanley Aronowitz, and Fredric Jameson (1984), pp. 178–209. Elaine Showalter, ed., The New Feminist Criticism: Essays on Women, Literature, and Theory (1985). Seyla Benhabib and Drucilla Cornell, eds., Feminism as Critique (1987). Russell Ferguson, Martha Gever, Trinh T. Minh-ha, and Cornel West, eds., Out There: Marginalization and Contemporary Cultures (1990).

Deborah G. Chay

OTHER WOMAN, The. For U.S. women writers, the charged phrase "The Other Woman" carries deeper, more complex, and less blameful meanings than it does in the culture at large. Whether they chronicle the agonies of women married to adulterous husbands, or the mixed emotions of women involved with married men, women writers anatomize grief and obsession. Women fiction writers chart a protagonist's intricate self-assessments which often turn upon comparisons of herself with the other women—wife or lover. The Other Woman thus becomes a catalyst which, however painful, allows a character to overturn myths of romantic love by which she had lived, hold the man responsible for his behavior, and understand—

and perhaps break—her emotional, social, and financial dependence upon men. Women poets who explore the theme not only address these concerns, but often project a figurative other woman, sometimes in the guise of a muse, who embodies elements of the psyche such as anger or sexual aggressiveness that women have repressed in order to survive in male-dominated society.

Nineteenth-century fiction writers often treat the theme not only with candor, but also with a resonant awareness of how *race and *class issues multiply the political dimensions of the situations they depict. In her short story "The Quadroons" (1842; rpt. Koppelman), Lydia Maria *Child details the seduction and abandonment of Rosalie, a graceful, cultivated, and virtuous mulatta. Elizabeth Stuart *Phelps, in "No News" (1869; rpt. Koppelman) demonstrates how exhaustion from housework and mothering prevents Harrie Sharpe from sharing the intellectual interests of her husband, who treats her as if she were a maid and falls in love with one of her unmarried friends. Charlotte Perkins *Gilman, on the other hand, in "Turned" (1911; rpt. Koppelman) charts the shift in Marion Marroner's consciousness from anger at the young maid whom her husband has impregnated, to sympathy and support for her. Nineteenth century women writers' tales of The Other Woman also frequently turn on family rivalries, as in Harriet Prescott Spofford's gothic story "The Amber Gods" (1863; rpt. Bendixen). Class issues also come to the fore in Elizabeth Stoddard's *The Morgesons* (1862), where Cassandra Morgeson falls in love with her married cousin Charles, who dies trying to protect her from a mad horse; toward the end of the novel, Cassandra's bankrupt father marries Charles' wealthy widow.

An interesting variant of the theme—the phantom other woman—illustrates the anguish that women suffer if they measure themselves against an impossibly perfect "ideal woman." Toni *Morrison's *Jazz* (1992), for example, begins when Joe Trace shoots his eighteen-year-old lover, Dorcas, "just to keep the feeling going." His wife, Violet, tries to learn everything she can about Dorcas, as if that knowledge could confer upon her the ideality that the girl attained only in death. In Alice Brown's short story "Natalie Blayne" (1904; rpt. Koppelman), Delia Gilbert grows deathly ill because she believes that Natalie Blayne, a women whom her husband once admired but now hardly remembers, has always cast a shadow upon their marriage. And in Alice *Walker's "Her Sweet Jerome" (*In Love and Trouble: Stories of Black Women*, 1973), the nameless protagonist, wielding an axe, confronts every woman in town and finally realizes that her husband has betrayed her for no woman, but for books on Black revolution. Walker's story, like others in which there is no other woman, not only underscores how a woman's obsession with the other arises from her own self-doubts, but also suggests that such feelings are perpetuated by the power imbalances of marriage. Thus, the phantom other woman is only an extreme manifestation of the anxiety and vulnerability often felt by women who ground their identities wholly upon men. In women's fiction, other women, however real they may be in terms of the story, become for the wives relentless spectres of the ideal woman.

And yet, because such impossible ideals have permeated U.S. culture, in women's fiction the other woman is often equally haunted. For her the wife also represents the ideal—whether of qualities she believes she lacks or of the comparative emotional security and social status conferred by marriage; sometimes, the other woman will even take on the wife's identity and lose all vestiges of her own. In Edith *Wharton's *Ethan Frome* (1911), Mattie Silver, whose grace and pleasantness counter the ill-humor of Ethan's sickly wife Zeena, becomes a petulant invalid whom Ethan must support along with his wife. In Nella *Larsen's *Passing* (1929), which questions power imbalances between races as well as gender inequities, Clare Kendry, passing as white, marries a wealthy racist; in a desperate bid to reclaim her lost culture and identity, she obsessively visits the home of her childhood friend, Irene Redfield, and begins an affair with Irene's husband. Rona Jaffe, in her short story "Rima the Bird Girl" (1960; rpt. Ferguson) and her novel *The Other Woman* (1972), details the terrifying stasis of other women who lose nearly all traces of their former selves. Gertrude *Stein, on the other hand, whether scrutinizing a love triangle among three women in *Q.E.D.* (1903) or two women and a man in "Melanctha: Each One as She May" from *Three Lives* (1909), leaves her characters' personalities intact; instead, she maps power shifts and role reversals between partners. And in Lorrie Moore's "How to Be an Other Woman" (*Self Help* 1985), the other woman discovers that the woman with whom her lover lives is not his wife, but also an "other woman." Moore's plot twist underscores the irony common to women fiction writers' treatment of the paradigm: At first envying a wife's security while blaming her for mistreating her husband, an other woman will discover that the wife feels as insecure as she does; although the husband's adultery has made them both "other women," their sense of inadequacy reflects their internalization of negative cultural attitudes toward women and exposes the double binds that divide the roles of "wife and mother" from that of "lover."

As Suzanne Juhasz has argued in *Naked and Fiery Forms* (1976), chief among the double binds against which women poets struggle are those between "poetry"—culturally defined as masculine creation, and "femininity"—culturally defined in terms of a woman's relationships. Women poets in the United States have adopted a variety of masks, or personae, which have allowed them to integrate "poet" and "woman" and speak of forbidden subjects such as anger, sexuality, and the very conflicts that generated the personae. Significantly, three twentieth century women poets well-known for their personae and their tropes of the double all had marriages that collapsed when their poet husbands left them for other, "more feminine" women. Many of the poems in Louise *Bogan's *Body of This Death* (1923) register her disillusionment with her first marriage and the pain she suffered when she learned that before the marriage her husband had slept with other women; in journal entries published in *Journey Around My Room* (1981), Bogan describes her discovery of her second husband Raymond Holden's adultery and contrasts his need for romance with her need not to be loved, but to love. *H. D.'s novels *Palimpsest* (1926) and *Bid Me to Live (A Madrigal)* (1960) offer veiled retellings of the dissolution of her marriage to Richard Aldington, who left her for another woman; many of the poems in *Heliodora* (1924) question love's sufficiency and obliquely elegize the marriage. Prose documentation of Sylvia *Plath's reaction to Ted Hughes' adultery is sparse, since the journals she kept at the time were destroyed by Hughes, but her poems develop a variety of responses: grief and anger, concern for her children, and self-renewal (*Collected Poems* 1981). Noteworthy treatments of the other woman's perspective are Elinor *Wylie's defiant lyrics (*Collected Poems* 1934); Anne *Sexton's "For My Lover, Returning to His Wife" and "You All Know the Story of the Other Woman" (*Love Poems* 1969); *Alta's *song of the wife, song of the mistress* (1969); and Louise *Glück's disquieting "Swans" (*Descending Figure* 1980) and "Marathon" (*The Triumph of Achilles* 1985). But whether they speak as lovers or as betrayed wives, the personae of women poets who explore the theme ultimately discover that the man desires an ideal—not their flesh and bones, but their image in the glass, as Helen Adam suggests in "The Hoose O' the Mirror" [*sic*] (*Ballads* 1964).

But women writers have also detailed ways to overcome emotional dependence on men and to develop a sense of self detached from bondage to the ideal. More constructive than the sexual excesses of *Henry and June* (1986) and *Incest* (1992), diary excerpts in which Anaïs *Nin flaunts her numerous liaisons, are narratives such as Ellen Lesser's novel *The Other Woman* (1988) that depict women who gain the courage to reconfigure their lives. In *The Other Woman: Stories of Two Women and a Man* (1984), editor Susan Koppelman includes work by such nineteenth century writers such as Helen Hunt *Jackson, and Mary E. Wilkins *Freeman, as well as material by lesser known twentieth century writers such as Ellen *Glasgow, Lee Yu-Hwa, and James Tiptree, Jr. (Alice Sheldon). The last story, "A Perfectly Nice Man" by Jane *Rule (1982), features the man's two ex-wives who become lovers and set up a household together. The joy and confidence which these two women share epitomizes the theme of Koppelman's collection, for the stories detail bonds between women and "leave readers with the knowledge that there is ... an independence, self-possession, and self esteem beyond pain" (xxv) available both to betrayed wives and to other women.

• Ferguson, Mary Ann, ed. *Images of Women in Literature.* Boston: Houghton Mifflin, 1973. Koppelman, Susan, ed. *The Other Woman: Stories of Two Women and a Man.* Old Westbury, NY: The Feminist Press, 1984. Stoddard, Elizabeth. *The Morgesons.* Eds. Lawrence Buell and Sandra A. Zagarell. 1862. Rpt. Philadelphia: U of Pennsylvania P, 1984. Bendixen, Alfred, ed. *Haunted Women: The Best Supernatural Tales by American Women Writers.* New York: Frederick Ungar, 1985.

Meg Schoerke

OZICK, Cynthia (b. 1928), poet, novelist, fiction writer, essayist, translator (from Yiddish), educator.

Born to Russian immigrants in New York City and raised in the Bronx, Ozick graduated from New York University in 1949 and earned a master's degree in English literature from Ohio State University in 1950. Defining herself as a covenanted Jew and as a Jewish writer, she foregrounds Judaism in her work and mines the intellectual and historical heritage of international Jewry. Ozick claims American English for the new Jewish language of a "New Yiddish" literature, and is a premier translator of Yiddish poetry; her many translations appear in three collections, including the *Penguin Book of Yiddish Verse* (1987). Although Ozick's own poems are relatively few and remain uncollected, her production of short fiction, novels, and essays is prodigious. Acclaimed for its cerebral imagination and story-telling acumen, her fiction typically weighs Hebraism against paganism to ponder a recurring ethical question: To what extent does the creation of art contravene the Second Commandment, which forbids idol making and idol worship?

Ozick's first published novel, *Trust* (1966), is about self-discovery through the search for the biological father. *The Messiah of Stockholm* (1987) links this theme to artistic production and complicates the question of literary idol making with the Nazis' murder of Jews. The Holocaust mediates two earlier short fictions published together as *The Shawl* (1989). Concerned with pedagogy, *The Cannibal Galaxy* (1983) studies post-Holocaust American Jewish assimilation.

Ozick's stories, two of which have garnered O. Henry First Prizes, anticipate or elaborate her novels' Jewish themes. Some are collected in *The Pagan Rabbi and Other Stories* (1971) and *Bloodshed and Three Novellas* (1976); *Levitation: Five Fictions* (1982) earned her a Guggenheim Fellowship. Ozick has published over a hundred essays and reviews, and two collections, *Art and Ardor: Essays* (1983) and *Metaphor and Memory: Essays* (1989). Distinguished by their intellectual breadth and authority, and Jamesian ambiguity, the essays address such topics as religion, literary criticism, language, social and political concerns, and feminism.

Succeeding the rise of American Jewish literature in Bellow, Roth, Singer, and Malamud, Ozick's literary maturation coincided with the second wave of feminism, of which she is suspicious. In "Literature and the Politics of Sex: A Dissent" (1977), she endorses the libertarian emancipation of women, but rejects what she calls the separatist classification "woman writer." She does proudly embrace the category "Jewish writer," and is one of the few women cited among American Jewish authors. Indeed, Ozick is hailed by Ruth R. Wisse in *Commentary* (1976) as leader of a pivotal movement in American Jewish literature characterized by writing based in the Jewish textual tradition and forged in Jewish visionary terms.

• Ruth R. Wisse, "American Jewish Writing, Act II," *Commentary* 61, no. 6 (June 1976): 40–45. Susan Currier and Daniel J. Cahill, "A Bibliography of the Writings of Cynthia Ozick," *Texas Studies in Literature and Language* 25, no. 2 (1983): 313–321. Harold Bloom, ed., *Cynthia Ozick: Modern Critical Views* (1986). Daniel Walden, ed., *The World of Cynthia Ozick: Studies in Jewish American Literature* (1987). Joseph Lowin, *Cynthia Ozick* (1988).

Ronna C. Johnson

P

PALEY, Grace (b. 1922), short fiction writer, poet. Grace Paley grew up in New York City, immersed in the stories told—in Yiddish and Russian, as well as English—in her extended Russian Jewish family and in the wider community of immigrants and ethnic minorities. Thus, the oral tradition was something that she took for granted. Paley considered herself a poet, however, while attending Hunter College and New York University, returning to the narrative form only later, in the fifties. Her first collection of stories, *The Little Disturbances of Man* (1959), based on her experiences in an army camp in World War II, garnered her reputation for gentle, comedic vision and an uncanny ability to capture a variety of urban voices. *Enormous Changes at the Last Minute* (1974), *Later the Same Day* (1985), and *Long Walks and Intimate Talks* (1991), long-awaited volumes of stories, have successively brought her even broader acclaim. In 1985, Paley published *Leaning Forward*, her first book of poems. The National Institute of Arts and Letters awarded Paley the literary award for short fiction in 1970; she was elected to the American Academy and Institute of Arts and Letters in 1980. Paley has two children, teaches creative writing at Sarah Lawrence College, and is a lifelong activist for feminism and world peace.

Paley's life and work draw on the family habit of political activism, born of her parents' socialist ideals and their memories of political exile—her father, to Siberia, her mother, to Germany. She also claims as influences Virginia *Woolf, James Joyce, Gertrude *Stein, Charlotte Brontë, and Elizabeth Gaskell. Her work explores the possibility of achieving the impossible in everyday life. The stories reverberate with wit and grace, with the human desire to forge connections against the odds of poverty, with the tenacity of communities in the face of violence and lack. Her characters are ordinary yet eccentric neighbors, and we, the readers, are eavesdroppers, as Paley in real life was: "That's what you listen for and what you expect when you are a kid: the next conversation will tell you what it's all about, if you only listen to it" (interview in *Caliban*, 1988). Perhaps Paley's ability to cut to the heart of what matters explains why a writer of relatively small output nonetheless is considered a major voice among contemporary feminist authors.

• Sara Poli, *Grace Paley* (1983). Barbara Eckstein, "Grace Paley's Community: Gradual Epiphanies in the Meantime," in *Politics and the Muse* (1989), pp. 124–141. Ulrich Halfmann and Philipp Gerlach, "Grace Paley: A Bibliography," *Tulsa Studies in Women's Literature* 8, no. 2 (Fall 1989): 339–354. Jacqueline Tayor, *Grace Paley: Illuminating the Dark Lives* (1990). Victoria Aarons, "Talking Lives: Storytelling and Renewal in Grace Paley's Short Fiction," *Studies in American Jewish Literature* 9, no. 1 (Spring 1990): 30–35.

Susan J. Zevenbergen

PAN-AFRICANISM. A complex intellectual, political, and cultural movement among Africans, African Americans, and Afro Caribbeans who regard or have regarded Africans and people of African descent as homogeneous. This movement contributes to a feeling of racial solidarity and a new self awareness, and causes African Americans and Afro Caribbeans to look upon Africa as their real homeland, without necessarily thinking of a physical return to Africa. Pan-Africanism also tries to create a bond between black people of Africa and of the Diaspora, recognizing that they are all linked to Africa through a common experience of oppression and slavery. Afrocentricism, a related intellectual movement, traces the origins of Western European civilization back to ancient Egypt and earlier African civilizations such as Kismet, rather than to ancient Greece and Rome.

Ideological Pan-Africanism began in the eighteenth century, when a few, Christianized, literate Africans living in Europe and the American colonies advocated a return to the West African coast, where they might convert the indigenous peoples to Christianity and establish independent settlements. The poet Phillis *Wheatley (1753–1784), though not interested in returning to Africa herself, did personally identify with her "sable race" in Africa and the American colonies. She advocated the Christianization of all blacks, as is evident in her most famous poem, "On Being Brought from Africa to America" (1773), and in several letters she wrote to her close friend Arbour Tanner, another black woman who worked as a servant in the home of James Tanner in Newport, Rhode Island.

During the 1830s, Maria Stewart, America's first black woman political writer, incorporated into her speeches to Boston's black community an Afrocentric argument that it not relent in the fight for its rights and liberty: "Yes, poor despised Africa was once the resort of sages and legislators of other nations, was esteemed the school for learning, and the most illustrious men in Greece flocked thither for instruction" (from "An Address Delivered at the African Masonic Hall," 1983).

During the late nineteenth century, the desire to help in the development and Christianization of the African continent gathered momentum among African Americans. Ida B. * Wells-Barnett (1863–1930), the journalist and antilynching activist, argued in a July 1892 essay entitled "Afro-Americans and Africa" in the A.M.E. Church Review that those enterprising black Americans who wished to go to Africa should be encouraged to go to Liberia, where there was a need to develop the abundant natural resources. Helen Curtis, an African-American teacher, social worker, missionary, and NAACP and YWCA/YMCA activist, was the widow of the former U.S. consul general to Liberia. She headed the industrial department at Monrovia College, Liberia, from 1924 to 1927. Among the early group of African-American missionaries sent to the Congo between 1890 and 1941 under the auspices of the southern Presbyterian church, five were women: Maria Fearing (1894–1915), Lillian Thomas DeYampert (1894–1915), Lucy Ganti Sheppard (1894–1910), Althea Brown Edmiston (1902–1937), and Annie Katherine Taylor Rochester (1906–1914). Though many of their husbands were the actual appointees to the American Presbyterian Congo Mission, these women nevertheless made a significant impact on the African women and children. The distinguished African-American educator Fannie Jackson Coppin traveled with her husband, a bishop of the African Methodist Church, to Capetown, South Africa, in 1902. Coppin developed missions among the black South African women. These missions in turn raised thousands of dollars to erect the Fanny Jackson Coppin Girls Hall at Wilberforce Institute, the A.M.E. school in Capetown.

Twentieth-century Pan-Africanism saw the convening of numerous congresses between 1900 and 1958 in Europe, the United States, and Ghana, which were attended by women and men from the African Diaspora. The feminist educator, scholar, and writer Anna J. * Cooper (1858–1964) attended the 1900 Pan-African meeting in London. Mrs. I. G. Hunt and Addie W. Hunton were on the international organizing committee for the 1921 Pan-African Congress, held concurrently in London, Brussels, and Paris. Hunton, a major leader in the black women's club movement, helped organize the Fourth Pan-African Congress in New York City in 1927.

Marcus Garvey and his first wife, Amy Ashwood Garvey, made Pan-Africanism—for a time limited to the urban elite—accessible to the masses of working people. They formed the Universal Negro Improvement Association (UNIA) in Jamaica in 1914, and in Harlem, New York, in 1916. UNIA promoted the spirit of race pride and love, with slogans like "Back to Africa" and "Africa for Africans." Garvey's second wife, Amy Jacques, was also very active in UNIA. Between 1925 and 1927, she actually ran the organization while Marcus Garvey was in jail. Several women held important positions in UNIA: Henrietta Vinton Davis directed UNIA's Black Star Lines, an international commercial and passenger steamship line, Queen Mother Moore (1898–1978) was active in the UNIA Harlem branch, and Mittie Maud Lena Gordon organized for UNIA in the Chicago area.

Cultural Pan-Africanism among African Americans began during the * Harlem Renaissance (or New Negro Movement) of the 1920s and 1930s. Women intellectuals, writers, and artists who made significant contributions to the study and appreciation of the Africanisms in African-American culture at the time were Jessie * Fauset, literary editor of the Crisis (1919–1926); Zora Neale * Hurston, folklorist and novelist who collected materials in the southern United States and Haiti; Shirley Graham Du Bois, second wife of W. E. B. Du Bois, who wrote a thesis for a master's degree in music history and criticism from Oberlin College in 1935 on "Survivals of Africanisms in Modern Music"; Josephine Baker, a dancer and entertainer who blended an exaggerated African motif into her performances; and Katherine Dunham, an anthropologist, choreographer, dancer, and school founder, who during the 1930s studied the peoples and cultures in Jamaica, Martinique, Trinidad, and Haiti on a Rosenwald Foundation travel grant. Subsequent African-American writers who have incorporated Pan-African themes into their work include Lorraine * Hansberry (A Raisin in the Sun, 1959), Alice * Walker ("The Diary of an African Nun," 1973, The Color Purple, 1982, and Possessing the Secret of Joy, 1992, Paule * Marshall (The Chosen Place, the Timeless People, 1969, and Praisesong for the Widow, 1983), and the 1970s poetry of Gwendolyn * Brooks, Mari * Evans, Nikki * Giovanni, and Sonia * Sanchez.

• Imanuel Geiss, *The Pan African Movement: A History of Pan-Africanism in America, Europe and Africa* (1974). Wilson Jeremiah Moses, *The Golden Age of Black Nationalism, 1850–1925* (1978). Sylvia Jacobs, ed., *Black Americans and the Missionary Movement in Africa* (1982). Robert Hill, ed., *Pan-African Biography* (1987). Marilyn Richardson, ed., *Maria Stewart, America's First Black Woman Political Writer: Essays and Speeches* (1987). Jessie Carney Smith, ed., *Notable Black American Women* (1992).

Alice A. Deck

PARKER, Dorothy (1893–1967), short story writer, poet, dramatist, essayist, critic. At one point considered the wittiest woman in America, Dorothy Parker was noted for her acerbic comments and epigrammatic style. A charter member of the Algonquin Club in the 1920s, she began her career publishing light verse, reviewing plays, and writing book reviews as the "Constant Reader" for the *New Yorker*. Born in West End, New Jersey, to J. Henry Rothschild, a Jewish clothing merchant, and Eliza A. Marston, a Scottish schoolteacher, Parker retained a lifelong image of herself as an outsider with a "mongrel" heritage. She attended the Blessed Sacrament Convent School in New York City until she was asked to leave for maintaining that the Immaculate Conception was "spontaneous combustion."

Well known for one-liners such as "Men seldom make passes at girls who wear glasses," Parker dismissed her "wise-cracking" image in a 1957 interview with Marion Capron. Never believing she had achieved the status of a major writer, she blamed the times: "Dammit, it *was* the twenties and we had to be smarty. . . . I should have had more sense." Parker's involvement with the Communist party in 1934 and her subsequent support for radical causes, which caused her to be blacklisted in 1949, reflect the times as well.

Her three volumes of light verse, *Enough Rope* (1926), *Sunset Gun* (1928), *Death and Taxes* (1931), and the collected edition, *Not So Deep As a Well* (1936), were best-sellers. She coauthored three plays: *Close Harmony* (1924), with Elmer Rice; *The Coast of Illyria* (1949), with Ross Evans; and *The Ladies of the Corridor* (1953), with Arnaud d'Usseau. She was openly contemptuous of the scripts and screenplays she wrote for Hollywood between 1925 and 1950. The body of her work now receiving the most critical attention is her short stories—*Laments for the Living* (1930), *After Such Pleasures* (1933), and *Here Lies* (1939).

Parker's sparse style, extensive use of dialogue, and pervasive irony reveal the pretensions and hypocrisies of society, and attack the constraining gender roles to which both sexes are subjected. Legendary for her difficulty in meeting deadlines, Parker found writing hard work. She told Capron, "I can't write five words but I change seven." Although Parker was dissatisfied with much of her work, her writing reveals a commitment to her craft and a belief in the power of language to address social inequity. She remains the most noted figure of the Algonquin group. She died alone in a New York hotel, leaving her papers to the National Association for the Advancement of Colored People.

• Marion Capron, "Dorothy Parker," in *Writers at Work*, ed. Malcolm Cowley (1957), pp. 70–82. John Keats, *You Might As Well Live* (1970). Arthur F. Kinney, *Dorothy Parker* (1978). Leslie Frewin, *The Late Mrs. Parker* (1986). Marion Mead, *Dorothy Parker* (1988).

Dianne Chambers

PARKER, Pat (1944–1989), poet, educator, health care worker, mother, lecturer, activist. When the African-American lesbian poet Pat Parker died on 17 June 1989, the gay and lesbian movement lost one of its most outspoken, respected activists. Parker's grass roots work has influenced the shaping of gay and lesbian literature and political work since the early 1970s, when she pounded the pavements of San Francisco and Oakland with coactivist Judy Grahn. Parker was one of the earliest contemporary poets and activists who was "out" about her lesbianism.

Parker spent the majority of her adult life in Oakland, California, partaking in her activism there through her poetry, speeches, and work with women's health networks throughout the Bay Area. While Parker fought against the unequal treatment of women in the health care system, it is terribly ironic that her own life came to an end much too soon because of breast cancer. Her struggle and death, however, exemplify the inseparability of her life's work and her writing.

Best known for her poetry, Parker's books include *Child of Myself* (1971), *Pit Stop* (1974 and 1975), *Womanslaughter* (1978), *Jonestown and Other Madness* (1985), and *Movement in Black: The Collected Poetry of Pat Parker, 1961–1978* (1990), which is a compilation of some of Parker's most powerful poems.

Through her words, Parker continually called into question the status quo, and she was quick to point out that the oppressor was not some larger-than-life monster, but was instead the white man in the business suit or even the lesbian in the closet. She often called attention to the highly controversial topics of racism and internalized homophobia within gay and lesbian circles, themes she addresses in her most widely anthologized poem, "Where Will You Be?" In *Jonestown and Other Madness*, Parker uses her experience as an African-American lesbian activist and women's health care worker to look at the classist, racist, homophobic sickness of society on a global scale.

Along with her poetry, Parker wrote numerous essays, including "Gay Parenting, or, Look Out, Anita" in *Politics of the Heart: A Lesbian Parenting Anthology* (1987) and "Revolution: It's Not Neat or Pretty or Quick" in *This Bridge Called My Back* (1983). Both her essays and poetry have come under the gay and lesbian academic critical eye and have been labeled "too brash" and "too angry." But, it is exactly within Parker's language of brutal honesty that we can find a political theory of lesbian activism that can be used, not only in academia, but in life. The essence of Pat Parker's material is about utilizing her words and vision as a guidebook to survival, and beyond that, to revolution.

• Anonymous, "In Memoriam," *Calyx: A Journal of Art and Literature by Women* 12, no. 1 (Summer 1989): 90–94. Brett Beemyn, "Bibliography of Works by and about Pat Parker (1944–1989)," *SAGE: A Scholarly Journal on Black Women* 6, no. 1 (Summer 1989):81–82.

Ardel Thomas

PARTON, Sara Payson Willis. *See* Fern, Fanny.

PASSING. A concept that existed before the term was formalized in African-American literature, *passing* refers to the act of moving permanently from identification with blacks to identification with whites; it enabled the minority to become a part of the majority. In the displays of power designed to keep black people "in their place," passing enabled them to subvert that power base and assume their own authority in naming and access. Based on lightness of skin coloring, "good hair," and Caucasoid features, obviously only a small portion of African Americans could effect this transfer. Made possible by the intermixture of the black and white races during slavery—and by their descendants for the several decades following slavery—passing was at once an advantage and a disadvantage. The advantage was that those inclined to pass gained unquestioned entry into American society and reaped the benefits of American democratic ideals; their "whiteness" assured that they acquired good jobs, lived in the better neighborhoods, and integrated into the social strata concomitant to middle-class American existence. The disadvantage was that those passing were forced to lose or voluntarily lost contact with their families; they had to listen on occasion to racist jokes about people they had known intimately; and they were forever in fear of being discovered. Loss of family is vividly illustrated in Langston Hughes's short story "Passing" (1933), in which a son has a fateful encounter with his mother.

From this initial definition of passing in the nineteenth and early twentieth centuries, the term in recent years has taken on overtones less related to color than to cultural identification. Today, passing refers to those African Americans, regardless of skin color, who elect to identify with Anglo-American culture and morality. This group will attend Ivy League schools, will get the best jobs that corporate America offers, and will otherwise disassociate itself from the African-American community.

The word *passing* is an apt term for describing the concept because it alludes to a history that has been "passed over," shrouded in lack of scholarly development—specifically, the sexual abuse and domination of black women by white men, both during and following slavery. This sleight of hand in scholarship, this trickery, is perhaps no more egregious than the actual practice of crossing racial boundaries. The combination of pride those who passed sometimes felt in the features that enabled them to do so, and the rejection or revulsion they showed toward blacks who could not pass, documents a fascinating moment in American race relations and the warped psychosexual politics that accompanied it.

Passing in its original sense did not always mean that those who crossed the line had abandoned their culture. For a part of the population, the lighter-skinned members of a family would move to a different town, pass on a good job during the day, and return to the black side of town at night. Kathryn Morgan, in her autobiographical *Children of Strangers* (1982), recounts that the "white" members of her family moved from Virginia to Philadelphia and passed in order to help the darker-skinned members financially. African-Americans who were light enough to do so also sometimes passed for a lark—for example, to get better accommodations on trains, as one of Morgan's aunts did, or simply for the thrill of knowing that they were being tricksters by playing a joke on those who had put Jim Crow statutes in place. On the more serious side, passing enabled Walter White, investigator for the NAACP, to move among and interview lynchers in the 1920s; the resulting work, "I Investigate Lynchings" (1929) was a strikingly revealing piece.

Expanded from its racial- and cultural-specific context, passing in recent years has taken on connotations in the gay community as well. Individuals who are "closeted" in professional and other work environments, sometimes to the detriment of those who are not, are said to be passing. In this context, clearly there is only room for negative applications of the word.

Instances of passing in the original sense of the word occur in African-American literature as early as 1853, when William Wells Brown published *Clotel; or, The President's Daughter*. In order to acquire passage in her escape to the North, Clotel poses as a young man of indistinct orgins, thus passing herself off as a man as well as a nonblack person. From this beginning, the theme dominated literature of the late nineteenth century, from Frances *Harper's *Iola Leroy* (1892), where the title character is light enough to pass but refuses to do so, to Charles W. Chesnutt's *The House behind the Cedars* (1900), where Rena Walden is convinced to join her brother in a passing escapade that backfires and eventually brings about her death.

Two of the most celebrated instances of passing in African-American literature are identified with *Harlem Renaissance writers. The first, James Weldon Johnson's *The Autobiography of An Ex-Colored Man*, was published anonymously in 1912. Reissued in 1927 at the height of the Renaissance, it recounts the exploits of an unnamed narrator who is the offspring of a mulatto woman and a father who has the "best blood" of the South in his veins. That distinction notwithstanding, the father still sends his lover and her illegitimate son to the North when he gets ready to marry and settle down. A culturally confused, morally inept, and sexually closeted man, the narrator eventually disappears into the white community instead of confronting the brutal history of African Americans. This is the first example in the literature where homosexual overtones coincide with the theme of passing.

The second work from a Renaissance writer featuring the passing theme is *Passing* (1929), by Nella *Larsen; it also marks the point at which the theme began to wane. Irene Redfield passes on occasions—when in restaurants and other public places. Her friend Clare Kendry has not only passed permanently, but she is married to a loathsome white racist who enjoys telling the ugliest of racist jokes. Not able to suppress her stereotypical beliefs about there being more rhythm and life in the black community, Clare resumes partying with Harlemites. When her husband follows her and discovers the nature of her diversion, she either leaps or is pushed from an apartment window.

These rather somber instances of passing from this period, mostly with tragic endings, are not the final word on the subject, however. In a delightful story that tests the ability of persons of Negroid ancestry to identify others who are, no matter how light their complexions, Langston Hughes puts two couples in a situation where all of their skills fail them. "Who's Passing for Who?" pokes fun at notions of racial identity and makes its characters far less sure of their ability to ferret out others of their race. A similar incident occurs in Toni *Morrison's *Sula* (1974), when Eva Peace claims that one of her boarders—known as Pretty Johnny to the neighbors, who think him to be black—is definitely not so; in humorous recognition of her ability to know others of her race, Eva nicknames him Tarbaby. These stories emphasize one of the primary "criteria" used to identify those who are passing—hair. "Good hair," reflective of the intermixture of black and white blood, will usually have some telltale signs of its Negroidness—if the examiner looks closely enough. (Recall the occasion at the conclusion of *Their Eyes Were Watching God* [1937] when black and white hurricane victims are identified and buried in pine boxes—or not—on the basis of the texture of their hair.)

An example of a more contemporary treatment of passing is Andrea *Lee's *Sarah Phillips* (1984), about a young black woman who goes to a prestigious northeastern school, then spends a promiscuous summer in France, where she has three roommates, all of whom are male. The sexual differentiation theme gets treated in works such as Rita *Dove's *The Siberian Village* (1991) and Brent Wade's *Company Man* (1992). In the former, a young man who has spent time in prison works hard to deny his attraction to his male cellmate, but that denial keeps manifesting itself in his out-of-prison experiences. In *Company Man*, the protagonist, hospitalized for a suicide attempt, reflects upon his relationship to his teenage best friend, who shocked his staid community by writing letters to everyone announcing his homosexuality. Although the narrator attends one of the "right" schools, marries into the "right" kind of family, and lives in the "right" neighborhood, he must ultimately confront the fact that his entire life has been an elaborate scheme of passing; his attraction for his friend endures more poignantly than any of his other encounters.

As this brief focus on passing indicates, a historical concept incorporated into a literature not only partly defined the direction of that literature for a period of several decades, but has now reentered the social realm, taken on new life and new meaning, and richly textured the connotations of its history as well as its current usage.

[See also Assimilation; Mixed Ancestry, Writers of; Ethnicity and Writing; Race; Whiteness.]

Trudier Harris

PATRIARCHY, the universal institutionalization of male privilege, is experienced most immediately as the power of the father within the biological-nuclear family. Its dominant cultural manifestation in the West continues to be humanistic individualism allied to capitalist economics.

The programmatic study of literature by and about women begun in the 1960s dissolves the boundary between aesthetics and politics to examine the inscription of patriarchal values in the form, content, and production of literary texts, as well as these texts' overt and subtle forms of resistance. This feminist criticism broadly defines patriarchy as sexual oppression. Its political agenda derives from landmark analyses of patriarchy, such as Mary Wollstonecraft's *A Vindication of the Rights of Woman* (1792), Margaret *Fuller's *Woman in the Nineteenth Century* (1845), and John Stuart Mill's *The Subjection of Women* (1869). Inspired by Enlightenment faith in reason, political democracy, and Romantic self-realization, these writers argue that the logic of humanistic individualism requires the opening of patriarchal privilege to women.

Most definitions of patriarchy address origins. Claude Lévi-Strauss (*Structural Anthropology,* 1963) derives patriarchy from the exogamy of prehistoric *kinship groups. Sigmund Freud builds his Oedipal theory of *gender identity upon an explanation of exogamy as originating in a psycho-mythic patricide that broke the father's control over the women of the clan. Feminists criticize the psychoanalytic application of Freud's theory as prescribing the meaning of *masculinity and *femininity in our culture, and reinscribing masculinity as the norm. Dorothy Dinnerstein (*The Mermaid and the Minotaur,* 1976) deploys *object-relations theory to locate patriarchy and its legitimization by the individual psyche in the outmoded techno-biological necessity that has given women responsibility for child care. Similarly focused on childhood, post-Freudians Jacques Lacan and Julia Kristeva shift the Oedipal moment from the infant's awareness of the penis or its absence to its acquisition of language. Kristeva's theory of a mother tongue precedent to the Oedipal break into the father's language has encouraged speculations on feminine language, such as Luce Irigaray's *Speculum of the Other Woman* (1985). Marxism tends to identify patriarchy with capitalism, subsuming sexual oppression under class oppression, reproduction under production. Socialist feminism attempts to synthesize Marxism's analysis of class and feminism's attack on sexual oppression. Radical feminist Catherine MacKinnon (*Toward a Feminist Theory of the State,* 1989) rejects this synthesis as

favoring Marxism, and indicts Marxist dialectic as patriarchal rationality. Her radical feminist equation of masculinity with patriarchy would eliminate masculinity as it currently exists.

Among postmodern challenges to the identification of the father with the truth, *deconstruction, a philosophy and a method of linguistic analysis, overturns the hierarchic oppositions—for example, man/woman, speaking/writing—that are the bases of Western thought. Michel Foucault's studies of knowledge and power explain how diverse forces shape any historical moment and how patriarchal power permeates society. However, just as feminists concerned with improving women's lives are uncomfortable with Kristeva's reduction of woman to a psychological principle and deconstruction's denial of truth, so they question the nihilism of Foucault's view that criticism not somehow in the service of patriarchy is impossible.

[*See also* Matriarchy.]

• Juliet Mitchell, *Psychoanalysis and Feminism* (1974). Zillah R. Eisenstein, ed., *Capitalist Patriarchy and the Case for Socialist Feminism* (1979). Irene Diamond and Lee Quinby, eds., *Feminism and Foucault: Reflections on Resistance* (1988). Mary Poovey, "Feminism and Deconstruction," *Feminist Studies* 14, no. 1 (Spring 1988): 51–65. Elizabeth Fox-Genovese, *Feminism without Illusions: A Critique of Individualism* (1991).

Virginia M. Kouidis

PEACE MOVEMENTS. *See* Antiwar Movements.

PERFORMANCE ART. The late 1960s and 1970s phenomenon, Performance Art, began in the 1950s with John Cage and Merce Cunningham energizing dancers, composers, and visual artists to collaborate in multimedia events. Unlike the fixed texts of conventional theater, Performance Art's commitment was to chance and indeterminacy. A "collage strategy" of various art forms made to impinge on each other, its structure was alogical and nonmatrixed. No director or writer stood between performer and task: Nonactors worked out tasks either alone or collaboratively.

By the late 1960s, many of the women artists, troubled by nonsymbolic representation, had broken away. Carolee Schneeman spoke against Cagean conceptualizing: " 'Chance method' is . . . a semantic contradiction which carries seeds of its own exhaustion in its hand clasp of chance-to-method" (*More Than Meat Joy,* 1979). Yvonne Rainer found that the strategy of indeterminacy went against her need for "selectivity and control" over her work.

The underlying disaffection was with modes established by a male-centered consciousness, the underlying need, a female-centered autonomy. The women's movement was important in both disaffection and need. Rachel Rosenthal: "Through the women's movement . . . I was able to take a new appraisal of my work and change it. . . . I redeemed my life by turning it into art" ("Interview," *Performance Art* 2, 1979). Schneeman: "My work would only be admitted into new kinds of aesthetic consciousness insofar as [it] conformed to [and supported] male expectations . . . In reexamining this isolation and . . . the trivialization of my own principles and energies—I . . . develop[ed] a private culture . . . based on an istory [sic] I devolved of lost women's image-making and artifacts."

The move to language for women artists and dancers was revolutionary. Instead of the earlier disjunction between movement and speech, words spoken were to be perceived as belonging to the performer speaking them. Language texts, though, did not imply linear narrative. By layering the languages of dreams, myths, everyday speech, and pop culture slogans, women artists explored in new ways the psychological purpose of collage strategy: to release the true language of the unconscious, to create new epistemologies. As Yvonne Rainer explained it in "Looking Myself in the Mouth": What "pushed me toward narrative . . . was 'emotional life.' . . . I was jettisoning a whole lexicon of formalized movement and behavior" (*October* 17, Summer 1981). Schneeman's need for texts grew from her involvement with "double knowledge," of both the received history of culture and the lost history of women's image making and artifacts. The then-recent work by women social scientists reinterpreting language and cultural distortions helped her make the leap from covert to overt language (*Homerun Muse* [1977] and *Interior Scroll* [1975]).

This feminist consciousness became central to women performance artists as they addressed specific women's issues and larger cultural aberrations. Until Schneeman's *Eye Body* (1963), the woman-as-nude had been the provenance of men. Schneeman's feminist-revolutionary act, concentrated on the primacy of female energy, was to reclaim her own body. Her task of challenging patriarchal myths and attendant cultural taboos qualitatively altered the character of performance art as it encouraged and energized other women to create politically freighted performances.

Schneeman's psychologically and symbolically autobiographical work inspired other women to investigate the undisclosed self. For a number of artists who turned to performance art—and to language—this investigation led to the creation of the alternate persona to speak for them.

These women, among them Colette, Lynn Hershman, and Theodora Skipitares, performing in alternate spaces—streets, restaurants, shops, hotels, buses—used their own dreams as a ground against which they pitched societal-cultural dreams. They often invested their performances with pop culture artifacts to call attention to the debased values of the patriarchy.

Colette's alternate persona, Justine (Little Miss Justice), would pose in tableaux, dressed in Victorian underwear to convey woman's imprisonment in the deadly environment of old values that continue to oppress women. The exotic and erotic environments she created evoked the multilayered image of boudoir-womb-cave. The 1990s pop star Madonna's use of underwear-as-armor is a complex gloss on Colette's text.

Hershman created the persona of Roberta Breitmore, who wore a three-piece dress from Goodwill, makeup to disguise the natural contours of her face, and a blond wig, because advertising convinced her that blondes have more fun. She joined Weight Watchers in her hunger to become the sylphic ideal of the culture. All of her attempts were doomed to failure because her dream of self was a dream of anonymity (*Lynn Hershman Is Not Roberta Breitmore*, 1978). In Hershman's "Roberta" comic strip, a nice irony is that Roberta's anonymity saves her from rape. The tasks Hershman performed as Roberta made her persona a trope of the woman victimized by pop culture values.

From Skipitares's earliest performance (*Mask Performance*, 1976) the mask of her face served as the alternate persona through whom she could speak the unspeakable. She created seventy-five masks of her face, from which she selected at random, and "spoke" in eclectic sounds motivated by the particular mask. Like her older "sisters" Rainer and Schneeman, she graduated from eclectic sounds to words, but words strung together in bizarre constructs.

Unlike the others, she removed her self from the scene. Experimenting with altered psychological states, Skipitares created *Mikropolis* (1981–1983). Motorized marionettes, all with her face and voice, dramatized in a complex of alogical structures Skipitares's feminist valuations of our culture. The dark comedy of the language of bizarre strings of pop culture clichés about rape either of body and mind, or of the environment, juxtaposed against the "lobotomized" mentality of the "speaker" in a minimal environment, enunciated Skipitares's radical vision of the patriarchy.

What all of these artists had in common, then, was that they worked from the centers of their specialness as women. They played off the mythos of being against cultural myths.

Schneeman's asserting the primacy of her gyno-centricity allowed other women, like Colette, Hershman, and Skipitares, to use their gynetic knowledge to enact the schizoid characteristics in contemporary society. Through their individually feminist explorations of chance and determinacy, of nonmatrixed events within alogical structures, they altered the shape and texture of performance art.

[NOTE: Performance Art since the 1980s bears little resemblance to its predecessor. The texts are fixed and rarely multimedia. Often the performers have had training in acting. Often there is a "literary" quality, regardless of how crude, because a number of performance artists of both genders are or began as writers. It is rare to find a performance artist who began as a visual artist or a dancer. The fresh spontaneity, the element of delighted surprise of both performer and audience is gone. All that remains is the unpolished quality, which had degenerated into crudity for its own sake.]

[See also Latina Drama; Lesbian Drama.]

• The Amazing Decade: Women and Performance Art in America 1970–1980, ed. Moire Roth. Astro Artz, LA, 1983. Heresy, July 1984, Women in Performance.

Kossia Orloff

PERFORMATIVITY. Performativity refers to the *doing* of language. It opposes more abstract conceptions of language as a structure of meaning or symbol system with an emphasis on the role of language in the concrete, particular transactions of speakers and hearers at specific sites. Performativity focusses on language as action and on meaning as the provisional, contingent, and inevitably partial effect of embodied processes of meaning-making.

J. L. Austin first articulated a performative sense of language in his lectures on speech act theory, *How to Do Things with Words* (1955). Austin posed "performative" utterances (saying as doing) against "constative" utterances (saying as stating). For Austin, performative speech is a form of action to which constative speech acts may refer. For example, one may report a wedding vow ("I heard them say 'I do'!") but the bride and groom actually *perform* the vow ("I do!"). The crucial difference between language as reference and language as performance, for Austin, is that while the former may be held to standards of truth and falsehood (did you really hear it? did they really say it?), the matter must be measured by its effects and consequences (e.g. the marriage). In this sense, performativity is also different from theatricality, which tends to characterize speech acts as something seen (a spectacle, scene, or show) rather than as something done.

The recent rediscovery of the Russian linguist, Mikhail Bakhtin, and developments in poststructural theory, complement Austin's sense of "performativity" with an emphasis on the "dialogic" and "intertextual" nature of both spoken and written transactions (see Bakhtin, "Discourse in the Novel," *The Dialogic Imagination*, 1984 and, for instance, Robert Scholes, *Protocols of Reading*, 1989). For Bakhtin, texts are born in dialogue. They are co-produced by authors and audiences. Their meanings are consequently emergent, unpredictable, context-specific, and multiple. Following Bakhtin, texts never sit still. They are always already interpenetrated by the other "texts," meanings, goals, and dispositions with which, in the process of dialogic interaction, they come into intimate contact. Whereas in Austin's model, the speaker retains control over his or her discourse, in Bakhtin that control is always tenuous, contested, and deflected by and through the "*other" to whom the discourse is addressed. Texts are, for Bakhtin, sites of struggle over who gets discursive control, whose meanings will be favored, and whose interests will be served by privileging one set of meanings over another.

Bakhtin shows us just how powerful the textual "other" may be in determining meaning or at least in putting given and dominant meanings into flux. He moreover shares with poststructural theorists like Homi Bhaba a tendency to see the "other" as already *in* the text—not waiting outside it (as if in critical ambush) but haunting its very constructions, disturbing its assertions, from the inside, as if the text were already undone by anticipation of its "other" (see Bhaba's introduction to *Nation and Narration*, 1990). Bhaba conceives of texts (especially those that contribute to discourses of nationality, race, gender, and class) as thus always on the edge of their own deconstruction—and yet, at the same time, filled with creative possibility. For Bhaba, the performative moment in discourse—the moment when it shows its deep ambivalence—is also the moment when it avails itself of revision, re-creation, and re-making. In contrast to much of the poststructural theory on which it nonetheless draws, Bhaba's sense of the performativity of language and narration thrills to the possibility of productive agency in the space of the "text."

Put simply: most conceptions of performativity assume that language as action entails a kind and degree of interaction that invites counter-agency. Following this model, performance becomes a site of transformation and even a paradigm for cultural resistance. To wit, social scientists are turning towards performance for explanation of the dialectics of power (see, for instance, James W. Fernandez, *Persuasions and Performances: The Play of Tropes in Culture*, 1986; and James C. Scott, *Domination and the Arts of Resistance: Hidden Transcripts*, 1990) and theatre scholars are increasingly committed to the rhetoric and politics of staged events (see, for instance, Philip Auslander, *Presence and Resistance: Postmodernism and Cultural Politics in Contemporary American Performance*, 1992; Sue-Ellen Case and Janelle Reinelt, eds., *The Performance of Power: Theatrical Discourse and Politics*, 1991; Jill Dolan, *The Feminist Spectator as Critic*, 1988; Lynda Hart and Peggy Phelan, eds., *Acting Out: Feminist Performances*, 1993; Peggy Phelan, *Unmarked: The Politics of Performance*, 1993). Performativity is thus also allied with the oral poetry movement in the late sixties and seventies, the rise of *performance art in the seventies and eighties (see Henry Sayre, *The Object of Performance*, 1989), developments in performance anthropology (see Victor Turner, *The Anthropology of Performance*, 1986), and the emerging field of Performance Studies generally.

Judith Butler's recent work on *gender as a performative construct (*Gender Trouble*, 1990) has made performativity an especially vital trope in the areas of women's studies and women's writing. Following on Joan Riviere's early articulation of "Womanliness as Masquerade" (*The International Journal of Psychoanalysis*, vol. 10, 1929), Butler defines gender as "an identity tenuously constituted in time, instituted in an exterior space through a *stylized repetition of acts*" (140). Her sense of gender as a performative process differs from both expressivist (gender as the reflection of essential characteristics) and constructivist (gender as a social fabrication) approaches in its emphasis on the dramatic and contingent aspects of gender identity. Most importantly, for Butler, considering gender as "a constituted *social temporality*" (141) means that it can be changed. It is in this regard that her work has been both highly influential and controversial.

Della Pollock

PERSONAL IDENTITY. *See* Identity.

PETRY, Ann (b. 1908), novelist, short fiction writer, author of young adult books. Ann Lane was born 12 October 1908 in Old Saybrook, Connecticut. The younger daughter of middle-class parents—Peter Clark Lane, Jr., was a pharmacist with his own drugstore, and Bertha James Lane was, among other occupations, a chiropodist and hairdresser—Ann grew up knowing few blacks outside her own home. But the Lane family was happy and close, and Ann's well-traveled uncles sparked her imagination

with stories of their adventures. The family penchant for story telling, combined with her insatiable reading, pointed Ann in the direction of a writing career.

Before becoming a professional writer, however, she graduated from the Connecticut College of Pharmacy (now part of the University of Connecticut) and began working at the family drugstore. In 1938, she married George Petry, moved with him to New York, and worked as a journalist for two weekly Harlem newspapers, at first selling ads for the *Amsterdam News*, and later reporting and editing for the *People's Voice*.

In the meantime, she had been submitting stories to magazines with little success. In 1943, she had a breakthrough when *Crisis* published "On Saturday the Siren Sounds at Noon." This publication led to a literary fellowship from Houghton Mifflin, which enabled her to write *The Street* (1946), her enormously successful first novel. The book sold over a million copies and garnered Petry popular and critical attention.

The Street remains Petry's best-known and most widely read work. Like Richard Wright's *Native Son* (1940), *The Street* is a naturalistic work examining the oppressive effects of racism and poverty on blacks. While *Native Son* focuses on a doomed young black man, *The Street* concerns Lutie Johnson, a doomed young black woman with an eight-year-old son. Lutie struggles valiantly against racism, sexism, and poverty in 1940s Harlem, but she finally turns to brutal violence as a way of expressing her rage at the circumstances her color and sex have forced her to endure.

Ann and George Petry returned to Old Saybrook after about nine years in New York. Petry published two more novels, *Country Place* (1947) and *The Narrows* (1953), both set in New England towns resembling Old Saybrook. The former deals with the lives of unhappy, often unscrupulous white people, while the latter concerns the troubles that arise when a black man falls in love with a white woman. Petry has also published a collection of short fiction, *Miss Muriel and Other Stories* (1971), and four books for children and young adult readers: *The Drugstore Cat* (1949), *Harriet Tubman: Conductor on the Underground Railroad* (1955), *Tituba of Salem Village* (1964), and *Legends of the Saints* (1970).

In the past decade, Petry has begun receiving more attention from critics. Her precise, rhythmic prose, her approach to race and gender, and the long span of her career make her an important presence in the canons of American, African-American, and women's literature.

The parents of one daughter, the Petrys still

live in Old Saybrook. Ann Petry's short story "The Moses Project" appeared in a 1986 issue of *Harbor Review*.

• Ann Petry's papers are at Boston University's Mugar Memorial Library. Vernon E. Lattin, "Ann Petry and the American Dream," *Black American Literary Forum* 12, no. 2 (1978): 69–72. Bernard Bell, "Ann Petry's Demythologizing of American Culture and Afro-American Character," in *Conjuring: Black Women, Fiction, and Literary Tradition*, eds. Marjorie Pryse and Hortense J. Spillers (1985), pp. 105–115. Marjorie Pryse, " 'Pattern against the Sky': Deism and Motherhood in Ann Petry's *The Street*," also in *Conjuring*, pp. 116–131. Nellie Y. McKay, "Ann Petry's *The Street* and *The Narrows*: A Study of the Influence of Class, Race, and Gender on Afro-American Women's Lives," in *Women and War: The Changing Status of American Women from the 1930s to the 1950s*, eds. Maria Diedrich and Dorothea Fischer-Hornung (1990), pp. 127–140.

Hilary Holladay

PHALLOCENTRISM,   Phallogocentrism. *See* Deconstruction and Feminism.

PHALLUS. *See* Psychoanalysis and Women.

PHELPS, Elizabeth Stuart (1815–1852), novelist, short story writer, juvenile author. Born on 13 August in Andover, Massachusetts, to Abigail Clark, a long-term invalid, and Moses Stuart, a professor of sacred literature at Andover Theological Seminary, Phelps was the fifth of nine children. By 1825, she was writing to amuse sisters and servants. Educated at Andover's Abbot Academy and Boston's Mount Vernon School (directed by the Rev. Jacob Abbott, author of the juvenile Rollo series), she first published brief religious articles during her teens under the name H. Trusta, an anagram of Stuart.

By 1834, Phelps developed the "cerebral disease" (headache, partial blindness, temporary paralysis), which eventually caused her death. Writing gave some relief, but she was never long without discomfort. In 1842, she married an Andover student called to a Boston pastorate, Austin Phelps. Her daughter, an author who later "wore" her mother's name, was born in 1844 and christened Mary Gray. After six years in Boston, Austin accepted an Andover faculty position and moved his family there. A first son, Moses Stuart, later a Smith College professor, was born in 1849, and a second, Amos Lawrence, who became a Congregational pastor, was born in 1852; Elizabeth's death followed in less than three months.

For three years, hers was a household name resulting from the wide popularity of her 1851 *The Sunny Side; or, The Country Minister's Wife*, a realistic novel exemplifying domestic trials and triumphs. Phelps's "Angel over the Right Shoulder," a separately published short story much anthologized for its feminist revelation of the cost to creative women of domestic responsibilities, appeared in 1852. Also published in 1852 was Phelps's favorite work, the partially autobiographical *A Peep at "Number Five"; or, A Chapter in the Life of a City Pastor* (reprint, 1971). In addition, Phelps wrote two posthumously published collections of short fiction, *The Last Leaf from Sunny Side* (1853), introduced by her husband's lengthy biographical "Memorial," and *The Tell-Tale; or, Home Secrets Told by Old Travellers* (1853). Framing her career were Sunday school books for children: the formulaic Kitty Brown series (1851–1853) and *Little Mary; or, Talks and Tales for Children* (1854).

Internationally translated, her domestic regional realism joined that of her Andover neighbor, Harriet Beecher * Stowe. The elder Phelps left a literary legacy to her daughter, as attested by the younger woman's novel, *The Story of Avis* (1877), and autobiography, *Chapters from a Life* (1896).

• Phelps's personal papers are housed at the Andover Historical Society. See also Margo Culley, "Vain Dreams: The Dream Convention and Women's Fiction," *Frontiers: A Journal of Women Studies* 1, no. 3 (1976): 94–102. Carol Farley Kessler, "A Literary Legacy: Elizabeth Stuart Phelps, Mother and Daughter," *Frontiers: A Journal of Women Studies* 5, no. 3 (1980): 28–33. Judith Fetterley, ed., *Provisions: A Reader from Nineteenth-Century American Women* (1985), pp. 203–215.

Carol Farley Kessler

PHELPS (WARD), Elizabeth Stuart, also Mary Adams (1844–1911), novelist, short story writer, essayist, juvenile author, poet. Boston-born daughter of author Elizabeth Stuart * Phelps (1815–1852) and minister Austin Phelps (1820–1890), Phelps moved to Andover, Massachusetts, in 1848 when her father joined the faculty of its theological seminary. After her mother's 1852 death, she "wore" her mother's name, although she had been christened Mary Gray after a maternal friend. She helped to raise the last two of her four brothers, as her autobiography *Chapters from a Life* (1896) indicates—one becoming Trotty, the hero of two juvenile books (1870, 1873).

The inspirations for her literary career were Elizabeth Barrett Browning (1806–1861), especially in her verse novel about a poet, *Aurora Leigh* (1856), and her own mother, whose *The Sunny Side; or, The Country Minister's Wife* (1851) anticipated the popularity of her daughter's "Gates" books. The most important of these was *The Gates Ajar* (1868; rpt., 1964), implying a utopian heaven as fulfillment for women. Phelps memorialized her mother's struggle to balance domesticity and art in *The Story of Avis* (1877; rpt., 1988). Influenced by Rebecca Harding *Davis's *Life in the Iron Mills* (1861), Phelps depicted the devastating 1860 Pemberton Mills fire in Lawrence, Massachusetts, in "The Tenth of January" (*Atlantic Monthly*, March 1868)—her first critical success. A Sunday school teacher for mill children, she had written two 1860s series for this audience: *Tiny*, and the more secular *Gypsy*. Also set in a mill town, *The Silent Partner* (1871; rpt., 1983) reveals women silenced in private as well as in public. Essays on women's rights and wrongs in the *Independent* and *Woman's Journal* (1871–1874) continued this theme, as does the heroine of *Doctor Zay* (1882; rpt., 1987), who may have derived from her friendship with physician Mary Briggs Harris.

Phelps belonged to the Boston literary circle surrounding Annie Adams *Fields (1834–1915) and was a Gloucester, Massachusetts, summer neighbor of reformer Mary Bucklin Davenport Claflin (1825–1896), and her educator/governor husband. Gloucester was the scene for the humorous *Old Maids and Burglars in Paradise* (1879, 1886). Five years after the accidental death of her favorite brother M[oses] Stuart, a Smith College professor, Phelps married a young journalist, Herbert Dickinson Ward (1861–1932); the marriage disappointed. After her father's death, she wrote *A Singular Life* (1895), whose temperance pastor memorialized his youthful ideals. A sensational novel, *Confessions of a Wife* (1902), appeared under the pseudonym Mary Adams, and was followed by antivivisection activism, including such fiction as *Trixy* (1904), one of Phelps's works with an antivivisection theme. Of some fifty-six titles, her best work had appeared by the mid-1880s. Charlotte Perkins *Gilman followed in her fictional footsteps. Dying alone in Newton, Massachusetts, Phelps arranged for her ashes to rest under a tombstone she designed.

• Ward's personal papers are housed at the Andover Historical Society, the Houghton Library at Harvard University, and the Beinecke Library at Yale University. See also Carol Farley Kessler, *Elizabeth Stuart Phelps* (1982). Lori Duin Kelly, *The Life and Works of Elizabeth Stuart Phelps, Victorian Feminist Writer* (1983). Susan Coultrap-McQuin, *Doing Literary Business: American Women Writers in the Nineteenth Century* (1990).

Carol Farley Kessler

PHILOSOPHERS. Philosophy in the United States has been defined almost exclusively by and in relation to formal academic institutions. Generally, in the period before the twentieth century, these institutions had little use for serious intellectual work by women. Because philosophy was considered among the most serious intellectual work of all, it is not surprising that today we are aware of few prominent women philosophers writing before the twentieth century. Indeed, in the United States, the term *philosophy*—which to the general reader connotes no more than written contemplation of life's deepest issues in a thorough, perhaps systematic, usually secular manner—has been so commandeered by the academy as to have little serious meaning outside of it.

Gertrude *Stein's writing, as an obvious example, reveals a profound engagement with the nature of mind, language, reality, freedom, and responsibility (all bona fide philosophical topics). Her work shows the clear influence of the American pragmatist movement, especially of William James, with whom she studied. Yet formal qualities of her works, and the intransigence of the philosophical academy, currently ensure that her writing can neither be considered philosophical nor studied formally in philosophy departments. It is precisely to these issues that feminist philosophers today, and feminist theorists more generally, turn their attention.

These thoughts lay the necessary groundwork for any discussion of philosophy by women in the United States, in large part because that history exists at present in only a nascent, archeological state—to some extent because the history of philosophy in the United States is itself in a similar state. According to Elizabeth Flower and Murray G. Murphey's authoritative *History of Philosophy in America* (1977), for example, pre-twentieth-century American philosophy has only one major exponent, the Puritan Jonathan Edwards, who read Calvinist doctrine through the writings of Newton and Locke. Thus, unlike in Europe, the women whose lives and philosophical works we no longer know were marginalized not in the shadows of towering figures like Kant and Hegel (or even Schilling and Fichte), but instead in those of minor philosophers like Edwards and even lesser lights.

Historians of women in philosophy have thus turned their attention to the philosophical tenor of works by writers not formally thought of as philosophers. Therese Boos Dykeman, for example, in her ground-breaking *American Women Philosophers, 1650–1930; Six Exemplary Thinkers* (1993), argues persuasively for the philosophical content of the works of Anne *Bradstreet (c. 1612–1672), best known as a founding American woman poet, and herself at least nominally part of American Puritanism. Alongside Bradstreet's better-known poetry, Dykeman points to her religious verse and the aphoristic *Meditations Divine and Moral* (1664), for searching, often feminist-leaning moral speculations.

Other early American women philosophers in Dykeman's history include Mercy Otis * Warren (1728–1814), a multifaceted writer and essayist who, in her time, was considered among the most important American political philosophers by her contemporaries Thomas Jefferson and John Adams; Judith Sargent * Murray (1751–1820), a political philosopher whose work included essays with a markedly feminist reading of gender relations; and Frances Wright (1795–1852), a woman of letters, playwright, and journalist who founded an experimental community and worked toward ending slavery and increasing rights and independence for women. These women included ethics and other philosophical speculations in their wide-ranging work.

In the mid-nineteenth century, the dominant philosophical mode in America was transcendentalism, itself an offshoot of European idealism. The leaders of the movement in America were, of course, Ralph Waldo Emerson and Henry David Thoreau. Among their circle, Sarah Margaret * Fuller (1810–1850, popularly known as Margaret) was the most prominent woman; her major work, *Woman in the Nineteenth Century* (1845), is still considered among the first American feminist manifestos. *Woman in the Nineteenth Century*, although not what we would recognize today as a work of philosophy, nevertheless follows the formal pattern of much work by transcendentalists by moving in and out of philosophical speculation. Fuller indicated her indebtedness to Emerson's philosophical "system" (such as it is), though she was not personally so beholden to the men of transcendentalism. Other women with roles in nineteenth-century transcendentalism include Elizabeth * Peabody (1804–1894), who briefly edited a periodical called *Aesthetic Papers*, and Sarah Helen Whitman (1803–1878), a poet and literary critic (and the "Helen" of Edgar Allan Poe's lyrics) who wrote an important contemporaneous essay on Emerson.

A crucial, sadly forgotten figure in the transition between nineteenth- and twentieth-century American philosophy is Mary Whiton Calkins (1863–1930), in her time one of the country's most prominent philosophers. Calkins trained under William James and Josiah Royce at Harvard University, and in 1895 James ranked her Ph.D. oral examination "above any that he had heard," according to Dykeman. The Harvard Corporation, however, did not award degrees to women, and thus Calkins continued writing and teaching at Wellesley College without the degree for more than

thirty years, rising to great prominence in the philosophical community. Calkins's work covered many philosophical topics, including the history of philosophy and the relations between philosophy and psychology. Her major works include four books—*An Introduction to Philosophy* (1901), *The Persistent Problems of Philosophy* (1907; revised five times), *A First Book in Psychology* (1909), and *The Good Man and the Good* (1918)—and many articles. She is one of only three academics to have held the presidencies of both the American Philosophical Society and the American Psychological Association. Yet at her death in 1930 and after two entreaties by distinguished colleagues, Harvard still refused to grant her the doctorate.

It is in the twentieth century that American women enter the philosophical canon with full force. In the first part of the century, women began being admitted into the academy and performing the professional work that had hitherto been done only by men. The most outstanding of these philosophers, and one who is still read today, was Susanne K. Langer (1895–1985). Langer distinguished herself as one of the few American writers to develop her own, original systematic philosophy. That philosophy, first aired in *Philosophy in a New Key* (1942) and *Feeling and Form* (1953), comprises a wholly original synthesis of aesthetics, symbol theory, logic, and psychology. Langer sees all human activity as fundamentally expressive and feeling-directed, and her philosophy receives its fullest statement in a three-volume major work, *Mind: An Essay on Human Feeling* (1967–1982). Langer's early writings are among the only pre-1950 works by any American philosopher remaining in print today.

The early part of the twentieth century also produced professional women philosophers. These include Alice Ambrose (b.1906), a student of Ludwig Wittgenstein; Hazel Barnes (b.1915), the renowned translator of Jean Paul Sartre's *Being and Nothingness* (1956) and an existentialist philosopher herself; Mary Twibell Clark, an Augustine scholar; Grace Mead Andrus De Laguna (1878–1978), primarily a Continental philosopher; Elizabeth Flower (b.1914), coauthor of the authoritative, two-volume *History of Philosophy in America;* Katherine Gilbert (1886–1952), an important aesthetician; Georgia Elma Harkness (1891–1974), a religious philosopher and historian; Christine Ladd-Franklin (1847–1930), like Mary Calkins, a prominent student of philosophy, logic, and psychology who found formal accreditation by the philosophical establishment difficult to obtain (she was granted the Ph.D. by Johns Hopkins University only in 1926); Edith Schipper (b.1909), a classicist who has written on logic, ethics, and aesthetics; and Marie Collins Swabey (1880–1966), a woman of wide-ranging intelligence who wrote on subjects as diverse as the nature of democracy, natural law, the nature of history, and relativity theory, among others.

All this being said, there is no denying that the influence of women writing philosophy has reached its fullest extent only in the latter part of the twentieth century. This influence has been felt primarily in two ways. The first is through the continuing work of professional women philosophers in the academy in addressing both traditional philosophical topics and the developing topics of feminist philosophy. More traditional philosophers include Marjorie Grene (b.1910), an important writer who has worked on existentialism (*Dreadful Freedom: A Critique of Existentialism*, 1948), on the relations between analytic and Continental philosophy (*Philosophy in and out of Europe*, 1976), and on the philosophy of biology (*The Understanding of Nature*, 1974); Ruth Barcun Marcus (b.1921), a logician and philosopher of language (ed., *The Logical Enterprise*, 1975); Ruth Garrett Millikan, a philosopher of mind and psychology (*Language, Thought, and Other Biological Categories*, 1984); Nancy Cartwright, an extremely influential philosopher of science (*How the Laws of Physics Lie* and *Nature's Capacities and Their Measurement*, 1989); and Susan Haack, author of numerous articles on language, realism, and other philosophical topics.

Feminist philosophers form the second broad area of women writing in philosophy departments today, and do so in part by challenging many aspects of traditional intellectual practice and the philosophical establishment. They have concentrated their work on developing "standpoint epistemologies," considerations of knowledge and its acquisition that insist on including the knower and his or her social context in epistemological theories; on feminist histories of philosophy; and on feminist revisions of philosophy of science. Especially important in these discussions are figures like Alison Jagger, whose *Feminist Politics and Human Nature* (1983) surveys different theories of human nature from feminist perspectives; Susan Bordo, whose *Flight to Objectivity* (1987) puts the feminist critique of traditional philosophy and epistemology in concise and powerful form; Marilyn Frye, author of *The Politics of Reality: Essays in Feminist Theory* (1993), a key text for feminist philosophy generally, as well as for the burgeoning field of lesbian philosophy; Sandra Harding, whose *Science Question in Feminism* (1986) and *Whose Science? Whose Knowledge? Thinking from Women's Lives* (1991)

combine sustained attention to both standpoint epistemologies and philosophy of science; and Helen Longino, author of a general and sophisticated rethinking of philosophy of science (*Science as Social Knowledge*, 1990). Readers interested in contemporary work should refer to philosophy journals, especially *Hypatia*, the main vehicle for feminist essays in philosophy, and the *American Philosophical Association Newsletter on Feminism and Philosophy*, as well as mainstream feminist journals such as *Signs*, *Feminist Studies*, and *differences* that include articles on feminist philosophy.

At the same time, the work of many contemporary feminist theorists not specifically identified as philosophers includes clearly philosophical features, and indeed this work is widely taught in feminist philosophy courses, if not in their "mainstream" counterparts. In this work an especially strong commitment to multicultural values and critical methodology makes itself fully apparent. This work also calls into question many of the traditional disciplinary and professional boundaries that, as we have seen, have worked to keep women out of the ranks of serious U.S. philosophical writers for at least three centuries. Among the many important works and writers under this heading, of special note are Judith Butler, trained as a Hegelian philosopher, but whose *Gender Trouble: Feminism and the Subversion of Identity* (1991) is read at least as widely by literary and cultural critics; Hortense Spillers, author of several searching essays on feminism and the African-American experience; Donna Haraway, a historian of science and cultural critic whose *Primate Visions* (1989) and *Simians, Cyborgs and Women* (1991) raise profound challenges to the masculinist subject of philosophical and scientific study; Evelyn Fox Keller, a sophisticated feminist critic of science (see especially her *Reflections on Gender and Science*, 1985, and *Secrets of Life, Secrets of Death*, 1992); and Gloria *Anzaldúa, a Chicana writer whose *Borderlands/La Frontera* (1987) contains profoundly philosophical speculations on the nature of identity, ethnicity, and nation.

• Sandra Harding and Merrill B. Hintikka, eds., *Discovering Reality: Feminist Perspectives on Epistemology, Metaphysics, Methodology, and the Philosophy of Science* (1983). Mary Ellen Waithe, ed., *A History of Women Philosophers*, 4 vols. (1987–). Ethel M. Kersey, *Women Philosophers: A Bio-Critical Source Book* (1989). Else M. Barth, *Women Philosophers: A Bibliography of Books through 1990* (1992). Linda Alcoff and Elizabeth Potter, eds., *Feminist Epistemologies* (1993).

David Golumbia

PIERCY, Marge (b. 1936), poet, novelist. Born during the Great Depression to working-class parents, Marge Piercy was the first of her family to go to college. She received her B.A. from the University of Michigan in 1957, and her M.A. from Northwestern in 1958. She began publishing poems in the sixties, and her first novel, *Going Down Fast*, was published in 1969.

Piercy says her influences are many, since she read widely during her adolescence, but she includes Emily *Dickinson, Walt Whitman, Muriel *Rukeyser, and Simone *de Beauvoir. Piercy credits her mother's and grandmother's *story telling, as well as myth and fairy tale, for her first notions about narrative.

Much of Piercy's work is concerned with the inequality she sees in America—economic, sexual, and racial. Critics sometimes accuse her of being transparently political, and of sacrificing craft for her political message. But Piercy's work does bring a feminist message to a wide audience.

Among her many volumes of poetry, *Circles on the Water* (1982) and *Available Light* (1988) are considered her best. Piercy's poems are almost always in her own voice, and again are often feminist and political. She says her poems are at once more personal and more universal than her fiction. For Piercy, poetry is a healing agent because it blends sound and rhythm, memory and dream, and many different kinds of knowledge. *Available Light* takes on the political issues present in everyday life, and is more carefully crafted than some earlier volumes.

Perhaps her best-known novel, *Woman on the Edge of Time* (1976) gives Piercy a vehicle in which to combine both her feminist theory and her story telling. A work of *science fiction, *Woman* remains important as one of the first feminist *utopias. Further, it boldly proposes an egalitarian system in which women are free of reproduction, no one owns property, and there are no gender-specific pronouns ("per" is the only pronoun). On another level, Piercy deals with a frightening present, in which psychiatrists try to alter the brains of poor people in a mental hospital. Her protagonist, Connie, must learn to fight the system, though she is poor and uneducated. As a work of science fiction, critics sometimes say *Woman* cannot be considered a serious work. But it is readily accessible to just the kind of audience Piercy wants to reach. Piercy's particular interest lies in getting people to cross boundaries of race, perception, or class they normally would not cross.

• Susan Kress, "In and Out of Time: The Form of Marge Piercy's Novels," in *Future Females: A Critical Anthology*, ed. Marlene S. Barr (1981), pp. 109–122.

Deborah Viles

PINCKNEY, Eliza Lucas (ca. 1722–ca. 1793), letter writer and agricultural pioneer. Eliza Lucas was born in Antigua, West Indies, and educated in England; she eventually settled near Charleston, South Carolina, where at twenty-two she married Charles Pinckney, a widowed lawyer more than twenty years her senior. Eliza was subsequently widowed at age thirty-five.

Pinckney's letters provide an important socio-historical illustration of an upper-class white woman's life in colonial and revolutionary times. They also provide testimony that the influence of the "southern belle" was never confined solely to the private sphere. Throughout her lifetime, for instance, Pinckney was often responsible for the supervision of her father's, husband's, and sons' plantations; during this time, she devoted herself to agricultural experiments, becoming legendary for her contribution to the development of indigo as a major Carolinian export.

The published *Letterbook* is divided into three parts depicting Pinckney's life as daughter, as wife, and as mother, respectively. The first section details her business enterprises and interests, her taste for classical literature, and her growing feelings for her future husband. Most of the second part contains letters directed to friends in South Carolina, and was composed while her husband served as a colonial agent in London. The letters that make up the final section represent those penned during her "luxury of grief" over her husband's sudden death as well as those written to and concerning her sons, Charles Cotesworth and Thomas, while they were enrolled abroad in English schools. Pinckney's letters aptly document romantic love ideology as well as the institution of Republican motherhood: wife/mother loving, sacrificing, and fighting for her family's survival before, during, and after wartime.

Pinckney believed in both the power of education and the power of women; an educated woman herself, she was a testament to that power and helped to spread it by educating others, including her sister, her daughter, and her family's slaves. Pinckney devoted herself to showing "how capable women are both of friendship and business." Her correspondence with women, which Pinckney once referred to as "an epistolary intercourse," reveals just how important she found women's lives, feelings, and opinions to be. Her female descendants shared her beliefs, as they were the ones responsible for collecting Pinckney's letters and composing her biography.

Pinckney owned slaves and was not free from the racist and Eurocentric biases of her era: she once called South Carolina the "primitive" other world. But as her resources grew, her pride in America strengthened. Like her adopted country, she, too, firmly believed in independence.

• Harriott Pinckney Holbrook, ed., *Journal and Letters of Eliza Lucas* (1850). Harriott Horry Ravenel, *Eliza Pinckney* (1896). Elise Pinckney, ed., *The Letterbook of Eliza Lucas Pinckney, 1739–1762* (1972). Anne Firor Scott, "Self Portraits: Three Women," in *Uprooted Americans: Essay for Oscar Handlin*, ed. Richard Bushman et al. (1979).

                                        Kazuko Watanabe

PIONEER WOMEN. Pioneer women were participants in a mass migration of Americans westward in search of better economic and social opportunities for themselves and their families. However, their stories—told in letters, diaries, journals, and fiction—have been largely absent from official histories of successive American frontiers. Until the 1970s, western history was told almost exclusively in terms of men and men's experiences. Women appeared, if at all, only as one-dimensional stereotypes.

Susan Armitage describes the field of western history as one dominated by "Hislanders," scholars writing stories of male adventure, rugged individualism, and the conquering of untamed land. Frederick Jackson Turner, whose "frontier thesis" (1893) still structures debates in western history, defined pioneering in terms of men and their activities—exploration, fur trapping, ranching, mining, farming, and lumbering. Subsequent critical debate continued along similar lines. This traditional account of pioneering had no place for women and women's labor—domestic production; homemaking; child rearing; the establishment of schools, libraries, churches, and hospitals.

The representations of pioneer women in literature and history, when they do appear, tend to be stereotypical. Sandra Myres identifies three prominent images of "westering women" from popular and official sources representing pioneering and early settlement: reluctant pioneer, loyal helpmate, and bad girl. The reluctant pioneer, ripped unwillingly away from the comforts of "civilization" and the support of her female friends and family, lives a life of toil, loneliness, and sorrow, being driven finally into insanity and early death by harsh frontier conditions. Fictional representations of the reluctant pioneer wife are found in Hamlin Garland's short fiction and O. E. Rölvaag's *Giants in the Earth* (1927). The helpmate to the enterprising pioneer, after James Fenimore Cooper's Esther, carries a gun in one hand to ward off wild beasts and hostile natives and her infant in the other. Plucky and determined, she is a "gentle tamer" of the wilderness, bringing "civ-ilization" in the form of churches and schools. She is a "Madonna of the Prairies," a description taken from the title of a 1921 painting by W. D. Koerner which shows a pretty young woman in a sunbonnet and lace collar, the bow of the covered wagon in which she is riding forming a halo around her head. Finally, there are bad girls—hard-drinking, gambling, guntoting women with shocking speech and manners who are often, but not always, prostitutes. Belle Starr and Calamity Jane fall into this category.

Real pioneer women are revealed through their own writings to be far more interesting, diverse, and nuanced characters. Although there are patterns in their lives, pioneer women were not a homogeneous group. They differed from each other by age, race, region, religion, ethnicity, class, level of education, marital status, and profession. Pioneer women tended to be young (under forty), but there were older women who went west as well. Most were Scandinavian, German, English, or Irish by extraction, although there were significant numbers from southern and eastern Europe as well. White middle-class women have left the most records, and African-American women, usually traveling as slaves, are almost invisible in the written record due to illiteracy. The lives of women already inhabiting the West when pioneers arrived—Native American and Mexican women—are only now being investigated in any detail.

The largest group of pioneer women were young, married white women with children who accompanied husbands west in search of farmland to better their economic and social fortunes. The lives of farm women centered around homemaking, child rearing, and domestic production. The labor of these women—their sewing, quilting, cooking, canning, gardening, keeping of livestock and poultry, soap making, cleaning, and laundry—maintained their own families, but also brought in money through the sale of these goods and services to others. In spite of the nineteenth-century doctrine of *separate spheres, pioneer women often found themselves doing "men's work"—helping to clear land, planting, harvesting, managing farms and ranches. Pioneer women were valued not only as guardians of home and hearth, but also as workers, since capitalism had not yet split the home from the world of "productive" work on the prairies and plains. Women who were single, widowed, divorced, or had husbands who were often away were independent agricultural entrepreneurs as well. Single women took up between 7 percent and 10 percent of all homesteads between 1890 and 1920.

Not all pioneer women, however, worked in agriculture; some worked in domestic service. They were cooks, washerwomen, and seamstresses, particularly in mining and cattle towns where there were large numbers of unmarried men. Women also owned and managed restaurants, hotels, and boarding houses or worked as waitresses and chambermaids in these institutions. They were milliners, dressmakers, and keepers of grocery and dry-goods stores. Still others were prostitutes, concentrating themselves in mining and cattle towns as madames, parlor girls, saloon girls, or streetwalkers.

Women with education had yet more options. Some combined their homemaking and child rearing with writing and journalism. Caroline * Kirkland, Eliza Farnham, and Mary Austin * Holley all wrote about their experiences on the prairies, offering entertainment and advice to would-be pioneers in the east. Educated women could, and often did, teach or give lessons. Catharine * Beecher led a campaign to send educated, single women west to teach in one-room schoolhouses. In addition, some of the women who were pioneers went west for religious reasons—as nuns or missionaries to Native Americans. A small number of women became lawyers and doctors.

Although many pioneer women began as reluctant emigrants, accompanying husbands who had decided to go west, they soon began to build lives which, although leaving the ideology of domesticity unchallenged in word, often challenged the separation of spheres in fact. Fictionalized representations of such women appear in the early novels of Willa * Cather in Alexandra Bergson of *O Pioneers!* (1913) and Ántonia Shimerda of *My Ántonia* (1918). Annette Kolodny argues that the white women who went west viewed the land differently than did their brothers and husbands. Where the men saw themselves conquering the virgin land, women fantasized planting a garden in the wilderness, creating a domestic space for family and community.

[See also Diaries and Journals; Exploration Narratives; Frontier Writing; Western Women's Writing.]

• Julie Roy Jeffrey, *Frontier Women* (1979). Sandra L. Myres, *Westering Women and the Frontier Experience 1800–1915* (1982). Lillian Schlissel, *Women's Diaries of the Westward Journey* (1982). Annette Kolodny, *The Land Before Her* (1984). Carol Fairbanks, *Prairie Women* (1986). Susan Armitage and Elizabeth Jameson, eds., *The Women's West* (1987). Glenda Riley, *The Female Frontier* (1988). Lillian Schlissel, Vicki Ruiz, and Janice Monk, eds., *Western Women: Their Land, Their Lives* (1988).

Erin A. Smith

PLATH, Sylvia (1932–1963), poet, novelist, and essayist. Sylvia Plath was born in Jamaica Plain, Massachusetts, the older child of Otto and Aurelia Schoeber Plath. Her father was professor of German and entomology (a specialist on bees) at Boston University; her mother, a high school teacher, was his student. Both parents valued learning. In 1940 Otto died of complications from surgery after a leg amputation, and Aurelia's parents became part of the household to care for the children when she returned to teaching.

Sylvia's interests in writing and art continued through her public school years in Wellesley, Massachusetts, and at Smith College, where she attended on scholarships. Her extensive publications of poems and fiction led to her selection for the College Board of *Mademoiselle* magazine in 1953. The depression that was endemic in her father's family troubled her during her junior year; when her mother sought treatment for her, she was given bi-polar electroconvulsive shock treatments as an out-patient. In August 1953, she attempted suicide by overdosing on sleeping pills.

Recovered after six months of intensive therapy, Sylvia returned to Smith and her usual academic success. A senior, she wrote an honors thesis on Dostoyevski's use of the double and graduated summa cum laude in English; she also won a Fulbright fellowship to study at Newnham College, Cambridge. In the fall of 1955, she sailed for England.

Plath studied hard but her life in England was also sexual. As her writing showed, she was angry about double-standard behavior, and claimed for herself the right to as much sexual experience as men had. She believed combining the erotic and the intellectual possible, and when she met Ted Hughes, a Cambridge poet, she felt that life with him would be ideal. The two were married in London on 16 June 1956, accompanied by Sylvia's mother.

After a honeymoon in Spain, the Hugheses set up housekeeping. Sylvia passed her examinations while Ted taught in a boys' school; in June they sailed for America. The next year Sylvia taught freshman English at Smith; in 1958 and 1959 they lived in Boston and wrote professionally. Ted's first poem collection, *The Hawk in the Rain*, won a major poetry prize; Sylvia's promise that she would make him a success seemed fulfilled. Unfortunately, giving such single-minded attention to Ted's work meant that developing her own voice as a writer was difficult. She visited Robert Lowell's class in poetry writing, where she met George Starbuck and Anne * Sexton; Sexton's work became an inspiration to her. Plath worked part-time as a secretary in the psychiatric division of Massachusetts General Hospital, transcribing patients' histories, which often included dreams. She also resumed therapy with the woman psychiatrist who had helped her after her breakdown.

The years in the States convinced Ted that he needed to live in England. After an autumn at Yaddo, the writers' colony, Ted and Sylvia sailed for London in December 1959. Sylvia was happy: she was writing good poems (she had written "The Colossus" at Yaddo, where she had discovered Theodore Roethke's poetry), and she was five months pregnant. Soon after Frieda's birth on 1 April 1960, they began looking for a country house to escape cramped, expensive London. In late summer of 1961, they moved to Devon, where Sylvia was ecstatic about their centuries-old manor house. Before that time, however, they wrote efficiently (sometimes in the borrowed study of poet W. S. Merwin), and Plath was able to finish most of *The Bell Jar*. Influenced by J. D. Salinger's *The Catcher in the Rye*, Sylvia's novel narrated a woman's life from adolescence, ending with a positive resolution of rebirth.

Ted wrote programs for the BBC and became a Faber author, in contact with T. S. Eliot and other important British poets; Sylvia was publishing new kinds of poems, content that William Heinemann had contracted to publish her book, *The Colossus and Other Poems*. Its publication in October 1960 was well received, and Alfred Knopf published the collection in the States.

Personal jealousies, differences in American and British views of gender roles, and a return of Sylvia's depression complicated the Plath-Hughes marriage. Despite their happiness when Sylvia became pregnant once more, after an earlier miscarriage, the marriage of two aspiring writers living in an isolated village with an infant and little money was difficult. After Nicholas's birth in January 1962, Sylvia faced the fact of Hughes's infidelity, expressing herself through increasingly angry—and powerful—poems. In contrast to such work as "The Rabbit Catcher" and "The Detective," her radio play for the BBC, "Three Women," is a beautifully wrought, somber poem about maternal choice. Plath had learned to find joy in her women-centered world, and the care of her children and friendships with other women were increasingly important. But she could not tolerate male irresponsibility. Living with the children in lonely Devon, Plath wrote many of the poems that later appeared in *Ariel*. Her so-called October poems, written during the month after Hughes had left her, are among her most famous: "Lady Lazarus," "Daddy," "Fever 103," "Purdah," "Poppies in July," "Ariel," and others. The magazines to which she sent these poems did not accept them; although the *New Yorker* magazine had a First Reading contract, its poetry editor refused all her late work except for a few lines.

Moving with the children to a London flat in December 1962, Plath tried to make a new life for herself, but the worst winter in a century added to her depression. Without a telephone, ill, and troubled with the care of the two infants, she committed suicide by sleeping pills and gas inhalation on 11 February 1963, just two weeks after the publication of *The Bell Jar* (written by "Victoria Lucas").

That novel, and the various collections of her poems that appeared during the next twenty years, secured for Plath the position of one of the most important women writers in the States. The mixture of comedic self-deprecation and forceful anger made her work a foreshadowing of the feminist writing that appeared in the later 1960s and the 1970s. Like *Friedan's 1963 *The Feminine Mystique*, Plath's *Bell Jar* followed in 1965 with the posthumously published collection *Ariel*, was both a harbinger and an early voice of the women's movement. As the posthumous awarding of the 1982 Pulitzer Prize for Poetry to Plath's *Collected Poems* showed, her audience was not limited to women readers, nor did her writing express only feminist sentiments.

Plath's work is valuable for its stylistic accomplishments—its melding of comic and serious elements, its ribald fashioning of near and slant rhymes in a free-form structure, its terse voicing of themes that have too often been treated only with piety. It is also valuable for its ability to reach today's reader, because of its concern with the real problems of our culture. In this age of gender conflicts, broken families, and economic inequities, Plath's forthright language speaks loudly about the anger of being both betrayed and powerless.

• The Sylvia Plath papers are housed at the Lilly Library, Indiana University, Bloomington, and at Smith College, Northampton, Mass. Ted Hughes published selections from her journals (*The Journals of Sylvia Plath*, ed. Frances McCullough, 1982) and some of the short fiction (*Johnny Panic and the Bible of Dreams, Short Stories, Prose and Diary Excerpts*, 1980); Aurelia Plath published *Letters Home by Sylvia Plath, Correspondence 1950–1963* (1975). Lynda K. Bundtzen, *Plath's Incarnations: Woman and the Creative Process*, (1983). Steven Tabor, *Sylvia Plath: An Analytical Bibliography* (1987). Linda Wagner-Martin, *Sylvia Plath, A Biography* (1987). Linda Wagner-Martin, ed., *Sylvia Plath: The Critical Heritage* (1988). Anne Stevenson, *Bitter Fame: A Life of Sylvia Plath*, (1989). Steven Axelrod, *Sylvia Plath, The Wound and the Cure of Words*, (1990).

Sheryl L. Meyering, *Reference Guide to Sylvia Plath* (1990).

Linda Wagner-Martin

PLAYWRIGHTS: 1975 TO PRESENT. Out of women's *consciousness-raising groups and the political and social upheaval of the 1960s emerged a rich variety of new women playwrights, each one voicing her perspective on those experiences, sometimes collectively, sometimes individually.

The appendix to *Women in American Theatre* documents the sudden swell of women playwrights from 1975 to present. Boosted by such new institutional honors as the American Theatre Association and the Susan Smith Blackburn awards, and encouraged by dozens of new feminist theaters, hundreds of unknown playwrights tried to find audiences in the 1970s. In 1978 the Women's Project of the American Place Theatre received 700 scripts when its founder Julia Miles put out a call for plays. This new generation of playwrights divides into two general groups: women in theater (those who work without a singularly political focus) and feminists (those who identify with an ideology and seek to effect social change with their plays). What both groups have in common is the difficulty of earning a living as a playwright, beginning with the pressure of finding critics and producers who will take their work seriously. There is also the question of the "female aesthetic," one that allows women to write from what they know, supports a link between the personal and political, and encourages some measure of self-determination. Because these new writers draw on an undervalued language and new forms of communication that are little understood in traditional theater, directors, producers and actors tend to dismiss their work or to distort the product beyond recognition.

Some playwrights, particularly those who choose not to take a strong political position, do enjoy commercial success. Notable are Pulitzer Prize winners Wendy *Wasserstein (b. 1950) for *The Heidi Chronicles* (1989), Beth *Henley (b. 1952) for *Crimes of the Heart* (1981), and Marsha *Norman (b. 1947) for *'Night Mother* (1983). Nevertheless, opportunities to work on Broadway, Off-Broadway, or Off-Off Broadway are rare and Pulitzer Prizes are still rarer. More women were writing plays for Broadway at the turn of the century than in 1992 because of lack of courage among the backers who underwrite Broadway productions. Given the high cost of production in New York City, playwrights without a track record of mass appeal have been simply considered too risky an investment.

Although the plays of contemporary women playwrights have reflected the political spectrum of women in America, this theater has been run largely by the feminists. Looking for alternatives to the frustration of working in mainstream theater, most feminist playwrights have chosen to trade the dubious lure of economic viability in commercial theater for the companionship and artistic stimulus of small theater companies—including both equity-aligned and community-based, nonprofit companies. As codirector of one of the oldest ongoing repertory companies, Judith Malina (b. 1926) of the Living Theatre in New York City is virtually an icon of the experimental and revolutionary theater that has inspired feminist theater in America. Other feminist activity in New York City was encouraged by writer and director Karen Malpede (b. 1945), who cofounded Brooklyn's New Cycle Theatre (1976–1983), and by Julia Miles, who opened The Women's Project at the American Place Theater with a Ford Foundation Grant in 1978. The Women's Project, one of the few feminist theater groups to survive that era, has produced musicals like *A . . . My Name is Alice* (1984), conceived by Joan Micklin Silver (b. 1935), and *Frida* (1992), with monologues by Migdalia Cruz (b. 1958) that appeal to nonfeminist professional theater across America.

Supporting networks like these ensembles become centers for writers in regional theater as well. Megan *Terry (b. 1932) and Jo Ann Schmidman of Omaha, Nebraska's Magic Theatre (established 1968) have both depended on and shaped these underground connections for their professional growth. Strong *feminism thrives economically at the Magic Theatre by avoiding fads, using in-kind communal support, and mounting the highly professional works of women such as Rochelle Owens (b. 1936), actress June Havoc (b. 1916), and Susan Yankowitz (b. 1941). Though chronically underfunded, these troupes attempt to provide work in theater for women; they also challenge the hierarchical values of male-dominated theater. Plays are written collectively, members share tasks of artistic director, stage manager, fundraiser, set designer, house manager, and actors, and much of the work is done on a volunteer basis.

Central to most feminist theater are themes about women's bodies. On a more trivial level these themes translate, for instance, into* humor about *body hair and advertising that attempts to define *beauty norms. When taken seriously, these themes become debates about cross-gender roles, discussions about food and weight, and scenes with battered or raped women, *incest, and *suicide. Performance artists Laurie *Anderson (b. 1947), Karen Finley (b. 1966?), and Madonna (Ciccone, b. 1959), using a specialized form of song and monologue in one-woman theater, interrogate the cultural constructions which condition the bodily image. Anderson accomplishes this with her androgynous hairstyle and dress. Finley, refusing power games drawn up by the male spectator, deliberately desecrates her nude female body with excrementlike matter; and Madonna takes charge of her own self-generated image by mocking the commodification of the female anatomy. Writing her own rules for sexual fantasy, Madonna flouts double standards that encourage only males to express their desires.

Plays written by one subgroup, the radical feminists, have attempted to empower women by discovering through art what is essential about womanhood. They often perform in communal *rituals that underscore the commonalities among women—namely their biological cycles, *motherhood, fertility, intuition, *spirituality, bonding, and nurturing. They celebrate their culture in small communities. Playwrights, often doubling as performers, employ female symbols and metaphors of women's early matrilineal systems and spiritual cultures that recognize women as possessors of the secret of life in dancing, singing and magical utterances. Radical feminists debunk male phobias, specifically men's fears about witches' power and mystery, herbal healing, and holistic medicine.

Closely allied with the radical feminists have been the lesbian playwrights who also confront male oppression and explore woman/woman sexual and nonsexual relationships. The most extreme form of this theater has been produced by separatists who protect participants in their theater—actors and audience—from the male gaze which fetishizes the female body. Lesbians critique *heterosexuality, and explore *eroticism within gay circles. More interested than most feminists in freeing up the voice that expresses sensual pleasure, lesbian theater experiments with celebrating the libidinal impulse and undermining the body as a stable referent, making it difficult for the audience to tell the truth about gesture or act. Like other feminist playwrights, lesbians such as performance artist Holly Hughes (b. 1965?) and Jane Chambers (1937–1983), with her *Last Summer at Bluefish Cove* (1980), wrestle with the images which have historically been used to represent their community. Lesbians question the essentialist concept of womanhood, that is, the assumption that women may be defined by core characteristics. Concerned that women are traditionally identified in opposition to the male as objects of desire, lesbian playwrights avoid stereotyping *femininity and *masculinity, seeking instead new forms to replace realistic drama that reinforces patriarchal assumptions. Writing cooperatively, many playwrights are in residence with companies like Split Britches at WOW (Women's One World) Cafe in New York City's East Village. A drama by Jane Wagner (b. 1935), *The Search for Signs of Intelligent Life in the Universe* (1986), performed by Lily Tomlin, is one play from the gay community that has won awards and realized commercial success.

Unlike the lesbians and radical feminist playwrights, the material feminists have found few allies in the United States, probably a legacy of the McCarthy era when playwrights were persecuted for their leftist political views. These are the Marxist and socialist feminists who emphasize *class, economic, and racial issues as they connect with *gender. Their plays promote audience participation with topics like ethnic pride, community power, and people's independence. They attack *ageism, *sexism, poverty, and institutional intimidation. Maxine Klein (b. 1934), playwright and director for the Little Flags Theatre Collective in Boston, is among the best known activist-authors in this movement.

African-American women, whose works are often distinctive for their blend of music, poetry, and dance that evoke musical rhythms, jazz forms, and storytelling from the black community, have also placed priority on racial discrimination, deprivation and division, but are more single-minded than most materialist feminists. Adrienne *Kennedy (b. 1931), for example, has led the way since the 60s and mid-70s in a theater that struggles to controvert sexist and racist *stereotypes. Women playwrights like Kim Hines (b. 1955) must often fight for the right to direct and create for male-dominated companies like Penumbra in Minneapolis, partly because ethnic themes take precedence over gender for most African-American playwrights. Notable for her innovation, Ntozake *Shange (b. 1948) has achieved international success with *for colored girls who have considered suicide / when the rainbow is enuf* (1976) and *Spell #7* (1979). Barbara Ann Teer (b. 1937), founder and director of the National Black Theatre, has been central to the African-American arts movement.

Limited by linguistic barriers, the works of Latina playwrights have not been widely circulated. In the 1970s, however, El Teatro de la Esperanza formed with the goal of being sensitive to the woman's place in a male-dominated Hispanic culture and featuring women playwrights. Joan Holden (b. 1939), playwright and director of the San Francisco Mime Troupe, has also made a substantial commitment to Latina writers. In Texas, playwright Estela *Portillo-Trambley (b. 1936) has earned a lasting reputation with her feminist ethnic and nonpolitical themes. The best-known playwright from the Hispanic community is Cuban-born Maria Irene Fornes (b. 1930) whose five Obie awards and polished productions have deservedly earned her a permanent place in American theater.

The Brooklyn-based Spiderwoman Theater, founded in 1975 by three Kuna-Rappahannock Indian sisters—Gloria and Muriel Miguel and Lisa Mayo—mines Native American culture for material. These sisters write wildly funny yet intensely serious plays—such as *Winnetou's Snake Oil Show From Wigwam City* (1989) and *Power Pipes* (1992)—that at once dignify their *folklore, defy male-constructed taboos about performing women, and mount assaults on mainstream stereotypes of the Native American community.

Since few early companies have survived to 1993, some playwrights have turned to more comprehensive, multimedia centers, such as the visionary Walker Art Center of Minneapolis, which sponsor works that continue to represent the woman's experience and create roles to be enjoyed by women, to stage relationships between women, and to explore the many reflections of the woman's self.

[*See also* Drama.]

• Maxine Klein, *Theatre For the 98%* (1978). Dinah Luise Leavitt, *Feminist Theatre Groups* (1980). Julia Miles, *The Women's Project* (1980) and *Women's Project 2* (1984). Helene Keyssar, *Feminist Theatre: An Introduction to Plays of Contemporary British and American Women* (1985). Helen Krich Chinoy and Linda Walsh Jenkins, *Women in American Theatre*, rev. and expanded ed. (1987). Sue-Ellen Case, *Feminism and Theatre* (1988). Sue-Ellen Case, ed., *Performing Feminisms: Feminist Critical Theory and Theatre* (1990). Emilie S. Kilgore, ed., *Contemporary Plays by Women: Outstanding Winners and Runners-up for the Susan Smith Blackburn Prize (1978–1990)* (1991).

Reade W. Dornan

POETRY. *This seven-part entry explores both the rich history of poetry by women in America and various thematic or formal categories that transcend chronological divisions within that body of work. Its divisions are:*

> 1650 to 1850
> 1850 to 1976
> Contemporary Women's Poetry
> Long Poem
> Love Poetry
> Religious Poetry
> Concrete Poems

The first essay describes the origins of women's poetry while the second charts what many see as the peak years of writing by women poets, from Emily Dickinson's remarkable work through the women poets of modernism and beyond. The essay on contemporary women poets covers the wealth of important work written since 1976. The essays on love poetry and religious poems speak of cohesive themes, while those on the long poem and concrete poems describe formalist patterns. For further information, please refer to the article on Poetry in the following entries: African-American Writing; Asian-American Writing; Chicana Writing; Jewish-American Writing; Latina Writing; Lesbian Writing; Native American Writing.

1650 to 1850

The first centuries of American poetry are often described as derivative. Much of what experimentation there was occurred in poetry written by women. Anne *Bradstreet's use of the sonnet and meditative mode for domestic and even romantic purposes was the first exploration of conventional poetic forms, but the eighteenth century too was filled with impressive work by women poets. As Emily Watts points out in *The Poetry of American Women from 1632 to 1945*, women's writing in poetry was consistently so innovative and diverse as to seem, at times, almost idiosyncratic.

The difficulty of reconstructing the earliest years of American literary history is complicated by the fact that many poems were circulated by *letter. When they were published, they appeared in newspapers and pamphlets rather than books. Retrieving this work is nearly impossible. Another issue is that many women wrote what has come to be known, derogatorily, as occasional verse—poems celebrating a historical or personal event. Literary critics sometimes objected to such a pragmatic focus, and refused to take the work seriously as "poetry." The two situations are interdependent: Women's poems appeared in newspapers precisely because they wanted to communicate to readers about real happenings. Women's poetry was popular because it spoke of recognizable human life.

In the time of Anne Bradstreet, however, much of women's writing was private. Few women committed themselves to print because—judging from the fate of Anne Hutchinson and a number of women hanged as witches in Salem—to be something other than conventionally religious and wifely was dangerous. But Bradstreet's legacy to such later writers as Anna Tompson Hayden, Jane Colman Turell, Elizabeth Sowle Bradford, Mercy Otis *Warren, Phillis *Wheatley, Sarah Wentworth *Morton, and Ann Eliza *Bleecker was the imaginative power to grasp existing poetic form and turn it to uses germane to women's lives and histories.

One of the earliest subjects in these women's works was their reassessment of what history had to say to them. Phillis Wheatley's re-enactment of the powerless position of the slave mother, who was often sold away from her own children, appeared to be a poem about a mourning woman from classical mythology. "Niobe in Distress for Her Children" becomes the metaphor for Wheatley's own black history.

Mercy Warren worked in a number of genres, but she achieved a kind of self-definition that made her spirited voice unmistakable. Ann Eliza Bleecker and her daughter, Margaretta Bleecker Faugeres, went a step further and created a nexus of themes that were of particular interest to women readers. Bleecker, for example, wrote about the activities of her children, commemorating events in their lives. Although many of her poems are lost because they were sent to friends and relatives, the knowledge of her lyric prowess and her ability to turn the terrors of frontier life into art had wide influence.

The real fruition of Bradstreet's collection, *The Tenth Muse Lately Sprung Up in America* (1650), the first published by an American poet of either sex, was the prominence during the nineteenth century of a number of talented and well-published women poets who were both recognized and valued. Some of these writers, in fact, made their living by the pen—no mean accomplishment for writers who did not write fiction. Were their writings extant, so that critical judgment could be based on evaluations of each woman's *oeuvre* (rather than on only the fragments and comments by contemporaries that are available), our perception today of what the earliest women's poetry was like—and for what reasons—might be entirely different.

Linda Wagner-Martin

1850 to 1976

A number of major poets work in this period; however, the model of a single women's tradition does not offer a viable approach to the variety of their poetry. While they may appeal to particular women predecessors, by and large the poets in this period develop their styles and register their voices within the traditions—shared by men and women—that define the parameters of the special discourse culturally distinguished as poetry. Because poetry is so tradition-bound, and because it can claim no clear referential relationship to social practices, factoring *gender into poetic history is not easy. Gender is crucial, however, in the ways these poets position themselves—as oppositional, subversive, marginal, or supplemen-

tary—within the common traditions they invoke to authorize themselves. For the most part, social *class is not a determinative variable; the poets discussed here enjoyed varying degrees of social and educational advantages—enough, at least, to situate them within the middle class.

Generalizing about the effect of gender on poetry is further complicated by how gender metaphors operate in figurations of poetic history. The binding tradition and its conventional imperatives place poetry as a "patriarchal" discourse; yet poetry's apparent exemption from immediate social practices genders it—especially after the eighteenth century—as a "*feminine" discourse, outside the male-gendered spheres of reason, utility, public activity, and power. Given the palimpsest of gender maps imposed on poetry, experimenting with traditional forms becomes useful for both men and women poets, although for different ends, to alleviate different kinds of anxieties. Through modernism at least, women poets experiment—whether by subverting canonical forms or current norms or abjuring them altogether—as much to signify their difference from popular, "female" verse as to resist the patriarchal authority inscribed in canonical forms.

Emily *Dickinson (1830–1886) is the key poet in the nineteenth century. A strong influence on many twentieth-century poets, men and women alike, many of her themes—love, death, renunciation, emotional excess—are common to nineteenth-century women's writing. But she challenges these norms as much as she questions patriarchal norms. Structurally and tonally, she is an ironic poet, who invokes yet subverts dominant paradigms and thus establishes new positions for poets to speak from. She is the first to exploit the opportunity marginality offers—to women and others—to examine the rules by which not only poems but central social discourses are constructed. Although she may use naive personae, she speaks with intellectual authority, and several important twentieth-century poets practice similar strategies, tapping the rhetorical privileges of an outsider's perspective on culturally discursive conventions.

Dickinson's strategic subversion of discursive conventions provides a model of how technical experimentation may be deployed for substantive cultural and ideological criticism. Her stylistic strategies include syntactic subversions to show the collusion of grammatical conventions with larger discursive orders; manipulations of scale to preclude consistent, totalizing perspectives and to highlight the presence of a specific speaker making a "poem"; semiotic game-playing that exploits accidents of lettering and other illegitimate ways of generating meaning to resist symbolic, idealizing economies; and mixing metaphors to skew analogical or allegorical ratios.

By the late nineteenth century, a feminist consciousness registers in more political poetry that challenges cultural gender arrangements. Elizabeth Bogart (1806–?) and Emily Foote Baldwin speak out against masculinist cultural values and the roles they assign women; Frances Ellen Watkins * Harper (1825–1911), an African American, begins writing abolitionist poems and continues to address both feminist and racial themes; Louise Imogen Guiney (1861–1920), a successful poet, searches other cultural traditions for alternatives; and Ella Wheeler Wilcox (1850–1919), also popular, addresses * sexuality in daring proto-feminist poems. Other poets include Helen Hunt * Jackson (1830–1885), Julia Ward * Howe (1819–1910) of "The Battle Hymn of the Republic," and Emily Pauline * Johnson (1861–1913), a Canadian Mohawk famous for her romantic treatments of Indian lore and oral literature. Emma Lazarus's (1849–1887) formally innovative work, important also for its Jewish perspective, and Lizette Woodworth Reese's (1856–1935) accomplished formal and imagistic precision anticipate early modernist aesthetic values.

With modernism, women poets' cultural position becomes complicated. While cultural conceptions of gender roles are more relaxed and offer greater opportunities for writers, certain poetic practices themselves become gendered, as the male modernists authorize their break with the Romantic-Victorian tradition by gendering it female. Thus major modernists Marianne * Moore (1887–1972) and * H. D. (1886–1961) occupy an odd position: although their technical experimentation and mythic recuperation are aligned with "male" strategies, they deploy them in fact to question the masculine authority inscribed in textual conventions. Experiments by women aim not only to revitalize a worn-out currency but to expose the constructedness of authoritative discourses and myths. Moore's experiments with syllabics, scale, and point of view function as a moral and political critique of discursive conventions, and H. D.'s mythic compositions aim for a female revision of myth and history. Gertrude * Stein's (1875–1946) radical textual practices also expose the larger orders underwriting, in her terms, "Patriarchal Poetry."

Thus modernist experimentalism offers wider formal and rhetorical choices for women, partly because it genders the Romantic-Victorian tradition. Someone like Moore, then, can be as idiosyncratic in her practice as Dickinson yet command cultural power, as witnessed by her influential career as a reviewer and as an editor of *The Dial;* she can place herself within a culturally privileged modernism while critiquing male-identified representations of experience. Yet a powerful position like hers requires avoiding or ironizing any subject clearly gendered female.

However, a number of widely read poets, writing in traditional forms, deal with such feminine subjects. In fact, the poets in this period may be classified as either * experimental—Amy * Lowell (1874–1925), Moore, * Stein, and H. D.—or traditional; arguably, poets with traditional aesthetic values are freer to speak from feminine and even openly feminist positions. Edna St. Vincent * Millay (1892–1950) addresses female sexuality and the * body in daring ways, speaking as a sexually liberated and politically committed woman. Yet her protests against social conventions do not engage literary conventions and authority; while this may be one strategy of legitimizing strong cultural opposition, it also dates her work and accounts for its marginality in predominantly modernist-biased figurations of this period. Also well-known were Sara * Teasdale's (1884–1933) accomplished romantic lyrics in spare, direct language with meter and rhyme, and Elinor * Wylie's (1885–1928) precision-crafted poems, combining antimodernist literary values with a forceful female voice.

After modernism, as free verse increasingly becomes the norm, neither experimental nor traditional forms carry the implications they do earlier in the century, and the alignment of traditional forms with feminine lyric subjects does not always hold. In fact, many poets in the thirties, forties, and fifties subscribe to the literary values of academic modernism and combine formally controlled verse with impersonal speakers, avoiding personal subjects to escape the label of "woman poet." Louise * Bogan (1897–1970) writes neither formally experimental verse nor feminine lyrics; though she clearly speaks as a woman, she addresses universal themes, maintains an intellectual distance, and is not entirely comfortable with the classification of a woman poet. Neither is Léonie Adams (b. 1899), whose formal verse similarly resists "female" sentiment. Elizabeth * Bishop (1911–1979) both considered herself a feminist and rejected categorization as a woman poet. She is the major poet of this period because of her ability to use traditional forms with a rhetorical distance and to question cultural and discursive constructions as fundamentally as Moore. Other poets who work primarily in traditional forms are May * Swenson (1913–1989), who writes as a naturalist, combining an interest in science and an intimacy with nature, May *Sarton (b. 1912), Josephine Miles (b. 1911), and Isabella Gardner (1915–1981). None writes feminine or feminist verse; all avoid explicitly personal or political poetry and uphold traditional esthetic values.

Some poets continue the experimental tradition. Laura *(Riding) Jackson (1901–1991) and Barbara Guest (b. 1923) share Stein's commitment to a philosophically deconstructive experimentalism. Objectivist-inspired Lorine Niedecker's (1903–1970) "ecological" poetry often addresses history, the natural environment, and their intersection, while Diane *Di Prima (b. 1934) is associated with the Beats. Denise *Levertov (b. 1923), whose mystical yet politically engaged celebrations of sensory experience and natural force aim to transform social consciousness, and Muriel *Rukeyser (1913–1980) give a lyric voice to leftist politics. Although these poets are all concerned with the position of the woman poet, they choose to define themselves primarily as poets rather than as women.

In the 1960s poets turn increasingly to personal subjects and openly invoke gender-specific experiences. Sylvia *Plath (1932–1963) and Anne *Sexton (1928–1974) address intimate emotional or personal experiences in rather sensational ways, at once using and protesting the voice of culturally constructed "women." Although Sexton is less accomplished than Plath, both have enjoyed wide popularity and influence on a rising feminist movement. Adrienne *Rich's (b. 1929) career, from its formalist beginnings to its personal-political development, has been important in developing a lesbian-feminist poetics. We see a sometimes violent confrontation between formal and discursive conventions and sexually, socially, and politically specific experiences in all three poets, who have helped articulate an increasingly political personal poetry as another model available to women.

The *Harlem Renaissance witnesses a resurgence of poetry and song by African-American women. Predominantly lyric poets, who also address sexual and racial subjects with varying degrees of explicit protest, are Georgia Douglas *Johnson (1886–1966), Angelina Weld *Grimké (1880–1958), Anne *Spencer (1882–1975), Gwendolyn *Bennett (1902–1981), Mae V. Cowdery (1909–1953), and Helene *Johnson (1907–?). The 1920s also mark the blues' rise to popularity, led by women songwriters and performers who have influenced both American poetry and subsequent blues history. Lyricists include the famous Gertrude "Ma" Rainey (1886–1939) and Bessie Smith (1898–1937); Ida Cox (1896–1967); Alberta Hunter (1895–1984); Victoria Spivey (1906–1976); Sippie Wallace (1898–1986); and Edith Wilson (1896–1981). Their

songs add a female inflection to traditional blues themes like love, sex, poverty, pain, and loneliness. In their call for social, sexual, and economic freedom, the larger, systemic repressions are exacerbated by what the speakers suffer at men's hands—neglect, betrayal, and even violence. The figure of a self-sufficient, self-assertive, confident woman emerges in this music.

Among post-Renaissance poets are Margaret *Walker (b. 1915), who begins publishing ballads and sonnets, as well as incorporating folk materials in forms drawn from African-American sources, and Margaret *Danner (b. 1915) and Gwendolyn *Brooks (b. 1917), who absorb modernist techniques. While Danner's language is largely literary, Brooks combines African-American diction and dialect with literary allusions, mixes free and canonical forms, and allows each to pressurize the other; for example, her use of sonnets—in sequences and within longer poems—invokes and politicizes both traditions. Her work becomes angrier and more polemical in the 1960s, when other African-American poets like Mari *Evans, Carolyn M. *Rodgers, Audre *Lorde (b. 1934), Sonia *Sanchez (b. 1935), June *Jordan (b. 1936), Lucille *Clifton (b. 1936), and Nikki *Giovanni (b. 1943) also begin to reject white literary models in favor of a poetry addressed to an African-American cultural community and its social and political concerns.

• Suzanne Juhasz, *Naked and Fiery Forms* (1976). Emily Stipes Watts, *The Poetry of American Women from 1632 to 1945* (1977). Sandra M. Gilbert and Susan Gubar, eds., *Shakespeare's Sisters: Feminist Essays on Women Poets* (1979). Diane Wood Middlebrook and Marilyn Yalom, eds., *Coming to Light: American Women Poets in the Twentieth Century* (1985). Mary K. DeShazer, *Inspiring Women* (1986). Alicia Suskin Ostriker, *Stealing the Language* (1986). Daphne Duval Harrison, *Black Pearls: Blues Queens of the 1920s* (1988). Maureen Honey, ed., *Shadowed Dreams: Women's Poetry of the Harlem Renaissance* (1989). Joanne Feit Diehl, *Women Poets and the American Sublime* (1990). Suzanne Clark, *Sentimental Modernism* (1991). Cheryl Walker, *Masks Outrageous and Austere* (1991).

Mutlu Konuk Blasing

Contemporary Women's Poetry

During the later 1960s to the present, "women's poetry" emerged as a category of poetic production and critical discussion, following the discovery that writing is not a gender-neutral site. Women's poetry became an intense manifesto, signifying women's cultural critique and political presence. The era is characterized by four intersecting practices: feminist-humanist poetries, recovery of forgotten women's poetries, poetries of female diversity, and poetries of "feminine" experimentalism.

The practice of an affirmative and analytic feminist-humanist poetry was exemplified by the work of Adrienne *Rich (b. 1929), who offered, in widely read poetry and essays, revisionary analyses critical of *gender norms. Feminist-humanist work is centrist in its formal nexus, its narrative or short-story basis, and its plainspoken, expressionist style. But it is decentered in treating "woman" (not "universal man"); domesticity, romance plots, maternality, struggles for self-expression, anatomies of *sexisms—all these and more were avidly explored themes. Some works explored autonomy and power, some made a frank and seriocomic anatomy of the female *body, some expressed rage at and satire of gender hierarchy, and affirmed kinds of *sisterhood among women.

A significant set of anthologies of women's poetry from the early 1970s—the most notable being Florence Howe and Ellen Bass's *No More Masks!": An Anthology of Poems by Women* (1973)—contained poems ripe for the thematic categorizing that was a sign of that stage of feminist criticism (called gynocriticism) which sees a woman writer culturally, socially, and psychologically marked by her status as a female, by gender asymmetry, by struggles for empowerment. Works treating illness as a stage on quests for self-integration seemed allegorical of women exiting from sexism. Sylvia *Plath (1932–1963) wrote searing analyses of female anger at emotional "purdah"; a sardonic picture of *marriage in "The Applicant"; an incantatory, wily lambasting of patriarchal power in "Daddy"; and a chant of a biographically compromised rebirth in "Lady Lazarus." Very interesting work emerged or was foregrounded on topoi such as *motherhood, *sexuality, and women in marriage and vocation—Gwendolyn *Brooks's ambiguous masterpiece "The Mother" (on *abortion); Anne *Sexton's nervy "The Abortion" and "Housewife"; and Muriel *Rukeyser's "Käthe Kollwitz," an exploration of woman as artist. Poets such as Susan Griffin, Sharon Olds, Marge *Piercy, Alicia Ostriker, Erica *Jong, and (Canadian) Margaret Atwood were, for many, avatars of the new frankness about sexuality, personal relations, and female struggle. For a number of women writers working out of a feminist critique, the invention of stories, images, and voices for the semisilenced, the unheard, the formerly invisible was a central creative practice.

Adrienne Rich had been a significant presence since her galvanic 1971 essay "When We Dead Awaken: Writing as Revision," which gave impetus to both critical revisionings and poetic explorations. Rich provided a manifesto for and a framing of the intense debate with cultural traditions and ideologies in which women writers had long been engaged. The term "revision" meant rewriting, revising, recasting, and demystifying certain (destructive) stories and ideas about women. Rich's poem "Diving into the Wreck," which postulated a journey and exploration by a brave female decoder into gender materials, became an instant classic; her earlier "Snapshots of a Daughter-in-Law" anatomized the social, cultural, psychological minefield of womanhood. Her poems "Power" and "Phantasia for Elvira Shatayev" had a solemn and evocative impact. During all her comings-out during this period (as feminist, mother, lesbian, Jew), Rich and her work remained touchstones of witness. Muriel *Rukeyser's poems proposed, in a ringing fashion, that there were unheard "truths," untold narratives of women as an underclass, and that speaking such truths would spark a revolutionary heightening of possibility. The words seemed prophetic; many poems were both apocalyptic and hopeful.

Culture seemed rife with inadequate stories constructing female experience which women writers were empowered to seize and transform in revisionary poetries of dissent and recreation. This dissent can propose social terms—with *class-based poetries such as those of Sharon Doubiago and Karen Brodine. But this revisionary impulse was especially pointed when faced with the products of what came to be called "patriarchal culture." Women poets boldly rewrote fairy tales (in Anne Sexton's brash, witty *Transformations* [1971], in work by Olga *Broumas). There were striking retellings of biblical legend and of Greek *myths (Demeter, Psyche, Medusa, and avatars of The Great Mother came in for particular attention). All stories and all heroes were put in question.

Revision involved rereading women's "experiences" and reframing these in representations, as well as rereading the cultural mythologies in which female figures were actors or acted upon. Revision also involved intense critical and creative discoveries of the work of earlier women authors, some only negligibly read and some ignored precisely because their works were treated as minor, quirky, derivative, inadequate—in short, woman's-poetry-as-lack. The recovery and reframing of women poets missing to literary history was a second practice central to this period. Here the study of the mythopoetic work of *H. D. holds a special place, as does the intense identification of female materials and narratives in the maenadic, much-mourned Sylvia Plath, but other notable discussions center around Emily *Dickinson, Elizabeth Barrett Browning, Gertrude *Stein,

Marianne *Moore, Mina Loy, Louise *Bogan, and Elizabeth *Bishop. There was increased appreciation of such older living writers as Gwendolyn Brooks, Denise Levertov, Carolyn *Kizer, June *Jordan, and May *Swenson. The recovery of undersung women writers and the identification of their gender-laden themes and strategies by feminist criticism had a real if diffuse influence on contemporary poetry, as well as an increasingly destabilizing influence on canonical literary modernism. The intensity of the rereadings had the effect of making many women poets—from the nineteenth century through the twentieth—the contemporaries of the present.

The 1974 National Book Award was accepted by Adrienne Rich collectively with the other women nominees Audre *Lorde and Alice *Walker "in the name of all the women whose voices have gone and still go unheard in a patriarchal world" with special attention to "the struggle for self-determination of all women, of every color, identification or derived class." This marks a shift in the totalizing of "woman" also characteristic of gynocriticism, and foregrounded critical interest in difference and diversity, commitment to multiracial subjectivities, and to writing from specific classes, religious cultures, and sexualities. The practice of poetries speaking to, and from, particular ethnic, racial, and cultural communities, including African-American, Native American, Hispanic, Asian-American, Jewish-American, and lesbian is a third practice which defines this period. This poetry sometimes has the analytic and affirmative quality of feminist-humanist poetry (indeed, many practitioners overlap) and often the mythic and spiritual aspirations of certain kinds of modernism. As with some feminist-humanist poetry, the "nationalistic" (or "cultural feminist") moment of nondialogic group affirmation and healing, the struggle against negative representations, and a separatist, oppositional stance to the "oppressor" are characteristic of certain fierce works. As with feminist-humanist poetries, the writer is seen as a cultural worker whose purpose surpasses self-revelation and self-expression. This multicultural poetry can be seen as acerbic social insight on the subject of white, heterosexual, or other mainstream hegemonies.

No matter what the minoritized group, certain themes recur. First is the desire to investigate one's communities and their cultural contradictions. Another central theme is border crossing, living in dialogue with several intersecting selves, and the "creolized" or "mestiza" identity that comes from several subject positions, and historical and linguistic claims. Bilingual or bidialectal materials are a source of both pain and resistant pride. All minoritized poets frame their identities in relation with empancipatory hopes, a sense of mission in a way similar to feminist writers—there are voices that must be heard, stories that must be told, language practices that must be rescued, historical particularities about despising and silencing that must be recovered, and communities that need the words and structures of representation for self-pride and self-understanding.

In Native American poetries there are themes and motifs seeking continuity with the ancestors, social anatomies, the deliberate engagement with traditional images and figures like coyote, the painful pleasure of "bearing cracked turquoise" (phrase from Wendy Rose) because of the multidimensional destruction of Native American culture by European-American culture. There is, as well, a fierce critique of European-American culture for its sometime tourism among the "Indian." These motifs can be seen in Joy Harjo, Diane *Glancy, Paula Gunn *Allen, Leslie Marmon *Silko, Linda *Hogan, Beth *Brant, and Wendy Rose.

African-American poetry by women had a period of intense flowering from its impetus in the *civil rights and black power movements, and the hope that black literature would "distill" (Gwendolyn Brooks's word) and contemplate the difference of black life from white life. There was a resurgent use of African language and *mythology. The writing had an unprecedented fervor and militancy from the intertwining of political and cultural aspirations. Writers of note include Audre Lorde, Sonia *Sanchez, Alice Walker, Nikki *Giovanni, Lucille *Clifton, Jayne *Cortez, Pat *Parker, Cheryl *Clarke, Carolyn *Rodgers, June *Jordan, Rita *Dove, and Toi Derricotte, as well as the older poets Margaret *Walker and Gwendolyn Brooks: all were (in Sanchez's words) looking "down the corridors/of our black birth." The feminist opera or "choreo-poem" by Ntozake *Shange *for colored girls who have considered suicide / when the rainbow is enuf* (1975) was a long-running hit play. Its affirmation out of pain marks it with the quest thematics of feminist-humanist poetry, but its textual practices join her to feminist *experimentalism; and it draws on many black rhetorical traditions (blues, signifying or playing the dozens, call and response, tricksterism—including the outtricking of male tricksters).

Women of color and lesbian women helped to deuniversalize a feminism overeager to assert a generalized "female tradition" or "women writer," claims which mute or ignore differences among women. Similar lists can be made of significant women writers from Asian-American cultures (Janice *Mirikitani, Ai,

Laureen Mar, Fay Chiang, Jessica *Hagedorn, Nellie Wong, Marilyn Chin), from Jewish-American culture (Irena Klepfisz, Chana Bloch), from Chicana and Hispanic cultures (Cherríe *Moraga, Lorna Dee *Cervantes, Ana *Castillo, Sandra *Cisneros). Lesbian Chicana Gloria *Anzaldúa's Spanish-English prose poem text called *Borderlands/La Frontera* is a rich *autobiography of coming to consciousness and writing within a minority culture. The exploration of lesbian and gay experience was a striking aspect of this period (writers such as Rich in "Twenty-One Love Poems," Broumas, Lorde, Marilyn *Hacker, Jan Clausen, Minnie Bruce Pratt). Judy *Grahn's astonishing elegy "A Woman Is Talking to Death" (1973) exemplified a stirring lesbian consciousness. *Women and Nature: The Roaring Inside Her* (1978) by Susan Griffin, a lesbian and cultural feminist, suggests the overdue death of "male culture" from its own technocratic hubris. The work is a revisionist rewriting of the Bible and thus a bold act of cultural critique. Finally, the prose-poem form of the work, its multiple discourses, and its collage and citation strategies, link this work to feminist experimental writing.

Feminist readers thus have had a critical, though not, for the most part, formally radical poetry available throughout this time. This poetry has now been offered the literary-political accolade of canonization—appearance on course syllabi, in anthologies, in articles, and in critical books. It is a poetry often in conformity with mainstream poetry's period style, although it is sometimes franker and more overtly abrasive, heightened, and aggressive in tone, and features a feminism of content. The poetry has a short-story quality, does not destabilize language, especially syntax, uses pointed metaphor and imagery as marks of invention, aims for thematic coherence. The poetry often is naturalistic, based on a single unitary "I," with a casual, conversational tone, raised appropriately to transcendence or epiphany. Some of the justifications for these rhetorical choices propose responsibility to a large audience, the idea of allowing all women to hear and understand without appeals to elite literariness. This—and it is problematic—may be summed up in a title of Rich: "The Dream of a Common Language." Feminist-humanist poetries and the related practices of minoritized poets such as Audre Lorde and Joy Harjo had stylistic parallels with the prize-winning poetries, neutral to feminism, of such women as Carolyn *Forché, Louise *Glück, and Jorie Graham. But these rhetorical and linguistic choices do not characterize all of women's poetry at this time.

In the 1960s, several women, influenced by

a Williams-Whitman (and "Beat" oppositional) nexus that played against the scenic mode of mainstream American poetry began writing highly individual work—among these Diane *Di Prima, Rochelle Owens, Denise *Levertov, and Diane *Wakoski; their themes were increasingly assimilable to general feminism, as in the avant-garde Anne Waldman's affirmative performance chant *Fast Speaking Woman* (1974). By the late seventies, the increasing number of writers using avant-garde or innovative language and structural practices within women's writing had been influenced by some or all of these factors: the growth of theory; the post-structuralist critical rupture of humanisms and notions of selfhood and identity; the psychoanalytic and linguistic sophistication of *French feminism imported to the United States; the influence of experimental modernisms in art, music, film, and fiction; and a growing critique of excesses of essentialist evocations of a total feminist "Woman." The rhetorical and formal strategies of such poetry depend on multiple voices, no unified "I" or single point of view, heteroglossias, conflictual citations of social discourses, nonlinear structures, cross-generic experiment, collage, nonnarrative play with subjectivity, temporality, and syntax. The fourth practice central to this period is experimental or innovative poetry, or what has been called "feminine" writing, in a feminist context ("l'écriture feminine" does not imply a gender of the speaker). Here women variously associated with the New York School, with Language Poetries, and with the *HOW(ever)* cohort can be noted, including Susan *Howe, Barbara Guest, Kathleen Fraser, Beverly Dahlen, Lyn Hejinian, Hannah Weiner, Rosemarie Waldrop, Carla Harryman, Tina Darragh, Rae Armantrout, Norma Cole, Bernadette Meyer, Maureen Owen, Rachel Blau DuPlessis, Johanna Drucker, Alice Notley, Marjorie Welish, Nicole Brossard (Canadian); some experimental writers come from "minority" backgrounds—Erica Hunt, Harryette Mullen, *Trinh Minh-Ha, Mei-Mei Berssenbrugge, Myung Mi Kim, Theresa Hak *Cha. Susan Howe's *The Liberties* (1980) sets Shakespeare's Cordelia and Swift's Stella in a theatrical space, and has them analyze their estrangling position as women and representations. Lyn Hejinian's *My Life* (1980, 1987) is a lambent prose-poem *autobiography avoiding fixed identity, even existing in two versions. Beverly Dahlen constructs an "endless" poem called *A Reading*, tracking otherness in memory, politics, and identity through a long chain of language associations.

• Suzanne Juhasz, *Naked and Fiery Forms: Modern American Poetry by Women, A New Tradition* (1976). Sandra M. Gilbert and Susan Gubar, eds., *Shake-*

speare's Sisters: Feminist Essays on Women Poets (1979). Dexter Fisher, ed., The Third Woman: Minority Women Writers of the United States (1980). Margaret Homans, Women Writers and Poetic Identity: Dorothy Wordsworth, Emily Bronte, and Emily Dickinson (1980). Erlene Stetson, ed., Black Sister: Poetry by Black American Women, 1746–1980 (1981). Marta Ester Sánchez, Contemporary Chicana Poetry: A Critical Approach to an Emerging Literature (1985). Paula Bennett, My Life A Loaded Gun: Female Creativity and Feminist Poetics (1986). Mary DeShazar, Inspiring Women: Reimagining the Muse (1986). Alicia Ostriker, Stealing the Language: The Emergence of Women's Poetry in America (1986). Jan Montefiore, Feminism and Poetry: Language, Experience, Identity in Women's Writing (1987). Joanne Feit Diehl, Women Poets and the American Sublime (1990). Betsy Erkkila, The Wicked Sisters: Women Poets, Literary History, and Discord (1992). Lynn Keller and Crisanne Miller, eds., Feminist Measures: Soundings in Poetry and Theory (1993). In addition, consult books and articles on specific authors, such as Rich, Brooks, Plath.

Rachel Blau DuPlessis

Long Poem

The long poem of American women writers has had an extended and varied history. From Anne *Bradstreet's Quarternions (1650) to Adrienne *Rich's Sources (1983), American women poets have experimented with the long poem for numerous purposes, turning to it as a means of demonstrating their erudition or solidarity with prevailing literary fashions, expressing their social and political concerns as well as their fantasies, attempting a national epic, revising *myth and history, or exploring their own experience. Such means in women's poetry have produced ends that are often subversive of the male literary tradition. For example, writing history, women can undermine the story of wars and destruction even when they appear to be merely imitative; writing long personal narratives, they can question the representative claims of male-centered narrative. Thus, women's long poems have had a development that is quite different from that of long poems written by men.

From the beginning, American women writing long poems have had to confront the idea that women were inadequate to the task even as they were demonstrating their poetic abilities, and, as a result, their work is of necessity double-voiced. Bradstreet's apologies for her "lowly pen" in the dedication to her father of her Quarternions (1650) might have led her to silence rather than to the writing of a spirited poem about nature in which the four elements of fire, air, earth, and water are figured as sisters in rivalry; or the four humors of choler, blood, melancholy, and phlegm are seen again as sisters in a debate won not by the most furious, but by the most conciliatory. Lowly though her pen may have been, it was not without its own imaginative power and independence from conventional hierarchies. Again, Bradstreet can use her "lowly pen" to write about the history of the world from the Assyrian Empire through the beginning of the Roman Empire in "Four Monarchies," depicting it as a story of war and destruction dominated by men where women are often the victims. Although Bradstreet's poem depends for its model on Guillaume Du Bartas's La Semaine (1579) and Sir Walter Raleigh's History of the World (1614), her modesty does not keep her from historical judgments that are quite different from theirs.

After Bradstreet, there were few long works by women until a century later when Phillis *Wheatley and Mercy Otis *Warren, representing two different classes of women and points of view, wrote long poems. Wheatley, an African slave brought to America when she was five or six years old, educated by John Wheatley in Boston, and finally freed in 1778, wrote poetry in the prevailing style, designed to celebrate the values of the emerging nation and derived from neoclassical models. Her "Liberty and Peace" (1784) was a poem of oratorical prophecy like the work of Philip Freneau or Hugh Henry Brackenridge's "The Rising Glory of America" (1771) or Joel Barlow's "The Prospect of Peace" (1778). Yet she was not without her innovative energy. Her longest poem was a revision of a mythological heroine, "Niobe in Distress for Her Children Slain by Apollo, from Ovid's Metamorphoses, Book VI, and from a View of the Painting of Mr. Richard Wilson" (1772) in which she depicts Niobe as a rebel against an established order, perhaps a veiled self-portrait. This poem is the beginning of a long line of women poets revising myths.

Unlike Wheatley, Mercy Otis Warren was at the center of society in the Republic—daughter of a prominent judge, wife of a general, and the lifelong friend of John and Abigail *Adams. Yet when she turned to the long poem, she used it for the same subversive purposes, writing political farces; blank-verse tragedies; and a mock-heroic celebration of the Boston Tea Party, "The Squabble of the Sea-Nymphs; or the Sacrifice of the Tuscararoes," in which women serve as revolutionary leaders. Joining Warren in treating contemporary political themes was Ann Eliza *Bleecker, whose poetry (published posthumously in 1793) included a long poem, "Written in the Retreat from Burgoyne," on the death of her daughter when the family had to leave their estate at the approach of British general John Burgoyne's forces in 1777.

Another member of the Boston aristocracy, Sarah Wentworth *Morton, published the first part of what was planned as a national epic,

Beacon Hill: A Local Poem, Historic and Descriptive (1797); but her most notable achievement was *Ouabi, or The Virtues of Nature: An Indian Tale in Four Cantoes* (1790), a poem celebrating the noble Indians and expressing strong anti-European sentiments. Morton's treatment of the Indian introduced a subject that was to reappear in long poems of the next century, especially in poems about Pocahontas. Lydia Huntley * Sigourney's "Pocahontas" (1841) and Mary Webster Mosby's *Pocahontas* (1840), two long sentimental poems celebrating the sacrifice or heroism of the Indian princess, are examples of this subgenre.

Unlike these women poets, whose works were actively engaged in political and social concerns, most nineteenth-century women writers used the long poem to narrate experience that was both private and fantastic. Maria Gowen Brooks, writing under the pen name of Maria del Occidente, produced a popular long narrative poem, *Zophiel, or the Bride of Seven* (1833), about the love of a fallen angel for a pure Hebrew maiden. Murdered prospective bridegrooms, rescue by a divinely appointed truly beloved, passages of erotic longing, all combined with footnotes on comparative religions and exotic regions, make this poem unusually provocative, expressive of the darker forces beneath the literary resurgence of midnineteenth century America.

By contrast, "The Sinless Child" (1843) by Elizabeth Oakes Prince * Smith owes a debt to Ralph Waldo Emerson's view of the child as a creature of nature. But Smith moves beyond Emerson in her development of the child, called Eva, who is more like a female Christ than a prelapsarian Eve, converting men by her innocence and released from an evil world by death.

From these private and sentimental long poems, American women poets at the end of the nineteenth century returned to public themes. "By the Waters of Babylon" by Emma Lazarus (1887), little poems in prose as she described them, was a controversial treatment of ghetto-seared Jews whom she saw in Eastern Europe. Moved by the pogroms in Russia during the 1880s, Lazarus turned from poetry influenced by Emerson to write about social issues. She also experimented with form, trying out the prose poem of Baudelaire. Both in form and content, Lazarus's work pointed to the new directions women poets were to take in the twentieth century. Ella Wheeler Wilcox's narrative *Three Women* (1897), written in predominantly rhyming anapestic tetrameter, also suggests the prosodic experimentation of long poems to be written by women. And her first long poem, *Maurine* (1888), introduced the new subject of an aggressive, independent, and intelligent woman artist who formed a contrast to a mother depicted as a passive and weak woman.

The experimental long poems written by women at the turn of the century did not entirely prepare readers for the burst of revolutionary poetry written by Gertrude * Stein, * H. D., Lola Ridge, Laura * Riding, and Mina Loy in the modernist period. More subversive than earlier work, the modernist experiments in women's poetry were more daring than the work of their male contemporaries. Writing before T. S. Eliot's *The Waste Land* or Ezra Pound's first *Cantos*, Stein created her prose poem, *Tender Buttons* (1914), which introduced some of the major innovations of the modernist long poem: the disappearance of the centered speaker, the disruption of the representational nature of words, and the discontinuity of the long work. In its resistance to referentiality, *Tender Buttons* is the most radical experiment of modernism. Stein worked to suggest that universal meaning is one of the oppressive illusions of patriarchal thinking, and perhaps, as a result, most of her poetry remained unpublished in her lifetime. Poems such as *Before the Flowers of Friendship Faded Friendship Faded* (1931) and pieces collected in *Bee Time Vine* (1953) and *Stanzas in Meditation* (1956) use rhythm, rhyme, alliteration, repetition, and other nonsemantic qualities as a means of collecting lines into a long form. She could also use coded language to celebrate taboo subjects such as lesbian passion in *Lifting Belly* (1915–1917) or she could be directly subversive as in *Patriarchal Poetry* (1927) which parodies poetry's repetitiveness.

The tension in Stein's work between a desire to experiment with language and a desire to express herself directly on social and political issues was exacerbated in the work of Laura Riding, which combines experimental language and social criticism. She pits herself against Whitman in "Disclaimer of the Person" (1938), which opens, "I say myself." She also wrote "Memories of Mortalities" (1938), a long poem about her childhood.

Also influenced by * Imagism and the Modernist experiments in language, Lola Ridge used the long form to write poetry of social commitment in "Red Flag" (1927), for example. Inspired by the execution of Sacco and Vanzetti, Ridge's book-length poem, *Firehead* (1929), retold the story of Christ in light of this event. Although she projected a poem cycle that would include *Firehead* along with treatments of central historical moments, Ridge never wrote it. By contrast, Mina Loy continued Stein's experimentation with Cubist techniques in her long poem, "Anglo-Mongrels and the Rose" (1923), not collected by Loy but valued by recent critics as one of the major poems of the twentieth century.

Although H. D. wrote during early modernism and produced a prose poem detailing her poetics in *Notes on Thought and Vision* (written in 1919 but not published until 1982), it was not until 1942 to 1946 that she turned to the long poem and wrote *Trilogy* in response to the disintegration of the world she saw during World War II. Fusing the virgin-mother and Magdalene in this reimagining of Christianity, H. D. proposes a matriarchal basis for western culture. Again in *Helen in Egypt* (1961), a three-part long poem in unrhymed *terza rima* with prose passages of summary, she revised the myth of Helen into an antiwar text that is also an examination of the roots of *violence against women, and particularly the mother. H. D.'s work extended the Modernist experiment with form to a topic of political, feminist awareness.

Poems of social commentary attracted black women poets. In 1942, Margaret *Walker's *For My People* was selected for the Yale Series of Younger Poets. In such longer poems as "Delta" and the prose poem of its title, as well as the ballads and lyrics, Walker writes the poems of protest that she was to continue into the *civil rights movement in *Prophets for a New Day* (1970) and dedicatory poems for "Harriet Tubman" of "Epitaph for My Father" (1973). Gwendolyn *Brooks also published her first volume of poetry in 1946. *Annie Allen* (1948) contains sequences such as the fifteen poems in *The Womanhood* or the forty-three stanzas of *The Anniad;* in 1968, Brooks published *In Mecca*, a dramatic poem about Chicago's black poor tenant dwellers.

Nonetheless, many of the immediate protégés of the Modernist women poets were intent on perfecting the lyric form and did not attempt the long poem at first. But even such a controlled lyricist as Elizabeth *Bishop moved toward the longer form as she began to write about her adopted land, Brazil. In "The Riverman" (1960) and "The Burglar of Babylon" (1964), she tried both narrative and ballad. "Crusoe in England" (1966) is another long poem that comments on civilization.

Strangely enough, it has been war more often than personal narrative that has inspired women poets to write long poems. Although a lyric poet of mystical intensity, Denise *Levertov tried the long poem in *The Sorrow Dance* (1966), an elegiac sequence for her sister Olga, a radical activist. Absorbed by protests against the Vietnam War, Levertov began to write long poems of political commentary. "From a Notebook: October '68–May '69" is one expression of her antiwar sentiment; *Relearning the Alphabet* is another long protest poem. She also could use the long form as a sequence of poems about personal relationships as in *Life in the Forest* (1978).

The beginning of the confessional movement in poetry written by men combined with the feminist movement to turn women poets increasingly toward an examination of their own experience and a new political awareness of the roles traditionally assigned to women. Although the confessional poems of Sylvia *Plath and Anne *Sexton were written as short lyrics, they were combined often in sequences such as Plath's bee poems or in a narrative of personal revelation that moved from poem to poem in Sexton's works. Sexton's attraction to the long poem led to the sequence that revised Grimms's fairy tales, *Transformations* (1971), exposing the conservative strain in the stories told to little girls. In this work, she gained a prophetic voice that was to dominate her late work.

Adrienne *Rich also took on the long form after a careful apprentice in the lyric. The title poem of *Snapshots of a Daughter-in-Law* (1963) marked a departure from her earlier work as she anatomized the fragmented lives of women who live through men. Like Levertov, she too was moved to write antiwar poems such as "The Burning of Paper Instead of Children" (1968) or "Shooting Script" (1971) in which Rich opens her line as she opens her subject to public themes. "From an Old House in America" (1974) turns to examine not just the history of American pioneering but the role of women in it. Moving toward the personal in a sequence of "Twenty-One Love Poems" (1978), Rich tries to relate the personal and public strains in her poetry as she examines the resources of her own language to express her experience. Finally, in *Sources* (1983) she enters into the long sequence through which she tries to come to terms with her relationships with her father, her husband, her life, as well as the place of women in the world.

The powerful presence of Rich's poetry has enabled younger women poets to try the long poem both as a form of self-expression and as a medium for commenting on history. Diane *Wakoski began to write long protest poems in the 1960s, including a series on George Washington, and continues to develop a confrontational style even in her poems of self-exploration. Audre *Lorde has written long poems such as "Black Studies" (1973) or *Need: A Choral of Black Women's Voices* (1979), which detail the conflicts and hopes of the urban world in which she lives. Jorie Graham takes history as her subject and carries on Rich's desire for accountability as she explores in a spare long poem "The Sense of an Ending" (1983). Carolyn *Kizer takes as her theme the independent woman in the sequence "Pro Femina" (1984). Tess Gallagher writes family history in a memorial to her childhood in the state of Washington in "Woodcutting on Lost Mountain" (1984) and "Amplitude" (1987).

The long poem has become a dominant form in the poetry written by women at the end of the twentieth century. From the earliest writing of women in America, the long poem has been an attractive form, but perhaps no period has been so receptive to the woman's long poem as the present one where women have assumed the conscience of their generation, commenting on social and political problems as well as on the private lives of women in a society that has become increasingly violent and dangerous.

• Caroline May, ed., *The American Female Poets* (1848). Rufus Griswold, ed., *The Female Poets of America* (1849). Thomas Buchanan Read, ed., *The Female Poets of America* (1849). Florence Howe and Elaine Bass, eds., *No More Masks! An Anthology of Poems by Women* (1973). Emily Stipes Watts, *The Poetry of American Women from 1632 to 1943* (1977). Alicia Suskin Ostriker, *Stealing the Language: The Emergence of Women's Poetry in America* (1986). Bonnie Kime Scott, ed., *The Gender of Modernism: A Critical Anthology* (1990). Jacqueline Vaught Brogan, *Part of the Climate: American Cubist Poetry* (1991).

Margaret Dickie

Love Poetry

What we recognize as love poetry—that which is inspired by, or directed to the object of, erotic or romantic desire—accounts for a comparatively small portion of the poetry written by women in the United States before the twentieth century. That definition, however, formed as it has been largely through examination of male models such as Petrarch and Shakespeare, is too narrow. Particularly in the nineteenth century, when the realm of sentiment was understood to be women's territory, women wrote poetry that was motivated by love but directed to their God, their children, and even their nation, as well as their lovers.

Love poetry in the Petrarchan tradition has always focused on the male lover's lack—the speaker uses his verse to woo the unwilling beloved, or to compensate or console himself. The lover never speaks from a position of plenitude or contentment; the beloved is unattainable, whether because of absence, disinclination, or social constraint (such as marriage). This Petrarchan model historically has been a vexed one for women for several reasons. First, the speaker of a conventional love poem is the lover, the one who pursues, and social convention of the nineteenth century made women the passive recipients of male attentions rather than active lovers. It would be seen as indecorous for an unmarried woman to declare her love for a man in print (which is to say, in public). But it is impossible to write a traditional love poem about one's spouse; the point of the poem is desire, which is predicated by lack. And a married woman writing about her desire for anyone but her husband would be adulterous.

This is not to say that no women in the United States wrote love poetry before the transgressive twentieth century. Rather, we must look for variations on the dominant form. Anne *Bradstreet provides an example of one set of possibilities. Her poems about love for her husband take for their occasions some actual or potential separation between them: "A Letter to Her Husband, Absent upon Public Employment," for instance, but also "Before the Birth of One of Her Children," in which she anticipates the possibility of dying in childbirth. In both cases, death is the imagined separation, and Bradstreet's piety prohibits any expression of regret at the prospect; around and beneath her submission to God's will, however, the modern reader still recognizes the human emotion.

Bradstreet also wrote about her love for her children, both literal and metaphorical. "The Author to Her Book" figures the book as a child "snatched" from its mother's side. The trope, not a new one even in Bradstreet's time, has enduring utility in allaying anxiety about female authorship; as maternal love is praiseworthy, and a conventionally acceptable topic in poetry by women, so love of writing can be represented as a form of maternal affection, as it is in Elizabeth Oakes *Smith's inscription to her long poem, *The Sinless Child*.

The nineteenth century saw an enormous increase in the volume of poetry published by women, and a proportional increase in love poetry, much of which continues to follow the patterns set by Bradstreet. Poems of love for children are prominent: Emma Embury's poem "To My First-Born" partakes of the same language in which she discusses marriage, as does Fanny Osgood's "A Mother's Prayer in Illness." The flowering of romantic friendships between women and the late-nineteenth-century social structure known as the Boston marriage both gave rise to love poetry from one woman to another. Embury's "Stanzas Addressed to a Friend on Her Marriage" is explicit about the speaker's jealousy and clearly depicts the bridegroom as her rival; Henrietta Cordelia *Ray, in "Verses to My Heart's-Sister," portrays her older sister as her life's companion.

Unmarried women were, within certain parameters, free to write about absent lovers: as a widow, Sarah Helen Whitman could write love poems for Edgar Allan Poe, who was by that time deceased. Edith M. Thomas, in "The Deep-Sea Pearl," describes love not as a having but as a "wound" that eventually produces a compensatory artistic "pearl"—imagery that conflates Petrarchan convention with Freudian theory. Some married women wrote about lovers other than their husbands (such as Frances Sargent Osgood in "Had We But Met"); some recall the time before they met (such as Anne Lynch Botta in "Love," with its overtones of Elizabeth Barrett Browning's *Sonnets from the Portuguese*).

In this century and throughout American history, there is little difference between love poetry by African-American women and that by European-American women. The lack of difference is perhaps not surprising, as Joan Sherman has observed; much of the rhetorical purpose of poetry by women of color, particularly in the nineteenth century, was to illustrate how much they had in common with their sisters in the dominant culture. Thus without anthology headnotes, Ray's and Mary Weston Fordham's love poems might be indistinguishable from Embury's or Whitman's.

The twentieth century opened many new possibilities for writing about erotic love; one consequence of new freedoms and frankness was a dwindling away of poems about other kinds of love. In the early part of the century, poets' reactions to the conventions of the nineteenth fall into two main categories. On the one hand, writers such as Sara *Teasdale, Elinor *Wylie, and Edna St. Vincent *Millay used traditional poetic forms, though the attitudes and relationships they depicted were often radically different from those of their predecessors. On the other hand, formally experimental poets like Mina Loy, Djuna *Barnes, and *H. D. made fragmentation and disruption of the lyric line of their resistance to the "nightingale" tradition.

Millay's love poems, many of which are in sonnet form, provide an excellent example of the first approach. While utilizing traditional Petrarchan modes, they also subvert them. In many cases, substituting a woman's voice for a man's as that of the active, desiring, speaking subject (as in the *carpe diem* sonnet, "When we are old, and these rejoicing veins . . .") is enough to startle conventional expectations. Millay also asserts that women feel lust as well as love, and sometimes separately ("I, being born a woman, and distressed . . ."), and claims her right to fulfill her physical desires without needing to apologize or disguise them as something other than they are. Finally, the witty cynicism of poems like "I shall forget you presently, my dear . . . ," which acknowledges from the beginning that even genuine love may be brief and transient, was part of the "modern" attitude

that contributed to Millay's enormous popularity in the late 1910s and early 1920s.

Because their poetry appeared more revolutionary in content than in form, poets such as Millay, Teasdale, and Wylie were often dismissed as sentimental by those who preferred the avant-garde. H. D.'s early, *imagist lyrics strive to escape all explicit emotion by focusing on concrete visual detail (such as the lover's footprint in "Pursuit" or the mirror in "Lais") and by stripping away the connective and affective elements. Mina Loy's "Love Songs" caused a sensation by taking anti-sentimentalism and fragmentation to an extreme.

Among all of these ground-breaking poets, the figure of Amy *Lowell still stands out. Lowell positioned herself among modernist innovators, but much of her poetry seems to belong to an earlier era. Just as her public persona was androgynous, so was her literary one; thus, the love poems to her companion, Ada Russell, partake of many of the conventions of heterosexual love lyrics written by men. Lowell's daringly sensual descriptions of the female body struck some contemporary readers as transgressive, but more recent critical practice must ask whether the shock comes from the text itself or from the reader's knowledge of the poet's gender. Gertrude *Stein's love poetry presents perhaps the opposite case: recent scholarship suggests that not only the comparatively explicit "Lifting Belly" but all her writing is unintelligible except as lesbian modernism; that for Stein, "sexual expression is intimately linked to linguistic expression" (Shari Benstock, *Women of the Left Bank*, 1986).

In the second half of the twentieth century, poets continue to struggle with the desire to write about their own experience of love without being labeled "sentimental" or "merely feminine." The rhetoric of the *women's movement in the 1960s and 1970s encouraged women not to be satisfied with the private, domestic sphere of love and family. The insight that "the personal is political" put love (and love poetry) under new scrutiny. One response has been a burst of explicitly lesbian love poetry from such poets as Adrienne *Rich, Marilyn *Hacker, and Olga *Broumas, the first two of these poets have engaged literary-historical politics by their choice of the traditional Petrarchan sonnet sequence.

The level of anxiety and discomfort that surrounds women's love poetry is also manifest in the choices of editors and anthologists, both male and female: love poetry is consistently underrepresented in both current and historical collections. Whatever the articulated principle of selection, the result has been to make the tradition less available to readers and poets alike.

[*See also* Romantic Love; Letters.]

• Cheryl Walker, *The Nightingale's Burden: Women Poets and American Culture before 1900* (1982). Joan R. Sherman, ed., *Collected Black Women's Poetry* (1988).

Lisa R. Myers

Religious Poetry

Religious is here considered as characterized by belief in God, however variously conceived; also by an awareness of supernatural forces. Anne *Bradstreet (c. 1612–1672), first of her sex to write poetry in the new land, is remembered for her picture of those New Englanders whose spiritual convictions she shared in the Massachusetts Bay Colony. Bradstreet expresses her faith in *The Tenth Muse Lately Sprung Up in America*, published in England in 1650 by her brother-in-law without her consent. "Contemplations" and "The Flesh and the Spirit" deserve the recognition brought them by John Berryman's *Homage to Mistress Anne Bradstreet* in the twentieth century.

The muse of Emily *Dickinson (1830–1886) likewise derives from Puritanism but goes its independent way. One cannot deny a place in this article to the author of "I never saw a moor," yet neither can wrestling with doubt be disavowed. Christ is important to the writer of Amherst but as the Crucified One, not the Risen Saviour. She speaks with God conversationally, her honesty before the Creator yielding a beauty comparable to that generated by strife in "The Windhover."

Elinor *Wylie in "Address to My Soul" and elsewhere presents a touch of spiritual *autobiography, as does Edna St. Vincent *Millay in "Recuerdo," which reads like a page out of the *Fioretti*. About the latter's "Renascence," Rosemary Sprague says in *Imaginary Gardens* (1969): "Her mind, fed by constant reading, had soared far above her chronological age, so that, young as she was, she could handle the most difficult philosophical and theological concepts with amazing ease." Devout Presbyterian that she was, Marianne *Moore fits into this essay only if her exquisitely observed birds and animals belong to the Book of the Creatures, an assumption justified by the end of "In Distrust of Merits": "Beauty is everlasting/and dust is for a time." Several of Josephine Jacobsen's poems—particularly "Ascetic's Soliloquy"—also show the way a poet's faith contributes to art.

Born in 1924 in Houston, Texas, Vassar Miller has continued to live in that city, struggling successfully against cerebral palsy to achieve the rank of major poet. A Protestant, she employs many Catholic allusions, for instance, saints (Augustine, Francis, Teresa of Avila) and the sacraments. Christmas, Holy Week, and Easter appear regularly in her work, treated with faith though at times in a questioning mode. Accomplished in the sonnet and villanelle, Miller nevertheless writes with freedom and surprise, her ingenuity in figures of speech breathtaking. The last word in her amusing title *If I Had Wheels or Love* (the collected volumes from *Adam's Footprints* on, 1991) should not mislead readers: they will find a realistic love of God in its pages.

Denise *Levertov is the daughter of an Anglican clergyman of Judaic ancestry. *Oblique Prayers* (1987) suggests telling the truth "slant," but in later volumes she seems to have caught fire from the first English poet, the monk Caedmon, as she reveals him in her monologue: she refines a transcendent explanation of life, using Christian imagery, though she belongs to no denomination. Mysticism may be defined as belief in what passes human comprehension. Hers is illustrated by her attitude in "The Showings: Lady Julian of Norwich, 1342–1416," wherein she accepts the miraculous easily, just as elsewhere she does with Jacob, or the serving-girl of Emmaus.

Phillis *Wheatley, a slave educated in New England, is the first African-American woman to write religious poetry in this country, composing such polished biblical narratives as "Goliath of Gath." Her successors are numerous, especially after the 1960s. Georgia Douglas *Johnson, a government employee in Washington, D.C., published four volumes between 1918 and 1962. June *Jordan brings together inner-city violence and Michelangelo in "The New Pietà: For the Mothers and Children of Detroit." Lucille *Clifton's 1972 *Good News about the Earth* is affirmative: as Don L. Lee writes in "Lucille Clifton: Warm Water, Greased Legs, and Dangerous Poetry": "To read her is to give birth to bright seasons" (Evans, 1984, p. 160). Nikki *Giovanni (cf. "Poem for Flora") offers a guide to black women poets in *Night Comes Softly*.

Alice *Walker, in "The Abduction of Saints," compares Malcolm X and Martin Luther King, Jr., with Christ as rebels in modern detail concerning the Crucifixion more effective than prayerbook praise. In addition to the poets mentioned, Anne *Spencer, Audre *Lorde, Sonia *Sanchez, Maya *Angelou, Gwendolyn *Brooks, and Mari *Evans exemplify religious themes.

As for Native American women, Berkeley professor Paula Gunn *Allen, herself one, explores the feminine in prose in *The Sacred Hoop*. Allen indicates in "Kospis'taya, A Gathering of Spirits" that she believes Native Americans are religious in their comprehension of the term "spiritual." An instance of what she means is Leslie * Silko's "Prayer of the Pacific," about which Mark Jarman in "Poetry and Religion" asserts: ". . . she has remade the religious imagination without asking us to accept it as part of an orthodoxy or institution." (McDowell 1991).

A Catholic, the Athabaskan Indian poet Mary Tall Mountain in "The Figure of Clay" relates how she fashions, then buries, a tiny girl made of cemetery earth until eventually, through meditation, it turns to an *alter ego* walking beside her in morning light equivalent to grace. Geary Hobson includes her lyric about the Blessed Virgin in his *The Remembered Earth*, but senses that a narrower classification is developing based on treatment of subject as well as ethnic roots; he feels that Tall Mountain and Joy Harjo are tending in that direction.

Nia Francisco, a Navajo, publishes bilingual poetry, a parallel to such practice in Ireland. *Star-Quilt* by Roberta Hill Whiteman of the Oneida tribe is only one of several recent significant collections. Wendy Rose, author of ten volumes, regards revelation in its deepest sense as a valid religious approach.

America, apart from Pound in *The Cantos*, has still to produce its (male or female) Dante. Mark Jarman, in "Poetry and Religion," writes: "Nevertheless, the religious impulse in poetry endures; many poems being written today show that urge to be tied to or united with or at one with a super-natural power that exists before, after, and throughout creation."

[*See also* Religion.]

• Arnold Adoff, ed., *The Poetry of Black America* (1973). Joseph Bruchac, ed., *Songs from This Earth on Turtle's Back: Contemporary Indian Poetry* (1983). Mari Evans, ed., *Black Women Writers, 1950–1980* (1984). Geary Hobson, ed., *The Remembered Earth: An Anthology of Contemporary Native American Literature* (1984). Steven Ford Brown, ed., *Heart's Invention: On the Poetry of Vassar Miller* (1988). Duane Niatum, ed., *Harper's Anthology of 20th Century Native American Poetry* (1988). Mark Jarman, "Poetry and Religion" in *Poetry after Modernism*, edited by Robert McDowell (1991), pp. 134–175. Linda Wagner-Martin, ed., *Critical Essays on Denise Levertov* (1991).

Bernetta Quinn, O.S.F.

Concrete Poems

Following World War II, poets in isolation or in groups in different parts of the world began to make what came to be called concrete poetry. Two major centers of activity developed in São Paulo, Brazil, around the Noigandres Group (Augusto de Campos, Haroldo de Campos, and Décio Pignatari), and in Switzerland with the publications and innovations of Eugen Gomringer. A chance meeting in 1955 between Pignatari and Gomringer marks the beginning of the international concrete poetry movement that flourished during the fifties and sixties in anthologies, little magazines, exhibitions and performances. Although the Noigandres Group conceived of their poems as "ideograms" and Gomringer called his "constellations," they settled on the general term *concrete poetry* for the movement to emphasize the kinship between the new poetry and the concrete art of Max Bill, Piet Mondrian, and others working along constructivist lines.

The concrete poem focuses upon the word (or syllable or letter) as a material object occupying space. In Gomringer's constellations single words are repeated or grouped with other words to be perceived first as a configuration (or image) on the page that imprints itself upon the mind as a picture. The Noigandres Group, influenced by Ezra Pound's use of the ideogramic method in the *Cantos* (based on study of the Chinese written character), juxtaposed words in spatial arrangements to be read as ideograms. Adding a third dimension—space— to the usual two-dimensional sound-meaning territory of the poem, they defined the space of the concrete poem as "verbivocovisual." There is so much similarity between Gomringer's constellations and Noigandres' ideograms that the terms are generally interchangeable. The goal in both is to balance to the highest possible degree the equation, form = context/content = form.

Although a great deal of concrete poetry was written in the favored constructivist/concrete mode, as the movement grew new forms proliferated. The label "concrete" became increasingly confusing and unsatisfactory. By 1970, during the comprehensive international exhibition "Concrete Poetry" at the Stedelijk Museum in Amsterdam, open rebellion against poetry in the constructivist tradition was in evidence. The movement was falling apart, although poets went on making visual and sound poetry. But the emergence of concrete poetry on a global scale following World War II cannot be written off as insignificant, for it would seem to be expressive of a human need for communication across national and linguistic boundaries following a cataclysmic worldwide breakdown in communication.

The concrete poetry movement never established a cohesive base in the United States. Whereas in Europe, Japan, and South America poets formed groups to sponsor publications, exhibitions and performances, in the States they worked mostly in isolation. Nevertheless the two major anthologies of the concrete poetry movement were edited by Americans and published in the United States. Emmett Williams, the first American to write concrete poetry as a member of the Darmstadt Circle in Germany (1957–1959), edited *An Anthology of Concrete Poetry* (1967). The work of twelve poets from the United States was included, one of whom was a woman, Mary Ellen Solt, whose first book, *Flowers in Concrete*, had been published in 1966. Solt edited the second major anthology, *Concrete Poetry: A World View* (1970). Both Williams and Solt, in addition to poems adhering to constructivist principles, included others exhibiting a strong calligraphic impulse, more allied with Expressionism, evidenced by intuitive manipulation of space and freer typographical choices. Solt's work was included in magazines, anthologies, and exhibitions in Europe, Japan, and South America and later in the United States. Her closest ties were with Ian Hamilton Finlay of Scotland, editor of the little magazine *Poor. Old. Tired. Horse*. In addition to conventional concrete poetry, she has written a long semiotic (or code) poem, "Marriage" (1976), and a book-length performance poem, "The Peoplemover. A Demonstration Poem" (1978).

By the time more poets in the United States began making poems along concrete lines, the international movement was essentially over. The new poets, many of them graphic designers, refused to work under the restrictions the early concretists had imposed upon themselves. For the most part they preferred to be called "visual." A prime mover in this freer direction was Richard Kostelanetz, poet, critic, and editor of *Imaged Words & Worded Images* (1970), *Text-Sound Texts* (1980), and other collections of new writing. In 1975 he curated a comprehensive exhibition, *Language & Structure in North America: The First Large Definitive Survey of North American Language Art*, for the Kensington Arts Association in Toronto.

Ruth Jacoby, Gay Beste Reineck, and Carol Bankerd are graphic artists whose visual poems present stunning images that enhance their sign qualities on the semantic level, whereas the work of poets Jane Augustine, Kathy Schenkel, and Adele Aldrich is focused on language. Augustine has experimented with the interchangeability of linguistic and mathematical signs. In her poem "2rde4ce" she combines numbers and letters to form words: 2l, 2th, 2lips, 2steppers. Schenkel's poems exhibit mastery of classic concrete techniques. The stress and boredom implied in the phrase "over and over" is conveyed by repeating it over and over

in a constellation with every other line printed upside-down except where in the nineteenth line the phrase "over again" intrudes as a climax of frustration and line 20 follows printed normally. The poem then proceeds with resumption of the alternating line pattern to the thirtieth and last ambiguous line: "over and over end." Visually the poem presents a form (ideogram) in the constructivist tradition: a functional object for contemplation created entirely by the structural organization of the materials. Aldrich, who refers to her poems as "visual" rather than "concrete," called her first book *Notpoems* (1975). In the third edition she intensified the sign quality of the poems by adding color and in some instances by changing the design. For example, beginning with the word "hate" in small, faint pink letters, she progresses by increasing letter size and intensity of hue until "hate" printed large is followed by "hated" even larger, the color having been intensified to a hot, reddish pink. The final word—"death"—is printed large in blue. The poem's full impact is felt when we realize that the word "death" was created by scrambling the same letters that occur in the word "hated." Aldridge employs word play to convey a powerful message with minimal means.

An important advance made by the concretists was to liberate the word from the page to find new existence as an object. Alison Sky has created sculpture poems using such new materials as translucent vinyl. In her sculpture poem "light," the word takes on new life as a many-faceted jewel. Joyce Cutler Shaw has made large ice sculptures of words.

The creation of sound poetry was a very important component of the international concrete poetry movement. Gertrude *Stein was acknowledged as a precursor. Several women in the United States have worked in this tradition, including Beth Anderson, Rosemarie Castoro, Harriet Zinnes, and Cindy Lubar. Others, for instance, Ellen Zweig and Judith Johnson Sherwin, have created performance texts. Terri Hanlon, Fern Friedman, and Nina Yankowitz have created texts for multiple voices. Arlene Schloss uses her voice as an "instrument" along with "audiotapes, video, slides, fire and print." Annea Lockwood employs words from several languages "with the intention of releasing their inherent sound-energy . . . one of the world's prime energies."

• Emmett Williams, ed., *An Anthology of Concrete Poetry* (1967). Jean-François Bory, ed., *Once Again* (1968). Eugene Wildman, ed., *Anthology of Concretism* (1969). Richard Kostelanetz, ed., *Imaged Words & Worded Images* (1970). Mary Ellen Solt, ed., *Concrete Poetry: A*

World View (1970. *Hispanic Arts,* 1968). Milton Klonsky, ed., *Speaking Pictures, A Gallery of Pictorial Poetry from the Sixteenth to the Present* (1975). Richard Kostelanetz, ed., *Text-Sound Texts* (1980). Ruth and Marvin Sackner, *The Ruth & Marvin Sackner Archive of Concrete and Visual Poetry 1984* (1986).

Mary Ellen Solt

POLISH-AMERICAN WRITING. The place of women of Polish descent is not secure in American letters. To this date, no Anzia * Yezierska, Maxine Hong * Kingston, Toni * Morrison, or Louise * Erdrich has appeared to give a feminine voice to an ethnic literary history that begins in the 1830s (and even earlier) but that has, until recently, resided in the hands of host-culture writers. Consequently, women of Polish descent who appear in American literature have been largely a reflection of cultural stereotypes and an expression of Europe's class system. Inevitably, they have been depicted as either princesses or peasants: as ladies of genteel birth, high culture, breeding, and aristocratic bearing or, beginning in the 1890s, as hardworking, simple, prolific toilers of the soil.

Even so, women writers of Polish descent have a recognizable literary history that begins in the 1920s in conjunction with the Polanie club in Minneapolis and the particular success of Monica Krawczyk and Victoria Janda. These and others of their generation, Polish-born or the children of immigrants, comprise the first stage of Polish literary ethnicity; that is, they introduced Polish culture, established identity markers, and recorded the rituals of assimilation from an ethnic point of view. Krawczyk's stories, written in the 1930s and 40s but published only in 1950 (in the collection *If the Branch Blossoms*), record the difficult transition from Pole to American. Krawczyk is the first to filter these events through the eyes of the ethnically Polish woman, whose frame of reference in the stories is essentially domestic. Nonetheless, Krawczyk's protagonists understand the social reorganization demanded by the New World experience and serve as bridges between two cultures. Similarly, Nellie Kowalczyk Musial's *The Little Worlds of Nellie Musial* (1954) documents the challenges to peasant women in an urban, industrialized New World landscape.

Helen Ogrodowski Bristol and Victoria Janda have somewhat different aims, although their work is also designed to introduce a minority culture. Born in Zyrardow, Bristol follows a family from Poland to Philadelphia in her verse novel, *Let the Blackbird Sing* (1952). She combines Old World legend, history, and customs with New World hopes and disappointments in a "typical" immigrant story of sentiment and disappointment. The poetry of Victoria Janda, *Star Hunger* (1942), *Walls of Space* (1945), and *Singing Furrows* (1953), employs the mysticism of Polish Catholicism, history, and folk-culture and celebrates Polish patriotism, as do Jona Konopka's novel, *Dust of Our Brothers' Blood* (1941), and other World War II–era works.

Wanda Kubiak and Anne Pellowski have written about the lives of ethnic farmers in turn-of-the-century Wisconsin. Pellowski's tetralogy—*Willow Wind Farm* (1981), *Stair Step Farm* (1981), *Winding Valley Farm* (1982), and *First Farm in the Valley* (1982)—follows four generations of a family from its immigration in the late nineteenth century to present times through the point of view of young girls coming to terms with their evolving ethnic identity. In *Polonaise Nevermore* (1962), Kubiak addresses the counterclaims of cultural isolationists and assimilationists and the religious controversy surrounding the establishment of Polish Catholicism in the United States.

Women of Polish descent have been especially active in the field of * children's literature. Anne Pellowski's tetralogy has attracted scholarly attention while Lois Lenski and Maia Wojciechowska have achieved international reputations. Neither Lenski nor Wojciechowska, both Newbery winners, write very much about the ethnic self, although Wojciechowska has published a collection of Polish legends, *Winter Tales from Poland* (1973), and Lenski has occasionally focused on the Polish-American community, as in *We Live in the North* (1965).

The work of contemporary women of Polish descent also appears in literary magazines and in anthologies such as *Concert at Chopin's House* (1987). In some cases, these writers have combined the search for the ethnic self with feminist concerns. In "Keeping My Name," Linda Mizajewski (*The Other Woman,* 1982) writes about the particular dilemma of the ethnically Polish woman who twice loses her identity—through cultural assimilation and again through marriage. Mizajewski states that she has always been "Mrs. Other," an outsider as ethnic and as woman. Other writers in *Concert at Chopin's House* explore connections between a culture almost lost and an ethnic self waiting to be born. Anna Wasecha is struck by the similarity of "her" Polish and Minnesota forests in "Babushka." In "About My Cousin," Margaret Szumowski escapes into the primeval forest of eastern Poland, to the beginning of "this long journey"; and Linda Nemec Foster (*A History of the Body*) writes about her Krakow grandmother cursing her Cleveland-born sons and her own fledgling love. Taken together, the works of these and other women writers of Polish descent offer insights into the complexities of dual cultures, gender, and the ethnically Polish experience.

[*See also* Assimilation; Citizenship; Ethnicity and Writing; European Immigrant Writing; Immigrant Writing; Irish-American Writing; Italian-American Writing; Jewish-American Writing.]

• Gladsky, Thomas S. *Princes, Peasants, and Other Polish Selves: Ethnicity in American Literature* (1992).

Thomas S. Gladsky

POLITE, Carlene Hatcher (b. 1932), African-American novelist. Polite has established herself as an experimental fiction writer with the publication of two novels, *Les Flagellents* (1966) and *Sister X and the Victims of Foul Play* (1975). Her innovative fiction embodies the rhetoric of black cultural revolution and resembles Ishmael Reed's stream-of-consciousness style.

Born 28 August 1932 to John and Lillian (Cook) Hatcher in Detroit, Polite attended public schools before becoming a student at Sarah Lawrence College in New York. After a brief stay, Polite left to study at the Martha Graham School of Contemporary Dance. During the 1950s, when she was a professional dancer and teacher of dance, a civil rights activist, and a teacher of yoga, Polite became increasingly aware of her need to write about the cultural revolution that was taking place. The 1960s found her immersed in freedom fighting and devoting her energies to political organizing.

Becoming an expatriate in 1964, Polite moved to Paris where she was encouraged by editor Dominique de Roux to write her first novel, *Les Flagellents*, also published in the States, which explores the lives of black men and women who are emotionally incapacitated in a sexist and racist society. The impressionistic novel focuses on two cerebral characters, Ideal and Jimson, who "flagellate" each other as they try to get beyond the narrow, prescriptive roles assigned to black men and women. Consisting of a spare plot and focused on the internalities of two lovers, *Les Flagellents* is an experimental novel.

Returning to the United States in 1971, Polite accepted a position as associate professor of English at the State University of New York, Buffalo, and began work on a second novel, *Sister X and the Victims of Foul Play*. Set in Paris, the central characters are expatriates who tell the story of a black exotic dancer who refuses to perform naked and dies after a mysterious fall from the stage; a French doctor reports that Sister X instead died of cancer. Polite suggests that blacks are victims of a cancerous society that destroys their dreams.

Polite's innovative spirit led her to seek a form that would allow her to express the unique psychological stresses placed upon black men and women. Polite's experiences as a Greenwich Village resident and later as an expatriate helped her to an acute understanding of the pain associated with otherness both in the United States and Europe. In order to give voice to characters who were individual and yet collective representations of blacks, Polite found it necessary to experiment with language and narrative in a manner unlike any of her black female contemporaries.

• Hammett Worthington-Smith, "Carlene Hatcher Polite" in *Afro-American Writers after 1955*, Dictionary of Literary Biography, vol. 33, eds. Trudier Harris and Thadious Davis (1984).

Elizabeth Brown-Guillory

POLITICAL ORGANIZATIONS. *This entry consists of three essays arranged historically to cover women's political organizations from the nineteenth century to the present:*

Nineteenth-century Organizations
1900 to 1960
1960 to the Present

For further information, please refer to Activism; Women's Movement.

Nineteenth-century Organizations

Within the course of the nineteenth century, women dramatically changed their relationship to the state. Even before the American Revolution, women shared both formal and informal roles as political actors: in the law, they were capable of giving testimony and were punishable for crimes; in certain civil proceedings, they could act as representatives for family members; as "deputy husbands" they could transact business arrangements and make contracts. Yet the Revolution unleashed both liberating and reactionary trends that altered women's assumed and actual functions in the new republican society. Common law secured its hold on American legal proceedings, and Blackstone's interpretation that married women were "civilly dead" soon became the prevalent political status applied to all women. Viewed as dependents, represented by their husbands, married women were denied the rights to sue, own property, make contracts, and, of course, vote.

Eighteenth-century "society" nevertheless assumed that middle-class women had an informal civic role through "polite intercourse" and "friendly visits." Moral and political obligations were involved when women performed such duties for the welfare of church and the *community. Much of women's early political engagement came through the establishment of various women's charitable societies. One of the first such societies in New York City was the Society for the Relief of Poor Widows with Small Children, organized in 1797 by Isabella Graham (1742–1814) and her daughter, Joanna Bethune (1770–1860). This mother and daughter team laid the foundation for a series of benevolent institutions, such as the Orphan Asylum, which was incorporated in 1807 and given state funding as early as 1811. Later, they opened a House of Industry for women, followed by the Female Union Society for the Promotion of Sabbath Schools. Through incorporation, female directors gained legal powers to sue, own property, and manage public monies and private donations. Yet Graham never claimed rights to political powers; instead, she gained privileges and patronage from the municipal government. Remarkably, Graham's activities were not concealed but celebrated in her published testimony, *The Power of Faith: The Life and Writings of the Late Mrs. Isabella Graham, of New York* (1816). More than a singular account of public service, Graham thus inscribed a visible place for benevolent women like herself within the public domain.

The political climate changed in the 1830s and 1840s, and women found themselves drawn into a diverse range of controversial campaigns. A new band of reformers battled prostitution, capital punishment, the severity of prison conditions, war, alcohol, and human slavery. Several women assumed editorships of several major reform periodicals: Lydia Maria * Child (1802–1880) oversaw the *National Antislavery Standard* from 1841 to 1843; Virginia Allen ran *The New York Pearl* (1846), one of the most popular temperance publications in New York City; Rebecca Eaton edited the *Friend of Virtue* for the New England Moral Reform Society (1836–1860); and Jane Swisshelm (1815–1884) started her own Pittsburgh newspaper, *Saturday Visitor* (1848–1857), which served as a forum for attacking slavery, the Mexican War, and the corrupt dealings of major politicians. In writing editorials, women acted as social critics and advocates, and increasingly they focused on social problems that demanded legal and political reform. The petition became their major political weapon, which reflected their appeal for redress from the government. Antislavery activists found themselves embroiled in a national controversy when Congress passed the "gag rule" that tabled such petitions between 1836 and 1844. Adopting a more militant style, and supporting divisive positions on political issues, women clearly had moved beyond the exercise of privileges, and instead they carved a new territory as a critical public that openly challenged both state and federal laws.

A decisively new direction emerged when a group of women mobilized around the issues of "woman's rights," a campaign that addressed a myriad of legal, religious, and political concerns. By organizing a series of public conventions, beginning in towns such as Seneca Falls, New York, in 1848, and followed by yearly "national" gatherings in Worcester, Massachusetts, in 1850 and 1851 and in Syracuse, Cleveland, Philadelphia, Cincinnati, and New York City from 1856 to 1860, these activists sought to demonstrate the ability of women to speak, deliberate, debate, and generate public opinion. Paulina Wright Davis (1813–1876) edited *The Una* (1853–1855), the official organ of the national movement, and Amelia Bloomer and somewhat later Mary Birdall operated *The Lily* (1849–1858), which published convention proceedings, speeches, social commentaries, and a new style of essay that engaged in a running debate with the editors of major journals. Elizabeth Cady * Stanton (1815–1902) wrote devastating rebukes of editorial columns of the *United States Magazine and Democratic Review*, *Harper's Weekly Magazine*, and even the *Southern Quarterly Journal*.

Although women's rights advocates called for suffrage as early as 1848, the movement encompassed a wide range of legal and political issues: improved divorce and child custody laws; married women's property rights; the right of contract, wages, and independent business ownership for married women; equal wages for women workers; and increased opportunities for women in education, medicine, law, and the ministry. Following the * Civil War, suffrage became a hotly contested issue, especially during the debates over the passage of the Fifteenth Amendment which granted black males the right to vote. Whether women should be included in the wording of the amendment divided the women's movement into two organizations. In 1869, Stanton and Susan B. * Anthony (1820–1906) formed the National Woman Suffrage Association, and in the pages of their new organ *The Revolution* (1868–1871) they called for a federal constitutional amendment for enfranchising women. Lucy Stone (1818–1892) and Henry Blackwell organized the American Woman Suffrage Association in the same year, edited *The Woman's Journal* (1870–1917), and they advocated a state-by-state suffrage campaign.

The nature of women's political involvement changed in the aftermath of the war, not only among suffrage supporters, but among other female reformers who increasingly directed their activities along partisan channels. Women began to organize around political districts, define themselves as a constituency, and address their demands to the attention of elected officials. The Women's Christian Temperance Union (WCTU) was organized in 1874, and under the guidance of Frances Willard (1837–1898), this new political association effectively established a strong local partisan base of support. Considered both president and "traveling ambassador" of the movement, Willard combined suffrage and temperance as twin issues, and like a party leader, she lectured around the country and kept her supporters informed through the distribution of WCTU organ, *The Union Signal* (1883–1903). By the end of the nineteenth century, women had entered modern politics as devoted partisans, simultaneously devoted to the interests of women and committed to local parties that supported the causes of temperance, woman suffrage, and the welfare of women.

[*See also* Activism; Women's Movement]

• Elizabeth Cady Stanton, Susan B. Anthony, and Matilda Josyln Gage, eds., *History of Woman Suffrage*, vol. 1 (1881). Edward T. James, Janet Wilson, and Paul S. Boyer, eds., *Notable American Women: A Biographical Dictionary*, 3 vols. (1971). Keith Melder, *The Beginnings of Sisterhood: The American Woman's Rights Movement, 1800–1850* (1977). Ellen Carol Dubois, *Feminism and Suffrage: The Emergence of an Independent Women's Movement in America, 1848–1869* (1978). Linda Kerber, *Women of the Republic: Intellect & Ideology in Revolutionary America* (1980). Ruth Bordin, *Woman and Temperance: The Quest for Power and Liberty, 1873–1900* (1981). Barbara Meil Hobson, *Uneasy Virtue: The Politics of Prostitution and the American Reform Tradition* (1987). Jean Fagan Yellin, *Women & Sisters: The Antislavery Feminists in American Culture* (1989). Barbara Bardes and Suzanne Gossett, *Declarations of Independence: Women and Political Power in Nineteenth Century America* (1990). Anne Firor Scott, *Natural Allies: Women's Associations in American History* (1991). Nancy Isenberg, "Women's Organizations," *Encyclopedia of American Society History* (1993).

Nancy G. Isenberg

1900 to 1960

The year 1900 was not a watershed for women in politics. The crusade for woman suffrage had entered a fourteen-year lull (ending in 1910) during which no state enfranchised its women. But 1900 served as a benchmark for noting a century of progress as women moved slowly away from legislatively enforced economic dependence and political invisibility. Despite their limited political strength, American women had enlarged their public influence and presence by 1900: the burgeoning industrial economy was absorbing more female labor; access to higher education gave a small but expanding group of women the emancipating option of a public, professional career; women had acquired limited voting privileges in several states and territories; and issues such as prohibition, pacifism, and woman suffrage beckoned many women into the political arena before they received the vote. In the era of progressive reform stretching from the latter decades of the nineteenth century to World War I, the celebrated * New Woman joined a variety of voluntary associations that met philanthropic, civic, and social interests; many of these organizations offered her the opportunity to acquire a political education.

Organized women frequently justified their assumption of the public role of reformer by asserting that they bore a special obligation as wives and mothers to combat social vices that threatened the welfare of the family. The success of the Woman's Christian Temperance Union (WCTU) evidenced the appeal of such a message. The WCTU, crusading under the banner of "home protection," still flourished after the loss of leader Frances Willard in 1898; in the early 1920s the union boasted roughly half a million members. The Young Women's Christian Association also drew several hundred thousand members dedicated to combatting vice (about 600,000 by the early 1920s). The organization endorsed female suffrage and international peace while honoring its primary mission to attend to the physical, intellectual, and spiritual needs of young women.

Many female reformers in the interwar period promoted the view that issues relating to home and family carried special relevance for women; similar logic supported the appointment of women (many of whom received political training as members of women's associations) to top administrative positions in federal agencies such as the Women's and Children's bureaus—but not the War Department.

Many American women denounced war—as they did prostitution and alcohol abuse—as a threat to civilized society and the sanctity of the home. In 1915 female pacifists, including Charlotte Perkins * Gilman and Jane * Addams, founded the Woman's Peace Party (later the Women's International League for Peace and Freedom). Preaching the message of peace proved a hazardous employment for female pacifists. They endured public vilification, particularly during wartime, and in the mid-1920s women's groups associated with the peace movement weathered a serious bout with red-baiting when a widely circulated "spider web" chart spuriously linked seventeen of them with communism.

The General Federation of Women's Clubs (GFWC) supported both prohibition and the Woman's Peace Party, but hesitated to adopt a prosuffrage stance until 1914. It did not endorse an equal rights amendment until 1944 (twenty-one years after its introduction). The women's *club movement continued to grow in the early decades of the century, but recruited primarily middle- and upper-middle-class women; the national organization, the GFWC, initially excluded African-American women from its membership. Unwelcome in many women's social and civic groups, black women formed separate associations at the local, state, and national levels. The National Association of Colored Women (NACW), organized in 1896, provided critically needed social services such as nurseries and health care instruction, and sponsored various other educational programs in black communities. Mary Church Terrell, a well-known lecturer, writer, and staunch civil rights advocate, served as the association's first president.

Black clubwomen led by the dynamic journalist and reformer Ida B. *Wells-Barnett also worked diligently for antilynching legislation. The Anti-Lynching Crusade (established 1922) received support from reform-minded white women in the Association of Southern Women for the Prevention of Lynching (1930–1942), but black activists and the ASWPL did not always agree on strategies and goals. African-American women also benefited from the leadership and national prominence of Mary McLeod *Bethune, a special adviser to Presidents Franklin Roosevelt and Harry Truman and founder of Bethune-Cookman College. Bethune remained president of the National Council of Negro Women, an organization she had established in 1935, for many years.

Many black women's organizations, including the NACW and the National Federation of Afro-American Women, added strength and mass to the suffrage cause; the leaders of National American Woman Suffrage Association (NAWSA), however, were ambivalent about blacks' participation. NAWSA had emerged out of the 1890 reconciliation of the two wings of the woman suffrage movement divided since 1869. After 1900 NAWSA's presidents were Dr. Anna Howard Shaw, a prominent member of the WCTU, and Susan B. *Anthony's chosen successor, the gifted organizer and orator Carrie Chapman *Catt.

Some members of NAWSA believed Catt's state-based strategy and the association's suasionist reform tactics retarded progress. Alice Paul and Lucy Burns, two of the dissenters, added a more militant agenda to the suffrage movement but consequently alienated themselves from NAWSA's moderate leaders. While still affiliated with NAWSA in 1913, Paul and Burns created the Congressional Union (CU); a few years later policy differences forced the CU to split from NAWSA. The CU formed the

Woman's party in 1916 (later named the National Woman's Party) while boldly continuing to confront the political establishment through frequent picketing of the White House, public burnings of President Wilson's speeches, and well-publicized hunger strikes by members jailed for the cause.

The National Women's Trade Union League (1903–1947) also added its voice to the suffrage crusade. The NWTUL was a successful attempt at collaboration between middle- and working-class women; it promoted organization and education among female laborers, demanded a "living wage," and lobbied for better health and safety standards in the workplace. Winning counsel in the landmark United States Supreme Court maximum hour case of *Muller* v. *Oregon* (1908) used studies conducted by the NWTUL and the National Consumer's League to demonstrate the impact of excessive working hours on women's health.

Philosophical rifts in the ranks of female activists persisted after the 1920 ratification of the Nineteenth Amendment. The National League of Women Voters (NLWV), NAWSA's postsuffrage nonpartisan progeny, and the National Woman's Party projected two distinct and sometimes conflicting visions of equal citizenship. The League remained the more moderate association, dedicating itself to citizenship training (including Americanization) and lobbying for a broad range of social reforms that often focused on the needs of women and children. Some members of the League viewed themselves as feminists but drew a sharp distinction between their definition of "equal" rights and that favored by the NWP. Both organizations supported the Sheppard-Towner Act (1921) and the Cable Act (1922), but remained fiercely divided over the Equal Rights Amendment and protective legislation for women. (The NLWV became a strong ERA proponent in the 1970s.)

Pledged to advocate absolute legal equality between the sexes, the NWP had unveiled the proposed amendment in 1923 and led lobbying efforts with the same vigor (some said brashness) it had displayed during the suffrage years. Members of the NWP would still be marching for the ERA in the 1970s, joined by some women's organizations initially antagonistic toward the cause.

The ERA collected more support from women's organizations after World War II. In the 1920s and 1930s, however, most of the principal members of the Women's Joint Congressional Committee (WJCC) denounced the ERA as a dangerous political design, arguing that the amendment would annul the special legislation for women that female reformers had worked decades to secure. Dubbed "the Women's Lobby on Capitol Hill," the WJCC was an effective coalition created at the close of the suffrage campaign to foster cooperation among organizations trying to promote Congressional action on women's issues. The WJCC never directly endorsed legislation; instead, its members formed subcommittees to work together on specific legislative projects. Major WJCC affiliates included the National League of Women Voters, WCTU, GFWC, NWTUL, American Association of University Women, National Federation of Business and Professional Women, and the National Council of Jewish Women.

The membership base of many women's political or politically active organizations began to contract in the interwar years as it became increasingly difficult to add new blood to the aging membership. Some organizations had dissolved by 1960; others assumed a lower profile in the more conservative post–World War II era. Women did not establish another major feminist organization until the creation of the National Organization for Women in 1966. Nevertheless, women's collective efforts to influence public policy did not become politically inconsequential. A dedicated core of female activists upheld the reform tradition that female voluntary organizations had shouldered for over a century, continuing to train leaders and fashion networks that would ably serve the women's movement in the 1960s and 1970s.

[*See also* Activism; Women's Movement.]

• Ida Husted Harper, ed., *The History of Woman Suffrage*, vols. 5 and 6 (1922). Inez Haynes Irwin, Appendices, *Angels and Amazons. A Hundred Years of American Women* (1933). Maud Wood Park, *Front Door Lobby*, edited by Edna Lamprey Stantial (1960). Aileen S. Kraditor, *The Ideas of the Woman Suffrage Movement, 1890–1920* (1965). Alfred M. Duster, ed., *Crusade for Justice. The Autobiography of Ida B. Wells* (1970). Susan D. Becker, *The Origins of the Equal Rights Amendment. American Feminism Between the Wars* (1981). Nancy F. Cott, *The Grounding of Modern Feminism* (1987). Leila J. Rupp and Verta Taylor, *Survival in the Doldrums: the American Women's Rights Movement, 1945 to the 1960s* (1987). Elizabeth Anne Payne, *Reform, Labor, and Feminism. Margaret Dreier Robins and the Women's Trade Union League* (1988). Louise M. Young, *In the Public Interest. The League of Women Voters, 1920–1970* (1989). Robin Muncy, *Creating a Female Dominion in American Reform, 1890–1935* (1991).

Candice Lewis Bredbenner

1960 to the Present

The changes that catapulted American women from their closely defined roles, mainly as support for the male-dominated workforce, to a revitalized and radical women's movement, began long before 1960. The changes started in the defense plants of World War II, where women were called upon to work to support their country in its struggle against fascism. The message to U.S. women was simply stated: at the end of the war they would return to their "natural" roles as homemakers and mothers. This message was hammered home by propaganda films showing female defense workers promising to relinquish their jobs in order to return to the roles that society prescribed for them. The changes in women's attitudes began when frustrated women started to read Betty * Friedan's *Feminine Mystique* (1963), and asked the same questions that Friedan did. They started to question the assumption that they must accept a future comprised of a suburban ranch house, 2.3 children, and intellectual challenges limited to home decoration or the PTA.

The sixties were a watershed era, not so much for the women's movement, but for the social and political changes that created doubt, anger, and activism in many segments of American society.

Beginning in the late 1950s women were prominent on picket lines around retail establishments that refused to serve African-Americans. As the decade of the sixties progressed, they were active participants in the Peace Corps, on * civil rights marches, the anti-war movement, and the social upheavals surrounding the hippies and yippies. For many women, the assumptions made by the men who defined women's role as a sexual and domestic convenience was upsetting. But with national issues of racial equality and ending the Viet Nam war taking political precedence, only small efforts were attempted to challenge traditional male behavior toward women.

While young women in the 1960s were searching for new directions for their lives, older women were searching too. Through the work of leaders like Friedan, by the mid-sixties the political scene was set for the founding of the National Organization of Women, NOW (1966).

In December 1961 the Kennedy administration encouraged women's political activism by establishing a Presidential Commission on the status of women. Pressure from the few women congressional members led to the creation of the Equal Employment Opportunity Commission (EEOC). Although the administration paid lip service to women's issues, little was done to enforce the EEOC. It was during a lunch break at a Washington meeting that Friedan and others founded the National Organization for Women (NOW). At its second national conference in 1967, NOW drew up a women's Bill of Rights. The demands included an equal rights constitutional amendment, enforcement of laws banning sex discrimination in employment, maternity leave rights in employment and in social security benefits, tax deduction for home and child care expenses for working parents, child care centers, equal and unsegregated * education, equal job training opportunities and allowances for women in poverty, and the right of women to control their reproductive lives.

Elements of the women's Bill of Rights, particularly those pertaining to * abortion rights, created considerable stress within the organization. Some blue collar women were against the ERA because their unions were against it. The abortion plank precipitated a walkout—partly due to religious groups hostile to choice, partly because some women believed that the passage of the bill would jeopardize the movement.

By the end of 1968 several moderate women's groups were formed. One was Women's Equality Action League (WEAL), which focused on cases of sex discrimination in higher education. Another, Federally Employed Women (FEW), pressured the Civil Service Commission to enforce the federal ban on sex discrimination.

More radically minded women formed both radical and socialist feminist groups by 1968. Despite their differences, moderate and radical feminists worked, organized, and demonstrated together on numerous occasions. America was shocked to see suburban housewives and hippies marching with signs that read "Eve Was Framed," and "End Human Sacrifice! Don't Get Married!!"

In 1970 the women's movement was confronted by another challenge—the demands of lesbians, who were dubbed by Friedan, "the lavender menace." Members of NOW were again torn between those who saw the visibility of lesbians as damaging to the cause, and those who demanded that the rights of these women also be represented.

During the 1970s difficulties encountered by black women who sought recognition within the movement often prevented a unified women's movement from coalescing. Some black women saw the bourgeois NOW as antithetical to Black Liberation. Others believed that their loyalty lay in building up the confidence of black men. Leaders such as Fannie Lou Hamer and Shirley Chisolm did cross the * class/color line. Hamer, a voting rights crusader, led the Mississippi Freedom Democratic Party to the 1964 Democratic convention, and Chisolm, after some soul searching, decided to support the National Abortion Rights Action League (NARAL), despite the fact that many black and hispanic women viewed birth control programs with distrust, suspecting their real purpose to be a means of controlling minority population growth. Even in the 1990s minority women's participation is rare at NARAL demonstrations.

Unhappily, the women's movement of the late twentieth century, like previous women's struggles in the United States, remains divided along class and ethnic lines. * Working class women often felt that their needs were underrepresented in the demands of NOW and radical feminists. This breach was addressed in 1974 by the formation of the Coalition of Labor Union Women (CLUE). By 1982 membership in CLUE had grown from 3000 to 16,000. Labor union women opted to work through a nonconfrontational stance with the AFL/CIO.

The most contentious facet of the women's movement in the late twentieth century is reproductive rights, an arena that has witnessed great success in the last twenty years, and yet is one of the most divisive in terms of class and ethnic affiliation.

The United States has enjoyed equal suffrage for women for almost 75 years, and yet far fewer U.S. women in the 1990s hold elective political posts than in Switzerland, which gave its women the right to vote only a few decades ago. It seems likely that until more women are serving in elective office and have time to build "old girl" networks to enable them to "work the system," American women will have to continue the struggle for greater opportunity and recognition of their abilities, self worth and basic rights.

• Gerda Lerner, ed., *Black Women in White America* (1973). William H. Chafe, *Women and Equality, Changing Patterns in American Culture* (1977). Sara Evans, *Personal Politics: The Roots of Women's Liberation in the Civil Rights Movement and the New Left* (1979). Linda K. Kerber and Jane DeHart Mathews, eds., *Women's America* (1982). Barbara Sinclair Deckard, *The Women's Movement* (1983). Judith Sealander and Dorothy Smith, "The Rise and Fall of Feminist Organizations in the 1970s: Dayton as a Case Study," *Feminist Studies*, Vol. 12, No. 2, Summer 1986. William H. Chafe, *The Paradox of Change* (1991).

Harriet Davis Kram

POLITICS AND WRITING. All writing by women is political, according to Myra Jehlen, because until very recently women were not supposed to write. Indeed, the conjunction of *politics* with *women's writing* might once have seemed a redundancy. Fredric Jameson, representing the beliefs of many Marxist critics, argues in *The Political Unconscious* (1981) that all writing is ultimately political, formed and informed by its sociohistorical context. Similarly, many contemporary feminist literary critics hypothesize, as Jehlen does, that all writing by women is to some degree women's writing: despite the writer's intentions, the material or psychic or social circumstances of her existence as a woman in a patriarchal society will be written into her work (see, for example, Sandra Gilbert and Susan Gubar's analysis of the "cover story" in *The Madwoman in the Attic*, 1979). Although these definitions of politics and women's writing are inclusive, perhaps overly so, they nevertheless illuminate the pervasive tendency of women writers in the United States to write their politics and politicize their writing.

Women's writing can be conceived more narrowly as writing by women conscious of their differences as women—whether the assumed source of those differences is biology, society, *race, sexual preference, economics, or other differences. Such differences, however, extend beyond differences from men; they include differences in perspective on particular structures of power that might actually place the woman writer on the side of hierarchical privilege; and they include differences among women—especially differences of race, economics, and sexual preference—that cause some writers inadvertently to recapitulate the very structures of oppression against which they write. The history of the conjunction between women's writing and politics manifests itself through centuries and across genres—in poetry, fiction, essays, autobiographies, treatises, historical and social studies, and most recently, in *feminist criticism.

In her influential manifesto *Sexual Politics* (1970), Kate *Millett redefines *politics* to include all relationships in which one group controls another. Hester Eisenstein suggests how Millett's expanded definition encompasses much writing by women; she notes in *Contemporary Feminist Thought* (1983), developing the feminist maxim "the personal is political," that any change in or displacement of woman's given position in society is likely to reverberate throughout the society.

For women writers, the personal has always been political: some critics argue that, in colonial history for example, the fact of Anne *Bradstreet's and Phyllis *Wheatley's poetry—as acts of personal expression forbidden, respectively, to a Puritan woman and to a slave—were profound acts of defiance. Creative works—poetry, narrative, and drama—have been the most common forum for women's personal expression of private politics, because social and political constraints encouraged, if not necessitated, imaginative constructions of resistance. Literary history in the United States is a history rich with women recording their private tragedies and their rebellions against enforced domesticity. Louisa May *Alcott, Elizabeth Stuart *Phelps, Elizabeth Stuart Phelps *Ward, Sarah Orne *Jewett, Kate *Chopin,

Edith *Wharton, Charlotte Perkins *Gilman, Susan *Glaspell, Mary *Austin, Dorothy Canfield *Fisher, Edith Summers *Kelley, and Tess *Slessinger are but a few of the women writers who explored and resisted the barriers imposed on their individuality. Many of their works record a discovery of identity in critique of politics of the domestic; many—the epitome being Gilman's *The Yellow Wallpaper* (1892)—explore the tension between domestic responsibilities and constraints and their need for an artistic outlet. Recording the constraints of domesticity is itself an act of defiance; such writing continues to be a mainstay of women's contemporary literature, as is clear in the work of Lillian *Hellman, Sylvia *Plath, Anne *Sexton, Marge *Piercy, Marilynne *Robinson, Beth *Henley and Anne *Tyler, to name only a few.

Minority women have similarly found a political voice in the literature of the private; however, their confronting multiple systems of oppression—sexism in addition to racism, homophobia, xenophobia—makes their writing doubly defiant, calling for or perhaps causing greater social upheaval. Autobiographies have provided women powerful critiques of both racism and domestic oppression, from Linda Brent (Harriet *Jacobs) and Ida B. *Wells-Barnett through Anne Moody, Maya *Angelou, Gloria *Naylor, Gayle *Jones, Leslie *Silko, and Maxine Hong *Kingston. The domestic worlds of pain and triumph have been movingly documented in poems, novels, and plays by Zora Neale *Hurston, Djuna *Barnes, Gwendolyn *Brooks, Lorraine *Hansberry, Toni *Morrison, Alice *Walker, Sherley Anne *Williams, and Louise *Erdrich. Women writers have continually transformed traditional genres into expressions of their own radical political locutions.

Of course, women have written very explicitly about politics for three centuries, and especially since their early involvement in movements against slavery. Discussing contemporary socialist feminist politics, Allison Jaggar notes in *Feminist Politics and Human Nature* (1983) that women's particular position as subordinated group gives them greater insight into related forms of oppression. Thus, as early as the 1830s, Angela and Sarah *Grimké were writing treatises comparing the plight of slaves to the restrictions placed upon women (see Angela Grimké, *Appeal to the Women of the South*, 1836). They quickly realized that women's position in society was not conducive to the political action necessary for the abolition of *slavery, resulting in Sarah Grimké's *Letters on the Equality of the Sexes, and the Condition of Women* (1837–1838). Other white, southern women writers followed suit, although in the form of novels exposing or recording both political and personal conflicts—Julia Peterkin's sensitive accounts of the Gullah Negroes, Ellen *Glasgow's depictions of women's victimage (*Virginia*, 1913) and of political conflicts in the South (*The Barren Ground*, 1925), Caroline *Gordon's similar accounts in *The Garden of Adonis* (1937) and *Women on the Porch* (1944).

The most famous novelistic account of and reaction against slavery is Harriet Beecher *Stowe's *Uncle Tom's Cabin* (1852), which she followed with *A Key to Uncle Tom's Cabin* (1853), documenting the real events she reproduced in the novel, and with another antislavery novel, *Dred: A Tale of the Great Dismal Swamp* (1856). Chapter thirteen in *Uncle Tom's Cabin* depicts Stowe's antipatriarchal politics: Rachel Halliday represents a vision of matriarchal *utopia, where *motherhood—not economics—serves as the most important human connection.

The woman suffrage movement, too, developed from women's growing sense of political powerlessness as they fought for *abolition. Lucy Stone founded the *Woman's Journal* in 1870 to provide a forum for both the antislavery movement and for woman suffrage. Susan B. *Anthony and Elizabeth Cady *Stanton pursued woman suffrage more aggressively after they were refused admission to an international abolitionists' conference because they were women. These women's political writings developed as accounts of their *activism: Anthony and Cady Stanton collaborated on the multivolume *History of Women's Suffrage* (1881–1887, 1900); Cady Stanton founded the journal *Revolution* (1868–1869) and wrote the two-volume *Women's Bible* (1895, 1898). The late nineteenth and early twentieth centuries saw a number of women activists who manifested in their writings the interdependence of the struggle for women's rights and the need for large-scale social changes. Rebecca Harding *Davis exposed political corruption and women's victimage in works such as "Life in the Iron Mills" (1861), *Margaret Howth* (1862), and *Silhouette of American Life* (1892); Nelly Bly (Elizabeth Cochrane Seaman) exposed corruption and oppression both in her articles for the New York *World* and in books like *Ten Days in a Madhouse* (1887); Jane *Addams took on social reform in *Democracy and Social Ethics* (1902) and *A New Conscience and an Ancient Evil* (1912).

Perhaps the most famous women political writers were those who saw the need for radical change in the entire social structure as requisite for the elimination of oppression. Although Margaret *Fuller's commitment to social revolution and Fourier's utopian society came only with her involvement in Italian politics the few

years before she died in 1850, her *Woman in the 19th Century* (1845) is considered the first truly feminist work in the United States. Writing at the same time as Emerson, Fuller advocated a "ravishing harmony" of the masculine and feminine spheres. She attacked the *class system in America for perpetuating radical divisions between men and women, as well as between women—prisoners and ladies of fashion: "Now I ask you, my sisters, if the women at the fashionable house be not answerable for those women being in prison? . . . Seek out these degraded women, give them tender sympathy, counsel, employment. Take the place of mothers, such as might have saved them originally." Charlotte Perkins *Gilman believed strongly in the need for women's economic independence, which she articulates in *Women and Economics* (1898); she also believed in the moral superiority of women and in male domination as an impediment to the evolutionary progression of human society to its perfection. She imagined a utopian society in *Herland* (1915), free from the domination of men, in which nature was respected and the innate talents of each individual used to the better development of the group. Emma *Goldman and Margaret Sanger theorized about utopian anarchic societies as they fought for women's rights to birth control (see, for example, Goldman's *Anarchism and Other Essays*, 1911, and Margaret Sanger's *Woman and the New Race*, 1920).

Women writers in the thirties drew on their experience in radical politics—and the Communist Front—to articulate their special party planks for women's causes. Meridel *Le Sueur's "Women on the Breadlines" (in *Harvest Song*, 1990) and her contributions to the *New Masses*, Josephine *Herbst's *Rope of Gold* (1939), Tillie *Olsen's unfinished *Yonnondio: From the Thirties* (1974), Fielding *Burke's *Call Home the Heart* (1932), and *Tess Slesinger's *The Unpossessed* (1934) all addressed working-class women's lives and the conjunction of economic politics and gender oppression. Zora Neale *Hurston's *Their Eyes Were Watching God* (1937) adds racial persecution to the consideration of proletarian and class positionality in American culture. (See Paula Rabinowitz's 1991 work, *Labor and Desire*, for a complete list of revolutionary thirties fiction.)

The most prominent conjunction of politics and women's writing in the contemporary United States is feminist writing. Allison Jaggar distinguishes among liberal, radical, and socialist feminist politics. Insofar as one can ascribe a politics to women's literature in the United States—and one can so only in retrospect, after the fact of criticism like Jaggar's—liberal feminist politics dominate women's writing up to, if not through, the second wave of feminism beginning with the Women's Liberation Movement of the 1960s. This politics, evolving from the work of Mary Wollstonecraft and John Stuart Mill, holds that rationality is the defining human characteristic and that women are as fully capable of rational thought as men. Consequently, liberal feminism argues for women's right to participate as fully in society as men, emphasizing the individual's power (given opportunity) for self-determination and autonomy. This is clearly the politics of the woman suffrage movement, and the ideal politics for women's literature, insofar as it is commonly conceived as the self-expression of a previously silenced voice (the basis of Jehlen's universal claim that women's writing is defiant).

The dominance of liberal feminism and of its emphasis on the individual has generated some internal politics, a politics within women's writing. Traditional Marxists (not necessarily women) have reduced all feminism to liberalism and condemned it as bourgeois. Jaggar analyzes liberalism as generally "somatophobic" (that is, in fear of the * body) because of its elevation of the rational. The basis of liberal feminism is the woman's ability to transcend the limitations arbitrarily imposed on her because of her body; under the skin, to the liberal feminist, men and women are alike. For the liberal feminist, then, literature becomes the perfect medium for expression of true self stifled by a body and the restrictions society forces upon it. This dismissal of the body as a "surface" difference also led to liberal feminists' frequent comparisons between their struggle and those of African Americans. Indeed, just as the fight for woman suffrage emerged from the abolitionist movement, the women's liberation movement (WLM) emerged—if only in its tactics—from the * civil rights movement. However, this dismissal of the body and this comparison of women with African Americans (not only ignoring the fact that many women are African American, but also ignoring those women—along with other minorities, including lesbians—and their accomplishments) led to several groups' disaffection with the WLM and the development of several alternative politics. Betty * Friedan is an example of a liberal feminist, leading women to fight for their freedom through social change in her 1963 The Feminine Mystique.

Radical feminist politics developed initially as a splinter group of the WLM. Ti-Grace Atkinson is generally regarded as the first radical feminist emerging from the WLM; however, commentators like Jaggar and Hester Eisenstein usually include Kate * Millett, Shulamith Firestone, and Germaine Greer in the category "radical" even though Millett's Sexual Politics and Greer's The Female Eunuch came early in the WLM and are usually strongly associated with it. However, Millett, Greer, and Firestone depart significantly from liberal feminist politics in their challenges to the power structure. * Liberal feminism sought women's rights within the political status quo; radical feminist politics began to challenge not only women's rights to access, but the very structures of society. Liberal feminism's "anything men can do, we can do better" attitude led to an implied ideal of androgyny (or, in Millett's terms, "unisex"); however, in her relatively early articulation of that ideal in Toward a Recognition of Androgyny (1973), Carolyn * Heilbrun clarified that androgyny meant not only that women could perform as well men, but also that men ought to behave more like women.

A second development in radical feminist politics, according to Jaggar, was the recognition that women could not so easily transcend their bodies: both Shulamith Firestone's The Dialectic of Sex (1970) and Susan Brownmiller's Against Our Will: Men, Women, and Rape (1976) challenged the liberal feminist assumption that the physical could become irrelevant. Radical feminist politics thus developed into a full-blown rejection of an increasingly monolithic conception of patriarchy. Jaggar views radical feminist politics as the first truly original politics in the history of women's rights, in its recognition that reality is a human construct, not a given, and that women need to create a new world, possibly even a new language. This new theory has been labeled social constructionism, a theory that suggests how * gender, * race, and * class categories are created through the language and relational systems which define the classifications.

Many radical feminists are poets or novelists who attempt, in both their creative work and in their social commentary, to forge a new language more closely tied to women's experience and even women's bodies. Among the best-known are Adrienne * Rich, Audre * Lorde, Andrea * Dworkin, Robin Morgan, and Joanna * Russ. Linguist and science fiction writer Suzette Hayden Elgin actually created her own language, called Laadan. Mary * Daly has similarly attempted to reclaim language and experience for (of) women, especially in her Wickedary (1987). Mainstream feminist literary criticism can generally be placed in the gap between liberal and radical—radical because usually woman-centered, liberal because generally places value on the individual.

Radical feminist separatists commonly believe that women can develop independently of patriarchal definitions of and impositions upon them only if men and women live separately. Consequently, there is significant overlap between radical and lesbian feminism. Ti-Grace Atkinson and Charlotte Bunch maintain that true feminists must be lesbian; Rita Mae *Brown, Adrienne Rich, and Mary Daly point to the utopian possibilities of lesbianism. Ironically, however, the literary writings of lesbian poets and novelists—excepting that of the most famous, like *Stein, *H. D., and Rich, who are frequently considered as artists quite apart from their sexual orientation—have been marginalized by mainstream (liberal) feminist literary critics. In her landmark essay "What Has Never Been: An Overview of Lesbian Feminist Literary Criticism" (*Feminist Studies* 7, no. 3, Fall 1981), Bonnie Zimmerman, following the example set by Jane *Rule in *Lesbian Images* (1975), critiques the *heterosexism of much feminist literary criticism, arguing for a criticism which accounts for lesbian experience and politics.

Women of color, and most predominantly African-American women, found themselves increasingly disenfranchised from both liberal and radical feminism and the literary criticism developing from them. The disenfranchisement of minority women from both liberal and radical traditions has been remarked by Barbara Smith, bell hooks, Deborah McDowell, Hortense Spillers, Bonnie Zimmerman, among others. In 1971, for instance, Toni *Morrison argued that the WLM was about white women's conflicts with white men and that the WLM was not interested in the very different racial and economic discrimination black women faced ("What the Black Woman Thinks About Women's Lib," *New York Times Magazine*, 22 August 1971, vol. 6). Angela *Davis faulted white feminist accounts of *rape as buying into racial *stereotypes about black men; their support for abortion, she contended, ignored the potential misuse toward genocide. Alison Edwards, Audre Lorde, Hortense Spillers, and bell hooks, among others, have demonstrated that both liberal and radical feminists define "woman" as the white, middle-class woman: the liberals in their acceptance of the eighteenth-century model of rationality, the radicals in their frequent tendency to posit some essence of women that some African-American women find foreign. Barbara Smith and Deborah McDowell have more specifically pointed to the omission of the work of women of color from what Elizabeth Meese, in *(Ex)tensions* (1990), terms Feminist Literary Criticism: that is, the liberal literary politics represented by white "gynocritics" like Elaine Showalter, Patricia Spacks, Ellen Moers, Nina Baym, and Sandra Gilbert and Su-

san Gubar. Smith, McDowell, and Susan Willis all point to the need to articulate a literary aesthetic that would be representative of African-American women's writing. Anthologies of critical writing similarly directed include *Sturdy Black Bridges* (1978), *Home Girls* (1983), and *This Bridge Called My Back* (1981), the latter representing other women of color as well.

Gayle Greene documents the major attributes of feminist fiction, such as those by Sylvia Plath in *The Bell Jar*, Sue Kaufman's *Diary of a Mad Housewife*, Marilyn *French's *The Women's Room*, and Marge Piercy's *Small Changes*: seeing feminist fiction as a "re-vision" (in Rich's sense) of "the tradition," Greene argues that feminist metafiction is also a characteristic of feminist political writing in the second wave of feminism. This metafiction "focuses on women as readers and writers, point[ing] to the key role of reading and writing in the women's movement. Versions of the feminist *Kunstlerroman* existed earlier in the century, but the genre reached its fullest expression during the second wave of feminism." These fictions also elaborate a critique of romance, are often self-reflexive and self-consciously realistic, but also alter dominant assumptions about representation.

According to Jaggar, socialist feminism is a very recent development that recognizes the differences between men and women (unlike liberal feminism), but that views these as the result of social, political, racial, and especially economic conditions. It therefore considers the causes of differences among women as well. It differs from radical feminism in its Marxist roots, generally rejecting the conception of patriarchy as monolithic or universal. Instead, it explores the specific forms of oppression women encounter in history and within given cultures, especially (in the U.S.) as a result of capitalism. Many socialist feminists—Jaggar, Hester Eisenstein, Nancy Chodorow, Angela Davis, Jean Elshtain, Zillah Eisenstein, Evelyn Fox Keller, Catherine MacKinnon, Lillian Rubin—tend to ignore literary production in favor of the specific changes in political, social, and legal structures necessary to eliminate oppression. Nevertheless, feminist literary critics as theoretically diverse as Lillian Robinson, Gayatri *Spivak, and Hortense Spillers explore the relations among literary productions, women's oppression, and the material circumstances that determine both.

[*See also* Authorship.]

• James D. Hart, ed., *The Oxford Companion to American Literature* (1965). James L. Cooper and Sheila McIsaac Cooper, eds., *The Roots of American Feminist Thought* (1973). Alison Jaggar, *Feminist Politics and Human Nature* (1983). Paul Lauter, ed., *Reconstructing*

American Literature: Courses, Syllabi, Issues (1983). Mary Eagleton, ed., *Feminist Literary Theory: A Reader* (1986). James D. Hart, ed., *The Concise Oxford Companion to American Literature* (1986). Lisa Tuttle, *Encyclopedia of Feminism* (1986). Gayle Greene, *Changing the Story: Feminist Fiction and the Tradition* (1991). Paula Rabinowitz, *Labor and Desire: Women's Revolutionary Fiction in Depression America* (1991).

Colleen Kennedy and Dale M. Bauer

PORNOGRAPHY. One of the greatest difficulties in discussing pornography is how to define the term. Where do we draw the line between porn, obscenity, and erotica? between hard and soft core? Former Supreme Court Justice Potter Stewart's definition of obscenity—that we know it when we see it—is frequently cited. But such an interpretation has its problems, particularly in leaving open to contention who, exactly, the "we" is that is doing the "seeing." The question extends not only to the seers who get to name and judge "porn" but to the voyeurs who enjoy and purchase it.

Within certain feminist circles, the pornographic spectator is decidedly male, the pornographic object decidedly female, and as a result, protesting pornography's dissemination becomes a decidedly feminist project. Anti-porn feminists, many of whom are involved in Women Against Pornography (WAP), often take as their motto the idea that pornography is the theory and *rape the practice. They argue that pornographic representations, with their graphic depiction of male domination and women's submission, are at the root of women's objectification and serve as a primary cause of male *violence against women.

Many of the most noted feminists who take this view have spelled out their positions in writing, including Kate *Millett in *Sexual Politics* (1969), Andrea *Dworkin in *Pornography: Men Possessing Women* (1981), Susan Griffin in *Pornography and Silence: Culture's Revenge Against Nature* (1981), Susanne Kappeler in *The Pornography of Representation* (1986), and Catherine MacKinnon in several essays, including those collected in her *Feminism Unmodified: Discourses on Life and Law* (1987). In general, these authors reject counter-arguments that porn is a free speech issue; most would insist instead that, through its vivid dehumanization of certain women, porn hurts all women and hence crosses over into the realm of harmful speech. Many of these writers have thus called for its *censorship or outright ban: Dworkin and MacKinnon, for instance, have been instrumental in establishing state and local ordinances against pornography, although these ordinances have thus far failed to hold up in court.

At the other end of the spectrum come theorists—feminists, civil libertarians, poststructuralists and/or combinations of each—who contend that pornography is representation and not reality, that it is not always and inevitably violence against women nor the cause of all evil, and that men are not the only ones to enjoy porn (not to mention sex). Typically, these theorists argue that there is no convincing proof that porn consumers commit violent crimes; they all concur that censorship is not the answer. Most who take this stance suggest that porn (as well as *sexuality) should be analyzed and explored rather than being automatically dismissed or repressed as filth.

It is such premises that motivate anthologies like *Caught Looking: Feminism, Pornography, and Censorship* (1987), a collection of articles dedicated to exploring not just porn but the volatile debate surrounding it; each essay is superimposed with questionably "pornographic" (the answer lies with the viewer) photos and images. Additional feminist studies that attempt to examine rather than vilify porn include Linda Williams's *Hard Core: Power, Pleasure, and the "Frenzy of the Visible"* (1989).

Within feminist circles, these two opposing stances and factions collided at the now-notorious Feminist IX "Towards a Politics of Sexuality" Conference hosted by Barnard College in 1982. There, feminists who defined sexuality as primarily a matter of pleasure, of danger, or a mixture of both exchanged ideas and at times insults. The issue of pornography proved a particularly inflammatory one for the conference, since pornography depicts sexuality's complex nature as both dangerous and pleasurable, often simultaneously so. Many of the papers generated for this conference are collected in Carole S. Vance's *Pleasure and Danger: Exploring Female Sexuality* (1984).

Feminist arenas are not the only places where porn is debated, of course. Erotic or lewd images have been around for as long as there have been viewers to enjoy them; the etymology of the word "pornography" shows that it originally meant "writing about (or by) prostitutes," and such writing has been with us since ancient times. Over time, as the concept broadened so that any sexualized representation (especially of women) would count as porn, writers as diverse as D. H. Lawrence, Virginia *Woolf, and Henry Miller have attempted to resolve the porn conundrum by taking sides. While both Lawrence and Miller argue for free expression and against any rigid attempt to categorically define porn, Woolf reveals an ambivalence many women share in her attempt to categorize certain works as pornographic and to stress their harmful effects (Hoff in *For Adult Users Only*).

Most historians of porn agree that while the written word may indeed be graphic, the pleasure found in porn often stems from its visual nature, from the freak shows and carnivals of the nineteenth century to the X-rated films and magazines of the twentieth. In fact, it is this visibility that frequently makes "porn" so stimulating to certain viewers and so offensive to others.

In the United States, a Puritan streak may be responsible for the visibility of not simply pornography but also of movements to suppress it. In the nineteenth century, the social purity movement was a powerful force against what its followers saw as corrupt and corrupting materials. Perhaps the most outspoken leader of this movement was Anthony Comstock, who led the drive to ban any lewd or obscene materials, which for Comstock included even information about birth control. Comstock's views on obscenity and morality are not dissimilar from those that motivate the contemporary anti-porn movements of the religious right.

Another highly visible contemporary force against porn has been the Meese Commission on Pornography. While an earlier panel formed under President Lyndon B. Johnson in 1970 had concluded that most obscenity laws should be repealed, the Meese Commission, formed under President Ronald Reagan in 1985, concluded the opposite: it found not only that existing laws against porn's production and distribution should be enforced, but that new laws should be written to eradicate any and all obscene and degrading representations and practices that would appeal to "prurient interests" (Pritchard in *For Adult Users Only*).

Legislation as a means of eradicating pornography has also been deployed in attempts to distinguish "porn" from "literature." Literary critics such as Susan *Sontag in "The Pornographic Imagination" have argued for such a distinction; for Sontag this difference is located in "literature's" attention to human feelings, emotions, and relationships versus "porn's" focus on the objectified body and particularly, the genital organs and their transactions (in *A Susan Sontag Reader*, 1982). Such theoretical distinctions, however, have traditionally not held sway in legal arenas, where numerous works that Sontag might classify as "literary" have been labeled obscene and faced with censorship due to their equation with the pornographic. These include James Joyce's *Ulysses* (1934; 1942), Radclyffe Hall's *Well of Loneliness* (1928), and Vladimir Nabokov's *Lolita* (1955). Also, although never challenged in a court of law, works including Kate *Chopin's *The Awakening* (1899) were met with social censure for their sexual explicitness, a disapproval that

in Chopin's case literally ended her writing career.

The fact that many of these works are now considered "classics" demonstrates the shifting, context-based nature of all attempts to define pornography definitively. If yesterday's "porn" is today's "high art," how can we be certain that today's "porn" will not come to mean something entirely different to future generations? But then again, as anti-porn feminists would contend, how can we be sure that those future generations are not so corrupted by today's porn that the very notion of a future is put in jeopardy? Clearly, debates about pornography—its meaning, function, and effects—are not esoteric or trivial pursuits but symbolically central to U.S. cultural and political practices. As such, whether or not we know it when we see it, porn will continue to figure as a force in the everyday life of U.S. men and women who grapple with both maintaining and changing gender roles and relations.

[*See also* Erotica; Censorship; Lesbian Pulp Fiction.]

• Joan Hoff, "Why Is There No History of Pornography?" in *For Adult Users Only: The Dilemma of Violent Pornography*, eds. Susan Gubar and Joan Hoff (1989), pp. 17–46. David Pritchard, "Beyond the Meese Commission Report: Understanding the Variable Nature of Pornography Regulation," in *For Adult Users Only*, pp. 163–177. Lynne Segal and Mary McIntosh, eds., *Sex Exposed: Sexuality and the Pornography Debate* (1993).

Cynthia J. Davis

PORTER, Katherine Anne (1890–1980), short story writer and novelist. Born in Indian Creek, Texas, Porter escaped her provincial native region as a young woman only to return to it time and again in her fiction. She endowed Miranda, the autobiographical heroine of her stories "Old Mortality" and "The Old Order," with the sensitivity and inquisitiveness she herself had possessed as a child. Attuned to cycles of birth, death, and regeneration in nature and well-versed in the legends and memory of family, Miranda, in the series of stories that chart her development, struggles to disentangle herself from her rural southern roots and "the badly cast fishing lines" of family to pursue a separate and self-determined identity. Compelled to leave the South, where as a woman writer she feared she would be regarded as a "freak," Porter wrote compassionately of family misfits and social outcasts in stories like "Holiday," "He," and "Noon Wine." The death of her mother when Porter was two, and her own struggles with tuberculosis and influenza as a young woman, exposed her early on to the death and illness that pervade her fiction.

But her ability to transform her experience

into fiction came only after a varied career in the performing arts and a long apprenticeship in journalism. She published her first collection of short stories, *Flowering Judas and Other Stories* (1930), when she was forty, although she placed individual stories in little magazines throughout the twenties. This collection includes the often anthologized stories "The Jilting of Granny Weatherall," "Theft," and "Rope," but consists primarily of stories set in Mexico, her "familiar country," where in 1920 she witnessed the country's political and artistic revolution. She lived in Europe during much of the thirties, publishing on her return to the United States *Pale Horse, Pale Rider: Three Short Novels* (1939) and *The Leaning Tower and Other Stories* (1944). A long period of artistic frustration followed as she attempted to complete an ambitious fictional account of her journey to Europe on the *Werra* in 1931. The novel, *Ship of Fools*, finally appeared in print in 1962 to great fanfare, million-dollar sales, and mixed critical reviews. *The Collected Stories of Katherine Anne Porter* received the National Book Award and the Pulitzer Prize for Fiction in 1966 and 1967.

Porter struggled to construct from a history of poverty, marital failures, and abject loneliness a more tolerable personal narrative: only with the publication of Joan Givner's biography, *Katherine Anne Porter: A Life* (1982), did readers learn of the extent to which Porter had glamorized the account of her life. Until recently her reputation as a consummate stylist steered critical attention away from her penetrating exploration of female experience and the indictment of patriarchal structures embedded in her fiction.

• Katherine Anne Porter, *The Collected Essays and Occasional Writings of Katherine Anne Porter* (1970). Jane Krause DeMouy, *Katherine Anne Porter's Women* (1983). Isabel Bayley, ed., *Letters of Katherine Anne Porter* (1990). Darlene Harbour Unrue, ed., *This Strange Old World and Other Book Reviews by Katherine Anne Porter* (1991).

Christine Hanks

PORTILLO-TRAMBLEY, Estela (b. 1936), dramatist, fiction writer, and educator. Born in El Paso, Texas, Estela Portillo grew up speaking Spanish at home and English in school. Despite the poverty they shared with all their neighbors, her parents nurtured her imagination and a belief in the American dream of success. She married after high school and then earned a B.A. from the University of Texas, El Paso, in 1957. While raising six children she managed a fourteen-year career as a high school English teacher and department chair, radio talk show host, and writer and host of a Chicano cultural television show, "Cumbres."

She began writing after her only son died at nine months of age; her first book, rejected by publishers, was a utopian vision combining Far Eastern philosophy with Western pragmatism. She reacted to the rejection by writing a play designed to sell—and it did, instantly. *The Day of the Swallows*, a story of a lesbian Chicana's struggle to act upon personal desire within a restrictive community, first appeared in 1971. Since then it has been included in at least four anthologies and is considered by many to be her best play.

Portillo-Trambley continued to work in theater, writing, acting, and directing: she was the resident dramatist at the Community College, El Paso, from 1970 to 1975. She has the distinction of being the first Chicana to write a musical comedy, *Morality Play*, which was first produced at the Chamizal National Theatre in El Paso in 1974. Four of her eleven plays are collected in the volume entitled *Sor Juana and Other Plays* (1983).

For her work in literature and theater she received the prestigious Quinto Sol Award in 1972. She edited a special issue of *El Grito* (vol. 7, no. 1, September 1973), the first issue of a major Chicano journal to concentrate exclusively on the works of women. In 1975 she published *Rain of Scorpions*, a collection of short stories that are feminist in the sense that they scrutinize women's potential for resisting victimization. She turned to novel writing with *Trini* (1986); her latest novel, *Masihani* (forthcoming), based on Toltec myth and history, provides a new positive image for La Llorona, the weeping woman of Chicano folklore.

Portillo-Trambley, a grandmother of eight children (one of whom she has adopted), is now director of fine arts in the El Paso schools.

• Juan Bruce-Novoa, *Chicano Authors* (1980). James G. Lesniak, ed., *Contemporary Authors, New Revision Series*, vol. 32 (1991).

Margaret A. Lukens

POST-COLONIALISM. In the field of literary criticism, the term *post-colonialism* is closely associated with the practice of *deconstruction and, in particular, that branch which is represented by Homi Bhabha, Abdul JanMohamed, and Gayatri Chakravorty *Spivak. Deconstruction itself is basically concerned with demonstrating the arbitrariness of binary oppositions commonly assumed to be natural or given, such as "self/other," "man/woman," and "East/West." Post-colonialism, understood as a critical stance and a deconstructive strategy for reading, aims at exposing the *race-, *class-, and *gender-specific determinations that inform each category of the above three bipolar models.

Although post-colonialism implies *the end of* or the period *after* colonialism, the term denotes a state in which colonial domination lingers on in areas other than the economic or administrative sector. For this reason, "post-colonialism" poses something of a conceptual problem for traditional political economists, since the end of colonialism marks the beginning of independence achieved through insurgent nationalism. But, as many political scientists have now pointed out, the emergence of nationalism in a colonial situation is, in fact, not separable from an often unperceived acceptance of the dominant colonial (that is, Western) values. Unlike the situation in Western countries, where the values that form the foundation of an independent nation are believed to have been generated from within their own indigenous culture, in colonized countries, which are implicitly conceived as "inferior," the new values are in fact taken from the world of the colonizers. By ignoring this race-encoded aspect of nationalism when it is applied to a non-Western country, existing discourses of political science expose the extent to which they falsely assume "universal" human experiences and values. These assumptions, however unintended, continue rather than counter colonial domination.

The term "post-colonialism," in contrast, provides the necessary conceptual framework for critiquing the resilience and logic of cultural imperialism. This might best be illustrated by the current debate on *multiculturalism and the growing interest in the "Third World" shown by academia in the U.S. The inclusion of African-American, Asian-American, and for that matter, women's and gay literature within the set curricula of many English departments, for example, may be considered the direct result of an increasing awareness of the cultural differences that are reflected within the complexity of human society. However, such an inclusion of hitherto "marginal" groups does not necessarily amount to a democratic move on the part of the hegemonic culture; ethnocentric tendencies in scholarly approaches to culture are far more pervasive than might be thought. The demand for recognition of "diversity" has only served to produce the somewhat cryptic formula "First-World theory/Third-World material." Not surprisingly, all developing countries are subsumed under the category "primitive" Third World, which then functions as the object of study for a theoretically "sophisticated" First World made up of the United States and selected European countries.

More than anything else, post-colonialism works to unravel power structures by criticizing the tools of representation provided by a hegemonic "First World" culture. As the indigenous but predominantly male-centered elite of colonies-turned-independent-states increasingly produce Western-acceptable self-images of "Third World" nations, a more rigorous examination of the cross-cultural exchange of knowledge, from which issues of race and gender are normally excluded, becomes absolutely mandatory. In other words, unlike a nationalist discourse, which believes that a term such as "Third World" grants non-Western countries an egalitarian status in the global arena, post-colonialism would arrest the silencing or misrepresentation of colonized voices.

In the attempt to explain the discriminatory aspect of existing cultural narratives, post-colonialism has turned to recent revisions in the theory of ideology. Basing itself on a definition of ideology that moves beyond the humanist notion of the self-contained thinking subject, post-colonialism takes into account an underlying and often repressed structure of domination within human consciousness. While conventional explications of ideology omit the question of desire and the complex process of *identity formation, a post-colonial notion of ideology emphasizes both these issues as examples of the repressed subtext of a hegemonic culture. At this level of understanding, post-colonialism as a theoretical discourse has benefitted from contemporary criticisms of Freudian *psychoanalysis as well as Marx's speculations on the question of value.

But perhaps the most productive approach to post-colonialism comes from that branch of deconstruction which not only takes into account issues of race and class, but also draws on feminist theory. Although the work of Gayatri Chakravorty Spivak is representative of a deconstructive/feminist approach to post-colonialism. Spivak's notion of *feminism bears little resemblance to mainstream Anglo-American feminist scholarship as exemplified, to name just one example, by the work of Elaine Showalter. Revealing subjectivity as the product of the larger socio-political structure, Spivak's brand of feminism rejects all *essentialist and individualistic notions that define "woman" or *femininity. Instead, she seeks to explore the complex ideological ramifications of race, class, and gender as they are perceived in history. Theoretically speaking, therefore, Spivak's approach to post-colonialism is informed by a critique of traditional epistemology, and post-colonialism is primarily a question of consciousness-raising, of understanding ideology as a complex operation that shapes and re-shapes a cultural, class, and gender-specific subjectivity. Spivak's conceptual approach is valuable because it shows the often unrecognized ethnocentric appropriation of non-Western women by mainstream Anglo-American and *French feminism. As Spivak shows, this is especially the case with the international representation of labor-power, where it is the uneducated and socially disenfranchised woman of non-Western cultures whose subjectivity is so very often omitted or erased. The incorporation of such issues of gender and race offers a theoretical framework that renders Spivak's work valuable to both feminism and deconstruction.

[*See also* Colonialism; Spivak, Gayatri; Third World Feminism, U.S.]

• Partha Chatterjee, *Nationalism and the Colonial World, A Derivative Discourse* (1987). Peter Collier and Helga Geyer-Ryan, eds., *Literary Theory Today* (1990). Abdul R. JanMohamed and David Lloyd, eds., *The Nature and Context of Minority Discourse* (1990). Gayatri Chakravorty Spivak, *The Post-Colonial Critic: Interviews, Strategies, Dialogues,* edited by Sarah Harasym (1990). Homi Bhabha, *Nation and Narration* (1991).

Ming-Bao Yue

POSTMODERN WRITING. While postmodernism's usefulness for feminism is debated in conference rooms and scholarly journals, the term *postmodernism* itself has become a catchphrase in the academy and in the popular media for any discourse that questions and subverts accepted notions of reality. Self-reflexive, contradictory, eclectic, and decentered, postmodernism's varying impulses range from the playful to the nihilistic, the polyphonic to the inarticulate. In literary terms, however, it is possible to narrow the concept of postmodernism to experimentation with writing's formal elements and textual practices: syntax, genre, closure, point of view, narrative voice, linear plot, etc. Postmodern writing not only refers to its own discursive processes but radically challenges language's ability to communicate experience and perception.

Until recently, this experimentation—alternatively called metafiction, fabulation, surfiction, or deconstructive fiction—has been associated almost exclusively with white male writers from the 1960s on, leading to the charge that there are no postmodern women writers. As Bonnie Zimmerman remarks in "Feminist Fiction and the Postmodern Challenge," "By the time postmodernism disrupted twentieth-century realism, it was generally accepted that men were writing the Great American Novels and women typing them" (*Postmodern Fiction: A Bio-Bibliographical Guide,* 1986). While women such as Virginia *Woolf, Gertrude *Stein, Mina Loy, and Djuna *Barnes were at the forefront of early twentieth-century modernist experimentation, feminism of the 1960s and 1970s seemed to call for realism to express

the growing consciousness of inequality and violence toward women, which Betty *Friedan in *The Feminine Mystique* (1963) labeled "the problem that has no name." Novels such as Sue Kaufman's *Diary of a Mad Housewife* (1967), Alix Kates Shulman's *Memoirs of an Ex-Prom Queen* (1969), Sylvia *Plath's *The Bell Jar* (1971), and Erica *Jong's *Fear of Flying* (1973) exposed the misogyny of American society, which most women were forced to confront daily. One slogan of the women's movement, "the personal is the political," validated the everyday experiences of white, middle-class housewives struggling to gain control of their own economic, sexual, and intellectual lives as important and interesting material for a new literary movement.

Yet when re-examined within a feminist framework, many of these so-called realist novels exemplify a postmodernism more thematically and stylistically innovative than that of male writers. As Ellen Friedman and Miriam Fuchs argue in *Breaking the Sequence: Women's Experimental Fiction* (1989), unlike male postmodernists, whose writing "display[s] a nostalgic yearning after and grieving for the comforting authority of linear narrative," women postmodernists "rupture[s] conventional structures of meaning by which the patriarchy reigns in order to give presence and voice to what was denied and repressed." Zimmerman's claim that women's experimental writing "usually serves the ultimate end of realism [for] it is women's real lives that defy the laws of the text" suggests not that realism is essentially a female literary form or that all women's writing demands realism, but that, for women, postmodern writing redefines realism in terms of the heterogenous nature of women's lived experiences. It is the complexity of women's lives that determines the textual necessity for new literary forms. Additionally, as Molly Hite points out, these innovations cannot be dismissed as the "natural" result of women's "difference," but are conscious artistic decisions (*The Other Side of the Story,* 1989).

While some critics such as Julia Kristeva and Hélène Cixous claim that all experimental writing is "feminine" writing, their analysis is most often focused on white male writers, disregarding women postmodernists' feminist imperative to expose inequalities of *gender, *race, *class, and *sexuality. In fact, feminist politics and postmodern aesthetics are often inextricably linked. Many women writers such as Paula Gunn *Allen, Toni Cade *Bambara, Toni *Morrison, June *Arnold, Sheila Ballantyne, Adrienne *Kennedy, Cynthia *Ozick, and Sheila Ortiz Taylor have abandoned a single, stable, reliable narrative voice in favor of multiple narrators, divided pronouns (I/she), or shifting points of view in order to emphasize the collective, relational nature of female identity. In Jong's *Fear of Flying*, for example, the blurred distinction between author, narrator, and character questions the "authorizing" of women's stories. Similarly, in *Dessa Rose*, Sherley Anne *Williams claims authorship for black women through the creation of what Marta Sánchez calls "the dialogizing voice" of a protagonist who is both omniscient narrator and first-person storyteller (*Genders* 15, 1992).

The connection between genre and cultural identity is explored by many women postmodernists, particularly women of color. For example, Maxine Hong *Kingston's *The Woman Warrior* (1976) blurs the boundaries between fiction, *autobiography, and history by revising Chinese *myth and "talk-story" to connect the dead "ghosts" of her cultural and familial past with the live "ghosts" of a hostile dominating world. Audre *Lorde calls her work *Zami: A New Spelling of My Name* (1982) a "biomythography" because it places her own life as a black lesbian poet in the context of a lesbian past that is always mythically creating its own history. In *Borderlands/La Frontera* (1987), self-described "Chicana *tejana* lesbian-feminist poet and fiction writer" Gloria *Anzaldúa combines multilingual poetry, historiography, myth, and autobiography to explore "la mestiza," the woman who bridges many cultures and identities. While writers such as Ntozake *Shange and Kathy *Acker create texts from a pastiche of folk stories, journal entries, poetry, and "borrowed" writings, Alice *Walker and Ana *Castillo have revised the *epistolary novel and Louise *Erdrich, Sandra *Cisneros, Helena María *Viramontes and others link short stories or vignettes into loosely novelistic form. Other writers such as Joanna *Russ, Sally Gearhart, Ursula *Le Guin, and Gloria *Naylor have turned to speculative fiction—science fiction, fantasy, *mystery, *gothic, or magical realism—to envision new worlds of possibility for women.

All of these works refuse the concept of a univocal, fixed female subjectivity and instead explore women's identities as multiplicitous, polyvocal, fragmented, contradictory, and resistant to coherence. However, some feminist theorists have cautioned that such a view of female subjectivity may foreclose the possibility of political agency for women by denying the power of collective identity and romanticizing madness and marginalization. Likewise, not all postmodern writings celebrate the "po-mo woman." Pamela Zoline's "The Heat Death of the Universe" (1967), for example, uses postmodern techniques to illustrate the domestic

dissatisfaction of a young, white, middle-class housewife named Sarah Boyle who can never remember how many children she has. "Heat Death" consists of fifty-four short sections that are numbered and sometimes titled. Some of the segments are simply words and their definitions, while others narrate Sarah's misguided attempts to create order out of domestic chaos by counting all of the "819 separate, moveable objects" in the living room, writing notes about the nitrogen cycle over the diaper pail, and fantasizing about cleaning the whole universe by scrubbing rocks and deodorizing caves. Sarah finally surrenders to the everpresent disorder of her household by going crazy in a kind of textual madness that disrupts linear syntax and narrative and warns that the fragmentation demanded by consumer culture traps women in an endless cycle of shopping, cleaning, and cooking.

As women writers continue to gain access to both mainstream and alternative presses, it is imperative to define their writing on its own terms. For example, is Leslie Marmon *Silko's "global" novel, *The Almanac of the Dead* (1991), with its non-linear chronology, numerous characters, and interwoven and unresolved stories, a postmodern novel? Similarly, anthologies such as *Resurgent: New Writing by Women* (1992) seek to collect individual and cooperative works lest "women writers be lost to a monolithic idea of the postmodern, as modernist women writers were obscured in their own time." An examination of the connections between these modernists and their postmodern sisters may ultimately reshape the "post" of postmodern in terms of female literary *collaboration rather than male rebellion.

[*See also* Experimental Writing; Fabulation, Feminist; Modernism; Science Fiction.]

Kayann Short

POSTSTRUCTURALISM. The principles that distinguish twentieth-century poststructuralism from the classical epistemology of the Enlightenment are most generally associated with three Frenchmen: psychoanalyst Jacques Lacan (1901–1981), philosopher-historian Michel Foucault (1926–1984), and philosopher Jacques Derrida (b. 1930). The relationship between Enlightenment ideas and poststructuralist tenets can perhaps best be illustrated by the lecture with which Derrida introduced poststructuralism into the United States. Presented at a 1966 conference on structuralism, "Structure, Sign, and Play in the Discourse of the Human Sciences" argued that the founding oppositions by which anthropologist Claude Lévi-Strauss defined structure—between center and margin or inside and outside—were actually not fixed oppositions but momentary stabilizations of the play of differences between and within terms that only seemed to be autonomous. From this, Derrida concluded not only that all apparently self-defining concepts are actually defined relationally, but also that the stabilization of any foundational concept—like center—depends upon the equally conventional stabilization of another concept—in this case margin—which seems to be the derivative term but is not. In so arguing, Derrida both placed his work within the logic of structuralism and overturned its fundamental organizing principles.

The epistemological shift in Derrida's critique of Lévi-Strauss is underwritten by the reconceptualization of language advanced by Ferdinand de Saussure in his *Course on General Linguistics* (1959). Saussure argued that words do not generate meaning by referring to things in a mimetic system of one-to-one correspondences, but relationally, through their similarity to and differences from other words. This non-referential theory of meaning has also facilitated other deconstructions of Enlightenment assumptions. Whereas Enlightenment epistemology considers consciousness and intention to be the origins of meaning and identity, for example, poststructuralist epistemology questions the very concept of origins and suggests that what we define as meaning and *identity are the effects of the conventions by which the play of difference is stabilized so that some signs can be privileged and others overlooked. Similarly, Lacan's claim that the differential system of language constitutes the apparent opposition between consciousness and unconsciousness deconstructs Freud's biologism; Foucault's genealogies of *madness and *sexuality revise teleological histories that chronicle a triumphant campaign of reason against repressive manifestations of power; and Derrida's readings of Western metaphysics expose the artifice by which speech has been assigned priority over writing, presence over absence, and master-text over commentary.

The relationship between poststructuralism and *feminism is as complex as poststructuralism's relationship to the Enlightenment. From one perspective, poststructuralism can be said to undermine feminism, for deconstructing identity deprives feminism of its founding concept—that women, by nature of their biology or experience, have some female identity that gives them common interests. From another perspective, however, feminism can be said to have performed a poststructuralist critique of "mankind" analogous to Derrida's *deconstruction of "structure." U.S. feminists demonstrated in the 1960s and 1970s that "mankind" is not a representative concept but achieves the appearance of universality by repressing the play of difference that privileges "man" by devaluing "woman." This idea has redefined what counts as knowledge in the same way that poststructuralism has revised the foundational logic of Enlightenment epistemology.

U.S. feminists have responded to the challenges of poststructuralism in a variety of ways. Some feminists have been critical of this theoretical turn, arguing, for example, that the fact that poststructuralism's dismantling of the rational subject coincides historically with the ability of increasing numbers of women to attain that subject position suggests that poststructuralism is essentially a strategy for containing women. Others, particularly women of color, have argued that the entire "race for theory," of which poststructuralism is perhaps the most arcane version, deflects attention from new writing by women and falsely attributes to women and people of color a marginality that is actually the effect of a white, masculinist perspective designed to overlook the writing by these groups that already exists. Among those more sympathetic to poststructuralism, some U.S. feminists have applauded the emphasis given to the subversive potential of the "feminine" position or "écriture feminine" identified by French feminists like Hélène Cixous (b. 1937), Luce Irigaray (b. 1939), and Julia Kristeva (b. 1941). Taking up the work of Foucault, some U.S. feminists have argued that sexual identity, which seems to be the basis of *gender, is also a notion only conventionally stabilized from a play of possible behaviors and postures. Other feminists have used poststructuralist strategies to construct histories and to imagine futures for feminism, arguing, for example, that the charge levied in the late 1970s by women of color and lesbians that U.S. feminism achieved its apparent unity by repressing the differences among women means that feminism is itself constituted only by repressing a constitutive play of differences.

Given the historical link between the Enlightenment notions of women's experience and agency and the political movement of feminism in the United States, the problem that must be addressed by every attempt to reconcile poststructuralism and feminism involves the relationships among definition, agency, and action. At one level, this problem surfaces in the repeated efforts to decide whether—or in what sense—men can "be" feminists. At another level, it appears in the theoretically dubious but—many women argue—historically crucial projects of identifying and preserving the contributions women have made to culture and exposing and challenging the disadvantages women experience because we are women. At still another level, it manifests itself whenever the interests of some women—women of color, women of different generations, women with different sexual orientations—conflict with the interests of women "in general." At stake in the problematic conjunction of feminism and poststructuralism are the theoretical and practical bases for women's participation in culture and politics and the usefulness of the concept of "woman."

[*See also* Deconstruction and Feminism; French Feminism; Psychoanalysis and Women, *article on* Jacques Lacan.]

• Michel Foucault, *Power/Knowledge* (1972; reprint, 1980). Jacques Lacan, *Écrits* (1977). Jacques Derrida, *Writing and Difference* (1978). Elaine Marks and Isabelle de Courtivron, eds., *New French Feminisms* (1981). Alice A. Jardine, *Gynesis: Configurations of Woman and Modernity* (1985). Teresa de Lauretis, ed., *Feminist Studies/Critical Studies* (1986). Alice A. Jardine and Paul Smith, eds., *Men in Feminism* (1987). *Feminist Studies* 14, no. 1 (1988). Judith A. Butler, *Gender Trouble* (1990). Joan Scott, "Women's History," in *New Perspectives on Historical Writing*, edited by Peter Burke (1991), pp. 42–66.

Mary Poovey

POUND, Louise (1872–1958), linguist and folklorist. The most prominent woman academician in the United States in the 1920s, Louise Pound was largely responsible for the unprecedented observation and recording of American English and American folkways during the first half of the twentieth century. Although she took her doctorate in Germanic philology at Heidelberg and taught and wrote about earlier periods of English language and literature throughout her career, Pound was always comfortable with her identity as a Nebraskan and an American; she described in hundreds of articles and speeches the regional, colloquial, spontaneous, and proscribed uses of language in the United States. H. L. Mencken, with whom Pound corresponded for more than three decades, acknowledged in his diary and in public tributes that Pound was the central figure in the investigation of American English.

Although Pound was professionally active for over half a century, it was in the 1920s that her scholarly interests and methods for encouraging and developing them coalesced most remarkably. During those years she published her influential *Poetic Origins and the Ballad* (1921); taught summer courses at Berkeley (1923), Yale (1928), and Chicago (1929); supported the founding of the Linguistic Society of America (1924); served as vice-president of the MLA (1925) and president of the American Folklore Society (1925–1927); cofounded (1925) and for five years served as main editor of *American Speech*; represented the United States as one of nine delegates to the International Council for English in London (1927); received an honorary degree from Smith College (1928); and began a long term on the advisory board of *American Literature*. Pound believed in organizations and was a founder, active member, and leader in many, serving as national president of the American Folklore Society, the American Dialect Society, and the Modern Language Association (1956).

Pound was a lifelong resident of Lincoln, Nebraska, where her parents had been among the first settlers. She was the middle child, between Roscoe (later Dean of Harvard Law School) and Olivia (later a Latin teacher and school administrator). The Pound children were taught at home by their mother, Laura Biddlecomb Pound, until they entered the university's two-year preparatory Latin school. At the coeducational state university where she received most of her formal education and taught for fifty years, Pound excelled in everything. An auburn-haired beauty who challenged and defeated the men's tennis champion, Pound was the golden girl of town and gown and inspired the adulation of everyone, including her younger schoolmate Willa *Cather. A woman of quick wit, engaging personality, and enduring friendships, Pound was a popular teacher who generously mentored her own students and others beginning careers, including the novelists Dorothy Canfield *Fisher and Mari Sandoz. Pound's athletic accomplishments led to her election as the first female member of the Nebraska Sports Hall of Fame.

• *Louise Pound*, MS 912, State Archives, Nebraska State Historical Society. See also *Selected Writings of Louise Pound* (1949).

Connie Eble

PREGNANCY. *See* Birth; Midwifery; Reproduction.

PREJUDICE. In current usage, *prejudice* most often designates an a priori judgment about a *gender, *class, *race, nationality, or other social grouping. Such judgments are pejorative and intended as negative prejudgments about capabilities, appearance, likes, or dislikes—anything that might be considered an identifying attribute or quality. Usually prejudices are openly negative, but they can also appear to be complimentary. For example, Victorian society idealized the white woman as "pure" (sexless) and "delicate" (physically and socially incapable). Social *stereotypes are composed of prejudices. Throughout U.S. history, women have been frequent objects of prejudicial statements. Women's intelligence, physical capability, emotional configuration, moral sense, social values, and sexuality have all been degraded in stereotypes that cast women as inferior to men, or women of color as inferior to white women, or capable independent women as threats to the social order.

Whether negative or seemingly positive, prejudice is more than ignorance. It is a belief that persists in spite of substantial evidence to the contrary. The still widely held belief that only men can be serious writers is one example. The existing literature by women, and the substantial recognition it has received in the last three decades, has had no effect on those who are prejudiced against women writers.

Prejudice is a complicated social phenomenon because it reverses our usual sense of cause and effect. For example, in the rationalization of *rape, women who are the recipients of *violence are seen as the cause of the violence done against them: if a woman is raped, it is because she deserved it. The male perpetrator is exonerated as an instrument of social or divine order, or as someone who was victimized by the illicit power of an immoral woman. This reversal of responsibility, which makes criminals innocent and victims guilty, characterizes the structure of prejudice in the U.S. Its origins can be traced to the variation in the explicit meanings of "prejudice" in colonial America.

In the seventeenth-century culture of New England, which strongly influenced the nature of prejudice in later U.S. history, the word *prejudice* also meant prognostication or religious prophecy. In this regard, negative prejudgments take on the quality of prediction, an ability to foretell the future through omens or revelations. Once rooted in religious creeds, prejudice expressed as prophecy actively coerces victims to behave in a way that will confirm the divinely sanctioned prophecy. Prophecy also rationalizes a highly selective choice of "evidence" to buttress prejudice, singling out arbitrary "signs" to predict and confirm the prophecy. For example, when Anne *Hutchinson was condemned and banished as a religious heretic in the Puritan colony of Massachusetts in 1637, this judgment against her was believed to be confirmed when she prematurely gave birth to a stillborn, grossly deformed fetus. This birth was interpreted as the "visible form" of her "misshapen opinions" on religion, a sign from God that proved the truth of the Puritans' judgment against her. Her minister, John Cotton, then predicted that her religious heresy would lead her to become an anarchic "sexual libertine." Such slander of her character, expressed as religious prophecy, typifies the mechanism for rationalizing prejudice against women who dissented from the political and religious opinions of the colony's male leaders. The negative judgments of men like Cotton carried the force of religious sanction, exonerating himself and blaming Hutchinson for the social disorder surrounding the controversy.

Prejudice was also used in the colonial U.S. as a verb meaning to enact material harm or injury to property or person. That is, prejudice not only resulted in acts of violent punishment that were sanctioned by religion; it also referred to the act of violence itself.

The link between social attitudes and physical harm, as well as the vindication of those who commit acts of violence, make it difficult to counteract prejudice. The documentation of violence in and of itself does not necessarily lessen prejudice in social attitudes. In documenting violent attacks on women such as rape, the violence of the deed is taken by feminists as self-evident proof of unjust social practice. However, for the prejudiced interpreter, the same documentation of violence results in the opposite conclusion: it is taken as sure evidence that the prejudice is true, a sanctioned act that simultaneously exposes and punishes the sins of female sexuality. Contemporary literature that addresses prejudice overtly, such as *This Bridge Called My Back* (1981), edited by Cherríe *Moraga and Gloria *Anzaldúa, not only documents violence against women but also engages the complex systems of interpretation that have assigned significance to those acts in differing and contradictory ways.

[*See also* Racism; Sexism; Homophobia.]

• Darrett B. Rutman, *Winthrop's Boston* (1965). David D. Hall, ed., *The Antinomian Controversy, 1636–1638* (1968). Ann Kibbey, *The Interpretation of Material Shapes in Puritanism* (1986).

Ann Kibbey

PRE-OEDIPAL STAGE. *See* Psychoanalysis and Women.

PRESSES, Women's. Since 1969, feminist presses have played an integral role in the establishment of feminist political movements in the United States. In 1978, Polly Joan and Andrea Chesman remarked, "More than any other movement in history, Feminism [has] been identified with publishing" (*Guide to Women's Publishing*, 1978). Given the suppression of women's words by traditional print and visual media, early *women's rights *activists eagerly gained access to whatever print technology was available, from mimeograph machines to letterpresses to offset printers. In fact, many early feminist presses, such as Diana Press, the Aunt Lute Book Company, and New Victoria Publishers, grew out of women's cooperative print shops. As Know, Inc., one of the first feminist presses in the United States, proclaimed: "Freedom of the Press Belongs to Those Who Own the Press!"

Despite a shared commitment to producing and distributing works by and about women, the early feminist presses chose diverse strategies to accomplish these goals. The first U.S. feminist publisher, Shameless Hussy Press, began in 1969 by printing the poems of its founder, *Griffin and Lyn Lyfshin, followed by an English translation of French writer George Sand and Ntozake *Shange's revolutionary play, *for colored girls who have considered suicide/when the rainbow is enuf.* In the same year, Know, Inc. was founded by nineteen Pittsburgh National Organization for Women members (NOW itself was then only three years old) to publish pamphlet reprints of essays, articles, and research studies, which sold for 10¢ to $1.00. The non-profit volunteer group later became a collective, publishing one or two non-fiction books a year, as well as five poetry volumes in 1974.

Also founded as a non-profit organization, The Feminist Press, the oldest U.S. feminist press still publishing today, is an educational press devoted to publishing texts for classroom use, including reprints of important nineteenth- and early twentieth-century fiction such as Charlotte Perkin *Gilman's *The Yellow Wallpaper,* Agnes *Smedley's *Daughter of Earth,* and Rebecca Harding *Davis's *Life in the Iron Mills.* They have also published nonsexist children's books, the *Women's Studies Quarterly,* educational curricula, biographies, and, most recently, anthologies of works by international women writers. Editor and co-founder Florence Howe attributes the continuing success of the Feminist Press to their twenty-year commitment to *multicultural scholarship with works such as the black women's studies collection, *All the Women Are White, All the Blacks Are Men, But Some of Us Are Brave* (1982).

The first book published by another early feminist press, the Women's Press Collective of Oakland, California, was produced on a mimeograph machine. *Woman to Woman* (1970), a lavender-paged collection of poems and drawings by women, was sold out of shopping bags until a donor contributed $500 to buy an antiquated offset press on which they printed Judy *Grahn's *Edward the Dyke* (1971). Even with the purchase of this equipment, many of the jobs such as collating and stapling were still done by hand, volunteer work that demanded "lots of spaghetti and coffee" (*Sinister Wisdom* 1, no. 2, Fall 1976).

Another early press, the Aunt Lute Book Company, began in 1972 as the Iowa City Women's Press, a lesbian press collective, and

survives today as a nonprofit educational foundation, publishing books such as Gloria *Anzaldúa's anthology of writing by women of color, *Making Face, Making Soul/Haciendo Caras* (1990). The Iowa City Women's Press was already publishing manuals on auto-mechanics and carpentry for women when members Joan Pinkvoss and Barb Wieser established the Aunt Lute Book Company as the press's publishing branch in 1982, increasing their book list with a novel and an anthology. Meanwhile, in 1978 Judith McDaniel and Maureen Brady founded Spinsters, Inc., in Argyle, New York, to provide women writers with an alternative to commercial publishers, beginning with their own works, Brady's novel *Give Me Your Good Ear* (1979) and McDaniel's critical essay on poet Adrienne *Rich. In 1983, Spinsters moved to San Francisco with a new editor, Sherry Thomas, and in 1986, merged with Aunt Lute, bringing together 28 feminist books that, according to an early mailing, were "so ahead of their times they will never sell out at Crown Books, or reach the *New York Times* bestseller list." In 1990, Aunt Lute and Spinsters separated into not-for-profit and for-profit entities, respectively, and in 1992, Sherry Thomas sold Spinsters Ink to Joan Drury, who moved the press to Minneapolis. Both presses maintain their tradition of publishing successful and innovative feminist books.

Another successful feminist press that began as a print shop in 1972 was Diana Press, Inc. Founded by a group of Baltimore *working-class women, Diana began with a 25-year-old Multilith 1250 and used profits to buy additional equipment. In late 1972, Rita Mae *Brown approached Diana with $300 for paper if the press would invest the labor to print 2,000 copies of her poems, *Songs for a Handsome Woman.* With women fronting their labor, the press continued to print several books a year. In early 1977, Diana moved to Oakland to join the Women's Press Collective in publishing a combined list of 11 books. On 25 October 1977, the press offices were vandalized. Paint, ink, and cleanser were poured into the presses, negatives and cover plates were ruined and typesetting was ripped up page by page. With both backlist and forthcoming books destroyed, including 5,000 copies of Rita Mae Brown's *A Plain Brown Rapper,* the press closed down its publishing program and established itself exclusively as a print shop in 1978. The demise of Diana was felt as a tremendous blow throughout the feminist print network.

Another influential feminist press established in 1972 was Daughters, Inc., originally based in Vermont, founded by June *Arnold and Parke Bowman to publish feminist-lesbian novels. In a controversial move, Daughters achieved commercial success by licensing mass-market paperback rights for one of their first novels, *Rubyfruit Jungle* by Rita Mae Brown, to Bantam Books for $750,000. By allowing the male literary establishment to make money from women's writing, many feminists felt that Daughters was breaking its commitment to work only with and for women. Daughters also published other groundbreaking novels, including Arnold's *Sister Gin* (1975), Bertha Harris's *lover* (1976), and a reprint of Penelope Mortimer's 1962 *The Pumpkin Eaters*, works that, according to Arnold, "are trying to shape a new tool for new uses, to reclaim language for ourselves with a very strong sense that we have been divided from it" (*Sinister Wisdom* 1, no. 2, Fall 1976).

Throughout the 1970s, feminist and lesbian presses were established to publish books for women that the mainstream presses would not consider. Some of these, such as Out and Out Books of Brooklyn, Metis and Womanpress of Chicago, Moon Books in Berkeley, and Persephone Press of Watertown, Massachusetts, are no longer in operation, yet all published works that were important to the establishment of feminist movements. Persephone Press, founded in 1976, was particularly legendary, not only for publishing best-sellers such as *This Bridge Called My Back* (1981) and *Nice Jewish Girls* (1982), but also for its above-industry royalties and lavish receptions. Like Diana Press's demise, Persephone's sudden closing in 1983 sent shockwaves throughout feminist communities.

However, other presses established in the 1970s continue to thrive. Naiad Press, formed in 1973, is the largest lesbian press today with nearly 200 titles in print. Alicejames books in Cambridge, Massachusetts, Eighth Mountain Press in Portland, Oregon, and Kelsey St. Press in Berkeley, California, continue to publish quality poetry and fiction by women. Seal Press, founded in Seattle in 1976 as a regional press for Northwestern women, is today recognized as an international leader in feminist books with its imprint, Women in Translation, now established as a separate, nonprofit press. Seal continues to publish groundbreaking works such as *Getting Free* (1982) and *The Black Women's Health Book* (1990), as well as important fiction and poetry.

Despite increased access for feminists to mainstream and academic publishing during the 1980s, the development of feminist presses continued throughout the decade as more and more readers supported their work. These presses expanded the groundwork laid by earlier presses by printing the words of women who were still denied a voice in both mainstream and alternative presses.

Kitchen Table: Women of Color Press, collectively formed in 1981, is devoted to publishing work that "is committed to producing and distributing the work of Third World women of all racial/cultural heritages, sexualities, and classes that will further the cause of Third World women's personal and political freedom." In addition to publishing poetry and fiction by individual writers, Kitchen Table published the anthologies *This Bridge Called My Back* (1983), with 75,000 copies now in print; *Cuentos: Stories by Latinas* (1983); and *Home Girls: A Black Feminist Anthology* (1983). They also published the Freedom Organizing Pamphlet Series, including the classic articulation of black feminist theory, "The Combahee River Collective Statement." According to publisher Barbara Smith, a Kitchen Table publication is chosen "not simply because it is by a woman of color, but because it consciously examines, from a positive and original perspective, the specific situation and issues that women of color face" (*Frontiers* 10, 1989).

Cleis Press, founded in 1980 and run bicoastally by Felice Newman in Pittsburgh and Frédérique Delacoste in San Francisco, has proven its dedication to "documenting women's resistance to oppression" by publishing books such as *AIDS: The Women* (1988), *The Power of Each Breath: A Disabled Women's Anthology* (1986) and *Sex Work: Writings by Women in the Sex Industry* (1987). Firebrand Press in Ithaca, New York, and Calyx Books in Corvalis, Oregon, both founded in the mid-1980s, also maintain a proven commitment to publishing writing by women of color, Jewish women, lesbians, older women, and working-class women. With its entire list of over fifty books still in print, Firebrand publishes books for a truly diverse community of women. Calyx Books follows the fine literary and artistic work begun by the journal *Calyx* in 1976. A non-profit organization, Calyx was the first feminist press to receive an NEA Advancement grant.

As feminist publishing survives into the 1990s, these presses are joined by numerous others, including Womyn's Braille Press (Minneapolis), Silverleaf (Seattle), Herbooks (Santa Cruz), Third Woman (Berkeley), Volcano (California), Chicory Blue (Connecticut), Mother Courage (Wisconsin), Sidewalk Revolution (Pittsburgh), Frog in the Well (San Francisco), Timely Books (Tennessee), ism (San Francisco), down there (California), Rising Tide (New York), Third Side (Chicago), and Crone's Own (North Carolina), in continuing the commitment to feminist politics initiated a quarter of a century ago. Given the capital-intensive nature of publishing, where production costs must be paid months before any sales revenue is received, a major challenge faced by all feminist presses today is finding the money to keep their backlists in print, for, unlike mainstream presses, feminist presses have a commitment to publishing books that are timely rather than trendy, books that will serve the ongoing needs of feminist and lesbian communities.

Feminist presses today have learned that they must integrate their political goals with astute business practices. To meet their cash flow problems, feminist presses have employed a variety of strategies, from nonprofit status and volunteer work to bank loans and private fundraising, to obtain the money necessary to thrive in difficult political and economic climates. More than any other source, however, the survival of feminist presses depends upon the support of a network of feminist readers reviewing, teaching, and buying their books.

[See also Authorship; Bookstores; Publishing Business.]

Kayann Short

PRISON WRITING. Women as subjects and authors of trial transcripts, confessions, * letters, * diaries, prison narratives and autobiographies, poems, and fictionalized accounts of imprisonment offer an understanding of American society that begins with the legal records of the prosecution of such women as Mary Dyer, Anne * Hutchinson, and the victims of the Salem * witchcraft trials.

The nineteenth century provides a surprising number of women's prison narratives. Several, including those of Rose Greenhow (1863) and Belle Boyd (1865), imprisoned as Confederate spies in the Old Capitol Prison in Washington, D.C., can be found in the American Culture Series (ACS). As Estelle Freedman explains (Their Sisters' Keepers: Women's Prison Reform in America, 1830–1930, 1981), the nineteenth century saw the creation of a class of women prison keepers; these women, from Sing Sing matrons Eliza Farnham and Georgiana Bruce Kirby (Years of Experience, 1887), to Caroline H. Wood (Woman in Prison, 1869, ACS), to twentieth-century official Mary B. Harris (I Knew Them in Prison, 1934), offer valuable material about themselves and their prisoners. Another nineteenth-century dynamic is the complex relationship of * narratives of captivity, imprisonment, and slavery, demonstrated most clearly in Harriet * Jacobs's Incidents in the Life of a Slave Girl (1861), a central text in H. Bruce Franklin's seminal discussion in The Victim as Criminal and Artist (1978).

The twentieth century offers autobiographi-

cal accounts of many women arrested for radical causes; among them are Emma * Goldman (Living My Life, 1931), Elizabeth Gurley Flynn (The Alderson Story, 1963), Kate Richards O'Hare (In Prison, 1920 and after), Tillie * Olsen ("Thousand Dollar Vagrant," 1934), Margaret Sanger (An Autobiography, 1938), and Agnes * Smedley ("Cell Mates," 1920). Ethel Rosenberg, executed with her husband for treason in 1953, left behind court transcripts and the letters she and her husband wrote during their ordeal. The 1960s produced accounts by civil rights activists; among the best known are Joan Baez's Daybreak (1968), Sally Belfrage's Freedom Summer (1965), and Barbara Deming's Prison Notes (1966, reprinted with other work in 1984 as Prisons That Could Not Hold). "Indians of All Tribes," claiming the island of Alcatraz as a center for Native Americans in 1969, saw the actual prison as the most fit symbolic expression of the treatment of Native Americans, and Janet Campbell Hale makes a similar argument in her novel The Jailing of Cecelia Capture (1985). If They Come in the Morning: Voices of Resistance (1971), by Angela * Davis "and other political prisoners" including poet Ericka Huggins, is a revolutionary account of Davis's case and a background of conflict and repression, including the history of the Black Panther Party. Davis also writes about her imprisonments in Angela Davis: An Autobiography (1974).

Although Tillie Olsen reported in Silences (1978) that women were overlooked even in areas that traditionally recovered the voices of the ordinary and the oppressed, the situation has been changing. The 1984 anthology The Light from Another Country: Poetry from American Prisons (edited by Joseph Bruchac) contains work by seven women—Carolyn Baxter, Diana Bickston, Yasmeen Jamal, Lorri Martinez, Michele Roberts, Jessica Scarbrough, and Terri Meyette Wilkins—and dozens of poets are represented in the anthologies and journals (Poppy, Prison Writing Review) published by prison writing groups. Jean Harris, convicted of murder and confined in the Bedford Hills Correctional Facility in New York, followed her They Always Call Us Ladies: Stories from Prison (1990) with a 1992 series of letters to journalist Shana Alexander. Patricia McConnel's 1989 Sing Soft, Sing Loud collects her autobiographical stories about women in prison; Katherine Dunn's short novel Attic (1969, republished 1990) is an antecedent.

Judith Scheffler's Wall Tappings: An Anthology of Writings by Women Prisoners (1986), not limited to American writers, offers an introduction to secondary works as well as an annotated bibliography of primary sources and a thematic anthology of readings. Scheffler omits accounts of the experience of Japanese Americans "interned" in concentration camps during World War II, which could easily be included in considerations of American imprisonment. Today most prison writers are still "celebrity" inmates, but the field offers many opportunities for research into the lives and works of American women such as "Girl Delinquent. Age Sixteen. An Undecorated Autobiography" (*Harper's*, 1932). In such works, the dominant culture's commitment to literacy ensures, albeit problematically, the survival of voices that would otherwise go uncaptured.

• David D. Hall, ed., *The Antinomian Controversy, 1636–1638: A Documentary History* (1968). Paul Boyer and Stephen Nissenbaum, eds., *The Salem Witchcraft Papers: Verbatim Transcripts of the Legal Documents of the Salem Witchcraft Outbreak of 1692* (1977). Him Mark Lai, Genny Lim, and Judy Yung, *Island. Poetry and History of Chinese Immigrants on Angel Island, 1910–1940* (1980). H. Bruce Franklin, *American Prisoners and Ex-Prisoners: Their Writings. An Annotated Bibliography of Published Works* (1982). Nicole Hahn Rafter, *Partial Justice: Women in State Prisons 1800–1935* (1985). Russell P. Dobash, R. Emerson Dobash, and Sue Gutteridge, *The Imprisonment of Women* (1986). Jolene Babyak, *Eyewitness on Alcatraz: Interviews with Guards, Familes and Prisoners Who Lived on THE ROCK* (1988). Ann M. Butler, "Still in Chains: Black Women in Western Prisons, 1865–1910," *The Western Historical Quarterly* 20, no. 1 (February 1989): 19–35. Barbara Harlow, *Barred: Women, Writing, and Political Detention* (1992).

Kathleen Burrage

PRO-CHOICE. *See* Abortion; Birth Control; Reproduction.

PROGRESSIVE ERA WRITING. The period in United States history commonly referred to as the Progressive Era, the last decade of the nineteenth century and first two to two-and-a-half decades of the twentieth, witnesses an extraordinary production of literature by women. Writing and publishing fiction during these years were Frances Ellen *Harper, Charlotte Perkins *Gilman, Alice *Dunbar-Nelson, Kate *Chopin, Amelia Johnson, Emma Kelley-Hawkins, Sarah Orne *Jewett, Pauline *Hopkins, *Zitkala-Ša, Edith *Wharton, Mary *Austin, Ellen *Glasgow, Gertrude *Stein, *Sui Sin Far, Onoto *Watanna, Willa *Cather, María Cristina Mena, Jessie Redmon *Fauset, Anzia *Yezierska, Edith Summers *Kelley, and Nella *Larsen. Heralding this period were writers in the 1870s and 1880s such as Elizabeth Stuart *Phelps, author of the middle-class white feminist novel about a woman artist, *The Story of Avis* (1877), and María Amparo Ruiz de Burton, author of the long political novel about the Mexican-American struggle for civil and property rights in California, *The Squatter and the Don* (1885). Just after this period came the work of such writers as Zora Neale *Hurston, who published her most famous novel, *Their Eyes Were Watching God*, in 1937, and Tillie *Olsen, whose novel *Yonnondio* was conceived in the 1930s, although it was not published until the 1970s.

Novels and collections of fiction by women at the turn of the century include a remarkable number of titles now regarded as among the most important in United States literary history. Representative texts include *Iola Leroy* (1892), "The Yellow Wallpaper" (1892), *The Country of the Pointed Firs* (1896), *The Goodness of St. Rocque* (1899), *The Awakening* (1899), *Contending Forces* (1900), *Old Indian Legends* (1901), *Of One Blood* (1902), *The Land of Little Rain* (1903), *The House of Mirth* (1905), *Three Lives* (1905–6), *Ethan Frome* (1911), *Mrs. Spring Fragrance* (1912), *O Pioneers!* (1913), "The Vine-Leaf" (1914), *Herland* (1915), *My Ántonia* (1918), *Hungry Hearts* (1920), *The Age of Innocence* (1920), *American Indian Stories* (1921), *Barren Ground* (1925), *Bread-Giver* (1925), *Cogewea* (1927), *Death Comes for the Archbishop* (1927), *Plum Bun* (1929), *Quicksand* (1928) and *Passing* (1929). Grouped, these titles (plus others) suggest an impressive, complicated body of work that is now beginning to be understood collectively. Literary production by women at the turn of the century indicates that the period was, for women, unusually hospitable. Conditions were particularly favorable to women writers with serious artistic and, in many cases, fused artistic/political ambitions, as is obvious from work by writers otherwise as different, for example, as Harper and Stein or Gilman and Zitkala-Ša.

However, to say that the turn of the century was a period in which United States women writers flourished is not to say that all women writers at the time enjoyed the same encouragement, prosperity, or success. Privileged white writers such as Edith Wharton, Ellen Glasgow, and Willa Cather were able to devote their lives to writing and publishing. Their novels sold well, in a number of instances becoming bestsellers, and their work was frequently singled out and praised for its artistic excellence. *Race and *class privilege offered no protection against hostile criticism for some white writers, as Kate Chopin's career demonstrates; but for many, building on a half century of successful authorship by white middle-class women, the turn of the century represented an era of remarkable opportunity. When the well-known literary critic Fred Lewis Pattee asked a group of readers in 1929 to name the "best"

American writers (regardless of *gender), the two figures who emerged at the top of the list were Edith Wharton and Willa Cather.

*Racism and ethnic discrimination created a quite different environment for turn-of-the-century women writers who were women of color. Pauline Hopkins, wishing to write primarily for fellow African-Americans, devoted incredible labor to editing the *Colored American Magazine,* which served as the outlet for most of her fiction, only to have her career virtually end when that journal changed ownership and moved from Boston to New York. The struggles of other African-American authors—Dunbar-Nelson's inability to get a novel published or Fauset's frustration with white editors' preconceptions of what black fiction "should" be like—testify to the difficulties of writing and publishing in a racist culture. Likewise, major obstacles faced *Native American writers such as *Humishuma, whose white collaborator both aided and altered her work, and *Asian-American authors such as Sui Sin Far and her sister Winnifred Eaton, the first of whom chronicled white abuse of Chinese Americans in her stories and the second of whom responded to virulent anti-Chinese discrimination by writing under the fake Japanese name Onoto *Watanna. One important theme in any discussion of turn-of-the-century women writers is the disparity between the situation of white women writers and writers who were women of color.

Yet if class, racial, and ethnic differences divide women writers of the Progressive Era, it is also true that serious fiction by U.S. women writers at the turn of the century forms a coherent body of work. Almost all of the writers named in this article, as well as many others, shared a number of perspectives. Their fiction shows them consciously concerned with issues of gender and silencing; questions of narrative form; the figure of the woman artist; the desire for connection with the world of one's mother, even as one journeyed farther and farther from that world into new territory; and the struggle with how to write one's presence into a tradition in many respects and for various reasons hostile to that presence. Texts as dissimilar as *The Country of the Pointed Firs, Of One Blood, The Age of Innocence, Me,* "The Vine-Leaf," and *American Indian Stories*—by writers as dissimilar as Sarah Orne Jewett, Pauline Hopkins, Edith Wharton, Onoto Watanna, María Cristina Mena, and Zitkala-Ša—speak to the constellation of issues named above. Repeatedly and perhaps most important, many women writers at the turn of the century—across all divisions of race and class—were determined to constitute themselves not just as writers but as artists, as creators entitled to full and equal voice with men in United States culture.

Supporting this changed attitude among women writers at the turn of the century were a number of social, economic, and political developments, many of which converged in the surge of vitality in *women's movements in the 1890s and the first two decades of the twentieth century. The campaign for women's suffrage, the possibility for more and higher *education, the accelerating power of the temperance movement, the proliferation of women's clubs, the participation of women in founding *civil rights organizations such as the NAACP or the Society of American Indians, the increasing success of dress reform and the growing social acceptance of the idea of *birth control: all reflected and produced a climate of female empowerment and struggle that, whether recognized by a given author or not, encouraged and promoted the work of women writers. For different individuals and for different groups of writers, the social and political realities could, to be sure, differ dramatically. But for women in general, the turn of the century represented a period of intense feminist agitation and contest, and that climate of challenge and change, then as now, both fostered and was reflected in the work of a significant number of artistically ambitious women writers from diverse backgrounds.

No one factor accounts for the relative decline in literary production by women after the 1920s, with women writers as a group not emerging in force again until the late 1960s and early 1970s. Certainly a major contributing factor, however, was the subsidence in widespread women's movements following the First World War and the accompanying resurgence in conservative ideologies about women. One thing that the vitality and brilliance of women's literary production at the turn of the century seems to illustrate is the crucial connection between political agitation and empowerment and art.

[*See also* Industrialization.]

• Hazel V. Carby, *Reconstructing Womanhood: The Emergence of the Afro-American Woman Novelist* (1987). Josephine Donovan, *After the Fall: The Demeter-Persephone Myth in Wharton, Cather, and Glasgow* (1989). Amy Ling, *Between Worlds: Women Writers of Chinese Ancestry* (1990). Elizabeth Ammons, *Conflicting Stories: American Women Writers at the Turn into the Twentieth Century* (1991). Claudia Tate, *Domestic Allegories of Political Desire: The Black Heroine's Text at the Turn of the Century* (1992).

Elizabeth Ammons

PROLETARIAN WRITING includes revolutionary *novels, *poetry, *reportage and theory produced primarily during the Great Depression era (1928–1940). Proletarian writing is specifically concerned with depicting workers' lives and class struggle, often through realist or documentary representations of factory and domestic labor, industrial strikes, racial *prejudice, *working-class militancy, middle-class decay, and "conversions" to communism. While the emergence of American proletarianism in the late 1920s was largely an emulation of the Soviet Union's official revolutionary aesthetic *(Proletcult)*, earlier incarnations of social critique by American women writers set the stage for a women's radical tradition in the United States. Works that anticipate some of the concerns of proletarian writers include Rebecca Harding *Davis's reformist depiction of "Life in the Iron Mills" (1861); the explicitly revolutionary political expression of turn-of-the-century radical Emma *Goldman; and the early-twentieth-century socialist writings of Charlotte Perkins *Gilman, Susan *Glaspell, and Vida Scudder.

Women's proletarian writing in the United States emerged in the distinctly masculine climate of the literary and political Left. Michael Gold's 1929 editorial "Go Left, Young Writers" described the new writer of proletarian literature as "a wild youth ... the son of working class parents, who himself works in the lumber camps, coal mines and steel mills ... he writes in jets of exasperated feeling and has not time to polish his work" (*New Masses*, January 1929). As Paula Rabinowitz notes in *Labor and Desire*, Gold's "equation of literary and political vitality with masculinity" excludes the possibility that any of these new writers might be women. In fact, radical women's literature actually pioneered some the generic conventions that became prototypically proletarian. The development of the strike plot is the most significant example: four of the six earliest strike novels, based on the dramatic events of a labor dispute at a textile mill in Gastonia, North Carolina, were written by women (Mary Heaton Vorse, *Strike!;* Fielding *Burke, *Call Home the Heart;* Grace Lumpkin, *To Make My Bread;* Myra Page, *Gathering Storm*). In his classic study of American revolutionary fiction *The Radical Novel in the United States* (1956), Walter Rideout implies women writers' ease within proletarian conventions by noting the receipt of Clara Weatherwax's novel *Marching! Marching!* of the 1935 *New Masses* prize for new novel on a proletarian theme; he called it the archetype of "doctrinal" proletarian fiction. Evelyn *Scott's novel *Calendar of Sin* (1931) is similarly emblematic of the proletarian theme of bourgeois decline.

Despite women writers' contribution to classic proletarian themes like the strike plot, working-class militancy, and middle-class decay, feminist critics have suggested that radical women writers disrupt, deform, and expand such conventions by introducing subject matter informed by *gender. *Short stories, novels, poems, non-fiction prose, and autobiographies by proletarian women writers explore themes specific to working-class female experience: the hardships of domestic labor and the "double day," gender-segregated labor pools, sexist unions, *sexual harassment in the factory, and the trivializing of women's issues (including domestic *violence, prostitution, *rape, *birth control, and *abortion) in Communist party policy. Women's depiction of unegalitarian relationships between working-class men and women in factories and families problematizes the proletarian fantasy of an ideal collectivity amongst workers and challenges the widespread critical assumption that proletarian literature is uniformly formulaic in its celebration of a perfectly homogenized class solidarity.

Since *class, rather than gender, was privileged as the central category of political difference by the (male) theoreticians of proletarian culture, women writers who addressed the specificity of female experience within that culture were vulnerable to the critique of being "suffragettes," belatedly caught up in middle-class reformist (rather than revolutionary) sentiment. In the Communist Party of the United States of America, *feminism was associated with the decadent, sexual bohemianism of the 1920s, while the proletarians' rejection of "personal" and transhistorical "aesthetics" in favor of socially engaged and collectively oriented cultural "work" relied on a logic that gendered the former feminine and the latter masculine. The feminization of allegedly bourgeois writing practices (such as the *domestic novel and experimental, modern poetry) by male theorists of proletarian writing betrays a skepticism about women's ability to write as historical subjects and agents of political change. The association of bourgeois values with a politically inert "feminine" sphere is perhaps most obviously articulated by Maxwell Bodenheim's poem "To a Revolutionary Girl," but appears in the writings of radical women as well as men, as evidenced by Muriel *Rukeyser's poem "More of a Corpse Than a Woman" and Lucia Trent's "Lady in a Limousine."

While most radical women writers followed Rukeyser's directive "Not Sappho, Sacco," regarding revolutionary subject matter, their attention to female experience in working-class life revised the traditional assumptions and priorities of proletarianism. Barbara Foley in

"Women and the Left in the Thirties" has suggested that, far from being anticollectivist, women's radical fiction actually produced "a proletarian heroism that is a good deal more communist and less bourgeois" than that of individualist male protagonists in men's novels; Meridel * Le Sueur's *The Girl* (1972) suggests the bond between mothers and children as the archetypal experience of communality, while "Stockyard Stella" (1935), a serialized novel written by several women workers, achieved a literal collectivization of the author function. Tillie * Olsen's *Yonnondio* (1974) and Ramona Lowe's "Woman in the Window" (1940) depict maternity and child rearing as political action rather than as biological destiny, emphasizing that comrades are made by mothers rather than merely reproduced by female bodies. Many radical women writers link the experience of women in the patriarchal family to that of workers under capitalism; in Agnes * Smedley's *Daughter of Earth* (1929) and Burke's *Call Home the Heart*, the protagonist's "conversion" to communism is premised upon her rebellion against a repressive household, while, in Le Sueur and Olsen, women's class consciousness is catalyzed by the experience of marital violence and sexual brutality. Black women writing in the proletarian tradition further refocus the genre; Lucille Boehm ("Two-Bit Piece," 1939) and Marita Bonner * Occomy ("The Whipping," 1939) explore the institutionalized poverty of black women, Ramona Lowe ("The Woman in the Window") writes about the commodification of black motherhood for white consumption and profit, and Elizabeth Thomas ("Our House," 1939) suggests the historically alienated nature of African-American labor.

The rearticulation of "standard" proletarian tropes (such as collectivism, unionism, communist conversion, and heroism) in the context of women's issues (such as child rearing, * patriarchy, and * sexual violence) does more than reject or "add-a-woman" to masculinist conventions; by extending proletarianism's radical critique to capitalism's social relations, women writers offer a corrective to the movement's privileging of economic production. Proletarian feminist theorists who challenge the reductive distinction between base and superstructure by examining the relationship between women's oppression and capitalism include Grace Hutchin (*Women Who Work*, 1935), Mary Inman (*In Women's Defense*, 1939), Rebecca Pitts ("Women and Communism," 1935), and Margaret Cowl ("We Must Win the Women," 1937). Women * journalists also revised and enriched the proletarian "urge to document" by recording women's lives in both capitalist and communist nations; those who traveled internationally include Josephine * Herbst (Cuba), Agnes Smedley (China), Anna Louise Strong (China/Spain), Ruth Gruber (Soviet Union), and Ella Winter (Soviet Union).

While it is impossible to provide a complete list, other proletarian women novelists, poets, theorists, and journalists who have not been mentioned above include Tess * Slesinger, Josephine Johnson, Myra Page, Genevieve Taggard, Margaret * Walker, Joy Davidman, Aunt Molly Jackson, Leane Zugsmith, Peggy Dennis, Dorothy * Day, Lauren Gilfillan, Ruth Lechlitner, and Ruth McKenney.

[*See also* Working-class Fiction; Class; Industrialization.]

• Paul Lauter, "Working-Class Women's Literature: An Introduction to Its Study," *Radical Teacher* 15 (1979): 16–26. Deborah Rosenfelt, "From the Thirties: Tillie Olsen and the Radical Tradition," *Feminist Studies* 7 (Fall 1981): 370–406. Alice Kessler-Harris and Paul Lauter, Introduction to *Call Home the Heart* by Fielding Burke (1985). Candida Ann Lacey, "Striking Fictions: Women Writers and the Making of a Proletarian Realism," *Women's Studies International Forum* 9, no. 4 (1986): 373–384. Deborah Rosenfelt, "Getting into the Game: American Women Writers and the Radical Tradition," *Women's Studies International Forum* 9, no. 4 (1986): 63–371. Charlotte Nekola and Paula Rabinowitz, eds., *Writing Red: An Anthology of American Women Writers* (1987). Barbara Foley, "Women and the Left in the Thirties," *American Literary History* 2 (Summer 1990): 150–169. Paula Rabinowitz, *Labor and Desire: Women's Revolutionary Fiction in Depression America* (1991). Barbara Foley, *Radical Representations: Politics and Form in U.S. Proletarian Fiction* (1994).

Jane C. Penner

PROPHESYINGS. Prophesying in the seventeenth century, as defined by the *Oxford English Dictionary*, was the act of speaking by divine inspiration, foretelling the future, or preaching to edify. The history of women's prophesyings in the United States traces back to Anne * Hutchinson and the * Antinomian controversy of 1636–1638. Hutchinson, a midwife and spiritual counselor of the Massachusetts Bay Colony, held informal biweekly meetings in her home to discuss spiritual matters. These meetings, attended largely by women, were tolerated by the Puritan ministers until she challenged their theology. Preaching a "covenant of grace," Hutchinson spoke of divine revelation and of hearing the inner voice of God, whereas her judges insisted that the Age of Prophesy had ended. A Synod of Elders met in 1637 and resolved that women could meet "to pray and edify one another," yet if any woman "in a prophetical way" began to expound on scripture or doctrine, the meeting would be disorderly and unlawful. Hutchinson was then brought to trial for her meetings and her prophesyings. Although she professed self-abnegation and the language of Christ speaking through her, the ministers perceived the woman asserting herself all the more vigorously. She was excommunicated from the church and banished from the colony, with many of her supporters following her.

Women's prophesyings had been much more common in England, particularly during the Interregnum when many women spoke at public gatherings and over 300 female visionaries published their prophetic writings. About 220 women of this literary group were Quakers, a religious sect believing that all people are equal "in the way of prophesy." As a result of such equality, women were the first Quakers to preach in London, Oxford, Cambridge, and finally, the New World. They began traveling to the Massachusetts Bay Colony in 1656 to prophesy and distribute their publications. Often, they were stripped and abusively searched for signs of *witchcraft, if not whipped or physically mutilated; always, they were fined or imprisoned, while their "heretical" tracts were burned publicly in the marketplace. As more and more Quakers arrived in Boston, the General Court levied fines against colonists who defended or secretly lodged Quakers and any Puritans who possessed Quaker literature. Yet the women did not stop their prophesying because of this harsh treatment. As Quakers, perceiving the body as the sacred vessel of divine revelation, several women went naked as a sign, while others appeared in sackcloth and ashes in the Puritan towns. Despite patriarchal opposition, they continued to preach at illegally held meetings, where they widely distributed their literature. Among the women returning to Boston as converted Quakers were Hutchinson's sister, Catherine Scott, and her Antinomian supporter, Mary Dyer; in 1660, Dyer became the only Quaker woman ever executed by the Puritan authorities.

These women expanded the boundaries of gender and prophecy in the New World. Challenging its lack of spiritual, sexual, or social toleration, they persisted in spreading their beliefs and thus ever increased the power of lay prophecy and the meaning of women's voices in colonial America.

• David D. Hall, ed., *The Antinomian Controversy, 1636–1638* (1968). Margaret Hope Bacon, *Mothers of Feminism: The Study of Quaker Women in America* (1969). Keith Thomas, *Religion and the Decline of Magic* (1971). Lyle Koehler, *A Search for Power: The "Weaker Sex" in Seventeenth-Century New England* (1980). Phyllis Mack, *Visionary Women* (1992).

Michele Lise Tarter

PROTESTANTISM. When Celie in Alice *Walker's *The Color Purple* (1982) writes letters to God because she feels unable to pray, she demonstrates a key sensibility among women in American Protestant culture. Although tradition effectively excluded women from doctrinal and homiletic writing until quite recently, Protestantism's theological commitment to each individual's divine calling, to personal interpretation of Scripture, and to institutional reform has empowered women to cast their religious visions in more secular forms of expression. American women writers have therefore stood in a reciprocal relationship to Protestant traditions, exerting profound pressures on religious doctrine and practice, but also absorbing elements of Protestantism into literary forms that have increasingly distanced themselves from orthodoxy.

The various manifestations of Calvinism that characterized pre-Revolutionary America encouraged religious self-scrutiny, but placed strict limits on self-expression, particularly for women. When Anne *Hutchinson advocated, at home meetings and then publicly, a relationship to Christ unmediated by the outer forms of Visible Sainthood, or good works, she was banished according to the biblical admonition "Let your women keep silence in the churches" (1 Corinthians 14: 34). However, Massachusetts allowed space for the poet Anne *Bradstreet to subtly negotiate her own Puritan experience— one ambivalent toward "vanity," satirical of disembodied spirit, and attuned to the idiosyncrasies of an American landscape quite apart from John Winthrop's millenarian injunction to be "as a city upon a hill." Hutchinson and Bradstreet form the foundation of a tradition of women in the first two centuries of American colonization whose spiritual *autobiographies that read life as supplementary Scripture and incorporate personal suffering and doubt into conventional narratives: Mary *Rowlandson's *The Narrative of Captivity and Restoration* (1682) resists the Puritan renunciation of mourning; *The Memoirs of Mrs. Abigail Bailey* (1815) challenges uncritical standards of propriety and Providence. By the Revolution, a new liberal rhetoric in American Protestant theology was pushing the bounds of what women could write. Phillis *Wheatley's poems skillfully shape this rhetoric to condemn *slavery and claim her own authority as "an Ethiop."

In the nineteenth century, dissenting voices like Anne Hutchinson's were more acceptable as the country itself became more diverse and as the idea of women's innate religiosity—apart from official doctrine and intimately connected to the home—accrued value as a way of popularizing Protestant social agendas. Liberal Cal-

vinist (later Episcopalian) Harriet Beecher
*Stowe's *Uncle Tom's Cabin* (1852), which Jane
Tompkins calls the "*summa theologica* ... of
America's religion of *domesticity*" (*Sensational Designs*, 1985), contains in the child Eva's
saintlike death the exemplum of the mid-century Protestant ethos: the mediation of political conflict, in this case *slavery, through
sentimentalized Christian charity at home. This
typology functions against lesser evils in the
period's other best-sellers, Presbyterian Susan
*Warner's *The Wide, Wide World* (1851) and
Unitarian Maria *Cummins's *The Lamplighter*
(1854), demonstrating a cultural and transsec-tarian consensus with a dual genealogy: liberal
Calvinist women novelists (such as Pheobe H.
Brown and Elizabeth Allen) who liberalized or-thodoxy from within, and New England Unitar-ians (such as Sarah A. Savage, Catherine *Sed-gwick, and Lydia Maria *Child) who chided it
from without.

A separate literary assault on Calvinism
came from *Southern women (such as Augusta
Evans *Wilson) characterizing the North as a
soulless man and the South as a compassionate
lady-savior of Africans, an attitude that
prompted Harriet *Jacobs to remark flatly in
Incidents in the Life of a Slave Girl (1861):
"There is a great difference between Christian-ity and the religion of the South." Whatever
their persuasion, these antebellum works uni-formly attest to the efficacy of narrative (even
prescriptive "how-to" books depended on en-gaging stories) over rigid doctrine delivered by
clergymen who, like Stowe's *stereotype in *The
Minister's Wooing* (1859), are "all logical, not in
the least aesthetic."

Such ministers were, of course, a dying
breed by the *Civil War; many clergy had
themselves abandoned strict theology and were
preaching and publishing stories similar to
those by women. But it would misrepresent the
total complexity of later-nineteenth-century
American Protestantism to say, in Ann Doug-las's terms from *The Feminization of American
Culture* (1977), that it had become "feminized."
Alongside the visions of domesticated heaven
(Lydia *Sigourney's poems and Elizabeth
Phelps *Ward's *Gates* novels) that capitalize on
mourning the Civil War dead, social gospel
works by both men and women (such as Marga-ret Sherwood and Katherine Woods) shift the
center of Protestant consciousness from the
home to the city, and call, in the absence of
Calvinist severity, for pragmatic social action,
patriotic evangelism, and heightened personal
accountability to an imminent Christ. Emily
*Dickinson's depictions of death and the after-life draw on these increasingly visible and secu-lar conceptions of divinity, but she retains alle-giance to an archaic idiom and, like
Hutchinson, to the conservative Protestant idea
of God as ultimately beyond representation.

Twentieth-century women writers have re-sponded to Protestant neo-orthodoxy—which
asserts theology over evangelism and resurrects
America's Puritan roots—by revising Protestant
history and doctrine in ways that challenge
both domestic sentimentality and evangelical
imperiousness. Willa *Cather (a convert from
Southern Baptism to Episcopalianism in 1922)
invests her literary faith in *Native American
and *Catholic landscapes that offer alternatives
to Protestant American religious history. Flan-nery *O'Connor (a devout Roman Catholic)
finds in the Southern Bible Belt a fallen land-scape ripe for a vision of grace that draws on
Catholic sacramentality as well as Calvinist ab-surdity, dread, and wonder. A secular neo-Calvinist sensibility operates in the poems of
O'Connor's friend Elizabeth *Bishop, who
charts pragmatic ground in a human world at
once ephemeral and, through Providence,
sturdy and interwoven. Alice Walker's Celie dis-covers through acts of writing and friendship in
her own fractured life a deity that modulates
Dickinson's occasionally blinding *whiteness
into the vibrant color purple. Toni *Morrison's
Beloved (1987) reconfigures the terms of
nineteenth-century Protestant society—*slav-ery, family, sacrificial children—from an
*African-American perspective offering no sen-timental, or simply Protestant, solutions.

• Barbara Welter, "Defenders of the Faith," in *Dimity
Convictions: The American Woman in the Nineteenth
Century* (1976), pp. 103–129. David S. Reynolds, "The
Feminization Controversy: Sexual Stereotypes and the
Paradoxes of Piety in Nineteenth-Century America,"
New England Quarterly 53, no. 1 (March 1980): 96–106.
David S. Reynolds, *Faith in Fiction: The Emergence of
Religious Literature in America* (1981). James A. Lev-ernier, "Phillis Wheatley and the New England
Clergy," *Early American Literature* 26, no. 1 (1991): 21–
38. Ann-Janine Morey, *Religion and Sexuality in Ameri-can Literature* (1992). Leo F. O'Connor, *The Protestant
Sensibility in the American Novel: An Annotated Bibliog-raphy* (1992). Kathleen M. Swaim, " 'Come and Hear':
Women's Puritan Evidences," and Ann Taves, "Self
and God in the Early Published Memoirs of New En-gland Women ," in *American Women's Autobiography:
Fea(s)ts of Memory*, ed. Margo Culley (1992), pp. 32–
56 and 57–74. Elisa New, "Feminist Invisibility: The
Examples of Anne Bradstreet and Anne Hutchinson,"
Common Knowledge 2, no. 1 (Spring 1993): 99–117.

Joseph Murphy

PROTEST WRITING. In her poem "Prologue"
(1650), Anne *Bradstreet complains of those
who think her "hand a needle better fits" than a
"poet's pen," and Alice *Dunbar-Nelson, in "I
Sit and Sew" (1927), expresses feelings of futil-ity because of similar *gender constraints.

Bradstreet, a white woman writing in the seventeenth century, and Dunbar-Nelson, a black woman writing in the twentieth, are but two of many American women whose writing demonstrates that women's oppression crosses cultural and racial, as well as spatial and temporal, boundaries. Southern antislavery advocate Sarah Moore *Grimké (1792–1873) describes such oppression as that "which woman has suffered in every age and country from her protector, man" (Letter IV, "Social Intercourse of the Sexes, 27 July 1837). One might think, then, that this shared oppression would result in a sisterhood that transcends other differences, but differences such as *race, *class, and sexual preference often are too deeply embedded. While no true sisterhood has flourished through the ages, there have been, and still are, countless instances in which nonwhite and white women, of all social, economical, and political backgrounds, have fought for the same causes, if not side by side, with equal intensity of purpose. Indeed, women's literature reflects a long tradition of activism, which shows that, despite everything, many women manage to move "beyond the sphere of [their] sex," to borrow a term from Margaret *Fuller's *Woman in the Nineteenth Century.*

The very act of writing has, historically, constituted movement beyond women's domestic sphere. Yet, the societal belief that they were not only stepping out of their own sphere but, worse, moving into an area of competition with men was a significant determinant for many early women writers. Although men slowly and reluctantly granted women "liberty" to write, as Mary E. Bryan states in her 1860 essay "How Should Women Write?" they did not grant "full freedom." Women, she argued, could "flutter" out of their cages "but . . . with clipped wings." Thus, when women did write, they were sometimes ambiguous about their own abilities. A feeling commonly held among them was expressed by Sarah Josepha *Hale, a successful editor in the mid-nineteenth century, and Grace *Greenwood, author and abolitionist, that even "true feminine genius" could not compare with "the Lords of creation" or "masters of the lyre."

These are a few of the reasons why early women writers frequently put into use the more "private" forms of writing as their means of expression. Private means here not written for publication, as was the case with most journals and *diaries. *Letters, too, even with their implied, albeit limited, audience, would fit into the taxonomy of private writing. Women used letters, journals, and diaries to express their views on many issues, among them the restrictions placed on them as writers, the debate over whether or not they should write, how they should write, and the question of subject matter.

That women chose methods more generally associated with their prescribed domain of domesticity does not mean that they always hid behind the "privacy" of letters and journals. Women often wrote candidly about themselves, their relations to and within society, and about their political views.

As Judy Simons argues in *Diaries and Journals of Literary Women from Fanny Burney to Virginia Woolf* (1990), the notion of a clear distinction between a private voice and a public voice is questionable. For example, the efficacy of Abigail *Adams's letters to her husband John Adams as political tools rather than as mere intimate appeals to a spouse becomes clearer when we consider his position as a delegate to the Continental Congress and as one of the framers of the Constitution. In a tone quite apart from what black playwright Lorraine *Hansberry would, two centuries later, call "parlor and bedroom wheedling of husbands," Abigail Adams asked that greater consideration be given to women, argued that men should not be given "unlimited power," and warned that women would rebel if they were not considered in the "new code of laws" (letter dated 31 March 1776).

For many women, letters served as a way around the difficulties of finding time and space to produce more "tolerable production[s]," in Elizabeth Cady *Stanton's words. In a letter to Susan B. *Anthony (1 December 1853), Stanton laments her inability to do research and to write because she was always "surrounded by children" and overburdened with various domestic chores. Fanny *Fern writes similarly of her mother, who was kept from "literary pursuits" because of a "fast-increasing family" (*Fanny Fern: A Memorial Volume,* 1873). They, like other women, voiced their feelings regarding the "woman question," confronting the many inequities suffered by their sex—and not just in regard to writing. Among their concerns were issues such as forced *marriage, societal stigmatization of the "old maid," and generally, the male "lust of dominion" over women that Sarah Moore *Grimké argues was the first consequence of the Fall.

Grimké used biblical scripture to protest male dominance—to show that men were equally guilty in the Fall and to demonstrate "that no supremacy was granted to man" (276 Letters II and XV, dated 17 July and 20 October 1837, respectively). She expressed these views in her letters to Mary Parker, president of the Boston Female Anti-slavery Society; these letters were first published in the *New England*

Spectator and later in a book entitled *Letters on the Equality of the Sexes and the Condition of Woman* (1838). Eliza Southgate Bowne, writing to her cousin Moses Porter, also addresses issues of inequality, which she believed were especially apparent in the matter of choosing a *marriage partner. She believed further that most women marry out of "gratitude" and that marriage was not essential to happiness. Stanton goes even further to imply that marriage is often a degradation. Moreover, in reading these letters, one gets the impression that the act of writing was as important to many of these women as their individual causes. The notion of writing as a means of self-salvation is generally implied or stated, as with Bowne, who wrote to Porter "... to sit down and unburthen [oppressive thoughts] on paper; it never fails to alleviate me."

Diaries and journals generally provide even greater insight into women's creativity, and they embody even more than letters the paradox of "private" writing. Simon uses the example of Russian diarist Marie Bashkirtseff, who stated that she wrote "as if no one in the world were ever to read it, yet with the purpose of being read." Journals were used for a variety of purposes: to record, for example, spiritual progress, life experiences, travels, political ideologies, or simply day-to-day engagements.

Women scholars studying such writings, like Judy Simons, have concluded that even the most fragmented journals and diaries offer particular insights into women's lives. Joanne Braxton argues in *Black Women Writing Autobiography* (1989) that Charlotte Forten *Grimké, for example, used her journals for political and artistic purposes as well as for self-evaluation. Likewise, Louisa May *Alcott's journals served the purpose of self-evaluation. On the surface, they seem to advocate Puritan ideals, but because her parents insisted on her journals being available for them to examine, Alcott's ability to be entirely honest is called into question. Simon, therefore, focuses on the "suppressed energies," on the obvious tension between Alcott's individual desire on the one hand and her parents' expectations on the other.

The religious experiences of Jarena *Lee, which were published in 1836 under the title "The Life and Religious Experience of Jarena Lee, A Coloured Lady," were based on her personal journals. In this and the expanded version, entitled *Religious Experience and Journal* (1849), both financed by Lee, she challenges the prescribed roles of women and the hypocrisy of black men in the black church. Jarena Lee's publications and those of Zilpha Elaw (*Memoirs of the Life, Religious Experiences and Travels of Mrs. Zilpha Elaw*, 1846), among others, function

to counter claims such as those made by Miriam Schneir in the introduction to *Feminism: The Essential Historical Writings* (1972) that what little writing by black women there is extant from the nineteenth century and prior is more concerned with *racism than *sexism. These writings do not focus on one more than the other; rather, they demonstrate the inextricability of the two. Indeed, they mark the beginning of a tradition of black women protesting the "double jeopardy" of being black and female. Black female *slave narratives, of which Harriet *Jacobs's *Incidents in the Life of a Slave Girl* (1861) is representative, and the speeches of black women activists such as Sojourner *Truth and Harriet Tubman, argue for the existence of outspoken black feminists in the nineteenth century.

Women's public speeches and essays attacking the social and political constraints imposed upon them have become part of women's literature and are available in various anthologies. Several volumes focusing exclusively on women—such as *Early American Women Writers: From Anne Bradstreet to Louisa May Alcott, 1650–1865* (1991), *The Norton Anthology of Literature by Women* (1985), *The Schomburg Library of Nineteenth-Century Black Women Writers* (1988 and 1991), and *Feminism: The Essential Historical Writings*, to name a few of the more comprehensive—reprint the speeches and essays of a wide range of women: Lucretia *Mott (1793–1880), a Quaker and member of the anti-slavery society and the women's movement; Sojourner Truth (1795–1883), a slave who never learned to read or write, but spoke as a traveling preacher for abolition, women's rights, and Christianity; Carrie Chapman *Catt (1859–1947), successor to Susan B. Anthony as president of the women's suffrage movement; Maria W. Steward, black female activist of the nineteenth century; and the women mentioned above—Adams, Grimké, Stanton, *Ashbridge—and numerous others. Individual volumes such as Charlotte Perkins *Gilman's famous *Women and Economics* (1898), which addressed women's economic dependence on men, added voice to the movement, and three of her other books—*Concerning Children* (1900), *The Home* (1903), and *Human Work* (1904)—address issues of women's domestic servitude.

Many women's autobiographical and semi-autobiographical narratives seek to revise traditional ways of seeing women and to present more accurate portrayals of their lives—thus, the significance of the *autobiography as personal history. Books such as Maxine Hong *Kingston's *The Woman Warrior* (1976) and Beverly Hungry Wolf's *The Ways of My Grandmothers* (1980) are representative of autobiographical narratives that seek to reconstruct not only female identities but cultural identities as well. Various critical studies have attempted to address the debates regarding women's writing as inevitably autobiographical and somehow inferior. In addition to those already named, a few noteworthy anthologies and critical studies that present and critique autobiographical writing by women are the following: *Redefining Autobiography in Twentieth-Century Women's Fiction* (1991), edited by Janice Morgan and Colette Hall; *The Ethnic American Woman: Problems, Protests, Lifestyle* (1978), by Edith Blicksilver; *Life/Lines: Theorizing Women's Autobiography* (1988), by Bella Brodzki and Celeste Schenck; and *A Poetics of Women's Autobiography: Marginality and the Fictions of Self-Representation* (1987), by Sidonie Smith.

In fiction, drama, and poetry, women writers—again, some of the same ones mentioned above—were no less committed to writing as a means to "unburthen" oppressive thoughts and to critique American society. The circumstances under which women have had to write, indeed, to live—considered anomalous, subjected to double standards, confronted with a male-dominated literary history—have meant that they have had to be especially creative and imaginative. As Emily Stipes Watts argues about women poets, in the introduction to *The Poetry of American Women from 1632 to 1945* (1977), women have not conformed to any monolithic theme or image. They have written on various topics, have created their own images, and have demonstrated stylistic originality.

When critics began reclaiming marginalized women's writings in the 1960s and 1970s, the need to find methods to deepen explications of their texts seemed especially pertinent. The *sentimental novel, for example, came to be associated, pejoratively, with women, because its characteristics—bathos, effusive emotion—were also associated with women. Novels such as Susannah *Rowson's *Charlotte Temple* (1791) and Harriet Beecher *Stowe's *Uncle Tom's Cabin* (1852), despite (or perhaps because of) their commercial success, were greatly criticized. However, in her essay "Sentimental Power," Jane P. Tompkins argues that Stowe's novel especially exemplifies the significance of sentimental fiction: that it is not limited to the domestic and that it offers powerful critiques of American society. And those black women's novels that have become available have had to recover from similar, if not worse, negative evaluations: Harriet *Wilson's *Our Nig* (1859), Frances W. *Harper's *Iola Leroy* (1892), Pauline *Hopkin's *Contending Forces* (1900), to name a few. Critics, especially black women critics,

have reconstructed the dialogue regarding black women's "sentimental" fiction in such books as *Invented Lives: Narratives of Black Women, 1860–1960* (1987), by Mary Helen Washington; *Conjuring: Black Women, Fiction, and Literary Tradition* (1985), edited by Marjorie Pryse and Hortense J. Spillers; and *Changing Our Own Words: Essays on Criticism, Theory, and Writing By Black Women* (1989), edited by Cheryl A. Wall.

Traditionally, critical examinations of women's writings have shown most of them conforming to the conventions and standards already established by men, even portraying women in similarly stereotypical ways. More recent critical studies, however, have begun to show that often when women seem to be working within tradition, they are in fact subverting it. Current feminist analyses favor wider ranges of reading possibilities, often by focusing on uncovering subtexts, like the "subpattern" of Charlotte Perkins *Gilman's yellow wallpaper—"a woman [or women] stooping down and creeping about behind that pattern"—in her famous protest fiction "The Yellow Wallpaper."

Women writers have consistently broken with tradition by examining issues outside the domain of the "feminine." They have dared to explore and critique male power vs. female powerlessness, reviewing specifically women's roles as wives and mothers. Annis Pratt's *Archetypal Patterns in Women's Fiction* (1981) offers an extensive discussion of such works as Sylvia *Plath's *The Bell Jar* (1963), Marge *Piercy's *Small Changes* (1973), and other texts that rewrite traditional love and marriage plots. Some women who have been read as adhering to tradition by writing genteel novels of manners are being reread as instead critiquing bourgeois values and suburban lifestyles, very often focusing on the tension between women's social roles and their struggles for freedom of expression and individuality: Edith *Wharton, for example, explores such issues in *The Age of Innocence* (1920); Shirley *Jackson in "The Lottery" carries the problem of conformity to its fatal conclusion. Black authors such as Nella *Larsen, in *Quicksand* (1928) and *Passing* (1929), and Jessie *Fauset, in *The Chinaberry Tree* (1931) and *Comedy: American Style* (1933), confront issues of race, class, and gender. Feminists have reread their texts as subversions of precursory white texts and as social satires.

One of the most daring ways in which women writers break with tradition is in their different treatments of women's *sexuality. Kate *Chopin's *The Awakening* (1899) depicts a woman's sexual development and growth instead of repression. Similarly, Zora Neale *Hurston's *Their Eyes Were Watching God*

(1937) explores a black female protagonist's sexual growth; Anne * Sexton's poetry deals directly with women's sexuality in poems such as "In Celebration of My Uterus"; and the poetry and other writings of Audre * Lorde and Adrienne * Rich deal explicitly with lesbianism.

In the last two decades, contemporary women writers have come into their own on a kind of new wave of feminism, claiming woman-identified voices and simultaneously protesting socially constructed images of women. Fiction such as Toni * Morrison's *Beloved* (1988), Alice * Walker's *The Color Purple* (1982), Joyce Carol * Oates's *Do With Me What You Will* (1973), Toni Cade * Bambara's *The Salt Eaters* (1980), Erica * Jong's *Fear of Flying* (1973), and Gloria * Naylor's *Mama Day* (1988), articulates the specific concerns of women in American society.

Finding Courage (1989), edited by Irene Zahava; Mary V. Dearborn's *Pocahontas's Daughters* (1986); Judith Fetterley's *Provisions: A Reader from Nineteenth-Century American Women* (1985); *Writing Red: An Anthology of American Women Writers, 1930–1940*, edited by Charlotte Nekola and Paula Rabinowitz (1987); and *Keeping the Faith: Writings By Contemporary Black American Women* (1974), edited by Pat Crutchfield Exum—these are a few books, along with some of those named above, that emerged from the 1970s and 1980s revival of women's texts. They not only make available the fiction and nonfiction of marginalized writers but also challenge the American literary * canon. These scholars are all concerned with presenting the differences between * myth and reality with regard to women's literature; they want to show that even when women writers seem to approve and perpetuate the status quo, the very act of their " * scribbling," as Nathaniel Hawthorn once termed it, becomes thereby an act of protest.

[*See also* Antiwar Movements; Activism; Women's Movement; Civil Rights Movement; American Indian Rights Movement; Political Organizations.]

• Helen Waite Papashvily, *All the Happy Endings* (1956). Helen Winter Stauffer and Susan J. Rosowski, *Women and Western American Literature* (1982). Dorothy Sterling, ed., *We Are Your Sisters: Black Women in the Nineteenth Century* (1984). Elaine Showalter, ed., *The New Feminist Criticism: Essays on Women, Literature, and Theory* (1985). Lucy M. Freibert and Barbara A. White, eds., *Hidden Hands: An Anthology of American Women Writers, 1790–1870* (1985). William L. Andrews, ed., *Sisters of the Spirit: Three Black Women's Autobiographies of the Nineteenth Century* (1986). Sandra Eagleton, ed., *Women in Literature; Lifestages through Stories, Poems and Plays* (1988). Sarah Moore Grimké, *Letters on the Equality of the Sexes and the Condition of Woman*, ed. Ann Bartlett (1988). Ann Allen

Schockley, ed., *Afro-American Women Writers 1746–1933: An Anthology and Critical Guide* (1988). Bonnie Kime Scott, ed., *The Gender of Modernism: A Critical Anthology* (1990). Katherine M. Rogers, ed., *The Meridian Anthology of Early American Women Writers* (1991).

Jacquelyn Y. McLendon

PSEUDONYMS. The tradition of anonymous and pseudonymous writing is a long one, stretching back to the beginnings of literary * authorship. Eighteenth- and nineteenth-century writers used pseudonyms to reflect their view of authorship as the avocation of a genteel amateur who was writing for the pleasure of family and friends, not for personal fame. In these early years, many men and women published anonymously or used same-sex or cross-sex pseudonyms. As authorship became a more respected vocation during the nineteenth century, the practice of literary disguise gradually diminished in the U.S., but it certainly has not yet disappeared. Women were and are probably somewhat more likely than men to use pseudonyms and cross-sex names (though there is some evidence to the contrary), but the use of male disguises by female writers has been less common in the U.S. than in England and France. Although pseudonyms have sometimes been chosen in reaction to negative social attitudes toward women writers, they have also been used as assertive strategies in women's literary careers.

Pseudonyms have been used for a variety of reasons by women writers. Because anonymity and pseudonymity was "proper" for writers and especially for women up through the early nineteenth century, a writer like Anne * Bradstreet published her poems as "A Gentlewoman." Some writers, like Sarah Orne * Jewett ("Alice Eliot") have used a pseudonym only briefly to gain the courage to begin a literary career. Mary Abigail Dodge ("Gail Hamilton") and Alice French ("Octave Thanet") expected their pseudonyms to help maintain their privacy and that of those who might seem to be discussed in their writings. Mary N. * Murfree ("Charles Egbert Craddock") hoped her name would keep critics' attention focused on her writing, not her sex. But, often a pen name piques readers' curiosity about the author, as it did about "Fanny * Fern" (Sara Jane Parton), and can then be used to sell books. In fact, writers like Helen Hunt * Jackson have developed multiple identities ("Saxe Holm" and "H.H.") for their own economic advantages. For its literary potential, writers like Marietta E. * Holley and Harriet Beecher * Stowe used pseudonyms to create personas ("Josiah Allen's Wife" and "Christopher Crowfield," respectively) to match their literary work.

The special attraction of pseudonymous writing for women is being able to name oneself outside of patriarchal, racist, and heterosexist limits. Women like Pauline Tarn ("Renée Vivien") become whomever they hope to be, even as in this case, a French poet. Contemporary poets "Ai" (Florence Anthony) and *"Alta" create themselves without any lineage. On the other hand, the Warner sisters adopted their grandmothers' names ("Elizabeth Wetherall" and "Amy Lothrop"), thus emphasizing their female heritage. And Toni Cade did the same by adding a signature (*"Bambara") that she found on a sketchbook in her great-grandmother's trunk. The power of self-naming has been crucial to women. With her name "Grace *Greenwood," Sarah Jane *Lippincott declared her love of the outdoors. With the names, *"Sui Sin Far" and "Ntozake *Shange," Edith Maud Eaton and Paulette Williams assertively declare their cultural heritage; "Elana Dykewomon" equally strongly asserts her sexuality with hers.

Whatever a writer's motives, a pseudonym is a reflection of the author's view of herself, her philosophy of life, and her attitudes toward her literary work.

• Charles Scott, "A Chapter on *Nom de Plumes*," *New England Magazine* 17 (October 1897): 185–192. Harry Smith, "The Science of Anonymity," *Living Age* 217 (April 1898): 40–47. Sandra Gilbert and Susan Gubar, "Ceremonies of the Alphabet: Female Grandmatologies and the Female Authorgraph," in *The Female Autograph*, ed. Donna C. Stanton, *New Literary Forum* 12–13 (1984): 23–52. Mary Kelley, *Private Woman, Public Stage: Literary Domesticity in Nineteenth Century America* (1990). Susan Coultrap-McQuin, *Doing Literary Business: American Women Writers in the Nineteenth Century* (1990).

Susan Coultrap-McQuin

PSYCHOANALYSIS AND WOMEN. *This four-part article describes and assesses the history and development of a crucial component of modern critical theory. Its divisions are*

Sigmund Freud
Early Dissent
Object Relations Theory
Jacques Lacan

For further information, see also Feminism; French Feminism; Literary Criticism.

Sigmund Freud

In his 1933 essay "Femininity," Freud stated that "Psycho-analysis does not try to describe what a woman is—that would be a task it could scarcely perform—but sets about enquiring how she comes into being, how a woman develops out of a child with a bisexual disposition."

To a substantial degree, Freud's thought was reproduced and carried on by women. Anna Freud first of all, but also Melanie Klein, Lou Andreas Salome, Helene Deutsch, Karen Horney, *H. D., Joan Riviere, Jeanne Lamplde Groot, Ruth Mack Brunswick, Princess Marie Bonaparte, and numerous other women on both sides of the Atlantic chose to follow him and also to create career paths for themselves.

It is nonetheless surprising that Freud found as many "daughters" as "sons" to continue (and/or modify) his line, since his patently patriarchal attitude colored his theory and perspective throughout his work. No other thinker before him, with the possible exception of Rousseau, seems to have inspired so many exceptional women. Not unlike Rousseau, Freud's often express misogyny, his energetic focus on the theory of fathering, and his formal incapacity to recognize the female role in cultural transmission in no way appears to have prevented dozens of women from appreciating him and sensing in his work (against his beliefs) a radical departure, some new element that would forever alter their status.

Freud's psychoanalysis granted "woman" two distinct and often diametrically opposed modes, one linked to her physicality—"female *sexuality"—and another, linked to something beyond the body and the symbolic orderings that negate it: "*femininity."

With respect to the female sexual *body, Freud found that since the conscious mind is primarily and originally constituted around the root form of negation (as prohibition, *taboo, or denial), culture is constructed by a paternal figure—that which primordially forbids certain enjoyments for the mutual benefit to be derived from the consequent formation and maintenance of a culture in common. The father function opposes the mother function: the site (like nature) of all possible enjoyments, the Mother nevertheless is also the end of these, since complete satisfaction is a form of death. Modeled on, but by no means strictly aligned with, real parental figures, these two functions had, for Freud, to be continuously and precariously balanced by the emerging ego of the new individual, independent of each. Here lay the start of the difficult placement of the female or feminine ego.

Since Freud's discovery of the unconscious originated in the observation of hysterical young women *(Studies in Hysteria)*, a link with women was forged from the beginning of psychoanalysis. So when Freud began to define the unconscious (which, "knowing no negation," operated side by side with and at cross-purposes to the "paternal" forces of civilization), it seemed to be aligned with the (lethal) forces of nature/mother/woman. Women could be thought of as existing more on the "unconscious" than the culturally "conscious" side of the radical division of the subject Freud had disclosed. Framed via the unconscious, the female as sexual is primarily the object of choice of a man who has developed Oedipally, because she represents the mother under three aspects ("The Theme of the Three Caskets"), all of which are forms of denying her ultimate claim on him (death). Furthermore, women who aligned themselves with the conceptual and analytical had themselves to identify with the scientific, rational, and therefore patriarchally structured side of the subject. They might appreciate the unconscious as a primary site of woman, but theoretically and practically they had to fit themselves into the masculine forms of discourse to operate as analysts.

Complications of this simplistic picture of Freud's "woman" arose, and continue to arise, however. First, despite his misogynist tone, Freud occasionally displayed genuine sympathy for women, for example in the empirical plight of mothers. He recognized disorders in the sexual enlightenment of young women. The moral censoring that afflicts the girl who enjoys a sexual relationship outside (or in) marriage also claimed his attention. Even the cornerstone to the differentiation of the sexes, the scene of genital comparisons of "boy" and "girl," is not, in fact, exclusively depicted by Freud as inevitably resulting in *penisneid*: on the contrary, Freud ran this scenario over and over with many variations, ranging from male denial of female castration (fetishism), male assimilation of female under male ("The Wolf-man" calls his sisters and playmates' genitals their "front bottom"), to the infamous remarks on penis envy in "Femininity."

Trouble between the female and Oedipus remains to the end of Freud's writing, however, and he never resolved the issues of female and male *homosexuality, both of which challenge genital (Oedipal) primary formalizations of biological and cultural reproduction. But in his essay on "Femininity," issues of biological and social distinctions between masculine and feminine begin to take second place to the question of pleasure. His discourse on femininity relates to woman outside "female sexuality." The latter always entails the parental dimension, or *reproduction; the former, that element in human sexuality Freud claimed took precedence over biological and cultural reproduction: pleasure. That there exists an entirely different line of sight in which woman re-appears in Freud via "femininity" has not been recognized sufficiently. It is certainly not without ambivalence, but it only tangentially participates in the oppressive reproductive schema.

In his essay on "Femininity," Freud makes plain that *male* and *female* refer biologically to the one who harbors either sperm or ovum; what constitutes "masculinity or "femininity," by contrast, "is an unknown characteristic which anatomy cannot lay hold of," though psychology might do so. Ways of conceiving the masculine/feminine distinction generally reduce to anatomy in common discourse (active/passive are tied to the motility of male sex-cells, for example, and to the "immobile" state of an ovum). Masculine "aggression" and "maternal instincts" are similarly reductive. Recourse to "*bisexuality" either physically (the presence of token opposite sex organs) or psychologically (aggressive women and passive men) is of no use in clarifying the distinctiveness of femininity. Nor is a preference for passive or active *aims* a basis for definition, for these are always influenced by and subject to societal aims.

Only the concept of pleasure begins to unlock the key to the riddle of femininity—and Freud himself did not face its ramifications. According to Freud's "Femininity" essay, girls are in every way the equal of boys with respect to the pleasures of the pre-oedipal oral, sadistic-anal, and phallic phases: "With their entry into the phallic phase the differences between the sexes are completely eclipsed by their agreements. We are now obliged to recognize that the little girl is a little man." Her clitoris is, like the penis, a phallus (both are phalluses by definition); its pleasures, sensitivity, "and at the same time, its importance" are what she must ultimately "hand over ... to the vagina," in order to take on the reproductive burdens societal order demands, becoming feminine" in part by this process, just as the boy becomes manly through accepting Oedipal limits.

But Freud decided that it is not society ("father") alone that lays the basis for the development of the little girl into a "woman." This is because the figure who forbids her certain enjoyments is not the father but the mother, who is, at the same time, the very source of such enjoyments: the mother's hygienic efforts on her behalf originally stimulated pleasurable sensations in the child's genitals. Now those pleasures are to be given up during her "phallic" (egalitarian) phase—and often it is the Mother who forbids her daughter genital pleasure. Whereas the boy, because his father is his rival for the mother, can throw the blame for the limits on his pleasure at him, and then trade places with him, the girl, equally powerfully attached to the mother, is prevented from this compensating identification with her rival: her beloved mother and her rival are one and the same. Thus, though the same holds for the boy, the mother's forbidding of similar pleasure in him does not, as Freud puts it, "alienate" him from the mother as it does the girl since he can re-attain figurative connection to this original source of pleasure by the proper female object choice.

The little girl, by contrast, already somewhat "lesser" in phallic proportions than the boy, is obliged, via the mother herself, to give up even that small(er) portion of pleasure she had taken for her own, and is further forbidden the figurative or transferential gratification later. Thus, there is only a "masculine libido" because it alone can be "accounted" for in the Oedipal system. Freud thus retreats, and terms the notion of "feminine libido" without justification. He turns on his own insight and reinscribes woman's sexual quiescence into "the aim of biology."

Unwittingly, however, Freud in this essay has actually freed femininity from predominantly moral and biological obligations, which have any way "been made to some extent independent of the consent of women."

Femininity can now be seen as the direct result of a contradiction or double-bind in woman's relation to her own *jouissance*, created by her structural relation to the mother; but it is potentially productive in effectively liberating her from the narrow band of choices granted her by an absence of "identification" (with the rival father). Woman's "choice" and consent remained narrow for Freud—she could basically choose her father or her brother. Nevertheless, structurally, Freud freed up the pleasurable rather than the purely reproductive aspects of her sexuality.

For Freud, "by thirty" woman's "libido" appears to have "taken up final positions and seems incapable of exchanging them for others." On this "unfriendly," not to say sour note, Freud tried to close the book on femininity, keeping it a mystery inside a riddle wrapped up in an enigma: a completely anesthetized, anesthetic posture. Yet, by his own account in his "Femininity" essay, the rigid version of "femininity" produced in women "by age thirty" is already the product of a "masculine" libido that has blunted the potential for development of an aesthetics of femininity resulting from the potential breadth of her range of choices for pleasurable objects beyond familial limits.

By aligning it with the aesthetic and pleasure, recent analysts have been able to regard femininity as a specific variant of the essence of Oedipus—the fending off of the lethal Maternal Thing (as Lucie Cantin put it in "The Feminine Thing," 1990)—a functional equivalent but very different from the masculine solution. It challenges patriarchal "cultural" presumptions that woman's "aesthetic object status" (her beauty) is a pure Pygmalionesque creation of male discourse, ensuring man's proper object-choice for reproductive purposes. The male stinting of the powers of choice inherit in "femininity" caused the feminism of the 60s, 70s, and 80s to reject it (as Susan Brownmiller did in *Femininity*, 1984) but in the work of Freud, "femininity" alone potentially counters the Oedipal version of women as crucial but unacknowledged operators of reproduction, uncompensated for their labor. "Femininity" could open the door to a system outside or beyond the phallus, where woman should not find her place precisely because man always wants to put her there.

• Sigmund Freud, *Dora: Fragment of an Analysis of a Case of Hysteria* (1905; reprint, 1963). Sigmund Freud, " 'Civilized' Sexual Morality and Modern Nervousness," in *Sexuality and the Psychology of Love*, edited by P. Rieff (1908; reprint, 1963), pp. 20–40. Sigmund Freud, "The Sexual Life of Human Beings," in *Introductory Lectures on Psychoanalysis* (1916; reprint, 1966), pp. 303–319. Sigmund Freud, "The Taboo of Virginity" (1918; reprint, 1963), pp. 70–86. Sigmund Freud, "From the Case History of an Infantile Neurosis," in *Three Case Histories* (1918; reprint, 1963). Sigmund Freud, *Civilization and Its Discontents*, edited by James Strachey (1930; reprint, 1961). Sigmund Freud, "Female Sexuality," in *Sexuality and the Psychology of Love* (1931; reprint, 1963). Sigmund Freud, "Femininity," in *New Introductory Lectures on Psychoanalysis* (1933; reprint, 1965), pp. 99–119. Ernest Jones, *The Life and Work of Sigmund Freud* (1953). Luce Irigaray, *This Sex Which Is Not One* (1977; reprint, 1985). Jacques Lacan, "God and the Jouissance of the Woman" and "Intervention on the Transference," in *Feminine Sexuality: Jacques Lacan and the école freudienne* (1982). Susan Brownmiller, *Femininity* (1984). Jacques Lacan, *Sémanaire VII: L'Ethique de la psychanalyse 1959–60* (1986). Melanie Klein, *Love, Guilt and Reparation and Other Works, 1921–45* (1988). Melanie Klein, *Envy, Gratitude and Other Works, 1946–63* (1988). Willy Apollon, Danielle Bergeron, and Lucie Cantin, *Traiter la psychose* (1990). Lucie Cantin, "The Feminine Thing," *The American Journal of Semiotics* 8, no. 3 (1990). Danielle Bergeron, "Femininity," *The American Journal of Semiotics* 8, no. 4 (1991). Juliet Flower MacCannell, "Mothers of Necessity: Psychoanalysis for Feminism," *American Literary History* 3, no. 3 (1991): 623–647.

Juliet Flower MacCannell

Early Dissent

When Sigmund Freud began one of his lectures on female sexuality by asking what women want, he may not have foreseen that many of his female disciples and critics would respond by arguing for a new theory of female sexuality, one that is less phallocentric and deterministic, one that removes women's psychosexual development from a male paradigm—where it is judged inferior and passive—and locates it within the social context that holds up the male model as *the* paradigm.

Feminism's revision or rejection of Freud is considered by many to be a relatively modern phenomenon, encouraged by the second wave of feminism as well as larger social movements and epistemic shifts. In France, it is associated with a group of Lacanian-influenced feminists, including Julia Kristeva, Luce Irigiray, and Hélène Cixous, who attack Freudian/Lacanian phallocentrism and typically invoke the female body as the basis for a different theory of sexuality. In the United States, the repudiation of Freud as sexist can largely be traced to Kate *Millett and her best-selling doctoral thesis *Sexual Politics* (1970), though surely such works as Betty *Friedan's *The Feminine Mystique* (1963) and Germaine Greer's *The Female Eunuch* (1971) also played a part.

These protests, however, could not have fomented had it not been for the work of some of Freud's early critics, particularly Helene Deutsch, Karen Horney, Melanie Klein, and Freud's daughter, Anna. To varying degrees, as Janet Sayers argues, these women typically accepted the "father's" emphasis on innate drives and the penis/phallus. And yet, they each took his theories of psychosexual development in new directions, often away from the phallus and toward the mother.

Of all the early disciples, Anna Freud was perhaps the most wedded to her father's theories. In pioneering child analysis, however, Anna Freud argued that some of her father's concepts, including free association, transference, and the pathology of ego defenses, while fine for adults, did not fit a child's psychic needs and abilities; she adapted her father's methods accordingly. Her later work in war nurseries and involvement in pediatric care resulted in substantial improvements in child care and child analytic training.

Anna Freud also remained the most fiercely loyal to a father-centered psychoanalytic focus, attacking the shift among other Freudian analysts not only towards a focus on the mother but towards the psychoanalyst-as-mother. Freud insisted this latter shift only extends the patient's fantasy of union with the mother, rather than, as is proper, interpreting it and encouraging more individuation.

Helene Deutsch, a disciple of Freud and prominent in his Vienna Society, managed to both retain Freud's father-focus and address the mother's role. Because she more or less espoused Freud's biologistic theories of sexuality, including the castration complex, and as she never truly questioned the prescriptions for normative womanhood built into psychoanalytic theory, many would discount her as an early critic of Freud. She is counted here as such because, unlike Freud, she devoted much of her attention to the role of the mother, drawing on her own experiences of mothering as well as her analysis of children to develop her theories of ego development, inauthenticity, lesbianism, and narcissism. Deutsch, one of the first psychoanalysts to focus on the mother's as well as the child's desire, also wrote the first psychoanalytic text on women's psychology, *The Psychology of Women's Sexual Functions* (1925), and later, in 1944, published her influential *The Psychology of Women*.

Posing contrast to Deutsch is Karen Horney, still celebrated by feminists as one of the first and most influential critics of Freudian phallocentrism and *essentialism. In essays collected in her book *Feminine Psychology* (1967), Horney points out the "masculine narcissism" lurking behind Freud's assumption that the female child sees her genitals as "lacking" when compared to the male. If girls do envy penises, Horney suggests, it is not simply a biologically based inferiority complex. As Juliet Mitchell argues, Horney continually stresses the psychological and social causes and effects of patriarchal sexual differences. Like Deutsch, Horney sees femininity as innate (although as her career progressed, she increasingly stressed the importance of parental and cultural influence) and emphasized the role of the mother in a girl's ego development. Unlike Deutsch, she countered Freud's penis envy with her own theory of male "womb envy," of men's envy of women's creative abilities. Horney's use of psychoanalysis to address problems in women's self-esteem remains highly influential today.

Yet another analyst, Melanie Klein, closely associated with Horney, is often credited as the founder, or at least a forerunner, of the object relations school of psychoanalysis. Throughout her career, Klein (one of the analysts Anna Freud criticized for her belief in the utility of the psychoanalyst-as-mother in transference) worked to illustrate the formative centrality of the mother internalized as object—of both love and hate—in a child's psychosexual development. Although for the most part embracing Freud's belief in the influence of anatomical difference, Klein's work with children and her recognition of the importance of interpersonal attachments led her to revise Freud's theories of sexuality. For Freud's authoritative patriarchal superego, Klein substituted the child's relation to the mother—even if only an internalized, fantasized version of the mother—in accounting for the formation of sexual differences in the Oedipal complex. In yet another revision, in her later work on depression, Klein suggested that this internalization occurs pre-Oedipally, beginning at birth. She argued that it is these internalized objects and projective identifications, not Freud's instincts and stages, that produce not only stable mental states but also illnesses such as depression and schizophrenia.

One more formative early critic of Freud should be mentioned in this context. Simone de * Beauvoir, in her *The Second Sex* (1949), attacks Freud for developing a theory that accounts for the differences between the sexes by assuming the male's superiority and normativeness without asking how or why patriarchal societal forces produce such discrepancies. Accounting for this production in *The Second Sex*, de Beauvoir also credits women with the ability to existentially choose their destiny through their actions and interactions rather than having it crudely determined for them by innate drives, anatomical "lacks," and "penis envy."

Nearly all of these early female critics attempted to apply Freud's theories, and in applying them, found them wanting—especially when it came to understanding women, mothering, and/or interpersonal relations. Although none dismissed Freud outright, each in her own way demonstrated that, in psychoanalytic theory as in other arenas, who is doing the theorizing makes as much if not more difference as what is being theorized. Although Freud often acknowledged this very fact, these women refused merely to acknowledge these biases and instead looked for methods of redressing them.

• Melanie Klein, et al., *Developments in Psycho-Analysis* (1952). Nancy Chodorow, *The Reproduction of Mothering: Psychoanalysis and the Sociology of Gender* (1978). Juliet Mitchell, *Psychoanalysis and Feminism* (1975). Janet Sayers, *Mothering Psychoanalysis* (1991). Janice Doane and Devon Hodges, *From Klein to Kristeva: Psychoanalytic Feminism and the Search for the "Good Enough" Mother* (1992).

Cynthia J. Davis

Object-Relations Theory

Freud, the father of psychoanalysis, in many ways also fathered its object relations school, even though this branch of psychoanalysis often defines itself in contradistinction to Freud's basic tenets. "Object relations" is a rubric that extends to cover numerous and often opposing psychoanalytic camps who nonetheless all share a focus on the role played by relations to the other/object in the formation of the self. In general, object relations analysts repudiate Freud's emphasis on innate drives; and yet, for all his "anatomy is destiny," Freud was not inattentive to the importance of such external factors as affective attachments in ego development. For instance, in his *Three Essays on the Theory of Sexuality* (1905), Freud acknowledges the role of the object when he argues that a child's relations are sexual from the outset since the objects involved—primarily the mother's breast and the mother herself—are always sexualized.

Additionally, object relations theorists have found Freud's theories on internalization and incorporation instrumental to their analysis of the formation of not only self but of superego as well. For example, a student of Freud's, Melanie Klein, who shared Freud's belief in the primacy of innate instincts in ego development, also is noted—among other things—for recognizing the foundational role of the internalized (m)other. For this and other theories involving interpersonal relations, Klein is often credited for founding psychoanalysis's object relations school. Others who receive credit include her student D. W. Winnicott, who drew attention not only to the internalized but also to the actual mother's role in development. Winnicott is also noted for theorizing the importance of "transitional objects," such as toys, dolls, or even pieces of cloth. Other important pioneers who in diverse ways address interpersonal relations include W. R. D. Fairbairn, Harry Guntrip, Harry Stack Sullivan, John Bowlby, Karen Horney, Clara Thompson, Erich Fromm, Frieda Fromm-Reichman, and, in America, Margaret Mahler and Heinz Kohut.

In the United States, object relations theory is perhaps best known to feminists through the work of Nancy Chodorow. Chodorow and her colleagues start from and with the psychoanalytic attention to the construction of (gendered) subjectivity and sexuality in early childhood. They reject, however, the Freudian-inspired emphasis on biological determinism and, in general, are silent regarding the Lacanian attention to language and signification. Instead, Chodorow focuses on how the infant's experiential interactions with others and others with them (not only in the Oedipal but, crucially for little girls, in the pre-Oedipal phase) produce the gendered individual.

Taking the patriarchal family structure not only as a given but as the most significant arena for identity formation, Chodorow argues that, because it is women who still primarily mother, it is women who remain the primary objects for both boy and girl infants. Since children of both genders, especially pre-Oedipally, forge their identities in relation to a female, the male infant's primary task becomes to differentiate his "self" from his m/other's, whereas the girl is never required to make such a sharp break. Because the girl thus forms her identity relationally and the boy through the rejection of relations, the girl, according to Chodorow, grows up with a greater potential for relations, empathy, and connectedness than does her male counterpart—hence the reproduction of mothering. Chodorow concludes that only after parenting ceases to be the asymmetrical—only after men and women take equal responsibility for parenting—will we produce children of both genders who will be less individualistic, less emotionally distant, more nurturing, more caring: in a word, more motherly.

Self-help groups and talk shows are filled with participants who trace their problems to their mothers. The increased tendency toward mother-blaming in this country might be thwarted were we as a nation to have a better grasp of mothering in the context of its social-psychological production within patriarchy. Object relation theorists like Chodorow represent one step away from mother-blaming and toward mother-understanding. As such, the importance of object relations theory for women should not be understated.

What's more, in a field attacked by such feminists as Kate *Millett and Luce Irigiray for its sexism/phallocentrism, object relations theory reintroduces women into the psychoanalytic picture as central. Although its assumption that it is women who mother has been confused with an implication that this is a "natural" state of affairs, and although it typically ignores homosexual relationships in its assumption of the nuclear family and of the necessity that boys grow up to desire girls and girls, boys, object relations theory provides a means of not only describing patriarchy but prescribing alternative social and interpersonal modes.

• Sigmund Freud, "Three Essays on the Theory of Sexuality," (1905), in *The Standard Edition of the Complete Psychological Works of Sigmund Freud*, 24 vols., translated and edited by James Strachey (1953–1974). Melanie Klein, et al., *New Directions in Psycho-Analysis* (1955). D. W. Winnicott, *Collected Papers: Through Paediatrics to Psycho-analysis* (1958). Nancy Chodorow, *The Reproduction of Mothering: Psychoanalysis and the Sociology of Gender* (1978). Robert Rogers, *Self and Other: Object Relations in Psychoanalysis and Literature* (1991).

Cynthia J. Davis

Jacques Lacan

The most important French psychoanalyst, Jacques Lacan (1900–1981), appears in this volume because, in the late 1970s and early 1980s, his work influenced a certain strand of American literary feminism.

The first major reclamation of psychoanalysis by a recognized feminist theorist, Juliet Mitchell's *Psychoanalysis and Feminism* (1974), follows Lacan's structuralist reinterpretation of Freud in order to render psychoanalysis useful to feminism. Her 1982 edition, with Jacqueline Rose, of a number of Lacanian texts in a volume entitled *Feminine Sexuality* actually reinscribes him as a "feminist theorist." A generation of British feminist intellectuals, coming of age and/or educated in the 1970s, studied Lacan as part of a feminist inquiry into female subjectivity. First through film theory and then through literary criticism, the British scholars exerted a significant influence upon North American academic feminism.

By 1980 the U.S. literary academy was focused on the question of poststructuralist theory and, as a consequence, academic feminism was polarized momentarily between so-called "American and *French feminism." The latter referred primarily to the mid-seventies writing of Hélène Cixous, Luce Irigaray, and Julia Kristeva. Central to the theorizing of these women was a Freudian psychoanalysis that had passed through Lacan's elaborate reconceptualization. Whether referring to these French women writers or to American poststructuralist feminist critics (Shoshana Felman, Alice Jardine, Naomi Schor), the reference to Lacan was central and obligatory. Hence, the second major path of Lacanian influence on American feminism is apparent. For a while, at least, it seemed as if fully half of academic feminism necessarily referred to Lacanian psychoanalysis.

Lacan's system is structuralist, his style poststructuralist. Both aspects, differently, contributed to his feminist reception. The first insured that gendered psychology is located in culture rather than nature, thus putting his analysis on the feminist side of identities as socially constructed. The second called into question the certitude, authority, objectification, and normativeness that had made psychoanalysis—like so many sciences and professions—objectionable to feminism.

Lacan formulated a basic congruity between Freud's discoveries and Ferdinand de Saussure's structural linguistics; he translated Freudian theory into linguistic terminology—two of his central concepts are the signifier and the subject. Freud's Oedipal and castration complexes, which sound as if they are about biology and family members, are retold as the drama of the subject's entry into language. The shift from biology into language parallels the feminist turn from sex to *gender. Emphasis on the difficulties of living in language is particularly resonant for literary feminism where struggle is waged both in and with patriarchal language.

A central term in Lacanian theory is the phallus, which has proved a stumbling block for some feminists, an attraction for others. Freudian psychology is already phallocentric, but Lacan makes it more explicitly so. Although this is likely to offend a liberal humanist conception of psychology, it has been argued that it is true to actual psychology in a phallocentric social order and that to struggle against phallocracy we must face how well and how pervasively it works. Insisting that the phallus is a signifier, not an organ, Lacan removes it from any natural status into the realm of culture.

Lacan's elusive, poetic style has proved alluring to many literary feminists, suggesting a science that would not be crudely reductive or mechanistically objectifying. In the 1950s Lacan was very critical of the American psychoanalytic establishment for service to what he called "the American way of life," specifically accusing the psychoanalysts of objectifying patients. This resonates with the feminist critique of the same period of psychotherapeutic practice.

One of Lacan's major theoretical contributions is his translation of the Freudian concept of transference into a relation to knowledge. For Lacan, transference is the projection of a "subject presumed to know." For academics this has particular interest, since we are not only in the knowledge-gathering business but also in the business of transmitting knowledge.

More teacher and lecturer than writer, Lacan's work is perhaps best gleaned from his yearly *Seminar*, many volumes of which have already been published and translated. The first issued and most influential is *The Four Fundamental Concepts of Psychoanalysis* (1978). Lacan did, however, author one actual book, *Ecrits*, an immense tome published in 1966, at the height of his French influence. In 1977 a much shorter *Ecrits: A Selection* was published in English, thus securing his Anglophone influence.

• John P. Muller and William J. Richardson, *Lacan and Language: A Reader's Guide to* Ecrits (1982). Jane Gallop, *The Daughter's Seduction* (1982). Catherine Clément, *The Lives and Legends of Jacques Lacan* (1983). Juliet Mitchell, *Women: The Longest Revolution* (1984). Jane Gallop, *Reading Lacan* (1985). Shoshana Felman, *Jacques Lacan and the Adventure of Insight* (1987). Elizabeth Grosz, *Jacques Lacan: A Feminist Introduction* (1990).

Jane Gallop

PUBERTY. See Adolescence; Girlhood.

PUBLISHING BUSINESS. The growth of publishing in this country has been steady, though the industry has remained until recently a small one. The first American press was established in Cambridge, Massachusetts, in 1639. Beginning as an adjunct to printing and bookselling, publishing was a cottage industry in which female members of a family sometimes participated. The early printer-publishers were authorized and controlled by the government; presses were used most often to publish government or religious documents. Literary works like Anne *Bradstreet's poems (1650) and controversial books were usually sent to England to be published.

In the eighteenth century, printing and publishing gradually expanded, not only in terms of the number of publishers (there were 50 printing offices in 1755) but also in the types of material published. By the late eighteenth century, literature was an increasing proportion of the output, second only to theology. Publishing was predominantly regional, centered in Boston, with Philadelphia and New York gaining prominence as the century passed. Women had begun publishing their writings, but it is difficult to know how many of them there were, since most works were published anonymously.

In the nineteenth century, publishing activity separated from bookselling and grew quickly. Between 1820 and 1850, the industry expanded tenfold in response to increasing national levels of *literacy, people's growing interest in reading as cheap entertainment, and an expanding railroad system that made the national distribution of books possible. Changes in printing technology, including the advent of the steam-powered cylinder press, the use of stereotyped plates, and cheaper methods of papermaking and binding, made possible the publication of less expensive books and created highly competitive markets. By mid-century two literary markets had emerged: the more traditional, "serious," literary one and the profit-oriented, "popular" one.

At mid-century, however, there were still only about 400 publishers, printers, and booksellers in the nation, concentrated in New York, Philadelphia, and, now to a lesser degree, in Boston. Virtually none of the 400 was a woman. Throughout the century, publishing firms were affected by national economic fluctuations between prosperity and depression; firms would suddenly disappear and mergers were common. Writers could find themselves without a publisher or with a new publisher overnight. In the second half of the century, publishing's growth did not keep pace with other types of manufacturing. Publishers often complained about how unprofitable publishing was. Women writers—mostly white, middle-class, and Protestant, like their publishers—made notable advances in the nineteenth-century literary marketplace, accounting for between 40 and 50 percent of the literature published at mid-century and three-quarters of the novels published by 1872. Writers from minority groups were also achieving some visibility by the end of the century, especially through their own presses.

The explosion of literary outlets provided opportunities for many writers, including women. In the popular market, the first paperback revolution began in the 1830s as a result of the technological advances making faster publication possible, the availability of foreign writings uncontrolled by copyright law, and a loophole in postal rates that enabled cheap papers and books to circulate at newspaper rates. This boom collapsed in 1843 with new postal regulations. Nevertheless, a wave of books written primarily by American authors followed in which many publishers offered books in cheap formats to large audiences. A second paperback boom began in the 1870s, spurred by a decline in the price of paper and by the appearance of even faster manufacturing processes. Many publishers issued cheap reprints of works by British and French authors, to the disadvantage of American writers. Because there still was no international copyright, publishers were not required to pay royalties, though some did make payments to foreign authors. This cutthroat competition resulted in the failure of many companies. The second boom ended with the passage of the International Copyright Law in 1891.

Magazine publication developed as an important outlet for writers by the mid-nineteenth century when publishers used their in-house magazines to serialize and advertise their books. Authors benefitted from the double exposure of their work and usually from increased compensation, but they had to conform to length and other requirements of serialization. These in-house publications gradually disappeared in the competition with independent, mass-market magazines at the end of the nineteenth century. Mass-market magazines often provided very good compensation for writers but were much more demanding in their requirements than the earlier magazines had been; many commissioned journalistic, "timely" articles and stories and encouraged an energetic, "masculine" literary style.

The first half of the twentieth century brought about the continued growth of the publishing industry spurred by a significant increase in population, a decrease in illiteracy, rising urbanization, and increasingly cosmopolitan tastes. The international book trade also grew. New printing types and design-making processes changed the physical appearances of books, while the 1930s invention of magazine rotary presses made higher-speed production possible, and synthetic glue for bookbinding facilitated the expansion of mass-market fiction. Approximately 900 publishers were listed in

Publishers Weekly Directory in 1945, although only 231 issued five or more books. There was some growth in the numbers of minority presses. For instance, eighteen African-American presses had been issuing books since the turn of the century.

The foundations for a third paperback revolution were laid early in the century with several successful lines of reprints. However, the twentieth-century paperback revolution that began at the end of the 1930s was the result of the innovation of category fiction, that is, fiction written in a fairly rigid pattern for a carefully identified audience. Beginning with Mercury Mysteries, published by American Mercury Books, category fiction was developed on a large scale by Pocket Books, Avon, Dell, and others who marketed books to a targeted audience. By the 1950s, when the popularity of * mysteries began to fade, publishers turned to * gothic novels. By the early 1970s, this category of fiction outsold all others; as interest began to wane, publishers turned to developing lines of romance fiction. For women writers seeking a popular audience, category fiction has provided many opportunities, albeit circumscribed by the requirements of the genre.

A great expansion of publishing occurred after World War II, with the number of titles released doubling between 1955 and 1977. This expansion was due to many factors, including the continuing boom in mass-market paperbacks and new capital generated by mergers and corporate takeovers. At the end of the twentieth century, many of the older, larger publishing houses have been absorbed by holding companies or merged with others; some have themselves become conglomerates. In this environment profit expectations are continually pushed higher; the sale and management of subsidiary rights—multimedia packages of books in hardcover, paperback, and film—and the promotion of authors on television have become very important. Chain stores exert pressures for fast-turnover titles and market their books like any other product. On the other hand, many small presses and university presses are flourishing around the country. There are approximately 5,000 small book and magazine presses publishing a wide variety of serious, often non-mainstream literature as well as non-fiction. A good number specialize in work by and for women and minorities; many of them support local and regional publication. Some university presses, of which there are now eighty-one, have picked up the publication of fiction and poetry. Small personal imprints within larger houses also help to maintain outlets for more experimental works. In fact, there are over 5,700 presses in *Book Publishers Direc-*

tory (1981). But alarms are frequently raised by the Authors Guild and others that publishing is becoming big business, there is an overemphasis on large sales and profits, and publishers are paying too little attention to serious fiction.

While changes over the past three centuries in the technology and economics of publishing have determined the ways in which writers could reach their public, changing attitudes of publishers and editors toward writers have also affected women's experiences and success. In the nineteenth century when publishing emerged as a distinct profession, the most respectable publishers like Charles Scribner, George P. Putnam, and Daniel Appleton espoused an ideal of the "Gentleman Publisher" who would develop trusting, paternalistic, and personal relationships with authors; who would have goals beyond commercial ones, to advance culture or provide a public service; and who would assume the role of moral guardian for society. Connections between authors and publishers were expected to be family-like and long term. Even the more profit-oriented publishers like Robert Bonner tried to appear to conform to this ideal. It is interesting to speculate whether these values, which were remarkably compatible with those espoused for/by women, facilitated the dramatic success of women writers in the mid-century marketplace.

Later in the century, the new ideal of the "Businessman Publisher" was more frequently expressed by publishers like S. S. McClure, Edward Bok, and Frank Munsey. They emphasized activity, efficiency, and profits. Instead of cultivating relationships with authors, these publishers focused their attention on managing books, requesting manuscripts on particular topics rather than just waiting to see what would come "over the transom." They were interested in audience appeal more than in moral guardianship. There was less emphasis by these publishers on their literary affinity with writers. In this new market, editors rather than publishers read the manuscripts; editors rather than publishers developed personal relationships with writers. Some have suggested that these publishers' values may have shut some women out. In any case, it was at this time that male and female writers began organizing themselves into "unions" meant to address their grievances against publishers.

In the twentieth century, even editors—many of whom are now women—are caught up in the economic web. Publishers in corporate offices—most of whom are still men—think of publishing in terms of market strategies, computer analysis, and entertainment, not in terms of personal relations, cultural service, or moral guardianship. Their editors, who at mid-

century might still have worked closely with authors, by the 1970s had also become economic managers—securing manuscripts but not editing them, negotiating with agents, or seeing authors only until the contract is signed. Enticed by larger salaries that come from mergers, some editors move from firm to firm, leaving behind authors with new editors who know nothing about them. As a result many writers have chosen to work with smaller houses or with editors who have personal imprints in order to partially recapture the ethos of relationships of the past.

Concomitant with other changes, publishers' methods of acquiring and paying for works have changed over the past three centuries. In the colonies, printer-publishers charged authors for typesetting, distribution, and royalties on each book. In the eighteenth century, manuscripts were more often pirated from England or other countries than secured from local authors. American authors continued to publish at their own risk, paying publishers for printing and distributing their works, or occasionally receiving copies of their own books, rather than royalties. This was certainly a more difficult situation for women, who generally did not control their own money, than for men, who did.

Gradually in the nineteenth century a half-profits system evolved under which about one-third of the retail price was split between the author and publisher. In other cases, authors paid for their own stereotype plates and then arranged with publishers for subsequent printings. By mid-century, currency was more stable than earlier and publishers could make a profit, so writers were less often asked to share the cost of publication. Outright purchase or royalty payments became common. Nevertheless, the use of contracts was not a regular practice until after the Civil War. Even then, contents were not standardized. It is difficult to judge whether women as a group received lower compensation than men because arrangements were worked out on an individual basis. Some company records reveal that the most successful women did receive royalties at the same rate as their male peers: 10 percent and/or author's risk in the 1940s, 15 percent and up in the 1850s, then back to the norm of 10 to 15 percent from 1850s to 1890s.

By the end of the nineteenth century, agents had become important in negotiations. Before this time writers themselves had made their arrangements with publishers or used friends and relatives as intermediaries to conduct their business. With the advent of agents came greater competition for authors and somewhat higher royalties. By the first decades of the twentieth century, some authors could demand extremely large advances for their work, but, for most writers, royalties were usually 10 percent. By World War I, many publishers began offering a sliding scale on royalties of 10 percent on the first 2,500 copies, 12.5 percent on the next 2,500, and 15 percent on all copies above 5,000 sold. In the 1950s advances for potential blockbusters topped the $100,000 mark, and in the 1970s reached as high as $2 million. But, again, most authors receive advances and royalties on a much smaller scale, particularly from small presses.

An author's success has always been affected by his or her publisher's approach to advertising and distribution; practices in these areas have also changed over time. Because the reading community was small in the colonies and authors often knew the subscribers/purchasers of their books, there was almost no advertising. Books were sold in bookshops, by book peddlers, and, late in the eighteenth century, by auctions. In the nineteenth century, most "Gentlemen Publishers" resisted flamboyant advertising in favor of more dignified announcements of publication in the papers, though some devised successful book promotion techniques, including planting favorable reviews in the newspapers. Occasionally their firms "puffed" novels that they thought would be popular successes, but they rarely worked to create a market. By contrast, the less respectable, more profit-oriented nineteenth-century publishers sought books that fit into previously established popular styles. The Beadle Brothers, T. B. Peterson, and others flooded the market with dime novels, story papers, and other diversionary reading, much of it in imitation of earlier successes. They experimented more freely with advertising, some of them spending more on one book than the respectable publishers spent in one year.

By the end of the nineteenth century, advertising had expanded dramatically—in advance of publication to build readership and after publication through news stories about the author or book, controversies, serialization, dramatic adaptations, and other techniques. Publishers tried many experiments including streetcar advertising and billboards; testimonials on books became common. The 1920s brought advertising on the radio. Though reviewers were more independent of publishers than they had been in the past, publishers still tried to cultivate them to write notices of their books. More and more advertising attention was and is focused on potential bestsellers. Advertising for mass-market fiction emphasizes the similarity of books marketed in a series. Rather than creating an audience, the mass market publisher taps a relatively predictable

one through book clubs, grocery stores, bookstore chains, and subscription sales. At the end of the twentieth century two different philosophies of advertising exist: the older one that assumed a book is unique and advertising will help it find its audience; and the newer one that focuses on sustaining the interest of previously identified readers in a particular type of literary work.

The development of copyright protection for writers and publishers was slow. The Act of 1790 provided some national copyright protection to the work of American authors for fourteen years with privileges of renewal, but this protection did not apply to works written by foreign nationals. In 1831 this protection was extended to twenty-eight years with renewal for fourteen more. The cutthroat competition of the paperback boom of the 1870s ultimately convinced enough publishers and authors to work for the passage of an International Copyright Law (1891) that granted to resident and nonresident writers copyright for twenty-eight years with the privilege of renewal for fourteen. The new law curtailed the cheap book business that was based on piracy and established the view that ideas were property that deserved protection. This law was revised in 1909 and again in 1976. The most recent law extends protection for the author's lifetime plus fifty years. American writers are also protected by the Universal Copyright Convention (1955) and other copyright treaties with countries around the world.

[*See also* Authorship; Presses, Women's; also see articles on African-American Publishing Outlets; Latina Publishing Outlets; Lesbian Publishing Outlets; Native American Publishing Outlets.]

• William Charvat, *Literary Publishing in America, 1790–1850* (1959). John Tebbel, *A History of Book Publishing in the United States,* 4 vols. (1972, 1975, 1978, 1981). Mary Kelley, *Private Woman, Public Stage: Literary Domesticity in Nineteenth-Century America* (1984). Janice A. Radway, "The Institutional Matrix: Publishing Romantic Fiction," in *Reading the Romance: Women, Patriarchy, and Popular Literature* (1984). Christopher P. Wilson, *The Labor of Words: Literary Professionalism in the Progressive Era* (1985). Elizabeth Long, "The Cultural Meaning of Concentration in Publishing," *Book Research Quarterly* 1, no. 4 (Winter 1985–1986): 3–27. Cathy N. Davidson, *Revolution and the Word: The Rise of the Novel in America* (1986). Susan Coultrap-McQuin, *Doing Literary Business: American Women Writers in the Nineteenth Century* (1990).
Susan Coultrap-McQuin

PUERTO RICAN WRITING, U.S. The writings of Puerto Rican women in the United States have become in recent years an important element of what is generally referred to as "Latina" literature. According to the 1990 U.S. census estimates, Puerto Ricans comprise 12.1% of the Latino population in the U.S., or the second-largest Hispanic-origin group in the country. The majority of the Puerto Rican population in the U.S., close to three million people, inhabit the southeastern sector of the country, although their presence is felt in the Midwest and as far away as Hawaii. Emigration has been a reality for Puerto Ricans since the island's invasion by the U.S. in 1898, but increased tremendously after World War II. The fact that Puerto Ricans have been U.S. citizens since 1917 has facilitated a back-and-forth migration pattern that continues to the present.

Given the impact of emigration on the island, it becomes problematic to identify authors as either "exile Puerto Rican," "U.S. Puerto Rican," or *Nuyorican*, a term used to describe authors of Puerto Rican origin who write in English. In general, however, U.S. Puerto Rican women writers are either "involuntary exiles" who have left the island for economic or social reasons, or the daughters and granddaughters of immigrants of working-class origin. Puerto Ricans face the common problems of racial and social discrimination with other ethnic groups that fall under the category of "non-whites" in the United States; although they share these common issues, U.S. Puerto Rican women authors are highly diversified and continue to evolve.

Despite the earlier presence in the U.S. of such important island poets as Clara Lair (1895–1974) and Julia de Burgos (1914–1953), the late 1960s and early 1970s represent the initiation of U.S. Puerto Rican writing with the emergence in New York of a number of young authors born and/or raised in the city who wrote in English. Instead of finding their inspiration in island literary traditions, these authors would be motivated by other esthetic and social concerns. The * civil rights movement of the 1960s sparked their desire to express formerly repressed cultural ideas and sensibilities in their own words. Mainly poets, these authors were influenced in style, tone, and theme by the militant * African-American writers who more directly reflected their own experiences in the marginalized sectors of their urban environments. The street imagery, the declamatory and musical quality of the verses, and the strongly denunciatory nature of African-American poetry were appealing to writers who identified with the call for national unity and ethnic and racial pride. Many of these poets did not have the advantages of a university background and would acquire their literary training in the language of the streets and the * oral tradition of their culture.

For women poets, however, the desire to reflect the complexities of their communities included the identification and denunciation of certain myths regarding Latina women and their stereotypical role within Hispanic patriarchal culture. Born in the Bronx, New York, Sandra María Esteves (b. 1948) is one of the few women poets to emerge at this juncture. Her poems, collected in *Yerba Buena* (1980) and in *Bluestown Mockingbird Mambo* (1990), defend, on the one hand, her Latina identity in the face of Anglo-American cultural discrimination and domination, and, on the other, critique the contradictions and limitations of this identity from within. Esteves's poetry creates a voice for the urban Latina woman that combines poetic militancy with the vibrant rhythms of salsa music.

Esteves and other writers took their poems to the people, reading in the cafés, the workshops, and the public performances that were popular at the time. The issue of language at first was troublesome; * biculturalism was still devalued and, as many of these writers switched from English to Spanish in different poems or within the same work, they were thus left open to the criticisms of purists with more traditional linguistic ideals. The pejorative term of "Spanglish" was often used to describe their efforts. Nevertheless, bilingual poetry became a popular vehicle for their poetic expression of the community they wished to represent. What was not recognized at the time was their creativity and the importance of their having given a voice to the masses of Puerto Rican immigrants who were not usually reflected in traditional literature.

During this same period, Nicholasa * Mohr (b. 1935) published her first work of prose fiction, *Nilda* (1973), followed by a collection of stories called *El Bronx Remembered* (1975). *Nilda* was greeted with critical acclaim and won several important literary awards. Thematically, it follows the trend of that period in that it describes a young girl's growing up as a member of a distinct racial or ethnic group in Anglo-dominated U.S. society. The protagonist must confront conflicts that include * racism, alienation, and the quest for cultural identity. The novel, however, is also a woman-centered text as it stresses the sexual differentiation in the socialization of Latina girls and the social contradictions with regard to women that begin in the early stages of development. Mohr's later works, *Felita* (1979) and *Rituals of Survival: A Woman's Portfolio* (1985), further develop this idea.

The influence of the international women's movement of the 1970s affected the growth and evolution of the writing of U.S. Puerto Rican women. The number of publications by women increased and the direction of their works changed. While political and social concerns and the issue of cultural identity remained, authors would include a distinctly female statement in many of their writings. Luz María Umpièrre (b. 1947) arrived from Puerto Rico in the 1970s and has remained in the U.S. where she has published a number of collections of poetry. Umpierre is a feminist author who explores the oppressive nature of *machismo* in Puerto Rican culture as well as the taboo of * lesbianism. Her bilingual collection of poetry, *The Margarita Poems* (1987), is defiant and rebellious as it broadens the dimensions of the discourse of contemporary Puerto Rican women.

Recent writings by U.S. Puerto Rican women have expanded the vision of a Latina-identified literature. Writers are increasing in numbers and are more dispersed geographically and more varied stylistically and thematically than before. Born in Puerto Rico and writing from her home in Georgia, Judith Ortiz * Cofer (b. 1952) produced an acclaimed novel, *The Line of the Sun* (1989), and a collection of personal narratives, *Silent Dancing: A Partial Remembrance of a Puerto Rican Childhood* (1990), which elaborate another perspective on "Puerto Ricanness" that is not limited to the New York scene. Ortiz Cofer writes in English but skillfully recreates her Puerto Rican childhood and the difficulties and lessons learned of immigration and living in two worlds in a style and tone reminiscent of contemporary Latin American narrative. Carmen de Monteflores (b. 1933) also reconstructs the Puerto Rico of her childhood from a female perspective in a novel that traces three generations of women whose lives are marked by racism and patriarchy in *Singing Softly/Cantando bajito* (1989). Monteflores lives in California and is also not a part of the New York *Nuyorian* literary movement, which had been generally perceived as representative of U.S. Puerto Rican writing. Likewise, Aurora Levins * Morales (b. 1954), born in Puerto Rico of a U.S. Jewish father and a New York Puerto Rican mother, has been living in the U.S. since an early age in Chicago and later California. *Getting Home Alive* (1986), the work she co-authored with her mother, the poet Rosario * Morales (b. 1930), is a collection of poetry and prose that explores the lives of two Puerto Rican women and addresses the complex issues of cultural and personal identity from a feminist and Third World perspective.

Critical attention has been less forthcoming. An important contribution to general issues on the culture and history of Puerto Rican women, both on the island and on the mainland, is the collection of essays edited by Edna Acosta-Belén, *The Puerto Rican Woman: Perspectives on Culture, History and Society* (1979); essays on Puerto Rican women in the United States as workers and as community leaders have led to a reevaluation of the historical role of women in U.S. society. An essay in the collection by Angela Jorge on "The Black Puerto Rican Woman in Contemporary American Society" is one of the first serious treatments of a topic often excluded from discussions of Puerto Rican identity.

Another work of note is the collection *Breaking Boundaries: Latina Writing and Critical Readings* (1989). Despite obvious differences among the groups of Latinas studied in the work in terms of class, race, and education, their collective perception in the U.S. as "minority" women unites them in significant ways. *Breaking Boundaries* reflects feminism's interest in non-hegemonic and counter-hegemonic discourse and the marginalization of nontraditional artists, as well as the recognition that whether she is an immigrant, exile, or "native Hispanic," a Latina's cultural identity continues to affect her writing even as it is produced from within the borders of Anglo-American society. Thus Puerto Rican women writers, however distinct their individual voices, remain in many ways united as a group with a common cultural heritage and a common struggle for recognition as a vital and integral part of contemporary U.S. literature.

[*See also* Latina Writing; Chicana Writing; Cuban-American Writing; Ethnicity and Writing; Assimilation.]

• Margarite Fernández Olmos, "From the Metropolis: Puerto Rican Women Poets and the Immigration Experience," *Third Woman* 1, no. 2 (1982): 40–51. Alma Gómez, Cherríe Moraga, and Mariana Romo-Carmona, eds., *Cuentos: Stories by Latinas* (1983). María del Carmen Boza, Beverly Silva, and Carmen Valle, eds., *Nosotras: Latina Literature Today* (1986). Evangelina Vigil, ed., *Woman of Her Word: Hispanic Women Write* (1987). Sandra María Esteves, "The Feminist Viewpoint in the Poetry of Puerto Rican Women in the United States," in *Images and Identities*, ed. Asela Rodríguez de Laguna (1987), pp. 171–178. Yamila Azize, "A Commentary on the Works of Three Puerto Rican Women Poets in New York," in *Breaking Boundaries*, ed. Asunción Horno-Delgado, et al. (1989), pp. 146–165. Eliana Ortega, "Poetic Discourse of the Puerto Rican Woman in the U.S.: New Voices of Anacaonian Liberation," in *Breaking Boundaries* (1989), pp. 122–135. Faythe Turner, ed., *Puerto Rican Writers at Home in the USA* (1991).

Margarite Fernández Olmos

PURITAN WRITING. *See* Colonial Era Writing.

Q

QUEER THEORY is an interdisciplinary approach to the study of *sexuality, making significant contributions to literary criticism, film and video criticism, philosophy, cultural studies, psychoanalysis, and legal scholarship. Queer theory builds on feminism and gay and lesbian scholarship. But as its own category assembling antihomophobic writing about sexuality, it is a recent phenomenon, having taken shape at the end of the 1980s. The format in which queer theory has been defined includes academic conferences and journals, books, and anthologies of writing on sexuality and cultural *activism.

Much of the antihomophobic writing defining queer theory was written in response to a series of events in the 1980s that signaled a backlash against gays and lesbians in the United States. These events include the 1986 Supreme Court decision supporting antisodomy laws *(Bowers vs. Hardwick)*, a 1989 law forbidding federal funding for art containing depictions of *homosexuality, and homophobic government and media handling of the *AIDS crisis. Faced with these events, antihomophobic writing and activism became imperative to those concerned with the politics and representation of sexuality.

The use of the word *queer* over a more conventional vocabulary of sexuality reflects several aspects of queer theory's project. The reappropriation of *queer*, a word that has been used homophobically, echoes the importance of reclaiming, rereading, and redefining texts to antihomophobic theory. In her introduction to a queer theory issue of the feminist journal *differences* (vol. 3, no. 2, Summer 1991), film theorist Teresa De Lauretis ascribes the use of *queer* to an attempt to address the limits of terms like gay, lesbian, bisexual, homosexual, and heterosexual. In setting the agenda for queer theory, many writers argue that this vocabulary participates in a narrow view of sexuality defined by the homo/heterosexual split, and that it can exclude other aspects of *identity that modify sexuality such as *race, *class, or *gender.

For lesbians this issue is of particular import because lesbianism has occupied an uneasy place within feminist theory, and femininity an uneasy place within gay studies. The relation between ethnicity and sexuality is an especially difficult issue for both feminist and gay and lesbian scholarship. The term *queer* has been useful for creating a conceptual space for the study of the ways in which gender, sexuality, and ethnicity interact. Nevertheless, the political efficacy of organizing around queer identity is contested and, much like feminism, queer activism and theory has been criticized for its reluctance to address race. An elaboration of both the limits and the benefits of queer identity can be found in essays by De Lauretis and in "Queer Nationality," co-authored by Lauren Berlant and Elizabeth Freeman (*boundary 2* 19, no. 1, 1992, 149–180).

The use of the word *queer* is furthermore a rejection of the residues of clinical diagnosis that cling to the word *homosexual*, a term that evolved from late-nineteenth-century scientific analysis of non-reproductive sexuality. The study of the development of sciences of sexuality (as in *psychoanalysis, or in the search for a biological origin of sex) is of keen interest to queer theory. French philosopher Michel Foucault's *History of Sexuality, Vol. 1: An Introduction* (1980) provides a powerful critical analysis of these systems of knowledge, and is one of queer theory's foundational texts. Foucault argues that sexuality is not a congenital condition existing prior to language and then expressed through it, but is instead an effect of language. In his critique of the repressive hypothesis, he similarly argues that sex is not repressed by prohibition or language, but is rather *produced* through prohibition and language. The social construction of *gender has been argued by feminists for decades. But Foucault's discussion of sex takes place within an analysis of the promotion of reproductive sexuality and attempts to leave behind any understanding of sex (and indeed the subject itself) as existing beyond language. As Eve Kosofsky Sedgwick writes in *Epistemology of the Closet* (1991), one of the axioms of queer theory is that while the study of gender and sexuality have much in common, they are not coextensive and, "correspondingly, antihomophobic inquiry is not coextensive with feminist inquiry."

Gayle Rubin explores the overlapping of gender and sexuality in her influential essay "Traffic in Women" (Rayna R. Reiter, ed., *Toward an Anthropology of Women*, 1975). The work of Foucault and Rubin has had a direct impact on the study of sexuality. Judith Butler makes use of both in her book *Gender Trouble* (1990) as does Eve Kosofsky Sedgwick in *Between Men* (1985). These two texts illustrate some of the different avenues for the study of sexuality. *Gender Trouble* is an explicitly theoretical work that focuses on psychoanalysis and feminist theory. In this book Butler uses Rubin's work to theorize the place of melancholia and the prohibition of homosexuality in gender identity, and provides a critique of fixed gender identity. *Between Men* is also a theoretical work, but a work that unpacks its ideas through a reading of the social bonds between men in English literature. Rubin's essay provides the foundation for Sedgwick's examination of the relationship between compulsory heterosexuality, *homophobia, and misogyny through the definition and exploration of male homosocial desire.

A recurring theme in definitions of queer theory is its uneasy relationship to theory itself. In part this is because it takes sexuality as its topic for critical analysis. The writings that define queer theory are not always recognizably "theoretical." Writing on queerness, politics, and cultural production draws much inspiration from (if it is not directly related to) the work of AIDS activists. The importance of cultural activism to queer theory is nowhere more urgent and apparent than in antihomophobic writings responsive to the AIDS crisis. Cindy Patton's book *Inventing AIDS* (1990) has done much to define the field of writing about AIDS while demonstrating how writing on a specific social issue can and must address such larger issues as homophobia, *sexism, and misogyny.

This brings us to another way in which theory gets queered by queers. Similar to the way in which some feminist scholars combine autobiographical writing with critical writing, some queer writers explore the borders between theory and other forms of written expression. Exemplifying this kind of work are Cherríe *Moraga's book *Loving in the War Years* (1983), and Gloria *Anzaldúa's *Borderlands/La Frontera* (1987), both of which theorize a relationship between queerness and writing while exploring the terrain of being Chicana and lesbian in the United States.

In "Traffic in Women," Gayle Rubin wrote that any social theory that fails to theorize gender and sexuality must be considered inadequate. This has been echoed more recently in a broad spectrum of writing on what queer theory aims to accomplish. Queer theory is not the theorization of a marginal lifestyle, but rather an argument for the centrality of its concerns to the study of Western culture. The interrogation of the homo/heterosexual definition is not something that can to be tacked onto cultural analysis. Queer theory's definitive texts aim to demonstrate that the incorporation of the study of sexuality into social theory requires that the very terms of that theory be altered.

[*See also* Lesbian Literary Theory; Literary Criticism; Lesbian Feminism.]

• Cherríe Moraga and Gloria Anzaldúa, eds., *This Bridge Called My Back: Writings by Radical Women of Color*, 2d ed. (1983). Douglas Crimp, ed., *AIDS: Cultural Analysis, Cultural Activism* (1988). Martin Bauml Duberman, Martha Vicinus, and George Chauncey, Jr., eds., *Hidden From History: Reclaiming the Gay and Lesbian Past* (1989). Diana Fuss, ed., *Inside/Out: Lesbian Theories, Gay Theories* (1991). Bad Object Choices, *How Do I Look?: Queer Film and Video* (1991). Cherry Smith, *Lesbians Talk Queer Notions* (1992). Montique Wittig, *The Straight Mind and Other Essays* (1992). Henry Abelove, Michèle Aina Barale, and David Halperin, eds., *The Lesbian and Gay Studies Reader* (1993).

Jennifer B. Doyle

QUILTING. *See* Needlework.

R

RACE. In the introduction to *"Race," Writing, and Difference* (1985), Henry Louis Gates, Jr., deconstructs the notion of "race" as a natural means of classification and demonstrates that it is a cultural construct. In spite of the fact that race is a trope or figure of speech, usages of race as a purportedly objective term of categorization still persist. Gates explains that cultural or ethnic differences or inclinations have been ascribed erroneously to "race"; indeed, language itself is implicated in the construction of race since language is the purveyor of a cultural order in which these supposedly natural or essential differences exist.

Historian Barbara Fields defines race as an ideological and historical construct. Not only must the factors involved in the construction of "race" be revealed, but the power relations concealed must be exposed. Why, for example, is "race" primarily used to categorize subdominant groups in society? Why is it not used more often in reference to "whiteness," as Hazel Carby points out in *Reconstructing Womanhood* (1987)? Carby asserts, "Work that uses race as a central category does not necessarily need to be about black women." Although a complete study of the ideological construction of various "races," including the "white race," is beyond the scope of this essay, ideally future work will address how various constructions of "race" interact with and help maintain one another.

In particular, a study of African-American women is informative since the construction of their race is integrally linked to the construction of their gender. Under *slavery, the black woman was subjected to all sorts of physical and psychological abuse. She was forced to perform as much hard labor as a male slave and was often sexually assaulted by her master, who used her as a sexual object and breeder. Since by law, children followed the condition of their mother, the slave woman became the unwilling perpetrator of the cycle of subjugation as she bore more slaves. She occupied the lowest position on the social scale and was subordinated on the basis of both her blackness and her femaleness.

In the late nineteenth and the twentieth centuries, the subordination of African-American women has taken a subtler form. African-American women have too often been subsumed under the larger categories of black and female, as implied by the title of the 1982 work, *All the Women Are White, All the Blacks Are Men, But Some of Us Are Brave*, edited by Gloria T. Hull, Patricia Bell Scott, and Barbara Smith. Certainly, as Gerda Lerner observes in *Black Women in White America: A Documentary History* (1972), black women have been "doubly invisible" since they are members of two groups that have been traditionally discriminated against in American society. However, Hull, Scott, and Smith complicate this reductive conclusion by showing that black women have also suffered discrimination *within* those marginalized groups by a racist women's movement that catered to white feminists and a sexist black rights movement that catered to black men. In the words of bell hooks, "No other group in America has so had their identity socialized out of existence as have black women . . . When black people are talked about the focus tends to be on black *men;* and when women are talked about the focus tends to be on *white* women" (*Ain't I a Woman*, 1981). Throughout most of American history, society has neither recognized nor listened to the voices of black women.

In addition, publishing houses, largely owned and operated by white males, traditionally have not encouraged black women writers. Even those writers who did have the good fortune of being published have frequently been forgotten soon thereafter. Only in recent years has there been an upsurge in the publication of black women's writing. Feminist and African-American scholars and writers are rediscovering and reviving important writers such as Harriet *Jacobs, Harriet E. *Wilson, Frances E. W. *Harper, Pauline *Hopkins, Nella *Larsen, Zora Neale *Hurston, and Ann *Petry. In effect, until the last two decades, black women had received little scholarly attention. Black historian Paula Giddings addresses this neglect in the preface to *When and Where I Enter: The Impact of Black Women on Race and Sex in America* (1984) and explains that her mission is "to tell a story largely untold." Giddings's "narrative history" of black women is a pioneering work intended to fill some of the glaring gaps in contemporary historiography.

Giddings's book is preceded by a number of

notable works. In 1970, *The Black Woman*, an anthology edited by Toni Cade, demonstrated the commitment black women have to defining themselves. A landmark year, 1970 also saw the publication of first novels by Toni *Morrison *(The Bluest Eye)* and Alice *Walker *(The Third Life of Grange Copeland)*. In 1974, Mary Helen Washington's influential essay, "Black Women Image Makers," was published in *Black World* and Alice Walker's renowned essay, "In Search of Our Mothers' Gardens," first appeared in *Ms.* magazine. The advent of black feminist literary criticism, however, was not to arrive until 1977 with the publication of Barbara Smith's landmark essay in *Conditions II*, "Toward a Black Feminist Criticism." In this essay, Smith calls for the creation of a critical approach that considers the intertwining forces of race, sex, and *class. Smith laments the omission or mishandling of black women writers by white feminist or black male critics as well as the omission of black lesbian writers or lesbian approaches from critical discourse.

However, one of the most significant if least elaborate sections of Smith's essay outlines some of the principles she thinks black feminist critics should use and asserts the presence of a "specifically Black female language." Yet Smith does not theorize how this language might actually come into play in literature. While she suggests that this common language arises from a shared experience of sexual and racial politics, she does not examine precisely how racial and sexual differences might be inscribed in discourse.

It is this ambitious project that Mae G. Henderson undertakes over a decade later in one of the most interesting theoretical articles available today concerning black women's writing, "Speaking in Tongues: Dialogics, Dialectics, and the Black Woman Writer's Literary Tradition." In this essay, Henderson rejects the critical posture that regards black women reductively as the "Other." Instead, she addresses the matrix of otherness in the self. This culturally fabricated matrix is, by her definition, the point at which one's race and gender intersect. Henderson's theory thus "seeks to account for racial difference within gender identity and gender differences within racial identity." Instead of separating race and gender and thereby ignoring the complexity of the multiple voices in black women's writing, Henderson insists upon the fusion of the two, emphasizing that the movement of voices is at once internal and external: "Black women's speech/writing becomes at once a dialogue between self and society and between self and psyche." Henderson explodes the binary opposition of public and private discourse elucidated by Deborah E. Mc-

Dowell in " 'The Changing Same': Generational Connections and Black Women Novelists" through a theory that accounts for the varied voices manifest in the dominant discursive order as well as the subdominant discursive order.

The multiple voices and discourses Henderson discusses in her article figure not only in her example from Zora Neale *Hurston's *Their Eyes Were Watching God* (1937), but also in other texts by black women. For example, in *Incidents in the Life of a Slave Girl* (1861, reprint 1973), Harriet *Jacobs represents her self in the narrative as Linda Brent, a woman who has "a woman's pride and a mother's love for my children." She speaks a discourse of gender identity to her avowedly white female audience by emphasizing her role as mother, a mother who will not leave her children and therefore spends seven years in a cramped attic before fleeing to freedom. Yet as Brent speaks this discourse of gender identity, she also speaks a discourse of racial difference. Indeed, she is painfully aware of the difference between herself and her white female reader, a difference that she must maintain in order not to alienate her audience. As a forerunner of the tragic mulatta figure that would emerge in late nineteenth-century African-American literature, Brent is positioned precariously between her white readership and her black slave past. She must treat the *taboo topic of miscegenation carefully and take responsibility for her intimate relationship with a white man without offending her white audience. Thus Brent frames her story as a confession or apology while she simultaneously asserts that, "the slave woman ought not to be judged by the same standard as others." Though she would speak a discourse of gender identity "to arouse the women of the North to a realizing sense of the condition of two millions of women at the South, still in bondage," yet Brent is painfully aware of her racial difference, a difference that has been ideologically constructed so that she is viewed primarily as an animal for breeding rather than a woman.

It is in reaction to this construction of the African-American woman as beast and breeder that black women wrote at the end of the nineteenth century. *Iola Leroy* (1892), in particular, is a refutation of *stereotypes of black women, a refutation ensconced within the accepted form of the domestic or sentimental novel. Harper travels a tenuous line between what her audience expects in the form of the domestic novel and her own personal desire to uplift her race *and* her sex by refuting prevailing notions of black womanhood.

As a mulatta heroine, Iola mediates between

whites and blacks. She is in racial limbo since she appears white and has been raised to have the refinement of "white civilization," yet is remanded to slavery when a racist cousin proves that she has "black blood." Iola then begins to acknowledge her bloodline, and consequently loses her social position as a virtuous "white" woman. She is threatened by her master's sexual advances but manages to escape to become a great spokesperson for the "race." Iola conforms to white standards of physical beauty and womanly virtues, yet she addresses the problems of black people and acts as a conduit for Harper's own ideas about racial uplift.

Whereas Iola's "white" and female * body is the site for racial uplift, the "black" body of the slave woman was the site of her oppression. The (ab)use of the slave woman as sexual object/breeder, field hand, and domestic resulted in a fusion of sexual and racial oppression in her body and being. In effect, the slave woman's body became a text of racial and sexual slavery from which one might "read" the story of her objectification and oppression.

It is this reading of the black female body as a text of racial and sexual oppression that has become the thematic focus of recent literature and criticism by such critics as Mae G. Henderson and Hortense Spillers. Contemporary versions of * slave narratives, including Gayl * Jones's *Corregidora* (1975), Octavia * Butler's *Kindred* (1979), Sherley Anne * Williams's *Dessa Rose* (1986), and Toni * Morrison's *Beloved* (1987), are giving rise to readings of the body as historical text. For these black women writers, the act of "re-membering," as Morrison calls it, is an act of recalling, revising, and restoring the black woman's body to her self. "Writing the body" for black women involves tracing the ideological path the black woman has had to follow from being an object to being a speaking subject. The process has involved placing black female protagonists at the center of texts and developing the rhetorical dexterity to manipulate a multiplicity of discourses. By showing how the slave woman was physically and psychologically "dis-membered" by slavery, African-American women writers are "re-membering" themselves and asserting their power to create their own identities.

The movement for self-determination is perhaps best expressed by one of the characters in Ntozake * Shange's powerful choreopoem, *for colored girls who have considered suicide/when the rainbow is enuf* (1975). The lady in red proclaims, "i found god in myself/ & i loved her/ i loved her fiercely." By rejecting a patriarchal notion of a deity and reconceptualizing god as black and female, Shange celebrates what it means to be black and female and part of a supportive sisterhood. In fact, it is through a * ritual of healing shared by women that the lady in red finds, "all the gods comin into me/ laying me open to myself . . . the holiness of myself released." This holiness, an affirmation of the beauty of being black and female, is a radical revision of racist and sexist ideology. Contemporary black women writers such as Shange laud their own transformative ability to write racial and sexual identities they can celebrate into being, into history. They are healing the deleterious effects of past constructions of race and gender by positioning black women at the center of their texts as well as by manipulating a multiplicity of discourses in order to subvert the dominant, "Master" discourse.

Although this discussion focuses on race as it relates to African-American culture and literature, the basic precepts can be extended to a discussion of * Native American, * Latina, * Asian-American, and * Jewish-American culture and literature. Recent scholarship on race has considered it primarily as it pertains to African Americans. However, this situation is changing as writers such as Maxine Hong * Kingston (*The Woman Warrior*, 1976; *China Men*, 1980; *Tripmaster Monkey*, 1989), Leslie Marmon * Silko (*Ceremony*, 1977; *Storyteller*, 1981; *Almanac of the Dead*, 1991), Anzia * Yezierska (*Hungry Hearts*, 1920; *Bread Givers*, 1925; *Red Ribbon on a White Horse*, 1950), and Sandra * Cisneros (*My Wicked, Wicked Ways*, 1987; *The House on Mango Street*, 1988; *Woman Hollering Creek*, 1991) are garnering critical attention. It should be noted that constructions of race are, by their very nature, multiple, arbitrary, and divisive. Any study of a "race" therefore should address how the category has been constructed in social, literary, and cultural history, and should illuminate how the complex interweavings of various constructions of race uphold and perpetuate the existing social order.

[*See also* Black Feminism; Cross-racial Friendship; Cross-racial Relations; Ethnicity and Writing; Mixed Ancestry, Writers of; Passing; Whiteness.]

• Barbara Christian, *Black Women Novelists: The Development of a Tradition, 1892–1976* (1980). Angela Davis, *Women, Race, and Class* (1981). bell hooks, *Ain't I a Woman: Black Women and Feminism* (1981). Barbara J. Fields, "Ideology and Race in American History," in *Region, Race, and Reconstruction*, ed. J. Morgan Kousser and James M. McPherson (1982), pp. 143–177. Barbara Omolade, "Hearts of Darkness," in *Powers of Desire: The Politics of Sexuality*, ed. Ann Snitow, Christine Stansell, and Sharon Thompson (1983), pp. 350–367. Gloria Wade-Gayles, *No Crystal Stair: Visions of Race and Sex in Black Women's Fiction* (1984). Mae G. Henderson, "(W)riting *the Work* and Working the Rites," *Black American Literature Forum* 23, no. 4 (1989): 631–660. Francoise Lionnet, *Autobiographical Voices: Race,*

Gender, Self-Portraiture (1989). bell hooks, *Yearning: Race, Gender, and Cultural Politics* (1990). Deborah E. McDowell, "'The Changing Same': Generational Connections and Black Women Novelists," in *Reading Black, Reading Feminist*, ed. Henry Louis Gates, Jr. (1990), pp. 91–115. Mae G. Henderson, "Speaking in Tongues: Dialogics, Dialectics, and the Black Woman Writer's Literary Tradition," also in *Reading Black, Reading Feminist*, pp. 116–142. Joanne V. Gabbin, "A Laying On of Hands: Black Women Writers Exploring the Roots of Their Folk and Cultural Tradition," in *Wild Women in the Whirlwind: Afra-American Culture and the Contemporary Literary Renaissance*, ed. Joanne M. Braxton and Andree Nicola McLaughlin (1990), pp. 246–263. Mae G. Henderson, "Toni Morrison's *Beloved*: Re-Membering the Body as Historical Text," in *Comparative American Identities*, ed. Hortense Spillers (1991), pp. 62–86.

Barnsley Brown

RACIAL IDENTITY. Since "race" is a cultural construct, racial identity is the construction of a self with respect to the elements of "race." In African-American women's writing, the construction of blackness gradually shifts from being primarily external to internal as writers begin to claim and reclaim a racial identity through writing. The claiming of a racial identity entails the simultaneous claiming of a sexual identity since the two are interconnected throughout history.

The eighteenth-century slave poets, Lucy *Terry and Phillis *Wheatley, were the first black women to achieve *literacy and thereby to write themselves into being. As Gloria *Naylor notes in "Love and Sex in the Afro-American Novel," "To attain literacy, then, was actually to attain 'being' within the social fabric, and that was an illegal existence until the abolition of *slavery." Blackness was synonymous with nonbeing, with the absence of reason and even, as Henry Louis Gates, Jr., discusses, the absence of "a collective, cultural memory." To write was to affirm one's presence in a Eurocentric world that privileged writing over speaking and considered blacks as children or beasts incapable of rational thought.

In the sexual arena, racist plantation *myths of black men and women as animal breeders and sexual demons were deeply ingrained in the white cultural consciousness by the 1850s. The nineteenth-century *cult of true womanhood propounded piety, purity, submissiveness, and domesticity as the four cardinal virtues of womanhood, as Barbara Welter has pointed out. A fifth virtue should be added, however—that of *whiteness; for the slave woman by virtue of her blackness did not dare aspire to any other status. As Harriet *Jacobs, who adopts the *pseudonym of Linda Brent, confides in *Incidents in the Life of a Slave Girl*

(1861, reprint 1973), "It is deemed a crime in her [the slave woman] to wish to be virtuous." Jacobs's narrative implicitly writes her self into being, creating what Jean Fagan Yellin terms "a heroic female figure," and explicitly calls for a new moral standard to be applied to the slave woman. Jacobs creates a protagonist who, like Frado in Harriet E. *Wilson's *Our Nig* (1859), elicits the sympathy of a white audience.

Indeed, *Incidents* and *Our Nig* are harbingers of the project of racial (and sexual) uplift that would characterize the writings of the late nineteenth century. Both Frances *Harper's *Iola Leroy* (1892) and Pauline *Hopkins's *Contending Forces* (1900) catered to a white audience by immortalizing light-skinned heroines whose outer and inner qualities corresponded to the accepted tenets of the cult of true (white) womanhood. Only as chaste and pious heroines who were beautiful according to white standards could these female characters perform their services as the instruments of moral and racial uplift.

In the twentieth century, literary constructions of racial identity became less determined by external conditions—the predominantly white audience and publishing world—and more celebratory of blackness. The development of the *Black Aesthetic during the *Harlem Renaissance of the 1920s and 1930s and its revival in the *Black Arts Movement of the 1960s ensured that blackness would be considered in its own Afrocentric right rather than in contrast to a Eurocentric tradition. Thematically, the return to Africa was manifest in a return to primitivism and *exoticism. Black women writers were less concerned with uplifting the race by creating ideal protagonists according to the tenets of true white womanhood. Nella *Larsen, for example, problematized racial identity in the form of Helga Crane, the protagonist of *Quicksand* (1928), who disdains the project of racial uplift and is often alienated from her race. Like Lutie Johnson in Ann *Petry's *The Street* (1946), Helga Crane is viewed frequently by others as a sexual object. Her racial identity as defined by others is at once a sexual identity, a modern-day version of the sexual temptress of plantation myths. The struggles of Helga Crane and Lutie Johnson to control their degree of sexual intimacy with others suggest what critic Mary Helen Washington designates as a fundamental issue in black women's literature, "whether or not women can exert control over their sexuality."

The struggle of contemporary black women writers to represent their own sexuality is thus also a struggle to claim and reclaim an empowering racial identity. In-depth explorations of female sexuality, such as in Paule *Marshall's *Brown Girl, Brownstones* (1959), Toni *Morrison's *The Bluest Eye* (1970) and *Sula* (1973), and Alice *Walker's *The Color Purple* (1982), attest to the fact that, as Gloria Naylor writes, "Modern black women writers have . . . stepped beyond the traditional restraints against females exploring their own sexuality." In particular, black women writers have exposed how oppressive racial ideologies have impacted on their sexuality. For example, in Gayl *Jones's *Corregidora* (1975), Ursa must make a journey of memory in which she confronts the psychological and sexual abuse her foremothers suffered at the hands of Corregidora, "the Portuguese slave breeder and whoremonger." Ursa must connect her own experience of abuse to theirs, but also transform it. While her foremothers have internalized and embodied the ideology of racial and sexual slavery, Ursa must construct a self and an identity that is not subject to the Corregidora legacy. Like Dana in Octavia *Butler's *Kindred* (1979), Ursa bears the responsibility for both writing and righting the past. While Dana actually journeys back in time to become a slave in *Kindred*, Ursa's journey of memory provides the impetus for her realization: "I have to make my own kind of life. I have to make some kind of life for myself." Her task is to fashion a self independent of her foremothers and their abuse, and thus, like Dana, to rupture the legacy of psychological and sexual abuse.

In effect, the narratives of *Corregidora* and *Kindred*, fashioned as the autobiographies of Ursa and Dana, suggest the struggle of contemporary black women writers to name and claim a racial and sexual identity by "re-membering" themselves into a collective past. However, as in *Corregidora* and *Kindred*, the writing/righting of that past involves exposing the gaps in history as it has been written and using that deficient past to construct a more liberating future. Journeys of memory and across time are the means by which Ursa and Dana are represented as making sense of the past and using it to construct a self and a life in the present. As narrative constructs, Ursa and Dana demonstrate how contemporary black women writers recollect oral history and write it into existence, dismembering racist and sexist ideologies through their own construction of a racial as well as sexual identity.

• Barbara Welter, *Dimity Convictions: The American Woman in the Nineteenth Century* (1976). Dorothy Sterling, ed., *We Are Your Sisters: Black Women in the Nineteenth Century* (1984). Henry Louis Gates, Jr., ed., *"Race," Writing, and Difference* (1985). Jean Fagan Yellin, "Texts and Contexts of Harriet Jacobs' *Incidents in the Life of a Slave Girl: Written by Herself*," in *The Slave's Narrative*, ed. Charles Davis and Henry Louis Gates, Jr. (1985), pp. 262–282. Hazel V. Carby, *Reconstructing Womanhood: The Emergence of the Afro-American Woman Novelist* (1987). Mary Helen Washington, *Invented Lives: Narratives of Black Women 1860–1960* (1987). Susan Willis, *Specifying: Black Women Writing the American Experience* (1987). Gloria Naylor, "Love and Sex in the Afro-American Novel," the *Yale Review* 78, no. 4 (1988): 19–31.

Barnsley Brown

RACISM permeates American society, a tragic legacy of the nation's history. With the arrival of Europeans on the continent, racism shaped the country's past, as colonialists displaced indigenous peoples, challenged their sovereignty and imported Africans as slaves. Throughout colonial and national history, for nearly four hundred years, racism has informed national and social identities, shaped American traditions, determined the distribution of wealth and power, and affected ways of seeing the world. Racism remains embedded in the sign systems, discourses, and institutions of United States culture, as assumptions about race inform language, perception, and conceptual frameworks of western culture. Isolating and alienating people, racism produces much of the societal violence directed at individuals and groups. At the end of the twentieth century the persistence of racism has created what Andrew Hacker calls *Two Nations: Black and White, Separate, Hostile, Unequal* (1992). Derrick Bell asserts, in *Faces at the Bottom of the Well: The Permanence of Racism* (1992), that "racism is an integral, permanent, and indestructible component of this society." Racism affects all Americans, but some groups and individuals suffer more directly than others.

Racial theories first emerged in the eighteenth century, although the term *racism* is relatively recent: indeed, its first entry in the *Oxford English Dictionary* dates from 1936. Social scientific studies in the mid-twentieth century distinguished between *prejudice (attitudes) and discrimination (behavior) and emphasized race relations as they examined presumed "laws" of racism. In the last decades, the persistence of racism, the effects of *postcolonialism, and theoretical work on culture have led to ongoing studies of racism, emphasizing historical formulations, the construction of racialized subjects, and effects of racism. Contemporary models for defining racism identify three linked forms: individualized, institutional, and ideological racism. Individual behaviors include placing racial epithets on public buildings, burning crosses, and fleeing urban neighborhoods. Individualized racism exists in a framework of institutional racism, meaning the policies, practices, and discursive forms, based on perceived racial differences, embedded in and sanctioned by society's institutions—including legal codes and judicial practices, educational systems, financial policies, labor practices, artistic forms, and linguistic constructions. Institutional racism pervades all systems of signification that convey meaning and shape perception of reality in U.S. society. Ideological racism provides supposed intellectual support for belief in white superiority; historically, such arguments have drawn upon reason, nature, and divine law. Racism functions in American society to oppress groups presumed inferior by those in power. Historically, conquering Indians provided "free" land and enslaving Africans provided cheap labor; racism served to divide white and black workers, making collective resistance difficult. Racism continues to affect economic, social, political, and legal relations in the nation, and psychological residues of racism affect both whites and nonwhites.

The meaning of racism and its effects on American society can best be understood historically. Two groups most profoundly affected by racism are indigeneous peoples and Africans brought involuntarily to North America. During the voyages to the western hemisphere, the Doctrine of Discovery justified conquest of the New World for European monarchs and denied indigenous peoples sovereignty and human rights. Robert Williams Jr., in *The American Indian in Western Legal Thought* (1990), writes, "The Doctrine of Discovery and its discourse of conquest assert the West's lawful power to impose its vision of truth on non-Western peoples through a racist, colonizing rule of law." Ninety percent of pre-contact populations in North America were soon decimated by European diseases and the effects of conquest. In *The Conquest of America* (1982), Tzvetan Todorov argues that the European conquerors of the New World perceived racial difference in terms of superiority and inferiority, not as differences that implied equality. Difference that implied inferiority legitimated exploitation. Though colonial and U.S. government Indian policies shifted over four hundred years, the effects were similar: wars, genocide, broken treaties, lost sovereignty, receding boundaries of Indian territory, and internalized oppression. The spread of white settlement and empire across the continent rested on the doctrine of Manifest Destiny—belief that Providence had chosen Anglo-Saxons to spread democracy and civilization over the globe.

The transatlantic slave trade brought ten million Africans to the western hemisphere. * Slavery in the United States, defined as inherited, lifetime servitude based on race, is distinguished from ancient forms by its racial base and inherited condition. The Constitution identified blacks as three-fifths of a person, and in 1857 the Supreme Court argued that African Americans could not claim the rights of * citizenship. After 246 years, the Thirteenth Amendment abolished slavery in 1865, but emancipation meant four million freed blacks faced other forms of subordination. * Sharecropping meant economic oppression, and Jim Crow laws legalized segregation in the South—a system the Supreme Court declared constitutional in *Plessy v. Ferguson* (1896). *De facto* segregation prevailed in the North, and lynchings and terror served as extralegal social control to oppress blacks in the North and South into the twentieth century. The * civil rights movement in the 1950s and 1960s challenged institutional racism, yet the legacy of slavery and Jim Crow continues to affect black and white Americans. Being black in America, writes Hacker, "bears the mark of slavery."

Other non-Anglo-Saxons have also been the target of systemic and institutional racism. Mexican Americans became objects of racism as Anglo-Saxon settlers and the United States government occupied and then conquered northern Mexico. The Mexican-American War (1846–1847) and the subsequent annexation of the Southwest by the United States were justified through the doctrine of Manifest Destiny. The occupation of Mexican land displaced thousands of Mexicans and subordinated them economically, politically, and culturally to Anglo-American domination. Anglo settlements and capital created a cultural hegemony in the region that persists to the present. From 1820 to 1975, roughly 47 million immigrants from Europe and Asia immigrated to the United States. Twentieth-century racial theories—such as those found in *The Passing of the Great Race* (1916) by anthropologist Madison Grant, claiming that mass * immigration threatened the original Anglo-American stock—contributed to the restrictive immigration legislation of the 1920s. These theories also activated undercurrents of * anti-Semitism and nativism then directed especially at Eastern and Southern European immigrant groups. European immigrants, however, never faced the racism reserved for Asians, which was evident in the Chinese Exclusion Act (1882), the war against Philippine independence (1898–1902), and Executive Order 9066 (1942) mandating the forced internment of 120,000 Japanese-Americans during World War II. Ultimately, * whiteness provided a visible barrier to the systematic racism reserved for people of color in United States history.

In *Playing in the Dark: Whiteness and the Literary Imagination* (1992), Toni *Morrison asks, "What does positing one's writerly self, in the wholly racialized society that is the United States, as unraced and all others as raced entail?" The literature of the United States, Morrison asserts, "has taken as it concern the architecture of a *new white man*," and positioned American readers generally as white. Morrison wants us to consider what effect this has had on the literary imagination in the last four hundred years. She denies this means an "investigation of what might be called racist or nonracist literature." Yet, consciousness of historical racism embedded in all cultural discourses will entail a rethinking of American literature. In a "wholly racialized society," writers may respond differently: they may reproduce racism, be victimized by racism, or resist racism.

Throughout U.S. history, writers articulated prevailing cultural discourses and so reproduced racism linguistically, metaphorically, or ideologically. Some women's suffrage advocates in the nineteenth century questioned black male suffrage when white (educated) women were denied the vote. In *Women, Race and Class* (1981), Angela *Davis examines the racist assumptions and language of that movement. Racist arguments also emerged in the early birth control movement, including the writings of Margaret Sanger. In the twentieth century, popularized fiction such as Margaret *Mitchell's *Gone With The Wind* (1936) perpetuates racial *stereotypes. Yet a reproduction of racism also emerges in more subtle forms when writers assume American readers to be white. Contributing to the twentieth-century women's movement, Betty *Friedan's *The Feminine Mystique* (1963) focused on the "problem with no name," and allegedly wrote of women's issues, but the book primarily addressed the condition of middle-class, suburban, married, white women. The pervasive practice of universalizing white women's experience appears in the title of a more recent work, *All the Women Are White, All the Blacks Are Men, But Some of Us Are Brave: Black Women's Studies* (1982).

In 1772 Phillis *Wheatley, a young African slave and the first English-speaking black poet, was called before eighteen of "the most respectable characters in Boston" to determine the authenticity of her poetry. The "Attestation" included in her first volume affirms that the poems "were (as we veribly believe) written by Phillis, a young Negro Girl, who was but a few Years since, brought an uncultivated Barbarian from Africa." Her African origins raised suspicions about the poetry's authenticity, demonstrating how racism may inform publication decisions, standards of worthiness, credibility, and value. These assumptions may operate unconsciously. The internalization of western European and American values, belief structures, and language by those who have been conquered, colonized, enslaved, or occupied represents another kind of victimization. For example, Toni Morrison's novel *The Bluest Eye* (1970) demonstrates the effect on a young black girl of racialized assumptions of *beauty, which represent blue eyes (signifying whiteness) as the object of desire. In her *autobiography, *Lakota Woman* (1990), Mary Crow Dog refers to this internalized oppression as being "whitemanized."

Women writers have also exposed and resisted racism. In the eighteenth and nineteenth centuries, black women focused much of their speaking and writing on the evils of slavery. *Black Women in White America: A Documentary History* (1972), edited by Gerda Lerner, reveals two centuries of black women's resistance to racism. In the early part of the twentieth century, works by Zora Neale *Hurston resist racism through emphasizing the persistence of black cultural traditions, for example *Mules and Men* (1935) and the novel *Their Eyes Were Watching God* (1937). Few white writers have attacked racism in American society, though abolitionists did, most notably Angelina and Sarah *Grimké. Harriet Beecher *Stowe's *Uncle Tom's Cabin* (1852), despite its racial stereotypes, attacked slavery directly when male writers of the period avoided it. In the twentieth century, Willa *Cather's *Sapphira and the Slave Girl* (1940) addresses slavery, and despite its limitations, Morrison notes, to Cather's "credit she did undertake the dangerous journey."

The last half of the twentieth century brings a flowering of writings by women of color resisting racism, representing all cultures and genres. Pioneering and collective efforts illustrate the shared struggle of women fighting racism, evident in *This Bridge Called My Back: Writings by Radical Women of Color* (1981), edited by Cherríe *Moraga and Gloria *Anzaldúa. Much of this writing explores cultural traditions and identity as one tool to resist hegemonic racist assumptions. Numerous writers resist racism directly by exposing its systemic and institutional forms, such as the dramatist Lorraine *Hansberry, whose award-winning play *A Raisin in the Sun* (1959) portrays three generations of a black family living in Chicago after World War II. Other African-American writers whose resistance to racism has been direct include the dramatist Ntozake *Shange; autobiographers such as Angela *Davis, Ann

Moody, and Maya *Angelou; the poets Gwendolyn *Brooks, Nikki *Giovanni, Audre *Lorde, and Sonia *Sanchez; and fiction writers Paule *Marshall, Gloria *Naylor, Toni Cade *Bambara, and the well-known and acclaimed Alice *Walker and Toni *Morrison. Native American writers also resist racism by affirming tribal traditions, for example, in Leslie Marmon *Silko's *Ceremony* (1977), which juxtaposes the destructive effects of racism on a young Indian male with the healing powers of Native American stories and *rituals. Autobiographers such as Mary Crow Dog (Lakota); poets such as Wendy *Rose (Hopi), Linda *Hogan (Chickasaw), Joy *Harjo (Creek), Paula Gunn *Allen (Laguna); and novelists such as Silko continue to expose racism while affirming traditional cultural identities. *American Indian Literatures: An Introduction, Bibliographic Review and Selected Bibliography* by A. LaVonne Brown Ruoff (1990) signifies the revitalization of these traditions and a resistance to racism.

A renaissance in Chicano literature began in 1965 and Chicana writers figured prominently. Cherríe Moraga's autobiography, *Loving in the War Years* (1983), and Gloria Anzaldúa's groundbreaking work, *Borderlands/La Frontera: The New Mestiza* (1987) and *Making Face, Making Soul: Haciendo Cara—Creative and Critical Perspectives by Women of Color* (1990), which Anzaldúa edited, deserve special mention in their resistance to racism and *sexism. *Chicano Literature: A Reference Guide* (1985), edited by Julio Martinez and Francisco Comeli, provides a meaningful sourcebook. The term *Asian-American* includes a number of groups from South and Southeast Asia; however, Asians are frequently discussed together for statistical purposes and to provide collective strength in the face of racism. Probably the most well-known Asian-American writer is Maxine Hong *Kingston, whose celebrated autobiographical work, *Woman Warrior* (1975) narrates the life of a young Chinese girl living among "ghosts." The rich and extensive writings of other Asian-American writers surface in the comprehensive collection *Making Waves: An Anthology of Writings By and About Asian American Women* (1989), edited by Asian Women United of California. Feminist scholars, such as bell hooks, resist racism by questioning its nature in the context of sexism, and by exploring the racist and sexist dimensions of post-colonialism, as do the works of Gayatri Chakravorty *Spivak.

[See also Prejudice.]

• Ron Takaki, *Iron Cages: Race and Culture in Nineteenth Century America* (1979). Henry Louis Gates, Jr., 'Race,' Writing and Difference* (1985). Peter Jackson, ed., *Race and Racism: Essays in Social Geography* (1987). Aldon Lynn Nielsen, *Reading Race: White American Poets and the Racial Discourse in the Twentieth Century* (1988). Paula Rothenberg, *Racism and Sexism: An Integrated Study* (1988). John Hope Franklin, *Race and History* (1989). Robert Miles, *Racism* (1989). bell hooks, *Yearning: Race, Gender and Cultural Politics* (1990). *Racism in the United States: A Comprehensive Classified Bibliography* (1990). David Theo Goldberg, *Anatomy of Racism* (1990).

Betty Ann Bergland

RAMSAY, Martha Laurens (1759–1811), diarist. One of the few American women idealized in nineteenth-century Protestant circles for the spiritual intensity and theological sophistication characterizing the portions of her private diary that were published posthumously in her *Memoirs*, Ramsay was born to Henry and Eleanor Laurens, leading citizens of Charleston, South Carolina, in 1759. Amid a family constellation constantly altered by death (an older sister died when she was five, her mother when she was eleven, her youngest brother when she was eighteen, her oldest brother in one of the last battles of the Revolutionary War), the earthly anchor of her life was devotion to her father. Traveling to England in 1775 with a sick uncle and aunt, and then to France, where she was trapped by the outbreak of war, Martha was finally privileged to serve in a public capacity as her father's hostess and secretary (the best he ever had, he told her biographer) during peace negotiations held in Europe in 1782–1783, to which Henry Laurens was one of three U.S. ambassadors.

Martha returned to Charleston in 1785, already twenty-five years old, well traveled and widely read. She had initiated a French village school, nursed her dying uncle and aunt, and tutored her own young sister. The physician attending her very ill and aged father, Dr. David Ramsay, already twice widowed and with an infant son, married her in January 1787. She viewed their republican marriage as a "matrimonial partnership" and bore him eleven children, eight of whom (four girls, four boys) were living when she died in 1811. Dr. Ramsay gave public credit to Martha for assisting him in medical and historical research, for her exemplary character, and for educational leadership, including her own curriculum for the children. She was enthusiastic about their friend Dr. Benjamin Rush's *Thoughts on the Education of Young Females* (1789).

Ramsay's presence on the new American literary horizon was engineered by her husband, himself one of the nation's first published historians. He assembled the *Memoirs of the Life of Martha Laurens Ramsay* (Philadelphia, 1811) around the private *diary she asked him to preserve as "a common book among the family" a few days before her death. His forty-six-page biography introduced it and four appendices completed it. Three of the appendices consisted of her letters or meditations and a fourth contained letters from Henry Laurens to Martha during the historic year 1776.

Since her writings were not originally intended for public consumption, the wording is intimate but abstract. She cast her passionate self-scrutiny in scriptural and theological terms, the highest psychologically analytic language available to her. The actual family and political events that gave rise to her internal dialogues with God must today be reconstructed from her husband's or father's papers. Her *Memoirs* reveal a literate, spiritually enlightened woman employing diary writing as a means of coping with life's daily trials: economic uncertainties, evangelical influences, illness and death, even a son's study habits at Princeton in 1810. The *Memoirs*, reprinted ten times up to 1845, were cited in popular religious magazines and other women's diaries as exemplary for the American woman.

• George C. Rogers, "Martha Laurens Ramsay," in *Notable American Women* (1971), pp. 111–113. Joanna B. Gillespie, "Many Gracious Providences: The Religious Cosmos of Martha Laurens Ramsay," *Colby Library Quarterly* 25, no. 3 (September 1989): 199–212. Joanna B. Gillespie, "Martha Laurens Ramsay: A Case Study of Diary as Autobiography," in *A Women's Diaries Miscellany*, ed. Jane Dupree Begos (1989). Joanna B. Gillespie, "Martha Laurens Ramsay: Prototypical Citizen in the Constitutional Era," in *A Selection of Papers from Women and the Constitution: A Bicentennial Perspective*, ed. Joyce M. Pair (1990). Joanna B. Gillespie, "1795: Martha Laurens Ramsay's Dark Night of the Soul," in *William and Mary Quarterly* 47, no. 1 (January 1991): 68–92.

Joanna B. Gillespie

RAND, Ayn (1905–1982), novelist, playwright, and philosopher. Alyssa (Alice) Rosenbaum, born and educated in St. Petersburg, Russia, created herself anew as Ayn Rand when she immigrated to the United States in 1926. Having experienced firsthand the effects of the Bolshevik revolution, Rand rejected the premises of communism on moral grounds, and became a lifelong advocate of capitalism. Through all her writings, both fiction and nonfiction, runs a basic theme of individualism, a rejection of collectivism.

Rand's earliest writing jobs were as a screenwriter; she lived in California during much of her early professional life. She first came to public attention, however, as a playwright. *Night of January 16th*, originally titled *Penthouse Legend*, had a successful Broadway run in 1935 and continues to be a staple of little theater. Taking place entirely in a courtroom, its most significant theatrical innovation is the

selection of a jury from the audience each night to decide the fate of the heroine.

We the Living (1936) and *Anthem* (1938), her first novels, attracted little attention, but *The Fountainhead* (1943) established her as a novelist of ideas and created an audience for further development of her philosophy, which climaxed in *Atlas Shrugged* (1957). *Atlas Shrugged* became the "bible" of an intellectual movement and the philosophy that Rand called "objectivism."

Though her philosophy is dismissed by the academic establishment and her novels deprecated by belles-lettres critics, her ideas have wide-ranging influence. A 1991 survey by the Library of Congress and the Book-of-the-Month Club found *Atlas Shrugged* second only to the Bible in a list of books that most influenced readers' lives. Many Libertarian leaders acknowledge her early influence, though she renounced their movement.

After the publication of *Atlas Shrugged*, Rand wrote no more fiction. During the sixties, she spoke on college campuses, wrote for *The Objectivist Newsletter* (later *The Objectivist*), and published several collections of essays. After her 1969 break with Nathaniel and Barbara Branden, who through the Nathaniel Branden Institute (NBI) created a national network of objectivist groups, she published *The Ayn Rand Letter* on an irregular basis until 1976. Important works from this era include *The Virtue of Selfishness* (1964), *Capitalism: The Unknown Ideal* (1966), *The Romantic Manifesto* (1969), and *Introduction to Objectivist Epistemology* (1979). The last book she worked on was *Philosophy: Who Needs It* (1982), published posthumously.

• William O'Neill, *With Charity Toward None* (1971). Mimi Reisel Gladstein, *The Ayn Rand Companion* (1984). Barbara Branden, *The Passion of Ayn Rand* (1986). Harry Binswanger, ed., *The Ayn Rand Lexicon* (1986). Ronald E. Merrill, *The Ideas of Ayn Rand* (1991).

Mimi Reisel Gladstein

RANTING. Throughout women's writings, a theme recurs: the need to break silence—not, as Tillie *Olsen (*Silences*, 1978) clarifies, natural silences, as of winter or gestation, but "unnatural silences" mandated by oppression. When a woman speaks her mind, criticizes, or talks back, she frequently is accused of bombast, *gossip, man bashing, *hysteria. No matter how measured her tones, she is likely to be reviled as a ranter, a wielder of wild, unruly, extravagant, unreasonable, and even violent verbiage. Yet, rant women must, for, as Audre *Lorde promised, our *silences will not protect us.

Representative "rantankerous" U.S. writers (and speakers) include Sojourner *Truth, Matilda Joslyn Gage, Elizabeth Cady *Stanton, Ida B. *Wells, Emma *Goldman, Kate *Millett, Robin Morgan, Valerie Solanas, Mary *Daly, Andrea *Dworkin, Catharine MacKinnon, June *Jordan, Gloria *Anzaldúa, Leslie *Silko, Paula Gunn *Allen, Cherríe *Moraga, Ntozake *Shange, Alice *Walker, and Toni *Morrison. Variously, they rail against atrocities of sex, *race, and *class; blaspheme against the male god/rod; storm against the wasting of the Earth; and rage against the silencing of all those who are *Other to *patriarchy. Anzaldúa refuses the orders of the white man to "stop speaking in tongues, stop writing left handed. Don't cultivate your colored skins nor tongues of fire if you want to make it in a right-handed world." Ranting back, she calls upon "third world women writers . . . [to] vomit the guilt, self-denial and race-hatred . . . force-fed us right back into [their] mouth."

Ranting women are seen as "unreasonable." To rant, as the dictionary defines it, is to "be in a rage," and ranting is the pure verbal expression of that passion. According to Mary Daly, women should not only proudly name themselves shrews, nags, scolds, harpies, and bitches, but should carefully nurture their passions against the seductions of psychic numbing. As she writes in *Pure Lust* (1984), "Rage is not 'a stage.' It is not something to be gotten over. It is transformative, focusing Force."

It is rage that fuels women's speaking out against atrocities such as *lynching and sexual abuse. For years, Ida B. Wells ran a one-woman crusade against lynching, daring openly to name the sexual abuse of African-American women by European-American men, and denouncing the lynch-legitimating lie that made all sexual contact between African-American men and European-American women *rape. So powerful were her words that in 1892 the offices of her newspaper, the Memphis *Free Speech*, were ransacked, and Wells herself was threatened with lynching. Wells clearly had succeeded in becoming (in the words of resplendent ranter June Jordan) a "menace to . . . [her] enemies."

For the past ten years, Andrea Dworkin and Catharine MacKinnon have run a two-woman crusade against *pornography, which, according to Dworkin, is "a discrete, identifiable system of sexual exploitation that hurts women as a class by creating inequality and abuse. This is a new legal idea, but it is the recognition and naming of an old and cruel injury to a dispossessed and coerced underclass. It is the sound of women's words breaking the longest silence." Some feminists accuse Dworkin and MacKinnon of censorial and antisex tendencies, insisting that pornography is speech, not practice. In

a 1991 novel, *Mercy*, Dworkin's protagonist, after years of sexual abuse, enunciates a political principle: "It is very important for women to kill men," and then does so. By explicitly advocating reverse gender terrorism in her fiction, Dworkin dares challenges from those who defend pornography as mere representation not connected to acts in the real world.

Women will be seen as most unreasonable and "rantankerous" when advocating violence against men. In 1968, another singular voice called for that necessity. Valerie Solanas opens the *Scum Manifesto* with this charge: "Life in this society being, at best, an utter bore and no aspect of society being at all relevant to women, there remains to civic-minded, responsible, thrill-seeking females only to overthrow the government, eliminate the money system, institute complete automation and destroy the male sex." In her riotous rant, Solanas eschews traditional political activism: "If SCUM ever marches, it will be over LBJ's stupid, sickening face. If SCUM ever strikes, it will be in the dark with a six inch blade." Many readers undoubtedly will reject Solanas's explicit directive toward political homicide, but may nonetheless delight in her unmatched invective as she anticipates some of the principal themes of radical *feminism: the fraudulent character of patriarchal literature and art, the connections between *patriarchy and necrophilia, mental illness, the trashing of the environment, sexual obsessiveness, and much more.

Solanas's hatred of her enemy is echoed in Alice *Walker's 1982 essay, "Only Justice Can Stop a Curse." It opens with a curse-prayer collected by Zora Neale *Hurston in the 1920s, an invocation of devastation so extreme that it causes Walker to sympathize temporarily with a revenge fantasy of nuclear holocaust against the white man's civilization (an emotion shared by Paula Gunn *Allen in her 1988 poem, "Molly Brant, Iroquois Matron Speaks"). Blasting the patriarchal European-based culture, Walker declares, "What they have done to the Old, they will do to the New. Under the white man every star would become a South Africa, every planet a Vietnam," and warns that "only justice to every living thing (and everything is alive) will save humankind."

In this essay, as in *The Color Purple* (1982), Walker invites her readers to consider the power of the curse-prayer, that rhythmic intonation of furious words so akin to ranting, in which the speaker calls upon fate to doom one's enemies and alter the course of events. In its best sense, ranting is not only a clarifying explosion of rage and truth, but also simultaneously a method of transmutation. Womanists use words to cast spells, to *Be-Speak*, defined by

Mary Daly and myself in *Webster's First New Intergalactic Wickedary of the English Language* (1987) as "bringing about a psychic and a material change by means of words; speaking into be-ing."

According to patriarchal grammar/language/reality, women are eternally silent things. Catharine MacKinnon sums up that dynamic as "Man fucks woman; subject verb object." Ranting or "talking back" radically disrupts and denies that progression, for women's verbal fire is no mere bombast, but is, as bell hooks avows, "the expression of our movement from object to subject—the liberated voice."

• June Jordan, "I Must Become a Menace to My Enemies," in *Things that I Do in the Dark* (1977), pp. 144–146. Audre Lorde, "The Transformation of Silence into Language and Action, in *Sister Outsider* (1978; reprint, 1984), pp. 40–44. Catharine A. MacKinnon, "Feminism, Marxism, Method, and the State: An Agenda for Theory," *Signs: Journal of Women in Culture and Society* 7, no. 3 (1982): 515–544. Gloria Anzaldúa, "Speaking in Tongues: A Letter to Third World Women Writers," in *This Bridge Called My Back: Writings by Radical Women of Color*, ed. Cherríe Moraga and Gloria Anzaldúa, 2d ed. (1983), pp. 165–173. Alice Walker, "Only Justice Can Stop a Curse," in *In Search of Our Mothers' Gardens* (1983), pp. 338–342. Andrea Dworkin, "Against the Male Flood: Censorship, Pornography, and Equality," in *Letters from a War Zone* (1985), pp. 253–275. Paula Gunn Allen, "Molly Brant: Iroquois Matron Speaks," in *Skins and Bones* (1988), pp. 10–13. bell hooks, *Talking Back* (1989).

Jane Caputi

RAP. The roots of rap can be traced from African bardic traditions to African-American secular and sacred traditions, such as toasts, sermons, blues, "the dozens," signifying, and jive (street) talk—all of which are delivered in a rhythmic chanted or poetic fashion. Since the 1920s, African-American artists—poets, jazz musicians, radio disc jockeys, comedians, ballad and funk-style performers—have occasionally interspersed traditional secular expressions, including jive talk and signifying, in their performances; the expressions were simply performed a cappella or loosely chanted over music. By the 1970s, chanting expressions in rhyming couplets to the rhythm of music was popularized among African-American youth of New York City as a distinct genre called rap music. It is defined as a quasi-song with rhyme and rhythmic speech, which draws on street language and is recited over an instrumental soundtrack.

In the early 1980s, major rap music performers were primarily males; but by the mid-1980s, a growing number of female artists expanded the roster. Among these were Roxanne Shante, The Real Roxanne, MC Lyte, Queen Latifah, Salt-N-Pepa, Yo-Yo, Nikki D., Harmony, Leshaun, Monie Love, and Sister Souljah.

• Tricia Rose, "Never Trust a Big Butt and a Smile," *Camera Obscura* 23 (May 1990): 109–131. Cheryl L. Keyes, *Rappin to the Beat: Rap Music as Street Culture among African Americans* (1992). Cheryl L. Keyes, " 'We're More Than a Novelty, Boys': Strategies of Female Rappers in the Rap Music Tradition," in *Feminist Messages: Coding in Women's Folk Culture*, ed. Joan N. Radner (1993), pp. 203–220.

Cheryl L. Keyes

RAPE. The project of tracing the thematic appearance of rape in American women's writing is complicated by cultural constraints that have discouraged women from articulating the threat of sexual violence, and by representational limitations that make it difficult to capture the experience of rape in words. The rapes that do appear in early American women's writing are seldom named as such. In the genre of the seduction novel, for example, the line between reluctant acquiescence and rape is frequently blurred. Susanna *Rowson's *Charlotte Temple* (1791), in which Montraville abducts the heroine and carries her off, unconscious, assigns responsibility for the "illicit love" that follows not to the man but to the woman, who has "forgot the respect due to herself."

Rape surfaces in nineteenth-century women's writing primarily in connection with the issue of slavery, which institutionalized the rape of black women by white men. Slave narratives such as Harriet *Jacobs's *Incidents in the Life of a Slave Girl* (1861) underline the immediate threat of rape in the everyday lives of slave women. Harriet Beecher *Stowe's novel *Uncle Tom's Cabin* (1852) traces the way in which Simon Legree's repeated rape and dehumanization of his slave, Cassy, transforms her faith into desperation and violence. In Pauline *Hopkins's novel *Contending Forces* (1899), much of the plot revolves around an incident in which a black man is lynched for raping a white woman; at the same time, a white man's rape of his black niece remains unpunished. A similar revelation of culture's double standards emerges in Sarah Winnemucca *Hopkins's *Life among the Piutes* (1883). This Native American perspective on frontier life reveals the Indian woman's fear of rape by white frontiersmen, and thus provides an important counter to a genre of Indian *captivity narratives in which the virtue of white women is repeatedly threatened by the savagery of their captors.

Many of the most interesting representations of rape in twentieth-century women's writing may be found in the work of *Latina, *Asian-American, *Native American, and

*African-American writers. These groups of women, who have traditionally confronted the barriers of race and ethnicity as well as gender, claim for themselves in their representations of rape the right to speak their own violation—and thus, frequently, the right to reclaim themselves from it. The increased statistical vulnerability of minority women to the violence of rape is a practical reality that is also a manifestation of a larger problem of maintaining identity in a hostile world; in the literature of minority women, rape is often a symbolic mark of oppression that also never ceases to exist as a concrete, physical fact. In "Poem about My Rights" (*Passion*, 1980), June *Jordan moves easily and naturally from her inability to step outside her door for fear of rape to the way in which her very identity is defined by violence: "I am the history of rape/ I am the history of the rejection of who I am. . . ." As an act in which physical and emotional violation converge, in which the external force of the violator is necessarily contained within the most intimate space of the victim, rape is an assault often imaged as self-destruction, an experience defined by the literal violation of the boundaries of anatomy and autonomy. Such an experience of fragmentation, as Jordan observes here, is also the fundamental experience of a woman attempting to claim an identity in a culture that defines her as the weakness against which to measure its own strength, or the absence that serves to mark its presence.

In *I Know Why the Caged Bird Sings* (1970), Maya *Angelou describes her own childhood experience of rape by observing, "The act of rape on an eight-year old body is a matter of the needle giving because the camel can't. The child gives, because the body can, and the mind of the violator cannot." In such a case, the victim's body becomes the imprint on which the rapist's identity is forcibly inscribed, her own being the mark of his desperate claim to power. In raping, therefore, the violator not only assaults his victim, but turns her presence into an absence that she herself may be unable to reclaim. The twelve-year-old rape victim in Cherríe *Moraga's play *Giving Up the Ghost* (1986) describes the rapist's attempt to penetrate her young body as a literal and figurative process of creating a hole where none existed before: "there was no hole/ he had to make it/ 'n' I see myself down there like a face/ with no opening/ a face with no features. . . . HE MADE ME A HOLE!" In rape, the apparent intimacy of physical closeness and the absolute denial of the victim's subjectivity converge to lend the rapist an awful power that the torturer/protagonist of Maria Irene Fornes's *The Conduct of Life* (1985) describes as "a desire to destroy and to

see things destroyed and to see the inside of them."

Just as Fornes, a Cuban-American writer, dramatizes the psychology of torture and rape to explore the psyche of the rapist, Chicana writers like Moraga, Sylvia Lizarraga, and Sandra Cisneros concentrate on the victim's experience of violation. In Lizarraga's short story "Silver Lake Road" (in *Requisa Treinta y Dos*, 1979), the rape of a single working mother pushes her to reconsider a traditional patriarchal relationship, as the need for protection suddenly looms larger than the desire for freedom. *Cisneros's short story "Red Clowns" (in *The House on Mango Street*, 1985) traces the impact of rape on a young girl haunted not only by the sour breath and brute force of the boy who rapes her, but by his corruption of the words of romance: "He wouldn't let me go. He said I love you, I love you, Spanish girl."

At times, the terrible intimacy of the act of rape is exaggerated by a victim's sense of complicity in her own violation. In *The Woman Who Owned the Shadows* (1983), Native American writer Paula Gunn *Allen explores a woman's self-fulfilling notion of her own powerlessness through a representation of rape that stresses Ephanie's inability to act out her resistance to a boyfriend's violence. As Louise *Erdrich explores in *Tracks* (1988), female power is not always a shield from male violence; in this novel, a strong and defiant young woman is raped by a group of men who attempt to reclaim through violence the patriarchal authority she has usurped.

The relationship between rape and power is also explored in the works of several Chinese-American women writers. Winnifred Eaton *Reeve's *Cattle* (1923) focuses on a young orphan girl who is raped by a cattle rancher determined to own and control not only his cattle, but his wife and his female servant. In Lin Tai-Yi's *War Tide* (1932), a Chinese woman is nearly raped by a Japanese soldier, and a twelve-year-old boy is forced to watch as his mother is raped and murdered. More recent fiction includes Diana *Chang's *A Passion for Life* (1961), a novel about a married woman's rape and subsequent pregnancy, and Amy *Tan's *The Joy Luck Club* (1989), which explores violence as a class and power issue by tracing the success of a wealthy man who forces An-Mei's widowed mother to be his concubine by "dishonoring" her through rape.

Contemporary African-American women writers whose works address the issue of rape include playwrights Adrienne *Kennedy (*Funnyhouse of a Negro*, 1964) and Ntozake *Shange (*for colored girls who have considered suicide/ when the rainbow is enuf*, 1975). Poet June Jordan reflects on rape as a personal and a political issue in "Case in Point," "Rape Is Not a Poem," and "Poem about My Rights" (*Passion*, 1980). The effect of rape or attempted rape on relationships between black and white women is addressed in Sherley Anne *Williams's *Dessa Rose* (1986) and Alice *Walker's "Advancing Luna—and Ida B. *Wells" (in *You Can't Keep a Good Woman Down*, 1981). The literal vision of rape victim and violator produce divergent perspectives on the experience of violation; in representations of rape, the reader may be subjected to the rhythms of the violator's pleasure, trapped within the confines of the victim's body, or afforded the luxury of the observer's detachment. While Maya Angelou, Ellease *Southerland (*Let the Lion Eat Straw*, 1979) and Alice Walker (*The Color Purple*, 1982) trace the experience of rape through the eyes of a child attacked by a trusted adult, Toni *Morrison (*The Bluest Eye*, 1970) focuses on the rapist's perspective to capture the emotional and physical turmoil underlying a father's rape of his daughter. In contrast, Gloria *Naylor's *The Women of Brewster Place* (1982) locks the reader within the victim's perspective during one of the most painful and sustained representations of violation in American literature.

The contributions of white women writers to the study of rape have also become increasingly visible in the last century. The issue of marital rape arises in several works that document the way in which the physical abuse of power is complicated by the manipulation of emotional ties. Both Meridel *Le Sueur's *The Girl* (written in 1939) and Marge *Piercy's *Small Changes* (1973) include scenes of marital rape. In Mari *Sandoz's nonfictional account of her abusive father's life, *Old Jules* (written in 1935), and Tillie *Olsen's novel, *Yonnondio* (written in the late 1930s), a daughter attempts to understand her father's brutality against her mother and women in general.

A number of novels published by white women in the 1970s explore the issue of rape as they reflect on related issues of power, gender, and violence. A focus on the aftermath of rape for the victim characterize J. M. Meier's *The Rape of Anne* (1976), Marilyn *French's *The Women's Room* (1977), and Gloria D. Miklowitz's *Did You Hear What Happened to Andrea?* (1979). Other novels of the seventies include Diane Johnson's *The Shadow Knows* (1975) and Lois *Gould's *A Sea Change* (1976), which blurs the line between fantasy and reality to focus on the experience of a woman raped with a gun by a man (real or imagined) she refers to familiarly as B.G., black gunman.

Poetic and dramatic reflections on rape include Adrienne *Rich's poem "Rape" (1972), which explores how the voice of authority in *patriarchy (in this case, a policeman responding to a rape victim) perpetuates violence against women; Ellen Bass's *Our Stunning Harvest* (1984), a dramatic reading that protests against male violence; and performance artist Karen Finley's collection *Shock Treatment* (1990). Susan Brownmiller's *Against Our Will* (1975) provides a fascinating and at times controversial reference source for the study of rape.

The works discussed here represent only a partial listing of women's writings on rape. Many early American works by women are only now being discovered and circulated, while portrayals of rape in many contemporary popular works, including the romance novel, raise questions of their own. Clearly, any analysis of women's writing on rape is more than a scholarly pursuit; it is one dimension of a larger effort to understand the origin and impact of rape, and ultimately to diminish the threat of such violence on women's lives.

[*See also* Incest; Sexual Harassment; Violence.]

• Maria Herrera-Sobek, "The Politics of Rape: Sexual Transgression in Chicana Fiction," *Americas Review* 15, nos. 3–4 (1987): 171–188. Elaine Showalter, "Rethinking the Seventies: Women Writers and Sexual Violence," in *Women and Violence in Literature*, ed. Katherine Anne Ackley (1990), pp. 237–254. Carolyn G. Heilbrun and Nancy K. Miller, eds., *Rape and Representation* (1991).

Laura E. Tanner

RAU, Santha Rama (b. 1923), novelist, essayist, travel writer. Santha Rama Rau was born in Madras, India. As the daughter of a diplomat, she traveled extensively, and was educated in England and the United States, graduating from Wellesley College in 1944. She accompanied her father to Tokyo when he was appointed independent India's first ambassador to Japan in 1947, and she taught English at Mrs. Hani's Freedom School in Japan. She also accompanied her father to the United States when he was appointed India's ambassador to the U.S., but she soon returned to Asia because she wanted to travel through the Far East. She has written memoirs, novels, travel books, and a cookbook.

In her first novel, *Remember the House* (1956), Baba, a young Indian woman, is seduced by the glamour of Western-style romance. She spurns the possibility of an arranged marriage and decides to fall in love with a schoolteacher who is already betrothed. Eventually, Baba learns about the different traditions and faces of love, and acknowledges the network of relationships of which she is a part.

Rau's first book, *Home to India* (1945), is autobiographical. It is the story of a young woman's return to her paternal grandmother's home after ten years of education in the West. *East of Home* (1950), another autobiographical work, begins with Rau's experiences in postwar Japan under the occupation. From Japan, she travels through cities and villages of China, Indochina, and Indonesia. It is a fascinating chronicle of a westernized Indian woman's gradual realization of herself and her country as integral and permanent parts of Asia. Many of Santha Rama Rau's works do read like travelogues, but in the best of her works, the reader finds compassionate and informative perceptions of the complex relationships that exist within and between families and cultures.

Santha Rama Rau's works are often difficult to find, and some are even out of print. This is a disservice to an important writer whose influence on younger, well-known South Asian–American women writers such as Meena *Alexander and Bharati *Mukherjee should not be underestimated.

• Roshni Rustomji-Kerns, "Expatriates, Immigrants and Literature: Three South Asian Women Writers," the *Massachusetts Review*, special issue entitled *Desh-Videsh: South Asian Expatriate Writing and Art* 29, no. 4 (Winter 1988–1989): 655–665.

Roshni Rustomji-Kerns

RAWLINGS, Marjorie Kinnan (1896–1953), novelist, essayist, and short story writer. Born and raised in Washington, D.C., Marjorie Kinnan graduated from the University of Wisconsin in 1918, married Charles Rawlings in 1919, and spent the next decade as a journalist in Rochester, New York. (She divorced Charles in 1933 and married Norton Baskin in 1941.)

A 1928 fishing trip changed the course of her life and her literary career. Enchanted by the north central Florida wilderness and its inhabitants, Rawlings purchased the farm and citrus grove later immortalized in her autobiographical *Cross Creek* (1942). Struggling to run the farm and grove, she found her spiritual home in the tiny rural community. "Cracker Chidlings" and "Jacob's Ladder" (*Scribner's Magazine*, 1931) began her lifelong commitment to writing about the region. She spent two months in the remote Big Scrub to research her first novel, *South Moon Under* (1933), a Book-of-the-Month Club selection. Her story about a backwoods woman betrayed by an unscrupulous husband, "Gal Young 'Un" won the 1933 O. Henry Memorial Short Story Contest. *The Yearling* (1937), a tale of a boy's coming-of-age in the isolated Florida frontier, brought her national celebrity and the 1938 Pulitzer Prize.

The success of *Cross Creek* inspired *Cross Creek Cookery* (1942), but also provoked a 1943 lawsuit by Zelma Cason for libel and invasion of privacy. In a highly publicized 1946 trial, neighbors and fellow writers rallied to support Rawlings. A jury ruled in her favor, but the Florida Supreme Court overruled the decision, awarding Cason nominal damages for the use of her name without permission. Although a landmark for the right of privacy in Florida, the decision has not served as a precedent for suits of other writers. Troubled by the trial, health problems, and the death of her trusted editor, Maxwell Perkins, Rawlings published little in the next decade. Research for a biography of her friend Ellen *Glasgow was cut short in 1953 when Rawlings died of a cerebral hemorrhage.

Although she repudiated *regionalism as a genre that exploits people's quaintness at the expense of their humanity, Marjorie Kinnan Rawlings became known for capturing the unique culture of a state increasingly stereotyped as a tourist resort. Focusing on isolated areas whose rough terrain inhibited commercial development, she depicted the poor white residents—with the exception of servants in *Cross Creek*, African Americans remain peripheral in her work—as fiercely independent pioneers, obeying a frontier ethic of respect for nature and mutual survival.

Rawlings other works are *Golden Apples* (1935); *When the Whippoorwill* (1940); *The Sojourner* (1953); *The Secret River* (1955); and *The Marjorie Rawlings Reader* (1956).

• Manuscripts and papers are located in the Marjorie Kinnan Rawlings Collection at the University of Florida Libraries' Rare Book Section. Additional collections are held at the University of Georgia Libraries, Athens; Alderman Library, University of Virginia, Charlottesville; Beinecke Rare Book and Manuscript Library, Yale University; and Scribner's Archives, Firestone Library, Princeton University. The *Marjorie Kinnan Rawlings Journal of Florida Literature*, begun in 1988 as the *Rawlings Journal* and renamed in 1990, has been the primary forum for criticism of her work. See also Gordon E. Bigelow, *Frontier Eden: The Literary Career of Marjorie Kinnan Rawlings* (1966). Gordon E. Bigelow and Laura V. Monti, eds., *Selected Letters of Marjorie Kinnan Rawlings* (1983). Elizabeth Silverthorne, *Marjorie Kinnan Rawlings: Sojourner at Cross Creek* (1988). Patricia Nassif Acton, *Invasion of Privacy: The* Cross Creek *Trial of Marjorie Kinnan Rawlings* (1988).

Jennifer Parchesky

RAY, Henrietta Cordelia (1849–1917), poet. Henrietta Cordelia Ray won public recognition in 1876 for her poem "Lincoln: Written for the Occasion of the Unveiling of the Freedmen's Monument in Memory of Abraham Lincoln." Born in New York, she was one of the three surviving daughters of Charles Bennett Ray, editor of the *Colored American* and later the pastor of the Bethesda Congregational Church. The Ray children were well educated: Charlotte Ray was the first woman lawyer to be admitted to the bar in the District of Columbia; Florence and Cordelia, as she preferred to be called, both had postgraduate degrees and careers as teachers.

H. Cordelia Ray wrote mainly sentimental lyrics on hackneyed themes, ignoring the current issues affecting her race. She and her sister Florence wrote *Sketch of the Life of the Rev. Charles B. Ray* (1887), her first book to be published. "To Our Father," a sonnet, is a moving tribute. The biography itself, however, is mainly a compilation of tributes, and gives no insight into its subject's character.

Sonnets, a collection of twelve poems, was published in 1893. These Petrarchan sonnets are on topics such as Niobe, life, aspiration, self-mastery, Shakespeare, Milton, Beethoven, and Raphael. Unfortunately, there are very few verses that display any complexity or innovation.

Ray published another collection of her verses in *Poems* (1910), which remained unavailable outside research libraries until its reprinting in *Collected Black Women's Poetry*, volume 3 in the Schomburg Library of Nineteenth-Century Black Women Writers (1988). The 145 poems are arranged in ten sections: A Rosary of Fancies; Meditations; Sonnets; Champions of Freedom; Ballads; Chanson D'Amours; Quatrains; The Procession of Seasons; and Heroic Echoes.

Ray was praised extensively by her contemporaries for her refined manners and classical learning. Hallie Quinn Brown in *Homespun Heroines and Other Women of Distinction* (1926) commended her on her "versatality, love of nature, classical knowledge, delicate fancy, and unaffected piety."

Ray's sheltered existence allowed her to nurture her literary skills, but also hampered her break from the genteel tradition. She lived in a cocoon, spinning her fanciful lyrics in intricate designs. It is not surprising then that she is remembered primarily for being an accomplished poet at a time when few black women could boast of such a distinction.

• S. Elizabeth Frazier, "Some Afro-American Women of Mark," *A.M.E. Church Review* 8 (April 1892): 373–386. William Henry Robinson, Jr., *Early Black American Poets* (1969). Joan R. Sherman, *Invisible Poets*, 2d ed. (1989).

Leela Kapai

READERSHIP. Women from the colonial period to the present have used their reading for pleasure and self-education. Reading gives women insight into their lives and their culture, mirrors their own experience and values, and creates a sense of community with authors, characters, and other women with whom they share their reading.

The majority of colonial American women had neither the education nor the leisure time to engage in extensive reading. Female children were taught only basic reading skills so that they could read the Bible. However, as E. Jennifer Monaghan notes, even limited reading skills would have been invaluable for a colonial woman, for time to read was time for herself and a departure from her multiple roles, all of which involved taking care of others. Having the power to read also enabled a woman to engage in her own religious devotions and to teach others to read. For the women writers of this period, reading one another's writing was crucial for their work and sense of themselves as artists. As Pattie Cowell notes in *Women Poets in Pre-Revolutionary America, 1650–1775* (1981), many colonial women poets corresponded with one another about their work, exchanged their poems, and wrote poems to one another.

Women readers in the Republican period benefited from improvements in women's *education and an expanding print world: *literacy levels rose, and changes in printing technology made more literature, particularly novels, available. The power of these texts in women's lives can perhaps best be measured by the vehemence with which social authorities protested against women reading fiction. Authorities encouraged women to avoid fiction's corrupting powers by reading history books instead. Yet as Linda K. Kerber observes in *Women of the Republic* (1980), the history texts of this period contained little about women's experience: if a woman sought a text that would mirror her life and her aspirations, she could only turn to a novel. Cathy N. Davidson argues in *Revolution and the Word* (1986) that novels of the early Republican period, such as *The Coquette* (1797) and *Charlotte Temple* (1791), became a source of self-education for the disenfranchised groups of the Republic, particularly women. Many of these novels also contained strong messages in support of women's education.

As the nineteenth century progressed, more women-authored texts appeared and women's readership grew. Susan K. Harris (*Nineteenth-Century American Women's Novels*, 1990) found evidence in the *letters and *diaries of nineteenth-century women that they often read *biographies of heroic women and were drawn to novels whose heroines provided them with role models for their own lives. Harris argues that although the "underplots" of nineteenth-century novels such as Catharine * Sedgwick's *A New-England Tale* (1822), Susan * Warner's *Queechy* (1852), and Louisa May * Alcott's *Work* (1873) conveyed traditional messages about female dependency, their "coverplots" presented women readers with models of independence—emotional, physical, and financial.

Barbara Sicherman's study of the Hamilton family of Indiana in the late nineteenth century provides further indication of reading's effect on women's sense of self. Drawn to plots that centered on adventurous and independent women who were involved in improving their communities and society, the young Hamilton women used these role models to articulate their career aspirations. Alice Hamilton was inspired to become a physician through reading Edmond O'Donovan's *The Merv Oasis* (1882), and Edith Hamilton's work with classic * myths and her skills as a storyteller were fostered by her love of historical novels and novels set in exotic places. In addition to helping each daughter develop her individual sense of self, the Hamilton family's reading strengthened the bonds of their community. Family members formed a reading club in which they read aloud from a variety of books. Their shared reading provided them with a shared language and ways to understand the world: when one of the women left home to attend school, she received a letter jointly written by seven of her relatives asking her to compare her experience with the depictions of boarding schools they had read in novels.

The Hamilton family's reading club continues to have descendants in the modern period. Elizabeth Long studied five Texan women's reading clubs in the 1980s and found that while the women used the categories designated by cultural authorities, such as "serious reading," to select their books, they used their reading for their own purposes. Ignoring issues such as the text's aesthetics, the women readers instead focused on their identifications with the characters in the books, using these to affirm their own choices or learn from people whose lives were different from their own. In so doing, the reading club members often valued the very aspects of women characters devalued by the culture at large.

Women readers also find "serious" meaning from their reading of popular literature. Janice Radway studied a group of romance readers (*Reading the Romance*, 1984) who described their reading of a genre criticized for being escapist trash as a rich and complex experience. Just as a colonial woman valued her time to read as time for herself, so too the twentieth-century romance readers viewed their reading as a break from the demands that they faced

as wives and mothers. Through the process of identifying with the romance's heroine, who came to be valued and nurtured by the male character, women readers experienced affirmation that they failed to receive in their role as the caretaker of others. Though the messages of the romance novels are not particularly radical—they do not challenge the social structure that creates and reinforces women's traditional roles—their effects are: women readers stated that their reading changed them by increasing their self-respect, which in turn enabled them to better assert themselves and their needs.

[*See also* Reading Circles; Women's Clubs; Libraries; Bookstores.]

• Elizabeth A. Flynn and Patrocinio P. Schweikart, eds., *Gender and Reading* (1986). Elizabeth Long, "Women, Reading, and Cultural Authority," *American Quarterly* 38, no. 4 (Fall 1986): 591–612. E. Jennifer Monaghan, "Literacy Instruction and Gender in Colonial New England," in *Reading in America: Literature and Social History*, ed. Cathy N. Davidson (1989), pp. 53–80. Barbara Sicherman, "Sense and Sensibility: A Case Study of Women's Reading in Late-Victorian America," in *Reading in America*, ed. Cathy N. Davidson (1989), pp. 201–225. Carl F. Kaestle et al., *Literacy in the United States: Readers and Reading since 1880* (1991).

Amy M. Thomas

READING CIRCLES. The term *reading circles* refers to social groups in which women read to pursue self-education. From the colonial period to the first years of the nineteenth century, reading circles were usually family-centered. Beginning in the 1830s, white and African-American women organized literary societies and reading clubs. Most prevalent between 1890 and 1940, they were part of a more general phenomenon—the club woman movement. In recent years, with increasing numbers of American women working outside the home, the club woman movement has languished, and with it the highly organized clubs typical of the previous period. Still, in most American cities today a multitude of informal groups of women meet regularly to discuss books and literary topics.

From the 1600s through the Revolution, women had no organizations to support their own reading, and they read or were read to within family circles. Most of their reading material came from the Bible, sermons, and godly books such as John Foxe's *Book of Martyrs*. Occasionally, women met to read socially with men. We know from the diary of Bostonian Samuel Sewall (1652–1730) that he joined a group of his fellow church members to read sermons and the biblical texts upon which they were based. In family circles and in church-based reading circles, the authority of fathers, husbands, and ministers ensured that social reading did not include bawdier popular tales like those of Chaucer, and that women's interpretations of Scripture confirmed the authority of the established government and rulers. As the 1637 interrogation of Anne *Hutchinson by the Massachusetts General Court shows, biblical interpretations that undermined New England Puritanism could result in church discipline and banishment.

Even though the Revolution brought with it new ways of thinking that promoted women's *education, few women in the early Republic had leisure time to organize reading circles outside their families. Northern and southern white women's diaries show women reading with and to sisters, mothers, and daughters as they darned, sewed, crocheted, or did needlepoint. Some families of the upper-middle and upper classes often spent literary evenings. The du Pont family of Wilmington, for example, read and enjoyed the plays of Corneille and Racine. Although the du Ponts were unusual because they spoke and read French during such evenings, they and many other well-educated families of the early Republic read secular works almost exclusively. For instance, by 1800 in southern Vermont, a median-size family library might have contained six books, among them a Bible and either schoolbooks, dictionaries, music books, travel books, philosophies, modern and classical literature, agricultural or scientific works, and books on politics and government. And by 1800, most American educators thought that women should read in all of these categories.

Historians theorize that women in family-based reading circles deferred to older, male participants. Often, deference was a necessity, since fewer than 60 percent of white women read in the northern states before the Revolution. Such deference would determine who chose the book to be read, who read it, and whose opinions prevailed in discussions of meaning. This interpretation gains reinforcement from the many sermons of the late-eighteenth and early-nineteenth centuries that decry women's practice of solitary reading and especially of reading novels. And women were reading novels, both alone and in the company of others. Diaries tell of women reading novels within female family circles and forming reading circles of friends. In both groups, women did *needlework and joint projects such as quilting while listening to novels.

During the antebellum period, among northern and midwestern white, middle- to upper-class women, extra-family reading circles usually had religious instruction or charitable work as their primary goal. If women had been touched by the message of evangelicalism, they often met in mothers' societies, benevolent associations, and education and missionary societies to read religious literature and advice about how to raise children and perform household responsibilities, and possibly also to sew and make quilts for the nearby or faraway needy. As the Strongsville (Ohio) Ladies Benevolent Society read from religious journals, letters from missionaries, *advice books, and magazine articles, its members sewed for the Home for the Friendless in New York City, the Ojibways in Minnesota, and fugitive slaves in Canada.

Among white working women and African-American women in antebellum America, reading circles had the purpose of complementing basic education and promoting self-improvement. Early-nineteenth-century *sentimental novels show factory girls organizing reading groups, and in Lowell, Massachusetts, in the 1830s, reading circles proliferated.

The first reading circle among African-American women known to historians is the Female Literary Society of Philadelphia (1831). Also in the 1830s, women in New York and Boston, cities with large free African-American populations, developed their own literary societies to help them gain the education often denied them by segregated common schools. While white Americans debated whether African Americans had a place in their society or whether they should be colonized in Liberia, African Americans found themselves unwelcome as speakers and patrons of learned societies and lyceums. So they formed their own associations for mental self-improvement in hopes of proving to white Americans that their achievements qualified them to live in free society. In Boston, the Afric-American Female Intelligence Society (1832) was founded by women who felt "actuated by a national feeling for the welfare of our friends" and so "thought it fit to associate for the diffusion of knowledge, the suppression of vice and immorality, and for cherishing such virtues as would render them happy and useful to society."

In the late 1860s, white middle-class women, with time to spare from household duties and child care, developed a new institutional public life by founding study and reading clubs. Although women's literary societies and *library associations existed before the *Civil War, the major period for the founding of reading clubs extends from the postbellum period through the first few decades of the twentieth century. In the late nineteenth century, reading clubs were controversial because of their association with woman's rights and because the word *club* previously had denoted organizations of men. Although most reading clubs were small—fewer than twenty-five members—so that meetings could be held at a member's home, thousands of women belonged to study clubs. After 1890, when reading clubs gained popularity in southern states, almost every American town and city had one, and large cities might have had as many as a dozen; to name a few: the Reading Club of Rockmart, Georgia; the Quiet Hour Club of Metuchen, New Jersey; the Fortnightly of Chicago; the Runcie Club of St. Joseph, Missouri; and the Ladies Literary Club of Salt Lake City.

For all but the summer months, a reading club usually met on a specified afternoon either bimonthly or monthly. For the year's work, a club would either adopt an author or devote themselves entirely to one topic, such as Shakespeare or the geography, history, and literature of a particular country. Each member prepared a paper in turn, and papers could be philosophical or practical. The Denver Fortnightly, for example, heard members deliver papers on "The Obligations of the Ideal to the Material" and "The Middle Period of Woman's Life: Its Advantages, Opportunities, and Capabilities." Most reading clubs had a written constitution; elected officers; adopted a club motto, color, and flower; and affiliated with the General Federation of Women's Clubs (1890).

In the postbellum period, reading clubs extended women's intellectual concerns and social life beyond their households. In the clubs of these days, reading matter was secular and the primary focus. Club constitutions usually banned discussions of religion and politics—topics that could destroy the comity of viable clubs. No longer was reading primarily religious or an accompaniment to domestic or charitable handiwork. Like the antebellum associations of African-American women, these reading clubs encouraged personal discipline, hard study, and the development of self-confidence. In their reading clubs, married women found opportunity to continue their education. As they researched topics and presented papers, they gained knowledge beyond their formal instruction in academies and high school and gained what may have been their first public speaking experiences.

Starting in the late 1880s, African-American middle- and upper-middle-class women also organized reading clubs and literary societies. In the South, these clubs often were founded by the women associated with one of the new institutions for higher education, as was the case, for instance, with the Tuskegee Women's Club (1895). Clubs followed southern African-American women's migration to northern cities and fulfilled that group's desire for an associa-

tional life aside from the churches. The Woman's Improvement Club of Indianapolis (WIC) (1903) came to be dominated by professionals, mostly teachers in the public school system, though clubs in other cities more closely resembled white clubs, with married members working primarily in their homes. Like the antebellum literary societies, the early-twentieth-century African-American clubs pursued high culture and tried to develop their members' race consciousness. The Coterie in Topeka read "the best known writers of this country and England," and WIC members learned about "Negro Inventions" and "Woman's Rights, and Especially of the Importance of Negro Women Being Alive to Their Opportunities."

Both white and African-American clubs involved themselves in their communities through philanthropy. A usual project for white clubs was the founding or raising of funds to support local, often segregated public libraries, while African-American clubs reached out to the less fortunate of their own race. The WIC of Indianapolis both founded a tuberculosis camp—the disease was epidemic among the urban poor—and sponsored public lectures by prominent African Americans such as Ida B. *Wells and W. E. B. Du Bois.

Since World War II, the highly organized women's reading club affiliated with a national club organization seems to have almost disappeared. Still, extra-domestic reading circles or clubs abound. City branches of the American Association of University Women sponsor study groups, and many white and African-American church women organize themselves for Bible study. Additionally, women in many American cities belong to informal reading circles. Almost none have constitutions; only a few have names. Some have met for a decade; others are ephemeral, coming together in response to an individual's or group's curiosity, and dissolving once it is satisfied. Whatever their form, most present-day clubs devote themselves to the study of women—either women's issues, literature, or history. This common interest shows that contemporary reading group members, usually college-educated women in their forties and fifties, use their associations to pursue knowledge that higher education of twenty to forty years ago did not offer. Elizabeth Long, a historian of modern-day reading clubs, points out that club discussions often give value to aspects of women's nature and experience ignored and devalued by the larger culture. Since the early Republic, women have used reading circles to direct their own education, and to integrate learning with their lives as mothers, wives, and workers.

[See also Women's Clubs; Readership; Libraries; Literacy; Education.]

• Jane Cunningham Croly, *The History of the Woman's Club Movement in America* (1898). Dorothy B. Porter, "Organized Educational Activities of Negro Literary Societies, 1828–1846," *Journal of Negro Education* 5 (1936): 555–576. Karen J. Blair, *The Clubwoman as Feminist: True Womanhood Redefined, 1868–1914* (1980). Helen H. Santmyer, ". . . And Ladies of the Club" (1982). Paula Giddings, *When and Where I Enter: The Impact of Black Women on Race and Sex in America* (1984). Elizabeth Long, "Women, Reading, and Cultural Authority: Some Implications of the Audience Perspective in Cultural Studies," *American Quarterly* 38 (1986): 591–612. Theodora Penny Martin, *The Sound of Our Own Voices: Women's Study Clubs, 1860–1910* (1987).

Louise L. Stevenson

REALISM. The term *realism* is derived from the Latin word *res*, meaning "thing." Realism therefore denotes a fundamental attachment to the things of this world without any transcendence. Before it was adopted into literary criticism, realism was commonly associated with materialism in philosophy. In the context of writing, realism is often envisaged in opposition to or as a reaction against romanticism. The term was first applied to literature in the French journal *Mercure de France* in 1826 to describe a type of writing that sought to imitate directly from nature rather than from previous artistic models, as had been customary. *Réalisme* was also the name of a review that appeared in Paris between July 1856 and May 1857; it proclaimed that art should give a truthful representation of the real world, that it should study contemporary life meticulously in order to provide an exact, complete, and sincere reproduction of the social milieu, and that it should do so dispassionately, impersonally, and objectively. *Madame Bovary* (1857), the masterpiece of the French novelist Gustave Flaubert, is a landmark in the development of realism for its portrayal of commonplace people in a dreary provincial environment.

The primary form for realism was narrative, which became increasingly accessible to a larger audience through the spread of literacy. In contrast to the dramatic adventures, high-flown sentiments, exotic settings, and cult of the past favored by the romantics, the realists focused on the middle reaches of life, the concrete problems and difficulties of ordinary people in an environment close at hand historically and geographically. The realists' emphasis on everyday life led to a far greater prominence for women both as writers and as central characters in fiction. In the portrayal of everyday life, domestic themes such as *marriage, money, family and social relationships, and tensions

and conflicts within a local *community play a vital part, fostering the new importance of women characters. Instead of ending with marriage and "they lived happily ever after," as had been the romantic tradition, realist novels opened with marriage, and examined its strains and stresses, which were particularly acute for women.

In the United States, realism coalesced with the tradition of *regionalist writing, which was well established in New England, the South, the Midwest, the Middle Atlantic states, and the West. Its emphasis on *local color fostered that observation of reality that is at the core of realism. The realists included numerous women writers. Harriet Beecher *Stowe though best known for *Uncle Tom's Cabin* (1852), also wrote the novels *The Minister's Wooing* (1859), *The Pearl of Orr's Island* (1862), *Oldtown Folks* (1869), and *Poganuc People* (1878), all of which dealt with religious observance by serious-minded people in small, tense New England communities. Sarah Orne *Jewett greatly admired the work of both Stowe and Flaubert; her best book, *The Country of the Pointed Firs* (1896), is a series of neat, unaffected sketches about the diverse inhabitants of a Maine town. Another novel of New England village life is *Pembroke* (1894) by Mary Wilkins *Freeman. The first novel of Elizabeth Drew Barstow *Stoddard, *The Morgesons* (1862), depicts family strife in pre–Civil War Massachusetts. Rebecca Harding *Davis exposes West Virginia industrial conditions in "Life in the Iron Mills," which appeared in the *Atlantic* in 1861, and political corruption in *John Andross* (1874). The most famous southern woman writer is *Kate Chopin, whose short story collections, *Bayou Folk* (1894) and *A Night in Acadie* (1897), preceded her novel *The Awakening* (1899). Of a later generation, Edith *Wharton and Willa *Cather were heirs to realism in their novels of social observation.

[See also Naturalism.]

• René Wellek, "The Concept of Realism in Literary Scholarship," in *Concepts of Criticism*, ed. Stephen J. Nichols, Jr. (1963), pp. 222–255. George J. Becker, ed., *Documents of Modern Literary Realism* (1963). F. W. J. Hemmings, ed., *The Age of Realism* (1974). George Levine, *The Realistic Imagination* (1981). Warner Berthoff, *The Ferment of Realism: American Literature, 1844–1919* (1981). John Vernon, *Money and Fiction: Literary Realism in the Nineteenth and Early Twentieth Centuries* (1985). Lilian R. Furst, *A Working Woman's Life* (1990). Lilian R. Furst, ed., *Realism* (1992).

Lilian R. Furst

RECIPE BOOKS. Through family recipes (or, in earlier times, "receipts"), women have shared their prime cooking secrets with friends and relatives. Gifts of love, recipes have throughout history been enclosed in personal letters or tucked into boxes of food. From the eighteenth century on, they have also been collected into booklets, printed, and either distributed or sold, with profits sometimes earmarked for the club or charity that designed the cookbook. This use of recipes as a gesture of friendship has also been one way women communicate with each other.

Sharing recipes was a means of salvaging something permanent from the almost constant labor of preparing food. Cooking was not like childrearing, where daily effort led to growth. The mundane and often physically difficult duties of growing or buying food, and then cleaning and cooking it, were unending. So whether families lived on farms or in mansions, in cities or on the frontier, women knew that other homemakers were interested, of necessity, in cookery.

The literally thousands of recipe books that have been published in the past two hundred years reflect women's interest in teaching about food. This educational mission appears in directions about choices among products, definitions of cookery terms, and comments about etiquette.

Even the earliest recipe books included a subjective element—writing about the author or her times that conveyed her personality to readers. When Edna Lewis, for example, describes a revival meeting in Virginia as a way of contextualizing her menu for that Sunday feast, a vivid sense of history flavors her recipes for sweet potato casserole and corn pudding. The author's pride in both her cooking and her writing is one reason recipe books are often titled with the writer's name—from *Miss Beecher's Domestic Receipt Book* (1846) to *Marion Harland's Cookery for Beginners* (1893) and *Miss Olive Allen's Tested Recipes* (1900). Both the use of the author's name and the evolution of recipe book series are still common practice.

Besides trying to give the buyer a wealth of information in a readable way, many recipe books aimed to save the cook time. *The Practical Cook Book* (a series from the 1850s) and *The Ideal Receipt Book, A Manual for Busy Housekeepers* (1898) were modeled on the same pattern as *The Efficient Epicure* (1982). Homemakers never had enough time to cook everything they wanted, so finding shortcuts to excellent meals was valuable. Saving money was another motif, and the word "economy" appears in countless titles.

In twentieth-century recipe collections, saving time and money became secondary to preserving one's health and the health of one's family. *The Metropolitan Life Cook Book* (1924)

led to a succession of insurance- or medical-industry-approved titles, some currently published by the American Heart Association. During the Second World War, a bevy of cookbooks used the appeal of improved health to convince readers of the need to conserve, and perhaps even grow, food: *Health for Victory Club Meal Planning Guide* (1943) was one of many titles.

The history of recipe books also suggests that buyers responded to *class cues. A popular series from the 1870s was *The White House Cook Book* collections; to eat the same food as the presidential family was surely to have risen in class. Many of the eighteenth-century books had the word "lady" in their title (e.g., *Lady's Receipt Book*, 1847), and others were coded to suggest that the homemaker might read cookbooks for the purpose of instructing her cook, because she herself, of course, would not work in the kitchen.

The best cooks were also seemingly the most scientific. In 1792, *New Art of Cookery* appeared, followed in 1807 with the *New System of Domestic Cookery*. Our recent century of "Good Housekeeping" titles suggests the American tendency to see a role for technology in all parts of homemaking. The myriad of cookbooks using recipes for mixers, blenders, freezers, electric skillets, outside grills, and microwave ovens attest to that fascination. Another hundred titles during this century include the word "modern," as if anything current would be inherently more scientific.

Most American cookbooks have still not targeted what we today consider the ethnic market. Only in the past twenty years have collections aimed at the various Hispanic, Asian-American, middle-European, Indian, and other cultures appeared. Ironically, so-called "regional" recipe books (particularly kinds of southern cooking—Creole, African-American) have long been popular. This pattern suggests that such specialization was also a function of class consciousness; most recipe book buyers used their menus as a way to convince people that their heritage, too, was that of the accepted Western European or British ancestry, considered the mark of the privileged.

Browsing the shelves of the cookbook section of any contemporary bookstore will satisfy the most avid cook—and the most interested social historian. The trend to reprint facsimile editions of long out-of-print recipe books gives the reader a window into history that has often been forgotten—the days when recipes were given in quantities to serve twenty people, or even fifty; when milking the cow oneself was the only way to be sure milk was truly sweet; and when a temperance household did not even read recipes that included liquor.

• Elizabeth Wason, *Cooks, Gluttons and Gourmets, a History of Cookery* (1962). Eleanor Lowenstein, *Bibliography of American Cookery Books, 1741–1860* (1972).

[*See also* Body and Health; Eating Disorders.]

Linda Wagner-Martin

RECONSTRUCTION is the period in American history immediately following the *Civil War. Traditionally its boundaries have been identified as the 1863 emancipation of the slaves and the 1877 accession to the presidency of Rutherford B. Hayes, whose withdrawal of federal troops from the South effectively put Reconstruction to an end.

During Reconstruction, three amendments were added to the Constitution to protect the rights of African Americans. The Thirteenth Amendment, ratified in 1865, outlawed *slavery. The Fourteenth Amendment (1868) extended federal citizenship to African Americans in response to the proliferation of "Black Codes," laws passed on the state and local levels to reinstate many of the same restrictions that had governed slaves. The Fifteenth Amendment, ratified in 1870 after much debate, gave black men the right to vote.

Reconstruction's effects on American women have been less easily identified. The Civil War and its aftermath rekindled the spirit of moral reform and inspired women to take active roles in their communities. The loss of over one million men in the conflict required women to enter the work force in significant numbers. The need for teachers to staff the growing public *education system encouraged women to seek out higher education. And the passage of the Fifteenth Amendment rejuvenated a flagging *suffragist movement anxious to secure similar rights for women.

The most pressing problem resulting from the Civil War was the welfare of the newly freed slaves. In 1865, the Freedmen's Bureau was established in order to oversee the integration of the newly freed slaves into American society. Frances *Harper, a noted poet, abolitionist, and feminist, toured the South during Reconstruction, lecturing to blacks and whites alike about reconciliation. Particularly concerned by the negative effects of slavery on the black family, she published *Sketches of Southern Life* in 1872; this poetry collection tells the story of Aunt Chloe, a former slave whose children were sold from her during slavery.

Her interest in the reconstruction of the black family mirrored the concerns of emancipated slaves. When the Civil War ended, several states instituted apprenticeship laws that bound black children to white "guardians" without the consent of parents or other family members. These apprenticeship laws were part of the Black Codes, as were laws restricting the rights of freed slaves to work for any employer and at any craft he or she wished. Mississippi passed legislation fining anyone who offered work to a black laborer already under contract to another employer; South Carolina permitted blacks to work only as farmers or domestic servants. The Fourteenth Amendment tried to counteract these codes by extending citizenship rights and equal protection to blacks, but in 1875 Congress felt the need to pass a Civil Rights Bill to expand the federal government's power to enforce blacks' right to equal protection under the law.

The emancipation of slaves created a significant demand for public education and qualified teachers, and gave women unprecedented access to higher education. Under the auspices of the Freedmen's Bureau, many women, white and black, joined the corps of teachers sent to the South to teach the emancipated slaves. In addition, the Morrill Land Grant Act of 1861 provided for the establishment of a network of state colleges and universities, many of which admitted women for both political and financial reasons. Several women's colleges were established, such as Vassar (1865), Wellesley (1875), and Smith (1875). And many newly founded black colleges, such as Fisk (1866) and Howard (1867), also admitted women. By 1880, almost one-third of college students were women.

Like teaching, writing was considered a respectable profession for women. In the South, the war had left many men dead and their wives and daughters responsible for supporting their families. Many women turned to writing in order to earn a living. Although there were no publishing houses in the South after the war, Southern writers found a market not only among Northern readers anxious to heal the wounds caused by the war, but also in several new literary magazines, such as *Scott's Monthly* and the *Sunny South*, founded during Reconstruction to reach Southern audiences.

As more women gained access to the work force, the inequality of women workers and the exploitation of women's labor became evident, leading women to organize a number of working women's groups, such as the Working Women's Association, formed in 1868. In addition, black working women, particularly those who worked as domestic laborers, organized in several states to stage strikes for better working conditions and higher wages.

While women were gaining access to both the work force and higher education, the feminist movement was trying to consolidate women's rights in the climate of profound social change wrought by Reconstruction. But in

1869, the suffrage movement divided over a disagreement concerning the Fifteenth Amendment, which guaranteed the vote for African-American men. Suffragist leader Elizabeth Cady *Stanton antagonized black women by refusing to endorse an amendment that enfranchised black men but not white women, and she alienated suffragists like Lucy *Stone and Julia Ward *Howe by linking the vote to an overarching program of feminist reforms of *marriage and the family. In 1869, Stone and Howe formed the American Woman Suffrage Association, while Stanton and Susan B. *Anthony formed the rival National Woman Suffrage Association.

Reconstruction ended when the Compromise of 1877 propelled the moderate Republican Rutherford B. Hayes into office after a hotly disputed election. Hayes's election symbolized the nation's strong desire to put a halt to the previous decade of tumultuous social change. One of his first acts as president was to authorize the withdrawal of federal troops from the South, in effect granting the South the privilege of home rule and allowing it to attempt to reconstruct itself according to the paternal ideology it had been forced to renounce.

As a result, Southern states were free to enact policies that severely restricted blacks' voting power. These policies included administering literacy tests, character tests, property tests, poll taxes, and grandfather clauses, which made it nearly impossible for most blacks to vote. Additional Jim Crow laws, which established racial segregation in all aspects of social and economic life, were affirmed in 1896 when the Supreme Court issued its decision in *Plessy v. Ferguson.* This ruling instituted the policy of "separate but equal"; that is, racial segregation was permitted as long as blacks were provided equal accommodations and services.

[*See also* Sharecropping; Antilynching Campaign.]

• Jay B. Hubbell, *The South in American Literature, 1607–1900* (1954). Anne Firor Scott, *The Southern Lady: From Pedestal to Politics* (1970). Ellen Carol DuBois, *Feminism and Suffrage: The Emergence of an Independent Women's Movement in America, 1848–1869* (1978). Dorothy Sterling, *We Are Your Sisters: Black Women in the Nineteenth Century* (1984). Jacqueline Jones, *Labor of Love, Labor of Sorrow: Black Women, Work, and the Family from Slavery to the Present* (1985). Barbara Miller Solomon, *In the Company of Educated Women: A History of Women and Higher Education in America* (1985). Eric Foner, *Reconstruction: America's Unfinished Revolution* (1988). Frances Smith Foster, ed., *A Brighter Coming Day: A Frances Ellen Watkins Harper Reader* (1990).

Wendy Wagner

REGIONALISM. From colonial times, the literature of the United States reflected geographic and ethnic diversity. Few countries were so large: life experience in the Florida Everglades differed radically from that in the Montana mountains or the Arizona deserts, and writing to some extent reflected such differences. Ethnic and racial differences were also related to regional situations—the existence of *slavery in the South, the concentration of Mexican and Mexican-American cultures in the Southwest, Jewish settlements in cities on both coasts, middle-European cultures along the East Coast and in the Midwest. In literary history, however, any description of writing as regional tends to limit, if not derogate. The political reality is that the writing of New England and the Atlantic coastal area has often been considered mainstream, while writing of other parts of the country has been marginalized by being called regional.

The concept of regionalism has recently been newly defined in an important 1992 collection of fiction by women writers, edited by Judith Fetterley and Marjorie Pryse. Their *American Women Regionalists, 1850–1910* defines the regional writer as one who cherished a locale and its people and who wrote from within the culture, rather than drawing it as odd, humorous, or idiosyncratic. Within these fictions, women's values of stability, love, and domesticity are set counter to the heroics of frontier expansion, and character becomes more significant than plot. Besides signaling the writers' affection for place, landscape is sometimes used, subtly, as a way to explore and mirror character.

Fetterley and Pryse also see the nineteenth-century concept of women's sphere as liberating rather than constraining. In effect, it freed such women writers as Sarah Orne *Jewett, Mary Wilkins *Freeman, Mary Noailles *Murfree, Rose Terry *Cooke, Kate *Chopin, Mary *Austin, Alice *Dunbar-Nelson, Willa *Cather, and others to shape a distinctive literary form that privileged women's voices as they recounted regional experiences.

[*See also* Local Color Fiction; New England Women's Writing; Southern Women's Writing; Western Women's Writing.]

Linda Wagner-Martin

RELIGION. *This is a two-part entry that addresses the origins and development of women's religious writing in the United States, from the beginnings to the present:*

To 1700
1700 to the Present

For further information, please refer to Catholic Writers; Exploration Narratives; Jewish-American Writing; Poetry, *article on* Religious Poetry; Spiritualism; Spirituality; Spiritual Narratives; Theologians.

To 1700

Any discussion of religion in America prior to 1700 and its relationship to women's writing in different disciplines poses a special historical and cultural dilemma because no American literature existed as such. Writings from this period reflected vastly different traditions of individuals who thought of themselves as colonists in new and savage lands. The colonists' hopes were to extend, expand, or reform their prior religious practices. Religious freedom often involved the exclusion of individuals with different views; physical and legal persecution of dissenters was commonplace. For example, *Native American religions were not recognized as such; colonists' records often contain Native references as "beast" and "devil."

Within these largely *Catholic and *Protestant contexts, women's role was clearly defined. In large measure, women were told to remain "subject to their husbands" and act accordingly. Women were discouraged from seeking public audiences for their works because modesty and humility were important virtues. And although women wrote poetry or kept *diaries, these works were viewed as primarily private, family documents.

Such traditions held fast through the early Spanish and French Catholic explorations in the New World, as well as the subsequent English ones. These explorations were primarily imperial activities designed to enhance the Spanish, French, and English empires. Through treaties, battles, and purchases, French and Spanish influence waned. We have little information, if any, about French, Spanish, and Native American women writers. New Orleans and New Spain gave way to the influence of New England.

English Protestants included Puritans, Baptists, and Quakers (Society of Friends); they came in search of the New Israel and new commercial enterprises. Early histories of the colonies, written by such men as William Bradford and John Winthrop, provide primarily religious, legalistic, political, and economic information about this period. Even well-educated Englishwomen continued in their roles as obedient helpmates to their husbands and virtuous models to their children. Embodying this dutiful spirit, Margaret Winthrop said to her husband John, "I shall always submit to what you shall think fit." Submission as an act of obedience was evidence of virtue.

The known women writers of this early period are few in number. Through their writings, these women expressed their perceptions of a world they believed was profoundly influenced by God's will and biblical teachings. Through this religious and spiritual framework, they reflected upon the meaning of their lives and shaped personal experiences into religiously artistic poems, prose, meditations, and letters. Additionally, women wrote two types of narratives: *Indian captivity and conversion. These works resulted in some of the earliest women's religious autobiographical and biographical writings.

The most prominent of these early women writers is Anne *Bradstreet, now regarded as America's first woman poet. Her work, steeped in the Protestant religious conventions of her time, includes a providential view of experience. She presents a traditionally theological outlook on marriage in "To My Dear and Loving Husband" when she writes, "If ever two were one, then surely we." Her other subjects, the death of her grandchildren and daughter-in-law and the reports of her illnesses and bouts of depression, all reflect her deeply felt sense of loss and isolation. Even in these painful reveries, however, Bradstreet turns back to the God who knows best and is good. Thus, in spite of her doubts and disappointments, she preserves the didactic, religious belief that God uses suffering and pain to instruct his earthly creatures. Like some other Protestants, she even hopes for reconciliation with other Christians; ultimately, she rejects this view because of the commonly held negative view of the papacy and because she feels she would be rejecting her father's religious beliefs.

She also presents domestic metaphors in her poetry and uses the didactic tradition to warn her children about becoming associated with "vulgars." In her "Prologue," she uses satirical comments to demand public acknowledgment of women's works; thus, she provides what has become some of the earliest known feminist writings. At the literal level, however, Bradstreet still reasserts the masculine mode of authority called for by her religious training. She is a faithful Puritan; consequently, she ends all her works by reaffirming the Protestant providential view often found in the biblical Psalms.

A second important woman writer of this era is Mary *Rowlandson, who is best known for her writing in another popular genre, the American Indian captivity narrative. Her narrative, often considered the first best-seller authored by an American woman, graphically portrays Mary's frightening capture by Indians, her subsequent captivity, and ultimate release. Narratives such as this one were encouraged for their religious as well as sensational values.

English audiences loved reading about the exploits of colonists among the "savages," while ministers such as Cotton Mather used the captivity tales as object lessons that reinforced the power of God to free those captives who held tenaciously to their faith.

Rowlandson's reports provide such a documentary. She found strength in prayer and Bible reading. Throughout her laborious tasks, her daily degradation, and her physical pain, she never lost her faith in God's power to redeem her. Even the tragic death of her young daughter could not sway her belief in redemption from her captors. Her theme—God's sustainment of her throughout her ordeal—became an important one. If the captives were freed, they became living examples of God's goodness, love, and justice. If the Indians killed their white captives, the Indians' cruelty could be used by the colonists to justify their own acts of revenge in exterminating the Indians.

While Bradstreet and Rowlandson were not persecuted for publishing their works, other women did not fare as well. Anne * Hutchinson, primarily known as a teacher and preacher, professed to divine revelations. After several trials, the Massachusetts Bay Colony Court convicted her of heresy and ultimately banished her. She continued her preaching, but was killed some time later by a band of Indians. William Bradford saw Hutchinson's assassination as a vindication of the earlier earthly verdict rendered by an all-male jury and court. Hutchinson's conviction, banishment, and death most certainly had a chilling effect on many women who might have otherwise sought a public audience for their views.

A handful of brave women writers remained undaunted, despite beatings, imprisonment, and death. These women were Quakers, the only religious group that treated women equally. They wrote about their own calls from God, which directed their conversions and sustained them through their persecution as converts. They also preserved the records of their sister Quakers' accomplishments in biographical writings, and wrote pamphlets, often while they were in jail, that remain a major source of women's writing in this early American period. The subject matter of the pamphlets cover a wide variety of issues, such as justifications for women's rights, the need for women to become preachers, and abuses of the state.

Mary Dyer was Anne Hutchinson's friend as well as follower. In 1657, she came to Boston from England to preach and was subsequently imprisoned for doing so. She wrote A Call from Death to Life (1660), in which she reports her last-minute reprieve from hanging. She contin-

ued her preaching, faced a second trial, and was hanged.

Quaker women often traveled in order to make converts. Unlike other women, they responded directly to God's call. Sometimes husbands would accompany their wives; if they chose not to, however, Quaker women would leave their husbands and families behind. Ann Curwen reported "the Lord made me willing to leave all," and so she began her life of Quaker preaching. She first made her way to Boston, and then traveled through America and the West Indies. She and her husband were beaten and imprisoned, as were many Quakers who persisted in preaching equality. Curwen defended the rights of slaves as well, and demanded they be allowed to attend Quaker meetings. She recalls many of her experiences in Relations of . . . (1680).

Other women missionaries include Joan Vokins, who visited colonies in the Americas and West Indies and wrote A Living Advertisement (1671); Mary Fisher, who traveled to Turkey and the West Indies and eventually settled in South Carolina, where she wrote False Prophets and Teachers Described (1652) with Elizabeth Hooton; and Hooten herself, who traveled to America twice. On her second voyage, she visited Boston and preached against persecution of the Quakers.

Through these early attempts to express their innermost feelings and beliefs, women demonstrated how deeply God's power to speak to them directly influenced their lives, vocations, and writing. For other women, religious beliefs sustained them in times of trial and tribulation, and offered them solace in their often hostile, painful, and difficult lives.

[See also Captivity Narratives; Exploration Narratives; Spiritualism; Spirituality; Spiritual Narratives.]

• Sydney E. Ahlstrom, Religious History of the American People (1972). Emily Stipes Watts, The Poetry of American Women from 1632–1945 (1977). Moira Ferguson, ed., First Feminists: British Women Writers: 1578–1799 (1985). Margaret Hope Bacon, Mothers of Feminism: The Story of Quaker Women in America (1986). Amy Schrager Lang, Prophetic Woman: Anne Hutchinson and the Problem of Dissent in the Literature of New England (1987). Elizabeth Potts Brown and Susan Mosher Stuard, Witnesses for Change: Quaker Women over Three Centuries (1989). Beth Doriani, " 'Then Have I . . . Said With David': Anne Bradstreet's Andover Manuscript Poems and the Influence of the Psalm Tradition," Early American Literature 24, no. 1 (Winter 1989): 52–70. Marilyn Westerkamp, "Anne Hutchinson, Sectarian Mysticism, and the Puritan Order," Church History 59, no. 4 (December 1990): 482–497. Lad Tobin, "A Radically Different Voice: Gender and Language in the Trials of Anne Hutchinson," Early American Literature 25, no. 3 (Fall 1990): 253–271.

Katharine M. Rogers, ed., *Early American Women Writers* (1992).

Adelaide P. Amore

1700 to the Present

Religion has played a complicated and at times contradictory role in the writings of American women over the last three centuries. In order to understand its significance, it is important to differentiate between the officially sanctioned attitudes that various religious groups have held with respect to women's roles and participation, and the personal religious beliefs of women themselves. These two aspects of religious faith, one authorized and the other experiential, have at times coincided and at times conflicted. But the relationship between the two has frequently been a central feature of women's literature.

Prior to the twentieth century, * Protestantism in its many forms was the dominant faith in the United States, and women consistently comprised the majority of the membership of churches. Although in most Protestant groups positions of authority such as the ministry were limited to men, the emphases on scriptural literacy and the primacy of personal religious experience offered many women the means to express their thoughts outside of the pulpit. Following in the Puritan tradition of spiritual self-scrutiny, Protestant women in the eighteenth and nineteenth centuries kept diaries and wrote letters describing their private religious experiences. This was particularly true among Protestant sects that stressed the equality of all believers before God, such as the Society of Friends, or Quakers, and some of the smaller sects that arose in the years following the Great Awakening of the mid-eighteenth century, such as the Universalists. In her 1774 autobiography, Elizabeth * Ashbridge described her early chafing under the male domination of the Anglican church and her first husband, and the subsequent freedom and sense of religious vocation she discovered after joining the Society of Friends. Similarly, Judith Sargent * Murray, a prominent New England essayist, attributed her commitment to female equality to her Universalist faith.

For the most part, women's writing before 1800 remained within the socially acceptable bounds of personal religious experience. By the mid-nineteenth century, both an increased access to higher * education and the rapid proliferation and distribution of periodical literature gave middle-class Protestant women the means to publish their works more widely. But it was

a renewed evangelical zeal, bolstered by the revivals of the Second Great Awakening in the first decades of the century, that motivated women to speculate more broadly about social issues. Harriet Beecher * Stowe, daughter of a Calvinist Presbyterian minister and a sister to seven siblings, offered the most famous religious critique of * slavery in her epic *Uncle Tom's Cabin* (1851). The novel was animated by both a fervent opposition to slavery and by a widespread antebellum commitment to the superior spiritual capacities of women. Stowe argued that women's domestic sphere of influence allowed them to exercise unique moral authority over the men in their lives; rather than desiring female equality in the public sphere, Stowe's work advocated a complementarity of roles, with women remaining in the home and providing spiritual inspiration for men. One of the most persistent images from her novel is the death of the Christian heroine, little Eva, whose sweet, gentle nature and spiritual maturity stir the souls of her entire household.

While the majority of white Protestant women in the nineteenth century probably agreed with Stowe's assertion of the superiority of female virtue, other women found in their personal spiritual commitments justification for condemning the religious institutions that initially had nurtured their faith. Sensing a disjunction between their own religious experiences and the sanctioned beliefs of the various Protestant churches, women such as Angelina and Sarah * Grimké, Emily * Dickinson, and Jarena * Lee used their writings to articulate alternative spiritual visions.

Opposition to slavery first attracted the literary talents of Angelina and Sarah Grimké, sisters born into a slaveholding South Carolina family. Distressed by their family's complicity in the slave system, the Grimké sisters moved to Philadelphia, joined the Society of Friends, and aligned themselves with the religiously inspired * abolitionism of William Lloyd Garrison. Both women drew upon the Bible and Quaker theology for their conviction of the spiritual equality of all human beings. In *Appeal to the Christian Women of the South* (1836), Angelina called upon women to "search the scriptures daily" in order to discern the sinfulness of slavery. Sarah turned her attention to women's rights in her most famous work, *Letters on the Equality of the Sexes and the Condition of Women* (1837). She likened "female slavery" within the domestic sphere to the bondage of African Americans, and buttressed her arguments with scriptural evidence. In challenging the sluggish response of the churches to the sinfulness of the slave system, the Grimkés increasingly questioned the authority of a male-dominated culture over the lives of women.

The religious protest of Emily Dickinson was far more private, although no less theologically radical. Like Stowe, Dickinson was born into a prominent and pious family in Amherst, Massachusetts. Although raised in the midst of religious revivals, Dickinson never experienced the conversion sought by her evangelical teachers and clergy, and she spent the bulk of her life in her house in Amherst, far from the social upheavals of evangelical reform. Yet her poetry reveals a perceptive and critical religious sensibility, one keenly tuned to a spiritual world removed from the Calvinism of her upbringing. Much of her verse is overtly anticlerical and anti-institutional, depicting a God hidden from the lives of humanity. Dickinson never left the Congregational church of her upbringing or the Protestant frame of reference that organized her writing, but within those structures, her skepticism and irreverence implicitly challenged ther most fundamental premises.

Protestantism was not just a religion of Euro-Americans. Both enslaved and free African Americans converted to Protestant Christianity in large numbers in the eighteenth and nineteenth centuries. Although many evangelical blacks during this period became well versed in the Bible, only a very small number attained full literacy, and thus written sources for their religious experiences and beliefs, and particularly for those of black women, are scarce. Phillis *Wheatley, a slave woman from Boston, was the most well known African-American poet of the eighteenth century. Although her work reflects a fairly orthodox Christian piety, Wheatley's worldview is troubling for contemporary readers because she expresses the conviction that bringing "pagan" Africans to a Christian nation was a blessing, and that servitude with Christian teachings was preferable to the freedom of the unbaptized. For Wheatley, evangelical faith was clearly a liberation from the bondage of ignorance, an enslavement more immediate to her than the physical bondage of fellow African-Americans. However, she also implored her readers to accept African-American Christians as the equals of whites.

Protestant piety also encouraged many African-American women to protest racial and sexual discrimination within their churches, and in the nineteenth century a growing number wrote published accounts of their lives. These autobiographies were often composed in the form of traditional Protestant conversion narratives, but they described spiritual journeys in which race and gender played prominent roles. Jarena Lee, born in Cape May, New Jersey, converted to Christianity at twenty-one and traveled as an itinerant preacher throughout the northeastern states, speaking to black and white audiences. She published her autobiography in order to alert others to the spiritual liberation that Christianity had given her, yet what stands out in her account is the resistance to her work she encountered from male clergy in the African Methodist Episcopal Church. Lee was one of a number of female itinerants who pressed the denomination to sanction the preaching of women, a cause that was defeated in 1852.

More recent female voices have fundamentally challenged the "blessings" of African Christianity. Although the African-American population in the twentieth century is still largely Christian, a growing number of women authors, including Zora Neale *Hurston, Toni *Morrison, and Alice *Walker, have begun to explore the historical mixing of African and Christian religious traditions in the United States. While acknowledging the positive influences that Christian piety has had on the personal lives of many blacks, the works of these women also explore the loss of African identity and the mixed legacy of the Protestant church in African-American history. Alternative traditions, such as the Muslim faith of Elijah Muhammed's Nation of Islam, have recently served as a vantage point for other writers to condemn the oppressive nature of Christianity, as is evident in the poetry of Sonia *Sanchez.

Only in the last century has religion figured largely as a topic of interest for Jewish-American and *Catholic women writers. Although both traditions, like Protestantism, are textually based and thus emphasize the importance of education for believers, Judaism and Catholicism place less priority on religion as personal experience. Whereas salvation within the Protestant tradition is viewed as a personal interaction between God and the individual, in both Catholicism and Judaism the means of divine redemption are mediated through the rituals of the religious group, which have historically been controlled by male leaders. Without an experiential basis to claim spiritual authority, and finding few means of reconciling personal faith with public protest, women within these traditions who are critical of male organizational structures have often condemned the beliefs and practices of the religious community as a whole, or have attributed their frustrations to personal failings.

The writings of Anzia *Yezierska, an immigrant from Russian Poland, reflect many of the religious themes common among Jewish and Catholic women writers in the modern era. In *Bread Givers* (1925), a semiautobiographical novel, Yezierska details the oppressive nature of Jewish ritual and patriarchal culture on the lives of women. Her heroine, Sara Smolinsky, struggles to reconcile life in the "new world" of America with the religious traditions of her past, but she is consistently held back by the unreasonable demands of a pious father who insists that she renounce her independence in order to support his Talmudic studies. Ultimately, Sara must choose between loyalty to her religious community and the dictates of her independent sense of self. Yezierska concludes that there can be no reconciliation between a woman's self-assertion and traditional religious structures.

In contrast, Flannery * O'Connor and Dorothy * Day both discovered radically novel means to express their deep-seated spirituality within the bounds of the Catholic faith. Reared in the postbellum South, O'Connor depicts a fictional world infused with a sense of the sacred, but renders it in vividly unsentimental and often strikingly violent terms. Day's involvement with the Catholic Worker Movement is detailed in her 1952 autobiography *The Long Loneliness*, which draws upon ordinary experiences to illuminate the mysteries of the religious life. Rather than accepting that access to the sacred remains within the hands of the clergy, both women explore the abilities of ordinary people, and women in particular, to experience God's grace directly and immediately.

Conversely, American Indian women in the twentieth century have explored the ways that a return to traditional religious beliefs and practices can restore cultural integrity, worn down by the historical incursions of Christian missionaries. Rather than viewing religious faith as an obstacle to self-fulfillment, as has been the case for many women in the Judeo-Christian tradition, Indian writers have more often characterized their religious heritage as a means of restoring personal and communal harmony. Because indigenous cultures are based upon oral traditions, it is only recently that Indians have attempted to bridge the gap between Euro-American culture and their own heritage. Gertrude Simmons Bonnin or * Zitkala-Ša, a Sioux, was one of the first women to express in writing the cultural dilemma faced by American Indians. In the *Atlantic Monthly* and other periodicals, she wrestled with themes of cultural displacement and Euro-American persecution. In an essay published in the December 1902 issue of the *Atlantic*, Bonnin asserted that she preferred the "pagan" world of nature to the dogma of the "pale-face missionary." In recent years, Leslie Marmon * Silko, raised on the Laguna Pueblo Reservation in New Mexico, has voiced similar themes in her highly praised novels and poetry. Unlike

the spiritual freedom experienced by Phillis Wheatley at the hands of Christian captors, recent American Indian literature focuses on a return to traditional religious practices as a liberation from the enslavement of Euro-Protestant culture.

[*See also* Catholic Writers; Poetry, *article on* Religious Poetry; Jewish-American Writing; Theologians; Spiritualism; Spirituality.]

• Barbara Welter, *Dimity Convictions* (1976). Ann Douglas, *The Feminization of American Culture* (1977). Nancy Cott, *The Bonds of Womanhood* (1977). Rosemary Radford Ruether and Rosemary Skinner Keller, *Women and Religion in America*, 2 vols. (1981–1983). William L. Andrews, ed., *Sisters of the Spirit: Three Black Women's Autobiographies of the Nineteenth Century* (1986). Charles H. Lippy and Peter W. Williams, eds., *Encyclopedia of the American Religious Experience*, 3 vols. (1988). Jean Fagan Yellin, *Women and Sisters: The Antislavery Feminists in American Culture* (1989). Paul Lauter et al., eds., *The Heath Anthology of American Literature*, 2 vols. (1990).

Laurie F. Maffly-Kipp

RELIGIOUS POETRY. *See* Poetry, article on Religious Poetry.

RELIGIOUS WRITING. *See* Catholic Writers; Theologians; Religion.

REPORTAGE. From the nineteenth-century to the present, women in the United States have published vivid, in-depth social, cultural, and political reports of the times in which they lived. In magazines, newspapers, and books, they documented the daily texture of massive political upheavals abroad and made visible the concrete effects of public policy at home. They anatomized the social order and mapped the signposts of social change for their fellow Americans.

The honor of being America's first woman foreign correspondent is generally accorded to Margaret * Fuller (1810–1850). Less well known is America's second woman foreign correspondent, African-American journalist Mary Ann Shadd Cary (1823–1893). During the early 1850s, shortly after Fuller filed her reports from Rome, Mary Ann Shad Cary published reportage about black life in Canada in the *(Ontario) Provincial Freeman* (a paper that reached readers in the northern United States), providing African Americans with images of what they were likely to encounter at the end of the underground railroad.

From the middle of the nineteenth century to the present, the reportage of American women foreign correspondents helped Americans understand revolutions, wars, and struggles for liberation as they happened. The stories that Margaret Fuller wrote between 1847 and

1849 for the New York *Tribune* about the Italian revolutionary movement helped introduce Americans to a cause whose fervor and idealism, Fuller felt, had affinities with the American Revolution. In the twentieth century, correspondents including Bessie Beatty (1886–1947) of the San Francisco *Bulletin*, Rheta Childe Dorr (1866–1848) of the New York *Mail* and Louise Bryant (1890–1936) of the Bell Syndicate, helped make Americans aware of the struggles and strivings of the revolutionary movement in Russia and how it transformed the fabric of ordinary life, particulary for women and children. In the 1930s, Josephine *Herbst (1892–1969) evoked vivid portraits of revolutionaries in Cuba, while Agnes *Smedley (1892–1950) and Anna Louise Strong (1885–1970) wrote about revolutionaries in China.

American women produced some memorable reportage during World War I. Rheta Childe Dorr and Bessie Beatty, for example, covered the Women's Battalion of Death on the Russian front, a story most of their male colleagues missed. (Before the Russian women could leave to fight the Germans in a battle in which half the women would be wounded or killed, they had to fend off attacks at the barracks from their fellow Russian soldiers, who tried to rape them.) Barred from the western front in Belgium in World War I, Mary Roberts *Rinehart (1876–1958) of the *Saturday Evening Post* managed to get there anyway, ahead of the men; the many exclusive stories she filed made grim European battlefield scenes real for American readers.

Martha *Gellhorn (b. 1908), writing for *Collier's* during the Spanish Civil War, evoked the tragedy of war by presenting vivid images of those rendered helpless or bewildered by the conflict. Marguerite Higgins's (1920–1966) award-winning reportage on the liberation of Dachau in May 1945 brought home the horrors of the concentration camps for readers of the New York *Herald Tribune*. Higgins went on to cover the Korean War and the Vietnam War, and Gellhorn covered the Vietnam War as well. In Vietnam, both Higgins and Gellhorn were critical of U.S. policies. Gloria Emerson (b. 1929) of the *New York Times* was another correspondent whose reports from Vietnam angered American officialdom: She blew the whistle on false body counts, observing, as Julia Edwards put it, "that women, children, and friendly villagers in the line of fire were counted as enemy soldiers killed, giving the impression that the U. S. Army was destroying the enemy at a time the Communists were gaining strength." Frances FitzGerald's (b. 1940) sensitive reportage on Vietnam in the *Atlantic* and other magazines (published in 1972 as *Fire in the Lake*) won a Pulitzer Prize and a National Book Award.

Americans' awareness of poverty and politics in Latin America have been shaped indelibly by the eloquent and meticulously researched reportage of Penny Lernoux (1940–1989) in the *Nation*, as well as in her award-winning 1979 book, *Cry of the People*.

On the domestic front, in the nineteenth and early twentieth century, women wrote reportage about such institutions as mental hospitals, sweatshops, and emergency rooms, and profiled the lives of mine workers, mill workers, strikers, and lynching victims. Margaret Fuller described in sharp vignettes in the New York *Tribune* in 1845 what she had seen at the Bloomingdale Asylum for the Insane. Both Winifred Black Bonfils ("Annie Laurie") (1863–1936) and Elizabeth Cochrane Seaman ("Nellie Bly") (1865–1922) feigned insanity to get into public asylums and share with readers the scenes they witnessed. Bonfils became a sweatshop and factory worker to record, in the New York *World*, a first-hand perspective on the lives of women workers; Seaman became a domestic servant and a shop girl to document in the San Francisco *Examiner* the experiences of women who really lived these lives. Marie Van Vorst (1867–1936) worked in a shoe factory and a cotton mill to gather information for the book of reportage she wrote with her sister-in-law Bessie in 1903, *The Woman Who Toils*.

The impassioned and massively documented 1890s reportage on lynchings that Ida B. Wells (1862–1931) published in African-American newspapers, including the New York *Age*, and in the pamphlets *Southern Horrors* and *A Red Record* remain an important source of our understanding of this chilling chapter of American history.

Reportage in the 1930s by Dorothy *Day (1897–1980) in the *Catholic Worker;* by Meridel *Le Sueur (b. 1900) in the *New Masses, American Mercury* and *Partisan Review;* by Tillie *Olsen (b. 1913) in *Partisan Review* and the *New Republic;* and by Mary Heaton Vorse (1874–1966) in the *New Republic* and *Working Woman* drew readers behind unemployment and poverty statistics into the texture of the lives of the poor, the hungry, the jobless, and the despairing. Also in the 1930s, while these white writers sketched Great Depression scenes of urban poverty, Zora Neale *Hurston (1891–1960) drew readers into the expressive life of rural black folk culture with an exuberant melange of reportage and *folklore, Mules and Men* (1935), and with her reportage on Haitian and Jamaican politics and folk traditions, *Tell My Horse* (1938).

In the 1960s and 1970s, Joan *Didion (b.

1934) published reportage on the counterculture and on life in California in the *Saturday Evening Post* and in the collections *Slouching toward Bethlehem* (1968) and *The White Album* (1979).

Whether documenting the fervor of a revolution, the pain of grinding poverty, or the anomie of contemporary life, the reportage written by American women in the nineteenth and twentieth centuries has helped illuminate dimensions of experience that might have otherwise remained invisible.

[*See also* Newspapers, Women's; Newspapers, Columns; Magazines, Women's; Little Magazines; Journals, Academic; Journalists.]

• I. Garland Penn, *The Afro-American Press and Its Editors* (1891; reprint, 1988). Ida B. Wells, *Crusade for Justice: The Autobiography of Ida B. Wells,* ed. Alfreda Duster (1970). Marion Marzolf, *Up from the Footnote: A History of Women Journalists* (1977). Zora Neale Hurston, *I Love Myself When I Am Laughing . . . and Then Again When I Am Looking Mean and Impressive: A Zora Neale Hurston Reader,* ed. Alice Walker (1979). Langdon Lynne Faust, ed., *American Women Writers: A Critical Reference Guide from Colonial Times to the Present* (1983). Barbara Belford, *Brilliant Bylines: A Biographical Anthology of Notable Newspaperwomen in America,* (1986). Charlotte Nekola and Paula Rabinowitz, eds., *Writing Red: An Anthology of American Women Writers, 1930–1940* (1987). Julia Edwards, *Women of the World: The Great Foreign Correspondents* (1988). Fritz Fleischmann, "Margaret Fuller," in *Classics in Cultural Criticism,* vol. 2 (1990). Margaret Fuller, *These Sad and Glorious Days: Dispatches from Europe, 1846–1850* (1991). Carla Peterson, *Doers of the Word: African-American Women Writers in the Ante-bellum North* (1994).

Shelley Fisher Fishkin

REPRODUCTION. The history of contraception, *abortion, and *childbirth in the United States has been a history of struggle since the nation began. During the colonial period, women depended on each other for assistance in childbirth, but with the importation of forceps in 1801 began an attempt to literally take reproductive control out of women's hands. Medical schools established at the end of the eighteenth century offered midwifery as their first specialization, and the American Medical Association (AMA), formed in 1848, consolidated power through a campaign to eliminate women *midwives through the legal restriction of abortion, and achieved the criminalization of abortion in every state by 1900. Over this same time period, the birthrate for white women fell from 7.04 live births per woman in 1800 to 3.56 in 1900, remaining near that number in the present day. Despite medicalization, regulation, and criminalization, large numbers of women have continued to control their fertility.

In her landmark history *Woman's Body,* *Woman's Right: Birth Control in America* (1976; rev. ed. 1990), Linda Gordon identifies four "peaks" in the reproductive control movement. The voluntary motherhood movement of the 1870s and 1880s insisted upon women's right to refuse sex with their husbands. The birth control movement of 1910–1920 enlisted radicals whose civil disobedience promoted contraception as a strategy of self-defense against the capitalist system, which failed to provide for the children of workers. The family planning movement beginning in the 1920s largely accomplished the official acceptance of birth control by neither specifically recognizing women's rights nor calling for any substantive social change. Instead, family planners framed reproductive control as a medical issue involving privileged white women and a method of population control targeting new immigrants and people of color. This platform accommodated both the government, which had launched a campaign against "race suicide," the disappearance of the white race through white women's refusal to reproduce, a decade before, and a medical organization, which sought exclusive professional control over reproductive services.

The fourth movement for reproductive freedom began as a singly focused call for women's right to choose for abortion and developed in 1960 with the marketing of oral contraceptives ("the pill"). The pill physically removed the act of sex from the act of contraception for women for the first time, symbolically separating sex and reproduction. The efficiency of the pill heightened women's expectations, making them less likely to accept unplanned pregancies. The call for abortion on demand framed these expectations as a claim by women for control over their own bodies. However, *Roe v. Wade,* the Supreme Court's 1973 decision to legalize abortion, translated this claim into the right to privacy, a right qualified by the judgment of a woman's private physician.

Pressure from a multiplicity of movements has expanded the reproductive freedom agenda to include issues such as gay and lesbian parenting, treatment for people with *AIDS, freedom from forced sterilization, affordable housing, and accessible health care. One precursor for this broader agenda comes from the mothers' rights movement of the first decades of the century. While suffragists hailed the vote as the entrance into full political participation for women, the momentum of the first wave of the *women's movement quickly dispersed. The first and perhaps only major use of women's franchise declared a healthy maternity every woman's right, and in 1921 forced the passage of the Sheppard-Towner Act, which provided health care for poor women and children. By the end of the decade, however, this movement dissipated, and medical opposition blocked further appropriations in 1929. In the 1960s, the National Welfare Rights Organization, among others, renewed the call for women's and children's health care, resulting in health care and food supplement programs begun in the 1970s and still in existence today. Nevertheless, a large percentage of women do not receive adequate prenatal care, and both infant and neonatal mortality are on the rise, disproportionately so for black infants.

Roe v. Wade elicited a second antiabortion movement, proving the right to privacy insufficient in guaranteeing reproductive freedom. The first partial victory of this movement came with the Hyde Amendment in 1977, which denied public insurance coverage of abortion. Poor women continue to have abortions at three times the rate of other women, but restrictions on access exact extreme economic sacrifice. In the 1980s and 1990s, further restrictions on access to abortion implemented at various levels included the omission of mention of abortion in federally funded clinics, mandatory parental notification for minors, state legislation against abortion in hospitals and clinics receiving federal funding, and spousal notification. This second movement to criminalize abortion differs from the first in the use of grass-roots tactics and a varied constituency that places the struggle against abortion in a broad perspective and frequently targets so-called nontraditional lifestyles as a threat to the sanctity of the family. Most significantly, for the first time, this movement values the rights of the fetus—designated the "right to life"—over those of pregnant women. In a balance of rights, the right to privacy has proven extremely vulnerable.

The concept of fetal rights has licensed increasing application of advanced technologies in childbirth where doctors believe the fetus in jeopardy, even when these technologies may endanger the pregnant woman. From forceps, Caesarean sections, and anesthesia, to fetal monitors, ultrasound scans, and in vitrio surgery, procedures appropriate for particular conditions become unnecessarily and often perilously generalized, protecting doctors from lawsuits while driving up the cost of delivery. Court orders protecting fetal rights have subjected women to these operations without their consent, targeting women of color in particular.

Regardless of public policy and medical practice, people have sought and found means to control their own bodies. "Jane," a diverse group of nearly 120 women in Chicago, performed over 11,000 underground abortions between 1971 and 1973. Byllye Avery of the Na-

tional Black Women's Health Project helped establish the Gainesville (Florida) Women's Health Center (1973) and Birthplace (1978) to provide poor women with the full range of reproductive options. Avery's philosophy of health care in "A Question of Survival/A Conspiracy of Silence: Abortion and Black Women's Health" (1990) also characterizes the challenge that taking control of reproduction has posed for women throughout U.S. history: health care not only represents a vital need, but "health offers all sorts of opportunities for empowerment."

[*See also* Birth Control; Birth.]

• Kristin Luker, *Abortion and the Politics of Motherhood* (1984). Richard W. Wertz and Dorothy C. Wertz, *Lying In: A History of Childbirth in America* (rev. ed., 1989). Barbara Katz Rothman, *Recreating Motherhood: Ideology and Technology in a Patriarchal Society* (1989). Rosalind Pollack Petchesky, *Abortion and Woman's Choice: The State, Sexuality, and Reproductive Freedom* (rev. ed., 1990). Byllye Avery, "A Question of Survival/ A Conspiracy of Silence: Abortion and Black Women's Health," in *From Abortion to Reproductive Freedom: Transforming a Movement*, ed. Marlene Gerber Fried (1990). Judith Wilt, *Abortion, Choice, and Contemporary Fiction: The Armageddon of the Maternal Instinct* (1990). Rickie Solinger *Wake Up Little Susie: Single Pregnancy and Race Before Roe v. Wade* (1992).

Celeste Fraser Delgado

RICH, Adrienne (b. 1929), poet, essayist, feminist theorist. There is no writer of comparable influence and achievement in so many areas of the contemporary women's movement as the poet and theorist Adrienne Rich. Over the years, hers has become one of the most eloquent, provocative voices on the politics of sexuality, race, language, power, and women's culture. There is scarcely an anthology of feminist writings that does not contain her work or specifically engage her ideas, a women's studies course that does not read her essays, or a poetry collection that does not include her work or that of the next generation of poets steeped in her example. In nineteen volumes of poetry, three collections of essays—*On Lies, Secrets and Silence* (1979), *Blood, Bread and Poetry* (1986), and *What Is Found There: Notebooks on Poetry and Politics* (1993)—the ground-breaking study of ** motherhood, *Of Woman Born: Motherhood as Experience and Institution* (1976), the editing of influential lesbian-feminist journals, and a lifetime of ** activism and visibility, the work of Adrienne Rich has persistently resonated at the heart of contemporary feminism and its resistance to ** racism, militarism, ** homophobia, and ** anti-Semitism.

Rich was born 16 May 1929 in Baltimore, Maryland, the elder of two daughters of Arnold Rich, a doctor and pathology professor at Johns

Hopkins University, and Helen Jones Rich, a gifted pianist and composer who had given up a possible professional musical career to raise a family. In her long autobiographical poem "Sources" (1983) and the essay "Split at the Root" (*Blood, Bread and Poetry*), Rich recalls her growing-up years as overtly dominated by the intellectual presence and demands of her father, while covertly marked by the submerged tensions and silences arising from the conflicts between the religious and cultural heritage of her father's Jewish background and her mother's southern Protestantism. Her relationship with her father was one of strong identification and desire for approval, yet it was adversarial in many ways. Under his tutelage Rich first began to write poetry, conforming to his standards well past her early successes and publications.

In 1951, Rich graduated from Radcliffe, and also won the prestigious Yale Younger Poets Prize for her first book, *A Change of World*. W. H. Auden, the judge of the award, wrote a preface for the book that acquired eventual notoriety for its classic tones of male condescension and paternalism to female artists. Yet, the preface accurately describes Rich's elegant technique, chiseled formalism, and restrained emotional content. Rich's early poems clearly announced in theme and style their debt to Frost, Yeats, Stevens, and Auden himself, and received their high acclaim on the basis of that fidelity.

In 1953, Rich married Alfred Conrad, a Harvard economist, and moved to Cambridge, Massachusetts, where she bore three sons in the next five years. As her journal entries from these years reveal, this was an emotionally and artistically difficult period; she was struggling with conflicts over the prescribed roles of womanhood versus those of artistry, over tensions between sexual and creative roles, love, and anger. Yet, in the late fifties and early sixties, these were issues she could not easily name to herself; indeed, they were feelings for which she felt guilty, even "monstrous," and for which there was as yet no wider cultural recognition, much less insight or analysis.

Rich's third book, *Snapshots of a Daughter-in-Law* (1963), which was eight years in the writing, stands as a watershed in her poetic development. For the first time, in language freer and more intimate and contextual, she situates her materials and emotions against themes of language, boundaries, resistance, escape, and moments of life-altering choice. As the poem "The Roofwalker" states, "A life I didn't choose/chose me," while "Prospective Immigrants Please Note" rhetorically asserts that the safety of enclosures and illusions must be abandoned for the claims of a risky but liberating reality.

The critical reaction to *Snapshots* was negative, with objections to its bitter tone and the shift away from her hallmarks of formalism and emotional control. Tellingly, feeling she had "flunked," Rich wrote *Necessities of Life* (1966) with a focus on death as the sign of how occluded and erased she felt when her own sense of coming into her rightful subject matter and voice was denied. *Necessities*, personally and poetically, was less a retreat than a pause. Coinciding with her personal and poetic evolution was the tremendous force of the historical moment. Rich's earlier, inchoate feelings of personal conflict, sexual alienation, and cultural oppression were finding increasing articulation in the larger social/political currents gathering force throughout the sixties, from the civil rights movements to the antiwar movement, to the emergent women's movement.

Rich moved to New York in 1966, when her husband took a teaching position at City College. She taught in the SEEK program, a remedial English program for poor, black, and third world students entering college, which was raising highly political questions about the collision of cultural codes of expression and the relation of language to power, issues that have consistently been addressed in Rich's work. She was also strongly impressed during this time by the work of James Baldwin and Simone de *Beauvoir. Though Rich and her husband were both involved in movements for social justice, it was to the women's movement that Rich gave her strongest allegiance. In its investigation of sexual politics, its linkage, as Rich phrased it, of "Vietnam and the lovers' bed," she located her grounding for issues of language, sexuality, oppression, and power that infused all the movements for liberation from a male-dominated world.

Rich's poetry has clearly recorded, imagined, and forecast her personal and political journeys with searing power. In 1956, she began dating her poems to underscore their existence within a context, and to argue against the idea that poetry existed separately from the poet's life. Stylistically, she began to draw on contemporary rhythms and images, especially those derived from the cinematic techniques of jump cuts and collage. *Leaflets* (1969), *The Will to Change* (1971), and *Diving into the Wreck* (1973) demonstrate a progressive coming to power as Rich contends against the desolation patriarchy enacts on literal and psychic landscape. Intimately connected with this struggle for empowerment and action is the deepening of her determination "to write directly and overtly as a woman, out of a woman's body and experience." In the poem "Tear Gas," she asserts "The will to change begins in the body not in the mind/My politics is in my body." Yet this tactic has not led Rich to a poetry that is in a way confessional. Rich's voice is most characteristically the voice of witness, oracle, or mythologizer, the seer with the burden of "verbal privilege" and the weight of moral imagination, who speaks for the speechless, records for the forgotten, invents anew at the site of erasure of women's lives.

With each subsequent volume—*Twenty-One Love Poems* (1976), *A Wild Patience Has Taken Me This Far* (1981), *The Fact of a Doorframe: Poems Selected and New* (1984), *Your Native Land, Your Life* (1986), *Time's Power* (1989), and most recently *An Atlas of the Difficult World* (1991)—Rich has confirmed and radicalized her fusion of political commitment and poetic vision. In her urging women to "revision" and to be "disloyal," she has engaged ever-wider experiences of women across cultures, history, and ethnicity, addressing themes of verbal privilege, male violence, and lesbian identity.

Over the years, Rich has taught at Swarthmore, Columbia, Brandeis, Rutgers, Cornell, San Jose State and Stanford University. Since 1976, she has lived with the writer and editor Michelle *Cliff. She is active in movements for gay and lesbian rights, reproductive freedom, and for the progressive Jewish movement New Jewish Agenda. In 1981, she received the Fund for Human Dignity Award of the National Gay Task Force. Her poetry has been honored with the National Book Award in 1974 for *Diving into the Wreck* (which she accepted jointly with Alice *Walker and Audre *Lorde in the name of all women who are silenced), two Guggenheim Fellowships, the first Ruth Lilly Poetry Prize, the Brandeis Creative Arts Medal, the Common Wealth Award, the William Whitehead Award for Lifetime Achievement, and the National Poetry Association Award for Distinguished Service to the Art of Poetry.

• David Kalstone, *Five Temperaments* (1977). Jane Cooper, *Reading Adrienne Rich: Reviews and Revisions, 1951–81* (1984). Deborah Pope, *A Separate Vision* (1984). Claire Keyes, *The Aesthetics of Power: The Poetry of Adrienne Rich* (1986). Paula Bennett, *My Life a Loaded Gun* (1986). Barbara C. Gelpi and Albert Gelpi, *Adrienne Rich's Poetry and Prose* (1993).

Deborah Pope

RIDING, Laura (1901–1991), poet, fiction writer, critic, publisher. Laura (Riding) Jackson was born Laura Reichenthal in New York City; she changed her name to Laura Riding Gottschalk when she married in 1922, publishing her first volume of poetry, *The Close Chaplet* (1926), under that name. She is best known as Laura Riding, the name she assumed in 1927 (after her 1925 divorce) and under which she published almost all of her poetry and much of her later prose. Riding renounced poetry in 1940 (after the 1938 publication of her *Collected Poems*) and, upon her remarriage in 1941 and her subsequent commitment to establishing a new lexicography, assumed the name of Laura (Riding) Jackson, the parenthesis indicating her relation to her earlier career as a poet. Given the quality of Riding's poetry, her elaboration of a clearly articulated and strongly argued poetics, and her associations with many of the major literary figures and movements of the past seventy years, her relative critical neglect can be explained only by her refusal to cede interpretive authority over her life and works. She has, for example, refused to allow her poems to be published in anthologies dedicated to women writers.

With the publication of her first poems, Riding gained immediate recognition from the Fugitives, a conservative group of southern critics and poets (including Allen Tate and Robert Penn Warren), later known as the New Critics. The Fugitives awarded her the Nashville Prize for most promising poet of the year in 1924, making her an honorary (and the only woman) member of their group in 1925. In 1926, Riding traveled to London, where she coauthored, with English poet Robert Graves, *A Survey of Modernist Poetry* (1927), a foundational text to the New Critical method of close reading. Riding and Graves, whose complicated and painful relationship lasted until 1940, moved to Mallorca, Spain, in 1929, taking with them the Seizin Press, established a year earlier. The Seizin Press primarily published works by Riding and Graves (including her 1928 essay collections, *Anarchism Is Not Enough* and *Contemporaries and Snobs*, and her 1935 *Progress of Stories*), but also Gertrude *Stein's *An Acquaintance with Description* (1929). They left Spain at the outbreak of the Spanish Civil War, and Riding returned to the United States in 1939.

Riding's 1940 renunciation of poetry—which she comments on in the preface to her 1970 *Selected Poems* and in the introduction to *The Poems of Laura Riding* (1980), a new edition of the 1938 collection—reflects her rigorous and even ascetic commitment to absolute linguistic "truth," which she also associated with a radical and impersonal individualism. Poetry's appeal to the senses, she came to believe, impeded a more "spiritual" apprehension of "the good in language." *The Telling* (1970), a prose "evangel," further articulates her commitment to an ultimately ahistorical universalism.

• Joyce Piell Wexler, *Laura Riding's Pursuit of Truth* (1979). Barbara Adams, *The Enemy Self: Poetry and Criticism of Laura Riding* (1990). K. K. Ruthven, "How to Avoid Being Canonized: Laura Riding," *Textual Practice* 5 (Summer 1991): 242–260. Jerome J. McGann, "Laura (Riding) Jackson and the Literal Truth," *Critical Inquiry* 18 (Spring 1992): 454–473. Jo-Ann Wallace, "Laura Riding and the Politics of Decanonization," *American Literature* 64 (1992): 111–126.

Jo-Ann Wallace

RIGHT TO LIFE. *See* Abortion; Birth; Birth Control; Reproduction.

RINEHART, Mary Roberts (1876–1958), novelist, short story writer, dramatist, journalist. Born on Pittsburgh's North Side, she entered nurses training in 1893, and in 1896 married Dr. Stanley M. Rinehart. In 1904, as a housewife, assistant in her husband's dispensary, and mother of three sons, Rinehart began writing short stories. More ambitious efforts led to serialized mysteries, beginning with *The Man in Lower 10* (1906). In 1908, Bobbs-Merrill published her first book, *The Circular Staircase*. By 1910, Rinehart had published three mystery novels and one romance, and her stories appeared in leading magazines such as *Munsey's*, *Lippincott's*, and the *Saturday Evening Post*. She even had a long-running play on Broadway, *Seven Days*, which she cowrote with Avery Hopwood.

Success brought Rinehart celebrity and wealth; her newly found independence of means fired her independence of spirit. World War I was a watershed; in January 1915, Rinehart went to France to provide unprecedented coverage of the French and English lines for the *Post* (April–June 1915).

In August 1920, two Rinehart-Hopwood plays opened on Broadway; *Spanish Love* ran for 307 performances, and *The Bat*, for 878. In 1922, Rinehart moved her family to Washington, D.C. Some of her stories and novels published during the 1920s offered a darker exploration of women's experiences in love and marriage, especially *Lost Ecstasy* (1927) and *This Strange Adventure* (1929).

Rinehart wrote in a variety of genres, but her major reputation rests with her *mystery writing, which during the Great Depression years and through the 1940s became an increasing preoccupation. Prices for Rinehart's serialized mysteries soared; the *Post* paid $60,000 for *The Album* (1933) and $65,000 for *The Wall* (1938).

Rinehart's autobiography *My Story* appeared in 1931 (it was expanded and republished in 1948), the year before Stanley Rinehart died. In 1935 she moved to New York,

summering in Bar Harbor, Maine, until fire destroyed her home in 1947. Although the postwar years saw a falling off of her popularity, she continued to publish until shortly before her death. Rinehart is buried with her husband in Arlington National Cemetery.

Rinehart provides a contradictory model of the woman writer. Middle-class values drove her to project an image of proper womanhood through autobiographical narratives that recast her professional life as a story of sacrifice for her family. At the same time, she sought independence and adventure both vicariously in fiction, especially in the stories of her spinster alter ego, Tish, and in fact, at the war front and in trips through the rugged American West. Nearly all of her writing reflects the contradictions in her own life, but the romances, now largely forgotten, provide the best mirror of Rinehart's attempt to embed a woman's ambition in the normative model of romance and marriage.

• The Rinehart Papers are housed in Special Collections, Hillman Library, University of Pittsburgh. G. Overton et al., *Mary Roberts Rinehart: A Sketch of the Woman and Her Work* (c. 1921). D. C. Disney and M. Mackaye, *Mary Roberts Rinehart* (1948). Jan Cohn, *Improbable Fiction: The Life of Mary Roberts Rinehart* (1980).

Jan Cohn

RITUALS AND CEREMONIES. From the seventeenth century onward, American women's writing has included rituals and ceremonies that commemorate events in women's lives, rather than traditionally male-oriented rites such as "conquering" new frontiers, hunting or killing, and discarding one's past. Female ceremonies observe birth, the complexities of love and courtship, and the regular performance of domestic work; they also focus on *community, the formation of *friendships with other women, and the discovery of one's own voice. These ceremonies are, of course, subject to change over time and across racial, ethnic, and class differences, and are frequently perceived as further means of oppression in women's lives. Thus, women's writing subverts and reenvisions rituals nearly as often as it acknowledges them.

Mid-nineteenth- through early twentieth-century writing by women of all colors lays claim to a variety of domestic rituals that serves to center women in the world, and establish their authority. Activities such as cooking, gardening, and sewing (especially quilting) emerge in the work of, among others, Harriet Beecher *Stowe, Louisa May *Alcott, Mary Wilkins *Freeman, Pauline *Hopkins, Sarah Orne *Jewett, Willa *Cather, and Susan *Glaspell. Also important are those texts that illustrate the thwarting of women's domestic rituals; Harriet *Jacobs's 1861 *Incidents in the Life of a Slave Girl* and Harriet *Wilson's 1859 *Our Nig* both reveal how the violent circumstances of *slavery continuously disrupt black women's attempts at domestic ceremony.

Home-centered rituals continue in the late twentieth century with Alice *Walker and Eudora *Welty, in whose work sewing, quilting, and communal feasts function to connect generations and allow for self-expression. Tillie *Olsen's *Tell Me A Riddle* (1961) not only includes domestic rites, but also incorporates the candle-lighting of the Jewish Sabbath. Much contemporary literature is concerned with the changing significance of domestic rites; the ceremonial aspects of food—cooking, handing down recipes, eating together—are redefined or subverted in the works of Margaret Atwood, Louise *Erdrich, Gloria *Naylor, Maxine Hong *Kingston, and Marilynne *Robinson.

Rites of passage are extraordinarily varied in American women's writing. Still, they often focus upon oral ritual as the discovery of identity, and upon the embracing or understanding of family and community. The anthology *Cuentos: Stories by Latinas* (1983) explores not only the rebelliousness of *adolescence, but also the more traditional rites of passage for a young Chicana, such as her *quincineros*—her fifteenth birthday celebration. Cherríe *Moraga's autobiographical *Loving in the War Years: lo que nunca pasó por sus labios* (1983) notes the presence of Catholic ceremony in *familia*: "The ritual of kissing and the sign of the cross with every coming and going from the home." Lorna Dee *Cervantes and Hisaye *Yamamoto both acknowledge the ceremonial power of finding an artistic voice for young girls, while Sandra *Cisneros and Paule *Marshall create the ritualized chants of women in communal spaces within the barrio and Barbadian communities, respectively. An interesting variation on such speech is the African-American "playing the dozens," a ritual of insult that marks a woman's powerful entry into the public sphere in Zora Neal *Hurston's *Their Eyes Were Watching God* (1937).

Rites of love and courtship are also common in women's writing. A recurrent motif of natural imagery marks the ritual of awakening sexuality in works like those of Kate *Chopin, Cather, Hurston, *Morrison, and Leslie Marmon *Silko. Silko's *Storyteller* (1981) and *Ceremony* (1977) both invoke the Laguna figure Yellow Woman in scenes of riverside trysts, thus emphasizing the Lagunas' connection with the earth. Similarly, Rayna Green's 1984 anthology

That's What She Said contains references to Native American ceremonies of female puberty, such as tattooing. On a less positive note, the constricting ceremonies of female adornment for attracting suitors are attacked in Edith *Wharton's *House of Mirth* (1905), as well as in Morrison's 1977 *Song of Solomon*.

The role of artist is sometimes offered as a counterattack to the more stultifying aspects of love and courtship rituals. Writers such as Alcott, Chopin, and Nella *Larsen document the various kinds of ceremonies that initiate a woman as an artist, such as sequestering herself from her daily world or connecting with other women artists. Also, religious ritual is evident in women's writing, from Anne *Bradstreet's and Phillis *Wheatley's eighteenth-century poetry to Morrison's *Beloved* (1987), Paula Gunn *Allen's *The Sacred Hoop: Recovering the Feminine in American Indian Traditions* (1986), and Julia Wolf Mazow's *The Woman Who Lost Her Names: Selected and Edited Writings of American Jewish Women* (1980). The variety of ceremony and ritual detailed in women's literature bears witness to rich, changing, living traditions important to women throughout United States history.

[*See also* Theologians; Spirituality.]

• Marjorie Pryse and Hortense J. Spillers, eds., *Conjuring: Black Women, Fiction and Literary Tradition* (1985). H. Nigel Thomas, *From Folklore to Fiction: A Study of Folk Heroes and Rituals in the Black American Novel* (1989). Ramón Saldívar, *Chicano Narrative: The Dialectics of Difference* (1990). Elaine Showalter, *Sister's Choice: Tradition and Change in American Women's Writing* (1991). Ann Romines, *The Home Plot: Women, Writing and Domestic Ritual* (1992).

Amy S. Gottfried

ROBERTS, Elizabeth Madox (1881–1941), poet, novelist, and short fiction writer. A native of Kentucky, the intensely felt setting of her work, Roberts published most of her twelve books during the last fifteen years of her life. Ill health and a teaching career delayed her college education, but she graduated with honors in 1921 from the University of Chicago, publishing her second volume of poetry, *Under the Tree*, the next year.

Her first novel, *The Time of Man* (1926), won international critical and popular acclaim, as did *The Great Meadow* (1930). Both works center on a young woman's growing consciousness of a self and spirit closely tied to nature; the first book involves a poor, illiterate daughter of an itinerant Kentucky farmer, and the second, an eighteenth-century Kentucky pioneer. Roberts wrote at her home in Springfield, Kentucky, where she was often confined by poor health but nevertheless wrote prolifically. She died of cancer as her final book was published and before she could complete her epic novel on Daniel Boone.

Roberts's work is characterized by its poetic realism, lyrical style, and affirmation of the recreation of self and order within the chaos of rural life. She was a careful aesthetician, concerned primarily with relationships within families and with nature. Her fiction makes use of a central consciousness, usually female, which she describes as rushing "out to the very edge of sense." Her realism is infused with poetic symbolism and musings, often on time, philosophical idealism, and the shaping of order from chaos. Frederick McDowell characterizes her novels as "symbolic parables illustrating the themes of psychic death and psychic restoration." The range and subtlety of her poetic talent are represented better in her fiction than in her poetry.

Her works that received less critical notice— novels *My Heart and My Flesh* (1927), *Jingling in the Wind* (1928), *A Buried Treasure* (1931), *He Sent Forth a Raven* (1935), and *Black Is My True Love's Hair* (1938); poetry collections *In the Great Steep's Garden* (1915) and *Sing in the Meadow* (1940); and short story collections *The Haunted Mirror* (1932) and *Not by Strange Gods* (1941)—have passed into obscurity. Limited through her classification by literary historians as a southern regionalist woman writer, though compared to writers such as William Faulkner, Robert Penn Warren, Emily *Dickinson, and Virginia *Woolf, Roberts has received little recent critical attention, even from feminist critics, although several of her novels were reprinted in the 1980s.

• Roberts's papers are at the Library of Congress. Harry Modern Campbell and Ruel E. Foster, *Elizabeth Madox Roberts: American Novelist* (1956). Earl H. Rovit, *Herald to Chaos: The Novels of Elizabeth Madox Roberts* (1960). Frederick McDowell, *Elizabeth Madox Roberts* (1963).

Ann M. Woodlief

ROBINSON, Marilynne (b. 1944), novelist, essayist. Marilynne Robinson was born in Sandpoint, Idaho, and grew up in northern Idaho and western Washington. She studied American literature and religion at Brown University in Rhode Island, and later did graduate work at the University of Washington. Robinson says she wrote narrative poetry from an early age, but gave up on it because it was "intractably bad," and started writing "little bits" of fiction (*Belles Lettres* interview, Fall 1990). She had no trouble getting her first novel (*Housekeeping*, 1980) published, however, and the book contin-

ues to generate critical acclaim. Robinson is married and has two children, whom she has referred to as "part of my research" for *Housekeeping*. In 1989, Robinson published *Mother Country*, a book-length essay about the history of Sellafield, the plutonium reprocessing facility in Great Britain.

Among her influences, Robinson names Melville's style and Emily *Dickinson's "temperament." The Bible and the philosophy of Emerson also played a role in her development as a novelist. "In Biblical literature, as in nineteenth-century American literature, the meeting place is between small, ordinary things and the most enormous, extended implications of significance," she explains (*Belles Lettres*, 1990). This influence manifests itself in *Housekeeping* as a preoccupation with the borders between the "housekeeping" pains of human civilization and the threatening, yet inviting, arms of encroaching nature. Critics have not resolved, however, whether nature represents some enveloping mother *goddess—and therefore an escape from patriarchal culture— or merely the rejection of all traditional human relationships for an asexual, genderless merging. By questioning and rejecting all social constructs, *Housekeeping* defies categorization by critics, refusing to advocate any philosophy, including a feminist one. At the same time, its evocation of the natural setting—a presence as strong as any character—its quirky and compelling female characters, and its rich prose justly make *Housekeeping* one of the most influential novels in recent memory.

Mother Country, on the other hand, has been dismissed as a polemical diatribe, but Robinson makes clear in her introduction that she welcomes this characterization, because her goal is to awaken Americans to the threat of plutonium pollution. Robinson assumed the journalist's role to demonstrate the absurdity of believing that a government puts benevolence above economics. This detour has changed Robinson's outlook on the role of fiction, making her unwilling to accept any art that merely "decorates" the grave state of the world (*Belles Lettres*, 1990).

• Joan Kirkby, "Is There Life after Art? The Metaphysics of Marilynne Robinson's *Housekeeping*," *Tulsa Studies in Women's Literature* 5, no. 1 (Spring 1986): 91– 109. Phyllis Lassner, "Escaping the Mirror of Sameness: Marilynne Robinson's *Housekeeping*," in *Mother Puzzles: Daughters and Mothers in Contemporary American Literature*, ed. Mickey Pearlman (1989), pp. 49–58. Sian Mile, "Femme Foetal: The Construction/Deconstruction of Female Subjectivity in *Housekeeping*, or Nothing Gained," *Genders* 8 (July 1990): 129–136. Maureen Tyan, "Marilynne Robinson's *Housekeeping*: The Subversive Narrative and the New American

Eve," *South Atlantic Review* 56, no. 1 (January 1991): 79–86.

Susan J. Zevenbergen

RODGERS, Carolyn M. (b. 1942), poet and literary theorist. Rodgers was born into a family that migrated from Arkansas to Chicago, Illinois, where she lived for the first fifteen years of her life. The youngest of four children, as a youth her activities were centered on those of the African Methodist Episcopal Church. She read avidly as a child and was active in the high school drama club. Though she began to write poems while still in high school, she did not begin to write seriously until she met Gwendolyn *Brooks during a reception at Roosevelt University, where Rodgers was an English major. Two years after meeting Brooks, Rodgers sent her some poems, which the elder poet praised. As a result of the influences of Brooks and Hoyt Fuller, the editor of *Negro Digest*, Rodgers self-published her first volume, *Paper Soul*, in 1968 to good reviews.

Rodgers then considered herself a full-time writer and began to attend writers' workshops and to read her poems on the college lecture circuit. She made important contributions as a founding member of both the Organization of Black American Culture, which published the literary magazine *Nommo*, and the Third World Press. She also wrote important articles on black poetry. In 1970 she published a second book, *Songs of a Blackbird*, which won the Poet Laureate Award of the Society of Midland Authors. She also received an award from the National Endowment for the Arts. Rodgers's influence became wider at this time because her poems were used in dramatic programs. In later years, this dramatic use of her poems was to continue with productions by Ruby Dee and Ossie Davis, as well as with an off-Broadway production by Woodie King, Jr., in 1982. Contacts made while attending the Phillis *Wheatley Conference in 1974 lead to Rodgers's publication by a major press. Doubleday brought out her volume *How I Got Ovah: New and Selected Poems*, a nominee for the National Book Award for 1976. In this book, Rodgers departs from the focus on black cultural nationalism that predominated in her earlier volumes to treat such themes as loneliness, love, and religion. In 1978, she published *The Heart as Ever Green* with Doubleday. Her next volume, *Translation* (1980), was published by means of a small grant from the Illinois Arts Council. Rodgers has continued to publish her own poetry, bringing out *Eden and Other Poems* in 1983, followed by *Finite Forms* (1985) and *Morning Glory: Poems* (1989).

• Eugene B. Redmond, *Drumvoices: The Mission of*

Afro-American Poetry—A Critical History (1976). Maria K. Mootry, "The OBAC Tradition: Don L. Lee, Carolyn Rodgers and the Early Years," in *Nommo: A Literary Legacy of Black Chicago, 1967–1987*, ed. Carole A. Parks (1987), pp. 2–10. Carolyn Rodgers, "Black Poerty—Where It's At," in *Nommo: A Literary Legacy of Black Chicago, 1967–1987*, ed. Carole A. Parks (1987), pp. 28–37.

Jon Woodson

ROE VS. WADE. *See* Abortion; Birth Control; Reproduction.

ROMAN CATHOLIC WRITERS. *See* Catholic Writers; Theologians.

ROMANCE NOVELS. Each year millions of women enter a world of fiction in which they leave behind daily cares and live out their secret desires and passions. Whether erotic or chaste, romance fiction chronicles changing and unchanging gender relations and patterns of desire. Representing 40 percent of popular book sales, American romance fiction epitomizes careful planning and marketing. Historically, women have dominated romance fiction as writers and readers. Middle-class women with some education wrote romance novels at home out of financial need and as an escape from problems. This entry surveys the origins and development of this form of women's writing.

When Kathleen Woodiwiss's best-seller, *The Flame and the Flower*, was published in 1972, it was the latest in a long line of books about love originally available through lending libraries and at fashionable spas in eighteenth- and nineteenth-century England. According to Nina Baym (*Women's Fiction: A Guide to Novels by and about Women in America, 1820–1870*, 1978), books with romantic motifs by popular writers Catharine Maria *Sedgwick and Susan *Warner appeared in post–Civil War America. These books embodied the rebellion against the theme of women's responsibilities to others that was central to women's fiction. Romance novels retained the earlier focus on the heroine's survival in a hostile world and her development into a strong woman while exploring women's inner life and their claims to pleasure.

In the early twentieth century, few new romance novels were published. Later, Edith M. Hull's *The Sheik* (1921), Margaret *Mitchell's *Gone with the Wind* (1936), and Kathleen Windsor's *Forever Amber* (1944) captured a large following with their romantic motifs. In the 1950s and 1960s, Victoria Holt and Mary Stewart wrote *gothic novels in which "innocent damsels" were terrorized in dreary mansions. Equally popular were historicals, which integrated romance with historical background, and regencies, which were situated in eighteenth-century England. In 1971, Harlequin Enterprises of Canada entered American romance publishing with its successful formula concept, featuring recurring plots and characters. Writers Janet Dailey and Alice Morgan made Harlequin the envy of publishers' row. *Sweet Savage Love* (1974) not only made Rosemary Rogers and Avon Books household words, but created the bodice-ripper romance, characterized by explicit sex and violence. By 1980, the "romance wars" were underway. Silhouette Books was formed to compete with Harlequin. Other publishers quickly developed romance lines. Writers Jude Deveraux and LaVryle Spencer introduced strong, independent heroines. Based on girls' school book club orders, in 1980 Scholastic Books developed *Wildfire*, the first teen romance-fiction series. Over a dozen publishers capitalized on Scholastic's success by issuing their own series. Later in the decade, Harlequin achieved control of the formula romance market by purchasing Silhouette.

Romance fiction continues to develop new categories of books and to widen its themes. Social issues vie with matters of the heart. The new office and erotic romances contain career-oriented heroines and more explicit sexuality. Once absent from romance fiction, African-American characters are featured in the Odyssey line. Naiad Press publishes romances for lesbian readers. Teen romance fiction now includes gothic and historical books, along with characters from several racial and ethnic groups. Through these developments, new readers are gained across ages and backgrounds.

Despite its popularity, romance fiction has only recently attained critical respectability. Early research condemned and dismissed romance fiction and its readers while barely noticing its contradictory qualities. Confined to textual analysis, this criticism equated all romance fiction with Harlequins or gothics. In one of the first critical essays, Joanna * Russ (*Journal of Popular Culture* 6 [1973]) analyzed how modern gothic romances promote women's passivity and glamorize marriage and domestic pursuits. Passive heroines dwelled in "justified paranoia" because of men bent on harming them. Ann Barr Snitow (*Radical History Review*, Spring/Summer 1979), Ann Douglas (*New Republic*, 30 August 1980), and Tania Modleski (*Loving with a Vengeance*, 1982) also argue that Harlequin and gothic romances are "dramas for dependency." Where Douglas views romance fiction as soft-core * pornography for women, Snitow identifies "a rebellious core of psychological vitality" associated with increasingly independent heroines. However,

Snitow believes the new heroines do not represent a breakthrough; they are surface accommodations to women's changing social positions. Douglas was the first to view romance fiction as a counterresponse to the success of the women's movement. Where Snitow considers romances to be "too pallid" to shape consciousness, Modleski regards consciousness-formation as the key component of this fiction: Gothics not only facilitate women's reflection on psychic conflicts with significant others, but are a protest against women's lack of power. However, the books neither question men's superiority nor the institutions of family and marriage. Romance fiction actually desensitizes readers to the evils of sexist society.

The major studies of romance fiction readers by Janice Radway (*Reading the Romance*, 1984), Carol Thurston (*The Romance Revolution*, 1987), and Linda K. Christian-Smith (*Becoming a Woman through Romance*, 1990) paint a more nuanced picture of romance fiction's double-edged qualities. Each study links the political economy of publishing with the personal and political implications of romance fiction reading. Christian-Smith develops Douglas's insight regarding romance fiction as counterresponse. She holds that teen romance fiction articulates the fears and resentments of the conservative New Right towards feminism and women's independence. Each study combines textual analysis with reader research. In the first adult reader ethnography, Radway interviewed and surveyed a group of midwestern women readers of nonformula romance fiction. Thurston conducted the only full-scale study of the new erotic romances with a national sample of readers. In the only full-scale study of teen romance fiction, Christian-Smith combines textual analysis with an ethnography of young women readers and their reading teachers in three urban, midwestern middle level schools.

As in the earlier research, these studies contain similar findings. Most readers were white and middle-class, although Christian-Smith identified some working-class, African-American, Hispanic, and Asian-American readers. In the Radway and Thurston surveys, many readers were married mothers with some postsecondary education; approximately half worked outside of the home. All readers discriminated in their book choices, preferring books with bright, strong, independent heroines and empathetic, vulnerable men. Additionally, teen readers chose books that were easily read, interesting, and with physically attractive characters. Reading provided relaxation, escape, personal private time, and a learning opportunity for all readers. The adult readers escaped the demands of nurturance and learned about distant places and times. Teen readers left behind home problems and the "boring" school day to learn about romance, dating, and boys. Women's reading also represented dissatisfaction with aspects of their relationships with men and with their social positions. However, Radway and Christian-Smith argue that escaping through fantasy forestalled demands for change in the real world. Radway's and Christian-Smith's textual analysis revealed a traditionalism that reconciled women to their social subordination. When teen readers substitute romance fiction for textbooks, they unwittingly limit their education and work possibilities, and funnel themselves toward domestic futures.

Despite this dark side, romance fiction is not totally conservative. According to Radway, reading romances represents a "mild protest" against women's devalued position, and a channel through which women claim their rights to pleasure and fantasy. Christian-Smith views the discourse of pleasure in teen romance novels as opening up a new space in adolescent fiction. For Thurston, erotic romances chronicle the evolution of the "liberated" American woman. Heroines who are both good and sexual with strong tendencies toward lives beyond the domestic context are important departures from traditional characters; this trend has been forced on publishers by women readers as critics. While the studies in this article demonstrate romance fiction's power to stimulate women's reflection on their femininities, these femininities are structured in relation to men despite the shifting ground of gender.

[See also Novel, Beginnings of the.]

Linda K. Christian-Smith

ROMAN MYTHOLOGICAL FIGURES. See Myths, article on Greek and Roman Mythological Figures.

ROMANTIC LOVE. Romantic love—in all its varieties, in all its pleasures and pains—figures prominently in the work of U.S. women writers of all colors, ethnicities, social classes, and sexual orientations. How could it be otherwise? From early age, women are socialized to think of romance as the summum bonum of existence and to believe that a life without love is not worth living.

Even writers whose biographies would seem to make them exempt from the craziness of love were not immune. Most obvious, perhaps, are Emily *Dickinson and Edith *Wharton. Although Dickinson's early biographers tried to make her seem like a prim Amherst maiden who spent her days lowering cookies in a basket

from her bedroom down to neighborhood children, Dickinson loved passionately and wrote with equal passion and pain. Her three "Master" letters to someone whose identity is still unknown are full of the same breath-stopping pain that characterizes her best poetry. Many biographers have tried to guess who this "Master" might have been: newspaper editor Samuel Bowles, judge Otis Phillips Lord, or minister Charles Wadsworth have all been named. Evidence suggests that the three extant letters are part of a larger correspondence that took place over the course of several years. The final two letters are intimate and heartbreaking. But "Master" was not Dickinson's only passion. She also wrote beautiful, glowing, ardent letters to Susan Gilbert, the woman who would become her sister-in-law, and some scholars have suggested that many of Dickinson's most powerful love poems were addressed to Gilbert.

The case of Edith Wharton is both more conventional and more tragic. Like many upper-class women of the late nineteenth century, Edith married when she was still a virgin and knew virtually nothing about the mechanics of sex. Her husband, Edward Robbins ("Teddy") Wharton, took no care to initiate her or, apparently, to give her pleasure. She thought of the events of her marriage night almost as a rape and insisted on separate bedrooms thereafter. For decades, literary historians wrote her off as "frigid," and even dismissed her work on those dubious grounds. In fact, we now know that Wharton later had a tempestuous, adulterous love affair. With Teddy increasingly jealous of her writing and determined to flaunt his emotional instability and his infidelities, Wharton turned for consolation to W. Morton Fullerton, an elegant seducer of both men and women. For the first time, Edith Wharton experienced love and sexual passion. In books such as *The Touchstone* (1900), *The House of Mirth* (1905), and *The Fruit of the Tree* (1907), Wharton had already written about competent, sensitive women in love with callow men, a plot she played out in her romance with Fullerton. After he broke off the affair with her without so much as a considerate Dear John, she grieved for years, then rewrote the plot of this affair in her masterwork, *The Age of Innocence* (1920), in which she was able to give her alter ego Ellen Olenska a far more dignified ending than Morton Fullerton had allowed her.

Reading the poetry, fiction, and plays of women writers alongside their biographies, one sees how often the literary work fictionalizes, enlivens, and even salvages the less satisfactory contours of real life. Even two of America's first novels, Susanna *Rowson's *Charlotte Temple* (1794) and Hannah Webster *Foster's *The Co-

quette (1797), are fictive works that reenact love tragedies. In the former, Rowson transforms the pain of her own marriage to a reprobate, ne'er-do-well, and profligate husband into a national allegory on the evils of seduction. In the latter, Foster tells the story of Elizabeth Whitman (to whom she was related by marriage), a poet and intellectual who had a child out of wedlock and died of childbirth alone in a local tavern. The story became the subject of many gossipy newspaper accounts, but Foster's version attempts to explain why a brilliant, mature woman would be taken in by someone who is a shallow and transparent seducer.

This, it seems, is one of the most important reasons women have written about romantic love: to explain its why and its how, both in exacting emotional terms and in larger sociological ones. When Zelda Sayre [*Fitzgerald] wrote love letters to F. Scott Fitzgerald, she was almost dizzy with self-destructive passion. When she fictionalized that love in *Save Me the Waltz* (1932), she anatomized the ways in which personal insecurities contributed to her madness in love. Had she poured less of herself into a debilitating marriage, she may well have produced more fiction. So, too, with Katherine Anne *Porter, whose entire writing career was crippled by demeaning bouts of love, often carried to histrionic excess, in which her writing shut down. To support herself, Porter worked as a copy editor, ghostwriter, and journalist. Virtually none of the men were worthy of her attentions and, from a literary perspective, none were worth the price of her sacrificed art.

For some, writing is the ultimate revenge for a love gone wrong. In her brilliant collection *In Mad Love and War* (1990), Muscogee Creek poet Joy *Harjo is especially adept at cataloging love's promises and pains. The blues sounds of her poetry—addressed, implicitly, to female lovers with lips and arms and false promises—seem as tough, smart, and sad as the tenor sax the author plays.

With so many personal and literary testimonials of love gone wrong, it is no surprise that feminists quickly elevated to the status of a classic Carroll Smith-Rosenberg's magisterial essay, "The Female World of Love and Ritual: Relations between Women in Nineteenth-Century America" (1985), which quotes from dozens of tender letters exchanged between nineteenth-century women, letters that declare love passionately, fondly, and generously.

• Carroll Smith-Rosenberg, "The Female World of Love and Ritual: Relations between Women in Nineteenth-Century America," in *Disorderly Conduct: Visions of Gender in Victorian America* (1985), pp. 53–76. R. W. Franklin, ed., *The Master Letters of Emily Dickinson* (1986). Linda S. Kauffman, *Discourses of Desire: Gender, Genre, and Epistolary Fictions* (1986). R. W. B. Lewis and Nancy Lewis, eds., *The Letters of Edith Wharton* (1988). Cathy N. Davidson, *The Book of Love: Writers and Their Love Letters* (1992).

Cathy N. Davidson

ROSCA, Ninotchka (b. 1941), novelist, short fiction writer, journalist, and political activist. Critics and reviewers placed Ninotchka Rosca within the magical-realist tradition of Gabriel García Márquez when her volume of short stories *Monsoon Collection* appeared in 1983. Rosca acknowledged the honor, but called her technique "supra-realism" instead. Her nonfiction *Endgame, The Fall of Marcos* (1987) shares some features of this embryonic style with her first novel, *State of War* (1988), and her latest work, *Twice Blessed* (1992). Her writings possess the texture of magical realism, but also evoke Philippine social-historical reality in the transparency of its inner excess.

Rosca, like many other *Filipino expatriate writers before her, regards Philippine history from an anthropological distance afforded by the West. But what distinguishes her journalism and fiction is a piercing eye developed from constant political displacement. Detained for six months for her political activism when Ferdinand Marcos imposed martial law in 1972, she fled from another arrest in 1976 with the help of a University of Iowa writing fellowship. Unable to return to the Philippines, she found refuge at the University of Hawaii, where she taught Tagalog until her move to New York in 1981.

These experiences of migrancy and persecution framed the conditions in which she wrote the *Monsoon* stories and her highly-praised first novel. They also furnished her with a multitude of narrative types, strategies, and structures. *State of War* and *Twice Blessed* elaborate the condensed contemplations on contemporary Philippine political culture pioneered by Linda *Ty-Casper. The novels are remarkable for imposing pattern and design on the riot of colors and seeming disorder in Philippine life that Ty-Casper, in her novellas, or Jessica *Hagedorn, in *Dogeaters* (1990), critiques and paints with verve.

For example, *Monsoon* follows the structure of the *Kundiman* (Filipino aria). But this collection also gives mimetic form to the suggestive *pasión* (a biblical chant recited ritually during the Philippine Lenten season) of Ty-Casper's *Awaiting Trespass* (1985) by syncopating nine pithy tales of social despair with nine episodes of the author's experiences of political torture. The stories take the rhythm of this canticle of Christly suffering by straining its power against and within autobiographical fragments. *State of*

War divides into three books of "Acts," "Numbers," and "Revelations," again alluding to Ty-Casper's tripartite description of the Filipino people's *pasión* in the preface to *Trespass*. Three major characters (Adrian Banyaga, Anna Villaverde, Eliza Hansen) allegorize the incestuous networks of relationships and dialectics of power in the Philippines. Colonizers from three countries (Spain, the United States, and briefly, Japan) had, at different times, intruded upon the three island groups (Luzon, Visayas, Mindanao) and left the archipelago and its people in a perpetual state of war. The geometry of historical determinism thus balances the Rabelaisian carnival that forms the basic action of the novel and plays out the inner conflicts of the characters. Rosca's aptitude for taut design was already evident in *Bitter Country and Other Stories* (1970) and the stories she published in the Philippines before her passage to the United States.

• Epifanio San Juan, Jr., *Toward a People's Literature* (1984). Epifanio San Juan, Jr., *Crisis in the Philippines* (1986). Paulino Lim, Jr., "Confronting Historical Pain in Rosca and Ty-Casper," *Pilipinas* 14 (Spring 1990): 1–5. Ninotchka Rosca, "Standards of Invisibility," *Filipinas Magazine* (May 1992): 9–10.

Oscar V. Campomanes

ROURKE, Constance (1885–1941), cultural historian, biographer, critic. Rourke was an advocate for the study of American folk traditions and popular culture. Arguing against the early writings of Van Wyck Brooks, who claimed that American society was hostile to the creation of art, Rourke insisted that the country possessed a vital cultural tradition adequate to the development of fine art. Rourke asserted throughout her career that folk arts were the necessary foundation to great art. Expanding the definition of culture to include such diverse traditions as frontier tales and vaudeville, Rourke matched extensive research with a popular writing style in an effort to make this American heritage accessible to as many readers as possible.

Born in Cleveland, Ohio, she moved to Grand Rapids, Michigan, at the age of three, at about the time her father died. She graduated from Vassar College in 1907 and taught primary school in Grand Rapids for a year before traveling through Europe on a William Borden Fellowship. After teaching at Vassar from 1910 to 1915, Rourke returned to Grand Rapids to devote herself to writing and lecturing.

Her first book, *Trumpets of Jubilee* (1927), recorded biographical portraits of five nineteenth-century figures who dramatized the American character: Lyman Beecher, Harriet Beecher *Stowe, Henry Ward Beecher, Horace Greeley, and P. T. Barnum. *Troupers of the Gold Coast; or, the Rise of Lotta Crabtree* (1928), a history portraying a close relationship between the frontier actress and her mother, is often read as Rourke's comment on a lifelong attachment to her own mother.

Rourke's best-known work, *American Humor: A Study of the National Character* (1931), argues that legends about the Yankee peddler, backwoodsman, minstrel, strolling actor, and comic poet attest to a native comic style available to writers as varied as Poe, Hawthorne, and Sinclair Lewis. Her other works include two juvenile biographies, *Davy Crockett* (1934) and *Audubon* (1936), and the critically admired *Charles Sheeler: Artist in the American Tradition* (1938). *The Roots of American Culture*, based on voluminous notes intended for a history of American culture, was edited by Brooks and published posthumously in 1942.

Rourke died after a fall on the icy porch of her home on 23 March 1941. As writer, lecturer, teacher, and community worker, she devoted her life to researching and acquainting Americans with the folk traditions that provided the foundation for an American culture not dependent on a European past, but unique in its own right.

• Stanley Edgar Hyman, "Constance Rourke and Folk Criticism," in *The Armed Vision*, 2d ed. (1955), pp. 114–131. Arthur F. Wertheim, "Constance Rourke and the Discovery of American Culture in the 1930s," in *The Study of American Culture: Contemporary Conflicts*, ed. Luther S. Luedtke (1977), pp. 49–61. Joan Shelley Rubin, *Constance Rourke and American Culture* (1980). Samuel I. Belman, *Constance M. Rourke* (1981).

Dianne Chambers

ROWLANDSON, Mary (c. 1635–1711), *captivity narrative writer. Mary, who was probably born in Somersetshire, England, migrated to the New World with John White, her father. She lived in Salem, Massachusetts, and later moved to Lancaster, Massachusetts, where she met Joseph Rowlandson, a minister, whom she married in 1656.

Suddenly, on the dawn of 10 February 1676, her life changed. During Joseph Rowlandson's absence from Lancaster, Matocomet, the Wampanoag Indian leader, burned Lancaster and took captive Mrs. Rowlandson, her three children, and others.

After Mary was in captivity for eleven weeks, her husband ransomed her for twenty pounds. After a long delay, the Rowlandsons secured the release of their two surviving children through the assistance of other colonists. The family moved to Wethersfield, Connecticut, where Joseph Rowlandson died in 1678. Mary married Captain Samuel Talcott on 6 August 1679; she resided in Wethersfield until her death on 5 January 1711.

Rowlandson's principal work, *The Soveraignty and Goodness of God, Together, with the Faithfulness of His Promises Displayed* (1682), chronicles her eleven-week captivity. Her firsthand narrative describes Matocomet's attack, the Indians' indiscriminate burning of homes, and the maiming and killing of twelve people: "It is a solemn sight to see so many Christians lying in their blood; . . . like 'a company of sheep torn by wolves.' . . ."

During her captivity, Rowlandson constantly demanded the return of her son Joseph and daughter Mary, whom the Indians had taken away. She also tried to tend to her wounded daughter Sarah; she writes that Sarah departed from life "like a lamb" on 18 February 1675. Later, the Indians sold Mary for a gun, but forced her son Joseph to join another group of Indians six miles away.

During her captivity, Rowlandson used her English houswifery skills to survive as a servant to Weetamoo, the wife of a subordinate Algonquin chief, Quinnapin. A tribesman gave her a Bible, which she read faithfully and quotes throughout her narrative.

Rowlandson reveals a profound spiritual transformation in this powerful and deeply moving piece of writing. A resourceful, feisty captive, she continued to believe in God's mercy while living in a "lively semblance of hell."

Her narrative provides the first detailed account of a woman's experience as an Indian captive. She emerges as a strong feminist voice filled with passion, integrity, and spirituality. Her heroic adventure found audiences in the New World and in England.

Mainstream writers who employed fictional variations of her narrative technique include James Fenimore Cooper (*Last of the Mohicans*, 1826), William Faulkner (*Sanctuary*, 1931), and Caroline * Gordon ("The Captive," 1945).

• Richard Slotkin, *Regeneration through Violence* (1973). Mitchell Robert Breitwieser, *American Puritanism and the Defense of Mourning: Religion, Grief, and Ethnology in Mary White Rowlandson's Captivity Narrative* (1990). Tara Fitzpatrick, "The Figure of Captivity: The Cultural Work of the Puritan Captivity Narrative," *American Literary History* 3, no. 1 (Spring 1991): 1–26.

Adelaide P. Amore

ROWSON, Susanna (1762–1824), novelist, actress, poet, lyricist, educator. When Susanna Haswell Rowson died in Boston in 1824, she was acclaimed as a prominent educator and writer of popular but instructive fiction. Today, her fame rests on her popular novel *Charlotte Temple, A Tale of Truth* (1791) and on her interest in women's education.

Born in Portsmouth, England, Susanna Haswell spent her childhood in the colony of Massachusetts. In London as a young woman she was attracted to the theater and in 1788 published *A Trip to Parnassus*, a poetic critique of the actors at the Covent Garden Theatre. That same year she married William Rowson, and together they tried but failed to make a living on the stage. Rowson supplemented her income by publishing four novels before she and her husband joined a group of other British actors and musicians in a move to the newly formed Philadelphia Theater Company, thus becoming artists in the new American Republic.

While acting in Philadelphia and then in Boston, Rowson also became known as a writer. She published song lyrics and two plays; republished two of her English novels, *Charlotte Temple* and *Rebecca; or, the Fille de Chambre* in 1794; and published a new novel, *The Trials of the Human Heart*, in 1796.

In 1797, at age thirty-five, Rowson changed careers, leaving the stage to found her own "young ladies' academies," which enabled her to put into practice the ideas about women's education she had developed in her novels. The themes of filial piety, acceptance of one's station in life, the nobility of the middle class, faith in virtue unrelated to rank, the strength and comfort derived from a community of women, and especially the need for a practical education for women had all contributed to the popularity of her novels. Her own schools enabled her to win a position in Boston society by offering these ideas to its daughters. At the same time she continued her writing—textbooks, poems, and three more novels.

Rowson's novels anticipated the surge of women's fiction in the nineteenth century, but she often countered the prevailing sentimental style by emphasizing rationality rather than romance. Many of her characters mirror the author's independence and her belief in the need for education and worldly wisdom. Rowson's career reflects the course of the arts and women's education during the important early development of the new United States.

• Rowson's papers are contained in the Barrett Collection at the University of Virginia. See also Susanna Rowson, *Charlotte Temple*, ed. Cathy N. Davidson (reprint, 1986). Patricia L. Parker, *Susanna Rowson* (1986).

Patricia Parker

RUIZ DE BURTON, María Amparo (1832–1895). María Amparo Ruiz was born in Baja California, in 1832, at the time California was joining the United States, an historical, political moment that, later, impacted every aspect of her personal and professional life. The granddaughter of Don José Manuel Ruiz, a former governor of Baja, whose lands in Ensenada were a small portion of the U.S. government's appropriation of Greater Mexico in the 1840s, Ruiz met her future husband, U.S. Captain Henry S. de Burton, when he arrived as commander of the U.S. forces sent to secure Baja California in 1847. Under the terms of protection afforded to U.S. supporters by the Treaty of Guadalupe-Hidalgo (1848), the sixteen-year-old Ruiz escaped with her family to relocate in Monterey, where, one year later, she crossed religious, ethnic, and national boundaries to marry the widowed, twenty-eight-year-old de Burton. The controversial, ultimately romanticized marriage was described in 1888 by Hubert Howe Bancroft in *A California Pastoral* and in a series of articles in California newspapers forty-four years later.

In 1859, Ruiz de Burton moved to New England with her husband, now a Brigadier-General of the Union Army, where she lived until 1869, when de Burton died of malaria, leaving her a widow of thirty-seven, with two children. Her tenure in New England led to the publication of *Who Would Have Thought It?* (1872), a biting satire upon Northern racism and religious hypocrisy which is remarkable in its narration by a Mexican child who has been adopted by the novel's abolitionist family. Years earlier, while in San Diego, Ruiz de Burton had written and produced *Don Quixote de la Mancha. A comedy in five acts taken from Cervantes novel of that name.*

Her second novel, *The Squatter and the Don* (1885), is a lengthy, politically complex historical romance attacking American social and political systems of the nineteenth century. Reissued by Arte Público Press with an excellent introduction by Rosaura Sánchez and Beatrice Pita, *The Squatter and the Don* is the first depiction published in English of the plight of the subordinated Californios, and the first narration of California history authored by a woman. Ruiz de Burton's own battles with "Anglo" squatters on her Jamul Ranch in San Diego County are the historical foundation of the novel's account of the struggles and ultimate dispossession of the fictional Don Marino Alamar family.

In another land battle, Ruiz de Burton grappled with her double identity as U.S. citizen and dispossessed Mexican, fighting unsuccessfully for years to reclaim the Ensenada tract in Baja California from U.S.-backed investors whom she identified as monopolist colonizers. Planning still another appeal, María Amparo Ruiz de Burton died in poverty in 1895.

• Hubert Howe Bancroft, *California Pastoral* (1888), pp. 330–331. María Amparo Ruiz de Burton, *The Squatter and the Don*, edited and introduced by Rosaura Sánchez and Beatrice Pita (1992).

Margot Sempreora

RUKEYSER, Muriel (1913–1980), poet, biographer, translator, essayist, critic, playwright, and novelist. Born in New York City to second-generation Jewish parents, Rukeyser attended Manhattan's School of Ethical Culture, the Fieldston School, Vassar College, and Columbia University. The daughter of a concrete salesman and a bookkeeper, she grew up emulating Joan of Arc, and by the age of thirteen, had decided to be a writer. Politically active throughout her life, Rukeyser allied herself with the Communist Party during the Depression; she attended the 1933 trial of the Scottsboro Boys in Alabama, traveled to Hanoi in 1972 with Denise *Levertov in protest of the Vietnam War, and in 1975, as the president of PEN American Center, she demonstrated against the imprisonment of the poet Kim Chi-Ha in Seoul, South Korea.

In 1935, her first collection of poems, *Theory of Flight*, won the Yale Younger Poets Prize. From 1935 to 1948 she published numerous essays and reviews as well as the biography of the physicist, Willard Gibbs, a three-act play, and four books of poems: *U.S. 1* (1938), *A Turning Wind: Poems* (1939), *Beast in View* (1944), and *The Green Wave* (1948). In 1945, Rukeyser moved to California, where she taught a poetry workshop at the California Labor School, and for two months was married to the painter Glynn Collins. In 1947, unmarried, she gave birth to her only child, (William) Laurie Rukeyser, whom she raised as a single parent. Though her political activity and productivity slowed somewhat after her son's birth, she continued to write and translate. In 1949, she published *Elegies, Orpheus,* and *The Life of Poetry,* her essential meditation on the place of poetry in society. In 1954, she moved back to New York and started teaching at Sarah Lawrence College. During the 1960s, she published her selected poems *Waterlily Fire* (1962), wrote the novel *The Orgy* (1966), continued teaching at Sarah Lawrence, translated and published the poems of Octavio Paz and Gunnar Ekelof, and completed the collection *Speed of Darkness* (1968). In the midst of this productive period, at the age of fifty-one, Rukeyser suffered her first paralyzing stroke.

Characterized by poems of great expansion, Rukeyser has often been compared to the poet Walt Whitman. Through the themes of silence and speech, Rukeyser's poems use the rhythms and music of language to create transformations in the physical, emotional, mythic, and political worlds. Rejecting and even mocking the despair of poets such as Sylvia *Plath, her poetry is generous and optimistic in spirit and vision, reflecting her political times as well as her personal experience as daughter, sister, mother, lover and friend, and as lesbian engaged in the changing world. During the last decade of her life, she published the biography *The Traces of Thomas Hariot* (1971), *Breaking Open* (1973), the translations of Octavio Paz's *Early Poems* (1973) and Brecht's *Uncle Eddie's Moustache* (1974), *The Gates* (1976), and *The Collected Poems of Muriel Rukeyser* (1979). With all of her books out of print for well over a decade, Rukeyser has long been known as one of the neglected, yet great and essential female voices of the twentieth century.

• Virginia R. Terris, "Muriel Rukeyser: A Retrospective," *American Poetry Review* 3 (May/June, 1974): 10–15. Louise Kertesz, *The Poetic Vision of Muriel Rukeyser* (1979). Kate Daniels and Richard Jones, eds., "Special Muriel Rukeyser Issue," *Poetry East* (1985): 6–228. Kate Daniels, ed., *Rukeyser Out of Silence, Selected Poems* (1992)

Jan Freeman

RULE, Jane (b. 1931), novelist, short story writer, essayist, social and literary critic, now retired. Born in Plainfield, New Jersey, to her mother, Jane, and businessman father, Arthur, Rule grew up in diverse parts of the U.S. She completed a B.A. in English at Mills College in California, and also studied at University College, London, and Stanford. She taught English from 1954 to 1956 at Concord Academy in Massachusetts, where she met Helen Sonthoff. They moved to Vancouver, where Rule adopted Canadian citizenship and taught English and creative writing at the University of British Columbia. After twenty years in the city, they relocated to their present home on Galiano Island, off the coast of British Columbia.

Rule's first and best-known novel, *The Desert of the Heart* (1964, filmed as *Desert Hearts*, 1985), broke with literary convention by presenting its lesbian protagonists positively and working beyond worn psychoanalytic assumptions in its portrayal of their developing love and commitment. It has been immensely important to lesbian readers since its publication. Rule has analyzed the politics of lesbian representation in *Lesbian Images* (1975), a groundbreaking study that combines a critique of institutional religion and psychoanalysis with biocritical analyses of twelve writers, from Radclyffe Hall and Willa *Cather to May *Sarton and Maureen Duffy.

While Rule is politically active, a contributor to gay and lesbian magazines (her essays are collected in *Outlander*, 1981, and *A Hot-Eyed Moderate*, 1985), and proudly lesbian, the fiction

after her second novel, *This Is Not For You* (1970), has not focused on lesbian sexuality. Rather, lesbian characters, as well as members of other marginalized groups such as the elderly, are woven into the inclusive social fabric depicted in novels such as *The Young in One Another's Arms* (1977) and *Memory Board* (1987). A favorite literary device is shifting point of view, which Rule uses to represent communities that incorporate difference, as in *Contract with the World* (1980), about a group of urban friends, and her twelfth book, *After the Fire* (1989), about an island community off the coast of British Columbia. Although the lesbian writer in *Contract* laments the lack of a language for lesbianism in terms that recall French feminist arguments, Rule herself works within an accessible mode of realism to subvert narrative, figurative, and conceptual conventions. Her short fiction, collected in *Theme for Diverse Instruments* (1975), *Outlander*, and *Inland Passage* (1985), is often more formally experimental.

• Special issue on Jane Rule, *Canadian Fiction Magazine* 23 (Autumn 1976). Marilyn Schuster, "Strategies for Survival: The Subtle Subversion of Jane Rule," *Feminist Studies* 7 (1983): 431–450. "Jane Rule" [bibliography] in Barbara Godard, ed., *Gynocritics/La Gynocritique* (1987), pp. 330–332.

Susan Brown

RURAL WOMEN. *See* Frontier Writing; New England Women's Writing; Pioneer Women; Southern Women's Writing; Western Women's Writing.

RUSH, Rebecca (1779–?), author of the 1812 novel *Kelroy*. Although she was born into the prominent Rush family of Philadelphia, very little information about Rebecca Rush is available. She was the eldest of five daughters born to the jurist Jacob Rush (younger brother of physician and essayist Benjamin), and Mary Wrench (Rench) Rush, who before her marriage was a miniature painter of some local fame. Although the extent of her own education is unknown, Rush grew up in an impressively educated and literate family. It is clear that she made frequent and sometimes lengthy visits with her uncle Benjamin and Aunt Julia, perhaps nursing their son Benjamin, during the years her father served as Third Circuit Court judge in Reading, Pennsylvania, some forty miles away. She was apparently still alive at the time of her father's death in 1820. After that, Rush disappears from the historical record.

Rush published *Kelroy, A Novel* in 1812, with little fanfare and virtually no critical notice. Despite the novel's merits, its advertisements were overshadowed by accounts of the United

States' skirmishes with the British—the war of 1812 was declared within a month of the publication of *Kelroy*. Her publishers, Bradford and Inskeep, expressed their confidence in the quality of *Kelroy*, paying $100 for the manuscript. The book was printed by Jane Aitkin, a successful Philadelphia printer who had taken over the business from her father and brother.

Kelroy is one of the most outstanding of early American novels. Predating the British *Pride and Prejudice* by a year, the plot complicates Austen's: What does a woman do who has made a "successful" marriage, only to have the husband die when she is past the age of remarriage, leaving her in poverty and with virtually no alternatives for support? *Kelroy's* Mrs. Hammond may seem to some a monster who attempts to "sell" her beautiful daughters to preserve her own expensive ways of living, but Rush creates a complicated character in the mother, who acts out of concern not only for herself, but also for her daughters.

If Rush creates a multidimensional "evil" mother, so, too, she complicates the virtue of the romantic protagonists, Emily and Kelroy. Although the two are morally elevated for their sensibility, they are not stalwart in it. In just this way, the novel is notable, as its handful of critics have observed, for its refusal to draw an artificially happy closure to the problems it surveys. All the main characters are caught in an ugly economy of conflicting interest, which cannot be resolved, the novel underscores, by a propitious marriage.

• Lillie Deming Loshe, *The Early American Novel* (1907). Henry Petter, *The Early American Novel* (1971). Harrison T. Meserole, "Some Notes on Early American Fiction: *Kelroy* Was There," *Studies in American Fiction* 5, no. 1 (1977): 1–12. Kathryn Zabelle Derounian, "Lost in the Crowd: Rebecca Rush's *Kelroy* (1812)," *American Transcendental Quarterly* 47–48 (Summer/Fall 1980): 117–126. Cathy N. Davidson, *Revolution and the Word: The Rise of the Novel in America* (1986).

Dana D. Nelson

RUSS, Joanna (b. 1937), novelist, short story writer, feminist critic. Joanna Russ was born and raised in New York City; she showed an early talent for science, winning the Westinghouse Science Prize in 1953. She attended Cornell University and the Yale School of Drama, and has taught women's studies and English since the mid-1960s, most recently at the University of Washington. Her books include several *science fiction novels, notably *The Female Man* (1975), *The Two of Them* (1978), and *Extra(ordinary) People* (1984), as well as the short story collections *Alyx* (1976) and *The Hidden Side of the Moon* (1987). Among feminist critics, Russ is appreciated for *How to Suppress Women's Writing* (1983), a wickedly funny attack on the methods used by the "literary" culture to marginalize work by women.

Since she believes her experience, as that of a woman, will never be considered "central," Russ says that she writes "realism disguised as fantasy, that is, science fiction" (*How to Suppress Women's Writing*). In science fiction, Russ, like many other feminist authors, can imagine the overthrow of patriarchal oppression. As a critic, Russ has traced the theme of the "rescue of the female child" in feminist utopian fiction: to "rescue" the female child for Russ means to remove the constraints of patriarchal society from her life, to bring her to a better society where she can find unlimited possibilities instead of "sexist restrictions, sexual objectification or even outright persecution" (*Future Females*, 1981). Kathleen Spencer sees this pattern as the underlying impulse throughout Joanna Russ's own fiction (*Science-Fiction Studies*, July 1990). Certainly Russ's heroines represent the coming-of-age of women, their coming into their power on a social level and as individuals.

Russ transforms the science fiction novel stylistically by experimenting with narrative structures built of myth, reverie, and meditative passages, as well as the more traditional elements. She received the Hugo Award for *The Female Man*, the story of a modern woman who travels between three alternate selves: the downtrodden woman of an imaginary past; an ambassador from an imagined, distant future; and a character from the time in between, from a world divided by war into Womanland and Manland. The novel has become an underground classic because, like much of Russ's fiction, it offers women a glimpse of their own possible evolution beyond oppressive structures, and, like one of Russ's adolescent heroines, they feel gratitude toward the female trailblazer who thus frees their imaginations.

• Marilyn J. Holt, "No Docile Daughters: A Study of Two Novels by Joanna Russ," *A Room of One's Own* 6, nos. 1–2 (1981):92–99. June Howard, "Widening the Dialogue on Feminist Science Fiction," in *Feminist Re-Visions: What Has Been and Might Be*, ed. Vivian Patraka (1983), pp. 64–96. Thelma J. Shinn, "Worlds of Words and Swords: Suzette Haden Elgin and Joanna Russ at Work," *Women Worldwalkers: New Dimensions of Science Fiction and Fantasy*, ed. Jane B. Weedman (1985), pp. 207–222. Samuel R. Delany, "Orders of Chaos: the Science Fiction of Joanna Russ," in *Women Worldwalkers: New Dimensions of Science Fiction and Fantasy*, ed. Jane B. Weedman (1985), pp. 95–123. Judith Spector, "The Functions of Sexuality in the Science Fiction of Russ, Piercy and Le Guin," in *Erotic Universe: Sexuality and Fantastic Literature*, ed. Donald Palumbo (1986), pp. 197–207.

Susan J. Zevenbergen

S

SAKSENA-NILSSON, Usha (also known as Usha Priyamvada), novelist, short story writer, educator. Usha Nilsson was born in Kanpur, India, to a financially impoverished family that was very active in the freedom movement. All the women in her family were avid readers, and Usha discovered English literature during her trips to the library to find books for her mother and her aunts. Nilsson's B.A., M.A., and Ph.D. are in English literature from Allahabad University, India. She minored in Hindi literature. Since 1977, she has taught in the Department of South Asian Studies at the University of Wisconsin, Madison.

Nilsson is a prolific writer, and has published short stories, novels, and scholarly essays since 1960. Unfortunately, her work rarely appears in anthologies and discussions of Asian-American writers. This is because, like many other important South Asian–American writers such as Kiran Patel, Sudha Chandola, Susham Bedi, Panna Naik, and Malathi Rao, Nilsson writes in a South Asian language—Hindi. She is presently working on a novel in English.

Nilsson's works deal with cultural complexities, which turn into everyday despair for her Indian-American characters. Women and men in her stories are constantly trying to come to terms with themselves within traditional, nontraditional, and often extramarital relationships.

In her short story "Such a Big Lie" (1986), Kiran, a traditional, seemingly happy wife and mother, returns to her home in America after a visit to India to discover that her lover Max has married his young student assistant. She quietly deals with her shock and her pain as she puts on her makeup, dresses in her favorite sari, and goes to an Indian restaurant with her husband and children. In a forthcoming short story, "Episode," a successful Indian-American doctor returns to India after her married Indian-American lover dies. She agrees to an arranged marriage with a widower, and tries to make sense of the fragments of her life while on her honeymoon. Nilsson's English-language work in progress is told from the point of view of an Indian-American couple and their friends. Again, the focus is on sexual tensions that underlie the intersecting patterns of relationships and cultural complications of her characters' lives.

Usha Nilsson's works need to be available in translation to a larger audience. She has a unique perception of the quiet inner dialogues, the seemingly routine relationships, the unexpected sexual relationships, and the fascinating courage of women who are trying to find their place in a mostly hostile world of men and conflicting cultures.

Roshni Rustomji-Kerns

SALEM WITCHCRAFT TRIALS. *See* Witchcraft.

SANCHEZ, Sonia (b. 1934), poet, playwright, activist, author. Sonia Sanchez, born Wilsonia Benita Driver on 9 September 1934 to Wilson L. Driver and Lena Jones Driver, spent her early years in Birmingham, Alabama. At the age of nine, she moved with her family to New York, where she attended public school and began writing poetry. In 1955, she graduated from Hunter College and studied at New York University with poet Louise * Bogan. Sanchez also has taught at several colleges and universities, beginning with San Francisco State between 1967 and 1969, where she played a significant role in establishing the first black studies program in the country. Having taught at the University of Pittsburgh, Rutgers University, and Amherst College, among others, Sanchez is currently a professor of literature and creative writing at Temple University, where she holds the Laura H. Carnell Chair in English.

Sanchez matured as a writer in America's turbulent 1960s, when a black power movement led by such political thinkers as Malcolm X, Stokely Carmichael, and Angela * Davis ushered in a change in race relations and challenged the social, economic, and political underpinnings of American institutions. This era shaped the mettle of the poet, and Sanchez became an armed prophet whose voice was at once a prod and a sword.

Through her preference for tightness, brevity, and gemlike intensity, Sanchez creates poetry that demonstrates a complex imagination and a serious social consciousness. In her eight volumes of poetry, which appeared between 1969 and 1987, Sanchez's voice is sometimes abrasive, but never as profane as the conditions she knows must be eradicated; her tone ranges greatly, yet her message is one of redeeming realism. Undergirding her poetic expression is an abiding concern for heritage; for the sovereignty of time, with all its ramifications of birth, change, rebirth, and death; for the impress of the past and memories; and for nurture, nature, and God.

In *Homecoming* (1969) and *We a BadddDDD People* (1970), Sanchez uses experimental language and typography to attack the dangers of the status quo and to empower black people. In these volumes, she also introduces her unmistakable signature: her singing/chanting voice. In *It's a New Day* (1971), a collection of poems "for young brothas and sistuhs," Sanchez, the mother of twin sons, reflects her deep interest in nurturing young minds. Her fourth volume, *Love Poems* (1973), includes poems that are collages of the images, sounds, aromas, and textures of woman-love. With the clarity and precision of Japanese ink sketches, Sanchez skillfully uses the haiku to evoke emotion.

A Blues Book for Blue Black Magical Women (1974) is a striking spiritual odyssey that reveals the poet's growing awareness of the psychological and spiritual features of her face. The work's scope is sweeping; though occasionally laden with the ideological doctrine of the Nation of Islam, it is, at its best, intimate, luminous, and apocalyptic. In 1978, she culled some of her best poetry in *I've Been a Woman: New and Selected Poems*. Six years later, Sanchez continued the quest begun in *A Blues Book* and went inside herself, inside her past, to pull out of her residual memory deeply personal experience. In *Homegirls and Handgrenades* (1984), she draws images that explode the autobiographical into universal truths. The predominant genre in this volume is the sketch, like those that stud Jean Toomer's *Cane*. Bubba, "the black panther of Harlem," lost in a sea of drugs and unfulfilled dreams; Norma, possessed of a black genius that remains unmined; or the old "bamboo-creased" woman in "Just Don't Never Give Up on Love" all live again and help Sanchez distill "sweet/astringent memories" from her own experience.

Distinguishing much of Sanchez's poetry is a prophetic voice that brings the weight of her experience to articulating the significant truths about liberation and love, self-actualization and being, spiritual growth and continuity, heroes, and the cycles of life. Her vision is original because it is both new and faithful to the origins of its inspiration. Therefore, it is not surprising that in her most recent volume of poetry, *Under a Soprano Sky* (1987), the mature voice of the poet is giving expression to the sources of her spiritual strength, establishing and reestablishing connections that recognize the family of man/womankind, and singing, as Billie Holliday did, of society's strange fruit sacrificed on the altars of political megalomania, economic greed, and social misunderstanding. Intense, deeply spiritual, and visionary, Sanchez moves her readers into her world, where ugliness is called by name and beauty is the greening of the universe.

Joanne V. Gabbin

SANCHEZ-SCOTT, Milcha (b. 1955), Chicana playwright. Although her subject matter, themes, and language reflect the bicultural reality of life in the southwestern United States and identify her as a Chicana playwright, Sanchez-Scott is the product of a more complicated background of cultural and ethnic influences. She was born in Bali to an Indonesian-Chinese mother and a Colombian-Mexican father. As a child, she divided time among England, Colombia, and Mexico before moving to California as a teenager with her family. She graduated from the University of San Diego with a degree in literature, philosophy, and theater, and premiered her first play, *Latina* (1980), several years later. Within her mixture of cultural experience, Sanchez-Scott traces the roots of her inspiration to South America and her heritage and childhood experiences there (*On New Ground*, 1987), but it is her experience of Chicano/a culture that has chiefly influenced her work.

Sanchez-Scott's plays feature a distinctive mix of magical realism and surrealism, often used to explore the specificity of women's experiences of Hispanic-American culture. *Latina* was inspired by the immigrant women the playwright met while working at an employment agency for maids in Beverly Hills. After premiering in 1980, *Latina* won seven *Dramalogue* awards and was later published in *Necessary Theater* (1989). Two of her one-act plays, *Dog Lady* and *The Cuban Swimmer*, were produced in 1984. *Dog Lady* was published in *Best Short Plays of 1986*, and both appeared in Theatre Communications Group's *Plays in Process* series (1985). *Roosters*, her best-known work, was first staged in 1987 and appeared in *On New Ground*, an anthology of contemporary Hispanic-American plays, and in *American Theatre*. Both *Stone Wedding* and *Evening Star* premiered in 1988, and *El Dorado* followed in 1991. Her oeuvre also features an adaptation of *Carmen*, Georges Bizet's opera of the same name.

Sanchez-Scott's work has established her as one of the most successful artists of Chicano theater; she is counted at the forefront of a growing number of Chicana playwrights receiving national recognition. Sanchez-Scott employs aspects of bilingualism and *biculturalism to sharpen her portraits of Hispanic-American life, and a distinctive visual imagery underscores her dialogue. Her themes, often treated satirically, include the tension between Hispanic and Anglo culture (frequently played out in the language choice of her characters), the dynamics of gender roles in patriarchal society, and an exploration of the family as a site of cultural and social struggle.

• Jon Bouknight, "Language as Cure: An Interview with Milcha Sanchez-Scott," *Latin American Theatre Review* 23, no. 2 (Spring 1990): 63–74.

Leigh H. Edwards

SANDOZ, Mari (1896–1966), biographer, novelist, and western historian, was born to Swiss immigrant homesteaders on the northwestern Nebraska frontier, near two Lakota reservations. When she was fourteen, the family moved southeast into the Nebraska sandhills, a mysterious area that both fascinated and frightened Mari. Her own childhood experiences and her early contacts with both Indian and settler storytellers gave Sandoz a unique understanding of her region's history, and was later augmented by extensive research. Although she lived most of her adult life in cities, the setting for her writing is usually the trans-Missouri region.

Sandoz's most significant work is her Great Plains series, comprised of *Old Jules* (1935), the biography of her father, a brutal man who was important in settling the region; her fine Indian biographies, *Crazy Horse* (1942) and *Cheyenne Autumn* (1953); and three books based on animal-human relations: *The Buffalo Hunters* (1954), *The Cattlemen* (1958), and *The Beaver Men* (1964). Other nonfiction includes *Love Song to the Plains* (1961), *The Battle of the Little Bighorn* (1966), and *These Were the Sioux* (1961).

While Sandoz's nonfiction receives high marks, her fiction varies in quality. As concerned about the present and future of America as she was about its past, she often wrote didactically; at times this didacticism overpowers the story. Her best novel, *Slogum House* (1937), set in the Nebraska sandhills, delineates the destruction caused by the rapacious, will-to-power Gulla Slogum, as she corrupts county officials, prostitutes her daughters, and abets murder to control her region. A story of western land-grabbing, the book is also an allegory representing the destruction caused by European dictators, particularly Hitler. A proletariat novel, *Capital City* (1939), and an antiwar story, *The Tom-Walker* (1947), are also allegorical.

Two novellas for young adults, *The Horsecatcher* (1957) and *The Story Catcher* (1963), re-create the ambience of life in Cheyenne and Lakota villages just prior to the coming of whites to the Plains in the mid-1800s.

Sandoz was concerned with style as well as content. Her language ranged from "barbed wire scratching on sand paper," as a critic said of her, to lyrical. Because she wrote her histories using story-telling devices and little conventional documentation, critics have had difficulty defining her nonfiction. Some historians now recognize her meticulous, detailed research and acknowledge using her material. Sociologists, anthropologists, and ethnologists also verify her writing. Western literary scholars and readers have long appreciated her work.

• The major collection of Mari Sandoz's work, including file cards, research notes, correspondence, maps, and manuscripts, is in the archives at Love Library, University of Nebraska, Lincoln. See also Mari Sandoz, *Hostiles and Friendlies: Selected Short Writings of Mari Sandoz* (1959). Helen Winter Stauffer, *Mari Sandoz, Story Catcher of the Plains* (1982). Barbara Rippey, "Toward a New Paradigm: Mari Sandoz's Study of Red and White Myth in *Cheyenne Autumn*," in *Women and Western American Literature*, eds. Helen Winter Stauffer and Susan J. Rosowski (1982), pp. 247–266. Betsy Downey, "Battered Pioneers, Jules Sandoz and the Physical Abuse of Wives on the American Frontier," *Great Plains Quarterly* 12, no. 1 (Winter 1992): 31–49. Helen Winter Stauffer, ed., *Letters of Mari Sandoz* (1992).

Helen Winter Stauffer

SANSAY, Leonora (fl. 1807–1823), novelist, was known to have written two anonymously published novels: *Secret History, or, The Horrors of St. Domingo, in a Series of Letters, Written by a Lady of Cap Francois, to Col. Burr* (1808), an epistolary novel, and *Laura* (1809), a sentimental romance. Recently two, perhaps three, additional anonymous novels were discovered, all published in London. *Zelica, the Creole* (1820) is a revised version of *Secret History*, expanded to three volumes. An advertisement in *Zelica* notes two forthcoming three-volume novels "by the same author"; these are *The Scarlet Handerchief*, published around 1823, and *The Stranger in Mexico*, which may not have been published with that title.

Sansay's birth and death dates are unknown, but she was probably born in the early 1780s, the daughter of Philadelphia innkeeper William Hassall. Around 1796, she began a romantic and intellectual relationship with Aaron Burr, which lasted about twenty years. Her social network was mostly Burr associates, and what is known of her derives mainly from Burr sources.

In 1800, she married Louis Sansay, an older French businessman, and in 1802, they traveled to St. Domingue (later Haiti), where she stayed about two years before fleeing the final expulsion of the whites by the black revolutionaries. She abandoned Louis, returned to Philadelphia, and later turned her adventures into her first novel.

In 1806, as Madam D'Auvergne, she was involved in Burr's alleged conspiracy and traveled with several Burr associates to New Orleans to await his expected arrival. Burr's plans failed, and she returned to Philadelphia where she completed *Secret History*. Her second novel was in preparation as *Secret History* rolled off the press.

Sansay's literary career was typically unremunerative. She reported earning only $100 for *Laura*. In 1809, she and Burr's colleague Erich Bollman established an artificial flower factory near Philadelphia. The last certain reference to her in Philadelphia is an 1813 letter to Burr.

Whether she pursued her later career in London or Philadelphia is unknown. However, the publisher notes that *Zelica* and the forthcoming novels were "transmitted . . . from America." Her later works are rare. There are only two recorded copies of *Zelica* in the United States, and none of *The Scarlet Handerchief*.

As is revealed in her letters and novels, Sansay was erudite, independent-minded, and vivacious. Her novels deal with the mistreatment of sensitive and intelligent women by men who cannot accept them as intellectual and moral equals. The recent discovery of her later novels makes her one of the more prolific early American woman novelists.

• "Laura—A New Novel," *The Port Folio* (January 1809): 68. "List of New Publications," *Monthly Magazine; or, British Register* (1 February 1821): 78. Lyle H. Wright, *American Fiction, 1774–1850* (1939), p. 172. Phillip Lapsansky, "Afro-Americana: Rediscovering Leonora Sansay," *The Annual Report of the Library Company of Philadelphia for the Year 1992* (1993).

Phil Lapsansky

SAPPHO (b. late seventh century B.C.), Greek/ Lesbian poet. Knowledge of her life is largely conjectural. She inhabited Lesbos, mostly Mitylene, except for an exile to Sicily. She was probably married, bore a daughter, Cleis, and was associated with a group of young aristocratic women. Of an estimated twelve thousand lines of verse attributed to her, virtually all is lost, much having been destroyed by the medieval Church: one complete poem, some citations, and fragments survive. Originally accompanied by lyre, her poetry included cultic hymns, mythological narrative, epithalamia, satire, and intensely passionate poetry about women. Sappho has been crucial to women writers, particularly poets. The single woman in the pantheon of classical authors, she provided a model for poets ranging from Emily *Dickinson to Rita Mae *Brown, and a point of departure or resistance for others, including Amy *Lowell and Muriel *Rukeyser. Although the four-line sapphic stanza is seldom employed in English, her writing has led to an association of women with the genres of the lyric and the fragment. The inevitable comparison of early women poets such as Aphra Behn or Lady Mary Wortley Montagu with Sappho was not always laudatory or purely literary: while her love for women was suppressed by early commentators and translators, rumors of unrestrained sexuality persisted.

Because so little is known of her, Sappho has provided an incredibly malleable figure for women exploring the cultural position of female, and, more recently, for lesbian artists. Ovid's unsubstantiated story, translated by Pope, of Sappho's leap from the Leucadian cliffs after being forsaken by the ferryman Phaon was formerly central to the construction of Sappho in Anglo-American literature; numerous nineteenth-century poets, including Felicia Hemans, Sarah Anna Lewis, Elizabeth *Oakes-Smith, and Sara *Teasdale, provide treatments of this heterosexual Sappho, often employing the *suicide to engage with tensions between love and artistic vocation, or to distance subjects like abandonment or sensuality. The notion of Sappho as homosexual, and the derivation of the word *lesbian* from her native island, while latent earlier, came to dominate Anglo-American constructions following the work of Baudelaire and Swinburne (who in France and England, respectively, shifted Sappho's sexual orientation from hetero- to homosexual/lesbian), strengthened by the increasing availability of Sappho's texts after the 1897 discoveries of papyrus fragments. Sapphic modernists Natalie Barney and Renée Vivien reworked the received myths and verses of Sappho, emulated Sappho's female artistic community by establishing a female salon in Paris, and sought to rematriate lesbianism to Lesbos. The *Imagists, particularly *H. D., were also strongly influenced; her Sapphic poems in *Sea Garden* (1916) and *Heliodora* (1924) join numerous nineteenth-and twentieth-century elaborations of Sappho's work.

The recent resurgence of feminism and interest in *lesbianism has produced a similar emphasis on Sappho. Judy *Grahn's (*The Highest Apple*, 1985) and Monique Wittig's ("Paradism," in *Homosexualities and French Literature*, eds. George Stambolian and Elaine Marks, 1979) placement of Sappho at the center of a suppressed woman-loving culture and the start of a lesbian literary tradition thus represents the latest development in the ongoing revision of this fluid female figure. Women writers continue to appropriate from dominant literary culture not a "historical" Sappho, but rather, shifting constructions of this paradigmatic female poet as a strategy of enablement in the assertion of a place within poetic tradition.

• Elaine Marks, "Lesbian Intertextuality," in *Homosexualities and French Literature*, ed. George Stambolian and Elaine Marks (1979), pp. 353–377. Anne Pippin Burnett, *Three Archaic Poets: Archilochus, Alcaeus, Sappho* (1983). Susan Gubar, "Sapphistries," *Signs: Journal of Women in Culture and Society* 10 (1984): 43–62. Joan de Jean, *Fictions of Sappho, 1546–1937* (1989). Jane McIntosh Snyder, *The Woman and the Lyre: Women Writers in classical Greece and Rome* (1989).

Susan Brown

SARTON, May (b. 1912), poet, novelist, diarist, essayist. May Sarton was born in Belgium to artist Mabel Elwes Sarton and science historian George Sarton. The family eventually settled in Cambridge, Massachusetts, where Sarton was educated, first at the Shady Hill School in Cambridge, and later at the High and Latin School. Against her family's wishes, Sarton refused to attend Vassar College, apprenticing instead at the Civic Repertory Theater in New York, under the direction of Eva Le Gallienne. In 1933, Sarton founded and directed her own company, the Apprentice Theater, until its failure during the Great Depression in 1936.

Sarton counts among her strongest influences her parents, who encouraged her creativity, the Shady Hill School, where she first began writing poetry, and her theater experience. Of the influences on her poetry, Sarton considers Yeats and Valery her classical training, and Amy *Lowell, *H. D., and Louise *Bogan among her more contemporary influences.

Though a prolific writer with nearly fifty books to her credit, Sarton has not garnered much critical acclaim until very recently. Writing in a variety of mediums, Sarton considers herself primarily a poet. Her poems are lyrical and often formal and/or rhymed, reflecting her belief that structure is critical both in life and art. Her poems express an essence, a moment, and explore such subjects as aging, the life of the creative woman, and Sarton's own creativity. For Sarton, poems are a way of communicating with the self.

Sarton's novels tackle more encompassing themes, delving into the way relationships grow and change. Her major themes are still apparent in this medium; she examines female friendships, creativity, aging, and the nature of solitude. *Mrs. Stevens Hears the Mermaids Singing* (1965), perhaps her most controversial novel, deals with a contemporary woman's

struggle to define herself both as an artist and as a lesbian at a time when neither theme was honored.

Sarton's critical acclaim began with her journals, her most popular writings, though she considers them minor work. Their popularity probably stems from her careful attention to the details of ordinary life. The journals, *Plant Dreaming Deep* (1968), *Journal of Solitude* (1977), and *At Seventy* (1984) among them, are candid accounts of a woman who relishes her solitude, a woman committed to her writing, a woman growing older.

Even after various health problems, including a stroke, Sarton remains committed to her work and the structure it provides, writing whenever she is able.

• May Sarton, *Collected Poems, 1930–1973* (1974). Lenora Blouin, *May Sarton: A Bibliography* (1978). Constance Hunting, ed., *May Sarton: Woman and Poet* (1982). Elizabeth Evans, *May Sarton Revisited* (1989). Peggy Whitman Prenshaw, ed., *Conversations with May Sarton* (1991).

Deborah Viles

SATIRE. *See* Humor.

SCHAW, Janet (fl. 1774–1776), travel writer. A Scots gentlewoman, Schaw resided briefly in Wilmington, North Carolina, and reported in serial *letters the customs and manners there and in Antigua to friends in Scotland. By the 1770s, the belletristic travel journal had become a distinct genre. Usually prepared in a fair copy, and often lavishly illustrated with watercolors, travel journals combined exercises in picturesque description with botanical observations, narratives, and sketches of exotic manners. Janet Schaw's *Journal of a Lady of Quality* (1774–1776) displayed a noteworthy belletristic talent in its evocations of people and places. She described the planters and slaves of Antigua with an almost anthropological precision, avoiding the West Indian caricatures popularized by Tobias Smollet. Schaw sympathized with the African slaves, informing her readers that the cruelty of their treatment by the sugar planters was hardly imaginable. North Carolinians she found bumptious and provincial. A Tory North Briton, Schaw saw the patriot activity in Wilmington as mob agitation. She claimed that she risked tar and feathers by dispatching her letters because of their metropolitan sentiments. This claim reveals more about Schaw's ability to dramatize herself than it does the political conditions in North Carolina. The journal provided an extraordinary theater in which Schaw could project her character.

Because of its Scottish audience, the journal

had no influence on the development of polite letters in America. Its value resides in its gendered dramatization of the clash of metropolitan sensibility with provincial circumstances. The manuscript was first published in 1921.

• The manuscript of Schaw's journal is housed in the British Library. See also Jay B. Hubbell, *The South in American Literature, 1607–1900* (1954). Robert Bain, "Janet Schaw," in *Southern Writers: A Biographical Dictionary* (1979).

David S. Shields

SCHOOLCRAFT, Jane Johnston (1800–1841), American Indian poet and writer of Ojibwe legends. The daughter of Irish fur trader John Johnston and Ozha-guscoday-way-quay, Jane Johnston Schoolcraft was educated at home in Sault Ste. Marie on the Canadian border between present-day Michigan and Ontario. Her father taught her literature, history, and the classics, and provided her with a large library. At the same time, her mother, daughter of the powerful Ojibwe leader Waub Ojeeb (White Fisher), gave Jane and her siblings a deep understanding of their tribe's beliefs, legends, and lore. Jane learned to speak Ojibwe as a child and remained fluent in the tongue her entire life. In 1809, her father took her to Ireland, where she completed her formal education.

When Henry Rowe Schoolcraft arrived at the Sault, the common name given to the area around the rapids of the St. Mary's River, in 1822 to begin his celebrated work in Indian languages, he found a raw frontier settlement. He also discovered the well-educated and articulate Jane Johnston when he boarded with her family. The two were married the following year. From the first, Jane and her family were instrumental in Schoolcraft's work. Even before their marriage, Jane assisted him in compiling his Chippewa vocabulary. Under her influence, Schoolcraft became fascinated with Ojibwe legends, and with her help began his collection of Native American tales.

The two began publication of the *Literary Voyager or Muzzeniegun*, a manuscript magazine, in the winter of 1826–1827. This weekly magazine was distributed in New York, Detroit, and other eastern cities, as well as in the Sault. It contained articles, legends, and poems, chiefly on American Indian themes. Lore, biographical sketches of prominent Ojibwes, and historical accounts were also included. In addition to the rich vein of Indian materials, the magazine carried the poetry and essays of Jane Schoolcraft under the pen names Rosa and Leelinau. Her essays depict the traditions and beliefs of her tribe. Schoolcraft's proximity to her sources guarantees her writings' authority and accuracy, and thus they are important documents. Her poetry is similar to that of American contemporaries, although she does experiment from time to time with rhyme and meter. Particularly poignant are the poems on her two-year-old son, William Henry, who died in 1827.

Jane Schoolcraft influenced other writers, in spite of her isolation in the North Woods. English author Anna B. Jameson, as well as Harriet Martineau and Thomas McKenney, traveled to the Sault to meet her. Indian materials in the *Literary Voyager* were used by Chandler R. Gilman in his works.

• Philip P. Mason, *The Literary Voyager or Muzzenyegun* (1962). Daniel F. Littlefield, Jr., and James W. Parins, *American Indian and Alaska Native Newspapers and Periodicals, 1826–1924* (1984).

James W. Parins

SCIENCE FICTION. Since its origin, women have written science fiction—fiction depending on cognitive estrangement derived from an imagined alteration in science and culture, and usually set in the future or on an alternate world. (See also * Utopia.) Mary Shelley's *Frankenstein* (1818) began a women's tradition in science fiction, a tradition that later incorporated the feminist technological utopia, popular in the nineteenth-century United States, and that was also influenced by travel narrative and scientific romance. All these influences may be seen in two early United States science fiction novels: Inez Haynes Irwin's *Angel Island* (1914), and Gertrude Barrows Bennett's *The Cerberus Heads* (1919, under the pen name Francis Stevens). Irwin's plot, drawing on the travel narrative and the feminist utopia, and anticipating her friend Charlotte Perkins * Irwin's 1915 *Herland*, satirizes the cult of the angel of the house: three men, shipwrecked on an island, capture and cut off the wings of three alien women who arrive there; when, years later, their daughters face a similar fate, the women rebel and force the men to let the daughters grow wings. Drawing on Shelley and the gothic, the scientific romances of H. G. Wells, and the dystopia, Bennett's story anticipates much pulp science fiction: By inhaling a powder invented by a mad scientist, three men and a woman arrive in an alternate Philadelphia, where a despotic government buttressed by state religion oppresses the masses. Satirizing the graft of Philadelphia's bosses, Bennett has her characters destroy the city and escape. Irwin's and Bennett's strong women characters differ markedly from those in men's writings at this time.

Although Bennett published in horror pulp magazines such as the *Thrill Book* (in 1919) and *Weird Tales* (in 1923), the first woman in the science fiction pulps was Clare Winger Harris, who won third prize in a short story contest in the pulp magazine *Amazing Stories* in June 1927 for "Fate of the Poseidonia." (Pulp magazines, on cheap paper, were the main avenue for publishing science fiction until the paperback novels of the 1950s.) Harris was also first to offer a female point of view, in "The Fifth Dimension" in *Amazing Stories* (1928). Other women writers soon followed with their short stories in the science fiction pulps: Sophie Wenzel Ellis, L. (Louise) Taylor Hansen, Lilith Lorraine (Mary Maude Wright), and Leslie F. Stone. Early women shared with male writers a romantic vision of science, perhaps because of the influence of the newly available college education in science for women. But unlike men, these women either extend women's sphere of influence to include women's control of government (as in Minna Irving's 1929 "The Moonwoman" in *Amazing Stories*, or Lilith Lorraine's 1930 "Into the 28th Century" in *Science Wonder Quarterly*) or advocate equal rights for women (as in Leslie Stone's 1929 *When the Sun Went Out*, or Louise Rice and Tonjoroff-Roberts's 1930 "The Astounding Enemy" in *Amazing Stories Quarterly*). Influenced by the feminist birth control campaigns of the 1920s, many women writers used science to eliminate *childbirth. Women writers also revised housekeeping through technology, paralleling the scientific homemaker promoted in the women's magazines from this time.

Women gradually disappeared from the 1930s pulps, being forced out by the Depression ethic against women working, by conservative editors, and by a growing "professionalization" (that is, masculinization) of science fiction. The few new women writers from this period, like C. L. Moore, published under initials or male pseudonyms. But Moore's contributions are significant: Through the Jirel of Joiry fantasies, she offered a model of the Amazonian hero; and in "No Woman Born" (1944), she updated the Frankenstein myth, making the monster a woman.

After World War II, women returned to the pulps, but were limited by an editorial rule that allowed only one female name to each issue, since white adolescent boys were the projected audience, even though other women might publish in the same issue under a male pseudonym. (In the 1940s, for example, in *Thrilling Wonder Stories*, Margaret St. Clair is the only woman writer published under a female name, although women who wrote under male names, like Leigh Brackett, published in the same issues with her.) Judith Merril, who helped shape a new realism in postwar science fiction, epitomized its advantages and pitfalls: "That Only a Mother" (1948) explores the effects of atomic

weapons on women's lives, and examines male prejudice against mutated children; *The Shadow on the Hearth* (1950), her novel about the atomic bombing of New York, includes explicit racism and a white heroine too feminine to act.

Conservative women with androgynous names—Andre Norton, Leigh Brackett, Marion Zimmer Bradley, and J. Hunter Holly—wrote near-future dystopias or space operas with macho male heroes for the paperback market in the 1950s. But they also made a secure place for women writers in the science fiction publishing industry. Many kept writing, and became pathbreakers in 1960s science fiction: Zenna Henderson offered reformed realism through utopian gender relations in her series on The People (1961–1967); Judith Merril introduced United States fans to the pleasures of fragmented, psychedelic "New Wave" techniques from British science fiction; Andre Norton offered witches as heroes in her long-running Witch World series (1962–present); and Marion Zimmer Bradley began the Darkover series (1964–present), featuring male homosexuals and, later, *Amazons and lesbians as heroes.

A strong women's tradition, often featuring the traditionally feminine trait of empathy as a special power, developed after 1960, and was evident in Norton's and Bradley's novels, and in later works by Anne McCaffrey, Sally Miller Gearhart, C. J. Cherryh, Mary Staton, and many others. The female hero in science fiction evolves from Norton's Jaelithe (*Witch World*, 1963) to *Russ's Jael (*The Female Man*, 1975) and Bradley's Jaelle (*The Shattered Chain*, 1976). By the late 1960s, science fiction was in conversation with *feminist theory and political issues through its critiques of dystopian patriarchies, as in the works of Pamela Zoline ("The Heat Death of the Universe," 1967) and Alice Sheldon, as James Tiptree, Jr. ("The Women Men Don't See," 1973), and in utopias by Ursula K. *Le Guin (*The Left Hand of Darkness*, 1969, and *The Dispossessed*, 1974), Joanna *Russ ("When It Changed," 1972, and *The Female Man*), Marge *Piercy (*Woman on the Edge of Time*, 1976), Suzy McKee Charnas (*Motherlines*, 1978), Alice Sheldon, again as James Tiptree, Jr. (*Up the Walls of the World*, 1978), and Sally Miller Gearhart (*The Wanderground*, 1979).

This feminist utopian revival was heralded by a developing feminist science fiction criticism, especially in essays by Russ and Le Guin. The utopias featured multicultural female heroes (Tiptree's black computer expert, Piercy's Hispanic Connie Ramos, and Russ's and Gearhart's lesbian main characters), gender equality, alternative family structures, anarchic governments, revised sciences, and debate over violence in achieving change. Indeed, Piercy's novel, interweaving the utopia of Mattapoisett with the dystopian story of a mental patient, became a kind of scripture for the women's movement of the 1970s. Feminist science fiction criticism flourished in the 1980s and 1990s, with books by Natalie Rosinsky, Marleen Barr, Sarah Lefanu, and Robin Roberts.

Writers of science fiction in the 1980s and 1990s continued former feminist trends with adventure stories (Melissa Scott's 1987 *The Kindly Ones*, which never identifies the gender of the industriously sexual first-person narrator, Janet Kagan's 1988 *Hellspark*, and Severna Park's lesbian 1992 *Speaking Dreams*), critiques of patriarchal society (Suzette Hayden Elgin's 1984 *Native Tongue* and Carol Emshwiller's 1990 *Carmen Dog*), and utopias (Joan Slonczewski's 1986 *A Door into Ocean*). Especially popular as a theme was reverse gender discrimination, countering the 1980s backlash, in novels like C. J. Cherryh's 1981 *The Pride of Chanur* and Cynthia Felice's 1986 *Double Nocturne*. Imagining a society where heterosexuality is a perversion, in *Ring of Swords* (1993), Eleanor Arnason extends this strategy to lesbian-gay discrimination. In addition, writers challenged assumptions of the 1970s feminist utopia with critiques of lesbian *separatism, as in Pamela Sargent's 1986 *The Shore of Women*, and Sheri S. Tepper's 1988 *The Gate to Women's Country*. Moreover, the black writer Octavia *Butler exposed the dystopic side of 1970s utopias in the Patternist series, through her exploration of mental telepathy as another means of creating hierarchy, and her treatment of the themes of *racism and imperialism in "Bloodchild" (1984) and her trilogy *Xenogenesis* (1987–1989).

Throughout the 1970s and 1980s, female science fiction fans have not only promoted women's science fiction, but have also changed the genre, pioneering feminist fanzines, collective writing, and K/S (Kirk/Spock) *pornography. While women science fiction writers exploit the freedoms of future or alternate settings to imagine women's lives as unconstrained, they also face particular generic problems: the cultural barriers of masculinist science, the convention of the woman as alien, and the dominance of male narrators in the genre. They write their ways around these barriers by creating utopian sciences, by moving the woman as alien from margin to center, and by resisting the male narrator with multiple narration or by using him to reform the males of their audiences.

[*See also* Fabulation; Postmodern Writing.]

• Joanna Russ, "What Can a Heroine Do? or Why Women Can't Write" and "The Image of Women in Science Fiction," in *Images of Women in Fiction*, ed. Susan Koppelman Cornillon (1972), pp. 3–20 and 79–94. Pamela Sargent, ed., *Women of Wonder* (1974). Ursula K. Le Guin, *The Language of the Night: Essays on Fantasy and Science Fiction*, ed. Susan Wood (1979). Natalie M. Rosinsky, *Feminist Futures: Contemporary Women's Speculative Fiction* (1984). Marleen Barr, *Alien to Femininity: Speculative Fiction and Feminist Theory* (1987). Sarah Lefanu, *Feminism and Science Fiction* (1989). Ursula K. Le Guin, *Dancing at the Edge of the World: Thoughts on Words, Women, Places* (1989). Anne Cranny-Francis, *Feminist Fictions: Feminist Uses of Generic Fiction* (1990). Robin Roberts, *A New Species: Gender and Science in Science Fiction* (1993). Jane Donawerth and Carol Kolmerten, eds., *Worlds of Difference: Utopian and Science Fiction by Women* (1994).

Jane Donawerth

SCIENCE WRITERS. Scientists traditionally publish their contributions to knowledge in the form of journal articles, reviews, book chapters, and books. Papers delivered at conferences may also be collected and edited under a single cover. Whereas writing in disciplines such as mathematics and physics might be unintelligible to all but the specialist, publications in anthropology, biology, and psychology may be enjoyed by a broad readership. Women's contributions to scientific literature have been significant, even if sometimes belatedly recognized. The rising interest in women in science has resulted in serious investigations of their early works. The most scholarly and comprehensive account of American women in science is Margaret Rossiter's *Women Scientists in America: Struggles and Strategies to 1940* (1982). Marcia Myers Bonta describes the lives of more than two dozen early naturalists and provides references to their works in *Women in the Field* (1991). Shirley Malcolm et al. summarize an important first conference for minority women in science in *The Double Bind: The Price of Being a Minority Woman in Science* (1976). A special issue of *Sage: A Scholarly Journal on Black Women* (1989) on science and technology documents the contributions and conflicts of African-American women in science, many of whom were "firsts" in their fields.

Jane Colden (1724–1766), a botanist and perhaps the best known of the colonial scientists, did not directly communicate her findings to the scientific community. This was done for her by her botanist father or his botanist friends. Her Linnaean classification and drawings of more than three hundred species, entitled *Jane Colden—Botanic Manuscript*, was finally published in 1963. A similar fate of patriarchal *sexism befell other women in scientific professions during the colonial period (see Joan Hoff Wilson, "Dancing Dogs of the Colonial Period," *Early American Literature* 7, Winter 1973). Popular works in botany were published by women during the eighteenth century, but the first important American woman scientist to publish scientific articles was the astronomer Maria Mitchell (1818–1889). Opportunities for women to study science began to increase after the establishment of women's colleges during the latter half of the nineteenth century, and when women were finally admitted to graduate schools.

Ann Fletcher (1838–1923) helped shape the study of American anthropology between 1880 and 1900 (see Joan Mark, *A Stranger in Her Native Land: Alice Fletcher and the American Indians*, 1988), but the classic works of Ruth Benedict (*Patterns of Culture*, 1934) and Margaret Mead (*Coming of Age in Samoa*, 1928) are better known because they spanned the period during which the discipline matured as a science. Benedict's *Race: Science and Politics* (1940) and *The Races of Mankind* (1943), written to combat the *racism of the time, are still relevant today.

Ellen Swallow Richards (1842–1911), chemist and pioneer ecologist, published her eleventh book, *Euthenics: the Science of a Controllable Environment*, in 1910. Naturalist Anna Botsford Comstock's (1854–1930) best-known work, *The Handbook of Nature Study* (1911), was translated into eight languages and is still in frequent use today. Biologist Libbie H. Hyman (1888–1969) received international acclaim for her five-volume treatise, *The Invertebrates* (1940–1967). Rachel *Carson (1907–1964) became a household name with the publication of *Silent Spring* (1962), her literate account of pesticide abuse. Evolution from our microbial ancestors is the subject of *Microcosmos* (1986) by microbiologist Lynn Margulis (coadvocator with James Lovelock of the Gaia theory of a living Earth) and coauthor Dorion Sagan. They also examine the evolution of sexuality in microorganisms and more complex forms of life in *Origins of Sex: Three Billion Years of Genetic Recombination* (1986).

Since the reemergence of feminism in the late 1960s and early 1970s, feminist thought has come to permeate almost every aspect of today's culture, including science. The result has been an outpouring of literature by feminist scientists, historians, philosophers, and sociologists. Their writings have tackled the institution of science itself and addressed questions of whether there is a feminist method or a feminist science (Ruth Bleier, ed., *Feminist Approaches to Science*, 1986; Nancy Tuana, ed., *Feminism and Science*, 1989; Sandra Harding, *Whose Science? Whose Knowledge?*, 1991).

*Gender and science are increasingly recognized as socially constructed categories (Evelyn Fox Keller, *Reflections on Gender and Science*, 1987; Helen E. Longino, *Science as Social Knowledge*, 1990). The scientific validity of so-called biologically-based sex differences has been seriously questioned (Anne Fausto-Sterling, *Myths of Gender: Biological Theories about Women and Men*, 1985). Indeed, biology has been misused to justify sexism and racism (Ruth Hubbard and Marian Lowe, eds., *Genes and Gender: II, Pitfalls in Research on Sex and Gender*, 1979; Ruth Hubbard, Mary Sue Henifin, and Barbara Fried, *Biological Woman—The Convenient Myth*, 1982; Ruth Bleier, *Science and Gender: A Critique of Biology and its Theories on Women*, 1984).

The women's mental health movement beginning in the early 1970s called for changes in traditional psychotherapy of women (Phyllis Chesler, *Women and Madness*, 1972; Jean Baker Miller, *Toward a New Psychology of Women*, 1976.) Eleanor Maccoby's *Psychology of Sex Differences* (1974), Carol Gilligan's *In a Different Voice* (1982), and Mary Field Belenky et al.'s *Women's Ways of Knowing* (1986) have also generated much discussion. Nine recent books on the psychology of women are discussed by Phyllis Grosskurth in her essay, "The New Psychology of Women," *New York Review of Books* 38, no. 17 (1991).

Primatology, or the study of the biology and behavior of nonhuman primates, has developed in the last two decades into one of the most active areas of scientific research and has made many earlier studies obsolete. Not only have these new studies been at the interface between biological and social sciences (sociobiology), they have also contributed to advances in evolutionary theory. It is interesting that this area of research has attracted many women from diverse scientific disciplines (Jane Beckman Lancaster, *Primate Behavior and the Emergence of Human Culture*, 1975; Sandra Blaffer Hrdy, *The Woman That Never Evolved*, 1981; Jane Goodall, *The Chimpanzees of Gombe: Patterns of Behavior*, 1986; Shirley C. Strum, *Almost Human: A Journey into the World of Baboons*, 1987; Barbara B. Smuts et al., eds., *Primate Societies*, 1987; Donna Haraway, *Primate Visions*, 1989).

Other relevant works by women in science are Ann E. Kammer et al., *Science, Sex and Society* (1979); Carolyn Merchant, *The Death of Nature* (1980); Zuleyma Tang Halpin, "Scientific Objectivity and the Concept of 'Other,'" *Women's Studies International Forum* 12, no. 3 (1989); Londa Schiebinger, *The Mind Has No Sex? Women in the Origins of Modern Science* (1989); Gabriele Kass-Simon and Patricia

Farnes, *Women of Science: Righting the Record* (1990); Carol Tavris, *The Mismeasure of Woman* (1992).

Evelyn M. Rivera

SCOTT, Evelyn (1893–1963), novelist, poet, essayist. A prolific author, Scott published eleven works of fiction and two autobiographies between 1919 and 1953; she also published over sixty poems, eight short stories, and dozens of essays and reviews in little magazines, as well as several pieces of juvenile literature.

Scott was born Elsie Dunn in Clarksville, Tennessee, a region that she describes in her 1937 autobiography *Background in Tennessee*. Economic conditions eventually caused the Dunns to move to New Orleans, where Elsie attended Sophie Newcombe School and then Tulane University. A self-proclaimed feminist from age fifteen, Elsie managed to break with her family and southern society by escaping to Brazil with Tulane professor Frederick Creighton Wellman, a married man. There they assumed new names: Dunn became Evelyn Scott and Wellman became Cyril Kay Scott. Despite her geographic remoteness, Scott managed to publish poetry in *Dial, Egoist,* and *Poetry* during this time; her innovative autobiographical work, *Escapade* (1923), chronicles these difficult years in Brazil.

The necessity of medical attention returned Scott to the United States, where she continued to publish her Imagist poetry; she brought out two volumes, *Precipitations* (1920) and *The Winter Alone* (1930). But it was fiction that established Scott's literary reputation. In her first novel, *The Narrow House* (1921), she unflinchingly portrays a deteriorating American family. It is the first element of a fictional trilogy completed by *Narcissus* (1922) and *The Golden Door* (1925).

The Scotts (spouses only by common law) settled for a time in Greenwich Village, where Evelyn reveled in the bohemian life-style. The Provincetown Players, in their 1920–1921 season, produced her play, *Love,* to less than rave reviews. In 1925, Scott, having left Wellman, legally married John Metcalfe, a fellow novelist.

Literary and popular success came with the publication of her Civil War novel, *The Wave* (1929), which chronicles the perceptions of over one hundred characters. Despite its lengthy, innovative content, the novel sold well. Scott went on to write five more novels, a number of which explored a recurring theme of the artist in society; however, they never matched her earlier success. Scott's literary alliances with other women are particularly significant; she

was close to Lola Ridge, Emma *Goldman, Kay *Boyle, and Jean Rhys. Scott moved frequently, residing at different times in New Mexico, Bermuda, New York, France, and England. She died in New York City, leaving four unpublished manuscripts of fiction and poetry.

• Evelyn Scott's personal papers and manuscripts are housed in the Harry Ransom Humanities Research Center at the University of Texas at Austin. Other Scott material is also contained in the Frederick Creighton Wellman Archive, housed at the same institution. See also D. A. Callard, *Pretty Good for a Woman: The Enigmas of Evelyn Scott* (1985).

Mary Wheeling White

SCRIBBLING WOMEN. Scribbling women are those who refuse to be silenced by critical standards that trivialize the subjects of women's lives, and who write with energy, intelligence, and commitment. The term was coined by Nathaniel Hawthorne on 19 January 1855, when from Liverpool, England, Hawthorne wrote to his New York publisher, William Ticknor, to report on various business matters and his plans for a new book. His publisher would not see a manuscript for some time, Hawthorne indicated, since "America is now wholly given over to a d——d mob of scribbling women, and I should have no chance of success while the public taste is occupied with their trash—and should be ashamed of myself if I did succeed." The oft-quoted phrase "d——d mob of scribbling women" typifies the critical response to generations of women writers. Works by fantastically popular writers, including *The Wide, Wide World* (1850) by Susan *Warner (Elizabeth Wetherell), *Ruth Hall* (1853) by Fanny *Fern (Sara Parton), *Uncle Tom's Cabin* (1852) by Harriet Beecher *Stowe, *The Lamplighter* (1854) by Maria Susanna *Cummins, *The Hidden Hand* (1859) by E.D.E.N. *Southworth, and *The Gates Ajar* (1868) by Elizabeth Stuart Phelps *Ward, have been dismissed and neglected as commercial fiction that addressed so-called domestic or *sentimental subjects rather than enduring themes. In recent years, feminist literary scholars have reevaluated and reclaimed much of this Anglo-American literary history, unleashing a firestorm of critical debate about the values that inform the traditional and male-dominated literary *canon.

• Ann Douglas Wood, "The 'Scribbling Women' and Fanny Fern: Why Women Wrote," *American Quarterly* 23, no. 1 (Spring 1971): 3–24. Jane Tompkins, *Sensational Designs: The Cultural Work of American Fiction, 1790–1860* (1985).

Mary Wyer

SEARS, Vickie L. (b. 1941), poet, short story writer, psychotherapist. Vickie Sears is a Cherokee/Spanish/English lesbian writer who was raised in the Pacific Northwest. Her short fiction and poetry have been anthologized in *A Gathering of Spirit* (1983), *Gathering Ground* (1984), *The Things That Divide Us* (1985), *Spider Woman's Granddaughters* (1989), *Dancing on the Rim of the World* (1990), *Talking Leaves* (1991), *Images of Women in Literature* (1991), and *Literature and Language* (1994). She has published a volume of short stories entitled *Simple Songs: Stories by Vickie Sears* (1990).

She is also the author of articles on sexual abuse (in *Changing Our Power*, 1987, and *She Who Was Lost Is Remembered*, 1991), lesbian relationships (*Lesbian Couples*, 1988), and ethics (*Feminist Ethics in Psychotherapy*, 1990). She makes her home in Seattle, Washington, where she practices the related arts of storytelling and feminist psychotherapy. She is, as well, the author of a screenplay and several teleplays.

Margaret A. Lukens

SEDGWICK, Catharine (1789–1867), novelist, short fiction writer, and one of the leading figures of early American literary culture. Sedgwick's novels, including *A New-England Tale* (1822), *Redwood* (1824), *Hope Leslie* (1827), and *The Linwoods* (1835), were widely praised by critics and reviewers as important contributions to the newly emerging body of American literature, and nineteenth-century literary historians placed her alongside figures such as Washington Irving and William Cullen Bryant as one of the country's first major writers. Although often dismissed by later critics who devalued the sentimental aspects of her work, Sedgwick has since reclaimed her status as one of the premier authors of the early national period.

A native of the Berkshire hills region in western Massachusetts, Sedgwick often drew upon local settings and customs in her writing. The success of her novels brought national attention to the region, and her home in Stockbridge became an important gathering place for established and aspiring writers from all parts of the country. Although her mother came from a powerful and wealthy New England family and her father was a staunch Federalist, Sedgwick grew to support a more Jacksonian brand of democracy, and, in novels such as *Clarence* (1830), she often satirized the privileged aristocracy to which her family belonged. Sedgwick's fiction was also influenced by a liberal religious upbringing. Her writings express strong anti-Calvinist sentiments, and the Unitarian flavor of works such as *A New-England Tale* and *Redwood* held great appeal for nineteenth-century liberal Protestants dissatisfied with the legacies of Puritanism.

Sedgwick's widespread popularity among both readers and critics resulted not simply from her critiques of aristocrats and Calvinists, but also from her success in creating active, vibrant female characters that were far more interesting and effective than those offered by male writers such as James Fenimore Cooper. In the historical romance *Hope Leslie*, Sedgwick's most famous novel, she merges an examination of the Puritans' treatment of Native Americans with a discussion of female *identity. Through the interaction of the two central characters, the Puritan woman Hope Leslie and the Native American woman Magawisca, Sedgwick engages in a rewriting of early American history that reveals the Puritans' brutal and unfair handling of Native Americans. *Hope Leslie* also revises traditional notions of submissive womanhood by arguing that women must recognize their domestic sphere as empowering and act as agents for the preservation and promotion of moral values.

• Mary Kelley, *Private Woman, Public Stage* (1984). Annette Kolodny, *The Land before Her: Fantasy and Experience of the American Frontiers, 1630–1860* (1984). Lawrence Buell, *New England Literary Culture: From Revolution through Renaissance* (1986). David S. Reynolds, *Beneath the American Renaissance: The Subversive Imagination in the Age of Emerson and Melville* (1989).

Paul Ryan Schneider

SEGREGATION. *See* Civil Rights Movements; Racism; Reconstruction.

SELF-HELP BOOKS. When, why, and by whom are self-help books considered to comprise a category? In *Revolution and the Word: The Rise of the Novel in America* (1986), Cathy N. Davidson argues that by the end of the eighteenth century, many works, both non-fiction and novels, were published in the U.S. which advocated self-education and self-help. At present, the genre relies heavily on targeting a specific audience, typically middle-class. For example, the self-reliance marketed as "new" may indeed be a new skill to those women who have certain privileges due to *race, *class, *ethnicity, and age, women raised in environments that encourage reliance and dependence on men of their social group rather than on themselves. By locating the problem(s) to be solved solely in the individual, self-help books, according to their critics, often neglect the influence of the social environment. In *I'm Dysfunctional, You're Dysfunctional: The Recovery Movement and Other Self-Help Fashions* (1992) Wendy Kaminer criticizes self-help movements for eliding differences among audience members, ignoring dissimilarities in suffering.

Works such as those included in *This Bridge*

Called My Back: Writings by Radical Women of Color (1981, second ed., 1983) edited by Cherríe *Moraga and Gloria *Anzaldúa, serve as acknowledgements and justifications of experiences of women of color. Both *Ain't I a Woman: Black Women and Feminism* (1981) by bell hooks and *Making Waves: An Anthology of Writings by and about Asian American Women* (1989), a work edited by Asian Women United of California, indict the *racism, classism, *homophobia and *sexism that seek to isolate and classify the myriad experiences of women of color. By promoting imagination and dignity, these authors demonstrate that personal growth is supported by community experiences.

The self-help philosophy of individual improvement can often ignore the situation of many women of color, poor women, disabled women, and lesbians. However, a recent bestseller in the self-help genre, Gloria *Steinem's *Revolution from Within: A Book of Self-Esteem* (1992), makes a point of not only addressing issues such as race, class, and sexual orientation but also reveals convergences between the individualistic aims of most self-help books and the collective, political goals of *feminism.

Multiple-authored self-help works can offer various views and different strategies. For example, the Boston Women's Health Book Collective notes the uneasiness felt by some members over the inclusion or rejection of certain topics in the revised edition of *The New Our Bodies, Ourselves* (1984). Additionally, in contrast to the first edition, the revised work relies less on a medical establishment for information and places greater emphasis on the knowledge and abilities of women themselves.

Ellen Bass and Laura Davis, authors of *The Courage to Heal: A Guide for Women Survivors of Child Sexual Abuse* (1988, rev. ed. 1992), advocate survival as a continual process that begins with the survival of the abuse. Survivors report to Bass and Davis that the abusive experiences become a part of one's life. In addition, books on sexual assault often relay various experiences through the voices of many women, even offering contradictory advice rather than a coherent program.

The indignation sometimes expressed when *gender and *women's studies texts are (still) categorized under "self-help" in several bookstores is noted concisely by Harriet Goldhor Lerner in "Problems for Profit?" *The Women's Review of Books*, April 1990. Lerner suggests that dominant members of society prefer to view self-help books as products for sickness rather than for individual and social change. Self-help books dealing with addiction are frequently modeled after Alcoholics Anonymous

and similar "12-step" recovery programs. As Cindy Patton notes in *Inventing *AIDS* (1990), the core of 12-step movements is acknowledging the individual's powerlessness over an addictive personality, thus discounting possible effects of an addictive-inducing environment. Harriet Goldhor Lerner notes that 12-step works can distort or support feminist ideals. Like Lerner, Susan Faludi, in *Backlash* (1992), and Jane Gallop, in *Around 1981* (1991), both discuss the distortion of feminism and the fear the movement has generated.

While the notion of "self" has changed, along with the feminist movement, the concept of self-improvement for women can continue to echo early etiquette guides where learning life skills means maintaining certain social standards. Self-help books can direct the audience to rely on an established authority or can encourage readers to question institutionalized power structures that often mislabel them as sick.

• Sasha Alyson, ed., *Young, Gay and Proud* (1985). Boston Women's Health Book Collective, *Our Bodies, Ourselves: A Book by and for Women* (1973). Del Martin, *Battered Wives* (1981). Suzanne Pharr, *Homophobia: A Weapon of Sexism* (1988). Linda Tschirhart Sanford and Mary Ellen Donovan, *Women and Self Esteem* (1984). Anne Wilson Schaef, *Co-dependence: Misunderstood and Mistrusted* (1986). Barbara Smith, ed., *Home Girls: A Black Feminist Anthology* (1983). *For Crying Out Loud: A Newsletter for Women Survivors of Child Sexual Abuse*, 3, no. 1 (Spring 1988) to 5, no. 4 (Winter 1990–1991).

Greta Ai-Yu Niu

SENECA FALLS CONVENTION. *See* Stanton, Elizabeth Cady; Suffrage Movement; Women's Political Organizations.

SENTIMENTAL NOVEL. *Sentimental* means mawkish, affected, or extravagantly emotional. For most of American literary history, virtually every nineteenth-century novel written by a woman has been routinely or even automatically described as sentimental, regardless of its actual content, tone, style, or themes, while virtually no novels written by men have been given this derogatory label. Even Ann Douglas's *The Feminization of American Culture* (1978), while paying new attention to nineteenth-century American women writers, argues that the work of these writers marks a decline from the intellectually strenuous and significant values that epitomized (male) Puritan culture. The popularity of sentimental women writers, she suggests, signaled the irreversible vitiation of American culture.

Subsequent feminist literary historians have taken Douglas and her many predecessors, from

F. O. Matthiessen to Perry Miller, to task on two different counts. First, scholars such as Nina Baym have shown that the term *sentimental novel* is often inexact, since nineteenth-century women wrote a wide range of novels. Baym's indispensable survey, *Woman's Fiction: A Guide to Novels by and about Women in America, 1820–1870* (1978), documents the variety and vitality of women's fiction. The second revaluation of the stereotypical use of the term *sentimental* comes from Jane Tompkins, in *Sensational Designs: The Cultural Work of American Fiction, 1790–1860* (1985), who argues that the evocation of emotion in fiction such as Harriet Beecher *Stowe's *Uncle Tom's Cabin* (1852) served as a powerful agent for social change and did not in and of itself warrant the pejorative label it received in the nineteenth century, nor the disapprobation under which it labored for most of the twentieth century. As Tompkins eloquently notes, in reacting against the success of nineteenth-century women writers, "twentieth-century critics have taught generations of students to equate popularity with debasement, emotionality with ineffectiveness, religiosity with fakery, domesticity with triviality, and all of these, implicitly, with womanly inferiority."

Tompkins and others have shown, by contrast, that the so-called sentimental novel marks one of the most powerful and interesting developments in American fiction. Beginning with America's first two best-sellers, Susanna *Rowson's *Charlotte: A Tale of Truth* (1791; later retitled *Charlotte Temple*) and Hannah Webster *Foster's *The Coquette* (1797), women writers focused simultaneously on sentiment (the tender emotions and perceptions of their fictional heroines) and the status quo (the harsh realities of life for women). As Cathy N. Davidson has shown in *Revolution and the Word: The Rise of the Novel in America* (1986), the sentimental novel was about and for the *femme covert* (Old French for "hidden woman"), a legal term indicating that a woman's rights were subsumed in her father's or husband's (and thus she did not need any legal rights of her own). In practice, late-eighteenth-century women also had far inferior educational opportunities than men, and were not allowed to attend universities. Finally, the sexual double standard supported men's rights to sexuality but condemned the "fallen woman," the woman who indulged in sexual relations outside of marriage. In view of the restrictiveness of women's lives, early sentimental novels served as cautionary tales, designed to show women how they could protect themselves against the wiles of seductive and unscrupulous men in a society that offered women few public protections.

As many critics have noted, by the beginning of the nineteenth century, the seduction plot became less important in women's fiction, but women writers continued to depict the harshness of the legal and social conditions that women had to face. Increasing emphasis was placed on women as social and political creatures who exerted an egalitarian, anti-industrial, spiritual force within a world motivated by greed, violence, and materialism. The nineteenth-century doctrine of *separate spheres enforced rigid gender distinctions between men and women as *industrialization and urbanization meant that paid labor outside the home replaced the older model of the self-sustaining farm or the cottage industry in which all family members (male and female, adults and children) took part. Men would earn wages in the factory or business; women would tend the hearth, raise children, and imbue the world with both aesthetic and religious harmony. The ideology of separate spheres was, of course, primarily middle class and white.

Historians have argued that the ideology of separate spheres conferred both benefits and restrictions on middle-class women, but the impact of this ideology on women's literary history is undeniable. Many a woman earned a living by her pen precisely because there were no other ways for her to earn a living. Such sentimental novelists as Rowson, Stowe, Louisa May *Alcott, and Susan *Warner were all primary breadwinners for their families, and all earned a living by writing.

Uncle Tom's Cabin (1852), Stowe's most famous novel, is not really about "woman's place" at all; yet, as Baym has noted, it is from this novel, more than any other, that the construct of the sentimental heroine was developed. The construct was based not on a woman character, but on a young girl, Little Eva, whose angelic qualities doom her to an early, tear-wrenching death. As Tompkins has shown, those tears were not idle. On the contrary, they moved a nation to sympathy for the enslaved, and, as much as any other book in American history, prompted hundreds of thousands of readers to become part of an enormous social movement, *abolitionism.

Maria *Cummins's *The Lamplighter* (1854) is another novel typically designated as sentimental. It, too, was a best-seller, selling up to five thousand copies a week at the height of its popularity, and it was this novel that provoked Hawthorne's infamous 1855 comment that "America is now wholly given over to a d——d mob of *scribbling women." Frustrated by his own relative lack of success, he asked, "What is the mystery of these innumerable editions of *The Lamplighter?*" Yet the success of the story is, as Elaine Ginsberg has noted, no real mystery. A skillful blend of some of the plots and devices used by the most popular British writers, Dickens and the Brontë sisters, *The Lamplighter* is the story of Gerty, an abused orphan who ultimately triumphs self-reliantly over adversity. The theme is Emerson's ideal transformed to the separate sphere of virtuous womanhood.

The Wide, Wide World (1850) by Susan *Warner was also a best-seller, even though it was originally rejected by several publishers. Here, too, a friendless young woman, Ellen Montgomery, must find her own way after the death of her mother. Perhaps closer to the stereotypical notion of the sentimental novel than any other book, *The Wide, Wide World* depends on tears as a crucial plot device, as Ellen weeps her way through various crises. Despite or because of this torrent of emotion, Ellen survives injustices and tyranny imposed on her by various male characters, often misguided father-figures. Matrimony ends Ellen's travails and allows her to enter into a sphere characterized by leisure, gentleness, and intellectual cultivation—a communal, loving adult world, and one in which Ellen is, so the ending portends, happy ever after. Yet, as Baym shrewdly observes, even this ending has an ideological ambiguity that the simple label "sentimental" would belie. The ideal family at the end of the book is emphatically not the standard, nineteenth-century nuclear family, but an extended collectivity of intelligent adults. The ending thus represents a new model of the happy family even as it poses an implicit (but severe) critique of the actual nineteenth-century patriarchal family, which, in this so-called sentimental novel, is portrayed as deficient if not downright violent and abusive.

A blistering attack on bourgeoise *marriage is offered in two African-American narratives that use elements of the sentimental tradition for subversive purposes. Harriet *Wilson's *Our Nig; or, Sketches from the Life of a Free Black, in a Two-Story White House, North* (1859) is a remarkable story that shows how life in that relatively affluent, New England "white house" is hardly the picture of civility or feminine virtue. Frado, an indentured servant with all the tender feelings of a sentimental heroine, is denied any expression of those feelings by a physically and emotionally cruel mistress. The man of the house is so passive that he does nothing to prevent this cruelty. In Harriet A. *Jacobs's *Incidents in the Life of a Slave Girl* (1861), a slave woman, Linda Brent, works to preserve her virtue against the lascivious sexual advances of her white master. Both books remind us that sentimentalism, whatever its merits or drawbacks, was an option only for middle-class white women. Jacobs even reminds us, overtly, of this by ending with a reversal, bordering on parody, of one of the most famous nineteenth-century women's novels, *Jane Eyre*. "Reader, my story ends with freedom; not in the usual way, with marriage," Linda Brent asserts.

It is important to emphasize that white as well as black writers challenged the sentimental tradition. Louisa May *Alcott wrote to support an extended family of men, women, and children. She wrote so much that she suffered paralysis in her writing hand. It seems particularly egregious that her work has been unthinkingly labeled sentimental. She authored a variety of books, including sensation novels, mysteries, detective stories, and realistic portrayals of working women. Even her most famous work, the best-selling novel *Little Women* (1868), is sentimental only if we stretch the definition to include, roughly, *any* mid-nineteenth-century novel written by a woman. But that's the point. The term has been applied arbitrarily and inaccurately and, until recently, always derogatorily. Anyone encountering it must be aware of its particular history in American literary criticism. Actual novels written by women from the late eighteenth century to the last third of the nineteenth century frequently offered more hardheaded analyses of the shortcomings of American society than did their so-called realistic male counterparts. It must be remembered that most sentimental novels were unsentimental indeed.

[*See also* Domestic Fiction; Novel, Beginnings of the; Romance Novels.]

• Elaine K. Ginsberg, "Maria Susanna Cummins," in *American Women Writers*, ed. Lina Mainiero (1979), pp. 436–437. Carl N. Degler, *At Odds: Women and the Family in America from the Revolution to the Present* (1980). Linda K. Kerber, *Women of the Republic: Intellect and Ideology in Revolutionary America* (1980). Nina Baym, *Novels, Readers, and Reviewers: Responses to Fiction in Antebellum America* (1984). Cathy N. Davidson, ed., *Reading in America: Literature and Social History* (1989). Ann Romines, *The Home Plot: Women, Writing, and Domestic Ritual* (1992). Shirley Samuels, eds., *The Culture of Sentiment* (1992). Cathy N. Davidson, "The Novel as Subversive Activity: Women Reading, Women Writing," in *Beyond the American Revolution: Explorations in the History of American Radicalism*, ed. Alfred F. Young (1993), pp. 283–316.

Cathy N. Davidson

SEPARATE SPHERES. The ideology of separate spheres, which developed in both the North and South from the time after the Revolutionary War through the first decades of the nineteenth century, held that each sex had its appropriate realm of activity and influence, which was determined by gender and divinely ordained. Men and women were different but equal, and their natures and roles were complementary to each other. Man's place was in the world—in commerce, the professions, and politics. Woman's place was in the home. The theory held that woman was morally superior to man and gave her an elevated role within the family—and, by extension, within society: In addition to the physical work necessary to maintain a comfortable home, she was responsible for meeting the family's emotional needs, providing moral guidance for her husband and children, and beginning and overseeing the children's education.

Because studies of the construct of separate spheres are based on written sources, they focus on the literate middle class, but it has been suggested the concept also affected the poorer class. However, one must question whether the image of woman enshrined in her home could have seemed anything but ironic to poorer working-class women of the industrialized North or the rural South, who were struggling to maintain subsistence—or to the slave working in the fields of the Southern plantation. Indeed, Sojourner *Truth's famous speech asserting her womanhood in the face of a man's admonition to women to stay in their sphere directly challenges the applicability of the doctrine to these nonprivileged groups.

In literature, the concept of separate spheres appears across a broad range of genres, most markedly from the 1830s through the 1850s. *Advice books advocate woman's sphere in promulgating guidelines for female behavior and defining the duties of girls and women. Adherence to woman's sphere is often assumed as a biographer's criterion for judging a female life worthy, and many female subjects are identified in terms of their relationships to men as mothers, wives, or daughters. In poetry, clear distinctions are assumed between men's and women's works. A woman poet should treat domestic materials, and, as Caroline May put it in *The American Female Poets* (1848), her "inspiration lies more in her heart than her head." Fiction was dominated by novels about domestic heroines, written by women for a predominantly female audience. In keeping with the concept of spheres shared by these authors and readers, these works highlighted family-based emotional ties and moral values. At the same time, of course, many women poets and novelists subverted or openly violated the boundaries of woman's sphere.

Consigning women to a separate sphere limited them, but it has been cogently argued that women also benefited. They gained in respect and self-esteem as the making of a home became a profession, and women's education came to be seen as essential preparation. Moreover, the boundaries of the sphere were expanded to include activities beyond the home. Participation in church-related charitable and self-improvement groups and in moral reform societies gave women a sense of shared gender identity, as well as organizational skills. Women moved into professions seen as appropriate to their sphere, such as teaching. For many women (though a minority) the stretching of the boundaries of woman's sphere finally enabled them to reject and move beyond it later in the nineteenth century.

[*See also* Domestic Ideology.]

• Anne Firor Scott, *The Southern Lady: From Pedestal to Politics, 1830–1930* (1970). Nancy F. Cott, *The Bonds of Womanhood: "Woman's Sphere" in New England, 1780–1835* (1977). Carl N. Degler, *At Odds: Women and the Family in America from the Revolution to the Present* (1980). Mary Kelley, *Private Woman, Public Stage: Literary Domesticity in Nineteenth-Century America* (1984). Sara M. Evans, *Born for Liberty: A History of Women in America* (1989).

Karen A. Dandurand

SEPARATISM. "Separatism," in the context of the second wave of the women's movement in the U.S., is generally understood by separatists as a politics which follows logically from feminist analysis of the situations of women, though some have ceded the label "*feminism" to the mainstream assimilationist feminists.

Lesbian separatist politics is eclectic and anarchic. It is a close relative of radical feminism. Many radical feminists of the late 60s and early 70s were, or became, separatists. Some themes common in separatist thought include: Male dominance is a "*class" relation between males and females which benefits all men, even those most abused by social relations among men; it is interwoven with systems of *race and economy and endures through sea-changes in them. Primary and interactive mechanisms that maintain male dominance are male *violence against women, the institution of female *heterosexuality, male control of meaning (language, image, value, *myth), and male control of material resources. These mechanisms both presuppose and coerce systematic cooptation of women's own energies and actions, without which the subordination of women to men would not be possible. The relations between women and men constitute a sort of class warfare which requires solidarity among women and nonfraternization with the enemy.

Generally, the separatist strategy is for women to place primary value on women and relations among women, which implies withdrawing from all forms of *collaboration in our own oppression or that of other women. In practice, this means cultivating autonomous bases of female social life. (U.S. separatists are not influenced by *French feminists, but there are some similarities between separatist thinking about lesbian community and French interest in a female symbolic, e.g., Irigaray.)

Women practicing such a politic, who may or may not adopt the name 'separatist', have in fact, from 1968 to 1993, created lives in which erotic bonds, economic cooperation, *friendship, self-made kin relations, and lesbian/gynocentric cultural production have created webs of female sociality within which women thrive and create themselves far more autonomously than is the norm within patriarchal institutions, and are dramatically less vulnerable to male violence, exploitation, and intellectual/emotional colonization. (Although most self-named separatists are lesbian and see lesbian eroticism as central to separatism, a minority opinion is that non-lesbian women might create lives external to the patriarchal institution of female heterosexuality and thus might be able to live according to a politics that is congruent with lesbian separatism.)

Writing by women who build this network of overlapping communities is to be found primarily in books and periodicals published by small independent publishers. The one work which is most widely read, world-wide, which articulates these values and politics is Mary *Daly's Gyn/Ecology. Many have learned of separatism through lesbian musicians, especially Alix Dobkin.

A very influential source of separatist thought is Jewish separatism. Jewish lesbians are central and influential members of separatist circles, and they commonly refer to the example of Jewish resistance to *assimilation. "I learned young the importance of struggling constantly against cultural/physical genocide; of naming the enemy; of maintaining an entirely separate way of life ... of refusing to be defined and absorbed by that enemy." Jewish *grandmothers are models: "Gentiles were not allowed in her home." Separatists also refer to Native American initiatives for cultural integrity and national autonomy and to African American separatist movements such as the movement led by Marcus Garvey, Black Muslims and Malcolm X, the Black Power movement, and the Black Panthers. African-American lesbian separatists also refer to the autonomous elaborations of female sociality and economic independence within the black families and communities of their childhoods.

Feminist or lesbian separatism has been the target of vitriolic denunciation by non-separatist feminists (including some whose own lives to a large extent enact separatism) who claim that separatism is racist, classist, escapist, utopian, man-hating (a characterization many separatists happily accept), fascist, anti-sex, elitist, essentialist, and various other things evil or thought to be so. Thoughtful and well-argued defenses against this hostile picture of separatism abound in separatist writing, but apparently are unread or unassimilated by these critics.

• For Lesbians Only: A Separatist Anthology, edited by Sarah Lusia Hoagland and Julia Penelope. Hypatia 7, no. 4 (Fall 1992): 212–222. Marilyn Murphy, Are You Girls Travelling Alone?

Marilyn Frye

SEXISM is a recent term, originating within the women's liberation movement of the 1960s. It was coined as a parallel to *racism and refers to the assumption that one sex is superior to the other. Marilyn Frye (The Politics of Reality, 1983) argues that in order to create and perpetuate the difference in status and power that such a belief implies, differences between men and women are created and highlighted so that distinct social groups are created and naturalized. This is partially the result of dichotomous thinking that constructs women as "other" to men rather than as similar to them by assigning opposite characteristics to each and then hierarchizing those characteristics so that those understood as male are superior to those understood as female.

The effects of sexism are both psychological and material. Although women are taught to be feminine—passive, nurturant, dependent—they also learn that those qualities are inferior to masculine characteristics—aggression, individual achievement, and independence. One consequence of this contradiction is low self-esteem. But the consequences of sexism are not only personal and psychological, nor is sexism simply a matter of one individual oppressing another. Instead, like racism, sexism structures our social institutions. For example, because women are thought to be especially suited for occupations that can be understood as compatible with *femininity and particularly with childbearing and childrearing, the majority of women are located within a few "female" job categories that are low in status and in pay. Though it is theoretically possible for women to be sexist, most scholars agree that while women or people of color may be prejudiced, because racism and sexism are primarily institutional rather than individual in nature, only members of dominant social groups, for whom and by whom such institutions are created, can be sexist or racist. Thus, sexism defines and limits women's roles based on their sex, when their sex is, in fact, irrelevant or should be irrelevant.

U.S. women writers both accommodate themselves to and challenge sexism in their writing.

This dynamic is evident in some of the earliest poetry written in the wake of the European occupation of North America. In "The Prologue to *The Tenth Muse Lately Sprung Up in America*" (1650), Anne *Bradstreet acknowledges that "I am obnoxious to each carping tongue / Who says my hand a needle better fits," and anticipates that whatever the quality of her verse, the (implicitly male) public will find a way to denigrate her skill. Yet Bradstreet also internalizes the sexism she perceives, and writes several lines down: "Men have precedency and still excel, / It is but vain unjustly to wage war; / Men can do best, and women know it well." Bradstreet, then, accommodates herself to the prevailing sexism of colonial society, but in so doing carves out a space for her writing.

In *Woman in the Nineteenth Century* (1843), Margaret *Fuller challenges the naturalness and rigidity of stereotypical sex roles: "Male and female represent two sides of the great radical dualism. But, in fact, they are perpetually passing one into another. Fluid hardens to solid, solid rushes to fluid. There is no wholly masculine man, no purely feminine woman." Fuller shows that the self-reliance valued by Henry David Thoreau and Ralph Waldo Emerson was in fact deprecated in women, who were expected to adhere to socially sanctioned codes of behavior rather than to develop independence in thought and behavior. She argues that women should be allowed to achieve independence as men are, and to enjoy their birthright to the "religious, the intelligent freedom of the universe to use its means, to learn its secret, as far as nature had enabled them, with God alone for their guide and judge."

The interdependence of racism and sexism is evident throughout *African-American women's writing. In many ways, African-American women were not considered women at all. Despite the sexist notion that women were fragile and economically dependent upon men, enslaved women endured backbreaking labor and corporal punishment. Moreover, unlike African-American men, African-American women were subject to white male sexual violence. As Harriet *Jacobs, writing under the pseudonym Linda Brent, describes it in *Incidents in the Life of a Slave Girl* (1861): "Slavery is a terrible thing for men; but it is far more terrible for women. Superadded to the burden common to all, *they* have wrongs, and suffering and mortification peculiarly their own." As Gerda Lerner has stated in her essay "Recontextualizing Differences Among Women," *Journal of Women's History* 1, no. 3 (Winter 1990), white women were able to minimize their own oppression on the basis of their sex with privilege based on race and, depending upon the their economic status, class. Brent's mistress's jealousy of her husband's interest in Brent shows the way that racism pits against each other those subject to sexism. This phenomenon is also clear in Harriet *Wilson's *Our Nig* (1859) in which it is the white mistress who is responsible for the suffering of the female protagonist, and the mistress's husband to whom she looks for help.

Charlotte Perkins *Gilman's *Herland* (1916) exposes cultural assumptions about female "nature" as ridiculous and unfounded by allowing the reader to join three male characters on a journey to Herland, a land without men. They are incredulous that there are no men in the obviously civilized country. They quickly learn, however, that the agricultural and other wonders that they see around them have been created by women, who, freed from the limitations imposed by men, have developed their abilities to perform traditionally male occupations. Gilman believed that women's limitations resulted from what she calls in *Women and Economics* (1898) excessive sex-distinction. She argues that women's economic dependence upon men forces women to rely upon their sexuality for a living. Thus, women's primary and secondary sexual characteristics are overdeveloped. Gilman suggests that a primary basis of sexism is the sexual enslavement of women to men. The results of this determines even the economic system. Since, Gilman argues, the economic dependence of women results in "sex-competition" between men, our entire economic system functions according to competition rather than cooperation.

Edith *Wharton, like Gilman, influenced by evolutionary thinking, demonstrates in *The House of Mirth* (1905) the tragic consequences of the economic dependence of women upon men. The wealthy Lily Bart has been fashioned by a combination of "early training" and "inherited tendencies" "to adorn and delight." Lacking an inheritance to complement her beauty in the marriage market and unable to adjust to any other environment, Lily commits *suicide.

Alice *Dunbar-Nelson's "I Sit and Sew" (1920) expresses the speaker's frustration with the passivity demanded of her while she aches to join men in war, with all its agony and its glory. Georgia Douglas *Johnson also decries the passivity and repression demanded of women, focusing particularly upon romantic relationships in *The Heart of a Woman* (1918) and *Bronze* (1922). Louise *Bogan's "Women" (1923) discusses women's passivity, or their lack of "wilderness," as well, but not in a poetic voice that identifies itself as experiencing such constriction. While some readers argue the poem is ironic, others argue that Bogan's internalized sexism results in a truly misogynistic poem.

Adrienne *Rich's "Compulsory Heterosexuality and Lesbian Existence" (*The Signs Reader*, 1983) calls such internalized sexism "male-identification." Rich's poetry, "Diving into the Wreck" (1972) and "Natural Resources" (1977) for example, suggests that despite this crippling legacy of sexism, female strengths endure. These poems, like others, metaphorize the position of women in a world of male violence. Like some of Rich's writing, Joanna *Russ's *science-fictional *The Female Man* (1975) suggests that female separatism—directing emotional, political, and erotic energy to women—is a crucial strategy for liberating women from a society in which they are socialized to exist for men. Like *Herland*, this novel exposes sexism by depicting a world without men, Janet's Whileaway. This world is juxtaposed with that of Jeanine, a 1960s in which neither World War II nor the subsequent social and economic transformations affecting women occurred; Jael's Manland, in which men and women engage in constant battle; and Joanna's world, our own 1969 in which men and women are superficially equal. Thus, as Tom Moylan argues in *Demand the Impossible* (1986), the novel constructs a "critical" *utopia and suggests the social forces necessary to create it.

Maxine Hong *Kingston's *The Woman Warrior* (1975) reveals the ways that language can be used both to perpetuate sexism and to fight against it. The Chinese-American protagonist is silenced by the stories her mother tells about daughters being sold into *slavery and daughters-in-law being tortured, and by her own experience of the low value placed upon daughters. However, her mother also tells her stories of female self-assertion that contradict the message that women are fated to be wives and slaves. Through the example of her mother and the *women warriors she tells her about, the protagonist learns that through language, by "talking-story," she too can actively shape her identity, rather than being passively shaped by her culture.

[*See also* Homophobia; Prejudice; Racism.]

• Judith Sargent Murray, "On the Equality of the Sexes," in *The Feminist Papers*, edited by Alice Rossi (1973), pp. 18–24. Sarah Grimké, *Letters on the Equality of the Sexes and Other Essays*, edited by Elizabeth A. Bartlett (1988). Emma Goldman, "The Tragedy of Women's Emancipation," *Anarchism and Other Essays* (1910; reprint 1969). Simone de Beauvoir, Introduction to *The Second Sex* (1953; reprint, 1974). Shirley Hill Witt, "Native Women Today: Sexism and the Indian Woman," in *Feminist Frameworks*, edited by Alison Jaggar and Paula S. Rothenberg, 2nd ed. (1984), pp. 23–31. Audre Lorde, "Age, Race, Class, and Sex: Women Redefining Difference," in Audre Lorde, *Sister Outsider: Essays and Speeches*. (1984). Cheris Kramarae and Paula A. Treichler, "Sexism," in *A Feminist Dictionary*, (1985). "Defining 'Racism' and 'Sexism,' " in *Race, Class, Gender in the United States*, edited by Paula S. Rothenberg, 2nd ed. (1992), pp. 5–8.

Angela E. Hubler

SEXTON, Anne (1928–1974), poet. Anne Harvey was born in Newton, Massachusetts, where she spent a tumultuous childhood in which her alcoholic father undermined Anne's self-esteem at every opportunity. In 1948, she eloped with Alfred (Kayo) Sexton, with whom she shared an often stormy relationship. Sexton bore two daughters—Linda in 1953, and Joyce in 1955—whose birth seemed the catalyst for Sexton's persistent depression, which led her to seek therapy. It was her therapist who encouraged her to begin writing as part of her treatment. Very soon poetry became a mainstay in Sexton's life.

Sexton's poetry explores the struggle between a woman's creativity and the conventions of her era. The disparity between the two pushed Sexton to the brink of suicide many times. She is often labeled a confessional poet and criticized for treating the subjects of the female body and her own madness too frankly. Sexton's work is meeting with renewed critical interest as feminist critics explore Sexton's themes, which include incest, motherhood, mental instability, and low self-esteem.

In 1957, Sexton formed what was to become the most important friendship of her life as well as the strongest influence on her poetry when she met Maxine *Kumin at a poetry workshop. Kumin and Sexton shared an intense correspondence, critiquing and encouraging each other's work.

To Bedlam and Part Way Back (1960), Sexton's first book, was written under the encouragement of Robert Lowell, who conducted a poetry workshop Sexton attended. As the title suggests, a good many of the poems focus on madness and recovery. Sexton won the Pulitzer Prize for *Live or Die* (1966), her third book, in which she examines her suicidal tendencies but also affirms life. The strong correlation between sexual desire and *suicide in this book suggests that Sexton may have been an *incest victim. In most of her later work, including *Mercy Street* (1969), Sexton's only published play, and *Transformations* (1972), Sexton's revisionist fairy tales, incest plays a central role. In numerous therapy sessions, Sexton accused both her father and live-in aunt of sexually abusing her as a child. Since her accounts are contradictory, there is some debate over whether such incidents occurred. Constant references to incest in her poetry, though, lend credence to her accusations.

Sexton committed suicide in 1974, finally succumbing to her mental illness and profound lack of self-esteem. Sexton's work chronicles an intense struggle against the debilitating effects of convention.

• *Anne Sexton: A Self-portrait in Letters*, ed. Linda Gray Sexton (1977). Anne Sexton, *Selected Poems of Anne Sexton*, eds. Diane Wood Middlebrook and Diana Hume George (1988). Caroline King Barnard, *Anne Sexton* (1989). *Critical Essays on Anne Sexton*, ed. Linda Wagner-Martin (1989). Diane Wood Middlebrook, *Anne Sexton: A Biography* (1991).

Deborah Viles

SEXUAL ABUSE. *See* Incest; Rape; Sexual Harassment.

SEXUAL HARASSMENT. According to *Sexual Harassment* (1991), an invaluable report in progress by the National Council for Research on Women, sexual harassment is defined, simply but unequivocally, as the unapproved and inappropriate sexualizing of a nonsexual relationship. Typically it is based on a real or perceived power imbalance, such as when an employer, coworker, colleague, or teacher demands sexual favors or sexual attention. Often power, not desire, is the real issue, as when a woman is harassed by her boss or a graduate student by her professor. Both are being told that they are worthwhile only as sexual objects, not as competent, intelligent human beings. A form of sexual victimization and discrimination, sexual harassment will be experienced, recent studies indicate, by 50 to 85 percent of American women during their working or academic life.

Harassers can be found in any walk of life, at all economic levels, and are typically married men, older than their victims, and of the same race as their victims. Like rapists whose psychological profiles do not distinguish them from the "normal" male population (except that they have committed *rape), a sexual harasser is often well respected and well liked in other aspects of his life and is usually regarded as a decent person even in his dealings with women other than the one he is harassing. His credibility makes it difficult for his victim to receive adequate redress. Indeed, most women do not report harassment for fear of not being believed, leading frequently to the woman's double victimization, first by the harasser, then by the system responsible for protecting her. In most cases, it is the woman victim, rather than her assailant, who transfers or quits her job to avoid further harassment.

Social activists such as Susan Brownmiller

(*Against Our Will: Men, Women, and Rape*, 1975) and legal scholars such as Catherine MacKinnon (*The Sexual Harassment of Working Women*, 1979) have done much to raise public awareness of the debilitating consequences of sexual harassment. They have stressed that there is an enormous difference between attraction and harassment. Just as it is unacceptable for a man to punch an employee or coworker with whom he is angry, it is unacceptable for a man to act out unwelcome sexual desires.

This seems like an elementary idea, but the first legal case on grounds of sexual harassment did not occur until the mid-seventies. Only in 1980 did the Equal Employment Opportunity Commission include in its "Guidelines on Discrimination" specific language indicating that sexual harassment was unlawful. In 1986, in a unanimous decision, the Supreme Court rejected the idea that harassment occurs only when the victim experiences "tangible economic harm" and upheld the EEOC guidelines that women in the workplace should be entitled to an environment free from intimidation, ridicule, and insult (*Meritor Savings Bank v. Vinson*, 1986). Five years later, Clarence Thomas's nomination to the Supreme Court was jeopardized when allegations of sexual harassment by former employee Anita Hill came to the attention of the Senate Judiciary Committee. However, her testimony was ultimately discounted. Fourteen white male senators grilled Professor Hill on national television, attacking her credibility and making thinly veiled innuendos about her personal life. Clarence Thomas currently sits on the Supreme Court.

Sexual harassment has been a theme in American fiction from the beginning. In the first best-selling novel in the United States, Susanna *Rowson's *Charlotte, a Tale of Truth* (popularly known as *Charlotte Temple*, 1794), the young English heroine is abandoned by the soldier who brings her to America. The soldier marries a "respectable" (and rich) woman and gives money to his friend Belcour to dispense to Charlotte. Belcour, however, withholds the money and then tries to extract sexual favors from Charlotte. Rather than submit to his advances, she flees, pregnant and friendless, into the night, and is taken in by poor people who feed her and deliver her child. She (of course) dies in childbirth. When Lily Bart in Edith *Wharton's *The House of Mirth* (1905) naively allows the husband of one of her friends to "speculate" for her on the stock market, she finds herself pressured for sexual favors in return for the money he has given her. She, too, escapes his unwarranted attentions but dies alone and friendless in a small rented room.

Sexual harassment goes hand in glove with

seduction stories, including the enormously popular "working girl" novels of late-nineteenth-century writer Laura Jean *Libbey. In her formulaic novels, a poor country girl comes to the city to find work and then becomes the target of salacious coworkers, employers, and other ravenous men. These young women are almost always saved from harassment or even rape by the intervention of a noble young man, often the factory owner's son. The virtue of the working heroine attracts him; they are married, and all is happy ever after. Yet these novels, even in their fantasies, dramatize the turn-of-the-century anxieties of working women, especially their powerlessness in the workplace. Analogously, the lesbian classic *Rubyfruit Jungle* (1973) by Rita Mae *Brown shows the relationship between power and sexual harassment. Whether waitresses or film school students, women must ward off the unwanted sexual advances of their "superiors."

The most egregious literary examples of sexual harassment occur in *slave narratives by both men and women, where slave women are shown to be totally at the mercy—by law and social custom—of their owners. Harriet A. *Jacobs, in her remarkable *Incidents in the Life of a Slave Girl* (1861), writes partly to stir white women into abolitionist action by transforming the familiar seduction narrative into a parable of the unparalleled sexual sadism that occurs under *slavery. In this fictionalized account, Linda Brent escapes from the harassment of Dr. Flint but does so by hiding out for years in her grandmother's attic. Two stories in the anthology *American Women Writers: Diverse Voices in Prose Since 1845* (1992), edited by Eileen Barrett and Mary Cullinan, also show women evading harassment. Louisa May *Alcott's "How I Went Out to Service" (1874) recounts the way she stood up to the demeaning and lascivious advances of a minister for whom she once worked as a maid. Paule *Marshall's "Brooklyn" (1961) is about a student who wards off the sexual harassment of her teacher, although, as Marshall notes, there was not even a term for his behavior when she was a college student in the fifties.

[*See also* Rape; Violence.]

• Barbara Gutek, *Sex and the Workplace* (1985). Jean O'Gorman Hughes and Bernice R. Sandler, *Peer Harassment: Hassles for Women on Campus* (1988). Michele Paludi, ed., *Working 9 to 5: Women, Men, Sex, and Power* (1991). Louise F. Fitzgerald, "Sexual Harassment: The Definition and Measurement of a Construct," in *Ivory Power: Sexual Harassment on Campus*, ed. Michele Paludi (1992). Louise F. Fitzgerald and A. J. Ormerod, "Breaking Silence: The Sexual Harassment of Women in Academia and the Workplace," *Handbook of the Psychology of Women* (1992).

Cathy N. Davidson

SEXUALITIES. In 1990, a collection of essays written by and for a multicultural community of women in the United States was published under the title *Women, *AIDS and Activism.* Among the book's contributors are self-identified African-Americans, Latinas, Asian-Americans, American Indians, Jews, Anglo-Americans, lesbians, bisexuals, and heterosexuals. Many of the writers discuss women's sexuality in the context of AIDS, targeting such subjects as AIDS-related gynecological disorders, negotiating safer sex, and the effects of living with AIDS-related restrictions on desire and sexual self-esteem. In so doing they collectively define contemporary sexuality as heterogeneous. Implicit in their writing are five other principles that are outlined below.

First, sexuality is always expressed in relation to *class, *ethnicity, *race, physical ability, and age. These expressions of the sexual mean that women's sexuality is no more reducible to their *gender than it is to their physiology. They also mean that female sexuality exists as an abstraction that readers must individualize if they are to understand whose sexuality is and is not implied in any discourse purporting to represent women's sexual life. Furthermore, all subcategories of female sexuality are also abstractions. By leveling off differences within a group or excluding differences from it, they produce the same false coherency on a micro level, as in: *the* Chicana lesbian, black women's sexuality, white working-class female heterosexuality of the 1920s, etc. One must ask which women of all those allegedly represented by any sexual group identity actually are represented by it and which are not.

Second, sexuality is embedded in history. The ways we think and talk about sex, the ways we experience sexual pleasure and construct sexual identities are all functions of our sociotemporal location; it thus follows that no aspect of contemporary sexuality should be assumed to apply transhistorically. The aspect of contemporary sexuality most often universalized is sexual identity. Because "lesbianism," "heterosexuality," and "bisexuality" are fundamental categories of the sexual as we now know it and because individuals generally experience their sexual identities as integral parts of themselves, and because the presence of what are now called lesbian, heterosexual, and bisexual behaviors has been documented throughout (American literary) history, the individuals who embody these behaviors seem to have been. Thus, although it has seemed possible—indeed necessary—to acknowledge sociohistorical differences within each identity group, it has seemed less possible to question the permanence of sexual identities as such.

This rule of permanence has met with two challenges. The first, which dates from the late 1960s and early 70s, combines a neo-Freudian understanding of sexuality as "polymorphously perverse" with a quasi-Marxist understanding of capitalism as an inherently repressive system that will "wither away" once subjects recognize the true nature of their desire and act accordingly. Generally speaking, proponents of this position understood sexual identity as a social control violently imposed upon human subjects whose sexual fluidity and freedom were thereby restricted and whose identities, once established, worked to set them against identities different from their own. The last of these effects was adduced in (partial) explanation of capitalism's continued success with subjects kept busy fighting each other instead of the system that represses them all.

The second challenge to the permanence of sexual identities was launched in the late 70s. Its earliest proponent was Michel Foucault, whose *A History of Sexuality, Volume One* (French publication, 1976; American, 1978) was rapidly followed by Jeffrey Weeks's *Coming Out: Homosexual Politics in Britain from the Nineteenth Century to the Present* (1977). Foucault's work, in particular, has prompted American scholars to look at sexuality in new ways. Those who adopt a Foucauldian approach to sexuality resemble the first wave of sexual challengers in that they also view sexual identities as social constructions. However, they differ with them fundamentally in their understanding of power. For Foucault, power does not repress sexuality so much as it produces sexuality *in toto*. Thus, polymorphous perversity can no more be a natural or authentic form of sexuality than sexual *identity can. On the contrary, both are cultural constructs as are all other aspects of sexual life. Foucault further argues that power is diffuse; that is, it does not emanate from a single source (be that capitalism or any other system).

These different understandings of sexuality and power yield a different comprehension of sexual identity. Basically, Foucauldians see sexual identity as a regulatory mechanism that subjects individuals to a set of rigid classifications. For example, even though sexual categories initially pathologized a group of individuals under the heading "lesbian" and they continue to mark lesbians as less psychosocially developed than heterosexuals, they also made it possible for early lesbians to speak of and for themselves and they continue to make it possible for them to organize on their own behalf.

Foucault locates the emergence of sexual identities in the late nineteenth century, which is when the term "lesbian" was coined. The coinage was adopted by members of a new branch of medicine called sexology. Like any emerging discipline, sexology was attempting to establish its necessity, in part by refining popular understandings of sexual disorder as a major cause of social disorder, and to extend its influence by virtue of its specialized knowledge. Sexologists' investigations of female "sexual disorders" led them to construct "the lesbian," whose invention produced "the heterosexual woman." Both figures are European constructs, neither of which made its way into the United States much before the twentieth century. In fact, "the lesbian" and her normative opposite, "the heterosexual woman," seem not to have been widely recognized by the American public much before the 1920s, which is approximately when these two figures were stabilized as identity formations.

The critical inference to be drawn from all these facts is that neither American women who had sex with other women nor those who had sex with men could have identified themselves as lesbians or heterosexuals prior to the emergence of either category. Yet one of the earliest national accounts of lesbianism, in the *Memphis Medical Monthly* of 1892, was a sensational story about a young white middle-class woman named Alice Mitchell who murdered Freda Ward, the woman she passionately loved. Over the next few decades, scattered reports on lesbians in "therapeutic" situations and prison settings appeared. Women who read these documents may well have come to the conclusion that a "lesbian" is what they were. No doubt the same shock of sexual recognition is a common experience of many lesbians and other sexual minorities today. In neither case need we assume that sexual representations *cause* sexuality; we need only accept their capacity to organize the sexual feelings we may already have into an identity we recognize as our own.

Generally speaking, the number of women who identify as any sexuality other than heterosexual depends upon the degree to which representations of sexual minorities are available and upon an array of other socioeconomic factors. Both the social conditions and sexual representations necessary to the formation of bisexual identity were unavailable until recently. In fact, for much of the twentieth century, bisexual women did not exist as a psychosocial identity, much less a political one. Instead, women who were erotically attracted to both sexes and/or had sex with women and men were assimilated into the sexual identities already established, thereby yielding the lesbian who was denying her sexuality in order to pass as heterosexual and the heterosexual who was going through a lesbian phase.

Third, if it is true that sexuality is both the effect of modern knowledge and the site of modern power, then it is also true that the coexistence of many sexualities at any historical moment does not mean that all sexualities are constructed as equal across American cultures or even within a particular sexual community. The deployment of sexuality has worked in a number of ways; for instance, it has awarded married heterosexual women cultural privileges and legal rights denied other women and it has accredited certain sexual representations as art and their producers as artists, while discrediting others as * pornography and their producers as pornographers. Because sexuality is, therefore, among the vehicles one group uses to gain sociopolitical ascendancy over others and because it is also used to establish cultural legitimacy, forge alliances, and build communities, it is not enough to ask what representations of sexuality mean; it is also necessary to ask how they function.

Fourth, the meanings of sexuality and the values ascribed to it are subject to change: because desire is fluid; because minority sexualities exist in tension with dominant sexualities by which they are affected and which they affect; and because historical events affect sexual life in manifold ways.

Fifth, and most comprehensively, sexuality does not exist apart from its modes of organization and representation, both of which are culturally and historically specific and both of which have manifold effects on what are commonly referred to as public and private life.

[*See also* Bisexuality; Heterosexuality; Lesbianism; Transexuality.]

Kate Cummings

SEXUAL REVOLUTION. *See* Lesbianism; Sexualities.

SHANGE, Ntozake (b. 1948), poet, playwright, author, educator, performance and installation artist, musician, actor, director.

Born Paulette Williams in Trenton, New Jersey, to a surgeon (father) and a psychiatric social worker–educator (mother), Ntozake Shange earned a B.A. in American Studies from Barnard College (1970) and an M.A. in American Studies from the University of Southern California (1973). In 1970, she abandoned her given name and embraced her African identity through adopting the Zulu names Ntozake (she who comes with her own things) and Shange ([one] who walks like a lion). Both names signify the particular emphasis in her work on language and redefinition as weapons of protest for women and African Americans specifically and for people of color generally.

Hailed as Off-Broadway's "first furious woman," Shange announced her presence in American theater with the acclaimed Broadway success, *for colored girls who have considered suicide/when the rainbow is enuf* (1976). Not only did that drama document the yet unconquered "metaphysical dilemma of bein' alive & bein' a woman & bein' colored," but it redefined the Eurocentric boundaries of theater, calling instead upon African cultural elements of song, music, dance, storytelling, improvisation, and poetry to create an emotional moment of self-actualization for the seven black women. Shange has published four other dramas in the choreopoem form—*Spell #7* (1979), *A Photograph: Lovers in Motion* (1979), *boogie woogie landscapes* (1979), *From Okra to Greens/ A Different Kinda Love Story: A Play/ With Music & Dance* (1985)—as well as a more conventional one-act play, *Daddy Says* (1989). She has written two novels, *Sassafrass, Cypress & Indigo* (1982) and *Betsey Brown* (1985), and two novellas, *Sassafrass* (1976) and *Melissa and Smith: A Story* (1985). Her poetry collections include *A Daughter's Geography* (1983), *from okra to greens: poems by ntozake shange* (1984), *Nappy Edges* (1987), *Ridin' the Moon in Texas: Word Paintings* (1987), and *The Love Space Demands: A Continuing Saga* (1991). Additionally, her essays about her writings are collected in *See No Evil: Prefaces, Essays & Accounts* (1984).

Shange's literary and feminist influences are many. To feminist poet Judy * Grahn she credits her artistic commitment to "killing the King's English." Literary influences include Amiri Baraka (LeRoi Jones) and Ishmael Reed. Shange continues the black female literary tradition of Zora Neale * Hurston, Alice * Childress, Sonia * Sanchez, Toni * Morrison, and Adrienne * Kennedy.

In her profession of "I write to fight," Shange declares herself "a war correspondent . . . in a war of cultural and aesthetic aggression." Her works evidence her passionate commitment to documenting and legitimizing the global struggles of those politically, socially, economically, and psychologically oppressed by racism, sexism, and capitalism. Rather than glorify victimization, Shange's works reestablish * rituals and * mythologies that accentuate the survival of the oppressed in their myriad complex realities. On the distinctly female voice in her writings, she comments: "I would hope that my choice of words, characters, and situations reflect my experience as a woman on the planet. . . . My perceptions and my syntax, my colloquialisms, my preoccupations are founded in race and gender." As to the specific audience for whom she writes, she says: "In most of my work, I'm talking to women because I'm talking to myself when I write." As a woman artist of color and as a feminist, Shange wages war on her own terms, creating in her works experiences that ". . . fill you up with something/ . . . make you swoon, stop in your tracks, change your mind, or make it up. . . . [experiences that] happen to you like cold water or a kiss."

Shange and her daughter reside in Philadelphia, where she is transforming *The Love Space Demands* into a performance piece, completing a novel *(Little Rich Colored Boy)*, and teaching *performance art and African literature in the New World at The Maryland Institute, College of Art. Recently she earned the title of the 1991 World Heavyweight Champion at the Taos Poetry Circus. While interviews with Shange, articles on her poetry and individual plays, and journalistic criticisms are available, no comprehensive book-length study that contextualizes Shange within appropriate African-American, feminist, and theatrical traditions exists.

• "Ntozake Shange Interviews Herself," *Ms.* (December 1977): 34–35, 70, 72. Claudia P. Tate, *Black Women Writers at Work* (1983). Stella Dong, *"Publishers Weekly Interviews Ntozake Shange," Publishers Weekly* (3 May 1985): 74–75. Andrea Stuart, " 'We Are Feeding Our Children the Sun': Talking with Ntozake Shange," *Spare Rib: A Women's Liberation Magazine* (May 1987): 14–17. "Women Playwrights: Themes and Variations," The *New York Times* (7 May 1989), section 2, pp. 1, 42.

Neal Lester

SHARECROPPING. A practice that emerged following the emancipation of African-American slaves, sharecropping came to define the method of land lease that would eventually become a new form of slavery. Without land of their own, many blacks were drawn into schemes where they worked a portion of the land owned by whites for a share of the profit from the crops. They would get all the seeds, food, and equipment they needed from the company store, which allowed them to run a tab throughout the year and to settle up once the crops, usually cotton, were gathered. When accounting time came, the black farmer was always a few dollars short of what he owed the landowner, so he invariably began the new year with a deficit. As that deficit grew, he found it impossible to escape from his situation by legal means. The hard, backbreaking work led to stooped, physically destroyed, and mentally blighted black people who could seldom envision escape for themselves or their children; their lives were an endless round of poor diet, fickle weather, and the unbeatable figures at the company store. Those with courage to match their imaginations escaped under cover of darkness to the North, that fabled land of opportunity.

As a theme in literature, sharecropping stretches from the late nineteenth century into the contemporary era. Charles W. Chesnutt would write in *The Wife of His Youth and Other Stories of the Color Line* (1900) as well as in his novels of the convict lease system that imprisoned black men in the same manner as sharecropping. Jailed on false charges of vagrancy, these men would in turn be hired out as cheap labor to local whites. This new prison environment was practically inescapable. Sterling Brown would paint equally vivid pictures of the inability of sharecroppers to escape their plight and of their paltry efforts to make do with what they had. His collection of poems, *Southern Road* (1932), documents the lives of rural blacks tied to unyielding soil and uncompromising landowners.

Sharecropping as an impetus to migrate north occurs in some of the works of Richard Wright and John O. Killens. A different kind of freedom is suggested in "A Summer Tragedy" (1933), a short story by Arna Bontemps, where a defeated elderly couple simply get into their car and drive into a river. The story therefore captures the spirit of despair that informs a lot of Wright's works. For most of the characters in his *Uncle Tom's Children* (1938), freedom is not something they can begin to visualize. Many of the characters in Ernest Gaines's works find themselves locked onto the Louisiana plantations where they were born, their futures dictated by local whites. Set from the 1940s to the 1970s, Gaines's works illustrate that not much had changed for black people in some parts of the South.

Alice *Walker's characters would find sharecropping equally inescapable in *The Third Life of Grange Copeland* (1970). Grange finally manages to steal away under cover of darkness, but his son Brownfield allows himself to become so damaged by the system that he kills his wife. Walker, born to sharecroppers in Eatonton, Georgia, drew upon firsthand knowledge of this practice when she wrote her novel.

In another literary portrait from this period, Jean Wheeler Smith's "Frankie Mae" (1968), a young girl who has learned rudimentary math skills finds that she is no match for the figures at the company store. When at thirteen Frankie Mae questions Mr. White Junior's addition, the landowner barely restrains himself from shooting her and her father. He sends her away with these words: "Long as you live, bitch, I'm gonna be right and you gonna be wrong. Now get your black ass outta here." This defeat leads to Frankie Mae's realization that education can never provide the way out of her family's predicament. She gives up school and slumps into the destructive existence that sharecropping engendered. At fifteen she has her first child; by nineteen she has three more. She dies giving birth to her fifth child. Several years after Frankie Mae's death, her father, inspired by the *civil rights movement, works for change by going on strike against Mr. White Junior.

Sharecropping reflected the power and ownership whites wielded over black people in spite of the Emancipation Proclamation. African-American writers have used this theme to texture their portraits of Southern culture, to perpetuate the cultural *myth (or warning) of the South as a place of death for black people, and to enhance their portraits of the realities of African-American life.

[See also Reconstruction.]

Trudier Harris

SHOCKLEY, Ann Allen (b. 1927), novelist, short story writer, critic, bibliographer, biographer, librarian. In all her bibliographical, biographical, critical, and creative works, Ann Allen Shockley has consistently committed herself to illuminating the experiences of African-American writers in general and of African-American women and lesbians in particular. Born in Louisville, Kentucky, she received a B.A. from Fisk University in 1948 and an M.S. in library science from Case Western Reserve University in 1959; after a career as journalist and teacher, she has been a librarian and archivist at Fisk University since 1969.

Shockley's writing, both nonfiction and fiction, has frequently been called pioneering. In compiling *Living Black Authors: A Biographical Directory* (1973), *A Handbook for Black Librarianship* (1977), and *Afro-American Women Writers (1746–1933): An Anthology and Critical Guide* (1988), she was among the first to recognize the fundamental need to make information—historical and contemporary—about black Americans available to the public. Whereas her directory and handbook are primarily research tools, her anthology of African-American women writers from the colonial period to the *Harlem Renaissance discusses the historical and social context for forty-one writers, establishing a black feminist literary tradition. In numerous periodical articles from the early 1960s, Shockley identified and discussed issues of significance to African-American studies, including black library collections, oral history, racism in children's literature, and antislavery materials. The majority of her periodical articles, however, have reflected her concern for black women and black lesbians.

While Shockley's early short stories, which were published in such leading black magazines as *Black World* and *Freedomways*, focused on racism, her creative work has come increasingly to focus on the triple jeopardy facing black lesbians—*racism, *sexism, *homophobia—as well as on their strategies for empowerment. Her 1974 novel, *Loving Her,* is the first black American lesbian novel as well as the first work written by an American describing a love affair between a black and a white woman. Of the ten stories in *The Black and White of It* (1980), all of which describe lesbian love, four concern white women, four black women, and one black and white women; "A Meeting of the Sapphic Daughters" addresses racism in the women's movement. Collectively these stories demonstrate the ubiquity of sexism and homophobia in American society, but they also powerfully project the destructive effects of such oppression in the black community.

Set almost wholly in the black community and using the rhetoric of black sermons, her most recent novel, *Say Jesus and Come to Me* (1982), describes the development of the love between two public women: the Reverend Myrtle Black, an evangelical preacher, and Travis Lee, a popular singer. If Ann Allen Shockley's fiction appears didactic, it resembles the writing of early black women writers who with similar courage and vision saw the necessity for social change.

• Barbara Smith, "Toward a Black Feminist Criticism," in *But Some of Us Are Brave,* eds. Gloria T. Hull, Patricia Bell Scott, and Barbara Smith (1982), pp. 157–175. Ann Allen Shockley, "The Black Lesbian in American Literature," in *Home Girls: A Black Feminist Anthology,* ed. Barbara Smith (1983), pp. 83–93. Helen R. Houston, "Ann Allen Shockley," in *Dictionary of Literary Biography: Afro-American Fiction Writers After 1955,* eds. Trudier Harris and Thadious M. Davis, vol. 33 (1984), pp. 232–236. Calvin Hernton, "The Sexual Mountain and Black Women Writers," in *Wild Women in the Whirlwind,* eds. Joanne M. Braxton and Andree Nicola McLaughlin (1990), pp. 195–212.

Elizabeth Schultz

SHORT STORY. There have been hundreds of U.S. women who published at least one volume of short stories between 1827, when Sally Wood published *Tales of the Night* in Portland, Maine, and mid-1993. The list of women who published at least one story between 1822 and 1993 is more than twice as long. Many of these women published enough stories to have filled several books, but their stories are, as yet, uncollected. (That is one of the ways that women's work is lost—it is published in ephemeral forms and never put between the covers of a book. The stories of writers such as Ada Jack Carver, Edwina Stanton Babcock, Pauline E. *Hopkins, and Elizabeth *Stoddard should be available to contemporary readers.) Despite this abundant and prolonged productivity, women's stories have been consistently underrepresented and misrepresented in historical considerations and representations of the genre. In anthologies that include any stories by women (about one-fourth of anthologies include no women at all), the ratio between women and men writers ranges from one in seven (Tillie * Olsen's figure) to one in eleven (based on my study of two hundred anthologies). Additionally, the themes that women most typically address in their short fiction are not represented; rather, it is the atypical stories, those that most closely resemble men's stories in their subject matter, or are written in a male voice, or most closely adhere to patriarchal myths about women that are available. Furthermore, the short story genre itself has undergone a loss of status, currently being viewed by many in the literary world as an apprenticeship genre, preparation for fiction writers on their way to tackling the greater task of writing novels. This view permeates despite the fact that many of our finest writers accomplished their greatest work in the short story genre.

The genre occupied a position of honor among readers, and its practitioners were highly esteemed by publishers from the 1820s until the * Civil War, and then again from the years following that war to those roughly corresponding with the overlapping burst of growth of the film industry—when many of the most talented or promising writers turned to script writing—and the Great Depression of the 1930s. After World War II, the genre diminished in popularity for various reasons; hence, stories by women have been further slighted because of the widespread ignorance about and indifference to the genre itself in the later half of the twentieth century. U.S. women's short stories are, therefore, still largely unknown, unexplored, unread, and unavailable.

The American short story was developed by a great many writers, women and men alike, from our nation's ethnic, racial, regional, and religious variety, and from all * classes and * sexualities. However, the earliest stories thus far uncovered were written by privileged Protestant white women who had educational and, often, in their early lives, financial advantages far greater than most. Nevertheless, as adults, these women wrote from financial necessity; they tried all the genres—from poetry to domestic management, child-rearing and * etiquette * advice, * children's literature, essays, plays, and novels—that might have enabled them to earn a "respectable" living. The fact that so many of them settled on the short story as the literary form in which to develop their greatest skills had as much to do with the popularity of the genre and their consequent greater financial

opportunities as it did with creative inclination. This conjunction of opportunity, need, and talent combined to produce the greatest assemblage of women's short stories ever written.

Catherine Maria * Sedgwick, her sister-in-law Susan Sedgwick, Lydia Maria * Child, Eliza Leslie, and Sarah Josepha * Hale began publishing stories in the mid-1820s. *The Atlantic Souvenir for 1826*, the first U.S. literary annual or gift book, published by Philadelphia publishers Matthew Carey (Leslie's brother-in-law) and Lea includes Sedgwick's "The Catholic Iroquois"; the 1827 *Souvenir* includes Sedgwick's "Modern Chivalry" and Child's "The Rival Brothers"; and soon thereafter Leslie's social satires began regular appearances. The literary gift books and annuals, which flourished between 1825 and 1865, were forerunners of three forms with us today: the short story anthology, the short story annual, and the * women's magazine. Women such as Leslie and Hale became editors and publishers and, in their successful bid for markets, exerted powerful influence over the shape and conventions of the developing short story. Hale is best known today as the editor who shaped * *Godey's Lady's Book*, one of the earliest successful women's magazines and periodical markets for short stories.

During these early decades, controversy arose among the practitioners of the developing genre about how a story ought to be shaped. The insistence among women writers that "life" and the life of a single although central character were not coterminous was reflected in the structure of stories. Life did not end with the death (or * marriage or betrayal, illness or bankruptcy, repented wickedness, repaired relationship, or indiscretion) of the protagonist, but with the consequences of the life choices that the character endured. Such insistence on the linking of characters' stories and the dynamic and continuing nature of consequences of actions and choices reflect a to-this-day unresolved literary argument about what constitutes an appropriate shape for the short story and, in particular, discussion as to when a story ends. The controversy also led to the invention of the linked story sequence. Hale's 1829 two-part story "The Village Schoolmistress" includes the jilting of the heroine as an important event in the shaping of her life, painful to be sure, but not more important than her love for her sister or her professional accomplishments. Caroline * Kirkland (1801–1864) may have been the initiator of the book-length linked story sequence in her 1839 *A New Home—Who'll Follow?; or, Glimpses of Western Life*. Her stories were connected through the medium of the experiences of her narrator. In Child's pioneering "tragic mullata" story, "The Quadroons" (1842 in *The Liberty Bell*, the first abolitionist literary annual), the consequences of *racism are traced across several generations. Alice *Cary's Ohio stories in the three volumes of *The Clovernook Papers* (1852–1854) develop the linked story sequence by focusing on consecutive and connected but not continuous episodes in the life of a single character. The *story cycle is enjoying renewed attention from writers and critics alike today. The convention seems to especially attract multicultural women writers, ranging from Martha *Wolfenstein's 1902 *Idylls of the Gass* to Gwendolyn *Brooks's *Maude Martha*, Alice *Childress's *Like One of the Family*, Maxine Hong *Kingston's *The Woman Warrior*, Louise *Erdrich's *Tracks*, to Andrea *Lee's *Sarah Phillips*.

Naturally, for a genre so young, few conventions existed. Child wrote some true stories and invented others, and collected both kinds in her 1846 *Fact and Fiction: A Collection of Stories*. A comparison of the apparently true and the invented stories reveals that the true stories are less tied to a crisis or any single event than are the invented stories. "True" stories, written in a conversational tone, are straightforward narratives of the flowing of life and lives. The invented stories, however, each contains a moment in the lives of the characters when the writer dramatizes rather than narrates events. This early fiction often relies on the conventions of oral *story telling, including the story-within-a-story framed telling and/or direct address to the reader.

The settings and themes of early stories reflect the struggle between respect and nostalgia for old-world traditions and the commitment to the creation of an indigenous American literature. There seem to be an equal number of stories set "over there" in romantic, often mythical evocations of the past, and stories set in what European immigrants thought of as "the New World." The old-world stories are less diverse in all ways than the new ones and were quickly replaced by the much more interesting and experimental American stories until the latter quarter of the nineteenth century, when "foreign" stories began to appear once again, but this time as a variant on the New World stories. Stories by such writers as Constance Fenimore *Woolson and Edith *Wharton, about American women visiting or living in Europe, were published during the same time that American literary *regionalism flourished. People were curious about aspects of the world far away from them, whether it be parts of the U.S. or parts of the Old World.

The early old-world stories (from the 1820s through the 1840s) use the conventions of heterosexual romance to evoke landscapes and fashions in clothing, speech, and manners unfamiliar to their readers. From the start, the New World stories present the much wider range of themes that have become characteristic of U.S. women's short stories: the relationships between women, especially *mother/daughter stories (see *Between Mothers and Daughters: Stories across a Generation*, ed. Susan Koppelman, 1985), *sister stories; women's *friendship stories (see *Women's Friendships: A Collection of Stories*, ed. Susan Koppelman, 1990); stories about interactions with the natural world (see especially stories by Appalachian women and Harriet Prescott *Spofford's 1860 "Circumstance," Mary Noailles *Murfree's—writing as Charles Egbert Craddock—1878 "The Star in the Valley," Katherine Sherwood *McDowell's—writing as Sherwood Bonner—1883 "On the Nine Mile"); stories about relationships across boundaries, especially those of *race and class (see the early *abolition stories by Child and *Dall and the contemporary *The Things That Divide Us*); stories about work both imposed by social expectation and work chosen, both necessary to the sustenance of life and necessary to the heart's and mind's fulfillment (of the chosen work stories there are the artist stories, such as Rebecca Harding *Davis's "Marcia," Dorothy Canfield *Fisher's 1937 "Babushka Farnham," Suzette Hayden Elgin's 1969 "For the Sake of Grace," and Sherry Thomas's 1979 "The Shape of Things to Come"), and stories about all the other kinds of work women could and chose to do, from the ministry (see Elizabeth Stuart *Phelps's "A Woman's Pulpit," 1879) to working as an arithmetician (Mary E. Wilkins *Freeman's "An Old Arithmetician," 1887), a typist (see Dorothy *West's "The Typewriter," 1926), a circus fat woman (Fannie *Hurst's "Even As You and I," 1919), a traveling saleswoman (Ruth Suckow's "A Great Mollie," 1931, and Edna *Ferber's stories about Edna McChesney), and a teacher (Mary Elizabeth Vroman's "See How They Run," 1951); stories about relationships with men—fathers, sons, husbands, lovers, and potential mates (women's stories that appear to be "only" about romance are usually stories about the quest for an adult identity or life-style and catalyze ethical problems); stories about "social problems" such as alcoholism (the many temperance stories of the last quarter of the nineteenth century), wife abuse (as in Alice Carey's 1859 "Passages from the Married Life of Eleanor Holmes" and Fannie Hurst's 1935 "Hattie Turner Vs. Hattie Turner"), or drug abuse (such as Louisa May *Alcott's 1869 "Perilous Play," Fannie Hurst's 1921 "She Walks in Beauty," or Sauda Jamal's 1980 "A Mother That Loves You"). The stories about *racism are so numerous and so constant that it must be seen as one of the major themes of women's short stories.

Women initiated or participated in the development of all of the subgenres of the short story. Eliza Leslie's 1832 "The Mysterious Gift" may have been the earliest woman's supernatural tale, and Gertrude *Atherton's 1905 "The Striding Place" one of the most famous early supernatural stories of this century. The tradition of women's work in fantasy, *ghost, and *science fiction stories has continued and blossomed in the late twentieth century with the work of C. L. Moore, Joanna *Russ, Carol Emshwiller, Vonda McIntyre, Kit Reed, James Tiptree, Jr. (Alice Sheldon), Ursula K. *Le Guin, Chelsea Quinn Yarbro, and others. *Mystery stories have always had great popularity. Among the most compelling are the 1895 lesbian locked-room murder story "The Long Arm" by Freeman, and Anna Katherine Green's stories of the first female detective, Violet Strange, who debuted in 1915.

Women have been couching social criticism in humorous stories from the time of Eliza Leslie. From Frances Whitcher's Widow Bedott stories in the 1850s to Marietta *Holley's stories of Josiah Allen's wife Samantha in the 1890s and Helen Reimensnyder Martin's early-twentieth-century stories of the Pennsylvania Dutch, women expressed criticisms of *sexism not only in *humor, but in a variety of regional and ethnic masks as well. Alice *Walker has continued the tradition in such stories as her 1980 "How Did I Get Away with Killing One of the Biggest Lawyers in the State? It Was Easy."

The Atlantic Souvenir, The Legendary, Affection's Gift, The Token, The Iris, and *The Gift* were not only commercially successful as remembrance books and annuals for various occasions (such as Christmas and New Year's) and as silent messengers in the gift exchange rituals of *friendship and courtship, but they also were used as fund-raisers for the *abolition and temperance movements and other causes, political and religious. With these annual volumes arose the literary subgenre known as the occasional story, which were stories written to celebrate or commemorate public, *community holidays or events. In particular, women embraced the opportunities for extralucrative publication at Christmas and Thanksgiving, making the writing of stories for these two holidays particularly important in their personal oeuvres. Alcott's "Mrs. Podger's Teapot" (1867) may have been the earliest occasional story, but Freeman probably wrote more Christmas stories than any other author, sometimes publishing three in one year. Fannie Hurst ran a close second (see *"May Your Days Be Merry and Bright" and Other Christmas Stories by Women,* ed. Susan Koppel-

man, 1988). Sarah Orne *Jewett was one of the most prolific Thanksgiving storytellers, although Zona *Gale's stories for this holiday may be the best, especially "Nobody Sick, Nobody Poor" (1909). Probably the most famous occasional story ever written is "The Perfect Tribute," the 1906 story by Mary Raymond Shipman Andrews about Lincoln's composing the Gettysburg Address—a story imagined for Memorial Day that has entered into history beside George Washington's cherry tree.

Along with Washington Irving and a few other men, these women invented the American short story. The creation of a literary genre is never the work of one individual; it is an antiphonal and collaborative work involving various levels of interaction among its creators, its audiences, its reviewers, and those who bring them together—the publishers. In the early days of the genre, many writers moved back and forth from one role to another.

In the decade of the 1830s, Hale, Delia Salter Bacon, Child, Leslie, Lydia *Sigourney, Sedgwick, Emma Embury, and Caroline Kirkland each published her first collection of stories for adults, all or most of the stories having been published earlier in either a periodical, a newspaper, or a literary gift book or annual. Many of these writers also had published earlier collections of stories and poems for children.

The 1840s saw continued publication by these women and also the first books of Fanny Forester, Hannah Flagg Gould, Mrs. A. J. Graves, Grace *Greenwood, Lucy Hooper, Caroline Mehetabel Sawyer, Ann Stephens, Harriet Beecher *Stowe, and Ellen Gould White. Besides the women publishing volumes of stories, there were those women whose stories were important in the development of both the genre and the audience for the genre whose stories still remain uncollected. These include (among others) Caroline Healey Dall, whose abolition stories were as important as Child's, and the female textile mill workers, such as Harriet Farley, Betsey Chamberlain, and Harriet Robinson, who wrote for the *Lowell Offering,* creating the first body of *working-class women's literature in the U.S. The next significant group of working-class women's stories were the temperance stories, most of them by women who wrote very little and whose work has never been collected. Then came such women as Gertrude Nafe, Voltairine De Cleyre, and Lillian Browne-Thayer, whose stories filled the pages of the radical magazines *Mother Earth* and *Masses* at the turn of the century. The most recent surge of working-class women's writing began with the publication by Judy *Grahn of *True to Life Adventure Stories.*

In the 1850s, the numbers of women publishing volumes of short stories increased with continued publication by these earlier women and the appearance of first volumes by a new generation of women writers, including Alcott, Caroline Butler, Cary, Caroline *Chesebrough, Julia Dumont, Mary Henderson Eastman, Caroline Lee *Hentz, Susan Pettigru King, Louise Moulton Chandler, Alice Neal, Elizabeth Stuart *Phelps (the mother), Frances Whitcher, and Mary Jane Windle. The publication of stories diminished dramatically during the decade of the *Civil War, but some women began their successful careers in this inhospitable time, including Davis, Elizabeth Stuart *Phelps (the daughter), and Stoddard. As peacetime enterprises were renewed in the 1870s, a new appetite for short stories burgeoned and the women writers who have often been cited by literary historians as the earliest important female practitioners of the genre finally began to publish—fifty years after the first publication of stories by important women short story writers.

As early as the 1830s, stories appeared in political newspapers such as the abolitionist *National Era;* literary newspapers such as the *New York Ledger,* a story weekly; religious denominational papers such as the *Trumpet* and the *Independent;* and regional papers such as the *Philadelphia Saturday Courier,* the *Southern Literary Messenger* and Ohio's first paper, the *Cincinnati Sentinel.* It was in these venues that writers such as Bacon and the Cary sisters, Alice and Phoebe, first published. In the mid-twentieth century, Sunday newspaper supplements contained short stories. In the late twentieth century, such feminist papers as *Sojourner* have continued the tradition of publishing women's short stories.

The growth of the magazine industry established an early inexhaustible market for stories oriented toward specific audiences, such as *Godey's Lady's Book,* among the earliest of women's magazines, and which relied heavily on Emma Embury's stories; *Russell's Magazine,* the preeminent antebellum Southern literary monthly for which Susan Pettigru King was the chief writer of fiction in the 1850s; the *Anglo-African Magazine,* the first African-American literary and general opinion magazine, and which featured Frances Watkins *Harper's story "The Two Offers" in 1859; and the *Occident and American Jewish Advocate,* in which Rebekah Hyneman began publishing in the 1860s. Other magazine stories were oriented toward general audiences, such as the *Atlantic Monthly,* begun in 1857 and including, by the publisher's request, a story by Rose Terry (later *Cooke), successful author of stories for women's magazines and Sunday school publications for children, who published the earliest lesbian story yet discovered, "My Visitation," in *Harper's New Monthly Magazine* in 1858. Love between women had not yet been pathologized, and such stories were not rare (see *"Two Friends" and Other Nineteenth-Century Lesbian Stories by U.S. Women,* ed. Koppelman, 1994). Others who published in magazines, including the various Harper periodicals, *Scribner's Monthly Magazine,* and *Lippincott's Magazine,* which were organs of book publishers, included Elizabeth Stuart Phelps (the daughter), Jewett, Helen Hunt *Jackson, Woolson, Alice French, Grace King, Mary Hallock Foote, Kate *Chopin, Sarah Barnwell Elliott, Alice *Brown, and many others who were considered in the last quarter of the nineteenth century by literary critics or historians under the rubric of *local colorists or literary regionalists.

Many of these writers published first in children's and/or women's magazines. Mary E. Wilkins (Freeman) published more than twenty-five stories in *Harper's Bazar,* a woman's magazine, before "graduating" to the "quality" magazines. Political magazines that published fiction, such as the liberal *Arena,* with stories by Will Allen Dromgoole, and feminist periodicals, such as *Una* and *Forerunner,* debuted (the latter was published, edited, and entirely written, stories included, by Charlotte Perkins *Gilman). The mass market magazines of the early twentieth century, such as *Cosmopolitan, Saturday Evening Post,* and *Redbook,* bid on the work of great short story writers. The so-called quality magazines in the middle fifty years of the century competed to define by their editorial policies "what a story should be." The *Atlantic* and *Harper's* continued to publish, the *New Yorker* was founded, and writers such as Nancy Hale, Dorothy *Parker, Mary *McCarthy, Frances Gray Patton, Jean *Stafford, and Hortense *Calisher found publication homes. Many of these magazines continue to publish stories today, including *Redbook* (with its special summer fiction issue), *Ms.,* and *Mademoiselle;* these magazines publish such established writers as Jessamyn West, Merrill Joan Gerber, Joyce Carol *Oates, Kristan *Hunter, Cynthia *Ozick, and Alice *Adams. These periodicals have been joined by important new ones—*Sinister Wisdom, 13th Moon, Hurricane Alice, Essence*—which publish newer writers such as Elana Dykewoman, Lee Lynch, Madelon Arnold, Leslea Newman, and others.

Stories by women writers from a variety of ethnic and racial groups began appearing early in the twentieth century in Anglo-American magazines for the first time; works were published by Hopkins, Wolfenstein, *Zitkala-Ša (also known by her Anglo name, Gertrude Bonnin), *Sui Sin Far (also known by her Anglo name, Edith Maude *Eaton), and Maria Christina Mena. How long women of varied races and ethnicities have been writing stories we do not yet know—but presumably much longer than Anglos have been publishing them. However, there have long been publications devoted to ethnic and racial groups, including *Crisis*, where Ann *Petry's stories appeared, *Black World*, with Jean Wheeler Smith, *Grito de Sol*, with stories by Sylvia Wood, and *De Colores*, featuring Rosalie Otero Peralta. Stories by Hisaye *Yamamoto also made their first appearance in periodicals.

By the turn of the century, editors of anthologies of the short story attempted both to define the form and create a *canon of stories they thought important. As one example, in 1922, Alexander Jessup published *Representative American Short Stories*, a collection of 74 pieces of writing he identified as short stories written between 1788 and 1921, including 58 stories by 48 male writers and 14 stories by 14 female writers (and 2 anonymously authored stories). His anthology included the most extensive bibliographical listing of short story writers ever assembled and the most apparently generous representation of women writers.

The first woman's story he included is from 1844: "The Schoolmaster's Progress," by Caroline Kirkland. Although most of her fiction centers on a woman protagonist who is the source of normative vision and the narrator of the life she observes in the frontier West, in selecting this story, Jessup gives the impression that Kirkland wrote about male figures. His choice of an 1844 story also suggested that there were either no, or no "good," earlier stories by women.

The second woman's story is the 1848 "The Belle; or, Love under the Rose," by Helen Irving. Jessup writes that "[this story] has been included not so much on account of its absolute literary value as to represent the sentimental effusions found so abundantly in the periodicals of the mid-century. . . . This story seems quite a charming example of a class noted rather for tediousness and insipidity than for charm. On the whole it seems a fitter representative of its class than the stories by better known writers that I have examined."

Thus the reader learns that this story isn't really a story, doesn't really count as literature, and should not be considered other than as an example of an enormous quantity of material—by better writers—that is better forgotten. Both the impression of Irving as an isolated figure and the idea that if women had written stories they were best forgotten are reinforced.

Jessup did include twelve other women—Stowe, Harriet Prescott Spofford, Charles Egbert Craddock (Mary Noailles Murfree), Wool-son, Freeman, Wharton, Jewett, Chopin, Annie Trumbull Slosson, Margaret Wade *Deland, and Katharine Fullerton Gerould. His patronizing tone and the fact that twelve of the stories included by women were published within only the last fifty years of the 133-year period the anthology represents give the reader the impression that women writers are interlopers on the literary scene and that they didn't start writing until men started showing them how.

Most of these women writers were characterized as local color or regional writers. Although Jessup includes them as representatives of the most recent past generation of writers, he ultimately dismisses their achievement by pointing out, at the close of his preface, that "a notable tendency in the American short story at the moment seems to be an increased emphasis on character." (The generally accepted but incorrect assumption about local color literature was that setting was a more important literary value than character and that local color literature was therefore of minor importance historically and certainly now passé.) He doesn't include any women writing the "new" kind of stories, with their supposed emphasis on character. Jessup's anthology is representative of the way in which women's stories have been treated, starting with the earliest collection (1869) up until today's most popular and most widely read anthologies.

[*See also* Ghost Stories; Magazines, Women's; Minimalist Fiction; Short-story Cycles.]

Susan Koppelman

SHORT-STORY CYCLES. The story cycle is a hybrid of the novel and the short-story collection, also known as the "story-novel" or "novelle," in which diverse prose pieces, often previously published in magazines, are sequenced in book form to replicate the structural cohesion of longer narratives. If the novel promises unity, assuring us that the last page clarifies the first, and the story compilation promises diversity, exposing us to different settings, times, and voices, the cycle offers a paradoxical experience—the "unified miscellany." Cohesion often depends less on formal elements, such as a linear plot or character development, than on the reader's ability to make imaginative connections between selections. Though only recently recognized as a genre, examples abound in American literature. Eliza Leslie's *Pencil Sketches* (1833), Catherine M. *Sedgwick's *Tales and Sketches* (1835), and Louisa May *Alcott's *Hospital Sketches* (1863) are three of the numerous collections that emulated the framing strategy of Washington Irving's *The Sketchbook of Geoffrey Crayon, Gent.* (1819–1820), the first commercially successful example of the form.

The cycle has special value for women writers. As feminist critics argue, *gender influences narrative style and structure. Rather than spotlight alienated heroes rebelling against society, women often focus on the relationships and rituals that weave a particular community together. While male writers rely on linear plots and climactic conclusions, women explore episodic experiences with indefinite resolutions. Given these differences, many women writers have wondered if the novel was the proper showcase for their talent. Sarah Orne *Jewett once told an editor that she was incapable of writing a long narrative: "I have no dramatic talent. The story would have no plot. I should have to fill it out with descriptions of character and meditations." She eventually wrote several novels, some of which, true to her fears, were criticized as plotless. But her masterpiece, *The Country of the Pointed Firs* (1896), exemplifies how the ensemble form complements the narratives of community that women compose.

In fact, a cycle can be thought of as a community of narratives in which each story, like a resident of a city block or rural village, exerts its individuality while simultaneously contributing to the distinctive character of its neighborhood. Not all communities are homogeneous, however. In some cycles, such as *The Country of the Pointed Firs*, a single character's perspective threads together larger narrative patterns. In others, varying points of view create an impressionistic patchwork effect. Nor does a cycle necessarily detail the lives of a single community. Instead, unity may derive from recurring story lines, allowing writers to explore formative experiences in heterogeneous settings.

Jewett alternately referred to her *Pointed Firs* stories as "sketches" and "chapters," alluding to the ambiguity of development inherent in the story cycle. A perceptive reader discovers an implicit plot: an outsider grows from observing to participating in the daily rituals of Dunnet Landing, an isolated village in Maine. To heighten that drama, Jewett makes her heroine a writer needing solitude to work, often putting her at odds with the congenial villagers, who place a high value on "seein' folks." During a funeral procession, for example, the narrator rushes away to write but soon regrets her haste. "I began to wonder if I ought not to have walked with the rest," she confesses. "I had now made myself and my friends remember that I did not really belong to Dunnet Landing." Under the aegis of her landlord, Almira Todd, she learns the customs that make the village unique: herb gathering, lobster fishing, and knitting are just a few of the activities whose indigenous rhythms pace these sketches. Subtle indications

mark her growing integration into the isolated society. Halfway through the sequence another seasonal visitor, Susan Fosdick, arrives in Dunnet Landing, and the narrator feels a tinge of jealousy over the attention given to her. Later, she ventures without her host as a guide, visiting a reclusive fisherman, Elijah Tilley, who has spent eight years mourning his wife's death. But the most important clue to her attitude is linguistic—in the late sketches, she speaks of "we" instead of "they."

The narrator's story is only a single thread in the tapestry of village life, however. Equally important, she provides an audience for the locals, who have their own narratives of alienation. Through these scenes we recognize what a valuable *ritual *storytelling itself is for creating *community. The bookish Captain Littlepage tells of being shipwrecked on a desolate Arctic island where he heard a Gothic tale of ghosts indifferent to the loneliness of lost sailors. Mrs. Todd and Mrs. Fosdick tell the story of "Poor Joanna," who exiled herself to a rocky, inhospitable island after her lover ran off to marry another woman. At the Bowden family reunion, which includes nearly everybody in the area, stories are passed like the sumptuous plates of food. In fact, the stories *are* literally food: the dessert cakes are topped with icing and pastries that chronicle family genealogy.

The Country of the Pointed Firs is a popular model for the story cycle. A number of other collections employ the single narrator device, including Katherine Anne *Porter's Miranda stories in *Pale Horse, Pale Rider* (1939) and *The Old Order* (1955), Jessamyn West's *The Friendly Persuasion* (1945) and *Cress Delahanty* (1953), Renata Adler's *Speedboat* (1976), and Sandra *Cisneros's *The House on Mango Street* (1985). But the homogeneous perspective has drawbacks. When one point of view dominates, only one side of the story is told. To convey the multiplicity of opinions that exist in a community, authors often write in a variety of voices.

Gloria *Naylor's *The Women of Brewster Place* (1982) is a perfect example of the multi-perspective cycle. The seven stories focus on the African-American women who live at Brewster Place, an urban housing unit. Two brief, lyrical descriptions of the neighborhood frame the narratives, their titles ("Dawn" and "Dusk") alluding to the cycles of hope and despair that characterize the lives of the residents. Unlike the Dunnet Landing villagers, Naylor's characters have little sense of community or support. They come to Brewster Place for different reasons—some because of economic necessity, some to hide, some to find ethnic solidarity. Like the buildings themselves, which have been tenanted and abandoned by generations of immigrants who earn their prosperity and move on, their lives are marked by abuse, betrayal, and isolation. Mattie Michael moves onto the block when her son jumps bail, forfeiting her house to the bondsman. Kiswana Brown takes a studio apartment to organize the residents into a political force, yet she must reconcile her revolutionary rhetoric with the comforts of her middle-class upbringing. In the cycle's most harrowing story, the bigotry of some residents against a lesbian couple, Theresa and Lorraine, escalates into a brutal assault. *Brewster Place* does contain flashes of communal hope: church services, community plays, tenants association meetings, and block parties bring the neighborhood together, but the connections are tenuous and momentary. In Dunnet Landing, life stories are community property, but at Brewster Place, they remain tangled in misunderstandings and confusions. When a street gang rapes Lorraine, she mistakenly kills the only tenant who befriended her, the building handyman Ben. None of the other women learns the truth.

As if to dramatize the fragmentation of the community, Naylor often switches perspectives within stories. In "Etta Mae Johnson," a woman who survives by her sexuality dreams of becoming the respectable wife of the local minister. When the point of view changes to the minister, who justifies their affair as a "temporary weakness of the flesh," we understand that Etta's hopes will never be realized. In "Louise Lucelia Turner," a mother tries to protect her daughter from an abusive lover; as the couple argues, we watch the child poke a fork into an electrical outlet. Finally, in "The Two," Lorraine's isolation from both her lover and the other women is complemented by a flashback to the day that Ben's wife ran off with another man. Their symbiosis is shattered after Lorraine's rape, when she bludgeons the handyman to death.

Other examples of the multiperspective cycle include Kate *Chopin's *Bayou Folk* (1894), Gertrude *Stein's *Three Lives* (1909), Eudora *Welty's *The Golden Apples* (1949), and Ruth A. Sasaki's *The Loom and Other Stories* (1991). Again, the cohesion of each cycle depends on the reader's ability to savor fragments of stories sprinkled like spices throughout the selections. An even more diverse type of ensemble explores a specific theme in a variety of settings. Examples include Willa *Cather's *The Troll Garden* (1905), *H. D.'s *Palimpsest* (1926), Flannery *O'Connor's *Everything that Rises Must Converge* (1965), and Paule *Marshall's *Soul Clap Hands and Sing* (1961).

Nor must we limit our understanding of the form specifically to *short* stories: with their interwoven family histories, Louise *Erdrich's Native American triptych *Love Medicine* (1984),

The Beet Queen (1986), and *Tracks* (1988) can be read as an extended ensemble that stretches across diverse volumes. As Erdrich's work demonstrates, the story cycle is a highly elastic form that can accommodate a variety of narrative types—even, one can imagine, a mixture of prose, poetry, and drama. Currently the popularity of the cycle is rising; publishers find that they generally sell better than short-story collections and offer a less risky investment than novels. Because relatively few studies of the genre are available, many interesting connections between the form and the characteristics of women's writing remain undeveloped. For both writers and critics then, the story cycle promises to be an exciting area of exploration and discovery.

[*See also* Short Story.]

• Forrest Ingram, *Representative Short Story Cycles of the Twentieth Century: Studies in a Literary Genre* (1971). J. Gerald Kennedy, "Towards a Poetics of the Short Story Cycle," *Journal of the Short Story in English* 11 (Autumn 1988): 9–25. Robert M. Luscher, "The Short Story Sequence: An Open Book," in *Short Story Theory at a Crossroads*, eds. Susan Lohaffer and Jo Ellyn Clarey (1989), pp. 148–170. Susan Garland Mann, *The Short Story Cycle: A Genre Companion and Reference Guide* (1989).

Kirk Curnutt

SHULMAN, Alix Kates (b. 1932), novelist. The only daughter and second child of first generation Russian-Polish secular Jewish parents, Alix Kates Shulman is a seriocomic feminist philosopher-novelist whose first novel, *Memoirs of an Ex-Prom Queen* (1972), a best-seller and National Book Award nominee, was hailed as the first important novel to emerge from the women's liberation movement. It ultimately sold more than a million copies and was adopted by the Literary Guild. It figured prominently on the syllabi of early women's studies courses.

Memoirs, recording a white middle-class heterosexual midwestern girl's coming of age, depicts Sasha Davis's emotionally painful, sexually active, and intellectually perplexed growing up trying to embody the ideal woman of the 1950s—sexy prom queen, proper wife, devoted mother. Structurally, Shulman combines the conventions of the classic bildungsroman and contemporary historical fiction.

Burning Questions (1978) is the fictional autobiography of an introspective rebel who awakens politically in the late 1960s. The novel chronicles the important changes in women's lives and consciousness wrought by contemporary feminism.

In *On The Stroll* (1981), Shulman explores the meaning and reality behind the images represented by the runaway teenage girl and the elderly homeless bag lady, prey to all the dangers of the city—alone, poor, abandoned, and victimized. She explores the possibilities for coalitions among women in situations that are symbolic of what women are conditioned to fear most if they abandon the hypothetical safety of "home."

In Every Woman's Life (1987) anatomizes the institution of marriage through the stories of three women friends. Shulman's signature portrayals of heterosexual eroticism from the perspective of lusty, humorous, sexually exacting women reaches its pinnacle in this book.

Born and educated in suburban Cleveland, Ohio, Shulman fled to New York City after graduation from Western Reserve University to escape the destiny dictated by the traditional sex roles in her world. She soon discovered that the pressures she fled were not restricted by geographical boundaries. Marriage and the birth of two children occupied her early New York years. As soon as both children entered nursery school, she began writing stories. In 1967, she became involved with the fledgling women's liberation movement as an early member of Redstockings. The radical feminist ideas developed in their consciousness-raising groups fueled her writing and ultimately, by giving her both a subject and an audience, enabled her to create a life of her own choosing. She has lectured, given readings, and taught writing and women's studies from Maine to Hawaii.

• Ellen Morgan, "Humanbecoming: Form and Focus in the Neo-Feminist Novel," in *Images of Women in Fiction: Feminist Perspectives,* ed. Susan Koppelman Cornillon (1972). Josephine Hendin, *Vulnerable People: A View of American Fiction Since 1945* (1978). Catharine Stimpson, *Where the Meanings Are* (1988). Alix Kates Shulman, "The Beat Queens," *Voice Literary Supplement* (June 1989). "The 'Taint' of Feminist Fiction" in *Critical Fictions: The Politics of Imaginative Writing* (1991) and in *Ms.* (December 1991).

Susan Koppelman

SIDHWA, Bapsi (b. 1938), novelist, active member in Pakistani women's organizations, educator. Born in Karachi, Bapsi Sidhwa was educated mainly at home in Lahore, Pakistan, because she had polio as a child. Apparently it was Louisa May *Alcott's *Little Women,* presented to her on her eleventh birthday, that opened up the world of fiction for her. The oral tradition of *storytelling, especially as carried on by women, was also an important influence. She received her B.A. from Kinnaird College for women in Lahore, Pakistan, and has taught at the University of Houston (1985), Rice University (1986), and Columbia University (1989). She resides in Houston and divides her time between Pakistan and the United States.

Most of Bapsi Sidhwa's early works are concerned not with the issues of expatriatism and immigration but with the issues of women in the context of the families and cultures of India and Pakistan. *The Crow Eaters* (1982) and *Cracking India* (1991) are both rooted in Sidhwa's own religious-ethnic community, the Parsis (Zoroastrians). *The Crow Eaters* is an interesting, often hilarious, saga of Faredoon (Freddy) Junglewalla's journey from a small village to the city of Lahore and then to London. Enjoyable as this novel is, the writing is sometimes careless and there seems to be a lack of convincing characters.

The Bride (1983) and *Cracking India* do not suffer from these weaknesses. Sidhwa was inspired to write *The Bride* during a visit to an army camp in the Karakoram mountains where she heard the story of a young Punjabi girl who had been married off to a man of the mountain tribal region. The bride ran away, but her husband's clan hunted her down and killed her. Sidhwa has skillfully rewritten the tragedy of the girl's marriage and murder, beginning with the communal violence of the 1947 partition of the subcontinent, during which her protagonist, a very young girl, is saved and adopted by a Muslim man.

Cracking India presents the history of India in the 1940s as observed and narrated by an eight-year-old Parsi girl, Lenny, who has polio and lives in Lahore. She tells us her story within the context of the story of her city and of the people surrounding her. The language, especially in the first half of the book, is often irritatingly explanatory regarding South Asian words and people. But this didacticism disappears when Sidhwa reaches the core of her narrative, where she presents the communal violence of the independence and partition era with uncompromising anger and sorrow.

In her first novel set in America, *An American Brat* (1993), the protagonist Feroza Ginwalla is sent to the U.S. from Pakistan by her family, who are alarmed by the influence fundamentalism has on her. Sidhwa describes Feroza's discovery of America and Americans with wonderful wit and compassion.

Bapsi Sidhwa has contributed to South Asian–American literature many unforgettable portraits of Pakistani women and fascinating examples of the Asian women's tradition of extending their family stories and gossip into the public domain of literature.

Roshni Rustomji-Kerns

SIGOURNEY, Lydia Huntley (1791–1865), educator, poet, prose writer. Raised an only child in Norwich, Connecticut, Lydia Huntley Sigourney was largely self-educated, encouraged to read and write by her mother and by her father's employer, Jerusha Lathrop. Aspiring to become a teacher, she began a school for women in 1811 that failed because of its remote location. In 1814, Daniel Wadsworth, son of a wealthy New England family, helped her successfully establish another school in more-populated Hartford. The following year he arranged to publish her first book of poems, *Moral Pieces*. Sigourney would become known for her poetry, but she would make her career writing as a teacher, a position she claimed was no less socially significant than that of a legislator.

Sigourney's work revered and embodied republican ideals, affirming a traditional economic class structure by appealing to powerful, privileged members of society to act on behalf of disenfranchised groups—Native Americans, slaves, the poor, the insane, and later, women. Marriage in 1819 seemed to guarantee support for these projects, but her husband saw writing mainly as an elegant pastime. Financial reverses in the late 1820s changed his mind, however, and soon Sigourney achieved a popularity that made her name a household word for decades, as she flooded the literary market through gift books, newspapers, and journals. In 1833 and 1834 alone she brought out twelve volumes of poetry and prose, publishing more than sixty-five volumes over six decades. Death was a common subject in her work—and a subject that sold—but income was not her only object, and elegy not always her attitude. Most characteristic of her collections is *Zinzendorff and Other Poems* (1833), whose title poem invokes the decimation of Native Americans in order to question American policy toward them in terms of a nonsectarian evangelical Christian vision—a vision in which death is not a private but a public concern.

In the 1840s, reprints and revisions financed her trip to Europe, recorded in *Pleasant Memories of Pleasant Lands* (1842), where she enjoyed her fame, meeting dignitaries and arranging for authorized versions of her works. Turning inward in *The Faded Hope* (1853), about the death of her son, and *Past Meridian* (1854), about aging, Sigourney continued to confide in her readers converting her private experiences into lessons in living. Her autobiography, *Letters of Life*, was published posthumously in 1866.

• Gordon Haight, *Mrs. Sigourney: The Sweet Singer of Hartford* (1930). Emily Stipes Watts, "Lydia Huntley Sigourney," *The Poetry of American Women from 1632 to 1945* (1977), pp. 83–97. Nina Baym, "Reinventing Lydia Sigourney," *American Literature* 62, no. 3 (Sep-tember, 1990): 385–404. Gary Wait and Everett Wilkie, eds., *Good Thoughts in Good Dress* (1992). The bulk of Sigourney's surviving letters is in the library of the Connecticut Historical Society and the Hartford Public Library.

Timothy H. Scherman

SILENCE DOGOOD (1706–1790), pseudonym for Benjamin Franklin, writer, printer, inventor, patriot, and statesman. In 1722, at the age of sixteen, Benjamin Franklin began his professional writing in his brother's Boston-based newspaper, *The New England Courant*. Fearing that his work might not be accepted, he submitted his essays under the guise of an opinionated Boston widow, adopting the *pseudonym Silence Dogood. Through his feminine persona he provided his readers with fourteen witty, opinionated views on the contemporary Boston scene. Silence Dogood satirically commented upon the hypocrisy and superficiality of contemporary Boston's culture. On education, Silence chided wealthy parents for foolishly spending money to educate their dull-witted children at Harvard; on poetry, Silence praised the half-excellencies of a piece; on pious elegies, Silence provided a recipe for writing generic ones.

At seventeen, Franklin ran off to Philadelphia and abandoned his feminine persona forever.

• Carl Van Doren, *Benjamin Franklin* (1938; reprint, 1973). Richard Amacher, *Benjamin Franklin, An American Man of Letters* (1964). Bruce Granger, *Benjamin Franklin* (1976). R. Clark, *Benjamin Franklin* (1983). L. Labaree, W. Willcox et al., eds., *The Papers of Benjamin Franklin*, 23 vols. (1959–1983).

Adelaide P. Amore

SILENCES. Tillie Olsen's landmark essay "Silences," which first appeared in *Harper's Magazine* in 1965, set up one of the most important intellectual constructs of literary *feminism of the 1960s and 1970s. Here Olsen distinguishes the painful incidents of writer's block that one can trace, for men as well as for women, throughout literary history from the particular silences to which women writers are singularly prey. These silences come from internalizing a definition of oneself as inferior (and therefore not worthy of self-expression), the exhaustion of raising a family and often working outside the home as well, the submissiveness of being a traditional wife and social hostess, and the subservience of defining oneself as ever and always handmaid to others: there to serve, never to be served; there to feed, never to be nourished or even to nourish one's inner resources. Writing historically about what silenced others and autobiographically about what silenced her,

Olsen, in a 1978 collection also called *Silences*, articulated the conditions and needs, the dreams and aspirations, of women who strove to write. More than that—by defining the problems, she inspired a generation of women to break through their own silences.

[*See also* Authorship; Collaboration; Gender and Writing.]

Cathy N. Davidson

SILKO, Leslie Marmon (b. 1948), novelist, poet, short fiction writer. Of mixed Laguna, Mexican, and white ancestry, Leslie Marmon was born in Albuquerque, New Mexico, and raised on the Laguna Pueblo Reservation. Though she speaks little of the Laguna language, she says, "what I know is Laguna. This place I am from is everything I am as a writer and human being."

Silko began writing as a little girl but did not decide to devote herself to it until after she had graduated from the University of New Mexico and attended several semesters of the university's American Indian law program. In 1974, she published *Laguna Woman*, her first book of poetry; that year she received an award for poetry from the *Chicago Review* and a writing fellowship from the National Endowment for the Arts. She spent two years in Ketchikan, Alaska, when she was provided with an artist's residence by the Rosewater Foundation-on-Ketchikan Creek.

Following her sojourn in Alaska she published *Ceremony* (1977), which brought her widespread acclaim; Frank MacShane wrote in the *New York Times Book Review* that "without question Leslie Silko is the most accomplished Indian writer of her generation." With the success of *Ceremony*, Silko began to receive more critical attention for her earlier writing, especially her short fiction. Her stories and poetry have been widely anthologized in *The Man to Send Rainclouds* (1974), *Carriers of the Dream Wheel* (1975), *Best Short Stories of 1975* (1976), *The Remembered Earth* (1979), *Earth Power Coming* (1983), *Spider Woman's Granddaughters* (1989), and *The Heath Anthology of American Literature* (1990), among others.

During the years 1978 to 1980, Silko corresponded with the American poet James Wright, who initiated the correspondence after he read *Ceremony*. Their letters to each other are collected in *The Delicacy and Strength of Lace* (1986), edited by Wright's widow, Anne Wright; much of Silko's view of herself as an author and of the craft of writing is revealed in the letters.

Her multigenre, semiautobiographical book *Storyteller* came out in 1981, the same year she was awarded the MacArthur Foundation Prize Fellowship of $176,000. This enabled her to work exclusively on artistic projects, including filmmaking with the Laguna Film Project and beginning the creation of her latest novel *Almanac of the Dead* (1991), a masterful "moral history of the Americas" told from a Native American perspective. Silko has been on the faculties of the University of New Mexico and the University of Arizona and now resides on a ranch outside of Tucson.

• Kathleen Mullen Sands, ed., *American Indian Quarterly* symposium issue, 5, no. 1 (1979). Dexter Fisher, ed., *The Third Woman* (1980). Per Seyersted, *Leslie Marmon Silko* (1980). Joseph Bruchac, ed., *Songs from This Earth on Turtle's Back* (1983). Hal May and Susan Trosky, eds., *Contemporary Authors*, vol. 122 (1988).

Margaret A. Lukens

SISTERHOOD. The term *sisterhood* describes the lines of affection, association, and influence that exist among women. While sisterhood implies mutuality, it also admits of difference and sometimes conflict. In women's history and literature, sisterhood has three overlapping senses: a bond developed among any group of women for support and the accomplishment of shared goals, often political; a society of women who, usually for religious and charitable reasons, take certain vows and live together under conventual rule; and the kinship relations between female siblings. Because sisterhood commonly arises in the context of traditional patriarchal systems of values and behaviors, the bonds of sisterhood may implicitly or explictly challenge the status quo. Thus the wish of an eighteenth-century writer for the *Free-thinker* to "have the whole Sisterhood of Canting Females banished to some Desert Island," and the reference to women's late nineteenth-century struggle for equal rights as the doings of a "Shrieking Sisterhood."

Although the purposes vary, in recent centuries women have joined together in sisterhood to achieve social or political reform. In the United States in the nineteenth and early twentieth centuries, for example, women organized to fight for abolition, temperance, and the vote; Sarah *Grimké—feminist, abolitionist, and Quaker—addressed women sharing her political commitments as "sister." Elizabeth Cady *Stanton and Lucretia *Mott organized women at the Seneca Falls Convention in 1848, launching the drive for suffrage as well as the modern women's movement. Margaret Sanger founded the American Birth Control League in 1921, a forerunner of International Planned Parenthood. The early twentieth century saw the formation of associations such as the League of Women Voters, the Women's Interim League for Peace and Freedom, and the Women's Trade Union League, all of which had parallels in

Great Britain and western Europe. Recently in the United States, the reform effort has been taken up by the National Organization for Women, founded in 1966 to achieve equal treatment of women in hiring and promotion. Implicit in such communities of women is the assumption of *gender difference, which often takes the form of affirming women's moral superiority over men's, and of values of hearth and home over those of the marketplace. These sisterly values are loudly proclaimed in nineteenth-century American and British domestic novels such as Charlotte Brontë's *Jane Eyre* (1847) and Harriet Beecher *Stowe's *Uncle Tom's Cabin* (1852), and are documented in social histories of female intimacy and friendship.

It would be inaccurate to characterize women's struggles for rights only with the examples of the United States, England, or western Europe. In Australia, for example, women's solidarity played a less crucial role in social reform and suffrage even though these movements occurred during similar time periods. In Argentina, upper-class women's organizations such as the Beneficent Society (1823–1948) and the Daughters of Mary (founded in 1908), which were closely tied to the Catholic Church, worked not for reform but for preservation of right-wing, patriarchal values to counter threatening socialism and *anarchism. And in regions of Shanghai, China, women in cotton mill factories between World War I and liberation in 1949 often pledged sisterhood to one another, marking their vows of loyalty with incense burning at Buddhist temples and celebratory meals. These sworn sisterhoods did not so much reflect challenges to *patriarchy brought about by a raised *working-class or female consciousness as they ensured women's basic survival against attack by gangs of men and bosses.

Sisterhoods can offer women safe haven without disrupting existing structures or values. Religious sisterhoods represent the largest number of women's groups organized in this way. Nuns are found in most world religions; in western culture, the term most commonly refers to the Christian communities of women living and working together, often in poverty, to serve the church. Traditionally, especially in the Middle Ages, religious orders provided women with respectable and economically viable alternatives to marriage or spinsterhood, as well as access to education, reading, and writing. Lay groups of religious women also further the work of their faith. Hadassah, the Women's Zionist Organization of America, for example, was founded in 1912 to promote health, education, and Jewish ideals in the United States and Israel. Although some may consider the Judeo-

Christian tradition, with its single male God and dichotomous view of women as Eve or Mary, incompatible with the concepts of shared power implied by sisterhood, many women have found room within these structures for cooperation and constructive action. They may even, as Isak Dinesen's short story, "The Blank Page" (1957), imagines, subvert the system while serving it. A more radical approach, however, is offered by feminist theologian Mary *Daly (*Gyn/Ecology*, 1978), who calls for the "Soul-Spark of sisterhood" to replace confining, patriarchal religions.

Sisterhood should not be conceived of as entirely free of conflict, competition, and coercive obligation. Although sororal bonds present a model of shared identity, sympathy, and cooperation, the differences among women are erased by a monolithic concept that ignores *race, economic and social *class, age, or sexual preference. African-American women, for example, may feel as much or more allegiance to African-American men, with whom they struggle against racial oppression, as they do with middle-class white women. Since historically African-American women have worked outside the home in low-paying jobs as well as inside the home as mothers, their issues of entry into the market economy are not the same as they are for white middle-class women who seek to exchange motherhood for well-paid careers. Lineage and kin-based sisterhoods are traditionally more central to Asian, African, and South American women than to European and North American women. Sisterhood may also have different meanings for lesbian and heterosexual women since it is used to refer to a continuum of female bonding, from the erotic to the collegial and professional.

The concept of sisterhood is supported by revisionist theories of Freud, which argue that the primary bonds between women are relational, empathic, and connected rather than autonomous and separate. Sisterhood is accordingly seen as a logical expression of women's experience. Some writers pursue this concept of a communal self through innovative techniques. Sandra *Cisneros, in *The House on Mango Street* (1984), and Amy *Tan, in *The Joy Luck Club* (1989), for example, create multiple voices and shared identities instead of a solitary narrative voice. Exploring individual identity and rivalry between natal sisters, cousins, and friends—common in women's writing from Jane Austen's *Sense and Sensibility* (1811) to Edith *Wharton's "The Old Maid" (1924) and Shirley *Jackson's *The Haunting of Hill House* (1959)—also works to a writer's advantage. Sisterly oppositions allow the representation of both socially approved and disapproved feminine behavior: "good" sisters are traditionally set against "bad" sisters. More importantly, however, each woman gains identity in contrast with the other; sisterhood thus provides a safe structure within which to explore misunderstood or complex aspects of feminine desire and behavior. Such is the case in Christina Rosetti's treatment of a sexually innocent and a sexually experienced sister in "Goblin Market" (1862) and in Toni *Morrison's depiction of the bonds between Sula and Nel in *Sula* (1973). Entire texts may even exist in sisterly relationship, for example, Charlotte Brontë's *Jane Eyre* and Jean Rhys's *Wide Sargasso Sea* (1966). Whether designed to accentuate difference or to reinforce solidarity, sisterhood is a significant, positive force in women's lives and a powerful trope in women's writing.

• Eileen Power, *Medieval English Nunneries* (1922). Robin Morgan, ed., *Sisterhood Is Powerful: An Anthology of Writings from the Women's Liberation Movement* (1970). Carroll Smith-Rosenberg, "The Female World of Love and Ritual: Relations between Women in Nineteenth-Century America," *Signs* 1, no. 1 (Autumn 1975): 1–29. Nancy F. Cott, *The Bonds of Womanhood: "Woman's Sphere" in New England, 1780–1835* (1977). Nancy Chodorow, *The Reproduction of Mothering: Psychoanalysis and the Sociology of Gender* (1978). Lillian Faderman, *Surpassing the Love of Men: Romantic Friendship and Love between Women from the Renaissance to the Present* (1981). Jean F. O'Barr, *Perspectives on Power: Women in Africa, Asia, and Latin America* (1982). Robin Morgan, ed., *Sisterhood is Global: The International Women's Movement Anthology* (1984). Margaret Forster, *Significant Sisters: The Grassroots of Active Feminism, 1839–1939* (1985). Emily Honig, *Sisters and Strangers: Women in the Shanghai Cotton Mills, 1919–1949* (1986). Elaine Showalter, *Sister's Choice: Traditions and Contradictions in American Women's Writing* (1991). Helena Michie, *Sororophobia: Differences among Women in Literature and Culture* (1992).

Carol J. Singley

SLAVE NARRATIVES are, at the most general level, written records of individual experience with the system of chattel *slavery. Such records range from anecdotal dictations and simple recollections of day-to-day life to highly stylized literary works employing sophisticated tropes and rhetorical strategies. But no matter what form the narrative assumes, it always relies upon personal experience to confront and contest slaveholding culture. Among slave narrators, the need to produce a written account of personal experience was intricately bound up with a conception of freedom, and writing became a way not only of affirming individual liberty but also of convincing others that slavery was a threat to the ideological and moral foundation of the United States.

White readers were often interested in accounts of former slaves, but they were also deeply suspicious of their truthfulness. Blacks were simply thought incapable of possessing the knowledge and ability to write accurate accounts of their own lives. Such *racism complicated the task of all former slaves who undertook to write narratives. A man such as Frederick Douglass labored in a restricted space: he could expect the authenticity of his works to be questioned exhaustively, and he knew his writings were subject to far more editorial control than anything his white contemporaries, male or female, might produce. Even as a black male, however, he did not occupy the lowest position in the hierarchy of nineteenth-century literary culture—that place was reserved for African-American women.

A woman who sought to record the experiences of her life as a slave faced the added obstacle of *sexism. She had to overcome the perceptions of white editors and readers who viewed her combined status as both female and African American as something less than human. Cultural prejudices dictated that she receive less support from abolitionist sponsors than her male counterpart. And even if she did manage to obtain financial support and secure the necessary sponsors to authenticate her work, she still had to overcome publishers and booksellers reluctant to promote it.

Still, the impressive body of literature left behind by women such as Harriet *Jacobs and Mary Prince provides compelling evidence of their struggle against slavery and the difficulties of writing and publishing. Narratives by African-American women now hold a significant place in studies of eighteenth- and nineteenth-century literature, and they form a critical part of the *autobiographical tradition that continues to influence literary production across boundaries of both race and sex in the United States today.

In the strictest sense, the term "slave narrative" refers only to those accounts of captivity and escape written by former slaves themselves. But the genre as a whole takes its energy from a variety of related sources including memoirs, oral *storytelling, *collaborations, *biographies, spiritual autobiographies, and interviews. Starting points for its history range from John Saffin's *Adam Negro's Tryall*, published in 1703, to *A Narrative of the Uncommon Sufferings and Surprising Deliverance of Briton Hammon, A Negro Man*, which first appeared in 1760.

Early texts often relied upon the conventions of the memoir to create rhetorical strategies that would become commonplace in subsequent works. Narratives such as that of Olaudah Equiano, first published in 1789, showed future writers how elements of personal experience, sometimes embellished and sometimes elided, could act as powerful tools in addressing a white audience. The events included in Equiano's narrative and the language he employs to describe his life story are carefully chosen to avoid alienating white readers, and his attempts to shape the way in which his memoir was received would inform the efforts of later narrators who faced suspicious and even hostile audiences.

Other early memoirs, including *A Narrative of the Lord's Wonderful Dealings with J. Marrant, a Black, Taken Down from His Own Relation* (1785) and *The Confessions of Nat Turner* (1831), are notable in part because they exemplify the practice of collaboration between black slaves and white amanuenses that also came to occupy a place in slave narrative tradition. One of the more intriguing examples of such collaboration is *Silvia Dubois, A Biography of the Slave Who Whipt Her Mistress and Gand Her Freedom* (1883), which is not strictly a *biography but rather a series of reminiscences resulting from interviews between Dubois, a former slave living in New Jersey, and Cornelius W. Larison, a white doctor.

Dubois's reminiscences exemplify the marginal role often assigned to former slaves by their white collaborators. While Larison does allow Dubois to have a voice within the text—he even preserves much of the character of her language by transcribing her remarks phonetically—the resulting series of anecdotes about everyday life and tirades against the morals and manners of the younger generation is by no means an autonomous narrative. Larison never allows Dubois to make the transition from dependent contributor to independent speaker, and it is impossible to know whether her reactions were genuine or if she simply told her questioner what he wanted to hear.

Among those African-American women who did have the opportunity to write their own narratives were the spiritual autobiographers. As early as the 1830s, free blacks such as Jarena *Lee, Zilpha *Elaw, Julia A. J. *Foote, and Nancy Prince began to publish accounts of spiritual and physical journeys that espoused Christian individualism as a way of combating racism and sexism. Although freeborn, the autobiographers nevertheless had firsthand experience with prejudices that denied the possibility of black spiritual identity, and their works sought to establish and celebrate spiritual as well as secular freedom for all African Americans. The accounts of their evangelical activities also provide a valuable perspective on the organization of religious life in nineteenth-century America.

Another famous autobiographical account from the nineteenth century is Elizabeth Keckley's *Behind the Scenes; or, Thirty Years a Slave and Four Years in the White House, as Mrs. Lincoln's Maid* (1868). Keckley was born a slave in Virginia but managed to purchase her freedom and move to Washington where her skills as a dressmaker brought her into contact with Mary Todd Lincoln. Since Keckley's narrative was influenced in part by a collaborator, James Redpath, it is difficult to determine how much of the text accurately reflects her own observations. The work does, however, provide a fascinating look at the Lincoln presidency and the family's domestic situation as well as information on Keckley's involvement with the Contraband Relief Association, an organization of African Americans that sought to provide economic assistance to former slaves during and after the Civil War.

Important biographical accounts of African-American women include such works as the *Narrative of Sojourner *Truth, A Northern Slave* (1850) and *Scenes in the Life of Harriet Tubman* (1869). Truth's and Tubman's biographers relate the stories of intensely courageous women who were committed to the abolition of slavery and the establishment of equal rights for all African Americans. Both were active throughout their lives in helping former slaves gain political and economic power, and each campaigned tirelessly for the women's suffrage movement—despite the fact that black women often faced discrimination and prejudice within the movement itself.

In addition to the many formal biographical works on famous figures, there also exist countless interviews and testimonies of other ex-slaves, many collected as part of the *Works Progress Administration Federal Writers' Project during the 1920s and 1930s. The interviews provide valuable information on the social and economic conditions and concerns of African-American men and women who lived through slavery and its aftermath.

Although the stories of former slaves were published in various forms ranging from collaboration to biography throughout the eighteenth and nineteenth centuries, the golden age of the slave narrative genre undoubtedly took place in the United States between approximately 1830 and 1860, corresponding roughly to the height of the abolitionist movement and other antislavery activity. With the founding of the *Liberator*, William Lloyd Garrison's antislavery newspaper, in January of 1831 and the organization of various abolitionist groups—including the first Female Anti-Slavery Society in 1832—an eager audience existed for African Americans who found the means to publish formal accounts of their own lives as slaves.

Since most whites conceived of African Americans as illiterate and, therefore, largely incapable of writing about their own lives, the question of authenticity hovered over nearly every slave narrative at some point. And the fact that a number of narratives, including Mattie Griffiths's *Autobiography of a Female Slave* (1857), were proved to be written by white authors made the publication of black writers even more difficult to accomplish. Narratives purported to be the creation of ex-slaves were subjected to intense scrutiny, and their presentations of people and events were often disputed, especially by the southern press.

Generally, in order to achieve publication, an African-American narrative had to be accompanied by some type of verifying document, usually written by a white abolitionist editor who authenticated the sources and endorsed the work as a worthwhile contribution to the fight against slavery. The original title page of Harriet *Jacobs's *Incidents In The Life of a Slave Girl* (1861), for example, proudly declares the editorship of abolitionist Lydia Maria *Child—even though Child herself stated that she had changed very little of the text.

One of the earliest women to overcome white prejudice and suspicion and publish her narrative was Mary Prince, a former slave from Bermuda whose work first appeared in London in 1831. Although Prince did not publish in the United States, her text created a model of form and language that future authors would rely upon to tell their own stories. Her impressive employment of the first-person narrative technique and the care she took to elucidate the horrors of slavery without overwhelming her audience mark Prince as one of the premier narrators of the nineteenth century.

But Prince did more than set technical standards; she was also the first narrator to expose the unique horrors suffered by black women under slavery. Earlier narratives written by men occasionally touch on the plight of slave women, but none fully explore, as Prince does, the problems of sexual abuse and the destruction of the family. Rather than simply present her readers with indirect references to sexual exploitation, Prince describes specific instances of harassment and abuse, and she voices her outrage at the system that sanctioned such treatment of women. She recounts the shame she felt at being forced to attend one of her masters as he took a bath and the inhuman manner in which female slaves, even pregnant ones, were whipped and beaten. In addition to exposing practices of sexual and physical brutalization, she also describes the pain and loss that resulted from the owners' common practice of splitting up slave families by selling off individual members to different buyers.

Prince's narrative is one of the first attempts to convince a white audience of the ability of blacks to truly know and understand their own desires and freedoms. Prince's claim of self-knowledge—that she knew what was best for herself—was a significant challenge to the prevailing white attitude that blacks needed slavery as a paternal framework. By thus broaching the topic of identity and arguing that blacks were something more than objects of white manipulation and exploitation, Prince began to articulate the kind of issues that would soon come to dominate the discourse on slavery in the United States.

One of the texts that enlarged upon Prince's work, and perhaps the most famous narrative by an African-American woman of the nineteenth century, is Harriet A. Jacobs's *Incidents in the Life of a Slave Girl*. First published anonymously in 1861, *Incidents* recounts Jacobs's personal history as a slave in Edenton, North Carolina, and her eventual escape to freedom in the North. Born around 1813 and orphaned at the age of six, Jacobs (Linda Brent in the narrative) nevertheless spends a happy childhood under the tutelage of a benevolent mistress who makes few demands and a free maternal grandmother who provides much support and comfort. When her mistress dies a few years later, however, the eleven-year-old Jacobs is willed to the family of Dr. James Norcom (Dr. Flint) and abruptly confronted with the violent reality of slave existence. Norcom subjects her to constant sexual overtures and threats of violence and forbids her to marry. To escape the harassment, Jacobs enters into a sexual relationship with another white man, Samuel Treadwell Sawyer (Mr. Sands). After more threats by Norcom, Jacobs is forced to spend the next seven years in hiding—much of it in a small attic space of her grandmother's home—cut off from her two children and isolated from the outside world. Incredibly, Jacobs manages to survive her ordeal, and the narrative ends with her escape to the North, where friends purchase her freedom.

Like Frederick Douglass's autobiographical writings, Jacobs's story embodies many of the central concerns of early African-American literature. It is revolutionary and confrontational as it employs incidents of individual experience to expose the hypocrisy of a nation founded on democratic principles yet tolerant of chattel slavery. But if Jacobs's story is personal, her message is ultimately addressed to a national audience. Linda Brent is not meant to represent just one person but an entire race, and Jacobs's intent is to coax readers into accepting all African Americans as intelligent, literate beings with talents and skills quite equal to those found in the white community.

Undergirding *Incidents* is the belief in the capacity of African-American women to exist as something other than the objects of white desire or derision. Jacobs's purpose is to create an active female persona endowed with the power to think and move independently in pursuit of individual goals. Linda Brent's battle of wits with Dr. Flint, which leaves him looking more like a bumbling fool than an all-powerful master, is one example of Jacobs's attempts to subvert traditional notions of black-white, female-male relationships and create a space for new conceptions of African-American identity.

The women in *Incidents* are imbued with a strength that allows them to break traditional stereotypes by refusing to be categorized as weak or inferior. Power is, in effect, redefined throughout the narrative as something which is not predicated on physical superiority but derived from familial bonds. Such bonds are largely maternal, and we can readily see how they lend support to the independence of Jacobs and her grandmother. Their strength—whether intellectual, emotional, or economic—is characterized in such a way as to show white readers that blacks were able not only to maintain a solid family structure but also to employ that structure as a means of surviving adversity.

Jacobs's desire to construct an identity for herself and other former slaves was frustrated in part by the constraints of a society that allowed little space for female authors and even less for those who happened also to be black. Jacobs's struggles exemplify the difficulties encountered by many ex-slaves who sought to bring their work before the public. She went through two different publishers, one of whom insisted that the text be prefaced with an endorsement from Lydia Maria Child, before finally managing to see her work into print. Even then she was forced to rely largely on her own energy and resources to help publish and promote the book.

In addition to the preface by Child, *Incidents* is also accompanied by letters of endorsement from Amy Post and George Lowther. Such endorsements were an expected part of any African-American publication, but, in a rare twist on common practice, Jacobs's letters were not written by white men but rather by a white woman and a black man. The fact that Jacobs was willing to risk public rejection by refusing to court white male verification shows how strongly she was committed to disrupting traditional patterns of patriarchal and racial domination.

Jacobs's goal of changing white perceptions of African Americans matches that of male slave narrators such as Frederick Douglass and William Wells Brown, but her desire to expose the complex system of sexual prejudice and violence that dominated the lives of enslaved women gives her narrative another dimension. She is able to give a firsthand account of the disastrous effects of the double standard that allowed slaveholders to worship their white wives even as they sexually abused their female slaves. Harassment and abuse were common practices, indeed expected privileges, for slave owners, and Jacobs's account of the behavior of Dr. Norcom shows she was intimately aware of the special terrors inflicted upon African-American women in the South. In addition to the propositions and threats they often endured on a daily basis, black women such as Jacobs often became pawns in power struggles between slaveholders and their wives. The actions of the jealous wife described in *Incidents* typify those of a mistress made resentful by her spouse's desires for a female slave. And, as Jacobs shows us, such resentment often found its outlet in further abuse and humiliation of slave women.

Despite the presence of institutionalized racism and sexism, Jacobs never allows her message to be controlled or compromised. It is important to remember that she writes *Incidents* out of a position of intense doubt and conflict—doubt in her audience's ability to understand her message and conflict over her own history and self-worth. Because she entered into a sexual relationship with Samuel Treadwell Sawyer outside of marriage—even though she did so to escape the threats of Dr. Norcom—she had to struggle through much culturally prescribed guilt. By including elements of her dilemma within the narrative, she manages to employ the experience to her own advantage. She comes to terms with her own past and then employs that personal history as a convincing argument against the impossible sexual standards that affected all African-American women.

As Jacobs shows us, the history of the slave narrative is, in effect, the history of a struggle for words, a fight to record the experiences of African-Americans who suffered under, adapted to, and worked against the institution that sought to deny them their identity. By communicating their stories, narrators were able to uncloak the injustice and hypocrisy of slaveholding culture and, by extension, call for that culture's extinction. Women such as Mary

Prince, Elizabeth Keckley, and Harriet Jacobs not only influenced the way their fellow African Americans viewed themselves, but they also helped begin the monumental task of reshaping conceptions of race and gender, a task that continues to characterize African-American literature in the twentieth century.

[*See also* Autobiography; Captivity Narratives.]

• Winthrop D. Jordan, *White Over Black: American Attitudes Toward the Negro 1550–1812* (1968). Arna Bontemps, ed., *Great Slave Narratives* (1969). Stephen Butterfield, *Black Autobiography in America* (1974). Charles L. Perdue, Jr., Thomas E. Barden, and Robert K. Phillips, eds., *Weevils in the Wheat: Interviews with Virginia Ex-Slaves* (1976). Dorothy Sterling, ed., *We Are Your Sisters: Black Women in the Nineteenth Century* (1984). Charles T. Davis and Henry Louis Gates, Jr., eds., *The Slave's Narrative* (1985). Jacqueline Jones, *Labor of Love, Labor of Sorrow: Black Women, Work, and the Family From Slavery to the Present* (1985). William L. Andrews, *To Tell a Free Story: The First Century of Afro-American Autobiography* (1986). William L. Andrews, ed., *Sisters of the Spirit: Three Black Women's Autobiographies of the Nineteenth Century* (1986). Henry Louis Gates, Jr., ed., *The Classic Slave Narratives* (1987). Harriet A. Jacobs, *Incidents In the Life of a Slave Girl* (1861; reprint edited and introduced by Jean Fagin Yellin, (1987). William L. Andrews and Henry Louis Gates, Jr., eds., *Six Women's Slave Narratives* (1988). C. W. Larison, *Silvia Dubois, A Biography of the Slave Who Whipt Her Mistres and Gand Her Fredom,* 1883; reprint edited and introduced by Jared C. Lobdell, 1988.) Blyden Jackson, ed., *A History of Afro-American Literature,* vol. 1 (1989).

—Paul Ryan Schneider

SLAVERY. Research on American slavery has often depicted this experience as a male event by focusing on its effects on the African-American man. A major reason for this incomplete history is that, until recently, much of the research on the subject has been produced by male scholars. With the reappearance of narratives of slave women and other written works of women of the nineteenth century through the Schomburg collection, a more authentic account of the African-American woman's slave experience has become available.

What is evident from these works is that the institution of slavery subverted and deformed all aspects of black female life in the attempt to colonize the African woman as worker and as producer of workers in a grand experiment of transportation of free labor. African women labored hard and long in their traditional societies before their enslavement. However, under slavery they were obliged both to take on the role of "surrogate men" and to become "breeders." Exploited to produce children who were themselves commodity items, the women found their traditional roles as mothers, daughters, and wives/lovers were perverted.

Because they had the power to reproduce the labor force for slavery, black women's subjugation was crucial to the smooth functioning of the Southern economy. This subjugation was maintained by a system of legalized sexual terror. Young adolescent and teenage girls were routinely abused by their masters and by other white men who had access to them. Because the law accorded all rights over property to slave masters and sanctioned the actions of virtually all white men with regard to blacks, slave women had no legal recourse against such violence.

The personal narratives of slave women are the best source of information about their experiences of slavery. These private lives have become public documents that retrieve black women's humanity from the brutal facts of chattel slave records. The narratives demonstrate the systematic perversion of all basic human relationships where the slave woman and her family were concerned. Thus, these women authors traced a shared pattern that attempted to give meaning and form to the random events that comprised their historical reality.

These acts of writing, therefore, testify to a "spiritual transcendence" that black women were able to sustain in the midst of their bodily captivity. As Henry Louis Gates, Jr., has observed in *The Signifying Monkey* (1988), the narratives allow them to become "speaking subjects ... by inscribing their voices in the written word." Their private voices enable the birth of a communal black female voice. In this manner, they "literally write themselves into being through carefully crafted representations in language of the black self." In brief, they function to gender the sociohistorical and economic experience of slavery.

One inherent characteristic of slavery, according to women's narratives, was the arbitrary and capricious separation of mothers and children. Death, sickness, incompetence, or irresponsibility on the part of the plantation master could, overnight, wrench loved ones from each other. Thus, slave families' security depended always on the master's whims. Mothering, a treasured role of nearly all African women, was deformed and circumscribed by the circumstances of the master and mistress. A slave woman had no legal rights to her children. Slave women were, in fact, commercial items, the "inventory" which, along with horses, cows, chickens, and pigs, constituted the slaveholder's net worth. The normal development of mother-child bonding was sabotaged by the buying and selling of family members without regard for the importance of natural human affections. This ambiguous designation of motherhood created contradictory emotions in the hearts of slave mothers, as Harriet Jacobs recounts in *Incidents in the Life of a Slave Girl:*

> When my babe was born, they said it was premature. It weighed only four pounds: . . . I had heard the doctor say I could not survive till morning. I had often prayed for death; but now I did not want to die, unless my child could die too. . . . For a year there was scarcely a day when I was free from chills and fever. My babe also was sickly. . . . Dr. Flint continued his visits, to look after my health; and he did not fail to remind me that my child was an addition to his stock of slaves.

First and foremost, the children of slave women were seen as additional assets whose value on the slave market was of paramount consideration. Property rights were a major factor in marriages and other male-female relations. Slave marriages were not legal, and the status of children was determined by the condition of the mother, a provision that always benefited the owners of slave women. The issue of property rights was important when slaves of different plantations married. Thus, many slave owners made every effort to "provide mates" for the men and women of their plantations. Annie L. Burton notes in her narrative "Memories of Childhood's Slavery Days" that

> If a slave man and woman wished to marry, a party would be arranged some Saturday night among the slaves. The marriage ceremony consisted of the pair jumping over a stick. If no children were born within a year or so, the wife was sold. At New Year's, if there was any debt or mortgage on the plantation, the extra slaves were taken to Clayton and sold at the court house. In this way families were separated.

In other instances, slave owners intervened violently to ensure their rights to any children born to their slave women. A primary motivating factor in the brutal beating of Frederick Douglass's aunt, as recounted in his narrative, was the fact that she loved a man from another plantation whom she refused to give up despite her master's warnings. In the same manner, Dr. Flint's refusal to allow Linda Brent to marry the man of her choice, as detailed in her narrative, can be seen as more than just the ravings of a jealous and lustful master when the issue of potential children from this union to a free black man is factored in.

Slave women's relationships with their children were disrupted in other ways as well. City dwellers with plantations in the countryside often sent the children of slave mothers to the country as soon as their mothers weaned them so that they would not be in the way, hindering the mother's work. The mothers might be allowed to visit them, perhaps only once a year.

Virtually all of the narratives of women slaves refer to this breach of the mother-child relationship either as it affected them directly or as they witnessed its effect on others. Mattie J. Jackson, in "The Story of Mattie J. Jackson," recalls an incident affecting her own family:

> We remained but a short time at the same residence when Mr. Lewis moved again to the country. Soon after, my little brother was taken sick in consequence of being confined in a box in which my mother was obliged to keep him. If permitted to creep around the floor her mistress thought it would take too much time to attend to him. He was two years old and never walked. His limbs were perfectly paralyzed for want of exercise. We now saw him gradually failing, but was not allowed to render him due attention. Even the morning he died she was compelled to attend to her usual work. She watched over him for three months by night and attended to her domestic affairs by day.

Other narrative accounts speak of slave women who suffered spontaneous abortions, miscarriages, sterility, and broken health because of their forced labor in the big house as well as in the fields.

Such perversion of women's roles as mothers often led slave women to harbor conflicting and sometimes destructive sentiments directly attributable to the absurd existence that was their lot under slavery. These paradoxical emotions were especially evident when the child in question was a female, as arbitrary separation of families, together with the unchallenged authority of the master, did not permit the safety given a white girl against the physical abuse of white men—masters, masters' sons, relatives, overseers, or others. As Eugene D. Genovese notes in *Roll, Jordan, Roll: The World the Slaves Made* (1972):

> Slaveholders deliberately assigned slave men to live and work as studs. The black women bore the transgressions of black men with much less equanimity than did the white men, whose indifference no doubt reflected a certain male camaraderie across class and racial lines. White men preferred to base their charge of black promiscuity on the alleged behavior of the women.

Nearly all slave narratives, those of men as well as those of women, speak of forced liaisons between slave women and white men. Frederick Douglass, Solomon Northrup, Moses Roper, and other male writers attest to this abuse of black women. Henry Bibb writes of how his own wife was forced to become a prostitute. Young slave girls were approached with bribes of clothing, money, and other gifts to solicit their sexual favors. If this method did not convince them to submit, they were brutally punished. For example, Louisa Picquet, like other beautiful mulatto and octoroon slave women, endured brutal beatings from her master, who tried in every way possible to force her to sleep in his room at night.

Enslaved women had no protection and little pity from their mistresses. The slave woman became the scapegoat in the domestic politics of the master. Nineteenth-century religious teachings labeled the woman as transgressor in all matters of illicit sex. Thus, the African woman, being associated with savagery and animal appetite, was blamed for her own victimization. Actual accounts from women slaves who worked as nurses, cooks, or maids indicate that their treatment was not necessarily less harsh than that of field slaves, for as a result of their proximity to their masters and mistresses, they were constantly subject to the lust of their masters and the brutal vengeance of their mistresses.

Persecution of slave women by their jealous mistresses is a situation echoed throughout the slave narratives, although there are references to occasional interventions on behalf of the black woman. Yet, the ambiguous role of the white woman and her marginalization within the patriarchal economy of slavery provoked in her the same kind of brutal responses as appeared in the men of her family and community. Generally, slave plantations were structured in such a way as to reflect a type of extended family. The master served as master-father to his own family as well as to his slaves, with his wife assuming the role of mistress-mother. Given their precarious positions within such a "dysfunctional" family, slave women experienced incestuous rape, child abuse, and neglect.

Slave mothers experienced particular stress where their daughters were concerned. As it was the parents who were primarily responsible for the moral training of their children, they often tried to prepare them for the inevitable dehumanization that awaited them. However, not many slave mothers could protect their daughters from abuse by white men or jealous mistresses, and the agony of mothers over the fate of their daughters is poignantly documented in the slaves' personal narratives. Bethany Veney, in "The Narrative of Bethany Veney: A Slave Woman," observes that

> you can never understand the slave mother's emotions as she clasps her new-born child, and knows that a master's word can at any moment take it from her embrace; and when, as was mine, that child is a girl, and from her own experience she sees its almost certain doom is to minister to the

unbridled lust of the slave-owner, and feels that the law holds over her no protecting arm, it is not strange that, rude and uncultured as I was, I felt all this, and would have been glad if we could have died together there and then.

In his classic study *The Slave Community*, John Blassingame observes that, "Few slave parents could protect their pretty daughters from the sexual advances of white men," but parents did try to "teach them values different from those their masters tried to instill in them, and give them a referent for self-esteem."

Consternation over the fate that awaited their children, especially their daughters, sometimes provoked mothers to commit abortion or infanticide. In 1856, Margaret Garner, together with her husband, four children, and several other slaves, escaped from Kentucky to Cincinnati, Ohio. They went into hiding on the *Underground Railroad but were discovered by their masters and local law officers. The fugitives fought bravely yet were overcome by their pursuers. The moment that they broke down the door of the house in which Margaret Garner was hiding, she took a butcher knife from the table and slit her small daughter's throat. Garner was taken to trial where she gained much sympathy. The child that she killed was, according to reports, a beautiful little girl, "near-white." There are conflicting reports about what happened to Garner after she was sold South and the boat on which she was traveling met with an accident. What seems to be clear, however, was her determination to kill all of her children and herself.

In her Pulitzer Prize-winning novel *Beloved*, Toni *Morrison revises the story of Margaret Garner with her heroine, Sethe, a fugitive slave who kills her baby daughter to prevent her from being returned to slavery. Through the spiritual and emotional struggles of the heroine and her reincarnated daughter, Beloved, Morrison foregrounds the plight of the slave mother forced to create a definition of motherhood deformed by the absurdities of the slave environment where property rights, ownership, and possession were of primary consideration. With her ambiguous attitude toward Sethe and her actions, Morrison seems to echo the sentiments of Brent, Veney, and other female slaves that the perversions of human relations fostered by slavery provoked behaviors in the slaves that cannot be clearly judged or understood from within the framework of traditional morality.

The issue of infanticide as a form of insurrection against the unmitigated arbitrary power of slave owners has been insufficiently researched, but that it occurred on a number of occasions and that it was considered on others is evident.

Linda Brent voices her own desperation over the situation of her children in regard to her long-time tormentor, Dr. Flint: "My children grew finely; and Dr. Flint would often say to me, 'These brats will bring me a handsome sum of money one of these days.' I thought to myself that, God being my helper, they should never pass into his hands. It seemed to me I would rather see them killed than have them given up to his power." In its determination to circumscribe a people's entire being into a series of simple prescribed texts of inferiority, the slavocracy created the myth of the black matriarch. This contention holds that black women dominated the home during slavery as a result of the repression of the black man by white masters. This *myth, as Dianne Sadoff notes in *Black Women in America* (1988), "originates in white resentment of the slave woman's seeming power through her sexual relationship with the master, when that relationship signifies instead her status as chattel."

Ironically, despite the fact that masters used sexual tyranny to suppress the black woman's resistance, she was, paradoxically, free from the constraints of submission imposed on Southern white women as a result of patriarchally contrived definitions of ladyhood. The black woman became a nebulous figure in the Southern slave society because of her role as laborer in a culture where ideals of femininity foregrounded domesticity. Thus, as Angela *Davis pointed out in 1971:

[The African-American woman] was a victim of the myth that only the woman, with the diminished capacity for mental and physical labor, should do degrading ... work. ... She was not sheltered or protected; ... She was also there in the fields, alongside the man, toiling under the lash. ... In order to approach its strategic goal—to exact the greatest possible surplus from the labor of slaves— the black woman had to be released from the chains of the myth of femininity.

In fact, as a result of her "nondesignation" as woman/slave, the black woman experienced a type of sexual equality with black men previously unknown in most European and African societies. A misreading of this mutual respect fostered by black men and women's situation of common oppression resulted in the development of an orthodoxy according to which the black woman assumed the role of domineering matriarch.

African women traditionally deferred to masculine authority. Their attitudes toward the home, housework, and child rearing did not promote the degrading of men. Even though the institution of slavery had bred strong women, according to Eugene D. Genovese most black women understood that the "degradation of their men represented their own degradation as black women and that of their children. They wanted their boys to grow up to be men. ... To do so, they needed the example of a strong black man."

In short, the female slave had to seek personal meaning and self-affirmation within herself because there were no avenues to it outside herself. Where these women were able to record the realities of their experiences, they retrieved black women's humanity from the public patriarchal documents in chattel records of slavery. These personal accounts represent acts of independence, both physical and spiritual, and attest to a psychic autonomy in which they were able to create spaces in their existence—"loopholes of retreat"—where they held on firmly to their inherent sense of worth.

[*See also* Abolition; Middle Passage; Underground Railroad.]

• Gerda Lerner, ed., *Black Women in White America: A Documentary History* (1973). John W. Blassingame, *The Slave Community: Plantation Life in the Antebellum South* (1972, 1979). Harriet Jacobs, *Incidents in the Life of A Slave Girl* (1973). Annie L. Burton, "Memories of Childhood's Slavery Days," in *Six Women's Slave Narratives* (1988). Angela Davis, "Reflections on the Black Woman's Role in the Community of Slaves," *Black Scholar* 3 (December 1971): 7. Henry Louis Gates, Jr., *The Signifying Monkey: A Theory of African-American Literary Criticism* (1988). Eugene D. Genovese, *Roll, Jordan, Roll: The World the Slaves Made* (1972, 1974). Rev. H. Mattison, "Louisa Picquet, The Octoroon: A Tale of Southern Slave Life," in *Collected Black Women's Narratives* (1988). Dianne F. Sadoff, "Black Matrilineage: The Case of Alice Walker and Zora Neale Hurston," in *Black Women in America: Social Science Perspectives*, eds. Micheline R. Malson, Elisabeth Mudimbe-Boyi, Jean F. O'Barr, and Mary Wyer (1988). Dr. L. S. Thompson, "The Story of Mattie J. Jackson," in *Six Women's Slave Narratives* (1988). Bethany Veney, "The Narrative of Bethany Veney: A Slave Woman," in *Collected Black Women's Narratives* (1988).

Joyce Hope Scott

SLESINGER, Tess (1905–1945), short story writer, novelist, screenwriter. Born in New York City to middle-class Jewish immigrant parents, Slesinger began writing and rebelling early, although she joked that her childhood had been too happy to contain anything valid to reject. Graduating from the Columbia School of Journalism in 1927, she moved from her job as assistant fashion editor for the *New York Herald Tribune* to assistant literary critic on the New York *Evening Post Literary Review*. In 1928, Slesinger married Herbert Solow, a leftist activist and writer, who cofounded *The Menorah Journal*, in which she published her first story (1928). Subsequently, she published fiction in such magazines as *American Mercury, Vanity Fair,* and *Forum.*

Her only novel, *The Unpossessed* (1934; reprint, 1966), concerns 1930s New York intellectuals. Well received, her satire was relished for its witty critique of contemporary society. Out of concern for economic and racial injustices, Slesinger marched in protests and delivered speeches as well as wrote. In 1935, she published a short-story collection, *Time: the Present;* the stories range in subject matter from abortion ("Missis Flinders") to a young woman's competing dependencies on both her mother and husband ("Mother to Dinner") to a failed strike attempt at an advertising agency ("The Mouse Trap"). The collection was republished in 1971 as *On Being Told That Her Second Husband Has Taken His First Lover, and Other Stories.* Her fiction pays close attention to the characters' inner thoughts and emotions, using stream of consciousness to expose hypocrisy, shallowness, and the ambiguities inherent in any important decisions.

Many contemporary reviews were gleeful that a leftist insider would expose her colleagues as Slesinger did: they interpreted her work as revealing the ultimate emptiness of radical intellectuals' rebellions and their alleged dissatisfaction with what they had created out of their lives. To some, her writing contains unrelenting malice and biting satire, while to others, compassion and sentimentality underlie her work. Above all, readers categorized her fiction as specifically feminine in its subject matter, technique, and appeal.

In 1935, Slesinger moved to Hollywood where she earned high salaries writing the screenplays for *The Good Earth* (1937) and *The Bride Wore Red* (1937). In 1936, she married Frank Davis, a film producer and writer. Together they wrote numerous successful scripts such as *Are Husbands Necessary?* (1942) and *A Tree Grows in Brooklyn* (1945). Helping to establish the viability of the Screenwriter's Guild, Slesinger remained politically active and, according to her unpublished papers, continued to satirically measure her social milieu and her era.

• Shirley Bagi, "Forgive Me for Dying," *Antioch Review* 35, nos. 2–3 (Spring-Summer 1977):224–236. Janet Sharistanian, "Tess Slesinger's Hollywood Sketches," *Michigan Quarterly Review* (Summer 1979):429–438.

Wendy M. DuBow

SMEDLEY, Agnes (1892–1950), novelist, journalist, biographer, and international champion of the working class. Born on a tenant farm in Missouri and raised in company-owned coal mining camps and towns in southern Colorado, Agnes Smedley was haunted by the memory of her mother's hands blackened by constant labor, and her song-loving father's desertions and crushed hopes for economic success. In 1908, she got her first break from a life of menial labor when she became a country school teacher. She briefly attended Tempe, Arizona, Normal School, and then by virtue of circumstance and her own writing, political organizing, vision, and pluck, she journeyed from California to New York to Berlin to Moscow and then to China, living and writing in the heart of the most radical intellectual and political circles of her day. She participated in the campaign for (Asian) Indian independence, was involved with the Berlin Freudians in the mid-1920s, campaigned with Margaret Sanger for *birth control rights (for which she was imprisoned), and was by 1928 and all through the 1930s an active participant in and reporter of the Chinese Revolution. She wrote hundreds of articles for socialist and progressive newspapers and journals, a classic working-class autobiographical novel, *Daughter of Earth* (1929), six books on China, including *Battle Hymn of China* (1943), and several pamphlets and collected editions. She included among her many friends or political comrades Emma *Goldman, Karin Michaelis, Käthe Kollwitz, Langston Hughes, Ding Ling, Nehru, Mao, and Zhou Enlai.

In her peripatetic and protean life, Agnes Smedley found the soil for revolutionary change in China rather than in the United States. Her style and language reflect both the bitterness of her impoverished youth and the lyrical beauty of her native Southwest. Critical of marriage and motherhood as institutions, skeptical of reformism and doctrinairism, she was convinced that writing, especially journalism, could be an agent for social change.

Returning to the United States in 1942, Smedley deservedly expected to establish herself as an expert on China, but her commitment to the Red Army and the peasants' perspective collided with publishers' ideological conservatism, and her writing was rejected. Falsely accused of being a Soviet spy, hounded by the FBI, she left the United States in November 1949, and died several months later in England at the age of fifty-eight after a purportedly successful operation. Her ashes are buried in China.

Her highly praised books fell victim to the anti-Communist hysteria of the 1950s and disappeared from libraries. Interest in Smedley was revived with the reprinting of *Daughter of Earth* (1973 and 1986) and *Portraits of Chinese Women in Revolution*, edited by Jan and Steve MacKinnon (1976).

• Arizona State University, Hayden Library, Tempe, is a primary source for Smedley letters and papers. See also Paul Lauter, "Afterword to *Daughter of Earth* (1973 edition). Lydia Sargent, stage adaptation of *Daughter of Earth* in *Playbook* (1986). Janice R. MacKinnon and Stephen R. Mackinnon, *Agnes Smedley: The Life and Times of an American Radical* (1988).

Janet Zandy

SMILEY, Jane (b. 1949), novelist, essayist, short story writer. Winner of the Pulitzer Prize and the National Book Critics Circle Award for her 1991 best-seller *A Thousand Acres*, Jane Smiley was born in Los Angeles and grew up in St. Louis. She earned a bachelor's degree from Vassar and her M.F.A. and Ph.D. from the University of Iowa. She is currently a professor of English at Iowa State University.

Smiley's fiction ranges broadly, from *The Greenlanders* (1988), a historical saga set in fourteenth-century Scandinavia, to *Barn Blind* (1980), a pastoral novel set during summer in the Midwest, and *Duplicate Keys* (1984), a mystery. Families—whether loving and cohesive or dysfunctional and abusive—occupy the center of her fiction. In *The Greenlanders*, a family curse is anticipated, feared, but never avoided through several generations. In *The Age of Grief* (1987), a collection of short stories, Smiley especially looks at matrimony and the loneliness of disparate love.

A Thousand Acres is her finest work to date. Rich in landscape and language, it is set on the Prairies, rolling and mythic, lyrical and violent. Her Zebulon County invites (and has received) comparison with Faulkner's Yoknapatawpha County, for Zebulon, too, is marked by complex relationships of kinship and history that pervade the personal interactions in the book. With an elegant prose style and a fine gift for description, Smiley makes the Prairie landscape almost as exotic—and as real—as medieval Scandinavia.

• "Smiley, Jane," in *Contemporary Authors*, ed. Frances C. Locher, vol. 104 (1982), p. 439. "Jane Smiley," in *Contemporary Literary Criticism*, eds. Donald G. Marowski and Roger Matuz, vol. 53 (1989), pp. 344–351. Thomas Wiloch and Jean W. Ross, "Smiley, Jane," in *Contemporary Authors New Revision Series*, ed. James G. Lesniak, vol. 30 (1990), pp. 409–413.

Cathy N. Davidson

SMITH, Anna Young (1756–1780), poet and saloniste. Anna Young was born in Philadelphia and orphaned when her mother, Jane Graeme Young, died from the complications of childbirth. The infant was raised by her aunt, Elizabeth Graeme, in Graeme Park, the estate of her grandfather, Dr. Thomas Graeme. There Elizabeth Graeme presided over a remarkable salon that met weekly for conversation. Throughout her childhood, Anna Young had contact with the most distinguished literary company that met in British America. Young's own ambitions as a poet were encouraged by her aunt. "An Ode to Gratitude, Inscribed to Miss Eliza Graeme by her Niece, Anna Young," testified to the care that Elizabeth Graeme lavished on the young writer.

Adopting the pseudonym "Sylvia," Anna Young began circulating manuscripts among Philadelphia's literary coteries in 1773 when she was seventeen. Her politics, like that of her grandfather and aunt, were Whig. "An Elegy to the Memory of American Volunteers" (1775) so captivated one of its readers that it was forwarded to the *Pennsylvania Magazine*, becoming the only work by Anna Young to see print during her lifetime. Like most provincial belletrists until the Revolution, she preferred the exclusive communication of manuscript writings to print. The incivility of print, evidenced by the asperity of the gazettes and the proliferation of unfeeling satire, disgusted her.

"On Reading Swift's Works" distilled her enmity toward the scabarous wit so often featured in print. Swift's abuse of Stella's charms, his frequent recourse to antifeminine scatalogy, provoked "Sylvia" to complain:

> . . . so oft filth chokes thy sprightly fire,
> We loathe one instant, and the next admire—
> Even while we laugh, we mourn thy wit's abuse,
> And while we praise thy talents, scorn their use.

Against Swift's sarcasm, Young championed compassionate feeling. Her "Ode to Sensibility" attributed divinity to an affective disposition, and pledged her allegiance to the power of emotion:

> Still may I feelingly alive
> To thy loved influence be.
> Oh may I ne'er thy power survive,
> Ne'er live bereft of thee.

Heeding the authority of her own emotions, she defied her father's wishes and married Dr. William Smith in 1775. Like her mother before her, Anna Young Smith died from the complications of childbirth on 3 April 1780.

• Manuscript of the "Elizabeth Graeme Ferguson Commonplace Book," are in the Dickinson College Library. Pattie Cowell, "Anna Young Smith," *Women Poets in Pre-Revolutionary America 1650–1775* (1981).

David S. Shields

SMITH, Lee (b. 1944), novelist, short story writer, educator. Born in Grundy, Virginia, Smith has transcended but never broken with the rural Appalachian heritage that runs through most of her work. After graduating from Hollins College, she turned her senior creative writing project into her first novel, *The Last Day the Dogbushes Bloomed* (1968), and for that novel won the first of many writing prizes.

Her early work, including *Something in the Wind* (1971), *Fancy Strut* (1973), *Black Mountain Breakdown* (1981), and *Cakewalk* (1981), a book of short stories, shows a writer developing her craft by exploring narrative uses of point of view and setting. Her fifth novel, *Oral History* (1983), marks Smith's emergence as a major voice in contemporary American literature. Her reputation has grown with subsequent works: *Family Linen* (1985), *Fair and Tender Ladies* (1988), *Me and My Baby View the Eclipse* [short stories] (1990), and *The Devil's Dream* (1992). Critics disagree about which of these is her best, but the consensus is that *Oral History* and *Fair and Tender Ladies* are superior to the others.

Smith's use of clearly delineated narrative voices is one of her strengths as a writer. Her point of view is limited omniscient (either third or first person), often shifting among various characters. In their distinctive voices, Smith's characters tell of their struggles with everyday problems, conflicts that focus the characters' finding, or failing to find, niches for themselves in their environments. The situations and perspectives the characters present are carefully, and frequently humorously, woven together into stories that combine linguistic vitality with richly textured settings.

Because of the strength of her powerful rural narrative voices and of the compelling physical details of her settings, Smith is frequently listed as a southern or regional writer, but her work requires broader attention and interpretation. Like many contemporary writers, especially southerners, Smith's use of ordinary people speaking colloquially and humorously of ordinary events makes her work appear superficial. Beneath the surface simplicity, however, run complex patterns of both actual and mythic cultural influences in conflict with individuals' (especially women's) psychological needs for self-expression and self-actualization. Critics are just beginning to mine those depths to develop commentaries not only on Smith's artistry but also on contemporary women's realities.

Smith juggles teaching creative writing and writing her own fiction, continuing to encourage the voices of emerging writers like Jill McCorkle, one of her former students, as well as to develop her powers as a writer and as a voice for the people about whom she writes.

• Lucinda H. MacKethan, "Artists and Beauticians: Balance in Lee Smith's Fiction," *Southern Literary Journal* 15, no. 1 (Fall 1982): 3–14. Anne Goodwyn Jones, "The World of Lee Smith," *Southern Quarterly* 22, no. 1 (Fall 1983): 115–139. Harriette C. Buchanan, "Lee Smith: The Storyteller's Voice," in *Southern Women Writers: The New Generation*, ed. Tonette Bond Inge (1990), pp. 324–345. Virginia A. Smith, "On Regionalism, Women's Writing, and Writing as a Woman: A Conversation with Lee Smith," *The Southern Review* 26, no. 4 (October 1990): 784–795. Dorothy Combs Hill, *Lee Smith* (1991).

Harriette C. Buchanan

SOCIAL COMEDY. In *A Very Serious Thing: Women's Humor and American Culture*, Nancy Walker discusses some of the reasons why women have traditionally been excluded from the study of American comic literature. Walker explains that while both male and female writers of humor are seen as "outsider" figures, usually observing the dominant system only to point out its flaws, the "outsider" role is especially important for the woman writer. "The humorist is at odds with the publicly espoused values of the culture, overturning its sacred cows, pointing out the nakedness of not only the Emperor, but also the politician, the pious, and the pompous," declares Walker. She goes on to assert that

> for women to adopt this role means that they must break out of the passive, subordinate position mandated for them by centuries of patriarchal tradition and take on the power accruing to those who reveal the shams, hypocrisies, and incongruities of the dominant culture. To be a woman and a humorist is to confront and subvert the very power that keeps women powerless, and at the same time to risk alienating those upon whom women are dependent for economic survival.

It is difficult to laugh openly at the boss, the father, the teacher—any figure who holds power directly over you. Dorothy *Parker, one of the most important writers of comic fiction and essays from the 1920s to the 1950s, argues that irreverence is essential for the creation of humorous prose: "There must be courage; there must be no awe.... There must be a disciplined eye and a wild mind." "Women use comedy," argues contemporary Pulitzer Prize-winning playwright Wendy *Wasserstein, author of the widely applauded Broadway hit, *The Heidi Chronicles:* "You use it to get a laugh but you use it deliberately, too."

There is a history of women humorists in America, although it has only recently been studied by feminist scholars. Writers such as Mercy Otis *Warren (1728–1814), "Fanny *Fern"/Sara Willis Parton (1811–72), Frances Miriam Berry Whitcher (1814–52), "Josiah Allen's Wife"/Marietta *Holley (1836–1926), Alice Duer Miller (1874–1942), Agnes Repplier (1855–1950), Helen Rowland (1875–1950), and Shirley

*Jackson (1919–65), should be added to the more contemporary list that would include Erica *Jong *(Fear of Flying)*, Nora Ephron *(Heartburn)*, Rita Mae *Brown *(Southern Discomfort)*, Ntozake * Shange *(for colored girls who have considered suicide/when the rainbow is enuf)*, Jane Wagner *(The Search for Signs of Intelligent Life in the Universe)*, and Cynthia Heimel *(Sex Tips for Girls)*, among others. From Louisa May *Alcott's short stories to Zora Neale *Hurston's *I Love Myself When I Am Laughing* to Anita *Loos's *Gentlemen Prefer Blonds* to Erma Bombeck's *Family—The Ties that Bind. . . . and Gag*, rebellion against the authority that men have historically possessed over women has always been a staple of women's humor. As Louisa May Alcott wrote of a harried female character in 1872, "[H]er sense of the ludicrous supported her through many trying scenes."

Some of the most powerful and provocative women writers of American literature are women of color, and their writing shows the strain, tensions, and rage of writing as an outsider who is even farther away from the center. Women writers of color have produced some of the wittiest satires on American life. Alice *Childress, a twentieth-century playwright and author, continually draws her audience's attention to the ironies of a life that says black women aren't fully human. As Mary Helen Washington tells us, the usual plot for the woman in fiction does not allow the heroine to triumph because to triumph is to undercut her supposedly frail femininity; in such a case the female protagonist "cannot savor the satisfaction of her actions because the very act of taking control of her life is also, for a woman, a fall from grace."

Often, submerged anger is covered or screened by humor, even though humor does not purge the writer's sense of distress. Flannery *O'Connor wrote in 1955 that "I am interested in making up a good case for distortion, as I am coming to believe it is the only way to make people see." O'Connor is, in this sentiment, echoing a history of women writers who felt a need to "distort" their truths in order to reach their audience. As nineteenth-century poet Emily *Dickinson coolly writes, "The Truth I do not dare to know I muffle with a jest." Dickinson also counseled her readers to "Tell the Truth, But Tell It Slant" since "Success in Circuit Lies."

Often the most profound forces of rage, recognition, and power were carefully concealed by women writers in order that their words not be suppressed completely. And in part because they told the truth "slanted" through humor, there is a great tradition of women's writing in America, going back to the colonial days of the mid-seventeenth century. At that time, for example, Anne *Bradstreet's poetry was published as the first collection of original poems produced in America. Bradstreet employs the sort of sly subversiveness that will be a characteristic of women's humor in America when she writes: "If what I do prove well, it won't advance. / They'll say it's stolen, or else it was by chance." Bradstreet's refusal to be treated as less able than her male contemporaries is another hallmark of American women's humor: wit is both evidence of—and born out of—a sense of defiance. Through intricate weavings of politics, aphoristic commentary, romance, and narrative, these works gain their profound power from small and large transgressions. These writers delightedly and unrelentingly expose the myths that have helped keep women "in their place." And they have begun to undo the system by refusing to participate within their assigned roles.

[*See also* Drama; Humor.]

• Dorothy Parker, *The Portable Dorothy Parker* (1973). Nancy Walker, *A Very Serious Thing: Women's Humor and American Culture* (1988). Nancy Walker and Zita Dressner, eds., *Redressing the Balance: American Women's Literary Humor from Colonial Times to the Present* (1988). Esther Cohen, "Uncommon Woman: An Interview with Wendy Wasserstein," in *Last Laughs: Perspectives on Women and Gender*, ed. Regina Barreca (1988). Reginia Barreca, ed., *New Perspectives on Women and Comedy* (1992).

Regina Barreca

SOCIOLOGISTS. Women have made important contributions to sociological writing since the discipline was formally established in U.S. universities in the late 1800s. However, because women sociologists often worked from bases outside the academy or from applied departments such as social work or home economics, their contributions to sociology have not been fully recognized. Revisionist scholarship, especially the works of Mary Jo Deegan (1988, 1991; Deegan and Hill 1987), Patricia Hill Collins (1990), and Paula Giddings (1984) have illuminated historical contributions by women to sociological thought and revealed common themes in the writings of women across sociological eras.

This essay reviews sociological writing by U.S. women in three eras: the late 1800s through the beginning of World War II; World War II to the rebirth of feminism in the early 1960s; and the mid-1960s to the present. Each period was marked by variations in women's status in universities and dominant modes of thought in the discipline. In the earliest period, women sociologists developed a distinctive approach to sociological writing that declined in the middle era. The contemporary period has produced an outpouring of scholarship by and about women, much of it reviving themes articulated by the earliest women sociologists. However, many contemporary writers are unaware of works of the founding sisters and regard the articulation of a distinctive women's approach to sociology as a recent phenomenon.

The Pre–World War II Era. When the University of Chicago opened the first U.S. sociology department in 1892, its faculty included the noted social reformer Jane *Addams and several other women. Addams and the women graduate students at Chicago were frequent contributors to the *American Journal of Sociology (AJS)*, initiated from the department in 1895. Marion Talbott, a faculty member, was one of the journal's early editors. Women were hired because at the time Chicago was regarded as a culturally impoverished region to be shunned by educated gentlemen.

Most women faculty, like Addams, had strong ties outside academia. Deegan credits the largely female staff and residents of Hull House with defining the substantive and methodological focus attributed to the men of the Chicago School of sociology. The *Hull House Maps and Papers*, published in 1893, provided a blueprint for the meticulous, empirical, activist-oriented field studies that characterized the Chicago department. The Hull House collective worked in nonhierarchical, collaborative research teams; focused inquiry on critical needs of women, children, and immigrants; and forged ties between researchers and Chicago philanthropists who funded reformist-oriented research. Other woman-centered collectives, for example one at Mount Holyoke College, produced significant research and fostered a distinctive woman's approach to sociology.

British sociologist Jennifer Platt has reported that women collected many of the "firsthand" accounts in the writings of male Chicago sociologists. Case history materials for W. I. Thomas's *The Unadjusted Girl*, for instance, came largely from files of female Chicago caseworkers or were collected by Thomas's graduate assistant, Jessie Taft, who now is remembered more as a social worker than as a sociologist.

Most women working in sociology departments were white, but Hill Collins and Giddings demonstrate the sociological relevance of writings of African-American women such as Maria Stewart, Anna Julia *Cooper, Sojourner *Truth, Mary McLeod *Bethune, and Ida B. *Wells-Barnett. The woman-centered collectives drew upon ideas of women of color and maintained ties to thinkers such as Wells Bar-

nett and Irene Diggs, but much work remains to be done to recover contributions of women of color writing outside of academia.

The work of early women sociologists usually was empirical, often quantitative. Demography was, in Deegan's terms, a "woman's corner" within sociology when mathematics was regarded as routine work suitable for women. However, early issues of *AJS* contained sophisticated quantitative papers by women. Amy Hewes, a Chicago student later on the Mount Holyoke faculty, published one of the earliest examples of mathematical modeling of social processes in *AJS* in 1899.

The empirical, social problems-oriented books and articles by women sociologists contrasted with the theoretical, abstract, and philosophical writings of men. A paper by Jane Addams in the first issue of *AJS* considered the "industry" of paid domestic employment. Addams wanted "to present the industry from the point of view of those women who are working in the households for wages." This work exemplified persistent themes in women's sociological writing: a focus on women's issues, preservation of voices of women subjects, and an explicit reform orientation—themes clearly reflected in ideas of contemporary feminist sociologists.

In the early 1900s, when Chicago and other universities attracted more male faculty, women were forced out of sociology into social work, home economics, or other applied areas, or out of academia altogether. In the East, women worked in women's colleges, government, or industry. Between 1920 and 1940 women publishing in *AJS* or in the more recently founded (1935) *American Sociological Review* were more likely than male authors to come from nonuniversity, nonsociology bases. Although women produced important sociology from these sites, their writings were ignored by sociologists.

Into the pre-World War II years the distinctive orientations of women sociologists of earlier generations persisted. One example was *Mothers of the South* by Margaret Jarman Hagood. As a government employee in the 1930s, Hagood produced the first systematic study of southern farm women. Although her richly detailed account usually is labeled demography, it resembles contemporary feminist case studies. The text preserves subjects' voices, and Hagood explicitly critiques public policies that are senseless from women's perspectives. Hagood reveals some of her personal biography and recounts in detail the nature of her relationships with subjects, who described her as "not so far from former country ways to be able to understand." Her research and the activism flowing from it addressed issues critical to women's well-being, such as access to reliable contraception.

World War II to the New Wave of Feminism. As World War II neared, women's sociological writings altered dramatically, partly in response to women's changing status in universities and shifts in the dominant forms of sociological research. Women's writing appeared in sociology journals slightly less frequently than in earlier years, and women's writing became more similar to men's. Many women coauthored with men of the same surnames, presumably their husbands. Almost invariably, women were the junior authors.

Women's involuntary departure from sociology departments in the 1920s left them with no secure institutional base from which to pass on women's distinctive forms of sociological writing. Jane Addams lost the considerable influence she held within sociology because of her pacifism in World War I. Male sociologists moved farther away from research on pressing social issues that had anchored sociology departments in the 1920s and became more concerned with "objective" applications of statistical techniques. Increasingly, sociological research cost money. Funding came from the military, other government agencies, and private companies, which favored male researchers and the research styles of men. Although women inside and outside the academy still collected and prepared data for statistical analysis, their perspectives rarely guided interpretations and their names rarely appeared on finished products.

The Columbia Bureau of Social Research employed many women in the 1950s, but only a few of them became prominent sociologists. Women scholars who published in *AJS* and *ASR* occasionally wrote on topics ignored by men, such as experiences of military women, but more often their work was indistinguishable from males' in content and form. After World War II, as returning military men flooded graduate programs, women's pursuit of advanced degrees in sociology diminished sharply.

Some of the freshest voices in sociology during this era were those of immigrant women such as Mirra Komarovsky. Her *Blue-Collar Marriage* (1964, with Jane Philips) illuminated experiences of women overlooked by social scientists. Although regarded as conservative by many contemporary feminists, Komarovsky's focus and methods were innovative for the times and served as the starting point for contemporary feminist analysis of women in families. Completing training and starting careers during this era were women sociologists, some of them wives of male sociologists, who became early leaders of the resurgence of feminist analysis in the mid-1960s. These included Jessie Bernard, Alice Rossi, and Helen Magill Hughes, who recounted their experiences in a 1973 special issue of *AJS* edited by Joan Huber that was an important landmark in feminist analysis. Rose Hum Lee, who authored several *AJS* articles on Chinese Americans, became the first Chinese-American chair of a sociology department at Roosevelt University.

Thus, although the distinctive voices of women sociologists were muted during this period that Deegan denotes "the dark era of patriarchal ascendancy," women formulated the beginnings of a broad-based critique of masculine bias in sociology that reached fruition in the next era.

The Second Wave of Feminism: The Mid-1960s to the Present. The rebirth of feminism in the United States produced a powerful critique of male bias in sociological writing. The aforementioned special issue of *AJS* and a collection entitled *Another Voice*, edited by Marcia Millman and Rosabeth Moss Kanter, were widely read, influential works. Feminist critics took sociologists to task for their exclusion, misrepresentation, and trivialization of women in universities and in society. Not all women sociologists regarded themselves as feminists nor responded to the feminist critique, but gender research increased dramatically. Women's enrollment in graduate programs also mushroomed in the 1970s.

New debates framed along gender lines emerged over appropriate topics, methods, conceptual frames, and applications of sociological work. Between 1974 and 1985 the amount of research by and about women published in major sociology journals more than doubled. Women's work exhibited distinctive patterns compared with men's. It was less apt to be quantitative or funded, but more apt to be coauthored. As in earlier eras, women sociologists collaborated across disciplines, with scholars in areas such as *women's studies or ethnic studies, and with persons outside universities. But now women sociologists worked to institutionalize feminist writing within academic sociology. Professional organizations, such as Sociologists for Women in Society (SWS), created professional development programs to teach scholars how to produce and publish feminist work. In collaboration with the new, rapidly growing section on sex and gender of the American Sociological Association, SWS launched *Gender and Society* as an outlet for feminist sociological research. Texts and readers on feminist sociological theory proliferated as courses on the sociology of women and gender prospered.

White women were most prominent initially in the resurgence of feminist sociology, but by the 1980s women of color—for the first time from within as well as outside universities—took part in criticism and redirection of the discipline. The Center for Research on Women at Memphis State University was the focal point for creation and distribution for new scholarship placing race, class, and gender at the center of sociological writing. *Gender and Society* is guided by a multiethnic editorial board and scholars representative of diverse feminist perspectives. Women sociologists increasingly analyzed women's experience cross-culturally, a trend strengthened by the influx of foreign women into American programs.

Women's sociological writing since the mid-1960s revives many of the themes of the pre-World War II era, but with greater sensitivity to diversity of experiences of women across race, ethnicity, nationality, social class, age, and sexual orientation. Scholars and activists work collaboratively in production of knowledge and promotion of social change. Sociologists probe the unknown realities of women's lives, often with an eye toward reform. Critical reflection on the research process and the writing of a feminist sociology to deconstruct male-biased accounts of social life are common themes.

Women's sociological writing, like women's writing in other disciplines, provokes criticism by opponents of diversity and multiculturalism in academia. Debates over appropriate standards for sociological research are aired in writings of sociologists and in the more private discourses surrounding hiring, promotion, and tenure in academic departments. Whether women's writings will alter sociology in fundamental ways, or develop as a separate line of inquiry, is still unresolved. At the moment, however, writings by women sociologists are on the upswing in volume and influence.

• Jane Addams, "A Belated Industry," *American Journal of Sociology* no. 1 (1885): 536–547. Amy Hewes, "Seminar Notes: Social Institutions and the Riemann Surface," *American Journal of Sociology* no. 5 (1899): 392–403. Margaret Jarman Hagood, *Mothers of the South: Portraiture of the White Tenant Farm Woman* (1939; reprint, 1977). Mirra Komarovsky and Jane Philips, *Blue-Collar Marriages* (1964). Joan Huber, ed., *American Journal of Sociology* Vol. 79, (1973). Marcia Millman and Rosabeth Moss Kanter, *Another Voice: Feminist Perspectives on Social Life and Social Science* (1975). Ann Firor Scott, Introduction to *Mothers of the South: Portraiture of the White Tenant Farm Woman* (1977) by Margaret Jarman Hagood. Rosalind Rosenberg, *Beyond Separate Spheres: The Intellectual Roots of Modern Feminism* (1982). Paula Giddings, *When and Where I Enter* (1984). Kathryn B. Ward and Linda Grant, "The Feminist Critique and a Decade of Published Research in Sociology Journals," *Sociological Quarterly* no. 26 (1985): 139–157. Mary Jo Deegan and Michael Hill, eds., *Women and Symbolic Interaction* (1987). Dorothy E. Smith, *The Everyday World as Problematic: A Feminist Sociology* (1987). Janet Saltzman Chafetz, *Feminist Sociology: An Overview of Contemporary Theories* (1988). Mary Jo Deegan, *Jane Addams and the Men of the Chicago School* (1988). Patricia Hill Collins, *Black Feminist Thought: Knowledge, Consciousness and The Politics of Empowerment* (1990). Mary Jo Deegan, *Women in Sociology: A Bio-Bibliographical Sourcebook* (1991). Linda Grant and Kathryn B. Ward, "Gender and Publishing in Sociology." *Gender and Society* no. 5 (1991): 207–223. Kathryn B. Ward and Linda Grant, "On a Wavelength of Their Own? Women and Sociological Theory," *Current Perspectives in Social Theory* no. 11 (1991): 117–140. Shulamit Reinharz, *Feminist Methods in Social Research* (1992).

Kathryn Ward

SONTAG, Susan (b. 1933), essayist, fiction writer, filmmaker, screenwriter, philosopher of culture. Sontag belongs to what Russell Jacoby defines in *The Last Intellectuals* (1987) as a rare class: the public intellectual. At North Hollywood High she shunned *Reader's Digest* assignments for the headier world of ideas in the *Partisan Review*. At twenty-six, she became a contributing editor of *Commentary*, entering the New York liberal intelligentsia that had already captured her imagination. Fascination with the ethics and aesthetics of modernism, especially its European forms, has inspired Sontag's prolific, often controversial, career.

With *Against Interpretation* (1966), she departed from the older New York liberalism, particularly its resistance to popular culture; "Notes on 'Camp' " drew criticism for its trendiness. To the contrary, this essay illustrates Sontag's ability to sense the intellectual roots of social movements. Constructing the essay in numbered sections, she connects "camp" with the European postmodernist trend toward fragmentation—a trend more familiar to her in 1966 than to her American critics. Walter Benjamin and Roland Barthes she considers kindred spirits.

On Photography (1977; National Book Critics' Circle Award) continues Sontag's exploration of the modernist aesthetic as modified and eventually molded by photographic imagery. Its power is insidious, she complains: "The camera doesn't rape, or even possess, though it may presume, intrude, trespass, distort, exploit, and, at the farthest reach of metaphor, assassinate—all activities that . . . can be conducted from a distance." Sontag's assertion that "[t]here is an aggression implicit in every use of the camera." anticipates feminist film critics' reactions against the aggressive masculine "gaze" of the camera eye.

Illness as Metaphor (1978), written after Sontag's breast cancer, breaks out of the abstraction marking her earlier essays. Yet it revisits a critical issue: the need to distrust totalizing schemes offered to explain complex realities (a need that modernism, for Sontag, promises and repeatedly fails to answer). She critiques the treatment of cancer as metaphor for moral fault. Shrouding the disease in mystery and theorizing "cancer personalities" is more than cruel, she asserts; it impedes recovery. Sontag's antidote, here as elsewhere, is demystification. The same theme informs *AIDS and Its Metaphors* (1989).

Sontag's politics defy labeling; she writes, she has said, out of grief. This impulse, she observes, is both radical, in wanting to right fundamental wrongs, and conservative, "because we know that ... so much is being destroyed" ("Nadine Gordimer and Susan Sontag: In Conversation," *Listener*, 23 May 1985, 16–17). Her restless, surprising career exemplifies the paradoxes of *modernism itself.

• Sohnya Sayres, *Susan Sontag: The Elegiac Modernist* (1990).

Sally Greene

SOUTH ASIAN–AMERICAN WOMEN WRITING. At this time in political history, the geographical-cultural area designated as South Asia consists of Bangladesh, India, the Maldive Islands, Pakistan, and Sri Lanka. Afghanistan is sometimes included as well. The cultural and political complexities and complications of South Asia are reflected in the different literary forms and languages of South Asian literature. The two volumes of *Women Writing in India* (Susie Tharu and K. Lalita, 1991 and 1993) make it clear that South Asian women writers are not a modern, Western-influenced phenomenon. Sucheta Mazumdar's introductory essay and Judy Young's appendix in *Making Waves: An Anthology of Writings By and About South Asian American Women* (1989) contain important information on the history of South Asian women in America.

The literary *canons of both Asia and the West have influenced the literary works of South Asian–American women writers. South Asian–American writing is also influenced, and often dominated, by the oral traditions of South Asian women's narratives, songs, instructions, and gossip. Santha Rama *Rau may be the earliest twentieth-century South Asian woman writer to have gained a large audience for her works, which are based on her experiences as a South Asian woman who lives in the West and has traveled widely. Besides the writers discussed in the individual essays in this volume, there are many other important South Asian women authors, including the poets Chitra De-

vakaruni (U.S.) and Uma Parameshwaran (Canada), leading novelists such as Anita Desai, and other writers from South Asia, such as Jean Arasanyagam from Sri Lanka, who have participated in the Iowa University Writer's Workshop. A number of well-known South Asian–American women writers write in their South Asian languages rather than in English. American literature written in Asian languages has a long history, but it has remained basically invisible in the on-going discourse regarding American identity and the creation of an American literature.

The choice between producing literature that is basically "interrogative," nourished by the ambiguities of unresolved issues, or literature that is basically "declarative," which states and describes issues with an apparently greater degree of self-assurance, takes on interesting dimensions in South Asian–American literature. The importance of this issue can be seen in the South Asian American authors' choice of geographic and cultural landscapes to form the narrative background and the underlying context of their works. In the first category are works by writers who live and write in the West but place their characters explicitly in South Asia. Within the narrative there is no acknowledgement of the author's own physical distance from South Asia, or of her possible emotional or intellectual dislocation from the landscape of her work. The works are created for a Western/Westernized audience. In this literature, which is often a declarative description of South Asia, the writer appears as a "middleperson," uninvolved with either side except as an interpreter. The temptation to use explanatory language, parentheses, footnotes, and appendices is difficult to resist or circumvent, and may contribute toward keeping this literature in the disastrous realm of "the exotic."

In the second category are works that portray South Asians who have lived in the West as *expatriates or *immigrants, and who return to South Asia either as residents or visitors. There is a nightmare quality in these works as women and men find themselves in the physical, cultural, and personal landscape where the once familiar has become confusingly alien and uncontrollable. This literature, which may also contain long descriptions and statements, is no longer a cultural offering translated for an alien audience. It is an attempt to understand the process of translating one's self to one's self without keeping an anxious eye on explaining one's self to the people of another culture.

The concluding chapter of Bapsi *Sidhwa's novel, *Cracking India* (1991), begins with a quote from Iqbal asking for "power to talk."

Meena *Alexander's novel, *Nampally Road* (1991), concludes with the protagonist looking at the raped woman she has helped, and stating that the woman's "mouth was healing slowly." The image of the spoken word and the mouth, either to empower or to confuse a woman, appears often in the works of South Asian–American women writers in all three categories. But it is in the third category of works in which many of the writers look toward healing their mouths and actively joining the voices of American literature.

The choice of locale in this third category of fiction is America. The writers now present people and events, the issues around cultural and personal identities, and the events that occur when cultures collide, not on Asian soil, but within the physical and cultural landscape of twentieth-century America.

The literature of the first category is mainly the literature of explanation based on the memory of public and private history. It may be a literature through which the South Asian woman reassures herself and her Western audience of her physical and cultural origins. The works in the second and third categories grope for explanations amid cultural confusion. The process of remembering and putting together the fragments of memories and realities of South Asia and America begins in the secondary category of works. In the third category the remembering becomes an attempt at revisioning and redefining the landscape, the people, and the events, as specifically South Asian–American. These three categories either merge or become polarized as the writers attempt to enter the "mainstream" of American literature.

The South Asian–American writer is seldom allowed to forget that she writes in the midst of an audience that generally views her as neither an authentic nor an important voice of the American experience. The South Asian–American writer who writes in English is aware that she has inherited the language of the colonizers of her mother country, a language that has taken on its own South Asian texture of sounds and meanings and that may disturb other English speakers. Given these complications, what English does the South Asian–American writer use? Does she write in the cadences of South Asian English? Does she assimilate into the English of the dominant American canon? Or does she manipulate the different languages of American discourse to forge her own language? How does she recreate her basically non-English world without allowing the use of English to diminish her world? For example, if she chooses to clip her stories short to suit twentieth-century literary canons of the U.S. and her American publisher's demands, she can injure the basic experience of time, space, and narrative, the essential language of her experience in Asia and America. And of course there is always the danger that in the process of possessing the language and the land, the writer herself may become possessed by the language and the land. This, in turn, may either enable her to create a vibrantly unique literature or force her to mold her works to fit existing canons.

As one reads with appreciation the increasing volume of works of South Asian–American women writers, one gains a growing respect for them as writers. They combine landscapes, cultures, and languages and transform them into a literature that is defiantly contemporary, one that insists on expanding our expectations of American literature.

[*See also* Asian-American Writing; Assimilation; Citizenship; Ethnicity and Writing; Immigrant Writing.]

• Maxine P. Fisher, *The Indians of New York City* (1980). Toronto South Asian Review, *A Meeting of Streams: South Asian Canadian Literature* (1985). Parmatma Saran, *The Asian Indian Experience in the United States* (1985). Roshni Rustomji, ed., *South Asian Women Writers: The Immigrant Experience*, special issue of the *Journal of South Asian Literature* 21, no. 1 (Winter–Spring 1986). Bharati Mukherjee and Ranu Vanikar, eds., *Writers of the Indian Commonwealth*, special issue of the *Literary Review* 29, no. 4 (Summer 1986). Ketu H. Katrak and R. Radhakrishna, eds., *Desh-Videsh: South Asian Expatriate Writing and Art*, special issue of the *Massachusetts Review* 29, no. 4 (Winter 1988–1989). Joan M. Jensen, *Passage from India: Asian Indian Immigrants in North America* (1988). Jane Singh, ed., *South Asians in North America: An Annotated and Selected Bibliography* (1988). Priya Agarwal, *Passage from India: Post-1965 Indian Immigrants and Their Children* (1991). Emmanuel S. Nelson, ed., *Writers of the Indian Diaspora* (1992). The Women of South Asian Descent Collective, eds., *Our Feet Walk the Sky: Women of the South Asian Diaspora* (1993).

Roshni Rustomji-Kerns

SOUTHEAST ASIAN-AMERICAN WRITING.

Before 1975 there was no Southeast Asian literature to speak of in the United States, let alone a literature produced by women coming from such background. But 1975 changed all that. With the fall of South Vietnam, Laos, and Cambodia there came a large influx of Vietnamese, Laotians, and Cambodians that has since grown to about a million even though in recent years the numbers of immigrants have fallen off.

The urge to express themselves in English surfaced first in schools, where almost overnight hundreds of thousands of children from these backgrounds turned up. To make them feel at home they were sometimes asked to write about themselves, their families, and their traditions—festivals, songs and dances, music and fashion, grandmother's tales, many of the things that women tend to be the repository of. If before 1975 there were only a couple of slim collections of Vietnamese tales written by women, such as Cong-Huyen Ton-Nu Nha-Trang's *Favorite Stories from Vietnam* and *More Favorite Stories from Vietnam*, after that watershed year there literally was a small flood. Among these works were *Beyond the East Wind* (1976), written by Duong Van Quyen in collaboration with Jewell R. Coburn; *Vietnamese Folktales* (1978), a cooperative product of Lan Nguyen and Lynne Burmark; *The Brocaded Slipper and Other Vietnamese Tales* (1982) by Lynette D. Vuong; and *Under the Starfruit Tree: Folktales from Vietnam* (1989) by Alice M. Terada, to supplement similar collections by men or previous well-known collections by American authors such as Gail B. Graham's *The Beggar in the Blanket and Other Vietnamese Tales* (1970) or Mona Ruoff's *From the Dragon's Cloud* (1979). This work parallels the work done by Vietnamese woman authors in Australia and elsewhere in the English-speaking world, such as Nguyen Thi Hong's *Five Vietnamese Folktales*, Tran My-Van's *Folk Tales from Indochina* (1987) and Morag Loh's *Stories and Storytellers from Indo-China* (1985). Jewell Coburn also collaborated with Lao and Cambodian informants to produce *Encircled Kingdom, Legends and Folktales of Laos* (1979) and *Khmers, Tigers, and Talisman: From the History and Legends of Mysterious Cambodia* (1978).

The life histories of Southeast Asian women were apparently also of great interest, as witnessed by their inclusion in such works as James A. Freeman's *Hearts of Sorrow: Vietnamese-American Lives* (1989), Al Santoli's *New Americans: An Oral History* (1988), or John Tenhula's *Voices from Southeast Asia: The Refugee Experience in the United States* (1991). But they could form the subject of whole books; Teeda Butt Mam's life story is retold in a volume by Joan D. Criddle and T. B. Mam, *To Destroy You Is No Loss* (1987), and her extended family is featured in Joan D. Criddle's *Bamboo and Butterflies: From Refugee to Citizen* (1992). The lives of Vietnamese women in the U.S. were made the subject of a movie by Trinh Thi *Minh Ha, who is now teaching film directing at the University of San Francisco, whereas the transition of Southeast Asian women to American life and their changing roles are being made the subject of a slide-and-photo presentation by Ang Robinson and Lisa Falk. But among such outstanding efforts at presenting Southeast Asian women and their traditions must be counted Amy Catlin's *Virgins, Orphans, Widows and Bards: Songs of Hmong Women* (1987), and *Textiles and Texts: Arts of Hmong Women from Laos,* co-authored by Amy Catlin and Dixie Swift (1987). The most poetic rendering of a Vietnamese woman's life is found in *Shallow Graves: Two Women and Vietnam*, a book-length poem by Wendy W. Larsen and Tran Thi Nga (1986), whereas Le Ly Hayslip's *When Heaven and Earth Changed Places* (1989), a best-seller soon to be made into a movie by Oliver Stone, is unfortunately a somewhat sensationalized version of her experience. But the most thoughtful, sometimes hilarious, but always poignant writings by Vietnamese women about their experience in America are being written in Vietnamese (and published here) by such authors as Tran Dieu Hang, Le Thi Hue, and especially Tran Kim Lan, a teacher in Boston and the author of *Gio Dem* ("Night Wind").

Concerned with the education of the second generation, many Southeast Asian women turned to writing for their children. Sivone Brahm, for instance, writes about Cambodia and retells Cambodian tales in English. Tran Kim Lan authored a book on *Tet, the New Year,* superbly illustrated by Vo-Dinh Mai (1992). Truong Anh Thuy went further and produced a little gem of a book, a bilingual small epic about Vietnam and Vietnamese children in America entitled *Truong Ca Loi Me Ru/A Mother's Lullaby* (1989).

Vietnamese women's writings are also found in translation, in such collections as James Banerian's *Vietnamese Short Stories* (1986) or the anthology edited by Nguyen Ngoc Bich, *War and Exile: A Vietnamese Anthology* (1989). A famous short work by Nha Ca, "A Story for Lovers," appears in both books but is translated by different hands. Earlier, Minh Quan's prize-winning story, "My Milk Runs Dry," appeared in *Stories from Asia* (1973). Pergamon Press in New York has published what is possibly the first translation into English of a Vietnamese novel by a woman writer, Minh Duc Hoai Trinh's *This Side, That Side,* a story about the Vietnamese women caught in the ideological war in Vietnam. Other Southeast Asian women, such as Lucy Nguyen Hong Nhiem, a faculty member at Amherst, work as translators of Vietnamese literature while Cong-Huyen Ton-Nu Nha-Trang has produced so far the most comprehensive survey of Vietnamese women's writing in English (in *Vietnam Forum*).

Vietnamese women have also made a mark in such fields as journalism and film. Tran Thi Tuong-Nhu, an anthropologist by training, is now a columnist for the *San Jose Mercury News,* and Vu Thanh Thuy, chosen a few years back as the Ortho Woman of the 21st Century, among others, works for the *San Diego Union* as Tu Anh-Huong did for the *Washington Post.* Kieu Chinh, the movie actress, is the subject of a multi-author bilingual Vietnamese-English retrospective, *Kieu Chinh: Hanoi-Saigon-Hollywood* (1991). Women's liberation under Communism is examined critically by Hoang Ngoc Thanh Dung in "To Serve the Cause of Women's Liberation" (in *To Be Made Over: Tales of Socialist Reeducation in Vietnam*, edited and translated by Huynh Sanh Thong, 1988). In criticism, Trinh Thi Minh Ha joins the ranks of the world's avant-garde with such works as *Un Art Sans Oeuvre* (1981); *African Spaces: Design for Living in Upper Volta*, written in collaboration with Jean Paul Bourdier (1985); *En Minuscules*, a book of poems (1987); *Woman, Native, Other*, on *post-colonialism and *feminism (1988); and *She, the Inappropriate Other* (1987), on postcolonial women as writing subjects.

[*See also* Asian-American Writing; South Asian–American Writing; Korean-American Writing; Japanese-American Writing; Chinese-American Writing; Filipino-American Writing; Polynesian-American Writing; Citizenship; Immigrant Writing; Ethnicity and Writing; Assimilation.]

Nguyen Ngoc Bich

SOUTHERLAND, Ellease (b. 1943), novelist, poet, essayist, and educator. Born in Brooklyn, Ellease Southerland has lived in Jamaica, Queens, New York, since she was nine. Her two novels, *Let the Lion Eat Straw* (1979) and *A Feast of Fools* (currently in manuscript), are rooted in the experiences of her own remarkable family. She writes about this family in the memoir, "I Got a Horn, You Got a Horn" for Alex Harris's *A World Unsuspected: Portraits of Southern Childhood* (1987): "we were in this world [New York], but not of this world."

While Southerland specifically refers to her parents' ties to the black South, her family was "not of this world" in other ways also. Like Kora in *Lion*, Ellease was the oldest daughter of fifteen children. And although there was plenty of hardship, what distinguishes both her family and the fictional Torch family is the intensity and creativity of their lives. There were morning exercises, full participation in their father's storefront church, and choral and instrumental performances. At ten, Southerland decided to be a poet and for years conducted monthly Poetry Sundays at her father's church. Ellease's mother's early death in 1965, the same year Southerland graduated from Queens College, left the family bereft and Ellease torn between her eagerness for independence and her sense of responsibility for her youngest siblings.

From 1966 to 1972 Southerland was a caseworker for New York City, and during that period she published her first poems. In 1974, she received an M.F.A. from Columbia. In 1975, her first book, the poetry collection *The Magic Sun Spins*, was published in London. Since 1973 she has taught at both the Borough of Manhattan Community College and at Pace University, where she is Poet-in-Residence. Such essays as "The Influence of Voodoo on the Fiction of Zora Neale *Hurston" (*Sturdy Black Bridges*, 1979), and "Egyptian Symbols and Contemporary Black Literature" (*Black Scholar*, Fall 1988), as well as her fiction, attest to her enduring interest in African cultural traditions and their relationship to African-American literature. With Egyptology, baking, travels to Africa—her last four trips to Africa have been to the Ibo Land of Nigeria—and music among her hobbies, she singles out hieroglyphs as something she likes better even than cake.

Let the Lion Eat Straw is Southerland's major publication to date. It has appeared in a Japanese edition, two British editions, and two more American editions. In telling the story of Abeba Torch, Southerland tells her own mother's story. Beautiful and moving to read, the novel is a stylistic achievement. It is accessible, as its having been voted by the American Library Association a "Best Book for Young Adults 1979" would suggest. Still, the scenes are represented with such brevity, intensity of images, and richness of allusion that the prose is akin to poetry. The chapter from *A Feast of Fools* that appears in *Breaking Ice: An Anthology of Contemporary African-American Fiction* (1990) promises comparable power and richness for this second novel. This time the main character is Kora Ada Torch, the eldest daughter from *Lion*. Southerland has referred to *Feast* as a "portrait of the artist" and as a celebration of Nigerian and African-American friendship.

• Jean W. Ross, *CA Interview with Ellease Southerland, in *Contemporary Authors*, ed. Hal May, vol. 107 (1983), pp. 481–482. Mary Hughes Brookhart, "Ellease Southerland," in *Dictionary of Literary Biography*, vol. 33: *Afro-American Fiction Writers after 1955*, eds. Thadious M. Davis and Trudier Harris (1984), pp. 239–244. "Southerland, Ellease," in *Black Writers: A Selection of Sketches from Contemporary Authors*, ed. Linda Metzger (1989), pp. 526–527.

Mary Hughes Brookhart

SOUTHERN WOMEN'S WRITING. Southern women writers have published poetry and drama, but the main body of their work has been in short and long fiction. Notable African-American poets include such writers as Frances Ellen Watkins *Harper (1825–1911), Anne *Spencer (1892–1975), Alice *Walker (b. 1944), and Nikki *Giovanni (b. 1943). Adrienne *Rich (b. 1929) is perhaps the best woman poet born in the South, but others—mostly forgotten today—are Margaret Junkin Preston (1820–1897), Lizette Woodworth Reese (1856–1935), and Beatrice Ravenel (1870–1956). Three distinguished women dramatists are Lillian *Hellman (1905–1984), Alice *Childress (b. 1920), and Beth *Henley (b. 1952).

Southern women writers began publishing in significant numbers from the 1830s to the 1860s, when the South was beginning to define itself as a separate section of the country. Many women wrote romantic, sentimental, melodramatic works that supported the slave-owning ideology of the South and sold in large numbers to an audience made up primarily of women; the novels are referred to as *domestic fiction. The women who wrote them generally published out of economic necessity. Among those writers are Caroline Gilman (1794–1888), Caroline *Hentz (1800–1856), E.D.E.N. *Southworth (1819–1899), and Augusta Evans Wilson (1835–1909). Gilman and Hentz were both born in New England and moved South with their husbands, Gilman to Charleston and Hentz to various posts in Kentucky, Alabama, and Georgia. Gilman's didactic works, such as *Recollections of a Southern Matron* (1838), made her the best-known southern woman writer from the 1830s to the 1850s. Among Hentz's many novels are two written to answer Harriet Beecher *Stowe's *Uncle Tom's Cabin* (1852); *The Planter's Northern Bride* (1851) and *Marcus Warland* (1852).

Southworth, the most prolific of the domestic novelists, published more than sixty novels, which earned her a generous income during her long life. Of all her works, the most popular was *The Hidden Hand* (1859). Wilson, too, was a popular novelist and a passionate Southerner who published her first novel at age twenty. Her most successful work was *St. Elmo* (1866), the story of the orphaned Edna Earl who becomes a famous writer and gives up her career to marry the Byronic hero, St. Elmo Murray, whom she reforms.

The domestic novelists dominated the sales of books during their period. At the same time two other women writers, Mary Boykin *Chesnut (1823–1886) and Harriet *Jacobs (1813–1897), were writing the records for which they later received recognition. Chesnut, the daughter and wife of slave-owners, was an intelligent, observant, and insightful recorder of her experiences in South Carolina and Richmond during the *Civil War. Readers can now consult her original diary for 1861 and 1865 in *The Private Mary Chesnut* (ed. C. Vann Woodward and Elisabeth Muhlenfeld, 1984) as well as her rewriting of the original diary some two decades after the war in *Mary Chesnut's Civil War* (ed. C. Vann Woodward, 1981). Harriet Jacobs's moving autobiography, which is set in North Carolina, *Incidents in the Life of a Slave Girl: Written by Herself*, was first published in 1861 under the *pseudonym Linda Brent and is now available in an edition by Jean Fagin Yellin (1987).

In the latter part of the nineteenth century the romantic novelists were replaced by writers with a more realistic vein whose fiction appealed especially to northern audiences after the Civil War. Much of this fiction was published in periodicals by well-born women who had traveled widely. Among those writers, who are generally labeled local colorists, are Sherwood Bonner (1849–1883) of Mississippi, Mary Noailles *Murfree (1850–1922) of Tennessee, Grace King (1852–1932) and Ruth McEnery Stuart (1852–1917) of Louisiana, and Constance Cary Harrison (1843–1920) of Virginia. Bonner published stories that included Negro dialect; she is credited with creating the Mammy character in fiction. Murfree, who published as Charles Egbert Craddock, earned excellent reviews for her first collection of stories set in remote communities, *In the Tennessee Mountains* (1884). King wrote of Louisiana Creoles to correct George Washington Cable's depictions, and Stuart set her humorous stories in Louisiana and in Arkansas. In many works Harrison depicted an idealized Virginia.

Kate *Chopin (1851–1904) is often included with the local colorists because of her fine short stories, which feature Creoles in Louisiana, but her work, particularly *The Awakening* (1899), transcends the genre. This novel, which realistically tells the story of the sexual awakening of Edna Pontellier and her attempt to emancipate herself from the cultural conventions of the Creoles, shocked contemporary reviewers. Rediscovered in the 1960s, *The Awakening* is considered a major text in American literature.

Ellen *Glasgow (1873–1945), whose career began as Chopin's ended, consciously reacted to the sentimental in her fiction and wrote realistically of her region. Glasgow employed her native Virginia materials in most of her nineteen novels, but, she explained, she applied "blood and irony" to them. Her large body of work, including such novels as *Barren Ground* (1925) and *The Sheltered Life* (1932), make her the first major woman writer of the South.

Glasgow's career began at the turn of the century, but her best work was published during the period from about 1920 to 1950, which is usually referred to as the Southern Literary Renaissance, when the national market was dominated by writers from the South. Glasgow, Katherine Anne *Porter (1890–1980), and Caroline *Gordon (1895–1981) are often included in discussions of the period. Porter wrote finely crafted short stories; among the best are those set in the South and featuring her autobiographical central character Miranda: "Old Mortality" (1935) and the stories in *The Old Order* (1955). Though not as well-known as Porter, Gordon published more fiction: six novels and three collections of short fiction. She is remembered for her short stories and for such novels as *Penhally* (1931) and *Aleck Maury, Sportsman* (1934).

Three other women writers associated with the Renaissance also excelled in the short story, though each published longer fiction: Eudora *Welty (b. 1909), Carson *McCullers (1917–1967), and Flannery *O'Connor (1925–1964). In her long career, Welty has published notable short stories in such volumes as *The Wide Net and Other Stories* (1943), excellent novels ranging from *Delta Wedding* (1946) to *The Optimist's Daughter* (1972), and an important autobiographical volume, *One Writer's Beginnings* (1984). Welty is the most distinguished living southern writer. McCullers' characters are most often about grotesques, lonely and searching for love. Two of her memorable works are the novel *The Member of the Wedding* (1946; adapted for the stage, 1950) and the novella *The Ballad of the Sad Cafe* (1951). O'Connor is known for her richly comic short stories, which often include bizarre elements as well as violence. Her work is shaped by her rural Georgia setting and her uncompromising religious beliefs. She published two novels, but her reputation rests primarily on the excellent short stories published in *A Good Man Is Hard to Find* (1955) and *Everything that Rises Must Converge* (1965).

Zora Neale *Hurston (1891–1960), whose work was ignored for many years, should be considered part of the Southern Renaissance. Now much respected as a novelist and folklorist, her best work is *Their Eyes Were Watching God* (1937). Other interesting work by women writers has not received much attention in discussions of the Renaissance. Frances *Newman (1883–1928) used southern materials to write two novels that are experimental in form and style, *The Hard-Boiled Virgin* (1926) and *Dead Lovers are Faithful Lovers* (1928). Evelyn *Scott (1893–1963) published many novels, among them a modernist work that told the story of the Civil War, *The Wave* (1929). Lillian Smith (1897–1966) wrote out of social commitment, as exemplified in her novel *Strange Fruit* (1944), which features miscegenation, and her autobiographical volume, *Killers of the Dream* (1949). Three proletarian novels, all set during the 1928 Gastonia textile strike, were written by southern women: Grace Lumpkin (b. 1892), *To Make My Bread* (1932); and Olive Tilford *Dargan,

who used the pseudonym Fielding Burke, (1869–1968), *Call Home the Heart* (1932); and Myra Page, *Gathering Storm* (1932).

The Southern Literary Renaissance is generally considered to have ended by about 1950, but there have been numbers of southern women publishing fine work since that time. Ellen Douglas, Elizabeth *Spencer, Shirley Ann Grau, and Doris *Betts form a bridge between the writers of the Renaissance and the great outpouring of fiction by southern women in the last two decades: among others, Alice *Walker, Lee *Smith, Bobbie Ann *Mason, Anne *Tyler, Ellen *Gilchrist, Beverly Lowry, Jill McCorkle, Gayl *Jones, Kaye Gibbons, Lisa Alter, Alice *Adams, Sherley Anne *Williams, Josephine Humphries, and Beth *Henley.

The history of southern women writers has not yet been written. In his 987-page *The South in American Literature: 1607–1900* (1954), Jay Hubbell devotes eight pages to a discussion of women writers between 1830 and 1865, including Augusta Jane Evans Wilson and Margaret Junkin Preston; Ellen Glasgow is covered in an epilogue on the twentieth century. Hubbell points out that "The place which Southern women writers made for themselves they made in spite of the disapproval of literary critics and often of timid and skeptical publishers."

In the last decade the history of southern women writers has been published in a number of books as women critics restructure a field that for many years emphasized the work of men. Anne Goodwyn Jones in *Tomorrow Is Another Day: The Woman Writer in the South, 1857–1936* (1981) analyzes the work of seven writers—from Augusta Evans Wilson to Margaret *Mitchell—with respect to each writer's responding to the "ideal of southern womanhood." In *Sacred Groves and Ravaged Gardens: The Fiction of Eudora Welty, Carson McCullers, and Flannery O'Connor* (1985), Louise Westling examines "the interrelations of a coherent, distinctively feminine literary tradition" by exploring the work of three writers who published their major work between 1940 and 1960. Lucinda MacKethan's study, *Daughters of Time: Creating Woman's Voice in Southern Story* (1990), traces the development in writers from Harriet Jacobs to Lee Smith in creating a distinctive female voice. Elizabeth Jane Harrison, in *Female Pastoral: Women Writers Re-Visioning the American South* (1991), looks at the work of seven writers, from Glasgow to Sherley Anne Williams, and identifies a female pastoral vision. Elizabeth Moss, in *Domestic Novelists in the Old South: Defenders of Southern Culture* (1992), studies the work of five popular novelists and argues that these writers "waged their ideological warfare" through their novels, a "form written exclusively by women for women."

In *Friendship and Sympathy: Communities of Southern Women Writers* (1992), Rosemary M. Magee brings together primary documents—letters, reviews, critical articles, interviews—that depict the interrelationships of a number of women writers, from Ellen Glasgow to Alice Walker and Anne Tyler. Two collections of essays—*Women Writers of the Contemporary South* (1984), edited by Peggy Whitman Prenshaw, and *Southern Women Writers: The New Generation* (1990)—edited by Tonette Bond Inge, provide articles on recent women. Mary Ellis Gibson edited a collection of short stories by contemporary women, *New Stories by Southern Women* (1989). These works are among those now being published that are telling the story of southern women writers by focusing on gender and reinterpreting southern letters, a field that has largely been defined in the past by white males. Gibson presents a fine, brief discussion in her introduction of the contemporary southern women writers who emphasize—among a number of commonalities—"dailiness" and "the nature of living within a social fabric," as well as families, communal occasions, and relationships between classes, women, family members.

Along with women critics re-examining women authors, the rediscovery of neglected works has enriched the *canon. The emergence of Kate Chopin's *The Awakening* (1899) in the 1960s, Zora Neale Hurston's *Their Eyes Were Watching God* (1937) in the 1970s, and Harriet Jacobs' *Incidents in the Life of a Slave Girl: Written by Herself* (1861) in the 1980s suggests that more forgotten masterpieces may yet be found. And with a broader definition of "literature" that includes domestic fiction, once dismissed as subliterary, and popular fiction, which includes such stupendous best-sellers as Mitchell's *Gone With the Wind* (1936) and Harper *Lee's *To Kill a Mockingbird* (1960), the role of women writers is enlarged. Gifted writers who have recently published their first novels—Dorothy Allison, *Bastard out of Carolina* (1992); Donna Tartt, *The Secret History* (1992); Elizabeth Dewberry Vaughn, *Many Things Have Happened Since He Died and Here Are the Highlights* (1990); Michael Lee West, *Crazy Ladies* (1990); and Dorie Sanders, *Clover* (1990)—suggest that significant literary accomplishments by southern women writers will continue well into the next century.

[*See also* Local Color Fiction; Regionalism.]

• Edwin Francis Alderman et al., eds., *Library of Southern Literature*, vol. 16 (1905–1913), pp. 145–155. Louis

D. Rubin, Jr. et al., eds., *A Bibliographical Guide to the Study of Southern Literature* (1969). Anne Firor Scott, *The Southern Lady: From Pedestal to Politics, 1830–1930* (1970). Minrose C. Gwin, *Black and White Women of the Old South: The Peculiar Sisterhood in American Literature* (1985). Kathryn Lee Seidel, *The Southern Belle in the American Novel* (1985). Louis D. Rubin, Jr. et al., eds., *The History of Southern Literature* (1985). Hazel Carby, *Reconstructing Womanhood: The Emergence of the African-American Woman Novelist* (1987). Joseph M. Flora and Robert Bain, eds., *Fifty Southern Writers After 1900* (1987). Helen Fiddyment Levy, *Fiction of the Home Place* (1992).

Dorothy M. Scura

SOUTHWORTH, E.D.E.N. (1819–1899), prominent, popular, and prolific author of sensational domestic and sentimental novels. Born to an old Virginia family, Emma Dorothy Eliza Nevitte grew up in Washington, D.C. After some years as a schoolteacher, she married Frederick Hamilton Southworth, an itinerant inventor, in 1840. The couple spent four years in Wisconsin where their two children, Richmond J. and Charlotte Emma, were born. In 1844, deserted by her husband, Southworth returned to Washington with her children, only to learn how few acceptable employment opportunities there were for middle-class women. After several years of extreme privation, she discovered that she could support her family with her writing. She achieved success with her first novel, *Retribution* (1849), and became established with her second, *The Deserted Wife* (1849). Over the next forty years, she wrote between fifty and sixty novels (multiple titles and editions make a precise count difficult). She made as much as $6,000 a year from her writing at the height of her career, and for overall sales she has been identified as the greatest publishing success in nineteenth-century America. She became a leading literary figure and counted Harriet Beecher *Stowe and John Greenleaf Whittier among her close friends. Committed to helping women support themselves, she encouraged many young women to become writers.

Her novels first were published in serial form in *The National Era* (1847–1859), *The Saturday Evening Post* (1849–1856), and the *New York Ledger* (1857–1886). Some of her most notable titles were *The Mother-in-Law* (1850); *The Discarded Daughter* (1852); *The Curse of Clifton* (1852); *India* (1853); *The Lost Heiress* (1854); *The Missing Bride* (1854); *The Hidden Hand* (1859); *In the Depths* and *Self-Raised* (serial pair, 1864); *Changed Brides* and *The Bride's Fate* (serial pair, 1867); *Only a Girl's Heart, The Rejected Bride, and Gertrude Hadden* (serial trio, 1875); *Em* and *Em's Husband,* (serial pair, 1877); *The Unloved Wife* and *Lilith,* (serial pair, 1882); *Her Mother's*

Secret and *For Woman's Love* (serial pair, 1883–1884); and *A Deed Without Name* (1886).

Though her novels contain a wide variety of settings, dilemmas, and characters, they possess several common elements. Usually they follow the life of a virtuous heroine who is forced to make her way alone. Christianity and domesticity are strong thematic undercurrents. The pacing is dramatic, sensational, and compelling, and the language ornate, descriptive, and often highly wrought. In spite of their frequent antebellum Southern settings, these novels are not apologias for *slavery, and *India* (1853) is unabashedly abolitionist. Though *The Hidden Hand* rightly remains her best-remembered work, her other novels deserve much more attention than they have received. E.D.E.N Southworth exposed the dark underside of *domesticity and, as such, revealed much about the realities women faced in her day.

• The Collected Papers are at Perkins Library, Duke University, and at the Library of Congress, Washington D.C. See also Regis Louise Boyle, *Mrs. E.D.E.N Southworth, Novelist* (1931). Nina Baym, *Woman's Fiction* (1978). Mary Kelly, *Private Woman, Public Stage* (1984). Susan Coultrap-McQuin, *Doing Literary Business* (1990).

Blythe Forcey

SPECULATIVE FICTION. *See* Fabulation, Feminist.

SPEECH COMMUNICATION PROFESSIONALS. Women in the speech communication professional community have never been voiceless. That community officially began in 1914, when seventeen male teachers whose primary interest was spoken English separated from the National Council of Teachers of English to form the National Association of Academic Teachers of Public Speaking. Today the national association, which numbers over 7,000, calls itself the Speech Communication Association (SCA). Roughly half of its members are women, who have, from the beginning, been actively involved in the organization. Women were members of the executive committee of SCA from 1916, and women's work was published from the outset, including three articles in the inital volume of the first journal. By 1917, that journal's third year, Maud May Babcock served on the editorial staff.

The membership has elected women to the presidency of SCA since 1932, when Henrietta Prentiss held the position. In the more than seventy-five years of the organization's history, eight other women have been elected: Maud May Babcock, Magdalene Kramer, Elise Hahn, Marie Hocmuth Nichols, Jane Blankenship, Anita Taylor, Beverly Long, and Patti Gillespie. Such inclusion can be viewed as a sign—even if a small one—of acceptance of women in all levels of the organization.

As noted, writing by women in speech communication has been published since SCA sponsored its first journal, the *Quarterly Journal of Public Speaking*, in 1915. The *Quarterly Journal of Speech (QJS)*, as it has been called since 1928, is sponsored by the national organization, along with *Communication Monographs* since 1934, *Communication Education* (formerly *Speech Teacher*) since 1952, *Text and Performance Quarterly* (formerly *Literature in Performance*) since 1980, and *Critical Studies in Mass Communication* since 1984. This essay addresses some historical trends in women's writing in these publications and several notable achievements and absences.

The history of women writing in the field of speech communication has varied in the topics covered and in the numbers of articles published. From those early years on, writing by women touched many of the interests embraced by the journals. In the pre–World War II period, women wrote primarily on "practical" issues such as speech therapy and forensics, the more "expressive" areas of oral interpretation and theater, and especially—as was to be the case for the next seven decades—on pedagogy at the elementary and secondary levels. By the 1960s, they had published research on discussion, voice science, public address, language development, interpersonal communication, conversation, and organizational communication. Little then was written by women that dealt with theoretical or political issues. Rhetoric, considered by some as the core research area of the field, was primarily the province of men.

Women have not enjoyed a consistently high level of representation in the field's journals. Although they were published in *QJS* in relatively large numbers from the beginning, the post-World War II era offered a different climate to women writing in the field. From 1950 to 1966, the percentage of articles written by women fell from 20 percent to 13 percent of the total. Since 1966, women have regained more space, publishing 27 percent of the articles from 1966 to 1990. Women, who number approximately 52 percent of the SCA membership, have written approximately 21 percent of the total articles published in the national journals to date, evidence of the continued discrepancy between women's presence in the professional community and the quantity of their published work. Furthermore, although women served on the executive committee of the national organization and as associate and assistant editors of the association's journals, only nine women have served as editors of these publications. Marie Hocmuth Nichols was the first woman appointed to edit *QJS*—in 1963, forty-eight years after the journal began. She was followed by Gladys Borchers and Mary Margaret Roberts for *Communication Education;* Martha Solomon, *QJS;* Margaret McLaughlin and Judee Burgoon, *Communication Monographs;* Beverly Long, Mary Frances Hopkins, and Kristin Langellier, *Text and Performance Quarterly;* and Sari Thomas, *Critical Studies in Mass Communication.*

Mary Margaret Roberts's tenure as editor (1973–1975) warrants special comment. During her term, *Communication Education* published twenty-five single-authored articles by women (38 percent of all single-authored articles), two co-authored by women, and fourteen co-authored by women and men. The work of forty-five women was represented during the three-year period, not including book reviews. Many of the articles written by women were among the earliest to deal with topics that reflected respect for diversity: speaking by American Indians, intercultural rhetoric, interpretation of ethnic texts, performing Chicano poetry and black drama, culture contact through performance, and interracial communication. One of the first articles to consider the influence of a woman speech educator focused on the achievements of Gertrude Johnson, contributor to the journals from 1919 until her death. During Roberts's editorship, *Communication Education* also published Jo Sprague's directive on reducing sexism in speech education, and "The Rhetoric of American Feminism: A Social Movement Course," the first article using "feminism" in its title (Wil Linkugel, 1974).

Speech communication historically has been an area sensitive to cultural difference. The field began as a person-centered study, and much of it, as Celeste Condit notes in *Transforming Visions: Feminist Critiques in Communication Studies* (1992), "has always been an oppositional practice; it has opposed the norms of the academy, and it has opposed the taken-for-grantedness of the mainstream of American political life." Articles dealing with difference were published in the journals as far back as the 1920s. The first article about a woman orator was published in 1929 and the first about African-Americans in 1935, both written by men. In 1936, an article dealing with the relationship between dominant and marginal cultures, also by a man, was published in *QJS.* Thus, while men clearly dominated the field, some of them evinced interest in and openness to difference from the outset.

Support of difference enhanced the possibility of women's publishing in the field's major journals, and allowed or encouraged them to publish articles on marginalized groups. For instance, it was a woman, Lois Buswell, who published in 1935 the first article about Native Americans. In a 1944 issue of *QJS*, Elaine MacDavitt was the first woman to write about an individual woman orator, Susan B. *Anthony. Earlier, a 1937 issue included the first article by a woman about a group of women, "Pioneer Women Orators of America," by Diane Yoakam. Yoakam not only focused on women speakers, but noted how their oratorical styles differed from those of males. The article celebrated those differences and argued for the contributions women made to American oratory. In a ringing conclusion, Yoakam took a distinctively feminist stance:

> In claiming the public platform for their use, the pioneer women orators set the precedent for, and helped to establish the propriety of, women as public speakers. By speaking and lecturing they exemplified women's true intellectual and physical capabilities, helped incite thought which led to the improvement of the legal, economic and educational status of women, and not only hastened, but helped to render inevitable, the ultimate emancipation and enfranchisement of American women.

Thus, although it did not happen often, at least some women were able to claim a political position near the beginning of the field's history. Also indicative of such a stance, Yoakam's comments on Angelina *Grimké and Sojourner *Truth are among the earliest on African-American women, a group whose practices and achievements remain underrepresented in women's writing today.

The past two decades have been years of great change for women writing in speech communication. Whereas in the early period, most of their articles were applicational, a recent shift to writing in the areas once dominated by men has occurred—specifically, in critical and rhetorical theory. Karlyn Kohrs Campbell's 1972 article, "The Rhetoric of Women's Liberation: An Oxymoron," in many ways pivotal for women in the field, set the tone and necessity for feminist theorizing.

In 1977, the increase in research by and about women led to a new journal (currently sponsored by a regional association), *Women's Studies in Communication.* While demonstrating the acceptance of a feminist voice, the publishing of feminist articles in feminist journals can also be interpreted as contributing to continued marginalization: the mainstream audience may not be exposed to and influenced by feminist perspectives.

Only a small number of articles by women in the association's national journals carry the words "woman," "women," "feminist," or "feminism" in their titles. In fact, during the journals' entire history, these words appear in article titles fewer than forty times. This paucity of articles that clearly claim a feminist perspective in their titles raises serious questions about the equity granted to—or won by—women within the speech communication community. The need to vigorously pursue such questions led Julia Wood and Gerald Phillips to initiate the National Conference on Gender and Communication Research (1984). The need prompted an issue of *Women's Studies in Communication*, "What Distinguishes Scholarship in Communication Studies?" (1988); and it led Lawrence B. Rosenfeld to devote an entire issue of *Communication Education* (January 1991) to "Gender Issues in the Communication Classroom." These questions are also actively engaged in the first comprehensive feminist critique of the speech communication discipline, Sheryl Perlmutter Bowen and Nancy Wyatt's *Transforming Visions*.

• Karl Wallace, ed., *A History of Speech Education in America* (1954). Karen Foss and Sonja Foss, "The Status of Research on Women and Communication," *Communication Quarterly* 31 (Summer 1983): 195–204. Carole Spitzack and Kathryn Carter, "Women in Communication Studies: A Typology for Revision," *Quarterly Journal of Speech* 73 (November 1987): 401–423. Lesley Steeves, "Feminist Theories and Media Studies," *Critical Studies in Mass Communication* 4 (1987): 95–135. Julia Wood, "Feminist Scholarship in Communication: Consensus, Diversity and Conversation Among Researchers," *Women's Studies in Communication* 11 (1988): 22–27. Barbara Bate and Anita Taylor, eds., *Women Communication: Studies of Women's Talk* (1988). Gerald Phillips and Julia Wood, eds., *Speech Communication: Essays to Commemorate the 75th Anniversary of the Speech Communication Association* (1990). Kay Capo and Darlene Hantzis, "(En)Gendered (and Endangered) Subjects: Writing, Reading, Performing, and Theorizing Feminist Criticism," *Text and Performance Quarterly* 11 (April 1991): 249–266. Sheryl Perlmutter Bowen and Nancy Wyatt, eds., *Transforming Visions: Feminist Critiques in Communication Studies* (1992).

Brooke DuPuy Baker and
Beverly Whitaker Long

SPENCER, Anne (1882–1975), poet. Traditionally, students and critics of African-American literature associate the black literary movement of the 1920s—the * Harlem Renaissance—with such prolific artists as Langston Hughes, James Weldon Johnson, Alain Locke, and Jean Toomer. When women writers do receive recognition, Zora Neale * Hurston and Nella * Larsen are the names mentioned. However, as black women writers began attracting popular and critical attention in the 1980s, poet Anne Spencer has begun to receive the attention she de-

serves. Her iconoclastic voice was rediscovered with J. Lee Greene's *Time's Unfading Garden: Anne Spencer's Life and Poetry* (1977), and critics are now acknowledging her substantial contribution to African-American arts and letters.

Born in Henry County, Virginia, on 6 February 1882, Annie Bethel Bannister was the only child of Joel Cephus Bannister and Sarah Louise Scales. After her tumultuous marriage ended, Sarah took Annie to Bramwell, West Virginia; subsequently, Sarah's financial exigencies forced her to place Annie in the home of William T. Dixie, an upstanding member of the black community. Reading dime-store novels and newspapers taught the precocious youngster about the power of language. While she was illiterate herself, Sarah Scales sent Anne to the Virginia Seminary in Lynchburg, and she graduated in 1899. This period was also significant because Anne met classmate Edward Spencer. The couple married on 15 May 1901 and had three children.

While Spencer befriended many Harlem Renaissance luminaries, her most fruitful relationship was with James Weldon Johnson. Not only did he discover her, but he also selected her pen name, Anne Spencer. Also, Johnson introduced her to H. L. Mencken who, like Carl Van Vechten, aided black writers. While Mencken helped Anne publish her first poem, "Before the Feast at Shushan," she later declined his patronage. Spencer published most of her poems during the 1920s in the period's most prestigious collections: James Weldon Johnson's *The Book of American Negro Poetry* (1922); Robert T. Kerlin's *Negro Poets and Their Poems* (1923); Louis Untermeyer's *American Poetry Since 1900* (1923); Alain Locke's *The New Negro* (1925); and Countee Cullen's *Caroling Dusk* (1925). One of her last poems, "For Jim, Easter Eve," was published in Langston Hughes and Arna Bontemps's *The Poetry of the Negro, 1746–1949* in 1948.

Many of Spencer's poems convey a romantic concern with the human search for beauty and meaning in a sordid universe, as well as people's futile attempts to impose order on God's earth. Poems in this vein include "At the Carnival" and "Change." However, Spencer cannot be viewed solely as a "nature" or "religious" poet, for her complex work resists such facile categorizations. "Black Man O' Mine," for instance, uses erotic imagery to celebrate black love. While Spencer did not write "protest" poetry— she wrote Johnson that "The Tom-Tom *forced* into poetry seems a sad state to me" (quoted in J. Lee Green's biography; author's emphasis)— she was aware of white oppression. The persona of "White Things" addresses racism metaphorically: "They [white things] turned the blood in a ruby rose/To a poor white poppy-flower." In addition she worked fervently with NAACP secretary Johnson and helped establish the Lynchburg chapter of that organization in 1918. Thus, an unequivocally black, feminist voice coexisted with one enamored of the earth's splendor.

Anne Spencer cultivated a garden that attracted several members of the black artistic community for over half a century: W. E. B. Du Bois, Langston Hughes, Georgia Douglas *Johnson, Paul Robeson, Gwendolyn *Brooks, and Maya *Angelou are just a few of the artists to visit her Lynchburg home. Her devotion to illuminating the beauty of God's garden and humankind's place in it anticipates writers such as Alice *Walker, who also sees a cosmic and spiritual relationship between human beings and the earth. Though many of her writings were lost, critics continue to rediscover the resonant voice of Anne Spencer—a voice that pulsates through black women's writing in the later half of the twentieth century.

• J. Lee Greene, *Time's Unfading Garden: Anne Spencer's Life and Poetry* (1977). Gloria T. Hull, "Afro-American Women Poets: A Bio-Critical Survey," in Sandra Gilbert and Susan Gubar, eds., *Skakespeare's Sisters* (1979). *Echoes from the Garden: The Anne Spencer Story*, documentary film (1980). Erlene Stetson, ed., *Black Sister: Poetry by Black American Women, 1746–1980* (1981). Maureen Honey, ed., *Shadowed Dreams: Women's Poetry of the Harlem Renaissance* (1989). Keith Clark, "Anne Spencer: Poet, Librarian," in *Notable Black American Women*, ed. Jessie Carney Smith (1992).

Keith Clark

SPENCER, Elizabeth (b. 1921), novelist, short story writer, and playwright. Born in Carrollton, Mississippi, Spencer matriculated at Belhaven College (1942), where she began an enduring friendship with Eudora *Welty. She earned an M.A. in English from Vanderbilt in 1943. Her thesis, "Irish Mythology in the Early Poetry of William Butler Yeats," analyzes Yeats's use of mythological symbolism to evoke a lost culture, a technique she later drew on in writing about the South.

Between 1943 and 1948, Spencer taught in small colleges in Tennessee and Mississippi, working briefly as a reporter for the *Nashville Tennessean*. In 1948 she published her first novel, *Fire in the Morning* (1948), and joined the English faculty of the University of Mississippi in Oxford. *This Crooked Way* (1952) advances the theme of her first novel: the difficulty of accommodating the Southern myth within a modernist universe.

In 1953, Spencer received a Guggenheim Fellowship and went to Rome. This move gave her an opportunity to gain detachment from the South, giving her Southern writing greater objectivity. She spent 1955 in New York revising *The Voice at the Back Door* (1956), a novel about racial confrontation. In 1956, in Cornwall, Spencer married John Rusher, an Englishman whom she had met in Italy in 1954.

In 1958 they moved to Montreal, and Spencer's work became more international. Set in Florence, *The Light in the Piazza* (1960), originally published in the *New Yorker*, featured her first female protagonist. The most commercially successful of her works, it was later filmed by MGM. *Knights and Dragons* (1965), also an Italian novella, and *No Place for an Angel* (1967), a novel that critiques America's materialism, continued her explorations of a Southern woman's life outside the South. In 1968 Spencer published her first story collection, *Ship Island and Other Stories* (1968). *The Snare* (1972), set in New Orleans, features Spencer's most complex and fully realized heroine.

In 1976 Spencer began teaching at Concordia University. She published *The Stories of Elizabeth Spencer* and *Marilee*, a story trilogy about a central protagonist, in 1981. With *The Salt Line* (1984), set in Biloxi, Mississippi, Spencer returned to a male protagonist, a man of honor set adrift in a corrupt society.

She was elected to the American Academy in 1985, and in 1986 she and Rusher returned to the U.S., and she joined the English faculty at UNC–Chapel Hill. In 1988 she published a story collection, *Jack of Diamonds*, and received an NEA Senior Fellowship. Her first play, *For Lease or Sale*, was produced in 1989. *The Night Travellers* (1991), a Vietnam era novel set in North Carolina and Canada, continues Spencer's portrayal of Southern women who earn and appreciate their strength.

• John Jones, "Elizabeth Spencer," in *Mississippi Writers Talking* (1982). Peggy Prenshaw, *Elizabeth Spencer* (1985). Adam Versenyi, "About the Playwright and the Play," playbill for *For Lease or Sale* (1989).

Marilyn Elkins

SPINSTERHOOD. The first recorded use of *spinster* dates from 1362 and indicated the occupation of thread spinner, regardless of the worker's gender. But the term eventually became so identified with women that by 1617 spinster had entered English Common Law as a legal category denoting a single woman, whether or not she worked to earn an income. Though non-Western and nonindustrial societies appear not to have had similar concepts, other European societies, particularly in the north, did develop analogous ideas. But for specific cultural-historical reasons, beginning with the disruptive impact of early modern industrial, economic, and cultural changes in English society, the Anglo-American *stereotype exhibits distinctive characteristics. With the growth of early capitalism, middle- and upper-class English women were discouraged from engaging in productive work while craftswomen were forced out of their guilds. The rise of *Protestantism, especially Henry VIII's dissolution of nunneries in 1537 and Puritanism's later anti-Catholic campaigns and emphasis on *marriage, probably created ripe conditions for the widespread acceptance of a new negative term for single women: old maid, which first appeared about 1530. Spinster and old maid were used almost synonymously by 1700, but a century later old maid had become more common, and spinsterhood began to be used by 1823 to designate the presumed characteristics of an unmarried woman, rather than a self-sufficient woman (Oxford English Dictionary, 2d ed., 1980). In the late twentieth-century United States, old maid is the more widely recognized term, used by men in jokes and stories based on old stereotypes.

The collection of traits associated with Anglo-American spinster/old maid stereotypes was in place before 1800: angularity and nearsighted awkwardness, crabbedness and constant ill nature, invasive curiosity and envy, gossiping and censoriousness, affection of youth and flirtatious pursuit of a husband. Fiction and nonfiction writers, as well as people in ordinary conversation, drew from these negative physical and psychological traits and constructed the "ridiculous" (or giddy) and the "sour" (or stern) old maid stereotype, serving as judgments, dismissals, and devaluations of undesirable women.

Similar constructs have also served as repositories of currently devalued but potentially positive traits, as Mary *Daly asserted in Gyn/Ecology: The Metaethics of Radical Feminism (1978). As a result, both real and fictional spinsters and old maids have, sometimes simultaneously, been envied and attacked by writers holding opposing perspectives on such potentially positive traits as independence and intelligence. Most often, however, the negative valuations of single women have won the cultural wars of representation, overwhelming both positive fictional valuations and acknowledgments of real women's experience.

The negative depictions of spinsters and old maids typical of the mid-nineteenth century led some American women writers—Rose Terry *Cooke prominent among them—to develop a positive counter-representation of single women congruent with both the ideology of *"true womanhood" and the fact that real unmarried women usually performed valuable if undervalued family services. This new genteel, or "sentimental," spinster (or "maiden lady") appeared in fiction and nonfiction by the mid-nineteenth century as a paragon of passive, sacrificial feminine virtue and was intended to counter the despicable traits of old maids in literature and folklore.

By the late nineteenth century, however, these attempts to correct the (mis)representations of spinsters in American literature seemed inadequate, if not irrelevant. The *suffrage movement and women's increasing roles in the paid labor force created the need for representations of single women other than as sour, silly, or genteel old maids, to redefine for real women struggling within new social and cultural circumstances a broader range of expression and action. The new ideal of womanhood, the New Woman—often identified as young and unmarried—was articulated in late-nineteenth- and early twentieth-century fiction, nonfiction, and social discourse in the context of other dialogues over massive changes in American culture. This prototype offered a comprehensive new vision of women as, simultaneously, self-sufficient, competent, and attractive, the last trait expressing social and cultural acceptance. In the midst of frequently rancorous debates about female identity, proponents of the New Woman, seeking a new term for themselves, attempted to reinvigorate the earliest gender-specific meaning of spinster as a capable, self-sufficient working woman. Their effort was not successful.

As the prototype of the New Woman was being elaborated, proponents of modern culture turned stern old maids into authoritarians to signify the repressiveness they objected to in Victorian society and culture (for example, Miss Watson in Twain's Huckleberry Finn). Defenders of tradition, including many writers for The Ladies' Home Journal, used genteel old maids as models of female virtue to counter the threatening figure of the independent, modern *New Woman; in contrast, humorist Marietta *Holley used her old maid character Betsy Bobbet to ridicule the sentimental absurdities of genteel culture. These uses of spinster/old maid stereotypes in the struggles between Victorian and modern culture spilled over into disputes over the "new womanhood." By the 1920s, New Woman social workers and teachers were often depicted as authoritarian old maids. Ellen *Glasgow in her Cosmopolitan story, "Ideals" (January 1926), focused on this irony when a genteel old maid finally makes the modern decision to live her own life, only to be trapped by her flapper niece's nostalgic expectations of her dedication to duty and sacrifice. Conflicting uses such as these make it impossible for readers then or now to expect stereotypes of spinsters or old maids to express any single, easily definable meaning.

The most effective counter to the attractive images of the New Woman at the turn of the twentieth century represented her as mannish in dress, ambition, and personality. This new formulation of the spinster/old maid overlapped with the emerging stereotype of the lesbian, especially in cautionary tales published in popular periodicals and aimed at girls who "wanted careers." These contests over female identity, symbolized positively by the New Woman and negatively by the "mannish woman," both including conflicting representations of old maids, focused to a large extent on defining "appropriate" dress and behavior for the increasing numbers of women entering the workforce. This process resulted in the new negative representation of the neurotic career woman, the twentieth-century old maid. Because she "effaced her sex" on the job by being competent and wearing man-tailored suits, she was presumed to possess repressed or disturbed sexuality—or no sexuality at all.

By this time, the crisis over the redefinition of womanhood had produced another new type, the " 'young' old maid," unique for her uncertain status. As the heroine of numerous popular magazine stories and movies, she was (and occasionally still is) depicted as a woman who, because of her flirtation with independence and achievement, is in danger (often melodramatically) of becoming neurotic: Will she be able to transform herself into a "real" woman who accepts "appropriate" modes of feminine appearance, behavior, and thought? Will she change in time to attract a man?

The years since the reemergence of the women's movement have brought new attempts to broaden the culturally approved definition of womanhood to make competence and self-sufficiency "attractive" female traits, the most positive meaning of spinsterhood. But this period has also seen the specter of old maidenism raised again (e.g., "Too Late for Prince Charming?" Newsweek, June 1986).

[See also Family; Kinship; Marriage; Widowhood.]

• Dorothy Yost Deegan, The Stereotype of the Single Woman in the American Novel (1951; reprint, 1969). Mary Daly, Gyn/Ecology: The Metaethics of Radical Feminism (1978). Lillian Faderman, Surpassing the Love of Men: Romantic Friendship and Love between Women (1981). Susan Koppelman, ed., Old Maids: Short Stories by Nineteenth Century U.S. Women Writers (1984). Leigh Chambers-Schiller, "Liberty, a Better Husband": Single Women in America, 1780–1840 (1984). Carroll Smith-Rosenberg, Disorderly Conduct (1985). Rosalind Urbach Moss, Reinventing Spinsterhood: Competing Images of "Womanhood" in American Culture, 1880–1960, Ph.D. diss., University of Minnesota (1988).

Rosalind Urbach Moss

SPIRITUALISM is the belief that mortals communicate with departed souls, usually through a medium by means of physical phenomena or abnormal mental states, such as trances. Attempts to communicate with the dead and with disembodied spirits through such seances have long been made throughout the world, in Africa, Haiti, Mexico, and among Native Americans, for example. Yet spiritualist practices were virtually unknown in mainstream U.S. society until March, 1848, when two young sisters in a farmhouse in New York State claimed to have communicated—through a coded system of raps—with the spirit of a peddler murdered by a previous owner of the house. News of the Fox sisters and of other spirit communications spread quickly.

Much of this interest was motivated by mere curiosity, but it also reflected a serious desire for change. As the mid-nineteenth century was overwhelmed by rapid industrial and cultural transformations, including scientific discoveries and theories of evolution, many Americans withdrew from Puritanistic doctrines of good against evil and embraced transcendentalism, Swedenborgianism, and spiritualism. It seems odd to contrast spiritualism with traditional Christianity, however. Why would people who believed that they could pray to a man who rose from the grave three days after his death and who in some denominations believed that they could pray to departed saints for intercession find it strange that in other cultures people believed in talking to spirits of the dead?

Certainly those most often ignored or oppressed by traditional Christianity in America were women of every color. Women became leaders in the spiritualist movement, including Kate and Margaret Fox, Emma Hardinge Britten, Victoria Woodhull, Cora Scott Hatch, Ada Hoyt Foye, and Julie Branch, and the movement became associated with women's rights. Mediumship offered women power by affirming life and a presumed equality after death, commanding respect of men and women, and providing financial independence. While the freedom or escape through spiritualism was interior, it was also quite exterior and tangible. Women could speak out and challenge authority, and they made their own places on earth and in the spiritual world in which they believed. The association of spiritualism with women led to accusations of its being unscientific, unintellectual, and unreasonable. Yet detractors could not entirely disarm spiritualists or dissuade the public's interest in the supernatural. Unlike the many women of the past who were persecuted as witches for threatening the patriarchal order, spiritualists commanded popular support and respect.

As a result of its popularity, spiritualism appears in the writings of many American women writers. Britten and Helene P. Blavatasky wrote extensively on spiritualism, while Hatch and Sarah Helen Whitman (one-time fiance of Edgar Allan Poe) wrote trance-inspired poetry. One finds spiritualist elements in the work of Elizabeth Stuart *Phelps, Lydia Maria *Child, Rosa Terry *Cooke, Louisa May *Alcott, Harriet Beecher *Stowe, Emily *Dickinson, Willa *Cather, Sarah Orne *Jewett, Edith *Wharton, Djuna *Barnes, Ellen *Glasgow, Flannery *O'Connor, Eudora *Welty, Shirley *Jackson, Alison Lurie, Sylvia *Plath, and Anne *Sexton.

While women involved in the spiritualist movement of nineteenth-century America were white, usually middle and upper-middle class, the influence of women as spiritualists in the African-American, Native American, and Hispanic communities has been more lasting. Women in these communities have commanded both respect and fear as voodoo priestesses, witches, shamans, and curanderas as they celebrate the idea that this world and the next are connected, that there is harmony between the physical and the spiritual. The strong oral traditions in these cultures have been an important factor in transmitting their spiritualist practices.

Many influential voices in the African-American, Native American, and Hispanic communities are lost in obscurity, but today the influence of spiritualism in writing is marked. Among African-American writers, important figures include Zora Neale *Hurston (whose *Tell My Horse* [1938] is probably the best-known book about voodoo in existence), Margaret *Walker, Gwendolyn *Brooks, Ntozake *Shange, *Alice Walker, and Toni *Morrison. Among Native American women writers one finds Leslie Marmon *Silko, Louise *Erdrich, Paula Gunn *Allen, and Wendy *Rose. And among Hispanic writers in America Pat Mora, Judy Lucero, Alma Villanueva, and Bernice Zamora reflect spiritualism in their works.

Women spiritualists share oppression as a way of life as well as concern for justice and equality, but they also share imagination defined as a nonrational, feminine spiritual value. Denied ownership of material wealth, denied ownership of their own bodies, women were and are forced inward to face their own interior selves, where ownership of their own spirits

cannot be denied. Religious zeal has long been associated with women, but not religious authority. Through spiritualism, women were and are able to turn their inner strength into an external force.

[*See also* Religion; Religious Writing; Spiritual Narratives; Spirituals.]

• R. Laurence Moore, *In Search of White Crows: Spiritualism, Parapsychology, and American Culture* (1977). Russell M. and Clare R. Goldfarb, *Spiritualism and Nineteenth-Century Letters* (1978). Houston A. Baker, Jr., *Workings of the Spirit: The Poetics of African-American Women's Writing* (1991).

Jeanne Campbell Reesman
and Michelle Powe

SPIRITUALITY. While feminism in the late 1960s and early 1970s tended to stress material and social issues ranging from equal pay for equal work to *sexual harassment, many contemporary feminists are paying increasing attention to women's spiritual issues. Feminist spirituality does not merely substitute a female godhead for a male but, rather, reevaluates the larger issues of faith, belief, community, and healing within the specific cycles of women's lives.

During the nineteenth century, too, women reevaluated their spiritual lives in light of feminist convictions. Suffragist Elizabeth Cady *Stanton's *The Woman's Bible* (1895) criticized the demeaning status accorded to women in the church's official Bible and proposed a new, woman-centered Old and New Testament that would be more nourishing to women's spiritual needs. Some nineteenth-century feminists dispensed with official church structures entirely and explored supernaturalism outside the confines of conventional religion. *Spiritualism, table-rapping, mediums, seances, and other para-natural phenomenon were all seen as alternative ways of knowing the world beyond the merely empirical. Howard Kerr and Charles L. Crow's *The Occult in America: New Historical Perspectives* (1986) is a good source book for studies of the paranormal, while Ann Braude's *Radical Spirits: Spiritualism and Women's Rights in Nineteenth-Century America* (1989) elucidates the relationship between spiritualism and late-nineteenth-century *feminism.

The contemporary "womanspirit movement" also attempts to bridge the national and supernatural, the rational and spiritual. This movement divides into two amorphous, sometimes overlapping, and sometimes conflicting camps: on the one hand are those who attempt to reform traditional religions to make them more woman-centered; on the other are those who reject all forms of patriarchal religion and who seek new forms through which to express female spirituality. In the first group, Christian feminists seek the feminist implications within Christ's teachings and argue that it was the early church fathers who imposed sexist codes on women's religion or that translations from ancient Greek or Hebrew arbitrarily posed masculine pronouns (God became "he") on terms that, in their original Biblical languages, were genderless. The main idea here is that returning to *true* religion allows one to be in touch with a spirituality that is not hopelessly misogynistic. A number of feminist theologians, including Rosemary Radford Ruether, Barbara Brown Zikmund, and Rosemary Skinner Keller, have surveyed the role of women in the Christian church, including reformers who work for the ordination of women as priests or ministers or who seek other ways of opening religious services and structures to women.

Some women have begun as religious reformers but ended up radicalized. Sonia Johnson, in *From Housewife to Heretic* (1981), *Going Out of Our Minds: The Metaphysics of Liberation* (1987), and *Wildfire: Igniting the She/Volution* (1989), moves from her role as a lifelong Mormon protesting against her religion's misogyny to someone who, after being excommunicated from her church, has issued a full declaration of religious independence. Similarly, Mary *Daly, whose *The Church and the Second Sex* (1968) critiqued the misogyny of Catholicism, has now moved to a far more radical position, with *Gyn/Ecology: The Metaethics of Radical Feminism* (1978) mapping out a spirituality far removed from organized, mainstream Catholicism.

Scholars including Cheryl Townsend Gilkes and Paula Giddings have analyzed the role of African-American women within various denominations of the black church. Vivian Jenkins Nelson, in "Women and Power," an interview in Theresa King O'Brien's *The Spiral Path: Essays and Interviews on Women's Spirituality* (1988), discusses the dynamics of power, femininity, and masculinity in African-American religious traditions while Sabrina Sojourner emphasizes the "goddess heritage of Black women." In her important study, *Moorings and Metaphors: Figures of Culture and Gender in Black Women's Literature* (1992), literary scholar Karla F. C. Holloway shows spiritual links between West African and African-American women's writings. It is through the writings of women, Holloway suggests, that indigenous matriarchal West African spiritual traditions have survived in black America.

Similarly, Jewish women have worked to reenvision the patriarchal base of Judaism. In *The Telling* (1993), novelist E. M. *Broner shows how the traditional Jewish seder has been transformed by a group of Jewish feminists and

activists who meet to affirm both ritual (their spiritual lives) and community (their activism in the world). With Naomi Nimrod, Broner has written "The Women's Haggadah." Here, the four questions asked on the first night of Passover are recast to account for the exodus of women. "Why on this night do we recline? We recline on this night for the unhurried telling of the legacy of Miriam." The Women's Haggadah ends with affirmation. The women follow Miriam, "her footsteps disappear in the sand. We find the map as we go along."

Those who seek spirituality outside traditional Western religions look for female divinity—worshiping the *Goddess, or various female incarnations of a guiding, universal spirit. Merlin Stone's *When God Was a Woman* (1976), Una Standard's *Mrs. Man* (1976), and Susan Griffin's *Woman and Nature: The Roaring Inside Her* (1978) were early, landmark books in the goddess tradition as well as important contributions to *ecofeminism. Annette Van Dyke's anthology *The Search for a Woman-Centered Spirituality* (1992) looks at literary evocations of women's spirituality in the work of Leslie Marmon *Silko, Paula Gunn *Allen, Audre *Lorde, Alice *Walker, Starhawk, Marion Zimmer Bradley, Sonia Johnson, and Mary Daly.

Lesbian scholars, theologians, and activists have been especially eloquent in reclaiming the body from the negative and often homophobic proscriptions imposed by organized religion. E. Ann Matter, in "My Sister, My Spouse," and Carter Heyward, in *Our Passion for Justice* (1984), have examined how lesbian women have been crippled by the burden of religiously sanctioned homophobia from medieval times to the present. Both lesbians and heterosexual women in the womanspirit movement have reaffirmed that the body is a vital part of woman's religious experience. Many womanspirit celebrations explicitly calibrate the cycles of women's lives, including *menstruation, *childbirth, and *menopause.

In two landmark anthologies, *Womanspirit Rising* (1979) and *Weaving Visions: New Patterns in Feminist Spirituality* (1989), Judith Plaskow and Carol P. Christ have documented the range and diversity of the new feminist theology and its wide influence in the culture at large. Women's spirituality informs New Age religious movements and has reached popular culture through women songwriters and performers, including Ferron, Ann Reed, Robin & Miriam, Starhawk, Terry Garthwaite, Mary Watkins, Jean Shinoda Bolen, Carole & Bren, and Kay Gardner.

The line between religion and anthropology has been irrevocably breached by the contemporary womenspirit movement. In the past, religion is what "we" (Western women, and for the most part middle-class, white women) practiced whereas "rituals" and "rites" were what "primitive" people indulged in. Increasingly, women have looked to those ancient religions and rites for guidance on how to live our spiritual lives. "Primitivism" has been embraced as a virtue in books such as Margot Adler's *Drawing Down the Moon: Witches, Druids, Goddess-Worshippers, and Other Pagans in America Today* (1979) or Clarissa Pinkola Estes's bestselling *Women Who Run with the Wolves* (1992).

The revitalization of traditional religion among Native American women reminds us of the matriarchal roots of many religions, especially Pueblo Indian religions, before white men arrived and imposed patriarchal Christianity and social structures on the indigenous population. Paula Gunn *Allen, in particular, has explored the role of women in Native American religion and expanded the implications of this matriarchy to all women in her influential *The Sacred Hoop: Recovering the Feminine in American Indian Traditions* (1986) and *Grandmothers of the Light: A Medicine Woman's Sourcebook* (1991). As she argues in the latter, the "ritual tradition is nothing new. It is at least as ancient as humankind." Feminists of the 1980s and 1990s have reclaimed that ancient humanity and celebrated the rituals that free woman's spirit.

[*See also* Religion; Rituals and Ceremonies; Theologians.]

• Carol P. Christ, *Diving Deep and Surfacing: Women Writers on Spiritual Quest* (1980). Sabrina Sojourner, "From the House of Yemanja: The Goddess Heritage of Black Women," in *The Politics of Women's Spirituality: Essays on the Rise of Spiritual Power Within the Women's Movement,* ed. Charlene Spretnak (1982). E. Ann Matter, "My Sister, My Spouse: Woman-Identified Women in Medieval Christianity," *Journal of Feminist Studies in Religion* 2, no. 2 (1986). Rosemary Radford Ruether and Rosemary Skinner Keller, eds., *Women and Religion in America: A Documentary History* (1986). Charlene Spretnar, "Wholly Writ," *Ms* (March–April 1993): 60–62.

Cathy N. Davidson

SPIRITUAL NARRATIVES. The spiritual narrative has been one of the forms of expression most available to ordinary American women over the past 350 years—available to them even when at times other public genres were not. In its basic form and language, the American spiritual narrative has usually been Christian—Protestant, in fact, though a wide variety of groups and individuals have used and adapted it. The narrative has varied considerably over time as well as among narrators, but its basic structure and key rhetorical elements have remained remarkably constant.

Spiritual narratives over three centuries tell much the same story: they usually begin with a period of relative indifference to things religious, and progress to a moment (or moments), usually during adolescence or young womanhood, when the narrator becomes aware of her need for religious awakening and salvation. (Such a moment is often provoked by a sudden shock—a frightening sermon, an illness, or the death of loved ones.) A period of struggle usually ensues, when the narrator persists in misunderstanding the nature of what is expected of her, or resists doing what she knows she must in order to be converted. The climax of the narrative comes with the event of conversion—when the narrator is finally able to acknowledge the helplessness of her situation: her inability to reform her thoughts or behavior, the futility of renouncing sin, and the pointlessness of trying to earn salvation on her own merits. She finally recognizes her absolute dependence on the grace offered by God. Once the conversion has taken place the narrator normally goes on to tell about the consequences of conversion: greater peace and happiness and a desire to inspire others to the same experience. The account may describe the later life of the narrator, often an alternation between periods of spiritual discouragement and renewed consecration, with the sense of consecration finally dominating.

Many narratives were originally offered orally, time after time at prayer and testimony meetings, before they were committed to writing. Sometimes the convert herself wrote the narrative down; other times a friend, family member, or pastor collected the letters, diaries, and records of memorable conversations with the convert (especially deathbed ones) and saw them into print. The narratives were published in a number of different forums: in pamphlets, newspapers, in magazines, in books privately printed or sponsored by tract societies and denominational publishing companies, even in hymns. They varied in length from a few sentences to hundreds of pages.

Because they might be recited so often, or simply because the narratives were not expected to exhibit originality, they tend to be formulaic: they employ similar plots and repeated phrases, including ample quotation from the Bible (usually the King James version).

The sources for the narratives—their forms and conventions and occasionally even their characteristic phrasings—reach back at least as far as apostolic times, with Paul's conversion on the road to Damascus being prototypical. The narratives reflect some knowledge of other early Christian sources, such as Augustine and the writings of medieval saints, but their most important roots are in the writings of seventeenth- and eighteenth-century English Puritans—both the spiritual narratives (most notably, John Bunyan's *Pilgrim's Progress* and *Grace Abounding to the Chief of Sinners*) and the devotional manuals delineating the progress of the spiritual life (such as Philip Doddridge's *Rise and Progress of the Soul*). The confessions of the early Methodists also served as models (for example, John Wesley's account of his Aldersgate experience and Hester Ann Rogers's *Account of the Experience of Hester Ann Rogers*).

The New England Puritans of the seventeenth and eighteenth centuries produced the first American forms. Prospective church members, both men and women, were often required to offer "spiritual relations" before they could join a congregation, and many of the most prominent New England ministers and political leaders left spiritual narratives. The form flourished particularly during the Great Awakening of the 1740s when Jonathan Edwards recorded the conversion stories of some of the women in his congregation *(A Narrative of Surprising Conversions)*. After a quiescent period during the Revolutionary era, the spiritual narrative revived in the nineteenth century, especially during times of religious excitement. In the twentieth century, the narrative has become more restricted, at least in its classic form, to religious subgroups—mostly to conservative Protestant evangelicals and pentecostals. Nevertheless, spiritual narratives of this and earlier centuries continue to be widely circulated—in traditional hymns, in the electronic media, and in books produced by trade publishers (especially the conversion stories of celebrities) and by conservative religious presses (such as, Revell, Zondervan, and Moody).

Though both men and women have related spiritual narratives over the centuries, it seems reasonable in the absence of quantitative measures to suppose that women found them particularly compatible, emphasizing as they did surrender to a male Father-God and to Christ as bridegroom. At first glance the narratives would seem simply to reinforce the standard socialization of women as passive, self-sacrificing, uncomplaining, and obedient daughters and wives. Certainly a large part of the conversion story is about surrender: narrators were expected to cap their account of a period of struggle, anger, resistance, and rebellion with a conclusion affirming their unconditional surrender. Nevertheless, the narratives appear to contain certain subtexts, of which the permission—even expectation—for girls and women to rebel, however temporarily, is one. More important, the conversion, while it was understood as a yielding to a superior will, at the same time encouraged converted women to undertake an active life, sometimes a daring and public one. As "instrumentalities" of God, converted women understood themselves as instructed to teach, to set up Sunday schools, to organize home and foreign mission societies, to sail as foreign missionaries, to proselytize, and even to enter the ordained ministry. And they were emboldened to proclaim what God had done in their lives in books and before substantial audiences. Finally, if God's will (as they interpreted it) conflicted with a father's, husband's, or brother's, it was God's will that was to prevail—surely a precept with revolutionary possibilities.

Protestant spiritual narratives have made an impact on groups originally far removed from such influence: African-American Christians, converts among Native Americans, and even Catholic and Jewish spiritual narrators. At the same time, there are of course spiritual narratives that more or less self-consciously break away from the Protestant pattern—current Native American narratives, for example, that emphasize the role of the female deity in creation and in sustaining the earth. And increasingly in the twentieth century the narrative has left its imprint on the tellers of "secular" narratives of transformation—on those who relate conversion to powerful political ideologies, to healing therapies (such as Alcoholics Anonymous), to causes (environmentalism, peace), and, particularly among women, to movements such as feminism and lesbianism. In fact, despite the importance in the twentieth century of slow evolutionary concepts of human development, conversion as a metaphor for personal and social experience persists in permeating American culture.

[*See also* Autobiography; Spiritualism; Spirituals.]

Virginia Brereton

SPIRITUALS. The African-American spiritual constitutes the earliest distinctive genre of the black sacred music tradition indigenous to America. Although some of the first scholarly commentators on spirituals disputed their African origins, the critical consensus has held sway in favor of this conclusion for very nearly a century. Evolving from the moans, chants, and cries of West African oral traditions under the duress of the *Middle Passage, spirituals like "Joshua Fit de Battle of Jerico" and "Didn't My Lord Deliver Daniel" record the American slaves' desperate desire to be freed from the onerous yoke of human bondage, expressed lyrically in the vivid, soteriological language of the Bible.

Because the early evolution of the African-American spiritual is owing significantly to congregational ritual in the "invisible institution" of the antebellum black church, the anonymity of individual influences on the genre and the ostensible singularity of sociocultural practices between bondsmen and bondswomen complicate the effort to identify women's unique contributions to the beginnings of a black sacred music tradition, particularly before Emancipation. However, if one woman's bearing on the African-American spiritual emerges from the obscurity of all of the others before Emancipation, then it is Harriet Tubman's. Tubman's example outlines the dual aesthetic and utilitarian function the spiritual played within the slave community.

According to her earliest biographer (Sarah H. Bradford, *Scenes in the Life of Harriet Tubman*, 1889), Tubman, the most famous conductor of the *Underground Railroad, sang from a carefully chosen personal repertoire of spirituals sotto voce in order to relay, through double meaning, arcane messages to frightened but anxious slaves ready to flee *slavery. That one of her standard selections for alerting potential fugitives was "Go Down, Moses" might easily explain the distinction given to her as "The Moses of Her People," as Georgia A. Ryder suggests ("Black Women in Song: Some Socio-Cultural Images," *Negro History Bulletin* 39, 1976). One can only wonder, then, how much Tubman's historical presence bears on the whole cycle of spirituals that herald the great biblical emancipator of Israel, Moses.

Other cycles in the corpus of African-American spirituals are more clearly associated with female imagery, if not female influence. Although no collector of the spirituals that this writer has been able to uncover has identified a Mary/Martha cycle as such, one has only to scan the lists of titles in a few collections of the texts of slave songs to discern this thematic possibility. "Oh Mary—Oh Marthy," "Mary Wept an' Marthy Moaned," and "Mary an' Martha Jes' Gone 'Long" evoke the two New Testament figures who, next to Jesus, are probably selected most often in the spirituals. Frequently, Mary, who is represented in the corpus as the Mother of Jesus or as Mary Magdelene as often as she is the mournful sister of Martha, is depicted singly, as in "Oh Mary Don't You Weep, Don't You Mourn" and "Mary Had a Baby."

Interestingly, motherhood on the one hand ("What You Going to Name That Pretty Little Baby?"), and the bitter angst of motherlessness on the other, figure as prominent motifs in the spirituals, whereas fatherhood figures only marginally. Among the most plaintive and emotive spirituals ever sung, perhaps none is more poignant than "Sometimes I Feel Like a Motherless Child":

Sometimes I feel like a motherless child
Sometimes I feel like a motherless child
Sometimes I feel like a motherless child
A long ways from my home;

or this doleful melody:

Yonder's my ole mudder
Been waggin' at de hill so long
'Bout time she cross over
Git home bime-by

In 1871, the Fisk Jubilee Singers—seven women and four men—introduced the African-American spiritual into highbrow cultural life in America and Europe. What had been formerly regarded as "barbaric chants and choruses" (Fanny *Kemble, *Journal of a Residence on a Georgia Plantation*, 1863) was "concertized" for public performance. "Sorrow songs," as W. E. B. Du Bois called the spirituals to the regret of Zora Neale *Hurston, were artistically arranged for full choruses, and some were newly composed for solo voices. The refined form, for the sake of European fastidiousness, ultimately betrayed much of the tradition's rootedness in African moans, chants, and cries. During this era, the female influence on the music form was entirely palpable. In 1927, the eminent African-American female composer and arranger Eva Jessye published two solo pieces. One of them, "I'm a Po' Lil' Orphan," underscores the theme of motherlessness so pervasive in the corpus of the spirituals. Florence B. Price and Undine Smith Moore are two more African-American women who followed in the tradition of Jessye.

After the Fisk Jubilee Singers in the late nineteenth century, it was Marian Anderson in the twentieth century whose moving renditions kept the African-American spiritual on the public stage in the United States and abroad. The standard-bearer in solo spiritual performance, Anderson was succeeded in this vain by such brilliant black voices as Mahalia Jackson, Leontyne Price, Jessye Norman, and Kathleen Battle.

The influence of the African-American spiritual on American cultural production has not been restricted to music or musical performance. Neither has black women's participation in the development and dissemination of the sacred music form been fixed therein. In the civil rights movement of the 1950s and 1960s, for instance, black women, though scarcely mentioned in the historiographies, belonged decidedly to the masses of civil dissidents who marched in nonviolent protest throughout the South singing adapted spirituals commonly called freedom songs. In black women's literature from Harriet *Jacobs's *Incidents in the Life of a Slave Girl* (1861) to Zora Neale Hurston's *Jonah's Gourd Vine* (1934) and *Moses, Man of the Mountain* (1939) to Toni *Morrison's *Beloved* (1987), spirituals have informed the aesthetic sensibilities of more than a few African-American women writers. In very recent years, the Alvin Ailey Dance Company has inspired dance audiences with a beautiful choreography of spiritual-based themes entitled "Revelations," with gender a critical distinction maintained within the text of the dance as well as in its interpretation.

In such a logocentric culture as ours, and despite the spiritual's humble origins among an illiterate class, its longevity and extended influence in the arts, literature, and politics attests to the irony that even if the enslaved creators of the spirituals—the women no less than the men—were not literate in the letter of God's Word, they had seized upon the spirit of it unmistakably.

[*See also* Spiritual Narratives; Spiritualism.]

• William Francis Allen, Charles Pickard Ware, Lucy McKim Garrison, eds., *Slave Songs of the United States* (1867; reprint, 1929). W. E. B. Du Bois, *The Souls of Black Folk* (1903). Mary Allen Grissom, ed., *The Negro Sings a New Heaven* (1930; reprint, 1969). James Weldon Johnson and J. Rosamond Johnson, eds., *The Books of American Negro Spirituals Including the Book of American Negro Spirituals and the Second Book of Negro Spirituals* (1940). Eileen Southern, *The Music of Black Americans: A History* (1971). Dena J. Epstein, *Sinful Tunes and Spirituals: Black Folk Music to the Civil War* (1977). Zora Neale Hurston, *The Sanctified Church: The Folklore Writings of Zora Neale Hurston* (1981).

M. O. Wallace

SPIVAK, Gayatri (b. 1942), literary critic, translator, academic, teacher, and trained singer of Indian classical music. Educated in her native India, with a B.A. in English from the University of Calcutta (1959), and in the United States, where she received her M.A. in English (1962) and Ph.D. in Comparative Literature (1967) from Cornell University, Spivak has continued her university career as professor of literature and critical theory at the Universities of Iowa and Texas, Emory, the University of Pittsburgh, and currently Columbia University. Variously identified as a "Third World feminist," a "high-ranking U.S. academic," and a "celebrated international lecturer," as well as a Marxist, a deconstructionist, and a "diasporic post-colonial," Spivak has herself referred to the difficult "question of what it is to be described adjectivally in terms of an ism" (*Oxford Literary Review* 13, 1–2 [1991]). Her intellectual influence, however, both within the United States and internationally, has been as wide-ranging—and, just as importantly, controversial—as these multiple epithets would even superficially indicate. The essays included in *In Other Worlds: Essays in Cultural Politics* (1987) trace a significant part of Spivak's intellectual and geopolitical itinerary. From the more disciplinarily identifiable English literary studies of Yeats, *Woolf, and Wordsworth (including her critiques of that discipline), of *French feminism, and the Marxist theorizing of value, to her analyses of selected stories by the contemporary Indian writer Mahasweta Devi, the volume marks both the theoretical conjunctures and the geographical locations that Spivak has traversed as writer and lecturer since her seminal English translation of and introduction to *Of Grammatology* (1974) by the French philosopher of *deconstruction Jacques Derrida. She has more recently continued that Benjaminian "task of the translator" in her renditions of Devi's stories, work that affiliates as well with her extended participation in the critical historiographies of Indian nationalism elaborated by the Subaltern Studies group in Australia and India (see *Selected Subaltern Studies*, eds. Ranajit Guha and Spivak, 1988). Her insistent interventions into the theories of post-colonialism are further exemplified in the interviews anthologized in *The Post-Colonial Critic: Interviews, Strategies, Dialogues* (1990), a collection that no less crucially identifies the interview itself as a genre specific to Spivak's intellectual practice. In just such an interview (*OLR*, 1991), she has since emphasized the directions—pursuing still the question "can the subaltern speak?"—of her current and projected work, at once academic and activist, on "feminism in decolonization," with special reference to Algeria, India, and Bangladesh. On a world political map riven with radical global realignments and in a United States academic milieu riddled by disciplinary skirmishes, Spivak's multifarious work—from Calcutta to Cornell to Columbia, in deconstruction and in decolonization—has challenged both the "correctness" of the *canon and the complacencies of those who support it.

• Gayatri Spivak, "Three Women's Texts and a Critique of Imperialism," *Critical Inquiry* 12, no. 1 (1985), reprinted in *The Feminist Reader: Essays in Gender and the Politics of Literary Criticism*, eds. Catherine Belsey and Jane Moore (1989) and in *Feminisms: Gender and Literary Studies*, eds. Diane Price Herndl and Robyn Warhol (1991). Gayatri Spivak, "Can the Subaltern Speak?," in *Marxism and the Interpretation of Culture*, eds. Cary Nelson and Lawrence Grossberg (1988). Gayatri Spivak, "In a Word," interview with Ellen Rooney, in *Differences* 1, no. 2 (1989). Gayatri Spivak, "French Feminism Revisited: Ethics and Politics," in

• *Feminists Theorize the Political,* eds. Judith Butler and Joan Scott (1992).

Barbara Harlow

SPOFFORD, Harriet Prescott (1835–1921), short story writer, novelist, essayist, and poet. When Thomas Wentworth Higginson advised Emily *Dickinson in 1862 to read the works of Harriet Prescott Spofford, she responded, "I read Miss Prescott's *Circumstance,* but it followed me in the dark, so I avoided her." And she added: "It is the only thing I ever read in my life that I didn't think I could have written myself." Dickinson's comments affirm not merely the power of Spofford's work, but also her striking originality in the literature of the nineteenth-century United States.

Harriet Elizabeth Prescott was born on 3 April 1835 in Calais, Maine. Throughout her childhood, Spofford's family struggled financially. Like many nineteenth-century women, Spofford began publishing anonymously in order to help support her family. The Boston papers paid badly, and Spofford worked long hours for little money. In 1858, Spofford sent a short story, "In a Cellar," to the *Atlantic Monthly,* where it was so unexpected that the editors suspected plagiarism. However, Higginson confirmed that "a demure little Yankee girl" had indeed written a tale about jewels and international diplomacy, and "In a Cellar" was published in February of 1859. It was the beginning of a long and lucrative career.

Harriet Prescott married Richard S. Spofford, Jr., in 1865. Although theirs was apparently an unusually happy marriage, many of Spofford's stories depict women's struggles for respect and equality within marriage. Spofford's first collection of short stories, *The Amber Gods and Other Stories,* was published in 1863. Perhaps her best-known work today, the title story disrupts conventional notions of form and content, anticipating twentieth-century techniques. Spofford's blasphemous, vain narrator stretches the boundaries of the nineteenth-century "heroine," and the spooky final line of "The Amber Gods" stretches the boundaries of narrative.

From the publication of "In a Cellar" in 1859 to *The Elder's People* in 1920, Spofford wrote hundreds of stories, poems, essays, and several novels, impressing writers as diverse as Henry James, Sarah Orne *Jewett, and Elizabeth Stuart *Phelps. In the pre- and post-Civil War period, in which writers and readers were increasingly turning to realism, Spofford retained the colorful drama and rhapsodic language of romance. Although her work is also informed by the *domestic fiction and *local color writings of her contemporaries, Spofford refused to abandon certain elements of romanticism. Today, the haunting quality that made her fiction popular throughout her lifetime is once again drawing attention to her work.

• Harriet Prescott Spofford, *A Scarlet Poppy and Other Stories* (1894). Harriet Prescott Spofford, *Old Madame and Other Tragedies* (1900). Harriet Prescott Spofford, *The Elder's People* (1920). Elizabeth K. Halbeisen, *Harriet Prescott Spofford: A Romantic Survival* (1935). Alfred Bendixen, ed. *"The Amber Gods" and Other Stories* (1989).

Jill C. Jones

STAFFORD, Jean (1915–1979), novelist and Pulitzer Prize–winning short story writer. Born in Covina, California, the youngest of four children, Jean Stafford felt unwanted by both her parents and her siblings. When she was five, her father, a curmudgeonly failed writer, uprooted his family from their Covina walnut ranch, moving to San Diego, where he succeeded in losing a substantial fortune on the stock exchange. Following this disaster, the Staffords lived in Colorado Springs and then in Boulder, where Stafford's mother ran a boardinghouse for female college students. An excellent student, Stafford was awarded both an A.B. and an A.M. degree in 1936 from the University of Colorado in Boulder; the next year, after receiving a fellowship, she studied philology at the University of Heidelberg.

From 1937 to 1938 Stafford taught English at Stephens College; she then moved to Massachusetts, working there on her first novel, *Boston Adventure* (1944). In 1940, Stafford married an aspiring poet, Robert Lowell, scion of the Boston Lowells. With the money she earned from *Boston Adventure,* she purchased a house in Damariscotta Mills in Maine, but soon after she and Lowell settled there, they separated. Suffering from depression and alcoholism, Stafford was hospitalized at Payne Whitney Psychiatric Hospital in New York City for almost a year. Her best novel, *The Mountain Lion* (1947), was published during this period. A recipient of two Guggenheim fellowships, Stafford began to publish short stories regularly in *The New Yorker.* In 1950, following her marriage to Oliver Jensen, a *Life* magazine writer, Stafford moved to Westport, Connecticut, where she was living when her third novel, *The Catherine Wheel* (1952), appeared. Her marriage to Jensen also ended in divorce; then, in 1959, she married *New Yorker* writer A. J. Liebling. After Liebling's death in 1963, Stafford lived in the house Liebling had purchased in The Springs, Long Island, except for the months in 1964 and 1965 when she was a fellow at Wesleyan University's Institute for Advanced Study and several months when she taught creative writing at Columbia University. Until she suffered a debilitating stroke in 1976, Stafford continued to support herself by her writing. In addition to book reviews and articles, she published *A Mother in History* (1966), based on her interviews with the mother of John F. Kennedy's assassin, Lee Harvey Oswald. In 1970, her *Collected Stories* was awarded the Pulitzer Prize.

Whether she was drawing on her early years in California and her troubled adolescence in Boulder in her first-rate *bildungsroman, *The Mountain Lion,* on her Wanderjahr in Germany during the rise of Hitler, or on her life in Massachusetts, Maine, New York City, or Connecticut, Stafford's beautifully crafted novels and short stories frequently are thinly disguised accounts of her own experience. Influenced by the fiction of Mark Twain, Henry James, Sarah Orne *Jewett, and Willa *Cather, Stafford wrote works that are notable for their irony, wit, sense of place, and poignant depictions of disaffected female characters who would have agreed with Mrs. Placer in Stafford's "In the Zoo" that life is "essentially a matter of being done in, let down, and swindled."

• The Jean Stafford Papers, are housed at the University of Colorado, Boulder. See also Wanda Avila, *Jean Stafford: A Comprehensive Bibliography* (1983). Mary Ellen Williams Walsh, *Jean Stafford* (1985). Maureen Ryan, *Innocence and Estrangement in the Fiction of Jean Stafford* (1987). David Roberts, *Jean Stafford: A Biography* (1988). Charlotte Margolis Goodman, *Jean Stafford: The Savage Heart* (1990). Ann Hulbert, *The Interior Castle: The Art and Life of Jean Stafford* (1992).

Charlotte Goodman

STANTON, Elizabeth Cady (1815–1902), suffragist, journalist, and lecturer. In 1840, twenty-five-year-old Elizabeth Cady Stanton met Philadelphia abolitionist Lucretia Mott at the World Anti-slavery Convention in London, which Stanton attended because her new husband, Henry B. Stanton, was a delegate. Mott, who had been forced into the visitors' gallery because the convention would not seat a woman delegate, talked with Stanton about the need for a women's rights movement in the United States. Eight years later they organized the first women's rights convention in Seneca Falls, New York. By this time Stanton had three children, and her experiences certainly shaped the *Declaration of Sentiments* she authored for that meeting. The *Declaration* called for higher education and professional opportunities for women, for married women's property rights, the right to divorce, and the right to custody of children; its most radical demand was for women's right to vote.

During the next ten years, Stanton gave birth to four more children, tried to attend women's rights conventions, and most importantly, in 1852, met her lifelong friend Susan B. *Anthony. An unmarried teacher, Anthony was much freer to travel and organize; therefore she watched the children while Stanton wrote speeches that Anthony then delivered. Stanton said of their working relationship, "I forged the thunderbolts and she fired them." During the fifties, both Stanton and Anthony also took the radical step of wearing the bloomer costume.

The 1860s were taken up with work for the Women's Loyal League, which raised funds for the Union Army. After the *Civil War, Stanton and other activists assumed that they had earned the right to vote along with the black men enfranchised by the fourteenth and fifteenth amendments. She worked with the American Equal Rights Association and was bitterly disappointed by the defeat of women's suffrage in Kansas in 1867. Continuing to insist on women's suffrage, in 1869 she and Anthony split away from Lucy Stone's American Woman Suffrage Association, which put aside women's suffrage to campaign for suffrage for black males. In New York, Stanton and Anthony established the National Woman Suffrage Association, which published a journal called the *Revolution,* and in addition to suffrage, championed the Working Women's Association in the 1860s.

During this decade, anger at the omission of women from the fourteenth and fifteenth amendments caused Stanton to begin to speak favorably of limiting the suffrage to educated men and women, thereby excluding most freed slaves and new immigrants. Her *racism was only slightly mitigated by her belief that all Americans had a right to a decent education and would thus eventually qualify to vote. Although they continued to campaign tirelessly for women's suffrage in the 1870s, Stanton and Anthony's small organization barely survived their support for the radical proponent of "free love," Victoria Woodhull, when she accused popular preacher Henry Ward Beecher of adultery in 1872. By 1890, it was clear that women's suffrage could not be won by a splintered organization, and the two major groups combined to become the National American Woman Suffrage Association (NAWSA) with Stanton as its first president. NAWSA survived thirty-two losses at the state level to become an organization of two million members by the time women's suffrage was won in 1920.

For the last third of her life, Elizabeth Cady Stanton grew increasingly more radical. She became a well-known journalist and lecturer, championing *suffrage, divorce and custody reform, equal pay, union membership, and voluntary motherhood (women's right to refuse sex to limit family size). Most radical was the 1895 publication of her *The Woman's Bible*, which challenged organized religion by including feminist interpretations of many passages. The *Woman's Bible* brought Stanton further censure by the press and even by the NAWSA.

But by now this grand old lady of American feminism weighed 250 pounds and hardly cared what others thought. In her last speech, the "Solitude of Self," delivered before the American Congress in 1892, ten years before her death, she ended with these words: "The strongest reason why we ask for woman a voice in the government; . . . in religion; . . . equality in social life; . . . a place in the trades and professions, . . . is because of her birthright to self-sovereignty; because as an individual, she must rely on herself."

• Harriot Stanton Blatch and Theodore Stanton, eds., *Elizabeth Cady Stanton as Revealed in Her Letters, Diary and Reminiscences* (1969; reprint of a 1922 edition). Mary Ann B. Oakley, *Elizabeth Cady Stanton* (1972). Ellen Carol DuBois, *Feminism and Suffrage: The Emergence of an Independent Women's Movement in America, 1848–1869* (1978). Ellen Carol DuBois, ed., *Elizabeth Cady Stanton, Susan B. Anthony: Correspondence, Writings, Speeches* (1981). Elisabeth Griffith, *In Her Own Right: The Life of Elizabeth Cady Stanton* (1984). Lois W. Banner, *Elizabeth Cady Stanton: A Radical for Women's Rights* (1987).

Laurie Crumpacker

STEIN, Gertrude (1874–1946), poet, novelist, playwright, essayist, librettist, biographer, and memoirist. One of the most innovative modern writers, Stein was the youngest child of Daniel and Amelia Keyser Stein, German Jews whose parents had emigrated to Baltimore. Leaving their clothing business in Allegheny, Pennsylvania, the Daniel Steins moved to Austria soon after Gertrude's birth and lived there and in Paris until returning to Oakland, California, in 1879. When Gertrude was eleven, her mother became ill with the cancer from which she was to die several years later; her father died suddenly when she was seventeen. She and Leo, the youngest brother, lived for a time with their oldest brother Michael, an executive with the San Francisco street railway system. Then, with her sister Bertha and Leo, Gertrude traveled back to Baltimore to live with her aunt's family.

When Leo transferred to Harvard, Gertrude decided she would attend Radcliffe. Her irregular schooling had been balanced by extensive reading, and she was accepted as a special student even though she had not graduated from secondary school. Studying philosophy and psychology with William James, Hugo Münsterberg, and others, she graduated magna cum laude in philosophy. From Radcliffe she went to Johns Hopkins Medical School, where her controversial stance on women's medicine caused problems with the male faculty. She chose not to graduate, and then worked on studies in the development of the brain with Llewelys Barker. Her published essays from her college years concern attention and the way fatigue affects it.

Lured by Leo's interest in art and his residence in Paris while he studied painting, Gertrude moved in 1903 to 27 rue de Fleurus. While Leo was a patron of the arts, purchasing Renoirs, Manets, and Cézannes, Gertrude became a writer. She observed people during their Saturday salons and then wrote late at night in the atelier, which was hung with pictures. Her earliest writing was the first version of *The Making of Americans*, her story of the "progress" of an American family; *Q.E.D.*, an account of her heartbreaking lesbian liaison in Baltimore; and *Fernhurst*, another treatment of power within a love triangle. In 1905 she began the collection of three "realistic" stories of common women—the German Anna and Lena, and the mulatto Melanctha—that would be privately published in 1909 as *Three Lives*. Distancing herself from the autobiographical, Stein relied on her knowledge of brain anatomy as she wrote with what she called "insistence." Her repetitions of syntax and language gave *Three Lives* a distinctively modern flavor. It was followed in 1912 by her word portraits of Matisse and Picasso, published in Alfred Stieglitz's *Camera Work*.

In 1907, Alice B. Toklas visited Paris, part of the group of Californians who admired Sarah and Mike Stein, also now living in Paris and collecting art—mostly works by Matisse. Once she and Gertrude formed their partnership, Alice became Gertrude's reader, typist, and critic. In 1910 she moved into the rue de Fleurus household and several years later Leo moved out—to Italy. Part of the dissension between the Steins stemmed from Leo's dislike of Cubism. Gertrude saw analogies between the Cubism of Picasso and Braque and her portraits and the poems of the 1914 *Tender Buttons*. Reminiscent of poetry by Apollinaire and Kandinsky, Stein's work seemed unique to American readers.

Finished with the 1000-page *The Making of Americans* in 1911 and excited by non-representational use of language, Stein wrote daily in French school notebooks. She published little. After she and Alice had lived in Spain for the first year of World War I, and then returned to France to work for the American Friends of the French Wounded (Stein driving a remodeled

Ford truck from 1916 to 1919), they concentrated on finding publishers for Stein's accumulating work, which now included plays and novels. Her fame as an avant-gardist brought her many visitors—Sherwood Anderson, Mabel *Dodge, Virgil Thomson, Carl Van Vechten—and she became a part of the Paris circle of expatriate Americans, including Sylvia *Beach, Natalie *Barney, Paul Bowles, Ernest Hemingway, Thornton Wilder, and others. In 1922 she published *Geography and Plays*, a collection of portraits and plays, and in 1925 Robert McAlmon published *The Making of Americans*.

After Edith Sitwell arranged for Stein to lecture in Oxford and Cambridge in 1926, the Hogarth Press published her lectures, *Composition as Explanation*, and she began to feel as if the "gloire" she had longed for might be possible. She was experimenting with longer poems ("Patriarchal Poetry" and "Stanzas in Meditation") and with essays about her aesthetic beliefs. Toklas began a publishing house called Plain Edition, publishing *Lucy Church Amiably* and other of Stein's books in the early 1930s.

After spending six weeks writing the memoir she slyly called *The Autobiography of Alice B. Toklas*, Stein found the recognition she hungered for. Serialized in the *Atlantic Monthly* and a Book-of-the-Month-Club selection, the *Autobiography* made Gertrude her first money (each of the Steins had lived on between $100 and $150 a month from a family trust fund). To capitalize on this fame, she toured the States lecturing, returning to the country of her birth for the first time since 1904. Between September 1934 and May 1935, Gertrude and Alice were fêted from New York to Richmond, San Francisco to Chicago. Their visit also coincided with performances of Stein and Virgil Thomson's opera *Four Saints in Three Acts*.

Returning to Paris, Stein wrote the second volume of her memoirs, *Everybody's Autobiography*, which Random House published in 1937, under their contract to bring out one book of Stein's each year. During the 1930s she published *Portraits and Prayers* (1934); *Lectures in America* and *Narration* (1935); *The Geographical History of America* (1936); *Picasso* (1938); and her first book for children, *The World Is Round* (1939).

When World War II became unavoidable, she and Toklas left Paris for the summer home they rented in Belley. Protected by the villagers of both Bilignin and Culoz, where they moved in 1944, they escaped the persecution that might have befallen them as Jews. Though life was hard, Stein continued writing. *Paris France* and *What Are Masterpieces* were published in 1940 and *Ida, A Novel* in 1941. The last book of her memoirs, *Wars I Have Seen*, appeared in 1945. As she had during World War I, Gertrude befriended the American soldiers she met, and her short life after peace was filled with speaking engagements and visiting with American G.I.s. One of her last books, *Brewsie and Willie* (1946), attempts to capture the soldiers' American idiom. She also finished *The Mother of Us All*, her opera based freely on Susan B. *Anthony's life, before dying in July 1946 of the intestinal cancer that had plagued her family. She left her estate to Toklas for as long as she lived. Most of Stein's manuscripts were published during the next fifteen years in a series of volumes by Yale University Press.

Criticism has only begun to analyze Stein's unique works. Diligent in her efforts to create a meaningful language, one that would reach the reader's consciousness in ways that most writing did not, Stein plumbed areas of communication that are as often non-verbal as linguistic. Her incorporation of *humor, sound, sex, and bawdiness, and unpredictable locutions and structures—always executed with the heightened consciousness of the observed performer—made her a pioneer of *postmodernism as well as a central figure of *modernism. Representative of the work being done by twentieth-century women artists, writers, and readers, Stein's writing gave readers an intimate sense of a woman's life and concerns. In a period when writers prided themselves on being able to shape language to new kinds of expressions, Gertrude Stein moved back into the most traditional relationship between writer and word: letting language find its own patterns, to express whatever meaning the reader might favor, viewing written art as a system of true and mutable communication.

• Stein's papers are at the Beinecke Library, American Literature Collection, Yale University; the Bancroft Library, University of California, Berkeley; and the Harry Ransom Humanities Research Center, University of Texas, Austin. See also W. G. Rogers, *When This You See Remember Me: Gertrude Stein in Person* (1948). Donald Gallup, ed., *The Flowers of Friendship: Letters Written to Gertrude Stein* (1953). John Malcolm Brinnin, *The Third Rose: Gertrude Stein and Her World* (1959). Alice B. Toklas, *What Is Remembered* (1963). Richard Bridgman, *Gertrude Stein in Pieces* (1970). James R. Mellow, *Charmed Circle: Gertrude Stein and Company* (1974). Wendy Steiner, *Exact Resemblance to Exact Resemblance: The Literary Portraiture of Gertrude Stein* (1978). Neil Schmitz, *Of Huck and Alice: Humorous Writing in American Literature* (1983). Shari Benstock, *Women of the Left Bank: Paris, 1900–1940* (1986). Harriet Chessman, *The Public Is Invited to Dance: Representation, the Body, and Dialogue in Gertrude Stein* (1989).

Linda Wagner-Martin

STEINEM, Gloria (b. 1934), author, editor, activist, and founder of *Ms. Magazine*. Born in

Toledo, Ohio, she spent her adolescence caring for her mentally ill mother after her parents divorced when she was seven. At seventeen, she entered Smith College on a scholarship, graduating with a B.A. magna cum laude in political science (1956). She did graduate work at the University of Delhi and the University of Calcutta, India (1957–1958). In India, she began writing for local newspapers, and became active in a group called the Radical Humanists, a peace-making team that tried to ease caste rioting in the villages.

Upon her return to the United States, Steinem began a successful career as a freelance writer and worked for the civil rights movement. In 1968, she and Clay Felker founded *New York Magazine*, to which she contributed a monthly column called "The City Politic." Steinem's early work was praised for its topicality and humor, but in 1969, when she published an article on *abortion and a follow-up article called "After Black Power, Women's Liberation," she began to receive harsh criticism from her male colleagues. Although the later article won the Penny-Missouri Journalism Award, she was discouraged from pursuing other feminist issues. When she found no publication that would accept her new work, she began to imagine a magazine directed toward a progressive female audience, in which all aspects of writing and production were controlled by women; in January of 1972, she founded *Ms. Magazine*.

From 1972 through 1989, Steinem spent much of her time meeting her editorial commitments to *Ms.*, but she managed to write articles and books, organize fund-raising projects, and attend speaking engagements. Her principal works are *Outrageous Acts and Everyday Rebellions* (1983), a collection of essays from her early years as a journalist; *Marilyn* (1986), a biography portraying Marilyn Monroe as a victim rather than a femme fatale; and *Revolution from Within: A Book of Self-Esteem* (1992), an exploration of the politics of self-love.

Steinem's prominence has made her both influential and vulnerable to criticism; she has been attacked from both sides of the feminist debate for either being too radical in her politics, or for representing only the more pleasant, mainstream aspects of *feminism. Currently living and working in New York, Steinem anticipates the publication of future writing projects.

• Betsy Carter, "Liberation's Next Wave," *Esquire* (June 1984): 202–206. "Gloria Steinem," in *Contemporary Literary Criticism* vol. 63, ed. Roger Matuz (1991), pp. 378–388. "Gloria Steinem," in *Contemporary Authors* vol. 28, eds. Hal May and James G. Leshiak (1991), pp. 443–445. Deirdre English, "She's Her Weakness Now," *New York Times Book Review* (2 February 1992): 13.

Traci Freeman

STEP-PARENTS AND STEPCHILDREN. By contrast with its British cousin, American writing lacks notable step-parent and stepchildren characters. While George Eliot, Charles Dickens, and William Makepeace Thackeray were capturing the economic and emotional undercurrents of Victorian family life in England, American women authors of the same period were writing a popular and sentimentalized account of the family, which frequently elided such complexities as second marriages (see Ann Douglas, *The Feminization of American Culture*, 1979). As much as they do appear, however, step-parent and stepchild relationships carry their greatest influence in the nineteenth-century and early-twentieth-century writing in which the sentimentalization of woman's domestic sphere masked her role in the rapidly changing economy.

In mid-nineteenth-century sentimental fiction the intrusion of a stepmother might disturb a daughter's control of the household economy, interrupt her growth into sexual maturity, and even threaten her life. In Adeline D. T. Whitney's childrens' story "My Mother Put It On," the narrator juxtaposes a childhood memory of a Christmas with her mother with an account of what her adult life has become. Burdened by unattractiveness, she never marries but continues to live with her stepmother after her father's death. The remembered Christmas gift of a "wax baby" and her father's remarriage when the girl is seventeen suggests that her ability to reach sexual maturity and motherhood in her own right has been curtailed by the appearance of a new mother. In Maria *Cummins's *The Lamplighter*, a father's remarriage to a woman of fashion disrupts the comfortable domesticity of his blind daughter and her female helpmate. The two women uncomplainingly suffer the noise and disorder created by the invasion of the stepmother and her two nieces (including a steamboat accident that almost results in their deaths) until rescued by the appropriate suitors.

Writing in the 1890s, Mary E. Wilkins *Freeman used the medium of a *ghost story to explore the more sinister side of the stepmother/stepdaughter relationship. The stepmother in the story allows her stepdaughter to die by neglecting to care for her during an illness. She is subsequently subject to nervous attacks brought on by the strange doings of the girl's ghost. Set in a small New England village in economic decline, "The Wind in the Rose-bush" emphasizes the stepmother's skill at retaining economic independence at the expense of her stepdaughter's life.

In "The Other Two" (1904) Edith *Wharton presents a modern-day situation of divorce and remarriage. Unusual in that it is told from the perspective of the stepfather, the story is set in an urban milieu in which dress and manners determine identity. Thrown into contact with his wife's first husband by the man's custodial visits to his stepdaughter, the stepfather gradually detects the cold-hearted ambition that lies behind his wife's show of motherly tenderness and social poise.

The relationships between step-parents and stepchildren in these texts become sites of economic and interpersonal tensions that pose a challenge to a popular version of the American family.

• Adeline D. T. Whitney, "My Mother Put It On," in *Under Twenty*, ed. Maria Lamberton Becker (1932). Ann Douglas, *The Feminization of American Culture* (1979). Mary E. Wilkins Freeman, *Selected Stories of Mary E. Wilkins Freeman*, ed. Marjorie Pryse (1983). Maria S. Cummins, *The Lamplighter* (1988). Edith Wharton, "The Other Two" in *The Heath Anthology of American Literature*, vol. 2 (1990).

Laura Byra

STEREOTYPES are textual or visual representations that depict an individual as a type by presenting selective, identifiable qualities ascribed to a real or constructed category of individuals. The term originated in eighteenth-century printing, where moulds were cast from hand-set type and were then used to cast identical sheets of letters and images that were used for the actual printing. The absolute correspondence between the cast and the original type led to the use of the term in regard to mental images during the mid-nineteenth century. This term stresses the fixed, unchanged form of the representation. Recently, other terms such as "image" and "mirage" have been proposed to avoid the association with the seemingly frozen representation.

The fixed aspect of the stereotype is a reflex of its origin. It represents the fantasy of a thought-collective about the essential nature and reality of members of another group. A thought-collective is any group of individuals who express a common identity through the use of a common discourse. Such thought-collectives can be "real" (i.e., embedded in or generating social institutions, such as science or the nobility), or they may be "imagined" (i.e., existing independent of such social institutions, such as ethnic groups that generate "imagined communities"). Thus in a patriarchal society, masculinist images of the "feminine" provide absolute definitions of the

woman as a means of generating an image that corresponds to the needs of the masculinist thought-collective. But at the same time such a "masculine" society provides alternative images of the "masculine" (such as the stereotype of the dangerous African-American male) as well as differentiated images of the "feminine" (such as the stereotypes of the whore and the mother) based on an ever-shifting need for control over the thought-collective's sense of cohesiveness.

A stereotype may seem to be positive or negative—that is, it may represent good or bad qualities of the collective in the form of the representation of an individual. No matter whether negative or positive, such images always disguise the desire to control the realities behind the categories so represented. Thus classic dichotomies of nineteenth-century Euro-American presentations of the woman—the bitch or the goddess and the whore or the mother—reflect positive and negative images of the female, yet all are means of reducing the complexity of female identity to categories generated by a patriarchal society when confronted with challenges to its own definitions of acceptable masculinity. As Nancy Walker states in "Reformers and Young Maidens" (1985), Ernest Hemingway's representations of the female define the limits of his own ambiguous sense of masculinity, while Mark Twain's images of female "virtue" simply reverse and domesticate existing images of female "vice." While the collectives stereotyped may or may not be capable of being so controlled, their images are clearly manipulable, since they are generated by the thought-collective. These images rarely permit any type of individuation. All thoughts, actions, and character development are understood in terms of the stereotype generated by the thought-collective.

All stereotypes are reflections of the inner life of the thought-collective that generates them. It is imposed upon those individuals who are seen, felt, or thought to belong to the category of the stereotype. Those stereotyped may even feel themselves as part of that thought-collective which generates the image applied to themselves, and share the symbolic vocabulary of their own representation. Thus the role that some Jewish women writers in the 1970s had in perpetuating and advocating the stereotype of the materialistic, sexually distant, and controlling J[ewish] A[merican] P[rincess] internalized many of the representations of the Jewish female present in the society in which they lived. Rather than contesting such masculine images, such as those present in the early work of the Jewish-American novelist Phillip Roth (*Goodbye, Columbus*, 1959), they saw these images as representing a sub-type, distant from their own self-representation. Such internalization may lead to the complex reevaluation or resistance to these images, often while employing them in ironic or contradictory ways. It can, however, also lead to a sense of self-abnegation in which these stereotypes are employed to represent the inner life of the author or artist. These images are usually triggered by visual clues in the depiction of the stereotype, so that the perception and representation of external realities are virtual clues to the internal life of the stereotyped character or image. Thus Sylvia * Plath's evocation of the anxiety generated by her Polish-German father (in "Daddy," 1962) is generated by those visual stereotypes specifically associated with the German after the Shoah. (The references in the poem to barbed wire, to the concentration camps, to "your neat mustache and your Aryan eye" all encapsulate the American image of the German as the figure of terror.)

As stereotypes are constructions of essential types, most stereotypes are polar. They represent the ends of a presumed spectrum, but few if any medial characters are to be found. Thus a stereotype is essentially "bad" or "good." And this dichotomy is understood to be a reflection of the essence of the type and is present in all aspects of the type. "Bad" is equated with a specific type of external "ugliness" and "good" with a perceived type of external "beauty." "Good" female characters, such as Harriet Beecher * Stowe's dying "little Eva" are associated with a type of ethereal beauty. "Bad" figures are associated with forms of deformity and ugliness. Ironic reversals are possible within such structures, so as to have the "inner beauty/goodness" of a character provide an alternative to the external "ugliness." The use of such figures in Carson * McCullers' *The Ballad of the Sad Café* (1951) is exemplary for such reversal.

Stereotypes can be either inclusive or exclusive. They can complement the nature of the thought-collective that is generating the image or they can be seen as separate from it. Thus a negative image can be clothed in a vocabulary that seems complimentary or at least not uncomplimentary, such as the representation of the "noble" prostitute in Bret Harte's "The Luck of Roaring Camp" (1870). All stereotypes are attempts to define the thought-collective, to construct a boundary for its inclusivity and exclusivity. In literary or visual forms these stereotypes are fixed representations of the imagined boundaries of the thought-collective that generates the image.

All thought-collectives generate stereotypes. Those with power generate them concerning those who seemingly threaten the retention and practice of power; those thought-collectives without power generate stereotypes of those with power as well as projections of their own powerlessness onto other stereotyped categories. (For example, as Milton A. Cohen explains in "Black Brutes and Mulatto Saints" [1984], Gertrude * Stein created an image of the mulatto as a liminal figure, neither black nor white, parallel to her own lesbian identity, understood as neither male nor female. Here the charge of nineteenth-century and early twentieth-century culture that marginal women are "destructive" rather than "creative" is internalized and reversed to stress the positive qualities of the liminal.) While a stereotype is a fantasy generated by one thought-collective and projected onto another, the group onto which this fantasy is projected is never neutral or passive in regard to the other group's fantasy. Thus the fantasy of a powerful group may well construct a group that otherwise does not comprehend itself as an entity (as in the construction of a regional identity out of a Romantic idea of place, e.g., the construction of the "Maine-man and woman" by Sarah Orne * Jewett); it may also reenforce a sense of identity or cohesion that exists within an already defined thought-collective (as in the literary construction of the * "flapper" in the work of F. Scott and Zelda * Fitzgerald). Groups so constructed may look in their midst for a sub-group that seems to possess the predominate defining qualities of the stereotype and thus project their sense of being controlled onto this group. (As Trudier Harris explains in "On *The Color Purple*, Stereotypes, and Silence" (1984), Alice * Walker's highly differentiated image of the African-American woman in *The Color Purple* (1982) is balanced by a projection of the negative qualities of the African American onto the African-American male.) Or indeed, they may well identify themselves with the qualities so delineated. This can lead to a form of self-hatred in which the negative stereotypes are taken as accurate labels for the identity of the group without power. This can be seen in the conservative image of the woman in the *Biography of Females* (1829) as well as *Letters to Young Ladies* (1833) of Lydia H. * Signourney. It can also lead to forms of resistance.

Resistance to stereotyping can take four identifiable forms. One form is an outright rejection of the categories applied to the group in which one is situated, a choice rarer in groups that see themselves as powerless and dependent on the toleration of the group with power. There can be a romantic reversal and transvaluation of categories, so that the representations of control applied to the stereotyped group are internalized and seen as positive attributes.

Kate *Chopin's image of the sexual awakening of a woman in *The Awakening* (1899) places at the center of her image the charge that women were fixated on their reproductive function and internalized it, stressing the woman's positive sexual life. There can be a universalization of the qualities, so that the qualities that are seen as attributes of a type or category are applied to all human beings. The stereotype of the sensitive female, often used to deny the ability of the woman to reason, is applied to both men and women in the fictive world of Edith *Wharton's *Ethan Frome* (1911). And finally there can be a recontextualization of such categories, so that traits are not made to fall into simplistic "positive" and "negative" categories. Charlotte Perkins *Gilman reinterprets the origin of her illness in *The Yellow Wallpaper* (1892) to have a social-psychological rather than a biological-physical cause. Biological explanations are often replaced by social explanations when liminal groups seek to explain the nature of their own identity in the late-nineteenth century, while in the mid-twentieth century social explanations are often replaced by biological ones. The antithesis of Gilman's presentation is to be found in Hannah Green's (that is, Joanne Greenberg) autobiographic novel, *I Never Promised You a Rose Garden* (1964).

The polar qualities of stereotypes are rooted in a social representation of an underlying psychological phenomena. All human beings internalize the presence of "good" and "bad" forces in the world as part of their coming to consciousness in the world. As in infancy one becomes aware of the difference between one's self and the external world, later one's psychic life centers about the control of the world about oneself. With maturity, one becomes more and more aware of the impossibility of controlling this external world and gives to the controllable elements "positive" qualities and to the uncontrollable "negative" qualities. These qualities become internalized representations of the world, which structure our stereotypes. Thus the underlying psychological structures associated with control or its absence is tied to the internalized representation of the world. The leap to generating images of control or its antithesis when confronted with a world perceived as being out of one's own control (or potentially so) draws upon the internalized, antithetical models of "good" (controllable) or "bad" (uncontrollable) images already present in the psyche. The human being imagines in images, in representations of the world that are already divided into polarities. Such fantasies are a means of controlling the world in which one must exist and which is, by its very nature, constructed randomly.

By empowering certain images with "good" or "bad" qualities, one can foresee their actions or natures or essences. They become controllable because one can sense what actions they will undertake, what views they will espouse, and what danger or benefit they will provide within one's sense of one's own thought-collective. Such images are the stuff of texts, as texts are themselves highly structured fantasies about the world. Contradictory stereotypes can and do exist simultaneously, even within the same textual representation. The coexistence seems contradictory until the referent group is defined. Each of these images is a model of control generated by a thought-collective. What seems contradictory is but the active drawing of the psychological boundaries of that thought-collective. All stereotypes are fluid and function to define the referent group; the perceived boundaries between stereotypes are arbitrary. What is equally fluid and arbitrary is what stands at the center—the constant self-defining of the thought-collective generating stereotypes to bound its otherwise difficult-to-define self.

Texts, in the most general sense, have evolved their own vocabulary of stereotypes and images. These images exist within the text, often generated by a specific social impulse in defining the boundaries of a thought-collective. Because they are seen as "real," as capturing "the kernel of truth," separate from their function in defining the referent group, these images can have a textual life of their own. The intertextual generation of stereotypes is an important moment in the seeming consistency of images. Images of the otherness of liminal groups can be easily traced over time through the seemingly constant attributes ascribed to their representations within textual traditions. Yet when this consistency is examined, it reveals itself to be a chimera. What is linked is the appropriation of sets of images that delineate the difference from the referent group. Thus qualities ascribed to one group can easily be expropriated by applying them to another even if there is no "kernel of truth" that might link both categories. Yet the qualities are of importance—not as much as bounding a single stereotype but in understanding what qualities are central to a given thought-collective's image of difference.

The older tradition of the study of literary images sought after a "kernel of truth" that lodged behind the stereotype. Often such studies were attempts to link the image of the literary stereotype with some "real" (positive or negative) quality of the collective represented. The objects examined were virtually always texts from the realm of "high" culture. The assumption was that the aesthetic value of the high cultural object provided proof for the reality of the stereotype. Those older studies, which sought to study the formal themes of literature either in terms of their archetypal patterns (such as Adam and Eve) or their literary traditions (such as Medea in Western drama), always sought to relate these themes to some type of social or cultural reality. Most often that reality was found by these critics in the specter of the autonomous work of art functioning independently of any historical or cultural context. Thus themes became the stuff of a "biological" or a "new critical" approach to literature and often remained in this venue.

In the past twenty years, the study of stereotypes has become the study of the group (and individual) fantasies of a culture. The objects themselves have shifted: no longer is the trinity "poem, play, novel" evoked. Objects from the "scientific" culture, from "popular" culture and "mass" culture, ranging from comics to sitcoms to medical textbooks have become the sources for the new studies of stereotype. The older sources have not been abandoned, but the new range of material has offered a more complex and nuanced set of studies that reflect our contemporary interest in questions shaped by class, national, racial, and gender identity. As a result the intent of the critic has also shifted.

No longer do critics of stereotypes seek after the "kernel of truth" in the image, rather, they use the image as a means of portraying the ever-shifting and often contradictory self-image of those whose fantasies are bound up with their use of images. The parallel study, that of the internalization of these images within the worldview of those represented, has become a substantial addition to this field through the work of feminist scholars and those scholars dealing with the image of racial difference, such as Elaine Showalter, Barbara Johnson, and Valerie Smith. The study of images, in its best and most coherent form today, is linked to the examination of the group and individual fantasies—both the fantasies of the group generating the images as well as those internalizing these images. Cultural artifacts serve to shape and focus these fantasies. They have no privileged status except as the means by which a society provides the context for the public expression of these fantasies. They provide access to these images. Different critical approaches have been applied to these fantasies (and the forces that shaped them).

But this new turning is also fraught with problems. Little attention has been paid to the strong tradition of the cultural artifact, the question of the genre, which itself helps shape and focus themes. There is no unmediated approach to the fantasy of groups and the mediation of the rules of each artifact (from opera to film to novel) must also be understood. The "rules" for representation, whether in the narrative or the visual tradition, must be analyzed, and the stereotype must not be seen as a "free-floating signifier" but as a social, historical, and literary phenomenon.

• Milton A. Cohen, "Black Brutes and Mulatto Saints: The Racial Hierarchy of Stein's 'Melanctha,'" *Black American Literature Forum* 18, no. 3 (Fall 1984): 119–121. Trudier Harris, "On *The Color Purple*, Stereotypes, and Silence," *Black American Literature Forum* 18, no. 4 (Winter 1984): 155–161. Alan Dundes, "The J.A.P. and the J.A.M. in American Jokelore," *Journal of American Folklore* 98, no. 390 (October–December 1985): 456–475. Nancy Walker, "Reformers and Young Maidens: Women and Virtue in *Adventures of Huckleberry Finn*," in *One Hundred Years of Huckleberry Finn: The Boy, His Book, and American Culture*, eds. J. Donald Crowley and Robert Sattlemeyer (1985), pp. 171–185. Sander Gilman, *Difference and Pathology: Stereotypes of Sexuality, Race, and Madness* (1985). Sander L. Gilman, *The Jew's Body* (1991).

Sander L. Gilman

STOCKTON, Annis Boudinot (1736–1801), one of the most frequently published women poets of the eighteenth century. Annis Boudinot Stockton was best known as the wife of Richard Stockton, signer of the Declaration of Independence. Stockton's friends and acquaintances knew she was a prolific writer, yet it was her social position rather than her poetry that seems to have brought her high regard. Born to Catherine Williams and Elias Boudinot in Darby, Pennsylvania, Annis Boudinot had the advantages that middling elite white status brought for young women and men. At a time when few women, even of her class, received much education, Annis Boudinot evidently received training in reading, writing, rudimentary ciphering, and the arts of sewing and dancing. In 1753, her father moved the family to Princeton, where Annis could circulate among that town's favored families. Annis Boudinot's marriage to Richard Stockton during the winter of 1757–1758 brought her into one of the oldest landed elite families of Princeton. Prior to the Revolutionary War, royal appointments for her husband created for Annis Stockton a high-profile life of social engagements. She bore six children, but time for writing was afforded her by the slaves and other workers used at Morven, the Princeton estate. During the American Revolution, the family estate was ransacked by Cornwallis and his troops, who used Morven as a central headquarters. Richard Stockton died in 1781, not long after the family returned to Morven. As a widow, Annis Stockton hosted some of the fêtes held by Congress when it met in Princeton in 1783, under the presidency of her brother Elias. She frequently entertained George and Martha Washington, and, over the course of several years, she hosted a number of members of the French, Italian, and Polish nobility, along with key American officials. Annis Stockton was proud of her family, and she worked hard to establish for herself and her children a set of social circumstances that would reflect her own favoring of high social class.

As a woman of the elite, she wrote poetry that indicated her strong attitudes about what was then considered good sense, decorum, and rationality modified by an appropriate amount of sensibility (a recognition of the emotional life and its relation to elements like friendship and poetic inspiration). Stockton was an energetic, prolific, highly stylized writer whose works number into the hundreds. A member of a writing circle that at various times included Elizabeth Graeme *Fergusson, Francis Hopkinson, John Dickinson, Philip Freneau, and Anna Young *Smith, Stockton wrote in the most common poetic forms of her day—odes, hymns, epithalamia, epitaphs, songs, and sonnets—on themes of friendship, the "battle" of the sexes, affairs of state, death, and religious beauty and belief. Stockton saw at least twenty-one of her poems published in the most prestigious newspapers and magazines. Like her lifelong Philadelphia friend Elizabeth Graeme Fergusson, Annis Stockton held "literary" meetings at her home and thus encouraged younger men, and especially women, to write.

• Annis Boudinot Stockton's MS poetry book is housed at the New Jersey Historical Society, Newark, New Jersey. See also Alfred Hoyt Bill, *A House Called Morven: Its Role in History*, rev. by Constance M. Greiff (1978). Carla J. Mulford, *The Poetry of Annis Boudinot Stockton* (1994).

Carla J. Mulford

STODDARD, Elizabeth Drew Barstow (1823–1902), novelist, short story writer, poet, literary journalist, and regionalist. Born into a prosperous family in Mattapoisett, Massachusetts, Stoddard moved to New York City in 1853 upon marrying poet Richard Stoddard. Quickly developing an idiosyncratic elliptical and vernacular mode of writing to explore the question of female subjectivity, she initially exulted in this iconoclasm, which put her out of step both with Richard's circle of genteel minor poets and with contemporary standards of decorum for women writers. In the semi-monthly columns of cultural-political commentary she wrote as the "Lady Correspondent" for the San Francisco

Alta (1854–1858), she relished commenting irreverently on subjects from *temperance to woman writers to relations between the sexes. The tensions between conventions and women's quest for selfhood were the subject of her fiction in the early 1860s. The protagonist of *The Morgesons* (1862) pursues a life encompassing sexuality, religious skepticism, and anger while her female friends and kin conform to repressive conventions. The energy with which *The Morgesons* mixes forms—female *Gothic, *bildungsroman, woman's fiction, regional fiction—reflects prevailing literary modes' inadequacy for Stoddard's subject as well as her own imaginativeness. Similarly, much of the short fiction she published in *Harper's* during this period calls attention to the confines of the formulas held proper for women authors and to the tension between her heroines' needs for selfhood and their prescribed fates, love and marriage.

The Morgesons sold poorly and by the mid-1860s it was clear that the Stoddards would succeed neither artistically nor commercially. Their finances were frequently precarious and their lives darkened by the early deaths of two of their three children. Elizabeth tried to adapt to contemporary tastes in *Two Men* (1865) and *Temple House* (1867); neither sold. Most of the short pieces she subsequently produced for magazines were slight, though a few and her book of children's stories, *Dolly Dinks' Doings* (1874), exhibit her hallmark intensity and generic originality. Only in letters, especially those to her lifelong friend and confidant Edmund Clarence Stedman (still largely unpublished), did she consistently express herself with forceful unconventionality. Her correspondence also reveals the deepening irascibility and abrasiveness of her later years, when bitterness at her failure and Richard's fueled envy of those who succeeded despite talents she judged far inferior. At the time of her death she had few admirers and no imitators. For years, literary historians and critics who mentioned her echoed William Dean Howells' glib assessment that she was a premature realist, but her originality and power have recently brought her the recognition she craved.

• Archival materials are located primarily in the American Antiquarian Society, Boston Public Library, Edmund Clarence Stedman Papers in Butler Library (Columbia University), Duke University Library, Colby College Library, Houghton Library (Harvard University), Middlebury College Library, New York Public Library, and Pennsylvania State University Library. See also James A. Matlack, "The Literary Career of Elizabeth Barstow Stoddard," Ph.D. diss., Yale University (1967). Lawrence Buell and Sandra Zagarell, eds., *"The Morgesons" and Other Writings, Published and Unpublished, by Elizabeth Stoddard* (1984). Sybil

Weir, "Our Lady Correspondent: The Achievement of Elizabeth Drew Stoddard," *San Jose Studies* 10 (1984): 73–91. Sandra A. Zagarell, "The Repossession of a Heritage: Elizabeth Stoddard's *The Morgesons*," *Studies in American Fiction* 13 (1985): 45–56. Susan Harris, *19th-Century American Women's Novels: Interpretive Strategies* (1990). Stacy Alaimo, "Elizabeth Stoddard's *The Morgesons*: A Feminist Dialogics of Bildung and Descent," *Legacy* 8, no. 1 (1991): 29–38. Sandra A. Zagarell, "Elizabeth Drew Barstow Stoddard: A Profile," *Legacy* 8, no. 1 (1991): 39–49.

Sandra A. Zagarell

STONE, Ruth (b. 1915), poet. Born in her grandparents' home in Roanoke, Virginia, Ruth Stone grew up in a household filled with music, poetry, and painting. The daughter of a drummer and the granddaughter of a state senator, Stone attributes her early love of poetry and her lyrical ear to her mother, Ruth Ferguson Perkins, who read Alfred Lord Tennyson's poetry aloud as she nursed her infant daughter. At the age of six, Stone moved with her family to her paternal grandparents' home in Indianapolis. It was here, in the midst of formal teas and evenings filled with dinner parties and humorous storytelling that Ruth Stone began writing poetry.

At the age of nineteen, Stone moved to Illinois with her first husband, a chemist. While living in Illinois, she met and later married the poet and novelist Walter Stone. In 1952, she moved with her husband and three daughters, Marcia, Phoebe, and Abigail, to Vassar College, where Walter Stone was offered a teaching position in the English department. At Vassar, Stone composed the poems for her first book, *In an Iridescent Time* (1959). During this period, she won *Poetry*'s Bess Hokin prize and the Kenyon Review Fellowship in Poetry. With the prize money from the Kenyon Review, Stone traveled alone to Vermont and bought a house where she could write and her family could spend the summers. Stone's life changed dramatically when, in 1959, on sabbatical from Vassar, Walter Stone moved with Ruth Stone and their young daughters to England. In England, Walter Stone committed suicide. For the next decade, Ruth Stone moved in and out of periods of deep depression and despair, and Walter Stone's life and death became a nearly constant presence in the poetry of Ruth Stone.

In 1963, Stone was awarded a two-year Radcliffe Institute fellowship, and from 1963 to 1965, she worked on poems for her second collection, *Topography and Other Poems* (1971), and developed close ties to other Radcliffe fellows, such as Maxine *Kumin and Tillie *Olsen. After the Radcliffe Institute, Stone taught creative writing at many universities throughout the United States, including Indi-

ana University at Bloomington; the University of California, Davis; New York University; and Old Dominion University. Currently she is Professor of English at the State University of New York at Binghamton. Between teaching engagements, Stone has lived in the Vermont house she purchased with the Kenyon Review Fellowship money in 1957. Known as the "mother poet" to many contemporary women writers, she is the recipient of numerous honors, including the Shelley Memorial Award (1964), two Guggenheim Fellowships (1971 and 1975), the Delmore Schwartz Award (1983), the Whiting Writer's Award (1986), and the Paterson Poetry Prize (1988). Returning over and over to the themes of loss and death, Ruth Stone's poems are ultimately emblems of survival. Combining lyricism with a poignant mix of humor and tragedy, she manipulates the emotions of her audience by opening them with laughter, then shocking them with sorrow. Stone is a feminist poet who uses poetry to boldly address the world of women and family, as well as issues such as aging, homelessness, and poverty. Interspersing astronomy, biology, physics, and botany into her poems, she calls attention to the largest and the smallest spheres, expressing the beauty of the natural world as she highlights the pathos of the human condition, and especially the female condition within the *patriarchal world. In addition to *Cheap* (1975), *Second-Hand Coat* (1987), and *Who Is the Widow's Muse* (1991), she has published several chapbooks, including *American Milk* (1986), *The Solution* (1989), and *Nursery Rhymes from Mother Stone* (1992).

• Harvey Gross, "On the Poetry of Ruth Stone: Selections and Commentary," *Iowa Review* 3 (1972): 94–106. Sandra M. Gilbert, "Interview: Ruth Stone," *California Quarterly* 10 (Autumn 1975): 55–70. Sandra M. Gilbert, Wendy Barker, Dorothy Gilbert, Diana O'Hehir, Josephine Miles, Tillie Olsen, Charlotte Painter, and Susan Gubar, "On Ruth Stone," *Extended Outlooks: The Iowa Review Collection of Contemporary Women Writers*, eds. Jane Cooper, Gwen Head, Adalaide Morris, and Marcia Southwick (1982): pp. 323–330. Robert Bradley, "An Interview with Ruth Stone," *A WP Chronicle* 23, no. 2 (October/November 1990): pp. 1–5. Wendy Barker, "Ruth Stone," *American Poets Since World War II, Second Series, Dictionary of Literary Biography*, vol. 105, ed. R. S. Gwynn (1990–1991): pp. 241–246.

Jan Freeman

STONEWALL. *See* Lesbian Feminism.

STORYTELLING. I began thinking of experience as stories we tell about ourselves the day I overheard my four-year-old son talking to himself about his life as he played alone in his room. That's when it occurred to me for the first time that if children say aloud what adults have learned to keep to themselves, then at that very moment I could be unwittingly composing an *autobiography to myself not unlike the one I could hear my son declaiming. That specific installment from Jesse's life story has since been forgotten, but not the scene in my mind's eye of the child interrupting his own play with odd bits of narration. Yet when I look on this scene, I am not only reminded that the past intrudes itself on the present. I am convinced that the child, now a young adult, is more likely to recall episodes from his autobiography than any part he played in transforming events into his experience.

So much conspires against Jesse's remembering that he is the narrator of his life. Everyone knows that people have experiences, which they then recall in speaking and writing. "You'll never guess what happened to me" announces an intent to recount something that is over and done with. It flies in the face of common sense to suggest that our anecdotes do not so much reconstitute as constitute experiences. We are taught to tell stories as if narration were incidental to experience. Yet if Jesse teaches himself to remember, as I and others have, that he is the narrator of his experience, there is a chance that what he learns about composing himself in the course of drafting his autobiography will challenge cultural practices that insist that experience is independent of self and that both self and experience are separate from their expression in language.

I learned about telling and listening to personal experience narratives from the women who gathered at my mother's kitchen table. That's where I was taught to find something interesting in even the most artless accounts, to side with the teller, and to accept events at face value. But it is also where I learned that a story about personal experience invites listeners to join the teller in reflecting on troubling events—a child's behavior, a parent or in-law's criticism, infidelity, pregnancy, unemployment, low wages, high prices, ill health. As I remember it, personal experience narratives posed rather than solved problems, which were explored and extended in either commentary or more narratives.

In more fanciful moments, I see my mother's kitchen as a parliament of narratives, the place where mothers met to legislate family life in the neighborhood. But that image came later, after *consciousness-raising groups had replaced the kitchen parliament, the *women's movement had begun publicizing stories of women's domestic lives, and the personal had become political—for me and a good many other women. Yet to this day I savor moments of *identity learned in my mother's kitchen and practiced

in women's groups, moments when being taken at my word and taking another woman at hers affirmed my membership in a *community of women. There is a sense in which identity with other women empowers those who recognize themselves in stories of women's experiences. As important as identity is to women, including myself, there is, however, a sense in which identity can be as dangerous to women as *sexism, sex-based discrimination, and *sexual harassment.

Just as representing experience as independent of teller and telling collapses distinctions between event and narration, political solidarity based on identity exchanges narratives of self for fetishes of the self, a bad bargain for any number of reasons, not least that ready-made selves fit most women about as well as ready-to-wear clothes. A fetishized self is a dangerously idealized woman, a standard that finds actual women lacking and that justifies excluding some women as not something: not feminine, not feminist. Identity fetishes of the self devalue the complex selves that emerge in narratives of personal experience, by offering to relieve us of the burden of composing ourselves in exchange for the illusion that we will always be the same, never different, as long as we identify ourselves as a kind of woman. Little wonder then that ready-to-wear identities make us even more anxious to deny everything about ourselves that differs from the fetish and encourage us to project that anxiety about the differences in ourselves onto others.

Some of the stories told in my mother's kitchen did little more than make a virtue of the *whiteness of the working-class women gathered there. I recall the women talking about not allowing their white children to swim in the town's public pool with black children (melanin was believed not to be indelible). I remember others reporting rumors of black families planning to buy or rent in what had been a poor but white neighborhood. And then there were the stories about unknown white girls whose reputations were ruined because they had been seen with a black boy (I remember there being many girls but only one boy), and there were rumors about white girls being sold into white *slavery and black women cruising white neighborhoods in search of white men and boys. Unlike the personal experience narratives that the women told about their own lives, the no-name children, adolescents, and adults fetishized in these accounts are black and white caricatures. Rather than posing problems for the women to discuss, these miscegenation stories terrorized and silenced the kitchen parliament.

Stories about the terrible sexuality of black

people represent white women not as the rightful legislators of domestic life but as the hapless victims of desegregation: they stand to lose their white children, white neighborhoods, good names, freedom, and husbands, sons, and brothers to miscegenation. The prefabricated stories that excluded black people from my mother's kitchen in fetishes of *whiteness and blackness recycled white supremicist propaganda, wherein political solidarity rests solely on white identity, on convincing white people that whiteness is itself so desirable that all black people wish to be white.

Because identity fetishes make a virtue of a single dimension of self (*race, color, *gender, *class, sexual orientation, *ethnicity, nationality, age, or religious affiliation), they devalue storytelling, which involves everyone in a process of composing themselves as the more or less multidimensional characters of their experiences. Identity fetishes cynically exclude those people on whom we project our differences even as they deny us a chance to explore differences within ourselves in narratives of experience. For it is difference, not identity, which links us to those not ourselves, those possible selves that are acknowledged and cherished only by people who can recall composing themselves when they narrate their experience.

[See also Orality; Folklore; Native American Oral Tradition; African-American Oral Tradition.]

• Mary Louise Pratt, "Natural Narrative: What Is 'Ordinary Language' Really Like?," in Toward a Speech Act Theory of Literary Discourse (1977), pp. 38–78. Minnie Bruce Pratt, "Identity: Skin Blood Heart," in Yours in Struggle: Three Feminist Perspectives on Anti-Semitism and Racism, edited by Elly Bulkin, Minnie Bruce Pratt, and Barbara Smith (1984), pp. 11–63. bell hooks, "Representing Whiteness: Seeing Wings of Desire," Z Magazine (February 1989):36–39. Iris Marion Young, Justice and the Politics of Difference (1989). Wendy Brown, "Feminist Hesitations, Postmodern Exposures," differences 5 (Spring 1991):63–84. Joan W. Scott, "The Evidence of Experience," Critical Inquiry 17 (Summer 1991):773–797.

Linda Brodkey

STOWE, Harriet Beecher (1811–1896), novelist, short fiction writer, essayist. Stowe's career and its critical reconsideration are marked by controversy and passion. She is remembered first and foremost for the inflammatory abolitionist novel Uncle Tom's Cabin (1852), but she also wrote prolifically on varied topics and in varied venues: regional sketches (The Mayflower [1843], Sam Lawson's Oldtown Fireside Stories [1872]), historical novels (The Minister's Wooing [1859], The Pearl of Orr's Island [1862], Oldtown Folks [1869]), and novels of manners

(My Wife and I [1871], Pink and White Tyranny [1871], We and Our Neighbors [1873]). Many of her works centered around domestic themes and women's issues: she provided household advice for the Atlantic (collected as Household Papers and Stories [1865]); co-wrote the domestic science manual An American Woman's Home (1869) with her sister Catharine; composed children's stories, poems, and hymns; and wrote essays on politics, women's rights, home decorating, and religion.

In all these works, she attempted a series of generative, if problematic, negotiations: between individual needs and *community responsibilities, between religious idealism and the hard-nosed practicality (usually associated with women) she called "faculty," between her ecumenical and egalitarian respect for others and her class- and race-bound constructions of them. The difficulties implicit in these balancing acts have led in her own time and in ours to widely differing interpretations of her works. She is seen as an apologist for *racism on the one hand, and as a champion of equal rights for blacks on the other; as a precursor for later feminists and as a conservative advocate of the domestic sphere. Both views are in a sense correct: the internal contradictions of her social vision domesticate even her own latent radicalism; because of this, Stowe simultaneously threatens and supports the culture out of which she wrote. Moreover, although at one time we imagined later regional and realist writing to be opposed to what was seen as naive and formulaic *sentimentalism, we now increasingly understand her subtle blend of the sentimental and the realist as an important model for later writers like *Jewett, Twain, Bret Harte, Rose Terry *Cooke, Mary Wilkins *Freeman, and Hamlin Garland.

Born in Litchfield, Connecticut, in 1811, Stowe was daughter, wife, sister, and mother to Protestant clergymen; not surprisingly, her earliest literary influences were the Bible, Bunyan, and Puritan theology and sermons, an austere diet that her evangelical father Lyman Beecher supplemented with generous helpings of Shakespeare, Byron, and Scott. Although he openly wished "Hattie had been a boy," he trained his daughters' minds as keenly as his sons'. The family recalled Stowe's mother, Roxanna Foote, who died when Harriet was five, as the idealized Victorian mother. Harriet grew up attempting to reconcile the paradox, as Mary Kelley has argued, of being committed to a public role by virtue of her profession, like her father, and to a private one by virtue of her gender, like her mother (Private Woman, Public Stage, 1984).

In 1832, the family moved to Cincinnati, a city divided by abolitionist and seccesionist fever, where Lyman took up the presidency of Lane Theological Seminary. Here Stowe's career began: her first stories were written and published, and she began assimilating the materials and anti-slavery beliefs that would catapult her to fame. She met and in 1836 married Calvin Ellis Stowe, an unprepossessing Biblical scholar of precarious means. Children quickly followed—seven in all between 1836 and 1850, the year the couple moved to Brunswick, Maine, where Calvin took a position at Bowdoin College. There among "the smell of sour milk, and sour meat, and sour everything," as Stowe had despairingly described housekeeping, she had a vision of an elderly black man being beaten to death.

That vision catalyzed *Uncle Tom's Cabin*, the nineteenth century's most famous and best-selling novel. Eventually translated into more than twenty languages, it was serialized in 1851 and 1852 and published as a book in 1852, to great acclaim and bitter criticism. Sensitive to Southern charges of inaccuracy, Stowe published *A Key to Uncle Tom's Cabin* (1854) to document the sources of her information; in 1856, she followed up on her success with a second anti-slavery novel, *Dred: A Tale of the Dismal Swamp*. Stowe's *sentimentalism forged formal equivalences between black and white characters and emotional connections between black characters and white middle-class readers, but it also presented the white experience as normative; Stowe's *abolitionism was radical in its demand for emancipation, but it relied upon racist assumptions of difference in its argument for colonization rather than integration. In doing so, the novel's "sentimental power," as Jane Tompkins calls it (*Sensational Designs: The Cultural Work of American Fiction*, 1985), continues to spark heated debates about *race and *racism in America.

Although she had incautiously sold the copyright to *Uncle Tom's Cabin* for $300 (enough, she claimed, to buy a good silk dress), by the late 1850s Stowe was internationally famous and the major breadwinner in the family. Her writing allowed the family to live comfortably in Andover, Massachussetts (1852–1864), and to build a rambling Victorian house in Hartford, Connecticut, which was her home until she died in 1896. During these years she wrote prolifically and sometimes carelessly, but with a shrewd sense of audience and a gift for capturing the vanishing culture of her childhood New England. Her historical New England novels celebrate the "pre-railroad" times of the early republic. *The Minister's Wooing* gently satirizes

Calvinism, celebrating its intellectual and moral integrity while critiquing its rigid theology; *Oldtown Folks* captures the religious, educational, cultural, and social rituals and institutions of post-Revolutionary New England. These novels and *The Pearl of Orr's Island* point to one of Stowe's most important legacies, particularly for younger women writers: sentimental moments are set among ordinary and faithfully recorded domestic experiences that resonate with symbolic importance. Stowe's regional eye and ear also undergird a subtle but sweeping redefinition of gender roles that extends to both men and women male-coded rights of leadership and female-centered responsibilities for community; if her female characters quilt and bake and navigate ships, her male characters practice law and hang curtains. Not as politically charged as her anti-slavery work, Stowe's New England novels have sometimes been overlooked, but they represent the aesthetic climax of her career.

As the 1870s arrived, Stowe's powers and her judgment began to fail. She published a scandalously received exposé of Lord Byron's sexual infidelities, *Lady Byron Vindicated*, which damaged her reputation as a moral author; to recover, she serialized a story in her brother Henry Ward Beecher's *Christian Century*. *My Wife and I* was followed by *Pink and White Tyranny* and *We and Our Neighbors;* set in fashionable New York, these novels have often, and in part rightly, been criticized as apologies for mass consumption. But Stowe's "Fifth Avenue princesses" also seek to reinvigorate what Stowe celebrated in her earlier works as precapitalist values of community responsibility, self-discipline, and charity—values that Stowe saw as countering consumer capitalism. While thematically and culturally fascinating, however, the New York novels uncouple sentimentalism from the realism that powered her earlier, more complex, aesthetic.

Stowe's artistic decline was paralleled by the final events in a series of personal tragedies, from the loss of an infant in 1849 to Calvin's death in 1886. She divided her time between Hartford and a Florida plantation, writing children's stories and hymns. At the end, Stowe cheerfully maintained that her mind was "nomadic"; her body occasionally wandered nocturnally through neighbors' houses. It is a fitting image for Stowe, who in her writing adapted her moral and spiritual expectations for American society to material domestic spaces.

• Edward Wagenknecht, *Harriet Beecher Stowe: The Known and The Unknown* (1965). Alice Crozier, *The Novels of Harriet Beecher Stowe* (1969). Marie Caskey,

Chariot of Fire: Religion and the Beecher Family (1978). Elizabeth Ammons, ed., *Critical Essays on Harriet Beecher Stowe* (1980). Milton Rugoff, *The Beechers* (1981). Eric J. Sundquist, ed., *New Essays on Uncle Tom's Cabin* (1986). Jeanne Boydston, Mary Kelley, and Anne Margolis, eds., *The Limits of Sisterhood: The Beecher Sisters on Women's Rights and Woman's Sphere* (1988). Lisa Watt MacFarlane, "The New England Kitchen Goes Uptown: Domestic Displacements in Harriet Beecher Stowe's New York," *New England Quarterly* 64, no. 2 (June, 1991): 272–292.

Lisa Watt MacFarlane

STRATTON-PORTER, Geneva (1863–1924), novelist, short story writer, columnist, illustrator, and photographer. Born in Wabash County, Indiana, Geneva Grace Stratton-Porter spent most of her life in the rural Indiana atmosphere that her art would immortalize. As the twelfth child of Mark and Mary Stratton, the young Gene relished watching her father, whom she idolized, care for her family, their land, and their community; an 1873 move to the city of Wabash left her unhappy and even rebellious. In 1883, she met and subsequently married Charles Porter, a successful druggist and businessman. The marriage, while lasting until her death, seems to have played a minor role in Stratton-Porter's life; she often lived independently of her husband. The couple's only child, Jeannette Helen Porter-Meehan, who would later write a sequel to one of her mother's most popular novels (*Freckles Comes Home*, 1929), was born in 1887. A year later, the family moved to Geneva, Indiana, where they built the first of several homes in which Stratton-Porter raised, sketched, and photographed birds and moths, the principal subjects of her nonfiction. The Porters eventually built Limberlost Cabin on the edge of the Limberlost Swamp, an area figuring prominently in the author's work. Living and working there and later on the banks of Sylvan Lake, Stratton-Porter moved to Los Angeles, California in 1920, where she continued writing and began producing motion pictures of her novels. When she was fatally injured in an automobile accident in 1924, Gene Stratton-Porter had written twenty-six books, over one hundred magazine articles, two book-length poems, and had illustrated, with watercolors and photographs, much of her own work. The overwhelming success of her five most popular books, which sold over eight million copies and were translated into fourteen languages, testifies to the strength of her public appeal.

As she herself noted, Gene Stratton-Porter sought to educate and morally elevate her reading public, especially with her avid conservationism. Her most popular novels (*Freckles*, 1904; *A Girl of the Limberlost*, 1908; *The Harvester*, 1911; *Michael O'Halloran*, 1915) cele-brate her beloved Limberlost, and Stratton-Porter herself often figures in these novels as the "Bird Woman," a naturalist whose benevolence and wisdom enable her protagonists. Her photographs, magazine articles, short stories, and wildlife books (she reached an agreement with Doubleday, her publisher, to alternate the publication of her nonfictional books about nature, which sold poorly, with her best-selling novels) all exhibit her determination to portray in a detailed and positive light the environments she loved.

• Jeannette Porter-Meehan, *Life and Letters of Gene Stratton-Porter* (1927; reprint 1972). James D. Hart, *The Popular Book: A History of America's Literary Taste* (1950). David G. Maclean, *Gene Stratton-Porter: A Bibliography and Collector's Guide* (1976). Bertrand F. Richards *Gene Stratton-Porter* (1980). Judith Reick Long, *Gene Stratton-Porter: Novelist and Naturalist* (1990).

Virginia B. Broaddus

STRUCTURALISM. *See* Poststructuralism.

SUBALTERN. The word *subaltern* denotes, in the words of the Oxford English Dictionary, "a person and or thing of inferior rank or status." It has signified as an adjective and a noun a person of lower rank in the British military, as in "a subaltern officer." In philosophical discourse, it also means the position of a proposition implied by another proposition—a subordinate proposition. In the twentieth century, *subaltern* has become a crucial term in social theory.

Subaltern was first used in theoretical writings on culture by the Italian Marxist Antonio Gramsci (1891–1937). Gramsci made interventions in Marxist theories of social structure and of social change. He initiated study of hegemony, resistance to hegemony, and of popular culture.

Continuing Gramsci's work on domination and subordination, the Subaltern Studies group of Southeast Asian scholars have used the term to name themselves and their project. In the preface to the first volume of the series *Subaltern Studies* published by Oxford University Press in 1982, Ranajit Guha says that the collective will use *subaltern* "as a name for the general attribute of subordination in South Asian society whether this is expressed in terms of class, caste, age, gender and office or in any other way." The general aim of the collective is to counteract the "tradition of elitism in South Asian studies." Guha suggests that their "emphasis on the subaltern functions both as a measure of objective assessment of the role of the elite and as a critique of elitist interpretations of that role."

The term has circulated from the work of

this collective into American critical discourse, and particularly into feminist discourse, largely through Gayatri Chakravorty *Spivak's work; this critic's books and essays on literature, philosophy, and cultural politics have been vitally important to the rethinking of American feminisms and Marxisms in light of third world exploitation. Spivak uses the term *subaltern* to denote the texts and peoples she studies. She supports the work of the Subaltern Studies collective, but when she looks at that project critically she argues that "a feminist historian of the subaltern must raise the question of woman as a structural rather than marginal issue" in analyses of cultures (*In Other Worlds*, 1987). She suggests that while the collective attends to *gender in their particular studies, they also need to see how gender structures the relations of domination and subordination they study.

Spivak's use of the term *subaltern* and her explication of the limits for *feminism of its prior uses has been essential for American feminist analyses of the position of women, the divisions among women, and the place, or displacement, of the third world in feminist critical discourse. Citing Spivak, Elspeth Probyn, for example, writing in the 1990 collection *Feminism/Postmodernism*, uses "subaltern" rather than the psychoanalytically charged term "Other" to refer to those women "excluded from multiple levels of empowerment." In that same collection, Judith Butler attends to Spivak's caveat on the "false ontology of women as a universal." Spivak's work on the subaltern has reminded American feminists of the many women around the world whose economic and geographic locations exclude them from the vision of first world theorists and the benefits of first world theory and the academy.

The term *subaltern* has been useful to women writers in describing the status of literary texts in relation to the *canon, in designating the political project of attending to the dominated, and in denoting the positions of different groups of women in male-dominated cultures. The term's colonial heritage, as well as its use in the discourse of logic, which has itself been a master discourse in the academy, makes it an especially charged term that carries with it, as Probyn writes, "a reminder of numerous nuances of oppression." Through Spivak's work on the subaltern, we are reminded that feminist writing itself can be the work of an elite and an elitist project. The term *subaltern* is a tool in the struggle to attend to gender without neglecting other structures of domination and subordination.

• Gayatri Chakravorty Spivak, "Imperialism and Sexual Difference," *Oxford Literary Review* 8 (1986): 225–240. David Forgacs, *An Antonio Gramsci Reader*

(1988). Cary Nelson and Lawrence Grossberg, eds., *Marxism and the Interpretation of Culture* (1988). Gayatri Chakravorty Spivak, *The Post-Colonial Critic* (1990).

Rebecca Ann Bach

SUBJECT, The. *See* Identity Politics; Subjectivity.

SUBJECTIVITY. Postmodernists undermine our confidence in the possibility or desirability of a unitary, rational subject. They claim there are no innate, transcendental, core, or fixed mental or subjective qualities. Rather, the subject is multiple and contradictory, constituted in and through complex, historically delimited forces such as knowledge, language, and power. Through careful historical or genealogical study, they show how beliefs in unitary conceptualizations of reason or even woman are effects of and dependent on particular discursive formations.

These critiques have had a powerful effect on Western feminists. Many of their claims for liberation have been dependent upon concepts such as rights, equality, freedom, and emancipation. The meaning and force of all these concepts arise out of and depend upon the same discursive formations in and through which the unitary subject was constituted. Furthermore, this subject has served as the ground and locus of these qualities. Their actualization has depended on its capacity for undetermined agency and knowledge.

Postmodernist writings have had an additional impact on white feminists. Their attention to *postmodernism in the mid-1980s coincided with the intensification of criticism by women of color of the race biases within white feminist theories and practices. The unity of the category of "woman" or a "feminist standpoint" was shown to depend upon the exclusion of the complexity of the determinants of the subjectivity of all women. *Race, geographical location, sexual identity, age, physical condition, and *class contribute in multiple and contradictory ways to the constitution of any woman's subjectivity and the meanings and nature of her practices.

Nonetheless, many feminists continue to argue that a decentered, multiple subjectivity cannot exercise the agency required for liberatory political action. They argue that emancipatory action and the very concept and hope of emancipation depend upon either a coherent self capable of autonomy, undetermined self-reflection, and the production of less false knowledge or the construction of a feminist standpoint grounded in and reflective of experiences widely shared by women. Possible candidates for such experience include *maternity;

female embodiment and/or sexuality; unique psychological characteristics such as relatedness to others; women's labor, especially in the reproduction of everyday life; and the objectification and victimization of women by male dominance.

Other feminists argue that a coherent self or the desire for a feminist standpoint is an unnecessary and dangerous mirage. The apparent existence of a coherent self is contingent upon the repression or denial of many other aspects of subjectivity. The devalued aspects are projected onto lesser "others." They can then be disavowed and the domination of inferiors justified. Even if a standpoint is conceived as a political construct built out of and reflecting struggle, this position still requires relatively straightforward relations between and homogeneity of experience, thinking, and practice. It necessarily requires that the experience of the oppressed is homogenous enough to ground a common position. This standpoint must have a privileged relation to reality so that its constructors will not generate new forms of domination as a necessary consequence of their emancipatory actions.

One view is that future feminist possibilities require caring for and encouraging decentered subjects. Only multiple selves can tolerate the ambiguity, ambivalence, complexity, and contradictions, and the simultaneously held positions of lack and surplus of power that pervade our increasingly multicultural world. Divided in and sometimes against themselves, such subjects' desire will include the struggle to let differences flourish rather than to exercise domination over unruly parts.

• Nancy C. M. Hartsock, *Money, Sex, and Power: Towards a Feminist Historical Materialism* (1985). Carole Pateman and Elizabeth Gross, eds., *Feminist Challenges: Social and Political Theory* (1987). Judith Butler, *Gender Trouble: Feminism and the Subversion of Identity* (1990). Patricia Hill Collins, *Black Feminist Thought: Knowledge, Consciousness and the Politics of Empowerment* (1990). Jane Flax, *Thinking Fragments: Psychoanalysis, Feminism and Postmodernism in the Contemporary West* (1990). Linda J. Nicholson, ed., *Feminism/Postmodernism* (1990). Chandra Talpade Mohanty, Ann Russo, and Lourdes Torres, *Third World Women and the Politics of Feminism* (1991).

Jane Flax

SUFFRAGE MOVEMENT. The struggle for woman suffrage spanned from 1848 to 1920. In Seneca Falls, New York, on 19–20 July 1848, antebellum reformers Elizabeth Cady *Stanton and Lucretia *Mott led the call for a Woman's Rights Convention. Stanton and Mott, active in the antebellum antislavery campaign, believed that women, like slaves, confronted the power of white men in seeking political, economic,

and legal rights. Denied access as delegates to the World Anti-Slavery Convention in London in 1840, Stanton and Mott realized they could not promote *abolitionism when they had no voice because they were women. Stanton and Mott at the Seneca Falls Convention drafted the "Declaration of Sentiments," modeling their document on the Declaration of Independence. The "Declaration of Sentiments" (1848) asserted women's right to vote, declaring "all men and women are created equal," as Stanton cites in *History of Woman Suffrage* (1881). Women's rights leaders believed in natural rights, arguing for women's autonomy in social relations. The group of women endorsing suffrage included educated women like Susan B. *Anthony and Lucy Stone. After Seneca Falls, in 1850 a national convention for women's rights met at Worcester, Massachusetts. To promote the cause, Paulina Wright Davis began publishing the monthly periodical *The Una*.

After the *Civil War, suffrage activists' abolitionist ties generated tensions. Republican Reconstruction politicians focused on black male suffrage, not woman suffrage. Passage of the Fourteenth Amendment (1866) excluded women from *citizenship and the ratification of the Fifteenth Amendment (1870) granting the vote to African-American men without mentioning sex represented major setbacks for woman suffrage advocates. Women suffrage leaders thought their abolitionist allies had abandoned them and thus organized for universal suffrage. Feminists and male antislavery leaders formed the American Equal Rights Association in 1866, ending the abolitionist phase of American feminism. A split developed between advocates of black suffrage and woman suffrage. Stanton and Anthony lobbied for woman suffrage, spearheading the independent feminist movement in America. Stanton opposed the Fifteenth Amendment, writing in *The Revolution*, a feminist newspaper founded in 1868 with the motto, "Men Their Rights and Nothing More—Women Their Rights, and Nothing Less." As an editor of *The Revolution*, Stanton disseminated her views on women's voting rights and often turned to racist and nativist rhetoric to obtain support for woman's ballot. Her critics like Lucy Stone and writer Julia Ward *Howe urged women to sacrifice the ballot in favor of black male franchise until after Reconstruction.

Conflicts emerged in the ideology of the suffrage leaders. In 1869, Stanton called for a woman suffrage amendment to the Constitution and asserted that women, not men, should hold leadership positions. Stanton and Anthony formed the National Woman Suffrage Association (NWSA), for women only, promoting their feminist goals of the vote for women and economic and political equality. The NWSA represented the first national feminist organization in the United States. Opposing the radical views of Stanton and Anthony, in 1869 Lucy Stone and her husband Henry Blackwell organized the American Woman Suffrage Association (AWSA), emphasizing the single issue of woman suffrage. The *Woman's Journal,* founded in 1870, became the organ of the more conservative AWSA.

The ideological split in the suffrage movement persisted in the 1870s and 1880s. In 1878 Stanton, seeking a federal constitutional amendment, had Senator A. A. Sargent of California introduce the "Anthony Amendment." The "Anthony Amendment," the basis for the Nineteenth Amendment, stated, "The right of citizens of the United States to vote shall not be denied or abridged by the United States or by any state on account of sex."

The Progressive Era from 1890 to 1920 marked the final phase of the woman suffrage campaign and involved new organizations, strategies, and rhetoric. The woman suffrage movement was part of progressivism, a widespread social, political, and economic reform effort. In 1890 the National American Woman Suffrage Association (NAWSA) was formed by merging the NWSA and the AWSA, unifying the suffrage associations. Initially led by Stanton and Anthony, the organization would soon be led by younger women. Middle-class reformers and suffrage supporters argued for women's voting rights as a way to achieve moral reforms and to clean up politics. Using imagery of woman as homemaking wives and mothers, suffrage proponents linked woman's ballot to *temperance, peace, labor, and urban reform in dramatic suffrage parades and speeches. Reformers encouraging woman suffrage included Frances Willard of the Women's Christian Temperance Union; Jane *Addams, founder of Hull House, author of *Twenty Years at Hull House* (1910), and later vice-president of NAWSA; Ida B. *Wells-Barnett of the *antilynching movement; and Charlotte Perkins *Gilman, feminist author of *Women and Economics* (1898).

The progressive ideal of women allied across class, race, and ethnic lines in the suffrage movement did not occur. Wells-Barnett founded the Alpha Suffrage Club in an effort to promote suffrage among black women in 1914, but she worried about white women in the suffrage movement who wanted to deny or restrict the black woman's vote. Harriot Stanton Blatch, daughter of Elizabeth Cady Stanton, established the Equality League of Self-Supporting Women in 1907 seeking to integrate

working-class women with middle-class professional women in suffrage activism. White middle-class women suffrists' alliance with working-class sisters was short lived as class divisions persisted. Writer and anarchist immigrant Emma *Goldman, although committed to equality, criticized suffrage leaders for ignoring the problems of working women and for upholding women as morally superior to men. Rural women in the Order of Patrons of Husbandry, known as the Grange, addressed domesticity and women's rights in the suffrage issue. Female Grange leaders asserted the order should support equal suffrage. Writing in periodicals like the *Grange Visitor,* Grange suffragists gained the order's support in 1893.

Antisuffrage sentiment became strongest during the Progressive Era. The countermovement consisted of white upper- and middle-class women who used the same imagery of homemaking used by suffragists but claimed women were unfit for the vote. Liquor industry interests, who feared women would vote for prohibition, especially opposed suffrage. Antisuffragists wanted to restrict women from men's spheres of business and politics.

The battle for woman suffrage intensified as some activists adopted militant tactics from the English suffragettes. Alice Paul organized the Congressional Union in 1913, holding the party in power, the Democrats, responsible for the suffrage amendment. The NAWSA withdrew support of Paul's more radical Congressional Union. To bolster the NAWSA, members elected Carrie Chapman Catt as president in 1915. Catt announced her "Winning Plan": to lobby for a state-by-state campaign for woman suffrage to gain President Wilson's support. In contrast, the National Woman's Party, including the Congressional Union, used militant tactics of radical demonstrations and marches. The National Woman's Party in 1917 picketed the White House and displayed the suffrage banner MR. PRESIDENT! HOW LONG MUST WOMEN WAIT FOR LIBERTY? Both radical and mainstream suffrage groups gained from the resultant publicity. Recognizing many women's patriotic support of the war effort, in 1918 President Wilson advised Democrats to support woman suffrage.

In 1919 both houses of Congress voted for the suffrage amendment. In 1920, after seventy-two years of struggle, the ratification of the Nineteenth Amendment granted women the right to vote.

[*See also* Political Organizations.]

• Elizabeth Cady Stanton, Susan B. Anthony, Matilda Joslyn Gage et al., eds., *History of Woman Suffrage,* vols. 1–6 (1881–1922). Eleanor Flexner, *Century of Struggle: The Woman's Rights Movement in the United States* (1959; reprint, 1973). Aileen Kraditor, *Ideas of the Woman Suffrage Movement, 1890–1920* (1965). Alfreda M. Duster, ed., *Crusade for Justice: The Autobiography of Ida B. Wells* (1970). Anne Firor Scott and Andrew MacKay Scott, *One Half the People: The Fight for Woman Suffrage* (1975; reprint, 1982). Ellen Carol DuBois, *Feminism and Suffrage: The Emergence of an Independent Women's Movement in America, 1848–1869* (1978). Mari Jo Buhle and Paul Buhle, eds., *The Concise History of Woman Suffrage: Selections from the Classic Work of Stanton, Anthony, Gage, and Harper* (1978). Alice Wexler, *Emma Goldman: An Intimate Life* (1984). Ellen Carol DuBois, "Harriot Stanton Blatch and the Transformation of Class Relations among Woman Suffragists," in *Gender, Class, Race, and Reform in the Progressive Era,* eds. Noralee Frankel and Nancy S. Dye (1991), pp. 162–179. Donald B. Marti, *Women of the Grange: Mutuality and Sisterhood in Rural America, 1866–1920* (1991).

Linda J. Borish

SUFFRAGIST PLAYS. One of the many elements of the woman suffrage movement that gave prosuffrage arguments a strong and public representation, suffragist plays dramatically articulated the benefits of women's rights, often through futuristic or allegorical settings that demonstrated the potential power of suffrage and blatantly ridiculed its opponents' arguments. While some of these plays reached the mainstream, "legitimate" theater, most were more in the tradition of parlor dramas—short, one-act plays often privately printed and intended for amateur performance. As such, suffragist plays could be put on as a part of rallies, meetings, and benefits. Little research has yet been done on suffrage plays in the United States, particularly their performance history, but an excellent starting point is Bettina Friedl's *On To Victory: Propaganda Plays of the Woman Suffrage Movement* (1987). Unless otherwise noted, the plays mentioned below are reprinted with an extensive introduction in this volume.

After the *Civil War, as issues of women's rights became increasingly visible, the popular stage presented burlesques that parodied women's rights by depicting among other things the supposedly absurd and unnatural consequences of women gaining the vote. The earliest play that overtly confronted these negative representations was Ella Cheever Thayer's *Lords of Creation: A Suffrage Drama in Three Acts* (1883). Thayer reverses the antisuffrage stereotypes by positively depicting an independent woman who successfully bails out her conservative father's business. Alice E. Ives's *A Very New Woman* (1896) also uses positive images of active women characters to refute the common claim that suffrage would hopelessly confuse traditional, gendered divisions between the public and private spheres.

As Friedl's collection shows, after the turn of the century suffrage plays became more numerous and took on a wide range of issues. Among Charlotte Perkins *Gilman's many contributions to the suffrage movement was her play *Something to Vote For* (1911), in which the members of a woman's club are persuaded that suffrage is necessary to protect a wide range of concerns for all women. Attacking the antisuffrage stance of the affluent classes was Emily Sargent Lewis's *Election Day: A Suffrage Play* (1912), another work which successfully undercuts antisuffragists by creating a devastatingly parodic portrayal of their position. After women won the vote in California, Kate Mills Fargo wrote *A Voting Demonstration* (1912), an instructional piece that showed women voters how to exercise their new rights. One of the most publically recognized suffragist playwrights was the stage actress Mary Shaw, who performed in the United States premier of *Votes for Women* (1909) written by the U.S.-born English actress Elizabeth Robins (not included in Friedl). Shaw wrote two works of her own—a satire called *The Woman of It; or, Our Friends the Anti-Suffragists* (1912) and an allegory entitled *The Parrot's Cage* (1913).

Suffrage plays were an attractive form of protest to many writers because of their power to construct scenarios that could directly refute negative *stereotypes by mocking them and replacing them with positive visions of an equitable future. Like parades, pageants, and speeches, they were an important part of the public action of the woman suffrage movement.

[*See also* Drama.]

• Friedl's collection includes reprints of sixteen suffragist plays, a handful of antisuffrage works, and an extensive bibliography. Albert Auster, *Actresses and Suffragists: Women in the American Theater 1890–1920* (1984). Dale Spender and Carole Hayman, eds., *How the Vote Was Won and Other Suffragette Plays* (1985).

Ted Hovet, Jr.

SUICIDE. A number of works by American women writers have dealt with suicide, or the possibility of it. Because many narratives are *bildungsromane*—stories of a young person's education—suicide as a possible choice occurs when the person's options narrow to nothing. Such narrowing is more likely in women's lives than in men's; accordingly, British and European fictions of the nineteenth and early twentieth centuries gave readers the characters of Emma Bovary, Anna Karenina, Tess Durbeyfield, Catharine Linton, Maggie Tulliver, Antoinette Cosway Rochester, Rachel Vinrace, and Septimus Smith, Mrs. Dalloway's surrogate in the novel named for her.

Eighteenth-century American fiction provided a range of fallen women who died in childbirth (as in Susanna *Rowson's *Charlotte Temple*) but women rarely committed suicide, perhaps because of religious taboos on the taking of one's own life. In her 1861 *Life in the Iron Mills*, Rebecca Harding *Davis's Hugh Wolfe— the impoverished iron worker who also sculpted—chose suicide rather than face the derogation of death in prison. Because so much about Wolfe was feminine, particularly his powerlessness and his sensitivity, readers saw his suicide as martyrdom. In 1872, Louisa May *Alcott's Christie Devon is rescued from suicide by a woman friend in *Work: A Story of Experience*, a bleak novel which brought home to readers how difficult life was for the working woman.

Suicide had long been one choice of black slave women, and in the various narratives about their lives, usually at least one woman committed suicide rather than face separation from her children, or the physical and sexual abuse common to *slavery. Taking one's life is a way of voicing protest against the conditions of living, and slaves—either of *race or *gender—have long considered it a viable option. But because literature existed in part to give moral instruction, the choice of suicide has been considered negative.

In 1899, when Kate *Chopin published *The Awakening*, readers found themselves confronted with the suicide of a beautiful and talented woman—who clearly chose to die rather than live as the wife of a patronizing man. Edna Pontellier swam nude to her death, defiant of the laws of society even while taking her own life. Even though Chopin had used the closure of suicide in "Desiree's Baby" and other of her earlier short stories, this novel took readers by the same kind of surprise as had Charlotte Perkins *Gilman's 1892 "The Yellow Wallpaper," where the protagonist ends mad rather than a suicide. In 1905, when Edith *Wharton chose the ambivalent route in her ironic *The House of Mirth*, with Lily Bart dying of an overdose of sleeping medicine, she had learned that too direct a message harmed sales. Her last chapter, during which Lily's would-be suitor Selden laments her death and mourns what might have been, is a cynical comment on the power of men who could act, but don't. Lily's may have been an accidental death, but Wharton never again chose to end a fiction in that way; for the next thirty years, her women characters knew enough to cut their losses and leave the man, or the country, that made their lives difficult.

Once the plotline of women's suicide had been introduced into American letters, authors resorted to it frequently. In her 1925 *Barren Ground*, Ellen *Glasgow suggested Dorinda Oakley's suicidal thoughts, only to have them turn to murder—and finally to the emotional suicide of complete sexual withdrawal. For every woman who considered suicide—in Nella *Larsen's *Quicksand* as well as Zora Neale *Hurston's "Sweat"—as many more either killed the men who were oppressing them (in Susan *Glaspell's *Trifles*, Ellen Glasgow's *The Sheltered Life*, or Kaye Gibbons's *A Cure for Dreams*) or learned to stay alive on their own terms (as did protagonists in Edith Wharton's *The Mother's Recompense*, Willa *Cather's *A Lost Lady*, and Marge *Piercy's *Woman on the Edge of Time*). Anger expressed toward others was becoming women's means of coping with the circumstances that previously had driven them to despair.

Even though Susan Faludi in *Backlash* (1991) points out that women's suicide rates peaked during the 1960s, according to women's writing, the threat of suicide tempers most female life stories. During the stable and conservative 1950s and 1960s, for example, several novels of suicide attempts gained best sellerdom. J. D. Salinger's *The Catcher in the Rye* in 1951 tried to save Holden Caulfield as he told of his frustration with, and alienation from, parents, teachers, and peers. A decade later both Sylvia *Plath and Joanne Greenberg recast Salinger's theme to tell the story of women's lives; Plath's *The Bell Jar* (1963) and Greenberg's *I Never Promised You a Rose Garden* (1964) gave positive endings to their accounts of adolescent women's suicide attempts. Unfortunately, Plath's own suicide in 1963, coupled with the eerie poem "Lady Lazarus" from her *Ariel* collection, undercut what she had intended as a positive, if realistic, novel about women's depression. Rather than being an encouraging writer, Plath became a cult figure to readers who saw suicide as positive. While Joan *Didion's protagonists usually survived her fictions, *Run, River* in 1963 and *Play It As It Lays* in 1970 also revealed the existential angst that underlay some suicides.

In 1976, Maxine Hong *Kingston published her mixed-genre *The Woman Warrior* and introduced the shamed, and unnamed, aunt who killed herself and her infant by jumping into the family well (and polluting the water supply). In each case, women who did not fit their society, women who had been made to feel outside and marginal, chose to take their own lives. The culmination of that strain in women's literature peaked with Marsha *Norman's 1983 play, *'night Mother*, with the daughter's suicide coming at the end of a dialogue both loving and argumentative with her aging mother.

Ntozake *Shange's answer to all this white woman suicide was her healthily corrective *for colored girls who have considered suicide/when* *the rainbow is enuf: a choreopoem.* Published in 1977 and performed widely (in 1976 on Broadway), Shange's intense amalgam of narratives of the lives of black women—most of whom stayed alive—gave the nod to other fragmented texts, mostly by other women of color, who also stressed the value of staying alive. Gloria *Naylor's *The Women of Brewster Place,* like her *Mama Day* and *Bailey's Cafe,* was an antisuicide fiction, as were Alice *Walker's *The Color Purple* and its sequels, *The Temple of My Familiar* and *Possessing the Secret of Joy.* Toni *Morrison's novels moved from the madness of the abused Pecola Breedlove in *The Bluest Eye* to the triumph of a range of women characters in *Beloved* and *Jazz.* Sandra *Cisneros's *Woman Hollering Creek* and *The House on Mango Street,* like Amy *Tan's *The Joy Luck Club* and *The Kitchen God's Wife,* also spoke to the endurance of both Chicana and Asian-American women. And in Lee *Smith's *Family Linen, Oral History, Fair and Tender Ladies,* and *The Devil's Dream,* like Jill McCorkle's *Tending to Virginia* and *Ferris Beach,* mainstream, middle-class white women also stayed alive, as they did in the 1990s poetry of Minnie Bruce *Pratt, Judy *Grahn, Rita *Dove, Adrienne *Rich, Susan Howe, Carolyn *Forche, Lucille *Clifton, Judith Ortiz *Cofer, Cathy Song, and countless other contemporary women poets.

For all the fiction and poetry published by women during the 1980s and the 1990s, it seems clear that the message of women's writing has become increasingly antisuicide. While women characters once reveled at having any kind of choice, female protagonists at the end of the twentieth century are insisting on not only more choice, but the choice to stay alive—and succeed on their own terms—in today's world.

[*See also* Body and Health.]

• A. Alvarez, *The Savage God: A Study of Suicide* (1972). Annis Pratt, *Archetypes of Women's Fiction* (1981). Marilyn Yalom, *Maternity, Mortality, and the Literature of Madness* (1985). George H. Colt, *The Enigma of Suicide* (1991). Susan Faludi, *Backlash, The Undeclared War Against American Women* (1991). Elisabeth Bronfen, *Over Her Dead Body, Configurations of Femininity, Death and the Aesthetic* (1992). Maud Ellmann, *The Hunger Artists, Starving, Writing, and Imprisonment* (1993).

Linda Wagner-Martin

SUI SIN FAR (Edith Eaton) (1865–1914), journalist, fiction writer, and author of *Mrs. Spring Fragrance* (1912), the first book-length collection by a Chinese/North American/Canadian writer. Sui Sin Far was born in Macclesfield, England, of a Chinese mother and English father during an era when England was invading China's interior and colonizing her people. The ambiguity that resulted is basic to her identity and to her stance as a writer. At age seven or eight, her national identity also crossed boundaries, when she migrated with her family to Montréal, Québec. Here she would suffer further levels of marginalization: as an eldest daughter taking on the role of second mother among thirteen siblings, as one member of a family plummeting from merchant to impoverished working class, as a child removed from school at age ten, and as a semi-invalid. In the 1880s and 1890s, Sui Sin Far began her career as a stenographer, a journalist on Montréal papers, and a writer of short fiction. In 1897, she moved for a year to Jamaica, then spent from 1898 to 1912 on the west and east coasts of the United States—supporting herself as a journalist and stenographer, squeezing writing time between cracks, and seeking publishing outlets. Despite the numerous obstacles standing between Sui Sin Far and creative achievement, none extinguished her "ambition to write a book," nor distracted her from the goal she recalled from childhood: to "fight [the] battles" of Chinese North Americans in print. Her most explicitly critical piece is "A Plea for the Chinaman," written for the *Montreal Daily Star* in 1896 in protest of a proposed $500 head tax for Chinese-Canadian immigrants. Two years after the publication of *Mrs. Spring Fragrance,* at age forty-nine in the midst of revising a novel for publication, she died of heart failure in Montréal's Royal Victoria hospital. She is buried in the Eaton family plot at Mont Royal cemetery.

Sui Sin Far's significance lies in several literary achievements. First, she presents portraits of turn-of-the-century North American Chinatowns, not in the mode of the "yellow peril" literature of her era, but with an insider's sympathy that has moved critics across the century to recognize her as a founder of Chinese-American literature. Second, she gives voice and protagonist roles both to the Eurasian perspective never before heard and to Chinese and Chinese North American women and children, thus breaking the *stereotypes of *silence, invisibility, and "bachelor society" that history has traditionally heaped on these populations. Third, she used the very divisions that society handed her to ground an identity and find strategies for her art that would communicate with a dual audience, experimenting with trickster characters and tools of irony that share a paradigm with other writers marginalized by *race, *class, or *gender who sought markets in the late nineteenth and early twentieth centuries. In the process, she left a literary legacy of the identity ambivalence so familiar to contemporary postcolonial writers and demonstrated what it means to be the child of an interracial union in a racist society.

Besides *Mrs. Spring Fragrance*, Sui Sin Far's located writings include approximately forty short stories, six essays, twenty-five journalistic pieces, and twenty-five letters. Unnumbered other pieces remain unlocated. No personal papers have been found. Many were destroyed in a trunk she lost in a train accident while crossing the continent in 1907.

• S. E. Solberg, "Sui Sin Far/Edith Eaton: First Chinese-American Fictionist," *MELUS* 8 (1981). Amy Ling, "Edith Eaton: Pioneer Chinamerican Writer and Feminist," *American Literary Realism* 16, no. 2 (1983): 287–298. Amy Ling, *Between Worlds: Women Writers of Chinese Ancestry* (1990). Xiao-Huang-Yin, "Between the East and West: Sui Sin Far—The First Chinese American Woman Writer," *Arizona Quarterly* 7 (Winter 1991): 49–84. Annette White-Parks, "Sui Sin Far: Writer on the Chinese-Anglo Borders of North America," Ph.D. diss., Washington State University (1991). Elizabeth Ammons, *Conflicting Stories: American Women Writers at the Turn into the Twentieth Century* (1991), pp. 105–120.

Annette White-Parks

SULERI, Sara, autobiographer, historian, literary critic, essayist, educator. Born in Pakistan, Sara Suleri received her B.A. from Kinnaird College, Lahore, Pakistan (1974), her M.A. from Punjab University, Lahore, Pakistan (1976), and her Ph.D. from Indiana University, Bloomington (1983). Her first book, a brilliant autobiographical novel, is titled *Meatless Days*. Her second book, *The Rhetoric of English-India*, is an exploration of *colonialism in India. Associate Professor of English at Yale University and an editor of the *Yale Journal of Criticism*, Suleri is also involved in a project to establish a program in Cultural Criticism at Yale University. Her next book, tentatively titled *Epistemologies of Elegance: Poetry and Politics in British India*, will be an introduction to the complexities of the Urdu poetic *ghazal*.

The personal and political memories of one woman's life in Pakistan are presented in *Meatless Days* in a narrative format that reflects the poetic construction of the *ghazal*. Each chapter is a separate piece of work yet the chapters can also be read sequentially as forming one work. Suleri claims that "there are no women in the third world," yet the book speaks continuously of women, describing with wry humor Pakistani women's intermittent questioning of themselves and their lives. Change and death link the portraits and episodes of the book. The three main women, Suleri's mother, *grandmother, and sister, are brought back to life for

us by the author's experience and discussion of their deaths.

The awareness of memory, the liveliness of sexuality in the personal and the political, and what Suleri calls the "idiosyncratic form of cultural history" are continued from the private arena of the personal memoir, *Meatless Days*, to the larger, more public, historical arena of *The Rhetoric of English-India*. The legends and memories of a colonized land, the multiplicity of the sexual imagery between the colonizer and the colonized, the dangers of looking at only the dominant or only the alternist views regarding the colonial process are presented in eight essays. Among the essays are discussions of the trial of Warren Hastings, the fiction of Kipling, Forster, and Rushdie, the diaries of nineteenth-century British women in India, and a discussion of Burke's patronizing, romantic defense of India.

In her refusal to remain the exploited, "the other" voice, Sara Suleri presents a convincing argument for Asian women as well as all colonized people as being integral members of any society, at any historical time.

Roshni Rustomji-Kerns

SUYIN, Han (b. 1917), novelist, autobiographer, biographer, essayist, and lecturer. Daughter of a Belgian mother and a Chinese father and fluent in French and Chinese, she has chosen English as her language. Christened Matilda Rosalie Elizabeth Chou, she has named herself Han Suyin. Wife of an Indian engineer, Vincent Ruthnaswamy, Han Suyin has family in India, Belgium, China, and the United States and maintains apartments in Lausanne, Beijing, and New York. Born in Henan, China, along the railroad which her father was building, Han Suyin was educated in China and Belgium, and she completed medical training in England. She practiced medicine for sixteen years before turning to writing. As her life has crossed national and political boundaries and her talent has bridged science and literature, so her writing encompasses many genres.

Her nine novels place the theme of interracial love into turbulent and various settings, such as China torn by war (*Destination Chungking*, 1942), Hong Kong during the Korean War (*A Many Splendored Thing*, 1952, popularized by the Hollywood film), Malaysia overthrowing English colonial rule (*And the Rain My Drink*, 1956), Nepal struggling for independence (*The Mountain Is Young*, 1958), Angkor Wat during a writers' conference and a murder (*Four Faces*, 1968), China and the United States from World War II to the 1980s (*Till Morning Comes*, 1982), and eighteenth-century Switzerland and Thailand at war (*The Enchantress*, 1985). Courageous and bold, Han Suyin does not avoid controversial subjects; her novella, "Winter Love," part of the volume *Two Loves* (1962), recounts the lesbian relationship between two students in London.

Because many of her novels are inspired by historical and autobiographical events, her four-volume *autobiography is intricately bound to history. It occasionally employs fiction. The first volume *The Crippled Tree* (1965) interweaves a variety of discourses and perspectives—historical background, family documents and letters, and fictional conjectures—to recreate her parents' courtship and marriage and her own birth and early childhood. The successive volumes, *A Mortal Flower* (1966), *Birdless Summer* (1968), and *My House Has Two Doors* (1980), bring the reader to the recent present. *Tigers and Butterflies* (1990) collects her essays and lectures on politics, culture and society.

Lambasted by some for blind partisanship, particularly visible in her biography of Mao Tse-tung and the Chinese Revolution, *The Morning Deluge* (1972) and *Wind in the Tower* (1976), and envied by others for her access into the highest circles of power, Han Suyin remains a controversial figure. Unperturbed, she energetically pursues her own path. She is presently working on a biography of Zhou Enlai.

• Han Suyin Papers are at the University of Massachusetts, Boston. See also Mimi Chan, *Images of Chinese Women in Anglo-American Literature* (1989). Aamer Hussein, Introduction to *Tigers and Butterflies: Selected Writings on Politics, Culture and Society*, by Han Suyin (1990). Amy Ling, *Between Worlds: Women Writers of Chinese Ancestry* (1990).

Amy Ling

SWENSON, May (1919–1989), poet, translator, dramatist, author of children's literature, editor, critic. Swenson achieved recognition as one of America's most visually inventive poets, with poetry exhibiting a range of formal and linguistic experimentation, as well as unconventional typography. She is best known for her "iconographs," poems arranged in the shape of their subject. Often classified as a nature poet, Swenson has also been praised for her precise observations of natural phenomena and her sensory, tactile poetry. In her attention to natural detail, she has been compared to Marianne *Moore and Elizabeth *Bishop, while her wordplay is reminiscent of e. e. cummings and Gertrude *Stein.

Born in Logan, Utah, the daughter of Swedish immigrants, Swenson earned a B.A. from Utah State University in 1939. After working as a reporter for a year, Swenson moved to New York, holding various jobs before becoming an editor for New Directions Press in 1959, resigning in 1966 to write poetry full time. She lived for the last twenty years of her life in Sea Cliff, New York, with her companion, R. R. Knudson, with whom she edited a collection entitled *American Sports Poems* (1989). Swenson earned numerous recognitions, including Guggenheim, Ford, and MacArthur fellowships, and membership in the National Institute of Arts and Letters and the Academy of American Poets.

Her first three volumes, *Another Animal* (1954), *Cage of Spires* (1958), and *To Mix with Time* (1963) introduce many of her characteristic themes: animal and human behavior, sexuality, death, and the nature of art and perception. *Cage of Spires* also introduces her first series of riddling poems, which grew out of her critique of the human need to name and define. Many of the poems in *Half Sun Half Sleep* (1967) turn on elaborate wordplay and visual patterning, techniques taken to the extreme in *Iconographs* (1970), typographically Swenson's boldest text. *New and Selected Things Taking Place* (1978) and *In Other Words* (1987), the last two volumes published before Swenson's death, showcase her examination of natural objects.

Swenson also published two collections of riddle poems for younger readers, a children's book, a play, three short stories, and a translation of the Swedish poet Tomas Tranströmer. *The Love Poems of May Swenson* (1991), published posthumously and including selections spanning her forty-year career, epitomizes Swenson's use of language as a vehicle for discovery, one which could palpably convey new perspectives on the human and natural worlds.

• May Swenson, *The Contemporary Poet as Artist and Critic* (1964). Karla Hammond, "An Interview with May Swenson," *Parnassus: Poetry in Review* 7, no. 1 (Fall/Winter 1978): 60–75. Alicia Ostriker, "May Swenson and the Shapes of Speculation," in *Shakespeare's Sisters: Feminist Essays on Women Poets*, ed. Sandra M. Gilbert and Susan Gubar (1979), pp. 221–233. Kenneth E. Gadomski, "May Swenson: A Bibliography of Primary and Secondary Sources," *Bulletin of Bibliography* 44, no. 1 (March 1987): 255–280.

Leigh H. Edwards

SYMBOLIC, The. *See* Psychoanalysis and Women, article on Jacques Lacan.

T

TABOOS, Literary. In the best of circumstances, we are inclined to believe that writers produce out of their own innate urges to create, inspired by whatever catches their fancy, free and accountable only to themselves. For writers who produce within a minority culture within a larger society, such facile expectations simply do not hold. A case in point is the history of *African-American writing. No matter how free any black writer professed to be, he or she was still bound by unspoken requirements of community, or publishers, or reviewers, indeed taboos that forced a conformity even when the writers professed that they were free of such strictures.

A case in point is the way black female characters have been portrayed in the literature over the past century. From ethereal Christian creatures such as those portrayed in William Wells Brown's *Clotel; Or, the President's Daughter* (1853) to those in Frances *Harper's *Iola Leroy* (1892) who are too pure to ever even use the bathroom, portraits of black women in the early- to mid-twentieth century depict them as generally long-suffering, bound by strictures of the church or the men in their lives, and not overly concerned about any urges to self-realization and self-fulfillment. And no matter how hard things became, they absolutely could not kill themselves. Sacrifice was the key trait for black women—sacrifice for parents, husbands, lovers, children (as with Aunt Sue in Richard Wright's "Bright and Morning Star," 1938).

Potentially rebellious Helga Crane in Nella *Larsen's *Quicksand* (1928) reaps her reward in marriage to a lascivious minister and in five pregnancies in about that many years. Zora Neale *Hurston's Nanny in *Their Eyes Were Watching God* (1937) can only hope that Janie will attain the fulfillment in life that has escaped her, and Janie does succeed in providing a bit of deviation from the expected norm of presentation by black writers. But the trend strongly continued in the 1950s with such critically acclaimed works as James Baldwin's *Go Tell It on the Mountain* (1953) and Lorraine *Hansberry's *A Raisin in the Sun* (1959). The women in Baldwin's novel bow to God, the church, and the men and children in their lives. One is expected to be forgiving when her educa-

tion is sacrificed for that of her brother, and another, gang-raped as a teenager, must live her life in the church, for that is the only remaining sanctuary to escape judgment and blame for the catastrophe that has befallen her. Hansberry's Mama Lena Younger is a paragon of strength and Christian virtue, a matriarch who guides the lives of her children with the same iron-willed strength that characterizes her prayers to God.

The general ranges and potential for black female character, therefore, operated on a set of unstated principles that black women writers post-1970 are only beginning to explode. Perhaps the first unwritten rule was the expectation that no black woman could be out of the church; in church was safety, out was damnation. Consider the fate of Esther in Baldwin's *Go Tell It on the Mountain*. She and Gabriel are involved in an extramarital affair, but she is the "scarlet lady," the "fallen" one, and the one who ultimately suffers and dies because of her "sin." Black female characters, then, were not usually depicted as being out of the church. "Slutty" black women were generally taboo.

Black women in the literature were usually exempted from going crazy. Other people might, but they had to hold on no matter the madness that prevailed around them. Toni *Morrison would explode that injunction in 1970 with the publication of *The Bluest Eye*, which depicts an eleven-year-old black girl driven crazy by lack of acceptance in her family and community. Alice *Walker would continue the trend in "Really, Doesn't Crime Pay?," one of the stories in her 1973 collection, *In Love and Trouble: Stories of Black Women*. Myrna is crazy enough—or sane enough—to try to chainsaw her husband's head off because he reminds her of the male oppression that has caused a man she presumed to be her friend to steal and publish one of her stories. Perhaps the crowning explosion of the injunction against insanity came in 1976, with Gayl *Jones's publication of *Eva's Man*. Now confined in a ward of a psychiatric hospital, Eva Medina Canada tells us how she has poisoned her lover and bitten off his penis because he kept her locked in a hotel room for his sexual pleasure. Once the taboo was broken, writers have not allowed it to be reimposed upon them. They have done as Mary

Helen Washington advocated in the introduction to *Black-Eyed Susans* (1975); they have killed the "sacred cow" of black female representation in the literature.

Two other taboos went hand in hand—black women could not have *abortions, and they could not abandon their children once they had given birth to them. The theme of sacrifice is again paramount. And again black women writers in the post-1970s period have claimed a right to depict black female character however the richness of their imaginations dictate. Eva Peace in Toni Morrison's *Sula* (1974) simply plops her children down in a neighbor's house and disappears for eighteen months, without explanation to anyone for her action. Instead of praying for her drug-addicted son, Plum, she burns him to death. And horror of horrors, Sula refuses to honor Eva by placing her in an old folks' home, the epitome of rejection and denial of parental responsibility in African-American communities.

Other characters do not allow the children to be born. Alice *Walker depicts *abortion in *You Can't Keep a Good Woman Down* (1981), and Ciel Turner, in Gloria *Naylor's *The Women of Brewster Place* (1982) has an abortion in an effort to save her failing marriage (the marriage fails anyway). Earlier in the literature, when Ruth Younger considered abortion in Lorraine Hansberry's *A Raisin in the Sun*, family, history, and morality were arrayed against her to get her to change her mind. In the 1980s, these female characters consider the choice their own, and they make it with or without assistance from others.

*Incest could also not be portrayed in the literature. Bold Ralph Ellison tried to deviate from that unwritten taboo in *Invisible Man* (1952), but he used language, history, personal narrative, *storytelling, and Freudian psychology as ways of distancing his readers from the reality of a father having engaged in sex with his daughter. There are no barriers to the pain of incest that Toni Morrison presents in *The Bluest Eye* (1970), or Alice Walker in *The Color Purple* (1982). And more recently, Marita Golden focuses on the subject; her *and do remember me* (1992) begins with a teenager's leaving home because she can no longer endure the pain and degradation of being her father's substitute wife—*with* her mother's knowledge. And the incident occurs in Mississippi; that usual territory of conflict between blacks and whites, therefore, becomes one of intraracial violence in the form of incest.

Perhaps the ultimate taboo in the literature, however, was the injunction against presenting lesbians or lesbian relationships. As Gloria Hull has shown, several of the *Harlem Renaissance women poets wrote lesbian poetry, though at times in conspicuously disguised ways. Fiction, however, was much more amenable to portraits of male homosexuals (as in Baldwin's *Giovanni's Room*, 1956, and *Another Country*, 1962) than to portraits of lesbians. The earliest blatant example in fiction is Ann Allen *Shockley's *Loving Her* (1974), which not only focuses on *lesbianism, but with an interracial couple. Shockley would continue her interest in the subject with a second novel (*Say Jesus and Come to Me*, 1982) and a collection of short stories (*The Black and White of It*, 1987). Of course the book that really made the topic one for public debate was Walker's *The Color Purple*.

The requirement to suffer through *everything* without consideration of suicide as an outlet came to an end in such works as Gloria Naylor's *Linden Hills* (1985), where a middle-class black woman not only commits *suicide, but does it in a strikingly artistic way by completing a perfect dive into an empty pool, and where another starves herself to death as the only protest against being the property of her husband. Morrison added her voice to the suicide option by having Sethe's mother kill herself in *Beloved* (1987) as a protest against *slavery, and J. California *Cooper made suicide for the same reason a kind of family tradition in *Family* (1991).

An explanation for the taboos outlined above is not long in coming. Early African-American writers were intent upon using the literature as an aid in getting equality for the black community. This goal-orientation that so defined the works of a writer like Charles W. Chesnutt was equally supported by the likes of W. E. B. Du Bois, who advocated a kind of "Best Foot Forward" literature. In a situation where African Americans were already being maligned from without the race, where lynchings, whippings, and other brutalities were commonplace, no race-concious writer wanted to be blamed for adding more fuel to the racist fire of attack—especially not in the depiction of female character. Black women had inherited a tradition of being considered more animalistic than human. For black writers to have shown them as immoral sluts, or as irresponsible mothers, or as drunkards, or as sexual "deviants," would have perhaps overburdened the budding literature if not led to its failure altogether. The fact that contemporary black women writers have broken out of these taboos is a testament to the *civil rights movement, the *black arts movement, the *women's movement, and perhaps an increased liberalism in the post-1950s twentieth century.

Trudier Harris

TAN, Amy (b. 1952), novelist. Amy Tan is a first-generation Chinese American born in Oakland, California. Formerly a freelance technical writer, she began to write short stories in 1985, some of which became chapters in her first novel, *The Joy Luck Club* (published 1989). Her second novel, *The Kitchen God's Wife,* was published in 1991.

Partially based on her own family history, Tan's novels interweave the voices of Chinese immigrant mothers and their American-born daughters. Like Maxine Hong *Kingston *(The Woman Warrior),* Monica *Sone *(Nisei Daughter)* and Canadian writers Joy Kogawa *(Obasan)* and Sky Lee *(Disappearing Moon Cafe),* Tan writes about the silences, distortions, and gaps in family history that fuel ambivalence and misunderstandings between *mothers and daughters. Reiterating a common theme among these writers, the breaking of silences in Tan's novels initiates the process of reclaiming lost histories and tracing intergenerational continuities.

Tan's significant departure from the pattern of the matrilineal literary tradition rests in her foregrounding of maternal subjectivity. *The Joy Luck Club* is a mosaic of seven voices: those of four mothers and three daughters. In *The Kitchen God's Wife,* a daughter's narration provides the frame for a story told from a mother's perspective. In both novels, mothers recount experiences of oppression, hardship, and loss in China. As transmitted from mothers to daughters, these stories become narratives of struggle and resistance; when set against their daughters' accounts of growing up in the United States, they suggest that identity is formed in relation to gender, cultural, and generational differences. Also, Tan skillfully captures the idiom and rhythms of a "mother tongue," a patois signaling the mothers' special "borderlands" positioning.

The intricate interweaving of narrative voices in *The Joy Luck Club* foregrounds *storytelling as a process. This structure also creates a complex network of resonances and thematic correspondences among individual stories, so that distinctions of identity and voice begin to blur. Melding generations and identities, Tan's vision is fully realized at the end of the novel: when one of the narrators is reunited with two long-lost half-sisters, the sisters see mirrored in each other their own faces and that of their mother. The resonant structure of the novel also involves the reader in actively unraveling the novel's multiple connections.

Tan's second novel has a more straightforward structure and draws more concretely on historical events. In it, a mother recounts her childhood and wartime experiences in China to her daughter. Alluding to a folk story about a male kitchen god, Tan revises the myth to center instead on the ordeals suffered by women so as to rewrite them as parables of strength and hope.

• Melanie McAlister, "(Mis)Reading *The Joy Luck Club,*" *Asian America* 1 (Winter 1992):102–118. Malini Johar Schueller, "Theorizing Ethnicity and Subjectivity: Maxine Hong Kingston's *Tripmaster Monkey* and Amy Tan's *Joy Luck Club,*" *Genders* 15 (Winter 1992):72–85. Marina Heung, "Daughter-Text/Mother-Text: Matrilineage in Amy Tan's *Joy Luck Club,*" *Feminist Studies* 19, no. 3 (Fall 1993):597–616.

Marina Heung

TAYLOR, Mildred Delois (b. 1943), novelist and educator. Born in Jackson, Mississippi, Taylor grew up in Toledo, Ohio. Even so, rural Mississippi remains the major setting for her work.

After earning a Bachelor of Education degree from the University of Toledo (1965) and two years in the Peace Corps teaching English and history in Ethiopia, she returned to the United States and served as a Peace Corps recruiter and instructor. After receiving the Master of Arts degree from the University of Colorado's School of Journalism (1968), she worked in the University's Black Studies and Black Education Programs before moving to Los Angeles, California, in 1971 to pursue her longstanding desire to write.

Song of the Trees (1975), chosen as *New York Times* Outstanding Book of the Year, begins the saga of the Logan family—a chronicle spanning the 1930s through the early 1940s in *Roll of Thunder, Hear My Cry* (1977), *Let the Circle Be Unbroken* (1981), *The Friendship* (1987), *Mississippi Bridge* (1990), and *The Road to Memphis* (1990). The more autobiographical *The Gold Cadillac* (1987) has its primary setting in Toledo, Ohio, during the 1950s.

A highly acclaimed writer of books for young readers, Taylor's books have garnered many awards. Honors include the Newbery Medal, *Boston Globe-Horn Book* Honor Book citation (1977), and Buxtehude Bulle Award (1985) for *Roll of Thunder, Hear My Cry;* Outstanding Book of the Year citation, *New York Times,* and Coretta Scott King Award (1982) for *Let The Circle Be Unbroken;* and the *Boston Globe-Horn Book* Award, Coretta Scott King Award (1988) for *The Friendship. The Road to Memphis* and *The Gold Cadillac* have respectively won the Coretta Scott King and the Christopher Awards, and in 1988 Taylor was honored by the Children's Book Council "for a body of work that has examined significant social issues and presented them in outstanding books for young readers."

The oral tradition undergirds Taylor's first-person *storytelling, with prototypes for several major black characters drawn from her own family. Readers follow the narration of outspoken, undaunted Cassie Logan from age eight to seventeen in all but two of the books.

Taylor's work depicts unity within the black family and the black community; realistic dialogue captures both black and white vernacular; adults and children confront bigotry with admirable strength and dignity; and the humorous antics of Cassie and others augment the optimistic spirit and hope for the future that characterize her writing. Taylor delves into race relations to entertain and to instruct.

• Adele Sarkissian et al., eds., *Something about the Author Autobiography Series*, vol. 5 (1988), pp. 267–286. Mary Turner Harper, "Merger and Metamorphosis in the Fiction of Mildred D. Taylor," *Children's Literature Association Quarterly* 13, no. 1 (Summer 1988): 75–79. Hal May and Deborah A. Straub, eds., *Contemporary Authors*, New Revision Series, vol. 25 (1989), pp. 440–441.

Mary Turner Harper

TEASDALE, Sara (1884–1933), poet. Born in St. Louis to wealthy parents, Sara Teasdale began writing poetry at a young age, publishing her first poems in 1902. She achieved considerable popularity as a poet of romantic love, with such collections as *Rivers to the Sea* (1915) and *Flame and Shadow* (1920), including the celebrated "I Shall Not Care" and "There Will Come Soft Rains." In 1918, she was awarded the Columbia Literary Prize (forerunner of the Pulitzer). Her *Collected Poems* (1937) underwent several reprintings, appearing in paperback in the 1960s.

Teasdale's life can be examined as dichotomous between artistic endeavor and social expectation. On the one hand, some sentiments in her poetry and letters reflect a desire to conform to the feminine ideal of her age. Indeed, she achieved great popularity with her familiar portraits of female beauty and maternity. On the other hand, Teasdale resisted social expectation, first in an illicit affair with the poet Vachel Lindsay, then in an abortion, and finally in a gradual estrangement from her husband Ernst Filsinger. Teasdale reflected that if marriage ever brought her ultimate bliss, it might rob her of creative energy; her marriage was not a happy one. Just prior to her divorce, Teasdale befriended Margaret Conklin, who would be her companion in her last years. After hearing of Vachel Lindsay's suicide in 1931, and haunted by fears of frail health and invalidism, Teasdale took her own life in 1933 in New York City, with an overdose of sleeping pills.

Teasdale's poetry reveals a profound commitment to art, inspired by her interest in the work of *Sappho and Christina Rossetti. Together with other female poets of the interwar period like Edna St. Vincent *Millay and Hilda Doolittle (*H. D.), Teasdale led a rediscovery of Sappho's works. Teasdale's writing is replete with classical allusions, and stylistically favors a controlled form and tone reminiscent of classical verse. Yet her poetry is modern in setting, favoring the subways and street lights of New York City; and modern in tone, reminiscent of the lyricism of W. B. Yeats and the tough-mindedness of Robert Frost. Her poems are calm on the surface, concealing intense anguish, often ending with solemn affirmation. New Critics generally disapproved of Teasdale's personal, emotional verse, but her poetry is now finding critical approval as an illustration of a woman grappling with the demands of the artist in a society steeped in Victorian views of womanhood.

• Margaret Haley Carpenter, *Sara Teasdale, A Biography* (1960). William Drake, *Sara Teasdale: Woman and Poet* (1979). Carl B. Schoen, *Sara Teasdale* (1986). Mary Ann Mannino, "Sara Teasdale: Fitting Tunes to Everything," *Turn-of-the-Century Women* 5, no. 1–2 (Summer/Winter 1990): 37–41.

Kelly D. Cannon

TEMPERANCE MOVEMENT. Temperance as an issue has been around as long as alcohol has been consumed. In the United States, the temperance movement began early in a sporadic fashion before the Revolutionary War. The first formal pledges to abstain appeared in New York State in 1808; total abstention (teetotalers) materialized in Boston in 1826. The rationale behind temperance ranged from the inexpediency of drink (influence on health, family stability, and employment) to drink as a sin.

Temperance participation reflected the contemporary social etiquette on *gender and *race. During the antebellum period, the antislavery and intersectional rivalries led to decline of the movement in the South. In the North, both white and black temperance unions denied admission to women. The World Temperance convention held in 1853 in New York City was the first to admit women (white), yet denied the admission of blacks. In New England, rare exceptions admitted blacks. Blacks, therefore, formed their own organizations. Due to its emphasis on Christian principles, the church was the first institution to feel the zeal of the reformers. In the black communities, temperance societies originated in the AME and AME Zion churches. Black temperance organizations usually denied admission to black women, although in New England some exceptions to this pattern existed, such as the Hartford Colored People's Temperance Society, which included thirty-two males and forty-five females in 1832. Black women, who saw the value of stable family life inherent in the temperance cause, formed their own groups, such as the Hudson Female Temperance Society (New York) and the Female E. C. Delevan Society (Lenox, Massachusetts).

During the *Civil War, social reforms became subordinated to the war effort. Temperance became a "conservation" effort, not a moral crusade. Following the war, however, the movement attempted again to reshape American society. The prohibition movement recognized that churches could no longer control human behavior, so voters demanded that government become the moral steward for society. Reflecting the religious mentality of the times, women and men became missionary crusaders holding revival meetings that told of ways to cure the evils of society. In the South, white temperance leaders courted the black vote through the churches, arguing that prohibition would enable the newly freed blacks to better achieve their goals and responsibilities. To white audiences, they presented temperance as a means to control the negative self-assertiveness of freedmen and prevent drunken attacks on white women. When prohibition amendments or local option laws failed to pass, the white leaders blamed blacks. Henceforth, prohibition and disfranchisement were linked in the South.

In the 1870s, women emerged from their church missionary societies to enter the saloons and beer halls. Within a decade, the Woman's Christian Temperance Union, under the leadership of Frances E. Willard, became the largest women's organization in size and importance. Most of the leaders were financially secure, married, white Protestants. The movement glorified the feminine virtues of superior morality, intuition, ladylike demeanor, and self-sacrifice. The WCTU stressed health concerns, prison reform, dress reform, peace, social purity, mothers' meetings, travelers' aid and the care of lower-class, needy or delinquent classes. They supported woman suffrage not as a right, but as a weapon to be used to protect the home and to improve the society.

Although WCTU leaders said that political rights should not be restricted by "accident of race, color, sex, or nationality," their rhetoric and writings reflected common academic perspectives, while catering to popular nativist or racist stereotypes in their efforts to gain supporters for their cause. Willard wrote in *Glimpses of Fifty Years* (1889) that the negative characteristics found in ethnic and racial groups resulted from environment, not biology. Yet, the literature and speeches of WCTU leaders disclosed stereotyping, especially of Irish, Swedish, German and African-American groups. The leaders accepted the supremacy of white, Anglo-Saxon, Protestant values, which were reflections of both leaders and membership.

During the late nineteenth century, the WCTU expanded its activities among various groups and geographical regions. The interest of black elites in family life, health, and morality had been demonstrated in the earlier temperance organizations formed during the antebellum years. Thus, black women responded to the call to join white women in the WCTU, and in the North, black women participated in a variety of temperance organizations. A few integrated with white women; some cooperated with black men; but most worked with other black women. White women from the South such as Sallie F. Chapin from Charleston organized their black sisters into segregated temperance societies. Known as "WCTU No. 2" or "colored work," the black temperance women participated because they believed in the goals and shared social values. Several became superintendents of "colored work": Jane M. Kenney (1881–1883), Frances E. Harper (1883–1891), J. E. Ray (1891–1895), Lucy Thurman (1895–1908), and Eliza E. Peterson (1908–?).

Participating in parallel activities in their own communities, the black women spoke in churches, circulated literature, and organized children into "Bands of Hope." In northern towns where blacks had not yet been disfranchised, the women assembled the prohibition vote. Some of these women, such as Frances Joseph and Amanda Smith, became international speakers for temperance. The National Association of Colored Women established a department for temperance as a result of speeches and writings by black women in the black press and periodicals.

Despite the stereotyping present in speeches and writings of the white leaders of the WCTU, few black or ethnically identified women spoke out against the negative characterizations. Ida B. *Wells-Barnett, a black journalist, created a backlash when she criticized Frances Willard's racism. Since most of the women who supported temperance shared the values of ladylike demeanor, few became critically assertive of the organization or leadership.

Women's campaign for reform was successful. By 1916, twenty-one states banned saloons and dry candidates won control of Congress. By 1919, the ratification of the Eighteenth Amendment, banning the production, sale, or transportation of intoxicating liquors, was achieved.

With the advent of woman suffrage the next year, however, the membership divided on the issue of women's role in politics, and the influence of the WCTU and temperance declined.

[*See also* Political Organizations; Religion.]

• E. Putnam Gordon, *Women Torch Bearers* (1924). E. H. Cherrington et al., *Standard Encyclopedia of the Alcohol Problem* (1926–1930). Joseph Timberlake, *Prohibition and the Progressive Movement* (1963). Rosalyn V. Cleagle, "The Colored Temperance Movement, 1830–1860," Master's thesis, Howard University (1969). Hanes Walton, Jr., and James E. Taylor, "Blacks and the Southern Prohibition Movement," *Phylon* 32 (Summer 1971): 247–259. Randall C. Jimerson, Francis Blouin, and Charles A. Isettes, eds., *Guide to the Microfilm Edition of the Temperance and Prohibition Papers* (1977). Ruth Bordin, *Women and Temperance* (1981). Dorothy Salem, *To Better Our World* (1990).

Dorothy C. Salem

TENNEY, Tabitha Gilman (1762–1837), author of satirical novel *Female Quixotism: Exhibited in the Romantic Opinions and Extravagant Adventures of Dorcasina Sheldon* (Boston 1801). She lived in Exeter, New Hampshire, all her life, except for several winters that she spent in Washington, D.C., with her husband, Samuel Tenney, a member of the United States Congress (1800–1807). She also compiled an anthology, *The Pleasing Instructor* (1799), and wrote *Domestic Cookery* (1808), but there are no known extant copies of either book. The later years of her life she devoted to fine needlework and charitable deeds.

Female Quixotism is a humorous response to late-eighteenth-century fears that novels, especially imported romances, would corrupt young female readers and divert them from realistic, domestic pursuits. Patterned roughly after Cervantes' *Don Quixote*, and Charlotte Lennox's *The Female Quixote*, Tenney's book portrays the foolish delusions and actions, springing from excessive indulgence in fiction, of plain-looking Dorcasina Sheldon through her nubile years to a disillusioned, unmarried old age. Ridiculing the literary sources of Dorcasina's novel mania, Tenney demonstrates her own familiarity with those very books, such as Richardson's *Sir Charles Grandisson* and Smollett's *Roderick Random*, that she mocks as dangerous to impressionable minds. Occasionally Tenney's rollicking Horatian satire takes a cruel Juvenalian twist.

Decidedly nationalistic and even xenophobic, Tenney also aims her barbs at Irish Catholicism, Jacobinism, Illuminationism, and atheism, which many patriots feared as threats to New England* Protestantism. Her ambiguous juxtaposition of admiration and condescension toward Dorcasina's African-American servant Scipio reflects ambivalent attitudes of Tenney's fellow citizens of New Hampshire. When Dorcasina extravagantly envisions herself as a universal liberating savior to the slaves, Tenney ridicules her heroine's abolitionism, and thus mirrors the Enlightenment dilemma of emancipating slaves without undermining established institutions. Above all, the Edenic purity of young women and early America must be preserved.

Contrasting sharply with *sentimental fiction of contemporaries William Hill Brown, Susanna *Rowson, and Hannah *Foster, *Female Quixotism* joins the satiric ranks of Royall Tyler's *Algerine Captive* and Hugh Henry Brackenridge's *Modern Chivalry*. With occasional mockery of popular *Gothic novels, Tenney is also a forerunner of sportive gothic writers such as Washington Irving. Sufficiently popular to go through at least five printings (1801, 1808, 1825, 1829, and 1841), *Female Quixotism* eventually declined into obscurity. Only recently has it reappeared (Scholars' Facsimiles and Reprints, 1988, and Oxford University Press, 1991) in company with other long-neglected women's writings from the nineteenth century.

• Evert A. and George C. Duyckinck, *Cyclopaedia of American Literature*, vol. 1 (1854; reprint, 1965), pp. 521–523. Henri Petter, *The Early American Novel* (1971). Candace K. B. Matzke, " 'The Woman Writes as if the Devil Was in Her': A Rhetorical Approach to Three Early American Novels," Ph.D. diss. (1983). Sally C. Hoople, "Tabitha Tenney: *Female Quixotism*," Ph.D. diss. (1985). Cathy N. Davidson, *Revolution and the Word: The Rise of the Novel in America* (1986).

Sally C. Hoople

TERRY, Lucy (1730–1821), balladeer and first known African-American poet. Born in West Africa, Lucy Terry was transported into New England and sold to Ebenezer Wells of Deerfield, Massachusetts, at age five. The Congregationalist minister of Deerfield taught her to read and write. She was sufficiently well versed in letters to compose "Bars Fight," a ballad memorializing the meadow slaughter that climaxed in an Indian raid on Deerfield in August 1746. The ballad, comprising twenty-six lines of rhymed couplets, differed in form and content from the most famous New England backcountry ballads—Tom Law's "The Rebel's Reward" about the Norridgewock expedition and "Lovewell's Fight" about the battle at Pigwacket. Those ballads lauded the violence and victory of colonial militias in *a b a b* quatrains; Lucy Terry's described the mayhem and dismay inflicted on Deerfield. The hardbitten remorse of her song contrasted with the exultation of Tom Law's. Only in its blunt imagery and vernacular language did "Bars Fight" resemble "Lovewell's Fight." Lucy Terry's sole known composition was probably designed to be sung or recited to a local audience. There is no indication that it was ever printed and distributed to the joint-stool singers of Boston or Portsmouth. Nevertheless, its local celebrity was such that it was published in 1855, over a century after its composition, as a sample of native folk balladry. Lucy Terry's life after the composition of "Bars Fights" is surprisingly well documented. Her liberty was purchased by Abijah Prince, a free black, who married her. They moved to Vermont, secured land in the new town of Sunderland, and raised six children. Lucy Terry was an ardent Whig. Her eldest son fought with Ethan Allen's Green Mountain Boys. Her faith in the United States government was vindicated when the U.S. Supreme Court found in her favor in a case in which a neighbor challenged her land title. She died at ninety-one, a local celebrity for her wit and skill at storytelling.

• George Sheldon, "Negro Slavery in Old Deerfield," *New England Magazine* (March 1893): 56. William H. Robinson, ed., *Early Black American Poets* (1969). Angelo Constanzo, "Three Black Poets in Eighteenth Century America," *Shippensburg State College Review* (1973).

David S. Shields

TERRY, Megan (b. 1932), playwright. Megan Terry is best known for her association with the New York's La Mama Theatre and the Open Theatre (of which she is a founding member) in the 1960s; her distinctive type of theatre, "transformational drama"; and her move in 1974 from New York City to Omaha, Nebraska, where she founded the Magic Theatre, where she is currently literary manager and playwright-in-residence. Her early association with * experimental, avant-garde theatre often distinguishes her from the more "mainstream" women playwrights, such as Beth * Henley, Marsha * Norman, and Wendy * Wasserstein.

Terry has written over sixty plays. Her most widely recognized work from the Open Theatre days is *Viet Rock* (1966), acclaimed as the first rock musical. During this era, Terry began to work with "transformational drama" as a stylistic approach and as a goal for audience response: "a dramatic action composed of brief sequences that are suddenly transformed into different sets of characters and circumstances" (Felicia Hardison Londre, "An Interview with Megan Terry," *Studies in American Drama, 1945–Present* 4). Terry's transformational drama has been widely influential in American theatre as it allows the playwright to present multiple perspectives and nonlinear structures which portray a postmodern sensibility.

Terry continues to explore in nontraditional, nonlinear, and * collaborative ways current social and psychological issues. A series in which she explores ways in which our words control our lives includes *The Tommy Allen Show* (1978), *Brazil Fado* (1978), and *American King's English for Queens* (1978). The "social action" series includes *Babes in the Bighouse* (1974), *Kegger* (1985), and *Amtrak* (1988). These plays confront issues of women in prison, child abuse, and teenage drinking. Virtually all musicals, they involve collaboration not only with the artists involved in the productions, but also with experts in particular fields (such as psychiatrists and neurosurgeons.).

Although born in Seattle, Terry's roots are in the Midwest; she has acknowledged that in establishing her theatre in Omaha she wished to regain those roots. One of her first productions after establishing the Magic Theatre was *100,001 Horror Stories of the Plains* (1975), a piece that, in celebration of the bicentennial, incorporates accounts of life on the plains. Terry has spoken of her move: "What drew me back? Sunlight. Endless sky. It's necessary for me to have light. Since living in Nebraska, I've written five times as much as any place I've lived" ("Anybody Is as Their Land and Air Is," *Studies in American Drama, 1945–Present* 4).

Terry's awards include an Obie for the best play of the 1969–1970 season, *Approaching Simone* (a biography of Simone Weil), Rockefeller grants, and a Guggenheim fellowship. Other plays in her vast repertoire are *Eat at Joe's; Calm Down, Mother; Keep Tightly Closed in a Cool, Dry Place;* and *Goona Goona.*

• June Schlueter, *"Keep Tightly Closed in a Cool Dry Place:* Megan Terry's Transformational Drama and the Possibilities of Self," *Studies in American Drama, 1945–Present* 2 (1987): 59–69. Kathleen Betsko and Rachel Koenig, eds., *Interviews with Contemporary Women Playwrights* (1987). Megan Terry, "Anybody Is as Their Land and Air Is," (speech), *Studies in American Drama, 1945–Present* 4 (1989): 83–90. Philip C. Kolin, "Megan Terry's *Amtrak:* An Iran-Contra Comedy," *Notes on Contemporary Literature* 20, no. 2 (March 1990): 3–5.

Kay K. Cook

TESTIFYING (or testifyin') denotes an expressive communication practice traditionally associated with African-American religious * ritual. Often moved by divine agency, individuals recount personal experiences as a way of affirming basic truths and shared assumptions of the community. Testifying, in either a sacred or secular context, can include narratives confirming the goodness of God as well as those attesting to the harsh realities and trials of daily life. Thus, testifying involves the appropriation of a specific verbal strategy, without regard to content or source of inspiration, which puts the speaker in the position of laying claim to Truth, with the anticipation of a reaffirming response, such as an "Amen" or "Uh-huh," from the audience. The ultimate power of the performance rests with the speaker's ability to dramatize—to reenact the experience—using language, gesture, and other paralinguistic devices in such a way that both speaker and audience relive that moment.

Testifying is so central to demonstrations of African-American verbal competence that it informs the structure and style of several other folk genres, including *spirituals and blues, sermons and rap. As if recognizing its privileged position, African-American authors also appropriate the strategies of testifying in written literature. The *slave narrative, for example, relies on this tradition, and Zora Neale *Hurston employs it to structure the inner narrative that re-creates Janie's journey to and from the horizon in *Their Eyes Were Watching God*. Whether in folk or literary contexts, testifying functions to affirm the cultural authority of the communication.

Adrienne Lanier Seward

TEXTBOOKS BY AND FOR WOMEN. Throughout the colonial period, American presses had habitually reprinted British "schoolbooks" (textbooks). In terms of authorship, the entire field was a male stronghold. After 1776, the Americans who began to compose textbooks in large numbers for their new nation remained overwhelmingly male.

In the area of English-language instruction, a handful of men wrote a few school texts for girls: Caleb Bingham composed an English grammar, *The Young Lady's Accidence* (1785); Ebenezer Bailey published *The Young Ladies' Class Book* (1831), a reader; and William Swan wrote *The Young Ladies Reader* (1851). But the most popular texts of the nineteenth century were written for both genders: the successive editions of William Holmes McGuffey's *Eclectic* series (1836 on).

There were a few isolated incidents of female authorship before 1880. *American Popular Lessons* (1820) was Eliza Robbins's compilation from the writings of Letitia Barbauld and Maria Edgeworth, who were, respectively, English and Irish. There were also Sarah Preston (Everett) Hale's *Boston Reading Lessons for Primary Schools* (1831) and Lydia *Sigourney's *The Boy's Reading-Book* (1839). A rare female author of spelling books was Mrs. S. A. Vaughan, with her *Vaughan's Speller, Definer, and Reader, for Beginners* (1853). A few women wrote "speakers": Anna Russell's *Young Ladies' Elocutionary Reader* (1845) was introduced by the editor and

textbook author William Russell; Anna Randall published her *Reading and Elocution: Theoretical and Practical* (1869). The need for readers for the Confederate South during the *Civil War inspired Marinda Branson Moore's *Dixie* series (1862).

After 1880, however, women began to write textbooks in increasing numbers. The widow of Lewis Monroe published a new edition of his readers, *Monroe's New Series* (1882), three years after his death. But it was Ellen Cyr who was the first woman to have a widely sold series. Her *Interstate Primer and First Reader* (1886) was revamped for Ginn as the primer of her *Children's Readers* (1891), later called the *Cyr Readers* (1899). In *Book Four* of the series she introduced excerpts from several women writers of prose and poetry. In 1887 Rebecca Pollard had a primer printed privately, *Busy Work for Little Fingers* (1887), as an antidote to the prevailing whole word method. Western Publishing House of Chicago subsequently put out her instructional manual, *A Complete Manual; Pollard's Synthetic Method of Reading and Spelling* (1889), as well as *Pollard's Synthetic Primer* and *Readers* (1889), *Pollard's Synthetic Speller* (1894), and her *First Book for Little Folks* (1898).

Even more influential was Sarah Louise Arnold, at one point the director of primary education for the public schools of Boston. Her series, with Charles Gilbert, *Stepping Stones to Literature* (1897), was popular, and her *Reading, How to Teach It* (1899) was a required text in many teacher-training courses. With Harvard professor George Lyman Kittredge, she wrote the *Mother Tongue* series (1900), and later became a coauthor of Ginn's *See and Say Series* (1913).

From the 1890s to 1920, women published reading instructional textbooks, in particular, with abandon. Like Cyr, many of them had their own names incorporated into the titles of the series: Helen Boyden's *Boyden's Readers* (1886), Adelaide Finch's *Finch* series (1897), Frances Lilian Taylor's *Taylor School Readers* (1900), and Sarah Sprague's *Sprague Classic Readers* (1902). Heath printed Emma Gordon's *Gordon Readers* (1910) as well as her methods text, *Comprehensive Method of Teaching Reading* (1902). Other textbooks were Maud Summers's *Summers Readers* (1908), Margaret Haliburton's *Haliburton* series (1911), Katharine Sloan's *New Sloan Readers* (1915) and Anna Magee's *Magee Readers* (1916). Mary Laing was coauthor with Andrew Edson of the *Edson-Laing Readers* (1920).

Between 1900 and 1920 women composed nearly all the new primers printed. They were also well represented in the movement to introduce children to literature as soon as possible (often through folk tales). Catherine Bryce was a junior author of the successful *Aldine Readers* (1907); Georgine Burchill was a coauthor of *Progressive Road to Reading* (1909); Margaret Free and Harriette Taylor Treadwell were coauthors of the *Reading-Literature* series (1912); and Ida Coe and Alice Christie were coauthors of the *Story Hour Readers* (1913). By the 1910s, it was actually difficult to find a complete series, such as James Fassett's *Beacon Readers* (1912) or William Elson's *Elson Readers* (1912), composed by men alone.

There were two other areas in which women seemed preeminent up to 1920: literacy for non-English speakers and adult literacy. Helen Cleveland composed *First Term's Work in Reading* for "very young or non-English speaking children" (1888); Maria Guilhermina Loureiro de Andrade, *Primeiro Livro de Leitura* (1894); Grace Mowry and others, *Spanish-American Readers* (1905); and Mary Sharpe, *A First Reader for Foreigners* (1911). The beginning of modern adult-literacy education dates from Cora Wilson Stewart's work at the "moonlight schools" of Kentucky and her *Country Life Readers* (1915) for rural illiterates.

By the 1920s, however, the scientific movement was beginning to alter the reading landscape. Research into reading fostered a flurry of professional textbooks, most of them by men. Nonetheless, women in public-school positions continued to write basal reading series. (These now forsook folk and fairy tales for realistic stories about children.) Emma Miller Bolenius was the sole author of Houghton-Mifflin's *Boys' and Girls' Readers* (1923). Clara Belle Baker and Edna Dean Baker composed the *Bobbs-Merrill Readers* (1923), and Martha Olsen and Eva Smedley, the *Smedley and Olsen Series* (1925). Emma Watkins wrote *Lippincott's Silent Reading for Beginners* (1925)—during the silent reading craze—and Catherine Bryce and Rose Lees Hardy, *The Newson Readers* (1927). Alberta Walker and Ethel Summy were the authors of Merrill's *Study Readers* (1928), and Mary Pennell and Alice Cusack teamed up for Ginn's *Children's Own Readers* (1929).

The year 1930 hinted at future change. This was the date of one of the earliest of Arthur Gates's many textbooks for Macmillan, *Peter and Peggy*. Arthur Gates had had no elementary-school teaching experience; his expertise stemmed from his experimental research in reading. That same year William S. Gray, an even more prolific reading researcher, joined William Elson as an author of Scott Foresman's *Elson Basic Readers*.

World War II (1939–1945) curtailed textbook publication, but of the six major new series published in the 1940s, women were senior or sole authors of three. However, in an updating of Scott, Foresman's earlier series, Gray became the senior author of *Basic Readers* (1940) and then *New Basic Readers* (1951). By this time he was the nation's most influential figure in a reading field that he helped to create. Between about 1940 and 1960, his so-called Dick and Jane readers outstripped all their rivals in popularity.

After 1950, women lost ground in the authorship stakes. Of ten basal reading series published between 1950 and 1965, not one woman was listed as a senior author. Women now appeared as junior authors to university men.

Interestingly, textbooks designed for the Catholic school system, whether adaptations of existing series or original works, were very likely to have female authors (often nuns). Examples are Mary Doyle's *Standard Catholic Readers by Grades* (1909); Honora Buttimer's anonymous *Ideal Catholic Readers* (1915); her primer was reprinted at least 18 times); Mother Emmanuel's revision of the *Curriculum Readers*, *Catholic Curriculum Readers* (1936); and the School Sisters of Notre Dame's *New American Readers for Catholic Schools* (1939). A late instance is Ginn's *Faith and Freedom* series (1952), coauthored by Sister Marguerite and Catherine Beebe.

In the publishing mainstream, the experience of one firm is instructive. The textbook-publishing house of Ginn was founded in 1867. In 1880 it printed Nelly Lloyd Knox Heath's English grammar, *Elementary Lessons in English*, probably the earliest Ginn textbook in any discipline to have female authorship. In 1887, Ginn published the primer of its first set of readers, in its "Classics for Children" series. Their author was Jenny Stickney, the principal of the Boston Training School for Teachers. Sara Lockwood, an English high school teacher, was invited to publish her *Lessons in English* (1888); it became a steady seller for years. As noted earlier, in 1891 Ginn launched Cyr's *Children's Readers*, which were successful enough to warrant a Spanish edition for Spanish-American schools. The firm then published Arnold's *Mother Tongue* series (1900), and the *Young and Field Advanced Literary Readers* (1916), by Walter Taylor Field and Ella Flagg Young, later superintendent of schools in Chicago. While the *Beacon Readers* (1912), by James Fassett, were the firm's greatest success of that decade, in the next decade Sister Mary Henry authored the *Rosary Readers* (1927), and Pennell and Cusack, respectively a former Missouri assistant superintendent of schools and a director of kindergarten and primary grades, wrote the *Children's Own Readers* (1929).

Significantly, in 1948 David Russell became

the senior author of the firm's flagship series, *Ginn Basic Readers* (1948 and 1961), with women as junior authors. Today the heir to the *Ginn Basic Readers* is Silver-Burdett and Ginn's *World Reading, Sterling Edition* (1991). Its eight authors are, in order of importance, three men, one woman, two men, and two women.

The reasons for the flowering of female textbook authorship after 1880 relate to the feminization of the teaching force: women became "experts" by default. Its decline may relate to the postwar "back to the home" movement of the 1950s. Changes in *education were also influential. Virtually all the women who wrote *literacy textbooks between 1880 and 1950 had once been classroom teachers. But the scientific movement produced (mostly male) educational psychologists like Gates and Gray whose primary interests lay in research. When publishers now chose authors for textbooks, they valued research expertise over classroom experience, and, all else being equal, men over women. Gender of *authorship thus mirrored traditional textbook content: "Dick" dominated "Jane." When content changed in response to the *civil rights movement of the 1960s, the gender of authors did not follow suit: in general, women continued to play a supporting role.

Today, for English-language textbooks other than basals, female authorship has greatly increased. In the area of English-composition texts, for instance, or developmental reading texts at the college level, the proportion of women who write textbooks has grown steadily over the past few decades.

[*See also* Literacy; Readership.]

• Thomas Bonaventure Lawler, *Seventy Years of Textbook Publishing: A History of Ginn and Company, 1867–1937* (1938). John Nietz, *Old Textbooks* (1961). Ruth Miller Elson, *Guardians of Tradition: American Schoolbooks of the Nineteenth Century* (1964). Wanda Dauksza Cook, *Adult Literacy Education in the United States* (1977). Nila Banton Smith, with a prologue by Leonard Courtney and an epilogue by H. Alan Robinson, *American Reading Instruction* (1986). Richard L. Venezky, introductory essay, *American Primers: Guide to the Microfiche Collection* (1990). E. Jennifer Monaghan, "Gender and Textbooks: Women Writers of Elementary Readers, 1880–1950," *Publishing Research Quarterly* (in press).

E. Jennifer Monaghan

THEATER. *See* Drama.

THEATER CRITICS. Theater criticism in the United States, like the commercial theater whose work the professional critic chiefly addresses, has been dominated by men since colonial times. Despite the social opprobrium attached to women attending theater in colonial America, a few women managed to publish

their responses to plays. One of the earliest, calling herself "Arabella Sly," wrote to the *Virginia Gazette* in 1756 inquiring about the "propriety" of laughing at a scene without shielding her face with a fan during a performance of *The Beaux Strategem.* Writing a few years later in the *Maryland Gazette,* "Clarinda" chastised the low-comic actors in a production of *Hamlet* who, being unsure of their lines, improvised vulgarities. Despite these occasional outbursts, women did not emerge as professional theater critics until the 1890s.

Mildred Aldrich contributed pieces on theater to *Arena* (1892, 1893), the *Boston Journal* (1894), and the *Boston Herald* (1895). Amy Leslie (née Lillie West) was the first important woman theater critic employed full time by a major metropolitan newspaper. A former light-opera singer and comedienne, in 1890 she wrote a review of a touring company's production of *Castles in the Air,* sold it to the *Chicago Daily News,* and was hired as the paper's drama critic, a position she held for forty years. *Some Players* collects sketches from her daily column, "What One Woman Sees." In *Ladies of the Press* (1936), Ishbel Ross briefly mentions four other women drama critics writing before 1936: Ada Patterson (*Theatre* magazine), Wilella Waldorf (*New York Post*), Carol Frink (*Chicago Herald Examiner*), and Leone Cass Baer (*Oregonian*).

The duo that significantly expanded opportunities open to theater critics in general, and women in particular, were Claudia Cassidy and Edith Isaacs. They began as reporters before being reassigned to the drama or arts desks of metropolitan newspapers. From the arts desk of the Chicago *Tribune,* Cassidy exerted a national influence. A midwesterner like Amy Leslie, Cassidy began as an arts reporter for the Chicago *Journal of Commerce* in 1925 and remained until 1941 as music and drama critic. She moved to the *Chicago Sun* and then to the desk of the Chicago *Tribune* where she remained for twenty-four years (1941–1965), writing a daily column called "On the Aisle" and later published *Europe—On the Aisle* (1954), an outgrowth of her summer travels. As the principal Chicago reviewer for drama, music, and dance, she influenced the direction and standards of the American commercial theater as she reviewed tryout productions scheduled for Broadway and touring companies bringing Broadway fare to the Midwest. Her name is part of the legendary success story of Tennessee Williams's *The Glass Menagerie,* which opened in Chicago in December 1944. When Chicago audiences failed to turn out for this exceptional play, Cassidy led the crusade to convince them of its importance. As a result of her efforts, *The Glass Menagerie* became a veritable hit, proceeded to

Broadway, and became a celebrated modern American play. Called a "brilliant phrasemaker," Cassidy campaigned against mediocrity in the theater and was only the second woman to serve as long-term theater critic for a large metropolitan newspaper. Sylvie Drake became the third in 1971 and Lloyd Rose for the *Washington Post* the fourth. Drake, employed as theater critic for the *Los Angeles Times*, following three years as critic for the Los Angeles *Canyon Crier* and freelance assignments for the *Times*, has exerted a major influence on West Coast theater.

Unlike Cassidy, Edith Juliet Rich Isaacs left the newspaper world and reviewed for the "small" magazines *Ainslee's Magazine* and *Theatre Arts*. In 1918 Sheldon Cheney invited her to join the latter's editorial board and in 1922, she was named editor. When she retired in 1946, she named her associate, Rosamond Gilder, as her successor. Isaacs expanded the magazine from a quarterly to a monthly and broadened the spectrum of interests to include dance, music, and mime. She supported such newcomers as Eugene O'Neill, Thornton Wilder, Martha Graham, Robert Edmond Jones, Jo Mielziner, Donald Oenslager, and many others. For twenty-five years, Edith Isaacs was a leading force as editor of this international magazine. Also, during the years between the two world wars, other women emerged as strong forces for change. Helen Deutsch, a press agent, single-handedly coerced New York drama critics to form a "Circle" to award a prize for the best new play by an American playwright produced in New York during the theater season. In 1938 Eleanor Flexner, a playwright and former contributor to *New Theatre* magazine, published *American Playwrights 1918–38*, an indictment of the failure of America's foremost dramatists to respond in their work to the social and economic conditions of the depression. Known as one of the few effective radical drama critics of her day, Flexner prepared the groundwork for women writers to promote social criticism in the arts.

Rosamond Gilder, founder of the International Theatre Institute, became the first woman to hold membership in the New York Drama Critics Circle; she, too, was an advocate of Flexner's sentiments that the critic has a social obligation to be a teacher and a guide. While her work with the international theater community frequently overshadowed her writing, she published a perceptive record of women in the history of acting (*Enter the Actress*, 1931) and a landmark performance study of *John Gielgud's Hamlet* (1937). She also expanded the role of the theater critic from observer to commentator/evaluator in her monthly *Theatre Arts* column entitled "Broadway in Review." Most important, she helped to define "dramatic" criticism for the American press. In her view, the drama critic's function, unlike the reviewer's, extended beyond responsibility to the individual artist. She wrote that critics must compel all concerned to "try to understand more clearly the satanic workings of the world around [them] and attempt at least to use their gifts to elucidate its meaning and thereby contribute . . . toward a better future" (*Theatre Arts*, 1945). Gilder's insistence on the critic's responsibility to the public influenced the next generation of women who were, in turn, to influence the American theater from the vantage point of such magazines as the *New Republic*, the *Nation*, the *New York Review of Books*, *Partisan Review*, the *New Yorker*, *Vogue*, *Evergreen Review*, *Mademoiselle*, and *Commentary*.

This next generation became nationally prominent figures in artistic and literary circles as critics, editors, novelists, essayists, and even filmmakers. Mary T. *McCarthy, following graduation from Vassar College, began writing book reviews for the *New Republic* and the *Nation*. In 1937, she joined the editorial staff of *Partisan Review*, where she wrote drama criticism until 1948. Some of her reviews were included in *Sights and Spectacles* (1956) and expanded in 1963 as *Mary McCarthy's Theatre Chronicles, 1937–1962*. She brought liberal politics and social awareness to her writing, arguing that the theater, "being sociable by nature, is a more sensitive register of time and its fleeting humors" than film. Her reviews registered American social history seen through two decades of theater. During the 1960s Elizabeth *Hardwick, the first woman to receive the George Jean Nathan award for dramatic criticism in 1967, wrote theater criticism for the *New York Review of Books* and *Vogue*. As one of its founding editors, she inveighed against the unprecedented power that the *New York Times* critics wielded over the Broadway theater. Hardwick's reviews of Broadway and Off Off Broadway were sharp and insightful, tending, like McCarthy's, more to literary and sociological concerns than to performance values. Susan *Sontag burst onto the arts scene with her 1964 "Notes on Camp" published in *Partisan Review;* her essay on camp, along with twenty-six other essays published on avant-garde theater, novels, and films between 1962 and 1965, were collected in *Against Interpretation* and nominated for the National Book Award. Sontag's criticism has focused on the avant-garde, especially the work of Antonin Artaud, Bertolt Brecht, and Peter Brook.

Such professional critics as Edith Oliver,

Margaret Croyden, Marilyn Stasio, Erika Monk, Alisa Solomon, and Bonnie Marranca write about theater for the *New Yorker, Cue Magazine,* the *Village Voice, Performing Arts Journal,* the *Drama Review, American Theatre, Changes, Ms. Magazine, Soho Weekly News, Newsday, Rolling Stone, Playbill,* and upon rare occasions the *New York Times.* Marranca, founding editor with her husband Gautam Dasgupta of the *Performing Arts Journal* and also a recipient of the George Jean Nathan award, has had a far-reaching impact on avant-garde theater and feminist writing. She has championed the American theatrical avant-garde of the last two decades, fostering in particular the works of Richard Foreman, Robert Wilson, Lee Breuer, Charles Ludlam, Maria Irene Fornes, and Sam Shepard. Edith Oliver, writing for the *New Yorker* magazine since 1968, also serves as a dramaturge at the Eugene O'Neill Theatre Center's new plays program in Waterford, Connecticut. Like Oliver, Marilyn Stasio encourages new playwrights in her capacity as critic for the *New York Post* (1978 to the present) and as drama reviewer for the weekly *Cue* magazine.

Writing formal theater criticism in the United States since 1890, a mere handful of women have shaped the public's understanding of the theater largely from the pages of major newspapers (with the exception of the *New York Times*) and small magazines. Women comprise twenty-three percent of the practicing theatrical critics in America today but they do so often far removed from theatrical centers. Frequently, their assignments were at the outset what Mary McCarthy in her *Theatre Chronicles* called "made-work" by editors, "like the W.P.A. jobs of the period." With the exception of those writing for metropolitan newspapers, women writing for weekly and monthly magazines turned away from the commodity-oriented commercial theater, nurtured newcomers to the theatrical scene, and fostered the avant-garde. Most importantly, they redefined the purpose of theater criticism to include critical responsibility to the creative artist, the public, and society. Indeed, the emergence of women in theater criticism has underscored more so than almost any other force the social and cultural diversity of the American theater.

[*See also* Drama.]

• Amy Leslie, *Some Players: Personal Sketches* (1899; reprint, 1906). Ishbel Ross, *Ladies of the Press: The Story of Women in Journalism by an Insider* (1936). Eleanor Flexner, *American Playwrights 1918–38: The Theatre Retreats from Reality* (1938, 1969). Rosamond Gilder, "Broadway in Review," *Theatre Arts* 29, no. 4 (April 1945): 197–207. Rosamond Gilder, "Broadway in Review," *Theatre Arts* 30, no. 5 (May 1946): 256–265.

Mary T. McCarthy, *Sights and Spectacles 1937–1956* (1956). Mary T. McCarthy, *Mary McCarthy's Theatre Chronicles 1937–1962* (1963). Susan Sontag, *Against Interpretation and Other Essays* (1966; reprint 1978). Marilyn Stasio, *Broadway's Beautiful Losers* (1972). Margaret Croyden, *Lunatics, Lovers and Poets: The Contemporary Experimental Theatre* (1974). Lehman Engel, *The Critics* (1976). M. E. Comtois, *Contemporary American Theatre Critics* (1977). Bonnie Marranca, *Theatre of Images* (1977). Bonnie Marranca, *American Dreams: The Imagination of Sam Shepard* (1981). Bonnie Marranca, *Theatrewritings* (1984). Helen K. Chinoy and Linda W. Jenkins, eds., *Women in American Theatre: Careers, Images, Movements. An Illustrated Anthology and Sourcebook,* revised edition (1987).

Milly S. Barranger

THEOLOGIANS. Apart from Mary Baker Eddy, whose *Science and Health* (1875) is the key text of her Christian Science church, and Ellen H. White, author of the nine-volume *Testimonies* for the Seventh-Day Adventist tradition, nineteenth-century women writers wrote mainly in the genres of pious writings and sermons.

In this century, women theologians have emerged in force and numbers since the late 1960s, when Mary *Daly's *The Church and the Second Sex* (1968) challenged the patriarchy of traditional Christianity and Catholicism in particular. This work was followed by *Beyond God the Father* (1973), which criticized the historical image of God as male. Daly also challenged the manner in which the Christian tradition wove antifemale images and interpretations in its doctrinal and liturgical elements. *Gyn/Ecology* (1978) explored the religiously justified antifemale practices of all Western and non-Western societies. In subsequent books, she examines the use/abuse of language and the negative use of words (e.g., witch, hag), in relation to women—words that once had positive meanings. Daly has moved to a post-Christian separatist stance.

Rosemary Radford Ruether, a *Catholic laywoman, has critiqued historical images of women in the Christian and Jewish traditions in *Religion and Sexism* (1974). Moving beyond these to invent a nonsexist Christianity led to her *Sexism and God-Talk* (1983). Biblical theologians such as Elizabeth Schussler-Fiorenza (*In Memory of Her*, 1983), Letty Russell, Phyllis Trible, and Virginia Ramey Mollenkott have focused on both a feminist reinterpretation of the Bible and a critique of its patriarchal attitudes toward women. A more conservative reinterpretation of women's role and place in Christianity is reflected in Alvera Mickelson's evangelical *Women, Authority and the Bible* (1986).

Ministerial roles and ordination questions are discussed in *Women Ministers* (1981), edited by Judith Weidman. Autobiographies by ordained women include Elizabeth Canham's *Pilgrimage to Priesthood* (1983) and the autobiographical and theological works of the lesbian Episcopal priest Carter Heywood, which shed light on women's call to ministry.

Women's *spirituality—in distinction to male-oriented understandings, experiences, and articulations—are explored in Joann Wolski Conn's *Women's Spirituality* (1986), in Christin Lore Weber's *Womanchrist* (1987), and in Janice Raymond's *A Passion for Friends: Toward a Philosophy of Female Friendship* (1986). A collection of essays that chronicles the personal transformation of a pioneer theologian and teacher is Nell Morton's *The Journey Is Home* (1985). In a similar vein, Barbara Walker's *The Skeptical Feminist: Discovering the Virgin, Mother and Crone* (1987) tells the story of her discovery of the *goddess tradition.

Women are addressing the issue of inclusive language in worship and in biblical translations noting the problems women encounter with not only male-oriented passages, but with the image of a male, patriarchal God. Attempts to move beyond gender images have created two approaches: finding feminine aspects of the divine in the Bible and, secondly, offering both a reinterpretation and a more positive view of the Jewish and Christian communities' understanding of women's role and place, particularly in the formative periods of the traditions. (See Mollenkott's *Women, Men and the Bible*, 1988; Elisabeth Tetlow's *Women and Ministry in the New Testament: Called to Serve*, 1980). For the Jewish tradition, Bernadette Brooten's *Women Leaders in the Ancient Synagogue* (1982) argues that women had important roles now historically overlooked. *Jewish Women in Historical Perspective* (1991), edited by Judith Baskin, and Susan Weidman Schneider's *Jewish and Female* (1985) offer historical and current interpretations of women in the tradition. Blu Greenberg's *On Women and Judaism* (1981) is more conservative in its assessment of women's role and place. In contrast, Susannah Heschel's *On Being a Jewish Feminist* (1983) is critical and transformative of the tradition, as is Judith Plaskow's *Standing Again at Sinai* (1990), which moves from the agenda of the Jewish women's movement to a new vision, if not version, of Judaism.

New *rituals are being created by women theologians. Inclusive language texts and rituals celebrating women's experiences include Miriam Therese Winter's *Womanword: A Feminist Lectionary and Psalter* (1990) and Ruether's *Womanchurch* (1985).

Women have also been revising the field of

ethics and morality. Discussions on issues of *sexuality, nonviolence, and social justice have found a feminist perspective in the writings of Beverly Wildung Harrison. Her *Making the Connections: Essays in Feminist Social Ethics* (Carol Robb, ed., 1985) and Lisa Sowle Cahill's *Between the Sexes; Foundations for a Christian Ethics of Sexuality* (1985) are revisionist examples of what constitutes ethical behavior and thought.

Women of color are addressing the problematic of white women theologians speaking for *all* women and are articulating their own experience of Christianity and reshaping it in dialogue among themselves and with white theologians. Much of the African-American women theologians' work is done in the context of story (e.g., theological reflections on Zora Neale *Hurston, Alice *Walker, and other women writers). Jacquelyn Grant's *White Women's Christ and Black Women's Jesus* (1989) dialogues with white feminist Christology in relation to a "womanist" theology for black people. Attempting to bridge the gap between the experiences of women of color and white women is Susan Thistlethwaite's *Sex, Race, and God: Christian Feminism in Black and White* (1989).

Hispanic women theologians' writings are both personal and autobiographical as well as analytical of the women's religious oppression. Ada Maria Isasi-Diaz and Yolanda Tarango's *Hispanic Women: Prophetic Voice in the Church* (1988) links women's positions in society and church with the themes of Latin American liberation theology.

Two sources that point to the creation of a new version of American Buddhism are: Sandy Boucher's *Turning the Wheel: American Women Creating the New Buddhism* (1988) and *A Gathering of Spirit: Women Teaching in American Buddhism* (1987), edited by Ellen Sidor.

Some women theologians have turned from Christianity to adopt and/or adapt a form of goddess religion or a modern version of wicca. The best example of the former is the autobiographical and theologically argued work of Carol Christ: *Laughter of Aphrodite: Reflections on a Journey to the Goddess* (1987); Starhawk's (Miriam Simos) *The Spiral Dance* (1979) is a good example of the latter. Women such as Christ refer to doing "thea-ology" as the feminine mode of "theo-logy." Starhawk attempts to uncover the nontextual tradition of wicca and to demonstrate its positive and holistic value for both men and women.

Rediscovering the feminine aspects of Native American religious traditions is the work of the literary critic, poet, and essayist Paula Gunn *Allen (*The Sacred Hoop: Recovering the*

Feminine in American Indian Tradition, 1986), who combines work in oral tradition and stories with theological interpretation.

[*See also* Catholic Writers; Poetry, article on Religious Poetry; Spirituality; Religion.]

• Rosemary Radford Ruether, *New Woman, New Earth: Sexist Ideologies and Human Liberation* (1975). Elisabeth Schussler Fiorenza, *Bread Not Stone: The Challenge of Feminist Biblical Interpretation* (1984). The Mudflower Collective (Katie G. Cannon et al.), *God's Fierce Whimsey: Christian Feminism and Theological Education* (1985). Paula M. Cooey, Sharon A. Farmer, and Mary Ellen Ross, eds., *Embodied Love: Sensuality and Relationship as Feminist Values* (1987). Katie G. Cannon, *Black Womanist Ethics* (1988). Anne E. Carr, *Transforming Grace: Christian Tradition and Women's Experience* (1988). Ursula King, *Women and Spirituality: Voices of Protest and Promise* (1989). Judith Plaskow and Carol P. Christ, eds., *Weaving the Visions: New Patterns in Feminist Spirituality* (1989). Tamar Frankiel, *The Voice of Sarah: Feminine Spirituality and Traditional Judaism* (1990). Mary E. Hunt, *Fierce Tenderness: A Feminist Theology of Friendship* (1992).

Mary Lea Schneider

THIRD WORLD FEMINISM, U.S. To link two apparently contradictory geographies in the term *U.S./third world feminism* as if together they can represent a single political locality is already to suggest the nature of this vital artistic, literary, academic, and political movement. The phrase enacts a geopolitical upheaval of nation-state, and a pulling together again under what is a transcultural and coalitional political vision. Under late twentieth-century, first world cultural conditions, U.S. third world feminism is a theory, method, and praxis permitting entry to a new mode of historical consciousness. It is a praxis which generates another kind of decolonizing subjectivity/citizenship across what were once considered "natural" boundaries of nation, *race, culture, sex, *gender, and *class.

This artistic, intellectual, and political movement arises in recent times, though there is a long history of alliances between women of color in the United States. Examples range from the councils held by Seminole, Yamassee, and African women during times of territorial *colonialism and *slavery, to the coalitions made among Chinese, Chicana, and African women in protective leagues and labor movement struggles of the 1920s, 1930s and 1940s. The contemporary formulation of U.S. third world feminism, however, is based in the great global struggles for decolonization of the nineteenth and twentieth centuries. These geopolitical struggles generated a new form of transnational alliance among peoples of color both outside of and within the United States as expressed in the demand for "Third World liberation." This term signified solidarity among new masses of peoples differentiated by nation, class, race, and culture but nevertheless allied by virtue of similar sociohistorical and colonial relations to dominant powers. This sense of solidarity guided the social movements of the 1960s and 1970s in the United States. Activists of color involved in the *civil rights, antiwar, black, Chicano, Asian, Native American, student, women's and gay liberation movements saw themselves as bonded, despite distinct and sometimes contrary aims and goals, in a coalitional form of consciousness opposed to dominating powers and oppressive social and racial hierarchies. To be a "third world liberationist" during this period did not mean to be committed solely to national and/or racial liberation. For U.S. people of color it meant to ally with what semiologists now identify as the "third" and repressed force that nevertheless constantly rises up through meaning systems, breaking apart two-term or binary divisions of human thought.

By 1971 a grass-roots movement of U.S. third world feminists began to form, bringing together women of color who, in spite of severe differences in historical relations to power, color, culture, gender, and sexual orientation, were surprised to recognize in one another profound similarities. A great number of newsletters, pamphlets, and books were produced by underground publishers from 1971 to 1974, including separate works by Janice *Mirikitani and Francis Beale, both entitled *Third World Women*, which were meant to affirm and develop the new kind of shared sisterhood/citizenship insistently emerging in the corridors and back rooms where women of color congregated. The burgeoning women's liberation movement, however, could not accept, recognize, or contain this new kind of female alliance. Beale's 1970 essay in *The Black Woman: An Anthology*, reprinted one year later in *Sisterhood is Powerful*, warned that women's liberation was fast becoming a "white women's movement" because it insisted on organizing along the gender demarcation male/female alone, when, as Sojourner *Truth had so eloquently stressed in 1851, people of color are often denied easy or comfortable access to either of these socially constructed categories. That same year, Chicana feminist Velia Hancock wrote in the *Chicano Studies Newsletter* that "white women focus on the maleness of our present social system" as if "a female dominated white America" will take a more reasonable course for people of color of either gender. In *Sula* (1973) Toni *Morrison suggested that women of color must understand that they are "neither white nor male, and that all freedom and triumph was forbidden to them," so "they had to set about creating something else to be." That "something else to be" was explored throughout the seventies by a growing number of U.S. third world feminist artists, writers, critics, theorists, and activists including Wendy *Rose, Leslie Marmon *Silko, Antonia Casteneda, Bea Medicine, Barbara Smith, Pat *Parker, Rosara Sanchez, Maxine Hong *Kingston, Lorna Dee *Cervantes, Judy Baca, Teresa Hak Kyung *Cha, Azizah Al-Hibri, and Margaret *Walker. As Barbara Noda put it, these feminists of color were "lowriding through the women's movement"; that is, they were developing the imagery, methods and theories necessary for the "cruising" through meaning systems which would become the hallmark of a distinctive U.S. third world feminism.

By the 1980s, U.S. third-world feminism had become a major intellectual force. In 1981 the National Women's Studies Association held the first U.S. conference on the troubled relationship between white and third world women, entitled "Women Respond to Racism." Three hundred women of color attended, and established the first "National Alliance of U.S. Third World Feminists," along with a statement of purpose arguing that U.S. third world feminism is organized according to a fundamentally different structure from that of a nationalist and hegemonic North American feminism. That same month, *This Bridge Called My Back, A Collection of Writings by Radical Women of Color* was released, edited by Cherríe *Moraga and Gloria *Anzaldúa. Here, as Toni Cade *Bambara put it, a growing number of U.S. third world feminists are "putting in telecalls to each other. And we're all on the line." *Bridge* quickly followed by the founding of Kitchen Table: Women of Color Press and the publication of a plethora of writings by feminists of color. These writings included Bernice Reagon's "Coalition Politics, Turning the Century" (1981), an explication of hegemonic white consciousness trapped in a prison-house of identity, making alliance across differences impossible, and Audre *Lorde's 1982 *Zami,* in which for women of color "it was a while before we came to realize that our place was the very house of difference rather than the security of any one particular difference." Angela *Davis, bell hooks, Maxine Baca Zinn, Aida Hurtado, Gayatri *Spivak, Beth *Brant, Janice Gould, and Barbara Christian are only a few of the many feminist writers and artists of color who made important contributions during this period.

Examination of their works reveal a U.S. third world feminism committed to generating a theory and method of consciousness-in-opposition to social hierarchy and capable of aligning a variety of social movements with one another across their differences of gender, race, class, and/or sexual orientation. The representation of this new theoretical structure is made possible by women of color because, as Paula Gunn *Allen puts it, so much has been taken away that "the place we live now is an idea"—and in this place new forms of identity, community, and solidarity become imaginable. In 1987, Gloria Anzaldúa published her famous work *Borderlands, La Frontera,* which defines U.S. third world feminism as "la conciencia de la mestiza," the consciousness of the mixed blood, born of life lived in "the crossroads" between worlds. This form of consciousness depends upon one's ability to read signs, "signifyin'," or "la facultad." Maria Lugones calls this activity of consciousness "world traveling." Patricia Hill Collins argues that its practitioners recognize "the outsider/within." Gayatri *Spivak writes about "shuttling" between meaning systems and the enactment of "strategic essentialism" as a mode of oppositional politics. Alice *Walker defines it as "Womanism," and I have argued that the processes of U.S. third world feminism generate the model for a new social movement theory of consciousness in opposition.

U.S. third world feminism is a theory and method of oppositional consciousness in the postmodern world. It can be understood as apprehending and organizing consciousness, aesthetics and politics around the following five points of resistance to U.S. social hierarchy: (1) the integrationist; (2) the revolutionary; (3) the supremacist or nationalist; (4) the separatist; and (5) the differential forms of U.S. third world feminism. It is the differential mode which allows the previous four to be understood and utilized as *tactics* for changing social relations. Under the differential theory and method of U.S. third-world feminism these modes of resistance, ideology, and political practice are seen and deployed as *technologies of power.* When enacted differentially, U.S. third-world feminism demands of its practitioners a commitment to the process of metamorphosis itself: the activity of the trickster who practices subjectivity-as-masquerade. This "morphing" is accomplished not simply for survival's sake, as in earlier times. It is a kind of conversion, rather, that allows movement through and over dominant systems of resistance, identity, race, gender, sex, and national meanings.

The field of U.S. third world feminism is not an easy terrain. Debates among feminists of color continue over which of these five forms comprise the most effective U.S. third world feminism, and how these feminisms should be distinguished. Contending U.S. names range from "transnational" or "transcultural" feminisms, where issues of race and ethnicity are sublimated, to "women-of-color-feminism," which emphasizes the exclusion of its population from legitimate state powers by virtue of color and/or physiognomy. Women-of-color-feminism, then, tends to commit to one or more of the five technologies of power as a means of increasing and reinforcing racial and tribal loyalties and self-determination. This focus tends to be more specific than that of "U.S. third world feminism," however, which is committed, above all, to the *differential* and poetic deployment of the technologies of power.

Differential consciousness views the five technologies of power as consensual illusions, transformable social narratives designed to intervene in reality for the sake of social justice. This sleight-of-consciousness creates a new space, a cyberspace where the transcultural, transnational leaps necessary to the generation of new forms of oppositional praxis are made possible. To identify a work as U.S. third world feminist is to find a work born of disruptions and of taking place, of immigrations and crossing borders, of traveling style, politics, poetics and procedures, of tactics, strategies, and movement, all produced with the aim of, as Merle Woo puts it in *Bridge*, equalizing power on behalf of the third world, the colonized, the class-, race-, gender-, or sexually subordinated. Ironically, given the history of U.S. third world feminism, the "flexibility of identity" demanded for living under colonial and subordinated conditions is currently demanded of every first world citizen affected by transforming global economies. This condition creates new grounds for coalition across borders in U.S. third world feminist praxis; that is, in an understanding of resistance that focuses on the differential deployment of consciousness in opposition.

[See also Feminism; Post-colonialism; Black Feminism.]

• Toni Cade Bambara, ed., *The Black Woman: An Anthology* (1970). Janice Mirikitani, ed., *Third World Women* (1973). Shirley Hill Witt, "Native Women Today: Sexism and the Indian Woman," *Civil Rights Digest* 6 (Spring 1974). Janice Mirikitani, ed., *Time to Greez! Incantations from the Third World* (1975). Anna Nieto-Gomez, "Sexism in the Movimiento," *La Gente* 6, no.4 (1976). Jane Katz, *I Am the Fire of Time—Voices of Native American Women* (1977). Dexter Fisher, ed., *The Third Woman: Minority Women Writers of the United States* (1980). Norma Alarcón, ed., *Journal of the Third Woman* (1980–). bell hooks, *Ain't I a Woman* (1981). Cherríe Moraga and Amber Hollibaugh, "What We're Rollin' Around in Bed with," *Heresies* (1981). Paula Gunn Allen, "Beloved Women: The Lesbian in American Indian Culture, *Conditions* 7 (1981). Gloria Hull, Patricia Bell Scott, and Barbara Smith, eds., *All the Blacks Are Men, All the Women Are White, but Some of Us Are Brave* (1982). Cherríe Moraga, *Loving in the War Years* (1983). Audre Lorde, *Sister Outsider* (1984). Beth Brant, ed., *A Gathering of Spirit: A Collection by North American Indian Women* (1988). Trin Minh Ha, *Woman Native Other* (1989). Gloria Anzaldúa, ed., *Haciendo Caras, Making Face, Making Soul: Writings by Feminists of Color* (1990). Chela Sandoval, "U.S. Third World Feminism: The Theory and Method of Oppositional Consciousness in the Postmodern World," *Genders* 10 (1991). Lourdes Torres and Chandra Mohanty, eds., *Third World Women and the Politics of Feminism* (1991).

Chéla Sandoval

THOMAS, Joyce Carol (b. 1938), poet, novelist, playwright, educator. Born in Ponca City, Oklahoma, Thomas moved with her family to the outskirts of Tracy, California, at age ten. Intrigued by language at an early age, she majored in Spanish and minored in French, receiving a Bachelor of Arts degree from San Jose State University (1966) and a Master of Arts degree from Stanford University (1967).

As an educator she taught French and Spanish in the California public schools, then achieved professorial status at San Jose State University, Contra Costa College (San Pablo, California), St. Mary's College (Moraga, California), Purdue University, the University of California at Santa Cruz, and the University of Tennessee at Knoxville. A former commissioner at Berkeley Civic Arts, and a visiting scholar during 1980 and 1981 at Stanford University's Center for Research on Women, she became a full-time writer in 1982.

Thomas's first book of published poetry, *Bittersweet* (1973), was followed by four others during the 1970s and 1980s, during which time she also produced her five plays in San Francisco, Berkeley, and Carson City, California.

A recipient of a Djerassi Fellowship for Creative Artists (Stanford, 1982, 1983), Thomas has written five novels for young adults. *Marked by Fire* (1982) received that year's Before Columbus Foundation Award and the American Book Award for children's fiction in paperback (in 1983); its sequel, *Bright Shadow* (1983), garnered the Coretta Scott King Citation. Both trace the joy and trauma of perceptive, gifted Abyssinia Jackson's life in Ponca City, Oklahoma. *The Golden Pasture* (1986), also set in Oklahoma, explores episodes from the life of young Carl Lee Jefferson, who also appears in *Bright Shadow*, with a lyric, fairy-tale quality. Tracy, California, becomes the setting for *Water Girl* (1986), which reveals young Amber Westbrooks's sensitivity to treatment accorded several American minorities as she embarks upon a discovery of self and heritage. *Journey* (1988), set in Berkeley, serves as a metaphor for the perils that await many contemporary black youths.

Thomas's love of language and perceptive grasp of both character and surroundings are apparent in the detailed, sensuous descriptions in her novels. Nuances of sound and sight blend with folk spirits and practices drawn from her own Oklahoma and California experiences as a black American. Comments Thomas, "I try to remember as I write my fiction that not only do we share the world with other races and nationalities but also with other creatures and critters. . . ." A "word-musician," she harmonizes *myth and fantasy with her love of nature, animals, and "critters" to celebrate the human experience.

• Joyce Nakamura et al., eds., *Something about the Author Autobiography Series,* vol. 7 (1989), pp. 299–311. *Children's Literature Review,* vol. 19 (1990), pp. 219–223. Linda Metzer et al., eds., *Black Writers* (1990), pp. 540–541.

Mary Turner Harper

THOMPSON, Dorothy (1893–1961), journalist and broadcaster. Born in Lancaster, New York, Dorothy Thompson was the daughter of a Methodist preacher. She was educated at Syracuse University (class of 1914) and found her first work as a publicist and organizer for woman suffrage. In 1920 she sailed to Europe, and for the next thirty years—first as a freelance correspondent and later as America's acknowledged expert on Middle Europe—she was undisputed queen of the national press corps, "the best journalist this generation has produced in any country," according to John Gunther, "and that is not saying anywhere near enough." In 1927 she married the novelist Sinclair Lewis and entered the world of "Lost Generation" celebrity. The union was marred from the outset by Lewis's alcoholism, by the pressures of Thompson's own success as a reporter and pundit, and by her sexual ambiguity, which led her, in the early 1930s, to a love affair with the German writer Christa Winsloe, author of *Mädchen in Uniform.* Thompson was not, in any sense, a lesbian activist, and apart from a strict notoriety she plays no role in the history of lesbian letters. But her sympathies were on the side of the individual passion—she argued movingly for "the right to love where my mind and heart admire"—and her best work was imbued with a strong, even apocalyptic moral purpose. In 1934 she became the first correspondent to be expelled from Berlin on the orders of Adolf Hitler: she was the loudest and strongest voice in American journalism against the menace of the Nazis. Her thrice-weekly column, "On the Re-

cord," was syndicated to hundreds of newspapers; she wrote a monthly essay for the *Ladies' Home Journal* and broadcast weekly, sometimes daily, on news topics over the NBC radio network. A cover story in *Time* magazine declared that Dorothy Thompson, in 1939, was the most influential woman in America after Eleanor Roosevelt.

Her career declined after World War II, when she argued for a "humane" peace with the defeated Germans and, later, took up the cause of the Palestinian Arabs in opposition to the State of Israel. "I refuse to become an anti-Semite by appointment," she declared, shocked that what she saw as an honest concern for human rights should lead to accusations of racism and betrayal. She looked around her at the America of the 1950s and saw a materialistic, dehumanizing culture, obsessed with "know-how" and devoid of reverence, a society composed, in her memorable phrase, of "literates illiterate in every higher sense," deprived of any authentic education or moral training, floundering in "an uncharted ethical miasma of 'being happy'" and suffering from "mental and spiritual rickets." Never conventionally religious, she was always deeply spiritual and appalled at the so-called march of progress in her time. Divorced from Lewis in 1942, she enjoyed a happy (and lusty) final marriage with the Czech painter Maxim Kopf (1892–1958). She died in Portugal in 1961 and left instructions for her epitaph: "Dorothy Thompson Kopf— Writer." She was unquestionably the preeminent woman journalist of her era—perhaps of all time in the United States.

• Mark Schorer, *Sinclair Lewis: An American Life* (1961). Vincent Sheean, *Dorothy and Red* (1963). Marion K. Sanders, *Dorothy Thompson: A Legend in Her Time* (1973). Peter Kurth, *American Cassandra: The Life of Dorothy Thompson* (1990).

Peter Kurth

TRAMBLEY, Estela Portillo. *See* Portillo-Trambley, Estela.

TRANSLATORS. Women's writing in the United States has long included translations. Until the last few years, however, women who translated were largely "invisible." Their work, like that of all translators, fell outside the scrutiny of critics, whose interest lay primarily in "original" authors and texts, even when they studied those texts in translation. In recent discussions, feminist critical practice, redefinitions of both literary originality and the text itself, and the questioning of mediation and alterity raised by cultural studies have all contributed to an unprecedented interest in translation. Translators have yet to be fully recognized and truly well compensated, but women translators are increasingly prominent. Numerous women figure among the most accomplished translators presently working in the United States and, even more important, women have been active participants in the current reevaluation of translation. They have also played significant roles in such professional organizations as the American Translators Association (ATA) and the American Literary Translators Association (ALTA).

Since the history of translation in the United States has never been chronicled, not to mention the history of women translators, it is only after considerable research, and a measure of chance, that one learns much about translations made even by well-known women writers. When those histories are written, they will no doubt echo the findings of Margaret Patterson Hannay and her contributors about Tudor women as translators and "marginal" writers (*Silent but for the Word*, 1985). They will also include discussions of such eighteenth-century translations as Phillis *Wheatley's version of *The Negro Equalled by Few Europeans* by Joseph La Vallée, marquis de Bois-Robert (published posthumously in 1801) and such nineteenth-century translations as Margaret *Fuller's versions of work by Goethe and others.

Although they are seldom isolated for study in their own right, the translations of twentieth-century writers such as Elizabeth *Bishop, Olga *Broumas, *H. D., M. F. K. Fisher, Carolyn *Forché, Heather McHugh, Muriel *Rukeyser, and Edna St. Vincent *Millay are readily accessible. What is more, many academic women are prolific translators, and a growing number of women work primarily as literary translators, among them Helen Lane, Barbara Wright, and Margaret Sayers Peden. That the very figure of the female translator intrigues women writers is evidenced by two recent novels in which she is a protagonist: Pat Goodheart's *The Translator* (1983) and Barbara Wilson's *Gaudí Afternoon* (1990). In Wilson's novel, translation itself becomes an exploration of sexuality and gender and is thus linked closely to the work of lesbian critics such as Alice Parker, who identifies translation with "passing" between language and sign systems.

One aspect of women's work in translation that has received sustained attention is the decision about which writers to translate. This is especially true of the last two decades and the commitment made by translators and scholars to familiarize readers in the United States with women writing in languages other than English. This commitment has occasioned both the introduction of countless "new" writers and highly innovative collaborative projects. George Sand's *Story of My Life* (1991), for example, resulted from work by sixty-five translators, and Zoë Angelsey's *Ixok Amar·Go: Central American Women's Poetry for Peace* (1987) includes contributions from over one hundred poets and translators. The commitment to translate women writers has also resulted in the creation of publishing enterprises devoted to the work of women writers. At least two university presses, SUNY and Nebraska, have created special series with their own editors and editorial boards, and many small and alternative presses have encouraged and published translations of writing by women. One of them, Seal Press, in 1984 established "Women in Translation," an imprint that has since become a separate publishing company. If at first the efforts and intentions of many translators were focused on the possibility of a universal women's "voice," changing definitions of identity have led translators and anthologists to appreciate and preserve distinct, individual voices, even within a given national tradition.

Intimately involved in the selection and publication of the work they translate, contemporary women translators have also begun to reflect critically on their interventions as language mediators and manipulators. Their examination often takes the form of introductory essays or afterwords, but the interrogation it encompasses surpasses the questions of word choice or annotation customarily discussed in translators' comments. Women translators and critics have begun to explore, for example, the effect on women of translating female, as opposed to male, writers. While not all of them would agree with Susanne de Lotbinière-Harwood's suggestion that a woman is inevitably damaged by translating a male writer (*Re-Belle et Infidèle/The Body Bilingual*, 1991), some will translate only work by women. Others, like Suzanne Jill Levine, who writes about her *collaboration with male writers (*The Subversive Scribe: Translating Latin American Fiction*, 1991), or Christina Zwarg, who studies Margaret Fuller's translations ("Feminism in Translation: Margaret Fuller's Tasso," *Studies in Romanticism* 29, 1990), discuss a female translator's work with male writers as a form of subversion and self-definition.

Additional issues explored by women translators include the conventional portrayal of translation as inevitable loss and (sexual) fidelity or betrayal, the selection of "representative" writers to translate and include in anthologies, and the choices made in the translation of culture-bound terms and referents, especially when texts from the "third" world are introduced into the language and literature of the "first." As they address each of those issues, women are exploring translation as an opportunity to question, and refuse, the dichotomies traditionally associated with translation and verbal expression in the West. In some instances, translators deliberately refrain from translating specific words or even entire sentences. In others, anthropologists consider the ethics of collecting, retelling, and retailing the life stories of "third" world women. In still others, such writers as Gloria *Anzaldúa, Sandra *Cisneros, and Jessica *Hagedorn could be said to trigger translation for their readers by writing in two languages or incorporating non-English words in their texts; their work points to an expanded definition of "translation" that includes the many intralingual translations that occur continually across cultures and genders within English itself. Finally, women are involved in efforts that reverse the direction translation usually follows in the United States. Ana *Castillo and Cherríe *Moraga, for example, are responsible for *Esta puente, mi espalda* (1988), a Spanish translation of *This Bridge Called My Back: Writing by Radical Women of Color* (1983), and Seal Press has recently published a bilingual edition of poems by North American poet Barbara Kingsolver with Spanish translations. In short, women translators are increasingly aware that the re-creation of a text in another language involves more than the transferal of words, and that each facet of translation contributes integrally to their practice.

• Margery Resnick and Isabelle de Courtivron, *Women Writers in Translation: An Annotated Bibliography, 1945–1982* (1984). Myriam Díaz-Diocaretz, *Translating Poetic Discourse: Questions of Feminist Strategies in Adrienne Rich* (1985). Sheryl St. Germain, ed., "Women in Translation," special issue of *Translation Review* 17 (1985). Maggie Humm, "Translation as Survival: Zora Neale Hurston and La Malincha," *Fiction International* 17, no. 2 (1987): 120–129. Gayatri Chakravorty Spivak, *In Other Worlds: Essays in Cultural Politics* (1987). Lori Chamberlain, "Gender and the Metaphorics of Translation," *Signs* 13, no. 3 (1988): 454–472. Daphne Patai, *Brazilian Women Speak: Contemporary Life Stories* (1988). Karen Van Dyck, ed., "Translation and Deterritorialization," special issue of *Journal of Modern Greek Studies* 8, no. 2 (1990). Anuradha Dingwaney and Carol Maier, "Translation as a Method of Cross-Cultural Teaching," in *Understanding Others: Cultural and Cross-Cultural Studies and the Teaching of Literature*, ed. Joseph Trimmer and Tilly Warnock (1992), pp. 47–62. Ruth Behar, *Translated Woman: Crossing the Border with Esperanza's Story* (1993). Alice Parker, "Under the Covers: A Synesthesia of Desire (Lesbian Translations)," in *Sexual Practice, Textual Theory: Lesbian Cultural Criticism*, eds. Susan J. Wolfe and Julia Penelope (1993), pp. 322–339.

Carol Maier

TRANSSEXUALITY refers to figures of mixed-gender identity, such as the Native American *berdache* or the Hawaiian *mahu*, as well as to transsexuals who have undergone sex reassignments through surgical intervention. A *berdache* is an anatomical male who has taken on an intermediate gender status, a female social role endowed with spiritual power rather than sexual stigma. The *mahu*, characterized by physical corpulence coded as female, are anatomical men who engage in *hula* dancing and form part of a gay urban subculture. Male spiritual roles are regendered in feminist fictions such as Maxine Hong *Kingston's *The Woman Warrior* (1975), where the swordswoman acts out of both filial piety and a desire to escape a restrictive gender role. In Lois *Gould's *A Sea-Change* (1975), the heroine turns into the black gunman she was raped by, thereby making sex the mutable category in order to understand the construction of gender. Lesbian-feminists like Janice Raymond in *The Transsexual Empire* (1979) address the implications of transsexualism by imagining the infiltration of such "pseudo-women" into the lesbian community, while the poet Sharon Olds in "Outside the Operating Room of the Sex-Change Doctor" (*Powers of Desire*, 1983) considers the meaning of the penises left after the operation. The lesbian mystery writer Barbara Wilson uses the discovery of a transsexual character to solve the magical-realist plot of *Gaudí Afternoon* (1990), while Judy Ruiz's autobiographical essay "Oranges and Sweet Sister Boy" (*Iowa Woman*, 1990) reexamines her own gender identity in light of her brother's sex reassignment.

[See also Bisexuality; Heterosexuality; Lesbianism; Sexualities.]

• Janice Raymond, *The Transsexual Empire: The Making of the She-Male* (1979). Walter L. Williams, *The Spirit and the Flesh: Sexual Diversity in American Indian Culture* (1986). Sandra Gilbert and Susan Gubar, "Cross-Dressing and Re-Dressing: Transvestism as Metaphor," in *No Man's Land: The Place of the Woman Writer in the Twentieth Century; Vol. 2: Sex Changes* (1989), pp. 324–376. Carol E. Robertson, "The Mahu of Hawai'i (an Art Essay), *Feminist Studies* 15, no. 2 (Summer 1989): 313–326. Marjorie Garber, "Spare Parts: The Surgical Construction of Gender," in *Vested Interests: Cross-Dressing and Cultural Anxiety* (1989), pp. 93–117.

Anne Herrmann

TRANSVESTISM. *See* Cross-dressing.

TRAVEL WRITING. A broadly defined genre, travel writing embraces *journals, guidebooks, sketches, essays, and books; in all these forms American women writers have made significant contributions. Paul Fussell in *Abroad* (1980) defines travel writing as "a sub-species of memoir in which the autobiographical narrative arises from the speaker's [sic] encounter with distant or unfamiliar data, and in which the narrative—unlike that in a novel or romance—claims literal validity by constant reference to actuality." Although Fussell's definition excludes guidebooks, it does reflect how travel writing conjoins the personal with the literal—a conjunction heightened in women's travel writing. A century and a half earlier, Mary Wollstonecraft suggested that attention to the personal distinguishes women's perspective from men's: "A man when he undertakes a journey, has in general, the end in view; a woman thinks more of the incidental occurrences, the strange things that may possibly occur on the road" (*A Vindication of the Rights of Woman*, 1792).

The *Narrative of the Captivity of Mrs. Mary Rowlandson* (1682) is perhaps the earliest example of American women's travel writing. *Rowlandson combines descriptions of her "removes" with an intimate account of her spiritual crisis. Unlike Rowlandson, whose journey was forced upon her, other women traveled by choice. In *The Journal of Madam Knight* (written in 1704), Sarah Kemble *Knight (1666–1727) records her journey from Boston to New York; like Rowlandson, she details colonial frontier life while revealing her "larger-than-life" character.

As the colonies matured into a nation, American women expanded their horizons with foreign travel. Louisa Catherine Johnson Adams (1775–1852) accompanied her husband John Quincy Adams on diplomatic missions abroad and wrote her *Narrative of A Journey from St. Petersburg to Paris, 1815* (1867); Elizabeth Cabot Cary Agassiz served as scribe to her husband Louis Agassiz on his expedition to Brazil, publishing her journal as *A Journey to Brazil* (1867). Blair Rice Niles (1880–1959) wrote *Our Search for a Wilderness* (1910) after traveling through the South Pacific and South America with her first husband; her second husband took the photographs included in her later books—*Casual Wanderings in Ecuador* (1923), *Colombia, Land of Miracles* (1924), and *Black Haiti* (1926). Niles researched each country before traveling; as a result, her books render the momentous and the ordinary in the lives of the common people.

Like Niles, Edith *Wharton (1843–1937) carefully researched the places she visited; although better known as a novelist, she brought a distinct art to travel writing—her essays in *Italian Backgrounds* (1905) combine evocative description with perceptive commentary, a blend also apparent in Mary *McCarthy's (1912–1989) *The Stones of Venice* (1959). Wharton recognized the opportunities the car gave to adventurous travelers; in *A Motor Flight Through France* (1908) she declares that "the motor-car has restored the romance of travel" by permitting a freedom not allowed by railroad timetables. She used that freedom well during a trip to Morocco at the end of World War I: *In Morocco* (1920) describes and critiques a society that entombs its women in the harem. Eleanor Roosevelt (1884–1962) also used her travels to examine non-Western societies; in *India and the Awakening East* (1953) her simplicity of style effectively captures the changing political climate of the East.

Wharton's contemporary Annie Peck Smith (1850–1935) recognized the advantages of modern transportation—she was a dedicated flier. An explorer, photographer, and mountaineer, at the age of eighty Smith toured South America by plane, and her subsequent book, *Flying Over South America* (1932) promotes the advantages of air travel. Many American women compiled standard travel guides, some specifically for women. Abigail May Alcott Nieriker, (1840–1879), the "Amy" of Louisa May *Alcott's *Little Women*, wrote the very practical *Studying Art Abroad, and How To Do It Cheaply* (1879) for women artists, enlivening basic information with social history; Nieriker's feminism corrects yet confirms the "Daisy Millerism" of the late nineteenth century. Blanche McManus Mansfield specialized in travel guides for women and children; *The American Woman Abroad* (1911) contains realistic advice given in detailed, economical prose akin to the drawings with which she illustrates her books. She also wrote and illustrated eight of the fifty titles in the Little Cousin series, which introduces American children to foreign geography, history, culture, and tourist attractions. Emily Kimbrough (1899–1989), widely known for *Our Hearts Were Young and Gay* (1942), a chronicle of a summer spent in Europe and written jointly with Cornelia Otis Skinner, wrote best-selling guides to England, Ireland, Italy, Portugal, France, and Greece; these books include "Michelin guide"-style information laced with anecdotes of people and places.

As Fussell's definition suggests, travel writing reveals as much—if not more—about the traveler than the travels; such is the case with Miriam Florence Folline Leslie (1863–1914). *In California: A Pleasure Trip from Gotham to the Golden Gate* (1877) portrays the grande dame's point of view. Although the book excels in sketches of Native Americans, Chinese immigrants, and Mormons, Leslie colors her observations with racism and intellectual snobbery. Eleanor Clark (b. 1913), in contrast, is receptive to sense of place: in *Rome and a Villa* (1952) she details the impact of Italy on her inner awareness. Kathryn Cavarly Hulme (1900–1981) also uses her travels to journey within; unlike the earlier *Arab Interlude* (1930), *Look a Lion in the Eye* (1974) documents Hulme's growing self-awareness, informed by Gurdjieff's mysticism. Similarly, China Galland's *Longing for Darkness* (1990) chronicles her search for self-acceptance, which takes her from Tibetan monasteries to Marian shrines in Poland.

Finally, a recently published anthology, *The House on Via Gombito* (1991), edited by Madelon Sprengnether and C. W. Truesdale, brings together the various strands of women's travel writing. Containing essays from previously published and never-published North American women writers, *The House on Via Gombito* includes spiritual quests, "psychic dislocations," and confrontations with historical, political, and economic realities. Journeys are prompted by the need to expand outer and inner horizons; travel writing—and especially women's travel writing—reflects the allure of the unknown, "the strange things that may possibly occur on the road."

[*See also* Exploration Narratives.]

• Paul Bowles, "Travel: The Challenge to Identity," *Nation* 186 (26 April 1958): 360–362. Michel Butor, "Travel and Writing," *Mosaic* 8, no. 1 (Fall 1974): 1–16. Helen Depar, ed., *The Discoverers: An Encyclopedia of Explorers and Exploration* (1980). Lina Mainiero, ed., *American Women Writers: A Critical Reference Guide from Colonial Times to the Present*, 3 vols. (1980). Catherine Barnes Stevenson, *Victorian Women Travel Writers in Africa* (1982). Virginia Scharff, *Taking the Wheel: Women and the Coming of the Motor Age* (1990). William Zinsser, ed., *They Went: The Art and Craft of Travel Writing* (1991).

Judith E. Funston

TRINH T. Minh-ha (b. 1952), writer, filmmaker, poet, and composer. Born in Vietnam, Trinh T. Minh-ha also teaches feminist and film theory as professor of cinema at San Francisco State University. Her versatility in several media can be understood as "interdisciplinary" in the radical sense of creating "a reality that involves the crossing of an indeterminate number of borderlines." In her writing this takes the form of a continuing redefinition of the boundaries of the political in relation to the personal, a project necessary for a postcolonial understanding and practice of subjectivity: "The challenge of the hyphenated reality lies in the hyphen itself: the *becoming* Asian-American; the realm in-between, where predetermined rules cannot fully apply." Evident in all her work is the critique of (imposed) identity as a mechanism by which women and third world people have been disenfranchised and censored. As she further writes, "To return to a denied identity and cultural heritage is also to under-

mine the very notions of identity and ethnicity" (*When the Moon Waxes Red*, 1991).

Anthropological filmmaking as a genre provoked her interest in the medium, in its "instrumental use of film *and people*" to project and maintain the status of the "all-knowing subject." This is practiced in "a form of legitimized (but unacknowledged as such) voyeurism . . . the pretense to see into or to *own* the others' *minds*, whose *knowledge* these others cannot, supposedly, have themselves." Her films are both a rigorous exploration of the apparatus (questioning the "ideology of the natural" in documentary conventions) and poetic, musical compositions sensitive to the flow between fact and fiction, subject and subjectivity. "I [as a filmmaker] do not *express* a reality more than a reality *impresses* itself on me. Expresses me."

Her work includes the books *Framer Framed: Film Scripts and Interviews* (1992), *When the Moon Waxes Red: Representation, Gender and Cultural Politics* (1991), *Woman, Native, Other: Writing Postcoloniality and Feminism* (1989), *En minuscules* (1987), *Un Art sans oeuvre* (1981), and the films *Shoot for the Contents* (on contemporary culture and politics in China, 1991), *Surname Viet Given Name Nam* (on identity and culture through the struggle of Vietnamese women, 1989), *Naked Spaces—Living Is Round* (on the relation between women, houses, and cosmos, West Africa, 1985), and *Reassemblage* (Senegal, 1982).

• Trinh T. Minh-ha, ed., *Discourse. Journal for Theoretical Studies in Media and Culture* 8 (Winter 1986–1987) and 11, no. 2 (Spring-Summer 1989). Russell Ferguson et al., eds., *Out There: Marginalization in Contemporary Culture* (1990). Marcia Tucker et al., eds., *Discourses: Conversations on Postmodern Art and Culture* (1990).

Linda Peckham

TRUE WOMAN. The term and concept of the True Woman pervaded antebellum nineteenth-century American culture, defining the proper role for middle-class white women. "The Cult of True Womanhood," as Barbara Welter named it in her influential essay of the same title, privileged the attributes of piety, purity, submissiveness, and domesticity. Among the media promulgating True Womanhood as the feminine ideal were *sentimental novels, conduct books, *advice manuals, sermons, and *women's magazines.

Piety, the foremost virtue of True Womanhood, required a devout belief in Christianity, stressing that woman was man's helpmeet, not his equal. A woman's duty was to serve her husband. Because she believed it to be ordained by God, a religious woman was unlikely to question her subordinate status.

Purity, a second virtue, demanded of women

chastity before *marriage and fidelity afterwards. The double standard of sexual morality held sway. Numerous men and women subscribed to the culturally sanctioned beliefs that reputable women (especially white) were less sexual by nature and that, therefore, they should act as exemplars of innocence, guiding the allegedly more sensual men to the path of righteousness.

Submissiveness required that a woman obey her parents and later her husband without question. Woman's passivity, dependence, self-effacement, and self-abnegation ensured that the patriarchal myth of male supremacy would remain in force. Although submission brought suffering for many women, they were schooled to view suffering as part of their lot and obediently accept it.

Domesticity promulgated the doctrine of *separate spheres, emphasizing that a woman's place was in the home and a man's place was in the world. Women were charged to center their lives on the home, immersing themselves in domestic tasks of housekeeping, child rearing, and providing comfort to/for their families. The home as both refuge for middle-class white men and proper sphere for their wives dominated much literature of the period. The tenets of True Womanhood explicitly circumscribed women's lives, limiting their participation outside the home to church-related activities. Women were to exercise power only through influencing their husbands and sons by their virtuous example.

Many women novelists during this period wrote sentimental fiction featuring heroines who possessed the traits associated with True Womanhood. Some historians have noted that the Industrial Revolution, which relied on the labor of both men and women, encouraged middle-class women to embrace the Cult of True Womanhood in order to emphasize their superiority to working-class and African-American women.

By the turn of the century, middle-class white women started to rebel against the concept of True Womanhood, while African-American women openly began to embrace it. In racist nineteenth-century America, African-American women were often unfairly stereotyped as wanton and sexually immoral. In an effort to reverse this stereotype, many middle-class African-American women organized clubs which were dedicated to the promulgation of the tenets of "True Womanhood."

Although the term "true woman" eventually disappeared from common parlance, making way for the "*new woman" of the 1890s, critics have linked its valorization of ideal femininity to the upsurge during the immediate post-war era of the "feminine mystique" and the neoconservative celebration during the closing quarter of the twentieth century of the "new chastity."

• Barbara Welter, "The Cult of True Womanhood," *American Quarterly* 18 (1966): 151–174. Nancy F. Cott, *The Bonds of Womanhood* (1977). Paula Giddings, *When and Where I Enter: The Impact of Black Women on Race and Sex in America* (1984). Mary Kelley, *Private Woman, Public Stage* (1984). Jane Tompkins, *Sensational Designs* (1985). Linda K. Kerber, "Separate Spheres, Female Worlds, Woman's Place: The Rhetoric of Women's History," *Journal of American History* 75 (1988): 9–39.

Cheri Louise Ross

TRUTH, Sojourner (ca. 1799–1883), black feminist abolitionist. The principal symbol of strength and blackness in the iconography of women's culture, the historic Sojourner Truth was illiterate. She herself initially created and purveyed the emblematic Sojourner Truth, which four educated white women publicists inserted into American memory. Together they created a figure who redefines gender identity.

Truth authenticated her message on the antislavery and women's rights circuits in the 1850s, 1860s, and 1870s by appealing to her own experience: Born Isabella, a slave in Ulster County, New York, she was emancipated by state law in 1827. In 1826–1827 she showed extraordinary initiative by leaving her master and choosing her own employer, going to court to secure the return of a child who had been illegally sold into slavery in the South, and becoming a Methodist after a Pauline conversion experience. Leaving Ulster County for New York City in the late 1820s, she joined a series of unorthodox religious groups, including the commune of the Prophet Matthias (Robert Matthews) in the early 1830s. In 1843, at the height of the widespread expectation inspired by William Miller of the apocalypse and Jesus' second coming, she renamed herself Sojourner Truth, paraphrasing her new vocation of itinerant preaching. At the utopian Northampton (Massachusetts) Association, she joined the ranks of feminist abolitionists. In Akron, Ohio, in 1851, she gave the speech which, despite—or because of—a crucial misquotation, is now her most famous; in Indiana in 1858, she bared her breast to prove that she was a woman.

To support herself, Truth dictated a *slave narrative—a product that was becoming commercially attractive—to her Northampton neighbor, Olive Gilbert, had the printer of the Boston *Liberator* publish it as *The Narrative of Sojourner Truth* in 1850, and sold it to her audiences for twenty-five cents. After Harriet Beecher *Stowe published *Uncle Tom's Cabin* in book form in 1852, Truth approached her for a publicity notice. The encounter produced both a blurb and Stowe's 1863 essay in the *Atlantic Monthly*, "Sojourner Truth, the Libyan Sibyl," which introduced Truth to a wide readership. Following Stowe, Frances Dana Gage, who had chaired the Akron meeting in 1851, published her own version of Truth's speech, which has become definitive, thanks to the dramatic, rhetorical question that Gage invented to express the import of Truth's speech: "And ar'n't *I* a woman?" In 1875–1878, Truth's Battle Creek, Michigan, neighbor, Frances Titus, reprinted the *Narrative* and added material from Truth's scrapbooks, including articles by Stowe and Gage. Gage's piece reappeared in volume 1 of Elizabeth Cady *Stanton et al., eds., *History of Woman Suffrage* (1881).

During and after the *Civil War, Truth worked with ex-slave refugees in and around Washington, D.C., deciding in the early 1870s that they should be resettled in the West. Her last public act was the circulation of a petition to Congress for the designation of federal lands for this purpose. After a long illness, she died in Battle Creek, Michigan, where she had lived since the mid-1850s.

• Jacqueline Bernard, *Journey toward Freedom: The Story of Sojourner Truth* (1967; 2d ed., 1990). Nell Irvin Painter, "Sojourner Truth in Life and Memory: Writing the Biography of an American Exotic," *Gender and History* 2, no. 1 (Spring 1990). "Sojourner Truth," in *Notable Black American Women*, ed. Jessie Carney Smith (1992). Nell Painter, "Sojourner Truth in Feminist Abolitionism: Difference, Slavery, and Memory," in *An Untrodden Path: Antislavery and Women's Political Culture*, eds. Jean Fagan Yellin and John C. Van Horne (1993).

Nell Irvin Painter

TY-CASPER, Linda (b. 1934), novelist, short story writer, lawyer. Linda Ty-Casper started writing while waiting for her Philippine bar examination results in the late 1950s. She eventually attended Harvard Law School, and her short stories appeared in *Asia Magazine, Antioch Review, New Mexico Quarterly, Southwest Review, Manila Review,* and *Solidarity,* among others. Her first collection, *The Transparent Sun and Other Stories,* came out in 1963, and *The Peninsulars,* a historical novel, in 1964. Law receded into the background as she found her voice and vocation in literature.

Ty-Casper's choice of short fiction as her first craft led to sustained experiments in writing novellas. Of her various books, only *The Three-Cornered Sun* (1979) qualifies as a full-length novel. All her other works delimit the expanse of the novel or expand the limits of the short story, averaging under two hundred printed pages in length. This economy of form conceals the astonishing scope of her historical vision, which now ranges from the 1850s Spanish Philippines to the apotheosis and decay of the Marcos regime (1965–1980s).

Claimed as a *Filipino-American writer, Ty-Casper also joins a long lineage of Filipino expatriate writers who transform extended residence outside the Philippines into imagined returns. Gerald Burns calls this the "repatriate theme" in Philippine literature, born out of colonial dispossession by Spain and the United States (*Philippine Studies* 40, First Quarter 1992). Many of these exiles, banished to the colonial capitals for dissent or by circumstances, would attempt reconnection while writing in Spanish and English, languages limited by the colonizers to the highly literate.

Ty-Casper allegorizes this predicament, its paralysis and possibilities of will, by transvaluing history in her works as the gain of perspective via distance and as the sign of loss for the dislocated. In fact, Ty-Casper revises the notion of culture bearing as the female task in Philippine culture by urging that women writers "bear history" to counter colonial myth and what she calls "the lesser self," or the self complicit with the colonizing powers.

Dread Empire (1980), *The Hazards of Distance* (1981), *Awaiting Trespass* (1985), *Fortress in the Plaza* (1985), *Wings of Stone* (1986), and *A Small Party in the Garden* (1988) dissect the culture of political corruption and atrophy fostered by the Marcoses. Resembling the roman à clef for political effect, they explore the links between recent immorality and abuses of power and the colonial past. Michelle Skinner's *Balikbayan* (1988), Sabina Murray's *Slow Burn* (1990), Jessica *Hagedorn's *Dog-eaters* (1990), and Ninotchka *Rosca's *Twice Blessed* (1991) implicitly draw their precedents from Ty-Casper's novellas. Rosca's *State of War* (1988) fabulates the rewriting of colonial history advanced by Ty-Casper's earlier novels on the Spanish conquistadores and the 1896 revolution against Spain, or *Ten Thousand Seeds* (1987), a novella on the American imperial moment in the Philippines (1898–1899).

• Bienvenido Lumbera, *Revaluation: Essays on Philippine Literature, Cinema and Popular Culture* (1984), pp. 227–240. Linda Ty-Casper, "Philippine Women: A Room Shared," *Pilipinas* 9 (Fall 1987): 27–33. Florentino Valeros and Estrellita Gruenberg, *Filipino Writers in English* (1987). Gerald Burns, "The Repatriate Theme in Philippine Second-Language Fiction," *Philippine Studies* 40 (First Quarter 1992): 3–34.

Oscar Campomanes

TYLER, Anne (b. 1941), novelist, short story writer. Born in Minneapolis, Minnesota, Anne Tyler was raised in a Quaker community outside Raleigh, North Carolina. She received her undergraduate degree in Russian studies at Duke University (1961) and did graduate work at Columbia University.

Tyler's experience with the Quaker community set her apart, something she thinks was necessary for her as a writer. Her novels, then, are a way of reconciling herself to the outside world, a world in which she, and her characters, are not entirely comfortable. Her characters are typically passive players in their own lives, reacting to circumstance rather than creating it.

Tyler was strongly influenced by Eudora *Welty's ability to capture the familiar, even the ordinary, and make it compelling. Tyler calls herself a "southern writer" because the texture of her stories comes from careful attention to her characters' regional speech patterns, gestures, and possessions, rather than what happens in the plot.

Critics often wonder at Tyler's choice of eccentric characters for her stories. In *The Accidental Tourist* (1985), for example, none of the characters copes well with the "accidents" of life. Macon Leary is trying to recover from the random murder of his son, and it is his obsessive quirkiness that makes him sympathetic. Tyler explores what it takes to heal the pain instilled by such a distressing event. Through his relationships with other odd characters, like Muriel and her son Alexander, Macon finds he can survive with patience and common sense. While critics sometimes call the novel sentimental and soap operatic, it is sincere and realistic. Though Macon may not be entirely healed, in the end he is able to make adult choices.

Breathing Lessons (1988) has received mixed critical response. Though it won the Pulitzer Prize in 1989, many critics feel it is not her best work, that it's "formula" Tyler. But the author does ask different questions in this novel. Tyler looks both at what it takes to make a marriage last, and how people deal with the passage of time. Her characters, particularly Maggie and Ira, seem shocked at their middle age, and the novel explores why. In the end, the reader, and to some extent Maggie, realize that time is a series of layers of memory and nostalgia, both of the present and future.

Common to the best of Tyler's work, including *Dinner at the Homesick Restaurant* (1983) and *Saint Maybe* (1991), are quirky characters and their daily lives. Eccentricity seems normal, and indeed, Tyler believes that even the most ordinary person has something unusual at his/her core.

• Anne Tyler, "Still Just Writing," in *The Writer on Her Work: Contemporary Women Reflect on Their Art and Situation*, ed. Janet Sternburg (1980), pp. 3–16. Ellen Pifer, "Anne Tyler, Medusa Points and Contact Points," in *Contemporary American Women Writers: Narrative Strategies*, eds. Catherine Rainwater and William J. Scheick (1985), pp. 119–152. Joseph C. Voelker, *Art and the Accidental in Anne Tyler* (1989). Alice Hall Petry, *Understanding Anne Tyler* (1990).

Deborah Viles

U

UNDERGROUND RAILROAD is the term generally used to refer to organized efforts to aid enslaved individuals in their attempts to escape to the northern states and to Canada during the decades preceding the *Civil War. Under this inclusive heading, successful escapes were credited by contemporaries and, later, historians to a network of "tracks," "conductors," and "stations" by which abolitionists and other sympathizers "conducted" the fugitives to the relative safety of the North. Although organized attempts to aid fugitive slaves date back to the beginning of the nineteenth century, estimates of the number of fugitives thus aided vary widely, ranging roughly from thirty thousand to one hundred thousand. There are varying stories also about the origin of the term *Underground Railroad*. In almost all versions, the term is coined by a befuddled slaveholder speculating on the successful escape of a slave. Among the many prominent African Americans and white abolitionists associated with the Underground Railroad are Harriet Tubman, Josiah Henson, Frederick Douglass, Frances E. W. *Harper, Charlotte L. Forten, Lydia Maria *Child, Laura S. Haviland, Lucretia Coffin *Mott, John Brown, and Sarah and Angelina *Grimké.

As the historian Larry Gara has argued in *The Liberty Line: The Legend of the Underground Railroad* (1961), the popular conception of the Underground Railroad as a coherent, well-organized system of operation is a mixture of fact and legend. Not only abolitionists but also antiabolitionists contributed to the legend before the Civil War, and a number of postwar books by participants and historians, especially in the 1880s and 1890s, secured the position of the Underground Railroad among the nation's folktales. In antebellum newspaper and magazine articles, in novels, narratives, and tracts, abolitionists and antiabolitionists alike both publicized and defined political tensions by representing the actual work being done regionally as the efforts of a single, mysterious institution, to the extent that any successful escapes— even those that relied on the individual heroism, ingenuity, and luck of the fugitive—often were credited to the Underground Railroad.

The legend has a firm basis in fact, for regional efforts to aid fugitives were often very well organized and effective. Conductors aided fugitives along established routes; in many cities, vigilance committees watched for "slave catchers" and other dangers; many antislavery organizations provided funding (though often not without considerable debate); sewing circles provided clothes to the fugitives; and secret modes of communication were established— most prominently, the songs and *spirituals that provided a coded language, by which "Follow the Drinking Gourd," for example, referred to the Big Dipper and the North Star.

However, the legend of a single institution, with its own president and a coherent, national system of secret codes and mysterious methods, has caused many to cast the fugitives themselves in a passive role, dependent on the efforts of white abolitionists for salvation from enslavement. Certainly, the efforts of such abolitionists as Levi Coffin and Thomas Garrett were significant. Still more significant were the efforts of those who returned to the land of their former enslavement to conduct others to safety; the most famous of these was Harriet Tubman, whose immeasurable heroism as an Underground Railroad conductor helped secure her fame (and offers of substantial rewards for her capture) as the "Moses of her people." But the legend of the Underground Railroad often renders invisible the many whose names are either unknown or unlisted in the register of official history—those who relied on their own courage and ingenuity. Long before they could find shelter in an underground station, or (in many cases) even discover the possibility of being conducted along an established route, many individuals had little more to base their hopes on than the North Star, along with whatever confidential associations with other fugitives and sympathizers they could form along the way.

If much of the Underground Railroad is legend, much of the legend of the Underground Railroad is a fact of political and cultural history, part of the struggle to define sides and to influence minds and hearts that characterizes the complex field of nineteenth-century African-American experience. The most famous story of the Underground Railroad, based on an actual account, is that presented in Harriet Beecher *Stowe's *Uncle Tom's Cabin; or, Life among the*

Lowly (1852), wherein Eliza Harris, having bounded across the ice on the Ohio river, is given refuge and conducted north by the Quaker Simeon Halliday. But while Stowe's novel was greatly influential, the most representative literary accounts of passage north, and of the continuing hazards one faced after reaching only relative freedom, are those by African-American women and men who, drawing from experience, focus on the heroism of the fugitive slaves, their friends, and their families themselves—for example, Harriet * Jacobs's *Incidents in the Life of a Slave Girl* (1861) and Lucy Delaney's *From the Darkness Cometh the Light; or, Struggles for Freedom* (c. 1891).

In the twentieth century, the legend of the Underground Railroad has been variously repeated and reshaped in works by a number of women writers—notably, in plays by Regina M. Andrews, May Miller, and Georgia Douglas * Johnson, and in juvenile fiction by Enid La Monte Meadowcroft, Ann * Petry, Frances William Browin, and Jeanette Winter. In many ways, the best representation of the fugitive's complex ordeal is that woven into the intricate fabric of Toni * Morrison's novel *Beloved* (1987), in which trust is both hazardous and, at times, necessary, and in which communal effort is formed from the individual experiences of African Americans themselves.

[*See also* Slavery; Abolition.]

• William Still, *The Underground Rail Road* (1872). Wilbur H. Siebert, *The Underground Railroad from Slavery to Freedom* (1898). Henrietta Buckmaster, *Let My People Go: The Story of the Underground Railroad and the Growth of the Abolition Movement* (1941; reprint, 1959). Horatio T. Strother, *The Underground Railroad in Connecticut* (1962). Benjamin Quarles, *Black Abolitionists* (1969). Stanley W. Campbell, *Slave Catchers: Enforcement of the Fugitive Slave Law, 1850–1860* (1970). Charles L. Blockson, "Escape from Slavery: The Underground Railroad," *National Geographic* (July 1984): 3–39. Charles L. Blockson, *The Underground Railroad* (1987).

John Ernest

UTOPIAS. Although utopian writing by American women has been doubly marginalized by both genre and gender, it affords a powerful perspective on developing feminisms in the United States. From the early nineteenth century (with Mary Griffith's "Three Hundred Years Hence," 1836) until the late twentieth, over two hundred utopian works by women were published, as Carol Farley Kessler notes in her most recent bibliography in *Utopian Studies* (vol. 1, 1990). Yet the most significant production of feminist utopian work falls into two periods: 1888–1919 and 1969–1990. Interestingly, the first phase coincides with the outpouring of utopian works by men at the turn of the century

in America, while the second phase stands alone. That this remarkable flood of work (at least 128 novels from 1969–1989) was ignored by scholars for nearly a decade speaks to the marginalization of women's writing and consequent distortion of generic histories. Ironically, for example, Frank and Fritzie Manuel (*Utopian Thought in the Western World*, 1979) lament the withering of utopian imagination in the twentieth century.

In the nineteenth century, both male and female utopists were influenced by the economic disparities of the Gilded Age and by one particularly effective text, Edward Bellamy's *Looking Backward* (1888), which prompted many imitations and responses. Women's utopian work, however, was distinctive in several ways. First, the issue of gender equity was more central and explored in far more detail, including the interrogation of the institution of marriage. As Kessler points out in her introduction to *Daring to Dream: Utopian Stories by U.S. Women, 1836–1919* (1984), the improvement of women's power within * marriage was more crucial to most of these utopists than was * suffrage. Second, women utopists radically revised domestic arrangements in order to ease women's labor, and, correlatively, represented the private sphere more fully than the public. Third, the revaluation of "mothering" or the importance of nurturing and * education became a central motivating value. Finally, the utopian works of the first phase often represented a drive toward spiritual growth and moral reform, grounded in a contemporary ideology of women's moral superiority. Perhaps the one distinctive aspect of form in women's work of this period is * humor. Parody of male pretensions, the delights of role reversal, and the deconstruction of gender * stereotypes inform much of this fiction. (See, for example, Mary Ford's "A Feminine Iconoclast," 1889; Lois Waisbrooker's *A Sex Revolution*, 1894; and Charlotte Perkins * Gilman's "Bee Wise," 1913.)

One of the best-known and most prolific utopian writers of this period, Gilman wrote three utopian novels and several short stories, all of which expose the limitations of current * gender hierarchies, the inefficiency of conventional domestic arrangements, the importance of women's economic viability, and the subversive power of female * friendship. Her best-known utopian work, *Herland* (1915) gains much of its power through ironic humor as her male protagonists wonder at the achievements of an all-female society. Although Herlanders privilege motherhood, Gilman's male narrator—and the reader—discover that the care and education of children are grounded not in biology, but reason.

Witty as this utopia is, it omits attention to women's erotic desire or differences of *race and *class. Indeed, most utopian novels of the period were written by upper-middle-class whites, and some are distinctly racist (See Mary Bradley Lane's *Mizora*, 1881). Yet *Unveiling a Parallel* by Alice Ilgenfritz Jones and Ella Merchant (1892) does conclude with a vision of a classless society that proclaims the equality of all races and religions.

The second phase of utopian writing by American women more fully addresses differences of class and race as well as gender, and envisions a range of social reform encompassing the public and private spheres. Certainly this change was influenced by the *civil rights movement of the sixties, the women's movement of the seventies, and increased immigration and ethnic diversity in late twentieth-century urban America. Conceptually, two broad and related areas of concern emerge from these varied texts: the redefinition of justice and power as well as the subversion of binary modes of thought long dominant in the Western tradition. As feminist utopists envision a better world in the late twentieth century, justice includes not only differences of ethnicity, race, and class, but representations of animals, the natural world, and even hybrid aliens. Power is figured not as dominance, but as the force released through the diversification of *subjectivity. Although the achievement of economic parity, valuation of the maternal, and emancipatory domestic arrangements remain important, sensual and creative pleasures also become part of the good life. Such conceptual revisions relate to the subversiveness inherent in many of these utopian projects, as categorical boundaries are transgressed—whether mind and body, heterosexual and homosexual, male and female, or even utopia and dystopia. For example, Alice *Walker's *The Color Purple* (1983) powerfully evokes a dystopian reality overcome by a utopian alliance of female support. An even more radical deconstruction of conventional boundaries is proposed by Octavia *Butler in her recent *Xenogenesis* series (see *Dawn*, 1987). In that work, too, the line between utopia and dystopia is blurred, but so is the distinction between human and machine. Butler's fictional utopian project figures hybrid subjects, just as Donna Haraway's feminist theory calls for new kinds of connections in a time of rapid technological development in "A Manifesto for Cyborgs" (*Socialist Review*, 1985). Similarly, Marge *Piercy, in her latest utopian/dystopian work (*He, She, and It*, 1991), reveals connections between medieval cabbalistic magic and twenty-first century cybernetics. The common drive, as it is depicted in these utopian projects, is the deconstruction of conventional discursive categories, including the category "human." Indeed, such writing encourages a continuous rethinking of identity.

One of Piercy's earlier works, *Woman on the Edge of Time* (1976), stands as a useful paradigm for many characteristics of postmodern feminist utopian fiction. Its protagonist is a woman, a poor Chicana, experienced in the multiple oppressions made likely by gender, class, and ethnic difference. In her time travel to utopia, Connie Ramos discovers a society made up of creative peoples of varied racial types and sexual preferences. One of the most startling technological advances in this utopia is the "brooder," which assures diversity by way of genetic engineering and ex utero birthing. Although parenting is highly valued as in earlier feminist utopias, it is undertaken regardless of gender by at least three persons. Therefore, the institution of marriage is no longer interrogated and "reformed," but abolished. Piercy's work, like many contemporary feminist utopias, is ambiguous, and the achievement of a better world uncertain.

Typically, contemporary utopias break away from the dominant conventions of the genre, such as a visitor/guide framework. Linguistic and structural experimentation characterize these works, including the invention of new words and languages (see Suzette Haden Elgin's *Native Tongue*, 1984, and *The Judas Rose*, 1987). Protagonists are almost always female, unlike the works of the first phase, and often not single, but clustered (See Joanna *Russ's *The Female Man*, 1974; Sally Miller Gearhart's *The Wanderground*, 1979; and Judy *Grahn's *Mundane's World*, 1988). Linear plot structure is largely abandoned in favor of discontinuous form, including the juxtaposition of different kinds of text within a work. (See Ursula *Le Guin's *The Dispossessed*, 1974, and *Always Coming Home*, 1985.)

Presented in innovative forms, the dreams of expanded social justice and the transgression of normative categories inform the postmodern feminist utopian imagination. The subversive potential of this fiction belies any attempt to dismiss it as merely essentialist or escapist. These feminist works are not blueprints for imitation but thought experiments with emancipatory power, mapping processes of personal and social transformation. Long neglected by scholars, this fiction is now recognized as the most exciting area of utopian studies and remains, as well, a continuing index to feminist desire.

• Anne K. Mellor, "On Feminist Utopias," *Women's Studies* 9, no. 3 (1982): 241–262. Lee Cullen Khanna, "Frontiers of Imagination: Women's Worlds," *Women's Studies International Forum* 7, no. 2 (1984): 97–102.

V

VAN DUYN, Mona (b. 1921), poet, critic, editor, and educator. Born in Waterloo, Iowa, Van Duyn received her B.A. from the University of Northern Iowa in 1942 and her M.A. from the University of Iowa in 1943, the same year she married Jarvis A. Thurston, the man with whom she would found and edit *Perspective, A Quarterly of Literature* (1947–1967). Van Duyn has taught at the University of Iowa (1943–1946), the University of Louisville (1946–1950), Washington University (1950–1967), the Salzburg, Austria, Seminar in American Studies (1973) and at Breadloaf. Winner of a number of prestigious awards, Van Duyn has earned *Poetry*'s Eunice Tietjens Memorial Prize (1956) and Harriet Monroe Award (1968), *Poetry Northwest*'s Helen Bullis Prize (1964 and 1976), the Bollingen Prize (1970), a National Endowment for the Arts grant (1966–1967), a Guggenheim Fellowship (1972–1973), Litt.D. degrees from Washington University (1971) and Cornell University (1972), a National Book Award for *To See, To Take* (1971), and the Pulitzer Prize for *Near Changes* (1991). In 1992, Van Duyn became the first female poet laureate of the United States, and the sixth American to hold that honor.

The title poem of *Valentines to the Wide World: Poems* (1959) examines the power of love and art to redeem moments, attitudes, and visions that otherwise are consumed by time's inexorable nature. The volume's final poem, "Toward a Definition of Marriage," suggests ironically that marriage resists definition by language but has the power to endure nonetheless. Van Duyn also explores complex relationships in *A Time of Bees* (1964). In the title poem, as in Sylvia * Plath's "Wintering," Van Duyn's bees are survivors that resist a couple's attempt to kill them. Even after they are banished to the garbage, the bees struggle, reproducing in death's face. The images define a female sensibility; the speaker is separate from "the men," and, as she accepts responsibility for voicing the story, her art emerges as crafted, but never forced.

In *To See, To Take* (1970), Van Duyn continues to wrestle with creation's mysteries. Poems such as "Leda" (which humorously revises Yeats's "Leda and the Swan") and "The Pietà,

Rhenish, 14th C., The Cloisters" testify to love's fierce powers of destruction and regeneration. In *Bedtime Stories* (1972), she uses her grandmother's voice to narrate the haunting stories of a first-generation American. *Merciful Disguises: Published and Unpublished Poems* (1973) includes selections from Van Duyn's earlier volumes and previously unpublished works from 1965–1973.

At this point in her career, Van Duyn had established herself as a poetic force; her wit and humor, coupled with masterful use of rhyme and form, are evidenced again in *Letters from a Father and Other Poems* (1982). Divided into four sections entitled "Last," "There," "Here," and "First," this volume's varied times and settings prove the poet's acute interest in the forces that shape character and voice. *Near Changes* (1990) includes poems of subtle rhyme whose subjects range from botanical and animal complexities, dedications to personal friends, newspaper trivia, and Van Duyn's longstanding fascination with the power of love.

Ann Walker

VIOLENCE encompasses battering, * rape, * incest, murder, * madness, * suicide, protest, resistance, and anger. Representations of violence in American women's writing—fiction and non-fiction—defy easy categorization. Contrary to cultural * stereotypes, and perhaps counterintuitively, neither the writers nor the characters that appear in the fictional texts share a specific, hence " * feminine," relation to violence. Rather, American women writing at different times, speaking from different locations of * race, * class, and * sexuality, and positing different concepts of agency, have produced a wide range of diverse, and sometimes unsettling, images.

As the work of recovering long-lost writings by women continues and as today's critical apparatus grows more sophisticated, it appears that women have consistently written about violence, albeit until the middle of our century, generally without graphic details. Even white middle-class women's writing through the nineteenth century, which seemed to present women only as the impotent victims of male violence and/or a sexist social order and very often ended with the heroine's death, suicide, or descent into madness, was, many recent studies suggest, more diverse than that. Thus, works by authors like Susanna *Rowson, Edith *Wharton, Charlotte Perkins *Gilman, and Kate *Chopin exist next to writings by Fanny *Fern, Mary Wilkins *Freeman, Harriet *Spofford, and others that emphasize women's strength and their determination to fight back even in defeat. With the beginning of the twentieth century, white American women begin to address violence with increasing directness: the home is exposed as a place of violence populated by husbands and fathers who batter and rape, or, at best, stifle the aspirations of the women in their families. Authors like Mary *Austin, Mari *Sandoz, Agnes *Smedley, Meridel *Le Sueur, and Tillie *Olsen, whose sympathies lie with the *working class, seem particularly open about the reality of family violence and, unlike middle-class identified writers, do not shy away from portraying it graphically. In these texts, the mothers—who usually suffer the brunt of brutality—are cowed into submission, while the daughters devise ways of resistance and rebellion. Two authors whose names are most commonly associated with stories of violence and who have been widely criticized for their "unfeminine" tales are Flannery *O'Connor and Joyce Carol *Oates. Oates, in particular, breaks with the tendency of presenting women only as the objects of violence; in her texts we also find women as perpetrators of violence, for instance, as abusive mothers.

Generally, however, the beginning of the contemporary debate on women and violence must be traced back to the early 1970s and the emerging *women's movement. As women took stock of their position in society, they realized the degree to which their lives were shaped by the experience of male violence. The women's publications of that time appropriately abound with stories of rape, incest, battering, and psychological abuse by fathers, brothers, uncles, and husbands. One text that has since been sharply criticized for its white, middle-class bias, but that was nevertheless crucial for focusing the debate and laying out the terms for any further discussion of women and violence was Susan Brownmiller's study of rape, *Against Our Will* (1975). Rape, Brownmiller argued, had to be understood as a form of misogynist violence that was directed against all women and that was moreover culturally sanctioned even as it was officially denounced. In the wake of *Against Our Will*, a whole body of analytical and imaginative writing on rape and battering

appeared that provided detailed evidence of women's historical victimization and overwhelmed many women with a sense of their powerlessness.

Today, as women reap the benefits of the struggles of the 1970s and 1980s, feminists feel more and more constrained by the conceptual legacy of those years. They question the implicit denial of agency that informs a good part of the older texts and casts doubt on women's ability to end their oppression. They also critique the continued gendering of violence, resistance, and agency as male, and reject as simplistic the correlation the older generation of feminists postulated between fiction/fantasy and reality. The most sustained criticism, however, has come from feminists of color, who have challenged the white middle-class bias of much of the writing and its erasure of the experiences of women of color.

Confronted with the everyday reality of racist and sexist violence, *African-American women have traditionally addressed violence much more directly than their white sisters. Starting in the nineteenth century with the beginning of sustained cultural production by African Americans and continuing into the present, there is a long line of texts that revolve around the experience of violence at the hands of white men and women. Such nineteenth-century writers as Harriet *Jacobs, Harriet *Wilson, Frances *Harper, and Pauline *Hopkins explore the suffering and brutalization of African Americans under *slavery and the virulently racist attacks on the community after Emancipation. One issue that from the 1890s onward commanded particular attention was *lynching. While the fight against lynching is most closely associated with the name of Ida B. *Wells, who was the first to attack unsparingly the practice and to accumulate proof of the state and federal authorities' collusion in its continuance, numerous women subsequently addressed themselves to the issue in articles, stories, and poetry. Because they were writing in times of intense struggle for *civil rights, twentieth-century African-American women through the 1970s focused mainly on violence engendered by *racism and its various displacements; sexist violence within the community, on the other hand, remained largely a *taboo topic. Though individual writers like Zora Neale *Hurston, Ann *Petry, and Toni *Morrison addressed the issue to some degree, it was centrally treated for the first time in 1982 in Alice *Walker's *The Color Purple*. Generally, what most distinguishes African-American women's writing on violence is an insistence on agency: the men and women who are represented do not allow themselves to be silently crushed by racist and sexist violence, but instead try, often successfully, to fight back. Thus the experience of violence does not become a sign of the community's or the individual's powerlessness, but rather testifies to strength and a will to survive.

Another group that in recent years has become embroiled in controversies are lesbian anti-antiporn writers. Writing from the premise of an unbridgeable gap that separates fantasy from reality, authors like Pat *Califia and Susie Bright produce pornographic texts that play with the fantasy of violence and explore women's pleasure in sadomasochistic (s/m) practices and the ritual infliction of pain. Rejecting the attacks of more orthodox lesbian and heterosexual feminists for whom s/m becomes indistinguishable from sexual violence, these writers emphasize s/m's consensual basis: the woman character, they argue, is never actually positioned as a victim, but instead at all times controls the fantasy. While violence is embraced as a vehicle of pleasure by lesbian "outlaws," mainstream lesbians have become progressively more critical of violence. In the 1970s, texts were dominated by the figure of the angry lesbian warrior who waged full-scale war against *patriarchy and did not shrink from resorting to violence (representative texts like *Sister Gin*, 1975, and *Angel Dance*, 1977, feature collectives that castrate and murder rapists and humiliate abusive men); the fictions of the 1980s, in contrast, allow only for defensive violence. Thematically, the focus has also shifted to instances of everyday violence addressing lesbians' experiences of incest, child abuse, rape, and gay bashing. Generally, what most distinguishes all lesbian writing on violence is a refusal to dwell on women's powerlessness.

[See also Rape; Incest; Sexual Harassment.]

• Melody Graulich, "Violence against Women in Literature of the Western Family," *Frontiers* 7, no. 3 (Spring 1984):14–20. Trudier Harris, *Exorcising Blackness: Historical and Literary Lynching and Burning Rituals* (1984). Alicia Ostriker, *Stealing the Language: The Emergence of Women's Poetry in America* (1986). Katherine Anne Ackley, ed., *Women and Violence in Literature: An Essay Collection* (1990). Bonnie Zimmerman, *The Safe Sea of Women: Lesbian Fiction 1969–1989* (1990). Sally Munt, ed., *New Lesbian Criticism: Literary and Cultural Readings* (1992).

Sabine Engel

VIRAMONTES, Helena María (b. 1954), fiction and screenplay writer, essayist, editor. For Helena María Viramontes, having time to do nothing but write is "an utter privilege" that few women of color possess. Born in East Los Angeles, Viramontes experienced early on the conflict between her need to write and the perpetual demands of caring for others. Her first collection of fiction, *The Moths and Other Stories* (1985), powerfully depicts the family as both a source of love and refuge in Chicano culture and as a patriarchal structure that requires absolute female submission. In the story "Growing," the limitations placed on girls at the onset of puberty are summed up in the father's condemnation, "Tú eres mujer."

Viramontes has received many awards, including a 1989 National Endowment for the Arts Fellowship grant. Her fiction has appeared in many Chicano/a and multicultural publications, including *Cuentos: Stories by Latinas* (1983) and *New Chicano/Chicana Writing* (1992). Viramontes has also coedited with María Hererra-Sobek two anthologies of Chicana creative and critical work, *Chicana Creativity and Criticism: Creating New Frontiers in American Literature* (1988) and *Chicana Writers: On Word and Film* (1993). Her second collection of short stories, *Paris Rats in E.L.A.* (1993), portrays barrio life through the eyes of a frightened young girl who lives for the infrequent attentions of her factory-working mother and her troubled older brother. In "Tears on My Pillow," as in "The Cariboo Cafe" from *Moths*, Viramontes revises the myth of *La Llorona, the wailing woman who searches for her dead children, as a metaphor for political and economic oppression.

Viramontes recently completed an M.F.A. at the University of California–Irvine, having previously left the program in 1981 due to lack of acceptance for her work. She is currently writing a novella, "Dogs," and a screenplay, "Modesta"; her teleplay of *Paris Rats in E.L.A.* is being produced by the American Film Institute. Viramontes is a former editor of *Xhisme Arte Magazine* and has read and lectured to academic and community audiences, including talks in New Delhi, China, and Venezuela. With her two young children providing an inspiration for the future, Viramontes believes, as she notes in "Why I Write" (1993), that language is a powerful tool for social change: "Through writing, I have learned to protect the soles of my feet from the broken glass. . . . Writing is the only way I know how to pray."

• Norma Alarcón, "Making 'Familia' from Scratch: Split Subjectivities in the Work of Helena María Viramontes and Cherríe Moraga," in *Chicana Creativity and Criticism: Charting New Frontiers in American Literature*, eds. María Hererra-Sobek and Helena María Viramontes (1988), pp. 147–159. Helena María Viramontes, "Nopalitos: The Making of Fiction," in *Breaking Boundaries: Latina Writing and Critical Readings*, eds. Asunción Horno-Delgado et al. (1989) and reprinted in *Making Face, Making Soul/ Haciendo Caras*, ed. Gloria Anzaldúa (1990), pp. 291–294. Roberta Fernández, " 'The Cariboo Cafe': Helena María Viramontes Discourses with Her Social and Cultural Contexts," *Women's Studies* 17 (1989): 71–85. Helena María Viramontes, "Why I Write," in *Chicana Writers: On Word and Film*, eds. Helena María Viramontes and María Herrera-Sobek (1994).

Kayann Short

VISUAL ART AND WRITING. In the mid-1970s, Martha Rosler's phototext *The Bowery in Two Inadequate Descriptive Systems* (1974–1975) indicated an emergent mode of interaction between writing and visual art. This emergence took two forms: formal refusal of previously established relations between image and caption, and growing acceptance of traffic between visual productions and theories of representation indebted to semiotics, psychoanalytic *film theory, and critical theory. Rosler's work—written and visual—exemplifies a critique of the stable relations encouraged by traditions of documentary photography within representational systems, and extends a conversation between visual art and critical or theoretical commentary. Alternating photographs empty of documentary subjects with nonnarrative text placards clearly incapable of "speaking for" absent documentary subjects, Rosler provided a starting point for an emergent discourse that was taken up by a number of women working in the visual arts in the late 1970s.

This essay examines two bodies of cultural production that rely upon interactions of written texts and images to destabilize conventions by which meaning is attributed by viewers. Separated by forces of cultural *racism operating in the art marketplace, art-critical practice, and U.S. political culture, common concerns over text-image relations and the deconstruction of mechanisms by which viewing subjects are centered, stabilized, or otherwise invited to assign meaning indicate convergent interests and strategies between the two groups despite differing critical attention and access to cultural space. Writing occupies a particularly salient position in the conceptual frameworks put to work by all of the women visual artists under consideration. Viewers are required to bring multiple literacies to bear when reading the text-image interactions. Text overlays, undermines, and often rewrites the visual images in this work, both compelling and simultaneously subverting possible readings.

The first body of work I will call feminist *postmodernist confrontational art in order to indicate the critical tradition that upholds Barbara Kruger, Jenny Holzer, and Silvia Kolbowski, as well as Marie Yates and Mary Kelly in the British context, as exemplary postmodernists, while situating their work within the historical context of its confrontational address,

indebted to Dadaist and Situationist agitprop and the second-wave feminist movement. One formation of this group as feminist postmodernists occurs in Craig Owens's essay "The Discourse of Others: Feminists and Postmodernism" in *The Anti-Aesthetic: Essays on Postmodern Culture* (1983). The critical conversation about this art owes much to film theory as an interdisciplinary mode of inquiry and critique of representation occurring in English through the British journal *Screen;* to the proliferation of Foucault's theory of discursive production of subjects in a variety of critiques of disciplinary knowledges and practices; and to the convergence of feminist psychoanalytic and semiotic approaches to cultural productions.

Site-specific art (park benches, buildings, and billboards) and photomontage are the main modes in which these artists work, using highly public forms that have been notably publicized throughout the 1980s. Much of this work has interventionist aims, particularly in regard to postmodern capitalism and the modes of subjection through which "consumers" are produced, and in the reproduction of gender through visual technologies. Conventional advertising and graphic design are treated as forms of visual assault, used to accomplish the delivery of messages and revealed as a highly effective means of subject positioning in the late twentieth-century United States. Confrontational strategies deployed by feminist postmodernist visual artists were taken up within the context of social movements, notably *AIDS treatment activism and feminist sexual politics. Barbara Kruger's work found a wide public, and is most usefully assessed in *Love for Sale: The Words and Pictures of Barbara Kruger* (1990) by Kate Linker.

The work accomplished by direct, public address in feminist postmodernist confrontational art occurs through the use of textual imperatives and interrogatives, two verbal forms that issue from a transcendent voice not traceable as the expression of a "self" configured through subjection. Kruger's use of pronouns problematizes the gender content of her messages, and certainly detaches address from racialized subjects. The voice-texts Kruger relied on in the early to mid-1980s refused not only "speaking for others" but "speaking for oneself," and were, I would argue, radically detached from expressivism, self-consciousness, and historical specificity. However, Kruger's work mounted a sustained critique of the subjection of women through capitalism, ideologies of romantic love, the gendered division of labor, mass media and commodification, and militarism within the historical context of late twentieth-century political culture. Her work has recently shifted toward increasing consideration of bodies within history, paralleling her involvement with poststructuralist theory that pays attention to the production of colonial and imperial subjects. In the introduction to *Remaking History* (1989), the fourth work published in the Dia Art Foundation Discussions in Contemporary Culture series, Kruger and coeditor Phil Mariani attend to the text as a site of struggle: "Texts empower; they grant authority, and their deconstruction from race-gender perspectives has become a kind of anti-imperialist strategy that has reverberations for political action." Thus, the use of text imperatives and interrogations is linked to an analysis of operations of power, knowledge, and political and economic privilege conferred through the "official discourses" mobilized and critiqued in feminist postmodernist confrontational art.

Visual representations and texts that oscillate between refusal and embrace of dominant modes of address abound in feminist postmodernist art, which tends to have a fairly adversarial relation to its viewers. The move to incorporate verbal texts strategically "trains" spectators to displace stable interpretations of either verbal or visual texts. The incommensurability of meanings between representational systems so aptly pointed out by Rosler's work on the Bowery—when text and image cannot be made to add up to coherently and comfortably overdetermined meanings—places pressure on conventions by which viewers attribute meaning within contemporary sign-systems. The handful of politicized women visual artists who exemplified postmodernism through the 1980s generated unprecedented attention to political art.

The production of reading-intensive art was by no means confined to the small group of feminist postmodernist artists who have been so widely held up as exemplars of confrontational art. Another body of contemporary visual work that relies upon writing has been produced by U.S. women of color working with modes of address and relations between text and image similar to the feminist postmodernists and other conceptual artists. This group of artists also uses text and narrative to foreground contradictory negotiations between self-identity, cultural identity, and historical processes that configure subjectivities and material relations. While artists such as Adrian Piper were working concurrently with or even preceding the mainly white feminist postmodernists, their work has appeared less often in the public sphere, or in art-critical assessments. U.S. women of color producing text-intensive visual art include Piper, Linda Nishio, Clarissa Sligh, and Celia Alvarez Munoz, all of whom

are mentioned in Lucy Lippard's compendium of African-American, Asian-American, Chicana, and Native American artists, *Mixed Blessings: New Art in a Multicultural America* (1990).

Narrative is frequently employed by this second grouping of artists as a means through which self-identity is articulated in conjunction and collision with marginalized cultural identities and material processes of historical disempowerment. Women's relations to dominant discursive constructions and cultural fictions are represented through relations to imposed second languages; institutional practices including desegregation, criminalization, family configurations, and childhood sexual abuse; and racial divisions of labor in the context of late capitalism. While their textual logic represents self-formations, it concentrates on formation of self—including racial and sexual formation—through often violent historical and political processes. Narrative is used as an often discontinuous, interrupted, antiexpressive vehicle through which self-identity is constructed rather than merely represented.

While the textual practices of these two groups of women visual artists rely on differing pragmatics, their alliances occur in the attempt to ground their deconstructions in historical contexts that take into account the positioning power of the large structures that exercise hold over subjects in late twentieth-century capitalist political culture.

• Benjamin H. D. Buchloh, "Allegorical Procedures: Appropriation and Montage in Contemporary Art," *Artforum* 20, no. 1 (September 1982): 43–56. Barbara Kruger, *We Won't Play Nature to Your Culture: Works by Barbara Kruger* (1983). Hal Foster, "Subversive Signs," in *Recodings: Art, Spectacle, Cultural Politics* (1985), pp. 99–118. Carol Squiers, "Diversionary (Syn)-tactics: Barbara Kruger Has Her Way with Words," *ArtNews* 86, no. 2 (February 1987): 76–85. Nancy Campbell, "The Oscillating Embrace: Subjection and Interpellation in Barbara Kruger's Art," *Genders* 1, no. 1 (Spring 1988): 57–74. David Deitcher, "Barbara Kruger: Resisting Arrest," *Artforum* 29, no. 6 (February 1991): 84–91. Judith Wilson, "In Memory of the News and of Ourselves: The Art of Adrian Piper," *Third Text* 16/17 (Autumn/Winter 1991): 39–64.

Nancy D. Campbell

VOCATIONAL ADVICE LITERATURE for and by women appears in every type of print media, including popular magazines, professional journals, political pamphlets, government publications, and newspapers. In addition to book-length studies assuming the guise of group biography, scientific research, journalistic exposé, memoir, and fiction, some periodical articles have been collected in volumes such as Anna Richardson's *The Girl Who Earns Her Own Living* (1905), which reprints several columns originally prepared for the *Woman's Home Companion* and the *Philadelphia Press,* and Catharine Oglesby's *Business Opportunities for Women* (1932), a compilation of articles previously published in *Ladies' Home Journal.*

In the United States, the term *vocation* operates within a secular context to describe and elevate gender-specific homemaking functions and to justify the feminization of various occupational specialities in the wage economy. In *The Young Lady's Friend* (1836), advice writer Eliza Farrar maintains that housekeeping alone constitutes woman's "peculiar calling," while acknowledging the importance of other pursuits, which she refers to as duties or occupations. However, Emma Willard bases her argument for state financing of women's colleges on the assumed legitimacy of teaching as a feminine vocation in *A Plan for Improving Female Education* (1819). As the ideal of universal public education became entrenched, an earlier understanding that equated vocation with a personal duty became subsumed under an emphasis on access to an expanding array of vocational choice via extended education or specialized training.

Vocational counseling itself gained professional status with the emergence of aptitude testing in the second decade of the twentieth century. Catherine Filene's *Careers for Women* (1920) includes two entries for this occupation, one on guidance counseling at the college level and another detailing its practice in high schools, and lists those colleges offering course work in vocational counseling as part of their teacher training curriculum. Indexing vocational guidance under "Social and Religious Workers and Counselors" in *The College Girl Looks Ahead to Her Career Opportunities* (1956), Marguerite Wykoff Zapoleon advises aspirants that they will need to obtain at least a master's degree in order to work in the field.

While the client population served by the guidance industry was initially conceived of as the young, by the mid-1950s, the subspecialty of vocational rehabilitation had emerged to assist those with special needs, such as prisoners and the disabled. In the 1960s, mature reentry women were recognized as comprising a group that faced unique barriers to full employment, and in the 1970s, women of color and displaced homemakers (that is, divorced, abandoned, or widowed women in midlife who must suddenly enter the workplace out of economic necessity, not choice) became the subjects of government manpower allocation strategies and intensified vocational services. The emphasis since the mid-1980s has been on dislocated, mid-career workers of both sexes.

Dissenting from the professionalized mainstream, some vocational advice writers have always maintained that capital accumulation rather than dignified employment is the ticket to economic independence and personal freedom. In her lectures on the labor market, collected in 1867, Caroline *Dall argues that women's economic insecurities stem not from a perceived lack of access to emerging job classifications, but rather from their failure to move from employee status to that of employer. Similarly, Anna Julia *Cooper addresses "Negro men of means" in *A Voice from the South by a Black Woman of the South* (1892) with the warning that neither superficial industrial training nor the prestige of classical education will alleviate the need to acquire land and investment capital. One of the earliest volumes to focus exclusively on vocational advice for women, Martha Rayne's *What Can a Woman Do?* (1883), explains how to take advantage of the preemption, homestead, and tree claim laws for personal gain, and offers guidelines for choosing a law school.

While the genre developed inconsistently and maintained an uneven relationship to economic fluctuations, all vocational advice writers confronted what Letty Cottin Pogrebin, in *How to Make It in A Man's World* (1970), calls the "double-dealing double standard" of a marketplace where gender-based wage and promotional disparities, on-the-job sexual harrassment and assault, and age discrimination are the norm. Like Pogrebin, many of these writers advocated the use of deceit and manipulation in self-defense while they discounted the potential remedy of unionization. Accounts such as Teresa S. Malkiel's *Diary of a Shirtwaist Striker* (1910) detailed the roles of ethnic and intergenerational ties in fostering effective resistance, yet most advice writers, like Frances Maule, who responds to the hard times of the Great Depression in *She Strives to Conquer* (1937), were more likely to prescribe regimes of grammatical improvement, wardrobe modification, and attitude adjustment to ameliorate traces of regional, class, or ethnic affiliation.

Under the influence of Helen Gurley Brown's *Sex and the Single Girl* (1962) and Betty *Friedan's *The Feminine Mystique* (1963), vocational advice literature flourished in the early 1970s, producing two notably comprehensive studies: Caroline Bird's *Everything a Woman Needs to Know to Get Paid What She's Worth* (1973) and Cynthia Fuchs Epstein's *Woman's Place: Options and Limits in Professional Careers* (1970). However, following the publication of Richard Nelson Bolles's best-selling *What Color is Your Parachute?* in 1972, vocational advice literature diverged into three distinct categories: the modified occupational catalog limited to one field of employment or sector of the economy (Baila Zeitz and Lorraine Dusky's *The Best Companies for Women*, 1988); manuals dealing exclusively with the techniques of job hunting (Monifa Azibo and Therese Crylen Unumb's *The Mature Woman's Back-to-Work Book*, 1980); and self-help books aimed at overcoming psycholog-ical barriers to success (Marjorie Hansen Shaevitz's *The Superwoman Syndrome*, 1984).

[*See also* Advice Books.]

Laura H. Roskos

VOTING RIGHTS. *See* Suffrage Movement.

W

WAKOSKI, Diane (b. 1937), American poet and educator, whose idiosyncratic work grew out of mid-century *confessional and deep image schools of poetry.

From the publication of her first book (*Coins and Coffins*, 1962) to her most recent (*Jason the Sailor*, 1993), Wakoski has written in a meditative style and distinctive voice about the role of imagination in the world that Wallace Stevens described as "completely physical." A typical long poem of hers may verge on or even include a letter, story, or essay, but it always seeks to transform mundane details from Wakoski's experiences of people and places by filtering them through a striking image or mythic figure, often drawn from her own mythological system. Some call her tone self-pitying, but others find it unrelentingly honest in her Stevensian task of sorting out desire from despair. Unwilling to join any political movement despite the obvious effects of patriarchal power on her own self-esteem, she has mined the inescapably political subject of greed, which she brilliantly redefines as the failure to choose—the problem of expecting to "have it all," so that no matter how much one has, it is never enough. Unlike Mark Twain and William Faulkner, who also indicted American rapacity, she scrupulously examines her own culpability.

Born into poverty in Whittier, California, Wakoski was no stranger to the desire for better things. Apart from the rocking provided by an uncle when she was a baby, occasional visits from her handsome father, and the piano lessons her mother provided, her family rarely satisfied her needs. Academic achievement, music, and poetry became substitutes for wealth and love. As a teenager and again as a student at the University of California–Berkeley (B.A., 1960), she had affairs that led to haunting pregnancies, births, and adoptions. After escaping to New York in 1960, she worked at a bookstore and taught in a junior high school, married twice for brief periods, and made her way into both avant-garde and academic circles by giving poetry readings. From 1966 to 1986, she published sixteen collections of poems, received several prestigious grants, and achieved full academic acceptance as a writer-in-residence at ten colleges and universities. In the 1980s, she joined the faculty at Michigan State University (1981), married Robert Turney (1982), and consolidated her work in *The Collected Greed* (1984) and *Emerald Ice: Selected Poems, 1962–1987* (1988). Despite her new security, she continues to assert the poet's right to see through our imperfections.

• Wakoski's manuscript collection is at the University of Arizona–Tucson. See also Philip Gerber and Robert Gemmett, eds., *A Terrible War: A Conversation with Diane Wakoski* (1970). Toby Olson, ed., "A Symposium on Diane Wakoski," *Margins* (January–March 1976): 90–129. Estella Lauter, "Diane Wakoski: Disentangling the Woman from the Moon," *Women as Mythmakers: Poetry and Visual Art by Twentieth-Century Women* (1984), pp. 98–113.

Estella Lauter

WALKER, Alice (b. 1944), novelist, essayist, short fiction writer, children's book writer, biographer, lecturer, educator. Alice Walker is arguably the most significant black American woman writer in the post-1950 era. Support for such a claim comes from the sheer volume of her publications, her popularity among the general public as well as the academic community, her international acclaim, and the consistently engaging nature of the topics about which she writes. Her focus on feminist issues within the black community, as well as upon intraracial violence and oppression, places her in a category of writers willing to confront the difficult problems of communities in transition, to complain about their male/female and parent/child relationships, and to cajole their members to renew their faith in each other for the sake of community survival. Her coining of the word *Womanist* to articulate her concept of black feminism has led to its own critical explosion. Her recent concentration on issues that affect women worldwide, particularly male oppression through female circumcision, illustrates that Walker refuses to compromise her effort to reform humanity and to sensitize human beings in general to the need to save the earth for future generations.

Walker was born on 9 February 1944 in Eatonton, Georgia, the eighth child of sharecroppers Willie Lee and Minnie Lou Grant Walker. The deprived setting and the perpetuation of the new slavery called *sharecropping would serve as the impetus for her first novel, *The*

Third Life of Grange Copeland, which she published in 1970. An accident with a BB gun at the age of eight (one of her older brothers shot her) caused Walker to lose sight in her right eye; it was covered by a scar. The problem was corrected when Walker was fourteen, but the result was that she felt ugly, a feeling that led her to the privacy of recording her thoughts in a notebook. The misfortune with the eye, which eventually led her to acquire a glass eye, served an immediate good purpose—it enabled her to attend Spelman College on a scholarship for disabled persons. After two years at Spelman, she transferred to Sarah Lawrence College where, under the guiding hand of Muriel *Rukeyser, she was able to get her early works published. Her relationship with Harcourt Brace Jovanovich continues today.

A trip to Africa during a summer from Sarah Lawrence led to the writing of several poems included in Walker's first collection, *Once* (1970). She was pregnant before the trip began, and the pregnancy only made her feel more at the mercy of her body, and suicidal. The writing of poems, she said, was a way for her to celebrate each day with the knowledge that she had not committed suicide the night before. She finished *Once* while she was waiting for friends to find an abortionist for her, which they succeeded in doing. Her second volume of poetry, *Revolutionary Petunias*, would appear in 1973. These early poetic efforts were succeeded by several more volumes of poetry, including *Good Night, Willie Lee, I'll See You in the Morning* (1979), *Horses Make a Landscape Look More Beautiful* (1984), and *Her Blue Body Everything We Know: Earthling Poems 1965–1990 Complete* (1991).

Walker's reputation as a fiction writer blossomed in the 1970s. *The Third Life of Grange Copeland* follows a man through his defeat at the hands of the white man for whom he share-crops, to further degredation in New York, to his return to Georgia as more sane, more whole, and more respectful of black women than he could have ever imagined being in his first life. *In Love and Trouble: Stories of Black Women* (1973) depicts various women who are at the mercy of the men in their lives, their own passions, forces of nature, or societal expectations of who and what they should be. In 1976, Walker published *Meridan*, which chronicles the sexual and racial politics of the civil rights movement. Walker herself was a participant in civil rights activities in Mississippi, where she worked from the late 1960s to the mid-1970s and where she married Mel Leventhal, a white civil rights lawyer; the couple had one child, a daughter named Rebecca. At Spelman, she says, she learned to appreciate all the young

stars involved in that movement, including Student Nonviolent Coordinating Committee leaders Julian Bond, John Lewis, and Ruby Davis Robinson; she also participated in demonstrations in Georgia.

Another endeavor for Walker in the 1970s was to assist in the process of recentering Zora Neale *Hurston in the literary world. She traveled to Eatonville, Florida, in search of Hurston's grave, and placed a marker at the site. She also wrote "In Search of Zora Neale Hurston" (1974) and the foreword to Robert E. Hemenway's biography of Hurston (1977). She would later edit a collection of Hurston's works entitled *I Love Myself When I Am Laughing . . . And Then Again When I Am Looking Mean and Impressive* (1979).

You Can't Keep a Good Woman Down, Walker's second collection of short stories, appeared in 1981. Her most feminist work to that point, it dealt with issues that grew out of the *civil rights and feminist movements. Interracial *rape, *abortion, sadomasochism, *pornography, and murder are a few of the powerful topics she treats. Some of the stories appear to be in the making, and one, "Advancing Luna—and Ida B. Wells," offered alternate endings.

The next year would bring Walker's most controversial work. Although she had started the novel in New York City, it was only when she divorced in 1977 and moved to California that the characters came freely and the finished product was achieved. *The Color Purple* (1982), a story of *incest and intraracial violence and abuse, drew a plethora of emotional responses from black communities as well as from black academics. Written in epistolary form, the novel recounts the initially tragic life and ultimate triumph of Celie, who moves from incest victim to lesbian love and entrepreneurship. Perhaps because of its controversial initial reception, the novel was widely read and discussed, and it has remained on college course lists since its publication. It was made into a movie and has been reissued at least twice since its original publication. Walker asserts that the story was based on that of her great-grandmother, who was raped and abused at the age of twelve. Celie's triumph over sexual abuse and physical beatings perhaps serves as a vicarious rewriting of Walker's great-grandmother's history. Celie's sister Nettie becomes a missionary in Africa, and it was the exploration of that link that would tie in to Walker's next two novelistic ventures.

In 1989, she published *The Temple of My Familiar*, which retains a couple of characters from *The Color Purple*, but without any obvious attempt at a sequel. What is important is that Walker's fascination for the African connection enables her to depict a woman, Lissie, who has spent numerous lives on that continent (Lissie has been reincarnated several times). The novel also provides, through lengthy conversations about the need to get in touch with one's spirit and one's spiritual past, a way for harassed contemporary African Americans to rediscover what is of value in themselves. Critics complained that the novel was too talky and too New Age, but it has found a faithful following among those who believe that harmony with the earth and all its creatures is of paramount concern. Spiritual guides, dead and alive, can aid in the process of that understanding.

In the spring of 1992, Walker published *Possessing the Secret of Joy*. Narrated from multiple voices, the story is that of another of the characters from *The Color Purple*. Tashi, who was Celie's daughter Olivia's best friend in the Olinka village, reappears as a woman scarred beyond reclamation by the physical and psychological trauma of female pharaonic circumcision—the complete removal of female genitalia and the sewing up of the vagina. Despite the quietness of her prose, Walker is clearly at war in the book—at war with a practice that has traumatized many women, but that is still practiced in many parts of the world. In an effort to further her cause for its demise, she includes a statement on the practice at the end of the novel, along with a reading list for interested persons.

Walker also has a well-deserved reputation as an essayist. Indeed, she is one of few African-American female writers who have published book-length collections of essays. To date, she has published two. The first, *In Search of Our Mothers' Gardens: Womanist Prose* (1983), was inspired by Walker's own mother as well as by Walker's reclaiming of Zora Neale Hurston. Walker has repeatedly suggested that the most significant influence upon her has been her mother; her image of her mother tending flowers in the many sharecropper shacks in which she was forced to live and making art out of that endeavor thus links the older and younger generations of creative artists. The second collection, *Living by the Word: Selected Writings, 1973–1987*, appeared in 1988.

Walker continues to live in the San Francisco area, where she established a small press, Wild Trees, for the purpose of publishing less well known writers. A film featuring her in her retreat was made in 1989; her popularity also extends to calendars, one of which, for 1986, featured photographs of Walker in gardening, relaxing, and working poses. She continues to be an impressively popular lecturer whose reading voice and power over her audiences are well celebrated.

• John O'Brien, *Interviews with Black Writers* (1974). Trudier Harris, "Folklore in the Fiction of Alice Walker: A Perpetuation of Historical and Literary Traditions," *Black American Literature Forum* 2 (Spring 1977): 3–8. Mary Helen Washington, "An Essay on Alice Walker," in *Sturdy Black Bridges*, eds. Roseann P. Bell, Bettye J. Parker, and Beverly Guy-Sheftall (1979), pp. 133–149. Barbara Christian, *Black Women Novelists: The Development of a Tradition, 1892–1976* (1980). Deborah McDowell, "The Self in Bloom: Alice Walker's *Meridian*," *CLA Journal* 24 (March 1981): 262–275. Mary Helen Washington, "Her Mother's Gifts," *Ms.* 10 (June 1982): 38. Mari Evans, ed., *Black Women Writers (1950–1980): A Critical Evaluation* (1983). Claudia Tate, "Alice Walker," in *Black Women Writers at Work* (1983), pp. 175–187. Trudier Harris, "On *The Color Purple*, Stereotypes, and Silence," *Black American Literature Forum* 14 (Winter 1984): 156–161. Melvin Dixon, *Ride Out the Wilderness: Geography and Identity in Afro-American Literature* (1987). Henry Louis Gates, Jr., *The Signifying Monkey: A Theory of Afro-American Literary Criticism* (1988). Louis H. Pratt and Darnell D. Pratt, *Alice Malsenior Walker: An Annotated Bibliography, 1968–1986* (1988). Elliott Butler-Evans, *Race, Gender, and Desire: Narrative Strategies in the Fiction of Toni Cade Bambara, Toni Morrison, and Alice Walker* (1989). bell hooks, "Writing the Subject: Reading *The Color Purple*" in *Reading Black, Reading Feminist: A Critical Anthology*, ed. Henry Louis Gates, Jr. (1990), pp. 454–470.

Trudier Harris

WALKER, Margaret (b. 1915), poet, novelist, essayist, critic, educator. Margaret Abigail Walker was born in Birmingham, Alabama. Her father, Sigismund C. Walker, was a minister, and her mother, Marion Dozier, a music teacher. Expected by her educated, ambitious parents to excel, Walker completed her B.A. in English at Northwestern University when she was only nineteen. In 1935, at the age of twenty, she joined the *Federal Writers' Project in Chicago, where she worked with Gwendolyn *Brooks and Richard Wright. In 1942, Walker received her master's degree in creative writing from the University of Iowa, where she completed her first volume of poetry, *For My People*. With the publication of this book, Walker became the first African-American to win the Yale Series of Younger Poets Award. In 1943, she married Firnist James Alexander, and together they had four children.

Walker has been an English professor since the early 1940s, first at West Virginia State College, then at Livingstone College in Salisbury, North Carolina. From 1946 to 1979, Walker taught at Jackson State University, where she also directed the Institute for the Study of the History, Life, and Culture of Black People. She received the Rosenwald Fellowship for Creative Writing in 1944, a Ford Fellowship at Yale University in 1954, and her Ph.D. in English at the University of Iowa in 1965.

Walker's writing career officially began with the publication of her first poem, "Daydreaming," in *Crisis* magazine in 1934. Her distinguished, prolific literary output includes four volumes of poetry, her novel *Jubilee* (1966), and an extensive array of essays, interviews, and speeches. Her devotion to writing has never flagged: Between 1988 and 1990, Walker, having reached her mid-seventies, produced three major works: a biography entitled *Richard Wright: Daemonic Genius* (1988), *This Is My Century: New and Collected Poems* (1989), and *How I Wrote* Jubilee *and Other Essays* (1990).

Walker has devoted her writing to celebrating African-American history and culture. She is probably best known for her poetry. "For My People," her signature poem, offers a hymn of praise for the dignity, the endurance, and the superhuman strength of African Americans, who are "singing their slave songs repeatedly," songs of transcendence that seek to make sense out of oppression. *Prophets for a New Day* (1970) identifies *civil rights leaders with biblical prophets.

Women play pivotal roles in Walker's poetry. "Lineage" enunciates Walker's connection with her matrilineal heritage, and folk ballads such as "Molly Means" suggest Walker's belief in conjure women's unparalleled power. Vyry, the protagonist of *Jubilee*, commemorates Walker's great-grandmother's strength in surviving *slavery and *racism.

Walker's literary influence derives from her compact, spare, accessible language and style. Numerous writers have admired and emulated her fierce commitment to reaching the widest possible audience with her work.

• Eugenia Collier, "Fields Watered with Blood: Myth and Ritual in the Poetry of Margaret Walker," in *Black Women Writers (1950–1980): A Critical Evaluation*, ed. Mari Evans (1984), pp. 499–509. Minrose C. Gwin, *Black and White Women of the Old South: The Peculiar Sisterhood in American Literature* (1985). R. Baxter Miller, ed., *Black American Poets between Worlds, 1940–1960* (1986). Jane Campbell, "Margaret Walker," in *African American Writers*, ed. Valerie Smith (1991), pp. 459–471.

Jane Campbell

WALTERS, Anna Lee (b. 1946), poet, fiction writer, technical writer, and publisher. Although she was born in Pawnee, Oklahoma, and is of Pawnee and Otoe-Missouria heritage, Anna Walters has devoted herself to life on the Navajo reservation in Tsaile, Arizona. She studied at the College of Santa Fe, New Mexico, and married a Navajo artist and museum curator named Harry Walters. Initially a technical writer, educational consultant, and curriculum

specialist at Navajo Community College, she went on to become an editor for and eventually director of Navajo Community College Press. She has used her influence as a publisher to encourage the production and publication of fiction by Native Americans; in her article "American Indian Thought and Identity in American Fiction" (*Coyote Was Here*, 1984), she says that creative fiction should not replace oral tradition and that it probably will not, but that a new place should be cleared for it alongside traditional tribal forms of literature. She is also tireless in urging Native Americans to become more actively involved in the technical side of marketing American Indian literature and to familiarize themselves with the media as a tool for changing and influencing outsiders' ideas about them.

Walters lectures on Native American life and literature, and writes primarily to an Indian audience, with an awareness of the multiplicity of tribes and traditions. It is her conviction that the narrative voice in American Indian fiction is a product of traditional tribal songs and *story telling, and even of *myth, and that its significance will be more apparent to people "attuned to a particular tribal memory experience."

She is the author of several works on Native American history and culture, including *Talking Indian: Reflections on Survival and Writing* (1992), *The Spirit of Native America: Beauty and Mysticism in American Indian Art* (1989), and *The Sacred* (1977), coauthored with Peggy Beck. She also edited a collection of Native writers' works entitled *Neon Powwow: New Native American Voices of the Southwest* (1993). Over the last twenty years, Walters's fiction, poetry, and articles have appeared in *The Man to Send Rain Clouds* (1974), *The Third Woman* (1980), *Spider Woman's Granddaughters* (1989), and *Talking Leaves* (1991), among others; she has published a collection of her own short fiction, *The Sun Is Not Merciful* (1985), a novel, *Ghost Singer* (1988), and a retelling of a traditional legend, *The Two-legged Creature: An Otoe Story* (1993).

• A. LaVonne Brown Ruoff, *American Indian Literatures* (1990).

Margaret A. Lukens

WARNER, Susan (1819–1885), novelist. Under the name Elizabeth Wetherell, Warner published *The Wide, Wide World*, the first American book to sell over a million copies. Warner grew up in a wealthy New York City household, but sudden financial losses in 1837 forced the Warner family to relocate to isolated Constitution Island, near West Point, New York. *The Wide, Wide World* (1851) was written in an attempt to earn money after twelve years of desperate poverty. Praised by critics for its realistic descriptions and spiritual quality, the novel was an immediate best-seller. Warner subsequently wrote twenty-nine additional adult novels and children's stories, including *Queechy* (1852), *Daisy* (1868), *Diana* (1877), *The Letter of Credit* (1881), and *Daisy Plains* (1885). She also coauthored sixteen children's books and edited a magazine for children, the *Little American* (1862–1864), with her sister, Anna Warner. Warner's works were well received, but her royalties were limited and her father's disastrous speculations continued to drain her finances. Warner remained at Constitution Island for the rest of her life.

Warner's novels combine an explicit Christian philosophy with realistic detail and humor. Her belief that true Christianity required complete submission and dedication to God's will is reflected throughout her work. Many of Warner's novels depict the spiritual education of a young woman who survives the loss of loved ones, financial hardships, and other difficulties and frustrations by cultivating Christian faith. In some cases, Warner represents these difficulties as tests of the heroine's submission to the divine will. In other instances, however, the heroine's adherence to Christian principles enables her to assert herself and resist wrongful human authorities, even parents and clergymen. Warner develops her spiritual dramas by using extensive descriptions of rural and urban locations and domestic tasks, and accurately recorded dialects. Although the settings of the various novels include Europe and Fiji, Warner situates her most successful works in New England and New York State, vividly depicting rigorous farm and household labor and stylish city life based on her own experiences.

The success of *The Wide, Wide World* inspired imitations, including religious novels such as Maria *Cummins's *The Lamplighter* (1854), Martha Finley's Elsie Dinsmore series (1867–1905), and *local color novels, which used dialect and regional descriptions to form their texture. Although none of Warner's later novels matched *The Wide, Wide World* in sales, Warner's reputation as a major American writer remained intact until the turn of the twentieth century.

• Anna Warner, *Susan Warner* (1909). Dorothy Hurlbut Sanderson, *They Wrote for a Living: A Bibliography of the Works of Susan Bogert Warner and Anna Bartlett Warner* (1976). Mabel Baker, *Light in the Morning: Memories of Susan and Anna Warner* (1978). Jane Tompkins, ed., Afterword to *The Wide, Wide World*, by Susan Warner (1987). Susan S. Williams, "Widening the World: Susan Warner, Her Readers, and the As-sumption of Authorship," *American Quarterly* 42, no. 4 (1990).

Jane Weiss

WAR NOVEL. By the end of the decade, there will be no exclusionary generalizations left to be made about the American war novel written by women. Particularly, the charge no longer obtains that "real" war writing, which concerns combat at the front, can only be written by the men who experienced it. The last exclusive male role—as a regular, combat, uniformed soldier—was taken on by women during the Gulf War, and surely by the end of the decade there will be more than one novel by a woman about the experience. Women, of course, have written as soldiers, dreaming themselves into the male experience, as in Harriette *Arnow's *The Kentucky Trace* (1974), concerning a Kentucky surveyor who is a soldier in the American Revolution. However, attempts by women to capture the war experience have been characterized as unconvincing, and even as crude ventures in cross-dressing. Frederick J. Hoffman, for instance, accuses Gertrude *Stein of interfering in a male domain with her war writing: "The perspective of an old-maid eccentric can scarcely be expected to yield large truths consistently." Edith *Wharton's *A Son at the Front* (1923) and *The Marne* (1918), Willa *Cather's *One of Ours* (1923), Katherine Anne *Porter's *Pale Horse, Pale Rider* (1939), all concerning World War I, have been damned as mawkishly sentimental and chauvinistic. Female domestic takes on the war experience have been found pale and irrelevant when measured against male combat views on war. The traditional *canon of the American war novel is decidedly male. For James Fenimore Cooper, Stephen Crane, Ernest Hemingway, Norman Mailer, James Jones, and others, combat is the crucible of manhood. In Richard Aldington's *Death of a Hero* (1929), for instance, soldiers who have experienced the front are transformed into a "new, curious race of men, the masculine men." They had been "where no woman and no half-man had ever been, could endure to be. They were Men."

Recently, feminist critics have challenged traditional assumptions concerning women writers and the war novel. The male perspective of war as being one of the "great" themes of fiction that a novelist engaged in producing "great" novels must experience has been effectively redescribed by feminists as parochial and chauvinistic. In this view, the fact that Jane Austen—to cross the Atlantic for a moment—did not describe the Napoleonic Wars raging during her lifetime, is no more an argument against her worth than the fact that Hemingway did not write a novel of manners is an argument against his. What was formerly described as mawkish and sentimental in Wharton, Cather, and Porter has been redescribed as domestic realism, providing insights into the home front at the time. Moreover, Aldington's "masculine men" are being measured against other views of those men. In her autobiographical novel *Bid Me to Live*, *H. D., who was married to Aldington, also portrays the husband-soldier on leave from the front as transformed. But for her, it is an alienating transformation. The protagonist, Julia, experiences her husband, Rafe, as so changed by warfare that she can no longer respond to him sexually. Moreover, American women's war novels, formerly banned and ignored, are being rediscovered, such as the book by the American nurse Ellen Lamotte, *The Backwash of War: The Human Wreckage of the Battlefield as Witnessed by an American Nurse* (1916). Indeed, reassessments of popular novels by women argue that these novels' cultural import may have been grossly underestimated by earlier critics who judged them as insignificant. For example, Jane Tompkins writes convincingly of Harriet Beecher * Stowe's *Uncle Tom's Cabin* (1852) making history: "It induced a nation to go to war and to free its slaves."

The voices of women writers of war are simultaneously terrifying, celebratory, visionary. Many concern the legacy of war. Cynthia * Ozick's novella *The Shawl* (1983) concerns a Jewish concentration camp survivor named Rosa, "a madwoman and a scavenger," who deludes herself that her infant daughter, Magda, thrown against an electrified fence by a guard, survived. In the end, Rosa surrenders the delusion for the promise of love in the here and now. Although Toni Morrison's * *Beloved* (1989) takes place right before the * Civil War, few would contend that it does not concern all-out war. Like *The Shawl*, however, *Beloved* has an ethics of hope. Morrison based *Beloved* on a * slave narrative about an escaped slave who murders her baby and threatens to murder all of her children rather than turn them over to the white man who owns her. The novel's protagonist, Sethe, the mother who commits the infanticide, undergoes a process of exorcising the literal ghost of her murdered daughter, Beloved. The ghost of Beloved embodies the meaning of * slavery for contemporary African Americans. Morrison suggests that just as Sethe does with Beloved, African Americans must come to terms with their slave past before they can project a real future. This future, according to Morrison, is dependent upon a balanced relationship between memory and hope. Obsession with the past, with ghosts and memory, as

Sethe is obsessed until the last pages of the narrative, breeds emotional self-mutilation. Sethe's lover, Paul D., tells her: "Me and you, we got more yesterday than anybody. We need some kind of tomorrow."

Jayne Anne Phillips in *Machine Dreams* (1984) and Bobbie Ann * Mason in *In Country* (1985) trace the effect on the families of the loss of a loved one in the Vietnam War. *Machine Dreams* follows a family from the marriage of the parents to two years after their son becomes missing in action; it depicts the baffling intersection of the national, the familial, and the individual. *In Country* concerns a family from Hopewell, Kentucky, who travels to the Vietnam War Memorial in Washington, D.C. Its particular focus is on the daughter of the dead soldier. She is set the difficult task of projecting a future for herself in the post-Vietnam world. *In Country* describes a condition that may persist into the new millennium: Although women have now participated as combat soldiers in the Gulf War, they are still left to deal with the legacy of male decision making.

[*See also* Violence.]

Ellen G. Friedman

WARREN, Mercy Otis (1728–1814), poet, playwright, and historian. Born the third of thirteen children of James and Mary Allyne Otis in Barnstable, Massachusetts, on 25 September 1728, Mercy received a similar education to her brothers. Her brother James instructed her in the classics, so she read Cicero and Brutus as well as Shakespeare, John Locke, Alexander Pope, and Walter Raleigh. Early, she concluded that historical events are imbued with moral significance—that God's patterns are revealed in historical actions.

Mercy Otis married James Warren, president of the Provincial Congress of Massachusetts. Through him, she met influential political figures such as George Washington, John and Abigail * Adams, and Samuel Adams. Her family's participation in the freedom movement enhanced her natural political interests; she established correspondences with political figures and made politics her subject.

She bore five sons in a happy, loving marriage. Her husband died on 27 November 1808, and she died on 19 October 1814. Her nephew Henry Warren wrote, "And thus, the frail reed is broken"; she was buried on Old Burial Hill in Plymouth, Massachusetts, beside her husband.

Warren's often satirical work dealt with political themes. During the early 1770s, she wrote poems and plays. In her poem "A Political Reverie," from *Poems, Dramatic and Miscellaneous* (1790), she spurred revolutionaries:

"Till every bosom feels a noble flame/And emulates a Lock's or Sydney's name." In her first satirical drama, *The Adulateur* (1772), published anonymously in the *Massachusetts Spy*, she peopled a fictional Upper Servia with Boston's leading citizens disguised as Romans. The central character, the ruler Rapatio, who suppresses the quest for freedom, is a thinly veiled version of Governor Thomas Hutchinson. In *The Defeat* (1773), Warren again depicts Rapatio's villainy and encourages Hutchinson's recall for misuse of taxpayer's monies.

Mercy's pamphlets found success as propaganda devices. John Adams expedited publication of *The Group* (1775), which satirized the mandamus councilors, who were Loyalists and who did not support the American revolutionary cause. Her *Observations on the New Constitution, and on the Federal Conventions* (1788) (by "A Columbia Patriot") aired objections to the new Constitution's lack of a bill of rights.

Her most influential work, the three-volume *History of the Rise, Progress, and Termination of the American Revolution* (1805), was the only contemporary history presenting a Republican viewpoint.

Warren enjoyed extraordinary opportunities to present her talents publicly. Throughout her life, she espoused the causes of liberty and woman's equality, and rejected the widespread notion of a deficiency in women's mental ability.

• Katharine Anthony, *First Lady of the Revolution: The Life of Mercy Otis Warren* (1958). Jean Fritz, *Cast for a Revolution: Some American Friends and Enemies, 1728–1814* (1972). Joan Hoff Wilson and Sharon L. Bollinger, "Mercy Otis Warren: Playwright, Poet and Historian of the American Revolution," in *Female Scholars: A Tradition of Learned Women before 1800*, ed. J. R. Brink (1980), pp. 161–182. Mary Anne Schofield, "The Happy Revolution: Colonial Women and the Eighteenth-Century Theater," in *Modern American Drama: The Female Canon*, ed. June Schlueter (1990), pp. 29–37.

Adelaide P. Amore

WASSERSTEIN, Wendy (b. 1950), dramatist and screenwriter. Born in New York, Wendy Wasserstein was educated at Mount Holyoke College, and many of her plays center on the uncertainties of well-educated affluent white women of her generation. She is particularly interested in the tension in the lives of women of the baby boom era between their conservative upbringing in the fifties and the liberating *feminism they experienced as college students in the sixties. Her plays attempt to negotiate these tensions with a comic touch.

Uncommon Women and Others (first pro-

duced in 1975; revised and enlarged in 1977) centers on a group of Mount Holyoke students who are both jubilant with feminist possibility and uncertain about their futures. *Isn't It Romantic* (first produced in 1981; revised in 1983) contemplates *marriage and the biological time clock (women rushing to have children before it's too late). Her most successful play, *The Heidi Chronicles* (first produced at Playwrights Horizons in 1988, and on Broadway at Plymouth Theatre in 1989), again examines the choices that affluent educated women make between careers and families. Focusing on art history professor Dr. Heidi Holland, it dramatizes her disillusionment as more and more of her feminist friends turn into crass career opportunists. The play ends with Heidi's adopting a baby—and posing for photos before an exhibition of works by Georgia O'Keeffe, perhaps the foremost symbol of the independent woman artist. Wasserstein's women, however, are seldom made of O'Keeffe's sterner stuff.

Wasserstein has been the recipient of numerous awards, including an Obie, a Tony, a Guggenheim Fellowship, a New York Drama Critics Circle Award, and a 1989 Pulitzer Prize for *The Heidi Chronicles*.

• Patricia R. Schroeder, "Wendy Wasserstein," in *Contemporary Authors Biographical Series*, edited by Matthew C. Rondané, vol. 3 (1989), pp. 379–384. Thomas Kozikowski, "Wasserstein, Wendy," in *Contemporary Authors*, ed. Susan M. Trosky, vol. 129 (1990), pp. 452–457. "Wendy Wasserstein," in *The Feminist Companion to Literature in English*, eds. Virginia Blain, Isobel Grundy, and Patricia Clements (1990), p. 1137. "Wendy Wasserstein: The Heidi Chronicles," in *Contemporary Literary Criticism*, edited by Roger Matuz, vol. 59 (1990), pp. 218–227.

Cathy N. Davidson

WATANNA, Onoto, also Winnifred Eaton (1875–1954), novelist, biographer, autobiographer, short-fiction writer, film scenarist, and dramatist. Born in Montreal to a Chinese mother and an English father, the eighth of fourteen children, Eaton knew poverty and prejudice and determined to achieve fame and fortune. To a large extent, she succeeded. Since her older sister, Edith Eaton (also *Sui Sin Far), was already writing about the Chinese in North America, and since the Japanese were then the admired Asians, Winnifred assumed a Japanese persona. She worked briefly as a journalist in Jamaica, West Indies, and as a stenographer in the Chicago stockyards. From 1901 to 1919 she lived in New York City, where she wrote the majority of her "Japanese" novels and moved in literary circles that included Mark Twain and Edith *Wharton. In 1917, she moved with her second husband to Calgary, Alberta, writing more realistic novels set in Canada, such as *His Royal Nibs* (1924) and *Cattle* (1925). From 1924 to 1931, she was chief scenarist at Universal Studios in Hollywood, after which she retired to Calgary.

Miss Nume of Japan (1899) was the first of her seventeen best-selling novels, the most famous of which, *A Japanese Nightingale* (1901), was translated into several European languages and received a lavish Broadway production to compete with *Madame Butterfly* (then a popular curtain raiser adapted from a story by John Luther Long). The most unusual Watanna novel was *The Diary of Delia* (1911), purportedly the diary of a maid written in Irish-American dialect. Often bearing flowery titles, such as *The Wooing of Wisteria* (1902), *The Heart of Hyacinth* (1903), and *The Love of Azalea* (1904), most Watanna novels were published with full-color illustrations and printed on predecorated papers. The books as objects, the stories themselves, and the author's persona all catered to the *orientalism then in vogue and accounted in some measure for their popularity. In each novel, Watanna followed the archetypal romance pattern, with the added spice of an exotic, mysterious, "oriental" heroine. To authenticate her fiction, Onoto Watanna claimed in *Who's Who* to have been born in 1879 in Nagasaki to a Japanese noblewoman.

Onoto Watanna may be dismissed as a literary hoax, but much may be gained from studying her career as a barometer of contemporary cultural prejudices and tastes. Japanese scholars themselves have read and approved of her work. And finally, her camouflage alerts us to the intensity of the battle being waged for recognition of ethnicity.

• Winnifred Eaton Reeve's papers are in the MacKimmie Library Archives at the University of Calgary, Calgary, Alberta, Canada. See also Amy Ling, *Between Worlds: Women Writers of Chinese Ancestry* (1990).

Amy Ling

WATKINS, Yoko Kawashima (b. 1934), children's fiction writer, lecturer. Watkins was born in Harbin, Manchuria, and enjoyed a comfortable childhood in Nanam, North Korea, where her father worked as a Japanese government official. In July 1945, as Japan's defeat in the Pacific War became imminent, Watkins, then eleven, fled with her mother and sixteen-year-old sister just as communist forces advanced on the town. *So Far From the Bamboo Grove* (1986), the story of Watkins's refugee experience written for children, covers a grueling escape by train and on foot to Seoul, the voyage to war-devastated Japan where Mrs. Kawa-

shima dies within two months after discovering her parents' home destroyed by bombing, the poverty and humiliations of Watkins and her sister as they struggle to feed themselves and stay in school, and the safe arrival of their older brother several months later. By the time Mr. Kawashima returned after a six-year imprisonment in Siberia, Watkins had studied English and was working as a typist and translator at Misawa Air Force Base in Aomori, where in 1953 she met and married American pilot Donald Watkins. They moved to the U.S. in 1958, living in Minnesota, Wisconsin, and Oregon before settling in Brewster, Massachusetts. They have four children, and raised two Taiwanese orphans with the help of Ko, Watkins' older sister, who lives in Cambridge, Massachusetts.

The writing of *So Far* was a painful process begun in 1976. Until then Watkins had never asked her brother about his escape, and he died within weeks after recounting it. When the book finally appeared ten years later, it won national praise and numerous awards from library, teacher, and children's literature organizations. Newspaper accounts of Watkins' lectures, which have taken her across the U.S. and to Guam, Kyoto, and Oxford, commend her storytelling gifts and rapport with children and teenagers, on whom she particularly wants to impress the necessity of sharing material wealth, not taking life's comforts for granted, and promoting world peace. Citing such details as Watkins' shrapnel wound in the chest, the unrelieved threat from roving soldiers, air attacks, and lack of provisions during the forty-five mile walk to Seoul, daily meals salvaged from garbage piles, and the girls' constant terror of being raped in the chaotic camps and train stations which became their homes in Japan, reviewers of the book unanimously praise its riveting and painful, but ultimately triumphant, narrative of resilience and hope.

Gayle K. Fujita Sato

WEINGARTEN, Violet (1915–1976), writer of fiction and nonfiction works. Violet Weingarten began her career in 1937 as a young reporter on the now defunct *Brooklyn Eagle*, where she remained for twelve years, turning her attention thereafter to the writing of films, short stories, and nonfiction works dealing largely with parents and children (an abiding interest throughout her life). These early works include *You Can Take Them with You: A Guide to Traveling with Children in Europe* (1961); *The Mother Who Works outside the Home* (1961); and *Life at the Bottom* (1965). She also wrote three "river books" for young people; *The Nile, Lifeline of*

Egypt (1964); *The Jordan, River of the Promised Land* (1967); and *The Ganges, Sacred River of India* (1969).

In 1968, Weingarten published her first novel, *Mrs. Beneker*, a witty account of a well-to-do suburban woman who, in her late forties (with children grown), sallies forth to pursue higher education and confront the burning social and political issues of the day. Impressed by the intricate and clearly authentic depiction of a woman intent on expanding her domestic horizons, one reviewer announced that "Mrs. Beneker is Mrs. America at mid-century."

Weingarten published three additional novels in the next eight years, all written in a meticulously lucid prose style and all centered on a Mrs. Beneker-like character, that is, a wife and mother—middle-aged, affluent, Jewish (highly assimilated), and "decent to the bone"—who is trying to take a human measure of her life and times. In *A Loving Wife* (1969), forty-two-year-old Molly Gilbert misses her son at college and feels "a kind of free-floating discontent" with a husband overinvolved in his work. In *A Woman of Feeling* (1972), Jo Baer, politically radical in her youth but now a middle-aged, middle-class liberal, is caught up in a generational struggle with her counterculture son and her socially aware daughter, who feels guilty about giving birth to her own child when there are so many needy children seeking adoption. In *Half a Marriage* (1976), the perfect couple is threatened by the husband's affair with a younger woman.

Weingarten's last book, *Intimations of Mortality* (1978), a *journal account of her two-year battle with cancer, was published posthumously. Heartbreaking and haunting, it is also transcendent in that Weingarten's unflinching honesty and generosity of spirit infuse every page.

• The *New York Times* (18 July 1976). *Publisher's Weekly* (26 July 1976).

Jacqueline Berke

WELD, Angelina Grimké. *See* Grimké, Sarah Moore and Angelina Grimké Weld.

WELLS, Helena, later Whitford (1760?–1824?), novelist and educator. Helena Wells was born in Charleston, South Carolina; her mother was Scottish and her father a Loyalist bookseller and publisher. Fleeing the imminent American Revolution, the family moved to England in 1774 or 1775. In 1789, Wells and her sister, Louisa, opened a boarding school for girls in London. Wells had retired by the time her first novel was published in 1798. Conflicting sources suggest she left the school either because of poor health or to become a private governess. Wells lived for a time in Yorkshire, married a man named Whitford in 1801, and bore four children, becoming ill after delivering her last child in 1806. The exact date of her death is unknown.

Well's fictional heroines fulfill certain gender *stereotypes while defying others. For instance, in Wells's first novel, *The Step-Mother* (1798), her orphan heroine mindfully fulfills her duties to her stepchildren, but in order to do so, she fires her lawyer and handles her own finances when her husband dies. Although Wells believed in women's independence of thought and pocketbook, she was not an ardent promoter of women's political rights. In her second novel, *Constantia Neville, or the West Indian* (1800), she even includes a criticism of Mary Wollstonecraft's *Vindication of the Rights of Women* (1792).

Wells's two other published works were nonfictional didactic treatises dedicated to her primary interest, women's *education. Wells advocated "religious practical education" that prepared women to handle their own finances, to communicate well, and to be "sensible and virtuous." *Letters on Subjects of Importance to the Happiness of Young Females* (1799), a series of epistles addressed to her students, outlines specific topics including "courteous demeanor" and "correct pronunciation and judicious choice of words." Both in *Letters* and in her final work, *Thoughts and Remarks on Establishing an Institution for the Education of Unportioned Respectable Females* (1809), Wells reveals her abiding concern for grammar and usage. In *Thoughts*, Wells criticizes uneducated teachers for "murdering" the English language, and proposes as a remedy the foundation of a women's teacher-training college to be sponsored by the Episcopal Church. *Thoughts* is, in effect, a manual for setting up such an institution, covering everything from physical plans for the buildings and grounds to subjects for instruction and recommendations for students' diet and exercise. Wells's proposals that all students should participate in the physical maintenance of the school, that tuition should be based on the student's financial standing, and that governesses should be rewarded "in proportion to what is generally awarded to a tutor of sons," reveal her ongoing awareness of and attention to the material bases of gender inequalities, both educational and cultural.

• Alexander Cowie, *The Rise of the American Novel* (1948). James A. Levernier and Douglas R. Wilmes, eds., *American Writers before 1800*, vol. 3 (1983). Janet Todd, ed., *A Dictionary of British and American Women Writers: 1660–1800* (1985). Cathy N. Davidson, *Revolution and the Word: The Rise of the Novel in America*

(1986). Virginia Blain, Patricia Clements, and Isobel Grundy, eds., *The Feminist Companion to Literature in English: Women Writers from the Middle Ages to the Present* (1990).

Catherine Taylor

WELLS-BARNETT, Ida B. (1862–1931), newspaper editor, antilynching campaigner, women's rights activist, lecturer, clubwoman. A schoolteacher turned newspaperwoman, Wells-Barnett committed her writing to the *antilynching cause in 1892 when Thomas Moss, a friend of hers, was lynched in Memphis because whites deemed that he was too outspoken and his business was too profitable to be owned by a black man. Wells wrote of the event in her newspaper, *The Free Speech and Headlight*, and advised blacks to leave Memphis for the West. After three months of exodus and editorials, Wells finally commented on the "thread bare lie" that black men raped white women, which had become the ostensible cause for lynching. Whites responded by burning her newspaper office, running her business manager out of town, and threatening to kill her if she returned to Memphis (she was vacationing in New York at the time).

Becoming even more committed to showing that economic and political justifications spawned more lynching than *rape did, Wells was uncompromising in uncovering brutality and in urging progressive Americans to bring about much-needed changes. She produced a seven-column article for T. Thomas Fortune's *The New York Age*, which she expanded and published in 1892 as *Southern Horrors: Lynch Law in All Its Phases;* the pamphlet included case studies of lynchings and offered "names, dates, and places of many lynchings for alleged rape." She continued her campaign against lynching with the publication in 1895 of *A Red Record: Tabulated Statistics and Alleged Causes of Lynching in the United States, 1892–1893–1894.* It was even more explicit in asserting that lynchings resulted when white women who willingly dated black men were caught and then screamed rape.

For a brief period in 1893 and for a more expanded time in 1894, Wells took her crusade to England in an effort to bring the influence she garnered there to bear on the lynching situation in the United States. A series of letters on her reception in England were published by the *Chicago Inter-Ocean.* Her last work on lynching was *Mob Rule in New Orleans*, published in 1900.

The daughter of slaves, Ida B. Wells was born in Holly Springs, Mississippi, on 16 July 1862. The oldest of eight children, she assumed responsibility for her surviving siblings when both her parents and the youngest child died in a yellow fever epidemic in 1878. Her attendance at Shaw University (later Rust College) had given her enough training to become a teacher, the profession she used to keep her family together until 1883, when the family was divided and she moved to Memphis to secure a better job.

Her refusal to accept second-class citizenship in America surfaced early. In Memphis in 1884, she refused to move from a regular passenger car on a train to the smoking car, where blacks were expected to ride. Bodily removed by the conductor and two white male passengers, she sued the railroad and won a five-hundred-dollar settlement, only to have a higher court reverse the lower court's decision.

In 1887, she submitted articles to a church newspaper, which led to her journalistic work and editorship of the Memphis *Free Speech and Headlight* (later *Free Speech*). Her articles critical of the "colored" schools in Memphis led to her dismissal as a teacher in 1891, and she became a full-time newspaperwoman. While antilynching work certainly required a major portion of her energy, she was also involved in the *women's club movement and other political issues central to African-American communities. With her relocation from Memphis to Chicago, she became involved in several projects there. When blacks were excluded from the Chicago World's Fair of 1893, Wells urged Frederick Douglass and others to join her in publishing *The Reason Why the Colored American Is Not in the World's Columbian Exposition.* She founded the Ida B. Wells Club of Chicago, and she served as a probation officer for young black men in Chicago. She also offered assistance to blacks migrating from the South into Chicago, and she was instrumental in the founding of the Chicago chapter of the NAACP.

Wells was married to Ferdinand L. Barnett, a Chicago lawyer, on 27 June 1895, and for a number of years she successfully combined careers as wife, mother, and *activist. She gave birth to two sons and two daughters and would take her babies on lecture engagements with the expectation that the local sponsors would provide the necessary child care for her. Wells completed an autobiography before she died on 25 March 1931.

Although a federal measure, the Dyer Anti-Lynching bill, was introduced in Congress many times, it never received enough support to pass. This failure was not due in any part to Wells-Barnett's lack of vigilance. As writer, lecturer, and surrogate lawyer, she fought to eradicate the evil of lynching from American society. The clarity of her vision and the power of her pen give her a place among the many black women writers, such as Anna Julia

*Cooper and Frances Ellen Watkins *Harper, who were intent upon showing the American public that black women too could use words effectively to transform the social and political situation of African Americans in the last decade of the nineteenth century.

• Ida B. Wells-Barnett's daughter, Alfreda M. Duster, edited and published Wells-Barnett's autobiography, *Crusade for Justice: The Autobiography of Ida B. Wells* (1970). Mildred I. Thompson, *Ida B. Wells-Barnett: An Exploratory Study of an American Black Woman, 1893–1930* (1990). Trudier Harris, comp., *Selected Works of Ida B. Wells-Barnett* (1991).

Trudier Harris

WELTY, Eudora (b. 1909), novelist, essayist, and short fiction writer. Born in Jackson, Mississippi, Eudora Welty was the only daughter and the eldest of three surviving children born to Christian Webb and Chestina Andrews Welty.

Her education included two years at the Mississippi State College for Women, completion of her B.A. at the University of Wisconsin in 1929, and courses in advertising at the Columbia University Graduate School of Business. These were cut short when her father became ill with leukemia and died in 1931. Welty returned to Mississippi, where she has lived ever since, and soon took a job as publicity agent for the Works Progress Administration (WPA), which allowed her to travel throughout the state and to pursue her hobby, photography. (In 1989 her book *Photographs* brought over two hundred of her "snapshots" to wide and appreciative public attention. The acuteness of perception and importance of the telling detail so characteristic of her stories are equally evident here.)

At the time of their marriage, Welty's father and mother made the unusual decision to leave their respective homes in Ohio and West Virginia to settle in Jackson, a location entirely new to them both. Reflected in Welty's fiction is a persistent concern with the experience of both outsiders and insiders, possibly resulting from her dual experience of the South's reluctant acceptance of newcomers and her lifelong residence there. Her earliest collection, *A Curtain of Green* (1941), emphasizes characters who live in isolation, whatever its cause, among them so many lonely people, misfits, and grotesque events (as in "Keela, the Outcast Indian Maiden," "Clytie," and "Petrified Man") that critics were quick to place her in the gothic tradition of Faulkner at his most bizarre.

Welty's fiction grew rapidly in sophistication during the 1940s. After a playful novella, *The Robber Bridegroom* (1942), that experimented with the genres of fairy tale, legend, and history, she published a second collection, *The Wide Net* (1943), in which she explored in greater depth her vision of the role of mystery in the human search for meaning. "First Love," "A Still Moment," and "The Winds" reveal Welty at her most subtle, evocative, and complex.

Delta Wedding (1946), Welty's first full-length novel, concerns events preceding a wedding in a large southern delta family and is the first of several texts reflecting a favorite theme: the gathering of families at such occasions as weddings, funerals, and reunions, when the characteristic dynamics of family relationships become, in Welty's view, most evident. These gatherings invariably entail a good deal of *sto-rytelling and allow Welty to express her fascination with the South's prevalent oral tradition. Her precision in depicting vernacular speech patterns and the dynamics of social interaction is a basic element in making her portrayals of southern life unforgettable.

Welty's own favorite among her works, a sequence of related stories entitled *The Golden Apples* (1949), is a tapestry of interwoven characters, incidents, images, and mythological allusions in which Welty continues her interest in wanderers and searchers and how they often fail to understand themselves enough to achieve their goals. Critics tend to agree that "June Recital," a key story in the collection, is one of the most beautifully rendered of American short stories, featuring the moving portrayal of a piano teacher whose ardent love for music causes her to place all of her hopes in the wrong pupil.

In 1954 Welty completed a light-hearted novella, *The Ponder Heart*, which she was soon to see brought to the New York stage. Another collection of stories, *The Bride of the Innisfallen*, followed in 1955, and then, for nearly fifteen years, no major work was published as Welty took on greater responsibility for her family, including her mother, who was ill for a long while preceding her death in 1966. Welty's imagination had been active, however: in 1970 she published *Losing Battles*, a loquacious comedy about a family reunion, and in 1972 she published *The Optimist's Daughter*, which was awarded the Pulitzer Prize. This novel, her most nearly autobiographical, explores themes and mythic allusions in ways that give it the intricacy of a well-wrought poem.

A collection of occasional pieces, *The Eye of the Story: Selected Essays and Reviews* (1978), shows Welty's critical perceptiveness and serves as a series of aesthetic statements that illuminate her own art. In 1984, three lectures Welty had given at Harvard on the childhood influences that led her to a career in writing were published in *One Writer's Beginnings,* a book that was on the *New York Times* best-seller list for forty-six weeks.

Welty and her fellow Mississippian, William Faulkner, wrote stories that reflected more closely and truly the experience of life in the South than had most writers before them. Each of their visions was unique, yet they reflected a power and vividness that seemed to authorize later writers in the region to recognize that truth was to be found in daily concerns, in the small, specific features of southern experience. Reynolds Price and Anne *Tyler, in particular, have said that the example of Welty's writing freed them to explore the immediate world about them. Thus, even as the nature of life in the South has rapidly changed, its many fine writers—especially Flannery *O'Connor and Carson *McCullers—have learned, and particularly from Welty, that the language, characters, and concerns of the South are valid materials for exploring universal human truths.

Welty has chosen in most of her fiction not to address directly the racial upheaval that tore apart the South and the country, especially in the 1960s. Her important essay "Must the Novelist Crusade?" is a response to those who felt southern writers must necessarily take a public position on contemporary social problems. She writes that the artist's task is to represent as faithfully as possible a vision and an understanding of life as it *is,* and she eschews the role of arguing what *ought to be* as not being the purview of a fiction writer. When *civil rights leader Medgar Evers was assassinated in Jackson in 1963, Welty wrote "Where Is the Voice Coming From?," a story that through its first-person narration by the murderer himself shows Welty's insight into the mindset of the type of southerner who reacts with violence to the prospect of integration. Welty's horror at the assassination led here (and in another fine story written a few years later, "The Demonstrators") to powerful examples of what she had meant about the artist making the complexities of life as she sees it comprehensible. Without a word of polemic, Welty makes vivid the distorted logic of the racist bigot.

The universal respect for Welty's achievement is reflected in an enormous number of awards, prizes, and honorary degrees given in recognition of her work. In addition to the Pulitzer Prize (1973), she has received Guggenheim Fellowships, several O. Henry Prizes for short fiction, the William Dean Howells Prize for Fiction, the National Institute of Arts and Letters Gold Medal, the President's Medal of Freedom, the National Medal for Literature, the Cleanth Brooks Medal, the Phi Beta Kappa Associates Award, the Common Wealth Award of the Modern Language Association, the American Book Award, the National Endowment for the Arts' National Medal of Arts, the Mississippi Institute of Arts and Letters Lifetime Achievement Award, the National Book Foundation Medal, the Peggy V. Helmerich Distinguished Author Award, and France's highest honor for a writer, the Chevalier de l'Ordre des Arts et Lettres—a particular favorite of Welty's because it constitutes knighthood.

One of the most celebrated of American writers, Eudora Welty lives alone and continues to write in her family home in Jackson. An intensely private person, she has chosen not to release most of her personal papers or to authorize a biography, feeling that her work should stand alone as the expression of her imagination.

• The most extensive collection of documents, photographs, and manuscripts on Welty is in the Mississippi Department of Archives and History in Jackson, and a second fine collection may be found at the Humanities Research Center at the University of Texas in Austin. See also Ruth Vande Kieft, *Eudora Welty* (1962), rev. ed. (1987). Eudora Welty, *The Collected Stories of Eudora Welty* (1980). Michael Kreyling, *Eudora Welty's Achievement of Order* (1980). Jennifer Lynn Randisi, *A Tissue of Lies: Eudora Welty and the Southern Romance* (1982). Albert J. Devlin, *Eudora Welty's Chronicle: A Story of Mississippi Life* (1983). Carol S. Manning, *With Ears Opening Like Morning Glories: Eudora Welty and the Love of Storytelling* (1985). Louise Westling, *Eudora Welty* (1989). Michael Kreyling, *Author and Agent: Eudora Welty and Diarmuid Russell* (1991). Peter Schmidt, *The Heart of the Story: Eudora Welty's Short Fiction* (1991).

Gail L. Mortimer

WEST, Dorothy (b. 1907), novelist, editor, and short-story writer. When she received an invitation to the 1926 *Opportunity* magazine writing awards dinner in New York, seventeen-year-old Dorothy West left her native Boston hopeful that she would win one of the coveted contest prizes and that her projected victory would launch her literary career. Her short-story entry, "The Typewriter," did indeed tie for second place with novelist-folklorist Zora Neale *Hurston's "Spunk," and though West was not the top prizewinner, her relative success convinced her parents that their daughter had enough talent to compete in the artistic renaissance then flourishing in Harlem. New York had long been West's idealized "Magic City" ever since she heard glamorous stories about it from composer Harry T. Burleigh, a family friend. Over the twenty years after she first came to New York, Dorothy West established herself as a competent writer of short stories and as founder and editor of two influential literary magazines, *Challenge* (1934–1936) and *New*

Challenge (1937). Later, after abandoning New York for Martha's Vineyard, she achieved her greatest literary success as author of the critically acclaimed autobiographical novel *The Living Is Easy* (1948).

West's short stories emphasize the irony of the black female urban experience, and many first appeared in *little magazines such as the *Messenger*, the *Saturday Evening Quill*, and *Opportunity*. From 1940 to 1960, she published about twenty-six stories in the *New York Daily News*, and in the 1980s, when the *News* donated its old files to the New York Public Library, these stories became property of the latter. West's editing career began in 1933, after a year-long trip to Soviet Russia, when she used forty dollars of her own to found the literary magazine *Challenge*, which ran for six issues before folding because of financial difficulties. She immediately followed this effort with *New Challenge* which, together with its predecessor, published original work by such Harlem Renaissance luminaries as Langston Hughes and James Weldon Johnson, and such younger writers as Ralph Ellison and Richard Wright. Indeed, Wright also coedited with West the one and only issue of *New Challenge*, which also fell prey to money problems. Thus, through her own writing, editing, and publishing, Dorothy West captured and embraced the aesthetic spirit and energy of the *Harlem Renaissance.

In 1945, after the Harlem Renaissance had long since exhausted itself, West left New York permanently for Martha's Vineyard, where she wrote her only published novel, *The Living Is Easy*. It originally appeared in 1948 and was reprinted in 1982 by the Feminist Press with an informative afterword by Adelaide M. Cromwell. West's South Carolina-bred mother, Rachel Pease Benson West, serves as the prototype for Cleo Judson, the novel's heroine; her blue-eyed father Isaac Christopher West for Cleo's husband Bart Judson; social activist and editor of the *Boston Guardian* Monroe Trotter for Simeon Binney; and West herself for Judy Judson. In describing the relationship between Cleo Judson and her daughter Judy, West virtually outlines a subconscious paradigm followed by many African-American mothers of tremendous strength, meanness, anger, frustration, imagination, and vitality. Unexpectedly, it educates as well as spiritually strengthens and sustains their dark-skinned young daughters in a society especially hostile to black females.

Most of the recent critical discussion about Dorothy West focuses on her novel and especially the protagonist Cleo Judson who, like Lillian Taylor of Chester Himes's novel *Third Generation* (1954), is marked by her capacity to destroy her family. Cleo's destructive behavior, however, stems more from a perverted love for her family than from the sort of deep-seated hatred that characterizes Lillian Taylor. Cleo's six-year-old daughter Judy serves as a foil to her destructive mother and watches impassively as Cleo breaks up the marriages of her sisters in order to compensate for a misconceived maternal rejection. On a personal level, *The Living Is Easy* becomes a means through which West tries to resolve her own conflicting feelings of admiration and anger toward Rachel West, with whom Dorothy West and other family members sparred for years because of the mother's penchant for interfering with their lives. Apparently, West's literary attempt at conflict resolution was successful. In an essay entitled "My Mother, Rachel West," published in *Invented Lives: Narratives of Black Women 1860–1960* (1987) after the death of Rachel West, Dorothy West reassesses their relationship and concludes that "some part of her was forever imbedded in our psyches, and we were not the worst [*sic*] for it."

• The Dorothy West Papers are held at the Mugar Memorial Library, Boston University; some earlier writings are part of the James Weldon Johnson Collection, Yale University. See also Walter C. Daniel, "Challenge Magazine: An Experiment That Failed," *College Language Association Journal* 19 (June 1976): 494–503. Mary Helen Washington, "I Sign My Mother's Name: Alice Walker, Dorothy West, Paule Marshall," in *Mothering the Mind: Twelve Studies of Writers and Their Silent Partners*, eds. Ruth Perry and Martine Watson Brownley (1984), pp. 142–163. Mary Helen Washington, "I Sign My Mother's Name: Maternal Power in Dorothy West's Novel, *The Living Is Easy*" in *Invented Lives: Narratives of Black Women 1860–1960* (1987), pp. 344–353. SallyAnn H. Ferguson. "Dorothy West," in *Dictionary of Literary Biography*, vol. 76, eds. Trudier Harris and Thadious Davis (1988), pp. 187–195.

SallyAnn H. Ferguson

WESTERN WOMEN'S WRITING. Literature by women in the American West began with the oral stories of indigenous women. The songs, stories, and legends women transmitted to their children constituted a cultural tradition, especially in matrilineal tribes such as the Pueblo Indians.

Starting in the second half of the nineteenth century, their writings—or the "as told to" accounts rendering aspects of their heritage—were inevitably shaped by the expectations of white male publishers. Because Native Americans were almost universally driven from their homelands, dispossessed, and massacred, writing became a means to perpetuate tradition in the face of cultural disintegration. Early examples of telling their side of the story include *Life Among the Piutes* (1883) by Sarah Winnemucca *Hopkins and *Old Indian Legends* (1901) by

*Zitkala-Ša, a Dakota Sioux. The first novel by an American Indian woman is *Cogewea—The Half-Blood: A Depiction of the Great Montana Cattle Range* (1927) by *Humishuma (Mourning Dove), born in Idaho in 1888.

The flowering of literature by Indian women did not come until the women's movement of the late 1960s and the 1970s, when many writers saw feminism as including a search for heritage as well as for a universal female voice. Writers presented narratives from past traditions: Kay Bennett Kaibah's *Recollections of a Navajo Girlhood* (1964), Elizabeth Cook-Lynn's *Then Badger Said This* (1977), Elizabeth Sullivan's *Indian Legends of the Trail of Tears and Other Stories* (1974), Judith Ivaloo Volborth's *Thunder-Root* (1977). Others challenged contemporary problems, often in the context of feminism, or gave special emphasis to language. Paula Gunn *Allen, Joy Harjo, Anita Endrezze-Danielson, Wendy Rose, Marnie Walsh, and other poets note that preliterate societies privilege the power of the word and that integral to the context is an audience to hear the story. Laguna novelist Leslie Marmon *Silko says in *Ceremony* (1977), "You don't have anything if you don't have the stories."

The writings of Native American women are filled with recurring images of land and landscapes, perhaps symbolic of all that has been lost, or a combination of the sense of loss and of hope, the power of survival.

The Spanish explorers of the sixteenth century brought their ballads, legends, and language, including *journals, diaries, and *autos*, religious plays passed on in the oral tradition. Written literature by women of Spanish or Mexican ancestry was slow to be accepted: these women were occupied with other work, their education was limited, and there were neither publishers nor market. Although a few writers were published in journals early in the century, books in English by Hispanic women did not appear until the mid-twentieth century: Fabiola Cabeza de Baca, Jovita Gonzáles, Josephine *Niggli, and Nina Otero all recognized that the spirit of a people resides in its folk beliefs and expressions.

The Chicano movement created and in part was created by the literary movements of the 1960s. Chicana writers typically use bilingual styles to present *folklore and legends, to further social protest, and to discuss their cultural positions. Their context is a long history that includes considerable political conflict and discrimination against them by other groups. The poetry of protest was the first genre to emerge, and poets have continued to examine *ethnicity and culture and to experiment with language. Chicana poets in the West such as Lorna Dee

*Cervantes, Sandra *Cisneros, Alicia Gaspar de Alba, Sylvia Alicia Gonzáles, Angela de Hoyos, Judy Lucero, Cherríe *Moraga, Victoria Moreno, Marina Rivera, Carmen Tafolla, Inés Hernández Tovar, and Marcela Christine Lucero-Trujillo have provided historical awareness and inspiration. Short fiction writers and dramatists include Gloria *Anzaldúa, Denise Chávez, Guadalupe Valdés Fallis, and Estela *Portillo-Trambley. Novelists have had a harder task in pleasing both Chicano and Anglo publishers and reaching a wide audience.

Travel books, journals, and diaries of westering white women comprise the beginning of western literature written in English, and contemporary scholars edit accounts and collect women's oral histories of mining camps, ranching, and pioneer life in general. Early writers who made successful use of western settings in their fiction include Helen Hunt *Jackson (*Ramona*, 1884), Mary *Austin (*The Land of Little Rain*, 1903), and Elizabeth Robins (*The Magnetic North*, 1904). Perhaps the best-known novels associated with place are Willa *Cather's *O Pioneers!* (1913), *My Ántonia* (1918), and *Death Comes for the Archbishop* (1927). Katherine Anne *Porter's short stories typically have southwestern settings; novelist Valerie Miner uses San Francisco. The contemporary writers who most often use a specific locale are the mystery writers: Sue Grafton's southern California, Marcia Muller's San Francisco, Katherine Forrest's Los Angeles, Barbara Wilson's Seattle, Antoinette Azolakov's Austin.

Women writers of the West Coast repeatedly suggest that the influence of the western setting is far-reaching. Novelist Jessamyn West and poet Josephine Miles respond consistently to the openness of a land where earth and sky meet. Several writers speak of the special social and political forces found in the West: Kay *Boyle, Tillie *Olsen, Susan Griffin, Judy *Grahn, and *Alta, for example, are associated with the antiwar and feminist movements of the seventies in the Bay area. Janet Lewis speaks of the appeal of the physical climate; science fiction writer Ursula *Le Guin says California has influenced her totally and utterly. Women writers have promoted the creation of independent presses and minority and regional journals in the West, such as Spokane poet Carolyn *Kizer's founding and editorship of *Poetry Northwest*.

*Asian Americans of the West Coast have been subjected to the control of immigration policies for a century, but especially since the feminist and *civil rights movements of the 1960s, these women's voices have emerged, contrasting a fabled cultural homeland with the present landscape and culture. Maxine Hong

*Kingston combines *autobiography with fiction in *The Woman Warrior* (1976). Other noted writers include Genny Lim, Laureen Mar, Janice *Mirikitani, Jade Snow *Wong, Nellie Wong, Hisaye *Yamamoto, Karen Tei Yamashita, and Wakako *Yamauchi.

Given the presence of minority women and the history of pioneering white women, much of the literature of women in the West invokes a determined will, persistence in the face of obstacles. Contemporary writers are the inheritors of a vigorous emphasis on language and the power of the word and continuing creators of an oral tradition. The relatively recent settlement as well as the physical landscape of space and openness add to the sense of possibility, of change, rather than adherence to a fixed and bound tradition.

It is the landscape of the region itself, from the plains to the mountains to the Pacific coast—and the big sky above—that most unites the voices of western women writers. However diverse their styles and life experiences, however distinct their messages, virtually all of the writers include a sense of place, for the American West is a vast and alluring region both in itself and in the cultural imagination of the world.

[*See also* Exploration Narratives; Frontier Writing; Native American Writing; Pioneer Writing; Regionalism.]

• Dexter Fisher, ed., *The Third Woman: Minority Women Writers of the United States* (1980). Cherríe Moraga and Gloria Anzaldúa, eds., *This Bridge Called My Back: Writings by Radical Women of Color* (1981). Marilyn Yalom, ed., *Women Writers of the West Coast* (1983). Vicki Piekarski, ed., *Westward the Women: An Anthology of Western Stories by Women*, 2d ed. (1988). Paula Gunn Allen, ed., *Spider Woman's Granddaughters: Traditional Tales and Contemporary Writing by Native American Women* (1989). Asian Women United of California, eds., *Making Waves: An Anthology of Writings by Asian-American Women* (1989). Amy Ling, *Between Worlds: Women Writers of Chinese Ancestry* (1990).

Lois A. Marchino

WETHERELL, Elizabeth. *See* Warner, Susan.

WHARTON, Edith (1862–1937), novelist and writer of short fiction, was born into the carefully guarded upper ranks of New York society. Both her father's and mother's lineage secured her a place in the New York Four Hundred (the size of which was determined by the capacity of Mrs. Vanderbilt's ballroom). Wharton would publish over thirty-five book-length works in her career as a writer, including eighty-six *short stories, eleven collections of short fiction, twenty-two works of longer fiction (both novels and novellas), two collections of poetry, books on architecture and gardens, *travel books (in-

cluding an account of the destruction along the French front while World War I was still being fought), a critical study called *The Writing of Fiction*, and an *autobiography, *A Backward Glance*. The rumors spread by some of her contemporaries that her brother's tutor had really been her father were part of a family romance invented to explain how such a remarkable novelist and intellectual could have been produced by such unimaginative parents and the New York aristocracy. The idea that a daughter of this set would become a writer was perhaps too bizarre to be imagined. Aside from Washington Irving, the chronicler of early New York and its Dutch settlers, few writers of fiction emerged from the nineteenth-century elite society into which Edith Newbold Jones made her debut.

Wharton was distantly related to Herman Melville, but he was considered a bohemian by the socially conservative denizens of Wharton's Old New York, where writing was considered to be somewhere between manual labor and the occult arts. In the nineteenth century, novelists—especially the growing number of influential female novelists—came from the settled ranks of the middle classes. Literature seemed to be the province of clergymen's daughters in particular—for example, Jane Austen, George Eliot, and Harriet Beecher *Stowe. The privileged world of Wharton's family devoted its leisure time to social rituals, which (in novels such as *The Custom of the Country* and *The Age of Innocence*) Wharton would describe as tribal practices incompatible with art. In the years following the *Civil War, a financial crisis caused the Joneses (like other families of their set) to move abroad, where they could live more cheaply. Between the ages of four and ten, in Paris and Florence, in German watering places and a still exotic Spain, Wharton was transformed by European culture and traditions. She would later insist that after she returned to New York at the age of ten, she "never felt otherwise than as in exile in America."

Wharton's mother, Lucretia Jones, represented the most repressive aspects of the American aristocratic class code. Yet despite her disapproval of her child's narrative aspirations, she did try to transcribe the stories that her precocious young daughter invented in an obsessive ritual called "making-up" in which the young Edith, although unable to read, would improvise stories as she stood holding a book. Wharton would later recall having had only two ambitions when she was a child: to be, like her mother, the best-dressed woman in New York, and to be a writer. She describes being caught between two opposing impulses, the desire "to make . . . pictures prettier" and the necessity of telling the truth, which she increasingly associated with books. Intellectually isolated during the "moral tortures" of her childhood, Wharton balanced her fears and attenuated her loneliness through the reading and writing that became the basis for what she would later describe as her "real life."

These conflicting polarities were intensely gendered. The world of decorative surfaces and politeness was ruled by her mother, whom she saw as standing in direct opposition to a darker masculine power called "God," which demanded the revelation of painful truths. These powerful oppositions between surface and depth, concealment and revelation, became in Wharton's work the codes for distinguishing between what she saw as the prettiness of sentimentalist fiction and the structural clarity of realist writing. At the age of fifteen she secretly wrote a thirty thousand-word novella called *Fast and Loose* under the pseudonym of Mr. Olivieri, accompanied by a savage review conceived for *The Nation* that compared the author to "a sick sentimental school-girl who has begun her work with a fierce and bloody resolve to make it as bad as Wilhelm Meister, Consuelo, and 'Goodbye Sweetheart' together."

When Wharton was sixteen, her mother had her poetry printed anonymously in a gesture that may have been meant to mark an end to such youthful pursuits. Fearing that she was becoming unattractively bookish, her parents hastened her debut into New York society just prior to her seventeenth birthday. When she married the sports-loving Teddy Wharton in 1885 at the age of twenty-three, Edith Wharton assumed the role of a young society matron. In 1889, she published three poems, and her first story appeared in *Scribner's* in 1891. In 1897 (with the architect Ogden Codman), she published *The Decoration of Houses*, which sought to elevate this field from the demeaning realm of dressmaking and ally it instead with architecture. In 1898, Wharton had a nervous breakdown; the prescribed cure, which required four months in almost complete isolation, released her from her exhausting life in society and resulted in a creative breakthrough that culminated in the publication of her first collection of stories, *The Greater Inclination*, in 1899. She described this as an event that broke "the chains that had held me for so long in a kind of torpor. For nearly twelve years, I had tried to adjust myself to my marriage; but now I was overmastered by the longing to meet people who shared my interests." Determined to write every day, Wharton began to live the life of a disciplined writer.

Wharton set her first novel, *The Valley of Decision* (1902), in eighteenth-century Italy. Critics complained that the characters were wooden and less important than the rich details about architecture, art, and religious and philosophical controversies. Henry James recommended that Wharton should "Do New York!," that she "must be tethered in native pastures, even if it reduces her to a backyard in New York." Wharton subsequently "did New York" in *The House of Mirth*. The serial publication of this best-selling novel taught Wharton the discipline of writing for deadlines and offered encouragement from a public impatient for each installment. Wharton's most powerful work as a novelist began with the publication of *The House of Mirth* in 1905 and closed with the publication of her Pulitzer Prize-winning novel, *The Age of Innocence*, in 1921. With *The Custom of the Country* (1913), the bitterly satirical novel that Wharton would call her "masterpiece," these novels contain Wharton's most devastating critiques of New York society. Declaring that a frivolous society may be judged by the value of what it destroys, Wharton chronicled in *The House of Mirth* the commodification and destruction of her heroine, Lily Bart.

In *The Custom of the Country*, Wharton shifted the source of destruction to a marauding heroine from the interior of America as the devouring Undine Spragg invades Old New York, an embattled world of tradition that Wharton calls "the Reservation." With her silver initials U.S. emblazoned on her pigeon-blood-colored stationary, Undine represents the nationalist and predatory aspects of her native country as she moves east from Manhattan to threaten the culture of the French aristocracy. Ellen Olenska of *The Age of Innocence* returns home from the old world of Europe to what she imagines is the more straightforward world represented by the allegorically named characters Newland Archer and May Welland. A historical novel that treats the world of Wharton's childhood, an "age of innocence" prior to the Great War, this novel reveals the tribal rituals of New York society as its members confirm their bonds by excluding a cousin who seems to bear the taint of European knowledge and experience.

These years in which Wharton produced her finest novels were also a difficult period of her life. Wharton had ceased having sexual relations with her husband after the first few weeks of their marriage—she would later admit that she had not known about sexual intercourse before she was married. At the age of forty-six, in the midst of a series of changes in her life, she began a passionate, yet finally unfulfilling, love affair with the journalist Morton Fullerton. In 1911, she separated from her husband and America, selling the New England home which she had built in 1902. Wharton, whom James had called "the great and glorious pendulum" because of her habitual trans-Atlantic crossings, became a permanent resident of France, where she would remain until her death twenty-six years later, returning to America only in 1913, the year of her French divorce, and briefly in 1923, when she received an honorary degree from Yale. During the war in France, Wharton organized relief efforts for the refugees and orphans displaced by the advancing German army. In 1916, Wharton was named a Chevalier of the Legion of Honor, the highest honor given to a foreigner in France.

In 1912, Wharton published *The Reef*, a novel about Americans living in France. Yet during this period she also wrote her New England novels *Ethan Frome* (1911) and *Summer* (1917). In these related works—*Ethan Frome* in its earliest version written in French was called "Hiver," and she referred to *Summer* as the "Hot Ethan"—Wharton explored a psychic landscape ruled by primal forces. One of her most autobiographical works, *Ethan Frome* can be seen as a terrifying description of what her life might have been like if she had not divorced her invalid husband. This purgatory, where a wounded man seems trapped in a New England farmhouse burdened by sickly and complaining women, is transformed in *Summer*, which Wharton wrote while surrounded by the destruction of the Great War. In her most lyrical and erotic novel, Wharton rewrites the story of virgin death, which destroyed the attractive female figures in *The House of Mirth* and *Ethan Frome*. Although troubling because the heroine ends up marrying the man who adopted her, *Summer* tells the story of inevitable fertility and the struggle to preserve human life. *Ethan Frome* and *Summer* also represent Wharton's ambivalent dialogue with the best of the domestic realists and the female local colorists, including Sarah Orne * Jewett and Mary Wilkins * Freeman, as she tried to imagine the fate of women and women's stories in America. In the 1920s, Wharton wrote a number of novels concerned with maternal questions, the best of which are *The Mother's Recompense* (1925) and *The Children* (1928). This group of novels is generally regarded as Wharton's weakest work; its subjects are criticized for seeming tailored to the tastes of the women's magazines of the period.

In her last completed novels, *Hudson River Bracketed* (1929) and *The Gods Arrive* (1932), Wharton attempts to tell the story of the American artist by chronicling the career of the writer Vance Weston who comes East to encounter both the past and fashionable literary movements. Although Wharton included this two volume opus among her personal favorites,

these novels are most interesting in the context of her ongoing effort to imagine the place and story of the American writer. From the publication of *The Touchstone* (1900), her first longer work of fiction, Wharton was concerned with the fate of the woman writer. In "Copy" (1901) a successful woman novelist describes herself as "a monster manufactured out of newspaper paragraphs, with ink in its veins" whose "keen sense of copyright is my nearest approach to an emotion." Both of these works depict the isolation of successful women novelists; both, like Wharton, have authored works called "Pomegranate Seed," evoking Wharton's lifelong identification of the woman writer with Persephone. The association of the woman writer with death is also apparent in Wharton's * ghost stories, which include some of her finest work in her last years. *Ghosts*, published posthumously in 1937, the year of Wharton's death, depicts female figures who are abandoned or imprisoned. Although many of the stories focus on strangling and silencing, some tell of women who are rescued from isolation and * silence long after their deaths by people who discover and decode their stories from written texts. The ghost stories provide a profound and psychically revealing account of Wharton's understanding of the place of the woman and the woman writer.

When Wharton published *The Reef*, James congratulated her by calling it Racinean, but others commended the novel by calling it Jamesian. From the beginning of her career, Wharton suffered in near silence praise from critics who could place her only as a female Henry James. Judged according to her * class background and condescended to because of her sex, Wharton has only recently begun to be appreciated as one of the most productive and gifted American writers of her generation. Deeply influenced by both American and European literature, including the classics, Wharton during her lifetime was a powerful presence to her contemporaries. Elizabeth Ammons argues that women "like Wharton, * Cather, and * Stein" were "the real giants against whom" writers such as Fitzgerald and Hemingway "needed to define themselves;" Wharton must also be considered among those Ammons refers to as the "turn-of-the century women writers [who] were imitated by Theodore Dreiser, Sherwood Anderson, and Sinclair Lewis." Categories such as realist, naturalist, or even sentimentalist describe different aspects of her work, but these terms are not adequate to describe her writing. By birth and inclination, Wharton was fated to occupy two worlds: not only Europe and America, but also, and perhaps equally dramatically, the nineteenth and twentieth centuries.

Her life began with the Civil War and ended on the eve of World War II. A culminating figure associated with the traditional and the past, Wharton is also particularly modern in her efforts to understand the place of women, artists, and America in the twentieth century.

• Blake Nevius, *Edith Wharton: A Study of Her Fiction* (1953). R. W. B. Lewis, *Edith Wharton: A Biography* (1975). Cynthia Griffin Wolff, *A Feast of Words: The Triumph of Edith Wharton* (1977). Elizabeth Ammons, *Edith Wharton's Argument with America* (1980). Sandra Gilbert, "Life's Empty Pack: Notes Toward a Literary Daughteronomy," *Critical Inquiry* 3, no. 11 (March 1985): 355–384. Elaine Showalter, "The Death of the Lady (Novelist): Wharton's *House of Mirth*," *Representations* 9 (Winter 1985): 133–149. Judith Fryer, *Felicitous Spaces: The Imaginative Structures of Edith Wharton and Willa Cather* (1987). R. W. B. Lewis and Nancy Lewis, eds., *The Letters of Edith Wharton* (1988). Josephine Donovan, *After the Fall: The Demeter-Persephone Myth in Wharton, Cather, and Glasgow* (1989). Susan Goodman, *Edith Wharton's Women: Friends and Rivals* (1990). Elizabeth Ammons, *Conflicting Stories: American Women Writers at the Turn into the Twentieth Century* (1991). Candace Waid, *Edith Wharton's Letters from the Underworld: Fictions of Women and Writing* (1991). Gloria Ehrlich, *The Sexual Education of Edith Wharton* (1992).

Candace Waid

WHEATLEY, Phillis (1753?–1784), poet and the first significant African-American writer. Wheatley arrived in Boston from West Africa on 11 July 1761 as a slave when she was about eight years old and was bought by John Wheatley, a Boston merchant. Little work was required of her, and from Mrs. Wheatley and her daughter she received a good education, even learning Latin. The Wheatleys were quite religious and Phillis became a pious Christian also, which is reflected in much of her poetry. Her abilities gained her increasingly wide recognition in Boston, especially after she began writing poetry at about age twelve. She was well acquainted with the works of Vergil, Horace, Ovid, Terence, and various English poets, especially Alexander Pope (and through Pope's translations, Homer). From these came certain influences on her poetry, especially the use of the neoclassical couplet and various classical subjects, allusions, and conventions.

In the spring of 1773, both for her frail health and in relation to publication of her book, she sailed to England with the Wheatleys' son. There she met many people important in religion, government, and society, and acquired books, including the works of Pope and John Milton. She would perhaps have been there when her book was published, but the dire ill health of Mrs. Wheatley led to Phillis's return to Boston on 13 September, sooner than had been planned. In the fall of 1773 after her return

to Boston, she was legally freed but remained in the Wheatley home. March 1774 saw the death of Mrs. Wheatley, Phillis's friend and protector who had also been the primary encourager and promoter of her poetry.

The location of the Wheatley house gave the poet easy witness to much that went on in Boston, including various events of the emerging American Revolution, which is reflected in a number of Wheatley's poems from that period. While her primary sympathies were for the patriots and the Revolution, she also maintained Loyalist and British contacts. With the British occupation of Boston in 1775, the Wheatleys fled the city, and from Providence, Rhode Island, Phillis Wheatley sent her George Washington poem to him. By the time she married John Peters on 1 April 1778, many of those who had befriended Wheatley were dead or departed, and Peters seems to have separated her from others, even moving his family to Wilmington, Massachusetts, during the early 1780s. Apparently her later years were full of personal, financial, and familial hardships. Though she had three children, her last surviving one was buried with her after her death in Boston on 5 December 1784.

During her lifetime Wheatley published at least forty-six poems and wrote a good many more, at least nine of which have also been recently published. We have twenty-two of her letters (1770–1779), and we know of others. Her earliest poem we know of is from 1765, and apparently her earliest published poem appeared in December 1767. Her 1770 poem on the death of the famous British preacher George Whitefield brought her wide recognition in both America and Britain, and in 1772 there was an attempt to publish a volume of her poems in Boston. However, with hope for more prestige and better financial return and with the encouragement and help of British religious acquaintances of the Wheatleys (especially the Countess of Huntingdon), her *Poems on Various Subjects, Religious and Moral* (also containing her portrait) was published in London in September 1773, the first book of poetry published by an African American. There were failed attempts in 1779 and 1784 to publish another volume of her poems.

Although many of her poems were written upon particular occasions (especially deaths) and often have religious emphases, there also are poetic focuses on such subjects as the American Revolution, Niobe, *education, *friendship, recollection, patronage, virtue, imagination, morning, evening, and a young African-American painter. Though her poetry does not often speak of *slavery and its wrongs, she did not ignore them, which is demonstrated in some poems and also in her letters. While the dominant mode in her poetry is neoclassical, there also is evidence to suggest some interest in other directions. More and more attention is being paid to what her works can reveal about her and themselves and how they relate to various concerns and newer ideas of both her time and ours (such as the sublime, romanticism, politics, *slavery and racial concerns, and *feminism). Though not now considered a poet of the first rank, Wheatley was more of that rank in her own times; and she remains of historical, aesthetic, and other interest both for African-American literature and for American literature as a whole.

• William H. Robinson, *Phillis Wheatley in the Black American Beginnings* (1975). William H. Robinson, *Phillis Wheatley: A Bio-Bibliography* (1981). William H. Robinson, ed., *Critical Essays on Phillis Wheatley* (1982). William H. Robinson, *Phillis Wheatley and Her Writings* (1984). John C. Shields, ed., *The Collected Works of Phillis Wheatley* (1988). Julian D. Mason, Jr., ed., *The Poems of Phillis Wheatley*, revised and enlarged edition (1989).

Julian Mason

WHITENESS. In many cultures, *racism manifests itself as *prejudice toward and/or discrimination against groups whose ethnic genealogy differs from that of the group that holds the reigns of power. In America, racists have taken "whiteness" to be the normative human condition, as expressed in their prejudice against various or sometimes all nonwhite groups. Ironically, contemporary antiracist or multicultural critics sometimes fall too easily into *identity politics, which can also relegate the nonwhite subject to the position of (racial) *Other. The result is literary Jim Crowism, where the categories "American literature" and "*African-American literature" exist separately but presumably not equally, a labeling analogous to (and as dubious as) that of "American literature" versus "women's literature." In either case, the implication is that the writing, whether by women of color or nonwhites of either gender, is somehow not truly American. "Whiteness," like "masculinity," is assumed to be synonymous with "American" and becomes the standard against which all other racial groups are configured.

In *Playing in the Dark: Whiteness and the Literary Imagination* (1992), Toni *Morrison interrogates the meaning of "whiteness" as a cultural and literary category. As she notes, the implied audience of most American literature (whether written by writers of European or African descent) is a white audience, so much so that simple terms such as "flesh-colored" can be used as if it described all flesh, not just Caucasian. Conversely, *"race" writing defines that written by nonwhite people, as if "whiteness" were not in itself a racial descriptor.

One literary consequence of the practice of viewing whiteness as "unraced" and thus in no need of explanation or exploration is that people of color are often rendered as *stereotypes in American literature. For example, in Mark Twain's *The Adventures of Huckleberry Finn* (1884) readers are asked to believe that "nigger Jim," a runaway slave, is either so ignorant or so little concerned with his own safety that he would go South, further into slave territory, in order to travel in the company of Huck, a lower-class white boy. To read the book even on the most basic level of plot requires us to deny full humanity to Jim, one of the book's two central characters. When Jim is viewed as a human being (rather than a stereotypical racial Other), the plot of the novel seems deeply flawed. Shelley Fisher Fishkin's important book *Was Huck Black? Mark Twain and African-American Voices* (1993) does not erase the central problem of Jim's implausibility as a character, but it greatly enriches our understanding of Twain by revealing how much he was influenced by and indebted to African Americans in the creation of both his black and white characters.

A second consequence of viewing whiteness as "unraced" is that nonwhite characters can be both present and invisible. In Kate *Chopin's *The Awakening* (1899), a variety of servants—black, octoroon, quadroon—allow the smooth functioning of social life among white, upper-middle-class Creoles, but we learn nothing of their lives or experiences, as if they were merely aspects of the local scenery. In both cases, potentially brilliant literary works are marred by an assumption that only white characters are worthy of being three-dimensional and consequential.

Morrison's intriguing counterassertion is that the very term "whiteness" needs to be destabilized in view of the enormous cultural and literary contribution of African-American culture to white culture, an influence that has occurred despite a heritage of white racism. As in Spike Lee's movie *Do the Right Thing*, some white people, with seemingly no sense of contradiction, can express overtly racist attitudes while imitating black street style and slang and idolizing black musicians and athletes. Because "whiteness" is assumed to be an independent and fixed identity, there is no acknowledgment of how (white) American culture is based on the contributions of nonwhite citizens.

In her study, Morrison reveals the racial substructure of American literature and society and the ways in which there can be no "white" culture without black culture—and vice versa.

Similar projects have been undertaken by a variety of literary critics such as Elizabeth Ammons (who shows the complex intertextual connections between a number of turn-of-the-century "white American women writers" and various women writers of color) and Dana D. Nelson (who looks at the ways in which white racism evolved in early American society as part of an ambivalent response to Native Americans and Africans). Historians, including Mary Beth Norton, Elizabeth Fox Genovese, and David R. Roediger, have traced similar patterns of racism in the face of cross-racial influence.

Increasingly, the term * "ethnicity" has been used to designate subdivisions within the general racial category of "white" and at other times to denote nonwhite writers as well as various writers who are white but not Anglo-Saxon. These varied uses of "ethnic" mark it as an inherently unstable category and one that changes according to which particular group is receiving recognition. * Irish Americans, * Italian Americans, and * Jewish Americans, for example, have all been defined as "ethnic," whereas virtually no work has been done on the ethnic contributions of French-American or Scandinavian-American writers. Yet Betty E. M. Ch'maj, in *Multicultural America: A Resource Book for Teachers of Humanities and American Studies* (1993), has recently defined her own ethnicity as Finnish American, and in *Ethnic Passages: Literary Immigrants in Twentieth-Century America* (1993), Thomas J. Ferraro breaks an implicit taboo of literary history by discussing "mainstream" American writers such as Theodore Dreiser and, in more detail, Henry Miller as ethnic, immigrant writers (both were of German ancestry but worked to conceal their ethnicity in their writing). Should we accuse Miller and Dreiser of ethnic * passing? Or is it better, as Ferraro prefers, to rethink the category "ethnic," as well as constructs of "American" and "white"?

In the introduction to *Sending My Heart Across the Years: Tradition and Innovation in Native American Autobiography* (1992), Hertha Dawn Wong notes that she had nearly finished her study when a relative revealed her family's long-concealed * Native American ancestry. Wong wonders how this revelation changes or fails to change her own identity politics. When asked if she is Native American, she says, ironically, that she now should answer, "Yes, kind of." The point, of course, is that "race" and "ethnicity" are ever-shifting categories, historically constructed and historically determined.

As anthropologists insistently observe, there are no objective biological markers for indicating where one race ends and another begins. Recent studies suggest, for example, that as much as fifteen to twenty percent of the so-called "white" population of the American South must have some * mixed ancestry (specifically African-American ancestry; the percentage is higher if one factors in a Native American genealogy). The further point is that in a country whose history of exploration, conquest, enslavement, * immigration, and * assimilation is as fluid and complicated as America's, all racial terms are, to some degree, arbitrary and historically constructed. Thus, it is important that we continue to challenge racial terminology, beginning with the most invisible yet unstable term of all, "whiteness."

[*See also* Ethnicity; Race; Writing.]

• Mary Beth Norton, *Liberty's Daughters: The Revolutionary Experience of American Women, 1750–1800* (1980). Werner Sollors, *Beyond Ethnicity: Consent and Descent in American Culture* (1986). Gloria Anzaldúa, ed., *Making Face, Making Soul: Haciendo Caras: Creative and Critical Perspectives by Women of Color* (1990). Kwame Anthony Appiah, "Racisms," in *Anatomy of Racism*, ed. David Theo Goldberg (1990), pp. 3–17. Ronald Takaki, *Iron Cages: Race and Culture in Nineteenth-Century America* (1990). Dana D. Nelson, *The Word in Black and White: Reading "Race" in American Literature* (1991). David R. Roediger, *The Wages of Whiteness: Race and the Making of the American Working Class* (1991). Elizabeth Ammons, *Conflicting Stories: American Women Writers at the Turn of the Century* (1991). Joyce W. Warren, ed., *The (Other) American Traditions: Nineteenth-Century Women Writers* (1993).

Cathy N. Davidson

WIDOWHOOD. Some of the earliest women's writing in America reflected challenges women face upon the death of a spouse and during the resulting period of widowhood. Prior to the twentieth century, young and middle-aged women were especially likely to become widowed (in the 1700s only half of all people born reached adulthood, and those that did lived to an average age of thirty-five). And while widowed men tended to remarry quickly, only wealthy widowed women were in a position to choose that option. Furthermore, because married women were commonly with children they endured arduous financial and social consequences upon loss of a spouse.

Early written accounts of widowhood were autobiographical. Plantation owner Eliza Lucas, young widow of Colonel Charles Pinckney, wrote letters in 1741 and 1742 describing her enthusiasm for farming, and her capable solo management of the plantation. More typical experiences, however, may have been those of Sarah Ripley Stearns, whose journal includes a detailed description of being widowed, lonely, and dependent in America in 1818. Autobiographical accounts of widowhood would again come into vogue in the mid-twentieth century, highlighted by books such as *On My Own* (1958) by Eleanor Roosevelt, *My Life with Martin Luther King, Jr.* (1969) by Coretta Scott King, and *Widow* (1974) by Lynn Caine.

*Biography has been another literary form in which women have described widowhood. Former slave Elizabeth Hobbs Keckley wrote the first insider's exposé by a resident of the White House in *Behind the Scenes; or; Thirty Years a Slave, and Four Years in the White House* (1868). A close confidant to Mary Todd Lincoln and her husband, President Lincoln, Keckley described Mrs. Lincoln's life after the 1865 assassination. Perhaps most controversial were revelations that the widowed Mrs. Lincoln was compelled to sell her clothing from her home in Chicago to raise money to support herself and her son.

Widowhood has been widely addressed in fiction. Indeed, widowhood was a theme of the first novel published in the United States by an African American: Harriet E. Adams *Wilson's 1859 book *Our Nig* described obstacles faced by one "frado," a single mother searching for a means of support after her spouse dies from yellow fever.

To support herself and six children after being widowed in 1883 at age thirty-two, Kate *Chopin began writing feminist fiction about unconventional heroines and the then *taboo subject of divorce. Her controversial short story "The Story of an Hour" described a woman's secret feelings of freedom upon hearing that her spouse had been killed in a railroad accident.

After World War II, widowhood began to receive serious attention from American researchers. By the 1970s social scientist Helena Z. Lopata had become the preeminent American scholar writing on the subject of widowhood. Her *Widowhood in an American City* (1973) and *Women as Widows* (1979) were ground-breaking books that brought the plight of ethnic and urban American widowed women into focus. Recently she completed *Widows* (1987), a series of works depicting widowhood in diverse American and world cultures.

[*See also* Family; Marriage; Spinsterhood.]

Robert C. DiGiulio

WILDER, Laura Ingalls (1867–1957), best known for her semiautobiographical Little House series (1932–1943), tells young readers what it meant to be a daughter of *pioneers. Her depiction of "Laura's" childhood and youth in the contexts of *family, *community, landscape, history, and the American *myths pioneers sought to manifest appears so convincing that the child internalizes the remembered past

as an experience and a truth. The critical adult reader must admit the fiction of Ingalls Wilder's *autobiography, her eight narratives that begin with *Little House in the Big Woods* (1932) and *Little House on the Prairie* (1935) and end with the adult Laura in *These Happy Golden Years* (1943). While Wilder's choice of a third-person narrative, always centered on Laura and growing linguistically with her, encourages the differentiation between author and character, Wilder herself nostalgically perpetuated the myth of her childhood.

Published during the Great Depression and the beginning of World War II, Wilder's narratives insist on American myths such as manifest destiny, self-reliant individualism, and progress. Such affirmations do not obscure the realistically presented ambiguities of family relationships or attitudes toward Native Americans nor do they deny economic hardships or the struggles in a harsh natural environment. The child reader may remember the "golden moments," but the adult is more likely to discern Wilder's social and political values.

Always coping with financial difficulties, Wilder began to write a column for the *Missouri Ruralist* in 1912. By 1919 she started a complicated *collaborative writing relation with her daughter Rose Wilder Lane (1886–1968), a novelist and journalist in her own right until she became fully absorbed in her mother's project. Both women were descendants of mothers strengthened by hard lives and rigid values; both shared conservative social and political views, but they differed in their emotional lives. Rose Wilder needed a loving acknowledgment that Laura Ingalls Wilder could not provide. As a writer, Wilder needed only to tap into the reservoir of her memories, but she depended on her daughter's skill for narrative continuity and style. The synthesis of lived memory and literary form they achieved has made the Little House books foundational for young readers' acceptance and eventual critique of the myths that inform American literature and culture.

• William Jay Jacobs, "Frontier Faith Revisited: The Little House Books of Laura Ingalls Wilder," *Hornbook Magazine* 41 (October 1965): 465–473. Rosa Ann Moore, "The Little House Books: Rose-Colored Classics," *Children's Literature* 7 (1978): 7–16. Anne Thompson Lee, " 'It is better farther on': Laura Ingalls Wilder and the Pioneer Spirit," *Lion and the Unicorn* 3 (1979–1980): 74–87. Janet Spaeth, *Laura Ingalls Wilder* (1987). Anita Clair Fellman, "Laura Ingalls Wilder and Rose Wilder Lane: The Politics of a Mother and Daughter Relationship," *Signs* 15 (Spring 1990): 535–561.

Hamida Bosmajian

WILLIAMS, Sherley Anne (b. 1944), essayist, critic, poet, novelist, educator. With her first book, *Give Birth to Brightness: A Thematic Study in Neo-Black Literature* (1972), Sherley Anne Williams articulates the principles that have come to underlie all her own writing, whether criticism, poetry, or fiction. Identifying the importance of historical continuity between contemporary black writers and their forebears as well as the importance of a dynamic connection between the personal and the communal experiences of black Americans, she argues that these writers discover and clearly reveal a culture that dignifies African Americans. By saturating her writing with the rhythms and resonances of black American speech and music, she effectively achieves this goal in her own work. A student of history and literature, with a B.A. from California State University at Fresno (1966) and an M.A. from Brown University (1972), she reflects in her works not only a knowledge and a skepticism of traditional texts but also a commitment to the reinterpretation of these texts through an examination of the realities of African-American experience. Born in Bakersfield, California, Williams, after studying and teaching in the East, is now a professor of literature at the University of California, San Diego. A children's book, *Working Cotton* (1992), is based on her childhood memories of growing up in California's Central Valley.

For her two books of poetry, *The Peacock Poems* (1975) and *Someone Sweet Angel Child* (1982), Williams draws on the experiences of her own life as a woman and a mother, on her family's struggles and strengths, and on African-American historical figures. Frequently anthologized, her poems often have the structure and theme of the blues; the tragedy they reveal is undercut by irony and a tough vitality. A continuing interest in the blues is reflected in Williams's essays, such as "The Blues Roots of Contemporary Afro-American Poetry" (*Massachusetts Review* 18, Autumn 1977) and "Returning to the Blues: Esther Phillips and Contemporary Blues Culture" (*Callaloo* 14, Fall 1991). Although she focused primarily on black American male writers to exemplify her perceptions in *Give Birth to Brightness*, in her poems and short stories she has increasingly been concerned with describing the lives of black women, all of whom "share the same legacy." With her first novel, *Dessa Rose* (1986), which evolved from a short story, "Meditations on History," and which critics now regard as a major text in black feminist studies, Williams challenges the racist and sexist views inscribed in traditional history. Through the novel's narrative she imagines the developing relationship between two historical women—the black slave Dessa Rose, who leads an uprising on a coffle, and the white plantation mistress Rufel, who provides a sanctuary for runaway slaves. Through the rich use of image and dialect Williams provides her characters and her readers with a liberating language. If, as Williams comments, black Americans "have survived by word of mouth—and made of that process a high art," it appears that she is determined to use African-American oral traditions effectively in her written words in order to reinterpret the history of black Americans and to contribute to their "high art."

• Interview with Williams in *Black Women Writers at Work*, ed. Claudia Tate (1983), pp. 205–213. Lillie P. Howard, "Sherley Anne Williams," in *Dictionary of Literary Biography: Afro-American Poets since 1955*, ed. Trudier Harris and Thadious M. Davis, vol. 41 (1985), pp. 343–350. Mae Gwendolyn Henderson, "Speaking in Tongues: Dialogics, Dialectics, and the Black Woman Writer's Literary Tradition," in *Changing Our Own Words: Essays on Criticism, Theory, and Writing by Black Women*, ed. Cheryl A. Wall (1989), pp. 16–37. Deborah E. McDowell, "Negotiating Between Tenses: Witnessing Slavery After Freedom—*Dessa Rose*," in *Slavery and the Literary Imagination*, eds. Deborah E. McDowell and Arnold Rampersad (1989), pp. 144–163.

Elizabeth Schultz

WILLIS, Sarah P. *See* Fern, Fanny.

WILSON, Harriet E. Adams (1828?–1870?), author of *Our Nig; or, Sketches from the Life of a Free Black, in a Two-Story House, North, Showing That Slavery's Shadows Fall Even There* (1859), a "fictionalized" autobiography, the first novel published by a black person in the United States, likely the first book published by a black woman in English.

Born in Milford, New Hampshire, Harriet E. Adams Wilson was probably the daughter of Charles Adams of New Ipswich, New Hampshire. Wilson suffered poor health, reportedly from long-term mistreatment probably related to servitude. By age twenty-two, she was living in Carpenter Samuel Boyles's household. Harriet Adams married Thomas Wilson 6 October 1851 in Milford, but he reportedly abandoned his wife prior to the birth of their son. In June 1852, Harriet Wilson gave birth to George Mason Wilson in the "county house," a paupers' facility. After the birth of his son, Thomas Wilson returned to his family, but he soon left again never to return. Ill and impoverished, Wilson briefly placed her son in the care of a couple but was able to retrieve him.

Economic hardship prompted Wilson to write *Our Nig*. She copyrighted and registered the book 18 August 1859 in the clerk's office, District Court, District of Massachusetts, and she published it 5 September 1859. The George C. Rand & Avery Company, Boston, printed the novel. Six months later, Wilson's son died of "fever."

Our Nig features a black man married to a white woman, a nineteenth-century fictional rarity. Frado, the couple's daughter and the novel's protagonist, suffers the death of her father and abandonment by her mother. Frado becomes an indentured servant in the home of the Bellmonts, a lower-middle-class white family, and suffers untold abuses by Mrs. Bellmont and her daughter. Frado briefly achieves independence and financial stability working as a milliner before marrying a black fugitive slave. However, he abandons his pregnant wife and later dies of yellow fever. At novel's end, Frado and her newborn child are homeless and abandoned.

Our Nig shares traits with *sentimental novels popularized by nineteenth-century American women writers, depicting long-suffering women protagonists. But as Henry Louis Gates, Jr., observes in his introduction to the 1983 edition, Harriet Wilson both borrows from and subverts the sentimental novel form. For example, Wilson's ending, spousal abandonment rather than a happy marriage, departs from the sentimental novel. In addition, Wilson tailors *race, sex, and *class issues in *Our Nig* to a black woman's experience. She also includes key *slave-narrative motifs: empowerment through *literacy and self-assertion, and a catalog of abuses inflicted upon slaves. "Authenticating" letters from white acquaintances, affixed to *Our Nig*, attest to the novelist's character, veracity, and social circumstances. Wilson's opening "apologia," a seemingly self-effacing strategy often included in slave narratives, cites her lack of literary refinement. By design, the strategy engendered sympathy from white readers and sold books.

But *Our Nig*'s fictional base distinguishes it from most slave narratives. Wilson's appeal to readers for patronage is a plea for financial assistance. And at the risk of offending some abolitionists, she unflinchingly exposes slave horrors in the North. Structurally, Wilson weaves intricate character development for Frado, the protagonist. Gates considers Wilson's ultimate contribution to the slave narrative form to be inventiveness in plot formation.

• Harriet A. Jacobs, *Incidents in the Life of a Slave Girl, Written by Herself*, ed. Jean Fagan Yellin (1987). William L. Andrews, *To Tell a Free Story: The First Century of Afro-American Autobiography, 1760–1865* (1988).

Helena Woodard

WINNEMUCCA, Sarah, also Thocmetony (1844–1891), diplomat, orator, teacher, and writer. Thocmetony was born into a band of Northern Paiutes led by her grandfather, Truckee, near Humboldt Lake in what is now Nevada. She lived through her tribe's first contact with white settlers as a little girl in the late 1840s, became educated in white ways and the English and Spanish languages, and assumed the name Sarah Winnemucca as an adolescent living among whites in Genoa, Nevada. After the death of her grandfather she grew into her role as interpreter between her people and U.S. military leaders and later the Indian agents who were employed to oversee the care of Indians on reservations.

In 1879 after the white-Indian conflict called the Bannock War, Winnemucca traveled to San Francisco to begin her series of appeals for peace and security. Newspaper headlines in San Francisco called her "The Princess Sarah," and her career as a lecturer was launched. She quickly attracted the attention of East Coast reformers of U.S. policy toward Indians; her own sense of mission took her to Washington, D.C., in 1880 to meet with President Hayes. In 1883 Winnemucca and her second husband, Lewis Hopkins, traveled to the East where she attracted large audiences and met an influential circle of people; however, finding that the lecture format frustrated her desire to tell the Paiutes' whole story, she decided to write a more complete account of their history with the editorial help of Mary Peabody Mann.

Life Among the Paiutes: Their Wrongs and Claims is the first known work published in English by a Native American woman. The eclecticism of the work makes it difficult to classify: it includes aspects of tribal history, personal narrative, political tract, *bildungsroman, and chronicle of white-Indian relations. Written with the political mission of reuniting her tribe on a single reserve of desirable land, it is a metaphor for her life, spent as it was as an interpreter and diplomat between the Paiutes, Shoshonis, and Bannocks and the U.S. government and military. The book attempts to reach the feelings of the average white reader by chronicling her unsuccessful efforts to gain a humane government response to the Paiutes' claims; it even contains a petition to the U.S. Congress at the end to enable the persuaded and sympathetic reader to take concrete action on behalf of the tribe. However, Winnemucca's petition to Congress met with no more success than any of her attempts to influence the U.S. government's policies toward her tribe.

Upon her return to Nevada in 1884, Winnemucca organized a school in the town of Lovelock where Indian children had the unique opportunity to learn in their own tongues (Sarah Winnemucca was fluent in three Indian languages) and where their own cultures would be valued and not erased. Her Peabody Indian School closed after four years, and she went to live in failing health with her sister Elma in Henry's Lake, Idaho. When Sarah Winnemucca died at age forty-seven, the *New York Times* carried her obituary. Despite the many apparent failures in her career, the vision and breadth of her attempt made her heroic.

• Edward T. James, ed., *Notable American Women 1607–1950*, vol. 3 (1971). Catharine S. Fowler, "Sarah Winnemucca," in *American Indian Intellectuals*, ed. Margot Liberty (1978). Gae Whitney Canfield, *Sarah Winnemucca of the Northern Paiutes* (1983). A. La-Vonne Brown Ruoff, *American Indian Literatures: An Introduction, Bibliographic Review, and Selected Bibliography* (1990). Margaret A. Lukens, "Sarah Winnemucca, Literary Ambassador," in *Creating Cultural Spaces*, diss. (1991), pp. 126–161.

Margaret A. Lukens

WISTER, Sally (1761–1804), Quaker diarist and poet. Sarah (Sally) Wister was born into an affluent Philadelphia family and educated at the Quaker School for Girls run by philanthropist Anthony Benezet, whose progressive curriculum helped foster her lifelong love of writing. When the British occupied Philadelphia in 1777, the Wisters, who were Patriots, took refuge with relatives in rural Gwynedd, Pennsylvania, until July 1780. During this time Wister began keeping a *journal for two close girlfriends. Usually called her Revolutionary journal, this is Wister's best-known work. Although she wrote the bulk of the Revolutionary journal in Gwynedd, she continued to make occasional entries at home in Philadelphia until 1781. But gradually the spirited, worldly extrovert so evident in the pages of that journal metamorphosed into the spiritual, unworldly introvert reflected in her later neoclassical poems and her devotional journal, kept from 1796 to 1797. Wister did not marry but lived at the family home and cared for her aging parents. She survived her mother by only two months and died, in her early forties, on 21 April 1804.

Wister's Revolutionary journal is an important historical document and a gem of early American women's literature because it provides rare insights into an adolescent female sensibility and because it is aesthetically noteworthy. While she wrote at a time of great national significance, she responded privately and individually, as did so many other contemporary women writers. Instead of taking a male view of the times by citing political events and battles, she took a female view of the Revolution and its aftermath. She displaces the war's fragmentation with the harmony of her family life and friendships, reduces macrocosmic events to microcosmic ones, emphasizes continuity and normalcy despite considerable disruption, and opts for a comic, optimistic tone instead of a pessimistic one.

Part of the Revolutionary journal was published for the first time in *The Pennsylvania Magazine of History and Biography* (1885–1886), and it has maintained a kind of underground reputation since then. A fuller edition was published in 1902, and portions were anthologized thereafter, but it was only in 1987 that a complete scholarly edition of Wister's journal and her other known writings appeared. Included in this edition is her devotional journal, where she documents her tormented spiritual crisis. Both of Wister's journals, as well as her other texts, define one Quaker woman's sense of her evolving spiritual, intellectual, political, emotional, and social identity.

• Sarah Wister, Revolutionary journal (Historical Society of Pennsylvania); devotional journal, 1796–1797, and correspondence, 1777–1779 (Wister Family Papers, Historical Society of Pennsylvania); poetry and prose (Eastwick Collection, American Philosophical Society). See also Kathryn Zabelle Derounian, ed., *The Journal and Occasional Writings of Sarah Wister* (1987).

Kathryn Zabelle Derounian-Stodola

WITCHCRAFT. Ancient Western beliefs about witchcraft differ markedly from the *stereotype put forward by modern Christianity. The earliest European sources identified the *witch by his or her capacity and desire to perform *maleficia*. *Maleficium* originally meant "an evil deed or mischief," but from the fourth century on, it involved magical practices (maleficia), "harm-doing by occult means," which were ascribed to both witches and sorcerers. The Old English *wicca/wicce*, the etymological root of *witch*, simply meant a man or woman who practiced magic and divination, either benevolent or malicious. *Maleficium* denoted only one kind of deed within a wide range of occult possibilities. Certain adversities were typical: natural disasters such as storms and fires that damaged grain, livestock, or households, or injured or killed people; and diseases in human beings or animals, particularly if they resulted in death.

The medieval concept of *maleficium* drew attention to a concrete event and its harmful effect, the supposed means (occult but not diabolic), and the implied motive (malice). It did not stereotype the supposed agents of these acts. Anyone with malicious intent and occult knowledge was capable of *maleficia*, and both men and women could be culpable. The Middle English *wicche* was used for both men and women and so, initially, was the modern English *witch*.

The modern belief that witches made pacts with Satan developed in continental Europe sometime in the fourteenth or fifteenth century. The Inquisition's attack on magicians and heretics was expanded to include witches per se, and Christian society concomitantly began to believe that most witches were women (despite the fact that significant numbers of men were also convicted). Adapting existing beliefs about magicians and heretical sects to incorporate symbolic images of women and reports of pagan religious practices among women, European clerics and lawyers produced a synthetic nightmare of powerful, dangerous, numerous, and distinctly female witches who paid homage to Satan and threatened all of society. At the height of witchcraft prosecution in Europe, from approximately 1550 to 1650, this new diabolic, sexualized image of the witch was a staple of trials that rationalized mass executions. People were convicted as much—or more—for spiritual and sexual relations with the devil as for any particular harm to other people.

The only large-scale trial and execution of witches in colonial America occurred in the Puritan town of Salem, Massachusetts, in 1692. It was also the last mass witchcraft trial in Euro-American history. Twenty people were executed, one-third of them men, and more than one hundred people were accused. At the center of attention were a group of teenage girls, many of them servants, who were supposedly "afflicted" by the witchcraft of their adult neighbors and who provided much of the "evidence" for conviction. As in Europe, the trials were initiated and conducted by the state. Also following the European pattern, the initially small number of accusations mushroomed after the accusation that there was a group of witches (all women) who had made a pact with the devil and held secret meetings. The evidence for conviction was based on the activities of "apparitions" who had been seen worshiping the devil or tormenting their neighbors (and especially tormenting the girls who were their primary accusers). That is, people were convicted for what their apparitions had done on the assumption that people controlled the activities of their apparitions.

In 1711, scarcely twenty years after the infamous trials, the state completely reversed its position, exonerating those who had been executed and paying restitution to their families. Thereafter, in the American colonies as in Europe the nature of supernatural mass culture shifted dramatically from witchcraft to Christian revivals, beginning in the colonies with the Great Awakening of 1720.

Both the great century of persecution in Reformation Europe and the witchcraft trials at Salem were marked first and foremost by the widespread executions for witchcraft through the mechanism of the legal process of the state. After all, people had believed in witchcraft for centuries, and private citizens had made informal accusations of witchcraft and punished witches for just as long. What was new in early modern Europe and what distinguished Salem in the New England history of witchcraft beliefs was the massive intervention of state authority to prosecute witchcraft as a widespread capital crime—and the subsequent epidemic of accusations and executions that this intervention produced. Witchcraft was not only heresy: it was the declared enemy of state power.

The emphasis placed on the symbolic female witch has made it easy to overlook the fact that witchcraft trials were very much about the power of male *sexuality as well. Men were responsible for the public articulation of the concept of the symbolic witch and for the social fact of widespread prosecution and execution. The lawyers and clerics who wrote the tracts, the laws, and the court procedures garnered power for themselves as a white male professional class through these mass prosecutions, creating a stark opposition between their own legal power and the illicit power of the female witch. Especially in the context of a Protestant religion that denied spiritual efficacy to the Virgin Mary and the female saints of Catholic tradition, female sexuality came to epitomize illegal power, irreligious beliefs, social chaos, and even mass destruction. Feminist historians view the Salem trials as the culmination of a century of misogyny. The legal history of New England shows many small and little-known cases of witchcraft prosecution in the seventeenth century in which women were repeatedly singled out as the scapegoats of male magistrates and clerics. Modern *feminists have also sought out the imaginative possibilities of the symbolic witch as the figure of the alienated woman whose power and knowledge place her outside the accepted conventions of society, but the attempt to recover a history of benevolent magical practices by women (including nontraditional medicine and *midwifery) is largely a speculative effort.

Contemporaneous narratives of witchcraft cases in colonial New England were collected for publication in the early twentieth century by George Lincoln Burr in *Narratives of the Witchcraft Cases* (1914). The depositions of the Salem trials were transcribed and made available to the public as a WPA project in the 1930s. These records were not published until 1977 (see Paul Boyer and Stephen Nissenbaum, eds., *The Salem Witchcraft Papers*). No court records other than the depositions have survived.

• Alan MacFarlane, *Witchcraft in Tudor and Stuart England* (1970). Keith Thomas, *Religion and the Decline of*

Magic (1971). H. C. Erik Midelfort, *Witch-hunting in Southwestern Germany* (1972). Paul Boyer and Stephen Nissenbaum, *Salem Possessed* (1974). Norman Cohn, *Europe's Inner Demons* (1975). Richard Keickhefer, *European Witch Trials* (1976). E. William Monter, *Witchcraft in France and Switzerland* (1976). Edward Peters, *The Magician, the Witch, and the Law* (1978). Ann Kibbey, "Mutations of the Supernatural," in *American Quarterly* (1982). Carol Karlsen, *Women and Witchcraft* (1987).

Ann Kibbey

WOLFENSTEIN, Martha (1869–1905), short story writer. Born in Insterburg, Prussia, the infant Wolfenstein immigrated with her parents Bertha Brieger and Samuel Wolfenstein to the United States. The family settled in St. Louis, Missouri, where Dr. Wolfenstein, the first man ordained a Reform rabbi in Europe, served Congregation B'nai El, the oldest and largest Reform Jewish congregation west of the Mississippi.

He was later drafted to administer the newly founded Cleveland Jewish Orphan Asylum, which housed many of the children orphaned by the typhoid epidemics of the 1870s. The family, which now included six children, moved to Cleveland, Ohio, in 1878, where they lived at the orphanage.

Martha Wolfenstein received her education in the Cleveland public schools. After her mother's death, Martha, then sixteen, assumed the duties of housekeeper for her father and younger siblings. She also served for a brief time as matron of the orphanage. She began to publish short stories in both Anglo-Jewish and secular periodicals. She appears to have been the first Jewish American woman to publish stories with Jewish characters and settings in secular general readership magazines. Her stories from *Lippincott's Magazine* and *Outlook* were collected and published under the title of one of them, *Idylls of the Gass* (The Alley) in 1901. Her stories from the *Cleveland Jewish Review and Observer* were published under the title *The Renegade and Other Stories* in 1905. She received praise and encouragement from, among others, Henrietta Szold, founder of Hadassah, and Israel Zangwill, prominent English Jewish novelist and Zionist.

By 1900 Wolfenstein was already frail from the tuberculosis that had killed her mother and would kill her six years later. The play she struggled to complete but never saw produced before her death seems to be lost. When she died the same year that her second book was published, no obituary appeared in the secular Cleveland papers.

Her early stories were based on her father's reminiscences of his childhood in a Moravian ghetto. It is primarily these stories that are collected in *Idylls of the Gass*. Her second collection gives voice to a variety of Jewish women whose stories reflect themes common to women writers: seduction and abandonment by an importunate, deceptive lover; the precarious life of a never-married woman in a society that values her only in terms of her usefulness to others; mother-son relationships; and women struggling to separate their spiritual lives from traditional patriarchal religious practices.

Susan Koppelman

WOMAN. *See* Gender Theory.

WOMAN CHIEF. While the existence of the *berdache*, the Indian male who preferred to live as a female, has been acknowledged for some time and been written about extensively in anthropological literature, only recently have scholars investigated the historical existence of Native American women who chose to act out traditional male roles. Valerie Sherer Mathes (1982) has assessed the lives of such Plains Indian women as "Woman Chief," a capable warrior whose success at hunting and war allowed her to take four wives who cooked, kept house, and tanned hides. Another Plains "woman chief," named Pine Leaf, early vowed that she would not marry until she had vanquished a hundred of her tribe's enemies, especially those responsible for killing her brother. Although at this point little more is known about these women warriors, it is important, as Mathes concludes, to reevaluate the stereotypical view of Native American women as "squaws," living virtually as slaves to their men. Many native societies, we now know, were matriarchal, and ethnographic data suggest that individual women were far more likely to stray from traditional (white) gender roles than was formerly believed to be the case.

[*See also* Amazon; Woman Warrior.]

• Carol Thomas Foreman, *Indian Woman Chiefs* (1976). Valerie Sherer Mathes, "Native American Women in Medicine and the Military," *Journal of the West* 21, no. 2 (April 1982): 41–48.

Arnold E. Davidson

WOMAN-IDENTIFIED WOMAN. In the spring of 1970, during the second Congress to Unite Women, a group calling themselves the Radicalesbians submitted a position paper entitled "The Woman-Identified Woman." Later anthologized in *Notes from the Third Year: Women's Liberation* (1971), the paper substitutes the term "woman-identified" for "lesbian" in part to render it less threatening to heterosexual (and homophobic) feminists. But semantic issues were not the only ones at stake: the authors sought to bring lesbian love out of the feminist closet by representing its practice and practitioners as ardently feminist.

Ultimately, the paper-cum-manifesto insisted that lesbians were not, among other myths, male-identified, sex-obsessed deviants and hence did not deserve to be persistently ghettoized within feminist circles and agendas. And yet, in order to convince reluctant hetero-feminists to accept lesbians in their midst, its authors downplay lesbianism as a matter of sexuality and define it primarily as political. Lesbianism, it is implied, could even be seen as the logical extension of the separatism and gynocentrism many hetero-feminists already engaged in or applauded and hence could, it was hoped, eventually be seen as feminism's best strategic hope for survival.

Although the paper does not altogether ignore the sexual aspects of lesbianism, it holds out the promise that all women, whether they slept with other women or not, could claim the adjective "woman-identified" so long as they acted with and on behalf of women. Also required would be a long overdue analysis of feminism's own blatant heterosexism and of the central role heterosexual relationships play(ed) in the continued oppression of women.

The influence of this paper has been far-reaching for feminist theory and writing in general. Only months after the Congress, the *New York Times* op-ed page solicited an essay from Ti-Grace * Atkinson, "Lesbianism and Feminism: Justice for Women as 'Unnatural,'" later included in Atkinson's *Amazon Odyssey* (1974), which strongly reaffirms the understanding of lesbianism as a political category and a vital feminist strategy.

Perhaps most notably, poet and author Adrienne * Rich has developed the concept of woman-identification in her theories of "the lesbian in us," "the lesbian continuum," and "lesbian existence." In these essays, Rich suggests that women are forced within patriarchal systems to repress our primary love and longing for women. In truth, she argues, all women fall somewhere along a continuum of woman-identified experiences and emotions and cannot be categorized as simply or solely hetero- or homosexual. Although Rich's argument has been challenged by lesbians for minimizing the erotic possibilities of woman-woman relationships, her frequently reprinted work has done much to advance discussions of woman-identification, its historic suppression, and its potential transformative power.

The woman-identified woman, of course, didn't just appear out of nowhere in 1970. In a more general sense, women have been identifying with, confiding in, and loving other women for centuries. In "The Female World of Love and Ritual," Carroll Smith-Rosenberg adapts Rich's "continuum" model to explain the ardent emotions exchanged in letters and in person among nineteenth-century girls (in her *Disorderly Conduct: Visions of Gender in Victorian America,* 1985). Also, in *Surpassing the Love of Men: Romantic Friendship and Love Between Women from the Renaissance to the Present* (1981), Lillian Faderman documents how many of these girls and the women they became shared an intimacy that was not simply implicitly sexual.

Nineteenth-century women's fiction also testifies to the tradition of woman-identification: in novels from Susan * Warner's *The Wide, Wide World* (1850) through Harriet * Jacob's *Incidents in the Life of a Slave Girl* (1857) to Louisa May * Alcott's *Little Women* (1868), female networks of nurturance and support occupy a vital place in women's lives. Modern fiction, ranging from Rita Mae * Brown's *Rubyfruit Jungle* (1973) through Marilyn * French's *The Woman's Room* (1977) to Toni * Morrison's *Sula* (1973) and *Beloved* (1987), also testify to the primacy of women-women relationships. Perhaps most explicitly, certain futuristic novels, including Charlotte Perkins * Gilman's *Herland* (1915) and Joanna * Russ's *The Female Man* (1975), adopt woman-identification with a vengeance and suggest that for women, * utopia just may be a world without men.

[*See also* Man-identified Woman; Separatism; Lesbian Feminism.]

• Adrienne Rich, *On Lies, Secrets and Silence: Selected Prose, 1966–1978* (1979). Adrienne Rich, *Blood, Bread and Poetry: Selected Prose, 1979–1986* (1986).

Cynthia J. Davis

WOMANISM. The term *womanist* has its intellectual roots in Alice * Walker's preface to her book of essays, *In Search of Our Mothers' Gardens: Womanist Prose* (1983). According to Walker, a "womanist" is a "black feminist or feminist of color" who possesses strength and persistence that facilitate personal development. She values the bonds between women, their "culture," their "emotional flexibility and [their] strength." Finally, as Tuzyline J. Allan notes in "Feminist and Womanist Aesthetics" (1991), the womanist follows the tradition of women who refuse * separatism and advocate an "emancipating ... ethos": wholeness and healing that transcend * gender, culture, * class, and * race.

Literary critics have tackled Walker's multifaceted term. The earliest critic, Chikwenye Ogunyemi, identifies the womanist tradition in novels by African and African-American women authors in which fictional black women move from physical or psychological enslavement to independence and freedom. Similarly, Harold Bloom, in *Alice Walker* (1989), argues that womanist writing captures the process: the movement from "confusion, resistance to the established order, and the discovery of a freeing order." Allan's "Feminist and Womanist Aesthetics" develops the most extensive definition and critique. Through a comparison to works by *Woolf, Drabble, and Emecheta, Allan calls *The Color Purple* the "paradigmatic womanist text," which reveals that "[t]he path to womanist victory in Walker's fiction is strewn with physically and psychically battered woman, victimized as much by self-hate as by an oppressive racist and sexist social system." While Allan's discussion is a persuasive beginning, literary criticism still lacks a provocative study that analyzes how Walker develops "womanism" in her later works and that further critiques Walker's works in conjunction with and/ or in opposition to "womanist" novels by other contemporary African-American women authors.

Walker does not limit her womanism to *The Color Purple*, but extends it in *The Temple of My Familiar* (1989) and *Possessing the Secret of Joy* (1992). Other novels that illustrate womanism are Gloria *Naylor's *Mama Day* (1988); Toni Morrison's novels (especially *Sula* and *Beloved*); and Sherley Anne *Williams's *Dessa Rose* (1986). Pre-Walkerian examples are evident in Harriet *Jacobs's *Incidents in the Life of a Slave Girl*, Zora Neale *Hurston's *Their Eyes Were Watching God* (1937), Alice *Childress's *Like One of the Family* (1956), Toni Cade *Bambara's *The Salt Eaters* (1980), and Naylor's *The Women of Brewster Place* (1980). Each of these novels resembles a womanist *bildungsroman, a black woman's physical and/or psychological journey and development.

Walker's term has also spurred discussion among historians and critics who have analyzed its implications in the context of white and black feminist ideologies. Historians argue that the black feminist movement arose from the belief that the white feminist ideology excluded the black woman's experience of *racism, *sexism, and classism. In *Talking Back* (1989), bell hooks rejects the belief that Walker coined the term to undercut feminist thought, because for hooks, womanism lacks "a tradition of radical political commitment to struggle and change." Conversely, in "Defining Black Feminist Thought" (1990), Patricia Collins defines the absent "tradition" by positing that Walker's womanism exemplifies the non-separatism and humanism underlying black feminist thought: "Black women's struggles are part of a wider

struggle for human dignity and empowerment."

While Allan applauds Walker's ideology, she considers it problematic in terms of the black/ white "feminist" debate. Allan asserts, "By foreclosing the possibility that womanist qualities can exist in the white female imagination, Walker creates an unbridgeable gulf between white and black feminist writers, a stance that is counterproductive to her womanist vision of racial and sexual equality." Thus, rather than reinstating philosophies of *separatism, white feminist and black womanist critics and authors must aim to recognize and incorporate the racial "other" into their ideologies of liberation.

• Alice Walker, *In Search of Our Mothers' Gardens: Womanist Prose* (1983). Chikwenye Ogunyemi, "Womanism: The Dynamics of the Contemporary Black Female Novel in English," *Signs: Journal of Women in Culture and Society* 11 (1985): 63–80. Harold Bloom, *Alice Walker* (1989). bell hooks, *Talking Back: Thinking Feminist, Thinking Black* (1989). Patricia H. Collins, "Defining Black Feminist Thought" in *Black Feminist Thought: Knowledge, Consciousness, and the Politics of Empowerment* (1990). Tuzyline J. Allan, "Feminist and Womanist Aesthetics: A Comparative Study," Ph.D. diss., State University of New York, Stony Brook (1991).

Deborah De Rosa

WOMAN QUESTION, THE is a general term denoting the multiplicity of concerns centering on the problematic status and condition of nineteenth-century middle-class women. Not limited to *suffrage, the woman question also focused on jobs, dress reform, marital rights, *birth control, and divorce. Engendering countless speeches, books, and newspaper and magazine articles, the controversy over women's rights dominated public discourse for decades. At stake for feminists was the legal and social recognition that women possessed equal abilities and, therefore, deserved status equal to that of men.

Although women had no legal standing, their power supposedly lay in influencing their husbands, brothers, and sons, who would then theoretically safeguard women's interests. The reality of nineteenth-century women's lives, however, demonstrated that the power implied in the concept of "influence" was, in most cases, negligible. Challenging patriarchal assumptions restricting women in every area of life, Sarah *Grimké's *Letters on the Equality of the Sexes* (1838) and Margaret *Fuller's *Woman in the Nineteenth Century* (1845) provided important early white feminist statements on the woman question.

In 1848 Elizabeth Cady *Stanton, Lucretia *Mott, and other white feminists organized the first women's rights convention at Seneca Falls, New York, where, with the support of Frederick Douglass, they issued the "Declaration of Sentiments," a document, based on the Declaration of Independence, which called for reform, targeting both law and custom regarding the culturally sanctioned inferior status of women. This document identifies many of the issues the woman question subsumed: property rights, educational and economic opportunities, loss of status/rights in marriage, divorce, child custody laws, and suffrage.

Realizing that much power rests with the enfranchised, both supporters and opponents of women's rights focused on women's suffrage. Although many women's rights advocates began as abolitionists, eventually a split occurred because some saw the plight of women and slaves as integrally linked, while others wanted to separate the two causes. Racial and class allegiancies led some early feminists to exclude African-Americans, immigrants, and poor women from their political agenda. Passage of the Fifteenth Amendment in 1870, which enfranchised African-American men and introduced the word "male" into the language of the Constitution, further complicated the woman question because it made female citizenship a debatable issue for the first time. While many women writers examined the role of women in society, they reached no consensus, creating models as different as the " * true woman" and the " * new woman." In general, the woman question provided the text or subtext for much of the literature produced from the 1850s until the passage of the Nineteenth Amendment in 1920. Frances E. W. * Harper's *Iola Leroy* (1892) and Henry James's *The Bostonians* (1886) are two of many novels that focus on the role of women in society.

[*See also* Suffrage Movement.]

• Eleanor Flexner, *Century of Struggle* (1959; reprint, 1975). Aileen S. Kraditor, *The Ideas of the Woman Suffrage Movement: 1890–1920* (1965; reprint, 1981). Paula Giddings, *When and Where I Enter: The Impact of Black Women on Race and Sex in America* (1984). Anne R. Shapiro, *Unlikely Heroines: Nineteenth-Century American Women Writers and the Woman Question* (1987). Jean Fagan Yellin, *Women and Sisters: Anti-Slavery Feminists in American Culture* (1989). Barbara Bardes and Suzanne Gossett, *Declarations of Independence: Women and Political Power in Nineteenth-Century American Fiction* (1990). Elizabeth Ammons, *Conflicting Stories: American Women Writers at the Turn into the Twentieth Century* (1991).

Cheri Louise Ross

WOMAN WARRIOR. In her semi-autobiographical novel *The Woman Warrior* (1976), Maxine Hong * Kingston uses the * Amazon image as a model for a distinctively feminine portrait of strength, autonomy, justice, and enormous empowerment. "Perhaps women were once so dangerous, that they had to have their feet bound." Her mother, Brave Orchid, told her she would grow up "a wife and a slave." At the same time her mother taught her "the song of the warrior woman, Fu Mu Lan." She decides she must grow up to be a female avenger.

In her fantasy, a seven-year-old Kingston follows a bird to the hut of an enigmatic old couple, who lead her through fifteen years of uninterrupted rigorous exercises. "Menstrual days did not interrupt my training. I was as strong as on any other day." At last a swordswoman, Kingston returns to her home to have her parents "carve revenge" on her back, incising "oaths and names" directly on her flesh. She leads an army to make right every abuse of power against her family and her village.

As a military commander, Kingston inspires and nurtures her men—feeding them and singing to them "glorious songs." Her army did not rape, loot, and plunder: they took food "only where there was an abundance. We brought order wherever we went."

In her vision, Kingston makes no sacrifice of her feminine strengths. She remains the unquestioned commander of her troops, even when her husband fights at her side. She continues to fight when she bears a son, adjusting the size of her armor to accommodate her belly, and later, her son nursing at her breast. "Marriage and childbirth strengthen the swordswoman, who is not a maid like Joan of Arc." Surveying the disparity between her life in American poverty and her dream vision of self as warrior, Kingston muses, "The swordswoman and I are not so dissimilar. She fights too, but her words are her weapons. The reporting is the vengeance."

[*See also* Amazon; Woman Chief.]

Abby Wettan Kleinbaum

WOMB ENVY, the male desire to give birth or to possess female sexual organs, is pervasive across human cultures. Couvade is perhaps the best-known instance of womb envy; the man takes to his bed and groans, simulating birth pains, while his wife gives birth.

Womb envy was expressed in Cyprus at the Festival of Ariadne, where priests imitated women in labor. The Yakut of Siberia believed their shamans actually could bear children. Galli priests of the goddess Astarte castrated themselves in order to become sexually like her. Subincision (the slitting of the penis) was practiced by priests in some ancient * goddess cultures and is still practiced today among central

Australian Aborigines. In the Naven tribe (New Guinea), boys are initiated into life by male sponsors who dress as pregnant women and cry out for their children in falsetto.

Religious *myths are full of men giving birth: Adam births Eve (from his rib); Zeus births Athena (from his head); the male god Earthmaker (of the Papagoes, southwest North America) makes people from his own body. In Christianity, the male father god metaphorically takes on female sex organs. Clement denigrates women's breasts as incapable of nourishing: ". . . the Father's breasts of love supply the milk." Paul said, "The man is not of the woman, but the woman of the man." Saint Gregory of Nyssa argued that the embryo was implanted in the female by the male. Cyprian wrote in 256 A.D., "The birth of Christians is in baptism." Puritan preachers constantly spoke of sucking at the "breasts of divine Providence," and Cotton Mather (in 1723) affirmed that ministers "travailed in birth" for their flocks.

In *Generation of Animals*, Aristotle contended that man actively supplies the form of the child and woman, passively, the matter. Neo-Aristotelians further described the father as the sole parent and the mother as a mere incubator. In the sixteenth century, Paracelsus contended that the "living child" created by alchemy would have "every member as well-proportioned as any infant in the womb." Some physicians today also contend that their stainless-steel wombs are better than the female's, which is "a dark and dangerous place."

Although psychologists do not make much of womb envy (Felix Boehm mentions "parturition envy" in 1930, Karen Horney "womb envy" in 1932, Bruno Bettleheim "vagina envy" in 1954), medical texts frequently exhibit pathological womb envy in four forms of antagonism toward female reproductive organs: those that blame the womb for almost all women's ailments; those that advocate mutilating or removing women's genitalia or reproductive organs; those that describe how to take over the birth process, making it more difficult for the woman to deliver; and those that advocate taking the birth function *entirely* away from women (using test tubes and artificial wombs).

[*See also* Birth.]

• Una Stannard, "The Male Maternal Instinct," *Trans-Action* (November–December 1970). Una Stannard, *Mrs. Man* (1977). Barbara Ehrenreich and Deidre English, *For Her Own Good* (1979). David Leverenz, *The Language of Puritan Feeling* (1980). Gena Corea, *The Mother Machine* (1986). Michelle Stanworth, ed., *Reproductive Technologies* (1988).

Gloria Kaufman

WOMEN'S CLUBS. Also known as literary, study, and culture clubs, hundreds of societies devoted to self-education and, eventually, civic reform were founded between the late 1860s and the 1900s. These all-female organizations led the early stages of the "women's club movement," which continued well into the twentieth century.

The late nineteenth-century women's clubs were not without precedent. As early as 1800 the Ladies' Literary Society of Chelsea had organized for religious and literary study, and several other discussion groups with literary emphases had surfaced in the decades preceding the war—notably Elizabeth Peabody's "Historical School" and Margaret *Fuller's "Conversations" gatherings in Boston, and the Edgeworthalean and Minerva Societies in Bloomington and New Harmony, Indiana. Both predominantly women and all women societies had flourished throughout the nineteenth century, and women had gained large-scale organizational experience in the United States Sanitary Commission during the *Civil War. But after the war large numbers of middle-class women found themselves in a new situation that fostered the rapid growth of study clubs. Experienced in work outside the home and less burdened by time-consuming domestic chores (because of numerous labor-saving inventions and mass production of consumer goods), they were frustrated by the prevailing "cult of *True Womanhood" that limited their "sphere of influence" to the home and prevented them from pursuing any form of higher *education. "Must I sew and trot babies and sing songs and tell Mother Goose stories, and still be expected to know how to write?" asked Julia Ward *Howe. "My fingers are becoming less and less familiar with the pen, my thoughts grow daily more insignificant and commonplace." Study clubs provided an outlet for thousands—eventually millions—of women without directly confronting the hypocrisies of Victorian *gender ideology.

Two of the most renowned groups, the New England Women's Club and Sorosis of New York (both founded in 1868), combined self-culture with a modest assertion of women's rights; they eventually took the lead in establishing the Association for the Advancement of Women (1873) and the General Federation of Women's Clubs (1890). Most of the clubs they led, however, remained focused on cultural and literary studies throughout the 1870s and 1880s. Though groups such as the Browning Society, the Catholic Women's Club, the Alternate Tuesdays Club, and the Four-Leaf Clover Club undoubtedly differed in priorities and procedures, these clubs, and hundreds more, had important similarities. A typical club was made up of 12 to 25 middle-class (almost never

* working-class or high society) women, most of them married and in their 40s and 50s. They would meet weekly, biweekly, or monthly for a program that would last about two hours and consist mainly of guest speakers or presentations from club members, followed by discussion. Members would conduct meetings according to parliamentary procedure, in some cases rotating executive positions frequently in order to give everyone leadership experience. In many cases the presentations evolved to allow for more active participation: a club might rely exclusively on "outside" lecturers for their first meetings, then start requiring members to teach each other, often working their way methodically through long-term courses of study. The reports themselves tended to progress over time from encyclopedic recitations to more original papers drawn from several sources to half-extemporaneous presentations from notes. Members usually researched literary, artistic, or historical subjects but occasionally dealt with women's issues.

Regardless of the topics, the experience of teaching themselves and each other in an egalitarian setting gave "clubwomen" a new sense of independence and confidence. While it was hardly revolutionary activity, researching, writing, and presenting papers on Shakespeare's England or the Pre-Raphaelites gave women an opportunity to express their opinions and to discover (or rediscover) the empowering sensation of writing.

Although few clubs made feminist claims or allied themselves with the suffrage movement prior to the 1900s, they still met with scattered opposition from the male establishment. The Rhode Island Women's Club was derisively called the "Society for the Prevention of Home Industry," and the amateurish nature of study club scholarship was often ridiculed, as in Sinclair Lewis's *Main Street* (1920). The clubs themselves insisted that their members remained devoted wives and mothers and, moreover, that their self-education benefited their families, since much of their study concerned home economy and since even the more academic knowledge they developed could be shared with their children. Nevertheless, these new women's clubs were more threatening to * patriarchy than the earlier benevolent societies had been, perhaps because they helped women to forge identities independently of their husbands.

The idea that the work of study clubs was consistent with True Womanhood provided more than a defense against male opposition; it also motivated clubs to become increasingly involved in social work. Club members gradually embraced the concept of "Municipal Housekeeping," reasoning that if women's moral purity was an essential influence on the Christian household (as True Womanhood's proponents maintained), it was also an essential influence on society as a whole. The shift in emphasis became apparent in the 1870s with the founding of the Association for the Advancement of Women, whose first congress featured papers on women's higher * education and "The Relation of Women's Work in the Household to Work Outside"; and the first Women's Educational and Industrial Union (Boston, 1877), which offered classes in typing, stenography, and bookkeeping and established an employment bureau.

An even more important turning point toward * activism came in 1890, when Sorosis, led by Jane C. Croly, succeeded in chartering the General Federation of Women's Clubs (GFWC). Croly recognized that the primary value in federation was the greater influence that a large, national organization could exert by direct action or lobbying. The GFWC was a great success: it grew rapidly, hosted elaborate biennial conventions, and, most significantly, led reform activity in such areas as child labor, education, the spoils system, and food and drug legislation. The women who directed the national organization—and who spoke for the club movement in books and periodicals—regarded Municipal Housekeeping as a logical extension of club members' self-education. The majority of small, local clubs, however, continued their traditional literature and culture programs while maintaining membership in the GFWC.

After World War I the General Federation's activism waned as women's clubs found a middle ground between self-culture and Municipal Housekeeping. By this time most of their civic reform and improvement projects had been subsumed by government at various levels; but if they no longer had to establish libraries or lobby for restrictions on child labor, clubs could still donate books and establish youth organizations. This modern version of the culture club remained popular through mid-century, enjoying an estimated total membership of 10,000,000 in 1954. Membership dropped off after the 1950s (*Time* magazine ran an article in 1988 describing women's clubs as an "endangered species") even as clubs became increasingly identified with conservative, leisure-class smugness.

Even in their most activist stages, the clubs were avowedly conservative. General Federation historian Mary I. Wood identified her organization's purpose in 1912 as the preservation of traditional family values in the wake of civilization's rapid progress, and virtually all of their reform activity, from temperance to child labor legislation, could be traced to that principle. Although the GFWC eventually endorsed women's right to vote (in 1914), in the 1890s and 1900s they presented themselves as an alternative to the "radical" suffragists. (There was, however, considerable debate on the issue throughout the Federation's history. Croly, for one, maintained that "the tongue and the pen [were] mightier than the ballot.") And while the General Federation's motto, "Unity in Diversity," seemed apt in reference to clubs with various interests, their diversity did not include women of color in its first decade, despite the existence of active African-American women's clubs. The most prominent societies generally excluded Jews and women of non–Western European descent (who, like black women, often formed their own clubs and tended to embrace reform work immediately). Women's clubs also tended to remain middle-class (or, later, "upper-middle-class") enclaves, largely because working-class women generally had less time to devote to self-culture or civic work.

It may be the clubs' unheroic stances on *race, *class, and women's issues that have led most historians to ignore or dismiss their work (even in books that focus on women's history). But a few scholars such as Karen J. Blair and Theodora Penny Martin have shown that clubs of the late nineteenth and early twentieth centuries cultivated a "domestic feminism" that contributed significantly to women's liberation. Study clubs enabled large numbers of women to achieve a new level of independence—first by helping them acquire the tools of self-expression and self-organization, and then by encouraging them to use those tools outside the home.

• Jane C. Croly, *The History of the Women's Club Movement in America* (1898). Mary I. Wood, *The History of the General Federation of Women's Clubs* (1912). Sophonisba P. Breckenridge, *Women in the Twentieth Century* (1933; reprint, 1972). Karen J. Blair, *The Clubwoman as Feminist: True Womanhood Redefined, 1868–1914* (1980). Helen Hooven Santmyer, ". . . And the Ladies of the Club" (1982; reprint, 1984). Anne Firor Scott, *Making the Invisible Woman Visible* (1984). Theodora Penny Martin, *The Sound of Our Own Voices: Women's Study Clubs, 1860–1910* (1987). Nancy R. Gibbs with Elaine Lafferty, "High Noon for Women's Clubs," *Time* 30 May 1988:72. Anne Firor Scott, "Most Invisible of All: Black Women's Voluntary Associations," *Journal of Southern History* 56, no. 1 (1990):3–22.

Scott Peeples

WOMEN'S MOVEMENT. Throughout America's past, women of all classes, races, ethnic and religious backgrounds, sexual preferences, and political beliefs have participated in organized activities to improve women's lives. This organizational life has been rich and diverse, including literary societies, *anti-lynching leagues, missionary societies, anti-saloon leagues, *suffrage associations, the Daughters of the American Revolution, Women of the Ku Klux Klan, and *consciousness-raising groups, as a sampling. When one speaks of "the women's movement," however, one is generally referring to the organized efforts of men and women to bring about equal rights for women in U.S. society. This story has been traditionally presented as a progressive, linear narrative of how courageous men and women in the past (mostly women) battled against backward-looking beliefs to bring about the relative equality of the present. The story of the women's movement in the United States, however, while almost always courageous, was not always progressive. All too frequently, hard-won gains turned into Pyrrhic victories during periods of retrenchment and reaction.

The various women's movements in America's past also labored under internal weaknesses. Women's movements frequently shared and utilized *essentialist arguments about women's innate and natural differences from men. While the use of these rationalizations often helped organizations to make important gains in the short run (such as women's suffrage), essentialist arguments can and are often used against women's equal treatment in society. (The Stop ERA campaign of the 1970s is a recent example.) In fact, it has been extremely difficult for woman's rights activists and feminists to get beyond the equality/difference dichotomy that feminist theorists have only recently begun dismantling. Also, women's rights activists have tended to come from white, middle-class, Protestant backgrounds, and the movements they founded spoke to this constituency. The inability to make a women's movement of all races, religions, and classes has been a continuing weakness of the mainstream women's movement.

Women's movements occurred during three separate periods in the history of the United States, although there was a great deal of continuity among the periods, and important and significant activity in the time between them. Each of the three movements was a significant part of a larger reform/social movement. They roughly coincide with the antebellum period (1830–1860), the *progressive era (approximately 1900–World War I), and the *civil rights movement and the student activism of the 1960s and early 1970s.

The First Women's Movement. Our American Enlightenment provided the intellectual origins of the first women's movement in the United States. The stage was set for a women's movement at the writing of the Declaration of Independence with the statement that "all men are created equal; that they are endowed by their Creator with certain inalienable rights; that among these are life, liberty and the pursuit of happiness." The desire of the Continental Congress to provide a justification for a revolt against tyranny prompted one of its member's wives, Abigail *Adams, to ask in a letter to her husband John, "in the new code of laws which I suppose it will be necessary for you to make, I desire you would remember the ladies and be more generous and favorable to them than your ancestors. Do not put such unlimited power into the hands of the husbands. Remember, all men would be tyrants if they could. If particular care and attention is not paid to the ladies, we are determined to foment a rebellion and will not hold ourselves bound by any laws in which we have no voice or representation" (31 March 1776).

The new republic's novel experiment in self-governance and rule of law in Western society required, according to those who were responsible for making it work, an educated, informed, moral citizenry—republican men and women. While many Americans were aware of *A Vindication of the Rights of Woman* by British writer and intellectual Mary Wollstonecraft (1792), most did not believe that women should, or even could, be educated equally to men. Nevertheless, many did argue for an educated female citizenry for the good of the nation and its future. Since it was commonly believed that it was the role of mothers to provide the early moral and educational training of their children, only educated, pious women could produce those boys who would become the best future citizens and leaders of the United States.

These immediate political changes in the United States overlay longer-term cultural attitudes about women that were changing as the United States began its shift to an industrial economy. The early nineteenth century saw the start of the shift from home-based production to shop- and factory-based production for most necessary goods and services. This revolutionary transformation altered attitudes about woman's "nature" and "sphere," and changed women's day-to-day lives, although the alteration varied by *class, *race, and region. Within the dominant culture (white, Anglo-Saxon, Protestant, middle and upper class), it was generally accepted that *"true" women were pious, pure, chaste, domestic, submissive, intuitive, emotional, peaceful, and physically weaker than men; they embodied qualities that were the exact opposite of, or complementary to, those of men. Because of these essential differences, men and women quite rightly inhab-

ited different spheres of existence, which for white, Anglo-Saxon, Protestant, middle- and upper-class women, revolved around female *rituals of visiting, births, illnesses, and other family crises or celebrations. Men labored in their competitive, public, masculine spheres while women remained in the domestic, private, feminine spheres. Strong bonds of womanhood or sisterhood not only revealed that women were relegated to a limited round of activities within an increasingly complex society, but also demonstrated how these women gave emotional meaning and fulfillment to their lives.

The first woman's movement in the United States occurred just as the existence of a women's sphere seemed to be limiting women's range of activities. The intellectual and organizational progress women made during the antebellum period grew out of the ferment of antebellum reform. Many of the early activists on behalf of women's rights, women such as the *Grimké sisters, Lucretia *Mott, Elizabeth Cady *Stanton, and Susan B. *Anthony, encountered and participated in one or more of the great causes of the day, such as religious revivals, *abolitionism, educational reform, temperance, and labor reform. *Abolitionism, in particular, provided the impetus for many women to venture beyond their spheres on behalf of this high and noble cause, only to be reminded by male leaders of abolitionist organizations that speaking in public, agitating, running meetings, handling money, and participating in mixed assemblies of men and women was not proper for ladies. Southern sisters Sarah and Angelina Grimké were early advocates for both abolitionism and women's rights. In her *Letters on the Equality of the Sexes and the Condition of Women*, Sarah Grimké wrote in 1837 that, "men and women were created equal; they are both moral and accountable beings, and whatever is right for man to do is right for woman."

Other reform and intellectual currents of the day also led women to expressions, both in print and in their behavior, of the desire for a change in gender roles. Scottish-born Frances Wright scandalized her New York City audience not only by being one of the first women to speak in public but also by tackling such subjects as labor reform, the gradual emancipation of slaves, and woman's emancipation. Margaret *Fuller, intellectual, writer, and one of the New England transcendentalists, also challenged all barriers to the fullest development of women. In her book *Woman in the Nineteenth Century* (1845), Fuller penned the famous line that women should be sea captains if they are so disposed. Invoking assumptions about natural rights, Fuller claimed, "We would have every arbitrary barrier thrown down. We would have every path laid open to Woman as freely as to Man." A "ravishing harmony of the sphere" would ensue when "inward and outward freedom for Woman as much as for Man shall be acknowledged as a *right*, not yielded as a concession. As the friend of the negro assumes that one man cannot by right hold another in bondage, so should the friend of Woman assume that Man cannot by right lay even well-meant restrictions on Woman."

The beginning of self-conscious, organized efforts on behalf of woman's rights is usually dated from 1848 to the famous women's rights convention at Seneca Falls, New York. This meeting identified most of the important activists for the nineteenth century, and also produced one of the most important documents of the woman's movement, the *Declaration of Sentiments and Resolutions*. The authors (including Elizabeth Cady Stanton and Lucretia Mott) rewrote the Declaration of Independence: "We hold these truths to be self-evident: that all men and women are created equal; that they are endowed by their Creator with certain inalienable rights; that among these are life, liberty, and the pursuit of happiness. . . ." The document went on to list dozens of grievances, "injuries and usurpations on the part of man toward woman, having in direct object an absolute tyranny over her." The various resolutions demanded that women be accorded equality in all matter of public life—political, religious, economic, and social.

Throughout mainstream U.S. society, the *Declaration of Sentiments and Resolutions*, like the movement it began, was at best ignored, at worst ridiculed. Small groups of activists conducted conventions, gave speeches, wrote tracts, and petitioned for the altering of laws that restricted married women's rights to own and dispose of their own property as well as the loosening of restrictions on divorce. In certain states, some of these legislative changes were enacted. However, aside from the major task of identifying women as a group experiencing deprivations and requiring a movement to undo the damage, no widespread improvement of women's condition ensued.

The Second Women's Movement. The second wave of activity on women's behalf proved more popular and successful, if ultimately more limited in its scope. Those men and women who participated in championing women's rights before the *Civil War continued in these efforts after the war, but their organizations were initially plagued by battles over tactics, ideology, and, most significantly, the issue of *race. Many women's rights activists, notably Eliza-

beth Cady Stanton and Susan B. Anthony, were profoundly disappointed and disillusioned that suffrage was not extended to women at the same time it was given to African-American men. In their postwar organization, the National Women's Suffrage Association (NWSA), these two women, while proposing equality for women in a wide variety of arenas and even attempting to make common cause (though unsuccessfully) with working-class women, invoked racist and ethnocentric rationales for female suffrage. If immigrant men and former slaves could vote, they argued, why not "respectable, white women"? While this rhetoric might have actually endeared them to many in U.S. society, other aspects of their program were too radical. They prohibited men from their organization; their journal, *Revolution*, explored all sorts of sensational issues of the day, including free love; and they called for a constitutional amendment to enfranchise women. The aims of the other women's rights organization, the American Women's Suffrage Association (AWSA), seemed more moderate. The people who formed this group after the Civil War— Lucy *Stone, Henry Blackwell, and Henry Ward Beecher—were more sanguine about putting women's suffrage on the "back burner" because the post–Civil War era was "the negro's hour." The AWSA advocated the use of state and local campaigns, in some cases for parital suffrage, to gradually win the vote for women. Both of these groups, however, were comprised of white, middle-class reformers, and neither was particularly successful until late in the century.

The merging of these two factions into the National American Women's Suffrage Association (NAWSA) in 1890 heralded many changes in the nature of women's movement activities. This merger occurred amid a great national debate about women's position in United States society that was prompted by the increasing appearance of women in the world of work (in many cases in unhealthy factories in growing urban areas), in the world of public benevolence and reform, in higher education, at the ballot box (in some western states), and even in organizations of socialists, communists, populists, anarchists, labor unions, and other "scandalous" organizations. At all levels of society, people argued "the woman question": where do women belong and what should they properly be doing?

There was no question that many women were transcending what was considered their appropriate sphere to participate in meetings of their women's clubs. White middle-class women, as well as African-American women, Jewish women, Catholic women, and women of a variety of ethnic groups came together in clubs for personal enrichment, cultural uplift, and important community work. Jane *Addams, college educated and committed to serving the community of humankind in some useful way, began a settlement house in a poor Chicago neighborhood. Hull House, which served primarily immigrant women and children, was the model for literally thousands of settlements to follow, as well as a beacon for educated white single women looking for purpose in their lives. Middle-class white women also joined the Women's Christian Temperance Union in large numbers during this period; in fact, * temperance was considered an important "women's issue." White middle-class reform women joined with working-class women to form the Women's Trade Union League to organize women workers throughout the United States.

At the same time, radical female intellectuals and activists, many of whom formed a coterie in Greenwich Village in New York City, were redefining the agenda of the women's movement. They were, in fact, giving birth to a set of ideals called * feminism. According to historian Nancy Cott (in *The Grounding of Modern Feminism*, 1987), the term *feminism* came into use in the 1910s to describe a wholly different, more controversial approach to activism on behalf of women. Feminism, according to Cott, was a movement committed to destroying sexual hierarchies, to uncovering the distinction between socially constructed gender roles and biologically determined sex roles, and to mobilizing women as a distinct social group with common aims and goals.

Feminist women of this group usually identified themselves as hyphenated radicals: anarchist-feminists like Emma *Goldman or socialist-feminists like Charlotte Perkins *Gilman and Margaret Sanger. In her writings and speeches, and in her own life, Goldman denounced institutional (governmental or religious) sanctions on free human relations, most notably *marriage. Women were naturally sexual beings, and women need only shed Victorian gender ideology and use *birth control to discover this for themselves. Goldman's advocacy of birth control contributed to Margaret Sanger's discovery of her own life's work: to make access to birth control available to all women. Gilman, in dozens of works of fiction and nonfiction, presented one of the most powerful and popular critiques of turn-of-the-century society. Her famous tract, *Women and Economics* (1898), a work influenced by social Darwinism, suggested that so-called women's nature has been conditioned by social evolution. Restricting women to domestic functions

in an isolated household, Gilman argued, stunted women's fullest development as human beings. To ameliorate this problem, Gilman proposed that the labor women had traditionally done in the private world of the home be done for pay in communal kitchens, laundries, nurseries, and so forth, thereby allowing all women a choice to pursue a wider variety of callings. Even though they held different ideas, Goldman, Gilman, and Sanger were suggesting new gender arrangements in what was considered the private sphere of home, family, and bedroom.

Ironically, while a small group of radical women undoubtedly experienced new freedoms (and challenges), most men and women were "coming around" to the idea of women's suffrage because of the increasingly racist and essentialist nature of the appeals. Suffrage was becoming acceptable to the mainstream. The *Woman Citizen*, the journal for the National American Women's Suffrage Association, stated on 7 July 1917, "That is exactly what the suffrage movement is today—bourgeois, middle-class, a great middle-of-the-road movement." The suffrage movement between 1900 and 1920, under the new leadership of Anna Howe Shaw and Carrie Chapman *Catt, was able to bring women from a wide variety of organizational affiliations into efforts to get the vote. Racial divisions were frequently exploited to attract white southern men and women into the suffrage ranks. If white women could vote, after all, this would ensure white supremacy in the south. Similar rhetoric was employed to persuade urban dwellers, who were concerned about swarming immigrants. Giving white, Anglo-Saxon, Protestant women the vote would counteract the influences of the large number of Catholic immigrants who were against temperance.

The newer converts to suffrage activity were also undoubtedly attracted by a significant shift in focus that Aileen Kraditor identified in her *Ideals of the Woman Suffrage Movement, 1890–1920* (1965) as "a change from the emphasis by suffragists on the ways in which women were the same as men and therefore had the *right* to vote, to a stress on the ways in which they differed from men, and therefore had the *duty* to contribute their special skills and experience to government" (emphasis Kraditor's). Since many of the philanthropic, religious, temperance, civic, and club activities of women were considered "social housekeeping" or "housekeeping on a grand scale," the vote would only help women shore up their gains in these acceptable areas. Because of the pervasive beliefs that women did possess a more passive, nurturing, caring, and domestically oriented nature, it was generally assumed that with the vote, women could eliminate child labor, abusive drinking, slums, poverty, tainted food, and even war. The NAWSA continued to use education, and state and local campaigns, to bring about gradual suffrage for women.

Some suffragists chafed under the constraints of both the ideology and tactics of this mainstream suffrage organization and broke away to form their own organization. Alice Paul and Lucy Burns, who were influenced by the militant tactics of the British suffrage movement, formed the Congressional Union in 1913, which by 1917 became the National Women's Party. These primarily younger women argued for a constitutional amendment to bring the vote to women, and they did so in a very "unladylike" way. They staged marches, demonstrations, and pickets; when arrested, they served their time and refused food.

Women's support and contributions to the Great War to preserve democracy in Europe undoubtedly added poignancy to this dramatic suffrage activity and signaled to many the need to extend democracy at home. By August 1920, the requisite number of states had ratified the constitutional amendment allowing women the right to vote. It was a great victory that many believed would bring fundamental changes (good or bad depending on one's perspective on women's rights) to United States society. The 1920s did appear to many to be a new era. It brought to mainstream, white, middle-class society a "revolution in manners and morals," which seemed to allow women greater sexual freedoms (heterosexual freedoms, really, since the 1920s saw the "discovery" of *lesbianism, but also witnessed enormous ambivalance toward and repression of lesbianism) and more opportunities in the world of work and education. The national government established the Women's Bureau in the Department of Labor to investigate the working conditions of women, and passed the Sheppard-Towner Maternity and Infancy Protection Act (1921) to provide prenatal and maternal nursing care and assistance for women throughout the country. The momentum prompted the National Women's Party to write the Equal Rights Amendment (E.R.A.) in 1923 and present it as the new item on the agenda of the Women's Movement.

But the promise of suffrage was unfulfilled. Much like those who followed in the 1980s, the young women coming of age in the 1920s found the efforts of their mothers and *grandmothers on behalf of women's rights unnecessary and even embarrassing. Since they could vote, smoke, drink (illegally), wear freer clothing, work for pay, and "pet," they felt that women were liberated. More important, the struggle

for suffrage had united enormously diverse groups of women that seemed to have little in common after the major battle had been won. Political cleavages plagued the mainstream, white, middle-class contingent. Many female activists were not enthusiastic about the E.R.A. because they felt it would undo decades of work for protective labor legislation designed to help women and children in the workplace. African-American women tried, in vain, to alert members of the National Women's Party to the fact that, because of the system of segregation and state voting restrictions, black women in the south (as well as black men) still could not vote. Alice Paul insisted that this was a "racial" issue, not a "feminist" issue. Race, class, political persuasions, regionalism, and debates about equality versus difference marred any possibility of unified action on behalf of all women.

The backsliding and state repression of the 1920s was followed quickly by the economic calamity of the 1930s, and then by the commitment to a total war effort during the first half of the 1940s. Gains in these decades did not result from any self-consciously described women's or feminist movement. Women's work, both inside and outside the home during these decades of crisis, was essential to the survival of their individual families as well as to the nation. And this was generally acknowledged, particularly during World War II, when "Rosie the Riveters" entered previously masculine factories and shops to contribute to the war effort. As World War II drew to a close, and it was clear that the mobilization of women's war work was coming to an end, only one organization remained to provide any continuity for women's rights issues. The Woman's Party "survived the doldrums" of the 1950s by keeping its ranks small, by lobbying national political leaders, and by focusing on the issue of the E.R.A.

But unlike the situation after World War I, when women's contributions to the war for democracy provoked an extension of democracy at home, the cry after World War II was for a return to "normalcy." Amid the unspeakable specters of the *Holocaust and nuclear weapons, Americans retreated to their private refuges in the emerging suburbs, escaping and seeking consolation in traditional gender roles and family life. The baby boom, the growth of suburbs, and early marriage age were all testaments to the power of this sentiment. Women's clearly defined and scientifically sanctioned role in this retreat was named and criticized in Betty *Friedan's influential book *The Feminine Mystique* (1963). Those most able to participate in this new feminine mystique—white, middle-class, suburban housewives—were unhappy, Friedan revealed. Their role servicing others allowed them no identity of their own. The solution was for them to take up fulfilling, self-identifying work.

Ironically, more women entered the labor force during the postwar era, and these women were older, married, and mothers. This slow increase in the labor force participation rate of women and its increasing demographic diversity contributed to what Alice Kessler-Harris in *Out to Work: A History of Wage Earning Women in the United States* (1982) calls "the radical consequences of incremental change." Undoubtedly, as more women made a lifetime commitment to wage work (even if they were thought of as "secondary" bread winners), issues of workplace equity and equal pay for equal work would become important for women of all class, racial, and ethnic backgrounds. In some progressive labor unions and in some state and local governments, women began to work for legislation to bring greater equity in the world of work. President John F. Kennedy's Commission on the Status of Women, convened in 1961, brought women's equity issues to the attention of the nation while providing an important forum for many of these female activists. The Equal Pay Act of 1963 reflected this concern.

The Third Women's Movement. A new era of great social change was about to begin. Building upon decades of painstaking legislative work, the NAACP was about to argue a case in the Supreme Court that would render a decision that would send shock waves throughout United States society. The 1954 decision in *Brown vs. the Board of Education of Topeka, Kansas* overturned the separate but equal doctrine that allowed for segregated public accommodations for African-Americans and whites. This decision not only alerted many white Americans to the plight of African Americans in the segregated South but also sparked a decade and a half of a wide variety of activities and organizations on behalf of the *civil rights of African Americans. These efforts provided the energy, ideology, and even personnel for other social movements of the 1960s and the 1970s, including a new women's movement. As in the 1830s, when the first woman's rights movement emerged from *abolitionism, the new women's movement of the 1960s, women's liberation, came from the civil rights as well as the student movements of the period.

The constituency of this new woman's movement resembled its foremothers. Those who identified themselves with the new women's liberation movement of the late 1960s were primarily white, middle-class, college-educated women, although unlike the previous periods, there were more notable exceptions. Many had come from left/progressive backgrounds. They encountered their own second-class status as women while participating in civil rights and antiwar, New Left organizations. Relegated to "women's work" (office work, housework), denied access to positions of power, and uncomfortable with the new sexual revolution, which seemed to promise more to men than women, these women began to formulate a critique of their position *as women.* Using tactics and ideologies from the social movements they had recently abandoned, New Left women separated themselves to formulate an analysis of their position in society. This was accomplished in small, decentralized, seemingly uncoordinated groups called *consciousness-raising groups. In these groups, women drew on their collective experiences to arrive at an understanding and a critique of their position in society, and to decide on a course of action. Numerous organizations and groups emerged from these discussions: guerilla theater groups, dance troupes, health collectives (like the collective that wrote the influential *Our Bodies, Our Selves*), *rape crisis centers, and day-care centers. A revival and a renewal of feminism emerged from this activity and its slogans were: "Look to your own oppression" and "the personal is political."

The vitality of the women's movement of the late 1960s and 1970s resulted from the uneasy alliance of these young women's liberationists with the women's rights activitists in the National Organization of Women (NOW), founded in 1966 by Betty Friedan and women from the various state commissions on the status of women. Modeled on the NAACP, NOW was committed to bringing about legislative changes to improve women's position in society. The organization attracted primarily older, white, professional, middle-class women who frequently did not extend their vision of women's liberation into the private spheres of sexuality and family life.

Nevertheless, both "wings" of the woman's movement of the late 1960s could unite to work on a number of important legislative and social issues of the day. Activists challenged and in many cases succeeded in dismantling artificial barriers to the fullest participation of women in public life. From professions to athletics to labor unions, women made new inroads into previously male preserves. Interest in the Equal Rights Amendment revived. And in 1973, the Supreme Court decision in *Roe v. Wade* guaranteed woman's reproductive choice during the first trimester of her pregnancy.

Women in both wings of the women's movement in the 1960s and 1970s could also participate in a new cultural/educational renaissance of women. A new woman's voice was heard in novels, poetry, song, and in nonfiction. Works of intellectuals like Kate *Millet, Germaine Greer, Gloria *Steinem (who founded *Ms. magazine), Shulamith Firestone, and all of the contributors to Robin Morgan's *Sisterhood Is Powerful* presented powerful critiques of partriarchial society and proposed new ways of thinking about the world. Creative writers like Adrienne *Rich, Toni *Morrison, Maya *Angelou, Marilyn *French, and Alice *Walker presented new women's voices, most importantly the voices of women of color, and by doing so, provoked a reconceptualizing of what constitutes a "literary *canon." Songwriters and singers like Holly Near, Meg Christian, and Margie Adams gave beautiful voices to women's issues and lesbian love in their music. Artists like Judy Chicago not only challenged conventional art forms with installations like *The Dinner Party*, but also taught the public important lessons from women's history. And, in the 1970s and continuing into the 1980s, *women's studies programs made their appearance in the academy.

The defeat of the E.R.A. in 1982, in part a result of a very successful Stop ERA campaign waged by Phyllis Schlafly, signaled to many the end of the most recent women's movement. Feminism did seem to fall into disrepute in the 1980s. The conservative political climate made feminism seem outdated and even unnecessary to many young people just as many of the gains of the recent women's movement came under attack. But there might be reason for cautious hope. Two extremely popular recent books, Susan Faludi's *Backlash* (1991) and Naomi Wolf's *The Beauty Myth* (1991), have alerted a new generation to the continuing problems facing women. Anita Hill's allegations of *sexual harrassment at Clarence Thomas's confirmation hearings for the Supreme Court as well as the William Kennedy Smith and Mike Tyson *rape trials have alerted the nation to the need for more work to make women truly safe and equal in our society. Recent Supreme Court decisions on *abortion have awakened reproductive rights groups to the need to remain vigilant on behalf of this fundamental human right for women. The realization that so-called women's issues (child care, family leave, health insurance, welfare, economic security, and choice) are national issues prompted a renewed effort to elect women to national office in 1992 and beyond. A new group, the Women's Action Coalition, recently formed in New York City and now extending to many larger cities throughout the nation, has committed itself to "direct action" on behalf of women's rights. It remains to be seen whether the 1990s will bring us our next "woman's movement."

[*See also* Activism; Political Organizations.]

• Eleanor Flexner, *Century of Struggle: The Woman's Rights Movement in the United States* (1959). Aileen S. Kraditor, *The Ideas of the Woman Suffrage Movement, 1890–1920* (1965). Gerda Lerner, *The Grimké Sisters from South Carolina: Pioneers for Woman's Rights and Abolition* (1966). Alice S. Rossi, ed., *The Feminist Papers: From Adams to de Beauvoir* (1973). Jo Freeman, *The Politics of Women's Liberation: A Case Study of an Emerging Social Movement and Its Relation to the Policy Process* (1975). Mari Jo Buhle and Paul Buhle, eds., *The Concise History of Woman Suffrage: Selections from the Classic Work of Stanton, Anthony, Gage, and Harper* (1978). Ellen Carol DuBois, *Feminism and Suffrage: The Emergence of an Independent Women's Movement in America, 1846–1869* (1978). Sara Evans, *Personal Politics: The Roots of Women's Liberation in the Civil Rights Movement and the New Left* (1980). Elizabeth Griffith, *In Her Own Right: The Life of Elizabeth Cady Stanton* (1984). Joan Hoff-Wilson, ed., *Rights of Passage: The Past and Future of the ERA* (1986). Nancy F. Cott, *The Grounding of Modern Feminism* (1987). Leila J. Rupp and Verta Taylor, *Survival in the Doldrums: The American Women's Rights Movement, 1945–1960* (1987).

Lisa M. Fine

WOMEN'S STUDIES PROGRAMS. Feminist scholarship is at heart an epistemological endeavor. It requires researcher and student alike to ask what we know about women and *gender systems, how we have come to know it, and what consequences flow from this view of the world. To engage in such an exercise, scholars need a place—an intellectual space in which to think about the world through the lens "women" and a social space in which they interact with others investigating similar questions. Women's studies programs in American universities have provided the institutional basis for such endeavors. They foster both the development of women's studies as an academic discipline and the creation of discipline-based scholarship that centers on women and gender. Outside the United States, research on women is often carried out in autonomous research centers and is less frequently made part of the core curriculum of universities.

Historically, women's studies courses emerged in the late 1960s and early 1970s as university after university began introducing the new scholarship into the curriculum. San Diego State University and Cornell are often cited as the first two schools to offer courses. In fact, more recent investigation shows that many colleges were responding to the same social and scholarly trends and starting to teach courses on women. In some instances, established scholars began teaching a course on "women and . . ." as a part of their regular responsibilities in their home departments. In other cases, a group of young scholars, usually joined by graduate students and community activists, put together the prototype of an introductory course for women's studies and offered it on an overload basis.

Whichever came first, the number of courses grew dramatically in the first half of the seventies and quickly began clustering into programs. Programs consisted of an interdisciplinary grouping of courses on women and gender, with an introductory and often a capstone course; a faculty member appointed to direct the interdisciplinary endeavor; space, budget, faculty, and staff in varying amounts; a calendar of events and/or a newsletter to distribute information about women's studies; public programming on campus and in the community to make others aware of the new scholarly developments; and a concentration, minor or major, in the field itself at both the undergraduate and graduate level in subsequent years.

By the 1990s, in just over twenty years, formal women's studies programs existed on almost 650 campuses and courses were offered on as many more. The National Women's Studies Association, based at the University of Maryland in College Park, Maryland, published the *1990 NWSA Directory of Women's Studies Programs, Women's Centers and Women's Research Centers*, giving statistics on the numbers of programs and suggesting that all three types of services played critical roles in the education for and about women.

The characteristics of programs varied considerably, depending on whether the campus also had a women's center to work with students on an individual basis on personal questions and on issues of campus climate; a research center that had external funding to bring visiting scholars to campus and fund research; a local or regional curriculum transformation project to foster new courses and revisions of existing ones; and the nature and scope of university resources available to the women's studies program. These variations aside, women's studies programs have been the institutional place where feminist scholarship has flourished. How has that been accomplished?

Women's studies programs foster feminist scholarship in both tangible and intangible ways. The first set of tangible activities relates to program basics. Urging faculty to offer courses on women often pushes faculty members to develop an emergent interest to the point where they feel comfortable calling themselves "experts" in the field. Advertising a series of courses already available on campus increases enrollments and puts participating faculty in communication with each other across departmental lines. Sponsoring seminar series in which faculty can hear about research in progress (as well as report their own) creates an intellectual milieu in which individual projects grow. Bringing visiting feminist scholars to campus (for a lecture, a day of visits to classes, or a more extended period of time) sets up networks of individuals who learn from each other. Some programs hold annual research conferences to showcase the work of both students and faculty. Other programs hold symposia that are more sustained opportunities for listening and exchanging. Still others have been the editorial homes for scholarly journals in women's studies.

All of these are the standard ways in which academic work proceeds. When done under the women's studies rubric, the activities are different in at least two aspects. First, women's studies is by definition an interdisciplinary endeavor and all of those who participate in it learn to talk across the jargon and paradigms of their disciplines. While doing so is often a personally painful and politically tricky endeavor, crossing disciplinary boundaries and studying neglected topics contributes directly to the vitality that is characteristic of women's studies. Second, women's studies is not usually content to let the academic status quo stand. Feminist scholarship insists that new subjects be investigated (for example, studying *violence against women) and that old disciplines be revised (for example, including the work of women authors, artists, and performers). Feminist scholars have been responsible both for new theoretical paradigms (for example, the gendered nature of the state, law, and public policy) as well as for significant shifts in disciplinary theory (for example, feminist literary criticism). Feminist scholarship has virtually transformed the tenets of every discipline and it is through the daily workings of women's studies programs that this scholarship has grown.

The second tangible area in which women's studies fosters feminist scholarship relates to teaching. Here the documentary record is much less extensive than the record of disciplinary change but the evidence is building. The first writings in women's studies as a discipline, published in a series of informal mimeographed booklets called *Female Studies*, emphasized the necessity of locating the academic subject in the experiences of the students. The latest discussion, recorded in *Liberal Learning and Arts and Sciences Majors*, the result of a three-year study of twelve majors by the Association of American Colleges, examines the ways in which students learn to validate their own voices and engage in critical thinking across the curriculum as a result of women's studies courses.

What characterizes women's studies approaches to teaching and how does it contribute to the development of feminist scholarship? Two recently published works, one edited by Jean F. O'Barr and Mary Wyer, *Engaging Feminism: Students Speak Up and Speak Out* (1992) and a study by the National Women's Studies Association called *The Courage to Question* (1992), begin to document the process. In each case, students describe how when teachers assume knowledge emanates only from their scholarly expertise, it does; how acknowledging the politics of knowledge construction propels students to participate in its building; how fusing theory with everyday experiences yields richer explanatory frameworks; and how collaborative rather than competitive teaching and learning styles work more effectively for many. Reading student accounts of their classroom experiences, it is clear that their voices have helped to shape the feminist research agenda by the questions they ask and the interests they express.

Many would argue that the intangible ways in which women's studies programs foster feminist scholarship are as important as the research and teaching projects they undertake. The contemporary university grows out of an academy that was based on the exclusion of women. While the campus climate may have grown less chilly in the years since feminist scholarship became a presence, it remains the case that women as faculty are few in number and women as students are relatively silent in the day-to-day operations of the campus (they do not have administrative leadership roles in significant numbers; their activities in sports, in social life, and in campus leadership tend to take second place to those of men; and studies of the effect of college life on women show a negative influence). Women's studies programs are variously described by women on campus as "homes," "havens," "safe places," and "a spot where I feel welcome and validated." By bringing feminist scholars, particularly women, together, by naming their inquiries into women's lives as legitimate, and by providing a means whereby they can further the projects that matter to them, women's studies programs provide intellectual, spiritual, and practical sustenance to the scholars who are doing feminist scholarship. Without that personal and professional support, they would be less likely to produce the growing number of presentations, articles, conference panels, and books that we have come to associate with a growing field of inquiry.

[*See also* Education.]

• Florence Howe, *Seven Years Later: Women's Studies Programs in 1976*, The National Advisory Council on Womens Educational Programs of the Women's Educational Equity Act in the Educational Amendments of 1974 (1976). Catharine R. Stimpson with Nina Kressner Cobb, *Women's Studies in the United States* (1986). Elizabeth Minnich, Jean O'Barr, and Rachel Rosenfeld, *Reconstructing the Academy: Women's Education and Women's Studies* (1988). Carol Pearson, Donna Shavlik, and Judy Touchton, eds., *Educating the Majority: How Women Are Changing Higher Education* (1989). Mariam Chamberlain, "The Emergence and Growth of Women's Studies Programs," in *The American Woman 1990–91: A Status Report*, ed. Sara E. Rix (1990).

Jean F. O'Barr

WOMEN WRITING ON MEN. Women critics in general and feminist women critics who work on the male *canon still confront a variety of problems, many of which come under the rubric of silencing—to borrow Tillie *Olsen's famous phrase—of both a literal and conceptual nature. The most apparent of these is the possibility of being silenced by external pressures. Because critical communities exercise their power by the threat of exclusion, the feminist critic has the potential of being treated as an outsider, completely or partially excluded from conference panels, editorial boards, or essay collections, or even in some instances, from access to research materials.

Moreover, since she has elected to ally herself, however marginally, with the predominantly white male scholarly community, the feminist critic working on a canonical male writer also finds her access to the emerging power structures of *gynocriticism problematic. Feminist scholars who work on women writers have been publishing and editing the much-needed texts of previously lost or marginalized women, creating new anthologies of writing by women, and setting up panels and conferences that attempt to redefine and expand the canon and validate previously devalued genres such as sentimental poetry, *local color writing, and popular romance. Yet, noting the ways in which the women who work exclusively on women writers have now developed their own networks and communities, those who concentrate on male writers and also think of themselves as feminists may sometimes feel that they have located themselves in an impossible middle zone between two theoretically and politically antithetical scholarly groups. Moreover, because of the gender politics involved, this constitutes more than simply non-alignment with one of the matrixes of power.

Awareness of these particular aspects of the politics of criticism provokes fundamental questions about the nature and purpose of the feminist critique of canonical male writers and thus about one's scholarly identity. If some of the feminists who work solely on female writers view askance those women who work on male writers as well, while the male community also at least partially excludes them, a critic can end by asking herself not only where she is but who she is.

Even within traditionally structured departments, some feminist critics believe it is as important to alter from within as it is to ally themselves and their work with that of the gynocritics; therefore, they are committed to scholarship and teaching on male writers like Faulkner, Hawthorne, and James. Thus, along with offering gender-based courses such as "Women in Literature" and "Women in Film," they also teach canonical courses such as "American Literature Survey" or "American Realism" with revised syllabi, and offer graduate seminars on such topics as "Sexual/Textual Politics in James, Wharton, and Glasgow," or "Faulkner: Feminism/Modernism." Stimulated by opportunities to teach courses that concentrate on feminist issues and female artists, they believe it is equally crucial to provide new perspectives on canonized male authors, to place them clearly in their cultural contexts, and, for further illumination, to play off their texts against those by women and by writers of color.

They have discovered, however, that proponents of the "classic canon" often find the decision to place women writers in the mainstream curriculum even more disruptive than a gynocritical approach. Yet clearly students' critical faculties are strengthened by the experience of juxtaposing the voices of canonized white male modernists with those of, for example, Zora Neale *Hurston, Edith *Wharton, Nella *Larsen, Gertrude *Stein, and Virginia *Woolf. Still, it is an uneasy situation, and in teaching as in research, feminists may feel torn between what appear as rival claims of "equality" and "difference," between the desire to be scholars of the canon occupying the center on equal terms with men and the wish to be different, to avoid the center by concentrating on women and minority writers still largely seen as marginal despite the ongoing attempts to retrieve them from marginality. Despite such conflicts, however, they believe that their critical thinking is enriched by a continued engagement with the variously feminine, feminist, and hegemonic voices of all these novelists.

The feminist frequently confronts important conceptual difficulties when she undertakes criticism of a male writer. To be sure, most feminist critiques have passed well beyond the taxonomic images-of-women stage and have moved toward a theory-based concern with topics such as voice and *silence, toward efforts to "hear" female (or black) characters, free of the usual patriarchal static that would ghettoize

them as irretrievably *Other, or toward relocating the authorial voice itself in diverse regions of the gender map, characterizing that voice as variously feminine, androgynous, bisexual, or even, perhaps, as lesbian. Feminist critiques have attempted to discern traces of silenced female voices in various male texts and to hear resistances in that female speech formerly heard as nonsense or *hysteria. They have also contextualized fiction and poetry, undertaking valuable efforts to read it through the lens of history and culture. The politics of sexuality itself has been reevaluated.

Nevertheless, a variety of inhibiting pressures affect some feminists at work on the male canon, in a few cases aborting their efforts. In the most vivid example of pressures of this sort, a women critic who has written extensively on both male and female writers said that the hostile, often personal attacks elicited by many of her recent feminist critiques makes her wonder whether silence might not be the appropriate tactic for the moment. Yet another woman, who has done extensive work on canonical male writers, notes that her criticism is often labeled (and sometimes assailed) as feminist, even when its approach to the literature neither grounds itself in the theory nor explores the issues commonly regarded as feminist; such labeling of criticism as feminist is among the forms of intellectual harassment cited in a 1991 MLA report. Other feminists report confronting more oblique but no less intimidating challenges, such as raising questions with themselves about the source and nature of their authority in relation to male texts, or wondering as whom, in gender terms, they speak.

To those women who live and work as feminists and are engaged by feminist theory, and who wish to speak from a position that coincides neither with the center nor the margins, it is necessary as well as enlivening to view the field of criticism as dialogic and carnivalesque, and the feminist critic as one who, in the words of Hélène Cixous, "doesn't annul differences but stirs them up." While the project of reexamining the traditional canon from a feminist vantage point may position the woman critic in an uncomfortable in-between space, it is a space whose occupation is crucial both to critical theory and practice and, ultimately, to the canon itself.

Judith L. Sensibar and
Judith Bryant Wittenberg

WONG, Jade Snow (b. 1922), autobiographer. The fifth child of seven, Jade Snow Wong was born and reared in San Francisco, in a strictly traditional Chinese home. That is, sons received preferential treatment; daughters were taught to subdue personal desires and expect nothing higher than the position of matriarch in a large family. American public schools, however, taught her individual rights, independence, and self-fulfillment. Culling the best from both worlds, Jade Snow Wong acknowledged the benefits of discipline, hard work, and self-sacrifice, yet asserted her independence by putting herself through college and creating her own ceramics business.

The struggle to resolve cultural conflicts found expression in her first *autobiography, *Fifth Chinese Daughter* (1950), in which the surface tone of respectfulness clashes with underlying, repressed anger at inequities suffered from both her family and the larger society. This tension epitomizes a major aspect of the Asian-American experience. Later writers, reading on the surface, have condemned Wong for her passive, assimilationist stance; others have found her book a model and an inspiration. Literary historians have seen *Fifth Chinese Daughter* as serving a political purpose in fulfilling the dominant society's need during World War II to distinguish Chinese allies from Japanese enemies.

In her second autobiography, *No Chinese Stranger* (1976), Jade Snow Wong continues her life story. With hindsight, she examines her early struggles to achieve a balance between Chinese filial piety and American self-assertion. She re-examines her relationship with her father, considering the losses and gains of his Old World child-rearing methods. She also recounts her marriage and family life, and most significantly, details her trip to Asia, which was sponsored by the U.S. State Department. To visit China as a Chinese American, born and educated in the United States, initially inspired trepidation and fear, but as the book's title states, the author ultimately discovered herself less of a stranger in a land she had never previously visited than in the country she calls home. Much of her comfort in China she attributes to the Chinese education her father had enforced, and much of the alienation she experiences in the U.S., she implies, is due to racial *prejudice.

Though Jade Snow Wong considers herself primarily a craftsperson in clay and enamels, her words have had wide influence. Even if her literary output has not been large, as a pioneer American-born Asian-American writer, her position and her early voicing of bicultural concerns make her work significant.

• Lowell Chun-Hoon, "Jade Snow Wong and the Fate of Chinese-American Identity," *Amerasia Journal* 1 (1971): 125–134. Elaine H. Kim, *Asian American Literature: An Introduction to the Writings and Their Social Context* (1982). Kathleen Loh Swee Yin and Kristoffer F. Paulson, "The Divided Voice of Chinese-American Narration: Jade Snow Wong's Fifth Chinese Daughter," *MELUS* 9, no. 1 (1982): 53–59. Karin Meissenburg, *The Writing on the Wall: Socio-Historical Aspects of Chinese American Literature, 1900–1980* (1986). Amy Ling, *Between Worlds: Women Writers of Chinese Ancestry* (1990).

Amy Ling

WOOD, S.S.B.K. (1759–1854), commonly known as Madam Wood, native-born Maine novelist and short fiction writer. Sarah Sayward Barrell Keating Wood grew up in the home of her affluent maternal grandfather, Judge Jonathan Sayward, and married his clerk, Richard Keating, who died in 1783, leaving her a widow with three children. She wrote four novels and several short stories before her marriage in 1804 to General Abiel Wood, who died in 1811. In 1827 *Tales of the Night* was published. Madam Wood was noted for wearing a high white ruffled headdress at home, or concealing her features behind a plain black bonnet outdoors. She died at the age of ninety-five.

Responding to prevailing moral strictures against fiction, Wood in her dedication for *Julia and the Illuminated Baron* (1800) explains her anonymity, apologizes for her literary shortcomings, and protests that in writing the book she has neglected no household duties. The preface to *Dorval; or The Speculator* (1801) asserts the value of domestic retreat. Wood further reinforces the stereotypical role of women as submissive homemakers by portraying passive, victimized heroines whose virtue prevails against terrifying evil. The orphaned Julia repulses the condescending advances of the Count de Launa, who offers to raise her social rank, through liaison with him, by presenting her as "a lovely ornament" (205). *Amelia; or, The Influence of Virtue* (1802) presents a meek heroine who uncomplainingly endures her philandering husband and his mistress, and even willingly raises his illegitimate children. In *Amelia* and in *Ferdinand and Elmira: A Russian Story* (1804), virtue ultimately brings happiness to the heroines and repentance to the heroes.

While America attempted to establish independence from Europe, Wood straddled both worlds. *Julia* takes place in England and France, an appropriate locale for the nefarious baron and his affiliation with illuminationism, which many patriotic Americans feared as a subversive alien ideology. *Ferdinand and Elmira* borrows mystery and *exoticism from its Russian setting. *Dorval*, however, is set in America and reflects the author's nationalistic thrust. "Storms and Sunshine," one of the *Tales of the Night* (1827), by "A Lady of Maine," takes place in Wood's native state. Set primarily in New

Hampshire, Wood's posthumously published *War the Parent of Domestic Calamity: A Tale of the Revolution* (1968) vividly depicts the disasters of violence.

Wood assumed a place among contemporary writers of sentimental tales who avowed their didactic intent to promote virtue, yet produced sensational melodramas laced with * gothic elements.

• William Gould, "Madam Wood, the First Maine Writer of Fiction," *Collections and Proceedings of the Maine Historical Society*, 2d ser., 1 (1890), pp. 401–408. Richard S. Sprague, ed., *A Handful of Spice: Essays in Maine*, 2d ser., 88 (1968), pp. 41–51. Henri Petter, *The Early American Novel* (1971). Lucy M. Freibert and Barbara A. White, eds., *Hidden Hands: An Anthology of American Women Writers, 1790–1870* (1985), pp. 51–67. William J. Scheick, "Education, Class, and the French Revolution in Sarah Wood's *Julia*," *Studies in American Fiction* 16, no. 1 (Spring 1988): 111–118.

Sally C. Hoople

WOOLF, Virginia (1882–1941), one of the premier modernist writers of this century. Daughter of British man of letters Sir Leslie Stephen, Virginia Stephen Woolf was educated at home and, in 1913, married Leonard Woolf, writer and publisher of The Hogarth Press. Several of her polemical works—the 1929 *A Room of One's Own* and the 1938 *Three Guineas*—have supplied some of the imagery and language for much of today's feminist thought and writing. In her insistence on the woman writer's need for independence—financially, geographically, and emotionally—Woolf foreshadowed current women writers' beliefs. Her fictional character Judith Shakespeare is even better known than characters from her beloved novels, *Mrs. Dalloway*, *The Waves*, and *To the Lighthouse*. Her parodic *Orlando: A Biography* has recently been made into a film.

An * incest survivor, Woolf suffered severe depressions. During World War II, with the threat of incarceration and execution imminent should England fall to Germany, she drowned herself in the river Ouse.

Linda Wagner-Martin

WOOLSON, Constance Fenimore (1840–1894), novelist, short-story writer, essayist, and poet. Despite the deaths from scarlet fever of three of her sisters only weeks after her birth, Constance Fenimore Woolson, great-niece of the novelist James Fenimore Cooper, spent a happy girlhood in the growing city of Cleveland, Ohio. She loved exercise and writing and was encouraged in both by her family and at school. Following her father's death in 1869, Woolson and her mother traveled along the eastern seaboard, frequently wintering in Florida. After her

mother's death in 1879, Woolson left America for Europe, never to return, although her lifelong dream was to retire to a cottage on the beach near St. Augustine.

In the spring of 1880, Woolson met the novelist Henry James in Florence and began what was one of the most important friendships of her life. Together the writers toured museums, dined, and discussed literature. Although there is scant evidence to support a love interest on either side, scholars have cited Woolson as the source for May Bartram in James's "The Beast in the Jungle," the famous story of a man who realizes only after May's death that she has loved him. In any case, though the relationship was probably platonic, it was clearly serious, and Woolson's and James's influence on each other's work is apparent.

Before leaving for Europe, Woolson wrote a children's novel, *The Old Stone House* (1872); travel sketches; essays; poetry; her first novel for adults, *Anne* (1880); and the short fiction in *Castle Nowhere: Lake Country Sketches* (1878) and *Rodman the Keeper: Southern Sketches*. However, most of her best work was completed abroad. Her late short-story collections, *Dorothy and Other Italian Stories* (1895) and *The Front Yard and Other Italian Stories* (1896), set in Europe, were written during Woolson's residence in various European cities. Set primarily in America, her novella *For the Major* (1883) and her three novels, *East Angels* (1886), *Jupiter Lights* (1889), and *Horace Chase* (1894), partake of both domestic and realistic traditions, featuring self-sacrificing heroines yearning for happy marriages and heroes adept at functioning in a market economy. Published posthumously, her last work, a collection of travel writing, was *Mentone, Cairo, and Corfu* (1896).

Suffering from inherited depression, worried about her finances, and believing * suicide a reasonable choice, Constance Fenimore Woolson may have designed her fatal fall from the second-story window of her Venetian apartments. Henry James believed Woolson a suicide and did not attend her funeral.

• The Western Reserve Historical Society, Cleveland, Ohio, holds the largest collection of Woolson's papers. See also John Dwight Kern, *Constance Fenimore Woolson: Literary Pioneer* (1934). Rayburn S. Moore, *Constance Fenimore Woolson* (1963). Joan Myers Weimer, ed., *Women Artists, Women Exiles: "Miss Grief" and Other Stories* (1988). Cheryl B. Torsney, *Constance Fenimore Woolson: The Grief of Artistry* (1989). Cheryl B. Torsney, ed., *Critical Essays on Constance Fenimore Woolson* (1992).

Cheryl B. Torsney

WORKING CLASS FICTION. *See* Class; Proletarian Writing.

WORKING-GIRL NOVEL. *See* Libbey, Laura Jean.

WRIGHT, Sarah Elizabeth (b. 1928), poet, novelist, lecturer, and social activist. Born the daughter of Willis Charles and Mary Amelia Moore Wright in Wetipquin, Maryland, Sarah Elizabeth Wright gained modest recognition when she co-authored with Lucy Smith a collection of poetry entitled *Give Me a Child* (1955), in which Wright wrote seven of seventeen poems about African-American survival in a racist land. In subsequent years, several of her short stories and essays have appeared in magazines such as *Freedomways* and *American Pen.* From 1945 to 1949, she was a student at Howard University, first under the tutelage of renowned poet-critic Sterling Brown and then of poet-novelist Owen Dodson. While at Howard she also was inspired by the example of Langston Hughes, who became a lifelong friend, and she became active in several literary and journalistic organizations. In 1949 Wright moved to Philadelphia where she eventually helped organize the Philadelphia Writers' Workshop to promote the work of black writers.

By 1957, she was drawn to New York and became actively involved with the work of the Harlem Writers' Guild, which then claimed as members such promising authors as John Oliver Killens, John Henrik Clarke, Alice Childress, and Paule Marshall. Wright credits the Guild for recognizing her own literary efforts as well as those of Rosa Guy, Lonnie Elder III, Ossie Davis, and Julian Mayfield. While still in New York during the mid-1960s, she joined with noted dramatist Aminata Moseka (Abby Lincoln), novelist Rosa Guy, and poet-actress Maya *Angelou to organize the Cultural Association for Women of African Heritage to promote self-esteem and human worth. A tireless activist in these and many other community and cultural activities over the years, Wright still is best known for the literary achievement of her one published novel, *This Child's Gonna Live* (1969), which chronicles the extraordinary fight of black mother Mariah Upshur against the poverty, bigotry, and death of her Maryland Eastern Shore community. Reprinted in 1986 by the Feminist Press with an essay by John Oliver Killens, *This Child's Gonna Live* is by far the most successful result of Wright's lifelong attempt to combine imaginative literary experimentation and social consciousness.

The novel achieves its greatest power from Wright's development of the complex protagonist Mariah Upshur, who, like Wright herself, grows up surrounded by the depressing and stultifying poverty of an Eastern Shore fishing community. In *Black American Literature and Humanism* (1981), critic Trudier Harris explores in some depth the irony that dominates this portrayal, focusing specifically on Wright's ability to evoke the reader's sympathy and concern for Mariah while simultaneously revealing the hypocrisy in her profession of religious piety. This hypocrisy, however, is a by-product of the defensive mechanism that African-American women have devised to cope both physically and spiritually with their often futile and illogical experiences in this country. In the protagonist's case, as Harris notes, "Mariah has reduced Jesus and God to the role of conversational buddies," who are very much like herself. Indeed, Jesus and God become extensions of her own personality, through which she verbalizes the elements of her life that would otherwise leave her speechless.

Another noteworthy irony in *This Child's* is suggested by the title itself, which alludes to the ambivalent relationship between Mariah and her children. Still unexamined by critics is the conflict between Mariah's repeated declarations that the unborn baby she is carrying will not die—as did her last child—and the fact that her son Rabbit does indeed die, perhaps with a little help from her mother. Moreover, Mariah's verbal and physical abuse of her already-born children, especially Rabbit, ironically undercuts her image as a heroic mother and points to psychological and social complexities in Wright's fictional portrayal of the mother-child relationship.

• Roger Whitlow, "Sarah E. Wright," in *Black American Literature: A Critical History* (1974), pp. 162–165. Anne Z. Mickelson, "Winging Upward: Black Women: Sarah E. Wright, Toni Morrison, Alice Walker," in *Reaching Out: Sensitivity and Order in Recent American Fiction by Women* (1979), pp. 112–124. Virginia B. Guilford, "Sarah Elizabeth Wright," *Dictionary of Literary Biography*, vol. 33, eds. Trudier Harris and Thadious Davis (1984), pp. 293–300. Burney J. Hollis, "The Race and the Runner: Female Fugitives in the Novels of Waters Turpin and Sarah Wright," in *Amid Visions and Revisions: Poetry and Criticism on Literature and the Arts* (1985), pp. 109–121.

SallyAnn H. Ferguson

WYLIE, Elinor (1885–1928), poet and novelist. Born Elinor Morton Hoyt of Somerville, New Jersey, she summered in Maine as a child and, at eighteen, spent a year with her grandfather traveling in Europe. Although Elinor never received a college education, she enrolled in Miss Baldwin's School, and in Bryn Mawr in 1882, and attended Miss Flint's in 1897 after her father became assistant attorney general and the family moved to Washington, D.C. Like Edith *Wharton, Wylie led a privileged life, but with those privileges came social expectations that Wylie could not meet. When she left her husband Philip Hichborn (who, it was later confirmed, was mentally unstable) and her only son to live with the married Horace Wylie in 1910, Elinor became a figure of scandal. In 1912, Philip Hichborn committed suicide, but, because of Katherine Wylie's refusal to grant her husband a divorce, Horace and Elinor were unable to marry until 1916. Like other women writers who deviated from society's expectations, Wylie and her work have been overlooked at least partly because of the spectacle of her life.

Printed privately, her first book, *Incidental Numbers* (1912), includes poems written during the years between 1902 and 1911; this early work shows Wylie's interest in technical virtuosity and demonstrates her ability to manipulate both word and line to meet the demands of poetic form. *Nets to Catch the Wind* (1921) won the Julia Ellsworth Ford prize that year—a significant award, because Edna St. Vincent *Millay, Marianne *Moore, and *H.D. all published volumes in 1921. These poems show that, like Yeats and others, Wylie was captivated by the idea that the art object was not prey to time, change, or human rejection and betrayal. The poems in *Black Armour* (1923) reinforced Wylie's reputation as a technically skilled poet and also explored the role of art in the speaker's life.

The dangers of excessive aestheticism, however, inform Wylie's fiction. In 1923, Wylie divorced Horace Wylie, married William Rose Benét and published *Jennifer Lorn*, whose title character is objectified by a husband who treats her like a possession valued for its beauty. Wylie uses satire to expose the problems inherent in the gothic romance plot. Similarly, *The Venetian Glass Nephew* (1925) reinforces the dichotomy between nature and art when a beautiful, vibrant woman becomes a porcelain figure out of her love for a man made of glass. Wylie's other novels, *The Orphan Angel* (1926) and *Mr. Hodge and Mr. Hazard* (1928), reflect her lifelong fascination with Shelley, who is the fictive subject of both works.

Trivial Breath (1928) begins and ends with poems to Shelley and addresses again the themes of artistic perfection and human frailty. *Angels and Earthly Creatures* (1929), a sonnet sequence published after Wylie's death from a stroke in 1928, rejects human love relationships for the solace of the spirit. With technical precision, Wylie's poems subtly reveal her Romantic and aesthetic preoccupations, while her novels develop those themes even more explicitly.

• The Hoyt family's collection of Wylie's correspondence and Horace Wylie's papers are housed in the Berg Collection at the New York Public Library. Yale University's Elinor Wylie Archive in the Beinecke Rare Book and Manuscript Library houses the papers of Wylie and William Rose Benét. See also *Collected Poems of Elinor Wylie* (1932). *Collected Prose of Elinor Wylie* (1933). *Last Poems of Elinor Wylie* (1943). Thomas A. Gray, *Elinor Wylie* (1969). Stanley Olson, *Elinor Wylie: A Life Apart* (1979). Judith Farr, *The Life and Art of Elinor Wylie* (1983).

Ann Walker

Y

YAMAMOTO, Hisaye (b. 1921), short story writer, essayist, and poet. One of the most highly regarded *nikkei* writers, Yamamoto was born in Redondo Beach, California to immigrant farmers from Kumamoto, Japan. Her residency in southern California was interrupted twice, from 1942 to 1945 when she was interned at Poston, Arizona, and from 1953 to 1955 when she joined a Catholic Worker farm in Staten Island, New York. In 1955 she married Anthony DeSoto, with whom she has five children. The best introduction to Yamamoto's work and its historical and literary contextualization is King-Kok Cheung's essay and bibliography in *Seventeen Syllables and Other Stories* (1988), which begins with Yamamoto's first major publication in *Partisan Review*, an essay on *sexual harassment, and concludes with a story about female friendship reprinted from *Hokubei Mainichi*, thus spanning forty years (1948–1988) of diverse achievement. Yamamoto recalls her early career in an essay entitled "Writing" (*Rafu Shimpo*, 20 December 1968), including teenage efforts under the pseudonym Napoleon, working as a reporter from 1945 to 1948 for a black weekly, and receiving in 1950–1951 one of the first John Hay Whitney Foundation Fellowship awards. Essays and poetry submitted regularly since the 1950s to Japanese-American newspapers such as *Rafu Shimpo* and *Hokubei Mainichi* afford an engrossing, revealing record of Yamamoto's life and development as a writer.

Yamamoto's reputation currently rests on a handful of stories, reprinted in the 1988 collection, which Cheung compares to the masterpieces of Katherine Mansfield, Flannery *O'Connor, Grace *Paley, and Ann *Petry. "Seventeen Syllables" (1949), "The Brown House" (1951), and "Yoneko's Earthquake" (selected for *Best American Short Stories: 1952*) depict the lives of prewar tenant farm communities, for which Yamamoto's work is particularly valued. These stories, as well as "The Legend of Miss Sasagawara" (1950) and "Wilshire Bus" (1950), which are set during and immediately after the war, delineate the shared and divisive stresses of American life as experienced by immigrant wives and husbands, conflict between parents and American-born children, and interactions between Japanese and other ethnic groups. They feature Yamamoto's celebrated deployment of multiple consciousnesses, double plots, and a supple ironic voice that permits a characteristic blend of indictment, forgiveness, questioning, and humor. Yamamoto's legacy is summarized in an unsurpassed interpretive essay bespeaking "tender regard" for *nisei* writer Toshio *Mori, and in tributes she receives in turn from younger writers like Yuri Kageyama, who recognizes from her example the artistry required beyond political rhetoric and factual knowledge to write "with truthfulness and integrity" as a Japanese-American woman.

• Hisaye Yamamoto, Introduction, *The Chauvinist and Other Stories* by Toshio Mori (1979), pp. 1–14. Dorothy Ritsuko McDonald and Katharine Newman, "Relocation and Dislocation: The Writings of Hisaye Yamamoto and Wakako Yamauchi," *MELUS* 7, no. 3 (Fall 1980): 21–38. Yuri Kageyama, "Hisaye Yamamoto—Nisei Writer," *Sunbury* 10 (1981): 32–42. William Satake Blauvelt, "Hisaye Yamamoto Recalls Miss Sasagawara," *International Examiner Literary Supplement* (19 July 1989): 19. Susan Schweik, *A Gulf So Deeply Cut: American Women Poets and the Second World War* (1991).

Gayle K. Fujita Sato

YAMAUCHI, Wakako (b. 1924), playwright. Born Wakako Nakamura in the town of Westmoreland in California's Imperial Valley, Yamauchi turned early to writing and reading as an escape from the isolation of farm life. Originally a short-story writer, Yamauchi acknowledges the influence of fiction writer Hisaye *Yamamoto, author of *Seventeen Syllables* (1988), who wrote unselfconsciously from a Japanese-American perspective. The two met as teenagers in Oceanside, California, where the Nakamura family moved to seek greater opportunity, her mother and father turning to work in the strawberry fields and later opening a boardinghouse. At the age of 17 she evacuated with her family to an internment camp in Poston, Arizona, where she spent a year and a half before obtaining permission to leave camp for Chicago, where she attended art school and supported herself working in a candy factory.

It was not until the late 1950s that she began to write following her marriage and birth of her daughter, Joy. "When I started to write . . . I had no intention of making it a vocation. I just wanted to write one story, one beautiful story." The result, "And the Soul Shall Dance," is regarded as a seminal work in Asian-American literature. She adapted the work for theater in 1974, and a number of productions followed. The play was adapted for television by PBS in 1977 and has been published in numerous collections including *Between Worlds* (1990), *Big Aiieeeee* (1991), and *Worlds of Literature* (1989).

With the exception of a recent work, *The Chairman's Wife (A Gang of One)* (1990), which focuses on events in China, Yamauchi's primary thematic concerns have been ordinary people and events. Her first two plays, *And the Soul Shall Dance* (1974) and *The Music Lesson* (1980), are lyrical and passionate dramas that depict the life of Japanese Americans during the prewar period. It is the small events of life—a bathhouse fire, an itinerant laborer with a passion for music—that serve as the point of departure for Yamauchi's plays. "When I write these stories they're really about very ordinary people. I think it's important because I'm an ordinary person. There's a lot of us doing ordinary things and yet there is courage in our lives." Other produced works of Yamauchi include *The Memento* (1986) and *12-1-A* (1982). She has also written *Not A Through Street* (1990), *Shirley Temple Hotcha-Cha* (1978), *Songs That Made the Hit Parade* (1985), and *The Trip* (1988). Her work has been produced by theaters such as the East West Players, the Pan Asian Repertory, Kumu Kahua, the Asian American Theater Company, the New York Shakespeare Festival Public Theater, and the Yale Repertory Theater.

Roberta Uno

YEZIERSKA, Anzia (ca. 1881–1970), novelist and short story writer known for her stories of Polish-Russian-Jewish immigrants crowding New York's Lower East Side in the early 1900s. Her novel, *Bread Givers* (1925, reprint 1975), about one such family and its daughter's rebellion against her father and the Old World patriarchal tradition, was rediscovered by contemporary feminists and social historians. They also prompted the publication of an Anzia Yezierska collection entitled *The Open Cage* (1979; 1984) and the reissue in the U.S. and Britain of Yezierska's *Red Ribbon on a White Horse* (1950, reprint 1981, current ed. 1987) and *Hungry Hearts and Other Stories* (1920, reprint 1985).

Yezierska migrated to this country from Poland with her family in 1890 when she was about nine years old. She lived with her parents, three sisters, and six brothers in an East Side tenement flat and from the age of sixteen worked in a sweatshop until she could escape at seventeen by winning a college scholarship. In later fictionalizing these experiences, she re-created the ungrammatical, half-Yiddish, half-English idiom of her ghetto characters, which critics and scholars often mistook for her own voice. Selling her first two books (*Hungry Hearts* and *Salome of the Tenements*, 1923) to Hollywood, she was widely publicized in the 1920s as "the sweatshop Cinderella" who had leaped overnight from a sewing machine to movie wealth.

In fact Yezierska graduated from Columbia University Teachers' College in 1904 and spent 10 years in teaching—she also married twice and had a daughter—before she began her writing career. She wrote seven books of fiction. The last book, *Red Ribbon on a White Horse*, was published when she was close to seventy, after an eighteen-year silence. Thereafter she wrote book reviews for the *New York Times* and short stories about old age that appeared in literary magazines but were not collected until after her death. Her early stories, most frequently "The Fat of the Land," named by Edward J. O'Brien as the Best Short Story of 1919, and "How I Found America," have been regularly reprinted in anthologies of American literature since their first publication.

Research after Yezierska's death, particularly by Jo Ann Boydston, director of the Center for Dewey Studies at Southern Illinois University, uncovered Yezierska's romantic relationship with the philosopher-educator John Dewey, who wrote several poems to her. Yezierska wrote about Dewey, disguising his identity, in two novels (*All I Could Never Be*, 1932, and *Red Ribbon on a White Horse*), and in some short stories.

• Anzia Yezierska Papers in Special Collections, Mugar Memorial Library, Boston University. Carol Schoen, *Anzia Yezierska* (1982). Jo Ann Boydston, ed., introduction to *The Poems of John Dewey*. Louise Levitas Henriksen, *Anzia Yezierska: A Writer's Life. How I Found America: The Collected Stories of Anzia Yezierska* (1991)

Louise Levitas Henriksen

Z

ZIONIST WRITING. *See* Holocaust Writing; Jewish-American Writing.

ZITKALA-ŠA, also Gertrude Simmons Bonnin (1876–1938), Sioux short story writer and Indian rights activist. Born as Gertrude Simmons on the Yankton Sioux reservation in South Dakota, Zitkala-Ša (Red Bird) spoke no English until age eight when she was sent east to the Quaker-run White's Manual Labor Institute in Wabash, Indiana. These early years preceding formal education were spent living with her mother in a wigwam, learning traditional Indian skills, and listening to older tribe members recount delightful stories that she later translated from Sioux into English in *Old Indian Legends* (1901). Their central figure is Iktomi, a duplicitous snare weaver (trickster), who is consistently outmaneuvered by those whom he intends to cheat. The spiritual Avenger also figures in these tales as a warrior who springs from a drop of buffalo blood in order to help the oppressed.

Her darker autobiographical sketches and short stories, first published in the *Atlantic Monthly* and *Harper's* (1900–1902), were later collected in *American Indian Legends* (1921). These vignettes of Indian life explore the paradoxical combination of Christian education and native Indian upbringing responsible for creating a sense of displacement that marred the lives of the author and her contemporaries. "The Soft Hearted Sioux," for example, is about the inability of a mission-educated son to oppose Christian doctrine by killing an animal that would provide meat necessary to his starving father.

Zitkala-Ša graduated from Earlham College in Richmond, Indiana, where she won awards for oratory. She studied music at the Boston Conservatory and played a violin solo at the Paris Exposition (1900), where she had traveled with the Carlisle Indian Band.

In 1902 she married Raymond Talesfase Bonnin, also a Sioux Indian. The couple's move to the Uintah and Ouray Reservation in Utah marked the beginning of Zitkala-Ša's political career. She served as secretary of the Society of American Indians (1916), edited the *American Indian Magazine* (1918–1919), founded the National Council of American Indians (1926), and remained its president until her death in 1938. She coauthored the important *Okla.'s Poor Rich Indians: An Orgy of Graft and Exploitation of the Five Civilized Tribes—Legalized Robbery* (1924) and traveled extensively lecturing on Indian rights, often dressed in native Sioux costume. With William Hanson, she wrote the opera *Sundance* (1913), which was notably successful because of her ability to portray authentic Sioux gesture and melody. Zitkala-Ša helped preserve native Indian culture when assimilation into white society threatened to end traditional oral patterns of transmitting Indian heritage from one generation to the next.

• Zitkala-Ša, "Impressions of an Indian Childhood" and "An Indian Teacher Among Indians," *Atlantic Monthly* (January, February, March 1900): 31–45, 185–194, 381–386. Zitkala-Ša, "Why I Am a Pagan," *Atlantic Monthly* 90 (December 1902): 802–803. Hazel W. Hertzberg, *The Search for an American Indian Identity* (1971). "Bonnin, Gertrude Simmons," in *Notable American Women 1607–1950*, vol. 1 (1971), pp. 198–200. Marion E. Gridley, *American Indian Women* (1974).

Terri S. Hayes

ca. 10,400 B.C.E.   A woman lived and died in what is now Midland, Texas. Her bones were unearthed in 1992. Although of unknown origins, she is perhaps representative as a member of one of numerous cultures that flourished on the continent until the time of the conquest.

1492   Native American population estimated at 25 to 45 million.

1492   Isabella (1451–1504) and Ferdinand (1452–1516) of Spain finance the first voyage of Christopher Columbus to the New World.

1587   Virginia Dare becomes the first child of English parents to be born on American soil.

1607   Pocahontas (1595?–1617) rescues Captain John Smith from captivity; two years later she became the first known Native American woman to marry a colonist when she married a captain "Kocuum."

1619   First African women—3 of 20 captives—arrive in Jamestown, Virginia, as indentured servants.

1620   First public library opens in Virginia.

1624   The first African-American child, William, is born to Isabel and Anthony of Virginia.

1636   Harvard College is founded, for men only.

1639   Mary Mandame is convicted of a "dallyance" with a Native American in Plymouth, Massachusetts, and after being whipped, is sentenced to wear a badge of shame on her sleeve.

1649   Goodwife Norman and Mary Hammon of the Massachusetts Bay Colony are tried for lesbianism; Norman is found guilty and Hammon is acquitted.

1655   Literacy among women is estimated at 50 percent.

1667   The "Massachusetts Queen," a squaw-sachem who governed the Massachusetts Confederacy from before 1620, dies, ending her long reign.

1676   Mary Rowlandson (1636–78) becomes the first woman captive released by Native Americans.

1692   Trials and executions of supposed witches in Salem, Massachusetts.

1715   Sybilla Masters, the first female inventor born in the newly settled colonies, invents a machine to prepare Indian corn.

1738   South Carolinian Elizabeth Timothy becomes the first woman to publish a newspaper, the *South-Carolina Gazette*.

1762   Ann Franklin (sister of Benjamin), becomes the first woman newspaper editor when she begins work at *Mercury* in Newport, Rhode Island.

1765   In Massachusetts, Jenny Slew, an African-American, sues for and wins her freedom.

1775–83   American Revolution: "Molly Pitcher" (possibly Mary Ludwig, Mary Hays, or Margaret Corbin) and Deborah Sampson are some of the women involved on the front lines; Anna Lee, a Shaker, becomes the country's first conscientious objector.

1776   Abigail Adams advises her husband, John (1735–1826), to "Remember the Ladies" when drafting the new government's laws.

1780s As many as 30 percent of all first births occur less than nine months after marriage, a figure not equalled until the present era.

1782   New England discontinues its use of the scarlet letter for adulterers.

TIMELINE OF U.S. WOMEN'S WRITING

Native American women of many tribes participated in storytelling, creating and continuing oral traditions that explained the creation and nature of the world; recorded their tribal and personal histories; taught skills, values, and beliefs; and provided humor and entertainment.

1645 Anne Hopkins, wife of the governor of Hartford, is taken to Boston for medical help for having "written many books" and lost her wits "by occasion of her giving herself wholly to reading and writing."

1650[1] Anne Dudley Bradstreet (1612?–72): *The Tenth Muse Lately Sprung Up in America*, first collection of verse produced in the New World and a bestseller in 17th-century London

1682 Mary Rowlandson (1636–78): *Narrative of the Captivity and Restoration of Mrs. Mary Rowlandson*

1701 Sarah Fiske (1652–92), spiritual autobiographer: *A Confession of Faith* (published posthumously)

1746 Lucy Terry (1730–1821): author of "Bars Fight, August 28, 1746," first African-American poet

1758 Elizabeth Sandwich Drinker (1734–1807): 1758–1787 journal published in 1937 as *Not So Long Ago*

1773 Phillis Wheatley (1753?–84): *Poems on Various Subjects, Religious and Moral*, first book of poems published by an African-American

1775 Mercy Otis Warren (1728–1814), playwright, poet, historian: *The Group*

1784 Hannah Adams (1755–1831), probably first professional woman writer in the United States: *Alphabetical Compendium of the Various Sects*

1. Date indicates publication of a significant work.

1783   First statutes are passed outlawing "crimes against nature" (including anal sex, fellatio, and buggery).

1787   Ratification of the U.S. Constitution, which denies suffrage to women and blacks and counts the latter as "three-fifths" of a person.

1790s Average age of marriage for white women is 22.

1790   U.S. African-American population equals 757,181; the vast majority, 697,624, are slaves; Africans are the second largest segment of the total U.S. population of 3,929,000.

1793   Mrs. Samuel Slater becomes the first U.S. woman to be granted a patent (for cotton sewing thread).

1800   Average of 7.04 children born to each American woman.

=

1812   War of 1812; Lucy Brewer, disguised as "George Baker," enlists as a marine.

1816   The African Methodist Episcopal Church (AME) is established.

1820   U.S. population totals 9.6 million; black women number 870,860 out of a total black population of 1,771,656; 750,010 of these women are slaves.

1825   The United Tailoresses Society of New York, the first women's labor organization, is formed.

1827   The first black newspaper, *Freedom's Journal*, is printed in New York.

1830s Cookstoves, as distinct from heating stoves, gain widespread use in America.

1831   The Female Literary Association of Philadelphia and the Afric-American Female Intelligence Society of Boston are formed.

1833   Lucretia Mott (1793–1880), abolitionist and suffragist, founds the Philadelphia Female Anti-Slavery Society.

1833   Oberlin College, the first co-educational, multi-racial college in the United States, is founded.

1835   New York's Mount Pleasant Female Prison, the nation's first women's prison, opens.

1836   Macon, Georgia's Wesleyan College, the first chartered women's college, opens.

1837   First Anti-Slavery Convention of American Women is held in New York City.

1837   Financial "Panic" caused by too much speculation in western lands, by unsound banking practices, and by overexpansion of transportation facilities, results in the closing of 600 banks.

1838   Cherokee Indians are expelled from the East Coast and begin the "Trail of Tears" toward reservations in the Midwest.

1839   Josephine Amelia Perkins becomes notorious as the first woman horse-thief on record in the United States.

1839   First married women's property act, allowing women to retain their personal property after marriage, passes in Mississippi; other states soon follow.

1840   The first issue of the *Lowell Offering*, a periodical featuring the articles and poetry of women employed by the Lowell Textile Mills, is published.

1840   Catherine E. Brewer becomes the first woman to graduate from college in the United States.

1846   The sewing machine is patented.

1848   Seneca Falls Convention, the first women's rights convention, is held.

1849   Harriet Tubman (c. 1821–1913), referred to as the "Moses of her people," escapes from slavery and spends the next decade helping other slaves to escape through "The Underground Railroad."

1850   U.S. population totals 23 million; black women number 1,827,550 out of a total black population of 3.2 million; 1,601,779 of these women are slaves.

1850   Average birth rate continues to decline to 5.42 children per married couple.

1850   Infant mortality among slaves is twice that for whites.

1850   The first national convention on woman suffrage is held in Worcester, Massachusetts.

1790 Sarah Wentworth Morton (1759–1846), the "American Sappho": *Ouâbi; or, The Virtues of Nature: An Indian Tale in Four Cantos*

1790 Judith Sargent Murray (1751–1820), essayist: "On the Equality of the Sexes"

1791 Susanna Rowson (1762–1824), novelist, playwright, educator: *Charlotte Temple*

1793 Ann Eliza Bleecker (1752–83), poet, short story writer, correspondent: *The Posthumous Works of Ann Eliza Bleecker* traces the toll of the American Revolution

1797 Hannah Webster Foster (1758–1840), novelist, educator: *The Coquette; or, The History of Eliza Wharton*

≡

1801 Tabitha Tenney (1762–1820), novelist, advice writer: *Female Quixotism*

1815 Lydia Sigourney (1791–1865), poet, novelist: *Moral Pieces in Prose and Verse*

1818 Hannah Mather Crocker (1752–1829), memoirist, poet, polemicist: *Observations on the Real Rights of Women*

1819 Emma Hart Willard (1787–1870), author of textbooks, advice books, and histories; poet: *Plan for Improving Female Education* published at her own expense

1824 Lydia Maria Child (1802–80): *Hobomok*

1825 Sarah Kemble Knight (1666–1727): *The Private Journal of a Journey from Boston to New York* (published posthumously)

1827 Catharine Sedgwick (1789–1867), novelist, biographer: *Hope Leslie*, controversial novel dealing with white/Native American relationships

1829 Frances Wright (1795–1852) begins publication of the newspaper *The Free Enquirer.*

1830 Frances Manwaring Caulkins (1795–1869) begins 30 years of writing for the American Tract Society.

1831 *The History of Mary Prince, a West Indian Slave*, dictated slave narrative

1835 American Female Moral Reform Society begins publication of *The Advocate.*

1836 Angelina Emily Grimké (1805–79), abolitionist, women's rights pioneer: *Appeal to Christian Women of the Southern States*

1837–77 Sarah Josepha Buell Hale edits *Godey's Lady's Book* and *American Ladies' Magazine.*

1839 Caroline Stansbury Kirkland (1801–64): *A New Home—Who'll Follow?* as "Mrs. Mary Claver, an Actual Settler"

1839 Frances Sargent Osgood (1811–50), poet: *The Casket of Fate*

1841 Ann Plato: *Essays*, first collection of essays by an African-American

1843 Catharine Beecher (1800–78), writer and advocate of female educational reform: *Treatise on Domestic Economy*

1845 Margaret Fuller (1810–50), essayist, editor of *The Dial: Woman in the Nineteenth Century*

1849 Jarena Lee publishes *Religious Experiences and Journal of Jarena Lee, Giving an Account of Her Call to Preach the Gospel*

1850 Caroline Lee Hentz (1800–56): *Linda; or, The Young Pilot of the Belle Creole*, novel

1850 Sara Jane Lippincott as "Grace Greenwood" (1823–1904), journalist, travel writer: *Greenwood Leaves*

1850 Sojourner Truth (1797–1883): *Narrative of Sojourner Truth*

1850   Lucy Sessions, the first black woman in the United States to earn a college degree, graduates from Oberlin College.

=

1851   Black activist Sojourner Truth (1797–1883) delivers her famous "Ain't I A Woman?" speech.

1851   Elizabeth Smith Miller invents the undergarments that would later come to be known as "bloomers," after being worn by feminist Amelia Bloomer.

1853   Antoinette Brown Blackwell (1825–1921), woman's rights reformer, theologian, and social scientist, becomes the first ordained woman minister in the United States.

1853–55   Pauline Davis publishes *The Una*, the first woman's suffrage paper.

1854   Lincoln University, originally called the Ashmum Institute, becomes the first black college in the United States.

1854   First microscopic observation of sperm and egg fusion proves women contribute equal genetic material in the reproductive process.

1855   The Woman's Hospital in New York is established by women as the first hospital for the treatment of women's diseases.

1855   Abolitionist Lucy Stone is the first U.S. woman to keep her maiden name after marriage.

1857   The U.S. Supreme Court upholds the Fugitive Slave Law and denies citizenship to blacks in the Dred Scott decision.

1860   Of approximately 35,000 Chinese in America, only 1,784 are women.

1861–65   Civil War: President Abraham Lincoln (1809–65) issues the Emancipation Proclamation in 1863, freeing all slaves in the Confederate states.

1862   The U.S. Department of Agriculture issues an annual report describing the typical farm woman as a "laboring drudge," working harder than her husband or any other farm hand or hired help.

1865   Thirteenth Amendment to the U.S. Constitution abolishes slavery.

1865   President Lincoln is assassinated: Mary E. Suratt becomes the first woman hanged by the U.S. government for her part in the conspiracy.

1866   The Young Women's Christian Association (YWCA) is formed in Boston.

1867   Dorothea Dix (1802–87), social reformer, tours the United States investigating mental hospitals, poor houses, and jails.

1868   Fourteenth Amendment grants citizenship and "due process" to all persons born or naturalized in the United States.

1869   St. Louis Law School becomes the first law school to admit women; Belle Mansfield, who read for the law on her own time, becomes the first practicing female attorney in the United States.

1869   Elizabeth Cady Stanton (1815–1902) and Susan B. Anthony (1820–1906) found the National Woman's Suffrage Association (NWSA).

1869   Disagreeing with the NWSA's tactics and programs, Lucy Stone founds the American Woman Suffrage Association (the two eventually merge in 1890).

1870   Fifteenth Amendment protects black males' rights to vote.

1870   Forty percent of black married women in the cotton belt are employed, mostly in field labor; 98.4 percent of white women in the same region have no recorded occupation.

1870   Sixty percent of all women workers are employed in domestic service jobs.

1870   The Philadelphia Colored Women's Christian Association is founded.

1871   Frances Elizabeth Willard (1839–98) becomes the first female college president when she is elected to head the Evanston College for Ladies.

1872   Victoria Woodhull runs for the office of President of the United States as the candidate of the Equal Rights Party.

1872   Sixteen women, including Susan B. Anthony, are arrested in New York for trying to vote in the presidential election.

1872   Charlotte E. Ray receives her diploma from Howard University's School of Law and becomes the first practicing black woman lawyer in the country.

1851 Susan Warner as "Elizabeth Wetherell" (1819–85): *The Wide, Wide World*, bestseller

1852 Alice Cary: *Hagar: A Story for Today*

1852 Elizabeth Stuart Phelps (1815–52): *The Angel Over the Right Shoulder*

1852 Harriet Beecher Stowe (1811–96), novelist, short story writer, abolitionist, author of domestic manuals: *Uncle Tom's Cabin*

1853 Paulina Davis begins publishing *Una*, the first women's rights newspaper in the United States

1853 Sara Payson Willis Parton as "Fanny Fern" (1811–72), novelist: *Fern Leaves from Fanny's Portfolio*

1854 Mary Ann Shadd Cary, first black woman editor, begins publishing an antislavery newspaper, the *Provincial Freeman*, in Canada

1854 Maria Susanna Cummins (1827–66): *The Lamplighter*

1854 Elizabeth Oakes Prince Smith: *Bertha and Lily; or, The Parsonage of Beech Glen*

1856 Frances Whitcher (1813–52), humorist: *The Widow Bedott Papers*

1857 Mary Seacole (1805?–81), free-born Jamaican Creole autobiographer: *Wonderful Adventures of Mrs. Seacole in Many Lands*

1859 Frances Ellen Watkins Harper (1825–1911), African-American poet, novelist, abolitionist, and advocate of women's rights: "The Two Offers," first short story published by a black person in America; *Iola Leroy* (1892), first novel about Reconstruction by an African-American

1859 E.D.E.N. Southworth (1819–99), author of more than 60 widely read novels: *The Hidden Hand*

1859 Harriet E. Wilson (1807?–70?): *Our Nig*, first novel by an African-American

1860 Caroline Wells Dall (1822–1912), advocate of coeducation and higher education for women: *Woman's Right to Labor; or, Low Wages and Hard Work*

1861 Rebecca Harding Davis (1831–1910): *Life in the Iron Mills*

1861 Julia Ward Howe (1819–1910), poet, dramatist, biographer, travel writer, feminist: "Battle Hymn of the Republic"

1861 Harriet Jacobs (1813–97): *Incidents in the Life of a Slave Girl*, first full-length slave narrative by a woman published in America

1862 On April 15, Emily Dickinson (1830–86), at the age of 31, sends four poems to Thomas Wentworth Higginson

1862 Elizabeth Drew Stoddard (1823–1902): *The Morgesons*, first of several novels and a children's book

1863 *Memoir of Old Elizabeth, a Coloured Woman*, slave narrative and spiritual autobiography

1863 Harriet Prescott Spofford (1835–1921): *The Amber Gods and Other Stories*

1867 Augusta Evans (1835–1909), prolific best-selling novelist: *St. Elmo*

1868 Louisa May Alcott (1823–88): *Little Women*

1868 Elizabeth Stuart Phelps (Ward) (1884–1911): *The Gates Ajar*

1868 Elizabeth Hobbs Keckley: *Behind the Scenes; or, Thirty Years a Slave, and Four Years in the White House*

1869 Sarah Elizabeth Hopkins Bradford: *Scenes in the Life of Harriet Tubman*

1872 Sarah Chauncey Woolsey as "Susan Coolidge" (1835–18905): *What Katy Did*, first in a series

1873 Marietta Holley (1836–1926), humorist: *My Opinions and Betsey Bobbet's*

1873 Celia Thaxter (1835–94), poet, short story writer: *Among the Isles of Shoals*, prose

1876 Eliza Andrews (1840–1931): *A Family Secret*, a bestseller

1876 Ella Wheeler Wilcox (1850–1919), poet, novelist, author of over 40 volumes: *Poems of Passion*

1873 Comstock Law is passed, making it illegal to send birth control information through the mails; the prohibition is not officially lifted until 1971.

1874 Women's Christian Temperance Union (WCTU) is founded.

1876 Harriet Purvis, an African American, is elected vice president of the National Woman Suffrage Association.

1876 Mary Baker Eddy (1821–1910) founds the Christian Science religion.

1876 Sarah Stevenson, physician and professor, becomes the first woman admitted to the American Medical Association (AMA).

1877 Helen Magill of Boston University becomes the first U.S. woman to earn a Ph.D.

1880 Approximately 2.5 million women are working for wages.

1880 The Native American population in the United States is estimated at 243,000; most are encamped in reservations.

1880 Impressionist painter Mary Cassatt (1845–1926) paints *Woman in Black at the Opera*.

1880–1910 Life expectancy for rural blacks, both men and women, is only 33 years.

1881 Atlanta Baptist Female Seminary, later Spelman Seminary (College), is founded.

1881 Clara Barton (1821–1912) founds the American Red Cross.

1881 Marion Talbot (1858–1948) establishes the Association of Collegiate Alumnae (renamed the American Association of University Women in 1921).

1885 Bryn Mawr College opens and becomes the first women's college to offer graduate studies.

1886 *Ladies' Home Journal* is first published.

1886 The number of divorces rises from 9,937 in 1867 to 25,535.

1886 Julia Richman becomes the first president of the newly established Young Women's Hebrew Association.

1886 Suzanna Madora Salter becomes the first woman mayor when she is elected in Argonia, Kansas.

1889 Jane Addams (1860–1935) establishes Hull House in Chicago with Ellen Gates Starr.

1890 Wyoming enters the Union and becomes the first state with full woman suffrage.

1890 Median age of marriage is 22.0 years for women and 26.1 for men.

1891 The word "feminist" is first used in a book review in the *Athenaeum*.

1893 Colorado's male voters are the first to grant women suffrage.

1893 The World's Columbian Expedition is held in Chicago, featuring a women's exhibition.

1893 Ida B. Wells-Barnett (1862–1931), journalist, teacher, and community organizer, becomes a prominent activist in the anti-lynching crusade.

1894 Radcliffe College is officially established.

1894 Elizabeth H. Bennett becomes the first woman to undergo a successful Caesarean operation.

1896 Mary Church Terrell becomes the founding prresident of the National Association of Colored Women.

1896 *Plessy v. Ferguson* rules "separate but equal" is a valid justification for segregation.

1896 Johnson & Johnson produces the first commercial disposable sanitary pads, called "Lister's Towels."

1897 Havelock Ellis, English psychologist and writer, publishes *Studies in the Psychology of Sex: Sexual Inversion*, which pathologizes same-sex love between women as "inverted."

1897 Alice McLellan Birney founds the Parent-Teacher Association and becomes its first president.

1900 An average of 3.56 children are born to each American woman.

1900 Women equal one-fifth of the American labor force, numbering some 5 million workers.

1877   Mary Putnam Jacobi (1842–1906), physician and author of fiction and nonfiction: *Question of Rest for Women During Menstruation*

1880   Lucretia Peabody Hale (1820–1900), novelist, humorist, author of children's books: *The Peterkin Papers*

1881   Rose Terry Cooke (1827–92), New England short story writer, poet: *Somebody's Neighbor*

1882   Emma Lazarus (1849–87), poet, translator: *Songs of a Semite;* her sonnet, "The New Colossus," inscribed on the pedestal of the Statue of Liberty in 1883

1883   Mary Hallock Foote (1847–1938), novelist, illustrator: *The Led-Horse Claim: A Romance of a Mining Camp*

1883   Sarah Winnemucca Hopkins (1844–91), Native American author: *Life Among the Piutes*

1883   Laura Jean Libbey (1862–1925), "working-girl novelist": *A Fatal Wooing*, one of some 80 novels during a 30-year career

1883   Frances E. Willard (1839–98), temperance reformer, advocate of women's rights, biographer: *Women and Temperance*

1884   Helen Hunt Jackson (1831–85), novelist, documenter of government injustices toward Native Americans: *Ramona*

1884   Mrs. Edward Mix (1832–84): *The Life of Mrs. Edward Mix, Written by Herself in 1880*, religious testament by antebellum free black woman

1884   Mary Noailles Murfree (1850–1922), regionalist short story writer: *In the Tennessee Mountains*

1885–86   Clarissa Minnie Thompson: *Treading the Winepress; or, A Mountain of Misfortune*, one of the first post–Civil War novels by an African-American woman

1886   Julia A. J. Foote (1823–1900): *A Brand Plucked from the Fire*, autobiography by black female evangelist

1886   Sarah Orne Jewett (1849–1909): *A White Heron and Other Stories*

1887   Mary E. Wilkins Freeman (1852–1930): *A Humble Romance and Other Stories*

1888   Grace Elizabeth King (1851–1931), New Orleans short story writer, novelist: *Monsieur Motte*, a collection of stories

1889   Mary Seymour Foot (1846–93) launches *Business Woman's Journal.*

1890   Mrs. Octavia Rogers Albert: *The House of Bondage; or, Charlotte Brooks and Other Slaves*, a collection of female slave narratives

1890   Roberts Brothers of Boston publishes a selection of 115 poems by Emily Dickinson

1890   Emily Pauline Johnson (1861–1913), begins a two-decade career performing her poetry in the United States, Canada, and England, under her Native name, Tehakionwake.

1891   Emma Dunham Kelley, African-American novelist: *Megda*

1892   Anna Julia Cooper (1859?–1964), educator and scholar: *A Voice from the South: By a Black Woman of the South*

1892   Charlotte Perkins Gilman (1860–1935): "The Yellow Wallpaper"

1893   Sophia Alice Callahan: *Wynema*, possibly first novel by a Native American woman

1894   First black women's newspaper, the *Woman's Era*, begun in Boston by the New Era Club

1895   Alice M. Brown (1857–1948), novelist, short story writer, dramatist, poet: *Meadow-Grass*, local color stories

1895   Alice Ruth Moore Dunbar-Nelson (1875–1935), African-American short story writer, poet, journalist, political and social activist: *Violets and Other Tales*

1895   Ida B. Wells-Barnett, African-American author: *A Red Record: Tabulated Statistics and Alleged Causes of Lynchings in the United States, 1892–1893–1894*

1895–99   *American Jewess*, first national Jewish women's magazine in United States, edited by Rosa Sonneschein

1898   Ida Husted Harper (1851–1931), journalist, suffragist: *The Life and Work of Susan B. Anthony*

1898   Harriet Jane Hanson Robinson: *Loom and Spindle; or Life among the Early Mill Girls*

1899   Kate Chopin (1851–1904): *The Awakening*

1900   Pauline E. Hopkins, black novelist, playwright, biographer: *Contending Forces: A Romance Illustrative of Negro Life North and South*

===

1902 Martha Washington (1732–1802) is the first American woman to be depicted on a postage stamp.

1904 Deaf mute Helen Keller (1880–1968) graduates cum laude from Radcliffe College.

1909 Approximately 20,000 women shirtwaist makers strike to protest oppressive "sweatshop" conditions, long hours, and low wages.

1909 The Negro National Committee (later, the National Association for the Advancement of Colored People, NAACP) is founded.

1910 An estimated 8 million immigrants arrive in the United States.

1910 Approximately 8 million women work outside the home.

1910 First woman suffrage parade is held in New York City.

1910 The White Slave Traffic Act (The Mann Act) is passed, outlawing the transportation of women across state lines for "immoral purposes."

1910 The Camp Fire Girls, an interracial, nonsectarian organization for girls, is formed.

1910 Ella Flagg Young becomes the first woman president of the National Education Association.

1911 A fire in Triangle Shirtwaist Company (New York City) kills 147 mostly female, immigrant employees.

1912 The Girl Scouts of America is founded.

1912 First electric washing machine is introduced.

1914 President Woodrow Wilson (1856–1924) declares the second Sunday in May "Mother's Day" and makes it a national holiday.

1915 Margaret Sanger and Emma Goldman are arrested for violating the Comstock Law.

1915 The Women's International League for Peace and Freedom (WILPF) is founded.

1915 Theda Bara (1885–1955), "The Vamp," becomes a star in *A Fool There Was*.

1915 With the invention of the metal lipstick container, mass production and purchase of lipsticks begin.

1916 Suffragists Alice Paul and Lucy Burns establish the National Woman's Party to oppose Woodrow Wilson and the Democratic presidential ticket.

1917 Jeannette Pickering Rankin (1880–1973), suffragist and pacifist, is sworn in as the first Congresswoman.

1917 The United States enters World War I.

1919 After her husband, Woodrow, suffers a stroke, Edith Bolling Wilson operates as acting president of the United States.

1920 The Nineteenth Amendment grants women the right to vote.

1920 The League of Women Voters is formed to continue the work of the now defunct National American Woman Suffrage Association.

1920 The U.S. Department of Labor establishes the Woman's Bureau to oversee wage-earning women's rights and interests with Mary Anderson as the first director.

1920 Approximately 21 percent of all adult female workers are white.

1920 Ethelda Bleibtrey becomes the first American woman to win a gold medal in the modern Olympic Games.

1921 Three black women, Georgianna R. Simpson (University of Chicago), Sadie Tanner Mossell (University of Pennsylvania), and Eva Dykes (Radcliffe College), become the first in the country to earn Ph.D. degrees.

1921 The first Miss America Pageant is held in Atlantic City, New Jersey.

1922 The Cable Act ensures women will no longer be deprived of citizenship upon marriage to a foreigner.

1922 Rebecca Latimer Felton becomes the first woman appointed to the U.S. Senate.

1922 Women's razors and depilatories are first advertised in Sears Roebuck catalogs.

1923 An Equal Rights Amendment is presented to Congress by Alice Paul of the National Woman's Party.

1901 Alice Hegan Rice (1870–1942), novelist, particularly of the urban poor: *Mrs. Wiggs of the Cabbage Patch*

1902 Helen Keller (1880–1968): *The Story of My Life*

1903 Mary Austin (1868–1934), ardent and vocal feminist and spokesperson for Native American and Hispanic traditions: *The Land of Little Rain*

1903 Kate Douglas Wiggin (1856–1923), children's author: *Rebecca of Sunnybrook Farm*

1905 Mary Boykin Chesnut (1823–86): *A Diary from Dixie* (published posthumously)

1905 Edith Wharton (1862–1937): *The House of Mirth*

1908 Mary Roberts Rinehart (1876–1958), novelist, detective fiction writer, playwright: *The Circular Staircase*

1932 Gertrude Stein (1874–1946): *Three Lives*

1910 Jane Addams (1860–1935), social worker, writer: *Twenty Years at Hull-House*

1911 Anna Botsford Comstock (1854–1930): *Handbook of Nature Study*

1911 Harriet Monroe (1860–1936), poet, editor; founds *Poetry: A Magazine of Verse*, for which she serves as editor for the next 24 years

1912 Mary Antin (1881–1949): *The Promised Land*, story of a young Jewish girl's odyssey from Russia to America

1912 Sui Sin Far (Edith Maud Eaton, 1865–1914), first Chinese-American author: *Mrs. Spring Fragrance*, a collection of short stories and articles

1913 Willa Cather (1873–1947): *O Pioneers!*

1913 Ellen Glasgow (1873–1945), Southern novelist, short story writer: *Virginia*

1914 Margaret Anderson (1886–1973) founds *Little Review*.

1915 Adelaide Crapsey (1878–1914), inventor of the cinquain, a five-line poetic form: *Verse*

1915 Alice Gerstenberg (1885–1972), playwright: *Overtones*, forerunner of later psychological drama, opens as a one-act play in New York

1915 Onoto Watanna (Winnifred Eaton), Chinese-American novelist and biographer: *Me*, anonymously published autobiography

1916 H. D. (Hilda Doolittle, 1886–1961): *Sea Garden*, volume of imagist poetry

1917 Dorothy Canfield Fisher (1879–1958), novelist, short story writer, critic, translator, advocate of Montessori education: *Understood Betsy*

1917 Grace Livingston Hill (1865–1947), author of 107 works, including contemporary romance, historical romance, mystery, and nonfiction: *The Witness*

1918 Georgia Douglas Johnson (1886–1966), poet: *The Heart of a Woman and Other Poems*, first black female writer to receive national recognition since Frances Harper

1919 Amy Lowell (1874–1925), poet: *Pictures of the Floating World*

1920 Zona Gale (1874–1938), novelist, short story writer, dramatist, poet, pacifist: *Miss Lulu Bett*

1920 Angelina Weld Grimké: *Rachel*, first drama published by a black woman and performed professionally by blacks

1921 Gertrude Simmons Bonnin (Zitkala-Ša, "Redbird," 1876–1938), Native American rights activist, daughter of a Sioux mother: *American Indian Stories*

1921 Susan Glaspell (1876–1948), prolific author of plays and fiction: *Inheritors*

1921 Louise Pound (1872–1958), teacher, sportswoman, editor, linguist: *Poetic Origins and the Ballad*

1922 Emily Post (1872–1960): *Etiquette in Society, in Business, in Politics, and at Home*

1922 Lillian E. Wood, African-American novelist: *Let My People Go*

1923 Louise Bogan (1897–1970), poet and long-time poetry critic for *The New Yorker*: *Body of This Death*

1923 Carrie Chapman Catt (1859–1947): *Woman Suffrage and Politics*

1923 Mina Loy (1882–1986): *Lunar Baedecker*, poetry

1923 Margaret Mead (1901–78): *Coming of Age in Samoa*

1923   Maidenform, Inc., founded by Ida Rosenthal (1889–1973), manufactures its first bra.

1924   Act of Congress grants American Indians citizenship.

1924   Ma Ferguson of Texas becomes the nation's first elected woman governor.

1925   The Women's World Fair, the first fair ever devoted to women's accomplishments, is held in Chicago.

1926   Violette N. Anderson becomes the first black woman to argue a case before the U.S. Supreme Court.

1926   Gertrude Bonnin becomes the founding president of the National Council of American Indians.

1926   Gertrude Ederle of New York becomes the first woman to swim the English Channel.

1927   Minnie Buckingham-Harper becomes the first black woman serving in the U.S. legislature when she is appointed to fill her husband's West Virginia congressional seat.

1929   U.S. stock market crashes, launching the Great Depression.

1929   The American publishers of Radclyffe Hall's lesbian novel, *The Well of Loneliness*, are tried and convicted of obscenity, although an appeals court overturns the verdict later that same year.

1930   "Mother" Jones (Mary Harris) (1830–1930), renowned labor organizer and agitator, who helped found both the Social Democratic Party and the Industrial Workers of the World, turns 100.

1930   Four million Americans are unemployed.

1930   Of the 45,200 Filipinos in America, 2,500 are women.

1930   Four-fifths of all households have electricity.

1930   Ellen Church becomes the first airline stewardess.

1931   Jane Addams becomes the first woman awarded the Nobel Peace Prize.

1933   Frances Perkins is named U.S. Secretary of Labor and becomes the first woman to hold a cabinet post.

1934   Hattie W. Carraway becomes the first woman elected to the U.S. Senate.

1935   Pearl S. Buck (1892–1973) becomes the first U.S. woman to be awarded a Nobel prize in literature.

1935   Mary McLeod Bethune becomes the founding president of the National Council of Negro Women.

1935–41   Under the Works Progress Administration of the second New Deal, women find economic relief from the Depression; overall, however, less than 20 percent of all WPA workers are female; 3 percent are black females.

1937   Amelia Earhart (1897–1937?), pilot, is lost en route in her attempt to fly around the world.

1938   A *Ladies Home Journal* poll finds that 79 percent of American women approve of the use of contraceptives.

1939   Start of World War II; the name "Rosie the Riveter" is coined to refer to women employed in the American defense industries.

1940   Ida Fuller of Vermont becomes the first person to receive a Social Security check.

1940   A little more than half of American households have built-in bathing equipment; one-third are still cooking with wood or coal, and only one-third have central heating.

1941   Fifty-two percent of American families have mechanical refrigerators and/or washing machines.

1942   Under President Franklin Roosevelt's (1882–1945) executive order, over 110,000 Japanese Americans are placed in internment camps.

1942   WAVES, the U.S. Navy Women's Corps; SPARS, the U.S. Coast Guard's Women's Corps; and WAAC, the Women's Army Auxiliary Corps (renamed WAC in 1943) are formed.

1942   The Congress of Racial Equality (CORE) is founded.

1942   Margaret Bourke-White (1906–71) becomes the first woman war correspondent.

1945   About 3.5 million U.S. women are union members.

1945   World War II ends; the following year, federal support of child care facilities, vital during wartime for women workers, is abruptly cut off.

1923 Edna St. Vincent Millay (1892–1950) wins a Pulitzer Prize for *The Ballad of the Harp-Weaver*, *A Few Figs from Thistles*, and sonnets in *American Poetry, 1922, a Miscellany*

1923 Genevieve Taggard (1894–1948): *Hawaiian Hilltop*, poems

1924 Marianne Moore (1887–1972): *Observations*

1925 Hallie Quinn Brown, African-American author: *Our Women: Past, Present, and Future* and *Tales My Father Taught Me*

1925 Babette Deutsch (1895–1982), poet, critic: *Honey Out of the Rock*

1925 Anita Loos (1893–1981), novelist, scriptwriter: *Gentlemen Prefer Blondes*

1925 Etsu Inagaki Sugimoto, Japanese-American novelist: *A Daughter of the Samurai*

1927 Dorothy Parker (1893–1967), leader of the Algonquin Round Table wits, begins writing stories and a book review column signed "Constant Reader" for *The New Yorker*.

1927 Mourning Dove (Hum-Ishu-Ma, 1888–1936), of Okanogan tribe: *Cogewea, The Half-Blood*

1928 Josephine Herbst (1897–1969), proletarian novelist: *Nothing Is Sacred*

1928 Nella Larsen, African-American novelist: *Quicksand*

1928 Julie Peterkin (1880–1961), specialist in the life and language of the Gullahs of South Carolina: *Scarlet Sister Mary*

1929 Mignon Eberhart (b. 1899): *The Patient in Room 18*, first of approximately 70 detective novels

1929 Jessie Redmon Fauset (1884?–1961), African-American novelist, editor: *Plum Bun: A Novel without a Moral*

1929 Agnes Smedley (1892–1950): *Daughter of Earth*, autobiographical novel

1929 Leane Zugsmith (1903–69), Jewish novelist: *All Victories Are Alike*

1930 Katherine Anne Porter (1890–1980): *Flowering Judas, and Other Stories*

1931 Fannie Hurst (1889–1968), African-American novelist: *Back Street*

1932 Pearl S. Buck (1892–1973): *The Good Earth*

1932 Zelda Fitzgerald (1899–1948): *Save Me the Last Waltz*

1932 Jovita Gonzalez, Chicana short story writer: "Among My People," in J. Frank Dobie, ed. *Tone the Bell Easy*

1932 Grace Lumpkin (b. 1903?), novelist of southern poor: *To Make My Bread*

1932 Dorothy Myra Page: *Gathering Storm*, fictional dramatization of significant events in American labor history

1932 Laura Ingalls Wilder (1867–1957): *Little House in the Big Woods*

1934 Ruth Benedict (1887–1948), one of the first U.S. women to become a professional anthropologist: *Patterns of Culture*

1934 Caroline Gordon (1895–1981), fiction writer, critic: *Aleck Maury, Sportsman*

1934 Lillian Hellman (1905–84), playwright, autobiographer: *The Children's Hour*, runs for 691 performances on Broadway

1934 Alice James (1848–92): *The Diary of Alice James*

1934 Tess Slesinger (1900–75): *The Unpossessed*, modernist novel

1934 Betty Smith (1904–72), novelist, playwright: *A Tree Grows in Brooklyn*

1935 Haruto Ishimoto, Japanese-American autobiographer: *Facing Two Ways: The Story of My Life*

1935 Meridel Le Sueur (b. 1900), novelist, journalist, poet: "Annunciation"

1935 Muriel Rukeyser (b. 1913): *Theory of Flight*, collection of poems

1935 Mari Sandoz (1896–1966), begins six-volume Great Plains series with *Old Jules*

1936 Djuna Barnes (1892–1982), experimental novelist, journalist, playwright: *Nightwood*

1936 Margaret Mitchell (1900–49): *Gone With the Wind*

1937 Zora Neale Hurston (c. 1901–60): *Their Eyes Were Watching God*

1937 Sara Teasdale: *Collected Poems* (posthumously published)

1938 Marjorie Kinnan Rawlings (1896–1953): *The Yearling*

1938 Laura Riding (b. 1901), poet, novelist, critic: *Collected Poems*

1948   Harry Truman (1884–1972) signs the Women's Armed (Services) Integration Act, granting women the opportunity to pursue careers in the military.

1948   As chair of the Commission on Human Rights for the United Nations, Eleanor Roosevelt (1884–1962) creates the Universal Declaration of Human Rights.

1949   Eugenie Moore Anderson becomes the first U.S. woman ambassador.

1949   The first bikini bathing suit makes its appearance.

1950   Approximately 25 percent of all black wives and 10 percent of all white wives are either separated, divorced, or widowed; for both groups, approximately 40 percent are heads of households with children.

1951   Marion Donovan begins marketing the product she created "out of a shower curtain and absorbent padding": disposable diapers.

1953   Ethel Greenglass Rosenberg and her husband Julius are executed in the electric chair at Sing Sing prison for allegedly passing atomic secrets to the Soviet Union.

1953   The Kinsey Report, "Sexual Behavior in the Human Female," is published.

1953   Hugh Hefner's *Playboy* magazine appears featuring Marilyn Monroe in the centerfold.

1954   *Brown v. Board of Education of Topeka* finds racial discrimination unconstitutional in schools.

1954   Three out of five households—about 29 million—own television sets, which have only been on the market since 1947.

1955   Rosa Parks is arrested after refusing to give up her seat to a white passenger on a Montgomery, Alabama, bus.

1955   Eight women in San Francisco found the Daughters of Bilitis (DOB), a group advocating social and civil rights for lesbians.

1957–75   During the Vietnam era, approximately 261,000 women serve in the U.S. Armed Forces, over 7,500 in Vietnam itself.

1958   Ethel Percy Andrews (1884–1967) founds the American Association of Retired Persons.

1960   Three million people receive benefits from Aid to Families with Dependent Children.

1960   Four-fifths of all whites and three-fifths of all non-whites use or have used contraceptives; 93 percent of all college-educated women have done so.

1961   Elizabeth Gurley Flynn (1890–1964) becomes the first woman chair of the U.S. Communist Party.

1961   Only 3.6 percent of law school students are women.

1940   Mildred Haun, Appalachian writer: *The Hawk's Done Gone*

1940   Carson McCullers (1919–67), novelist, short story writer, playwright: *The Heart Is a Lonely Hunter*

1941   Eudora Welty (b. 1909), prolific Southern author of novels, short stories, memoirs: *A Curtain of Green*

1942   Mary McCarthy (b. 1912), essayist, fiction writer: *The Company She Keeps*

1942   Margaret Walker (b. 1915), African-American poet, novelist: *For My People*

1943   Jane Bowles (1917–73): *Two Serious Ladies*

1943   Ayn Rand (1905–82), Russian-born novelist: *The Fountainhead*

1943   Phyllis Whitney, popular author of children's and adult mysteries, and Gothic romances: *The Red Carnelian*

1944   Lillian Smith (1897–1966), novelist, civil rights advocate: *Strange Fruit*

1945   Josephina Niggli (1910–83): *Mexican Village*, collection of stories; perhaps first work of fiction by a Mexican American to reach a large audience

1945   Santha Rama Rau, Asian-Indian-American autobiographer, novelist: *Home to India*

1945   Jessamyn West (1902–84), novelist, short story writer: *The Friendly Persuasion*

1946   Elizabeth Bishop (1911–79): *North and South*

1946   Fannie Cook (1893–1949): *Mrs. Palmer's Honey*, winner of the first George Washington Carver Memorial Award

1946   Denise Levertov (b. 1923), poet: *The Double Image*

1946   Ann Petry (b. 1908), African-American novelist: *The Street*

1948   Shirley Jackson: "The Lottery" appears in *The New Yorker*

1950   Gwendolyn Brooks (b. 1917), African-American poet, and novelist: *Annie Allen* wins Pulitzer Prize

1950   Anzia Yezierska (1882?–1970), Polish-born novelist, short story writer: *Red Ribbon on a White Horse*

====

1952   Patricia Highsmith as Claire Morgan: *The Price of Salt*, one of the best-selling lesbian novels of all times

1952   Flannery O'Connor (1925–64), Southern novelist, short story writer: *Wise Blood*, novel

1953   Monica Sone, Japanese-American autobiographer: *Nisei Daughter*

1954   Harriette Arnow (b. 1908), Appalachian novelist: *The Dollmaker*

1954   Alice B. Toklas (1877–1967): *The Alice B. Toklas Cook Book*

1956   Eileen Chang, Chinese-American novelist: *The Naked Earth*

1957   Ann Bannon, lesbian novelist: *Odd Girl Out*

1959   Lorraine Hansberry (1930–65): *A Raisin in the Sun*, first Broadway play written by a black woman

1959   Paule Marshall (b. 1929), African-American novelist, short story writer: *Brown Girl, Brownstones*

1959   Grace Paley (b. 1922): *The Little Disturbances of Man*

1959   Mona Van Duyn (b. 1921), poet: *Valentines to the Wide World*

1960   Harper Lee: *To Kill a Mockingbird*

1960   Sylvia Plath (1932–63): *The Colossus and Other Poems; The Bell Jar*, published under the name "Victoria Lucas," appears in 1963

1960   Anne Sexton (1928–74): *To Bedlam and Part Way Back*, poetry

1961   Tillie Olsen (b. c. 1912), feminist, social activist, fiction writer, retriever of many "lost" works by women: "Tell Me a Riddle"

1962   Rachel Carson (1904–64), marine biologist, writer: *The Silent Spring* awakens people to the dangers of insecticides for the environment

1962 An estimated 46.5 million viewers watch on all three major networks as Jacqueline Kennedy leads a tour of the White House.

1963 Martin Luther King, Jr. (1929–68) delivers his "I Have a Dream" speech during a civil rights march on Washington, D.C.

1963 Federal Judge Sarah Tilghman Hughes swears in Lyndon B. Johnson (1908–73) aboard Air Force One following the assassination of John F. Kennedy (1917–63).

1964 Civil Rights Act is passed; Title VII bans sex discrimination in employment.

1965 The federal program Project Head Start is established to assist and educate impoverished children.

1965 *Griswold v. Connecticut* becomes noteworthy for overturning a statute that made using birth control or giving out information about its use illegal.

1965 The Moynihan Report, "The Negro Family: The Case for National Action," places blame for the poverty and alleged pathology of the black community on black single mothers.

1965 A study conducted in New York State finds that, in the years before abortions are decriminalized, black and Puerto Rican women represent 80 percent of all deaths from illegal abortions.

1966 The National Organization of Women (NOW) is founded by 28 feminists.

1966 The mini-skirt is in, with skirt lengths rising 4 to 7 inches above the knee.

1967 *Loving v. Virginia* allows interracial marriage and revokes anti-miscegenation laws in Virginia.

1968 Shirley Chisholm (b. 1924), becomes the first black woman elected to the U.S. House of Representatives.

1968 Martin Luther King, Jr., is assassinated; Coretta Scott King is voted Most Admired Woman by college students.

1969 The first Women's Studies baccalaureate degree program is offered at San Diego State University.

1969 The Woodstock Music and Art Fair, held August 15 to 18 on a farm in upstate New York, draws some 300,000 to 400,000 people.

1969 Stonewall riots in New York City mark the beginning of the gay liberation movement and the founding of the Gay Liberation Front (GLF).

1970 Women's employment is 31.2 million, compared to 18.4 million in 1950.

1970 Approximately 17 percent of white women and 6 percent of black women hold college degrees.

1970 California enacts the Western world's first completely no-fault divorce law.

1970 A Princeton University study finds that 20 percent of all black and Chicana married women have been permanently sterilized.

1971 *Ms.* magazine is launched in Gloria Steinem's living room in New York City; its first issue hits the newsstand in 1972.

1972 The Equal Rights Amendment is sent to the states for ratification after passing Congress.

1972 The first rape crisis center opens in Washington, D.C.; five years later, 150 centers operate nationwide.

1972 In St. Paul, Minnesota, the first battered women's shelter opens; six years later, 300 shelters have opened and the National Coalition Against Domestic Violence has been formed.

1973 *Roe v. Wade* strikes down all state laws prohibiting abortion on any grounds during the first trimester.

1973 Sex-segregated help wanted ads are outlawed by the U.S. Supreme Court.

1973 Marian Wright Edelman founds the Children's Defense Fund.

1974 The Lesbian Herstory Archives is founded in New York.

1974 American Psychiatric Association removes homosexuality from its list of mental disorders.

1974 President Gerald Ford (b. 1913) signs legislation allowing girls to play Little League baseball.

1975 U.N. International Women's Year conference is held in Mexico City with 6,300 women attending; it leads to the U.N. Decade for Women.

1962   Wylma Dykeman (b. 1920), novelist, biographer, historian of Appalachia: *The Tall Woman*

1962   Madeleine L'Engle (b. 1918), writer of fantasy for children, autobiographer: *A Wrinkle in Time*

1963   Betty Friedan (b. 1921): *The Feminine Mystique*

1963   Elizabeth Hardwick founds *The New York Review of Books.*

1963   Linda Ty-Casper, Filipina-American fiction writer: *The Transparent Sun and Other Stories*

1964   Shirley Ann Grau (b. 1929), novelist, short story writer: *The Keepers of the House*, Pulitzer Prize–winning novel

1964   Qöyawayma Polingaysi (b. 1892): *No Turning Back*, autobiography of life as a Hopi Indian and leader in the education of Native Americans

1964   Jane Rule (b. 1931): *Desert of the Heart*, lesbian novel

1964   Under the pseudonym Amanda Cross, Carolyn Heilbrun begins the Kate Fansler series of mystery novels with *In the Final Analysis.*

1965   May Sarton: *Mrs. Stevens Hears the Mermaids Singing*, novel

1966   Alice Adams, novelist, short story writer: *Careless Love*

1966   Silveria Baltasar, Filipina-American writer: *Your House Is My House*, nonfiction

1966   Anaïs Nin begins the publication of *The Diary of Anaïs Nin 1931–1966.*

1967   Joyce Carol Oates (b. 1938), prolific novelist, short story writer: "Where Are You Going, Where Have You Been?" and *A Garden of Earthly Delights*

1967   Diane Wakoski, poet: *The George Washington Poems*

1968   Joan Baez (b. 1941), Chicana autobiographer, folk singer: *Daybreak*

1968   Joan Didion: *Slouching Towards Bethlehem*

1968   Nikki Giovanni (b. 1943), African-American poet: *Black Feeling, Black Talk*

1969   Ursula K. LeGuin (b. 1929), science fiction and fantasy writer, essayist: *The Left-Hand of Darkness*

1970   Maya Angelou (b. 1928), prolific African-American novelist, poet, autobiographer: *I Know Why the Caged Bird Sings*

1970   Gail Godwin (b. 1937): *The Perfectionists*

1970   Germaine Greer (b. 1939): *The Female Eunuch*

1970   Audre Lorde (1934–92): *The First Cities*, poetry by black feminist lesbian

1970   Robin Morgan: *Sisterhood Is Powerful*

1970   Radicalesbians: *The Woman-Identified Woman*

1970   Sonia Sanchez (b. 1934): *We a BaddDDD People*

1971   Bharati Mukherjee, Asian-Indian-American novelist: *The Tiger's Daughter*

1972   Jessica Hagedorn, Filipina fiction writer, poet, dramatist: *Chiquita Banana*

1972   Willyce Kim, Korean-American poet: *Eating Artichokes*

1972   Alix Kates Shulman, novelist: *Memoirs of an Ex-Prom Queen*

1972   Kathleen E. Woodiwiss: *The Flame and the Flower*, influential popular romance

1973   Rita Mae Brown (b. 1944): *Rubyfruit Jungle*

1973   Erica Jong (b. 1942): *Fear of Flying*

1973   Maxine Kumin (b. 1925): *Up Country: Poems of New England*, Pulitzer Prize–winning collection

1973   Adrienne Rich (b. 1929), lesbian poet, essayist, activist: *Diving into the Wreck*, winner of National Book Award in 1974

1974   Alison Lurie (b. 1926): *The War Between the Tates*

1974   Nicholasa Mohr (b. 1935): *Nilda*, semi-autobiographical story of a Puerto Rican girl growing up in the Bronx

1975   Joy Harjo (b. 1951), Creek poet: *The Last Song*

1975   Angela de Hoyos, Chicana poet: *Arise Chicano* and *Chicano Poems for the Barrio*

1975   Gayl Jones (b. 1949), African-American novelist, poet: *Corregidora*

1975   In *Taylor v. Louisiana*, the U.S. Supreme Court outlaws automatic exclusion of women from jury duty.

1977   Hyde Amendment prohibits Medicaid-funded abortions.

1977   Eleanor Holmes Norton, chair of the Equal Employment Opportunity Commission (EEOC), authors federal guidelines on sexual harassment in the workplace.

1977   National Women's Studies Association (NWSA) is founded.

1978   The first year that all seven sister colleges—Barnard, Bryn Mawr, Mount Holyoke, Radcliffe, Smith, Vassar, Wellesley—have female presidents.

1978   Faye Wattleton becomes the first black president of Planned Parenthood Federation of America.

1979   For the first time more women than men enter college in the United States.

1979   Lesbians and gays march on Washington for their rights.

1979   Two of the U.S. hostages in the U.S. Embassy in Teheran, Iran, are women: Kathryn Koob and Elizabeth Ann Swift.

1980   Over 40 percent of the total workforce is female; women with children at home constitute 20 percent of the total workforce.

1980   Approximately 1.9 million Asian-American women are living in the United States.

1980   Population of Native Americans is approximately 1 million; the estimated life expectancy of contemporary Native Americans averages 45 years; estimated unemployment is between 60 and 90 percent.

1980   The U.S. Census allows that "the head of the household" need not be the husband.

1981   Sandra Day O'Connor becomes the first woman justice on the U.S. Supreme Court.

1982   The Equal Rights Amendment is defeated.

1982   With 27 percent of all Filipino women holding college degrees, they are better educated than any other U.S. population group, male or female.

1983   There are 444 Women's Studies programs in colleges and universities nationwide.

1983   Sally Ride becomes the first American female astronaut in space.

1984   A *Glamour* survey finds that more women would be happier about weight loss than about success in work or in interpersonal relations.

1984   The Democratic Party names Congresswoman Geraldine Ferraro as its vice-presidential nominee.

1985   Approximately 15,000 people die of AIDS; in 1986, the Women's AIDS Project is formed in Los Angeles.

1985   Median age of marriage for women is 23.2 years; for men, 25.5 years.

1986   Unanimous decision by the U.S. Supreme Court finds that sexual harassment is illegal job discrimination.

1986   The space shuttle *Challenger* explodes, killing all seven crew members including schoolteacher Christa McAuliffe and astronaut Judith Resnik.

1986   Full-time working women make only about 64 cents to a man's dollar.

1986   Seventy-two percent of childhood sexual abuse is perpetrated by fathers and stepfathers.

1987   Congresswoman Patricia Schroeder announces that a shortage of funds will prevent her from seeking the Democratic presidential nomination in 1988.

1987   Wilma Mankiller becomes the first woman elected head of the Cherokee Nation.

1987   Dr. Mae Jemison becomes NASA's first black woman astronaut.

1987   Eighty-five percent of U.S. counties offer no abortion services.

1988   Women cast 10 million more ballots than men in the presidential election; New Alliance Party Candidate Lenora Fulani becomes the first woman and first black whose name appears on all 50 states' ballots as a presidential candidate.

1988   More than 2 million women have had breast implants; 100,000 have had liposuction.

1988   Study calculates that on any given night in the United States, there are 735,000 homeless.

1989   *Webster v. Reproductive Health Services* returns to states the authority to limit a woman's right to a legal abortion.

1975 Joanna Russ (b. 1937), novelist, short story writer, especially of science fiction: *The Female Man*

1975 Jade Snow Wong: *No Chinese Stranger*, Chinese-American autobiography

1976 Lori Higa, Japanese-American dramatist: *Calamity Jane Meets Sushi Mama and the BVD Kid; or, . . . Lady Murasaki Rides the Wild Wild West*

1976 Maxine Hong Kingston (b. 1940), Chinese-American author: *The Woman Warrior*

1976 Marge Piercy: *Woman on the Edge of Time*

1976 Anne Rice (b. 1941), novelist who also writes erotica under A. N. Roquelaire and Anne Rampling: *Interview with a Vampire*

1976 Ntozake Shange (b. 1948): *for colored girls who have considered suicide / when the rainbow is enuf*, a choreopoem, and *Sassafrass, Cypress and Indigo*, a novel

1976 Bernice Zamora (b. 1938), Chicana author: *Restless Serpents*, poetry

1977 Meena Alexander, Asian-Indian-American poet, novelist, playwright, scholar: *I Root My Name* and *Without Place*, poetry; and *In the Middle Earth*, a one-act play

1977 Marilyn French: *The Women's Room*

1977 Toni Morrison (b. 1931): *Song of Solomon*, wins National Book Critics' Circle Award and National Book Award

1977 Marcia Muller introduces Sharon McCone, a female private detective, in *Edwin of the Iron Shoes.*

1977 Leslie Marmon Silko (b. 1948), Native American poet and novelist: *Ceremony*

1978 E. M. Broner, Jewish-American author: *A Weave of Women*, lyric novel

1978 Mary Daly (b. 1928): *Gyn/Ecology*

1978 Beth Henley (b. 1952): *Crimes of the Heart*, a play

1978 May Wong, Chinese-American poet: *Superstitions: Poems*

1979 Octavia E. Butler (b. 1947), African-American science fiction writer: *Kindred*

1980 Toni Cade Bambara: *The Salt Eaters*, a novel

1980 Ann Beattie (b. 1947): *Falling in Place*, a novel

1980 Michelle Cliff: *Claiming an Identity They Taught Me to Despise*

1980 Rita Dove, African-American poet: *The Yellow House on the Corner*

1980 Velina Hasu Houston, black-Japanese-American dramatist: *Asa Ga Kimashita (Morning Has Broken)*

1981 Lorna Dee Cervantes, poet: *Emplumada: Poems*

1982 Marion Zimmer Bradley: *The Mists of Avalon*, best-selling rewriting of the Arthurian legend from the perspective of female characters

1982 Bobbie Ann Mason (b. 1940), Southern author of short stories and novels: *Shiloh and Other Stories*

1982 Gloria Naylor (b. 1950), African-American novelist: *The Women of Brewster Place*, winner of the American Book Award

1982 Two highly successful series of mystery novels featuring female detectives are launched: Sara Paretsky's *Indemnity Only*, with V. I. Warshawski, and Sue Grafton's *"A" is for Alibi*, with Kinsey Millhone.

1982 Cathy Song, Korean-American poet: *Picture Bride*

1982 Sheila Ortiz Taylor, Chicana novelist: *Faultline*

1982 Anne Tyler (b. 1941), novelist and short story writer: *Dinner at the Homesick Restaurant*

1982 Alice Walker (b. 1944), African-American novelist, short story writer, essayist: *The Color Purple*, wins American Book Award and a Pulitzer Prize

1983 Becky Birtha (b. 1948), African-American lesbian short story writer, poet: *For Nights Like This One: Stories of Loving Women*

1983 Patricia Enrado, Filipina fiction writer: *House of Images*

1983 Cherríe Moraga, Chicana short story writer: *Loving in the War Years: Lo que nunca pasó por sus labios*

1983 Marsha Norman (b. 1947), playwright: *'night Mother*

1990   Sharon Pratt Dixon becomes the first black woman to be elected mayor of a major U.S. city (Washington, D.C.).

1990   Women hold 25 seats (4.7%) in the U.S. Congress; 23 are in the House of Representatives and 2 are in the Senate.

1990   Act for Better Child Care (ABC) becomes law, enacting comprehensive child care legislation.

1990   With the appointment of Justice Sandra Gardebring, the Minnesota Supreme Court becomes the first powerful legal institution to employ a majority of women.

1990   A record 3.1 million women hold two jobs at once.

1991   Clarence Thomas is appointed to the U.S. Supreme Court despite allegations of sexual harassment by law professor and former EEOC colleague Anita Hill.

1991–92   By the end of the Persian Gulf War, 13 U.S. women fighters have been killed and 2 taken prisoner.

1992   Women represent two-thirds of all poor American adults; more than 80 percent of all full-time working women earn less than $20,000 a year and the gender-based pay gap is worse in the United States than in any other country in the developed world.

1992   U.S. Navy investigates allegations of the sexual harassment of 26 women at its annual Tailhook Association conference.

1992   Two much-watched rape trials: William Kennedy Smith, nephew of Senator Ted Kennedy, is acquitted; boxer Mike Tyson is convicted and sentenced to ten years in jail.

1992   Women hold only 4.5 percent of all seats on the boards of Fortune 500 companies.

1992   In *Planned Parenthood v. Casey*, the U.S. Supreme Court affirms the constitutionality of abortion but allows individual states to place restrictions that do not "unduly burden" the woman.

1992   William Clinton is elected president; Hilary Rodham Clinton is the first president's wife to hold a professional degree.

1992   Of the 106 women who run for the House of Representatives, 47 win seats; 5 of the 11 women Senate candidates win seats, including the first black woman Senator, Carol Moseley Braun from Illinois.

1992   Seventy percent of all wives outlive their husbands.

Compiled by Cynthia Davis

1983 Lee Smith (b. 1944), Southern novelist, short story writer: *Oral History*

1983 Estela Portillo Trambley, Chicana playwright, fiction writer: *Sor Juana and Other Plays*

1984 Sandra Cisneros (b. 1954), Chicana-American novelist, short story writer, poet: *The House on Mango Street*

1984 Louise Erdrich (also writes as Chippewa, b. 1954), Native American novelist, poet: *Jacklight*, poetry; and *Love Medicine*, novel

1984 Ellen Gilchrist (b. 1935), novelist, short story writer, poet: *The Annunciation*, and novel; and *Victory Over Japan*, collection of short stories

1984 Roberta Hill Whiteman (b. 1947), Native American woman of the Oneida tribe: publishes *Star Quilt*

1985 Jamaica Kincaid: *Annie John*

1986 Kathy Acker: *Don Quixote*

1986 Ana Castillo, Chicana novelist, poet: *The Mixquihuala Letters*, poetry

1986 Tama Janowitz (b. 1957): *Slaves of New York*, collection of short stories

1986 Pat Mora, Chicana poet: *Borders*

1986 Sherley Ann Williams (b. 1944), African-American novelist: *Dessa Rose*

1987 Lucille Clifton, African-American poet, memoirist, children's writer: *Good Woman: Poems and a Memoir: 1969–1980*

1987 Fannie Flagg: *Fried Green Tomatoes at the Whistle Stop Cafe*

1987 Kaye Gibbons (b. 1960), Southern novelist: *Ellen Foster*

1987 Toni Morrison: *Beloved*, wins Pulitzer Prize and Robert F. Kennedy Book Award

1988 Hisaye Yamamoto, Japanese-American short story writer: *Seventeen Syllables and Other Stories*

1989 Terry McMillan, African-American novelist: *Disappearing Acts*

1989 Susan Sontag: *AIDS and Its Metaphors*

1989 Amy Tan, Chinese-American novelist: *The Joy Luck Club*

1989 Wendy Wasserstein: *The Heidi Chronicles*, first female author to win a Tony Award for Best Play

1993 Maya Angelou reads "On the Pulse of the Morning" at Presidential Inauguration.

1993 Toni Morrison wins the Nobel Prize for Literature.

Compiled by Kathryn West

BIBLIOGRAPHY

Guides to Research and Teaching

Addis, Patricia K. *Through a Woman's I: An Annotated Bibliography of American Women's Autobiographical Writings, 1946–1976.* Metuchen, NJ: Scarecrow P, 1983.

Allen, Paula Gunn, ed. *Studies in American Indian Literature: Critical Essays and Course Designs.* New York: MLA, 1983.

Arata, Esther Spring. *More Black American Playwrights: A Bibliography.* Metuchen, NJ: Scarecrow P, 1978.

Arata, Esther Spring, and Nicholas John Rotoli. *Black American Playwrights, 1800 to the Present: A Bibliography.* Metuchen, NJ: Scarecrow P, 1976.

Armitage, Susan, et al., eds. *Women in the West: A Guide to Manuscript Sources.* New York: Garland, 1991.

Bataille, Gretchen M., ed. *Native American Women: A Biographical Dictionary.* New York: Garland, 1993.

Bataille, Gretchen M., and Kathleen Mullen Sands. *American Indian Women: A Guide to Research.* New York: Garland, 1991.

Baym, Nina. *Woman's Fiction: A Guide to Novels by and about Women in America, 1820–1870.* Urbana: U of Illinois P, 1993.

Blair, Virginia, Isobel Grundy, and Patricia Clements, eds. *The Feminist Companion to Literature in English: Women Writers from the Middle Ages to the Present.* New Haven, CT: Yale UP, 1990.

Brumble, H. David, III. *An Annotated Bibliography of American Indian and Eskimo Autobiographies.* Lincoln: U of Nebraska P, 1981.

Buck, Claire, ed. *The Bloomsbury Guide to Women's Literature.* New York: Prentice Hall, 1992.

Buhle, Mari J. *Women and the American Left: A Guide to Sources.* Boston: G. K. Hall, 1983.

Butler, Deborah A. *American Women Writers on Vietnam: Unheard Voices: A Selected Annotated Bibliography.* New York: Garland, 1990.

Candelaria, Cordelia, ed. *Multiethnic Literature of the United States: Critical Introductions and Classroom Resources.* Boulder: U of Colorado P, 1989.

Chapman, Dorothy Hilton, comp. *Index to Poetry by Black American Women.* Westport, CT: Greenwood P, 1986.

Cheung, King-Kok, and Stan Yogi. *Asian American Literature: An Annotated Bibliography.* New York: MLA, 1988.

Chinoy, Helen Krich, and Linda Walsh Jenkins. *Women in the American Theatre: Careers, Images, Movements: An Illustrated Anthology and Sourcebook.* Rev. ed. New York: Theater Communications Group, 1987.

Ch'maj, Betty E. M., ed. *Multicultural America: A Resource Book for Teachers of Humanities and American Studies; Syllabi, Essays, Projects, Bibliography.* Lanham, MD: UP of America, 1993.

Colonnese, Tom, and Louis Owens. *American Indian Novelists: An Annotated Critical Bibliography.* New York: Garland, 1985.

Cordasco, Francesco. *The Immigrant Women in North America: An Annotated Bibliography of Selected References.* Metuchen, NJ: Scarecrow P, 1985.

Coven, Brenda. *American Women Dramatists of the Twentieth Century: A Bibliography.* Metuchen, NJ: Scarecrow P, 1982.

Cronin, Gloria L., Blaine H. Hall, and Connie Lamb. *Jewish-American Fiction Writers: An Annotated Bibliography.* New York: Garland, 1991.

Cunningham, Nella, ed. *Multicultural Women's Sourcebook: Materials Guide for Use in Women's Studies and Bilingual Multicultural Programs.* Newton, MA: Women's Educational Equity Act Publishing Center and Education Development Center, 1982.

Dance, Daryl Cumber, ed. *Fifty Caribbean Writers: A Bio-Bibliographical Critical Sourcebook.* Westport, CT: Greenwood P, 1986.

Davis, Gwenn, and Beverly A. Joyce, comps. *Personal Writings by Women to 1900: A Bibliography of American and British Writers.* Norman: U of Oklahoma P, 1989.

Duke, Maurice, Jackson R. Bryer, and M. Thomas Inge, eds. *American Women Writers: Bibliographical Essays.* Westport, CT: Greenwood P, 1983.

Eger, Ernestina N., comp. *A Bibliography of Criticism of Contemporary Chicano Literature.* Berkeley, CA: Chicano Studies Library Publications, 1980.

Elwell, Ellen Sue Levi, and Edward R. Levenson, eds. *The Jewish Women's Studies Guide.* Fresh Meadows, NY: Biblio P, 1982.

Erisman, Fred, and Richard W. Etulain, eds. *Fifty Western Writers: A Bio-Bibliographical Sourcebook.* Westport, CT: Greenwood P, 1982.

Foster, David William, ed. *Sourcebook of Hispanic Culture in the United States.* Chicago: American Library Association, 1982.

French, William P., Michel J. Fabre, Amritjit Singh, and Genevieve E. Fabre. *Afro-American Poetry and Drama, 1760–1975: A Guide to Information Sources.* Detroit: Gale, 1979.

Gabaccia, Donna, comp. *Immigrant Women in the United States: A Selectively Annotated Multidisciplinary Bibliography.* Westport, CT: Greenwood P, 1989.

Gibaldi, Joseph, ed. *Introduction to Scholarship in Modern Languages and Literatures.* 2nd ed. New York: MLA, 1992.

970

Glikin, Ronda. *Black American Women in Literature: A Bibliography, 1976 through 1987.* Jefferson, NC: McFarland, 1989.

Green, Rayna. *Native American Women: A Contextual Bibliography.* Bloomington: Indiana UP, 1983.

Harris, Trudier, and Thadious M. Davis, eds. *Afro-American Fiction Writers after 1955.* Vol. 33 of *Dictionary of Literary Biography.* Detroit: Gale, 1984.

———. *Afro-American Poets since 1955.* Vol. 41 of *Dictionary of Literary Biography.* Detroit: Gale, 1985.

———. *Afro-American Writers, 1940–1955.* Vol. 76 of *Dictionary of Literary Biography.* Detroit: Gale, 1988.

———. *Afro-American Writers after 1955: Dramatists and Prose Writers.* Vol. 38 of *Dictionary of Literary Biography.* Detroit: Gale, 1985.

———. *Afro-American Writers before the Harlem Renaissance.* Vol. 50 of *Dictionary of Literary Biography.* Detroit: Gale, 1986.

———. *Afro-American Writers from the Harlem Renaissance to 1940.* Vol. 51 of *Dictionary of Literary Biography.* Detroit: Gale, 1987.

Hatch, James V., and Omanii Abdullah, eds. *Black Playwrights, 1823–1977: An Annotated Bibliography of Plays.* New York: Bowker, 1977.

Holte, James C. *The Ethnic I: A Sourcebook for Ethnic-American Autobiography.* Westport, CT: Greenwood P, 1988.

Howard, Sharon M. *African American Women Fiction Writers, 1859–1986: An Annotated Bibliography.* New York: Garland, 1989.

Hull, Gloria T., Patricia Bell Scott, and Barbara Smith, eds. *But Some of Us Are Brave: Black Women's Studies.* Old Westbury, NY: Feminist P, 1981.

Jacobson, Angeline, comp. *Contemporary Native American Literature: A Selected, Partially Annotated Bibliography.* Metuchen, NJ: Scarecrow P, 1977.

James, Edward T., ed. *Notable American Women.* Cambridge, MA: Belknap P of Harvard UP, 1971.

Kanellos, Nicolas, ed. *Biographical Dictionary of Hispanic Literature in the United States: The Literature of Puerto Ricans, Cuban Americans, and Other Hispanic Writers.* Westport, CT: Greenwood P, 1989.

Kramarae, Cheris, and Paula A. Treichler. *A Feminist Dictionary.* Boston: Beacon P, 1985.

Lomeli, Francisco A., and Carl R. Shirley, eds. *Chicano Writers: First Series.* Vol. 82 of *Dictionary of Literary Biography.* Detroit: Gale, 1989.

———. *Chicano Writers: Second Series.* Vol. 122 of *Dictionary of Literary Autobiography.* Detroit: Gale, 1992.

Mainiero, Lina, ed. *American Women Writers: A Critical Reference Guide from Colonial Times to the Present.* 4 vols. New York: Frederick Ungar, 1979–1982.

Manning, Beverley. *Index to American Women Speakers, 1828–1978.* Metuchen, NJ: Scarecrow P, 1980.

———. *We Shall Be Heard: An Index to Speeches by American Women, 1978–1985.* Metuchen, NJ: Scarecrow P, 1988.

Martínez, Julio A., and Francisco A. Lomelí. *Chicano Literature: A Reference Guide.* Westport, CT: Greenwood P, 1985.

Peterson, Bernard L., Jr. *Contemporary Black American Playwrights and Their Plays: A Biographical Directory and Dramatic Index.* Westport, CT: Greenwood P, 1988.

Reardon, Joan, and Kristine A. Thorsen. *Poetry by American Women, 1900–1975: A Bibliography.* Metuchen, NJ: Scarecrow P, 1979.

Rhodes, Carolyn H., ed. *First Person Female American: A Selected and Annotated Bibliography of the Autobiographies of American Women Living after 1950.* Vol. II of *American Notes and Queries Supplement.* Troy, NY: Whitston, 1980.

Robinson, Doris. *Women Novelists, 1891–1920: An Index to Biographical and Autobiographical Sources.* New York: Garland, 1984.

Rock, Roger O., comp. *The Native American in American Literature: A Selectively Annotated Bibliography.* Westport, CT: Greenwood P, 1985.

Roses, Lorraine Elena, and Ruth Elizabeth Randolph. *Harlem Renaissance and Beyond: Literary Biographies of 100 Black Women Writers, 1900–1945.* Boston: G. K. Hall, 1990.

Ruoff, A. LaVonne Brown. *American Indian Literatures: An Introduction, Bibliographic Review, and Selected Bibliography.* New York: MLA, 1990.

Ruoff, A. LaVonne Brown, and Jerry W. Ward, Jr. *Redefining American Literary History: Committee on Literatures and Languages of America.* New York: MLA, 1990.

Schwartz, Narda Lacey. *Articles on Women Writers: A Bibliography.* Santa Barbara, CA: ABC-Clio, 1986.

Shockley, Ann Allen, ed. *Afro-American Women Writers, 1746–1933: An Anthology and Critical Guide.* Boston: G. K. Hall, 1988.

Sicherman, Barbara, and Carol Hurd Green, eds. *Notable American Women: The Modern Period.* Cambridge, MA: Belknap P of Harvard UP, 1980.

Sims, Janet L., comp. *The Progress of Afro-American Women: A Selected Bibliography and Resource Guide.* Westport, CT: Greenwood P, 1980.

Tierney, Helen, ed. *Women's Studies Encyclopedia.* Westport, CT: Greenwood P, 1990.

Walden, Daniel, ed. *Twentieth-Century American-Jewish Fiction Writers.* Vol. 28 of *Dictionary of Literary Biography.* Detroit: Gale, 1984.

Walker, Robbie Jean, ed. *The Rhetoric of Struggle: Public Address by African American Women.* New York: Garland, 1992.

White, Barbara A. *American Women's Fiction, 1790–1870: A Reference Guide.* New York: Garland, 1990.

———. *American Women Writers: An Annotated Bibliography of Criticism.* New York: Garland, 1977.

Williams, Ora. *American Black Women in the Arts and Social Sciences: A Bibliographic Survey.* 1973. Rev. ed. Metuchen, NJ: Scarecrow P, 1977.

Women Talking and Writing about Women

Balassi, William, et al., eds. *This Is about Vision: Interviews with Southwestern Writers.* Albuquerque: U of New Mexico P, 1990.

Bell, Roseanne P., Bettye J. Parker, and Beverly Guy-Sheftall. *Sturdy Black Bridges: Visions of Black Women in Literature.* Garden City, NY: Anchor P/Doubleday, 1979.

Betsko, Kathleen, and Rachel Koenig, comps. *Interviews with Contemporary Women Playwrights.* New York: Beech Tree Books, 1987.

Binder, Wolfgang, ed. *Partial Autobiographies: Interviews with Twenty Chicano Poets.* Erlangen, West Germany: Palm and Enke, 1985.

Braden, Maria. *She Said What?: Interviews with Women Newspaper Columnists.* Lexington: UP of Kentucky, 1993.

Brandt, Kate. *Happy Endings: Lesbian Writers Talk about Their Lives and Work.* Tallahassee, FL: Naiad P, 1993.

Bruce-Novoa, Juan D. *Chicano Authors: Inquiry by Interview.* Austin: U of Texas P, 1980.

Bruchac, Joseph. *Survival This Way: Interviews with American Indian Poets.* Tucson: U of Arizona P, 1987.

Chamberlain, Mary, ed. *Writing Lives: Conversations between Women Writers.* London: Virago P, 1988.

Coltelli, Laura. *Winged Words: American Indian Writers Speak.* Lincoln: U of Nebraska P, 1990.

Evans, Mari, ed. *Black Women Writers (1950–1980): A Critical Evaluation.* Garden City, NY: Anchor P/Doubleday, 1984.

Jordan, Shirley M., ed. *Broken Silences: Interviews with Black and White Women Writers.* New Brunswick, NJ: Rutgers UP, 1993.

Melhem, D. H. *Heroism in the New Black Poetry: Introductions and Interviews.* Lexington: UP of Kentucky, 1990.

Pearlman, Mickey. *Listen to Their Voices: Twenty Interviews with Women Who Write.* New York: Norton, 1993.

Pearlman, Mickey, and Katherine Usher Henderson, eds. *Inter/View: Talks with America's Writing Women.* Lexington: UP of Kentucky, 1990.

Plimpton, George, ed. *Women Writers at Work.* New York: Penguin, 1989.

Sternburg, Janet, ed. *The Writer on Her Work.* New York: Norton, 1980.

——. *The Writer on Her Work, Volume II: New Essays in New Territory.* New York: Norton, 1991.

Swann, Brian, and Arnold Krupat, eds. *I Tell You Now: Autobiographical Essays by Native American Writers.* Lincoln: U of Nebraska P, 1987.

Tate, Claudia, ed. *Black Women Writers at Work.* New York: Continuum, 1983.

Todd, Janet, ed. *Women Writers Talking.* New York: Holmes and Meier, 1983.

Webber, Jeannette L., and Joan Grumman, eds. *Woman as Writer.* Boston: Houghton Mifflin, 1978.

Yalom, Marilyn, ed. *Women Writers of the West Coast: Speaking of Their Lives and Careers.* Santa Barbara, CA: Capra P, 1983.

Criticism

Aguero, Kathleen, ed. *Daily Fare: Essays from the Multicultural Experience.* Athens: U of Georgia P, 1993.

Allen, Mary. *The Necessary Blankness: Women in Major American Fiction of the Sixties.* Urbana: U of Illinois P, 1976.

Allen, Paula Gunn. *The Sacred Hoop: Recovering the Feminine in American Indian Traditions.* Boston: Beacon P, 1986.

Alpern, Sara, et al. *The Challenge of Feminist Biography: Writing the Lives of Modern American Women.* Urbana: U of Illinois P, 1992.

Ammons, Elizabeth. *Conflicting Stories: American Women Writers at the Turn into the Twentieth Century.* New York: Oxford UP, 1991.

Andrews, William L. *To Tell a Free Story: The First Century of American Autobiography, 1760–1865.* Urbana: U of Illinois P, 1986.

Anzaldúa, Gloria, ed. *Making Face, Making Soul/ Haciendo Caras: Creative and Critical Perspectives by Women of Color.* San Francisco: Aunt Lute Foundation, 1990.

Awkward, Michael. *Inspiriting Influences: Tradition, Revision, and Afro-American Women's Novels.* New York: Columbia UP, 1989.

Baker, Houston A., Jr., ed. *Three American Literatures: Essays in Chicano, Native American, and Asian-American Literature for Teachers of American Literature.* New York: MLA, 1982.

——. *Workings of the Spirit: The Poetics of Afro-American Women's Writing.* Chicago: U of Chicago P, 1991.

Bakerman, Jane S., ed. *And Then There Were Nine— More Women of Mystery.* Bowling Green, OH: Bowling Green U Popular P, 1985.

Bardes, Barbara, and Suzanne Gossett. *Declarations of Independence: Women and Political Power in Nineteenth-Century American Fiction.* New Brunswick, NJ: Rutgers UP, 1990.

Bargainnier, Earl F., ed. *10 Women of Mystery.* Bowling Green, OH: Bowling Green State U Popular P, 1981.

Barr, Marleen S. *Feminist Fabulation: Space/Postmodern Fiction.* Iowa City: U of Iowa P, 1992.

Barr, Marleen S., and Nicolas D. Smith, eds. *Women and Utopia: Critical Interpretations.* Lanham, MD: UP of America, 1983.

Barolini, Helen, ed. *The Dream Book: An Anthology of Writings by Italian-American Women.* New York: Schocken Books, 1985.

Barreca, Regina, ed. *New Perspectives on Women and Comedy.* Philadelphia: Gordon and Breach Science Publishers, 1992.

Bartkowski, Frances. *Feminist Utopias.* Lincoln: U of Nebraska P, 1989.

Bataille, Gretchen M., and Kathleen Mullen Sands. *American Indian Women, Telling Their Lives.* Lincoln: U of Nebraska P, 1984.

Baym, Nina. *Feminism and American Literary History: Essays.* New Brunswick, NJ: Rutgers UP, 1992.

Bedrosian, Margaret. *The Magical Pine Ring: Culture and Imagination in Armenian-American Literature.* Detroit: Wayne State UP, 1991.

Bell, Bernard W. *The Afro-American Novel and Its Tradition.* Amherst: U of Massachusetts P, 1987.

Bennett, Paula. *My Life, a Loaded Gun: Female Creativity and Feminist Poetics.* Boston: Beacon P, 1986.

Benstock, Shari. *Feminist Issues in Literary Scholarship.* Bloomington: Indiana UP, 1987.

———. *The Private Self: Theory and Practice of Women's Autobiographical Writings.* Chapel Hill: U of North Carolina P, 1988.

———. *Textualizing the Feminine: On the Limits of Genre.* Norman: U of Oklahoma P, 1991.

———. *Women of the Left Bank: Paris, 1900–1940.* Austin: U of Texas P, 1986.

Berkowitz, Gerald M. *America Drama of the Twentieth Century.* New York: Longman, 1992.

Bevilacqua, Winnifred Farrant, ed. *Fiction by American Women: Recent Views.* Port Washington, NY: Associated Faculty P, 1983.

Bloom, Harold, ed. *American Women Poets.* New York: Chelsea House, 1986.

Brantley, Will. *Feminine Sense in Southern Memoir.* Jackson: UP of Mississippi, 1993.

Braxton, Joanne M. *Black Women Writing Autobiography: A Tradition within a Tradition.* Philadelphia: Temple UP, 1989.

Braxton, Joanne M., and Andrée Nicola McLaughlin. *Wild Women in the Whirlwind: Afro-American Culture and the Contemporary Literary Renaissance.* New Brunswick, NJ: Rutgers UP, 1989.

Brodhead, Richard H. *Cultures of Letters: Scenes of Reading and Writing in Nineteenth-Century America.* Chicago: U of Chicago P, 1993.

Broe, Mary Lynn, and Angela Ingram. *Women's Writing in Exile.* Chapel Hill: U of North Carolina P, 1989.

Brown, Dorothy H., and Barbara C. Ewell. *Louisiana Women Writers: New Essays and a Comprehensive Bibliography.* Baton Rouge: Louisiana State UP, 1992.

Brown, Janet. *Feminist Drama: Definition and Critical Analysis.* Metuchen, NJ: Scarecrow P, 1979.

———. *Taking Center Stage: Feminism in Contemporary U.S. Drama.* Metuchen, NJ: Scarecrow P, 1991.

Brown-Guillory, Elizabeth. *Their Place on the Stage: Black Women Playwrights in America.* Westport, CT: Greenwood P, 1988.

Bruce-Novoa, Juan D. *Chicano Poetry: A Response to Chaos.* Austin: U of Texas P, 1982.

Brumble, H. David, III. *American Indian Autobiography.* Berkeley: U of California P, 1988.

Budd, Elaine. *13 Mistresses of Murder.* New York: Frederick Ungar, 1986.

Butler-Evans, Elliott. *Race, Gender, and Desire: Narrative Strategies in the Fiction of Toni Cade Bambara, Toni Morrison, and Alice Walker.* Philadelphia: Temple UP, 1989.

Campbell, Karlyn Kohrs. *Man Cannot Speak for Her.* 2 vols. Westport, CT: Greenwood P, 1989.

Candelaria, Cordelia. *Chicano Poetry: A Critical Introduction.* Westport, CT: Greenwood P, 1986.

Carby, Hazel V. *Reconstructing Womanhood: The Emergence of the Afro-American Woman Novelist.* New York: Oxford UP, 1987.

Casey, Daniel J., and Robert E. Rhodes, eds. *Irish-American Fiction: Essays in Criticism.* New York: AMS Press, 1979.

Chin, Frank, et al., eds. Introduction: "Fifty Years of our Whole Life." *Aiiieeeee! An Anthology of Asian-American Writers.* 1974. Washington: Howard UP, 1983.

Christian, Barbara. *Black Feminist Criticism: Perspectives on Black Women Writers.* New York: Pergamon P, 1985.

———. *Black Women Novelists: The Development of a Tradition, 1892–1976.* Westport, CT: Greenwood P, 1980.

Clark, Suzanne. *Sentimental Modernism: Women Writers and the Revolution of the World.* Bloomington: Indiana UP, 1991.

Cooper, Helen M., Adrienne Auslander Munich, and Susan Merrill Squier. *Arms and the Woman: War, Gender, and Literary Representation.* Chapel Hill: U of North Carolina P, 1989.

Cordova, Teresa, et al. *Chicano Voices: Intersections of Class, Race, and Gender.* Austin: U of Texas P and Center for Mexican American Studies, 1986.

Coultrap-McQuin, Susan. *Doing Literary Business: American Women Writers in the Nineteenth Century.* Chapel Hill: U of North Carolina P, 1990.

Cranny-Francis, Anne. *Feminist Fiction: Feminist Uses of Generic Fiction.* New York: St. Martin's P, 1990.

Culley, Margo. *American Women's Autobiography: Fea(s)ts of Memory.* Madison: U of Wisconsin P, 1992.

Daly, Brenda O., and Maureen T. Reddy, eds. *Narrating Mothers: Theorizing Maternal Subjectivities.* Knoxville: U of Tennessee P, 1991.

Davidson, Cathy N., ed. *Reading in America: Literature and Social History.* Baltimore: Johns Hopkins UP, 1989.

———. *Revolution and the World: The Rise of the Novel in America.* New York: Oxford UP, 1986.

Davidson, Cathy N., and E. M. Broner, eds. *The Lost Tradition: Mothers and Daughters in Literature.* New York: Frederick Ungar, 1980.

Davis, Charles T., and Henry Louis Gates, Jr., eds. *The Slave's Narrative.* New York: Oxford UP, 1984.

Dearborn, Mary V. *Pocahontas's Daughters: Gender and Ethnicity in American Culture.* New York: Oxford UP, 1986.

DeShazer, Mary K. *Inspiring Women: Reimagining the Muse.* New York: Pergamon P, 1986.

De Weever, Jacqueline. *Mythmaking and Metaphor in Black Women's Fiction.* New York: St. Martin's P, 1992.

Diehl, Joanne Feit. *Women Poets and the American Sublime.* Bloomington: Indiana UP, 1990.

Di Pietro, Robert, and Edward Ifkovic, et al., eds. *Ethnic Perspectives in American Literature: Selected Essays on the European Contribution.* New York: MLA, 1983.

Dixon, Melvin. *Ride Out the Wilderness: Geography and Identity in Afro-American Literature.* Urbana: U of Illinois P, 1987.

Dodd, Elizabeth. *The Veiled Mirror and the Woman Poet: H. D., Louise Bogan, Elizabeth Bishop, and Louise Glück.* Columbia: U of Missouri P, 1992.

Donaldson, Laura E. *Decolonizing Feminisms: Race, Gender, and Empire-Building.* Chapel Hill: U of North Carolina P, 1992.

Donovan, Josephine. *New England Local Color Literature: A Women's Tradition.* New York: Frederick Ungar, 1982.

Drake, William. *The First Wave: Women Poets in*

America, 1915–1945. New York: Macmillan: 1987.

DuPlessis, Rachel Blau. *Writing beyond the Ending: Narrative Strategies of Twentieth-Century Women Writers.* Bloomington: Indiana UP, 1985.

Du Pont, Denise, ed. *Women of Vision.* New York: St. Martin's P, 1988.

Elliott, Emory, et al., eds. *Columbia Literary History of the United States.* New York: Columbia UP, 1988.

Elliott, Emory, et al., eds. *The Columbia History of the American Novel.* New York: Columbia UP, 1991.

Erkkila, Betsy. *The Wicked Sisters: Women Poets, Literary History, and Discord.* New York: Oxford UP, 1992.

Fabre, Genevieve. *European Perspectives on Hispanic Literature of the United States.* Houston: Arte Publico P, 1988.

Fairbanks, Carol. *Prairie Women: Images in American and Canadian Fiction.* New Haven, CT: Yale UP, 1986.

Fisher, Dexter. *The Third Woman: Minority Women Writers of the United States.* Boston: Houghton Mifflin, 1979.

Foster, Frances Smith, ed. *Witnessing Slavery: The Development of the Ante-Bellum Slave Narratives.* Westport, CT: Greenwood P, 1979.

Freedman, Diane P. *An Alchemy of Genres: Cross-Genre Writing by American Feminist Poet-Critics.* Charlottesville: UP of Virginia, 1992.

Gates, Henry Louis, Jr., ed. *Reading Black, Reading Feminist: A Critical Anthology.* New York: Meridian Book, 1990.

Gelfant, Blanche H. *Women Writing in America: Voices in Collage.* Hanover, NH: UP of New England, 1984.

Gilbert, Sandra, and Susan Gubar. *The Madwoman in the Attic: The Woman Writer and the Nineteenth-Century Literary Imagination.* New Haven: Yale UP, 1979.

Gilbert, Sandra M., and Susan Gubar. *No Man's Land: The Place of the Woman Writer in the Twentieth Century.* New Haven, CT: Yale UP, 1988.

Gould, Jean. *American Women Poets: Pioneers of Modern Poetry.* New York: Dodd, Mead, 1980.

——. *Modern American Women Poets.* New York: Dodd, Mead, 1984.

Grahn, Judy. *The Highest Apple: Sappho and the Lesbian Poetic Tradition.* San Francisco: Spinsters, Ink, 1985.

Gray, Nancy. *Language Unbound: On Experimental Writing by Women.* Urbana: U of Illinois P, 1992.

Greene, Gayle, and Coppelia Kahn, eds. *Making a Difference.* New York: Methuen, 1985.

Gwin, Minrose C. *Black and White Women of the Old South: The Peculiar Sisterhood in American Literature.* Knoxville: U of Tennessee P, 1985.

Hanson, Elizabeth I. *Forever There: Race and Gender in Contemporary Native American Fiction.* New York: Peter Lang, 1989.

Harris, Marie, and Kathleen Aguero, eds. *A Gift of Tongues: Critical Challenges in Contemporary American Poetry.* Athens: U of Georgia P, 1987.

Harris, Susan K. *19th-Century American Women's Novels: Interpretive Strategies.* Cambridge, England: Cambridge UP, 1990.

Harris, Trudier. *From Mammies to Militants: Domestics in Black American Literature.* Philadelphia: Temple UP, 1982.

Harrison, Elizabeth J. *Female Pastoral: Women Writers Re-Visioning the American South.* Knoxville: U of Tennessee P, 1991.

Hart, Lynda, ed. *Making a Spectacle: Feminist Essays on Contemporary Women's Theater.* Ann Arbor: U of Michigan P, 1989.

Heller, Dana A. *The Feminization of Quest-Romance: Radical Departures.* Austin: U of Texas P, 1990.

Herndl, Diane Price. *Invalid Women: Figuring Feminine Illness in American Fiction and Culture, 1840–1940.* Chapel Hill: U of North Carolina P, 1993.

Hernton, Calvin C. *The Sexual Mountain and Black Women Writers: Adventures in Sex, Literature, and Real Life.* Garden City, NY: Doubleday, 1987.

Herrera-Sobek, Maria, ed. *Beyond Stereotypes: The Critical Analysis of Chicana Literature.* Binghamton, NY: Bilingual P/Editorial Bilingue, 1985.

Herrera-Sobek, Maria, and Helena Maria Viramontes, eds. *Chicana Creativity and Criticism: Charting New Frontiers in American Literature.* Houston: Arte Publico P, 1988.

Hirsch, Marianne. *The Mother/Daughter Plot: Narrative, Psychoanalysis, Feminism.* Bloomington: Indiana UP, 1989.

Hogue, W. Lawrence. *Discourse and the Other: The Production of the Afro-American Text.* Durham, NC: Duke UP, 1986.

Holloway, Karla F. C. *Moorings and Metaphors: Figures of Culture and Gender in Black Women's Literature.* New Brunswick, NJ: Rutgers UP, 1992.

hooks, bell. *Talking Back: Thinking Feminist, Thinking Black.* Boston: South End P, 1989.

Horno-Delgado, Asuncion, et al., eds. *Breaking Boundaries: Latina Writing and Critical Readings.* Amherst: U of Massachusetts P, 1989.

Howe, Florence, ed. *Tradition and the Talents of Women.* Urbana: U of Illinois P, 1991.

Huerta, Jorge A. *Chicano Theater: Themes and Forms.* Ypsilanti, MI: Bilingual P, 1982.

Huf, L. M. *Portrait of the Artist as a Young Woman.* New York: Frederick Ungar, 1983.

Hull, Gloria T. *Color, Sex and Poetry: Three Women Writers of the Harlem Renaissance.* Bloomington: Indiana UP, 1987.

Inge, Tonette Bond, ed. *Southern Women Writers: The New Generation.* Tuscaloosa: U of Alabama P, 1980.

Jackson, Blyden. *A History of Afro-American Literature.* Baton Rouge: Louisiana State UP, 1989.

Jara, Rene, and Nicholas Spadaccini, eds. *1492–1992: Re/Discovering Colonial Writing.* Minneapolis: U of Minnesota P, 1989.

Jimenez, Francisco, ed. *The Identification and Analysis of Chicano Literature.* New York: Bilingual P/Editorial Bilingue, 1979.

Jones, Anne Goodwyn. *Tomorrow Is Another Day: The Woman Writer in the South, 1859–1936.* Baton Rouge: Louisiana State UP, 1981.

Jordan, Cynthia S. *Second Stories: The Politics of Language, Form, and Gender in Early American*

Fictions. Chapel Hill: U of North Carolina P, 1989.

Kanellos, Nicolas. *A History of Hispanic Theatre in the United States: Origins to 1940.* Austin: U of Texas P, 1990.

Kelley, Mary. *Private Woman, Public Stage: Literary Domesticity in Nineteenth-Century America.* New York: Oxford UP, 1984.

Kestler, Frances Roe, comp. *The Indian Captivity Narrative: A Woman's View.* New York: Garland, 1990.

Kim, Elaine H. *Asian-American Literature, an Introduction to the Writings and Their Social Context.* Philadelphia: Temple UP, 1982.

Kolodny, Annette. *The Land Before Her: Fantasy and Experience of the American Frontiers, 1630–1860.* Chapel Hill: U of North Carolina P, 1984.

———. *The Lay of the Land: Metaphor as Experience and History in American Life and Letters.* Chapel Hill: U of North Carolina P, 1975.

Krupat, Arnold. *The Voice in the Margin: Native American Literature and the Canon.* Berkeley: U of California P, 1989.

Kubitschek, Missy Dehn. *Claiming the Heritage: African-American Women Novelists and History.* Jackson: UP of Mississippi, 1991.

Lauter, Paul. *Canons and Contexts.* New York: Oxford UP, 1991.

Leavitt, Dinah Luise. *Feminist Theatre Groups.* Jefferson, NC: McFarland, 1980.

Lee, Lawrence L., and Merrill E. Lewis, eds. *Women, Women Writers, and the West.* Troy, NY: Whitston, 1979.

Levy, Helen Fiddyment. *Fiction of the Home Place: Jewett, Cather, Glasgow, Porter, Welty, and Naylor.* Jackson: UP of Mississippi, 1992.

Lichtenstein, Diane. *Writing Their Nations: The Tradition of Nineteenth-Century American Jewish Women Writers.* Bloomington: Indiana UP, 1992.

Lifshin, Lyn, ed. *Ariadne's Thread: A Collection of Contemporary Women's Journals.* New York: Harper and Row, 1982.

Lim, Shirley Geok-lin, and Amy Ling, eds. *Reading the Literatures of Asian America.* Philadelphia: Temple UP, 1992.

Lincoln, Kenneth. *Native American Renaissance.* 2nd ed. 1983. Los Angeles: U of California P, 1985.

Ling, Amy. *Between Worlds: Women Writers of Chinese Ancestry.* New York: Pergamon P, 1990.

Logsdon, Loren, and Charles W. Mayer. *Since Flannery O'Connor: Essays on the Contemporary Short Story.* Macomb: Western Illinois UP, 1987.

Lyon, Thomas, and J. Golden Taylor, eds. *A Literary History of the American West.* Fort Worth: Texas Christian UP, 1987.

MacKethan, Lucinda H. *Daughters of Time: Creating Woman's Voice in Southern Story.* Athens: U of Georgia P, 1990.

Magee, Rosemary M., ed. *Friendship and Sympathy: Communities of Southern Women Writers.* Jackson: UP of Mississippi, 1992.

Manning, Carol, ed. *Female Tradition in Southern Literature.* Urbana: U of Illinois P, 1993.

Martin, Wendy. *An American Triptych: Anne Bradstreet, Emily Dickinson, Adrienne Rich.* Chapel Hill: U of North Carolina P, 1984.

McClave, Heather, ed. *Women Writers of the Short Story: A Collection of Critical Essays.* Englewood Cliffs, NJ: Prentice-Hall, 1980.

McDowell, Deborah E., and Arnold Rampersad, eds. *Slavery and the Literary Imagination.* Baltimore: Johns Hopkins UP, 1989.

McNall, Sally Allen. *Who Is in the House? A Psychological Study of Two Centuries of Women's Fiction in America, 1795 to the Present.* New York: Elsevier North Holland, 1981.

Meese, Elizabeth A. *Crossing the Double-Cross: The Practice of Feminist Criticism.* Chapel Hill: U of North Carolina P, 1986.

———. *(Ex)tensions: Re-figuring Feminist Criticism.* Urbana: U of Illinois P, 1990.

Michie, Helena. *Sororophobia: Differences among Women in Literature and Culture.* New York: Oxford UP, 1992.

Middlebrook, Diane Wood, and Marilyn Yalom, eds. *Coming to Light: American Women Poets in the Twentieth Century.* Ann Arbor: U of Michigan P, 1985.

Miller, R. Baxter, ed. *Black American Poets between Worlds, 1940–1960.* Knoxville: U of Tennessee P, 1986.

Miner, Madonne M. *Insatiable Appetites: Twentieth-Century American Women's Bestsellers.* Westport, CT: Greenwood P, 1984.

Mirande, Alfredo, and Evangelina Enriquez. *La Chicana: The Mexican-American Woman.* Chicago: U of Chicago P, 1979.

Mobley, Marilyn Sanders. *Folk Roots and Mythic Wings in Sarah Orne Jewett and Toni Morrison: The Cultural Function of Narrative.* Baton Rouge: Louisiana State UP, 1991.

Moers, Ellen. *Literary Women.* Garden City, NY: Doubleday, 1976.

Mohr, Eugene. *The Nuyorican Experience: Literature of the Puerto Rican Minority.* Westport, CT: Greenwood P, 1983.

Montefiore, Jan. *Feminism and Poetry: Language, Experience, Identity in Women's Writing.* New York: Pandora, 1987.

Moraga, Cherríe, and Gloria Anzaldúa, eds. *This Bridge Called My Back: Writings by Radical Women of Color.* Rpt. New York: Kitchen Table: Women of Color P, 1983.

Munt, Sally, ed. *New Lesbian Criticism: Literary and Cultural Readings.* New York: Columbia UP, 1992.

Murphy, Brenda. *American Realism and American Drama, 1880–1940.* Cambridge, England: Cambridge UP, 1987.

Mussell, Kay. *Fantasy and Reconciliation: Contemporary Formulas of Women's Romance Fiction.* Westport, CT: Greenwood P, 1984.

Natalle, Elizabeth J. *Feminist Theatre: A Study in Persuasion.* Metuchen, NJ: Scarecrow P, 1985.

Nelson, Dana D. *The Word in Black and White: Reading "Race" in American Literature, 1638–1867.* New York: Oxford UP, 1992.

Neuman, Shirley. *Autobiography and Questions of Gender.* Portland: Frank Cass, 1991.

Newton, Judith, and Deborah Rosenfelt, eds. *Feminist Criticism and Social Change: Sex, Class, and Race in Literature and Culture.* New York: Methuen, 1985.

Norwood, Vera. *Made from This Earth: American Women and Nature.* Chapel Hill: U of North Carolina P, 1993.

Norwood, Vera, and Janice Monk, eds. *The Desert Is No Lady: Southwestern Landscapes in Women's Writing and Art.* New Haven, CT: Yale UP, 1987.

Olauson, Judith. *The American Woman Playwright: A View of Criticism and Characterization.* Troy, NY: Whitston, 1981.

Ostriker, Alicia Suskin. *Stealing the Language: The Emergence of Women's Poetry in America.* Boston: Beacon P, 1986.

———. *Writing Like a Woman.* Ann Arbor: U of Michigan P, 1983.

Payne, James Robert, ed. *Multicultural Autobiography: American Lives.* Knoxville: U of Tennessee P, 1992.

Pearlman, Mickey, ed. *American Women Writing Fiction: Memory, Identity, Family, Space.* Lexington: UP of Kentucky, 1989.

———. *Mother Puzzle: Daughters and Mothers in Contemporary American Literature.* Westport, CT: Greenwood P, 1989.

Pope, Deborah. *A Separate Vision: Isolation in Contemporary Women's Poetry.* Baton Rouge: Louisiana State UP, 1984.

Pratt, Annis, et al. *Archetypal Patterns in Women's Fiction.* Bloomington: Indiana UP, 1981.

Prenshaw, Peggy Whitman, ed. *Women Writers of the Contemporary South.* Jackson: UP of Mississippi, 1984.

Pryse, Marjorie, and Hortense J. Spillers, eds. *Conjuring: Black Women, Fiction, and Literary Tradition.* Bloomington: Indiana UP, 1985.

Rabinowitz, Paula. *Labor and Desire: Women's Revolutionary Fiction in Depression America.* Chapel Hill: U of North Carolina P, 1991.

Rainwater, Catherine, and William J. Scheick, eds. *Contemporary American Women Writers: Narrative Strategies.* Lexington: UP of Kentucky, 1985.

Roberts, Robin. *A New Species: Gender and Science in Science Fiction.* Urbana: U of Illinois P, 1993.

Rocard, Marcienne. *The Children of the Sun: Mexican-Americans in the Literature of the United States.* Tran. Edward G. Brown, Jr. Tucson: U of Arizona P, 1989.

Rodríguez de Laguna, Asela, ed. *Images and Identities: The Puerto Rican in Two World Contexts.* New Brunswick, NJ: Transaction, 1987.

Roller, Judi M. *The Politics of the Feminist Novel.* Westport, CT: Greenwood P, 1986.

Romines, Ann. *The Home Plot: Women, Writing and Domestic Ritual.* Amherst: U of Massachusetts P, 1992.

Saldivar, Ramon. *Chicano Narrative: The Dialectics of Difference.* Madison: U of Wisconsin P, 1990.

Samuels, Shirley, ed. *The Culture of Sentiment: Race, Gender, and Sentimentality in Nineteenth-Century America.* New York: Oxford UP, 1992.

Sanchez, Marta Ester. *Contemporary Chicana Poetry: A Critical Approach to an Emerging Literature.* Berkeley: U of California P, 1985.

Sanders, Leslie Catherine. *The Development of Black Theater in America: From Shadows to Selves.* Baton Rouge: Louisiana State UP, 1988.

Saxton, Marsha, and Florence Howe, eds. *With Wings: An Anthology of Literature by and about Women with Disabilities.* New York: Feminist Press at the City University of New York, 1987.

Schöler, Bo, ed. *Coyote Was Here; Essays on Contemporary Native American Literary and Political Mobilization.* Aarhus, Denmark: SEKLOS, 1984.

Schweik, Susan. *A Gulf So Deeply Cut: American Women Poets and the Second World War.* Madison: U of Wisconsin P, 1991.

Seller, Maxine Schwartz, ed. *Ethnic Theatre in the United States.* Westport, CT: Greenwood P, 1983.

———. *Immigrant Women.* Philadelphia: Temple UP, 1980.

Shapiro, Ann R. *Unlikely Heroines: Nineteenth-Century American Women Writers and the Woman Question.* Westport, CT: Greenwood P, 1987.

Shinn, Thelma J. *Radiant Daughters: Fictional American Women.* Westport, CT: Greenwood P, 1986.

Showalter, Elaine. *Sister's Choice: Tradition and Change in American Women's Writing.* Oxford: Clarendon P, 1991.

Shuffelton, Frank, ed. *A Mixed Race: Ethnicity in Early America.* New York: Oxford UP, 1993.

Simonds, Wendy, and Barbara Katz Rothman. *Centuries of Solace: Expressions of Maternal Grief in Popular Literature.* Philadelphia: Temple UP, 1992.

Simonson, Rick, and Scott Walker. *The Graywolf Annual Five: Multi-Cultural Literacy.* St. Paul, MN: Graywolf P, 1988.

Smith, Sidonie, and Julia Watson, eds. *De/colonizing the Subject: The Politics of Gender in Women's Autobiography.* Minneapolis: U of Minnesota P, 1992.

Smith, Valerie. *Self-Discovery and Authority in Afro-American Narrative.* Cambridge, MA: Harvard UP, 1987.

Sochen, June. *Consecrate Every Day: The Public Lives of Jewish American Women, 1880–1980.* Albany: State U of New York P, 1981.

———, ed. *Women's Comic Visions.* Detroit: Wayne State UP, 1991.

Sollors, Werner. *Beyond Ethnicity: Consent and Descent in American Culture.* New York: Oxford UP, 1986.

———, ed. *The Invention of Ethnicity.* New York: Oxford UP, 1989.

Sommers, Joseph, and Tomas Ybarra-Frausto, eds. *Modern Chicano Writers: A Collection of Critical Essays.* Englewood Cliffs, NJ: Prentice-Hall, 1979.

Spillers, Hortense J., ed. *Comparative American Identities: Race, Sex, and Nationality in the Modern Text.* New York: Routledge, 1991.

Spivack, Charlotte. *Merlin's Daughters: Contemporary Women Writers of Fantasy.* Westport, CT: Greenwood P, 1987.

Staicar, Tom, ed. *The Feminine Eye: Science Fiction and the Women Who Write It.* New York: Frederick Ungar, 1982.

Stauffer, Helen Winter, and Susan J. Rosowski, comps. *Women and Western American Literature.* Troy, NY: Whitston, 1982.

Stout, Janis P. *Strategies of Reticence: Silence and Meaning in the Works of Jane Austen, Willa Cather, Katherine Anne Porter, and Joan Didion.* Charlottesville: UP of Virginia, 1990.

Tate, Claudia. *Domestic Allegories of Political Desire: The Black Heroine's Text at the Turn of the Century.* New York: Oxford UP, 1992.

Tatum, Charles M. *Chicano Literature.* Boston: Twayne, 1982.

Taylor, Helen. *Gender, Race, and Region in the Writings of Grace King, Ruth McEnery Stuart, and Kate Chopin.* Baton Rouge: Louisiana State UP, 1989.

Tompkins, Jane P. *Sensational Designs: The Cultural Work of American Fiction, 1790–1860.* New York: Oxford UP, 1985.

Treichler, Paula A., Cheris Kramarae, and Beth Stafford, eds. *For Alma Mater: Theory and Practice in Feminist Scholarship.* Urbana: U of Illinois P, 1985.

Trujillo, Roberto G., and Andres Rodriguez, comps. *Literatura Chicana: Creative and Critical Writings through 1984.* Oakland, CA: Floricanto, 1985.

TuSmith, Bonnie. *All My Relatives: Community in Contemporary Ethnic American Literatures.* Ann Arbor: U of Michigan P, 1993.

Urgo, James R. *Novel Frames: Literature as Guide to Race, Sex, and History in American Culture.* Jackson: UP of Mississippi, 1991.

Vizenor, Gerald, ed. *Narrative Chance: Postmodern Discourse on Native American Literatures.* Albuquerque: U of New Mexico P, 1989.

Wade-Gayles, Gloria. *No Crystal Stair: Visions of Race and Sex in Black Women's Fiction.* New York: Pilgrim P, 1984.

Wagner, Lilya. *Women War Correspondents in World War II.* Westport, CT: Greenwood P, 1989.

Wagner-Martin, Linda. *The Modern American Novel, 1914–1945: A Critical History.* Boston: Twayne, 1990.

Walker, Cheryl. *Masks Outrageous and Austere: Culture, Psyche, and Persona in Modern Women Poets.* Bloomington: Indiana UP, 1991.

———. *The Nightingale's Burden: Women Poets and American Culture before 1900.* Bloomington: Indiana UP, 1982.

Walker, Nancy A. *Feminist Alternatives: Irony and Fantasy in the Contemporary Novel by Women.* Jackson: UP of Mississippi, 1990.

———. *A Very Serious Thing: Women's Humor and American Culture.* Minneapolis: U of Minnesota P, 1988.

Wall, Cheryl, ed. *Changing Our Own Words: Essays on Criticism, Theory, and Writing by Black Women.* New Brunswick, NJ: Rutgers UP, 1989.

Warren, Joyce W., ed. *The (Other) American Traditions: Nineteenth Century Women Writers.* New Brunswick, NJ: Rutgers UP, 1993.

Washington, Mary Helen, ed. *Invented Lives: Narratives of Black Women, 1860–1960.* Garden City, NY: Anchor P, 1987.

Watson, Carole McAlpine. *Prologue: The Novels of Black American Women, 1891–1965.* Westport, CT: Greenwood P, 1985.

Waugh, Patricia. *Feminine Fictions: Revisiting the Modern.* New York: Routledge, 1989.

Waxman, Barbara Frey. *From the Hearth to the Open Road: A Feminist Study of Aging in Contemporary Literature.* Westport, CT: Greenwood P, 1990.

Weixlmann, Joe, and Houston A. Baker, Jr., eds. *Studies in Black American Literature, Volume III: Black Feminist Criticism.* Greenwood, FL: Penkevill, 1988.

Westling, Louise. *Sacred Groves and Ravaged Gardens: The Fiction of Eudora Welty, Carson McCullers, and Flannery O'Connor.* Athens: U of Georgia P, 1985.

White, Barbara A. *Growing Up Female: Adolescent Girlhood in American Fiction.* Westport, CT: Greenwood P, 1985.

Wiget, Andrew, ed. *Critical Essays on Native American Literature.* Boston: G. K. Hall, 1985.

———. *Native American Literature.* Boston: Twayne, 1985.

Willis, Susan. *Specifying: Black Women Writing the American Experience.* Madison: U of Wisconsin P, 1987.

Winter, Kari J. *Subjects of Slavery, Agents of Change: Women and Power in Gothic Novels and Slave Narratives.* Athens: U of Georgia P, 1992.

Winter, Kate H. *The Woman in the Mountain: Reconstructions of Self and Land by Adirondack Women Writers.* Albany: SUNY-Albany, 1988.

Wittig, Monique. *The Straight Mind and Other Essays.* Boston: Beacon P, 1992.

Yamada, Mitsuye, and Sarie Sachie Hylkema, eds. *Sowing Ti Leaves: Writings by Multi-Cultural Women.* Irvine, CA: Multi-Cultural Women Writers of Orange County, 1990.

Yellin, Jean Fagan. *Women and Sisters: The Antislavery Feminists in American Culture.* New Haven, CT: Yale UP, 1989.

Young, Mary E. *Mules and Dragons: Popular Culture Images in the Selected Writings of African-American and Chinese-American Women Writers.* Westport, CT: Greenwood P, 1993.

Yorke, Liz. *Impertinent Voices: Subversive Strategies in Contemporary Women's Poetry.* New York: Routledge, 1991.

Zandy, Janet, ed. *Calling Home: Working-Class Women's Writings: An Anthology.* New Brunswick, NJ: Rutgers UP, 1990.

Compiled by Dianne Chambers

DIRECTORY OF EDITORS AND ADVISERS

Editors in Chief

CATHY N. DAVIDSON Professor of English at Duke University and Editor of *American Literature*, has published many books, including *Revolution and the Word: The Rise of the Novel in America; Reading in America: Literature and Social History; The Book of Love: Writers and their Love Letters;* and *Thirty-six Views of Mount Fuji: On Finding Myself in Japan.* She is the General Editor for Oxford University Press's *Early American Women Writers* series and is the President of the American Studies Association.

LINDA WAGNER-MARTIN Hanes Professor of English and Comparative Literature at the University of North Carolina at Chapel Hill, is the author or editor of more than thirty-five books in the fields of modern American literature, women's literature, and biography. She has received grants from the Guggenheim Foundation, the Rockefeller Foundation, the National Endowment for the Humanities, the American Council of Learned Societies, the Bunting Institute, and others. Currently President of the Ernest Hemingway Foundation, Wagner-Martin is contemporary section editor for *The D. C. Heath Anthology of American Literature.* Recent books include *Telling Women's Lives: The New Biography,* and a biography of Gertrude Stein.

Editors

ELIZABETH AMMONS Professor of English and American Literature, Tufts University. Author of *Conflicting Stories: American Women Writers at the Turn into the Twentieth Century* and *Edith Wharton's Argument with America.* Editor of *Critical Essays on Harriet Beecher Stowe; Short Fiction by Black Women, 1900–1920;* and (with Annette White-Parks) *Tricksterism and Multicultural Turn-of-the-Century U.S. Writers.*

AMY LING Associate Professor of English, Director of Asian American Studies Program, University of Wisconsin at Madison. Author of *Between Worlds: Women Writers of Chinese Ancestry; Chinamerican Reflections,* a chapbook of poems and paintings; and numerous articles and bibliographies on Asian American authors. Editor of six books on multicultural and Asian American literature.

TRUDIER HARRIS Augustus Baldwin Longstreet Professor of American Literature, Emory University. Author of *From Mammies to Militants: Domestics in Black American Literature; Exorcising Blackness: Historical and Literary Lynching and Burning Rituals;* and *Black Women in the Fiction of James Baldwin.* Her most recent book-length critical work is *Fiction and Folklore: The Novels of Toni Morrison.* She has co-edited three volumes of the *Dictionary of Literary Biography* series on African American writers and edited three additional volumes. Presently, Harris is co-editing *The Oxford Companion to African American Literature.*

ANN KIBBEY Professor of English, University of Colorado at Boulder. Author of *The Interpretation of Material Shapes in Puritanism: A Study of Rhetoric, Prejudice, and Violence.* Founding Editor and Editor-in-Chief of *Genders,* an interdisciplinary journal about gender and sexuality in art, literature, film, and mass media. Editor of *Sexual Artifice: Persons, Images, Politics.* Author of articles on African-American literature, women and criminality in colonial America, and feminist theory. Kibbey is presently writing a book about film and feminism.

JANICE RADWAY Professor of Literature, Program in Literature, Duke University. Author of *Reading and Romance: Women, Patriarchy, and Popular Literature.* Radway is presently completing *The Book of the Month Club and the General Reader.* She has co-edited, with Toril Moi, a volume of the *South Atlantic Quarterly* on materialist feminism, and is co-editing, with Carl Kaestle, volumes on the twentieth century for *The American Antiquarian Society's Collaborative History of the Book in the United States.*

Advisers

FRANCES R. APARICIO Associate Professor of Romance Languages and Literatures, Program in American Culture/Latino and Latina Studies, University of Michigan. Author of *Versiones, interpretaciones, creaciones: instancias de la traducción literaria en Hispanoamerica en el siglo veinte.* Editor and translator of *Canto de la locura y otros poemas/Song of Madness and Other Poems* (by Francisco Matos Paoli) and editor of *Writers of America: Latina and Latino Voices.*

JUDITH BUTLER Professor of Rhetoric and Comparative Literature, University of California at Berkeley. Author of *Bodies That Matter: On the Discursive Limits of Sex; Gender Trouble: Feminism and the Subversion of Identity;* and *Subjects of Desire: Hegelian Reflections in Twentieth-Century France.* She is co-editor (with Joan W. Scott) of *Feminists Theorize the Political.*

CORDELIA CANDELARIA Professor of English, Arizona State University. Author of *Chicano Po-*

etry: A Critical Introduction; Seeking the Perfect Game: Baseball in American Literature; and a collection of poems, *Ojo de la cueva/Cave Springs.* She is currently working on a new collection of poems, *Rainbow in Black and White.*

WILLIAM H. CHAFE Alice Mary Baldwin Professor of History, Duke University. Author of *The Paradox of Change: American Women in the Twentieth Century; The American Woman: Her Changing Social, Economic, and Political Roles, 1920–1970; Women and Equality: Changing Patterns in American Culture; Civilities and Civil Rights: Greensboro, North Carolina, and the Black Struggle for Freedom;* and *Never Stop Running: Allard Lowenstein and the Struggle to Save American Liberalism.*

LEE CHAMBERS-SCHILLER Professor of History, University of Colorado at Boulder. Author of *Liberty, A Better Husband: Single Women in America: The Generations of 1780–1840* and a contributor to *New Research on Women.* She is working on a biography of Maria Weston Chapman and her family.

LIZA FIOL-MATTA National Council for Research on Women and Instructor of English, La-Guardia Community College (CCNY); Director, Ford Foundation Curriculum, Mainstreaming and Teaching Initiative. She is co-editor of *Women of Color in the Multicultural Curriculum: Transforming the College Classroom.*

DIANA FUSS Associate Professor of English, Princeton University. Author of *Essentially Speaking: Feminism, Nature, and Difference* and editor of *Inside/Out: Lesbian Theories, Gay Theories.* She has also published essays on gay and lesbian theory, feminist theory, and fashion.

JOY HARJO Professor of English, University of New Mexico. Author of several collections of poems, including *She Had Some Horses; What Moon Drove Me to Do This?; In Mad Love and War;* and *The Woman Who Fell from the Sky* (forthcoming). She has co-authored the prose work *The Last Song: Secrets from the Center of the World* (with Steven Strom) and film scripts, such as "Origin of the Apache Crown Dance."

KARLA F. C. HOLLOWAY Professor of English, Duke University. Author of *The Character of the World: The Texts of Zora Neale Hurston; New Dimensions of Spirituality: A Biracial and Bicultural Reading of the Novels of Toni Morrison* (with Stephanie Demetrakopoulos); *Moorings and Metaphors: Figures of Culture and Gender in Black Women's Literature;* and *Codes of Conduct: Reflections on Ethics and Ethnicity* (forthcoming).

ALISON M. JAGGAR Professor of Women's Studies, University of Colorado at Boulder. Author of *Feminist Politics and Human Nature* and co-editor of *Feminist Frameworks: Alternative Theoretical Accounts of the Relations between Women and Men* and *Gender/Body/Knowledge: Feminist Reconstructions of Being and Knowing.*

LINDA K. KERBER May Brodbeck Professor in the Liberal Arts and Professor of History, The University of Iowa. Author of *Federalists in Dissent: Imagery and Ideology in Jeffersonian America* and *Women of the Republic: Intellect and Ideology in Revolutionary America.* She is the editor of *Revolutionary Generation: Ideology, Politics and Culture in the Early Republic* and co-editor of *Women's America: Refocusing the Past.*

ELAINE H. KIM Professor of Asian American Studies, University of California at Berkeley. Author of *Asian American Literature: An Introduction to the Writings and their Social Context* and co-author (with Janice Otani) of *With Silk Wings: Asian American Women at Work.*

WENDY ROSE Professor of American Indian Studies, Fresno City College. Author of several volumes of poetry, including *Hopi Roadrunner Dancing; Lost Copper; Long Division, A Tribal History; The Halfbreed Chronicles and Other Poems; Academic Squaw: Reports to the World from the Ivory Tower; What Happened When the Hopi Hit New York;* and *Bone Dance: New and Selected Poems.*

A. LAVONNE BROWN RUOFF Professor of English, University of Illinois, Chicago Circle. Author of *American Indian Literatures: An Introduction, Bibliographic Review, and Selected Bibliography,* editor of *Three Nineteenth-Century American Indian Autobiographers,* and co-editor (with Jerry Ward) of *Redefining American Literary History.*

KATHLEEN M. SANDS Professor of English and Folklore, Arizona State University. Author of *Charreria Mexicana: An Equestrian Folk Tradition.* She is editor of *Circle of Motion: Arizona Anthology of Contemporary American Indian Literature; Autobiography of a Yaqui Poet;* and *People of Pasqua;* and co-editor (with Gretchen M. Bataille) of *American Indian Women: A Guide to Research* and *American Indian Women: Telling Their Lives.*

CATHARINE R. STIMPSON Director, MacArthur Foundation, and Professor of English, Rutgers University. Author of *Where the Meanings Are* and *Women's Studies in the United States.* Editor of *Women and the "Equal Rights" Amendment: Senate Subcommittee Hearings on the Constitutional Amendment* and co-editor of *Women and the American City; Women, Households, and the Economy;* and *Women—Sex and Sexuality.*

MARGARET B. WILKERSON Professor and Chair of Afro-American Studies, University of California at Berkeley. Author of *Nine Plays by Black Women* and co-editor of the theater issue of *Black Scholar.* She has published articles on Lorraine Hansberry, Toni Morrison, and other women of color.

SAU-LING C. WONG Associate Professor of Ethnic Studies, University of California at Berkeley. Author of *Reading Asian American Literature: From Necessity to Extravagance,* as well as articles on Maxine Hong Kingston, Chinese immigrant literature, immigrant autobiography, second language acquisition, and educational rights for immigrants.

INDEX

Abbott, Edith, **3**
Abel, Elizabeth, 334–35
Abinader, Elmaz, 61
Abolition, **3–5**
  black feminism and, 888–89
  Maria Weston Chapman and,
    162
  Lydia Maria Child and, 177
  Grimké sisters and, 367
  Frances Watkins Harper and,
    378–79
  journalism and, 628, 757
  liberal feminism and, 517, 755,
    860, 930, 934
  political activity and, 686, 691
  racism and, 737
  religion and, 755
  roots of movement, 58
  short stories and, 801, 802
  sisterhood and, 808
  slave narratives and, 810, 811,
    888–89
  Elizabeth Cady Stanton and,
    845, 860
  suffrage dispute and, 517, 930
  Underground Railroad and, 757,
    842, **891–92**
Abortion, **5–6**
  as birth control, 114
  as black literary taboo, 868
  Chicana rights and, 176
  fetal rights and, 760
  legalization of, 5, 759–60, 939
  liberal feminism and, 517
  as political issue, 690, 693
  writings about, 6, 113
Abu-Jaber, Diana, 61, 62
Academic journals. *See* Journals,
  academic
Acadian writing. *See* Creole and
  Acadian writing
Acker, Kathy, **6–7**, 294
Acosta-Belén, Edna, 485
Activism, **7–8**
  African-American writers and,
    28–29, 35–36
  antiwar movements, **58–60**, 687
  autobiography and, 88
  black women and, 28
  Chicana rights and, **175–77**
  Chinese-Americans, 184
  feminist approach to, 936
  immigrant women and, 418,
    435–36, 443
  labor-related, 422
  Native American, 46, **47–48**
  New York writers and, 632
  sisterhood and, **808–10**
  third world liberationist, 880

  women's clubs and, 932–33
  See also specific causes
Adams, Abigail, 4, **8–9**, 13, 203,
    265, 523, 713, 934
Adams, Alice, **9**, 802, 830
Adams, Elizabeth Laura, 156, 213
Adams, Hannah, **9–10**, 389
Adams, Harriet S., 180, 597
Adams, Louisa Catherine, 886
Adams, Margie, 939
Adams, Mary. *See* Phelps (Ward),
    Elizabeth Stuart
Addams, Jane, **10–11**, 422, 491–92,
    822, 823, 861, 936
Adell, Sandra, *as contributor*, 31–
    34
Adelman, Marcy, 511
Adler, Felix, 548
Adler, Margot, 840
Adler, Renata, 804
Adnan, Etel, 60, 61
Adolescence, **11–12**
  eating disorders and, 269
  flapper and, **325**
  girlhood and, **350–52**
  romance novels, 766–68
  See also Bildungsroman and
    künstlerroman
Adultery, 646–48
Advertising, book, 726
Advice books, **12–15**
  beauty, 98
  colonial era, 204
  etiquette, **285–86**
  health, 15, 43, 128, **381–83**, 786
  housekeeping, **400–401**
  marriage, 14, 382–83, **547–48**
  motherhood, **585–86**
  newspaper columnists, 451, 627
  self-help, **785–86**
  True Woman and, 887
  vocational, **899–901**
  youth market, 178–79, 181, 350
Advocacy writing. *See* Protest
  writing
Advocate magazine, 499
Africa. *See* Pan-Africanism
African-American oral tradition,
    15–16, 24, 644
  first known poem, 36
  folklore and, 325–26
  Zora Neale Hurston and, 16,
    325, 377–78
  testifying, **873–74**
African-American publishing
  outlets, **16–20**, 21, 137, 376,
    540, 724
African-American reading
  network, **20–22**

African Americans
  children's literature and, 182
  citizenship and, 190, 736, 751,
    752, 860
  domestic workers, 401
  education and, 272, 273, 523,
    751
  libraries for, 519
  male suffrage, 517, 737, 751, 752,
    860
  matriarchy myth, 817
  migration and, 567
  Pan-African movement, **650–52**
  quiltmaking tradition, 624
  race and, 731
  reading circles, 747, 933
  Reconstruction and, **751–52**
  religion and, 756, 811, 839, 867,
    873–74, 879
  separatist movements, 790
  temperance movement and,
    870–71
  True Womanhood and, 888
  women scientists, 782
  women's clubs, 17, 18, 19, 21, 25,
    35, 377, 392, 399, 519, 911, 933
  women's movement and, 937
  See also Black feminism; Civil
    rights movement; Racism;
    Reconstruction; Slavery
African-American writing, **22–40**
  academic journals and, 454
  advice books, 285–86
  anthologies, 33, 34, 36, 52–53,
    141, 732
  antisuicide, 863–64
  ba-ad woman in, **91**
  beauty standards in, 98, 99
  bildungsroman, 105
  bilingual-bicultural, 107
  black aesthetic and, **117–19**
  Black Arts Movement and, **119–
    22**
  Black English and, **122–23**
  black feminism and, 123, 124
  black migration and, 566, 567
  Chicago Renaissance, **165–67**,
    575
  civil rights movement and, **191–
    92**
  collaborative, 201
  in colonial era, 919–20
  community in, 210
  conjure woman in, 213
  diaries and journals, 246, 375
  drama, **29–31**, 257, 258, 375
  fashion and, 304
  on fathers, 306
  on female double jeopardy, 714